TWENTY-FOURTH

KOVELS'
Antiques &
Collectibles
PRICE LIST

For the 1992 Market

ILLUSTRATED

CROWN PUBLISHERS, INC.   NEW YORK

BOOKS BY RALPH AND TERRY KOVEL

American Country Furniture 1780–1875
Dictionary of Marks—Pottery & Porcelain
A Directory of American Silver, Pewter and Silver Plate
Kovels' Advertising Collectibles Price List
Kovels' American Silver Marks
Kovels' Antiques & Collectibles Price List
Kovels' Antiques & Collectibles Fix-It Source Book
Kovels' Book of Antique Labels
Kovels' Bottles Price List
Kovels' Collector's Guide to American Art Pottery
Kovels' Collector's Source Book
Kovels' Depression Glass & American Dinnerware Price List
Kovels' Guide to Selling Your Antiques & Collectibles
Kovels' Illustrated Price Guide to Royal Doulton
Kovels' Know Your Antiques
Kovels' Know Your Collectibles
Kovels' New Dictionary of Marks—Pottery & Porcelain
Kovels' Organizer for Collectors
Kovels' Price Guide for Collector Plates, Figurines, Paperweights,
and Other Limited Editions

Published by Crown Publishers, Inc., 201 East 50th Street,
New York, New York 10022. Member of the Crown Publishing Group.
CROWN is a trademark of Crown Publishers, Inc.
Manufactured in the U.S.A.
Library of Congress Catalog Card Number: 83-643618

ISBN 0-517-58472-7
10   9   8   7   6   5   4   3   2   1
First Edition

DEAR READER,

Amid discussions of a depression or recession, a rising unemployment rate, and the news of Desert Storm, the antiques and collectibles market slogged through the year. In the East there were many reports of poor sales at shows and lower auction prices. In other parts of the country the sales seemed steady and there were high prices for top-quality antiques.

The news media favored three stories: the newly discovered Van Gogh painting that sold for $1.43 million, the print of the Declaration of Independence found in back of a flea market picture that sold for $2.42 million, and the Honus Wagner baseball card auctioned for almost a half-million dollars. But collectors were interested in other record prices.

"Investment potential" is still making headlines. Record prices are reported in newspapers and on television because they are surprising to the noncollector. Those who follow the antiques market know dozens of records are set each year as collectors find new interests and as changing values of money, silver, and stocks influence prices.

Over the years we have read millions of prices and used thousands of pictures in *Kovels' Antiques & Collectibles Price List*. Prices listed here include a random selection of pieces offered for sale *this* year. We report on everyday antiques like pressed glass and oak furniture, exotic Tiffany and Lalique, and uncommon skorps and roemers. The smallest item this year is probably a pair of silver earrings, 7/8-inch long, that sold for $110. The largest is a 28-foot-long post office wall that brought $6,500. We do not list the top of the market but concentrate on the average pieces in any category. We will often add one high-priced piece in a category so you will realize that some of the rarities are quite valuable. For example, Ohr pottery can sell for $300 to $22,000. Most pieces we list are under $10,000. A few pieces of Rookwood, Galle, and Pairpoint sold for very high prices this year, but these records are not included in the general category listings. The highest price in this book is an ebonized vanity table for $18,000. The lowest price is a 25¢ plastic Coca-Cola glass. We even list the weird and wonderful, and this year you can find prices for a human skeleton, a firkin, and a niddy-noddy.

The book is changed slightly each year. Categories are added or omitted to make it easier for you to find your antiques. The book is kept to about 800 pages because it is written to go with you to sales. We try to have a balanced format—not too much glass, pottery, or collectibles, not too many items that sell for over $5,000. The prices are *from* the American market *for* the American market. Few European sales are reported. We take the editorial privilege of not including any prices that seem to result from "auction fever."

The computer-generated index is so complete it amazes us. Use it often. An internal alphabetical index is also included. For example, there is a category for "Celluloid." Most items will be found there, but if there is a toy made of celluloid, it will be listed under "Toy" and also indexed under "Celluloid."

All pictures and prices are new every year, except pictures that are pattern examples shown in "Depression Glass" and "Pressed Glass." Pictured antiques are not museum pieces, but items offered for sale.

The hints are set in easy-to-notice special type. Leaf through the book and learn how to wash porcelains, store textiles, guard against theft, and much more. Old *Kovels'* price books should be saved for future reference, tax, and appraisal information.

RECORD PRICES

In 1989 a lithographed tin sign picturing a flag made of Campbell's soup cans sold for $44,000. In 1990 a similar sign brought a record $93,000 at auction. This was not the only collectible to sell for a surprisingly high price. An American Express violet credit card from 1959 sold privately for $400, and an Eagle Scout medal was auctioned for $2,500. An unused feather golf ball made about 1840 sold for $25,900, but the sports item of the year was the Honus Wagner T-206 cigarette card auctioned for $451,000.

Toys continued to be a collecting field of great interest. A 1907 Lehmann Autobus set a record at $9,250. The German-made Mickey Mouse tap dancer toy sold for $17,600. In June of 1991 at an important toy sale, many high prices were recorded—including $104,500 for a German clockwork Christmas toy. It was a goat-drawn tin sleigh holding a wooden Santa dressed in crepe paper made in the late 1800s.

Furniture always sells well and records were set, although nothing came near the $15.2 million cabinet sold last year. An American carved-mahogany card table made around 1760 in Philadelphia brought $1,045,000. Lannuier, the New York cabinetmaker, made a brass-mounted gilt-trimmed table with a marble top about 1815, and it sold in 1991 for $704,000. Queen Anne furniture set records with a New England carved-mahogany bonnet-top highboy made around 1760 that sold for $247,000. A Shaker pine-work counter with original red paint, c.1830, brought $220,000. John Belter is still the highest-priced Victorian furniture manufacturer. A carved-rosewood bed he made brought a record $101,750 and a laminated rosewood dresser was $42,350. A nine-piece set of Stanton Hall pattern parlor furniture by J. & J. W. Meeks, another Victorian cabinetmaker, was $51,700.

The ceramics market is still strong, and there were two records this year for American art pottery: a Saturday Evening Girls (Paul Revere Pottery) bowl made in 1913 brought $10,175 and a green Rookwood vase with copper fish decorations sold for $198,000. There was an auction of a major collection of spatterware where prices were very high. The record bid was $39,600 for a set of five cups and saucers in the fish pattern. A stoneware four-gallon churn made in the mid-nineteenth century, marked N. Clark & Co., decorated with a cobalt-blue slip decoration of a long-eared spaniel, brought $47,500. A desirable shaving mug depicting a doctor at a patient's bedside set a record of $8,360. KPM plaques have been rising in price for several years, and a record $47,300 was paid for a plaque showing a group of ladies watching a dancing couple in a ballroom.

It is no surprise when a Tiffany lamp or window sells for a high price. A triple-panel window picturing purple wisteria vines on a trellis brought $440,000. A Tiffany lamp with a dragonfly shade was $275,000. And few were surprised when a Clichy basket-shaped paperweight sold for $258,500, and a Stradivarius violin made in 1720 brought $1,760,000.

Some records are surprising. A Patek Philippe astronomic watch with triple date and moon phases was $851,400; a Shaker yellow-painted pine bucket made in 1869 was $4,400; and a sixteenth-century gold thimble set with rubies was $35,000. Several duck decoys set records at a Massachusetts auction. A Stevens factory wigeon drake was $18,245, a Lem and Steve Ward pintail hen $30,800, and a George Warin goose $24,200.

But baseball was the star of the year. It was not just the Honus Wagner that brought big prices. A Currier and Ives print of "The American National Game of Base Ball at the Elysian Fields, Hoboken, N.J." sold for $44,000. And "Shoeless" Joe Jackson, the "Black Sox" baseball player, made news again when his autograph sold for $23,100.

The prices in this book are reports of the general antiques market, not the record-setting examples. Each year, every price in the book is new. We do *not* estimate or "update" prices. Prices are the actual asking price, although the buyer may have negotiated to a lower figure. No price is an estimate. *We do not ask dealers and writers to estimate prices.* Experience has shown that a collector of one type of antique is prejudiced in favor of that item, and prices are usually high or low, but rarely a true report. If a price range is given, it is because at least two identical items were offered for sale at different times. The computer records prices and prints the high and low figures. Price ranges are found only in categories like "Pressed Glass," where identical items can be identified. Some prices in *Kovels' Antiques & Collectibles Price List* may seem high and some may seem low because of regional variations. But each price is one you could have paid for the object.

If you are selling your collection, do *not* expect to get retail value unless you are a dealer. Wholesale prices for antiques are from 20 percent to 50 percent less than retail. Remember, the antiques dealer must make a profit or go out of business.

ACKNOWLEDGMENTS

Special thanks should go to those who helped us with pictures and deeds: Antique Exchange, Antique Market, Antiques Warehouse Inc., Arman's of Newport Inc., Noel Barrett, Bill Bertoia, Frank H. Boos Gallery, Butterfield & Butterfield, Christie's, Christie's East, Marvin Cohen Auctions, Samuel Cottone Auctions & Appraisals, DeFina Auctions, William Doyle Galleries, Richard & Eileen Dubrow Antiques, DuMouchelle's, Robert C. Eldred Company Inc., Garth's Auctions Inc., Gemini Galleries, Mike Glad, Glass-works Auctions, Morton M. Goldberg Auction Galleries Inc., Gene Harris Antique Auction Center, Greenwich Auction Room, Graham's Antiques, Guernsey's, Harmer Rooke Galleries, Norman Heckler & Co., Willis Henry Auctions, Lelands, Leslie Hindman Auctioneers, Marlene's Antique Market, Neal Auction Company, Oliver's Auction Gallery Inc., Richard Opfer, Phillips, David Rago, Lloyd Ralston, Sandy Rosnick, Skinner Inc., Sotheby's, Theriault's, Uwe Breker, Wolf's Auctioneers & Appraisers, and Woody Auction Company. Lee Markley and Rachel Davis gave special help.

To the others in the antiques trade who knowingly or unknowingly contributed prices or pictures to this book, we say "Thank you!" We could not do it without you. Some of you are: Jerry Alingh, American Breweriana Association, American Carnival Glass News, The American Indian Shop, American Pie, Antique Affaire Ltd., Antique Bottle & Glass Collector, Antique Market Report, Antique Treasury, Antiques & Collectibles Buyer, Antiques & Collecting, Antiques At 805, Florence Archambault, Theresa Baier, Birchland Antiques, Benedict J. Blachowicz, Bobin's Antiques, Richard A Bourne Co. Inc., Bud and Sally's Antiques, Cel-ebration!, Cerebro, Childhood Memo Inc., Circa, The Coca-Cola Collectors News, Russ Cochran's Comic Art Auction, Cohen's Auction Gallery, The Collector's Marketplace, Cookies, Crown Jewels of the Wire, Decoys Unlimited, Dynastic Ivory Factory, Encore, Federation Glass Works, Forever Fun, Fox & Fox, French Connection Antiques, Hayward/Hall, Stan & Peggy Hecker, Heisey News, Roslyn L. Herman, David Hernandez Art & Antiques, Hesson Collectibles, The Hickory Club Mart, The Hobstar, Tom Horvitz, Hummel Collector's Club Inc., Imperial Half Bushel, Jack & Scottie Imrie, Michael Ivankovich Antiques, George Kamm, Klingenberg's, Sheldon J. Lewis, Lloyd Ralston Toys, Howard Lowery, Lyons Ltd., Lynda's Attic, Maundy International, Mike's General Store, Montgomery Auction Exchange Inc., The Mouse Man Ink, Musical Box Society, The Mystic Light of the Aladdin Knights, National Cambridge Collectors Inc., National Shaving Mug Collectors' Association, The New Glaze, Gerald Newman, Old Store Front Antiques, Optimistic Pezzimist, The Oriental Corner, Paper Collectors' Marketplace, Paper Pile Quarterly, Parker Enterprises, Les Paul's, Pen Fancier's Magazine, Pettigrew's, Carol J. Pinney, Ross Porter,

Judy Posner, Powder Puff, Red Wing Collectors Newsletter, Charlie Reynolds, Riba Auctions, Ronin Gallery, Ruth and Earl's Antiques, Robert F. Schneider, Kennth E. Schneringer, Jack Seiderman, Bill Shawver, Bill Smith, The Stained Finger, Stangland, Swann Galleries Inc., Team Antiques, Temple's Antiques, Emma Terry, Barry Thomsen, Tools Ads, Toothpick Bulletin, Town and Country Auctions, Toy Scouts Inc., Toy Shop, Don Treadway, The Upside World of an O. J. Collector, Earl Wallis, Larry D. Wells, West Monument Street, Wheel Goods Trader, Howard Whitlow, Richard W. Withington, Inc., Tom Witte's Antiques, Wodyn Inc., World's Fair Collectors Society Inc., Lynda Wright, YesterDAZE Toys, Les Zakarin.

MORE ANTIQUE PRICE NEWS

Need to know the latest prices? We write a newsletter for collectors who want to know the latest news, trends, and prices for the antiques and collectibles market. *Kovels on Antiques and Collectibles* is an easy-to-read, 12-page, picture-filled newsletter about antiques of interest to collectors and dealers. It includes sale reports, reviews of price books, information about what to buy and sell, and articles on marks, fakes, care, security, and more. For more information about *Kovels on Antiques and Collectibles*, send a double-stamped, self-addressed envelope to Kovels, P.O. Box 22200-K, Beachwood, Ohio 44122.

Our television series, "Collector's Journal with Ralph and Terry Kovel," can be seen on The Discovery Channel. The show includes news, prices, and information. Watch us to see collectors and collections.

HOW TO USE THIS BOOK

There are a few rules for using this book. Each listing is arranged in the following manner: CATEGORY (such as Pressed Glass or Furniture), OBJECT (such as vase), DESCRIPTION (as much information as possible about size, age, color, and pattern). Some types of glass are exceptions to this rule. These are listed CATEGORY, PATTERN, OBJECT, DESCRIPTION. All items are presumed to be in good condition and undamaged, unless otherwise noted.

Several special categories were formed to make a more sensible listing. For instance, "Tool" includes special equipment because the casual collector might not know the proper name for an "adze." Masonic has been put into the larger category "Fraternal." New categories include "American Dinnerware," "Arts & Crafts," "Kay Finch," "Jukebox," "Kosta," "Motorcycle," "Rosemeade," "Sascha Brastoff," and "Scientific Instruments." The index can help you locate items.

Several idiosyncrasies of style appear because the book is printed by computer. Everything is listed according to the computer alphabetizing system. This means words such as "Mt." are alphabetized as "M-T," not as "M-O-U-N-T." All numerals are before all letters, thus 2 comes before A. A quick glance will make this clear, as it is consistent throughout the book

We made several editorial decisions. A bowl is a "bowl" and not a dish unless it is a special dish, such as a pickle dish. A butter dish is a "butter." A salt dish is called a "salt" to differentiate it from a saltshaker. It is always "sugar and creamer," "never "creamer and sugar." Where one dimension is given, it is the height; or if the object is round, the dimension is the diameter. Height of a picture is listed before width. Glass is clear unless a color is indicated.

Every entry is listed alphabetically, but the problem of language remains. Some antiques terms, like "Sheffield" or "snow baby," have two meanings. Be sure to read the paragraph headings to know the meaning used. All category headings are based on the language of the average person at an average show, and we use terms like "mud figures" even if not technically correct.

This book does not include price listings of fine art paintings, books, comic books, stamps, coins, and a few other special categories.

All pictures in *Kovels' Antiques & Collectibles Price List* are listed with the prices asked by the seller. "Illus" (illustrated nearby) is part of the description if a picture is shown.

There have been misinformed comments about how this book is written. We *do* use the computer. It alphabetizes, ranges prices, sets type, and does other time-consuming jobs. Because of the computer, the book can be produced quickly. The last entries are added in June; the book is available in October. This is six months faster than would be possible any other way. But it is human help that finds prices and checks accuracy. We read everything at least twice, sometimes more. We edit from 100,000 entries to the 50,000 entries found here. We correct spelling, remove incorrect data, write category headings, and decide on new categories. We sometimes make errors. Information in the paragraphs is reviewed and updated each year.

Prices are reports from all parts of the United States and Canada (translated to U.S. dollars at the rate of 82¢ U.S. to $1 Canadian) between June 1990 and June 1991. A few prices are from auctions, most are from shops and shows. Every price is checked for accuracy, but we are not responsible for errors.

It is unprofessional for an appraiser to set a value for an unseen item. Because of this, we cannot answer your letters asking for specific price information. But please write if you have any requests for categories to be included in future editions or any corrections to information in the paragraphs.

When you see us at the shows, stop and say hello. Since our television show has been on The Discovery Channel in all parts of the country, we find we can no longer be anonymous buyers. It may mean the dealers know us before we ask a price, but it has been wonderful to meet all of you. Don't be surprised if we ask for your suggestions for the next edition of *Kovels' Antiques & Collectibles Price List*. Or you can write us at P.O. Box 22200-K, Beachwood, Ohio 44122.

RALPH & TERRY KOVEL
Senior Members, American Society of Appraisers
July 1991

◆◆◆◆◆◆◆◆◆◆◆◆◆◆◆◆◆◆◆◆◆◆◆

If you move glass in cold weather, be sure to let it sit at room temperature for several hours before you try unpacking it. The glass will break more easily if there is an abrupt temperature change.

◆◆◆◆◆◆◆◆◆◆◆◆◆◆◆◆◆◆◆◆◆◆◆◆

A. Walter, Salt, Pate–De–Verre, 1 In.

Almaric Walter made pate–de–verre glass under contract at the Daum glassworks from 1908 to 1914. He started his own firm in Nancy, France, in 1919. Pieces made before 1914 are signed *Daum, Nancy* with a cross. After 1919 the signature is *A. Walter Nancy.*

A. WALTER, Dish, Figural, Lizard, Defenseless Bee, Signed, c.1925, 10 5/8 In. 9900.00
   Dish, Figural, Wave Washing Over Fish, c.1925, 7 1/8 In. 4400.00
   Figurine, Mermaid, Kneeling, Pate–De–Verre, Signed, 1925, 4 1/4 In. 715.00
   Figurine, Sparrow, Signed, c.1925, 3 7/8 In. 770.00
   Figurine, Woman On Green Bench, Draped Dress, Signed, 8 In. 2500.00
   Inkwell, Berried Vines, Pate–De–Verre, c.1925, 6 1/4 In. 880.00
   Jar, Chestnut Finial, Chestnut Leaves, Signed, c.1925, 6 1/4 In. 1760.00
   Pendant, Molded Scarab, Wooden Beads, 17 1/4 In. 1980.00
   Pendant, Roses Bouquet, Rust Buds, Cord, 15 1/2 In. 1100.00
   Perfume Bottle, Scene, Atomizer, No Bulb, Gold Plated Top 1200.00
   Salt, Mottled Turquoise & Sea Green, Roses & Vines, Signed, 1 In. 1255.00
   Salt, Pate–De–Verre, 1 In. ....*Illus* 1155.00
   Vase, Faience Pattern Top & Base, Silver Base, 3 1/2 In. 450.00
   Vase, Frog On Lily Pad Leaves, 6 In. 6500.00
   Vase, Trumpet, Lizard Above Base, c.1920, 8 5/8 In. 9900.00

ABC plates, or children's alphabet plates, were most popular from 1780 to 1860, but are still being made. The letters on the plate were meant as teaching aids for children learning to read. The plates were made of pottery, porcelain, metal, or glass.

ABC, Dish, Feeding, Divided, Animals, Orange Bakelite, Silver Base, Box, 1930s 18.00
   Dish, Feeding, Shenango 35.00
   Dish, Santa Claus, Children 125.00
   Mug, Kewpie, O'Neil 140.00
   Plate, 2 Boys Playing Banjos, English 75.00
   Plate, 3 Black Men Raising Glasses, Rule of Three, 8 In. 195.00
   Plate, Alphabet Border, Administration Bldg., Chicago Fair, 6 1/4 In. 225.00
   Plate, Arrival of General McClellan 375.00
   Plate, Bluebird, Eggs In Nest, On Branch, Tin, Ohio Art, 6 1/4 In. 10.00
   Plate, Boy Scouts In Woods, c.1920, 7 1/4 In. 125.00
   Plate, Buster Brown, 6 1/4 In. 85.00
   Plate, Cat & Fiddle, Playing Dog, Dancing Cow, Staffordshire, 5 In. 75.00
   Plate, Chickens, Polychrome Enamel, Staffordshire, Black, 6 1/4 In. 110.00
   Plate, Children, Many Sayings, Cobalt, Staffordshire, 7 In. 145.00
   Plate, Clock & Alphabet, Glass, Small 15.00
   Plate, Crusoe, Making Boat, Staffordshire 110.00

Plate, Etched Child's Head Center, Glass 35.00
Plate, Girl Swinging, Tin, Ohio Art, 8 1/4 In. 45.00
Plate, Hickory Dickory Dock, Underwood High Chair Co., Crescent Shape 110.00
Plate, Jumbo, Tin, 6 1/8 In. 125.00
Plate, Kitten & Pup In Creamers, Germany 40.00
Plate, Kittens Playing Center, Red & Yellow, Tin, 4 1/4 In. 55.00
Plate, Little Bo Peep, Staffordshire 55.00
Plate, Little Miss Muffet, Staffordshire 80.00
Plate, Major General George G. Meade 350.00
Plate, Mary Had A Little Lamb, Tin, 8 In. .... 150.00 To 160.00
Plate, Nativity Scene, Tin, 4 In. 20.00
Plate, Nursery Rhymes, Aluminum 25.00
Plate, Polly Flinders, Nursery Rhyme, Tin 35.00
Plate, Quilted Center, Alphabet Rim, Beads With Numerals 55.00
Plate, Scene of 2 Children Playing Hoops, Tin, 2 7/8 In. 100.00
Plate, Seal Hunters, Elsmore, 7 In. 135.00
Plate, Seesaw Margery Daw, Staffordshire 125.00
Plate, Sioux Indian Chief, Brown Transfer, 7 3/8 In. 150.00
Plate, Souvenir, Greenville, Ohio, Milk Glass 125.00
Plate, Washington, Tin, 5 5/8 In. 145.00
Plate, Who Killed Cock Robin, Tin, 7 7/8 In. .... 60.00 To 100.00
Plate, Zebra, Black Transfer, Staffordshire, 6 1/8 In. 85.00

Abingdon Pottery was established in 1934 by Raymond E. Bidwell as the Abingdon Sanitary Manufacturing Company. The company made art pottery and other wares. Sixteen varieties of cookie jars are known. The factory ceased production of art pottery in 1950.

ABINGDON, Bookends, Stylized Flat–Nosed Bust, Black Glaze, Pair 95.00
Bowl, Acanthus Leaves Interior, Oval, Turquoise, 16 In. 12.00
Bowl, Art Deco, Blue Glaze, No. 543 .... 12.00
Bust, Trojan Head, Art Deco 145.00
Candlestick, Double, White 15.00
Console Set, 2–Light Candlesticks, Green 25.00
Console Set, Flowers, Gold Trim, 3 Piece 20.00
Cookie Jar, 3 Bears .... 75.00 To 90.00
Cookie Jar, Clock .... 45.00 To 69.00
Cookie Jar, Cookie Time .... 40.00 To 60.00
Cookie Jar, Granny 100.00
Cookie Jar, Hobby Horse .... 95.00 To 175.00
Cookie Jar, Humpty Dumpty .... 75.00 To 125.00
Cookie Jar, Jack–In–The–Box .... 159.00 To 175.00
Cookie Jar, Jack–O–Lantern 350.00
Cookie Jar, Little Old Lady, Black 375.00
Cookie Jar, Little Old Lady, White 85.00
Cookie Jar, Locomotive 52.00
Cookie Jar, Mary & Lamb 138.00
Cookie Jar, Miss Muffet 190.00
Cookie Jar, Money Sack, White 70.00
Cookie Jar, Mother Goose 185.00
Cookie Jar, Three Bears .... 65.00 To 92.00
Cookie Jar, Train Engine, White, Green 78.00
Cookie Jar, Windmill 175.00
Cornucopia, Blue Glaze, 4 1/2 In. 15.00
Cornucopia, Green Glaze, No. 996, 7 In. 10.00
Figurine, Horsehead, Black 25.00
Figurine, Kangaroo, No. 605 .... 40.00
Planter, Mexican Cactus 30.00
Vase, Beige, Paper Label, 8 In. 75.00
Vase, Blue Glaze, Handles, No. 142, 5 1/2 In. 14.00
Vase, Blue Glaze, No. 320, 9 In. 17.00
Vase, Cover, Coolie, Pink Design 65.00
Vase, Eggshell, No. 520 .... 15.00
Vase, Laurel, Green, 8 In. 45.00

Vase, Urn Shape, Pink, 10 In.	10.00
Vase, Urn Shape, Pink, 13 In.	55.00
Wall Pocket, Calla, No. 586	30.00
Wall Pocket, Daisy, Red Glaze	70.00
Wall Pocket, Figural, Apron, Black & Pink Glaze	75.00
Wall Pocket, Figural, Carriage, Charteuse Glaze, No. 711	55.00
Wall Pocket, Lily, No. 377, 8 1/2 In.	20.00

Adams china was made by William Adams and Sons of Staffordshire, England. The firm was founded in 1769 and is still working. All types of tablewares and useful wares have been made through the years. Other pieces of Adams will be found listed under Flow Blue.

ADAMS, Birds of America, Canvasback Duck, England	35.00
Birds of America, Cedar Waxwing, England	35.00
Bowl, Fairy Villages, Flow Blue, 10 1/4 In.	175.00
Plate, Cries of London, 8 1/2 In.	30.00
Plate, Kyber, Flow Blue, 10 In.	120.00
Platter, Bowl, Vegetable, Dr. Syntax, Blue & White, Open	99.00
Toddy Plate, English Scene, Boat, Dark Blue, 6 In.	65.00

The old country store with the crackers in a barrel and a potbellied stove is a symbol of an earlier, less hectic time. The advertisements, containers, and products sold in these stores are now all collectibles. We have tried to list items in the logical places, so large store fixtures will be found under the Architectural category, enameled tin dishes under Graniteware, etc. Listed here are many of the advertising items. Other similar pieces may be found under the product name such as Planters Peanuts.

ADVERTISING, see also Paper

ADVERTISING, Ashtray, Armstrong, Rubber Tire, Rhino	18.00
Ashtray, Baseball Mitt Shape, Colonial Premier Co., Chicago	30.00
Ashtray, Breyer's Ice Cream, 1941	15.00
Ashtray, Doe–Wah–Jack	17.00
Ashtray, Esso, Humble Oil, German Shepherd	20.00
Ashtray, Fatima Cigarettes	55.00
Ashtray, Firestone, Texas Centennial, 1936	100.00
Ashtray, Fly Piper Planes, Embossed Plane & Letters, Metal	20.00
Ashtray, General Tire, Glass Insert, Embossed Slogan, 5 In.	20.00
Ashtray, General Tire, Rubber Tire, Glass Insert With Saying	35.00
Ashtray, Goodrich, Silvertown Tire	18.00
Ashtray, Goodrich, Tire, 100th Anniversary, Box	45.00
Ashtray, Harold's Club, Black Amethyst	20.00
Ashtray, Harrah's Club, Iridescent, 1950s	10.00
Ashtray, John Deere, Van Brunt Drills, Sample	15.00
Ashtray, Kelly Heavy–Duty, Tire, Green Insert	30.00
Ashtray, Kentucky Colonel	8.00
Ashtray, Michelin Man, Bakelite	65.00 To 85.00
Ashtray, Michigan State Fair, 1909, Horsehead, Cast Iron	12.00
Ashtray, Neuweiler, Blue, White, Ceramic Stein In Center, 7 In.	48.00
Ashtray, Nipper & Horn, Liconia, New Hampshire, Ceramic, c.1930	125.00
Ashtray, Old Judge Coffee, Tin	90.00
Ashtray, Rainier Pale Beer, Roseville Pottery Co.	35.00
Ashtray, RCA, Cast	115.00
Ashtray, Shu Linkou Air Station, Brass, 1930s, 5 Piece Set	40.00
Ashtray, Sierra Beer, Reno, Spur On Copper	35.00
Ashtray, Smokey Bear	95.00
Ashtray, Taittinger Champagne, France	75.00
Ashtray, Viceroy	6.00
Bag, Bull Durham, Cigarette Roll Paper, Cloth	22.00
Bag, Flour, Dakota Maid, Cloth, Indian Maid Picture	23.00
Bag, Flour, Lined, Drawstring, 10 Lb.	6.00
Bag, Flour, Lined, Drawstring, 25 Lb.	7.50

Bag, Flour, Snow White Flour, Snow White Rolling Dough 20.00
Bag, Flour, Southern Mills, Uncut Girl Doll, Cloth, 50 Lb. 20.00
Bag, Jewel Tea, Paper, Victory Package, 1 1/2 Lb. 20.00
Banana Split Set, Chiquita, Banana Shape, Spoon, Book, 1971 .... 30.00
Banner, Circus, Riverside Amusement Park, Chicago 750.00
Banner, Fairies Starch, Canvas, 1910s, 14 x 30 In. 12.00
Banner, Federal Tires, Felt, 1900s, 28 x 11 1/2 In. 57.00
Banner, Star Tobacco, Lithograph On Fabric, 89 In. 110.00
Bean Pot, Heinz 57 Logo, Brown Glaze, 3 In., Pair 12.50
Bin, Beechnut Tobacco 450.00
Bin, Blanke's Coffee, 2 Ft. 175.00
Bin, English Curved Tobacco 350.00
Bin, Great Stars Coffee, 25 Lb. 192.50
Bin, High Grade Coffee, WW. Manning, Boston 100.00
Bin, Jersey Coffee, Painted, 120 Lbs. 250.00
Bin, Johnson's Peacemake Coffee, Tin Lithograph, 24 In. 445.00
Bin, Ojibwa, Fine Cut, Tin Top & Bottom 475.00
Bin, Proctor & Gamble Soap, Metal, Large 175.00
Bin, Spice, Handock 3200.00
Bin, Sterling Tobacco, Dark, Round 150.00
Bin, Sure Shot Tobacco 545.00
Bin, Sweet Burley Dark, Red, Black & Gold 200.00
Bin, Sweet Burley Light, Yellow 55.00
Bin, Sweet Mist Chewing Tobacco, Cardboard, Tin Top & Bottom 155.00
Bin, Tea, Edwin J. Gillies & Co., Revolving Bar For Teas 220.00
Bin, Thomson & Taylor Roasted Coffee, Tin, 19 1/2 In. 65.00
Bin, Tiger Chewing Tobacco, 5 Cent Packages, Blue 363.00
Bin, Tiger Chewing Tobacco, Cardboard, Tin Top & Bottom, Red 134.00
Bin, Trolley Chewing Tobacco, Lithograph On Tin, 10 1/2 In. 1600.00
Blackboard, Nehi, Tin 75.00
Blender, Barroom, Southern Comfort Liquor, Electric 225.00
Blotter, Aetna Dynamite, Unused 8.00
Blotter, After Every Meal For Life, Wrigley's, 3 1/2 x 7 In. 8.00
Blotter, Allison & Co. Steel Forgings, Chester, Pa., 1900s 5.00
Blotter, Brown & Bigelow, Paul Webb Signed, 9 In. 7.00
Blotter, Garland Stove, Woman, With Logo Fan 8.00
Blotter, Minnesota Business College, Indian, Whispering Leaves 10.00
Blotter, Mulford's Antitoxin Glass Syringe, Unused, 6 x 3 In. 6.00
Blotter, Royal Corona, Kitchen Range 9.00
Blotter, Venetian Lamplighter 60.00
    ADVERTISING, BOOK, see Paper, Book
Book Bag, Kool–Aid, Canvas 10.00
Booklet, Child's, Hood's Sarsaparilla, Palette Shape, 1894 .... 45.00
Booklet, Coloring, Heinz, Kindergarten, 1905 .... 15.00
Booklet, Eclipse Starch, Mother Goose, 16 Pages 10.00
Booklet, Fable, Orange Crush 18.00
Booklet, Gold Dust Twins, Die–Cut, 1908 .... 40.00 To 45.00
Booklet, Kellogg's Mother Goose, 1933 .... 15.00
Booklet, Magic, Sapolio Soap, Witch Cover, 1800s 20.00
Booklet, National Tile Co., 24 Ceramic Tiles, Salesman's, 1915 .... 85.00
Booklet, New Book of Songs, Hamlin's Wizard Oil, Early 1900s 5.00
Booklet, ONT Thread, Rhymes, Palmer Cox Illustrations 18.00
Booklet, Pop–Up, Sears Roebuck, 1933 .... 18.00
Booklet, Theatrical Costume Fabric, Samples, 1920 .... 15.00
    ADVERTISING, BOTTLE, see Bottle
    ADVERTISING, BOTTLE OPENER, see Bottle Opener
Bowl, L. Mankowitz Cloaks, Chicago, Pressed Glass 38.00
Bowl, Wheaties, Baseball Players Silhouettes, Milk Glass 18.00
    ADVERTISING, BOX, see also Box
Box, Arbuckles Sugar, Wooden, Bridge Picture 2 Sides 75.00
Box, Argo Starch, 4 In. 20.00
Box, Aunt Jemima Pancake, Picture, Contents, Open, 1930s 62.00
Box, Baker's Chocolate, Wooden 20.00

Box, Beechnut Chewing Gum, Cardboard, 6 In. 44.00
Box, Blumers 5 Cent Shirt Waist Starch, 1906 .... 30.00
Box, Briggs Smoking Tobacco, Wooden, 7 In. 12.00
Box, Broxie Buddies Candy, Elves Playing In Snow, Tin, 5 Lb. 68.00
Box, Captain Crunch, Boats, 1950s 4.50
Box, Carmen Complexion Powder 30.00
Box, Carte Blanche Tobacco, Casket, Edgeworth, Tin, 3 x 2 In. 23.00
Box, Cigar, Old Virginia Cheroots, 1883, Picture of Black Man 48.00
Box, Cigar, Old Virginia Cheroots, Black Man Picture, 1926 .... 150.00
Box, Cigar, Swann & Co., Tampa, 2 Drawers 65.00
Box, Cigar, Tom Moore, Souvenir, Tin Lithograph, Hinged Cover 13.00
Box, Cigar, Yellow Kid, Graphics 550.00
Box, Cigar, Young Trumpes, 1883 .... 85.00
Box, Colgate's Fab Soap, Sea & Sunrise Picture, 1940, Sample 20.00
Box, Delivery, Boston Dairy, Wooden, Sheet Metal, Holds 2 Qt. 145.00
Box, Diamond Safety Matches, Small 5.00
Box, Display, Pall Mall Cigarettes 65.00
Box, Display, Sen–Sen, 1900s 42.00
Box, Display, Vaseline Hair Tonic 35.00
Box, ET Cereal 95.00
Box, Faultless Starch, Sample 25.00
Box, Fish Shape, Tobacco, Wooden, Relief Carving, 6 5/8 In. 75.00
Box, Ghostbusters Cereal 55.00
Box, Gold Brand Coffee, 7 In. 8.00
Box, Gold Dust Cleanser 27.50
Box, Gold Dust, Full, Unopened, 9 In. 38.00
Box, Golden Pheasant Condoms, Bird On Each, 1 Gross 20.00
Box, Grandpa's Soap, With Soap 18.00
Box, Grant's Hygienic Crackers, Flattened, 1920, 9 x 6 1/4 In. 18.00
Box, Griesedieck Beer, Wooden, Hinged Lid 60.00
Box, Hercules Powder Co., Wood, Sliding Lid, 5 x 3 5/8 x 3 In. 12.00
Box, Hohner Harmonica, 4 Tier Accordion Style, Wooden, Germany 95.00
Box, Howard Johnson's Cigar, Boy & Pieman Logo 25.00
Box, Kroger's Apricots, Wooden 21.00
Box, Montgomery Ward Clothespins, 4 In., 40 Piece 20.00
Box, New York Knife Co., Pocket Knife, 2 1/2 x 4 3/4 x 2 In. 35.00
Box, Old Virginia Cherrots, Lorillard, Cigar, Black Man, 1926 .... 30.00
Box, Page's Tested Flower Seeds, 16 Sections, 16 1/2 x 14 In. 75.00
Box, Paints & Varnishes, Boston, Mass., Wooden, 19 x 11 In. 25.00
Box, Peters High Velocity, Shells For Hunting, 2 Piece 35.00
Box, Philip Morris Tobacco, Cardboard, Flat 50s 18.50
Box, Popcorn, Butter–Kist, Paper, 6 1/2 In. 10.00
Box, Post Toasties Cereal, Mickey Mouse, 1934 .... 675.00
Box, Quaker Oats Cereal, Mother's Carnival, Fiesta Premium 68.00
Box, Quisp Cereal 60.00
Box, Recipe, Gold Medal, Dovetailed Wood, 1930s 23.00
Box, Remington Arms Co., 12 Gauge Shells, Pat. May 1892, 2 Pc. 35.00
Box, Rices Popular Flower Seeds, Paper Litho, 11 In. 95.00
Box, Seed, Primitive, Pine, Red, 9 Sections, Sliding Lid, 11 In. 75.00
Box, Seed, Thurber's, Label In Lid, 1800s 235.00
Box, Snicker's, Graphics 15.00
Box, Soap, Frank Sidall, Wooden, Lithograph 125.00
Box, Sunshine Biscuits, Cover 21.00
Box, Swift & Co. Soap, Color Label 20.00
Box, Thread, Clarks Mile End, English Wood 35.00
Box, United States Cartridge Co., 12 Gauge Shot Shells, 2 Pc. 25.00
Box, Whalebone, Ivory Bear Finial, W. W. Dodson, 1968, 3 x 4 In. 550.00
Box, Wheaties Cereal, 1940s War Theme 18.00
Box, Wheaties Cereal, Pete Rose 45.00
Box, Winchester Jr. Rifle Corps, For Rifle Kit, Shipping 95.00
Box, Winchester Shot Gun Shells, Cardboard, Pair 24.00
Box, Zagnut Bars, 5 Cent 15.00
Brace, Screen Door, Drink Moxie 85.00

◆◆◆

"A stitch in time" helps with repairs, too. If, while you are cleaning it, a small piece of veneer falls from a piece of furniture, put it in an envelope immediately, mark where it came from, and put it in the drawer (or tape it to the piece), to be reglued when you have time. Reglue as soon as possible.

◆◆◆

Bread Box, Rice's Pan–Dandy Bread, Enamel Sign, Wooden	275.00
Bread Box, Truth Bread, George Washington Scenes	225.00
Bread Plate, Pioneer Flour Mills	45.00
Bread Plate, White Wings Flour, 90th Anniversary	60.00
Broom Rack, Gold Medal Flour, Tin, 41 In.	165.00
Broom Rack, Merkle's Blu–Jay, Color	875.00
Brush, Essmueller Mill Furnishing, St. Louis, Celluloid	20.00
Brush, Mirror, Andy Gump, Miniature	50.00
Bucket, Sunnyfield Lard, 4 Lb.	28.00
Bust, Raleigh Cigarettes, Pressed Cardboard, 15 In.	77.00
Butler, Moxie, Carved Wood, Painted, 35 In.	220.00
Butler, Phillips 66	55.00
Cabinet, Baker's, Maple, Multi–Drawers, Original Hardware	845.00
Cabinet, Belding, Heminway Sewing Silks	1400.00
Cabinet, DeLaval Parts, Tin Lithograph Front, 18 x 26 x 10 In.	635.00
Cabinet, Diamond Dye, 4 Drawers On Side, Wood Case	660.00
Cabinet, Diamond Dye, Evolution of Woman, Tin Front	895.00
Cabinet, Diamond Dye, Governess, Children, Tin Front	450.00 To 950.00
Cabinet, Diamond Dye, Mansion, Tin Front, 30 In.	1570.00
Cabinet, Diamond Dye, Maypole Balloon Scene, Tin Front	1015.00
Cabinet, Diamond Dye, Slant Front, Wooden, Tin	875.00
Cabinet, Diamond Dye, Woman Dyeing Clothes, Tin Front	660.00
Cabinet, Dy–Ola, Wooden Front, 17 x 13 In.	192.00
Cabinet, Eveready Mazda Auto Lamp, Tin	115.00
Cabinet, Feen A Mint, Tin	525.00
Cabinet, Lorillard, Glass, Drawers, Dates 1760–1883, 31 x 43 In.	4345.00
Cabinet, Munyon Homeopathic, Rear Drawers, Tin, 20 x 14 In.	495.00
Cabinet, Peerless Dyes, Train, Camels, Wood, Tin, Sliding Doors	8745.00
Cabinet, Pratts Food Co., Veterinary, 23 x 9 1/2 In.	990.00
Cabinet, Putnam Dye, Slant Front, Wooden, Tin Face	225.00
Cabinet, Putnam Dye, Small	95.00
Cabinet, Putnam Dye, Tin	135.00
Cabinet, Putnam Dye, Wooden Box, Tin Litho, General Putnam	340.00
Cabinet, Putnam Fadeless Dyes, 150 Packets, Metal	95.00
Cabinet, Rainbow Dye	550.00
Cabinet, Rit Dye, Woman Front, Tin, Wooden Drawer In Back	195.00
Cabinet, Spool, Clark, Mile–End, Slant Lift Top, Oak, 36 x 25 In.	350.00
Cabinet, Spool, Clark, O. N. T.	525.00
Cabinet, Spool, Heminway, Oak, Stenciled	475.00
Cabinet, Spool, J & P Coats, 2 Drawers	250.00
Cabinet, Spool, J & P Coats, Slant Front, Tin, Glass, Small	95.00
Cabinet, Spool, Kerr & Co., 6 Drawers	550.00
Cabinet, Spool, Nonotuck Silk Company, On Legs	375.00
Cabinet, Spool, Willimantic, 3 Drawers	245.00
Cake Pan, Py–O–My	8.00
Can Opener, Pet Milk, Embossed Hand, Holding Can, Cow	15.00
Candy Container, Metal, Glass, Slant Front, Brach, 7 x 18 In.	35.00
Candy Dish, Pickering's Carpets–Furniture, Cut Glass	20.00
ADVERTISING, CANISTER, see Advertising, Tin	
ADVERTISING, CARD, see Card, Advertising	
Carrier, 7–Up, Aluminum, 12 Bottle	50.00

Carton, L & M Long Lights Complimentary Cigarettes, Contents 25.00
Carton, Stride Menthol Cigarettes, Contents 25.00
Case, Blatz Beer, Wooden, Hinged Lid 35.00
Case, Good Old Hoosier Beer, S. Bend Brewing, Wooden, Bottles 55.00
Case, Our Family Tea, Tin Lined, Wooden, Held 40-1/2 Lb. Pkgs. 55.00
Case, William Clarke & Sons, 2 Drawer, Needle, Oak 145.00
Casserole, Moxie, China 75.00
Chair, Piedmont Cigarette, Folding, Porcelain Insert, 32 In. 93.00
Chair, Seal Plug Cut, Embossed, Wooden, Folding, 37 In. 99.00
    ADVERTISING, CHANGE RECEIVER, see also Advertising, Tip Tray
Change Receiver, Old Rippy Whiskey, Copper 35.00
Charm, Good Luck, Orange Crush, 1930s 35.00
Charm, Roi-Tan Cigars, Car 35.00
Charm, Speedy Alka Seltzer, Sterling 55.00
Cigar Box, Hambone 110.00
Cigar Cutter, Bone, Soligen 18.00
Cigar Cutter, Harvard, Colorful, Key Wind 290.00
Cigar Cutter, Swift 30.00
Cigar Cutter, Yankee 300.00
Cleanser, Babbitt's Cleanser, Paper, Tin, 4 In. 4.00
Cleanser, Old Dutch, Paper, Tin Top & Bottom, 5 In. 12.00
    ADVERTISING, CLOCK, see Clock
Cloth, 1905 Calendar, Bemis Bag Co., Sporting Dogs 140.00
Coaster, Ruppert Beer, Tin, Set 22.00
    ADVERTISING, COFFEE GRINDER, see Coffee Grinder
Compote, Sunkist, Pink, Depression Glass, 12 In. 88.00
Cookie Sheet, Betty Crocker Bisquick, Tin 6.50
Cooler, Bottle, Derby Hat, Gordon's Gin 20.00
Cooler, Curtis & Moore's Orangeade 65.00
Cooler, Schlitz, 1950s 25.00
Corkscrew, Anheuser-Busch, Eagle Facing Leaf, Looks At Label 53.00
Corkscrew, Drink Lemp, St. Louis, Bullet Shape, Metal 25.00
Crate, Blatz Beer, Wooden, 12 x 18 x 11 In. 30.00
Crate, Taggarts Bread, Wooden, Worn Green Paint 18.00
Creamer, Dolly Madison Dairy, Red Cameo 1 Side, 1 3/4 In. 12.00
Creamer, F. B. B. Co., Dairy, Embossed, 2 Oz., 2 1/2 In. 10.00
Creamer, Kellogg's Cereal 20.00
Creamer, Lone Oak Farm, Embossed 2 Oz., 2 3/8 In. 10.00
Creamer, Marten's Dairy, Reddish Brown, 1 15/16 In. 14.00
Creamer, Post Cereal, Measured 20.00
Creamer, Schmidt's Guernsey, Orange, Beaver Dam, Wis., 2 1/4 In. 21.00
Crock, Heinz's Apple Butter, Label 90.00
Crock, Heinz's Gurkin Sweet Mixed Pickles, 12 In. 85.00
Crumber Set, Mendalia Flour, 2 Piece 65.00
Cup, Chock Full 'O Nuts Coffee, Says Heavenly Coffee, In Cloud 20.00
Cup, Dunkin' Donuts Coffee, Donut Boy Picture 25.00
Cup, Measuring, Kellogg's, Green Glass, 3 Spouts 17.00
Cup, Measuring, Kellogg's, Pink Glass, 3 Spouts 22.00
Cutout, Circus, Nehi, 1929 .... 100.00
Decal, Window, Orange Crush, 1943, Large, Set of 3 .... 150.00
Dish, Schraft's Chocolates 22.00
Dispenser, Buckeye Root Beer Syrup 695.00
Dispenser, Buckeye Root Beer, Cola Nut & Mug, c.1915 .... 1870.00
Dispenser, Buckeye Root Beer, Dancing Devils ....875.00 To 1265.00
Dispenser, Cherry Smash, 5 Cent, Glass, Original Pump 2500.00
Dispenser, Cherry Smash, Ruby Glass 400.00
Dispenser, Dixie Cup, Metal 70.00
Dispenser, Dr Pepper 7100.00
Dispenser, Grape Julep, Pump Marked, 14 In. 935.00
Dispenser, Hires Root Beer, No Pump 150.00
Dispenser, Hires Root Beer, Original Pump 192.00
Dispenser, Hires Syrup, Hourglass, Pump ....800.00 To 850.00
Dispenser, Howel's Orange Julep, 5 Cent, 15 In. 990.00

Dispenser, Lash's Syrup, Spigot, Embossed Green Glass Globe 185.00
Dispenser, Malt, Hamilton Beach, Arnold, Green Porcelain Base 450.00
Dispenser, Mission Orange Syrup, Green Glass 175.00
Dispenser, Mission Real Fruit, Green Glass 175.00
Dispenser, Nesbitt's Hot Chocolate, Frosted Glass, 18 In. 220.00
Dispenser, Oak Barrel Soda Fountain, Richardson Lemon–Lime 198.00
Dispenser, Orange Crush, Painted Crushie, Glass, Chrome, 30 In. 1150.00
Dispenser, Richardson Root Beer, Barrel, Claw Feet 200.00
Dispenser, Ward's Lime Crush ....975.00 To 1278.00
Dispenser, Ward's Orange Crush, Large 550.00
Dispenser, Zig–Zig Cigarette, Papers, Tin Litho, 6 In. 35.00
Dispenser, Zipp Root Beer, Barrel Shape 1875.00
Display Cabinet, Dr. Scholl's, Counter Top, Glass Front 225.00
Display Case, Chicklets Gum Box, Glass Litho, 10 In. 140.00
Display Case, Conklin Pen, Counter Top 400.00
Display Case, Dr. Jackson's Remedies, Wood, 26 In. 395.00
Display Case, Eveready Battery, Battery–Shaped Top, Tin 55.00
Display Case, Freihoffers Quality Cakes, Tin Litho, 22 In. 225.00
Display Case, Genco Razor, With 8 Razors, Tin Litho, 14 In. 245.00
Display Case, Priwleys, California Fruit & Pepsin Gum, Etched 500.00
Display Case, Royal Coffee, Painted Wood, Glass Front, 29 In. 77.00
Display Case, Scheaffer Lead & Pen Points 65.00
Display Case, Sidewell Collars, 14 Display Collars, Oak, 47 In. 745.00
Display Model, China Airlines, Boeing 40.00
Display Rack, Campbell Soups, Metal, 1930s, 22 x 18 In. 75.00
Display Rack, St. Joseph's Aspirin, Tin, 12 Cent, 7 In. 165.00
Display, Auto Lite Spark Plugs 200.00
Display, Boye Needles, Shuttles, Bobbins, Tin Litho, 16 In. 160.00
Display, Cashmere Bouquet, Die–Cut Tin 2970.00
Display, Doll Dealer, Googly–Eyed Doll Peeking Out, 3 x 4 In. 225.00
Display, Dr Pepper, Santa, Vinyl Face, 30 In. 64.00
Display, Eveready Flashlight 200.00
Display, Feen–A–Mint Laxative, Mirror 295.00
Display, Geo. Washington Cut Plug, Cardboard, 11 x 26 In. 45.00
Display, Greyhound Bus, Stand–Up, Die–Cut, 1940s, 19 In. 125.00
Display, James Dean Shady Character Sunglasses, Figural 100.00
Display, LaBoobs, Painted, Wooden, Easel Back, France, 20 In. 195.00
Display, Lincoln Distilling Co., Inc., Cardboard, 19 In. 355.00
Display, Mazda Light Bulb, Fan Shape, Maxfield Parrish, Lighted 645.00
Display, Mechanical, Gem Damaskene Razor, Poem, 1910 .... 3575.00
Display, Poll Parrot Shoes, Tin 12.00
Display, Sinclair, Dino Dealer, Plastic, Blow–Up, 1930s, 30 In. 40.00
Display, Sir Walter Raleigh, Dummy Can, Picture of Raleigh 45.00
Door Pull, Occident Flour, Brass 85.00
Door Pull, Texaco, Figural, Logo, Double, Plastic, 1960s 45.00
Door Push, Foot, Schultze Shoemakers, Brass, 1900s, 3 x 10 In. 77.00
Door Push, Hires Root Beer 60.00
Door Push, Kellam's Teas & Coffees 50.00
Door Push, Majors Cement, Porcelain 225.00
Door Push, Orange Crush 75.00
Door Push, Perry's Quality Beverages, Tin 45.00
Door Push, Pictures Bottle, 5–Color, 1940s, 4 x 10 In. 13.00
Door Push, Red Fox Beverages, 1950s, 4 x 13 1/2 In. 14.00
Door Push, Salada Tea 70.00
Door Push, Salada Tea, Porcelain 80.00
Door Push, Sweetheart Flour, Porcelain 85.00
Door Push, Tru–Ade Orange Drink 45.00
Door Push, Vicks Cough Drops 85.00
Door Push, With Bottle, Canada Dry 45.00
Dustpan, Ryger's Produce & Hatchery, Chicks, Metal, Long Handle 42.00
Earrings, Wendy's, Where's The Beef 10.00
Egg Holder, Milk Glass, Williams Poultry Food, Metal, 5 In. 195.00
Egg Separator, Buffalo Times 12.50

ADVERTISING, FAN, see Fan, Advertising

Figure, Baker's, La Belle Chocolatiere Lady, Metal, 3 In.	125.00
Figure, Bear, Coveralls, Int'l. Harvester, 1944, Iron, 5 In.	85.00
Figure, Beefeater Gin, Composition, Wood Base, 17 In.	49.00
Figure, Bottle, Display, Carter's Ink, Stoneware	1200.00
Figure, Camel, Crane & Breed Casket Co., Cast Iron, 1 1/2 In.	70.00
Figure, Child, Molded Shoes, Movable Arms, 1914, 39 In.	475.00
Figure, Columbia All, Black Boy, Cigar, Striker, Majolica, 7 In.	310.00
Figure, Dog, Chief Watta Pop, Plaster, Headdress of Lollipops	495.00
Figure, Dog, Hush Puppy	6.00
Figure, Dog, Nipper, RCA, Glass, Miniature	15.00
Figure, Dog, Nipper, RCA, Papier–Mache, 36 In.	1000.00
Figure, Dr. Miles Heart Cure, Cardboard, c.1902, 22 In.	250.00
Figure, Drum Major, General Electric, Wooden, Jointed, 18 In.	990.00
Figure, Duquesne Beer	40.00
Figure, Hamm's Bear, By Campfire, Fish In Pan	49.00
Figure, Horse, Carved, Black Paint, Jos. Cobb & Son, 72 x 64 In.	1000.00
Figure, Horse, Columbia Gall Salve, Chalkware, 14 x 16 In.	425.00
Figure, Ice Cream Cone, Lyons' Pola Maid Ice Cream, 4 Ft.	2500.00
Figure, Kessler, Yellow, Red Robe, Plaster, 12 In.	10.00
Figure, Marilyn Monroe, Niagara, Royal Orleans	175.00
Figure, Mennen, Hard Hat Man	15.00
Figure, Michelin Tires, Plaster Figure, 33 In.	9750.00
Figure, Mortar & Pestle, Electric Motor, Revolves, 32 In.	357.00
Figure, Old Dutch Beer, Plaster, 14 In.	120.00
Figure, Pabst Blue Ribbon, White Metal, Painted, 15 In.	72.00
Figure, Pig, Best Pig Vorceps, Reimers, Davenport, Glass, 7 In.	225.00
Figure, Pug Dog, Pug Cigars, 5 Cent, Plaster, 16 In.	775.00
Figure, Reddy Kilowatt, Die Cut, Orange Red & Ivory, 6 In.	25.00
Figure, Stephenson Underwear, Figure, Tin, 35 1/2 In.	465.00
Figure, Tiger, Used On Esso Station's Roof, Large	247.50
Figure, William Penn, Cigar Box, Standing, Papier–Mache, 4 Ft.	605.00
Figure, Wilton Armetale	30.00
Figure, Wizard of O's, Campbell Soup, 7 In.	14.50
Figure, Woman, Children, Yardleys, Lavender, Chalkware, 14 In.	345.00
Flashlight, 7–Up Bottle Shape	35.00
Glass, Bromo–Seltzer, Cobalt Blue	35.00
Globe, Double Sided, Nation Bohemian, National Beer, 16 In.	380.00
Glove Stretcher, Woman's, Pownes	48.00
Goblet, Duz Soap, Amber	6.00
Hanger, For Coal Shovel, Coal Company, Tin, Wall, 1920s	69.00
Harness, Horse, Single, Brass Tags, Sunshine Biscuits	135.00
Hat Stand, Selz Shoe Store Crest, Victorian Style	85.00
Helmet, Child's, Red Goose	45.00
Hike–O–Meter, Wheaties	30.00
Holder, Cigar Box, Glass Lid, Brass Hinges	55.00
Hotplate, Nestle's Hot Chocolate, Standing Metal Sign, 12 In.	95.00
Humidor, Briggs Smoking Tobacco, Barrel Shape, Wooden	20.00
Humidor, Hayner Cigars, Dayton, Ohio	95.00
Ice Pick, Winchester	55.00 To 110.00
Ice Tongs, New State Ice Co.	35.00
Ice Tongs, Norman Ice & Fuel Co.	35.00
Jar, Bagdad Tobacco, China, Cover	600.00
Jar, Barrel Shape, Hormel Pig's Knuckles, Bail Handle	22.00
Jar, Borden's Malted Milk	250.00
Jar, Dairymaid Cream Caramel Toffee, Label On Clear Glass	27.50
Jar, Elephant Peanuts, Salted, Embossed On Side	495.00
Jar, Globe Tobacco, Barrel, Amber, Wooden Bail, Oat. 1882, 9 In.	60.00
Jar, Gum, Dis–Me, Kis–Me Gum Co., 9 1/2 In.	45.00
Jar, Heinz, Apple Butter, Stoneware, Label, Amethyst Glass Lid	425.00
Jar, Kis–Me Gum, Louisville, Ky.	45.00
Jar, Kis–Me Gum, Paper Label	125.00
Jar, Lance Cracker, Metal Top	50.00

Jar, Squirrel Brand Salted Nuts, Glass, Clear, 13 In. 110.00
Jar, W & S Cough Drops, Mascotte Pattern On Base & Lid 400.00
Jar, Whiz Auto Body Polish, Car & Pixies, 1 Pt. 50.00
Kaleidoscope, Campbell's Soup Can 25.00
Kit, Fingernail File, Michigan Bell Telephone, Paper, 1940s 13.00
Kite, Hagan Ice Cream, Pat. April 24, 1923 .... 25.00
Knife, Demand Tuf Nut Work Clothes, Barlow, Pocket 45.00
Knife, King Oscar Sardines, Pocket 20.00
Label, American Derby Cigar, Horse Race, Jockey, 1892 .... 30.00
Label, Arctic Hero, Cigar Box, Naval Commander & Arctic Scenes 20.00
Label, Belle of Virginia, Cigar Box, Lady With Fan 28.00
Label, Bluette Cigar, Young Woman, Light Blue Hues 7.00
Label, Buckingham Pear, Cowboy Rides Pig, 1920s, 8 x 11 In. 5.00
Label, Bumblebee Cherries, Bees On Clover, 1910, 4 x 13 1/2 In. ..../ 3.00
Label, Camel, Arab On Camel In Desert, Cigar 7.50
Label, Chief Okee Cigar, Indian Chief, 1912 .... 30.00
Label, Duke of Navarre Cigar, Bust, Medieval Battle, 1907 .... 4.00
Label, First Banner Cigar, Washington, Large 7.50
Label, Golden Flower Cigar 4.00
Label, Jackie Boy Apples, Sailor Kid, 1925, 9 x 10 In. 3.00
Label, Kentucky Cardinal Apples, 1918 .... 16.00
Label, La Paledo Cigar, Horses Flank Eagle 2.00
Label, Liberty Bond Cigar, Promoting American Bones 6.00
Label, Miss Wisconsin, 1937, 4 Piece 20.00
Label, Nightingale Apples, Bird & Apples, 1910, 7 x 10 In. 9.00
Label, Old Black Joe Gin, Black Man, Jug, 1930s, 3 1/2 x 4 In. 3.00
Label, Overland Cigar, Streamliner Train & Old Pre–1890 Train 7.50
Label, Quabaug Water, Indian Chief, 1890s, 9 x 12 In. 5.00
Label, Red Dancer Cigar, 1920s Woman, Red Turban 6.00
Label, Red Rose Raisin, 1890, 8 1/2 x 13 In. 20.00
Label, Star of Beauty Cigar, Woman's Bust, Blue Borders 8.00
Label, Westwood Tomatoes, Old Time Golfer, 1920s, 4 x 11 In. 4.00
Label, Wide Awake Cigar, Uncle Sam, Eagle, c.1900, 6 x 10 In. 8.00
Label, Wm. Penn Cigar, White Letters 12.00
Label, Woodrow Wilson Cigar, Bust of President 9.00
Label, Ziegler's Chocolate Giant Bars, Milwaukee, 1920, 14 In. 7.50
Lamp, Hanging, National Cigar, Mica 4400.00
Lamp, Schmidt Beer, Canvas Tepee 150.00
Lighter, Hamm's Beer, Bear On Log 25.00
ADVERTISING, LUNCH BOX, see Lunch Box
Manicure Kit, Cutex, Hinged Lid, Tin, 1920s 13.00
Marbles In Mesh Sock, Weather–Bird Shoes 7.00
Mask, Circus, Muffets, Shredded Wheat Cereal, 1930–40, 16 Piece 75.00
Mask, Indian, Drink Herbo, Made From Indian Herbs, Colorful 75.00
Mask, Pinocchio, Gillette, Envelope, 1939, Pair 30.00
Match Holder, Diamond, Black Family Scene, Gas Light Cover, Tin 300.00
Match Safe, Drink E. Robinsons Pilsener Lager Beer, 1892 .... 51.00
Match Safe, Val. Blatz Brewing Co., Trademark On Reverse 35.00
Matchbook Holder, Abe Burnett & Co., 1 1/2 x 2 1/4 In. 50.00
Matchsafe, Schiltz 55.00
Menu Board, 7–Up, Tin, 1940s 65.00
Menu Board, Alka Seltzer, Tin, Wooden Framed, Drug Store 175.00
Menu Board, Butter Nut Bread, Fiberboard, Diecut Loaf Top 140.00

Pocket mirrors range in size from 1 1/2 to 5 inches in diameter.
Most of these mirrors were given away as advertising promotions.

Mirror, Angelus Marshmallows, Cherubs, Pocket ....50.00 To 100.00
Mirror, Aunt Jemima Breakfast Club, Pocket 35.00
Mirror, Bell Roasted Coffee, Picture of Bell, Pocket, 2 In. 20.00
Mirror, Big Jo Flour, Pocket, 2 In. 18.00
Mirror, Buckingham Bros. Cigars, Convex Spheres, 12 In. 235.00
Mirror, Capital Building, St. Paul, Minn., Pocket 15.00
Mirror, Carmen Complexion Powder, Pocket 38.00

Mirror, Cascarets Laxative, Angel, Celluloid, 2 In. .... 42.00 To 65.00
Mirror, Compass, Japan, Pocket 15.00
Mirror, Crane Whiskey, Pocket 60.00
Mirror, Duffy's Malt Whiskey, Pocket, 2 3/4 In. 15.00
Mirror, Farm Machinery, Political, North Dakota, Oval, Pocket 70.00
Mirror, Globe Casket Mfg., Round, Pocket 45.00
Mirror, Greenwood's Pianos, Meek Co., Pocket 35.00
Mirror, Holeproof Hosiery, Pocket, 2 1/2 In. 15.00
Mirror, Horlick's Malted Milk, Maid With Cow, Celluloid, 2 In. 125.00
Mirror, Huyler's Candy, Beautiful Woman, Pocket 48.00
Mirror, Mascot Cut Tobacco, Pocket, 2 In. .... 11.00 To 48.00
Mirror, Natures Remedy, Pocket 25.00
Mirror, Nebraska Telephone Co., Pocket, 1 3/4 In. 50.00
Mirror, Office Outfitters, Paperweight, Pocket, 3 1/2 In. 20.00
Mirror, Old Reliable Coffee, Hand 75.00
Mirror, Paperweight, Artistic Weaving Co., New York, 1939 .... 25.00
Mirror, Parry Manufacturing Co., Indianapolis, Oval, Pocket 165.00
Mirror, Queen Quality Shoes, Pocket 25.00
Mirror, Roberts & Co., Utica, Hand, 1917, Miniature 30.00
Mirror, Standard Remington, Typewriter, Pocket, 3 1/2 In. 65.00
Mirror, Star Coffee, Round, Pocket 22.00
Mirror, Starrett Tools, Pocket 18.00
Mirror, Studebaker Vehicle Works, South Bend, Ind., Pocket 195.00
Mirror, Traveler's Insurance, Railroad Men's Reliance, Pocket 85.00
Mirror, Weingarten 5 Cent Cigars, Pocket .... 35.00 To 40.00
Mirror, Wisconsin Funeral Convention, Pocket, 1911 .... 25.00
Mirror, Worth Blend Coffee, Vinnedge Co., Hotels, Cafes, Pocket 55.00
Mold, Brown's Mule Tobacco 18.00
Mold, Mother's Oats, Aluminum, Ring Type 46.00
Mug, A & W Root Beer, Embossed, 3 1/4 In. 2.00
Mug, A & W Root Beer, Tall 3.00
Mug, A & W, Arrow Logo, Glass, 3 1/2 In. 10.00
Mug, Augsburger Beer, Logo, Commemorative, 5 3/16 In. 20.00
Mug, Ballantine Beer, Sing Along, 5 1/4 In. 15.00
Mug, Budweiser Beer, 1980 .... 175.00
Mug, Budweiser Beer, Sun Valley, Wade, Large 25.00
Mug, Clipper, The Light Dark Beer, Blue Logo, 5 1/16 In. 5.50
Mug, Coors Herman, Joseph Black, Irish Creme 15.00
Mug, Coors, State Fair, 1939 .... 25.00
Mug, Culmbacher Beer, East St. Louis 135.00
Mug, Dad's, Have A Dad's Black Cow, Red & Yellow, 5 In. 6.00
Mug, Dog & Suds, Glass 8.00
Mug, Dove Ginger Ale, Dove Picture, Ornate Handle, Green, Brown 145.00
Mug, Edelweiss Beer, Ceramic, 4 1/2 In. 16.00
Mug, Falstaff Beer, Glass, Embossed Trademark, 7 In. 25.00
Mug, Frostop Root Beer 10.00
Mug, GE Nasa Nimbus Observatory 10.00
Mug, Graf's Beer, Since 1873, 4 3/4 In. 6.00
Mug, Hamm's Beer, Red, Logo, 5 5/8 In. 25.00
Mug, Hershey, World Map, 6 Piece 17.50
Mug, Hires Root Beer, Since 1876, Red & White, 3 1/4 In. 7.00
Mug, Hires Root Beer, Stoneware, Hourglass Shape 22.00
Mug, Manderscheid Co., Sioux City, Iowa, Miniature 48.00
Mug, Moxie, Handle, 5 In. 45.00
Mug, Nathan Dohrmannu Co., San Francisco, Salt Glaze, 3 Handles 100.00
Mug, Nestles Quik, Rabbit 13.00
Mug, Nestles, Around The World, Set of 6 .... 25.00
Mug, Nestles, Etched 10.00
Mug, Old Colony Brewing Co., Boston, Stoneware, Blue, 5 In. 45.00
Mug, Ponderosa, Tin 6.50
Mug, Red Wind, Pre Prohibition 145.00
Mug, Richardson's Root Beer, Ornate Etched Glass 62.00
Mug, Richardson's Root Beer, Rochester, N. Y., 6 5/8 In. 37.00

Advertising, Pitcher,
Dr. Harter's Wild Cherry Bitters, 13 In.

◆◆◆◆◆◆◆◆◆◆◆◆◆◆◆◆◆◆◆◆◆◆◆◆
The best time to buy an antique
is when you see it.
◆◆◆◆◆◆◆◆◆◆◆◆◆◆◆◆◆◆◆◆◆◆◆◆

Mug, Rochester Root Beer, Etched, 6 1/8 In. .... 12.00 To 20.00
Mug, Schlitz Beer, Blue & Gray, Impressed Design, 4 1/2 In. 60.00
Mug, Stewart Root Beer 4.75
Mug, Stroh's Beer, Tall 9.50
Napkin Holder, Lionstone Restaurant, Geneva, N. Y., Metal 15.00
Napkin Holder, Rolling Rock Beer, Mountain Stream Picture 20.00
Needle Dispenser, Sewing Machine, Wood Vials, Boyce Brand 52.00
Night Light, G. E. 15.00
Pack, Tobacco, Happy Jim Chewing Tobacco, 15 Cents, 6 In. 40.00
Pail, Armour Peanut Butter, Nursery Characters 150.00
Pail, Barbour's Peanut Butter, Tin 105.00
Pail, Bluehill Coffee, Tin Lithograph, 10 1/2 In. 105.00
Pail, Buffalo Brand Peanut Butter, Tin Lithograph, 4 In. 100.00
Pail, Clark's Peanut Butter, Canadian, Graphics, 8 1/2 In. 285.00
Pail, Climax Peanut Butter, 1 Lb. .... 65.00 To 75.00
Pail, Esskay Pure Lard, Wire Handle, Tin Lithograph, 5 In. 38.00
Pail, Jack & Jill Peanut Butter, Gold, Black, Canadian, 5 Lb. 50.00
Pail, Jack & Jill Peanut Butter, Red, White, Blue, Canadian 120.00
Pail, Lovell & Covel Historical Candy 110.00
Pail, Luzianne Coffee, Black Mammy Picture 65.00
Pail, Minneopa Peanut Butter, Indian Scenes 420.00
Pail, Monarch Teenie Weenie Peanut Butter .... 145.00 To 250.00
Pail, Monarch Teenie Weenie Popcorn 350.00
Pail, Morris Supreme Peanut Butter, Graphics, 8 1/2 In. 165.00
Pail, Mrs. Tucker's Shortening, Tin Lithograph, 7 In. 45.00
Pail, Niagara Peanut Butter, Kids Playing 285.00
Pail, Nigger Hair Tobacco, Tin Lithograph, 6 1/2 In. .... 275.00 To 385.00
Pail, Pedro Tobacco, Playing Card Design 65.00
Pail, Prairie Queen Baking Powder, Tin 95.00
Pail, Pure Lard 25.00
Pail, Shedd's Peanut Butter, 5 Lb. 15.00
Pail, Southern Rose Shortening, Tin 20.00

◆◆

A drawer that is stuck can be helped by heat. Remove any nearby
drawers, then aim a blow dryer set on medium at the wood. Once
the drawer is opened, rub the runners with soap or a candle.

◆◆

Pail, Sunbeam Peanut Butter, Children At The Beach 550.00
Pail, Swift's Lard, Silverleaf Brand, 8 Lb. 30.00
Pail, Swift's Peanut Butter, Wizard of Oz 35.00
Pail, Toyland Peanut Butter, Tin, 1 Lb. 110.00
Pail, White Swan Peanut Butter, 1 Lb. 100.00
Pail, Yankee Peanut Butter 125.00
Pancake Turner, Rumford Baking Powder, Green Wooden Handle 13.00
Patch, Ask For Walter's Beer, Embroidered, Large 25.00
Pen Dispenser, Budweiser, White, Plastic, 6 1/2 x 3 1/2 In. 15.00
Pencil, Reddy Kilowatt 10.00
Pencil, Regal Pale Beer, With 1951 Yearly Calendar 15.00
Pin, Elsie, Borden's, Plastic 22.00
Pin, Kellogg's, Little Joe Character, 1947 .... 8.00
Pin, Miller High Life, Celluloid, Die Cut, Pin Back, 1905 .... 75.00
Pin, Pickle, Heinz, Green Plastic 8.00
Pin, Vote For Phillip Morris, With Johnnie, Pinback 23.00
Pitcher, A & W Root Beer, Orange, White & Brown Bear, 8 1/8 In. 22.00
Pitcher, Champale Beer, Red On White, 10 1/2 In. 15.00
Pitcher, Dr. Harter's Wild Cherry Bitters, 13 In. ....*Illus* 325.00
Pitcher, Heilman's Special Export Beer, Red, 9 1/8 In. 9.50
Pitcher, Miller Beer, Nasty Havit Pub, Logo On Side, 6 7/8 In. 12.00
Pitcher, Pabst Blue Ribbon Beer, Blue, 9 1/8 In. 70.00
Plate, General Telephone, 9 1/2 In. 35.00
Plate, Mobil Oil, Logo, 7 In. 35.00
Plate, Pioneer Flour Mill, San Antonio 45.00
Plate, Remington, Smoke Signal 30.00
Platter, Horn & Hardart Baking Co., Oval, 1920s, 8 1/2 x 6 In. 20.00
Pouch, Climax Plug Tobacco 22.00
Pouch, Hambone Tobacco, Full 198.00
Punch Set, Old Crown, Gold Trim, 10 Cups, Ladle 150.00
Punchboard, Old Gold, Camel, Penny Cigarettes, Unpunched 35.00
Rack, Blu "J" Brooms, Merkle Broom Co. 50.00
Rack, Display, Brach's Candy Shop, Tin 30.00
Rack, Prince Albert, Wall, Wire 45.00
Rattle, Baby's, Heinz 57 .... 15.00
Rolling Machine, Bugler Tobacco, Box 25.00
Ruler, Autoline, Robosoco Oils, Folding, Celluloid, 1910, 12 In. 25.00
Ruler, NuGrape, Wooden, 12 In. 10.00
Sack, Bull Durham Tobacco, Roll Your Own, Yellow Tie String 17.75
    ADVERTISING, SALT & PEPPER, see Salt & Pepper
    ADVERTISING, SCALE, see Scale
School Multiplier, Rex Bitters, Chicago, 4 3/4 In. ....*Illus* 90.00
Scoop, Forest City Bakery, Tin 12.00
Sewing, Thimble, Borden's, Metal 8.50
Shade, Fulton's Ice Cream Parlor, Leaded Glass 550.00
Shaker, Horlicks, Lum & Abner 35.00
Shaker, Ovaltine, Aluminun 10.00
Shaker, Ovaltine, Plastic 15.00
Shoehorn, Florsheim Shoe 50.00
Shoehorn, Kirn Beer, 19 In. 15.00
Shoehorn, Long Wear Shoes 70.00
Shoehorn, Shinola 70.00
Shoes, Bob Smart Shoes For Young Men, Salesman's Sample, Box 50.00
Shot Glass, Old Fitzgerald Straight Bourbon, 2 3/8 In. 4.00
Shot Glass, Playbow, Key Girl Center, 2 15/16 In. 3.50
Sign, A Moxie Girl, Moxie Nerve Food, Tin Lithograph, 31 In. 4650.00
Sign, A. M. McGregor, Wooden Horseshoe, 45 x 36 In. 750.00
Sign, Acme Motor Finishes, Tin, 12 x 14 In. 525.00
Sign, Advance Thresher Co., Tin, Self–Framed, 1900, 18 x 26 In. 565.00
Sign, Akron Brewing Co., Building, Decal On Wood, 36 x 24 In. 137.50
Sign, Amoco, Double–Sided, Porcelain, 17 x 20 In. 375.00
Sign, Anheuser–Busch, Bevo, Tin, 27 x 13 In. .... 170.00 To 225.00
Sign, Anheuser–Busch, Custer's Last Stand, 32 x 36 In. 275.00

Sign, Anheuser–Busch, Malt Nutrine, Tin, 13 1/2 In. 230.00
Sign, Arm & Hammer Birds of America, 1917, 36 x 24 In. 65.00
Sign, Armour's Light House Family Soap, Porcelain, 13 In. 10.00
Sign, Army & Navy Goods, Tin Over Wood, Sailor, 68 In. 1340.00
Sign, Ath–Lo–Pho–Ros Ointment, Stand Up, Cardboard, 28 1/2 In. 185.00
Sign, Atwater Kent Radio, Metal, Glass, 12 In, ... 225.00
Sign, Axes of The World Ar Collins, Cardboard, 10 x 20 In. 45.00
Sign, Back Bay Guide Service, Duck In Center, 19 x 26 1/2 In. 350.00
Sign, Ballantines Brews, Tin Lithograph, Self–Framed, 31 In. 480.00
Sign, Banjo Tobacco, Wooden Frame, 16 In. 240.00
Sign, Barber Shears, Working, Wooden, 11 In. 150.00
Sign, Barber Shop, Painted Tin, Wooden Frame, 18 x 54 In. 235.00
Sign, Bartels Brewing Co., Paper, Framed, 40 x 28 In. 1210.00
Sign, Be Sociable Serve Pepsi, Metal, 8 x 16 In. 45.00
Sign, Beech Nut Gum, Trolley, Frame, 10 3/4 x 20 3/4 In. 75.00
Sign, Behrs Varnish, Black & White, Tin, 24 x 18 In. 27.50
Sign, Berry Bros. Lion Oil, Log Cabin, Wooden, 21 x 12 x 10 In. 245.00
Sign, Beymer Bauman White Lead Paint, Dutch Boy, 20 x 14 In. 4400.00
Sign, Big Kick Scrap, Diecut, Cardboard, 1940s, 8 x 12 In. 5.00

Advertising, School Multiplier, Rex Bitters,
Chicago, 4 3/4 In.

◆◆◆◆◆◆◆◆◆◆◆◆◆◆◆◆◆◆◆◆◆◆◆

Any lithographed can with a picture is of more value to the collector than a lithographed can with just names. Any paper–labeled can that can be dated before 1875 is rare. Any ad that pictures an American flag or a Black has added value. Known brand names are also of greater value.

◆◆◆◆◆◆◆◆◆◆◆◆◆◆◆◆◆◆◆◆◆◆◆

Advertising, Sign, Brown's Iron Bitters, Girl,
Paper, 14 7/8 In.

Advertising, Sign, Coles Peruvian,
Enamel On Metal, 6 x 16 In.

Sign, Blatz, Art Deco, Red, Blue, White, Glass, Round, 10 1/2 In. 130.00
Sign, Blatz, Lighted, Reverse On Glass, 13 x 9 In. 25.00
Sign, Blue Beason Coal, Embossed Tin, 20 x 13 1/2 In. 495.00
Sign, Blue Boar Tobacco, Stand–Up, Tin Lithograph, 14 In. 250.00
Sign, Blue Jay Brooms, Tin, Framed, 11 x 15 In. 155.00
Sign, Boot Trade, Painted, Wooden, 17 In. 230.00
Sign, Boot, 3–D, Black Paint, c.1900, 21 In. 2250.00
Sign, Boschee's German Syrup, Tin Litho, Wood Frame, 19 1/2 In. 2200.00
Sign, Brandreth Pills, Wood Frame, 34 In. 245.00
Sign, Breining's Pure Linseed Oil, Porcelain, 12 x 20 In. 500.00
Sign, Brooke Bond Tea, Porcelain On Steel, 4 x 2 Ft. 15.00
Sign, Brown's Iron Bitters, Girl, Paper, 14 7/8 In. ....*Illus* 400.00
Sign, Buckeye Beer, American Artworks, Tin Lithograph, 20 In. 93.00
Sign, Budweiser, Attack On Overland Stage, Cardboard, 30 In. 33.00
Sign, Bull Durham, Blacks Kissing Through Umbrella, 35 In. 1800.00
Sign, Bull Durham, Package, Lithograph On Cardboard, 35 In. 445.00
Sign, Bull Durham, Relief Figures, Tin, 11 1/2 x 16 In. 380.00
Sign, Bull Durham, Tin, Figures In Relief, 11 x 16 In. 380.00
Sign, Buster Brown & Tige, Buster In Shoe, Tige Pulling, 40 In. 5500.00
Sign, Butcher Boy, Milk Glass, Maroon Ground, White Letters 165.00
Sign, Cadillac Service, Double–Sided, Porcelain, 42 In. 1495.00
Sign, Cadillac, Porcelain, 20 In. 525.00
Sign, Campbells Soup, Curved Porcelain 3400.00
Sign, Campbells Vegetable Soup, Porcelain, 22 x 14 In. 1500.00
Sign, Cannon Ball Cigar, Indian Maiden, Tin, 11 1/2 x 14 In. 285.00
Sign, Cannon Ball Cigar, Tin Lithograph, Self–Framed, 14 In. 440.00
Sign, Cetacolor Dye, Paper On Canvas, 36 x 24 In. 185.00
Sign, Cherry Cola, Perry's Quality Beverages, Tin, 14 x 20 In. 40.00
Sign, Chesterfield Cigarettes, Bob Hope, 1930s, 20 x 43 In. 75.00
Sign, Chew Rose Leaf Tobacco, Ivory, Majolica, Round, 9 In. 325.00
Sign, Chickering & Sons Piano Fortes, Reverse Painted, 42 In. 825.00
Sign, Cigar, Call Again, A Welcome Smoke, Tin, 1930s, 12 x 36 In. 38.00
Sign, Cliquot Club, 2–Sided, Cardboard, 1930s, 2 1/4 x 7 In. 3.00
Sign, Coburgen Beer, Maiden, Painted Tin, 20 x 16 In. 110.00
Sign, Coles Peruvian, Enamel On Metal, 6 x 16 In. ....*Illus* 350.00
Sign, Colts Patent Fire Arms Mfg. Co., Schoonover, 32 x 19 In. 440.00
Sign, Cook's Beer, 2–Sided Fence, 1940s, 14 x 28 In. 22.00
Sign, Cream of Wheat, World's Fare, Brewer, 1923, 8 x 11 1/2 In. 27.50
Sign, Cudahy's Ham, Tin, Late 1800s, 31 3/4 x 25 1/2 In. 715.00
Sign, Cuesta, Rey & Co., Tin Lithograph, Gesso Frame, 27 In. 110.00
Sign, D. Horsely Lawyer, Stenographer–Notary, Wood, 12 x 36 In. 135.00
Sign, Dan Patch Rye, Reverse On Glass, 34 x 24 In. 3850.00
Sign, Danville Stove Works, Tin Lithograph, 28 In. 525.00
Sign, DeLaval, Porcelain, Original Paper, 12 x 16 In. 90.00
Sign, Denby Cigars, Counter, Cardboard, 5 1/2 x 10 1/2 In. 65.00
Sign, Dentyne Chewing Gum, Porcelain, 9 In. 120.00
Sign, Diamond Dye, Embossed Tin Lithograph, Wood Frame, 30 In. 320.00
Sign, Dispenser, Cut Chewing Tobacco, Tin Lithograph, 10 1/2 In 55.00
Sign, Doctor Stork, Malt Nutrine, Tin Lithograph, 12 1/2 In. 70.00
Sign, Dolly Madison Cigars, Tin, 6 x 20 In. 20.00
Sign, Dr Pepper, Bottle & Cock, Tin, 1940s 140.00
Sign, Dr Pepper, Victorian Gentleman, Cardboard Lithograph 4640.00
Sign, Dr. Hands Remedies, Print, Wood Frame, 22 In. 685.00
Sign, Dr. P. Halls Remedy, 42 In. 160.00
Sign, Dr. P. Halls Remedy, Print, Cardboard, Framed, 43 In. 140.00
Sign, Dr. Seigert's Angostura Bitters, Framed, 30 In. 525.00
Sign, Dr. Swett's Root Beer, Tin, 56 1/2 x 32 In. 35.00
Sign, Dr. Swetts Root Beer, 5 Cents, 2–Sided, Die Cut Tin, 6 In. 245.00
Sign, Dr. D. Jaynes, Reverse On Glass, 12 1/2 x 14 In. ....*Illus* 850.00
Sign, Dr. H. A. Stribley, Gold Letters, Double Sided, 12 x 27 In. 425.00
Sign, Dr. Laneville–Chiropractor, Appointment Only, 24 In. 145.00
Sign, Drink Hires In Bottles, Metal, 1920s, 5 x 14 In. 160.00
Sign, Drug Store Est'b 1842, 2 Sides, Painted Wood, 72 In. 700.00

Sign, Drugs, White & Sanded Black, Signed Crown, 11 x 49 In. 225.00
Sign, Dub–L–Valu Root Beer, Tin, 1930s, 11 x 18 In. 15.00
Sign, Dupont Gunpowder, Tin, Paper Label, 6 In. 35.00
Sign, E. L. Spellman & Co., Tin, Frame, 19 1/2 x 27 3/4 In. 1980.00
Sign, Ed Dot Cigar, Cigar Shape, Full Color, 1930s, 34 x 6 In. 18.00
Sign, Empire Soap, Black Children, 1887, 26 1/2 x 19 In. 600.00
Sign, Engesser Brewing & Malting Co., Tin, 27 x 20 In. 4675.00
Sign, Exchange Brewery, Auld Lang Syne, Celluloid, 14 x 11 In. 285.00
Sign, Exide Batteries, Figural, Tin, 34 x 22 In. 345.00
Sign, Fairy Soap, Double–Sided, Metal, 18 x 12 1/4 In. 7150.00
Sign, Fairy Soap, Framed Print, N. K. Fairbank & Co. 21 In. 445.00
Sign, Fairy Soap, Girl, Box of Soap, Paper Lithograph, 22 In. 165.00
Sign, Falstaff Beer, Tin Lithograph, 22 1/2 x 30 1/2 In. 3520.00
Sign, Fatima Turkish Blend Cigarettes, Metal, Oval, 22 x 16 In. 650.00
Sign, Firestone, Double–Sided, Porcelain, 14 x 19 In. 495.00
Sign, Fish, Chew Black Bass Navy, Tin Lithograph, 20 In. 330.00
Sign, Ford Genuine Parts, Porcelain, Oval, 36 In. 250.00
Sign, Fordson Tractors, Painted Tin, 12 x 36 In. 425.00
Sign, Fox Head Beer, Porcelain, 26 x 40 In. 175.00
Sign, Fresh Eggs, Green & Black On White, Wooden, 12 x 26 In. 125.00
Sign, Friedman & Keiler, Brook Hill, Dog, Tin, 39 x 28 1/2 In. 525.00
Sign, Gander Cooking & Salad Oil, Tin Lithograph, 19 In. 565.00
Sign, Garden Tea Room, Scalloped, Wooden, 18 1/2 x 30 1/2 In. 275.00
Sign, Garfield Tea, Old Gentleman, Tin, 26 1/2 x 18 3/4 In. 935.00
Sign, Garrett Wine, Uncle Sam & Miss Liberty, Tin, 18 x 26 In. 7425.00
Sign, GE TV Tubes, Tin, Blue, 11 x 9 In. 25.00
Sign, Genesse Lager Beer, Tin Lithograph, 22 x 14 In. 300.00
Sign, Gerber Baby, Color, 3–D, Framed, 9 x 11 In. 45.00
Sign, Giant Grip Shoes & Calks, Embossed Tin, 13 1/2 x 20 In. 100.00
Sign, Gluek Beer, Vitrolight, Curved, 16 x 23 In. 775.00
Sign, Goodrich Tires, Porcelain, Flange, 2 Sides, 1930s, 24 In. 195.00

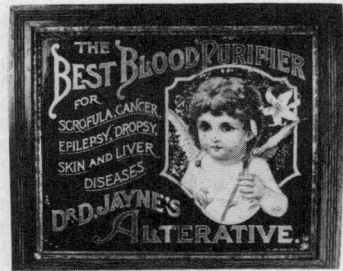

Advertising, Sign, Dr. D. Jaynes,
Reverse On Glass, 12 1/2 x 14 In.

Advertising, Sign, Paine's Celery Compound,
Tin, 14 x 10 In.

Sign, Goodrich, Rubber Footwear, Akron, Oh., 2 Sides, 24 In. Dia. 275.00
Sign, Goodyear, 2 Sides, Porcelain, 24 In. 350.00
Sign, Grape Nuts, Girl, Dog, Framed, Tin, 19 x 24 In. ....665.00 To 1500.00
Sign, Gravel Springs Mineral Water, Tin, 19 x 13 1/4 In. 195.00
Sign, Great American Insurance Co., Tin, Frame, 26 3/4 x 11 In. 65.00
Sign, Green River Whiskey, Tin Lithograph, Black Mule, 24 In. 800.00
Sign, Green River Whiskey, Tin Lithograph, Black, Frame, 42 In. 1750.00
Sign, H. W. Johns, Asbestos Liquid, Blue, Frame, 12 x 46 In. 55.00
Sign, Hamm's Beer, Electric Light, Scene Moves, 31 x 30 In. 100.00
Sign, Hand, The Independent, Carved Wood, Painted, Koch, 44 In. 1200.00
Sign, Hat, Richardson Hats & Caps, Sheet Metal, c.1840 .... 1850.00
Sign, Henry George 5 Cent Cigar, Tin Lithograph, Oval, 15 In. 350.00
Sign, Hercules Powder Co., 17 1/2 x 12 In. 145.00
Sign, Hiawatha Porridge Oats, Cardboard, 10 x 14 In. 150.00
Sign, Hires Improved Root Beer, Paper, 13 1/2 x 16 1/2 In. 2475.00
Sign, Honey Moon Smoking Tobacco, Paper, Framed, 11 x 21 In. 575.00
Sign, Hood's Ice Cream, Tin Lithograph, 22 In. 143.00
Sign, Hoosier, Original Paint, 8 x 66 In. 525.00
Sign, Horseshoe Tobacco, Double–Sided, Porcelain, 1910, 18 In. 110.00
Sign, Hupmobile, Double–Sided, Porcelain, 16 x 30 In. ....495.00 To 895.00
Sign, Husemann's Soda, Black On Yellow, Tin, 1920s, 13 x 19 In. 20.00
Sign, Hustins Beer, Matted & Framed, Oval, Tin 665.00
Sign, I. W. Harper Whiskey, Dog, Indoor Scene, Frame, 17 x 23 In. 495.00
Sign, In The Mood, Dancing Figure, Neon, 56 x 29 1/2 In. 665.00
Sign, Independent Lock Company, Tin Lithograph, 32 In. 44.00
Sign, International Stock Food, 28 1/2 In. 45.00
Sign, J. Estey & Co., Organs, Matted & Framed, 28 x 20 In. 275.00
Sign, J. I. Case Threshing Machine Co., Tin, 13 1/4 x 20 In. 5060.00
Sign, Jos. Doelgert's Sons Lager, Tin Lithograph, 25 1/2 In. 150.00
Sign, Kaiser Approved Service, Frazer, Porcelain, 58 In. 357.50
Sign, Keen Kutter, Tin, 10 x 28 In. ....48.00 To 65.00
Sign, Kendall Oil, Roadside Sign, Wood, Round, 24 In. 285.00
Sign, Kendall, Double–Sided, Porcelain, 24 In. 145.00
Sign, King Midas Flour, Girl In Bonnet, Tin, 1910s, 13 x 39 In. 250.00
Sign, Kis Me Gum, Woman In Yellow, Cardboard, 9 1/2 x 13 In. 72.00
Sign, Knapsack Rye, Reverse Glass, Soldier, Frame, 25 x 18 In. 9900.00
Sign, Lawrence Garrett Cigars, Porcelain, 24 x 32 In. 1450.00
Sign, Lee Overalls, Die Cut, Standup, Cloth Overalls, 8 x 3 In. 9.00
Sign, Lee Work Clothing Dept., Tin, Wooden Frame, 6 In. x 5 Ft. 245.00
Sign, Lily of The Valley Coffee, Lithograph, 6 1/4 In. 82.50
Sign, London Life Cigarettes, Self–Framed, Tin, 1910, 34 In. 1045.00
Sign, Lose–Wiles Nobility Chocolates, Diecut Tin, 30 In. 9075.00
Sign, Martinette, Drink That Refreshes, Tin, 9 x 4 1/2 In. 1.50
Sign, Mason & Hamilin, Tin Lithograph, Wood Frame, 32 In. 1500.00
Sign, Mayo's Plug, Porcelain, 13 In. 330.00
Sign, Mercedes–Benz, Parts, Porcelain, 22 x 30 In. 425.00
Sign, Merchants Gargling Oil, Framed, 36 In. 670.00
Sign, Mobil Gas, Pegasus, Metal, 89 x 70 In. 240.00
Sign, Mobil Oil, Flying Pegasus, Porcelain On Steel, 4 Ft. 150.00
Sign, Mobilene Motor Oil, Porcelain, 16 x 54 In. 185.00
Sign, Moxie, Tin Lithograph, Oval, 28 x 19 1/2 In. 110.00
Sign, Moxie, Tin, Round, 23 In. 77.00
Sign, Murad Cigarette, Tin Lithograph, 39 1/2 In. 280.00
Sign, National Farm Loan Assoc., Porcelain, 3 x 1 1/2 Ft. 75.00
Sign, National Mazda Lamps, Reverse On Glass, 8 1/2 In. 55.00
Sign, National Merchandising, Reverse On Glass, 23 In. 82.50
Sign, Nichol 5 Cent Kola, Multicolor, 1930s, 12 x 36 In. 100.00
Sign, Nichol Kola, Embossed Bottle, Tin, 38 x 15 In. 82.50
Sign, Nickel King Cigars, Cardboard, 16 x 18 In. 35.00
Sign, Northwestern Mutual Life Insurance, Tin, 31 x 22 In. 110.00
Sign, Nu–Grape, Bottle Shape, Tin, 14 In. 85.00
Sign, Nu–Grape, Yellow & Blue, March 9, 1920, Tin 100.00
Sign, O'Keefe Beer, Open–Closed, 9 x 14 In. 45.00

◆◆

A fresh ink stain on wood can be removed by washing with water and then applying lemon juice.

◆◆

Sign, OilMax Cement, Oil Wells, Metal, Yellow, 14 x 28 In.	58.00
Sign, Old Colony Beverages, Embossed Tin, 1938, 39 x 12 In.	100.00
Sign, Old Crow, Hard Rubber, Self Framed, 16 In.	180.00
Sign, Old Darling Bourbon & Rye, Reverse On Glass, 34 x 24 In.	467.00
Sign, Old Export, Scene, Plaster, 14 In,	150.00
Sign, Old German Lager Beer, Painted On Glass, 28 In.	20.00
Sign, Old Granddad Whiskey, Tin Lithograph, 28 In.	280.00
Sign, Old Reading Beer, Cardboard, Wood Frame, 34 In.	55.00
Sign, Olds Service, Double–Sided, Porcelain, 60 In.	1395.00
Sign, Optometrist, Glasses, Painted Eyes, Cast Iron	1000.00
Sign, Orange Crush, Framed, 1924, 14 x 22 In.	10.00
Sign, Orange Crush, Tin, 1940, 14 x 22 In.	125.00
Sign, Orange Crush, Tin, 1940, 3 x 24 In.	40.00
Sign, Pabst Blue Ribbon, Boxing Jim Corbett, 3–D, 14 x 20 In.	200.00
Sign, Pabst Extract, Woman On Front, Wood, 36 In.	66.00
Sign, Padlock Key, We Cut Finest Keys, Sheet Iron, 16 x 34 In.	150.00
Sign, Paine's Celery Compound, Tin, 14 x 10 In. ....*Illus*	325.00
Sign, Parke Davis, Factory Scene, Frame, 17 1/2 x 31 In.	132.00
Sign, Patton's Auto Gloss, Wheel, Painted Wood, 22 In.	2395.00
Sign, Pawnbroker 2nd Ave., Blue & White Enamel, 56 x 135 In.	450.00
Sign, Pe–Ru–Na For Catarrh, Wooden Frame, 15 1/2 In.	725.00
Sign, Pears Soap, Impudent Hussies, 1902, 19 1/2 x 24 1/2 In.	80.00
Sign, Pepsi–Cola, Tin, 7 1/2 x 27 In.	55.00
Sign, Pfeiffer's Beer, Horse War Admiral, Metal, 14 x 18 In.	65.00
Sign, Philip A. Wood, Dentist, Wooden, 2 Sides, 21 x 33 1/2 In.	100.00
Sign, Pickwick Ale, Tin Lithograph, Wood Frame, 24 In.	130.00
Sign, Pocket Watch, Painted Sheet Metal, Iron Frame, 21 1/2 In.	225.00
Sign, Poll Parrot Shoes, Outlined In Green Neon, 3 Ft.	2750.00
Sign, Polly Stamps, Parrot, Electric, Box, 13 x 25 In.	85.00
Sign, Powell Muffler, Carbon Monoxide, Tin, 13 1/4 x 10 In.	225.00
Sign, Priscilla Ware, Aluminum Utensils, Box, 10 x 5 1/4 In.	35.00
Sign, Providence Washington Insurance Co., 1799, 26 x 20 In.	450.00
Sign, R. C. Cola, Coed Drinks Cola, Cardboard, 1940s, 11 x 28 In.	20.00
Sign, Racine Tires, Painted Tin, 10 x 31 In.	350.00
Sign, Radio, Sales & Service, Blue Mirror, Wall, Round, 30 In.	1250.00
Sign, Radio, Sparton, Authorized Dealer, Porcelain, 12 x 18 In.	875.00
Sign, Radiola, Gold Background, Framed, c.1935, 14 x 19 In.	175.00
Sign, Railway Inn, Steward & Patterson Ltd., Framed, 33 x 43 In	330.00
Sign, Raspberry Charms, c.1920, 22 x 12 In.	200.00
Sign, RCA Victor, Record Shape, Composition Board, 47 In.	225.00
Sign, Recruit Cigars, 1909, 9 1/2 x 14 1/2 In.	715.00
Sign, Red Dot Cigar, Cardboard, 5 1/2 x 37 In.	27.00
Sign, Red Goose Shoes, 2 Sides, Neon, 8 Ft.	700.00
Sign, Red Goose Shoes, Outlined In Neon, 2 Ft.	2145.00
Sign, Red Man Chewing Tobacco, Tin Lithograph, 5 In.	45.00
Sign, Redfern's Rubber Heels, Tin Lithograph, Wood Frame, 16 In	190.00
Sign, Roman's Tonic Liver Pills, Cardboard In Frame, 29 In.	245.00
Sign, Romance Chocolates, N. Rockwell, Linen, 1920, 20 x 40 In.	1550.00
Sign, Royal Blue Seltz Shoe, Reverse Glass, 19 1/2 x 16 In.	357.50
Sign, Runkel Brothers Cocoa, Graphic, Tin, 13 1/2 x 19 In.	3400.00
Sign, Russells Ale, Tin Lithograph, 29 In.	180.00
Sign, Saiz De Carlos Elixir, Embossed, Tin Lithograph, 20 In.	330.00
Sign, Sam Clay Hand Made Sour Mash Whiskey, Tin, 18 x 26 In.	330.00
Sign, San Felice Cigar, Tin Lithograph, 13 In.	166.00
Sign, Schlitz Beer, Reverse On Glass, Metal Frame, 12 x 12 In.	38.00

Sign, Schmidt's Beer, Reverse Painted, 8 In. 35.00
Sign, Sebastopol, Home of Gravenstein Apples, Metal, 14 1/2 In. 45.00
Sign, Seneca Cameras, Indian, Embossed, Tin 3500.00
Sign, Shell Gasoline, 3 Dimensional Shell Form Letters, 17 In. 275.00
Sign, Sherwin Williams Paint, Enamel, 20 x 30 In. 355.00
Sign, Shield Shape, Wooden Frame, Red, White & Blue, 34 x 30 In. 150.00
Sign, Sinclair Gasoline, Dinosaur, Porcelain, 12 x 13 1/2 In. 70.00
Sign, Sinclair Restroom, With Rack 250.00
Sign, Sinclair, Opaline, 16 x 60 In. 225.00
Sign, Smile Soft Drink, Embossed Tin, 4 1/2 x 13 1/2 In. 95.00
Sign, Smoke Camels, Pack Pictured, Tin, 20 x 2 1/2 In. 15.00
Sign, Social Club Whiskey, Reverse Glass, Frame, 13 x 19 In. 2145.00
Sign, Stillwell Ham, Wood Frame, 16 In. 170.00
Sign, Stop–Police, Wooden, White Letters On Black, 28 x 18 In. 85.00
Sign, Street, 15 MPH, Porcelain, 18 x 24 In. 395.00
Sign, Sunbeam Mixmaster, Electric, Mixes, Blinks, Tin, 25 In. 295.00
Sign, Sunbeam Toaster, Electric, Raises & Lowers, 22 In. 325.00
Sign, Swan Fire Extinguisher, Tin Lithograph, 22 In. 25.00
Sign, Tetley Tea, 1906, Woman 3500.00
Sign, Texaco Fire Chief, Porcelain, 18 x 12 In. 175.00
Sign, Texaco Sky Chief, Porcelain, 18 x 12 In. 175.00
Sign, Texaco, Free Crankcase Service, Porcelain, 30 x 30 In. 200.00
Sign, Texaco, Porcelain, 15 In. 88.00
Sign, Texas Brewing Co., Factory, Paper, Framed, 40 x 27 In. 2860.00
Sign, Thieme & Wagner Beer, Porcelain, Round, 18 In. 895.00
Sign, Torrance Drug Co., Mortar, Pestle, Metal, 23 x 12 In. 69.00
Sign, Trade, Boot, Gilded Tassels, Cast Iron Ring, Wood, 33 In. 3025.00
Sign, Trade, Farrier, Painted Wood, 45 x 36 In. 475.00
Sign, Tuttle's Elixir, Tin, 4 1/4 x 19 3/4 In. ....*Illus* 200.00
Sign, Uneeda, 3–Way, Changes As You Move 1200.00
Sign, Union 76, 4 Color, Porcelain, 24 In. 350.00
Sign, Union Leader Cut Plug Togacco, Uncle Sam, 22 x 30 In. 5390.00
Sign, United Motor, Cardboard, 24 x 33 In. 495.00
Sign, Van Camp's Soup, Die Cut Tin, 32 x 20 1/2 In. 1450.00
Sign, Vaseline, Woman With Tube, c.1920, 22 x 12 In. 275.00
Sign, Velvet Tobacco, Steel, Double Sided, 13 1/2 In. 650.00
Sign, Vermo Stomach Bitters, Tin, 6 1/2 x 9 1/4 In. ....*Illus* 160.00
Sign, Viceroy, Come In, Tin, 11 x 25 In. 20.00
Sign, Walkover Shoes, Man In Tux, Cardboard, c.1910, 20 x 6 In. 8.00
Sign, Walkover Shoes, Man One Side, Woman Other, Tin, 27 1/2 In. 1875.00
Sign, Walter Baker Chocolate, Gold Frame, 45 x 22 In. 335.00

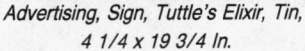

Advertising, Sign, Tuttle's Elixir, Tin,
4 1/4 x 19 3/4 In.

Advertising, Sign, Vermo Stomach Bitters,
Tin, 6 1/2 x 9 1/4 In.

Sign, Waltham Watches, Reverse On Glass, Eagle, 23 x 16 In. 137.00
Sign, Warner's Safe Yeast, Print, 29 In. 155.00
Sign, We Give Polly Stamps, Poll Parrot, Electric, 13 x 25 In. 85.00
Sign, We Sell MacWythe Wire Rope, Glass, 18 x 10 In. 100.00
Sign, Wells Fargo & Co., Stage Depot, Wooden, 14 x 34 In. 50.00
Sign, Westinghouse Mazda Lamps, Cardboard, 26 x 19 In. 1295.00
Sign, Wetherills Paint & Varnish, Tin, 24 In. 80.00
Sign, White Star Gasoline, Porcelain, 1920s, 30 In. 395.00
Sign, Whitman's Chocolates & Confections, Porcelain, 40 In. 99.00
Sign, Whitman's Chocolates, Green, Porcelain, 13 1/2 x 39 1/2 I 90.00
Sign, Whitman's Chocolates, Metal, 9 In. 50.00
Sign, Wilcox & White, Reverse Painted, Birds, Lizards, 19 In. 525.00
Sign, Williamson Cat Market, Wooden, N. Y., 1850, 78 x 30 In. 2200.00
Sign, Winchester Rifles, Neon Light–Up, Metal Frame, Stand 750.00
Sign, Wm. Younger & Co., Scotch Ale, Dye Cut Sign, 13 In. 225.00
Sign, Wolf's Head, 1 x 6 In. 100.00
Sign, Wonder Orange, Soda Pop, Colorful 150.00
Sign, Wooden Ball, Iron Twisted Link Hanger, J. Moore, 9 In. 575.00
Sign, Woolson Spice Co., New Crop Tea, Tin Lithograph, 6 In. 27.50
Sign, Woolworth, Gold Lettering, Red Glass, Frame, 14 In. 255.00
Sign, Yale Brewing, Reverse On Glass, Factory, 23 1/2 x 32 In. 2850.00
Soap, Packer's Healing Tar, 1919 .... 5.00
Soap, Palmolive, Cake Type, Wrapper, 1940s, Sample 10.00
Soda Set, A & W Root Beer, Pitcher & 8 Tall Glasses 65.00
Spittoon, Pony Express Chewing Tobacco 350.00
Spittoon, Pony Express Tobacco, Pictures Rider, Brass 35.00
Spittoon, Red Skin Brand Chewing Tobacco, Brass, 11 In. 125.00
Spittoon, Top Stone Cigars, White & Blue, Porcelain, 9 1/4 In. 125.00
Spoon & Fork, Skippy 25.00
Spoon, Bakers Breakfast Cocoa, Silver, Raised Writing, Lady Top 25.00
Spoon, Grand Union Tea Co., Headquarter's In Bowl, Silver 25.00
Spoon, Kellogg's, Wooden, 13 In. 13.00
Spoon, Knotts Berry, California, Sterling, Demitasse 8.00
Spoon, Quaker Tea, Figural Man Handle, Pouring Tea, Demitasse 35.00
Spoon, Towles Log Cabin Syrup 15.00
Spoon, Walker's Grape Juice, Figural Bottle Handle 20.00
Spy Kit, Capt. Crunch Seadog 20.00
Stickpin, Burk Pork Packers, Pig, 1900 .... 35.00
Stickpin, John Deere, Gilt, Leaping Deer 35.00
Straw Holder, Depression Glass, Green 575.00
Straw Holder, Flint Glass, Square 135.00
String Dispenser, Red Goose Shoes, Painted Iron, 14 1/2 In. 1100.00
String Holder, Dixon Hosiery 3500.00
String Holder, Post Toasties, Tin Front, Round 50.00
String Holder, Red Goose, Cast Iron, Repainted 1150.00
String Holder, SSS For The Blood, Cast Iron 150.00
Sugar & Creamer, Ken–L Ration 34.00
Table, Ice Cream, Breyers, Porcelain, 30 1/2 In. 225.00
     ADVERTISING, THERMOMETER, see Thermometer
Thermos, Clarke's Pure Rye, 1908 .... 80.00
Tie Clasp, Reddy Kilowatt, Red Enamel On Brass, 2 1/2 x 1 In. 24.00

 The English language is sometimes confusing. Tin cans or canisters were first used commercially in the United States in 1819 and were called *tins*. Today the word *tin* is used by most collectors to describe many types of containers, including food tins, biscuit boxes, roly poly tobacco containers, gunpowder cans, talcum powder sprinkle–top cans, cigarette flat–fifty tins, and more. Beer cans are listed in their own section. Things made of undecorated tin are listed under Tinware.

Tin, 3 Knights Condom 95.00
Tin, 4 Roses Tobacco, Upright, Pocket, Green 50.00
Tin, Abbey Tobacco, Pictures Cathedral, Blue, Pocket 150.00

Tin, Advance Agent Cigars, Round, 6 x 4 In. 275.00
Tin, After Glow Coffee, 4 Lb. 30.00
Tin, Alliance Coffee, Paper, Tin Ends, Canister, 6 In. 29.00
Tin, American Beauty Coffee, Paper With Tin Ends, 6 x 3 In. 25.00
Tin, American Eagle Chewing Tobacco, Flat, Pocket 1100.00
Tin, American Rifle Team Coffee, Tin Lithograph 110.00
Tin, Angelus Marshmallows, 12 Oz. 22.00
Tin, Angelus Marshmallows, 5 Lb. 30.00
Tin, Atwoods Coffee, Blue, 10 x 7 1/2 In. 65.00
Tin, Aunt Jemima Cooking & Salad Oil, Picture, 5 Gal. 1500.00
Tin, Bag, Tetley Tea, Silver & Blue 5.00
Tin, Bagdad Tobacco, Pictures Turk, Pocket 135.00
Tin, Bagdad Tobacco, Plain Top, Pocket 70.00
Tin, Bagley's Compass, Small Top, Paper Label 95.00
Tin, Bambino, Pocket, 4 x 2 In. 1800.00
Tin, Bambino, Tobacco 1800.00
Tin, Beechnut, Factory Scene, Indian Scene, 11 x 12 1/2 x 6 In. 45.00
Tin, Belfast Tobacco, 4 x 6 In. 48.00
Tin, Between The Acts Cigars, Embossed, Man In Black, 5 1/2 In. 145.00
Tin, Bixby's Satinola Shoe Polish, Box Shape, Black Man, Box 35.00
Tin, Black Fox Cigars, Canada, Round, 6 x 4 In. 675.00
Tin, Blanke's Happy Thought Coffee, Tin Lithograph, 9 In. 25.00
Tin, Blue Bird Coffee, 12 x 8 In. 110.00
Tin, Blue Ribbon Spice, Red, White & Blue 6.00
Tin, Borated Talc, Blue 15.00
Tin, Bowl of Roses Tobacco, Pocket ....70.00 To 175.00
Tin, Box, Hinged, Snow Flake Crackers, 9 x 9 In. 50.00
Tin, Breakfast Call Coffee, 3 Lb. 35.00
Tin, Bridal Brand Coffee, 1 Lb, ... 835.00
Tin, Brigg's Tobacco, Hand Holding Pipe, Pocket, 3 x 2 In. 25.00
Tin, Brigg's Tobacco, When A Feller Needs A Friend, Round, Wood 21.00
Tin, Bright Tiger, Paper Side, 11 1/2 In. 82.00
Tin, Brook's Spoon Cotton, Tin Lithograph, 1 1/2 In. 44.00
Tin, Buckingham Tobacco, Paper Label, Pocket 30.00
Tin, Buckingham Tobacco, Tin Lithograph, Pocket, 4 x 2 In. 115.00
Tin, Bulldog Tobacco, Bulldog, Pocket, 4 x 2 In. ....200.00 To 415.00
Tin, Burley Boy Tobacco, 4 x 2 In. 770.00
Tin, Burley Tobacco, Tin Lithograph, 6 1/2 In. 93.00
Tin, Cadette Talc, Gray 80.00
Tin, California Nugget, Chop Cut, 4 x 2 In. 105.00
Tin, Calumet Baking Powder, 1 Lb. 9 Oz. 8.00
Tin, Calumet Baking Powder, 5 Lb. 17.50
Tin, Campfire Marshmallow, 1 Lb. 37.50
Tin, Campfire Marshmallows, Glass Top, 5 Lb. 35.00
Tin, Caraja Coffee, Paper Lithograph Label, 6 In. 38.00
Tin, Carlings Brewery, Pictures Policemen Drinking, Tin 145.00
Tin, Carlton Club Tobacco, Blue Coat of Arms, Pocket, 4 x 2 In. 175.00
Tin, Carlton Club Tobacco, Red Coat of Arms, Pocket, 4 x 2 In. 175.00
Tin, Carr Co., 14 Member Family At Dinner, Santa, Biscuit 125.00
Tin, Carter Typewriter Ribbon 8.00
Tin, Cashmere Bouquet Talc, Sample 22.00
Tin, Caswells Coffee, Woman Lithograph, 3 Lb., 12 x 4 In. 52.00
Tin, Caswells Kona Coffee, Gold Lithograph, 7 1/4 In. 16.50
Tin, Caswells National Crest Brand Coffee, Eagle, 2 1/2 Lb. 35.00
Tin, Central Union Tobacco, Face, Quarter Moon, 8 x 6 x 3 In. 325.00
Tin, Checkers Tobacco, 1910 Tax Stamp, Contents, Pocket 800.00
Tin, Checkers Tobacco, Pocket, 4 x 2 In. 150.00
Tin, Chesterfield, Flat, Pocket 10.00
Tin, Chocolate, Fish Shape, 4 In. 20.00
Tin, Cigar, Bayuk Perfecto, 1930 .... 18.00
Tin, City Soda Crackers, Natonal Biscuit Co., 6 Lb. 40.00
Tin, Climax Plug Tobacco, Lithograph, 12 In. 13.50
Tin, Coach & Four Tobacco, Stagecoach, Pocket, 4 x 2 In. 350.00

◆◆◆◆◆◆◆◆◆◆◆◆◆◆◆◆◆◆◆◆◆◆

Tin signs and cans will fade from the ultraviolet rays coming in a window or from a fluorescent light. Plexiglass UF–1 or UF–3 will cover the window and keep the rays away from your collection. There are also plastic sleeves to cover fluorescent tubes.

Advertising, Tin, Half & Half Tobacco, Pocket ◆◆◆◆◆◆◆◆◆◆◆◆◆◆◆◆◆◆◆◆◆◆◆

Tin, Colonial Dame Coffee, Lithograph, 6 x 3 In.	88.00
Tin, Columbia, Cut Plug Tobacco, Slip Lid, Round	113.00
Tin, Comrade Coffee, 3 Lb., 8 x 5 In.	50.00
Tin, Continental Cubes Tobacco, Pocket, 8 x 6 In.	390.00
Tin, Country Doctor Pipe Mixture, 8 Oz.	45.00
Tin, Courthouse Mixture Tobacco, Pittsburgh, Pocket	175.00
Tin, Cream of Sweets Marshmallow Drops, Large Breadbox Size	85.00
Tin, Crowing Rooster Cigar, Black, Orange, Half–Spanish, 6 In.	45.00
Tin, Cut Plug Granulated, Pocket	1175.00
Tin, Dactylis Talcum, Colgate	40.00
Tin, Dash Little Cigars, Pocket	65.00
Tin, Dauntless Coffee, Label, Full, 1 Lb.	88.00
Tin, Derby Tobacco, Flat, Pocket	40.00
Tin, Dilling's Lemon Drops, Paper Label, 4 Lb.	17.50
Tin, Dixie Kid Cut Plug Tobacco, Black Child	225.00
Tin, Dixie Kid Tobacco, Black, 6 x 5 x 5 In.	195.00
Tin, Dixie Queen Plug Cut Tobacco, Basketweave	175.00
Tin, Dixie Queen, Knob Top, Dark Blue, 6 x 4 x 3 In.	495.00
Tin, Dixie Salted Peanuts, 10 Lb.	990.00
Tin, Dixie, Chopcut Plug, Tin Lithograph, 4 1/2 In.	175.00
Tin, Dr. Johnson's Educator Crackers, Lithograph Top	28.00
Tin, Dr. Wiley's Scalp Treatment	45.00
Tin, Dr. Scholl's Foot Balm, Sample	9.00
Tin, Droste's Cocoa, 1 Lb.	20.00
Tin, Dryer–Kiss Talc	12.00
Tin, Dupont Bulk Smokeless Powder, Paper Label	20.00
Tin, Eatons Sun Glow Spice, Cream, Red, Black, 4 In.	9.00
Tin, El Capital Coffee, Lithograph, 6 x 3 In.	33.00
Tin, El Toro Cigars, Paper Lithograph, 5 1/4 In.	38.50
Tin, Elm Cigars, Embossed Tin Lithograph, 5 1/4 In.	75.00
Tin, Empress Spice, Full Lithograph, 9 In.	26.00
Tin, Epicure Tobacco, Leaves To Top, Pocket	100.00
Tin, Epicure Tobacco, Man Smoking Long Pipe, Pocket	310.00
Tin, Estabrooks Red Rose Coffee, 5 Lb.	75.00
Tin, Etoile De Franc Talc, Tin Lithograph, 6 In.	28.00
Tin, Extons Oyster & Butter Crackers, Glass Front	825.00
Tin, Falk's Highest Grade Tobacco, Dome Top, Red, 4 x 2 In.	152.00
Tin, Famous Cake Box Mixture Tobacco, Lithograph, 4 1/2 In.	18.50
Tin, Faneuil Hall Cigar, Round, 4 x 3 In.	137.00
Tin, Fast Mail, Tin Lithograph, 5 In.	33.00
Tin, Favorite Marshmallows, 5 Lb.	25.00
Tin, Fisher's Peanuts, 15 Lb.	85.00
Tin, Fishmuth Tobacco, Pocket	2250.00
Tin, Fitts Violet Talc, Art Nouveau	20.00
Tin, Flick & Flock Cigars, Dogs Inside Top	192.00
Tin, Forest & Stream Tobacco, 2 Men In Canoe, Pocket, 4 x 2 In.	500.00
Tin, Four Roses Tobacco, Green, Pocket, 4 x 2 In.	750.00

Tin, Four Roses Tobacco, Silver, Flip Lid, Pocket .... 55.00 To 60.00
Tin, Frontenac Peanut Butter, Red, White, Blue & Gold, 1930s 20.00
Tin, Gail & Ax, Smoking & Chewing Tobacco, Small Top, 6 x 4 In. 170.00
Tin, German Cottage, Heinrich Haeberlein, 7 In. ....*Illus* 110.00
Tin, Ghiridelli Chocolate, Eagle, 6 x 3 In. 12.00
Tin, Globe Tobacco, Red & Black, Pocket, Small 350.00
Tin, Gold Leaf Tobacco, Paper Label, 2 x 8 In. 635.00
Tin, Gold Medal High Grade Blend Coffee, Canister, Paper 30.00
Tin, Gold Standard Spice, Red, White & Blue 8.00
Tin, Golden Crown Brand Coconut, Tin Lithograph, 6 In. 4.00
Tin, Golden Wedding Coffee, 1 Lb. 25.00
Tin, Granger Tobacco, Pointer & Tobacco Leaf, Tin, Pocket 25.00
Tin, Gwan Bee Tea, Oriental Child Lithograph 30.00
Tin, Gypsy Boy Coffee, Embossed, Flat, 1 Lb. 35.00
Tin, Half & Half Tobacco, Pocket ....*Illus* 1.00
Tin, Hercules Bull's–Eye Smokeless Powder, Label 45.00
Tin, Hiawatha Straight Cut Tobacco, Green, 4 x 6 In. 115.00
Tin, Hiawatha, Yellow, Red & Black, 3 x 5 In. 75.00
Tin, High Grade Typewriter, Upright Rectangular 15.00
Tin, Hindoo Tobacco, Hindoo Smoking Pipe, Pocket 875.00
Tin, Hoffman's Old Time Coffee, 1 Lb, ... 140.00
Tin, Holyrood Palace Candy, Edinburgh Picture, 6 x 3 1/2 In. 15.00
Tin, Honest Labor Cut Plug, Paterson Tobacco Co., 5 In. 55.00
Tin, Honey Moon Tobacco, 2 On The Moon, Pocket, 4 x 2 In. 450.00
Tin, Honey Moon Tobacco, Man Leaning On Moon 75.00
Tin, Hoosier Coffee, Little Boy Holding Bucket of Paint, Label 330.00
Tin, Hudson's Bay Tea, 8 1/2 x 6 x 6 In. 65.00
Tin, Huntley & Palmer, Creel, Embossed Litho, Biscuit, 7 1/2 In. 302.00
Tin, Huntley & Palmers, Binocular Shape, 7 In. 55.00
Tin, Huntley & Palmers, Biscuit Shape 165.00
Tin, Huntley & Palmers, Book Carrier Shape, Litho, 4 1/4 In. 110.00
Tin, Huntley & Palmers, China Cabinet, Lithograph, 7 1/4 In. 252.00
Tin, Huntley & Palmers, Egyptian Scene, Biscuit, 8 3/4 In. 95.00
Tin, Huntley & Palmers, Lantern, Embossed Litho, Biscuit, 9 In. 170.00
Tin, Huntley & Palmers, Laundry Basket, Litho, Biscuit, 6 In 220.00
Tin, Huntley & Palmers, Leather Bound Book 495.00
Tin, Huntley & Palmers, Purse, Embossed, Litho, Biscuit, 7 In. 33.00
Tin, Huntley & Palmers, Suitcase, Lithograph, Biscuit, 8 In. 72.00
Tin, Huntley & Palmers, Toby Jug, Lithograph, Biscuit, 6 1/2 In. 330.00
Tin, Idle Hour, Napoleon, World's Fair, Box 242.00
Tin, Imperial Smoking Mixture 145.00
Tin, In–Between–The–Acts Cigars, 8 x 3 x 1 In. 185.00
Tin, Indian Rifle Gun Powder, Paper Lithograph, 5 In. 40.00
Tin, Innerclean Herbal Laxative 7.75
Tin, Japo–Borax Cleanser, Paper Label 27.50
Tin, Jayne's Expectorant Tablets 65.00
Tin, Jenny Lee Potato Chip, Red, White & Blue, 1 Lb. 15.00
Tin, Jim Dandies Peanuts, Baseball Scene, 1916, 11 In. 1650.00
Tin, Johnson's Wax, 1920s, 3 1/2 Oz. 32.00
Tin, Jumbo Peanut Butter, Black Boy Eating Peanut 450.00
Tin, Kake Kan Koffee, 3 Lb. 35.00
Tin, Karo Syrup, Sample, 1906 .... 36.00
Tin, Katahdin Tobacco, Pocket 1800.00
Tin, Kennebec Cigars, Lithograph, 8 1/2 In. 60.00
Tin, Kentucky Club Mixture, Pocket 10.00
Tin, Kentucky Club, Pocket 4.00
Tin, Kentucky Club, Round 15.00
Tin, Kim–Bo Tobacco, Paper Lithograph, Pocket, 4 1/4 In. 100.00
Tin, King Edward Cigars, Canada, Pocket 575.00
Tin, King Powder Co., Semi–Smokeless Powder, Light Green, 1 Lb. 70.00
Tin, King Syrup, Tin Lithograph, 3 In. 13.00
Tin, Kleenal, Cleanses Everything, Cardboard, 1926, 4 In. 15.00
Tin, Koin Pack Condoms 25.00

Tin, Kovah Spice, Egg Salt, Full Lithograph, 8 1/2 In. 29.00
Tin, Kybo Coffee, 1 Lb. 30.00
Tin, La Paulina Cigar, Gold, Tin Lithograph, 5 In. 6.00
Tin, LaBara Bath Powder 18.00
Tin, Layman's Quality Aspirin, Man With Headache 50.00
Tin, Lipton's Tea, Gold 15.00
Tin, London Sherbet Tobacco, Tin Lithograph, 4 1/4 In. 82.50
Tin, Lord Tennyson Puritano Cigars, Lithograph, 5 1/4 In. 60.00
Tin, Lotus Peanuts, 10 Lb. 220.00
Tin, Louisiana Perique Tobacco, Edward Hen, Pocket 225.00
Tin, Louisiana Tobacco, Graduate, 3 x 2 1 1/2 In. 55.00
Tin, Loving Cup, Embossed, Lithograph, Elizabethan Couple 120.00
Tin, Loyal Coffee, Lithograph, 6 In. 22.00
Tin, Lucky Duck Cigars 1100.00
Tin, Lucky Strike Roll Cut Tobacco, Pocket, 4 x 2 In. 60.00
Tin, Luzianne Coffee, 3 Lb. .... 79.50 To 85.00
Tin, Luzianne Coffee, Mammy, Bail Handle, 3 Lb. 135.00
Tin, Luzianne Coffee, Mammy, Lithograph, White Ground, 1 Lb. 90.00
Tin, Luzianne Coffee, Red, Sample 95.00
Tin, Luzianne Coffee, White, 1 Lb. 65.00
Tin, Luzianne, Coffee & Chicory, Black Mammy, 1 Lb. 40.00
Tin, Macfarlane, Lang & Co., Anvil, Tin Litho, 6 1/2 In. .... *Illus* 192.00
Tin, Macfarlane, Lang & Co., The House That Jack Built, Biscuit 170.00
Tin, Macfarlane, Lang & Co., Yule Log, Biscuit, 6 In. 247.00
Tin, Machwitz Coffee, 3 Black Boys 100.00
Tin, Malkin's Spice, Red, White, Blue, 8 1/2 In. 8.00
Tin, Mammoth Peanut Butter, Elephant, 5 Lb. 250.00
Tin, Mammy's Coffee, Lid & Bail, 4 Lb. 200.00
Tin, Mammy's Favorite Brand Coffee, 4 Lb. 175.00
Tin, Mariposa Tobacco, Pocket, 3 x 2 In. 1200.00
Tin, Marshmallow Drops, Gold Crown, Tin Lithograph, 6 In. 28.00
Tin, Mary Garden Talc, Woman's Face In Medallion 15.00
Tin, Maryland Maid, Pure Sugar Candy, Tin Lithograph, 7 In. 33.00
Tin, Mazawattee Tea, Grandma & Granddaughter, Dressed Alike 125.00
Tin, McLaughlin Mocha Java, 1 Lb. 22.00
Tin, Meadow Gold Milk Box 35.00
Tin, Meerschaum Cut Plug, Lithograph, 5 In. 60.00
Tin, Mellow Sweet, Fine Cut, Light, 2 x 8 In. 225.00
Tin, Mennen Talcum, Sample 25.00
Tin, Mentholatum, Trial Size 8.00
Tin, Merkel's Tooth Powder, Red, Black & Gold, Sample, 1917 .... 18.00
Tin, Mione Soap 20.00
Tin, Modern Tex Prophylactic 30.00
Tin, Monarch Cocoa, 16 Oz. 25.00
Tin, Monogram Brand Coffee, Paper Lithograph, 6 x 3 In. 46.00
Tin, Moseman's Peanut Butter, Sample 175.00
Tin, Mount Cross Coffee, Milk Pail 85.00
Tin, Muriel Cigars, Tin Lithograph, 6 In. 60.00
Tin, Murray's Hair Dressing Pomade, 1 1/2 x 3 In. 6.00
Tin, Mustard Plaster, 4 Original Mustard Plasters, Litho, 3 In. 13.00
Tin, Nestor Gianadis Cigarettes, Lithograph, 6 In. 145.00
Tin, Nigger Hair Smoking Tobacco, 6 1/2 In. 350.00
Tin, Nigger Hair Tobacco, Cardboard Lithograph, 6 1/2 In. 175.00
Tin, No-To-Bac, Sterling Products, Inc., Pocket 34.00

♦♦

A rolltop on a rolltop desk can be repaired with window–shade
material. Glue the slats to the material with white glue. Be careful;
this is not an easy repair and slats must be spaced properly.

♦♦

Tin, North Pole Tobacco, Oval Top, 6 x 6 x 4 In. 175.00
Tin, North Star, Flat, Pocket, 6 x 2 x 2 In. 455.00
Tin, O–Cedar Mop, 1920s 21.00
Tin, Oil, Deering Harvester, Norton Bros., Chicago, Orange 195.00
Tin, Old Abe "Bright" Chewing Tobacco, Round, 8 1/4 In. 495.00
Tin, Old Abe Chewing Tobacco, Flat, Pocket 1430.00
Tin, Old Chum Tobacco, Canada, 1919, 5 x 3 x 2 In. 85.00
Tin, Old Colony Tobacco, Curved Body, Pocket 115.00
Tin, Old Colony Tobacco, Cyldrical, Ashtray Top 110.00
Tin, Old Colony Tobacco, Pocket 120.00
Tin, Old Rip Tobacco, Dark Red, 2 1/8 x 3 1/4 In. 105.00
Tin, Old Squire Tobacco, Blue, Pocket, 8 1/2 In. 2250.00
Tin, Omar Cigarettes, Metal, 6 x 8 In. 40.00
Tin, Opera Beauties, Adelina Patti, Flat, Pocket 200.00
Tin, Opera Beauties, Gray–Green, Lithograph Top, Pocket 115.00
Tin, Optimus Condom 80.00
Tin, Orcico Cigars, 6 x 6 x 4 In. 210.00
Tin, Oysters, Fishing Boat, Blue & White, 1 Gal. 17.50
Tin, Park & Tilford Nuts & Fruits, Fan Shape, Flowers, 2 Lb. 25.00
Tin, Pat Hand Tobacco, Picture of Hand, Pocket 175.00
Tin, Paul Jones Tobacco, Blue, Pocket 950.00
Tin, Paul Jones Tobacco, Red, Pocket 2500.00
Tin, Peanut, Brownie Broad, 10 Lb. 135.00
Tin, Peek Frean & Co., Horseshoe, Embossed Litho, 6 1/2 In. 88.00
Tin, Peter Pan Peanut Butter, Lithograph, 6 1/4 In. 45.00
Tin, Pettits & Smith's Cough Drops, Lithograph, 8 1/2 In. 82.50
Tin, Pilot–Knob Coffee, Bower Bros., 5 Lb. 70.00
Tin, Plee–Zing Coffee, 3 Lb. 25.00
Tin, Possum Cigars, Red, 6 x 6 In. 44.00
Tin, Powder, Dead Shot, American Powder Mills, Litho, Brass Lid 88.00
Tin, Prairie Flower, Flat Pocket 755.00
Tin, Pride of Virginia, Aqua, Brown, Pat. 1879, 6 In. 25.00
Tin, Prince Albert, Crimp Cut, 5 In. 40.00
Tin, Pulverized Cream Tartar, Blue, Gold Stenciled, 5 x 7 In. 85.00
Tin, Pure Brown Mustard, 8 In. 77.00
Tin, Purse, Courtship Scene, Lithograph, Biscuit, 6 In. 38.00
Tin, Qboid Granulated Plug, Lithograph, 4 1/4 In. 210.00
Tin, Queed Tobacco, Pocket 195.00
Tin, Queen Nuts, 3 Large Snakes Pop Out 20.00
Tin, Quezal Coffee, 1 Lb. 49.50
Tin, Real Skin Prophylactic, Lion Picture, Unopened 15.00
Tin, Red Dot Cigar, 3 1/2 x 5 1/2 In. 40.00
Tin, Red Jacket, Pocket, 4 x 2 In. 25.00
Tin, Red Wolf Coffee, 1 Lb. 60.00
Tin, Regal Cube Cut Tobacco, Pocket 92.00
Tin, Revelation Tobacco, Sample, 2 x 1 In. 75.00
Tin, Richelieu Orange Peko Tea, Japanese Woman, 4 Oz. 9.00
Tin, Rock Castle Tobacco, Pocket, 3 x 2 In. 575.00
Tin, Roly Poly, Clown, Green, Red Buttons, Ruffle, Germany, 5 In. 145.00
Tin, Roly Poly, Mammy, Mayo Tobacco 500.00
Tin, Roly Poly, Satisfied Customer .... 195.00 To 225.00
Tin, Roly Poly, Satisfied Customer, Mayo's 650.00
Tin, Roly Poly, Singing Waiter, Mayo 575.00
Tin, Roly Poly, U. S. Marine, Mammy 600.00
Tin, Rose–O'Cuba Cigars, Lithograph, 5 1/2 In. 77.00
Tin, Royal Dutch Coffee 44.00
Tin, Royal Shield Spice, Red, White, Blue, Gold, 8 1/2 In. 8.00
Tin, Royaline Liver Regulator, 2 1/4 In. 10.00
Tin, Rumford Baking Powder, Sample 50.00
Tin, S. Henderson & Sons, Log Cabin, Litho, Biscuit, 6 1/2 In. 150.00
Tin, Saf–T–Way Condoms 45.00
Tin, Schraft's Candy, Roses, Needlepoint Design, 1 Lb. 18.00
Tin, Seal of North Carolina, Plug Cut, Small Top, 6 x 3 In. 350.00

Advertising, Tin, Wm. Crawford, Globe, Biscuit, 8 In.; Advertising, Tin, German Cottage, Heinrich Haeberlein, 7 In.; Advertising, Tin, Macfarlane, Lang & Co., Anvil, Tin Litho, 6 1/2 In.

Tin, Seal of North Carolina, Sample, 2 x 2 5/8 In. 715.00
Tin, Sears Roebuck Coffee, 12 In. 125.00
Tin, Sensation Smoking Tobacco, 5 In. 12.00
Tin, Shaeffer's, Contains Eraser, Blue & White 6.00
Tin, Sheik Condom 15.00
Tin, Shubs Tobacco, Pocket 1500.00
Tin, Sir Walter Raleigh, Portrait, Pocket 4.00
Tin, Sir Walter Raleigh, Smoking Tobacco, Pocket 10.00
Tin, Skippy Peanut Butter, 1 Lb. 150.00
Tin, Snake Charmer Cigarettes, Lithograph, 4 1/2 In. 75.00
Tin, Snow Flake Crackers, Red, Hinged, 9 x 8 x 7 In. 49.00
Tin, Snow King Baking Powder, Sample 65.00
Tin, Stag Tobacco, Oval 55.00
Tin, Stanwix Tobacco, 1917 Tax Stamp, Contents, Pocket 1400.00
Tin, Stanwix, Ground Plug, Blue, Pocket 325.00
Tin, Star & Crescent Cigars, Tin Lithograph, 5 In. 88.00
Tin, Steamer Trunk, Tin Lithograph, Biscuit, 4 1/2 In. 38.00
Tin, Stephano Brothers Cigarettes, Paper Label, 5 1/2 In. 22.00
Tin, Strong–Heart Coffee, Lithograph, 5 3/4 In. 330.00
Tin, Sultan, Pocket, 3 x 2 In. 39.00
Tin, Sweet Burley Tobacco, Red, Tin 125.00
Tin, Sweet Cuba Tobacco, Dark Brown, Round, 14 x 8 In. 95.00
Tin, Sweet Cuba, Light, 2 x 8 In. 53.00
Tin, Sweet Mist Chewing Tobacco, Lithograph, 11 1/2 In. 71.50
Tin, Sweet Mist Tobacco, Gray, Blue, 2 x 8 In. 125.00
Tin, Sweet Violet Tobacco, Pocket, 4 x 2 In. 1250.00
Tin, Syrup, Towle's Log Cabin, 6 In. 132.00
Tin, Talc, Motif Cosmetics, 12 Oz. 18.00
Tin, Three Feathers Tobacco, Pocket, 4 x 2 In. 400.00
Tin, Tiger, Hold On To Your Tigers, Red, Gold, 48 Pkg., Round 265.00
Tin, Timur Coffee, 1 Lb, ... 2100.00
Tin, Tip Top Tire Patch, Contents, Color 8.00
Tin, Tom Moore Cigars, Hinged Lid, Tin Lithograph 14.00
Tin, Traders Spices, Maryland Mills, Paper Lithograph, 9 In. 22.00
Tin, Trout–Line Tobacco, Fisherman, Pocket, 7 x 5 In. 750.00
Tin, Trout–Line Tobacco, Tin Lithograph, Pocket, 3 3/4 In. 295.00
Tin, Tudor House, Lithograph, Biscuit, 6 1/4 In. 44.00
Tin, Turtle Food, Also For Lizards, Turtle Picture, 1930s 20.00
Tin, Tuxedo Spice, Yellow, 8 In. 9.00
Tin, Tuxedo Tobacco, Curved Body, Pocket 185.00
Tin, Twin Oaks Tobacco, Pocket 25.00

Tin, Two Orphans Cigars 100.00
Tin, Typewriter Ribbon, Art Deco, Black & White 23.00
Tin, U. S. Marine Tobacco, Pocket, 4 x 3 In. .... 160.00 To 195.00
Tin, Uncle Daniel, Dark Red, 2 x 8 In. 154.00
Tin, Uncle Sam Tobacco, Canada, Pocket, 4 x 2 In. 2600.00
Tin, Union Leader Tobacco, Uncle Sam, Pocket .... 50.00 To 85.00
Tin, United Happiness Candy Stores, 1 Lb. 575.00
Tin, Velvet, Pipe & Cigarette, Pocket 10.00
Tin, Virginia Dare, Leda & Swan, Square Corners 138.00
Tin, Virginity Tobacco, Girl & Factory, 3 3/4 x 4 1/2 x 7 In. 175.00
Tin, W & R Jacob & Co., Coach On Wheels, Biscuit, 9 In. 137.00
Tin, W. H. Baker Bet Cocoa, 3 3/4 In. 210.00
Tin, Watkin's Baking Powder, 1930s 12.00
Tin, Watkin's Malted Milk, 1930s, Sample 42.50
Tin, Watkin's Spice, Black, 9 1/2 In. 10.00
Tin, Whip Tobacco, Green, Man With Whip & Horse, Pocket 400.00
Tin, Whip, Lithograph, 5 1/2 In. 198.00
Tin, White Manor Tobacco, Picture of Mansion, Pocket 300.00
Tin, White Manor Tobacco, Pocket 225.00
Tin, White Rose Tea Balls 22.00
Tin, White Star Spice, Red, Green 7.00
Tin, Whitman's White Caps Mints, 4 In. 12.50
Tin, Who Can Beat It Coffee, Lithograph, 9 In. 27.50
Tin, Willem II Cigars, Picture of Willem, Flat Pocket 12.00
Tin, Willoughby Taylor, Oval, Lift Lever, Pocket 20.00
Tin, Winner, Cut Plug, Small Top 95.00
Tin, Wm. Crawford & Sons, Globe, Lithograph, Biscuit, 8 In. 152.00
Tin, Wm. Crawford, Globe, Biscuit, 8 In. ....*Illus* 152.00
Tin, Y & S Old Fashioned Lozenges, Viewing Panel, 7 3/4 In. 45.00
Tin, Yankee Boys Tobacco, Pocket, Blond, 4 In. 575.00
Tin, Yankee Boys Tobacco, Pocket, Brunette, 4 In. 575.00
Tin, Yummy Malt, 1920s, 1 Lb. 35.00
Tin, Yunan's Black Tea, Tea Pickers, 4 Oz. 5.00
Tin, Zanzibar Brand Black Pepper, Lithograph, 9 1/2 In. 38.00
Tin, Zulu Stogies 73.00

A tip tray is a decorated metal tray less than 5 inches in diameter. It was placed on the table or counter to hold either the bill or the coins that were left as a tip. A change receiver could be made of glass, plastic, or metal. It was kept on the counter near the cash register and held the money passed back and forth by the cashier.

ADVERTISING, TIP TRAY, see also Advertising, Change Receiver

Tip Tray, ABC Bread, Palace of Varied Industries 35.00
Tip Tray, Andrew White Cigars 175.00
Tip Tray, Apollinaris Water, Polly Cartoon 75.00
Tip Tray, Bartel Lager, Ale & Porter 70.00
Tip Tray, Clover Brand Shoes, Black Boy Eating Watermelon 250.00
Tip Tray, Cottolene, Black Woman, Boy Picking Cotton ....58.00 To 165.00
Tip Tray, Dixie Loan Co., Money When You Need It, Gold Letters 70.00
Tip Tray, Everwess, Blue & Red, Cream Ground, Rectangular, 6 In. 35.00
Tip Tray, Fairy Soap, Tin Lithograph, 4 1/4 In. .... 38.00 To 88.00
Tip Tray, Globe-Wernicke Furniture & Undertakers 30.00
Tip Tray, Globe-Wernicke, Sectional Bookcase 75.00
Tip Tray, Gold Brand Chocolate & Cocoa 55.00
Tip Tray, Gold Seal Champagne, Product Scene 85.00
Tip Tray, Grain Beltbeers 25.00
Tip Tray, H. Wagener, Bottle With Label Picture 253.00
Tip Tray, Hydroler Whiskey, Tin Litho., 4 1/2 In. .... 25.00 To 60.00
Tip Tray, King's Pure Malt 70.00
Tip Tray, Light Horse Squadron Cigars 105.00
Tip Tray, Miller High Life, 1952 .... 10.00
Tip Tray, MiLola Cigars 80.00
Tip Tray, Moxie, Purple Flower 250.00

Tip Tray, National Brewing Co., Cowboy Holding Beer Bottle 715.00
Tip Tray, Oak Stove, Round 55.00
Tip Tray, Oakville Co., Hand Holding Safety Pin, Oval 55.00
Tip Tray, Old Angus Scotch 10.00
Tip Tray, Old Boone Whiskey, Tin Lithograph, 4 1/4 In. 185.00
Tip Tray, Opia Cigars, Girl Spaced Out On Opium 585.00
Tip Tray, Plymouth Cigar, Tin Lithograph, 3 3/4 In. 44.00
Tip Tray, Prudential 40.00
Tip Tray, Red Raven 145.00
Tip Tray, Rock Island Brewing Co., Lily A Beverage 65.00
Tip Tray, Rubsam & Hormann Brewing Co. 440.00
Tip Tray, Schlitz, 1955 .... 10.00
Tip Tray, Sea Pipers Scotch 10.00
Tip Tray, Seagrams 7 Crown 10.00
Tip Tray, Sears Roebuck 50.00
Tip Tray, Slade's Peanut Butter 32.00
Tip Tray, Sterling Beer, 1930s 18.00
Tobacco Cutter, Barnes, Smith & Co., With Lighter, Brass Plated 1045.00
Tobacco Cutter, Brown's Mule, Reynold's 50.00
Tobacco Cutter, El Palencia, Nickel Plated, Iron, 1889, 6 In. 125.00
Tobacco Cutter, Imp 145.00
Tobacco Cutter, King Alfred 10 Cents, Iron, 14 1/4 In. 795.00
Tobacco Cutter, Lorillard 55.00
Tobacco Cutter, Reynolds 68.00
Tobacco Cutter, Silhouette, Horse, Rider, Iron, Handle, 19 In. 275.00
Tobacco Cutter, Star Plug Tobacco 55.00
Tobacco Cutter, Star, Save The Tags, Cast Iron, Calibrated To 2 .... 75.00
Tray, Adolph Coors, Mountain Trademark, 13 In. 140.00
Tray, Alta–Vista Ice Cream, Victorian Lady 275.00
Tray, Anheuser–Busch, Tin Lithograph, 15 1/2 x 18 In. 1925.00
Tray, Baker's Chocolate, Round, Large .... 350.00 To 422.50
Tray, Baker's Chocolate, Tin, 16 1/2 x 14 In. 132.00
Tray, Bornheim Style Beer, Tivoli Brewing Co., Brass, 12 In. 95.00
Tray, Budweiser, Louis Levy 150.00
Tray, Buffalo Brewery, Sacramento, Round, 12 In. 192.50
Tray, Buffalo Brewing Co., Indian, On Horse, Dish–Type, Deep 525.00
Tray, Calumet Baking Powder, 7 x 11 In. 10.00
Tray, Central Brewing Co. 715.00
Tray, Champagne Velvet Beer, Terre Haute, Indiana 412.50
Tray, Champlain Ale, Enamel, 12 In. 50.00
Tray, Cherry Blossoms, Oblong 145.00
Tray, Clement Cycles & Autos 100.00
Tray, Consumers Beer, Round, 14 In. 50.00
Tray, Crystal Spring Brewing Co., 2 Country Girls, At River 1100.00
Tray, Dawsons Ale & Beer 80.00
Tray, Deer Brand, August Schell Brewing Co., 14 In. 100.00
Tray, Deer Park Brewing Co., Lithograph, 11 1/2 In. 165.00
Tray, Diogenes Breing Co., Oval, Stamped Figure, Brass 325.00
Tray, Doe Wah Jack Stoves, Small 24.00
Tray, Dr Pepper, Woman, Rectangular 225.00
Tray, Echo Springs Whiskey, Wood Grain, 13 In. 52.00
Tray, Edelweiss Beer, Pretty Red–Headed Woman, 1913 .... 120.00
Tray, Emmerling Grossvater Beer, Rectangular 345.00
Tray, Enterprise Beer, Picture of Woman, 1905 .... 200.00
Tray, Falls City Lager Beer, Oval 150.00
Tray, Falstaff Lemp Brewery, 1908, 24 In. 375.00
Tray, Falstaff Lemp Brewery, 1910, 24 In. 275.00
Tray, Franks' Pale Dry Ginger Ale, Soda Bottle, 1930s 65.00
Tray, Ginsing Beverages, Lithograph of Woman On Rickshaw 110.00
Tray, Green River Whiskey, Black Man, Mule In Front of Inn 275.00
Tray, Hampden Brewing Co., Tin Lithograph, 13 In. 185.00
Tray, Hap, Cast of Trust Game, Copper, 1930, 12 1/2 x 16 1/2 In. 110.00
Tray, Havensteins, Blue, Gold, Red, Round, 14 In. 110.00

Tray, Heim Beer, Factory Scene, 16 1/2 x 13 1/2 In. .... 750.00 To 880.00
Tray, Hires Root Beer, Haskell Coffin Girl, 13 x 10 In. 210.00
Tray, Iroquois Indian Head Beer, Indian Picture, Round 95.00
Tray, J. Leisy Brewing Co., Tin Lithograph, 15 1/2 x 18 In. 2200.00
Tray, Jersey Cream, Victorian Girl, 13 In. .... 145.00 To 175.00
Tray, Julia Marlow, Various Roles, Tin, 16 1/2 x 13 1/2 In. 145.00
Tray, Lemp Brewing Co., Logo In Sunburst, Tin, 1905, 12 In. 90.00
Tray, Liberty Beer, Rochester, N. Y., Indian Maiden, 12 In. 82.50
Tray, Malt Rainier Beer, Friends, 1905 .... 125.00
Tray, Miller Beer, Girl On Moon, 13 1/4 In. .... 30.00 To 45.00
Tray, Miller High Life, Oval 65.00
Tray, Monroe Brewing Co., Picture of King, c.1912, 12 In. 135.00
Tray, Nu–Grape, Girl With Bottle 95.00
Tray, Old Dutch Cleanser, Porcelain, 14 x 20 In. 225.00
Tray, Olympia Beer, Cavalier, c.1915 .... 65.00
Tray, Olympic Beer, Girl Perched On Bottle 45.00
Tray, Orange Julep Drink, Tin Lithograph, 13 In. 59.00
Tray, Pacific Beer, Mt. Tacoma, 1912, 12 In. 50.00
Tray, Page's Ice Cream, Brownies, Lithograph, 13 x 10 3/4 In. 247.00
Tray, Pennzoil, 100% Pure Pennsylvania, 25 x 31 In. 95.00
Tray, People Beer & Old Derby Ale, Oshkosh, Wis., 13 1/2 In. 72.00
Tray, Peter Dolger Beer, 17 In. 220.00
Tray, Red Raven, Bird In Bottle, Round 200.00
Tray, Red Ribbon Beer, Tin Lithograph, 13 In. 330.00
Tray, Ropkins Hartford, Interior Bay Scene 1150.00
Tray, Rowes Ice Cream, Pretty Girl 295.00
Tray, Ruppert Beer, Art Deco By Hans Flato 95.00
Tray, Scotch Whiskey, Copper, Bar Top, Engraved, 8 1/2 In. 55.00
Tray, Sheridan Beer, Cowboy, Bucking Horse 65.00
Tray, Sparks, Perfect Health Porcelain, Gold Frame, 21 In. 600.00
Tray, Straight Whiskey, Tin Lithograph, 12 In. 160.00
Tray, Superior Beer, Indian Maiden 45.00
  ADVERTISING, TRAY, TIP, see Advertising, Tip Tray
Tray, Virginia Dare, American Wines, Tin Lithograph, 12 In. 245.00
Tray, Walter Brewing Co., Eau Claire, Wis., Factory, Brass, 1910s 295.00
Tray, Watt's Glycerine Jelly, Lillie Langtry, 17 x 11 1/2 In. 715.00
Tray, Weld's Ice Cream, Round, 13 1/4 In. 55.00
Tray, Welz & Zerweck Brewery, Brooklyn, 13 1/2 x 16 1/2 In. 165.00
Tray, Zipp's Cherri–O, Round, 12 In. 770.00
Tumbler, A & W Cream Soda, Frosted Glass, Metal Holder, 5 In. 7.00
Tumbler, American Brewing Co., St. Louis, Mo., Eagle, 6 1/2 In. 39.00
Tumbler, Anaconda Brewing Co., Anaconda, Montana 798.00
Tumbler, Anheuser–Busch, A Logo, Eagle, Purple Glass, 5 3/8 In. 30.00
Tumbler, Atlas Prager, Red Enameled Glass, 4 3/4 In. 20.00
Tumbler, Berghoff, Est. 1898, Enameled Glass, 4 7/8 In. 2.00
Tumbler, Blatz, Blue Enameled Glass, 4 3/4 In. 2.00
Tumbler, Buckeye Beer, Ohio 60.00
Tumbler, Burger King, Star Wars 2.75
Tumbler, Chicklets, Metal, Glass 85.00
Tumbler, Coors, Centennial, 1959 .... 15.00
Tumbler, Dr Pepper, Happy Days, Fonz, 6 1/8 In. 3.00
Tumbler, Dr Pepper, I'm A Pepper, Richard Gittus, Red, 5 In. 3.00
Tumbler, DuBois Budweiser, Etched 45.00
Tumbler, Esser's Best, Cross Plains, Wisconsin 305.00
Tumbler, Fountain, Cliquot Club Cyc–Cola, 5 In. 24.00
Tumbler, Gentleman Brewing, Etched Glass 35.00
Tumbler, Gleuck's Beer, Minnesota 43.00
Tumbler, Hygela Spring Water, Etched 10.00
Tumbler, Measuring, Frigidaire, Div. General Motors, 4 5/8 In. 2.00
Tumbler, Measuring, General Electric, Tblsp. To Pint, 4 3/4 In. 4.00
Tumbler, National Bohemian Beer, One–Eyed Man, 5 13/16 In. 9.00
Tumbler, Old Milwaukee Beer, Logo In Circle, 3 1/4 In. 3.00
Tumbler, Pizza Hut, All Time Bronco Greats, 1 of 4, 4 1/8 In. 4.00

Tumbler, Popeye's Fried Cicken	25.00
Tumbler, Sally's New York Sheraton Hotel, Figural Nude, Tall	15.00
Tumbler, Schlitz, Brown Enameled Name, Glass, White, 3 1/8 In.	7.00
Tumbler, Wendy's, 10th Ann. Convention, 1985, Crystal, 6 5/8 In.	5.00
Tumbler, Wolfman, Universal Pictures	35.00
Tumbler, Yes We Can, McDonald's, Gr. Opening, May 1982, 4 3/4 In.	4.00
Umbrella, John Neher Clothing For Horses & Mules, 25 In.	55.00
Vase, Lord Calvert, 2–Sided, China, 12 In.	15.00
Wall Pocket, Cool Cigarette, Tin	25.00
Whistle, Blow For Harvest Bread	12.50
Whistle, Butter–Nut Bread, 1920s	17.00
Whistle, Figural, Oscar Mayer	12.00
Whistle, Yoerg's Beer, Cave Aged, Aluminum, Thimble Shape	20.00
Window, Budweiser Faust, Leaded, c.1890, 47 x 31 In.	4950.00
Window, Phoenix Beer, Stained Glass, 69 x 31 In.	880.00
Yard Stick, John Deere, 4 Sides	8.00
Yard Stick, Moxie	185.00

Agata glass was made by Joseph Locke of the New England Glass Company of Cambridge, Massachusetts, after 1885. A metallic stain was applied to New England Peachblow and the mottled design characteristic of agata appeared.

AGATA, Finger Bowl, Splotches, Tracery	695.00
Toothpick, Cactus, Red	175.00
Tumbler, Mottled	450.00
Tumbler, New England, 3 3/4 In.	550.00
Tumbler, Water, Gold Oily Mottling, 3 7/8 In.	795.00
Vase, Lily, Folded Tricorner Rim, Flower Form, 5 3/4 In.	1000.00
Vase, Trumpet, Pale Mottling, 8 3/4 In.	440.00
Water Set, 6 Piece	3200.00

Akro agate glass was made in Clarksburg, West Virginia, from 1932 to 1951. Before that time, the firm made children's glass marbles. Most of the glass is marked with a crow flying through the letter A.

AKRO AGATE, Ashtray, Floor Model, Parts Light Up	95.00
Bell, Cobalt Blue, 5 1/2 In.	75.00
Bowl, Green, Graduated Dart, 3–Footed, 5 1/4 In.	35.00
Candlestick, Pumpkin, Pair	145.00
Coaster, Transparent Blue, Westite	90.00
Creamer, Marbelized Blue & White	15.00
Cup, Green	9.00
Cup, Pumpkin	12.00
Flowerpot, Green, Blue Marbelized, 2 3/4 In.	9.00
Flowerpot, Green, Orange Marbelized, 2 1/4 In.	7.00
Flowerpot, Pumpkin, 4 In.	85.00
Flowerpot, Ribbed Top, Cobalt Blue, 2 1/2 In.	12.00
Lamp, Custard Glass, 23 In.	35.00
Pitcher, Water, Blue, Stacked Disc & Interior Panel	85.00
Planter, Orange, White, 6 In.	14.00
Plate, Light Blue, Raised Daisy	15.00
Powder Jar, Colonial Lady, Pink	45.00
Powder Jar, Concentric Ring, Green Marbelized	30.00
Powder Jar, Mexicali, Orange Marbelized	45.00
Powder Jar, Scotty Dog Cover	55.00
Saucer, Turquoise	4.00
Saucer, Yellow	4.00
Saucer, Yellow, Raised Daisy	12.00
Tea Set, Child's, Jadite, Box	450.00
Tea Set, Child's, Raised Daisy, Box, 13 Piece	210.00
Tumbler, White, Stacked Disc & Interior Panel	50.00
Water Set, Transparent Green, 7 Piece	70.00

◆ ◆

A white ring on a table top is in the finish, a black ring is in the wood. It is easier to remove a damaged finish than a wood stain.

◆ ◆

Alabaster is a very soft form of gypsum, a stone that resembles marble. It was often carved into vases or statues in Victorian times. There are alabaster carvings being made even today. Because the alabaster is very porous, it will dissolve if kept in water, so do not use alabaster vases for flowers.

ALABASTER, Bowl, Carved Base, 13 3/4 x 5 1/4 In.	30.00
Bust, Woman, Renaissance Style, Marble Base, 16 In.	400.00
Bust, Young Boy, Cap & Lace Collar, Marble Plinth, 14 In.	605.00
Figurine, Child, Reclining On Cushion, Holding Doll, 10 x 19 In.	495.00
Figurine, Young Girl, Seated On Cushion, 14 1/2 In.	550.00
Group, Birth of Venus, On Scallop Shell, 19th Century, 17 In.	440.00
Lamp, Birds, 19 In.	375.00
Lamp, Classic Draped Woman, Fountain, 20 1/2 x 16 x 19 1/2 In.	500.00
Lamp, Rebecca At The Well, Holding Urn of Water, 44 In.	4180.00
Tazza, Grapevine Design Rim, Italy, 19th Century, 10 x 9 1/2 In.	121.00

Alexandrite is a name with many meanings. It is a form of the mineral chrysoberyl that changes from green to red under artificial light. A man–made version of this mineral is sold in Mexico today. It changes from deep purple to aquamarine blue under artificial light. The Alexandrite listed here is glass made in the late nineteenth and twentieth centuries. Thomas Webb & Sons sold their transparent glass shaded from yellow to rose to blue under the name Alexandrite. Stevens and Williams had a cased Alexandrite of yellow, rose, and blue. A. Douglas Nash Corporation made an amethyst–colored Alexandrite. Several American glass companies of the 1920s made a glass that changed color under electric lights and these were called Alexandrite, too.

ALEXANDRITE, Bowl, Honeycomb Pattern, Fold–In Top, 2 1/2 x 3 1/4 In.	715.00
Toothpick, Hat	150.00
Toothpick, Honeycomb, Straight Rim, 2 1/8 In.	495.00
Toothpick, Ruffled Rim, 2 1/2 In.	700.00

Alhambra is a pattern of tableware made in Vienna, Austria, in the twentieth century. The geometric designs are in applied gold, red, and dark green. Full sets of dishes can be found in this pattern.

ALHAMBRA, Plate, 10 In.	40.00
Sugar & Creamer	100.00
Cup & Saucer, Austria	50.00

Aluminum was more expensive than gold or silver until the 1850s. Chemists learned how to refine bauxite to get aluminum. Jewelry and other small objects were made of the valuable metal until 1914 when an inexpensive smelting process was invented. The aluminum collected today dates from the 1930s through 1950s. Hand–hammered pieces are the most popular.

ALUMINUM, Ashtray, Wendell August Forge	40.00
Basket, Flowered Handle, Rodney Kent, 5 x 7 In.	15.00
Basket, Hammered, Blue Ridge Plate Insert	25.00
Basket, Hand Finished, Fruits & Flowers, 8 x 11 In.	15.00
Bowl, Fruit, Handle, Rodney Kent, 3 1/2 x 10 In.	25.00
Bowl, Grape Clusters Around Edge, Westbend, 14 In.	5.00
Bowl, Incised Flowers & Leaves, Palmer Smith, Small	6.00
Bowl, John Finley	15.00

Bowl, Shallow, Looped Handles, Wilson	14.00
Bread Basket, Cover, Bamboo Pattern, Handle, Everlast, 8 x 9 In.	20.00
Bun Warmer	70.00
Cake Plate, Pedestal Style, 8 1/2 In.	15.00
Candleholder, Lotus Leaf, Art Deco, Wendell August Forge, Pair	70.00
Cocktail Shaker	45.00
Crumb Set, Art Nouveau Design	17.00
Dish, Lobster, Bruce Fox	55.00
Fruit Bowl, Pedestal	45.00
Ice Bucket, Bamboo Pattern, Everlast	19.00
Ice Bucket, Everlast, Lid Knob, Side Handles	19.00
Ice Bucket, Insulated, Everlast, 5 1/2 x 9 In.	30.00
Ice Bucket, Wendell August Forge	120.00
Lazy Susan, 4 Sections, Everlast	10.00
Match Holder, Arthur Armor	30.00
Pancake & Corn Set, Russel Wright, Chass Brass	245.00
Pitcher, Mum Pattern, Continental	50.00
Pitcher, Water, Everlast	22.00
Plate, Limoges Plate Interior, 2 Handles, Farber & Shlevin	46.00
Sherbet, Glass Liner, 8 Piece	20.00
Snack Server, 3 Sections, Electric, Chase Brass	125.00
Table Set, Child's, Serving Spoon, Solingen, Germany, 6 Piece	90.00
Tray, 5 Sections, Continental	20.00
Tray, Canterbury Arts, Handle, 7 1/2 x 17 1/4 In.	20.00
Tray, Chrysanthemum Pattern, Round, 14 In.	45.00
Tray, Curved Handles, Lilies	5.00
Tray, Hammered, Floral, 2 Handles, Keystone, 14 In.	16.00
Tray, Hammered, Geese, Arthur Armour, 11 x 17 In.	45.00
Tray, Harmony House, 10 In.	15.00
Tray, Lake & Boat Dock Scene, Cromell, 13 x 21 In.	12.50
Tray, Pine Pattern, Swirled Ridges, Square	5.00
Tray, Tidbit, 2 Fan–Shaped Sections, Center Handle, Rodney Kent	15.00
Tumbler	2.50
Vase, Hammered, Arthur Armour, 12 In.	75.00
Warmer, Tile Inset	250.00
Waste Basket, Arthur Armour	15.00
Water Set, Mayfair, 9 Piece	155.00

AMBER, see Jewelry

Amber glass is the name of any glassware with the proper yellow–brown shading. It was a popular color just after the Civil War and many pressed glass pieces were made of amber glass. Depression glass of the 1930s–1950s was also made in shades of amber glass. All types are being reproduced.

AMBER GLASS, Box, Salt	130.00
Canister, Tea	65.00
Jug, Claret, French Pewter Holder, 11 1/2 In.	265.00
Salt & Pepper	20.00
Vase, Orange Berries, Leaves, White, Dragonfly, Footed, 5 In.	40.00

AMBERETTE, see Pressed Glass, Amberette

Amberina is a two–toned glassware made from 1883 to about 1900. It was patented by Joseph Locke of the New England Glass Company, but was also made by other companies. The glass shades from red to amber.

AMBERINA, see also Baccarat; Plated Amberina

AMBERINA, Bowl, Daisy & Button, Boat Shape, 8 1/2 x 10 1/4 In.	450.00
Bowl, Diamond–Quilted, Scalloped Rim, 5 In.	355.00
Bowl, Inverted Thumbprint, Boat Shape, Meriden Holder, 14 1/2 In.	425.00
Bowl, Pressed Daisy & Button, Hobbs, Brockunier, Boat Shape, 10 In.	450.00
Butter, Cover, Enameled, Blue, Large	595.00
Canoe, Daisy & Button, Silver Plated Holder, 8 In.	550.00
Castor, Pickle, Swirled Raised Rib Design, Cherubs On Frame	395.00

Celery Vase, Diamond–Quilted, Square Scalloped Top, 6 1/2 In. 325.00
Celery Vase, New England, Square Top, 6 1/4 In. 495.00
Celery Vase, Thumbprint Panels 285.00
Compote, Diamond–Quilted, Fuchsia, Amber, Mt. Washington, 8 1/2 In. 665.00
Creamer, Square Top, Neck & Shoulder, Amber Handle, 4 1/4 In. 385.00
Cruet, Inverted Thumbprint, New England 595.00
Cruet, Inverted Thumbprint, White Flowers, Square Base, 8 1/4 In. 450.00
Cruet, Wine, Swirl, Pedestal, Amber Double Loop Handle, 11 1/4 In. 295.00
Decanter, Russian, Libbey, 7 1/2 In. ....*Illus* 1200.00
Decanter, Swirl, Double Loop Handle, Amber Stopper, 11 1/4 In. 295.00
Dish, Daisy & Button, Cranberry, Orange, Yellow, 6 In. ....*Illus* 55.00
Dish, Ice Cream, Blown–Out Ribs, Scalloped Rim, 9 1/4 x 6 1/2 In. 295.00
Dish, Scalloped Rim, Russian, 5 3/4 In. 55.00
Eyecup .... 18.00 To 25.00
Ice Bucket, Inverted Thumbprint, Tab Handles, 4 3/4 x 6 3/4 In. 705.00
Liquor Set, 6 Piece 400.00
Pitcher, Hobnail, Amber Handle, 6 3/4 In. 815.00
Pitcher, Inverted Thumbprint, Ruffled, Amber Handle, 9 1/2 In. 265.00
Pitcher, Milk, Amber Handle, 7 3/8 In. 195.00
Pitcher, Milk, Coin Spot, Ribbed Handle, Square Mouth, 4 1/2 In. 330.00
Pitcher, Russian, Libbey, 12 In. ....*Illus* 2200.00
Pitcher, Tankard Shape, Optic, Amber Handle, 7 In. 425.00
Pitcher, Water, Design 400.00
Pitcher, Water, Inverted Thumbprint, Amber Handle, 7 In. 395.00
Pitcher, Water, Ribbed, Amber Handle, 10 1/4 In. 265.00
Salt & Pepper, Blue & White Daisies, Original Top, 3 1/2 In. 255.00
Saltshaker, Silver Plated 1950.00
Spooner, Daisy & Button, 5 In. 255.00
Sugar, Cover, Daisy & Button, Amber Base, 5 1/2 In. 540.00
Toothpick, Coin Dot, Ruffled 250.00
Toothpick, Daisy & Button 385.00
Toothpick, Daisy & Button, Footed 275.00
Toothpick, Diamond–Quilted Optic, Mt. Washington 250.00
Toothpick, Diamond–Quilted, Tricorner Rim, New England Glass Co. 225.00
Toothpick, Venetian Diamond, Square Mouth 225.00
Tumbler, Baby Thumbprint .... 59.00 To 75.00
Tumbler, Diamond–Quilted, Belltone, 3 3/4 In. 95.00
Tumbler, Reverse Thumbprint, Etched 95.00
Tumbler, Russian, 3 Piece ....*Illus* 3135.00
Vase, Cylindrical, 8 3/8 In. 125.00
Vase, Drape Pattern, 9 Blown–Out Panels, Flared, 6 1/2 In. 250.00

Amberina, Dish, Daisy & Button, Cranberry, Orange, Yellow, 6 In.; Amberina,
Decanter, Russian, Libbey, 7 1/2 In.; Amberina, Pitcher, Russian, Libbey, 12 In.;
Amberina, Tumbler, Russian, 3 Piece

Vase, Draped, 9 Fluted Panels, Fuchsia To Amber, 6 1/2 In. 250.00
Vase, Embossed Leaves At Base, Embossed Swirl, 8 3/8 In. 125.00
Vase, Jack-In-The-Pulpit, Swirl, Amber Feet & Trim, 12 In. 445.00
Vase, Swirl, Enameled Mums, Green Leaves, Amber Edging, 9 7/8 In. 325.00
Vase, Trumpet, Applied Wafer Base, Pink Ring At Junction, 7 In. 475.00
Water Set, 5 Piece 325.00
Water Set, Swirl, Stemmed, 7 Piece 325.00

The American Art Clay Company of Indianapolis, Indiana, made a variety of art pottery wares, especially vases, from about 1930 to after World War II. The company used the mark AMACO, as well as the company name. Do not confuse this company with an earlier art pottery firm from Edgerton, Wisconsin, called the American Art Clay Works.

AMERICAN ART CLAY CO., Figurine, Cheetah, Blue, 5 In. 75.00
Vase, Deco, Red, White, 7 In. 80.00
Vase, Green, 8 In. 85.00
Vase, Green, Drip Glaze, 8 In. 75.00
Vase, Green, Metallic, 9 In. 110.00

Ceramic dinnerware made in the United States from the 1930s through the 1950s is called *Depression dinnerware* or *American dinnerware* by collectors. Most was made in potteries in southern Ohio, West Virginia, and California. Dishes were sold in gift shops and department stores, or were given away as premiums. Many of these patterns are listed in this book in their own sections such as Autumn Leaf, Coors, Fiesta, Franciscan, Harker, Harlequin, Red Wing, Riviera, Russel Wright, Vernon Kilns, and Watt. For more information, see *Kovels' Depression Glass & American Dinnerware Price List.*

AMERICAN DINNERWARE, Ashtray, Pate Sur Pate, Teal, Harker 3.00
Bowl, Apple & Pear, Blue Ridge, 8 In. 6.00
Bowl, Rancho, Green, French Saxon, 5 1/2 In. .... 2.50 To 3.00
Bowl, Vegetable, Tickled Pink, Blue Ridge 18.00
Bowl, Woodvine, Universal, 6 1/2 In. 5.00
Cake Server, Spoon, Fork, Mexicana, Homer Laughlin 150.00
Candlestick, Ring, Green, Bauer 15.00
Chop Plate, California Provincial, Metlox, 12 In. 25.00
Cookie Jar, Mar-Crest, Western Stoneware .... 20.00 To 22.00
Creamer, Lu-Ray, Pink, Taylor, Smith & Taylor 4.00
Cup & Saucer, Hacienda, Homer Laughlin 4.00
Cup & Saucer, Homestead Provincial, Metlox 8.00
Cup & Saucer, Rhythm, Yellow, Homer Laughlin 7.00
Cup & Saucer, Woodvine, Universal 5.50
Cup, After Dinner, Mayflower, Blue Ridge 10.00
Cup, Ballerina, Dove Gray, Universal Potteries 3.00
Currier & Ives, Bowl, 9 In., Royal China 7.00
Currier & Ives, Pepper Shaker, Royal China 5.00
Mixing Bowl, Ring, Dark Blue, Bauer, 1 1/2 Pt. 17.50
Mug, Red Rooster, Metlox .... 15.00 To 18.00
Pie Baker, Silhouette, Crooksville 25.00
Pie Plate, Cat-Tail, Universal Potteries, 10 In. 8.00
Pitcher, Rhythm Rose, Homer Laughlin, 5 1/2 In. 9.00
Plate, Caliente, Green, Paden City, 9 In. 10.00
Plate, Crab Apple, 6 In., Blue Ridge .... 2.25 To 3.00
Plate, Crab Apple, 10 In., Blue Ridge .... 6.00 To 10.00
Plate, Lu-Ray, Blue, Taylor, Smith & Taylor, 6 In. 3.00
Plate, Lu-Ray, Green, Taylor, Smith & Taylor, 10 In. 15.00
Plate, Petalware, Light Green, W. S. George, 7 In. 2.50
Plate, Petalware, Yellow, W. S. George, 6 In. 1.50
Plate, Rancho, Maroon, French Saxon, 9 In. .... 4.00 To 4.50
Plate, Virginia Rose, 9 In., Homer Laughlin 5.00
Plate, Wildflower, 9 In. 10.00

Plate, Woodfield, Coral, Steubenville, 10 1/2 In. 5.00
Plate, Yorktown, Terra–Cotta, Knowles, 9 In. ....5.00 To 10.00
Platter, Organdy, Homer Laughlin, 12 In. 12.50
Salt & Pepper, Mexicana, Homer Laughlin 65.00
Soup, Coupe, Sunny, Blue Ridge 5.00
Soup, Dish, Old Curiosity Shop, Green, Royal China 3.00
Sugar & Creamer, Cover, Red Rooster, Metlox .... 10.00 To 20.00
Sugar & Creamer, Tickled Pink, Blue Ridge 20.00
Sugar, California Provincial, Metlox 11.00
Sugar, Old Curiosity Shop, Pink, Royal China 3.00
Teapot, Cover, Woodfield, Gray, Steubenville 20.00
Teapot, Sunny, Blue Ridge 45.00
Tumbler, Ring, Yellow, Bauer, 3 Oz. 15.00
Tureen, Cover, Virginia Rose, Homer Laughlin 35.00

The American Encaustic Tiling Company was founded in Zanesville, Ohio, in 1875. The company planned to make a variety of tiles to compete with the English tiles that were selling in the United States for use in fireplaces and other architectural needs. The first glazed tiles were made in 1880, embossed tiles were added in 1881, faience tiles in the 1920s. The firm closed in 1935 and reopened in 1937 as the Shawnee Pottery.

AMERICAN ENCAUSTIC TILING CO., Tile, Art Deco, 4 Piece 125.00
Tile, Fish, Waves, 4 Colors, 2 x 4 In. 65.00
Tile, Floral, Blue, 6 In. 25.00
Tile, Malibu, 6 In. 25.00
Tile, Multicolor, 6 In. 25.00
Tile, Tudor, 6 In. 25.00

Amethyst glass is any of the many glasswares made in the dark purple color of the gemstone called amethyst. Included in this section are many pieces made in the nineteenth and twentieth centuries. Very dark pieces are called black amethyst and are listed under that heading.

AMETHYST GLASS, Candlestick, Hexagonal, 7 5/8 In. 320.00
Compote, Loop Pattern, Flint 1300.00
Cordial Set, Silver Overlay, Sterling Tag, 6 Piece 65.00
Plate, 6 In., 4 Piece 28.00
Vase, 8 In. 14.00
Vase, Chalice, Controlled Bubbles Stem, Intaglio, 12 In. 87.00
   AMPHORA, see Teplitz
   ANDIRON AND RELATED FIREPLACE ITEMS, see Fireplace

Stuffed animals or fish, rugs made of animal skins, and other similar collectibles are listed in this section. Collectors should be aware of the endangered species laws that make it illegal to buy and sell some of these items. Any eagle feathers, many types of cats, such as leopard, and many forms of tortoiseshell can be confiscated if discovered by the government.

ANIMAL TROPHY, Badger, Rampant, With Whiskey Bottle 55.00
Bear, Black, Standing, Naturalistic Base ....*Illus* 2750.00
Bear, Brown, 6 Ft. ....*Illus* 3850.00
Birds, Moss, Beetles, Dome Case, c.1860 ....*Illus* 650.00
Buffalo, Head, Mounted 1500.00
Moose Head, 36 x 41 In. 770.00
Moose Head, 51 x 45 In. 465.00
Rug, Bear Skin 395.00
Rug, Bearskin, 54 x 74 In. 375.00
Rug, Zebra Skin, 10 Ft. x 6 Ft. 7 In. 495.00
Skull, Alligator, 7 In. 95.00
Skull, Baboon, Adult Male, Fangs 125.00
Skull, Impala, 20–In. Horns 45.00
Skull, Monkey, Jaws & Teeth 45.00

Skull, Walrus, Nose Plate, Teeth, 14–In. Tusks	650.00
Skull, Wolf, Jaw & Teeth	95.00
Turtle, Stuffed, Large	55.00
Tusk, Walrus, 21 x 2 3/4 In. Diam.	295.00
Tusk, Warthog, Curved, 9 x 1 1/4 In. Diam.	25.00
Wolf's Head, Snarling, Showing Teeth	375.00

Animation cels are painted drawings on celluloid that are needed to make an animated cartoon. Hundreds of cels are made, then photographed in sequence to make a cartoon showing moving figures. Early examples made by the Walt Disney Studios are popular with collectors today.

ANIMATION ART, Cel, Alice In Wonderland, Matted, Framed, 8 x 5 3/4 In.	2200.00
Cel, Alice In Wonderland, Crawling	1500.00
Cel, Alice In Wonderland, Sketch of Red Rose	250.00
Cel, All Dogs Go To Heaven, Green Gator Holds Charlie	200.00
Cel, Aristocats, O'Malley & Duchess, 5 1/2 x 8 1/2 In.	544.00
Cel, Aristocats, Tom O'Malley, Eyes Wide Open	300.00
Cel, Bambi, Thumper, 6 x 5 In.	1815.00
Cel, Bedknobs & Broomsticks, King Leonidas, Robe & Crown	225.00
Cel, Ben & Me, Kneeling Ben Franklin	500.00
Cel, Berenstain Bears, Family Scene, Papa Reading To Cubs	100.00
Cel, Betty Boop, Baby Boop & Pudge	650.00
Cel, Borden's, Elmer & Son, Commercial	165.00
Cel, Brave Little Tailor, Matted & Framed, 1938, 7 x 6 3/4 In	4400.00
Cel, Bugs Bunny, Unmentionables, Framed, Friz Freleng, 1963	750.00
Cel, Cinderella, Duke On Chandelelier, 1950, 9 x 10 1/4 In.	990.00
Cel, Cinderella, Prince Charming, 9 x 10 In.	907.00
Cel, Donald Duck, Matted, 1950s, 9 x 6 In.	770.00
Cel, Donald Duck, Officer Duck, In Uniform	425.00
Cel, Donald Duck, Ready To Fight, Matted, 1945, 8 1/2 x 10 In.	2090.00

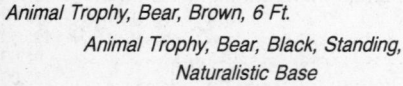

Animal Trophy, Bear, Brown, 6 Ft.
Animal Trophy, Bear, Black, Standing,
Naturalistic Base

Animal Trophy, Birds, Moss, Beetles,
Dome Case, c.1860

Cel, Donald Duck, Sailor Suit, 7 1/4 x 4 In. 1028.00
Cel, Duck Laugh, Daffy Laughing, 1930s, 6 1/2 x 5 In. 1320.00
Cel, Duck Tales, Descending Stairs, Matted, 1970s, 7 x 10 In. 880.00
Cel, Dumbo, Sad, Timothy On His Trunk 1000.00
Cel, Eeyore & Piglet, A Day For Eeyore 500.00
Cel, Elroy & George Jetson, 1960s 325.00
Cel, Fantasia, 3 Cherubs Floating Over Garland of Flowers 1600.00
Cel, Fantasia, Mickey Mouse & Pluto, 8 x 11 In. 665.00
Cel, Fantasia, Pastoral Symphony, 12 x 15 In. 847.00
Cel, Fawn & Bluebird, Snow White 4000.00
Cel, Ferdinand The Bull, Picador On Horse, 1938, 8 x 11 In. 605.00
Cel, Flintstones, Barney On Bike 100.00
Cel, Flintstones, Barney With Space Suit 100.00
Cel, Flintstones, Fred & Barney With Dinosaur & Policeman 110.00
Cel, Fox & Hound, Standing On Hind Legs To Drink 300.00
Cel, Geppetto Holding Pinocchio, Framed, 1939, 8 x 9 In. 8800.00
Cel, Great Mouse Detective, Basil At Microscope 300.00
Cel, Great Mouse Detective, Ratigan Looking Evil 325.00
Cel, Great Mouse Detective, Ratigan, 12 Henchmen 250.00
Cel, Gulliver's Travels, Tied Down, 12 1/4 x 16 3/4 In. 7700.00
Cel, Heidi's Song, At Cottage, Signed 225.00
Cel, Huey, Dewey, Louie, Top Hats, 5 x 5 1/2 In. 786.00
Cel, Hunting Instinct, Chip & Dale, Holding Acorns, 2 x 5 In. 605.00
Cel, Jerry Mouse, In Spacesuit, 1950s 150.00
Cel, Jiminy Cricket, Holding Hat In Hand 400.00
Cel, Jungle Book, Baloo, 8 x 10 1/2 In. 786.00
Cel, Jungle Book, Baloo, Mowgli, 7 x 10 In. 1940.00
Cel, Jungle Book, Mowgli Battling Kaa's Tail 600.00
Cel, Jungle Book, Mowgli, Dancing, 1967, 6 In. 675.00
Cel, Jungle Book, Mowgli, Dancing, Matted, 1967, 8 In. 675.00
Cel, Lady & The Tramp, 9 x 12 In. 1573.00
Cel, Lady & The Tramp, Framed, 1955, 5 1/2 x 13 1/4 In. 1980.00
Cel, Lady & Tramp, 4 x 8 In. 1998.00
Cel, Lady & Tramp, Lady Running With Ball In Mouth 1500.00
Cel, Lady Tremaine With Cane, Evil Pose 1000.00
Cel, Ludwig Von Drake, Dressed As Gaucho, Dancing, Singing 400.00
Cel, Make Mine Music, 1946, Framed, 7 1/2 In. 1100.00
Cel, Mary Poppins, Members of Pearly Band, 12 x 14 In. 968.00
Cel, Mickey Mouse Club, TV Show, 1950s, 7 3/4 x 7 3/4 In. 4400.00
Cel, Ninja Turtles 110.00
Cel, One Hundred & One Dalmatians, 1961, 7 3/4 x 9 3/4 In. 1430.00
Cel, Pebbles, On Stone Floor, Hand–Inked, Master Ground 495.00
Cel, Peter Pan, Indian Princess Tiger Lily, 12 x 15 In. 910.00
Cel, Peter Pan, John With Umbrella In Hand 500.00
Cel, Peter Pan, Tinkerbell, Framed, 9 3/4 x 12 In. 1100.00
Cel, Peter Pan, Wearing Headdress, 6 x 6 In. 1695.00
Cel, Pink Panther, With Camera, Hand–Inked, Matted 275.00
Cel, Pinocchio, Carrying Apple, 6 x 6 In. 4710.00
Cel, Pinocchio, Figaro The Cat 2300.00
Cel, Pinocchio, Jiminy Cricket, Framed, 1940 .... 600.00
Cel, Pinocchio, Stromboli, 7 x 7 In. 575.00
Cel, Pixie & Brownie, Shadows, c.1940, 6 1/2 x 5 In. 475.00
Cel, Pixie & Pup, Jumping Through Air, c.1940, 6 1/2 x 5 In. 475.00

◆◆

As a general rule, the drawer bottom of an 18th–century chest was made of 2 or 3 pieces of wood, the Victorian drawer bottom was made from a single piece. The Victorian bottom was often screwed in place.

◆◆

Cel, Porky Pig, In Sailor's Uniform, 1930s, 7 x 6 In. 1595.00
Cel, Robin Hood, Little John, Sherwood Green, 9 x 13 In. 650.00
Cel, Shanghaied, Mickey, Minnie, Peg–Leg, 8 x 10 In. 575.00
Cel, Sherlock Daffy, Daffy Duck As Detective, 9 x 11 In. 910.00
Cel, Sleeping Beauty, 3 Fairies, 12 x 16 In. 8715.00
Cel, Sleeping Beauty, 3 Fairies, Framed, 1959, 9 1/2 x 10 3/4 .... 1430.00
Cel, Sleeping Beauty, Aurora As Briar Rose, 8 x 10 In. 2175.00
Cel, Sleeping Beauty, Lackey, 6 x 6 In. 605.00
Cel, Sleeping Beauty, Prince Philip Kneels On Ground 175.00
Cel, Sleeping Beauty, Prince Phillip, 8 x 10 In. 1210.00
Cel, Smurfs, 2 Smurfs In Tree, 1 Blowing Horn 100.00
Cel, Smurfs, Smurfette 110.00
Cel, Snow White & 7 Dwarfs, Framed, 1937, 9 1/2 x 8 In. 2090.00
Cel, Snow White & 7 Dwarfs, Framed, 5 x 5 1/4 In. 385.00
Cel, Snow White & Seven Dwarfs, 6 x 8 In. 1936.00
Cel, Snow White, Waist Up, Eye Open 2500.00
Cel, Song of The South, 9 Story Drawings, 11 x 13 In. 1450.00
Cel, Sound Your F, Ratz Brothers Singing, 8 x 11 In. 930.00
Cel, Star Trek 300.00
Cel, Sword In The Stone, Merlin Examing His Specs 700.00
Cel, Ugly Duckling, Air–Brush Ground, 8 x 10 1/2 In. 3500.00
Cel, Who Framed Roger Rabbit, 8 x 13 In. 2425.00
Cel, Winnie The Pooh, On The Way To School, 9 x 12 In. 910.00
Cel, Winnie The Pooh, Sad Eeyore, 4 1/2 x 5 In. 1450.00
Cel, Woody Woodpecker, Building, Front End of Car, 8 x 11 In. 605.00
Cel, Yellow Submarine, 1968, 11 x 15 In., Pair 4430.00
Cel, Yellow Submarine, George & Paul, Blue Meanie, 7 x 9 In. 2055.00
Cel, Yellow Submarine, Matted, Framed, 1968, 12 x 32 In. 2750.00
Cel, Yellow Submarine, Nowhere Man, Blue Meanie, 8 x 12 In. 910.00

Anna Pottery The Anna Pottery was started in Anna, Illinois, in 1859 by Cornwall and Wallace Kirkpatrick. They made many types of utilitarian wares, bricks, drain tiles, and gift ware. The most collectible pieces made by the pottery are the pig–shaped bottles and jugs with special inscriptions, applied animals and figures. The pottery closed in 1894.

ANNA POTTERY, Castle, Gray, Blue Highlights, c.1882, 10 3/8 x 11 In. 3500.00
Pig, Embossed Railroad Lines, Cities, c.1882, 7 In. 5750.00
    APPLE PEELER, see Kitchen, Peeler, Apple

Arc–en–ciel is the French word for rainbow. A pottery factory named Arc–en–ciel was founded in Zanesville, Ohio, in 1903. The company made art pottery for a short time, then became the Brighton Pottery in 1905.

ARC–EN–CIEL, Vase, Gold Purple Luster, Rough Finish, 10 In. 200.00
Vase, Iridescent Gold, 6 In. 75.00

This section includes a variety of collectibles, usually very large, that have been removed from buildings. Hardware, backbars, doors, paneling, and even old bathtubs are now wanted by collectors. Pieces of the Victorian, Art Nouveau, and Art Deco styles are in greatest demand.

ARCHITECTURAL, Altar, Catholic, 2 Piece, 1890s, 6 x 8 Ft., 2 Piece 400.00
Back Bar, Mirror, Paneled, Brass Fixture, Tiger Oak, 10 Ft. 6500.00
Backbar, Marble Work Space, 1910s, 8 x 12 Ft. 3500.00
Banister Railing, Carved Spindles, Oak, 164 In., 3 Piece 605.00
Bath Tub, Tin, Design On Metal Legs, Oak Trim 400.00
Bathtub, Lobed Rim, Copper, 29 x 70 In. 825.00
Birdbath, Shell Bowl, Bird Design, Putto Support, Lead, 31 In. 275.00
Bracket, Horse Leg, Corner Protector, 25 In. 455.00
Cage, Bank Teller, Tennessee Marble, 5 Stations, 30 Ft. 4000.00
Column, Fluted, Pine, 67 In., Pair 495.00
Diorama, House, Wood, Metal, Plaster & Paper, 27 1/4 x 31 In. 412.50

Door, Relief Carved Figures, Nigeria, Yoruba, 52 In. 225.00
Doorknob, Clear Glass, Pair 12.00
Figure, Angel, Terra–Cotta, c.1870, 3 Ft. 8500.00
Finial, Acanthus Form, Copper, 41 1/2 In., Pair 465.00
Finial, Ball Above Spire, Spanish Brown Paint, Zinc, 39 In. 357.00
Finial, Flame–Top, Tin, 1 White, 1 Green, 27 In., Pair 110.00
Finial, Flame–Top, Tin, Double Stepped Base, 32 In., Pair 90.00
Finial, Fruit & Foliate Cluster, White & Brown, 27 In. 440.00
Finial, Pineapple Shape, Cast Iron, Green Finish, 20 1/2 In. 350.00
Finial, Pineapple, Applied Scroll, Copper, 24 In., Pair 440.00
Finial, Pineapple, Green Paint, Cast Iron, 21 In. 300.00
Finial, Spire, Banner Cut–Out Reads E. J., Tin, 67 In., Pair 660.00
Finial, Stylized Pineapple, Copper, 18 1/2 In., Pair 495.00
Finial, Terra–Cotta, American, 40 In. 465.00
Finial, Tulip, Painted & Verdigris, Copper, 27 In., 4 Piece 1985.00
Fireplace, Victorian, White Marble, 4 x 6 Ft. 6500.00
Fountain, Garden, Fiske, Center & 4 Side Spouts 8500.00
Fountain, Garden, Pan With Pipes, Lead, Shell Base, 30 In. 995.00
Gate, Cast Iron 950.00
Gate, Diamond Design, Scrolled Supports, Iron, 68 In., Pair 385.00
Gate, Spread Wing Eagle, Iron & Parcel Gilt, 88 In., 4 Piece 2875.00
Gate, Stylized Figure of Cockeral, Wrought Iron, 1925, 4 Ft. 650.00
Gatepost, Iron, Ear of Corn, Black, Green, Yellow, 44 In., Pair 800.00
Hitching Post, Horse's Head, Iron, 20th Century, 13 In., Pair 110.00
Ionic Capital, Painted, Terra–Cotta, Painted, 26 In. 110.00
Lion's Head, 3/4 Bodied Head, Zinc, 32 1/2 x 73 In. 3400.00
Louver, Fan Shape, Green & White Paint 750.00
Mantel, Pine, Country 135.00
Mantel, Polar, Incised & Applied Carving 52.50
Mantel, Quartersawn Oak, Plain 100.00
Marble, George III, Sienna, Swags, 43 x 46 In. 9350.00
Ornament, Cornucopia, Zinc, c.1880, 6 x 9 In., 4 Piece 225.00
Ornament, Eagle, Molded Zinc, Late 19th Century, America 1760.00
Ornament, Flame Finial On Pyramidal Base, Zinc. 33 In., Pair 385.00
Ornament, Gate, Lion, Cast Iron 95.00
Ornament, Roof, Flame Top, Zinc & Tin, 38 1/4 In., 4 Piece 995.00
Ornament, Stylized Pineapple, Copper, 16 1/2 In., Pair 440.00
Panel, Leaded, Alternating Brown & Tan Slag, 78 x 24 In., Pr. 175.00
Plaster Molding Sample Boards, 2 Sides, 19th Century, 7 Pc. 850.00
Post Office, Oak, Brass Box, Cage, Frosted Glass, 7 x 28 Ft. 6500.00
Post, Temple, Carved Foo Dogs, Birds, China, Giltwood, 96 In. 175.00
Railing, Floral Scroll, Cast Iron, 2 Sections, 37 1/2 In. 120.00
Railing, Wooden, Fire–Fender Type, Turned Posts, White, 35 In. 45.00
Showcase, Cashier's Station, Swinging Doors, Beveled Mirror 8500.00
Showcase, Penny Candy, Slant Front 425.00
Soda Fountain, 13 Chrome Stools, Freezer, Marble Top, 25 Ft. 4000.00
Soda Fountian, Marble, Foot Rests, 13 Chrome Stools, 25 Ft. 4000.00
Spire, Ball Finial, Ecclesiastical Forms, Iron, 84 In. 85.00
Sundial, Garden, Pedestal, Cast Iron & Cast Stone, 41 In. 2475.00
Telephone Booth, Public Telephone Sign, Pressed Tin Lined 1500.00
Teller's Cage, Tennessee Marble, 5 Stations, 30 Ft. 4000.00
Toilet Seat & Cover, Oak, Knott Mfg. Co., Salesman Sample 450.00
Vent, Barn, Star Center, Iron Hinges & Latch, 41 x 48 In. 450.00
Watch Case, Jeweler's, 6 Small Drawers, Watch Parts 350.00
Wood Carving, Faces In Foliage, J. Melchers, 21 x 24 In., Pr. 3400.00

Arequipa Pottery was produced from 1911 to 1918 by the patients of the Arequipa Sanitorium in Marin County Hills, California.

AREQUIPA, Pot, Green, Blue, Brown, Leaf Design, 5 In. 400.00
Vase, Carved Chestnut Tree Branches, Marked, c.1915, 6 1/4 In. 995.00
Vase, Molded Leaves, Multicolor, 3 x 5 In. 600.00
Vase, Vertical Fluted Design On Corners, c.1915, 8 1/8 In. 665.00
    ARGY–ROUSSEAU, see G. Argy–Rousseau

右
田

Arita is a port in Japan. Porcelain was made there from about 1616. Many types of decorations were used, including the popular Imari designs, which are listed under Imari in this book.

ARITA, Bottle, Trees, Houses, Red, Blue, 7 In.	550.00
Bowl, Chrysanthemums, Ribbon, Green, Red, Turquoise, Gold, 7 In.	1200.00
Vase, Flowering Trees, Flaring Ruffled Rim, 8 1/2 In., Pair	45.00
Vase, Stylized Flowers, Red, Blue, 10 In.	750.00

Art Deco, or Art Moderne, a style started at the Paris Exposition of 1925, is characterized by linear, geometric designs. All types of furniture and decorative arts, jewelry, book bindings, and even games were designed in this style.

ART DECO, see also Furniture; various glass categories; etc.

ART DECO, Ashtray, Figural, Nude, Metal, Floor, Bronze Finish, 26 In.	445.00
Ashtray, Woman, Nude, Standing, Metal, 8 In. Brass Tray, 26 In.	345.00
Box, Cigarette, Lighter, Chrome, Enameled, Ronson, 1930, 3 x 8 In.	110.00
Box, Hinged Lid, Cloisonne, 2 Stylized Horses, 1 1/2 x 4 3/4 In.	55.00
Compote, Cast Bronze, White Metal, Verdigris, Oscar Bach, 14 In.	200.00
Figurine, Woman, Winter Clothes, Schaubau Kunst	110.00
Flower Holder, Figural, Nude, Red Ceramic, 9 In.	49.00
Ice Bucket, Figural, Cockatoo, Metal, Glass Eyes, 15 In.	79.00
Jar, Cover, Porcelain, Bullet Stepped, 4 Medallions, Germany, 8 In.	44.00
Lamp, Gilt Caryatids Support Alabaster Dish, 21 In. ....*Illus*	6400.00
Mirror & Brush Set, Green Bakelite, 2 Piece	45.00
Sugar Shaker, Chrome Top & Bottom Spout, Clear Glass, Dated 1931	55.00
Tray, Burgundy, Micarta, Geometric, Westinghouse, Round, 15 In.	247.00
Vase, Biscuit Porcelain, Sculpted, Heinrich, 1930, 23 1/2 In.	770.00
Vase, Enameled, 14 In.	275.00
Vase, Flamingo	40.00
Wall Pocket, Head, Porcelain, Pair	75.00

Art Deco, Lamp, Gilt Caryatids Support Alabaster Dish, 21 In.

Art glass means any of the many forms of glassware made during the late nineteenth century or early twentieth century. These wares were expensive and production was limited. Art glass is not the typical commercial glass that was made in large quantities, and most of the art glass was produced by hand methods. Later twentieth–century glass is listed under Contemporary Glass or by the factory name.

ART GLASS, see also separate heading such as Burmese; Cameo Glass; Tiffany; etc.

ART GLASS, Basket, Band of Vaseline, White Rim, Thorn Handle, Blue, 7 1/2 In.	355.00
Basket, Pink & Yellow Spatter, Applied Thorn Handle, 7 In.	145.00
Basket, Rose Glass, Clear Glass Handles	140.00
Basket, Thorn Handle, White Spatter & Mica Interior, 8 1/4 In.	280.00
Bowl, Crystal, Random Bubbles, Littala, K. Franck, Small	90.00
Bowl, Frosted Flowers, St. Helaire, 6 3/4 In.	330.00
Bowl, Iridescent Gold Pulled Feather, Baluster, 7 x 5 1/8 In.	325.00
Bowl, Leaded, 8 Pointed Open Cutouts, Art France, 15 x 5 In.	150.00
Bowl, White Gridwork Interior, Kosta, Signed, 3 1/2 x 5 In.	165.00
Branch, Maroon, Gold Enameled, Hanging Flowers, Moser–Type, 7 In.	250.00
Centerpiece, Daum Glass, Silver Flecks, Amber, Metal Frame, 10 In.	865.00
Cordial, Crystal, Hunting Scene, Lobmeyer	140.00
Cranberry, Clear Overlay, Acid Cutback Flowers, 7 x 3 In.	135.00
Decanter, Blown, Built–In Jewels	65.00
Dish, Wafer, Red & White Pedestal Twist Around Blue, 4 1/2 In.	324.00
Figurine, Flying Eagle, Geometric Metal Base, Bolae, 59 x 43 In.	4250.00
Figurine, Polar Bear, Maleris, Signed, 2 In.	95.00
Goblet, Blue Lithophane Type Portraits, Etched, Pair	4000.00
Lamp, River Landscape, Metal Mounts, Michel, c.1915, 14 1/2 In.	3100.00
Night–light, Flowering Branches, Touchard, c.1900, 8 1/2 In.	995.00
Perfume Bottle, Cut Swirls, Facets & Gothic Arches, 9 In.	445.00
Perfume Bottle, Lily Blossoms, Saint Louis, c.1900, 6 7/8 In.	600.00
Pitcher, Double Gourd, Trellised Roses, Marcel Goupy, 1920, 9 In.	550.00
Pitcher, Peach Blow Coloring, Amber & Cranberry Leaf, 8 3/4 In.	1000.00
Powder Jar, Figural, Nude, With 2 Dogs, Green	75.00
Punch Cup, Palmer Cox Brownie, Cat, Napoli 5, 2 1/4 x 3 1/4 In.	2250.00
Rose Bowl, Allover Martele, Gold Flowers, Burgen & Schverer	5750.00
Salt, Chartreuse To Clear, Silver Plated Basket Frame, 4 In.	185.00
Sculpture, Black, White Interior, 4 Flared Arms, 18 In.	100.00
Shade, Alternating Art Deco Panels, Jefferson, 16 In.	440.00
Shade, Scalloped Bottom Edge, Calcite, 2 1/2 x 5 In., Pair	250.00
Shade, Trumpet Shape, Calcite, 2 1/4 x 4 In.	135.00
Sugar & Creamer, Leaf Design, Red, Orange, Summit	45.00
Urn, Malachite, 9 In., Pair ....*Illus*	605.00
Vase, Amber Butterflies, Blue Leaves, Crystal, 8 In.	310.00
Vase, Art Deco, Purple, Gray, Charder, 8 In.	550.00
Vase, Berry–Laden Branches, Ovoid, St. Louis, c.1920, 9 7/8 In.	1100.00
Vase, Bulbous, Internal Striations, Gold, Bramhal, 1977, 10 In.	83.00
Vase, Cornucopia, Pearl Iridescent, Footed, Green Foot, 10 In.	325.00
Vase, Crystal, Allover Etched Farmer, Wheat, Forest, Karhula, 9 In.	150.00
Vase, Enameled Birds, Flowers, Butterscotch To White, 7 In., Pair	345.00
Vase, Enameled White Spatter, Red Stripes, Boda, B. Vallier, 3 In.	75.00
Vase, Gold Enameled Butterfly, Blue Overlay, 11 1/4 In.	550.00
Vase, Gooseberry Leaves, Fruits, Weis, c.1920, 11 3/8 In.	660.00
Vase, Green, Etched Sailboat Design, Flaring Form, 7 In.	50.00
Vase, Green, Gold, Trevaise, 9 1/4 In.	1100.00
Vase, Heron & Frog, Frosted Finish, c.1884, 4 1/2 In.	395.00
Vase, Honesdale, Regeletto Pattern, Gold Design	445.00
Vase, Labino, Blue Sculpted Glass, Mauve, Signed, 5 1/2 In.	475.00
Vase, Marbelized Gold, Spherical, Long Cylindrical Neck, 10 In.	70.00
Vase, Overall Floral & Scrolling, Oval, Peynaud, 10 In.	335.00
Vase, Poppy, Orange, Paul D'Avesn, 9 In.	725.00
Vase, Rolled Rim, Bulbous, Trapped Geometric, M. Harris, 1968, 6 In.	137.00

Art Glass, Urn, Malachite, 9 In., Pair

Vase, Royal Blue, Gilt Metal Mount, Austrian, c.1900, 17 In.	1430.00
Vase, Stipled Design, Gold Rim, Maroon Streaks, 6 1/4 In.	165.00
Vase, Stretched Millefiori Canes, Cobalt Blue, St. Louis, 9 In.	1980.00
Water Server, Double Spout, Blenko, Amber	10.00

Art Nouveau is a style of design that was at its most popular from 1895 to 1905. Famous designers, including Rene Lalique and Emile Galle, produced furniture, glass, silver, metalwork, and buildings in the new style. Ladies with long flowing hair and elongated bodies were among the more easily recognized design elements. Copies of this style are being made today. Many modern pieces of jewelry can be found.

ART NOUVEAU, see also Furniture; various glass categories; etc.

ART NOUVEAU, Ashtray, Woman, Brass	32.00
Candlestick, Brass, 12 In.	175.00
Holder, Photograph, Bronze, 3-D Insects, 26 x 21 In.	725.00
Plaque, Woman's Head, Silver Plate Over Pewter, 20 In.	595.00

The first American art pottery was made in Cincinnati, Ohio, during the 1870s. The pieces were hand thrown and hand decorated. The art pottery tradition continued until the 1920s when studio potters began making the more artistic wares.

ART POTTERY, see also under factory name

ART POTTERY, Bowl, Bjorn Wimblad, 5 In.	10.00
Bowl, Comical Harlequin Portrait Inside, Bjorn Winblad, 4 In.	95.00
Bowl, Leaf, Black Glaze, Green Inside, W. Gregory, 1920, 1 5/8 In.	83.00
Bowl, Yellow–Green Glaze, Brown Edge, Square, Natzler, 4 3/4 In.	825.00
Charger, Woman, Combing Hair, White, Henry Varnum Poor, 11 In.	825.00
Ewer, Arabesque, Charlotte Rhead, 15 In.	255.00
Ewer, Corn Design, Mt. Olympia, 7 1/2 In.	80.00
Figurine, Horse, Art Deco, Wiener Werkstatte, 4 1/2 x 5 In.	950.00
Jardiniere, Dragon, Turquoise Glaze Interior, Korean, 17 In.	110.00
Jardiniere, Footed, Norse, 6 In.	75.00
Lemonade Set, Cow On Pitcher, Edwin & Mary Scheier, 5 Piece	795.00
Lion, Seated On Rocky Base, Glass Eyes, Scotland, 9 1/2 In., Pr.	330.00
Mottled Gold Ground, Indian Type Design, C. Rhead, 5 5/8 In.	195.00
Mug, Grotesque Face, Matte Brown To Green, Walley, 5 1/2 In.	467.00
Pitcher Set, Gray Animals, White Ground, Scheier, 10 Piece	1100.00
Pitcher, Gold Adventurine, Mahogany Flambe, Jervis, 4 x 5 In.	350.00
Pitcher, Hydrangea, Charlotte Rhead, 7 3/4 In.	255.00
Pitcher, Stylized Woman, Potter, Cream, Maija Grotell, 5 1/2 In.	3850.00

◆◆◆

Cigarette burns on wooden furniture are difficult to conceal. Rub the burn with scratch–cover polish. If that does not help, rub the burn with a paste of rottenstone (found in most hardware stores) and linseed oil.

◆◆◆

Pitcher, Trellis Pattern, Gold Trim, Charlotte Rhead, 8 1/2 In.	195.00
Planter, Bust, Person, Beret, White Glaze, Wieselthier, 9 3/8 In.	192.00
Plaque, Autumn Leaves, Charlotte Rhead, 14 1/4 In.	225.00
Plaque, Geometric Designs, Charlotte Rhead, 12 3/4 In.	225.00
Plaque, Geometric Interior Design, Maria Opouli, 6 In., Pair	770.00
Plaque, Manchu Pattern, Charlotte Rhead, 14 1/4 In.	225.00
Plate, Blue Glaze, Red Clay, E. & M. Scheier, 7 1/2 In., 8 Piece	83.00
Platter, Poisson Fond Blanc, Pablo Picasso, 13 x 16 1/2 In.	6860.00
Vase, Rushmore, Green Drip, 6 In.	35.00
Vase, 2 Molded Trout, Walley Pottery, Marked, Label, 12 1/4 In.	2530.00
Vase, Abstract Head Figures, Bulbous, Brown, Scheier, 7 1/2 In.	415.00
Vase, Apple Green Top, Black & Brown Flambe, Cabat, 4 x 3 In.	192.00
Vase, Applied Brown Broad Leaves, Walley, Bulbous, 7 x 6 In.	1430.00
Vase, Band of Gold Flowers, Blue Centers, Paul Dachsel, 8 In.	495.00
Vase, Blue, Applied Sprig, Cincinnati, 6 In.	175.00
Vase, Blueberries, Multicolored Leaves, J. Imlay, 10 1/2 In.	60.00
Vase, Bud, Floral, Cream, Hand Painted, Nillsjo, Label, 4 1/2 In.	15.00
Vase, Bud, Striated Burgundy, Gold, Gray, Green, Walley, 4 1/2 In.	110.00
Vase, Byzantine Pattern, Charlotte Rhead, 7 7/8 In.	165.00
Vase, Crabapple Blossoms, Blue Mottled Ground, Bennett, 14 In.	5280.00
Vase, Crucible, Bulbous, Green Over Brown Flambe, Chicago, 7 In.	247.00
Vase, Enameled Band of Florals, Blue, French Deco Studio, 3 In.	850.00
Vase, Flambe Purple Layers, Ribbed, Bulbous, Primavera, 16 In.	125.00
Vase, Flowers, Lavender, Charlotte Rhead, 7 3/4 In.	220.00
Vase, Geometric Design, Black Ground, Marie & Julienne, 6 In.	795.00
Vase, Geometric, Blue Gloss, WPA, 1933–36, 6 In.	140.00
Vase, Incised Floral, Light Blue, Bottle Shape, 7 1/2 In.	90.00
Vase, Incised Linear, Matte Green, Studio Pottery, 1913, 6 In.	110.00
Vase, Landscape Design, Hand Painted, Spencer Edge, 8 3/4 In.	82.50
Vase, Manchu, Dark Green Dragon, Charlotte Rhead, 10 1/2 In.	195.00
Vase, Manchu, Dragon, Gold Trim, Charlotte Rhead, 8 1/4 In.	195.00
Vase, Massier, Purple & Gold Butterflies, Signed, 5 3/4 In.	775.00
Vase, Matte Green, Spade Design, Greek Key Border, 4 In.	247.00
Vase, Matte Green, White, Black Frieze of Squares, Jervis, 5 In.	2200.00
Vase, Modernistic Designs, Alfred Stellmacher, 10 3/4 In.	357.50
Vase, Mustard Glaze, Double Gourd, Linthorpe, Dresser, 8 In.	550.00
Vase, Orange Flowers, Blue, Yellow Trim, Charlotte Rhead, 7 In.	165.00
Vase, Red Drip Glaze, Chelsea Keramic, 9 In.	400.00
Vase, Reticulated Grasshoppers, Green, P. Dachsel, 1904, 16 In.	990.00
Vase, Rose & Pink, Speckled Blue Ground, H. Ruggles, '25, 6 In.	467.00
Vase, Speckled Blue & Green Glaze, Ovoid, Robinson, 12 In.	82.50
Vase, Stork, Teal To Peach Ground, Flared Lip, France, 13 In.	110.00
Vase, Textured, Stoneware, Black, Maija Grotell, c.1950, 23 In.	8800.00
Vase, Trellis, Lustred Flowers, Brown Lining, Rhead, 8 In.	185.00
Vase, Twisted Handles, Green, Mountainside Pottery, 6 1/2 In.	135.00

The Arts & Crafts movement in American decorative arts was from 1894 to 1923. In the 1970s collectors began to rediscover Mission furniture, art pottery, metalwork, linens, and light fixtures from this period. The interest has continued. Today everything from this period is collectible, including jewelry, graphics, and silverware.

ARTS & CRAFTS, see also Furniture; various glass categories; etc.

Arts & Crafts, Lantern, Copper,
Caramel Slag Glass, 16 In.

ARTS & CRAFTS, Bookends, Copper, Brass, Geometric	50.00
Bowl, Raised Geometric Designs, Copper, 8 In.	45.00
Humidor, Attached Pipe Rest, Matchbox Holder, Copper	90.00
Jardiniere, Pale Green, Blue, Brown, 10 1/2 In.	315.00
Lantern, Copper, Caramel Slag Glass, 16 In. ....*Illus*	475.00
Table Runner, Embroidered Silk, Linen, 48 x 15 In.	175.00

AURENE   Aurene glass was made by Frederick Carder of New York about 1904. It is an iridescent gold or blue glass, usually marked *Aurene* or *Steuben.*

AURENE, Bowl, 3–Footed, Signed, 10 1/4 In.	610.00
Bowl, Blue, Footed, Flower Frog, Signed	750.00
Bowl, Pinched Top, 8 1/2 In.	1200.00
Candlestick, Baluster & Ring Turned Shaft, Marked, 8 1/4 In., Pair	770.00
Candlestick, Blue, Signed, 8 1/2 In., Pair	1265.00
Candlestick, Gold, 10 In., Pair	1150.00
Compote, Pedestal, Iridescent Blue, 7 In.	522.50
Goblet, Bulbous Center, Blue Mirror Finish Inside	350.00
Jardiniere, Blue, Signed, 6 1/2 In.	900.00
Lamp, Blue, Steuben, 17 In.	2650.00
Perfume Bottle, Gold	775.00
Perfume Bottle, Gold, Atomizer, 6 In.	575.00
Perfume Bottle, Gold, Dauber, 10 In.	895.00
Salt, Gold .... 215.00 To	300.00
Shade, Dome, Zipper, Applied Platinum Band, 7 1/2 In.	2150.00
Shade, Green, Platinum Feather, Signed, 5 In.	595.00
Shade, Platinum Feather, Green, Gold Lined, Signed	750.00
Shade, Rippled Green, Calcite Interior, Pair	395.00
Shade, Trumpet, Calcite, Gold, Swags, Signed, 5 1/2 In., Pair	450.00
Tumbler, Gold Iridescent, Flared, 3 7/8 In.	275.00
Tumbler, Iced Tea, Gold, Signed, 6 1/2 In.	425.00
Vase, Blue, 10 In. .... 750.00 To	1350.00
Vase, Blue, Shade Shape, Fluted Rim, Signed, 5 1/4 In.	595.00
Vase, Calcite Exterior, Trumpet Shape, Gold, Ruffled, 6 In.	375.00
Vase, Calcite, Gold Vines & Leaves, 6 In.	1150.00
Vase, Flared Scalloped Rim, Twisted Stem, Signed, 12 In.	2255.00
Vase, Flower Form, Bluish–Gold, Signed, 12 1/4 In.	2750.00
Vase, Gold Peacock Eyes, Swirling Threads, Signed, 7 3/4 In.	2975.00
Vase, Gold, 3 Prong, Blue Highlights, 6 In.	1050.00
Vase, Gold, Floriform, 4 1/2 In.	525.00
Vase, Jack–In–The–Pulpit, Gold, 6 1/2 In.	850.00

Vase, Peacock Blue, 10 In.	1250.00
Vase, Ribbed, Flared, Blue, 5 1/2 In.	675.00
Vase, Rose–Red With Blue Exterior & Interior, Ruffled, 8 x 8 In.	1050.00
Vase, Stick, Blue, 8 In.	325.00
Vase, Stump, Signed, 6 1/4 In.	880.00

AUSTRIA, see Royal Dux; Kauffmann; Porcelain

Auto parts and accessories are collectors' items today. Gas pump globes and license plates are part of this specialty. Prices are determined by age, rarity, and condition.

AUTO, Badge, Chauffeur, Ohio, Tin, 1940	14.00
Badge, Osterr Automobile Club, Enameled, c.1935	175.00
Banner, Ford, Showroom, Car, 2 Engines, Ford Emblem, 1951, 4 x 3 In., Set	325.00
Banner, Skelly's 2 New Gasolines, Cloth, Skelly Man's Face, Logo	50.00
Banner, Studebaker, Showroom, 1953, 38 x 52 In.	85.00
Banner, Veedol, Oil Can Picture, Cloth, Colorful	35.00
Box, Coil, Model T, Wooden	29.00
Catalog, Buick, Diarama, 1955, 8 Pages	14.00
Catalog, Chevrolet, Fold–Out, Color, 1948, 11 1/2 x 8 In.	13.00
Clock, Dashboard, Elgin	80.00
Dealer's Promotion Fold–Out, 1957 DeSoto	20.00
Emblem, Radiator, Dodge, Enameled	25.00
Encyclopedia, Gilmore Oil Lubrication, 1937, 12 x 9 In.	325.00
Fender Skirt, Cadillac, Box, 1968, Pair	170.00
Gas Pump Globe, Ashland	400.00
Gas Pump Globe, Atlantic Hi–Arc	225.00
Gas Pump Globe, Cities Service Oils, Metal Frame, 1929, 15 In.	350.00
Gas Pump Globe, D–X Marine	325.00
Gas Pump Globe, Dixie Premium, Yellow Ground, Red Logo, Plastic Body	175.00
Gas Pump Globe, Gulf, 1 Piece	375.00
Gas Pump Globe, Gulf, Etched That Good Gulf	600.00
Gas Pump Globe, Gulf, Restored	400.00
Gas Pump Globe, Imperial	175.00
Gas Pump Globe, Penzoil Ethyl Gas, All Glass	400.00
Gas Pump Globe, Phillips 66	395.00
Gas Pump Globe, Quaker Gasoline	1425.00
Gas Pump Globe, Sinclair	175.00
Gas Pump Globe, Skelly	175.00
Gas Pump Globe, Texaco, See Gauge, Complete, 1930s	45.00
Gas Pump Globe, Tydol	325.00 To 375.00
Gas Pump Globe, Valvoline Marine	175.00
Gas Pump Globe, Vickers	110.00
Gas Pump Globe, White Eagle, Milk Glass	875.00
Gas Pump Globe, White Rose, Glass Body, 13 1/2 In.	375.00
Gloves, Driving, Canvas, Battery–Powered Turn Signals On Left, 1900s	412.00
Headlight, Buick, 1929, Pair	145.00
Headlight, Model A, Chrome Frame, Pair	200.00
Heater, Motor	45.00
Holder, Credit Card, Texaco Service You Can Trust	20.00

AUTO, HOOD ORNAMENT, see also Lalique

Hood Ornament, Bulldog, Mack Truck	35.00
Hood Ornament, Cadillac, 1932	450.00
Hood Ornament, Dodge Ram, 8 In.	35.00
Hood Ornament, Eagle, Bronze	50.00
Hood Ornament, Figural Head, Lindbergh, Chrome, c.1927	990.00
Hood Ornament, Flying Swan	55.00
Hood Ornament, Greyhound, Ford, 1934	45.00
Hood Ornament, Lion, Dated 1924	30.00
Hood Ornament, Ram, Horns Curved Out & Around	20.00
Hood Ornament, Ram, Horns Tight To Body	15.00
Hood Ornament, Rocket	15.00
Hood Ornament, Terraplane	50.00
Hood Ornament, Triomphe, F. Bazin, Bronze, c.1927, 8 In.	4000.00

Hood Ornament, Winged Goddess, Chrome, 1964 Ford 70.00
Hood Ornament, Winged Lady Hood, Aluminum 50.00
Horn, Ooga, Old Claxon Type 55.00
Horn, Taxi, Brass 15.00
Jack, Pierce-Arrow 50.00
Jar, Wm. Penn Motor Oil, World War II, 1 Qt. 20.00
Lamp Kit, Mazda, Tin Case 35.00
License Plate, Alabama, 1938 .... 85.00
License Plate, Illinois, 1968, Pair 3.00
License Plate, Iowa, 1937 .... 65.00
License Plate, Japan Occupation, Black, Yellow, Pair 110.00
License Plate, Louisiana, 1977, Magnolia Center 6.00
License Plate, Massachusetts, 1921, Pair 20.00
License Plate, New York, 1906, Leather, Brass Tag 395.00
License Plate, Ohio, 1925 .... 7.00
License Plate, Ohio, 1929 .... 7.00
License Plate, Ohio, 1933 .... 7.00
License Plate, Ohio, 1940, Chauffeur 14.00
License Plate, South Dakota, Mt. Rushmore, 1955 .... 8.00
Luggage Rack, Running Board, Model T, Clamp On 25.00
Manual, Guide To Your New 1953 Chevrolet 23.00
Manual, Nash Technical Service, 1940 .... 35.00
Manual, Owner's, Chevrolet, 1936 .... 30.00
Map Rack, Texaco Touring Service 40.00
Padlock, Ford, With Key 60.00
Rack, Bottle, Mobil, N. O. S., Tin, 1930s 28.00
Radiator Cap, Model T 15.00
Radiator Emblem, Hupmobile Nash 25.00
Radiator Emblem, Willys Knight 25.00
Radiator Grill, Rolls Royce, 1930s 900.00
Radio, Ford, 1955 .... 50.00
Repair Kit, Goodrich Tires, Tin, Blue, White, 1920s 50.00
Sign, Champlin, Car Streaking Through Sky, Cardboard, 1930, 22 x 28 In. 65.00
Tiger, S Tail, A Tiger Under The Hood, Package, 1950s 6.00
Tin, Falcon Oil, 1 Qt. 8.00
Tool Box, Fordson Tractor 45.00
Vase, Carnival Glass, Marigold, Metal Holder 25.00

Autumn Leaf pattern china was made for the Jewel Tea Company beginning in 1933. Hall China Company of East Liverpool, Ohio, Crooksville China Company of Crooksville, Ohio, Harker Potteries of Chester, West Virginia, and Paden City Pottery, Paden City, West Virginia, made dishes with this design. Autumn Leaf has remained popular and was made by Hall China Company until 1978. Some other pieces in the Autumn Leaf pattern are still being made. For more information, see *Kovels' Depression Glass & American Dinnerware Price List.*

AUTUMN LEAF, Bean Pot, 1 Handle 495.00
Bean Pot, 2 Handles 140.00
Berry Bowl, 5 1/2 In. 4.00
Bowl, Fruit, Hall 3.00
Bowl, Jewel Tea, 8 In. 35.00
Bowl, Vegetable, Oval, 10 1/2 In. 15.00
Butter, 1 Lb. 295.00
Butter, 1/4 Lb. 165.00
Cake Plate, Jewel Tea 8.00
Cake Stand 125.00
Casserole, Jewel Tea, 2 Qt. .... 10.00 To 12.00
Coffeepot, Drip, Hall 16.00
Cookie Jar, Big Ear 120.00
Creamer, New Style, Hall 7.00
Cup & Saucer .... 6.00 To 9.00
Cup, Hall 4.00

Custard, Hall 7.00
Jar, Hall 100.00
Jug, Ball 20.00
Mug, Cone 55.00
Mug, Irish Coffee 100.00
Mug, Irish Coffee, 4 Piece 350.00
Percolator, Electric 275.00
Pitcher, Hall, 5 1/2 In. 15.00
Plate, 9 In. 7.00
Plate, Hall, 7 1/4 In. 4.00
Plate, Harker, 6 In. 5.00
Platter, Hall, 13 1/2 In. 14.00
Salt & Pepper, Handle, Hall 20.00
Saucepan, Jewel Tea 35.00
Saucer, Hall 2.00
Soup, Cream 20.00
Soup, Dish, Hall 10.00
Tablecloth, Jewel Tea, Sailcloth, 54 x 64 In. 100.00
Teapot, Aladdin .... 32.00 To 35.00
Teapot, Club .... 395.00 To 400.00
Teapot, Newport, Jewel Tea, 1930s 125.00
Tidbit, 3 Tiers 65.00
Tray, Tidbit 75.00
Trivet, Tin, Oval, 10 3/4 In. 10.00
Trivet, Tin, Round, 7 1/4 In. 8.00
Tumbler, Juice 20.00
Bowl, Vegetable, Round, 9 In. 55.00
    AVON, see Bottle, Avon

BACCARAT

Baccarat glass was made in France by La Compagnie des Cristalleries de Baccarat, located 150 miles from Paris. The factory was started in 1765. The firm went bankrupt and began operating again about 1822. Cane and millefiori paperweights were made during the 1860 to 1880 period. The firm is still working near Paris making paperweights and glasswares.

BACCARAT, Bottle, Cognac, Crystal, Stopper, 11 In. 135.00
Bottle, Perfume, Turtle Form, Pair, 3 In. 358.00
Box, Clear, Amber Buttons, Signed, 4 x 3 1/2 In. 125.00
Box, Knob Finial, Rose Teinte, Round, Marked, 5 x 3 5/8 In. 88.00
Box, Lift–Off Lid, Rose Teinte, Embossed Swirl, 2 x 3 In. 75.00
Candlestick, Rose Tiente, Swirl, Scalloped Foot & Top, 7 In. 125.00
Cellarette, Baroque Mounts, 3 Decanters, 15 Cordials, c.1900 .... 9000.00
Clock, Mantel, Child Top, Enameled Dial, Oval Case, 16 1/4 In. 5775.00
Decanter, Cranberry, Marked, 12 In., Pair .... *Illus* 550.00
Dresser Set, Pale Green Overlay, Etched, Blossoms, Gilt, 6 Piece 4290.00
Figurine, Black Cat 175.00
Figurine, Frog, Signed, 2 1/2 In. 75.00

Baccarat, Decanter, Cranberry, Marked,
12 In., Pair

◆◆◆◆◆◆◆◆◆◆◆◆◆◆◆◆◆◆◆◆◆◆

Antique glass should be handled as if it has been repaired and might fall apart. Hold a pitcher by the body, not the handle. Pick up stemware by holding both the stem and the bowl. Hold plates in two hands, not by the rim.

◆◆◆◆◆◆◆◆◆◆◆◆◆◆◆◆◆◆◆◆◆◆

Figurine, Horse, Jumping, 9 In.	185.00
Figurine, Pelican, Signed, 6 1/2 In.	110.00
Figurine, Turtle, Signed, 4 In.	65.00
Figurine, Wild Boar, Signed	145.00
Goblet, Sulphide Portrait of St. Jacques, Hexagonal, 4 1/2 In.	605.00
Hat, Basket Weave, Clambroth, c.1860	150.00
Jar, Diagonal Diamond, Amberina	20.00
Lamp, Fairy, Rose Tiente, Sunburst Swirl, Saucer Base, 4 In.	245.00
Paperweight, Blue Sulphide, Depicting Bull, 2 3/4 In.	30.00
Paperweight, Concentric Millefiori, Blue Ground, 1 15/16 In.	716.00
Paperweight, Concentric Millefiori, Translucent Blue, 2 9/16 In.	715.00
Paperweight, Dog, Running, Scroll & Foliage, Amber Flash, 2 3/4 In.	400.00
Paperweight, Iceberg Shape, 2 1/2 In.	75.00
Paperweight, Mica, Green Glass, Rock–Like Inclusions, 1 3/4 In.	125.00
Paperweight, Millefiori, Rooster, Deer, Dog, Horse, Canes, 2 9/16 In.	1870.00
Paperweight, Mushroom, Millefiori, Blue & White, Star–Cut Base	522.00
Paperweight, Mushroom, Multicolored, Blue Over White, 3 3/16 In.	1045.00
Paperweight, Pink Snake On Upset Muslin Ground, 3 3/16 In.	9790.00
Paperweight, Purple & Yellow Pansy, Clear Ground, 2 1/2 In.	660.00
Paperweight, Sulphide, Abe Lincoln, Deep Blue Ground, 2 3/4 In.	440.00
Paperweight, Sulphide, Bull, 8 x 2 3/4 In.	35.00
Paperweight, Sulphide, Eisenhower, Clear Fan–Cut Base, 2 7/8 In.	330.00
Paperweight, Sulphide, Eustace Tilley, Blue, 2 3/4 In.	2650.00
Paperweight, Sulphide, Geo. Washington, Blue Waffle, 2 13/16 In.	385.00
Paperweight, Sulphide, John F. Kennedy, Green Flash, 2 13/16 In.	220.00
Paperweight, White Clematis, Outer Ring, Clear Ground, 2 13/16 In.	2310.00
Perfume Bottle, Paneled, Cut, 5 1/2 In.	32.00
Punch Bowl Set, Orange & Black Enameled Design ....Illus	1430.00
Punch Set, Tray, Frosted Granular Texture, Gilt Accent, 10 Piece	1435.00
Shot Glass, Millefiori, Flared Rim, Paperweight Base, 2 1/4 In.	225.00
Toothpick, Clear, c.1900, Embossed Mark	75.00
Tumble–Up Set, Rose Teinte, Embossed Swirl Pattern, 7 3/4 In.	225.00
Tumbler, Gold Flowers, Amberina, Paper Label, 3 3/4 In.	230.00
Tumbler, Rose Teinte, Sunburst Pattern, Marked, 4 In.	55.00
Urn, Ribbon Crest Panel, Bronze Holder, 13 In.	715.00
Vase, Butterflies, Flowers, Opalescent, 6 In.	135.00
Vase, Colonial Pattern, 3 In.	25.00
Vase, Curving Elephant Trunks Form Handle, 10 In.	88.00
Vase, Prima Vera, 8 In.	95.00
Vase, Swirl Cut, 5 In.	195.00
Vase, Swirl Cut, 7 1/2 In.	225.00

Baccarat, Punch Bowl Set, Orange & Black Enameled Design

Vase, Swirl Cut, 10 In. 325.00
Wine, Amberina, Gold Scroll Enamel, 4 1/2 In., Pair 75.00
Wine, Cut, Set of 6 .... 300.00

Badges have been used since before the Civil War. Collectors search for examples of all types, including law enforcement and company identification badges. Well–known prison or law enforcement badges are most desirable. Most are made of nickel or brass. Many recent reproductions have been made.

BADGE, Air Force Security Police 45.00
  Austrian Republic, Grand Golden Honor Badge & Star, 1952 .... 800.00
  C. R. I. & P. Railway, Special Police, 6–Pointed Star 195.00
  Cap, Aloha Airlines 350.00
  Chauffer, Ohio, 1937 .... 25.00
  Chauffeur, Memphis, Tenn., 1917 .... 30.00
  Chicago Police, Presented To Sammy Davis, Jr., Gold Color 850.00
  Highway Patrol, Kentucky State Highway Commission 185.00
  Hungarian, Order of Medjidje, Worn Around Neck 100.00
  Key West Police Dept., Florida 73.00
  Major Bowes, Honorary Police Chief, Nashville 550.00
  Police, Paramount Studio, With Hat, 1940s 198.00
  Romanian, Order of The Star, Worn Around Neck 280.00
  Serbian, Order of St. Sava II, Worn Around Neck 175.00
  Serbian, Order of White Eagle, Grand Officer's, 1903–15 .... 700.00
  Slave, John Joseph Lafar, Charleston, S. C., 1823, 2 3/4 In. 3300.00
  Special Police, Indianapolis, 1950 .... 25.00
  Tennessee Highway Patrol, Captain's 120.00
  Wells Fargo, Security 65.00
  Willys Overland Motors, Employee's 35.00
  Worker's, Allis Chalmers, Bronze Oval, Dated 1919 .... 30.00
BAG, BEADED, see Purse

Metal banks have been made since 1868. There are still banks, mechanical banks, and registering banks (those which show the total money deposited on the face of the bank). Many old banks have been reproduced since the 1950s in iron or plastic.

BANK, 2 Faces, Painted Cast Iron, 4 1/4 In. 120.00
  3 Little Pigs, Cast Iron, Original Paint 155.00
  Addams Family, Thing 55.00
  Andy Gump, Cast Iron, 4 3/8 In. 600.00
  Arabian Safe, Cast Iron 150.00
  Auto, Armored Car, Japan, Box 195.00
  Auto, Cast Iron, No Paint, 5 3/4 In. 150.00
  Balking Mule, Lehmann 375.00
  Barrel, Baxter Springs, Kan., Chrome 10.00
  Barrel, St. Bernard Bank & Trust Co., Arabi, La., Wooden 25.00
  Baseball Player, Cast Iron .... 135.00 To 295.00
  Baseball Player, Standing, c.1910, 6 In. 275.00
  Baseball, Glass 45.00
  Battleship, Oregon, 5 In. 195.00
  Bear, Hamm's Beer 450.00
  Beehive, Cast Iron, 2 3/8 In. 145.00
  Beehive, Yellow & Green, Cast Iron, 2 3/8 In. 450.00

◆◆

Date wicker furniture from the label. Wakefield Rattan Co. was used from 1855 to 1897; Heywood–Wakefield Co., 1868–1897; Heywood Bros. & Wakefield Co., 1897–1921; Heywood–Wakefield Co. after 1921.

◆◆

Bench, Black, Gold Trim, Brass Pins, Handmade, J. Honons, 5 1/8 In. 155.00
Big Boy, Vinyl 8.00
Billiken On Throne, Cast Iron 95.00
Birdcage, Traces of Gold, Cast Iron, 4 In. 30.00
Black Boy, 2 Faces, Black & Gold, Cast Iron, 5 1/4 In. 90.00
Black Boy, 2 Faces, Cast Iron, 4 1/8 In. 75.00
Black Boy, 2 Faces, Floppy Hat, Cast Iron, Painted, 4 3/16 In. 250.00
Black Sharecropper, Cast Iron 135.00
Black Woman, Benne Wafers, Tin 10.00
Bokar Coffee, Black Ground 14.00
Buffalo, Cast Iron, Original Paint 137.50
Building, Bank of Columbia, Cast Iron, Worn Nickel Plate, 5 1/2 In. 85.00
Building, Bank of Columbus, Nickel Plated Cast Iron, 5 1/2 In. 80.00
Building, Hexagonal, Dark Japanning, Cast Iron, 2 1/2 In. 155.00
Building, Independence Hall, Clear Pattern Glass, Tin Base, 7 1/4 In. 85.00
Building, Ohio Mutual Bldg. & Loan Co., Cast Iron 450.00
Building, People's Bank, Grand Rapids, Mich., Cast Iron 450.00
Building, Skyscraper, Silver & Gold, Cast Iron, 3 5/8 In. 25.00
Building, State Bank, Cast Iron, Moore, 4 1/8 In. 45.00
Buster Brown & Tige, Cast Iron 165.00
Captain Kidd, Cast Iron, 5 5/8 In. 295.00
Cat & Dog, Crank, Bells Ring, Kyset & Rox, Cast Iron, 1880s 545.00
Cat's Head, Pottery, White, Green Glaze, 3 In. 95.00
Cat, Grapette, Clear Glass, Metal Cap 25.00
Cat, With Ball, Cast Iron 285.00
Cat, With Ball, Chalkware, 8 In. 250.00
Charlie Tuna, Starkist, Figural, Ceramic, 9 In. 29.00
Chest, Empire, 3 Drawers, Scroddleware, England, 5 1/2 In. 65.00
Chicken, Cast Iron, 1930s 65.00
Chuck E. Cheese 9.00
Church Window, Safe, Brown Japanning, Cast Iron, 3 1/8 In. 45.00
Church, Star Island Chapel, Isle of Shoales, N. H., Mahogany, 12 1/4 In. 130.00
Clown, China, Moveable Eyes, 7 In. 55.00
Coffin, Windup, Box .... 39.00 To 42.00
Colonel Sanders, Figural, 10 In. 20.00
Conoco Man, Plastic, Green, 5 1/2 In. 60.00
Conoco Truck 250.00
Cook Stove, Cast Iron 45.00
Coors Lite Beer Can, Aluminum 5.00
Cow, Gray, Cast Iron, 5 In. 48.00
Crock, Acorn Stove 60.00
Davy Crockett, Figural, Metal 25.00
Deer, Large Antlers, Cast Iron, 9 In. 110.00
Dime Register, Bayfield, Wi., Metal, Dark Green, 1930 .... 17.50
Dime Register, Cast Iron, 4 3/4 In. 30.00
Dime Register, Cast Iron, 5 1/2 In. 55.00
Dime Register, Gem, Eagle 15.00
Dime Register, Popeye, Tin, 1956 .... 35.00 To 48.00
Dime Register, Trunk 125.00
Dime Register, Western Savings, Buffalo, Blue Metal, Key 7.50
Dog's Head, Scottie, Green Glaze, 3 3/8 In. 55.00
Dog, Beagle, Ford Motor Co. Credit Union 30.00
Dog, Boston Bull Terrier, Cast Iron, 5 1/4 In. 95.00
Dog, Boxer, Sitting, Cast Iron 75.00
Dog, Bulldog, Metropolitan Bank, Cast Iron 165.00
Dog, Bulldog, Seated, Cast Iron, 4 3/8 In. 65.00
Dog, Cast Iron, 7 1/2 In. 100.00
Dog, English Bulldog, Standing, Black & White, Cast Iron 95.00
Dog, Fido, Cast Iron .... 65.00 To 75.00
Dog, Fido, On Pillow, Polychrome Paint, Cast Iron, 5 1/4 In. 200.00
Dog, Hush Puppy, Rubber 25.00
Dog, Irish Setter, Iron, 5 1/2 In. 125.00
Dog, Newfoundland, With Pack, Cast Iron, 5 1/2 In. 330.00

Dog, Retriever, With Pack, Brown Japanning & Gold, Cast Iron, 5 1/2 In. 40.00
Dog, Retriever, With Pack, Cast Iron, 3 3/8 In. 50.00
Dog, Scotty 125.00
Dog, Seated, Cast Iron, Gold, Red Collar 65.00
Dog, Snoopy On Ball, Pottery 20.00
Dog, Snoopy, Clear Glass 14.00
Dog, St. Bernard, Backpack, Iron 95.00
Donald Duck, Cowboy Hat, Neckerchief, On Treasure Chest, Plastic, 9 In. 35.00
Donkey, Cast Iron, 7 In. 130.00
Drum, Ohio Art 15.00
Dutch Girl, Pottery, 4 3/4 In. 50.00
Eagle & Eaglets, Book of Knowledge 95.00
Eagle & Shield, Cast Iron 950.00
Egg, Red Goose Shoes, Plastic 18.00
Electrolux, Box 35.00
Elephant, Blue, Cast Iron, 4 In. 48.00
Elephant, Gold & Red, Tin Wheels, Cast Iron, 4 In. 180.00
Elephant, Hubley, Cast Iron 150.00
Elephant, On Tub, Cast Iron, 5 3/8 In. 95.00
Elephant, On Wheels, Cast Iron, 4 x 4 1/2 In. 425.00
Elephant, Standing, Blanket, Pottery, White, Green Glaze, 5 1/2 In. 40.00
Elf's Head, White Clay, Brown Glaze, 3 3/8 In. 55.00
Elmer Fudd, Bugs Bunny, Talking, 1970s 35.00
English Throne, Aluminum 80.00
Eveready, Black Cat, Plastic, 1981 .... 18.00
Ferris Wheel, Nickel Plate, 4 1/2 In. 1025.00
Foxy Grandpa, Cast Iron, 5 1/4 In. 125.00
Frankenstein Head 20.00
Fred Flintstone, Ceramic, 20 In. 30.00
French Stove, Brown Enamel & Nickel Plate, 4 1/4 In. 50.00
Gas Pump, Sinclair, RD–119, Tin 17.00
Gas Stove, Black, Traces of Gold, Cast Iron, 5 1/2 In. 125.00
General Butler, Cast Iron, 6 1/2 In. 900.00
Glass Block, Corning Glass, 1 3/4 x 3 x 3 In. 25.00
Globe, Aqua, Gold Trim, White Metal, 4 In. 5.00
Globe, Tin, Ohio Art, 7 In. 8.00
Golliwog, Black, Non–Ferrous Cast Metal, 6 1/4 In. 45.00
Graf Zeppelin, Cast Iron, 6 3/4 In. 145.00
Grandpa's Hat, Cast Iron, 2 1/4 In. 205.00
Gum Machine, Fred Flintstone 25.00
Horse, Gold Paint, Cast Iron, 5 1/2 In. 80.00
Horse, Prancing, Cast Iron, 4 3/4 In. 45.00
Horse, Silver Paint, Cast Iron, 4 In. 25.00
House, 1 Story, Cast Iron, 2 7/8 In. 45.00
House, Glass, Pittsburgh Paints 50.00
Huckleberry Hound Candy Factory, Box 225.00
Ideal Dog & Cat Food, Tin, Full Size Can 20.00
Ideal Trust, Bronze Finish, Cast Iron, 7 1/8 In. 115.00
Indian, With Tomahawk, Cast Iron 100.00
James Salt Water Taffy, Tip Top, Papier–Mache, 7 In. ....6.00 To 20.00
Jester Head, Majolica, 3 In. 94.50
John Deere, Cast Iron 1000.00
John F. Kennedy 15.00
Jolly Nigger, Cast Aluminum 123.00
Jolly Nigger, Original Paint, Cast Iron 1430.00
Jug, Pottery, Reddish Clay, Primitive House & Trees, 4 1/4 In. 125.00
Junior Cash, Nickel Plated Cast Iron, 4 1/4 In. 70.00
Liberty Bell, Glass, 4 1/2 x 4 In. 22.00
Liberty Bell, Wooden Base, White Metal, 7 1/8 In. 95.00
Lincoln, Glass, Tin Top 30.00
Lion, Cast Iron, 2 1/2 In. 80.00
Lion, Ears Up, Cast Iron, 4 1/2 In. 5.00
Lion, Gold Paint, Cast Iron, 2 1/2 In. 60.00

Bank, Mechanical, Bad Accident, Cast Iron, 10 In.

Lion, Standing, Cast Iron 75.00
Listerine, Frog Razor Blades 25.00
Little Audrey, Blue Dress, Black Shoes, USA, Ceramic, 9 In. .... 120.00 To 145.00
Long John Silver 12.50
Lucky Joe, Snow Crest, Clear Glass, Metal Top, 7 In. .... 25.00 To 35.00
Lulu 15.00
Magic Chef 12.50
Mailbox, Raised Figural Eagle, Cast Iron, 5 In. 65.00
Mammy, Hands On Hips, Hubley, Cast Iron, 5 1/4 In. ....65.00 To 120.00
McDonald's, Grimace, Ceramic, Box 14.00
McDonald's, Wastebasket 3.00

 Mechanical banks were first made about 1870. Any bank with moving parts is considered mechanical. The metal banks made before World War I are the most desirable. Copies and new designs of mechanical banks have been made in metal or plastic since the 1920s.

Mechanical, Artillery, Cast Iron, 8 In. 1210.00
Mechanical, Artillery, Confederate Soldier 975.00
Mechanical, Artillery, Nickel Plated 1750.00
Mechanical, Artillery, Union Soldier 1850.00
Mechanical, Bad Accident, Cast Iron, 10 In. ....*Illus* 2200.00
Mechanical, Bill E. Grin 550.00
Mechanical, Billy Goat 990.00
Mechanical, Boy & Bulldog 440.00
Mechanical, Boy Milking Cow, Book of Knowledge 175.00
Mechanical, Boy On Trapeze 1265.00
Mechanical, Boy Robbing Bird's Nest 7920.00
Mechanical, Cabin, Cast Iron ....385.00 To 550.00
Mechanical, Circus, Cast Iron, 6 In. ....*Illus* 1760.00
Mechanical, Clown's Head, Lever–Action Tongue, Tin, Chein 85.00

Mechanical, Darktown Battery, 10 In. .... 1050.00 To 7600.00
Mechanical, Darky & Cabin, Green Cabin 750.00
Mechanical, Dentist, With Black Boy, Cast Iron 145.00
Mechanical, Dinah 425.00
Mechanical, Dog On Turntable 300.00
Mechanical, Eagle & Eaglets, Cast Iron, 6 1/8 In. 425.00
Mechanical, Eagle & Eaglets, Cast Iron, J. & E. Stevens, 6 1/8 In. 357.50
Mechanical, Elephant, On Pedestal, 3 Clowns, Iron, 6 In. 1760.00
Mechanical, Elephant, Sitting On Drum, Coin On Trunk, Raises, Chein 80.00
Mechanical, Frog, Cast Iron, Patent 1875, 4 1/2 x 9 1/4 In. 175.00
Mechanical, Frogs, Two, Painted Cast Iron, 8 1/2 In. 725.00
Mechanical, Gem, Cast Iron, 5 1/2 In. 300.00
Mechanical, Hall's Excelsior, Painted Cast Iron, 5 In. 170.00
Mechanical, Hall's Liliput, Yellow, Red Dome, J. & E. Stevens, 4 1/2 In. 525.00

Bank, Mechanical, Oriental Fortune Teller,   *Bank, Mechanical, Circus, Cast Iron, 6 In.*
Cast Iron, 8 In.

Bank, Mechanical, Monkey With Bell,   *Bank, Mechanical, Peg Leg Beggar,*
Cast Iron, Painted, 6 In.   *Cast Iron, 5 In.*

Mechanical, Hen & Chick 2250.00
Mechanical, Hippopotamus, Metal, Box 40.00
Mechanical, Hometown Baseball, Cast Iron 145.00
Mechanical, Humpty Dumpty, Book of Knowledge 125.00
Mechanical, I Always Did 'Spise A Mule, Cast Iron 1430.00
Mechanical, Indian & Bear 165.00
Mechanical, Indian & Bear, Feathers Intact 5390.00
Mechanical, Jolly Nigger, Cast Iron, Polychrome Paint, 8 3/8 In. 450.00
Mechanical, Jolly Nigger, High Hat, Cast Iron, 4 3/4 In. 415.00
Mechanical, Jonah & The Whale 495.00
Mechanical, Leap Frog, Cast Iron 145.00
Mechanical, Lilliput, Cast Iron, 4 3/8 In. 375.00
Mechanical, Lion & Monkeys, Cast Iron, Polychrome, 9 1/2 In. 600.00
Mechanical, Lion Hunter, 1950s 50.00
Mechanical, Lion Hunter, Dated 1910 .... 5600.00
Mechanical, Magician, Cast Iron .... 145.00 To 165.00
Mechanical, Mailbox, Rural, With Flag, Tin, 7 In. 20.00
Mechanical, Monkey With Bell, Cast Iron, Painted, 6 In. ....*Illus* 4290.00
Mechanical, Monkey, Tips Hat, On Barrel, Tin, Chein ....65.00 To 195.00
Mechanical, Organ Grinder & Monkey 495.00
Mechanical, Oriental Fortune Teller, Cast Iron, 8 In. ....*Illus* 4620.00
Mechanical, Owl, Turns Head, Blue Eyes, Cast Iron, 1880 .... 200.00 To 240.00
Mechanical, Paddy & The Pig 2640.00
Mechanical, Panorama, Revolving Lithographed Landscapes, Cast Iron 9350.00
Mechanical, Peg Leg Beggar, Cast Iron, 5 In. ....*Illus* 1870.00
Mechanical, Professor Pug Frog, Cast Iron, 3 1/4 In. 250.00
Mechanical, Punch & Judy, Cast Iron .... 495.00 To 990.00
Mechanical, Rooster, Cast Iron, 6 1/8 In. .... 175.00 To 325.00
Mechanical, Savings Bank, Tin, Slot In Chimney, Yellow, 5 1/2 In. 275.00
Mechanical, Seal 250.00
Mechanical, Southern Comfort, Confederate Soldier, 1950s ....75.00 To 150.00
Mechanical, Speaking Dog, Painted Cast Iron, 7 1/2 In. .... 525.00 To 950.00
Mechanical, Stump Speaker, Cast Iron .... 1980.00 To 3750.00
Mechanical, Tabby Bank, Cast Iron, 4 1/2 In. 475.00
Mechanical, Tammany Bank, Cast Iron, Dec. 23, 1878, 5 3/4 In. .... 350.00 To 975.00
Mechanical, Tank & Cannon 850.00
Mechanical, Teddy & Bear, Flat Hat 3500.00
Mechanical, Teddy & The Bear, Book of Knowledge 82.50
Mechanical, Teddy & The Bear, Cast Iron .... 145.00 To 550.00
Mechanical, Wild West 45.00
Mechanical, William Tell, Cast Iron, 10 1/2 In. .... 605.00 To 800.00
Mechanical, World's Fair 650.00
Merry–Go–Round, Cast Iron 88.00
Merry–Go–Round, Gray Iron Casting Co., Nickel Finish, 1925, 4 1/2 In. 155.00
Metz Beer, Ceramic, Barrel Shape 22.00
Middy, Cast Iron 165.00
Monkey, Chein 35.00
Mutt & Jeff, Cast Iron 95.00
Oliver Hardy, Plastic, 13 3/4 In. 42.00
Oscar In An Airplane, Ceramic 18.00
Our Kitchener, Cast Iron 185.00
Overland Circus, Horses, Driver, Bear, Cast Iron, USA, 14 In. 200.00
Pig, 2–Tone Marbelized Glaze, Austria, Pottery, 4 1/4 In. 25.00
Pig, Cast Iron, 4 x 2 In. 30.00
Pig, Crying, Chalkware 25.00
Pig, Earthenware, Brown Glaze, Yellow Dots, 6 In. 40.00
Pig, Earthenware, Brown Glaze, Yellow Splotches, Ohio, 3 5/8 In. 125.00
Pig, Laughing, Polychrome Paint, Cast Iron, 5 1/4 In. 100.00
Pig, Seated, Cast Iron 50.00
Pig, Sleek, Bronze, 7 In. 45.00
Pig, Smiley, 6 In. 27.50
Pig, Smiling, Tower Federal Savings & Loan 65.00
Pinocchio, Iron 150.00

Pinocchio, Vinyl	15.00
Pirate, On Treasure Chest, Cast Iron	65.00
Pirate, On Treasure Chest, Pot Metal	65.00
Pizza Hut Pizza Man, Hard Plastic, 7 1/2 In.	40.00
Poppin' Fresh Dough Boy, Ceramic	25.00
Porky Pig, Cast Iron	265.00
Prancing Horse, Gold, Cast Iron, 4 3/8 In.	40.00
Prudential, Light Green, Glow-In-Dark, Shape of Rock of Gibralter	20.00
Punch & Judy, Book of Knowledge	95.00
Punch & Judy, Tin, 2 7/8 In.	200.00
Puzzle, County Bank, W. P. To F. M., Handmade, Wooden, 1877, 5 1/2 In.	80.00
Rabbit, Cast Iron, 6 1/2 In.	250.00
Radio, 10–Dime, Viz, White & Brown Plastic, 1949	12.00
Radio, Majestic, Bronze Finish, Tin Back, Cast Iron, 4 1/2 In.	45.00
Radio, Nickel Plated Door, Kenton, Cast Iron, 4 1/2 In.	110.00
Red Circle Coffee, Tin	15.00
Redware, Knob Finial, Mottled Brown Glaze, Slashes of Black, 6 In.	145.00
Refrigerator, Electrolux	35.00
Register, Adding, 3 Coins, Tin, Schonk Works, Red, Gold, Black, 5 1/2 In.	90.00
Rexal Drugs, Camera, 1960, 4 In.	20.00
Rival Dog Food, Tin	10.00
Riverboat, Paddle Wheel, Arcade, 7 1/2 In.	325.00
Rockingham House, Pottery, 5 x 3 In.	175.00
Rooster, Cast Iron	110.00
Safe, Daisy, Cast Iron, 3 1/2 In.	25.00
Safe, Fidelity Trust, Wood Interior With Drawer, Cast Iron, 8 1/2 In.	95.00
Safe, Floral Relief Design, Cast Iron, 4 5/8 In.	120.00
Sailor, Cast Iron, 5 1/4 In.	130.00
Santa Claus, Flocking, White Metal, 5 7/8 In.	50.00
Santa Claus, Papier–Mache, 9 In.	95.00
Santa Claus, Plaster, 1950s	25.00
Santa Claus, Polychrome Paint, White Metal, 6 1/4 In.	45.00
Save & Smile Money Box, Cast Iron, 4 1/4 In.	325.00
Seaman's Savings, Seaman, Duffel Bag, Ceramic	10.00
Security Safe Deposit, Black, Brass Dial, Cast Iron, 4 3/4 In.	85.00
Security Safe, Cast Iron	30.00
Sharecropper, Cast Iron	25.50
Sixpenny Piece Bank, Aluminum, 3 1/8 In.	80.00
Smokey The Bear, Pottery	12.50 To 20.00
Snoopy Doghouse, Pottery	20.00
Stan Laurel, Plastic, 1972	32.00
Star Wars Imperial Guard, Box	20.00
Star Wars Princess Kaneesha, Box	20.00
Statue of Liberty, Cast Iron	115.00 To 195.00
Switch To Dodge, Auto Barrel, Tin	50.00
Tank, World War I, Cast Iron	135.00
Thing, Addams Family, Box	35.00
Three Wise Monkeys, Cast Iron, 3 1/4 In.	250.00
Thrifty Dial, Wood Wheels, Tin	35.00
Thrifty Elf, Chein	80.00
Throne, Bronze Finish, Cast Iron, 8 1/4 In.	105.00
Throne, Coronation of Queen Elizabeth, Cast Iron, 1953, 8 1/4 In.	105.00
Treasure Chest, Cast Iron	14.00
Tri–Coin, Calendar, Gerett, Freeport, Illinois, Box	45.00
Troll Boy	29.00
Troll Man, 1964	29.00
Troll, 8 In.	25.00
Troll, Dam, Label On Clothes, 8 In.	45.00
Trunk, Nickel Plated Cast Iron, 3 1/2 In.	25.00
Turkey, Brown Japanning With Red, Cast Iron, 4 1/4 In.	285.00
Turkey, Cast Iron, 3 1/2 In.	55.00
Tweety Bird	55.00
Tweety Bird On Cage, Dakin	20.00

U. S. Mail, Metal	30.00
U. S. Mailbox	15.00
Uncle Sam, Milk Glass, Painted, 1940, 5 x 7 In.	30.00
Uncle Sam, Rozane	89.00
Watch Me Grow, Tin	40.00
Wolf's Head Oil Can, Small	16.00
Woody Woodpecker, Pottery	20.00
World, Rooster On Top Crows When Cranked, Tin Lithograph, 17 In.	95.00

 There is much confusion about the terms Banko, Korean ware, and Sumida. We are using the terms in the way most often used by antiques dealers and collectors. Korean ware is now called *Sumida Gawa* and is listed in this book under that heading. Banko is a group of rustic Japanese wares made in the nineteenth and twentieth centuries. Some pieces are made of mosaics of colored clay, some are fanciful teapots. Redware and other materials were also used.

BANKO, Teapot, Elephant	85.00
Teapot, Seven Gods, Vivid Colors, Small	225.00
Vase, Trees, Pagoda, Brown Glaze, Matte Front, 5 1/2 In.	50.00

 Barbershop collectibles range from the popular red and white striped pole that used to be found in front of every shop to the small scissors and tools of the trade. Barber chairs are wanted, especially the older models with elaborate iron trim.

BARBER, Backbar, 3 Stations, Beveled Mirrors, Marble Top, Oak, 8 x 14 Ft.	5000.00
Chair, Child's, Chrome & Enameled, 1930s	1750.00
Chair, Child's, Pony, Sits In Saddle, Stein & Goldstein	7500.00
Chair, Hydraulic, Patent 1907	1800.00
Pole, 6 Star Modern Service, Metal, Enameled, 4 Ft.	130.00
Pole, Black & White, Acorn Ends	413.00
Pole, Black, White & Red Paint, Iron Brackets, Wooden, 30 3/4 In.	325.00
Pole, Electric, 1920s	750.00

◆◆◆

Different types of furniture polish give different finishes. Liquid, oil polish, or paste wax leave a high luster. Cream polish and spray wax leave a medium luster.

◆◆◆

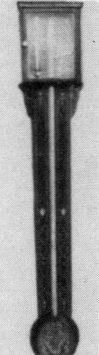

◆◆◆◆◆◆◆◆◆◆◆◆◆◆◆◆◆◆◆◆◆◆◆◆

To clean lithographed tin banks, try using Sani–wax and 0000–grade steel wool, but use with extreme caution.

◆◆◆◆◆◆◆◆◆◆◆◆◆◆◆◆◆◆◆◆◆◆◆◆

Barometer, English, Croce, York

Pole, Koken, Wall, Acorn Cap, Red & White Glass 1000.00
Pole, Red, White & Blue Repaint, Turned Wooden, 41 In. 300.00
Pole, Turned & Rope Carved, Red & White Repaint, 34 1/2 In., Pair 400.00
Pole, Turned Wood, Paint Traces, Added Base, 77 In. 275.00
Pole, Turned Wood, Polychrome Repaint, 89 1/2 In. 900.00
Sign, Barber Shop, Flange, Porcelain, Red, White & Blue, 2 Sides 155.00
Wildroot Hair Tonic, Professional Use Only, Tin 60.00

Barometers are used to forecast the weather. Antique barometers with elaborate wooden cases and brass trim are the most desirable. Mercury column barometers are popular with collectors. It is difficult to find someone to repair a broken example, so be sure your barometer is in working condition.

BAROMETER, Brass Face, Charles Wilder, Bird's-Eye Walnut, 1860, 37 5/8 In. 900.00
Carved Sculptures, Dog, Dead Game, Walnut, c.1880, 36 In. 885.00
Clock, Copper Clad, Footed Plinth, Signed, Loehr 132.00
English, Croce, York ....*Illus* 1050.00
Germany, 1900s 65.00
Hepplewhite, Star Flowers, Silvered Dial, F. Giobbi, 39 1/2 In. 400.00
Marine, Wood Cistern, English, Brass, Mahogany, c.1870, 38 In. 1650.00
Regency, Lione & Co., Clock, Thermometer, Mahogany, 45 1/2 In. 1870.00
Sawfish, Cartilage Rostrum, Jas. W. Queen, c.1880, 34 In. 3200.00
Silvered Faces, A. Buserya, English, Mahogany Veneer, 39 In. 600.00
Stick, Etched Ivory Gauge, Dublin, Mahogany, 36 In. 305.00
Stick, Mahogany Case, London, 1825–50 .... 990.00
Stick, Rosewood Case, London, 1825 .... 2475.00
Thermometer, Altitude Adjustment, Short & Mason, Mahogany, 20 In. 125.00
Wheel, Thermometer, G. Minola, London, Mahogany, c.1800, 38 In. 880.00

Basalt is a special type of ceramic invented by Josiah Wedgwood in the eighteenth century. It is a fine-grained, unglazed stoneware.

BASALT, Bowl, Footed, Black, Wedgwood, 7 In. 660.00
Candlestick, Muses, Wedgwood, 7 In., Pair 250.00
Creamer, Neoclassical Figures, Squared Handle, c.1815, 4 In. 55.00
Pitcher, Allover Design, Wedgwood, Bulbous, 5 1/2 In. 135.00
Teapot, Wedgwood, Black, Small 350.00
BASEBALL, see Card, Baseball; Sports

Baskets of all types are popular with collectors. Indian, Japanese, African, Shaker, and many other kinds of baskets can be found. Of course, baskets are still being made; so the collector must learn to tell the age and style of the basket to determine the value.

BASKET, Bentwood, Rectangular, Radiating Ribs, 7 x 16 x 11 In. 45.00
Berry, Star On Bottom, Wooden, 4 In. 95.00
Blue Woven Band, Bentwood Handle, Round, 5 1/4 x 7 1/2 In. 35.00
Buttocks, Splint, Bentwood Handle, 3 1/2 x 6 1/2 In. 155.00
Buttocks, Splint, Bentwood Handle, 6 x 10 x 11 In. 200.00
Buttocks, Splint, Bentwood Handle, 6 x 12 1/2 In. 150.00
Buttocks, Splint, Bentwood Handle, 11 x 12 In. 55.00
Buttocks, Splint, Bentwood Handle, 17 x 20 In. 45.00
Buttocks, Splint, Bentwood Handle, Ernest Everett, 11 1/2 In. 165.00
Buttocks, Splint, Bentwood Handles, Cover, 9 x 14 x 15 In. 75.00
Buttocks, Splint, Green Paint, 5 3/4 x 11 1/2 In. 175.00
Buttocks, Split Oak, 10 x 12 In. 90.00
Cheese, Splint, 7 1/2 x 21 1/2 In. 275.00
Cheese, Splint, Scrubbed Finish, 30 In. 400.00
Drying, Splint, Wire Bottom, Branded Dr. Webb, 14 1/2 x 15 In. 70.00
Egg, Splint, Radiating Ribs, Bentwood Handle, 13 x 14 In. 200.00
Flower, Splint, Tall Bentwood Handle, 6 In. 85.00
Gathering, Bentwood Rim Handles, Perpendicular Handle, 20 1/2 In. 145.00
Gathering, Splint, Bentwood Handle, 13 In. 200.00
Grass, Knobbed Lid, Polychrome Design, Eskimo, c.1900, 7 3/4 In. 115.00
Herb Drying, Splint, 20 1/2 x 21 In. 355.00

Laundry, Splint, Bentwood Rim Handles, Round, 21 x 10 In. 65.00
Laundry, Splint, Rim Handholds, Laced With Copper Wire, 20 In. 155.00
Laundry, Splint, Rim Handholds, Oval, 12 1/2 x 22 x 27 In. 105.00
Laundry, Splint, Wooden Base, Bentwood Rim Handle, 19 x 27 In. 55.00
Loom, Hanging, Splint, 17 x 14 1/2 In. 350.00
Loom, Hanging, Splint, 2 Sections, 11 In. 300.00
Loom, Splint, 7 1/2 In. 250.00
Nantucket, 1 Egg, Signed Note F. Sylvaro, '97, 2 7/8 x 3 5/8 In. 715.00
Nantucket, 19th Century, 5 1/2 x 13 In. 1450.00
Nantucket, Cane & Splint, Swivel Handle, 7 1/4 x 12 1/2 In. 850.00
Nantucket, Mitchell Ray, Nantucket, Mass., Label, 8 1/4 In. 1900.00
Nantucket, Shaped Swing Handle, W. D. Appleton, 7 3/4 x 12 In. 1875.00
Nantucket, Splint, 1 Egg 1250.00
Nantucket, Splint, Bentwood Swivel Handle, 9 3/4 x 20 3/4 In. 1000.00
Picnic, Splint, Oval, 13 1/4 x 16 1/2 In. 25.00
Potato Field, Heavy Wire Bail Handle 20.00
Raffia, Handle, 3 1/2 x 1 1/4 In. 85.00
Reed, Melon Rib Cover, Double Swivel Handles, Oval, 15 In. 85.00
Splint, Bentwood Handle, 9 1/2 x 16 1/2 In. 75.00
Splint, Bentwood Handle, Black Paint Under Brown, 7 x 10 In. 150.00
Splint, Bentwood Handle, Green Paint, 10 1/2 x 15 In. 105.00
Splint, Bentwood Handle, Handle Marked Gilpin, 16 1/4 In. 65.00
Splint, Bentwood Rim Handles, 12 x 27 x 31 In. 250.00
Splint, Bentwood Rim Handles, 3 1/2 x 10 In. 200.00
Splint, Bentwood Rim Handles, 3 1/2 x 6 1/4 In. 350.00
Splint, Bentwood Rim Handles, Small Attached Basket, 18 In. 105.00
Splint, Bound Rim Design, Bentwood Handle, 13 x 19 In. 235.00
Splint, Dark Green Potato Print Designs, 10 x 13 In. 175.00
Splint, Dark Interior, Bentwood Handle, 9 1/4 In. 260.00
Splint, Goose Feather, 12 In. 20.00
Splint, Goose Feather, Cover, 24 In. 20.00
Splint, Green Web Shoulder Straps, 19 In. 25.00
Splint, Laundry, Reinforcing Bands, 13 x 25 In. 75.00
Splint, Light Blue Paint, Bentwood Handle, Round, 13 In. 330.00
Splint, Natural & Faded Red, Bentwood Rim Handles, 15 In. 275.00
Splint, Natural, Bentwood Rim Handles, Red, Blue, 15 x 5 In. 70.00
Splint, Oak Swing Handle, 19th Century, 16 In. 350.00
Splint, Open Lattice Bottom, 12 1/2 x 17 1/2 In. 95.00
Splint, Open Rim Handholds, Round, 6 1/4 x 9 1/4 In. 25.00
Splint, Painted Floral, Bentwood Rim Handles, 8 1/4 In. 300.00
Splint, Potato Print Design, 4 1/2 x 7 In. 55.00
Splint, Potato Print, Red & Blue Watercolor, 8 x 10 In. 155.00
Splint, Potato Print, Red & Blue, 12 1/4 x 13 1/4 x 5 1/4 In. 325.00
Splint, Potato Print, Stylized Flowers, Brown, Green, 9 x 3 In. 75.00
Splint, Radiating Ribs, 2–Tone Weaving, Bentwood Handle, 8 In. 235.00
Splint, Radiating Ribs, 6 x 11 x 14 In. 95.00
Splint, Rectangular Base, Oval Rim, Flared, 11 x 20 x 10 In. 195.00
Splint, Red & Black Watercolor Polka–Dot Design, 15 1/2 In. 35.00
Splint, Red Paint, Fixed Wooden Handle, Round, 6 x 5 x 5 3/4 In. 935.00
Splint, Rim Handholds, Wooden Feet, 12 x 15 In. 65.00
Splint, Satchel Shape, Bentwood Handle, 13 x 13 1/2 In. 200.00
Splint, Splint–Wrapped Swivel Handle, 10 x 15 In. 120.00
Splint, Square Base & Cover, c.1845, Round, 12 1/2 x 20 In. 300.00
Splint, Storage, Cover, Geometric Hearts & Arrows, American Indian 250.00
Splint, String Reed Wrapping, 5 3/4 x 8 1/4 In. 20.00
Splint, Swivel Handle, 11 x 11 1/2 In. 90.00
Splint, Swivel Handle, Round, 5 1/4 x 10 In. 225.00
Splint, Swivel Handle, Round, 5 x 8 1/2 In. 435.00
Splint, Swivel Handle, Round, 7 x 10 In. 165.00
Splint, Swivel Handle, Round, 12 1/2 x 7 1/2 In. 375.00
Splint, Swivel Handle, Worn Brown Varnish, 15 x 9 In. 375.00
Splint, Wooden Frame, Bentwood Rim Handles, 18 x 21 In. 300.00
Splint, Wooden Handle, Double Wrapped Rim, Round, Small 55.00

Splint, Wrapped Rim Handles, Oval, 10 x 13 x 8 In.	105.00
Straw, Heart Shape, 3 1/2 x 3 1/2 In.	100.00
Wire Bale Handle, 1/2 Bushel, 14 3/4 In., 4 Piece	140.00
Woven Bear Grass, Knob Lid, Linear Design, Eskimo, 1940s	195.00

BATCHELDER Ernest Batchelder made ceramic and copper items in Los Angeles,
LOS ANGELES California. He died in 1957.

BATCHELDER, Bowl, Green, 3 x 10 In.	100.00
Tile, Ivy, Green, Blue, Matte, 8–In. Square	50.00
Tile, Trees In Landscape, Brown, Green, 8 In.	175.00
Vase, Grapes, Leaves, Matte, 12 In.	95.00

Batman and Robin are characters from a comic strip by Bob Kane
that started in 1939. In 1966, the characters became part of a
popular television series. There have been radio and movie serials
that featured the pair. In 1989 a full–length movie was made.

BATMAN, Bank, Ceramic	95.00
Bank, Figural, Porcelain	45.00 To 85.00
Batcycle, Pedal Tricycle, Mid–1970s	45.00
Batmobile, 1966, Worchester	100.00
Batmobile, Avon	75.00
Batmobile, Batboat & Trailer, Die–Cast Metal, 1966, Corgi, 5 In.	575.00
Batmobile, Battery Operated, Azrak–Hamway, 1974, 10 In.	250.00
Batmobile, Corgi, 1966	195.00
Batmobile, Corgi, 1973	65.00
Batmobile, Gyro, 1973	45.00
Belt, Box, 1966	95.00
Bicycle Ornament, On Card	85.00
Bicycle Siren, 1978, 5 In.	25.00
Book, Big Little Book, Cheetah Caper	19.75
Bookends, 1966, Box	250.00
Bracelet, Charm, Card Back	125.00
Button, Batman & Robin Society, 1960s, 3 In.	15.00
Card, Bubble Gum	5.00
Clock, Talking Alarm, 1966	55.00 To 65.00
Clock, Talking Alarm, Batman & Robin, 1974	90.00 To 125.00
Colorforms, 1966	35.00 To 100.00
Coloring Book	10.00
Coloring Book Poster, 1960s, Hollway Candy, 17 x 22 In.	85.00
Comic Book, No. 163	8.50
Contact Paper, 1970s, 8 x 18 In.	45.00
Costume & Mask, Ben Copper, 1973	45.00
Costume, Box, 1966	150.00
Costume, Unused, Box, 1970	75.00
Credit Card	6.00
Cup, Taco Bell	5.00
Doll, 1977, Mego, 8 In.	40.00
Doll, 1977, Mego, 12 In.	95.00
Doll, Cloth, 15 In.	250.00
Doll, Robin, 1973, Mego, 9 In.	45.00
Doll, Walking, Inflatable, 18 In.	175.00
Doll, Walking, Mary Wiu, 1966	125.00
Escape Gun, Lincoln, 1966	45.00
Figure, Cardboard, Joint Action, Package, 1977, 36 In.	7.00
Figure, Cloth Outfit, Vinyl Boots, Stand, Applause, 17 In.	25.00
Game, Board, Denys Fisher, 1976	30.00
Game, Shooting Arcade, Marx, 1966	25.00
Game, Target Set, Japan, 1960s	550.00
Gun, Grenade, 1966, 16 1/2 In.	175.00
Hairbrush, Figural, Avon, 1979	15.00
Lamp, Cave, Figural	75.00
Lobby Card, Movie, 1949	85.00
Lunch Box, Thermos, 1966	125.00 To 225.00

Marble	10.00
Marbles, Robin Comic, 1966	21.00
Model Kit, Aurora, Unbuilt, 1966	175.00
Model Kit, Batmobile, Ertl	9.95
Model Kit, Billikin	65.00
Model Kit, T.V. Version, Plastic, 1960s	30.00
Mug, 1982	10.00
Mug, Batman & Joker, England	30.00
Mug, Black Picture, White, 3 1/4 In.	12.00
Mug, White, Fire–King	40.00
Paint By Number Book, Whitman, 1966	35.00
Paint Set, Stardust, Hasbro, 1966	45.00
Pen, Empire Pencil Co., 1966	75.00
Pencil Case, 1966	45.00 To 75.00
Pennant, Batman & Robin, 1966	20.00
Pez, Batman, Soft Head	21.00
Pez, Hard Head	10.00
Pez, With Cape	135.00
Poster, Movie, 1966	125.00
Poster, Penguin, Cat Woman, Bert Ward, France, 1966, 44 x 61 In.	450.00
Puzzle, Batman, Riddler, Penguin, Joker, Wooden Frame, Playskool	15.00
Puzzle, Hand Held, 1976	5.00
Puzzle, Jigsaw, Box, 1966	25.00
Puzzle, Whitman, 150 Piece, 1966	25.00
Radio, Figural	12.00
Record, Batman & Robin, 33 1/3, Colorful Jacket, 1966	25.00
Record, Scarecrow Image	5.00
Ring, Brass, Enamel, Bat Logo, 1966	65.00
Road Racing Set, 1976, Batmobile, Jokermobile	245.00
Robot, Cloth Cape, Vinyl Head, Tin Lithograph, Japan, 1964, 12 In.	3200.00
Skates, 1966	50.00
Sleeping Bag, 1974	35.00
Spoon & Fork Set, 1966	75.00
Sticker, Batman & Robin, On Card	4.00
Sticker, Bumper, 1960s	1.25
Tie, Yellow Bat Logo, 1966	45.00
Toy, Batman On Motorcycle, Robin In Sidecar, 1976, Plastic, 10 In.	45.00
Toy, Car, Duncan	25.00
Toy, Riding, Marx, 1966	50.00
Toy, Soakie, Bandai, 8 In.	20.00
Toy, Tin, Windup, Box	125.00
Trading Cards, Special Series, 1960s	250.00
Trash Can, 1966	35.00
Tumbler, Batgirl, Pepsi–Cola, 1976, 6 1/4 In.	18.00
Tumbler, Batman, Pepsi–Cola, 1976, 6 1/4 In.	6.00 To 12.00
Utility Belt, Handcuffs, Communicator, Decoder, Watch, 1979, Remco	145.00
View-Master, Talking, 3–D Cartridge, Box	10.00
Wallet, Comb, Nail File, Wallet Card, Coin Holder, 1966	65.00
Wristwatch, 1977, Red Ground, DAB	225.00
Wristwatch, Black Band, D. C. Comics, 1977	50.00
Wristwatch, Box, 1977	195.00
Wristwatch, Emblem, Black Band, Quartz, Quintel	25.00
Wristwatch, Gilbert, 1966	295.00
Wristwatch, Plastic Helmet Type, Cowel	45.00
Zoomcycle, 1977, Battery, Box	75.00

Battersea enamels are enamels painted on copper and made in the Battersea district of London from about 1750 to 1756. Many similar enamels are mistakenly called *Battersea.*

BATTERSEA, Box, Cosmetic, Yellow Enamel, Mirror, Oval, 1 1/8 x 1 3/4 In.	350.00
Box, Hinged Cover, House Scene, Bird Reading	150.00
Box, Hinged Cover, Medallion On Lid, A Friend's Gift, 1 3/4 In.	265.00
Box, Hinged White Cover, Bluebird In Foliage, Oval, 1 1/2 In.	275.00

Box, Patch, Woman's Torso Shape, Cover Is Head, 3 In.	1650.00
Doorknob, Historical Portrait, 4 Pairs	5500.00
Knob, Mirror, Painted Porcelain Face, 1 3/4 In. Diam., Pair	275.00
Needle Case, Gold Frame Around Flowers, Blue, 2 1/2 In.	600.00
Needle Case, Green Behind Flowers, Yellow, 2 1/2 In.	600.00

J. A. Bauer moved his Kentucky pottery to Los Angeles, California, in 1909. The company made art pottery after 1912 and dinnerwares after 1929. The factory went out of business around 1958.

BAUER, Ashtray, Yellow	3.00
Bowl, Batter, Ring, Orange	75.00
Bowl, Ringware, 12 In.	42.00
Bowl, Vegetable, Monterey, Cobalt Blue	12.00
Butter, Cover, Ring, Orange	75.00
Carafe, Ring	25.00
Casserole, Individual, Cover	15.00
Casserole, Ring, Cover, 7 1/2 In.	25.00
Casserole, Yellow, Cover, 1 1/2 Qt.	25.00
Coffee Server, Red & Orange, Wooden Handle, 8 Cup	45.00
Coffee Server, Wooden Handle, Cover	18.00
Cookie Jar, Yellow	30.00
Cup, Ring, Blue	30.00
Mug, Green, After Dinner	40.00
Pitcher, 1 1/2 Pt.	15.00
Plate, Yellow, Ring, 6 1/2 In.	10.00
Platter, Ring, Turquoise, 13 In.	23.00
Saucer, El Chico, Green	6.00
Saucer, Monterey, Blue	5.00
Stein, Beer	45.00
Teapot, Aladdin, Olive Green, 4–Cup	38.00
Teapot, Burgundy	40.00
Teapot, Cobalt Blue	18.00
Teapot, Monterey, Burgundy, 2–Cup .... 20.00 To	30.00
Teapot, Monterey, Cobalt Blue	45.00
Tumbler, Monterey, Cobalt Blue	10.00
Tumbler, Wooden Handle, Various Colors, 4 Piece	45.00
Vase, Figural, Green, 7 1/2 In.	20.00

Porcelains of all types were made in the region known as Bavaria. In the nineteenth century, the mark often included the word *Bavaria.* After 1871, the words *Bavaria, Germany,* were used. Listed here are pieces that include the name Bavaria in some form, but major porcelain makers such as Rosenthal are listed in their own categories.

BAVARIA, Cake Plate, Roses, Pierced Handles, Luster, 11 In.	22.00
Celery, Pale Lavendar Flowers, Cream Ground, 13 In.	35.00
Chocolate Pot, Multicolored Floral, Portrait, Cobalt Blue, 11 In.	195.00
Chop Plate, Gold Trim	30.00
Pitcher, Rose Garlands, 3 5/8 In.	12.00
Plate, Blues, 6 In.	10.00
Plate, Hand Painted Floral Border, Silver Overlay, 1900, 9 3/4 In.	75.00
Powder Jar, Perfume Bottle, Woman, Figural, Pair	65.00
Powder Jar, Woman, Figural	35.00
Relish, Narcissus, Gold, Handle, Art Nouveau	25.00
Sugar & Creamer, Allover Pink, Gold	35.00
Vase, Biscuit Porcelain, Geometric, Henrich, Square, 15 3/4 In.	104.00
Vase, Floral, Signed, Gold Handles, 13 In.	130.00

The Beatles became a famous music group in the 1960s. They first appeared on American network television in 1964. The group disbanded in 1971. Collectors search for any items picturing the four members of the group or any recordings. Because these items are so new, the condition is very important and top prices are paid only for items in mint condition.

BEATLES, Bandana, Triangular 25.00
Bank, Plastic, 1964 .... 20.00
Banner, Beatles Written Script, Royal Blue Felt, White 35.00
Binder, 3 Ring, White Vinyl 75.00
Book, Beatles Greatest Hits, With Notes, 1977, 96 Pages 30.00
Book, Hard Day's Night, Paperback, 1st Edition 28.00
Book, Recorded Hits, 1963 .... 55.00
Bracelet, Charm, Card 35.00
Button, 1964 .... 10.00
Button, Flasher, Paul, Red Ground, Black, Large 25.00
Button, I'm A Beatles Booster 1.50
Cake Set, Blue, 4 Figures, Original Box 40.00
Cake Set, Box 95.00
Candy Dish, John Lennon In Center, England, China, 5 In. 165.00
Candy Dish, Paul McCartney In Center, England, China, 5 In. 165.00
Card, Bubble Gum 10.00
Coin Purse, John Lennon, 1960s, Canada 30.00
Color Set, Yellow Submarine, Sealed 175.00
Comb, Giant, 1960s, Plastic, 14 In. 100.00
Comic Book, Yellow Submarine 30.00
Concert Ticket, Boston, Aug. 18, 1966 .... 20.00
Costume, Blue Meanie, No Mask, Box 175.00
Costume, George, Mask, Box 150.00
Diary, 1964, Topps, 49 Cards 450.00
Disk–Go–Case, Yellow, 1966 .... 110.00
Display, Sgt. Pepper, Die–Cut, 1967 .... 25.00
Doll, John Lennon, Remco, Box 110.00
Doll, Ringo, Remco 45.00
Doll, Vinyl, Inflatable, With Instruments, Nems Ltd., Box, Set of 4 .... 125.00
Dolls, Remco, Set of 4 .... 275.00
Game, Flip Your Wig, Milton Bradley, 1964 .... 100.00
Game, Flip Your Wig, Some Missing Pieces, Box, 1964 .... 65.00
Jacket, World Tour, Satin 550.00
Key Chain 15.00
Lunch Box, Blue 175.00
Lunch Box, Yellow Submarine .... 115.00 To 475.00
Magazine, Playboy, Feb. 1965 .... 20.00
Magazine, Yellow Submarine, 1968 .... 25.00
Nodder, Plastic, Hong Kong, 5 In., 4 Piece 75.00
Paint Set, Ringo Canvas, Paint By Number, 11 x 14 In. 125.00
Paperweight, Glass, Enclosing Beatles Litho, Yellow, Black, Gray 65.00
Photograph Album, Sgt. Pepper 30.00
Pillow 100.00
Pin, Flasher, 3 In. 22.00
Popout Book, Yellow Submarine, 1968 .... 25.00
Puzzle, Yellow Submarine, Jayman, 1958 .... 95.00
Record Album, I Want To Hold Your Hand, Capital, 1st Pressing 35.00
Record Catalog, Apple, 12 Pages, 1973 .... 15.00
Record, Hey Jude/Revolution, Flexi–Disc, Plain Sleeve, 4 In. 375.00
Ring Set, Late 1960s 20.00
Scarf, Nems, Pink 35.00
Stage Suit, Wool Sharkskin, Paul McCartney, c.1963 .... 6325.00
Submarine, Yellow, Corgi, 1968, Box 450.00

◆◆

Don't ship furniture from a hot to a cold climate, if it can be avoided.

◆◆

Switch Plate, Yellow Submarine, 1968, 6 1/2 x 10 1/2 In. 35.00
Toy, Ringo, With Drum, Remco 55.00
Wall Hanging, Linen, White, Burgundy, Black, Violet, 31 x 20 In. 275.00
Whistle, Help 6.00

Plates marked *R. K. Beck* were made by Buffalo Pottery and others. R. K. Beck was an artist who specialized in wildlife paintings. Many of his designs were reproduced on decals which were applied to plates.

BECK, Plate, Fish, Flowers, 10 In. 50.00

Beehive, Austria or *Beehive, Vienna,* are terms used in English-speaking countries to refer to the many types of decorated porcelain bearing a mark that looks like a beehive. The mark is actually a shield, viewed upside down. It was first used in 1744 by the Royal Porcelain Manufactory of Vienna. The firm made porcelains, called *Royal Vienna* by collectors, until it closed in 1864. Many other German, Austrian, and Japanese factories have reproduced Royal Vienna wares, complete with the original shield or *beehive* mark. This listing includes the expensive, original Royal Vienna porcelains and many other types of beehive porcelain. The Royal Vienna pieces include that name in the description.

BEEHIVE, Figurine, Barometer Bearer, Tricorn, c.1760, 8 3/8 In. 885.00
Figurine, Sausage Seller, Vienna, c.1765, 7 13/16 In. 1000.00
Figurine, Vintner, Conical Hat, c.1765, 7 3/4 In. 1100.00
Figurine, Woodsman, Leaning On Ax, c.1760, 6 1/4 In. 885.00
Group, Gallant & Pug, Red Cloak, c.1770, 7 7/8 In. 1210.00
Plaque, Lassitude, Art Nouveau Flowers, Marked, 10 In. 1750.00
Plaque, Punishment of Cupid, Giltwood Frame, c.1880, 25 x 25 In. 1320.00
Plate, Angelus, Gold Trim, 9 In. 38.00
Plate, Cabinet, Figural Scene, Beaded Border, 10 7/8 In., 10 Piece 1775.00
Plate, Die Melonenesser, 9 1/2 In. ....*Illus* 302.00
Plate, Echo, Signed Wagner, 10 In. ....*Illus* 1595.00
Plate, Madonna Della Sedia, Gilded Frame, Marked, 9 1/2 In. 475.00
Plate, Mythology Scene, Green & Gold Border, A. Kauffmann, 8 In. 135.00
Plate, Nymph Plucking Grapes, Signed Wagner, 9 1/2 In. 1650.00
Plate, Nymph Seated On Stone Bench, 9 1/2 In. 1650.00
Plate, Picture of Ruth, 10 1/2 In. ....*Illus* 825.00
Platter, Court Scene, Cobalt & Gold Border, Oblong, 11 1/4 In. 137.50
Tea Set, Woman Portraits Surrounded By Jewels, 1900, 13 Piece 6600.00
Urn, Red, Gilt Scrolling, Royal Vienna, 20 1/2 In. ....*Illus* 1100.00
Urn, Stand, Allegorical Figures, Parcel Gilt, Cover, 20 1/4 In., Pair 6050.00
Urn, Woman Beside Sea, Woman With Cupid, Maroon & Blue, 9 3/4 In. 515.00
Vase, 2 Handles, Kauffmann, Beehive Mark, 8 In. 325.00
Vase, Girl, With Candle, Scrolls, Cobalt Blue, 3 3/4 In. 60.00
Vase, Portrait, Woman, Raised Flowers, Gold Border, c.1880, 7 In. 1765.00
Vase, Rose, Maroon Ground, Portrait Preciosa, Marked, 8 In. 950.00

Beehive, Plate, Die Melonenesser, 9 1/2 In.
Beehive, Plate, Echo, Signed Wagner, 10 In.
Beehive, Plate, Picture of Ruth, 10 1/2 In.

Beehive, Urn, Red, Gilt Scrolling,
Royal Vienna, 20 1/2 In.

Vase, Woman Portrait, Scrolled Handles, Signed Wagner, 15 In. 5500.00
    BEER BOTTLE, see Bottle, Beer

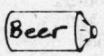

Beer was sold in kegs or returnable bottles until 1934. The first patent for a can was issued to the American Can Company in September of that year; and Gotfried Kruger Brewing Company, Newark, New Jersey, was the first to use the can. The cone–top can was first made in 1935, the aluminum pop–top in 1962. Collectors should look for cans in good condition, with no dents or rust. Serious collectors prefer cans that have been opened from the bottom.

BEER CAN, ABC Ale, August Wagner 2.00
    Acme 4.50
    Alpine, General, ... 6.00
    Amana, Cold Spring 3.00
    Atlas Prager, Drewery's, South Bend 5.00
    Augustiner, Wagner 3.00
    Aulder Brau, Walter's 8.00
    Ballantine Light Lager 8.00
    Ballantine Premium, Pulltab 7.00
    Banner, Cumberland 10.00
    Bavarian Select, Bavarian, Evansville 7.00
    Bergoff, Walter's 8.00
    Big Cat, Pabst 5.00
    Bilow's Gardens Tate Light 14.00
    Brewer's Best Premium Bavarian Type, Walter 10.00
    Brown Derby Pilsner, Salem Brewery Assoc. 25.00
    Brut, Lone Star 15.00
    Budweiser Oktoberfest, Bank Top 10.00
    Canadian Ace, Cone Top, 12 Oz. 30.00
    Champagne Velvet, G. Heileman 6.00
    Chief Oshkosh, People's 7.00
    Coburger, Old Dutch 5.00
    Cold Brau, Drewry's 10.00
    Gilley's Beer, Closed, Steel, 1987 .... 5.00

Bells have been made of porcelain, china, or metal through the centuries. All types are collected. Favorites include glass bells, figural bells, school bells, and cowbells. Be careful not to buy a bell made from an old glass goblet.

BELL, Amethyst Glass, Square, Crowing Rooster Painted On Top Handle 350.00
    Avon, Cape Cod, Red, Dated 1979 .... 15.00
    Boxing Ring, Brass, Trip Hammer, 10 In. 75.00
    Brass, Domed Brass, Iron Tap, Pat. 1863 .... 35.00
    Brass, Embossed Warrior's Heads, Design, 4 1/2 x 5 In. 95.00
    Brass, Knight Handle, Words Around Base, 6 7/8 In. 125.00
    Colonial Woman, Brass, 3 1/4 In. 20.00
    Counter, Tortoise Shape, Cast Iron, Press Tail To Ring, Victorian 140.00
    Cow, Copper, Handmade, Large 30.00
    Cranberry Glass, Yellow Handle, Large 95.00
    Desk, Mother-of-Pearl, Brass, Marble, Victorian 200.00
    Duck Sitting On Handle Top, Brass, Engraved, 6 x 3 1/2 In. 44.00
    Embossed Warrior's Heads, Designs, Brass, 5 x 4 1/4 In. 95.00
    Gong, S. Stickley, Copper, Oak Frame, Copper Straps, c.1904, 37 In. 1540.00
    Grace Hopkin's Dance Studio, Cleveland, Small 6.00
    Horsehead Set, Red Plume, Christmas Ribbons 55.00
    Liberty Foundry, St. Louis, Cast Iron 50.00
    Madame Pomadour, Brass, 1915, 6 1/2 In. 65.00
    Madame Pompadour, Bronze Finish, 6 1/2 In. 188.00
    Monastery, Latin Inscription, Brass, Wall Hung, 16 In. 195.00
    Owl, Brass, Tap To Ring, 7 1/2 In. 25.00
    R. A. F., Heads of Churchill, Roosevelt, Stalin, Aircraft Metal, 5 In. 60.00
    School, B. C. Taylor, Dayton, Ohio, Cast Iron, 18 x 27 In. 475.00

School, Brass, Turned Maple Handle, Marked No. 6, 6 1/2 In. 65.00
School, Cypress Lake Senior High School, Brass 125.00
School, Turned Maple Handle, 10 3/4 In. 79.00
Sheep, Brass, Iron Clapper, Leather Strap, Pair 95.00
Sleigh, Iron Strap, 4 Graduated Sizes, Shaft 45.00
Sleigh, Nickel Plated, 3 Clappers Each 4 Bells, Arched Strap, 12 In. 45.00
Sleigh, With Yoke, Large 470.00
Trolley Car 200.00
Victorian Lady, Silver Plate, Lunt 25.00

 Belle Ware glass was made in 1903 by Carl V. Helmschmied. In 1904 he started a corporation known as the Helmschmied Manufacturing Company. His factory closed in 1908 and he worked on his own until his death in 1934.

BELLE WARE, Vase, Opaque White Glass, Clear Beads, 6 In. 385.00
Vase, Pink Florals, Textured White, Scalloped Top, 15 In. 95.00

Belleek china is made in Ireland, other European countries, and the United States. The glaze is creamy yellow and appears wet. The first Belleek was made in 1857. All pieces listed here are Irish Belleek. The mark changed through the years. The first mark, black, dates from 1863 to 1890. The second mark, black, dates from 1891 to 1926 and includes the words *Co. Fermanagh, Ireland.* The third mark, black, dates from 1926 to 1946 and has the words *Deanta in Eirinn.* The fourth mark, same as the third mark but green, dates from 1946 to 1955. The fifth mark, green, dates from 1955 to 1965 and has an R in a circle added in the upper right. The sixth mark, green, dates after 1965 and the words *Co. Fermanagh* have been omitted. The seventh mark, gold, was used after 1980 and omits the words *Deanta in Eirinn.*

BELLEEK, see also Ceramic Art Co.; Haviland; Lenox; Ott & Brewer; Willets

BELLEEK, Basket, Latticework, Floral & Vine Border, Oval, 9 x 7 x 3 1/2 In. 220.00
Basket, Latticework, Floral & Vine Border, Rope Foot, 7 1/4 x 9 In. 245.00
Basket, Latticework, Heart Shape, Flowers, Rope Foot, Case, 5 In. 198.00
Bowl, Shells & Coral, Oval, 1st Mark, Black, 3 1/4 In. 175.00
Butter, Cottage Form, Cover, 6 5/8 x 5 1/8 In. 100.00
Candleholder, Cherub On Dolphin, Gold Mark .... 115.00 To 150.00
Coffeepot, Basket Weave & Shamrock, Twig Handle, 3rd Mark, Black 250.00
Compote, Tri–Horse Pedestal, 1st Mark, Black 2250.00
Creamer, Girl, Figural, 4 1/2 In. 55.00
Creamer, Grapes & Face, Black Mark 135.00
Creamer, Hexagonal, Gold Rim, 2nd Mark, Black 70.00
Creamer, Shamrock, Green Mark 35.00
Creamer, Shell, 2nd Mark, Black 120.00
Creamer, Swirl, Applied Flowers, 3rd Mark, Black 250.00
Cup & Saucer, Basket Weave & Shamrock, 3rd Mark, Black 50.00
Cup & Saucer, Shamrock, 3rd Mark, Black 80.00
Eggcup Set, Sydney, Holder, 6 Cups, 4th Mark, Green 195.00
Figurine, Leprechaun On Mushroom, 3rd Mark, Black, 5 1/2 In. 295.00
Honey Pot, Stand, Grassware, 1st Mark, Black 425.00
Mug, Shamrock, 3rd Mark, Black 95.00
Pitcher, Aberdeen, Left Handed, 2nd Mark, Black, 7 1/2 In. 350.00
Plate, Basket Weave & Shamrock, 3rd Mark, Black, 7 In. 60.00
Plate, Christmas, Gaelic, 1971 .... 21.00
Plate, Limpet, 3rd Mark, Black, 8 In. 38.00
Plate, Shamrock, 3rd Mark, Black, 8 1/4 In. 48.00
Salt Dish, Shell, 1890s 65.00
Saucer, Basket Weave & Shamrock, 2nd Mark, Black 40.00
Saucer, Tridacna, Pink Trim, Gold Edge, 4th Mark, Green 25.00
Spill, Lily, 4th Mark, Green, 6 1/2 In. 75.00
Sugar & Creamer, Ivory, Green Mark 70.00
Sugar & Creamer, Lotus, 3rd Mark, Black .... 70.00 To 85.00

  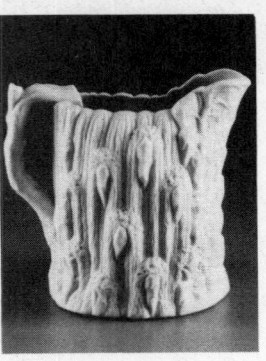

Bennington, Figurine, Swiss Lady, Flint Enamel Glaze, 7 In.   *Bennington, Jug, J. & E. Norton, Cobalt House, 3 Gal., 16 In.*   *Bennington, Pitcher, Cascade, Smear Glaze, 8 1/4 In.*

Sugar & Creamer, Ribbon, 3rd Mark, Black	75.00
Sugar & Creamer, Shell, 5th Mark, Green	75.00
Sugar, Lotus, 3rd Mark, Black	60.00
Sugar, Shell, Green Mark	100.00
Swan, 3rd Mark, Black	155.00
Tea Kettle, Tridacna, Pink, 2nd Mark, Black	325.00
Tea Set, Neptune, Tray, 2nd Mark, Black, 8 Piece	2800.00
Tea Set, Shamrock, 2nd Mark, Green	510.00
Teapot, Green Mark	94.00
Teapot, Limpet, 3rd Mark, Black	225.00 To 350.00
Teapot, Shamrock, Green Mark	125.00
Tray, Grape Cluster, Grapevine Handles, Black Mark, 13 x 6 1/4 In.	295.00
Vase, Aberdeen, Raised Florals, 3rd Mark, Black, 9 1/4 In., Pair	660.00
Vase, Applied Flowers, Leaves, Ivory, Scalloped, Handles, 12 3/4 In.	150.00
Vase, Fish, Lavender Highlights, Black Mark, 7 3/8 In.	110.00
Vase, Frog, 2nd Mark, Black, 4 1/2 In.	160.00
Vase, Gold & Rust Violets, 5 In.	395.00
Vase, Nile, Green Leaves, Orchid, 1st Mark, Black, 10 In.	295.00
Vase, Nile, Protruding Lilies, 2nd Mark, Black, 13 1/8 In.	595.00
Vase, Sunflower, 3rd Mark, Green, 7 1/2 In.	50.00

Bennington ware was the product of two factories working in Bennington, Vermont. Both firms were out of business by 1896. The wares include brown and yellow mottled pottery, Parian, scroddled ware, stoneware, graniteware, yellowware, and Staffordshirelike vases.

BENNINGTON, Bank, Globular Form, Short Stem, Spiral Finial, 7 In.	165.00
Bedpan, Brown Crackle Glaze, 18 In.	20.00 To 22.50
Bottle, Coachman, c.1850, 8 1/2 In.	660.00 To 675.00
Bowl, Mixing, Relief Modeled Design, 8 1/2 In.	95.00
Box, Cupid Asleep On Lid, Parian	175.00
Candlestick, 9 1/2 In.	415.00
Candlestick, Flint, Enamel, Pair	1550.00
Candlestick, Rockingham Blaze, 9 In.	300.00
Change Cover, Swiss Woman, Cream Glaze, Green Overglaze, 7 In.	2550.00
Change Cover, Toby Type	1650.00
Cuspidor, Diamond Pattern, Scroddle, 4 1/2 x 6 1/4 In.	495.00
Cuspidor, Diamond Pattern, Scroddle, 5 1/4 x 7 In.	550.00
Cuspidor, Flint Enamel, Embossed Diamond Design, 8 1/2 In.	275.00
Cuspidor, Shell, Scalloped Rim	60.00
Cuspidor, Shell, Side Vent	90.00

Dinner Set, Service For 4	50.00
Doorknob, Brown Pottery, Set	12.00
Figurine, Swiss Lady, Flint Enamel Glaze, 7 In. ....*Illus*	2530.00
Jug, J. & E. Norton, Cobalt House, 3 Gal., 16 In. ....*Illus*	6380.00
Pitcher, Acanthus, Marked, 5 1/2 In.	55.00
Pitcher, Alternate Rib Pattern, 1849 Mark, 10 In.	935.00
Pitcher, Cascade, Smear Glaze, 8 1/4 In. ....*Illus*	110.00
Pitcher, Charter Oak, Graniteware Glaze, Marked, 9 11/16 In.	195.00
Pitcher, Charter Oak, Smear Glaze, Marked, 9 1/2 In.	195.00
Pitcher, Charter Oak, U. S. Pottery, 7 1/2 In.	247.00
Pitcher, Charter Oak, Unglazed Interior, Marked, 9 1/2 In.	220.00
Pitcher, Daffodil, 11 In.	137.00
Pitcher, Ivy Vine, c.1849, 9 1/2 In.	440.00
Pitcher, Leaf & Flower, Fenton Works, 9 1/4 In.	275.00
Pitcher, Paul & Virginia, Blue & White, 9 1/2 In.	357.00
Pitcher, Paul & Virginia, U. S. Pottery, 10 1/4 In.	220.00
Pitcher, Pond Lily, Marked, 8 1/4 In.	110.00
Pitcher, Pond Lily, U.S. Pottery, 7 3/4 In.	193.00
Pitcher, Pond Lily, U.S. Pottery, 8 1/4 In.	165.00
Pitcher, Rosebud, Fenton Works, 9 3/4 In.	165.00
Pitcher, Sunflower, U.S. Pottery, 7 3/4 In.	193.00
Pitcher, Tulip & Sunflower, Marked, 8 In.	150.00
Pitcher, Wild Rose, 9 7/8 In.	235.00
Pitcher, Wild Rose, Glazed Interior, Marked, 9 1/2 In.	88.00
Pitcher, Wild Rose, Shiny Glaze, 10 1/4 In.	85.00
Snuff Jar, Toby Type	1100.00
Soap Dish, Drain, Marked Lyman & Fenton, Flint	150.00
Tobacco Jar, Mottled Brown, Large	135.00
Toby Jug, Ben Franklin	825.00

Berlin, a German porcelain factory, was started in 1751 by Wilhelm Kaspar Wegely. In 1763, the factory was taken over by Frederick the Great and became the Royal Berlin Porcelain Manufactory. It is still in operation today. Pieces have been marked in a variety of ways.

BERLIN, Plaque, Urchins Eating Fruit, Dog Watches, 9 7/8 x 12 1/4 In.	5500.00
Platter, 3 Insects Amid Floral Bouquet, c.1780, 14 7/8 In.	220.00
Vase, Cover, Painted Leaves & Insects, 1890s, 24 1/2 In., Pair	2200.00

John Beswick started making earthenware in Staffordshire, England, in 1936. The company is now part of Royal Doulton Tableware, Ltd. Figurines of animals, especially dogs and horses, Beatrix Potter animals, and other wares are still being made.

BESWICK, Ashtray, Puppy, 6 In.	18.00
Figurine, Dogs, Spaniel, White, Luster Trim, 6 In., Pair	65.00
Figurine, Horse, Mare	54.00
Figurine, Horse, Stallion	54.00
Figurine, Hunter, On Stallion, 10 In.	95.00
Figurine, Rabbit In Top Hat, 4 In.	35.00
Figurine, Rabbit With Apron, 4 In.	35.00
Mug, Captain Cuttle	45.00
Pitcher, Palm Trees, Blown–Out, 7 In.	55.00
Teapot, Peggotty	40.00
Vase, Palm Trees	40.00

Betty Boop, the cartoon figure, first appeared on the screen in 1931. Her face was modeled after the famous singer Helen Kane and her body after Mae West. In 1935 a comic strip was started. Although the Betty Boop cartoons were ended by 1938, there has been a revival of interest in the Betty Boop image in the 1980s and new pieces are being made.

BETTY BOOP, Animated Drawing, With Popeye, M. Fleischer, 8 1/2 x 11 1/2 In.	522.00
Animation Cel	140.00

◆◆

Examine a piece of furniture and look for unexplained holes, stains, and fade marks. They may indicate a fake.

◆◆

Bank, With Top Hat 20.00
Cards, Playing 75.00
Clock, Alarm, With Koko Clown 50.00
Doll, Black Dress, Heart Label, Fleischer Studios 850.00
Doll, Kalluss 850.00
Doll, M–Toy, Box, 12 In. 35.00
Light Bulb, Christmas, Figural, 1930s 125.00
Marble 15.00
Perfume Bottle 22.00
Purse, Shoulder, Portrait 40.00
Tumbler, Red Enameled, Frosted Glass, 6 In. 10.00
Wristwatch 10.00

The bicycle was invented in 1839. The first manufactured bicycle was made in 1861. Special ladies' bicycles were made after 1874. The modern safety bicycle was not produced until 1885. Collectors search for all types of bicycles and tricycles. Bicycle–related items are also listed here.

BICYCLE, Bell, Cast Brass, Eagle, Nickel Plated 85.00
Columbia, 52 In. 2800.00
Dutch, J. Winrix, Antwerpen, Black, 35 x 77 In. 82.00
Elgin, Boys, 1960s 2200.00
Highwheeler, 54 In. 1650.00
J. C. Higgins, Streamlined Color Flow, Silver & Blue, 39 x 71 In. 440.00
Motor, Whizzer, Balloon Tire, Bolt–On Motor 4000.00
Phantom, Boy's, Green, 6–Hole Carrier 480.00
Pioneer, Gendron, Rubber Tires, Wire Spokes, 29 x 11 In. 175.00
Plate, French Cycle Co., Baltimore, Enameled Brass 23.00
Raleigh, 3 Speed, Balloon Tires, 1954 .... 700.00
Roadmaster, Luxury Liner, Woman's, Metallic Blue, 1945, 26 In. 350.00
Schwinn, Black Phantom ....850.00 To 2500.00
Schwinn, Black Phantom, Restored 1950.00
Schwinn, Delivery, Large Basket, U.S. Mail Model, 1940s 1500.00
Schwinn, Girl's, Pink & Chrome, 1965 .... 25.00
Schwinn, Red & White, 40 In. 55.00
Shelby, Super Deluxe, Woman's, Blue, Chrome, Lights, 1953, 26 In. 850.00
Star, Large Wheel 6200.00
Tire Rims & Fenders, Wood & Metal, Fenders, 40 1/2 x 72 In. 305.00
Tribune, Model 86, Shaft Drive, 1903 .... 800.00
Tricycle, Air Flow 495.00
Tricycle, Junior Rocketrike, AMF, 1938 .... 225.00
Velocipede, 3 Wheels 550.00
Velocipede, Gendron Wheel Co., Cloth Seat, 1855, 45 x 31 In. 1400.00
Velocipede, Push & Pull, Orange, Black Pinstriping, 24 In. 5000.00
Western Flyer, Boy's, Batmobile Picture Both Sides, 1950s, 26 In. 700.00

Bing and Grondahl is a famous Danish factory making fine porcelains from 1853 to the present. Underglaze blue decoration was started in 1886. The annual Christmas plate series was introduced in 1895. Dinnerwares, stoneware, and figurines are still being made today. The firm has used the initials B & G and a stylized castle as part of the mark since 1898.

B & G
KJØBENHAVN
MADE IN
DENMARK

BING & GRONDAHL, Coffeepot, Seagull, Gold Trim 150.00
Creamer, Seagull, Gold Trim 40.00
Cruet, Blue & White 40.00

Cup & Saucer, Seagull, Gold Trim	40.00
Figurine, Ballerina, No. 2300, 12 In.	295.00
Figurine, Boy & Girl, Dancing, No. 2385	250.00
Figurine, Boy & Girl, Kissing, No. 2162	240.00
Figurine, Boy & Girl, Seated, Reading, No. 1567	175.00
Figurine, Boy On Bench, No. 1213	145.00
Figurine, Boy With Rabbit, No. 2319	145.00
Figurine, Bulldog, Gray & White, 1910, 6 x 6 In.	450.00
Figurine, Cat, No. 2256, 7 In.	110.00
Figurine, Child, With Doll, No. 2400	145.00
Figurine, Child, With Pup, No. 1747	145.00
Figurine, Clown, No. 2353	125.00
Figurine, Colonial Man & Woman Skating, Overglaze, No. 8022	850.00
Figurine, Dancing Lesson, No. 1845	275.00
Figurine, Four Aches, Tummy, Head, Ear, Tooth	150.00
Figurine, Girl Lying Down Reading Book, No. 2304	160.00
Figurine, Girl With Ball	85.00
Figurine, Girl With Ball, No. 239	145.00
Figurine, Girl With Doll, No. 1721, 7 In.	181.50
Figurine, Gold Crested Kinglet, No. 2458	45.00
Figurine, Parrot, No. 2019	125.00
Figurine, Peacock, No. 1628, 15 In.	425.00
Figurine, Penguin, No. 1822, 9 1/2 In.	185.00
Figurine, Sandman, Mo. 2055	150.00
Figurine, Shoemaker, 8 x 6 In.	265.00
Figurine, Silver Pheasant, No. 1784	900.00
Figurine, Spilt Milk, Weeping Girl, No. 2246 .... 130.00 To	150.00
Figurine, Woman Milking Cow, Cat, 7 1/2 x 7 In.	550.00
Gravy Boat, Seagull, Attached Tray, Gold Trim	150.00
Plaque, Shell Shape, Exposition Universelle, Paris, 1900	500.00
Plate, Christmas, 1927	75.00
Plate, Christmas, 1952	65.00
Plate, Christmas, 1956	65.00
Plate, Christmas, 1960	90.00
Plate, Christmas, 1967	40.00
Plate, Christmas, 1969	15.00
Plate, Christmas, 1970	28.00
Plate, Christmas, 1972	25.00
Plate, Christmas, 1975	28.00
Plate, Christmas, 1979	35.00
Plate, Christmas, 1981	20.00
Plate, Christmas, 1987	49.00
Plate, Dog & Puppies, 1969	380.00
Plate, Jubilee, 1970	15.00
Plate, Jubilee, 1975	25.00
Plate, Little Viking	39.00
Plate, Mother's Day, 1969	300.00
Plate, Seagull, Gold Trim, 9 5/8 In.	40.00
Plate, White House, 1987	17.00
Plate, Williamsburg, 1986	80.00
Platter, Seagull, Gold Trim, 16 x 11 In.	175.00
Sugar, Cover, Seagull, Gold Trim	75.00
Thimble, Velvet Box, 1979	25.00

All types of old binoculars are wanted by collectors. Those made in the eighteenth and nineteenth centuries are favored by serious collectors. The small, attractive binoculars called opera glasses are listed in their own section.

BINOCULARS, Bausch & Lomb, Compass On Hard Leather Case	150.00
Debonair, 3 1/2 x 20 In.	6.00
Tom Corbett	65.00

Old birdcages are collected for use as homes for pet birds and as decorative objects of folk art. Elaborate wooden cages of the past centuries can still be found. The brass or wicker cages of the 1930s are popular with bird owners.

BIRDCAGE, 4 Feeders, Shell Design Door, Shells Each Side of Cage, 1920s	30.00
Brass, Octagonal Black Marble Foot, Riband Pedestal, 70 In.	770.00
Brass, Stand, 1910	150.00
Chateau Form, French, c.1880, Large	3800.00
Hendryx, Brass	50.00
House Shape, Gabled Roof & Base, Deer Head Over Door, Tin, 1873	125.00
Oriental Style, Octagonal	3250.00
Pagoda Form, Brass	125.00
Parakeet, Celluloid, Weighted	18.00
Schmid Bros., Musical, Bird On Perch Dances To Music, 8 In.	15.00
Taj Mahal Design, Wire Pattern, Victorian	300.00
Wicker, 17 In.	75.00
Wire, Wooden Frame, Pull Out Copper Tray, Black Paint, 21 3/4 In.	160.00
Wood & Twisted Wire, Whalebone & Baleen Inlay, Dated 1862	4987.50
Wood & Wire, Chateau Style, Stand, France, c.1870, 75 x 75 In.	3500.00
Wood & Wire, Slant Roof, 15 In.	95.00
Wood & Wire, White Paint, Blue Trim, 20 In.	75.00
Wrought Iron & Wire, 1 Door Over Lower Shelf Base, 6 Ft. 6 In.	990.00

Bisque is an unglazed baked porcelain. Finished bisque has a slightly sandy texture with a dull finish. Some of it may be decorated with various colors. Bisque gained favor during the late Victorian era when thousands of bisque figurines were made. It is still being made.

BISQUE, see also named porcelain factories

BISQUE, 2 Blond Girls In Wicker Basket, 4 3/4 x 3 1/4 In.	135.00
Box, 2 Cats On Pillow Cover, Glazed Bisque, Germany	125.00
Bust, Boy, Metal Fly On Nose, Bib, Tam, Padded Top, Box, 3 1/2 In.	265.00
Bust, Woman & Man, 19th Century, Germany, Pair	575.00
Dish, Dog On Basket, With Bone, France, 5 3/4 x 6 1/2 x 9 In.	550.00
Egg, Black Boy Breaking Out, Head 1 Side, Rear At Other, 2 In.	95.00
Figurine, Bear, Skiing, Holding Skis, Schneider, 8 In.	155.00
Figurine, Bride & Groom, 1950s, 4 1/2 In.	18.00
Figurine, Cleopatra, With Lyre, White, Green Base, 4 x 4 1/2 In.	65.00
Figurine, Googly–Eyed Child, Holding Teddy Bear, Germany, 5 3/4 In.	58.00
Figurine, Googly–Eyed Child, Holding Teether, Germany, 5 1/2 In.	48.00
Figurine, Jackie Coogan, The Kid, 6 1/2 In.	300.00
Figurine, Neoclassical Man & Woman, Copenhagen, 12 3/4 In., Pair	4675.00
Figurine, Rachel, Marked J. G., Glass Dome, 15 In.	440.00
Figurine, Small Boy, Sailor Hat, Sword, 4 3/4 In.	45.00
Figurine, Victorian Man & Woman, Tinted, Pair	75.00
Jar, Woman, Dunking Roll In Coffee Cup, Bouffes–Parisiens, 13 In.	185.00
Night–Light, Figural, Cat's Head, White, Green Glass Eyes, 3 1/4 In.	145.00
Pitcher, Open Pod Shape, Stig Lindenberg, 1935–40, 5 In.	247.00
Vase, French Period Couple Scene, Scrollwork, Triangular, 3 1/2 In.	45.00

Black amethyst glass appears black until it is held to the light, then a dark purple can be seen. It has been made in many factories from 1860 to the present.

BLACK AMETHYST, Box, Patch, Hinged, White Flowers, 1 1/8 x 2 1/8 In.	90.00
Compote, Shell, Westmoreland, 6 In.	55.00
Flowerpot, Underplate, 4 1/2 In.	20.00
Mug, Lacy, Medallion, Souvenir	55.00
Powder Jar, Metal Lid, 2 Lovebirds	40.00
Toothpick	18.00
Tray, 9 3/4 In.	38.00
Vase, Boy, Fishing Pole & Fish, Mary Gregory, 11 3/4 In.	245.00
Vase, Embossed Dancing Maidens, 2 Handles, c.1935, 7 In.	75.00

Vase, Enameled Flowers, Gold Rim Top & Bottom, 8 In., Pair	150.00
Vase, Trumpet, Gold Design On Rim	75.00
Vase, Victorian Dancing Girls, Blown, Painted, 12 In., Pair	235.00

> Black memorabilia has become an important area of collecting since the 1970s. Any piece that pictures a black person is included in this category and objects range from sheet music to salt and pepper shakers. The best material dates from past centuries, but many recent items are of interest even if not yet expensive.

BLACK, Ashtray, Coon Chicken Inn, 6 In.	145.00
Ashtray–Match Holder, Wash On Line	35.00
Ashtray–Nodder, Black Boy, With Cigar, Die Cast	75.00
Bank, Aunt Jemima, Cast Iron, Large	148.00
Book, Amos 'n Andy, 1929	40.00
Book, Black Diaper Dan, 1949	30.00
Book, Little Black Sambo, 1935	50.00
Book, Little Black Sambo, Hardback, Helen Bannerman	30.00
Book, Little Black Sambo, Illustrated, 1939	82.50
Book, Little Black Sambo, Unused, 1959	30.00
Book, Little Brown Koko, 1959	30.00
Book, Ten Little Colored Boys, Dated 1942	85.00
Book, Topsy, c.1800	150.00
Bowl, Watermelon, Black Figural Handle, Enameled	200.00
Bread Plate, Coon Chicken Inn	100.00
Brooch, Black Women, Plastic	32.00
Brush, Figural, Woman, Wood Top, Rounded Brush Base, New Orleans	35.00
Card, Birthday, Girl, Singing, Dancing, Cloth Dress, Unused, 1930s	15.00
Card, Birthday, Pickaninny, Rhyme In Dialect	15.00
Card, Get Well, Boy, Yo' Is Feelin In De', 1941, Hallmark, 4 In.	10.00
Card, Thanksgiving, Pickaninny, When Ah Wishes, Ah's Talking Turkey	15.00
Card, Valentine, Moving Man, Honey Get A Move On, 1941, 4 In.	10.00
Chopping Board, Mammy, Reckon Ah Needs, Wooden Peg	40.00
Clothes Brush, Bellboy, Green, 8 In.	27.00
Clothes Brush, Mammy, 7 In.	16.00
Doll, Baby, Bisque	30.00
Doll, Baby, Celluloid, Turtle Mark, 3 1/4 In.	45.00
Doll, Bisque, Movable String–Tied Arms & Legs, Japan, 1930s, 4 1/2 In.	50.00
Doll, Celluloid, Feathers, Necklace, Earrings, Japan, 7 In.	35.00
Doll, Child, Bisque, Closed Mouth, Swivel Neck, Jointed, 5 In.	850.00
Doll, Cloth, 18 In.	175.00
Doll, Composition Socket Head, 5–Piece Body, Clothes, A. M., 11 1/2 In.	198.00
Doll, Dancing, Carved, Polychromed, Articulated Limbs, 10 In.	75.00
Doll, G. I. Joe, Box	70.00
Doll, Handmade, Mammy, Sewn On Eyes & Mouth, Polka Dot Dress, 10 In.	135.00
Doll, Knitted, Red Pants & Hat, Green Shirt, 1880–90, 15 In.	245.00
Doll, Mammy, Black Cloth, Red Dress, Painted Face	35.00
Doll, Mammy, Cloth, Mask Face, Stands On Boots, Dress, 14 1/2 In.	231.00
Doll, Mammy, Rag, I'se Your Honey Girl, Printed Fabric, Mill, N. Y.	275.00
Doll, Mammy, Walker, Windup	240.00
Doll, Man, Painted Eyes, Molded Hair, Shoulderhead, 16 In.	550.00
Doll, Nut Head, Mammy, Clothes Basket, 10 In.	65.00
Doll, Painted Oilcloth, Ethnic Features, 12 In.	695.00
Doll, Rag, Girl, Over Bottle, Stuffed Clothes, Yarn Hair, 18 1/2 In.	125.00
Doll, Rag, Silk Face, Babyland	550.00
Doll, Uncle Mose, Envelope, 1949	68.50
Doll, Wade & Diana, Oil Cloth, 1950s	75.00
Doorstop, Aunt Jemima, Full–Bodied, Cast Iron, 11 1/4 In.	115.00
Egg Timer, Black Chef, Porcelain, Germany	48.00
Egg Timer, Mammy	148.00
Fan, Black Man, Carver	25.00
Figurine, Black, Pushing, Outhouse, Wheels, My Old Country Seat, Bisque	50.00
Figurine, Jazz Musician, Nodders, German, 4 In., Pair	175.00
Fishing Lure, Sambo, Box	35.00

Game, Amos 'n Andy Acrobat, Box, 1930s	95.00
Game, Little Black Sambo	85.00
Game, Target, Black Sambo, Tin, Wyandotte, Tall	95.00
Half Doll On Pincushion	65.00
Holder, Potholder, Mammy, Wooden	16.00
Holder, Scouring Pad, Hanging, Mammy, Coventry Pottery	55.00
Holder, Scouring Pad, Mammy, Wall, Ceramic	68.00
Hose Caddy, Garden, Enameled Black Man, Sheet Steel, 29 In.	65.00
Humidor, Mammy, Figural Head	275.00
Lamp, Blackamoor, Pottery, Electric	75.00
Lamp, Woman's Head, Pottery	95.00
Laundry Bag, Mammy	90.00
Light Pull, Aunt Jemima, Breakfast Club	15.00
Magazine Cover, Child, Muff, Red Dress, Judge, Christmas 1897	365.00
Mammy, Walker	69.00
Mannequin, Child, Plaster, Clockwork, Cloth Sunday Suit & Tie	1925.00
Match Holder, Boy, Carrying Watermelon, Majolica	200.00
Match Holder, Grotesque Black Man, Watermelon, Chalkware	25.00
Match Holder, Man On Leaf, Majolica	250.00
Memo Board, Says We Needs	26.00
Menu, Coon Chicken Inn, Small	35.00
Menu, Pickaninny Center, Menu Fans Around	8.00
Noisemaker, Black Man, Tin	40.00
Note Pad, Wall, Aunt Jemima	60.00
Nutcracker, Carved Wood, Painted Lips, Glass Eyes, 11 In.	495.00
Outhouse, Black Boy Inside, 1 Waiting Outside	25.00
Pail, Luzianne Coffee & Chicory, Mammy, 1928	75.00
Painting, Oil, Portrait, Black Man, From South Carolina, 1900	375.00
Perfume Bottle, Golliwog, 3 In.	85.00
Perfume Bottle, Golliwog, Stopper, 2 In.	40.00
Photochrome Gravure, Young Woman, E. W. Kemble, 1897, 9 1/4 x 12 In.	300.00

Black, Puppet, Painted Wood & Cloth, 13 In.

◆◆◆◆◆◆◆◆◆◆◆◆◆◆◆◆◆◆◆◆◆◆◆

Don't repaint old metal toys. It
lowers the value.

◆◆◆◆◆◆◆◆◆◆◆◆◆◆◆◆◆◆◆◆◆◆◆

Photograph, Sutro Baths Amusement Center, San Fran., 1890, 8 x 10 In. 95.00
Pie Bird, Chef, Stoneware, Green 100.00
Pie Bird, Chef, Stoneware, Yellow 85.00
Pie Bird, Young Black Girl, Stoneware 95.00
Pin, Head, Tin Lithograph, Tug Cord To Spin Eyes, 2 1/2 In. 45.00
Pincushion, Mammy, Figural 39.00
Pitcher, Figural, Black Man's Head, Brown & Black Albany Slip, 10 In. 2800.00
Pitcher, Syrup, Aunt Jemima 30.00
Pitcher, Syrup, Aunt Jemima, F & F Mold 50.00
Place Mat, Aunt Jemima 37.00
Plaque, Potholder, Aunt Jemima, Tin, Wall, 7 x 10 In. 45.00
Plate, Coon Chicken Inn 145.00
Plate, Coon Chicken, Head of Winking Man 200.00
Playing Cards, Little Black Sambo, 2 Decks, Box 20.00
Postcard, Caddy, Boy, Carrying Larger Bag of Golf Clubs, 1907 .... 9.00
Postcard, Comic, Linen, Color, 1940, 6 Different 12.00
Postcard, Relaxed Man, Smoking Pipe, Thiele, 1907 .... 35.00
Postcard, White Baby, In Tub, Black Golliwog, Suspended Over Tub, 1907 .... 20.00
Postcard, Woman, Comic Saying, Artist's Logo, Postmark 1903 .... 14.00
Potholder, Doll, Crocheted 10.00
Print, Cable Car Turntable, San Fran., Ralph Wilson, 1950, 10 x 8 In. 85.00
Print, Pastel, Man With Hat, B. Neutz, Framed, 8 x 11 In. 450.00
Print, Truckin', Couple Dancing, G. Duncan, Watercolor, 1935, 8 In. 2000.00
Puppet, Painted Wood & Cloth, 13 In. ....*Illus* 115.00
Recipe Box, Mammy, Red .... 130.00 To 169.00
Recipe Pamphlet, Aunt Jemima 5.00
Rocker, Mammy's, 1860s 2000.00
Salt & Pepper, Aunt Jemima & Uncle Mose, Red, F & F, 5 In. .... 60.00 To 75.00
Salt & Pepper, Aunt Jemima, F & F Mold, 5 In. 60.00
Salt & Pepper, Aunt Jemima, Louisiana, Green Apron, F & F ....90.00 To 165.00
Salt & Pepper, Chef & Mammy, Occupied Japan 30.00
Salt & Pepper, Jungle Boys, Wood 35.00
Salt & Pepper, Mammy & Butler 75.00
Salt & Pepper, Mammy & Chef .... 30.00 To 45.00
Salt & Pepper, Man & Woman, Cellulite, Press Button, 1940s 20.00
Salt & Pepper, Pickaninny Babies, Stacking, Ceramic 85.00
Salt & Pepper, Southern Belle & Mammy, Plantation Tray 39.50
Salt & Pepper, Valentine Couple 95.00
Shopping Peg Board, Reckon Ah Needs 60.00
Sign, Table, Coon Chicken Inn, 2–Sided Easel, 1930s, 4 x 5 In. 9.00
Smoke Set, Boy Sitting On Basket, Floppy Hat, Eating Melon, 6 x 6 In. 325.00
Soap, Figural, Baby, Paris Perfume Co., 1920s, Box, 4 In. 35.00
Spice Jar, Ginger, Clove, Allspice, Aunt Jemima 25.00
Spice Set, Aunt Jemima 150,.00
Spoon Holder, Mammy, Ceramic, 5 In. 65.00
Spoon, St. Augustine, Crocodile, Wrapped Around Boy Handle, Sterling 65.00
String Holder, Black Girl 195.00
String Holder, Mammy, Japan 100.00
String Holder, Mammy, Usa 95.00
String Holder, Smiling Black Lady, Full–Bodied, Painted, 7 In. 58.00
Sugar & Creamer, Aunt Jemima, Green, F & F 130.00
Sugar & Creamer, Aunt Jemima, Yellow, F & F .... 100.00 To 160.00
Swizzle Stick, Ubangi Woman, 15 Goes To Droopy 40 Years, 6 Piece 45.00
Swizzle Stick, Zulu Lulu, On Card 25.00
Syrup, Aunt Jemima, Plastic .... 35.00 To 55.00
Tablecloth, Mammys Dancing 85.00
Tape Measure & Pincushion, Mammy, Lithograph On Wood 55.00
Thermometer, Brown Boy Behind 30.00
Thermometer, Diaper Dan, Pants Change Color, Dated 1949, 5 1/2 In. 29.00
Toaster Cover, Mammy 20.00
Towel Set, 7 Days of Week, Mammy, Embroidered, 7 Piece 165.00
Towel, Mammy, Appliqued 65.00
Towel, Mammy, Washing Floor 39.00

◆◆◆

Fakers sometimes make a round table with leaves from a square table with leaves because it would have more value. This can be spotted if you carefully examine the overall proportion of the table and the edges of the top.

◆◆◆

Toy, Alabama Coon Jigger, Lithograph, Painted, Lehmann, 10 In.	330.00
Toy, Amos & Andy, Animated, 1929	40.00
Toy, Amos & Sandy, Acrobats, Box	75.00
Toy, Black Andy, Wooden Jointed, 6 In.	250.00
Toy, Black Sambo, Animated	95.00
Toy, Jazzbo Jim, Mechanical, Tin Lithograph, Unique Art, 9 1/2 In.	330.00
Toy, Jigger, Composition, Wood, Cloth Dress, American, 10 In.	2400.00
Toy, Mammy, Tin Lithograph, Lindstrom, 8 In.	210.00
Toy, Minstrel, Tin, Top Hat, Original Paint, Germany, 9 In.	990.00
Wall Pad, Mammy, Celluloid	39.00
Whirligig, Man, Arms & Legs Jointed, Dances As Propellor Turns	495.00
Wood Carving, Black Woman, Painted, Life–Size, 19th Century	3685.00

Blown glass was formed by forcing air through a rod into molten glass. Early glass and some forms of art glass were hand blown. Other types of glass were molded or pressed.

BLOWN GLASS, Bottle, Amber, 20 Swirled Ribs, Globular, 6 In.	95.00
Bottle, Ludlow, Olive, 5 1/2 In.	85.00
Bottle, Toilet Water, 3 Mold, Tam–O–Shanter Stopper, Blue, 6 In.	155.00
Bowl, Clear, 11 x 6 1/2 In.	150.00
Bowl, Clear, Folded Rim, 11 1/4 x 10 1/2 In.	100.00
Bowl, Zanesville, Diamond, 4 1/2 In. _Illus_	660.00
Canister, 2 Applied Rings, Domed Finial Cover, 11 1/2 In.	175.00
Canister, Knobbed Cover, 2 Applied Rings, 10 1/2 In.	90.00
Carafe, Rayed & Geometric, Aqua, 3 Mold, 1815–40, 8 In.	1500.00
Club, Bottle Shape, Aqua, 7 3/4 In.	65.00
Compote, Applied Trumpet Foot, Clear, 13 1/4 In.	175.00
Cordial, Cut Floral Design On Bowl, 3 1/8 In.	10.00
Creamer, Zanesville, Petal Footed, 1815–1830, 5 In. _Illus_	440.00
Decanter, 3 Mold, 3 Applied Rings, Crystal, 8 In.	70.00

◆◆◆◆◆◆◆◆◆◆◆◆◆◆◆◆◆◆◆◆◆◆◆

Never allow water to evaporate in a glass vase. It will leave a white residue that may be impossible to remove.

◆◆◆◆◆◆◆◆◆◆◆◆◆◆◆◆◆◆◆◆◆◆◆

Blown Glass, Bowl, Zanesville, Diamond, 4 1/2 In.

Blown Glass, Creamer, Zanesville, Petal Footed, 1815–1830, 5 In.

Demi-John, Green, 23 1/2 In.	50.00
Feeder, Hummingbird, Cobalt Blue Finial, 5 1/4 In.	95.00
Figure, Santa Claus, Applied Legs & Feet, Early 1900s	65.00
Jar, Apothecary, Domed Cover, Knob Finial, Flared Foot, 14 In.	75.00
Jar, Aqua, 20 Swirled Ribs, Fold Lip, 4 1/4 In.	50.00
Jar, Domed Lid, Scene, Paper Label	145.00
Jar, Green, Folded Lip, Cylindrical, 9 7/8 In.	20.00
Mug, Copper Wheel Engraved 2 Hearts, 6 5/8 In.	150.00
Mug, Shield-Shaped Medallion, Words Remember Me, 4 3/4 In.	245.00
Pitcher, Clear, Applied Handle, Ground Pontil, 7 7/8 In.	45.00
Pitcher, Enameled Scene, Words, Applied Handle, Germany, 13 In.	65.00
Pitcher, Light Green, Crudely Applied Handle, 5 5/8 In.	50.00
Pitcher, Olive Amber, 5 1/2 In.	2900.00
Pitcher, Oval, Flared Bulbous, Handle, Murano, 1912, 11 In.	300.00
Salt, Sapphire Blue, Footed, 3 1/4 In.	225.00
Tumbler, Copper Wheel Engraved 2 Hearts, 7 In.	400.00
Tumbler, Copper Wheel Engraved Basket of Flowers, 4 In.	35.00
Tumbler, Copper Wheel Engraved Basket of Flowers, Green, 7 In.	175.00
Tumbler, Flip, McKearin GII-33 Pattern, 1830, 5 1/2 In.	99.00
Vase, Enameled Lily-of-The-Valley, Green, 11 1/2 In., Pair	145.00
Vase, Hyacinth, Applied Ring, Amethyst, 7 1/2 In.	225.00
Vase, Trumpet, Baluster Stem, Folded Rim, Amethyst, 9 1/2 In.	475.00
Whimsey, Folded Rim, Hat Shape, Zanesville, Amber, 10 3/8 In.	200.00
Wine, Copper Wheel Engraved Bowl, Crystal, 5 In.	22.50
Wine, Knop Stem, Panel Cut, Peacock Green, 5 1/8 In.	100.00
Witch's Ball, Deep Amethyst, 5 3/4 In.	25.00

BLUE AMBERINA, see Amberina
BLUE GLASS, see Cobalt Blue
BLUE ONION, see Onion

 Blue Willow pattern has been made in England since 1780. The pattern has been copied by factories in many countries, including Germany, Japan, and the United States. It is still being made. Willow was named for a pattern that pictures a bridge, birds, willow trees, and a Chinese landscape.

BLUE WILLOW, Bowl, Center Pattern, Beaded Rays, 9 In.	5.00
Bowl, Fruit, 5 In.	4.50
Bowl, Vegetable, Meakin, Oval, 8 1/2 In.	35.00
Bread Plate, Japan	4.00
Coffeepot, Japan, Demitasse	10.00
Cup & Saucer, Japan	15.00
Cup & Saucer, Occupied Japan	17.00
Cup, Child's, Empress Litho	14.00
Cup, Japan	9.50
Cup, Jumbo, 5 x 8 3/4 In.	100.00
Dinner Set, Occupied Japan, 16 Piece	135.00
Eggcup, Footed	10.00
Eggcup, Single, Flat, Wood & Sons	17.50
Gravy Boat, Ridgway	40.00
Grill Plate, Grimwades, Dark Blue	35.00
Grill Plate, Japan	12.00
Jar, Rington's Ltd. Tea Merchant's, 8 In.	115.00
Luncheon Plate, Japan	10.00
Mug, Japan	10.00
Pitcher	32.50
Pitcher, Booth, 1 Qt.	65.00
Plate, Allerton, 9 In.	20.00
Plate, England, 9 In.	8.00
Plate, Gold Trim, 10 In.	12.00
Plate, Gold Trim, Staffordshire, 8 In.	25.00
Plate, Myott & Son, 8 In.	8.00
Plate, Myott & Son, 9 3/4 In.	10.00
Plate, Ruffled, Allerton, 9 1/4 In.	15.00

Plate, Wedgwood, 8 In. 6.00
Platter, Bista, Noritake, 12 In. 23.00
Platter, Japan, 12 1/2 In. 45.00
Platter, Myott & Son, 14 1/2 In. 50.00
Platter, R. H. & Co., 17 3/4 In. 95.00
Platter, Woods Ware, 11 3/4 In. 35.00
Relish, 3 Sections, 11 In. 50.00
Salt & Pepper, Ceramic, Wood 15.00
Salt & Pepper, England 35.00
Soup, Dish, Allerton 25.00
Sugar & Creamer, Marked Copeland, 3 1/4 In. 200.00
Sugar, 1792–1832 .... 60.00
Sugar, Japan 25.00
Tea Set, Child's, Japan, Box, 23 Piece 250.00
Tea Set, Child's, Occupied Japan, 12 Piece 125.00
Teapot, Buffalo Pottery 125.00
Tray, Royal, Flange Rim, 12 In. 12.00
Tureen, Cover, Allerton, Marked, 8 x 12 In. 135.00
Tureen, Occupied Japan 75.00
Waste Bowl, Myott & Son 18.00
     BLUERINA, see Amberina

The Boch Freres factory was founded in 1841 in La Louviere in eastern Belgium. The wares resemble the work of Villeroy & Boch. The factory is still in business.

BOCH FRERES, Charger, Man Smoking, Dutch Scene, Blue & White, Oval 195.00
Jug, Art Deco Penguin Shape, Metallic Black, Stamped, 10 In. 225.00
Lamp, Art Deco Design, 14 In. 295.00
Lamp, Art Deco, Orange, Yellow & Black 230.00
Lamp, Crackle Glaze, Art Deco Panels, 1920s, Octagonal, 12 In. 135.00
Lamp, Lime, Blue & Rust On White, Charles Catteau, 8 1/2 In. 375.00
Vase, Figural, Snowman, Art Deco, White, 9 In. 85.00
Vase, Yellow Flambe, Over Blue-Green, Bottle Shape, 10 In. 170.00

Osso China Company was reorganized as Edward Marshall Boehm, Inc., in 1953. The company is still working in England and New Jersey. In the early days of the factory, dishes were made, but the elaborate and lifelike bird figurines are the best known ware. Edward Marshall Boehm, the founder, died in 1961; but the firm has continued to design and produce porcelain. Today, the firm makes both limited and unlimited editions of figurines and plates.

BOEHM, Box, Fluted, Rectangular, Green, Marked, 3 1/2 x 6 In. 145.00
Bust, Madonna, White Bisque, Porcelain Base 175.00
Figurine, Baby Goldfinch, No. 448 .... 195.00
Figurine, Baby Robin, No. 437G 55.00
Figurine, Baby Wood Thrush, No. 444C 195.00
Figurine, Barn Owl 4950.00
Figurine, Black Capped Chickadee, 8 1/2 In. 160.00
Figurine, Camillia, Helen Boehm 600.00
Figurine, Canada Geese With Goslings, No. 408 .... 695.00
Figurine, Canadian Warbler & Butterfly 1000.00
Figurine, Cat & 2 Kittens, Enameling, 5 1/4 In. 110.00
Figurine, Catbird 1200.00
Figurine, Firebird, Ballet Classic, White Bisque 175.00
Figurine, Frog On Lily Pad 85.00
Figurine, Goldfinches On Thistle 1000.00
Figurine, Lapwing 3000.00
Figurine, Lovers, Lucite Case, 7 In. 85.00
Figurine, Mallards In Flight, No. 406, 11 x 11 1/2 In. 695.00
Figurine, Pope John XXIII 500.00
Figurine, Prince Charming, Gold Slippers, White, 7 1/2 In. 145.00
Figurine, Roadrunner 2200.00
Figurine, Royal Blessing 950.00

Figurine, Wood Thrush 110.00
Figurine, Woodcock, No. 413 .... 1500.00
Mask, King Tut 1850.00
Plate, Wild Turkey 40.00
Vase, Shasta Daisies, Metallic Gold, 12 In. 295.00

Bohemian glass is an ornate overlay or flashed glass made during the Victorian era. It has been reproduced in Bohemia, which is now a part of Czechoslovakia. Glass made from 1875 to 1900 is preferred by collectors.

BOHEMIAN GLASS, Bowl, Ruby Cut To Clear, Large 150.00
Celery, Washington D. C. Scene, Ruby Flashed, 9 In. ....*Illus* 745.00
Decanter, City Hall Scene, Ruby Flashed, 10 In. ....*Illus* 2750.00
Decanter, Copper Wheel Floral, Clear, Red Amber, 15 3/4 In. 136.00
Decanter, Etched Deer & Bird, Stopper, Ruby, 11 In. 80.00
Decanter, Grape Design, Stopper, Ruby Flash, 12 In. 75.00
Decanter, Red & Gold 75.00
Dish, Powder, Ruby Stain, Clear & Frosted, Bird, Domed Cover 55.00
Goblet, Capitol, Washington, D. C., Brock's Monument, Pair 690.00
Goblet, Fairmount Water Works, Ruby Flashed ....*Illus* 495.00
Goblet, Ruby Flashed, Battle Monument, 7 In. ....*Illus* 495.00
Goblet, Ruby Flashed, Exposition Palace, 6 In. ....*Illus* 495.00
Goblet, Ruby Flashed, Patent Office View, 7 In. ....*Illus* 935.00
Mug, President's House, Washington, D. C., 4 3/4 In. 410.00
Pitcher, Water, Floradora, Cranberry, Gold Trim 250.00
Pokal, Capitol Building, Niagara Falls, 16 In., Pair 1900.00
Tumble–Up, Flowers, Ruby Cut To Clear .... 65.00 To 75.00
Vase, Castle, Deer, Bird, Ruby, 11 x 9 In. 150.00
Vase, Engraved Flowers, Amber Cut To Clear, 11 In. 295.00
Vase, Etched Animals, Blue, 6 In. 200.00
Vase, Girard's Bank, City Hall, N. Y., 4 1/2 In., Pair 1210.00
Vase, Iron Springs Hotel, Maniton, Colorado, 7 1/2 In. 413.00
Water Set, Stag Design, Green, 6 Piece 325.00

Bone dishes were considered a necessary part of a table setting for the Victorian table. The crescent–shaped dish was kept at the edge of the dinner plate so the bones removed from the fish could be stored away from the uneaten food. Some bone dishes were made in more fanciful shapes and many resemble fish.

BONE DISH, Black Transfer, Houses 30.00
Fish Shape, Blue, Orange 75.00
Flow Blue, Shanghai 25.00
Flow Blue, Trees and Houses 25.00
Hand Painted Flowers, Curved 35.00

Bookends have probably been used since books became inexpensive. Early libraries kept books in cupboards, not on open shelves. By the 1870s bookends appeared, especially homemade fret–carved wooden examples. Most bookends listed in this book date from the twentieth century.

BOOKENDS, Abraham Lincoln, Bronze 75.00
African Black Couple, Playing Drums, Mahogany 25.00
Angel Fish, Ceramic, Czechoslovakia, 5 In. 42.00
Bucking Horse & Cowboy, Syroco 16.00
Bust of Buccaneer, Chalkware, Herzel 265.00
Child Cowering From Frog, S. Morani, Cold Painted Metal 25.00
Colonial Woman, Sitting, Black, Occupied Japan, 4 1/2 In. 35.00
Constitution Clipper Ship, Cast Iron 35.00
Dancing Frogs, In Tails, Top Hats, Rack, Metal, 1920s 50.00
Dancing Girl, Art Deco, Bronze, 7 1/2 In. 150.00
Dianna, With Hound, Sciarroca Wood, 5 x 6 In. 28.00
Dog, Boston Bull Pup, Hubley, 6 x 4 1/2 In. 100.00
Elephant, Maroon Glaze, Cliftwood 95.00

End of The Trail, Bronze 115.00
End of Trail, Bronze 115.00
Foo Dogs, Blue Glazed, 10 x 5 In., Pair 795.00
Football Players, Bronzed Iron, 1920, 6 In. 75.00
Girl's Head, Expandable 40.00
Hartford Fire Insurance Co., Bronze, Dated 1933 .... 75.00 To 85.00
Hartford Fire Insurance, Bronze, 1935 .... 75.00
Hartford Insurance Co., 1935 .... 35.00
Head, Woman's, Sleeping, Long Hair, Black Base, Chalkware, 7 In. 75.00
Horse, Clear Glass 12.50
Horse, Grazing, Cast Iron 20.00
Horse, Saddled, Head Down, Cast Iron 30.00
Indian Head, Bronze 155.00
Indian On Horse, End of Trail, Bronzed Pot Metal 65.00

Bohemian Glass, Goblet, Fairmount Water Works, Ruby Flashed
Bohemian Glass, Decanter, City Hall Scene, Ruby Flashed, 10 In.
Bohemian Glass, Celery, Washington D. C. Scene, Ruby Flashed, 9 In.

Bohemian Glass, Goblet, Ruby Flashed, Battle Monument, 7 In.
Bohemian Glass, Goblet, Ruby Flashed, Patent Office View, 7 In.
Bohemian Glass, Goblet, Ruby Flashed, Exposition Palace, 6 In.

Indian, Cast Iron 22.00
Indian, Full Headdress, Cast Iron, Copper Finish 75.00
Joan of Arc, Painted Bronze Finish, Cast Iron 30.00
Kraftsman Studios, Laguna Beach, Handmade, Copper 45.00
Leda & The Swan, Art Deco, Gold, Cast Iron, 8 x 4 1/2 In. 85.00
Lincoln, Giving Gettysburg Address, Bronze 45.00
Lions, Pompeian, Bronze 195.00
Log Cabin, Tall Pines, Moonlit Night, Cast Iron, 1920s, 6 x 4 In. 45.00
Lovers, Art Deco, Cast Metal 50.00
Mayflower, Iron 27.00
Nude Man, Wrestling Lion, Art Deco, Pierced, Bronzed Iron, 6 In. 37.00
Nude On Horseback, Art Deco, Glass, 6 In. 65.00
Offraude, Nude Man & Woman Kneeling, Bronze, Hoffman, 10 3/8 In. 220.00
Penguin, Leaning On Base, Pottery, Black, Cream, France, 8 1/2 In. 302.00
Poodle, Black Ceramic, 1950s 35.00
Rearing Horse, Glass, Amber, L. E. Smith 40.00
Roman Soldier, With Horse, Cast Iron 30.00
Scotty Looking Over Floral Fence, Hubley 140.00
Ship Design, Burgundy With Intaglio Bakelite 30.00
Ship, Cast Iron 12.00
Sun Bonnet Babies, 6 In. 100.00
Woman Archer, Hunting Dog, Art Deco, Sirocco Wood, 7 In. 33.00

Bookmarks were originally made of parchment, cloth, or leather. Soon woven silk ribbon, thin cardboard, celluloid, wood, silver, tortoiseshell, and metals were used. Examples made before 1850 are scarce, but there are many to be found dating before 1920.

BOOKMARK, Acorn, Pretty Little Girl, Cardboard 5.00
Butterfly, Figural, Souvenir, GGIE 15.00
Declaration of Independence, Woven Silk, Signing Scene 85.00
Medicinal Advertising, Woman & Lily Pond, Art Nouveau, 1905 .... 30.00
Muskingum County Fair, 1899 .... 10.00
Nazi, Castle & Stadium At Nuremberg, Silk, 1966 .... 150.00
Poole Piano, Celluloid 15.00
Tarzan, 1930 .... 60.00

      BOSTON & SANDWICH CO., see Lutz; Sandwich Glass

As soon as the commercial bottle was invented, the opener to be used with the new types of closures became a necessity. Many types of bottle openers can be found, most dating from the twentieth century. Collectors prize advertising and comic openers.

BOTTLE OPENER, Alligator, Green, Rhinestone Eyes, 3 In. 35.00
Alligator, Head Down 95.00
Alligator, Head Up, Bronze 125.00
Alligator, Iron, Painted, John Wright Co., 5 In. 125.00
Bar Bum, Comes Apart, Bar Tools Inside, Opener In Hat 85.00
Beer Drinker, Cast Iron 38.00
Black Face, Cast Iron 75.00
Black Man, Cast Iron, 4 3/8 In. 55.00
Black Man, Riding Alligator, Cast Iron 180.00
Bulldog, White, Green Collar, Cast Iron, 4 1/8 In. 25.00
Clown, Cast Iron, 4 3/8 In. 100.00
Cocker Spaniel, Black, Cast Iron, 3 3/4 In. 65.00
Cowboy, At Signpost, Iron, Painted, John Wright Co., 4 1/2 In. 125.00
Cowboy, Guitar, San Antonio, Texas, John Wright Co., 4 7/8 In. 225.00
Cowboy, With Cactus, Cast Iron 170.00
Crocodile, Brass 25.00
Devil, Reclining, Chrome, Body of Woman With Head of Devil 188.00
Dinky Dan, Cast Iron 275.00
Dog, Cocker Spaniel, John Wright Co. 30.00
Dog, Setter, Brown & White, Cast Iron 80.00
Donkey, Cast Iron, 3 5/8 In. .... 10.00 To 25.00
Donkey, Polychrome Paint, Cast Iron, 3 1/8 In. 35.00

Donkey, Seated, Ears Back, Iron, Wilton, 3 5/8 In. .... 30.00 To 60.00
Drunk At Palm Tree, Bald Head, Painted, Wilton, 4 1/8 In. 55.00
Drunk At Signpost, 1000 Islands, Wilton, 4 In. 15.00
Drunk At Signpost, Sequoia Park, J. Wright, 4 In .... 25.00 To 50.00
Duck Head 18.00
Elephant, Cast Iron, 3 5/8 In. 15.00
Elephant, Chrome, Germany 95.00
Elephant, Pink, Cast Iron 45.00
Elephant, Polychrome Paint, Cast Iron, 3 3/4 In. 145.00
Elephant, Seated, Iron, Black Paint, Marked W. H. R., 3 1/2 In. 15.00
Elephant, Seated, Iron, Painted, Wilton, 3 5/8 In. 35.00
Elephant, Walking, Worn Silver Paint, Wilton, 3 1/4 In. 145.00
Eskimo, Cliquot Club Soda, Brass 88.00
Eskimo, Kentucky Tavern Whiskey 198.00
False Teeth 55.00
Fish, Brass 10.00
Fisherman 52.00
Fleer's Gum 30.00
Foundryman 40.00
Four-Eyed Man, Cast Iron 65.00
Frank Jones 7.00
Frostie 8.00
Gaynola 20.00
Girl By Lampost, Painted, John Wright, 4 1/4 In. 32.00
Goat's Head, Cast Iron 52.00
Goat, Cast Iron 65.00
Gray Squirrel, Cast Iron 145.00
Hand Shape, Cast Iron 20.00
Helmet, Bell Telephone 12.00
Hooker, At Lightpost, On Ashtray 15.00
Horse On Pedestal 40.00
Horse's Rear End 65.00
Lobster, Brass, France .... 10.00 To 15.00
Lobster, Cast Iron, Red Paint .... 10.00 To 35.00
Mallard Duck, Brass 10.00
Man, Standing, Blue With Red & Black, Cast Iron, 6 In. 50.00
Man, Wearing Derby, 1 Glass Eye Open That Blinks 35.00
Mickey Mouse, Brass 10.00
Miss Four Eyes 80.00
Monkey, Aluminum 12.00
Monkey, Cast Iron 130.00
Mother Goose, Painted Aluminum 45.00
Mr. Peanut, Original 550.00
Nu-Icy 20.00
Nude, Brass, Art Deco 40.00
Nude, Cast, Plated Bronze 10.00
Parrot On Perch, Iron, 5 In. 110.00
Parrot, Cast Iron, Painted 165.00
Parrot, Chrome, Corkscrew Back 15.00
Parrot, On Peach, Polychrome Paint, Cast Iron, 4 3/8 In. 25.00
Parrot, Polychrome, 5 In. 65.00
Parrot, Round Base, Cast Iron, 3 In. 50.00
Pelican, Cast Iron 65.00
Pelican, Polychrome Paint, Cast Iron, 3 3/8 In. 25.00
Pelican, Solid Brass 115.00
Pheasant, Aluminum 12.00

◆◆

For a pollution-free furniture cleaner, use a mixture of 1 cup olive or vegetable oil and 1/2 cup lemon juice.

◆◆

Pig's Behind 28.00
Pointer, Polychrome Paint, Cast Iron, 4 1/2 In. 35.00
Rooster, Cast Iron .... 45.00 To 65.00
Rooster, Polychrome Paint, Cast Iron, 3 1/4 In. 75.00
Sailor 158.00
Sea Gull, Cast Iron 80.00
Sea Horse, Polychrome Paint, John Wright Inc., 4 1/8 In. 25.00
Seagull, On Stump, Brass 15.00
Shark, Aluminum 15.00
Shark, Brass 10.00
Shovel, Brass 10.00
Skunk, Polychrome, Cast Iron, 2 7/8 In. 55.00
Springer Spaniel, Enameling On Lead 30.00
Sprite Boy, Wall 12.00
Squirrel, Cast Iron 90.00
Tennis Racket, Brass .... 10.00 To 20.00
Trout, Cast Iron 60.00
Winking Man 25.00

Bottle collecting has become a major American hobby. There are several general categories of bottles, such as historic flasks, bitters, household, and figural. For modern bottle prices and more old bottle prices, see the book *The Kovels' Bottles Price List* by Ralph and Terry Kovel.

BOTTLE, Ale, Old Crown, Empty & Sealed, Dinner Gift, With Dated 1939 Letter 325.00
Apothecary, Blown Glass, Clear, 9 1/2 In. 45.00

Avon started in 1886 as the California Perfume Company. It was not until 1929 that the name *Avon* was used. In 1939, it became Avon Products, Inc. Each year Avon sells figural bottles filled with cosmetic products. Ceramic, plastic, and glass bottles are made in limited editions.

Avon, Alligator, Sweet Pickles, 1978 .... 4.00
Avon, Ben Franklin, 1974 .... 4.00
Avon, Canada Goose 3.00
Avon, Casey's Lantern, Amber 40.00
Avon, Cologne, Apple Blossom, 2 Oz. 4.00
Avon, Cologne, Calico Cat 2.25
Avon, Cologne, Charisma Ultra, 2 Oz. 5.00
Avon, Cologne, Field Flowers 8.00
Avon, Cologne, Timeless, Ultra Mist 5.00
Avon, Cologne, Topaze, 1974 .... 1.50
Avon, Cologne, Unspoken, 1 Oz. 4.00
Avon, Fire Truck, Red Sentinel 8.00
Avon, French Telephone, Box 18.00
Avon, Pepperbox Pistol, 1976 .... 4.00
Avon, Pony Post, 1966 .... 3.50
Avon, Pot Belly Stove, 1970 .... 2.50
Avon, Pyramid of Fragrance 15.00
Avon, Town Pump 2.00
Avon, Tractor, Harvester, 1973 .... 10.00
Avon, Windjammer, Man's World, 1969 .... 4.00
Bar, Swirled Enamel, Buster Brown, Rye 55.00
Barber's, Noonan's, Light Green 60.00
Barber, Blown-Out Pattern, Pink & White Spatter 125.00
Barber, Enameled Flowers, Amethyst, 7 3/4 In. 160.00
Barber, Fern & Daisy, Vaseline Opalescent 175.00
Barber, Frosted Turquoise, White Floral Design, 5 In. 125.00
Barber, Honey Amber Satin, Rolled Lip, T. Noonan Barber Supplies 110.00
Barber, Honey Amber, Cut Flutes On Neck, Circles At Base 110.00
Barber, Inverted Thumbprint, Amber, 8 In. 160.00
Barber, Inverted Thumbprint, Sapphire Blue 110.00
Barber, Painted Woman On Horseback 125.00

Bottle, Cologne, Gothic Arches,
Clear To Dark Cobalt, 9 In.

Bottle, Cologne, Ribbed Petticoat Shape,
Clear To Cobalt, 7 In.

Barber, Reversed Raised Swirls, White Opalescent	125.00
Barber, Vegederm, Enameled Nouveau Women, Amethyst, Pair	475.00
Barber, Wildroot Cream Oil, For Professional Use Only, 1940s, Full	20.00

Beam bottles are made to hold Kentucky Straight Bourbon, made by the James B. Beam Distilling Company. The Beam series of ceramic bottles began in 1953.

Beam, Blue Jay, 1969	12.00
Beam, Caboose, Red, 1980	51.00
Beam, Corvette, Black, 1984	138.00
Beam, Corvette, Red, 1984	70.00
Beam, Decanter, Sailfish, No Label, 1957	20.00
Beam, Oldsmobile, 1904	45.00
Beam, Volkswagen, Red, 1973	39.00
Beer, Alpen Brau, Label Says Buy War Bonds, Contents	20.00
Beer, Anhauser–Busch, 12 In.	12.00
Beer, Minck Brewing Co., Richmond, Ind., Aqua	11.00
Beer, Schlitz, Ruby, Label	15.00
Bitters, Atwood's Quinine Tonic, Square, Aqua	65.00
Bitters, Begg's Dandelion, Sioux City, Iowa, c.1870	215.00
Bitters, Cabin, Medium Amber	1200.00
Bitters, Canoe, Figural, Tippecanoe, Honey Amber, 1870, 9 In.	65.00
Bitters, Chamberlain's Curacoa, Contents, Amber	65.00
Bitters, Charles London Cordial Gin, Blue Green, 8 In.	75.00
Bitters, Dingens Napoleon Cocktail, Drum Shape, Yellow Amber	2860.00
Bitters, Doperaille House, Black Glass, Shoulder Seal	165.00
Bitters, Dr. George Pierce's Indian Restorative	65.00
Bitters, Dr. Harter's Wild Cherry, Embossed Cherries, Amber	175.00
Bitters, Dr. Henley's Wild Grape Root, Rectangular, Olive Amber	650.00
Bitters, Dr. J. Hostetter's, Amber	24.00
Bitters, Dr. Lovegood's Family	825.00
Bitters, Dr. Petzold's, Light Amber, Small	80.00
Bitters, Dr. Von Hopfs Curacoa, Amber, Rectangular	75.00
Bitters, Drake's Plantation, 4–Label Panels, Medium Amber	395.00
Bitters, Drake's Plantation, 6 Log, Puce	110.00
Bitters, Electric Brand	12.50
Bitters, Fish, Amber	130.00
Bitters, Jackson's Aromatic Life	975.00
Bitters, Lash, Amber	22.00
Bitters, Lediard's Celebrated Stomach, Greenish Blue	400.00
Bitters, Litthauer Stomach, Milk Glass	125.00

Bitters, Log Cabin, Light Amber 160.00
Bitters, National, Amber 225.00
Bitters, Niagara Star 225.00
Bitters, Old Sachem, Barrel, Aqua 1760.00
Bitters, Pinkerton's Wahoo & Calisaya 200.00
Bitters, Pond's Kidney & Liver, Amber 50.00
Bitters, Prune Stomach & Liver, Amber 65.00
Bitters, Simon's, Figural, Military Man Bust, Amber 1850.00
Bitters, Stockton's Port Wine Bitters 150.00
Bitters, Sunny Castle Stomach, Milwaukee, Light Amber 150.00
Bitters, Vermo Stomach, Clear 45.00
Calabash, Jenny Lind, Iron Pontil, Aqua, 9 3/4 In. .... 105.00 To 155.00
Chestnut, New England, Thousands of Bubbles, Deep Green, 6 In. 395.00
Chestnut, New England, Vertical Ribs, Olive, c.1825, 1/2 Pt. 125.00
Coal Oil, Ornate Glass, Unusual, 1900 .... 200.00
BOTTLE, COCA-COLA, see Coca-Cola, Bottle
Cologne, Gothic Arches, Clear To Dark Cobalt, 9 In. ....*Illus* 220.00
Cologne, Ribbed Petticoat Shape, Clear To Cobalt, 7 In. ....*Illus* 330.00
Cordial, Floral & Human Figure Pontil, Bohemian, 5 1/4 In. 195.00
Cork, Man, Tam O'Shanter 12.00
Cosmetic, Palmer's Vegetable Lotion, Crooked Neck, Clear, 5 In. 5.00
Cream, Separator, Colorless, Red Pyroglazed, Square, 1 Qt. 385.00
Decanter, Blown Three-Mold, Yellowish Green 5000.00
Dresser, Ribbon, Stopper, 1917 .... 125.00
Ezra Brooks, African Lion, 1981 .... 22.50
Ezra Brooks, Bengal Tiger 25.00
Ezra Brooks, Clown, Cowboy Hat 20.00
Ezra Brooks, Grandfather Clock 9.00
Ezra Brooks, Kachina Doll, No. 1, 1972 .... 71.00
Ezra Brooks, Kachina Doll, No. 2, 1973 .... 45.00
Figural, Bear, Opaque White, 11 In. 77.50
Figural, Black Waiter, Frosted Body, 15 In. 365.00
Figural, Black Waiter, Frosted Body, Removable Head, 15 In. 445.00
Figural, Clanky Syrup Spaceman, Vinyl, 1950s 50.00
Figural, Madonna, Cobalt 40.00
Figural, Pig, Good Old Bourbon In A Pig 65.00
Figural, Sweet Potato, Ceramic, For Sneaking Whiskey, 7 In. 65.00
Figural, Violin, Amethyst, 10 In. 20.00
Flask, A Little More Grape, Captain Bragg, Copper Color 2200.00
Flask, Applied Figure of Indian Chief, Clark & Fox, Stoneware, 1829 .... 1100.00
Flask, Baltimore Glass Works, Anchor, Aqua, Applied Top, 1 Pt. 85.00
Flask, Bull's-Eye, Blown Glass, Amethyst, 6 In. 25.00
Flask, Cannon & Union, Clasped Hands, F. A. & Co., Aqua, 7 3/4 In. 75.00
Flask, Carved Coconut, Silver Mounts, Musical Instruments, Flags 258.00
Flask, Double Eagle, Aqua, 8 7/8 In. 75.00
Flask, Double Eagle, Olive Amber, 1820s, 1 Pt. 250.00
Flask, Double Eagle, Pittsburgh, Pa., In Oval, Aqua, 9 In., 1 Qt. 55.00
Flask, Eagle & Union, Clasped Hands, Aqua, 7 1/2 In. 55.00
Flask, Eagle With Pittsburgh, Union, Clasped Hands, Aqua, 7 5/8 In. 65.00
Flask, Eagle, Concentric Ring, Light Green, c.1820 .... 4000.00
Flask, Fells Point, Baltimore, Aqua, 1 Qt. 60.00
Flask, For Pike's Peak, Eagle With Banner, Aqua, 8 7/8 In. 50.00
Flask, For Pike's Peak, Eagle With Credo, Aqua, 8 7/8 In. 75.00
Flask, Gen. Taylor Never Surrenders, More Grape, Aqua, 1/2 Pt. 125.00
Flask, General Washington, Eagle, Aqua, 1 Pt. 105.00
Flask, Honest Measure In Arch, Full Pint Below, Clear, 8 In. 10.00
Flask, Lafayette, Emerald Green, 1/2 Pt. 800.00
Flask, Lafayette, Golden Yellow, 1/2 Pt. 2800.00
Flask, Lafayette, Golden Yellow, 1 Pt. 250.00
Flask, Lafayette, Liberty Cap Reverse, Golden Yellow, 1 Pt. 425.00
Flask, Lafayette, Liberty Cap Reverse, Light Olive Yellow, 1/2 Pt. 3250.00
Flask, Lafayette, Masonic Reverse, Light Olive Amber, 1/2 Pt 1200.00
Flask, Lafayette, Masonic Reverse, Olive Green, 1 Pt. 1500.00

Flask, Masonic, Eagle, Greenish Aqua, 1820, 1 Pt. 525.00
Flask, McK GII–60, Eagle, Amber To Brown, 1820–35, 1/2 Pt. 350.00
Flask, Pistol, Dog & Flying Eagle, Brass Top, 4 1/2 In. 65.00
Flask, Railroad Lowell, Eagle, Olive Amber, 5 3/8 In. 130.00
Flask, Sailboat, Star, Greenish Aqua, 1846, 1/2 Pt. 245.00
Flask, Santa Claus Label Under Glass, Merry Christmas, New Year 1600.00
Flask, Scroll, Aqua, 7 In., 1 Pt. 25.00
Flask, Sheaf of Grain, 1 Qt. 137.50
Flask, Shot, Hawksley, Deer, Foliage, Copper 225.00
Flask, South Carolina Dispensary, Jo–Jo, Monogram 25.00
Flask, Spring Blossom Whiskey Blend, Embossed 1/2 Pint 10.00
Flask, Success To The Railroad, Golden Amber, 1 Pt. 165.00
Flask, Urn & Cornucopia, McK GII–4, Olive Amber, 6 1/2 In., 1 Pt. 65.00
Flask, Urn & Cornucopia, Olive Green, 1/2 Pt. 50.00
Flask, Washington & Jackson, Dark Amber 495.00
Flask, Washington, Taylor Portrait, 1840s, 1 Qt. 2970.00
Flask, Washington, Taylor, Aqua, 1/2 Pt. 55.00
Flask, Zachary Taylor, Gen. Taylor Never Surrenders, c.1850, 1 Pt. 2090.00
Flask, Zachary Taylor, Rough & Ready, Corn, World, Green, 1850, 1 Pt. 5250.00
Forni's Heil Oil Liniment, 5 5/8 In. 9.00
Fruit Jar, Dome Top, 1/2 Gal. 900.00
Fruit Jar, Fruit Keeper, Spider Leg Clamp, Aqua, 1/2 Gal. 125.00
Fruit Jar, Mason, 1 Qt. 1356.00
Fruit Jar, Mason, 1/2 Gal. 165.00
Fruit Jar, Mason, Golden State, Triangle With S, Amethyst, 1/2 Gal. 300.00
Fruit, Atlas Mason, Olive, Zinc Cover, 1 Pt. 18.00
Harrison Columbian Ink, Aqua, 1 Gal. 1760.00
Ink, Barrel Shape, Floral Design, Light Blue Green 2200.00
Ink, Carter's, Cats Walking Back Fence At Midnight, 1940s 35.00
Ink, Carter's, Cobalt Blue, Cathedral, 1 Qt. 135.00
Ink, Carter's, Cone, Amber, Label, 1897 .... 30.00
Ink, Harrison's Columbian, Aqua, Label, 12 Sides, 1 Gal. 1760.00
Ink, Harrison's Columbian, Cobalt Blue, Master, Small 900.00
Ink, Harrison's Columbian, Rolled Mouth, Small 375.00
Ink, Harrison's, Green, Octagonal, Small 1225.00
Ink, House Shape, Aqua, 6 1/2 x 5 In. 715.00
Ink, Mason & Co., 8–Sided Umbrella, 2 1/2 In. 165.00
Ink, Pitkin Type, Tooled Double Mouth 525.00
Ink, Thompson, Troy, Fine Black Ink, Yellow–Amber 2860.00
Ink, Umbrella, 8–Sided, Steel Pen Ink Label, Green, 1845, 2 1/2 In. 100.00
Ink, Waters, Small 950.00
Ink, Who's Ink? Firmin's, Wilkinsburg, Penna, Clear, 7 1/2 In. 12.50
Jar, Borden's Milk, Milk Glass, Cover, 1920s 10.00
Jar, Enameled, Pink Over Clear Cutback, 5 In., Pair 460.00
Lemon Flavoring, HICO, Clear, Cap, 8 Oz. 6.00
Lemon Flavoring, Watkins, Clear, Yellow Cap, 4 1/2 Oz. 4.00
Lionstone, Boxer, 1975 .... 24.00
Lionstone, Cardinal 21.00
Lionstone, Johnny Unitas 55.00
Lionstone, Roadrunner 23.00
Lionstone, Valley Forge, 1975 .... 16.00
Ludlow, Olive Green, 5 1/4 In. 85.00
Lydia E. Pinkham's Vegetable Compound, Green 8.00
Medicine, Blondels Specific Preventative & Cure, Open Pontil 100.00
Medicine, Bonpland's Fever & Ague Remedy, Open Pontil 55.00
Medicine, Bragg's Arctic Liniment 60.00
Medicine, Celro–Kola, In Script, Portland, Oregon, Amber, Square 65.00
Medicine, Clarke's Genessee Liniment 90.00
Medicine, Cod Liver Oil, Fish Shape, Amber, 6 1/4 In. 20.00
Medicine, Curtis & Perkins Cramp & Pain Killer 30.00
Medicine, Dr. Browder's Compound Syrup of Indian Turnip 65.00
Medicine, Dr. Curtis, Inhaling Hygean Vapor, N. Y., Complete Label 35.00
Medicine, Dr. Davis' Depurative, Blue–Green, Bubbly 915.00

Medicine, Dr. Fahrney, Raised Letters, Tin Lid 15.00
Medicine, Dr. J. Hedges, Fever & Ague Annihilator, N. Y., 7 1/2 In. 180.00
Medicine, Dr. J. F. Churchill's Specific Remedy For Consumption 200.00
Medicine, Ever Ready Drug Co., Hollywood, Amber, 5 3/4 In. 65.00
Medicine, Golden X Remedy For Man & Beast, Indian Brave, 1900s 25.00
Medicine, Great Shoshonee's Remedy 85.00
Medicine, Himalya, Kola Compound, Cures Asthma 12.00
Medicine, Langenbach's Dysentery Cure, Embossed, Label 25.00
Medicine, Martha Washington Hair Restorer, 7 In. ....*Illus* 160.00
Medicine, Mrs. Mettler's Restorative Syrup, Rectangular, 8 1/2 In. 225.00
Medicine, Piso's Cure, Emerald Green, 5 1/4 In. 9.00
Medicine, Spark's Perfect Health, Embossed Man 150.00
Medicine, Vick's Drops, Cobalt Blue, Cap, Sample 20.00
Medicine, Warner's Safe Liver & Kidney Cure, Amber 20.00
Milk, Baby Face, Voegels, Minn., 1 Qt. 65.00
Milk, Cream Top, Baby Face, 1 Qt. 65.00
Milk, Layton Park Dairy, Milwaukee, Wisc., 1/2 Gal. 15.00
Milk, Molded Baby's Head, 10 In. 40.00
Milk, Ohleen's Milk, Minneapolis, Buy War Bonds, Painted, 1 Qt. 28.00
Milk, Premium Quality, Amber, 1 Qt. 6.50
Milk, St. Paul Milk Co., Pilgrim's Picture, Painted, Round, 1 Qt. 22.00
Milk, Thatcher, Absolutely Pure Milk, Man Milking Cow, 1 Qt. 305.50
Milk, To Be Washed & Returned, Handle, A. G. Smalley, 1/2 Pt. 440.00
Milk, V. M. & I. Co., Amber, 1 Qt. 50.00
Milk, Wanzer & Sons, Chicago, Raised Lettering, Purplish Tint, 1 Qt. 12.00
Milk, Woodrow Wilson's Dairy, Palmyria, Wisc., 1 Pt. 10.00
Nurser, Acme, Lay Down 60.00
Nurser, Fire–King, Blue .... 15.00 To 18.00
Nurser, Grip Tite, Teat & Valve, Box 25.00
Nursing, Evenflo, Rubber Nipple, Plastic Screw Top, 1950s, 3 In. 14.00
Owl Drug 10.00
Pedigo's Fishing Bait, Clear, White Cap 3.75
BOTTLE, see Perfume Bottle
Pickle, Cathedral, Rolled Lip, Aqua, 9 1/4 In. 75.00
Pickle, Gothic Arch, Iron Pontil, Aqua, 11 3/8 In. 175.00
Pickle, Shaker Brand 357.50
Poison, Bowman's Drug, Cobalt Blue 350.00
Poison, Coles Patent, England, Cobalt Blue 175.00
Poison, Dutcher's Dead Shot For Bed Bugs 325.00
Poison, Mulford, Cobalt Blue, Skull & Crossbones 18.00
Poison, Skull, Crossed Bones On Base, Cobalt Blue, 4 1/8 In. 1430.00
Red & Gold Medallion, Men, Spears, Engraved, 10 In. 2600.00
Root Beer, Jobethco, Peoria, Ill. 8.00
Seltzer, Big Chief, Stockton, Calif., Clear, Red Print 85.00
Seltzer, Irwin Beverages, Penna., Sapphire Blue, Czechoslovakia 95.00
Seltzer, Quinnipiac Spring Water, Indian Swastika Emblem 20.00
Seltzer, Standard Bottling Co., Salt Lake, Utah, Clear 45.00
Shampoo, Dog, Figural, Shampoodle, Cobalt, 1940s, 10 In. 45.00
Snuff, 2 Brass Sitting Gods, Incised China 250.00
Snuff, Carnelian, Malachite Cover, Flattened Ovide, 2 1/2 In. 165.00
Snuff, Carved & Tinted Figures, Garden Setting, Jade Top, 2 3/4 In. 385.00
Snuff, Carved Figures, Spoon In Top, China, c.1900, 4 In. 145.00
Snuff, Carved Glass & Coral, Urn & Figure, China, 3 1/4 In. 1400.00
Snuff, Carved Ivory Faces Allover, Spoon 250.00
Snuff, Carved Jade, Squash Form, 2 1/2 In. 330.00
Snuff, Design of Elders, Ivory, 2 1/2 In. 410.00
Snuff, Figural, Mouse, Jadeite, Wood Stand, Chinese, 2 1/2 In. 522.50
Snuff, Lorilards Maccoboy, Olive, 1845–60, 4 1/2 In. ....*Illus* 75.00
Snuff, Rose Quartz, Jade Cover, Flattened Ovid, 2 1/2 In. 170.00
Snuff, Stoneware, Blue Gray, Bird On Branch, Wooden Stopper 200.00
Soda, Allen's Red Tame Cherry, 4 In. 500.00
Soda, Big Boy 1.50
Soda, Carpenter & Cobb Knickerbocker, 10–Sided, Sapphire 665.00

Bottle, Snuff, Lorilards Maccoboy, Olive, 1845–60, 4 1/2 In.

Bottle, Soda, J. A. Dearborn, N. Y., Cobalt Blue, Blob Top,
7 1/4 In.

Bottle, Whiskey, McK GVII–3,

E. G. Booz's, Honey Amber,
7 3/4 In.

Bottle, Medicine, Martha Washington Hair Restorer, 7 In.

Soda, Chas. Cable & Son Po'keepsie Premium Sarsaparilla & Lemon	660.00
Soda, Cierinc & Bros., Youngstown, Ohio, Inside Closure, Blob Top	12.00
Soda, Crystal Palace, Emerald Green	465.00
Soda, Dr. Townsend's Sarsaparilla, Albany, N. Y., Embossed M, Green	45.00
Soda, Dr. Wilcox's Compound Extract, Reverse S In Wilcox, 9 1/2 In.	875.00
Soda, Epperson's Carbonated Beverage Co., Kansas City, Missouri	60.00
Soda, Ginger Ale, Betheseda Pale Dry, Waukesha, Wis.	13.00
Soda, Hires, Enamelled Syrup Line	18.00
Soda, I. D. Bull's Extract, Open Pontil, Aqua	225.00
Soda, J. A. Dearborn, N. Y., Cobalt Blue, Blob Top, 7 1/4 In. ....*Illus*	450.00
Soda, Mason Root Beer	18.00
Soda, Masury's Compound, V & T Hanks, Rochester, N. Y., 11 1/4 In.	330.00
Soda, Nehi Orange, Contents, 10 Oz.	6.00
Soda, Sarsaparilla, Cooke's, Cobalt Blue	2400.00
Soda, U–Ly–Kit, Pat. 1923	15.00
Soda, Virginia Dare	20.00
Toilet Water, Cobalt Blue 3–Mold, Tam–O–Shanter Stopper, 5 3/8 In.	265.00
Water, Moses Poland, Clear White	28.00
Water, Pluto Spring Water, Green, Contents, 2 1/4 Oz.	17.00
Wheaton, Apollo	25.00
Whiskey, Applegate & Sons, Louisville, Clear	8.00
Whiskey, E. G. Booz's, Cabin Shape, Green	275.00
Whiskey, Green River, 7 1/2 In.	33.00
Whiskey, J. F. Cutter, Light Olive Amber, No Star In Base	150.00
Whiskey, McK GVII–3, E. G. Booz's, Honey Amber, 7 3/4 In. ....*Illus*	900.00
Whiskey, McLean's Strengthening Cordial, Whittled, Aqua	25.00
Whiskey, Roth & Co., San Francisco, Amber	37.00
Whisky, Buster Brown Rye, Back Bar, Swirled, Enameled	55.00
Whisky, Painted Baseball Player, A's Uniform, Unopened, 1950s, 6 In.	98.00

 Boxes of all kinds are collected. They were made of thin strips of
inlaid wood, metal, tortoiseshell, embroidery, or other material.

**BOX, see also Advertising, Box; Ivory, Box; Porcelain, Box; Shaker, Box;
and various Porcelain categories.**

BOX, Applied Brass Initials, J. G., Interior Marbelized, 2 Nudes, 21 In.	35.00
Baleen, Cover, Engraved Patriotic Objects, Round, 3 5/8 x 8 3/8 In.	445.00
Band, Decoupage Cover, Indian Princess, Floral, Oval, 20 In.	1550.00
Band, Floral Design, Wallpaper Covered Bentwood, 1847, 17 In.	400.00
Band, Hunt Scenes, Wallpaper On Cardboard, 13 x 16 1/2 In.	135.00
Band, Polychrome Flowers On Sides, Horse & Rider, Bentwood, 18 In.	2050.00
Band, Tropical Birds, Wallpaper Covered Cardboard, 16 In.	300.00

◆◆◆

Gilt frames can be cleaned with beer.

◆◆◆

Band, Wallpaper Covered, H. S. Spaulding, 1850s, 9 1/2 x 12 1/2 In. 5500.00
Band, Wallpaper Covered, Landscape Scenes, A. F. Miller, 13 1/2 In. 750.00
  BOX, BATTERSEA, see Battersea, Box
Bentwood, Cover, Medium Green Paint, 11 1/2 x 22 In. 900.00
Bentwood, Eagle, Shield, Stars, Green Paint, Round, 10 1/4 In. 235.00
Bentwood, Laced Seams, Floral, German Inscription On Lid, 16 1/2 In. 850.00
Bentwood, Laced Seams, Oval, 12 In. 125.00
Bentwood, Laced Seams, Salmon Pink Paint, Polychrome Tulips, 14 3/8 In. 1350.00
Bentwood, Single Finger Construction, Copper Tacks, 7 7/8 In. 275.00
Bentwood, Single Finger Construction, Oval, 5 1/2 In. 200.00
Bentwood, Single Finger Construction, Oval, Cover, 11 1/2 In. 95.00
Bentwood, Spring Lid, Laced Seams, Natural Pine & Paint, 12 3/4 In. 175.00
Bentwood, Star Design On Cover, Black Paint, Round, 5 3/4 In. 375.00
Bentwood, Whiting Creamery On Lid, Green Paint, 10 In. 150.00
Bible, Iron Hinges & Edge Bands, Wash Red & Brown, 19 x 15 1/2 In. 185.00
Bible, Walnut, Inlaid Hearts, Tulips & Date, 1799 .... 3100.00
Bible, Wooden, 1850 .... 230.00
Black & Yellow Striping, Floral Design, Pine, 12 1/2 In. 150.00
Blue, Bail Handle, Bentwood, Round, 9 In. 170.00
Bob Hope Shirt 20.00
Book, Chinese, Camphor Wood, c.1880 .... 880.00
Branded Geometric Designs, Bentwood, Round, 4 x 9 1/2 In. 55.00
Brass Tacks & Lock, Ring Handle, Leather Covered, Paper Lining, 8 In. 45.00
Bread, Tin, Glass Top 16.00
Bride's, Couple Walking Dog, House Design On Sides, Bentwood, 18 In. 625.00
Bride's, Pine, Gray Paint, Red Striped. Floral, Bentwood Sides, 16 In. 550.00
Bride's, Stylized Floral, Polychrome Paint, Pine, 17 3/4 In. 1400.00
Bunny Shape, From Solid Walnut Log, 6 1/2 In. 70.00
Burl Walnut, Brass Corners, Hinges & Handles, Dutch, 17th Century 1300.00
Camel Cigarettes, Cardboard 25.00
Camphorwood, Lift Top, Brass Bail Handle, 19th Century, 15 1/2 In. 145.00
Candle Dryer & Storage, Painted Black 695.00
Candle, England, Mahogany, c.1810 .... 595.00
Candle, Molded Sliding Lid, Red Paint, Pine, 16 In. 345.00
Candle, Poplar, Red Paint, Raised Frame Slide Cover, 15 1/2 x 9 In. 225.00
Candle, Slant Lid, Leather Hinge, Sage Green, c.1820, 7 x 9 x 12 1/2 In. 395.00
Candle, Sliding Cover, Birch With Red Stain, 9 In. 175.00
Candle, Sliding Lid, 1 Drawer, Walnut, 15 In. 1900.00
Candle, Sliding Lid, Hex Designs, Salmon Paint, Thomas Wein 1823, 15 In. 2300.00
Candle, Sliding Lid, Old Blue Paint, Hardwood, 11 In. 275.00
Candle, Sliding Lid, Old Red Finish, 7 x 12 x 6 In. 150.00
Candle, Walnut, Pennsylvania, 2-Part Interior, Chest, 8 1/2 x 13 1/2 In. 235.00
Candle, Wooden, Red Paint 175.00
Cartridge, Various Marks, Dated, German, Leather 70.00
Charles X, Arched Top, Steel Bound, Lemonwood & Burl, c.1825, 7 1/2 In. 415.00
Checkers, Backgammon, Primitive, Pine, Walnut Inlay, Opens 13 x 14 In. 100.00
Chest, Coffer, Metal, Medieval, Glass Jewels, Late 19th Century, 10 In. 125.00
Church, Chip Carved Oak, Pinwheel 3 Sides, I. H. S., 5 x 10 x 5 3/4 In. 495.00
Cigarette, Drum Shape, With Ashtray, Metal, Maroon Bakelite, Chase 125.00
Cigarette, Nickel Silver, 4 Buttress Legs, L. & M. T. Co., 2 3/4 x 6 In. 165.00
Desk, Curly Maple, Paper Lined, Printed Lathrop & Willard, 10 In. 165.00
Dish, Tabletop, Beaded Edge On Lid, Pine, 23 1/2 x 26 1/4 In. 425.00
Document, Asphaltum Ground, Swags & Leaf, Tin, 1830s, 6 1/4 x 9 1/2 In. 550.00
Document, Asphaltum Ground, Swags, Red Berries, Tin, 4 3/4 x 8 In. 330.00
Document, Brass Bail Handle, Vinegar Paint 495.00
Document, Green, Red & Yellow Design, Cover, 8 x 14 In. 525.00

Document, Lift Lid, Iron Strap Hinges, Walnut, 10 1/2 x 25 In. 4100.00
Document, Reddish–Brown Surface, Lock, c.1830, 9 3/4 x 25 x 11 In. 170.00
Dome Top, Iron Escutcheon & Side Handles, Vinegar Painted, 13 1/4 In. 825.00
Dome Top, Iron Hasp & Lock, Yellow Sponge, Red Striped 860.00
Dome Top, Oval Reserves of Birds & Flowers All Sides, Pine, 13 In. 2300.00
Dome Top, Painted Portrait On Lid, 7 In. 85.00
Dome Top, Pine, Yellow & Black Traces of Paint, Lock & Key, 22 In. 175.00
Dome Top, Poplar, Red & Black Grained, Stenciled, Lock & Hasp, 30 In. 125.00
Dome Top, Poplar, Red Paint, Wrought Iron Lock & Hasp, 30 In. 80.00
Dome Top, Red Paint, Black Border, Stenciled Foliage, 18 In. 600.00
Dough, Brown Graining On White, Iron Thumb Latch, 35 3/4 x 46 In. 425.00
Dough, Pine, Red Paint, Iron Side Handles, Leather Hinges, 25 1/2 In. 115.00
Dough, Poplar, Dovetailed 225.00
Dovetailed, Iron Strap Hinges, Yellow Striping, Pine, 12 In. 145.00
Dowry, Hand Painted, France, 18th Century 695.00
Dresser, 3 Drawers, Bow–Shape, Flower & Leaf, Menuit, 5 1/2 x 8 In. 250.00
Dresser, Bell Shape, Frosted Satin, Hinged Lid, 5 1/2 x 8 1/2 In. 250.00
Dresser, George IV, Brass Bound, Fitted, Inlaid Mahogany, 24 x 10 In. 1320.00
Dresser, Man's, Carved Walnut, 2 Standing Deer Cover, Austria, 1880 .... 500.00
Embossed Brass Rooster At Key Hole, Brass Handle, Cherry, 10 In. 125.00
Enameled Cover, Coral Finial, Wood Lining, 4 Paw Feet, Brass, Apollo 60.00
Finger Construction On Lid, Side Handles, Bentwood, 13 In. 185.00
Fish, Figural, Painted Silk Over Molded Body, Back Lid, 1880, 13 1/2 In. 350.00
Geometric & Urn Design, Tortoiseshell & Gold, 2 7/8 In. 355.00
Green & White Edge Stripe, Floral Design, Oval, Bentwood, 8 1/4 In. 150.00
Hanging, 1 Drawer, Arched Crest, Walnut & Cherry, 15 1/2 x 14 1/2 In. 1900.00
Hanging, Carved Bird On Sliding Lid, Floral All Sides, Oak, 13 1/2 In. 600.00
Hanging, Lift Lid, Cutout Crest, Drawer 175.00
Hat, Cavanagh, N. Y. C. 10.00
Hat, Promonade, Graphic, 1830 .... 500.00
Hat, Wallpapered, Marked H. S. Spalding 5500.00
Hinged Lid, Cast Iron Bracket Feet, American, Tiger Maple, 15 1/4 In. 770.00
Hinged Lid, Fall Front, Brass Medallions, Rosewood Veneer, 15 1/2 In. 500.00
Inlaid Star On Cover, Divided Interior, Bird's–Eye Maple, 12 1/4 In. 302.00
Jewelry, Poplar, Carved Flowers, Name Addie, 4 Swing Trays, 12 1/4 In. 200.00
Knife, Brass Handle, Mahogany, 9 x 14 1/2 In. 175.00
Knife, Dovetailed, Mahogany, 12 x 18 1/2 In. 175.00
Knife, Dovetailed, Varnish Finish, Cherry, 14 1/4 x 9 3/4 In. 100.00
Knife, George III Style, Urn Form, American, Mahogany, 1920s, 27 In. 665.00
Knife, Georgian, Inlaid Wood, Full Interior, England, Pair 1600.00
Knife, Hanging, Black Striping, Stenciled Design, Poplar, 14 In. 600.00
Knife, Hinged Top, Cross Banded Design, Mahogany, 14 In. 195.00
Knife, Mahogany, Satinwood, Pair 2450.00
Knife, Peg Construction, Cutout Handle, Pine, 8 In. 275.00
Knife, Pine, Dark Finish, 2 Sections, 18 x 28 In. 35.00
Knife, Pine, Dovetailed, 8 1/2 x 16 1/2 In. 105.00
Knife, Pineapple Finial, Carved & Painted Mahogany, c.1825, 27 In., Pair 5500.00
Knife, Red Graining On White Ground, Poplar, 23 x 13 1/2 In. 150.00
Knife, Stenciled Yellow Floral, Poplar, 9 x 13 In. 155.00
Knife, Turned Handle, Divided Interior, Curly Maple, 13 1/4 In. 275.00
Knife, Walnut, Divider With Cutout Handle, Mid–19th Century, 23 3/4 In. 225.00
Knife, Walnut, Red Paint Over Black, Pennsylvania, 9 3/4 x 15 In. 125.00
Knife, Walnut, Worn Red Paint, Scalloped, Pennsylvania, 9 3/4 x 15 In. 100.00
Knife, Woven Splint, Divided, Polychrome Floral, 9 x 12 In. 225.00
Letter, Domed Top, Marked Slot, Circular, Brass Mounted, 17 In. 3575.00
Lid Held By Wooden Spring Clips, Laced Seams, Bentwood, 14 1/2 In. 150.00
Lid, Bentwood Swivel Handle, 6 x 9 1/2 In. 65.00
Lift Lid, Bracket Feet, 1 Drawer, Poplar, 12 1/2 x 14 3/4 In. 275.00
Louis XIV, Cover, Brass, Pewter & Tortoiseshell Marquetry, 6 5/8 In. 7150.00
Marx, For Dare Devil Flyer, No. 700 .... 28.50
Military Powder, God Bless America Long May It Wave, 48–Star Flag 15.00
Music, Kitty Cucumber, Winter Wonderland 25.00
Nesting, Bentwood, Shaker Type, Copper, 5 3/4 To 9 3/4 In., 4 Pc. 280.00

Box, Singing Bird, German, Enamel, c.1900, 4 In.

Nesting, Refinished, 5 1/2, 6 3/4 & 7 3/4 In., 3 Piece 165.00
Painted Flower On Lid, Copper Tacks, Bentwood, Round, 6 In. 75.00
Pantry, Baleen, Engraved House, Ship, Vine, Green Paint, Oval, 6 7/8 In. 303.00
Pantry, Wood Burned, 7 1/2 In. 35.00
Pencil, Jackie Coogan 35.00
Pencil, Jungle Book, Empire Co., 1966 .... 30.00
Pencil, Regular Fellers 30.00
Pencil, Space Patrol Earth, 1940s 55.00
Pencil, Wood Burned ABC, Bear, Deer, Fox 35.00
Pill, Abalone Inlaid Top 60.00
Pine, Bride's, Floral, Blue Paint, German Inscription, Laced, 19 In. 625.00
Pine, Dome Top, Landscapes, Buildings, 4 3/8 In. 95.00
Pipe, Dovetailed Drawer, Scalloped Rim, Pine, 16 7/8 In. 825.00
Poplar, Sliding Lid, Divided Interior, 15 In. 150.00
Powder, Diamond–Quilted, Ornate Brass Lid 55.00
Rat Tails Cigars, Black Boy On Rat's Tail 155.00
Relief Carved Indian Head On Lid, Walnut & Pine, 8 In. 105.00
Repository, Chip Carved, Brown Paint, 14 In. 990.00
Ring, Floral, Blue Ground, Wooden, c.1800, 5 1/2 x 3 1/2 x 2 1/4 In. 250.00
Salt, Lift Lid, Dovetailed Case & Drawer, Poplar, 9 3/4 In. 105.00
Shoe Form, Hinged Lid, Carved Birds, Fleur–De–Lis, Seated Man, 5 3/4 In. 400.00
Shoeshine, Shinola, Carrying Strap, Brushes 60.00
Silver Crest, Bronze, Sterling Design, Wooden Lined 125.00
Silver, Cutout Handle, Pine, American, 13 1/4 x 9 3/4 In. 45.00
Singing Bird, German, Enamel, c.1900, 4 In. ....*Illus* 3740.00
Spice, 7 Drawers, Unusual 350.00
Steiff, Christmas, Unused, 1950s 15.00
Storage, Red & Black Graining, 10 In. 475.00
Storage, Stave Constructed, Pine, Hardwood Bands, 6 1/4 x 13 In. 125.00
Strong, Lift Lid, 3 Drawers, Side Handles, Brass & Walnut, 14 3/4 In. 110.00
Strong, Striping, 3 Drawers, Safe Shape, Wilbur M. J. Doehla, Pine, 15 In. 100.00

Tack, Original Red & Gold Paint 210.00
    BOX, TEA CADDY, see Tea Caddy
Thistle On Brass Handle, Brown Vinegar Graining, Poplar, 19 3/4 In. 325.00
Tie, Pyrographic, Man & Woman Ice Skating 20.00
Tree Trunk Type, Carved Knots 1100.00
Wall, Heart Cutout, Dovetailed, Ochre Paint, 19th Century, 10 In. 600.00
Wallpaper Covered Cardboard, Geometric Floral, Dated 1800, 4 x 6 In. 350.00
Wallpaper, Cover, Polychrome Floral, Round, 4 1/4 x 3 1/8 In. 230.00
Walnut, Hanging, Scalloped Edge Design, Wire Nail, 12 In. 105.00
Walnut, Inlaid Hinged Lid, Dovetailed, Divided, Coin Tray, 18 In. 300.00
Woman's, Godey's, 1844 .... 65.00
Wood, Sleigh Style, Empire, Brown Paint, Black Striping 400.00
Wooden Spring Latch Lid, Bentwood, Oval, 13 3/4 In. 110.00
Wooden, Floral Design, Red Paint, Threaded Lid, 4 x 3 In. 55.00
Wooden, Landscape & Animal Design, Copper, 19th Century, 22 x 15 In. 70.00
Wooden, Smoke Design 28.50
Writing, Mahogany, Brass Bound, Fitted, W. Esser 1844, England, 20 In. 350.00

The Boy Scout movement in the United States started in 1910. The
first Jamboree was held in 1937. Collectors search for any material
related to scouting, including patches, manuals, and uniforms. Girl
Scouts are listed under their own heading.

BOY SCOUT, Badge, Round–Up Ranchers, Tin 14.00
Bank, Cast Iron 135.00
Bank, Cast Iron, 5 3/4 In. 60.00
Bank, Sardine Can, Says 4th Jamboree 28.00
Binoculars 25.00
Book, Capturing A Spy, 1913 .... 25.00
Book, Painting, No. 8, 1907 .... 15.00
Booklet, Boy Scout Jamboree, 1952 .... 8.00
Button, Jacket, 6 .... 12.00
Camera 25.00
Canteen, Box 16.00
Canteen, Original Strap & Cover, Official, 1920s 25.00
Car, Lobby, Tex Rides With Boy Scouts 50.00
Drum, Toy, Tin 50.00
Figure, Box, 1965 .... 5.00
Game, Progress, Board, 1926, 7 Pieces 65.00
Handbook, 1945 .... 12.00
Handbook, 1982 .... 6.00
Handkerchief, Boy Fishing, 1915 .... 22.00
Kit, Beadcraft, 1940s 30.00
Knife, Jack 32.50
Knife, Pocket, Tuxedo Can 7.00
Knife, Remington .... 65.00 To 70.00
Medal, 1953 Jamboree 35.00
Medal, Eagle Scout, Sterling Silver 250.00
Mug, Jamboree, 1973 .... 35.00
Night–Light, Revolving, 1950 .... 175.00
Print, Calendar, Forward America, Norman Rockwell, 22 x 27 In. 22.00
Print, Calendar, Reverence, Norman Rockwell, 16 x 21 In. 18.00
Print, Calendar, Right Way, Norman Rockwell, 16 x 21 In. 18.00
Puzzle Box, Cub Scout 24.00
Radio, Blinker, Telegraph, 1922 .... 125.00
Sheet Music, Boy Scout Dream & Boy Scout Parade, 1912, 1915, Pair 25.00
Tab, I Gave 5.00
Token, Good Turn, Metal 7.00
Wallet, Cub Scout, 1950s 15.00

Walter Hubbard and his brother–in–law, Nathaniel Lyman Bradley,
started making cast iron clocks, tables, frames, andirons, lamps,
chandeliers, sconces, and sewing birds in 1854 in Meriden,

Connecticut. The company became Bradley & Hubbard Manufacturing Company in 1875. Charles Parker Company bought the firm in 1940. Their lamps are especially prized by collectors.

BRADLEY & HUBBARD, Bookends, Science & Study 45.00
   Chandelier, 12–Light, Oil, Cast Iron, c.1870, 40 In. 1215.00
   Clock, Black Minstrel, Banjo, Glass Eyes, Iron, 15 In. 695.00
   Desk Set, Art Deco, 5 Piece 125.00
   Doorstop, Flower Basket 175.00
   Doorstop, Gate, Cast Iron 150.00
   Humidor, Copper 40.00
   Inkwell, Double, Stamp Drawer, Pen Rack, Art Deco 115.00
   Lamp, Banquet, Oil 200.00
   Lamp, Hand Painted Shade, Electric, Signed, 37 In. 395.00
   Lamp, Oil, Bracket Handles, Copper & Brass, 17 In. 110.00
   Lamp, Store, Hanging, Brass Font, Brass, c.1890, 52 In. 600.00
   Letter Holder, Victorian Gilt Metal, Stags, Hounds, 9 In. 70.00
   Plaque, Woman, Carrying Bundle of Sticks, 8 1/2 In. 250.00
   Tray, Calling Card, Girl, Birds, Bronze, Signed, 7 1/2 In. 265.00
   Tray, Girl With Flowing Hair, 7 1/2 x 4 In. 165.00

Brass has been used for decorative pieces and useful tablewares since ancient times. It is an alloy of copper, zinc, and other metals.

   BRASS, see also Bell; Tool; Trivet; etc.
BRASS, Anvil, 2 3/4 In. 10.00
   Bed Warmer, Engraved & Pierced Lid, Curly Maple Handle, 48 1/2 In. 250.00
   Bed Warmer, Engraved Foliage On Cover, Wooden Handle, 45 In. 275.00
   Bed Warmer, Impressed Floral Design, Painted Handle, 42 1/2 In. 410.00
   Bed Warmer, Pierced & Tooled Lid, Foliage Designs, Wooden Handle 325.00
   Bed Warmer, Star Flower Tooled Lid Design, Wooden Handle, 41 3/4 In. 300.00
   Bed Warmer, Turned Handle, Engraved Cover, 41 1/2 In. 150.00
   Bowl, Allover Design, Carved Teakwood Tripod Holder, India 135.00
   Box, Knob On Side, Lock With Key & Keeper, 4 1/2 x 8 In. 45.00
   Box, Tobacco, 1800 .... 295.00
   Bucket, Ansonia, Iron Bail, 1851 .... 105.00
   Bucket, Spun, Iron Bail Handle, Ansonia Brass Co., 13 1/4 x 9 In. 45.00
   Candle Snuffer 40.00
   BRASS, CANDLESTICK, see Candlestick
   Chest, Carved Stone Inserts, 9 1/2 In. 55.00
   Cigar Clipper 17.50
   Cigar Clipper, New Bachelor, Brass 18.00
   Clock Jack, G. Slater & Co., 12 1/2 In. 85.00
   Dipper, Elongated Bowl, Wrought Iron Handle, 20 In. 95.00
   Dish, Ember, Tripod Scrolled Feet, Turned Wooden Handle, 8 1/4 In. 55.00
   Door Knocker, Eagle, Banner & Arrows In Claws, Spread Wings, Cast 35.00
   Door Knocker, Hammer & Anvil 68.00
   Door Knocker, Lion's Head, 1890s 75.00
   Door Knocker, Lion's Head, England, 8 In. 24.00
   Door Knocker, Stratford, 4 1/2 In. 15.00
   Door Knocker, Woman's Hand, Lace & Beaded Cuff, Striker Plate, 6 In. 125.00
   Drawer Pull, Colonial, 1920s, 6 Piece 40.00
   Dresser Jar, Red & Black Leaf Design, Glass Liner, Chase 45.00
   Figurine, Becky Thatcher 65.00
   Figurine, Dog, Feeding On Platter, England, 4 3/4 In. 45.00
   Figurine, Figure, Reclining, Teak Stand, 4 5/8 In. 40.00
   Flower Holder, Squatty, India 90.00
   Hibachi, Loop Handles, Overall Florals, Brass, Japanese, 14 In. 275.00
   Incense Burner, Chalice Type, Colorful 95.00
   Incense Burner, Foo Dog, 4 3/8 In. 75.00
   Kettle Stand, English, 12 x 16 1/2 In. 450.00
   Mask, Harlequin, Woman's, Ireland 16.00
   Measure, Dry, N. Y. & Eagle Marks, Graduated, c.1850, 6 Piece 2100.00
   Mortar & Pestle, Brass, 5 x 5 1/2 In. 85.00

Pail, Bail Handle, 11 3/4 In.	40.00
Pail, Iron Bail Handle, Spun, Haydens Patent, 6 x 9 1/2 In.	65.00
Pan, Jam, c.1820	150.00
Plant Stand, Paw Feet, 23 In.	75.00
Plate, Portrait, Man, Woman, Porcelain Insert, 18th Century, 15 In., Pr.	250.00
Samovar, Marks Depicting Russian Coins, Russia, 18 1/2 In.	55.00
Scissors, Wick Trimmer, Tray, 9 1/2 In.	85.00
Shelf, Kettle, Reticulated Top, England, 9 In.	70.00
Shelf, Kettle, Reticulated Top, Oval, 13 3/4 In.	85.00
Spyglass, Leather Bound, 2–Segment Type, Sunshade On End	95.50
Stand, Umbrella, Woven Open Worked Panels, Hexagonal, Europe, 23 In.	247.00
Stencil, Star Mark, For Feed Sacks & Crates, Pat. 1868 & 1871, 13 In.	105.00
Table, Tilt Top, 6 3/4 In.	50.00
Tea Kettle, Jugendstil, Jan Eisenloffel, 1910	2500.00
Teapot, Bulbous Form, Carved Wooden Handle, Tibetan, 1890s, 11 1/2 In.	250.00
Teapot, Bulbous Form, Demon Handle, Tibetan, 19th Century, 9 3/4 In.	145.00
Telescope, Celestial, Jos. Parkes & Son, England, 56 In.	3740.00
Telescope, Mahogany, G. Richardson, London, Day, Night, Opens To 3 Ft.	345.00
Telescope, Pocket, Black, Wollensak, Rochester, Opens To 4 3/4 In.	95.00
Telescope, Pocket, Leather, SW Type, Opens To 6 5/8 In.	110.00
Telescope, Wooden Tripod, 19th Century	715.00
Tray, Louis XV, Classical Children Dancing, Silvered, 10 x 13 In.	495.00
Umbrella Stand, Lion Head Ring Handles, Square, 21 1/2 In.	82.50
Vase, Cloisonne Bands, Oriental, 10 1/2 In.	60.00
Weight, Grave Short & Funner, London, 1 To 56 Lb., 1870, 7 Piece	2200.00
Weight, West Riding, Spherical, 1908, 4 Oz. To 56 Lb., 16 Piece	3300.00
Writing Stand, 4 Canisters, Candleholder & Bell, 7 In.	375.00

BRASTOFF, see Sascha Brastoff
BREAD PLATE, see Silver, porcelain factories, and various Pressed Glass Patterns

Glass bride's baskets or bride's bowls were usually one–of–a–kind novelties made in American and European glass factories. They were especially popular about 1880 when the decorated basket was often given as a wedding gift. Cut glass baskets were popular after 1890. All brides' baskets lost favor about 1905.

BRIDE'S BASKET, Celery Green Inset, Ruffled, Child's, 5 3/4 In.	225.00
Crimped Rim, Silver Over Pewter Frame, 11 1/4 In.	250.00
Pink Overlay Glass, Plated Holder, Cherubs, Austria	650.00
Ruffled, Enameled Center, Cranberry Cased In White, 10 In.	250.00
BRIDE'S BOWL, Enameled Flowers, 1 Trumpet, Silver Plated Holder, 16 In.	350.00
Enameled Flowers, Lacy Ormolu Stand, 11 1/8 x 10 1/2 In.	550.00
Pink To Green, Yellow Flowers & Design, Pink, 8 x 10 In.	295.00
Sandwich Overlay, Rubina Shading, Footed Holder	400.00
Silvered Pedestal Stand, Satin Glass, Forget–Me–Nots, 12 In.	350.00

Bristol glass was made in Bristol, England, after the 1700s. The Bristol glass most often seen today is a Victorian, lightweight opaque glass that is often blue. Some of the glass was decorated with enamels.

BRISTOL, Biscuit Jar, Birds & Foliage, Tan, Plated Fittings, 7 3/4 In.	195.00
Biscuit Jar, Ostrich, Stork On Opposite Side, 7 x 4 1/4 In.	270.00
Dish, Sweetmeat, Ducks & Cranes, Cow Finial, 4 In.	350.00
Lamp, Chimney, 16 1/2 In.	95.00
Perfume Bottle, Ball Stopper, Gold Stars & Dots, Green, 4 1/4 In.	88.00
Sweetmeat, Silver Lid, Opaque Cream, Enameled Floral, 5 1/2 In.	125.00
Vase, Coach & Horses Medallion, 14 In.	110.00
Vase, Deer Scenes, Peach	30.00
Vase, Enameled Butterfly, Blue, 3 In.	75.00
Vase, Enameled Flowers, Beaded, Silver Plated Holder, 14 1/2 In.	275.00
Vase, Enameled Flowers, Butterly, Blue, 7 1/2 In., Pair	88.00
Vase, Hand Painted, Frosted, 9 5/8 x 3 1/2 In., Pair	85.00

BRITANNIA, see Pewter

Bronze is an alloy of copper, tin, and other metals. It is used to make figurines, lamps, and other decorative objects.

BRONZE, Ashtray, Bull's Head 45.00
  Ashtray, Deer Stands Over Fallen Hunter 45.00
  Ashtray, Lady's Face, Deco 45.00
  Beaker, Wine, Geometric Design, Chinese, 7 1/2 In. 55.00
  Box, Cricket Cage, With Mouse, Oriental, Wooden Stand, 5 3/4 In. 350.00
  Box, Foliate & Berry Finial, Hinged Lid, C. Sorenson, 6 3/4 x 4 In. 55.00
  Brazier, Incised Floral Designs, 19th Century, Japan, 16 In. 192.50
  Bulldog, E. K. H., Marble Base, Collar Marked, 1920, 7 In. 375.00
  Bust, A. Carrier–Belleuse, Maiden, Flowing Hair, 24 In. .... 2000.00 To 2200.00
  Bust, Boris Aronson, Rasputin, c.1916, 27 In. 8250.00
  Bust, Donatello, Young Man, 16 In. 275.00
  Bust, E. H. Dumaige, Young Woman, Pan Pipe & Straw Hat, 17 In. 715.00
  Bust, Febrari, Young Girl, Bonnet, 24 In. ....*Illus* 2100.00
  Bust, Hagenauer, Nubian Woman, Early 20th Century, 14 3/8 In. 2200.00
  Bust, Italy, King Emanuel, Waist Up, With Hands 1500.00
  Bust, Jean–Baptiste II Lemoyne, Louis XV, Armor & Cloak, 15 3/4 In. 4125.00
  Bust, Mars, Bearded, Helmet, Classical Designs, Wooden Base, 12 In. 220.00
  Bust, Max Kalish, Portrait Bust, Marble Base, 8 In. 2420.00
  Bust, Moreau, 2 Female Royal Personages, Silvered, 20 In., Pair 3000.00
  Bust, Rembrandt, Bronze Plinth, 30 In. ....*Illus* 1200.00
  Bust, Van Der Straeten, Girl In Hat, 15 In. 660.00
  Candelabrum, 6–Light, Napoleon III, Marble Base, Bronze, 33 In., Pair 1100.00
  Candelabrum, Rouge Marble & Ormolu Base, 41 In., Pair ....*Illus* 6050.00
  Centerpiece, 3 Caryatid, Ormolu Swans & Lyres, 19 3/4 In. ....*Illus* 3190.00
  Clock Lamp, M. Tarmler, 2–Light, Reclining Nude, Metal Flowers 450.00
  Desk Clip, Adam & Eve Under Tree, Snake, Bird, 3 1/4 In. 65.00
  Desk Set, Enamel, Red Flowers, Berries, Buffalo Arts & Crafts, 4 Pc. 995.00
  Door Knocker, Long Horn Bull & Spur, Western Type 275.00

◆◆

If a piece of paper becomes stuck to the finish of a dresser top, try this method of removal. Soak the paper with mineral oil. Let it sit a few hours, then rub with a rough cloth. Repeat until the paper is removed.

◆◆

Bronze, Bust, Febrari, Young Girl, Bonnet, 24 In.

Bronze, Bust, Rembrandt, Bronze Plinth, 30 In.

Drinking Horn, Gilt, Wooden Base, 19th Century, 27 In. 687.00
Ewer, Fluted & Geometric Design, Scroll Handle, Tibetan, 13 1/4 In. 165.00
Figurine, A. Carrier, Allegorical Figure of Diana, 27 1/2 In. 5225.00
Figurine, A. Carrier, King Charles I, 28 3/4 In. 2750.00
Figurine, A. Falquiere, Boy With Rooster, 31 1/4 In. 2475.00
Figurine, A. Rodin, Wounded Lion, Signed, 1881, 10 7/8 x 13 7/8 In. 6020.00
Figurine, A. E. Gaudez, David, c.1860, 30 In. 1980.00
Figurine, Angelo Negretti, Nude Maidens, c.1910, 15 1/4 In. 880.00
Figurine, Arthur Putnam, Sleeping Lion, Marble Plinth, Signed, 11 In. 1985.00

Bronze, Candelabrum,
Rouge Marble & Ormolu Base, 41 In., Pair

Bronze, Centerpiece, 3 Caryatid,
Ormolu Swans & Lyres, 19 3/4 In.

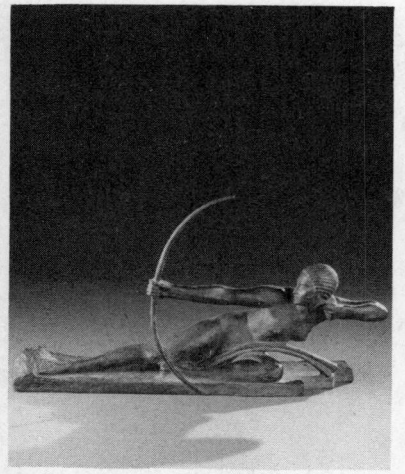

Bronze, Figurine, Bouraine, Female Archer,
c.1925, 19 In.

Bronze, Figurine, Fratin, Horse, Standing,
1842, 12 7/8 In.

Figurine, B. P. Vonnoh, Girl With Butterflies, c.1900, 13 1/4 In. 7000.00
Figurine, Barye, Lion, Walking, Green-Black Patina, 16 In. 1650.00
Figurine, Barye, Tiger, 4 x 8 In. 775.00
Figurine, Belloc, Warrior, Rearing Horse, Green Patina, 26 1/2 In. 990.00
Figurine, Bosio, Henri IV, As Child, 4 Ft. 1 In. 2200.00
Figurine, Bouraine, Female Archer, c.1925, 19 In. ....*Illus* 990.00
Figurine, Boy, Examining Sole of Foot, Marble Base, 18 In. 385.00
Figurine, Brink, Little Meter Maid, Square Onyx Plinth, 16 1/4 In. 450.00
Figurine, Bruno Zach, Woman Smoking, Loose Jacket, c.1925, 15 In. 1100.00
Figurine, Bufano, Owl, Square Wooden Plinth, 6 3/4 In. ....275.00 To 305.00
Figurine, Bufano, Wolf, Wooden Plinth, Signed, 4 In. 100.00
Figurine, C. Podolak, Skater, Full Stride, 9 1/2 x 14 In. 660.00
Figurine, Cartier, Indian Being Attacked By Mountain Lion, 26 In. 1765.00
Figurine, Cavacos, Nude Dancer, Marble Base, c.1925, 19 1/4 In. 2500.00
Figurine, Chana Orloff, Peasant Woman, Silvered, c.1925, 8 In. 1430.00
Figurine, Charol, Golfer, Stylized Form, Club In Hand, 18 1/8 In. 2750.00
Figurine, Chiparus, Egyptian Dance, c.1925, 28 1/2 In. 6050.00
Figurine, Chiparus, Waking Woman, c.1925, 12 1/4 In. 1980.00
Figurine, Chiparus, Woman With Lion, c.1925, 10 x 16 3/4 In. 5500.00
Figurine, Cyrus Edward Dallin, Scout, 23 1/2 In. 7975.00
Figurine, Cyrus Edward Dallin, Signal of Peace, 12 3/4 In. 2310.00
Figurine, Delagrange, Loie Fuller, Standing, Cape, 16 3/4 In. 8800.00
Figurine, Dubois, Mandolin Player, 24 In. 1870.00
Figurine, E. Lansere, Cossack After Hunt, Russia, 15 x 11 x 5 In. 6950.00
Figurine, E. Picault, Roman Soldier, Honor Patria Base, 63 1/4 In. 1400.00
Figurine, E. T. Hurley, Turtle, Hinged Back, 6 In. 715.00
Figurine, Eagle, Flag Pole Finial, 10 x 8 In. 145.00
Figurine, Edith B. Parsons, Terrier, 4 In. 3300.00
Figurine, Elephant, 5 x 7 In. 300.00
Figurine, Ernest Trova, Gox #2, 1987, 11 x 8 x 3 In. 1980.00
Figurine, Eugene Deplechin, Amphitrite, On Dolphin, c.1893, 10 In. 935.00
Figurine, F. Halnon, Nude Female, Green Marble Base, 14 In. 1980.00
Figurine, F. Pautrot, Pointer, Hunting Hare, 5 1/2 In. 275.00
Figurine, Franz Bergman, Centerpiece, Intwined Flowers, 12 3/4 In. 2650.00
Figurine, Fratin, Horse, Standing, 1842, 12 7/8 In. ....*Illus* 1100.00
Figurine, Frishmuth, Nymph, The Vine, c.1921, 11 3/4 In. 5225.00
Figurine, Frishmuth, The Star, Metallic Plinth, 1914, 19 1/4 In. 4675.00
Figurine, Gemito, Neopolitan Street Urchin, 10 3/4 In. 2200.00
Figurine, Guillemin, Samurai, Silvered Bronze, 8 1/4 In., Pair 3300.00
Figurine, Gustave, Dore, Knight In Armor, Leaps Over Monk, 13 3/4 In. 4620.00
Figurine, H. G. Danzniany, Dancer, Exotic Attire, c.1925, 21 1/4 In. 825.00
Figurine, Harriet Frishmuth, The Star, 18 7/8 In. 8250.00
Figurine, Henri Ple, Woman, Holding A Bird, 34 In. 6050.00
Figurine, Huzel, Classical Woman In Grecian Attire, c.1860, 11 In. 995.00
Figurine, I. Bonheur, Bull, 23 1/2 In. 5225.00
Figurine, James Andrey, Roaring Lion, Marble Plinth, Signed, 21 In. 600.00
Figurine, Jean Lambert-Rucki, St. Francis, 20th Century, 16 1/2 In. 5500.00
Figurine, Kaan, Peasant Woman With Sicklel, Marble Plinth, 18 In. 660.00
Figurine, Kalish, Floyd B. Odlum, 1935, 17 1/2 In. 2200.00
Figurine, Kalish, Goldminer, 7 3/8 In. 2420.00
Figurine, Kalish, Road Worker, Marble Base, 1930, 18 In. ....7000.00 To 7700.00
Figurine, Kalish, Seated Figure, 13 In. 1650.00
Figurine, Kauba, Harem Dancer, Marble Pedestal, 7 1/2 In. 1650.00
Figurine, Kauba, Sharpshooter, Marble Base, 8 3/4 In. 1320.00
Figurine, Korschann, Woman, Head Bowed, c.1900, 13 In. 1100.00
Figurine, Lansere, Mother With Child, Russia, 12 x 12 x 5 In. 5950.00
Figurine, Liebrich, Bear & Cossack, Russia 7500.00
Figurine, Lorenzl, Dancer, Poised On Toes, c.1920, 13 1/2 In. 660.00
Figurine, Luca Madrassi, 2 Lovers, Standing, Large 1980.00
Figurine, Lucy Currier Richards, Pierrette, c.1915, 19 1/2 In. 1870.00
Figurine, M. Amodie, Mercury, Messenger of The Gods, Napoli, 20 In. 700.00
Figurine, M. De Lisio, Portrait of Virgil Thompson, 1980, 13 In. 4000.00
Figurine, M. Guiraud Riviere, Dancer, Marble Pedestal, 18 7/8 In. 1320.00

Bronze, Figurine, Sino–Tibetan Goddess,   *Bronze, Figurine, Venus De Milo, 24 In.*
Lotus Base, 56 In.

Figurine, MacMonnies, Baccante & Infant Fawn, 1894, 33 1/4 In. 5000.00
Figurine, Male, Draped Lower Body, Roman, 2nd Century, 4 1/2 In. 600.00
Figurine, Marcel Bouraine, Woman, Bobbed Hair, c.1925, 14 1/2 In. 1650.00
Figurine, Maurice Guiraud Riviere, Tennis Player, 18 1/2 In. 2100.00
Figurine, Mene, 2 Horses, 17 In. 2500.00
Figurine, Moigniez, Woodcock, Onyx Base, 10 1/2 In. 650.00
Figurine, Mother Pig & Babies, Signed, 3 1/2 In. 45.00
Figurine, Nude, Contemporary, Dark Green Marble, 19 In. 275.00
Figurine, Old Golfer, In Knickers, Small 50.00
Figurine, Pigalle, Nude Youth, Lionskin Over Shoulder, 25 In. 1500.00
Figurine, Rochard, Branch, Chrome Plated Cranes, Marble Base, 20 In. 325.00
Figurine, Rodin, Tet De Jeune Femme, Marble Base, 7 In. 2860.00
Figurine, Russia, Traveler With Pack Horse, 1875, 5 1/2 x 6 1/2 In. 1325.00
Figurine, Salome, Allegorical, Rose, Marble Plinth, 30 1/2 In. 1925.00
Figurine, Sauvage, Venus De Milo, 22 1/2 In. 335.00
Figurine, Schaper, Bismarck, Brown Patina, 12 1/2 In. 1300.00
Figurine, Schenk, Young Peasant Woman, 37 In. 3400.00
Figurine, Scotty Dog, 2 In. 70.00
Figurine, Seated Buddha, Lotus Plinth, Tibetan, 6 1/4 In. 475.00
Figurine, Seated Lions, 47 In. 2500.00
Figurine, Seated Noble, Character Seal Mark, 3 In. 555.00
Figurine, Seikoju, Elephant, 19th Century, 13 In. 357.50
Figurine, Sino–Tibetan Goddess, Lotus Base, 56 In. ....*Illus* 200.00
Figurine, Venus De Milo, 24 In. ....*Illus* 175.00
Figurine, Verdigris, Flying Goose, Upraised Wings, 31 x 27 In. 1900.00
Figurine, Victor Salmones, Trajectory, 47 x 45 x 33 1/2 In. 8250.00
Figurine, Victor Siefert, Woman, Carrying 2 Buckets, c.1875, 7 In. 595.00
Figurine, Vienna, Cat Band, 1880–1910, Miniature, 10 Piece 950.00
Figurine, Vienna, Mice Band, 1880, Miniature, 4 Piece 225.00
Figurine, Vienna, Monkeys On Pillow, Couple Embracing, 13 x 10 In. 3100.00
Figurine, Virion, Stork 595.00
Figurine, Wan Lien, Fat God of Happiness, Ming, 1473–1620, 11 1/2 In. 7900.00
Figurine, Wan Lien, Manjusri Seated On Lion, Ming, 1573–1620, 12 In. 9500.00
Figurine, Winder, Standing Buffalo, Ivory Horns, 1893, 10 x 13 In. 885.00
Group, Carrier, Woman, Flowing Drapery, Child At Foot, 21 In., Pair 3850.00
Group, Chalon, Equestrian, Flying Woman Astride, Marble, 23 3/8 In. 6050.00
Group, Delabrierre, Lion Attacking Serpent, 15 1/2 In. 1100.00
Group, Eugene Lanceray, Equestrian, Horseman Roping Horse, 25 In. 4400.00
Group, Fonderia Nelli Roma, Perseu, With Head of Medusa, 31 1/2 In. 4125.00
Group, Horse & Whippet, 1890s, 16 x 19 In. 715.00
Group, Lanceray, 3 Horses, Russia, Dated 1875, 8 1/2 x 9 In. 1100.00

Group, Laurent, Doe & Her Young, c.1900, 7 1/2 In. 990.00
Group, Moreau, Allegorical, 28 In. 7150.00
Group, Picault, Allegorical, Winged Horse, Red Marble, 37 1/2 In. 6050.00
Head, After Greek Prototype, Metal Stand, 13 In. 995.00
Incense Burner, Foo Dog, Japan, 6 In. 395.00
Incense Burner, Seated Foo Dog Cover, Cloud Design, 8 1/2 In. 465.00
Incense Holder, Altar, Reclining Buffalo Form, Indian, 1 3/4 In. 125.00
Ivory, Bottle, Snuff, Chinese Wise Man, Colorful Robe 95.00
Jar, Champleve, 2 Ogre Head Handles, Cloud Ground, China, 22 In. 450.00
Jar, Dragons, Foo Dog, China, 14 5/8 In. 165.00
Jar, Lotus Shape, Oriental, 9 1/2 In. 60.00
Jar, Oriental, Colored Metal Inlaid, 12 In. 725.00
Jardiniere, Gustav Gurschner, Art Deco, 3 Handles, 3 In. 185.00
Lamp Base, Hagenauer, Stylized Nude Figure, Against Tree, 14 1/4 In. ....,.... 2200.00
Lamp Bracket, Worn Gold Paint, 18 x 24 1/2 In., Pair 675.00
Lamp, Austrian, Arab Men Playing Chess, Electric, 20 1/2 In. 1100.00
Mask, Charles Sykes, Couple Embracing, Green Marble Base, 9 7/8 In. 4950.00
Mold, For Pewter Spoons, 8 In. 250.00
Mortar & Pestle, 5 In. 35.00
Pencil Holder, Scotty Dog 40.00
Pitcher, Relief Figure of Young Woman, Reclining, C. B. Peron, 9 In. 165.00
Plant Stand, Napoleon III, Pendant Chains, c.1870, 44 In., Pair 3650.00
Plaque, Barye, Eagle, Attacking Snake & Goat, 4 In., Pair 2640.00
Plaque, L. Hottot, Woman, Man, Arab Attire, Cold Painted, 25 In., Pair 2475.00
Plaque, M. Herter Fecit, Portrait, Boy, Brown Patina, 13 x 11 In. 110.00
Plaque, William Zorach, The Dance, 9 1/4 x 8 3/4 In. 1875.00
Schimmelphfennig, Sun Butterfly–Girl, Brown Patina, 1899, 19 In. 990.00
Seal, Squirrel, Grapes & Leaves, Oriental 450.00
Spur, Horsehead, Single 60.00
Tray, Art Nouveau, Mermaid & Merboy, 6 In. 88.00
Tray, Gustave Gurschner, Horseshoe & Female Design, 9 In. 330.00
Umbrella Stand, Oriental 350.00
Urn, France, Crystal, Silver Band, 23 In. 1450.00
Vase, 4 Birds & Flowers, Japan, c.1920, 12 In. 595.00
Vase, Applied Floral & Avian Design, Lamp Mounted, Japan, 12 In. Pr. 400.00
Vase, Gilt Flowers, Japan, c.1920, 11 In. 160.00
Vase, Koichi, Gun Metal Finish With Silver & Copper, 7 In. 250.00
Vase, Serpent Mask & Loose Ring Handles, Ch'ing Dynasty, 22 In. 660.00

Brownies were first drawn in 1883 by Palmer Cox. They are characterized by large round eyes, downturned mouths, and skinny legs. Toys, books, dinnerware, and other objects were made with the Brownies as part of the design.

BROWNIES, Basket, Etched Design of Brownies, Candy Ad, Silver Plate, 6 In. 85.00
Creamer, Verse, Reading Little Boy Blue, Gold Trim, Palmer Cox 75.00
Cup & Saucer 59.00
Cup, Palmer Cox, 3 Different Scenes, 3 1/4 In. 65.00
Mold, Ice Cream, Brownie, Pewter, Hand In Pocket, Palmer Cox, 5 In. 100.00
Mold, Ice Cream, Pewter, Palmer Cox, 5 In. 90.00
Nodder, Winking Brownie, Happy, 5 In. 135.00
Plate, 19 Different Brownies, Silver Plate, Palmer Cox, 8 1/2 In. 125.00
Plate, Fluted Swirl Border, Palmer Cox, 8 1/2 In. 75.00
Puzzle, Skating, Palmer Cox, Frame, 20 Pieces, 10 1/2 x 12 1/2 In. 95.00
Saltshaker, Brownie, Dancing With Golliwog, Egg Shape, Pewter Lid 95.00

George Brush started working in 1901 in Zanesville, Ohio. He started his own pottery in 1907, but it burned to the ground and he joined McCoy in 1909. After a series of name changes, the company became The Brush Pottery in 1925. Collectors favor the figural cookie jars made by this company.

BRUSH, Cookie Jar, Bear, Feet Apart ....60.00 To 125.00
Cookie Jar, Bear, Feet Together 125.00
Cookie Jar, Bunny, Gray 175.00

Cookie Jar, Bunny, White .... 50.00 To 80.00
Cookie Jar, Cat Finial, Pink 48.00
Cookie Jar, Chicken, White, On Nest 60.00
Cookie Jar, Cinderella's Pumpkin .... 69.00 To 165.00
Cookie Jar, Clock 65.00
Cookie Jar, Covered Wagon 400.00
Cookie Jar, Cow, Brown .... 60.00 To 90.00
Cookie Jar, Cow, Purple .... 650.00 To 800.00
Cookie Jar, Davy Crockett .... 128.00 To 235.00
Cookie Jar, Donkey, With Cart .... 100.00 To 200.00
Cookie Jar, Formal Pig 225.00
Cookie Jar, Formal Pig, Green 100.00
Cookie Jar, Girl With Cookie 95.00
Cookie Jar, Granny, Green Dress 65.00
Cookie Jar, House 65.00
Cookie Jar, Humpty Dumpty .... 110.00 To 125.00
Cookie Jar, Little Angel 785.00
Cookie Jar, Little Boy Blue, Gold Trim 610.00
Cookie Jar, Little Boy, Blue 300.00
Cookie Jar, Little Girl 265.00
Cookie Jar, Little Red Riding Hood .... 300.00 To 500.00
Cookie Jar, Old Woman's Shoe 115.00
Cookie Jar, Panda Bear .... 99.00 To 115.00
Cookie Jar, Peter Pan .... 290.00 To 450.00
Cookie Jar, Peter Peter Pumpkin Eater .... 185.00 To 225.00
Cookie Jar, Squirrel On Log .... 40.00 To 65.00
Cookie Jar, Treasure Chest .... 78.00 To 85.00
Flowerpot, Sculptured Mushrooms, Tan Treebark, Label, 4 1/2 In. 9.00
Jardiniere, Pompeian, 6 1/2 In. 35.00
Lantern, Patio, 2 Sides 24.00
Pitcher, Avenue of Trees 60.00
Planter, Ostrich 15.00
Vase, Pillow, Princess, 7 In. 20.00
　　　BRUSH MCCOY, see McCoy

Buck Rogers was the first American science fiction comic strip. It
started in 1929 and continued until 1965. Buck has also appeared in
comic books, movies, and, in the 1980s, in a television series. Any
memorabilia connected with the character Buck Rogers is collectible.

BUCK ROGERS, Attack Ship 35.00
Badge, Solar Scout, 1935 .... 45.00 To 75.00
Boat, Battle Cruiser, Tootsietoy, 1930s 150.00
Book, Big Little Book, Buck Rogers Doom Comet 45.00
Doll, Box, 1979 .... 18.00
Gun, Sonic Ray, 1950s 68.00
Holster, Brown Leather, 1930s, 8 In. 25.00
Lunch Box 18.00
Pistol, Atomic 110.00
Pistol, Automatic 180.00
Pistol, Disintegrator, Leather Holster, Daisy, c.1936 .... 375.00
Pistol, Rocket, 1934 .... 85.00
Ring, Picture 395.00
Robot, Twiki, Walking 50.00
Space Ranger Kit, Sylvania Toy Premium, 1952 .... 175.00
Space Ship, Suction Tip, Bomb Sight, 1942 .... 70.00
Watch, Pocket, Lighting Bolt Hands, Ingraham, 1936 .... 750.00

Buffalo pottery was made in Buffalo, New York, after 1902. The
company was established by the Larkin Company, famous
manufacturers of soap. The wares are marked with a picture of a
buffalo and the date of manufacture. Deldare ware is the most
famous pottery made at the factory. It is khaki–colored transfer–
decorated ware.

BUFFALO POTTERY DELDARE, Bowl, Fallowfield Hunt, The Start, 9 In. 625.00
Bowl, Fruit, Village Tavern Scene 295.00
Bowl, Ye Village Tavern, 1908, 9 1/4 In. 445.00
Bowl, Ye Village Tavern, 1924, 9 1/2 In. 435.00
Charger, Evening At Lion Inn, 12 In. 475.00
Chop Plate, An Evening At Ye Lion Inn, 14 In. 425.00
Cup & Saucer, Fallowfield 250.00
Cup & Saucer, Ye Olden Days .... 195.00 To 245.00
Figurine, Dr. Syntax, Emerald, 12 x 9 In. 1050.00
Hair Receiver, Ye Village Street 325.00
Mug, Ye Lion Inn, 4 1/2 In. .... 225.00 To 375.00
Pitcher, Breaking For Cover, 10 In. 350.00
Pitcher, Breaking For Cover, 1908, 7 In. 375.00
Pitcher, Fallowfield Hunt, 6 In. 425.00
Pitcher, Fallowfield Hunt, Hunt Supper, 1909, Tall 775.00
Pitcher, Fallowfield Hunt, Octagonal 800.00
Pitcher, Fallowfield Hunt, The Return, 8 In. 650.00
Plaque, Ye Lion Inn, 1905, 12 In. 500.00
Plate, An Evening At Ye Lion Inn, c.1908, 14 In. 595.00
Plate, At Ye Lion Inn, 6 1/4 In. 300.00
Plate, Breaking For Cover, 1908, 10 In. 225.00
Plate, Fallowfield Hunt, 10 In. 165.00
Plate, Fallowfield Hunt, The Start, 14 In. 525.00
Plate, Fallowfield Hunt, The Start, 9 1/2 In. 160.00
Plate, Yankee Doodle 1700.00
Platter, Fallowfield Hunt, The Start, 14 In. 195.00
Soup, Dish, Green Body, Ye Olden Days, 6 In., 4 Pc. 250.00
Sugar & Creamer, Cover, Ye Olden Days .... 400.00 To 475.00
Tankard, Annual Rent, 8 In. 625.00
Tea Tile, Traveling In Ye Olden Days 500.00
Tea Tray, 13 3/4 x 10 1/4 In. 450.00
Teapot, Breaking Cover 425.00
Teapot, Ye Village Inn, Signed, 6 In. 450.00
Tray, Calling Card, Fallowfield Hunt, 1909 .... 425.00
Tray, Card, Mr. Pickwick Addresses The Club 750.00
Tray, Dresser, Dancing Ye Minuet .... 700.00 To 850.00
Tray, Rural Sport, 8 x 10 In. 1450.00
BUFFALO POTTERY, Ashtray, Chesapeake & Ohio R.R. 100.00
Chocolate Pot, Emerald 1700.00
Cup & Saucer, Blue Willow 30.00
Dish, Feeding, Campbell Kids, 7 1/2 In. 40.00
Pitcher, Emerald, Dr. Syntax 1700.00
Pitcher, Mariner, 9 1/4 In. 400.00
Pitcher, Pilgrim, Dated 1903 .... 695.00
Pitcher, Rip Van Winkle 535.00
Pitcher, Robin Hood, Stag, Verse, c.1906, 8 In. .... 275.00 To 550.00
Pitcher, Roosevelt Bear Scenes, Brown Transfer, 1907, 8 In. 1000.00
Pitcher, Their Manner of Telling Stories 400.00
Pitcher, Whaling 395.00
Plate, Christmas, 1952 .... 25.00
Plate, Gunner 125.00
Tankard, Sailboats, Abino, 12 In. 1750.00

♦♦

If you accidently dust off a bit of veneer, a loose screw, a piece of metal mounting, immediately put it in an envelope and tape or pin it to the back of the furniture. When you have time, decide if you or an expert should do the needed restoration. These small pieces should be carefully saved because they can never be exactly duplicated.

♦♦

Teapot, Gold Band, Ivory 35.00

Burmese glass was developed by Frederick Shirley at the Mt. Washington Glass Works in New Bedford, Massachusetts, in 1885. It is a two–toned glass, shading from peach to yellow. Some have a pattern mold design. A few Burmese pieces were decorated with pictures or applied glass flowers of colored Burmese glass.

BURMESE, see also Gunderson

BURMESE, **Bonbon,** Shiny Finish, Mt. Washington, 5 x 2 3/4 In. 585.00
  Bowl, Painted Brown Leaves, Fluted Top, 4 x 8 3/4 In. 375.00
  Bowl, Silver Plated Holder, 8 In., Pair 4000.00
  Bride's Basket, Enameled Forget–Me–Nots, Meriden Frame 750.00
  Cookie Jar, Shaded Water Lillies, Opal Lining, Mt. Washington 775.00
  Cracker Jar, Oakleaf & Acorn, Mt. Washington 700.00
  Cruet Set, 2 Bottles, Salt & Pepper, No Stoppers 1500.00
  Cruet, Melon–Ribbed, Mushroom Stopper, Mt. Washington, 6 1/2 In. 1065.00
  Lamp, Fairy, Berry & Leaf Design, Clarke Insert, 3 1/2 In. 1750.00
  Lamp, Fairy, Burmese Bowl & Candle Cup, Double Skirted, Crimped 2450.00
  Lamp, Fairy, Floral Shade, Clarke Insert, 3 1/2 In. 605.00
  Lamp, Fairy, Tapestry Flower Bow Base, Clarke Insert, 6 1/2 In. 950.00
  Perfume Bottle, Lay Down, Mistletoe, Leaves, Berries, 4 7/8 In. 1250.00
  Pitcher, Mt. Washington, 11 In. 1155.00
  Pitcher, Squat, Mt. Washington, 7 1/2 In. 900.00
  Pitcher, Water 1200.00
  Saltshaker, Begonia Leaf, Ribbed 250.00
  Saltshaker, Caladium Leaf Design, Mt. Washington 250.00
  Saltshaker, Silver Plated Top, Mt. Washington, 3 7/8 In. 275.00
  Sugar Bowl & Creamer, Yellow, 2 x 3 1/2 In. 750.00
  Toothpick, 6–Sided Top, Mt. Washington 425.00
  Toothpick, Lavender Pansies, Square Mouth 350.00
  Toothpick, Tri–Corner Top, 1 3/4 In. 412.50
  Tumbler, Fern Fronds, Mt. Washington 585.00
  Tumbler, Yellow Roses, Mt. Washington, 3/4 In. 565.00
  Vase, 8 Yellow Ribs Rising From Base To Top, Pedestal, 4 1/4 In. 475.00
  Vase, Daisy Blossoms, Foliage, Handles, Mt. Washington, 12 1/2 In. 1950.00
  Vase, Double Gourd, 6 3/4 In. 300.00
  Vase, Double Gourd, Allover Maidenhair Fern, Mt. Washington, 7 In. 900.00
  Vase, Floral Design, Silver Plated Frame, 8 1/4 In. 515.00
  Vase, Flying Storks, Gourd Shape, Mt. Washington, 10 In. 3525.00
  Vase, Jack–In–The–Pulpit, Berries & Leaves, 5 In. 715.00
  Vase, Jack–In–The–Pulpit, Crimped, Mt. Washington, 14 1/2 In. 985.00
  Vase, Leaves & Berries, Dimpled On All Sides, 6 In. 385.00
  Vase, Lily Shape, c.1880, 12 In. 495.00
  Vase, Lily, Sterling Base, 7 1/4 In. 165.00
  Vase, Prunus Blossoms, Mt. Washington 345.00
  Vase, Robert Burns Verse, Mt. Washington, 8 x 6 1/4 In. 3450.00
  Vase, Squatty, Square Neck, 2 1/2 In., Pair 445.00
  Vase, Thomas Hood Verse, Mt. Washington, 13 In. 2310.00
  Vase, Trefoil Top, Bowling Pin Shape, Mt. Washington, 12 1/2 In. 685.00
  Wall Hanger, Green 145.00

BURMESE, WEBB, see Webb Burmese

Buster Brown, the comic strip, first appeared in color in 1902. Buster and his dog Tige remained a popular comic and soon became even more famous as the emblem for a shoe company, a textile firm, and others. The strip was discontinued in 1920, but some of the advertising is still in use.

BUSTER BROWN, **Badge,** Secret Service, Raised Lettering 10.00
  Bandana 50.00
  Book, Me & My Bubble, R. F. Outcault, 1903 .... 245.00
  Button, Buster & Tige, Vacation Days Carnival, 1946, 2 1/2 In. 35.00
  Button, Pinback, Shoes 20.00
  Card, Playing, Buster & Tige, Comics Reverse, 1904, Miniature 58.00

Certificate, Guarantee 28.00
Cigar Bands, 5 Piece 20.00
Clicker 15.00
Comic Book, 1954 .... 10.00
Comic Page, A Trip To Chinatown, Color, 1909, 16 x 20 In. 50.00
Comic Strip, Sunday Newspapers, 1920 .... 25.00
Cup & Saucer 40.00
Cup, Germany, Early 1900s 75.00
Hook, Coat 28.00
Mannekin, With Tige, Composition, 30 In. 500.00
Mirror, Child's, Buster Brown Shoes 140.00
Mustard 110.00
Noisemaker, Wood & Metal 15.00
Pencil Clip, Buster Brown Shoes, Foxed 15.00
Periscope .... 18.00 To 20.00
Pin, Secret Service 27.50
Postcard, 1905 .... 18.00
Postcard, Buster Brown Shoes, Illustrated, c.1930 .... 15.00
Postcard, Buster, Tige & Yellow Kid, Over Bounding Main, 1903 .... 45.00
Poster, 4 Ft. 165.00
Ruler 8.00
Sign, Hardboard, Buster & Tige, 14 x 14 In. 110.00
Socks Box, With Logo 20.00
Tablet 26.00
Tin, Buster Brown Cigar, Buster & Tige, Early 1900s 5775.00
Tin, Spice, Mustard, Buster Brown 55.00
Tin, Spice, Pickling, Buster Brown 52.00
Tin, Spice, Red Pepper, Buster Brown 55.00
Wagon, Buster Brown Health Shoes, Wooden, Red, Black, 35 In. 350.00

Butter chips, or butter pats, were small individual dishes for butter. They were in the height of fashion from 1880 to 1910. Earlier as well as later examples are known.

BUTTER CHIP, Argyle, Grindley, Flow Blue 28.00
Ayr, W. & E. Cord, Flow Blue 30.00
Belmont, Meakin, Flow Blue 30.00
Byzantine, Wood & Sons, Flow Blue 30.00
Chinese, Wedgwood, Flow Blue 25.00
Diana, Meakin, Flow Blue 27.50
Duchess, Flow Blue 22.00
Grace, Flow Blue .... 28.00 To 30.00
Holland, Flow Blue 17.50
Iris, Flow Blue 18.00
Marechal Neil, Flow Blue 28.00
Marie, Flow Blue 25.00
Melbourne, Grindley, Flow Blue 27.50
Raleigh, Burgess & Leigh, Flow Blue 17.50
Touraine, Flow Blue 28.00
Verona, Flow Blue 28.00
BUTTER MOLD, see Kitchen, Mold, Butter

Buttons have been known throughout the centuries, and there are millions of styles. Gold, silver, or precious stones were used for the best buttons, but most were made of natural materials like bone or shell, or from inexpensive metals. Only a few types are listed for comparison.

BUTTON, Cameo, Czechoslovakia, On Card, 12 Piece 35.00
Coral, Rose Carved, Box, 8 Piece 150.00
Gold Metal, Shank, English Scroll, 1930s, Card, 4 Piece 12.00
Malachite, Gilt Mount, Paris Label, Box, 10 Piece 250.00
Marcasite, Enameled Roses, Victorian, 12 Piece 150.00
Pewter, English Print Engraved McGreery, 1920s, Card, 4 Piece 9.00
Pharoah Head, Brass Repousse, Brown Bakelite 75.00

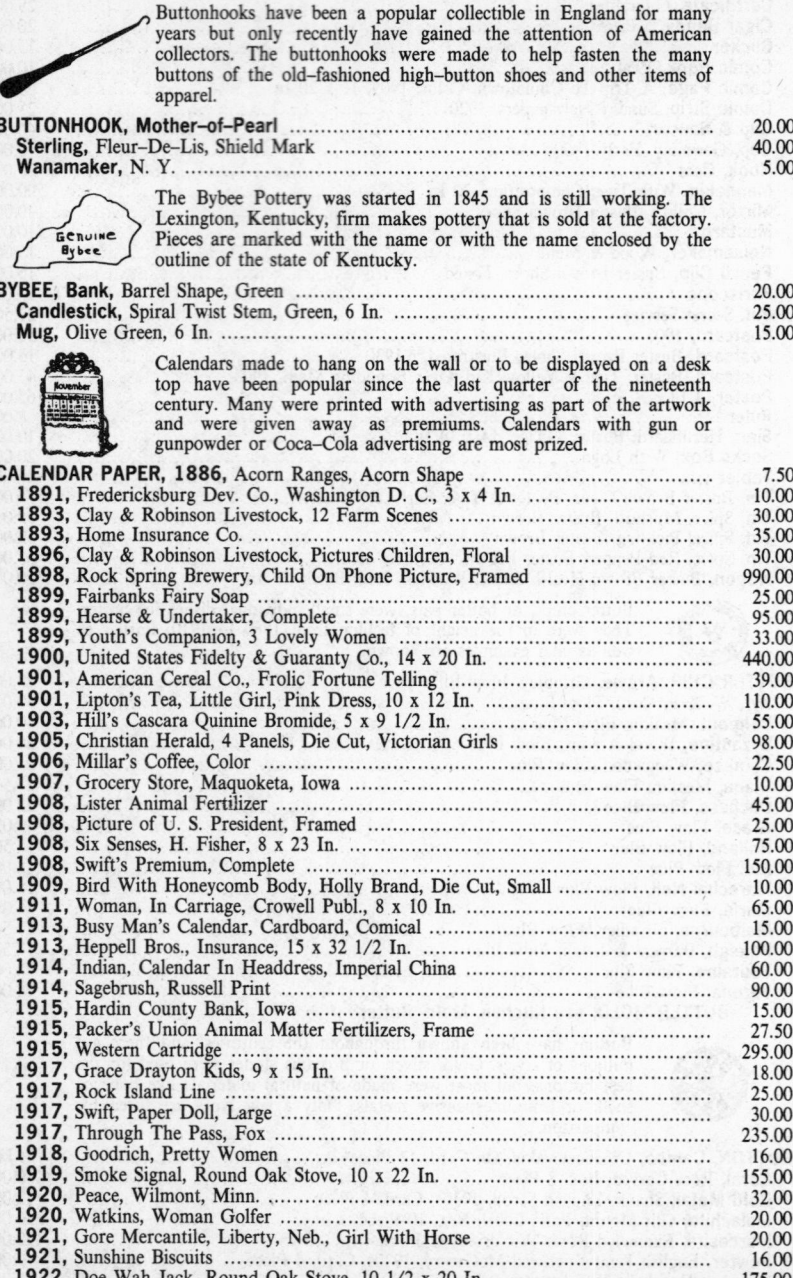

Buttonhooks have been a popular collectible in England for many years but only recently have gained the attention of American collectors. The buttonhooks were made to help fasten the many buttons of the old–fashioned high–button shoes and other items of apparel.

BUTTONHOOK, Mother–of–Pearl	20.00
Sterling, Fleur–De–Lis, Shield Mark	40.00
Wanamaker, N. Y.	5.00

The Bybee Pottery was started in 1845 and is still working. The Lexington, Kentucky, firm makes pottery that is sold at the factory. Pieces are marked with the name or with the name enclosed by the outline of the state of Kentucky.

BYBEE, Bank, Barrel Shape, Green	20.00
Candlestick, Spiral Twist Stem, Green, 6 In.	25.00
Mug, Olive Green, 6 In.	15.00

Calendars made to hang on the wall or to be displayed on a desk top have been popular since the last quarter of the nineteenth century. Many were printed with advertising as part of the artwork and were given away as premiums. Calendars with gun or gunpowder or Coca–Cola advertising are most prized.

CALENDAR PAPER, 1886, Acorn Ranges, Acorn Shape	7.50
1891, Fredericksburg Dev. Co., Washington D. C., 3 x 4 In.	10.00
1893, Clay & Robinson Livestock, 12 Farm Scenes	30.00
1893, Home Insurance Co.	35.00
1896, Clay & Robinson Livestock, Pictures Children, Floral	30.00
1898, Rock Spring Brewery, Child On Phone Picture, Framed	990.00
1899, Fairbanks Fairy Soap	25.00
1899, Hearse & Undertaker, Complete	95.00
1899, Youth's Companion, 3 Lovely Women	33.00
1900, United States Fidelty & Guaranty Co., 14 x 20 In.	440.00
1901, American Cereal Co., Frolic Fortune Telling	39.00
1901, Lipton's Tea, Little Girl, Pink Dress, 10 x 12 In.	110.00
1903, Hill's Cascara Quinine Bromide, 5 x 9 1/2 In.	55.00
1905, Christian Herald, 4 Panels, Die Cut, Victorian Girls	98.00
1906, Millar's Coffee, Color	22.50
1907, Grocery Store, Maquoketa, Iowa	10.00
1908, Lister Animal Fertilizer	45.00
1908, Picture of U. S. President, Framed	25.00
1908, Six Senses, H. Fisher, 8 x 23 In.	75.00
1908, Swift's Premium, Complete	150.00
1909, Bird With Honeycomb Body, Holly Brand, Die Cut, Small	10.00
1911, Woman, In Carriage, Crowell Publ., 8 x 10 In.	65.00
1913, Busy Man's Calendar, Cardboard, Comical	15.00
1913, Heppell Bros., Insurance, 15 x 32 1/2 In.	100.00
1914, Indian, Calendar In Headdress, Imperial China	60.00
1914, Sagebrush, Russell Print	90.00
1915, Hardin County Bank, Iowa	15.00
1915, Packer's Union Animal Matter Fertilizers, Frame	27.50
1915, Western Cartridge	295.00
1917, Grace Drayton Kids, 9 x 15 In.	18.00
1917, Rock Island Line	25.00
1917, Swift, Paper Doll, Large	30.00
1917, Through The Pass, Fox	235.00
1918, Goodrich, Pretty Women	16.00
1919, Smoke Signal, Round Oak Stove, 10 x 22 In.	155.00
1920, Peace, Wilmont, Minn.	32.00
1920, Watkins, Woman Golfer	20.00
1921, Gore Mercantile, Liberty, Neb., Girl With Horse	20.00
1921, Sunshine Biscuits	16.00
1922, Doe Wah Jack, Round Oak Stove, 10 1/2 x 20 In.	175.00

1923, Round Oak Stove, Indian & Squaw, 10 1/2 x 21 In. 145.00
1924, Calgary Brewing 185.00
1924, Red Man's Wireless, Osborne 48.00
1925, G. W. Herrington's Drug Store, Texas, 14 x 8 1/2 In. 16.00
1925, Yeast Foam, Pretty Woman 20.00
1926, Statue of Liberty, Amer. Inst. Citizen., 14 x 6 In. 12.50
1928, Firestone, Hunting Dogs 27.50
1929, Girl In Glass Picture, Atlanta, Kansas 20.00
1929, NuGrape, Full Pad 235.00
1929, Winchester, Snowshoes 165.00
1930, Goodyear Tire, Scene of Baby In Tub 18.00
1933, Keen Kutter 90.00
1936, Great Northern Railroad, Indian Art 68.00
1936, Tucson Saddle Shop, Russell Print 95.00
1937, Henry Ford, Reprint, Folded, 12 x 18 In. 12.00
1937, Woman With Roses 20.00
1940, Columbian Manila Rope 40.00
1940, Keen Kutter 60.00
1942, Texaco, Pinup 38.00
1943, Dunkirk Lumber & Coal, Maxwell Parrish, 12 x 24 In. 55.00
1943, Endicott Johnson Shoes 20.00
1943, Federal Motor Truck Co., Metal Bands, 34 x 16 In. 155.00
1945, American Way, Norman Rockwell 50.00
1945, Calif. Grocery Store, Girl & Dog Looking, Army Plane 17.50
1945, How Nong Chinese Herb Co., Oakland, Ca., 10 x 16 In. 12.50
1945, Pinup, Forever Yours, Rolf Armstrong, 16 x 33 In. 150.00
1946, Audubon, 4 Prints 50.00
1946, Evening Star, Full Figured Nude, E. Moran, 16 x 33 In. 175.00
1946, Orange Crush 150.00
1947, Pepsi–Cola 85.00
1947, Petty, Fawcett Publications, Envelope 50.00
1948, Dr Pepper 95.00
1949, Grapette 24.00
1949, Pinup, Miss Mercury, Rolf Armstrong, 16 x 33 In. 135.00
1949, Speedway Oil 7.50
1950, John Deere 90.00
1950, Pinup, Irresistible, Rolf Armstrong, 11 x 23 In. 75.00
1950, TWA 20.00
1951, Arkansas Cotton Oil Co. 25.00
1951, Union Pacific 20.00
1953, Allis Chalmer, Unopened 18.00
1953, Esquire, Complete 24.00
1955, Marilyn Monroe, Golden Dreams 75.00
1955, Stepping Out, Girl, Evening Dress, Elvgrin, 16 x 33 In. 85.00
1957, Field & Stream, Hunting & Fishing Pictures 75.00
1957, Meadow Gold 8.50
1957, Sun Crest Cola 28.00
1960, Jayne Mansfield, Studio Secrets 40.00
1961, Chessie Railroad 12.00
1964, 6 Landscape Prints, Boxed, Image Size, 10 x 10 In. 345.00
1971, Trolley Cars, 8 1/2 x 11 In. 20.00
1980, Vargo 45.00

Calendar plates were very popular in the United States from 1906 to 1929. Since then, plates have been made every year. A calendar and the name of a store, a picture of flowers, a girl, or a scene were featured on the plate.

CALENDAR PLATE, 1906, Indian, Calendar Headdress Center, Imperial China 60.00
1908, Dog 55.00
1908, Dog Portrait Center 55.00
1908, Roses 55.00
1909, Baker, Jeweler, Iowa Falls, Iowa 35.00
1909, Cerro Gordo, Illinois, Grocery Store 18.00

1909, Compliments of Graham & Johnston, Kansas City, Mo.	30.00
1909, Horsehead Center, Green Calendar	22.00
1909, Queen Louise Portrait	26.00
1909, Scenic	25.00
1910, Boxer Dog Portrait, 7 1/2 In.	45.00
1910, Gibson–Type Girl Portrait, Carnation–McNichol	30.00
1910, Lighthouse, Pope Gosser, Advertising	30.00
1910, Motor Girl	38.00
1910, Swimming Hole Scene	32.00
1910, Woman, Elaborate Hat, Abbottstown, Globe China, 6 In.	30.00
1911, Bird Dogs Center	35.00
1911, Cherub Center, Cash Grocery Store, Hoopston, Ill.	40.00
1911, Irises & Christmas Scenes	25.00
1911, Lincoln's Portrait	75.00
1912, Airplanes, Peterson Bros., Hawley, Minn.	25.00
1913, Nuremburg, Penna., Cherubs & Floral	30.00
1914, Roses, Ed. Bernhard, Baltimore, Md., Dresden	30.00
1915, Panama Canal, Ark House Furnishing, Calif., 6 1/4 In.	35.00
1916, 2 Birds, Edwin Magargee, Family Liquor Store	37.50
1917, Cat	25.00
1919, Flag	35.00
1919, Ship Scene	25.00
1920, American Eagle & Victory, Great World War, Minn.	32.00
1920, Victory–Peace	35.00
1923, Hudsonville, Mich., Advertising	35.00
1928, Deer	50.00
1930, Dutch Boy With Dog	50.00
1954, Fiesta	20.00
1962, Merry Christmas, Gately's	15.00
1964, Pebbleford, Pink, Advertising	8.00
1969, God Bless Our House, Meakin	8.00
1973, Meakin, Blue	8.00
1977, Pink, Meakin	8.00

Camark Pottery started in 1924 in Camden, Arkansas. Jack Carnes founded the firm and made many types of glazes and wares. The company was bought by Mary Daniel, who still owns the firm. Production was halted in 1983.

CAMARK, Pitcher, Parrot Handle, Blue, Gold, 6 1/2 In.	45.00
Pitcher, Parrot Handle, Green	45.00
Salt & Pepper, Man, Woman, Green, Red	20.00
Vase, Red, Glossy, 6 1/2 In.	50.00
Wall Pocket, Window Box, Burgundy	10.00

Cambridge art pottery was made in Cambridge, Ohio, from about 1895 until World War I. The factory made brown glazed decorated wares with a variety of marks including an acorn, the name *Cambridge,* the name *Oakwood,* or the name *Terrhea.*

CAMBRIDGE POTTERY, Tile, Night, Morning, Large, Pair	400.00
Vase, Green, Brown, Yellow, Acorn Mark, 8 In.	95.00
Vase, Green, Brown, Yellow, Oakwood, 7 In.	75.00

Cambridge Glass Company was founded in 1901 in Cambridge, Ohio. The company closed in 1954, reopened briefly, and closed again in 1958. The firm made all types of glass. Their early wares included heavy pressed glass with the mark *Near Cut.* Later wares included Crown Tuscan, etched stemware, clear and colored glass. The firm used a C in a triangle mark after 1920.

CAMBRIDGE, see also Depression Glass

CAMBRIDGE, Apple Blossom, Candlestick, Amber, 5 In., Pair	40.00
Apple Blossom, Candlestick, Pair	25.00

Apple Blossom, Candlestick, Pink, 5 In., Pair	70.00
Apple Blossom, Claret	28.00
Apple Blossom, Nut Cup, Footed, Yellow, 3 In.	45.00
Apple Blossom, Plate, Yellow, 6 In.	8.00
Apple Blossom, Plate, Yellow, 8 1/2 In.	9.00
Apple Blossom, Salt & Pepper, Yellow	85.00
Apple Blossom, Sherbet, Yellow	18.00
Apple Blossom, Sugar & Creamer, Pink	45.00
Apple Blossom, Wine	25.00
Arcadia, Bowl, Flared, Oblong, 11 x 13 In.	25.00
Aurora, Sherbet, Green	10.00
Bashful Charlotte, Flower Frog, 8 1/2 In.	65.00
Bookends, Eagle, Pair	150.00
Buzz Saw, Compote, Nearcut, Ruffled Edge, Signed, 6 In.	20.00
Buzz Saw, Nappy, Nearcut, 6 In.	17.50
Calla Lily, Candlestick, Gold, Pair	40.00
Calla Lily, Candlestick, Green, 6 1/2 In., Pair	65.00
Caprice Alpine, Candy Box, Cover, 3–Footed, 6 In.	30.00
Caprice, Ashtray, Gold, 3 In.	5.00
Caprice, Bowl, 12 In.	180.00
Caprice, Bowl, 4–Footed, Blue, 12 1/2 In.	65.00 To 70.00
Caprice, Bowl, 4–Footed, Oval, 11 In.	50.00
Caprice, Bowl, 4–Footed, Silver Overlay, 13 1/2 In.	58.00
Caprice, Bowl, Emerald, 13 In.	55.00
Caprice, Bowl, Ruffled, Blue, 10 In.	65.00
Caprice, Box, Cigarette, Blue, Cover, Small	27.50
Caprice, Box, Cigarette, Blue, Dolphin	43.00
Caprice, Box, Cover, Moonlight Blue, 3 1/2 x 2 1/2 In.	37.50
Caprice, Candleholder, Blue, 7 In., Pair	75.00
Caprice, Candleholder, Pair	50.00
Caprice, Candlestick, 3–Light, Blue, Pair	500.00
Caprice, Cocktail	15.00
Caprice, Compote, Blue, 6 In.	95.00
Caprice, Compote, Silver Design, Footed, 7 In.	30.00
Caprice, Cup & Saucer, Blue	40.00
Caprice, Cup & Saucer, Mocha	25.00
Caprice, Cup & Saucer, Pistachio	30.00
Caprice, Dish, Mayonnaise, Blue, Spoon	65.00
Caprice, Pitcher, Juice, Blue	250.00
Caprice, Plate, 9 1/2 In.	35.00
Caprice, Plate, Blue, 7 1/2 In.	18.00
Caprice, Plate, Blue, 8 1/2 In.	22.00
Caprice, Plate, Blue, 9 1/2 In.	95.00
Caprice, Relish, 3 Sections, 8 In.	35.00
Caprice, Rose Bowl, Blue, 8 In.	150.00
Caprice, Sugar & Creamer, 3 In.	45.00
Caprice, Sugar & Creamer, Blue, Individual	35.00
Caprice, Tumbler, 5 Oz.	16.00
Caprice, Tumbler, Juice, Blue	15.00
Caprice, Tumbler, Pink, 10 Oz.	50.00
Chantilly, Candlestick, Pair	60.00
Chantilly, Candy Dish, 3 Sections, Sterling Silver Knob	50.00
Chantilly, Compote, 5 In.	30.00 To 34.00
Chantilly, Cruet, Oil	30.00
Chantilly, Dish, Divided, Sterling Base, 6 In.	35.00
Chantilly, Goblet, 7 3/4 In.	20.00
Chantilly, Salt & Pepper, Sterling Top	22.00
Chelsea, Butter, Cover	50.00
Chelsea, Vase, Violet, Cut Flowers, 4 5/8 In.	50.00
Cleo, Bowl, 10 In.	45.00
Cleo, Cup & Saucer	12.00
Cleo, Ice Tub, Green	48.00
Cleo, Plate, Amber, 9 1/2 In.	20.00

◆◆◆

If you reupholster an antique piece of furniture, save some of the original fabric. Put it in an envelope and tape it to the bottom of the seat so future owners know more about the original appearance. When selling a piece, this sort of history will add to the value.

◆◆◆

Cleo, Tray, 11 In.	13.00
Colonial, Butter, Cover, Child's, Blue	20.00
Colonial, Sugar, Cover, Child's, Blue	20.00
Colonial, Toothpick, Blue	30.00
Colonial, Toothpick, Green	15.00
Crown Tuscan, Ashtray	295.00
Crown Tuscan, Ashtray, 3–Footed, 4 In.	14.00
Crown Tuscan, Bowl, Ivy Ball, Footed, 8 In.	50.00
Crown Tuscan, Candelabra, Amber, Pair	40.00
Crown Tuscan, Candleholder, Cambridge, Keyhole Stem	45.00
Crown Tuscan, Candleholder, Dolphin	125.00
Crown Tuscan, Candlestick, 2–Light, Dolphin, Pair	245.00
Crown Tuscan, Candlestick, 2–Light, Keyhole Stem	45.00
Crown Tuscan, Candlestick, Shell, Dolphin	40.00
Crown Tuscan, Candy Dish, 3 Sections	65.00
Crown Tuscan, Candy Dish, Cover, 3 Sections	95.00
Crown Tuscan, Candy Dish, Cover, 3 Sections, Gold Trim	48.00
Crown Tuscan, Candy Dish, Shell Cover, Footed, Label	110.00
Crown Tuscan, Compote, Footed, 6 In.	35.00
Crown Tuscan, Dish, Cover, 3 Sections	45.00
Crown Tuscan, Ivy Ball, Amber	175.00
Crown Tuscan, Ivy Ball, Keyhole Stem, 7 1/2 In.	50.00
Crown Tuscan, Pitcher, Ball, Gold Encrusted, Portia, 64 Oz.	180.00
Crown Tuscan, Relish, 3 Sections, 3 Handles, 8 In.	25.00
Crown Tuscan, Swan, Gold Design, 8 1/2 In.	125.00
Crown Tuscan, Vase, Red Flower, Shell, 7 1/2 In.	125.00
Daffodil, Relish, 2 Sections	30.00
Decagon, Cup & Saucer, Green	15.00
Decagon, Plate, Center Handle, Gold, 11 In.	45.00
Decagon, Plate, Green, 7 1/2 In.	10.00
Decagon, Sugar & Creamer, Gold	15.00
Diane, Goblet	20.00
Diane, Ice Bucket	65.00
Diane, Jug, Ball, 80 Oz.	140.00
Diane, Keg Set, Barrel Tumblers, Tray, Amber, Black, 8 Piece	200.00
Diane, Relish, 5 Sections, Etched	30.00 To 44.00
Diane, Tumbler, Iced Tea, 12 Oz.	20.00
Diane, Vase, Gold Inlay, 10 In.	85.00
Draped Lady, Flower Frog	95.00
Draped Lady, Flower Frog, Dianthus Pink, 13 In.	175.00
Draped Lady, Flower Frog, Frosted, 8 1/2 In.	225.00
Draped Lady, Flower Frog, Green, 8 In.	120.00
Draped Lady, Flower Frog, Peachblow, 13 In.	150.00
Draped Lady, Flower Frog, Pink, 9 In.	100.00 To 125.00
Elaine, Cocktail Shaker, Metal Top	85.00
Everglade, Vase, Violet	85.00
Feather, Cake Plate, 9 1/2 In.	17.50
Fernland, Cruet	40.00
Gadroon, Relish, 3 Sections, 10 In.	30.00
Georgian, Tumbler, Amethyst, 9 Oz.	12.50
Georgian, Tumbler, Gold, 2 1/2 Oz.	15.00
Gloria, Candlestick, Pink, Pair	65.00

Gloria, Vase, Amber, 11 In.	100.00
Heatherbloom, Goblet	425.00
Heatherbloom, Plate, 6 In.	5.75
Heatherbloom, Plate, 8 1/2 In.	7.25
Heirloom, Plate, Green, 12 1/2 In.	15.00
Heirloom, Sugar & Creamer, Individual	28.00
Heirloom, Urn, Green, 9 1/2 In.	60.00
Heron, Bowl & Flower Frog, Large	135.00
Heron, Cruet	75.00
Heron, Flower Frog	45.00
Heron, Plate, Asparagus	20.00
Honeycomb, Compote, 8 In.	125.00
Hunt Scene, Claret, Pink, Gold Encrusted	40.00
Hunt Scene, Finger Bowl, Peachblow	27.50
Hunt Scene, Goblet, Pink, Gold Encrusted	40.00
Hunt Scene, Sherbet, Pink, Gold Encrusted	30.00
Jenny Lind, Basket, Amber	75.00
King Edward, Pitcher, Water, Cut, Sterling Silver Foot	95.00
Krystol, Bowl, Ivy Ball, Gold, Footed, 4 1/2 In.	20.00
Lorna, Tumbler, Royal Blue, 12 Oz., 5 Piece	220.00
Marjorie, Champagne, Etched	10.00
Marjorie, Cruet	35.00
Marjorie, Cup, 5 Oz.	4.25
Marjorie, Napkin Ring	25.00
Marjorie, Napkin Ring, Nearcut	18.00
Martha, Plate, Deviled Egg, 10 In.	25.00
Modern, Sherbet, Willow Blue, 3 1/2 In.	28.00
Mt. Vernon, Celery, Footed, Oval, 10 3/4 x 4 1/2 In.	20.00
Mt. Vernon, Compote	22.00
Mt. Vernon, Cordial Set, Decanter, 6 Cordials	75.00
Mt. Vernon, Decanter, Forest Green, Crystal Stopper, 40 Oz.	60.00
Mt. Vernon, Ice Bucket, Chrome Handle & Tongs	45.00
Mt. Vernon, Salt, 2 Handles, Amber	25.00
Mt. Vernon, Vase, Flared, Footed, 6 1/2 In.	25.00
Nautilus, Vase, Footed, Crown Tuscan, 11 In.	85.00
Nude Stem, Bowl, Ivy Ball, Cobalt	225.00
Nude Stem, Cocktail, Amethyst	70.00
Nude Stem, Cocktail, Carmen Bowl	140.00
Nude Stem, Cocktail, Ebony, Clear Bowl	125.00
Nude Stem, Compote, Carmen Bowl	175.00
Nude Stem, Compote, Cobalt, 8 In.	225.00
Nude Stem, Compote, Crown Tuscan, 5 In.	120.00
Nude Stem, Compote, Cupped Top, Carmen, 7 In.	160.00
Nude Stem, Compote, Green, Shell, Tall	550.00
Nude Stem, Compote, Shell Bowl, 6 In.	125.00
Nude Stem, Goblet, Cobalt	140.00
Nude Stem, Goblet, Green	85.00
Optic, Cruet, 2 Oz.	15.00
Orange Blossom, Tumbler, Footed	15.00
Portia, Relish, 3 Sections, 3 Handles, Gold Encrusted, 8 In.	20.00
Pristine, Cup & Saucer, Green, Etched, Demitasse	15.00
Ribbon Candy, Spooner, Ruby Stained	48.00
Rose Point, Bell	68.00
Rose Point, Bonbon, 2 Handles	25.00
Rose Point, Bonbon, Gold Border	35.00
Rose Point, Butter, Cover, Round, 5 In.	160.00
Rose Point, Cake Plate, 14 In.	85.00
Rose Point, Candleholder, 2–Light, Keyhole	30.00
Rose Point, Candlestick, 3–Light, Pair	80.00
Rose Point, Celery & Relish, 12 In.	35.00
Rose Point, Compote, Cheese, 3 x 5 7/8 In.	30.00
Rose Point, Cordial, 1 Oz.	55.00
Rose Point, Creamer	30.00

Rose Point, Cruet 149.75
Rose Point, Cup 30.00
Rose Point, Cup & Saucer 42.50
Rose Point, Dish, Honey 295.00
Rose Point, Goblet 25.00
Rose Point, Ice Bucket, Tongs .... 120.00 To 125.00
Rose Point, Marmalade, Footed 60.00
Rose Point, Plate, 10 1/4 In. 115.00
Rose Point, Plate, 6–Sided, 8 In. 20.00
Rose Point, Plate, 7 1/2 In. 15.00
Rose Point, Plate, 8 In. 15.00
Rose Point, Plate, Scalloped, 8 In. 20.00
Rose Point, Relish, 3 Sections, 6 1/2 In. 34.00
Rose Point, Relish, 3 Sections, 10 3/4 In. 52.00
Rose Point, Relish, 3 Sections, Gold 65.00
Rose Point, Salt & Pepper, Footed 55.00
Rose Point, Saucer 7.00
Rose Point, Server, Center Handle, 11 In. 110.00
Rose Point, Sherbet, 6 1/2 In. 19.00
Rose Point, Sherbet, Low 24.50
Rose Point, Sherbet, Stemmed 20.00
Rose Point, Spooner, 3 1/2 In. 35.00
Rose Point, Torte Plate, 14 In. 90.00
Rose Point, Tray, Square, 6 x 6 In. 150.00
Rose Point, Vase, Footed, Gold, 10 3/4 In. 85.00
Sea Gull, Figurine 34.00
Seashell, Box, Cigarette, Cover, Green, 4 1/2 x 3 1/2 In. 75.00
Seashell, Centerpiece 85.00
Seashell, Torte Plate, 14 In. 45.00
Swan, Carmen, 3 In. 115.00
Swan, Ebony, 3 1/2 In. 50.00
Swan, Milk Glass, 3 In. 125.00
Swan, Milk Glass, 8 1/2 In. 400.00
Swan, Mocha, Signed, 3 1/2 In. 75.00
Swan, Royal Blue, 3 In. 125.00
Tally–Ho, Cocktail Shaker, Gray Cutting 85.00
Tally–Ho, Compote, Crystal, 6 1/2 In. 10.00
Tally–Ho, Compote, Forest Green, Crystal Stem, 6 In. 45.00
Tally–Ho, Goblet, Amber, 14 Oz. 15.00
Tally–Ho, Jug, Amber, 74 Oz. 45.00
Tally–Ho, Mug, Carmen 38.00
Tally–Ho, Plate, Carmen, 9 1/2 In. 28.00
Tally–Ho, Punch Cup, Red 17.50
Tally–Ho, Sugar & Creamer 50.00
Valencia, Relish, 3 Sections, 2 Handles, 10 In. 30.00
Wildflower, Candleholder 20.00
Wildflower, Candlestick 45.00
Wildflower, Candy Dish, Cover, Gold Trim 68.00

 Cameo glass was made in much the same manner as a cameo in jewelry. Parts of the top layer of glass were cut away to reveal a different colored glass beneath. The most famous cameo glass was made during the nineteenth century.

CAMEO GLASS, see also under factory names, such as De Vez or Galle
CAMEO GLASS, Bowl, Violets & Leaves, Blue & White Ground, 3 1/4 In. 770.00
Egg, Lid, Dark Brown On Yellow Ground, Raspillar, 4 7/8 In. 1200.00
Jam Jar, White Flowers & Leaves, Blue, England, 5 1/4 In. 1625.00
Perfume Bottle, Butterfly & Floral, Sterling Lid, England 3080.00
Plate, Oriental Pagoda Scene, Intaglio Cut, England, 8 In. 1320.00
Rose Bowl, Multicolor Floral, Silver Flecked Body, England 885.00
Vase, 2 Colors, Purple Leaves & Limbs, Moda, 6 1/4 x 6 In. 750.00
Vase, Arabian Landscape, France, 15 In. 2200.00
Vase, Beige To Yellow Ground, Cut Foliage, Signed, 9 In. 795.00

Vase, Carved Clematis Branch, Front & Back, England, 7 1/2 In. 3750.00
Vase, Cut White Flowers Over Front Half, Apricot, England 3500.00
Vase, Flowers & Leaves, Citron & White, England, 6 3/4 In. 1395.00
Vase, Landscape, Lighthouse On Hill, Girhen, c.1925, 12 3/4 In. 665.00
Vase, Leaf Cluster, Gold, Ruby Overlay, Stourbridge, 16 1/4 In. 775.00
Vase, Leaves & Flowers, Pink, White Interior, England, 4 7/8 In. 850.00
Vase, Opaque Flowers & Leaves, Citron, England, 3 5/8 In. 850.00
Vase, Opaque Leaves & Flowers, Pink, England, 4 7/8 In. 850.00
Vase, Orange & Green Mums, Textured Ground, France, 10 In. 775.00
Vase, Pods & Leaves On Gold, Verrerie D' Art, 4 1/4 In. 995.00
Vase, Poppy Blossoms, Inverted Teardrop Shape, 8 1/4 In. 1835.00
Vase, Sailboats On Orange & Olive, J. Michel, 10 1/4 In. 1430.00
Vase, Shiny & Acid Finish Nudes, Erotic Positions, Green, 8 In. 665.00
Vase, White Butterflies, White Trim, Red, England, 2 3/4 In. 1100.00
Vase, White Carved Leaves & Flower, Pink, England, 4 7/8 In. 850.00
Vase, White Cut To Green Ground, Forest Green, Gem, 3 1/4 In. 3600.00
Vase, White To Vaseline Morning Glories, Ruffled, 5 x 6 In. 1100.00

CAMPAIGN, see Political

The Campbell Kids were first used as part of an advertisement for the Campbell Soup Company in 1906. The kids were created by Grace Drayton, a popular illustrator of the day. The kids were used in magazine and newspaper ads until about 1951. They were presented again in 1966; and in 1983, they were redesigned with a slimmer, more contemporary appearance.

CAMPBELL KIDS, Card, Tally, Campbell Kids Standing, 5 Different 20.00
  Cookie Jar, Bobber 355.00
  Cookie Jar, Davar, Nodder Head 195.00
  Doll, Campbell Soup 35.00
  Doll, Checked Shirt, Chef's Hat, Apron, Ideal, c.1953, 16 In. 97.50
  Doll, Girl, Cloth, 1982, 16 In. 22.00
  Doll, Googly, AM 210 .... 275.00
  Doll, Ideal, 8 In. 22.00
  Doll, Kids, Pair 18.00
  Doll, Scottish, 1960s 60.00
  Doorstop, Campbell's Soup Kid, Girl, Cast Iron, G. A. Drayton 305.00
  Game, Puzzle, Box 35.00
  Magazine Ad, Kids With Limericks, 1915 .... 8.00
  Magazine Ad, Kids, Color, Drayton, 1920s 10.00
  Mixer, Muro, Box 80.00
  Money Clip, Campbell's Soups 50.00
  Potholder, Pair 25.00
  Puzzle, Jaymar 12.00
  Salt & Pepper, Figural .... 14.00 To 45.00
  Tumbler, Campbell Soup Co., Modesto Plant, Smoky, 4 1/8 In. 18.00

Camphor glass is a cloudy white glass that has been blown or pressed. It was made by many factories in the Midwest during the mid–nineteenth century.

CAMPHOR GLASS, Candlestick, 5 In., Pair 20.00
  Creamer, 3 1/2 In. 25.00
  Plate, Flowers, 7 1/2 In. 30.00
  Rose Bowl, Violets, Green Leaves, c.1910 .... 50.00
  Vase, Hands, Holding Vase, Aqua, Pair 75.00

A candlestick is designed to hold one candle; a candelabrum has more than one arm and holds many candles. The eccentricity of the English language makes the plural of candelabrum into candelabra.

CANDELABRUM, 10–Light, Putti Figures Playing Flutes, 19th Century, Pair 9500.00
  11–Light, Gilt Bronze, Onyx, Putto Support Urn, 36 In., Pair 6050.00
  3–Light, Crimped Drip Pan, Copper, Silver Wash, 15 In., Pair 302.00
  3–Light, Cut Glass, Rococo, Bronze, Grape Vine, 18 1/2 In. 110.00
  3–Light, Scroll Arms, Silver Plate, 19 1/2 In 175.00

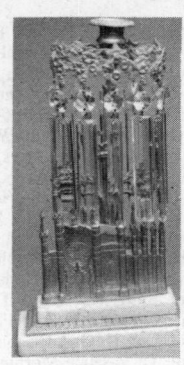

Candlestick, Brass, Bigelow Chapel,
Wm. F. Shaw, 14 1/2 In., Pair

Candelabrum, 4–Light, Bronze Dore, c.1900,
18 In., Pair

4–Light, Attached Snuffer & Shears, France 385.00
4–Light, Bronze Dore, c.1900, 18 In., Pair ....*Illus* 1700.00
5–Candle, Silver Plated, Glass, Orivit, Germany, 16 1/4 In., Pair 1900.00
5–Light, French Style, Putti, Gilt Bronze, 23 1/2 In., Pair 950.00
5–Light, Regency, Gilt Bronze, Cage Form Branches, 25 In., Pair 2200.00
5–Light, Slate & Marble Base, Bronze, Claw Feet, 19 In., Pair 70.00
6–Light, Bronze, Putto Supports, Electrified, 38 In. 2200.00
6–Light, Louis XV, Gilt Bronze, Foliate Scrolled, 26 In., Pair 2750.00
7–Light, Ormolu & Patinated Bronze, c.1810, 27 1/2 In. 4850.00
Regency, Gilt, Bronze & Crystal, 20 In., Pair 6050.00

 Candlesticks were made of brass, pewter, Sandwich glass, sterling silver, plated silver, and all types of pottery and porcelain. The earliest candlesticks, dating from the sixteenth century, held the candle on a pricket (sharp pointed spike). These lost favor because in times of strife the large church candlesticks with prickets became formidable weapons, so the socket was mandated. Candlesticks changed in style through the centuries and designs range from classic to rococo to Art Nouveau to Art Deco.

CANDLESTICK, Blue & White Latticinio Swirl Shade, Brass, 5 In. 345.00
  Brass, Baluster, Diamond Knop, Queen of Diamonds, 11 In., Pr. 275.00
  Brass, Baluster–Turned Stem, Geo Grove, 8 1/2 In., Pair 3025.00
  Brass, Beehive, 16 In. 295.00
  Brass, Bigelow Chapel, Wm. F. Shaw, 14 1/2 In., Pair ....*Illus* 303.00
  Brass, Bulbous Bobeche, Circular Foot, 12 1/2 In., Pair 715.00
  Brass, Bulbous Bobeche, Cirle Foot Stem, 11 1/2 In., Pair 110.00
  Brass, Bulbous Bobeche, Narrow Ring Stem, 12 1/2 In., Pair 715.00
  Brass, Conical Socket, Short Standard, Disc Base, 6 In., Pair 275.00
  Brass, Disc Bobeche, Disc Base, Jarvis, c.1905, 11 1/4 In., Pair 1325.00
  Brass, Disc Foot, Removable Ring Bobeches, 14 1/4 In., Pair 825.00
  Brass, Dolphin, Art Nouveau, 1890, 7 1/8 In. 185.00
  Brass, Dutch, Wide Mid–Drip Pan, 10 1/2 In. 700.00
  Brass, England, Pair 300.00
  Brass, Flared, Cylindrical Socket, Chase Brass, 8 7/8 In., Pair 275.00
  Brass, George II, Detachable Bobeches, 10 In., Pair 3700.00
  Brass, Georgian, Flaring Bobeche, Incised Knop, 9 In., Pair 4500.00
  Brass, Lamp Mounted, Pricket, Italian Neoclassical, 24 In., Pair 550.00
  Brass, Neoclassical, Pushup, 6 3/4 In., Pair 150.00
  Brass, Open Spiral Stem, 13 In., Pair 300.00
  Brass, Push–Up, 7 1/2 In., Pair 90.00
  Brass, Push–Up, 8 1/2 In., Pair 85.00

Brass, Push–Up, Beehive & Diamond Quilted, 8 In., Pair 110.00
Brass, Push–Up, Victorian, 10 3/4 In., Pair 130.00
Brass, Queen Anne, 1720, Pair 975.00
Brass, Queen of Diamonds, Insert, Pair 300.00
Brass, Short Foot, Square Base, 7 7/8 In., Pair 1600.00
Brass, Side Mounted Push–Up, Spike Ended Handle, 6 In. 300.00
Brass, Side Push–Up, 8 /4 In. 85.00
Brass, Spade Shaped Design, Circular Base, Jarvie, 14 x 6 In. 1650.00
Brass, Stem Screws Into Square Base, 8 7/8 In., Pair 90.00
Brass, Tree of Life Design, Gilt 90.00
Brass, Victorian, Diamond–Quilted, Pushup, 10 In., Pair 170.00
Brass, Woman, Gown, Candle Over Head, Art Nouveau, 10 In., Pair 195.00
Bronze, Battery Operated, Handle, Pat. 9/7/1915, 6 In. 95.00
Bronze, Disc Foot, Stylized Poppy Bud, Jarvie, 13 3/4 In. 2420.00
Bronze, Female Figure Support, Swirled Hair, c.1900, 9 3/4 In. 550.00
Bronze, Jarvie, Lota, Pair 6050.00
Bronze, Prisms, 1850, 12 In., Pair 300.00
Bronze, Robert Jarvie, Tapering Standard, c.1910, 13 7/8 In. 2200.00
Bronze, Sconce, Louis XVI, 2–Light, Ribbon Form, 12 1/2 In., Pair 375.00
Chrome, Art Deco Style, Red, Butterscotch Bakelite, Pair 95.00
Gilt Metal, Floral, Figural, Marble Base, Prisms, 15 1/2 In., Pr. 100.00
Gilt–Bronze, Portrait Head of Standard, Raingo, 11 In., Pair 2475.00
Iron, Hog Scraper, Push–Up, Hanger Missing, 6 1/2 In. 85.00
Iron, Hogscraper, Push–Up, Brass Ring, 8 In. 275.00
Iron, Hogscraper, Push–Up, Lip Hanger, 6 1/2 In. 125.00
Iron, Spiral Push–Up, Turned Wooden Base, 6 3/4 In. 225.00
Oak, Open Twist, 6 In., Pair 65.00
Oak, Twist, 12 In., Pair 85.00
Polished Stainless Steel, Geometric, 3 In., Pair 110.00
Sterling, Navarre, Pair 275.00
Tin, Saucer, Deep Dish, Flat Ring Handle, Thumb Lift, 9 x 4 In. 175.00
Turned Walnut, Brass Insert 15.00
    CANDLEWICK, see Imperial; Pressed Glass

 Candy containers have been popular since the late Victorian era. Collectors have long favored the glass containers; but now all types, including tin and papier–mache, are collected. Probably the earliest glass container sold commercially was the Liberty Bell made in 1876 for sale at the Centennial Exposition. Thousands of designs were made until the cost became too high in the 1960s. By the late 1970s, reproductions were being made and sold without the candy. Containers listed here are glass unless otherwise described.

CANDY CONTAINER, Airplane, Liberty Motors 3500.00
Airplane, No. 5 .... 20.00
Airplane, Spirit of Goodwill, Glass 175.00
Airplane, Spirit of Goodwill, Red Propeller .... 125.00 To 140.00
Airplane, Spirit of St. Louis, Painted Letters 665.00
Alarm Clock, Candy 225.00
Apple 68.00
Army Bomber 38.00
Army Tank, 2–Gun 30.00
Auto 75.00
Auto, Amos 'N' Andy .... 330.00 To 450.00
Auto, Limousine, Glass Wheels ....80.00 To 100.00
Auto, Rear Trunk, Red Wheels 115.00
Auto, Sedan, Glass 25.00
Baby Chick, Standing 65.00
Baby Deer 22.00
Baby's Bottle, Nipple, Contents 15.00
Baseball 32.00
Baseball Player, On Base, Red & Gold Paint 535.00
Battleship 32.00
Battleship, On Waves 228.00

◆ ◆

If you see any numbers or letters on the frame of a wooden piece of furniture, do not remove or erase them. They may refer to a catalog; and, eventually, you may be able to attribute the piece to the proper manufacturer.

◆ ◆

Battleship, On Waves, Clear, Original Closure	150.00
Belsnickle, Carrying Feather Tree, Papier–Mache, 7 1/2 In.	310.00
Belsnickle, Cloak, Mica Flakes, Papier–Mache, 6 1/2 In.	145.00
Belsnickle, Mica Flakes, Papier–Mache, 12 3/4 In.	500.00
Belsnickle, White Outfit, Papier–Mache, 10 In.	385.00
Billiken, Clear	100.00
Boat, 5 1/2 In.	18.00
Boot, Christmas	12.00
Boy With Snowball, Bisque, Heubach	525.00
Bugle, Glass, Brass Handle, 6 In.	65.00
Bulldog Puppy, Red Tongue, Nub Tail, Neck Closure, 5 In.	55.00
Bulldog, Black & Gold, Original Closure	50.00
Bulldog, Gold Collar	55.00
Camera On Tripod	235.00
Camera, Wooden Bulb, Tripod	275.00
Candlestick Telephone, Glass	18.00
Candy Cane, Mercury Glass, Gold	35.00
Cannon, Red Carriage & Wheels, Candy	475.00
Cannon, Tin, Glass, West Bros.	225.00
Cat, 3 In.	90.00
Cat, Cloth Dress, Glass Eyes, 6 In.	198.00
Chef, On Egg, German, 4 In.	110.00
Chick In Eggshell Auto	250.00
Chick Pull Cart, Papier Mache, Wood, Nodding Girl, 9 In.	205.00
Chicken, Wing Closure, Glass Eyes, Feather Tail, 10 In.	65.00
Child Dressed As Rabbit, Eyes To Side, Bisque, 7 In.	375.00
Child, Naked	35.00 To 65.00
Circus Dog, Hat, Clear	18.00
Circus Wagon	90.00
Clock	32.00
Clown, Rabbit, Clowns Feet, Nodding, Glass Eyes, 10 In.	1775.00
Desk Telephone, Glass	12.00
Dirigible, Los Angeles	150.00 To 200.00
Dog, Beagle, Nodder Head, Brown & White, Germany	140.00
Dog, Glass	9.00
Dog, Paper Hat With Plume, Glass	18.00
Dog, Scotty, Bottom Closure	7.00
Dog, Scotty, Top Closure	12.00
Donkey & Cart, Ceramic	10.00
Drug Store	18.00 To 20.00
Duck, Blue Dress, Pink Hat, Glass Eyes, 4 1/2 In.	55.00
Dutch Windmill	50.00
Dutch Windmill, Yellow Glass	75.00
Easter Egg, 12 x 15 In.	150.00
Elephant, Swallowtail Suit, Tin Cap	200.00
Elf, Papier–Mache With Wood, Cloth & Paper, 7 1/4 In.	125.00
Father Christmas Astride Burro, Composition, Wood, 11 In.	3425.00
Fido	25.00
Fire Engine, 5 In.	70.00
Fire Engine, Blue Glass	90.00
Fire Engine, Glass	14.00
Fire Engine, Large Boiler	50.00

Fire Station, Tin, 1914	40.00
Fish, Papier–Mache, Glass Eyes, Germany, 7 1/2 In.	187.00
Foxy Grandpa, Riding Rabbit, Papier–Mache	675.00
Gas Pump	150.00
Gene Autry, Guitar	75.00
George Washington, Bisque Head, On Horse, Germany, 11 In.	775.00
George Washington, On Horse, Composition & Wood	995.00
Globe, On Stand, Glass, Pot Metal, 4 1/2 In.	457.00
Grandpa, Mohair Rabbit, Glass, Blue Suit, Yellow Hat, 7 In.	495.00
Gun, Contents	38.00
Gun, Glass, 8 In.	35.00
Gun, Metal	59.00
Hat, Dresden	42.00
Hat, Tin Brim, Candy	125.00
Henny Penny, Yellow Body, Dotted Kerchief, Germany, 5 In.	50.00
Horn, 3–Valve	100.00
Horn, Glass, Large	18.00
Horse, Pulling Cart	8.50
Hot Doggie, Amber, Some Original Paint, 1925	350.00
House of Glass, Original Closure	150.00
Independence Hall	350.00
Iron, Electric	60.00
Jack–O'–Lantern, Papier–Mache	45.00
Jack–O'–Lantern, Papier–Mache, 4 In.	35.00
Jackie Coogan	950.00
Kewpie By Barrel	45.00
Kitten, Gray, Stripes, Glass Eyes, Crouching, 6 In.	125.00
Koala Bear	45.00
Lantern, Brass Closure	12.00
Lantern, Dietz	45.00
Lantern, Glass	35.00
Lantern, Glass & Tin, Avon, Small	18.00
Lantern, No. 391	20.00
Lantern, Red & Black Top, Contents	15.00
Liberty Bell, Amber	75.00
Liberty Bell, Green	75.00
Mailbox, Souvenir of Monroe, N. J. .... 200.00 To	215.00
Mau–U–Moon, Papier–Mache, Germany, 7 In.	225.00
Moon Mullins, Shaker Top	30.00
Mule, Pulling Barrel	80.00
Mule, Pulling Wagon	45.00
Opera Glasses, Clear, Gold, Lids	65.00
Pear	68.00
Peter Rabbit, Pull Toy, 1952	46.00
Pez, Angel	4.00
Pez, Barney Bear, Free Watercolor Paint Set	25.00
Pez, Boy, Blue Cap, Blond Hair	20.00
Pez, Camel, Whistle Head	30.00
Pez, Captain Hook	20.00
Pez, Casper	64.00
Pez, Cat With Derby, Orange Hat, Black Face	20.00
Pez, Cocoa Marsh Space Man, Navy Blue	100.00
Pez, Crocodile	50.00
Pez, Dalmations, Canada, 1989	8.00
Pez, Doctor	25.00
Pez, Duck With Flower, Green Face, Yellow Lips, Red Flowers	25.00
Pez, Easter Bunny	15.00
Pez, Engineer	35.00
Pez, Fireman	15.00
Pez, Football Player, Red Helmet, Face Mask, Box	140.00
Pez, Football Player, White Stripe, Face Mask, Mouth Guard	90.00
Pez, Frankenstein	150.00
Pez, Garfield	10.00

Pez, Gorilla, Dark Brown Face, Red Eyes	12.00
Pez, Indian Chief	40.00
Pez, Indian Squaw	33.00
Pez, Joker, Soft Head	50.00
Pez, Knight, Red Plume	60.00
Pez, Lamp, Whistle Head	17.00
Pez, Lion With Crown	20.00
Pez, Little Bad Wolf	30.00
Pez, Maharajah	20.00
Pez, Mary Poppins	250.00
Pez, Mexican	36.00
Pez, Monkey Sailor	15.00
Pez, Monster Octopus, 1970s	30.00
Pez, Mr. Ugly	5.00
Pez, Nurse, Blonde	25.00
Pez, Penguin, Whistle Head	18.00
Pez, Pirate	40.00
Pez, Policeman	12.00 To 15.00
Pez, Raven, Black Head, Yellow Beak, Red Glasses	8.00
Pez, Ringmaster	25.00
Pez, Robot, Full–Bodied	125.00
Pez, Rooster, White Face	15.00
Pez, Sheik	40.00
Pez, Sheriff	30.00
Pez, Spiderman	8.00
Pez, Totem Fireman	25.00
Pez, Uncle Sam	33.00
Pez, Wonder Woman, Soft Head	20.00
Pez, Yappy Dog, Green	100.00
Pez, Zombi, Soft Head	65.00
Pig, Germany	145.00
Pig, Papier–Mache, Germany	98.00
Pistol, 8 In.	30.00
Pistol, Glass	7.50
Plane, Tin Wing & Prop, Candy, Label	85.00
Pony Cart, Glass	8.00
Porky Pig, Papier–Mache	65.00
Potato, 5 1/2 In.	40.00
Princess Theater	26.00
Pug, Glass Eyes, Germany, 3 1/2 In.	286.00
Pug, With Blanket, Glass Eyes, Germany, 5 In.	300.00
Pumpkin Man, 3 In.	140.00
Pumpkin, Papier–Mache, 9 In.	20.00
Puppy	12.00
Rabbit In Carriage, Fur–Covered, Twig Cart	3500.00
Rabbit In Egg, Germany	58.00
Rabbit, Ears Back	50.00
Rabbit, Emerging From Pink Egg, Gold	40.00
Rabbit, Glass Eyes, Wooden Legs, 11 In.	195.00
Rabbit, Millstien	20.00
Rabbit, Nibbling Carrot	30.00
Rabbit, Nodder, Papier–Mache, Germany	25.00
Rabbit, On Accordion, Papier–Mache, Cloth, Radish, 10 In.	1980.00
Rabbit, Papier–Mache, Germany, 9 In.	22.00
Rabbit, Pulling Babies, Pull Toy	40.00
Rabbit, Pushing Cart	425.00
Rabbit, Pushing Wheelbarrow, Original Closure	135.00
Rabbit, Running On Log	175.00 To 240.00
Rabbit, Seated, Glasses, German, 5 In.	250.00
Rabbit, Sitting, Wood Stake Legs, Neck Closure, 8 In.	80.00
Rabbit, White Fur, Glass Eyes, Lithographed Ears, 6 1/2 In.	80.00
Reindeer, Antlers, Painted Eyes, 6 In.	105.00
Rocking Horse, Clear	175.00

Rooster Head	175.00
Rooster, Japan	75.00
Santa Claus Head, Papier–Mache, 3 3/4 In.	715.00
Santa Claus, Bisque Head, Cloth & Papier–Mache Body, 8 In.	615.00
Santa Claus, Blue Pants, Black Boots, Fur Face, 7 In.	295.00
Santa Claus, Christmas Colors, Unused, 1920s	18.00
Santa Claus, Cotton, Body Separates, Occupied Japan	89.00
Santa Claus, Feather Tree Sprig, Germany, 5 1/2 In.	215.00
Santa Claus, German, 9 In.	340.00
Santa Claus, In Car, Wood Wheels	275.00
Santa Claus, Leaving Chimney, Original Closure	90.00
Santa Claus, Long Coat, Fur, Holding Feather Tree, 8 In.	310.00
Santa Claus, Nodder, Papier–Mache, 14 In.	50.00
Santa Claus, Nodding, 14 In.	24.00
Santa Claus, Painted Glass, Original Closure, 5 In.	220.00
Santa Claus, Papier–Mache, 10 In.	48.00
Santa Claus, Red Coat, Mittens, Germany, 1920s, 8 1/4 In.	140.00
Santa Claus, Sleigh & Reindeer, Fur, Log Sled, 10 In.	995.00
Santa's Boot, Candy & Label	20.00
Santa's Face, Chenille	70.00
Scotty	12.00
Snowman	35.00
Space Gun	45.00
Spark Plug, The Horse, Glass	125.00
Stage Coach, Crystal	127.00
Station Wagon .... 35.00 To 38.00
Submarine, Glass, Tin Litho, 5 1/2 In.	380.00
Suitcase, Clear Glass	50.00
Suitcase, Milk Glass	50.00
Suitcase, Tin Closure, Wire Handle	70.00
Tank, No. 724 .... 22.00 To 30.00
Taxi, 6 Vents, Yellow Glass	60.00
Train, Glass	25.00
Train, Tin Cap	120.00
Trophy, 3 Handles, Gold Gilt	121.00
Truck, Gasoline	35.00
Trunk, Gold Trim, Milk Glass	135.00
Tune In Radio	85.00
Turkey, Back Closure, 5 1/2 In.	43.00
Turkey, Candy	140.00
Turkey, Molded, Metal Feet, Neck Closure, 6 In.	65.00
Turkey, Painted Detail, Bottom Closure, 4 In.	20.00
Ugly Duckling	121.00
Vegetable Person, With Glasses, Purse, Germany, 3 1/2 In.	210.00
Wheelbarrow, Red	75.00
Wooly Dog, Basket of Toys, Germany, 5 1/2 In.	100.00
World Globe, No Stand, No. 276	200.00

Canes and walking sticks were used by every well–dressed man in the nineteenth century, but by World War I the style had changed. Today canes are used by few but the infirm. Collectors prize old canes made with special features such as hidden swords, whiskey flasks, or risque pictures seen through peepholes. Examples with solid gold heads or made from exotic materials such as walrus vertebrae are among the higher priced canes.

CANE, 9K Gold Knopped Head, Name & Date, Simons Bro., Ebonized, 35 In.	330.00
African Head Handle, Carved, Tree Root Shaft, Brass Tip ....*Illus*	95.00
Bird Handle, Carved, All 1 Piece, Brass Tip ....*Illus*	300.00
Bird's Head, Carved, Blackthorn, All 1 Piece ....*Illus*	185.00
Boxers, Carved Portraits, American, 1900, 37 In.	1650.00
Caricature Head, Don Quixote–Type, Large	575.00
Carnival, Elephant Head, Ball & Claw Foot, Japan	75.00
Child's, Ivory & Bone Handle, 19 In.	65.00

Dog Head Handle, Malacca Shaft, Sterling Ferrule ....*Illus*   160.00
Dog Head, Carved, 34 1/2 In. 85.00
Duck Handle, Iron, Caps 125.00
Eagle, Snakes, Figures, Carved Allover, Mustard Paint 750.00
Engraved Silver Head, Horn Tip, Rosewood, 36 In. 300.00
Glass, Aqua, Twisted Handle & Tip, 30 In. 110.00
Glass, Burgundy Swirl Stripes, Baton Top, 58 In. 225.00
Glass, Honey Amber, Ribbed Handle, Square Body, Corkscrew Base, 33 In. 195.00
Gold Plate, Engraved P. I. Perrin, 35 In. 265.00
Hand Clutching An Ivory Rod, Carved 350.00
Head, Ivory, Carved Eagle & Shield, Gilt Ferrule, 36 In. 300.00
Horn Handle, Carved Trotter Nancy Hanks, Signed T. W. Moore, 35 In. 1540.00
Indian Chief's Head, Deer Head, Elf, Old Dutch Girl, 38 In. 200.00
Man With Mustache, Carved, Handle, Black Walnut Shaft ....*Illus*   400.00
Parade, American Legion Convention, Milk Glass Dome Lights Up, 1940 ....   85.00
Puzzle, Ball Handle, Snake Entwined Shaft, S. S. A., Dated 1861, 37 In. 330.00
Puzzle, Pig, Eats, Corn Ear, Herbert Borders, Late 19th Century, 39 In. 6600.00
Puzzle, Wooden, T–Shaped Handle, America, Late 19th Century, 35 In. 495.00
Reeded Head, Ebonized Shaft, Horn Tip, Late 19th Century, 33 1/2 In. 247.50
Rosewood, Whale's Tooth Handle, 30 3/4 In. 65.00
Silver Plate, Band Engraved E. P. Morrill, Manchester, N. H., 35 1/2 In. 190.00
Skull, Metal, White 195.00
Stag, Ivory, Ebonzied Shank, Ivory Button Knotholes, 36 In. 175.00
Sword, Greyhound Handle 115.00
Sword, Lion Head Finial, Ivory, Brass Handle 150.00
Walking Stick, Amethyst Head, Pierced Gold Borders, Ebony, 32 In. 275.00
Walking Stick, Bamboo Turnings, Silver Cap, Walnut, Dated 1812, 34 In. 120.00
Walking Stick, Blue & Brown Swirls, Blown Glass, 43 1/2 In. 30.00
Walking Stick, Curly Maple, Brown Patina, 36 1/4 In. 55.00
Walking Stick, Engraved Christmas 1885, Gold Handle 180.00
Walking Stick, Engraved Sallie Burton, Lignum Vitae, 33 3/4 In. 75.00
Walking Stick, Glass, Spiral Threading, Glass, 44 1/4 In. 115.00
Walking Stick, Head, Ivory, Bears Attacking Man & Woman, 34 1/2 In. 400.00
Walking Stick, Hound With Hunting Cap 85.00
Walking Stick, Indian Head, Ivory, Headdress, Ivory Tip, 34 1/2 In. 500.00
Walking Stick, Ivory Head of Bearded Man, Carved, Walnut, 34 1/4 In. 100.00
Walking Stick, Man, Carved, Fleur–De–Lis, H. S. Nimz, S. D., 1917, 37 In. 715.00
Walking Stick, Miller With Sack of Grain, Carved, c.1840, 83 In. 650.00
Walking Stick, Silver Handle, Art Nouveau Flowers, 36 1/4 In. 110.00
Walking Stick, Silver Handle, Horn Tip, Rosewood, 37 1/4 In. 125.00
Walking Stick, Sterling Silver Handle, Eagle, Glass Eyes, 38 In. 335.00

Cane, African Head Handle, Carved,
Tree Root Shaft, Brass Tip
Cane, Dog Head Handle, Malacca Shaft,
Sterling Ferrule

Cane, Bird Handle, Carved, All 1 Piece, Brass Tip
Cane, Man With Mustache, Carved, Handle,
Black Walnut Shaft
Cane, Bird's Head, Carved, Blackthorn, All 1 Piece

Walking Stick, Tortoiseshell, Gold Handle, Continental, 34 In. 1100.00
Walking Stick, Whale's Tooth Handle, Rosewood, 30 3/4 In. 65.00
Walking Stick, Woman's, Coin Silver Maiden's Head Handle, 34 1/4 In. 255.00
Walking Stick, Woman's, Wilver Repousse Handle, 35 1/2 In. 110.00
Whale Ivory, Fist With Coiled Snake Shape, Tapered Shaft, 34 3/4 In. 650.00
White Twisted Ribbon Inside, Crook Handle, Glass, 18 1/2 In. 125.00

Caneware is a tan–colored, unglazed stoneware that was first developed by Josiah Wedgwood about 1770. It has been made by many companies since that time and is often used for cooking or serving utensils.

CANEWARE, Basket, Twisted Handle, Woven Sides, 8 In. 150.00
Game Dish, Cover, Hare Finial, Wedgwood, Oval, c.1865, 5 5/8 x 8 In. 415.00
Game Dish, Strap Handle, Grape Vines, Wedgwood, 8 x 10 1/2 In. 525.00
Tureen, Cover With Rabbit, c.1810 .... 350.00

Canton china is blue–and–white ware made near Canton, China, from about 1785 to 1895. It is hand decorated with Chinese scenes.

CANTON, Basket, Undertray, Reticulated 275.00
Bowl, Scalloped Rim, 4 1/2 x 10 1/2 In. 575.00
Bowl, Square 825.00
Box, Cover, Rectangular, 7 1/4 In. 1100.00
Candlestick 1265.00
Coffeepot, Fruit Finial, Intertwined Handle, 7 In. 800.00
Creamer, Helmet Shape, 5 In. 400.00
Dish, Cover, Almond Shape, Blue & White, 8 In. 100.00
Dish, Cover, Chinese River Scene, Blue & White, 7 3/4 x 9 1/4 In. 250.00
Dish, Cover, Embossed Finial, Boar's Head Handles, 7 In. 450.00
Dish, Cover, Fruit Finial, Almond Shape, 10 1/4 In. 500.00
Dish, Cover, Fruit Finial, Insert, 11 In. 900.00
Dish, Cover, Fruit Finial, Rectangular, 8 3/8 In. 375.00
Dish, Diamond Shape, 10 In. 275.00
Dish, Serving, Cover, Landscape, 11 1/2 In. ....*Illus* 550.00
Dish, Shrimp 2035.00
Fish Tank, Floral, Carved Wooden Stand 6875.00
Ginger Jar, Blue & White, Porcelain, Floral, Wood Base, 8 In. 495.00
Pen Box, Rectangular, Blue & White, 7 1/4 In. 1100.00
Pitcher, Cider, Cover, 19th Century, 6 3/4 In. 1045.00
Plate, Hot Water, 9 1/8 In. 200.00
Plate, Kidney Shape 385.00
Plate, Scalloped, 9 1/4 In. 770.00

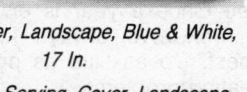

Canton, Platter, Landscape, Blue & White, 17 In.

Canton, Tureen, Cover, Boar's Handle, Landscape, 13 In.

Canton, Dish, Serving, Cover, Landscape, 11 1/2 In.

Platter, 14 1/2 In. .... 325.00 To 350.00
Platter, 19 5/8 In. 600.00
Platter, Birds, Butterflies & Floral, Gilt Rim, 11 1/4 x 15 In. 470.00
Platter, Canted Corners, 16 x 12 1/2 In. 302.00
Platter, Landscape, Blue & White, 17 In. ....*Illus* 450.00
Platter, Native Temples & Houses On Lakeside, 17 1/2 x 14 In. 330.00
Platter, Oval, 18 1/2 In. 825.00
Platter, Village Scene, Cloud Border, 9 1/2 x 12 In. 195.00
Platter, Well & Tree, 19th Century, 15 1/2 x 12 1/2 In. 305.00
Sauceboat, Rain Cloud Border, Scalloped, 7 1/2 In. 300.00
Spittoon, Blue & White, 8 In. 2420.00
Sugar, Cover, Fruit Finial, Intertwined Handles, 5 1/8 In. 100.00
Tea Caddy, Cover, Octagonal, 6 1/2 In. .... 2500.00 To 2750.00
Tea Caddy, Village Scene, Cloud Border, 1860s, 6 1/2 In. 2200.00
Teapot, Berry Finial, Intertwined Handle, Floral Ends, 6 In. 650.00
Teapot, Village Scene, Cloud Border, 1850s, 5 1/2 In. 165.00
Tile, Tea, Village Scene, Crisscross Border, 4 7/8 In. 355.00
Tray, Leaf Shape, 7 1/2 In. 250.00
Tray, Quaterfoil, 7 3/4 In. 250.00
Tray, Quatrefoil, 11 x 9 In. 575.00
Tureen, Cover, Boar's Handle, Landscape, 13 In. ....*Illus* 715.00
Tureen, Embossed Finial, Boar's Head Handles, 12 in. 1325.00

N

Capo–di–Monte porcelain was first made in Naples, Italy, from 1743 to 1759. The factory moved near Madrid, Spain, reopened in 1771, and worked to 1834. Since that time the Doccia factory of Italy acquired the molds and is using the N and crown mark. Societe Richard Ceramica is a modern–day firm often referred to as Ginori or Capo–di–Monte. This company uses the crown and N mark.

CAPO–DI–MONTE, Bowl, Gilt Floral Swags, 3 Surrounding Dancing Maids, 8 In. 495.00
Box, Dresser, Green, Gold, Pink & Yellow 110.00
Box, Jewelry, Brown & Ivory, 4 Curved Feet, Roses Inside 80.00
Clock, Mantel, Putto Finial, Floral Case, Late 19th Century 550.00
Cup & Saucer, 2 Handles, c.1860 .... 165.00
Dinner Set, Napoleon & Josephine, Bee Mark 1265.00
Figurine, African Crowned Crane, Plants, G. Armani, 14 In. 175.00
Figurine, Chestnut Vendor, Urchin, G. Armani, 8 x 10 In. 250.00
Figurine, Chestnut Vendor, Woman, Stove, G. Armani, 8 x 10 In. 250.00
Figurine, Fisherman, Tasseled Cap, Smoking Pipe, 10 1/2 In. 175.00
Figurine, Hunter, With Dog, Large 275.00
Figurine, Young Photographer, Marked, 9 1/2 x 8 1/2 In. 125.00
Ginger Jar, Court Scene, 12 In. 225.00
Urn, Cover, Cherub Handles, Nymphs & Cherubs Panels, 20 In. 650.00
Urn, Cover, Cherubs, Grapes, Bacchus Head Handles, 7 x 15 In. 450.00
Urn, Cover, Fruit Finial, Allegorical Figures, 20 In., Pair 525.00
Urn, Figural Landscape & Geometric Design, 11 1/4 In. 45.00
Urn, Figural Landscape, Geometric, Scroll Handles, 11 1/4 In. 40.00
Urn, Hand Painted Scenes, Crown Mark, 22 x 11 In., Pair 3500.00
Urn, Molded Cherubs & Grapes, Head Handles, 15 x 7 1/2 In. 375.00
Urn, Seminude Women & Men, Gold Loop Handles, 13 1/2 In. 325.00
Urn, Winged Cherub Handles, Nymphs & Cherubs, 12 x 20 In. 650.00
Vase, Ram's Head Handles, Pedestal, 7 1/2 In. 275.00

◆◆◆

Infrequent waxing of furniture is best. Once a year is enough. Go heavy on elbow grease; light on wax....We always knew lazy housekeeping with antiques is the best. Do as little as possible to clean and shine pieces and avoid creating problems.

◆◆◆

Captain Marvel was introduced in February 1940 in Whiz comic books. An orphan named Billy Batson met the wizard Shazam and whenever he said the magic word he was transformed into a superhero. A movie serial was released in 1940. The comic was discontinued in 1954. A second Captain Marvel appeared in 1966, a third in 1967. Only the original was transformed by shouting *Shazam*.

CAPTAIN MARVEL, Bank, Dime	150.00
Book, Coloring, 1941	85.00
Book, Coloring, Giant Comic, 1975	12.00
Card, Membership Club, 1940	75.00
Magic Flute	40.00
Paper Dolls, 3 Flying Marvels, Envelope, Unused	100.00
Punch–Out, Captain Marvel, Jr., Paper, Envelope	16.00
Sheet, Secret Message	25.00
Toy, Captain Marvel, Jr., Ski Jump	45.00
Watch, Box, 1948, Unused	750.00
Whistle, Power Siren, 2 1/3 In.	25.00

Captain Midnight began as a radio show in September 1940. The first comic book appeared in July 1941. Captain Midnight was really the aviator Captain Albright, who was to defeat the Nazis. A movie serial was made in 1942 and a comic strip was published for a short time. The comic book Captain Midnight ended his career in 1948. The radio premiums are the prized collector memorabilia today.

CAPTAIN MIDNIGHT, Bank, Magic Dime Saver, Tin, Octagonal	145.00
Book, Riddle	25.00
Book, Trick & Riddle	40.00
Decoder Badge, Secret Squadron	80.00
Decoder, 1945	60.00 To 110.00
Decoder, 1949	25.00
Medal, Flight Patrol	25.00
Ring, Secret	65.00
Secret Squadron Decoder Key, Manual, 1949	200.00
Whistle, Code–O–Graph	65.00

CARAMEL SLAG, see Chocolate Glass

The cards listed here include advertising cards, greeting cards, baseball cards, playing cards, valentines, and others. Color pictures were rare in the nineteenth century, so companies gave away colorful cards with pictures of children, flowers, products, or related scenes that promoted the company name. These were often collected and stored in albums. Greeting cards are also a nineteenth–century idea that has remained popular. Baseball cards also date from the nineteenth century when they were used by tobacco companies as giveaways. The gum cards were started in 1933, but it was not until after World War II that the bubble gum cards favored today were produced. Today over 1,000 cards are issued each year by the gum companies.

CARD, see also Postcard

CARD, Advertising, Arbuckle Coffee, Map of Alaska, 5 Scenes, 5 x 3 In.	5.50
Advertising, Ayers Cherry Pectoral, Penn's Treaty, 1883, 2 1/2 x 4 In.	7.00
Advertising, Barr Dry Goods Store, Girl, Dolls, 1880, 4 1/4 x 3 In.	7.50
Advertising, Canfield Dress Shields, Woman, Open Blouse Shows Shields	12.00
Advertising, Dr. Thomas Electric Oil, Woman With Roses, 5 x 6 1/2 In.	10.00
Advertising, Duke Cigarettes, Man, Coon, 1889, 1 1/2 x 2 3/4 In.	15.00
Advertising, Estey Organ Co., Girl With Harp, 1885, 3 x 5 In.	12.50
Advertising, Flasher, Post Corn Flakes, Danny Thomas Winks Eye, 1950s	24.00
Advertising, Gail Borden Eagle Brand, Girl In Pink Pointing To Can	10.00
Advertising, Greatest 10 Cent Show On Earth, 1885, 4 x 2 1/2 In.	20.00
Advertising, Hires Root Beer, Little Boy, 1898	50.00

Advertising, J & P Coats Thread, Boy Delivering Box To Spinster, 1900	15.00
Advertising, J. J. Bamburg & Co., Clothiers, 1882, 4 1/2 x 5 1/2 In.	27.50
Advertising, Lorillard's 5 Cent Anti Fine Cut Tobacco, Girl, 1880s	4.00
Advertising, Merrick Thread, Angel, Driving Butterflies, 1882	6.00
Advertising, Rice's Seeds, Choice Radish Seeds, 1880, 3 x 4 1/2 In.	12.50
Advertising, Rubifoam For The Teeth, Color, 1890	20.00
Advertising, Summerfield & Roman, Clothiers, Child, 4 1/4 x 6 1/2 In.	10.00
Advertising, Thomas Electric Oil, Lovely Woman, Hat, 1888, 4 1/4 In.	10.00
Advertising, W. J. Wilson & Son, Die Cut, Child, Umbrella, 8 x 6 1/2 In.	10.00
Advertising, Yeast Foam, Black Cook, Large	55.00
Baseball, Al Rosen, Topps, 1953	22.00
Baseball, Babe Ruth, Autographed	3850.00
Baseball, Bill Ripkin, Error F Face	45.00
Baseball, Bob Feller, Bowman, 1952	65.00
Baseball, Bob Gibson, Topps, Rookie, 1959	90.00
Baseball, Brooklyn Dodgers Pennant Team, Autographed, 1955	1210.00
Baseball, Brooks Robinson, Fleer, 1963	20.00
Baseball, Casey Stengel, Bowman, 1950	75.00
Baseball, Cy Young, Autographed	2475.00
Baseball, Dave Winfield, Donruss, 1985	.50
Baseball, Don Newcombe, Bowman, 1951	20.00
Baseball, Duke Snider, Bowman, 1953	145.00
Baseball, Hank Bauer, Bowman, 1954	10.00
Baseball, Joe Garagiola, Bowman, 1951	110.00
Baseball, Lou Gehrig, Big League Chewing Gum, No. 55	220.00
Baseball, Mickey Mantle, Rookie of The Year, Topps, 1952	7150.00
Baseball, Mike Schmidt, Topps, Rookie, 1973	150.00
Baseball, Pete Rose, Topps, No. 207	90.00
Baseball, Phil Rizzuto, Topps, 1954	50.00
Baseball, Set, Topps, 1960, 572 Piece	875.00
Baseball, Ted Williams, Bowman, 1950	375.00
Baseball, Whitey Ford, Topps, 1961	18.00
Baseball, Willie Mays, Topps, 1958	120.00
Baseball, Yogi Berra, Topps, 1964	40.00
Boxer, 4 Different Photos, 1920–30, 3 1/2 x 5 1/2 In., 4 Piece	26.00
Boxer, Marciano, Sugar Ray, 3 1/2 x 5 1/2 In., 1950s, 8 Piece	34.00
Christmas, Children At Beach, Message On Back, Die Cut, c.1888	6.50
Christmas, Floral Design, Scalloped Edges, Inside Verse, c.1890	10.00
Christmas, Kind Regards, Joyful Christmas To You, 2 1/2 x 3 1/2 In.	4.00
Christmas, Santa Claus, In Plane, Children, Balcony, John Winsch, 1913	20.00
Christmas, Stream, Forest, Christmas Greetings, Raphael Tuck & Sons	7.50
Christmas, U. S. S. Arkansas, Ship Photo, 1918	15.00
Christmas, Yellow Roses In Gold Basket, c.1899, 3 1/2 x 4 1/2 In.	6.50
Cigarette, Builders of The Empire, Lithograph, c.1898, 50 Piece	235.00
Cigarette, Poker Hands, 1920s, 52 Piece	100.00
Easter Greeting, Country Store, Punch–Out, 1920	10.00
Easter, String For Hanging, Germany, 1918	10.00
Golf, Nicklaus, 1981	10.00
Gum, Addams Family, 10 Piece	20.00
Gum, Dark Shadows, 10 Piece	15.00
Gum, Rat Patrol, 36 Piece	25.00
Gum, U. N. C. L. E., 24 Piece	30.00
Hockey, Rookie Wayne Gretzky, Topps, No. 18	275.00
Lobby, All Through The Night, Bogart, Warner Bros., 1941, 14 x 22 In.	475.00
Lobby, Big Broadcast of 1938, Hope, Lamour, Paramount, 14 x 22 In.	975.00
Lobby, Fiend of Dope Island, 1950s	75.00
Lobby, First Space Ship On Venus, 1962	75.00
Lobby, Greta Garbo, Two–Faced Woman, 1941	350.00
Lobby, John Wayne, Wyoming Outlaw, 1939	400.00
Lobby, Little Rascals, Shrimps For A Day, Black & White, 11 x 14 In.	22.50
Lobby, Loves of Carmen, Rita Hayworth, 1948	55.00
Lobby, Magnetic Monster, Appliances Gone Beserk, 1950s	75.00
Lobby, Miracle On 34th Street, 1947	25.00

Lobby, Mole People, Monster, 1964 .... 45.00
Lobby, Radio Stars On Parade, Frances Langford, Ralph Edwards, 1945 .... 35.00
Lobby, Sing Baby Sing, Alice Faye, Fox, 1936, 14 x 22 In. 250.00
New Years, May Your New Year Be Happy & Bright, 4 3/4 x 5 In. 6.50
Pacific Far East Line, Ship Interiors, Black Bartender, 1960s, 2 Part 3.00
Player's Tobacco, An Album of Aeroplanes, Full Album, 1934 .... 95.00
Player's Tobacco, Kings & Queens of England, Full Album, 1935 .... 95.00
Playing, Atlantic City, In Suede Book, With Clasp, Miniature 8.00
Playing, Barbie, Mattel, c.1979 .... 6.00
Playing, Beechnut Lifesavers 15.00
Playing, Cherchez La Femme, Large Size Nudes 45.00
Playing, Diamond Crystal Salt, Logo, St. Clair, Mich. 25.00
Playing, Gold Medal Flour, Eventually, Picture, 1910s, Box 34.00
Playing, Halls Cough Drops, Doctor, With Doll, Norman Rockwell 3.50
Playing, Hoyle, Norman Rockwell, 2 Decks, Box, 1940s 48.00
Playing, King Kong, Joker, Box 30.00
Playing, Marilyn Monroe 10.00
Playing, Marilyn Monroe, Box, 1950s 90.00
Playing, Mazda Lamps 50.00
Playing, Nile Fortune Cards, Box, 1900 .... 50.00
Playing, North Western Railroad, Union Clip, 1944 .... 12.00
Playing, Pan–American Exposition, Box, 1901 .... 50.00
Playing, Petty Girl, Art Deco Faces of Eccentrics of Day, 1933, Box 18.00
Playing, Playboy Club 10.00
Playing, Pleasure Pals, Norman Rockwell, Double, Box, 1930–40 .... 75.00
Playing, Rock Island Railroad, Box, Seal, 1940s 20.00
Playing, Seedy Alka–Seltzer 30.00
Playing, Southern Pacific Railroad, Golden West Souvenir, 1910 .... 45.00
Playing, Southern Pacific Railroad, Mission Scene 25.00
Playing, Tourist, 1933 .... 10.00
Playing, W. C. Fields, How To Win At Poker, 2 Decks, Unopened 16.00
Playing, Yukon Route & White Pass 150.00
Valentine, 3 Figures, Foldout, Red Pleated Crepe Paper, 12 In. 25.00
Valentine, 4 Figures, Flowers, Silver, Crepe Paper, Pastel, 1900s, 8 In. 30.00
Valentine, Comic, Car & Accident, Early 1900s, Large 25.00
Valentine, Cut–Work, Verse, Dark Ground, Framed, Square, 15 1/2 In. 192.00
Valentine, Dolly Dingle, Eyes Go From Side To Side, Box, 6 x 6 In. 35.00
Valentine, Honey Comb 3D, Cupid, Hearts & Flowers, Set of 6, 4 In. 8.00
Valentine, Kids In Planes, Cars, 1920, Set of 105 .... 12.00
Valentine, Little Red Riding Hood, Honeycomb Tissue 4.00
Valentine, Pull Down Front, Boy With Hoop Steps Out 30.00
CARDER, see Aurene; Steuben

Carlsbad, Germany, is a mark found on china made by several factories in Germany. Most of the pieces available today were made after 1891.

CARLSBAD, Humidor, Silver Plated Pipe On Cover, Woman & Cupid, Signed 385.00
Inkstand, Lion's Paw Feet, Shepherd & Shepherdess, Quill Holders 1800.00
Pitcher, Hand Painted Flower, Ivory Ground, 9 In. 55.00
Pitcher, Twisted Gold & Silver Handle 165.00
Salt, White, Gold Inside, Flowers, Handle, 3 3/4 x 1 3/4 In. 30.00

Carlton ware was made at the Carlton Works of Stoke-on-Trent, England, about 1890. The firm traded as Wiltshaw & Robinson until 1957. It was renamed Carlton Ware Ltd. in 1958.

CARLTON WARE, Biscuit Jar, Multicolored Floral, Cobalt Blue Trim, 9 1/2 In. 110.00
Bowl, Tree In Black, Orange Flowers, Yellow Ground, 3 In. 280.00
Charger, Girl With Hoop Skirt, Parasol, 15 1/2 In. 1500.00
Dish, Leaf, Green 40.00
Hatpin Holder 42.00
Tray, Leaf 45.00

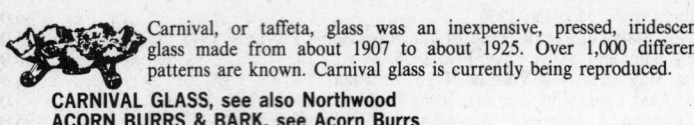 Carnival, or taffeta, glass was an inexpensive, pressed, iridescent glass made from about 1907 to about 1925. Over 1,000 different patterns are known. Carnival glass is currently being reproduced.

CARNIVAL GLASS, see also Northwood
ACORN BURRS & BARK, see Acorn Burrs
CARNIVAL GLASS, Acorn Burrs, Berry Set, Purple, 7 Piece 400.00
Acorn Burrs, Bowl, Green, 5 In., 6 Piece 295.00
Acorn Burrs, Creamer, Marigold 60.00
Acorn Burrs, Pitcher, Water, Amethyst 475.00
Acorn Burrs, Punch Cup, Ice Green 55.00
Acorn Burrs, Punch Set, Green, 7 Piece .... 1700.00 To 1800.00
Acorn Burrs, Punch Set, Marigold, 11 Piece 675.00
Acorn Burrs, Tumbler, Amethyst 50.00
Acorn Burrs, Tumbler, Green 45.00
Acorn Burrs, Water Set, Marigold, 5 Piece 650.00
Acorn Burrs, Water Set, Purple, 9 Piece 675.00
Acorn, Bowl, Marigold, 7 1/2 In. 95.00
Acorn, Bowl, Red, 7 1/2 In. 500.00
AMARYLLIS, see Tiger Lily
AMERICAN BEAUTY ROSES, see Wreath of Roses
Apple Blossom Twigs, Bowl, Peach, 9 In. 135.00
Apple Tree, Pitcher, Blue 495.00
Apple Tree, Tumbler, Marigold .... 30.00 To 50.00
AURORA, see Flowers
Autumn Acorns, Bowl, Green, 8 3/4 In. 75.00
Banded Drape, Pitcher, Blue 300.00
Banded Drape, Water Set, Marigold, 7 Piece 395.00
Banded Drape, Water Set, Marigold, 7 Piece 450.00
BANDED MEDALLION & TEARDROP, see Beaded Bull's Eye
Basket, Basket, Ice Green, Open Edge, Square 195.00
BATTENBURG LACE NO. 1, see Hearts & Flowers
BATTENBURG LACE NO. 2, see Captive Rose
BATTENBURG LACE NO. 3, see Fanciful
Beaded Bull's Eye, Vase, Purple, 11 In. 100.00
Beaded Cable, Rose Bowl, Amethyst, 4 In. 70.00
Beaded Cable, Rose Bowl, Aqua .... 235.00 To 300.00
Beaded Cable, Rose Bowl, Ice Blue 750.00
Beaded Cable, Rose Bowl, Marigold 135.00
BEADED MEDALLION & TEARDROP, see Beaded Bull's Eye
Beaded Shell, Mug, Blue 125.00
Beaded Shell, Mug, Marigold 125.00
Beaded Shell, Mug, Purple 95.00
Beaded Shell, Spooner, Blue 35.00
Beaded Shell, Tumbler, Amethyst 47.50
Beaded Shell, Tumbler, Blue 115.00
Beaded Shell, Tumbler, Purple .... 50.00 To 80.00
Birds & Cherries, Bowl, Ruffled, Blue, 9 1/2 In. .... 475.00 To 495.00
Birds & Cherries, Bowl, Ruffled, Purple, 9 1/2 In. 40.00
BIRDS ON BOUGH, see Birds & Cherries
BLACKBERRY & CHECKERBOARD, see Blackberry Block
BLACKBERRY A., see Blackberry
BLACKBERRY B., see Blackberry Spray
Blackberry Block, Tumbler, Marigold .... 25.00 To 30.00
Blackberry Spray, Hat, Red .... 300.00 To 375.00
Blackberry Wreath, Bowl, Green, 10 In. 110.00
Blackberry Wreath, Bowl, Marigold, 8 In. 80.00
Blackberry, Hat, Red .... 400.00 To 450.00
Blossomtime, Compote, Purple 125.00
Broken Arches, Punch Set, Purple, 7 Piece 350.00
Brooklyn Bridge, Bowl, Scalloped, Marigold, 8 3/4 In. 275.00
BUSHEL BASKET, see Basket
Butterfly & Berry, Berry Set 200.00

Butterfly & Berry, Bowl, Footed, Amethyst, 10 In. 110.00
Butterfly & Berry, Bowl, Footed, Marigold, 5 In. .... 25.00 To 30.00
Butterfly & Berry, Creamer, Cobalt Blue 90.00
Butterfly & Berry, Creamer, Marigold 40.00
Butterfly & Berry, Table Set, Marigold, 4 Piece .... 325.00 To 350.00
Butterfly & Berry, Tumbler, Marigold 15.00
Butterfly & Berry, Vase, Crimped Top 50.00
Butterfly & Berry, Vase, Green 125.00
Butterfly & Berry, Vase, Red 275.00
    BUTTERFLY & CABLE, see Springtime
Butterfly & Fern, Pitcher, Marigold 195.00
Butterfly & Fern, Tumbler, Blue 35.00
Butterfly & Fern, Tumbler, Green .... 50.00 To 55.00
Butterfly & Fern, Water Set, Green, 7 Piece 925.00
    BUTTERFLY & GRAPE, see Butterfly & Berry
    BUTTERFLY & PLUME, see Butterfly & Fern
    BUTTERFLY & STIPPLED RAYS, see Butterfly
Butterfly & Tulip, Bowl, Footed, Marigold, Square 400.00
Butterfly & Tulip, Bowl, Marigold, Whimsey 800.00
Butterfly, Bonbon, Green .... 55.00 To 65.00
Butterfly, Bonbon, Marigold 45.00
Butterfly, Bonbon, Purple .... 195.00 To 275.00
    CABBAGE ROSE & GRAPE, see Wine & Roses
    CACTUS LEAF RAYS, see Leaf Rays
Captive Rose, Bowl, Green, 9 In. 65.00
Captive Rose, Plate, Amethyst, 9 1/4 In. 1200.00
Captive Rose, Plate, Blue, 9 In. .... 160.00 To 225.00
Captive Rose, Plate, Marigold, 9 In. 195.00
Carolina Dogwood, Bowl, Blue .... 200.00 To 320.00
    CATTAILS & FISH, see Fisherman's Mug
    CATTAILS & WATER LILY, see Water Lily & Cattails
    CHERRIES & HOLLY WREATH, see Cherry Circle
    CHERRIES & MUMS, see Mikado
Cherry & Cable, Creamer, Marigold 70.00
Cherry Chain, Bowl, Orange Tree Exterior, Purple, 8 In. 225.00
Cherry Circles, Bonbon, Marigold 45.00
Cherry Circles, Bonbon, Vaseline 345.00
    CHERRY WREATHED, see Wreathed Cherry
Cherry, Saucer, Ruffled, Marigold, 6 In. 25.00
Cherry, Spooner, Marigold 60.00
    CHRISTMAS CACTUS, see Thistle
    CHRISTMAS PLATE, see Poinsettia
Chrysanthemum, Bowl, Footed, Blue, 10 In. .... 155.00 To 200.00
Coin Dot, Bowl, Amethyst, 9 1/2 In. 60.00
Coin Dot, Bowl, Red, 7 1/2 In. 950.00
Concave Diamonds, Tumbler, Coaster, Ice Blue 35.00
Cosmos & Cane, Berry Set, White, 5 Piece 170.00
Cosmos Variant, Bowl, Ruffled, Blue, 10 In. 80.00
Cosmos, Bowl, Marigold, 9 In. 45.00
Country Kitchen, Table Set, Amethyst, 4 Piece 650.00
Crab Claw, Tumbler, Marigold 65.00
Crackle, Water Set, Marigold, 7 Piece .... 80.00 To 100.00
Dahlia, Creamer, Amethyst 55.00
Dahlia, Creamer, White 125.00
Dahlia, Tumbler, White 85.00
    DAISY & LATTICE BAND, see Lattice & Daisy
Daisy & Plume, Rose Bowl, Footed, Amethyst 75.00
Daisy & Plume, Rose Bowl, Footed, Marigold 50.00
    DAISY BAND & DRAPE, see Daisies & Drape
    DANDELION VARIANT, see Paneled Dandelion
Dandelion, Mug, Aqua .... 450.00 To 575.00
Dandelion, Mug, Marigold 290.00
Dandelion, Pitcher, Green 675.00

◆◆

A stained glass window is probably more stable than it looks. Small cracks in the glass, even a bowed window, is usually not a problem. Cracked solder joints between pieces of glass should be repaired.

◆◆

Dandelion, Pitcher, Marigold	375.00
Dandelion, Tumbler, Purple	65.00
Diamond & Rib, Vase, Marigold, 9 1/2 In.	35.00
Diamond & Rib, Vase, Marigold, 17 In.	25.00
Diamond Lace, Pitcher, Amethyst	265.00
Diamond Lace, Pitcher, Purple	220.00
Diamond Lace, Tumbler, Amethyst	30.00
Diamond Lace, Tumbler, Purple	40.00
Diamond Lace, Water Set, Purple, 7 Piece	345.00
DIAMOND POINT & DAISY, see Cosmos & Cane	
Diamond Point Columns, Bowl, Marigold, 5 x 2 1/2 In.	20.00
Diamond Point Columns, Creamer, Marigold	35.00
Diamond Point Columns, Vase, Blue, 16 In.	250.00
Diamond Point Columns, Vase, Green, 8 In.	40.00
Diamond Point Columns, Vase, Marigold, 6 In.	42.00
Diamond Point Columns, Vase, Purple, 7 In.	40.00
Diamond Point Columns, Vase, White, 10 In.	65.00 To 135.00
DOGWOOD & MARSH LILY, see Two Flowers	
Dogwood Sprays, Bowl, Footed, Peach, 9 In.	100.00
Double Dutch, Bowl, Footed, Purple, 9 In.	150.00
Double Dutch, Bowl, Marigold, 5 In.	20.00
Double Star, Tumbler, Green	30.00
Double Star, Tumbler, Green, 6 Piece	200.00
Double–Stem Rose, Bowl, Amethyst, 8 In.	68.00
Dragon & Lotus, Bowl, 3–Footed, Lime Green, 7 In.	300.00
Dragon & Lotus, Bowl, Ice Cream, Red, 9 In.	1000.000 To 1500.00
Dragon & Lotus, Bowl, Marigold, 9 In.	42.00 To 65.00
Dragon & Strawberry, Bowl, Blue, 9 In.	550.00
DRAPE & TIE, see Rosalind	
Drapery, Candy Dish, Ice Blue	150.00 To 160.00
Drapery, Candy Dish, Purple	135.00
Drapery, Candy Dish, White	115.00 To 135.00
Drapery, Rose Bowl, Ice Blue	600.00 To 1300.00
Drapery, Rose Bowl, Marigold	385.00
Drapery, Rose Bowl, Purple	260.00
Drapery, Vase, Ice Blue, 8 In.	60.00
Drapery, Vase, Ice Blue, 10 In.	185.00
EGYPTIAN BAND, see Round–Up	
Embroidered Mums, Bonbon, Stemmed, White	1150.00
Embroidered Mums, Bowl, Amber, 9 In.	1000.00
Embroidered Mums, Bowl, Purple	1600.00
Embroidered Mums, Plate, Ice Green	1650.00
Estate, Creamer, Peach	65.00
Estate, Sugar & Creamer, Aqua	150.00
FAN & ARCH, see Persian Garden	
Fanciful, Plate, Purple, 9 In.	160.00
Fashion, Pitcher, Marigold	125.00
Fashion, Punch Cup, Marigold	20.00
Fashion, Punch Set, Marigold, 9 Piece	230.00
FEATHER & HOBSTAR, see Inverted Feather	
Feather Stitch, Bowl, Blue	65.00
FENTON'S BUTTERFLY, see Butterfly	
Field Flower, Pitcher, Green	120.00
Field Flower, Pitcher, Marigold	125.00

Field Flower, Tumbler, Marigold 25.00
Field Flower, Water Set, Marigold, 5 Piece 245.00
    FIELD ROSE, see Rambler Rose
Fine Cut & Roses, Candy Dish, Blue 350.00
Fine Cut & Roses, Candy Dish, White ....95.00 To 206.00
Fine Cut & Roses, Rose Bowl, Amethyst 75.00
Fine Cut & Roses, Rose Bowl, Ice Blue 300.00
Fine Rib, Bowl, Green, 10 In. 75.00
Fine Rib, Bowl, Purple, 7 In. 30.00
Fine Rib, Vase, Blue, 12 In. 40.00
Fine Rib, Vase, Marigold, 7 In. 15.00
    FINECUT & STAR, see Star & File
    FISH & FLOWERS, see Trout & Fly
Fisherman's Mug, Mug, Amethyst 90.00
Fisherman's Mug, Mug, Purple 75.00
    FISHERMAN'S NET, see Treebark
Fishnet, Epergne, Peach 295.00
Fishnet, Epergne, Purple 195.00
Fishscale & Beads, Plate, Amethyst, 7 1/2 In. 595.00
Fleur De Leis, Bowl, Ruffled, Green, 10 In. 225.00
    FLORAL & DIAMOND POINT, see Fine Cut & Roses
Floral & Grape, Pitcher, Marigold 100.00
Floral & Grape, Tumbler, Blue 35.00
Floral & Grape, Water Set, Amethyst, 6 Piece 425.00
Floral & Grape, Water Set, Blue, 7 Piece 285.00
    FLORAL & GRAPEVINE, see Floral & Grape
Floral & Optic, Cake Plate, White 60.00
    FLOWER POT, see Butterfly & Tulip
    FLOWERING ALMONDS, see Peacock Tail
Flowers, Rose Bowl, White 195.00
    FLUFFY BIRD, see Peacock
Flute, Water Set, Amethyst, 7 Piece 110.00
Folding Fan, Compote, Peach 65.00
Four Flowers, Bowl, Peach, 10 In. 85.00
Fruit & Flowers, Berry Set, Marigold, 7 Piece 175.00
Fruit & Flowers, Berry Set, Purple, 7 Piece 600.00
Fruit & Flowers, Bonbon, Green 75.00
Fruit & Flowers, Bonbon, Ice Blue ....425.00 To 500.00
Fruit & Flowers, Bonbon, Marigold 55.00
Fruit & Flowers, Bonbon, White 400.00
Fruit & Flowers, Bowl, Blue, 7 In. ....175.00 To 185.00
Garden Path Variant, Bowl, Peach, 6 In. 70.00
Garland, Rose Bowl, Blue 60.00
Garland, Rose Bowl, Marigold 45.00
God & Home, Tumbler, Blue 275.00
Golden Harvest, Decanter, Wine, Marigold 75.00
Good Luck, Bowl, Green 350.00
Good Luck, Bowl, Marigold ....125.00 To 145.00
Good Luck, Plate, Emerald Green 5000.00
Good Luck, Plate, Purple 400.00
Grape & Cable, Banana Boat, Amethyst, 11 3/4 In. 225.00
Grape & Cable, Bonbon, Marigold 55.00
Grape & Cable, Bowl, 3–Footed, Marigold, 8 In. 85.00
Grape & Cable, Bowl, Amethyst, 10 In. 85.00
Grape & Cable, Bowl, Blue, 10 1/2 In. 350.00
Grape & Cable, Bowl, Green, 7 1/2 In. 75.00
Grape & Cable, Bowl, Ice Cream, Green, 11 In. 325.00
Grape & Cable, Bowl, Marigold, 8 1/2 In. 60.00
Grape & Cable, Bowl, Persian Medallion Interior, Blue, 9 In. 230.00
Grape & Cable, Bowl, Purple, 7 1/2 In. 45.00
Grape & Cable, Butter, Cover, Marigold 145.00
Grape & Cable, Butter, Cover, Purple 210.00
Grape & Cable, Compote, Cover, Amethyst 430.00

Grape & Cable, Cookie Jar, Amethyst 85.00
Grape & Cable, Creamer, Green 125.00
Grape & Cable, Decanter, Whiskey, Marigold .... 200.00 To 475.00
Grape & Cable, Hatpin Holder, Marigold 150.00
Grape & Cable, Hatpin Holder, Purple 185.00
Grape & Cable, Orange Bowl, Blue, 10 1/2 In. 325.00
Grape & Cable, Perfume Bottle, Stopper, Purple 625.00
Grape & Cable, Plate, Green, 9 In. 295.00
Grape & Cable, Plate, Marigold, 10 In. 125.00
Grape & Cable, Powder Jar, Cover, Marigold 130.00
Grape & Cable, Powder Jar, Purple 115.00
Grape & Cable, Punch Bowl, Ameythst, 2 Piece 675.00
Grape & Cable, Punch Cup, Aqua 675.00
Grape & Cable, Punch Cup, Blue 80.00
Grape & Cable, Punch Cup, Marigold 18.50
Grape & Cable, Punch Set, Green, 11 Piece 750.00
Grape & Cable, Punch Set, Purple, 10 Piece 1050.00
Grape & Cable, Shot Glass, Marigold 160.00
Grape & Cable, Spooner, Green 110.00
Grape & Cable, Table Set, Marigold, 4 Piece .... 265.00 To 595.00
Grape & Cable, Tray, Dresser, Aqua 1600.00
Grape & Cable, Tray, Dresser, Marigold 175.00
Grape & Cable, Tray, Dresser, Purple 200.00
Grape & Cable, Tumbler, Marigold 15.00
Grape & Cable, Water Set, Amethyst, 7 Piece .... 445.00 To 495.00
Grape & Cable, Water Set, Marigold, 9 Piece 400.00
Grape & Gothic Arches, Tumbler, Blue 75.00
Grape Arbor, Pitcher, Water, Tankard Shape, Ice Blue 2750.00
Grape Arbor, Tumbler, White 135.00
Grape Arbor, Water Set, Marigold, 7 Piece .... 295.00 To 475.00
  GRAPE DELIGHT, see Vintage
Grape Delight, Rose Bowl, Amethyst .... 55.00 To 70.00
Grape Delight, Rose Bowl, Purple 135.00
Grape Leaves, Bowl, Green, 9 In. 95.00
Grape, Bowl, Amber, 5 In. 20.00
Grape, Bowl, Ruffled, Purple, 9 In. 75.00
Grape, Decanter, Stopper, Amethyst, 12 In. 210.00
Grape, Fernery, 3-Footed, Blue, 5 1/2 x 3 1/2 In. 65.00
Grape, Fernery, 3-Footed, Green, 5 1/2 x 3 1/2 In. 65.00
Grape, Pitcher, Marigold 75.00
Grape, Pitcher, Water, Purple 145.00
Grape, Punch Cup, Marigold 10.00
Grape, Tobacco Jar, Purple .... 450.00 To 900.00
Grape, Water Set, Marigold, 6 Piece 150.00
Grape, Wine, Amethyst 37.50
  GRAPEVINE DIAMONDS, see Grapevine Lattice
Grapevine Lattice, Bowl, White, 6 In. 55.00
Grapevine Lattice, Pitcher, Amethyst 595.00
Grapevine Lattice, Tankard Set, Purple, 7 Piece 600.00
Grapevine Lattice, Tumbler, Marigold 50.00
Greek Key, Tumbler, Purple 85.00
Harvest Poppy, Compote, Marigold 195.00
  HARVEST TIME, see Golden Harvest
Hattie, Bowl, Marigold, 8 In. 35.00
Heart & Vine, Bowl, Green, 8 In. 95.00
Heart & Vine, Plate, Blue 225.00
Hearts & Flowers, Bowl, Marigold 395.00
Hearts & Flowers, Bowl, Ruffled, Ice Blue .... 373.00 To 550.00
Hearts & Flowers, Compote, White 160.00
Heavy Grape, Bowl, Marigold, 9 In. 25.00
Heavy Grape, Bowl, Ruffled, Purple, 11 In. 400.00
Heavy Grape, Plate, Marigold, 11 1/2 In. 145.00
Heavy Grape, Plate, Purple, 7 In. 75.00

HERON & RUSHES, see Stork & Rushes
HOBNAIL, see also Hobnail category
Hobnail, Bell, Marigold 15.00
Hobnail, Bell, Peacock 15.00
HOBSTAR & TORCH, see Double Star
Hobstar, Cookie Jar, Marigold, 8 In. 55.00
Hobstars & Arches, Vase, Marigold, 9 1/2 In. 75.00
Holly & Berry, Nappy, Purple 50.00
HOLLY SPRAY, see Holly Sprig
Holly Sprig, Bonbon, Marigold .... 55.00 To 65.00
Holly Sprig, Bowl, Green, 8 In. .... 70.00 To 80.00
Holly Sprig, Bowl, Ruffled, Green, 8 1/4 In. 135.00
Holly, Bowl, Amber, 10 In. 250.00
Holly, Bowl, Amethyst, 10 In. 40.00
Holly, Hat, Red .... 450.00 To 850.00
Holly, Plate, Amethyst 685.00
Holly, Plate, Blue 450.00
Holly, Plate, White 150.00
Holly, Sherbet, Blue 55.00
Holly, Toothpick, Green 45.00
HONEYCOMB COLLAR, see Fishscale & Beads
Horse Medallion, Nut Bowl, Marigold 95.00
Horse Medallion, Plate, Marigold, 8 In. 150.00
HORSE MEDALLIONS, see Horses' Heads
Horses' Heads, Plate, Marigold, 7 1/2 In. 145.00
Horses' Heads, Plate, Marigold, 8 In. 195.00
INTERIOR OF CHERRIES & MUMS, see Mikado
Inverted Feather, Cracker Jar, Green .... 225.00 To 335.00
Inverted Feather, Table Set, Green, 4 Piece 150.00
Inverted Feather, Water Set, Gold Trim, Green, 7 Piece 175.00
Inverted Strawberry, Bowl, Green, 7 In. 125.00
IRISH LACE, see Louisa
Kangaroo, Bowl, Crimped Edge, Australian, Purple, 9 1/2 In. 150.00
KIMBERLY, see Concave Diamonds
Kittens, Cup & Saucer, Marigold 245.00
Kittens, Saucer, Marigold 175.00
Kittens, Toothpick, Marigold .... 145.00 To 175.00
LABELLE POPPY, see Poppy Show
LABELLE ROSE, see Rose Show
Lattice & Daisy, Tumbler, Marigold 25.00
Lattice & Grape, Tumbler, Blue 25.00
Lattice & Grape, Water Set, Marigold, 7 Piece .... 275.00 To 395.00
LATTICE & GRAPEVINE, see Lattice & Grape
Leaf & Beads, Candy Dish, Rayed Inside, Green, 8 1/2 In. 65.00
Leaf & Beads, Rose Bowl, Amethyst 75.00
Leaf & Beads, Rose Bowl, Aqua .... 225.00 To 1100.00
Leaf & Beads, Rose Bowl, Blue 145.00
Leaf & Beads, Rose Bowl, Green 65.00
Leaf & Beads, Rose Bowl, Marigold 125.00
Leaf & Beads, Rose Bowl, Purple 85.00
LEAF MEDALLION, see Leaf Chain
LEAF PINWHEEL & STAR FLOWER, see Whirling Leaves
Leaf Rays, Nappy, Marigold 20.00
Leaf Rays, Nappy, Peach 155.00
Little Fishes, Bowl, Footed, Marigold, 8 1/2 In. 60.00
Little Flowers, Bowl, Green, 10 In. 85.00
Little Stars, Bowl, Amethyst, 7 In. 85.00
Little Stars, Bowl, Green, 7 In. 180.00
Loganberry, Vase, Marigold, 10 In. 125.00
LOOP & COLUMN, see Pulled Loop
Lotus & Grape, Bowl, Footed, Amethyst, 7 In. 35.00
Louisa, Rose Bowl, Aqua 125.00
Louisa, Rose Bowl, Green 55.00

Louisa, Rose Bowl, Marigold, 9 In. .... 40.00 To 45.00
Louisa, Rose Bowl, Purple, 9 In. 37.00
Lustre Rose, Bowl, Marigold, 8 In. 39.00
Lustre Rose, Bowl, Purple, 7 1/2 In. 30.00
Lustre Rose, Rose Bowl, Amber 85.00
Lustre Rose, Table Set, Marigold, 4 Piece 250.00
Lustre Rose, Tumbler, Purple 35.00
    MAGNOLIA & POINSETTIA, see Water Lily
Many Fruits, Punch Cup, Marigold 12.00
Many Fruits, Punch Set, Marigold, 8 Piece 375.00
Maple Leaf, Marigold 6 Piece 200.00
Maple Leaf, Purple, 7 Piece 500.00
Marilyn, Tumbler, Amethyst 90.00
Mary Ann, Vase, 3 Handles, Marigold 450.00
    MARYLAND, see Rustic
    MAYFLOWER, see Four–70–Four
    MELINDA, see Wishbone
    MELON & FAN, see Diamond & Rib
Memphis, Punch Cup, White 45.00
Mikado, Compote, Blue, Large 130.00
Milady, Tumbler, Blue 85.00
    MULTI FRUIT & FLOWERS, see Many Fruits
Multi Fruit & Flowers, Dessert, Stem, Green 750.00
Multi Fruit & Flowers, Tumbler, Green 1050.00
Nippon, Bowl, Ice Blue 275.00
Octagon, Pitcher, Milk, Marigold 160.00
Open Rose, Bowl, White, 9 In. 115.00
    ORANGE TREE & SCROLL, see Orange Tree Variant
Orange Tree, Bowl, 3–Footed, Fluted, Blue, 10 In. 185.00
Orange Tree, Bowl, 4–Footed, Blue, 10 In. 195.00
Orange Tree, Bowl, Berries Inside, White, 8 In. 325.00
Orange Tree, Bowl, Green, 8 1/2 In. 185.00
Orange Tree, Bowl, Marigold, 8 1/2 In. 65.00
Orange Tree, Bowl, White, 8 1/2 In. 135.00
Orange Tree, Butter, Blue 63.00
Orange Tree, Goblet, Marigold 35.00
Orange Tree, Loving Cup, Handles, Blue 225.00
Orange Tree, Loving Cup, Handles, Green 130.00
Orange Tree, Loving Cup, Handles, Marigold .... 225.00 To 250.00
Orange Tree, Mug, Aqua 100.00
Orange Tree, Mug, Red .... 375.00 To 575.00
Orange Tree, Pitcher, Water, Blue 1700.00
Orange Tree, Pitcher, Water, White 675.00
Orange Tree, Plate, Blue, 9 1/4 In. 295.00
Orange Tree, Punch Bowl, White 850.00
Orange Tree, Punch Set, Blue, 7 Piece 395.00
Orange Tree, Punch Set, Marigold, 5 Piece 275.00
Orange Tree, Rose Bowl, Green 135.00
Orange Tree, Sherbet, Stem, Blue 25.00
Orange Tree, Sherbet, Stem, Marigold 20.00
Oriental Poppy, Pitcher, Purple 695.00
Oriental Poppy, Pitcher, Water, Tankard Shape, Green 825.00
Oriental Poppy, Tumbler, Purple .... 30.00 To 40.00
Oriental Poppy, Tumbler, White 170.00
Oriental Poppy, Water Set, Purple, 5 Piece 875.00
Oval & Round, Bowl, White, 9 In 25.00
Palm Beach, Water Set, White, 7 Piece 400.00
    PANELED BACHELOR BUTTONS, see Milady
Pansy, Bowl, Marigold, 9 In. 125.00
Pansy, Creamer, Amber 85.00
Panther, Berry Set, Marigold, 7 Piece 550.00
Panther, Bowl, Footed, Marigold, 5 3/4 In. 40.00
Peach & Pear, Banana Boat, Marigold 85.00

Peach, Tumbler, White 45.00
Peacock & Dahlia, Bowl, Ruffled, Marigold, 7 In. 35.00
Peacock & Grape, Bowl, Marigold, 9 In. 50.00
Peacock & Grape, Bowl, Ruffled, Amber, 9 In. 220.00
Peacock & Urn, Bowl, Ice Cream, Ice Blue, 10 In. 900.00
Peacock & Urn, Bowl, Ice Cream, Marigold, 6 In. 150.00
Peacock & Urn, Bowl, Ice Cream, Marigold, 10 In. .... 275.00 To 375.00
Peacock & Urn, Bowl, Marigold, 8 1/2 In. 95.00
Peacock & Urn, Plate, White, 9 In. 400.00
Peacock At The Fountain, Butter, Amethyst 140.00
Peacock At The Fountain, Pitcher, Purple 475.00
Peacock At The Fountain, Punch Bowl, Blue 1250.00
Peacock At The Fountain, Punch Cup, Blue 35.00
Peacock At The Fountain, Punch Cup, Purple 30.00
Peacock At The Fountain, Punch Set, Blue, 7 Piece 625.00
Peacock At The Fountain, Spooner, Purple 90.00
Peacock At The Fountain, Table Set, Amethyst, 4 Piece 575.00
Peacock At The Fountain, Table Set, Blue, 4 Piece 2100.00
Peacock At The Fountain, Tumbler, Blue 45.00
Peacock At The Fountain, Tumbler, Purple 35.00
Peacock At The Fountain, Water Set, Marigold, 7 Piece 575.00
    PEACOCK EYE & GRAPE, see Vineyard
    PEACOCK ON FENCE, see Peacock
Peacock Tail, Bowl, Ice Cream, Red, 7 1/2 In. 850.00
Peacock, Bowl, Amethyst, 8 3/4 In. .... 425.00 To 650.00
Peacock, Bowl, Aqua, 8 3/4 In. 600.00
Peacock, Bowl, Purple, 8 3/4 In. 380.00
Peacock, Plate, Green, 9 In. 1800.00
Peacock, Plate, Ice Green, 9 In. .... 425.00 To 525.00
Peacock, Plate, Marigold, 9 In. 315.00
Perfection, Tumbler, Amethyst 250.00
Persian Garden, Fruit Bowl, Base, Ruffled, White 500.00
Persian Medallion, Bonbon, Blue 65.00
Persian Medallion, Bonbon, Green 55.00
Persian Medallion, Bonbon, Marigold 28.00
Persian Medallion, Bonbon, Red .... 400.00 To 925.00
Persian Medallion, Bowl, Purple, 8 In. 65.00
Persian Medallion, Chop Plate, Blue, 10 In. 1050.00
Persian Medallion, Compote, Green 325.00
Persian Medallion, Plate, Marigold, 6 In. 38.00
Petal & Fan, Berry Set, Peach, 7 Piece 450.00
    PINE CONE WREATH, see Pine Cone
Pine Cone, Bowl, Marigold, 6 In. 29.00
Pineapple, Creamer, Purple 45.00
Plaid, Bowl, Red, 8 3/4 In. 2500.00
    POINSETTIA & LATTICE, see Poinsettia
Poinsettia, Pitcher, Milk, Green 145.00
Poinsettia, Pitcher, Milk, Marigold 55.00
Pond Lily, Bonbon, Blue 65.00
    PONY ROSETTE, see Pony
Pony, Bowl, Ice Green, 8 1/2 In. 850.00
Pony, Bowl, Marigold, 8 1/2 In. 65.00
Poppy Show, Plate, Marigold, 9 1/2 In. 375.00
Prayer Rug, Nappy, Marigold 450.00
    PRINCESS LACE, see Octagon
Pulled Loop, Vase, Peach 50.00
Question Marks, Bonbon, Marigold 32.00
Raindrops, Bowl, Amethyst, 9 In. 50.00
Raindrops, Bowl, Footed, Purple, 9 In. 50.00
Rambler Rose, Water Set, Blue, 7 Piece 370.00
Raspberry, Pitcher, Green 225.00
Raspberry, Pitcher, Marigold 145.00
Raspberry, Tumbler, Marigold 28.00

◆◆◆

Mildew, fungus, stains, and odors can be removed from the wooden parts of furniture by using a commercial mildew remover found at the supermarket. Wipe the entire piece or it will have a lighter spot where it was cleaned.

◆◆◆

Raspberry, Tumbler, Purple	40.00
Rays & Ribbons, Bowl, Fluted, Green, 9 In.	115.00
Ripple, Vase, Marigold, 11 1/2 In.	45.00
Ripple, Vase, Purple, 11 In.	55.00
Rising Sun, Pitcher, Pedestal Base, Marigold	650.00
ROBIN RED BREAST, see Robin	
Robin, Mug, Marigold	50.00
Rosalind, Bowl, Amethyst, 9 1/2 In.	250.00
Rosalind, Bowl, Marigold, 10 In.	150.00
Rosalind, Bowl, Purple, 8 In.	400.00
ROSE & RUFFLES, see Open Rose	
Rose Show, Bowl, Aqua	1000.00
Rose Show, Bowl, Marigold	525.00
Rose Show, Plate, Blue, 9 In.	1400.00
Rose Show, Plate, White, 9 In.	385.00
Roses & Fruit, Bonbon, Amethyst	525.00
Round-Up, Bowl, Ruffled, White, 9 In.	195.00
Round-Up, Plate, Purple, 9 In.	235.00
Rustic, Vase, Funeral, Blue, 18 1/2 In.	950.00
Rustic, Vase, Funeral, Blue, 20 In.	800.00
Rustic, Vase, Funeral, Marigold	325.00
SAILBOAT & WINDMILL, see Sailboats	
Sailboats, Bowl, Ice Cream, Blue, 5 1/2 In.	45.00
Sailboats, Goblet, Marigold	145.00
Sailboats, Plate, Marigold, 6 In.	400.00
Sailboats, Wine, Blue	90.00 To 95.00
Sailboats, Wine, Marigold	40.00
Scroll Embossed, Plate, Green, 9 In.	80.00
Scroll, Bowl, Purple	45.00
SCROLL-CABLE, see Estate	
SEA LANES, see Little Fishes	
Seaweed, Bowl, Amethyst, 10 1/2 In.	350.00
Singing Birds, Butter, Cover, Amethyst	350.00
Singing Birds, Mug, Amethyst	100.00
Singing Birds, Mug, Green	275.00 To 325.00
Singing Birds, Mug, Purple	65.00
Singing Birds, Tumbler, Green	50.00 To 55.00
Singing Birds, Water Set, Green, 6 Piece	550.00
Singing Birds, Water Set, Marigold, 7 Piece	500.00
Single Flower, Bowl, Peach, 9 In.	45.00
Ski Star, Berry Set, Peach, 5 Piece	160.00
Ski Star, Bowl, Marigold, 10 In.	42.00
Ski Star, Bowl, Peach, 10 In.	275.00
Ski Star, Bowl, Purple, 10 In.	125.00
Ski Star, Plate, Dome-Footed, Peach	225.00
Smooth Rays, Bowl, Green, 7 In.	55.00
Soda Gold, Candlestick, Marigold, 3 1/2 In., Pair	50.00
Soldiers & Sailors, Plate, Blue	1300.00
SPIDER WEB, see Soda Gold	
Springtime, Tumbler, Marigold	45.00
Stag & Holly, Bowl, Clambroth, 9 1/2 In.	325.00
Stag & Holly, Bowl, Footed, Amethyst, 9 1/2 In.	225.00

Stag & Holly, Bowl, Footed, Red, 8 In. 2200.00
Stag & Holly, Bowl, Pink, Footed 120.00
Stag & Holly, Rose Bowl, Marigold 295.00
Star & File, Creamer, Marigold 28.00
Star Medallion, Tumbler, Marigold 15.00
    STIPPLED CLEMATIS, see Little Stars
    STIPPLED DIAMOND & FLOWER, see Little Flowers
    STIPPLED LEAF & BEADS, see leaf & Beads
    STIPPLED POSY & PODS, see Four Flowers
Stippled Rays, Bonbon, Red 350.00
Stippled Rays, Bowl, Amethyst, 7 In. 60.00
Stippled Rays, Bowl, Marigold, 9 In. 35.00
Stippled Rays, Bowl, Marigold, 10 In. 35.00
Stippled Rays, Bowl, Red, 6 In. 875.00
Stippled Rays, Candy Dish, Amethyst 35.00
Stippled Rays, Plate, Green, 7 In. 45.00
    STIPPLED RIBBONS & RAYS, see Rays & Ribbons
Stork & Rushes, Mug, Marigold 30.00
Stork & Rushes, Punch Cup, Marigold .... 16.00 To 17.00
Stork & Rushes, Tumbler, Blue 40.00
Stork & Rushes, Tumbler, Cobalt Blue 45.00
Strawberry Scroll, Tumbler, Blue 55.00
Strawberry, Bonbon, Blue .... 65.00 To 75.00
Strawberry, Bonbon, Marigold 160.00
Strawberry, Epergne, Purple 225.00
Strawberry, Plate, Amethyst, 9 In. 140.00
Strawberry, Plate, Green, 9 In. 135.00
Strawberry, Plate, Purple, 9 In. 175.00
    SUNFLOWER, see Dandelion
    SUNFLOWER & WHEAT, see Fieldflower
Swan, Salt, Aqua 225.00
Swirl, Pitcher Set, Marigold, 9 Piece 125.00
Target, Vase, Marigold, 11 1/2 In. 15.00
    TEARDROPS, see Raindrops
Ten Mums, Bowl, Green, 10 In. 75.00
Ten Mums, Tumbler, Marigold 55.00
Ten Mums, Water Set, Blue, 7 Piece 1000.00
Ten Mums, Water Set, Marigold, 7 Piece 450.00
Thin Rib, Vase, Ice Green, 11 In. 200.00
Thistle, Bowl, Purple, 8 In. 55.00
Three Fruits, Bowl, Amethyst, 9 In. 165.00
Three Fruits, Bowl, Aqua, 9 In. 1200.00
Three Fruits, Bowl, Blue, 9 In. 195.00
Three Fruits, Plate, Blue 275.00
Three Fruits, Plate, Purple, 9 In. .... 125.00 To 200.00
Tiger Lily, Pitcher, Green 250.00
Tiger Lily, Pitcher, Marigold 145.00
Tiger Lily, Tumbler, Purple .... 45.00 To 55.00
Tiger Lily, Water Set, Marigold, 7 Piece 300.00
Tree Bark, Pickle Jar, Green 22.00
Tree Bark, Pitcher, Water, Marigold 40.00
Tree Bark, Water Set, Marigold, 7 Piece 80.00
Tree Trunk, Vase, Aqua, 10 1/2 In. 550.00
Tree Trunk, Vase, Blue, 10 1/2 In. 65.00
Tree Trunk, Vase, Funeral, Blue, 19 1/2 In. 2800.00
Tree Trunk, Vase, Funeral, Purple, 14 In. 125.00
Tree Trunk, Vase, White, 10 1/2 In. 85.00
Trout & Fly, Bowl, Marigold 450.00
Trout & Fly, Dish, Fluted, Purple 800.00
Two Flowers, Bowl, Blue, 10 1/2 In. 1400.00
Two Flowers, Bowl, Spatula Footed, Amber, 8 In. 1925.00
Two Flowers, Sauce, Marigold, 4 3/4 In. 100.00
Vineyard, Pitcher, Marigold .... 65.00 To 90.00

Carousel, Horse, Charles Dare, Dapple Gray, c.1890, 3 1/2 Ft.

Vineyard, Water Set, Marigold	260.00
Vintage, Bowl, Blue, 9 In.	48.00
Vintage, Epergne, 1–Light, Green	165.00
Vintage, Fernery, Blue	50.00 To 55.00
Waffle Block, Creamer, Marigold	55.00
Water Lily & Cattails, Tumbler, Marigold	40.00 To 95.00
Water Lily, Bowl, Footed, Green, 10 1/2 In.	95.00
Water Lily, Bowl, Footed, Marigold, 9 In.	40.00
Water Lily, Bowl, Footed, Marigold, 10 In.	45.00 To 65.00
Water Lily, Sauce, Ruffled, Red	600.00
Whirling Leaves, Bowl, Marigold, 11 In.	65.00
Whirling Star, Punch Cup, Marigold, 6 Piece	65.00
Wide Panel, Candy Dish, Cover, Red	400.00
Wide Panel, Vase, Red, 10 1/2 In.	380.00 To 450.00
WIDE SWIRL, see Swirl	
WILD GRAPES, see Grape Leaves	
WINDMILL MEDALLION, see Windmill	
Windmill, Bowl, Marigold, 7 In.	45.00
Windmill, Pitcher, Marigold	65.00
Wine & Roses, Wine, Marigold	95.00
Wishbone, Bowl, Amethyst, 10 1/2 In.	175.00
Wishbone, Bowl, Footed, Marigold, 9 In.	50.00 To 85.00
Wishbone, Bowl, Marigold, 8 In.	48.00 To 58.00
Wishbone, Bowl, Ruffled, Purple, 10 In.	135.00
Wishbone, Plate, Footed, Marigold, 8 1/2 In.	2000.00
WISTERIA & LATTICE, see Wisteria	
Wisteria, Tumbler, Ice Blue	325.00
Wreath of Roses, Bonbon, Handle, Stem, Green	75.00
Wreathed Cherry, Banana Boat, Amethyst, 12 1/2 x 10 In.	125.00
Wreathed Cherry, Bowl, Oval, Marigold 13 1/2 In.	85.00
Wreathed Cherry, Spooner, White	80.00

Carriage, Baby Buggy, Convertible Top, Light Green, American

Wreathed Cherry, Tumbler, Marigold	30.00
Wreathed Roses, Bonbon, Stem, Blue	85.00

The first carousel or merry–go–round figures carved in the United States were made in 1867 by Gustav Dentzel. Collectors discovered the charm of the hand–carved figures in the 1970s and they were soon classed as folk art. Most desirable are the figures other than horses, such as pigs, camels, lions, or dogs. A jumper is a figure that was made to move up and down on a pole, a stander was placed in a stationary position.

CAROUSEL, Coach, Cinderella, Bayol, 1905	5000.00
Horse, 3rd Row, Herschel, Late 1920s	4200.00
Horse, Allan Herschell, All Wood, 1925	3500.00
Horse, Black Saddle, Glass Eyes, Braided Tail, American, 53 In.	525.00
Horse, Cast Zinc, Red & Black Paint, 40 In.	65.00
Horse, Charles Dare, Dapple Gray, c.1890, 3 1/2 Ft. ....*Illus*	1650.00
Horse, Glass Eyes, Horsehair Tail, 56 x 58 In.	8250.00
Horse, Herschel, 3rd Row, Late 1920s	4200.00
Horse, Hershell, Aluminum, 1950s	1200.00
Horse, Jumper, 2nd Row, Striped, Illion	4725.00
Horse, Jumper, Brass Pole, C. W. Parker	4000.00
Horse, Jumper, C. W. Parker, Brass Pole, Mid–Position	4000.00
Horse, Jumper, Parker, Brass Pole	4000.00
Horse, Laminated Wooden Body, Old Repaint, 61 In.	500.00
Horse, Looff, Natural Wood	4500.00
Horse, Prancer, Heyn, Restored, 1870	2625.00
Horse, Spooner, England	6825.00
Horse, Tucked Head, Parker	7800.00
Jeep, Ride Car, 1950s	150.00
Mirror, Painted, 8 Light Bulbs Around Oval Mirror, 38 In., Pair	715.00
Pig, Brass Pole, Hand Carved, 47 In.	600.00
Pig, Carved & Painted Wood	1705.00
Pig, Hand Carved, Brass Pole, 47 In.	600.00
Rooster, Cast Aluminum, Repaint, Iron Standard, 39 1/2 In.	375.00

The word *carriage* has several meanings, so this section lists baby carriages, buggies for adults, horse–drawn sleighs, and even strollers. Doll–sized carriages are listed under *Toy.*

CARRIAGE, Baby Buggy, Convertible Top, Light Green, American ....*Illus*	440.00
Baby Buggy, Green Wicker	375.00
Baby Buggy, Heywood Wakefield, Dark Brown	400.00

Baby Buggy, Storkline, Black Leather, Chrome Trim, Full Size	200.00
Baby Buggy, Storkline, Black Leather, Chrome, Folding Hood, c.1940	200.00
Baby Buggy, Wicker, Large Iron Bound Wooden Wheels, Silk Parasol	633.00
Baby Buggy, Wicker, Scrolled Type, 4 Large Wheels, Painted	595.00
Baby Buggy, Wicker, Victorian, Heywood, 46 x 34 x 21 In.	330.00
Baby Buggy, Wood, Leather & Iron, Velvet Seat, Carpet Footrest	650.00
Market Wagon, Studebaker	1320.00
Mule Cart, Pale Gray Paint, 5-Ft. Red Wheels, Hardware	225.00
Perambulator, Victorian, Collapsible Leather Top	605.00
Pony Cart, Wicker, Painted Red	2200.00
Pram, Burgundy & White, Snow Cover, England	25.00
Pram, Victorian, Wicker, Rubber Wheels, Umbrella, 50 x 21 x 59 In.	995.00
Push Cart, Child's, 2 Wheels, Black, Vinyl Convertible Top, 36 In.	192.00
Sleigh, Bi-Wing, Paris, Maine	425.00
Sleigh, Child's, Bright Orange	990.00
Sleigh, Iron Tipped Runners, Floral, Striping, Wooden, 37 1/2 In.	450.00
Sleigh, Mixed Hardwoods, Original Paint, Velvet, Handle, 1860	625.00
Sleigh, Push, Wooden, Steel, Bentwood Runners, Red & Green, 44 In.	175.00
Sleigh, Red Glaze, Velvet Upholstery, Wood Runners, 63 In.	605.00
Sleigh, Rosemaling, Rear Tool Box, Snow Screen, Norwegian, c.1800	4800.00
Sleigh, Stenciled Irish, Figural End Runners, 1880	700.00
Sleigh, Stenciled, Quebec, Canada, Small	375.00
Sleigh, Wooden, Pin Stripe, Victorian, 23 x 36 In.	600.00
Stroller, Covered Back & Seat, Rattan Sides, Iron Frame, Maple	330.00
Stroller, Wicker, Parsol, 1860s	2100.00
Wagon, 3 Upholstered Seats, Green Blue, Yellow Striped, Red Wheels	1375.00
Wagon, Horse, Wooden Wheels, Blue Milk Paint, Iron Fittings	700.00

An eye on the cash was a necessity in stores of the nineteenth century, too. The cash register was invented in 1884. John and James Ritty invented a large clocklike model that kept a record of the dollars and cents exchanged in the store. John Patterson improved the cash register with a paper roll to record the money. By the early 1900s, elaborate brass registers were made. About World War I, the fancy case was exchanged for the more modern types.

CASH REGISTER, Barber, Oak	215.00
Imperial	600.00
Michigan, Rings To 20. 00	295.00
Model 2, Candy Store, Scroll Work	375.00
National, 6 Drawer, Nickel Over Brass, Floor	2000.00
National, Floor Model	1400.00
National, Model 313, Ice Cream Parlor, Brass .... 450.00 To 850.00
National, Model 317, Candy Store, Brass	600.00
National, Model 332	995.00
National, Model 332, Brass	650.00
National, Model 452, Brass	375.00
National, Model 522-EL-ZC, Tiger Oak, Burnished Brass	2200.00
National, Model 582, 4 Drawers	950.00
National, Owned By Biedenharn Candy Co., 1902	2500.00
National, Serial No. 401700	400.00
National, White Marble Shelf Over Drawer, Brass	875.00
St. Louis, Register Up To 1.95, 16 1/2 x 16 3/4 In.	145.00

Castor sets holding just salt and pepper castors were used in the seventeenth century. The sugar castor, mustard pot, spice dredger, bottles for vinegar and oil, and other spice holders became popular by the eighteenth century. These sets were usually made of sterling silver. The American Victorian castor set, the type most collected today, was made of silver plated Britannia metal. Colored glass bottles were introduced after the Civil War. The sets were out of fashion by World War I. Be careful when buying sets with colored bottles; many are reproductions.

CASTOR SET, see also various Porcelain and Glass categories
CASTOR SET, 3–Bottle, Cranberry, Silver Plated Holder, 5 1/2 In. 185.00
  3–Bottle, Mustard & Pepper Shaker, Open Salt, Cranberry, 5 In. 195.00
  4–Bottle, Pewter Frame, Marked I. Trask, 8 In. 300.00
  5–Bottle, Revolving, Silver Plate, Roswell Gleason 1100.00
  Jumbo Pattern, Pressed Glass, Complete 550.00

The pickle castor was a glass jar about six inches in height, held in a special metal holder. It became a popular dinner table accessory about 1890. The jar had a top that was usually silver or silver plate. The frame, also of a silver metal, had a handle that arched above the jar and a hook that held a pair of tongs. By 1900, the pickle castor was out of fashion. Many examples found today have reproduced glass jars in old holders.

CASTOR, PICKLE, see also various Glass categories
CASTOR, Pickle, Amberina, Egg Shape, Hobnail Pattern, Greyhound At Base 650.00
  Pickle, Bubble Lattice Pattern, Silver Frame, Blue, 10 1/2 In. 335.00
  Pickle, Burmese, Applied Flower, Square, Middletown Frame 200.00
  Pickle, Cased Cone, Tufts Frame 200.00
  Pickle, Clear Paneled Glass, Round Hinged Lid, Fork, 2 Glass Tongs 185.00
  Pickle, Cone, Ruby Glass Insert, Brooklyn Frame, 11 3/4 In. 450.00
  Pickle, Coreopsis, Raised Flowers 200.00
  Pickle, Cranberry Barrel Insert, Dog Feet, Figural Frame 395.00
  Pickle, Crane, Homan Frame 90.00
  Pickle, Daisy & Button Insert, Silver Plated Frame, Tongs 185.00
  Pickle, Daisy & Button, Sapphire Blue, Stand 275.00
  Pickle, Double, Lead Crystal, Silver Holder, Lids, Fork, Reed & Barton 225.00
  Pickle, Elk's Head Finial, Double 145.00
  Pickle, Enameled Florals, Cranberry Glass Insert, Footed Frame 225.00
  Pickle, Florals & Lily–of–The–Valley, Frame, Sapphire Blue 250.00
  Pickle, Frame Slides, Cherubs On Front & Frame, Rogers 735.00
  Pickle, Hobnail, Cranberry Opalescent 300.00
  Pickle, Inverted Thumbprint Insert, Silver Frame, Tongs & Lid 480.00
  Pickle, Leafy Vines On Clear, Silver Plated Frame & Tongs 110.00
  Pickle, Little River, Monarc Frame 100.00
  Pickle, Melon Swirl Jar, Pairpoint 100.00
  Pickle, Opalescent Swags Insert, Robin's Egg Blue Threading, Frame 325.00
  Pickle, Pear Shape, Flowers, Plated Frame, Sapphire Blue, 9 1/4 In. 435.00
  Pickle, Pink Florette, Tufts Frame 150.00
  Pickle, Raspberry, Diamond–Quilted, Meriden Frame, Ball Feet, Tongs 325.00
  Pickle, Rubena, Enameled Flowers, Silver Frame 300.00
  Pickle, Victorian, Cloverleaf, Ornate, Tongs 155.00
  Pickle, Victorian, Threaded Glass, Tongs 140.00
  CATALOG, see Paper, Catalog
  CAUGHLEY, see Salopian

The firm Cauldon Limited worked in Staffordshire, Great Britain, and went through many name changes. John Ridgway made porcelain at Cauldon Place, Hanley, until 1855. The firm of John Ridgway, Bates and Co. of Cauldon Place worked from 1856 to 1859. It became Bates, Brown–Westhead, Moore and Co. from 1859 to 1862. Brown–Westhead, Moore and Co. worked from 1862 to 1904. About 1890, this firm started using the words *Cauldon* or *Cauldon ware* as part of the mark. Cauldon Ltd. worked from 1905 to 1920, Cauldon Potteries from 1920 to 1962.

CAULDON, see also Indian Tree
CAULDON, Cup & Saucer, Cobalt Blue, Flowers, Gold 35.00
  Plate, Hunt Scene, 7 1/2 In. 55.00
  Plate, Landscape Scene, 10 3/4 In. 65.00
  CEL, see Animation Art, Cel

Celadon is a Chinese porcelain having a velvet–textured green–gray glaze. Japanese, Korean, and other factories also made a celadon–colored glaze.

CELADON, Bowl, Trellising Vine, Floral Banding, 7 1/4 In.	2000.00
Box, Cover, Soap, Allover Birds & Butterflies, 4 3/4 x 5 1/2 In.	165.00
Cup, Paneled Bowl, Flaring Stem, 4 1/2 In., Pair	45.00
Jar, Temple, Foo Lion Finial, Baluster Form, 42 In., Pair	935.00
Jardiniere, Polychrome Floral, Octagonal, 10 1/4 In.	75.00
Planter, Raised Floral, Chinese Characters, Green, 10 1/4 In.	365.00
Plate, Enamel Floral, Bird Design, 8 1/2 In.	125.00
Vase, Gu–Form, Mounted As Lamp, 10 1/2 In., Pair	137.00
Vase, Petals At Shoulder, Ch'ing Dynasty, 8 In.	275.00
Vase, White Embossed Design, Crazed, Stand, Chinese, 23 1/2 In.	95.00

Celluloid is a trademark for a plastic developed in 1868 by John W. Hyatt. Celluloid Manufacturing Company, the Celluloid Novelty Company, Celluloid Fancy Goods Company, and American Xylonite Company all used Celluloid to make jewelry, games, sewing equipment, false teeth, and piano keys. Eventually, the Hyatt Company became the American Celluloid and Chemical Manufacturing Company—the Celanese Corporation. The name *Celluloid* was often used to identify any similar plastic. Celluloid toys are listed under toys.

CELLULOID, Box, Dresser, Amber, 3 x 2 In.	8.00
Box, Music, Radio, Marbelized, Footed, Art Deco, 7 In.	150.00
Bracelet, Carved Pastel Flowers	35.00
Brush & Comb Set, Pink, Hand Painted Flowers, Box, 1920s	40.00
Brush, Dresser	30.00
Crumb Set, Ivory	15.00
Dresser Set, Black Travel Case, 12 Piece	95.00
Figure, Rabbit Doctor, 5 In.	40.00
Figurine, Nellie Fox	100.00
Letter Opener, Jockey	35.00
Mirror, Dresser	30.00
Mirror, Hand, Red Bakelite Handle, Stylized Lady, Logo, Small	30.00
Necklace, Amber Chain, Hanging Flowers & Leaves	65.00
Penholder, Desk, Dog On Point	20.00
Portrait, Madonna, Child, Signed, Miniature	135.00
Powder Box, Art Deco, Green	45.00
Rattle, Baby Face In Center, Colored	50.00
Rattle, Bear	85.00
Soap Dish	30.00
Spoon, Scottye Embossed Handle, Beetleware, 5 In.	10.00
Stork, Baby In Diaper, Hanging From Beak, 1930s, 10 In.	50.00
Tape Measure, Fruit Basket	38.00
Tape Measure, Owl	30.00
Toothpick, Sterling Case	23.00

The Ceramic Art Company of Trenton, New Jersey, was established in 1889 by J. Coxon and W. Lenox and was an early producer of American Belleek porcelain. It became Lenox, Inc. in 1906. Do not confuse this ware with the pottery made by the Ceramic Arts Studio of Madison, Wisconsin.

◆◆◆

Never buy a repainted chair if you can buy one with original paint. Never strip all the paint from a chair if you can restore the original paint.

◆◆◆

CERAMIC ART CO., Mug, Gibson Girl Monochrome Portrait, 5 In. 135.00
Mug, Plums, Leaves, 5 1/2 In. 150.00
Vase, Flowers, Green, Pink, Palette Mark, 12 In. 550.00

Ceramic Arts Studio was founded in Madison, Wisconsin, by Lawrence Rabbett and Ruben Sand. There most popular products were expensive molded figurines. The pottery closed in 1955. Do not confuse these products with those of the Ceramic Art Co. of Trenton, New Jersey.

CERAMIC ARTS STUDIO, Ashtray, Elf 25.00
Figurine, Boy Fishing, No Pole 30.00
Figurine, Maurice 22.00
Figurine, Oriental Boy 15.00
Figurine, Polish Girl 28.00
Figurine, Wee Dutch Boy 17.00
Figurine, Zorina 22.00
Head Vase, Lotus ....30.00 To 45.00
Head Vase, Manchu 45.00
Head Vase, Mei–Ling, 8 1/4 In. 55.00
Plaque, , Shadow Dancers, 7 In., Pair 48.00
Plaque, Dutch Boy & Girl, Pair 75.00
Plaque, Shadow Dancer 55.00
Shelf Sitter, Maurice & Michele, Pair 38.00
Shelf Sitter, Michelle 14.00
Vase, African Man's Head, 1950s, 8 In. 90.00
Vase, Head, Bonnie 28.00
Vase, Oriental Couple, Triple Bud 60.00
Wall Plaque, Arabesque 45.00
Wall Plaque, Attitude 45.00

Chalkware is really plaster of Paris decorated with watercolors. One type was molded from Staffordshire and other porcelain models and painted and sold as inexpensive decorations in the nineteenth century. Figures of plaster, made from about 1910 to 1940 for use as prizes at carnivals, are also known as chalkware.

CHALKWARE, Bank, Apple, Mid–1800s 135.00
Bank, Beaver 10.00
Bank, Cupid 15.00
Bank, Ferdinand 20.00
Bank, Santa Claus, 12 In. 28.00
Bank, Seated Cat, Full–Bodied, Polychrome Paint, 9 1/2 In. 200.00
Bank, Sgt. Bilko, 12 In. 30.00
Building, Steeple, Candlelight, Stained Glass, 27 3/4 In. 100.00
Bust, General MacArthur 40.00
Bust, Young Girl, Polychrome Paint, 11 In. 215.00
    CHALKWARE, FIGURINE, see also Kewpie
Figurine, 3 Black Children 325.00
Figurine, Bulldog, 10 1/2 In. 20.00
Figurine, Cat, Lying, Black & Yellow, 2 1/2 x 4 In. 165.00
Figurine, Cat, Mouse In Mouth, Oval Pillow Base, 4 In. 375.00
Figurine, Cat, Nodding Head, Red & Black Paint, 8 1/2 In. 300.00
Figurine, Cat, Pipe In Mouth, Polychrome Paint, 10 1/4 In. 235.00
Figurine, Cat, Sitting, 18th Century 4200.00
Figurine, Cat, With Ball, Polychrome Paint, 9 In. 230.00
Figurine, Cat, With Pipe, Polychrome Paint, 10 1/4 In. 230.00
Figurine, Charles Dickens, Seated 15.00
Figurine, Coliseum, Olympic, 1932 .... 40.00
Figurine, Dog, Full–Bodied, Red & Black Paint, 10 x 8 3/4 In. 300.00
Figurine, Dog, Seated, Polychrome Traces, 5 1/4 In. 65.00
Figurine, Dog, Seated, Smoke Yellow Varnish, 8 3/8 In. 100.00
Figurine, Dog, Standing, Red & Black, 6 7/8 In. 165.00
Figurine, Dog, With Pipe, Coin Slot In Head, 8 1/2 In. 10.00
Figurine, Drum Majorette, 15 In. 18.00

Figurine, Horse & Rider, Black, Red & Blue Green, 6 7/8 In. 450.00
Figurine, Lamb, Polychrome Paint & Varnish, 11 In. 150.00
Figurine, Lamb, Polychrome Traces, 4 3/4 In. 45.00
Figurine, Lion, On Ball, Large 45.00
Figurine, Little Black Sambo, Hanging, 8 In. 26.00
Figurine, Mother & Daughter, Yardley Perfume, 14 x 9 In. 295.00
Figurine, Owl, Original Paint, 19 1/2 In. 800.00
Figurine, Parrot, On Ball Base, Embossed Feathers, 7 3/4 In. 270.00
Figurine, Parrot, On Plinth, Polychrome Paint, 8 1/4 In. 250.00
Figurine, Rooster, Polychrome Paint, Yellow, Black & Red 2090.00
Figurine, Rooster, Red, Black & Olive Brown, 9 In. 90.00
Figurine, Snow White 40.00
Figurine, Snow White, 14 1/2 In. .... 35.00 To 40.00
Figurine, Squirrel, Polychrome Paint, 6 1/4 In. .... 300.00 To 350.00
Figurine, Urn, Fruit Filled, 6 1/2 In. 137.00
Figurine, Women's Army Corp, 14 In. 35.00
Nodder, Rabbit, Black & Red Paint, 5 3/4 In. 950.00
Potholder, Boy & Girl Holding Umbrellas, Pair 60.00
String Holder, Cat 28.00
String Holder, Cat With Ball of Yarn 23.00
String Holder, Chef 28.00
String Holder, Girl, With Blue Bonnet 45.00
String Holder, Red Apple, On Branch, With Blackberries 16.00
String Holder, Yellow Pear, Purple Plums & Leaves 16.00
Urn of Fruit, Polychrome Paint, 12 1/2 In. 750.00
Urn of Fruit, Polychrome Paint, 15 In. 550.00
Watch Holder, Cherub, Architectural, 11 1/2 In. 200.00

Charlie Chaplin, the famous comic and actor, lived from 1889 to 1977. He made his first movie in 1913. He did the movie *The Tramp* in 1915. The character of the Tramp has remained famous and is in use today in a series of television commercials for computers. Dolls, candy containers, and all sorts of memorabilia picture Charlie Chaplin. Pieces are being made even today.

CHARLIE CHAPLIN, Box, Hanky, Wood, Pirp-Art, Square, 6 In. 45.00
Candy Container 140.00
Candy Container, Charlie Chaplin Next To Barrel 145.00
Comic Book, 1917 .... 20.00
Doll, 22 In. 35.00
Figurine, Marked Reel Mirthfully Yours, 9 1/2 In. 75.00
Glove Holder, 9 In. 45.00
Joker, Card, Playing, 1 Card Only 6.75
Paper Doll, 1921, Uncut 75.00
Postcard, Wood Pirp-Art 45.00
Poster, Floor Walker, Otis Lithograph, 1920, 40 x 80 In. 4800.00
Poster, Foreign Film 65.00
Poster, The Cure, Export & Import Film, 1923, 40 x 80 In. 2900.00
Poster, Thief Catcher, Orange, Brown, Gray, 1920, 28 x 41 In. 900.00
Sheet Music, Charlie Chaplin Walk 16.50
Toy, 7 In. 60.00
Wristwatch, Bradley, Backwards 140.00

Charlie McCarthy was the ventriloquist's dummy used by Edgar Bergen from the 1930s. He was famous for his work in radio, movies, and television. The act was retired in the 1970s.

CHARLIE MCCARTHY, Card, Birthday, Blockheads, 1938 .... 40.00
Card, Birthday, Charlie, Edgar Bergen, Envelope, 1938 .... 12.50
Cutout, Charlie McCarthy, Standard Brands, 1938, 4 In. 6.00
Cutout, Edgar Bergen, Standard Brands, 1938, 4 In. 5.00
Doll, 1977, Large 16.00
Doll, Black Tuxedo, Movable Mouth 40.00
Doll, Ventriloquist, 31 In. 250.00
Doll, Ventriloquist, Composition Head, Hands, Suit, 20 In. 79.00

Doll, Wood, Pull String, 12 In.	175.00
Dummy, Summer Suit, White Shoes & Slacks, F & B, 16 In.	285.00
Game, Flying Hats, Original Can, Instructions	35.00
Pin, Die Cut	45.00
Portrait, Cardboard, Tab Moves Eyes & Mouth, 18 In.	275.00
Print, Charlie At CBS Mike, Coke, 1949	85.00
Puppet, Hand	65.00
Radio, Majestic, Charlie McCarthy	125.00
Salt & Pepper	45.00
Scarf, The Dude Cowboy, Silk, Graphics	89.00
Spoon, Profile, Monocle On Handle, Silver Plate, 6 In.	28.00
Spoon, Silver Plate, Duchess	15.00
Toy, Mortimer Snerd Tricky Auto, Tinplate, Marx	825.00
Toy, Mortimer Snerd, With Drum, Tinplate, Marx, 1939, Box	1870.00
Toy, Tin Lithograph, Mouth Drops, Marx, 8 1/2 In. ....*Illus*	220.00
Toy, Windup, Walker, 1930s	350.00
Yo-Yo, Charlie's Head, Pull Cord & Mouth Opens, 1968	15.00

 Chelsea grape pattern was made before 1840. A small bunch of grapes in a raised design, colored with purple or blue luster, is on the border of the white china plate. Several factories made this pattern but most of the pieces are unmarked. The pattern is sometimes called *Aynsley* or *Grandmother*. Chelsea sprig is similar but has a sprig of flowers instead of the bunch of grapes. Chelsea thistle has a raised thistle pattern. Do not confuse these patterns with pieces made by the Chelsea factory of London in the eighteenth century.

CHELSEA GRAPE, Bowl, 6 In.	27.00
Coffee Cup, Large	25.00
Creamer	20.00
Cup & Saucer	30.00
Egg Cup	25.00
Plate, 8 In.	20.00
Teapot, Octagonal, 6 Cup	120.00
CHELSEA KERAMIC ART WORKS, see Dedham	
CHELSEA SPRIG, Bowl, 7 In.	20.00
Butter Chip	10.00
Creamer	55.00
Cup & Saucer	25.00
Plate, 10 In.	25.00
Plate, 8 In.	20.00

 Chelsea porcelain was made in the Chelsea area of London from about 1745 to 1784. Ceramic designs were borrowed from the Meissen models of the day. Pieces were made of soft paste. The gold

Charlie McCarthy, Toy, Tin Lithograph, Mouth Drops, Marx, 8 1/2 In.

◆ ◆ ◆ ◆ ◆ ◆ ◆ ◆ ◆ ◆ ◆ ◆ ◆ ◆ ◆ ◆ ◆ ◆ ◆ ◆

American carousel figures are more heavily carved on the right side because they went around counterclockwise. The left side is more ornate for European carousel figures because the carousel turned the other way. American figures sell for more money.

◆ ◆ ◆ ◆ ◆ ◆ ◆ ◆ ◆ ◆ ◆ ◆ ◆ ◆ ◆ ◆ ◆ ◆ ◆ ◆

anchor was used as the mark but it has been copied by many other factories. Recent copies of Chelsea have been made from the original molds.

CHELSEA, Dish, Leaf Shape, Green, Yellow, Brown, Anchor Mark 8 In. 750.00
Figurine, Dog, Gold Anchor, 2 1/2 x 3 1/2 In. 185.00
Figurine, Woman, Flower Decorated Dress, c.1760, 8 In. 1550.00
Relish, Leaf Shape, White, Butterflies, Insects, Anchor, 9 1/2 In. 605.00
Soup, Dish, Gold Phoenix In Flight, Shrubbery, c.1754, 9 1/8 In. 2750.00

Chinese export porcelain comprises all the many kinds of porcelain made in China for export to America and Europe in the eighteenth and nineteenth centuries.

CHINESE EXPORT, see also Canton; Celadon; Nanking; Rose Medallion
CHINESE EXPORT, Bowl, Blue & White, 19 In. 357.00
Bowl, Blue Border, Gold, Monogram, 5 In. 99.00
Bowl, Blue Design, c.1850 .... 550.00
Bowl, Egg & Spinach Glaze, 18th Century, 5 1/2 In. 550.00
Bowl, Enameled Scenes, 4 3/4 x 11 1/2 In. 275.00
Bowl, Famille Rose, Figural Scenic Groupings, 11 3/4 In. 965.00
Bowl, Floral Enameling, Blue Underglaze, 8 In. 425.00
Bowl, Goldfish Design, 19th Century, 4 x 11 In. 385.00
Bowl, Mandarin Courtyard Scenes, Gilt Rim, 5 /2 In. 412.00
Bowl, Mandarin Palette, Diaper Ground, 10 In., Pair 1435.00
Bowl, Salad, Blue, 9 1/2 In. 1540.00
Bowl, Scenes, Underglaze Blue & Enamel, 11 1/4 In. 350.00
Candlestick, Famille Rose, Floral, Insect, 8 1/4 In., Pr. 335.00
Chestnut Basket, Under Tray, Basket Is 10 1/2 In. 1875.00
Chocolate Pot, Burnt Orange & Gilt Floral Spray, 9 1/2 In. 525.00
Chop Plate, Eagle & Banner, BLP Initials, 1815, 16 1/4 In. 850.00
Creamer, Helmut, Famille Rose 265.00
Cup & Bowl, Tea, Handleless, Stars, Blue, Gold, Set of 8 .... 660.00
Cup & Saucer, Armorial Crest, Purple Bowknot, Blue Trim 467.50
Custard Cup, Cover, Strap Handles, Fitzhugh, 8 Sets 2900.00
Dish, Cover, Medallion, Famille Rose Interior, 9 1/2 In. 220.00
Dish, Cover, Shaped, Blue, 19th Century, 13 In. 1650.00
Dish, Crest Center, Blue Border, Flowerettes, 6 In. 412.00
Dish, Hot Water Base, Blue Border, Monogram, 1833, 9 1/2 In. 600.00
Dish, Warming, Opposing Spouts, Trace of Gold, 10 In. 110.00
Figurine, Birds of Paradise, 1820–30, 16 In., Pair 2500.00
Figurine, Parrot, Porcelain, 8 1/4 In., Pair 445.00
Figurine, Samurai Warrior, Seated, Holding Sword, Porcelain 165.00
Garden Seat, 4–Claw Dragon, White Ground, c.1870, 13 In. 2450.00
Holder, Joss Stick, Famille Rose, Elephant Form, Pair 5500.00
Jar, Cover, Famille Rose, Double Circle Mark, 18 In. 825.00
Jar, Ginger, Famille Rose, Figures In Procession, 13 In. 100.00
Jug, Cider, Cover, Blue, 19th Century, 11 1/2 In. 2650.00
Jug, Cider, Foo Dog Finial, Floral, Striping, 11 1/4 In. 1500.00
Mug, American Eagle, 5 In. 1350.00
Pitcher, Hot Cider, Covered Spout, c.1770 .... 4600.00
Planter, Blue, White, 19th Century, 14 x 10 In. 1895.00
Planter, Famille Rose, Phoenix Birds, 5 3/4 In. 335.00
Plate, Armorial, Floral & Insect Rim, 9 1/4 In., 9 Piece 6700.00
Plate, Butterfly & Trellis Rim, Center Medallion, 9 1/2 In. 55.00
Plate, Dutch Hongs, 9 1/4 In. 7500.00
Plate, Floral Enameling With Birds, 9 In. 55.00
Plate, Floral, Pomegranate Rim, 9 1/2 In. ....*Illus* 400.00
Platter, Birds & Flowers, 19th Century, 12 1/4 In. 225.00
Platter, Blue Fitzhugh, 18 1/2 x 16 1/4 In. 825.00
Platter, Coat of Arms, Lion, 18 1/2 In. ....*Illus* 1595.00
Platter, Famille Rose, Floral Border, 8 1/4 x 10 3/4 In. 275.00
Platter, Lake Scene, 19th Century, 12 In. 225.00
Platter, Mandarin Palette, Figures At Lake, 17 1/2 In. 1100.00

Platter, Medallion, Floral Panels, 14 1/2 x 11 3/4 In. 305.00
Platter, Rose Medallion Enameled Design, 8 1/4 x 6 1/2 In. 550.00
Pot, Hot Water, Cover, Village Scene, 9 1/2 In. ....*Illus* 650.00
Salad Bowl, Center Medallion, Floral Panels, 9 1/2 In. 880.00
Saucer, Famille Rose, Yogzheng, 1723 .... 1870.00
Soup, Dish, Center Medallion, Floral Panels, 9 5/8 In., 8 Pc. 415.00
Soup, Dish, Famille Rose, Quan Yin Scene, 8 1/2 In., Pair 1045.00
Tea Caddy, Blue Border, Gold, Monogram, 5 In. 305.00
Tea Caddy, Landscape, 4 Pewter Containers, Lacquer, 6 In. 275.00
Tea Pot, Berry Design, Cover, 5 In. 275.00
Tea Pot, Blue Band, Berry Design, Pedestal Base, 6 In. 715.00
Tea Set, Blue & Gilt Border, 53 Piece 4500.00
Teapot, 19th Century, 5 3/4 In. 525.00
Teapot, Famille Rose, Armorial 2000.00
Teapot, Gold Design of Mars & Venus, Seen By Cupid, 4 In. 1155.00
Teapot, Lotus & Faux Bois, 5 1/2 In. 1980.00
Teapot, Marriage, Famille Rose, Armorial 825.00
Tray, Central Pagoda Scene, Footed, c.1810, 10 In. 1650.00
Tureen, Cover, Garden Scenes, Animal Form Handles, 12 In. 835.00
Tureen, Cover, Under Tray, Blue, 13 In. 3520.00
Tureen, Cover, Under Tray, Blue, 6 1/2 In. 1100.00
Tureen, Flower Finial, Armorial Design, 13 3/4 In. 2200.00
Tureen, Sauce, Sunflower Finial, Twisted Handles, 8 1/4 In. 550.00
Tureen, Soup, Floral Finial, Coat of Arms, 18th Century 9250.00
Vase, Famille Rose, Court & Military Scene, c.1900, 25 In. 330.00
Vase, Famille Rose, Geometric & Floral Design, 9 In. 135.00
Vase, Famille Rose, Immortal, Attendants, 1920s, 24 In. 1650.00
Vase, Yellow, Green Dragon Design, Pottery, 29 In. 302.00
Wash Basin, Famille Rose, Figural Scene, 1880s, 15 In. 165.00

 Chocolate glass, sometimes mistakenly called caramel slag, was made by the Indiana Tumbler and Goblet Company of Greentown, Indiana, from 1900 to 1903. Fenton Art Glass Co. also made chocolate glass from about 1907 to 1915. A few recent reproductions have been made.

CHOCOLATE GLASS, Box, Dolphin Cover, Sawtooth Rim, 4 3/4 In. 55.00
Butter, Cactus, Cover 185.00
Butter, Cover, Beaded Swag 50.00
Butter, Cover, Cactus, Greentown 395.00
Butter, Cover, Leaf Bracket 75.00
Butter, Open, Dewey, 4 In. 65.00
Compote, Jelly, Pleat Band 145.00
Creamer, Cactus 72.00
Creamer, Shuttle, 6 In. 175.00
Cruet, Cactus, Original Stopper 140.00
Cruet, Cord Drapery 165.00
Crust, Cactus 140.00

Chinese Export, Plate, Floral,
Pomegranate Rim, 9 1/2 In.
Chinese Export, Pot, Hot Water, Cover,
Village Scene, 9 1/2 In.

Chinese Export, Platter, Coat of Arms, Lion,
18 1/2 In.

Dish, Dolphin, Fish Finial Cover, Beaded Rim 295.00
Dish, Sweatmeat, Cover, Cactus 450.00
Goblet, Ribbed Palm, Flint 30.00
Mug, Robin 15.00
Mug, Tavern Scene, 6 In. 125.00
Mug, Tavern Scene, 8 In. 395.00
Pitcher, Water, Jubilee 225.00
Plate, Troubador, Greentown, 6 1/4 In. 135.00
Salt & Pepper 90.00
Salt & Pepper, Cactus 90.00
Sugar, Cover, Diamond Cut With Leaf, Amber 60.00
Sugar, Cover, Leaf Bracket, 6 1/2 In. .... 22.50 To 68.00
Syrup, Cord Drapery 275.00
Syrup, Strigal 135.00
Table Set, Leaf Bracket, 4 Piece 375.00
Toothpick, Cactus .... 25.00 To 125.00
Tray, Venetian, Comb & Brush 175.00
Tumbler, Cosmos 30.00
Tumbler, Geneva, 3 7/8 In. 85.00
Tumbler, Shuttle 95.00

The first decorated Christmas tree in America is claimed by many states, including Pennsylvania (1747), Massachusetts (1832), Illinois (1833), Ohio (1838), and Iowa (1845). The first glass ornaments were imported from Germany about 1860. Dresden ornaments were made about 100 years ago of paper and tinsel. Manufacturers in the United States were making ornaments in the early 1870s. Electric lights were first used on a Christmas tree in 1882. Character light bulbs became popular in the 1920s, bubble lights in the 1940s, twinkle bulbs in the 1950s, plastic bulbs by 1955. In this book a Christmas light is a holder for a candle used on the tree. Other forms of lighting include light bulbs.

CHRISTMAS TREE, Feather, 3 Ft. .... 245.00 To 300.00
Feather, 4 1/2 Ft. 345.00
Feather, Germany, 18 In. .... 140.00 To 155.00
Feather, Germany, 21 In. 285.00
Feather, Germany, 22 In. 165.00
Feather, Gold Paint, Electrified 60.00
Feather, Red Berries, Tin Candle Sockets, 39 In. 200.00
Feather, Red Berries, Wooden Base, 16 In. 175.00
Feather, Spruce, Red Berries, 14 1/2 In. 150.00
Feather, White, 12 Limbs, Germany, 17 In. 135.00
Fence, Box 90.00
Fence, Gate, 21 x 21 In. 65.00
Fence, Picket, Front Gate, White, Green Trim, Square, 18 In. 125.00
Fence, Red Rails, Green Posts, 2 Gates, 8 16-In. Sections 95.00
Glass Rod Candles, Electric Bulb Base, 1940s 30.00
Holder, Tin, Different Santa Scenes, 14 In. 73.00
Icicles, 1930s 7.50
Light Bulb, Andy Gump 27.00
Light Bulb, Candle, Bubble 10.00
Light Bulb, Clown, Double-Faced, White Mask, Ruffle Collar 22.00
Light Bulb, Diamond-Quilted, Amethyst, 2 7/8 In. 75.00
Light Bulb, Fairy, Nursery Rhyme Figures, England, Box, 1930s 160.00
Light Bulb, Father Christmas, With Toys, Japan 135.00
Light Bulb, GE, Colors, Noma Cord, 59 Piece 200.00
Light Bulb, Girl's Head, Double-Sided, Gold Hair, 1 1/2 In. 18.00
Light Bulb, Japanese Lantern Shape, 1940s, String of 10 .... 80.00
Light Bulb, Noma, Dated 1939, Box 22.00
Light Bulb, Santa Claus, 2 Sides 20.00
Light Bulb, Santa, 3 In. 20.00
Light Bulb, Smitty 60.00
Light Bulb, Snow-Covered Cottage, Pane Windows, 2 In. 10.00

◆◆

Rearrange lamps, figurines, vases, and other knicknacks on table tops. If you don't, the exposed wood will be lighter than the covered sections under the ornaments.

◆◆

Light Bulb, Snowman, Stick In Hand, Red Cap, 2 1/2 In.	12.00
Light Bulb, Zeppelin, Patriotic	100.00
Oranment, Boy & Girl, Movable, Papier–Mache, Germany, 4 In.	135.00
Ornament, Al Jolson's Head, Blown Glass, 3 1/4 In.	300.00
Ornament, Angel, Noma, Original Box, Blue Robe, 8 In.	18.00
Ornament, Apple, Cotton, Red, Large	28.00
Ornament, Apple, Red Cotton, Large	28.00
Ornament, Balloon, Double, Wire Wrapped	60.00
Ornament, Banana Horn, Paper, Wood, Dresden, 7 In.	60.00
Ornament, Bead Roping, Glass, 4 Strands, 100 In.	130.00
Ornament, Beaded Fringe, Czechoslovakia, 16 In.	50.00
Ornament, Bell, Interior Scene	10.00
Ornament, Bird, Blown Glass	15.00
Ornament, Bird, Papier–Mache	8.00
Ornament, Bird, Spring Clip, Spun Glass Tail, Green, 6 In.	7.00
Ornament, Boat, With Tinsel, 5 3/4 In.	10.00
Ornament, Camel, Dresden	95.00
Ornament, Camel, Flocked, Glass Eyes, Putz, 2 1/2 In.	18.00
Ornament, Candy Cane, Blown Glass	15.00
Ornament, Candy Cane, Cobalt & Gold Stripes, 6 1/2 In.	8.00
Ornament, Carousel	35.00
Ornament, Carrot, Orange, 4 In.	42.50
Ornament, Cat, Blown Glass	10.00
Ornament, Child Sitting On Ball, Holding Bear, Blown Glass	60.00
Ornament, Christ Child, Mohair Wig, Golden Halo, Wax, Box	150.00
Ornament, Christmas Face On Pine Cone	48.00
Ornament, Clown, Flesh Face, Red Suit, Gold Buttons, 4 In.	40.00
Ornament, Clown, Yellow, 3 1/2 In.	45.00
Ornament, Cornucopia Candy Container, 9 In.	40.00
Ornament, Dancing Couple, Jointed, Papier–Mache, 2 In.	65.00
Ornament, Double Balloon, Wire Wrapped	60.00
Ornament, Elf, Bisque, Japan, Box, 12 Piece	35.00
Ornament, Father Christmas Embossed On Leaf	85.00
Ornament, Father Christmas Face, On Pinecone	48.00
Ornament, Father Christmas Indent On Leaf	48.00
Ornament, Father Christmas, With Staff, 6 Bulb	50.00
Ornament, Fish, Candle Clip	18.00
Ornament, Football Player, Crepe Paper Clothes	45.00
Ornament, Fruit With Bug, 2 7/8 In.	80.00
Ornament, Gazebo	35.00
Ornament, Girl With Composition Face, Crepe Dress, Cotton	72.00
Ornament, Horn	20.00
Ornament, Horse, Jumping, Papier–Mache, 4 x 3 In.	50.00
Ornament, House, Silver, Red Door, Pine Trees, 3 In.	15.00
Ornament, Humming Birds, Gold Nest, Glass Tails, 2 Pc., 5 In.	45.00
Ornament, Icicle, Gold Glass, 12 In.	35.00
Ornament, Icicle, Spun Cotton, White, Mica, Hanger, 5 In.	15.00
Ornament, Kugle, Green, 2 1/2 In.	25.00
Ornament, Kugle, Silver, 1 1/2 In.	18.00
Ornament, Lamb, Woolly	30.00
Ornament, Pear, Cotton, Green, Large	28.00
Ornament, Pear, Frosted Glass, 2 In.	25.00
Ornament, Pickle, Green Paint, 4 1/2 In.	10.00
Ornament, Rabbit, Papier Mache	42.00

Ornament, Santa Airship, Germany, Felt, 6 In.	132.00
Ornament, Santa Claus, Bisque Face, Felt Costume, 9 In.	65.00
Ornament, Santa Claus, Chenille Arms & Legs	60.00
Ornament, Santa Claus, Chenille Arms & Legs, Composition	60.00
Ornament, Santa Claus, Chenille Boot, Celluloid Face, 6 In.	165.00
Ornament, Santa Claus, Flying, Polychromed Wood, 13 In.	50.00
Ornament, Santa Claus, Holding Bubble Light	30.00
Ornament, Santa Claus, Plastic, 1940s, Box, 3 In., 6 Piece	45.00
Ornament, Santa Claus, Red Clothes, Dresden Belt, 8 In.	275.00
Ornament, Santa Claus, Red, Silver Pearl, Spring Clip	50.00
Ornament, Santa Claus, Roly Poly, Red, Celluloid, 3 In.	15.00
Ornament, Santa's Head, Mica, Papier-Mache, Germany, 1930s	25.00
Ornament, Shepherd Boy, Red Pants, Papier-Mache, 3 In.	15.00
Ornament, Slipper, Tinsel	25.00
Ornament, Snowball, Spun Cotton, With Mica, 2 1/2 In.	20.00
Ornament, Snowman, Holding Bubble Light	35.00
Ornament, Stork, Blown Glass	12.00
Ornament, Stork, Cotton Batting, 6 In.	95.00
Ornament, Swan, Tinsel & Feathers, 6 In.	20.00
Ornament, Teardrop, Glass, Frosted, Pearl, Box, 6 In., 6 Piece	125.00
Ornament, Tree On Clip	32.00
Ornament, Zeppelin, U. S. Flag, Spun Glass Tail, 1920s	85.00
Stand, Cast Iron, c.1890	65.00
Stand, Santa Claus, Cast Iron	400.00
Stand, Snow Village Design, Tin Litho, 18 In.	30.00

 Almost anything connected with Christmas is collected. Ornaments, feather trees, tree stands, santa claus figures, special dishes, even games and wrapping paper. A Belsnickle is a nineteenth-century figure of Father Christmas. A kugel is an early, heavy ornament made of thick blown glass, lined with zinc or lead, and often covered with colored wax.

CHRISTMAS, Bank, Santa, Chalkware, Ringing Bell, Holding Bag, 1940s	45.00
Bells, Red Cellophane, Cluster of 4, Box	10.00
Belsnickle, Red Robe, Snow Base, 7 In.	695.00
Belsnickle, Santa Claus, Open Coat, Feather Tree, 9 1/2 In.	495.00
Box, Candy, Figural, Santa Claus	85.00
Button, Santa Claus, Auto, Pinback, Celluloid, 1911, 1 1/4 In.	40.00
Candleholder, Santa Claus, Papier-Mache	30.00
Candles, Cardboard, Mica, Tinsel, 1920-30	35.00
Candy Container, Boot, Kentucky Tavern, Papier-Mache, 9 In.	18.00
Candy Container, Christmas Tree, Papier-Mache, 9 In.	143.00
Candy Container, Red Suit, Feather Tree, Germany, 6 In.	185.00
Candy Container, Santa In Chimney, Papier-Mache, Cardboard, 9 In.	357.00
Cup, From Santa Claus At Siegel Cooper Co., New York Store	58.00
Doll, Baby, Creche, Wax Head, 18th Century	200.00
Fence, 2 Fixed Gates, 18 Sections, Wooden, Red & Green	75.00

Christmas, Plaque, Santa, Chalk, 22 In.

◆◆◆◆◆◆◆◆◆◆◆◆◆◆◆◆◆◆◆◆◆◆◆

If you are a collector of old Christmas tree ornaments or Christmas lights, use these on the tree. Do not use burning candles. It is too dangerous.

◆◆◆◆◆◆◆◆◆◆◆◆◆◆◆◆◆◆◆◆◆◆◆

Figure, Santa Claus In Moss–Covered Sled, 5 1/2 x 9 In. 435.00
Figure, Santa Claus, Stuffed, 24 In. 125.00
Figure, Skier, Skater, Santa, Horse Drawn Sleigh, Barclay, 12 Pc. 180.00
Manger Set, Plates, Painted, Instructions, Box, Dated 1933 .... 87.00
Mask, Parade–Type, Santa Claus, Papier–Mache, Whole Head, Germany 350.00
Mask, Santa 20.00
Mask, Santa, Painted Wire, Horsehair, 8 In. 143.00
Mold, Ice Cream, Father Christmas, Pewter, Small 125.00
Mold, Santa, Iron, Griswold 450.00
Paperweight, Snow Dome, Brick Chimney, Santa, On Fireplace 20.00
Plaque, Santa, Chalk, 22 In. ....*Illus* 165.00
CHRISTMAS, PLATE, see Collector Plate
Putz, Horse, Tan, Glass Eyes, Mane, Saddle, 5 In. 48.00
Reindeer, Modder, Green Saddle, Glass Eyes, F. A. O. Schwarz, 17 In. 400.00
Santa Claus, Gold Face, White Ground, 1950s, 23 x 16 In. 55.00
Santa Claus, In Bell, Cardboard, Stand–Up, 1920–30, 9 x 13 In. 75.00
Santa Claus, In Plastic Snow Dome 14.00
Santa Claus, In Sleigh, Reindeer, Cardboard, 1920s, 10 x 13 In. 125.00
Santa Claus, Mechanical, 30 In. 150.00
Santa Claus, On Sparkling Snow Base, 8 x 11 In. 75.00
Santa Claus, Par–T–Pak Beverages, Die Cut, 32 x 36 In. 28.00
Santa Claus, Red Hood, Holly Wreath On Head 8.00
Santa Claus, Reindeer, Cardboard, Plaster Face, Japan, 13 In. 110.00
Seals, 1933 To 1947, 700 Piece 20.00
Seals, Red Cross, Winter Scene, Full Sheet of 100, 1934 .... 14.00
Sleigh, Santa's, Wood, Paper Litho, 12 In. 1925.00
Spoon, Santa In Chimney, Bag of Toys, Sterling, Demitasse 95.00
Stable, 3 Candleholder Top, Jesus In Crib, 2 Children, Handmade 40.00
Toy, Santa Claus & Reindeers, Windup, Strauss, Late 1800s 2100.00
Toy, Santa Claus & Sled, Windup, Tin & Celluloid, Japan, 6 3/4 In. 27.50
Toy, Santa Claus & Sleigh, Occupied Japan 68.00
Toy, Santa Claus, Battery Operated, Alps Co. 145.00
Toy, Santa Claus, On Nodding Donkey, Mohair, Glass Eyes, 10 In. 550.00
Toy, Santa Claus, On Scooter, Battery Operated, Box 65.00
Toy, Santa Claus, Reindeer & Sleigh, Pull Toy, Hubley 1155.00
Toy, Santa Claus, Riding Deer, Tin, Windup, 5 1/2 In. 150.00
Toy, Santa Claus, Stuffed, 1940s, 8 In. 23.00
Toy, Santa Claus, Vinyl Face, Hands & Boots, Plush, My–Toy, 24 In. 45.00
Toy, Santa Claus, Walker, Cloth Dressed, Wood Legs, 9 In. 357.00
Toy, Santa Claus, Walking, 2 Sides, Paper, 12 In. 95.00
Toy, Santa's Sleigh & Reindeer, Windup, Tin, Strauss, 11 1/4 In. 1900.00

Art Deco chrome items became popular in the 1930s. Collectors are most interested in high–style pieces made by the Connecticut firms of Chase Brass and Copper Company and Manning Bowman.

CHROME, Bookends, Cat, Arched Back, Tail In Air, Chase Brass, 8 1/2 In. 130.00
Bottle Opener & Jigger, Combination, Chase 20.00
Bowl, Bakelite Handle 12.30
Box, Dresser, Celluloid Handles, Chase Brass 47.50
Candlestick, Chase Brass, Wooden Bottom, Pair 20.00
Candlestick, Nude Woman, Art Deco, Krome–Kraft, Farber, 9 In., Pair 100.00
Candy, Bronze & Brass Color, Rose Knob, Glass Insert 40.00
Cigarette Box, Bakelite Bottom, Dolphin Handle, Chase Brass 40.00
Cigarette Case, Indian Chief Profile 15.00
Cocktail Mixer, Chase 22.50
Cocktail Set, Bell Shape, Art Deco, 4 Red Glass Goblets, Tray, 6 Pc. 225.00
Cocktail Shaker, Glass, Chrome Lid 20.00
Cocktail Shaker, Musical, 2 Chrome Tumbler, Plays How Dry I Am 125.00
Cocktail Shaker, Penguin, Napier, 1936, 11 3/4 In. 330.00
Coffee, Urn, Bakelite Handle & Tap, Electric 28.00
Cookie Cannister, Lucite Knob, Eveready 20.00
Corkscrew & Shot Glass 10.00
Decanter Set, Farberware, Amber, 7 Piece 98.00

Decanter, Wine, Ebony Glass, Krome Kraft 125.00
Figurine, Borzoi, Standing, Metal, Chrome Plated, Hagenauer, 10 In. 3300.00
Figurine, Woman, Nude, Standing, Metal, Plated, Hagenauer, 9 1/8 In. 1650.00
Gravy Boat, Undertray, Chase Brass 35.00
Ice Bucket, Rockwell Kent .... 500.00 To 715.00
Lazy Susan, Amber Glass, Krome Kraft 135.00
Martini Mixer, Chase Brass 22.50
Pitcher, Plastic Handle, Plated, L. B., 12 1/2 In. 120.00
Pitcher, Water, Arcadio, Chase Brass 45.00
Salt & Pepper, Chase Brass 40.00
Server, Folds Out To 1 On Top, 2 On Bottom, Chase Brass, 11 x 7 In. 55.00
Server, Hot & Cold, Penguin, Westbend 12.50
Shaker, Cocktail, Farberware, 6 Wines, Amber Inserts 65.00
Silent Butler, Amber Glass, Wood Handle, Farberware 50.00
Silent Butler, Art Deco, Farberware 20.00
Smoking Stand, Art Deco 55.00
Tea Set, Willow, England, Bakelite Covers & Handles, 5 Piece 125.00
Teapot, Ball, Bakelite Handle, Chase 75.00
Toaster, Red Bakelite 48.00
Torchiere, Half–Moon Shade, Cylindrical, Stepped, 1930, 67 In., Pair 440.00
Vase, Portuguese Man of War, Sea Designs, Ikora, WMF, 7 3/4 In. 275.00
Waffle Maker, Art Deco, Top Opens When Handle Lowers 18.00

Carved wooden or cast iron figures were used as advertisements in front of the Victorian cigar store. The carved figures are now collected as folk art. They range in size from counter type, about three feet, to over eight feet high.

CIGAR STORE FIGURE, Indian Chief, Headdress, Dagger In Hand, 70 1/4 In. 2650.00
Indian Princess, Carved Wood, Polychrome, 87 In. 3200.00
Indian, Feathered Headdress, Carrying Book, 5 Ft. 1 In 8500.00
Indian, Solid Wood, 1920s, 6 Ft. 4 In. 6000.00
Princess, Headdress, Green Costume, Pine, c.1875, 79 In. 10450.00
Squaw, Wooden, Tall 3500.00

Cinnabar is a vermilion or red lacquer. Some pieces are made with hundreds of thicknesses of the lacquer that is later carved.

CINNABAR, Bottle, Snuff, Figural, Landscape, 2 3/4 In. 50.00
Box, Cover, Carved, Square, 4 In. 35.00
Cache Pot, Reserves of Flowers & Vines, Hexagonal, 10 In., Pair 2450.00
Ginger Jar, Cover, 5 Scenes 65.00
Vase, 9 In. 55.00

Civil War mementos are important collector's items. Most of the pieces are military items used from 1861 to 1865.

CIVIL WAR, Bayonet, Confederate, Triangular 30.00
Belt, Cartridge, U. S. Cavalry, Leather 375.00
Book, Music, Drum, Fife & Bugle Calls 75.00
Boots, Wooden Pegs, Serial Numbered 290.00
Buckle, U. S., 1855 .... 135.00
Bugle, Not Original Mouthpiece 275.00
Drum, Artillery, Cannon Behind U. S. Shield, 32 Stars, c.1858 .... 1875.00
Drum, Calf Skin Heads, Ordnance Mark, 9 x 15 1/2 In. 550.00
Drum, Large Eagle, A. Rogers, Flushing, L. I. 2970.00
Drum, Snare, Eagle On Flagstaff, Flag Banner, Rim Hooks 1650.00
Drum, Snare, Star Designs, Bird's–Eye Maple, Rawhide Skin 880.00
Flag, 34 Stars 1045.00
Lantern Globe, Presentation, Ohio, Name, Rank & Unit 1850.00
Matches, Issue, Full Pack, Dated 1861 .... 35.00
Matchsafe, With Matches, Fitted Into Knapsack 25.00
Medal of Honor, To James Woodsom, Discharge Papers 2750.00
Medal, Grant & Lee, Centennial, 2 1/2 In. 48.00
Photograph, Sailors, Ship, Albumen, J. W. Black, 1864, 16 x 11 In. 660.00
Razor, Dated 1865 .... 25.00

Shaving Mug, Side Pocket For Brush, Tin, 4 x 4 1/2 In.	75.00
Spurs, Cavalry	75.00
Strop, Razor, Cavalry	2.00
Uniform, Colonel, Caped Coat, Vest & Jacket, 3 Piece	1980.00
Uniform, Union	1800.00

CKAW, see Dedham

Clambroth glass, popular in the Victorian era, is a grayish color and is semiopaque like clambroth.

CLAMBROTH, Bowl, Crab Claw, Aqua Opalescent, Collar Base, 9 In.	100.00
Candlestick, Loop & Petal, Black Ash Streaks, 6 3/4 In., Pair	130.00
Goblet, Button Arches, Endicott, N. Y.	30.00
Lamp, Scotty Dog, 1930s	58.00
Spill, Horn of Plenty	550.00
Sugar, Cover, Gothic Arch, 5 1/4 In.	200.00

Clarice Cliff
NEWPORT POTTERY
ENGLAND

Clarice Cliff was a designer who worked in several English factories after the 1920s. She died in 1972.

CLARICE CLIFF, Biscuit Jar, Bizarre Ware, Rattan Handle, 9 1/4 In.	255.00
Bone Dish, Tonquin	18.00
Bowl, Serving, Tonquin, Brown	20.00
Bowl, Soup, Devonshire	9.00
Bread Plate, Tonquin, Brown	8.00
Cookie Jar, Tonquin, Blue & White	95.00
Creamer, Art Deco	30.00
Creamer, Cow, Laughing, Brown Transfer	60.00
Cup & Saucer, Plate, Floral, Art Deco, 3 Piece	35.00
Dinner Set, Tonquin, Blue, 49 Piece	275.00
Dish, Jam, Celtic Harvest, Chrome Handle, Spoon, Marked, 5 In.	55.00
Dish, Soup, Devonshire	10.00
Dish, Tonquin	9.00
Flower Frog, Autumn Crocus, Bizarre	350.00
Pitcher, Cream, Sailboat Scene, Burslem, 1932, 2 3/8 In.	192.00
Pitcher, My Garden, Floral Handle, Bizarre, 9 In.	355.00
Plate, Asparagus	65.00
Plate, Banana	65.00
Plate, Coronation, Queen Elizabeth	40.00
Plate, Cotswold, 11 In.	30.00
Plate, Day By Day	65.00
Plate, Peas	65.00
Plate, Salad, Tonquin, Brown	8.00
Plate, Tonquin, Brown	10.00
Sugar & Creamer, Bizarre, Ovoid, Gold Stars In Sky	250.00
Sugar & Creamer, Floral, Cream Ground, Art Deco, 3 3/8 In.	65.00
Sugar & Creamer, Spoon, Red Scene	18.00
Vase, Embossed Flowers & Handle, Marked, 8 3/4 In.	88.00
Vase, In My Garden, Melon Sections, Marked, 7 In.	95.00
Vase, Lovebirds, Yellow Ground, 12 1/4 In.	225.00

Clewell ware was made in limited quantities by Charles Walter Clewell of Canton, Ohio, from 1902 to 1955. Pottery was covered with a thin coating of bronze, then treated to make the bronze turn different colors. Pieces covered with copper, brass, or silver were also made. Mr. Clewell's secret formula for blue patina bronze was burned when he died in 1965.

CLEWELL, Vase, Blue Patinated Over Bronze, Marked, 12 3/4 In.	1000.00
Vase, Bronze Patina, 18 In.	650.00
Vase, Bulbous, Signed, 4 1/2 In.	400.00
Vase, Copper–Clad, 12 In.	1600.00

Clews pottery was made by George Clews & Co. of Brownhill Pottery, Tunstall, England, from 1806 to 1861.

CLEWS, see also Flow Blue

CLEWS, Candlestick, Chameleon Ware, Mottled Brown, White, Cobalt Glaze, 6 In. 60.00
Plate, Landing of Lafayette, Staffordshire, 10 In. 165.00
Plate, Moral Maxims, Black Transfer, 1817–37 .... 8.00

Clifton Pottery was founded by William Long in Clifton, New
Jersey, in 1905. He worked there until 1908 making a line called
Crystal Patina. Clifton Pottery made art pottery. Another firm,
Chesapeake Pottery, sold majolica marked *Clifton ware.*

CLIFTON, Bowl, Pitcher Form, Indian, Signed, 6 1/2 In. 185.00
Humidor, Indian Ware 90.00
Humidor, Indian Ware, Cover 95.00
Teapot, Black Indian Style, Dark Rust Ground, 5 In. 70.00
Teapot, Crystal Patina 100.00
Teapot, Green, Flat Stylized, Crystal Patina 180.00
Teapot, Indian 85.00
Vase, Indian Studio, W. L. 40.00

Clocks of all types have always been popular with collectors. The
eighteenth-century tall case, or grandfather's clock, was designed to
house a works with a long pendulum. In 1816, Eli Terry patented a
new, smaller works for a clock; and the case became smaller. The
clock could be kept on a shelf instead of on the floor. By 1840,
coiled springs were used and even smaller clocks were made.
Battery-powered electric clocks were made in the 1870s.

CLOCK, Act of Parliament, English 2750.00
Advertising, Admiral Appliances, 1940s 150.00
Advertising, Baird, Key & Pendulum, 6 Advertisers 1870.00
Advertising, Breyers Ice Cream, Light–Up 90.00
Advertising, Bud Light, 14 x 14 In. 20.00
Advertising, Cadillac, Neon, 18 In. 900.00
Advertising, Calumet Baking Powder, Calendar, Sessions 300.00
Advertising, Calumet Baking Powder, With Calendar 800.00
Advertising, Canada Dry, Electric 135.00
Advertising, Cape Cod Hearth Lighter 25.00
Advertising, Carhartt Overalls, Neon 475.00
Advertising, Champion Spark Plug 265.00
Advertising, Chevrolet Rear Window, Neon, 1937 .... 750.00
Advertising, Chevrolet, Neon 600.00
Advertising, Dickey's Indian Blood & Liver Pills, Victorian, 27 In. 725.00
Advertising, Dr Pepper 22.50
Advertising, Dr Pepper, 20 x 33 In. 125.00
Advertising, Dr Pepper, Bottle Shape, Tin 140.00
Advertising, Dr Pepper, General Electric, Logo 225.00
Advertising, Dr Pepper, Light–Up, 1950s 90.00
Advertising, Dr Pepper, Pam, Glass Face 75.00
Advertising, Enna Jettick Shoes, 8 Sides 600.00
Advertising, Ever–Ready Safety Razor, Man Shaving, 18 In. .... 650.00 To 880.00
Advertising, Fehr's Beer, Plastic, It's Always Fehr Weather 22.50
Advertising, Fisherman, Fish Jumps On Second 145.00
Advertising, Gem Damaskeene Razor, Man, Holding Child, Soap On Face 3200.00
Advertising, Gem Razor, 1904 .... 1850.00
Advertising, Guerin Chocolate, Japy Freres, France 125.00
Advertising, Imperial Bread, Time To Buy, Large 195.00
Advertising, J. F. Krieft, Cast Iron & Zinc, c.1880 .... 3800.00
Advertising, Keebler Elf, Alarm, Windup 30.00
Advertising, Kleenatub & Wrigleys Scouring Soap, Key, Oak, 34 In. 1650.00
Advertising, Marigold Dairy Products, Double Face, Lights Up 130.00
Advertising, Marlboro 33.00
Advertising, Monarch Foods, Lion 275.00
Advertising, Nesbitt, Flourescent 100.00
Advertising, Nu Grape, Light–Up, Bottle Shape, 1940s 150.00
Advertising, Old Drum Whiskey, Marching Players, Drum, 11 1/4 In. 450.00
Advertising, Pabst Blue Ribbon, Electric .... 20.00 To 30.00

Advertising, Pearl Beer, Neon 385.00
Advertising, Pennzoil, Light–Up 225.00
Advertising, Pepsi–Cola, 1940s 275.00
Advertising, Pepsi–Cola, Electric, 1930s 175.00
Advertising, Pet Dairy Foods, Light–Up 50.00
Advertising, Purina Chows, Light–Up, 1940s 180.00
Advertising, Red Goose Shoes, Gilbert, Shelf, Small 225.00
Advertising, Royal Crown Cola, Glass Front, Square, 15 In. 30.00
Advertising, Schlosser's Ice Cream, Neon, Octagon, 1940s 750.00
Advertising, Schwinn Bicycles, Neon 550.00
Advertising, Sealtest, Neon 350.00
Advertising, Sheehan Mere Co., Liquors, House, Iron, 13 x 8 In. 165.00
Advertising, Sparton Radio, Telechron, Wall, Exclusive Dealer, 12 In. 550.00
Advertising, Sweet Orr Work Clothes, Lighted, Pam 245.00
Advertising, Teddy Snow Crop, Blinking Eye 90.00
Advertising, Time Is On Our Side, Electric Neon Clock Co., 30 In. 412.50
Advertising, U. S. G. Harness Oil, Reverse Stencil On Window 775.00
Advertising, Walker Muffler & Pipes, Tin 20.00
Advertising, Ward's Orange Crush, Regulator, 1908 .... 1600.00
Advertising, Weather Bird, Electric, Neon Lights, Metal, 18 1/2 In. 495.00
Advertising, Westinghouse, Listen & You'll Buy A Westinghouse Radio 400.00
Advertising, Whistle Beverages 425.00
Advertising, Wings Perfume, Detroit, Hoof Feet, Iron, 15 x 14 In. 195.00
Alarm, Bugs Bunny, 1974 .... 18.00
Alarm, Raggedy Ann & Raggedy Andy, Talking, Box 100.00
Alarm, Snoopy, Blessing, 1970 .... 45.00 To 75.00
Alarm, Snoopy, Chases Butterfly With Net, 1958 .... 150.00
Alarm, Sylvester & Tweety, Bird Cries For Help As Alarm Rings, 1970s 115.00
Alarm, Telechron, Clear Lucite Block, Brass Band Around Face, 1940s 80.00
Animated, Alarm, Woody Woodpecker, 1959 .... 175.00
Animated, Owl, Carved, Japan 125.00
Animated, Standing Girl, Eyes Roll With Strike of Hour, Iron, 17 In. 1765.00
Animated, Woody Woodpecker, 1959 .... 120.00
Ansonia, 8–Day, Chime, Royal Bonn Case, Late 1800s 350.00
Ansonia, Boudoir, Royal Bonn 250.00
Ansonia, Bronze & Gilt Design, c.1923, 66 In. 950.00
Ansonia, Fisher & Hunter Statue 1000.00
Ansonia, Kitchen, Walnut Case 220.00
Ansonia, La Roca, Royal Bolin, Germany, 4 1/2 In. 295.00
Ansonia, Mantel, 8–Day, Hour & 1/2 Hour Strike, 1885 .... 165.00
Ansonia, Mantel, Black Enameled Iron, Bronze Fittings, c.1910, 18 In. 110.00
Ansonia, Mantel, No. 167, Metal Case, 8–Day, Enamel Dial 195.00
Ansonia, Mantel, Renaissance Revival, Black Iron, Bronze, 13 x 18 In. 100.00
Ansonia, Mantel, Westminster Chimes 45.00
Ansonia, Regulator, Depot Type, Date Hand, Maple, 30 1/2 In. 375.00
Ansonia, Regulator, Queen Elizabeth 500.00
Ansonia, School, Time Only .... 165.00 To 200.00
Ansonia, Wall, 8–Day, Strikes On Gong 200.00
Art Deco, Black & Gray, Glass Face Lights Up 150.00
Arts & Crafts, Hammered Copper, European Design, New Haven, 11 In. 445.00
Aunt Jemima, Table 375.00
Banjo, Brass Works, Metal Face, Mahogany Case, 34 In. 1800.00
Banjo, Eglomise & Mahogany, American Eagle, 19th Century, 38 1/2 In. 550.00
Banjo, Ingram, 8–Day 100.00

◆◆

Some Shaker chairs have a number impressed on the top of the front leg or back post. This indicated where the chair belonged. Each room had a number.

◆◆

Clock, Banjo, New England, Weight Drive,   *Clock, Black Girl, Eyes Roll, Iron, 17 1/2 In.*
8–Day

Banjo, J. Stowell, Reverse Painting, Com. Perry's Victory, 41 1/2 In. 1250.00
Banjo, Lemuel Curtis, Mahogany, Banded Veneer, Reverse Painted, 32 In. 2100.00
Banjo, New England, Weight Drive, 8–Day ....*Illus*   825.00
Banjo, S. Williard 3300.00
Banjo, Seward, Federal, Mahogany 1980.00
Banjo, William M. Bacon, Mahogany, Reverse Painted, 8–Day, 42 In. 770.00
Beehive, Painted George Washington, Grain Painted, c.1840, 15 In. 1500.00
Black Girl, Eyes Roll, Iron, 17 1/2 In. ....*Illus* 1765.00
Blinking Eye, Santa Claus 200.00
Bracket, 2 Train Fusee, 8–Day, James Hanna, Quebec, 15 1/2 x 9 1/2 In. 2750.00
Bracket, Carved Mask Crest, Gilt Bronze, Oak, 27 In. 1500.00
Bracket, Kirkwood, George III, Mahogany, Domed Case, 16 1/2 In. 2640.00
Bracket, William & Mary, Gilt Metal Face, Ebonized Wood Case, 14 In. 3200.00
Brass Works, Metal Face, Reverse Glass of J. C. Brown, 17 1/2 In. 230.00
Brewster & Ingraham, Steeple, Etched Glass Door, 8–Day, c.1844, 19 In. 700.00
Brewster & Ingraham, Steeple, Etched Glass Panel, c.1844, 3/4 Size 800.00
Carriage, Brass & Glass, France, 1870s 160.00
Carriage, Brass, Glass, 1870, France 160.00
Carriage, Repeater, Carrying Case, France 950.00
Carriage, Time & Alarm, Flower Garland Dial, France 300.00
Cartier, Desk, Gold, Agate & Enamel, Cabochon Sapphire, c.1930 .... 3575.00
Cartier, Desk, Gold, Jade & Enamel, c.1930 .... 6600.00
Cartier, Desk, Quarter Repeating, Blue Enamel On Rayed Ground, c.1915 .... 4675.00
Cartier, Green Agate 1650.00
Cast Metal, Girl, Gilt Zephyr, Green Onyx Base, France, 24 1/4 In. 175.00
Charles X, Portico, Ebonized, Ormolu Mounted, c.1820 .... 600.00
Chelsea, Ship, Silvered Dial, Brass Trimmed Case, 10 In. 1400.00
Cuckoo, 30–Hour, Chain Wind, Breitinger, c.1890, 21 In. 800.00
Cuckoo, Birds With Glass Eyes, Nest of Baby Birds, 3–Tune Music Box 875.00
Cuckoo, Miniature, Deebler, Box 58.00
Cuckoo, Schmeckenbecker, Germany, 6 In. 58.00
Desk, Chronoscope, Marble, Lucerne, Ruby Arrow, c.1930 .... 3300.00
Detex–Newman, Watchman's, Complete, With Key 150.00
Directoire Style, Floral Porcelain Dial, Oval Case, France, 10 In. 550.00
Dutch, Oak, Wall, Arched Hood, Applied Spandrels, Chimes, Pendulum 825.00
E. Howard, Washington Hook & Ladder Co. Presentation On Glass 2250.00
E. N. Welch, Wall, Figure 8, Time, Pat. Aug. 30, 1870 .... 275.00
Egyptian Revival, Mantel, Paris Porcelain, c.1880 .... 5000.00
Eli Terry, Ithaca Calendar, Black Upper Dial, Walnut, 1875, 20 In. 3100.00
Eli Terry, Pillar & Scroll, c.1818, 31 In. 1800.00
Eli Terry, Pillar & Scroll, Painted Scene 2450.00
Eli Terry, Pillar & Scroll, Shelf, Reverse Painted Glass, Label 2600.00
Eli Terry, Shelf, 30–Hour, Wooden Dial, Weight Driven 685.00
Eli Terry, Shelf, Wooden Works & Face, Reverse Glass, Mahogany, 30 In. 175.00
Ephraim Downes, Pillar & Scroll, Reverse Painted Ship, 31 1/4 In. 800.00
Francois Moreau, Figural, Matching Urn, 3 Piece 375.00
Garniture, Gilt Bronze, Medieval Figures, 13 3/4 In., 3 Piece 2200.00

Garniture, Louis XVI, Marble, White Metal, 20 1/2 In., 3 Piece 335.00
Garniture, Renaissance Revival, 4–Light, Japy Freres, 20 In., 3 Piece 775.00
General Electric, Banjo Style, Picture of Mt. Vernon 65.00
General Electric, Catalin, Brown Swirl, 5 x 5 3/4 In. 75.00
Gilbert, Depot, Large 1100.00
Gilbert, Wall, LaReforma 350.00
Guberlin, Chronoscope, Desk, Red Marble, Onyx Panels, c.1930 .... 3300.00
Gustav Becker, Westminster, Chimes, Brass, Mahogany, 13 x 30 In. 500.00
H. Coehler Co., Cat, Eyes Move, Hanging, Acorn Weights, Wooden, 7 In. 82.50
Haddon, Hall, Moving Grandmother In Rocker, Electric, Lights Up 65.00
Haddon, Teeter–Totter, Moves 110.00
Hamilton, Quartz 75.00
Hammond, Alarm, Bakelite, 1930 .... 35.00
Howard Miller, Atom, 12 Radiating Arms, Spheres, G. Nelson, 13 1/2 In. 275.00
Ingraham, Calendar, Kitchen, Gila 220.00
Ingraham, Mantel, Copper Clad Feet, 8 Copper Columns 145.00
Ingraham, Mantel, Copper Footed & Columns 145.00
Ingraham, Regulator, Wabash R.R. 350.00
Ingraham, School, Long Drop 265.00
Iron, Eagle, Shield & Flags, Paper Face, 13 In. 135.00
Ithaca, Calendar, Chronometer On Glass, 36 In. 2500.00
Ithaca, Calendar, Double Dial, Rosewood 850.00
Ithaca, Calendar, Walnut, Pat. 1865 & 1866, 21 1/4 In. 575.00
Ithaca, Wall, Time & Strike, Oak 300.00
Ives, Black Dancers 1200.00
Jacob Benedle, 30–Day, Porcelain Dial, Satinwood Inlay, 1840s, 46 In. 7500.00
James Murray, Lancelot Style, Inlaid Mahogany Case, c.1825, 10 In. 2500.00
Jerome & Darrow, Shelf, Bouquet, Black & Gold, 35 In. ....*Illus* 325.00
Joe Lewis 425.00
John Skirving, Bracket, Silvered Dial, Anchor Escapement, 1750, 22 In. 6800.00
Krober, Wall, Oak, Large 900.00
L. & J. G. Stickley, Tall Case, Beveled Top, Stepped–In Center, 78 In. 9350.00
Lantern, Brass, Dragons, Baluster Columns, Weights, Japan, 8 In. 2200.00
Lantern, Single Train Fusee, E. Jones, London, c.1686 .... 852.50
Louis XVI Style, Mask & Sunburst Over Lyre, Gilt Bronze, 13 In. 495.00
Lux, 3–Day, Pendulette, Large, Unused 100.00
Lux, Black Boy Shining Shoes 310.00
Lux, Cottage, Green Roof, 8–Day 110.00
Lux, Fountain of Youth 100.00
Lux, Mammy Smoking Pipe 105.00
Lux, Organ Grinder 295.00
Lux, Peanut Roaster 400.00
Lux, Spinning Wheel ....98.00 To 125.00
Mantel, Alabaster, Ormolu & Porcelain Mounted, Putti, France, 22 In. 1540.00
Mantel, Berger, Napoleon III, Ormolu, Boy, Garden Tools, Strike, 14 In. 330.00
Mantel, Brass & Champleve Enamel, Time & Strike, Marti & Cie, France 2100.00
Mantel, Brass Overlay On Wood, 8–Day, Sculpture On Top & Door, France 1325.00
Mantel, Cast Metal, Mother, Child, Slate Base, French–Style, 19 In. 145.00
Mantel, Champleve, Cherubs Support, Gilt Bronze, Enameled, 12 1/2 In. 1650.00
Mantel, Cuckoo, Walnut Case Resembles Castle, 19th Century, 14 In. 775.00
Mantel, F. L. Hausburg, Gilded Cast Metal, Black Slate Base, 22 1/4 In. 525.00
Mantel, Figures Playing Checkers On Base, Time & Strike, 18 1/2 In. 3300.00
Mantel, French Boulle, Brass Face & Mount, Floral, Dragons, 28 In. 1350.00
Mantel, Gilbert Florence, Claw Feet 85.00
Mantel, Gilt Bronze, Allover Floral, Nude Man, French Style, 17 In. 450.00
Mantel, Gustav Becker, Tambour Model, Westminster Chimes, c.1914 .... 275.00
Mantel, Herschede, Grand Prize Panama Pacific Exposition, 1915 .... 545.00
Mantel, Krober, 8–Day, Iron Case 175.00
Mantel, Louis Philippe, Bronze, Marble, Allegorical Figures, 30 In. 4400.00
Mantel, Louis XVI, Allegorical Figures, Gilt Bronze, Marble, 21 In. 4125.00
Mantel, Louis XVI, Fruitwood, Bronze, 13 In. 485.00
Mantel, Manning Bowman, Chrome, Tortoiseshell Bakelite, 9 1/2 x 8 In. 110.00
Mantel, Napoleon III Bust, Gilt, Bronze, Eagle Plinth, 1850, 26 1/2 In. 3575.00

Clock, Jerome & Darrow, Shelf, Bouquet,
Black & Gold, 35 In.

Clock, Shelf, Federal, Mahogany,
Farm Scene, c.1830, 17 1/4 In.

Mantel, Napoleon III, Bronze, Time & Strike, G. Philippe, 15 In.	220.00
Mantel, Ogee, Reverse Painted View of Broadway, N. Y., 26 1/2 In.	605.00
Mantel, Quentin, Floral, Reserves, 8–Day, Time & Strike, 13 3/16 In.	440.00
Mantel, Skeleton Design, Electric, Brass & Glass	35.00
Mantel, Spaulding, Rococo–Style, Gilt Bronze, France	605.00
Mantel, Telechron, Westminster Chime, 15 x 9 In.	325.00
Mantel, Tortoiseshell, Ebony & Ormolu Trim, France, 1850, 12 1/2 In.	1500.00
Mantel, Vale, George III, Mahogany, Music, Gilt Metal, 1770, 22 1/2 In.	7150.00
Minneapolis 77, Thermostat, Wall, Jeweled, 1920s	85.00
Morbier, Brass, Porcelain, Time & Strike, 8–Day Repeater, 4 Ft. 6 In.	1325.00
Morgan, Tall, Mahogany, Edinburgh	1210.00
Neon, 2–Sided, Say–It–In–Neon Co., 1940s	3000.00
New Haven, Banjo, 30–Day, Oval Bottom	500.00
New Haven, Elfreda, Wall, Oak	650.00
New Haven, Gallery, 8–Day, Square Pendulum	85.00
New Haven, Gold Plated Bronze, Garden Scene On Dial, 8–Day	495.00
New Haven, Kitchen, Mayflower Model, Walnut	195.00
New Haven, Parlor, 8–Day, Scene On Dial, Gold Plated Bronze, c.1885	575.00
New Haven, Parlor, Gold Plated Bronze, Garden Scene On Porcelain	450.00
New Haven, Regulator, Wall, Vamoose, 30–Day	450.00
New Haven, School, Time, Calendar	285.00
New Haven, Tambour, Large	175.00
Oeil De Boeuf, Strikes Hour Twice, Again In 2 Minutes, France, c.1800	495.00
Peter Shutz, Ribbed Quarter Columns, Chippendale Feet, Penna., 1808	2750.00
Phinney–Walker, Alarm, Rhinestone, Germany	32.00
Pillar & Scroll, Wooden Works, Ephraim Downes, Mahogany, 31 1/4 In.	1350.00
Plique–A–Jour & Gilt, Inset Multicolored Glass, France, 17 In.	6050.00
Pratt, Jr., Gallery, Octagonal, Gold Leafed Case, Rosewood, 1840, 26 In.	2200.00
Regulator, Crystal, Enameled Face, Mercury Pendulum, France, 10 In.	200.00
Regulator, Enamel Face, Mercury Pendulum, France, 10 In.	225.00
Regulator, Enamel, Beveled Glass, Brass, France, 11 1/4 In.	350.00
Regulator, Master, Self–Winding, Oak, 3 Volt, c.1890, 5 Ft.	3500.00
Repeating, Brass, Early 20th Century, France, 7 In.	415.00
Richard Parsons, George III, Music, Ebonized, Painted, 1770–80, 21 In.	3850.00
Riley Whiting, Cherry, Mahogany, Masonic Dial, 1810	4900.00
Riley Whiting, Federal, Pillar & Scroll, 1820, 30 x 17 x 4 1/2 In.	885.00
Robbie The Robot, Waist High, Clock In Breastplate, Barometer Visor	1925.00
S. B. Terry, Regulator, Wall, Mahogany Veneer Case, c.1850, 30 In.	1800.00
Sessions, Airplane, Propeller, Wooden, Rubber Tires, Electric, 21 In.	65.00
Sessions, Shelf, Strikes Hour & 1/2 Hour, Original Dial & Glass, 1903	82.50
Seth Thomas, Alarm, 4 Jewel, Bakelite Case, 1 3/4 x 1 3/4 In.	65.00

Seth Thomas, Alarm, 8–Day, Automatic Shut Off	185.00
Seth Thomas, Banjo, Treasure Island	465.00
Seth Thomas, Cathedral, Strike, Key, Wood & Brass, 13 x 9 In.	165.00
Seth Thomas, Copper Wash Metal Case, Classical Figurals Top & Sides	425.00
Seth Thomas, Mantel, 8–Day, Chime, 2 Lions & Pillars, Early 1900s	400.00
Seth Thomas, Mantel, Arch Form, Chimes, Mahogany Case, 9 1/2 In.	65.00
Seth Thomas, Mantel, Bim Bam, Tambour	45.00
Seth Thomas, Mantel, Mahogany, Arch Form, Chimes, 18 x 4 x 9 1/2 In.	60.00
Seth Thomas, Pillar & Scroll, Reverse Painted House, 31 In.	3850.00
Seth Thomas, Regulator, No. 2, Rosewood Case	765.00
Seth Thomas, Rosewood, Double Dial, 8–Day, 27 1/2 In.	770.00
Seth Thomas, Shelf, Athens, Time & Alarm	225.00
Seth Thomas, Shelf, Metal Face, Reverse Glass, Pot of Flowers, 25 In.	145.00
Seth Thomas, Ship's Wheel, Brass, 8–Day, 7 Jewels, Patent 1921	305.00
Seth Thomas, Ship's, c.1890	350.00
Seth Thomas, Triple Decker, 8–Day, Weights	525.00
Seth Thomas, Wall, Marine, Outside Bell, 30–Hour, Silvered Dial, 1915	445.00
Seth Thomas, Wall, Railroad Station, 1 Weight, 68 In.	1400.00
Shelf, Empire, Reverse Painted Decoupage, Kellogg Lithograph, 32 In.	500.00
Shelf, Federal, Mahogany, Farm Scene, c.1830, 17 1/4 In. ....*Illus*	1045.00
Silas Hoadley, Pillar & Splat, Reverse Glass, Dated 1810	975.00
Sinbad The Sailor, Ceramic, Gold Trimmed Turban, 12 x 8 In.	57.00
Skeleton, Gothic Spires, Painted Dial, Dome, 19th Century, 14 In.	475.00
Sperry & Co., Cottage, Reverse Painted Door, 30–Hour, 1850, 12 In.	195.00
Standard, Master, Oak, Bell, Round Top, 1916, 5 In.	600.00
Steeple, Double Decker, Brass Works, Mahogany Veneer, 23 1/2 In.	450.00
Steeple, Double Decker, Reverse Painted Glass, Mahogany, 26 1/2 In.	2100.00
Stromberg, Electric, Beveled Glass, Oak Case, 1915	875.00
Stromberg, Master Regulator, Cherry, 5 In.	600.00
Stromberg, Master Regulator, Oak, Beveled Glass, 5 In.	600.00
Table, Time & Strike, 1/4–Hour Repeat, Robert & Couvoissier, c.1750	3000.00
Tall Case, A. Girooust, Brass Dial, Mahogany, c.1760, 7 Ft. 7 1/2 In.	6875.00
Tall Case, A. Loggan, Inlaid, Brass Works, Eagle Finial, 87 In.	2550.00
Tall Case, A. Twiss, Canada, 6 Ft. 10 In.	1485.00
Tall Case, Andrew Eyster, Broken Arch Top, Moon Dial, Cherry, c.1830	8000.00
Tall Case, Andrew Rich, Moving Figure of Father Time, c.1820	7400.00
Tall Case, Arched Dial, Lunar Dial, Mahogany, c.1790, 88 1/2 In.	3000.00
Tall Case, Barton Stillman, Allover Ova Inlay, Cherry, 1814, 7 Ft.	8400.00
Tall Case, Barton Stillman, Inlaid, Numbered 4, Dated 1814	8000.00
Tall Case, Bombay Oak, Trapezoidal Door, Bracket Feet, Dutch, 83 In.	600.00
Tall Case, Brass Dial, 30–Hour Weight Driven, Walnut, England, c.1750	1100.00
Tall Case, Calendar, Moon Phase, Iron Face, Cherry, 96 1/2 In.	7000.00
Tall Case, Cavell, George III, Etched Brass Face, Striking, 7 Ft. 3 In.	5500.00
Tall Case, Cherry, Dovetailed Bonnet, Brass Works, Weights, 86 In.	1050.00
Tall Case, Chinoiserie, Oriental Landscape, England, 88 1/2 In.	2365.00
Tall Case, Chippendale, Red, Bonnet, Weight Driven, Late 1700, 7 Ft.	1800.00
Tall Case, Curly Maple, Cherry, Walnut, Bonnet, Pendulum, 99 3/4 In.	700.00
Tall Case, Daniel Balch, Brass Dial & Finials, c.1760, 7 Ft. 9 In.	5500.00
Tall Case, David Charles Worth, Tiger & Bird's–Eye Maple Inlay	7500.00
Tall Case, E. Duffield, Roman & Arabic Numerals, c.1745, 88 1/2 In.	9350.00
Tall Case, Ephraim & Thomas Clark, 8–Day	8600.00
Tall Case, F. Wingate, No. 82, Moon Dial, Mahogany, 1811, 7 Ft. 4 In.	9900.00
Tall Case, George Hoff, Brass Face, 1750s, 88 In.	9250.00
Tall Case, Girod, Carved Fruit, Maple & Fruitwood, 77 1/4 In.	522.00
Tall Case, Gustav Stickley, Brass Face, Copper Numerals, 70 3/4 In.	8250.00
Tall Case, Hepplewhite, Fretwork Crest, Brass Works, Cherry, 91 In.	2500.00
Tall Case, Herschede, Canterbury & Westminster Chimes, 7–Tube	6500.00
Tall Case, Hershede, Moon Dial	425.00
Tall Case, Hillam & Son, Painted Dial, Mahogany Case, 91 In.	1100.00
Tall Case, Hutchinson, Mahogany	5060.00
Tall Case, J. Ratcliffe, Engraved Brass Face, Strikes Hour, 1735	2800.00
Tall Case, J. W. Hoogeneen, Enamel Face, 1 Weight, Second Hand, 83 In.	660.00
Tall Case, Jacob Cope, 30–Hour, Compass Inlay, Cherry, 1830, 8 Ft.	9500.00

Clock, Tall Case, Thomas Beggs, Mahogany,
  Brass Works, 1840, 76 In.

◆◆◆◆◆◆◆◆◆◆◆◆◆◆◆◆◆◆◆◆◆◆◆

Fakers sometimes "marry" a
clock works and a clock case.
Examine a clock carefully to be
sure the parts are all original.

◆◆◆◆◆◆◆◆◆◆◆◆◆◆◆◆◆◆◆◆◆◆◆

Tall Case, John Key, Seconds & Calendar Dials, Walnut, Scotland	1200.00
Tall Case, John Meredith, Federal, Mahogany Case, c.1790, 96 In.	9900.00
Tall Case, Larkin, Oak	435.00
Tall Case, Lewis Truscott, Foliate Enamel Dial, Japanned, 89 1/4 In.	770.00
Tall Case, Louis XV, Fruitwood Parquetry, Bronze Mounted, 86 In.	5720.00
Tall Case, Louis XVI, Arched Glazed Door, Enamel Face, Walnut, 111 In.	660.00
Tall Case, Mallett, William & Mary, Walnut, Seaweed, 7 Ft. 4 In.	9350.00
Tall Case, Miller, Thomas & Son, Brass Dial, Oak, c.1775	5500.00
Tall Case, Mirror & Ivory Inlay, Brass Works, England, 86 In.	1900.00
Tall Case, Mission Oak	2200.00
Tall Case, Moon Dial, 8–Day, Tiger & Bird's–Eye Maple, c.1830, 9 Ft.	5100.00
Tall Case, Moon Dial, Inlaid Rosettes, Walnut Case, c.1890, 95 In.	8750.00
Tall Case, New England, Cherry, 7 Ft. 5 In.	4400.00
Tall Case, New England, Painted Dial, Inlaid Cherry, 1810, 90 3/4 In.	5500.00
Tall Case, P. Bergsten, Brass Works, Metal Dial, 1758, 85 1/2 In.	575.00
Tall Case, Pagoda Top, Moon Phase, Date & Day, Dutch, 97 In.	5225.00
Tall Case, Painted Iron Face, Moon Dial, Cherry, c.1800, 96 1/2 In.	7000.00
Tall Case, Pine, Red Painted, American, Signed Tho's Lift	1800.00
Tall Case, Queen Anne, Inlaid Walnut, Arched Glazed Door, 91 1/2 In.	9900.00
Tall Case, S. Thomas, Plymouth, Gilt Trim, Fluted Bonnet, Pine, 84 In.	1200.00
Tall Case, S. Whalley, George III, Brass Dial, Date, Oak, 85 In.	825.00
Tall Case, Silas Hoadley, Masonic Designs On Dial, Pine	1500.00
Tall Case, Thomas & Hoadley, Wood Dial, 1815, 7 Ft. 7 In.	3300.00
Tall Case, Thomas Beggs, Mahogany, Brass Works, 1840, 76 In. *Illus*	2200.00
Tall Case, Thomas Ellicott, Georgian, Red Lacquer, Brass Works, 8 Ft.	8800.00
Tall Case, Thomas Hutchinson, 8–Day, Moon Dial, Mahogany, 1816	5060.00
Tall Case, Thomas Lumpkin, Fretwork, Glazed Walnut, c.1745, 89 In.	7150.00
Tall Case, Thomas Steel, Enamel & Foil Dial, Mahogany, 7 Ft. 4 In.	5800.00
Tall Case, Thos. Smith, 3 Weights, Brass Dial, No Pendulum	2300.00
Tall Case, W. Tomlinson, William & Mary, Marquetry, London, 83 In.	6600.00
Tall Case, Walter Durfee, Westminster Chimes, Cathedral Frame, c.1896	6875.00
Tall Case, William Cowan, Sea Captain On Dial, Mahogany, 7 Ft. 6 In.	6100.00
Tall Case, Wilson & Osborn, Birmingham, Moon Phase, Cherry, 94 1/2 In.	5000.00
Tall Case, Wooden Face, Imitation Figured Wood, Pine, 82 In.	1550.00
Telechron, Pink Mirror	65.00
Terry, Pillar & Scroll, Shelf	1870.00
Terry, Pillar & Scroll, Wood Face, Reverse Painted Glass, 29 1/2 In.	1000.00
Terry, Shelf, Empire, Gold Stenciled Floral, Mahogany Case, 33 3/4 In.	175.00
CLOCK, TIFFANY, see Tiffany, Clock	
Topsy, Watermelon Eater	88.00
Turnbull & Young, Keyhole, Seconds, Calendar Dials, 2–Weight, Scotland	1540.00
United, Stagecoach, Animated Driver & Horses, Metal, 1950s, 20 In.	87.00
Wag–On–Wall, Floral Wooden Face, Brass Gears, 17 3/4 In.	375.00
Wag–On–Wall, Painted Wooden Face, Weight, Pendulum, 9 1/4 In.	350.00
Wall, 8–Day, Repousse Brass, Strikes On Gong, Square Dial, 19 1/4 In.	1400.00
Waltham, Banjo, Eagle Finial, Brass Bezel, 8–Day Weight, 43 In.	2310.00
Waltham, Banjo, Lever Platform Movement, Gilt Front, 1820s, 42 In.	2300.00

Waltham, Banjo, Weight Driven 1200.00
Waltham, Vanguard, Winding Indicator 750.00
Waterbury, Banjo, Reverse Painted Glass, Brass Finial, 41 In. 715.00
Waterbury, Mantel, 8–Day, Enameled Dial, Marble, 1857 .... 250.00
Waterbury, Romance Statue 550.00
Waterbury, Ship's, Ship's Wheel Spokes Case, 20th Century, 10 In. 750.00
Waterbury, Wall, Cambridge 525.00
Welch, Gingerbread, Oak, 8–Day, 1/2–Hour Strike, 22 1/2 In. .... 145.00 To 160.00
Welch, Mantel, 8–Day, 1/2–Hour Strike, 22 In. 88.50
Welch, Patti Series, Glass Design, Dual Spring, c.1830, 20 In. 1500.00
Welch, School, Long Drop 300.00
Welch, Wall, Figure 8 Shape, Time Only, 1870 .... 275.00 To 300.00
Westclox, Andover, Alarm, Chrome Case, Blue Glass, Silver & Ivory Dial 150.00
Westclox, Sambo 55.00
Willard, Banjo, Reverse Painted Glass, c.1820 .... 7000.00
Willard, Banjo, Reverse Painted Glass, Naval, Mahogany, c.1825, 33 In. 5500.00

Cloisonne enamel was developed during the tenth century. A glass enamel was applied between small ribbonlike pieces of metal on a metal base. Most cloisonne is Chinese or Japanese. Pieces marked *China* are twentieth–century examples.

CLOISONNE, Ashtray, Multicolored Flowers, Turquoise Ground, 4 1/4 In. 30.00
Bowl, Floral Exterior, Polychrome Elephant Interior 1320.00
Bowl, Geometric, Floral & Animal Design, 19th Century, 7 In. 495.00
Box, Hinged Cover, Geometric Design, 4 3/4 In. 75.00
Box, Stamp, Double, 2 3/4 x 2 3/4 In. 110.00
Box, Stamp, Hinged Lid, Floral, 3 In. 60.00
Candlestick, Spade Shape, 3 In. Diam. 98.00
Chamberstick, Butterfly Design, Saucer, 5 1/2 In. 225.00
Charger, Bird & Flowers, Turquoise Ground, Japan, 12 In. 395.00
Charger, Fan–Shaped Reserves of Finch & Crane, Japan, 18 In. 305.00
Clock, c.1880, 7 1/2 x 7 1/2 In. 650.00
Compote, Floral, Scalloped, Pedestal, China, 5 1/2 x 9 1/2 In. 225.00
Cup & Saucer, Demitasse 65.00
Ginger Jar, Powder Blue, Green & Red Roses, 7 In. 250.00
Incense Burner, Bird Shape, Pair 275.00
Napkin Ring 4.50
Plate, 2 Herons, Flowers, 11 3/4 In. 200.00
Powder Box, Aqua Floral 45.00
Teapot, Crane Scene, Hexagonal Shape, China, 8 In. 195.00
Teapot, Miniature .... 105.00 To 150.00
Teapot, White Ducks, Blue Ground, 5 In. 220.00
Tray, Art Nouveau, Lotus Birds, Japan, c.1900, 7 In. 137.50
Tray, Prunus Blossoms, Bird, Blue Ground, 4 3/4 x 3 1/4 In. 60.00
Urn, With Clock Inset, Victorian, England, 1890 .... 3200.00
Vase, Blue Fish Scale Pattern, 12 5/8 In., Pair 60.00
Vase, Blue Ground, China, 24 In. ....*Illus*   880.00
Vase, Cloud Scrolls, Yellow Dragon, Red Flames, 8 1/2 In., Pair 250.00
Vase, Colored Fish, Blue Ground, 6 1/4 In. 95.00
Vase, Florals & Animals In Bands, Gold Stone Panels, 9 3/4 In. 850.00
Vase, Flowers & Flying Bird, Enameled Interior, 10 In. 495.00
Vase, Hexagonal Shape, Floral, Foliate & String Inlay, 14 In., Pr. 225.00
Vase, Irises In Pond, 19th Century, 4 3/4 In. 715.00
Vase, On Silver, Scrolls, Dragon, Iris, Blue Ground, 3 1/2 In., Pair 665.00
Vase, Pink & White Roses, Deep Red, 2 1/2 In., Pair 275.00
Vase, Pink Flowers, Black, 7 In. 87.50
Vase, Pink, White, Roses, Silver Wires, Akasuke, 4 In. 85.00
Vase, Reserve of Flowers & Crane, Black Ground, 7 1/4 In. 385.00
Vase, Scenic Panels, Double Gourd Shape, China, 9 1/2 In., Pair 350.00
Vase, Yellow & White Flowers, Green Foliage, Blue Ground, 11 In. 275.00

◆◆

Sometimes when there has been damage, an armchair is reworked into a side chair. The new chair can be detected because an armchair would be wider than a side chair and the incorrect proportions tell it's a fake.

◆◆

Antique and collectible clothes of all types are listed in this section. Dresses, hats, shoes, underwear and more are found here. Other textiles are to be found in the Coverlet, Quilt, Textile, World War I, and World War II sections.

CLOTHING, Bathing Costume, Midi–Blouse, Knickers, Cotton Stockings, Black	40.00
Bathing Suit, Man's, Black & White Wool	65.00
Blouse, Battenburg Lace	125.00
Blouse, Green Silk, Beaded	65.00
Blouse, Victorian, White, Fancy	35.00
Blouse, Western Type, Taupe, 2 Black Horseheads Front, Small	68.00
Bonnet, Leghorn, Hand Braided Trim, Silk Lining, 1830s	85.00
Booties, Baby's, Soft Leather, Blue, 1910	25.00
Bowler, Man's	45.00
Burial Foot Dress, Woman's, Elastic, McCamish Co., Box, 1930s	25.00
Camisole Drawers, Silk, Lace Net Inserts	30.00
Cap, Beaded, Hand Sewn Shell Beads, Sequins, 1925	32.00
Cape, Allover Jet Beaded, 1890s	95.00
Cape, Black Lace, Victorian, Beaded	150.00
Cape, White Silk, Yellow Silk Lining, Embroidered Lilies, Symbols	85.00
Christening Gown & Underdress, Silk & Lace, c.1900	165.00
Cloche, Woman's, Iridescent Black Feathers, Jos. Magnin, 1920s, Box	45.00
Coat, Evening, Black Velvet, 1940s	118.00
Coat, Evening, Red Satin, White Satin Lining, Mary Pickford's	200.00
Coat, Girl's, Blue Linen	62.00
Coat, Mink, Woman's, Tannish Brown, Size 12	60.00
Coat, Mouton Fur	50.00
Coat, Multicolored Silk Thread, New York, Medium	135.00
Coat, Persian Lamb, Fur Collar, Medium	95.00
Coat, Seal Fur, Muff	80.00

Cloisonne, Vase, Blue Ground, China, 24 In.

◆◆◆◆◆◆◆◆◆◆◆◆◆◆◆◆◆◆◆◆◆◆◆◆

Glassware, old or new, requires careful handling. Stand each piece upright, not touching one another. Never nest pieces. Wash in moderately hot water and mild detergent. Avoid wiping gold or platinum banded pieces while glasses are hot. Never use scouring pads or silver polish on glass. For an automatic dishwasher be sure the water temperature is under 180 degrees.

◆◆◆◆◆◆◆◆◆◆◆◆◆◆◆◆◆◆◆◆◆◆◆◆

Collar, Battenburg, Ecru 15.00
Collar, Link, Gold Wash, Whiting Davis 80.00
Collar, Pearls, Art Deco, 1 1/4 In. Wide 35.00
Corset, Nubone 30.00
Dress & Slip, Baptism, 41 In. 65.00
Dress & Slip, Baptism, 57 In. 80.00
Dress, Baby's, Pre–1930s 25.00
Dress, Beaded, Chiffon, Green 125.00
Dress, Black Net, 1916–19 .... 125.00
Dress, Black Satin, Beige Battenburg Lace Trim, 1920, Size 12 .... 65.00
Dress, Black Velvet, Gold Studs On Sleeves, Ankle–Length, 1920s 95.00
Dress, Black Velvet, Long Sleeves, Ecru Lace, Mid–Length, 1920s 60.00
Dress, Boy's, White, Victorian, 1893 .... 80.00
Dress, Child's, Victorian, White Linen, Sailor Style, Size 4–6 .... 88.00
Dress, Christening, Embroidered Cotton Eyelet, Slip, 32 In. 55.00
Dress, Christening, Eyelet Trim 60.00
Dress, Christening, Tucked Panel Front, Ruffle, White, 40 In. 95.00
Dress, Courting, Black Knit Lace, Pink Satin Lined, 1915 .... 125.00
Dress, Evening, Burgundy Velvet, 1920s 85.00
Dress, Flapper, Beaded, Amber 250.00
Dress, Green Velvet, Wide Belt, Skirt Dips In Back, 1930 .... 125.00
Dress, Hand–Done Cut Work, Linen, Full–Length, 1920s 750.00
Dress, Satin, Beaded, 1920s 150.00
Dress, Satin, Black & White Paisley, Trim, Mid–Victorian, 2 Piece 250.00
Dress, Wedding, All Lace, Hoop Skirt 125.00
Dress, Wedding, Battenburg Lace, Handmade, Re–Embroidered, 6 Yds. 350.00
Dress, Wedding, Cream Silk, 1800s 100.00
Dress, Yakima, 1900–20 .... 1200.00
Dressing Gown, Edwin Booth, Velvet, Gold Brocade, Quilted Lining 770.00
Dressing Gown, White Silk Brocade, Floor Length, 1950s, Size 12 ..... 65.00
Garters, Man's, 1930s, Box 22.00
Garters, Man's, Leather, Metal & Rubber, 1930s, Box 12.00
Garters, Victorian, Lace 15.00
Girdle, Playtex, Rubber 15.00
Gloves, Child's, Leather 35.00
Gloves, Woman's, Black Rayon, Cotton, Elastic Cinch Wrist, 10 In. 15.00
Gloves, Woman's, Leather 6.50
Gloves, Woman's, White Eyelet Cotton, Elastic Cinch Wrist, 11 In. 15.00
Gloves, Woman's, White Rayon, Cloth Label, 10 1/2 In. 10.00
Hat, Beaver, French Label, Wooden Box 75.00
Hat, Derby, Box 15.00
Hat, Gaucho, Woman's, Coffee Brown, Wool Felt 65.00
Hat, Helmet, Woman's, Dark Brown Mink, Wool Jersey Ties 45.00
Hat, Pillbox, Jackie Kennedy's Style, 1960 .... 25.00
Hat, Rabbit Fur, White 15.00
Hat, Sheer Brown, Glass Ball & Orange Floral Trim, 1918 .... 55.00
Hat, Taupe, Feathers, Designer's, Box 15.00
Hat, Top, Beaver, Austin Neale, 1877 .... 55.00
Hat, Top, Black, Original Leather Box 120.00
Hat, Top, Silk & Beaver, Leather Box 80.00
Hat, Woman's, Black Wool, Wide Brim, Robinson's, Box, 1940s 40.00
Headdress, Lace, Quimper, Brittany, Box 55.00
Hoop Skirt, Elliptical, Wire & Tape, Civil War 75.00
Jacket, Crystal Fox, Fingertip Length, Face Framing Collar 375.00
Jacket, Dress, Uniform, Silver Washed Buttons, America, 1820 .... 2530.00
Jacket, Norwegian Fox 375.00
Kimono, Birds, Flowers, Fans, Red, Silver & Gold, Display Rod, 70 In. 200.00
Kimono, Family Crest, Black Silk 90.00
Kimono, Peach Silk, Heavy Gold–Threaded Dragon 150.00
Muff, Purse, Fox Fur, Brocaded 75.00
Neckpiece, Silver Fox, 2 Perfectly Matched Pieces, 1940s 45.00
Neckpiece, Whole Mink, 4 Piece 20.00
Nightcap, Purple Silk, Lace 20.00

Nightdress, Raw Silk, Cream, Flowers, Drawstring Tassel, 1930s 45.00
Nightgown, Blue–Gray, French Lace, Bergdorf Goodman 35.00
Nightgown, Wedding, Lace Trim, Victorian 95.00
Obi, Blue Stripe, Red & White Embroidery 25.00
Obi, Butterflies, Beige 60.00
Obi, Gray & Beige Silk 65.00
Obi, Mountains, Beige 60.00
Obi, Purple & Beige Embroidery 25.00
Opera Cape, Blue Velvet, 1920s 95.00
Opera Coat, Black Velvet, Rabbit Trim, Full–Length, 1920s 125.00
Pantaloons, Child's, Solid Rows of Lace Ruffles 35.00
Pants, Football, Men's, Brown, Wooden Stays Sewn In 25.00
Petticoat, Lacy, Ruffled, Trouseau 75.00
Robe, 3 Floral & Butterfly Medallions, Chinese Red, Kesi 1300.00
Robe, Overall Foliate, Gold Ground, Silk, China, 7 Ft. 6 In. 195.00
Scarf, Mourning, Watercolor On Velvet, John Bacon, 1807 .... 2310.00
Scarf, Paisley, Double Face, 54 x 67 In. 450.00
Shawl, Embroidered Flowers, Fringe, Tassels, Beige Silk, 18 In. 125.00
Shawl, Gray Wool On Cotton Ground, India, 64 x 70 In. 12.50
Shawl, Multicolored Design, Ivory Ground, India, 74 x 90 In. 25.00
Shawl, Paisley, Black Center, Dark Red, Square, 5 1/2 Ft. 250.00
Shawl, Paisley, Red Ground, Kashmir, 72 x 64 In. 175.00
Shawl, Paisley, Woven Design, Embroidered Patches, 68 x 68 In. 375.00
Shawl, Patchwork Paisley, Embroidered Fringe Gates, Europe, 6 Ft. 330.00
Shawl, Repeating Paisley, Orange & Red, Square, 5 1/2 Ft. 225.00
Shoes, Baby's, High Button, White Kid 26.00
Shoes, Baby's, Leather High Top, 1930s 20.00
Shoes, Child's, High Button, Brown Leather 30.00
Shoes, Child's, Leather, 1910, Box 35.00
Shoes, Man's, Button Type 27.00
Shoes, Mary Janes, Brown & Cream 26.00
Shoes, Woman's, High Top, 1890s 42.50
Shoes, Woman's, High Top, Lace Up 20.00
Slip, Half, Cotton, String Waist, Lace Bottom 35.00
Slip, Peach Silk Satin, Adjustable, Full, Large Lace Hem, 1930s 45.00
Slippers, Wedding, White Satin, Flower & Fringe Trim 50.00
Slippers, Wedding, White Satin, Tulle Rose 30.00
Snowshoes, Child's, Red 150.00
Spats, Pre–1930s 12.00
Spats, Woman's, 9–Button, Black 12.00
Stockings, Baby's, Black, Pink Top 20.00
Stockings, Imperial Lisle, Full–Fashioned, White, Pair 10.00
Stockings, Lisle 4.50
Stockings, Silk, Woman Pictured On Box, 1920s 45.00
Suit, Black Velvet, Ecru Lace Trim, 1920s 75.00
Suspenders, Child's, Red Ryder 15.00
Swim Cap, Frilly, Package, 1950s 8.00
Tea Gown, Mauve Silk, Sleeveless, Venetian Glass Beads, Fortuny 1100.00
Tea Gown, Pleated Green Silk, Venetian Glass Beads, Fortuny 1650.00
Tie, Jack Benny's, Polyester Black & White, Dan Lopez 275.00
Underwear, Long Johns, Cotton, Drop Seat 15.00
Uniform, British Military, Wool Jacket, Vest, Trousers, Epaulets 275.00
Union Suit, Child's, Cotton Plisse, Bone Buttons, 1930s, Box 28.00
Vestment, Ecclesiastical, Silk Brocade, Gilt Floral, 1850s 225.00
Vestment, Ecclesiastical, Silk Brocade, Polychrome & Gilt Floral 440.00

 Cluthra glass is a two–layered glass with small air pockets that form white spots. The Steuben Glass Works of Corning, New York, made it after 1903. Kimball Glass Company of Vineland, New Jersey, made Cluthra from about 1925. Victor Durand signed some pieces with his name.

CLUTHRA, see also Steuben
CLUTHRA, Bowl, Black–Gray, Swirling Bubbles, Steuben, 15 In. 880.00

Bowl, Blue To White, Steuben, 12 1/2 In. ....*Illus*	550.00
Bowl, Futuristic Shape, Steuben, 4 x 7 In.	695.00
Lamp Base, Rose & Green, Crystal Handles, Steuben, 12 In.	2500.00
Vase, Blue & White, 11 In.	2000.00
Vase, Green & White, England, 10 In.	120.00
Vase, Mottled Purple, Random Bubbles, Steuben, 8 In.	1700.00
Vase, Raspberry Colored, Signed, Steuben, 11 In.	1650.00

Coalbrookdale was made by the Coalport porcelain factory of England during the Victorian period. Pieces are decorated with floral encrustations.

COALBROOKDALE, Candlestick, Polychrome Flowers & Leaves, 5 1/2 In., Pair	45.00
Dish, Cover, Flowers & Leaves, Oval, 9 In.	85.00
Ewer, Applied Flowers, White Ground, 8 In., Pair ....*Illus*	300.00
Jar, Ginger, Cover, Polychromed Flowers, Leaves, 6 1/4 In.	110.00
Potpourri, Trumpet, Flowers, Leaf Handle, 8 In. ....*Illus*	1500.00
Urn, Cover, Flowers On Body & Lid, Domed Foot, 7 In.	45.00

Coalport ware has been made by the Coalport Porcelain Works of England from 1795 to the present time. Early pieces were unmarked. About 1810–1825 the pieces were marked with the name *Coalport* in various forms. Later pieces also had the name *John Rose* in the mark. The crown mark has been used with variations since 1881.

COALPORT, Bell, White, Green Handle	40.00
Berry Set, Allover Multicolored Floral, Server, Sugar & Creamer	110.00
Berry Set, Sugar, Creamer & Bowl, Allover Multicolored Floral	125.00
Candlestick, White Rococo, Applied Flowers, Leaves, 6 In., Pair	40.00
Cup & Saucer, Small Red & Yellow Flowers, Silver Resist Rims	35.00
Dish, Flowers, Leaves, Oval, Coalbrookdale, 9 In.	80.00
Figurine, Allison, Ladies of Fashion	35.00

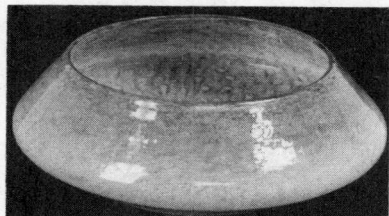

Cluthra, Bowl, Blue To White, Steuben, 12 1/2 In.

♦♦♦♦♦♦♦♦♦♦♦♦♦♦♦♦♦♦♦♦♦♦♦

If you receive a package of glass antiques during cold weather, let it sit inside for a few hours before you unpack it. The glass must return to room temperature slowly or it may crack.

♦♦♦♦♦♦♦♦♦♦♦♦♦♦♦♦♦♦♦♦♦♦♦

Coalbrookdale, Ewer, Applied Flowers, White Ground, 8 In., Pair

Coalbrookdale, Potpourri, Trumpet, Flowers, Leaf Handle, 8 In.

♦♦♦♦♦♦♦♦♦♦♦♦♦♦♦♦♦♦♦♦♦♦♦

If the name "England" (or that of some other country) appears, the dish was made after 1891, but it may have been made as early as 1887. The words "made in England" (or some other country) indicate the piece was made after 1914.

♦♦♦♦♦♦♦♦♦♦♦♦♦♦♦♦♦♦♦♦♦♦♦

Figurine, Bridesmaid, Blue Crinoline Dress, 8 In.	95.00
Figurine, June, 5 In.	38.00
Figurine, Miss Prudence	95.00
Ginger Jar, Applied Flowers, Leaves, Baluster, Cover, Coalbrookdale	100.00
Jug, Armorial, Youth In Black Hat, Red Jacket, 1796–1800, 8 1/4 In.	770.00
Platter, Corn Flowers & Poppy, Poppy & Vine Border, 24 In.	990.00
Urn, Flowers, Double Handle, Baluster, Coalbrookdale, 7 In.	40.00
Urn, Hunting Scene, J. H. Plant, Painter, Green Ground, 27 In., Pair	9350.00
Vase, Jeweled, Pink Ground, Gilt Scrolling Handles, 7 5/8 In.	770.00
Vase, Overall Pate–Sur–Pate, Marked, 8 In.	775.00

Cobalt blue glass was made using oxide of cobalt. The characteristic bright dark blue identifies it for the collector. Most cobalt glass found today was made after the Civil War.

COBALT BLUE, Bottle, George Washington, Jacquin	35.00
Bowl, Basketweave, 7 In.	25.00
Box, Hinged Lid, Flowers, Leaves, White Beading, 1 3/4 x 3 In.	90.00
Box, Raised White Flowers On Top, White Beading, 2 x 2 3/4 In.	50.00
Eyecup	18.00
Figurine, Bluebirds	18.00
Ice Tub, Sailboat, Chrome Holder	65.00
Jug, Fleischman Co., Flat Sided	125.00
Pitcher, Applied Gold Floral, Large	75.00
Plate, 12 Days of Christmas, Imperial, 9 In.	25.00
Reamer, Long Handle	35.00
Salt & Pepper	15.00 To 35.00
Saltshaker, 5 1/2 In.	15.00
Spoon Holder	39.00
Stein, Wedding, Blown, Enameled Floral, Deer Thumblift, 1 Liter	1041.00
Vase, Allover Leaves & Vines, Silver Deposit, Boda, 4 1/2 In.	105.00
Vase, Fluted, Large	20.00
Vase, Souvenir, Seven Falls, Cheyenne, Cannon, Elaborate Handles	20.00
Vase, White Scroll, Wall Wire Rack	45.00

Coca–Cola was first served in 1886 in Atlanta, Georgia. It was advertised through signs, newspaper ads, coupons, bottles, trays, calendars, and even lamps and clocks. Collectors want anything with the word *Coca–Cola,* including a few rare products like gum wrappers and cigar bands. The famous trademark was patented in 1893, the *Coke* mark in 1945. Many modern items and reproductions are being made.

COCA–COLA, Ad, Baseball, 1914	15.00
Ashtray, White Glass, Drink Coca–Cola Light, Belgium	6.00
Bank, Cardboard, Thirst Knows No Season, Atlanta, 3 1/2 x 4 In.	2.00
Bank, Owl, Red Plastic, Drink Coca–Cola, 4 1/4 In.	4.00
Bank, Pig, Red Plastic, Drink Coca–Cola, 2 3/4 x 4 1/2 In.	4.00
Bank, Piggy	10.00
Banner, 1984 Olympics Stadium, U. S. Athletes, 18 x 22 In.	45.00
Banner, Canvas, 16 x 11 In., 1911	1200.00
Barrel, Syrup, Label, 1930s, 10 Gal.	195.00
Beanie, Felt, 1950s	5.00
Blotter, 1913	35.00
Blotter, 1918–20	49.00
Blotter, 1928	85.00
Blotter, Girl In Bathing Suit, 1942	15.00
Blotter, L'Heure Du Coke, French Canada, Corner Picture, 1955	15.00
Blotter, Thirst Come, 1934	85.00
Book Cover, Football Design, 1957	10.00
Book, When You Entertain, 1930s	24.00
Bookcover, Basketball, Cheerleader & Referee Signals, 1960	3.00
Bookcover, Coke Adds Life, Hobbleskirt On Bottle, Cartoon, 1976	2.00
Bookends, Bottle, Bronze, 1963	375.00
Bookmark, Flip–Clip, Office, Enjoy Coca–Cola, Blue Steel	2.00

Bookmark, Hilda Clark, 1903 .... 250.00
Bookmark, Hilda Clark, Heart Shape, Celluloid, 1899 .... 900.00
Bottle Holder, 1950s 9.00
Bottle, Coca–Cola Bottling, Superior, Wisc. 15.00
Bottle, Holly Springs, Missouri 50.00
Bottle, Jonesboro, Arkansas 200.00
Bottle, Los Angeles 5.00
Bottle, Seltzer, Blue, Pump 250.00
Bottle, Seltzer, Coke Top 120.00
Bottle, Straight Side, Label, 1905 .... 175.00
Bottle, Syrup, No Cap, 1920s 350.00
Bowl, Pretzel, 1930s 135.00
Box, 5 Cent Coin–Operated, Holds 12 Bottles, 16 x 16 x 13 In. 2900.00
Brass, With Black Watch Fob, 1912 .... 195.00
Brass, With Red Watch Fob, 1920s 125.00
Button, Red & White, Tin, 12 In. 130.00
Calendar, 1904, Frame, 8 x 15 In. 855.00
Calendar, 1913, Hamilton King, 3 Folds, No Pad 1900.00
Calendar, 1914, Betty, Full Pad 1320.00
Calendar, 1918, June, Caprice 160.00
Calendar, 1921, Autumn Girl, Glass .... 255.00 To 325.00
Calendar, 1927, Framed, 30 x 17 In. 340.00
Calendar, 1929 .... 375.00
Calendar, 1937, N. C. Wyeth, Matted & Framed, 24 1/2 x 12 1/2 In. ... 550.00
Calendar, 1939, Girls, Frame 595.00
Calendar, 1942 .... 125.00
Can. 6–Pack, Tin, Small, 1950s 525.00
Can, Large Diamond, 1960 .... 65.00
Cap, Baseball, Felt, 1940s 8.00
Cap, Beanie, 1930s 25.00
Card Table, Gold Bottle Embossed In Each Corner, c.1927 .... 140.00
Card, Lilian Nordica, Coke Ad, 1905 .... 115.00
Card, Playing, 1943 .... 65.00
Card, Playing, 1950 .... 37.50
Card, Playing, Coca–Cola Trivia, Silhouette Girl, Coke Banner 6.00
Card, Playing, Enjoy Diet Coke, Sealed, Box 5.00
Card, Playing, Poster & Calendar Art, 1 1/2 x 2 In., 40 Piece 8.00
Card, Trolley, Santa Claus 155.00
Carrier, Plastic, 24–Hole, Small 15.00
Chair, Folding, Wooden 42.00
Cigarette Lighter, Miniature 15.00
Clock & Menu Board, Fishtail 375.00
Clock, Counter, Lights Up, 1950s 650.00
Clock, Electric Watch, 1950 .... 275.00
Clock, Electric, Gilbert, 1931 .... 395.00
Clock, Fishtail, Lighted .... 125.00 To 150.00
Clock, Gilbert, Gibson Girl, Regulator, 1910 .... 4000.00
Clock, Light–Up, Square, 1950s .... 135.00 To 175.00
Clock, Plastic Enjoy Coke, Lighted 25.00
Clock, Regulator, 1970s 235.00
Clock, Regulator, Chimes On Hour, Oak, 3/4 Mini., 1940s 695.00
Clock, Silhouette Girl, Metal, Round, 1939 .... 385.00
Clock, Skate Refreshed, Light Up, 1950s, Large 395.00
Clock, Wall Frame, 1948, 36 In. 350.00
Clock, Wood Frame, 1939 .... 250.00
Coaster, Aluminum, 6 Piece 25.00
Coin–Operated Machine, Model 51 .... 205.00
Coin–Operated Machine, Vendo, Model 44 .... 2900.00
Cookie Jar, Coke Can, U. S. A. 25.00
Cooler, 1960, Red, Green, White, Square 55.00
Cooler, Airline, 12 In. 160.00
Cooler, Floor Model, Holds 27 Cases of Soda, 10 Ft. 1925.00
Cooler, Model GBV–50, Glasco 950.00

Cooler, Picnic, Coke, 1950s 45.00
Dish, Pretzel, Aluminum, 1930s .... 195.00 To 225.00
Display, Santa Claus, Battery Operated, Cardboard, 1969, 5 Ft. 200.00
Door Pull, Bottle Shape, Plastic, 1950s ...:.. 160.00
Door Pull, Bottle, Aluminum, 1930s ....:... 175.00
Door Push, Aluminum, 1905 .... 295.00
Door Push, Silhouette Girl, 1939 .... 395.00
Door Push, Sundrop Golden Girl 30.00
Figure, Girl With Bottle, Hand Shaped Plaster, Color, 12 1/2 In. 65.00
Figurine, Santa Claus, Royal Orleans, Box, 1983 .... 100.00
Fly Swatter, 1942 ....8.00 To 12.00
Game, Checkers, 1970s, Box 50.00
Game, Coke Kwiz King, 1970s 30.00
Goblet 25.00
Harmonica, Enjoy Coca-Cola, Hohner 20.00
Hat, Driver's, 1930s 100.00
Ice Pick, Bottle Opener, 1930s 15.00
Ice Pick, Wooden Handle, 1939 .... 12.00
Jug, Label, Clear Glass, 1 Gal. 10.00
Jug, Syrup, 1940s 50.00
Kazoo, Coke Is It, Red, 1982 .... 2.00
Kite, American Flyer, Framed, 1930s 500.00
Knife 6.00
Knife, Pocket, Figural, Woman's Leg, Brass 10.00
Lamp, Leaded Glass, c.1918 .... 4950.00
Letter Opener, Bronze 15.00
Lighter, Bottle Shape 10.00
Lighter, Cigarette, Bottle Shape 12.00
Loveseat, Upholstered Seat, Sides & Back, From Coolers, 1950s 2000.00
Machine, Bike, Box 395.00
Machine, Vendo, Model 59 .... 600.00
Marble, White Glass, Square Red Logo, 1 In. 1.00
Matchstriker, Porcelain, Red, White, Yellow, Black, Canada, 1938 .... 122.00
Medallion, Corinth Classic, 10,000 Meter Run, May, 1985, 1 1/2 In. 4.00
Menu Board, Tin, Girl, 1940 .... 75.00
Mirror, 1906, Pocket 220.00
Mirror, 1909, Pocket 395.00
Mirror, Calendar, Celluloid, 1932 .... 145.00
Mirror, Celluloid, Pocket 125.00
Mirror, Pocket, 1907 .... 475.00
Money Clip 275.00
Music Box, Cooler, Miniature, 1940s 195.00
Note Pad, 1905 .... 145.00
Palm Press, Porcelain, Red, White, Yellow, Canada, 1940s, 11 x 4 In. 88.00
Paper Doll, Punch-Out Sheet, Season's Greetings, 9 x 11 1/2 In. 3.00
Paper Dolls, Cardboard, Punch-Out, 1950s, 9 x 11 In. 5.00
Paperweight 25.00
Pen & Pencil Set, Cross, 12K Gold Filled, Box, 1960s 115.00
Pencil Case, Complete, 1940s ....60.00 To 67.50
Pin, Lapel, Coca-Cola Collectors Intl. Club, Ariz., Brass 3.00
Pitcher, Declaration of Independence, Red Over White, 9 3/4 In. 7.00
Pitcher, Fountain Glass Shape, Coke, Godfather's Pizza, 9 3/4 In. 1.00

◆◆◆

The eighteenth-century bookcase had shelves that were placed sym-
metrically. If the bottom shelf is 8 inches from the bottom, the top
shelf should be 8 inches from the top. If the permanent grooves for
the shelves are not spaced this way, look carefully to be sure you
have an antique piece.

◆◆◆

Plate, Santa Claus, Royal Orleans, 1983	35.00
Pop Case, 1950, Wood	28.00
Poster, Football Players, Referee's, Folds To Book Cover, 1949	20.00
Poster, Your Thirst Takes Wings, 1940, 35 x 20 In.	350.00
Punch Board, Unused, 1940s, 7 x 8 In.	18.00
Push Plate, Have A Coke, Small, 1930s	295.00
Pushbar, Porcelain, Red, Yellow, White, Canada, 1940s, 3 x 30 In.	110.00
Puzzle, Wooden, Norman Rockwell, 1932	500.00
Rack, Wire, Take Home A 6 Pack	120.00
Radio, Cooler Shape	575.00
Ruler, Figural, Coca–Cola, Red & White, 7 In.	1.00
Ruler, Jackson, Tenn., 75th Anniversary, Wooden, 1905–1980	4.00
Score Pad, Gin Rummy, Drink Coca–Cola, Refreshed, Rules, 1951	5.00
Sewing Kit, Red, White, Vinyl, Compliments of Coca–Cola Bottling	1.00
Sheet Music, Ben Bold, Front & Back, Color, 1906	1200.00
Sign, Bottle, Die Cut, 16 In.	85.00
Sign, Bottle, Tin, 6 Feet	700.00
Sign, Button, Porcelain, 36 In.	175.00
Sign, Button, With Bottle, Round, 8 In.	85.00
Sign, Coca–Cola Case Rack, Robinson, 1933, 8 x 12 In.	295.00
Sign, Coca–Cola Case, Masonite, 1940s, 54 In.	550.00
Sign, Coca–Cola Curb Service, Porcelain, 2 Sided, 1942	2400.00
Sign, Coca–Cola Fountain Service, 2 Sided, 1934, 22 x 26 In.	550.00
Sign, Die Cut Bottle, Tin, 16 In.	85.00
Sign, Eddie Fisher, Cardboard, 1954	50.00
Sign, Girl Holding Bottle, Tin, 1927, 8 1/2 x 11 In.	1100.00
Sign, Girl In Yellow, Tin, 12 x 34 In.	195.00
Sign, Hobbleskirt Bottle, Porcelain, 21 x 6 1/4 In.	38.00
Sign, Man & Women Drinking Coke, Tin, 66 x 29 In.	150.00
Sign, Menu Board, Light Up, 1950	100.00
Sign, Picture of Bottle, Tin, 1951, 17 x 57 In.	175.00
Sign, Play Refreshed, Cardboard, 2 Sides, Sports, 20 x 36 In.	245.00
Sign, Policeman, Slow School Zone, Base, 1954	1400.00
Sign, Rack, Sign of Good Taste, Tin, c.1960, 15 x 16 In.	50.00
Sign, Round Cap, Tin Litho, 25 In.	59.00
Sign, Scottish Girl Cutout, Cardboard, 53 In.	500.00
Sign, Service, Fountain, Porcelain	225.00
Sign, Small Flange, 1970s	50.00
Sign, Sold Here, Straight–Sided Bottle, Embossed Tin, 1907	2090.00
Sign, State Bird, Festoon, Cardboard, 1950s	495.00
Sign, Tin, Raised, 1950s	10.00
Sign, Woman, Large Picture Hat, Die Cut Pasteboard	110.00
Sofa, Upholstered Seat, Sides & Back, From Coolers, 1950s	2000.00
Sticker, It's The Real Thing Coke, 1969, Round, 3 In.	.50
Straw Holder, Glass	150.00
Swizzle Stick, Coca–Cola 19th Hole, Golf Flag & Tee	.50
Table, Card, c.1927	325.00
Tally Card Set, Bridge, Drink Coca–Cola, Refreshed, 1950, 8 Piece	50.00
Tape Measure, Retractable, Barlow, Metal, Box, Round, 6 Ft.	8.00
Thermometer, Bottle Shape, 1950s, 17 In.	45.00
Thermometer, Bottle Shape, Gold, 1950s, 7 In.	18.00
Thermometer, Coke 1950s Flat Bottle, Tin	95.00
Thermometer, Coke Bottle, Oval, Pat. Dec. 25, 1923	50.00
Thermometer, Dec. 25th, Anniversary, 1923	55.00
Thermometer, Masonite, 1944	350.00
Thermometer, Outdoor, Logo Collage, Metal Casing, Round, 12 In.	18.00
Thermometer, Things Go Better, 1964, 12 In.	85.00
Thermometer, Tin, Butter, 1950, 9 In.	140.00
Thermometer, Wooden, 1908, 5 x 21 In.	195.00
Thimble, Red Glass	25.00
Tip Tray, 1909, Coca–Cola Girl	220.00
Tip Tray, 1912, Girl In Hat, Hamilton King	200.00 To 365.00
Tip Tray, 1914, Betty	93.50 To 195.00

Tip Tray, 1917, Elaine .... 135.00 To 165.00
Tip Tray, Tome Sprite El Refresco, Mexico, 1964, 6 1/2 x 8 In. 3.00
Toaster, Sandwich 995.00
Toy, Dispenser, Tumblers, 1950s 52.00
Toy, Truck, 20 In. 185.00
Toy, Truck, Mack, Cardboard, 16th Collectors Convention, 18 In. 8.00
Tractor, With Trailer, Chinese, Box 25.00
Training Kit, Sales, 1940, 20 In. 77.00
Tray, 1904, Woman's Picture, Oval 2585.00
Tray, 1909, World's Fair Girl, Large 3520.00
Tray, 1909, World's Fair Girl, Small 2310.00
Tray, 1914, Betty, Oval 935.00
Tray, 1914, Betty, Rectangular 495.00
Tray, 1917, Elaine 400.00
Tray, 1921, Summer Girl 175.00
Tray, 1924, Smiling Girl .... 135.00 To 225.00
Tray, 1925, Girl At Party 135.00
Tray, 1926, Sports Couple 687.50
Tray, 1927, Girl With Bobbed Hair 635.00
Tray, 1929, Girl In Swimsuit Holding Bottle .... 175.00 To 235.00
Tray, 1929, Girl In Swimsuit Holding Glass 467.50
Tray, 1930, Girl With Telephone 220.00
Tray, 1931, Farm Boy With Dog, Rockwell 1430.00
Tray, 1933, Frances Dee 467.50
Tray, 1935, Johnny Weissmuler & Maureen O'Sullivan 1375.00
Tray, 1936, Girl In Evening Gown, Seated, 13 x 10 In. 185.00
Tray, 1936, Hostess Girl 412.50
Tray, 1937, Running Girl 175.00
Tray, 1938, Girl In The Afternoon ....95.00 To 110.00
Tray, 1939, Springboard Girl 85.00
Tray, 1939, Springboard Girl, 13 In. 265.00
Tray, 1939, Springboard Girl, Spanish Version 88.00
Tray, 1940, Sailor Girl .... 100.00 To 187.00
Tray, 1941, Girl Ice Skater .... 100.00 To 275.00
Tray, 1942, Two Girls At Car .... 110.00 To 300.00
Tray, 1948 .... 30.00
Tray, 1948, French Version 55.00
Tray, 1953, Madge Evans 165.00
Tray, 1957, Umbrella Girl, France 285.00
Tray, Buvez Coca–Cola Glace, Porcelain, Round, 12 In. .... 300.00 To 325.00
Tray, Coca–Cola, Served With Wicker Cart 25.00
Tray, Picnic Cart, 1958, 20 1/2 x 13 1/4 In. 12.00
Truck, Marx, 20 In. 185.00
Truck, Matchbox, 9 1/2 In. 40.00
Truck, Metal Craft 425.00
Tumbler, Etched, 1931 .... 55.00
Tumbler, Holly Hobbie Happy Talk, Tasks Done With Love, 6 In. 2.00
Tumbler, Kollect–A–Series, Logo, Brutus Character, 5 7/8 In. 8.00
Tumbler, Plastic, Classic & Hardee's Moose In Hammock, 6 3/4 In. .... .25
Tumbler, Plastic, Classic & McDonalds, Plaid, 6 3/4 In. .... .25
Tumbler, Plastic, Coke & Taste of Colorado Festival, 5 In. .... .25
Tumbler, Santa, Rockwell, December 4, 1920, 6 In. 4.00
Tumbler, Spirit of 1776, Washington Crossing Delaware, 5 5/8 In. 4.00
Watch Fob, Bulldog 120.00
Whistle, Cardboard, 1920 .... 265.00
Whistle, Official's, Metal Hasp, Red Nylon Necklace 8.00
Whistle, Wooden, 1920s 55.00

 Coffee grinders of home size were first made about 1894. They lost
favor by the 1930s. Large floor–standing or counter model coffee
grinders were used in the nineteenth–century country store. The

renewed interest in fresh–ground coffee has produced many modern electric and hand grinders, and reproductions of the old styles are being made.

COFFEE GRINDER, Arcade, No. 3, Wall Mount, Crystal 165.00
Arcade, No. 708, Cast Iron 50.00
Arcade, Telephone, Oak Box 195.00
Arcade, Wall 95.00
Brighton Queens, Wall Mount 175.00
C. Parker Co., No. 450, Wall Mount, Patent 1876 .... 60.00
Designs, Tin & Brass, 10 1/4 In. 95.00
Diamond Cut, Wall 70.00
Diamond, Table Top 70.00
Drawer, Wooden Base, Pewter Hopper, Iron Handle, 6 1/4 In. 105.00
Drawer, Wooden Base, Red, 12 1/2 In. 525.00
Enterprise, Painted Design, Cast Iron, 1873, 12 1/2 In. 175.00
G. & L. Dartt, New London, Tin & Cast Iron 60.00
Golden Rule, Wall Mount 195.00
Goldenberg, Tin 50.00
Kitchen Aid, 1936 .... 60.00
L. F. & C., Clamp–On, Cast Iron 45.00
Landers, Frary, Clark, Iron, Drawer, Marked 11 .... 285.00
Lane Brothers, Counter Top, Red & Black Paint 2200.00
Lap, Adams, Pat. 1840 .... 78.00
Lap, Harah Muhle, Pine, 5 In. 55.00
Lil Tot, Child's, 2 1/2 x 2 1/2 In. 85.00
National Specialty Co., Double Wheel, 1875, Large 375.00
Parkers, Original Finish, 1900 .... 85.00
Universal No. 014, Wall, Tin, Dated 1909 .... 70.00
Universal, No. 110, Tin 50.00
Wooden, Dovetailed 38.00
Wooden, Dutch Scenes On Tin 75.00

Coin spot is a glass pattern that was named by the collectors. It features coinlike spots as part of the glass. Colored, clear, and opalescent glass was made with the spots. Many companies used the design in the 1870–90 period. It is so popular that reproductions are still being made.

COIN SPOT, Bottle, Barber, Cranberry, 7 1/4 In. 140.00
Bowl, Amberina, 4 3/4 In. 45.00
Bowl, Cranberry, 2 3/4 x 4 1/2 In. 55.00
Lamp, Finger, Kerosene, Aqua Opalescent 295.00
Lamp, Fluted, Ruffled Beige Shade, Cranberry, 30 In. 160.00
Lamp, Oil, Hand, Chimney, Blue Green, 9 3/4 In. 465.00
Pitcher, Aqua Opalescent 185.00
Pitcher, Enameled Flowers & Leaves, 5 In. 95.00
Pitcher, Milk, Amethyst, Blue, Gold Spots, 7 1/2 In. 160.00
Pitcher, Water, Blue, Fenton 150.00
Pitcher, Water, Optic, Lime Green, Fenton 150.00
Saltshaker, Amberina, 3 In. 65.00
Syrup, Blue 190.00
Syrup, Canary Color 300.00
Syrup, Cranberry Opalescent 395.00
Syrup, Opalescent, Original Top 125.00

The vending machine is an ancient invention dating back to 200 B.C. when holy water was dispensed in a coin–operated vase. Smokers in seventeenth–century England could buy tobacco from a coin–operated box. It was not until after the Civil War that the technology made modern coin–operated games and vending machines plentiful. Slot machines, arcade games, and dispensers are all collected.

COIN–OPERATED MACHINE, 1 Cent Catch N Match, Berger 595.00

A. B. T. Challenger, Pistol Shooting Gallery, 1950s 350.00
Baby Grand, Golden Oak 65.00
Baseball, 1 Cent 300.00
Baseball, Arcade, 1 Cent 675.00
Baseball, Miniature, 1 Cent 500.00
Candy, Hershey's, 1 Cent, Wall Mount 350.00
Candy, Wilber's Chocolate, Tall Metal Case 250.00
Candyette, Wall Mounted 150.00
Card, Sittman & Pitt, Marquee & Award Cards 2200.00
Cigarette, Counter Model, Cast Aluminum, 15 Cent 250.00
Cigarette, Wings, 1 Cent 425.00
Cinch, Shine Cloth 20.00
Coin Changer, Hopking & Robinson, 1883 .... 575.00
Digger, Buckley 1600.00
Digger, Iron Claw, Exhibit Supply, 5 Cent 2500.00
Dispenser, Cigarette, Camels 235.00
Dispenser, Sanitary Shield Toilet Paper 3575.00
Fortune Teller, Three Wise Owls 700.00
Gambling, Best Hand 850.00
Game, Pikes Peak 450.00
Gum, Bubble, Rex 2900.00
Gum, Chiclets, Porcelain 950.00
Gum, Clown's Head Shape, Plastic, 1 Cent 40.00
Gum, Fleer's Pepsin 2800.00
Gum, Niagara Pepsin, Clockwork Mechanism, 1 Cent 7700.00
Gum, Orbit 350.00
Gum, Pulver Yellow Kid, Animated, Oak Cabinet 5000.00
Gum, Pulver, Clockworks, Clown Figure, c.1930 .... 775.00
Gum, Pulver, Cop Directing Traffic .... 725.00 To 750.00
Gum, Pulver, Hot Chv., Column Vendor 150.00
Gum, Stick, Zeno, Oak, 1893 .... 1000.00
Gum, Tutti Frutti, Key, Oak Case 1320.00
Gumball, Acorn, Oak 40.00
Gumball, Ad–Lee E–Z, Globe, Sticker 525.00
Gumball, Advance, Football Globe 175.00
Gumball, Atlas Masters, 5 Cent 45.00
Gumball, Atlas, 1950s 45.00
Gumball, Baby Grand Deluxe, Victor, Golden Oak, 1951 .... 75.00
Gumball, Columbus, Dart Gambling 2000.00
Gumball, Columbus, Dart, Barrel Lock .... 2200.00 To 2500.00
Gumball, Columbus, Model A, Round Globe 170.00
Gumball, Ford Vending Machine Co., 1919 .... 200.00
Gumball, Ford, 1919 .... 125.00
Gumball, Ford, 1950 .... 55.00
Gumball, Fred Flintstone, Hard Plastic, Hasbro, 1968 .... 30.00
Gumball, Metal, 1 Cent 195.00
Gumball, Northwestern, Red Porcelain, 1933 .... 150.00
Gumball, Rex 1050.00
Gumball, Samco Bendor, Octagonal Shape Globe 55.00
Gumball, Topper, 1 Cent 125.00
Gumball, Victor, Baby Grand 45.00
Gumball, Victor, Baby Grand Model, Oak, Glass Front 35.00
Gumball, Victor, Universal, 1940s 65.00
Gumball, Victor, Yellow Jacket, 1940s 75.00
Gunball, Victor, Model K, 1 Cent 300.00
Hand Lotion, Decals On Glass Globe, 1 Cent, 1930s 350.00
Horse Race 5000.00
Horse Race, Table Top, c.1929 .... 5000.00
Keeney's Twin Bonus, Super Bell, 2 Players, 5 Coins 3500.00
Kicker, Catcher Football, 1 Cent, 1933 .... 500.00
Lighter Fluid Dispenser 425.00
Mansfield, Automatic Clerk 800.00
Match Dispenser, Rosebud, Northwestern, 1 Cent, Key 250.00

Match, 1 Cent, Cast Iron & Wood 275.00
Match, Cast Iron 195.00
Match, Diamond 245.00
Matchbox Dispenser, 1 Cent 350.00
Mutoscope, Art Deco, Crank, Floor Model 2200.00
Mutoscope, Card Holder, 1 Wheel, Iron Floor Model 2500.00
Mutoscope, Crank Movie Machine, Floor Model 2200.00
Mutoscope, Digger 4200.00
Mutoscope, Floor Model, Cast Iron, Shell Casting Top 2500.00
Mutoscope, Strength Tester, Tungo 1500.00
National Target, Penny Flip, Cast Aluminum 250.00
Nickelodeon, Coinola Cupid, 1915 .... 8500.00
Nickelodeon, Seeburg, Model L Jr., Oak 5895.00
Nut, Master Fantail 1100.00
Nut, Northwest Deluxe, 1 & 5 Cent 100.00
Nut, Silver King, Glass Light-Up Top, 5 Cent 150.00
Nut, Stewart & McGuire, 1935 .... 125.00
Peanut, Advance, Bigmouth, 1923 .... 225.00
Peanut, Advance, Football Globe 130.00
Peanut, Atlas, Bantam, 5 Cent, Key ....75.00 To 125.00
Peanut, Atlas, Bantam, Octagon Glass Globe, 5 Cent 130.00
Peanut, Butterkist Toasted 775.00
Peanut, Columbus, Model A 300.00
Peanut, Double Nugget, 1930s 175.00
Peanut, Hance, Cast Iron, 1 Cent 700.00
Peanut, Hawkeye, 1940s 75.00
Peanut, Little Nut Vendor, 1 Cent, Green, Red House 475.00
Peanut, Little Nut Vendor, Lansing, Mich. 475.00
Peanut, Northwestern, Cast Iron, 1933 .... 175.00
Peanut, Northwestern, Frosted Globe 300.00
Peanut, Northwestern, Model 33, Frosted Globe, Locks 350.00
Peanut, Northwestern, Painted Cast Iron 125.00
Peanut, Northwestern, Painted White Cast Iron, Globe 150.00
Peanut, Prize King, Cast Iron 75.00
Peanut, Silver King Deluxe, 1930s 85.00
Peanut, Simpson, Claw Feet 1100.00
Peanut, Sun, 5 Cent 55.00
Peanut, Victor, Model V, 1 Cent, 1940s .... 65.00 To 75.00
Peep Show, Esco, Sultans Harem Viewer, 1 Cent 700.00
Pinball, Gottlieb, Alice In Wonderland 900.00
Pinball, Gottlieb, Buckeroo 550.00
Pinball, Gottlieb, Cinderella 750.00
Pinball, Gottlieb, Roller Coaster 350.00
Pinball, Gottlieb, Straight Shooter 350.00
Pinball, Gottlieb, World Champ 750.00
Pinball, Hayburner, Williams Mfg. Co. 500.00
Pinball, Star Skill Cards, Counter Top 195.00
Pinball, Williams, Lucky Strike 250.00
Playing Cards 2200.00
Popcorn, Dunbar 1000.00
Popcorn, French Fried, 1933 World's Fair, Advance 2000.00
Popcorn, Manley 500.00
Popcorn, Star, Floor Model, 1929 .... 400.00
Racehorse, Table Top, c.1929 .... 5000.00
Shermack, Double Stamp 45.00
Shocker, Spear The Dragon 6800.00
Slot, 1 Arm Bandit, Comet, 1 To 5 Cent, 1930s 1395.00
Slot, Bally, Clover Bell 2000.00
Slot, Bally, Double Bell, 5 & 25 Cent 3000.00
Slot, Bally, Triple Bell, Dimes, Nickels, Quarters 605.00
Slot, Caille, Ben Hur 4500.00
Slot, Dutch Boy, 5 Cents 1675.00
Slot, Jennings, Club Chief, Light-Up, 5 Cent, 1940s 1800.00

◆◆◆◆◆◆◆◆◆◆◆◆◆◆◆◆◆◆◆◆◆

Always use a metal polish on the metal it was made for. Don't clean silver with pewter or chrome polish. The wrong formula may scratch the metal.

◆◆◆◆◆◆◆◆◆◆◆◆◆◆◆◆◆◆◆◆◆

Coin–Operated Machine, Slot, Jennings,
Twenty–Five Cent Play

◆◆◆◆◆◆◆◆◆◆◆◆◆◆◆◆◆◆◆◆◆◆◆◆◆◆◆◆◆◆◆◆◆◆◆◆◆◆

Plastic should be cleaned gently. Wipe with a damp cloth, then dry. Do not use an abrasive cleaner. Soapy water can be used.

◆◆◆◆◆◆◆◆◆◆◆◆◆◆◆◆◆◆◆◆◆◆◆◆◆◆◆◆◆◆◆◆◆◆◆◆◆◆

Slot, Jennings, Lifesaver, Diecast & Wood, 5 Cents	900.00
Slot, Jennings, Little Duke, With Gumball Dispenser	1500.00
Slot, Jennings, Silver Moon, 5 Cent	1050.00
Slot, Jennings, Silver Moon, Console, 5 Cent	950.00
Slot, Jennings, Tic–Tac–Toe, 5 Cent	2000.00
Slot, Jennings, Twenty–Five Cent Play ....*Illus*	1100.00
Slot, Keeney, Twin Bonus Super Bell, 1 To 5 Coins	3500.00
Slot, Mills, Black Cherry, Dime Slot, c.1947	1800.00
Slot, Mills, Bursting Cherry, 25 Cents, 1941	2000.00
Slot, Mills, Q–T Firebird	1500.00
Slot, Mills, Skyscraper	1025.00
Slot, Pace, Twin Reels, 5 & 10 Cent, 1940s	825.00
Slot, Quarter, Wood & Diecast, Mills	800.00
Slot, Watling, Baby Bell, Fortune Teller Reels	2250.00
Slot, Watling, Rol–A–Top, Bonus Jackpot, 5 Cent	5100.00
Slot, Zipper Ball, 10 Cents	200.00
Stamp, Shipman, Blue Porcelain	50.00
Stereoscope Viewer, Rosenfield, Mild Erotic Cards	600.00
Stimulator, Poker, Caille Quintette, 25 Reels, 1901	8500.00
Target, Indian Penny Drop	725.00
Trade Stimulator, Dice, 1920s	500.00
Trade Stimulator, Fairest Wheel, Glass Base, Cigars	750.00
Trade Stimulator, Imperial, Gumball, 1940s, 5 Cent	185.00
Trade Stimulator, Play Ball	1050.00
Trade Stimulator, Try–Skill	235.00
Trade Stimulator, Winner Spiral	1800.00
Vendor, Dr Pepper, Vendo, No. 81, Green, 10 Cent	2500.00
Vendor, Soda Pop, Dr Pepper, No. 81, 10 Cent	2500.00
Whitting, Sculptoscope	600.00

Collector plates are modern plates produced in limited editions. Some will be found listed under the factory name, such as Bing & Grondahl, Royal Copenhagen, Royal Doulton, and Wedgwood.

Pictures and more price information can be found in Kovels' Price Guide for Collector Plates, Figurines, Paperweights and Other Limited Editions.

COLLECTOR PLATE, Avon, Tenderness Commemorative, 1974, Box	40.00
Crown Parian, Freddie's Shack, 1980	60.00
DeGrazia, Los Ninos, 1976	1100.00
DeGrazia, Spring Blossoms, 1987	36.00
Knowles, Grandma's Courting Dress, 1984	25.00
Knowles, Grandpa Plays Santa, 1985	30.00
Knowles, Pintail, 1986	52.00
Knowles, Scarlett, 1978	250.00
Rockwell & Cobbler, 1978	55.00
Rockwell, Christmas, 1975	32.50
Rockwell, Cobbler, 1978	120.00
Rockwell, Horse Trader, Gorham, 1979	40.00
Rockwell, Music Master, 1981	20.00
Rockwell, River Shore, 1977	28.00
Rockwell, Toymaker, 1977	145.00
Rockwell, Toymaker, 1980	40.00
Rockwell, Traveling Salesman, Gorham, 1977	40.00
Rockwell, Tycoon, 1982	32.50
Schmid, Raggedy Ann, Christmas, 1977	6.00
Viletta, Sabina In Grass, 1979	95.00

Comic art, or cartoon art, is a relatively new field of collecting. Original comic strips, magazine covers, and even printed strips are collected. The first daily comic strip was printed in 1907. The paintings on celluloid used for movie cartoons are listed in this book under Animation Art.

COMIC ART, Barney Google, Bille DeBeck, Strip, May 13, 1931, 4 1/2 x 18 In.	245.00
Boob McNutt, Chicago Herald, Page, 1925	18.00
Book, Vault of Horror, Cover, No. 25, June, July	1650.00
Buz Sawyer, Roy Crane, Strip, Apr. 26, 1947, 5 x 16 In.	300.00
Dick Tracy, Chester Gould, Dec. 1, 1940, 26 x 19 In.	1950.00
Li'l Abner, Al Capp, Oct. 10, 1954, 21 x 21 In.	485.00
Phantom, Ray Moore, Strip, Mar. 25, 1937, 6 x 28 In.	4400.00
Pogo, Walt Kelly, Strip, 4 1/2 x 17 In.	850.00
Prince Valiant, Hal Foster, Aug. 26, 1956, 34 x 23 In.	2370.00
Tarzan, Burne Hogarth, Dec. 12, 1943, 27 x 20 In.	2200.00
Thimble Theater, Popeye, E. C. Segar, Strip, 1936, 4 1/2 x 20 In.	800.00
Vault of Horror, About Face, Johnny Craig, 8 Pages	735.00

Commemorative items have been made to honor members of royalty and those of great national fame. World's fairs and important historical events are also remembered with commemorative pieces.

COMMEMORATIVE, see also Coronation; World's Fair

COMMEMORATIVE, Bank, Crown Shape, Elizabeth II, Iron, 1953	25.00
Beaker, Victoria, Diamond Jubilee, Brown & White	165.00
Beaker, Victoria, Queen of Great Britain, Ireland, 1887, 4 In.	95.00
Mug, George V & Mary Silver Jubilee, 1910–35, Pottery	35.00
Mug, Wedding, Charles & Diane	22.00
Pendant, Edward VII & Alexandra Picture, Silver, 1901	25.00
Pin Tray, Elizabeth II, Silver Jubilee, 4 1/4 In.	15.00
Pitcher, Tennyson, Burslem, Blue & White, Gold, 1892	265.00
Pitcher, Victoria, Lambeth, High Gloss, 1897	285.00
Plate, Charles & Diana Wedding, 8 1/4 In.	20.00
Plate, Prince Charles & Diana, Wedding, Royal Albert	30.00
Plate, Queen Elizabeth & King George VI's Visit U. S., 1939	42.00

A woman did not powder her face in public until after World War I. By 1920 the beauty parlor, permanent waves, and cosmetics had become acceptable. A few companies sold cake face powder in a box with a mirror and a pad or puff. Soon the compact was being designed by jewelers and made of gold, silver, and precious materials. Cosmetic companies began to sell powder in attractive compacts of less valuable metal or plastic. Collectors today search for Art Deco designs, commemorative compacts from world's fairs or political events, and unusual examples. Many were made with companion lipsticks and other fittings.

COMPACT, 3 Men Riding Elephant On Cover, Siam Silver	80.00
Agate Inset, Engraved, Sterling Silver	95.00
Art Deco Shape, Empire State Building	30.00
Art Deco, Bakelite	20.00
Art Nouveau, Embossed Silver, Change Holder On Chain, Germany, Box	110.00
Art Nouveau, Finger Ring	25.00
Arthur Murray On Top, To Elinor Kilpatrick, Murray Dancers Photo	16.00
Bakelite, Breen, Art Deco	24.00
Blue Guilloche Enamel, Sun Ray & Fleur–De–Lis, Sterling	385.00
Bourjois, Evening In Paris, Square, 2 1/4 In.	25.00
Brushed Gold, High Gloss, Flat, DT Monogram, 4 1/2 In.	25.00
Carryall, Light Blue Enameled, Fitted, Mesh Wrist Loop	80.00
Coty, Flower Center, Textured Silver, Square, Envelope, 2 1/4 In.	25.00
Coty, Red Bull's–Eye, 1950	23.00
Designed As Telephone, Red, White & Black Enamel, Round	25.00
Elgin, American, Box	16.00 To 27.00
Elgin, Basket of Flowers, Sterling Silver, Signed	60.00
Elgin, Gold Mesh Base, Goldtone Cover, Floral, M Monogram, 3 In.	35.00
Elgin, Silver & Goldtone	26.00
Elgin, Sterling, American	50.00
Elizabeth Arden, Light Blue Enameled	80.00
Elizabeth Arden, Sifter Style, Scroll Design, Gilt, 3 3/4 In.	40.00
Embossed Flowers, Celluloid, 4 1/2 In.	22.00
Estee Lauder	21.00
Evans, Black & White Applied Figure, White Enameled Mesh Pouch	60.00
Evans, Carryall, Compartments For Powder, Lipstick, Comb, Goldtone	125.00
Evans, Hand Painted Cloisonne Cover, Gold Mesh Bottom	58.00
Evans, Roses On Enamel	25.00
Evening In Paris	30.00
Georg Jensen, Sterling Silver	375.00
Girey, Confetti, Kamra Pak, Eagle Emblem Cover	45.00
Gorham, Sterling Silver, 1955, 3 In.	40.00
Green Glass, Cut Design, Cambridge	45.00
Hand Mirror Shape, Black Bakelite	40.00
Henriette	30.00
Hingeco, Heart Shape, Sterling, Navy Logo On Cover	50.00
Illinois Watch Center, Gold	75.00
Limoges, Goldtone, Hand Mirror	50.00
Lucite, Sterling Lovebirds Inset, Square, 3 In.	28.00
Lydia Pinkham	20.00
Map of Massachusetts	15.00
Max Factor, Mother–of–Pearl	8.00
Mondaine, Rhinestone Clasp	10.00
Monogrammed, Ivory Colored Celluloid	15.00
Needlepoint, Multicolored Flowers On Back, Square, 2 3/4 In.	35.00
New York World's Fair, 1936, Needlepoint Lid, Mirror & Puff	100.00
Norida, Sifter & Hinged Stand–Up Mirror	20.00
Nude Silhouette, Art Deco	25.00
Pilcher, Wooden, Horse's Head Cover, Janet Inscribed On Back	50.00
Prince Machiavelli, Red, Gold Crown	14.00
Purse, Beautiful Woman, Mother–of–Pearl, 5 Sections, 1880s, 4 In.	295.00
Revlon, Black Enamel, Gold, 1950s	10.00
Revlon, Ultima, Goldtone	8.00
Rex, Etched Silver & Tortoise	20.00
Rex, Silver Plate	18.00
Richard Hudnut, Blue Enameled	31.00

Richard Hudnut, Goldtone, Handle, 2 1/2 x 3 In.	20.00
Schuco, Monkey	250.00
Seated Cat, Celluloid	20.00
Silver Color, Enameled Flowers, Sifter	40.00
Silver Plate, Blue Enameled, Flowers, Art Deco, Finger Ring	90.00
Silver, Chased Design, Mexico	85.00
Silver, Germany, Dated 1925, 2 In.	14.00
Silvered Repousse, Mirror, Powderette	325.00
Slots For Coins, Rhinestone Dollar Sign On Front	35.00
Snakeskin, Brown, Argentina	20.00
Souvenir of Israel, Zipper Closure, Engraved Scenes, Goldtone	8.00
Souvenir, Camp Ripley, Minn., Hand Painted	15.00
Statue of Liberty	40.00
Sterling, Braided Chain	65.00
Sterling, Doves On Front, Plastic, 1940s	60.00
Sterling, Mexico, Square	90.00
Sterling, Pastel Floral Enameled, White Ground, 2 1/8 In.	95.00
Sterling, With Chain & Finger Ring, ARC Monogram, Small, Round	50.00
Stratton, Black Roses On Red Top, Goldtone	20.00
Stylized Wave Pattern On Cover & Sides, Diamonds, 14K White Gold	1320.00
Tre–Jur, 2 Sections	45.00
Truart, Goldtone, Round, 3 1/2 In.	15.00
Volupte, Gold, Basketweave, Square, Slim, 1930s, Box	30.00
Volupte, Musical	90.00
Volupte, Pastel Rhinestones In Lid, Goldtone, Square, 2 1/2 In.	110.00
Volupte, Raised Goldleaf & Rhinestones On Cover	15.00
Yardley of London, 2 Slide–Out Compartments, 1930s	15.00
Yardley, Lipstick Holder On Side	15.00
Yellow Enamel, Flowers, 2 Compartments	40.00

Consolidated Lamp and Glass Company of Coraopolis, Pennsylvania, was founded in 1894. The company made lamps, tablewares, and art glass. Collectors are particularly interested in the wares made after 1925, including black satin glass, Martele (which resembled Lalique), and colored glasswares. The company closed for the final time in 1967.

CONSOLIDATED GLASS, Bowl, Dancing Nude, Crystal, 8 In.	60.00
Compote, Orchid, Green, 10 In.	175.00
Fish Bowl, Martele, Amethyst	350.00
Fish Bowl, Martele, Green	400.00
Plate, Dancing Nude, Crystal, 10 1/2 In.	75.00
Plate, Fruit Leaf, Green, 12 In.	125.00
Vase, Bird of Paradise, Blue, Crystal	300.00
Vase, Catalonian, 7 In.	30.00

The term *contemporary glass* refers to art glass made since 1950. Some contemporary glass factories, such as Baccarat or Orrefors, are listed under their own categories. Earlier glass may be listed in the Art Glass section and Italian glass may be found in the Venetian Glass and Venini sections.

CONTEMPORARY GLASS, Bowl, Crystal, Shell Design, 9 3/4 x 5 1/2 In.	60.00
Ewer, Pink Satin To Clear, Etched, 13 1/4 In., Pair	70.00
Ice Bucket, Crystal, Pinched Ring Handles, 9 1/2 In.	85.00
Vase, Blue Feathers On Red, C. Lotton, 1984, 2 In.	195.00
Vase, Blue Sculptured Glass, Labino, 5 1/2 x 5 1/2 In.	475.00
Vase, Crystal, Cofrac Art Verrier, France, 9 1/4 In.	120.00
Vase, Crystal, Cristal Clear, Romsit Advertising, 10 In.	45.00
Vase, Threading, White & Pink, C. Lotton, 1980, 7 In.	350.00
Vase, Trumpet, Crystal, Stewart Pattern, 12 In.	90.00
Vase, White, Red Flower, C. Lotton, 8 3/4 In.	357.00

Cookbooks are collected for various reasons. Some are wanted for the recipes, some for investment, and some as examples of advertising. Cookbooks and recipe pamphlets are included in this section.

COOKBOOK, 20 Lessons By Calumet Baking, 1916 .... 15.00
All Manner of Food, Michael Field, 1970, 382 Pages 7.00
American Woman, 1947 .... 10.00
American Woman, Berolzhimer 20.00
Anyone Can Bake, Royal Baking Powder, 100 Pages, 1928 .... 20.00
Baker's Best Chocolate, 1932 .... 18.00
Best of All Cookbook, Brobeck, 1960, 512 Pages 7.00
Better Homes & Garden, 1953 .... 15.00
Black Mammy 45.00
Calumet Baking Book 7.00
Calumet, Reliable Recipes 15.00
Calumut, Master Cake Baker, 107 Pages, 1927 .... 15.00
Canning & Recipe Book, Prof. Blits, Unusual, 189 .... 38.00
Central College, Lexington, Mo. 8.00
Ceresota, Color Lithograph, 1912 .... 15.00
Clabber Girl 8.00
Complete Western Cookbook, 1964 .... 7.50
Cook It In A Casserole, 1943 .... 5.00
Eat, Drink & Be Merry In Maryland, 1932 .... 15.00
Edison Electric, With Movie Stars, 1950 .... 12.00
Electric Refrigerator Recipes, General Electric, 1927 .... 13.00
Famous Old New Orleans Recipes, 1900 .... 8.50
Fascinating Foods From The Deep South, Van Duzor, 1963, 117 Pgs. 7.00
Favorite Recipes From Kraft 3.00
Favorite Recipes From Lutheran Brotherhood, 1970, 182 Pages 7.00
Gold Cookbook By Master Chef Louis P. DeGouy, 1960 .... 18.00
Gone With The Wind, Pebeco, 1940, 48 Pages 48.00
Hawaiian, 75th Anniversary, 1966 .... 7.00
Historical Cooking of The Black Hills 8.00
Home Comfort Stoves 25.00
Home Comfort, Testimonials, Household Hints, 200 Pages 20.00
Hood's Practical Cookbook, 349 Pages, 1897 .... 20.00
Jell-O Girl Entertains, Rose O'Neill, 8 Illustrations 16.00
Jell-O, 1918 .... 10.00
Jell-O, Norman Rockwell Print 35.00
Jell-O, Parrish 40.00
Karo Kookery, 1942 .... 9.00
Kate Smith, 1940, 46 Pages 7.00
KC Baking Powder, War Department Recognition 18.00
La Cuisine Creole, 1885 .... 350.00
Ladies Aid, 1917 .... 8.50
Liberace Cooks, 1970 .... 20.00
Lippencott's Housewifery, 353 Pages, 1921 .... 15.00
Little Brown Coco 15.00
Look No Further, Autographed 5.00
Lowneys, Boston, Hard Cover, 1912 .... 8.00
Martha Dixon 10.00
Mary Dunbar Waterless Cooker, Jewel Tea, 20 Pages, 1926 .... 12.00
Nature Cure, 1918 .... 36.00
Navy Mother's Cookbook, Oakland, Calif., Navy Mothers Club, 1940s 8.00
New Orleans Recipes, Aunt Jemima Picture, 1932 .... 40.00
One Hundred Prize Dinners, 78 Pages, 1900 .... 20.00
Pennsylvania Cookbook, 1936 .... 15.00
Peter Pauper Press Casserole 6.00
Ralston Mother Goose Recipe, Illustrated By C. M. Burd, 1919 .... 16.00
Recipe Cards, Log Cabin, Original Envelope, 1920s 25.00
Royal Cookbook 5.00
Rumford, Blond Child On Cover, 1909 .... 35.00

Rumford, Common Sense 10.00
Saginaw, No Covers, 1890 .... 40.00
Saturday Evening Post, Soft Cover, 1979, 8 1/2 x 11 In. 20.00
Savannah, 1933 .... 12.50
Seattle's Bride Cookbook, 1890s, 104 Pages 30.00
Secrets of Southern Cooking, 1956 .... 12.00
Sensational Salads, Ventura 4.00
Sheraton World Cookbook, 1982 .... 12.00
Southern Cookbook, Profile of Mammy On Wooden Cover 60.00
Soy Bean Magic, Gwen Mallard, 1976, 80 Pages 1.50
Taber, Stillmeadow, 1965 .... 23.00
Thousand Ways To Please A Husband, 1917 .... 25.00
Victory Wartime Cooking 15.00
Vincent & Mary Price, Recipes From All Over World, Calorie Chart 20.00
Wearever 8.00
Western, 1936 .... 6.00
Westinghouse 5.00
World's Greatest Recipes, James Beard, 1976 .... 13.00

 Cookie jars with brightly painted designs or amusing figural shapes became popular in the mid–1930s. Many companies made them and collectors search for cookie jars either by design or by maker's name. Listed here are examples by the less common makers. Major factories are listed under their own names in other sections of the book, such as Abingdon; Brush; Hull; McCoy; Red Wing; Shawnee. See also Black and Disneyana.

COOKIE JAR, Aunt Jemima, F & F .... 225.00 To 325.00
Balloon Lady, Pottery Guild .... 90.00 To 140.00
Bambi, American Bisque, USA 400.00
Barn, Old MacDonald, Regal China 140.00
Bear With Cookie, American Bisque 35.00
Bear With Hat, American Bisque 45.00
Bear, Avon 50.00
Bear, Drummer, Colorful 35.00
Bear, Girl, Metlox 35.00
Bear, Regal China 59.00
Bear, Twin Winton 40.00
Bear, With Dots 55.00
Bear, With Flower, American Bisque 40.00
Bear, With Golf Hat, American Bisque 65.00
Betsy Ross, Enesco 95.00
Betty & Barney Rubble's House 725.00
Betty Boop, With Top Hat 30.00
Big Bird, California Originals 52.00
Black Chef 140.00
Black Chef, Japan 250.00
Black Chef, National Silver 275.00
Black Chef, Pearl China .... 400.00 To 600.00
Black Coffeepot, George & Martha, American Bisque 18.00
Black Engine 95.00
Black Girl, Vegetables Gathered In Her Dress 135.00
Black Little Girl, Green Dress, Patch Heart, Treasure Craft 88.00
Black Mammy, Mixing Bowl, Yellow, Metlox 130.00
Black Man's Bust, Straw Hat, Tie, Large Face, Wisecarver 119.00
Black Man, Banjo, Girl Behind, Wisecarver 119.00
Black Santa, Bag of Toys, Wisecarver 135.00
Black Santa, Metlox 250.00
Black Woman's Bust, Earrings, Large Face, Wisecarver 119.00
Black Woman, Jazz Singer, Clay Arts 49.00
Blackboard Clown, , American Bisque 125.00
Blackboard Clown, American Bisque 100.00
Blackboard Saddle, American Bisque .... 110.00 To 135.00
Blue Bonnet Sue, Advertising, Box 40.00

Boots, American Bisque .... 75.00 To 192.00
Boy Duck, Royal 35.00
Boy Graduate, Cardinal 65.00
Boy Pig, American Bisque .... 60.00 To 70.00
Boy With Skirt, Pottery Guild 65.00
Brown, Flower & Dots, Mar–Crest 40.00
Bugs Bunny 175.00
Butler, Brown, Japan 200.00
C3PO, Roman Ceramics 135.00
Carousel, USA 25.00
Casper, USA 700.00
Cat On Basket, Japan 25.00
Cat On Beehive, American Bisque .... 32.00 To 38.00
Cat, Black 40.00
Cat, Dog 65.00
Century 21 House, Little People In House 250.00
Chef, Gold Trim, Pearl China 415.00
Chef, Pearl China 385.00
Chef, Salad Bowl, Regal China 185.00
Chicken, Fabco 40.00
Chicken, Iron Cover 49.00
Chicken, Napco 50.00
Chicken, Pottery Guild 35.00
Cinderella, Box 140.00
Cinderella, Napco .... 50.00 To 70.00
Clown 80.00
Clown On Stage, American Bisque 180.00
Clown, American Bisque .... 27.50 To 50.00
Clown, Ball & Seal 150.00
Coffeepot, Brown, Treasure Craft .... 30.00 To 47.00
Cookie Monster Chef 85.00
Cookie Monster, California Originals .... 30.00 To 75.00
Cookie Trolley, Treasure Craft 16.00
Cookie Truck, American Bisque .... 38.00 To 70.00
Cookies, Nut On Lid, Japan 40.00
Cooky, Pearl China 350.00
Corner Jar, American Bisque 160.00
Cow Over The Moon, American Bisque .... 145.00 To 150.00
Darth Vader .... 135.00 To 140.00
Davy Crockett, American Bisque .... 150.00 To 250.00
Davy Crockett, Ransberg 80.00
Davy Crockett, Regal China .... 168.00 To 185.00
Diaper Pin Pig, Regal China 275.00
Dino, Golf Bag, American Bisque .... 480.00 To 625.00
Dino, Metlox 60.00
Dog In Basket, American Bisque .... 25.00 To 35.00
Dog In Doghouse, Bird On Roof, American Bisque 90.00
Dog, Purina, Yellow Plastic 125.00
Donald Duck and Pumpkin, California Originals 250.00
Donkey, Milk Wagon, American Bisque .... 55.00 To 75.00
Dove, Doranne 40.00
Drummer Bear 29.00

◆◆

To remove the musty smell from a closed cupboard or box, try using rice. Parch several handfuls of uncooked rice in a shallow pan in the oven. Then put the pan and rice in the musty drawer. You may have to repeat the parching to keep the moisture and mildew from reappearing.

◆◆

Dutch Boy & Girl, Pottery Guild, Pair 75.00
Dutch Boy, Brown Pants, Pottery Guild 38.00
Dutch Boy, Pottery Guild 50.00
Dutch Boy, With Sailboat 15.00
Dutch Girl, American Bisque 58.00
Dutch Girl, Pottery Guild .... 75.00 To 80.00
Eeyore, California Original 15.00
Elephant, Royal 35.00
Elephant, Sitting Up, American Bisque 48.00
Elephant, With Ball Cap, American Bisque 40.00
Elf, With Pixie Face, Green Hair 55.00
Elsie The Cow, F & F 145.00
Elsie, In Barrel, Pottery Guild 118.00
Ernie 25.00
Ernie, California Originals 35.00
European Girl, Pottery Guild 140.00
Fish, Metlox 150.00
Fred Flintstone 49.00
Fred Flintstone & Pebbles, Vandor .... 59.00 To 75.00
French Chef Head, Cardinal 85.00
Frog, Legs Crossed 40.00
Frontier Family 40.00
Girl Pig, Dotted Dress, American Bisque .... 45.00 To 50.00
Girl Pig, Metlox 69.00
Girl, Has Vegetables In Dress, Wisecarver 125.00
Goldilocks, Regal China .... 120.00 To 250.00
Granny, American Bisque 45.00
Granny, Napco 45.00
Granny, With Bonnet 55.00
Head of Little Boy, Marked Engineer, Japan 35.00
Hen, With Chicks, Morton 42.00
Hopalong Cassidy 150.00
House, Blue & White, Stair, Balcony, Otagiri 66.00
Hubert Lion, With Bank, Wire Rim Glasses, Regal China ...... 225.00 To 425.00
Humpty Dumpty, Red Brick Wall, Gold Trim, Regal China 165.00
Ice Cream Cone, U. S. A. 30.00
Jazz Singer 45.00
Jug, Monmouth 25.00
Jukebox, Vandor .... 49.00 To 65.00
Ken–L–Ration Pup, Plastic, F & F 105.00
Keystone Cop, Marsh of California 60.00
Kids In Shoe House, Green Trim, Red & Brown, Japan 35.00
Kitchen Witch 50.00
Kraft Bear, Regal China .... 90.00 To 135.00
Kraft Marshmallow, 15 In. 125.00
Lady Pig, American Bisque 60.00
Lamb Head, Metlox 80.00
Las Vegas Slot Machine, Doranne of California 60.00
Liberty Bell, Crystal 30.00
Lion, Belmont .... 25.00 To 60.00
Little Bopeep, Ransburg 85.00
Little Girl Lamb, American Bisque 45.00
Little Girl, Green Dress, Patch Heart, Box, Treasure Craft 49.00
Little Red Riding Hood, Pottery Guild .... 74.00 To 120.00
Ludwig Von Drake, Matching Mugs 180.00
Luzianne 510.00
Majorette, American Bisque 85.00
Majorette, Gold Trim, Regal China 99.00
Mama, Holding Rolling Pin, Apron, Cat Against Leg, N. S. Gustin 95.00
Mammy 500.00
Mammy, Churn & Child, Wisecarver 119.00
Mammy, F & F 195.00
Mammy, Metlox, Red Dots 190.00

Mammy, Mosaic, Blue 350.00
Mammy, Mosaic, Yellow 500.00
Mammy, National Silver .... 175.00 To 240.00
Mammy, Pearl China .... 125.00 To 725.00
Mammy, Plastic, F & F .... 330.00 To 360.00
Mickey Mouse & Minnie Mouse, Turnabout 85.00
Mickey Mouse The Baker, Hoan Ltd. 50.00
Money Sack, White, Pink Letters, Abingdon 49.00
Monk 35.00
Monk, Treasure Craft 35.00
Monk, Twin Winton 40.00
Mother Rabbit, With Baby 65.00
Mother's Best, Cleminson 35.00
Oatmeal, Regal 85.00
Owl 16.00
Owl, Royal 25.00
Paddington Bear, Toscany 98.00
Panda Bear, Metlox 45.00
Parrot, Metlox .... 79.00 To 95.00
Peasant Woman, Multicolors, Brayton Laguna 125.00
Peek-A-Boo, Regal China, Van Telligen Mark 295.00
Peek-A-Boo, Van Telligen Mark 475.00
Pelican, California Original 39.00
Pig, American Bisque .... 25.00 To 65.00
Pig, With Shamrocks, American Bisque .... 55.00 To 65.00
Pillsbury Doughboy, Premium, Box 30.00
Pillsbury Doughboy, Signed, Dated 1973 .... 60.00
Pinocchio, Metlox 190.00
Pinocchio, Metlox, Paper Label 450.00
Pinocchio, Walt Disney 475.00
Poodle, Fifi, Regal 250.00
Poodle, Green Trim 65.00
Popeye Head, American Bisque 650.00
Porky Pig, Duncan, Warner Bros., 1975 .... 150.00
Puppy In Basket 20.00
Puppy, Pot, American Bisque 85.00
Purple Cow, Metlox 70.00
Quaker Boy 100.00
Quaker Oats, Regal 85.00
Quaker Oats, Regal China .... 80.00 To 95.00
Queen of Hearts, Alice In Wonderland, Maddux 95.00
R2D2 .... 85.00 To 150.00
Rabbit 'N Basket, Royal 35.00
Rabbit In Hat, American Bisque .... 50.00 To 70.00
Radio, 1950's Style, Vandor 29.00
Rag Doll, Polka Dot Dress, Hands Raised, Starnes of California 75.00
Raggedy Andy, Metlox 95.00
Raggedy Andy, Twin Winton 20.00
Raggedy Ann 45.00
Ring Bell For Cookies, American Bisque 25.00
Rooster Decal, Hexagonal 25.00
Rooster, American Bisque 49.00
Rubble House, Flintstones, American Bisque 395.00
Sadiron, American Bisque 50.00
Sailor Elephant, Treasure Craft 30.00
Sailor Elephant, Twin Winton 50.00
Sambo The Chef 175.00
Sandman, American Bisque 48.00
Santa Claus Bust, Plastic, Dated 1973 .... 32.00
Santa Claus Face, Plastic, Red & White, Empire .... 33.00 To 39.00
Santa Claus, 1952, Jamar 175.00
Santa Claus, Bag of Toys, Wisecarver 135.00
Santa Claus, California Originals 75.00

Santa Claus, With Bell, Holly On Hat, Gold Buckles	60.00
Santa Claus, Word Cookies On Front, Plastic, Empire	40.00
Santa's Cookie House, Santa Climbing On Roof, Otagiri, 1980	175.00
Sheriff, Hole In Hat	30.00
Sheriff, Marsh Ceramics	65.00
Sheriff, No Hole In Hat	27.00
Snoopy	140.00
Space Ship, American Bisque	85.00
Squirrel, On Nut, Metlox	39.00
Squirrel, On Pine Cone, Metlox	50.00 To 65.00
Stagecoach, Sierra Vista	188.00 To 275.00
Star Wars 1 Side, Darth Vader Other Side, Metlox	100.00
Star Wars, R2–D2, Advertising, Tin, Uneeda Biscuit	12.00
Stella Strawberry, Peedee	60.00
Superman, California Originals	285.00
Tat–L–Tale, Voice Box In Lid	350.00
Thou Shalt Not Steal, Twin Winton	35.00
Three Bears, Abingdon	90.00
Tiger	95.00
Tom & Jerry, MGM	129.00 To 145.00
Toy Soldier	30.00
Toy Soldier, American Bisque	55.00
Train	16.00
Train Engine, Abingdon	90.00
Transformer	60.00
Trolley Car, Treasure Craft	55.00
Tudor House, Treasure Craft	35.00
Tugboat, USA	25.00
Tuggles	65.00
Turkey, Morton	75.00
Turnabout Bear, Royal	40.00
Turtle With Butterfly, Maurice of California	60.00
Turtle, Rabbit Finial	50.00
Umbrella Kids, American Bisque	95.00 To 125.00
White Chick, American Bisque	30.00
Wilma Flintstone, Talking On Phone, American Bisque	250.00 To 375.00
Windmill, Fabco	20.00
Winnie The Pooh	40.00
Winnie The Pooh, Walt Disney Productions	85.00
Wizard, Clay Arts	49.00
Woman & Balloons, Pottery Guild	65.00
Woman, Children In Shoe	85.00
Yarn Doll, American Bisque	55.00 To 85.00
Yogi Bear, American Bisque	75.00
Yogi Bear, Felt Tag, American Bisque	225.00

COORS U.S.A. Coors ware was made by a pottery in Golden, Colorado, owned by the Coors Beverage Company. It was produced from the turn of the century until the pottery was destroyed by fire in the 1930s. The name *Coors* is marked on the back. For more information, see *Kovels' Depression Glass & American Dinnerware Price List.*

COORS, Bowl, Pudding, Floral, Thermo	30.00
Bowl, Rosebud, Handle	30.00
Container, Malted Milk	85.00
Mortar & Pestle, Porcelain	45.00
Plate, Rosebud, Burgundy, 10 In.	10.00
Tumbler, Rosebud, Handle, Yellow	26.00
Vase, Art Deco, High Gloss Yellow, Handles Form Circle, 5 In.	40.00

COPELAND SPODE ENGLAND Josiah Spode established a pottery at Stoke–on–Trent, England, in 1770. In 1833, the firm was purchased by William Copeland and Thomas Garrett and the firm mark was changed. In 1847, Copeland became the sole owner and the mark changed again. W. T.

Copeland & Sons continued until a 1976 merger when it became Royal Worcester Spode. Pieces are listed in this book under the name that appears in the mark. Copeland Spode, Copeland, and Royal Worcester have separate listings.

COPELAND SPODE, Bowl, Italian Scenes, Black & White, 9 1/2 In. 150.00
    Dinner Set, Stoneware, Buttercup Pattern, 76 Piece 275.00
    Dresser Set, Ringtree, Candleholders, Tray, Leaf Pattern 325.00
    Pitcher, Frank E. Burley Design, Salt Glaze, 8 3/8 In. 300.00
    Pitcher, Hunt Scene, White, Green, Beige 145.00
    Plate, Audubon Bird, 6 In. 12.00
    Plate, Red Tower, 6 1/4 In. 8.00
    Plate, Red Tower, 7 3/4 In. 10.00
    Platter, Floral, Foliate & Geometrics, 19 1/2 In. 550.00
    Soup, Dish, Red Tower, 7 3/4 In. 12.00
    Sugar & Creamer, Cover 125.00
    Sugar & Creamer, White Figural Design, Blue & White 25.00
    Teapot 160.00
    Tureen, Cover, Red Tower, 11 x 9 x 6 In. 75.00
    Urn, On Revolving Tray, Red & White, 13 x 17 1/2 In. 275.00
COPELAND, Butter Chip, Blue, Yellow & Purple, c.1878, 4 Piece 275.00
    Pitcher, Embossed Hunt Scenes, White, Salt Glaze, 4 7/8 In. 30.00

Utilitarian items, such as teakettles and cooking pans, have been handcrafted from copper in America since the days of the early colonists. Copper became a popular metal with the Arts and Crafts makers of the early 1900s and decorative pieces such as bookends and desk sets were made. Other pieces of copper may be found in the Bradley & Hubbard, Kitchen, and Roycroft categories.

COPPER LUSTER, see Luster, Copper
COPPER, Ale Muller, 1800 .... 125.00
    Bed Warmer, Floral Engraved Cover, Turned Handle, 40 In. 125.00
    Bed Warmer, Floral Engraved, Pierced Cover, Turned Handle, 42 In. 225.00
    Bed Warmer, Hot Water, Copper, Wooden Handle, 40 In. 45.00
    Bed Warmer, Pierced & Tooled Lid, Turned Handle, 44 1/2 In. 95.00
    Bed Warmer, Tooled Pinwheel Lid, Black Paint, 42 1/2 In. 160.00
    Box, Enameled Peacock Cover, Boston Arts & Crafts, Round, 6 3/4 In. 660.00
    Candle Sconce, Wall, Stylized Floral, Mission, 9 1/2 x 3 1/2 In. 165.00
    Cannister, Snuff, Griffins, Angels, Camels, Tinned 85.00
    Chamberstick, Gustav Stickley, C Handle, Bowl Shaped Base, 9 In., Pr. 1100.00
    Cigar Cutter & Ashtray, Brass Pelican, 6 1/2 x 3 3/4 x 4 7/8 In. 60.00
    Cigar Cutter, Straiton & Storm, Bouquet Seegars 3575.00
    Dutch Oven, Brass Bail, Copper Ears, Ribbed Bands, 15 x 16 In. 275.00
    Figure, Cat, Jan & Joel Martel, Marble Pedestal, c.1925, 16 1/8 In. 1650.00
    Flask, Shot, Embossed Eagle, US, Clasped Hands, 10 In. 90.00
    Funnel, 1870 .... 125.00
    Horn, Coachman's, 48 1/2 In. 80.00
    Jardiniere, Hammered Urn Top, Double Brass Handles, 31 1/2 In., Pair 885.00
    Kettle, Apple Butter, Dovetailed 215.00
    Kettle, Bulbous, Hinged Handle, 19th Century, Dayton, Stutsman, 10 In. 1430.00
    Kettle, Candy, Dovetailed, Iron Handles, 19 1/2 x 9 1/2 In. 135.00
    Measure, 1800, 1/2 Gal. 350.00
    COPPER, MOLD, see Kitchen, Mold
    Pail, Handle, Cylindrical, 2 3/8 In. 60.00
    Pail, Spout, Wooden Handle, Brass Handle For Pouring, 12 1/4 In. 55.00
    Pan, Warming, Brass Cover, Grain Painted Handle, 10 x 41 In. 165.00
    Pitcher, Haystack, American, 2 Gal. 125.00
    Pot, Dovetailed, Iron Side Handles, Tripod, Round, 22 1/2 In. 75.00
    Pot, Nesting, Brass Handles, France, 3 Piece 55.00
    Sauce Pan, Cover, Long Handle, Dovetailed 145.00
    Sauce Pan, Dovetailed, Wrought Copper Handle, 8 1/4 In. 45.00
    Saucepan, Cast Iron Handle, J. Van Range Co., Cinci., O., 7 In. 40.00
    Sconce, Hammered, Almond Shape Back, Candle Holder Center, Pair 82.50

Tea & Coffee Set, 4 Piece 275.00
Tea Kettle, Bird On Spout 35.00
Tea Set, Tray, 1900, 5 Piece 795.00
Teakettle, Stamped F. Miller, 12 In. 800.00
Teakettle, Swing Handle, Stamped GT Rissler, 12 In. 625.00
Teakettle, William Bailey, York, Penna., 12 In. 1300.00
Teapot, Whistling Bird 25.00
Vase, Arts & Craft Style, Hammered, Manning & Bowman, 10 In. 125.00
Vase, Dirk Van Erp, Warts, Brown & Black Patina, Globular, 9 x 6 In. 2970.00
Vase, Jack-In-The-Pulpit Design, Theodore Pond, c.1912, 17 1/4 In. 330.00
Vase, Karl Kipp, 3 Triangular Riveted Buttresses, 7 x 3 1/4 In. 550.00

Coralene glass was made by firing many small colored beads on the outside of glassware. It was made in many patterns in the United States and Europe in the 1880s. Reproductions are made today.

CORALENE, Box, Domed Lid, 4 Free Form Reserves In Floral, 4 1/4 In. 115.00
CORALENE, JAPANESE, see Japanese Coralene
Rose Bowl, 6-Crimp Top, White Lining, Amber Feet, 3 x 4 1/2 In. 375.00
Vase, Burmese, Handle, 8 In. 395.00
Vase, Pink Nasturiums, Leaves, Brown, Small Handles, 8 1/4 In. 410.00
Vase, Wheat Design, Diamond-Quilted, 10 1/2 In. 1070.00

Boleslaw Cybis was one of the founders of the Cordey China Company in 1942 in Trenton, New Jersey. The firm produced gift shop items. In 1969 it was acquired by the Lightron Corp. and operated as the Schiller Cordey Co., manufacturers of lamps. About 1950 Boleslaw Cybis began making Cybis porcelains which are listed in their own section in this book.

CORDEY, Bust, Man 45.00
Bust, Woman, No. 8039, 15 In. 175.00
Bust, Woman, With Flowers, No. 5054 .... 95.00
Figurine, Bird, On Stump 150.00
Figurine, Bluebird, On Tree Stump 150.00
Figurine, Female Torso, 9 In. 75.00
Figurine, Grape Harvester, 16 1/2 In. 105.00
Figurine, Woman & Man Playing Mandolin, Lace Trim 375.00
Lamp, Colonial Lady, Bonnet, Basket of Flowers, 24 In. 195.00
Lamp, Girl In Pink, Bonnet, Tulip Shade 185.00
Vase, Wall, Figural, Full Face, Woman With Wide Brim Hat 120.00

There has been a need for a corkscrew since the first bottle was sealed with a cork, probably in the seventeenth century. Today collectors search for the early, unusual patented examples or the figural corkscrews of recent years.

CORKSCREW, Figural, Waiter, Head Holds Tool 37.50
Monkey, Brass 22.00
Naughty Boy, Bronze, 1940s 15.00
Schlitz 35.00
Wire Spring Type, Wooden Handle 10.00
Wooden Case, Pocket 15.00

Coronation cups have been made since the 1800s. Pottery or glass with a picture of the monarch and date have been souvenirs for many coronations. The pieces that mention King Edward VIII, the king who was never crowned, are not rare; and collectors should be sure to check values before buying.

CORONATION, see also Commemorative
CORONATION, Bank, Cast Iron, Throne, Queen Elizabeth, 1953, 8 1/4 In. 105.00
Bank, Elizabeth, Nickel Plated Steel, 3 3/8 In. 5.00
Beaker, Czar Nicholas, Enamel On Tin. 1896 .... 85.00
Bonbon, Edward VII & Alexandria, Pleated, 1902, 7 In. 58.00
Book, George VI, Sphere Coronation Issue, London, 1937 .... 20.00
Booklet, Coronation of Her Majesty Queen Elizabeth II 12.50

Cup & Saucer, Edward VII, Royal Doulton	65.00
Cup & Saucer, Queen Elizabeth, Royal Standard	25.00
Cup, Edward VII, Royal Doulton	100.00
Cup, George V, Winton	100.00
Dish, Shell Shape, Queen Elizabeth, Bone China, 1953	20.00
Mug, Elizabeth & George VI, Moorcroft	125.00
Mug, Queen Elizabeth's Coronation, Cream Ground, Midwinter	18.00
Paperweight, Queen Elizabeth & Duke, Baccarat, 2 13/16 In.	348.00
Paperweight, Queen Elizabeth II, 1953, 3 1/8 In.	990.00
Plate, Edward VIII, Square, 8 In.	35.00
Plate, Elizabeth II, 9 In.	25.00
Plate, Elizabeth II, Scottish Attire, Square, 9 In.	30.00
Plate, Queen Elizabeth, 1953	30.00
Program, Royalty, England, May 12, 1937	75.00
Spoon Set, Monarchs 1837–1937, Figural, Sterling, Case, 8 Piece	225.00
Tin, Chocolate, George VI & Elizabeth, Red, 1937	15.00
Tumbler, 1937	12.00

Cosmos is a pressed milk glass pattern with colored flowers made from 1894 to 1915 by the Consolidated Lamp and Glass Company. Tablewares and lamps were made. A few pieces were also made of clear glass with painted decorations.

COSMOS, Butter, Cover, Pink Band	195.00 To 245.00
Lamp, Clear, Painted, Miniature	45.00
Lamp, Fishnet Ground, Blue Band, Miniature	60.00
Lamp, Milk Glass, White, 16 1/2 In.	550.00

Linen or wool coverlets were made during the nineteenth century. Most of the coverlets date from 1800 to 1850. Four types were made: the double woven, jacquard, summer and winter, and overshot. Later coverlets were made of a variety of materials. Quilts are listed in this book in their own section.

COVERLET, Double Weave, Blue & White, 68 x 78 In.	250.00
Double Weave, Geometric Design, 19th Century, 95 x 80 In.	115.00
Double Weave, Geometric Design, Pine Tree Borders, 68 x 76 In.	175.00
Double Weave, Geometric Floral Design, 19th Century, 82 x 80 In.	120.00
Double Weave, Medallions, Red, Green, Blue, Wool, D. Cosley, 1850	885.00
Double Weave, Navy & Cream, Reversible, 72 x 84 In.	425.00
Double Weave, Optical Pattern, 68 x 86 In.	475.00
Double Weave, Red, Cream & Black, J. Packer, 1839, 40 x 37 In.	6500.00
Double Weave, Snowflake & Pine Tree, 76 x 88 In.	225.00
Double Weave, Snowflake & Pine Tree, Fringed, 70 x 84 In.	225.00
Double Weave, Snowflake & Pine Tree, Navy & Natural, 72 x 89 In.	325.00
Double Weave. Geometric, Bird Design, Henry Moll, 1838, 90 x 79 In.	300.00
Jacquard, 4 Rose Medallions, D. Cosley, Ky., 1861, 78 x 82 In.	325.00
Jacquard, 4 Rose Medallions, Vintage Border, 1860, 68 x 90 In.	400.00
Jacquard, Birds, Christian & Heathen Borders, 82 x 84 In.	850.00
Jacquard, Birds, Urns, Christian & Heathen Border, 68 x 86 In.	500.00
Jacquard, Blue & White Flower Heads, Floral Border, 90 x 76 In.	495.00
Jacquard, Blue & White, A. J. Siegenthaler, Wooster, Ohio, 1858	550.00
Jacquard, Blue, Red & White, Corners Dated 1848, 74 x 90 In.	300.00
Jacquard, Center Birds & Flowers, Building Border, 84 x 88 In.	100.00
Jacquard, Christian & Heathen Border, Flowers, Bird, 82 x 88 In.	100.00
Jacquard, Eagle & Bird Borders, Gabriel Rausher, 1850, 73 x 92 In.	1400.00
Jacquard, Floral Design, E. Longanecker, 1845, 82 x 99 In.	625.00
Jacquard, Floral Design, Eagle & Star Border, L. Hesse, 1842	750.00
Jacquard, Floral Medallions, Bird Border, 70 x 76 In.	200.00
Jacquard, Floral Medallions, Double Vine Border, 86 x 92 In.	1800.00
Jacquard, Floral Pattern, Peter Lorenz, 86 x 98 In.	385.00
Jacquard, Floral, 2 Piece, 80 x 93 In.	115.00
Jacquard, Floral, Bird Border, John Klinhinz, 1851, 70 x 87 In.	165.00
Jacquard, Floral, Bird Border, Leucinda Swoyer, Ohio, 76 x 92 In.	800.00
Jacquard, Floral, Foliate, Star, Rachel M. Wilson, 1845, 85 x 77 In.	825.00

*Coverlet, Jacquard, Peter Lorenz, 1837,
86 X 96 In.*

Jacquard, Floral, Geometric, Eagle Corners, 1837, 98 x 68 In.	95.00
Jacquard, Floral, Marked 1846, 2 Piece, 76 x 84 In.	1000.00
Jacquard, Floral, Navy, Tomato Red, Natural, 2 Piece, 70 x 80 In.	100.00
Jacquard, Flowers & Birds, W. & J. M. Cright, 1855, 82 x 82 In.	650.00
Jacquard, Flowers, Liberty Coins, Center Medallion, 78 x 92 In.	1500.00
Jacquard, Geometric Floral, Birds, 72 x 91 In.	200.00
Jacquard, Geometric Floral, Corners Dated 1843, 76 x 96 In.	300.00
Jacquard, Geometric Floral, Stars Border, 72 x 76 In.	200.00
Jacquard, House & Pot of Flowers, Corner Eagles, 72 x 76 In.	350.00
Jacquard, Medallions, Wreaths, Blue, White, 1845, 73 x 101 In.	300.00
Jacquard, Memorial Hall, Amer. Eagles, Orange, White, 78 x 82 In.	225.00
Jacquard, Memorial Hall, Centennial 1776–1876, 82 x 82 In.	325.00
Jacquard, Parrot Design, Peter Lorenz, 1839, 84 x 80 In.	660.00
Jacquard, Peter Lorenz, 1837, 86 x 96 In. *Illus*	935.00
Jacquard, Red Wool, Cotton, Urn & Scrolls, Absalom Klinger, c.1855	550.00
Jacquard, Rose & Star, Bird Borders, E. A. Angel, 1893, 84 x 86 In.	600.00
Jacquard, Rose Design, Triple Bird Border, 82 x 98 In.	1000.00
Jacquard, Signed Peter Seibert, 1850–1867, 88 x 66 In.	750.00
Jacquard, Star & Floral Medallion Center, 85 x 91 In.	400.00
Jacquard, Star & Floral Medallion, Floral Border, 78 x 96 In.	600.00
Jacquard, Star Center, Bird Border, 66 x 88 In.	325.00
Jacquard, Sunburst & Lily, D. Cosley, Xenia, Ohio, 1847	1215.00
Jacquard, Washington In Red & White, 74 x 74 In.	200.00
Jacquard, Washington On Horseback, J. Cunningham, 78 x 88 In.	800.00
Jacquard, Wool, Red & Natural, 66 x 74 In.	225.00
Jacquard, Wool, Red, White, Blue & Green, 19th Century, 80 x 86 In.	225.00
Liberty Design, M. Klein, State of Ohio, Montgomery County, 1850	1430.00
Overshot, Blue & White, 70 x 92 In.	125.00
Overshot, Blue, Red & Green, 82 x 82 In.	50.00
Overshot, Geometric Design, Pine Tree Border, 76 x 98 In.	115.00
Overshot, Geometric, Wool, Blue & Red, Fringed 2 Sides	335.00
Overshot, Navy & Natural, Openwork Border, Fringed, 96 x 105 In.	200.00

Overshot, Optical Pattern, 88 x 96 In.	100.00
Overshot, Optical Pattern, Blue, Red, Natural, 84 x 96 In.	300.00
Overshot, Optical Pattern, Red, Black & White, 85 x 96 In.	200.00
Overshot, Optical Pattern, Woven & Tied Fringe, 80 x 96 In.	225.00
Overshot, Red & Natural White, Fringe, 64 x 86 In.	150.00
Overshot, Red & Navy Blue, 76 x 90 In.	200.00
Overshot, Red, Blue & Green, 76 x 88 In.	250.00
Overshot, Wool, Rust, Olive & Cream, 19th Century, 85 x 72 In.	195.00
Wool, Embroidered, Madder Homespun, Blues, Greens, Pinks & Yellows	1350.00

Guy Cowan made pottery in Rocky River, Ohio, a suburb of Cleveland, from 1913 to 1931. The Cowan Pottery made art pottery and wares for florists. A stylized mark with the word *Cowan* was used on most pieces. A commercial, mass–produced line was marked *Lakeware.* Collectors today search for the Art Deco pieces by Guy Cowan, Viktor Schreckengost, Waylande Gregory, or Thelma Frazier Winter.

COWAN, Bowl, Blue Luster, Marked, 7 1/2 x 21 1/2 In.	75.00
Bowl, Pumpkin Glaze Interior, Green Exterior, Handles, 16 In.	145.00
Bowl, With Flower Holder, Nude, 6 1/2 In.	165.00
Candleholder & Flower Frog, Nude, Scarf Dancer, 3 Piece	175.00
Candleholder, Ivory, 4 In.	14.00
Candlestick, Luster, 3 In., Pair	25.00
Charger, Fish, Seaweed & Sea Creatures, Dark Blue Ground, 11 1/2 In.	495.00
Decanter, King Chess Figure, Oriental Red & Black, c.1929, 12 In.	475.00
Flower Frog, Nude Woman, 10 In. .... 150.00 To	255.00
Flower Frog, Nude Woman, White, 6 1/2 In.	75.00
Flower Holder, Nude Woman, White, 6 1/2 In.	85.00
Melon Bowl, Blown Out, Turquoise, Green, Marked, 4 3/8 In., 4 Piece	65.00
Vase, Pillow Shape, Blue Luster, 7 1/2 In.	85.00
Vase, Portrait Medallion, Postgate, 6 x 5 In.	160.00
Vase, Turquoise Glaze, Bulbous, 9 1/2 In.	115.00
Vase, Underseas Design, Deep Blue, Alexander Blazys, c.1930, 6 1/2 In.	2000.00

Cracker Jack, the molasses–flavored popcorn mixture, was first made in 1896 in Chicago, Illinois. A prize was added to each box in 1912. Collectors search for the old boxes and toys and advertising materials. Many of the toys are unmarked.

CRACKER JACK, Badge, Police, Metal	12.00
Baseball Score Counter	35.00
Bat	45.00
Bear	10.00
Bookmark, Puppy, Litho, Metal, 2 3/4 In.	30.00
Fire Truck, Tin	20.00
Flip Book, Charlie Chaplin	75.00
Game Counter	18.00
Game, Board	25.00
Knife, Pocket, Jack Embossed On Side	200.00
Letterhead, Borden's Cracker Jack, Picture, Unused	15.00
Lunch Box	25.00
Mirror, Pocket, Advertising, Celluloid	135.00
Postcard, Bear, No. 10	55.00
Sheet, Baseball Players, Color, 1914–15, Uncut	200.00
Top, Logo, Tin	25.00
Watch, Pocket, Tin	20.00
Whale	10.00
Wheelbarrow, Tin Lithograph	25.00

Crackle glass was originally made by the Venetians, but most of the ware found today dates from the 1800s. The glass was heated, cooled, and refired so that many small lines appeared inside the glass. It was made in many factories in the United States and Europe.

CRACKLE GLASS, Creamer, Clear Applied Handle, 5 In.	60.00
Pitcher, Electric Blue, 9 1/2 In.	75.00
Spooner, Enameled Stork & Flowers, Turquoise	150.00
Urn, Bronze Mounts, Swan Handles, Amethyst, c.1810, 10 1/2 In.	250.00
Vase, Auto, Metal Holder	25.00
Water Set, Marigold Carnival, Imperial, 7 Piece	110.00

Cranberry glass is an almost transparent yellow–red glass. It resembles the color of cranberry juice. The glass has been made in Europe and America since the Civil War. It is still being made and reproductions can fool the unwary.

CRANBERRY GLASS, see also Northwood; Rubena Verde; etc.

CRANBERRY GLASS, Basket, Clear Shell Feet, Clear Handle, 6 x 6 In.	165.00
Basket, Crystal Ribbed Handle, 12 x 9 In.	250.00
Biscuit Jar, Brass Lid, White Overshot Craquelle, 7 In.	400.00
Bottle, Barber, 7 In.	225.00
Bowl, Hobbs–Brockunier, Applied Ribbon Rim, 10 x 3 In.	135.00
Box, Cover, Sanded White Leaves, Grapes, Footed, 4 3/4 In.	165.00
Box, Hinged Cover, European Village Scene, 3 3/4 In.	295.00
Castor, Pickle, Meriden Frame, Tongs	295.00
Celery, Inverted Thumbprint, Enameled Design, 6 1/2 In.	90.00
Decanter, Wine, Inverted Thumbprint, 7 1/2 In.	595.00
Epergne, Opalescent, 3 Flowers	495.00
Epergne, Trumpet, Ruffled, Overshot, Gilt Mount, 22 1/2 In.	165.00
Ewer, Applied Vaseline Handle, 5 In.	25.00
Ewer, Blue, Pink & White Flowers, Scroll Designs, 12 In.	265.00
Jar, Cover, Crystal Trim, Flowers & Scrolls, 9 In.	425.00
Jug, Claret, Pewter Mountings, French, 11 1/4 In.	295.00
Jug, Claret, Silver Encased, c.1840, 14 1/2 In.	900.00
Lamp, Finger, Ribbed, Clear Applied Handle, 5 1/4 In.	195.00
Night–Light, Handled Ormolu Holder, France, 6 1/4 In.	195.00
Pitcher, Daisy & Fern, Ruffled Neck, Everted Rim, 9 1/2 In.	235.00
Pitcher, Floral & Gold Designs, Clear Handle, 11 In.	165.00
Pitcher, Hobnail, 5 In.	75.00
Pitcher, Ice Bladder, 3–Petal Top, 10 In.	325.00
Pitcher, Inverted Thumbprint, Clear Handle, 5 3/4 In.	95.00
Pitcher, Inverted Thumbprint, Clear Handle, 6 3/4 In.	120.00
Pitcher, Inverted Thumbprint, Reeded Handle, 6 1/4 In.	125.00
Pitcher, Inverted Thumbprint, Square Mouth, 7 1/2 In.	150.00
Pitcher, Optic, Clear Handle, 5 In.	68.00
Pitcher, Overshot	400.00
Pitcher, Reverse Swirl, 8 /12 In.	275.00
Pitcher, Thumbprint, Design	595.00
Pitcher, Water, Allover Enameled Flowers & Leaves	100.00
Pitcher, Water, Swirl, Opalescent, Clear Handle, 8 1/2 In.	150.00
Relish, Oblong	18.00
Salt & Pepper, Inverted Baby Thumbprint, Enamel Design	70.00
Sugar Shaker, Inverted Coin Spot	110.00
Sugar Shaker, Leaf Umbrella	250.00
Sugar Shaker, Pressed Panels, Resilvered Top, 5 1/2 In.	65.00
Table Set, Ruffled Rims, Blown Glass, 4 Piece	475.00
Toothpick, Leaf Mold, White & Clear	70.00
Tumbler, Gold Band, Multicolored Daisies, 3 3/4 In.	75.00
Tumbler, Hand Painted Purple Flowers	45.00
Vase, Overshot, Clear Rim Ruffled, Appliqued Floral, 11 In.	295.00
Vase, Partridges Amid Flowers, 10 3/4 In., Pair	460.00
Vase, Sanded White Scallops, Ormolu Feet, 5 3/4 In., Pair	225.00
Vase, Spiral Optic, Pulled Crimped Top, 11 1/2 In.	115.00
Vase, Threaded, Metal Butterfly Base	125.00
Vase, Thumbprint, Orchid, White Flowers, 3 In.	70.00
Vase, White Flowers, Blue, Green Leaves, Footed, 6 3/4 In.	85.00

Creamware, or queensware, was developed by Josiah Wedgwood about 1765. It is a cream–colored earthenware that has been copied by many factories.

CREAMWARE, see also Wedgwood

CREAMWARE, Basket, Chestnut, Stand, Overall Design, Floral Swags, 10 1/4 In.	2315.00
Bowl, Brick Red & Green Flower Band, 8 In.	225.00
Bowl, Figures & River Landscape, 1830s, 6 5/8 In.	335.00
Bowl, Underplate, Basket Weave Design, Marked, 6 3/4 In.	175.00
Compote, Oriental Design, 9 1/2 x 11 In.	800.00
Condiment Set, Green Marbelizing, Pewter Lids, 4 Piece	320.00
Cup & Saucer, Cow, Landscape & Floral, c.1810	85.00
Cup & Saucer, Figures Seated At River, Church, c.1840	100.00
Cup & Saucer, Floral, Geometric Design, c.1810	55.00
Cup, Present From Caroline, Hooped Handle, c.1810, 2 1/8 In.	210.00
Flask, Scallop Shell Form, Multicolored Design, 6 3/4 In.	995.00
Mug, Sailing Ship, Flanked By Sailors, 1820s, 4 In.	205.00
Pitcher, Flared Rim, Intertwined Handle, Florals, 5 1/4 In.	150.00
Pitcher, Milk, Figures In Oriental Landscape, c.1810, 6 In.	175.00
Pitcher, Milk, Fox In Chicken Coop, c.1810, 6 In.	175.00
Pitcher, Thomas Aspinall, St. Louis, Mo., America, 8 3/8 In.	1980.00
Plate, Armorial, Motto Pax In Bello, c.1780, 9 1/8 In.	665.00
Plate, Embossed & Reticulated Rim, 9 1/2 In.	175.00
Plate, Enamel Design, c.1830, 8 In.	330.00
Plate, Orange Tree In Tub, Couple In Profile, 10 1/8 In.	425.00
Plate, Prince & Princess William V of Orange, Leeds, 9 1/2 In.	750.00
Puzzle Jug, Handle, Leeds, 7 In.	605.00
Teapot, Acanthus, Overall Strawberry & Foliate, 11 1/2 In.	525.00
Teapot, Floral Bouquet Flanking Spout, c.1780, 4 3/8 In.	385.00
Teapot, Flower Finial, Oriental Design, 4 3/4 In.	350.00
Teapot, Fred. Prussia, Rex Inscription, Small	2860.00

Credit cards, credit tokens, metal charge plates, and other similar collectibles are now part of the numismatic collecting hobby.

CREDIT CARD, American Airlines, 03/86	6.00
American Express Gold, 8/83	35.00
American Express, 4/65, Violet	120.00
American Oil Company, 11/69	17.00
Amoco Oil Company, 12/85	6.00
ARCO, White Stripe, Silver, Colored Logo, 11/75	8.00
BankAmerica, First & Merchants National Bank, 6/73	18.00
BankAmericard, Chase Manhattan, 6/75	15.00
BankAmericard, First National Bank of Arizona, 03/70	45.00
Citgo Petroleum, Gold	6.00
Conoco, White With Red Stripe	8.00
Diamond Shamrock, Blue Sky, No Mag Stripe, 08/84	8.00
Diner's Club, Booklet, 140 Pages, Green Cover, May 31, 1960	165.00
Diner's Club, Booklet, Eastern Section, 112 Pages, 11/30/58	175.00
Eastern, 10/84	6.00
Marshall Field's	6.00
MasterCard, Community First Bank, 7/83	6.00
MasterCard, First National, Kansas City, Pre–Hologram, 07/84	10.00
MasterCard, FirstCity Bank, Astro Baseball Team	20.00
MasterCard, FirstCity, 11/88	8.00
MasterCard, FirstCity, Pre–Hologram, 11/84	10.00
Midwest Bank Card, Harris Bank, 3/70	16.00
Neiman Marcus, Gold Princess	6.00
Saks Fifth Avenue, Brown Princess	4.00
Sears, Sears In Box	4.00
Southwestern Bell Calling Card, Thin	3.00
United Airlines, 03/87	4.00
Visa, Bank One, Pre–Hologram, Red Back, 10/85	15.00
Visa, BankAmericard, 7/84	7.00

◆◆◆◆◆◆◆◆◆◆◆◆◆◆◆◆◆◆◆◆◆◆◆◆◆◆

Spray the inside of a glass flower vase with a non-stick product made to keep food from sticking to cooking pots. This will keep the vase from staining if water is left in too long.

◆◆◆◆◆◆◆◆◆◆◆◆◆◆◆◆◆◆◆◆◆◆◆◆◆◆

Crown Milano, Biscuit Jar,
Plated Lid & Handle, Signed CM, 6 In.
Crown Milano, Biscuit Jar, Purple, Pink,
Blue, Marked CM 520, 6 In.

Visa, BankAmericard, Pre–Hologram, 06/84	....	10.00
Visa, FirstCity, Pre–Hologram, 08/85	....	10.00

 A faience factory was established at Creil, France, in 1794. The company merged with a factory in Montereau in 1819. The firm made stoneware, mocha ware, and soft paste porcelain. The name Creil appears as part of the mark on many pieces. The Creil factory closed in 1895.

CREIL, Creamer, Pink, Maroon Flowers, 6 In.	....	65.00
Plate, Playful Peasants, 1846	....	100.00
Plate, Yellow With Black Floral Design, 10 In.	....	85.00

Crown Derby is the nickname given to the works of the Royal Crown Derby factory, which began working in England in 1859. An earlier and more famous English Derby factory existed from 1750 to 1848. The two factories were not related. Most of the porcelain found today with the Derby mark is the work of the later Derby factory.

CROWN DERBY, see also Derby; Royal Crown Derby

CROWN DERBY, Garniture Set, Imari Colors, Witches Pattern, 1810, 3 Piece	....	2000.00
Tray, Imari Pattern, 19th Century, 18 1/2 In.	....	300.00

 Crown Milano glass was made by Frederick Shirley at the Mt. Washington Glass Works about 1890. It had a plain biscuit color with a satin finish. It was decorated with flowers and often had large gold scrolls.

CROWN MILANO, Biscuit Jar, Clusters of Apple Blossoms, Bail, 6 In.	....	685.00
Biscuit Jar, Enameled Mums, Gold Leaves, Silver Fittings	....	650.00
Biscuit Jar, Gold Fern Leaves, Marked	....	495.00
Biscuit Jar, Plated Lid & Handle, Signed CM, 6 In.	...................................*Illus*	600.00
Biscuit Jar, Purple, Pink, Blue, Marked CM 520, 6 In.	...............................*Illus*	500.00
Box, Dresser, Hand Painted Roses, Leaves, Signed, 5 In.	....	395.00
Castor, Pickle, Begonia Leaves, Flowers, Pairpoint Holder, Tong	....	1875.00
Cracker Jar, Hand Painted, Harbor Scene	....	425.00
Dish, Cover, Melon Ribbed, Center Gold Scrolls, 5 1/4 In.	....	850.00
Dish, Turtle Finial, Diagonal Bands, Spider Mums, 7 In.	....	1025.00
Ewer, Raised Gold Laurel Wreath, Shepardess, Birds, 10 1/2 In.	....	1450.00
Ewer, White Neck & Body, Sepia Scrolls & Florals, 12 In.	....	1750.00
Jam Jar, Blown Out, Pearlized Cactus, 4 In.	....	650.00
Jam Jar, Turtle On Cover, Swirled & Jeweled Design, 4 1/2 In.	....	550.00
Pitcher, 2 Tumblers, Albertine	....	1500.00
Pitcher, Syrup, Mount Washington Glass Co., Acorns, Leaves	....	985.00
Rose Bowl, Enameled Acorns, Leaves Outlined In Gold, 16 In.	....	650.00
Sugar Shaker, Vertical Ribs, Daisy Blossoms, Pewter Top	....	435.00
Syrup, Gold & Brown Daisies On Panels, 4 In.	....	485.00
Tumbler, Gold Floral Garland & Trim, White Opaque, 3 3/4 In.	....	550.00
Vase, Cover, Ivy Leaves & Vines, Outlined In Gold, 10 1/2 In.	....	2280.00

Vase, Gold Beads, Double Eagle Medallion, Green, 9 In. 650.00
Vase, Gold Leaves & Scrolls, Thorn Handle, Marked, 7 1/2 In. 2695.00
Vase, Gold Leaves & Vines, Shadow Circles, Marked, 13 In. 1925.00
Vase, Orange Mums, Shadow Leaf Ground, Flared Rim, 5 7/8 In. 935.00
Vase, Overall Vines, Scrolls & Flowers, Petal Top, 9 3/4 In. 1700.00
Vase, Slit Rim, Brown Swirled Devices, Gold Outlines, 15 In. 1200.00
Vase, Tableau of 2 Children, Colonial Dress, 8 1/2 In. 1350.00
Vase, Thistle Design, Thorny Handle, Mt. Washington, 7 1/2 In. 1200.00
    CROWN TUSCAN, see Cambridge

Cruets of glass or porcelain were made to hold vinegar, oil, and other condiments. They were especially popular during Victorian times but have been made in a variety of styles since the eighteenth century.

    CRUET, see also Castor Set
CRUET, Amber, Blue Stopper 95.00
  Amberina, Stopper 295.00
  Cranberry Glass, Clear Handle, Stopper 75.00
  Cut Glass, Pineapple & Fan 55.00
  Daisy & Button, Amber 95.00
  Daisy & Fern, Blue 95.00
  Daisy & Fern, Yellow 95.00
  Diamond–Quilted Satin Glass, Blue, Frosted Stopper & Handle 165.00
  Diamond–Quilted, Mother–of–Pearl, Gold, Frosted Handle, Stopper, 8 In. 585.00
  Dice & Block, Amber 95.00
  Georgia Gem, Clear, Stopper 55.00
  Glass, Forest Green, Stopper 30.00
  Grape, Green 75.00
  Inverted Panel, Amber 150.00
  Jewel & Tassel, Blue 90.00
  Leaf Bracket, Chocolate, Stopper 175.00
  Milton, Amber 90.00
  Pinch Bottle, Amber 95.00
  Thumbprint, Amber 90.00
  Thumbprint, Green 90.00
  Vinegar, Scalloped 6 Point, Ruby Stain, Stopper, 6 3/4 In. 125.00

Cup plates are small glass or china plates that held the cup while a gentleman of the mid–nineteenth century drank his coffee or tea from the saucer. The most famous cup plates were made of glass at the Boston and Sandwich factory located in Sandwich, Massachusetts. There have been many new glass cup plates made in recent years for sale to the gift shops or the limited edition collectors. These are similar to the old plates but can be identified.

CUP PLATE, Pink Luster Trim, Registry Mark 15.00
  Sandwich Glass, Amber 750.00
  Youth & Old Age, Child With Kite, Man Looking At Tombstone 135.00

Currier & Ives made the famous American lithographs marked with their name from 1857 to 1907. The mark used on the print included the street address in New York City, and it is possible to date the year of the original issue from this information. Earlier prints were made by N. Currier and used that name from 1835 to 1847. Many reprints of the Currier or Currier & Ives prints have been made. Many collectors also buy the insurance calendars that were based on the old prints. The words large, small, or medium folio refer to size.

CURRIER & IVES, American Farm Yard, Evening, Medium Folio 2100.00
  American Farm Yard, Morning, Large Folio 2420.00
  American Homestead, Spring, Frame, 12 1/2 x 16 1/2 In. 325.00
  American Homestead, Summer, Frame, 12 1/2 x 16 1/2 In. 350.00
  American Homestead, Winter, Frame, c.1868, 8 x 12 1/2 In. 330.00
  American Homestead, Winter, Framed, 1868, 8 x 12 1/2 In. 660.00
  American Winter Scene, Evening, Frame, 23 3/4 x 30 3/4 In. 195.00

◆◆◆

To remove wet glass rings from furniture, first try rubbing in a little
cigar ash to open the finish lightly. If this doesn't work, thoroughly
rub in a non–drying oil such as lemon or almond oil. Follow with a
regular wax paste. The same procedure can be used to remove
white marks caused by heat.

◆◆◆

Battle of Buena Vista, Framed, Small Folio	100.00
Battle of Gettysburg, PA., July 3rd, 1863, Small Folio	210.00
Bouquet of Fruit, Frame, 1875, 15 1/4 x 19 1/2 In.	65.00
Burning of Chicago, 1871, Small Folio	350.00
Camping Out, Some of The Right Sort, 1856, 19 x 27 1/4 In.	1045.00
Celebrated Stallions, 1866, Mounted, 20 1/4 x 28 3/4 In.	750.00
Chicago, As It Was, Framed, Small	850.00
Crack Team, Large Folio	1215.00
Darktown Fire Brigade, Slightly Demoralized, 17 x 21 In.	150.00
Darktown Tournament, Close Quarters. 14 1/2 x 18 3/4 In.	200.00
Death Shot, Colored, 8 1/2 x 12 1/2 In.	85.00
Flora Temple, Mounted, 1860, 20 3/4 x 28 In.	550.00
Fording The River, Frame, 14 x 17 3/4 In.	65.00
Fruit & Flowers, Gilded Frame, 19 3/4 x 15 1/4 In.	125.00
Fruits, Autumn, Framed, 1871, 12 3/4 x 16 1/2 In.	125.00
Fruits, Summer Varieties, Published 1871, 15 1/2 x 19 In.	200.00
Good Luck To Ye, Trade Card	75.00
Henry Clay of Kentucky, Framed, 14 1/4 x 18 1/4 In.	150.00
Home In The Wilderness, 1870, Small Folio	440.00
Hudson River, Crow's Nest, Frame, 1873, 15 x 18 1/2 In.	250.00
Increase In Family, Rosewood Veneer Frame, 21 x 17 In.	135.00
Ivy Bridge, Crisscross Frame	75.00
John Wesley Preaching On His Father's Grave	45.00
Life of A Fireman, Metropolitan, 1848–62, 17 x 26 In.	1450.00
Life of A Fireman, New Era, 1861, Framed, 17 x 26 In.	1350.00
Life of A Sportsman, Colored, 8 1/2 x 1 2 1/2 In.	165.00
Life of Sportsman, Camping In Woods, 1872, 12 x 15 3/4 In.	350.00
Little Brothers, Cherry Frame, 17 x 13 In.	50.00
Little Brothers, Shadowbox Frame, 18 1/2 x 14 1/2 In.	35.00
Little Daisy, Frame, 10 x 15 In.	80.00
Little Snowbird, Poplar Frame, 16 1/2 x 12 1/2 In.	175.00
Mayflower Saluted By The Fleet, Frame, Large Folio	775.00
Mazeppa, Mahogany Veneer Frame, 12 1/2 x 16 1/2 In.	30.00
Midnight Race On The Mississippi, Frame, 13 x 16 In.	450.00
Minnehaha Falls, Minnesota, Framed, 11 3/8 x 15 3/4 In.	225.00
Morning of Life, Child, Crisscross Frame	75.00
My Little White Bunnies, Framed, 11 1/2 x 15 1/2 In.	175.00
National Game, Three Outs & One Run, Small Folio	1985.00
New Excursion Steamer Columbia, Large Folio	2750.00
Night By The Camp Fire, Framed, 1861, 10 1/4 x 15 In.	330.00
Noontide, A Shady Spot, Small Folio	145.00
Old Oaken Bucket, Cherry Frame, 1872, 15 1/2 x 19 1/2 In.	250.00
On The St. Lawrence, Indian Encampment, Small Folio	275.00
Peaceful River, Small Folio	175.00
Pickerel, Curly Maple Frame, 1872, 15 1/2 x 19 1/2 In.	425.00
Preparing For Market, Bird's–Eye Frame, 27 3/4 x 35 In.	850.00
Sailor's Return, Cherry Frame, 16 1/2 x 12 1/2 In.	75.00
Saratoga Lake, Matted & Framed, 16 x 19 In.	195.00
Scenery of Wissahickon, N. Y., 1857–73, 8 1/2 x 12 1/2 In.	650.00
See My New Boots, Gilded Frame, 1856, 29 x 22 1/4 In.	150.00
Sleigh Race, Medium Folio	900.00

Soldier's Adieu, 1847, 15 1/4 x 12 In. 70.00
Squirrel Shooting, Beveled Frame, 12 1/4 x 16 1/4 In. 250.00
Squirrel Shooting, Colored, Framed, 11 1/2 x 15 1/2 In. 150.00
Summer Fruits, Shadow Box Frame, 18 3/4 x 23 In. 300.00
Trotting Cracks On Snow, 1858, 19 1/2 x 29 3/4 In. 1900.00
Trotting Stallion Phallas, Frame, 1883, 29 1/2 x 39 1/2 In. 700.00
Vase of Flowers, Beveled Cherry Frame, 17 1/4 x 13 1/4 In. 125.00
Washington's Reception, Gilt Frame, 15 x 4 3/4 In. 55.00
Washington's Reception, Ladies, 1845, 18 1/4 x 14 1/4 In. 100.00
Wedding Day, Bird's-Eye Maple Frame, 15 1/2 x 13 1/2 In. 65.00
Western Farmer's Home, Frame, 13 1/2 x 17 1/2 In. 375.00

Custard glass is an opaque glass sometimes called *buttermilk glass.*
It was first made in the United States after 1886 at the La Belle
Glass Works, Bridgeport, Ohio. It is being reproduced.

CUSTARD GLASS, Argonaut Shell, Berry Set, 7 Piece 575.00
Argonaut Shell, Butter, Cover, Signed 250.00
Argonaut Shell, Cruet, Gold 395.00
Argonaut Shell, Cruet, No Stopper 75.00
Argonaut Shell, Pitcher Set, 5 Piece 495.00
Argonaut Shell, Sugar, Cover, Gold 195.00
Beaded Circle, Creamer 125.00
Beaded Circle, Spooner .... 35.00 To 139.00
Beaded Swag, Goblet, Souvenir 60.00
Cherry Sprig, Berry Set, Northwood, Oval Master Bowl, 7 Piece 500.00
Chrysanthemum Sprig, Berry Bowl, Master 160.00
Chrysanthemum Sprig, Berry Bowl, Oval, Master 150.00
Chrysanthemum Sprig, Butter, Signed 245.00
Chrysanthemum Sprig, Celery, Blue 1200.00
Chrysanthemum Sprig, Compote, Jelly 40.00
Chrysanthemum Sprig, Creamer 40.00
Chrysanthemum Sprig, Cruet, Amber Stopper 80.00
Chrysanthemum Sprig, Cruet, Blue 650.00
Chrysanthemum Sprig, Cruet, Green, Gold Trim 295.00
Chrysanthemum Sprig, Salt & Pepper 475.00
Chrysanthemum Sprig, Saltshaker 135.00
Chrysanthemum Sprig, Saltshaker, Blue 162.00
Chrysanthemum Sprig, Sugar, Cover, Blue, 7 In. 325.00
Chrysanthemum Sprig, Sugar, Cover, Blue, Gold Trim, 7 In. 325.00
Chrysanthemum Sprig, Table Set, 4 Piece 320.00
Chrysanthemum Sprig, Toothpick, Signed 250.00
Chrysanthemum Sprig, Tumbler, 6 Piece 265.00
Chrysanthemum Sprig, Tumbler, Blue, 5 Piece 350.00
Delaware, Celery Vase 85.00
Diamond With Peg, Creamer 85.00
Diamond With Peg, Pitcher, 5 In. 90.00
Diamond With Peg, Toothpick, Painted Roses, Souvenir 50.00
Diamond With Peg, Toothpick, Rose, Souvenir, Krystol Mark 45.00
Diamond With Peg, Tumbler 50.00
Diamond With Peg, Wine 35.00
Everglades, Berry Bowl, Boat Shape, Large 165.00
Everglades, Berry Bowl, Gold & Green Trim 200.00
Fluted Scroll, Berry Bowl, With Flower, 7 1/2 In. 145.00
Fluted Scroll, Water Set, 5 Piece 295.00
Fruit & Flowers, Dish 72.00
Geneva, Banana Boat, Green Design 125.00
Geneva, Berry Bowl, Oval, Green Design, 8 1/2 In. 85.00
Geneva, Spooner, Green & Red Design 100.00
Geneva, Sugar, Open 75.00
Geneva, Toothpick, Gaudy Gold 70.00
Geneva, Tumbler 55.00
Georgia Gem, Celery Vase 135.00
Georgia Gem, Cruet, Green 225.00

Georgia Gem, Spooner, Floral .... 55.00 To 65.00
Grape & Cable, Berry Bowl, Northwood 26.00
Grape & Cable, Tumbler, Nutmeg Stain, 6 Piece 300.00
Grape & Gothic Arches, Goblet 35.00
Grape & Gothic Arches, Spooner, Northwood 55.00
Heart & Thumbprint, Sugar & Creamer, Metal Fittings 175.00
Intaglio, Bowl, Footed, 8 1/2 In. 175.00
Intaglio, Spooner .... 85.00 To 90.00
Intaglio, Table Set, Green Gold Trim, 4 Piece 500.00
Inverted Fan & Feather, Butter, Cover 235.00
Inverted Fan & Feather, Spooner 120.00
    IVORINA VERDE, see Winged Scroll
Jackson, Cruet 100.00
Jackson, Cruet, Goofus Clear Stopper 125.00
    LITTLE GEM, see Georgia Gem
Lotus & Grape, Bonbon, Green Stain, 2 Handles 65.00
Louis XV, Banana Bowl 118.00
Louis XV, Berry Bowl, Oval, Master 110.00
Louis XV, Creamer .... 55.00 To 65.00
Louis XV, Pitcher, Water, Green, Gold Trim 145.00
Louis XV, Spooner, Gold Trim 55.00
Louis XV, Sugar, Cover 45.00
Louis XV, Sugar, Cover, Green, Gold Trim 95.00
Louis XV, Table Set, Gold Trim, 4 Piece .... 475.00 To 500.00
    MAIZE, see Maize category
Maple Leaf, Butter, Cover .... 200.00 To 225.00
Maple Leaf, Spooner .... 35.00 To 105.00
Ram's Head, Table Set, Mask Spout, Initials AD, 4 Piece 275.00
Ribbed Drape, Spooner 85.00
Ribbed Drape, Sugar, Cover 165.00
Ribbed Thumbprint, Tumbler 42.50
Ring Band, Breakfast Set 425.00
Tarentum's Victoria, Sauce Dish, Pea Green, Footed 75.00
Tarentum's Victoria, Sugar, Green 90.00
Tiny Thumbprint, Toothpick .... 18.00 To 55.00
Vermont, Creamer, Blue Design 95.00
Vermont, Toothpick, Green Design 135.00
Winged Scroll, Butter, Cover 160.00
Winged Scroll, Dish, Olive 45.00
Winged Scroll, Dish, Olive, Gold Trim 110.00
Winged Scroll, Toothpick 85.00
Winged Scroll, Tray, 6 Scrolls, Gold Trim, 6 x 3 1/2 In. 45.00

Cut glass has been made since ancient times, but the large majority of the pieces now for sale date from the brilliant period of glass design, 1880 to 1905. These pieces have elaborate geometric designs with a deep miter cut. Modern cut glass with a similar appearance is being made in England and Ireland. Chips and scratches are often difficult to notice but lower the value dramatically.

CUT GLASS, see also listings under factory name
CUT GLASS, American Brilliant, Pitcher, Water, Flowers, Vines, 8 In. 155.00
Banana Boat, Allover Cutting, 6 3/4 x 10 In. 450.00
Banana Boat, Royal, Hunt, 4 1/2 x 8 1/4 x 11 1/4 In. 545.00
Basket, Berlyn, 3 Step–Up Pedestal Base, 8 x 5 1/2 In. 365.00
Basket, Checkerboard, Fan, Triple Knotched Handle, 7 1/2 In. 165.00
Basket, Double Dolbys & Step Cutting, Basketweave 2600.00
Basket, Hobstars, Strawberry Diamonds, Handle, 20 In. ....*Illus* 1870.00
Bell, Dinner, 8–Sided, Hobstar & Strawberry Diamond Vesicas 110.00
Berry Bowl, Juno, Bergen, 4 1/2 x 8 In. 650.00
Biscuit Jar, Silver Plated, England, 6 In. 148.00
Bonbon, Hobstars, Cane & Crosshatch, Loop Handle, 7 3/4 In. 265.00
Bonbon, Stars, Pinwheels, Diamond Cuts, Sawtooth Rim 65.00
Bottle, Bitters, Renaissance, Dorflinger, Sterling Top 275.00

Bottle, Sauce, Geometric & Floral, Hoare, 6 1/2 In. 395.00
Bottle, Sauce, Hobstars, Fans, Prism Cut Neck, 9 In. 110.00
Bottle, Venetian & Encore, Fluted Throat, Ovoid, Straus, 9 In. 325.00
Bottle, Whiskey, Georgia, Higgins & Seiter, 14 In. 595.00
Bottle, Whiskey, Swirled Cut Lip, Prism Cut Stopper, 11 3/4 In. 585.00
Bottle, Worcestershire Sauce, Henry VIII, Clark, 8 In. 285.00
Bowl, Brilliant, Fan & Diamond, Serrated Rim, 8 1/2 In. 165.00
Bowl, Buttons With Hobstars, Prism Cuts, Hoare, 10 In. 305.00
Bowl, Buzz Stars, Hobstars, Sawtooth Rim, 8 1/4 In. .... 125.00 To 165.00
Bowl, Carolyn, Triangular, 3 1/4 x 9 1/2 In. 495.00
Bowl, Center, Houndstooth Rim, Diamond Cut, 12 In. 120.00
Bowl, Center, Houndstooth Rim, Geometric, 9 1/2 In. 130.00
Bowl, Cobalt To Clear, 18 Panels, Hobstars, Germany, 4 x 9 In. 280.00
Bowl, Expanding Star, 10 In. 325.00
Bowl, Geometric & Diamond Cut, Bulbous, 9 1/2 In. 50.00
Bowl, Geometric & Diamond Design, 9 1/2 In. 55.00
Bowl, Harvard Border, Step Cut Center, 7 3/4 In. 170.00
Bowl, Harvard Variant, Sawtooth Rim, 8 In. 465.00
Bowl, Hobstar Pineapple, 8 x 11 1/2 In. 495.00
Bowl, Hobstars & Ovals, Cobalt Blue To Clear, Germany, 4 x 9 In. 280.00
Bowl, Houndstooth Rim, Diamond, Geometric & Floral, 10 In. 130.00
Bowl, Houndstooth Rim, Geometric & Diamond, Circular, 10 In. 80.00
Bowl, Pinto, 6–Lobed, 10 In. 1350.00
Bowl, Pinwheels, Fan & Relief Diamond, Scalloped Rim, 8 In. 125.00
Bowl, Quatrefoil Rosette, Clark, 4 x 9 5/8 In. 2450.00
Bowl, Strawberry Diamond, Hoare, 4 1/2 x 12 In. 550.00
Box, Florence Star, Prism Top, Hobstars, Silver Plated Collar 445.00
Box, Handkerchief, Double Row of Punties, Crossing Miters, 7 In. 695.00
Butter Tub, Hobstars, Fan Tabs, Scalloped Rim, 4 3/4 x 5 1/2 In. 165.00
Butter, Cover, Buzz Stars, Polished Leaves, Miter Cuts, 5 x 4 In. 125.00
Butter, Cover, Center Handle, Hobstars, Crosshatch, 5 In. 165.00
Butter, Finial & Teardrop Cover, Strawberry Diamond 250.00
Candlestick, Diamond & Hobstar Body, Hobstar Base, 12 In. 950.00
Candlestick, Honeycomb, Intaglio, 6–Petal Flowers, 10 In., Pair 595.00
Candlestick, Teardrop Stem, Flowers, Leaves, 7 5/8 In., Pair 525.00
Candy Dish, Cane & Fan, Serrated Edges, Brilliant, 6 In. 75.00
Candy Dish, Russian, Shield Shape, Rayed Bottom, 5 1/4 In. 140.00
Candy Dish, Star Design, 2 Handles, Rolled Rim, 9 1/2 In. 185.00
Canoe, Harvard, 11 In. 260.00
Celery Tray, 24–Point Hobstar Center, 10 3/4 x 5 In. 215.00
Celery Tray, Greek Key, 12 3/4 x 5 1/4 In. 1195.00
Champagne Cooler, Arcadia–Like Pattern, 7 In. 1475.00
Champagne, Amber Bowl, Blue Stem & Foot, Dorflinger, 6 1/4 In. 75.00
Champagne, Kalana Lily, Dorflinger, 5 1/4 In. 100.00
Champagne, Russian, Star Buttons, Teardrop Stem, 4 3/4 In. 85.00
Coffeepot, Alhambra, Wilcox Silver Top, 8 In. 4500.00
Compote, Brilliant, Teardrop Stem, 7 In. 95.00

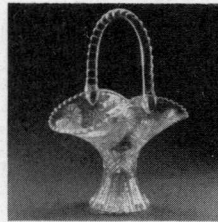

Cut Glass, Basket, Hobstars,
Strawberry Diamonds, Handle, 20 In.

To test the age of engraving on
glass, place a white handkerchief on the inside. If the engraving is old, the lines will usually
show up darker than the rest of
the glass. New engraving has a
bright powderlike surface.

Compote, Cobalt To Clear, Pedestal, Germany, 9 x 11 In. 350.00
Compote, Fruit, Buffalo, 8 5/8 x 8 In. 350.00
Compote, Hobstars & Fans, Scalloped Rim, Notched Stem, 7 In. 195.00
Compote, Straus Drape, 9 In. 550.00
Cordial Set, Fants, Bull's-Eyes, Stars, Emerald, Stopper, 7 Piece 100.00
Cordial, Royal, Stemmed, Dorflinger 110.00
Creamer, Russian, Thumbprint Cut Handle, 5 In. 550.00
Cruet, Alternating Hobstars & Crossed Fans, 6 3/4 In. 160.00
Cruet, Brilliant, Cut Allover, Double-Notched Handle, 8 In. 85.00
Cruet, Hobstars, Panels of Crosshatch, 3-Corner Rim 85.00
Cruet, Venetian, Hawkes, 6 3/4 In. 345.00
Cup, Hobstars, Fans & Strawberry Diamond Bars, Hoare, 3 In., 8 Pc. 450.00
Decanter Set, Ball Stoppers, Wooden Case, Lock, Dorflinger, 12 In. 600.00
Decanter, Aberdeen, Stopper Cut In Pattern, 13 In. 2600.00
Decanter, Croesus, J. Hoare, 12 1/2 In. 2885.00
Decanter, Green Cut To Clear, Dorflinger 2700.00
Decanter, Harvard Cut, Brilliant, 16 1/2 In. 325.00
Decanter, Harvard, Bulbous Body, Intaglio Flower, 13 In. 290.00
Decanter, Hobstar, Rosettes, Fans, Flutes On Neck, 12 1/2 In. 475.00
Decanter, Monarch, Hoare, 12 In. 250.00
Decanter, Scotch, Clark, Pattern Cut Stopper, 7 In. 425.00
Decanter, Whiskey, Thistle, Gorham Sterling Stopper 395.00
Dish, 18-Point Star Footed, Panel & Crosscut, 3 1/2 In. 100.00
Dish, Cracker, Flowers, Stems & Cane, Double Handles, 10 1/2 In. 115.00
Dish, Ice Cream, Russian, Rayed Buttons, 6 In. 55.00
Dish, Leaf Shape, Clear Button Hobstars, 16 1/2 x 4 In. 795.00
Dish, Olive, Egginton, 8 x 4 In. 95.00
Dish, Pinwheel & Star, 8 1/2 In. 35.00
Epergne, Sterling Base, 20 3/4 In. 325.00
Fernery, Allover Cutting, Footed 165.00
Fernery, Butterfly & Daisy, Footed, 7 1/2 In. 125.00
Flower Center, Drape, Straus, 10 In. 900.00
Flower Center, Hobstars & Fans, Step Cut Neck, 7 x 12 In. 665.00
Fruit Bowl, Button & Star Cut, 8 In. 120.00
Globe, Russian Cut, Chain Hanger, 6 In. 295.00
Goblet, Buckle, 6 In. 100.00
Goblet, Fox Hunt Scene, Hollow Stem 95.00
Hair Receiver, Buzz Stars, Crosshatch 135.00
Holder, Sugar Cube, Wheat & Sunflowers 37.00
Horseradish Jar, Bull's-Eye Top & Bottom, Hollow Stopper, 5 In. 195.00
Humidor, Colonial, Dorflinger, 9 1/2 In. 1200.00
Ice Bucket, Carolyn, Tab Handles, J. Hoare, 5 3/4 x 6 In. 565.00
Inkwell, Cane Base, Gorham Top, 3 1/4 x 2 1/2 In. 290.00
Jar, Crisscross, Star, Clear To Cranberry, 4 3/4 In. ....*Illus* 195.00
Jar, Horseradish, Cover, Allover Hobstars & Fans 95.00
Jug, Whiskey, Strap Handle, Cane, Hobstar Base, Dorflinger 1150.00
Knife Rest, Cane & Nailhead, 6 In., Pair 85.00
Lamp, Boudoir, Pressed & Wheel Cut, Persian Domed Shade, 13 In. 247.00
Lamp, Brilliant, Mushroom Shade, Buzz Star, Prisms, 9 x 17 1/2 In. 1650.00
Lamp, Daisy & Diamond, Cut Globe, Crystal Prisms, 15 1/2 In. 935.00
Lamp, Harvard & Pinwheel, 17 In. 2200.00
Lamp, Hobstar & Fan, Prisms, 21 In. 2900.00
Liquor Set, Notched Prism, Cranberry, Decanter & 6 Shot Glasses 450.00
Mayonnaise Set, Cover, Hobstars, Brilliant, American 215.00
Mayonnaise Set, Gladys, Flutes At Base, 6 1/2-In. Bowl 350.00
Mayonnaise Set, Harvard, 16-Point Hobstar Tray, 6 1/8 x 4 In. 425.00
Mayonnaise Set, Russian, Rayed Buttons, 3 x 7 In. 315.00
Mustard Pot, Crosscut Diamond, Silver Top & Handle, Clark 225.00
Napkin Ring, Brilliant, Pair 85.00
Nut Bowl, Crosscut Diamond & Fan, Dorflinger, 4 In. 125.00
Nut Set, Hobstar & Notched Cane, Boat-Shaped Bowls, 7 Piece 295.00
Perfume Bottle, Hobstars, Fans, Diamond Point, Green, Clear, 7 In. 275.00
Perfume Bottle, Sterling Collar & Stopper, Amethyst, Pair 450.00

Pitcher Set, Brilliant, American, 7 Piece	335.00
Pitcher, Champagne, Brilliant, 15 In.	950.00
Pitcher, Champagne, Button Russian, Ovoid, Allover Cut, 14 In.	2000.00
Pitcher, Harvard, J. K. Berger, 6 1/2 In.	825.00
Pitcher, Harvard, Triple Step Cut Handle, Fluted Spout, 8 3/4 In.	330.00
Pitcher, Hobstars, Fans, Stars In Diamond Field, Bergen, 10 In.	165.00
Pitcher, Pedestal, Handle, Hobstars, Taylor Bros., 10 3/4 In.	795.00
Pitcher, Water, Allyn, Bergen	325.00
Pitcher, Water, Pinwheel Cut, 16 In.	140.00
Plate, Acme, Hoare, 7 In.	135.00
Plate, Brilliant With Intaglio Cutting, 9 In.	160.00
Plate, Drape, Straus, 7 In.	215.00
Plate, Intaglio Cuttings, Brilliant, 9 In.	160.00
Plate, Prima Donna, Signed, 8 In.	340.00
Plate, Propellar, 7 In.	395.00
Plate, Royal, Heart Shape, Hunt, 7 In.	325.00
Plate, Triple Square, Dentil Edge, Clark, 9 In.	495.00
Powder Boy, Harvard, 6 1/2 In.	115.00
Punch Bowl, Hampton, J. D. Bergens, 2 Piece	2600.00
Punch Bowl, Stand, Sawtooth, Zipper, Hobstar, 12 In. ....*Illus*	853.00
Punch Cup, Hobstars Over Sides & Base, Signed Galatea, 11 Piece	450.00
Punch Set, Tiffany, Pedestal, Bergen, 15 3/4 In., 12 Piece	3400.00
Relish, Hobstar Fan, Crossbar Base, 3 x 7 1/2 In.	125.00
Relish, Ribbon Star, 4 Sections, Handles, 9 In.	480.00
Rose Bowl, Allover Hobstars, Strawberry Diamond, Fan, 5 In.	185.00
Rose Bowl, Vessica Cutting, Outlined With Prisms, Pedestal, 5 In.	280.00
Salt, Zipper	12.00
Sugar & Creamer, Cane & Fan, Pitkin & Brooks, 3 1/2 In.	110.00
Sugar & Creamer, Cluster, Egginton, 3 1/2 x 4 In.	345.00
Sugar & Creamer, Diamond & Floral, Scroll Handles	55.00
Sugar & Creamer, Propellor Pattern, 3 3/4 In.	425.00
Sugar & Creamer, Russian, 2 1/2 x 4 1/2 In.	575.00
Sugar, Cover, Russian, Marked NN, 7 1/2 In.	550.00
Sugar, Strawberry, Double Handles, Sawtooth Rim, P & B	38.50
Syrup, Hinged Lid, Pinwheels, Miters & Crosshatch, 5 1/2 In.	135.00
Syrup, Strawberry, Diamonds & Fan, Silver Collar, 4 In.	145.00
Tankard, Brilliant, 12 In.	150.00
Tobacco Jar, Hobstar Cover, 8-Sided Hobstar & Fan Body	285.00
Toothpick, Diamond & Fan	38.00
Tray, Chrysanthemum, Hawkes, Oval, 10 In.	775.00
Tray, Ice Cream, Empress Eugenie, Bergen, 14 1/2 x 8 In.	2600.00

Cut Glass, Jar, Crisscross, Star,
Clear To Cranberry, 4 3/4 In.

◆◆◆◆◆◆◆◆◆◆◆◆◆◆◆◆◆◆◆◆◆

To ship small pieces of glass, try this trick. Put the glass in a styrofoam cup, then wrap in bubble wrap or several layers of paper. Stuff sides and bottom of a large box with styrofoam trays. Then put the antiques on the trays. Pack more styrofoam around them. Maybe you can get extra trays at your grocery store.

◆◆◆◆◆◆◆◆◆◆◆◆◆◆◆◆◆◆◆◆◆

Tray, Ice Cream, Wedgemere, 12 In. 2700.00
Tray, Ice Cream, Wheeling, 12 In. 750.00
Tray, Pinwheels, Hobstars, Cane, Fan, Clark, 15 In. 550.00
Tray, Royal, Hunt, 12 In. 1250.00
Tray, Tiffany, 13 In. 1800.00
Tumbler, Hindoo, Hoare 50.00
Vase, Allover Geometric Cutting, 14 1/4 In. 985.00
Vase, American Brilliant, Dorflinger, 1900s, 16 In. 350.00
Vase, Brilliant Period, Cut Leaves, Birds & Flowers, 13 In. 175.00
Vase, Brilliant, 16 In. 98.00
Vase, Brilliant, Floral, 1900, 12 In. 220.00
Vase, Clear, Star Cut Base, Diamonds & Fans, Webb, 8 In. 75.00
Vase, Corset, Elmira 100, Geometric Cutting, 9 In. 325.00
Vase, Crosscut Diamond & Pinwheel, 8 In. 145.00
Vase, Diamond Point & Fan, Amethyst, 7 1/2 x 5 In. 160.00
Vase, Fan, Brilliant Period, 9 3/4 x 4 1/2 In. 1350.00
Vase, Flower & Harvard, Sawtooth Rim, Hourglass Shape, 16 1/4 In. 450.00
Vase, Geometric Cutting, Unusual Shape, 12 1/2 In. 795.00
Vase, Geometric Iris, Clark, 10 In. 295.00
Vase, Green To Clear, Dorflinger, 12 In. 3200.00
Vase, Harvard Variation, Knobbed Ball Stem, 13 In. 375.00
Vase, Harvard, Corset Shape, 12 In. 295.00
Vase, Hobstars, Bowling Pin Shape, 15 3/4 x 7 5/8 In. ....*Illus* 1750.00
Vase, Kalana Poppy, Flared Rim, Dorflinger, 6 In. 275.00
Vase, Montrose, Emerald Green Cut To Clear, Dorflinger, 18 In. 5500.00
Vase, Nordel, Urn Shape, Square Footed Pedestal, 11 In. 2395.00
Vase, Overlaid With Green, Dorflinger, 11 3/4 In. ....*Illus* 935.00
Vase, Triple Notched Hobstars & Cane, Handles, 9 3/4 x 8 1/2 In. 1475.00
Vase, Trumpet, Fan & Sunburst, Emerald Green, 22 In. 100.00
Vase, Trumpet, Hobstars, Notched Rim, Starburst Base, 14 In. 225.00
Vase, Trumpet, Russian Cutting, Rayed Buttons, 9 In. 295.00
Water Set, Flower & Harvard, 14 1/2 In., 6 Piece 290.00
Water Set, Hobstar Chains In Diamond Field, Carafe, 5 Tumblers 525.00
Wine, Parisian, Tear Drop Stem, Dorflinger, 4 1/2 In. 95.00

◆◆◆

Try this method to remove white water stains from wood. Put a piece
of blotter paper over the spot, press with a warm iron. The spot
should vanish. If it does not, rub it with lemon oil.

◆◆◆

Cut Glass, Punch Bowl, Stand, Sawtooth, Zipper, Hobstar, 12 In.
Cut Glass, Vase, Hobstars, Bowling Pin Shape, 15 3/4 x 7 5/8 In.
Cut Glass, Vase, Overlaid With Green, Dorflinger, 11 3/4 In.

Cybis, Bust, Eskimo Child, 7 1/2 In.
Cybis, Bust, Indian Boy, 1975, 10 In.
Cybis, Bust, Indian Boy, Signed, 12 In.

Cybis, Figurine, 2 Colts, 1969, 8 In.

 Boleslaw Cybis came to the United States from Poland in 1939. He started making porcelains in Long Island, New York, in 1940. He moved to Trenton, New Jersey, in 1942, as one of the founders of Cordey China Co. and started his own Cybis Porcelains about 1950. The firm is still working. (See also Cordey.)

CYBIS, Bust, Eros	225.00
Bust, Eskimo Child, 7 1/2 In. ....*Illus*	110.00
Bust, Indian Boy, 1975, 10 In. ....*Illus*	200.00
Bust, Indian Boy, Signed, 12 In. ....*Illus*	110.00
Bust, Madonna	128.00
Creamer, Rose, Light Yellow Spatter, Octagonal, 5 1/2 In.	27.50
Figurine, 2 Colts, 1969, 8 In. ....*Illus*	175.00
Figurine, Baby Owl	80.00
Figurine, Ballerina, On Cue	175.00 To 450.00
Figurine, Betty Blue	200.00
Figurine, Bunny Snowball	75.00
Figurine, Burro Fitzgerald	175.00
Figurine, Chantilly Cat	225.00
Figurine, Chelsea Cat	225.00
Figurine, Christopher	250.00
Figurine, Cinderella	600.00
Figurine, Colonial Flower Basket	5500.00
Figurine, Deer Mouse	125.00
Figurine, Duckling Baby Brother	80.00
Figurine, Elephant	4000.00
Figurine, Elizabeth Ann	250.00 To 275.00
Figurine, Eskimo Mother	1800.00
Figurine, Exodus	1350.00
Figurine, First Flight	100.00
Figurine, Flight Into Egypt	1000.00
Figurine, Goldilocks & 1 Bear	175.00
Figurine, Great White Heron	1500.00
Figurine, Gretel	175.00
Figurine, Guinevere	850.00
Figurine, Heidi	175.00
Figurine, Jeannie With Light Brown Hair	500.00
Figurine, Juliet	2000.00
Figurine, Little Blue Heron	1000.00
Figurine, Little Bo Peep	300.00
Figurine, Little Princess	130.00
Figurine, Little Princess, 1970	550.00
Figurine, Madonna, Queen of Angels	150.00
Figurine, Madonna, With Bluebird	235.00
Figurine, Mandy The Lamb	100.00
Figurine, Melissa	375.00
Figurine, Pegasus	1900.00

Figurine, Peter Pan	600.00
Figurine, Pollyanna	150.00
Figurine, Rapunsel, Pink	400.00
Figurine, Rapunzel, Lilac, No. 801	450.00
Figurine, Rebecca	225.00
Figurine, Springtime	275.00
Figurine, Squirrel, 7 3/4 In.	110.00 To 120.00
Figurine, Thumbelina	125.00
Figurine, Wendy	175.00
Figurine, Windflower	135.00
Figurine, Wood Wren & Dogwood	250.00

There are some collectibles that are identified by the name of the country, not a factory mark. Anything marked *Czechoslovakia* is popular today. The name, first used as a mark after the country was formed in 1918, appears on glass and porcelain and other decorative items. The name is still used in some trademarks.

CZECHOSLOVAKIA, Creamer, Figural, Moose	17.00
Creamer, Parrot, 4 1/2 In.	25.00
Decanter, Crystal, 4 Sections	65.00
Dresser Set, Amethyst Cut To Clear, Stoppers, 4 Piece	595.00
Lamp, Ball, Crystal, White Flowers, Pair	55.00
Lamp, Dark Blue Flowers, Handle, Crystal, 8 In.	350.00
Lamp, Perfume, Blue Glass Ball, Cut Design	50.00
Perfume Bottle, Cobalt Blue, Atomizer, 5 In.	50.00
Perfume Bottle, Dog Head Dauber	240.00
Plate, Floral Center, Gold Encrusted Rim, 10 3/4 In., 12 Pc.	180.00
Vase, Amber Glass, Enameled, 6 x 5 In.	40.00
Vase, Art Deco, Enameled Woman On Black Amethyst, 8 In.	165.00
Vase, Black Amethyst, Silver Overlay, Bird On Twig, Signed	60.00
Vase, Cobalt Blue Threading, Coin Dots Cut Allover, 8 In.	185.00
Vase, Colored Bird, Gold Butterfly, Blown Glass, Blue, 7 In.	65.00
Vase, Green, Black Trim Top, 13 In.	145.00
Vase, Mottled, 8 1/2 In.	50.00
Vase, Orange & Silver Peacock, 10 1/8 In.	75.00
Wall Pocket, Bird On Fruit & Bird At Well	25.00
Water Set, Orange, Clear, Silver Deposit Bird, Rockett, 6 Pc.	250.00

D'Argental is a mark used in France by the Compagnie des Cristalleries de St. Louis. The firm made multilayered, acid-cut cameo glass in the late nineteenth and twentieth centuries. D'Argental is the French name for the city of Munzthal, home of the glassworks. Later they made enameled etched glass.

D'ARGENTAL, Box, Domed Lid, Berried Leafy Branches, Signed, c.1920, 5 1/2 In.	995.00
Lamp Base, River Landscape, Gilt Bronze, Signed, 1920, 16 5/8 In.	1550.00
Lamp, Scent, Forget-Me-Nots, Leaves, Frosted, Signed, 6 1/4 In.	2310.00
Lamp, Scent, Red Sailboats, Water & Sky, Signed, 7 In.	1595.00
Vase, 3 Cuttings, Amethyst To Purple To Frosted, 7 In.	950.00
Vase, Amethyst Jonquils, Frosted Ground, Signed, 10 1/2 In.	825.00
Vase, Burgundy On Blue, Signed, 6 In.	650.00
Vase, Cameo Acorns, Foliage, Bulbous	1075.00
Vase, Iris Blossoms, Leaves, Signed, c.1815, 11 3/4 In.	3300.00
Vase, Landscape, Trees In Foreground, Signed, c.1915, 9 3/4 In.	2310.00
Vase, Lighthouse, Ocean, Rocky Shore, Signed, . 5 In.	725.00
Vase, River Landscape, Signed, c.1915, 6 In.	1045.00
Vase, Thistle, Maroon, Burgundy & Yellow Frost, Signed, 9 1/2 In.	2500.00
Vase, Tulip Blossoms, Leaves, Signed, c.1915, 9 3/8 In.	1210.00
Vase, Woman & Children, Tree, Pink & Cream, Signed, 13 3/4 In.	3100.00
Vase, Woman Reaching Into Tree, Pink & Cream, Signed, 13 3/4 In.	2850.00

Daum Nancy, Box, Cameo, Enameled, 6 In.
Daum Nancy, Vase, Art Deco, Ice Blue, 16 1/2 In., Pair
Daum Nancy, Vase, Orange & Yellow, Overlaid With Scene, 7 1/4 In.

Jean Daum started a glassworks in Nancy, France, in 1875. The company, now called *Cristalleries de Nancy*, is still working. The *Daum Nancy* mark has been used in many variations. The name of the city and the artist are usually both included.

DAUM NANCY, Ashtray, Air Bubbles, Green, Signed, 2 1/5 x 10 In.	185.00
Base, Internal Mottled Streaks, Signed, c.1920, 11 3/4 In.	550.00
Bowl, Desert Scene, 4 Colors, 3 1/2 x 6 In.	3000.00
Bowl, Draped Upper Section, 4 Lobes, Signed, 1960s, 8 1/2 In.	550.00
Bowl, Dutch Winter Seascape, Signed, c.1910, 3 1/2 In.	6050.00
Bowl, Etched Geometric, Golden Amber, 11 1/2 In.	2860.00
Bowl, Etched, Smoke Gray, Undulating Geometric, Footed, 11 In.	2860.00
Bowl, Flaring Lip, Tiers of Triangles, Signed, c.1935, 12 In.	880.00
Bowl, Gray Walls, Grapes & Leaves, Signed, 4 3/4 In.	'320.00
Bowl, Leaves, Buds, Variegated Ground, Cushion Foot, 7 1/2 In.	1650.00
Bowl, Red Honeysuckles, Stems, Amber Ground, Tab Handles, Signed	3575.00
Bowl, Ships At Sea, Canary & Orange, Swollen Cylinder, 5 1/2 In.	4400.00
Bowl, Summer Scene, 7 3/4 In.	4000.00
Bowl, Wheat Thistles, Leaves, Gray Ground, Signed, 1910, 9 3/4 In.	825.00
Box, Cameo, Enameled, 6 In. *Illus*	8800.00
Box, Cover, Berried Leafy Branches, Signed, c.1910, 4 1/4 In.	1980.00
Box, Cover, Poppy Blossoms, Enameled, Signed, 3 x 5 1/2 In.	6875.00
Box, Cover, Red Berries, 6 1/2 In.	5500.00
Box, Domed Lid, Clover Blossoms, Signed, c.1900	2640.00
Box, Domed Lid, Fir Boughs, Berries, Signed, c.1910, 3 1/2 In.	2475.00
Box, Winter Scene, Handle, Silver Mounted, 5 1/2 x 6 3/4 In.	3250.00
Chandelier, Rose Blossoms, Glass & Wrought Iron, 1925, 26 In.	1870.00
Creamer, Cross of Lorraine, Floral & Leaves, Signed, 2 3/4 In.	1000.00
Cruet, Cross of Lorraine Cameo, Signed, 7 1/4 In.	1600.00
Decanter, Streaked & Mottled Charcoal Gray, Signed, 1930, 11 In.	330.00
Ewer, Small Blossoms, Peach & White Ground, Handle, Cameo, 12 In.	9350.00
Figurine, Elephant, Seated, Ears & Trunk Extended, Signed, 9 In.	275.00
Lamp, Cameo Glass, Waisted Domical Shade, Iron Base, 16 In.	6380.00
Lamp, Gray, Blue & Orange, Scrolled, 3–Sided, Signed, 6 In.	1540.00
Lamp, Winter Scene, 20 In.	20000.00
Perfume Bottle, Blossoms, Red, Yellow & White, Stopper, 4 3/4 In.	4950.00
Pitcher, Riverside Landscape, Tooled Handle, Signed, 10 1/2 In.	1765.00
Rose Bowl, Summer Scene, Oblong	7000.00
Rose Bowl, Winter Scene	2700.00
Salt, Bucket Form, Trees By Tranquil Lake, Signed, 1 7/16 In.	880.00
Salt, Enameled Venetian Lagoon, Ovoid, Signed, c.1910, 1 1/2 In.	1100.00

Sculpture, Flying Waterfowl, Chrome Stem, Signed, 8 In. 225.00
Toothpick, Inside Grooving, Oval, c.1960, 2 1/2 In. 95.00
Toothpick, Rose Blossoms, Buds, Leaves, Thorns, Enameled, 2 In. 485.00
Toothpick, Sprig of Single–Petaled Rose, Thorned Stem, 2 In. 485.00
Tumbler, Gold & White Enamel On Vaseline Frost, 5 In. 325.00
Tumbler, Thistle, Green To Clear, Gold Designs, Signed, 4 1/2 In. 425.00
Vase, 3 Textured Rings, Amber Sphere, Signed, 3 3/4 In. 330.00
Vase, Art Deco, Ice Blue, 16 1/2 In., Pair ....*Illus* 10450.00
Vase, Art Deco, Mottled Russet To Dark Gray, 22 1/2 In. 1500.00
Vase, Autumn Trees At Lake Side, Tapered, Signed, 6 In. 4025.00
Vase, Berluze, Footed, 6 In. 2000.00
Vase, Berluze, Footed, 36 In. 4500.00
Vase, Black Enameled Cougar, Burnt Orange Frosted, 2 1/2 In. 2100.00
Vase, Blossoms, Mottled Orange, Inverted Trumpet, 11 3/4 In. 8900.00
Vase, Blown Into Geometric Iron Mount, Signed, c.1925, 12 In. 1650.00
Vase, Cameo, Green & Amethyst Flowers & Ferns, Gilded, 4 3/4 In. 1200.00
Vase, Cameo, Leafy Branches, Polished Berries, Signed, 12 In. 8250.00
Vase, Daylily Blossoms, Leaves, Signed, c.1910, 7 7/8 In. 9350.00
Vase, Enameled Winter Forest Landscape, Signed, 4 13/16 In. 2425.00
Vase, Etched Budding & Blooming Lilies, Signed, 3 1/2 In. 2530.00
Vase, Etched Horizontal Bands, Turquoise, Spherical, 7 1/2 In. 2250.00
Vase, Ferns, Birds, Mottled Yellow, Egg Shape, Cameo, 5 1/2 In. 4500.00
Vase, Floral & Dragonfly, 3 1/2 In. 1100.00
Vase, Forest & Lake Scene, 6 1/2 x 6 1/2 In. 3000.00
Vase, Geometric Reticulated Iron, Amber, L. Majorelle, 12 In. 3520.00
Vase, Green & Orange Over Amethyst & White, Signed, 16 1/2 In. 6250.00
Vase, Interior Enameled Landscape, Trees, Signed, 14 In. 7050.00
Vase, Landscape Scene, Signed, 4 1/2 x 6 In. 715.00
Vase, Leafy Fruiting Branches, Signed, c.1910, 11 In. 6050.00
Vase, Marsh Landscape, Flowers, Grasses, Signed, c.1910, 12 In. 7750.00
Vase, Mottled Green Leafage, Anemone Blossoms, Signed, 7 7/8 In. 4450.00
Vase, Orange & Yellow, Overlaid With Scene, 7 1/4 In. ....*Illus* 5060.00
Vase, Orange To Green Brown, Pate–De–Verre, 5 In. 750.00
Vase, Paneled, Mottled Colors, Signed, c.1910, 25 1/2 In. 3200.00
Vase, Red Star Flowers, Textured Ground, Signed, 5 1/2 In. 1050.00
Vase, River Landscape, Distant Mountains, Signed, c.1910, 12 In. 3850.00
Vase, River Landscape, Leafy Trees, Signed, c.1910, 5 1/2 In. 5500.00
Vase, River Landscape, Village In Distance, c.1910, 3 1/8 In. 1925.00
Vase, Scalloped Rim, Controlled Bubbles, Apricot, 8 x 9 In. 595.00
Vase, Sprays of Leafy Wildflowers, Signed, c.1910, 9 7/8 In. 4125.00
Vase, Spring Landscape, Leafy Trees, Signed, c.1910, 3 3/4 In. 2750.00
Vase, Spring Scene, 4 In. 2800.00
Vase, Spring Scene, Signed, 14 In. 5650.00
Vase, Storks In Flight, Peach & White, Bulbous, 6 1/4 In. 5500.00
Vase, Sunset Riverscape, Dark Green & Black, Signed, 3 1/2 In. 1100.00
Vase, Teardrop Form, Bird On Branch, Signed, c.1920, 14 1/4 In. 2000.00
Vase, Thistle, 4 3/4 In. 955.00
Vase, Thistle, Enamel Tracery, Gold Streaking, 19 In. 7750.00
Vase, Tulips & Leaves, Purple Overlay, Signed, c.1910, 18 7/8 In. 6650.00
Vase, Wildflowers & Leaves, Signed, c.1910, 9 In. 3125.00
Vase, Winter Forest Landscape, Signed, c.1910, 7 1/8 In. 4675.00
Vase, Winter Landscape, Yellow & Orange, Signed, 1910, 4 1/2 In. 2475.00
Vase, Winter, Snow Scene, Ovoid, Signed, 4 1/2 In. 1925.00
Wine, Etched Thistle Blossoms, Gold Rim, 5 1/2 In., Set of 6 .... 1525.00

DAVENPORT
LONGPORT
STAFFORDSHRE

Davenport pottery and porcelain were made at the Davenport factory in Longport, Staffordshire, England, from 1793 to 1887. Earthenwares, creamwares, porcelains, ironstone, and other ceramics were made. Most of the pieces are marked with a form of the word *Davenport.*

DAVENPORT, Dinner Set, Child's, Amoy, Flow Blue, 1844, 43 Piece 6500.00
Plate, Cyrus, Black Transfer, Anchor Mark, 1850, 8 1/2 In. 60.00
Platter, Bride of Lammermoor, Magenta, 15 x 19 In. 225.00

Sauce, Amoy, Flow Blue 65.00
Teapot, Strawberry, Vine Border, 5 1/2 In. 55.00

Davy Crockett, the American frontiersman, was born in 1786 and died in 1836. He became popular again in 1954 with the introduction of a television series about his life. Coonskin caps and buckskins became popular and hundreds of different Davy Crockett items were made.

DAVY CROCKETT, Bank, Figural, Copper, Metal 45.00
Belt, Leather, On Card, 1950s 55.00
Billfold .... 12.00 To 15.00
Billfold, Box 80.00
Book, 1955 .... 6.00
Bowl, Fire–King 10.00
Candy Box, 1950s 48.00
Clock, Wall, 1950s, Original Box 300.00
Coaster Wagon, 1950s 110.00
Cookie Jar, Brush .... 128.00 To 225.00
Cookie Jar, Gold On Name, Regal .... 168.00 To 185.00
Cookie Jar, Head, McCoy 375.00
Cookie Jar, In Bushes, American Bisque .... 150.00 To 250.00
Cookie Jar, McCoy 700.00
Cookie Jar, Ransburg 80.00
Decals, Iron–On, Card 35.00
Display, Billfold 175.00
Doll, Boy & Girl, Madame Alexander, 1955, Pair 750.00
Doll, Cloth, Hat 18.00
Doll, Woolworth, Box 40.00
Fix–It Stage Coach, Alamo Express, Ideal, 15 In. 145.00
Game, Target, Indian, Keystone, 7 Figures, Repeater Rifle, Box 145.00
Iron–On Scenes, 4 Different Pgs., 1959, Unused, 7 x 3 1/2 In. 10.00
Jacket, Vinyl 40.00
Knife, Pocket, 1950s .... 35.00 To 39.00
Knife, Pocket, Picture 26.00
Knife, Tomahawk, Fess Parker, 1950s, Pocket 50.00
Lamp, Davy Holding Knife & Rifle, Metal 165.00
Lamp, Desk, 18 In. 160.00
Lamp, Figural, Copper, Metal, Tall 145.00
Lamp, Original Shade 135.00
Lunch Box, Davy Crockett At Alamo, Thermos .... 60.00 To 95.00
Mug, Brush 42.00
Mug, Figural, Pottery, Young Davy 45.00
Mug, Red, Fire–King 14.00
Nodder 25.00
Outfit, Frontier, Cap, Vest, Belt, Keystone Bros., 1950s 38.00
Penlight 25.00
Plate, Display, Graphic 45.00
Play Set, At The Alamo 300.00
Powder Horn, Belt & Compass, On Card 85.00
Powder Horn, Offical Disneyland, Daisy 50.00
Record, Ballad of Davy Crockett, 45 Rpm, Peanut Butter, 1950s 15.00
Ring, Full Head, Brass Plating 32.00
Target Set, Indian, Keystone, Box 125.00
Tie & Lariat, On Card 15.00
Tie Clasp, On Card 25.00
Tie Slide, Figural, Cast Metal 9.00
Toy, Indian, Davy, Yellow & Brown, 4 3/4 In. 9.00
Tumbler, Davy Had A Creed That Said, Capitol, 4 1/4 In. 4.00
Wallet, Vinyl, 1950s, Unused .... 10.00 To 25.00
Watch, Original Card 18.00
Watch, Toy, 1950s, Card 7.00
Wristwatch, Price Sticker 100.00

William de Morgan made art pottery in England from the 1860s to 1907. He is best known for his luster–glazed Moorish–inspired pieces. The pottery used a variety of marks.

DE MORGAN, Charger, Red, Black Luster, Geometric, 16 In. 2000.00
Tile, Flowers, Leaves, Green, Red, 8 In. 300.00

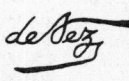 E. S. Monot founded a glass company near Paris in 1851. The company changed names many times. De Vez was a signature used on cameo glass made by this firm after 1910. Mt. Joye, another glass by this factory, is listed in its own section.

DE VEZ, Box, Cover, Oriental Scene, Pine Branches, Signed, Round, 5 1/4 In. 825.00
Lamp, Cows On Hillside, Forest, Houses, Purple, Blue & Gold, 12 In. 9500.00
Lamp, Hanging, Yellow & Brown Shade, Silk Cord 550.00
Vase, Blue Butterflies On Leaves, Yellow Ground, Signed, 8 1/4 In. 900.00
Vase, Bridge & Mountains On Base, Vines On Neck, Signed, 14 In. 1925.00
Vase, Castle Scene, Russets & Yellow, Signed, 8 In. 2250.00
Vase, Mountain, Cottage & Lake, Orange Ground, Signed, 10 In. 1800.00
Vase, River Landscape, Leafy Trees, Signed, c.1920, 6 In. 1150.00
Vase, Trees, Island & Cottage, Signed, 9 In. 1800.00

 Decoys are carved or turned wooden copies of birds or fish. The decoy was placed in the water or propped on the shore to lure flying birds to the pond for hunters. Some decoys are handmade, some are commercial products. Today there is a group of artists making modern decoys for display, not for use in a pond.

DECOY, Black Bass, Wooden, Leather Fins, Painted, Glass Eyes, Stand, 12 In. 150.00
Black Duck, A. Elmer Crowell, Glass Eyes, 6 1/2 x 16 1/2 In. 990.00
Black Duck, A. T. Maxwell, Glass Eyes, 17 In. 85.00
Black Duck, Balsa Body, Wooden Head, Glass Eyes, 15 1/2 In. 145.00
Black Duck, Bowman 9900.00
Black Duck, Dodge Factory, 16 In. 225.00
Black Duck, Ed Coradetti 500.00
Black Duck, Elmer Crowell, c.1915 .... 2700.00
Black Duck, Flying, Gus Wilson, Weathered 2300.00
Black Duck, Gunderfinger, 1930s 225.00
Black Duck, Harry Conklin, Branded, 17 1/2 In. 250.00
Black Duck, Hollow, Original Paint, Glass Eyes, 17 1/2 In. 85.00
Black Duck, Ken Anger 1250.00
Black Duck, Mason, Original Paint, Shot Scars, 16 1/4 In. 95.00
Black Duck, Primitive, Cork, Wooden, Painted, 17 1/4 In. 15.00
Black Duck, Primitive, Glass Eyes, 13 1/2 In. 75.00
Black Duck, Reeves, 15 5/8 In. 125.00
Bluebill Drake, Glass Eyes, 11 1/2 In. 55.00
Bluebill Drake, Hollow Body, Oversized Glass Eyes 65.00
Bluebill Drake, Ira Hudson, Old Repaint, Tack Eyes, 13 1/4 In. 205.00
Bluebill Drake, Primitive, Painted, Tack Eyes, Wis., 12 1/2 In. 55.00
Bluebill Drake, Relief Carved Detail, 14 In. 165.00
Bluebill Drake, Turk Libensperger 475.00
Bluebill Duck, Comb Feather, Coombs, 1930s 495.00
Bluebill Hen, Irving Miller, 11 1/2 In. 150.00
Bluebill Hen, Stylized Silhouette, Samuel E. Squires, 14 In. 250.00
Bluebill, Hollow Carved, Lou Rathmell, 1944, Pair 8800.00
Bluebill, Primitive, Hollow, Worn Paint, Glass Eyes, 13 3/4 In., Pair 130.00
Brandt, R. C. Orcutt, Original Paint, Glass Eyes, 16 In. 95.00
Bufflehead Drake, 10 3/4 In. 65.00
Bufflehead Drake, Contemporary, R. Dunn, 11 3/4 In. 45.00
Bufflehead, Doug Jester, Pair 8250.00
Bufflehead, Sleeper, Glass Eyes, Mid-20th Century, Primitive, 10 In. 105.00
Canada Goose, Cork Body, Wooden Head & Keel, Bill Enright, 24 1/2 In. 500.00
Canada Goose, Joe Haines, Wood, Wire & Canvas, 23 3/4 In. 145.00
Canada Goose, Joe Lincoln, Repainted, 12 x 22 In. 385.00
Canada Goose, Lowell Strayer, Cork Body, Wooden Head, 20 3/4 In. 65.00

Canada Goose, Preener, Tack Eyes, Steel Rod Legs, Contemporary, 24 In. 300.00
Canada Goose, Snake Head, Glass Eyes, 23 1/2 In. 325.00
Canvasback Drake, Balsa Body, Wooden Head, Glass Eyes, Herter, 15 In. 85.00
Canvasback Drake, Bobtail, Glass Eyes, 14 1/4 In. 105.00
Canvasback Drake, Glass Eyes, 14 1/2 In. 95.00
Canvasback Drake, High Head, Glass Eyes, Marked Duck Inn, 16 1/2 In. 175.00
Canvasback Drake, Hollow, Charles Schoenhider Jr., 15 3/4 In. 175.00
Canvasback Drake, Madion Mitchell, 1960, 16 In. 200.00
Canvasback Drake, Mason, Seneca Model, Hollow, Glass Eyes, 15 3/4 In. 175.00
Canvasback Drake, Tack Eyes, Muskie Manor, 13 1/4 In. 250.00
Canvasback Hen, Ben Schmidt, Original Paint, Glass Eyes, 15 1/2 In. 400.00
Canvasback Hen, Bobtail, Glass Eyes, Michigan, 15 1/2 In. 150.00
Canvasback Hen, Glass Eyes, Charles Bean, 14 3/4 In. 225.00
Canvasback Hen, Glass Eyes, Upper Chesapeake Bay, 16 In. 65.00
Canvasback Hen, Madison Mitchell, Original Paint, 14 1/2 In. 125.00
Canvasback, High Neck Troller, Maryland, 1920 .... 245.00
Canvasback, Milton Watson 595.00
Canvasback, Stevens, Oversized, 1890 .... 6600.00
Coot, Glass Eyes, Gus Nelow, 14 1/2 In. 95.00
Coot, Glass Eyes, Old Paint, 1950s, 10 1/4 In. 145.00
Coot, Glass Eyes, Repaint, 12 1/4 In. 55.00
Coot, Glass Eyes, White Trim, Ontario, Canada, 12 In. 85.00
Coot, Raft-Type Base, 11 In. 20.00
Coot, Turned Head, Glass Eyes, Hollow, 11 In. 60.00
Coot, Worn Paint, Hollow, Glass Eyes, 10 In. 205.00
Crow, Black Paint, Glass Eyes, Papier–Mache, 16 1/4 In. 12.50
Crow, Primitive, Old Black Repaint, 11 In. 80.00
Dove, White, Curt Duff, Glass Eyes, Feather Wings, 1930, 11 3/4 In. 65.00
Drake, Bluebill, Arthur Wellington, Glass Eyes, 14 1/2 In. 175.00
Drake, Bluebill, c.1920s, 12 x 6 x 5 In. 65.00
Drake, Carved Wings, Turned Head, European, 11 1/2 In. 70.00
Drake, Cast Iron, Old Paint, 13 3/4 In. 250.00
Duck, General Fibre Co. 30.00
Eider Hen, Preening, Gus Wilson 9900.00
Fish, Bass, Tack Eyes, 6 Metal Fins, Mr. X, c.1890, 8 In. 1430.00
Fish, Brook Trout, "15" Painted On Fin, Kenneth Brunning, 7 In. 1430.00
Fish, Brook Trout, Leather Tail, Harry Seymour, 1880s, 7 In. 2310.00
Fish, Brown Trout, Leather Tail, 4 Metal Fins, 6 3/4 In. 605.00
Fish, Cast Aluminum, Sletten, Unused, 1950s 22.00
Fish, Crappie, Olive Green, Metal Fins, 6 1/2 In. ....*Illus*   88.00

Decoy, Fish,
Crawdad, Red,
Black, Wood,
10 In.

Decoy, Fish,
Wooden,
Burn Markings,
Metal Fins,
7 3/4 In.

Decoy, Fish, Trout, Red, Orange, Black Speckles, 7 In.
Decoy, Fish, Trout, Black, Red, Metal Fins, 8 In.
Decoy, Fish, Crappie, Olive Green, Metal Fins, 6 1/2 In.

◆◆

Try to rearrange your furniture once a year to avoid noticeable sun
fading.

◆◆

Fish, Crawdad, Red, Black, Wood, 10 In. ....*Illus*   77.00
Fish, Driftwood, Carl Christiansen, Polychrome, Glass Eyes, 29 In. 30.00
Fish, Herring, 6 Metal Fins, Isaac Goulette, 1930s, 6 1/2 In. 440.00
Fish, Inchworm Line Ties, 2 Metal Fins, Leroy Howell, 6 3/4 In. 298.00
Fish, Leather Tail, Spots On Body, Harry Seymour, 1970s, 7 In. 1925.00
Fish, Louis Leach, Red, White & Black, Slitter, 7 1/4 In. 25.00
Fish, Mickey Mouse, Black Wood Body, Tin Legs, 4 In. 675.00
Fish, Muskie, Wood & Tin, 17 3/4 In. 90.00
Fish, New York Perch, 1870s, 9 In. 4125.00
Fish, Oliver Reigstad, 1960 ....   17.00
Fish, Perch, Brass Tack Eyes, 6 Metal Fins, Civil War Era, 9 In. 4125.00
Fish, Shiner, Wood & Black On Back, 4 Metal Fins, c.1890, 8 In. 605.00
Fish, Spearing, Ice Fishing, Wooden, Tin Fins, 13 In. 110.00
Fish, Steelhead, Carved Mouth & Gill, Gold Paint, c.1900, 6 In. 1100.00
Fish, Sucker, Carved Gills, 6 Metal Fins, Oscar Peterson, 8 1/2 In. 1320.00
Fish, Trout, Black, Red, Metal Fins, 8 In. ....*Illus*   110.00
Fish, Trout, Iridescent Gold Sides, Oscar Peterson, 7 1/2 In. 2530.00
Fish, Trout, Metal Tail, 4 Metal Fins, 1890s, 8 In. 665.00
Fish, Trout, Red, Orange, Black Speckles, 7 In. ....*Illus*   55.00
Fish, Turtle, Lead Head, Legs & Tail, 14 In. 175.00
Fish, White, Red Head, 3 Fins, Wooden, Ice Fishing, c.1930s, 8 In. 65.00
Fish, Wooden, Burn Markings, Metal Fins, 7 3/4 In. ....*Illus*   143.00
Fish, Wooden, Tin, Painted, 9 1/2 In. 60.00
Goldeneye Drake, Worn Repaint, 13 1/2 In. 75.00
Goldeneye Duck, Mason Factory, Glass Eyes, 15 1/2 In. 900.00
Goldeneye Hen, D. K. Nichol, 1900 ....   7150.00
Goldeneye, Mason, Glass Eyes, Slope Breasted, 15 1/2 In. 990.00
Goose, Field, Detachable Wings, Tin & Wood, 1920s 400.00
Goose, Foldout Cardboard 25.00
Goose, Hollow, Repainted, Brant, 17 1/2 In. 150.00
Goose, Missouri River, 1920s 65.00
Goose, Stick–Up, Wooden, Removable Head, Glass Eyes, 1920s 90.00
Goose, Swimming, Hollow Body, Glass Eyes, W. R. G., 22 In. 45.00
Goose, Tin & Wood 400.00
Grebe, Glass Eyes, Clarence Krieser, 9 3/4 In. 325.00
Green Wing Teal, Vergie Hodge & Chas. Moore, 14 In., Pr. 330.00
Mallard Drake, Feeding Position, Dowel Legs, 19 In. 225.00
Mallard Drake, Feeding Position, Metal Tail Feather, 17 In. 105.00
Mallard Drake, Glass Eyes, Ken Harris, 16 In. 125.00
Mallard Drake, Illinois River, 16 1/2 In. 95.00
Mallard Drake, Layers of Worn Paint, Glass Eyes, 17 1/2 In. 40.00
Mallard Drake, Paul LeFavre, Hawks Bay, Canada, 13 1/2 In. 30.00
Mallard Drake, Sleeper, Original Paint, Al Wragg, 14 3/4 In. 185.00
Mallard Hen, Glass Eyes, Cliff Reinsager, 1967, 14 1/2 In. 45.00
Mallard Hen, Hector Whittington, Hollow, Turned Head, 17 1/4 In. 225.00
Mallard Hen, Hollow, Repaint, Illinois River, 13 In. 65.00
Mallard Hen, Mason's Premier, Hollow, Original Paint, 17 1/4 In. 300.00
Mallard, High Head, Tack Eyes, Bill Enright, 1973, 17 In., Pair 600.00
Mallard, Preening, Chas. Moore, '80, 14 1/4 In., Pair 300.00
Mallard, Tack Eyes, Original Paint, Mason, c.1920, Pair 550.00
Merganser Drake, Mason, Glass Eyes, 17 In. 155.00
Merganser Drake, Winnebago Decoys, Michael J. Helf, 17 In. 45.00
Merganser, Primitive, Worn Repaint, 16 In. 105.00
Pintail Drake, Ganderfinger 400.00
Pintail Drake, Glass Eyes, Chas Moore '90, 19 1/4 In. 50.00
Pintail Drake, Glass Eyes, Repaint, 16 1/2 In. 85.00
Pintail Drake, Leslie Rondau, Original Paint, Glass Eyes, 19 3/4 In. 35.00
Pintail Drake, Painted, Tack Eyes, 18 In. 175.00
Pintail Drake, Von Vick, Original Paint, 17 1/2 In. 65.00
Pintail Drake, Weeks, Original Paint, Glass Eyes, 16 1/2 In. 90.00
Pintail Duck, Preener, Hollow Body, Mike Barrett, 13 3/4 In. 200.00
Pintail Hen, Painted, Glass Eyes, Don Zeng, Chicago, 1965, 13 1/2 In. 375.00
Pintail Hen, Stevens Factory, Weedsport, N. Y. 6050.00

Plover, Carved & Painted, Peg Bill, 9 In.	250.00
Plover, Crowell, 1900	4400.00
Red–Breasted Merganser, Ben Smith	9950.00
Red–Breasted Merganser, Capt. P. A. Wright	6600.00
Redhead Drake, Cecil Johns, Ontario, Canada, 13 1/2 In.	95.00
Redhead Drake, Glass Eyes, Mason, 13 1/2 In.	150.00
Redhead Drake, Madison Mitchell, 13 In.	300.00
Redhead Drake, Relief Carving, Glass Eyes, 1940s, 12 1/4 In.	135.00
Redhead Drake, Sleeper, Hollow, Repaint, St. Clair Flats, Ill., 14 In.	105.00
Redhead Drake, Tom Avera, Turned Head, Glass Eyes, 14 1/2 In.	25.00
Ringneck Drake, Original Paint, Glass Eyes, California, 15 1/4 In.	55.00
Ruddy Duck, Glass Eyes, 10 3/4 In.	135.00
Sanderling Peep, Sleeping, c.1900	185.00
Sea Gull, Gus Wilson, Weathered	715.00
Shorebird, Inserted Bill, 9 In	210.00
Shorebird, Original Paint, Glass Eyes, 9 1/2 In.	65.00
Shorebird, Original Paint, Glass Eyes, Shot Marks, 11 1/2 In.	450.00
Shorebird, Roothead, Driftwood Base, Original Paint, 13 In.	135.00
Swan, Contemporary, Jimmy Bowden, Original Paint, Glass Eyes, 36 In.	250.00
Teal Hen, Glass Eyes, Pete Peterson, Virginia, 1979, 13 1/2 In.	85.00
Trout, Wooden, Metal Fins, Glass Eyes, 7 3/4 In.	100.00
White Wing Scoter, Capt. C. Bailey, c.1930, Canvas Cover, 24 3/4 In.	220.00
Wigeon Drake, Primitive, Mid–20th Century, Currituck Sound, 16 In.	65.00
Wood Duck Drake, Jack Sweet, Original Paint, Glass Eyes, 11 3/4 In.	80.00

 Chelsea Keramic Art Works was established in 1872 in Chelsea, Massachusetts, by members of the Robertson family. The firm used the mark *CKAW.* The factory closed in 1889 and was reorganized as the Chelsea Pottery U.S. in 1891. It became the Dedham Pottery of Dedham, Massachusetts, in 1895. The factory closed in 1943. It was famous for its crackleware dishes, which picture blue outlines of animals, flowers, and other natural motifs.

DEDHAM, Ashtray, Magnolia, Stamped, 4 In.	220.00
Bacon Rasher, Rabbit	1215.00
Bonbon, Cover, Elephants	950.00
Bowl, Elephant, 9 In.	990.00
Bowl, Porridge, Rabbit, Signed, 4 1/2 In.	195.00
Bowl, Rabbit, 5 1/4 In.	195.00
Bowl, Rabbit, Marked, 7 In.	385.00
Bowl, Serving, Rabbit, Ruffled Edge	1100.00
Butter Pat, Wild Rose	450.00
Candlestick, Rabbit, Signed, Pair	395.00
Card Holder, Rabbit	775.00
Charger, Dolphin	2310.00
Creamer, Rabbit, Marked, 5 1/8 In.	465.00
Creamer, Tankard, Rabbit, Signed	110.00
Cup & Plate, Bouillon, Duck, Marked, 6 In.	440.00
Cup & Saucer, Grape	210.00
Dish, 5–Sided, Early 20th Century, 7 In.	525.00
Dish, Vegetable, Cover, Mushroom	1200.00
Dish, Vegetable, Cover, Rabbit	1255.00
Eggcup, Polar Bear, Marked, Double, 2 3/4 In.	305.00
Eggcup, Rabbit, 1 1/2 In.	220.00
Knife Rest, Rabbit, 3 1/4 In.	467.00
Moth, 8 In.	550.00
Mug, Chick	2090.00
Mustard, Rabbit	1100.00
Pitcher, Owl & Moon 1 Side, Barnyard Fowl & Sun Other, White, 5 In.	600.00
Pitcher, Rabbit Band, Crackled, Handle, Marked, 4 3/4 x 6 In.	357.00
Pitcher, Rabbit, Miniature	2425.00
Pitcher, Striated Green & Brown Glaze, CKAW, c.1885, 9 In.	110.00
Pitcher, Tankard, Signed, 3 In.	260.00
Plate, Begging Scotty Dog, Marked, 10 In.	2650.00

Plate, Birds In Potted Orange Tree, 8 In. 825.00
Plate, Cat, 6 In. 6820.00
Plate, Cherry, 9 6/8 In. 145.00
Plate, Dolphin, Marked, 7 1/2 In. 715.00
Plate, Duck, 8 1/2 In. 345.00
Plate, Duck, Blue Ink Mark, 8 1/2 In. 275.00
Plate, Grape, Sharply Outlined, Maude Davenport, 9 3/4 In. 385.00
Plate, Horse Chestnuts, 8 1/2 In. 225.00
Plate, Iris, 20th Century, 10 In. 165.00
Plate, Iris, Blue Ink Mark, 9 3/4 In. 385.00
Plate, Iris, Blue, 8 1/2 In. 180.00
Plate, Moth, 8 In. 550.00
Plate, Mushroom, Crackled, Square Ink Mark, 8 1/2 In. 225.00
Plate, Oak Leaf, Unglazed 450.00
Plate, Owl, 10 In. 1750.00
Plate, Pineapple, 10 In. 795.00
Plate, Polar Bear, Marked, 10 In. 465.00
Plate, Poppy, 8 In. 550.00
Plate, Quail, 9 In. 6050.00
Plate, Rabbit, Crackled Center, Marked, 8 1/2 In. 82.00
Plate, Rabbit, Crackled, 12 In. 450.00
Plate, Rabbit, Deep Blue, 8 1/2 In. 180.00
Plate, Rabbit, Pink Glaze 200.00
Plate, Tapestry Lion, 10 In. 3740.00
Plate, Turkey, 10 In. .... 245.00 To 660.00
Plate, Turkey, Crackled, Ink Mark, 9 3/4 In. 385.00
Plate, Turtle 3190.00
Saltshaker, Rabbit, Crackled, 2 3/4 x 2 1/2 In. 110.00
Stein, Rabbit, Marked, 5 1/4 In. 240.00
Tankard, Rabbit, 1 Pt. 795.00
Tile, Tea, Rabbit, Circular Design, Crackled White, Marked, 5 1/2 In. 357.00
Tile, Tea, Rabbit, Square, Dated 1931, 4 5/8 In. 330.00
Toothpick, Boot Shape 1600.00
Vase, Crackleware, Swollen Form, Narrow Neck, CKAW, 1880s, 7 In. 275.00
Vase, Elongated Neck, Tapering To Base, Oxblood, 8 1/4 In. 1100.00
Vase, Hugh C. Robertson, 1890s, 2 In. 550.00
Vase, Mauve Drippled Glaze, Squat, Baluster, Robertson, 6 1/4 In. 1760.00
Vase, Oviform Body, Flowing Glaze, Hugh C. Robertson, 1890s, 9 In. 275.00
Vase, Short Neck, Squat Bulbous Form, CKAW, 6 In. 1760.00
Vase, Stylized Plant & Floral Design, c.1885, 6 1/8 In. 2535.00
Vase, Swollen Form, Marked CKAW, 7 In. 275.00

John and Elizabeth Degenhart started the Crystal Art Glass of Cambridge, Ohio, in 1947. Quality paperweights and other glass objects were made. John died in 1964 and his wife took over management and production ideas. Over 145 colors of glass were made. In 1978, after the death of Mrs. Degenhart, the molds were sold. The D in a heart trademark was removed, so collectors can easily recognize the true Degenhart piece.

DEGENHART, Figurine, Lamb On Basket, Crown Tuscan 65.00
Figurine, Robin On Nest, Crown Tuscan 125.00
Paperweight, Lime Green Flash Over Lily In Window, 3 1/8 In. 715.00

Degue is a signature found acid–etched on pieces of French glass made in the early 1900s. Cameo, mold blown, and smooth glass with contrasting colored rims are the types most often found.

DEGUE, Vase, Geometric Medial Frieze, Flared Oval, Signed, 6 1/4 In. 305.00
Vase, Pink Streaked, Chrysanthemums, Leaves, Signed, c.1925, 12 3/8 In. 1325.00
Vase, Stylized Blossoms, Leaves, Signed, c.1925, 9 1/2 In. 885.00

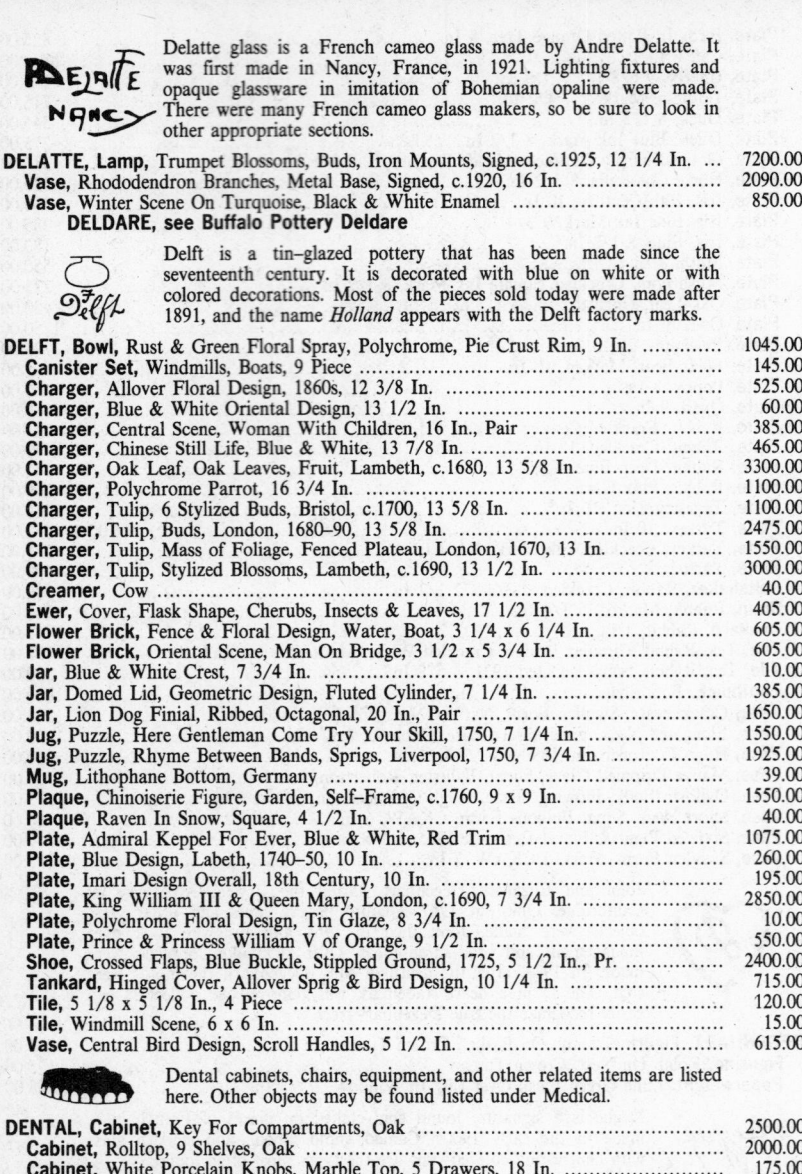

Delatte glass is a French cameo glass made by Andre Delatte. It was first made in Nancy, France, in 1921. Lighting fixtures and opaque glassware in imitation of Bohemian opaline were made. There were many French cameo glass makers, so be sure to look in other appropriate sections.

DELATTE, Lamp, Trumpet Blossoms, Buds, Iron Mounts, Signed, c.1925, 12 1/4 In. ...	7200.00
Vase, Rhododendron Branches, Metal Base, Signed, c.1920, 16 In.	2090.00
Vase, Winter Scene On Turquoise, Black & White Enamel	850.00

DELDARE, see Buffalo Pottery Deldare

Delft is a tin-glazed pottery that has been made since the seventeenth century. It is decorated with blue on white or with colored decorations. Most of the pieces sold today were made after 1891, and the name *Holland* appears with the Delft factory marks.

DELFT, Bowl, Rust & Green Floral Spray, Polychrome, Pie Crust Rim, 9 In.	1045.00
Canister Set, Windmills, Boats, 9 Piece	145.00
Charger, Allover Floral Design, 1860s, 12 3/8 In.	525.00
Charger, Blue & White Oriental Design, 13 1/2 In.	60.00
Charger, Central Scene, Woman With Children, 16 In., Pair	385.00
Charger, Chinese Still Life, Blue & White, 13 7/8 In.	465.00
Charger, Oak Leaf, Oak Leaves, Fruit, Lambeth, c.1680, 13 5/8 In.	3300.00
Charger, Polychrome Parrot, 16 3/4 In.	1100.00
Charger, Tulip, 6 Stylized Buds, Bristol, c.1700, 13 5/8 In.	1100.00
Charger, Tulip, Buds, London, 1680–90, 13 5/8 In.	2475.00
Charger, Tulip, Mass of Foliage, Fenced Plateau, London, 1670, 13 In.	1550.00
Charger, Tulip, Stylized Blossoms, Lambeth, c.1690, 13 1/2 In.	3000.00
Creamer, Cow	40.00
Ewer, Cover, Flask Shape, Cherubs, Insects & Leaves, 17 1/2 In.	405.00
Flower Brick, Fence & Floral Design, Water, Boat, 3 1/4 x 6 1/4 In.	605.00
Flower Brick, Oriental Scene, Man On Bridge, 3 1/2 x 5 3/4 In.	605.00
Jar, Blue & White Crest, 7 3/4 In.	10.00
Jar, Domed Lid, Geometric Design, Fluted Cylinder, 7 1/4 In.	385.00
Jar, Lion Dog Finial, Ribbed, Octagonal, 20 In., Pair	1650.00
Jug, Puzzle, Here Gentleman Come Try Your Skill, 1750, 7 1/4 In.	1550.00
Jug, Puzzle, Rhyme Between Bands, Sprigs, Liverpool, 1750, 7 3/4 In.	1925.00
Mug, Lithophane Bottom, Germany	39.00
Plaque, Chinoiserie Figure, Garden, Self-Frame, c.1760, 9 x 9 In.	1550.00
Plaque, Raven In Snow, Square, 4 1/2 In.	40.00
Plate, Admiral Keppel For Ever, Blue & White, Red Trim	1075.00
Plate, Blue Design, Labeth, 1740–50, 10 In.	260.00
Plate, Imari Design Overall, 18th Century, 10 In.	195.00
Plate, King William III & Queen Mary, London, c.1690, 7 3/4 In.	2850.00
Plate, Polychrome Floral Design, Tin Glaze, 8 3/4 In.	10.00
Plate, Prince & Princess William V of Orange, 9 1/2 In.	550.00
Shoe, Crossed Flaps, Blue Buckle, Stippled Ground, 1725, 5 1/2 In., Pr.	2400.00
Tankard, Hinged Cover, Allover Sprig & Bird Design, 10 1/4 In.	715.00
Tile, 5 1/8 x 5 1/8 In., 4 Piece	120.00
Tile, Windmill Scene, 6 x 6 In.	15.00
Vase, Central Bird Design, Scroll Handles, 5 1/2 In.	615.00

Dental cabinets, chairs, equipment, and other related items are listed here. Other objects may be found listed under Medical.

DENTAL, Cabinet, Key For Compartments, Oak	2500.00
Cabinet, Rolltop, 9 Shelves, Oak	2000.00
Cabinet, White Porcelain Knobs, Marble Top, 5 Drawers, 18 In.	175.00
Chair, Dentist, Metal, Vinyl Seat	5.00
Chair, Ridder, Hydraulic, 1922	2500.00
Cup, Spittle, Gold Bands, Insert, Funnel Shape, China	110.00
Mold, False Teeth, Brass	55.00
Pliers, 1980s	12.00
Pliers, Tooth Puller, Brass	15.00
Tooth Sample Set, Eiber Dental Lab., 125 Teeth On Cards, 1890	75.00

William Long of Steubenville, Ohio, founded the Lonhuda Pottery Company in 1892. In 1900 he moved to Denver, Colorado, and organized the Denver China and Pottery Company. This pottery worked until 1905 when Long moved to New Jersey and founded the Clifton Pottery. Long also worked for Weller Pottery, Roseville Pottery, and American Encaustic Tiling Company.

DENVER, Vase, Black Matte Glaze, 5 In.	150.00
Vase, Green Matte, 6 In.	125.00
Vase, Violets, Leaves, Green, 4 1/2 In.	450.00

Depression glass was an inexpensive glass manufactured in large quantities during the 1920s and early 1930s. It was made in many colors and patterns by dozens of factories in the United States. The name *Depression glass* is a modern one. For more descriptions, history, pictures, and prices of Depression glass, see the book *Kovels' Depression Glass & American Dinnerware Price List.*

ACCORDION PLEATS, see Round Robin

DEPRESSION GLASS, Adam, Ashtray, Green, 4 1/4 In.	8.00
Adam, Bowl, Green, 4 3/4 In.	6.00 To 10.00
Adam, Bowl, Pink, 5 1/2 In.	10.00
Adam, Bowl, Pink, 6 3/4 In.	18.00
Adam, Butter, Cover, Pink	62.00 To 70.00
Adam, Cake Plate, Footed, Pink, 10 In.	15.00
Adam, Cake Plate, Green	17.00
Adam, Candleholder, Pink, 4 In., Pair	65.00
Adam, Cup & Saucer, Green	20.00
Adam, Cup & Saucer, Pink	18.00 To 20.00
Adam, Cup, Pink	15.00
Adam, Grill Plate, Green	12.00
Adam, Pitcher, Pink, 8 In.	27.00
Adam, Plate, Crystal, Square, 9 In.	16.00
Adam, Plate, Pink, 6 In.	2.50
Adam, Plate, Square, Pink, 7 3/4 In.	10.00
Adam, Relish, Divided, Pink	6.00
Adam, Saucer, Green	3.50
Adam, Saucer, Pink	2.50
Adam, Tumbler, Footed, Pink, 5 1/2 In.	33.00 To 45.00
Adam, Water Set, Green, 7 Piece	120.00
Alice, Cup & Saucer, Blue	6.00
Alice, Cup & Saucer, Jadite	2.50 To 4.00
Alice, Plate, Blue, 8 1/2 In.	9.00
Alice, Plate, Jadite, 8 1/2 In.	10.00

AMERICAN BEAUTY, see English Hobnail

American Pioneer, Bowl, Handle, 5 In.	12.00
American Pioneer, Bowl, Handle, Crystal, 9 In.	13.00
American Pioneer, Candlestick, Crystal, 6 1/2 In., Pair	65.00
American Pioneer, Coaster, Pink, 3 1/2 In.	20.00
American Pioneer, Cup & Saucer, Crystal	5.00 To 7.50
American Pioneer, Cup & Saucer, Green	12.00
American Pioneer, Cup & Saucer, Pink	9.50
American Pioneer, Goblet, Crystal, 4 In.	30.00 To 40.00
American Pioneer, Goblet, Crystal, 6 In.	35.00
American Pioneer, Mayonnaise, Green, 4 1/4 In.	65.00
American Pioneer, Plate, Crystal, 8 In.	6.00
American Pioneer, Plate, Pink, 8 In.	5.00 To 6.00
American Pioneer, Sherbet, Crystal, 3 1/2 In.	14.00
American Pioneer, Sugar, Pink, 2 3/4 In.	13.00
American Sweetheart, Bowl, Monax, 6 In.	8.00 To 10.00
American Sweetheart, Bowl, Monax, 9 In.	30.00 To 45.00
American Sweetheart, Bowl, Pink, 9 In.	22.00 To 27.50
American Sweetheart, Bowl, Vegetable, Oval, Pink, 11 In.	30.00
American Sweetheart, Creamer, Monax	6.00

◆◆

Use one type of furniture polish. If you switch from an oil polish to a wax polish, the surface will appear smudged.

◆◆

American Sweetheart, Cup & Saucer, Monax .... 7.50 To 8.50
American Sweetheart, Cup & Saucer, Pink .... 10.00 To 15.00
American Sweetheart, Cup, Red 25.00
American Sweetheart, Plate, Monax, 6 In. 4.00
American Sweetheart, Plate, Monax, 8 In. 6.00
American Sweetheart, Plate, Monax, 9 In. 13.00
American Sweetheart, Plate, Monax, 10 1/4 In. 13.00
American Sweetheart, Plate, Monax, 12 In. .... 9.00 To 12.00
American Sweetheart, Plate, Pink, 12 In. .... 8.00 To 13.00
American Sweetheart, Plate, Pink, 6 In. 2.00
American Sweetheart, Plate, Red, 15 1/2 In. 250.00
American Sweetheart, Platter, Oval, Monax, 13 In. 42.00
American Sweetheart, Salt & Pepper, Monax, Footed 200.00
American Sweetheart, Salt & Pepper, Pink, Footed 250.00
American Sweetheart, Saltshaker, Footed, Monax 105.00
American Sweetheart, Saucer, Monax 2.50
American Sweetheart, Sherbet, Monax, 4 1/4 In. 18.00
American Sweetheart, Soup, Cream, Pink, 4 1/2 In. 35.00
American Sweetheart, Soup, Dish, Pink, 9 1/2 In. .... 28.00 To 35.00
American Sweetheart, Sugar & Creamer, Cover, Red 175.00
American Sweetheart, Sugar & Creamer, Monax .... 10.00 To 15.00
American Sweetheart, Sugar, Monax 6.00
American Sweetheart, Tidbit, 2 Tiers, Monax .... 45.00 To 50.00
  ANGEL FISH, see Sportsman Series
Anniversary, Bowl, Crystal, 4 7/8 In. 2.00
Anniversary, Butter, Cover, Crystal 22.00
Anniversary, Butter, Cover, Pink .... 40.00 To 47.00
Anniversary, Cup & Saucer, Crystal 2.50
Anniversary, Cup & Saucer, Iridescent 4.00
Anniversary, Plate, Crystal, 6 1/4 In. 1.25
Anniversary, Plate, Crystal, 9 In. 5.50
Anniversary, Sugar & Creamer, Cover, Pink 25.00
Anniversary, Sugar & Creamer, Open, Crystal 4.00
Anniversary, Vase, Crystal, 6 1/2 In. 6.00
Anniversary, Wine, Crystal 3.50
Anniversary, Wine, Pink .... 8.00 To 11.00
  APPLE BLOSSOM, see Dogwood
Aunt Polly, Bowl, Handles, Green, 5 1/2 In. 14.00
Aunt Polly, Butter, Cover, Blue .... 70.00 To 125.00
Aunt Polly, Compote, 2 Handles, Iridescent 18.00
Aunt Polly, Creamer, Green 24.00
Aunt Polly, Plate, Blue, 6 In. .... 7.50 To 9.00
Aunt Polly, Salt & Pepper, Blue 195.00
Aunt Polly, Sherbet, Blue .... 7.00 To 12.00
Aunt Polly, Sherbet, Iridescent 11.50
Aunt Polly, Sugar, Cover, Green 35.00
Aunt Polly, Vase, Blue, 6 1/2 In. 45.00
Aurora, Bowl, Blue, 5 3/8 In. 8.00
Aurora, Bowl, Green, 5 3/8 In. 6.50
Aurora, Bowl, Pink, 5 3/8 In. 6.00
Aurora, Cup, Blue 5.00
Aurora, Plate, Blue, 6 1/2 In. 6.00
Aurora, Tumbler, Blue, 4 3/4 In. 14.00
Avocado, Creamer, Footed, Green .... 24.00 To 38.00
Avocado, Cup & Saucer, Green 55.00

Avocado, Plate, Green, 6 3/8 In. .... 10.00 To 13.00
Avocado, Plate, Pink, 6 3/8 In. 10.00
Avocado, Saucer, Pink 20.00
Avocado, Soup, Dish, Crystal 7.00
   B PATTERN, see Dogwood
   BALLERINA, see Cameo
Bamboo Optic, Cup & Saucer, Green 6.50
Bamboo Optic, Cup, Pink .... 4.00 To 5.00
Bamboo Optic, Plate, Green, 12 3/4 In. 10.00
Bamboo Optic, Plate, Server, Center Handle, Green 25.00
Bamboo Optic, Sugar & Creamer, Green 7.50
Bamboo Optic, Sugar, Pink 10.00
   BANDED CHERRY, see Cherry Blossom
   BANDED PETALWARE, see Petalware
   BANDED RAINBOW, see Ring
   BANDED RIBBON, see New Century
   BANDED RINGS, see Ring
Baroque, Bowl, Flared, Yellow, 12 In. .... 25.00 To 27.00
Baroque, Candleholder, Yellow, 5 1/2 In., Pair 28.00
Baroque, Cup & Saucer, Blue 25.00
Baroque, Goblet, Yellow, 6 3/4 In. .... 22.00 To 27.50
Baroque, Plate, Blue, 7 In. .... 9.00 To 14.00
Baroque, Plate, Crystal, 7 In. .... 4.00 To 6.00
Baroque, Punch Bowl Set, Blue, 12 Cups 1500.00
   BASKET, see No. 615
Beaded Block, Bowl, Iridescent, 6 1/2 In. 11.00
Beaded Block, Bowl, Lily, Iridescent, 4 1/2 In. 15.00
Beaded Block, Bowl, Round, Crystal, 4 1/2 In. 15.00
Beaded Block, Creamer, Blue 17.50
Beaded Block, Creamer, Pink 10.00
Beaded Block, Pitcher, Crystal, 5 1/4 In. .... 47.00 To 52.00
Beaded Block, Plate, Iridescent, 7 3/4 In. 10.00
Beaded Block, Plate, Square, Amber, 8 In. 8.00
Beaded Block, Plate, Vaseline, 7 3/4 In. 5.00
Beaded Block, Soup, Cream, Amber 18.00
Beaded Block, Sugar & Creamer, Blue 65.00
Beaded Block, Sugar & Creamer, Vaseline 65.00
Beaded Block, Vase, Blue, 6 In. .... 17.00 To 20.00
Beaded Block, Vase, Pink, 6 In. .... 10.00 To 14.00
   BERWICK, see Boopie
   BEVERAGE WITH SAILBOAT, see White Ship
   BIG RIB, see Manhattan
   BLOCK, see Block Optic
Block Optic, Berry Bowl, Green, 4 1/4 In. 5.00
Block Optic, Butter, Cover, Green 35.00
Block Optic, Creamer, Flat, Pink 10.00
Block Optic, Cup & Saucer, Green .... 9.50 To 13.00
Block Optic, Cup, Green 5.00
Block Optic, Plate, Green, 8 In. 3.00
Block Optic, Plate, Green, 9 In. 13.00
Block Optic, Salt & Pepper, Footed, Green 25.00
Block Optic, Saltshaker, Green 11.00
Block Optic, Sherbet, Green, 3 1/4 In. 4.00
Block Optic, Sherbet, Green, 4 3/4 In. 18.00
Block Optic, Sherbet, Pink, 4 3/4 In. .... 4.00 To 9.00
Block Optic, Sugar & Creamer, Green 12.00
Block Optic, Wine, Crystal, 4 1/2 In. 12.00
Boopie, Tumbler, Footed, Crystal, 3 1/2 In. 2.00
Boopie, Tumbler, Footed, Green, 3 7/8 In. 4.00
Boopie, Tumbler, Footed, Royal Ruby, 3 1/2 In. 5.50
   BORDETTE, see Chinex Classic; Cremax
   BOUQUET & LATTICE, see Normandie
Bowknot, Bowl, Green, 4 1/4 In. 12.00

Bowknot, Plate, Crystal, 7 In. 7.50
Bowknot, Plate, Green, 7 In. 5.00
Bowknot, Tumbler, Green, 5 In. 14.00
    BRIDAL BOUQUET, see No. 615
Bubble, Bowl, Blue, 5 1/4 In. .... 6.00 To 7.00
Bubble, Cup & Saucer, Blue 4.00
Bubble, Grill Plate, Blue, 9 3/8 In. 7.00
Bubble, Plate, Blue, 6 3/4 In. 2.00
Bubble, Plate, Blue, 9 In. 5.00
Bubble, Soup, Dish, Blue .... 7.50 To 9.00
Bubble, Soup, Dish, Crystal 4.00
Bubble, Sugar, Green 7.00
Bubble, Tumbler, Juice, Red, 6 Oz. 6.50
Bubble, Water Set, Red, 9 Piece 90.00
    BULLSEYE, see Bubble
Burple, Bowl, Crystal, 8 1/2 In. 3.00
Burple, Bowl, Green, 4 1/2 In. 2.00
Burple, Cocktail, Green, Crystal Foot 7.50
Burple, Sherbet, Green, Footed, 3 5/8 In. 4.00
    BUTTERFLIES & ROSES, see Flower Garden with Butterflies
    BUTTONS & BOWS, see Holiday
By Cracky, Plate, Octagonal, Amber, 8 In. 2.00
By Cracky, Plate, Octagonal, Green, 6 In. 1.50
By Cracky, Sherbet, Green 3.00
By Cracky, Snack Tray, Amber 4.00
    CABBAGE ROSE, see Sharon
    CABBAGE ROSE WITH SINGLE ARCH, see Rosemary
Cameo, Bowl, Soup, Rimmed, 9 In. 25.00
Cameo, Cookie Jar, Cover, Green .... 35.00 To 38.00
Cameo, Goblet, Footed, Green, 6 In. 35.00
Cameo, Grill Plate, Green, 10 1/2 In. 7.50
Cameo, Pitcher, Green, 5 3/4 In. 135.00
Cameo, Tumbler, Footed, Yellow, 5 In. 12.00
Cameo, Tumbler, Green, 5 In. 18.00
Cameo, Tumbler, Pink, 5 In. 75.00
Cameo, Wine, Green, 4 In. 45.00
Candlewick, Basket, Handle, Crystal, 6 1/2 In. 32.00
Candlewick, Bowl, Handles, Blue, 7 In. 45.00
Candlewick, Bowl, Heart, Handle, Crystal, 6 In. 18.00
Candlewick, Candleholder, 3–Light, Crystal, Pair 95.00
Candlewick, Cup & Saucer, Crystal, After Dinner 14.00
Candlewick, Nappy, Crystal, 5 In. 10.00
Candlewick, Plate, 2 Handles, Black 60.00
Candlewick, Plate, Crystal, 6 In. 6.50
    CAPRICE, see Cambridge Glass category
    CHAIN DAISY, see Adam
Chantilly, Bowl, Tab Handle, Crystal, 11 1/2 In. 30.00
Chantilly, Candlestick, 3–Light, Crystal, 6 In. 38.00
Chantilly, Dish, Mayonnaise, Ladle, Crystal 25.00
Chantilly, Vase, Bud, Crystal, 10 In. 25.00
Chantilly, Wine, Crystal, 2 1/2 Oz. 35.00
Cherry Blossom, Butter, Cover, Pink 45.00
Cherry Blossom, Coaster, Pink 10.00
Cherry Blossom, Cup & Saucer, Green 19.00
Cherry Blossom, Cup, Green 13.50
Cherry Blossom, Pitcher, Flat, Green, 8 In. .... 32.50 To 50.00
Cherry Blossom, Plate, Green, 7 In. 15.00
Cherry Blossom, Platter, Pink, 13 In. 28.00
Cherry Blossom, Sandwich Tray, Pink, 10 1/2 In. 12.50
Cherry Blossom, Saucer, Pink 2.50
Cherry Blossom, Sugar, Cover, Pink 18.00
Cherry Blossom, Tumbler, 4 1/2 In. 22.50
Cherry Blossom, Tumbler, Footed, Green, 4 In. .... 16.00 To 28.00

Cherry Blossom, Tumbler, Footed, Pink, 3 3/4 In. 12.00
Cherry Blossom, Tumbler, Footed, Pink, 4 1/2 In. 22.00
    CHERRY, see Cherry Blossom
    CHERRY–BERRY, see also Strawberry
Cherry–Berry, Bowl, Crystal, 7 1/2 In. 16.00
Cherry–Berry, Bowl, Green, 6 1/4 In. 32.00
Cherry–Berry, Dish, Olive, Green, Handle, 5 In. 32.00
Cherry–Berry, Sherbet, Green 6.00
Chinex Classic, Bowl, Ivory, 5 3/4 In. 4.00
Chinex Classic, Bowl, Ivory, With Decal, 5 3/4 In. 6.00
Chinex Classic, Creamer, Ivory With Decal 6.00
Chinex Classic, Plate, Ivory With Decal, 9 3/4 In. 6.00
Chinex Classic, Plate, Ivory, 9 3/4 In. 5.00
Chinex Classic, Sherbet, Footed, Ivory 8.00
Chinex Classic, Sugar & Creamer, Ivory 12.00
Circle, Champagne, Green .... 9.00 To 9.50
Circle, Creamer, Pink 18.75
Circle, Pitcher, Green, 80 Oz. 30.00
Circle, Plate, Pink, 8 1/4 In. 11.50
Circle, Sherbet, Crystal, Green Stem 12.00
Circle, Sherbet, Green, 3 1/8 In. 5.50
    CIRCULAR RIBS, see Circle
    CLASSIC, see Chinex Classic
    CLEO, see Cambridge Glass category
Cloverleaf, Creamer, Yellow 11.00
Cloverleaf, Cup & Saucer, Pink 6.00
Cloverleaf, Sherbet, Pink 7.50
Colonial, Butter, Cover, Green 30.00
Colonial, Tumbler, Crystal, 4 In. 10.00
Columbia, Butter, Cover, Crystal 15.00
Columbia, Chop Plate, Crystal, 11 In. 6.00
Columbia, Plate, Crystal, 6 In. 2.00
Columbia, Plate, Crystal, 9 1/2 In. 6.00
Columbia, Saucer, Crystal 2.00
    CRISS CROSS, see X Design
    CUBE, see Cubist
Cubist, Butter, Cover, Green 75.00
Cubist, Candy Jar, Cover, Footed, Pink 12.00
Cubist, Cup & Saucer, Green 7.50
Cubist, Plate, Green, 8 In. 3.50
Cubist, Sherbet, Footed, Green 6.00
Cubist, Sherbet, Footed, Pink 4.00
Cubist, Sugar & Creamer, Pink, 2 In. 4.00
Cubist, Sugar, Pink, 2 In. 2.50
Cubist, Sugar, Pink, 3 In. 3.00
Cupid, Creamer, Green 35.00
    DAISY, see No. 620
    DAISY PETALS, see Petalware
    DANCING GIRL, see Cameo
Della Robbia, Bowl, Crystal, 5 1/2 In. 4.00
Della Robbia, Butter, Cover, Crystal 18.00
Della Robbia, Cup & Saucer, Crystal 6.00
Della Robbia, Plate, Crystal, 10 1/2 In. 25.00
Della Robbia, Sugar & Creamer, Crystal 12.00
    DIAMOND, see Windsor
    DIAMOND PATTERN, see Miss America
    DIAMOND POINT, see Petalware
Diamond Quilted, Sherbet, Green 5.00
Dogwood, Bowl, Pink, 5 1/2 In. 16.50
Dogwood, Bowl, Pink, 8 1/2 In. 40.00
Dogwood, Creamer, Pink 13.75
Dogwood, Cup & Saucer, Pink, Thick 15.00
Dogwood, Cup & Saucer, Pink, Thin 14.00

Dogwood, Cup, Pink 9.50
Dogwood, Grill Plate, Pink, 10 1/2 In. .... 12.00 To 13.50
Dogwood, Plate, Pink, 12 In. 18.50
Dogwood, Plate, Pink, 6 In. 3.00
Dogwood, Plate, Pink, 8 In. 5.00
Dogwood, Platter, Oval, Pink, 12 In. 325.00
Dogwood, Saucer, Pink 3.00
Dogwood, Sugar & Creamer, Pink 17.50
Dogwood, Sugar, Pink 10.00
Doric & Pansy, Cup & Saucer, Ultramarine 20.00
Doric & Pansy, Plate, Ultramarine, 6 In. 7.00
    DORIC WITH PANSY, see Doric & Pansy
Doric, Butter, Cover, Green 55.00
Doric, Salt & Pepper, Green 15.00
    DOUBLE SHIELD, see Mt. Pleasant
    DOUBLE SWIRL, see Swirl
    DRAPE & TASSEL, see Princess
    DUTCH ROSE, see Rosemary
    EARLY AMERICAN ROCK CRYSTAL, see Rock Crystal
    ENGLISH HOBNAIL, see also Miss America
English Hobnail, Bowl, Crystal, 4 1/2 In. 6.00
English Hobnail, Box, Cigarette, Crystal 25.00
English Hobnail, Candy Dish, 15 In. 50.00
English Hobnail, Cruet Set, Blue, 3 Piece 59.00
English Hobnail, Goblet, Crystal, 3 Oz. 15.00
English Hobnail, Plate, Crystal, 6 In. 4.00
English Hobnail, Salt & Pepper, Crystal 60.00
English Hobnail, Saltshaker, Crystal 22.50
English Hobnail, Sherbet, Crystal 3.50
English Hobnail, Sherbet, Pink 12.00
English Hobnail, Sugar & Creamer, Red 17.50
English Hobnail, Tumbler, Crystal, 9 Oz. 8.50
    EVERGLADE, see Cambridge Glass category
    FAN & FEATHER, see Adam
Federal, Refrigerator, Amber, 8 x 8 In. 12.00
    FINE RIB, see Homespun
Fire–King, Bowl, Measuring, Blue, 16 Oz. 27.50
Fire–King, Butter, Jadite 5.00
Fire–King, Casserole, Cover, Blue, Individual 10.00
Fire–King, Measuring Cup, Ivory 10.00
Fire–King, Mixing Bowl, Blue, 6 7/8 In. 9.00
Fire–King, Mixing Bowl, Jadite, 8 In. 6.00
    FLAT DIAMOND, see Diamond Quilted
Floragold, Bowl, Crystal, 4 1/2 In. 3.50
Floragold, Bowl, Iridescent, Ruffled, 5 1/2 In. 7.50
Floragold, Bowl, Iridescent, Ruffled, 9 1/2 In. 7.50
Floragold, Cup & Saucer, Iridescent 12.00
Floragold, Cup, Crystal 5.00
Floragold, Pitcher, Iridescent, 64 Oz. .... 25.00 To 28.00
Floragold, Plate, Iridescent, 8 1/2 In. 22.00
Floragold, Platter, Pink, 11 1/4 In. 20.00
Floragold, Sugar, Cover, Iridescent 13.00
    FLORAL RIM, see Vitrock
Floral, Bowl, Green, Oval, 9 In. 12.00
Floral, Creamer, Flat, Green ....8.00 To 10.00
Floral, Salt & Pepper, Footed, Green 42.00
Floral, Sugar, Green 6.00
Florentine No. 1, Creamer 5.00
Florentine No. 1, Creamer, Pink 7.50
Florentine No. 1, Cup, Yellow 6.00
Florentine No. 1, Sherbet, Green 5.50
Florentine No. 1, Sugar, Pink, Ruffled 10.00
Florentine No. 2, Ashtray, Yellow 16.00

Florentine No. 2, Grill Plate, Yellow, 10 1/4 In. 8.00
Florentine No. 2, Plate, Green, 10 In. 7.50
Florentine No. 2, Plate, Green, 8 1/2 In. 5.00
Florentine No. 2, Relish, 3 Sections, Pink 14.00
Florentine No. 2, Sherbet, Green, 6 In. 2.00
Florentine No. 2, Soup, Cream, Green 9.00
Florentine No. 2, Soup, Cream, Pink 10.00
Florentine No. 2, Sugar & Creamer, Yellow 15.00
Florentine No. 2, Tumbler, Footed, Green, 4 1/2 In. 15.00
Florentine No. 2, Tumbler, Yellow, 4 In. 14.00
    FLOWER & LEAF BAND, see Indiana Custard
    FLOWER BASKET, see No. 615
    FLOWER GARDEN, see Flower Garden with Butterflies
Flower Garden With Butterflies, Bonbon, Black, 6 5/8 In. 350.00
Flower Garden With Butterflies, Candy Dish, Cover, Blue 150.00
    FLOWER RIM, see Vitrock
Forest Green, Cup & Saucer, Green 3.50
Forest Green, Cup, Green 6.50
Forest Green, Pitcher, Green, 22 Oz. 15.00
Forest Green, Pitcher, Green, 3 Qt. 20.00
Forest Green, Punch Set, Green, 13 Piece 27.00
Forest Green, Punch Set, Green, 18 Piece 70.00
Fortune, Bowl, Handle, Pink, 4 1/2 In. 2.25
Fortune, Bowl, Pink, 4 In. 3.00
Fortune, Tumbler, Pink, 3 1/2 In. 5.00
    FROSTED BLOCK, see Beaded Block
Fruits, Cup & Saucer, Green 6.00
Fruits, Plate, Pink, 8 In. 4.00
Fruits, Sherbet, Green 9.00
Georgian, Sugar, Cover, Green, 4 In. 40.00
    GLADIOLI, see Royal Lace
    GLORIA, see Cambridge Glass category
    HAIRPIN, see Newport
    HANGING BASKET, see No. 615
Harp, Cake Plate, Footed, Crystal, Gold Trim, 9 In. 14.00
Harp, Cake Stand, Crystal, 9 In. 12.00
Harp, Coaster Set, Crystal, 4 Piece 12.50
Harp, Plate, Crystal, 7 In. 4.50
Harp, Tray, Crystal, Handle 18.00
Heritage, Bowl, Crystal, 10 1/2 In. 10.00
Heritage, Creamer, Footed, Crystal 18.00
Heritage, Cup & Saucer, Crystal 4.00
Heritage, Plate, Crystal, 9 1/4 In. 7.00
    HEX OPTIC, see Hexagon Optic
Hexagon Optic, Pitcher, Green, 5 In. 10.00
Hexagon Optic, Salt & Pepper, Green 12.00
Hexagon Optic, Tumbler, Footed, Iridescent, 5 3/4 In. 5.00
Hexagon Optic, Whiskey, Green, 2 In. 12.00
    HEXAGON TRIPLE BAND, see Colony
    HINGE, see Patrician
    HOBNAIL, see also Moonstone
Hobnail, Cup & Saucer, Pink 5.00
Hobnail, Goblet, Crystal, 13 Oz. 14.50
Hobnail, Plate, Pink, 8 1/2 In. 1.50
Holiday, Pitcher, Pink, 18 Oz. 45.00
Homespun, Cup, Pink 5.00
Homespun, Plate, Pink, 9 1/4 In. 9.50
Homespun, Tumbler, Flared Top, Pink, 4 In. 8.00
Homespun, Tumbler, Pink, 5 1/4 In. 20.00
    HONEYCOMB, see Hexagon Optic
    HORIZONTAL FINE RIB, see Manhattan
    HORIZONTAL RIBBED, see Manhattan
    HORIZONTAL ROUNDED BIG RIB, see Manhattan

HORIZONTAL SHARP BIG RIB, see Manhattan
HORSESHOE, see No. 612
Indiana Custard, Bowl, Ivory, 4 7/8 In. 4.00
Indiana Custard, Creamer, Ivory 10.00
Indiana Custard, Sugar & Creamer, Cover, Ivory 32.50
     IRIS & HERRINGBONE, see Iris
Iris, Bowl, Crystal, 11 1/2 In. 10.00
Iris, Bowl, Crystal, 5 In. 7.00
Iris, Bowl, Crystal, Ruffled, 9 1/2 In. 20.00
Iris, Candy Jar, Cover, Crystal 75.00
Iris, Goblet, Iridescent, 4 In. 16.00
Iris, Pitcher, Crystal, 9 1/2 In. 22.00
Iris, Plate, Crystal, 8 In. 35.00
Iris, Sherbet, Iridescent, 2 1/2 In. 4.00
Iris, Sugar & Creamer, Crystal 21.00
Iris, Tumbler, Footed, Crystal, 6 In. 13.50
Iris, Tumbler, Footed, Iridescent, 6 In. 14.00
     JADITE, see also Jane–Ray
Jadite, Bowl, Batter, Green 20.00
Jadite, Bowl, Green, 4 1/4 In. 2.50
Jadite, Dish, Refrigerator, Cover 10.00
Jadite, Eggcup, Green 4.50
     JANE–RAY, see also Jadite
Jane–Ray, Bowl, Jadite, 6 In. 4.00
Jane–Ray, Cup & Saucer, Jadite 2.00
Jane–Ray, Plate, Jadite, 10 In. 3.50
Jubilee, Cake Tray, Handle, Yellow, 11 In. 24.00
Jubilee, Mayonnaise Set, Yellow, 3 Piece 195.00
Jubilee, Plate, Yellow, 7 In. 12.00
Jubilee, Sugar & Creamer, Yellow 35.00
     KATY BLUE, see Lace Edge
     KNIFE & FORK, see Colonial
     LACE EDGE, see also Queen Mary
Lace Edge, Bowl, 3–Footed, Crystal, 10 1/2 In. 152.00
Lace Edge, Bowl, 3–Footed, Pink, 10 1/2 In. 110.00
Lace Edge, Butter, Cover, Pink 40.00
Lace Edge, Candy Jar, Cover, Ribbed, Crystal 45.00

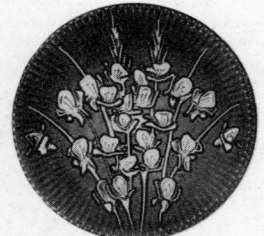

Depression glass, Iris, Beaded Edge

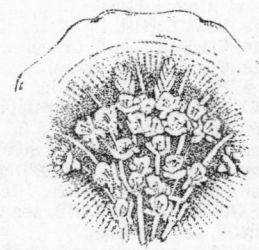

Depression glass, Iris, Ruffled Edge

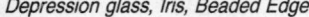

White water spots on table tops can be a problem. Mix 2 table-spoons of white vinegar in a pint of mineral oil. Rub on the table top. Test a small spot before starting because a few finishes may not accept this mixture.

Lace Edge, Grill Plate, Pink, 10 1/2 In. 6.00
Lace Edge, Plate, Crystal, 8 1/4 In. 8.00
Lace Edge, Relish, 3 Sections, Pink, 7 1/2 In. 40.00
    LACY DAISY, see No. 618
Lake Como, Bowl, Opaque White, 6 In. 15.00
Lake Como, Salt & Pepper, Opaque White 30.00
Lake Como, Soup, Dish, Opaque White 100.00
Laurel, Bowl, Jade, 5 In. 3.00
Laurel, Creamer, Jade .... 5.00 To 6.50
Laurel, Cup, Jade 4.50
Laurel, Saucer, Ivory 2.00
Laurel, Sherbet, Jade 4.00
Laurel, Tumbler, Ivory, 4 1/2 In. 24.00
Lido, Cocktail, Green 25.00
Lido, Compote, Crystal, 5 1/2 In. 20.00
Lido, Sugar & Creamer, Crystal, Large 30.00
    LILY MEDALLION, see American Sweetheart
    LINCOLN DRAPE, see Princess
Lincoln Inn, Cup & Saucer, Blue 30.00
Lincoln Inn, Tumbler, Ruby, Footed, 4 Oz. 12.00
    LINE 300, see Peacock & Wild Rose
    LITTLE HOSTESS, see Moderntone Little Hostess
    LOOP, see Lace Edge
    LORAIN, see No. 615
    LORNA, see Cambridge Glass category
    LOUISA, see Floragold
    LOVEBIRDS, see Georgian
    LYDIA RAY, see New Century
MacHob, Pitcher, Crystal, 75 Oz. 30.00
Madrid, Bowl, Pink, 5 In. 4.00
Madrid, Bowl, Vegetable, Oval, Amber, 10 In. 10.00
Madrid, Creamer, Amber 3.40
Madrid, Jell-O Mold, Amber, 2 1/8 In. 8.00
Madrid, Pitcher, Ice Lip, Amber, 8 1/2 In. 50.00
Madrid, Plate, Blue, 7 1/2 In. 20.00
Madrid, Soup, Dish, Amber 8.00
Madrid, Soup, Dish, Amber, 6 Piece 28.00
Madrid, Tumbler, Amber, 5 1/2 In. .... 12.50 To 15.00
    MAGNOLIA, see Dogwood
Manhattan, Bowl, Open Handles, Pink, 9 1/2 In. 20.00
Manhattan, Candy Dish, Pink 8.00
Manhattan, Compote, Pink, 5 3/4 In. 35.00
Manhattan, Sugar, Pink 5.00
Manhattan, Tray, 5 Inserts, Green, 14 In. 45.00
Manhattan, Vase, Crystal, 8 In. 12.00
Manhattan, Wine, Crystal, 3 1/2 In. 5.00
    MANY WINDOWS, see Roulette

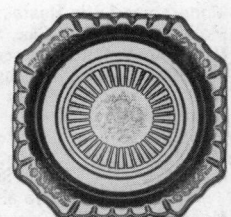

Depression glass, Laurel   *Depression glass, Madrid*   *Depression glass,*
Mayfair Open Rose

Depression glass, Miss America

Depression glass, Moderntone

MAYFAIR, see Mayfair Open Rose

Mayfair Federal, Bowl, Vegetable, Oval, 10 In.	20.00
Mayfair Federal, Cup & Saucer, Amber	8.00
Mayfair Federal, Grill Plate, Crystal	11.00
Mayfair Open Rose, Bowl, Pink, 7 In.	15.00
Mayfair Open Rose, Candy Dish, Cover, Pink Frosted	40.00
Mayfair Open Rose, Celery, Divided, Blue, 10 In.	35.00
Mayfair Open Rose, Cup, Blue	35.00
Mayfair Open Rose, Cup, Pink	9.00
Mayfair Open Rose, Decanter Set, Pink, 6 Piece	200.00
Mayfair Open Rose, Plate, Center Handle, Green, 12 In.	20.00
Mayfair Open Rose, Plate, Center Handle, Oval, Blue, 12 In.	45.00

MEADOW FLOWER, see No. 618
MEANDERING VINE, see Madrid
MISS AMERICA, see also English Hobnail

Miss America, Bowl, Green, 6 1/4 In.	10.00
Miss America, Coaster, Crystal, 5 3/4 In.	11.00
Miss America, Cup, Green	12.50
Miss America, Goblet, Crystal, 4 3/4 In.	12.00
Miss America, Grill Plate, 10 1/4 In.	7.00
Miss America, Salt & Pepper, Pink	50.00
Miss America, Saucer, Green	15.00
Miss America, Tumbler, Green, 4 1/2 In.	16.00
Miss America, Tumbler, Pink, 5 3/4 In.	47.50

MODERNE ART, see Tea Room

Moderntone Little Hostess, Plates, Set of 5	15.00
Moderntone Little Hostess, Tea Set, Multicolored, 16 Pc.	45.00
Moderntone, Cobalt Blue, Sugar & Creamer	16.50
Moderntone, Cup & Saucer, Amethyst	9.00
Moderntone, Plate, Amethyst, 10 1/2 In.	15.00
Moderntone, Plate, Cobalt Blue, 7 3/4 In.	6.00
Moderntone, Tumbler, Cobalt Blue, 9 Oz.	22.00
Moondrops, Cocktail Shaker, Amber	20.00
Moondrops, Cup & Saucer, Amber	9.50
Moondrops, Wine, Metal Stem, Ruby, 5 1/2 In.	12.00

MOONSTONE, see also Hobnail

Moonstone, Goblet, Crystal, 10 Oz.	13.00

MT. VERNON, see Cambridge Glass category

Mt. Pleasant, Bowl, 2 Handles, Black, Square, 8 In.	22.00
Mt. Pleasant, Candlesticks, 2–Light, Black, Pair	30.00
Mt. Pleasant, Dish, Mayonnaise, Blue, 3–Footed, 5 1/2 In.	24.00

Depression glass, Mt. Pleasant   Depression glass, No. 612   Depression glass, Normandie

Mt. Pleasant, Platter, Blue, 2 Handles, 10 In. 45.00
    NAUTILUS, see Cambridge Glass category
Navarre, Champagne, Blue, 5 5/8 In. 24.00
Navarre, Plate, Crystal, 8 1/2 In. 17.50
Navarre, Tumbler, Blue, 5 7/8 In. 27.50
    NEW CENTURY, see also Ovide
New Century, Cup, Amethyst 15.00
New Century, Plate, Crystal, 8 1/2 In. 7.00
New Century, Salt & Pepper, Green 20.00
New Century, Tumbler, Blue, 9 Oz. 18.00
Newport, Creamer, Cobalt Blue 8.00
Newport, Plate, Amethyst, 11 1/2 In. 12.00
Newport, Plate, Amethyst, 8 1/2 In. 8.00
Newport, Plate, Cobalt Blue, 8 1/2 In. 3.25
Newport, Soup, Dish, Cobalt Blue 12.00
Newport, Sugar, Cobalt Blue 8.00
Newport, Sugar, White 8.00
Newport, Sugar, White, Platonite 5.00
Newport, Tumbler, Amethyst, 4 1/2 In. 21.00
    NO. 601, see Avocado
No. 612, Cup & Saucer, Green .... 8.00 To 9.00
No. 612, Cup, Green 6.50
No. 612, Grill Plate, Green, 11 In. 50.00
No. 612, Relish, 3 Sections, Footed, Yellow 29.00
No. 612, Sugar & Creamer, Green 15.00
No. 615, Bowl, Green, Deep, 8 In. 70.00
No. 615, Bowl, Yellow, 6 In. 35.00
No. 615, Compote, Crystal 20.00
No. 615, Creamer, Footed, Yellow 16.00
No. 615, Sugar, Footed, Yellow 16.00
No. 616, Cup, Green 8.00
No. 618, Cake Plate, Handle, Crystal, 10 In. 38.00
No. 618, Creamer, Amber 10.00
No. 620, Bowl, Vegetable, Amber, Oval, 10 In. 12.00
No. 620, Cup & Saucer, Green 6.00
No. 620, Cup, Amber 4.50
No. 620, Plate, Amber, 11 1/2 In. 9.00
No. 620, Plate, Amber, 6 In. 1.75
No. 620, Plate, Amber, 7 3/8 In. 5.00
No. 620, Plate, Sandwich, Crystal 6.00
No. 620, Soup, Cream, Amber .... 6.00 To 8.00
No. 620, Sugar & Creamer, Green 14.00
No. 620, Tumbler, Footed, Amber, 12 Oz. 25.00
    NO. 622, see Pretzel
Normandie, Bowl, Iridescent, 5 In. 4.00
Normandie, Creamer, Iridescent 4.00
Normandie, Creamer, Iridescent 6.50

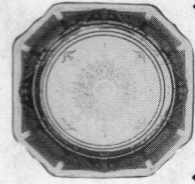

♦♦♦♦♦♦♦♦♦♦♦♦♦♦♦♦♦♦♦♦♦♦♦♦♦

American brilliant period cut
glass will fluoresce a pale lime
green under a black light. Newly
cut glass will look purple–pink
under the same light.

♦♦♦♦♦♦♦♦♦♦♦♦♦♦♦♦♦♦♦♦♦♦♦♦♦

Depression glass,   *Depression glass,*
Patrician   *Princess*

Normandie, Cup, Iridescent	5.00
Normandie, Grill Plate, Iridescent, 11 In.	12.00
Normandie, Plate, Iridescent, 6 In.	2.00
Normandie, Saucer, Iridescent	1.50 To 3.00
Normandie, Sugar, Iridescent	6.50
Old Cafe, Bowl, Pink, 5 In.	2.50
Old Cafe, Candy Dish, Ruby, 8 In.	10.00

OLD FLORENTINE, see Florentine No. 1
OPALESCENT HOBNAIL, see Moonstone
OPEN LACE, see Lace Edge
OPEN ROSE, see Mayfair Open Rose
OPEN SCALLOP, see Lace Edge
OPTIC DESIGN, see Raindrops
ORANGE BLOSSOM, see also Indiana Custard
OREGON GRAPE, see Woolworth
ORIENTAL POPPY, see Florentine No. 2
OVIDE, see also New Century

Ovide, Bowl, Green, 5 In.	2.50
Ovide, Salt & Pepper, White	7.00
Ovide, Saucer, Black	4.00
Oyster & Pearl, Bowl, Deep, Ruby, 6 1/2 In.	14.00
Oyster & Pearl, Bowl, Handle, Ruby, 5 1/2 In.	9.00
Oyster & Pearl, Bowl, Heart, Fired-On Green, 5 1/4 In.	5.00

PANEL, see Sheraton
PANELED ASTER, see Madrid
PANELED CHERRY BLOSSOM, see Cherry Blossom
PANSY & DORIC, see Doric & Pansy
PARROT, see Sylvan

Parrot, Butter, Green	35.00
Parrot, Sugar, Cover	100.00
Patrician, Cookie Jar, Cover, Crystal	60.00
Patrician, Cup & Saucer, Green	12.00
Patrician, Cup, Pink	6.00
Patrician, Dish, Jam, Green, 6 1/2 In.	25.00
Patrician, Grill Plate, Crystal, 10 1/2 In.	10.00
Patrician, Plate, Amber, 10 1/2 In.	4.00
Patrician, Plate, Green, 9 In.	6.00
Patrician, Platter, Amber, 11 1/2 In.	18.50
Patrician, Salt & Pepper, Amber	42.00
Patrician, Sherbet, Amber	6.50
Patrician, Tumbler, Amber, 4 In.	16.00
Patrician, Tumbler, Crystal, 4 In.	22.00

PEACOCK & ROSE, see Peacock & Wild Rose

Peacock & Wild Rose, Plate, 2 Handles, Pink, 10 3/8 In.	32.00

PEBBLE OPTIC, see Raindrops
PETAL, see Petalware
PETAL SWIRL, see Swirl

Petalware, Bowl, Crystal, 9 In. 7.00
Petalware, Cup & Saucer, Cremax, Gold Trim 5.00
Petalware, Juice Set, Pink, 5 Piece 65.00
Petalware, Plate, Cremax, 11 In. 6.50
    PINEAPPLE & FLORAL, see No. 618
    PINWHEEL, see Sierra
Pinwheel, Salt & Pepper, Pink 30.00
    POINSETTIA, see Floral
    POPPY NO. 1, see Florentine No. 1
    POPPY NO. 2, see Florentine No. 2
Pretzel, Bowl, Crystal, 7 1/2 In. 7.00
Pretzel, Cup & Saucer, Crystal 4.50
Pretzel, Plate, Crystal, 9 3/8 In. 5.00
Primo, Cup & Saucer, Green 8.00
Primo, Grill Plate, Green, 10 In. 7.50
Primo, Tumbler, Yellow, 5 3/4 In. 13.00
    PRIMUS, see Madrid
Princess, Bowl, Oval, Green, 10 In. 20.00
Princess, Candy Dish, Cover, Green 40.00
Princess, Cup & Saucer, Green 12.00
Princess, Cup, Green 7.00
Princess, Cup, Topaz 4.50
Princess, Cup, Yellow 5.00
Princess, Grill Late, Yellow, 10 1/2 In. 8.00
Princess, Plate, Green, 5 1/2 In. .... 4.00 To 6.00
Princess, Saltshaker, Green 12.00
Princess, Sherbet, Pink 11.00
    PRISMATIC LINE, see Queen Mary
    PROVINCIAL, see Bubble
    QUEEN MARY, see also Lace Edge
Queen Mary, Bowl, Pink, 6 In. 15.00
Queen Mary, Bowl, Pink, 7 In. 20.00
Queen Mary, Cigarette Jar, Crystal, 2 x 3 In. 5.00
Queen Mary, Creamer, Crystal, ... 3.50
Queen Mary, Cup, Pink 2.75
Queen Mary, Plate, Crystal, 12 In. 5.00
Radiance, Vase, Crimped, Cobalt Blue, 7 In. 8.00
Raindrops, Cup, Crystal 4.00
Raindrops, Plate, Sherbet, Green 1.50
    RASPBERRY BAND, see Laurel
    RIBBED, see Manhattan
    RIBBON CANDY, see Pretzel
Ribbon, Plate, Green, 8 In. 3.00
Ribbon, Sherbet, Footed, Crystal 4.50
Ribbon, Tumbler, Green, 6 In. 16.00
Ring, Creamer, Footed, Crystal 2.50
Ring, Sugar, Footed, Crystal 4.50
Ring–Ding, Bowl, Crystal, 5 In. 3.00
Ring–Ding, Whiskey, Crystal 4.50
Rock Crystal, Bowl, Footed, Green, 10 1/2 In. 48.00
Rock Crystal, Candlestick, Crystal, 5 1/2 In., Pair 30.00
Rock Crystal, Cocktail, Tall, Crystal, 3 1/2 Oz. 10.00
Rock Crystal, Pickle, Crystal, 7 In. 15.00
Rock Crystal, Plate, Crystal, 8 1/2 In. 5.00
Rock Crystal, Plate, Crystal, 10 1/2 In. 20.00
Rock Crystal, Plate, Red, 7 1/2 In. 15.00
Rock Crystal, Relish, 6 Parts, Crystal, 14 In. .... 22.00 To 25.00
Rock Crystal, Saucer, Crystal 4.00
Rock Crystal, Sherbet, Green 15.00
Rock Crystal, Spooner, Crystal, 7 In. 16.00
Rock Crystal, Wine, Red, 2 Oz. 35.00
Rose Cameo, Tumbler, Green, 5 In. .... 9.00 To 12.00
    ROSE LACE, see Royal Lace

◆◆◆

You can't win! Homes in cold areas with central heating must be humidified to keep the furniture from drying and cracking. Homes in warm areas must be dehumidified to keep condensation from rotting the wood.

◆◆◆

ROSEMARY, see also Mayfair Federal
Rosemary, Soup, Cream, Amber	9.00
Roulette, Cup, Green	2.75
Roulette, Plate, Green, 6 In.	1.75
Roulette, Tumbler, Footed, Green, 5 1/2 In.	15.00 To 17.50
Round Robin, Cup & Saucer, Green	6.00
Round Robin, Plate, Iridescent, 6 In.	1.50
Royal Lace, Bowl, Footed, Blue, 10 In.	55.00
Royal Lace, Butter, Cover, Amethyst	60.00
Royal Lace, Butter, Cover, Green	120.00
Royal Lace, Cookie Jar, Green	60.00
Royal Lace, Cookie Jar, Pink	45.00
Royal Lace, Pitcher, Water, Pink, 8 1/2 In.	60.00
Royal Lace, Salt & Pepper, Amethyst	45.00
Royal Lace, Salt & Pepper, Crystal	39.00
Royal Lace, Sugar & Creamer, Amethyst	43.00
Royal Lace, Water Pitcher, Pink, 8 In.	60.00
Royal Lace, Water Set, Crystal, 7 Piece	100.00
Royal Lace, Water Set, Pink, 7 Piece	115.00
Royal Ruby, Cup	10.00
RUSSIAN, see Holiday	
S Pattern, Cup	3.00
S Pattern, Cup & Saucer, Crystal	3.50
S Pattern, Cup & Saucer, Gold Band	3.50
S Pattern, Plate, Amber, 8 1/4 In.	2.50
S Pattern, Sugar, Platinum Band	4.00
S Pattern, Tumbler, 4 3/4 In.	3.00
SAIL BOAT, see White Ship	
SAILING SHIP, see White Ship	
Sandwich Anchor Hocking, Bowl, Crystal, 9 In.	15.00
Sandwich Anchor Hocking, Cookie Jar, Cover, Forest Green	16.00
Sandwich Anchor Hocking, Cup, Amber	3.00
Sandwich Anchor Hocking, Custard Cup, Crystal	2.50
Sandwich Anchor Hocking, Plate, Gold, 9 In.	5.00
Sandwich Anchor Hocking, Punch Set, Crystal, 11 Piece	35.00
Sandwich Anchor Hocking, Tumbler, 9 Oz.	4.50 To 6.00
Sandwich Indiana, Bowl, Amber, 4 1/4 In.	4.00

Depression glass, Royal Lace

Depression glass, Sharon

Depression glass, Swirl

Sandwich Indiana, Butter, Crystal 85.00
Sandwich Indiana, Cup 12.00
Sandwich Indiana, Plate, Oval, Crystal, 8 In. 12.00
Sandwich Indiana, Snack Plate, Cup, Crystal, Oval 5.00
Sandwich Indiana, Sugar & Creamer, Red 50.00
Sandwich Indiana, Tumbler, Crystal, Footed, 12 Oz. 22.00
    SAWTOOTH, see English Hobnail
    SHAMROCK, see Cloverleaf
Sharon, Bowl, Amber, 6 In. 11.00
Sharon, Bowl, Amber, 8 1/2 In. .... 4.00 To 7.50
Sharon, Butter, Cover, Green 68.00
Sharon, Candy Dish, Yellow 25.00
Sharon, Creamer, Pink .... 10.00 To 13.00
Sharon, Cup, Pink 10.00
Sharon, Plate, Amber, 9 1/2 In. 7.00
Sharon, Plate, Green, 6 In. 4.50
Sharon, Plate, Pink, 6 In. 2.00
Sharon, Saucer, Pink 2.00
Sharon, Sugar, Cover, Green 35.00
    SHELL, see Petalware
Sierra, Bowl, Green, 8 1/2 In. 14.00
Sierra, Bowl, Pink, 5 1/2 In. 7.00
Sierra, Butter, Cover, Green 50.00
Sierra, Creamer, Green 14.50
Sierra, Tray, Serving, Pink, 10 1/2 In. 9.00
    SMOCKING, see Windsor
    SNOWFLAKE, see Doric
    SPIRAL OPTIC, see Spiral
Spiral, Ice Bucket, Green 35.00
Spiral, Sherbet, Green 4.00
Spiral, Sherbet, Pink 3.00
    SPOKE, see Patrician
    SPORTSMAN SERIES, see also White Ship; Windmill
Sportsman Series, Tumbler, Fish, 5 Oz. 6.00
Starlight, Sherbet, Crystal 4.00
Starlight, Sugar, Crystal 4.00
    STIPPLED ROSE BAND, see S Pattern
    STRAWBERRY, see also Cherry–Berry
Strawberry, Bowl, Green, 7 1/2 In. 31.50
Strawberry, Pitcher, Pink, 7 3/4 In. 100.00
Sunflower, Cake Plate, Pink, 10 In. 9.00
Sunflower, Sugar, Cover, Green 13.50
    SWEET PEAR, see Avocado
Swirl, Bowl, Ultramarine, 5 1/4 In. 7.00
Swirl, Candy Dish, Open, Ultramarine 10.00
Swirl, Platter, Oval, Ice Blue, 12 In. 24.00
Swirl, Salt & Pepper, Ultramarine 19.00
Swirl, Sugar & Creamer, Delphite 14.00
Swirl, Sugar, Ultramarine 8.00
Swirl, Vase, Footed, Ultramarine, 8 1/2 In. 18.00
Swirl, Vase, Ultramarine, 8 1/2 In. 18.00
    SWIRLED BIG RIB, see Spiral
Sylvan, Plate, Green, 7 1/2 In. 17.00
Sylvan, Sherbet, Green 17.00
    TASSELL, see Princess
Tea Room, Goblet, Pink, 9 Oz. 50.00
Tea Room, Ice Bucket, Green 38.00
Tea Room, Sugar & Creamer, Amber 185.00
Tea Room, Sugar, Footed, Green, 4 1/2 In. 13.00
Tea Room, Sugar, Pink, 4 In. 13.00
Tea Room, Vase, Ruffled, Crystal, 9 1/2 In. .... 10.00 To 13.00
Thistle, Bowl, Pink, 10 1/2 In. 190.00
Thistle, Cake Plate, Green, 13 In. 80.00

Thistle, Plate, Green, 8 In.	12.00
Thistle, Saucer, Pink	8.00
THREE PARROT, see Sylvan	
TIERED SEMI OPTIC, see Line 191	
TREE OF LIFE, see Craquel	
Tulip, Console Set, Amethyst, 3 Piece	68.00
Tulip, Sugar, Green	10.00
VERNON, see No. 616	
VERTICAL RIBBED, see Queen Mary	
Victory, Cup & Saucer, Green	9.00
Victory, Plate, Amber, 7 In.	5.00
Victory, Plate, Black, 8 In.	11.00
Victory, Plate, Pink, 9 In.	15.00
Vitrock, Cup, White	3.25
Vitrock, Soup, Dish, White, 9 In.	15.00
VIVID BANDS, see Petalware	
WAFFLE, see Waterford	
WAFFLE KEG, see Victorian	
Waterford, Bowl, Pink, 4 3/4 In.	9.00
Waterford, Cake Plate, Handles, 10 1/4 In.	5.00
Waterford, Goblet, Pink, 5 1/2 In.	60.00
Waterford, Plate, Salad, Crystal	1.50
Waterford, Salt & Pepper, Crystal	5.50
Waterford, Sugar & Creamer, Crystal	5.00
Waterford, Sugar, Cover, Crystal	2.75
Waterford, Tumbler, Footed, Pink, 4 7/8 In.	14.00
WEDDING BAND, see Moderntone	
Whirly–Twirly, Pitcher, Green, 3 Qt.	27.00
Whirly–Twirly, Tumbler, Green, 12 Oz.	7.00
WHITE SAIL, see White Ship	
White Ship, Cocktail Shaker, Blue, Stirrer	30.00
White Ship, Plate, Blue, 9 In.	30.00
White Ship, Tumbler, Blue, 4 7/8 In.	10.00
White Ship, Tumbler, Blue, 5 Oz.	6.00
WILD ROSE, see Dogwood	
WILD ROSE WITH APPLE BLOSSOM, see Flower Garden with Butterflies	
WILDFLOWER, see No. 618	
WINDSOR DIAMOND, see Windsor	
Windsor, Bowl, Boat Shape, 7 x 11 3/4 In.	10.00
Windsor, Candlestick, 3 In., Pair	12.50
Windsor, Cup, Pink	4.00 To 6.00
Windsor, Tumbler, Crystal, 7 1/4 In.	6.00
Windsor, Tumbler, Pink, 4 In.	10.00
WINGED MEDALLION, see Madrid	
X Design, Butter, Cover, Crystal, 1 Lb.	15.00
X Design, Butter, Cover, Green, 1 Lb.	25.00
X Design, Reamer, Orange, Pink	175.00

To clean wax from glass candle-sticks, scrape with a wooden stick, then wash off the remaining wax with rubbing alcohol.

Depression glass,
Sylvan

Depression glass,
Windsor

Derby, Box, Dove, Purple & White, c.1800, 7 1/2 In.

◆◆◆◆◆◆◆◆◆◆◆◆◆◆◆◆◆◆◆◆◆◆◆◆◆

Is it cut or pressed glass? Feel
the edges of the design of the
glass. Cut glass has sharp
edges; pressed-glass designs
are molded into the glass.

◆◆◆◆◆◆◆◆◆◆◆◆◆◆◆◆◆◆◆◆◆◆◆◆◆

Derby porcelain was made in Derby, England, from 1756 to the
present. The factory changed names and marks several times.
Chelsea Derby (1770–1784), Crown Derby (1784–1811), and the
modern Royal Crown Derby are some of the most famous periods
of the factory.

DERBY, see also Chelsea; Crown Derby; Royal Crown Derby

DERBY, Box, Dove, Purple & White, c.1800, 7 1/2 In. ....*Illus*	880.00
Dish, Scalloped, Red & Yellow Apple, Insects, Sprig, c.1760, 9 9/16 In.	4675.00
Figurine, Taylor & His Wife, c.1840, Pair	900.00
Fish Plate, Red Transfer, Fish Center, Marked, 9 3/8 In., 6 Piece	305.00
Tureen, Soup, Kings Pattern, Oval, c.1850, 3 Piece	3500.00
Vase, Girl Standing On Rocky Peak, Goat, Blue On Yellow, 7 3/4 In.	5025.00

The DeVilbiss Company has made atomizers of all types since 1888
but no longer makes the perfume bottle tops so popular with
collectors. These were made from 1920 to 1968. The glass bottle
may be by any of many manufacturers even if the atomizer says
DeVilbiss. More atomizer bottles are listed in the perfume bottle
section.

DEVILBISS, Atomizer, Cranberry	45.00
Perfume Bottle, Art Deco, Black, Orange Floral, Dauber, 4 3/4 In.	40.00
Perfume Bottle, Atomizer, Green Enameled	75.00
Perfume Bottle, Peach, Atomizer, Box	42.00
Perfume Bottle, Silver Crackle Glass, Plunger	27.00

The comic strip *Dick Tracy* started in 1931. He was the hero of
movies from 1937 to 1947, starred in a radio series in the 1940s and
a television series in the 1950s. Memorabilia from all these activities
is collected.

DICK TRACY, Airplane, Wooden, Box	27.00
Badge, Club, Leather Pouch	75.00
Badge, Crime Stoppers, Metal, 1940s Premium, 1/2 In.	15.00
Badge, Detective Club, Brass	25.00
Badge, Secret Service Patrol	18.00
Badge, Secret Service Patrol, Member, Brass, 1939, 1/2 In.	15.00
Book, Big Little Book, 1933	18.00
Book, Big Little Book, and Boris Arson Gang, 1935	25.00
Book, Big Little Book, Stolen Bonds	45.00
Book, Celebrated Cases of, Chester Gould, 1st Edition, 1931–51	100.00
Book, Dick Tracy Meets The Night Crawler, Book Jacket	25.00
Book, Paint	55.00
Book, Punch–Out	125.00
Box, Doll's, Bonnie Braids	60.00
Button, Pin Back	20.00
Candy Box, 1940s	85.00

Car, Copmobile ....55.00 To 150.00
Car, Squad, Friction, Light & Siren, Machine Gun, Marx, 11 1/4 In. 250.00
Car, Squad, Windup, Tin Litho, Yellow Flashing Light, Marx, Box 800.00
Car, Tin Litho, Battery Operated, Marx, 11 In. 105.00
Card, Series 121 Through 144, 1934, 96 Cards 48.00
Cartoon Kit, 1968 .... 15.00
Certificate, Service Patrol, Quaker Puffed Wheat, 1938, 14 In. 15.00
Comic Book, Harvey Publications 75.00
Comic Book, No. 100 .... 50.00
Comic Book, Popped Wheat, 1940, 16 Pages 15.00
Detective Kit, Dick Tracy Jr., Uncut, 1962 .... 65.00
Document, Membership, Junior G–Man, 8 x 10 In. 35.00
Doll, Applause, 14 In. 19.50
Doll, Bonny Braids, Walker, Plastic, 1951, Charmore Company 125.00
Doll, Honeymoon, Box, Ideal 375.00
Doll, With Stand, 9 In. 15.00
Doll, With Stand, 14 In. 25.00
Eyeglasses 5.00
Figural Set, Dick, Jr., Chief Brandon, Lead, 2 In., 3 Piece 65.00
Game, Board, Selchow & Righter, 1960s 65.00
Game, Card, 1934 .... 50.00
Game, Crime Stoppers, 1963 .... 50.00
Game, Master Detective, Box 28.00
Gun, Cap 25.00
Hairbrush, 1939 .... 25.00
Holster, Leather, Shoulder, 1930s 145.00
Iron On Transfer, 8 x 10 In. 18.00
Knife, Pocket ....50.00 To 60.00
Light Bulb, Figural, Christmas, Milk Glass, 1930s ....50.00 To 125.00
Lunch Box, 1967 .... 225.00
Lunch Box, Thermos .... 75.00 To 95.00
Membership Kit, Crime Stoppers, Brass Badge, 1940s 40.00
Model, Aurora, Box 125.00
Model, Space Coupe, Box 150.00
Mug, Figural Handle .... 13.00 To 20.00
Pillow, 1960 .... 25.00
Pin, Pep 25.00
Pistol, Sparkling Pop, Marx, 1940s, 8 In. 220.00
Poster, Now On The Screen, Scarface, RKO, 1945, 27 x 71 In. 300.00
Puppet, Hand, Vinyl Head, Cloth Body, Ideal, 1961 .... 85.00
Puzzle, Man Hunt, Jaymar 18.00
Radio, Wrist, 2–Way, Box 125.00
Rubb'rniks, Tracy, Junior, Flat Top, Jo Jitsu, 1968, 6 In. 145.00
Salt & Pepper, Dick Tracy & Junior 35.00
Secret Detecto Kit 65.00
Suspenders, Box .... 35.00 To 95.00
Target Set, On Card 12.00
Toy, B. O. Plenty, Walker, Windup, Tin Litho, Box .... 250.00 To 450.00
Toy, Soaky 35.00
Tube, Detective Ink 15.00
Tumbler, Black Word Shaky, Picture, Frosted Glass, 5 In. 75.00
Tumbler, Blue Word Vitamin Flintheart, Picture, Frosted, 5 In. 83.00
Wrist Radio, Box, Instructions, 1956 .... 160.00 To 325.00
Wristwatch, Points Gun, Steel, Tonneau Case, Pigskin Strap 399.00
Wristwatch, TV, On Card 12.00
        DICKENS WARE, see Royal Doulton; Weller

The Dionne quintuplets were born in Canada on May 28, 1934. The
publicity about their birth and their special status as wards of the
Canadian government made them famous throughout the world.
Visitors could watch the girls play, reporters interviewed the girls

and the staff, and thousands of special dolls and souvenirs were made picturing the quints at different ages. Emilie died in 1954, Marie in 1970. Yvonne, Annette, and Cecile still live in Canada.

DIONNE QUINTUPLETS, Ad, B/W Electrolux 5.00
Ad, Palmolive, Colored 10.00
Book, Protecting The Dionnes, Lysol, 1936, 24 Pages 20.00
Book, Soon We'll Be Three, Sticker Mark On Front 7.00
Booklet, Administering Angels, Mdme. Legros, 1936 .... 89.00
Calendar, 1942 .... 32.00
Calendar, 1942, Paper 27.00
Card, Lobby, 1936 .... 20.00
Card, Playing 30.00
Doll Set, Plastic, Moveable, Japan, Box, 1930s, 2 1/2 In. 85.00
Doll, 1930s 210.00
Doll, Sun Outfits, Madame Alexander, 7 In., 5 Piece 1045.00
Doll, Yvonne, Composition, Madame Alexander, 7 1/2 In. 165.00
Fan 12.00
Magazine, Modern Screen, April, 1936 .... 45.00
Paper Doll, Merrill, Uncut, 1935 .... 240.00
Paper Doll, No. 3488, 1939, Uncut 195.00
Paper Doll, With Cars, Cut 100.00
Postcard, 1940 .... 15.00
Soap Set, Box, 1934 .... 125.00
Spoon Set, 5 Piece 125.00
Spoon, Emilie 25.00

Walt Disney and his company introduced many comic characters to the world. Collectors search for examples of the work of the Disney Studios and the many commercial products modeled after his characters. These collectibles are called *Disneyana.*

DISNEYANA, Ashtray, 3 Little Pigs, Playing Instruments, Lusterware, Japan 95.00
Ashtray, Mickey Mouse, Lusterware, 1930 .... 125.00
Bank, Donald Duck, Disney Ceramics 48.00
Bank, Donald Duck, Glass 50.00
Bank, Mechanical, Mickey Mouse, 10th Anniversary Disney World 75.00
Bank, Mechanical, Mickey Mouse, Wolverine 17.00
Bank, Mickey Mouse Club, Large, 1950s 15.00
Bank, Mickey Mouse, Combination Bookends, Cast Iron, 5 In. 32.50
Bank, Treasure Chest, Mickey Mouse, Moving Head, Crown Toy, 1930s 350.00
Baton Twirler, Donald Duck, Fisher–Price 250.00
Bingo Wheel, Disney Characters 40.00
Birthday Party Set, Plastic, 51 Piece 110.00
Book, Big Little Book, Mickey Mouse, Foreign Legion 50.00
Book, Big Little Book, Mickey Mouse, Pluto To The Racer 50.00
Book, Big Little Book, Mickey Mouse, Sacred Jewel, 1936 .... 40.00 To 50.00
Book, Coloring, Mickey & Minnie Mouse, 1933 .... 50.00
Book, Coloring, Mickey Mouse, 1957 .... 15.00
Book, Mickey Mouse, David McKay Series, 1931, 48 Pages, 10 In. 85.00
Book, Pinocchio, Cocomalt, 1939 .... 10.00
Book, Pinocchio, Whitman, No. 709, 1939 .... 55.00
Book, Pop–Up, Cinderella, Puppet Show 30.00
Book, Pop–Up, King Neptune, Babes In Woods, W. D. E., 1934 .... 575.00
Book, Pop–Up, Mickey Mouse, 1933 .... 325.00 To 500.00
Book, Snow White & The 7 Dwarfs, Whitman, 1938 .... 45.00
Bookend, Doc & Grumpy, 7 Dwarfs, LaMode Studios Inc., 1938 .... 250.00
Bottle Opener, Mickey Mouse 10.00
Bowl, Mickey Mouse, Red Beetleware, Post Bran Flakes, 1930s 15.00
Box, Candy, Zorro, With Cartoon Panel On Back 48.00
Box, Jewelry, Music, Donald Duck & Nephews 200.00
Box, Mickey Mouse Sunshine Straws, Hertz Mfg., 1950s 10.00
Box, Pinocchio, Libbey Safedge Tumblers, Omar Flour, 1940s, 17 In. 65.00
Brush, Clothes, Mickey Mouse, 1930s 55.00

Bubble Pipe, Mickey Mouse, Red & Silver, Plastic, Lido 18.00
Bus, Lady & The Tramp, Tin, Friction, 1966, 5 x 13 In. 295.00
Button, Disneyland Mickey Mouse Club, 3 In. 10.00
Cake Nodders, Donald, Mickey, Goofy, Pluto, Marx 100.00
Camera, Donald Duck, Instructions, Box 250.00
Cane, Composition Mickey Mouse's Head, W. D. E., Borgfeldt 225.00
Car, Mickey Mouse 50th Anniversary, Lionel, Box 400.00
Card, 3 Little Pigs, 1930 .... 45.00
Card, Playing, Old Maid, Mickey Mouse, Box 150.00
Card, Playing, Snow White, Goofy Joker, Rules, 1930s, Box .... 60.00 To 80.00
Card, Valentine, Circus, Hallmark 10.00
DISNEYANA, CEL, see Animation Art
Charm, Mickey Mouse, Celluloid, 1930s, 3/4 In. 20.00
Clock, Alarm, Bugs Bunny, Talking 25.00
Clock, Alarm, Ingersoll U. S. Time Corp., Box 200.00
Clock, Alarm, Mickey & Donald, Vantage, Germany 350.00
Clock, Alarm, Mickey & Goofy, Red Metal, 1970s, Bradley 100.00
Clock, Alarm, Mickey Mouse, Bradley 50.00
Clock, Alarm, Mickey, Bradley, Box, 1970s, Large .... 75.00 To 85.00
Clock, Cinderella, Wall, Elgin 30.00
Clock, Dome, Plays Mickey Mouse March, Bradley, Box 200.00
Clock, Mickey Mouse, Ingersoll, Electric 577.00
Clock–Radio, Mickey Mouse 125.00
Coin, Mickey Mouse Club Birthday, Wards 27.50
Comic Strip, Mickey Mouse, Sunday Newspaper, 1934 .... 25.00
Cookie Jar, Donald Duck 125.00
Cookie Jar, Donald Duck & Nephews, Disney 75.00
Cookie Jar, Donald Duck, Turnabout .... 60.00 To 125.00
Cookie Jar, Donald Duck, Walt Disney Co., Hoan Ltd. 125.00
Cookie Jar, Dumbo, Turnabout, Walt Disney 75.00
Cookie Jar, Mickey & Minnie Mouse, Disney 125.00
Cookie Jar, Mickey Mouse Baker, Rolling Pin & Chef Hat 48.00
Cookie Jar, Mickey Mouse, Bum Train, Treasure Craft 40.00
Cookie Jar, Mickey Mouse, Hoppity Ball 50.00
Cookie Jar, Mickey Mouse, On Drum, Disney 250.00
Cookie Jar, Pinocchio 325.00
Cookie Jar, Tigger, Walt Disney Productions .... 125.00 To 250.00
Cookie Jar, Winnie The Pooh 72.00
Costume, Halloween, Dumbo, 1950s 25.00
Costume, Mickey Mouse, Worn Over Play Clothes, Box 500.00
Crayons, Character, Giant, Box, Disney, 1949, 10 Piece 45.00
Creamer, Donald Duck, 6 In. 68.00
Creamer, Dumbo, Gold Trim, 1940s, 6 In. .... 25.00 To 35.00
Creamer, Mickey Mouse, Tail Handle, Mouth Pourer, Japan 20.00
Cufflinks & Tie Clasp, Mouseketeers, Brass, Enameled, 1960s 35.00
Cufflinks, Mickey Mouse, 1 In. 50.00
Cup, Snow White, Plastic 8.00
Decal, Iron On, Mickey Mouse, Full Figure, 1940s 6.00
Desk, Light Up Drawing, Mickey Mouse 40.00
Dish, Feeding, Hot Water, Donald Duck, Leeds, 1940s 80.00
Display, Wristwatch, Lorus, Mickey Mouse, Plastic, Metal, 12 In. 145.00
Doll, Donald Duck, Gay Caballero, Plastic, Mavco, Box, 1960s 175.00
Doll, Donald Duck, Knickerbocker, 13 In. 450.00
Doll, Donald Duck, Walker 20.00
Doll, Jiminy Cricket, Moveable Head, Knickerbocker, 10 In. 425.00
Doll, Mickey Mouse Club, Horsman 40.00
Doll, Mickey Mouse, Black Plush, Walt Disney Prod., 14 In. 93.00
Doll, Mickey Mouse, Jointed, Wood, Lollipop Hands, 7 In. 1200.00
Doll, Mickey Mouse, Steiff, 10 In. 1850.00
Doll, Mickey Mouse, Steiff, 14 In. 3520.00
Doll, Mickey Mouse, Steiff, 1931, 5 In. 1000.00
Doll, Mickey Mouse, Steiff, 9 In. 975.00
Doll, Mickey Mouse, Talks, Pull String, Walt Disney Prod., 1973 .... 19.00

Doll, Minnie Mouse, Steiff, 14 In.	3520.00
Doll, Mousketeer, Boy, Girl, Vinyl, Horseman, 9 In., Pair	300.00
Dollhouse, Metal, Marx	65.00
Dollhouse, Mickey Mouse, O. B. Andrews, Box, 1933	725.00
Doorstop, Mickey Mouse	90.00
Doorstop, Mickey Mouse, Pie–Cut Eyes, Wooden	65.00
Drawing, Mickey's Rival, Full Figure, Black, Red, Matted, 1936	500.00
Drawing, Mickey's Surprise Party, Pluto, 1939, 8 1/2 x 11 1/2 In.	990.00
Drawing, Practical Pig of Fiddler & Fifer, 1939	125.00
Drummer, Donald Duck, Plastic & Tin, Marx, Box	475.00
Eggcup, Dopey, Glazed, Japan, 2 3/4 In.	95.00
Figurine, 100 & 1 Dalmatians, Parents & 3 Children, Disney	89.50
Figurine, Baby Bambi, American Pottery Co., 4 1/2 In.	75.00
Figurine, Dancing Elephant, Fantasia, Vernon Kilns, 1940, 5 In.	250.00
Figurine, Donald Duck's Nephew, Chalkware, 3 In.	19.00
Figurine, Donald Duck, Bugle, Bisque, 1930s, 3 In.	125.00
Figurine, Donald Duck, Chalkware, 13 1/4 In.	55.00
Figurine, Dumbo, Ceramic, American Pottery	60.00
Figurine, Ferdinand The Bull, Black, Bisque, 1930s	28.00
Figurine, Ferdinand, Bisque, 3 In.	55.00
Figurine, Happy, 7 Dwarfs, Hagen–Renaker, 1950s	95.00
Figurine, Mickey Mouse, Bisque, Playing Saxophone, 3 1/2 In.	85.00
Figurine, Mickey Mouse, Holding Flag, 1930s, 3 3/4 In.	275.00
Figurine, Mickey Mouse, Playing Banjo, Bisque, 1930s, 3 1/4 In.	350.00
Figurine, Mickey Mouse, Wooden, Wire Arms & Legs, 5 In.	50.00
Figurine, Minnie Mouse, Donald Duck, Rifle, Bisque, Disney, 3 In.	135.00
Figurine, Minnie Mouse, Porcelain, 4 In.	85.00
Figurine, Pinocchio, Chalkware, 14 In.	45.00
Figurine, Snow White & 7 Dwarfs, E. K. Shaw, American Pottery	785.00
Figurine, Snow White, Chalkware, 14 In.	65.00
Figurine, Snow White, Yellow Dress, Walt Disney Prod., 1960, 5 In.	25.00
Figurine, Thumper, American Pottery	65.00
Figurine, Tinker Bell, Ceramic, Marked, Japan, 3 In.	45.00
Game, Board, Rescue Race, Box	95.00
Game, Card, Snow White & 7 Dwarfs, 1948	15.00
Game, Donald Duck Bean Bag, Parker Bros., Box, 1939	135.00
Game, Donald Duck, Tricky Toe, 1950s	25.00
Game, Mickey Mouse Library of Games, Russell Mfg., 1946	110.00
Game, Mickey Mouse, Parker Bros.	15.00
Game, Mickey Slugaroo, 1950s	25.00
Game, Pin The Tail On Mickey, Paper, Marks Bros., Envelope, 1930s	85.00
Game, Pluto, Board, Box, 1977	15.00
Game, Rickety Bridge, Mickey Mouse, 3d, Complete	15.00
Game, Riverboat, W. C. P, 1960	30.00
Game, Sleeping Beauty, Board, Parker Bros., 1959	50.00
Game, Target, Mickey Mouse, Lithograph Board, Marx Bros., Co.	110.00
Game, Tiddley Winks, 1963, Whitman	25.00
Game, Walt Disney's Fantasyland, Parker Brothers, 1956	35.00
Guitar, Mouseketeers, Box	65.00
Handkerchief, Mickey Mouse, Colorful, 3 Piece	36.00
Hanger, Stocking, Mickey Mouse, Hallmark, Box	20.00
Holder, Pencil, Donald Duck, Brass	28.00
Holder, Toothbrush, Mickey Mouse, Bisque	85.00
Holder, Toothbrush, Mickey, Minnie & Donald Duck, Bisque, 1930s	210.00
Ironing Board, Snow White & 7 Dwarfs	30.00
Jukebox, Mickey Mouse, c.1973	65.00
Knife, Fork & Spoon, Mickey Mouse, Stainless Steel, 1959, 3 Piece	195.00
Knife, Mickey Mouse, 2 Blades, Imperial, Pocket	75.00
Lamp & Music Box, Sleeping Beauty, Bakelite	85.00
Lamp, Bambi Story Book, Figural, Plastic, Dolly Toy Co., 1970s	30.00
Lamp, Bambi, Walt Disney Products	32.00
Lamp, Ceiling Fixture, Mickey Mouse, Pluto, Donald Duck, Glass	375.00
Lamp, Donald Duck, Sailor, No Shade, 1940s, Leeds, 11 1/2 In.	225.00

Light Bulb Set, Christmas, 7 Different 70.00
Light Bulb Set, Christmas, Noma, Mickey Mouse, W. D. Ent., Box 295.00
Locket, Disneyland, Heart Shape, Gold Metal, 1 In. 15.00
Lunch Box, Aladdin, Walt Disney World 10.00
Lunch Box, Black Hole, Thermos .... 20.00 To 40.00
Lunch Box, Disney Express, Thermos 20.00
Lunch Box, Disneyland Castle, Thermos 145.00
Lunch Box, Dome Shaped, Disney Characters, 1960 .... 45.00
Lunch Box, Firefighter, Dome Shaped 100.00
Lunch Box, Junglebook, Thermos, 1966 .... 50.00
Lunch Box, Magic Kingdom 25.00
Lunch Box, Magic Kingdom, Aladdin 15.00
Lunch Box, Magic Kingdom, Wonderful World, Walt Disney 20.00
Lunch Box, Mickey Mouse Club, 1970s 15.00
Lunch Box, Mickey Mouse, World's Fair 20.00
Lunch Box, School Bus, Dome Shaped, Disney, Thermos 75.00
Lunch Box, Snow White & The 7 Dwarfs, Ohio Art 15.00
Lunch Box, Snow White, Made In Belgium, 1938 .... 650.00
Lunch Box, Snow White, With Spinner 15.00
Lunch Box, Zorro 52.00
Magic Slate, Mickey Mouse, Color, Box, Unused 60.00
Map, Disneyland, 1964 .... 45.00
Map, Disneyland, 1970s 12.00
Marble, Donald Duck 12.50
Marble, Mickey Mouse 10.00
Marionette, Alice In Wonderland 95.00
Marionette, Donald Duck, Composition, England, Box, 10 In. 75.00
Marionette, Dopey, Composition, England, Box, 20 In. 275.00
Marionette, Grumpy, Composition, Madame Alexander, 9 In. 185.00
Marionette, Jiminy Cricket, Gund, Label 75.00
Marionette, Mickey & Minnie, Papier–Mache Head, Pair 700.00
Marionette, Mickey Mouse, Composition, England, Box, 23 In. 275.00
Marionette, Minnie Mouse, Composition 200.00
Marionette, Minnie Mouse, Pelham, Box, 12 In. 125.00
Marionette, Pinocchio, 14 In. 155.00
Marionette, Pinocchio, 1930 .... 70.00
Mask, Pinocchio, Gillette Razor Premium 15.00
Mask, Wheaties Cereal Box Back, 2 Piece 18.00
Matchbox Holder, 3 Little Pigs 72.00
Mickey Mouse Club Mousekartooner Set 28.00
Mickey Mouse, Target, Marks, Box, 1934 .... 400.00
MouseGetar, 4 Strings, Paper Lithograph, 1950s, Mattel 55.00
Moviejector, Mickey Mouse, 1938 .... 175.00
Mug, Breaktime, Mickey Mouse 10.00
Mug, Mickey Mouse Club, Plastic, 1950s, 4 In. 18.00
Musical Sweeper, Dopey, Fisher–Price 95.00
Necklace & Ring, Minnie Mouse, Box 20.00
Nodder, Donald Duck, Ceramic, 6 In. .... 65.00 To 90.00
Nodder, Mickey Mouse 65.00
Nodder, Mickey Mouse, Marx, Package, 3 In. 5.00
Nodder, Pluto 65.00
Paint Box, Cinderella, 1925 .... 55.00
Paint Box, Donald Duck, Transogram, 1938 .... 55.00
Paint Set, Mickey Mouse & Donald Duck, Tin, 1950s 40.00
Panchito Rooster, c.1940 .... 50.00
Paper Doll, 7 Dwarfs, Missing Sneezy & Snow White, 1938 .... 45.00
Peanut Machine, Mickey Mouse 1350.00
Pencil Box, Mickey Mouse, Red, Blue & White, 10 1/2 x 6 In. 135.00
Pencil Box, Mickey, Minnie, Donald, Dixon, 1930s .... 60.00 To 65.00
Pencil Sharpener, Dopey, Ceramic, 4 In. 40.00
Pencil, Inkograph, Mechanical, Mickey Mouse Head, Decal, 1930s 125.00
Perfume Bottle, Mickey Mouse 119.00
Phonograph & Projector, Records & Film, Walt Disney Ent. 900.00

Phonograph, Mickey Mouse, His Arm Plays Records 85.00
Pin, Disneyland Tomorrowland, Donald As Astronaut, Enamel, 1 In. 20.00
Pin, Disneyland, 35 Years of Magic, Mickey As Wizard, 3 In. 25.00
Pin, Mickey Mouse, 60 Years Flashing, Enameled 20.00
Pin, Mickey Mouse, Celluloid, Mickey Holds Sign, 7th Birthday 125.00
Pin, Pinocchio, Celluloid 25.00
Pitcher, Dumbo, 8 In. 23.00
Pitcher, Mickey Mouse, Japan, 7 In. 135.00
Planter, Bambi, Ceramic, Walt Disney Productions .... 45.00 To 50.00
Planter, Donald Duck, Santa Suit, Pastel 85.00
Planter, Dumbo 22.00
Plate, Souvenir, Disney, 1966, 9 1/2 In. 18.00
Poster, Fantasia, Re-Release Movie, 1960s, 27 x 41 In. 85.00
Poster, Skyfest Balloon Salute 30th Year, Disney 20.00
Print, Snow White & 7 Dwarfs, Watercolor, E. Tyler, 28 x 24 In. 115.00
Print, The Black Hole, Disney, 21 x 21 In. 75.00
Projector, Mickey Mouse, Keystone, 1935 .... 225.00 To 500.00
Puppet, Donald Duck, Gund, Box 55.00
Puppet, Hand, Ferdinand The Bull, Composition Head, Crown, 1938 .... 50.00
Puppet, Hand, Lady & Tramp, Gund, Pair 55.00
Puppet, Hand, Tinker Bell, 1950s 20.00
Puppet, Jiminy Cricket, String, Gund 110.00
Puppet, Lady & The Tramp, 1955 .... 25.00
Puppet, Pinocchio, Gund 15.00
Puppet, Pinocchio, Instructions, Booklet, Pelham 55.00
Purse, Coin, Enameled Mickey & Minnie, Chain, 1932, 3 x 3 In. 265.00
Puzzle, Cold Blooded Penguin, Walt Disney, Box 14.00
Puzzle, Flying Donkey, Walt Disney, Box 14.00
Puzzle, Lady & The Tramp 15.00
Puzzle, Mickey Mouse, 1950s 20.00
Radio, Mickey Mouse, 1932 .... 1800.00
Rattle, Mickey Mouse, Blue Celluloid 150.00
Record, Dumbo, RCA, 78 RPM, 1940s, 3 Piece 22.00
Record, Mickey & The Beanstalk, Book, Capital, 78 RPM, 1947, 3 Pc. 35.00
Record, Mickey Mouse, Album, LP, 1947 .... 20.00
Record, Pinocchio, RCA, 78 RPM, 3 Piece 22.00
Ring, Mickey Mouse Club Sticker, 1950s 9.00
Ring, Mickey Mouse, Goofy & Pluto, Engraved Aluminum, 1950s 20.00
Rocker, Mickey Mouse, c.1935, Wood, Mengel Company, 34 In. 450.00
Safety Patrol, Mickey Mouse, Fisher-Price 125.00
Salt & Pepper, Donald Duck 45.00
Salt & Pepper, Dumbo 15.00
Salt & Pepper, Mickey & Minnie Mouse 25.00
Salt & Pepper, Mickey & Minnie Mouse, Leeds, 1940s 18.00
Salt & Pepper, Mickey Mouse & Beanstalk, Box 12.00
Salt & Pepper, Pluto 25.00
Salt & Pepper, Thumper, Leeds, 1940s 20.00
Scooter, Mickey Mouse, Windup, Masudaya, Box 32.00
Scrapbook, Mickey Mouse, Walt Disney Ent. 45.00
Sheet Music, A Dream Is A Wish, Cinderella, 1949 .... 12.00
Sheet Music, Whistle While You Work, Snow White, 1937 .... 15.00
Shelf Sitter, Tinker Bell, Hagen-Renaker, 1950s 425.00
Shovel, Snow, Donald Duck, Mickey's Nephews, 1930, Ohio Art, 27 In. 350.00
Sled, Mickey Mouse, Walt Disney Enterprises, S. L. Allen & Co. 165.00
Snack Set, Mickey Mouse, Box, 3 Piece 22.00
Soap Set, Snow White & 7 Dwarfs, Figural, Box, 1938 .... 225.00
Soap, Mickey Mouse, Walt Disney, Box 130.00
Spoon, Mickey Mouse, Silver Plate, Post Toasties, 1930s 18.00
Spoon, Pinocchio, Donkey, Silver Plate, Duchess, 1940 .... 16.00
Stamp Set, Pinocchio, 1939 .... 35.00
Sticker Book, Aristocats, U. S. A., 225 .... 32.00
Sticker Book, Great Mouse Detective, U. S. A., 225 .... 40.00
Sticker Book, Snow White & 7 Dwarfs, 225 .... 32.00

Disneyana, Toy, Pinocchio, Tin Lithograph,
Eyes Blink, Marx, 8 In.

Disneyana, Toy, Pluto Pup, Tin Lithograph,
Linemar, Japan, 6 In.

Stool, Donald Duck, 3–Legged	20.00
Stove, Snow White, Wolverine	25.00
Sweeper, Donald Duck	75.00
Tambourine, Mickey Mouse Club	22.00
Tape, Hot Iron, Pluto, 3 Appliques, 1946	20.00
Target Set, Zorro, T. Cohn, Box	135.00
Tea Set, Cinderella, 16 Piece	385.00
Tea Set, Donald Duck, Tan & White, Luster Trim, 18 Piece	425.00
Tea Set, Mickey & Minnie Mouse, Plastic, 14 Piece	25.00
Tin, Shoe Polish, Mickey Mouse	15.00
Tool Chest, Mickey Mouse, Tin Litho, Hamilton, 1935	325.00
Toothbrush Set, Mickey Mouse, Battery Operated, Box	18.00
Top, Mickey Mouse, Tin, Chein	14.00 To 20.00
Toy, 7 Dwarfs, Sieberling Rubber, Akron, Ohio, 1938	500.00
Toy, Donald Duck, Marching	12.00
Toy, Donald Duck, On Tractor, Friction, Plastic	16.00
Toy, Donald Duck, On Tricycle, Battery Operated, Box	120.00
Toy, Donald Duck, Squeak, Rubber, Dell, 10 In.	25.00
Toy, Donald Duck, Talking, Fisher–Price, No. 765	75.00
Toy, Donald Duck, Windup, Schuco, Box	325.00
Toy, Donald Duck, With 3 Nephews, Walker, Marx	25.00
Toy, Drummer, Mickey Mouse, Windup, Tin	9680.00
Toy, Ferris Wheel, Mickey Mouse, Chein	285.00
Toy, Fire Truck, Mickey Mouse, Donald Duck, Sun Rubber	65.00 To 100.00
Toy, Fire Truck, Mickey Mouse, Sun Rubber	75.00
Toy, Goofy, Spinning Tail, Head Bobs, Windup, Linemar, 1950s	500.00
Toy, Hand Car, Mickey Mouse Figures, Pie–Eyed, Lionel, Box	2310.00
Toy, Handcar, Mickey Miner, Orange Steel, Key Wind, Lionel, 8 In.	632.00
Toy, Handcar, Mickey Mouse, Lionel, No Nose On Mickey	357.00
Toy, Hopper, Donald Duck, Remote Control, Tin Litho, Linemar, 1950s	375.00
Toy, Jiminy Cricket, Rubber Controller, Tin Lithograph, Linemar	200.00
Toy, Kaleidoscope, Mickey Mouse, Cardboard, Lithograph, 9 In.	99.00
Toy, Mickey & Minnie Mouse, Tin Cart, Celluloid, Occupied Japan	7700.00
Toy, Mickey Mouse Choo Choo, Fisher–Price No. 485, 1949	85.00
Toy, Mickey Mouse Dipsy Car, Linemar, Tin, 1950s	742.00 To 825.00
Toy, Mickey Mouse, Felt, Steiff	950.00
Toy, Mickey Mouse, In Airplane, Rubber, Sieberling	75.00
Toy, Mickey Mouse, Playing A Xylophone, Mechanical, 11 In.	250.00
Toy, Mickey Mouse, Pull, Hill Brass Co., N. Y., 1930s	725.00
Toy, Mickey Mouse, Riding Tricycle, Japan	30.00
Toy, Mickey Mouse, Rubber, 1960, 12 In.	44.00

Toy, Mickey Mouse, Stick, 1930s, 10 In. 65.00
Toy, Mickey Mouse, Straw Filled, Composition Feet, 10 In. 300.00
Toy, Mickey Mouse, Waddler, Windup, Celluloid, 1934 .... 5400.00
Toy, Mickey Mouse, Wood, Flexible Tail, 1926 .... 170.00
Toy, Mickey Mouse, Wooden, Fun–E–Flex, 1930s, 3 3/4 In. 175.00
Toy, Minnie Mouse, In Rocker 750.00
Toy, Minnie Mouse, In Rocker, Windup, Tin, Marx, 1950s 475.00
Toy, Minnie Mouse, Playing Mandolin, Bisque, 1930s, 4 In. 89.00
Toy, Pinocchio, Tin Lithograph, Eyes Blink, Marx, 8 In. ....*Illus* 100.00
Toy, Pinocchio, Waddler, Box 450.00
Toy, Pinocchio, Windup, Marx, 1950s, 5 In. 350.00
Toy, Pinocchio, Xylophone Player, Battery Operated, Box 112.00
Toy, Plaster Casting Set, Donald Duck, Box 195.00
Toy, Pluto Pup, Tin Lithograph, Linemar, Japan, 6 In. ....*Illus* 412.00
Toy, Pluto, Rubber Ears, Tin Lithograph, Windup 75.00
Toy, Pluto, Windup, Linemar, 1950s 250.00
Toy, Pop–Up Kritter 35.00
Toy, Puddle Jumper, Mickey Mouse, Fisher–Price, No. 310 .... 105.00
Toy, Ride 'Em Jumping Ball, Donald Duck, Large 25.00
Toy, Roly Poly, Minnie Mouse, Musical 20.00
Toy, Sand Pail, Pinocchio, Tin Lithograph, Red, 1940s 165.00
Tractor, Mickey Mouse, Late–1940s 105.00
Train, Circus, Mickey Mouse, Tin Lithograph, Lionel, Box .... 1540.00 To 1815.00
Tray, Disneyland, Tin Lithograph, 12 1/2 x 17 In. 25.00
Tumbler Set, Snow White, 1920s, 4 3/4 In., 8 Piece 150.00
Tumbler, Bashful, 7 Dwarfs, Red, 1930s, 4 3/4 In. 18.00
Tumbler, Cinderella & Prince, Walt Disney Prod., 5 1/4 In. 9.00
Tumbler, Donald Duck, Blue, Walt Disney Prod., 1950s, 3 3/8 In. 17.00
Tumbler, Mickey Mouse Club Logo, 1970s, 3 5/8 In. 5.00
Tumbler, Mickey Mouse Club Logo, 1970s, 4 3/4 In. 8.00
Tumbler, Mickey Mouse, Black, 1920, 4 3/8 In. 40.00
Tumbler, Mickey Mouse, Bosco, Black, 1930s, 3 3/8 In. 40.00
Umbrella, Mickey Mouse, 1940 .... 75.00
Viewer, Camera, Mickey Mouse, Box 35.00
Wall Pocket, Bambi, Disney 58.00
Wallet, Mickey Mouse, Vinyl, 1950s, Unused 25.00
Watch Fob, Mickey Mouse .... 125.00 To 240.00
Watch, Mickey Mouse Bicentennial, Pocket, Box 100.00
Watch, Pocket, Mickey Mouse, Ingersol 375.00
Watering Can, Donald Duck, Tin, Walt Disney, 1938 .... 30.00
Watering Can, Mickey Mouse, Tin Litho, Ohio Art, 1930s, 6 In. 85.00
Wristwatch, Cinderella, 1955 .... 100.00
Wristwatch, Cinderella, 3 Bands, Miniature Comic Book, Box, 1967 .... 100.00
Wristwatch, Cinderella, In Slipper 400.00
Wristwatch, Cinderella, With Statue, 1958 .... 130.00
Wristwatch, Donald Duck Commemorative, 1983, Box 250.00
Wristwatch, Donald Duck, Black Band, Arms Move, Quartz, Lorus 25.00
Wristwatch, Donald Duck, U. S. Time 150.00
Wristwatch, Girl's, Jessica Rabbit, Armitron 80.00
Wristwatch, Goofy, Backwards, Brown Band, Arms Move, Quartz 275.00
Wristwatch, Goofy, Helbros, Box, 1972 .... 980.00
Wristwatch, Man's, Mickey Mouse, Elgin, 17 Jewel, 1969 .... 195.00
Wristwatch, Man's, Mickey Mouse, Elgin, 17 Jewels, 1969 .... 195.00
Wristwatch, Man's, Mickey Mouse, Helbros, 17 Jewel, 1972 .... 185.00
Wristwatch, Man's, Mickey Mouse, Helbros, 17 Jewels, 1972 .... 185.00
Wristwatch, Mickey & Minnie Mouse, Red Band, Quartz, Lorus 25.00
Wristwatch, Mickey Mouse & Donald, Lorus, Walt Disney Prod., Box 95.00
Wristwatch, Mickey Mouse, 1940s 75.00
Wristwatch, Mickey Mouse, Avon, Box 25.00
Wristwatch, Mickey Mouse, Ingersoll, 1938 .... 500.00
Wristwatch, Mickey Mouse, Ingersoll, 1946 .... 255.00
Wristwatch, Mickey Mouse, Ingersoll, Metal Band, 1933 .... 450.00
Wristwatch, Mickey Mouse, Leather Band, 1936 .... 350.00

Wristwatch, Mickey Mouse, Red Hands & Strap, Steel 139.00
Wristwatch, Mickey Mouse, Thru The Years, Tan Band, Quartz, Lorus 100.00
Wristwatch, Mickey Mouse, Train On Back, Bradley, Case, Pocket 45.00
Wristwatch, Snow White, Original Strap 125.00
Wristwatch, Snow White, Timex, Red Strap, 1960s 85.00
Wristwatch, Snow White, White Band, Golden Anniversary, Lorus 45.00
Wristwatch, Woman's, Mickey Mouse, Helbros, 17 Jewel 170.00
Xyophone, Donald Duck, Paper Lighto, Wood, Fisher–Price, 13 In. 200.00
Yo–Yo–Video Action, Box 15.00
    DOCTOR, see Medical; Dental

Doll entries are listed by marks printed or incised on the doll, if
possible. If there are no marks, the doll is listed by the name of the
subject or country.

DOLL, A & M, Dream Baby, Playpen, Bottle & Diaper, 8 In. Head, Box, Austria 350.00
A. B. G. 1361, Chunky Baby Body, 25 In. 1400.00
A. B. G., Walker, Blue Sleep Eyes, Ball–Jointed, Clothes, 25 In. 575.00
A. M. 20, Open Mouth, Upper Teeth, Wood & Composition, Jointed, 42 In. 1875.00
A. M. 200, Googly, All Original, 11 In. 950.00
A. M. 323, Bisque Head, Googly Eyes, Closed Mouth, Brown Wig, 12 In. 1540.00
A. M. 323, Googly, 5 Piece Body, White Dress, 7 In. 275.00
A. M. 325, Rosie Baby, Bisque, 12 In. 425.00
A. M. 353, Oriental Baby, Bisque, Bent Limb Body, 16 1/2 In. 1320.00
A. M. 353, Oriental, Bisque Head, Painted Hair, Bent–Limb Body, 19 In. 990.00
A. M. 362, Black, Molded Features, 11 1/2 In. 700.00
A. M. 370, Child, Bisque, 4 Teeth, Kid Body, Marked, 24 In. 390.00
A. M. 370, Dancer, Mechanical, 27 In. 2700.00
A. M. 390, Bisque Head, Fully Jointed Body, Sleep Eyes, Wig, 24 In. 200.00
A. M. 390, Bisque Head, Open Mouth, Fully Jointed Composition Body 175.00
A. M. 390, Ringlet Style Hair, Original Clothes, Box 775.00
A. M. 971, Character, 17 In. 600.00
A. M., Bisque Head, Glass Eyes, Open Mouth, Germany, 18 In. 275.00
A. M., Bisque Shoulder Head, Open Mouth, Jointed Kid Body, Cloth Legs 150.00
A. M., Dream Baby, 10 In. 150.00
A. M., Floradora, 19 In. 295.00
A. M., Floradora, Kid Body, Bisque Lower Arms, Dressed, 25 In. 275.00
A. M., Girl, Black, Stationary Eyes, Jointed Body & Limbs, 17 1/2 In. 665.00
A. M., Just Me, Glass Eyes To Looking To Side, 9 In. 700.00
A. M., Kid Body, Bisque Shoulder Head, Dress, 21 1/2 In. 192.00
A. M., Oriental, Painted Hair, Bent Limb Composition Body, 13 In. 825.00
A. M., Socket Head, Ball–Jointed, Brown Human Hair, 42 In. 1210.00
Advertising, Big Boy Set, Dolly, Big Boy & Nuggett, 3 Piece 9.00
Advertising, Big Boy, Vinyl 15.00
Advertising, Blue Bonnet Sue 15.00
Advertising, Burger King, 21 In. 25.00
Advertising, Burger King, Cloth, 12 In. ....5.00 To 12.00
Advertising, Burger King, Cloth, 1960–70, 13 1/2 In. 13.00
Advertising, Burger King, Cloth, 24 In. 15.00
Advertising, Burger King, Magical, Knickerbocker, 1980, Box 15.00
Advertising, Campbell's Soup, Scottish Outfit 48.00
Advertising, Capt' Crunch, Stuffed, 1978, 15 In. 45.00
Advertising, Chiquita Bananna, Cloth, 16 In. 10.00
Advertising, Choo Choo Charlie, Good 'N' Plenty 24.00
Advertising, Colonel Sanders, Kentucky Fried Chicken 6.00
Advertising, Count Chocula, Vinyl 24.00
Advertising, Elf, Ernie Keebler 18.00
Advertising, Elsie 50.00
Advertising, Elsie The Cow, 15 In. ....38.00 To 45.00
Advertising, Eskimo Pie, Cloth, 1960–70, 16 In. 13.00
Advertising, Freckles The Frog, Kelloggs, 1935, 13 x 17 In., Uncut 50.00
Advertising, General Electric, Radio Man 450.00
Advertising, General Mills, 6 In. 12.50
Advertising, Gerber Baby, 10 In. 15.00

Advertising, Goldilocks, Cocoa Wheats, Cloth, 1940s .... 37.50 To 45.00
Advertising, Green Giant Sprout, Cloth, 12 In. 10.00
Advertising, Green Giant Sprout, Vinyl 15.00
Advertising, Gretchen, Coco-Wheats, Uncut Cloth 50.00
Advertising, Hans The Nestle's Chocolate Man, Vinyl, 1969, 12 1/2 In. 95.00
Advertising, Hotpoint, Wooden, Large 750.00
Advertising, Jack Frost Sugar, Playing Drums 15.00
Advertising, Jolly Green Giant, Cloth, 1960-70, 16 In. 10.00
Advertising, Kellogg's Clown, In Barrel 5.00
Advertising, Kellogg's Freckles, 1935 .... 25.00
Advertising, Kelloggs, Oilcloth, Uncut, 1945 .... 20.00
Advertising, Korn Krisp, Cloth, Uncut, November 1899, 35 x 26 In. 375.00
Advertising, Magic Chef, Vinyl 18.00
Advertising, McDonald Hamburglar 20.00
Advertising, McDonald, Professor, Gadget 15.00
Advertising, Miss Curity, Counter Figure 95.00
Advertising, Miss Revlon 75.00
Advertising, Mr. Magoo, Baseball Player, Cap Marked GE, 28 In. 85.00
Advertising, Mr. Salty Pretzel Man, Cloth 20.00
Advertising, Nestle's Quick Rabbit, Stuffed, Canada, 1982, 22 In. 19.00
Advertising, Northern Tissue, Box, 1988 .... 18.00
Advertising, Phillips 66 Buddy Lee 350.00
Advertising, Pillsbury Doughboy, Terrycloth, Stuffed, 12 1/2 In. 26.00
Advertising, Ronald McDonald 7.50
Advertising, Ronald McDonald, Rag, 4 In. ....5.00 To 10.00
Advertising, Ronald McDonald, Whistle, 21 In. 30.00
Advertising, Sambo's Restaurant, Cloth, Dakin 15.00
Advertising, Texaco, Ventriloquist, Uniform, Composition, Large 225.00
Advertising, Toucan Sam, Stuffed, Fruit Loops, 1960s 45.00
Advertising, Wendy, Cloth, 14 In. 9.00
Advertising, Western Union, 6 In. 15.00
Albert Alligator, Vinyl, Walt Kelly, 1969, 5 In. 8.00
  DOLL, ALEXANDER, see Doll, Madame Alexander
Amberg 1362, 20 In. 375.00
Amberg, Baby Peggy, Socket Head, Smiling, Closed Mouth, 18 In. 2500.00
Amberg, Pouty Baby, 11 In. 395.00
Amelia Earhart, Bisque, 5 In. 145.00
American Character, Mama, Composition, Cloth Body, Yellow Dress, 21 In. 220.00
Amish, Clothespin, Ohio 115.00
Andy Gibb, Disco, Box 48.00
Angela Cartwright, Make Room For Daddy, 15 In. 35.00
  DOLL, ARMAND MARSEILLE, see Doll, A. M.
Automaton, Ballerina, Bisque Head, Wire & Paper Body, 16 1/8 In. 1100.00
Automaton, Walking Her Baby Carriage, Papier-Mache Head 2090.00
Averill 1005/3652, Bonnie Babe, Dome Head, Cloth Body, Clothes, 18 In. 357.00
Baby, Boy, Composition, Blue Rompers, Round White Hat, Dated 1920 .... 130.00
Baby, Celluloid, Glass Eyes, Turtle Mark, 12 In. 225.00
Baby, Creche, 1820 .... 1200.00
Bahr & Proschild 585, Baby, Composition, Sleep Eyes 900.00
Bahr & Proschild, Baby, 15 1/2 In. 425.00
Bahr & Proschild, Bisque, Bent Limb, 12 1/2 In. 400.00
  DOLL, BARBIE, see Doll, Mattel, Barbie
Bebe Phenix, Chemise, Blue Paperweight Eyes, Wig, 17 In. 3900.00

◆◆

A video inventory is being offered in some cities. It is a color video cassette recording done in your home with your voice describing the antiques. Keep it in a safe deposit box for a permanent record of your collection.

◆◆

Bebe, Bisque Head, Paperweight Eyes, Closed Mouth, 1880s, 16 3/8 In.	5500.00
Bebe, Original Chemise, 17 In.	5600.00
Bebe, Pressed Bisque Head, Wooden Body, Key Wind Music Box, 17 In.	6600.00
DOLL, BERGMANN, see also Doll, S & H; Doll, Simon & Halbig	
Bergmann, Child, Bisque, Open–Close Eyes, Original Clothes, 32 In.	950.00
Bergner, 3–Face, Bisque Flange Neck, String–Crier, Cloth, 15 In.	1045.00
Bisque Head, 5–Piece Composition Body, Molded Hair, 6 1/2 In.	350.00
Bisque Head, Molded Hair, Painted Googly Eyes, 5–Piece Body, 6 1/2 In.	375.00
Bisque, 3 Face, Old Clothes, 15 In.	1500.00
Bisque, Jointed At Shoulders, Buster Brown Type Clothes, 1910, 7 In.	75.00
Bisque, Swivel Neck, Glass Eyes, Closed Mouth, 12 In.	585.00
Bisque, Weighted Eyes, Open Mouth, Parasol, Germany, 12 In.	85.00
Bride & Groom, Bisque, Crepe Paper Rose O'Neill Dress, Japan, Pair	165.00
Bride & Groom, Germany, Box, 3 1/2 In.	350.00
Bride, Blond Human Hair Wig, Stuffed Cloth Body, Wax Arms, Legs, 20 In.	550.00
Brooke Shields, 1982, 12 In.	18.00
Bru Jne No. 10, Brown Eyes, Blond, Ball–Jointed, Clothes, 23 1/2 In.	7500.00
Bru Jne, Fashion Lady, Closed Mouth, Original Dress, 15 1/2 In.	3800.00
Bru Jne, Fashion, Smiling, Original Clothes, Bisque, 16 In.	3500.00
Buddy Lee, Cowboy	160.00
Buddy Lee, Flossie Flirt, Plastic, 22 In.	200.00
Bugs Bunny, Talking, Box	25.00
Bullwinkle, Talking, 10 In.	35.00
Bye–Lo, Baby, Brown Eyes, Original Outfit, Box, 8 1/2 In.	575.00
Bye–Lo, Baby, Composition Head, Cloth Body, Marked Blanket	300.00
Bye–Lo, Bisque, Blue Eyes, Celluloid Hands, 15 1/2 In.	850.00
Bye–Lo, Bisque, Brown Eyes, Old Clothes, Celluloid Hands, 12 1/2 In.	500.00
Bye–Lo, Bisque, Brown Eyes, Tag, Original Clothes, 17 In.	1000.00
Bye–Lo, Brown Eyes, Celluloid Hands, 13–In. Diam. Head	750.00
Cameo, Kewpie, Hot 'N Tot, Black, Vinyl, 10 In.	85.00 To 150.00
Cameo, Kewpie, Rubber, Glass Eyes, Signed Rose O'Neill	75.00
Cameo, Little Miss Peep, Box	45.00
Campbell Kids, Kid Body, Bisque Hands, Side Eyes, 10 1/2 In.	250.00
Captain Action	95.00
Celluloid Shoulderhead, Sleep Eyes, Stuffed Kid Body, 22 In.	105.00
Celluloid, Blond Braids, Maroon Dress, Apron, Turtle Mark, 11 1/2 In.	22.00
Celluloid, Boy, Molded Hair, Glass Eyes, Cloth Body, Germany, 18 In.	125.00
Celluloid, Braids, Painted Eyes, Taffeta Skirt, Turtle Mark, 12 In.	49.50
Celluloid, Toddler, Molded Hair, Glass Eyes, Germany, 13 In.	115.00
Chad Valley, Long John Silver, Glass Eyes	1200.00
Chad Valley, Princess Marie, 18 In.	400.00
Chad Valley, Sailor, Composition, 1940	100.00
Chase, Baby, Sateen Body, Original Dress, 14 In.	425.00
Chase, Boy, Cloth, Textured Painted Blond Hair, 26 In.	990.00
Chase, Boy, Muslin & Stockinette, Blond, Painted Face, Romper, 13 In.	143.00
Chase, Stockinette, Molded & Painted Blond Hair, Sateen Body, 12 In.	425.00
Chase, Stockinette, Painted Blond Hair, Cotton Sateen Body,	450.00
Chemtoy, Juro, John Travolta, 1977, 12 In.	45.00
China Head, Legs & Arms, Lace Trimmed Dress, Germany, 6 3/8 In.	150.00
China, Cloth Body, Bisque Arms, Legs, Molded Hair, Dress, Germany, 6 In.	38.50
China, Flat Top, 8 In.	350.00
Cloth, Emma & Marietta Adams, Painted, World's Columbian Fair, 1893	1870.00
Cloth, Stitched Black Hair, Eyes, Red Lips, Hands, 16 In.	70.00
Cochran, Cowboy, Closed Mouth, 15 In.	650.00
Commando, Schwarzenegger, Box, 16 In.	75.00
Connie Lynn	325.00
Dakin, Pebbles, Flintstone	11.00
Danel, Paris, Bebe, Jumeau Jointed Body, Pearl Earrings, 16 In.	3575.00
Dawn, Fashion, Box	25.00
Demacol, Glass Eyes, Googly, 11 In.	650.00
Dennis The Menace, Plastic, 12 1/4 In.	22.00
DEP 13, Bisque, Hair, Jointed Composition, Old Clothes, 28 In.	600.00
DEP, Bisque, Brown Human Hair Wig, Original Dress, Socks, French, 14 In.	995.00

DEP, Composition Ball–Jointed Body, Sleep Eyes, Pierced Ears, 19 In.	650.00
DEP, Tete Jumeau, Pull String, 25 In.	1600.00
Dolly Dingle, Dickie Dingle, Pair	100.00
Dolly Madison, China Head, Blond, 21 In.	495.00
Dr. Doolittle, Rex Harrison	45.00
Dr. Little Chap, 2 Outfits In Packages	50.00
E. D. Depose, Wooden & Composition Body, Blown Glass Eyes, 16 In.	1000.00
E. D., Jumeau Body, Brown Paperweight Eyes, 21 In.	995.00
Effanbee, Abraham Lincoln, Box	67.50
Effanbee, Alfalfa	50.00
Effanbee, Ann Shirley, Blond Braids, Dressed, 15 In. .... 150.00 To 375.00
Effanbee, Art Carney	150.00
Effanbee, Baby Grumpy	85.00
Effanbee, Baby, Bisque, Lenox Head, Chemise & Sweater, 1919, 10 In.	250.00
Effanbee, Boy, Just Friends, Dutch	25.00
Effanbee, Bubbles, Original Heart Locket, Bent Limb, 16 In.	175.00
Effanbee, Buckwheat	40.00
Effanbee, Dorothy, Tinman, Lion, Strawman, 4 Piece	135.00
Effanbee, Dwight Eisenhower, Box	67.50
Effanbee, Flower Girl & Ring Bearer, 1966, Pair	125.00
Effanbee, Gibson Girl	195.00
Effanbee, Harry Truman .... 65.00 To 75.00
Effanbee, Heather	90.00
Effanbee, John Wayne, Box, 17 In.	150.00
Effanbee, Little Lady, String Hair, Composition, 21 In.	195.00
Effanbee, Marionette, Lucifer, Black	250.00
Effanbee, Mark Twain, Box	75.00
Effanbee, Mary Poppins, Box	55.00
Effanbee, Most Happy Family, In Living Room, Box, 1957, 3 Piece	195.00
Effanbee, Patsy, Composition, 11 In.	175.00
Effanbee, Rosemary, Dress, Hat, Shoes, Composition, 26 In.	195.00
Effanbee, Skippy, Composition, Cloth Body, Keep 'Em Flying, 14 In.	1017.00
Effanbee, Suzette, Black, Composition, Native Costume	275.00
Effanbee, Suzette, Composition, Bridal Dress, 14 In.	85.00
Effanbee, W. C. Fields, Centennial, 1980	100.00
Evangeline, Baby–Type, 1895	88.00
F & B, Babe Ruth, Box	150.00
F & B, Jackie Gleason & Art Carney, Box, Pair	250.00
F. G., Fashion, Bisque Swivel Head, Cotton Dress, Shoes, 22 In.	4000.00
F. G., Fashion, Kid Body, Blue Eyes, 14 In.	1800.00
Felix The Cat, Composition, 8 1/2 In.	100.00
Fish Vendor, French, Terra Cotta, c.1920, 9 1/2 In.	65.00
Flip Wilson, Flip Side Geraldine .... 22.00 To 45.00
Football Player, Cloth, Vinyl Head	8.00
Fred Sanford, Rag	32.00
Freddy Krueger, Poseable, Box, 9 In.	50.00
Freddy Krueger, Talking, Matchbox, 18 In.	50.00
French, Black Hair, Powder Blue Lace Dress, Anchor Mark	800.00
French, Fashion, Bisque Swivel Head, Kid Body, Paperweight Eyes, 1870s	2145.00
French, Fashion, Bisque Swivel Head, Pierced Ears, Dressed, 15 In.	1100.00
French, Fashion, Brown Paperweight Eyes, Antique Clothes, 15 1/2 In.	1995.00
French, Fashion, Girl, Bisque Swivel Head, Kid Body, Dressed, 15 1/8 In.	3740.00
French, Fashion, Kid Body, Black Gown, Marked MX4, 14 In.	2700.00
French, Glass Eyes, Bamboo Teeth, Original Clothes, 36 In.	1350.00
French, Kid Leather Body, Striped Dress, Hat, Shoes, Marked F. G., 22 In.	4000.00
French, Walking, Cork Pate, Sleep Eyes, Throws Kisses, Voice Box, 22 In.	990.00
Frozen Charlie, Blond, 15 In. .... 385.00 To 485.00
Frozen Charlotte, Black Hair, China, Dress, 4 1/4 In.	55.00
Frozen Charlotte, White Bisque, 3 In.	20.00
Fulper, Porcelain, Open Close Eyes, Blond, Kid–Jointed, Dressed, 21 In.	1250.00
Fulper, Toddler, 20 In.	525.00
G. I. Joe, Black Adventurer, Dog Tag, Life–Like Hair, 12 In.	108.00
G. I. Joe, Man of Action, Talking	34.00

G. I. Joe, Marine Camouflage Shirt, Field Pack, Painted Hair, 12 In. 48.00
G. I. Joe, Pilot's Orange Jumpsuit, Boots, Blond Painted Hair, 12 In. 58.00
G. I. Joe, Tagged, Booklet, Box, 1964 .... 110.00
G. I. Joe, Talking Man of Action 85.00
DOLL, GEBRUDER HEUBACH, see also Doll, Heubach
Gebruder Heubach 399, Black, 13 In. Head, Large 950.00
Gebruder Heubach 6692, Cloth Body, Bisque Lower Arms & Legs, Dressed 395.00
Gebruder Heubach 9058, Googly, Painted Eyes, Shoes & Socks, 7 In. 400.00
Gebruder Heubach, 7612, Character, Flocked Hair, 5 Piece Body, 11 In. 500.00
Gebruder Heubach, 8420, Child, Pouty Mouth, Ball–Jointed, 14 In. 1100.00
Gebruder Heubach, Baby, Mechanical, In Basket, Rotating Action, 8 In. 650.00
Gebruder Heubach, Brown Sleep Eyes, Kid Body, 26 In. 500.00
Gebruder Heubach, Child, Molded Hair, Intaglio Eyes, 8 1/4 In. 350.00
Gebruder Huebach, Googly, 5 Piece Body, Painted Eyes, Shoes, 6 1/4 In. 285.00
Georgene, Composition, Pink Dress, Tags, Labels, Box 475.00
Germany, American School Boy, Bisque, Glass Eyes, Closed Mouth, 18 In. 375.00
Germany, Bisque, Dressed, 4 In., Pair 90.00
Germany, Character Toddler, Flirty Eyes, Bisque Socket Head, 17 In. 467.00
Germany, Girl, Sleep Eyes, Human Hair, Toddler Body, Turtle Mark, 19 In. 250.00
Germany, Santa Claus, Glass Eyes, Composition Face & Hands, 26 In. 275.00
Ginny, Prince Charming, Strung, Box 425.00
Gladdie, Original Clothes, 17 In. 895.00
Goggly, Hug Me Kiddie, Brown Eyes, Felt Body, Dress, Mask Face, 1911 .... 600.00
Golliwog, England, 14 1/2 In. 95.00
Gottschalk & Co., Baby, Bisque, Bent Limb Body, Wobble Tongue, 19 In. 350.00
Grace Putnam, Bye–Lo, Baby, Black, Germany 1400.00
Grace Putnam, Bye–Lo, Baby, Germany 1200.00
Gruelle, Raggedy Ann, Wooden Heart, Pat. Sept. 7, 1915 .... 2500.00
GSP, Bye–Lo, Clear Blue Sleep Eyes, Original Clothes, 12 In. Head 450.00
Gund & RCA, Ludwig Von Drake, Talking, Box 380.00
Gunzel, Boy, Vinyl Head, Stretch Velour Body, Brown Human Hair, 28 In. 165.00
Hagara, Amanda 150.00
Hallmark, Amelia Earhart 10.00
Hallmark, Babe Ruth 20.00
Hallmark, Winifred Witch 15.00
Handwerck 69, Bisque, Brown Human Hair Wig, Original Dress, 25 In. 950.00
Handwerck 109, Almond Shaped Sleeping Brown Eyes, Lawn Dress, 18 In. 475.00
Handwerck 109, Bisque Socket Head, Open Mouth, Blond Wig, 19 In. 1430.00
Handwerck 109, Sleep Eyes, Ball–Jointed, White Dress & Hat, 18 In. 475.00
Handwerck 109–15, Blond Wig, Sleep Eyes, Open Mouth, Teeth, 28 In. 935.00
Handwerck, Bebe Reclame, 1898, Box 975.00
Handwerck, Bisque Head, Open Mouth, Fully Composition Body, 23 In. 225.00
Handwerck, Bisque Head, Open Mouth, Pierced Ears, Original Wig, 21 In. 400.00
Handwerck, Bisque Head, Sleep Eyes, Ball–Jointed, Open Mouth, 20 In. 385.00
Handwerck, Bisque Shoulder Head, Open Mouth, Kid Body & Legs, 30 In. 200.00
Handwerck, Blond Hair, Socket Head, Ball–Jointed, Tucked Dress, 29 In. 3025.00
Handwerck, Brown Sleep Eyes, Blond Mohair, Old Clothes, 20 In. 400.00
Hasbro, Flying Nun, 12 In. 100.00
Hasbro, Kelly, Charlie's Angel, 1977, 8 1/2 In. 25.00
Hazelle, Fairy Princess, Marionette, Moveable Mouth, 15 In. 65.00
Head, China, Dark Hair, Blue Eyes, Red Eyeliner, 1880s Style, 5 In. 60.00
Head, China, Blond, 1880s Style, Embossed Necklace, 3 In. 50.00
Heebee Shebee, Bisque, Sticker, 7 1/8 In. 750.00
Heidi Ott, Baby, Awake, 19 In. 655.00
Heidi Ott, Baby, Pink & White Outfit, 19 In. 565.00
Heidi Ott, Baby, Sleeping, 19 In. 655.00
Heidi Ott, Black Baby, Vinyl Head, Curly Hair, Playsuit, Box, 13 In. 385.00
Heidi Ott, Clown, Bravo, With Violin, 19 In. 625.00
Heidi Ott, Clown, She Love Me Not, 19 In. 625.00
Heidi Ott, Clown, She Loves Me, 19 In. 625.00
Heidi Ott, Eric, Alpine Suit, 19 In. 655.00
Heidi Ott, Erika, Blond, 20 In. 655.00
Heinrich Handwerck, Child, 27 In. 550.00

Hendren, Infant, Composition & Cloth, Painted Eyes, Molded Hair 65.00
Henry, Comics, Bisque 60.00
DOLL, HEUBACH, see Doll, Gebruder Heubach
Heubach Koppelsdorf 264, Bisque Head, Set Eyes, 14 In. 325.00
Heubach Koppelsdorf 267, Character Baby, Bisque, Curly Hair, 18 In. 425.00
Heubach Koppelsdorf 320–12, 5 Piece Body, 2 Upper Teeth, 30 In. 550.00
Heubach Koppelsdorf, Baby, Teeth, Breather Nostrils, Gauze Suit, 15 In. 395.00
Heubach Koppelsdorf, Boy Chef, Bisque, 6 In. 165.00
Heubach Koppelsdorf, Character Baby, 18 In. 650.00
Heubach Koppelsdorf, Child, Composition, Sleep Eyes, Dutch, 6 In. 135.00
Heubach Koppelsdorf, Coquette Girl, Bisque, Kid Body, 11 1/2 In. 475.00
Heubach Koppelsdorf, Girl, Bisque, Socket Head, Human Wig, 30 In. 715.00
Heubach Kopplesdorf 275, Bisque Head, Blond Wig, Leather Body, 18 In. 265.00
Heubach, Bisque Head, 5–Piece Papier–Mache Body, Closed Mouth, 8 In. 1295.00
Heubach, Bisque Head, Glass Sleep Eyes, Mohair Wig, 23 In. 100.00
Horsman, Baby Dimples, 20 In. 99.50
Horsman, Cindy, Long Gown, Matching Ruffled Hat, 15 In. 90.00
Horsman, Composition, Cloth Body, Tin Eyes, 20 In. 40.00
Horsman, Crier, Composition Head 100.00
Horsman, Ella Cinders, 18 In. 62.50
Horsman, He Bee, She Bee, Pair 62.50
Horsman, Mary Poppins, Handbag, 1964, 12 In. 50.00
Horsman, Poor Pitiful Pearl, Booklet, Extra Clothes, Box 150.00
Horsman, Tessie Talk, Ventriloquist Doll, 18 In. 48.50
Horsman, Twins, Vinyl Head & Limbs, Cloth Body, Sleep Eyes, 13 In., Pr. 99.00
Horsman, Walker, 1964, 27 In. 30.00
Hoyer, Composition, Brown Saran Wig, Sleep Eyes, Ballerina, 14 In. 93.00
Ideal, Baby Snooks, Composition 250.00
Ideal, Betsy McCall, 36 In. 200.00
Ideal, Betsy McCall, All Original, 8 In. 110.00
Ideal, Bonnie Braids, Hard Plastic, Vinyl Head, 1951, 13 In. 65.00
Ideal, Bye–Bye Baby, Dressed, 25 In. .... 350.00 To 455.00
Ideal, Crissy, Orange Dress & Shoes 35.00
Ideal, Fannie Brice, Composition, Dressed, 1938 .... 200.00
Ideal, Gro–Hair Tressy 45.00
Ideal, Kissy, Box, 1961, 30 In. 75.00
Ideal, Miss Revlon, Sunglasses & Pearls, 19 In. 125.00
Ideal, Patti Playpal, Original Clothes, Box, 36 In. .... 250.00 To 275.00
Ideal, Saucy Walker, 1960, 32 In. 50.00
Ideal, Snow White, Box, 18 In. 500.00
Ideal, Tammy B, Clothes & Stand 45.00
Ideal, Toni, Nurse Dress, 19 In. 180.00
Illya, Man From U. N. C. L. E., Box 190.00
DOLL, INDIAN, see Indian, Doll
Indiana Jones 200.00
DOLL, J.D.K., see also Doll, Kestner
J. D. K. 10, Baby, Bald Head, 13 In. 500.00
J. D. K. 13, Baby, Painted Hair, Solid Dome Head, 14 In. 1000.00
J. D. K. 221, Googly–Eye, Ball–Jointed Toddler Body, 15 In. 3410.00
J. D. K. 257, Character Baby, 5 Piece Body, Curly Blond, Dress, 23 In. 825.00
J. D. K. 260, Character, 32 In. 1200.00
James Bond, Action, Thunderball, Complete Accessories, 1965, 12 In. 155.00
Jane Withers, 20 In. 950.00
Joe Ellis, Pewter Feet 500.00
Joey Stivic, Archie Bunker's Grandson, Box 50.00
John Wayne, Cowboy, Box 85.00
Jumeau 1180, Brown Paperweight Eyes, Clothes, 13 In. 4995.00
Jumeau 1907, Bisque, Upper Teeth, Jointed Body, Pink Silk Dress, 14 In. 1430.00
Jumeau, Bisque Head, Brown Wig, Original Outfit, Shoes, Purse, 29 In. 3200.00
Jumeau, Bisque Head, Stationary Eyes, Open–Close Mouth, 11 1/2 In. 5500.00
Jumeau, Bisque Socket Head, Blue Paperweight Eyes, Open Mouth, 20 In. 2200.00
Jumeau, Bisque Socket Head, Rose Silk & Lace Dress, Bonnet, 11 In. 7700.00
Jumeau, Bisque, Open Mouth, Open–Close Eyes, Dress, Lace Trim, 29 In. 2300.00

Jumeau, Bisque, Teeth, Blond Ringlets, Silk Underwear, 29 1/2 In. 2950.00
Jumeau, Closed Mouth, Original Wig & Clothing 2400.00
Jumeau, Human Hair Wig, Dressed, 1907, 20 In. 2000.00
Jumeau, Poured Bisque Head, Cork Pate, Composition Body, 11 In. 2750.00
Juro, Jerry Mahoney, Dummy, 1967 .... 45.00
Jutta, Brown Glass Eyes, Open Mouth, Ball–Jointed, Eyelet Dress, 27 In. 445.00
K * R 100, Brown Sleep Eyes, Ball–Jointed, 39 In. 2950.00
K * R 101, Bisque Head, Black Character Doll, Painted Eyes, 9 1/4 In. 400.00
K * R 101, Character, Jointed, Composition, Bisque Head, 8 1/2 In. 1045.00
K * R 114, Character, Intaglio Eyes, Pouty Mouth, Dressed, 8 1/2 In. 1320.00
K * R 114, Pouty, Original Clothes, 7 In. 1650.00
K * R 114/13, Character Child, Blond Wig, Pouty Mouth, Jointed, 13 In. 1045.00
K * R 116A, Baby, Bisque, Tongue, Crocheted Outfit, 16 1/2 In. 1950.00
K * R 116A, Baby, Brown Sleep Eyes, Dimples, 14 1/2 In. 1650.00
K * R 117A, Bisque, Open Close Eyes, Long Curls, Dressed, 17 1/2 In. 4500.00
K * R 121, Character Baby, Bisque Head, 5 Piece Body, Bonnet, 24 In. 660.00
K * R 126, Character Baby, Sleep Eyes, Christening Gown, Bonnet, 23 In. 795.00
K * R 126, Character Toddler, Bisque, Ball–Jointed, Underwear, 24 In. 522.00
K * R 126, Flirty Eye, Bisque, 19 In. 595.00
K * R 131, Googly Eyes, Watermelon Smile, Ball–Jointed, 15 In. 6050.00
K * R 39, Bisque Socket Head, Ball–Jointed, Open Mouth, 15 In. 550.00
K * R, Bisque, Ball Jointed, Original Wig, Old Clothes, 25 1/2 In. 1050.00
K * R, Character Baby, Flirty Glass Eyes, Open Mouth, 13 In. 1100.00
K * R, Character Toddler, Bisque Head, Sleep–Flirty Eyes, 13 In. 400.00
K * R, Toddler, Flirty Eye, Open Mouth, 14 In. 1900.00
Kaiser, Baby, 12 In. 450.00
Kammer & Reinhardt 100, Boy, Bisque, Painted Hair, Dressed, 18 In. 950.00
Kammer & Reinhardt 117A, Girl, Mein Liebling, Dressed, 17 1/2 In. 4500.00
Kammer & Reinhardt, 127, Boy, Molded Brown Painted Hair, 12 In. 1150.00
Kammer & Reinhardt, Girl, Braided Buns, Crocheted Dress, 11 In. 3500.00
Karl Hatman, Bisque Head, Jointed Body, 27 In. 435.00
Kathe Kruse, Boy, Brown Wig, Celluloid Face, 1970s, 10 1/2 In. 190.00
Kathe Kruse, Girl, Plastic Head, Muslin Body, Blond Braids, 19 In. 225.00
Kathe Kruse, Hula Dancer, Bisque, Painted Black, Sleep Eyes, 7 1/2 In. 75.00
Kathe Kruse, Ilsebill & Friedebald, Box, 1986, Pair 1600.00
    DOLL, KESTNER, see also Doll, J.D.K.
Kestner 7, Bisque Swivel Head, Blond, Original Clothing, 18 In. 935.00
Kestner 143, Bisque Socket Head, Ball–Jointed, Bobbed Hair, 16 In. 715.00
Kestner 143, Character Child, Blue Sleep Eyes, 2 Upper Teeth, 20 In. 605.00
Kestner 148, Brown Open–Close Eyes, Brown Silk Dress, 21 In. 425.00
Kestner 152, Baby, Closed Mouth, Tongue, Glass Sleep Eyes, 11 In. 300.00
Kestner 154, Bisque, Sleep Eyes, Kid Body, Plaster Pate, 21 In. 385.00
Kestner 164, Bisque, Sleep Eyes, Composition Ball–Jointed Body, 25 In. 485.00
Kestner 172, Gibson Girl, Antique Outfit, Fur Piece, 18 In. 2695.00
Kestner, Bisque Head, Glass Sleep Eyes, Original Mohair Wig, 14 In. 650.00
Kestner, Bisque, Jointed Head, Arms, Legs, Sleep Eyes, Pink Boots, 9 In. 985.00
Kestner, Bye–Lo, Baby, Bisque, Jointed, Wrapper, 4 1/2 In. 165.00
Kestner, Child, 14 In. 400.00
Kestner, Closed–Mouth, Bisque, Unmarked, 27 In. 3000.00
Kestner, Turned Shoulder Head, Jointed Kid Body & Legs, 19 In. 400.00
Kestner, Tyrolean Clothes, Jointed Kid Body, Marked, 15 In. 300.00
    DOLL, KEWPIE, see Kewpie, Doll
King George VI, Felt & Velvet Outfit 145.00
Kley & Hahn 161, Character Boy, 18 In. 1650.00
Kley & Hahn 526, Character, Blue Paperweight Eyes, Bisque, 20 1/2 In. 4500.00
Kley & Hahn, Bisque, Composition Ball–Jointed Body, 19 1/2 In. 400.00
Knickerbocker, Barney, Cloth, 17 In. 65.00
Knickerbocker, Flintstone, Cloth, 17 In. 65.00
Knickerbocker, Grumpy, 9 In. 115.00
Knickerbocker, Pinocchio, Composition, c.1939, 14 In. 385.00
Knickerbocker, Pixie & Dixie, Plush, 1959, Pair 68.00
Knickerbocker, Raggedy Andy 17.00
Knickerbocker, Raggedy Ann & Raggedy Andy, 1961, Set 170.00

◆◆

Be careful about putting antique china or glass in the dishwasher.
Glass will sometimes crack from the heat. Porcelains with gold overglaze decoration often lose the gold. Damaged or crazed glaze will
sometimes pop off the plates in large pieces.

◆◆

Knickerbocker, W. C. Fields, Talking	85.00
Konig & Wernicke, Toddler, 19 In.	700.00
Kreuger, Love Me, Box	105.00
Kreuger, Timmy Luke, Brunette, Knee Socks, Saddle Shoes, 21 In.	154.00
Laurel & Hardy, Bisque Head, Pair	50.00
Laverne & Shirley, 1977, 12 In., Pair	125.00
LeConte, Lenci–Type Body, Bisque, Replaced Blond, Pink Dress, 24 In.	220.00
Lenci, Bettina, With Bunny, Box	125.00
Lenci, Black Mohair Wig, Painted Blue Eyes, 15 In. ....*Illus*	38.50
Lenci, Easter Outfit, Holding Basket, c.1924, 18 In.	795.00
Lenci, Felt, Holding Chicken, 10 In. ....*Illus*	33.00
Lenci, Flirty Eyes, Painted Mouth, Coat, Skirt & Hat, 19 In.	935.00
Lenci, Girl, Felt Body, Painted Features, 9 1/2 In.	40.00
Lenci, Mascotte Girl, Floppy Hat, 10 In. ....*Illus*	104.50
Lenci, Painted Features, Orange Gauze Dress, Hat, Felt, 23 In.	1320.00
Lenci, Peasant, Felt, Blond, Painted Blue Eyes, 14 In. ....*Illus*	550.00
Lenci, Starry–Eyed, c.1940, 10 In.	325.00
Lenci, Violetta, 21 In.	275.00
Limbach, Bisque Head, Jointed Composition Body, Sleep Eyes, 26 In.	275.00
Limbach, Bisque, Jointed, Painted, Blond Hair, 5 In.	38.50
Limoges, Blue Paperweight Eyes, Teeth, Auburn Wig, Clothes, 27 In.	1250.00
Lindstrom, Dancing Lassie, Working, 1930s, 8 In.	100.00
Maberg, Baby, Frog Body, Brown Eyes, Celluloid Hands, 12 1/2 In.	450.00
Madame Alexander, Alice, Cloth, Mask Face, Painted, Yarn Hair, 20 In.	121.00
Madame Alexander, Carmen Miranda, Original Clothes, Label, 7 1/2 In.	80.00
Madame Alexander, Carnival In Rio, Porcelain, Box	385.00
Madame Alexander, Cissy, All Original, 21 In.	280.00
Madame Alexander, Cissy, Black Taffeta Dress, Tag	225.00
Madame Alexander, Cissy, Hard Plastic Head, Blue Sleep Eyes, 20 In.	1017.00
Madame Alexander, Cissy, Pink Taffeta Gown, Tag, 1957	525.00
Madame Alexander, Coco Melanie, Wrist Tag, 1966	1450.00
Madame Alexander, Cornelia, 1976, 21 In.	400.00
Madame Alexander, Elise Bride, 17 In.	110.00
Madame Alexander, Huggums, Box, 25 In.	145.00
Madame Alexander, Little Betty, Hawaiian Outfit, 1937, 9 In.	100.00
Madame Alexander, Little Shaver, Cloth, Buckram Face, Brown Wig, 15 In.	175.00
Madame Alexander, Little Women, 11 In., 5 Piece	275.00 To 350.00

Doll, Lenci, Mascotte Girl, Floppy Hat, 10 In.
Doll, Lenci, Black Mohair Wig, Painted Blue Eyes, 15 In.
Doll, Lenci, Peasant, Felt, Blond, Painted Blue Eyes, 14 In.
Doll, Lenci, Felt, Holding Chicken, 10 In.

Madame Alexander, Madame, Box, 1968, 14 In.	180.00
Madame Alexander, Magnolia, 21 In.	240.00
Madame Alexander, Mary Ellen, Hard Plastic, 1954, 31 In.	300.00
Madame Alexander, Natasha, Russian Type Brocade Clothes	330.00
Madame Alexander, Portrait, Madame Alexander, Pink, Box	300.00
Madame Alexander, Pussy Cat, Box, 1965	80.00
Madame Alexander, Rubber, 1950s, 14 In.	55.00
Madame Alexander, Sarah Bernhardt, Brown Velvet Dress	225.00
Madame Alexander, Scarlett O'Hara, Dress, Shoes, 21 In.	350.00
Madame Alexander, Scarlett O'Hara, Hard Plastic, 1950s, 12 In.	475.00
Madame Alexander, Scarlett, Brown, Green Eyes, Print Dress, 14 In.	66.00
Madame Alexander, Sonja Henie, Dressed, Accessories, 1941, 14 In.	180.00
Madame Alexander, Sonja Henie, Ski Outfit, 1930s	330.00
Madame Alexander, Sweet Tears, Black Hair	75.00
Madame Alexander, Winnie Walker, Hard Plastic, 1953, 23 1/2 In.	250.00
Mae Starr, Talking, With Cylinders	875.00
Magilla Gorilla, 1964	120.00
Marionette, Horse, Wooden, Polychrome, Cloth, Fiber, 10 1/2 In.	17.50
Marionette, Little Red Riding Hood, Pelham, China Head & Hands	75.00
Martha Chase, Cloth, Hard–Pressed Head, Dress, Stockings, Shoes, 16 In.	715.00
Marvel Toy, Talker, Walker, Hard Plastic, Lever Action, Box, 26 In.	150.00
MASH, Klinger, In Dress, 4 In., Set of 7	80.00
Mattel, Barbie, American Girl, Bathing Suit	275.00
Mattel, Barbie, American Girl, Blond	350.00
Mattel, Barbie, Astronaut, Brunette, No. 4	335.00
Mattel, Barbie, Blond Ponytail, Pearl Earrings, Stand, Box, 1962	225.00
Mattel, Barbie, Blond, 18 In.	150.00
Mattel, Barbie, Blond, No. 3	225.00
Mattel, Barbie, Bride, Porcelain	350.00 To 400.00
Mattel, Barbie, Brunette, No. 4, Box	225.00
Mattel, Barbie, Bubble Cut, Bent Knee, De La Renta Costume	65.00
Mattel, Barbie, Bubble Cut, Blond, Nighty Negligee, Dog, 1963	122.00
Mattel, Barbie, Bubble Cut, Brunette, 1962	30.00
Mattel, Barbie, Bubble Cut, Red, Black & White Striped Swimsuit, 1961	104.00
Mattel, Barbie, Enchanted Evening	250.00
Mattel, Barbie, Eskimo	125.00
Mattel, Barbie, Happy Holidays, Germany, Box	110.00
Mattel, Barbie, Happy Holidays, Red, 1988	100.00
Mattel, Barbie, Happy Holidays, White, 1989	60.00
Mattel, Barbie, Music Lovin'	30.00
Mattel, Barbie, No. 4, Brunette Ponytail	225.00
Mattel, Barbie, Parisian, International, Box	175.00
Mattel, Barbie, Sears 100th Anniversary	50.00
Mattel, Barbie, Skipper, Trunk With Extra Outfits	125.00
Mattel, Barbie, Sleep Eyes	185.00
Mattel, Barbie, Solo In The Spotlight	250.00
Mattel, Barbie, Sun Gold Malibu, Box	35.00
Mattel, Buffy & Mrs. Beasley, Box, 2 Piece	95.00
Mattel, Cheryl Ladd, Box	45.00
Mattel, Donny Osmond, 8 In.	25.00
Mattel, Ken, Brunette, 1962	20.00
Mattel, Ken, Straight Legs, Black Hair, 1962	50.00
Mattel, Marie Osmond, 1976, 12 In.	25.00
Mattel, Midge, Bendable Legs	275.00
Mattel, Peaches & Cream, Black, 1984	30.00
Mattel, Pepper, Tammy's Sister, Box	30.00
Mattel, Scooter, Brown Hair	55.00
Mattel, Skater, Windup, 1980	20.00
Mattel, Skipper, Accessories, Box, 1963	80.00
Mattel, Skipper, Bendable Legs, 1965	65.00
Mattel, Skipper, Original Clothes, Stand, Box, 1963	70.00
Mattel, Twiggy, Box	100.00
Mattel, Twirly Curls, Black, 1982	20.00

Maude Tousey Fangel, Cloth, Signed, 16 1/2 In. 750.00
Max Shulman, Two–Faced Bisque Head, Intaglio Eyes, Jointed, 7 3/4 In. 310.00
Mego, Action Jackson, Box 25.00
Mego, Action Jackson, Dressed, Box, 8 In. 18.00
Mego, Bodey, From Starsky & Hutch 18.00
Mego, Captain & Tenille 70.00
Mego, Captain America, 12 In. 45.00
Mego, Captain Kirk, Star Trek, Poseable, 12 1/2 In. 55.00
Mego, Cat Woman 50.00
Mego, Cher 35.00
Mego, Chips, Ponch 18.00
Mego, Diana Ross 55.00
Mego, Dorothy, Wizard of Oz, Box, 8 In. 35.00
Mego, Dukes of Hazard, Card, 8 In. 10.00
Mego, Glinda, Wizard of Oz, Box, 8 In. 35.00
Mego, Huggy Bear 24.00
Mego, LaVerne & Shirley 80.00
Mego, Spiderman, 8 In. 15.00
Mego, Suzanne Somers, 1978, 12 In. 45.00
Mego, Tarzan, 8 In. 95.00
Mego, Wizard of Oz, Package 15.00
Mego, Wonder Woman 30.00
Merry Thought, Rag, Tag On Foot, 1940 .... 25.00
Milliner's Model, Original Clothes, 16 1/2 In. 550.00
Morimura Bros., Bisque Socket Head, Composition Baby Body, 14 1/2 In. 315.00
Morimura, Bisque Shoulder Head, Jointed Oil Cloth Body, 17 In. 110.00
Nancy Ann Storybook, Baby, Hard Plastic, Sleep Eyes, Tag 65.00
Nancy Lee, Velvet Dress, Tags, Labels, 21 In. 475.00
Norah Wellings, Boy, Tan Skin, 8 In. 45.00
Norah Wellings, English Schoolboy, Felt, Mask Face, 14 1/2 In. 93.00
Norah Wellings, Mountie 110.00
Norah Wellings, Sailor 110.00
Ohio State Fair, Annie 50.00
Opryland U. S. A., Alison, 1986 .... 375.00
Our Pet 992, Toddler Body, All Original, Germany, 1915, 10 In. 695.00
    DOLL, PAPER, see Paper Doll
Parian, Blond, Snood, Gold Trim, 12 In. 200.00
Parian, Boy, Cloth Body, Molded Hair, Shirt & Bowtie, 16 1/2 In. 300.00
Parian, Lower Wooden Arms, Augusta, 23 In. 1200.00
Paris 60, Harem Girl, Painted Eyes, All Original 495.00
Peasant, Cloth, Stitched Faces, Italy, 15 & 17 In., Pair ....*Illus* 82.50
Pee Wee Herman, Vinyl, Cloth, Carousel, J. C. Penney, 41 In. 175.00
Penny, Carved, Articulated, Painted, Insam Family, Germany, 11 1/2 In. 45.00
    DOLL, PINCUSHION, see Pincushion Doll
Poland, Cloth, Composition, Braids, Dressed, 12 In. 38.00
Poor Pitiful Pearl, 1950s, 13 In. 60.00
President Hayes Wife, China Head, Fancy Hair, 17 In. 335.00

Doll, Peasant, Cloth, Stitched Faces, Italy,
15 & 17 In., Pair

◆◆◆◆◆◆◆◆◆◆◆◆◆◆◆◆◆◆◆◆◆◆

Save your doll's packaging, tags,
and inserts. These can triple the
price when the doll is sold.

◆◆◆◆◆◆◆◆◆◆◆◆◆◆◆◆◆◆◆◆◆◆

Puppet, Alligator, Hand, Steiff 60.00
Puppet, Bulldog, Steiff 35.00
Puppet, Dr. Doolittle, Hand, Talker 30.00
Puppet, Dutch Boy Paint, Package 38.00
Puppet, Dutch Boy, Package, 1956, 12 In. 45.00
Puppet, Eddy Baby, Steiff 65.00
Puppet, Farfel, Hand, Jimmy Nelson On Sides, Box 225.00
Puppet, Floyd Patterson, Boxing 25.00
Puppet, Grandpa Munster 150.00
Puppet, Gumby, Hand 15.00
Puppet, Herman Munster, Talking, Hand 285.00
Puppet, Lion, Steiff 65.00
Puppet, Little Red Riding Hood, Hand 12.50
Puppet, Mr. Ed, Talking Horse 85.00
Puppet, Mr. Magoo, Hand, Vinyl Head, Cloth Body, 1962 .... 85.00
Puppet, Mr. Magoo, Vinyl Head, Cloth Body, Blue, Green Cloth 35.00
Puppet, Shadow, Leather Parchment, Penile Bone Handles, Framed, Large 290.00
Puppet, Spark Plug, Hand, Vinyl Head, Cloth Body, 1960s, Gune 65.00
Puppet, Wolf, Steiff 75.00
Puppet, Yosemite Sam, Hand 10.00
Puss–In–Boots, Blond Mohair, Jointed, Embroidered Muzzle, 16 5/8 In. 55.00
Putnam, Baby, Dome Head, Celluloid Hands, White Clothes, 16 1/2-In. Head 440.00
Queen Louise, Sleep Eyes, Mohair Wig, Antique Clothes, 18 In. 350.00
Rag, Boy George, LIN, 14 In. 125.00
Rag, Mammy, Painted Leather Face & Forearms, Button Eyes, 32 In. 200.00
Ravca, Immigrant Man, Paris 45.00
Ravca, Immigrant Woman, Paris 45.00
Remco, Grandpa Munster, Addams' Family 235.00
Remco, I Dream of Jeannie, Accessories, Pink Bottle, 1967, 6 1/2 In. 200.00
Remco, Lurch, Addams' Family, 1964 .... 120.00
Rose O'Neill, Talcum Powder Dispenser, 1913 .... 110.00
Russia, Composition, Blue Sleep Eyes, Original Clothes, 18 1/2 In. 295.00
    DOLL, S & H, see also Doll, Bergmann; Doll, Simon & Halbig
S & H 1040, Brown Sleep Eyes, Blond, Dressed, Kid Body, 19 In. 350.00
S & H 1159, Lady, Brown Sleep Eyes, Original Clothes, 22 In. 2400.00
S. F. B. J. 10, Kisses, Pull Strings, 24 In. 1325.00
S. F. B. J. 25, Tete Jumeau, Bisque, Open Mouth, Red Hair, Dress, 20 In. 1500.00
S. F. B. J. 227, Boy, Bisque Head, Painted Hair, 6 Teeth, 16 3/4 In. 550.00
S. F. B. J. 235, Boy, Bisque, 14 In. 1200.00
S. F. B. J. 235, Boy, Molded Hair, Blue Glass Eyes, 2 Upper Teeth, 15 In. 1210.00
S. F. B. J. 236, Bisque, Upper Teeth, Brown Wig, Nursing Gown, 20 In. 1750.00
S. F. B. J. 236, Toddler, Bisque Head, Smiling Mouth, Dressed. 20 In. 1795.00
S. F. B. J. 236, Toddler, Bisque, Open–Close Mouth & Eyes, 20 In. 1750.00
S. F. B. J. 247, Twirp, 25 In. 2800.00
S. F. B. J. 251, Toddler Boy, Wobbly Tongue, Original Clothes, 21 In. 1600.00
S. F. B. J. 251, Toddler, Tongue, Blue Sleep Eyes, Clothes, 25 In. 2400.00
S. F. B. J. 252, Bisque, Closed Pouty Mouth, Satin Dress, 11 In. 4500.00
S. F. B. J. 252, Pouty, Composition Jointed Body, Wool Dress, 11 1/2 In. 4500.00
S. F. B. J. 252, Pouty, Human Hair, Ball–Jointed, Dressed, 13 In. 1500.00
S. F. B. J. 252, Pouty, Original Wig, Dress, 13 1/2 In. 6000.00
S. F. B. J. 252, Toddler, Ball–Jointed, 13 In. 165.00
S. F. B. J. 301, Bisque, Open Close Eyes, Jointed, Silk Dress, 24 1/2 In. 1100.00
S. F. B. J. 301, Bisque, Upper Teeth, Jointed Body, Underclothes, 29 In. 1350.00
S. F. B. J. 301, Open Mouth, Cotton Floral Chemise, Label, Box, 29 In. 1980.00
S. F. B. J. 301, Walker Type Body, Blue Eyes, Clothes, 21 1/2 In. 895.00
S. F. B. J., Bisque, Upper Teeth, Jointed Body, Underclothes, 21 1/2 In. 1250.00
S. F. B. J., Boy, Bisque Head, Composition, Jointed, Satin Dress, 21 In. 1250.00
S. F. B. J., Character Toddler, Open–Close Mouth, Velvet Dress, 20 In. 1210.00
S. F. B. J., Joan of Arc, 15 In. 400.00
S. F. B. J., Tete Jumeau, Open Mouth, Pierced Ears, 19 7/8 In. 350.00
Sasha, Baby, In Basket 175.00
Schilling, Papier–Mache, Dressed, 1894 .... 390.00
Schmidt 1293, Boy, Bisque Head, Sleep Eyes, Jointed, 1920s, 13 1/2 In. 715.00

Schoenau & Hoffmeister, Automaton, Child, Reclining, Head, Eyelids Move 900.00
Schoenau & Hoffmeister, Automaton, Jester, Arms Move, Bells, 9 In. 1750.00
Schoenau & Hoffmeister, Viola, Dutch Bob, Boy's Clothing, 22 In. 450.00
Schoenhut 310, Original Paint, Wig, Sailor Girl Outfit, 16 In. 1300.00
Schoenhut, Baby Face, 17 In. 600.00
Schoenhut, Bareback Rider, Bisque Head, 8 In. 350.00
Schoenhut, Boy, Molded Hair, 15 1/2 In. 750.00
Schoenhut, Character Baby, Wooden, Mohair Wig, Painted Features, 14 In. 300.00
Schoenhut, Character Girl, Pouty, White Wool Sailor Outfit, 18 In. 950.00
Schoenhut, Girl, Carved & Painted Wood, c.1914, 14 1/2 In. 385.00
Schoenhut, Girl, Carved Wooden Socket Head, Mohair Wig, 17 In. 1750.00
Schoenhut, Girl, Molded Hair, 14 1/2 In. 750.00
Schoenhut, Hilda, Walker 1200.00
Schoenhut, Pumpkin Head, Wax, 1840, 29 In. 750.00
        DOLL, SHIRLEY TEMPLE, see Shirley Temple
        DOLL, SIMON & HALBIG, see also Doll, Bergmann; Doll, S & H
Simon & Halbig 3, Bisque Socket Head, Ball–Jointed, Blond, 24 In. 330.00
Simon & Halbig 5, Flapper, Bisque, Ball–Jointed, Bobbed Hair, 14 In. 605.00
Simon & Halbig 15, Bisque Head, Sleep Eyes, Open Mouth, 23 In. 200.00
Simon & Halbig 719, Paperweight Eyes, Ball–Jointed, Composition 1980.00
Simon & Halbig 759, Black Feather Boa 1100.00
Simon & Halbig 927–11, Character Child, 25 In. 1200.00
Simon & Halbig 949, Bisque Head, Kid Body & Legs, 24 1/2 In. 1430.00
Simon & Halbig 1010, Fashion, Pierced Ears, 16 In. 525.00
Simon & Halbig 1078, Pale Bisque, French Body, Rose Dress, 26 In. 1200.00
Simon & Halbig 1079, Blond Mohair, Pierced Ears, White Dress, 30 In. 705.00
Simon & Halbig 1079, Old Clothing, 18 In. 650.00
Simon & Halbig 1159, Lady Body, Gibson Girl Dress, 14 In. 1200.00
Simon & Halbig 1159, Young Girl, Original Wig, 12 1/2 In. 950.00
Simon & Halbig 1249, Bisque Head, Glass Sleep Eyes, 20 In. 300.00
Simon & Halbig 1249, Bisque, Blue Eyes, Wood & Composition, 19 In. 770.00
Simon & Halbig 1329, Chinese Child, Brown Sleep Eyes, 14 In. 2400.00
Simon & Halbig 1329, Oriental Girl, Pierced Ears, Open Mouth, 15 In. 1100.00
Simon & Halbig, Ball–Jointed Composition Body, Brown Wig, 32 In. 1095.00
Simon & Halbig, Ball–Jointed, Black Brocade Gown, Hat, Parasol, 32 In. 1450.00
Simon & Halbig, Bisque Head, Glass Sleep Eyes, Open Mouth, 13 1/2 In. 357.00
Simon & Halbig, Bisque Head, Open Mouth, Scandinavian Costume, 19 In. 225.00
Simon & Halbig, Bisque Head, Pierced Ears, Open Mouth, 17 1/2 In. 750.00
Simon & Halbig, Bisque Lady, Brown Wig, 4 Teeth, Pierced Ears, 17 In. 1295.00
Simon & Halbig, Bisque, Blond Curly Hair, Shiny Body, 21 In. 420.00
Simon & Halbig, Bisque, Upper Teeth, Dress, Underclothes, 32 In. 895.00
Simon & Halbig, Blue Sleep Eyes, Open Mouth, 22 In. 330.00
Simon & Halbig, Farmer, Original Clothes, 11 In. 895.00
Simon & Halbig, Uncle Sam, 12 1/2 In. 1750.00
Skeezix, Oilcloth, 12 In. .... 35.00 To 68.00
Skookums, Indian Man, Woman & Papoose, 3 Piece 100.00
Soupy Sales, Box 225.00
Spoon, Washer Girl, Yarn Hair, 14 In. 235.00
Star Trek, Set of 6, 8 In. 300.00
Steiff, Betina, Blue Eyes, Blond Ponytails, Sailor Dress, 21 In. 132.00
Steiff, Clown, Coloro, White Tag 140.00
Steiff, Soldier, World War I 1150.00
Steiner, Automaton, Rolls On 3 Wheels, Moving Arms, Key Wind, 15 In. 4000.00
Steiner, Bebe Le Parisien, Closed Mouth, Box, 23 In. 6750.00
Steiner, Bisque Head, Fully Jointed Composition Body, Open Mouth 200.00
Steiner, Bisque, Cork Pate, Paperweight Eyes, Jointed Body, 8 In. 1320.00
Steiner, Bisque, Dots At Eye Corners, Jointed, Wool Pants, 33 In. 5225.00
Steiner, Jointed French Body, Pierced Ears, Cardboard Pate, 24 1/2 In. 5225.00
Steiner, Mechanical, Baby, Kicking & Crying, Keywind, 17 In. 2250.00
Steiner, Mechanical, Bisque Head, Cardboard & Muslin Body, 22 In. 1650.00
Strange Man, Standing, 1880–90, 15 In. 295.00
Swain, Character Baby, Bisque Dome Head, 5 Piece Body, Blond, 9 In. 467.00
Sweet Sue, Clothes, 23 1/2 In. 150.00

Doorstop, Basket of Flowers, Cast Iron, 10 In.

Doorstop, Basket of Flowers, Cast Iron, 11 1/2 In.

Doorstop, Pot of Tulips, Cast Iron, 8 In.

Terri Lee, Ballerina, Auburn, Tutu	325.00
Terri Lee, Brownie Dress, No Belt	195.00
Terri Lee, Brownie Outfit	195.00
Terri Lee, Girl Scout Outfit	195.00
Terri Lee, Hawaiian Outfit	285.00
Tete Jumeau 11, Bisque Head, Jointed Wrists, Chunky Body, 25 In.	705.00
Tete Jumeau, Bisque Socket Head, Jointed, Navy–Type Clothes, 26 In.	1485.00
Tete Jumeau, Bisque, Closed Mouth, 4 Piece Wardrobe, 16 In.	4200.00
Tete Jumeau, Blue Paperweight Eyes, Bisque, 23 1/2 In.	5200.00
Tete Jumeau, Lace Dress & Bonnet, Signed, 20 In.	3200.00
Tete Jumeau, Mechanical Music, Bisque, Dressed, Velvet Fez, 20 In.	4500.00
Tiny Tears	30.00
Tipsy Tumbler, Box, 1960	50.00 To 55.00
Tod–L–Tot, Rubber, Drinks, Wets, Squeaker, Glassene Eyes, Sun Rubber Co.	50.00
Toodles, Walker, Composition, New Outfit, Spring Action, 1937, 33 In.	135.00
Topsy Turvy, Awake & Asleep, 1960	20.00
Tutti, Pink Sunsuit, Box	50.00
Unis 149, Bisque, Light Brown, Composition, 16 In.	850.00
Unis 301, Open Mouth, Bisque Head, Open Close Eyes, Dressed, 28 In.	1250.00
Unis, Bisque, Brown Skin, Composition, Glass Eyes, Marked, 10 In.	200.00
Unis, Black, French, 10 In.	275.00
Unis, Sleep Eyes, 8 In.	229.00
Van Berg, Baby, Bisque Head, Cloth Jointed, Celluloid Arms, Bottle	450.00
Ventriloquist, Dummy, Talking Tessie, Red Hair	30.00
Vogue, Baby Dear, Painted Eyes, Tuft Hair, 18 In.	95.00
Vogue, Ginny, Plastic, Brown Hair, Organdy Dress, 1950s, 7 1/2 In.	132.00
Vogue, Ginny, Plastic, Straight Legs, Sleep Eyes, Blond, 1950s, 7 1/2 In.	55.00
Vogue, Ginny, Walker, Auburn Hair, Pink Taffeta Dress, 8 In.	75.00
Vogue, Jack & Jill, Clothes, Pair	365.00
Vogue, Jill, With Tin Trunk & 3 Outfits, 1957	150.00
Vogue, Toodles, Composition	365.00
Walking, Molded & Glazed China Shoulder Head, Cardboard Body, 10 In.	300.00
Walkure, Bisque Head, Sleep Eyes, Jointed Composition Body, 18 In.	195.00
Walkure, Blue Sleep Eyes, Ball–Jointed, Original Clothes, 34 In.	1395.00
Walkure, Flapper, Blue Glass Eyes, 28 In.	1295.00
Walnut–Head, Painted Features, Clothes, 9 1/2 & 12 In., Pair	137.00
Wax, Over Papier–Mache, Wooden Arms & Legs, Hair, 9 In.	60.00
Wayne Gretsky, Hockey Player, Box	60.00
Winky Dink, Inflatable, Header Card	35.00
Wooden, Penny, Pegged Arms & Legs, Painted Hair & Face, 12 In.	80.00
Woods, Jane Eyre, Bride	115.00
Yolando Bello, Matthew, Box	125.00
Yolando Bello, Sarah, Box	125.00

DONALD DUCK, see Disneyana

Iron doorstops have been made in all types of designs. The vast majority of the doorstops sold today are cast iron and were made from about 1890 to 1930. Most of them are shaped like people, animals, flowers, or ships.

DOORSTOP, Amish Man, 9 In.	100.00
Aunt Jemima, Cast Iron	275.00
Aunt Jemima, Full Figure, Hubley, 12 In.	150.00
Basket of Flowers, Cast Iron, 10 In. ....*Illus*	126.00
Basket of Flowers, Cast Iron, 11 1/2 In. ....*Illus*	275.00
Black Man On Cotton Bale, Cast Iron	2250.00
Cape Cod Cottage	135.00
Cat, Licking Paw, Cast Iron, Waverly Studio, 1926, 7 3/4 In.	175.00
Cat, Sleeping, Rose Medallion, Porcelain	35.00
Charleston Dancers, Cast Iron	1200.00
Christmas Tree .... 125.00 To 135.00	
Cockateil, Cast Iron, 1930	95.00
Cockatoo, Cast Iron, 1930	198.00
Cockatoo, Cast Iron, 4 1/2 x 14 In.	125.00
Comic Mother With Punch & Judy Babies, Brass, 11 1/8 In.	125.00
Cosmos Vase, Cast Iron, Large	1250.00
Covered Wagon, Cast Iron ....75.00 To 120.00	
Covered Wagon, With Oxen, Cast Iron	165.00
Dog, Airedale, Full Figure, Cast Iron, 8 1/2 In.	100.00
Dog, Airedale, Full Figure, Cast Iron, 9 1/4 In.	150.00
Dog, Birddog, On Point, Cast Iron	35.00
Dog, Boston Terrier, Cast Iron, Cold Painted, 8 1/2 In.	70.00
Dog, Bulldog, 1 1/4 x 1 5/8 In.	155.00
Dog, Bulldog, Full Figure, Black & White Enameled, 7 5/8 In.	85.00
Dog, Bulldog, Full Figure, Cast Iron, 9 3/4 In.	75.00
Dog, Bulldog, Full Figure, Cast Iron, Painted, 9 In.	95.00
Dog, Chocolate Brown Glaze & Mottled Base, Dalton Pottery	350.00
Dog, Cocker Spaniel, Painted	175.00
Dog, Collie, Chalkware	30.00
Dog, Fox Terrior, Full Figure, Cast Iron	150.00
Dog, French Bulldog, Cast Iron, Hubley	115.00
Dog, German Shepherd, Sitting, Hubley .... 100.00 To 125.00	
Dog, New York Brass Co., No. 136, Dated 1928	65.00
Dog, Pointer, Full Figure, Cast Iron, Black & White Paint, 15 In.	85.00
Dog, Seated, Cast Iron, Black Paint, 7 7/8 In.	75.00
Dog, Seated, Cast Iron, Black, Glass Eyes, Greenblatt, 1928, 13 In.	120.00
Dog, Setter At Point, Painted	110.00
Dog, St. Bernard, Barrel In Mouth, Painted	145.00
Dog, Terrier, Cast Iron	80.00
Dog, Wolfhound, Cast Iron, Full Figure, White Paint, 15 1/4 In.	85.00
Dog, Wolfhound, Folk Art Repaint, Full Figure, Cast Iron, 9 In.	125.00
Doll, Hubley	190.00
Dolphins, Cast Iron, 1922	165.00
Dutch Girl, Cast Iron, 10 x 9 In.	145.00
Dutch Girl, Original Paint	230.00
Dutch Girl, Wearing Shoulder Yoke, Buckets, Gold, Blue, Green, 8 In.	85.00
Eagle, Cast Iron, 7 In.	75.00
Eagle, Cast Iron, Gilt, 6 x 10 In.	220.00
Elephant & Palm Tree, Cast Iron	115.00
Elephant, 6 1/2 In.	50.00
Elephant, Cast Iron, Full Figure, Worn Gray Paint, 8 1/4 In.	70.00
Elephant, Red ....85.00 To 100.00	

◆◆◆

Don't clean coins. Collectors want coins with the patina unchanged.

◆◆◆

Fisherman, Cape Cod, 5 In. 125.00
Flower Basket, Cast Iron, Polychrome, 10 1/4 In. 65.00
Flower Basket, Cast Iron, Polychrome, USA, 8 1/2 In. 65.00
Flower Basket, Cast Iron, Twisted Handle 78.00
Flower Pot, Hubley, 9 In. 100.00
Football Player, 5 1/2 In. 50.00
Footman, Cast Iron 800.00
Footman, Cast Iron, Small 350.00
Frog, Bronze, Open Mouth, Green Paint, 8 In. 95.00
Frog, Cast Iron 70.00
Frog, Cast Iron, Realistic Repaint, 5 1/2 In. 25.00
Frog, Standing, Cast Iron 357.50
Geese, Three, Hubley, 8 In. 210.00
Geese, Two, Cast Iron 340.00
Geisha, Cast Iron, Hubley 125.00
Gettysburg Battlefield Eternal Light, Cast Iron, 1936 .... 70.00
Girl, Art Deco, Cast Iron 165.00
Girl, With Fruit Basket, 9 In. 150.00
Gnome, Cast Iron 150.00
Golfer, Putting, Painted 325.00
Halloween Girl, White Cape, Jack-O'-Lantern, Cast Iron 2800.00
Heron, Cast Iron 75.00
Horse, On Base, Cast Iron, Black, 3 x 6 x 6 In. 60.00
Horseshoe, Bar For Scraper, Clown Cigarettes, Cast Iron, 8 In. 175.00
Indian, Standing, Painted 325.00
Iris, Cast Iron 165.00
Kettle, Open Fireplace 100.00
Kitten, Sitting 100.00
Leghorn Hen 175.00
Lighthouse, 6 In. 100.00
Lighthouse, Cast Iron 185.00
Lilies of The Valley, Hubley 175.00
Lion, Cast Iron, 11 1/2 x 9 In. 195.00
Little Miss Muffet, 8 In. 150.00
London Stagecoach, Cast Iron 65.00
Mammy, 13 1/2 In. .... 150.00 To 250.00
Messenger Boy, Cast Iron 700.00
Milkmaid, Cast Iron 220.00
Monkey, Long-Tail, Cast Iron 242.00
Nasturtiums, Hubley .... 50.00 To 85.00
Old Salt, 6 1/2 In. 100.00
Oriental Child, With Ball, Cast Iron, 8 3/4 In. 75.00
Owl, Cast Iron, Glass Eyes 160.00
Owl, Polychrome, Cast Iron, 5 3/4 In. 75.00
Parlor Maid, Cast Iron 1400.00
Parrot, Cast Iron, 12 In. 175.00
Parrot, Cast Iron, 14 In. 165.00
Peacock, Painted 195.00
Penguin, Full Figure, Cast Iron, 10 1/2 In. 215.00
Pheasant, Hubley, Signed Fred Everett, 8 1/4 In. 500.00
Pirate, Full Figure, Cast Iron, Worn Gilding, 7 In. 25.00
Polly, Hubley 95.00
Pot of Tulips, Cast Iron, 8 In. ....*Illus* 137.00
Punch & Judy, Cast Iron 247.50
Pup, Dolly Dingle's, Wooden, Bee Stinging Hip, 5 x 7 In. 35.00
Rabbit, Cast Iron, White Paint, 10 1/2 In. 247.00
Rabbit, Full Figure, Cast Iron, 10 3/4 In. 200.00
Rabbit, Full Figure, Cast Iron, 11 3/4 In. 125.00
Rabbit, With Top Hat, Cast Iron 700.00
Ram & Ewe, Cast Iron, 9 x 7 1/2 In. 530.00
Red Fox, Hunt Clothes, Holding French Horn, Flat Back 40.00
Santa Claus, Original Paint, Cast Iron 2000.00
Sheep, Black, Cast Iron, 7 x 9 In. 270.00

Shepherd, Sitting, Bronzed Iron, 9 In. 95.00
Ship, Cast Iron, Original Paint 65.00
Ship, The Nina, Cast Iron, Painted, 10 x 11 In. 90.00
Spanish Dancer, 9 In. 375.00
Squirrel, Cast Iron 160.00
Stag, Cast Iron, Polychrome, Glass Eyes, 19 In. 475.00
Sunbonnet Girl, Cast Iron, 6 In. 95.00
Tiger, Cast Iron 1450.00
Top Hat, Cast Iron 192.50
Tulips, Cast Iron 50.00
Turtle, Cast Iron, 5 1/2 x 7 In. 220.00
Washington, Cast Iron, Dark Patina, 12 In. 200.00
White Rabbit 225.00
Windmill, Polychrome, Cast Iron, 7 In. 95.00
Woman, Cast Iron, Grecian Robes, Dog On Leash, Apple In Hand 110.00
Zinnias, Cast Iron, Hubley 150.00

Doulton pottery and porcelain were made by Doulton and Co. of Burslem, England, after 1882. The name *Royal Doulton* appeared on their wares after 1902. Other pottery by Doulton is listed under Royal Doulton.

DOULTON, Bottle, Comical Embossed Scenes, Stoneware, 7 1/4 In. 150.00
Bowl, Watteau, Flow Blue, 9 3/4 In. 80.00
Bowl, Watteau, Flow Blue, Round, 8 1/4 In. 95.00
Cookie Jar, Arundel, Flow Blue 150.00
Ewer, Blue Crocus, Cobalt Blue & Gold Trim, Burslem, 6 3/4 In. 150.00
Figurine, Cat, Flambe, 12 In. 275.00
Jardiniere, Morrisian, Burslem, Flow Blue, Bulbous, 5 In. 110.00
Jug, Raised Blue Ground, Lambeth, 5 1/4 In. 320.00
Lamp, Saucer Base, Metal Stem, Umbrella Shade, Lambeth, 12 1/4 In. 600.00
Meat Server, Watteau, Well & Tree, Cover, Cutout Handles, Flow Blue 395.00
Pitcher & Bowl, Oyama, Flow Blue 625.00
Pitcher, Floral, Turquoise Jewels, Cream Ground, Burslem, 5 In. 195.00
Pitcher, Indian 2 Sides, Spout & Handle, Edward Kemeys, 5 1/2 In. 335.00
Plate, Artful Dodger, 10 1/2 In. 105.00
Plate, Banff National Park, 10 1/2 In. 35.00
Plate, Fox Hunting, Ruffled, Comedic Man In Tree, 10 1/2 In. 125.00
Plate, Golfing, Losers Leave To Speak, Winners To Laugh, 10 3/4 In. 400.00
Teapot, Pomegranate, Goldfinches & Fruit, Burslem 95.00
Toothpick, Burslem 175.00
Tumbler, Victoria Golden Jubilee, Lambeth, 5 In. 125.00
Vase, Allover Flowers, Inside Design, Green, Faience, 11 1/2 In. 495.00
Vase, Incised Horses, Beaded Borders, Lambeth, H. Barlow, 11 In. 395.00
Vase, Leaf, Lambeth, 10 1/2 In., Pair 585.00
Vase, Peonies, Dark Blue, Lambeth, Elise Simmance, 7 1/2 In. 495.00
    DR. SYNTAX, see Adams; Staffordshire

Moriage is a type of decoration on Japanese pottery. Raised white designs are applied to the ware. Dragonware is a form of moriage pottery. White dragons are the major raised decorations. The background color is gray and white, orange and lavender, or orange and brown. It is a twentieth–century ware.

DRAGONWARE, Chocolate Set, Pot, Sugar, Creamer, 6 Cups and Saucers 225.00
Creamer, Gray & Black 25.00
Cup & Saucer, Lithophane, Girl 15.00
Cup, 4 Piece 30.00
Plate, 9 In. 20.00
Tea Set, Lithophane Teacups, 15 Piece 195.00
Tea Set, Moriage, 14 Piece 115.00
Vase, Orange Luster Trim, 9 In. 100.00

Dresden, Figurine, Man, Lady, Courtly Dress,
Marked, 12 In.

Dresden china is any china made in the town of Dresden, Germany. The most famous factory in Dresden is the Meissen factory. Figurines of eighteenth–century ladies and gentlemen, animal groups, or cherubs and other mythological subjects were popular. One special type of figurine was made with skirts of porcelain–dipped lace. Do not make the mistake of thinking that all pieces marked *Dresden* are from the Meissen factory. The Meissen pieces usually have crossed swords marks and are listed under Meissen.

Maroon and yellowish chrome green were never used to decorate porcelain during the eighteenth century. Almost all the eighteenth–century figures had brown eyes.

DRESDEN, Bidet, Hand Painted, 2 3/4 x 4 3/4 x 3 In.	250.00
Bowl, 4 Cherubs, Supported, 13 x 10 In.	475.00
Bowl, Hand Painted Flowers, Gold Trim, c.1860, 10 1/2 In.	250.00
Bowl, Relief Flowers, Reticulated, Side Handle, Square, 9 1/4 In.	150.00
Candelabra, 3–Light, Figure Flanked By Floral Design, 11 In., Pair	100.00
Chocolate Pot, Floral, Cream Ground	45.00
Compote, Floral, Reticulated, Gilt, Marked, 8 1/2 x 5 In.	85.00
Compote, Reticulated Border, Flowers, Schumann, 5 1/2 x 7 In.	125.00
Figurine, Flower Couple, Man & Woman, Carl Thieme, 9 In., Pair	250.00
Figurine, Girl Playing Mandolin, Boy Beside Her, 6 In.	245.00
Figurine, Gypsy Woman, Seated, With Goat, Crown, 8 x 10 1/4 In.	450.00
Figurine, Man, Lady, Courtly Dress, Marked, 12 In. ....*Illus*	187.00
Figurine, Monkey, Sitting Cross Legged, Pipe, 1910, 6 In.	495.00
Fruit Bowl, Open Lattice Work, Pedestal, Flowers, 8 1/2 In.	350.00
Group, Man Playing Piano, Woman Playing Cello, 1930s, 13 In.	395.00
Group, Ring Around Rosy, 3 Girls, Dancing, 8 1/2 x 6 1/2 In.	450.00
Group, Tailor Riding Billy Goat, With Scissors & Iron, 12 In.	410.00
Holder, Placecard, Pink Roses, Set of 12	150.00
Lamp, Figural, Children Among Flowers, Shade, 20 In.	275.00
Lamp, Lithophane of Nudes, Flowers, Cherubs At Base	1895.00
Plate, Floral, Gold Trim, Scalloped Rim, 9 1/2 In.	125.00
Teapot, Flowers, Schumann	45.00
Vase, Gold, Scenic Period Medallion, Cobalt Blue, Marked	325.00

Duncan & Miller is a term used by collectors when referring to glass made by the George A. Duncan and Sons Company or the Duncan and Miller Glass and Miller Glass Company. These companies worked from 1893 to 1955, when the use of the name *Duncan* was discontinued and the firm became part of the United of the United States Glass Company. Early patterns may be listed under Pressed Glass.

DUNCAN & MILLER, 3 Chrysanthemum, Dish, Frosted, Signed, 16 In.	125.00
Astaire, Tumbler, Flat, Ruby, 10 Oz.	15.00
Barred Oval, Butter, Cover, Frosted	50.00
Bassettown, Sugar & Spooner, Cover	245.00
Beaded Swirl, Butter, Cover	110.00
Beaded Swirl, Butter, Cover, Green, Gold Trim	125.00
Beaded Swirl, Creamer, Green, Gold Trim	65.00

Beaded Swirl, Table Set, Green, Gold Trim, 4 Piece	375.00
Canterbury, Box, Cigarette, Cover	28.00
Canterbury, Cup & Saucer	48.00
Canterbury, Plate, Chartreuse, 7 1/2 In.	5.00
Canterbury, Tumbler, Blue	35.00
Caribbean, Cup	6.00
Caribbean, Luncheon Set, Underplate, 12 Cups, Ruby Handles	250.00
Caribbean, Punch Bowl, 10 In.	65.00
Celtic Cross, Goblet	35.00
Daisy & Button, Canoe, 13 In.	65.00
Diamond Ridge, Punch Bowl, Pedestal, 10 1/2 In.	160.00
Duck, Box, Cigarette, Cover, 6 In.	40.00
First Love, Basket, Crystal, 12 In.	28.00
First Love, Cocktail	21.00
First Love, Pitcher, Martini	145.00
First Love, Wine, 3 Oz.	21.00
Georgian, Sherbet, Green	9.00
Grandee, Candlestick, 3–Light, No. 14	45.00
Heron, Paper Label	110.00
Hobnail, Goblet, 6 In.	9.50 To 11.00
Hobnail, Hat, Blue, 8 In.	60.00
Hobnail, Sugar & Creamer	15.00
Hobnail, Vase, Ruffled, Pink, 6 1/2 In.	70.00
Language of Flowers, Goblet, 10 Oz.	18.00
Mardi Gras, Champagne	25.00
Mardi Gras, Toothpick, Gold Trim	28.00
Near Cut, Vase, 10 In.	32.50
Radiance, Pitcher, Sapphire Blue, 1/2 Gal.	95.00
Radiance, Pitcher, Sapphire Blue, 16 Oz.	85.00
Radiance, Vase, Black, 9 In.	55.00
Raindrop, Champagne	12.00
Raindrop, Water Set, 7 Piece	65.00
Sandwich, Ashtray, Duck, 8 In.	18.00
Sandwich, Basket, Handle, Oval, 10 In.	70.00
Sandwich, Bowl, 5 In.	5.00
Sandwich, Bowl, Salad, Deep, 10 In.	25.00
Sandwich, Cake Stand, Pedestal, 13 In.	50.00
Sandwich, Candlestick, Bobeches, Prisms, Pair	98.00
Sandwich, Cruet Set, 2 Bottles, Tray	60.00
Sandwich, Dish, Ice Cream, 5 Oz.	6.00
Sandwich, Lily Bowl, 10 In.	44.00
Sandwich, Pitcher, Ice Lip, 64 Oz.	115.00
Sandwich, Plate, 8 In.	7.00 To 9.00
Sandwich, Plate, 13 In.	35.00
Sandwich, Plate, Deviled Egg, 12 In.	45.00
Spiral Flutes, Cup & Saucer, Amber, After Dinner	20.00
Spiral Flutes, Cup & Saucer, Green	11.00
Spiral Flutes, Goblet, Green, 7 Oz.	12.00
Spiral Flutes, Plate, Green, 6 In.	3.00
Spiral Flutes, Plate, Green, 7 1/2 In.	4.00
Spiral Flutes, Plate, Green, 8 1/4 In.	4.50 To 8.00
Spiral Flutes, Tumbler, Green	8.00
Stippled Star, Celery	38.00
Swan, 3 1/2 In., Pair	45.00
Swan, 10 1/4 In.	45.00
Swan, 3 1/2 In., Pair	45.00
Swan, Green, Large	85.00
Swan, Large	85.00
Swan, Small	35.00
Swordfish	45.00
Sylvan, Swan, Blue Opalescent, Open Back	170.00
Sylvan, Swan, Pink Opalescent, 5 1/2 In.	110.00
Teardrop, Candleholder, 4 In.	8.00

Teardrop, Cocktail, Pink	15.00
Teardrop, Dish, Heart Shape, Divided	15.00
Teardrop, Goblet, 9 Oz.	13.00
Teardrop, Pickle, Oval	12.00
Teardrop, Relish, 3 Sections	12.00
Teardrop, Sugar & Creamer, Tray, Individual	18.00
Teardrop, Tumbler, 12 Oz. ....8.00 To	10.00
Teardrop, Wine, Pink	15.00
Three–Face, Cake Plate, 8 x 11 In.	250.00
Vermont, Soup, Dish, 8 3/4 In.	45.00

Durand glass was made by Victor Durand from 1879 to 1935 at several factories. Most of the iridescent Durand glass was made by Victor Durand, Jr., from 1912 to 1924 at the Durand Art Glass Works in Vineland, New Jersey.

DURAND, Compote, Bowl, Red, Pulled Flower Center, Yellow Stems & Base, 6 In.	660.00
Compote, King Tut, Gold, Gold Stem & Base, 5 1/2 In.	925.00
Compote, Red, Scalloped, 10 Rib, Ambergris Twisted Stem, 6 1/4 In.	305.00
Cup & Saucer, Gold Iridescent	375.00
Ginger Jar, Cover, Gold Threading, 9 1/4 In.	1750.00
Ginger Jar, Cover, Lily Pad Leaves, Gold Interior, Signed, 8 1/4 In.	1350.00
Jar, Hearts & Vines, Amber Rosette On Lid, Signed, 9 1/2 In.	4125.00
Lamp, Table, Directoire Style Shade, Garden Scene, Signed, 16 In.	3100.00
Parfait, White Pulled Feather, Fern Band, Amber Stem, 5 1/2 In.	715.00
Plate, Opalescent Peacock Feathers, Cut Center, 8 In.	170.00
Plate, Sapphire Blue, 10 Ribs, Opaque Edge, Signed, 10 3/4 In.	195.00
Plate, White Pulled Feather Floral, Cross–Hatched Center, 6 In.	125.00
Torchere, Gold Glass Walls, White Crackle Overlay, 18 In., Pair	775.00
Torchere, Swan Embellished Cage, Vasiform Shade, 70 In.	1100.00
Urn, King Tut, Orange & Green	1150.00
Vase, Allover White Heart & Vine, Iridescent Blue, 6 3/4 In.	550.00
Vase, Blue Bulb Body, Elongated Neck, Mirror Base, 18 1/2 In.	2200.00
Vase, Blue Opalescent	650.00
Vase, Blue, Black	475.00
Vase, Egyptian, Green & White Feather Design, Crackle, 8 3/4 In.	965.00
Vase, Feather Design, Cranberry & Tangerine	875.00
Vase, Gold Threading, Flared Top, 7 In.	550.00
Vase, Gold Threading, Iridescent, Blue Aurene, Signed, 6 x 5 In.	750.00
Vase, Green Crystal, Double Gourd Neck, Squatty Base, 8 x 12 In.	225.00
Vase, Green Pulled Feathers, Gold Threads, Signed, 8 1/2 In.	1350.00
Vase, Intaglio Cut, Ambergris, Signed, 4 In.	370.00
Vase, King Tut, Blue & White, Gold Interior, 9 1/2 In.	750.00
Vase, King Tut, Blue Loop Designs, Ivory Ground, 10 1/2 In.	495.00
Vase, Lily Pads, Gold Thread Design, Signed, 8 In.	650.00
Vase, Pulled Feathers, Gold Threading, Gold, 9 1/2 In.	1100.00
Vase, Random Color Variation, Blue Iridescent, Signed, 4 In.	500.00
Vase, Silver Blue, Iridescent, 10 In.	850.00
Vase, Spherical Bowl, Orange To Opal, Leaf & Vine, 6 1/2 x 8 In.	1540.00
Vase, Transparent Amethyst Crystal, 16 Ribbed Body, Signed, 10 In.	195.00
Vase, White Feathers, Iridescent Blue, 8 In.	225.00
Vase, White Hearts & Vines, Iridescent Blue, 9 In.	750.00
Vase, White Spider, Gold Tinge, Blue, 8 1/2 In.	1200.00

Elfinware was made from about 1918 to 1940. It is a Dresden–like porcelain that was sold in dime stores and gift shops. Many pieces were decorated with raised flowers. The small pieces are marked with the name *Elfinware* or with a crown and M mark. The words *Germany* or *Made in Germany* also appear on some pieces.

ELFINWARE, Basket, 2 3/4 In.	15.00
Basket, 3 In.	38.00
Bowl, Oval, 4 In.	85.00
Box, Cover With Massed Flowers, Square, 3 1/2 In.	55.00
Box, Forget–Me–Not, Roses, Heart Shape, 3 In.	25.00

◆◆

Let your baskets share the bathroom with you when you take a shower. The hot, moist air is good for the basket.

◆◆

Holder, Card, Wicker Baskets, Green, Fan Shape, 13 Piece	200.00 To 235.00
Holder, Card, Wicker Baskets, Pale Green, Fan Shape, 12 Piece	175.00
Pitcher, 2 In.	55.00
Shoe, Dutch, 4 In.	95.00
Shoe, High Heeled, Forget–Me–Not, Roses	28.00
Teapot, Allover Moss, Forget–Me–Not, Roses, 3 In.	40.00
Vase, 2 1/2 In.	38.00
Vase, Handles, 2 1/2 In.	75.00
Watering Can	25.00

Elvis Presley, the famous singer, lived from 1935 to 1977. He became famous by 1956. Elvis appeared on television, starred in twenty–seven movies, and performed in Las Vegas. Memorabilia from any of the Presley shows, his records, and even memorials made after his death are collected.

ELVIS PRESLEY, Book, Song, Large	15.00
Bust, Frosted Glass, 12 In.	65.00
Bust, Goebel	50.00
Calendar, Pocket, RCA, Color, 1969, 2 1/2 x 4 In.	9.00
Calendar, Pocket, RCA, Singing, 1971, 2 1/2 x 4 In.	8.00
Card, Bubble Gum, Pair	15.00
Cover, TV Guide, Sept. 8, 1956	145.00
Decanter, Aloha, Box	200.00
Decanter, Karate, Box	250.00
Doll, Black Clothes, Box, World	95.00
Doll, Elvis In Concert, Box	140.00
Eyecup	18.00
Hat, Black Gabardine, Song Titles, Signed Photo, Dated 1956	69.00
Lamp, Bust, 36 In.	110.00
Magazine, Look, Elvis, 1971	25.00
Phonograph Player, Automatic Changer	450.00
Picture, Publicity Still, Autographed	775.00
Poster, Clambake	35.00
Poster, Easy Come Easy Go	35.00
Poster, Paradise Hawaiian Style, 13 x 30 In.	35.00
Sheet Music, As Long As I Have You, Blue–Tone Photo	21.00
Sheet Music, Don't Leave Me Now, Blue–Tone Photo, 9 x 12 In.	21.00
Sheet Music, Heartbreak Hotel, Blue–Tone Photo, 9 x 12 In.	41.00
Sheet Music, Stuck On You, 1960	12.00
Shirt, Red Puffed Sleeve, With Photograph, 1970	2750.00
Tape Measure, Heart, Elvis, Love Me Tender	9.00
Walking Stick, Gold Dagger Inside, Eagle Head, Plaque, 40 In.	3025.00

In the eighteenth and nineteenth centuries, workmen from Russia, France, England, and other countries made small boxes and table pieces of enamel on metal. One form of English enamel is called *Battersea* and is listed under that name. There was a revival of interest in enameling in the thirties and a new style evolved.

ENAMEL, Ashtray, Black, White Crackle, Ed Winter, 6 In.	75.00
Beaker, Victorian, Nellio	390.00
Box, Cigarette, Green–Gold Geometric, Blue, E. Winter	120.00
Box, Dresser, Woman & Man Under Tree With Lamb, France, 5 In.	1925.00
Box, Patch, France	155.00
Charger, City, River Scene, Scalloped Rim, China, c.1900, 11 1/2 In.	275.00
Cup, Women, Cherubs, Pink, Vienna, 10 In. ....*Illus*	2200.00

Dresser Set, Guilloche, Cut Glass, Sterling Mounts, 10 Piece 465.00
Etui, Yellow, Floral Reserves, Brass Mounted, France, 2 1/2 In. 165.00
Ewer, Underplate, Red & Yellow, Stylized Flowers, France, 3 1/2 In. 825.00
Letter Holder, Gold Washed Stylized Floral, France, 4 3/4 In. 275.00
Plaque, 3 Mice, Pink, Thelma Winter, 11 In. 215.00
Plaque, Cavalier, Artist, France, 8 1/4 x 4 In. 605.00
Plaque, On Copper, Village & Lake, Faure–Limoges, Framed, 8 x 10 In. 1210.00
Salt, Ball Feet, Blue, Russia, Marked BH 1884, 2 1/2 In. 325.00
Salt, Red & White Fish Scale, Gilt Metal, Spoon, Russia 35.00
Sugar Scoop, Russia, Signed Klingert, 5 In. 675.00
Sugar Shaker, Rust Floral, Yellow Cased Glass, Silvered Top, 7 In. 70.00
Tazza, Child Astride Dolphin Support, Castles, France, 4 In. 1250.00
Tile, Children Figures, Fern Coles, 1950, Set of 4 .... 100.00
Vase, Bust Length Woman, Forest & Lake, France, 5 1/2 In. 2970.00
Vase, Dancing Woman & Cherub, Wooded Landscape, France, 6 1/4 In. 1650.00
Vase, Full Figure of Woman, Wooded Ground, Fern, 4 In. 600.00
Vase, Full Length Man, 18th Century Dress, France, 8 In. 990.00
Vase, Woman, Holding Rose On Garden Terrace, France, 6 1/2 In. 990.00
Vase, Young Woman, Floral Headband, Green Ground, France, 7 1/4 In. 2200.00

ES Germany porcelain was made at the factory of Erdmann
Schlegelmilch from 1861 to 1925 in Suhl, Germany. The porcelain
was sold decorated or undecorated. Other pieces were made at the
factory in Saxony, Prussia, and are marked *ES Prussia.* Reinhold
Schlegelmilch, a brother, made the famous wares marked *RS
Germany.*

ES GERMANY, Figurine, Woman, Large Feathered Hat, 9 1/2 In. 32.00
Plate, Floral Trim, 6 In. 25.00
Plate, Women In Forest Center, Blue Boarder, 8–Sided, 8 3/4 In. 175.00

All types of Eskimo artifacts are collected. Carvings of whale or
walrus teeth are listed under Scrimshaw. Baskets are in the Basket
category. All other types of Eskimo art are listed here.

ESKIMO, Blanket, Button, Dark Gray & Red Trade Cloth, 44 x 35 In. 600.00
Box, Tool, Carved Ivory Handles On Lid, Bentwood, Oval 1900.00
Carving, Owl, On Its Prey, Mottled Gray Soapstone, Signed, 9 In. 335.00
Cribbage Board, Ivory, Many Scenes Allover, Dark Pigment, 12 1/4 In. 3520.00
Cribbage Board, Walrus Tusk, Ship, Whales, Walruses, 1900 .... 1600.00
Door Knocker, Figural, Eskimo, Wooden 134.00
Figure, Eskimo In Kayak, Seal, Basalt 198.00
Figure, Eskimo, Large Fish, Basalt 143.00
Figure, Eskimo, With Ax, Basalt 176.00
Figure, Face of Man, Basalt, Large 66.00
Figure, Hunting Scene, Ivory Carving, Paul Nattanguk, 1973, 28 In. 2090.00
Figurine, Man Holding A Salmon, Green Jadite, 5 In. 65.00
Group, Dog Sled, Sled Runner, Bone, Ivory Carved, 4, 5 & 11 In., 3 Pc. 110.00
Kasaka & Pants, Elkskin, Sinew Sewn, 1905 .... 1000.00

*Enamel, Cup, Women, Cherubs, Pink, Vienna,
10 In.*

◆ ◆

If you have to pack or store an
oddly shaped antique try this
trick. Get a damp polyurethane
sponge, preferably the two layer
type with a stiffer bottom layer.
Put the piece on the wet sponge.
It will make the proper shaped
indentation and when the
sponge dries, the piece will be
held safely in one position.

◆ ◆

Knife, Presentation, Ivory, Black Pigment Engraving, 14 In.	1870.00
Moccasins, Beaded, Alaska	160.00
Moccasins, Child's, Beaded Bird Design, Alaska	175.00
Picture, Dancing Birds, Stonecut, Tissue, Pitscolak, 1971, 13 x 20 In.	275.00
Picture, Owl & Geese, Brown & Blue, Jamasie Teevee, 15 1/2 x 13 In.	82.50
Pipe, Ivory, Dogs, Wolves, Walrus & Seal, Flared Bowl, 12 In.	1100.00
Pipe, Ivory, Sea Mammals, Kayak, Curved Expanding Stem, 8 3/8 In.	660.00
Skin Stencil, Tissue, Wrestling 2 Spirits, Kaikshut, 19 x 23 In.	165.00
Spear, Bird, Wooden Shaft, Barbed Bone Prongs Mid-Shaft, 65 In.	522.00

Etling glass is very similar in design to Lalique and Phoenix glass.
It was made in France for Etling, a retail shop. It dates from the
1920s and 1930s.

ETLING, Bowl, Nude Women Dancing, 14 In.	150.00
Bowl, Opalescent White Fern Fronds, 12 In.	75.00

ФАБЕРЖЕ
КФ

Faberge was a firm of jewelers and goldsmiths founded in St.
Petersburg, Russia, in 1842, by Gustav Faberge. Peter Carl Faberge,
his son, was jeweler to the Russian Imperial Court from about 1870
to 1914.

FABERGE, Bowl, Waste, Chased Shells & Foliage, c.1900, 6 1/2 In.	1100.00
Box, Pill, Gem Stones In Catch, Gold Wash Interior, Marked, 3 In.	2650.00
Compact, Diamond Set Wreath, Enameled Rim, c.1910, 1 3/4 In.	5225.00
Compact, Hinged Cover, Silver-Gilt & Translucent, c.1900, 4 In.	6600.00
Fork, Spatulate Handle, Swans & Cornucopia, c.1900, 6 Piece	990.00
Kovsh, Enameled Imperial Eagles, c.1910, 3 1/2 In.	3575.00
Pencil Holder, 3 Sections, Gold & Enamel, c.1890, 4 3/8 In.	2200.00
Waiter, Reeded Border, Band of Anthemion, c.1885, 6 1/2 In.	1320.00

Definitions of the words differentiating the types of pottery and
porcelain are difficult because there is so much overlapping of
meaning. Faience is tin-glazed earthenware, especially the wares
made in France, Germany, and Scandinavia. It is also correct to say
that faience is the same as majolica or Delft, although usually the
term refers only to the tin-glazed pottery of the three regions
mentioned.

FAIENCE, Bowl, Magenta & Green Enamel, Gilt, Reticulated, 6 1/4 In.	115.00
Bowl, Underplate, Polychrome Flowers, 9 1/4 In.	25.00
Box, Cover, Apple Shape, Calyx, Stem, Strasbourg, 1750, 2 3/16 In., Pr.	7975.00
Box, Cover, Apple Shape, Veined Leaves, c.1760, 3 1/8 x 4 In.	3575.00
Box, Cover, Artichoke, Overlapping Leaves, Blue Interior, 5 1/2 In.	6600.00
Chamberstick, Snuffer, Tobacco Leaf Design, St. Clement, 5 1/2 In.	82.50
Dish, Shell Shape, Tulip Amid Floral Spray, c.1770, 9 In., Pair	3575.00
Dish, Tompe-l'oeil, Carrots, Turnips, Scallions, 1890s, 16 5/8 In.	1925.00
Figurine, Man, Playing Guitar & Woman, Holding Fan, 40 In., Pair	2200.00
Inkstand, Blue & White, France, 7 In.	55.00
Inkwell, Clover Leaf Shape, Glazed, France, 2 Piece	60.00
Lavabo, Brass Spigot, Multicolored Bird & Scroll, 27 x 18 In.	357.00
Pitcher, Parrot, Beak Pouring, France	180.00
Plate, Floral, Bird & Eel Center	95.00
Plate, Floral, Red Border, 9 In.	55.00
Plate, Sunflower, France, 8 In.	18.00
Stein, Jagged Glaze Crazing, Pewter Lid & Base Ring	306.00
Teapot, Animal Head Spout, Foliate Handle, c.1750, 5 5/8 In.	770.00
Tile, Bird	175.00
Tureen, Asparagus, Bound With Brown Cords, Sceaux, 1775, 6 5/8 In.	4950.00

Fairings are small souvenir china boxes and figurines that were sold
at country fairs during the nineteenth century. Most were made in
Germany. Reproductions of fairings are being made, especially of
the famous *twelve months of marriage* series.

FAIRING, Box, Child Looking In Mirror, Cover, 4 In.	95.00
Box, Man With Dog, Cover	40.00

Box, Red Riding Hood, Wolf, Cover, 4 In. 60.00
Box, Sleeping Child In Highchair, Cover, 4 In 120.00
Box, Tree Stump, Bird On Top, Wings Spread 80.00
Box, Trunk, Match Strike On Bottom 35.00
Figurine, Kiss Me Quick 165.00
Figurine, Last To Bed Put Out The Light, 3 1/2 In. 250.00
Figurine, Married For Money, 3 1/2 In. 175.00
Figurine, Married, Trouble Begins, 3 1/2 In. 225.00
Figurine, Nip On The Sly, 4 In. 225.00
Figurine, The Power of Love 225.00
Figurine, Three O'clock In The Morning, 3 1/2 In. 300.00
Figurine, Twelve Months After Marriage 250.00
Figurine, Welsh Tea Party 350.00

FAIRYLAND LUSTER, see Wedgwood
FAMILLE ROSE, see Chinese Export

Fans have been used for cooling since the days of the ancients. By the eighteenth century, the fan was an accessory for the lady of fashion and very elaborate and expensive fans were made. Sticks were made of ivory or wood, set with jewels or carved. The fans were made of painted silk or paper. Inexpensive paper fans printed with advertising were giveaways in the late–nineteenth and early–twentieth centuries. Electric fans were introduced in 1882.

FAN, Advertising, 7–Up, Art Deco Style Bathing Beauty, Cardboard, 1931 .... 12.50
Advertising, Conrad Motor Car Co., Dodge, Plymouth, Cardboard, 1930 .... 10.00
Advertising, Kikkoman Soy Sauce, Stick, 1940s 15.00
Advertising, Maytag, Washing Machine Picture 45.00
Advertising, Moxie, Boy On Moxiemobile, Cardboard, 1922, 7 x 8 In. 85.00
Advertising, Moxie, Muriel Ostriche Portrait, Cardboard, 1918 .... 75.00
Advertising, Putnam Dyes 40.00
Advertising, Putnam Dyes, Gen. Putnam, Escape Dragoons, Cardboard, 8 In. 25.00
Advertising, SAS Air Line, Black Silk, White Marigold, 1940s 25.00
Advertising, Shiro's Ice Cream & Candy, Major League Mgrs., From 1913 .... 3080.00
Advertising, Snyder Drug Store, Tums & Nature's Remedy, Children, Wagon 20.00
Advertising, Zig–Zag Candy 40.00
Aqua Silk, In Hand Painted Oriental Box 35.00
Battery Operated, Knapp, Exposed Armature & Coil, 6 In. Blades 425.00
Battery Operated, Little Hustler 250.00
Black Feather, Tortoiseshell Frame 75.00
Black Lace, Plum Ground, Scalloped, Wooden, Floral, Metal Handle 55.00
Black Satin, Chantilly Lace, Pheasant Center, Tortoiseshell, Large 45.00
Calendar, 1892 .... 50.00
Dr Pepper, 1931 .... 60.00
Electric, Desk, Signal, Horizontal Blades 650.00
Electric, General Electric, Brass Blades, Large 300.00
Electric, General Electric, Coin–Operated 250.00
Electric, General Electric, Oscillating, Art Deco 65.00
Electric, General Electric, Polished Brass Blades, Large 45.00
Electric, Little Hustler, Exposed Armature & Coil, 4 In. Blades 275.00
Electric, Polar Club, Brass Blades 65.00
Electric, Polar Cub, 2 1/2 In. Brass Blades 85.00
Fidelity Bank, Dunmore, Penna., 3–Fold, Dogs, Birds, Babies, 1920s 20.00
Fold–Away, Purse Size, 1940s, Box 8.00
Folding, 1917 .... 2.00
Folding, Silver, Gold Tassle, Elaborate, Stick, 1800s, 8 1/2 In. 45.00
Hand Painted On Black Silk, A. Thomasse, 12 1/2 In. 165.00
Holly, 4 Girls, No Year Or Date, Hollyberries, Closed – 4 1/2 x 10 In. 95.00
Mannequin Head, Stylistic, 1930s, 14 In. 125.00
Mother–of–Pearl, Hand Painted Religious Scene 330.00
Mother–of–Pearl, Hand Painted, 1/2 Circle Glass Front Frame, Danzel 500.00
Ostrich Feathers, Black Carved Sticks, 11 x 23 In. 85.00
Ostrich Feathers, Tortoiseshell, Edwardian, Black 50.00
Ostrich Plumes, Black, Mother–of–Pearl Sticks, Tassel 45.00

Ostrich Plumes, Blue, Tortoiseshell Handles	60.00
Painted Figures With Sheep, Carved Ivory Struts, Frame	155.00
Painted Silk, Sequins, Wooden Ribs, Frame, 14 3/4 x 19 3/4 In.	75.99
Palace Shoes, Paddle Type, Child & Horseshoe, 1900s, Large	8.00
Peacock Feathers, Pink, White Lattice Handle	20.00
Tortoiseshell & Lace, 18K Gold Hook, 13 1/2 In.	200.00
U. S. World Trade Fair, For Japan, Child, Dated April 14, 1957, Paddle	35.00
Woodrow Wilson, Heart Shape, Washington, Lincoln & Wilson Portraits	30.00
Woven Splint, Turned Handle, Red Ribbon, 10 3/4 In.	45.00

Federzeichnung is the very strange German name for a pattern of mother-of-pearl satin glass. The pattern had irregularly shaped sections of brown glass covered with a pattern of gold squiggle lines. It was first made in the late-nineteenth century.

FEDERZEICHNUNG, Vase, Gold Band Around Top, White Lining, 10 1/4 In.	1695.00
Vase, Gold Design, Tricorner Interior, 5 3/4 In.	2200.00
Vase, Pearl Air Traps, Pink Lining, Enameled, 6 In.	2125.00

Fenton Art Glass Company, founded in Martins Ferry, Ohio, by Frank L. Fenton, is now located in Williamstown, West Virginia. It is noted for early carnival glass produced between 1907 and 1920. Many other types of glass were also made.

FENTON, Alley Cat, Figurine, Red	42.00
Apple Blossom Crest, Bowl, Heart Shape	42.50
Aqua Crest, Plate, 12 In.	28.00
Aqua Crest, Tidbit, 3 Tiers	38.00
Aqua Crest, Vase, 8 In.	21.00
Aqua Crest, Vase, Triangular, 5 In.	35.00
Aqua Crest, Vase, Tulip, 8 In.	100.00
Bear Cub, Figurine, Sitting, White	17.00
Bicentennial, Patriots, Red	22.50
Black Crest, Bonbon, Handles	45.00
Blue Ridge, Pitcher Set, 7 Piece	150.00
Bubble Optic, Vase, Honey Amber, 11 1/2 In.	125.00
Burmese, Bell, 6 In.	25.00
Burmese, Creamer, Hand-Painted Flowers	50.00
Butterfly, Figurine, Topaz	27.00
Butterfly, Finger Bowl, Underplate, White	225.00
Coin Dot, Bowl, Crimped, Topaz, 6 1/2 In.	30.00
Coin Dot, Bowl, Ruffled, Topaz, 8 1/2 In.	27.00
Coin Dot, Bowl, Scalloped, Topaz, 7 In.	27.00
Coin Dot, Creamer, Blue, 4 In.	45.00
Coin Dot, Lamp, Cranberry, Miniature	195.00
Coin Dot, Lamp, Topaz, Tall	125.00
Coin Dot, Rose Bowl, Pinch Top, 3 x 4 In.	75.00
Coin Dot, Vase, 7 In.	45.00
Coin Dot, Vase, 8 1/2 In.	35.00
Coin Dot, Vase, Cranberry, 4 1/2 In.	30.00
Coin Dot, Vase, Cranberry, 6 In.	40.00
Coin Dot, Vase, Topaz, 10 1/2 In.	95.00
Coinspot, Vase, Cranberry, 7 1/2 In.	75.00
Coinspot, Vase, Ruffled, Cranberry, 10 In.	75.00
Coinspot, Water Set, 7 Piece	195.00
Daisy & Button, Boot, Amethyst	15.00
Daisy & Button, Candy Jar, Green	50.00
Daisy & Fern, Bottle, Barber	110.00
Daisy & Fern, Lamp, Cranberry, 21 In.	550.00
Deer, Reclining, Red Slag	50.00
Dolphin Handle, Compote, Amethyst	25.00
Dolphin Handle, Vase, Fan, Jade	20.00
Dolphin, Bowl, Etched	45.00
Dot Optic, Pitcher, Reed Handle, Green	175.00
Dragon & Lotus, Bowl, Purple Iridescent, 9 In.	80.00

Emerald Crest, Bowl, Salad, 10 In.	48.00
Emerald Crest, Flowerpot	40.00
Emerald Crest, Flowerpot, Attached Saucer	50.00
Emerald Crest, Vase, 4 1/4 In.	28.00
Fern, Cruet, Blue & White	85.00
Gold Crest, Bowl, 6 In.	10.00
Gold Crest, Bowl, 12 In.	27.50
Gold Crest, Top Hat, Crimped, 4 In.	40.00
Gold Crest, Vase, Fan, 7 In.	20.00
Hobnail, Basket, Handle, 4 1/2 In.	38.00
Hobnail, Bonbon, Ruffled, Blue	12.00
Hobnail, Bowl, Ruffled, Blue, 10 In.	60.00
Hobnail, Cruet, Blue	45.00
Hobnail, Fruit Bowl	45.00
Hobnail, Jug Set, Blue, 6 Tumblers	35.00
Hobnail, Jug, Milk Glass, 80 Oz.	65.00
Hobnail, Pitcher & Bowl Set, Milk Glass	55.00
Hobnail, Pitcher, Cranberry, Squat, 5 In.	120.00
Hobnail, Pitcher, Squat	45.00
Hobnail, Vase, 8 In.	60.00
Hobnail, Vase, Fan, 6 1/4 In.	22.00
Hobnail, Vase, Fan, Blue, 8 In.	35.00
Ivory Crest, Bowl, Ruffled, Hand Painted, 5 In.	40.00
Ivory Crest, Vase, 10 In.	55.00
Jamestown, Basket, 8 1/2 In.	35.00
Jamestown, Cake Plate, Footed, Blue	35.00
Lamp, Student's, Coin Dot, Honeysuckle, 21 In.	150.00
Lincoln Inn, Cup & Saucer, Cobalt Blue	25.00
Lincoln Inn, Plate, Pink, 8 In.	10.00
Lincoln Inn, Tumbler, Footed, 5 In.	19.00
Lincoln Inn, Water Set, Amethyst, 7 Piece	145.00
Peach Crest, Basket, Milk Glass Handle	47.50
Peach Crest, Bowl, Double Crimped, 13 In.	90.00
Peach Crest, Candlestick, 5 In.	25.00
Peach Crest, Creamer, 4 In.	30.00
Peach Crest, Jug, Squat, 5 1/2 In.	55.00
Peach Crest, Vase, 6 In.	27.50 To 30.00
Peach Crest, Vase, 8 1/2 In.	68.00
Peach Crest, Vase, Double Crimped, 5 1/2 In.	30.00
Rose Crest, Bonbon	12.50
Rose Crest, Bowl, 7 In.	20.00
Rose Crest, Vase, 6 1/2 In.	19.00
Rose Crest, Vase, 11 In.	65.00
Rosealene, Vase, Bud	29.00
Silver Crest, Bonbon, Metal Center Handle, Ruffled	10.00
Silver Crest, Compote, Violets, 8 In.	20.00
Silver Crest, Epergne, 12 In.	125.00
Silver Crest, Epergne, 3–Light	85.00
Silver Crest, Tidbit, 2 Tiers	22.00
Silver Crest, Vase, 4 1/2 In.	3.50
Silver Crest, Vase, Beaded Melon, 6 In.	15.00
Silver Crest, Vase, Violets, 6 In.	20.00
Snow Crest, Flowerpot, Emerald Green, Underplate	55.00
Spanish Lace, Pitcher, Aqua, 6 In.	58.00
Spiral Optic, Jug, Handle, 5 1/4 In.	40.00
Spiral Optic, Vase, 7 In.	50.00
Swan, Bonbon, Green, 7 1/2 x 7 In.	16.00
Swirl, Cruet, Green	90.00
Vintage, Bowl, Caramel, 6 1/2 In.	39.00
Water Lily & Cattails, Bowl, Amethyst, 10 1/2 In.	58.00
Water Lily & Cattails, Pitcher, Water, Amethyst	300.00

fiesta

Fiesta, the colorful dinnerware, was introduced in 1936 by the Homer Laughlin China Co., redesigned in 1969, and withdrawn in 1973. It was reissued again in 1986 in different colors. The simple design was characterized by a band of concentric circles, beginning at the rim. Cups had full–circle handles until 1969, when partial–circle handles were made. Harlequin and Riviera were related wares. For more information and prices of American dinnerware, see the book *Kovels' Depression Glass & American Dinnerware Price List.*

FIESTA, Bowl, Fruit, Ivory, 5 1/2 In.	10.00
Bowl, Fruit, Rose, 4 3/4 In.	22.00
Bowl, Gold, Ironstone, 6 1/2 In.	4.00
Bowl, Green, Ironstone, 5 1/2 In.	3.00
Bowl, Green, Ironstone, 9 In.	10.00
Bowl, Light Green, 4 1/2 In.	10.00
Bowl, Medium Green, 8 1/2 In.	45.00
Bowl, Mixing, No. 1, Red	40.00
Bowl, Mixing, No. 3, Red	35.00
Bowl, Mixing, No. 5, Yellow	26.00
Bowl, Salad, Yellow	30.00
Bowl, Yellow, 6 In.	15.00
Carafe, Red	95.00
Casserole, Light Green, Kitchen Kraft, 8 In.	40.00
Casserole, Turquoise, Cover	95.00
Casserole, Yellow, Cover	195.00
Chop Plate, Ivory, 15 In.	55.00
Chop Plate, Light Green, 13 In.	20.00
Chop Plate, Red, 15 In.	27.50
Chop Plate, Rose, 13 In.	32.50
Coffeepot, Light Green	38.00
Coffeepot, Light Green, After Dinner	95.00
Creamer, Dark Green	14.00
Creamer, Stick Handle, Red	20.00
Creamer, Yellow	9.00
Cup, Chartreuse	25.00
Cup, Medium Green	22.00
Cup, Turquoise	18.00
Ewer, Spherical Body, Stepped Domed Foot, Blue, Cover, 10 In.	27.50
Gravy Boat, Dark Green	55.00
Gravy Boat, Turquoise	18.00
Grill Plate, Ivory	10.00
Jam Jar, Gold, Ironstone	35.00
Mustard, Cobalt Blue, Cover	115.00
Nappy, Gray, 8 1/2 In.	32.00
Nappy, Gray, 9 In.	30.00
Nappy, Light Green	12.00
Nappy, Rose	29.00
Nappy, Yellow, 8 1/2 In.	20.00
Pie Plate, Yellow, Kitchen Kraft, 10 In.	30.00
Pitcher, Disc, Dark Green	100.00
Pitcher, Disc, Green	45.00
Pitcher, Disc, Ivory	30.00
Pitcher, Disc, Red	75.00
Pitcher, Disc, Red, 30 Oz.	85.00
Pitcher, Disc, Water, Ivory	40.00
Pitcher, Water, Red, Disk	75.00
Plate, Chartreuse, 7 In.	9.00
Plate, Chartreuse, 9 In.	12.00
Plate, Chartreuse, 10 In.	35.00
Plate, Cobalt Blue, 10 In.	18.00 To 24.00
Plate, Dark Green, 10 In.	35.00
Plate, Good Luck, Ivory, 1955, 9 1/2 In.	35.00
Plate, Gray, 6 In.	7.00

Plate, Gray, 7 In. .... 9.00 To 9.50
Plate, Green, 9 In. 12.00
Plate, Ivory, 9 In. 45.00
Plate, Ivory, 10 In. 20.00
Plate, Light Green, 10 In. 17.00
Plate, Medium Green, 6 In. 9.50
Plate, Orange, 10 In. 10.00
Plate, Red, 10 In. 18.00
Plate, Rose, 9 In. 12.00
Plate, Rose, 10 In. 35.00
Plate, Salad, Medium Green, Individual 60.00
Plate, Turquoise, 9 In. 10.00
Plate, Turquoise, Compartment 15.00
Plate, Yellow, 10 1/2 In. 10.00
Platter, Chartreuse 35.00
Platter, Cobalt Blue, Kitchen Kraft, Oval 60.00
Platter, Light Green 16.00
Platter, Medium Green 32.00
Platter, Rose, 12 In. .... 25.00 To 35.00
Platter, Yellow 16.00
Popcorn Set, Metal 65.00
Refrigerator Set, Red, Cover, 3 Piece 185.00
Relish, Center Handle, Yellow 25.00
Salt & Pepper, Teapot Shape 55.00
Saucer, Chartreuse 4.00
Shaker, Medium Green 16.00
Skillet, Yellow, Cover 125.00
Soup, Cream, Green 25.00
Soup, Cream, Ivory 25.00
Soup, Onion, Cobalt Blue, Cover 195.00
Sugar, Turquoise 20.00

◆◆

Watch out for exploding antiques! Any type of gun, shell, powder can, nitrate movie film, and some chemicals possibly left in old bottles or cans are dangerous. If you don't know about these items, contact your local police or fire department for help.

◆◆

◆◆◆◆◆◆◆◆◆◆◆◆◆◆◆◆◆◆◆◆◆◆◆

Shallow nicks and rough edges on glass can sometimes be smoothed off with fine emery paper.

◆◆◆◆◆◆◆◆◆◆◆◆◆◆◆◆◆◆◆◆◆◆◆

Findlay Onyx, Toothpick, White Floral, Ruby, Globular, 2 1/2 In.

Findlay Onyx, Mustard Pot, White Floral & Leaf, Ruby, 3 3/4 In.

Syrup, Turquoise 140.00
Tray, Utility, Turquoise 20.00
Vase, Bud, Yellow 27.00
Vase, Bud, Yellow, 6 In. 15.00
Vase, Rose, 6 In. 12.00
    FINCH, see Kay Finch

Findlay, or onyx, glass was made using three layers of glass. It was manufactured by the Dalzell Gilmore Leighton Company about 1889 in Findlay, Ohio. The platinum, ruby, or black pattern was molded into the glass. The glass came in several colors, but was usually white or ruby.

FINDLAY ONYX, Berry Bowl, Master 400.00
Bowl, Cover, Ruby, Bulbous, 5 1/2 In. 578.00
Bowl, Platinum Luster, Floral Designs In Silver Luster, 7 In. 193.00
Bowl, Ruby, Opalescent White Flowers and Leaves, 4 In. 853.00
Box, Domed Cover, Ruby, 6 In. 1760.00
Caster, Platinum Luster, Floral and Leaf Design, 5 1/2 In. 220.00
Celery Vase, 7 In. .... 200.00 To 275.00
Celery Vase, Platinum & Silver Luster, 6 1/2 In. 248.00
Creamer 485.00
Creamer, Ruby, Bulbous, Fluted Neck, 4 5/8 In. 1265.00
Dish, Purple, Cushion Shape, 4 In. 1100.00
Mustard Pot, White Floral & Leaf, Ruby, 3 3/4 In. .... *Illus* 1100.00
Pitcher, Platinum Luster, Bulbous, 8 In. 660.00
Spooner, Platinum Blossoms, 4 1/4 In 245.00
Sugar Shaker .... 195.00 To 400.00
Sugar Shaker, Platinum Luster Flowers, 5 1/2 In. 395.00
Toothpick, White Floral, Ruby, Globular, 2 1/2 In. .... *Illus* 715.00
Tumble–Up, Platinum Luster, Snowflakes, Bulbous, 8 3/4 In. 550.00
Tumbler, Platinum Luster Flowers, Barrel Shape, 3 3/4 In. 395.00
Tumbler, Platinum Luster, Straight Sides, 3 5/8 In. 385.00
Tumbler, Ruby, White Flowers & Leaves, 3 5/8 In. 770.00
Vase, Amber, White Flowers & Leaves, Bulbous, 4 3/8 In. 440.00
Vase, Ruby, Cylindrical Fluted Neck, Bulbous, 6 1/2 In. 825.00

It is said that every little boy wanted to be a fireman or a train engineer 75 years ago and the collectors today reflect this interest. All types of firefighting equipment are wanted, from fire marks to uniforms to toy fire trucks.

FIREFIGHTING, Alarm Box, Chicago, Cast Iron, 1900 .... 250.00
Alarm Box, On Iron Stand 475.00
Ax, Parade 235.00
Banner, Muster Welcome To Cortland, Fireman Pictured, c.1880 .... 750.00
Bucket, Banner & Foliage, A. Morse, 12 1/4 In. 600.00
Bucket, Banner, No. 1 Citizens Fire Society 1824, 13 In. 1000.00
Bucket, Banner, No. 2 Citizens Fire Society 1824, 13 In. 275.00
Bucket, Ceremonial, Enterprise Fire Club, Leather, 1810, 13 In. 3025.00
Bucket, Leather, Red Paint, Black Trim, No. 3, 11 In. 300.00
Bucket, Little Giant, Falmouth 660.00
Extinguisher, Phoenix, Lithograph On Tin, 21 3/4 In., Pair 145.00
Extinguisher, Texaco, Brass, 1930s 50.00
Fire Mark, Mutual Ins. Co., Angel Over Charleston, 9 1/2 In. 65.00
Firemark, Eagle, Banner, Eagle Ins. Co., Cincinnati, 8 x 12 In. 935.00
Firemark, F. A., Polychrome, 7 3/8 x 11 1/2 In. 210.00
Firemark, Hose & F. A., Cast Iron, 11 1/4 x 7 1/4 In. 100.00
Firemark, Man With Horn, Cast Iron, 11 1/4 x 8 3/4 In. 65.00
Firemark, Pumper, City Insurance Co., Cin., 9 1/2 x 12 1/2 In. 715.00
Firemark, Pumper, Fire Dept. Insurance, Iron, 8 x 11 1/2 In. 415.00
Grenade, Harden Improved, Iron Clamp, Label, 1880s, 5 In. 275.00
Grenade, Red Comet 5.00
Grenade, Red Comet, Holder, Contents 40.00
Hat, Parade, Franklin Hose Company, Franklin Pictured, 1838 .... 6275.00

◆◆

Never move an object that might explode. Call the local police bomb squad. Many accidents are caused by old souvenir hand grenades and firearms.

◆◆

Hat, Parade, Gilt Paint, Northern No. 1 Liberty, 1756, 6 In. 3650.00
Hat, Parade, Painted, Fairmount, Philadelphia, 6 In. 9350.00
Helmet, Oilcloth, Shield, Niagara 3 Brunswick, 5 1/2 In. 1100.00
Jacket, Fireman's, 1880s 80.00
Lamp, DeVoursney Bros., Blue, Red, Clear Glass, 1886, 19 In., Pr. 2310.00
Lantern, La France, Dietz 300.00
Ribbon, Fame & Franklin Fire Companies, Penna., Silk, 1894 .... 32.00

 The fireplace was used to cook and to heat the American home in past centuries. Many types of tools and equipment were used. Andirons held the logs in place, firebacks reflected the heat into the room, and tongs were used to move either fuel or food. Many types of spits and roasting jacks were made and are listed under Kitchen.

FIREPLACE, Andirons, Baseball Players, Traces of Paint 3850.00
Andirons, Bell Metal, Lemon Finial, Baluster Shaft, 13 In. 665.00
Andirons, Bell Metal, Urn Top 2000.00
Andirons, Brass, America, 1830, 18 In. 225.00
Andirons, Brass, Colonial Revival, Urn Legs, Ball Feet, 26 In. 385.00
Andirons, Brass, Dolphin, Foliate Base, 24 In. ....*Illus* 1200.00
Andirons, Brass, Federal, Steeple Top Plinth, c.1810, 20 1/2 In. 1100.00
Andirons, Brass, Georgian Style, Ball Finial, Arched Feet, 18 In. 198.00
Andirons, Brass, Iron Dogs, 22 In. 2200.00
Andirons, Brass, Iron, Ball Finial, Outward Scrolling Feet, 26 In. 60.00
Andirons, Brass, Iron, John Molineux, Boston, c.1800, 14 In. 525.00
Andirons, Brass, Iron, Signed I. C., Late–18th Century, 17 In. 445.00
Andirons, Brass, Iron, Swag & Tassel Atop Column, 26 1/4 In. 1650.00
Andirons, Brass, Iron, Urn Finial, Wittingham, c.1790, 22 In. 3300.00
Andirons, Brass, Knife Blade, Penny Feet, Urn Finials 450.00
Andirons, Brass, O. Hillips, New York, 23 In. 1540.00
Andirons, Brass, Open Scrolled Support, Dutch, 22 In. 2750.00
Andirons, Brass, Renaissance Revival, Tool Set, 23 In. 160.00
Andirons, Brass, Richard Wittingham, c.1800, 18 1/2 In. 995.00
Andirons, Brass, Steeple Top, 15 1/2 In. 200.00
Andirons, Brass, Turned Finial, Baluster Shaft, 1830, 7 In. 550.00
Andirons, Brass, Urn & Ribbed Finials, Shovel, Tongs, 18 In. 225.00
Andirons, Brass, Urn–Shaped Finial, Engraved Urns & Disks 8500.00
Andirons, Bronze, Sea Serpent Bases, Figures At Top 4500.00
Andirons, Bronze, Sphinx On Base, Gilt & Patinated, 15 In. 6600.00

Fireplace, Andirons, Brass, Dolphin, Foliate Base, 24 In.

◆◆◆◆◆◆◆◆◆◆◆◆◆◆◆◆◆◆◆◆◆◆◆◆

Have your chimney cleaned if you move into an old house or if you burn wood regularly. A creosote buildup can cause an explosion. Nesting animals can cause fire or smoke.

◆◆◆◆◆◆◆◆◆◆◆◆◆◆◆◆◆◆◆◆◆◆◆◆

Andirons, Bronze, Steeple Top, Faceted & Ball Feet, c.1800 .... 100.00
Andirons, Bronze, Stylized Dolphins, Flaming Torches, 24 In. 605.00
Andirons, Chrome, Art Deco, Clear Crystal, 11 In. 55.00
Andirons, Double Lemon Top, Pierced Gallery, c.1825, 22 In. 3500.00
Andirons, Federal, Matching Tools 110.00
Andirons, Iron, Figural, Hessian Soldiers, Black Paint, 19 In. 300.00
Andirons, Iron, Fir Tree, Half Round, 18 In. 935.00
Andirons, Iron, Hand Wrought, 10 In. 250.00
Andirons, Iron, Hessian Soldier, 20 In. 180.00
Andirons, Iron, Hessian, Hand On Saber, 18th Century, 19 In. 1210.00
Andirons, Iron, Horseshoe 86.00
Andirons, Iron, Knife Blade, Swan Head Finials, 19th Century 500.00
Andirons, Iron, Penguin Form, R. C. Murphy 1450.00
Andirons, Iron, Penny Feet, Faceted Finials, 20 1/4 In. 225.00
Andirons, Iron, Penny Feet, Oval Ring Finials, 14 In. 215.00
Andirons, Iron, Post & Ball, Tooled Feet, G. Stickley, 28 x 26 In. 2310.00
Andirons, Iron, Ratchet Posts, 26 In. 150.00
Andirons, Iron, Seated Dogs, Richard Clancy, 13 3/4 In. 850.00
Andirons, Iron, Sunflower Finials, Foliate Feet, c.1886 .... 4950.00
Andirons, Louis XVI, Screen, 3 Tools 1550.00
Andirons, Stacked Balls, Lion Chenets, Stand, Tools, Dutch 145.00
Andirons, Wrought Iron, Cabriole Curved Legs, Tool Set, 20 In. 110.00
Basket, Grate, Man In The Moon, Cast Iron 250.00
Bellows, Chip Carved, 18th Century 875.00
Bellows, Freehand & Stenciled Fruit & Foliage, 17 1/2 In. 250.00
Bellows, Turtle Back, Floral Design, Brass Nozzle, 18 In. 125.00
Bellows, Turtle Back, Gold Design, Brass Nozzle, 17 In. 200.00
Box, Log, Brass, Figural Design, 22 x 32 x 14 1/2 In. 88.00
Box, Log, Brass, Figural Relief Design, 32 x 14 1/2 x 22 In. 80.00
Bracket, Mantel, Brass, Holds Bottle Jack In Fireplace 150.00
Broiler, 4 Fleur–De–Lis On Top, Rotary, Wrought Iron, 27 1/2 In. 200.00
Broiler, Drip Holes, Iron 265.00
Broiler, Forged, 4–Footed, 13 In. Handle, 10 x 11 In. 130.00
Broiler, Rotary, Concave Frame, Wrought Iron, 17 3/4 In. 215.00
Broiler, Rotary, Handle Stamped J. B. Turner, Iron, 27 In. 100.00
Broiler, Rotary, Wrought Iron, 12 x 21 In. 145.00
Broiler, Rotary, Wrought Iron, 15 In. 175.00
Broiler, Rotary, Wrought Iron, 25 1/4 In. 55.00
Broiler, Upright, Urn Finial, Adjustable Rack, Iron, 27 3/4 In. 825.00
Carrier, Log, Brass, Half–Cylindrical Form, Claw Feet, 20 x 13 In. 35.00
Chenet, Louis XV, Foliate Acanthus Scrolls, 14 In., Pair 770.00
Coal Bin, Brass Cover, 1895 .... 597.00
Coal Carrier, Sliding Lid, Wooden Handle, Sheet Iron, 37 1/2 In. 325.00
Coal Carrier, Sliding Lid, Wooden Handle, Sheet Iron, 41 In. 300.00
Coal Chest, Gothic Style, Hinged Top, Allegorical Figures, Brass 198.00
Coal Hod, Hammered Brass, Early 20th Century, 28 In. 75.00
Fender, Brass Top Rail Over Wire Posts, Wire Scrollwork, 56 In. 2100.00
Fender, Brass, Federal Style, 1870, 53 1/2 x 14 1/2 x 4 In. 215.00
Fender, Brass, Paw Feet, 49 In. 350.00
Fender, Brass, Wire Grill, Iron Frame, 3 Finials, 52 1/2 In. 550.00
Fender, Bronze & Gilt Bronze, Reclining Lions At Ends, c.1810 .... 1650.00
Fender, Bronze, Shell Carving, Corner Figures, Pierced, 60 In. 1545.00
Fender, Galvanized Metal, Ball Finials, 24 In. 35.00
Fender, Gilt Metal, Regency, St. Bernard Dogs Sides, 1820, 46 In. 3575.00
Fire Basket, Iron, Goosehead Finials, Cabriol Legs, 18th Century 1250.00
Fire Guard, Iron, Art Deco, Marble, 2 Shelves, 26 x 83 x 10 In. 2200.00
Fireback, Cast Iron, Elihu Vedder, 3 Piece 5100.00
Fireback, Cast Iron, French Couple, Period Costumes, 21 1/2 In. 225.00
Fireboard, Oil On Canvas, Floral, 38 x 43 In. 3500.00
Fork, 3 Prong, Hanging Eye, 22 3/4 In. 65.00
Fork, Meat, c.1800, 32 In. 125.00
Fork, Roasting, 3 Prongs, Cutout Heart In Handle, Iron, 27 1/2 In. 250.00
Fork, Roasting, Brass Inlay, Iron, 18 1/4 In. 235.00

◆◆◆◆◆◆◆◆◆◆◆◆◆◆◆◆◆◆◆◆◆◆

When the weather is bad, the auction will probably be good. Brave storms and cold and attend the auctions in bad weather when the crowd is small and the prices low.

◆◆◆◆◆◆◆◆◆◆◆◆◆◆◆◆◆◆◆◆◆◆

Fireplace, Screen, Needlepoint,
Shield Shape, 44 1/2 x 25 In.

Fork, Roasting, On Stand, Heart Handle, 25 In.	145.00
Fork, Tooled Ram's Horn Finial, Iron, 17 1/4 In.	135.00
Gate, George III, Columnar Serpentine Form, Brass & Iron, 31 In.	550.00
Grate, Brass, Regency, Serpentine & Columnar Form, 28 1/2 In.	465.00
Gridiron, 3 Hearts On Cross Members, Handwrought	365.00
Guard, Brass, Velvet Upholstered Seat, Plinth Base, 53 In.	330.00
Guard, Fluted Crest Rail Over Spindles, Marble Top, 83 In.	2000.00
Hanger, 8 Skewers, Wrought Iron	195.00
Kettle Tilter, Serpentine Handle, Wrought Iron, 19 In.	275.00
Mantel, Side Columns, Gas Heater, Heart–Shaped Fire Bricks	285.00
Pan, Transfer Hot Coals, Brass Bowl, Copper Rivets, Russia, 1890	395.00
Peel, Heart Handle, 36 In.	195.00
Peel, Oven, Wrought Iron, Ram's Horn Handle, 43 In.	75.00 To 135.00
Peel, Wrought Iron, 43 1/4 In.	65.00
Rack, Roasting, Wrought Iron, Adjustable, Tripod Base, 30 1/4 In.	550.00
Roaster, Gamebird, Rizzler, Plymouth, Hand Forged, 30 In.	375.00
Rotisserie, Windup, Cast Iron, c.1830	395.00
Screen, 2 Panels, Chinese Painted Panels, Court Scenes, 42 In.	825.00
Screen, 3 Panels, Folding, Carved Wood, Art Deco, 30 x 48 In.	1295.00
Screen, 3 Sliding Panels, Oriental Design, Silk Damask, 43 In.	165.00
Screen, 3 Steel Mesh Panels	25.00
Screen, 8 Panels, Iron, G. Stickley, 2 Handles, 27 1/2 x 40 In.	4500.00
Screen, Acanthus & Scrolled Crest, Brocade Screen, 45 In.	250.00
Screen, Biblical Figures, Gros & Petit Point Panel, 51 In.	770.00
Screen, Geometric Design, Victorian, Brass & Glass, 30 In.	495.00
Screen, George III, Seated Woman, Mahogany, c.1810, 46 x 22 In.	9500.00
Screen, Iron, Stylized Clouds, Rising Sun, Sea Gull, 36 1/4 In.	3575.00
Screen, Louis XV, Gilt Bronze & Mesh	1450.00
Screen, Louis XV, Petit Point Upholstery, Walnut, 38 x 23 In.	265.00
Screen, Needlepoint Panel On Trifid Base, Mahogany, 62 In.	357.00
Screen, Needlepoint, Shield Shape, 44 1/2 x 25 In. *Illus*	135.00
Screen, Overall Geometric Design, Walnut & Stained Glass, 37 In.	357.50
Screen, Petit Point Panel of Angel & Child, Gesso & Giltwood	305.00
Screen, Pole, Adjustable, Mahogany, c.1875, 59 In.	198.00
Screen, Pole, Bellflower Carving, Snake Feet, Mahogany, 58 In.	275.00
Screen, Pole, Mahogany, 58 In.	825.00
Screen, Pole, Needlepoint, Arms of England, Rosewood	850.00
Screen, Pole, Rectangular Screen, Lacqueed, Papier–Mache, 52 In.	550.00
Screen, Regency, Mahogany, Bronze, Pleated Silk, 55 1/2 In.	7750.00
Screen, Serpentine, 3 Brass Finials	2300.00
Screen, Steel Triangular Devices, Wire Screen, Bronze, 5 Ft. 3 In.	880.00
Screen, Tabletop, Petit Point Tabby Cat, Rosewood, 17 In.	715.00
Screen, Victorian, Grosse Point Landscape, Rosewood, 38 In.	415.00
Screen, Wallpaper On Wood, Stenciled	650.00
Scuttle, Coal, Brass Mounted, Mahogany, With Shovel, England	145.00
Scuttle, Coal, Helmet Form, Brass	65.00
Skimmer, Starflower Shaped Holes, Iron Handle, Brass, 18 1/4 In.	55.00

Tilter, Stationary, Penny Feet, Wrought Iron, 22 In. 65.00
Toaster, Twisted Detail, Wrought Iron, 16 In. 125.00
Toaster, Twisted Handle, Wooden Grip, Iron, 25 x 12 In. 75.00
Toaster, Wooden Handle, Wrought Iron, 18 In. 75.00
Tongs, Toggle, Forged Iron, Expanding, 18th Century, 8 1/2 In. 175.00
Tongs, Wrought Iron, 27 In. 25.00
Tool Set, Arts & Crafts, Hammered, Urn Form, Scroll, c.1910, 8 Pc. 445.00
Tool Set, Bronze, Art Nouveau Cherub Handles, Stand, 1890, 3 Piece 1025.00
Trammel, Hooks In Shape of Human Heads, Copper & Brass, 1797 .... 875.00
Trammel, Sawtooth, Bottom Eye For Hook, Wrought Iron, 26 In. 100.00
Trammel, Sawtooth, Wrought Iron, Scroll On End, 45 In. 89.00
Trivet & Fork, Combination, Iron, 43 x 25 In. 175.00
Wafer Iron, Engraved Crown, Initials & Date 1759, 33 1/2 In. 65.00

MF Porcelain was made in Herend, Hungary, by Moritz Fischer. The factory was founded in 1839 and continued working into the twentieth century. The wares are sometimes referred to as *Herend* porcelain.

FISCHER, Bowl, Blue Garden, 7 1/2 In. 75.00
Dish, Pierced, Circular, 4 3/4 In. 35.00
Figurine, 2 Peacocks, 8 1/4 In. 110.00
Figurine, Folk Dancer, No. 5491, 11 1/2 In. 395.00
Figurine, Rabbit, White Glaze, 4 x 5 In. 110.00
Figurine, Sea Horse, Double, Gray, Coral 185.00
Holder, Card, Chickens On Leaves, Set of 8 .... 175.00

Fishing reels of brass or nickel were made in the United States by 1810. Bamboo fly rods were sold by 1860, often marked with the maker's name. Metal lures, then wooden and metal lures were made in the nineteenth century. Plastic lures were made by the 1930s. All fishing material is collected today and even equipment of the past thirty years is of interest if in good condition with original box.

FISHING, Book, Facts & Useful Hints Relating To Fishing & Shooting, 1874 .... 25.00
Box, Bait, Side Fish Cutouts, Screen Lining, Wood, 24 x 11 In. 145.00
Box, Belt Loops, Stenciled Fish & Lures, Tole, 6 In. 7.50
Box, Tackle, B. F. Meek 539.00
Box, Tackle, Child's, Enameled Tin, Lift-Out Tray, Scenes, 5 x 3 In. 275.00
Box, Tackle, Filled With Fishing Needs, Wooden, 24 In. 175.00
Box, Tackle, Winchester 65.00
Bucket, Minnow, Green, Gold Striping, Cream City, Tole, 8 1/4 In. 95.00
Bucket, Minnow, Jones, Green Paint 325.00
Catalog, Fishing Tackle, 1941, 112 Pages 9.00
Creel, Slant Top, Center Hole, Half Round, Lid Hinges 100.00
Creel, Split Willow, Center Hole, Boat Belly Shape, 10 1/2 In. 220.00
Creel, Wicker .... 65.00 To 72.00
Creel, Wicker, Leather Straps 125.00
Creel, Wicker, Trout, Leather Straps, Collapsible Net In Sheath 87.00
Creel, Willow, Iron Hinges & Clasp, Center Lid Hole, Wooden Legs 275.00
Creel, Woven Reed, 13 1/2 In. 25.00
Creel, Woven Splint, Red Paint, 11 3/4 In. 175.00
Display, Country Store, 21 Lures, 21 x 14 In. 600.00
Dryer, Line, Black Enamel, Brass Fitted, Clamp, Round, 13 In. 38.50
Fly Case, 21 Hand-Tied Flies, Leatherized 55.00
Fly Rod, Gateway Deluxe, Split Bamboo, 2 Tips, 8 1/2 In. 45.00
Fly Rod, Herter's Grand Deluxe, Handmade, 9 Ft. 250.00
Fly Rod, Oris Impregnated, Bamboo, 7 Ft. 525.00
Fly Rod, Shakespeare, Split Bamboo 28.00
Gaff, Salmon, Telescoping, W. Brown, Scotland, 19th Century, 27 In. 450.00
Hook, Automatic Spring Loader, 5-In. Jaw Spread When Cocked 38.50
Hooks, Occupied Japan, Package 20.00
Lure, Brown's Fisherette, Wood, Metalworn Polychrome Paint, 5 In. 20.00
Lure, Bug Spoon, Pfleuger May, 1890, 2 3/4 In. 1540.00
Lure, Bug-Type, Surface, Revolving Red Head, Decker, 1 7/8 In. 330.00

◆◆◆

When buying antiques, beware of stickers, magic marker numbers, and other dealer added labels that may damage the antique. Any type of sticky tape or label will leave marks on paper or paint finishes. Metal with an oxidized finish is damaged when ink marks are removed. Pencil or pen notations often leave indentations.

◆◆◆

Lure, Carved Wood, Painted, 3 Set of Hooks, American, 9 In.	195.00
Lure, Chugger Jr., Heddon, Plastic	32.00
Lure, Crazy Crawler, Heddon	16.00
Lure, Creek Chub, Dingbat, Wooden	25.00
Lure, Fish, Cast Lead Fins, Aluminum Tail, 13 In.	110.00
Lure, Fish, Metal Fins, Oscar Peterson, 8 In.	600.00
Lure, Frog, Black Bead Eyes, Rotating Front Legs, Carved, 9 1/2 In.	75.00
Lure, Frog, Double Jointed Hind Legs, Flotation Tubes, 4 1/2 In.	65.00
Lure, Frog, E & S, 8 In.	150.00
Lure, Glowbody Minnow, Glass & Metal, Abbey & Imbrie, 3 1/4 In.	75.00
Lure, Minnow, Creek Club Pikie, No. 701W, Box	25.00
Lure, Minnow, Hollow Metal, Leaf Blade, J. B. McHarg, 3 1/2 In.	135.00
Lure, Minnow, Miller, Reversible, 1916, 4 1/4 Ft.	1650.00
Lure, Northern Pike, 4 Metal Fins, Otto Bishop, 4 3/4 In.	195.00
Lure, Paw Paw Bullhead, Tack Eyes, Wooden	75.00
Lure, Pike, Rotating Tail, A. J. Downey, 14 1/2 In.	300.00
Lure, Red & White Deer Tail, Teardrop Shape, 8 In.	20.00
Lure, Spinner, Scalloped–Edge Blade, Chapman & Sons, Snap Swivel	120.00
Lure, Sunfish, Glass Eyes, 5 1/2 In.	45.00
Minnow Trap, Camp, Glass	50.00 To 60.00
Mold, Sinker, Palmer	15.00 To 25.00
Net, Landing, Wooden Frame, Label, 23 1/2 In.	50.00
Outboard Motor, Neptune, 1 7/8 H. P.	75.00
Plug, Jumpin' Jo	7.50
Reel, Abercrombie & Fitch, No. 80	35.00
Reel, Airex, Box	45.00
Reel, B. F. Meek & Sons, No. 33, Silver & Nickel Plated, Bluegrass	110.00
Reel, B. F. Meek & Sons, No. 44	5500.00
Reel, Everol Special, Big Game, Line, Box	255.00
Reel, Hardy 3/0, Cascapedia, Salmon Red, 1930s	7150.00
Reel, Hawks & Ogilvy, Brass Ball Handle, Walnut Hand Control	250.00
Reel, Horton, No. 3, Bluegrass	125.00
Reel, Humphrey	16.00
Reel, J. F. & B. F. Meek, Casting, 3 Numbered Screws, Brass	5500.00
Reel, Julius Vom Hofe	150.00
Reel, Meek & Milam, Casting, No. 3, Sliding Click & Drag, Brass	665.00
Reel, Meisselbach Tripart	35.00
Reel, Ocean City Free Spool, No. 250	35.00
Reel, Pennell, No. 80, Jeweled	55.00
Reel, Pflueger Supreme	20.00
Reel, Pflueger, No. 1558, Sal–Trout	25.00
Reel, Shakespeare	12.00
Reel, South Bend	12.00
Reel, South Bend, No. 550	35.00
Reel, Talbot Reel & Mfg. Co., Comet, German Silver Bit	465.00
Reel, Trout, H. I. Leonard, German Silver Handle & Foot, Pat. 1913	1760.00
Reel, Winchester, No. 2242	95.00
Reel, Wm. H. Talbot, No. 3, German Silver, Ivory Grip, Patent 1901	1870.00
Rod & Reel, Game, Thigh Rest, Adjustable Brake, Cast Alloy, 5 Ft.	110.00
Rod, Bamboo, Nickel–Plated Fittings, Aluminum Case, 68 In.	25.00
Rod, Hadley, Trout, 2 Tip, Amhurst Rod Co., 8 Ft.	245.00

Rod, Heddon, Cast Split Bamboo, Agate Eyes, Case, 5 Ft.	150.00
Rod, J. C. Higgins, Engraved Reel	18.00
Rod, Jim Payne, Casting, Staggered Ferrule, Agate Guides, Model 303	1155.00
Rod, Leonard, Trout, Hunt 50–4, 8 Ft.	5500.00
Rod, Wye, Salmon, Locking Ferrules, 2–Handed, Canvas Case, 12 1/2 Ft.	275.00
Saw & Chisel, Ice Hole, Wooden Handle, Cast Iron Frame	305.00
Seat, Canoe, Cane Seat & Back, Folding	115.00
Sign, Izaak Walton League of America, Tin, 18 x 12 In.	198.00
Spear, Iron, Wooden Handle, 56 In.	30.00
Spearhead, Iron, 10 1/2 In.	25.00
Stone, Sharpening, Fish On Cover, Pike	250.00
Trap, Minnow, Camp, Glass	52.50
Trap, Minnow, Checotah, Oklahoma	80.00
Trap, Minnow, Orvis, Glass	68.50

FLAG, see Textile, Flag

Flash Gordon appeared in the Sunday comics in 1934. The daily strip started in 1940. The hero was also in comic books from 1930 to 1970, in books from 1936, in movies from 1938, on the radio in the 1930s and 1940s, and on television from 1953 to 1954. All sorts of memorabilia are collected, but the ray guns and rocket ships are the most popular.

FLASH GORDON, Big Little Book	40.00
Book, Pop–Up	255.00
Cap Gun, Diecast, 1981	45.00
Compass, Wrist, On Original Card, 1950s	45.00
Gun, Arresting Ray	195.00
March of Comic Book, Funny Box Socks, No. 118	75.00
Postcard, Flash Gordon, K. F. S. Promotion	12.00
Ray Gun, Arresting, Marx	135.00
Rocket Fighter, Marx	575.00
Stun Gun, 1979	35.00

Florence Ceramics were made in Pasadena, California, from World War II to 1977. Florence Ward created many colorful figurines, boxes, candleholders, and other items for the giftshop trade. Each piece was marked with an ink stamp that included the name Florence Ceramics Co. The company was sold in 1964 and although the name remained the same the products were very different. Mugs, cups, and trays were made.

FLORENCE CERAMICS, Figurine, Abigail, Godey Costume	95.00
Figurine, Ann, Green & Gold Trim, 6 1/4 In.	55.00
Figurine, Bea	65.00
Figurine, Blynkin	75.00
Figurine, Charmaine, 8 1/2 In.	80.00
Figurine, Choir Boy	40.00
Figurine, Claudia, 8 In.	85.00
Figurine, Delia & Mate, White, Gold Trim, Pair	160.00
Figurine, Delia, 7 3/4 In.	85.00 To 90.00
Figurine, Diane, 8 1/2 In.	85.00 To 95.00
Figurine, Elaine & Jim, White, Gold Trim, Pair	135.00
Figurine, Elaine, Godey Costume, 6 In.	45.00 To 65.00
Figurine, Giselle	80.00
Figurine, Jim, Green & Gold Trim, 6 1/4 In.	50.00 To 55.00
Figurine, John Alden	140.00 To 150.00
Figurine, John Alden & Priscilla, Pair	250.00
Figurine, Laura	95.00
Figurine, Lea	65.00
Figurine, Lila	75.00
Figurine, Lillian, Godey Costume, Gold Trim, 8 In.	95.00
Figurine, Louis XVI & Marie Antoinette, 10 In., Pair	325.00
Figurine, Madame Pompadour, White	187.00
Figurine, Margaret	425.00

Figurine, Marie Antoinette 150.00
Figurine, Marsie 60.00
Figurine, Matilda, Godey Costume, 8 1/2 In. .... 60.00 To 95.00
Figurine, Melanie, 7 1/2 In. .... 50.00 To 60.00
Figurine, Nita 85.00
Figurine, Oriental Holding Vase, Blue, 8 In. 15.00
Figurine, Our Lady of Grace, Pasadena, ... 65.00
Figurine, Parakeet 28.00
Figurine, Peter 110.00
Figurine, Pinkie & Blue Boy, 12 In., Pair .... 350.00 To 390.00
Figurine, Priscilla 120.00
Figurine, Rebecca 110.00
Figurine, Rose Lillian, 8 In. 50.00
Figurine, Sarah 95.00
Figurine, Story Hour, Woman, Boy & Girl 325.00
Figurine, Victor 110.00
Figurine, Victoria 80.00
Figurine, Vivian, Godey Costume, 10 In. .... 90.00 To 110.00
Figurine, Wynkin 75.00
Flower Holder, Oriental Couple, 8 In., Pair 30.00
Head Vase, Pink & Green 150.00
Lamp, Dear Ruth, Green Dress, Red Hair, Seated On Bench 225.00
Planter, Girl 35.00
Plaque, Bust, Figural 45.00
Plaque, Woman, Standing, Pink 60.00
Platter, Chinese Boy & Girl, Black & White 65.00

Flow blue, or flo blue, was made in England about 1830 to 1900. The plates were printed with designs using a cobalt blue coloring. The color flowed from the design to the white plate so that the finished plate has a smeared blue design. The plates were usually made of ironstone china.

FLOW BLUE, Berry Bowl, Linda 35.00
  Berry Bowl, Marechal Niel 35.00
  Bone Dish, Belmont, Meakin 45.00
  Bone Dish, Bolingbroke, Ridgway 45.00
  Bone Dish, Lotus, Grindley 20.00
  Bone Dish, Marechal Niel 40.00
  Bone Dish, Marie, Grindley, 6 Piece 195.00
  Bowl & Pitcher, Shell 1150.00
  Bowl, Blue Rose, Grindley, 6 1/4 In. 40.00
  Bowl, Brazil, Cover, 11 In. 250.00
  Bowl, Cashmere, 8 3/4 x 10 3/4 In. 495.00
  Bowl, Catherine Mermet, Grindley, 10 In. 95.00
  Bowl, Chapoo, Wedgwood, 8 In. 40.00
  Bowl, Clifton, Cover, 11 In. 165.00
  Bowl, Conway, New Wharf, 9 In. 90.00
  Bowl, Corea, Slotted Cover, Underplate, 11 In. 225.00
  Bowl, Cover, Carlton, Rose Finial, Alcock 395.00
  Bowl, Cover, Dainty, Maddock, Oval 275.00
  Bowl, Cover, La Belle, Raised Flowers Rim, 10 1/4 x 8 1/4 In. 250.00
  Bowl, Cover, Locarno, Gibson & Son, 9 In. 70.00
  Bowl, Cover, Vegetable, Clover, Grindley, Oblong, 11 In. 250.00
  Bowl, Cover, Vegetable, Hong Kong 275.00
  Bowl, Crossed Bands, Heart Shape, Cutout Handles, Ridgway, 11 In. 225.00
  Bowl, Del Monte, Gold & Blue Design, Johnson Bros., 9 1/2 In. 55.00
  Bowl, Denton, Grindley, Small 20.00
  Bowl, Florida, Grindley, 10 In. 125.00
  Bowl, Florida, Grindley, Oval, 6 In. 35.00
  Bowl, Fruit, La Belle, Scalloped 275.00
  Bowl, Gainsborough, Ridgway, 9 1/2 In. 145.00
  Bowl, Geisha, Upper Hanley Potteries, 9 3/4 In. 175.00
  Bowl, Hofburg, Open Handles, 11 In. 110.00

Bowl, Holland, Meakin, Cover, 11 In. .... 150.00 To 160.00
Bowl, Idris, 10 1/2 In. 29.00
Bowl, Kelvin, Meakin, Oval, 6 3/4 x 8 1/2 In. 110.00
Bowl, Kenworth, Johnson Bros., Oval, 8 3/4 In. 75.00
Bowl, La Belle, Cover, 11 In. 285.00
Bowl, La Belle, Gold Rim, 9 1/2 In. 110.00
Bowl, La Belle, Scalloped, Gold Trim, Deep Blue Florals, 11 In. 190.00
Bowl, La Hore, Phillips, 8 1/4 x 6 1/4 In. 250.00
Bowl, Lorne, Cover, 10 1/2 In. 195.00
Bowl, Maria, Cover, Lacy Handles 155.00
Bowl, Melbourne, Cover, 10 1/2 In. 275.00
Bowl, Olympia, 9 In. 80.00
Bowl, Oyster, La Belle, 9 In., 6 Piece 360.00
Bowl, Persian Moss, 10 In. 90.00
Bowl, Pitcher, Brooklyn 850.00
Bowl, Pitcher, Montrose 695.00
Bowl, Spinach, 4 1/4 In. 65.00
Bowl, Temple, Podmore & Walker, Oval, 9 1/2 In. 95.00
Bowl, Touraine, 7 x 9 1/2 In. 95.00
Bowl, Touraine, Stanley, Cover 295.00
Bowl, Vine, Wedgwood, 4 1/2 In. 30.00
Bowl, Waste, Shell, Challinor 75.00
Bowl, Watteau, New Wharf, 10 1/2 In. 170.00
Bowl, Watteau, Oblong, 9 1/4 In. 85.00
Box, Toothbrush, Madras, c.1876 .... 275.00
Butter, Cover, Holland, Meakin 190.00
Butter, Cover, Olympia, Grindley 105.00
Cake Plate, Cyprus, Pedestal, Ridgway, Bates, 12 In. 395.00
Cake Plate, Non Pareil, 11 In. 235.00
Casserole, Cover, Idris 59.00
Celery, La Belle, 13 x 6 1/4 In. 175.00
Chamber Pot, Cover 150.00
Chamber Pot, Gainsborough, Ridgway, 5 1/2 x 9 1/2 In. 275.00
Chamber Pot, Lucerne 90.00
Charger, Camellia, Wedgwood, 12 1/2 In. 395.00
Charger, Chatsworth, 11 In. 145.00
Charger, Chusan, Wedgwood 350.00
Charger, La Belle, 11 In. 95.00
Charger, La Belle, 13 In. 110.00
Coffeepot, Lily, 9 In. 125.00
Coffeepot, Lustre Band, E & F 475.00
Compote, Formosa, 8 Sides, Handles, Ridgway, 9 In. 950.00
Cracker Jar, Rose 195.00
Creamer, Chusan, Clementson 325.00
Creamer, Conway, New Wharf 140.00
Creamer, Daisy, Societe Ceramique, 12 1/4 In. 160.00
Creamer, Davenport, Wood .... 75.00 To 85.00
Creamer, Hamilton, Meakin 95.00
Creamer, Iris 50.00
Creamer, La Belle, Wheeling 95.00
Creamer, Marechal Niel .... 145.00 To 150.00
Creamer, Neopolitan 125.00
Creamer, Non Pareil 150.00
Creamer, Oriental, Alcock 290.00
Creamer, Scinde, Walker 325.00
Cup & Saucer, Amoy, Handleless, Davenport 135.00
Cup & Saucer, Celia 45.00
Cup & Saucer, Clover, Grindley 60.00
Cup & Saucer, Dahlia 90.00
Cup & Saucer, Geisha, Ford & Sons 90.00
Cup & Saucer, Grenada, Alcock 75.00
Cup & Saucer, Indian, Handleless 125.00
Cup & Saucer, Indian, Pratt 100.00

Cup & Saucer, Kenworth, Johnson Bros.	60.00
Cup & Saucer, Kyber, Handless	135.00
Cup & Saucer, Lancaster	75.00
Cup & Saucer, Landscape, Wedgwood, Demitasse	65.00
Cup & Saucer, Portman	65.00
Cup & Saucer, Rose, Grindley	75.00
Cup & Saucer, Simla, c.1860	85.00
Cup & Saucer, Spinach	78.00
Cup & Saucer, Touraine, Stanley	75.00 To 78.00
Cup Plate, Arabesque	95.00
Cup Plate, Carlton, Alcock	75.00
Cup Plate, Chapoo	95.00
Cup Plate, Excelsior, Fell	100.00
Cup Plate, Hong Kong	115.00
Cup Plate, Indian	100.00
Dinner Set, Holland, Meakin, Service For 10	3000.00
Dish, Honey, Athens, Meigh	65.00
Drainer, Chusan, Wedgwood, 12 1/4 In.	450.00
Eggcup, Dainty, Maddock	100.00
Gravy Boat, Albany	75.00
Gravy Boat, Athens, Meigh	200.00
Gravy Boat, Brazil, Underplate	125.00
Gravy Boat, Chatsworth	65.00
Gravy Boat, Colonial	65.00
Gravy Boat, Dundee, Ridgway	95.00
Gravy Boat, Ebor, Ridgway	95.00
Gravy Boat, Florida, Grindley	100.00
Gravy Boat, Halford, F & Sons	25.00
Gravy Boat, Hamilton, Underplate, Meakin	125.00
Gravy Boat, Holland	160.00
Gravy Boat, Hong Kong, Meigh, 1845	145.00
Gravy Boat, Iris, Grindley	85.00
Gravy Boat, Keswick	65.00
Gravy Boat, Olympia, Underplate, Grindley	85.00
Gravy Boat, Poppy, Grindley	90.00
Gravy Boat, Scinde, Alcock	475.00
Gravy Boat, Tivoli	145.00
Gravy Boat, Vermont, Underplate	125.00
Holder, Shaving Brush, Hawthorne, Dunn Bennett & Co.	75.00
Jardiniere, Dog Rose, Gold Outlined Rim, Ridgway, 12 x 12 1/2 In.	350.00
Mug, Blue Blossom, Ridgway	295.00
Mug, Wagon Wheel, Child's	135.00
Mug, Whampoa, 4 1/8 In.	295.00
Nurser, Infant, WT & C, 3 x 6 In., Pair	85.00
Pitcher & Bowl, Pansy, c.1890	750.00
Pitcher, Bowl, Soap Dish, Chamber Pot, Alhambra, Meakin, 4 Piece	975.00
Pitcher, Clarence, 6 In.	195.00
Pitcher, Gainsborough, Ridgway, 2 1/2 Qt.	225.00
Pitcher, Gironde, Grindley, 1 Qt.	175.00
Pitcher, Jesmond, 7 In.	150.00
Pitcher, La Belle, 2 Qt.	275.00
Pitcher, Madras, Doulton, 5 1/2 In.	195.00
Pitcher, Milk, La Pavot	260.00 To 265.00
Pitcher, Peking, F. & Sons, 6 1/2 In.	75.00
Pitcher, Water, Hong Kong	360.00
Pitcher, Water, Mandarin	395.00
Pitcher, Waverly, Maddock, 1 1/2 Qt.	300.00
Plate, Alaska, Grindley, 7 3/4 In.	35.00
Plate, Alaska, Grindley, 10 In.	60.00
Plate, Amoy, 9 1/2 In.	85.00 To 90.00
Plate, Amoy, 10 1/2 In.	70.00 To 100.00
Plate, Amoy, c.1850, 7 1/4 In.	55.00
Plate, Arabesque, Mayer, 10 In.	125.00

Plate, Avon, Booth, 9 1/4 In. 75.00
Plate, Belmont, Meakin, 7 1/2 In. 30.00
Plate, Bentick, Meakin, 6 1/2 In. 30.00
Plate, Bentick, Meakin, 10 In. 65.00
Plate, Catherine, 9 In. 50.00
Plate, Catherine, 10 In. 52.00
Plate, Chain of States 65.00
Plate, Chinese, Allerton, 9 In. 28.00
Plate, Chinese, Dimmock, 9 In. 85.00
Plate, Cincinnati, 10 In. 40.00
Plate, Claremont, Scalloped, 10 In. 50.00
Plate, Clover, Grindley, 5 3/4 In. 30.00
Plate, Clover, Grindley, 9 In. 45.00
Plate, Clytie, Grindley, 9 3/4 In. 70.00
Plate, Clytie, Wedgwood, 10 In. 69.50
Plate, Conway, 10 In. 75.00
Plate, Conway, New Wharf Pottery, 9 In. 45.00
Plate, Country Scene, Wood, 9 In. 40.00
Plate, Daisy, Societe Ceramique, 9 1/4 In. 100.00
Plate, Daytona, Florida, 10 In. 50.00
Plate, Dover, Grindley, 5 7/8 In. 25.00
Plate, Eagle, Shield, Arrows 125.00
Plate, Empress, 10 1/2 In. 90.00
Plate, Excelsior, Fell, 10 1/2 In. 115.00
Plate, Farm, Ford, 10 In. 58.00
Plate, Formosa, Mayer, 9 3/4 In. 115.00
Plate, Fortuna, Johnson Bros., c.1900, 10 In. 95.00
Plate, Gem, Hammersley, 9 3/4 In. 165.00
Plate, Grace, 9 3/4 In. 60.00
Plate, Grace, Grindley, 10 In. 68.00
Plate, Hong Kong, 10 1/4 In. 125.00
Plate, Indian, 10 1/4 In. 110.00
Plate, Janette, Grindley, 8 In. 60.00
Plate, Japan, T. Feil, c.1860, 9 In. 75.00
Plate, Kelvin, 9 In. 45.00
Plate, Kelvin, Meakin, 6 3/4 In. 36.50
Plate, Kelvin, Meakin, 8 In. 46.50
Plate, Kelvin, Meakin, 9 In. 56.50
Plate, Kenworth, Johnson Bros., 7 1/2 In. 39.50
Plate, Kenworth, Johnson Bros., 9 In. 49.50
Plate, La Belle, 9 In. 55.00
Plate, La Belle, 10 In. 75.00
Plate, La Hore, 9 1/2 In. 110.00
Plate, Larch, Hancock & Sons, 10 1/2 In. 79.50
Plate, Linda, John Maddock & Son 45.00
Plate, Madras, 8 3/4 In. 70.00
Plate, Marie, 9 In. 37.00
Plate, Marquis, Grindley, 10 In. 200.00
Plate, Martha Washington 65.00
Plate, Non Pareil, Burgess & Leigh, 8 3/4 In. 75.00
Plate, Oregon, Mayer, 9 1/2 In. 115.00
Plate, Oriental, Ridgway, 5 3/4 In. 28.00
Plate, Paris, New Wharf Pottery, 9 In. 49.50
Plate, Percy, Morley, 9 1/2 In. 90.00
Plate, Poppy, Grindley, 9 In. 35.00
Plate, Portman, Grindley, 8 In. 45.00
Plate, Raleigh, Burgess & Leigh, 9 3/4 In. 42.50
Plate, Richmond, Johnson Bros., 10 In. 55.00
Plate, Richmond, Meakin, 9 In. 50.00
Plate, Rose & Ivy, Brown–Westlead & Moore & Co., 10 1/2 In. 49.75
Plate, Scinde, 12 Sides, 7 In. 75.00
Plate, Scinde, T. Walker, 9 1/2 In. 65.00
Plate, Shanghai, 10 In. ....82.00 To 125.00

Plate, Shell, Challinor, 9 3/4 In. 90.00
Plate, Sylph, 10 In. 85.00
Plate, Sylph, Pountneys, 10 1/2 In., Pair 85.00
Plate, Temple, 1850, 9 1/4 In. 75.00
Plate, Temple, Podmore & Walker, 8 5/8 In. 90.00
Plate, Temple, Podmore & Walker, 9 3/4 In. 125.00
Plate, Togo, 9 3/4 In. 65.00
Plate, Tonquin, Heath, 10 1/2 In. 135.00
Plate, Touraine, 10 In. 75.00
Plate, Touraine, 7 3/4 In. 55.00
Plate, Touraine, 8 3/4 In. 65.00
Plate, Turin, Johnson Bros., 10 In. 45.00
Plate, Verona, Wood & Sons, 8 In. 35.00
Plate, Vine, Wedgwood, 8 In. 34.00
Plate, Waldorf, New Wharf Pottery, 10 In. 75.00
Plate, Washington St., Boston, 10 In. 50.00
Plate, Watteau, 9 In. 170.00
Plate, Watteau, 10 1/2 In. 75.00
Plate, Watteau, Doulton, 7 1/4 In. 75.00
Plate, Yedo, 9 1/4 In. 65.00
Platter, Alaska, Grindley, 16 In. 195.00
Platter, Amoy, 18 In. 325.00
Platter, Argyle, Grindley, 12 3/4 In. 165.00
Platter, Argyle, Grindley, 15 1/4 x 10 1/2 In. 150.00
Platter, Argyle, Grindley, 17 1/3 x 12 In. 175.00
Platter, Ashburton, Grindley, 10 x 15 In. 250.00
Platter, Beaufort, Grindley, 14 In. 150.00
Platter, Beaufort, Grindley, 25 In. 175.00
Platter, Buccleuch 550.00
Platter, Camellia, Wedgwood, 18 1/2 In. 475.00
Platter, Canton, Maddox Ironstone, 17 In. 585.00
Platter, Carlton, c.1850, 15 x 12 In. 225.00
Platter, Chapoo, Wedgwood, 13 1/2 x 10 1/2 In. 275.00
Platter, Chinese, Dimmock, 15 1/2 In. .... 285.00 To 295.00
Platter, Clover, Grindley, 14 1/4 In. 150.00
Platter, Clover, Grindley, 16 1/2 In. 160.00
Platter, Conway, 10 In. 70.00
Platter, Davenport, 10 x 14 In. 70.00
Platter, Delmar, 12 In. 50.00
Platter, Duchess, 14 In. 110.00
Platter, Florida, Grindley, 10 1/3 In. 125.00
Platter, Flower, Heath, 13 1/2 In. 350.00
Platter, Formosa, Mayer, 13 1/4 In. 295.00
Platter, Fox Hunt, Staffordshire, c.1830, 14 1/2 x 11 1/2 In. 305.00
Platter, Geneva, Doulton, 14 In. 225.00
Platter, Georgia, Johnson Bros., 10 1/2 x 14 In. 210.00
Platter, Grace, 21 In. .... 345.00 To 395.00
Platter, Hawthorne, Mercer Pottery Co., 19 1/4 In. 250.00
Platter, Holland, 12 1/2 In. 125.00
Platter, Holland, 16 In. .... 135.00 To 175.00
Platter, Holland, Johnson, 14 In. 145.00

◆◆

Having trouble with stain in a glass bottle or vase? Sometimes this type of stain can be removed. Fill the bottle with water, drop in an Alka–Seltzer and let it soak for about 24 hours. Then, rub the ring with a brush or a cloth. If the deposit is a chemical deposit, this treatment should remove it. If the ring is actually caused by etching of the glass, it can not be removed unless the bottle is polished.

◆◆

Platter, Horticultural, Wedgwood, 1880, 13 1/2 x 10 In. 95.00
Platter, Indian Jar, 22 In. 1150.00
Platter, Indian, Pratt, 13 1/4 x 10 1/4 In. 225.00
Platter, Iris, Art Nouveau, Oval, 12 In. 95.00
Platter, Iris, Grindley, 11 1/2 x 8 1/2 In. 65.00
Platter, Jewel, Johnson Bros., 14 1/2 x 10 1/2 In. 95.00
Platter, Kelvin, Meakin, 8 1/2 x 12 1/2 In. 150.00
Platter, Kenworth, Johnson Bros., 11 x 14 In. 172.50
Platter, Kew, 17 In. 70.00
Platter, La Belle, 11 1/2 x 8 In. 105.00
Platter, La Francais, 15 In. 100.00
Platter, La Hore, Phillips, 15 1/2 x 12 In. 450.00
Platter, Lancaster, New Wharf Pottery, c.1890, 9 1/4 x 12 1/2 In. 95.00
Platter, Marechal Niel, Grindley, 9 x 12 1/2 In. 90.00
Platter, Marie, 12 In. 95.00
Platter, Marie, 13 1/2 In. 195.00
Platter, Melbourne, Grindley, 12 x 18 In. 245.00
Platter, Melrose, Doulton, 12 x 18 In. 245.00
Platter, Oregon, Mayer, 10 1/2 In. 225.00
Platter, Paris, Edge Malkin & Co., 11 x 14 1/4 In. 130.00
Platter, Penang, Ridgway, 13 1/2 x 10 1/2 In. 375.00
Platter, Raleigh, Burgess & Leigh, 13 1/2 x 17 3/4 In. 195.00
Platter, Rock, 10 In. 125.00
Platter, Rose Festoon, Alcock, 16 1/2 In. 395.00
Platter, Scinde, 16 x 12 In. 425.00
Platter, Scinde, Walker, 17 3/4 In. 495.00
Platter, Shanghai, Grindley, 12 1/2 x 8 3/4 In. .... 75.00 To 95.00
Platter, Sobraon, 16 x 12 In. 425.00
Platter, St. Louis, 16 In. 140.00
Platter, Temple, 16 x 12 In. 425.00
Platter, Togo, Colonial Pottery, 12 In. 125.00
Platter, Touraine, 10 1/2 In. 100.00
Platter, Touraine, 12 1/2 In. 125.00
Platter, Trellis, Grindley, 12 1/2 In. 75.00
Platter, Wildrose 130.00
Potty, Yuan, Wood & Sons, 5 x 11 In. 95.00
Relish, Abbey, Jones & Sons, 5 1/2 x 10 1/2 In. 120.00
Relish, Bute, 3 Sections, Bond & Sons, 12 In. 190.00
Relish, Clover, Grindley, 7 1/2 In. 65.00
Relish, Colonial, Meakin .... 55.00 To 60.00
Relish, Devon 75.00
Sauce, Amerillia, Underplate, Podmore & Walker 735.00
Sauce, Argyle, Grindley 30.00
Sauce, Vermont, Burgess & Leigh, 5 In. 22.00
Saucer, Chapoo, Wedgwood 21.00
Saucer, Florida, Johnson Bros. 30.00
Saucer, Holland 25.00
Saucer, Jewel, Johnson Bros., 4 Piece 98.00
Saucer, Waldorf 24.00
Server, Warwick, Ruffled Gold Rim, 6 1/2 In. 60.00
Slop Jar, Cover, Marble Variant 900.00
Soap Dish, Triumph, Maddock, 3 Piece 80.00
Soup, Dish, Alaska, Flanged, 9 In. 55.00
Soup, Dish, Alaska, Grindley .... 45.00 To 49.00
Soup, Dish, Brazil 75.00
Soup, Dish, Circassia, 10 1/2 In. .... 45.00 To 125.00
Soup, Dish, Clarence, Grindley, 9 In. 55.00
Soup, Dish, Clover, Grindley, 7 3/4 In. 40.00
Soup, Dish, Florence, George Jones, 9 1/4 In. 95.00
Soup, Dish, Gironde, 7 1/2 In. 30.00
Soup, Dish, Indian, 10 1/2 In. 110.00
Soup, Dish, Marechal Niel, Grindley, 7 3/4 In. 60.00
Soup, Dish, Touraine, Stanley, 7 1/2 In. 145.00

Soup, Dish, Touraine, Stanley, 8 3/4 In. 65.00
Sugar & Creamer, Chinese, Wedgwood, Child's 250.00
Sugar & Creamer, Cover, Glentine 150.00
Sugar & Creamer, Ferrar, Wedgwood 225.00
Sugar & Creamer, Franklin's Tomb, E. & G. Phillips, c.1822 .... 550.00
Sugar & Creamer, Gravy Boat, Plate, Mongolia, Johnson, 3 Piece 375.00
Sugar & Creamer, La Belle 350.00
Sugar, Cover, Chapoo, 1860, 9 1/4 In. 225.00
Sugar, Cover, Chen–Si 295.00
Sugar, Cover, Olympia, Grindley 90.00
Syrup, La Belle, Sprint Lid 195.00
Syrup, Pewter Cover, La Belle, Floral, Grindley 350.00
Table Setting, Corey Hill, Rust, E. Walley, 1845, 5 Piece 180.00
Teapot, Amoy .... 265.00 To 350.00
Teapot, Chapoo 595.00
Teapot, Chapoo, Wedgwood, 9 1/2 In. 325.00
Teapot, Manilla 625.00
Teapot, Orchid, Maddock 325.00
Teapot, Oregon 595.00
Teapot, Troy 695.00
Toothbrush Holder, Bluebell, Cover 350.00
Toothbrush Holder, Doreen, c.1891 .... 120.00
Toothbrush Holder, Oban 60.00
Tray, Lonsdale, Samuel Ford & Co., c.1898, 10 x 8 In. 85.00
Trivet, Floral, Warwick, 6 1/2 In. 125.00
Tureen, Amerillia, Underplate, 7 In. 650.00
Tureen, Celtic, Grindley, Cover 225.00
Tureen, Clarissa, Johnson Bros., Cover 175.00
Tureen, Eastern Vines, Meigh, Cover, Underplate, 7 In. 395.00
Tureen, Ellesmere, Furnivals, 9 In. 265.00
Tureen, Geranium, Ridgway, Cover 1000.00
Tureen, Grace, Cover 225.00
Tureen, Hague, Johnson Bros., Cover, Underplate, 8 1/4 x 6 1/2 In. 245.00
Tureen, Linden, Bluebirds, Cover 275.00
Tureen, Lonsdale, Ridgway 350.00
Tureen, Mandarin, Maddock, Cover 450.00
Tureen, Melsary, Booth, Cover, Underplate 150.00
Tureen, Morning Glory, Wood & Hughes, Gold Trim, 9 In. 295.00
Tureen, Nonpareil, Rectangular, Burgess & Leigh, Cover 475.00
Tureen, Oriental, Ridgway, Cover 350.00
Tureen, Osborne, Ridgway, 9 In. .... 375.00 To 400.00
Tureen, Scinde, 7 In. 675.00
Tureen, Scinde, Ladle, Underplate, Alcock, 7 In. 1195.00
Tureen, Tillenberg, Clementson, Cover, Underplate 1000.00
Tureen, Tivoli 1950.00
Vase, Venetia, Hexagonal, Blue, Barker Bros., 8 1/2 In. 235.00
Wash Set, Fashoda, 5 Piece 695.00
Waste Bowl, Argyle 110.00
Waste Bowl, La Belle, 6 In. 50.00
Waste Bowl, Tonquin 325.00
Waste Bowl, Waldorf 150.00

FLYING PHOENIX, see Phoenix Bird

Folk art is listed in many sections of the book under the actual name of the object. See categories such as Box; Cigar Store Figure; Weather Vane; Wooden; etc.

FOLK ART, Acrobats, On Ladder, Wooden, 52 In. 225.00
Airplane, Wooden, 4–Ft. Wingspan, Moving Wheels & Propeller 125.00
Ashtray Holder, Bellhop, Wooden, Blue & Gold Uniform, 23 In. 85.00
Band, Piano Player, 20 Black Figures, Wooden, 16 x 23 In. 975.00
Birdhouse, Church Form, Original Paint 375.00
Birdhouse, Log Cabin 140.00
Birdhouse, Victorian, Wooden, 19th Century ....*Illus* 625.00

Folk Art, Birdhouse, Victorian, Wooden, 19th Century
Folk Art, Santo, Madonna & Child, Angels, Demon, 27 1/2 In.
Folk Art, Santo, Saint, Standing, Pierced Nimbus, 39 1/2 In.
Folk Art, Whirligig, Man Sawing Wood, On Sawhorse, 23 In.

Birdhouse, Weathered Poplar, Yellow–Green, 26 In.	250.00
Birdhouse, White Clapboard, Gabled Roof, Weathered, 24 In.	200.00
Birdhouse, Wren, Curved Base, 10 x 6 In.	20.00
Black Man Carrying Fish, Signed, Cherry, Carving	225.00
Bowl, Little Black Sambo, Umbrella, Mother, Pancakes, Wood, 12 In.	150.00
Box, Carved & Painted, Glazed Window, Locking Door, 11 1/2 In.	245.00
Box, Display, Hanging, Carved Stars, Center Beads, 17 1/2 In.	110.00
Carousel, Horse & Swan Boats, Riders, Tin Flag, 51 x 33 In.	450.00
Carousel, Ride, Tin Buckets, 4 Figures, Tin Flag, 56 In.	325.00
Chariot, Horse, 2 Tribal Figures, 4 Walking Figures, 21 In.	475.00
Church, Polychrome, Wood, 6 In.	468.00
Cigar Store Figure, Indian, Wood, Outstretched Hand, 26 In.	775.00
Circus Ring, 13 Figures, 5 Horses, 4 Riders, Wooden, 43 In.	525.00
Clown, Circus, Carved Wood, Polychrome, 20th Century, 73 In.	550.00
Coat Hanger, Carved Cow Horns, Shield Shape, 35 x 12 x 8 In.	125.00
Deer, Salmon Color, Wood Body, Green Base, Rollers, 42 x 59 In.	7700.00
Ferris Wheel, Wooden, 36 In.	475.00
Figure, Bird, Long Neck, On Ball Atop Plinth, Wooden, 16 1/2 In.	525.00
Figure, Cardinal, 6 3/8 In.	100.00
Figure, Cat, Sitting, Full–Bodied, Lumber Camp, 1910, 16 In.	850.00
Figure, Convict, Unhappy, Carnival Game, Hand Carved, 12 In.	325.00
Figure, Dancing Man, Smooth Wood, Painted, 10 1/4 In.	275.00
Figure, Fat Man, 10 In.	45.00
Figure, Horse, Polychrome Paint, Wooden, 10 3/4 In.	65.00
Figure, Medusa Head, From Circus Wagon, Polychrome Paint, 19 In.	550.00
Figure, Mermaid, Added Base, Made From 1 Piece Of Wood, 15 1/2 In.	925.00
Figure, Parrot, On Perch, Polychrome Paint, 3 5/8 In.	225.00
Figure, Policeman, Tip–Up, Tin, 1920s, Blue, Gold, 7 x 9 In.	40.00
Figure, Townspeople, Carved, Polychrome, 6 In., 24 Piece	525.00
Finch, Carved Wooden, Gold, Mounted On Hemlock Bark, 7 In.	250.00
Frame, Weathered Wood, Gate Door Effect, Silver, 13 x 9 In.	90.00
Grapes, Bunch, Stone, Wooden Stem, Off–White, 10 x 4 x 4 In.	40.00
Grasshopper, Iron Legs, Wooden, 20th Century, 23 In.	425.00
Head, Popeye Reed, Sandstone, Hole For Hanging, E. Reed, 3 3/8 In.	150.00
Horse's Head, Circus, Wooden, Carved, Painted, 20th Century, 25 In.	195.00
Indian's Head, Sandstone, E. Reed, 9 1/2 In.	275.00
Indian, Bow, Arrow & Bear, Silhouette, Sheet Metal, 62 x 60 In.	325.00
Indian, With Bow, Cutout, Relief Carving, Weathered Paint, 45 In.	350.00
Lamp, Made From Popsicle Sticks, 24 In.	75.00 To 95.00
Lamp, Wooden Stirrup, Cow Brands Sides, 1940s, Paper Shade, 9 In.	40.00
Man, Humorous, High Boots, Playing Guitar, Dog, Carving, 8 In.	135.00
Mandolin, Pine, Cherry, Stars & Moon, Pierced, Tom Phillips, c.1910	475.00
Mat, Cornhusk, Hand Braided, 12 In.	35.00
Numerals, Wooden, Hand Carved, Used To Mark Sheep, 5 1/2 In.	35.00
Nut Shell, Tropical, Relief Carved, Compote of Flowers, 4 5/8 In.	25.00
Rooster, Polychrome Paint, 15 1/4 In.	105.00
Santo, Madonna & Child, Angels, Demon, 27 1/2 In. ....*Illus*	600.00

Santo, Saint, Standing, Pierced Nimbus, 39 1/2 In. ....*Illus*   1100.00
Santo, St. Mary, Crown, Polychrome, Wooden, Added Base, 9 1/2 In. 85.00
Santo, St. Mary, Tin Halo, Wooden, Polychrome, 16 1/2 In. 285.00
Santo, St. Rochus, Wooden, Polychrome, Small Figure, Dog, 15 In. 225.00
Stagecoach, Burnt Wood, 1904, 20 In. 175.00
Totem Pole, Animal, Bird, Polychrome Paint, 1930s, 27 In. 200.00
Towel Bar, Figures of Horses, Woman's Head, 1920s 30.00
Turtle, Horn Tail, Glass Eyes, Green, Wooden, 21 In. 195.00
Wagon, Circus, Animals, Drivers, 2–Horse Teams, Wooden 4000.00
Whirligig, 2 Men On Seesaw, Wood, Sheet Metal, Painted, 22 In. 25.00
Whirligig, 3 Figures Sawing Wood, Doing Laundry, Chopping, 9 In. 193.00
Whirligig, Abraham Lincoln 1100.00
Whirligig, Airplane 45.00
Whirligig, American Officer, Saber Paddles, American, 19th Century 9350.00
Whirligig, Bearded Farmer, Hat, Sawing Log, 16 x 15 x 12 In. 125.00
Whirligig, Bicycle, Polychrome Wood, Cyclist Pedals, 20 In. 880.00
Whirligig, Clown, 19 1/4 x 49 In. 450.00
Whirligig, Comic Black Man & Chinaman, 2 Propellers, 20 x 25 In. 525.00
Whirligig, Girl Churning Butter, Wood, Sheet Metal, 16 1/2 In. 35.00
Whirligig, Hessian Soldier, Polychrome Iron, 35 In. 495.00
Whirligig, Horse Race, Stenciled Wood, Propellers Turn, 2 Horses 330.00
Whirligig, Indian & Tepee, Wood, Tin, Painted, 11 In. 25.00
Whirligig, Mammy, Child, Man, Wood, Sheet Metal, Painted, 35 In. 45.00
Whirligig, Man Climbing Ladder, Wood, Tin, Polychrome, 60 In. 50.00
Whirligig, Man Sawing Wood, On Sawhorse, 23 In. ....*Illus*   55.00
Whirligig, Man Sawing Wood, Wood, Sheet Metal, Painted, 18 In. 45.00
Whirligig, Painted Wood, Farmer Milking Cow, 20 In. 275.00
Whirligig, Policeman, Black & White Paint, 12 3/4 In. 1200.00
Whirligig, Sailboat 685.00
Whirligig, Surfer, On Surfboard, Painted, 1930s, 26 x 24 1/2 In. 1980.00
Whirligig, Uncle Sam, 19 In. 75.00
Whirligig, Witch, Stenciled Wood, Flying Witch, Broom Turns, 13 In. 249.00
Whirligig, Woman Churns As It Turns 65.00
Whirligig, Woman, With Washboard, Polychrome Repaint, 28 In. 325.00
Whirlygig, Ferry Boat, Litho, Painted Tin, Sidewheeler, 8 1/2 In. 450.00
Whirlygig, Row Boat, Tin Litho, Painted Sailor, Germany, 6 In. 605.00

Cold feet have been a problem for generations. Our ancestors had many ingenious ways to warm feet with portable foot warmers. Some warmers held charcoal, others held hot water. Pottery, tin, and soapstone were the favored materials to conduct the heat. The warmer was kept under the feet, then the legs and feet were tucked into a blanket, providing welcome warmth in a cold carriage or church.

FOOT WARMER, Cast Iron Top Plate, Heart & Quatrefoil Cutout, 11 x 13 In. 225.00
  Diamond & Circle Designs, Cherry Frame, 8 3/4 In. 150.00
  Henderson's, Stoneware 165.00
  Pierced Diamond Design, Tin & Birchwood, 8 x 9 In. 190.00
  Pierced Tin Hearts, Cooling Pan, Cherry Case, 5 3/4 x 9 In. 285.00
  Punched Circle & Heart Design, Tin & Wood, 9 1/4 x 7 3/4 In. 200.00
  Scratch Dated 1846 ....   225.00
     FOOTBALL, see Card, Football; Sports

Fostoria glass was made in Fostoria, Ohio, from 1887 to 1891. The factory was moved to Moundsville, West Virginia, and most of the glass seen in shops today is a twentieth–century product. The company was sold in 1983; new items will be easily identifiable, according to the new owners, Lancaster Colony Corporation.

     FOSTORIA, see also Milk Glass
FOSTORIA, Alexis, Wine 10.00
  American Lady, Goblet 30.00
  American Lady, Goblet, Amethyst 27.50
  American Lady, Iced Tea 18.00

American Lady, Sherbet, Amethyst	20.00
American, Banana Boat, 9 In.	145.00
American, Boat, 8 1/2 In.	12.00
American, Bottle, Bitters	45.00
American, Bottle, Condiment, Stopper	105.00
American, Bowl, Flower Frog, Cupper, 7 In.	50.00
American, Butter, Cover, Round	85.00 To 100.00
American, Cake Plate, Round, 10 In.	75.00
American, Cake Stand, Square, 7 x 10 In.	75.00
American, Candy Dish, Cover, 3 Sections	65.00
American, Candy Dish, Cover, Footed	40.00
American, Cheese & Cracker Set	45.00 To 55.00
American, Compote, Cover, 9 In.	30.00
American, Cruet	18.50
American, Cup & Saucer	10.00 To 12.00
American, Decanter, Whiskey	80.00
American, Goblet, 8 Piece	120.00
American, Goblet, Low	9.00
American, Ice Bucket, Liner	42.00
American, Ice Tub, 5 5/8 In.	35.00
American, Ice Tub, 6 1/2 In.	45.00
American, Mayonnaise Set, 3 Piece	30.00 To 45.00
American, Pitcher, Glass Cover, 1/2 Gal.	500.00
American, Pitcher, Ice Lip, 8 1/2 In.	60.00 To 85.00
American, Pitcher, Lemonade	250.00
American, Plate, 8 1/2 In.	8.00 To 10.00
American, Plate, 9 In.	18.00 To 22.00
American, Plate, Torte, 18 In.	95.00
American, Platter, Oval, 12 In.	140.00
American, Powder Box, Metal Top, 3 x 8 In.	70.00
American, Punch Bowl, Footed	125.00
American, Relish, 2 Sections, Oval	30.00
American, Rose Bowl, 5 In.	22.00
American, Salt & Pepper, Tray, Small	20.00 To 35.00
American, Sandwich Server, 12 In.	25.00
American, Sherbet, Flared	10.00
American, Straw Jar, Cover	250.00
American, Sugar & Creamer	15.00
American, Sugar & Creamer, Green	125.00
American, Sugar Shaker, Pontil Mark	30.00
American, Toothpick	27.00
American, Tumbler, 3 3/8 In.	12.00
American, Vase, Flared, 10 In., Pair	159.00
American, Vase, Flared, 9 1/2 In.	60.00 To 78.00
American, Wine, Hexagonal Foot, 2 1/2 Oz.	8.00
Baroque, Bonbon, 3-Footed, Blue	95.00
Baroque, Bowl, Handle, 10 1/2 In.	12.99 To 22.00
Baroque, Candlestick, Topaz, 5 In., Pair	30.00
Baroque, Compote, Topaz, 4 3/4 In.	22.50
Baroque, Cruet, Stopper	60.00
Baroque, Cruet, Stopper, Topaz	295.00
Baroque, Cup & Saucer	12.00
Baroque, Cup & Saucer, Blue	25.00
Baroque, Ice Bucket	22.00
Baroque, Plate, 7 In.	6.00
Baroque, Plate, Blue, 9 1/2 In.	49.50
Baroque, Plate, Topaz, 7 In.	9.50
Baroque, Plate, Topaz, 9 1/2 In.	42.50
Baroque, Plate, Torte, Blue, 14 In.	65.00
Baroque, Punch Cup, Blue	25.00
Baroque, Salt & Pepper, Blue	100.00
Baroque, Sherbet, Blue	18.00
Baroque, Sweetmeat, Cover, Blue	395.00

◆◆

Be careful where you put a fresh pumpkin or gourd. Put a plastic liner underneath them. A rotting pumpkin will permanently stain wood or marble.

◆◆

Beverly, Bouillon, Amber	12.50
Beverly, Bouillon, Saucer, Green	16.00
Beverly, Creamer, Amber, Footed	20.00
Beverly, Goblet	24.00
Beverly, Mayonnaise, Square	20.00
Beverly, Soup, Cream, Amber	12.50
Buttercup, Bowl, Handle, 10 In.	30.00
Buttercup, Console, Oval, 11 In.	47.50
Buttercup, Cup & Saucer	18.00 To 25.00
Buttercup, Goblet	25.00
Buttercup, Plate, 9 1/2 In.	35.00
Buttercup, Tumbler, Iced Tea	24.00
Century, Bonbon, 3–Footed, 7 1/4 In.	10.00 To 22.50
Century, Candlestick, 4 1/2 In., Pair	50.00
Century, Cruet, Stopper	45.00
Century, Cup & Saucer	6.00 To 12.50
Century, Pitcher, Ice Lip, 7 1/8 In.	80.00
Century, Plate, 7 1/2 In.	12.00
Century, Plate, 9 1/2 In.	14.00
Century, Plate, Snack, 8 1/2 In.	30.00
Century, Platter, Oval, 12 In.	15.00
Century, Sugar & Creamer	17.50
Century, Sugar & Creamer, Footed, 4 In.	18.00
Chintz, Bonbon, 3–Footed	35.00
Chintz, Candy Dish, Cover, 3 Sections	95.00
Chintz, Cocktail, Stem, 4 Oz.	24.50
Chintz, Goblet, 9 Oz.	20.00
Chintz, Plate, 7 1/2 In.	12.00
Chintz, Plate, 9 1/2 In.	45.00
Chintz, Relish, 3 Sections, 7 x 12 In.	30.00
Chintz, Sugar & Creamer, 3 3/4 In.	20.00 To 25.00
Chintz, Sugar & Creamer, Tray, Individual	75.00
Christiana, Goblet, 6 3/8 In.	10.00
Christiana, Sherbet, 4 3/8 In.	10.00
Coin, Ashtray, 4 Coins, Olive Green	17.50
Coin, Ashtray, Red	27.50
Coin, Bowl, Oval, Olive Green, 9 In.	30.00
Coin, Bowl, Oval, Red, 9 In.	25.00
Coin, Cake Stand, Footed, Amber	85.00
Coin, Candlestick, Olive Green, 4 In., Pair	125.00
Coin, Candy Dish, Cover, Amber, 6 In.	30.00
Coin, Candy Dish, Cover, Olive Green	45.00
Coin, Candy Dish, Cover, Red	48.00 To 85.00
Coin, Candy Jar, Cover, Amber, 6 In.	27.50
Coin, Goblet, Olive Green	55.00
Coin, Lamp, Courting, Amber	90.00
Coin, Sugar & Creamer, Cover, Amber	30.00
Coin, Sugar, Cover, Olive Green	60.00
Coin, Urn, Cover, Olive Green	95.00
Coin, Urn, Cover, Red, Tall	125.00
Colonial Dame, Cordial, Green, 3 1/4 In.	25.00
Colonial Dame, Goblet, Green, 10 Oz.	15.00
Colonial Dame, Tumbler, Iced Tea, Green, 12 Oz.	16.00
Colonial Dame, Wine, Green, 4 5/8 In.	15.00

Colonial Mirror, Cordial, 1 Oz. .... 12.00 To 14.00
Colonial Mirror, Oyster Cocktail 8.00
Colony, Candleholder, 8 Prisms, 7 1/2 In. 40.00
Colony, Candlestick, 10 Prisms, Blue, Crystal Tops, 14 1/2 In., Pair 245.00
Colony, Candy Dish, Cover, Footed .... 35.00 To 50.00
Colony, Celery Vase, Flared, 7 1/2 In. 35.00
Colony, Cocktail, 4 In. 12.00
Colony, Console Set, Amber, 9–In. Candlesticks, 3 Piece 350.00
Colony, Creamer, 3 In. 5.00
Colony, Cup & Saucer 8.00
Colony, Oyster Cocktail, 3 3/8 In. 15.00
Colony, Plate, 6 In. 6.00
Colony, Plate, 7 In. 9.50
Colony, Plate, 8 In. 5.00
Colony, Plate, 9 1/2 In. 18.00
Colony, Plate, Cupped, 12 In. 30.00
Colony, Punch Cup 20.00
Colony, Relish, 2 Sections 14.00
Colony, Salt & Pepper, Individual, 2 5/8 In. 12.00
Colony, Sugar & Creamer, Tray, Individual .... 18.00 To 27.50
Colony, Vase, Cornucopia 110.00
Colony, Vase, Flared, 7 1/2 In. .... 35.00 To 37.50
Contour, Butter, 1/4 Lb. 25.00
Contour, Candlestick, 6 In., Pair 30.00
Contour, Goblet 22.50
Contour, Mayonnaise, Ladle 25.00
Contour, Relish, 2 Sections 20.00
Contour, Sugar & Creamer, Tray, Individual 25.00
Contour, Tumbler, Iced Tea 24.00
Coronet, Bonbon, 3–Footed 17.50
Coronet, Cruet, Oil, 5 Oz. 20.00
Coronet, Mayonnaise, 2 Sections 22.50
Coronet, Plate, 9 In. 18.00
Coronet, Relish, 4 Sections 22.50
Coronet, Sugar & Creamer, Tray, Individual 20.00
Cynthia, Cordial, 3/4 Oz. 20.00
Diadem, Candy Dish, Cover, 1/2 Lb. 22.00
Dolly Madison, Champagne, 6 Oz. 16.00
Dolly Madison, Cocktail, 3 3/4 Oz. 15.00
Dolly Madison, Goblet, 9 Oz. .... 16.00 To 17.50
Dolly Madison, Tumbler, Iced Tea, 12 Oz. 17.50
Fairfax, Ashtray, Amber, 2 1/2 In. 15.00
Fairfax, Bonbon, Blue 22.50
Fairfax, Bouillon, Amber, Footed 12.50
Fairfax, Bowl, Amber, 5 In. 9.50
Fairfax, Butter, Cover, Green 85.00
Fairfax, Candy Dish, Cover, Amber 45.00
Fairfax, Candy Dish, Cover, Green 65.00
Fairfax, Celery, Amber, 11 1/2 In. 15.00
Fairfax, Cocktail, Amber 19.50
Fairfax, Cup & Saucer, Flat, Amber 12.50
Fairfax, Cup & Saucer, Flat, Green 12.50
Fairfax, Cup & Saucer, Green, After Dinner 15.00
Fairfax, Cup & Saucer, Orchid, After Dinner 22.00
Fairfax, Cup & Saucer, Pink 8.50
Fairfax, Cup & Saucer, Topaz, After Dinner 22.00
Fairfax, Dish, Pickle, Amber, 8 3/4 In. 12.50
Fairfax, Goblet, 10 Oz. 16.00
Fairfax, Goblet, Amber, 10 Oz. 17.50
Fairfax, Grill Plate, Green, 10 1/4 In. .... 25.00 To 37.50
Fairfax, Grill Plate, Orchid, 10 1/4 In. 35.00
Fairfax, Grill Plate, Rose, 10 1/4 In. 35.00
Fairfax, Oyster Cocktail, Amber 16.00

Fairfax, Pitcher, Topaz 100.00
Fairfax, Pitcher, Water, Amber 125.00
Fairfax, Pitcher, Water, Blue 150.00
Fairfax, Plate, Amber, 6 In. 4.00
Fairfax, Plate, Amber, 7 1/2 In. 5.00
Fairfax, Plate, Blue, 8 3/4 In. 12.00
Fairfax, Plate, Topaz, 7 1/2 In. 5.00
Fairfax, Sugar & Creamer, Orchid 20.00
Fairfax, Sugar, Cover, Rose 35.00
Fairfax, Tumbler, Iced Tea, Blue 24.00
Fairfax, Whiskey, Amber 15.00
Figurine, Horse, 4 In. 45.00
Figurine, Mermaid 60.00
Figurine, Polar Bear, Frosted 40.00
Georgian, Sherbet, 6 Oz. 10.00
Georgian, Tumbler, Juice, 4 Oz. 10.00
Heirloom, Bowl, 12 In. 40.00
Heirloom, Candlestick, Blue Opalescent, 9 In. 30.00
Heirloom, Plate, Torte, 13 In. 40.00
Heirloom, Tumbler, Iced Tea 20.00
Hermitage, Tumbler, Wisteria, Footed, 8 Oz. 15.00
Holly, Cordial, 3 7/8 In. 17.50
Holly, Mayonnaise, 3 Piece 45.00
Jamestown, Butter, Blue, 1/4 Lb. 65.00
Jamestown, Goblet, Amber, 5 3/4 In. .... 9.50 To 15.00
Jamestown, Goblet, Green, 5 3/4 In. 35.00
Jamestown, Pitcher, Water, Blue, 3 Pt. 145.00
Jamestown, Plate, Amber, 8 In. 19.00
Jamestown, Plate, Blue, 8 In. 20.00
Jamestown, Plate, Green, 8 In. 14.00
Jamestown, Sherbet, Amber .... 7.00 To 15.00
Jamestown, Sugar & Creamer, Green 35.00
Jamestown, Tumbler, Iced Tea, Amber, Footed, 6 In. 17.00
Jamestown, Tumbler, Iced Tea, Blue, Footed, 6 In. 20.00
Jamestown, Wine, Amber, 4 5/16 In. 20.00
Jenny Lind, Pitcher, Milk, Blue, 8 1/4 In. 118.00
June, Bouillon Cup, Saucer, Rose 60.00
June, Bowl, Whipped Cream 18.00
June, Candlestick, 3 In. 18.00
June, Cheese Dish 25.00
June, Cocktail, 5 1/4 In. 27.00
June, Cocktail, Topaz, 5 1/4 In. 40.00
June, Cup & Saucer 22.00
June, Cup & Saucer, Blue 47.50
June, Cup & Saucer, Rose 42.50
June, Cup & Saucer, Topaz 28.00
June, Cup, Rose, After Dinner 75.00
June, Dish, 3–Footed, Topaz 24.00
June, Goblet, 8 1/4 In. 25.50
June, Ice Bucket, Blue 98.00
June, Ice Bucket, Topaz 56.00
June, Parfait, Topaz, 5 1/4 In. 48.00
June, Pitcher, Water 285.00
June, Pitcher, Water, Rose 495.00
June, Plate, Blue, 7 In. 15.00
June, Plate, Blue, 9 In. 45.00
June, Plate, Liner, 6 In. 5.00
June, Plate, Rose, 6 In. 12.00
June, Plate, Topaz, 6 In. 5.00
June, Plate, Topaz, 7 In. .... 8.00 To 8.50
June, Platter, 12 In. 35.00
June, Platter, Blue, Oval, 12 In. 145.00
June, Salt & Pepper, Blue, Footed 200.00

June, Salt & Pepper, Footed 33.00
June, Sherbet, Blue 29.00
June, Sugar & Creamer, Individual 95.00
June, Sugar & Creamer, Topaz, Individual 47.50
June, Sugar, Cover, Rose 275.00
June, Sugar, Topaz 23.00
June, Sweetmeat, Loop Handle, Blue 42.50
June, Tumbler, Iced Tea, Rose, 6 In. 55.00
June, Whiskey, 2 1/2 In. 35.00
Lafayette, Champagne, Wisteria 27.50
Lafayette, Cup & Saucer, Wisteria 20.00
Lafayette, Goblet, Wisteria 47.50
Lafayette, Plate, Wisteria, 6 In. 12.50
Lafayette, Plate, Wisteria, 7 1/2 In. 17.50
Laurel, Goblet, 9 Oz. 17.50
Laurel, Sherbet, 6 Oz. 15.00
Laurel, Wine, 3 1/2 Oz. 15.00
Lido, Cocktail, Blue, 3 1/2 Oz. 25.00
Lido, Compote, 4 3/4 In. 22.50
Lido, Cruet, Stopper, Blue 450.00
Lido, Goblet, 9 Oz. 17.50
Lido, Mayonnaise, 2 Sections, 6 1/2 In. 15.00
Mayflower, Cup & Saucer 12.00
Meadow Rose, Cake Plate, Handle, 10 In. .... 28.00 To 45.00
Meadow Rose, Cake Plate, Handle, Blue, 10 In. 75.00
Meadow Rose, Candlestick, 2–Light, Pair 50.00
Meadow Rose, Champagne, 5 5/8 In. 12.00
Meadow Rose, Cup & Saucer, Footed 25.00
Meadow Rose, Mayonnaise Set, Ladle, 3 Piece 45.00
Meadow Rose, Nappy, Handle, 5 In. 18.00
Meadow Rose, Pitcher, 9 3/4 In. 350.00
Meadow Rose, Plate, 9 1/2 In. 40.00
Meadow Rose, Plate, Torte, 14 In. 45.00
Meadow Rose, Relish, 2 Sections 29.50
Meadow Rose, Sauce, Underplate 125.00
Meadow Rose, Sugar & Creamer 25.00
Meadow Rose, Sugar, Individual 17.50
Meadow Rose, Tumbler, Iced Tea, Blue, 5 7/8 In. 40.00
Midnight Rose, Cordial, 1 Oz. 45.00
Midnight Rose, Goblet, 9 Oz. 24.00
Midnight Rose, Relish, 2 Sections, Handle 25.00
Midnight Rose, Tumbler, Iced Tea, 12 Oz. 24.00
Millefleur, Whiskey, 2 Oz. 20.00
Navarre, Champagne, Blue, 6 Oz. 24.00
Navarre, Champagne, Pink, 6 Oz. 17.00
Navarre, Creamer, Individual 15.00
Navarre, Goblet, Pink, 10 Oz. 35.00
Navarre, Plate, 7 In. 14.00
Navarre, Relish, 3 Sections, 10 1/2 In. 45.00
Navarre, Sherbet 17.00
Navarre, Sugar & Creamer 35.00
Navarre, Vase, 5 In. 75.00
Oakleaf, Cake Plate, Green, Footed 125.00
Oakleaf, Candlestick, 2 In., Pair 40.00
Oakleaf, Candlestick, Black, 3 In., Pair 65.00
Oakleaf, Candy Dish, Cover, Rose 175.00
Pine, Bonbon, 6 7/8 In. 30.00
Pine, Butter, Cover, 1/4 Lb. 45.00
Pine, Relish, 2 Sections, 7 3/8 In. 35.00
Rogene, Tumbler, Footed .... 14.00 To 17.00
Romance, Cocktail, 3 1/2 Oz. .... 18.00 To 19.50
Romance, Cup & Saucer 25.00
Romance, Oyster Cocktail 25.00

Romance, Plate, 9 In. 40.00
Romance, Sherbet, Low, 6 Oz. 16.00
Romance, Tumbler, Juice, 5 Oz. 19.50
Rose, Sugar & Creamer, Tray 35.00
Royal, Ashtray, Green, 4 In. 45.00
Royal, Bouillon, Flat, Green 16.00
Royal, Bowl, Green, 6 In. 18.50
Royal, Candlestick, Amber, 9 In. 100.00
Royal, Candy Dish, Cover, Amber 125.00
Royal, Candy Dish, Cover, Green 95.00
Royal, Finger Bowl, Amber 20.00
Royal, Goblet, Green 25.00
Royal, Plate, Amber, 8 In. 7.50
Royal, Plate, Green, 6 In. 4.50
Royal, Plate, Green, 7 In. 4.50
Royal, Platter, Amber, 10 1/2 In. 27.50
Royal, Soup, Cream, Amber 14.50
Royal, Soup, Dish, Amber, 8 In. 22.50
Royal, Soup, Dish, Green, 8 In. 8.50
Royal, Whiskey, Green, 2 1/2 Oz. 37.50
Seascape, Sugar & Creamer, Pink .... 45.00 To 65.00
Seville, Champagne, Amber 18.00
Seville, Claret, Amber 25.00
Seville, Cordial, Amber 60.00
Seville, Oyster Cocktail, Amber 18.00
Seville, Underplate, Amber, 6 In. 3.00
Shirley, Champagne, Saucer, 6 Oz. 18.50
Shirley, Cordial, 3/4 Oz. 40.00
Shirley, Mayonnaise, 3 Piece 135.00
Shirley, Plate, 7 In. 7.00
Shirley, Soup, Cream 24.00
Shirley, Vase, Flame, 10 In. 75.00
Trojan, Bonbon, Yellow 29.50
Trojan, Cup & Saucer, Topaz .... 15.00 To 20.00
Trojan, Goblet, Topaz, 10 Oz. 20.00
Trojan, Plate, Topaz, 6 In. 6.00
Trojan, Plate, Topaz, 8 In. 9.50
Trojan, Salt & Pepper, Topaz 45.00
Trojan, Tumbler, Iced Tea, Topaz, 12 Oz. 22.00
Vernon, Ashtray, Green, 4 In. 45.00
Vernon, Bowl, Vegetable, Green, Oval, 9 In. 60.00
Vernon, Candy Dish, Cover, Blue 195.00
Vernon, Creamer, Green, Footed 25.00
Vernon, Finger Bowl, Underplate, Blue 35.00
Vernon, Saltshaker, Green 60.00
Vernon, Sherbet, Blue, Low, 6 Oz. 25.00
Vernon, Sherbet, Green 15.00
Vernon, Tumbler, Blue, 5 1/4 In. 27.50
Versailles, Bonbon, Blue 42.50
Versailles, Bouillon, Topaz 22.00
Versailles, Bouillon, Underplate, Blue 47.50
Versailles, Bouillon, Underplate, Rose 29.50
Versailles, Bowl, Green, 9 In. 65.00
Versailles, Candlestick, Scroll, Blue, 5 In. 35.00
Versailles, Chop Plate, Blue, 13 In. 125.00
Versailles, Cocktail, Rose, 3 Oz. 35.00
Versailles, Compote, Rose, 7 In. 47.50
Versailles, Compote, Topaz, 5 In. 35.00
Versailles, Console, Green, 12 In. 45.00
Versailles, Creamer, Green, Large 35.00
Versailles, Creamer, Rose, Individual 47.50
Versailles, Cup & Saucer, Topaz, After Dinner 49.50
Versailles, Finger Bowl, Underplate, Green 38.00

Versailles, Goblet, Blue, 8 1/4 In.	40.00
Versailles, Ice Bucket	65.00
Versailles, Ice Bucket, Rose	125.00
Versailles, Mayonnaise, Blue, 3 Piece	150.00
Versailles, Plate, Blue, 10 In.	75.00
Versailles, Plate, Green, 10 In.	49.50
Versailles, Platter, Blue, 12 In.	125.00
Versailles, Saltshaker, Green	60.00
Versailles, Sugar & Creamer, Blue, Individual	175.00
Versailles, Sugar Pail, Green	150.00
Versailles, Sugar, Cover, Rose	135.00
Versailles, Sugar, Rose, Individual	22.00
Versailles, Sugar, Topaz, Individual	47.50
Vesper, Candlestick, 2 In., Pair	37.50
Vesper, Candy Dish, Amber, Cover	145.00
Vesper, Candy Dish, Cover, 3 Sections, Green	65.00
Vesper, Chop Plate, Green, 15 In.	55.00
Vesper, Cup & Saucer, Footed, Amber	22.50
Vesper, Cup & Saucer, Green	22.50
Vesper, Ice Bucket, Green	75.00
Vesper, Plate, Amber, 6 In.	5.00
Vesper, Plate, Amber, 7 In.	7.50
Vesper, Plate, Amber, 8 In.	9.50
Vesper, Platter, Amber, Oval, 15 In.	150.00
Vesper, Soup, Cream, Footed, Green	17.50
Vesper, Tumbler, Iced Tea, Green, 12 Oz.	29.50
Victoria, Sherbet, Low	14.50
Victoria, Toothpick	55.00
Wildflower, Compote, Green, 3 In.	25.00
Wildflower, Syrup, Cover, Green	95.00
Willowmere, Champagne, Saucer, 6 Oz.	16.00
Willowmere, Cocktail, 3 1/2 Oz.	22.50
Willowmere, Cup & Saucer	16.00
Willowmere, Relish, 2 Sections	12.00
Willowmere, Relish, 3 Sections, 10 In.	30.00 To 35.00
Willowmere, Sherbet, Low	16.00
Willowmere, Tray, Lunch, Handle	35.00
Willowmere, Tumbler, Footed, 9 Oz.	18.00
Willowmere, Tumbler, Iced Tea, 12 Oz.	29.50
Woodland, Claret	5.00
Woodland, Pitcher	50.00

FOVAL, see Fry Foval
FRAME, PICTURE, see Furniture, Frame

Gladding, McBean and Company started in 1875. The company grew and acquired other potteries. They made sewer pipes, floor tiles, dinnerwares, and art pottery with a variety of trademarks. In 1934 dinnerware and art pottery were sold under the name Franciscan Ware. They made china and cream-colored, decorated earthenware. Desert Rose, Apple, El Patio, and Coronado were best sellers. The company became Interpace Corporation and in 1979 was purchased by Josiah Wedgwood & Sons. The plant was closed in 1984 but a few of the patterns are still being made. For more information, see *Kovels' Depression Glass & American Dinnerware Price List.*

FRANCISCAN, Ashtray, Apple	6.00
Bowl, Apple, 7 1/2 In.	10.00
Bowl, Cereal, Desert Rose, Flared	9.00
Bowl, Cereal, Strawberry Fair	6.50
Bowl, Mug & Plate, Desert Rose, Child's, 3 Piece	85.00
Bowl, Vegetable, Apple, Divided, Round	10.00 To 17.50
Bowl, Vegetable, Duet, Oval	12.00
Butter, Apple	18.00

Canister, Tea, Desert Rose	55.00
Chop Plate, Apple, 14 In.	35.00
Clock, Desert Rose	35.00
Coffeepot, Coronado, Ivory, After Dinner	45.00
Cookie Jar, Apple	90.00
Creamer, El Patio, Redwood Brown	8.00
Cup & Saucer, Apple	7.50 To 8.00
Cup & Saucer, Autumn	4.50
Cup & Saucer, Coronado, After Dinner	12.00
Cup & Saucer, Desert Rose	7.00
Cup & Saucer, Starburst	5.00
Eggcup, Desert Rose	10.00
Gravy Boat, Desert Rose	18.00
Mug, Desert Rose, 12 Oz.	15.00
Place Setting, Apple, 5 Piece	45.00
Plate, Apple, 6 1/2 In.	3.00
Plate, Apple, 8 In.	5.25 To 8.00
Plate, Apple, 10 1/2 In.	7.50
Plate, Coronado, Aqua, 10 In.	3.50
Plate, Desert Rose, 10 In.	8.00
Plate, Dinner, Autumn	5.50
Plate, Dinner, Desert Rose	5.00
Plate, Dinner, Duet	6.00 To 8.00
Plate, Dinner, Starburst, 10 1/2 In.	6.00 To 8.00
Plate, Starburst, 8 In.	4.00
Platter, Apple, 14 In.	18.50
Platter, Meadow Rose, 14 In.	35.00
Salt & Pepper, Apple, Tall	18.00
Salt & Pepper, Starburst	20.00
Saucer, Apple	2.00 To 4.25
Soup, Dish, Apple	8.50
Sugar & Creamer, Apple, Cover	17.50
Teapot, Apple	35.00
Teapot, Desert Rose	45.00
Thimble, Desert Rose	10.00
Tray, Starburst, Loop Handle	18.00
Tumbler, Desert Rose	16.00

Francisware is a named glassware made by Hobbs, Brockunier and Company of Wheeling, West Virginia, in the 1880s. It is a clear or frosted hobnail or swirl pattern glass with amber–stained rim. Some pieces were made by a pressed glass method, others were mold blown.

FRANCISWARE, Butter, Cover, Amber, Frosted	75.00 To 95.00
Toothpick, Frosted, Amber Top	45.00
Toothpick, Hobnail, 2 1/2 In.	50.00

Frankart, Inc., New York, New York, mass–produced nude *dancing lady* lamps, ashtrays, and other decorative Art Deco items in the 1920s and 1930s. They were made of white lead composition and spray–painted. *Frankart Inc.* and the patent number and year were stamped on the base.

FRANKART, Ashtray, Crane, Stylized Verde Green, No Insert, 8 x 6 In.	150.00
Ashtray, Kneeling Nude	350.00
Bookend, Boy, Carrying Sailboat, Dog, Crackled Finish, 7 In.	65.00
Bookends, Dog, Scotty	150.00
Bookends, Dog, Scotty Head, Silver On Black Base, 6 In., Pair	110.00
Bookends, Dog, Setter, Standing	175.00
Bookends, Dog, Terrier	125.00
Bookends, Double Horsehead	30.00
Bookends, Horsehead	50.00
Bookends, Woman With Flowers In Hair	125.00
Bust, Meditating Woman, Bronze Patina, 7 3/4 In.	250.00

Figurine, Dog, Setter, Bronze, 7 1/2 x 5 In. 200.00
Figurine, Nude, Kneeling, Holding Ray, Gunmetal Gray, 9 x 9 In. 295.00
Figurine, Nude, Leaning Back, Iridescent Green Paint, 9 1/2 In. 295.00
Inkwell, Nude, Seated, Pen Tray At Side 350.00
Lamp, 3 Glass Columns 1300.00
Lamp, Nude, Dancing, Silhouette, Frosted Glass Panel 375.00
Lamp, Nude, Standing, Holding Carved Glass Shade 155.00
Lamp, Nude, Standing, Silhouette, Frosted Pink Glass, 9 1/2 In. 825.00
Lamp, Shriner's, Dated 1927 .... 150.00

 Frankoma Pottery was originally known as The Frank Potteries when John F. Frank opened shop in 1933. The factory is now working in Sapulpa, Oklahoma. Early wares were made from a light cream-colored clay, but in 1956 the company switched to a red burning clay. The firm makes dinnerwares, utilitarian and decorative kitchenwares, figurines, flowerpots, and limited edition and commemorative pieces.

FRANKOMA, Ashtray, Kansas, 1970, 3 3/4 In. 8.50
Bookends, Charger Horse, Dark Greens, Marked 200.00
Bowl, Flower, Brown 16.00
Bowl, Plainsman, Green, 11 In. 8.00
Butter, Aztec, Green 7.00
Casserole, Wagon Wheel, Green, Cover, 3 Qt. 36.00
Casserole, Wagonwheel, Green, Cover, 2 Qt. 10.00
Decanter, Stopper, Red, Janice Frank 65.00
Decanter, Stopper, Red, John Frank 77.00
Figurine, Boy & Girl, Pair 125.00
Figurine, Cat, Seated, Green & Brown 48.00
Figurine, Dog, English Setter, 5 In. 35.00
Figurine, Dog, Irish Setter, Miniature 60.00
Figurine, Dog, Pointer, Green & Brown, 3 1/4 In. 48.00
Figurine, Fan Dancer, 11 1/2 x 13 1/2 In. 185.00
Figurine, Fan Dancer, Blue, Brown Highlights, 11 1/2 x 13 1/2 In. 275.00
Figurine, Fan Dancer, Green, Brown Highlights, 11 1/2 x 13 1/2 In. 235.00
Figurine, Fan Dancer, In Bowl 195.00
Figurine, Flower Girl, No. 700 .... 65.00
Figurine, Gardener Boy 90.00
Figurine, Horse, Blue, 4 1/2 In. 48.00
Figurine, Puma, No. 116, Ivory Glaze, 9 In. 50.00
Figurine, Swan, Miniature 45.00
Figurine, Trojan Horse, Blue, Miniature 60.00
Figurine, Woman, Nude, Seated, Prairie Green, 10 In. 80.00
Jug, Burgundy, Cork Stopper 35.00
Jug, Green, Stopper, 1/2 Gal. 25.00
Masks, Tragedy & Comedy, Pair 95.00
Mug, Cowboy, Red, 1977 .... 10.00
Mug, Cowboy, White, 1977 .... 10.00
Mug, Donkey, 1985 .... 3.00
Mug, Donkey, Brown, 1979 .... 20.00
Mug, Donkey, Yellow, 1975 ....4.00 To 25.00
Mug, Elephant, Nixon-Agnew, Flame, 1969 .... 70.00
Mug, Gray, Horse Decal, 18 Oz. 12.00

◆◆

When using antiques on a holiday table, be careful. Wax from candles can stain a cloth. Dishes may stain from cranberry or other fruits. Flower containers are easily water stained. Vases and plants often stain wood; be sure to use a coaster or dish. Greens draped on pictures or marble can stain. Cellophane tape will leave a mark.

◆◆

Pitcher, Handle, 7 1/2 In. 15.00
Plaque, Indian Chief, Rust, 1962 .... 10.00
Plaque, Indian Warrior, Prairie Green, 5 In. 20.00
Plaque, Will Rogers, Green Border, St. Clair 125.00
Plate, Christmas, 1968 .... 20.00
Plate, Christmas, 1974 .... 20.00
Plate, Easter, Oral Roberts, 1972 .... 15.00
Plate, Easter, White, 1972, 7 In. 15.00
Plate, Good Will Towards Men, 1965 .... 125.00
Plate, Statue of Liberty 12.00
Salt & Pepper, Bulls 35.00
Salt & Pepper, Oil Derrick 10.00
Trivet, Cherokee Alphabet 20.00
Trivet, Eagle 10.00
Trivet, Five Nations 20.00
Wall Pocket, Phoebe 95.00
Wall Pocket, Phoebe, Brown 60.00

The Fraternal section lists objects that are related to the many different fraternal organizations in the United States. The Elks, Masons, Odd Fellows, and others are included. Furniture is listed in the Furniture section.

FRATERNAL, see also Shaving Mug

FRATERNAL, American Legion, Ring, Auxiliary, 10K Gold, Black Onyx 40.00
Eastern Star, Pin, Diamond 140.00
Elks, Pin, Elk Head, B. P. O. E., 10K Gold 40.00
Elks, Pin, Woman's, 10K Gold 40.00
Elks, Plate, Mt. Hood, Elk At River, Tin Lithograph, 1912 .... 75.00
Elks, Ring, Raised Head & Antlers, 14K Gold 175.00
Elks, Stickpin, Elk Head, B. P. O. E., Gold Filled 45.00
Elks, Wristwatch, Elgin, Elk On Face, 6 Sides 90.00
F. O. E., Pin, Delegate, Brass & Copper, Eagle, Enameled, 1913 .... 25.00
Knights of Columbus, Match Safe, 1919 .... 15.00
Knights of Columbus, Sword 45.00
Knights of Columbus, Watch, Gold Filled, Wheeler Movement 85.00
Knights of Pythias, Drinking Set, Christmas, Tankard & 6 Mugs 950.00
Knights Templar, Mug, Carnival Glass, Ice Blue 350.00
Masonic, Book, Free Masonry In Wisonsin, 480 Pages, 1823–52 .... 15.00
Masonic, Champagne, New Orleans 1910 Souvenir 165.00
Masonic, Coverlet, Jacquard 1200.00
Masonic, Goblet, Schooner, Eagle In Wreath, Symbols, 6 1/2 In. 745.00
Masonic, Goblet, St. Paul, 1908 .... 65.00
Masonic, Letter Opener, Wooden Handle, Insignia 20.00
Masonic, Mug, Altoona, Penna. 50.00
Masonic, Mug, Atlantic City, Picture Each Side, 1904 .... 40.00
Masonic, Mug, Tankard Shape, Lulu, Atlantic City, 1904 .... 48.00
Masonic, Notebook, Black Woman Pictured, 1902 .... 35.00
Masonic, Plate, 5–Pointed Star, Hanging 25.00
Masonic, Plate, Los Angeles, May, 1906, 6 In. 45.00
Masonic, Ring, 10K Gold 145.00
Masonic, Ring, 3/4 Carat Diamond, 1890 .... 575.00
Masonic, Ring, Gold, 1915 .... 60.00
Masonic, Shaving Mug, Wheel With Calipers & T. Square 110.00
Masonic, Shelf, Carved Walnut, Old Varnish, 19 In. 375.00
Masonic, Spoon, Silver, Toledo, 1906 .... 22.00
Masonic, Thermometer, Veiled Prophet, Atop Dragon, 1901 .... 250.00
Masonic, Tumbler, Colored Milk Glass, Pittsburgh, 1918 .... 135.00
Masonic, Watch Chain, With Fob 45.00
Masonic, Watch Fob, Gold 25.00
Masonic, Watch Fob, Gold 45.00
Masonic, Watch Fob, Hook & Locket, Emblem On Locket, c.1890 .... 80.00
Masonic, Watch Fob, Yellow Gold 40.00
Masonic, Watch, 14K Gold, 17 Jewels, Hunting, Waltham, Pocket 999.00

Odd Fellows, Apron, Sheepskin Panel, Symbol, Compass, 16 x 13 In. 55.00
Odd Fellows, Axe, Ornamental, Pair 100.00
Odd Fellows, Badge, I. O. O. F., Iowa, 1910 .... 20.00
Odd Fellows, Book, Paperback, Convention, 1922, Large 25.00
Odd Fellows, Symbol, Heart & Hand, Carved Wooden Hand 1265.00
Odd Fellows, Uniform, Ceremonial, Black, Decorative Circles 65.00
Order of Moose, Pin & Medal, Milwaukee Convention, Silver, 1914 .... 17.50
Order of Moose, Pitcher Set, 6 Mugs, 12–In. Pitcher 148.00
Shriner, Bank, Figural, Wearing Fez, Bobbing Head, 1960s 40.00
Shriner, Bobbing Head 45.00
Shriner, Bottle, Crippled Children, Child, Lionstone .:....................................... 75.00
Shriner, Champagne, Rochester, N. Y., 1911 .... 75.00
Shriner, Champagne, Tobacco Leaf, Louisville, 1909 .... 60.00
Shriner, Emblem, Hanging, Metal, Dated 1920, 12 x 12 x 3/4 In. 85.00
Shriner, Fez, 1930s 25.00
Shriner, Fez, 1940s 35.00
Shriner, Fez, Red, Emblems, Tassel 10.00
Shriner, Goblet, 1911 .... 75.00
Shriner, Goblet, St. Paul, Minn., Ruby, 1908 .... 50.00 To 55.00
Shriner, Mug, Raised Indian, Scimitar Handle, Souvenir, 1904 .... 55.00
Shriner, Mug, Saratoga Indian, 1903 .... 65.00
Shriner, Plate, Shenango Pottery 65.00
Shriner, Salt Glass, Symbol, Syria Temple, Pittsburgh, 1908 .... 165.00
Shriner, Spoon, Embossed 38.00
Shriner, Toothpick, Barrel, Niagara Falls, 1905 .... 35.00
Shriner, Tray, Nile Temple, Seattle, Glass, 1974 .... 25.00

Fry glass was made by the H. C. Fry Glass Company of Rochester, Pennsylvania. The company, founded in 1901, first made cut glass and other types of fine glasswares. In 1922, they patented a heat–resistant glass called *Pearl Oven glass.* For two years, 1926–1927, the company made Fry Foval, an opal ware decorated with colored trim. Reproductions of this glass have been made. The company also made Depression glass and some pieces of cut glass are listed in those sections.

FRY FOVAL, Bowl, Fruit, Blue Rim & Stem Connector, 12 In. 575.00
Candlestick, Blue Opalescent, 9 1/2 In., Pair 295.00
Compote, Opalescent Bowl, Blue Stem, Flared Rim, 7 In. 275.00
Cup & Saucer, Opalescent, Jade Handle 50.00
Ice Bucket, Green, Wicker Handle 195.00
Perfume Bottle, Jade 200.00
Pitcher Set, Lemonade, Cobalt Handles, Cover, 7 Cups 550.00
Pitcher, Pedestal, Blue Handle, 8 In. 250.00
Tea Set, Pearl Glass, Green Jade Handles, Spout & Finials, 3 Pc. 335.00
Teapot, Jade Green Handle, Spout & Knob, 6 1/4 In. 260.00
Vase, Body of Graduated Circle Form, Green Knob, 7 3/4 In. 160.00
Vase, Flared Rim, Blue Pedestal Base, 9 1/2 In. 165.00
Vase, Flored Top, Blue Disc Foot, 10 In. 325.00
FRY, Baker, 9 x 5 x 3 In. 15.00
Bowl, Cut Glass, Stars, Crosshatching, Center Flower On Base, 9 1/2 In. 100.00
Casserole, Opalescent 20.00
Clock, Cut Glass, Signed, 5 1/2 x 4 In. 450.00
Coffeepot, Rochester, Opalescent 40.00
Pie Pan, Opalescent, 9 1/2 In. 12.50
Pie Plate, Opalescent, 9 1/2 In. 8.00
Sugar & Creamer, Cut Glass, Pinwheels, Vesicas, Strawberry Diamond 135.00
Teapot, Blue Handle, Spout & Finial, 3 Cup 325.00
Toothpick, Opalescent, 3 In. 25.00
Tray, Ice Cream, Cut Glass, Nelson Pattern 275.00

Fulper is the mark used by the American Pottery Company of Flemington, New Jersey. The art pottery was made from 1910 to 1929. The firm had been making bottles, jugs, and housewares from

1805. Doll heads were made about 1928. The firm became Stangl Pottery in 1929. Fulper art pottery is admired for its attractive glazes and simple shapes.

FULPER, Bean Pot, Brown	40.00
Bookends, Book Shape, Maroon	150.00
Bookends, Nude, Figural	78.00
Bookends, Peacock, Purple	395.00
Bookends, Sphinx, Matte Green, Label	200.00
Bowl, Artichoke, Medium Green Flowing Flambe, Mahogany, 5 x 8 In.	770.00
Bowl, Blue Crystalline To Brown Flambe, 3 Ball Feet, 5 x 11 In.	330.00
Bowl, Bulb, 10 Sides, Brown Drip Over Caramel, 2 1/2 x 8 3/4 In.	127.50
Bowl, Creamy Mustard Glaze, Mottled, 7 1/2 In.	50.00
Bowl, Effigy, 3 Figures, Blue–Green To Butterscotch Flambe, 10 In.	825.00
Bowl, Green & Black, Footed, Black Stamp, 8 In.	90.00
Bowl, Lavender, Flambe, 8 1/2 In.	650.00
Bowl, Mottled, Green, Brown, Gold & Black Shades, 3 1/4 x 10 1/2 In.	135.00
Bowl, Periwinkle Blue Glaze, Honey Interior, Shallow, 10 1/2 x 3 In.	137.00
Bowl, Red Matte, Apple Green Interior, Flared, Open, 6 1/2 x 12 In.	770.00
Bowl, Stepped Disc Base, 3 Effigy Supports, Marked, 7 1/4 x 10 In.	440.00
Bowl, Trumpet Shape, Blues, Footed, 10 In.	200.00
Candleholder, Flared Bobeche, Brown To Gray Flambe, 16 In., Pair	2090.00
Candleholder, Hooded, Blue Flambe	200.00
Candlestick, Flame Pull–Up, 10 3/4 In., Pair	600.00
Candlestick, Luster Drip Over Matte Blue Wisteria Glaze, 5 3/4 In.	95.00
Centerpiece, 3 Applied Candleholders Rim, Brown Flambe, 7 x 11 In.	220.00
Centerpiece, Urn Shape, Hammered Olive On Green, Pedestal, 10 In.	1760.00
Centerpiece, Urn Shape, Scroll Feet, Green Glaze, c.1915, 10 1/2 In.	1600.00
Console Set, Burgundy Matte, 3 Piece	265.00
Console Set, Rose Glaze, Turquoise Trim, 3 Piece	265.00
Console Set, Rose Matte, Turquoise Trim, Ribbed Bowl, 3 Piece	250.00
Flower Frog, Boy, Nude	60.00
Jardiniere, Greek Handles, Pink, 6 In.	325.00
Lamp, Conical Domed Base, Brown Matte, Cylindrical Standard, 16 In.	357.00
Lamp, Conical Leaded Glass Shade, Dark Brown Glaze, 14 In.	4180.00
Lamp, Perfume, Art Deco Girl	165.00
Lamp, Perfume, Art Deco, Woman, Orange Skirt, Black Hair	145.00
Lamp, Perfume, Cytharia, Woman, In Ballgown, 12 In.	900.00 To 950.00
Lamp, Slag Glass Shade	425.00
Lamp, Vasecraft, Green & White, 13 1/2 In. *Illus*	3080.00
Pitcher, Coiled, Green & Charcoal Glaze, Stamped, c.1907, 5 1/4 In.	195.00
Rose Bowl, French Blue, Shiny Glaze, 7 In.	150.00
Urn, Green Crystalline Glaze, Marked, c.1915, 13 In.	1870.00
Urn, Striated Green Matte Crystalline Glaze, 2 Handles, 12 x 11 In.	995.00
Vase, 7–Sided, Yellow & Blue Flambe, 9 In. *Illus*	275.00
Vase, Black Mirror, Blue Lava Glaze, 5 In.	125.00
Vase, Black Mirror, Gun–Metal Glaze, Marked, 8 In.	150.00

Fulper, Lamp, Vasecraft, Green & White,
13 1/2 In.

Fulper, Vase, Cat's–Eye Glaze, Mustard Matte, 5 In.
Fulper, Vase, 7–Sided, Yellow & Blue Flambe, 9 In.

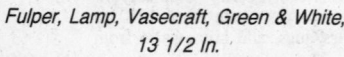

Vase, Black Over Chinese Blue Flambe, Tapering, Bulbous, 13 1/2 In. 935.00
Vase, Blue Crystalline Glaze, Scrolled Handles, c.1920, 13 In. 1210.00
Vase, Blue Drip Over Tan, 7 x 4 In. 145.00
Vase, Blue Matte, 2 Handles, Flared Base, Cylindrical Neck, 11 In. 300.00
Vase, Bowl Shape, Brown, Green, Handles, 6 1/2 x 10 In. 950.00
Vase, Bowl Shape, Gold Flambe Glaze, Stamped, c.1915, 5 1/2 In. 250.00
Vase, Brown & Caramel Flambe, Green Ground, 2 Handles, 9 1/2 In. 275.00
Vase, Brown–Black Drip Glaze Over Blue, Baluster, 12 1/4 In. 3850.00
Vase, Buttress, Brown Mirror, 8 In. 350.00
Vase, Cat's-Eye Glaze, Mustard Matte, 5 In. ....*Illus* 110.00
Vase, Copper Crystalline, Geometric, Flared Cylinder, 11 1/4 In. 4620.00
Vase, Crystalline Blue Glaze Over Cream, 7 1/4 In. 145.00
Vase, Crystalline Glaze, c.1915, 9 In. 110.00
Vase, Drip, Handle, 6 1/2 x 8 In. 530.00
Vase, Famille Plum, 11 3/4 In. 495.00
Vase, Famille Rose, Green Matte Base, Shouldered Handles, 6 In. 275.00
Vase, Flag, Metallic Green Flambe, 4 Pinched Openings, Bulbous, 8 In. 715.00
Vase, Flambe, Green & Blue Over Pink, Rafco, 4 In. 95.00
Vase, Flower, Trumpet, Black Over Copper, 8 In. 110.00
Vase, Flowing Butterscotch Flambe, Bulbous Base, 13 1/2 x 7 In. 935.00
Vase, Greek Handles, Matte Purple, 9 In. 550.00
Vase, Green & Eggplant Glaze, 2 Loop Handles, Wide Mouth, 6 3/4 In. 247.00
Vase, Green–Blue Drip Glaze, Bulbous, Handles, 8 In. 295.00
Vase, High Shoulders, Green & Aqua Glaze, 8 In. 250.00
Vase, Leopard Skin, 8 3/4 In. 300.00
Vase, Matte Green, Hammered, Wishbone Handles, Bulbous, 9 x 9 In. 550.00
Vase, Molded Cattails 2420.00
Vase, Plum Mirror, Sticker, Bulbous, 7 In. 275.00
Vase, Ribbed, 3 Twist Handles, Brown, 7 In. 135.00
Vase, Sea Foam, 3 Handles, 7 In. 210.00
Vase, Sea Foam, With Crystals, 3 Handles, 7 In. 165.00
Vase, Shaded Green To Rose, Swollen Form, Label, c.1918, 11 1/2 In. 445.00
Vase, Twig Sticks, Stamped, c.1915, 8 1/2 In. 225.00

All types of furniture are listed in this section. Examples dating from the seventeenth century to the 1950s are included. Prices for furniture vary in different parts of the country. Oak furniture is most expensive in the West; large pieces over eight feet high are sold for the most money in the South where high ceilings are found in the old homes. Condition is very important when determining prices. These are NOT average prices but rather reports of unique sales. If the description includes the word *style,* the piece resembles the old furniture style but was made at a later time. It is not a period piece.

FURNITURE, Armchair, see also Furniture, Chair
FURNITURE, Armchair Set, Foliate Frame, Musical Instruments, Upholstered, 6 .... 8250.00
Armchair, Acanthus Crest, Interlocking Strapwork, Mahogany 9350.00
Armchair, Art Nouveau, Fruitwood, Floral Upholstery 770.00
Armchair, Balloon Back, Scrolling Arms, Walnut 192.50
Armchair, Banister Back, Cockscomb Crest, Early 18th Century 900.00
Armchair, Banister Back, Pierced Heart & Crown Crest, c.1725 .... 2650.00
Armchair, Biedermeier, Ebonized Bronze Mounted, 19th Century 525.00
Armchair, Biedermeir, Upholstered Back & Seat, Fruitwood, Pair 2530.00
Armchair, Carved Eagle & Cherubs, Cane Back, Upholstered Seat 220.00
Armchair, Carved, Cane Seat & Back, England 450.00
Armchair, Carved, Medallion Back, Upholstered Seat, Oak 325.00
Armchair, Chinese Chippendale, Pierced Splat Back, Slip Seat 660.00
Armchair, Circular Back, Adams Style, Mixed Wood, Pair 1045.00
Armchair, Cow Horn Legs, Arms & Top Back Upholstered 275.00
Armchair, Curved Crest, 9 Spindles, Shaped Seat 1150.00
Armchair, Dutch Rococo, Walnut, Crest, Upholstered Back, Seat, Pr. 635.00
Armchair, Floral Carved Crest, Tapestry Upholstered Seat, 44 In. 1650.00
Armchair, Floral Design, Red & Black Graining, Rush Seat, 37 In. 200.00

Armchair, French Empire, Gilt Bronze Rosette, Fruitwood, Pair 3100.00
Armchair, French Style, Cane Back & Sides 35.00
Armchair, George III Style, Needlepoint Upholstered Back, Pair 4125.00
Armchair, George III, Gilt Wood, c.1775, Pair 2300.00
Armchair, George III, Mahogany, Lyre Back, Serpentine, Upholstered 3850.00
Armchair, George III, Mahogany, Serpentine, Pierced Splat 1450.00
Armchair, George III, Over-Upholstered Seat, Satinwood, 1800 .... 2200.00
Armchair, Green Striping, Stenciled Crest, Mahogany Arms 55.00
Armchair, Grotto, Carved Silver Arms 3200.00
Armchair, Horn, American, Upholstered In Cow Hide, c.1880 .... 3100.00
Armchair, L. & J. G. Stickley, No. 836, Tall Back, Open Arms, Seat 302.00
Armchair, L. & J. G. Stickley, Adjustable Back, Cushion, 40 In. 1650.00
Armchair, Laminated Surround, Upholstered, Josef Hoffmann, c.1905 .... 8800.00
Armchair, Library, Padded Arms, Carved Handholds, Mahogany, Pair 8800.00
Armchair, Louis XIII, Upholstered Back, Square Seat, Oak 550.00
Armchair, Louis XVI Style, Laurel Crest, Blue Velvet ....*Illus* 400.00
Armchair, Louis XVI Style, Leaf-Tip Frame, Giltwood, Pair 1320.00
Armchair, Mahogany, Needlepoint & Petit Point, Italy ....*Illus* 825.00
Armchair, Mother-of-Pearl & Bone Inlay, Upholstered, Syrian 3025.00
Armchair, Mother-of-Pearl Inlay, Carved Arms, Stone Seat, Teak 465.00
Armchair, Open Balloon Back, Demon Carved Backsplat, Yew, Pair 1045.00
Armchair, Ornate Carved, Gold Floral Upholstery, Overstuffed 85.00
Armchair, Painted Chinese Figures In Landscape, Chinese Export 8800.00
Armchair, Pilgrim Style, Sausage Turned, Slat Back 275.00
Armchair, Queen Anne, Walnut, Octagonal Back, Upholstered 3850.00
Armchair, Tubular Chrome U-Shaped Legs, Red Upholstery, 1930, Pr. 110.00
Armchair, Vase & Ring Turned Brace Back, Mixed Woods 8250.00
Armoire, Biedermeier, 2 Doors, Figured Walnut 2530.00
Armoire, Chippendale, Pennsylvania, Walnut, c.1770, 7 Ft. 4 In. 3300.00
Armoire, Faux Marble Top, Painted Scrolling Foliage, 72 In. 225.00
Armoire, French Provincial, Carved Flower Basket, Oak, 89 In. 2600.00
Armoire, French Provincial, Crown Molding, Fruitwood, 1890, 96 In. 4000.00
Armoire, French Provincial, Panel Doors, Stained Oak, 77 In. 445.00
Armoire, French Provincial, Paneled Carved Doors, Oak, 89 In. 2850.00
Armoire, Fruitwood, French Style, Beveled Glass Door, 37 x 90 In. 1200.00
Armoire, Himmelmayer, Single Door, Curly Maple, c.1850 .... 4400.00
Armoire, Lion Heraldic Crest, Allegorical Doors, Oak, 10 Ft. 2 In. 4200.00
Armoire, Louis XV Style, 2 Mirrored Doors, Walnut, 94 3/4 In. 1760.00
Armoire, Louis XV, Carved Paneled Doors, Iron Hinges, Oak, 90 In. 715,.00
Armoire, Victorian, Rosewood, Mirrored Door, Base Drawer, 10 Ft. 1850.00
Baker's Rack, Scroll & Pierced Design, Iron & Brass, 74 1/2 In. 550.00

Furniture, Armchair, Louis XVI Style,
Laurel Crest, Blue Velvet

Furniture, Armchair, Mahogany,
Needlepoint & Petit Point, Italy

◆◆◆◆◆◆◆◆◆◆◆◆◆◆◆◆◆◆◆◆◆◆◆◆◆◆◆◆◆◆◆◆◆◆◆◆◆◆◆

Never put a cast iron cooking pan in the dishwasher. Do not soak it for long. Excess water will remove the "seasoning" and the pan will not cook as well.

◆◆◆◆◆◆◆◆◆◆◆◆◆◆◆◆◆◆◆◆◆◆◆◆◆◆◆◆◆◆◆◆◆◆◆◆◆◆◆

Banquette, Iron, White, Upholstered, France, Early 1800s	4500.00
Bassinet, Wicker, Wheels, c.1915	140.00
Beau Brummel, Federal, Bird's Eye Maple, 1790	825.00
Bed & Dresser, Victorian, Walnut, Marble Top, 2 Piece	4800.00
Bed Step, Turned Front Legs, Graining, Pine & Poplar, 22 1/2 In.	600.00
Bed Step, William IV, Mahogany, Turned Tapered Feet, 1830, 27 In.	2300.00
Bed, Canopy, Hepplewhite, Inlaid Serpentine Tester	4125.00
Bed, Canopy, Mahogany, Fishnet Tester, 51 x 73 x 66 In.	650.00
Bed, Canopy, Paneled Headboard, Maple, c.1840	1775.00
Bed, Canopy, Reeded Posts, Cherry, c.1830	3200.00
Bed, Canopy, Sheraton, Curly Maple	1870.00
Bed, Canopy, Sheraton, Maple	2000.00
Bed, Canopy, Sheraton, Maple & Birch, c.1820	1200.00
Bed, Canopy, Sheraton, Red Wash, Shaped Canopy, c.1820	3630.00
Bed, Canopy, Silk Panel, 2 Carved Posts, Mahogany, 8 Ft. 2 In.	4125.00
Bed, Day, Sleigh Ends, Walnut, 26 x 78 In.	600.00
Bed, Faux Bamboo, Turned Finials, Maple, c.1880, 72 1/2 In.	825.00
Bed, Federal, Four–Poster, Arched Canopy, Poplar, c.1800	2425.00
Bed, Federal, Four–Poster, Crossbanded Birch & Pine, c.1810	2750.00
Bed, Federal, Low Post, Painted Red, Mushroom Finials, 75 x 49 In.	225.00
Bed, Field, Sheraton, Mahogany, Rope Turned	2000.00
Bed, Folding, Spring, c.1910, 7 1/2 x 7 In.	275.00
Bed, Four–Poster, Federal, Maple, 6 Ft. 8 In.	2750.00
Bed, Four–Poster, Jenny Lind	110.00
Bed, Four–Poster, Mahogany, Acanthus, 1840, Large	2000.00
Bed, Four–Poster, Mahogany, Finials On Post, 1840, 7 Ft. 2 In.	1995.00
Bed, Four–Poster, Mahogany, Wooden Slats, Single	135.00
Bed, Four–Poster, Rope, Acorn, Maple	650.00
Bed, Four–Poster, Smoke Grained Frame, c.1815, Miniature	5600.00
Bed, French Restauration, Rosewood, Inlaid, c.1830 ....*Illus*	880.00
Bed, Gustav Stickley, No. 923, Oak, Tapered Posts, 59 x 78 x 42 In.	440.00
Bed, Half–Tester, Child's, Carved Walnut, c.1860	1650.00
Bed, Iron, Rounded Head & Footboard, Medallion Type Designs	135.00
Bed, Majorelle, Marquetry, Wisteria, Walnut, c.1900, 5 Ft. 3 In.	9900.00
Bed, Marriage, Painted Woman & Man Headboard, German, Pine, 1842	4675.00
Bed, Oak, Copper, Rollicking Cherub Panels, 42 x 81 x 29 In.	400.00
Bed, Paneled Head & Footboard, Marquetry, Mahogany Veneer, 69 In.	495.00
Bed, Rope, Acorn Finials, Cherry, 52 x 75 In.	65.00

Furniture, Bed, French Restauration, Rosewood, Inlaid, c.1830

Furniture, Bench, Garden, Iron, Renaissance Revival, 41 x 40 In.

Furniture, Bench, Garden, Iron, W. McHose & Co., 35 x 57 In.

Bed, Rope, Blanket Rail, Curly Maple, 52 x 45 In.	550.00
Bed, Rope, Brown Vinegar Graining, Blanket Bar, 58 x 68 In.	4000.00
Bed, Rope, Cannonball, Scalloped Headboard, Male, 53 x 74 3/4 In.	375.00
Bed, Rope, Curly Birch, Curly Maple, Bird's-Eye Maple, 73 1/2 In.	800.00
Bed, Rope, Paneled Headboard, Curly Maple & Poplar, 76 In.	300.00
Bed, Rope, Poplar, Red-Brown Graining Over Gray, 42 x 72 x 36 In.	200.00
Bed, Rope, Scrolled Headboard, Curly Maple, 80 x 60 X72 In.	3000.00
Bed, Rope, Tall Post, Pine Headboard, Birch, 67 1/2 x 76 x 40 In.	1350.00
Bed, Rope, Turned Posts, Blanket Rail, Poplar, 59 1/2 x 75 1/2 In.	150.00
Bed, Scroll Cut Head & Foot Board, Pine, 19th Century, 36 3/4 In.	225.00
Bed, Sleigh, Carved Rosewood, c.1850	2100.00
Bed, Sleigh, Curved Side Rails, Louis Philippe, Cherry, 74 In.	1200.00
Bed, Sofa When Closed, Pillar & Scroll	3950.00
Bed, Tall Post, Maple, Rope, New England, 1835, 64 x 53 x 74 In.	1210.00
Bed, Tall Post, Pine Headboard, Maple, 61 x 72 3/4 In.	2850.00
Bed, Tester, Inlaid Mahogany, Shaped Canopy, 54 In.	6600.00
Bed, Trundle, Rope, Wooden Caster Wheels, Poplar, 49 x 38 1/2 In.	325.00
Bed, Turned Posts, 53 x 77 In.	3500.00
Bed, Victorian, Carved Foliate Over Headboard, Mahogany, Double	1980.00
Bed, Walnut, Acorns & Circles Headboard, 19th Century, 7 Ft.	700.00
Bed, Youth, Maple, Folding, Wooden Slats, Castors	285.00
Bed, Youth, Tiger Maple, 4 Tapering Square Posts, c.1830	1760.00
Bedroom Set, Bakelite & Brass Handles, Etched Mirror, 4 Piece	1100.00
Bedroom Set, Bed, Marble Topped Dresser, Cheval Mirror, Walnut	2675.00
Bedroom Set, Burl Walnut Overlay, Solid Walnut, 1870, 3 Piece	6950.00
Bedroom Set, Carved, Marble On Dresser & Commode, Walnut, 3 Piece	5000.00
Bedroom Set, Chippendale, Mahogany, Kling Furniture Co., 5 Piece	625.00
Bedroom Set, Four-Poster Canopy Bed, Dresser, Washstand, Cherry	4000.00
Bedroom Set, Single Bed, Nightstand & Armoire, Iris Inlay, France	1600.00
Bedroom Set, Sleigh Bed, Highboy, Chest, Walnut	400.00
Bedroom Set, Sleigh Bed, Vanity, 2 Mirrored Dressers, Walnut	1800.00
Bedroom Set, Sleigh Furniture Co., 3 Piece	2500.00
Bedroom Set, T. B. Brooks, Bed Dresser, Marble Top, Walnut, 3 Piece	5750.00
Bedroom Set, Victorian, Carved Florals, Walnut, 3 Piece	7100.00
Bench, 3 Drawers Under Seat, Pennsylvania, 6 Ft.	1895.00
Bench, Adirondack	75.00
Bench, Beaded Apron Edges, Original Red Paint, Pine, 78 In.	275.00
Bench, Brazilian, Arched Crest, Carved Hardwood, 50 1/2 x 47 In.	365.00
Bench, Bucket, Pennsylvania, Red Paint, 1840, 70 1/2 x 42 1/4 In.	6500.00
Bench, Bucket, Traces of Gray Paint, Pine, 36 x 45 1/2 In.	550.00
Bench, Courting, Amish, Pine, Brown Combed, Lift-Lid Seat, 52 In.	450.00
Bench, Cutout Feet, Dark Patina, Pine, 16 x 72 In.	125.00
Bench, Dutch Scenes, Gold Floral Designs, Black, Rush Seat, 47 In.	900.00
Bench, Egyptian, Classical Revival, Sphinx Arm, Cane Seat, 59 In.	2100.00
Bench, Empire, Brown & Black Striping, Foliage, 79 3/4 In.	2300.00
Bench, Garden, Cast Stone, Female-Form Bases, 4 Ft. 10 In., Pair	2100.00
Bench, Garden, Cast Stone, Leaf-Tip Supports, 55 1/2 In.	1100.00

Bench, Garden, Cast Stone, Scrolled Legs, 37 1/2 In. 2750.00
Bench, Garden, Cast Stone, Seat Molded With Leaf Tips, 50 In. 990.00
Bench, Garden, Floral, Owl Head Arms, White Paint, Iron, 42 In. 850.00
Bench, Garden, Geometric Design, Iron, c.1880, 4 Ft. 8 In. 3850.00
Bench, Garden, Iron, Center Mask Over Pierced Pattern, 44 In. 935.00
Bench, Garden, Iron, Double Chair Back, James Carr, 40 In. 4500.00
Bench, Garden, Iron, Fern Design, White Paint, 55 In. 700.00
Bench, Garden, Iron, Renaissance Revival, 41 x 40 In. ....*Illus* 880.00
Bench, Garden, Iron, Twig Form, 2 Armchairs, 4 Ft. 2 In. 6050.00
Bench, Garden, Iron, Urn of Flowers Crest Rail, 41 x 40 In. 880.00
Bench, Garden, Iron, Vintage Pattern, 19th Century, 34 In. 250.00
Bench, Garden, Iron, W. McHose & Co., 35 x 57 In. ....*Illus* 2200.00
Bench, Garden, Iron, White, 1900 .... 425.00
Bench, Garden, Leaves, Iron, c.1860, Pair 1900.00
Bench, Garden, Wire, Black Paint, 52 In. 375.00
Bench, Garden, Wire, Twisted, White Paint, 40 In. 55.00
Bench, Garden, Wire, White Repaint, Victorian, 55 In. 225.00
Bench, Gustav Stickley, No. 286, Square Spindled Back, 1907, 4 Ft. 8800.00
Bench, Jacobean Style, Hinged Seat, Carved Oak, 45 x 44 In. 770.00
Bench, Jeweler's, Roll Top, Oak 1800.00
Bench, Kneeling, Green & Red, Bamboo Turned Legs, 36 3/4 In. 325.00
Bench, L & N Railroad, Oak 310.00
Bench, Lift–Lid Seat, Low Back, Scrolled Arms, Pine, 62 1/2 In. 500.00
Bench, Limbert, Window, 4 Side Cutouts, 1907, 24 In. 4950.00
Bench, Louis Xv, Serpentine Mahogany Apron, 31 x 18 x 21 In. 80.00
Bench, Louis XV, Upholstered, Serpentine Mahogany Apron, 31 In. 88.00
Bench, Louis XVI, Walnut, Guilloche Molded Skirt, 6 Legs, 53 In. 330.00
Bench, Majorelle, Clematis Pattern, Carved Arm Rests, c.1900 .... 6600.00
Bench, Mammy's, Gold Stenciling, Painted, Homespun Seat, c.1850 .... 1695.00
Bench, Mammy's, Red & Black Graining, Removable Guard, 60 In. 1500.00
Bench, Mammy's, Stenciled, Baby Guard, Black Paint, 46 1/2 In. 700.00
Bench, Mammy's, Yellow Striping, Gold Stenciling, 56 1/4 In. 800.00
Bench, Mammy, Arrow–Back Splats 500.00
Bench, Milk, Shaker, Paneled Doors, Wooden Latches, Poplar, 48 In. 1400.00
Bench, Mortised, Cutout Apron, Bootjack Ends, Dry Paint, 60 In. 750.00
Bench, Mortised, Red Paint, Softwood, 19th Century, 37 In. 720.00
Bench, Pencil Post Legs, Gray Paint, Poplar, 16 x 35 In. 175.00
Bench, Pine, American Southwest, 18th Century 6600.00
Bench, Pine, Green Paint, 11 3/4 x 86 In. 150.00
Bench, Primitive, Pine, Paint Layers, 12 x 70 x 19 In. 135.00
Bench, Scalloped Apron, Cut Corners, Pine, 18 x 12 x 60 In. 500.00
Bench, Settee, Garden, Iron, Foliage Scrolls, 37 In. 175.00
Bench, Shaped Arms, Slat Back, Hopsack Upholstered, Birch, 60 In. 250.00
Bench, Splayed Legs, Pine, 14 x 48 In. 300.00
Bench, Standing Bear Supports, Walnut, Switzerland, 36 In. 4125.00
Bench, Vanity, Wicker, White Paint, 1890s 425.00
Bench, Water, 3 Tiers, Green Paint, 3 Ft. 250.00
Bench, Water, Bootjack Feet, 2 Step–Back Shelves, Pine, 49 In. 750.00
Bench, Water, Bootjack Sides, Red Paint, 2 Shelves, 1880s 650.00
Bench, Water, Gallery, Pine, 31 x 43 1/2 In. 145.00
Bench, Water, Step–Back Top Shelf, Pine, 42 3/4 x 39 In. 350.00
Bench, Water, Walnut, Weathered, 37 x 18 x 36 In. 150.00
Bench, White Painted Cast Iron Twig 1050.00
Bench, Window, Regency, Ebonized, Parcel Gilt, Caned, 1810, 43 In. 4400.00
Bench, Windsor, Bamboo, Green Repaint, 17 1/4 x 23 1/4 In. 575.00
Bench, Windsor, Comb Back, Paper Label, Seat, 18 1/2 In. 350.00
Bench, Windsor, D–Shaped Seat, c.1800, 35 1/4 In. 4200.00
Bench, Windsor, Plank Seat, 4 Medallion Back, Bamboo, 72 1/2 In. 1900.00
Bench, Windsor, Plank Seat, Bamboo Spindles, Crest, Black Paint 575.00
Bench, Windsor, Scrolled Arms, Spindle Back, Mahogany, 48 1/2 In. 2100.00
Bench, Work, Tray Top, Salmon Paint, Mixed Woods, 29 x 41 In. 2900.00
Bin, Baker's, Amish, Lift Lid, Burl Painted, Poplar, 50 1/2 In. 475.00
Bin, Seed, 12 Bins, Walker Bin Co., Oak, 6 Ft. 3 In. 1000.00

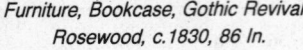

Furniture, Bookcase, Gothic Revival,   Furniture, Bookcase, Oak, 7 Sections, c.1900
Rosewood, c.1830, 86 In.

Blanket Chest, Hepplewhite, Pine, 2 Drawers, New England	950.00
Bookcase, Beidermeier, Gothic Arched Doors, Birch Veneer, 68 In.	1985.00
Bookcase, Carved Floral Arched Opening, French, Oak, 95 x 45 In.	1350.00
Bookcase, Federal, Mahogany, Glass Doors, 1810	7500.00
Bookcase, George III Style, Breakfront, Japanned, Scarlet Ground	935.00
Bookcase, Georgian Style, 5 Sections, Lower Doors, Stained, 88 In.	1450.00
Bookcase, Georgian Style, Mullioned Doors, Mahogany, 80 x 49 In.	885.00
Bookcase, Gothic Revival, Rosewood, c.1830, 86 In. ....*Illus*	3520.00
Bookcase, Gustav Stickley, 1 Door	4125.00
Bookcase, Gustav Stickley, 2 Doors, 12 Panes, c.1912, 56 In.	4100.00
Bookcase, Gustav Stickley, 2 Doors, Gallery, c.1905, 56 1/2 In.	4400.00
Bookcase, Gustav Stickley, Single Door	4125.00
Bookcase, Italian Baroque, Grilled Door, Walnut, c.1790, 8 Ft.	8250.00
Bookcase, L. & J. G. Stickley, 1 Door, 3/4 Gallery, 55 x 24 In.	2750.00
Bookcase, Limbert, 3 Doors, Gallery, Black, 46 x 48 x 11 In.	1450.00
Bookcase, Limbert, No. 350	3025.00
Bookcase, Limbert, Single Door	4950.00
Bookcase, Mahogany & Mahogany Crotch–Grain Veneer, 88 In.	6600.00
Bookcase, Mullion Glazed Doors, 5 Shelves, Mahogany, 88 x 43 In.	1430.00
Bookcase, Oak, 7 Sections, c.1900 ....*Illus*	1100.00
Bookcase, Open Shelf, Lion–Form Stiles, Rosewood, c.1820, Dwarf	5500.00
Bookcase, Stickley Bros., 2 Doors, 8 Panes Glass,, 52 x 48 In.	1750.00
Bookcase, Stickley Bros., Glazed Double Door, Oak, 35 3/4 In.	1700.00
Bookcase, Stickley, 2 Doors, Mission Oak	1500.00
Bookcase, Stickley, No. 321, Mission Oak, 3 Shelves, Glass Doors	3500.00
Bookcase, Victorian, Walnut, Crest, 2 Glass Doors, 2 Drawers	3250.00
Bookshelf, Double, Open, France, Mahogany, c.1930, 6 Ft. 7 In.	1100.00
Box, Blanket, Dated 1723, English Oak	400.00
Box, Blanket, Pine, Blue Paint, Open Till, 32 x 47 x 18 1/2 In.	3400.00
Box, Blanket, Poplar, Red & Black Sponged, c.1800	300.00
Bracket, George III, Gilt Wood, Dolphin Head, 16 In., Pr.	5500.00
Breakfront, 4 Glazed Doors, 4 Drawers, Mahogany, 90 In.	1655.00
Breakfront, Scrolled Columns, 16 Pane, Walnut, c.1830, 96 x 50 In.	1300.00
Bucket, Peat, Brass Bound, Liner, Mahogany, c.1800, 13 1/2 In.	1980.00
Bucket, Peat, George III, Brass Bound, 15 In.	995.00
Buffet, 3 Drawers, 2 Cupboards, Shaped Apron, Walnut, 64 In.	1350.00
Buffet, Oak, Serpentine, Claw Foot, Applied Carvings	110.00
Buffet, Serpentine Top, 2 Drawers, 3 Cupboards, Walnut, 80 In.	775.00
Bureau Bookcase, George III, Mahogany, Slant Front, 92 In., 2 Part	9350.00
Bureau, Chippendale, Swell Front, Tiger Maple Facings, Pine	4000.00
Bureau, Federal, Bow Front, Mahogany Veneer, 4 Drawers, 39 1/4 In.	1765.00

Bureau, Federal, Mahogany Veneer, Graduated Drawers, New England 1430.00
Bureau, Parquetry, Marquetry & Burl Inlay, Flant Front 7750.00
Bureau, Serpentine Front, Graduated Drawers, Mahogany 2750.00
Bureau, Serpentine Front, Inlaid Mahogany, c.1790, 37 1/4 In. 9500.00
Cabinet On Chest, Cherry, Victorian, 3 Short Over Drawer, 73 In. 485.00
Cabinet, Apostle, Stand, 10 Interior Drawers, Painted, 64 In. 3100.00
Cabinet, Bar, Art Deco, Laminated Blond Mahogany, Berlin, 48 In. 165.00
Cabinet, Bar, Flip Top, 2 Doors, Fruitwood, 31 1/4 x 40 In. 275.00
Cabinet, Bedside, Handles Over Tambour, Mahogany, 28 1/2 In. 2750.00
Cabinet, Blueprint, Cherry, Multiple Drawers, 1890s 450.00
Cabinet, Book, G. Stickley, Open Top, 1 Door, Eastwood Label, 40 In. 2850.00
Cabinet, Chest, Bow Front, Mahogany, Veneer, 1810, 40 x 43 1/2 In. 1100.00
Cabinet, China, Bombe, Hand Painted, Gilded, France 2100.00
Cabinet, China, Bow Front, Glass Door & Sides, Oak, 72 x 44 In. 825.00
Cabinet, China, Bow Front, Oak, Claw Foot, 4 1/2 Ft. 325.00
Cabinet, China, G. Stickley, 1 Door, Backsplash, 63 x 36 x 15 In. 3650.00
Cabinet, China, Mahogany, Faux Mullion Doors, 34 In. 230.00
Cabinet, China, Mahogany, Individual Glazed Doors, America, 1920 .... 675.00
Cabinet, Classical, Mahogany Veneer, 10 Base Drawers, 1820, 74 In. 3750.00
Cabinet, Continental, 3 Faux Drawers, Fruitwood Parquetry, 34 In. 1210.00
Cabinet, Corner, Demilune, 2 Doors, Shelves, Pine, 50 x 33 In. 360.00
Cabinet, Corner, Oak, 2–Over–2 Doors, Walnut Stain 300.00
Cabinet, Curio, French Style, Polychrome, Ormolu Trim, 66 In. 475.00
Cabinet, Curio, Gold Paint, Floral & Ormolu, Curved Glass, 67 In. 550.00
Cabinet, Curio, Gold Repaint, Painted Scenes, Curved Glass, 56 In. 250.00
Cabinet, Curio, Louis XVI, Gilded, Ormolu, Curved Glass, 57 In. 1000.00
Cabinet, Curio, Vernis Martin, Corset Shape, Large 1250.00
Cabinet, Doors Fitted With Leather Books, Mahogany, 4 Ft. 10 In. 3350.00
Cabinet, Filing, Walnut, Early 20th Century, 34 1/2 x 19 In. 65.00
Cabinet, Fretwork, Mullioned Doors, Mahogany, c.1900 .... 225.00
Cabinet, Hanging, 2 Paneled Doors, c.1875, 19 x 25 In. 335.00
Cabinet, Hanging, Eastlake, Carved Ebony, 1 Door 225.00
Cabinet, Hanging, Floral Painted, Scandinavia, 33 x 21 x 12 In. 330.00
Cabinet, Hanging, Stepped Pediment, Glass Door, Drawers, Pine 250.00
Cabinet, Hoosier Style, 2 Green Glass Doors 450.00
Cabinet, Jewel, Rosewood, Mother–of–Pearl, 3 Drawers, Desk, 14 In. 1895.00
Cabinet, Kitchen, Boone, 2 Frosted Doors, Porcelain Work Top 300.00
Cabinet, Lacquer, Chinese, Cafe Au Lait, Flower Branches, 69 In. 6650.00
Cabinet, Leaded Doors, Gold Silk Lining, Ebony, c.1870, 83 In. 2500.00
Cabinet, Magazine, G. Stickley, No. 79, Cutouts At Top, Oak, 1910 .... 995.00
Cabinet, Music, 7 Short Drawers, Mahogany, 41 x 20 1/2 In. 225.00
Cabinet, Music, Brass Banded, Bow Front Door, Marquetry, Mahogany 175.00
Cabinet, Music, Mirror, Satinwood Interior, Rosewood 995.00
Cabinet, Music, Spanish Style, 2 Doors, Painted Design, 65 1/2 In. 495.00
Cabinet, Oak, 1 Drawer, Carved Doors, 17th Century, 34 1/2 In. 1350.00
Cabinet, Oak, Leaded Glass Curio Top, 68 x 52 x 23 In. 1045.00
Cabinet, Red Lacquered, Gilded, 2 Doors, Chinese, 18 x 12 x 9 In. 137.00
Cabinet, Regency, Mahogany, Brass, Inlaid, Hairy Paw Feet, 4 Ft. 4950.00
Cabinet, Renaissance Revival, Ebonized, Marble Top, Germany 450.00
Cabinet, Screws, 96 Drawers, Mahogany, Octagonal, 42 In. 2500.00
Cabinet, Sheraton, Satinwood, Pediment Top, 74 x 36 In. 5000.00
Cabinet, Storage, 4 Rows of 5 Drawers, Mirrored Fronts, Oak, 5 Ft. 2400.00
Cabinet, Tobacco, Brass Trim, Drawers, Burl Walnut, 12 1/2 In. 665.00
Cabinet, Victorian, Beveled Mirror, With Coal Scuttle, Small 245.00
Candlestand, 2–Light, Adjustable Accordian Arm, Iron, 40 In. 550.00
Candlestand, Adjustable, Animal–Head Ornament, Iron, 58 1/2 In. 500.00
Candlestand, Ball–Turned Pedestal, Dish Top, Walnut, 26 In. 3200.00
Candlestand, Cherrywood, Eliphalet Chapin, Tripod, Snake Feet 665.00
Candlestand, Chippendale, Ink Graining, Maple, 25 3/4 In. 2500.00
Candlestand, Chippendale, Piecrust Top, Carved Base 500.00
Candlestand, Curly Maple Legs, Banded Edge Inlay, 29 In. 375.00
Candlestand, Curly Maple, 28 3/4 In. 130.00
Candlestand, Curved Legs, Cutter, Mt. Union, Walnut & Cherry 60.00

Candlestand, Dish Top, Chester County, Walnut, 23 In.		2750.00
Candlestand, Federal, Cherry, Square Top, 1790, 27 x 16 3/4 In.		1320.00
Candlestand, Federal, New England, Birch, c.1810, 28 In.		770.00
Candlestand, Federal, Oval Tilt Top, Mahogany, 29 3/4 In.		1430.00
Candlestand, Federal, Serpentine Top, Birch, 26 3/4 In.		1320.00
Candlestand, Federal, Tiger Maple, New England, 27 x 19 x 16 In.		1650.00
Candlestand, Federal, Tilt Top, Duncan Phyfe, c.1815, 28 In.		9350.00
Candlestand, Federal, Tilt Top, Quatrefoil, Serpentine Top, c.1785		2200.00
Candlestand, Federal, Tilt Top, Tiger Maple, 27 3/4 x 21 x 17 In.		2200.00
Candlestand, Gallery, Curly Maple, 27 In.		1350.00
Candlestand, George III, Tilt Top, Japanned, 27 In.		660.00
Candlestand, Gilt Stenciled Compote of Fruit, Poplar, 28 1/4 In.		250.00
Candlestand, Hepplewhite, Oval Tilt Top, Mahogany, 27 3/4 In.		1600.00
Candlestand, Hepplewhite, Oval Tilt Top, Walnut, 27 In.		650.00
Candlestand, Hepplewhite, Oval Top, Cherry, 28 1/4 In.		800.00
Candlestand, Hepplewhite, Spider Legs, Cherry, 28 1/4 x 17 In.		1000.00
Candlestand, Mahogany Veneer, Tilt Top, Cock-Beaded, R. I., 28 In.		2100.00
Candlestand, Mahogany, Octagonal Top, America, 1810-20		975.00
Candlestand, Maple, Tripod, Ovoid Rectangular Top, 26 x 20 In.		200.00
Candlestand, Octagonal Top, Outscrolling Base, Maple, 27 1/2 In.		525.00
Candlestand, Oval Tilt Top, Inlaid Mahogany, c.1800		1600.00
Candlestand, Ovoid Rectangular Top, Maple, 29 1/4 In.		225.00
Candlestand, Rosewood, Grain Painted, New England, 25 1/4 In.		2310.00
Candlestand, Snake Feet, 1 Board Top, Cherry & Birch, 27 1/2 In.		400.00
Candlestand, Spider Legs, Cherry & Stripe Grain Walnut, 30 In.		360.00
Candlestand, Square Top, 3 Scroll Cut Legs, Maple, 28 In.		665.00
Candlestand, Square Top, Fretwork Gallery, Mahogany, 28 In.		150.00
Candlestand, Square Top, Stringing, Birch & Cherry, 27 3/4 In.		2550.00
Candlestand, Tiger Maple, Square Top, Tripod, New England, 24 In.		1450.00
Candlestand, Tilt Top, Birch & Mahogany, c.1805, 30 1/2 In.		9900.00
Candlestand, Tilt Top, Handkerchief Top, Snake Foot		1750.00
Candlestand, Tilt Top, Joseph Short, Mahogany, c.1800, 27 1/2 In.		8250.00
Candlestand, Tilt Top, Serpentine Top, Snake Foot		1600.00
Candlestand, Tilt Top, Spade Foot, Mahogany		2400.00
Candlestand, Walnut & Fruitwood, c.1830, 23 1/2 In.		1400.00
Candlestand, Walnut, Clover-Form Top, 3 Cutout Legs, 17 x 28 In.		60.00
Candlestand, Whittled Feet, Breadboard Top, Pine, 30 In.		700.00
Candlestand, Windsor, Round Top, Poplar, 27 1/2 In.		350.00
Candlestand, Wood, 2 Metal Holders, Red, 18th Century, 50 In.		385.00
Canterbury, Carved Walnut, Victorian, England, c.1855		3520.00
Canterbury, George III, Mahogany, 2 Drawers, 22 x 20 x 16 In.		1100.00
Canterbury, Georgian Style, 4 Compartments, Mahogany, 19 x 19 In.		525.00
Canterbury, Mahogany, 1 Long Drawer, 18 1/4 x 14 x 19 1/2 In.		187.00
Canterbury, Mahogany, 1 Lower Drawer, Ivory Pulls, 20 x 26 In.		357.50
Canterbury, Mahogany, American, c.1850, 18 1/2 In.		1045.00
Canterbury, Regency, Mahogany, Latticework, Frieze Drawer, 21 In.		6325.00
Canterbury, Rosewood, 4 Sections, Lifting Handle, Drawer, 21 In.		5500.00
Canterbury, Sheraton, Mahogany, 1 Drawer, England, 14 x 19 3/4 In.		850.00
Canterbury, Victorian, Burl Walnut, Fruitwood Inlaid, Tray, 1860		2500.00
Canterbury, Walnut, 4 Compartments Over Drawer, 19 1/4 x 14 In.		198.00
Canterbury, William IV, Frieze Drawer, Rosewood, c.1840, 20 In.		3575.00
Case, Gun, Brassbound Corners, Mahogany, 20 In.		315.00
Cellarette, 4 Cut Glass Decanters, Tin Ice Compartment, England		615.00
Cellarette, Divided, Palmette Finial, Mahogany, 29 x 32 In.		2970.00
Cellarette, Limbert, No. 751, 1 Drawer, Copper Pulls, 36 x 25 In.		1100.00
Cellarette, Mahogany, Shelves, Marquetry Butterfly, Galle, 45 In.		4650.00
Cellarette, Pullout Surface, Tin, Copper Cooler, Oak, 35 1/2 In.		335.00
Cellarette, Regency, Brassbound, Hexagonal, Mahogany, 27 In.		880.00
Cellarette, Sliding Lid, Barnes, Bellaire, Ohio, Cherry, c.1820		3500.00
Cellarette, Stand, George III, Mahogany, Hexagonal, Hinged, 27 In.		2550.00
Chair Set, American Empire, Mahogany, Urn Back Splat, Pierced, 4		325.00
Chair Set, Andre Arbus, Cherrywood, c.1950, 6		9200.00
Chair Set, Andre Arbus, Leather Upholstered, Rosewood, 1930, 8		5500.00

Chair Set, Baltimore Style, Original Paint, 1840, 6 .... 1950.00
Chair Set, C. Eames Style, White Vinyl, Fiberglass, Wire Frame, 4 .... 195.00
Chair Set, Captain's, Plank Seat, Painted Pine, 4 .... 115.00
Chair Set, Chippendale Style, Comb Splat, Slip Seat, Mahogany, 6 .... 775.00
Chair Set, Chippendale, Pierced Splat, Slip Seat, Mahogany, 8 .... 2000.00
Chair Set, Chromed Steel, Painted Wood, Leather, Breuer, 8 .... 4125.00
Chair Set, Classical Carved Mahogany, 1820–30, 35 In., 6 .... 4675.00
Chair Set, Demi Arms, Walnut, Burl Veneered Trim, 1860–80, 4 .... 600.00
Chair Set, Dining, Arched Crest, Pierced Splat, Mahogany, 7 .... 425.00
Chair Set, Dining, Arched Crest, Pierced Urn Splat, Mahogany, 10 .... 1100.00
Chair Set, Dining, Directoire, Fruitwood, 2 Armchairs, 10 .... 1100.00
Chair Set, Dining, George III, Out–Turned Arms, c.1800, 4 .... 4125.00
Chair Set, Dining, Georgian Style, Ribbon Back, Mahogany, 7 .... 385.00
Chair Set, Dining, Gustav Stickley, 3 Horizontal Slats, c.1907, 6 .... 3410.00
Chair Set, Dining, Jacobean Style, Cane Panel, Oak, 6 .... 335.00
Chair Set, Dining, L. & J. G. Stickley, No. 1340, c.1910, 12 .... 1875.00
Chair Set, Dining, Leather Upholstered Back, Floral Frame, 10 .... 3575.00
Chair Set, Dining, Pierced Vasiform Splat, Slip Seat, Mahogany, 6 .... 665.00
Chair Set, Dining, Queen Anne, Urn Shaped Splat, Slip Seat, 6 .... 1325.00
Chair Set, Dining, Rolled Crest Rail Over Tub Back, Mahogany, 12 .... 3100.00
Chair Set, Dining, Shaped Rail, Vasiform Splat, Mahogany, 6 .... 2850.00
Chair Set, Dining, Shell & Serpent, French, Mahogany, c.1900, 10 .... 2100.00
Chair Set, Dining, Spindle Back, Rush Seat, Ash, 6 .... 825.00
Chair Set, Dutch, Vasiform Splat, Balloon Seat, Shell Knees, 6 .... 3520.00
Chair Set, Elizabethan Revival, Grain Painted, 3 .... 275.00
Chair Set, Empire, Balloon Back, America, Carved Rosewood, 10 .... 3575.00
Chair Set, Fiddleback, Carved Mahogany, America, c.1840, 6 .... 1000.00
Chair Set, Fiddleback, Cream & Green Stenciling, 19th Century, 6 .... 1525.00
Chair Set, Fiddleback, Yellow Outline Stencils, Kentucky, 6 .... 775.00
Chair Set, G. Nelson, Curved Back Rail, Round Cushion Seat, 10 .... 3630.00
Chair Set, Garden, Atlanta Stove Works, Cast Iron, 3 .... 335.00
Chair Set, George III, Mahogany, Satinwood Inlaid, 2 Armchairs, 4 .... 1550.00
Chair Set, George III, Mahogany, Serpentine Pierced Crest, 8 .... 1875.00
Chair Set, George III, Parcel Gilt, Ebonized, Caned Seat, 1800, 4 .... 1350.00
Chair Set, George III, Scroll On Crest, 2 Armchairs, 8 .... 8150.00
Chair Set, Georgian Style, Carved Mahogany, 8 .... 1800.00
Chair Set, Georgian Style, Painted Brown, Gilt Design, 6 .... 5500.00
Chair Set, Half Spindle, Stenciled, Flame Grain Mahogany, 6 .... 1500.00
Chair Set, Hepplewhite, Mahogany, Brocade Slip Seat, Armchair, 6 .... 750.00
Chair Set, Hitchcock, Rabbit Ear, Stenciled, 6 .... 2400.00
Chair Set, Hongmu, Pierced & Carved Back, 30 1/2 In., 4 .... 775.00
Chair Set, Iron, Vinyl Upholstered Cushion, Medallion Back, 4 .... 1000.00
Chair Set, Jacobean Style, Carved Back, Grapes & Birds, c.1890, 4 .... 495.00
Chair Set, Ladder Back, 3 Slats, Turned Finials, Rush Seat, 6 .... 150.00
Chair Set, Ladder Back, Gustav Stickley, 6 .... 3575.00
Chair Set, Ladder Back, Red & Black Graining, Cane Seat, 6 .... 550.00
Chair Set, Ladder Back, Red & Black Graining, Floral On Crest, 4 .... 900.00
Chair Set, Ladder Back, Rush Seat, Maple, 2 Armchairs, 4 .... 600.00
Chair Set, Louis XV, Walnut, Upholstered Serpentine Seat, 8 .... 1350.00
Chair Set, Louix XV, Walnut, Upholstered Back, Padded Seat, 8 .... 1550.00
Chair Set, Pennsylvania, Gray, Black & Yellow Striping, Rose, 6 .... 1200.00
Chair Set, Plank Bottom, Painted Rose Design, 1860, 4 .... 900.00
Chair Set, Plywood & Tubular Steel, Herman Miller, 1946, 5 .... 1485.00
Chair Set, Press Back, Oak, Refinished, 4 .... 400.00
Chair Set, Pub, English, Yew Wood, Plank Bottom, 4 ....*Illus* 800.00
Chair Set, Queen Anne, Walnut, 1880–1900, 8 .... 6325.00

◆◆◆

Old heating grates of iron have a new use. Put them on the outdoor
mat to be used as mud scrapers.

◆◆◆

Furniture, Chair Set, Sheraton, Curly Maple, Caned Seats, 6

Chair Set, Rabbit Ear, Curly Maple, 1820–40, 4 ....*Illus*   825.00
Chair Set, Regency, Brass & Ebony Inlay On Crest, Slip Seat, 6 ....   450.00
Chair Set, Regency, Brass Inlaid Rosewood, 2 Armchairs, 6 .... 4675.00
Chair Set, Regency, X–Form Splat, Mahogany, 2 Armchairs, 8 .... 7800.00
Chair Set, Rope & Turned Crest Rail, Caned Seat, Curly Maple, 6 .... 7000.00
Chair Set, Rope Turnings Around Crest & Over Arms, 4 .... 2200.00
Chair Set, Rose Carved Crest Rail, Saber Legs, Maple, 4 ....   165.00
Chair Set, Sheraton, Bamboo Style, Painted Yellow, c.1810, 5 .... 1350.00
Chair Set, Sheraton, Curly Maple, Caned Seats, 6 ....*Illus* 6600.00
Chair Set, Sheraton, Faux Rosewood, 6 ....   632.50
Chair Set, Sheraton, Worn Black, Gold Striping, 2 Armchairs, 12 ....   900.00
Chair Set, Shield Back, Wheat Sheath Splat, Mahogany, 4 ....   775.00
Chair Set, Slipper, Rectangular Back & Seat, 4 ....   615.00
Chair Set, Spindle Back, Yellow & Green Striping, Gold Stencil, 6 ....   600.00
Chair Set, Spindle Rod Back, Wavy Crest Rail, Shaped Seat, 5 .... 1100.00

Furniture, Chair Set, Pub, English, Yew Wood, Plank Bottom, 4

Furniture, Chair Set, Rabbit Ear, Curly Maple, 1820–40, 4

Furniture, Chair Set, Wallace Nutting, Queen Anne, Mahogany, 4

Chair Set, Square Back, 7 Slats, Arts & Crafts, Oak, 6 .... 715.00
Chair Set, Thumb Back, Sponge Painted Seats, Painted Design, 6 .... 4900.00
Chair Set, Tub Shape, South America, Twig & Leather, 4 .... 145.00
Chair Set, Vase Splat, Shaped Crest, Cane Seat, Maple, 4 .... 1000.00
Chair Set, Wallace Nutting, Ladder Back, 5 Slats, Sausage, 4 .... 1045.00
Chair Set, Wallace Nutting, Queen Anne, Mahogany, 4 ....*Illus* 2090.00
Chair Set, Wicker, Cabriole Legs, 4 .... 950.00
Chair Set, William IV, Curved Crest, Upholstered Seat, 4 .... 3100.00
Chair Set, Windsor Style, Spindle Back, Vasiform Splat, 5 .... 550.00
Chair Set, Windsor, Arrow Back, Bamboo, Black Paint, Striping, 4 .... 340.00
Chair Set, Windsor, Bamboo, 5 .... 550.00
Chair Set, Windsor, Bamboo, Arrow Slat, Refinished, 6 .... 600.00
Chair Set, Windsor, Bow Back, 9 Spindles, 4 .... 4250.00
Chair Set, Windsor, Bow Back, 9 Spindles, Saddle Seat, 3 .... 1650.00
Chair Set, Windsor, Bow Back, Plank Set, E. Tebbets, c.1820, 6 .... 2475.00
Chair Set, Windsor, Fan Back, New England, c.1790, 6 .... 4700.00
Chair Set, Windsor, Step Down, Rake Back, c.1790, 6 .... 2950.00
Chair Set, Windsor, Yew Wood, England, 4 ....*Illus* 1000.00
Chair Table, Mustard Paint, Sponged Design, c.1830 .... 2300.00
Chair Table, New England, Remnants of Original Paint 4500.00
Chair Table, Paneled Back, Center Drop–Down Table, Pine, 71 In. 495.00
Chair Table, Pine, Lift Top, Hudson Valley, Green Paint, Small 2300.00
Chair, , McHugh, Oak, 2 Horizontal Slat, Rush Seat, 1 Stretcher 300.00
Chair, 1/2 Spindle, Gold & Black Over Yellow Paint 210.00
Chair, Adirondack, Arms, Pair 695.00
Chair, Adirondack, Rhododendron Root, Arms .... 450.00 To 632.50
Chair, American Gothic, Stump Work Upholstery 605.00
Chair, Arrow–Back, Rabbit Ears, Bamboo Turning, Plank Seat, Brown 100.00
Chair, Arrow–Back, Yellow & Orange Striping, Child's, 18 1/2 In. 125.00
Chair, Balloon Back, Needlepoint Upholstery, Mahogany, Pair 385.00
Chair, Balloon Back, Walnut, Fruit Carvings, Velvet Seat 125.00

Furniture, Chair Set, Windsor,
Yew Wood, England

Furniture, Chair, Ladder Back, 18th Century
Furniture, Chair, Bookkeeper's, Windsor, 21 In.

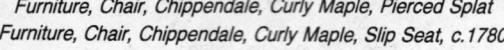

Furniture, Chair, Chippendale, Curly Maple, Pierced Splat
Furniture, Chair, Chippendale, Curly Maple, Slip Seat, c.1780

Furniture, Chair, Chippendale,
Mahogany, c.1760

Chair, Bamboo, Black Repaint	55.00
Chair, Banister Back, Gold Freehand Painted, Black	3850.00
Chair, Banister Back, Maple, Rush Seat, Turned Legs & Posts	250.00
Chair, Banister Back, Open Crest, Spanish Feet, Rush Seat, N. H.	1100.00
Chair, Banister Back, Rush Seat, Painted Maple, 1750s	1250.00
Chair, Banister Back, Sausage Turnings, Shaped Arms, Rush Seat	700.00
Chair, Banister Back, Scrolled Arms, Split Spindles	950.00
Chair, Banister Back, Shaped Crest, Black Paint, Rush Seat	200.00
Chair, Barrel Back, Gilt Lion, 12 Spindles, Walnut, c.1735, Pair	10000.00
Chair, Barrel Back, Tapered Spindles, Dipped Seat, Walnut	1350.00
Chair, Bookkeeper's, Oak, Barrel Back, Cane Seat, Tapering Legs	198.00
Chair, Bookkeeper's, Windsor, 21 In. _____*Illus*	165.00
Chair, C. Rohlfs, Tall Art Nouveau Back, Overhanging Seat, 52 In.	7700.00
Chair, Captain's, Bentwood Arms	55.00
Chair, Carved, Northwind Face, Mahogany, c.1890	350.00
Chair, Ceremonial, Twisting Dragons, Ivory Eyes, Oriental	2450.00
Chair, Charles Eames, Molded Plywood, c.1946, Pair	850.00
Chair, Charles Eames, Molded Plywood, Pair	852.50
Chair, Child's, Bliss, Alphabet	325.00
Chair, Child's, Carved Acanthus Leaves, Foot Rest, Mahogany	1650.00
Chair, Child's, Ladder Back, 2 Slats, Splint Seat, Arms 18 In.	85.00
Chair, Child's, Ladder Back, Arms Red, Gold, Black, 19 In.	75.00
Chair, Child's, Ladder Back, Rush Seat, American, 19th Century	65.00
Chair, Child's, Plank Seat, Spindle Back, Arms	85.00
Chair, Child's, Rattan, Fan Back	345.00
Chair, Child's, Victorian, Embroidered Horsehair Cover, Rosewood	385.00
Chair, Child's, Windsor, Bow Back, 25 In.	200.00
Chair, Child's, Windsor, Bow Back, Light Blue, Yellow Striped	1980.00
Chair, Child's, Windsor, Elm, Oak, England, 1800	1984.00
Chair, Child's, Windsor, Fan Back, Knuckle Arm, 18th Century	2475.00
Chair, Chippendale, Carved Mahogany, Molded Ears	3520.00
Chair, Chippendale, Carved Mahogany, Upholstered Seat, 1790, Pair	550.00
Chair, Chippendale, Cherry, Refinished, New England, 1770–1800	385.00
Chair, Chippendale, Curly Maple, Pierced Splat _____*Illus*	2090.00
Chair, Chippendale, Curly Maple, Slip Seat, c.1780 _____*Illus*	715.00
Chair, Chippendale, Gothic Pierced Splat, Mahogany, c.1760	2420.00
Chair, Chippendale, Gothic Splat, Ball & Claw Feet	4675.00
Chair, Chippendale, Mahogany, 3 Ribbon Back, Serpentine Seat, 1790	885.00
Chair, Chippendale, Mahogany, c.1760 _____*Illus*	550.00
Chair, Chippendale, Mahogany, Rush Seat, 1770–1800, Pair	1980.00
Chair, Chippendale, Mahogany, Upholstered Seat, Refinished	2860.00
Chair, Chippendale, Mahogany, Upholstered, Raked Molded Ears	330.00
Chair, Chippendale, Maple, New England, 1770–1800	525.00
Chair, Chippendale, Pierced Interlaced Strapwork, Mahogany, 1760	4650.00
Chair, Chippendale, Pierced Splat, Shell Carvings, Mahogany	3750.00
Chair, Chippendale, Raked Molded Ears, Rush Slip Seat, 1760–95	715.00
Chair, Chippendale, Red & Black Graining, Rush Seat	715.00

Chair, Chippendale, Rush Seat, Massachusetts, 1770, Pair 995.00
Chair, Chippendale, Scalloped Apron, Shell Crest, Mahogany 4500.00
Chair, Chippendale, Slip Seat, Cherry, 19th Century 275.00
Chair, Commode, Comb Back, Saddle Seat, Grain Painted, 19th C. 65.00
Chair, Commode, Corner, Arms Over Pierced Splats, Mahogany 1045.00
Chair, Commode, Roundabout, Chippendale, Refinished 2200.00
Chair, Commode, String Painted, High Comb Back, 19th Century 60.00
Chair, Commode, Windsor, Yellow Over Blue, Removable Hole Cover 255.00
Chair, Comode, Queen Anne, Vase-Shaped Splat, Walnut 6000.00
Chair, Corner, 2 Slats, Cane Seat, Flared Rabbit Ear Posts 175.00
Chair, Corner, 2 Vasiform Pierced Splats, Rush Seat, Oak, 28 In. 715.00
Chair, Corner, 2 Vasiform Splats, Out-Turned Arms, Walnut 995.00
Chair, Corner, Balloon Seat, Pierced Slats, Walnut 3100.00
Chair, Corner, Chippendale, Mahogany, Carved Knees, England 1350.00
Chair, Corner, Chippendale, Slip Seat, Hard & Soft Woods 650.00
Chair, Corner, Curved Arm Rail, Rush Seat, Hardwoods, 29 1/2 In. 400.00
Chair, Corner, George II, Urnform Splats, Mahogany, 1740 .... 2640.00
Chair, Corner, Georgian Style, Carved Arms, Mahogany, Pair 775.00
Chair, Corner, High Comb Back, Pierced Backsplat, Rush Seat 250.00
Chair, Corner, Maple, Rush Seat, Refinished, Curved Armrail 225.00
Chair, Corner, Paper Rush Seat, Maple 600.00
Chair, Corner, Square Legs, Pierced Vase Splats, Rush Seat, Maple 2400.00
Chair, Corner, Woven Split Seat, Black Paint, Hardwood 450.00
Chair, Cottage, Cane Seat, Hand Painted Back 40.00
Chair, Curved Back, Brass Inlaid Ebony, Scrolled Arms, Pair 2200.00
Chair, Dark Mahogany, Scrolled Arms, c.1840 .... 1225.00
Chair, David Coutant, New York City, Painted Black, c.1780 .... 3550.00
Chair, Desk, Child's, Light Oak, 14 1/2 In. 55.00
Chair, Dressing, Shaker, Mt. Lebanon, Varnish, Taped Seat, 1930 .... 525.00
Chair, Eileen Gray, Tubular Chromed Steel & Leather, c.1930, Pair 8850.00
Chair, Empire Revival, Walnut, Inlaid, Goose Turnings, Upholstered 475.00
Chair, Federal, Child's, Saber Legs, Bird's-Eye Veneers 445.00
Chair, Federal, Shield Back, Pair 357.00
Chair, Ferdinand Kramer, Black Painted Beechwood, c.1927, Pair 1350.00
Chair, Folding, Victorian, Bamboo, Painted, Carpet Upholstery 60.00
Chair, Formed As Swan, Upholstered Seat, Italian, Walnut 2550.00
Chair, Frank Lloyd Wright, Rolled Arms, Loose Cushion, c.1917 .... 4675.00
Chair, Garden, Iron, Foliage, Black Repaint 200.00
Chair, Garden, Iron, Lily of Valley, Barrel Back, W. McHose & Co. 1500.00
Chair, George III, Ladder Back, Mahogany, Over-Upholstered Seat, 4 .... 4400.00
Chair, George III, Pierced Back Headed By Pagoda, Japanned 2200.00
Chair, George III, Shaped Ears, Gothic Splat, Mahogany 1200.00
Chair, George III, Shaped Rectangular Back, Scrolled Arms 3950.00
Chair, George III, Shield Back, Arms, Painted, Upholstered, c.1780 .... 4950.00
Chair, George III, Upholstered Back & Seat, Mahogany, Pair 9900.00
Chair, Green Paint, Black Striping, Black Floral, Plank Seat, Pair 150.00
Chair, Green, Gold & Red Floral, Black Paint, P. Wilder, c.1860 .... 650.00
Chair, Grotto, Leaf Pine, Dolphin Arms, Italian, Pair ....*Illus* 3200.00
Chair, Gustav Stickley, 4 Curved Splats, Arms, No. 324, Oak, c.1907 .... 665.00
Chair, Gustav Stickley, Fixed Back, Arms, 5 Vertical Slats, c.1904 .... 1430.00
Chair, Gustav Stickley, No. 338, Inlaid Oak, Rush Seat, 3 Slat Back 3850.00
Chair, Harden, Oak, Upholstered Seat, Arms 150.00
Chair, Hepplewhite, Slip Seat, Dark Varnish, Cherry, 39 In. 60.00
Chair, High Back, Spindle, Baker 90.00
Chair, Hitchcock Type, Yellow & Green Striping, Balloon Seat 175.00
Chair, Hitchcock, Black Paint, Gold Fruit Stencil, 1820s 500.00
Chair, Hitchcock, Plank Seat, Burgundy Paint, Stenciled Fruit 125.00
Chair, Hoffmann, Upholstered Back, Ebonized Ash, 1905 .... 6650.00
Chair, Hoffmann, Upholstered, 8 Spindled Arms, Beechwood, c.1905 .... 1100.00
Chair, Horn, Fur Covered Seat, America, 1890 ....*Illus* 1100.00
Chair, Hunzinger, Lollipop 650.00
Chair, Hunzinger, Photographer's, Gold Incised 4675.00
Chair, Hunzinger, Pipe-Like Spindles 550.00

Chair, Iron Arms, Fern Pattern, 19th Century 440.00
Chair, J. & J. W. Meeks, Stanton Hall, Arms, Rosewood, c.1860 .... 3745.00
Chair, Jacobean, Carved Lion Head Finials, Upholstered, Hardwood 250.00
Chair, L. & J. G. Stickley, Pair 147.00
Chair, Ladder Back, 18th Century ...._Illus_ 550.00
Chair, Ladder Back, 2 Slats, Rush Seat, Arms 275.00
Chair, Ladder Back, 3 Slats, Rush Seat, Brown Finish 85.00
Chair, Ladder Back, 3 Slats, Woven Split Hickory Seat 65.00
Chair, Ladder Back, 4 Arched Slats, Paper Rush Seat, 41 3/4 In. 275.00
Chair, Ladder Back, 4 Graduated Slats, Added Rockers, Rush Seat 175.00
Chair, Ladder Back, 4 Slats, Bentwood Arms, Splint Seat 70.00
Chair, Ladder Back, 4 Slats, Ram's Horn Scroll Arms, Rush Seat 600.00
Chair, Ladder Back, 4 Slats, Shaped Arms, Rush Seat, 46 3/4 In. 275.00
Chair, Ladder Back, 5 Arched Slats, Arms, Splint Seat, Pair 3450.00
Chair, Ladder Back, 5 Arched Slats, Bulbous Stretcher, Arms, Maple 4250.00
Chair, Ladder Back, 5 Slats, Bulbous Stretcher, Arms, Maple 3960.00
Chair, Ladder Back, Ash, Mushroom Finials, x Form Stretcher, Arms 1650.00
Chair, Ladder Back, Painted, Inscribed Father Freedom 1818 .... 175.00
Chair, Ladder Back, Rush Seat, Black Over Red, Pair 350.00
Chair, Ladder Back, Sausage Turned, Grain Painted, 1890s 2600.00
Chair, Ladder Back, Shaker, No. 7 .... 1980.00
Chair, Laminated Cardboard, Compressed Scroll, Gehry, 1970, Pair 5300.00
Chair, Leather Upholstery, Soriana, c.1970, Pair 1350.00
Chair, Library, Regency, Opens To Form Steps, Mahogany 5000.00
Chair, Lily of The Valley, Cast Iron, 33 x 27 In. ...._Illus_ 1650.00

Furniture, Chair, Grotto, Leaf Pine,
Dolphin Arms, Italian, Pair

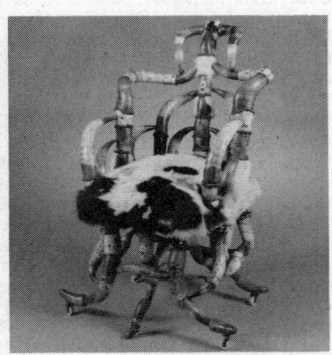

Furniture, Chair, Horn, Fur Covered Seat,
America, 1890

Furniture, Chair, Lily of The Valley, Cast Iron,
33 x 27 In.

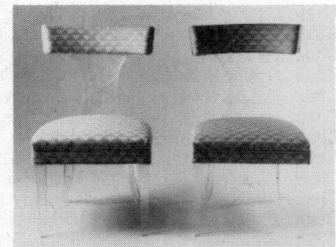

Furniture, Chair, Lucite, Upholstered Seat,
35 1/2 In.

Chair, Limbert, 5 Slats, Oak, Box Spring, Pair 480.00
Chair, Limbert, No. 81 .... 6600.00
Chair, Limbert, Tall Trapezoidal Cutout Back, 45 In. 2450.00
Chair, Lolling, Edwardian, Mahogany, Scrolling Out Arms, England 225.00
Chair, Lolling, Edwardian, Scrolling Arms, Mahogany, England 250.00
Chair, Lolling, Federal, Mahogany, Molded Arms, Upholstered, c.1800 .... 5600.00
Chair, Lolling, Green Silk Brocade Upholstery, Mahogany 275.00
Chair, Lolling, Green Silk Upholstery, Mahogany Frame 500.00
Chair, Lolling, Hepplewhite, Mahogany, Upholstered, String Inlay 2100.00
Chair, Louis XVI–Style, Laurel Carved Back, Fluted Legs 335.00
Chair, Lounge, Harry Bertoia, Steel Wire, Black Plastic Coating 137.00
Chair, Lounge, Molded Fiberglass, Leather Covered, Italy, 1969 .... 1100.00
Chair, Lucite, Trapezoidal Upholstered Seat, Shield Back, Jackson 3550.00
Chair, Lucite, Upholstered Seat, 35 1/2 In. ....*Illus* 412.00
Chair, Mahogany, New England, Upholstered Seat, 18th Century 2750.00
Chair, Martha Washington Style, Silk Upholstery, Mahogany 2425.00
Chair, Molded Crest Over 3 Uprights, Mahogany, c.1790, Pair 1650.00
Chair, Moravian, Plank Seat, Carved Back Scrolls, 1830 .... 115.00
Chair, Moravian, W–Shaped Splats, Hardwood, Pair 400.00
Chair, Morris, Gustav Stickley, Adjustable Back, Flat Arm, c.1910 .... 3800.00
Chair, Morris, Gustav Stickley, Drop Arms, Spindle 9350.00
Chair, Morris, Gustav Stickley, Flat Arm Over 5 Slats, c.1912 .... 4620.00
Chair, Morris, Gustav Stickley, No. 2342, Arms, Adjustable Back 6380.00
Chair, Morris, Gustave Stickley, No. 332 .... 5500.00
Chair, Morris, Gustav Stickley, No. 332, Adjustable Back, Flat Arm 4100.00
Chair, Morris, Gustav Stickley, Spindled 8250.00
Chair, Morris, L. & J. G. Stickley, Adjustable, Flat Arm, 1912–1918 .... 825.00
Chair, Morris, Limbert, Broad Slanted Arms, Corbel–Type Feet 5225.00
Chair, Morris, Limbert, No. 510, Flat Arm Over 5 Slats, 1912 .... 1750.00
Chair, Music, Lacquered & Mother–of–Pearl Inlay, 2 Piece 605.00
Chair, Nakashima, Square Spindles, Cherry, c.1960, Pair 550.00
Chair, Oak, Carved, Arms, Needlework Seat & Back 225.00
Chair, Oak, Carved, Arms, Vulcan At Forge, Kirk By Kendal, 54 In. 475.00
Chair, Office, Oak, Swivel Seat, Slat Back 120.00
Chair, Outward Turned–Down Arms, Mahogany, c.1900 .... 55.00
Chair, Pilgrim, c.1680 .... 3200.00
Chair, Queen Anne, Banister Back, Ash Split Seat, 1770–1810, Pair 800.00
Chair, Queen Anne, Mahogany, Slipper Foot, Upholstered Seat 3850.00
Chair, Queen Anne, Nut Brown, Duck Feet, Vase Splat, 19th Century 175.00
Chair, Queen Anne, Reeded Banister Back, Rush Seat, N. H. 950.00
Chair, Queen Anne, Rush Seat, Vase Splat, Black Repaint 75.00
Chair, Queen Anne, Vase–Shaped Splat, Walnut 2640.00
Chair, Queen Anne, Walnut, Leather Upholstery, 1750, 41 In. 9350.00
Chair, Ram's Head Mounts, Cowhide Upholstery, Silver Plated 1000.00
Chair, Recliner, Oak, Mission, Beast Heads, Royal Chair Co. 500.00
Chair, Recliner, Victorian, Black Horsehair, Large 175.00
Chair, Regency Style, Curved Crest Rail, Slip Seat, Brass 1045.00
Chair, Regency, Green Painted, Open Arms, Caned Seat, Pair 3300.00
Chair, Regency, Mahogany, Caned Tub–Shaped Back, Upholstered Seat 4500.00
Chair, Regency, Painted, Caned, Cushion, Open Arms, 1810, Pair 6100.00
Chair, Renaissance Revival, Walnut, Rectangular Tufted Back, Seat 155.00
FURNITURE, Chair, Rocker, see Furniture, Rocker
Chair, Rococo Revival, Rosewood Laminated, 1860 ....*Illus* 425.00
Chair, Rococo, Arched Shell–Carved Crest, Portugal, Walnut 385.00
Chair, Rosewood Laminated, Upholstered Seat, c.1860 ....*Illus* 400.00
Chair, Roycroft, 1 Slat Back, Leather Seat, 44 x 17 In. 650.00
Chair, Roycroft, Ladder Back, Tacked–On Leather, Brown Finish 1100.00
Chair, Roycroft, Macmurdo Feet, Leather Seat, Dark, Wilder, No. 35 .... 550.00
Chair, Rush Seat, Curly Maple With Tiger Stripes, 19th Century 775.00
Chair, Rush Seat, Painted Design, 1815–1825, Pair 650.00
Chair, Saber Leg, Pierced Back Splats, Tiger Maple, Pair 150.00
Chair, Sack Back, Allover Black Paint, Gold Striping, 1770–1790 .... 2000.00
Chair, Sack Back, Horseshoe–Shaped Seat, Black, Maple & Pine 1100.00

Furniture, Chair, Rosewood Laminated,
Upholstered Seat, c.1860

Furniture, Chair, Rococo Revival,
Rosewood Laminated, 1860

Furniture, Chair, Windsor,
Continuous Arm,
Spindle Back, Black

◆◆

Remove the rust from iron by soaking the piece in kerosene for
twenty–four hours or use any one of several commercial prepara-
tions made for the removal of rust. Wash, dry, and coat the piece
with a light oil to protect it.

◆◆

Chair, Sack Back, Windsor, 7 Spindles, Tapering Legs, 1780	3850.00
Chair, Savonarola, Griffin Pierced Splats, Italy, Walnut, Pair	715.00
Chair, Scrolled Arms, Saber Legs, Vase Splat, Cane Seat, Maple	100.00
Chair, Scrolled Rail, Pierced Splat, Scrolled Arms, Stanton	195.00
Chair, Seymour, Pointed Arch Back Splats, Pair	6600.00
Chair, Shaker, Arms, Maple, Presentation, 1910–1920	9350.00
Chair, Shaker, Cherry, Red Stain	5500.00
Chair, Shaker, No. 7, Ivory & Orange Tape, Arms	750.00
Chair, Shaker, Tilter, Harvard, Mass.	4200.00
Chair, Shaker, Watervliet	3000.00
Chair, Shell Crest, Vasiform Splat, Slip Seat, Mahogany, c.1760	550.00
Chair, Sheraton, Black Grain, Stencil, Balloon Painted Rush, Pair	350.00
Chair, Sheraton, Mustard Painted Design, Cane Seat, 1815, Pair	1675.00
Chair, Sheraton, Rope & Turned Crest Rail, Splint Seat	275.00
Chair, Shield Back, Philadelphia, Mahogany, c.1790	2200.00
Chair, Slat Back, Arms, Hudson River Valley, Splint Seat, c.1680	6800.00
Chair, Slat Back, Arms, Red Over Black Paint, Rush Seat	2310.00
Chair, Slipper, Belter, Corset Back, Rosewood, c.1840	2600.00
Chair, Snowshoe, Bentwood, Arms, Leather Webbed, Trestle, 35 In.	415.00
Chair, Spindle Back, Spring Cushion Seat, 1912, 32 1/2 In.	825.00
Chair, Spindle Splats, Caned Seat, Bamboo Turned Pine	330.00
Chair, Splat Back, Paw Front Feet, Arms, Oak	65.00
Chair, Square Open Work Back, X–Form Splat, Bowed Arms, Painted	465.00
Chair, Stag Horn, Upholstered, Arms	1000.00
Chair, Steer Horn, 14 Horns Each, Pair	1500.00
Chair, Streamlined, Metal Frame, Red Vinyl, Royal Chrome, 1938	165.00
Chair, Swan, Molded Fiberglass Shell, Orange Upholstery, Jacobsen	110.00
Chair, Thonet, Hoffman, Brown Beech, Leather, 1905	2250.00
Chair, Upholstered Back & Seat, Black Forest, Walnut, 37 In.	885.00
Chair, Vase–Form Splats, Balloon–Shaped Seat, Red Walnut, Pair	2750.00
Chair, Victorian, Balloon Back, Grape & Floral Crest	90.00
Chair, Victorian, Balloon Back, Upholstered Seat	55.00
Chair, Victorian, Mahogany, Balloon Back, Arms, Black Needlepoint	350.00
Chair, Victorian, Walnut, Balloon Back, Floral Crest, Needlepoint	90.00
Chair, Wainscot, Carved Rosettes & Geometrics, Oak, 17th Century	2750.00
Chair, Walnut Prie–Dieu, Beadwork Seat & Back, England, 1885	395.00
Chair, Wicker, Square Back, Rounded Arms	198.00

Chair, Wicker, Yoke Back, Arms, Deep Apron	115.00
Chair, Wicker, Yoke Back, Deep Apron, x Stretcher, Arms	105.00
Chair, William & Mary, Banister Back, Dark Varnish, Splint Seat	1045.00
Chair, William & Mary, High Back, Arms, Walnut, 17th Century	825.00
Chair, William & Mary, Leather Back & Seat, Boston, c.1735	5500.00
Chair, Windsor, Added Rockers, Windsor, Bow Back	250.00
Chair, Windsor, Arms, Firehouse, Swivel, Painted	4125.00
Chair, Windsor, Arms, Needlepoint Seat, Early 20th Century	135.00
Chair, Windsor, Arrow Spindles Over 1/2 Spindles, Saddle Seat	275.00
Chair, Windsor, Bamboo Turnings, Saddle Seat, 16 1/2 In.	300.00
Chair, Windsor, Bamboo, 7 Spindles, Shaped Seat	475.00
Chair, Windsor, Bamboo, Bow Back, 9 Spindle, Saddle Seat	200.00
Chair, Windsor, Bamboo, Double–Comb Crest, Saddle Seat	475.00
Chair, Windsor, Birdcage, 1820s	750.00
Chair, Windsor, Birdcage, Round Crest Medallions, 1800–30, Pair	1100.00
Chair, Windsor, Bow Back, 7 Spindles, Bamboo Turnings, Saddle Seat	450.00
Chair, Windsor, Bow Back, 7 Spindles, Saddle Seat, H Stretcher	275.00
Chair, Windsor, Bow Back, 7 Spindles, Splayed Base, Saddle Seat	225.00
Chair, Windsor, Bow Back, 9 Spindles, Saddle Seat	600.00
Chair, Windsor, Bow Back, 9 Spindles, Saddle Seat, Arms	300.00
Chair, Windsor, Bow Back, 9 Spindles, Splayed Base, Saddle Seat	375.00
Chair, Windsor, Bow Back, Bamboo Turnings, 9 Spindles	200.00
Chair, Windsor, Bow Back, Bamboo Turnings, Saddle Seat, Arms	550.00
Chair, Windsor, Bow Back, Cherry Arms, Hard & Softwood	1300.00
Chair, Windsor, Bow Back, H Stretcher, Arms, Black Repaint	750.00
Chair, Windsor, Bow Back, Oval Seat, Spindle Back, 36 1/2 In.	500.00
Chair, Windsor, Bow Back, Refinished	175.00
Chair, Windsor, Bow Back, Saddle Seat, Scrolled Arms	450.00
Chair, Windsor, Bow Back, Striping, Brushed Grain, Added Rockers	700.00
Chair, Windsor, Brace Back, Leather Saddle Seat, Arms	900.00
Chair, Windsor, Brace Back, Refinished, England, 14 1/2 In.	75.00
Chair, Windsor, Brace Back, Saddle Seat, Curved Arms, Pair	600.00
Chair, Windsor, Brace Back, Turned Spindles, Saddle Seat	400.00
Chair, Windsor, Carved Ear, Fanback, 7 Spindles	1050.00
Chair, Windsor, Carved Ear, Fanback, 9 Spindles, Black Paint	1900.00
Chair, Windsor, Child's, Sack Back, Black Paint, Late 18th Century	1100.00
Chair, Windsor, Comb Back, 9 Spindles, Elliptical Seat, Green	5775.00
Chair, Windsor, Comb Back, Knuckle Arms, Carved Ear Crest Rail	4850.00
Chair, Windsor, Comb Back, Molded Edge Seat, Black Paint	650.00
Chair, Windsor, Comb Back, Oval Saddle Seat, Black Paint	3000.00
Chair, Windsor, Continuous Arm, Saddle Seat	115.00
Chair, Windsor, Continuous Arm, Spindle Back, Black ....*Illus*	6500.00
Chair, Windsor, Continuous, Black Paint, New York, 1785–1800	1100.00
Chair, Windsor, Double–Bobbin Turned, Black Paint, c.1830	1150.00
Chair, Windsor, Fan Back, Arms, Saddle Seat	550.00
Chair, Windsor, Fanback, 7 Spindles, Carved Ears, 18th Century	2900.00
Chair, Windsor, Fanback, 7 Spindles, Saddle Seat, Black, Trumble	2310.00
Chair, Windsor, Fanback, 9 Spindles, Vase Turnings, 18th Century	7700.00
Chair, Windsor, Fanback, Bowed Crest, Bamboo Legs, 36 In.	1100.00
Chair, Windsor, Fanback, Gray Traces, Conn. River Valley, Pair	775.00
Chair, Windsor, Fanback, Red Paint, 1790–1800, New England	1775.00
Chair, Windsor, I. C. Tuttle	3400.00
Chair, Windsor, Low Back, 9 Spindles, Saddle Seat, Green Repaint	650.00
Chair, Windsor, Medallion Back, Bamboo	125.00
Chair, Windsor, New England, 1800–1820, 36 1/2 In.	1760.00
Chair, Windsor, Rod Back, 6 Spindle, Green Painted, Pair	675.00
Chair, Windsor, Rod Back, Refinished, Pair	275.00
Chair, Windsor, Sack Back, 7 Spindles, 38 In.	3850.00
Chair, Windsor, Sack Back, Knuckle Arms	460.00
Chair, Windsor, Sack Back, Lancaster County	4510.00
Chair, Windsor, Sheet Steel & Tin, Blue Paint	450.00
Chair, Windsor, Spindle Back, Arms, Elm & Fruitwood	225.00
Chair, Windsor, Spindle Back, Shaped Seat	100.00

Chair, Windsor, Writing Arm, J. C. Hubbard 3975.00
Chair, Windsor, Writing Arm, Sack Back, 1 Drawer, 7 Spindles 3575.00
Chair, Wing Back, Hepplewhite, Red & White Upholstery, Mahogany 2200.00
Chair, Wing, Child's, Pine, Brown Paint, 1880, 19 In. 135.00
Chair, Wing, Chippendale, America, 19th Century 675.00
Chair, Wing, Chippendale, Outward Scrolling Arms 225.00
Chair, Wing, Federal, Rope Legs, Carved Arms, Upholstered 6325.00
Chair, Wing, Green & Ivory Striped Upholstery, Fruitwood 825.00
Chair, Wing, Pine Base, Upholstered In Floral Design, 42 In. 700.00
Chair, Wing, Queen Anne, Crewel Upholstery, Knee Shells, Mahogany 3400.00
Chair, Wing, William & Mary, Elmwood, Cabriole Legs, 1700 .... 9900.00
Chair, Wire Mesh, Sculpted Back & Arms, 1944, 27 1/2 In. 275.00
Chair, Writing Arm, Drawer Under Seat & Arm, Comb Back 2000.00
Chair, York, Maple, Faux Rosewood Graining, Replaced Rush Seat 1320.00
Chaise Lounge, French Style, Upholstered, Cream Frame, 62 In. 220.00
Chaise Lounge, Wicker, Pink 1195.00
Chaise Lounge, Wicker, Scrolled Arms, Painted, 4 Ft. 11 In. 4120.00
Chaise Lounge, Wicker, White, 1930s 260.00
Chest, 2 Drawers, George III, Hinged Top, Oak, c.1785, 27 x 48 In. 440.00
Chest, 2 Drawers, Pilgrim Century, Replaced Ball Feet, Brasses 4400.00
Chest, 2 Over 4 Drawers, Bracket Feet, Walnut, 21 In. 3500.00
Chest, 2 Over 4 Drawers, Salmon Grain Paint, c.1810, 38 In. 5830.00
Chest, 3 Drawers, 4 Drawers, Facade, Maple, 43 x 35 3/4 In. 1600.00
Chest, 3 Drawers, Empire, Curly Maple, Pilasters, 16 x 8 x 18 In. 1300.00
Chest, 3 Drawers, Pine, Red Grained, Block Feet, 36 x 19 x 33 In. 55.00
Chest, 3 Drawers, Poplar, Grain Painted Mahogany, 37 x 38 In. 715.00
Chest, 3 Drawers, Traces of Old Black, Pine, 38 1/4 x 38 1/2 In. 800.00
Chest, 3 Over 5 Drawers, Walnut, c.1800 .... 6650.00
Chest, 4 Cock-Beaded Drawers, Fluted Quarter Columns, Mahogany 3900.00
Chest, 4 Drawers, Bird's-Eye Veneer, Sheraton, Maple, 38 In. 1125.00
Chest, 4 Drawers, Bronze Wreath Handles, Marble Top, 32 x 35 In. 4950.00
Chest, 4 Drawers, Cherry, Brass, All Original, 1824 .... 650.00
Chest, 4 Drawers, Cherry, Curly Maple & Walnut, 45 1/2 In. 475.00
Chest, 4 Drawers, Child's, Black Vinegar Graining, Pine & Poplar 625.00
Chest, 4 Drawers, Chippendale, Curly Maple 325.00
Chest, 4 Drawers, Chippendale, Dovetailed Case, Maple, 34 3/4 In. 2250.00
Chest, 4 Drawers, Chippendale, Serpentine Front, Mahogany, c.1780 .... 10000.00
Chest, 4 Drawers, Chippendale, Serpentine, Lighthouse Brasses 10000.00
Chest, 4 Drawers, Cock-Beaded, Curly Maple & Birch, 34 3/4 In. 1450.00
Chest, 4 Drawers, Cock-Beaded, George III, Mahogany, 29 x 44 In. 445.00
Chest, 4 Drawers, Cock-Beaded, Hepplewhite, Poplar, 40 x 18 In. 800.00
Chest, 4 Drawers, Cock-Beaded, Tiger Maple, c.1790 .... 7150.00
Chest, 4 Drawers, Cottage, Pine, Grained, Gallery & Shelf, 41 In. 225.00
Chest, 4 Drawers, Curly Maple & Cherry, c.1820, 43 1/4 In. 880.00
Chest, 4 Drawers, Curved Front Supports & Feet, Painted, 46 In. 2600.00
Chest, 4 Drawers, Dovetailed, Cherry, Square Corner Posts, 42 In. 550.00
Chest, 4 Drawers, Dovetailed, Empire, Curly Maple, 42 x 44 In. 650.00
Chest, 4 Drawers, Dovetailed, Sheraton, Cherry, Gallery, 44 3/4 In. 900.00
Chest, 4 Drawers, Drop Front, Cherry, Fluted Corners, Ogee Feet 1870.00
Chest, 4 Drawers, Empire, Cherry & Walnut, 44 1/2 x 43 In. 850.00
Chest, 4 Drawers, Empire, Maple With Curl, Poplar, Cherry, 41 In. 700.00
Chest, 4 Drawers, Federal, Bow Front, Inlaid Cherry, c.1810, 37 In. 4450.00
Chest, 4 Drawers, Federal, Bow Front, Mahogany, 34 In. 6050.00
Chest, 4 Drawers, Figured Drawer Fronts, Tiger Maple 1350.00
Chest, 4 Drawers, George III, Bow Front, Mahogany, c.1800, 33 In. 2200.00
Chest, 4 Drawers, George III, Serpentine Front, Mahogany, 34 In. 3575.00
Chest, 4 Drawers, Graduated, Cherry, Overhanging Top, 29 In. 3300.00
Chest, 4 Drawers, Graduated, Chippendale, Brasses, 1780s, Medium 8650.00
Chest, 4 Drawers, Graduated, Chippendale, Escutcheons, Brass Rings 2310.00
Chest, 4 Drawers, Graduated, Federal, Reeded & Shaped Legs, 1820 .... 1950.00
Chest, 4 Drawers, Graduated, Federal, Serpentine, 1790 .... 6050.00
Chest, 4 Drawers, Graduated, Hepplewhite, Cherry, Original Brasses 2500.00
Chest, 4 Drawers, Graduated, Serpentine Front, Cherry, 38 In. 7750.00

Chest, 4 Drawers, Graduated, Sheraton, Bow Front, Cherry, 39 In.	850.00
Chest, 4 Drawers, Graduated, Walnut, 42 x 37 1/2 In.	750.00
Chest, 4 Drawers, Hepplewhite, Flame Birch	3100.00
Chest, 4 Drawers, Hepplewhite, French Feet, Walnut, c.1800, 41 In.	4250.00
Chest, 4 Drawers, Hepplewhite, Inlaid Fronts, c.1785	5200.00
Chest, 4 Drawers, Hepplewhite, Scalloped Apron, Cherry, 37 3/4 In.	400.00
Chest, 4 Drawers, Hepplewhite, Scalloped, Mahogany, 37 1/2 In.	2000.00
Chest, 4 Drawers, Long, Shaped Skirt, Painted Red, Pine, 45 In.	1550.00
Chest, 4 Drawers, Overlapping, Cherry & Walnut, Miniature	300.00
Chest, 4 Drawers, Ring Pulls, Dark Red Paint, Pine, Miniature	200.00
Chest, 4 Drawers, Rope-Carved Feet, Mahogany Veneer, 41 1/2 In.	850.00
Chest, 4 Drawers, Sheraton, Curly Maple, Cherry, c.1820 ....Illus	880.00
Chest, 4 Drawers, Sheraton, Edge Beading, Walnut, 39 1/4 In.	1200.00
Chest, 4 Drawers, Sheraton, Pine & Poplar, 50 In.	350.00
Chest, 5 Drawers, Chippendale, Edge Beading, Mahogany, 35 x 39 In.	1000.00
Chest, 5 Drawers, Chippendale, Figured Maple, 45 5/8 In.	7150.00
Chest, 5 Drawers, Chippendale, Mahogany, England, 32 1/4 In.	1150.00
Chest, 5 Drawers, Cock-Beaded, Sheraton, Cherry, 43 1/4 In.	775.00
Chest, 5 Drawers, Empire, Cherry, Curly Maple, Pilasters, 50 In.	900.00
Chest, 5 Drawers, Original Brass Pulls, Poplar, Miniature	325.00
Chest, 5 Drawers, Sheraton, Curly Maple, c.1820, 45 In. ....Illus	2300.00
Chest, 5 Drawers, Sheraton, Reeded Stiles, Walnut, 47 x 40 In.	850.00
Chest, 5 Graduated Drawers, Ohio, Curly Maple, c.1820, 45 In.	2300.00
Chest, 6 Board, Blue, Carrying Handles, 18th Century, 18 x 43 In.	995.00
Chest, 6 Board, Green Paint, Rufus Porter Style Trees, 43 In.	2090.00
Chest, 6 Drawers, Acorn Finials, Scrolled Crest, Walnut, 73 In.	468.00
Chest, 6 Drawers, Chippendale, Walnut, 41 1/2 x 32 1/2 In.	1200.00
Chest, 6 Drawers, Curly Maple, Bracket Base	3850.00
Chest, 6 Drawers, G. Stickley, No. 902, Reverse-V Splash, 52 In.	4675.00
Chest, 6 Drawers, Graduated, Birch, Pine, 55 x 36 In.	8500.00
Chest, 6 Drawers, New England, Maple, c.1790, 36 In.	3100.00
Chest, 6 Drawers, Tiger Maple Banding, Walnut, 57 x 39 In.	4000.00
Chest, 6 Drawers, Yellow, Red Top, Cherry, 51 1/4 x 40 1/4 In.	4200.00
Chest, 7 Drawers, Chippendale, Curly Maple, c.1780, 59 1/2 In.	8800.00
Chest, 7 Drawers, Cock-Beaded, Cherry, 21 x 42 x 47 1/2 In.	800.00
Chest, 7 Drawers, Curly Maple Facade, Maple, 48 1/4 In.	4000.00
Chest, 7 Drawers, Graduated, Chippendale, Maple, 60 1/4 In.	6600.00
Chest, 8 Drawers, Chamfered Corners, Chestnut, 57 x 39 In.	7250.00
Chest, 8 Drawers, Cock-Beaded, Shaped Apron, Cherry, c.1810, 64 In.	7000.00
Chest, 8 Drawers, Diamond Banding, Curly Walnut, c.1790, 70 In.	9500.00
Chest, 8 Drawers, Federal, Mahogany, c.1790, 66 x 40 In.	2800.00
Chest, 8 Drawers, Hepplewhite, Cherry, 63 1/2 x 38 3/4 In.	7000.00
Chest, 8 Drawers, Oval Brass, Walnut, c.1790, 68 In.	7750.00
Chest, 9 Drawers, Arched Top Drawers, Bracket Feet	2700.00
Chest, 9 Drawers, Cock-Beaded, Figured Cherry, 44 In.	3100.00
Chest, 9 Drawers, Original Brasses, Walnut, c.1790, 60 In.	5250.00
Chest, 9 Drawers, Quarter Columns, Walnut, 18th Century, 40 In.	7000.00

Furniture, Chest, 4 Drawers, Sheraton, Curly Maple, Cherry, c.1820

Furniture, Chest, 5 Drawers, Sheraton, Curly Maple, c.1820, 45 In.

Furniture, Chest, Empire, Mahogany, 32 1/2 x 32 1/2 In.

Chest, 9 Drawers. Chippendale, Walnut, Fret Frieze, 66 In. 5000.00
Chest, Arched Top, Embossed Designs, Iron, North Africa, 58 In. 1650.00
Chest, Bachelor's, 3 Drawers, Bracket Feet, Walnut, 24 1/2 In. 715.00
Chest, Bachelor's, 3 Drawers, Pull–Out Trivet, Mahogany 198.50
Chest, Bachelor's, Block Front, Pull–Out Slide, Mahogany 500.00
Chest, Bachelor's, Bow Front, Pull–Out Slide, Mahogany, 35 In. 2650.00
Chest, Bird's–Eye Veneer Drawers, Birch, 37 3/4 x 41 5/8 In. 2000.00
Chest, Blanket, 1 Drawer, Green, Original Brass, 1820, 48 x 33 In. 1500.00
Chest, Blanket, 2 Drawers, Bracket Feet, Walnut, 29 x 43 3/4 In. 2250.00
Chest, Blanket, 2 Drawers, Fishtail Hinges, Striped Walnut, c.1800 .... 6950.00
Chest, Blanket, 2 Drawers, Original Brass, Rhode Island, Chestnut 775.00
Chest, Blanket, 2 Drawers, Original Paint & Brasses, New York 1850.00
Chest, Blanket, 2 Drawers, Strap Hinges, Crab Lock, Cherry 1000.00
Chest, Blanket, 3 Drawers, 19th Century, Miniature 935.00
Chest, Blanket, 3 Drawers, Chippendale, Pine, 49 x 22 x 30 In. 675.00
Chest, Blanket, 3 Drawers, Iron Hinges & Till, Walnut, 50 3/4 In. 2900.00
Chest, Blanket, 3 Drawers, Lift Lid, Till, Castors, Poplar, 49 In. 175.00
Chest, Blanket, 3 Drawers, Red & Black, Softwood, c.1830, 50 In. 8000.00
Chest, Blanket, 4 False Drawers, 2 Real, Cotter Pins, Black Paint 2950.00
Chest, Blanket, Alligatored Brown Graining, Green Trim, Miniature 875.00
Chest, Blanket, Black & Gray Graining, Poplar, 46 1/4 In. 225.00
Chest, Blanket, Bracket Feet, Scrolled Front, Tiger Maple 1800.00
Chest, Blanket, Brown Graining Over Blue, Till, Poplar, 37 1/2 In. 480.00
Chest, Blanket, Chippendale, Till, Bracket Feet, Cherry, 37 1/2 In. 600.00
Chest, Blanket, Crimson Red Case, Gold Stenciled I Y 1855, 41 In. 1200.00
Chest, Blanket, Drawer, Scrolled Apron, Cherry, 34 1/2 x 46 In. 455.00
Chest, Blanket, Drawer, Till, Staple Hinges, Red Paint, Pine, 33 In. 250.00
Chest, Blanket, Flowerpots On Panels, 2 Tills, Pine, 63 1/4 In. 2300.00
Chest, Blanket, Grain Painted, Ocher, 38 x 38 x 17 3/8 In. 1550.00
Chest, Blanket, Grain Painted, Small 695.00
Chest, Blanket, Green & Iron–Red Paint, Mid–1800s 1600.00
Chest, Blanket, Green Paint, Forged Iron Side Handles, 49 In. 950.00
Chest, Blanket, Hinged Lid, Inside Drawer, Walnut, 1790, Miniature 880.00
Chest, Blanket, Hinged Lid, Poplar, 38 In. 75.00
Chest, Blanket, Hinged Top, Scrolled Brackets, Walnut, 59 In. 990.00
Chest, Blanket, Lid, Red Paint & Black Graining, Pine, 43 3/8 In. 400.00
Chest, Blanket, Lift Lid, Till, Iron Strap Hinges, Pine, 52 In. 650.00
Chest, Blanket, Ogee Feet, Fish Tail Hinges, Walnut, 38 In. 1250.00
Chest, Blanket, Old Green Paint, Bear–Trap Lock 400.00
Chest, Blanket, Pennsylvania, Orange–Red & Green Paint, 1840s 1600.00
Chest, Blanket, Pennsylvania, Pine, Brown Vinegar Graining, 50 In. 1300.00
Chest, Blanket, Pine, Red Finish, Till, Strap Hinges, 39 x 24 In. 225.00
Chest, Blanket, Poplar, Flame Graining, Till, 44 x 20 x 23 In. 450.00
Chest, Blanket, Poplar, Natural Refinished, Till, 50 x 22 x 28 In. 200.00
Chest, Blanket, Raised Panel Front & Sides, Feather Paint, c.1830 .... 1800.00
Chest, Blanket, Red & Black Paint, Signed & Dated MH 1882, 43 In. 3100.00
Chest, Blanket, Red Comb Graining, Till, Pine, 20 3/4 x 33 1/2 In. 800.00
Chest, Blanket, Red Flame Graining, Till, Poplar, 19 x 40 In. 1000.00
Chest, Blanket, Red Paint, Green & Yellow Striping, 37 In. 1850.00
Chest, Blanket, Red Paint, Signed & Dated EZ 1857, 37 In. 1300.00
Chest, Blanket, Reeding Along Edge of Lid, Deep Skirt 1400.00
Chest, Blanket, Sheraton, Red Painted Pine & Poplar, 25 1/2 In. 675.00
Chest, Blanket, Soap Hollow, Penna., Poplar, 22 1/4 x 41 1/2 In. 900.00
Chest, Blanket, Square Corner Posts, Till, Walnut, 21 1/2 x 37 In. 400.00
Chest, Blanket, Staple Hinges, Till, Red Paint, Pine, 45 In. 350.00
Chest, Blanket, Strap Hinges, Bear–Trap Lock, Till, Oak, 46 1/2 In. 485.00
Chest, Blanket, Striped Red & Orange Case, 19th Century, 37 In. 1300.00
Chest, Blanket, Vinegar Graining, Poplar, 28 x 45 In. 750.00
Chest, Block Front, 3 Drawers, Cherry, 32 x 38 In. 3000.00
Chest, Bowfront, 4 Drawers, Dust Shelves, Cherry, 38 x 41 In. 2200.00
Chest, Bowfront, 4 Drawers, Edge Beading, Mahogany, 40 3/4 In. 750.00
Chest, Bowfront, Curly Maple Drawer Fronts, Cherry, 39 1/2 In. 900.00
Chest, Bowfront, Flame Veneer, Walnut Stiles, Cherry, 36 1/2 In. 1300.00

Chest, Bowfront, French Feet, Mahogany, c.1800, 38 x 40 In. 2600.00
Chest, Bowfront, Inlaid Corner Fans, 4 Drawers, Cherry, 37 In. 6750.00
Chest, Bowfront, Portsmouth, Contrasting Veneers, 36 1/4 In. 8800.00
Chest, Brass Bound, Red Pigskin Facings, Camphor, 36 In. 1500.00
Chest, Brass Covered, Embossed Scenes, Wheels, 1850s, 17 x 20 In. 325.00
Chest, Butler's, Carved Acanthus Leaf & Scroll, Mahogany, c.1835 .... 1875.00
Chest, Captain's, Lid, Rope Handles, Camphorwood, 41 1/2 In. 390.00
Chest, Carpenter's, Poplar, 2 Drawers, 17 x 27 In. 200.00
Chest, Chippendale, 3 Short, 3 Long Drawers, England, Mahogany 2450.00
Chest, Chippendale, 3 Short, 5 Long Drawers, Walnut, c.1770, 63 In. 6325.00
Chest, Chippendale, Oxbow Front, Mahogany, c.1770, 32 1/4 In. 10000.00
Chest, Curly Maple Half-Turned Columns, Cherry, c.1830, Miniature 3200.00
Chest, D Front, Line Inlay, Mahogany Veneer, Cherry, 42 3/4 In. 1350.00
Chest, Dower, Dark Pine, 2 Bottom Drawers 450.00
Chest, Dower, Original Green Paint, 26 1/2 x 45 1/4 In. 1540.00
Chest, Dower, Top Lock, Covered Till, Pennsylvania, Walnut, 55 In. 2400.00
Chest, Empire, Bird's-Eye & Tiger Maple, Twisted Pillars, Canada 1800.00
Chest, Empire, Butternut, Poplar, Pine, Dovetailed Drawers, 13 In. 150.00
Chest, Empire, Cherry, 17 In. 880.00
Chest, Empire, Cherry, Walnut, Woods, Varnish, 22 x 12 3/4 x 25 In. 400.00
Chest, Empire, Crotch Panels, 31 In. 700.00
Chest, Empire, Mahogany, 32 1/2 x 32 1/2 In. ....*Illus* 880.00
Chest, Empire, Raised Panel Ends, 4 Drawers, Butternut, Miniature 450.00
Chest, Federal, Deep Top Drawer, Mahogany, c.1800, 45 3/4 In. 4450.00
Chest, Federal, Maple, Bird's-Eye Maple Veneer, 1800, 42 In. 1100.00
Chest, Fire Gilt Brass Fittings, Mahogany, 35 x 39 In. 6875.00
Chest, Flame Mahogany, Marble Top, France 1375.00
Chest, Gustav Stickley, Chamfered, Inverted-V Backsplash, 42 In. 4125.00
Chest, Gustav Stickley, Iron Hinges, c.1901, 25 1/4 In. 6000.00
Chest, Hepplewhite, 2 Over 4 Drawers, Mahogany, 45 In. 1675.00
Chest, Hepplewhite, Cherry & Poplar, Dated 1824, 40 1/2 x 40 In. 2000.00
Chest, Hepplewhite, Inlaid Escutcheons, Walnut, c.1810, 39 In. 2500.00
Chest, Hepplewhite, Line Inlay In Drawer Fronts, Walnut, c.1800 .... 2250.00
Chest, Hepplewhite, T Nails, Pine Secondary Wood, Cherry 2800.00
Chest, Hinged Cover, Painted Coaching Scenes, Pine, 49 In. 990.00
Chest, Hinged Lid, Foliate Corners, Korean, Stained, 23 x 40 In. 198.00
Chest, Immigrant's, Dome Top, Pine, Brown Flame Graining, 38 In. 160.00
Chest, Jacobean Style, Hinged Top Opening, Oak, 47 x 21 1/2 In. 825.00
Chest, Kneehole Dressing, Serpentine Fronted, Mahogany, c.1770 .... 6050.00
Chest, Lift Lid, Fall Front, Oyster Veneer, Brass Bound, 12 In. 1320.00
Chest, Louis XV, Marble Top, Gilt Metal Trim 1800.00
Chest, Louis XV, Morocco Leather Top, Carved Walnut, 1870, 60 In. 2000.00
Chest, Mahogany Drawer Fronts, Maple Banding, c.1800, 38 In. 8850.00
Chest, Mahogany, 2 Short Over 4 Graduating Drawers, 1900s 160.00
Chest, Mule, 2 Drawers, Vinegar Graining, Pine, 40 x 43 1/4 In. 2400.00
Chest, Mule, Brown Flame Graining, 2 Drawers, 39 x 40 1/2 In. 250.00
Chest, Mule, Lift Lid, Scalloped Base, Cherry, 29 x 35 In. 650.00
Chest, Mule, Lift Lid, Staple Hinges, Pine, 40 1/4 x 38 3/4 In. 650.00
Chest, Mule, Pennsylvania, Pine, Brown Graining, 39 x 18 x 38 In. 1700.00
Chest, Mule, Scalloped Base, 3 Drawers, Pine & Poplar, 41 1/2 In. 300.00
Chest, Oak, Swivel Mirrors, 2 Short Over 4 Long Drawers, 72 In. 200.00
Chest, Oyster Veneer, Brass, Interior Baize Trays, 18 1/2 In. 2200.00
Chest, Paneled Ends, Cock-Beaded Drawers, Tiger Maple, 37 1/2 In. 2500.00
Chest, Pine, Cutout Feet, Scalloped Apron, 39 x 40 x 16 In. 575.00
Chest, Queen Anne, Walnut Oyster Veneer, Brass, 10 x 18 In. 2000.00
Chest, Reeded Stiles, 10 Drawers, Cherry, c.1830, 73 1/2 In. 3000.00
Chest, Rope Carved Feet, Curly Maple Facade, Cherry, 46 1/2 In. 500.00
Chest, Sheraton, 2 Over 3 Drawers, Cherry, 26 In. 4070.00
Chest, Sheraton, Bird's-Eye Maple Drawers, c.1830, 40 In. 605.00
Chest, Sheraton, Bird's-Eye Veneer, Maple & Cherry, 44 In. 2400.00
Chest, Sheraton, Bow Front, Tiger Maple, 43 x 38 In. 1900.00
Chest, Sheraton, Poplar, 22 In. 2200.00
Chest, Spice, Walnut, Ogee Feet, Raised Panel Door, 15 3/4 In. 850.00

Chest, Stenciled J. K., Soap Hollow, Penna., Cherry, 48 In. 900.00
Chest, Stickley Bros., Swivel Mirror, 2 Drawers, c.1912, 66 In. 440.00
Chest, Sugar, Cherry, 45 1/2 x 36 1/2 In. 522.50
Chest, Sugar, Divided, Drawer, Poplar & Cherry, 30 1/2 In. 1765.00
Chest, Sugar, Hepplewhite, Cherry, Kentucky 8900.00
Chest, Sugar, Hepplewhite, Walnut, Inlaid, Divided Interior, 40 In. 900.00
Chest, Sugar, Hinged Lid, Poplar, 27 3/4 x 32 1/2 In. 350.00
Chest, Tiger Maple, 2 Recessed Short Over 4 Long Drawers, 53 In. 350.00
Chest, Walnut, 5 Short & 4 Long Drawers, 18th Century, 66 In. 3960.00
Chest-On-Chest, 4 Drawers, Empire, Glove Drawers, Wooden Pulls 210.00
Chest-On-Chest, 5 Drawers, Mahogany, c.1775, 5 Ft. 10 In. 4125.00
Chest-On-Chest, 6 Drawers, George III, Mahogany, 6 Ft. 2 In. 3300.00
Chest-On-Chest, 9 Drawers, Cock-Beaded, Walnut, 71 In. 4200.00
Chest-On-Chest, Child's, Georgian, England, c.1770, 50 x 36 In. 3500.00
Chest-On-Chest, Chippendale, 9 Drawers, Cherry, c.1900, 88 1/2 In. 550.00
Chest-On-Chest, Flat Top, Maryland, c.1755, 65 In. 6600.00
Chest-On-Chest, George III, Mahogany, 5 Over 3 Drawers, 79 In. 3025.00
Chest-On-Chest, George III, Upper 5 Drawers, Lower 3 Drawers 8000.00
Chest-On-Chest, Huntly Furniture Co., Mahogany, 51 In. 75.00
Chest-On-Frame, 7 Drawers, Queen Anne, Walnut, 58 1/2 In. 1150.00
Chest-On-Stand, Long Drawer Over 3 Small Drawers, Oak, 70 In. 1545.00
Chiffonier, Limbert, No. 485 .... 2200.00
China Cabinet, Louis XV, 2 Panel Doors, Oak, 95 1/2 x 56 1/2 In. 3600.00
China Cabinet, Stickley, Side & Front Panes, Overhanging Top 3850.00
Coach, Fainting, Victorian, Eastlake Design, 69 In. 165.00
Coal Holder, Rosewood, Victorian, Marquetry, Beveled Mirror, 1840 .... 650.00
Coat Rack, Brass Trim, Walnut, 1880s 275.00
Coat Rack, Eastlake, Walnut, Brass Trim, 3 Legs, 1880 .... 275.00
Coat Rack, Oak, Hanging, 4 Hooks, Beveled Mirror 75.00
Coffer, Paneled Hinged Top, Carved Design, English Oak, 29 In. 2200.00

◆◆◆

An ivory should never be washed, especially if it is tinted. The best way to clean an ivory is with a soft brush. If you have a friend whose hands perspire profusely, have him handle the ivory, as it will add to the patina and coloring. An ivory should be kept in high humidity, so it is always best to keep an open cup of water or a plant nearby.

◆◆◆

Furniture, Commode, Gentleman's,
Mahogany, 38 x 26 In.

Furniture, Commode, Louis XV,
Figural Mounts, Marble Top, 44 In.

Commode, 3 Drawers, Leaf Pulls, Splashback, Walnut 400.00
Commode, Classical Revival, Mahogany Veneer, 39 x 25 x 19 In. 990.00
Commode, Gentleman's, Mahogany, 38 x 26 In. ....*Illus* 1200.00
Commode, Louis Philippe, Cylindrical Case, Burl & Walnut, 29 In. 375.00
Commode, Louis XV, Figural Mounts, Marble Top, 44 In. ....*Illus* 750.00
Commode, Louis XV, Serpentine Top, 3 Drawers, Fruitwood, 31 In. 4400.00
Commode, Rosewood, Marble Top, Stenciled J. Dessoir Maker, c.1840 .... 1650.00
Commode, Victorian, Step, Hinged Lid, Mahogany, Chamber Pot, Lid 265.00
Confessional Booth, Carved, Germany, Oak, 11 Ft. x 8 Ft. 10 In. 8500.00
Console, Frank Lloyd Wright, Beaded, Rectangular Panels, c.1917 .... 1320.00
Console, Jackson, Blond Mahogany Top, Base, Lucite, Glass, 48 In. 7700.00
Cooler, Wine, Regency, Inlaid Mahogany, Pinecone Finials, 34 In. 3850.00
Costumer, L. & J. G. Stickley, Adjustable Mirror, Handcraft, Oak 2600.00
Costumer, Stickley Bros., 4 Iron Hooks, Cross Stretcher, 68 In. 247.00
Couch, Fainting, Victorian, Soft Blue Upholstery 950.00
Cradle Cover, Shaker, Poplar Frame, 3 Bentwood Hoops, 15 x 35 In. 25.00
Cradle, Doll's, Scrolled Edges, Poplar, 25 3/4 In. 105.00
Cradle, Dovetailed, Heart Cutout 1 End, Red Repaint, 41 In. 175.00
Cradle, Hooded, Mahogany 440.00
Cradle, In Frame, Dovetailed, Butternut, 37 3/4 x 45 In. 550.00
Cradle, Post & Panel, Red Paint Over Cherry, c.1840 .... 850.00
Cradle, Rocking Horse, Grain Painted, 19th Century, 18 x 42 In. 335.00
Cradle, Scalloped Ends, Heart Cutouts, Poplar, 39 In. 250.00
Cradle, Shaped Sides, Cutout Rockers, Cherry, 41 In. 125.00
Cradle, Square Posts, Turned Finials, Poplar, 41 In. 65.00
Cradle, Swing, Maple, Spindle 795.00
Cradle, Victorian, 4–Poster, Turned Legs & Spindles, Springs 280.00
Cradle, Victorian, Heart–Shaped Handles, 26 x 41 In. 137.50
Cradle, Whittled Finials On Posts, Pine, 36 In. 100.00
Cradle, Wicker 125.00
Cradle, Wrought Iron, 19th Century, 35 x 41 In. 475.00
Credenza, 6 Paneled Drawers, 2 Pairs of Doors, Walnut, 7 Ft. 6 In. 9900.00
Credenza, Black Marble Top, 4 Doors, Gilt Metal Insets, 30 In. 385.00
Crib Settle, Gustav Stickley, 13 Slats, Leather Seat, Oak, c.1902 .... 4500.00
Crib, Folding, Maple 170.00
Crib, Spool, Walnut 330.00
Cupboard, 16 Panes, 2 Drawers, c.1820, 2 Piece 4500.00
Cupboard, 2 Drawers, 2 Doors, 8 Panes, Walnut, 88 x 49 3/4 In. 1100.00
Cupboard, 3 Drawers In Base, Pie Shelf Top, Maple, 86 1/2 In. 4500.00
Cupboard, 3 Drawers, 2 Tilt–Out Bins, 3 Doors, Tin, 1900s, 44 In. 350.00
Cupboard, 3 Overhanging Drawers, 12 Panes, Candle Drawer, Cherry 6000.00
Cupboard, 4 Panes, Old Paint, Softwood, 30 In. 5280.00
Cupboard, 9 Panes, Bracket Feet, H Hinges, Walnut, Small 3900.00
Cupboard, Apothecary, Pine, Poplar, 6 Drawers, 25 x 11 x 24 In. 375.00
Cupboard, Bedside, George III, Carrying Handles, 2 Doors, Mahogany 4675.00
Cupboard, Child's, Curly Maple, 2 Drawers & Doors, 21 In. 500.00
Cupboard, Child's, Kitchen, 4 Doors, Pots & Pans, c.1920 .... 250.00
Cupboard, Chimney, Beading Around Door, 4 Shelves, Walnut 3500.00
Cupboard, Chimney, Raised Panels, Rosehead Nails, c.1710 .... 2600.00
Cupboard, Chippendale, 3 Drawers, Bottom Doors, Walnut, 62 In. 1200.00
Cupboard, Connecticut, Barrel Back, Arched Top Door, 7 Ft. 9 In. 5500.00
Cupboard, Continental, Scrolls On Doors, Hardwood, 35 1/4 In. 525.00
Cupboard, Corner, 1 Drawer, Orange & Red Paint, Softwood, 7 Ft. 6500.00
Cupboard, Corner, 3 Drawers, Split Panel Doors, Figured Cherry 4500.00
Cupboard, Corner, 5 Drawers, Carved Surfaces, Walnut, 92 x 57 In. 4900.00
Cupboard, Corner, 9 Panes, H Hinges, Walnut, 2 Piece, 27 In. 4600.00
Cupboard, Corner, 12 Panes, 2 Drawers, Walnut, 7 Ft. 5 In. 6600.00
Cupboard, Corner, 12 Panes, 3 Convex Drawers, Poplar, c.1825 .... 3850.00
Cupboard, Corner, 12 Panes, Bracket Feet, Walnut, 19th Century 7040.00
Cupboard, Corner, 12 Panes, Butterfly Shelves, Softwood 2400.00
Cupboard, Corner, 12 Panes, Raised Panel Doors, 77 x 48 In. 4100.00
Cupboard, Corner, 12 Panes, Walnut, 19th Century 5000.00
Cupboard, Corner, 16 Panes, Flush Beaded Panels, Cherry 4620.00

Cupboard, Corner, Arched & Cathedral Doors, Walnut, 1820s, 8 Ft.	6250.00
Cupboard, Corner, Arched Swan Neck, 1 Glass Door, Walnut, 90 In.	445.00
Cupboard, Corner, Baltimore, 2 Base Doors, Glass Door	4250.00
Cupboard, Corner, Barrel Back, Butterfly Hinges, Pine, 75 1/2 In.	1250.00
Cupboard, Corner, Barrel Back, Pine, 101 x 54 3/4 In.	500.00
Cupboard, Corner, Beaded Framed Doors, Pine & Poplar, 85 In.	2400.00
Cupboard, Corner, Blind Arched Door, Walnut, c.1800, 85 In.	9900.00
Cupboard, Corner, Blind Door, Red Paint	4620.00
Cupboard, Corner, Blind Door, Walnut, Early 19th Century	6250.00
Cupboard, Corner, Cathedral Doors, 3 Drawers, Walnut, 7 Ft. 6 In.	8600.00
Cupboard, Corner, Curly Maple, 3 Drawers, 4 Doors, 48 x 79 In.	2700.00
Cupboard, Corner, Empire, 3 Convex Drawers, Cherry, 2 Piece	4000.00
Cupboard, Corner, Federal, Flower Inlay, Walnut, c.1800, 8 Ft.	9075.00
Cupboard, Corner, Flame Graining, Pine & Poplar, 81 x 47 In.	4750.00
Cupboard, Corner, Georgian, Hanging, Mahogany, 1820	2778.00
Cupboard, Corner, Glazed Doors, Drawer, Pine, 89 In.	615.00
Cupboard, Corner, Grain Painted, Poplar, 84 x 57 In.	5500.00
Cupboard, Corner, Hanging, 1 Flat Paneled Door, Tiger Maple	3750.00
Cupboard, Corner, Hanging, Astragal Glazed Door, Mahogany	1200.00
Cupboard, Corner, Hanging, Brass Hinges, Red Paint, Poplar, 41 In.	1000.00
Cupboard, Corner, Hanging, Paneled Door, Mahogany, 31 In.	525.00
Cupboard, Corner, Hanging, Paneled Door, Pine, 36 1/2 x 34 In.	650.00
Cupboard, Corner, Inset Corner Columns, 12 Panes, c.1820	6200.00
Cupboard, Corner, Latches, Curly Maple, Cherry, Walnut, 85 In.	3800.00
Cupboard, Corner, Paneled & Mullioned Doors, Walnut, 95 1/2 In.	6250.00
Cupboard, Corner, Paneled Doors In Base, Open Top, Pine, 79 In.	600.00
Cupboard, Corner, Paneled Doors, 8 Panes, Cherry, 92 3/4 In.	57.50
Cupboard, Corner, Paneled Doors, Band of Inlay, Walnut, 87 1/2 In.	2600.00
Cupboard, Corner, Paneled Doors, Butternut Drawers, Poplar, 83 In.	1150.00
Cupboard, Corner, Paneled Doors, Shelves, Pine, 87 1/2 In.	335.00
Cupboard, Corner, Pine, Fluted Pilasters, 2 Doors, England, 77 In.	1300.00
Cupboard, Corner, Pine, One Piece, Cutout Feet, 84 x 42 In.	550.00
Cupboard, Corner, Pine, Tombstone Doors Top, America, 6 Ft. 1 In.	1350.00
Cupboard, Corner, Raised Panel Doors, Walnut, 1840s, 7 Ft. 5 In.	6500.00
Cupboard, Corner, Raised Panel Doors, Walnut, 90 1/4 In.	4000.00
Cupboard, Corner, Reeded Pilasters, Painted, c.1820, 90 In.	3850.00
Cupboard, Corner, Shaker, Sabbathday Lake	1450.00
Cupboard, Corner, Split Panel Doors, 9 Panes, Poplar, 28 In.	2175.00
Cupboard, Corner, Step Back, 12 Panes, Cutout Feet & Apron, Cherry	4600.00
Cupboard, Corner, Turn Buckles, Poplar, 81 3/4 x 50 1/2 In.	1200.00
Cupboard, Corner, Walnut, 1820s, 6 Ft. 8 In.	3000.00
Cupboard, Corner, Walnut, 2 Glass Over 2 Solid Doors, 7 Ft.	1000.00
Cupboard, Doors Hinged To Returns, 16 Panes, Walnut	3100.00
Cupboard, Dutch, 5 Spice Drawers, Painted Softwood	2600.00
Cupboard, Dutch, Convex Candle Drawers, Walnut, 19th Century	4200.00
Cupboard, Dutch, Paneled Ends, Cherry	7800.00
Cupboard, Dutch, Shaped Shelves, Cutout Plate Rails, Softwood	6750.00
Cupboard, Dutch, Spoon Cutouts, Plate Rails, Maple	4450.00
Cupboard, False Drawer, Secret Compartment, 12 Panes, Varnish	2900.00
Cupboard, Federal, Tiger Maple, 2 Base Doors, 73 x 45 In.	3850.00
Cupboard, Hanging, 1 Drawer, Iron Hinges, Europe, Pine, 37 In.	400.00
Cupboard, Hanging, 1 Drawer, Pennsylvania, Walnut, 41 In.	900.00
Cupboard, Hanging, 2 Drawers, Blue Paint, 19th Century, 30 In.	975.00
Cupboard, Hanging, Cornice Molding, Wood Knob, Cherry, 24 1/4 In.	900.00

◆◆◆

Never wind an old clock counterclockwise. Clocks that are wound
from the back should be wound counterclockwise because that is
really clockwise from the front of the clock.

◆◆◆

Cupboard, Hanging, Fitted Interior, Pigeon Holes, Poplar, 30 In. 450.00
Cupboard, Hanging, Paneled Door, Rattail Hinges, Walnut, c.1755 .... 4070.00
Cupboard, Hanging, Pine, Worn Black Paint, Door, 12 x 17 x 29 In. 150.00
Cupboard, Hanging, Red Flame Graining, 2 Drawers, Pine 600.00
Cupboard, Hoosier, Oak, Signed 795.00
Cupboard, Jelly, 2 Drawers Over 2 Blind Doors, Curly Cherry, 1850 .... 875.00
Cupboard, Jelly, 2 Drawers Over 2 Doors, Blue–Gray Paint 550.00
Cupboard, Jelly, Double Door, Red Paint, Paneled Sides, Softwood 3850.00
Cupboard, Jelly, Double Door, Walnut 2700.00
Cupboard, Jelly, Double Doors, Traces of Blue, Poplar, 36 x 48 In. 85.00
Cupboard, Jelly, Paneled Door, Metal Latch, Poplar, 40 In. 485.00
Cupboard, Jelly, Paneled Doors, Cherry & Poplar, 50 1/2 In. 875.00
Cupboard, Jelly, Pine, Raised Panel Doors, 58 In. 500.00
Cupboard, Jelly, Poplar, Red Paint, Paneled Doors, 1 Drawer, 60 In. 350.00
Cupboard, Jelly, Primitive Landscape On Doors, 38 x 13 x 52 In. 1600.00
Cupboard, Jelly, Red Paint, Softwood, 19th Century 1450.00
Cupboard, Jelly, Walnut, Mustard Yellow Repaint, Ohio, 39 3/4 In. 1250.00
Cupboard, Kitchen, Pine, 4 Shelves, Heart, Bracket Feet, 8 1/2 Ft. 600.00
Cupboard, Molded Arch & Keystone, Pine & Poplar, 95 In. 3500.00
Cupboard, Open Top Shelves, 2 Doors, Red Paint 2200.00
Cupboard, Paneled Doors, Enclosed Shelves, Fruitwood, 83 x 46 In. 825.00
Cupboard, Paneled Doors, Open Shelf, Painted Pine, 1880s, 78 In. 120.00
Cupboard, Pennsylvania Dutch, 12 Paneled Doors, Maple, c.1830 .... 4500.00
Cupboard, Pennsylvlania Dutch, Overhanging Drawers, Softwood 4600.00
Cupboard, Pewter, 1 Board Door, Scalloped Top, Pine, 80 1/2 In. 1600.00
Cupboard, Pewter, Batten Door, Open Top, Pine, 72 1/2 In. 1000.00
Cupboard, Pewter, Olive Green, Blue Wash Interior, Pine, 76 In. 900.00
Cupboard, Pewter, Open, Walnut, Worn Blue Paint, 42 x 10 x 64 In. 150.00
Cupboard, Pewter, Primitive, Poplar, Open, 1 Door, 38 x 77 In. 1800.00
Cupboard, Pine, Cornice, 1 Base Door, Open Shelves, 76 In., 2 Piece 900.00
Cupboard, Pine, Frieze, Door, Scalloped Apron, 41 x 35 x 16 In. 385.00
Cupboard, Poplar, Graining, Hanging, Cornice, 1 Door, 24 x 35 In. 500.00
Cupboard, Red Wash, New England, Early 19th Century, 78 x 50 In. 3550.00
Cupboard, Scalloped Apron, 8 Paneled Doors, Poplar, 89 In. 1400.00
Cupboard, Scalloped Base, Paneled Doors, Pine, 84 In., 2 Piece 950.00
Cupboard, Shaker, 1 Large Door, 3 Graduated Drawers Base, 7 Ft. 7500.00
Cupboard, Shaker, Enfield, Softwood, Natural Honey, 6 Ft. 4 In. 7150.00
Cupboard, Shaker, Hanging, Pine, Brown, Paneled Door, 29 x 62 In. 700.00
Cupboard, Sheaf of Wheat Carved On Door, c.1860 .... 250.00
Cupboard, Slant Back, New England, Green, Glass Pulls, 18 In. 3190.00
Cupboard, Spice, Primitive, Green Paint, 35 Drawers, 17 1/4 In. 295.00
Cupboard, Splashboard, 2 Drawers, Painted & Grained Pine, c.1825 .... 1650.00
Cupboard, Step Back, 2 Drawers, H Hinges, Walnut, 30 In. 2800.00
Cupboard, Step Back, 4 Doors, 3 Drawers, Red Paint, Wisc., 1800s 2200.00
Cupboard, Step Back, 6 Drawers, 24 Pane, Walnut 4840.00
Cupboard, Step Back, 8 Paneled Doors, 2 Drawers, Cherry, 84 In. 3500.00
Cupboard, Step Back, Cherry, 2 Glass–Top Doors, 2 Drawers 1850.00
Cupboard, Step Back, Glazed Doors, Shelves, English, Pine, 86 In. 1050.00
Cupboard, Step Back, Paneled Doors, 3 Drawers, Poplar, 85 1/4 In. 2250.00
Cupboard, Step Back, Pine, 1870 .... 1500.00
Cupboard, Step Back, Pine, Glass Top Doors, Square Nails, 70 In. 850.00
Cupboard, Step Back, Red Wash, Raised Panel Doors, New Hampshire 2475.00
Cupboard, Step Back, Tiger Maple, Pegged & Mortised, 2 Piece 8600.00
Cupboard, Step Back, Walnut, 2 8–Paneled Over 2 Blind Doors 700.00
Cupboard, Step, Blind Front, Curly Maple, 83 In. 7700.00
Cupboard, Tramp Art, Polychrome Paint, N. Y., c.1900 ....*Illus* 7150.00
Cupboard, Wall, Open, Red Stain, Poplar, 79 x 43 3/4 In. 600.00
Cupboard, Wall, Painted, Mirrored Door, Drawer, Late 19th Century 550.00
Cupboard, Wall, Paneled Doors, 3 Drawers, Pie Shelf, Pine & Poplar 3100.00
Cupboard, Welsh, 3 Dovetailed Drawers, Open Top, England, 76 In. 2600.00
Cupboard, Welsh, Georgian, 4 Drawers, Oak, c.1830, 87 In. 2200.00
Cupboard, Welsh, Oak, Elm Inlaid, 18th Century, 82 x 86 In. 7500.00
Cupboard, Welsh, Oak, George III, 81 x 72 x 14 In. ....*Illus* 5500.00

Furniture, Cupboard, Tramp Art,
Polychrome Paint, N. Y., c.1900

Furniture, Cupboard, Welsh, Oak, George III,
81 x 72 x 14 In.

Daybed, Black Over Red Paint, Adjustable Back, Maple, 68 In. 9000.00
Daybed, Blue, Late 19th Century, Fancy Form, Small 675.00
Daybed, Charles X, Gilt Foliate Trim, Fretwork, France, c.1840 .... 5000.00
Daybed, Federal, Crest Rail, Lyre Splat, Silk Upholstered, 70 In. 825.00
Daybed, Federal, Mixed Woods, c.1825, 74 In. 495.00
Daybed, L. & J. G. Stickley, Prairie, Upholstered, 1908, 80 In. 4125.00
Daybed, L. & J. G. Stickley, Mission Oak 1900.00
Daybed, L. & J. G. Stickley, Seat Over Slats, Oak, 1910, 6 Ft. 4 In. 660.00
Daybed, L. & J. G. Stickley, Seat Rail Slides Out, c.1908 .... 2975.00
Daybed, L. & J. G. Stickley, Seat Slides Out, c.1912, 77 In. 1750.00
Daybed, Lacquered, Caned Seat, Cast Iron Hardware, Japan 5775.00
Daybed, Pine, Black & Brown-Red, Jigsaw, Cutout Brackets, 74 In. 50.00
Daybed, Rush Seat, Adjustable Back Rest, Hardwood, 23 x 68 In. 9000.00
Daybed, Sheraton, Rolled Crest Rails, Mahogany, 73 In. 220.00
Daybed, Stained Pine, Carved Eagle, Lyre Form Splat, 70 In. 825.00
Daybed, Walnut, Dark, Square Cutout Legs, Mortised, 25 x 70 In. 85.00
Daybed, William & Mary, Framed Cane Center Head Rest 600.00
Daybed, Windsor, Yellow Paint, Stenciled, 1820s, 49 x 80 5/8 In. 1760.00
Desk & Chair, Art Nouveau, Marquetry Burl Walnut & Fruitwood 5500.00
Desk & Chair, L. & J. G. Stickley, No. 610 & 913, Kneehole, 1912 .... 605.00
Desk & Chair, Welbilt, No. 928 & 908a, Oak, Inlaid, 1920, 42 In. 330.00
Desk On Frame, Drop Front, Interior Drawers, Maple, 34 1/2 In. 4000.00
Desk On Frame, Pine, Early 19th Century, 46 1/2 x 34 x 23 In. 475.00
Desk, 1 Long, 2 Small Drawers, Copper Pulls, c.1912, 30 x 60 In. 412.50
Desk, 2 Drawers, Scalloped Crest, Pine, 37 3/4 x 39 In. 275.00
Desk, 4 Drawers, Fitted Interior, Banded Inlay, Cherry, 44 In. 5500.00
Desk, Architect's, George III, Mahogany, Leather, 3 Drawers, 1 Door 9350.00
Desk, Butler's, 6 Drawers, Paneled End, Curly Maple, c.1830 .... 1125.00
Desk, Butler's, Cathedral Glass Doors, Mahogany, 40 In. 2200.00
Desk, Butler's, Federal, Inlaid Mahogany, c.1805, 44 1/2 In. 3850.00
Desk, Butler's, Mahogany, Desk Compartment Over 3 Drawers 200.00
Desk, Butler's, Pull-Out Desk, 3 Drawers, Walnut, 46 1/4 In. 1100.00
Desk, Butler's, With Built-In Lockside Chest 2500.00
Desk, Child's, Blackboard, Pressed Frame, Multicolored Scroll 175.00
Desk, Child's, Oak, Slant Front, Bunny Silhouette, Gallery, 27 In. 195.00
Desk, Child's, Pigeonhole Between Top Drawers, 4 Ft. 2500.00
Desk, Chippendale, Drop Front, Mahogany, 4 Drawers, American 1600.00
Desk, Chippendale, Slant Front, 4 Drawers, Curly Maple, 41 1/2 In. 3600.00
Desk, Chippendale, Slant Front, Curly Maple, c.1760, 41 1/4 In. 4675.00
Desk, Chippendale, Slant Front, Maple, 17 Drawers, 43 In. 1800.00
Desk, Clerk's, Slant Front, Lift Lid, 1 Drawer, Pine, 55 In. 450.00
Desk, Country School, Slant Top, Lift Lid, Pine, 44 x 28 1/2 In. 400.00
Desk, Cylinder Top, Prudent Mallard, Carved Rosewood, c.1860 .... 7775.00
Desk, Cylinder, Federal, Scrolled Drawers, Cherry, 40 1/8 x 42 In. 1350.00
Desk, Cylinder, Painted Center Medallion, Satinwood, 44 1/2 In. 4675.00
Desk, Double Pedestal, Leather Top, 3 Drawers, Burl Walnut, 30 In. 1210.00
Desk, Drop Front, Gustav Stickley, No. 706, Oak, Paneled, 44 In. 2420.00

Desk, Drop Front, Tiger Maple 6000.00
Desk, Empire, Slant Front, Mahogany 275.00
Desk, Fall Front, 2 Outer Drawers, Walnut, 1730s, 37 1/2 In. 1980.00
Desk, Federal, Fall Front, Mahogany Veneer, Inlay, Cylinder, 90 In. 3350.00
Desk, Field, Folding, Leather Interior, Mahogany, 22 1/2 x 24 In. 1500.00
Desk, George III, Bombe, Leather Surface, 4 Drawers, Elm, 54 In. 3500.00
Desk, Governor Winthrop, Woman's, Serpentine Drop Front 247.50
Desk, Hepplewhite, Lift Lid, Fitted Interior, 1 Drawer, Walnut 175.00
Desk, Kneehole, Carved Pen & Ink Tray, 2 Banks of 4 Drawers, Oak 525.00
Desk, Kneehole, Leather Panels, 1 Long, 6 Short Drawers, 43 In. 110.00
Desk, Kneehole, Recessed Cupboard, Mahogany, 1790s, 30 x 29 In. 935.00
Desk, Lady's, Dutch Marquetry, Serpentine Lid, 1 Drawer 2450.00
Desk, Lady's, Pierced Gallery, Leather Top, Mahogany, 35 x 45 In. 615.00
Desk, Lap, Brass Bound, Walnut, England, March 2, 1877 .... 220.00
Desk, Lap, Brass Diamond Inlay, Pen Wells, Mahogany, 20 1/2 In. 357.00
Desk, Lap, Fitted Interior, Lacquered, Chinese, 19th Cent., 16 In. 335.00
Desk, Lap, Front Opening, 2 Drawers, England, Oak, 9 1/2 x 20 In. 110.00
Desk, Lap, Inlaid Mother-of-Pearl Floral, Rosewood, 11 In. 55.00
Desk, Lap, Inlaid Star, Crescent & Leaf, Lined, Rosewood, c.1815 .... 2000.00
Desk, Lap, Mother-of-Pearl & Ebony Inlay, 2 Wells, Scotland 545.00
Desk, Lap, Tambour Opens To Fitted Interior, Mahogany, 20 1/2 In. 665.00
Desk, Library, Mission Style, Tall Back, 1 Drawer, Side Shelves 225.00
Desk, Merchant's, Lift Top, 13 Drawers, 2 Doors, Cherry 5000.00
Desk, Moore, Walnut, Bird's-Eye Maple Drawers, Gallery, Dated 1878 .... 8100.00
Desk, Partner's, George II, Mahogany, Pedestal, Leather, 9 Drawers 4450.00
Desk, Partner's, Gustav Stickley, Wooden Pulls, 1902, 60 x 40 In. 7700.00
Desk, Partner's, Leather Top, Turned Columns, Mahogany, 48 In. 5750.00
Desk, Partner's, Tooled Leather, Double Pedestals, Oak & Burl Elm 1045.00
Desk, Partner's, Walnut, Pedestal, Serpentine, Leather Top, 6 Ft. 9900.00
Desk, Pedestal, 9 Drawers, Leather Insert, Mahogany, 30 x 48 In. 1150.00
Desk, Queen Anne, Drop Front, Figured Maple, c.1740 .... 6650.00
Desk, Queen Anne, Secret Hiding Place, Mahogany, c.1820 .... 1500.00
Desk, Regency, Mahogany, 3 Drawers, Tilt Top, England, 31 1/2 In. 1100.00
Desk, Ripple Front, Felt Writing Surface, Mahogany, 77 1/2 In. 825.00
Desk, Roll Top, Globe Wernicke, c.1900, 72 In. 2500.00
Desk, Roll Top, Quartersawn Oak, Raised Panels, 54 In. 1600.00
Desk, Roll Top, S Roll, Leaf Carved, Walnut ....*Illus* 935.00
Desk, Roll Top, Single Pedestal, Swivel Chair, Oak, 44 x 44 In. 665.00
Desk, Roll Top, Slide-Out Writing Surface, Walnut, 2 Glass Doors 2950.00
Desk, S Roll Top, Chair, Mahogany, 60 In. 1200.00
Desk, Schoolmaster's, 2 Interior Drawers, Walnut, c.1830 .... 600.00
Desk, Schoolmaster's, Diamond Escutcheon, Cherry, 31 1/2 In. 450.00
Desk, Schoolmaster's, Hepplewhite, Cherry, 3 Drawers, 37 x 39 In. 675.00
Desk, Schoolmaster's, Lift Top, Dark Red Paint, Poplar, 34 In. 400.00
Desk, Schoolmaster's, Lift Top, Pine, 30 x 50 In. 225.00
Desk, Schoolmaster's, Pine, Dark Finish, 28 x 23 x 32 1/2 In. 150.00
Desk, Schoolmaster's, Tiger Maple, 6 Interior Drawers, 1805 .... 2200.00

Furniture, Desk, Roll Top, S Roll,
Leaf Carved, Walnut

Furniture, Desk, Slant Front,
Maple, c.1780, 41 In.

◆◆

To test a piece of jade to see if it is real, use a small pen knife. Rub the tip of the knife across the bottom of the piece until there is a mark. A white line means the knife scratched the stone and it is not jade. A black line means the stone scratched the blade and it is probably jade.

◆◆

Desk, Shaker, Double School Type, Mixed Woods, Refinished	2850.00
Desk, Slant Front, 4 Drawers, Mahogany, c.1825, 41 In.	3350.00
Desk, Slant Front, 4 Drawers, Pigeon Holes, Cherry, 41 1/2 In.	2000.00
Desk, Slant Front, Bird's-Eye Maple Fronts, Tiger Maple, c.1830	1250.00
Desk, Slant Front, Bombe Shape, Marquetry, Dutch, Matching Chair	3950.00
Desk, Slant Front, Chippendale, Ball & Claw, Massachusetts, 1780	5600.00
Desk, Slant Front, Chippendale, Block Front, 42 x 36 x 19 In.	3100.00
Desk, Slant Front, Chippendale, Carved Tiger Maple, 42 1/2 In.	9350.00
Desk, Slant Front, Chippendale, Cherry, Conn., 1760-1800, 42 In.	3080.00
Desk, Slant Front, Chippendale, Pull-Out Center Case, Walnut	9240.00
Desk, Slant Front, Dovetailed Case, 5 Drawers, Maple, 42 1/2 In.	3500.00
Desk, Slant Front, George II, Mahogany, Pigeonholes, 1740, 42 In.	4950.00
Desk, Slant Front, Inlaid Interior, Cherry, c.1790, 38 In.	6050.00
Desk, Slant Front, Inlaid Patera, Cherry, c.1800, 41 x 40 In.	2865.00
Desk, Slant Front, Maple, Bracket Base, Graduated Drawers, 40 In.	1430.00
Desk, Slant Front, Maple, c.1780, 41 In. ....*Illus*	1650.00
Desk, Slant Front, Maple, Old Brasses, Rhode Island, 1800, 43 In.	4125.00
Desk, Slant Front, Open Compartments, Tiger Maple, c.1780, 42 In.	5225.00
Desk, Slant Front, Original Red Stain, Maple, c.1810	3600.00
Desk, Slant Front, Oxbow, Ball & Claw Feet, Birch, 45 3/4 In.	3750.00
Desk, Slant Front, Pay Master's, Walnut, 49 x 73 In.	1150.00
Desk, Slant Front, Queen Anne, Fitted Interior, Walnut, c.1725	6050.00
Desk, Slant Front, Queen Anne, Maple, c.1750, Child's	4950.00
Desk, Slant Front, Sheraton, Curly Maple, 5 Drawers, 39 3/4 In.	1800.00
Desk, Slant Front, Stand Up, Writing Slide, 2 Drawers, Pine, c.1830	2250.00
Desk, Slant Front, Step-Down Interior, Mahogany, c.1790, 37 In.	7700.00
Desk, Slant Front, Tiger Maple	3300.00
Desk, Slant Front, Walnut, c.1800, 41 In.	2000.00
Desk, Slant Front, Walnut, Pigeon Holes, 4 Drawers, 1800	3410.00
Desk, Stand Up, Miller's, 3 Drawers, Walnut, 19th Century, 7 Ft.	1750.00
Desk, Table Top, Lift Top, Dovetailed Case, 38 1/2 x 18 1/2 In.	350.00
Desk, Table Top, Slant Top Lift Lid, 3 Drawers, Pine, 13 x 17 In.	650.00
Desk, Tambour, Biscuit Corners, Tiger Maple, Turned Pilasters	8500.00
Desk, Tambour, Cylinder, Fitted Interior, Anglo-Indian, 43 1/2 In.	6650.00
Desk, Tambour, Hepplewhite, Inlaid Mahogany	6050.00
Desk, Tambour, Hepplewhite, Mahogany, 2 Drawers, Fitted, 1890s	1475.00
Desk, Thonet, A. J. Hoffman, Brown Beech, Leather, 1905	5500.00
Desk, Wall, Chautauqua, Rotating Scroll	170.00
Desk, Wicker, Heywood Wakefield, Painted, 42 1/2 x 37 x 75 In.	880.00
Desk, Woman's, 4 Drawers, Oval Brasses, Mahogany, 52 3/4 In.	3000.00
Desk, Woman's, Drop Front, Larkin Label	325.00
Desk, Woman's, Federal Style, Mahogany Veneer, 1929	2850.00
Desk, Woman's, Frieze Drawer Over 2 Drawers, Burl, Walnut, 30 In.	750.00
Desk, Woman's, Larkin Style, Bird's-Eye Maple	550.00
Desk, Woman's, Larkin, Drop Front, Beveled Mirror, Open Front	350.00
Desk, Writing Slide, French, Rosewood, Mahogany, 1930, 29 1/2 In.	1650.00
Dining Set, Baroque Style, Walnut, Warriors, Maidens, Birds, 9 Pc.	9900.00
Dining Set, F. Hansen, Modern Danish, Round Laminated Top, 5 Pc.	550.00
Dining Set, Frieze, Leather Upholstery, Walnut, c.1900, 5 Piece	2750.00
Dining Set, Laminated Cardboard, 4 Easy Edges Chairs, Gehry	6600.00
Dining Set, Oak, Reflector Leaf, 9 Piece	975.00

Dining Set, Sheraton Style, Table, Chairs, Buffet, Server, Cabinet 950.00
Dining Set, Walnut, 6 Acorn–Type Legs Table, Leaves, 1920s, 5 Pc. 350.00
Dresser, Carved Nudes On Front & Sides of Mirror, Mahogany 2400.00
Dresser, Child's, 3 Drawers, Tilt Mirror, Glove Box, Oak 200.00
Dresser, G. Stickley, 2 Top Drawers, 4 Lower Drawers, Mirror 2000.00
Dresser, L. & J. G. Stickley, Adjustable Mirror, No. 101, c.1912 .... 2400.00
Dresser, Louis XVI Style, Marble Top, Oak, 33 x 50 1/2 In. 1600.00
Dresser, Marble Top, Carved Walnut, c.1860, 86 1/2 x 57 In. 2200.00
Dresser, Marble Top, Mirror, 2 Drawers, Shelves, Eastlake 345.00
Dresser, Swivel Mirror, 2 Small Over 2 Long Drawers, Oak 190.00
Dry Sink, 2 Doors, Hunter Green Over Apple, 1840, 43 x 22 In. 1500.00
Dry Sink, 2 Drawers, Paneled Doors, Poplar, 44 3/4 x 45 In. 1600.00
Dry Sink, Graining Over Red, Pine, 32 x 49 In. 125.00
Dry Sink, Hutch, Pine, Mortise & Tenon Construction, 2 Doors 1650.00
Dry Sink, Lift Lid, Mustard Graining, Iron Latches, Pine, 33 In. 1150.00
Dry Sink, Lift Top, 1 Drawer, Oak Graining, 19th Century, 34 In. 750.00
Dry Sink, Oak, Cupboard Top, Glass Doors, Pullout Section 2650.00
Dry Sink, Original Red Paint, 2 Doors Up & 2 Down 700.00
Dry Sink, Pine, 35 1/2 x 27 In. ....*Illus* 1100.00
Dry Sink, Pine, Red & Blue Repaint, Removable Ball Finial, 35 In. 725.00
Dry Sink, Poplar, Light Blue Paint, Paneled Doors, 30 3/4 In. 975.00
Dry Sink, Single Board Door, Iron Latch, Pine, 29 3/4 x 38 In. 350.00
Dry Sink, Spoon Carved, Poplar, 1 Dovetailed Drawer, 2 Doors 275.00
Dry Sink, Swing–Out Shelf, Iron Latch, Poplar, 26 x 33 In. 350.00
Dumbwaiter, Circular, 3 Cabriole Legs, Mahogany, 30 x 25 In. 120.00
Etagere, 3 Galleried Shelves, Mahogany, 42 1/2 In. 715.00
Etagere, Heywood Wakefield, No. 3919, Wicker, 3 Shelves, 36 1/4 In. 275.00
Etagere, Inlaid, Rosewood, England, c.1890 .... 7500.00
Fainting Couch, Openwork Back 935.00
Fauteuil, Fruitwood, Balloon Back, Allover Floral, French Style 95.00
Footstool, Brown Paint, Upholstered Leather Top, 10 x 14 In. 175.00
Footstool, Carved, Bun Feet, Red Cotton Upholstery, 1814, Pair 3500.00
Footstool, Chenille–Shirred Wool Cover, 18 1/2 x 12 In. 2400.00
Footstool, Cowhorn Legs, Red Plush Upholstery, 11 x 14 In. 48.00
Footstool, Curly Maple, 5 1/2 x 9 1/2 x 14 1/2 In. 175.00
Footstool, Cutout Ends, Star Design On Apron, Walnut, 15 In. 145.00
Footstool, George III, Mahogany, Needlepoint, 6 1/2 x 4 x 30 In. 110.00
Footstool, George III, Upholstered Seat, Mahogany, 1780s 465.00
Footstool, Georgian Style, Upholstered Cushion, 15 x 25 In. 175.00
Footstool, Gustav Stickley, 7 Spindles End, Leather, 15 x 20 In. 2750.00
Footstool, Iron Base, Needlepoint Cover 70.00
Footstool, Legs Mortised Through Cutout Top, 9 1/4 x 20 1/2 In. 115.00
Footstool, Limbert, Oak, Original Leather Seat, Label 75.00
Footstool, Louis XV, Upholstered Seat, Mahogany, 15 x 22 In. 145.00
Footstool, Mahogany, Needlepoint, Vanderley Brothers, 17 x 14 In. 95.00
Footstool, Pine, Refinished, 9 1/2 x 18 x 13 1/2 In. 45.00
Footstool, Roycroft, Drop–In Leatherette Cushion, 14 x 17 In. 550.00

Furniture, Dry Sink, Pine, 35 1/2 x 27 In.

◆◆◆◆◆◆◆◆◆◆◆◆◆◆◆◆◆◆◆◆◆

Serious collecting of antique furniture began in the 1920s. Fakers began to make great pieces
from average pieces. Butterfly
tables were made from tavern
tables, block–front bureaus from
plain bureaus, inlaid eagles and
other designs were added to furniture and clocks. Plain highboys
were "improved" with scroll tops.

◆◆◆◆◆◆◆◆◆◆◆◆◆◆◆◆◆◆◆◆◆

Furniture, Highboy, Queen Anne,
Cabriole Legs, Duck Feet, 71 In.

Furniture, Highboy, Queen Anne,
Curly Maple, c.1750, 67 1/2 In.

Footstool, Splayed Base, Turned Legs, 8 1/4 x 14 3/4 In. 70.00
Footstool, Splayed Legs, Decal On Top, 8 x 12 3/4 x 7 1/4 In. 85.00
Footstool, Stenciled & Freehand Floral Top Design, 12 In. 75.00
Footstool, Upholstered Top, X–Form Legs, Italy, 19 x 20 In. 1760.00
Footstool, Upholstered, Gilt Leaf–Form Legs, Mahogany, 1835, Pr. 9900.00
Footstool, Victorian, Bamboo, Square, Cotton, Saber Legs, Pair 6000.00
Footstool, Victorian, Needlepoint Upholstery, Cast Iron 95.00
Footstool, Victorian, Rococo, Cast Iron 450.00
Footstool, Walnut, Cutout Feet, Old Varnish, 14 In. 65.00
Footstool, Walnut, Floral Tapestry, Cabriole Legs, Lion Masks 3350.00
Footstool, Windsor, Bamboo Turning, Oval, Black Paint Over Red 200.00
Footstool, Windsor, Splayed Base, Green Repaint, Oval, 10 3/4 In. 225.00
Footstool, Windsor, Striped Legs, Oval Top, Pine, 13 1/2 x 8 In. 225.00
Footstool, Windsor, Upholstered Top, Oval, 12 3/4 In. 90.00
Frame, Gilt, Gesso, c.1860, 24 x 36 In. 400.00
Garden Seat, Ceramic, Elephant, Howdah, Oriental, 22 3/4 In. 225.00
Garden Seat, Multicolored Birds & Flowers, Porcelain, 18 In. 445.00
Garden Seat, Reserves of Dragon & Phoenix, Porcelain, 18 In., Pr. 1100.00
Garden Set, Settee, 2 Armchairs, Fern & Leaves, Cast Iron 3850.00
Hall Stand, Arts & Crafts, Mirror, Hooks, Bench, Oak, 74 1/2 In. 120.00
Hall Stand, Drawer, Mirror, Oak 300.00
Hall Stand, Lifetime, Umbrella, Brown, Copper Tray, 72 In. 225.00
Hall Stand, Light Fixture, Beveled Mirror, 6 Hooks, France, 6 Ft. 885.00
Hall Stand, Marble Top, Pier, 2 Drawers, Lord Byron Cameo, Walnut 7500.00
Hall Stand, Mirror, Oak, 4 Ornate Hooks, Applied Carvings 375.00
Hall Stand, Planter, Paris Label, Carved Oak, 9 Ft. 9 In. 3200.00
Hall Tree, Acanthus–Carved Post, 15 Supports, Maple, 79 In. 1320.00
Hall Tree, Carved Crest, Brass Hooks, Hinged Seat, Oak, 81 In. 470.00
Hall Tree, New Drip Pan, England, 1880 .... 2200.00
Hall Tree, Stick-and-Ball Design, Oak 900.00
Hall Tree, Thonet, Bentwood 467.00
High Chair, Arrow Back, Brown Over Red Paint, Yellow Striping 125.00
High Chair, Cane Seat, Oak, 1890s 175.00
High Chair, Converts To Stroller, Pressed Back, Oak 595.00
High Chair, George III, Acanthus Over Splat, c.1875 .... 5500.00
High Chair, Green Painted, Rush Seat, New Jersey, 39 1/2 In. 770.00
High Chair, Ladder Back, Arched Slats, Maple & Hickory, 35 In. 600.00
High Chair, Ladder Back, Board Seat, 35 1/2 In. 700.00
High Chair, Ladder Back, Splayed Legs, Woven Seat, 18th Century 1870.00
High Chair, Ladder Back, Splint Seat, 33 1/2 In. 110.00
High Chair, Ladder Back, Woven Splint Seat 100.00

*Furniture, Kas, Cherry, Raised Panel Doors,
58 x 76 In., 2 Piece*

◆◆◆◆◆◆◆◆◆◆◆◆◆◆◆◆◆◆◆◆◆◆◆◆

Slightly damaged wooden furniture will look better if it is waxed with a high–quality paste wax. Do not use spray or liquid wax because it has other chemicals that may cause problems. Apply the wax with a tightly woven soft cotton cloth, not cheesecloth because it may snag. Wax only once a year. Buff monthly.

◆◆◆◆◆◆◆◆◆◆◆◆◆◆◆◆◆◆◆◆◆◆◆◆

High Chair, Low Spindle Back, Bentwood Arm, 29 1/2 In.	200.00
High Chair, Pine & Hardwood, 30 In.	55.00
High Chair, Serpentine Back, Carved Acanthus Leaves, Mahogany	5000.00
High Chair, Spindle Back, Black Paint, 33 In.	75.00
High Chair, Spindle Back, Tray, Oak	100.00
High Chair, Spindle Black, Red Repaint, 34 3/4 In.	150.00
High Chair, Stave Constructed Barrel–Type Front, Wing Back, Pine	65.00
High Chair, Tulip Ended Arms, Caned Seat, Saber Legs	245.00
High Chair, Victorian, Stenciled Crest Rail	160.00
High Chair, Windsor, 31 In.	365.00
High Chair, Windsor, Bamboo Turned, 35 3/4 In.	450.00
Highboy, 4 Apron Drawers, 9 Top Drawers, Maple, 78 1/2 In.	8000.00
Highboy, Flame & Urn Finials, Mahogany, c.1870, 87 In.	3960.00
Highboy, George III, 5 Drawers, Slide, Mahogany, 72 1/2 In.	3080.00
Highboy, Queen Anne, 9 Dovetailed Drawers, Maple, 69 1/2 In.	7500.00
Highboy, Queen Anne, 9 Overlapping Drawers, Maple, 69 1/2 In.	6000.00
Highboy, Queen Anne, Cabriole Legs, Duck Feet, 71 In. ....*Illus*	5500.00
Highboy, Queen Anne, Curly Maple, c.1750, 67 1/2 In. ....*Illus*	7700.00
Highboy, Queen Anne, Dovetailed, New England, 2 Piece	3100.00
Highboy, Queen Anne, Flat Top, New England, c.1760, 6 Ft. 1/2 In.	7700.00
Highboy, Queen Anne, Maple, Connecticut, 1750, 6 Ft.	7000.00
Highboy, Queen Anne, Maple, Flat Top, America	3600.00
Huntboard, 2 Drawers, Small Center Drawer, Yellow Pine, 56 In.	2400.00
Huntboard, 2 Drawers, Yellow Pine, 19th Century, 47 x 51 In.	3400.00
Hutch, 3 Open Shelves, Base Paneled Doors, Pine, 1880s, 70 In.	885.00
Hutch, 3 Shelves, 1 Long Over 2 Aligned Drawers, Cherry, 36 In.	210.00
Hutch, Child's, Arts & Crafts, 1 Door, 3 Drawers, c.1920, 23 In.	275.00
Ice Cream Set, 4 Chairs	325.00
Ice Cream Set, Table & 2 Chairs, Wooden	195.00
Ice Cream Set, Table, Heart–Shaped Chair Back	450.00
Kas, Cherry, Raised Panel Doors, 58 x 76 In., 2 Piece ....*Illus*	4000.00
Kas, Chippendale, Shelves, Red Paint, Pine, 73 1/2 x 39 In.	750.00
Letter Rack, G. Stickley, 4 Sections, Leather Cover, 12 5/8 In.	1320.00
Library Steps, Leather Inset, Hinged Front Door, Mahogany, 27 In.	715.00
Library Steps, Regency, Tooled Leather Top, Mahogany, 24 1/2 In.	3350.00
Linen Press, 2 Drawers In Base, Painted, Pine, 75 x 46 1/2 In.	900.00
Linen Press, 2 Drawers, 2–Door Top, 6 Panes, Cherry, 72 In.	1100.00
Linen Press, 4 Drawers, Inlaid Banding, Walnut, 95 x 43 1/2 In.	5250.00
Linen Press, Doors, 2 Short Over 2 Long Drawers, Mahogany, 49 In.	1750.00
Linen Press, Federal, Mahogany, 2 Doors, 3 Base Drawers, 82 In.	1550.00
Linen Press, Orignal Base, Pulls & Cornices, Cherry, c.1830	2750.00
Linen Press, Paneled Doors, 4 Shelves, Mahogany, 79 1/2 In.	1200.00
Linen Press, Pierced Tin Panels, 4 Drawers, Hardwood, 72 1/4 In.	2500.00
Linen Press, Regency, Ebony Stringing, Ireland, c.1820, 84 In.	5000.00
Love Seat, Arched Tufted Upholstered Back, Bowed Arms, 57 In.	155.00
Love Seat, John Henry Belter, Rosalie Pattern	8250.00
Love Seat, Louis XV, Needlepoint, Reupholstered, Walnut, 1925	900.00

Love Seat, Renaissance Revival, Tufted Upholstered Back, 57 In. 140.00
Love Seat, Sheraton, Boston Origin, c.1830 .... 1850.00
Love Seat, Triple–Arched Crest Rail, Carved Leaf & Nut, 67 In. 275.00
Love Seat, Victorian, Fruit Carved Back, Upholstered, Claw Feet 500.00
Lowboy, Chippendale, Mahogany, 2 Short Over 1 Long Drawer, 32 In. 467.00
Lowboy, Chippendale, Mahogany, Wallace Nutting ....*Illus* 2100.00
Lowboy, Drawer, Shaped Apron, Scrolled Feet, Oak, 28 In. 357.00
Lowboy, George II, Shaped Apron, 1 Drawer, Walnut, 27 x 31 In. 3000.00
Lowboy, George II, String Inlay, Oak, 18th Century, 28 1/4 In. 3850.00
Lowboy, Queen Anne Style, Long Drawer Over 3, Cherry, 30 x 30 In. 470.00
Lowboy, Queen Anne, 1 Drawer, 1 Board Top, Walnut, 27 x 29 3/4 In. 2600.00
Lowboy, Queen Anne, 1 Long, 3 Short Drawers, Curly Maple, c.1750 .... 7150.00
Lowboy, Queen Anne, 2 Drawers, Curly Maple, 35 3/4 In. 1600.00
Lowboy, Queen Anne, 4 Drawers, Fan & Thumb Top, Walnut & Maple 8000.00
Lowboy, Queen Anne, 4 Drawers, Scrolled Apron, Curly Maple, 30 In. 6750.00
Lowboy, Queen Anne, 4 Lipped Drawers, Walnut, Miniature 5600.00
Lowboy, Queen Anne, Cherry, 1 Long Drawer Over 3 Short, 27 In. 9625.00
Lowboy, Queen Anne, Inlaid Fan, New England, 18th C., Mahogany 4650.00
Lowboy, Queen Anne, Molded Top, Shell Carved Drawer, Cherry 6700.00
Lowboy, Trifid Feet, Walnut, 18th Century, 29 x 30 In. 7000.00
Lowboy, William & Mary Style, Frieze Drawers, Oak, 27 In. 275.00
Lowboy, William & Mary Style, Paneled Drawer, Oak, 19th Century 775.00
Mirror, Acanthus Leaf & Pierced Cut Design, 48 1/2 x 27 In. 110.00
Mirror, Applied Rosettes, Gilt Wood, Italy, c.1840, 34 x 29 In. 250.00
Mirror, Beveled Pine Frame, 7 1/8 x 10 1/4 In. 75.00
Mirror, Biedermeier, Triangular Pediment, Germany, c.1820, 72 In. 2000.00
Mirror, Bull's–Eye, Federal, Eagle Pediment, Allover Gilt, 29 In. 2200.00
Mirror, Carved & Pierced, Dragons On Top, Oriental, 32 x 21 In. 380.00
Mirror, Charles II, Gilt Wood, Silvered, Putti Crest, 1660, 46 In. 9350.00
Mirror, Cheval, Gilt Brass Design, Walnut, France, c.1870, 75 In. 2000.00
Mirror, Cheval, Oval Beveled Glass, Amboyna Wood, 1925, 5 Ft. 9 In. 1650.00
Mirror, Cheval, Trestle Base, Bun Feet, Mahogany, 74 In. 935.00
Mirror, Chippendale, Bird & Urn Crest Over Mirror, 44 x 22 In. 275.00
Mirror, Chippendale, Curly Maple, 27 x 15 In. ....*Illus* 495.00
Mirror, Chippendale, Gilt Eagle, Mahogany, 29 1/4 x 15 1/4 In. 475.00
Mirror, Chippendale, Gold Liner & Eagle, 33 x 16 3/4 In. 350.00
Mirror, Chippendale, Mahogany Frame, 20 x 12 In. 125.00
Mirror, Chippendale, Mahogany Veneer On Pine, 30 x 15 1/4 In. 475.00
Mirror, Chippendale, Molded Frame, Gilt Liner, 27 x 14 3/4 In. 450.00
Mirror, Chippendale, Parcel Gilt Walnut, c.1770, 45 x 24 1/4 In. 5775.00
Mirror, Chippendale, Phoenix, 35 In. 3200.00
Mirror, Chippendale, Pierced & Carved Crest, c.1750, 29 x 18 In. 775.00
Mirror, Chippendale, Scroll, Mahogany Veneer, 26 1/2 x 14 3/4 In. 400.00
Mirror, Chippendale, Sheaf of Wheat At Top, c.1790, 23 1/2 In. 357.00
Mirror, Classical, Gilt Wood, Eglomise Tablet, America, 39 x 19 In 550.00
Mirror, Classical, Gilt, Eglomise Panel 2650.00
Mirror, Continental, Book Matched Walnut Veneer Crest, 48 In. 2000.00

Furniture, Lowboy, Chippendale, Mahogany,
Wallace Nutting

◆ ◆ ◆ ◆ ◆ ◆ ◆ ◆ ◆ ◆ ◆ ◆ ◆ ◆ ◆ ◆ ◆ ◆ ◆

To remove a smell from a drawer. Sprinkle the inside of the drawer with baking soda and leave it there for a week. Vacuum. Repeat if necessary. If the smell is from an animal, try washing the wood with a solution of neutroleum alpha found in pet stores.

◆ ◆ ◆ ◆ ◆ ◆ ◆ ◆ ◆ ◆ ◆ ◆ ◆ ◆ ◆ ◆ ◆ ◆ ◆

Mirror, Convex, Candle Arms, Eagle At Top, c.1820 .... 2650.00
Mirror, Convex, Candle Arms, Gilt Frame, 21 In., Pair 1300.00
Mirror, Convex, Carved Gilt Wood, 19th Century, 34 3/4 x 22 In. 2850.00
Mirror, Convex, Spread–Wing Eagle Top, Gilt Wood, c.1820, 49 In. 3410.00
Mirror, Convex, Wood & Gesso Frame, 23 1/2 In. 300.00
Mirror, Courting, Eglomise Fruit Crest, Continental, 17 x 11 In. 415.00
Mirror, Courting, Reverse–Painted Glass, Flowers, 15 x 10 In. 525.00
Mirror, Crest Ornament, Mahogany Veneer Frame, 7 x 19 1/4 In. 275.00
Mirror, Divided, Carved Gilt Wood, D. Fraser, 1838, 42 x 21 In. 775.00
Mirror, Double Beveled, Gilt Rococo Frame, 21 x 18 1/2 In. 405.00
Mirror, Dressing Table, Ivory, Cherubs, Coat of Arms, 33 x 26 In. 7150.00
Mirror, Dressing, Block–and–Ring Supports, Mahogany, 1835, 34 In. 1350.00
Mirror, Dressing, Regency, Inlaid Mahogany, c.1810, 25 1/2 In. 1750.00
Mirror, Dressing, Robed Figure, Nudes At Sides, Bronze, 33 1/2 In. 2750.00
Mirror, Dressing, Swing Mirror, Stepped Base, Mahogany, 27 1/2 In. 135.00
Mirror, Eagle On Sheaf of Acanthus Leaves, Giltwood, 4 Ft. 6 In. 6050.00
Mirror, Eagle Pediment, Bellflower Border, Oak, 54 x 20 In. 465.00
Mirror, Empire, Burled Walnut, 18 x 24 In. 35.00
Mirror, Empire, Red, Yellow Grained, Reverse Painted, 21 x 13 In. 500.00
Mirror, Empire, Reverse Glass of Girl With Bird, 34 x 15 1/2 In. 275.00
Mirror, Empire, Reverse Painting of Boy & Rabbit, 33 1/4 In. 85.00
Mirror, Federal, Acanthus Carved Pilasters, Mahogany, 34 x 17 In. 325.00
Mirror, Federal, Architectural, Reverse Glass, 33 x 19 1/2 In. 325.00
Mirror, Federal, c.1820, 38 In. ....*Illus* 1045.00
Mirror, Federal, Carved Gilt Wood & Eglomise, c.1810, 5 Ft. 3 In. 4450.00
Mirror, Federal, Convex, Eagle At Top, Gilt Wood, c.1815, 39 1/2 In 2750.00
Mirror, Federal, Gilt & Eglomise Pier, c.1800, 60 1/4 x 29 In. 8500.00
Mirror, Federal, Gilt Sprays, Mahogany, c.1795, 60 1/2 In. 5500.00
Mirror, Federal, Gilt Wood & Gesso, Eglomise Panel, 1805 .... 880.00
Mirror, Federal, Gilt, Eagle Finial, Bull's–Eye, 54 x 32 1/4 In. 3600.00
Mirror, Federal, Mahogany, Gilt Gesso Eagle, 51 x 24 In. 415.00
Mirror, Federal, Mahogany, Shaped, Crest, Gilt Eagle, 63 x 30 In. 305.00
Mirror, Federal, Reverse Painted War of 1812, Gilt, 49 x 23 In. 1200.00
Mirror, Female Figure, Flowers, Silver Frame, 1902, 71 3/4 In. 3300.00
Mirror, Figured Birch, Top Panel, Zoar, Oh., 61 x 28 In. ....*Illus* 990.00
Mirror, Fret Scroll, Gilt, Carved Rondel, Mahogany, 39 x 22 In. 1300.00
Mirror, Garland & Bowknot, Bisque Plaque, Gilt Wood, 48 x 19 In. 1875.00
Mirror, George II, Beveled Glass, Walnut, c.1745, 4 Ft. 2 In. 4950.00
Mirror, George II, Carved Leaf Tips Frame, Walnut, c.1745, 49 In. 9950.00
Mirror, George II, Walnut, Parcel Gilt, C–Scrolls, 56 In., Pair 4950.00
Mirror, George III, Pierced Crest, Vines, Gilt Wood, 4 Ft. 5 In. 9900.00
Mirror, George III, Tree Trunk, 3 Ho–Ho Birds, Pine, 4 Ft. 11 In. 7775.00
Mirror, Gilt Liner & Phoenix, Mahogany, 35 1/2 x 20 1/2 In. 1575.00
Mirror, Gilt Wood & Verre Eglomise, c.1790, 36 1/2 x 19 In. 775.00
Mirror, Gilt Wood & Wirework Crest, c.1795, 59 1/2 In. 2750.00
Mirror, Gilt Wood Frame, Scrolled Leaves, Fruits, 4 Ft. 3 In., Pair 6675.00
Mirror, Gold Repaint, Gesso Eagle, Garlands, Mahogany, 36 x 21 In. 275.00

Furniture, Mirror, Chippendale, Curly Maple, 27 x 15 In.

Furniture, Mirror, Federal, c.1820, 38 In.

Furniture, Mirror, Figured Birch, Top Panel, 61 x 28 In.

Furniture, Mirror, White Porcelain, Gilt Floral, 26 x 18 In.

Furniture, Parlor Set, Renaissance, Walnut, 6 Piece

Mirror, Gustav Stickley, No. 910, Oak, Hooks, Chain, 23 x 35 In. 1450.00
Mirror, Hepplewhite, Inlaid Banded Frame, 38 3/4 x 19 1/2 In. 550.00
Mirror, Hepplewhite, Inlaid Frame, Mahogany, 38 x 18 3/4 In. 550.00
Mirror, Ice Cream Parlor, Free Standing, Mahogany, 1900 .... 900.00
Mirror, Iron Frame, Bust of Washington, Franklin, 19 1/2 In., Pr. 1600.00
Mirror, Italian Baroque, Foliage At Corners, Parcel Gilt, 33 In. 715.00
Mirror, Italian Neoclassical, Gilt Wood, Augustus Bust, 43 In. 1750.00
Mirror, Louis XVI, Bird Crest, 48 x 34 In. 660.00
Mirror, Mahogany, Scroll, Gilt, England, 36 x 19 3/4 In. 450.00
Mirror, Nutting, Cottage With Roses, 10 1/2 x 27 In. 225.00
Mirror, Pagoda Shape, Reverse Plaque, Oval, 45 1/2 x 41 1/2 In. 3575.00
Mirror, Paint & Metal Trim, Folding Case, Mexico, 24 3/4 In. 200.00
Mirror, Pier, Shell Carved, Gilt, c.1855, 83 In. 1000.00
Mirror, Pierced Shell & Scroll Crest, Gilt Wood, 51 x 25 In. 665.00
Mirror, Plateau, Beveled Glass, Silver Plated, 11 3/4 In. 75.00
Mirror, Plateau, Beveled Glass, Silver Plated, 12 1/4 In. 125.00
Mirror, Plateau, Pitkin & Brooks, 10 In. 225.00
Mirror, Queen Anne Style, Mahogany & Parcel Gilt, 58 x 22 In. 335.00
Mirror, Queen Anne, Japanned, Beveled Glass, 12 x 16 1/4 In. 4650.00
Mirror, Queen Anne, Mahogany Veneer, 30 1/4 x 12 5/8 In. 600.00
Mirror, Queen Anne, Walnut Veneer, Ogee Frame, England, 37 In. 425.00
Mirror, Queen Anne, Walnut, Gilt, 1710 .... 4900.00
Mirror, Red Flame Graining Frame, 17 3/4 x 12 3/4 In. 400.00
Mirror, Reverse Painting of House, Pine, 24 1/4 x 15 In. 165.00
Mirror, Reverse Painting, 2-Part Fluted Frame, Gold, 18 1/2 In. 115.00
Mirror, Reverse Painting, Fluted Frame, Pine, 18 1/2 x 13 In. 55.00
Mirror, Reverse Painting, House, Trees, Gilt Frame, 23 x 10 In. 550.00
Mirror, Rococo Style, C-Scrolled Frame, Gilt Wood, 33 In., Pair 2250.00
Mirror, Scroll, Crest, Mahogany Veneer On Pine, 17 x 9 3/4 In. 675.00
Mirror, Scroll, Eagle On Crest, Mahogany, 31 1/2 x 16 1/4 In. 1450.00
Mirror, Scroll, Inlaid Frame, Gilded Liner, Mahogany, 31 x 17 In. 400.00
Mirror, Scroll, Line Inlay On Frame, 21 3/4 x 12 3/4 In. 150.00
Mirror, Scroll, Mahogany Veneer On Pine, Frame, 35 1/2 x 19 In. 500.00
Mirror, Scroll, Marked J. W. Adams, 1865, 17 7/8 x 11 3/8 In. 275.00
Mirror, Scroll, Shell, Mahogany & Parcel Gilt, 53 1/8 In. 9350.00
Mirror, Shaving, 1 Drawer, Beveled Glass, Mahogany, 16 1/2 In. 350.00
Mirror, Shaving, 2 Drawers, D Front, Mahogany 575.00

◆◆◆

Don't wear jewelry when swimming. Both salt and chlorine damage
some types of stones like opals or emeralds. Sand will scratch coral,
pearl, opal, lapis, turquoise, and other stones. Base metals will
corrode.

◆◆◆

Furniture, Pedestal, Woman Figure, Mahogany, 11 x 39 1/2 In.

◆◆◆◆◆◆◆◆◆◆◆◆◆◆◆◆◆◆◆◆◆◆◆◆

It is safe to use spray or paste wax on your furniture but be careful about changing brands. It is okay to put paste wax over spray wax. It is not safe to put spray wax over paste wax becaue it may soften the paste wax and spoil the finish.

◆◆◆◆◆◆◆◆◆◆◆◆◆◆◆◆◆◆◆◆◆◆◆◆

Mirror, Shaving, Adjustable, 3 Drawers, Mahogany, 22 x 23 1/4 In.	150.00
Mirror, Shaving, Adjustable, Ball Feet, 1 Drawer, Mahogany, 19 In.	200.00
Mirror, Shaving, Bowfront, 2 Drawers, Mahogany Veneer, 19 1/2 In.	275.00
Mirror, Shaving, Bowfront, Mahogany On Pine, 21 x 19 1/4 In.	150.00
Mirror, Shaving, D Front, 3 Drawers, Ivory Feet, 28 1/2 In.	800.00
Mirror, Shaving, Dark Finish, Hardwood, 12 1/4 x 7 1/2 In.	150.00
Mirror, Shaving, Empire, Cross–Banded Veneer, Mahogany, 19 In.	75.00
Mirror, Shaving, Mahogany, 3 Dovetailed Drawers, Oval, 22 1/2 In.	150.00
Mirror, Shaving, Ring–Turned Stiles Support, Mahogany, 30 In.	75.00
Mirror, Shaving, Wall, Walnut, Victorian, For Comb & Brush Base	95.00
Mirror, Swan's Neck Cresting, Parcel Gilt, Mahogany, 4 Ft. 3 In.	3575.00
Mirror, Swivel Frame, Abalone Shell Inlay, Teak, 15 3/4 In.	125.00
Mirror, Vanity, Double Glass, Brass, 13 x 11 In.	125.00
Mirror, Venetian, Rococo, Flowers, Rope Rim, 49 1/2 x 57 1/2 In.	825.00
Mirror, Wall, Remember The Maine, Metal Frame	52.50
Mirror, Wall, Twin Birds Head, Putti Head On Apron, 52 x 34 In.	1100.00
Mirror, White Porcelain, Gilt Floral, 26 x 18 In. ....*Illus*	2000.00
Mirror, William & Mary, Oyster Veneered Walnut, 41 In.	1350.00
Mirror, Wrought Iron, Spiral Flowers Frame, c.1925, 17 3/4 In.	1650.00
Parlor Set, Baroque, Settee, Armchair, 2 Side Chairs, Upholstered	850.00
Parlor Set, Eastlake Design, Double Back Love Seat, Armchair, 4	250.00
Parlor Set, Egyptian Revival, Bronze Mounts, 1850s, 5 Piece	3850.00
Parlor Set, Egyptian Revival, Original Tapestry, Settee, 4 Chairs	4500.00
Parlor Set, Jeliff, Renaissance Revival, Walnut, 3 Piece	7150.00
Parlor Set, M. Kammerer, Bentwood, Settee, 2 Armchairs, c.1910	9350.00
Parlor Set, Renaissance, Walnut, 6 Piece ....*Illus*	1200.00
Pedestal, Brass Design, Brass Mounted, Alabaster, 40 In.	335.00
Pedestal, Hexagonal, Square Top, Walnut, 33 x 17 1/2 x 16 3/4 In.	100.00
Pedestal, Limbert, Oak, Inlaid Pedestal, 13–In. –Square Top	1550.00
Pedestal, Victorian, Cherry, Ball & Claw Feet, Marble	1225.00
Pedestal, Woman Figure, Mahogany, 11 x 39 1/2 In. ....*Illus*	1600.00
Pew, Church, Oak, Slightly Curved, 7 Ft.	115.00
Pie Safe, 3 Tins, Punched, 2 Upper Drawers, Walnut, 48 In.	850.00
Pie Safe, 8 Tins, Blue, Miniature	950.00
Pie Safe, 12 Tins, Punched, Double Doors, Pine & Poplar	950.00
Pie Safe, 12 Tins, Soldiers, Mason's Trowels, Stars, c.1840	3200.00
Pie Safe, 12 Tins, Tall Leg, 2 Drawers, Refinished	355.00
Pie Safe, 8 Tins, Star Design, Red Paint	875.00
Pie Safe, Bottom Doors, Pinwheel Design, Walnut, 65 x 42 In.	1100.00
Pie Safe, Cherry & Poplar, 19th Century, 61 x 42 In. ....*Illus*	1980.00
Pie Safe, Double Doors, Screen Inserts, Poplar, 47 x 49 1/2 In.	500.00
Pie Safe, Double Doors, Star–Punched Panels, Butternut & Poplar	700.00
Pie Safe, Empire, Punched Urn Tins, 1 Drawer, Softwood	1000.00
Pie Safe, Hanging, Poplar, Tin, Red Paint, 36 x 27 3/4 In.	200.00
Pie Safe, Potted Flower Tins, Red Wash	1600.00
Pie Safe, Punched Horse Design	1500.00
Pie Safe, Punched Peafowl Design	2650.00

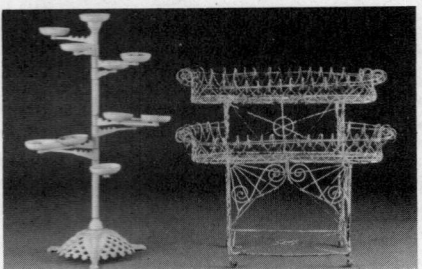

Furniture, Plant Stand, Iron, Movable Arms, 42 In.

Furniture, Plant Stand, Wirework, 31 In.

Pie Safe, Walnut & Mixed Woods, Mid 19th Century, 6 Ft.	6500.00
Plant Stand, Iron, Movable Arms, 42 In. ....*Illus*	55.00
Plant Stand, Wirework, 31 In. ....*Illus*	137.00
Planter, Faces, Garlands, Rectangular, Marble	2600.00
Planter, Regency, String Inlay, Lion Ring Handles, 5 In., Pair	75.00
Rack, Magazine, Wooden Hearts Applied, 16 x 14 x 14 In.	225.00
Rack, Spoon, Drawer, Lidded Compartment, Oak, 27 x 13 3/4 In.	250.00
Recamier, Belter, Rococo, Rosewood, Rosalie Without The Grapes	5500.00
Recamier, Caned, Black Lacquer, Upturned Foot Rest, c.1825, 7 Ft.	5500.00
Recamier, Scrolled Ends, America, Mahogany, c.1820, 7 Ft. 3 In.	1980.00
Rocker & Potty, Cherry & Walnut, 24 In.	35.00
Rocker, Arms, Horsehair, Gold & Yellow Striping	150.00
Rocker, Bamboo, Windsor, Spindle Back, Arms	400.00
Rocker, Bentwood, Cut Velvet Fabric Fitted Back, Thonet	775.00
Rocker, Boston, Grain Painted, 1825–35, 39 In.	410.00
Rocker, Boston, Maple, Scrolling Arms, 19th Century, America	175.00
Rocker, Boston, Old Repaint, Stenciled	45.00
Rocker, Boston, Rosewood Graining, Stenciled, 1835, 44 In.	245.00
Rocker, Button–Turned Arm Posts, 4 Slats, Paper Rush Seat	210.00
Rocker, Carved Back Splats, Rush Seat, America, Oak	120.00
Rocker, Carved Floral & Grape Crest Rail, Upholstered Seat, Oak	133.00
Rocker, Carved Mask & Berry Branches Frame, Walnut, c.1880	4675.00
Rocker, Cheboygen Chair Co., Caned Back, Upholstered Seat	88.00
Rocker, Child's, Cane	120.00
Rocker, Child's, Carpet	125.00
Rocker, Child's, Carpet Covered	125.00
Rocker, Child's, Dark Paint, Traces of Striping & Stencil, 14 In.	105.00
Rocker, Child's, Ladder Back, Pine Birch, Brown Stain, Splint Seat	195.00
Rocker, Child's, Painted Crest Rail Design, Caned Seat, Loop Arms	180.00
Rocker, Child's, Painted Crest Rail, Caned Seat & Back, Loop Arms	165.00
Rocker, Child's, Painted, 19th Century, 21 In.	390.00

◆◆◆◆◆◆◆◆◆◆◆◆◆◆◆◆◆◆◆◆◆◆◆◆◆

Furniture, Pie Safe, Cherry & Poplar,
19th Century, 61 x 42 In.

Slightly scratched or damaged wooden furniture will look better if it is waxed with a high–quality paste wax. Do not use spray or liquid wax because it has other added chemicals that may cause probems. Apply the wax with a tightly woven soft cotton cloth, not cheesecloth because it may snag. Wax only once a year. Buff monthly.

◆◆◆◆◆◆◆◆◆◆◆◆◆◆◆◆◆◆◆◆◆◆◆◆

Rocker, Child's, Plank Seat, Curly Maple 115.00
Rocker, Child's, Pressed Back, Oak, Dated 1899 .... 325.00
Rocker, Child's, Shaker, Arms, Refinished 1225.00
Rocker, Child's, Shaker, Button Arms, Label, 19th Century 1300.00
Rocker, Child's, Stenciled, Stamped CH Baltimore 350.00
Rocker, Child's, Thonet, Wicker Back & Seat 750.00
Rocker, Child's, Wicker .... 100.00 To 150.00
Rocker, Child's, Wicker, Cane Seat 350.00
Rocker, Comb Back, Arrow Slats, Gold Striping, Arms 150.00
Rocker, Comb Back, Bamboo Turnings, Mahogany Arms 800.00
Rocker, Comb Back, Yellow Paint, Freehand Painted Design 1100.00
Rocker, Faces Carved In Arm Rests, Leather Seat, Oak 325.00
Rocker, G. Stickley, 4 Back Slats, Flat Arm Over 5 Slats, c.1907 .... 1650.00
Rocker, Gustav Stickley, Flat Arms Over 5 Vertical Slats, 1904 .... 1875.00
Rocker, Gustav Stickley, No. 311 1/2, V Back, Fabric Seat, 1907 .... 550.00
Rocker, Gustav Stickley, No. 323 .... 2860.00
Rocker, Hunzinger, Arms, Carved & Incised Walnut, c.1870 .... 465.00
Rocker, J. P. Wilder 88.00
Rocker, L. & J. G Stickley, Concave Rail Over 6 Slats, c.1912 .... 440.00
Rocker, L. & J. G. Stickley, 6 Slats, Spring Cushion, c.1910 .... 355.00
Rocker, Ladder Back, 4 Slat, Arms, Rush Seat, Dark Finish 150.00
Rocker, Ladder Back, Arms, Red Wash, Old Splint Seat, 43 1/2 In. 1045.00
Rocker, Ladder Back, Half Arms, 4 Slats, Splint Seat 255.00
Rocker, Ladder Back, Maple, c.1800 ....*Illus*   605.00
Rocker, Ladder Back, Painted Cloth, Twine Seat, 24 1/2 In. 88.00
Rocker, Ladder Back, Red & Black Paint, Arms 150.00
Rocker, Ladder Back, Shaker No. 7 .... 1980.00
Rocker, Ladder Back, Splint Seat, Arms 175.00
Rocker, Ladder Back, Woven Splint Seat, Arms 85.00
Rocker, Ladder Back, Yellow String, 3 Slats, Rush Seat 50.00
Rocker, Limbert, 4 Horizontal Slats, Front Seat Rail, c.1910 .... 2000.00
Rocker, Limbert, Inlaid Ebony 2090.00
Rocker, Limbert, No. 819, Flat Open Arms, Leather Back & Seat, 1910 .... 2200.00
Rocker, Lincoln, Cane Seat & Back 100.00
Rocker, Lincoln, Curly Maple, Crest Rail, Caned Seat & Back 220.00
Rocker, New England, Salmon Paint, 18th Century 575.00
Rocker, Oak, Floral & Grape Crest, Scrolled, America 120.00
Rocker, Peru Chair Co., Mission Style, Oak 60.00
Rocker, Platform, Child's, Leather Seat & Back 225.00
Rocker, Platform, Scroll & Carved Design, Oak 135.00
Rocker, Platform, Spoon Carving, Porcelain Casters 210.00

*Furniture, Rocker, Ladder Back, Maple,
c.1800*

*Furniture, Rocker, Shaker,
Arms With Mushroom Caps, Rush Seat*

Rocker, Platform, Wicker, Arms, Original Finish 850.00
Rocker, Pressed Back, Mahogany Stain 105.00
Rocker, Pressed Back, Oak, Spindle Back & Sides 45.00
Rocker, Sewing, Arrowback, Split Plank Seat 40.00
Rocker, Sewing, Gustav Stickley, No. 303, Canvas Seat, c.1904 .... 412.50
Rocker, Sewing, Oak, Caned Seat & Back 90.00
Rocker, Sewing, Seat Hip Rests, Cand Back, Carved Crown 150.00
Rocker, Sewing, Shaker, New Lebanon, No. 8, Original Seat 650.00
Rocker, Shaker, Arms With Mushroom Caps, Rush Seat ....*Illus* 440.00
Rocker, Shaker, Arms, Slat Back, Maple, c.1840, 44 In. 2900.00
Rocker, Shaker, Mount Lebanon, Rush Seat, Mushroom Cap On Arms 1400.00
Rocker, Shaker, New England, Arms, Maple, c.1840, 44 In. 3200.00
Rocker, Shaker, No. 0, Child's, Mt. Lebanon 125.00
Rocker, Shaker, No. 0, Mt. Lebanon, Splint Seat, c.1880 .... 995.00
Rocker, Shaker, No. 2, Mt. Lebanon, Black & Tan Tape Seat 412.00
Rocker, Shaker, No. 3, Mt. Lebanon, N. Y., Tape Seat, c.1880 .... 605.00
Rocker, Shaker, No. 3, Original Finish, Tape Seat 300.00
Rocker, Shaker, No. 6, Mount Lebanon 1895.00
Rocker, Shaker, No. 6, Mushroom Arm Caps, 4 Slats, Paper Rush Seat 750.00
Rocker, Shaker, No. 7, Mushroom Arm Caps, Shawl Bar, 42 In. 400.00
Rocker, Shaker, No. 7, Original Tape Seat & Back, Arms 1950.00
Rocker, Shell Back & Seat, Parcel Gilt & Painted, Venetian 3300.00
Rocker, Shop of The Crafters, Cincinnati, Labeled, Mission Oak 175.00
Rocker, Spindle Back, Stenciled Crest 175.00
Rocker, Thonet, Arched Rail, Velvet Back, Armrests & Seat, 53 In. 770.00
Rocker, Thonet, Foot Rest, c.1890 .... 1800.00
Rocker, Upholstered In Olive Green Linsey–Woolsey 770.00
Rocker, Victorian, Carved Crest, Tufted Ruby Upholstery 200.00
Rocker, Wicker, c.1890 .... 1870.00
Rocker, William & Mary, Banister Back, 1650–1720 .... 950.00
Rocker, Windsor, Bow Back, Arms, Bamboo, Old Red & Black Graining 125.00
Rocker, Windsor, Comb Back, Oval Seat, Arms 300.00
Rocker, Windsor, Rod Back, Black Paint, New England, 19th Century 110.00
Rocker, Windsor, Step Down 335.00
Rocker, Windsor, Traces of Paint, Elm, 1830s 385.00
Screen, 2–Panel, Beveled Mirror, Laminated Wood, 103 In., Pair 120.00
Screen, 2–Panel, Fish, Plants, Leon Jallot, 1930, 5 Ft. 7 1/4 In. 9900.00
Screen, 2–Panel, Oak, Ball & Stick Design, No Fabric 22.59
Screen, 3 Panels, Heraldic Crest, Griffins, Oak, 70 x 64 In. 665.00
Screen, 3–Panel, Floral Design, Batik, 71 1/2 In. 135.00
Screen, 3–Panel, Gadroon, Acanthus, Floral Carving, France, 71 In. 995.00
Screen, 3–Panel, Hand Painted Pheasants, Trees, Black Leather 1800.00
Screen, 3–Panel, Lake & Game Bird, Silk Panels, Japan, 67 In. 495.00
Screen, 3–Panel, Leaded Glass, Matthew Bros., Oak, 67 1/2 In. 7775.00
Screen, 3–Panel, Needlepoint, Biblical Scenes, Mahogany, 85 In. 2250.00
Screen, 3–Panel, Painted Venetian Scene, England, 69 In. 225.00
Screen, 3–Panel, Reticulated Panels, Europe, Pine, 79 x 60 In. 330.00
Screen, 3–Panel, Walnut, Rococo, V. Martin, 19 x 71 In. 900.00
Screen, 4 Panel, Floral & Fruit, Center Gilt Scene, 78 In. 2450.00
Screen, 4–Panel, Beveled Mirror, Laminated Wood, 103 In., Pair 210.00
Screen, 4–Panel, Birds, Fruit, Embossed & Painted Leather, 84 In. 1000.00
Screen, 4–Panel, Black Lacquer, Polychrome Design, 70 In. 150.00
Screen, 4–Panel, Blue & Gold Damask, 4 Ft. 7 In. x 17 3/4 In. 8900.00
Screen, 4–Panel, Cranes In Wooded Landscape, Japan, 34 1/2 In. 135.00
Screen, 4–Panel, Crewel Oriental Garden Scene, 67 In. 1320.00
Screen, 4–Panel, Embroidered Landscape, Oriental, 68 1/2 In. 155.00
Screen, 4–Panel, Landscape, Silk Brocade On Reverse, 84 In. 225.00
Screen, 4–Panel, Painted Cranes, Gold, Oriental, 38 x 59 In. 55.00
Screen, 4–Panel, Queen Anne, Needlepoint, Allegorical Woman, 6 Ft. 2250.00
Screen, 6–Panel, Ivory & Mother–of–Pearl Inlay, China, c.1900 .... 9700.00
Screen, 6–Panel, Oriental, Birds & Flowers, 18K Gold Leaf, 1930s 1000.00
Screen, 6–Panel, Scenes, Children At Play, China, 72 x 114 In. 605.00
Screen, 8–Panel, Black Lacquer, Relief Carved Scene, 128 x 84 In. 175.00

Furniture, Secretary Bookcase, Cherry,
Drop Front, 72 In.

Furniture, Secretary Bookcase, Walnut, 9 Ft.

Screen, Candle, Petit Point Floral, Mahogany, 17 1/4 In. 150.00
Screen, Embroidered Birds, Ebonized Frame, 45 x 43 In. 1320.00
Screen, Ivory, Rosewood, Emperor, China, 30 x 30 In. ....*Illus* 725.00
Screen, Pole, Black & White Beadwork, Roman God, Blue, Victorian 615.00
Screen, Pole, Chippendale, Mahogany, Dark Finish, 60 In. 275.00
Screen, Pole, Painted & Penwork, Brass Mounted, c.1810, 4 Ft. 8 In. 1650.00
Screen, Pole, Regency, Mahogany, Rebecca At Well, England, 61 In. 250.00
Screen, Table, Woman In Palace Garden, 6 Panel, Paper, 34 1/2 In. 1100.00
Secretary Bookcase, 7 Drawers, Mahogany, 88 1/2 In. 2700.00
Secretary Bookcase, Block Front, A. Keesecker, Mahogany, 95 In. 3100.00
Secretary Bookcase, Brass Eagle Finial, Inlaid Mahogany, c.1810 .... 6700.00
Secretary Bookcase, Carved Mahogany & Cherrywood, c.1825, 8 Ft. 2350.00
Secretary Bookcase, Cherry, Drop Front, 72 In. ....*Illus* 1500.00
Secretary Bookcase, Eastlake Style, Walnut, 89 In. 1155.00
Secretary Bookcase, Faux Marble Floral, 2 Doors, Painted Pine 2200.00
Secretary Bookcase, Flame Mahogany, Marble Insert, 1830, 7 Ft. 2300.00
Secretary Bookcase, George III, Inlaid Mahogany 5625.00
Secretary Bookcase, Grill Insets, Satinwood, c.1800, 6 Ft. 7 In. 6650.00
Secretary Bookcase, Hepplewhite, Mahogany Inlay, 5 Drawer, 87 In. 3100.00
Secretary Bookcase, Mirrored Doors, 2 Domes, Walnut, 92 1/2 In. 7975.00
Secretary Bookcase, Mullioned Doors, Fall Front, Mahogany, c.1900 .... 7425.00
Secretary Bookcase, Regency, Arched Doors, Rosewood, 71 In. 3400.00
Secretary Bookcase, Rosewood, Glass Doors, 1860, 9 Ft. 2 In. 5300.00
Secretary Bookcase, Top Glass Doors, 39–In. Writing Height 775.00
Secretary Bookcase, Walnut, 9 Ft. ....*Illus* 2200.00

Furniture, Screen, Ivory, Rosewood, Emperor,
China, 30 x 30 In.

◆◆◆◆◆◆◆◆◆◆◆◆◆◆◆◆◆◆◆◆◆◆◆

If the screw holding a hinge is
loose, try this old–fashioned
remedy. Break the heads off
several large wooden kitchen
matches. Put the wooden strips
in the hole with some glue, then
screw the old screw back into
place.

◆◆◆◆◆◆◆◆◆◆◆◆◆◆◆◆◆◆◆◆◆◆◆

Secretary Desk, Plantation Style, Cherry & Tiger Maple	1800.00
Secretary, Biedermeier, Drop Front, Walnut, Marble Top	2850.00
Secretary, Cylinder, Burled, Walnut, 1880s, 11 Ft. 11 In.	8500.00
Secretary, Empire, Glass Top, Tiger Maple	1815.00
Secretary, Fall Front, Fitted Interior, Rosewood, 4 Ft. 11 In.	4400.00
Secretary, Fall Front, Marble Top, Biedermeier, Walnut, 58 In.	2860.00
Secretary, Federal, Mahogany, C Scroll Attached Mirror, Boston	7150.00
Secretary, Georgian, Mahogany, Swan Pediment, Ogee Bracket Feet	4125.00
Secretary, Hepplewhite, Drop Front, Mahogany, 2 Drawers, Large	5225.00
Secretary, Mahogany, 4 Drawers, Glass Doors, Pediment Top, 7 Ft.	4200.00
Secretary, Mahogany, Bird's-Eye Maple, 2 Doors, 3 Drawers, 1810	6500.00
Secretary, Mirrored Doors, Painted & Gilt, 103 1/2 x 46 In.	9500.00
Secretary, On Frame, 12 Interior Drawers, Maple, 82 1/2 In.	1700.00
Secretary, Tambour, Satinwood Ovals, Drop Panel, Cherry, c.1830	5800.00
Secretary, Wooton, Fall Front, Trestle Feet, Walnut & Maple, 6 Ft.	10000.00
Server, 3 Drawers, Scalloped Crest, Curly Maple, 36 1/2 In.	3750.00
Server, Eastlake, Walnut, Pierced Backsplash, Acorn Finial, 71 In.	495.00
Server, Gustav Stickley, 3 Drawers, Backsplash, Shelf, 39 x 48 In.	2550.00
Server, Gustav Stickley, No. 802	4125.00
Server, Paneled Doors, 3 Drawers, Pine, 56 1/2 x 47 In.	600.00
Server, Pine, 3 Shelves, Refinished, Canada, 18th Century	1045.00
Server, Sheraton, Brass Gallery, Walsh & Egerton Label	6650.00
Settee, Acanthus Rail, Putti Supports, Gilt Wood, 53 In.	775.00
Settee, Adirondack	1700.00
Settee, Camel Back, Scrolled Arms, Damask Upholstered, 63 In.	1875.00
Settee, Carved Dolphin Arms, America, Mahogany, c.1825	2325.00
Settee, Carved Teak, Dragons, Flowers, Birds, Chinese, 49 1/4 In.	1000.00
Settee, Double Back, Pierced Lattice Sides, Marble, India, 43 In.	7700.00
Settee, Edwardian, Pineapple Finials, Inlaid Mahogany, 49 In.	880.00
Settee, Federal, Mahogany, Silk, Mass., 1810, 66 In.	6325.00
Settee, Floral & Shell Carved Crest, Upholstered, Walnut, 78 In.	220.00
Settee, George III, Leather Upholstery, Gilt Wood, 1785, 69 In.	5500.00
Settee, Harden, Oak, Upholstered Seat	200.00
Settee, Herter Brothers, Brass Inlay, Inlaid Rosewood, c.1880	1980.00
Settee, Hoof Feet, Carved Walnut, France, LRC, c.1840, Pair	2860.00
Settee, J. & J. W. Meeks, Stanton Hall, Carved, Laminated Rosewood	5775.00
Settee, Knuckle Arms, Painted, T. Mason, 18th Century	3850.00
Settee, Light Green, Stenciled, 19th Century, 32 x 15 x 72 In.	825.00
Settee, Louis XIV Style, Gilt, Gold & Ivory Upholstery, 50 In.	550.00
Settee, Louis XVI Style, Oval Back, Brocade Upholstery, Gilt Wood	1200.00
Settee, Meeks, Rococo, Henry Ford Pattern, Laminated Rosewood	5775.00
Settee, Outward Turned-Down Arms, Mahogany, c.1900, 52 In.	110.00
Settee, Quadruple Back, Caned, Cushioned, Mahogany, 6 Ft. 3 In.	3410.00
Settee, Rosette Carved Crest Rail, Curved Arms, Silk Upholstery	1200.00
Settee, Roycroft, Oak, Vertical Slats, 2 Drawers, c.1910, 63 In.	5225.00
Settee, Satinwood & Abalone Inlaid Rosewood, 61 In.	885.00
Settee, Sheraton, Black, Red & Gold Design, Rush Seat	2300.00
Settee, Sheraton, Camelback, Carved Bellflowers, Mahogany, 80 In.	1650.00
Settee, Tiger Maple, Cane Seat, Arms	1980.00
Settee, Triple Chair Back, Caryatid Arms, Lacquered, 60 In.	440.00
Settee, Twig & Root, c.1910	1250.00
Settee, Victorian, Arched Back, Serpentine Seat, Walnut, 65 In.	335.00
Settee, Victorian, Floral Carved Arched Back, Mahogany, 72 In.	225.00
Settee, Victorian, Floral Crest, Button Tufted Back, Oak, 72 In.	325.00
Settee, Windsor, Red, Bamboo Spindles, Penna., 1800, 6 Ft. 6 In.	3650.00
Settee, Windsor, Rod Back, 8 Legs, Outswept Arms, c.1800, 77 In.	4950.00
Settee, Windsor, Rod Back, Allover Brown Paint, 78 In.	2550.00
Settee, Windsor, Spindle Back, Plank Seat, 41 1/2 In.	450.00
Settle Bench, Fireside, Flame Stitch Cushion, 60 x 47 In.	55.00
Settle, Brooks, Square Spindled Even Arm, Dark Brown, 41 x 94 In.	1925.00
Settle, Curved, 1690–1750, 8 Ft.	300.00
Settle, Curved, Dark Green Paint, 62 In.	1100.00
Settle, G. Stickley, 8 Vertical Back Slats, Cushion Seat, c.1907	8500.00

◆◆◆

To remove a musty odor from a book, sprinkle talcum powder between the pages, then wrap the book and store it for a few months. When you open it again, brush out all the powder and the musty smell will be gone.

◆◆◆

Settle, G. Stickley, No. 208, 8 Slats, Cushion Seat, 76 In.	9350.00
Settle, Gilt Stenciled Design, Plank Seat, Black Paint, 85 In.	375.00
Settle, Gray Paint, Striped, Floral, Angel Wing, Plank Seat, 70 In.	1600.00
Settle, Gustav Stickley, Even Arm, 8 Slats, Spring Seat, 76 In.	8250.00
Settle, L. & J. G. Stickley, No. 281, Even Arm, Oak, c.1906, 76 In.	6000.00
Settle, L. & J. G. Stickley, 7 Vertical Slats, Spring Cushion, 1912	2535.00
Settle, Limbert, 9 Vertical Slats, Cushion, c.1910, 84 3/4 In.	3850.00
Settle, Limbert, Upholstered Seat, 5 Ft.	3250.00
Settle, Oak, Dark Finish, Curved, England, 72 x 59 1/2 In.	950.00
Settle, Paneled Back, Double–Hinged Seat, Pine, 69 x 73 1/2 In.	475.00
Settle, Philadelphia, Red & Black Graining, Rush Seat, 48 In.	900.00
Settle, Pine, Curved Hooded Back, Branded N. Price, 61 1/2 In.	1450.00
Settle, Plank Seat, Scrolled Arms, Spindle Back, 78 1/2 In.	1800.00
Settle, Rolled Arms, Olive Green, Copper & Black Stencil Design	4800.00
Settle, Spindle Back, Penna., Blue Paint Over Red, 1830, 6 Ft.	495.00
Settle, Spindle Back, Plank Seat, 2 Boards, Curved Arms, 90 In.	575.00
Settle, Wide Plank Seat, Scrolled Arms, 3–Slat Back, 70 3/4 In.	325.00
Settle, William & Mary, Carved Back, Oak	3850.00
Settle, William & Mary, Carved Lunette, 17th Century, 58 1/2 In.	3855.00
Settle, Windsor, Rockers, Bamboo Turnings, Shaped Seat, 34 In.	400.00
Shelf, Corner, Hanging, Diamond On Base, Red Varnish, 36 3/4 In.	700.00
Shelf, Corner, Painted Pine, 3 Paneled Shelves, Zoar, Ohio, 46 In.	1200.00
Shelf, Hanging, Butterfly Form, Orange, Black, Yellow, 12 x 13 In.	60.00
Shelf, Hanging, Scalloped Ends, 3 Shelves, 29 x 21 3/4 In.	255.00
Shelf, Mahogany, Whale End, 4 Graduated Shelves, 34 x 25 In.	715.00
Shelf, Open, Pine Shelves, Walnut Facings, Walnut, 58 3/4 In.	475.00
Sideboard, 3 Drawers Over 2 Doors, Beveled Mirror, Oak	2000.00
Sideboard, 3 Drawers, Cupboards, Inlaid Mahogany, 1790, 70 1/4 In.	6150.00
Sideboard, 3 Drawers, Figured Mahogany Veneer, Cherry, 73 1/4 In.	1000.00
Sideboard, 5 Drawers, Double Doors, Mahogany, 39 3/4 x 67 5/8 In.	2500.00
Sideboard, Adirondack, 3 Drawers, 2 Doors, 1915, 54 x 43 x 25 In.	825.00
Sideboard, Backboard, Carved, English, Mahogany, c.1850	975.00
Sideboard, Bowfront, 4 Drawers, Kneehole, Mahogany, 4 Ft. 3 In.	8250.00
Sideboard, Brass Plate Rack, Serpentine Top, Mahogany, 78 In.	1350.00
Sideboard, Crotch Grain Front, Mahogany, c.1800, 66 In.	5400.00
Sideboard, Curved Glass, Beveled Mirror, Holland	1200.00
Sideboard, Cutlery Drawer, 2 Doors, Line Inlay, Mahogany, 71 In.	4500.00
Sideboard, Drawer In Pedestal Sides, Mahogany, 1820, 7 Ft. 10 In.	9950.00
Sideboard, Ebonized & Leaded Glass, E. A. Tayler, c.1905, 6 Ft.	8850.00
Sideboard, Empire, Mahogany, 3 Drawers & 4 Doors, 67 x 44 In.	500.00
Sideboard, Federal, Inlaid Mahogany Veneer, 1 Drawer, 1790, 67 In.	8250.00
Sideboard, Flame Veneer, Oval Banding, Mahogany, 68 1/2 In.	4000.00
Sideboard, G. Stickley, 1 Long, 2 Short Drawers, 1907, 45 5/8 In.	1800.00
Sideboard, G. Stickley, Gallery, Metal Pulls, 2 Doors, 48 In.	3850.00
Sideboard, George III, Mahogany, Bowfront Center Section, 1790	9900.00
Sideboard, Georgian Style, Baker, 4 Drawers, Walnut, 82 In.	2250.00
Sideboard, Georgian Style, Inlaid Mahogany, England	3400.00
Sideboard, Hepplewhite, Bowfront Center, Mahogany, 60 In.	1000.00
Sideboard, Hepplewhite, Line & Fan Inlay, Mahogany, 40 x 71 In.	2850.00
Sideboard, Hepplewhite, Potthast Brothers	7600.00
Sideboard, Hepplewhite, String Inlay, Mahogany, c.1800, 72 In.	5390.00
Sideboard, J. & T. Seymour, Mahogany Veneer, c.1790, 6 Ft. 2 In.	10000.00

Sideboard, Lifetime Furniture, Mirrored Back, c.1910, 60 1/2 In.	550.00
Sideboard, Limbert, Oak, 8–Leg Prairie, 1908–12 ....*Illus*	4400.00
Sideboard, Limbert, Plate Rail, 3 Drawers, Oak, c.1912	4000.00
Sideboard, Line & Bellflower Inlay, Mahogany, 40 x 65 1/2 In.	3200.00
Sideboard, Line Inlay, 7 Drawers, Mahogany, 84 In.	1500.00
Sideboard, Line Inlay, Flame Veneer, Mahogany, c.1800, 68 In.	4000.00
Sideboard, Lion Brass Pulls, Cellaret Drawers, England, c.1820	3500.00
Sideboard, Mahogany, Upper Shelf, Mirror, 2 Doors, 7 Drawers	1500.00
Sideboard, Marble Top, 4 Doors, 3 Drawers, Mahogany, 73 1/2 In.	1200.00
Sideboard, Mirror, England, Burl Mahogany, 5 Ft. 5 In. x 7 Ft.	2250.00
Sideboard, Oak, Marble Top, Drawers, 4 Doors, Mirror	5995.00
Sideboard, Oak, Marble Top, Winged Griffin Crest, Mirror	5995.00
Sideboard, Stickley Bros., Oak, 60 In.	1200.00
Sideboard, Victorian, 4 Drawers, 2 Cupboards, Walnut, 72 1/2 In.	825.00
Sofa Bed, Pillar & Scroll	3960.00
Sofa Bed, Style of Carl Johan, c.1820	1550.00
Sofa, Aesthetic Movement, Walnut & Burl Walnut	1045.00
Sofa, Arched Back, Scrolling Arms, Leather & Mahogany, 76 In.	250.00
Sofa, Belter, Rosalie, Double Diamond Tuft, 58 In.	6500.00
Sofa, Bolsters, Cornucopia Arms, Eagle Carved, Hairy Paw, 1800s	1500.00
Sofa, Camelback, George III, Scrolled Arms, Loose Cushion, 7 Ft.	5500.00
Sofa, Camelback, George III, Upholstered Crest, Seat, 6 Ft. 11 In.	3300.00
Sofa, Camelback, Navy Blue Wool Upholstery, 1930s, 76 In.	400.00
Sofa, Camelback, Rolled Arms, Velvet Upholstery, 1930s, 84 In.	775.00
Sofa, Carved, Rosewood, 1890	2100.00
Sofa, Chippendale Style, Camelback, Flame Stitch Upholstery	1600.00
Sofa, Chippendale, Fluted Block Legs, Leather Upholstered, 7 Ft.	2300.00
Sofa, Chrome, Gray & Pink Vinyl, Bench Type, 1935	100.00
Sofa, Dunbar, Cotton Upholstery, Metal Legs, 1955, 97 In.	385.00
Sofa, Empire, Camel Back, Tufted Arms, Down Pillow, Mahogany Trim	3500.00
Sofa, Federal, Arms Over Arrow Supports, Mahogany, 1810, 75 In.	2250.00

Furniture, Sideboard, Limbert, Oak, 8–Leg Prairie, 1908–12

Furniture, Sofa, Federal, Mahogany, Satinwood Inlay

Sofa, Federal, Carved Mahogany, Upholstered, 38 x 76 x 26 In. 1350.00
Sofa, Federal, Eagle Head Carving, Upholstered 1980.00
Sofa, Federal, Mahogany, Satinwood Inlay ....*Illus* 900.00
Sofa, Figured Maple, Upholstered, 1850s, 7 Ft. 885.00
Sofa, Geometric & Floral Upholstery, Down Cushions, 90 In. 665.00
Sofa, Herman Miller, Upholstered Foam, Chrome Legs, 1954, 72 In. 715.00
Sofa, Jeliff, Open Arm, Walnut, Female Busts, Stylized Foliage 1900.00
Sofa, Mahogany Frame, Brass Feet, Brocade Upholstery, 71 1/4 In. 1000.00
Sofa, Mahogany Frame, Lyre Frame, Swan's Head Crest, Upholstered, 80 In. 250.00
Sofa, Mohair Wool Cover, Chrome, Metal Bands, c.1970, 8 Ft. 1100.00
Sofa, New England, Mahogany Inlay, c.1800, 33 1/2 x 69 In. 3750.00
Sofa, Ormolu Mounts, 2 Seater, Russia, c.1820 .... 2000.00
Sofa, Sheraton, 8 Legs, Reeded Legs & Arms 3600.00
Sofa, Sheraton, Ebony Inlay At Arms, Mahogany & Satinwood, 72 In. 7000.00
Sofa, Sheraton, Mahogany, Gold & Ivory Striped Brocade, 77 In. 1300.00
Sofa, Triple Medallion Back, Rosewood, c.1880 .... 1000.00
Sofa, Victorian, Red Velvet Upholstery, c.1860 .... 2850.00
Sofa, Victorian, Winged Lions Carved In Mahogany Frame 4500.00
Sofa, Windsor, Bow Back, Black & Green Paint, Shaped Arms 2100.00
Stand, 1 Drawer, 1–Board Top, Cherry & Birch, 28 In. 500.00
Stand, 1 Drawer, 2–Board Top, Cherry, 28 1/2 x 21 1/2 In. 350.00
Stand, 1 Drawer, 2–Board Top, Drop Leaf, Curly Maple, 30 In. 300.00
Stand, 1 Drawer, Cock–Beaded, Hepplewhite, Walnut, 28 3/4 In. 550.00
Stand, 1 Drawer, Curly Maple, America, 29 In. 1760.00
Stand, 1 Drawer, Cut–Out Top, Connecticut, Cherry, 26 1/4 In. 850.00
Stand, 1 Drawer, Dovetailed, Cherry, 2 Board, Turned Legs, 28 In. 235.00
Stand, 1 Drawer, Dovetailed, Oval Brasses, Curly Maple, 27 1/2 In. 650.00
Stand, 1 Drawer, Dovetailed, Sheraton, Cherry, 28 1/4 x 19 In. 575.00
Stand, 1 Drawer, Dovetailed, Southern Pine, 28 3/4 In. 700.00
Stand, 1 Drawer, Grain Painted, 1820–30 .... 2200.00
Stand, 1 Drawer, Hepplewhite, 1–Board Top, Cherry, 26 3/4 x 18 In. 375.00
Stand, 1 Drawer, Hepplewhite, 2–Board Top, 1850s, 27 3/4 In. 275.00
Stand, 1 Drawer, Hepplewhite, Cherry, Beaded, 18 3/4 x 20 x 29 In. 425.00
Stand, 1 Drawer, Hepplewhite, Curly Maple & Cherry, 28 x 18 In. 1200.00
Stand, 1 Drawer, Hepplewhite, Square Legs, Pine, 28 3/4 In. 275.00
Stand, 1 Drawer, Sheraton, Curly Maple, 17 1/2 x 21 1/2 x 30 In. 550.00
Stand, 1 Drawer, Sheraton, Walnut, Miniature 455.00
Stand, 1 Drawer, Square Legs, Poplar, 28 3/4 x 23 3/4 In. 500.00
Stand, 1 Drawer, Square Top, Spindle Legs, Cherry, 27 In. 175.00
Stand, 1–Board Pine Top, Hickory Base, 27 1/2 In. 200.00
Stand, 2 Drawers, Cherry, Curly Maple Veneer, 28 1/2 In. 300.00
Stand, 2 Drawers, Dovetailed, 1–Board Top, Maple, 28 1/2 In. 500.00
Stand, 2 Drawers, Dovetailed, 2–Board Top, Ash, 29 1/2 In. 350.00
Stand, 2 Drawers, Drop Leaf, Walnut, 20 x 16 In. 225.00
Stand, 2 Drawers, Drop Leaves, Tiger Maple, 1820 .... 1250.00
Stand, 2 Drawers, Empire, Drop Leaf, Maple, 29 1/2 x 22 In. 450.00
Stand, 2 Drawers, Scalloped Base Shelf, Curly Maple, 28 3/4 In. 550.00
Stand, 3 Drawers, Curly Maple Fronts, 27 1/2 x 19 x 21 1/2 In. 250.00
Stand, Basin, Mid–Platform Drawer, Mahogany, 33 In., Pair 1760.00
Stand, Book, George II, Adjustable, Tripod, c.1735, 32 In. 3850.00
Stand, Carved Teak, Soapstone Insert, China, 18 x 16 1/2 In. 375.00
Stand, Chinese Chippendale, 3 Shelves 375.00
Stand, Cookie Corners, Pineapple Turned Legs, Mahogany, c.1830 .... 1155.00
Stand, Corner, Adirondack, Black, Red & Gold Daubs, Varnish, 62 In. 210.00
Stand, Dictionary, Casters, Mahogany, 32 1/2 In. 55.00
Stand, Ebonized, 3 Legs, c.1895 ....*Illus* 825.00
Stand, Federal, Carved Walnut, Rectangular Top, 28 x 30 x 21 In. 2750.00
Stand, George I, Tripod, Removable Top, Yew Wood, 20 1/4 In. 3850.00
Stand, George III, Cylindrical Gallery, Brass, c.1885, 33 In. 550.00
Stand, Hepplewhite, 1–Board Top, Red Paint, Pine, 26 In. 200.00
Stand, Hepplewhite, Drawer, Beaded Edge, Ovolo Corners, Cherry 1075.00
Stand, Hepplewhite, Pencil Post Legs, Pine, 32 x 21 3/4 In. 350.00
Stand, Hepplewhite, Pine, Poplar, Refinished, 2–Board Top, 29 In. 175.00

Furniture, Stand, Ebonized, 3 Legs, c.1895   Furniture, Stand, Umbrella, Bear, Victorian

Stand, Lift Top, Writing Surface, Cherry & Tiger Maple, c.1835 .... 3850.00
Stand, Magazine, G. Stickley, 4 Shelves, Cutout Handles, 40 In. 1550.00
Stand, Magazine, Glazed Doors On Bamboo Legs, Lacquered, 46 In. 445.00
Stand, Mahogany, Arts & Crafts, Lower Shelf, Splayed Legs, 24 In. 82.50
Stand, Music, Hepplewhite, Mahogany, Pullout Shelves, 33 In. 150.00
Stand, Music, Rococo Revival, Mounted On Table, Drawer, Low Shelf 950.00
Stand, Penna., Walnut, Red Stained, 2 Drawers, 22 x 25 x 30 In. 100.00
Stand, Phone, Limbert 2200.00
Stand, Pine, Red Repaint, 3 Tiers, Pennsylvania, 29 3/4 In. 500.00
Stand, Pitcher & Bowl, America, Mahogany, c.1840 .... 275.00
Stand, Plant, Adirondack, Green, Orange & Gold, 14 x 52 x 40 In. 550.00
Stand, Plant, Adirondack, Rhododendron, Black Paint, 28 In. 375.00
Stand, Plant, Art Deco, Glass Top, Metal Shell Base, 1930, 32 In. 247.00
Stand, Plant, Circular Geometric Form, Wicker, 1910s, 18 1/2 In. 35.00
Stand, Plant, Gilt Iron, Pine Cone Finial, Scrolled Arms, 86 In. 30.00
Stand, Plant, Globular Vase, Painted Wirework, 31 In. 110.00
Stand, Plant, Pierced Carved, Marble Top 455.00
Stand, Plant, Pine Cone Finial, Scrolling Branch Arms, 86 1/2 In. 55.00
Stand, Plant, Romanesque Style, White Repaint, Pedestal, 36 In. 95.00
Stand, Plant, Turned Wood, Mahogany Finish, Pedestal, 37 In. 85.00
Stand, Plant, Twisted Wire, 3 Tiers, Trellis Top, White, 73 In. 175.00
Stand, Plant, Wire, 3 Tiers 135.00
Stand, Plant, Wire, On Casters, Folding, 27 x 32 1/2 In. 135.00
Stand, Queen Anne, Circular Top, Tripod Arched Cabriole Legs 1320.00
Stand, Red Wash Over White, Pine, Butternut & Poplar, 29 3/4 In. 250.00
Stand, Roycroft, Little Journey, Keyed Tenons, 26 x 14 In., Pair 1100.00
Stand, Sewing, 2 Drawers, Side Compartments, Mahogany, c.1790 .... 3200.00
Stand, Sewing, Classical, Mahogany Veneer, 1820s, 29 x 21 x 19 In. 220.00
Stand, Sewing, Empire, 2 Drawers 300.00
Stand, Sewing, Empire, Fitted Interior 467.00
Stand, Sewing, Hepplewhite, String Inlays On Legs, Burl Veneers 1100.00
Stand, Sewing, Lift Top, Tambour Door, Mahogany, 29 x 24 3/4 In. 3850.00
Stand, Sewing, Mahogany Veneer, 19 Section, 1830, 21 x 15 In. 845.00
Stand, Sewing, Martha Washington, Cherry, Curly Maple, 3 Drawers 715.00
Stand, Sewing, Martha Washington, Mahogany, Pedestal, Bowed End 525.00
Stand, Sewing, Shaker, Cherry, Tiger Maple, Butternut, 21 3/4 In. 7750.00
Stand, Sewing, Stickley Bros., Blue Shellack, Label 425.00
Stand, Shaving, 2 Drawers, Lower Cupboard, Grained, Rosewood 1980.00
Stand, Shaving, Adjustable Mirror, 2 Drawers, Mahogany, 62 In. 357.00
Stand, Shaving, Carved Wood 137.50
Stand, Sheraton, Cherry Drawers, Maple, 30 x 22 1/2 In. 420.00
Stand, Smoking, Adirondack, Log Cabin, 26 In. 35.00
Stand, Smoking, Chrome, Mahogany Bakelite, Belmet, 1930, 20 3/4 In. 192.00
Stand, Smoking, Figural, Black Man In Tails, Cast Iron, 35 1/2 In. 350.00
Stand, Tea, Maple, Round Top, Snake Feet, Turned Pedestal, 1780 .... 995.00
Stand, Telephone, Center Cupboard, 2 Side Cupboards, Maple, 45 In. 550.00
Stand, Tilt Top, Serpentine Top, Boston, Mahogany, 26 3/4 In. 2200.00

◆◆◆◆◆◆◆◆◆◆◆◆◆◆◆◆◆◆◆◆◆◆◆◆

Cover scratches on dark cherry
or mahogany by rubbing them
with a bit of cotton dipped in iodine. Lighter woods can be covered by cotton dipped in a solution of equal parts iodine and
alcohol.

◆◆◆◆◆◆◆◆◆◆◆◆◆◆◆◆◆◆◆◆◆◆◆◆

Furniture, Stool, Turned Wood, Oak & Maple,
18th Century, 20 In.

Stand, Turned Pull, Maple, c.1820, 30 In.	1100.00
Stand, Umbrella, Arts & Crafts, Compartments, 33 x 9 1/2 x 22 In.	330.00
Stand, Umbrella, Bear, Victorian ....*Illus*	2000.00
Stand, Umbrella, Gustav Stickley, No. 54, 4 Square Posts, 33 In.	6050.00
Stand, Umbrella, Hat, Marble Top, Coalbrookdale, Iron, 85 In.	2700.00
Stand, Umbrella, Jack & Beanstalk, Green, Iron, England, 33 In.	400.00
Stand, Umbrella, Tree Trunk Design, Birds, Terra–Cotta	275.00
Stand, Victorian, 3 Shelves, Inlaid Alabaster, Brass, 46 In.	145.00
Stand, Wash, Cherry, Refinished, Gallery, Drawer, 23 x 19 x 28 In.	400.00
Stool, Brown Leather Upholstery, Nailhead Trim, Oak, 15 x 20 In.	775.00
Stool, Dressing, 6 Spindles Each End, Frank Lloyd Wright, c.1917	5775.00
Stool, Dressing, Foliate Carved Legs, Slip–In Seat, Mahogany	4125.00
Stool, Fluted Apron, Block Feet, Carved Oak, 19 x 18 In.	335.00
Stool, Gout, Adjustable Legs, Parcel Gilt & Painted, 17 In.	605.00
Stool, Gout, Folding	28.00
Stool, Louis XIV Style, Tasseled, Loose Velvet Cushion, Pair	3300.00
Stool, Mahogany, Upholstered Seat, 16 In.	2200.00
Stool, Milking, Blue Repaint, 11 1/2 In.	45.00
Stool, Organ, Adjustable, Ball & Claw Feet	85.00
Stool, Piano, Circular Turning Seat, Claw & Ball Feet, 19 In.	55.00
Stool, Piano, Duncan Phyfe, Carved Legs	825.00
Stool, Pine, Brown Grain Painted, 19 In.	250.00
Stool, Shaker, Pine, Painted Bottom, 8 x 13 x 5 3/4 In.	185.00
Stool, Shaped Top, Gadrooned Edge Over Scroll, Oak, 18 x 32 In.	385.00
Stool, Turned Legs, Splint Seat, 11 x 12 1/2 In.	35.00
Stool, Turned Wood, Oak & Maple, 18th Century, 20 In. ....*Illus*	1320.00
Stool, Weaver's, Connecticut	995.00
Stool, William & Mary, Walnut, Tooled Leather Cover, 18 1/2 In.	1650.00
Stool, William IV Style, Cushion, Brass Caps, Walnut, 57 In.	935.00
Stool, Windsor, Green Paint, 27 In.	175.00
Stool, Woven Cane Seat, Bamboo Turned Legs, 9 x 12 In.	25.00
Stool, Z, Troy Sunshade, Round Black Cushion, Chrome, 1930, 23 In.	450.00
Swing, Porch, Oak	90.00
Swing, Porch, Side Magazine Racks, Wicker, 1890s, 86 In.	850.00
Swing, Wicker, Woven Band, Lattice, Wrapped Frame, 1920, Extra Long	950.00
Table, 1 Drawer, Red Paint, Softwood, 19th Century, Top, 20 In.	1100.00
Table, 1 Drawer, Scroll Cut Apron, English Oak, 1730s, 27 1/2 In.	1250.00
Table, 1–Board Top, Cut Out Ovolo Corners, Cherry, 27 3/4 In.	200.00
Table, 2 Drawers, Acanthus Carved Standards, Rosewood, 4 Ft. 2 In.	5225.00
Table, 2 Frieze Drawers, Jacaranda Wood, Brazil, 68 In.	275.00
Table, 2 Tiers, Hoof Feet, Chinese, Brown Lacquer, 32 In.	2450.00
Table, 2 Tiers, Rosewood & Mahogany, France, c.1925, 29 3/4 In.	550.00
Table, Altar, Marble Top, Mother–of–Pearl Inlay, China, Teak	605.00
Table, Altar, Pierced Apron, Carved Teakwood, China, 51 In.	1400.00
Table, Architect's, George III, Mahogany	4400.00
Table, Art Deco, Burl, Ebonized, Stepped Base, 26 x 27 In., Pair	220.00
Table, Art Deco, Mirror Top, Columnar Base, Painted Pine, 29 In.	65.00

Table, Banquet, Acanthus Carved Legs, 3 Leaves, Walnut, 29 In. 1875.00
Table, Banquet, Hepplewhite, Mahogany, c.1800 .... 4500.00
Table, Banquet, Hepplewhite, Mahogany, D End, Extends To 108 In. 800.00
Table, Banquet, Sheraton Type, Mahogany 1350.00
Table, Bentwood, J. & J. Kohn, Black Beechwood, 1905 .... 2675.00
Table, Blackamoor Base, Carved Wood, Dark Finish, Round Top 1450.00
Table, Bouillotte Style, Fruitwood, Tole Shade, Brass, 56 In. 110.00
Table, Breakfast, Drop Leaf, Mahogany, Hairy Legs, Paw Feet, 38 In. 1250.00
Table, Breakfast, Regency, Rosewood, Brass Inlay, 1820, Round, 4 Ft. 3575.00
Table, Breakfast, Regency, Tilt Top, Mahogany, 46 In. 1980.00
Table, Breakfast, Tilt Top, Mahogany Veneer, England, 44 x 29 In. 100.00
Table, Breakfast, Victorian, Carved Pedestal, Burl Walnut, c.1850 .... 675.00
Table, Breakfast, William IV, Carved Animal Paw Feet 2450.00
Table, Butterfly, New England, Maple, Square Stretcher 1100.00
Table, Butterfly, Pegged, Worn Red Paint, 1 Drawer, 19th Century 695.00
Table, Card, Baize Inset, 1 Drawer, Maryland 2200.00
Table, Card, Bellflower Inlay, Mahogany, c.1800, 36 In. 4300.00
Table, Card, Biedermeier, Swivel Top, Ash, 30 3/4 x 34 1/4 In. 310.00
Table, Card, Carved Foliage Supports, Mahogany, c.1820, 32 3/4 In. 4200.00
Table, Card, Chippendale, Drawer, Red, Birch, 16 1/4 x 34 3/4 In. 700.00
Table, Card, Classical, Mahogany, Lyre, Paw Feet, Casters, 1820–30 .... 3900.00
Table, Card, Console, Maple, c.1800, 36 1/2 In. ....*Illus* 660.00
Table, Card, D–Shaped Apron, Mahogany Veneer, Cherry, 28 x 43 In. 650.00
Table, Card, Demilune Top, Rayed & Satinwood Fan Inlay, c.1790 .... 4510.00
Table, Card, Demilune, Mahogany, 28 x 35 1/2 In. 900.00
Table, Card, Empire, Isaac Vose 800.00
Table, Card, Empire, Mahogany & Flame Grain Veneer, Brass Inlay 1200.00
Table, Card, Federal, Figured Veneer Apron, Mahogany, 28 3/4 In. 1200.00
Table, Card, Federal, Mahogany Veneer, Fited Drawer, 22 x 14 In. 4400.00
Table, Card, Federal, Mahogany Veneer, New England, 29 x 36 In. 825.00
Table, Card, Federal, Mahogany, Serpentine, Philadelphia, 1820 .... 880.00
Table, Card, Federal, Sawtooth Inlay, Mahogany, c.1810, 31 3/4 In. 7150.00
Table, Card, Folding Top, Swing Leg, Figured Veneer, Mahogany 2350.00
Table, Card, George II, Long Drawer, Walnut, c.1735, 28 1/2 In. 2090.00
Table, Card, George III, Mahogany, Hinged Molded Top, 36 x 17 In. 440.00
Table, Card, Griffins With Lyres, Mahogany, c.1830, 36 1/2 In. 2750.00
Table, Card, Hepplewhite, Inlaid, c.1800, 35 In. 2000.00
Table, Card, Hepplewhite, Inlaid, Tiger Maple 2500.00
Table, Card, Hepplewhite, Ovolo Corners, Mahogany, 27 1/2 x 36 In. 8750.00
Table, Card, Lyre Base, Mahogany, Early 19th Century, 36 In. 1200.00
Table, Card, Mahogany, D Shape, 37 1/2 In. 2300.00
Table, Card, Serpentine Corners, Mahogany, c.1790, 34 1/4 In. 3200.00
Table, Card, Serpentine Front, Inlaid Frieze, Mahogany, c.1810 .... 2750.00
Table, Card, Serpentine Front, New England, Mahogany, 1810, 30 In. 1350.00
Table, Card, Sheraton, Inlaid, Birch, 30 x 35 1/2 In. 800.00
Table, Card, Sheraton, Shaped Front, Turned & Reeded Legs 2400.00
Table, Card, Sheraton, Shaped Top, Carved Legs, Mahogany & Birch 4100.00

Furniture, Table, Card,
Console, Maple, c.1800,
36 1/2 In.

Furniture, Table, Drop Leaf,
Maple, c.1900, 30 1/2 In.

Furniture, Table, Drum,
Mahogany, Tooled Leather
Insert, 30 In.

Table, Card, Tapered Rope Twist Legs, Maple, c.1800, 36 1/2 In. 665.00
Table, Card, Tiger Maple, Cherry, Shaped Skirt, Ovolo Corners, 1820 .... 2200.00
Table, Center, Eastlake Design, Marble, Casters, 27 x 19 x 30 In. 110.00
Table, Center, Pineapple Pedestal, Mahogany, Paw Feet, Mid–1800 .... 800.00
Table, Center, Renaissance Revival, Pedestal 1500.00
Table, Center, Victorian, Mahogany, Carved Apron, Base, 42 In. D. 1950.00
Table, Center, William IV, Pearwood & Elmswood, Oval, 40 x 28 In. 6600.00
Table, Chalet, Limbert, Spade–Shape Cutout Flat Leg, Octagonal 2420.00
Table, Cherry, Drop Leaf, Gateleg, 19th Century, 44 x 16 x 29 In. 400.00
Table, Classical Revival, Stenciled & Raised Painted Design 4510.00
Table, Coffee, Glass Tray Top, Elephant Carved Legs, Walnut 248.00
Table, Coffee, Mirrored Top, Fruitwood, 40 x 38 In. 65.00
Table, Coffee, Serpentine, Hinged x Base, Glass, Wood, 1955, 28 In. 192.00
Table, Console, Gilt Leaf Tips At Knees, Mahogany, 5 Ft. 2 In. 4400.00
Table, Console, Marble Top, Garlands, Rosette Frieze, Fruitwood 1000.00
Table, Console, Sheraton, Gateleg, Cherry, 1 Leaf, 29 x 51 In. 440.00
Table, Demilune Console, Inlaid Apron, Mahogany, 44 1/2 In. 1100.00
Table, Demilune, Maple, Inlaid, Turned Legs, Secret Drawer, 40 In. 750.00
Table, Demilune, Unfolds Into Round Top, Walnut, 50 1/2 In. 300.00
Table, Dining, 4–Column Supports, Paw Feet, Mahogany, 136 1/2 In. 8250.00
Table, Dining, Carved Single Pedestal, Seats 18, Mahogany, c.1880 .... 8500.00
Table, Dining, Crossbanded Top, 2 Pedestals, Mahogany, 77 In. 880.00
Table, Dining, D. Pabst, Carved, Walnut, c.1860, 4 Ft. 10 In. 4950.00
Table, Dining, Draw Leaves, Brass Feet, Austria, Mahogany, c.1910 .... 2750.00
Table, Dining, Drexel, 2 Leaves, Mahogany 2090.00
Table, Dining, Drop Leaf, 3 Leaves, Mahogany, 73 In. 110.00
Table, Dining, Drop Leaf, Chippendale, Swing Leg, Cherry, 40 In. 3750.00
Table, Dining, Drop Leaf, Extension, Inlaid Mahogany, 4 Ft. 2 In. 3300.00
Table, Dining, Federal, Lyre Pedestals, Mahogany, 2 Leaves, 72 In. 825.00
Table, Dining, G. Stickley, Pedestal, 6 Leaves, Round, 60 In. 5500.00
Table, Dining, George IV, 2 Pedestal, Mahogany, Paw Casters, 8 Ft. 9350.00
Table, Dining, Georgian, Mahogany, 3 Sections, D–Shaped Ends 9900.00
Table, Dining, Gustav Stickley, No. 632, Oak, 4 Leaves, 29 x 48 In. 6050.00
Table, Dining, L. & J. G. Stickley, No. 720, 4 Leaves, 1912, 54 In. 265.00
Table, Dining, L. & J. G. Stickley, 5 Legs, 4 Leaves, c.1912, 54 In. 2400.00
Table, Dining, L. & J. G. Stickley, 5 Square Legs, 2 Leaves, 48 In. 1485.00
Table, Dining, Limbert, Arched Skirt, Square Legs, c.1910, 51 In. 1210.00
Table, Dining, Majorelle, Extension, Walnut, c.1900, 4 Ft. 10 In. 1100.00
Table, Dining, Queen Anne, Drop Leaf, Curly Maple, c.1760, 28 In. 2310.00
Table, Dining, Regency, 4 Columns, Lion Paw Feet, Walnut, 60 In. 5500.00
Table, Dining, Regency, Drop Leaf, 3 Leaves, Mahogany, 27 x 50 In. 3300.00
Table, Dining, Rounded Corners, Santo Domingo Mahogany, 42 In. 4300.00
Table, Dining, Sheraton Style, Drop Leaf Mahogany, 49 x 54 In. 1200.00
Table, Dining, Trestle, Mid–19th Century, 2 Leaves, Extends 10 Ft. 8250.00
Table, Dressing, 2 Short, 1 Long Drawer, Mahogany, 28 x 32 In. 2640.00
Table, Dressing, Kneehole, 2 Banks of Drawers, Mirrored, Bench 145.00
Table, Dressing, Kneehole, George III, Mahogany, c.1850, 30 1/2 In. 2200.00
Table, Dressing, Kneehole, Slide, 3 Drawers Each Side, Mahogany 4950.00
Table, Dressing, Original Brasses, Painted Cherry, c.1830, 32 In. 935.00
Table, Dressing, Painted, Black & Brown Striping, Pine, 40 1/4 In. 2800.00
Table, Dressing, Porcelain Mounted, Mahogany, c.1880, 41 x 55 In. 7700.00
Table, Drop Leaf, 6 Swing Legs, Oval Top, Walnut, 48 x 19 3/4 In. 175.00
Table, Drop Leaf, 6 Swing Legs, Walnut, 17 3/4 x 43 3/4 In. 175.00
Table, Drop Leaf, Birch, 1 Drawer, Tapering Legs, 35 3/4 In. 355.00
Table, Drop Leaf, Cherry, 1 Drawer, Cutout Corners 250.00
Table, Drop Leaf, Chippendale, Carved Walnut, c.1725, 51 1/2 In. 3520.00

◆◆

Ivory, opals, and pearls need to "breathe." Do not store wrapped in plastic; keep in a cloth bag.

◆◆

Table, Drop Leaf, Double Swing Leg, Cherry, Old Red Paint 750.00
Table, Drop Leaf, Duncan Phyfe, Pedestal, 1 Drawer 450.00
Table, Drop Leaf, Federal, Drawer, Early 1800s 850.00
Table, Drop Leaf, Federal, Mahogany, Hairy Paw Legs, 89 x 24 In. 800.00
Table, Drop Leaf, Figured Bird's–Eye Maple, 42 x 42 In. 8800.00
Table, Drop Leaf, Gateleg Support, Oak, England, 28 3/4 In. 150.00
Table, Drop Leaf, Gateleg, Oval Top, Mahogany, Open, 5 Ft. 2 In. 4400.00
Table, Drop Leaf, George II, Hinged Leaves, Mahogany, c.1745 .... 2200.00
Table, Drop Leaf, Maple, c.1900, 30 1/2 In. ....*Illus*   275.00
Table, Drop Leaf, Oval, Walnut, 5 Leaves, 1880s 800.00
Table, Drop Leaf, Pine, 12 Sides, Scissors Base, America, 32 In. 275.00
Table, Drop Leaf, Pullout Supports, Cherry Base, Pine, 60 In. 3900.00
Table, Drop Leaf, Queen Anne, Pad Feet, Maple, c.1760, 49 In. 4400.00
Table, Drop Leaf, Queen Anne, Walnut, c.1780, 48 1/2 In. 1650.00
Table, Drop Leaf, Sheraton, Birch, Scrubbed Top, Red, 21 x 54 In. 850.00
Table, Drop Leaf, Sheraton, Cherry, 1810 .... 695.00
Table, Drop Leaf, Stylized Carved Spanish Feet 935.00
Table, Drop Leaf, Tiger Maple 1400.00
Table, Drop Leaf, Tiger Maple, Gateleg, 1790–1800, 48 In. Open 1350.00
Table, Drop Leaf, Walnut, Refinished, Turned & Rope Legs, 21 In. 250.00
Table, Drum, Georgian Style, Brass Castors, Oak, 29 x 38 In. 187.00
Table, Drum, Mahogany, Tooled Leather Insert, 30 In. ....*Illus*   2860.00
Table, Drum, Regency, Mahogany, Leather Top, 4 False & 4 Drawers 7700.00
Table, Eileen Gray, Glass Top, Tubular Metal Frame, Adjustable 275.00
Table, Empire, Mahogany, Ill. Governor's Mansion Label, 7 x 4 Ft. 1650.00
Table, Farm, 3 Drawers, 3–Board Top, Walnut, 19th Century, 5 Ft. 2600.00
Table, Farm, Hepplewhite, 2 Boards, 1 Drawer 1000.00
Table, Farm, Pine, 2 Lipped Drawers, Red Paint, Yellow Top, Penna. 2100.00
Table, Felt–Lined Drawer, Step–Down Crest, Curly Maple, 31 In. 2350.00
Table, Figured Tilt Top, Carved Scroll Legs, Mahogany, 28 In. 105.00
Table, Fold Top, Gilt Bronze Mounted, Ebony & Boulle, 30 x 34 In 1430.00
Table, Folding, Sawbuck, Hardwood, Late–19th Century, 36 x 82 In. 200.00
Table, Galle, 2 Tier, Inlaid Fruitwood, Signed, c.1900, 29 1/2 In. 880.00
Table, Galle, 3 Tier, Marquetry, Fruitwood, c.1900, 41 1/4 In. 6650.00
Table, Galle, Mahogany, Triangular, Marquetry Cock, Poppies, 28 In. 2650.00
Table, Galle, Marquetry Flowering Branches, c.1900, 25 3/4 In. 4450.00
Table, Game, Contemporary, Square Top, Painted & Granite, 41 In. 550.00
Table, Game, George III, Marquetry, D Shape, Satinwood, 36 In. 4450.00
Table, Game, George III, Painted Flowers, Vines, Satinwood, c.1790 .... 7150.00
Table, Game, Italian Rococo, Pad Feet, Walnut, 31 1/4 x 43 In. 3550.00
Table, Game, Louis XVI Style, Brass & Tortoiseshell Inlay, 30 In. 155.00
Table, Game, Mahogany, England, 19th Century 1900.00
Table, Game, Sheraton, Serpentine, McIntyre Type, Rope Twist Legs 1400.00
Table, Game, Stenciled, Carved Mahogany, S. & J. Dawson, c.1825 .... 1200.00
Table, Game, Triple–Fold Top, Game, Writing, Inkwell, Mahogany 3200.00
Table, Game, William IV, Rosewood, Brass Inlaid, 35 x 17 In., Pair 6650.00
Table, Gateleg, Drawer, Drop–Leaf Oval Top, Mahogany, 41 1/2 In. 525.00
Table, Gateleg, Maple & Other Woods, 28 1/4 X 40 1/2 In. 600.00
Table, George II, Walnut, Cabriole Legs, Gray Marble Top, 7 Ft. 7800.00
Table, George III, Spider Gateleg, Mahogany, c.1800, 39 In. 4125.00
Table, Glass Top Over Ship's Wheel, Brass & Oak, 21 x 30 In. 275.00
Table, Gold Aurene Rows, Glass Tiles, Steuben, 19 1/2 In. 1980.00
Table, Gustav Stickley, 4 Cut–In Leg Posts, c.1902, 28 x 30 In. 1200.00
Table, Gustav Stickley, Arched Cross Stretcher, c.1908, 48 In. 3350.00
Table, Gustav Stickley, No. 446, Medium Brown, Decal, c.1905 .... 2550.00
Table, Gustav Stickley, Poppy Top, Key Through Tenons, 24 In. 1875.00
Table, H. Miller, Rosewood Veneer, Aluminum, Chrome, 1972, 78 In. 665.00
Table, Half Round, Empire, Marble Top, Mahogany, 28 3/4 x 36 In. 250.00
Table, Harvest, Breadboard Ends, Pine & Birch, 34 x 84 In. 1000.00
Table, Harvest, Drawer Each End, Pine & Poplar, 59 3/4 In. 300.00
Table, Harvest, Drop Leaf, Birch & Poplar, 29 x 72 In. 1100.00
Table, Harvest, Pine, 19th Century, 41 x 108 x 60 In. ....*Illus*   3630.00
Table, Hepplewhite, Pembroke, Mahogany, Inlaid, 18 x 28 In. 700.00

Furniture, Table, Harvest, Pine, 19th Century,
41 x 108 x 60 In.

Furniture, Table, Sewing, Drop Leaf,
Mahogany, 2 Drawers, c.1835

Table, Hepplewhite, Square Legs, 1 Drawer, Butternut, 28 In.	325.00
Table, Hickory Furniture Co., 47 1/2 In.	900.00
Table, Hunt, D Shape, Hinged Leaves, Mahogany, 51 x 22 In.	187.50
Table, Hunt, Mahogany, Irish	7700.00
Table, Hutch, 1 Drawer, 3–Board Top, Maple & Pine, 36 x 42 1/2 In.	500.00
Table, Hutch, Converts To Settle, Poplar	1000.00
Table, Hutch, Cutout 1–Board Ends, Pine, Board Seat, 66 In.	700.00
Table, Hutch, Hinged Lid, Cutout Ends, Pine, 27 1/2 x 69 In.	275.00
Table, Hutch, Round Top, Lift Seat, Pine, 28 x 48 3/4 In.	4750.00
Table, Hutch, Seat Mortised Through Ends, Pine, 63 1/2 In.	3700.00
Table, Iron, Glass Top, Square	550.00
Table, Jacobean, Oak, Molded Top, Pierced Brackets, 30 x 22 In.	137.00
Table, Kitchen, Blond–Faux Laminate, 4 Double Chrome Legs, 54 In	85.00
Table, Kneeling Blackamoor Support, Marble Top, 37 In., Pair	5500.00
Table, Lamp, Glass Ball-and–Claw Feet, Oak	90.00
Table, Lamp, Square Top, Paw Feet, c.1870	185.00
Table, Lazy Susan, Poplar, Red Traces, 2 Drawers, 52 3/4 In.	500.00
Table, Leaves, 6 Legs, Oak, Square, 42 In.	450.00
Table, Library, 1 Drawer, Square Legs, Double Pedestal, Oak	155.00
Table, Library, 2 Drawers, Leather Top, Mahogany, 37 1/2 In.	800.00
Table, Library, C. F. Kade, Mission, Reverses To Billard–Pool, 1914	1250.00
Table, Library, G. Stickley, No. 636, Chamfered Legs, Round, 48 In.	1550.00
Table, Library, G. Stickley, No. 675, 2 Drawers, Shelf, Keyed Tenons	500.00
Table, Library, Gustav Stickley, No. 428, Oak, Arched Apron, 49 In.	2000.00
Table, Library, Gustav Stickley, No. 652, Copper V Pull, Oak, 36 In.	1200.00
Table, Library, Inlaid Top, Carved Ends, 2 Drawers, Walnut, 47 In.	500.00
Table, Library, Painted, 3 Drawers, Brass Pulls, 45 3/4 In.	350.00
Table, Library, Renaissance Revival, Mahogany, 4 Drawers, 59 In.	1450.00
Table, Library, Slotted Cash Drawer, Walnut, 18th Century, 50 In.	8000.00
Table, Library, Victorian, Walnut, 60 In.	2850.00
Table, Limbert, No. 147, Cutout	6100.00
Table, Limbert, No. 153, Turtle Top, Cutout Sides, Shelf, 48 In.	2000.00
Table, Limbert, Pedestal, Cutout	6325.00
Table, Limed Oak, 1 Drawer, Lower Shelf, Ranch Oak & Co., 20 In.	93.50
Table, Louis XV, Marquetry, 3 Drawers, Marble Top, 1925, 29 In.	500.00
Table, Lucite, Glass Top, Tapered Legs, Jackson, 1942, 26 In., Pair	4450.00
Table, Mahogany, Inlaid, Marquetry Design of Cock & Poppies	1700.00
Table, Majorelle, Inlaid Mahogany, 2 Tiers, 29 1/2 x 18 In.	4100.00
Table, Marble Oval Top, Floral Frieze, Rosewood, 1850s, 4 Ft. 5 In.	5775.00
Table, Marble Top, Brass Arrows With Knotted Rope Base, 28 In.	3850.00
Table, Marble Top, Foliate Scrolls, Seashell, Gilt, 4 Ft. 5 In.	6100.00
Table, Mission, Oak, 4 Triangular Chairs Nest Into 38–In. Table	900.00
Table, Mosaic & Marble Top, Italy, Walnut, 18 x 16 In.	6500.00
Table, Mottled Marble Top, Stylized Border, Mahogany, 43 In.	4950.00
Table, Nesting, Century Furniture Co., 24 1/2 In., 3	445.00
Table, Nesting, Dragon Head Feet, Gilt Design, Scarlet Lacquer, 5	5500.00
Table, Nesting, Inlaid, Marquetry, Galle, 4 Piece ....*Illus*	4000.00

Furniture, Table, Nesting, Inlaid, Marquetry,
Galle, 4 Piece

Furniture, Table, Sewing, Lacquered, Japan,
31 In.

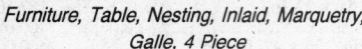

Table, Nesting, J. Hoffmann, Handles, Fabric Under Glass, 1910, 4	4125.00
Table, Nesting, Mahogany, England, 4 Piece	825.00
Table, Nesting, Orange Lacquer, Dragons, 12 x 21 x 26 In., 4	100.00
Table, Nesting, Pierced & Carved Frieze, China, 28 x 20 In.	465.00
Table, Oak, Green Slag Glass Panels, Stepped Base, 26 In.	385.00
Table, Oval Inlaid Top, Mahogany, 27 In.	1875.00
Table, Painted Landscape, Figure Before Pavilions, Dutch, 44 In.	5500.00
Table, Parlor, Rococo, Turtle, Rosewood, Flame Inlaid, 1850, 4 Ft.	1750.00
Table, Pedestal, 4 Leaves, Walnut, Large	1100.00
Table, Pembroke, Card & Tassle, Bookend Inlays, Mahogany, c.1790	7800.00
Table, Pembroke, Chippendale, Drop Leaves, Drawer, Mahogany, 1770	6050.00
Table, Pembroke, Chippendale, Hinged Leaves, Mahogany, c.1775	3850.00
Table, Pembroke, Cock–Beaded Drawer, Mahogany, 28 3/4 In.	500.00
Table, Pembroke, Cross–Banded Top, Casters, Oval, Mahogany, 28 In.	8800.00
Table, Pembroke, Drawer, Curly Maple Legs, Cherry, 27 3/4 In.	475.00
Table, Pembroke, Drop Leaf, 1 Drawer, Brass Pull	6600.00
Table, Pembroke, Drop Leaf, Drawer On Each End, Small	1550.00
Table, Pembroke, Drop Leaves, Carved Walnut, c.1760, 44 1/4 In.	6600.00
Table, Pembroke, Drop Leaves, Casters, Mahogany, c.1770, 28 In.	4125.00
Table, Pembroke, Edge Beading, Shaped Leaves, Mahogany, 28 1/2 In.	800.00
Table, Pembroke, Floral, Foliate & Acorn Inlay, Mahogany, Pair	5000.00
Table, Pembroke, Folding Apron Wings, Maple, 28 x 36 1/4 In.	1250.00
Table, Pembroke, George III, Drawer, Inlaid Mahogany	5500.00
Table, Pembroke, Hepplewhite, 1 Drawer, 26 3/4 In.	1000.00
Table, Pembroke, Hepplewhite, Shaped Leaves, Mahogany, c.1790	4000.00
Table, Pembroke, Line Inlay, Cherry, c.1800, 35 In.	550.00
Table, Pembroke, Line–Edge Inlay On Drawer, Mahogany, 28 3/4 In.	1300.00
Table, Pembroke, Mahogany, Satinwood Banded, 1 Long Drawer, 24 In.	200.00
Table, Pembroke, Mahogany, String Inlay & Banding, 1790, N. Y.	2950.00
Table, Pembroke, Sheraton, Alligatored Varnish On Base, Cherry	500.00
Table, Pembroke, Sheraton, Drop Leaf Top, Cherry, 17 1/2 x 40 In.	400.00
Table, Pennsylvania, 2 Drawer, Washed Top	1175.00
Table, Pier Over Mirror, Empire, White Marble Top, Carved	3500.00
Table, Pier, Alabaster Pilasters, Ormolu Columnar, Marble	6600.00
Table, Pier, Brass Inlaid Frieze, Marble Top, Mahogany, c.1820	6875.00
Table, Pier, Mahogany, Bronze Mount, c.1820	2000.00
Table, Pier, Mahongany, Carved and Stenciled, White Marble Top	4125.00
Table, Pier, Marble Top, Egyptian–Style Supports, Mahogany	1900.00
Table, Pier, Pillar & Scroll, Marble Top, Mirrored, Mahogany, 1840	885.00
Table, Pier, Stencil Design, Carved Acanthus & Paw Supports	5500.00
Table, Pine Breadboard Top, Hardwood Base, Secret Compartment	425.00

Table, Poker, Tilt Top, Cast Iron Base, Early 1900s 625.00
Table, Queen Anne, Drop Leaf, Rounded Leaves, 48 In. 1925.00
Table, Queen Anne, Drop Leaf, Swing Leg, Maple, 27 1/2 x 49 In. 2200.00
Table, Queen Anne, Drop Leaf, Swing Leg, Maple, 28 x 41 3/4 In. 6000.00
Table, Queen Anne, Duck Feet, 1 Drawer, Walnut, 27 3/4 x 29 In. 800.00
Table, Queen Anne, Inlaid Walnut, D Shape, 1 Drawer, 24 1/2 In. 7750.00
Table, Queen Anne, Mahogany, Tilt Top, Birdcage, 18th Century 750.00
Table, Queen Anne, Pad Feet, Pennsylvania, Walnut, c.1750 .... 6700.00
Table, Queen Anne, Porringer Top, Curly Maple & Pine, 26 3/4 In. 7000.00
Table, Refectory, 3 Drawers, Scrolled Supports, Walnut, 80 1/2 In. 2250.00
Table, Refectory, Stuart, Columnar Supports, Oak, 6 Ft. 1 In. 8250.00
Table, Removable Top, Old Red Repaint, Pine, 27 3/4 x 24 1/4 In. 675.00
Table, Rose Marble Top, Carved Frieze, Hardwood, China, 32 In. 165.00
Table, Sawbuck, 3–Board Pine Breadboard Top, 30 1/2 x 51 In. 225.00
Table, Sawbuck, Beaded Edge, Pine, 28 x 29 In. 450.00
Table, Sawbuck, Pine Base, Walnut Top, 29 3/4 x 60 3/4 In. 800.00
Table, Sawbuck, Pine, Black Paint Base, Natural Top, 23 x 49 In. 400.00
Table, Scalloped Apron, Poplar, 27 x 39 3/4 In. 175.00
Table, Scalloped Top, Astrological Designs, Cast Iron, 29 In. 5500.00
Table, Scrolled Legs, Base Shelf, 1 Drawer, Mahogany, 27 1/2 In. 295.00
Table, Serving, Fret Carved, Splashboard, Mahogany, 7 Ft. 6 In. 5500.00
Table, Serving, George III, Mahogany, Serpentine, 1780, 5 Ft. 8 In. 5500.00
Table, Serving, Gustav Stickley, No. 802, Apron, 2 Drawers, 39 In. 4650.00
Table, Serving, Regency, Inlaid Mahogany, 5 Ft. 6 1/2 In. 8250.00
Table, Serving, Sheraton, Ivory Escutcheons, 1810–20, 68 In. 1650.00
Table, Sewing, 1 Dovetailed Drawer, Oak & Pine, 30 x 27 1/2 In. 245.00
Table, Sewing, 2 Drawers, American Classical, Mahogany, c.1825 .... 525.00
Table, Sewing, 2 Drawers, Brass Pulls, Red & Black Paint, c.1820 .... 3190.00
Table, Sewing, 2 Drawers, Removable Top, Poplar, 62 1/2 In. 925.00
Table, Sewing, 2 Drawers, Rope–Turned Legs, Mahogany, 29 In. 275.00
Table, Sewing, 2 Drawers, Writing Slide, Bird's–Eye Maple, 30 In. 9500.00
Table, Sewing, Bag On Slide, Biedermeier, Walnut, 29 1/2 In. 385.00
Table, Sewing, Classical Revival, Mahogany, c.1825, 29 1/2 In. 1200.00
Table, Sewing, Contrasting Grain Paint, 3 Drawer, Half Spindles 680.00
Table, Sewing, Drop Leaf, Mahogany, 2 Drawers, c.1835 ....*Illus* 350.00
Table, Sewing, Ebonized, Brass, 1 Drawer, Pullout Bin, France, 23 In 450.00
Table, Sewing, Federal, 2 Serpentine–Shaped Drawers, 27 In. 3100.00
Table, Sewing, Federal, S. F. McIntire, Carved Mahogany, 28 1/2 In. 2750.00
Table, Sewing, Federal, Serpentine, 2 Drawers, America, 18 x 14 In. 2800.00
Table, Sewing, Federal, Walnut, c.1810, 26 1/4 x 19 1/4 In. 225.00
Table, Sewing, Fitted Drawer, Mahogany, c.1830 .... 700.00
Table, Sewing, Fitted Interior, Roses On Support, Rosewood, c.1844 .... 1100.00
Table, Sewing, Gallery, 2–Board Top, Pine, 30 1/4 x 40 1/2 In. 400.00
Table, Sewing, Gallery, 3 Drawers, Smoke–Grained Top, 33 x 25 In. 2450.00
Table, Sewing, Hepplewhite, Ash, 2–Board Top, 1 Drawer, 33 x 47 In. 200.00
Table, Sewing, Ivory Inlay, Tortoiseshell Mounted, 1820s, 29 In. 3350.00
Table, Sewing, Lacquered, Japan, 31 In. ....*Illus* 330.00
Table, Sewing, Lacquered, Lift Top, Trestle, 1 Drawer, Japan, 31 In. 350.00
Table, Sewing, Lift Top, Drawer, Flame Grain Mahogany, 28 x 20 .... 275.00
Table, Sewing, Lift Top, Drawer, Tiger Maple, c.1830 .... 500.00
Table, Sewing, Mahogany Veneer, Drawer, Silk Bag, 1820–30, 40 In. 2000.00
Table, Sewing, Mahogany, Lift Top Compartment, 2 Drawers, Shelf 325.00
Table, Sewing, Pine, Cherry, Drawer On Each End, Shelf, 26 x 18 In. 1100.00
Table, Sewing, Poplar Base, Scrubbed–Pine Top, 32 x 51 In. 150.00
Table, Sewing, Queen Anne, Walnut, 2 Drawers, 33 x 57 x 30 In. 400.00
Table, Sewing, Regency, Hinged Top, Inlaid Mahogany, c.1815, 29 In. 1550.00
Table, Sewing, Removable Top, 2 Drawers, 32 1/2 x 60 In. 1485.00
Table, Sewing, Rosewood, Fitted Maple Interior, c.1845 .... 495.00
Table, Sewing, Sewing Bag, Tiger Maple, Cherry, 3 Drawers 885.00
Table, Sewing, Victorian, Sliding Work Basket, Rosewood, c.1850 .... 3400.00
Table, Sewing, Writing Surface, Tambour Sides, Mahogany, 1815 .... 6700.00
Table, Sewing, Yellow & Red Paint, 1–Board Top, 21 In. 2100.00
Table, Shaker, Trestle, Shoe–Foot, 74 x 32 In. 5225.00

Table, Sheraton, Cookie Corners, 1 Drawer, Tiger Maple, 34 1/2 In. 3960.00
Table, Sheraton, Pembroke, 1 Drawer, Shaped Top, Cherry, 28 In. 850.00
Table, Sheraton, Poplar, 2–Board Cleaned Top, Varnish Base, 29 In. 175.00
Table, Sheraton, Tiger Maple, Cookie Corners, 3 Drawers ....*Illus* 3950.00
Table, Silver, Fret–Carved Gallery, Mahogany, 30 x 34 In. 6700.00
Table, Smoking, Naked Woman Cutout Support, 10–Sided Top, 26 In. 175.00
Table, Sofa, Marble Top, Lyre Form Pedestal, Walnut, 34 1/2 In. 495.00
Table, Sofa, Regency, Mahogany, Drop Leaf, England, 1810, 55 In. 3450.00
Table, Supper, Scalloped, Molded Angular Legs, Mahogany, 25 In. 2750.00
Table, Swing Leg, Drop Leaf, Mahogany, Early 20th Century, 39 In. 400.00
Table, Tavern, 2 Drawers, Removable Top, Walnut, 33 x 41 In. 1350.00
Table, Tavern, Breadboard Ends, Drawer, Maple, 38 In. 2420.00
Table, Tavern, Breadboard Top, Trace of Red, Maple, 26 1/2 In. 400.00
Table, Tavern, Cherry, Splayed, Square Legs, Drawer, 31 x 26 In. 600.00
Table, Tavern, Chippendale, Drawer, Walnut, 44 1/4 In. 150.00
Table, Tavern, Curly Maple, 27 1/2 x 35 1/2 In. 595.00
Table, Tavern, Cutout Apron, Curly Maple, 26 x 31 3/4 In. 6000.00
Table, Tavern, Delaware Valley, Walnut 4620.00
Table, Tavern, Drawer, Maple Base, Pine Top, 25 1/4 x 35 3/4 In. 800.00
Table, Tavern, Drawer, Removable 1–Board Top, Pine & Poplar 275.00
Table, Tavern, Drawer, Yellow Pine, c.1725 .... 4200.00
Table, Tavern, Hepplewhite, 1 Drawer, 1–Board Top, Maple, 27 In. 7000.00
Table, Tavern, Jacobean, Oak, Box Stretcher, 56 x 29 x 28 In. 550.00
Table, Tavern, Jacobean, Turned & Blocked Legs, Oak, 56 1/2 In. 600.00
Table, Tavern, Lipped Drawer, Scalloped Apron, Walnut 7700.00
Table, Tavern, New England, Honey Shade, 2 Breadboard Top 4950.00
Table, Tavern, Pine, Maple, 36 x 25 In. ....*Illus* 770.00
Table, Tavern, Pine, Worn Red Finish, Round, England, 31 In. 350.00
Table, Tavern, Queen Anne, 1 Drawer, Breadboard Top, 42 In. 500.00
Table, Tavern, Queen Anne, 2–Board Top, Maple, 26 1/2 In. 750.00
Table, Tavern, Queen Anne, Drawer, Pine Top, Cherry, 40 1/4 In. 2900.00
Table, Tavern, Queen Anne, Oval Top, Maple & Birch, 1750–75 .... 5500.00
Table, Tavern, Queen Anne, Oval Top, Maple, 24 1/2 x 26 x 30 In. 3500.00
Table, Tavern, Queen Anne, Pine Apron & Top, Birch Stretchers 1900.00
Table, Tavern, Scalloped Apron, Red Paint, Softwood, 28 1/2 In. 6700.00
Table, Tavern, Tilt Top, Oak, Shoe Feet, Pine Top, France, 42 In. 500.00
Table, Tavern, Tilt Top, Pine, Oval Top, Trestle, 28 x 36 In. 1100.00
Table, Tavern, William & Mary, 3 Drawers, Walnut, c.1780, 54 In. 5500.00
Table, Tavern, William & Mary, Pine, c.1710, 22 1/2 In. 5500.00
Table, Tea, Birdcage, Philadelphia, Mahogany, 30 In. 4500.00
Table, Tea, Cedarwood, Revolving, 1780 .... 1045.00
Table, Tea, Chippendale, Tip Top, Mahogany, c.1770, 28 x 34 In. 1000.00
Table, Tea, Chippendale, Wallace Nutting, Mahogany ....*Illus* 3950.00
Table, Tea, Fold Top, Mahogany, 30 x 38 In. 665.00
Table, Tea, Frieze Drawer, Side Slides, Yew Wood, 28 1/2 In. 605.00
Table, Tea, George II, Carved Knees, Ireland, Mahogany, 28 1/2 In. 6100.00
Table, Tea, George III, Square Tilt Top, Mahogany, 28 x 24 In. 885.00

Furniture, Table, Sheraton,
Tiger Maple,
Cookie Corners, 3 Drawers

Furniture, Table, Tavern,
Pine, Maple,
36 x 25 In.

Furniture, Table,
Tea, Chippendale,
Wallace Nutting, Mahogany

Furniture, Table, Trestle,
Revival, Oak, Scrolled Feet,
c.1880

Furniture, Table, William &
Mary, Wallace Nutting, Oak,
39 1/2 In.

Furniture, Table, Work,
Mahogany, 19th Century

◆◆

One antique earring can still be used. Have the jeweler make it into
a stickpin, a tie tac or a ring. If it is clip–on, use it like a lapel pin; or
if it is for pierced ears, attach it through the knit of a sweater. Some
earrings can be hung in the center of a strand of pearls, an old–
fashioned adaptation of the new "pearl enhancers."

◆◆

Table, Tea, George III, Tilt Top, Oak, 28 x 29 3/4 In.	225.00
Table, Tea, Maple, Refinished, Rhode Island, 1740–90, 37 x 25 In.	3350.00
Table, Tea, Pierced & Carved Aprons, Tibet, 28 x 11 1/2 In.	250.00
Table, Tea, Queen Anne, Candle Slides, Tray, Mahogany, 26 1/2 In.	1100.00
Table, Tea, Queen Anne, Pad Feet, Rhode Island, c.1740	4675.00
Table, Tea, Rhode Island, Maple, 26 x 36 7/8 In.	3300.00
Table, Tea, Tilt Top, America, Walnut, 29 x 33 In.	660.00
Table, Tea, Tilt Top, Arched Legs, Mahogany, 27 In.	465.00
Table, Tea, Tilt Top, Bird's–Eye Veneer, John B. Miller, Pine	900.00
Table, Tea, Tilt Top, Chippendale, Claw & Egg Feet, Mahogany	2475.00
Table, Tea, Tilt Top, Chippendale, Late 18th Century, 34 x 33 In.	1650.00
Table, Tea, Tilt Top, English, Oak Base, Mahogany Top, 27 In.	400.00
Table, Tea, Tilt Top, New England, Curly Maple, c.1770, 26 1/4 In.	3850.00
Table, Tea, Tilt Top, Papier–Mache Tray, Black, 18 3/4 x 30 In.	300.00
Table, Tea, Tilt Top, Trifid Base, Mahogany, 27 x 30 1/2 In.	825.00
Table, Tea, Tilt, Curly Maple, Tripod, 3–Board Top, 24 In. Diam.	775.00
Table, Tea, Vase Column, Carved Knees, Mahogany, 33 In.	7150.00
Table, Tilt Top, Chippendale, Mahogany, Tripod, 24 x 26 x 27 In.	800.00
Table, Tilt Top, Connecticut, Cherry, c.1780	1400.00
Table, Tilt Top, Mahogany, Signed Tobey	550.00
Table, Tilt Top, Mother–of–Pearl Design, Papier–Mache, 36 1/2 In.	1760.00
Table, Tilt Top, Painted Game Board Top, 28 1/2 In.	6600.00
Table, Tilt Top, Scalloped Circular Top, Tripod, Mahogany, 28 In.	2750.00
Table, Tilt Top, Tiger Maple, Birdcage, 32 In. Diam. Top	1900.00
Table, Tray, Sheraton, Pierced Gallery, Mahogany, c.1840, 25 In.	550.00
Table, Trestle, L. & J. G. Stickley, No. 594, c.1910, 72 In.	4010.00
Table, Trestle, L. & J. G. Stickley, No. 593, Cut Corner, 84 x 30 In.	935.00
Table, Trestle, Revival, Oak, Scrolled Feet, c.1880 ......*Illus*	2000.00
Table, Tric–Trac, Mahogany, Ebony, Bone Inlaid, Continental, 1800	4450.00
Table, Tripod, English Oak, Arched Feet, 27 x 31 In.	220.00
Table, Victorian, Marble Top, 4 Arched Legs, 34 x 22 In.	70.00
Table, Vintage Design, Blue Paint, Board Insert, Iron, 24 x 16 In.	160.00
Table, Walnut, 2 Board Top, 34 x 29 In.	125.00
Table, Wicker, Heywood & Co., Paper Label, 28 3/4 In.	1350.00
Table, William & Mary Style, Bun Feet, Oak, 33 x 24 3/4 In.	495.00

Table, William & Mary, Book–Matched Veneer Apron, Walnut, Small 1300.00
Table, William & Mary, Trestle Base, Pine, 1730s, 8 Ft. 8250.00
Table, William & Mary, Wallace Nutting, Oak, 39 1/2 In. ....*Illus* 600.00
Table, William IV, Rosewood Grained, Gilt Metal, Casters, 19 In. 3350.00
Table, Work, Mahogany, 19th Century ....*Illus* 303.00
Table, Work, Queen Anne, American, 32 1/2 x 60 In. ....*Illus* 1485.00
Table, Writing, Dutch, Marquetry, Walnut, 1780s 3450.00
Table, Writing, Frieze Drawer, Carved Legs, Korea, Elm & Pine 80.00
Table, Writing, George III, Mahogany, Gilt–Tooled Leather, 1800 .... 6650.00
Table, Writing, Inlay Over Frieze, Marquetry, Walnut, 29 3/4 In. 3350.00
Table, Writing, Regency, Inlaid Rosewood, 19th Century ....*Illus* 5500.00
Table, Writing, Regency, Mahogany, 2 Drawers, Gillows, 1820, 38 In. 6600.00
Table–Bed, Mission Oak, Library Table, Converts To Bed, Feather 175.00
Tabouret, Gustav Stickley, No. 603, Round, Cross Stretcher, 1907 .... 825.00
Tabouret, Gustav Stickley, No. 660, Square Top, Canted Legs, 19 In. 935.00
Tabouret, Gustav Stickley, Round, Straight Legs, c.1912, 18 In. 475.00
Tabouret, L. & J. G. Stickley, Octagonal, Cross Stretcher, 1912 .... 825.00
Tabouret, L. & J. G. Stickley, Octagonal, Arched Stretchers, 18 In. 1210.00
Tabouret, Louis XVI, Beechwood, Needlepoint Round Cushion, 17 In. 220.00
Tabouret, Oak, Cambridge Tiles, Lower Shelf, Keyed Tenons, 19 In. 165.00
Tabouret, Roycroft No. 11, Macmurdo Feet, 3–Slat Ends 1650.00
Tabouret, Roycroft No. 49, Macmurdo Feet, 3–Slat Ends, 20 x 14 In. 1875.00
Tailoring Counter, Shaker, Pumpkin, Stain, Pine, Poplar, 8 Drawers 8800.00
Tea Cart, Mahogany 340.00
Tray, Black Lacquer, Papier–Mache, Bamboo–Turned Stand, 30 In. 3850.00

Furniture, Table, Work, Queen Anne, American, 32 1/2 x 60 In.

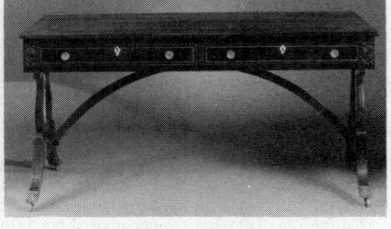

Furniture, Table, Writing, Regency, Inlaid Rosewood, 19th Century

Furniture, Vanity, Ebonized Wood, Meissen Porcelain, 59 In.

Furniture, Washstand, George II, Mahogany, Round Shelves, 32 In.

Tray, Breakfast, Stickley Bros., Folds Flat, 16 x 24 In. 200.00
Tray, Butler's, Dovetailed Mahogany, 21 1/2 x 33 In. 600.00
Tray, Butler's, Stand, Mahogany 950.00
Tray, Floral Mother–of–Pearl & Ebony, c.1830, 18 x 24 In. 495.00
Tray, Galle, Inlaid Floral, Wood 1500.00
Tray, Galle, Marquetry 2100.00
Tray, Galleried Top, Cut–Out Handles, Walnut, 22 x 36 x 23 In. 550.00
Tray, Gilt & Black Lacquer, Papier–Mache, Stand, 1825, 32 1/2 In. 7150.00
Tray, Papier–Mache, Stand, Bamboo Shoots, Floral, 1860s, 30 1/4 In. 2200.00
Tray, Papier–Mache, Stand, Black Lacquer, Lad Fishing, 31 In. 3200.00
Tray, Papier–Mache, Stand, Painted Foliage, c.1850, 26 x 31 In. 6600.00
Tray, Woven Splint, Green Paint, Bentwood Handle, 7 x 9 1/2 In. 200.00
Trolley, Sheraton, 4 Tiers, Mahogany, Ebony Inlaid, England, 16 In. 1250.00
Valet, Art Deco, Reticulated Geometric, Stepped, Brass, 57 In. 225.00
Vanity, Art Deco, Waterfall, Mahogany Veneer, 4 Drawers, Mirror 250.00
Vanity, Ebonized Wood, Meissen Porcelain, 59 In. ....*Illus* 18000.00
Vanity, Louis XV, Ormolu Mounted, Inlaid Florals, Kingwood 4500.00
Vanity, Metal, Demilune Top, Frameless Mirror, Glass, 1930, 42 In. 440.00
Vanity, Split Marble Top, Footrest, Bowed Front, Tilt Mirror 3500.00
Vitrine, Carved & Mirrored, Shelves, Eastlake, c.1890, 62 x 40 In. 330.00
Vitrine, Edwardian, Mahogany, Standing, Inlaid, c.1890 .... 880.00
Vitrine, Glazed Inset Panels, Landscape Scene, Stand, 4 Ft. 2 In. 3575.00
Vitrine, V. Martin Style Painted Panels, Bronze Mounts, France 1430.00
Walker, Baby's, Tray, Bamboo 605.00
Wall Shelf, Country French, 3 Tier, Center Plate Support, 49 .... 550.00
Wardrobe, G. Stickley, 2 Doors, Copper Pulls, c.1907, 60 1/8 In. 5500.00
Wardrobe, Mirror, Oak, 1 Door 130.00
Wardrobe, Pine, Brown Graining, 1 Door, Wooden Hooks, 46 x 74 In. 325.00
Wardrobe, Roane Co., Tenn., 2 Doors, Dull Grain Paint 1400.00
Wash Stand, Oak, Victorian,, 2 Doors, Chestnut Handles, 30 In. 325.00
Washstand, 1 Drawer, Chestnut Handles, Wooden Casters, Oak, 35 In. 360.00
Washstand, 1 Drawer, Gallery, Scalloped Edge, Poplar, 30 In. 150.00
Washstand, 3 Drawers, Towel Bars, Crotch–Grain Mahogany, c.1830 .... 675.00
Washstand, Combed Graining, Alligator Finish, Poplar, 29 1/2 In. 600.00
Washstand, Corner, Curly Cherry Front, Rope Twist Legs, Cherry 950.00
Washstand, Corner, Cutout For Bowl, Mahogany, 46 1/2 In. 225.00
Washstand, Corner, Federal, Inlaid Mahogny, Satinwood, c.1810 .... 1320.00
Washstand, Corner, Hepplewhite, Back Splash, 2 Shelves, Mahogany 220.00
Washstand, George II, Mahogany, Round Shelves, 32 In. ....*Illus* 800.00
Washstand, Lift Top, Basin Fitting, Towel Rack, Walnut, 32 In. 410.00
Washstand, Marble Top, 1 Long & 2 Small Drawers, Walnut, 37 In. 198.00
Washstand, Shaker, Pine, Red Wash Under Varnish, 1830, 31 In. 6600.00
Washstand, Shaker, Putty Paint, High Backboard 5500.00
Washstand, Sheraton, Brown Vinegar Graining, Pine, 30 3/4 In. 200.00
Washstand, Sheraton, Drawer In Base, Gallery, Cherry, 28 x 19 In. 300.00
Washstand, Sheraton, Paneled, Cherry Gallery, Tiger Maple, 29 In. 825.00
Washstand, Sheraton, Stepped, Grained 300.00
Washstand, Walnut, Burl Walnut, Marble Top, Drawer & 2 Doors 285.00
Wastebasket, Gustav Stickley, Slat Sided, c.1912, 14 In. 935.00
Wastebasket, Oak, Arts & Craft, Applied Knobs In Corners, 15 In. 250.00
Whatnot, 3 Tiers, Chinese Style, Parcel Gilt, Lacquer, 21 In. 2750.00
Whatnot, Corner, Graduated Shelves, Walnut, Standing 180.00
Whatnot, Victorian Style, Walnut, 5 Tiers 495.00
Window Seat, George III, Carved Acanthus Leaves, Gilt Wood 6650.00
Window Seat, George III, Painted, Upholstered, Arms, 41 1/2 In. 2250.00
Window Seat, Regency Style, Cabriole Legs, Painted Green, 37 In. 550.00
Window Seat, S–Scrolled Ends, Inlaid Brass, Mahogany, 45 In. 4950.00
Wine Cooler, Urn Shape, England, Mahogany, 32 In., Pair 3300.00
Wine Cooler, William IV, Mahogany, c.1835 .... 885.00
Wine Cooler, William IV, Mahogany, Lined, 1845, 20 x 37 x 28 In. 2475.00

Galle Pottery, Basket,
Egyptian Style, Molded
Signature, 8 In.

Galle Pottery, Candlestick, Blue,
Rien Sans Amour, 10 In.

Galle Pottery, Centerpiece,
Enamel Scarab, Dragonfly, Gilt,
14 In.

Galle, Egg, Gray, Overlaid
and Cameo Cut, Gray, Green,
10 In.

Galle, Vase, Gray, Overlaid
Green, Wisteria, Star Mark,
17 In.
Galle, Vase, Gray, Pink,
Overlaid Lavender,
Green, Hydrangea, 12 In.

Galle, Vase, Enameled In Pink,
White & Green, Spider Mark,
14 In.

A porcelain works was started in Furstenberg, Germany, in 1747. It is still working. Many of the modern products are made in the old molds.

FURSTENBERG, Candlestick, Raised Flowers, Leaves, 1850, 10 In. 200.00
Figurine, Girl With Lamb, c.1820, 8 In. 385.00

G-ARGY-ROUSSEAU   Gabriel Argy-Rousseau, born in 1885, was a French glass artist who produced a variety of objects in the Art Deco style. His mark, *G. Argy-Rousseau,* was usually impressed.

G. ARGY-ROUSSEAU, Box, Cover, Cornflowers, Pate-De-Cristal, c.1925, 3 1/8 In. 5500.00
Paperweight, Pate-De-Verre Cube, Blue & Green, 1 7/8 In. 1750.00
Shade, Gas, Cameo Drip Design, Lavender, Signed, 5 1/2 In. 465.00
Shot Glass, Triangular Peaks, Signed, 3 In. 1210.00
Vase, Spiders In Webs, Flowering Branches, 1925, 4 5/8 In. 1340.00

Emile Galle, the famous French designer, made ceramics after 1874. The pieces were marked with the initials *E.G.* impressed, *Em. Galle Faiencerie de Nancy,* or a version of his signature. Galle is best known for his glass, listed in the next section.

GALLE POTTERY, Basket, Egyptian Style, Molded Signature, 8 In. ....*Illus* 3850.00
Basket, Open Work Body, Medallion Centered Flowers, 10 In. 575.00
Candlestick, Blue, Rien Sans Amour, 10 In. ....*Illus* 550.00
Centerpiece, Enamel Scarab, Dragonfly, Gilt, 14 In. ....*Illus* 4290.00
Ewer, Romantic Minstrel Scene, Freeform, 8 In. 1250.00

Figurine, Cat & Dog, Lady & Tramp, Signed, 12 In., Pair 6100.00
Vase, Blue, Purple, Yellow, 6 1/2 In. 305.00
Vase, Man Holding Sword, Figures, Signed, 11 In. 1100.00

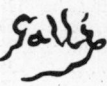

Galle was a designer who made glass, pottery, furniture, and other
Art Nouveau items. Emile Galle founded his factory in France in
1874. After Galle's death in 1904, the firm continued to make glass
and furniture until 1931. The name *Galle* was used as a mark, but it
was often hidden in the design of the object. Galle Pottery is listed
above and his furniture is listed in the Furniture section.

GALLE, Ashtray, Rose Glass, Martele, Crescent–Moon Shape, Engraved 4650.00
Bowl, Incurved Lip, Fuchsia Blossoms, Buds, Signed, c.1910, 6 1/2 In. 6600.00
Bowl, Intaglio Berried Leaves, Signed, c.1885, 5 1/2 In. 3850.00
Bowl, Padded Iris, Hammered Ground, Signed, 6 1/2 In. 9350.00
Box, Brown & Green Lake Scene, White Frosted, Cameo, Triangular, 5 In. 3080.00
Box, Cover, Wildflower Sprays, Leaves, Green, Signed, c.1900, 5 1/8 In. 2750.00
Centerpiece, Egyptian Style, Enameled Scarab & Dragonfly, 14 In. 4295.00
Charger, Red & Burgundy Roses, Frosted Ground, Footed, 13 1/2 In. 6100.00
Decanter, Blossoms, Buds, Leaves, Stopper, Signed, c.1900, 10 1/8 In. 7150.00
Dish, Bird Finial, Underplate, Foliage, Signed, c.1880, 4 3/4 In. 5500.00
Egg, Gray, Overlaid and Cameo Cut, Gray, Green, 10 In. ....*Illus* 7260.00
Figurine, Dog, Pug–Type, Seated, Hearts & Circles, Signed, 15 In. 1650.00
Fixture, Ceiling, Magnolia Blossoms, Buds, Signed, c.1900, 13 1/2 In. 9900.00
Lamp Base, Alsatian Mountain Landscape, Signed, c.1900, 13 3/8 In. 3850.00
Lamp Base, Marguerite Blossoms, Buds, Leaves, Signed, c.1900, 9 1/4 In. 1750.00
Lamp, 3–Layer Dome Shade, Signed 4600.00
Lamp, Blue & Purple Blossoms, Yellow, White, Baluster Base, 12 In. 885.00
Lamp, Boudoir, 3 Burgundy Butterflies, Iron Base, Signed, 4 In. 1250.00
Perfume Bottle, Cameo, Nasturitium Blossoms, Buds, Signed, 6 3/4 In. 1550.00
Perfume Bottle, Deep Blue Clematis, White, Bulbous, Stopper, 5 1/4 In. 2850.00
Perfume Bottle, Flowering Branches, Teardrop Form, c.1900, 6 7/8 In. 1985.00
Perfume Bottle, Shaded Blossoms & Leafy Stem, Yellow, 6 In. 825.00
Perfume Bottle, Sycamore Branches, Signed, c.1910, 4 1/4 In. 2750.00
Perfume Bottle, Violet Blossoms, Teardrop, Signed, 1900, 8 3/4 In. 2100.00
Powder Jar, Wisteria In Brown & Purple, Frosted Ground, Signed, 4 In. 1435.00
Rose Bowl, Clematis Vines, Blossoms, Signed, c.1900, 7 1/2 In. 9900.00
Shade, Floral Design, Butterflies, Signed, 8 1/2 In. 3200.00
Sherbet, Red Cherries, Green & White Leaves, Gold Chain, 2 3/4 In. 495.00
Tumbler, Water Set, Whimsical Woman & Man, Signed, 3 Piece 3500.00
Vase, 3 Colors, Fire Polished, 7 1/4 In. 1100.00
Vase, 3 Colors, Green Vines & Grapes, 4 x 7 In. 950.00
Vase, 3 Colors, Orchids, Amethyst To Orange Base, 7 1/4 In. 1100.00
Vase, Alsatian Mountain Landscape, Ovoid, Signed, c.1900, 11 In. 4180.00
Vase, Amber Floral & Leaf On Green, White & Frost, Signed, 13 3/4 In. 4000.00
Vase, Amethyst & Green Blossoms & Leaves, Signed, 6 3/4 In. 1350.00
Vase, Banjo, 3 Colors, 5 In. 1200.00
Vase, Berries, Holly Leaves, Flaring Neck, Signed, c.1900, 14 1/8 In. 6050.00
Vase, Black–Eyed Susans Above Leaves, Signed, c.1900, 6 3/4 In. 7700.00
Vase, Blossoms, Birds & Leafy Stems, Signed, 6 1/4 In. 1045.00
Vase, Blown–Out Okra Design, Signed, 6 5/8 In. 7000.00
Vase, Bottle, Trees, Fence & Water, Brown Shades, Signed, 6 3/4 In. 1600.00
Vase, Brown Flowers & Leaves On White, 4 In. 895.00
Vase, Brown Forest Scene, Frosted Green, Trumpet, 18 1/2 In. 5500.00
Vase, Brown Pods On Gold, Signed, 5 1/2 In. 935.00
Vase, Bud, Cobalt Blue On Frosted, 6 In. 900.00
Vase, Bud, Green On Frost, Unusual Shape, 5 3/4 In. 850.00
Vase, Burgundy Flowers & Leaves, Gold Ground, Signed, 7 3/4 In. 995.00
Vase, Canoe Form, Waterlilies, Lily Pads, Dragonfly, 4 3/4 In. 5500.00
Vase, Carved, Hyalite, 10 In. 2300.00
Vase, Clematis Blossoms, Leaves, Bulbous Base, Signed, 1900, 5 3/4 In. 2200.00
Vase, Cover, Blossoms, Egg Shape, White Frosted, Cameo, 6 In. 4180.00
Vase, Enameled Blossoms, Citrine, Swollen Cylinder, 10 In. 6050.00
Vase, Enameled In Pink, White & Green, Spider Mark, 14 In. ....*Illus* 7920.00

Vase, Ferns, Gray, Green & Khaki Overlay, c.1900, 7 1/4 In. 775.00
Vase, Fishing Boats, Distant Sea Gulls, Signed, c.1900, 20 5/8 In. 5500.00
Vase, Flask Form, River Landscape, Trees, Signed, c.1900, 5 3/4 In. 4180.00
Vase, Floral & Leaf Design, Signed, 7 In. 1100.00
Vase, Floral & Vines, Butterflies, Stand–Up Collar, Signed, 6 In. 1295.00
Vase, Floral Designs, Winged Insect, Shell Ornaments, 3 5/8 In., Pair 3635.00
Vase, Flowering Leafy Vines, Conical Neck, Signed, c.1900, 6 3/8 In. 3750.00
Vase, Flowering Trees, Purple Cut To Opaque, Signed, 6 1/2 In. 350.00
Vase, Flowers, Leaves, Opaque White, 3 1/2 In. 795.00
Vase, Fuchsia Design On Yellow, 5 1/4 In. 1125.00
Vase, Fuchsia Flowers & Leaves, Tricorner Top, 8 In. 3200.00
Vase, Gold Trees, River Scene, Frosted Gold Ground, Signed, 14 1/4 In. 7150.00
Vase, Gray, Overlaid Green, Wisteria, Star Mark, 17 In. ....*Illus* 2310.00
Vase, Gray, Pink, Overlaid Lavender, Green, Hydrangea, 12 In. ....*Illus* 3410.00
Vase, Green Fern On Amber Ground, Signed, 4 In. 665.00
Vase, Heraldic Scene, Clear Taupe, Bulbous, Waisted Neck, 10 1/2 In. 7700.00
Vase, Hyalite, Carved, 10 In. 375.00
Vase, Hydrangea Blossoms, Blue & Green, Signed, 1904, 5 7/8 In. 1980.00
Vase, Iris & Butterfly, Lavender & White, Large 4500.00
Vase, Iris Design, Light Green & Amethyst, Frosted, Signed, 4 3/4 In. 1750.00
Vase, Landscape, Lotus Blossoms, Signed, c.1900, 5 1/2 In. 2100.00
Vase, Layered Blossoms, Buds & Leafy Stems, Flared Rim, Label, 3 In. 995.00
Vase, Leaves & Berries, Frosted, Amethyst, Signed, 6 1/4 In. 1400.00
Vase, Leaves, Vines, Bellflowers, 3 Colors, 13 1/2 In. 3000.00
Vase, Lion's Paw Handles, Wildflowers, Gilt, Signed, 6 1/2 In. 305.00
Vase, Maple Leaves, Ocher Ground, Signed, 5 1/4 In. 995.00
Vase, Mountainous Landscape, Flattened Ovoid, Signed, 1900, 7 5/8 In. 2975.00
Vase, Mountains & Trees, Amethyst & Blue, Signed, 6 1/2 In. 1900.00
Vase, Multiple Flowerheads, Buds, Signed, c.1900, 13 1/4 In. 3300.00
Vase, Off–White Pine Cones & Needles, Browns, 8 In. 2500.00
Vase, Oriental Style, Leaf & Pod Cuttings, Gold, Signed, 17 3/4 In. 2035.00
Vase, Pendant Blossoming Clematis Vines, Signed, c.1900, 15 In. 5500.00
Vase, Pendant Squash Blossoms, Leaves, Signed, c.1925, 7 1/2 In. 7150.00
Vase, Pilgrim Shape, Clematis, Lavender To Frost, Signed, 6 In. 1500.00
Vase, Pink, Double Overlaid With Green & Lavender, Signed, 13 3/4 In. 3550.00
Vase, Pods & Leaves On Orange To Frosted Ground, Signed, 18 In. 2200.00
Vase, Poppy Blossoms, Leaves, Gray, Signed, c.1900, 4 3/4 In. 2475.00
Vase, Purple Flowers, Vines, 3 7/8 x 2 In. 600.00
Vase, Red & Yellow Poppies, Green–Yellow, Cameo, Bulbous, 4 1/4 In. 3850.00
Vase, Red Cherry Design, Yellow & White Ground, 3 In. 950.00
Vase, Red Floral On Frosted Gold, Signed, 6 1/4 In. 1450.00
Vase, River Landscape, Docked Row Boats, Signed, c.1900, 15 In. 6600.00
Vase, Scenic, Cylinder, 5 In. 1500.00
Vase, Small Flowers & Whirling Leaves, Purple To Gold, 7 In. 2800.00
Vase, Smoky Swirled Body, Enameled & Etched Wildflowers, 13 In. 3100.00
Vase, Spider Chrysanthemums, Signed, c.1900, 13 3/8 In. 3850.00
Vase, Spray of Wildflowers, Buds, Leaves, Signed, c.1900, 7 1/2 In. 1875.00
Vase, Spray of Wildflowers, Leaves, Signed, c.1900, 6 1/2 In. 2200.00
Vase, Stick, Carved Leaves In Mahogany, Signed, Miniature 390.00
Vase, Stylized Thistle, Cross of Lorraine On Reverse, Signed, 18 In. 8250.00
Vase, Vines, Leaves, Flowers, Buds, Purple, 3 7/8 x 2 3/4 In. 650.00
Vase, Violet & Green Flowers, Neutral Ground, 4 1/2 In. 475.00
Vase, Wildflowers & Leaves, Truncated Baluster Form, Signed, 5 In. 1650.00
Vase, Wildflowers, Long Neck, Everted Lip, Signed, c.1900, 6 In. 1980.00
Vase, Woodland Landscape, Teardrop Form, Signed, c.1900, 5 In. 2850.00

 Game plates are plates of any make decorated with pictures of birds, animals, or fish. The game plates usually came in sets consisting of twelve dishes and a serving platter. These sets were most popular during the 1880s.

GAME PLATE, Dogs In Field, Gold Trim, Limoges, 10 In. 35.00
Geese, Green Transfer, Coronet, 10 In. 65.00
Grouse, Gold Trim, Limoges, 9 In. 65.00

Pheasant, Gold Rim, Limoges, 10 In. 75.00
GAME SET, Fish, Majolica, Platter, England, 12 Piece 400.00
Game Birds, Gold Trim, Pierced Border, 12 Plates, Platter 265.00

Children's games of all sorts are collected. Of special interest are any board games or card games. Other games may be found listed under Card, Toy, or the name of the character or celebrity featured in the game.

GAME, 20, 000 Leagues Under The Sea .... 20.00 To 25.00
20, 000 Leagues Under The Sea, Electric Quiz, Jaymar, 1953 .... 50.00
3 Musketeers, 1900s, Strategy 65.00
A Merry Christmas, Santa Claus In Gift–Laden Auto, Milton Bradley 660.00
Abbott & Costello's Who's On First, Selchow & Richter, 1978 .... 25.00
Across The Continent, Board, 1952, Parker Brothers 50.00
Across The Continent, U. S. Map Board, Wallace Reid Film, 1924, 8 In. 17.50
Addams Family, Card Game .... 30.00 To 45.00
Addams Family, Ideal, 1964 .... 175.00
Air Mail Race, Standard Industries, 1927 .... 170.00
Airways Pinball, 1930s 55.00
Alfred Hitchcock's Why Game 15.00
Alfred Hitchcock's Why, Board, 1961, Milton Bradley 50.00
Alien 20.00
Alien, Board, 1979 .... 25.00
All In The Family 8.00
Alox Agates Marble, 1930s 25.00
Alphabet, Underdog, Gordy, 1975 .... 10.00
Amos & Andy, Acrobat, Box, 1930s 95.00
Annette's Secret Passage, Board, Parker Bros. 50.00
Anzio, Avalon Hills, Board, 1969 .... 35.00
Apba Major League Baseball, Board 60.00
Around The World In 80 Days 45.00
As The World Turns 25.00
Assembly Line, Selchow, 1953 .... 20.00
Autobridge, Board, Papers, 1938 .... 30.00
Away We Go, Board, Jackie Gleason, 1954 .... 120.00
Badminton Set, Ken Davidson, Rackets, Shuttlecocks, Box 20.00
Ball Toss, Santa Claus, Boardwalk At Ashbury Park, 1920s 1650.00
Barbie, Queen of The Prom, Board, Mattel, 1960 .... 35.00 To 50.00
Barney Google & Spark Plug, Milton Bradley, 1923, Box, 18 In. 95.00
Basketball, Baldwin, Brooklyn, Box 55.00
Bat Masterson, Gene Barry Twirling Cane 35.00
Beany & Cecil Match It, Mattel, 1961 .... 35.00
Beat The Clock, 1954 .... 25.00
Beat The Clock, Milton Bradley, Box, 1969 .... 100.00
Beatles Flip Your Wig, Board 100.00
Ben Casey, MD 35.00
Beverly Hillbillies, 1963 .... 30.00
Beverly Hillbillies, Board 30.00
Bewitched 30.00
Big Jitters, Tin Lithograph, Plastic Overlay, Marx 25.00
Big Rail, John Wayne Film, 1930, Parker Bros., Board 375.00
Billiard, Folding Mahogany Case, 9 Ivory Balls, Cue Stick, 33 1/2 In. 3900.00
Bing Crosby, Board, 1947 .... 110.00
Bingo, Little Rascals, Our Gang, Gabriel Co., 1958 .... 70.00
Bionic Crisis, Parker Brothers, Sealed, 1975 .... 20.00
Black Hole Space Alert 15.00
Black Sambo, Target, Tin 95.00
Blocks, Numbers, Gem Puzzle, Box, 3 3/4 x 3 3/4 In. 7.50
Blondie, Card Game, 1941 .... 45.00
Board, 1 Side 64 Squares, Reverse 144 Squares, 28 3/4 x 18 3/4 In. 275.00
Board, Black & Red, Plywood, 2900, 20 x 26 1/2 In. 165.00
Board, Black Paint, 13 Iron Hooks, Pine, 44 In. 125.00
Board, Blocks Numbered, Play By Mail, Red, White, Black, 18 x 16 In. 795.00

Board, Breadboard, Bag of Checkers, Handle, 16 x 27 1/2 In. 145.00
Board, Checkers & Backgammon, Folding Box Type, Egyptian Scenes 350.00
Board, Cribbage, Le Count No. 3, Metal & Wood, Early 1900s, Box 37.50
Board, Dart, Tim Holt, Box 275.00
Board, Dart, Wall Hanging, Anheuser–Busch, Oak Case, 21 3/4 x 16 In. 95.00
Board, Inlaid Birch, Square, 18 1/2 In. 135.00
Board, Ouija 15.00
Board, Parcheesi, Red, Green & Off–White Original Paint 655.00
Board, Yellowed Varnish, Brown Squares, 19 x 29 In. 155.00
Bonanza Poler 35.00
Caddy, Poker Chip, Inlaid Mahogany, 12 1/4 In. 275.00
Cage, Chuck–A–Luck 295.00
Call Me Lucky, Parker Bros., Board, 1954 .... 40.00
Camelot, Parker Brothers, 1930 .... 59.00
Candid Camera, Target Game, Square, 16 In. 135.00
Captain Gallant, Transogram, 1955 .... 80.00
Captain Kangaroo, Tic Tagaroo 45.00
Captain Video, Space T. V., Box, 1950 ....60.00 To 150.00
Car 54 Where Are You, Allioson, Board, 1961 .... 100.00
Card, Authors, Case, 1940s 6.00
Card, Bewitched, 1965 .... 27.00
Card, Blondie, 1941 .... 45.00
Card, Charlie Chan, 1939, Sidney Toler As Chan 30.00
Card, Fortune Telling, Whitman, 1940 .... 15.00
Card, Funny Monsters, You'll Die Laughing, 66 Cards 25.00
Card, Green Hornet, 1966, Sealed 20.00
Card, Illya Kuryakin, Man From U. N. C. L. E., Milton Bradley, Box 20.00
Card, License To Kill, 1967 .... 60.00
Card, Mad Magazine, 1979 .... 8.00
Card, Pinocchio, Box, 1939 .... 22.00
Card, Tarot, James Bond, 007, Box, 1974 .... 50.00
Card, Tootie Kazootie 25.00
Card, Touring, Parker Bros., 1926 .... 17.50
Card, Touring, Parker Bros., 1933 .... 28.00
Card, Wings, Parker Brothers, 1928 .... 80.00
Cards & Poker Chips, Leather Covered Case 37.00
Case, Card, Floral Carving, 4 1/2 In. 235.00
Casper Jumping Bean, 1959 .... 30.00
Casper The Ghost, 1970s 12.00
Casper, Glow In The Dark 18.00
Casper, Milton Bradley, Board 30.00
Charlie's Angels, 1977 ....10.00 To 12.00
Checkerboard, Alligatored Yellow, Black, Brown, Wood Square, 16 1/2 In. 150.00
Checkerboard, Black & Mustard Graining, Poplar, 22 1/2 x 15 1/2 In. 125.00
Checkerboard, Carved, Game On Reverse, Pine, 15 1/2 x 24 In. 205.00
Checkerboard, Painted Red & Black, Striping, Pine, 17 1/4 x 18 In. 350.00
Checkerboard, Pine, Pumpkin & Black Grid, 23 1/2 x 17 3/4 In. 170.00
Checkerboard, Pine, Red, Black K7 Blue Paint, 28 x 15 3/4 In. 250.00

◆◆

Pearls have gone up in value dramatically. If you own pearls that are more than 10 years old, have them reappraised. Care is important. Don't put them in a box with sharp objects. Don't let them touch perfume or hair spray. Perspiration is bad, so wipe the pearls after each wearing. Don't wash too often, the water may weaken the string. Never store them in airtight warm places like safe deposit boxes or plastic bags. Long periods of airtight storage will ruin the pearls' luster.

◆◆

Checkerboard, Red & Black Paint, Poplar, 14 x 18 In. 200.00
Checkerboard, Red & Black Repaint, 18 1/4 x 30 1/2 In. 200.00
Checkerboard, Red & Black, Gray Border, Playwood, 1900, Square, 17 In. 145.00
Checkerboard, Red & Black, Green & Black Border, Painted, 17 1/2 In. 1210.00
Checkerboard, Red & Natural, Stripes, Poplar, 16 1/4 x 16 1/2 In. 375.00
Checkerboard, Reverse Painted, Gold Leaf, Black, Framed, 21 x 21 In. 100.00
Checkerboard, Scalloped Edges, 7 Iron Hooks, Pine, 24 1/2 In. 95.00
Checkerboard, Wooden, Yellow & Black Paint, 17 x 27 In. 250.00
Chess Set, Carved Ivory, China, Late 17th Century, 26 Piece 3700.00
Chess Set, Hawks & Doves, Pres. L. Johnson, J. L. King, Ceramic, 1968 .... 3000.00
Chess Set, Ivory, Fitted Silk–Lined Box Opening To Chess Board 990.00
Chess Set, Ivory, Non–Figural, Turkey, 18th Century 800.00
Chess Set, Silver, Bronze & Gold Plated, Green Onyx Board, Small 5885.00
Chess Set, White, Red Players, Ivory, Lacquered Board, China, 3 3/4 In. 165.00
Chess Set, Wood Carved, Wood Box 45.00
Chinese Checkers, Checker Game On Reverse Side, Ohio Art 20.00
Chinese Checkers, Milton Bradley, Wooden 23.00
Chinese Chi Chi Fortune Telling, Bamboo Sticks, Rules, Box 35.00
Chitty Chitty Bang Bang 40.00
Chitty, Chitty, Bang, Bang, Board, Milton Bradley 12.00
Chutes & Ladders, 1956 .... 20.00
Cinderella, Parker Bros., Pink Board, 1965 .... 25.00
Cities, 1940s 20.00
Clue, Parker Brothers, 1950 .... 90.00
Columbo 10.00
Combat Pinball, Marx 25.00
Cootie, Giant, 1960s 30.00
Cowboy Roundup, Board, 1952 .... 16.00
Cribbage, Milton Bradley, Board, Box 20.00
Crosby Derby, Bing Crosby, Board, H. Fishlove Co., 1947 .... 150.00
Dark Shadows, Board 35.00
Dark Shadows, Whitman, 1968 .... 35.00
Dark Shadows, With Teeth 50.00
Dating Game, TV Show, Hasbro, 1967 .... 25.00
Dave Garroway's Today, Sealed Box 25.00
Dave Garroway's Wide Wide World License Bingo, Box 10.00
Dennis The Menace, Tiddly Winks 45.00
Diamonds & Hearts, Board, McLoughlin Bros. 95.00
Diplomacy, Board, 1961 .... 40.00
Disney Frontierland, Parker, 1955 .... 20.00
Dominoes, Carved Bone Ebony, Inlaid Box With Deer & Lion Scene 110.00
Dominoes, Ivory, 1800s 225.00
Dominoes, Railroad Design, Box 25.00
Dominoes, Van Nostrand's Bunker Hill Lager 45.00
Dominos, Bulwark Cut Plug Toabcco, Tin Lithograph Case, Tin Tiles 210.00
Down & Out Marble, Box 50.00
Down You Go, Selchow & Righter, 1954 .... 40.00
Dr. Busby, Board, 1905 .... 20.00
Dr. Kildare, 1962 .... 28.00
Dragnet, 1955 .... 45.00
Easy Money, Milton Bradley, 1936 .... 50.00
Ellery Queen Mystery Game, Ideal, 1967 .... 35.00
Emergency, Tv Show 18.00
Escalado, Chad Valley, Box 250.00
Escape From Death Star, Kenner, Board, Box 18.00
Family Affair, Board, 1973 .... 48.00
Fantasyland 8.00
Fat Albert, 1937 .... 27.50
Fat Albert, Board 20.00
Feed The Elphant, Board 18.00
Felix The Cat, Board 15.00
Fibber McGee & Molly's Wistful Vista Mystery Game, 1940 .... 20.00 To 30.00
Fish Pond, Disneyland, McLoughlin Bros. 100.00

Fish Pond, Milton Bradley, Box	12.00
Five Jacks, Penny Flip, Cast Aluminum Front, Oak Case	875.00
Flash Gordon, 1960s	15.00
Flash Gordon, Board, 1960s	15.00
Flintstones Tumble Race, 1962, Transogram	85.00
Flintstones, Milton Bradley, 1971	15.00
Flintstones, Stone Age, 1961, Transogram, 9 x 17 In.	65.00
Flying Nun, Board	25.00 To 45.00
Football, Tom Hamilton, 1935	85.00
Fortune Telling Game, Parker Bros., Cards, 1890	50.00
Fortune Telling, Mystiscope, 1925	40.00
French Horse Race, Wood Die Cast Riders	175.00
Game of District Messenger Boy, McLoughlin	175.00
Game of India, Milton Bradley, 1936	30.00
Game of India, Transogram, 1938	25.00
Game of Knowledge, Trade Is Power, Paper Lithograph, Wood	75.00
Game of Yertle, Dr. Seuss, Revell, 1960	170.00
Gee Whiz, Horse Race, Wolverine, Tin	45.00 To 100.00
Get Smart	45.00
Giant Cootie, Board	75.00
Giant Wheel, Remco	65.00
Gilligan's Island	15.00
Go To Head of Class, Milton Bradley, c.1956	20.00
Gomer Pyle, Board, Transogram	75.00
Gomer Pyle, Transogram, Complete	75.00
Greatest Show On Earth, Board, Saalfield, 1942	20.00
Green Ghost	25.00
Gumby Playful Trails	20.00
Happy Days	8.00
Happy Days, Board	7.00
Harlem Globetrotters, 1971	65.00
Hasimoto Sam, Board	20.00
Have Gun Will Travel, Board, Parker Brothers, 1959	35.00
Hawaiian Punch, Mattel, 1978	40.00
Heckle & Jeckle, 3–D, Target, Box	20.00
Hippety Hop, Board, Corey Game Co., 1940	115.00
Hit The Beach, Milton Bradley, 1965	35.00
Hogan's Heroes, Board, Transogram, 1966	65.00
Honey West, 1965, Ideal	100.00
Horse Race, Wood Board, Snap Cover Case, 1942, 4 1/2 x 4 1/2 In.	12.00
Horse Racing, Mechanical, Jeu De Course, France	425.00
I Spy, Board, Ideal, 1965	85.00
I Spy, Starring Culp & Cosby, Ideal, 1965	85.00
Incredible Hulk, Board	19.00
Interpol Calling, Board	20.00
Jackie Gleason & Away We Go, Transogram, 1956	150.00
James Bond 007 Secret Agent, Milton Bradley, 1964	12.00
James Bond Road Race, Slot Car Set, Astin–Martin, Mustang, 1965	650.00
Jerry Lewis, Dean Martin, Puppet Show	45.00
Jolly Darkie, Target, Milton Bradley	275.00
Juggler, Popeye, Tin, 1928	50.00
Kellogg's Wheel of Knowledge, 1930	20.00
Kentucky Derby	250.00
Kicker Catcher, Baseball, 1 Cent	300.00
Kitty Kat Marble, Box	90.00
Knock Down Target, Pistol, Rubber Tipped Darts, Marx	65.00
Knockout Electronic Boxing, Northwestern Products, Battery Operated	125.00
Kreskins ESP, Board, Milton Bradley, 1966	30.00
Kukla & Ollie, Board, 1962	50.00
Landmark FBI, Transogram, 1960s	25.00
Lassie, Board, 1965	35.00
Laverne & Shirley, Board	10.00
Leave It To Beaver, Ambush	25.00

Leave It To Beaver, Board, Ambush Game 35.00
Lie Detector, Interrogation Box, Bell Rings, Mattell 45.00
Life of The Party, Board, Rosebud Art Co. 20.00
Little Black Sambo, Board, 1945 .... 90.00 To 125.00
Little Kittens Tiddlywinks, Spears, Box, 1920s 40.00
Looney Tunes, Board, 1968 .... 42.00
Lost In Space, Board, 1966 .... 65.00
Lost In Space, Milton Bradley, 1965 .... 65.00 To 75.00
Lotto, Playing Cards, Wooden Tokens, Green Wooden Box, 8 x 9 5/8 In. 10.00
Lucy Show, Transogram, 1962 .... 150.00
Mad Magazine, Screwball, Board, 1960 .... 50.00
Mad's Spy Vs Spy, Board, Milton Bradley 10.00
Magic Hoops, Label, Milton Bradley, Oak Box 100.00
Mah Jong, Ivory, Wooden Box, Brass Trim, 1900s 250.00
Man In The Moon, McLoughlin Brothers, c.1900 .... 3850.00
Marble, Pitfalls of Pinocchio, Whitman 95.00
Margie, Milton Bradley, 1961 .... 75.00
Mary Poppins' Magic Wheel, 1960 .... 25.00
McHale's Navy, 1964 .... 25.00
McHales Navy, Transogram, 1962 .... 30.00
Mental Whoopee, Board, Simon & Schuster, 1933 .... 30.00
Midway, Board, Avalon Hill, 1964 .... 35.00
Mighty Mouse Playhouse Rescue Game, 1956, Unused 50.00
Mighty Mouse Skill Roll, Terrytoons Characters, 1960s, 14 x 16 In. 125.00
Mighty Mouse Spin Targets, 1950, Aldon, 9 x 11 In. 45.00
Milton The Monster, Board 25.00
Monkees, Board, Tran Co., 1967 .... 100.00
Mork & Mindy 8.00
Motor Carriage, Box 35.00
Mouse Trap, Board, 1963 .... 35.00
Mouse Trap, Ideal 25.00
My Favorite Martian, Board 50.00
Nancy Drew Mystery, 1957 .... 35.00 To 40.00
Napoleon Solo, The Man From U. N. C. L. E., Board, Ideal, Box 65.00
Nixon's, Box 15.00
No Respect, Board, Milton Bradley, 1985 .... 15.00
Nodding Nancy, Mammy Pipe Toss, Wooden Platform, 4 Pipes, 4 Rings 210.00
Old Maid, Circus Characters, Whitman 20.00
Olympic Runners, Mechanical, Tin, Wolverine, 1930s 100.00
Outlaw & Posse, Board, Milton Bradley, 1978 .... 15.00
Outlaws, T. V., Transogram, 1961 .... 25.00
Owl Game, Chicago, Board, 2 Sides, Square, 1901, 28 1/2 In. 155.00
Panorama of Europe, J. & E. Wallis, Case, 1815, 24 1/2 x 18 5/8 In. 550.00
Partridge Family, Board 30.00
Patty Duke, Board, Milton Bradley, 1963 .... 20.00 To 35.00
Perry Mason, Board 25.00
Perry Mason, Transogram, 1959 .... 70.00
Petticoat Junction 35.00
Pin The Tail On Mickey, Mickey Mouse 192.00
Pinball, Happi Time, Sears 38.50
Pinball, Home Run King, 1940s, 2 1/2 x 4 1/2 In. 7.00
Pinball, Marbles, Wolverine 15.00
Pinball, Nutty Mad 45.00
Pinball, Poosh–Em–Up 52.00
Pinball, Poosh–Em–Up, 1930s 35.00
Pinball, U. N. C. L. E., Marx 20.00
Ping Pong, Box, 1932 .... 45.00
Pinocchio, Board, 17 x 14 In. 35.00
Pit, Bull & Bear Edition, Parker Bros., 1903 .... 10.00
Pitch–Em, Horseshoe, Wolverine 32.00
Play Your Hunch, T.V., Transogram, 1960 .... 18.00
Poker Chips, Airplane, Composition, Box, 100 Piece 69.00
Poker Chips, Lorillard Plug Tobacco, Slate, Pair 10.00

Pony Express, Board, 1947 .... 30.00
Poor Jenny, Board, Pieces, Box, 1927 .... 33.00
Popeye The Juggler, Tin, King Features, 1929 .... 75.00
Prince Valiant, Board 45.00
Punch Board, Uncle Sam, Our Uncle, 25 Cent Per Play 60.00
Puzzle, 007, Thunderball, Milton Bradley, Box 40.00
Puzzle, Baseball Size, Wooden, Round 25.00
Puzzle, Chase & Sanborn Tea, Ceylon Girl Picking Tea, 1890s 37.50
Puzzle, Creature Glow In Dark, Box 175.00
Puzzle, David Cassidy, 1972, 500 Piece 26.00
Puzzle, Dixie Crystals, Girl Baking, Dog Begging, 1930s, 18 x 15 In. ... 65.00
Puzzle, Elsie's Dexterity, Bordens, 1941 .... 90.00
Puzzle, Felix, 1949 .... 29.00
Puzzle, Greyhound Bus, Wooden, 1930s 30.00
Puzzle, Halloween, Jigsaw 20.00
Puzzle, Hood's Rainy Day, 2 Sides 85.00
Puzzle, Hunter, With Rifle, 1948 .... 20.00
Puzzle, Inner Sanctum, No. 1, Peter Arno 65.00
Puzzle, Kellogg's, Girl With Flowers, Cardboard, 1933, 6 x 8 In. 38.00
Puzzle, Little Black Sambo, Wooden, Round, Box, 7 1/2 In. 145.00
Puzzle, Little Red Riding Hood, Milton Bradley, Box, c.1900 .... 145.00
Puzzle, Locomotive, McLoughlin Bros. 350.00
Puzzle, Make Me, Jigsaw 17.00
Puzzle, Mary Poppins, Box 10.00
Puzzle, MASH 10.00
Puzzle, Michael Jackson, Paper Doll, Uncut .... 15.00 To 25.00
Puzzle, Mummy, Jaymar, 1963, Box 90.00
Puzzle, Munsters, Box 45.00
Puzzle, Night Before Christmas Santa Claus Cube, McLoughlin, 1890s ... 4400.00
Puzzle, Prince, Slipper On Cinderella's Foot, Jigsaw, Jaymar, 1950s 18.00
Puzzle, Rifleman, Tray, 1960 .... 20.00
Puzzle, Rootie Kazooti, 3 Puzzles, Box 35.00
Puzzle, Space 1999 .... 12.00
Puzzle, Space Patrol, Frame Tray 45.00
Puzzle, St. Nicholas, McLoughlin, 1890s 360.00
Puzzle, Vargas Beauty, Tuco, 1933 .... 22.00
Puzzle, Wagon Train 20.00
Puzzle, Wells Fargo, 1959 .... 23.00
Puzzle, Whittlemore Shoe Polish, 2 Sides 75.00
Quick Draw McGraw, 1960 .... 45.00
Rat Patrol, Board, 1965 .... 55.00
Red Ryder, Target, Box, 1939 .... 125.00
Rich Uncle, Parker Bros., 1959 .... 35.00
Rifleman, Board, 1959, Milton Bradley .... 30.00 To 45.00
Rifleman, Board, Box, 1959 .... 40.00 To 45.00
Rip Van Winkle, Box, 1929 .... 47.00
Rivals, Parker Bros. 350.00
Road Runner, 1968 .... 30.00
Roadrace, James Bond, 1965, Gilbert 500.00
Robin Hood, Milton Bradley, 1937 .... 75.00
Round The Clock Golf, 12–In. Tin Lithograph, Box, 1920s 195.00
Royal Jackstraws, Colored Wooden Sticks, Milton Bradley, 1936 .... 12.50
Rudolph The Red–Nosed Reindeer, Cadaco, Board, 1977 .... 30.00
Sea Hunt, Board, 1961 .... 55.00
Sea Hunt, Lowell, 1961 .... 75.00
Senior Combination, Board, 14 Games, Box, 1920s 60.00
Sergeant Preston 30.00
Sergeant Preston, Board, 1956, Milton Bradly 25.00
Shooting Gallery Target, 2 Chickens, Iron, Trigger, 10 1/4 x 16 In. 50.00
Shooting Gallery, Bulldog, Metal Marbles, Wood & Cst Iron, Arcade, 1920 ... 150.00
Shooting Gallery, Gun & Box, Wyandotte 135.00
Six Million Dollar Man, Board, Parker Bros. 15.00
Skunk, Board, 1953 .... 15.00

Slalom, Battery	125.00
Slime Monster, Mattel, Box, 1977	25.00
Snake Eyes, No. 27, All Cards, Chips & Dice, Box	50.00
Snoopy & Red Baron, 1970	28.00
Space Pilot, Board, 1951	75.00
Speedway Classic Motorcycle, Lights Up With Batteries	38.50
Spin–It Marble, Box	55.00
Spiro T. Agnew American History Challenge, Gabriel, 1971	25.00
Squeeze Your Bippy, Laugh–In, Box, 1968	65.00
Stagecoach, Milton Bradley, 1958	40.00
Standard Red Crown, Board, Cars, Spinner	38.00
Star Trek, Ideal, 1967	85.00
Star Wars, Escape From Death Star, Box, Kenner, 1977	40.00
Star Wars, Parker Brothers	25.00
States, Board, 1954	15.00
Stepplechase, McLoughlin, Box	135.00
Stockade Cowboy & Indian, Selchow & Righter, 1930s	35.00
Swarm of Bees, Bixby's Royal Polish, Cardboard	40.00
Talk To Cecil, Cecil The Seasick Sea Serpent Puppet, 1961	150.00
Tell It To The Judge, Eddie Cantor	60.00
That Girl, 1969, Remco	68.00
Three Little Pigs, Walt Disney, Lithographed Paper, 1933, 10 x 14 In.	55.00
Thunderball 007, 1965	25.00
Tim Holt, Target Game, Box	55.00
Tin Can Alley, Chuck Connors, Board	50.00
Tomorrowland, Parker Brothers	40.00
Tootsie Roll, Astronaut Target, 1940	40.00
Uncle Wiggily, Board, Parker Bros. .... 12.00 To 29.00	
Undersea World of Cousteau, 1968	22.00
Untouchables, Elliot Ness, Box, 1961	50.00
Voyage To The Bottom of The Sea, Board	35.00
Wanted Dead Or Alive, Steve McQueen On Cover, Lowell	165.00
Watermelon Patch, Board, McLoughlin Brothers, 1890s	2475.00
Welcome Back Kotter	10.00
Wells Fargo	32.00
Wheel, Metal Stand, Red Border, White Dice, Blue Ground, 20 In. Diam.	395.00
Wheel, Yellow, Green, Blue & Salmon, White Letters, 20 In. Diam.	295.00
Winky Dink T. V. Kit, 1954	30.00
Wizard of Oz, 1930s	350.00
Yacht Race, Board, Parker Brothers, 1961	40.00
Yankee Doodle, Board, McLoughlin	550.00
Yastrzemski Baseball	55.00
Yogi Bear Ball Toss, Transogram, 1960	60.00
You Bet Your Life, Groucho Marx	60.00

ГАРДНЕРㆍ The Gardner porcelain works was founded in Verbiki, outside Moscow, by the English–born Francis Gardner in 1766. Gardner made porcelain tablewares, figurines, and faience.

GARDNER, Figurine, Dancing Peasant Woman, Porcelain, 8 1/8 In.	995.00
Figurine, Peasant Woman, Headress of Flowers, Porcelain, 8 1/8 In.	775.00
Figurine, Young Woman, Garland In Hair, Porcelain, 8 1/8 In.	335.00
Group, 3 Carousing Men, Porcelain, 10 1/4 In.	2100.00
Group, Man & Boy, Performing Bear, Porcelain, 6 In.	1650.00

 Gaudy Dutch pottery was made in England for America from about 1810 to 1820. It is a white earthenware with Imari–style decorations of red, blue, green, yellow, and black. Only sixteen patterns of Gaudy Dutch were made: Butterfly, Carnation, Dahlia, Double Rose, Dove, Grape, Leaf, Oyster, Primrose, Single Rose, Strawflower, Sunflower, Urn, War Bonnet, Zinnia, and No Name. Other similar wares are called *Gaudy Ironstone* and *Gaudy Welsh.*

GAUDY DUTCH, Bowl, Butterfly Variant, 6 1/4 In.	688.00

◆◆◆

Rub amber beads on a wool carpet, then hold the beads over a small scrap of paper. The amber will collect static electricity and pick up the paper. Glass will not. Sometimes when amber is rubbed, it smells a bit like pine resin.

◆◆◆

Bowl, Butterfly Variant, 6 3/8 In.	880.00
Bowl, Dahlia, 6 1/4 In.	358.00
Bowl, Grape, Luster Trim, 6 1/2 In.	385.00
Bowl, Wash Basin, Butterfly Variant, 12 In. ....*Illus*	11,000
Coffeepot, Single Rose, Domed, 11 In. ....*Illus*	5725.00
Coffeepot, Sunflower, 9 1/2 In.	1650.00
Creamer, Butterfly Variant, 3 1/2 In.	660.00
Creamer, Butterfly Variant, 3 3/4 In.	1320.00
Creamer, Butterfly Variant, 3 5/8 In.	660.00
Creamer, Butterfly Variant, Barrel Shape, 4 1/2 In.	990.00
Creamer, Carnation, 4 3/4 In.	605.00
Creamer, Double Rose, 4 3/4 In.	935.00
Creamer, Double Rose, 5 1/4 In.	633.00
Creamer, Dove, 4 1/2 In.	715.00
Creamer, Dove, 4 1/4 In.	413.00
Creamer, Oyster, 3 3/4 In.	138.00
Creamer, Single Rose	550.00
Creamer, Single Rose, 4 1/2 In.	605.00
Creamer, Sunflower, 3 3/4 In.	110.00
Creamer, Sunflower, 4 1/2 In.	853.00
Creamer, War Bonnet	550.00
Cup & Saucer, Dark Blue, Rust, Lime Green	325.00
Cup & Saucer, Handleless, Grape Pattern	250.00
Cup & Saucer, Handleless, Single Rose	250.00
Cup & Saucer, Single Rose	220.00
Cup & Saucer, Urn, 2 3/8 In.	413.00
Cup Plate	275.00
Dish, Butterfly Variant, 10 In.	1320.00
Dish, Butterfly Variant, 9 7/8 In.	990.00
Dish, Butterfly Variant, Deep, 8 3/8 In.	303.00
Dish, Butterfly Variant, Deep, 9 7/8 In.	990.00
Dish, Carnation, Deep, 10 In.	1210.00
Dish, Single Rose, Deep, 10 In.	632.00 To 688.00
Dish, Single Rose, Riley, Deep, 10 1/8 In.	660.00
Dish, War Bonnet, Deep, 9 1/2 In.	825.00
Dish, War Bonnet, Deep, 9 5/8 In.	1540.00
Jug, Double Rose, Mask Spout, Dark Beard, 6 1/16 In.	1705.00

Gaudy Dutch, Bowl, Wash Basin, Butterfly Variant, 12 In.
Gaudy Dutch, Coffeepot, Single Rose, Domed, 11 In.

Gaudy Dutch, Pitcher, War Bonnet, 5 3/4 In.
Gaudy Dutch, Teapot, Butterfly, 7 In.
Gaudy Dutch, Teapot, Carnation, 6 1/2 In.

Gaudy Dutch, Plate,   *Gaudy Dutch, Plate,*   *Gaudy Dutch, Plate,*
Urn, 9 7/8 In.   *Sunflower, 9 3/4 In.*   *Single Rose, 9 3/4 In.*

Jug, Double Rose, Mask Spout, Light Beard, 6 1/4 In.	550.00
Pitcher, Double Rose, 8 1/4 In.	1430.00
Pitcher, Grape, 8 In.	2420.00
Pitcher, War Bonnet, 5 3/4 In. ....*Illus*	220.00
Plate, Butterfly Variant, 10 In.	578.00 To 633.00
Plate, Butterfly Variant, 9 3/4 In.	715.00 To 825.00
Plate, Butterfly Variant, 9 7/8 In.	688.00 To 935.00
Plate, Carnation, 9 7/8 In.	550.00 To 1155.00
Plate, Double Rose, 10 In.	715.00
Plate, Dove, 10 In.	770.00
Plate, Dove, 8 1/8 In.	633.00
Plate, Dove, 9 3/4 In.	385.00 To 715.00
Plate, Dove, 9 7/8 In.	750.00
Plate, Grape, 9 3/4 In.	495.00
Plate, Grape, 9 5/8 In.	633.00
Plate, Oyster, 9 7/8 In.	633.00
Plate, Primrose, Riley, 9 7/8 In.	2640.00
Plate, Single Rose, 8 1/2 In.	220.00
Plate, Single Rose, 8 1/4 In.	330.00
Plate, Single Rose, 9 3/4 In. ....*Illus*	1045.00
Plate, Strawflower, Riley, 10 In.	2750.00
Plate, Sunflower, 9 3/4 In. ....*Illus*	1155.00
Plate, Urn Variant, 5 5/16 In.	385.00
Plate, Urn Variant, 7 3/16 In.	413.00
Plate, Urn Variant, 8 1/4 In.	660.00
Plate, Urn Variant, 9 7/8 In.	660.00
Plate, Urn, 9 7/8 In. ....*Illus*	550.00
Plate, War Bonnet, 8 1/4 In.	375.00
Plate, War Bonnet, 9 3/4 In.	425.00 To 578.00
Plate, Zinnia, Riley, 10 In.	660.00 To 1155.00
Platter, Double Rose, 10 1/2 In.	2970.00
Platter, Double Rose, 11 5/8 In.	3630.00
Platter, Double Rose, 15 In.	3630.00
Sugar, Dove, 5 1/4 In.	633.00
Sugar, Single Rose, Round	688.00
Teapot, Butterfly Variant, 5 3/4 In.	1320.00
Teapot, Butterfly, 7 In. ....*Illus*	715.00
Teapot, Carnation, 6 1/2 In. ....*Illus*	660.00
Teapot, Dove, 7 1/2 In.	660.00

Some collectors have named the ironstone wares with the bright Gaudy Dutchlike patterns *Gaudy Ironstone*. It was made in England for the American market. There may be other examples found in the listing for Ironstone or under the name of the ceramic factory.

GAUDY IRONSTONE, Cake Plate, McCartney, 12 In.	165.00
Cup & Saucer, Strawberry, Handleless, Floral, 6 Sets	360.00
Plate, Flow Blue, 9 1/4 In.	120.00
Plate, Strawberry Design, 9 1/2 In., 2 Piece	230.00
Plate, Strawberry, 12 Sides, 8 1/2 In.	95.00
Platter, Floral, Blue & Purple Underglaze, 12 3/8 In.	145.00
Sugar Bowl, Floral Design, Luster, 7 1/4 In.	85.00
Teapot, Floral, Luster, Fruit Finial, Walley, 9 1/2 In.	235.00

Gaudy Welsh is an Imari–decorated earthenware with red, blue, green, and gold decorations. Most Gaudy Welsh was made in England for the American market. It was made after 1820.

GAUDY WELSH, Bowl, 3 x 5 1/2 In.	65.00
Bowl, Oyster, 6 In.	30.00
Bowl, Polychrome Floral, Footed, 5 1/2 x 10 In.	400.00
Creamer, Oyster	45.00
Cup & Saucer, Oyster	35.00
Mug, 2 7/8 In.	55.00
Pitcher, 4 In.	125.00
Pitcher, 8 3/4 In.	250.00
Pitcher, Oyster, 5 In.	75.00
Plate, Oyster, 7 In.	17.50
Plate, Oyster, 9 In.	25.00
Serving Set, China Handles, 2 Piece	145.00

In the late–nineteenth century, Geisha Girl porcelain was made in Japan for export. It was an inexpensive porcelain often sold in dime stores or used as free premiums. Pieces are sometimes marked with the name of a store. Japanese ladies in kimonos are pictured on the dishes. There are over 125 recorded patterns. Borders of red, blue, green, gold, brown, or several of these colors were used. Modern reproductions are being made.

GEISHA GIRL, Biscuit Jar, Cover	45.00
Cup & Saucer	150.00
Plate, 8 In.	150.00
Teapot, Melon Shape	40.00
Toothbrush Holder, Red Trim	45.00
Wall Pocket, Figure With Basket On Back For Flowers	45.00

Gene Autry was born in 1907. He began his career as the *Singing Cowboy* in 1928. His first movie appearance was in 1934, his last in 1958.

GENE AUTRY, Badge, Club	12.00
Book, Big Little Book, Law of The Range	30.00
Book, Punch–Out	175.00
Book, Song	10.00
Boots, Cowboy, Box	160.00
Boots, Rubber, Box	150.00
Cap Gun, Box	150.00
Cap Gun, Pearl Grips, Kenton	55.00
Cap Pistol, Cast Iron, Small	125.00
Costume	200.00
Game, Bandit Trail, 1939	100.00
Guitar, Emenee, Box	125.00 To 175.00
Guitar, Melody Ranch, Wood, Case	150.00
Guitar, Song Book, 1955, Plastic	195.00
Gun & Holster Set	350.00
Gun & Holster Set, Double, Box	650.00

Gun & Holster, Double, Leslie Henry, Box 300.00
Gun, Bang, Tour Souvenir, 1950s 5.00
Horn, Bike, Box 125.00
Magic Slate 20.00
Outfit, With Cap Guns, Box 275.00
Plaque, Laminated, 1940s 25.00
Record Album, Stampedo, 2 Records, 1949 .... 25.00
Reel, For Viewmaster, Gene & Champion 12.00
Repeating Cap Pistol, Kenton, Box, 1940s 185.00
Ring, American Flag 85.00
Sheet Music, Phantom Empire 15.00
Song Folio, Autry's Photos, 28 Songs, 1934, 64 Pages 15.00
Vest, Hat & Chaps, Box 200.00
Watch 195.00
Watch, Gilbert, 1964, Bix 325.00

Black–and–blue decorated Gibson Girl plates were made in the early 1900s. Twenty–four different 10 1/2–inch plates were made by the Royal Doulton Pottery at Lambeth, England. These pictured scenes from the book *A Widow and Her Friends* by Charles Dana Gibson. Another set of twelve 9–inch plates featuring pictures of the heads of Gibson Girls had all–blue decoration. Many other items also pictured the famous Gibson Girl.

GIBSON GIRL, Book, No. 1, 100 Gibson Girl Prints, Large 65.00
Plate, A Quiet Dinner With Dr. Bottles 98.00
Plate, Miss Babbles Brings A Copy, 10 1/2 In. 88.50
Plate, Miss Babbles, The Authoress, Calls, 10 1/2 In. 95.00
Plate, She Decides To Die, 10 1/2 In. 95.00
Plate, Winning New Friends, 10 1/2 In. 88.50

GILLINDER   Gillinder pressed glass was first made by William T. Gillinder of Philadelphia in 1863. The company had a working factory on the grounds at the Centennial and made small, marked pieces of glass for sale as souvenirs. They made a variety of decorative glass pieces and tablewares.

GILLINDER, Bust, Washington, Centennial 375.00
Figurine, Buddha, Seated, Amber, Signed, 6 In. 150.00
Mug, Ruth The Gleaner 125.00

The Girl Scout movement started in 1912, two years after the Boy Scouts. It began under Juliette Gordon Low of Savannah, Georgia. The first Girl Scout cookies were sold in 1928. Collectors search for anything pertaining to the Girl Scouts, including uniforms, publications, and old cookie boxes.

GIRL SCOUT, Book, Brownie, 7th Printing 5.00
Doll, Effanbee, 1966, 11 In. 45.00
Handbook, 1932 .... 15.00
Mess Kit 20.00
Ring, Sterling, Green Enamel 18.00
Sash, 14 Badges 17.00
Tin, Cashew, Girl Scout Holding Flower Bouquet Picture 35.00
Uniform, Dress, Trim, c.1930 .... 50.00
    GLASS, CONTEMPORARY, see Contemporary Glass

Eyeglasses, or spectacles, were mentioned in a manuscript in 1289 and have been used ever since. The first glasses with rigid side pieces were made in London in 1727. Bifocals were invented by Benjamin Franklin in 1785. Lorgnettes were popular in late–Victorian times. Opera glasses are listed in their own section.

GLASSES, Goggles, American, Optical, Aluminum Frames, Green Lenses, Pilot's 150.00
Lorgnette, Curb Link Chain, Opals, Rock Crystal Rondels, 14K Gold 1100.00
Lorgnette, Folding, Cat's–Eye Shape, Rhinestones 55.00
Lorgnette, Gold, Amethyst, Garnet & Diamond, c.1900 .... 3750.00

Lorgnette, Iridescent Mother–of–Pearl Inlay, France, 1880 .... 125.00
Lorgnette, Sterling Silver, Chain 125.00
Spectacles, J. Owen, Sterling Silver, c.1830 .... 195.00

W. Goebel Porzellanfabrik of Oeslau, Germany, now Rodental, West Germany, has made many types of figurines and dishes. The firm is still working. The pieces marked *Goebel Hummel* are listed under Hummel in this book.

GOEBEL, Bell, White Angel, 1976 .... 10.00
Bust, No. 3, Sister Hummel, Painted 140.00
Condiment Set, Monk, 4 Piece 160.00
Creamer, Monk, Stylized Bee, 2 1/2 In. 30.00
Creamer, Musicians, 4 1/2 In. 30.00
Egg Timer, Friar Tuck, Stylized Bee 40.00
Figurine, Ballet Classique, Man, White Bisque, No. 7501 .... 100.00
Figurine, Blue Martin, Box 155.00
Figurine, Boy, Girl, Ball–Jointed, Red Hair, Charlot, 1957, 11 In., Pr. 150.00
Figurine, Charlot By, 1957 .... 40.00
Figurine, Chick Girl 75.00
Figurine, Chirping Sparrow 95.00
Figurine, Cowardly Lion, Miniature 100.00
Figurine, Donald Duck, Fishing, 1970s, 5 In. 75.00
Figurine, Donkey, Full Bee, 2 1/2 x 3 In. 85.00
Figurine, Dresden Dancer, ... 75.00
Figurine, Figaro, With Ball, No. 125, Full Bee 225.00
Figurine, Friar Tuck 95.00
Figurine, Gnomes, Boy Holds Objects, 8 1/2 x 9 In., 5 Piece 250.00
Figurine, Goldfinch, Stylized Bee, 5 x 7 In. 75.00
Figurine, Mitzi, 1963 .... 50.00
Figurine, Palomino Horse, 8 x 7 In. 50.00
Figurine, Pigs, Dozing, 4 1/2 In. 24.00
Figurine, Precious Years, Miniature 100.00
Figurine, Prince Charming, Kneeling, Goebel, 1980s, 4 1/2 In. 75.00
Figurine, Red Winged Blackbird, Miniature 100.00
Figurine, Seagull, 3 Line Mark, 5 x 8 1/2 In. 35.00
Figurine, Tinker Bell, Stylized Bee, 8 1/2 In. 155.00
Figurine, Valentine Gift, Boy 150.00
Figurine, Valentine Gift, Girl 350.00
Head, Kennedy, Bisque, Box 25.00
Music Box, Holy Family 100.00
Pendant, Valentine Gift 125.00
Pitcher, Friar Tuck, Full Bee, 4 In. 45.00
Pitcher, Friar Tuck, Stylized Bee, 2 1/2 In. 22.00
Pitcher, Monk, Full Bee, Large 85.00
Plate, 12 Tribes of Israel, Ispanky, 1978 .... 200.00
Salt & Pepper, Friar Tuck 30.00
Salt & Pepper, Friar Tuck, Stylized Bee 22.00
Salt & Pepper, Lobster, With Cage 45.00
Salt & Pepper, Monk .... 35.00 To 45.00
Salt & Pepper, Monk, Red Clothes 60.00
Salt & Pepper, Rabbits, Thumper, Full Bee, 2 1/2 In. 85.00
Sign, Dealer, Friar Tuck 65.00
Sign, Merchant 30.00
Sugar & Creamer, Cover, Monks 35.00
Sugar & Creamer, Red Cardinal, 4 1/2 In. 275.00
Sugar & Creamer, Tray, Friar Tuck, Full Bee, 3 Piece 90.00
Sugar, Cover, Friar Tuck 35.00
Sugar, Creamer, Tray, Friar Tuck, Crown Mark 65.00

Porcelain has been made by three branches of the Goldscheider family. The family left Vienna in 1938 and started factories in England and in Trenton, New Jersey. The New Jersey factory started in 1940 as Goldscheider–U.S.A. In 1941 it became

Goldscheider–Everlast Corporation. From 1947 to 1953 it was Goldcrest Ceramics Corporation. In 1950 the Vienna plant was returned to Mr. Goldscheider and the company continues in business. The Trenton, New Jersey, business is now Goldscheider of Vienna and imports all of the pieces.

GOLDSCHEIDER, Bust, Madonna, Wooden Base	85.00
Bust, Madonna, Wooden Base, 9 1/2 In.	75.00
Figurine, Apple Showers, 6 3/4 In.	37.50
Figurine, Bird, Toucan, On Stump	40.00
Figurine, Colonial Lady, Pink Gown, 7 In.	35.00
Figurine, Lady, Beautiful Morning, Porcher, 7 In.	70.00
Figurine, Madonna, 8 1/2 In.	55.00
Figurine, Oriental Man, With Musical Instrument, 11 1/4 In.	150.00
Figurine, Rabbit, White, Pair	80.00
Figurine, Woman Clown, Mandolin, Thamasch, 13 1/2 In.	660.00
Figurine, Woman With Umbrella, 11 1/2 In.	85.00
Figurine, Woman, Holding Basket of Flowers, 7 1/2 In.	45.00
Figurine, Woman, Pink Gown, Fan, 12 In.	195.00
Figurine, Woman, With Umbrella, 11 1/2 In.	95.00

GOLF, see Sports

Lawton Gonder opened Gonder Ceramic Arts, Inc., in 1941. He worked in the old Peters and Reed pottery in Zanesville, Ohio. Gonder pieces include lamp bases marked *Eglee* and many wares with Oriental–type glazes.

GONDER, Bowl, Pedestal, Gold Crackle	30.00
Figurine, Puma, Reclining, 19 In.	90.00
Figurine, Rooster, Turquoise, Craquelle Glaze, 11 1/2 In.	45.00
Vase, Flower Form, Aqua & Brown Spatter, Pink Interior	3.50
Vase, Leaf Shape, Mottled Pink Interior, 9 In.	9.00

Goofus glass was made from about 1900 to 1920 by many American factories. It was originally painted gold, red, green, bronze, pink, purple, or other bright colors. Many pieces are found today with flaking paint and this lowers the value.

GOOFUS GLASS, Plate, Child's, This Little Pig Went To Market, 6 In.	125.00
Powder Jar, Gibson Girl	45.00
Rose Bowl, 5 Sides	75.00
Rose Bowl, Gold, Red	23.00

Goss china has been made since 1858. English potter William Henry Goss first made it at the Falcon Pottery in Stoke–on–Trent. The factory name was changed to Goss China Company in 1934 when it was taken over by Cauldon Potteries. Production ceased in 1940. Goss china resembles Irish Belleek in both body and glaze. The company also made popular souvenir china, usually marked with local crests and names.

W. H. COSS

GOSS, Bottle, Canterbury	22.00
Bottle, Sir William Wallace	30.00
Building, Eddystone Lighthouse	50.00
Building, Huet's House	200.00
Building, St. Nicholas Chapel	195.00
Bust, Wordsworth, Parian, 6 In.	275.00
Creamer, Arundel	25.00
Creamer, Heraldic	55.00
Ewer, Allied Flags, 2 In.	30.00
Jug, St. Albans Abbey	30.00
Urn, St. Andrews University	25.00

Pottery has been made in Gouda, Holland, since the seventeenth
century. Two firms, the Zenith pottery, established in the eighteenth
century, and the Zuid–Hollandsche pottery, made the brightly
colored wares marked *Gouda* from 1880 to about 1940. Many pieces
featured Art Nouveau or Art Deco designs.

GOUDA, Basket, 8 In.	100.00
Basket, Bridge, Art Deco Floral, Black, White, Oval, 4 In.	75.00
Bottle, Plazuid, 10 In.	35.00
Bowl Vase, Art Nouveau Floral, Green & Blue Ground, 3 1/2 In.	80.00
Bowl, Ivora, 5 In.	25.00
Box, Cover, Art Deco, Green & White Ground, 1928, 1 1/2 x 5 x 4 In.	120.00
Candlestick, Donier, Blue & Yellow Designs, Label, 3 In.	95.00
Candlestick, Green, Gray, Cream & Orange, 7 In., Pair	125.00
Compote, Aroe, Stylized Floral Bands, Black, Light Gray, 5 1/2 In.	80.00
Compote, Trudy, Art Deco Floral, Turquoise, White, Black, 4 1/2 In.	70.00
Console Set, Multicolored Geometrics, Attached Bobeches, 3 Piece	185.00
Decanter, Ata, Stylized Floral, Light Gray, Stopper, 10 In.	80.00
Dish, Lydia, Divided, Art Deco Floral, Black, White, 1 1/2 In.	55.00
Figurine, Shoe, Stylized Floral, White, Dark Blue Interior, 3 1/2 In.	25.00
Ginger Jar, High Glaze, 10 In.	575.00
Humidor, Pedestal, Signed	265.00
Ink Stand, Floral, Art Nouveau	60.00
Inkwell, Kelat, Stylized Floral, Gray, Green, Insert, 9 3/4 In.	100.00
Lamp, Kelot, Candlestick Shape, Cobalt & Green, Marked, 18 In.	80.00
Match Holder, Striker On Bottom	50.00
Pitcher, Floral, Signed, 9 In.	230.00
Pitcher, Stylized Floral, Black & Light Blue Ground, 6 1/2 In.	100.00
Vase, Conventional Floral, 2–Tone Blue Ground, High Gloss, 7 In.	400.00
Vase, Damascene, 9 1/2 In.	250.00
Vase, Delf Pattern, Art Deco Floral, Black Ground, 6 1/2 In.	60.00
Vase, Disconta, Art Deco Floral, White & Black, 7 5/8 In., Pr.	280.00
Vase, Distel Bird, 10 In.	650.00
Vase, Floral Design, Handle, 6 In.	60.00
Vase, Golota, Pedestal, Floral, Art Deco Shape, 7 1/2 In.	80.00
Vase, Marken, Stylized Design, Green, 2 Handles, 9 In.	150.00
Vase, Ortolman, Stylized Floral, Black & Gray, 1928, 6 In.	70.00
Vase, Padua, Art Deco Floral, Black, Arnhem, Holland, 8 In.	45.00
Vase, Peppy, 2 Tiny Handles, Stylized Floral, Green, 5 In.	70.00

Graniteware is an enameled tinware that has been used in the
kitchen from the late–nineteenth century to the present. Earlier
graniteware was green or turquoise blue, with white spatters. The
later ware was gray with white spatters. Reproductions are being
made in all colors.

GRANITEWARE, Baker, Green, Florets, Cover, Oval	60.00
Bedpan, Cobalt Blue Swirl	95.00
Biscuit Cutter, Onyx	298.00
Boiler, Double, Child's, Red, White	30.00
Bottle, Milk, Farm Fresh Tools, Rooster Picture	35.00
Bread Box, Blue–Gray Speckled	88.00
Bread Riser, Black & White Mottled	57.50
Bucket, Berry, Child's, Blue & White	52.00
Bucket, Berry, Doll's, Gray	48.00
Bucket, Cover, Berry, Child's, Gray	65.00
Bucket, Cover, Wire Bail, Green Shading To Lighter Green	85.00

◆◆

The ladies pictured on old cameos often have long thin noses. The
cute turned up nose is seen on modern cameos.

◆◆

Bucket, Gray, Oval, 3 Piece 125.00
Bucket, Gray, Rectangular, Complete 165.00
Bucket, Marbelized Blue & White 40.00
Bucket, Water, Brown & White Swirl, Large 98.00
Cake Pan, Blue & White Swirl, Molded Handles, 10 x 14 In. 140.00
Chamber Bucket, Cover, White & Black 20.00
Coffee Boiler, Green & White Swirl, Cobalt Handle 375.00
Coffee Boiler, Turquoise & White Swirl, 1 1/2 Gal. 35.00
Coffeepot, Bird In Flower, Pewter Gooseneck Spout, White 195.00
Coffeepot, Blue & White 185.00
Coffeepot, Blue & White Swirl, 9 In. 128.00
Coffeepot, Blue & White, Swirl, 10 1/2 In. .... 145.00 To 175.00
Coffeepot, Blue Swirl ....85.00 To 145.00
Coffeepot, Blue–Gray Body, White Specks, Blue Trim, Hinged Lid 49.50
Coffeepot, Brown Speckle, Pewter Hand, Spout & Cover, 1900 .... 225.00
Coffeepot, Brown Swirl 180.00
Coffeepot, Copper Band Around Rim, Gray 165.00
Coffeepot, Gray, 7 In. 35.00
Coffeepot, Mottled Turquoise & White 50.00
Coffeepot, Percolator, Apple Green, 3 Piece 20.00
Coffeepot, Percolator, White, Black, Flintstone, Label 28.00
Coffeepot, White & Blue, Tin Top, Wood Handle 155.00
Colander, Blue & White 60.00
Colander, Blue & White Swirl 67.50
Colander, Brown, White Splotches, 11 In. 30.00
Colander, Gray, 3 Legs 45.00
Colander, Red To Orange, Gray Interior, Large 55.00
Cream Pail, Gray, Tin Lid, 6 1/4 In. 125.00
Creamer, Child's, White, Gold Trim, Tiny 55.00
Cup, Gray, Loop Handle 5.00
Dinner Bucket, Miner's, Round 195.00
Dish, Serving, Blue & White 20.00
Dish, Soap, Hanging, Blue Swirl 110.00
Dishpan, Blue & White Swirl, 17 In. 38.00
Dishpan, Colored Swirl, Black Handles & Rim, 17 1/2 In. 125.00
Dishpan, Handle, Cobalt Blue & White Swirl, 19 In. 95.00
Dishpan, White & Red 20.00
Dishpan, White Inside, Black Trim, Wire Handles, 13 In. 75.00
Double Boiler, Cover, Cream, Green Trim 45.00
Double Boiler, Cream & Green 12.00
Double Boiler, Mottled Grays, 3 Piece 24.00
Dough Riser, Blue & White Mottled, Large 260.00
Dough Riser, Gray 150.00
Dustpan, Gray & White Mottled 88.00
Feeder, Chick, Blue & White 45.00
Feeding Set, Child's, Blue Duck, 3 Piece 58.00
Feeding Set, Duck, Blue, 3 Piece 65.00
Fish Cooker, Insert, Gray, Large 125.00
Flask, Blue, 1850s 165.00
Foot Tub, Gray Mottling, Rolled Edges, 16 x 19 In. 55.00
Fruit Bowl, Multicolor, 12 In. 25.00
Funnel, Blue & White Swirl, Diamond Ware, Squat 75.00
Funnel, Brown & White Speckled 20.00
Funnel, Child's, Blue Trim, Tiny 48.00
Funnel, Gray ....8.00 To 26.00
Grater, Gray Mottled, Ideal 345.00
Heater, Gas, White & Black, Clipper Ship, Footed, 15 x 10 In. 47.00
Ladle, Blue Swirl 62.50
Ladle, Cocoa, Gray, Hollow Handle 225.00
Ladle, Cocoa, Gray, Tubular Handle 200.00
Ladle, Gray 10.00
Ladle, Pickle, Yellow, Green Rim 45.00
Loaf Pan, Gray 10.00

Lunch Pail 45.00
Measure, Dry, Gray, 1 Qt. 25.00
Measure, Red & White, 8 In. 60.00
Measure, White, Vollrath Label, 2 Cup 18.00
Mold, Food, Fluted, Gray 45.00
Mold, Grey, Ruffled, With Corn 160.00
Mold, Ribbed Melon, Gray, Marked Extra Agate, No. 50 .... 70.00
Muffin Pan, 12 Hole, Gray 58.00
Muffin Pan, 6 Hole, Gray 35.00
Muffin Pan, Gray, 12 Hole 35.00
Muffin, Gray, Round, Individual, Set of 6 .... 295.00
Mug, Gray & Black Spatter, Red Trim 12.00
Pail, Berry, Powder Blue, Black Handle & Trim, 5 x 5 3/4 In. 32.00
Pail, Child's, Gray Mottle, Small 165.00
Pail, Diaper, Gray, Cover, Wooden Handle, Label 40.00
Pan, Baking, Gray, 2 Handles, Large 10.00
Pan, Bread, Green 42.50
Pan, Cake, Blue & White Swirl, 13 x 9 In. 85.00
Pan, Gray, Cover, Deep, 2 Handles, 9 In. 10.00
Pan, Gray, Label, Huge 50.00
Pan, Ladyfingers, Gray 295.00
Pan, Loaf, Gray 24.00
Pan, Roasting, Red 65.00
Pan, Sauce, Blue & White Swirl 25.00
Pancake Turner, Gray 45.00
Pickle Dipper, Yellow 55.00
Pie Plate, Cobalt Blue & White, Swirl 30.00
Pie Plate, Gray ....7.00 To 12.00
Pie Plate, Green & White 23.00
Pie Plate, Swirl Teal Green, 9 In. 45.00
Pitcher & Bowl, Child's, Confetti Pattern 250.00
Pitcher, Measuring, Gray Mottled, 1 Pt. 40.00
Pitcher, Milk, Blue & White Swirl, 7 5/8 In. 115.00
Pitcher, Milk, Blue Swirl, Small 110.00
Plate, Blue Marbelized, 13 3/4 In. 55.00
Plate, Center Bird, Red & Blue Flowers, White, 8 1/2 In. 45.00
Plate, Dinner, Gray 20.00
Plate, Gray, Dark Blue Spatter, Black Rim, Set of 8 .... 40.00
Pot, Handles, Blue & White, 9 In. 65.00
Pot, Handles, Blue & White, 11 In. 85.00
Pot, Speckled Snowflake, Wooden Handle, 14 In. 35.00
Potty, Light Blue, Solid, Small 12.50
Roaster, Child's, Gray Mottled 68.00
Roaster, Cover, Blue 65.00
Roaster, Cover, Blue & White 20.00
Roaster, Cover, Gray, Red 30.00
Roaster, Dark Green, Rectangular, 10 3/4 x 7 3/4 In. 15.00
Roaster, Vented Cover, Emerald Green Swirl, 17 In. 250.00
Sauce Pan, Blue & White Swirl 35.00
Sauce Pan, Yellow, Florets, Stick Handle, Cover 45.00
Scoop, Gray, Square 78.00
Skillet, Green & White 65.00
Skimmer, Blue & White Swirl 65.00
Soap Dish, Brown & White Swirl, Hanging 155.00
Soap Dish, Cobalt, White Swirl 95.00
Spoon, Mixing, Mottled Blue & White 28.00
Strainer, Gray, 8 Sides, Attached Drain Pan, Handle 300.00
Strainer, Gray, Drain Pan, Octagonal, 3 Legs, Side Handle 375.00
Strainer, Triangular, Cream, Green Banding, 1930s 24.00
Sugar & Creamer, Red & White Swirl, 1950s 95.00
Sugar, White, Small 55.00
Table & Chairs, Child's, Noah's Ark, Alphabet 295.00
Table, Child's, Noah's Ark 130.00

Tea Set, Brown & White, Pewter Trim 1700.00
Tea Set, Child's, Light Blue, Dark Blue Trim, 7 Piece 295.00
Tea Set, Red, Blue & White Panel, c.1900, 11 Piece 395.00
Tea Set, Relish Pattern, White Interior, Brown & White, 4 Piece 1700.00
Tea Steeper, Cover, Blue Swirl 220.00
Tea Strainer, Gray 48.00
Tea Strainer, White, Fancy 30.00
Teakettle, Turquoise, Wire & Wood Bail 150.00
Teapot, Black & White Flecks, 8 1/2 In. 67.00
Teapot, Blue & White, Large 55.00
Teapot, Flowers & Bulrushes, Pewter Spout, White 170.00
Teapot, Fruit 25.00
Teapot, Red Marbelized, Tall 65.00
Tray, Bakery, White, Blue Trim, 12 x 17 In., 6 Piece 50.00
Tray, Peach, Pear & Grapes, Round, 18 In. 48.00
Tub, Foot, Dark Gray, Oval 95.00
Urinal, Woman's, Traveling, Allover Blue & White Sponge 85.00
Washboard, Cobalt Blue .... 48.00 To 59.00
Washpan, Gray, Salesman's Sample, Royal, 6 In. 75.00
Water Carrier, Gray, Bail, Strap Handle On Back 95.00
Water Carrier, Hinged Cover, 1 Handle Over Top, 1 At Back, Oval 325.00

 Greentown glass was made by the Indiana Tumbler and Goblet Company of Greentown, Indiana, from 1894 to 1903. In 1899, the factory name was changed to National Glass Company. A variety of pressed, milk, and chocolate glass was made.

GREENTOWN, see also Chocolate Glass; Custard Glass; Holly Amber; Milk Glass; Pressed Glass

GREENTOWN, Bowl, Teardrop & Tassel, Emerald Green, 8 1/2 In. 225.00
Box, Cat On Hamper Cover, Opaque White Glass, 5 In. .... 275.00 To 330.00
Box, Dolphin Cover, Golden Agate Glass, Beaded, 4 1/2 In. 275.00
Box, Dolphin Cover, Nile Green, Beaded Rim, 4 1/2 In. 1980.00
Bust, Dewey, Emerald Green, Ribbed Base 275.00
Butter, Cover, Overall Lattice 35.00
Compote, Cord Drapery, Amber, 9 In. 225.00
Compote, Holly, Hollow Pedestal, Crystal, 7 1/2 In. 110.00
Creamer, Indian Head, Nile Green, 5 3/4 In. 220.00
Creamer, Overall Lattice 22.00
Mug, Drinking Scene, Nile Green 145.00
Mug, Overall Lattice 12.00
Mug, Serenade, Blue 25.00
Pitcher, Water, Austrian, Crystal 175.00
Pitcher, Water, Fleur–De–Lis 65.00
Pitcher, Water, Squirrel, Crystal 125.00
Saltshaker, Pleat Band, Pair 35.00
Tumbler, Bands of Holly & Opalee Glass, Beaded, 4 In. 1870.00
Tumbler, Brazen Shield 45.00
Tumbler, Holly, White Agate, Beaded Design At Base, 4 In. 935.00

 Grueby Faience Company of Boston, Massachusetts, was incorporated in 1897 by William H. Grueby. Garden statuary, art pottery, and architectural tiles were made until 1920. The company developed a matte green glaze that was so popular it was copied by many other factories making a less expensive type of pottery. This eventually led to the financial problems of the pottery.

GRUEBY, Bowl, Applied Broad Leaves, Cucumber Green Glaze, Flared, 5 x 8 In. 1430.00
Bowl, Molded Leaf Design, Wilhelmina Post, c.1898, 3 1/2 x 6 In. 385.00
Bowl, Overlapping Pointed Leaves, Cucumber Glaze, Low, 10 1/2 In. 1210.00
Bowl, Yellow Blossoms Alternate Leaf Rows, A. Lingley, Squat, 9 In. 7150.00
Lamp Base, Bigelow & Kennard Shade, 3 Arm Supports, c.1915, 14 In. 7150.00
Lamp, 3–Light, Tooled 3–Petaled Flowers, Signed, c.1905, 24 1/4 In. 3575.00
Paperweight, Scarab, c.1905, 2 1/2 In. 410.00
Paperweight, Scarab, Marked, c.1905, 3 1/8 In. 110.00

Paperweight, Winged Scarab, Dark Ochre, c.1905, 2 5/8 In. 220.00
Tile, Figural, Cherub & Cornucopia, Marked, c.1910, 6 In. 250.00
Tile, Geometric Shape, Matte Glaze, No Design, 20 Piece 400.00
Tile, Polar Bear, Blue Ground, 5 5/8 x 7 In. 385.00
Tile, Polar Bear, Rectangular, White On Deep Blue Ground, 5 x 7 In. 385.00
Vase, Alternating Flowers On Stems & Broad Leaves, c.1907, 5 In. 1700.00
Vase, Broad & Thin Leaves, Earthy Green Matte, 10 x 4 1/4 In. 2200.00
Vase, Broad Leaves Alternate Yellow Buds, R. Erickson, 11 x 8 In. 7700.00
Vase, Cucumber Glaze, Vertical Ribs, Baluster, R. E., 7 5/8 In. 2530.00
Vase, Daffodils, 11 In. 4125.00
Vase, Gourd Form, Stylized Petals, Marie A. Seaman, 8 3/4 In. 2600.00
Vase, Green & Yellow Matte Glaze, Tapered Bulbous, W. Post, 5 In. 1870.00
Vase, Green Glaze, Leaves, Cylindrical Neck, Bulbous, 11 3/4 In. 2200.00
Vase, Green, Large Leaves, Buds, 5 In. 1000.00
Vase, Leaf Design, Glazed Exterior, Green Interior, c.1905, 6 In. 410.00
Vase, Leaf Design, Oatmeal Glaze, Marked, c.1902, 8 In. 385.00
Vase, Molded Design, Green Glaze, c.1902, 7 In. 715.00
Vase, Molded Leaf, Dark Green, W. Post, c.1898, 4 1/2 In. 880.00
Vase, Overlapping Curved Leaves, Cucumber Matte Green Glaze, 9 In. 825.00
Vase, Repeating Broad Leaf Design, A. Lingley, 6 x 5 In. ....:....... 935.00
Vase, Sculpted Leaves & Flowers 5225.00
Vase, Wide Leaves Alternate, Stems & Buds, Light Blue, Bulbous, 8 In. 1760.00

 Included in this category are shotguns, pistols, and other antique firearms. Rifles are listed in their own section. Be very careful when buying or selling guns because there are special laws governing the sale and ownership. A collector's gun should be displayed in a safe manner, probably with the barrel filled or a part missing to be sure it cannot be accidentally fired.

GUN, Air Pistol, Winchester, No. 363 .... 145.00
BB, Daisy, Red Rider, Box, 1960s 50.00
BB, Daisy, Side Logo, Patent Dates 1808 & 1915 .... 65.00
BB, Targeteer, Daisy, Model 118, Box 95.00
Carbine, Military, Iron Swivel, British, 21–In. Barrel 450.00
Carbine, Steyer, Model 95, Military, Side–Mounted Sling Swivels 145.00
Colt 45, Six–Shooter, General Zapatas, Pearl Handle, Nickel Plated 750.00
Colt, Civil War, Walnut Grips, Brass Frame, Pocket Model 370.00
Long, Pennsylvania, Maple Stock, Signed A. Kopp 2640.00
Luger, S/42 Semi–Automatic, Leather Case, Extra Clip, Papers, 1939 .... 700.00
Matchlock, Incised Brass Mounts, Japanese, 18th Century, 50 1/2 In. 1760.00
Musket, Enfield, Full Stock, 39–In. Barrel 485.00
Musket, Flintlock, Barnett, London, c.1800 .... 350.00
Musket, Matchlock, Chinese Inscription, 42 1/2–In. Barrel 375.00
Percussion Blunderbuss, Spanish, 1–Piece Wood Stock 295.00
Pistol, Belgian Browning, No. 404342, Holster & Carrying Case, 4 3/4 In. 225.00
Pistol, Colt, Automatic, 45 Caliber, Nickel Plated 295.00
Pistol, Colt, Combat Commander 285.00
Pistol, Colt, Python 290.00
Pistol, Flintlock, Carved Full Stock, Inlaid, Europe, 19 1/4 In. 185.00
Pistol, Radam, 9 mm., Leather Holster, Extra Clip 425.00
Pistol, U. S. Army Issue, . 45 .... 275.00
Pistol, Walther, PPK, 32 Caliber, Leather Case 510.00
Revolver, D. Moore, 7 Shot, Side Load, Octagonal Barrel, c.1860 .... 605.00
Revolver, Military Size, 12 mm., Civil War Era, 12 In. 235.00
Revolver, Pin Fire, Civil War 300.00
Revolver, Smith & Wesson, 6 Shot, Pearl Handle 165.00
Shotgun, Browning, 12 Gauge, Automatic, 5 Shot 380.00
Shotgun, Double Barrel, Fox 240.00
Shotgun, Double Barrel, Percussion, c.1850, 34 In. 175.00
Shotgun, Presentation, Middle Eastern, Carved, Precious Metal 2200.00
Shotgun, Savage, 20 Gauge, Double Barrel, Walnut Stock 235.00
Shotgun, Winchester, M94, Canadian Centennial 240.00
Shotgun, Winchester, Model 12, Single Shot, 16 Gauge Pump, Walnut Stock 400.00

Shotgun, Winchester, Model 12–16	440.00
Shotgun, Winchester, Model 21, Double Barrel, 16 Gauge, Case	1485.00
Stevens, Repeater, Cross Bolt, 12 Gauge, Model 124	95.00
Stevens, Tip–Up, Nickel Plated Frame, Pocket, Pre–1912	150.00
Winchester Model 12, 16 Gauge Pump, Case	350.00
Winchester Model 21, Double Barrel, 16 Gauge, Case	1350.00
Winchester, Model 43–410	550.00

Gunderson glass was made at the Gunderson–Pairpoint Glass Works of New Bedford, Massachusetts, from 1952 to 1957. Gunderson Peachblow is especially famous.

GUNDERSON, Cup & Saucer, Peachblow	175.00
Tumbler, Peachblow	160.00
Vase, Peachblow, 4 1/2 x 3 In.	75.00

The Gustavsberg ceramics factory was founded in 1827 near Stockholm, Sweden. It is best known to collectors for its twentieth-century art wares, especially a green stoneware with silver inlay.

GUSTAVSBERG, Ashtray, Rectangular, Silver Ship, Green, Argenta	35.00
Bowl, Triangular Silver Insets, Green, Argenta, 2 In.	75.00
Bowl, Triangular Silver Insets, Green, Argenta, 3 In.	85.00
Box, Cigarette, Silver Ship, Green	95.00
Jar, Boat Design On Cover, Argenta, 5 1/2 In.	850.00
Vase, Carved Stylized Leaves, Light Blue, Mottled, 1930, 7 In.	300.00
Vase, Large Swimming Fish, Bubbles, Green, c.1940, 7 In.	1400.00

Gutta–percha was one of the first plastic materials. It was made from a mixture of resins from Malaysian trees. It was molded and used for daguerreotype cases, toilet articles, and picture frames in the nineteenth century.

GUTTA–PERCHA, Case, Constitution & Law, Eagle & Scroll, 3 x 2 1/2 In.	75.00
Case, Gentleman, Fireman Scene On Covers, 3 3/4 x 3 1/4 In.	95.00
Case, Man With Soldier's Cap, 1850s, 2 3/4 x 2 1/4 In.	65.00
Case, Presentation of The Yams, 1/4 Plate	260.00
Mirror, Hand, Sailboat, Shell, Tree of Life Around Edge	37.00

Haeger Potteries, Inc., Dundee, Illinois, started making commercial art wares in 1914. Early pieces were marked with the name *Haeger* written over an *H.* About 1938, the mark *Royal Haeger* was used. The firm is still making florist wares and lamp bases.

HAEGER, Bookend–Planters, Green, Paper Label	20.00
Figurine, Gazelle, Leaping, Curved Horns, 13 In.	35.00
Figurine, Gazelle, Stylized, 17 In.	55.00
Figurine, Panther, 18 In.	15.00
Figurine, Pheasant, Gold Tweed	40.00
Figurine, Rendezvous, Male & Female, Back To Back, 20 In.	80.00
Flower Frog, Black Swan	20.00
Lamp, Antelope, Leaping, Black, Gold Fiberglass Shade, 20 In.	57.00
Lamp, Birds On Limb Over Lamp, Planter Base, Green	25.00
Lamp, Figural, Siren of Sea, Fiberglass Shade, 17 In.	65.00
Lamp, T.V., Panther, Facing Left, Brown & Greens, 8 x 13 In.	75.00
Planter, Mouse Standing By Cheese	22.50
Planter, Swan, Blue	17.00
Planter, Swordfish, Green	18.00
Vase, Clown Drummer, Pink, 9 In.	27.50
HALF–DOLL, see Pincushion Doll	

HALL'S SUPERIOR QUALITY KITCHENWARE — Hall China Company started in East Liverpool, Ohio, in 1903. The firm made all types of wares. Collectors search for the Hall teapots made from the 1920s to the 1950s. The dinnerwares of the same period, especially Autumn Leaf pattern, are also popular. The Hall

◆◆◆

To repair or restring a broken seed pearl necklace, use monofilament fishing line. It is strong, fine, and stiff enough to use without a needle. The original Victorian pieces were strung on horsehair.

◆◆◆

China Company is still working. Autumn Leaf pattern dishes are listed in their own category in this book. For more information, see *Kovels' Depression Glass & American Dinnerware Price List.*

HALL, Bean Pot, Brown, Individual	6.00
Bean Pot, Radiance, Handle	60.00
Bowl Set, Mixing, Red Poppy, 3 Piece	40.00
Bowl, Berry, Mt. Vernon	2.50
Bowl, Red Poppy, 9 In.	14.00
Bowl, Silhouette Medallion, 7 1/2 In.	15.00
Bowl, Vegetable, Red Poppy, Round, 9 In.	15.00
Cake Plate, Radiance	30.00
Canister Set, Radiance, 4 Piece	370.00
Casserole, Cover, Green Turtle	75.00
Casserole, Cover, Red Poppy	30.00
Casserole, Cover, Red Tab Handle	15.00
Casserole, Cover, Rose White	36.00
Casserole, Cover, Silhouette	25.00
Casserole, Cover, Sunshine, No. 488	30.00
Casserole, Morning Glory	40.00
Casserole, Poppy, 9 In.	50.00
Casserole, Red Poppy, Cover, 7 In.	18.00
Casserole, Sundial, Red	30.00
Cheese Bowl, Metal Plate, Kraft	12.00
Chocolate Pot, St. Louis, Cobalt Blue, 2 Cup	20.00
Coffee Set, Philadelphia, Stock Green, Gold, 3 Piece	65.00
Coffeepot, Amory, Cobalt Blue	45.00
Coffeepot, Arch	25.00
Coffeepot, Bellevue, 2 Cup	55.00
Coffeepot, Chinese Red, Drip	53.00
Coffeepot, Colonial	190.00
Coffeepot, Colonial, Mini–Floral	20.00
Coffeepot, Drip, Morning Glory	165.00
Coffeepot, Drip, Red Poppy	28.00 To 32.00
Coffeepot, Drip–O–Lator, Trellis	25.00
Coffeepot, Electric, Zeisel, Mulberry Decal	70.00
Coffeepot, Heather Rose, Step–Down	25.00
Cookie Jar, Poppy	45.00
Cookie Jar, Sheriff, Box	25.00
Cookie Jar, Sundial, Red	100.00 To 200.00
Cookie Jar, Zeisel, Pink	30.00
Cookie Jar, Zeisel, Pink, Gold Trim	50.00
Creamer, Lipton, Black	10.00
Creamer, Red Poppy	10.00
Cup & Saucer, Cameo Rose	5.00
Gravy Boat, Fantasy, Eva Zeisel	10.00
Jug, Ball, Green	25.00
Jug, Ball, No. 5, Red	30.00
Jug, Chinese Red Bands, 1 1/2 Pt.	10.00
Jug, Poppy & Wheat, Medium	40.00
Jug, Radiance	20.00
Jug, Rose Parade, Ball Type	35.00
Leftover, Poppy	60.00
Mug, Irish Coffee, 4 Piece	10.00

Percolator, Electric, Pheasant Decal	120.00
Pitcher, Milk, Green, 48 Oz.	25.00
Pitcher, Red Poppy	20.00
Pitcher, Schenley, Maroon	22.50
Plate, Cameo Rose, 8 1/2 In.	8.00
Plate, Cameo Rose, 10 In.	9.00
Plate, Crocus	12.00
Plate, Heather Rose, 7 1/2 In.	3.00
Plate, Salad, Tulip, Pastel	30.00
Plate, Tulip, 6 In.	1.50
Punch Set, Old Crow, Ladle, Gold Trim, 10 Cups, 12 Pieces	155.00
Rolling Pin, Taverne	110.00
Salt & Pepper, Blue Blossom, Handles	40.00
Salt & Pepper, Chinese Red, Banded	15.00
Salt & Pepper, Radiance	85.00
Salt & Pepper, Wildfire, Teardrop	10.00
Stack Set, Morning Glory, Pastel	125.00
Sugar & Creamer, Boston, Maroon, Gold Handle & Spout	45.00
Sugar & Creamer, Cover, Cameo Rose	15.00
Sugar & Creamer, Cover, Heather Rose	12.00
Sugar & Creamer, Cover, Maroon, Gold Bands	60.00
Sugar & Creamer, Cover, New York	29.00
Sugar & Creamer, Lipton, Warm Yellow	18.00
Sugar & Creamer, New York, Stock Brown, Gold Band	45.00
Sugar & Creamer, Philadelphia, Black & Gold	38.00
Sugar, Cover, Sani–Grid, Chinese Red	12.00
Teapot, Airflow, Cobalt Blue	45.00
Teapot, Airflow, Emerald Green, Gold	45.00
Teapot, Aladdin, Black	40.00
Teapot, Aladdin, Black Luster, Gold Trim	25.00
Teapot, Aladdin, Black, Gold, Round Infuser	45.00
Teapot, Aladdin, Turquoise, 6 Cup	30.00
Teapot, Aladdin, Yellow	40.00
Teapot, Albany, Brown, Gold	30.00
Teapot, Baltimore, Maroon, Label	45.00
Teapot, Basket	110.00
Teapot, Basket, Canary, Silver Trim	95.00
Teapot, Basketball, Chinese Red	460.00
Teapot, Basketball, Yellow, Trim, No Cover	55.00
Teapot, Bellevue, Marine Blue	25.00
Teapot, Birdcage, Maroon, Gold	265.00
Teapot, Birdcage, Red	350.00
Teapot, Boston, Blue, Gold Label, 6 Cup	30.00
Teapot, Boston, Brown, Individual	6.50
Teapot, Boston, Emerald Green, 2 Cup	24.00
Teapot, Boston, Maroon, 2 Cup	24.00
Teapot, Boston, Maroon, Gold Trim	25.00 To 32.00
Teapot, Boston, Mauve	25.00
Teapot, Boston, White, Brushed–Gold Handle, 3 Cup	15.00
Teapot, Buchanan, Dark Green	35.00
Teapot, Cameo Rose	35.00
Teapot, Canary Parade	25.00
Teapot, Caraway, Cadet, 2 Cup	35.00
Teapot, Cleveland, Emerald Green	20.00
Teapot, Daffodil, Twin Spout	50.00
Teapot, French, 2 Cup	12.50
Teapot, French, Mustard Yellow, 2 Cup	24.00
Teapot, Gold Dots	35.00
Teapot, Gold Flowers, French, Yellow, 2 Cup	30.00
Teapot, Gold Flowers, Yellow, 2 Cup	30.00
Teapot, Hollywood, Ivory	18.00
Teapot, Hollywood, Ivory, Gold, 6 Cup	30.00
Teapot, Hollywood, Maroon	39.00

Teapot, Hook, Blue 25.00
Teapot, Hook, Yellow 25.00
Teapot, Lipton, Warm Yellow 25.00
Teapot, Los Angeles 30.00
Teapot, Los Angeles, Cobalt & Gold, 6 Cup 45.00
Teapot, Los Angeles, Yellow, Gold 35.00
Teapot, McCormick 15.00
Teapot, McCormick, Blue, Green 27.50
Teapot, Melody, Chinese Red 59.00
Teapot, Melody, Stick, Green, White, 2 Cup 12.00
Teapot, Moderne, Yellow 13.00
Teapot, New York, Brown, Gold Trim .... 12.00 To 14.00
Teapot, New York, Cobalt Blue, Gold Band 68.00
Teapot, New York, Yellow, 2 Cup 24.00
Teapot, Parade, Yellow 40.00
Teapot, Parade, Yellow, Gold Label 27.50
Teapot, Philadelphia, Cobalt Blue, Gold 40.00
Teapot, Philadelphia, Rose 22.00
Teapot, Poppy 145.00
Teapot, Regal, Apple Green 70.00
Teapot, Rhythm, Chinese Red 110.00
Teapot, Ronald Reagan .... 35.00 To 50.00
Teapot, Rutherford, Eggshell Swag 75.00
Teapot, Sanka, 2 Cup 17.00
Teapot, Streamline, Black, 6 Cup 40.00
Teapot, Sundial, Yellow 60.00
Teapot, Thorley Grape, Yellow 60.00
Teapot, Victorian, Birch, Ivory 22.50
Teapot, Windshield, Maroon 20.00
Teapot, Windshield, Polka Dot, Ivory & Gold, Label 25.00
Tray, Red Poppy, Rectanglar 40.00
Tricolator, Coffee Queen, Yellow, 6 Cup 20.00
Vase, Trumpet, Daffodil, Yellow 8.50

Halloween is an ancient holiday that has been changed in the last 200 years. The jack–o'–lantern, witches on broomsticks, and orange decorations seem to be twentieth–century creations. Collectors started to become serious about collecting Halloween–related items in the late 1970s. The papier–mache decorations, now replaced by plastic, and old costumes are in demand.

HALLOWEEN, Box, Baby Ruth Candy Bars, 2 Cents, Children In Costume 45.00
Candleholder, Black Cat, Porcelain, Germany, Pair 125.00
Candy Container, Pumpkin, Plastic 14.00
Candy Container, Pumpkin, Scarecrow, Plastic 18.00
Cat, Black, Papier–Mache, German 135.00
Cat, Stand–Up Cardboard, Black, 12 In. 9.00
Clacker, Scenes, Orange, Wooden, 8 1/2 In. 25.00
Clicker, Tin 14.00
Costume, Annie Oakley 225.00
Costume, Batgirl, Box, 1976 .... 18.00
Costume, Blondie, Box, 1950s 20.00
Costume, Bozo The Clown, Box, 1970 .... 12.00
Costume, Bugs Bunny, Box, 1955 .... 32.00
Costume, Casper The Ghost 15.00
Costume, Darth Vader 35.00
Costume, Deputy Dawg, 1962 .... 60.00
Costume, Electronic Man Robot, Fibre–Bilt Toys, Box, 1950s 125.00
Costume, G. I. Joe, Box 45.00
Costume, Jeannie, Hanna Barbera, 1974 .... 15.00
Costume, Knight, Metal Armor, Plastic Helmet, Marx, 8 Piece 95.00
Costume, Laurel & Hardy, Box 30.00
Costume, Linus The Lionhearted, Box, 1965 .... 60.00
Costume, Marshall's Outfit, Wyatt Earp Type, Vest, Shirt, Pants 80.00

Costume, Monkees 25.00
Costume, Monster, Box, 1963 .... 30.00
Costume, Mr. Spock, 1976 .... 18.00
Costume, Mr. Spock, From Star Trek, Mas, Paramount Pictures, 1975 .... 50.00
Costume, Phantom 40.00
Costume, Pirate, 1940s 28.00
Costume, Playsuit, Clarabelle, Wonderland 125.00
Costume, Snake Charmer, Box, 1960 .... 20.00
Costume, Snoopy, Box 25.00
Costume, Spider–Man, Box, 1972 .... 18.00
Costume, Star Wars, Double Mask, Box 45.00
Costume, Steve Canyon 75.00
Costume, Tarzan, Box, 1967 .... 60.00
Costume, U. S. Astronaut, Box, 1961 .... 32.00
Costume, Wagon Train, Western, Leslie, Henry 225.00
Costume, Wonder Woman, Ben Cooper, Box, 1978 .... 8.00
Costume, Zorro, Ben Cooper, Box 125.00
Costume, Zorro, Box 65.00
Costume, Zorro, Cape, Belt & Mask, Box 69.00
Costume, Zorro, Walt Disney, Box 55.00
Jack–O'–Lantern, 2 Faces, 10 In. 55.00
Jack–O'–Lantern, Lithograph, Tin 50.00
Jack–O'–Lantern, Metal, Bats, Owls Lithograph, 1930–40 .... 34.00
Jack–O'–Lantern, Papier–Mache, 8 In. 35.00
Jack–O'–Lantern, Papier–Mache, Scary Face, 10 In. 82.00
Jack–O'–Lantern, Papier–Mache, With Inserts, 10 In. 45.00
Jack–O'–Lantern, Surprised Expression, Cardboard, 1930–40, 25 In. 55.00
Jack–O'–Lantern, Tin, Witches, Goblins, Candlelight, 5 In. 22.00
Lantern, 2–Tone Papier–Mache, Buffalo, N. Y. 125.00
Lantern, Cardboard Frame, Blue Tissue Behind Cutouts, 10 1/2 In. 75.00
Lantern, Cat's Head, Wire Bail, Orange, 5 1/4 In. 70.00
Lantern, Orange Cardboard Frame, Tissue, Square, 5 x 10 1/2 In. 38.00
Lantern, Skull, Foldout, 1940s, 10 x 5 In. 60.00
Lantern, Skull, Milk Glass, Metal, Crown Mark, Japan, 6 1/2 In. 125.00
Lantern, Skull, Red Insert, 4 3/4 In. 260.00
Lantern, Witch's Head, Celluloid, Box 160.00
Mask, Fu Manchu, Stiffened Gauze 6.00
Mask, Jimmy Carter 45.00
Mask, Moe, of 3 Stooges 80.00
Mask, Richard Nixon 45.00
Mask, Skeleton, Stiffened Gauze 6.00
Noisemaker, 5–Tier, Pumpkin Face, Germany, 5 1/2 In. 70.00
Noisemaker, Clown Face, Tin 35.00
Noisemaker, Goblet, Hand Carved Handle 85.00
Noisemaker, Pumpkin Head, Pope, Germany, Lack, Blue, 6 In. 19.00
Noisemaker, Rachet, Devil, Wood 95.00
Noisemaker, Wooden, Dark Patina, 12 In. 30.00
Nut Cup, Witch's Caldron, Crepe Paper 6.00
Placard, Witch & Crescent Autumn Moon, Orange, 1930s, 21 x 7 In. 35.00
Postcard, John Winsch, 1911 .... 45.00
Pumpkin Man Soldier, German, Embossed 40.00
Pumpkin, Papier–Mache, 5 In. 20.00
Pumpkin, Papier–Mache, Different Sizes, 4 Piece 48.00
Sparkler, Cat, Lithographed Tin, Chein, Box, 1930s 85.00
Tambourine, Pumpkin Face 45.00
Whistle, Trick Or Treat, Celluloid 10.00
Witch, Bowl, Papier–Mache, Dress, Wooden Legs, Germany, 10 In. 770.00
Witch, Caldron Nut Cups, Crepe Paper 6.00
Witch, Paper–Mache, 3 In. 18.00

Hampshire pottery was made in Keene, New Hampshire, between 1871 and 1923. Hampshire developed a line of colored glazed wares as early as 1883, including a Royal Worcester–type pink, olive

green, blue, and mahogany. Pieces are marked with the printed
mark or the impressed name *Hampshire Pottery* or *J.S.T. & Co.,
Keene, N.H.* Many pieces were marked with city names and sold as
souvenirs.

HAMPSHIRE, Bowl, Leaves Alternating With Buds, C. Robertson, c.1909, 10 In. 330.00
Lamp Base, Morning Glory Leaves, Vines, Trumpet Shape, 14 3/4 In. 195.00
Pitcher, Water, Green Matte Finish 245.00
Stein, Green ....: 155.00
Teapot, Black 500.00
Vase, Lily Pad, Pinched, Green, 3 x 5 In. 135.00
Vase, Mauve Glaze, Bud & Trailing Stems, Marked, 6 3/4 In. 247.50
Vase, Mottled Glaze Forms Veni Pattern, Marked, c.1909, 3 1/4 In. 105.00
Vase, Repeating Molded Lilies, Matte Green, 8 1/2 In. 350.00

 Philip Handel worked in Meriden, Connecticut, from 1885 and in
New York City from 1893 to 1933. His firm made art glass and
other types of lamps. Handel shades were made not only of leaded
glass in a style reminiscent of Tiffany but also of reverse painted
glass. Handel also made vases and other glass objects.

HANDEL, Humidor, Bear Design, Green On Rust, Opalescent Glass 650.00
Lamp, 2 Bands of Overlapping Petals, Signed, 12 In. 355.00
Lamp, 3–Light, Poinsettia Blossoms, Leaded Shade, 28 In. 1540.00
Lamp, 4 Petal Feet, Painted Bridge, Landscape, Signed, 18 In. 5060.00
Lamp, 6–Panel Orange Shade, Bronze Base, Signed, 7 In. 2090.00
Lamp, Autumn Leaves, Reverse Painted Cone Shade, Signed, 21 1/2 In. 3300.00
Lamp, Bronze, Green Glass, 18 In. ....*Illus* 3740.00
Lamp, Candlestick, Teroma, Bobeche Socket Rim, Signed, 8 1/4 In. 665.00
Lamp, Cased Shade, Wild Roses, Stems, Textured Ground, Signed, 18 In. 2750.00
Lamp, Desk, Pine, 6–Panel Orange Shade, 7 In. ....*Illus* 2090.00
Lamp, Dogwood Leaded Shade, Petal Form Base, Marked, 25 In. 3850.00
Lamp, Domical Shade, Tree Trunk Bronze Supports, Signed, 1916, 22 In. 6500.00
Lamp, Double Lakeside Scene, Blue Clouds, Signed, 15 In. 1765.00
Lamp, Interior Painted Parakeets, Signed, 13 1/2 In. 4625.00
Lamp, Leafy Trees Tuck–Under Domed Shade, Stepped Base, 15 In. 357.00
Lamp, Obverse Floral & Scroll, Porcelainized Shade, Signed 2175.00
Lamp, Painted Reverse & Obverse, Lakeside, Signed, 13 In. 1430.00
Lamp, Reverse & Observe Goldenrod Clusters, Signed, 21 1/2 In. 2200.00
Lamp, Reverse Painted, Signed Palme, 18 In. 2250.00
Lamp, Reverse–Painted Domed Shade, Enameled Landscape Shade, 18 In 3850.00
Lamp, Reverse–Painted Scenic Shade, Signed, 18 In. 3300.00
Lamp, Reverse–Painted Shade, Leaf & Berries, 18 1/2 In. 660.00
Lamp, Reverse–Painted Shade, Mountainous Landscape, 14 In. 2200.00
Lamp, Reverse–Painted Shade, Red–Orange, 7 In. ....*Illus* 4620.00
Lamp, Reverse–Painted Teroma Dome Shade, Signed, 20 1/2 In. 3300.00
Lamp, Reverse–Painted Tree, Mountain Scene, 13 1/2 In. 1900.00
Lamp, Ribbed–Glass Dome, Reverse Painted, Panorama, Signed, 21 In. 2850.00

Handel, Lamp,
Bronze, Green Glass,
18 In.

Handel, Lamp, Desk,
Pine, 6–Panel Orange
Shade, 7 In.

Handel, Lamp,
Reverse–Painted
Shade, Red–Orange,
7 In.

Handel, Lamp, Table,
Shade Signed Handel
5487R, 18 In.

Lamp, Rocky Shoreline, Domed Shade, 2–Light, Reverse Painted, 20 In. 1370.00
Lamp, Slag Shade, Lighted Base 750.00
Lamp, Table, Shade Signed Handel 5487R, 18 In. ....*Illus* 5060.00
Lamp, Textured Leaves, Cylindrical Shade, Adjustable, 8 In. 770.00
Lamp, Textured Pine Trees, Interior Trees, 14 In. 2475.00
Nightlight, Floral Ribbed, Egg Shape, Pair 2000.00
Shade, Hexagonal, Red Diamonds, Green Piping, 6 x 4 1/2 In. 200.00
Shade, Leaded Green Panel, Windowpane Grillwork, 7 x 16 In. 985.00
Vase, Chipped Glass Foot, Cypress, Lake, Mountains, c.1906, 10 In. 2100.00
Vase, Teroma, Bird In Flight, 11 In., Pair 8500.00
HARDWARE, see Architectural

Harker Pottery Company of East Liverpool, Ohio, was founded by Benjamin Harker in 1840. The company made many types of pottery but by the Civil War was making quantities of yellowware from native clays. They also made Rockingham–type brown–glazed pottery and whiteware. The plant was moved to Chester, West Virginia, in 1931. Dinnerwares were made and sold nationally. In 1971 the company was sold to Jeanette Glass Company and all operations ceased in 1972. For more information, see *Kovels' Depression Glass & American Dinnerware Price List.*

HARKER, Ashtray, Queen Mary 3.25
Bowl, Amy, 9 In. 20.00
Bowl, Clover, Green, 8 In. 15.00
Bowl, Vegetable, Pate–Sur–Pate, Teal 8.00
Cake Plate, Cameoware 6.00
Cake Plate, Pink Roses 20.00
Cake Plate, Rose, Matching Server .... 30.00 To 35.00
Cake Set, Pine Cone, 8 Piece .... 40.00 To 45.00
Cake Set, Pine Cone, Lifter, 8 Piece 25.00
Cake Set, Victorian Couple, Square, Server, Plate, 8 Piece 18.00
Cake Stand, Modern Tulip 10.00
Creamer, Cameoware, Blue 7.00
Creamer, Cameoware, Cover 7.50
Dish, Feeding, Blue Cameo, Chrome Holder, Hot Water, 3 Sections 20.00
Feeder, Baby's, Cameoware, Pink, Round, Bartsch Metal Frame 15.00
Flowerpot, Bambi 22.00
Jar, Cigarette, Queen Mary, Crystal 2.25
Jug, Cover, White Rose, Blue 30.00
Luncheon Set, Pate–Sur–Pate, Teal, 8 Piece 25.00
Mug, Daniel Boone 22.00
Mug, Hound Handle 48.00
Mustard, Petalware, Cobalt Blue 5.50
Plate, Cameoware, 9 In. 4.00
Plate, Clover, Green, 10 In. 6.00
Plate, Rooster, Yellow, 7 In. 2.50
Platter, Cameo Ivy, Green, Large 12.00
Platter, Red Apple, Coral, 13 In. 2.00
Rolling Pin, Basket With Fruits & Flowers 38.00
Rolling Pin, Blue Ceramic 35.00
Rolling Pin, Gold, White Handles 80.00
Rolling Pin, Kelvinator 85.00
Rolling Pin, Mallow 80.00
Rolling Pin, Modern Tulip 35.00
Rolling Pin, Morning Glory 85.00
Rolling Pin, Petit Point Rose 65.00
Rolling Pin, Pink Cameo 85.00
Rolling Pin, White, Flowered Edge 85.00
Spoon & Lifter, Apple, 2 Piece 15.00
Teapot, Cameo, Pink 20.00
Teapot, Red Apple 30.00

Harlequin dinnerware was produced by the Homer Laughlin Company from 1938 to 1964, and sold without trademark by the F. W. Woolworth Co. It has a concentric ring design like Fiesta, but the rings are separated from the rim by a plain margin. Cup handles are triangular in shape. For more information, see *Kovels' Depression Glass & American Dinnerware Price List.*

HARLEQUIN, Bowl, Red, 5 1/2 In. 7.00
  Casserole, Mauve, Blue 30.00
  Creamer, Mauve 10.00
  Creamer, Novelty 13.00
  Eggcup, Double, Spruce 14.00
  Eggcup, Red 15.00
  Eggcup, Yellow 12.00
  Figurine, Lamb, Green 65.00
  Figurine, Penguin, Yellow .... 25.00 To 65.00
  Gravy Boat, Turquoise 11.00
  Jug, Water, Ball, Mauve 23.00
  Nut Dish, Spruce 7.00
  Penguin, Blue 45.00
  Pitcher, Red 28.00
  Plate, Chartreuse, 9 In. 8.00
  Plate, Gray, 6 1/4 In. 4.00
  Plate, Gray, 9 In. 10.00
  Plate, Maroon, 9 In. 10.50
  Plate, Yellow, 9 In. 6.50
  Platter, Turquoise, 11 In. 10.00
  Platter, Yellow, 13 In. .... 12.00 To 13.50
  Sugar, Cover, Chartreuse 12.00
  Sugar, Cover, Red 12.00

Hatpins were fashionable from 1860 to 1920 when the large, heavy hat required special long-shanked pins to hold it in place. Naturally, hatpin holders were made during the same years. The hatpin holder resembles a large saltshaker, but it often has no opening at the bottom as a shaker does. Hatpin holders were made of all types of ceramics and metal. Look for other prices under the names of specific manufacturers.

HATPIN HOLDER, Arcadian, Crested Ware 48.00
  Pink, Green & White Dots, Japan, Green Mark, 4 1/2 In. 50.00

Hatpins were popular from 1860 to 1920. The long pin, often over four inches, was used to hold the hat in place on the hair. The tops of the pins were made of all materials from solid gold and real gemstones to ceramics and glass. Be careful to buy original hatpins and not recent pieces made by altering old buttons.

HATPIN, Amethyst Glass 20.00
  Butterfly & Stone, 12 In. 22.50
  Goldtone Metal, Brillants, Blue Stone, Concealed Puff In Top 1400.00
  Hiawatha & Minnehaha, Sterling Silver, Pair 550.00
  Rhinestone & Amber, 1 1/2 x 10 In. 80.00
  Rhinestone, 1 1/2 In. Head, Faceted Amber, 10 In. Shank 80.00
  Scarab, Moire 22.00
  Scorpion, Pearl & Filigree Brass, 3 In. 125.00
  Silver Metal Head, Large Purple Faceted Stone, 2 In. 70.00

HAVILAND & CO. Haviland china has been made in Limoges, France, since 1842. The factory was started by the Haviland Brothers of New York City. Pieces are marked H & Co., Haviland & Co., or Theodore Haviland. It is possible to match existing sets of dishes through dealers who specialize in Haviland china. Other factories worked in the town of Limoges making a similar chinaware. These porcelains are listed in this book under *Limoges.*

HAVILAND, Bowl, Fruit, Pink Roses, Gold, Rectangular 50.00
  Bowl, Vegetable, Apple Blossom, Oval 45.00
  Chocolate Pot, Rouen Mold, Roses, 9 1/2 In. 125.00
  Chocolate Set, Floral Design, Ribbon Handle, 10 In., 6 Piece 400.00
  Chocolate Set, Ribbon Handle, Flowers, Double Mark, 6 Piece 425.00
  Chocolate Set, Ribbon Handle, Flowers, Scalloped, 6 Piece 375.00
  Coffeepot, Duck 165.00
  Creamer, Duck 100.00
  Cup & Saucer, Allover Blue & Lavender Flowers, Demitasse 40.00
  Dish, Pastel Flowers 15.00
  Eggcup, Border Pattern, Large 85.00
  Hair Receiver, Yellow Floral, Factory Design 65.00
  Pitcher, Goose, Large 165.00
  Pitcher, Goose, Small 100.00
  Plate, Cherubs, Flowers, 8 In. 20.00
  Plate, Princess, 7 1/2 In. 6.00
  Plate, Ransom, 9 1/2 In. 10.00
  Plate, Scene, Roses & Gold Border, Factory Design 45.00
  Platter, Fish 86.00
  Soup, Dish, Oxford, Rim 12.00
  Sugar, Duck 75.00
  Tea Set, Plaisance Pattern, 27 Piece 375.00

T. G. Hawkes & Company of Corning, New York, was founded in 1880. The firm cut glass blanks made at other glassworks until 1962. Many pieces are marked with the trademark, a trefoil ring enclosing a fleur-de-lis and two hawks. Cut glass by other manufacturers is listed under either the factory name or the general category Cut Glass.

HAWKES, Berry Bowl, Queens, 5 In. 135.00
  Bonbon, Russian, Starred Button, Pedestal, 2 3/4 x 6 In. 325.00
  Bowl, Cardinal, Bird Medallions In Crosscut Diamonds, Signed, 9 In. 675.00
  Bowl, Crimped, 4 x 12 In. 1950.00
  Bowl, Etched Floral, Light Green, Metal Rim & Handle, Signed 185.00
  Bowl, Grecian, Rolled-In Sides, Signed, 8 1/2 In. 1350.00
  Bowl, Marquis 1950.00
  Bowl, Theodora 3100.00
  Bowl, Venetian, Triangular Shape, Signed, 9 In. 650.00
  Butter Pat, Maple Leaf Shape, Signed 45.00
  Candleholder, Intaglio Floral Garland Above Bulb, 3 1/2 In., Pair 165.00
  Candlestick, Fine Block With Oval Punties, Teardop Stem, 8 In., Pair 450.00
  Carafe, Cut Glass, Venetian 250.00
  Carafe, Teutonic, Signed, 7 In. 305.00
  Casserole, Cover, Russian, Signed, 8 In. 1800.00
  Celery, Gravic, 11 In. 225.00
  Cocktail Shaker, Etched & Gilt Dragon, Plated Top, Signed, 8 1/2 In. 275.00
  Cocktail Shaker, Owl In Tree With Moon, Sterling Top, 8 1/2 In. 135.00
  Cruet, 3-Pour Spout, Signed, 6 In. 165.00
  Dish, Grecian, Heart Shape, 6 x 11 In. 595.00
  Electrolier, Majestic, 21 1/2 In. 4200.00
  Lamp, Boudoir, Strawberry Domed, 18 In. 1600.00
  Perfume Bottle, Teutonic, 6 1/2 In. 255.00
  Perfume Bottle, Venetian 375.00

◆◆◆

Clean aluminum with fine steel wool or steel wool soap pads. To remove discoloration boil two teaspoons of cream of tartar and a quart of water in the utensil. The acid from cooking tomatoes or rhubarb in the pot may also remove the stain.

◆◆◆

Perfume Bottle, Venetian, Pattern Wraps Around Base, 7 In.	375.00
Plate, Canton, Signed, 7 In.	210.00
Plate, Venetian, 9 In.	350.00
Punch Bowl, Nautilus, 13 In.	4400.00
Punch Bowl, North Star, Signed	3600.00
Ring Tray, Etched Gracia Pattern, Signed, c.1920, 4 x 3 In.	75.00
Rose Bowl, Brunswick, On Pedestal, 4 3/4 In.	545.00
Rose Bowl, Chrysanthemum Pattern, 6 1/2 x 8 In.	825.00
Shot Glass, Cut, Signed, 8 Piece	325.00
Sugar & Creamer, Cut Stars, Shooting Stars	125.00
Sugar & Creamer, Intaglio Flowers & Leaves, Signed	150.00
Tankard, Nail Head Diamond Hobstar, Zippered Lip, Signed, 11 In.	695.00
Tray, Gravic Iris, 12 In.	950.00
Tray, Holland Pattern, Signed, 6 1/2 x 10 In.	450.00
Tray, Late Devonshire, Signed, 13 In.	1200.00
Vase, Blue, Signed, 11 In.	250.00
Vase, Brazilian, Corset Shape, 10 In.	335.00
Vase, Carnation, Gravic Style, Signed, 2 Part, 16 1/2 In.	2150.00
Vase, Crystal, Silver, Ribbons, Floral, 14 In.	180.00
Vase, Fan, Engraved Leaves, Green Foot, Signed, 7 1/2 In.	150.00
Vase, Garlands of Flowers, Gravic, Marked, 11 3/4 In.	260.00
Vase, Hobstars Alternating With Swirl Prisms, Signed, 18 In.	325.00
Vase, Iris, To Harold Tabbert, Boston, 12 1/2 In.	800.00
Vase, Trumpet, Greek Key Border, Hexagonal, Starburst Foot, 14 In.	210.00
Vase, Trumpet, Teutonic, Scalloped Hobstar Base, 12 1/2 In.	675.00
Vase, Vernay, Bulbous Stem, Signed, 12 1/2 In.	210.00
Wine, Queen's, Square Base, Signed, 6 1/2 In.	225.00

Figural vases, generally showing a woman from the shoulders up, were used by florists primarily in the 1950s and 1960s. Head vases, made in a variety of sizes and often decorated with imitation jewelry and other lifelike accessories, were manufactured in Japan and the U.S. Less elaborate examples were made as early as the 1930s. Religious themes, babies, and animals are also common subjects.

HEAD VASE, African Man, C. A. S., 8 In.	135.00
Black Woman, Paper Label	23.00
Black Woman, Turban, Striped Bandana, 4 3/4 In.	60.00
Black, Gold Eyes	28.00
Blond, Pearl Necklace, Earring, 6 In.	35.00
Cocker Spaniel	25.00
Doris Day	20.00
Girl With Umbrella	22.50
Girl, Pigtails	17.50 To 26.00
Girl, Pigtails, Becky	32.00
Girl, With Umbrella, Pigtails	40.00
Ivory Woman, Wide Brimmed Hat, 8 1/2 In.	45.00
Jackie Kennedy, 1964, 6 In.	95.00 To 110.00
Little Girl	20.00
Lucille Ball	20.00
Madonna, Occupied Japan	12.50
Mucha–Type, Art Nouveau, Impressed L, 10 x 6 In.	144.00
No. 1067, Inarco, 1960s	20.00
Oriental Girl, Bobbin Head	20.00
Polynesian Girl, Shawnee	30.00
Poodle, White	16.00
Raggedy Ann Type	12.00
Red Haired Child, Full Body	15.00
Woman, Brimmed Hat, Full–Length Right Arm, Open Hand, Flowers	40.00
Woman, Hat Brim, 2 1/2 In.	25.00
Woman, Hat Brim, 5 3/8 In.	40.00
Woman, Inarco, 1963	15.00
Woman, Large Rolled Rim Pink Hat, Gold Necklace, Black Bangs	17.50
Woman, Off–The–Shoulder Dress, Coy Expression, Bisque, Small	12.50

Woman, Upswept Hairdo, Yellow Rose On Pink Hat 25.00
Woman, Wide Brimmed Hat, Ivory 30.00

Heintz Art Metal shop made jewelry, copper, silver, and brass in Buffalo, New York, from 1906 to 1935. The most popular items with collectors today are the copper desk sets and vases made with applied silver designs.

HEINTZ ART, Ashtray, Matchbox Attached, Silver On Bronze 65.00
Humidor, Cover, Applied Silver Griffins, Cylindrical, 8 x 5 In. 247.00
Inkstand, Bird, Bronze, Silver Overlay 175.00
Lamp, Reticulated Shade, Bublous Base, Silver Overlay, 10 In. 660.00
Smoking Set, Bronze, Nested, Set of 3, 12 In. 95.00
Vase, Floral Sterling Design, Green Patina, Bronze Body, 5 In. 225.00
Vase, Sterling On Bronze, 7 1/2 In. 120.00

Heisey glass was made from 1896 to 1957 in Newark, Ohio, by A. H. Heisey and Co., Inc. The Imperial Glass Company of Bellaire, Ohio, bought some of the molds and the rights to the trademark. Some Heisey patterns have been made by Imperial since 1960. After 1968, they stopped using the *H* trademark. Heisey used romantic names for colors such as *Sahara.* Do not confuse color and pattern names.

HEISEY, see also Custard Glass; Ruby Glass
HEISEY, Albemarie, Champagne, Saucer, 5 Oz. 22.50
Albemarie, Compote, Sahara, 7 In. 45.00
Apple, Marmalade, Cover, Cut, Ladle 135.00
Arch, Tumbler, Amber 75.00
Arch, Tumbler, Sahara 45.00
Aristocrat, Candlestick, Floral Etch, 7 In. 65.00
Asiatic, Figurine, Pheasant, Crystal 295.00
Athena, Candelabra, 2–Light, Pair 110.00
Athena, Plate, Torte, 14 In. 50.00
Athena, Salad Bowl, 10 1/2 In. 30.00
Banded Flute, Candlestick 65.00
Banded Flute, Chamberstick 39.50
Banded Flute, Cruet, Stopper, 4 Oz. 30.00
Banded Flute, Jar, Horseradish, Stopper 40.00
Banded Flute, Matchbox 150.00
Banded Picket, Basket, Flamingo 295.00
Barbara Fritchie, Brandy, 3/4 Oz. .... 85.00 To 95.00
Barbara Fritchie, Brandy, Cobalt, 3/4 Oz. 450.00
Barbara Fritchie, Cordial, 1 Oz. 85.00
Basket, Etched, 13 In. 225.00
Beaded Panel & Sunburst, Compote 125.00
Beaded Panel & Sunburst, Cracker Jar 295.00
Beaded Panel & Sunburst, Decanter, Wine, Handle, 10 Oz. 125.00
Beaded Panel & Sunburst, Punch Bowl, Stand 195.00
Beaded Panel & Sunburst, Sugar, Individual 35.00
Beaded Panel & Sunburst, Toothpick, Gold Trim 85.00
Beaded Swag, Cake Server, 10 1/2 In. 65.00
Beaded Swag, Goblet, Dow City, Iowa 50.00
Beaded Swag, Pitcher, Ruby Stained 105.00
Beaded Swag, Pitcher, Water 125.00
Beaded Swag, Spooner 40.00
Beaded Swag, Sugar, Cover 50.00
Beaded Swag, Table Set, Crystal, Gold Trim, 4 Piece .... 205.00 To 225.00
Beaded Swag, Table Set, Gold Trim, 4 Piece 195.00
Beaded Swag, Table Set, Gold, Red Flashed, 4 Piece 100.00
Bonnet, Basket, 15 1/2 In. 265.00
Bookend, Frosted 95.00
Box, Cigarette, Horsehead Finial, Crystal 110.00
Cabochon, Candleholder, 2–Light, Pair 120.00
Cabochon, Compote, Jelly, Footed, Bell–Air Cut, 5 In. 32.50

Cabochon, Plate, 8 In. 18.00
Cabochon, Sugar & Creamer, Marked, Dawn 85.00
Candlestick, No. 4, 1902–21, Pair 125.00
Candlestick, Orchid Etched 90.00
Candy Jar, 22K Gold Overlay, Cobalt Enameled Inside, 10 1/2 In. 300.00
Carcassonne, Goblet, Short Stem, Alexandrite, 11 Oz. 90.00
Carcassonne, Tumbler, Bar, 2 Oz. 10.00
Cascade, Candlestick, 3–Light, Orchid Etch, Pair 165.00
Cathedral, Vase, Flared Artic Etch 225.00
Charter Oak, Candleholder, 3–Light, Flamingo, Pair 155.00
Charter Oak, Compote, Moongleam, 7 In. 75.00
Charter Oak, Sherbet, Marked, Flamingo, 6 Oz. 20.00
Charter Oak, Sherbet, Marked, Moongleam, 6 Oz. 25.00
Classic, Candelabrum, 1–Light, Prism, 7 1/2 In. 250.00
Coarse Rib, Celery, Flamingo, 12 In. 25.00
Coarse Rib, Celery, Flamingo, Marked, 9 In. 37.50
Coarse Rib, Mustard, Gold Flashed, Marked 40.00
Coarse Rib, Plate, 8 In. 12.00
Coarse Rib, Plate, Marked, Flamingo, 7 In. 12.00
Cobel, Cocktail Shaker, Antarctic Etch, 1 Qt. 130.00
Coleport, Cordial, 1 Oz. 10.50
Coleport, Tumbler, Marked, Crystal, 8 Oz. 15.00
Colonial, Bowl, Crystal, 3 1/2 x 9 In. 68.00
Colonial, Bowl, Fruit, Cover, 2 Qt. 215.00
Colonial, Champagne, Saucer, 4 Oz. 22.00
Colonial, Goblet, Footed, 7 Oz. 12.50
Colonial, Jam Jar, Cover, Ladle, Cut Base & Cover, Marked 95.00
Colonial, Jelly, Footed, Handle 24.00
Colonial, Pitcher, 2 Qt. 95.00
Colonial, Powder Box, Silver Cover, Marked 65.00
Colonial, Punch Bowl, Base, Footed 160.00
Colonial, Sherbet, Footed, 4 1/2 Oz. 58.00
Colonial, Tankard Set, Silver Deposit, 5 Piece 145.00
Columbia, Candlestick, 1–Light, 3 1/2 In., Pair 65.00
Continental, Pitcher, Water 145.00
Continental, Toothpick, Marked 60.00
Creole, Bar Glass, Alexandrite, 1 Oz. 200.00
Cross Lined Flute, Tumbler, Marked, 8 Oz. 18.00
Crystolite, Box, Cigarette, Cover, 4 In. 20.00
Crystolite, Candleholder, 4 1/2 In. 12.00
Crystolite, Coaster, 4 In. 6.00
Crystolite, Cocktail Shaker, 36 Oz. 245.00
Crystolite, Holder, Cigarette, Round Footed 20.00
Crystolite, Ice Bucket, Marked 75.00
Crystolite, Jam Jar, Marked, 7 In. 72.50
Crystolite, Jelly, 2 Sections, Handle, 6 In. 21.50
Crystolite, Mustard, Marked 52.50
Crystolite, Nut Seat, Leaf, 5 Piece 38.00
Crystolite, Powder Box, Cover, Marked, 4 3/4 In. 65.00
Crystolite, Saltshaker 17.50
Crystolite, Sherbet, 6 Oz. 19.00
Crystolite, Sugar & Creamer 20.00
Crystolite, Sugar & Creamer 17.50
Crystolite, Sugar & Creamer, Tray, Individual 27.50
Crystolite, Tray, Dresser, Oblong, 13 In. 75.00
Double Rib & Panel, Basket, Moongleam 175.00
Duquesne, Tumbler, Tangerine, 5 Oz. 1456.00
Elephant Handled Mug, Amber 600.00
Empress Etch, Goblet, Water, Sahara 35.00
Empress, Bowl, Console, Moongleam 98.00
Empress, Bowl, Dolphin Footed, Sahara, 9 In. 30.00
Empress, Bowl, Sahara, 2 Handles, 10 In. 60.00
Empress, Celery, Moongleam, 13 In. 35.00

Empress, Cruet, Oil, Stopper, Moongleam, 3 Oz.	130.00
Empress, Cup & Saucer, Beaded, Sahara	30.00
Empress, Lamp, Stick, Etched Stem Base	145.00
Empress, Nut Dish, Sahara, Individual	27.50
Empress, Plate, 10 In.	35.00
Empress, Plate, Orchid Etch, 8 In.	25.00
Empress, Relish, 2 Sections, Moonglow, 13 In.	25.00
Empress, Sugar & Creamer, Sahara	45.00 To 60.00
Fairacre, Goblet, Marked	17.50
Fancy Loop, Bowl, Crimped, Footed, Crystal, 8 In.	80.00
Fancy Loop, Cruet	35.00
Fancy Loop, Sugar, Green	30.00
Fancy Loop, Toothpick	60.00 To 65.00
Fandango, Cruet	40.00
Fandango, Toothpick	30.00
Favor, Vase, Cobalt Blue, Diamond Optic	225.00
Figurine, Airdale	700.00
Figurine, Asiatic Pheasant	325.00 To 425.00
Figurine, Bull	1195.00
Figurine, Colt, Balking	225.00
Figurine, Colt, Standing	95.00
Figurine, Colt, Standing, Amber	550.00
Figurine, Colt, Standing, Carmel	35.00
Figurine, Cygnet	175.00 To 190.00
Figurine, Donkey	200.00
Figurine, Elephant, Large	325.00 To 425.00
Figurine, Elephant, Small	250.00
Figurine, Filly, Head Turned, Verde Green, Marked	600.00
Figurine, Flying Mare	1500.00
Figurine, Giraffe, Head Back	190.00 To 225.00
Figurine, Goose, Wings Halfway Up	75.00 To 90.00
Figurine, Goose, Wings Up	100.00 To 105.00
Figurine, Hen	365.00
Figurine, Horsehead, Child Toy	75.00
Figurine, Kingfisher, Hawthorne	240.00
Figurine, Madonna	90.00
Figurine, Mallard, Wings Halfway Up	165.00
Figurine, Mallard, Wings Up, Carmel	30.00
Figurine, Piglets	60.00
Figurine, Pony, Kicking	150.00 To 175.00
Figurine, Pony, Standing	95.00
Figurine, Pouter Pigeon	950.00
Figurine, Ringneck Pheasant	130.00 To 145.00
Figurine, Rooster, Fighting, 8 In.	85.00
Figurine, Scotty	110.00
Figurine, Sow, Black, Marked	500.00
Figurine, Sparky	110.00
Figurine, Sparrow	95.00 To 105.00
Figurine, Tropical Fish	1495.00
Figurine, Wood Duckling, Floating, Marked	110.00
Figurine, Wood Duckling, Standing	160.00
Finesse, Claret, 5 Oz.	9.00
Finesse, Cocktail, 4 Oz.	9.00
Finesse, Cocktail, Hollow Stem, Crystal, 3 Oz.	25.00
Fish, Bookends, Crystal	225.00
Flamingo, Bonbon, Marked, Individual, 4 Piece	48.00
Flamingo, Goblet, 9 Oz.	30.00
Flamingo, Ice Tub, Octagonal, Marked	105.00
Flamingo, Relish, Divided, 2 Handles	22.00
Flat Panel, Horseradish	45.00
Flat Panel, Toothpick, Cutting	65.00
Gascony, Sherbet, Tangerine	160.00
Gayoso, Goblet, Flamingo	25.00

Glenford, Goblet, Soda, 12 Oz.	30.00
Grape, Candlestick, Pair	145.00
Greek Key, Bowl, 7 1/2 In.	90.00
Greek Key, Candy Jar, 2 Lb.	175.00
Greek Key, Compote, Jelly, Handle, 5 In.	39.50
Greek Key, Cruet, 6 Oz.	125.00 To 128.00
Greek Key, Cruet, Silver Overlay, 6 Oz.	105.00
Greek Key, Dish, Banana Split	22.00
Greek Key, Nappy, 5 In.	30.00
Greek Key, Nappy, 8 In.	60.00
Greek Key, Nut Cup, Marked, 6 Piece	138.00
Greek Key, Punch Cup	12.50
Greek Key, Punch Cup, Flamingo	28.50
Greek Key, Sherbet, 4 Oz.	10.00
Greek Key, Soda, Marked, 5 Oz.	30.00
Greek Key, Tankard, 3 Footed, Marked	168.00
Greek Key, Tankard, 3 Pt.	188.00
Groove & Slash, Humidor, Art Nouveau Cover, Crystal	175.00
Hartman, Candy Dish, Painted Design, 1/2 Lb.	50.00
Hartman, Tumbler, Flared Optic, Marked, 4 Oz.	11.00
Horsehead, Bookends, Frosted	95.00
Horsehead, Box, Cigarette, 6 In.	50.00
Ipswich, Bowl, 5 x 11 In.	65.00
Ipswich, Candle Vase, Insert	65.00 To 190.00
Ipswich, Plate, Square, Sahara, 8 In.	28.00
Ipswich, Sherbet, Marked, 4 Oz.	12.50
Ipswich, Tumbler, Moongleam, Footed, 8 Oz.	105.00
Kalonyal, Butter, Cover	195.00
Kenilworth, Goblet, Water	45.00
Kimberly, Goblet, Water	22.00
King Arthur, Goblet, Marked, Flamingo. 10 Oz.	30.00
Lafayette, Compote, Yellow, Etched Figures, Marked, 6 x 8 1/2 In.	90.00
Lafayette, Goblet, Marked	25.00
Lariat, Ashtray, Crystal	7.50
Lariat, Basket, 8 1/2 In.	150.00
Lariat, Bonbon, 7 1/2 In.	45.00
Lariat, Bowl, 8 1/2 In.	25.00
Lariat, Bowl, Flared, 4 x 9 In.	40.00
Lariat, Bowl, Ruffled, 12 In.	28.00
Lariat, Bowl, Silver Overlay, 7 In.	35.00
Lariat, Box, Cigarette, Cover, 4 In.	48.00
Lariat, Candleholder, 2–Light, Pair	45.00
Lariat, Candleholder, 3–Light, Pair	55.00
Lariat, Coaster, 4 In.	7.00
Lariat, Coaster, 4 In.	9.00
Lariat, Cordial, Moonglo Cut	100.00
Lariat, Cup & Saucer	38.00
Lariat, Goblet, Moonglo Cut	24.00
Lariat, Plate, Etched, 12 In.	40.00
Lariat, Punch Set, 15 Piece	325.00
Lariat, Relish, Divided, Round, 7 In.	25.00
Lariat, Sherbet, Moonglo Cut	20.00
Lariat, Sugar	12.00
Lariat, Sugar & Creamer, Tray, Crystal	22.00
Lariat, Torte Platter, 15 In.	55.00
Lariat, Tumbler, Juice	10.00
Lariat, Vase, Crimped, Footed, 7 In.	32.00
Lariat, Vase, Fan, Footed, 7 In.	30.00
Lariat, Wine, Moonglo Cut	24.00
Legionnaire, Cocktail, Amber Stem, 3 Oz.	50.00
Legionnaire, Cordial, 1 Oz.	75.00
Little Squatter, Candleblock, 1 1/4 In., Pair	20.00
Locket On Chain, Cake Stand	85.00

◆◆◆

Tin cookie cutters can be dated by the construction methods. Old ones are soldered in spots, not a long thin solder joint. If the solder joins the cutting–edge piece to the back by a thin, barely visible line, it is less than 50 years old.

◆◆◆

Locket On Chain, Cake Stand	125.00
Locket On Chain, Nappy, 4 In.	29.00
Locket On Chain, Shade, Gas, Crimped	150.00
Lodestar, Bowl, Alexandrite, 13 In.	135.00
Lodestar, Bowl, Dawn, 8 In.	55.00
Lodestar, Pitcher, Dawn, 1 Qt.	155.00
Lodestar, Vase, Star Bottom, Marked, 8 In.	350.00
Mercury, Candlestick, Orchid Etch, Pair	85.00
Minuet, Champagne, Etch	30.00
Minuet, Champagne, Saucer	22.00
Minuet, Cocktail, Etch	45.00
Minuet, Goblet, Water, Etch	40.00
Minuet, Tumbler, Iced Tea, Etch	40.00
Monte Cristo, Cordial, 1 Oz.	85.00
Moongleam Empress, Plate, 8 In.	18.00
Moongleam, Celery, Marked, 13 In.	30.00
Moongleam, Sugar & Creamer, Half Circle	150.00
Moonglo, Cocktail	15.00
Moonglo, Plate, 8 In.	14.00
Moonstone, Bowl, Crimped, 7 3/4 In.	10.00
Moonstone, Cup	6.50
Moonstone, Plate, Dessert, Crimped	6.50
Moonstone, Sugar	6.00
Moonstone, Vase, Bud	9.00
Narrow Flute, Banana Split	27.00
Narrow Flute, Celery, Rim, 12 In.	25.00
Narrow Flute, Dish, Pickle, Metal Frame, Marked, Sahara	65.00
Narrow Flute, Jar, Preserve, Cover, Footed	42.00
Narrow Flute, Jug, 12 Oz.	40.00
Narrow Flute, Pickle	28.00
Narrow Flute, Pitcher, 6 1/2 In.	65.00
Narrow Flute, Plate, Moongleam, 7 In.	7.50
Narrow Flute, Plate, Moongleam, 10 In.	35.00
Narrow Flute, Sugar & Creamer, Copper Wheel Cutting	45.00
Narrow Flute, Sugar Tray, Domino, Marked	50.00
National, Soda, Tally Ho Etch, 12 Oz.	35.00
National, Whiskey, Tally Ho Etch, 1 1/2 Oz.	22.00
New Era, Tumbler, Soda, 5 Oz.	22.00
Oceanic, Cocktail, Oyster, Orchid Etch	60.00
Octagon, Bonbon, Moonglo, Empress Etch, 6 In.	32.00
Octagon, Celery, Rim, Marked, Moongleam, 12 In.	40.00
Octagon, Plate, Flamingo, 7 In.	7.00
Octagon, Tray, Handle, Cut, 10 In.	37.50
Old Colony, Goblet, Low	22.50
Old Colony, Plate, Sahara, Square, 7 In.	18.00
Old Colony, Sherbet, Sahara	22.00
Old Colony, Sugar & Creamer, Sahara	95.00
Old Glory, Cordial, Renaissance Etch, Marked	80.00
Old Glory, Parfaits	30.00
Old Sandwich, Ashtray, Cobalt Blue	35.00
Old Sandwich, Ashtray, Square, Individual	7.50 To 9.00
Old Sandwich, Bowl, Yellow	22.00

Old Sandwich, Candlestick, Yellow, 6 In. 85.00
Old Sandwich, Cruet, Stopper, Sahara 27.50
Old Sandwich, Decanter, Sherry, 18 Oz. 90.00
Old Sandwich, Goblet, Footed, Sahara, 10 Oz. 37.50
Old Sandwich, Sherbet, Sahara, 6 Oz. 20.00
Old Sandwich, Tumbler, Bar, 1 1/2 Oz. 120.00
Old Williamsburg, Candlestick, 1–Light, 11 In. 100.00
Old Williamsburg, Candlestick, 9 In., Pair 140.00
Old Williamsburg, Decanter, 32 Oz. 100.00
Old Williamsburg, Decanter, Flamingo, 18 Oz. 245.00
Optic Tooth, Tumbler, Moongleam, 12 Oz. 30.00
Orchid Etch, Candlestick, 2–Light, Pair 130.00
Orchid Etch, Compote 45.00
Orchid Etch, Goblet, Water 35.00
Orchid Etch, Salt & Pepper 75.00
Orchid Etch, Saucer 12.50
Orchid, Cigar Jar, Cover 90.00
Orchid, Goblet, Water 35.00
Orchid, Ice Bucket 210.00
Orchid, Relish, 3 Sections, Oblong, 11 In. 65.00
Orchid, Sugar & Creamer, Individual 45.00
Park Avenue, Cordial, Signed 95.00
Patrician, Candleholder, Marked, 1904, 7 1/2 In., Pair 125.00
Patrician, Candlestick, 5 In., Pair 50.00
Peerless, Compote, Jelly, Gold, 5 In. 47.50
Peerless, Decanter, 20 Oz. 85.00
Peerless, Jug, 1 Qt. 70.00
Peerless, Toothpick .... 25.00 To 38.00
Petal, Creamer, Moongleam 27.50
Petal, Sugar, Moongleam 27.50
Pied Piper, Goblet, 13 Piece 240.00
Pillows, Spooner 87.50
Pineapple & Fan, Berry Set, 8–In. Master Bowl, 5 Piece 350.00
Pineapple & Fan, Bowl, Emerald Green, 9 In. 50.00
Pineapple & Fan, Butter, Cover, Crystal 95.00
Pineapple & Fan, Celery, 11 In. 25.00
Pineapple & Fan, Grape Bowl, Crystal 55.00
Pineapple & Fan, Sugar, Hotel 32.00
Pineapple & Fan, Toothpick, Crystal, Gold Trim 50.00
Pineapple & Fan, Toothpick, Gold Fan 80.00
Pinwheel & Fan, Hair Receiver, Crystal 65.00
Pinwheel & Fan, Hair Receiver, Metal Top 42.00
Pinwheel & Fan, Jug, 3 Pt. 125.00
Pinwheel & Fan, Pitcher 235.00
Plantation, Bowl, 9 In. 125.00
Plantation, Bowl, Scalloped, 7 3/4 x 3 In. 80.00
Plantation, Candy Dish, Cover, Footed, 8 In. 150.00
Plantation, Champagne, 6 Oz. 22.00
Plantation, Compote, Footed, 7 x 4 In. 60.00
Plantation, Cruet, Stopper 90.00
Plantation, Cup & Saucer 35.00
Plantation, Dish, Divided 28.00
Plantation, Fruit Bowl, 9 In. 140.00
Plantation, Jelly, 2 Handles 32.00
Plantation, Mayonnaise Set, Ivy Etch, 3 Piece 110.00
Plantation, Plate, 7 In. 11.00
Plantation, Plate, 8 1/2 In. .... 22.50 To 32.00
Plantation, Relish, 5 Sections 140.00
Plantation, Sherbet 22.00
Plantation, Sugar & Creamer, Footed .... 65.00 To 95.00
Pleat & Panel, Compote, Cover, Flamingo 90.00
Pleat & Panel, Plate, Marked, Flamingo 16.00
Portsmouth, Goblet, 9 Oz. 30.00

Prince of Wales Plumes, Celery, Crystal, 10 In. 30.00
Prince of Wales Plumes, Compote, 10 In. 75.00
Prince of Wales Plumes, Compote, Jelly, Footed, Gold, 5 In. 72.50
Prince of Wales Plumes, Tumbler, Gold Trim, 5 Piece 150.00
Priscilla, Sherbet, 3 Oz. 10.00
Prison Stripe, Nappy, 10 In. 60.00
Provincial, Candlestick, Purple, Pair 35.00
Provincial, Sherbet, Green 5.00
Provincial, Sherbet, Purple 8.00
Provincial, Sugar & Creamer 35.00
Provincial, Tumbler, Juice, Purple 6.50
Punty & Diamond Point, Punch Cup, Crystal 20.00
Punty & Diamond Point, Sugar Shaker 75.00
Puritan, Celery Vase, Marked 65.00
Puritan, Claret, 3 1/2 Oz., 5 In. 25.00
Puritan, Ice Bucket .... 49.00 To 50.00
Puritan, Ice Tub, Drainer 85.00
Puritan, Jelly, Footed, 4 1/2 In. 39.00
Puritan, Jug, Squat, Marked, 3 Pt. 85.00
Puritan, Nappy, 11 In. 45.00
Puritan, Nappy, 4 3/4 In. 10.00
Puritan, Plate, 13 In. 47.50
Puritan, Sherry, 2 Oz. 18.00
Puritan, Wine, Burgundy, 3 1/2 Oz. 12.50
Queen Ann, Bowl, Minuet Etch, 11 In. 50.00
Queen Ann, Bowl, Orchid Etch, 9 In. 70.00
Queen Ann, Candlestick, 7 1/2 In., Pair 175.00
Queen Ann, Cruet, Artic Etch 60.00
Queen Ann, Ice Bucket, Footed, Arctic Etch 130.00
Queen Ann, Mustard, Cover 32.00
Queen Ann, Nappy, Crimped, 9 In. 62.00
Queen Ann, Plate, Minuet Etch, 7 In. 20.00
Queen Ann, Plate, Minuet Etch, 8 In. 22.00
Queen Ann, Relish, 3 Sections, Orchid Etch 60.00
Queen Ann, Sugar & Creamer, Footed, Minuet Etch 75.00
Queen Anne, Candlestick, Prisms, Orchid, Pair 200.00
Rabbit, Paperweight .... 120.00 To 165.00
Recessed Panel, Candy Jar, Crystal, 3 Lb., Pair 285.00
Renaissance, Goblet, Water 25.00
Rib & Panel, Goblet, Moongleam, 9 Oz. 25.00
Rib & Panel, Mayonnaise, Moongleam, 2 Handles 19.00
Rib & Panel, Nappy, Moongleam, 5 In. 15.00
Ridge & Star, Plate, Flamingo, 7 1/2 In. 12.50
Ridgeleigh, Bowl, Silver Overlay, 10 In. 85.00
Ridgeleigh, Box, Cigarette, Cover, 4 In. 22.00
Ridgeleigh, Candelabrum, 1–Light, Prisms, Pair 150.00
Ridgeleigh, Candle Vase, Zircon, 6 In. 130.00
Ridgeleigh, Candleholder, 5 1/2 In., Pair 25.00
Ridgeleigh, Coaster Set, Sahara, 8 Piece, Box 160.00
Ridgeleigh, Coaster, Sahara, 3 1/2 In. 12.00
Ridgeleigh, Cocktail Shaker 195.00
Ridgeleigh, Compote, Jelly, 3 Handles, Marked, 6 1/2 In. 22.00
Ridgeleigh, Holder, Cigarette, 2 7/8 In. 20.00
Ridgeleigh, Mustard, Cover, Marked 47.50
Ridgeleigh, Plate, Square, 6 In. 12.50
Ridgeleigh, Plate, Square, 8 In. 25.00
Ridgeleigh, Relish, 5 Sections 38.00
Ridgeleigh, Salt 8.00
Ring Band, Toothpick, Orange Flowers, White Daisies, Gold 55.00
Ring Band, Tumbler, Custard, Decorah, Iowa 85.00
Rococo, Plate, 7 In. 15.00
Rococo, Plate, Frosted Design, Marked, 12 In. 40.00
Rooster, Cocktail, Stem .... 59.00 To 70.00

Rooster, Decanter, 4 Rooster Head Wines 215.00
Rooster, Vase 75.00
Rose Etch, Goblet, Water, 9 Oz. 40.00
Rose Etch, Platter, Sandwich, Handles 170.00
Rose Etch, Salt & Pepper 95.00
Rose Etch, Tumbler, Iced Tea 47.50
Rose, Bowl, Crimped, 12 In. 50.00
Rose, Dish, Dressing, Etch, Divided, Marked, 6 1/2 In. 65.00
Rose, Goblet, 9 Oz. 55.00
Rose, Plate, 7 In. 28.00
Rose, Sherbet, 6 Oz. 17.00
Rose, Sherbet, 6 Oz. 34.00
Sailboat Carving, Soda, 8 Oz. 55.00
Saturn Rings, Vase, Ball Foot, 8 1/2 In. 50.00
Sawtooth Band, Toothpick 50.00
Southwind, Sherbet 20.00
Spanish, Champagne 15.00
Spanish, Champagne, Cobalt Blue 60.00
Spanish, Champagne, Tangerine 145.00
Star & Zipper, Nappy, 8 In. 40.00
Star & Zipper, Nappy, 9 In. 38.00
Star, Relish, 5 Sections 35.00
Star, Relish, Normandie Etch 75.00
Stepped Octagon, Plate, Marked, Moongleam, 8 In. 12.00
Sunburst, Candlestick, Flamingo, Square, 3 1/2 In., Pair 95.00
Sunburst, Dish, Pickle, Oblong, 9 In. 30.00
Sunburst, Mug, Beer, Drinking Scene, 16 Oz. 115.00
Sunburst, Nappy, Gold, 4 In. 22.50
Sunburst, Punch Bowl, Base & Ladle 170.00
Symphone, Cordial, Crinoline Etch 87.50
Symphone, Goblet, Minuet Etch, 9 Oz. 35.00
Symphone, Tumbler, 12 Oz. 15.00
Tally Ho, Ice Bucket, Carmen 95.00
Tally Ho, Ice Bucket, Green 58.00
Tally Ho, Sugar & Creamer 50.00
Touraine, Table Set, Ruby, Gold Etch, 4 Piece 175.00
Trident, Candlestick, Orchid Etch, Pair 95.00
Trident, Candlestick, Rose Etch, Pair 175.00
Trident, Candlestick, Sahara, Pair .... 110.00 To 135.00
Tudor, Compote, 6 1/2 In. 35.00
Tudor, Compote, Jelly, Footed, 5 In. 17.50
Twentieth Century, Sherbet, Sahara 20.00
Twist, Bowl, Nasturtium, Moongleam, 8 In. 70.00
Twist, Bowl, Pink, Cupped, 9 In. 50.00
Twist, Candlestick, Moongleam, Pair 65.00
Twist, Celery, Marigold, Marked 40.00
Twist, Ice Bucket, Moongleam 80.00
Twist, Ice Bucket, Silver Plated Handle, Marked 155.00
Twist, Ice Tub, Handles 60.00
Twist, Mustard, Underplate, Crystal 45.00
Twist, Plate, Marigold, 9 In. 20.00
Twist, Relish, Moongleam, 12 In. 32.00
Twist, Soup, Cream 55.00
Twist, Syrup, Cream 55.00
Tyrolean, Champagne, Orchid Etch, Stem 40.00
Tyrolean, Wine, Orchid Etch, 3 Oz. 72.50
Victorian Belle, Bell, Frosted .... 68.00 To 75.00
Victorian Belle, Bell, Gold Design, Frosted 85.00
Victorian, Compote, 3 1/2 In. 30.00
Victorian, Cruet, 3 Oz. 30.00
Victorian, Glass, Bar, 2 Oz. 15.00
Victorian, Goblet 27.00
Victorian, Punch Cup 10.00

Victorian, Sugar & Creamer 35.00
Victorian, Toothpick 28.00
Victorian, Tumbler, Bar, 2 Oz. 17.00
Victorian, Tumbler, Old–Fashioned, 3 Oz. 13.00
Wabash, Goblet, Frontenac Etch 15.00
Wabash, Sherbet, Frontenac Etch 12.00
Wampum, Candlestick, Pair .... 28.00 To 30.00
Warwick, Candlestick, 2–Light, Sahara, Pair 145.00
Warwick, Candlestick, Pair 30.00
Warwick, Vase, 8 1/2 In. 50.00
Warwick, Vase, Cobalt Blue, 5 In. 195.00
Warwick, Vase, Cornucopia, 9 In. 175.00
Warwick, Vase, Horn of Plenty, Crystal, Marked, 7in. 35.00
Waverly, Bowl, Seahorse Feet, Rose Etch, 11 In. 125.00
Waverly, Butter, Cover, Orchid, Square, 6 In. 125.00
Waverly, Candy Dish, Cover, Seahorse Handles, Orchid Etch 225.00
Waverly, Flower Bowl, Orchid Etch, 13 In. 60.00
Waverly, Plate, Orchid Etch, 7 In. 17.50
Waverly, Sugar & Creamer, Orchid Etch 58.00
Waverly, Tray, Sandwich, Center Handle 50.00
Whirlpool, Candy Dish, Cover, Marked 125.00
Whirlpool, Champagne 8.00
Whirlpool, Goblet, Water 15.00
Whirlpool, Mayonnaise, 3 Handles 125.00
Whirlpool, Plate, 8 In. 5.00
Whirlpool, Punch Set, 11 Piece 150.00
Whirlpool, Smoke Set, Covered Cigarette Box, 4 Square Ashtrays ... 60.00
Whirlpool, Tray, 12 1/2 In. 25.00
Whirlpool, Tumbler, Iced Tea 30.00
Whirlpool, Tumbler, Marked, 9 Oz. 20.00
Whirlpool, Wine, 2 1/2 Oz. 10.00
Williamsburg, Decanter, Moongleam, Crystal Stopper, 18 Oz. 245.00
Williamsburg, Marmalade, Cover, 8 Oz. 90.00
Windsor, Candlestick, 7 In. 65.00
Winged Scroll, Butter, Cover, Emerald Green 75.00
Winged Scroll, Cruet, Crystal 125.00
Winged Scroll, Cruet, Custard Glass 200.00
Winged Scroll, Pitcher, Gold Trim 197.00
Winged Scroll, Table Set, 4 Piece 325.00
Yeoman, Dish, Cheese, Footed, Hawthorne 65.00
Yeoman, Goblet, Flamingo, 9 Oz. 25.00
Yeoman, Goblet, Moongleam, Marked, 8 Oz. 30.00
Yeoman, Plate, Diamond Optic, 10 In. 55.00
Yeoman, Server, Center Handle 20.00
Yeoman, Sugar Shaker & Creamer, Pink 80.00
Yeoman, Tray, 3 Sections, Marked, Moongleam, 11 In. 42.00
Yorktown, Cocktail, Stem, Ivy Etch, 3 1/2 Oz. 28.00
Zodiac, Ashtray, Marked 2.50
Zodiac, Bowl, Amber, Footed, 11 In. 60.00
    HEREND, see Fischer

Gebruder Heubach, a firm working in Lichten, Germany, from 1840
to 1925, is best known for bisque dolls and doll heads, their
principal products. They also manufactured bisque figurines,
including piano babies, beginning in the 1880s, and glazed figurines
in the 1900s. Dolls are not listed here, but are listed in the Doll
section. Another factory, Ernst Heubach, working in Koppelsdorf,
Germany, also made porcelain and dolls.

HEUBACH, DOLL, see Doll, Gebruder Heubach
    HEUBACH, DOLL, see Doll, Gebruder Heubach; Doll, Heubach
HEUBACH, Figurine, 2 Children Playing Dress Up, Mirror In Hand, 10 In. 735.00
  Figurine, Baby, Crawling, Marked, 5 1/2 In. 175.00
  Figurine, Baby, Sitting, Holding Foot, 8 In. 400.00

Figurine, Ballerina, 8 In. 125.00
Figurine, Boy & Girl Fishing At Beach, 13 In. 895.00
Figurine, Dutch Girl, 4 In. 95.00
Figurine, Dutch Girl, Attached Basket, 7 1/2 In. 325.00
Figurine, Girl Holding Dove To Breast, 11 In. 550.00
Figurine, Girl, Holding Skirt Out, Blond, Flowers, Marked, 8 1/2 In. 158.00
Figurine, Girl, Sitting, Holding Hands, Marked, 4 1/2 In. 95.00
Figurine, Lady, Holding Dove On Shoulder, 8 In. 135.00
Figurine, Piano Baby, Hand To Face, 9 1/2 In. 500.00
Tray, Molded Seagull On Rim, Sailboat Center, 8 1/2 x 5 In. 75.00
Vase, Pink Roses On Blue, Yellow & Green, 8 3/4 In. 48.00

Higbee glass was made by the J. B. Higbee Company of Bridgeville, Pennsylvania, about 1900. Tablewares were made and it is possible to assemble a full set of dishes and goblets in some Higbee patterns. Most of the glass is clear, not colored.

HIGBEE, see also Pressed Glass
HIGBEE, Cake Stand, Paneled Thistle 27.00
Cake Stand, Pinecut Star & Fan 27.00
Ladle 25.00
Punch Cup, Crystal 12.00
Table Set, Arrowheads In Ovals, 4 Piece 75.00
HISTORIC BLUE, see factory names such as Adams, Clews, Ridgway, Staffordshire

Hobnail glass is a pattern of glass with bumps in an allover pattern. Dozens of hobnail patterns and variants have been made. Clear, colored, and opalescent hobnail have been made and are being reproduced. Other pieces of hobnail are also listed under Carnival Glass, Hobnail.

HOBNAIL, see also Fenton; Francisware
HOBNAIL, Celery Vase, Pink To Cream, 7 In. 220.00
Cookie Jar, Milk Glass, Cover, Handle, 7 x 8 In. 35.00
Cruet, Blue Opalescent, Faceted Stopper 225.00
Cruet, White Opalescent 45.00
Dish, 3 Sections, Opalescent 18.50
Mustard, Blue Opalescent, Clear Glass Spreader 35.00
Newel Post, Knob, Opalescent, Pair 125.00
Pitcher, Cranberry Opalescent 550.00
Pitcher, Milk, Cranberry Opalescent 450.00
Pitcher, Pink Opalescent, Clear Handle, Square Mouth, 5 1/8 In. 125.00
Pitcher, Water, Vaseline Opalescent 495.00
Rose Bowl, Cranberry Opalescent 85.00
Table Set, Ruffled, Blue Opalescent, Blown 295.00
Tumbler, Amberina, 7 In. 15.00
Vase, Cranberry, 5 In. 50.00

Hochst, or Hoechst, porcelain was made in Germany from 1746 to 1796. It was marked with a six-spoke wheel. Be careful when buying Hochst; many other firms have used a very similar wheel-shaped mark.

HOCHST, Cup & Saucer, Chateau Center of Saucer, Carriage, 1760, 4 7/8 In. 1650.00
Figurine, Boy & Girl, Horse, Flowers, 7 In. 500.00
Figurine, Boy & Girl, Standing, 4 3/4 In., Pair .... 160.00 To 175.00
Figurine, Two Children With Rabbit, c.1780, 5 1/2 In. 2475.00
Figurine, Two Children, Boy Taking Flowers, c.1780, 5 9/16 In. 2475.00

Holly amber, or golden agate, glass was made by the Indiana Tumbler and Goblet Company of Greentown, Indiana, from January 1, 1903, to June 13, 1903. It is a pressed glass pattern featuring holly leaves in the amber-shaded glass. The glass was made with shadings that range from creamy opalescent to brown-amber.

HOLLY AMBER, Butter, Cover 985.00

Creamer, 4 1/2 In.	350.00
Relish, Oval	375.00
Salt & Pepper	475.00
Sauce, 4 1/2 In.	220.00
Spooner, 4 In.	485.00
Syrup	1200.00
Toothpick	345.00 To 475.00
Tumbler	350.00
Tumbler, Beaded	275.00

 Hopalong Cassidy was named William Lawrence Boyd when he was born in Cambridge, Ohio, in 1895. His first movie appearance was in 1919, but the first Hopalong Cassidy film was not until 1934. Sixty–six films were made. In 1948, William Boyd purchased the television rights to the movies, then later made fifty–two new programs. In the 1950s, Hopalong Cassidy and his horse, named *Topper,* were seen in comics, records, toys, and other products. Boyd died in 1972.

HOPALONG CASSIDY, Badge, Sheriff's, Brass	18.00 To 20.00
Ballpoint Pen, Box	24.00
Bank, Blue, Plastic	70.00
Bedspread & Rug	250.00
Binoculars, Metal	45.00 To 95.00
Birthday Card, Inset Photo Pinback	35.00
Blotter, Hoppy, Gabby Hayes, Jimmy Ellison	25.00
Book, Coloring, Shoe Premium	45.00
Book, Mechanical, T.V., Hoppy & Danny	55.00
Book, Mechanical, T.V., Hoppy & Lucky At Copper Gulch	75.00
Book, Pop–Up	82.00
Book, Song, Hoppy, Photos, 1951	45.00
Book, T.V., Mechanical	60.00
Book, Two Young Cowboys	20.00
Bottle, Milk, Dairylea	38.00
Calendar, 1956, Complete	225.00
Camera, Box	155.00 To 200.00
Camera, Instamatic Shape, Black Case	65.00
Canasta Set, Box	95.00
Card, Greeting, Hopalong & Metal Boots	18.00
Cards, Playing, Canasta, Box	38.00
Chair, Canvas, Wooden, 1950s	350.00
Clock, Alarm, U. S. Time	100.00
Clothes Hamper	250.00
Coloring Book, Large	55.00
Coloring Book, Unused	30.00 To 35.00
Compass, Hat & Ring	225.00
Compass, Wrist	45.00
Cookie Jar, Cookie Corral	250.00 To 475.00
Costume, Cowboy, Box	225.00
Costume, Cowgirl	150.00
Costume, Cowgirl, Box	165.00
Cup, Hopalong, Horse, Blue Enameled, Milk Glass, 3 1/16 In.	16.00
Dart Game, 2–Sided Target, Tin, Box, Missing Darts	227.00

◆◆

To clean dirt and corrosion from lamps and lanterns, use brass pol- ish and steel wool. Or, to avoid rubbing off the nickel plating, first clean the surface with Fantastic or 409. Then apply Naval jelly with a brush. Rub for several minutes with the brush. Let stand for 30 min- utes and wash it off. Let it dry, polish gently with steel wool.

◆◆

Display, Butter–Nut Bread Loaf 95.00
Doll, Ideal, 1949, 21 In. 125.00
Face Mask, Latex, Box 450.00
Field Glasses, Box ....112.00 To 190.00
Figure, Hoppy & Horse Topper, Box, 6 In. 225.00
Figure, Lead 125.00
Filmstrip, T.V., With Chain & Film 65.00
Flashlight 85.00
Game, Board, Cowboy Heroes, Hoppy, Box, 1950 .... 65.00
Game, Canasta, Box 90.00
Game, Puzzle, Set of 3, Box 70.00
Game, Puzzle, Set of 3, Box 125.00
Game, Shooting Gallery, Box, 1950s 200.00
Glass, Milk Glass 40.00
Guitar, Box 195.00
Gun & Holster Pin 50.00
Gun & Holster, Box 650.00
Gun, Zoomerang, Red 80.00
Hair Trainer, 4 Oz. 30.00
Hat Ring 125.00
Hat, Gray 175.00
Hoppy & Topper, Rocking Base, Tin Lithograph, Windup, Marx 425.00
Horseshoe, Good Luck, Plastic 12.00
Knife, Pocket, Full Picture of Hoppy On Horse On Handle 75.00
Knife, Pocket, Hoppy On Topper, Graphic 85.00
Lamp, Bullet, Shade 850.00
Lamp, Roto View 165.00
Lobby Card, 1941 .... 20.00
Lunch Box, Lithograph, T. V. Screen, 1954 ....85.00 To 100.00
Lunch Box, Square Decal, Red, 1951 ....65.00 To 70.00
Magazine, Look, August 29, 1950 .... 18.00
Mug, Bowl & Plate, Chuck Wagon, Transfer, W. S. George. 82.50
Mug, Glass 12.50
Mug, Red Letters ....18.00 To 25.00
Mug, White, Green 20.00
Napkins, Unopened 42.00
Night–Light, Holster, Milk Glass 150.00
Outfit, Cowgirl, Box 175.00
Paint Set 150.00
Paper Plates, Unopened 21.00
Pencil Sharpener, Blue 25.00
Pencil Sharpener, Yellow 30.00
Photo Album 50.00
Pillow, Satin, 1950s 175.00
Plate, Dinner, W. S. George, 3 Piece Set 75.00
Plate, Ivan Anderson Signed, 1983 .... 120.00
Postcard, Chrysler, 1942 .... 14.00
Poster, Dairylea Milk, Picture of Hoppy 69.00
Poster, Riders of The Dead Line, Movie, 1940s 35.00
Radio, Black 600.00
Radio, Red, Arvin ....125.00 To 250.00
Record Album, Hoppy, Calif. & Lucky, Photos, 2 Records 75.00
Record Album, Square Dance Holdup & Bozo's Party, Book 25.00
Record Album, Square Dance Holdup, 17 Pages of Photos 45.00
Record, Capital, Hoppy On Front, 1950s 28.00
Reel, For Viewmaster, Hoppy & Topper 12.00
Ring, Face 40.00
Rocker, Child's, T.V. 395.00
School Bag 175.00
Shooting Gallery, Tin Lithograph, Windup, Box 275.00
Sleeping Bag 300.00
Slide, Neckerchief 35.00
Spurs 125.00

Stationery, 21 Cards, 17 Envelopes, Box, Buzza Cardoza 175.00
Stationery, 25 Folders 18.00
Stationery, Unopened, 24 Pages 95.00
Storybook, Hoppy, Danny 18.00
Sweater, Gray 125.00
Sweater, Picture of Hoppy On Front 125.00
Target, 2–Sided, Tin Lithograph 58.00
Thermos .... 25.00 To 45.00
Tie & Holder 50.00
Transogram, 1950, Coloring Outfit, Box 285.00
Tumbler, 5 In. 25.00
Tumbler, Black Letters 21.00
Tumbler, Hoppy & Horse, Black, Milk Glass, 4 7/8 In. 31.00
Tumbler, Milk Glass 32.00
Watch, 1958 .... 85.00
Watch, Original Strap .... 75.00 To 95.00
Watch, Pocket 295.00
Wood Burning Set, Box 225.00
Wristwatch, Box 300.00

Howdy Doody and Buffalo Bob were the main characters in a
children's series televised from 1947 to 1960. Howdy was a
redheaded puppet. The series became popular with college students
in the late 1970s when Buffalo Bob began to lecture on the
campuses.

HOWDY DOODY, Chair, Musical 65.00
Bank, Ceramic, Bust, 1950 .... 300.00 To 400.00
Bank, Head, Vandor .... 90.00 To 95.00
Bank, Riding Pig, Ceramic 175.00
Belt Buckle 25.00
Book, Howdy Doody Fun 20.00
Book, It's Howdy Doody Time, Little Golden Book 14.00
Camera, Flub–A–Dub, Box 100.00
Car, Nylint 480.00
Catalog, Merchandise, 1955 .... 50.00
Chair, Musical 65.00
Clock, Alarm, Talking, Bob Smith's Wake–Up Voice, Box 135.00
Clock, Time Teacher, Package 40.00
Comic Book 20.00
Cookie Jar .... 250.00 To 700.00
Cookie Jar, Brush 500.00
Cookie Jar, Cookie–Go–Round 85.00
Cookie Jar, Vandor 150.00
Cutout Detective Disguises, Poll Parrot Shoes, Uncut 20.00
Doll, Cloth Body, Rubber Face, Moving Mouth, Goldberger, 1950s 90.00
Doll, Cloth, Clothes, 10 1/2 In. 15.00
Doll, Composition, Original Clothes, Brown Sleep Eyes, 1940s 275.00
Doll, Composition, Sleep Eyes, Effanbee, 19 In. 195.00
Figure Set, T. V. Show, Plastic, Box, 5 Piece 135.00
Figure, Jointed, Front of N. B. C. Mike 145.00
Flashlight Ring 95.00
Game, Bean Bag, Kagran 125.00
Game, Board, Howdy Doody's T.V., Milton Bradley .... 25.00 To 35.00
Game, Card 24.00
Game, Flip–A–Ring, Flub–A–Dub, Package 95.00
Key Chain, Box 9.00
Key Chain, Puzzle 20.00
Lunch Box, Dome Cover, Plastic 8.00
Lunch Box, Howdy, Princess & Chuck Wagon, 1958 .... 125.00
Marionette, 1950s .... 100.00 To 250.00
Marionette, Princess Summerfall Winterspring 125.00
Night–Light, Figural .... 95.00 To 135.00
Placemat, 8 Piece 55.00

Placemat, Paper, Kagran, 13 x 9 1/2 In.	10.00
Plaque, Howdy & Santa Claus, Lighted, Box	125.00
Plaque, Howdy's, Mr. Bluster & Clarabell Faces, 3 Piece	115.00
Plate, Mug & Bowl Set, Graphic, 3 Piece	175.00
Puppet Set, Howdy & Clarabell, Cloth, Vinyl, Mary Hartline, Pair	185.00
Puppet Show, Plastic Figures, On Card, 5 Piece	115.00
Puppet, Hand	38.00
Record Player, Box	200.00
Ribbon, NBC, 36 In.	10.00
Ring, Flasher, Gray Back, 8 Piece	85.00
Ring, Flashlight	95.00 To 125.00
Ring, Flicker	15.00
Rocker, Child's	65.00
Salt & Pepper, Howdy's Face	95.00 To 115.00
Spoon, Silver Plate	20.00
Tin, Cookie–Go–Round	165.00
Toy Set, 5 Plastic Characters, Movable Mouths, Box	80.00
Toy, Circus Wheel, Paper, Poll Parrot Shoe	25.00
Toy, Howdy Doody Band, Box	1550.00
Tumbler, Clarabell, Red, 1930s, 4 3/8 In.	35.00
Tumbler, Dilly Dally Is Circus Big Shot, White, Blue, 4 1/4 In.	8.00
Tumbler, Doodyville Elephant Squirts Clarabell, 4 1/4 In.	10.00
Tumbler, Hey Kids, Come On Along, Welch's Sure Helps, 4 1/8 In.	12.00
Tumbler, Hey Kids, On Land, Sea, Welch's Tastes Best, 4 1/8 In.	8.00
Wristwatch, 40th Anniversary, Box	45.00
Wristwatch, Moving Eyes, Box, 1954	450.00

Hull pottery was made in Crooksville, Ohio, from 1905. Addis E. Hull bought the Acme Pottery Company and started making ceramic wares. In 1917, A. E. Hull Pottery began making art pottery as well as the commercial wares. For a short time, 1921 to 1929, the firm also sold pottery imported from Europe. The dinnerwares of the 1940s, including the Little Red Riding Hood line, the high gloss artwares of the 1950s, and the matte wares of the 1940s, are all popular with collectors. The firm officially closed in March 1986.

HULL, Ashtray, Blue, Metal Afghan Dog Center Finial, Round, 5 In.	15.00
Ashtray, Serenade, 13 x 10 1/2 In.	30.00
Ashtray, Unicorn, Red & Green	20.00
Bank, Little Red Riding Hood	210.00
Basket, Bow–Knot, Blue, 12 In.	995.00
Basket, Bow–Knot, Pink, 12 In.	995.00
Basket, Butterfly, Cream, Turquoise	40.00
Basket, Capri, Seagreen, 6 3/4 In.	45.00
Basket, Crab Apple, Hanging	300.00
Basket, Ebb Tide, 6 1/2 In.	38.00
Basket, Open Rose, Pink & Green, 6 In.	150.00
Basket, Parchment & Pine, 16 1/2 In.	50.00 To 70.00
Basket, Tokay, 10 1/2 In.	80.00
Basket, Tokay, Green & White, 10 1/2 In.	45.00
Basket, Wildflower, 16 x 10 1/2 In.	120.00
Basket, Woodland, Glossy, Green & Blue, 8 3/4 In.	48.00
Bowl, Ebbtide, 15 3/4 In.	190.00
Bowl, Sunglow, 9 1/2 In.	12.00
Bowl, Water Lily, Cream & Green, 13 1/2 x 21 In.	90.00
Butter, Cover, Little Red Riding Hood	150.00 To 235.00
Candleholder, Open Rose	125.00
Candlestick, Bow–Knot, Pair	50.00
Candlestick, Magnolia, Pair	48.00
Clock, Birdhouse, Sessions	225.00
Console Bowl, Bow–Knot, 13 In.	175.00
Console Bowl, Iris	35.00
Console Bowl, Water Lily, Brown	125.00

Console Set, Butterfly, Window Box, Candlesticks, Glossy White 55.00
Console Set, Magnolia, Blue & Pink, 3 Piece 90.00
Console Set, Parchment & Pine 65.00
Console Set, Water Lily, Brown, 3 Piece 125.00
Console, Calla Lily, Handle 60.00
Cookie Jar, Barefoot Boy 350.00
Cookie Jar, Big Red Apple 35.00
Cookie Jar, Butterfly, Window Box, 12 In. 20.00
Cookie Jar, Duck, Logo 45.00
Cookie Jar, Floral, No. 48 .... 38.00
Cookie Jar, Gingerbread Boy, Brown .... 45.00 To 52.00
Cookie Jar, Little Red Riding Hood, Closed Basket, Poinsettias 120.00
Cookie Jar, Little Red Riding Hood, Gold Snowflakes 110.00
Cookie Jar, Little Red Riding Hood, Gold Trim 120.00
Cookie Jar, Little Red Riding Hood, Open Basket 145.00
Cookie Jar, Little Red Riding Hood, Yellow Basket, Blue Trim Apron 130.00
Cornucopia, Bow-Knot, Pink & Blue, 6 1/2 In. 55.00
Cornucopia, Butterfly, 6 1/2 In. 40.00
Cornucopia, Calla Lilly, 8 x 9 In. 50.00
Cornucopia, Calla Lily 35.00
Cornucopia, Dogwood, 3 3/4 In. 40.00
Cornucopia, Parchment & Pine .... 15.00 To 22.50
Cornucopia, Wildflower, Pink & Blue, 7 x 7 1/2 In., Pair 90.00
Creamer, Little Red Riding Hood, Pour Through Head 175.00
Creamer, Magnolia 25.00
Cup, House & Garden 2.00
Ewer, Bow-Knot 60.00
Ewer, Dogwood, 11 1/2 In. 245.00
Ewer, Dogwood, Label, 8 1/2 In. 85.00
Ewer, Dogwood, Peach, 4 3/4 In. 35.00
Ewer, Wildflower, 8 1/2 In. 72.00
Figurine, Dachshund, Black, 6 x 14 In. 49.00
Figurine, Dancing Girl, Pink, 1940s, 7 In. 40.00
Figurine, Swan, White, 8 In. 22.00
Flowerpot, Bow-Knot 48.00
Flowerpot, Butterfly, 5 x 6 In. 35.00
Flowerpot, Sueno Tulip, 6 In. 55.00
Grease Jar, Little Red Riding Hood 975.00
Jardiniere, Water Lily, 5 In. 125.00
Lamp, Ewer, Woodland, Gloss 285.00
Lamp, Poppy, Factory 375.00
Lamp, Woodland 600.00
Lavabo Set, Blue 95.00
Lavabo, Butterfly 85.00
Match Holder, Little Red Riding Hood, Unpainted 330.00
Mug, Beer, Embossed, 1920 .... 25.00
Mug, Beer, Happy Days Are Here Again 20.00
Mustard, Spoon, Little Red Riding Hood 195.00
Pie Pan, Nuline, Blue 17.50
Pitcher & Mug, Brown, White, 6 Piece 15.00
Pitcher, Ebb Tide, 14 In. 58.00
Pitcher, Milk, Little Red Riding Hood, 8 In. 135.00
Pitcher, Open Rose, 13 In. 225.00
Pitcher, Serenade, Blue Ground 60.00
Pitcher, Serenade, Chickadees, Blue, 10 1/2 In. 50.00
Pitcher, Wildflower, White, 13 1/2 In. 275.00
Pitcher, Woodland, Glossy, 6 1/4 In. 15.00
Planter, Art Deco Woman, 7 1/2 In. 4.50
Planter, Boy On Fence 15.00
Planter, Duck, 9 x 10 In. 95.00
Planter, Duck, Green & Pink 25.00
Planter, Figural, Swan, Signed, 7 1/2 In. 7.50
Planter, Giraffe 30.00

Planter, Kitten 30.00
Planter, Kitten & Spool 15.00
Planter, Knight 34.00
Planter, Madonna 20.00
Planter, Madonna, Yellow 15.00
Planter, Poodle 10.00
Planter, Poppy, 6 1/2 In. 100.00
Planter, Rooster 14.00
Planter, Swan, Figural, Green, High Gloss, Signed, 7 1/2 In. 7.00
Planter, Windmill, White, Gold Trim 21.00
Plaque, Bow-Knot 200.00
Plaque, Bow-Knot, 10 In. 425.00
Salt & Pepper, House & Garden, Small 15.00
Salt & Pepper, Little Red Riding Hood, 3 1/2 In. .... 18.00 To 25.00
Salt & Pepper, Little Red Riding Hood, 5 1/2 In. .... 60.00 To 75.00
Salt & Pepper, Pig 20.00
Stein, Elk's Head, B. P. O. E. Logo, 6 In. 25.00
Stein, Happy Days Are Here Again 18.00
Sugar & Creamer, Little Red Riding Hood 160.00
Sugar, Little Red Riding Hood 55.00
Sugar, Magnolia 20.00
Tea Set, Blossom Flite, 3 Piece 65.00
Tea Set, Butterfly, 3 Piece 38.00
Tea Set, Magnolia 89.00
Tea Set, Water Lily, Peach 165.00
Teapot, Bow-Knot ....90.00 To 100.00
Teapot, Dogwood 129.00
Teapot, Little Red Riding Hood 295.00
Teapot, Magnolia ....90.00 To 100.00
Teapot, Magnolia, Blue 72.00
Teapot, Royal 45.00
Teapot, Serenade, Pink 85.00
Teapot, Water Lily, Brown 75.00
Teapot, Water Lily, Pink 110.00
Tokay, Basket 5.00
Vase, Bow-Knot, 8 1/2 In. 85.00
Vase, Bow-Knot, Blue To Pink, 8 1/2 In. 175.00
Vase, Bow-Knot, Pink, 6 1/2 In. 80.00
Vase, Butterfly, 7 In. 28.00
Vase, Calla Lily, 5 In. 45.00
Vase, Granada, 9 In. 30.00
Vase, Magnolia, 5 1/2 In. 12.00
Vase, Magnolia, 6 1/2 In. 25.00
Vase, Magnolia, Matte, 15 In. 260.00
Vase, Magnolia, Matte, Pink, 6 1/2 In. 38.00
Vase, Magnolia, Pink & Blue, 8 1/2 In. 55.00
Vase, Mardi Gras, 9 1/2 In. 35.00
Vase, Open Rose, Hand, 8 1/2 In. 125.00
Vase, Open Rose, Wing Handles, 6 1/2 In. 6.00
Vase, Orchid, Blue, 8 1/2 In. 95.00
Vase, Pansy, Blue Matte, 6 In. 65.00
Vase, Parchment & Pine, Kitten Head 35.00
Vase, Pinecone, Blue, 6 1/ 2 In. 68.00
Vase, Planter, Strawberry, Footed, 6 1/2 In. 8.00
Vase, Poppy, 8 1/2 In. 70.00
Vase, Red Strawberries, Scalloped, Gold Trim, Handles, 6 1/2 In. 17.00
Vase, Reindeer, 8 In. 65.00
Vase, Rosella, Pink, Glossy, 15 x 8 1/2 In. 45.00
Vase, Sueno Tulip, Blue, 8 1/2 In. 60.00
Vase, Tokay, 8 1/4 In. 40.00
Vase, Water Lily, 6 1/2 In. 35.00
Vase, Water Lily, Matte, 10 1/2 In. 60.00
Vase, Water Lily, Pink & Aqua, Label, 10 1/2 In. 65.00

Vase, Water Lily, Pink, Green, 6 1/2 In. 32.00
Vase, Wildflower, 7 1/2 In. .... 40.00 To 45.00
Vase, Wildflower, Cream & Pink, 5 1/2 In., Pair 55.00
Vase, Wildflower, Cream & Pink, 5 x 6 1/2 In. 45.00
Vase, Wildflower, Yellow & Rose, 15 x 10 1/2 In. 85.00
Vase, Woodland, 7 1/2 In. .... 20.00 To 45.00
Vase, Woodland, Double, Pink, Green, 8 1/2 In. 40.00
Vase, Woodland, Pink, 16 x 8 1/2 In. 47.50
Vase, Woodland, Yellow, Green, Matte, 8 1/2 In. 65.00
Wall Pocket, Bow–Knot, Wiskbroom, Blue, 8 In. 65.00
Wall Pocket, Butterfly, Whiskbroom Shape, 8 1/2 In. 7.00
Wall Pocket, Cup & Saucer, Bow Knot, Blue 75.00
Wall Pocket, Cup & Saucer, Sunglow, Pink 55.00
Wall Pocket, Geese, Pink & Gray, Pair 60.00
Wall Pocket, Little Red Riding Hood 200.00
Wall Pocket, Sunglow, Pitcher Shape, Pink, Gold Trim 20.00
Window Box, Butterfly, Glossy 25.00
Window Box, Serenade .... 28.00 To 35.00
Window Box, Woodland 18.00
Window Box, Woodland, 10 x 14 In. 30.00

Hummel figurines, based on the drawings of Berta Hummel, are made by the W. Goebel Porzellanfabrik of Oeslau, Germany, now Rodenthal, West Germany. They were first made in 1934. The mark has changed through the years. The following are the approximate dates for each of the marks: *Crown* mark, 1935 to 1949; *U.S. Zone, Germany,* 1946 to 1948; *West Germany,* after 1949; *full bee* with variations, 1950 to 1959; *stylized bee,* 1960 to 1972; *three line mark,* 1968 to 1979; *vee over gee,* 1972 to 1979; *new mark, West Germany* 1979 to 1990; and the *Goebel, Germany,* mark introduced in 1991.

HUMMEL, Ashtray, Happy Pastime, No. 62, Stylized Bee 75.00
Ashtray, Joyful, No. 33, Stylized Bee 150.00
Bell, Annual, 1978 .... 25.00
Bell, Annual, 1979 .... 25.00
Bell, Annual, 1981 .... 50.00
Bell, Annual, 1984 .... 35.00
Bookends, Book Worm, Boy & Girl, Full Bee 395.00
Bookends, Goose Girl, Stylized Bee 125.00
Calendar, 1969 .... 35.00
Calendar, 1970 .... 30.00
Calendar, 1977 .... 15.00
Calendar, 1984 .... 10.00
Candleholder, No. 24/I, Lullaby, Full Bee 195.00
Candleholder, No. 24/I, Lullaby, Stylized Bee 139.00
Candleholder, No. 24/III, Lullaby, Vee Over Gee 398.00
Candleholder, No. 37, Herald Angels, Stylized Bee 200.00
Candleholder, No. 439, A Gentle Glow 130.00
Clock, No. 422, Chapel Time 725.00
Figurine, No. 1, Puppy Love, Full Bee 245.00
Figurine, No. 1, Puppy Love, Stylized Bee 225.00
Figurine, No. 2/0, Little Fiddler, Stylized Bee 165.00
Figurine, No. 2/II, Little Fiddler, Vee Over Gee 500.00
Figurine, No. 3/II, Book Worm, Vee Over Gee .... 300.00 To 565.00
Figurine, No. 5, Strolling Along, Stylized Bee 125.00
Figurine, No. 6/0, Sensitive Hunter, Full Bee 180.00
Figurine, No. 6/I, Sensitive Hunter, Vee Over Gee 125.00
Figurine, No. 7/0, Merry Wanderer, Crown Mark 495.00
Figurine, No. 8, Book Worm, Full Bee 100.00
Figurine, No. 8, Book Worm, Stylized Bee 115.00
Figurine, No. 9, Begging His Shore, Stylized Bee 195.00
Figurine, No. 10/I, Flower Madonna, Full Bee 210.00
Figurine, No. 10/I, Flower Madonna, Stylized Bee 225.00
Figurine, No. 11/0, Merry Wanderer, Stylized Bee 108.00

Figurine, No. 11/2/0, Merry Wanderer, Full Bee 155.00
Figurine, No. 12/I, Chimney Sweep, Full Bee 175.00
Figurine, No. 12/I, Chimney Sweep, Vee Over Gee 94.00
Figurine, No. 15/0, Hear Ye, Hear Ye, Full Bee 200.00
Figurine, No. 16/2/0, Little Hiker, Stylized Bee 85.00
Figurine, No. 18, Christ Child, Stylized Bee 110.00
Figurine, No. 20, Prayer Before Battle, Full Bee 175.00
Figurine, No. 21/0, Heavenly Angel, Full Bee 130.00
Figurine, No. 28/II, Wayside Devotion, Crown Mark 695.00
Figurine, No. 32, Little Gabriel, Full Bee 170.00
Figurine, No. 43, March Winds, Full Bee 140.00
Figurine, No. 47/0, Goose Girl, Full Bee .... 250.00 To 275.00
Figurine, No. 47/3/0, Goose Girl, Stylized Bee 119.00
Figurine, No. 49/0, To Market, Stylized Bee 175.00
Figurine, No. 50/2/0, Volunteers, Vee Over Gee 120.00
Figurine, No. 50/I, Volunteers, Full Bee 800.00
Figurine, No. 51/2/0, Village Boy, Three Line Mark 65.00
Figurine, No. 52/I, Going To Grandmas, Vee Over Gee .... 318.00 To 400.00
Figurine, No. 53, Joyful, Full Bee 80.00
Figurine, No. 53, Joyful, Stylized Bee 55.00
Figurine, No. 57/0, Chick Girl, Crown Mark 400.00
Figurine, No. 58/0, Playmates, Crown Mark 275.00
Figurine, No. 63, Singing Lesson, Stylized Bee 58.00
Figurine, No. 65, Farewell, Crown Mark 525.00
Figurine, No. 65, Farewell, Full Bee 255.00
Figurine, No. 67, Doll Mother, Stylized Bee 165.00
Figurine, No. 68, Lost Sheep, Full Bee 250.00
Figurine, No. 68/0, Lost Sheep, Vee Over Gee 90.00
Figurine, No. 71, Stormy Weather, Stylized Bee 440.00
Figurine, No. 71, Stormy Weather, Vee Over Gee 200.00
Figurine, No. 71/2/0, Stormy Weather 180.00
Figurine, No. 72, Spring Cheer, Crown & Full Bee 198.00
Figurine, No. 79, Globe Trotter, Full Bee 255.00
Figurine, No. 79, Globe Trotter, Stylized Bee 92.00
Figurine, No. 80, Little Scholar, Full Bee 175.00
Figurine, No. 80, Little Scholar, Stylized Bee 125.00
Figurine, No. 81, School Girl, Crown Mark 329.00
Figurine, No. 81/2/0, School Girl, Crown & Full Bee 275.00
Figurine, No. 84/0, Worship, Full Bee 165.00
Figurine, No. 85/II, Serenade, Vee Over Gee 195.00
Figurine, No. 95, Brother, Stylized Bee 95.00
Figurine, No. 109/II, Happy Traveler, Stylized Bee 325.00
Figurine, No. 119, Postman, Stylized Bee 150.00
Figurine, No. 123, Max and Moritz, Full Bee 170.00
Figurine, No. 124/0, Hello, Full Bee 250.00
Figurine, No. 127, Doctor, Full Bee 140.00
Figurine, No. 131, Street Singer, Full Bee 160.00
Figurine, No. 135, Soloist, Full Bee .... 120.00 To 150.00
Figurine, No. 136/V, Friends, Vee Over Gee 500.00
Figurine, No. 141/3/0, Apple Tree Girl, Full Bee 120.00
Figurine, No. 141/I, Apple Tree Girl, Stylized Bee .... 160.00 To 162.00
Figurine, No. 142/3/0, Apple Tree Boy, Stylized Bee 70.00
Figurine, No. 142/I, Apple Tree Boy, Vee Over Gee 108.00
Figurine, No. 143, Boots, Full Bee 350.00
Figurine, No. 143/0, Boots, Full Bee 160.00
Figurine, No. 143/0, Boots, Vee Over Gee 80.00
Figurine, No. 150/II/A, Happy Days, Full Bee 110.00
Figurine, No. 152/11/B, Umbrella Girl, Vee Over Gee 750.00
Figurine, No. 152/II/A, Umbrella Boy, Vee Over Gee 650.00
Figurine, No. 152/II/B, Umbrella Boy, Vee Over Gee 750.00
Figurine, No. 152/II/B, Umbrella Girl, Vee Over Gee 650.00
Figurine, No. 153/0, Auf Wiedersehen, Stylized Bee 165.00
Figurine, No. 153/0, Auf Wiedersehen, With Hat, Full Bee 3000.00

◆◆

To protect your investment in household furnishings, rewire any
lamps in your home that are 15 or more years old. Cords crack and
are a fire hazard.

◆◆

Figurine, No. 153/I, Auf Wiedersehen, Vee Over Gee	195.00
Figurine, No. 154/0, Waiter, Vee Over Gee	95.00
Figurine, No. 170/III, School Boys, Vee Over Gee	1000.00 To 1500.00
Figurine, No. 171, Little Sweeper, Stylized Bee	80.00
Figurine, No. 172/II & 173/II, Festival Harmony, Vee Over Gee, Pair	500.00
Figurine, No. 177/III, School Girls, Vee Over Gee	1025.00 To 1500.00
Figurine, No. 178, Photographer, Three Line Mark	160.00
Figurine, No. 179, Coquettes, Full Bee	295.00
Figurine, No. 184, Latest News, Stylized Bee	162.00 To 300.00
Figurine, No. 185, Accordian Boy, Vee Over Gee	75.00
Figurine, No. 195/2/0, Barnyard Hero, Full Bee	165.00 To 175.00
Figurine, No. 196/0, Telling Her Secret, Three Line Mark	160.00
Figurine, No. 196/I, Telling Her Secret, Vee Over Gee	273.00
Figurine, No. 197/2/0, Be Patient, Vee Over Gee	130.00
Figurine, No. 198, Home From Market, Full Bee	215.00
Figurine, No. 200/0, Little Goat Herder, Three Line Mark	130.00
Figurine, No. 200/0, Little Goat Herder, Vee Over Gee	95.00
Figurine, No. 201/I, Retreat To Safety, Vee Over Gee	150.00
Figurine, No. 217, Boy With Toothache, Full Bee	135.00
Figurine, No. 218/2/0, Birthday Serenade, Stylized Bee	295.00 To 350.00
Figurine, No. 220, We Congratulate, Three Line Mark	60.00 To 80.00
Figurine, No. 220/2/0, We Congratulate, Full Bee	450.00
Figurine, No. 226, The Mail Is Here, Stylized Bee	450.00
Figurine, No. 257, For Mother, Three Line Mark	88.00
Figurine, No. 258, Which Hand?, Three Line Mark	90.00
Figurine, No. 311, Kiss Me, Three Line Mark	500.00
Figurine, No. 317, Not For You!, Three Line Mark	185.00
Figurine, No. 319, Doll Bath, Three Line Mark	150.00
Figurine, No. 321, Wash Day, Three Line Mark	165.00
Figurine, No. 332, Soldier Boy, Three Line Mark	295.00
Figurine, No. 333, Blessed Event	230.00
Figurine, No. 345, A Fair Measure, Vee Over Gee	113.00
Figurine, No. 346, Smart Little Sister, Three Line Mark	165.00
Figurine, No. 347, Adventure Bound, Vee Over Gee	2000.00
Figurine, No. 348, Ring Around The Rosie, Vee Over Gee	1000.00 To 1100.00
Figurine, No. 385, Chicken–Licken, Vee Over Gee	129.00
Font, No. 91B, Angel At Prayer	65.00
Font, No. 147, Angel Shrine, Three Line Mark	48.00
Lamp, No. 56A, Culprits, Crown Mark	350.00
Lamp, No. 56A, Culprits, Vee Over Gee	175.00
Plaque, No. 180, Tuneful Good Night, Vee Over Gee	180.00
Plaque, No. 92, Merry Wanderer, Crown Mark	295.00
Plaque, No. 93, Little Fiddler, Crown Mark	295.00
Plate, Anniversary, 1975	65.00 To 80.00
Plate, Anniversary, 1980	50.00 To 125.00
Plate, Annual, 1971	695.00
Plate, Annual, 1973	70.00
Plate, Annual, 1974	40.00
Plate, Annual, 1981	30.00
Plate, Christmas, 1974	42.50
Plate, Mother's Day, Rabbits, 1975	40.00
Plate, No. 736, Daisies Don't Tell	120.00
Plate, No. 738, Valentine Gift	120.00

Hutschenreuther Porcelain Company of Selb, Germany, was established in 1814 and is still working. The company makes fine quality porcelain dinnerwares and figurines. The mark has changed through the years, but the name and the lion insignia appear in most versions.

HUTSCHENREUTHER, Candlestick, Cupids Holding Torches, Signed, 6 3/4 In., Pr. ...	275.00
Centerpiece, Geometric Shapes Supporting Nude, 15 In.	77.00
Cigarette Lighter, Pin Tray, Pastel Roses	18.00
Coffeepot, Richelieu, Cover, 9 1/2 Cup	125.00
Cup & Saucer, Richelieu	45.00
Cup & Saucer, Sylvia, 8 Sets	195.00
Figurine, Brennertown Band, 8 1/4 In.	345.00
Figurine, Cat, Sitting, White, Green Eyes, 7 In.	165.00
Figurine, Dachshund, Standing On Hind Legs, White, 7 In.	165.00
Figurine, Dancers, Purple & Yellow Costumes, 8 1/4 In.	345.00
Figurine, Elephant	95.00
Figurine, Nude Woman, Holding Gold Ball, Signed, 10 In.	395.00
Figurine, Nude Woman, On Gold Ball Base, 9 In.	115.00
Figurine, Panda	95.00
Figurine, Polar Bear On Gold Ball, 4 In.	145.00
Figurine, Spaniel	95.00
Flower Frog, Cupid Standing On Gold Bowl, 7 1/2 In.	725.00
Ginger Jar, Cobalt Blue, 8 In.	95.00
Group, Woman & Man Dancers, Werner, 8 1/4 In.	345.00
Plate, Dinner, Richelieu	50.00
Plate, Roses of Redonte, Box, 8 Piece	260.00
Plate, Silver–Wash Figures, Birds, 10 3/4 In., 10 Piece	225.00
Platter, Kensington, Oval, 15 x 11 In.	80.00
Teapot, Cover, Demitasse	20.00

An icon is a special, revered picture of Jesus, Mary, or a saint. These are usually Russian or Byzantine. The small icons collected today are made of wood and tin or precious metals. Many modern copies have been made in the old style and are being sold to unsuspecting tourists in Russia and Europe.

ICON, Anastasis, Resurrection & Descent Into Hell, Russia, 14 x 12 1/2 In.	2090.00
Brass Oklad, Gilt Frame, Shadowbox, Russia, 8 1/2 x 6 3/4 In.	375.00
Christ Pantocrator, Russia, 1908, 5 x 5 1/2 In.	440.00
Christ Pantocrator, Silver Gilt Engraving, Russia, 1899, 7 x 9 In.	885.00
Christ Pontocrator, Cloisonne, Moscow, 1895, 12 x 10 In. ....*Illus*	4180.00
Decollation of Saint John, Russia, 14 x 12 In.	990.00
Deisis, Crowned Christ, Virgin, John The Baptist, Greece, 14 x 20 In.	825.00
Doors Conceal Porcelain Assumption, Metal, 8 In.	375.00
Entombment of Christ, Russia, 19th Century, 14 1/4 x 17 1/4 In.	1350.00
Entry Into Jerusalem, Christ, Donkey, Followers, Russia, 11 x 13 In.	1550.00
Kazan Mother of God, Russia, 18th Century, 11 3/4 x 10 In.	1215.00

Icon, Christ Pontocrator, Cloisonne, Moscow, 1895, 12 x 10 In.

Madonna & Child, Russia, 2 1/4 x 2 1/2 In. 125.00
Mother of God Bogolubskaya, Virgin, Scroll, Russia, 11 x 14 In. 1540.00
Mother of God, Russia, 18th Century, 13 1/2 x 11 1/4 In. 1200.00
Pokrov, Saints In Borders, Russia, 19th Century, 17 1/2 x 14 3/4 In. 2860.00
Presentation of Christ In Temple, Russia, 17 1/2 x 17 3/8 In. 825.00
Prophet Elijah, Inscribed Scroll, Ivory Ground, Russia, 10 x 12 In. 2520.00
Resurrection With Feasts, 12 Festivals, Russia, 15 1/2 In. 525.00
Resurrection, Descent, Hell, Christ's Passion, Russia, 17 x 21 In. 1650.00
Saint, Silver, A. Sev'Yer, Russia, 2 1/2 x 2 1/4 In. 325.00
Saint, St. Petersburg, Silver, Russia, 1896–1908, 2 1/2 x 2 1/4 In. 357.50
Saints Antip, Basil & Tikhon, Russia, 12 3/4 x 11 1/4 In. 1870.00
Saints Gregory, Basil & John, Russia, 12 1/4 x 10 3/8 In. 1650.00
St. Elijah, Hagiograpical, Scenes, Russia, c.1780, 14 x 12 In. 1650.00
St. Euphronia, Standing In Cloud, Buildings, Russia, 10 x 12 In. 495.00
St. George, Slaying Dragon, Russia, 16 1/4 x 13 1/4 In. 1870.00
St. Nicholas, Oil & Gilt On Panel, Russia, 13 1/2 x 11 1/2 In. 880.00
St. Trifon, Silver Gilt, Moscow, c.1900 .... 2200.00
Tikhvin, Mother of God, 6 Various Saints, Russia, 10 x 12 In. 1870.00
Virgin & Child, Russia, 19th Century, 12 1/4 x 10 1/4 In. 825.00
Virgin of Kazakstan, Repousse Silver, Gilt Oklad, Russia, 12 1/4 In. 850.00

Imari patterns are named for the Japanese ware decorated with
orange and blue stylized flowers. The design on the Japanese ware
became so characteristic that the name *Imari* has come to mean any
pattern of this type. It was copied by the European factories of the
eighteenth and early–nineteenth centuries.

IMARI, Bowl, 18th Century, Shallow, 9 1/2 In. 160.00
Bowl, 9 1/2 In. 175.00
Bowl, Cover, Red & Turquoise Foliate, 3 1/2 In. 225.00
Bowl, Floral Reserves On Blue Ground, 11 In. .... 275.00 To 330.00
Bowl, Floral, Blues, Reds, Greens, Orange, 8 1/2 In. 235.00
Bowl, Garden Scenes, Birds, Lion Mask & Ring Handles, 12 3/8 In. 1980.00
Bowl, Hexagonal, 19th Century, 13 1/2 x 5 1/4 In. 300.00
Bowl, Panels of Birds, Flowers, 11 In. 135.00
Bowl, Scalloped Edge, 19th Century, 2 3/4 x 7 1/2 In. 195.00
Bowl, Shallow, 18 1/4 In. 375.00
Charger, Blue & White, 16 3/4 In. 90.00
Charger, Blue & White, Red Enameled & Gilt, 16 1/4 In. 250.00
Charger, Floral & Urn Design, 19th Century, 12 In. 385.00
Charger, Reds, Blues & Gold, 13 In. 175.00
Charger, Scalloped Border Design, 12 In. 100.00
Charger, Vase With Vining Flowers, Gold Outlined, 13 5/8 In. 375.00
Dish, Fish Form of A Pair of Fish, 10 1/4 In. 467.50
Dish, Scalloped Edge, 19th Century, 8 In. 110.00
Dish, Scalloped Edge, 19th Century, 8 1/2 In. 140.00
Figurine, Cat, 11 3/4 In. 75.00
Figurine, Foo Dogs, Polychrome, 15 1/2 In., Pair 110.00
Figurine, Seal, Porcelain, 9 In. 50.00
Headrest, Cat, 13 In., Pair 110.00
Planter, Cobalt Blue & Red, Gold Highlights, 7 1/4 x 9 1/4 In. 385.00
Planter, Undertray, Paneled Floral Designs, 13 3/4 In., Pair 885.00
Punch Bowl, Garden Scene Panels, Center Medallion, 10 1/2 In. 605.00
Vase, Blue & White, 14 1/4 In., Pair 430.00
Vase, Floral Landscape, Foo Lions, Ruffled, Baluster, 32 3/4 In. 770.00
Vase, Gilt, 9 5/8 In. 245.00

Imperial Glass Corporation was founded in Bellaire, Ohio, in 1901.
It became a division of Lenox, Inc., in 1977 and was sold to Arthur
R. Lorch in 1981. It was sold again in 1982. It went bankrupt in
1982 and some of the molds and assets have been offered to other
companies. The Imperial glass preferred by the collector is stretch
glass, art glass, carnival glass, and the top–quality tablewares.

IMPERIAL, Cake Stand, Cape Cod 65.00

Candlewick, Ashtray, Round, 4 In.	4.00
Candlewick, Basket, 11 In.	75.00
Candlewick, Bowl, 3 Footed, 8 1/2 In.	95.00
Candlewick, Bowl, Blue, Footed, Etched	45.00
Candlewick, Bowl, Floral Etch, Sterling Base, 5 In.	45.00
Candlewick, Butter, Individual, 4 1/2 In.	8.00
Candlewick, Candleholder, Double, Pair	30.00
Candlewick, Candlestick, Arched, Pair	175.00
Candlewick, Candlestick, Square	30.00
Candlewick, Creamer	8.00
Candlewick, Cup & Saucer	7.00
Candlewick, Cup Plate, Off–Center Ring, 6 In.	6.00
Candlewick, Fruit Tray, 10 1/2 In.	130.00
Candlewick, Lazy Susan, 3 Piece	200.00
Candlewick, Plate, 6 In.	3.00
Candlewick, Plate, 7 In.	8.00
Candlewick, Plate, Advertising, 1937, 4 In.	18.00
Candlewick, Plate, Birthday, 14 In.	235.00
Candlewick, Plate, Deviled Egg, Center Handle	48.00
Candlewick, Platter, 13 In.	14.00
Candlewick, Platter, 16 In.	175.00
Candlewick, Relish, 3 Footed	50.00
Candlewick, Relish, 3 Sections, Rectangular, 10 In.	45.00
Candlewick, Relish, 4 Sections, 8 1/2 In.	18.00
Candlewick, Relish, 4 Sections, 12 In.	40.00 To 45.00
Candlewick, Server, Deviled Egg	70.00
Candlewick, Soup, Dish	8.00
Candlewick, Sugar & Creamer, Individual	18.00
Candlewick, Sugar, Cover	11.00
Candlewick, Tray, Center Handle, Round, 8 In.	30.00
Candlewick, Tray, Handles, Round, 14 In.	50.00
Candlewick, Tray, Pastry, 11 1/2 In.	38.00
Candlewick, Vase, Fan, 6 In.	40.00
Candlewick, Wine, Yellow	30.00
Cape Cod, Bowl, Footed, 10 In.	50.00
Cape Cod, Cake Plate, Footed, Round	48.00
Cape Cod, Cake Plate, Footed, Square	77.00
Cape Cod, Cordial, Red	30.00
Cape Cod, Cup & Saucer, Red	30.00
Cape Cod, Goblet, Water, Red	20.00
Cape Cod, Sherbet, Red	15.00
Cape Cod, Sugar & Creamer, Square	40.00
Catawba Grape, Compote	20.00
Cathay, Lamp, Wedding, Jade Green, Crystal Globe, Pair	174.00
Colonial, Goblet, Lemonade, Handle, Marigold	45.00
D'Angelo, Pitcher, Crystal	60.00
Delaware, Tankard, Green	90.00
Figurine, Man, Sitting, Chicken On Knee, 2 1/4 x 3 1/2 In.	60.00
Jewels, Vase, Marked, 6 In.	185.00
Katy, Plate, Amber, 9 In.	8.00
Mt. Boys, Mug, Granny, Paul Webb	40.00
Owl, Sugar & Creamer, Cobalt Blue	36.00
Paneled, Rose Bowl, Cobalt Blue	15.00
Poinsetta, Pitcher, Milk	55.00
Robin, Water Set, Helios Green, 7 Piece	140.00
Shell, Bowl, Purple, 7 In.	27.00
Tree Bark, Pitcher, 2 Tumblers	49.50
Windmill, Plate, Cobalt Blue	35.00
Zippered Heart, Bowl, Amethyst, 5 In.	50.00
Zippered Heart, Sauce, Purple	29.00
Zodiac, Compote, Peacock	15.00

Indian Tree is a china pattern that was popular during the last half of the nineteenth century. It was copied from earlier Indian textile patterns that were very similar. The pattern includes the crooked branch of a tree and a partial landscape with exotic flowers and leaves. Green, blue, pink, and orange were the favored colors used in the design.

INDIAN TREE, Bowl, Cereal, Scalloped, Coalport	20.00
Compote, Fruit, Coalport, 9 1/2 In.	150.00
Cup & Saucer, Coalport	28.00
Plate, Scalloped, Coalport, 6 3/4 In.	20.00
Sugar & Creamer, Coalport	125.00
Sugar & Creamer, Cover, Crown–Clarence, Large	15.00
Teapot, Coalport	165.00
Tray, Scalloped, Coalport, 10 1/2 In.	85.00

Indian art from North America has attracted the collector for many years. Each tribe has its own distinctive designs and techniques. Baskets, jewelry, pottery, and leatherwork are of greatest collector interest. Eskimo art is listed in another section in this book.

INDIAN, Bag, Cheyenne, Bandolier, Beaded, 1880	8800.00
Bag, Chippewa, Floral Beadwork Design On Black Velvet	2750.00
Bag, Nez Perce, Corn Husk	1150.00
Bag, Nez Perce, Corn Husk, Embroidered, Morning Star, Handles, 15 In.	715.00
Bag, Nez Perce, Corn Husk, Red, Green & Black, c.1890	1600.00
Bag, Plains, Trade Beads Various Patterns, Flap Cover, 5 x 4 In.	295.00
Bag, Woodlands, Bandolier, Floral Beadwork, 45 1/2 x 16 1/2 In.	750.00
Basket, Algonquin, Birch Bark, Scraped Leaf Designs, 13 x 24 1/2 In.	200.00
Basket, Apache, Flaring Sides, Geometric Design, c.1920, 15 In.	1045.00
Basket, Atsuqewi, Twisted Beargrass & Redbud, Twined Band, 6 1/2 In.	250.00
Basket, Cherokee, Oak Splint, Wooden Handle, B. Jannper, 12 1/2 In.	82.50
Basket, Cherokee, Presentation, 4 x 6 In.	225.00
Basket, Hopi, Wicker, 1920, 12 In.	165.00
Basket, Hupa, Acorn Storage, Twined Beargrass, 7 1/2 x 10 In.	75.00
Basket, Nootka, Cover, For Glass Float Balls, Cedar, 6 1/4 In.	105.00
Basket, Northwest, Root, Twined Spruce, Cover, Swing Handle, 5 In.	357.00
Basket, Ottawa, Porcupine Quill Applique In Foliage Pattern	70.00
Basket, Papago, 1910, 18 In.	225.00
Basket, Papago, 3 1/2 x 7 In.	125.00
Basket, Papago, Berry Picking, Birchbark, 22 x 14 In.	400.00
Basket, Papago, Cover, Flying Bat Figure, 3 1/2 x 4 1/2 In.	200.00
Basket, Papago, Dark Brown, 3 1/2 x 8 1/2 In.	88.00
Basket, Papago, Dark Brown, 3 x 10 In.	180.00
Basket, Papago, Dark Brown, Black Trim, 4 1/2 x 10 In.	260.00
Basket, Papago, Friendship, 4 x 9 In.	200.00
Basket, Papago, Golden Brown, 14 1/2 x 11 In.	160.00
Basket, Papago, Light Brown, 3 x 7 1/2 In.	80.00
Basket, Pima, Lightning Bolt Design, 11 In.	1100.00
Basket, Pima, Prehistoric–Type Braid Rim, 4 1/2 x 7 1/2 In.	325.00
Basket, Pima, Round Center, 4 Petal Tips Form Rim, c.1910, 7 1/2 In.	412.50
Basket, Pima, Round, 14 In.	98.00
Basket, Pomo, Northern, Boat Shape, 1890	2200.00
Basket, Salishan, Berry, Bowl Shape, Braided Rim, Beargrass, 6 In.	85.00
Basket, Sewing, Braided Sweetgrass, Dyed Splint, Square, 1930	45.00
Basket, Southwest, Geometric Design, 17 1/4 In.	770.00
Basket, Washo, Beaded, 1910–1920, Small	2800.00
Basket, Woodland, Lid, Potato Print Designs, 18 1/2 x 18 1/2 In.	275.00
Belt Buckle, Shoshone, Beaded	75.00
Belt, Plains, Beaded & Tacked Hide, 1 In. Wide, 59 In.	495.00
Blanket, Navajo, Browns, 4 x 6 Ft.	*Illus* 415.00
Blanket, Navajo, Chief's, 57 x 66 In.	3080.00
Blanket, Navajo, Chief's, Homespun, Second Phase 12 Spot, 48 x 68 In.	2420.00
Blanket, Navajo, Child's, Handspun Wool, 60 Threads Per Inch, 1880	6500.00

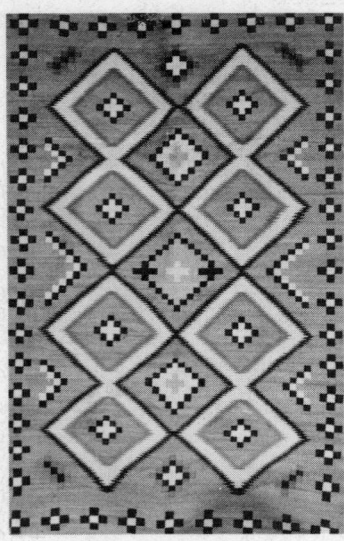

Indian, Blanket, Navajo, Browns, 4 x 6 Ft.

*Indian, Blanket, Navajo, Diamond Medallion,
Brown, Red, 5 x 7 Ft.*

Blanket, Navajo, Diamond Medallion, Brown, Red, 5 x 7 Ft. ....*Illus*   550.00
Blanket, Navajo, Saddle, Corner Design, Double, 30 x 58 In., Pair 200.00
Blanket, Navajo, Saddle, Diamond–Twill Pattern, Double, 32 x 53 In. 55.00
Blanket, Navajo, Saddle, Double 250.00
Blanket, Navajo, Saddle, Homespun, Shaded Gray Ground, Fred Harvey 220.00

◆◆

Clean leather chairs, sofas, and tabletops regularly to avoid polish
buildup. Wipe with a mixture of 1/4 cup vinegar and 1/2 cup water.
Then wash the leather with saddle soap and rub briskly with a soft
cloth.

◆◆

Indian, Bowl, Acoma, Black, Geometric Design, 7 In.

Bow Case, Northern Plains, Double Quiver, Bow & 3 Arrows, 1890 .... 795.00
Bowl, Acoma, Black, Geometric Design, 7 In. ....*Illus* 305.00
Bowl, Apache, Coiled, Human & Animal Figures, 17 1/2 In. 1500.00
Bowl, Hopi, Black On Yellow–Orange, Parrot, Prehistoric, 8 1/2 In. 467.00
Bowl, Hopi, Pale Yellow, Black & Red, Band, Compressed, 7 1/2 In. 110.00
Bowl, Hopi, Tadpoles, Mottled Dark Orange, Yellow Interior, 11 In. 1100.00
Bowl, Pima, Coiled Basketry, Black Diamonds, Bars, Willow, 11 x 6 In. 302.50
Bowl, Southwest, Polished Brick, Carved Plumed Serpent, 9 x 5 In. 825.00
Bowl, Washo, Coiled Basketry, Bracken Fern, Willow Ground, 8 3/4 In. 685.00
Bowl, Washo, Coiled Basketry, Flared, Redbud & Willow, 5 x 10 1/2 In. 550.00
Bowl, Zuni, Dough 8800.00
Box, Chippewa, Birch Bark, Sweet Grass, Porcupine Quills, 14 x 9 In. 125.00
Box, Hip Roofed Cover, Hand Painted, Brass Edges, 8 x 12 x 10 In. 110.00
Box, Micmac, Porcupine Quill & Spruce Root On Birchboard, 1850 .... 1400.00
Box, Navajo, Silver, Large Turquoise Stone Lid, Rectangular, 3 In. 302.00
Bracelet, Navajo, Silver & 19 Bezel–Set Turquoise Stones, 2 3/4 In. 495.00
Breastplate, Sioux, Man's, 76 Hair–Pipe Beads 1050.00
Breeches, Crow, Child's, Beaded Hide, 1910 .... 2500.00
Buckle, Shoshone, Beaded 70.00
Carving, Northwest, Cedar, Shaman, Standing, Bear Robe, Weapon, 11 In. 440.00
Case, Parfleche, Plains, Geometric Painted, 30 x 14 3/4 In. 1430.00
Chaps, Navajo, Leather, Silver Conchos 225.00
Coat, Osage, Wedding, Red Broadcloth, Embroidery, Silver Brooches 3500.00
Cradle Board, Iroquois, Bentwood, Bird & Crown, Dated 1888, 27 In. 3300.00
Cradle Board, Iroquois, Carved & Painted, Birds & Flowers, 1888 .... 3300.00
Cradle Board, Navajo, Pine 200.00
Cradle Board, Ojibway, Green Wood, Heart Cutout, Red Sack, c.1900 .... 1650.00
Cradle, Woodland, Doll's, Woven Splint, Natural, Blue, 7 1/2 In. 25.00
Doll, Hopi, Kachina, Cottonwood, 10 3/8 In. 7000.00
Doll, Hopi, Kachina, Painted Cottonwood, Horsehair, Feathers 2100.00
Doll, Hopi, Maiden Costume, 15 1/2 In. 165.00
Doll, Mojave, Beaded Yoke, By Mrs. A. Fields, c.1930 .... 1500.00
Doll, Plains, Beaded & Fringed Hide, Trade Cloth Body, 13 In. 220.00
Doll, Seminole, Costume, Beads, 15 1/2 In., Pair 95.00
Doll, Sioux, Squaw & Papoose, Leather Beaded Clothes 25.00
Doll, Woodland, Man & Woman, c.1910, 12 In., Pair 195.00
Dress, Apache, Beaded & Fringed Buckskin, Poncho, 23 3/4 x 34 In 2090.00
Dress, Crow, Child's, Cowrie Shells, 1880 .... 1250.00
Dress, Nez Perce, Individually Tied Down Cowrie Shells, c.1890 .... 5000.00
Dress, Sioux, Girl's, Beaded Yoke, 1895–1905 .... 5000.00
Drum, Hopi, Rawhide Head, Cottonwood, 10 3/4 x 8 In. 85.00
Drum, Sioux, Ghost Dance, Painted Horse & Warrior, Beadwork Strips 3000.00
Figure, Cochiti, Dog, Pottery 275.00
Figure, Cochiti, Missionary, Rosary, Rancher Clothes, Pottery, 1900 .... 5775.00
Gauntlets, Cree, Doeskin, Beaded Foliage Cuffs 295.00
Gauntlets, Nez Perce, Floral Beading, Fringed Cuffs, 15 In. 210.00
Gun Scabbard, Crow, Fringed, Beaded Panels On The Butt & Point 5000.00
Jar, Acoma, Cream Slip Over Clay, Crosshatched Geometrics, 6 1/2 In. 220.00
Jar, Cochiti, Black Over Ivory Slip, Geometric, H. Cordero, 9 1/2 In. 220.00
Jar, Hopi, Seed, Concentric Swagged, Carinated Form, 10 In. 715.00
Jar, San Ildefonso, Polychrome, Signed Marie & Julian, 8 In. 850.00
Jar, San Ildefonso, Redware, Plumed Serpent, 5 x 6 3/4 In. 3740.00
Jar, Santa Clara, Carved, Teresita Naranjo, 9 1/4 In. 1400.00
Jar, Southwest, Blackware, Bear Paw Design, Gun Metal, 2 7/8 x 4 In. 440.00
Jar, Southwest, Blackware, Stylized Wing Design, 3 x 4 1/4 In. 880.00
Jar, Storage, Cordage Lugs, 6 1/2 x 9 1/2 In. 350.00
Jar, Zuni, Heartline, c.1920, 8 In. 985.00
Jar, Zuni, White Slip Over Pink Clay, Dotted Geometric, 7 In. 220.00
Kachina, Zuni, Bracelet, Animal Fur Tail, Beadwork Necklace, 17 In. 195.00
Marriage Stick, Delaware, Wood, Split Fork, Incised Face End, 23 In. 1127.00
Martingale, Crow, Turquoise, Pink, Red & Yellow Beads, Brass Bells 7500.00
Mask, Cherokee, Buffalo Hunter's, c.1870 .... 3000.00
Mask, Cherokee, Face, 1930s 990.00

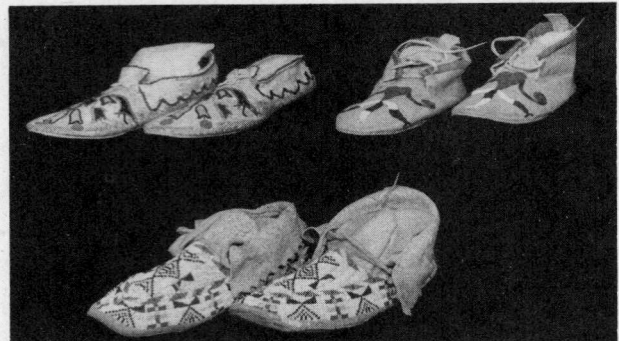

Indian, Moccasins, Woodland, Beaded, Flowers, 10 In.   *Indian, Moccasins, Plains, Beaded, 11 In.*   *Indian, Moccasins, Woodland, Beaded, Hearts, 11 In.*

◆◆◆

To clean an old coffee grinder, grind white rice through the mill. When the rice appears to be clean, the grinder is clean enough to use.

◆◆◆

Mask, Iroquois, Big Lips, Copper & Horsehair, Wooden, 11 1/2 In.	250.00
Mitts, Northern Plateau, Beaded, Red, Gingham Lining, 12 In.	250.00
Moccasins, Alaskan, Child's, Beaded	50.00
Moccasins, Apache, Beaded Hide, Deerskin Uppers, 9 1/2 In., Pair	880.00
Moccasins, Beaded Sealskin	200.00
Moccasins, Cheyenne, Beaded Hide, Sinew, Geometric, 11 In., Pair	484.00
Moccasins, Cheyenne, Child's, Red Uppers, Colored Cross, 7 1/4 In.	55.00
Moccasins, Cheyenne, Multicolored Beadwork, c.1890	750.00
Moccasins, Crow, Beaded	165.00
Moccasins, Crow, Red Beads, High Tops, Glass Button Fasteners, 9 In.	195.00
Moccasins, Kiowa, Beaded, Ochre Paint & Cobalt Laundry Dye	2500.00
Moccasins, Navajo, Rabbit Face Beadwork, Leather	75.00
Moccasins, Plains, Beaded, 11 In. *Illus*	412.00
Moccasins, Sioux, Beaded Hide, Sinew, Colored, 10 1/2 In.	512.00
Moccasins, Sioux, Quilled	1800.00
Moccasins, Sioux, Sinew–Sewn Beadwork, Red Heart, White, 10 1/2 In.	350.00
Moccasins, Sioux, Sinew–Sewn, Beaded Hide	715.00
Moccasins, Woodland, Beaded, Flowers, 10 In. *Illus*	204.00
Moccasins, Woodland, Beaded, Hearts, 11 In. *Illus*	143.00
Model, Canoe, Northwest, Cedar, 2 Indian Figures, 34 1/2 In., 3 Piece	220.00
Necklace, Navajo, Squash Blossom, 17 Pieces of Turquoise, Silver	375.00
Necklace, Osage, Wampum & Bone Bead, Pre 1850	7500.00
Necklace, Woodlands, Bearclaw	9900.00
Necklace, Woodlands, Bearclaw, Hide Strung, 16 3/4 In.	9000.00
Olla, Acoma, White Slip Over White Clay, Geometric, 11 In.	1980.00
Olla, Chemehuevi, Geometric Design, Ann Land, c.1900, 5 3/4 In.	3500.00
Olla, Santo Domingo, Geometric Pattern	1050.00
Painting, Navajo, Shepherdess, On Paper, H. Begay, 1917, 11 x 14 In.	935.00
Parka, Alaskan, Baby's, Sealgut	550.00
Pipe Bag, Arapaho	1000.00
Pipe Bag, Sioux, Beaded, Fringed Hide, Geometric, White Ground, 22 In.	880.00
Pipe Bag, Sioux, Beaded, Quilled & Fringed Hide, 22 In.	1430.00

Pipe Bag, Sioux, Beaded, Quilled, Fringed Hide, Sinew–Sewn, 18 1/2 In. 550.00
Pipe Bag, Sioux, Quilled Hide, 1860s 7150.00
Pipe Bag, Sioux–Arapaho, Beaded, Quilled & Fringed Hide, 17 1/2 In. 1045.00
Pipe, Sioux, Red Catlinite Head, Lead Inlay, Yellow Stem 1250.00
Pipe, Woodlands, Catlinite, Figural, Red & Green Pigment Traces 3850.00
Plate, San Ildefonso, Black On Black, Stylized Parrots, 12 1/4 In. 5280.00
Postcard, Chippewa In Tribal Dress, Peace Pipes, 1913 .... 27.50
Pouch, Apache, Black & White Pony Beads, Hide, 1850s 4180.00
Pouch, Erie, Beaded Flowers, Foliage, Bands, Black Ground 195.00
Pouch, Ottawa, Beaded Pattern, Black Ground, 4 In. 115.00
Purse, Shoshone, All Beaded 95.00
Rattle, Iroquois, Turtle, 1940s, 18 In. 250.00
Rattle, Northwest, Carved Head, Abalone Inset, 2 Sections, 10 In. 440.00
Rug, Navajo, Ganado & Klagetoh Feather Pictorial, 36 x 56 In. 375.00
Rug, Navajo, Ganado With Teec Nos Pas Border, Wool, 38 x 55 In. 500.00
Rug, Navajo, Geometric Stripe Pattern, 36 x 59 In. 200.00
Rug, Navajo, Geometric, Natural Ground, 2 Gray Hills, 74 x 47 In. 402.50
Rug, Navajo, Interlocking Stepped Diamonds, Gray Ground, 64 x 24 In. 220.00
Rug, Navajo, Pictorial, Sand Painting, c.1936, 47 1/2 x 66 3/4 In. 2000.00
Rug, Navajo, Red, Black & Gray, 37 1/4 x 69 In. 1100.00
Rug, Navajo, Serrated Design, White Ground, 38 x 70 In. 200.00
Rug, Navajo, Serrated Diamond Design, White Ground, 1930, 46 x 74 In. 300.00
Rug, Navajo, Storm Pattern, Light Gray Ground, 71 x 46 In. 467.00
Rug, Navajo, Storm Pattern, Red Ground, c.1915, 40 x 59 In. 325.00
Saddlebag, Northern Plains, Beaded, Pair 2530.00
Serving Set, Northwest, Figural Raven Handles, Cedar, 2 Piece 187.00
Shield, Sioux, Painted Rawhide, Feathers, c.1920 .... 225.00
Shirt, Cree, Buckskin, c.1880 .... 1500.00
Snowshoes, Northeast Woodlands, Beaver–Tail Style, Tassels, 28 In. 880.00
Souvenir, Beaded Bird, Branch & Cherries, 1917 .... 82.00
Spear Point, Obsidian 65.00
Spoon, Northwest, Wooden, Flat Back, Red & Black, Totemic, 12 In. 605.00
Staff, Delaware, Wood, Split Fork End, Incised Face, Painted, 9 In. 825.00
Suit, Apache, Woven Cotton, Human Hair Trim 330.00
Totem Pole, Northwest Coast, Carved 9900.00
Totem Pole, Northwest, Cedar, Multicolored Paint, 20th Century, 9 Ft. 5775.00
Totem, Northwest, Cedar, Incised, Paint Remnants, 17 1/2 In. 990.00
Tray, Apache, Coiled, Animal & Human Figures 1500.00
Tray, Papago, Star, 8 In. 110.00
Tray, Papago, Star, 12 In. 250.00
Trunk, Cascades–Plateau, Imbricated, Coiled, Rectangular, 6 x 11 In. 770.00
Trunk, Mohawk, Covered In Red Trade Cloth, Clear Trade Beads 5500.00
Vase, Acoma, Wedding, 5 In. 325.00
Vase, Santa Clara, Wedding, Carved Redware, Serpent Design 1400.00
Vase, Zia, Brown On Cream Slip, 5 In. 325.00
Vest, Sioux, Child's, Beaded Hide, Geometric Devices, 13 1/2 In. 1100.00
Vest, Sioux, Child's, Beaded With Horses On Front, Buffalo On Back 7500.00
Wearing Blanket, Navajo, Indigo & Ivory Diamonds, Red Ground 9900.00
Weaving, Navajo, Geometric, Sand Ground, 1950, 59 x 53 In. 330.00
Weaving, Navajo, Geometric, Tan Ground, 1950, 71 1/2 x 38 1/2 In. 412.50
Weaving, Navajo, Sand Painting, Ivory Ground, 1936, 47 1/2 x 67 In. 2200.00

An inkstand was made to be placed on a desk. It held some type of container for ink, and possibly a sander, a pen tray, a pen, a holder for pounce, and even a candle to melt the sealing wax. Inkstands date to the eighteenth century and have been made of silver, copper, ceramics, and glass.

INKSTAND, Brass, Drop Front, Dog Head Hinged Lid, Calendar, 1893, 6 1/2 In. 250.00
Dog Seated Next To Game Bag & Rabbit, Bronze, c.1880, 4 1/2 In. 445.00
Double, Embossed Flowers, Pen Tray At Top, Glass Wells, Cast Iron 98.00
Griffin, Copper, Clam Shell Tray, 2 Red Glass Wells, 11 x 6 In. 350.00
Iron, Victorian, Lacy, 2 Bottles On Axis, 4 x 5 6 1/2 In. 95.00
Little Eva & Uncle Tom, Attached Sander, Porcelain 145.00

Monkey's Head Form, Glass Eyes, Walnut, England, 4 1/2 In.	550.00
Nest Lid, 2 Pots, Carved Leaves, Acorns, Walnut, 12 1/2 x 10 In.	165.00
Papier-Mache & Mother-of-Pearl, Victorian, 11 3/4 x 9 1/2 In.	205.00
Porcelain, Pump Style, Gilt Metal Snakes, Pen Rack, 5 x 7 In.	495.00
Pottery, Birds & Flowers, 2 Wells, France, 5 5/8 x 7 x 3 3/4 In.	200.00
Rosewood, Brass Inlaid, 2 Bottles, Drawer, 1840, 12 In.	715.00
Waterford Glass Inkwell, Silver, John Smyth, 1863	3430.00
Woman's Head Lid, Brass, Art Nouveau	195.00

Inkwells, of course, held ink. Ready-made ink was first made about 1836 and was sold in bottles. The desk inkwell had a narrow hole so the pen would not slip inside. Pottery, glass, pewter, silver, and other materials were used to make inkwells. Look in other sections for more listings of inkwells.

INKWELL, 2 Bronze Elephants, Onyx, 11 x 19 In.	2000.00
4 Quill Holes, Bottle, Wooden, Silliman, Chester, Conn., 3 1/2 In.	150.00
Black Glass, Marked Property of U. S. Navy	30.00
Blown Three Mold, Cylindrical, Amber, Disc Mouth, c.1830, 2 In.	231.00
Blown Three Mold, Olive Green, Keene, N. H., 1 1/2 x 2 1/4 In.	260.00
Blue Glass, Art Deco, Chrome	95.00
Bulldog Form, Glass Eyes, Ivory Teeth, Fruitwood, England, 5 In.	305.00
Crab, Brass, Says M. J. L. 1895, Friendship Inside, Removable Inkwell	85.00
Crumpled Boot, Amber Glass	50.00
Cut & Pressed Glass, Cane Pattern, Holds 1 Tsp. of Ink, Tiny	50.00
Cut Glass, Pyramid Top, Diamond Shape, 3 1/2 In.	235.00
Cut Glass, With Watch, Sterling Cover, Birmingham, England, 1908	1900.00
Dog, Boxer, Glass Eyes, Fruitwood, England, 4 3/4 In.	605.00
Elephant, Glass Cup, Bronze Finish, Cast Metal, Germany, 5 3/8 In.	45.00
Floral Design, Champleve Enamel, France, 3 x 7 In.	120.00
Fostoria, Colony, Crystal, Lid, 2 1/2 x 1 1/2 In.	40.00
Horseshoe Shaped Pen Holder, Carved, Molded Base, Glass, 1880s	125.00
Lion, Hinged Well In Corner, Bronze, Marble Base	395.00
Lion, White Marble Base, Well In Corner, Bronze, 11 In.	445.00
Man With Cane, Smoking, Before Envelope Holder, Iron	205.00
Millefiori Base & Stopper, Red, White & Blue, Whitefriars, 6 In.	935.00
Millefiori, Stopper, 4 1/2 In.	175.00
Oriental Seated On Base, Hat Cover, Pen Ledge, 4 In.	80.00
Papier-Mache, Mother-of-Pearl Inlaid Design	300.00
Pen Tray, Bakelite, Swirled Caramel, Dickinson, England, 11 1/2 In.	110.00
Pewter Hinged Lid, Swirl Pattern	55.00
Pewter, Ceramic Insert, 1 7/8 In.	40.00
Pewter, Wide Flat Base, 7 3/4 In.	65.00
Pewter, Wide Flat Base, Ceramic Insert, 6 In.	55.00
Police Dog Form, Glass Eyes, Pine, England, 3 1/4 In.	330.00
Porcelain, Intaglio, Brass Hinged Lid, Handpainted, 4 In.	95.00
Rooster & Hen, Hens As Well Covers, Wooden, 16 In.	385.00
Saucer, Cat On 1 Side, Dog Other, Vienna Bronze, Cut Glass Well	295.00
Souvenir, Michigan, Clear Glass, Tin Top & Base, 1 1/4 x 1 1/2 In.	15.00
Stamp Box In Cover	65.00
Suitcase, Traveling	79.00
Truncated Pyramid, Hinged Cover, Crystal, Sterling Fittings, 2 In.	235.00
Umbrella Mushroom, Green, Blue & Red, Stopper, Millville, 9 1/2 In.	605.00

Insulators of glass or pottery have been made for use on telegraph or telephone poles since 1844. Thousands of different styles of insulators have been made. Most common are those of clear or aqua glass, most desirable are the threadless types made from 1850 to 1870.

INSULATOR, AGM, Medium Amber	12.00
Armstrong, 51 C3, Dark Brown	8.00
Armstrong, Root Beer Amber	9.00
Brookfield 83, Fulton Street, Light Aqua	11.00
Brookfield, D On Dome, Light Purple	18.00

Brookfield, Dark Olive, Root Beer Swirls	40.00
Brookfield, Lime Green, New York	5.00
Brookfield, Medium Aqua	3.00
Cable, S. D. P., Dark Aqua, Threaded Skirt	40.00
California Electric Works, Misshapen, Light Aqua	225.00
Canadian Pacific Railway Co., Steel Blue, Light Purple, Amber	35.00
Chambera, Aqua	175.00
Columbia, Aqua	55.00
Columbia, Wide Groove Style	125.00
Diamond, Backward 15, Medium Purple	14.00
Dominion, Light Green	7.00
Duquesne, Cornflower	37.00
F. M. Locke, No. 5, 5 Patent Dates, Aqua	60.00
F. M. Locke, No. 15, Dark Blue Aqua	10.00
F. M. Locke, No. 20, Blue Aqua	10.00
Fall River Police, Aqua	40.00
Gayner, No. 90, Blue	5.00
Grand Canyon, Steely Tinted Clear	20.00
Hawley, Aqua	15.00
Hemingray, Coolie Hat	75.00
Hemingray, No. 9, Valvoline	10.00
Hemingray, No. 16, 1/3 Clear, 2/3 Blue	48.00
Hemingray, No. 19, Orange Amber, Milkr. D. P.	96.00
Hemingray, No. 40, Emerald Green	5.00
Hewingray, No. 14, Misspelled, Aqua	11.00
Jeffery, Upside–Down Embossing, Aqua	65.00
Kerr, Clear	5.00
Kerr, No. 2, Clear	2.00
Lynchburg, No. 2, Cable, Aqua	10.00
Lynchburg, No. 43, SDLP, Light Aqua	7.00
M. F. G. Co., Aqua	6.00
Maydwell, U. S. A., Clear	5.00
McLaughlin, No. 16, "7", Green	16.00
McLaughlin, No. 16, Small RDP, Clear, Straw Tint	8.00
McLaughlin, No. 19, Light Green	5.00
McLaughlin, No. 20, Pale Green	7.00
McLaughlin, Steel Blue	5.00
Muncie, Deep Blue	30.00
Pennyquick, Dark Aqua	22.00
Prism, Blue Aqua	30.00
Prism, Pat. 90, Deep Aqua	15.00
Provo, Aqua	20.00
Ramshorn, Goodyear Rubber, No Wood Block	25.00
Segmented Thread, Base Emblem NAT, Blue Aqua	100.00
Star, Light Green, Outer Skirt Underpour	10.00
T. S., No. 3, Carnival	135.00
T. T. P. Tel. Co., Double Struck Emblem, Aqua	9.00
Threadless, Black Glass, CD 738	2200.00
W. F. G. Co., Denver, Ice Aqua	10.00
W. F. G. Co., Medium Delft Blue	15.00
W. G. M. Co., Black	65.00
Wade, Bubbly Blue Aqua	135.00
WE Mfg., 1871, Green	18.00
Whitall Tatum, No. 5, Aqua	5.00
Whitall Tatum, No. 5, Clear	2.00

IRISH BELLEEK, see Belleek

Iron is a metal that has been used by man since prehistoric times. It is a popular metal for tools and decorative items like doorstops that need as much weight as possible. Items are listed here or under other appropriate headings such as Architectural, Bookends, Doorstop, Kitchen, or Tool. The tool that is used for ironing clothes, an iron, is listed under Kitchen, Iron; or Kitchen, Sadiron.

◆ ◆

Leather needs care. Keep it in a room with high humidity. Leave tabs
and other stress points unsnapped to lessen tearing. Don't hang
leather saddles, holsters, etc., over sharp nails; use large diameter
poles. Don't display near a heat source or in direct sunlight. Don't
use neat's foot oil, use an appropriate leather product.

◆ ◆

IRON, Birdbath, Sprinkler, Figural, Bird, Repainted, 1900s	350.00
Birdhouse, Made In Fashion of Main Residence	687.50
Boot Scraper, Lyre, Oval Scalloped Base, 11 1/4 x 9 1/2 In.	100.00
Boot Scraper, On Pan, With Griffins, Worn Paint, 13 x 17 1/2 In.	215.00
Boot Scraper, Scotty, Wooden Base, Flat	55.00
Boot Scraper, Top Scrolled, Screw Mount, Hand Forged, 9 x 9 In.	225.00
Boot Scraper, Walking Cat Form, Tail Upright, 10 x 10 In.	395.00
Bootjack, Cricket, Orange, Black, Extra Large Eyes	195.00
Bootjack, Naughty Nellie, Polychrome, 10 In.	205.00
Buggy Step, Heart Cutout, Maine	65.00
Door Knocker, Parrot On Branch, Oval, 4 x 3 In.	75.00
Eagle, Large	600.00
Eagle, Looking Down, To Be Mounted On Post, 31 In. Wingspan	115.00
Eagle, Outstretched Wings, 1870	2800.00
Fawn, American, Late 19th Century, 4 Ft. 3 In.	3190.00
Fence, 58 x 33 1/2 In.	225.00
Figurine, 2 Reindeer, Pulling Sleigh, Woman, Holding Reins, 14 1/2 In.	660.00
Figurine, Dwarf, Carrying Bucket, 29 In.	250.00
Figurine, Rabbit, Garden, Kramer Bros. Fdy., Dayton, White, Pink, 11 In.	200.00
Finials, Pineapple, Leaf, Brown Paint, 35 Lbs, 20 x 8 In., Pair	365.00
Flowerpot, Fluted Bowl, Square Base, Painted, 13 x 18 In.	88.00
Grate, Ceiling, Ornate, Cast Iron, Pat. 1897	30.00
Grate, Floor, Pinwheel Center, Square, 10 1/2 In.	125.00
Hitching Post, Double Minerva Head Finial, Fluted Column, 45 In.	1300.00
Hitching Post, Horse Head, c.1850, White & Black Glaze, 60 In.	220.00
Hitching Post, Horse Head, Wooden Base, 20th Century, 11 1/2 In.	25.00
Hitching Post, Tree Form, 43 In., Pair	950.00
Hitching Post, Treelike, Multiple Branch Stumps, Bark Texture, 67 In.	175.00
Horse Head, For Hitching Post, 10 In.	75.00
Latch, Spring, Elbow Handles, 4 x 9 1/2 In.	95.00
Lock, Box, Folding Key, 3 x 5 In.	35.00
Lock, Bronze Mechanism, Brass Knobs, 3 3/4 x 6 In.	125.00
Lock, Chevron Shape, Small	10.00
Lock, Dutch Box, Elbow Handle & Keeper, 4 1/4 x 6 In.	45.00
Mailbox, Scrollwork, Peephole	40.00
IRON, MATCH HOLDER, see Match Holder	
Model, Bicycle, Brass, 8 1/2 x 11 In.	247.00
Plant Holder, White Repaint, 21 3/4 x 20 In.	100.00
Plant Stand, Tiered, Rococo Style, 6 Pierced Trays, Painted, 39 1/2 In.	2870.00
Planter, Caryatid–Type Child, Supporting Oval Basket, 45 In.	2600.00
Plaque, Horse Head, Black Paint, Round, 18 1/2 In.	100.00
Plate Rack, Triangular Tier, 7 Graduated Shelves, 59 In.	250.00
Post Cap, For Hitching Post, Victorian Style, Ball Top, 2 Rings, 8 In.	85.00
Rack, For Clay Pipe, To Stand In Fireplace, 18th Century	247.00
Rack, Key, Luther, Milwaukee, 12 x 9 In.	45.00
Rack, Plate, Hooks For Utensils, 55 In.	200.00
Ram's Head, Old Paint, 12 In.	12.00
Rush Light Holder, Diamond Shape Counterbalance, 9 In.	400.00
Rush Light Holder, Primitive, Candlesocket Counterbalance, 11 In.	300.00
Safe, H. D. Cary & Son, Scenic Panel, Gold Striping	880.00
Shelf, Vining Open Work Floral Design, 10 x 13 3/4 In.	175.00

Shooting Gallery Target, Jumping Squirrel, Red Paint, 9 x 5 In.	85.00
Shooting Gallery Target, Tom Turkey, Silver & Red, 7 x 4 In.	165.00
Sink, Gothic Revival Base, Black Paint, 16 1/2 x 29 x 30 In.	225.00
Sprinkler, Lawn, Wood Duck Shape	1500.00
Statue, Draped Woman, Spring, France, 1850, 6 Ft.	9995.00
Street Light, Cast Iron, Globe, 1890s	425.00
Target, Shooting Gallery, Bird Shape, 2 5/8 In.	49.50
Urn, Foliage, Mask Faces On Bowl, Kramer Bros. Fdy., 52 1/2 In.	700.00
Urn, Garden, Black, Kramer Bros., 21 In., Pair	550.00
Urn, Garden, Campana Form, White Paint, Victorian, 36 x 39 In., Pair	1100.00
Urn, Garden, Kramer Bros., Dayton, 37 In. ....*Illus*	1100.00
Urn, Griffin & Dolphins, Noah H. Baker, 41 x 35 In. ....*Illus*	1100.00
Urn, Removable Base, White Repaint, 27 In., Pair	850.00
Utensil Rack, 4 Hooks, Scrolled Crest, 13 3/4 In.	95.00
Watch Holder, Helmets & Armor, Gold, 4 Ivory Boar Tusks, 10 1/2 In.	95.00
Wedge Doorstop, Heron, Brass	225.00
Weight, Gate, Clenched Fists, 6 In., Pair	1320.00
Wick Trimmer, Hand Forged, Scissor Shape	35.00
Wick Trimmer, Lamp, Scissor Shape, 6 In.	35.00
Windmill Weight, 1913 Model, Challenge Company, Batavia, 30 In.	1000.00
Windmill Weight, Bobtail Horse	400.00
Windmill Weight, Bull, Black	1100.00
Windmill Weight, Bull, Hereford	1100.00
Windmill Weight, Chicken, Hummer, 10 In.	350.00
Windmill Weight, Eclipse	250.00
Windmill Weight, Elgin Rooster, No. 2 On Tail, 10 Ft.	1400.00
Windmill Weight, Horse, Dempster Bobtain	400.00
Windmill Weight, Horse, Short Tail	425.00
Windmill Weight, Hummer Chicken, 10 In.	350.00
Windmill Weight, Rooster, Barnacle Eye	4300.00
Windmill Weight, Rooster, Hummer, Long Stem	450.00
Windmill Weight, Rooster, Hummer, White Paint	500.00
Windmill Weight, Rooster, Red & White Paint, 19 1/4 In.	1200.00
Windmill Weight, Rooster, Screw Leg	5500.00
Windmill Weight, Rooster, Woodmanse, Gray Paint	2200.00
Windmill Weight, Squirrel	1500.00
Window Grate, Scroll Top, Block Bottom, Large	350.00

Ironstone china was first made in 1813. It gained its greatest popularity during the mid–nineteenth century. The heavy, durable, off–white pottery was made in white or was decorated with any of

Iron, Urn, Garden, Kramer Bros., Dayton, 37 In.

Iron, Urn, Griffin & Dolphins, Noah H. Baker, 41 x 35 In.

Ironstone, Tureen, Amherst Japan Pattern, Cover, 14 In.

 hundreds of patterns. Much flow blue pottery was made of ironstone. Some of the decorations were raised. Many pieces of ironstone are unmarked but some English and American factories included the word *Ironstone* in their marks.

IRONSTONE, see also Chelsea Grape; Chelsea Sprig; Flow Blue; Gaudy Ironstone; Moss Rose; Staffordshire; Tea Leaf Ironstone

IRONSTONE, Bowl, Vegetable, Cover, White, 10 In.	25.00
Casserole, Wedgwood, 1790–1800	120.00
Chamber Pot, Corn & Oats, Cover, White	90.00
Chamber Pot, Corn & Oats, White	120.00
Chamber Pot, Floral, Foliate & Geometric Design, Scroll Handles	38.50
Chowder Set, Child's, 13 Piece	65.00
Compote, Boote, 4 1/4 x 8 1/4 In.	45.00
Cup Plate, Little Palm	10.00
Dessert Set, Orange, Blue, Mason, c.1835, 15 Piece	1325.00
Feeder, Infant	6.00
Garniture, Double Landscape, Gilt Handles, Mason, c.1840, 3 Piece	1450.00
Gravy Boat, Corn & Oats, White	25.00
Gravy Boat, White	15.00
Jar, Brine, Asiatic Pheasants Pattern, 12 x 13 In.	215.00
Mold, Food, Fish, White	65.00
Pitcher & Bowl, Floral & Foliate Design Overall, Ivory Ground	110.00
Pitcher, Black Transfer, Bust of Washington, Elsmore, 9 3/8 In.	200.00
Pitcher, Civil War Scenes, Eagle & Serpent, White, 9 In.	550.00
Pitcher, Gaudy Floral, Allerton's Persian Ware, 9 In.	25.00
Pitcher, Royal Chintz Pattern, 12 In.	55.00
Pitcher, Tinturn Pattern, Meakin, 9 In.	49.00
Pitcher, White, Round, 13 In.	70.00
Plate, Bowknot & Clover, 8 3/4 In.	20.00
Plate, Ceres, Orange Luster, 9 1/2 In.	48.00
Plate, Floral Design, Mason, c.1820, 9 3/8 In., 7 Piece	415.00
Platter, Blue Feather Edge, 14 1/4 In.	55.00
Platter, Floral Design, Blue Spatter Rim, 13 1/2 In.	150.00
Platter, Floral In Underglaze, Enameling & Luster, 13 5/8 In.	65.00
Platter, Medina Pattern, Cotton & Barlow, 12 x 15 1/2 In.	135.00
Platter, Overall Floral, 19th Century, 18 x 14 1/2 In., Pair	385.00
Platter, Presidential Transfer, Presidents Border, 13 6/8 In.	140.00
Platter, Red & Blue Cherry Center, Red & Blue Stripes Rim, Large	165.00
Platter, White, T. & R. Boote, Oval, Large	65.00
Platter, White, Wedgwood, Oval, Large	65.00
Spittoon, Woman's, Moss Rose	65.00
IRONSTONE, TEA LEAF, see Tea Leaf Ironstone	
Teapot, Arms of Pennsylvania, 8 1/2 In.	465.00
Toothbrush Holder, Diana, Meakin, 4 1/2 In.	35.00
Tureen, Amherst Japan Pattern, Cover, 14 In. ....*Illus*	400.00
Wash Set, Gold Band, 4 Piece	185.00

Ivory, Figurine, Buddhist Lion, Traces of Gilt, 3 In.

 Laszlo Ispanky began his American career as a designer for Cybis Porcelains. In 1966, he established his own studio in Pennington, New Jersey; and, since 1976, he has worked for Goebel of North America. He works in stone, wood, or metal, as well as porcelain. The first limited edition figurines were issued in 1966.

ISPANSKY, Figurine, Antony, Roman Suit, Eagle Helmet In Hand, 1978, 11 In.	850.00
Figurine, Artist Girl	600.00
Figurine, Isaiah	500.00
Figurine, Swan Lake	1000.00

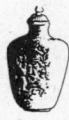 The tusk of an elephant is ivory and to many that is the only true ivory. To most collectors, the term *ivory* also includes such natural materials as walrus, hippopotamus, or whale teeth or tusks, and some of the vegetable materials that are of similar texture and density. Other ivory items are listed under Scrimshaw or Netsuke. Collectors should be aware of the recent laws concerning the buying and selling of ivory.

IVORY, Ball, Figures of Rabbits, Dragons & Monkeys, 2 In.	120.00
Box, Jewelry, Pierced & Engraved, Walrus, Russia, 8 3/4 In.	1320.00
Box, Ornately Carved	95.00
Box, Taj Mahal, Painted, Inlaid, Ebony, Indian, 19th Century, 4 x 6 In.	95.00
Brush, Clothes, Horsehair, Engraved Handle, Ferrule Date 1878, 7 In.	45.00
Candlestick, Egyptian Caryatid Stem, 9 In., Pair	160.00
Chest, Lift Top, Mortal Remains of Capt. T. Witham, 21 1/2 In.	2200.00
Figurine, Bear, Standing, Growling, Baleen Base, Alaska, 4 3/4 In.	250.00
Figurine, Buddha, Surrounded By Laughing Children, Japan, 7 In.	275.00
Figurine, Buddhist Lion, Traces of Gilt, 3 In. ....*Illus*	242.00
Figurine, Fisherman & Wife, Japanese, 1950s, 12 In.	1600.00
Figurine, God of Longevity, White Beard, Ju–I Scepter, 12 1/2 In., Pr.	2250.00
Figurine, Goddess, Standing, Holding Lotus Spray, c.1900, 14 1/4 In.	335.00
Figurine, Hunter With Prey Strapped On Back, Africa, 7 1/2 In.	110.00
Figurine, Lady, Fan, Flowers, Signed Min–Gyoku, 6 In.	105.00
Figurine, Men & Women Around Table, 11 In.	1210.00
Figurine, Napoleon, Opens To A Triptych,, 19th Century, 8 5/16 In.	745.00
Figurine, Oriental Man, Standing, With Monkey, Signed Ippo, 4 1/4 In.	155.00
Figurine, Oriental Man, Standing, With Monkey, Signed Ryuosan, 5 In.	95.00
Figurine, Oriental Old Man, Pipe & Staff, Carved Ebony Base, 8 In.	950.00
Figurine, Warrior Riding Horse–Drawn Chariot, 8 x 10 In.	600.00
Figurine, Woman, Reclining On Bench, Holding Child, 10 In.	1000.00
Inro, Phoenix 1 Side, Reverse Has Dragon, 3 Case	850.00
Jackknife, Victorian Lady's Shoe	75.00
Paper Knife, Silver Mounted, Unger Brothers, c.1900, 11 In.	440.00
Tankard, Bacchanalian Revelry Allover, c.1870	7370.00
Tusk, Elephant, Carved, 2 x 21 In.	245.00
Tusk, Walrus, Skull, Nose, Teeth, 14 In.	650.00

Tusk, Woman On Front, Elephant, Deer & Trees, 10 1/2 In.	6500.00
Vase, Bud, Oriental, 5 In., Pair	30.00
Whiskbroom, Carved Handle, 11 1/2 In.	40.00

Jack Armstrong, the all–American boy, was the hero of a radio serial from 1933 to 1951. Premiums were offered to the listeners until the mid–1940s. Jack Armstrong's best–known endorsement is for Wheaties.

JACK ARMSTRONG, Airplane, Ranger	150.00
Answer Box	45.00
Flashlight, Black Torpedo	45.00
Flashlight, Blue	25.00
Hike–O–Meter	35.00
Pedometer .... 17.00 To	20.00
Telescope	30.00
Telescope, Explorer	12.00

Jack–in–the–pulpit vases were named for their odd trumpetlike shape that resembles the wild plant called jack–in–the–pulpit. The design originated in the late Victorian years. Vases in the jack–in–the–pulpit shape were made of ceramic or glass.

JACK–IN–THE–PULPIT, Vase, Cranberry, Vaseline Rigaree Stem, Deep Red Rim	95.00
Vase, Flower Top, Petal Feet, White Ground, 7 In.	110.00

Jackfield ware was originally a black glazed pottery made in Jackfield, England, from 1750 to 1775. A yellow glazed ware has also been called Jackfield ware. Most of the pieces referred to as *Jackfield* today are black–glazed, red–clay wares made at the Jackfield Pottery in Shropshire, England, in Victorian times.

JACKFIELD, Creamer, Cover, Cow, Gold Trim	90.00
Creamer, Cow, Black & Gold	150.00
Pitcher, 5 In.	40.00
Sugar & Creamer, Figural, Cat, Painted Facial Features	95.00

Two different minerals, nephrite and jadeite, are called jade. Nephrite is the mineral used for most early Oriental carvings. Jade is a very tough stone that is found in many colors from dark green to pale lavender. Jade carvings are still being made in the old styles, so collectors must be careful not to be fooled by recent pieces. Jade jewelry is found in this book under Jewelry.

JADE, Box, Lotus Blossoms, Dragons, White, Green, 5 In.	950.00
Figurine, Boy, 2 3/4 In.	35.00
Figurine, Horse, Mutton Fat, 5 1/2 In.	250.00
Figurine, Immortal With Lute, Gray–Green, 6 In.	1200.00
Figurine, Reclining Horse, Head Turned, Hind Hoof In Mouth, 8 1/2 In.	3520.00
Figurine, Tang Horse, Mottled Green, Chinese, 4 1/3 x 3 3/4 In.	75.00
Ring, Burma, Oval, 9/16 x 3/4 In.	500.00
Ring, Cabochon, Silver Floral, Applied Gold, Arts & Crafts	275.00

Japanese Coralene is a ceramic decorated with small raised beads and dots. It was first made in the nineteenth century. Later wares made to imitate coralene had dots of enamel. There is also another type of coralene that is made with small glass beads on glass containers.

JAPANESE CORALENE, Bowl, Countess Anna Potocka Portrait, Pierced, 12 In.	3400.00
Vase, Flowers, Pink, Green, Gold Dots, 8 In.	200.00
Vase, Flowers, Red, Rust, White Dot Trim, 12 In.	550.00
Vase, Turquoise, Dragons, Flowers, White Dot Trim, 15 In.	350.00
JAPANESE WOODBLOCK PRINT, see Print, Japanese	

There are two types of jasperware. Some pieces are made from colored clay with raised designs of the same or contrasting colored clay. Other pieces are made by decorating the raised portions with a glaze.

JASPERWARE, see also various art potteries; Wedgwood

JASPERWARE, **Box**, Radford	55.00
Carving, Drunken Poet, Red, Serpentine, Chinese, 18th Century	1200.00
Cheese Dish, Blue, White, Dome Cover, 1880–1890 ....*Illus*	225.00
Pitcher, Milk, Tilt Lid, Dark Blue, Wedgwood, 1920s	130.00
Sweet Dish, Silver Jubilee, 1977, Wedgwood	48.00
Teapot, Art Nouveau, S & V	140.00
Toothpick, Etruria, Dark Blue, Wedgwood	120.00
Urn, White Classic Figures, Blue, Germany, 2 1/4 In.	35.00

Jewelry, if made from gold and precious gems or plastic and colored glass, is still popular with collectors. Values are determined by the intrinsic value of the stones and metal and by the skill of the craftsmen and designers. Victorian and older jewelry has been popular since the 1950s. More recent interests are Art Deco and Edwardian styles, Mexican and Danish silver jewelry, and beads of all kinds. Copies of almost all styles are being made.

JEWELRY, **Bar Pin**, 3 Bezel Set Turquoise, Yellow Gold, 1 13/16 In.	65.00
Bar Pin, Art Deco, 3 Diamonds, 18K Gold	110.00
Bar Pin, Center Diamond, White Gold	110.00
Bar Pin, Pearls, Gold, Georg Jensen	550.00
Bar Pin, Platinum, Set With Diamonds, Sapphires, 1930 ....*Illus*	7700.00
Bar Pin, Round Center Diamond, Diamond Each End, 18K White Gold	3300.00
Bar Pin, Victorian, 3 White Sapphires, 14K Yellow Gold, 1 7/8 In.	85.00
Bracelet & Earring Set, Sterling, Curvilinear & Bead, H. Aguilar	330.00
Bracelet, 5 Oval Turquoise Stones, Lebolt, 14K Gold, 7 3/4 In.	2200.00
Bracelet, Art Deco, 4 Cabochon Tourmalines, 10K Gold Filled	85.00
Bracelet, Art Deco, Hinged Plaques, F. W., 14K Yellow Gold, 7 1/4 In.	137.50
Bracelet, Bamboo Style, Bangle, Florentine Finish	495.00
Bracelet, Bangle, Victorian, 14 Carved Shell Cameos, Gold	495.00
Bracelet, Blue Glass & Pearl, Fancy Clasp, Miriam Haskell	125.00
Bracelet, Cameo, 6 Rows of Open–Link Chain, 14K Gold	440.00
Bracelet, Center Enamel Plaque of Peasant Woman, Gold Frame, 1900	2750.00
Bracelet, Charm, Disney Characters, 14K Gold, 7 In.	605.00
Bracelet, Cobra, Double, 3 Sapphires, 20 Pt. Diamond	175.00
Bracelet, Coral, Enameled Gold Geometric, 9 Blue Links, 14K Gold	150.00
Bracelet, Cuff, Ivory	40.00
Bracelet, Cuff, Orange Bakelite, 1 1/2 In., 1920s	9.00
Bracelet, Cuff, Sterling Silver, Arts & Crafts, Hammered, Gorham	121.00
Bracelet, Double–Row Rope Design, 14K Yellow Gold, 7 In.	305.00
Bracelet, Floral Engrving, Yellow Gold Filled, 1/2 In.	200.00
Bracelet, Gold Link, Faceted Bars, Tiffany, 14K Gold	1045.00

Jasperware, Cheese Dish, Blue, White, Dome Cover, 1880–1890

Bracelet, Golf Bag, Sterling 25.00
Bracelet, Hinged, Tooled Leaf Scrolls, Sterling, Mexico 65.00
Bracelet, Jet, Covered Clear Rhinestones, 2 1/4 In. 125.00
Bracelet, Onyx & Rose Gold, Wire Twist Highlights, Pair 1870.00
Bracelet, Pebbled, Pressure Clasp, 14K Yellow Gold 325.00
Bracelet, Rhinestone, Amber, Blue & Gray, Hinged, 1 5/8 In. Wide 75.00
Bracelet, Rhinestone, Blue, Lavender, Weiss 50.00
Bracelet, Rhinestones, Eisenberg 120.00
Bracelet, Rose Cut Diamonds, Niello, Austro–Hungary, 18K Gold, 1880 .... 4000.00
Bracelet, Round Diamonds, Baguette & Triangular Emeralds, 7 In. 1700.00
Bracelet, Siam, Silver, 1 1/2 In. 40.00
Bracelet, Silver, Alternating Links, Georg Jensen, 7 1/4 In. 475.00
Bracelet, Snake Form, Inset Ruby Eyes, 14K Yellow Gold, 7 In. 410.00
Bracelet, Snake, Mesh, Whiting Davis 45.00
Bracelet, Snake, Silver, Upper Arm, Whiting Davis 75.00
Bracelet, Solid Link, Black Onyx Stone, 3 Diamonds, 14K White Gold 375.00
Bracelet, Solid Triangular Links, 14K Gold, 3/8 In. Wide 305.00
Bracelet, Tapered Brickwork, Florentine Finish, 18K Gold 440.00
Bracelet, V–Shaped Sterling Links, Taxco, 8 In. 110.00
Bracelet, Vauxhall Glass, Lapis Lazuli Colored Medallions, Box 100.00
Brooch, Cameo, Gold Mount, Synthetic Rubies, Garnets ....*Illus* 2860.00
Brooch, Donkey With Man, Silver, Mexico 26.00
Brooch, Platinum, Diamonds, c.1920 ....*Illus* 1650.00
Buckle, Jet Beadwork, Square, 1900s, 3 x 2 1/2 In., Box 25.00
Buckle, Rhinestones, Heart Shape, Kendall & Marcus, 4 In. 90.00
Cameo, 14K Gold, Filigree, Diamond Pendant, 2 1/4 x 2 In. ....*Illus* 1210.00
Charm, 1967 Chevrolet, 14K Gold 65.00
Charm, Bourbon Street Lamp, 14K Gold, Lights Up 60.00
Charm, Coffee Mill, 14K Gold 40.00
Charm, Owl, 14K Gold 34.00
Chatelaine, Art Nouveau, Egyptian Design, Perfume Container 185.00
Chatelaine, Needlework, 5 Attachments, Late 1800s, England 695.00

◆◆

To remove a dried cork that has fallen inside a bottle, try this. Pour some household ammonia in the bottle. Let it sit for a few days. Most of the cork should dissolve and can easily be removed.

◆◆

Jewelry, Bar Pin, Platinum,
Set With Diamonds, Sapphires, 1930
Jewelry, Brooch, Cameo, Gold Mount,
Synthetic Rubies, Garnets
Jewelry, Brooch, Platinum,
Diamonds, c.1920

Jewelry, Cameo, 14K Gold,
Filigree, Diamond Pendant,
2 1/4 x 2 In.

Dream Antiques

A Stradivarius violin, a baseball autographed by Babe Ruth, a set of Haviland china, a fabulous Victorian desk...These are the antiques of our fantasies. Some of these dreams are great rarities priced beyond our means, some are affordable and available for less than $300.

Who hasn't heard about a Stradivarius violin, probably the most famous musical instrument in the world? Antonio Stradivari made 1,116 violins, cellos, and violas in Italy in the early 1700s, and 705 are known to exist in the world today. Musicians consider it a privilege to play a Stradivarius and many of these valuable stringed instruments are used by concert musicians. The most expensive Strad ever sold at auction brought $1.76 million in 1990 at Sotheby's, London, so owning a Strad will remain a dream for most of us. But a "lost" Strad was rediscovered in the 1980s in the estate of a penniless musician who had been using it for many years. Several other instruments disappeared during World War II and may now be unidentified and unnoticed in an attic or a high school band.

Baseball cards fill the dreams of old and young collectors. Many

The Honus Wagner T-206 cigarette card is the dream of every baseball card collector. The locations of about 40 of the 1910 cards are known. One sold in 1991 for almost a half million dollars. Courtesy Joshua Evans of Leland's, New York

This diamond-studded championship boxing belt was presented to Jack Dempsey after he won the heavyweight crown in a fight against Jess Willard in 1919. The belt buckle is made of 14-carat gold set with diamonds. The added historic and nostalgic value made it an $8,250 dream at auction in 1990. Courtesy Sotheby's

yearn for their own childhood box of cards discarded in a cleaning frenzy years ago. The rarest card, the Honus Wagner T-206 cigarette card of 1910, sold at Sotheby's, New York, in 1991 for $441,000, making one collector's dream come true. Wagner was a ball player who did not smoke, and he objected to the unauthorized use of his picture for a cigarette ad. The card was withdrawn and fewer than 40 exist today. This dream card has gone up in price dramatically. In 1972 a Wagner card was sold for $1,500; in 1977 another brought $3,876. The price was up to $25,000 by 1983, $115,000 in 1989. But you can buy other rarities such as a Mickey Mantle card for $49,500 or a common Roger Clemens for under $1.

Perhaps you dream of owning other sports memorabilia. A baseball signed by Babe Ruth auctioned in 1990 in New York City for $1,980; Jack Dempsey's 1919 belt with a gold buckle decorated with diamonds was $8,250. A feather golf ball brought $11,500 in 1989; a brown patent "rake iron" golf club made in 1900 set a record at $90,000 in 1989. A limited budget may make you dream for less exotic wooden-handle golf clubs that can be found in attics or basements. These sell for $5 to $500 each.

Who hasn't wished that Grandma's painting hanging in the living room is really a long-lost masterpiece worth hundreds of thousands of dollars? A Milwaukee couple had this dream come true in 1991. A small painting of a vase of flowers they were given in 1960 was noticed by Leslie Hindman Galleries during a routine appraisal of home furnishings. It was identified as an 1886 picture by Vincent Van

Above: If a full-sized quilt is too large for your dreams, perhaps this crib quilt is proper. This pieced silk quilt made around 1880–1900 cost $440. Courtesy Christie's

◆ ◆ ◆ ◆ ◆ ◆ ◆ ◆ ◆ ◆ ◆ ◆ ◆ ◆ ◆ ◆

◆ ◆ ◆ ◆ ◆ ◆ ◆ ◆ ◆ ◆ ◆ ◆ ◆ ◆

Below: A dramatic Tiffany lamp with leaded-glass shade and bronze base might be your dream. This peony lamp, 29 inches high, 22 inches in diameter, is signed "Tiffany Studios New York." It sold for $220,000 in 1990. Courtesy Christie's

◆ ◆ ◆ ◆ ◆ ◆ ◆ ◆ ◆ ◆ ◆ ◆ ◆

Left: One collector's realized dream. This 16¼-by-13-inch oil painting of a vase of flowers hung in a home for years until it was discovered and sold at auction. The Van Gogh painting brought $1.43 million at the 1991 Leslie Hindman sale in Chicago, Illinois.

Above: *Little Orphan Annie has gained fame through comic strips, radio, movies, and stage. Many dream of their childhood cups made of Beatleware by the makers of Ovaltine. The cups were a radio premium.*

◆ ◆

Left: *The mysterious French firm of Halopeau made this 23-inch-high doll in the nineteenth century. The record price of $100,000 bought it in 1990 at an auction by Theriault's.*

◆ ◆

Below: *Almost too beautiful to use. This American inlaid-maple-and-walnut pool table sold for $14,300. Courtesy Sotheby's*

Gogh and was auctioned by the Chicago firm for $1.43 million.

Louis Comfort Tiffany was an American designer, painter, glass artist, and jeweler. Electric lighting had just been invented in the 1880s when Tiffany Studios began to make lamps that held light bulbs. Shades were made of iridescent gold glass, or were colorful stained-glass depictions of flowers and other designs. The bronze lamp bases were shaped like leafy plants or stylized pillars. Collectors pay the highest prices for the lamps with leaded-glass shades, but any marked Tiffany is of value. The most expensive Tiffany lamp ever sold at auction, the magnolia-pattern floor lamp, brought $528,000 in 1984. Bargain-hunters can buy other Tiffanys at much lower prices. Dreams come in all price ranges and today Tiffany lamps sell from $900 for a desk lamp to $220,000 for a peony leaded-glass and bronze table lamp.

Quilts bring back memories of childhood and comfort. Examples are found at every antiques show or tucked away in storage at Grandma's house. The record price for a full-sized quilt is $176,000, set in 1987 for an 1840 Baltimore album quilt of colorful flowers and railroad scenes. But dreamers can look for quilts that are more affordable; a patchwork quilt from the 1930s could sell for $100.

Old toys of all types bring memories of earlier, carefree years, and collectors have been paying high prices for the toys of their child-hood. A replacement for the mechanical bank, pedal car, teddy bear, doll, or Christmas toy discarded by parents can be found today at shops and shows. An old worn teddy bear can sell for $50 to $86,350, the record price paid in London in 1989. Theriault's, an auction house specializing in dolls, sold a French doll in 1990 for a record-breaking $100,000. The highest-priced doll sold at auction before 1991 was a Kammer & Reinhardt bisque character doll made in Germany about 1909. It was sold in London in 1989 for $169,576. But dolls can sell for just a few dollars and many twentieth-century dolls are still stored in boxes at home.

Even large "toys" are part of our dreams. Old pool tables have become so popular there are reproductions of the ornate old styles being made. Last year an original inlaid-maple-and walnut pool table made around 1880 sold at auction for $14,300. Memories of the 1940s prompted bidders this year to phone from all over the country to a Boston auction house. The winning bidder for a 1941 Wurlitzer 850 with its spinning disks and colored lights had to pay $15,400.

Nostalgia has created dreams of many things previous generations threw away. Want an orphan Annie cup? You might have to pay $30. And don't forget old cereal boxes selling for 25¢ to $100, lunch boxes for $1 to $400, or fast food glasses for under 50¢. Since the 1970s the dream kitchens seen in decorating magazines have included store memorabilia. Today the old boxes, cans, and signs are seen in every part of a collector's home. But the ultimate advertising collectible is now as valuable as a rare oil painting. In 1990 a tin sign advertising Campbell's soup sold for $93,500.

Who doesn't dream of the comics and cartoons of preteen years? Old comic books, toys related to comics, and anything from a three-little-pigs toothbrush holder made in 1936 ($85) to a Roger Rabbit stuffed toy ($25) is part of some child's or adult's dreams. One serious collector fulfills his dreams by buying old posters of comics and the original celluloid pictures used to make the animated cartoons we see at the movies. The 1935 cartoon "The Band Concert" was the first

◆ ◆ ◆ ◆ ◆ ◆ ◆ ◆ ◆ ◆ ◆ ◆ ◆ ◆ ◆ ◆

Music, lights, and fun join for memories with this 1941 Wurlitzer 850 jukebox. It featured a multicolor spinning film that gave it the glow. Bidders with memories of the forties fought for this dream until one succeeded with a bid of $15,400. Courtesy Skinner Auctioneers and Appraisers, Boston

A determined bidder paid $93,500 in 1990 for the lithographed tin Campell's Soup flag sign setting a record for this type of collectible. The 36-by-48-inch sign is one of five known. Campbell's recalled the signs shortly after they were introduced in 1905 because they felt the design was disrespectful to the flag. This sign sold for $5,000 in 1981; a similar one brought $11,000 in 1986, and another $44,000 in 1989. The cost of dreams is rising. Courtesy Richard Oliver's Auction Gallery, Kennebunk, Maine

❖ ❖ ❖ ❖ ❖ ❖ ❖ ❖ ❖ ❖ ❖ ❖ ❖ ❖ ❖ ❖ ❖ ❖

Anything picturing Mickey Mouse is sought after by collectors. Old celluloids used to make the animated cartoons are rare, and those dated before 1940 are almost impossible to find. This image from "The Band Concert" is the oldest color cel of Mickey known today. Courtesy Mike and Jeanne Glad

❖ ❖ ❖ ❖ ❖ ❖ ❖ ❖ ❖ ❖ ❖ ❖ ❖ ❖ ❖ ❖ ❖ ❖

Mickey Mouse cartoon in color. A cel from that cartoon is worth over $100,000 today.

A home filled with antiques and memories of past years is the dream of many. A collector paid $93,500 for a mission-style settle by Gustav Stickley in 1988 and $44,000 for a painted corner cupboard in 1983. Who hasn't heard of a Chippendale-style chair? But few of us can afford an original. A Chippendale chair with carved hairy-paw feet made in Philadelphia about 1770 sold in 1982 for $275,000. The most expensive piece of American furniture ever sold at auction was a mahogany desk-bookcase made in 1760. It brought $12,100,000 in 1989. Dreams differ. Some of us want a Wooton desk, today worth well over the 1979 record price of $18,000. Others covet a wicker chair that will cost less than $300. And those who prefer twentieth-century collectibles want a piece of Frank Lloyd Wright furniture, perhaps the 1950s aluminum chair sold in 1990 for $26,400.

◆ ◆ ◆ ◆ ◆ ◆ ◆ ◆ ◆ ◆ ◆ ◆

Elaborate wicker chairs are so popular they are being made again today, but collectors dream of owning an original old example. This gentleman's chair was made about 1900 and can be purchased for less than $500.

The Wooton desk with its cubby holes and locks was the desk of the rich when produced in the late-nineteenth century. This "Extra-Grade Wooton Patent Secretary" was made in Indianapolis about 1875. It is the dream of many collectors. Courtesy Richard and Eileen Dubrow Antiques, Inc.

◆ ◆ ◆ ◆ ◆ ◆ ◆ ◆ ◆ ◆ ◆ ◆ ◆ ◆ ◆ ◆ ◆ ◆

If you can't get a Frank Lloyd Wright house, perhaps you can dream with a piece of his furniture. Wright designed this hexagonal aluminum chair for the H. C. Price Company Tower in Bartlesville, Oklahoma, about 1953. It sold in 1990 for $26,400. Courtesy Christie's

❖ ❖ ❖ ❖ ❖ ❖ ❖ ❖ ❖ ❖ ❖ ❖ ❖ ❖ ❖ ❖ ❖ ❖ ❖ ❖

Beautiful glass is the dream of some—everything from pressed-glass goblets to 1950s contemporary wares. Lalique, an expensive glass made in France since the 1890s, entices many. In 1979 the record price of $26,000 was paid for a frosted Lalique vase with frogs. In 1988 an identical vase brought $210,000. This year a peony-decorated vase sold for $10,120. Even more expensive are pieces of French cameo glass made in the nineteenth century. Layers of colored glass are formed into a single piece, then the designs are made by cutting away parts of the glass. A Galle lamp shaped like three

Oran *is the French name for this blue-stained 10½-inch-high peony-decorated glass vase by Rene Lalique et Cie. It is marked "R. Lalique, France," a mark used before the death of Lalique in 1945. Recent auction price was $10,120. Courtesy Christie's*

❖ ❖ ❖ ❖ ❖ ❖ ❖ ❖ ❖ ❖ ❖ ❖ ❖ ❖ ❖ ❖ ❖ ❖ ❖ ❖

mushrooms sold in 1989 for $1,100,000. But dreamers can find a small cameo glass vase for less than $500.

Everyone wants beautiful dishes for the table. The name Haviland is probably the best-known word in the vocabulary of those who look back to dinner on Sunday-best dishes with grandparents. During the nineteenth and twentieth centuries, "best" dishes were made in Limoges, France, by the Haviland factory. A set of Haviland was the wedding gift preferred by every bride. It is so popular today, shops carry many patterns so a collector can fill in an inherited set or buy an

Pablino diaz Kowa is the Indian pictured by Grace Young on the 1901 Rookwood vase. Only vases are known to have a full-length Indian portrait, so the dream of owning one is remote. This 14½-inch example sold for $18,150.

A spider spins her web on this Galle Cameo glass vase of purplish red and red glass. The web is etched, the spider of applied glass on a 13¾-inch vase. It is signed "E. Galle Crisallerie Nancy" in a part of the web. The 1990 price at auction was $34,100. Courtesy Wolf's, Cleveland, Ohio

Hot cocoa and cookies and a Haviland tea set are memories of years gone by. This chocolate set in "Marseille" is marked in green "H & Co. L France." The L is for Limoges. The tray for this set is 14 inches square, the chocolate pot is 9 inches high. Shanahan Collection featured in Mary Frank Gaston's Haviland Collectibles and Objects of Art, Collector Books, 1984

This majolica fish must have enticed many children with its gurgle when the milk was poured. It is made of the bright tin-glazed pottery wanted by many collectors.

❖ ❖ ❖ ❖ ❖ ❖ ❖ ❖ ❖ ❖ ❖ ❖ ❖ ❖ ❖ ❖ ❖

Above: Viktor Schreckengost made several different "jazz" bowls for the Cowan Pottery about 1931. The first "jazz" bowl was made on order for First Lady Eleanor Roosevelt. This yellow example was one of those made later for sale in gift shops. Art Deco collectors dream of finding pottery with such strong design, even at the over-$40,000 price range.

◆ ◆

◆ ◆ ◆ ◆ ◆ ◆ ◆ ◆ ◆ ◆ ◆ ◆ ◆

Left: George Ohr poked, pinched, and squeezed this black-glazed 5-inch-high vase that sold at auction for $5,000. It was made about 1900 in a shape that was unlike the work of any other potter. Courtesy David Rago

◆ ◆

Right: The green-matte-glazed art pottery of the early 1900s is the dream of many Arts and Crafts collectors. It looks right on a mission table. This Teco vase was designed by William J. Dood and made by Gates Potteries around 1910. The 11½-inch-high vase had a 1990 worth of $16,500. Courtesy Christie's

assembled set. Service for twelve is about $500. If you prefer a more colorful look, try majolica, a tin-glazed earthenware decorated in bright colors. English, French, and American-made dishes mimic fruit, leaves, birds, and animals. An attractive pitcher costs $75 to $100, a rare English game dish sold in 1990 for $3,200.

American art pottery has become popular again, and a green vase for flowers or a shelf of rare pieces is part of the collector's dreams. The pottery that most fascinates collectors is Rookwood, the Cincinnati, Ohio, pottery made from 1880 to 1960. A vase with a full-length Indian pictured on the brown glaze sold for $3,600 in 1978. A similar one sold in 1990 for $18,150. The record price for an Indian-decorated Rookwood vase is $32,000 set in 1980. But the top price for any Rookwood is $198,000 for a vase sold in June 1991. Other popular art pottery in this decade is the Massachusetts-made Dedham pottery (a wolf and owl plate brought $69,300) and Grueby pottery (a two-color vase with jonquils sold for $30,800. This year's favorite is Teco, made by Gates Potteries of Michigan with a record price of $44,000. Dreamers will find it difficult to find a good example for under $5,000. About five years ago, works by George Ohr, an eccentric Mississippi potter, became the favored collectible of the modern artists in New York. Record price set in 1990 was $22,000 for a black-glazed vase. Deco designs are now part of the dreams of the "thirty-something" generation. The very important "jazz" bowl made in the 1930s by Cowan potteries of Ohio has sold for over $40,000.

One collector made his dream come true when he bought this record-priced toy for $104,500 in April 1991. The sleigh and goats are of painted tin. Santa is made of wood with a composition face and crepe paper clothing. The nineteenth-century Christmas toy was made by Althof-Bergmann of Germany. It is 18 inches long. Courtesy Ron Bello Studio, New York City, Noel Barrett Antiques and Auctions, Carversville, Pennsylvania

◆ ◆

But sometimes collectors keep chasing a dream antique for years, watching the price rise and supply dwindle. We first saw our dream, a Martinware bird, in London years ago priced at $600, far too much we thought. A few years ago we actually bid $2,000 for a bird, only to see it sell for over $6,000. In 1990 a 14-inch bird brought $17,600 while a smaller example was $9,350. For us, owning a piece of Martinware is still a dream. But all collectors know that often that special treasure seems to be waiting for just the right owner at just the right price. And we keep dreaming that a bargain-priced Martinware figure will join our collection some day.

Our dream, Martinware bird vessels. The heads come off to become cups, the bodies hold the liquid. The 14-inch bird sold for $17,600, but the smaller 11-inch bird was $9,350. Both birds were made between 1887–1889 and are signed and dated. Courtesy Christie's

Cigarette Case, Diamond Monogram, Sapphire Thumbpiece, 14K Gold 715.00
Cigarette Case, Sapphire Thumbpiece, 18K Gold 1210.00
Clip, Fur, Swallow, Clear Stones, Red Eyes, Unger Bros. 45.00
Clip, Green Bakelite 28.50
Clip, Sweater, Rabbit, Sterling Siler 35.00
Collar Button, Black Enamel, 18K Yellow Gold, Pair 45.00
Comb, Shell Trim, Haskell 35.00
Cross, Amethyst, 18K Yellow Gold 1650.00
Cuff Links, Bombe Shape, Textured Surface, 14K Gold 135.00
Cuff Links, Lapis Lazuli, Band of Platinum, Rose–Cut Diamonds 935.00
Cuff Links, Lapis Lazuli, Octagonal, Inlaid Platinum 935.00
Cuff Links, Plaque of Gold In Quartz, 14K Gold Mounting 605.00
Earrings, Cameo, 14K Gold, Screw Type 35.00
Earrings, Cameo, 2 Cameos In Each, Gold Mountings 275.00
Earrings, Carved Ivory, 14K Gold Posts 20.00
Earrings, Dangle, Black Stone In Top, Rhinestone In Dangle, Hobe 20.00
Earrings, Drop Design, 14 Diamonds, 14K Yellow Gold 825.00
Earrings, Drop, Diamond & Emerald, Yellow & White Gold 2000.00
Earrings, Loops, Inlaid With Turquoise, Screw Type 25.00
Earrings, Oval–Cut Center Sapphires, Diamonds Around, 14K Gold 325.00
Earrings, Pearl, Surrounded By Emeralds & Diamonds, Mabe, 14K Gold 880.00
Earrings, Silver, Beaded Oval, Georg Jensen, 7/8 In. 110.00
Earrings, Silver, Beaded, Oval, Georg Jensen, 1945, 1 1/2 In. 110.00
Earrings, Silver, Mexico 85.00
Earrings, Sterling Silver, Blue Jasper, Wedgwood 65.00
Hairpin, Bakelite, 1930s, Box 8.00
    JEWELRY, HATPIN, see Hatpin
    JEWELRY, INDIAN, see Indian
Lavaliere, Cameo, 18 Seed Pearls, Center Pearl Drop, 10K ....90.00 To 110.00
Lavaliere, Carved Gourd, Exotic Bird, Jadeite, 14K Gold 5500.00
Lavaliere, Center Emerald, Pearl Drop, 14K Gold 165.00
Locket, Chain, Pearl Trim, Miriam Haskell, 19 In. 60.00
Locket, Heart Shape, Opens To Place Perfume, Sterling Silver 225.00
Locket, Mourning, 1877 .... 250.00
Locket, Victorian, Allover Engraved, Center Diamond, 14K Gold 115.00
Neck Chain, Twisted Leaf Design, Gold Circles, Haskell, 60 In. 55.00
Necklace & Brooch, Cultured & Seed Pearls, Floral Links 1300.00
Necklace & Earrings, Mughal Style, Emeralds, Pearls & Rubies 2310.00
Necklace, 30 Oval– & Round–Cut Sapphires, 14K Yellow Gold 305.00
Necklace, Bakelite, Coin–Shaped Buttons, Navy, White, 5/8 x 53 In. 150.00
Necklace, Bead, Victorian, 15 In., 14K Yellow Gold 135.00
Necklace, Bracelet, Earrings, White Opaque Glass, Rhinestone, Hobe 90.00
Necklace, Cabochon, Stylized Grapes, Silver, Arts & Crafts, 17 In. 357.00
Necklace, Carnelian Agate, Graduated, 26 In. 195.00
Necklace, Carved Jet, Art Deco, Whitby, England 350.00
Necklace, Cherry Amber, Art Deco, 16 In. 45.00
Necklace, Choker, Bakelite Rondels, Alternating Faceted Crystals 25.00
Necklace, Choker, False Pearl, 2 Strand, Miriam Haskell 85.00
Necklace, Choker, False Pearls & Rhinestones, Trifari 35.00
Necklace, Chunky Black & Pink Stones, Sarah Coventry 125.00
Necklace, Coral Beads, Tibetan, 18 In. 440.00
Necklace, Double Circular Links, 18K Yellow Gold, 18 In. 825.00
Necklace, Earrings, Amethyst, Sterling, Geometric Pattern, Spratling 950.00
Necklace, Enamel, Sterling, Brown Egyptian Figures, Margot, Taxco 500.00
Necklace, Freshwater Pearls, 5 Strands, 14K Gold Bead & Clasp 175.00
Necklace, Gold Plated, Black & White Cameo, Victorian 100.00
Necklace, Hair, 2 Strands, Gold–Filled Clasp, 13 1/2 In. 85.00
Necklace, Indian Silver, Turquoise Pendant, Iverson, 2 1/2 In. 350.00
Necklace, Jade, Slide Clasp, 14K Yellow Gold, 20 In. 135.00
Necklace, Oval Lapis Lazuli Pendant, Continental Silver 135.00
Necklace, Pearl, Baroque, 74 Beads, 14K Clasp, c.1910, 24 In. 420.00
Necklace, Pendant of Wheat & Birds, Georg Jensen, Chain, Box, 27 In. 500.00
Necklace, Pink Stone Set In Marcasite, Chain 35.00

Necklace, Red Coral, Victorian .... 85.00 To 95.00
Necklace, Sapphire, 30 Sapphires, 14K Gold 275.00
Necklace, Silver, Victorian, 15 In. 145.00
Necklace, Sterling, Stylized Acorns & Oak Leaves, Kalo, 15 1/2 In. 195.00
Pendant Set, Large Citrine, 14K Yellow Gold, Cartier 357.00
Pendant, Cabochon, Cut Outs, Sterling & Coral, T. H. S., 18 1/2 In. 660.00
Pendant, Carved Lapis Lazuli, 14K Yellow Gold Chain & Mount 30.00
Pendant, Filigree Gold, Emerald Glass Stones, Art Nouveau, 2 In. 35.00
Pendant, Jade, 18K Gold, Chain, Peru 35.00
Pendant, Marcasite, Large Hematite Center, Sterling Silver 105.00
Pendant, Mughal Style, Etched Emeralds, Enameled 1980.00
Pendant, Plique–A–Jour, Art Nouveau, Gold, 19th Century 800.00
Pendant, Woman's Head, Lily In Hair, Large 65.00
Pin & Earrings, Multi–Pastel Rhinestones, Weiss, 2 In. 40.00
Pin, 10 Full Cut Diamonds, Yellow Gold 410.00
Pin, 3 Robins, Ruby Eyes, Cartier, 18K Gold 2900.00
Pin, Art Nouveau Woman's Head, Gold Over Copper 70.00
Pin, Bakelite, Red Butterfly, 9 Dangling Berries 165.00
Pin, Bee, Ruby Eyes, Tiffany, 18K Gold 440.00
Pin, Bicolor Gold, 2 Pink, 2 Yellow Circles, Paul Flato, 1940s 3080.00
Pin, Black Woman, Flapper Type, White 125.00
Pin, Bow, 8 Round Diamonds, 12 Round Rubies, 14K Gold, 1940s 1320.00
Pin, Bowknot, 18K Gold, Diamonds, 3 In. 590.00
Pin, Bumblebee, Sterling, Joseff of Hollywood, 1 1/4 In. 175.00
Pin, Cabochon, Silver, Mother–of–Pearl, Arts & Crafts, 1 1/2 In. 137.00
Pin, Cameo, Coral, Seed Pearls, 14K Yellow Gold 535.00
Pin, Cameo, Italian, 14K Gold Bezel, 1 x 1 1/2 In. 85.00
Pin, Cameo, Lava, 14K White Gold Mounted, Filigree 160.00
Pin, Cameo, Openwork, Gold Tone Edge, 2 1/4 In. 48.00
Pin, Cameo, Ornate Mounting, 2 3/4 x 1 1/4 In. 85.00
Pin, Carnelian Center, Lotus Leaves & Beads, Maru Gage, 1 5/8 In. 220.00
Pin, Carnelian, Sardonyx Overlay, Seed Pearl, 21K Gold 145.00
Pin, Carved Ivory, Floral, Victorian 36.00
Pin, Cat, Arched Back, Emerald Eyes, Ruby Mouth 165.00
Pin, Cat, Sterling Silver, Jewelart Art Moderne 25.00
Pin, Center Crystal Surrounded By Rhinestones, Eisenberg 140.00
Pin, Center Oval Sapphire, Surrounded By Rose–Cut Diamonds 7000.00
Pin, Cherub With Child Swinging, Sterling Silver 220.00
Pin, Diamond Crescent & Star, European & Brilliant Diamonds 1980.00
Pin, Dog, Emerald Eyes, Cartier, 18K Gold 1760.00
Pin, Dragonfly Shape, Sterling, Gorham, 2 1/2 x 1 1/2 In. 165.00
Pin, Dragonfly, Black Onyx Eyes, Cellion, 18K Gold 660.00
Pin, Dragonfly, Cabochon Body, Emerald Eyes, Diamonds, 18K Gold 1320.00
Pin, Enameled Floral, Victorian, Gold, Back Hair Section, 1863 .... 357.00
Pin, Filigree, Florentine, 4 Diamond, 2 Sapphire, 14K Gold, 1920s 235.00
Pin, Fish, Marlin, 14K Gold, 4 In. 495.00
Pin, Floral Bow, Rhinestones, 2 1/2 x 3 1/4 In. 42.00
Pin, Floral, Hand Carved Ivory, Victorian 35.00
Pin, Flying Goose, Bakelite, Amber, 3 In. 65.00
Pin, Garnet & 9 Mabe Pearls, 14K Gold 330.00
Pin, Geometric Design, Silver & Enamel, E. David, Marked 935.00
Pin, Glass & Enameled Willow Scene, 18K Gold, 18th Century 595.00
Pin, Gold Elephant, Standing On Ivory Tusk, Kenneth Lane 45.00
Pin, Gone With The Wind, Cameo, Lux Premium 75.00
Pin, Gutta Percha, Victorian, Gold 65.00
Pin, Horse & Carriage Painted, Paperweight Type, 1800s, 1 1/2 In. 45.00
Pin, Horse's Head, Caramel Bakelite, Carved Applied Eye, 1920s 65.00
Pin, Lobster, Rhinestone, Thelma Deutsch, 4 In. 85.00
Pin, Maple Leaf Shape, Gold–Toned Openwork, Rhinestones, Trifari 32.00
Pin, Memorial, Miniature On Ivory, Mary Queen of Scots, Box 357.50
Pin, Mourning, Basketweave Hair Ground, Framed, 2 x 1 12 In. 90.00
Pin, Mourning, Portrait of Woman, Frame, 3 1/2 x 3 In. 300.00
Pin, Mourning, Urn & Weeping Willow, 1 x 1 1/8 In. 65.00

Pin, Mourning, Woven Hair, Dated 1857	100.00
Pin, Oil On Porcelain, 2 Lovers	55.00
Pin, Oval & Round Coral Cabochons, Floral, Georg Jensen, Silver	505.00
Pin, Oval Plaque of Flowers, Gold Frame, Memorial Locket	412.00
Pin, Oval, Pietra Dura, Silver Mounting, 1 1/2 In.	115.00
Pin, Pietra Dura, Oval, 14K Gold Mount	120.00
Pin, Plique-A-Jour, Enameled Berries & Leaves	185.00
Pin, Pretty Woman, Repousse, Sterling, Hollow	65.00
Pin, Rampant Lion, Pave Set, Rose-Cut Stones, Cartier, 1880, Pair	4400.00
Pin, Retractable Plique-A-Jour Enamel Wings, Ruby, Emerald, Gold	440.00
Pin, Rhinestone, Spray, Dark Green, Clear Stones, Hobe	40.00
Pin, Rhinestones, Spells Out U. S. A., 45 Stones	29.00
Pin, Rose Diamond & Enamel, French, 18K Gold, Pair	770.00
Pin, Sardonyx Cameo, Gold Frame, Wirework, Victorian	660.00
Pin, Silver, Floral & Leaf Design, Georg Jensen, 1 7/8 In.	110.00
Pin, Silver, Floriform Design, Arts & Crafts, Austrian, 2 1/4 In.	55.00
Pin, Silver, Openwork, Georg Jensen, 1946, 1 3/4 In.	247.00
Pin, Snowflake, Covered With Tiny Baroque Pearls, Haskell, 2 In.	85.00
Pin, Songbird Shape, Sapphire Eye, Turquoise Plumage, Cartier	2700.00
Pin, Sterling Silver, Blue Jasper, Wedgwood	60.00
Pin, Sterling Silver, Oval Citrine, 2 Moonstones, 2 1/8 In.	605.00
Pin, Sterling, Design In Block, Black Ground, FHB, 1 5/8 In.	192.00
Pin, Stylized Bird On Top of Wreath, Georg Jensen	95.00
Pin, Tussie Mussie, Silver Plate	95.00
Pin, Woman At Window, Flowing Hair, Flowers, Sterling Silver	70.00
Pin, Woman Wearing Hat, Plumes, Beads, Mary Gregory, 1 1/4 In.	295.00
Pin, Wreath, Rhinestone, Prong Set, Joseph Warner	28.00
Pin-Pendant, Cameo, Heart Shape, 14K Gold	95.00
Ring, 9 Oval Cut Opals, Mexican Silver Band	250.00
Ring, Amber, Fossilized Ant, 12K Yellow Gold	88.00
Ring, Amethyst, Carved, Victorian, Pink Gold	70.00
Ring, Blue Sapphire, Oval, 14K Gold	125.00
Ring, Blue Topaz & Diamonds, 14K Yellow Gold	215.00
Ring, Brilliant-Cut Emerald, Stepped Filigree Mounting, 14K Gold	410.00
Ring, Buckle, Brickwork Band, Rubies & Diamonds, Tiffany, c.1940	880.00
Ring, Center Lapis Lazuli, Floral Frame, Georg Jesen, Marked	275.00
Ring, Center Oval Turquoise, Surround of 12 Diamonds, 18K Gold	715.00
Ring, Class, Mitchell, So. Dakota, 14K Gold, 1915	30.00
Ring, Cocktail, 9 Full Cut Diamonds, Contemporary Design, 14K Gold	330.00
Ring, Cultured Pearl, 7 Single Cut Diamonds, White Gold	155.00
Ring, Dinner, 14K Yellow Gold, 1 Round Cut Diamond & 4 Smaller	180.00
Ring, Dinner, Smoky Coral, 14K Yellow Gold	110.00
Ring, Filigree, Rubies, Diamonds, 1 x 3/4 In.	535.00
Ring, Garnet, Rose Gold Plated Silver, Marked 925	70.00
Ring, Garnet, Victorian, Seed Pearls, 14K Gold	75.00
Ring, Man's, Star Sapphire, 3 Diamonds, 14K Gold	100.00
Ring, Marquise Amethyst, 14K Gold	135.00
Ring, Moonstone, Stylized Silver Leaf & Bead, Georg Jensen	220.00
Ring, Opal, 14K Yellow Gold, 2 mm. Diam.	255.00
Ring, Opal, 2 Rubies Each Side, 14K Gold	155.00
Ring, Orange Corundum, Seed Pearls, Victorian, 10K Gold	70.00
Ring, Oval Amethyst, Flanked By 6 Small Diamonds, Yellow Gold	775.00
Ring, Pearl Center, 18 Rubies, Beaded Openwork, 18K Gold	380.00
Ring, Pink Sapphire, 14K Gold	125.00
Ring, Red Bakelite, Carved Dome, Art Deco	45.00
Ring, Round Cut Center Sapphire, Filigree Setting, 18K White Gold	110.00
Ring, Silver, Beaded Oval, Georg Jensen, 1945	93.00
Ring, Snuff, Gold, Enameled, Lisez Et Croyez	250.00
Ring, Square Cut Rubies, Diamonds, Platinum Mounting, Cartier	5500.00
Ring, Sterling & Swiss Lapis, Insect Design Shank, Marked	85.00
Ring, Wedding Band, 26 Square Cut Rubies, Platinum	550.00
Ring, Wedding, Gold, 8 Sides, Dated 1873	125.00
Stickpin, Artic Circle, World Globe	18.00

John Rogers, Group, John Alden & Priscilla,
c.1855, 22 In.

◆◆◆◆◆◆◆◆◆◆◆◆◆◆◆◆◆◆◆◆◆◆◆◆◆

Rogers groups or other plaster figures should not be cleaned with water or chemicals. Remove the dirt with an art gum eraser. If the finish is destroyed, repaint the figure with a watercolor paint in a shade matching the original.

◆◆◆◆◆◆◆◆◆◆◆◆◆◆◆◆◆◆◆◆◆◆◆◆◆

Stickpin, Cameo, 4 Seed Pearls, Gold	75.00
Stickpin, Case Plow Works, Sunburst, Hand Holding Plow Blade	55.00
Stickpin, Death To Rum, Nickel Hatchet, Enameled Letters	30.00
Stickpin, Dog's Head, Celluloid, Rhinestone Eyes	17.50
Stickpin, Emerson Footlift Farm Implements, Plated Foot	37.00
Stickpin, Lion Buggy, Bronze Lion	30.00
Stickpin, Lucky Strike, Green Enameled Package	28.00
Stickpin, Man In Moon, Diamond Eye, Ruby Cigar End, Yellow Gold	375.00
Stickpin, Owl, Pave Diamond Face, Garnet Eyes, Platinum & Gold	1045.00
Stickpin, Pharoah's Head, French, 18K Gold	250.00
Stickpin, Plow, Copper Oval	38.00
Stickpin, Round Oak Range, Doe–Wah–Jack Profile, Bronze	45.00
Stickpin, Shell Cameo, 14K Gold	65.00
Stickpin, United Munitions Co., Copper Arrow	24.00
Stickpin, Victorian, Solid Gold, Diamond & Seed Pearls	50.00
Stud Set, Cufflinks & 3 Studs, Moonstone, 14K Yellow Gold	125.00
Tie Tack, General George Washington, Battersea, 1 1/2 In., Pair	1550.00
JEWELRY, WATCH, see Watch	
Watch Chain, Carved & Roped Links, Watch Fob Compass	100.00
Watch Chain, Elongated Hammered Links, Yellow Gold Filled, T Bar	27.00
Watch Chain, Opals In Slide, Gold Filled	100.00
Watch Chain, Railroad Conductor's, Solid Gold	340.00
Watch Chain, Sport, Fob	16.00
Watch Chain, Woman's, Heart Slide	75.00
Watch Chain, Yellow–Gold Filled, Silver Fob of Madonna & Child	42.00
JEWELRY, WRISTWATCH, see Wristwatch	

John Rogers statues were made from 1859 to 1892. The originals were bronze, but the thousands of copies made by the Rogers factory were of painted plaster. Eighty different figures were made. Similar painted plaster figures were made by some other factories. Never repaint a Rogers figure because this lowers the value to collectors.

JOHN ROGERS, Group, A Frolic At The Old Homestead, Gray, 27 x 23 In.	850.00
Group, Charity Patient, 1866, 22 In.	550.00
Group, Checkers Up At The Farm, 1875, 20 In.	450.00
Group, Coming To The Parson, 1870, 22 In.	325.00
Group, Country Post Office, News From The Army, 1864, 20 In.	1600.00
Group, Elder's Daughter, 1887, 21 1/2 In.	1300.00
Group, Fetching The Doctor, Copper Coated, 1881, 16 In.	1500.00
Group, Fighting Bob, Pewter Pistols, 1889, 34 In.	1540.00
Group, Football, Painted, 1891, 15 In.	1800.00
Group, Frolic At The Old Homestead, 1887, 22 1/2 In.	700.00
Group, Going For The Cows, 1873, 11 1/2 In.	425.00
Group, Ha, I Like Not That, Othello, Booth, Salvini, 1882, 22 In.	275.00
Group, Is It So Nominated, Merchant of Venice, 1880, 23 In.	357.50
Group, John Alden & Priscilla, c.1855, 22 In. ....*Illus*	600.00

Group, King Lear, Signed, 1885, 19 In.	1100.00
Group, Mail Day, 1864, 16 In.	1200.00
Group, Neighboring Pews, 1883, 18 1/2 In.	525.00
Group, Peddler At The Fair, 1878, 20 In.	1200.00
Group, Photographer & Sitter, Set, 1878, 17 & 18 1/2 In.	2500.00
Group, Politics, 1888, 18 In.	1900.00
Group, Rip Van Winkle At Home, Signed, 1871, 21 x 12 In.	355.00
Group, Rip Van Winkle On The Mountain, Signed, 21 1/4 In.	350.00
Group, Rip Van Winkle Returned, Signed, 1871, 21 1/4 In.	1155.00
Group, Rip Van Winkle, On The Mountain, Signed, 1871, 21 1/4 In.	385.00
Group, Shaughraun and Tatters, April, 1875, 20 In.	250.00
Group, Washington, 1875, 30 In.	2200.00
Group, Watch On The Santa Maria, 1892, 15 1/2 In.	2300.00
Group, We Boys, 1872, 17 In.	550.00
Group, Wounded To The Rear, One More Shot, 1865, 23 1/2 In.	550.00
Group, You Are A Spirit I Know, 1885, 19 In.	650.00

Any memorabilia that refers to the Jews or the Jewish religion is collected. Interests range from newspaper clippings that mention eighteenth- and nineteenth-century Jewish Americans to religious objects, such as menorahs or spice boxes. Age, condition, and the intrinsic value of the material, as well as the historic and artistic importance, determine the value.

JUDAICA, Book, Megilla, Silver Filigree	1000.00
Lamp, Hannukah, Hebrew Inscription, German Silver, 13 1/4 In.	9000.00
Megilla, Esther, Illuminated, Haman, Mordechai On Box	3400.00
Torah Set, Finials, Shield, Pointer, German Silver, 18th Century	9000.00
Watercolor, On Paper, Torah With Sabbath Candelabra, Folk Art	695.00

Jugtown Pottery refers to pottery made in North Carolina as far back as the 1750s. In 1915, Juliana and Jacques Busbee set up a training and sales organization for what they named *Jugtown Pottery.* In 1921, they built a shop at Jugtown, North Carolina, and hired Ben Owen as a potter in 1923. The Busbees moved the village store where the pottery was sold and promoted to New York City. Juliana Busbee sold the New York store in 1926 and moved into a log cabin near the Jugtown Pottery. The pottery closed in 1958. It reopened and is still working near Seagrove, North Carolina.

JUGTOWN, Bowl, Rice, Frogskin, 5 In., Pair	85.00
Jug, Frogskin Green Glaze	35.00
Mug, Frogskin, Large, Pair	85.00 To 145.00
Plate, Tobacco Spit Brown, Raised Sides	25.00
Teapot, Orange	35.00
Vase, Chinese Blue, 4 In.	90.00 To 125.00
Vase, Chinese Blue, Red Glaze, 6 1/2 In.	600.00
Vase, Inkwell, Chinese Blue, Red	90.00
Vase, Jug, Tobacco Brown, 4 1/2 In.	50.00

The first coin-operated phonograph was demonstrated in 1889. In 1906 the *Automatic Entertainer* appeared, the first coin-operated phonograph to offer several different selections of music. The first electrically powered jukebox was introduced in 1927. Collectors search for jukeboxes of all ages, especially those with flashing lights and unusual design and graphics.

JUKEBOX, Aerion, No. 1200-A	950.00
Bimbo, Animated Monkeys	2800.00
Ristaucrat, 100 Selections	795.00
Rock-Ola, Model 1426	8000.00
Rock-Ola, Model 403, Wall, Restored	1950.00
Rock-Ola, No. 424	750.00
Seeburg Nickelodeon, Model L Jr., Oak	5895.00
Seeburg, 1939	3500.00
Seeburg, Model 222	1600.00

Seeburg, Model 9800	1000.00
Victory	9500.00
Wall, Capehart, Cast Iron	250.00
Williams, Music Mite, Stand	1500.00
Wurlitzer, Model 61, Counter Top 2500.00 To	3500.00
Wurlitzer, Model 750, 1941	5300.00
Wurlitzer, Model 1015	7600.00
Wurlitzer, Model 1100	6500.00
Wurlitzer, Model 1600	1275.00
Wurlitzer, Model 1800	2650.00
Wurlitzer, Model 2000, Pages	2750.00
Wurlitzer, Model 2304	1175.00
Wurlitzer, Model 800	6500.00

Kate Greenaway, who was a famous illustrator of children's books, drew pictures of children in high–waisted Empire dresses. She lived from 1846 to 1901. Her designs appear on china, glass, and other pieces. Figural napkin rings depicting the Greenaway children may also be found listed under Napkin Ring, Figural.

KATE GREENAWAY, Card Holder, Silver Plate	325.00
Figurine, Girl, Bonnet, Boy, With Gun, 6 In., Pair	125.00
Figurine, Girl, Tennis Player, Ruffled Cap, Long Dress, 4 In.	40.00
Figurine, Little Boy & Girl On Potty, She Is Worried	50.00
Lamp, Pastel Childen, White Porcelain	350.00
Salt & Pepper, Boy & Girl	140.00
Toothpick, With Baker Boy, Cap, Long Apron, 1900, 5 1/2 In.	50.00

Kauffmann refers to the type of work done by Angelica Kauffmann, a painter and decorative artist for Adam Brothers in England between 1766 and 1781. She designed small–scale pictorial subjects in the neoclassic manner. Most porcelains signed *Kauffmann* were made in the 1800s. She did not do the artwork on all pieces signed with her name.

KAUFFMANN, Bowl, Cupids, Flowers, Red, Green, Gold, 10 In.	95.00
Box, Child and Maiden, Lilacs, Leaves, 5 In.	75.00
Cup & Saucer, Dark Blue, Gold, Green	100.00
Cup & Saucer, Greek Maidens In Field of Flowers	75.00
Jardiniere, , Mythology Figures, 2 Handles, 9 x 14 In.	195.00
Plate, Classical Scene of Dancing Girls, Burgundy Border, 10 In.	85.00
Plate, Greek Maidens Dancing, Cobalt Border, 10 In.	85.00
Tray, Classical Scene, Transfer, Gold, Round, 17 In.	112.00
Vase, 4 Maidens In Field, 18 In.	395.00

Kay Finch
CALIFORNIA

Kay Finch Ceramics were made in Corona Del Mar, California, from 1935 to 1963. The hand–decorated pieces often depicted whimsical animals and people. Pastel colors were used.

KAY FINCH, Candlestick, Planters, Brown, Pair	40.00
Figurine, Angel Head, Hand Painted	15.00
Figurine, Angel, Head With Wings	29.00
Figurine, Angel, Praying, Blonde, 4 In.	40.00
Figurine, Boy With Pig, 6 In.	50.00
Figurine, Cat, 5 1/2 In.	34.00
Figurine, Cat, 6 In.	175.00
Figurine, Cat, Hand Painted, 5 1/2 x 7 In.	40.00
Figurine, Cocker Spaniel, 8 In.	125.00
Figurine, Duck, Hand Painted	22.00
Figurine, Godey Couple, Hand Painted	75.00
Figurine, Kitten, 7 x 5 In.	60.00
Figurine, Lamb, Pink, 5 3/4 In.	23.00
Figurine, Owl, Hand Painted, 3 3/4 In.	22.00
Figurine, Peasants, Pair	150.00
Figurine, Rabbit, Hand Painted	30.00
Figurine, Rooster & Hen, Hand Painted, Pair	60.00

Old leather saddles and other antiques can be safely cleaned and reconditioned at home. Wash the leather in warm water and glycerine soap. Rub with an old soft cloth diaper. Keep replacing the dirty water. Don't be surprised at how much clean water is needed. A saddle takes about ten gallons. Reshape any bent or creased sections while the leather is damp. Dry the leather overnight, away from sunlight. Next rub olive oil or almond oil into the leather. Dry for 6 hours, apply more oil. A final polish can be added with carnuba wax applied with your fingertips. Buff with a soft cloth.

Teapot, Magnolia	90.00

KAYSERZINN, see Pewter

KELVA Kelva glassware was made by the C. F. Monroe Company of Meriden, Connecticut, about 1904. It is a pale, pastel–painted glass decorated with flowers, designs, or scenes. Kelva resembles Nakara and Wave Crest, two other glasswares made by the same company.

KELVA, Box, Blue Daisies, Pink Ground, Lined, 3 3/4 x 4 x 5 1/2 In.	540.00
Box, Cover, Enameled Dots, Flowers, Brass Feet & Mounts, 3 1/2 In.	395.00
Box, Cover, Lilies, Lined, Signed, 6 1/2 In.	135.00
Box, Dresser, Dark Green	285.00
Box, Dresser, Painted Wild Roses, Mottled Green Ground, Marked, 4 In.	385.00
Box, Hinged Cover, Enameled Dots, Brass Feet & Mounts, 3 1/2 In.	395.00
Box, Hinged Lid, 6 Sides, Enameled Dots, Pink Flowers, 3 1/2 In.	395.00
Box, Jewelry, Hinged Cover, Pink, White Flowers, Marked, 3 3/4 x 8 In.	650.00
Box, Wild Roses, Fuchsia Trim, White Dots, 3 1/2 x 6 In.	690.00
Dish, Sweetmeat, Pink Floral, Mottled Green Ground, Marked	357.50
Humidor, Cigar, Pink Flowers, Word Cigars On Front, Blue Ground, 5 In.	550.00
Saltshaker, Scroll Waves, Pink To White	85.00
Tray, Pin, Pink Flowers	90.00

Kemple glass was made by John Kemple of East Palestine, Ohio, and Kenova, West Virginia, from 1945 to 1970. The glass was made from old molds. Many designs and colors were made. Kemple pieces are usually marked with a K on the bottom. Many milk glass pieces were made with or without the mark.

KEMPLE, Candlesticks, Dolphin, Pair	45.00
Dish, Dog Cover	55.00
Dish, Rooster Cover, 7 In.	35.00
Dish, Turkey On Basket	50.00
Figurine, Rooster, Milk Glass, Large	85.00
Rooster Cover, Amber, 8 In.	55.00

The Kenton Hills Pottery made art wares, including vases and figurines that resembled Rookwood, probably because so many of the original artists and workmen had worked at the Rookwood plant.

KENTON HILLS, Bowl, Aventurine, 6 In.	200.00
Vase, Glossy Red, 4 In.	200.00
Vase, Green, Blue, Hentschel, 7 In.	350.00

KEW-BLAS Kew Blas is the name used by the Union Glass Company of Somerville, Massachusetts. The name refers to an iridescent golden glass made from the 1890s to 1924. The iridescent glass was reminiscent of the Tiffany glass of the period.

KEW BLAS, Vase, King Tut, Scalloped, Gold & Opalescent, Signed, 9 3/4 In.	950.00

Vase, Overall Snakeskin, Gold Iridescent, Signed, 4 1/2 In.	650.00
Vase, Pulled Feather, Gold, Signed, 5 In.	500.00
Vase, Scalloped, Green Pulled Design, Gold, Signed, 10 1/4 In.	610.00
Vase, Zipper Pattern, Green Swags, Gold Interior, Signed, 7 3/4 In.	995.00

Kewpies, designed by Rose O'Neill, were first pictured in the *Ladies' Home Journal.* The pixielike figures were a success, and Kewpie dolls started appearing in 1911. Kewpie pictures and other items soon followed. Collectors search for all items that picture the little winged people.

KEWPIE, Bank, Fat Kewpie, Chalkware, 12 In.	25.00
Bank, Kewpie, With Wings, Chalkware, 12 In.	68.00
Book, Christmas	15.00
Book, Paper Doll	35.00
Candy Container, Glass, 6 In.	75.00
Card Tray, Bronzed	50.00
Creamer, Leapfrog, R. Rudolstadt, Rose O'Neill	165.00
Display, Cardboard, Red Santa Hat, Rose O'Neill, 1912, 12 In.	45.00
Doll, Bisque, Heart Label, Signed Rose O'Neill, 6 In.	300.00
Doll, Bisque, Painted Blue Wings, Blond Topknot, Rose O'Neill, 6 In.	82.50
Doll, Bisque, Rose O'Neill, 1920s, 6 In.	220.00
Doll, Bisque, Rose O'Neill, 9 In.	350.00
Doll, Bisque, Rose O'Neill, Tiny	60.50
Doll, Boy & Girl, Christmas Clothes, 1987, 10 1/2 In., Pair	55.00
Doll, Buttonhole, Seal, Rose O'Neill, 2 In.	200.00
Doll, Celluloid, Heart Sticker, 9 1/2 In.	100.00
Doll, Character Baby, Bisque, Sleep Eyes, Nippon, 13 In.	135.00
Doll, Composition, 13 1/2 In.	200.00
Doll, Composition, Blue Wings, Rose O'Neill, 1913, 12 In.	38.50
Doll, Lawyer, Rose O'Neill, 3 3/4 In.	375.00
Doll, Vinyl, Jointed Neck, Arms & Hips, 9 In.	50.00
Figurine, Bisque, In Swing, Metal	45.00 To 49.00
Figurine, Movable Arms, Frozen Legs, 6 1/2 In.	150.00
Figurine, Reader, 1913	95.00
Figurine, Rose O'Neill, 1936, 2 1/2 In.	35.00
Figurine, Thinker, Carnival, Tall	25.00
Figurine, Thinker, Rose O'Neill	25.00
Hatpin Holder, Heart Shape	149.00
Holder, Place Card, Reading Book, Rose O'Neill, 2 1/2 In.	200.00
Hugger, Rose O'Neill, 2 1/2 In.	175.00
Hugger, Sitting, Mandolin, 2 In.	250.00
Match Pack, Kewpie Hotels, Kewpie Picture	15.00
Notes, Rose O'Neill, Box	10.00
Ornament, Christmas, 10 Piece	25.00
Paper Dolls, In Kewpieland, 1960s, Uncut	20.00
Paperweight, Kewpie & Purdue Foundry In Relief, Cast Iron	150.00
Pill Box, Tin, Kewpie On Swing	100.00
Plate, Christmas, 1971	12.00
Plate, Floral Border, Action, Prussian Soldier, Rose O'Neill	80.00
Plate, Leapfrog, R. Rudolstadt, Rose O'Neill	175.00
Plate, Portrait, Rose O'Neill	100.00
Plate, R. Rudolstadt, 7 In.	75.00
Plate, Santa Claus & 11 Kewpies, 1973, 10 1/2 In.	39.00
Postcard, Valentine, Signed Rose O'Neill	35.00
Ring, Official	55.00
Shaving Mug, Milk Glass	100.00
Stationery, Rose O'Neill, Box	10.00
Tea Rest, Germany	105.00
Thimble, Marked Kewpie	35.00
Tray, Bobwhite Ice Cream, 1920s	225.00

KIMBALL, see Cluthra
KING'S ROSE, see Soft Paste

All types of kitchen utensils, from eggbeaters to bowls, are collected today. Handmade wooden and metal items, like ladles and apple peelers, were made in the early–nineteenth century. Mass–produced pieces, like iron apple peelers and graniteware, were made in the nineteenth century. Other kitchen wares are listed under manufacturers' names or under Advertising; Tool; or Wooden.

KITCHEN, Apple Corer & Sectioner, 2 Side Handles, Silver Plate, c.1890	75.00
Apple Parer, Wooden, Handled Blade, Wooden Pegged Crank Handle	350.00
Ashtray, Match Holder, Griswold	15.00
Baller, Fruit, Wooden Handle, Germany	7.00
Basket, Egg Boiling, Wire, Arched Twisted Handle, 1820, 3 1/2 In.	95.00
Basket, Egg, Wire, Collapsible, 5 In.	23.00
Beater Jar, Milk Glass, Hazel Atlas, 1923	20.00
Beater, Whippo Super Whipper, Iron & Glass, 2 Piece	50.00
Blender, Mastercraft	20.00
Blender, Oster, Glass, Chrome, Pulp Juicer, Instruction Book, 1961	38.00
Board, Bread, Inset Braces On Back, Poplar, 22 In. Plus Handle	55.00
Board, Bread, Single Piece of Poplar, 20 1/2 x 27 In.	35.00
Board, Cutting, Pig, Wire Tail, 13 x 8 In.	25.00
Bottle, Water, Refrigerator, 1930s	15.00
Bottle, Water, Refrigerator, Bubble, Aluminum Ice Lid	15.00
Bowl, Butter, With Paddle	85.00
Bowl, Butter, Wooden, 16 In.	8.00
Box, Scouring, Square Nail Construction, Pine, 33 3/4 In.	200.00
Bread Box, Truth Spices, Picture of George Washington	165.00
Bread Maker, Universal, 1906	35.00
Bread Raiser, Cover, Tin, N. Y., Large	25.00
Broiler, Manning Bowman, Electric	50.00
Broiler, Revolving, Iron	100.00
Broom, Splint Ash, Braided Band, Early 19th Century, 54 In.	195.00
Bucket, Mince Meat, Wooden, Partial Paper Label, 5 Lb.	68.00
Butcher Block, Maple, 1900s, 35 x 35 In.	450.00
KITCHEN, BUTTER MOLD, see Kitchen, Mold, Butter	
Butter Paddle, Curl In Bowl, Turned Top For Hook, Maple, 10 1/2 In.	65.00
Butter Paddle, Curly Maple, Worn Dark Patina, 9 1/4 In.	55.00
Butter Paddle, Gray Scrubbed Finish, 9 In.	500.00
Butter Paddle, Maple, Hanging Hook On Handle, 9 In.	45.00
Butter Paddle, Primitive, Wooden	12.00
Butter Stamp, 3 Strawberries, Leaves, Knob Handle, 2 1/2 In.	175.00
Butter Stamp, Bird, Cased, 4 1/2 In.	90.00
Butter Stamp, Cow, 3 1/2 In.	35.00
Butter Stamp, Double Flower & Leaves, 3 3/4 In.	100.00
Butter Stamp, Double Sheaf of Wheat, c.1830, 2 x 4 In.	85.00
Butter Stamp, Double Thistle & Leaves, Elongated Knob, 1830, 5 In.	350.00
Butter Stamp, Double Thistle & Leaves, Knob Handle, 5 In.	350.00
Butter Stamp, Eagle & Shield, Turned Handle, 3 5/8 In.	125.00
Butter Stamp, Eagle & Star, Turned Handle, Scrubbed, 4 1/4 In.	125.00
Butter Stamp, Eagle, 3 1/8 In.	200.00
Butter Stamp, Eagle, Turned Handle, 4 In.	175.00
Butter Stamp, Eagle, Turned Handle, Round, 4 1/2 In.	300.00
Butter Stamp, Eagle, With Foliage & Star, 4 5/8 In.	450.00
Butter Stamp, Fish, Primitive, 3 In.	150.00
Butter Stamp, Floral Design, Primitive, 3 3/8 In.	45.00
Butter Stamp, Floral, Semicircular, 3 1/2 x 7 In.	185.00
Butter Stamp, Floral, Turned Handle, 3 7/8 In.	110.00
Butter Stamp, Flower & Leaf	65.00
Butter Stamp, Flower & Leaf, Square, Wooden	55.00
Butter Stamp, Flower, 2 Leaves, Round, 3 3/4 In.	50.00
Butter Stamp, Flower, Lollipop, 8 1/2 In.	275.00
Butter Stamp, Foliage Design, Long Turned Handle, 3 3/4 In.	30.00
Butter Stamp, Foliage, Oblong, 4 x 6 1/2 In.	150.00
Butter Stamp, Geometric Design, Octagonal, Reversible, 3 7/8 In.	50.00

Butter Stamp, Heart Design, Foliage, Cross Hatched, 4 3/8 In. 300.00
Butter Stamp, Lollipop, Primitive Tulip, Star Flower, 8 In. 400.00
Butter Stamp, Medallion of Tulips, Sawtooth Border, 4 1/2 In. 220.00
Butter Stamp, Pineapple, Turned Handle, 4 3/8 In. 30.00
Butter Stamp, Pinwheel, 3 3/4 In. 115.00
Butter Stamp, Pomegranate, 3 5/8 In. 30.00
Butter Stamp, Sheaf of Wheat 75.00
Butter Stamp, Star Flower & Heart, On 2 Sides, Wooden, 4 7/8 In. 350.00
Butter Stamp, Star Flower, 4 5/8 In. 90.00
Butter Stamp, Star Flower, Lollipop, 6 1/8 In. 265.00
Butter Stamp, Star Flower, Lollipop, 8 1/4 In. 175.00
Butter Stamp, Star Flower, Rectangular, 3 1/4 x 3 7/8 In. 20.00
Butter Stamp, Sunflower & Leaves, 4 1/4 In. 430.00
Butter Stamp, Swan 85.00
Butter Stamp, Thistle 75.00
Cake Pan, Heart Shape, Tin, Individual, Rolled Edge, 1830, 4 x 5 In. 75.00
Cake Safe, Japanned Tin, Handles 25.00
Can Opener, Edlund Jr., Steel, Wooden Knob, Handle, Pat. 1925, 1929 .... 8.00
Can Opener, Fish, Gold & Red, Large 19.00
Can Opener, Keen Kutter, Iron 18.00
Can Opener, Winchester 30.00
Canister Set, Dutch Boy & Girl, Metal, 4 Piece 40.00
Canister Set, Salt Box, Pink–Purple Pansies, Mepoco, Germany, 8 Pc. 200.00
Carpet Beater, Wire 7.00
Carrier, Butter, Wire Bail, Red Paint, c.1850, 7 1/2 x 11 1/2 In. 225.00
Carving Set, Bone Handles, Box, 3 Piece 25.00
Cheese Ladder, Mortised & Pinned, Early 1800s, 10 1/2 x 22 In. 75.00
Cheese Press, Hand Carved Dog, 12 In. 110.00
Cherry Pitter, Enterprise 35.00
Chopper, Food, 6 Bell Shaped Blades, Keen Kutter, Wood Handle, 8 In. 45.00
Chopper, Food, Crescent Blade, Wooden Handle 30.00
Chopper, Food, Keen Kutter 12.00
Chopper, Food, Wooden Handle, Single Blade, 6 3/4 x 9 1/2 In. 135.00
Chopper, Nut, Hazel Atlas .... 6.00 To 8.00
Churn, Crank Type, Round 105.00
Churn, Dazey, 1 Qt. 350.00
Churn, Dazey, 2 Qt. 185.00
Churn, Dazey, 4 Qt. 145.00
Churn, Dazey, 6 Qt. 175.00
Churn, Dazey, Allover Daisies, Dated 225.00
Churn, Dazey, High Top, 1 Qt. 1000.00
Churn, Dazey, No. 4, Original Paint On Crank 70.00
Churn, Wooden Bands, Stave Extension Handle, 19 In. Plus Handle 325.00
Churn, Wooden Dasher, Conneaut, Ohio, 1 Gal. 40.00
Cider Press, Iron Works 275.00
Clothes Washer, Hand, Perfect, Pat. Oct. 13, 1985, Tin, 15 x 15 In. 95.00
Clothesline Reel, Indoor, Red, Box 12.00
Clothespin, 4 1/2 In. .... .50
Clothespin, Flat Shape, 8 Piece 4.00
Clothespin, Hollywood Pinups, Colored Aluminum, Card of 10 .... 12.50
Clothespin, Rogers Clean Grip, Bakelite, Face Design, 24 Piece 12.50
KITCHEN, COFFEE GRINDER, see Coffee Grinder
Coffeepot, Iron, Brass Finial, Iron Handle, Lid, No. 1647, 10 5/8 In. 400.00
Coffeepot, White Enamel, Dark Blue Trim 9.00
Colander, Footed, 19 In. 25.00
Cookie Board, 2 Hearts One Side, 1 On Other, 8 3/4 x 20 1/4 In. 485.00
Cookie Board, 2 Pomegranates, 2 Tulips, Cherry, 4 1/2 x 2 In. 120.00
Cookie Board, 6 Carved Animals, People, Worm Holes, 4 x 20 1/4 In. 110.00
Cookie Board, 6 Carved Figures, 18 x 5 1/2 In. 150.00
Cookie Board, 9 Relief Carved Figures, 3 3/4 x 30 1/2 In. 200.00
Cookie Board, Carved 2 Faces, Basket of Flowers, Tulips, 6 x 7 In. 495.00
Cookie Board, Carved Horse, Rider, Rooster On Reverse, 13 x 10 In. 175.00
Cookie Board, Chicken, Tin Edging, 10 1/4 x 6 3/4 In. 425.00

Cookie Board, Circles, Man With Long Nose, 6 Sections, 21 3/4 In. 275.00
Cookie Board, Eagle & Banner, In God We Trust, 12 3/4 x 6 3/8 In. 400.00
Cookie Board, Figure In Alpine Costume, 39 1/2 x 10 3/4 In. 50.00
Cookie Board, Flower Design, 27 x 5 In. 40.00
Cookie Board, Fox & Goose 1 Side, Dog On Other, 2 3/8 x 3 3/4 In. 55.00
Cookie Board, Geometrics 1 Side, Thistle Obverse, 7 1/2 In. 125.00
Cookie Board, Heart, Basket of Flowers, Natural, 10 x 12 In. 350.00
Cookie Board, Man 1 Side, Woman Other, Wooden, 4 3/4 x 11 3/4 In. 255.00
Cookie Board, People, Mermaid, 8 Carved Sections, 27 1/2 x 5 In. 95.00
Cookie Board, Reindeer Pulling Sleigh, Santa Claus, 4 1/2 In. 260.00
Cookie Board, Rooster, Dark Finish, 9 3/4 x 10 3/4 In. 125.00
Cookie Board, Scrubbed, Carved, 7 3/4 x 6 3/4 In. 60.00
Cookie Board, Springerle, 12 Designs, 4 5/8 x 7 7/8 In. 125.00
Cookie Cutter, Animal, Child's, Tin, 4 Piece 24.00
Cookie Cutter, Bear, Seated, Strap Handle, 3 x 3 1/2 In. 25.00
Cookie Cutter, Bird, In Flight, Folded Handle, 2 1/4 x 3 1/2 In. 22.00
Cookie Cutter, Bird, Wooden Back, Tin, 19th Century, 5 x 4 In. 250.00
Cookie Cutter, Blondie, Box 135.00
Cookie Cutter, Blondie, With Puppies, 1948 .... 125.00
Cookie Cutter, Cartoon, Tom & Jerry, Droppy, 1956, 6 Piece 30.00
Cookie Cutter, Cat, Inset Eyes, Tin, 19th Century, 8 x 4 In. 650.00
Cookie Cutter, Cat, Tin, Strap Back 15.00
Cookie Cutter, Chicken, Tin 5.00
Cookie Cutter, Cornucopia, Strap Handle, Tin 45.00
Cookie Cutter, Dagwood & Blondie, Box, 1948 .... 125.00
Cookie Cutter, Dog, Collie, Folded Handle, 2 1/2 x 4 In. 30.00
Cookie Cutter, Dog, Tin 10.00
Cookie Cutter, Duck, Tin, Handle 10.00
Cookie Cutter, Eagle, 19th Century, 9 x 3 In. 500.00
Cookie Cutter, Fireman, 19th Century, 4 x 7 In. 200.00
Cookie Cutter, Fish, Tin 50.00
Cookie Cutter, Fish, Tin, Strap Back 15.00
Cookie Cutter, Hand, Tin, 4 3/4 In. 150.00
Cookie Cutter, Heart, Handle, 4 1/2 x 3 1/2 In. 28.00
Cookie Cutter, Heart-In-Hand, Strap Handle, 3 x 5 1/2 In. 525.00
Cookie Cutter, Horse, Tin, Large 140.00
Cookie Cutter, Indian Girl, Long Skirt, 19th Century, 6 x 17 In. 475.00
Cookie Cutter, Indian, Deep Edge, 19th Century, 8 x 4 In. 250.00
Cookie Cutter, Indian, Threatening, 4 x 7 In. 550.00
Cookie Cutter, Man On Horseback, Blowing Horn, 19th Century 450.00
Cookie Cutter, Mermaid, 19th Century, 6 x 5 In. 450.00
Cookie Cutter, Moose, 19th Century, 7 x 8 In. 300.00
Cookie Cutter, Old Man, Walking Stick, 19th Century, 4 x 7 In. 275.00
Cookie Cutter, Peacock, Handmade, 4 x 3 1/2 In. 45.00
Cookie Cutter, Peafowl, Tin, No Handle, 1840, 5 x 6 In. 220.00
Cookie Cutter, Protesting Pioneer, 19th Century, 4 x 8 In. 175.00
Cookie Cutter, Reddy Kilowatt, Box 35.00
Cookie Cutter, Reindeer, 19th Century, 12 x 9 In. 775.00
Cookie Cutter, Rooster, Tin, Wooden Back, 19th Century, 6 x 5 In. 750.00
Cookie Cutter, Runaway Slave, Inset Eye, 19th Century, 7 x 12 In. 7400.00
Cookie Cutter, Santa Claus 6.50
Cookie Cutter, Santa Claus, Holding Tree, 19th Century, 11 x 15 In. 800.00
Cookie Cutter, Santa Claus, Pack On Back, 19th Century, 6 x 9 In. 375.00
Cookie Cutter, Santa Claus, Tin, Copper, 8 In. 95.00
Cookie Cutter, Santa Claus, Tin, Copper, T. Mill, Philadelphia, 6 In. 65.00
Cookie Cutter, Scotty 3.00
Cookie Cutter, Set, Doll Size, In Tin Box 55.00
Cookie Cutter, Snowman, Corncob Pipe, Stovepipe Hat, 8 In. 65.00
Cookie Cutter, Snowman, Tin 30.00
Cookie Cutter, Stag With Antlers, Tin, 5 3/4 In. 178.50
Cookie Cutter, Stylized Woman, Tin, 7 1/2 In. 85.00
Cookie Cutter, Tulip, Leafed Stem, Tin, 7 x 4 In. 600.00
Cookie Cutter, Turkey, Tin, 2 1/2 In. 115.00

Cookie Cutter, Uncle Sam, 19th Century, 3 x 12 In.	725.00
Cookie Cutter, Uncle Sam, Mounted On Candle Sconce, 4 x 12 In.	3000.00
Cookie Press, 3 Patterns, Cylinder, Swing Handle, 1870	18.00
Cookie Press, Cake Decorator, Popeil, Box, 1950	8.00
Corer & Slicer, Apple, Homemade, Made To Fasten To Bench, 18 In.	65.00
Corer, Grapefruit, Pumpkin, Bakelite	7.50
Cup, Measuring, Horlick's	9.00
Cup, Measuring, Seville, 2 Spouts, Yellow	195.00
Curler, Electric, Wood, Metal, Accessories, Instructions, Box, 1940	18.00
Curling Iron, Folding Handle	9.50
Curling Iron, Sterling Handle, Small	35.00
Cutter, Board, Cabbage, Walnut, 4–Lobed Cutout	60.00
Cutter, Cabbage, Arcade, Oak	150.00
Cutter, Cabbage, Circular Cut–Out Crest, 8 x 25 1/2 In.	95.00
Cutter, Cabbage, Wooden	6.00
Cutter, Cabbage, Wooden, Shield Shape, 14 In.	55.00
Cutter, Cabbage, Wooden, Sliding Box Top	36.00
Cutter, Doughnut, Cottolene, Tin	8.00
Cutter, Doughnut, Tin, Stick Type, Heavy, 3 1/2 In.	15.00
Cutter, Doughnut, Turned Elongated Handle, Wooden	130.00
Cutter, Pasta, Germany, c.1880	160.00
Deep Fryer, Automatic, Fryyte, Chrome, 1950s	20.00
Dispenser, Dixie Cup, Metal	50.00
Dough Box, 1–Board Cover, Poplar, 29 x 40 1/2 In.	275.00
Dough Box, Dovetailed Box & Lid, Brown Grained Paint, 29 x 39 In.	300.00
Dough Box, Dovetailed, Red Paint, Softwood, 19th Century, 44 In.	1500.00
Dough Box, Hepplewhite, 1–Board Lid, Poplar, 28 x 41 In.	450.00
Dough Box, Louis XVI, Walnut, Serpentine Lid, 38 x 48 x 21 In.	1550.00
Dough Scraper, Cast Iron	35.00
Dough Scraper, Iron Blade, Engraved Copper, 18th Century, 3 1/2 In.	95.00
Drain Board, Cast Iron, Wooden Tongue In Groove Tray	35.00
Drying Cage, 3 Pullout Trays, Screen Cover, Wood, 17 x 16 In.	100.00
Duster, Turkey Feather	35.00
Dutch Oven, Griswold No. 9, Cover	45.00
Dutch Oven, Griswold No. 833	60.00
Egg Beater, Wire, A & J, Dated 1923	20.00
Egg Fryer, Griswold	35.00
Egg Timer, Aluminum	17.00
Eggbeater, 2 Speed, Black & White Worn Paint, Art Deco Style	17.50
Eggbeater, Dover, 1891	20.00
Eggbeater, Fits On Tumbler, Dated 1923	20.00
Eggbeater, Glass Bottom, Dated 1923	20.00
Eggbeater, Made In The U. S. American, Red Handle, Patent 1925	3.00
Eggbeater, Silvers & Co., New York, Glass, Cast Iron, Wire Whip	145.00
Eggcup, Bride & Groom, Cleminson, Pair	10.00
Firkin, Wooden, Cover, Quince Jelly Label	125.00
Flue Cover, Cherub, Angel, Litho, Pink & White Border, 9 1/4 In.	65.00
Flue Cover, Children, 9 1/2 In.	35.00 To 40.00
Flue Cover, Pretty Girl	28.00
Flue Cover, Pretty Woman, Wide Gold Border, 7 1/2 In.	25.00
Flue Cover, Roses, 9 1/2 In.	25.00
Flue Cover, Woman, See–Thru Blouse, Hands Behind Head, 7 3/4 In.	40.00
Fly Swatter, Merry	14.00
Food Mill, Foley, Red Handle	12.00
Frying Pan, Griswold, No. 0	65.00
Frying Pan, Self Basting Lid, Griswold, No. 5	32.00
Funnel, Canning, Crystal	8.00
Funnel, Nut Brown Pie Funnel, White	50.00
Grater, Hand, Tin Handle, Oval	15.00
Grater, Nutmeg, Everett	75.00
Grater, Rapid, Metal	8.00
Griddle, Griswold, No. 14, Bail Handle, Round	95.00
Grinder, Brass, Lighthouse Shape, Allover Geometric, 13 1/2 In.	30.00

Grinder, Climax	3.00
Grinder, Food, Keen Kutter	22.00 To 25.00
Grinder, Food, Lorraine, Box	25.00
Grinder, Food, Russwin, Drops Open For Cleaning, Cast Iron, 1902	30.00
Grinder, Food, Universal, Wooden Box	5.00
Grinder, Herb, Wooden Trough & Roller, 18th Century, 11 In.	795.00
Grinder, Keystone, Galvanized, Boyertown, No. 307n, Handle, 1920	47.50
Grinder, Meat, Griswold, No. 2	25.00
Grinder, Meat, Griswold, No. 4	53.00
Grinder, Meat, Griswold, Puritan No. 10	45.00
Grinder, Meat, Keen Kutter	6.00
Grinder, Meat, Winchester	40.00
Grinder, Sausage, Enterprise, On Wooden Bench, Cast Iron, 37 In.	25.00
Heater, Catalytic, Winchester	45.00
Heater, Stewart, Hard Coal, 96 Mica Windows, Nickel, 6 Ft.	4500.00
Holder, Ice Cream Cone, Child's, Molded	35.00
Holder, Ice Cream Cone, Octagonal, Copper & Glass	475.00
Hot Plate, Edison Co., 1914	30.00
Ice Cream Freezer, Peerless, 6 In.	125.00
Ice Cream Freezer, Reliable, Blue Paint	100.00
Ice Cream Freezer, White Mountain Junior, Label, 6 1/4 In.	275.00
Ice Cream Freezer, White Mountain, Miniature	300.00
Ice Crusher, Rival	20.00
Ice Pick, Winchester No. 9502	30.00
Ice Shaver, Arctic No. 33, Cast Metal	12.50
Ice Shaver, Gilchrist, No. 78	40.00
Icebox, 3 Doors, Brass Hardware, Century Brand	650.00
Icebox, 3 Doors, Golden Oak	650.00
Icebox, 3 Doors, Golden Oak, Brass Hardware, Restored	600.00
Icebox, Country, Zinc Lined, Tray, O. G. Tinkham, 16 1/2 x 12 1/4 In.	190.00
Icebox, Simmons Siberia, Oak, Original Hardware	900.00
Iron, Charcoal, Wooden Handle	35.00
Iron, Child's, AOW, No. 2, Iron, 4 In.	39.00
Iron, Child's, Attached Handle, Cast Iron	35.00
Iron, Coleman, Gas, Box, Unused	45.00
Iron, Fluting, Geneva, Pat. 1886	75.00
Iron, Fluting, Trivet, Streeter, Dated 1878	55.00
Iron, Gas Can, Pump, Coleman, No. 4	50.00
Iron, Gas, Coleman, Blue Enamelware	40.00
Iron, Gas, Enamelware, Blue	40.00
Iron, Gasoline, Pump & Fuel Can, Trivet	40.00
Iron, Tailor's, Electric	35.00
Iron, Tailor's, Electric, Gross–Star, Stand Cord	85.00
Iron, Traveling, Sunbeam, Metal Case, 12/22/25	75.00
Ironing Board, Folding, Wooden	8.00
Jar, Spice, Cover, Basketweave, Cinnamon, Stoneware	200.00
Jar, Spice, Cover, Basketweave, Cloves, Stoneware	200.00
Jug, Batter, Cover, Green Glass, Jenkins, Floral Etch	225.00
Juicer, Figural, Duck, Pour Spout Mouth, Japan	35.00
Juicer, Handy Andy	25.00
Juicer, Sunkist Juicit, Electric	20.00
Kettle, Griswold, No. 00, 3 Legs, Bail	150.00
Kettle, Gypsy, Marked Car Roy 1/2 Gal., Iron, 6 x 6 3/4 In.	65.00
Knife Sharpener, Dazey, Cast Iron	25.00

◆◆◆

It is best to wash marble with distilled water. Any trace of acid or iron in the water will cause deterioration or stains. Use soft soap, a bit of ammonia, and a plastic container.

◆◆◆

KITCHEN, MATCH SAFE, see Match Safe

Measure, Bentwood, 7 3/4 x 14 1/2 In.	105.00
Measure, Ideal, Pour Shape, Crystal, May 26, 1896	20.00
Measure, Round Bentwood, Turned Handle, Copper Tracks, 7 x 7 In.	250.00
Meat Grinder, Griswold, No. 1111	30.00
Meat Slicer, Cast Iron, Dated 1918	25.00
Meat Tenderizer, Arched Handle, Iron, Rectangular, 2 x 3 In.	35.00
Milk Shake Machine, Gilbert, No. B2	80.00
Milk Shake Machine, Gilchrist, No. 22	120.00
Milk Shake Machine, Gilchrist, With Cup, 1926	65.00
Milk Shake Machine, Hamilton Beach, Adjustable Column, 14 1/2 In.	55.00
Milk Shake Machine, Hamilton Beach, No. 17	125.00
Mixer, Hamilton Beach, Marble Base, Adjustable Column, 14 1/2 In.	55.00
Mixer, Hamilton Beach, Onyx Base	125.00
Mixer, Sunbeam, Jadite Bowl, Attachments	65.00

KITCHEN, MOLD, see also Pewter, Mold; Tinware, Mold

Mold, Baking, Rabbit, Griswold, 11 In., 2 Piece	90.00
Mold, Butter, 4 Designs, Sheaf, Berries, Ear of Corn, 4 x 13 In.	175.00
Mold, Butter, 8 Square Designs, Rectangular, 5 1/2 x 11 In.	225.00
Mold, Butter, Acorn, Wood, 2 1/2 In.	20.00
Mold, Butter, Cow, c.1820, 5 In.	350.00
Mold, Butter, Cow, Case Plunger, 2 1/3 In.	395.00
Mold, Butter, Double Acorn, Turned Handle, 4 x 7 In.	135.00
Mold, Butter, Pineapple Print, Pat. 1866	92.00
Mold, Butter, Pineapple, 1 Lb.	65.00
Mold, Butter, Pineapple, Wooden, 3 3/4 In.	50.00
Mold, Butter, Pomegranate, Round, 5 In.	75.00
Mold, Butter, Print–Lines Pattern, 2 Piece	55.00
Mold, Butter, Sheaf Design, Gray–Scrubbed Finish, 4 1/2 x 8 1/4 In.	55.00
Mold, Butter, Ship, Wood, 2 1/2 In.	20.00
Mold, Butter, Swan, Maple, c.1830, 4 In.	220.00
Mold, Cake, Lamb, Cast Iron, 2 Sections, 8 x 13 In.	110.00
Mold, Cake, Lamb, No. 866	100.00
Mold, Cake, Lamb, Schaab Stove & Furniture Co., Iron	125.00
Mold, Cake, Rabbit, Griswold .... 150.00 To	325.00
Mold, Cake, Santa Claus, Cast Iron, Griswold	450.00
Mold, Cake, Santa Claus, Griswold .... 285.00 To	550.00

KITCHEN, MOLD, CANDLE, see Tinware, Mold, Candle

Mold, Candy, 3 Hearts, 31 1/2 In.	245.00
Mold, Candy, Clark Bar, Multiple	25.00
Mold, Candy, Easter Bunny With Basket, Tin, 12 In.	65.00
Mold, Candy, Hearts & Stars, Wooden, 23 1/2 In.	45.00
Mold, Candy, Lamb, Tin, France	35.00
Mold, Candy, Maggie & Jiggs, Pair	25.00
Mold, Candy, Primitive Rooster, Dark Patina, 6 1/4 x 11 5/8 In.	295.00
Mold, Candy, Rabbit, Tin, 1930s, 18 In.	125.00
Mold, Chocolate, 4 Chickens, 11 1/2 6 1/2 In.	125.00
Mold, Chocolate, 8 Hens, Nest, Tin, Steel Frame, 9 1/2 x 10 1/2 In.	25.00
Mold, Chocolate, Egg, 8 In.	125.00
Mold, Chocolate, Elephant	60.00
Mold, Chocolate, Fish, Tin, France, 16 In.	45.00
Mold, Chocolate, Pig, Standing, 3 In.	45.00
Mold, Chocolate, Rabbit Pushing Baby In Carriage, Pewter, 8 In.	275.00
Mold, Chocolate, Rabbit, 8 In.	145.00
Mold, Chocolate, Rabbit, 9 In.	150.00
Mold, Chocolate, Rabbit, Double, 6 In.	125.00
Mold, Chocolate, Rabbit, Holding Egg, Double, 7 In.	125.00
Mold, Chocolate, Rabbit, Holding Flowers, Anton Reiche, 3 In.	150.00
Mold, Chocolate, Rabbit, Sitting, 9 In.	50.00
Mold, Chocolate, Rabbit, Sitting, Side Clamps, 8 1/4 In.	60.00
Mold, Chocolate, Rooster, 4–In. Frame	75.00
Mold, Chocolate, Setting Hen, Tin	38.00
Mold, Chocolate, Turkey, Tin	48.00

Mold, Chocolate, Wedding, Double Lovebird, Large 150.00
Mold, Chocolate, Wedding, Groom 68.00
Mold, Chocolate, Wedding, House 62.00
Mold, Chocolate, Winged Chicken, Clips, 4 1/2 In. 70.00
Mold, Cookie, Basket of Flowers, Grapes, Iron, 1830s, 5 1/2 x 6 In. 260.00
Mold, Cookie, Basket of Fruit, Holly Border, 1800s, 4 1/2 x 6 In. 165.00
Mold, Fish, Sculpted Scales & Fins, Copper, c.1890, 10 x 11 In. 30.00
Mold, Food, Eagle, Tin & Copper, 6 1/4 In. 275.00
Mold, Food, Geometric Design, Copper, 9 1/2 In. 45.00
Mold, Food, Mother's Oats, Ring, Aluminum 45.00
Mold, Food, Turtle Shape, Blue & White, Pottery, Germany, 8 1/2 In. 80.00
    KITCHEN, MOLD, ICE CREAM, see Pewter, Mold, Ice Cream
Mold, Maple Sugar, 6 Crimped Cups, Tin, 5 1/2 x 9 In. 55.00
Mold, Muffin, Flowers, Iron, Handles 85.00
Mold, Pudding, Acorn, 2 Piece 16.00
Mold, Pudding, Kreamer, 5 In. 35.00
Mold, Pudding, Rabbit, Fluted, Oval, Tin, 3 x 4 In. 9.00
Mortar & Pestle, Burl Maple, 19th Century, 7 1/2 x 8 3/4 In. 192.00
Noodle Roller, Tiger Maple 24.00
Numbers, Birthday Cake, Wooden, Germany, 10 Piece 29.00
Nut Chopper, Univorm, Tin Top, Bowl 30.00
Pan, Bread Stick, Griswold, No. 22, Box 38.00
Pan, Bread, Ideal, Blackened Tin, Hinged Lid, Torpedo Shape, Pat. 1897 .... 15.00
Pan, Copper, Dovetailed, Iron Handle, Coat of Arms, 23 In. 145.00
Pan, Corn Stick, Cast Iron, Wagner 25.00
Pan, Corn Stick, Griswold No. 262 .... 65.00
Pan, Corn Stick, Wagnerware, Tea Size .... 40.00 To 54.00
Pan, Crispy Corn Stick, Griswold 75.00
Pan, French Roll, Griswold 35.00
Pan, Muffin, 8 Holes, Marked Pillsbury Health Bran 16.00
Pan, Muffin, Bear, Dated 1924, Large 65.00
Pan, Muffin, Egg Shape, Cast Iron, 11 Holes 25.00
Pan, Popover, Griswold, No. 18, 6 Holes 90.00
Pan, Swedish Pancake, Griswold No. 34 .... 40.00
Pastry Jigger, Carved Maple, Shaft, Ball End, Early 1800s, 6 In. 150.00
Pea Sheller, Clamp–On Type 35.00
Peel, 2 Hearts, Iron 170.00
Peel, Chip Carved Compass & Star, Both Sides, 19 3/8 In. 190.00
Peel, Ram's Horn Handle, Iron, 42 3/4 In. 95.00
Peeler, Apple, 2 Hearts, 8 Gears 50.00
Peeler, Apple, L. C. Hudson, 1882 .... 50.00
Peeler, Apple, White Mountain, Box 25.00
Peeler, Apple, White Mountain, Box 20.00
Peeler, Apple, White Mountain, Goodell Co., Antrim, N. H., Cast Iron 45.00
Peeler, Apple, Whitemore, Mechanical, Cast Iron 70.00
Peeler, Apple, Wooden, On Bench, 45 1/2 In. 25.00
Pestle, Curly Maple, 9 In. 175.00
Pie Bird, Bird, All Yellow, China 12.00
Pie Bird, Bird, Blue, Yellow & Black Design, 4 1/4 In. 22.00
Pie Bird, Bird, White, Green, Pink & Yellow Design, China, 4 3/4 In 18.00
Pie Bird, Bird, Yellow & Brown, China 12.00
Pie Bird, Black Chef, Dressed In Yellow, Figural, China 65.00
Pie Bird, Black Chef, Yellow Outfit, Hat 80.00
Pie Bird, Black Girl, Figural, China 52.00
Pie Bird, Black Mammy, Arms Outstretched, Figural, China 55.00
Pie Bird, Black Man Holding Pie, Painted Blackbird Flying Out 55.00
Pie Bird, Black, White Base 24.00
Pie Bird, Blackbird 15.00
Pie Bird, Blue Willow Pattern, China 15.00
Pie Bird, Brass, Old Red Paint 26.00
Pie Bird, Brown Owl On Stump 50.00
Pie Bird, Chicken .... 48.00 To 49.00
Pie Bird, Cottage, Figural, China 47.00

Pie Bird, Duck	49.00
Pie Bird, Duck, Blue, China	21.00
Pie Bird, Duck, Rose, China	21.00
Pie Bird, Dutch Girl, Figural	54.00
Pie Bird, Elephant, Marked Cardinal China	135.00
Pie Bird, Elephant, Standing On Rear Feet, White	50.00
Pie Bird, English Bobby, Blue Uniform, Figural, China	54.00 To 55.00
Pie Bird, English Lady In Chair With Cup Tea, China	52.00
Pie Bird, Funnel Type, Redware Pottery	15.00
Pie Bird, Humpty Dumpty, Figural, China	52.00
Pie Bird, Mammy Holding Rolling Pin	55.00
Pie Bird, Man Followed By 3 Children, White Funnel, Yellow Top	50.00
Pie Bird, Mouse, Holding Broom In Front, Tail In Back	52.00
Pie Bird, Owl On Stump, White	50.00
Pie Bird, Owl, Brown, Perched On Stump, China	45.00
Pie Bird, Penguin, Green Scarf & Hat	55.00
Pie Bird, Rooster, Blue Willow Pattern, China	20.00
Pie Bird, Rooster, Brown, Yellow, Green, China	35.00
Pie Bird, Woman Holding Pie	50.00
Pie Crimper, Brass & Wrought Iron, 7 5/8 In.	325.00
Pie Crimper, Engraved Iron, Wooden Handle, 8 In.	85.00
Pie Crimper, Green Bakelite	12.50
Pie Crimper, Primitive, Tin, Pierced Hearts, Fluted, Handle, 1875	45.00
Pie Crimper, S–Shaped Handle, All Wood, c.1800, 8 In.	75.00
Pie Lifter, Brass Ferrule, Wooden Handle, Hanging Ring, 2 Tine	55.00
Pie Pan, California Pies, Marked 10–Cent Deposit, Tin	20.00
Plunger, Butter Mold, 1868	48.00
Popcorn Popper, Hot Plate Base, Green & Ivory Metal	15.00
Popcorn Popper, Mazola By Karo	75.00
Popcorn Popper, Poppin' Pete	38.00
Potato Masher, Child's, Wooden Handle	8.00
Potato Masher, Twisted Wire, Wooden Handle	10.00
Potato Masher, Wooden	4.50
Press, Meat Juice, H. F. Osborne, Cast Iron, Patent 1884	145.00
Rack, Drying, 2 Sections, Pine, 24 x 32 In.	300.00
Rack, Drying, 3 Horizontal Bars, Pine & Poplar, 39 1/2 x 32 In.	125.00
Rack, Drying, Canvas Hinge, Pine, 41 1/2 x 25 1/2 In.	75.00
Rack, Drying, Cherry, Maple, Straight Legs, 1840–60, 60 x 42 In.	195.00
Rack, Drying, Folding, Pine, 3 Sections, 34 x 72 In.	65.00
Rack, Egg Storage, Yellow Paint, Red Stiping, 20 x 14 In.	200.00
Rack, Hanging, Scalloped, Wire Nail Hooks, European, 17 x 28 In.	120.00
Rack, Plate, Hanging, Leaded Glass Doors, Tiger Oak Grain, 40 In.	522.00
Rack, Utensil, Spearpoint Finials, Spike Ends, Iron, 11 1/2 In.	45.00
Raisin Seeder, Enterprise	50.00
Raisin Seeder, Everett, Instructions	70.00
KITCHEN, REAMER, see Reamer	
Refrigerator, General Electric, Motor On Top, 1930s, 64 In.	350.00
Refrigerator, General Electric, Unit On Top, 1930s	75.00
Roaster, Coffee Bean, Slide Cover, Tin, Cylindrical, 35 In.	350.00
Rolling Pin, Blue & White Stripe	150.00
Rolling Pin, Cookie, N. Y. State, Flowers, Geometric Border, c.1800	295.00
Rolling Pin, Curly Maple, 18 1/2 In.	55.00
Rolling Pin, Glass, Aqua, Blown, 6 In.	40.00
Rolling Pin, Glass, Aqua, Wooden Handles	110.00
Rolling Pin, Glass, Dark Amber, Blown, 13 1/2 In.	65.00
Rolling Pin, Jadite, Shaker End	395.00
Rolling Pin, Morning Glory, Harker	85.00
Rolling Pin, Munising, Green Handle	16.00
Rolling Pin, Nailsea Type, Freeblown, Dark Olive Amber, 13 1/4 In.	88.00
Rolling Pin, Noodle, R. H. Crafts, Rochester, N. Y., 8 1/2 In.	45.00
Rolling Pin, Roll Rite, Pink, Metal Cap	33.00
Rolling Pin, Stoneware, Colonial Pattern	775.00
Rolling Pin, Stoneware, Forest City, Iowa	250.00

Rolling Pin, Tiger Maple 22.00
Rolling Pin, Walnut, Double 85.00
Rolling Pin, Wizard, Milk Glass 45.00
Rolling Pin, Yellowware 95.00
Sadiron, Child's, Dover, Red Handle 28.00
Sadiron, Child's, Pat. 1900 .... 48.00
Sadiron, Simplex, Pat. Boston 1825, Wooden Handle, Electric, 13 Lb. 100.00
KITCHEN, SALT & PEPPER, see Salt & Pepper
Sausage Grinder, On Plank 125.00
Scoop, Cranberry, Wood, Tin, Canvas, Chandler's Improved, 1906, 19 In. 85.00
Scoop, Gilchrist 40.00
Scoop, Gilchrist, Wooden Handle 45.00
Scoop, Hamilton Beach, Model 67 .... 15.00
Scoop, Ice Cream, Cast Aluminum, 1 Piece 9.00
Scoop, Ice Cream, Conical, Tin, Brass & Wood, c.1880 .... 75.00
Scoop, Ice Cream, Conical, Tin, c.1830 .... 55.00
Scoop, Ice Cream, Erie, Round, 1908, Size 16 .... 85.00
Scoop, Ice Cream, Geer Clipper Disher 250.00
Scoop, Ice Cream, Gem, Wooden Handle, Size 10 .... 25.00
Scoop, Ice Cream, Gilchrist 25.00
Scoop, Ice Cream, Gilchrist, No. 31, Brass Scoop, Oak Handle 42.00
Scoop, Ice Cream, Gilchrist, No. 31, Size 40 .... 110.00
Scoop, Ice Cream, Gilchrist, No. 33 .... 85.00
Scoop, Ice Cream, Hamilton Beach, No. 65, Bakelite Handle, 9 1/2 In. 8.00
Scoop, Ice Cream, Indestructo No. 3, Round, Size 16 .... 78.00
Scoop, Ice Cream, Keiner Williams, Steel, Patent 1905 .... 25.00
Scoop, Ice Cream, Kingery 150.00
Scoop, Ice Cream, Kingery, 1894 .... 175.00
Scoop, Ice Cream, Kingery, Squeeze Handle, Size 12 .... 210.00
Scoop, Ice Cream, New Gem, No. 12, Brass, Nickel Plated 15.00
Scoop, Spice, Carved Carry, Short Handle, Early 1800s, 2 1/2 In. 44.00
Sieve, Heart Shape, Ring Fret, Tin, 4 3/4 In. 125.00
Sieve, Pot Rim Hook, Handle, Copper, 8 1/4 In. 85.00
Sieve, Wooden, Adjustable, 18 In. 65.00
Sifter, Flour, Addy's Store, 2 Cup 8.00
Sifter, Flour, McKenney Produce, Dunlop, Iowa 8.00
Sifter, Foley, Paper Label, 1 Cup 9.00
Siphon, Economy Cream Extractor, Box 12.00
Siphon, Magic Cream Remover, Used In Milk Bottle, Box 10.00
Skillet, Cast Iron Handle, Copper, 8 In. 65.00
Skillet, Chef's, Wagner, Sloped Sides, 9 In. 25.00
Skillet, Egg, Griswold, Square, 4 1/2 In. 35.00
Skillet, Griddle Cover, Wagner 37.50
Skillet, Griswold, No. 2 .... 90.00
Skillet, Griswold, No. 3 .... 25.00
Skillet, Griswold, No. 4 .... 12.50 To 35.00
Skillet, Griswold, No. 4, Iron, Logo 45.00
Skillet, Griswold, No. 6 .... 20.00 To 22.00
Skillet, Griswold, No. 8 .... 22.00
Skillet, Griswold, No. 8, Smoke Ring, Large Logo 30.00
Skillet, Griswold, No. 9 .... 20.00
Skillet, Griswold, No. 12 .... 50.00
Skillet, Wagner Sidney-O, No. 3 .... 10.00
Skillet, Wagnerware No. 3 .... 20.00
Slicer, Carrot, Center Hole Slides Over Blade, Birch, 7 3/4 In. 75.00
Slicer, Meat, Cast Iron, Sterling No. 10 .... 30.00
Slicer, Table Top, Hand Crank, Iron, The Eagle 40.00
Smoothing Board & Roller, 19th Century 100.00
Sock Stretcher, Wooden, Pair 15.00
Spice Box, 7 Boxes Inside, Wooden, November 17, 1868, 7 3/4 In. 295.00
Spice Box, 8 Canisters, Stenciled Labels, Bentwood, 9 1/2 In. 225.00
Spice Box, 8 Interior Canisters, Bentwood, 9 1/4 In. 65.00
Spice Box, Lock Front, c.1820 .... 1025.00

Spice Cabinet, 8 Drawers, 10 x 16 In.	245.00
Spice Cabinet, Open, 2 Lower Sections, Mahogany, c.1739, 28 1/2 In.	1210.00
Spice Set, Rack, 1930s	45.00
Spoon Rack, Primitive, Hanging, Oak, Brown Traces, 17 x 10 1/2 In.	125.00
Spoon, Rack, House Shape, Three 4–Spoon Racks, Wooden, 16 In.	275.00
Spoon, Stirring, Heart–Shaped Holes	35.00
Strainer, Tea, Brass Wire, Germany	10.00
String Holder, Apple	19.00
String Holder, Apple & Worm, Chalkware	25.00
String Holder, Cat, Ceramic	29.00
String Holder, Colonial Girl	45.00
String Holder, Dutch Girl, Chalkware	25.00
String Holder, Embossed Leaf Designs, Cast Iron, 9 3/4 In.	75.00
String Holder, Hula Girl	45.00
String Holder, Kitty, 6 x 4 In.	50.00
String Holder, Mexican, Chalkware	25.00
String Holder, Strawberry Face	27.00
String Holder, Victorian Girl, Full Figure, Japan	35.00
Teakettle, Goose Neck Spout, Iron Handle, No. 004, 4 1/2 Pints	95.00
Teakettle, Goose Neck Spout, Kenrick & Sons, 3 Pints, 9 In.	135.00
Teakettle, Goose Neck Spout, Wire Bale, Tin Lid, Iron, 3 5/8 In.	155.00
Teakettle, Griswold, 5 Qt.	22.00
Teakettle, Wagner, 5 Qt.	24.00
Teapot, Queen Anne Style, Tin, Wooden Handle	170.00
Tenderizer, Meat, Pottery Head, Oak Handle	132.00
Thermometer, Meat, Taylor Instrument, White Graniteware, Box	16.00
Thermos Server, Lift–Out Mercury Glass Liner, Dated 1910	25.00
Toaster, Art Deco, 1940s	30.00
Toaster, Bread, Tin	3.00
Toaster, Chrome & Bakelite, Hand Operated	10.00
Toaster, Edison, 1914	75.00
Toaster, Hot Point, Cut–Out Design	35.00
Toaster, Knoblock, Pyramid, Tin, USA	42.00
Toaster, Wire, Folds Over, Twisted Handle, 6 x 8 1/2 In.	72.00
Toaster, Wrought Iron, 15 x 11 In.	105.00
Travel Drying Kit, 12 Small Clothespins, Rope, Unused, Card, 1920s	10.00
Tray, Cake Cooler, Wireware, 12 1/2 In.	25.00
Tray, Wooden, Pink Flamingos	22.00
Trivet, Horseshoe, Good Luck, Iron	41.00
Tub Rack & Wringer, Household Brand, Wooden	35.00
Tub, Wooden, Rooster Label, Tongue & Groove, Bail, 14 x 6 1/2 In.	85.00
Vacuum Cleaner, Regina, Pneumatic, 1907	100.00
Vacuum Cleaner, Thompson, Canister Type	35.00
Vegetable Washer, Glass Bead Design, Wireware, 13 In.	25.00
Wafer Iron, Church 1 Side, Plants On Other, Iron, 28 In.	400.00
Waffle Iron, Geometric Pattern, E. C. Simmons	80.00
Waffle Iron, Griswold No. 8	100.00
Waffle Iron, Hearts & Stars, Griswold	175.00
Waffle Iron, Iron, 3 Footed, 1900s	125.00
Waffle Iron, Keen Kutter, Logo, 4 Sections	160.00
Waffle Iron, Stand, Wooden Handles, Stratton Junior No. 8, Miniature	110.00
Waffle Iron, Stove Top, Wagner, Wood Handles, Cast Iron, 1892	80.00
Waffle Iron, Stover Junior	75.00 To 90.00
Waffle Maker, Griswold, Cast Iron, Base, 1900	68.00
Waffle, Turn Table, Griswold No. 8	45.00
Wash Stick, Wooden, 25 In.	95.00
Washboard, Blue Graniteware	110.00
Washboard, Blue Porcelain	30.00
Washboard, Corrugated, Soap Pocket, 22 x 13 In.	95.00
Washboard, Gray Speckled Graniteware	125.00
Washboard, National Glass	17.50
Washboard, Primitive, 30 1/2 x 10 1/2 In.	170.00
Washboard, Rockingham Insert, Pine, 25 1/2 x 12 3/4 In.	525.00

◆◆

The marble top of a table can be shined with putty powder (zinconium oxide) from a cemetery monument works. Put the powder on a piece of damp felt and rub the marble until it shines.

◆◆

Washboard, Star Flowers On Crest, Cast Iron, 21 1/2 x 12 In.	475.00
Washboard, Whittled Ribs, Cut–Out Handle, Pine, 6 5/8 x 3 1/4 In.	40.00
Washboard, Wood Rollers	95.00
Washboard, Wooden, Carved Corrugated, Soap Pocket, 13 x 21 1/2 In.	95.00

In the 1960s, the United States government passed a law that required knife manufacturers to mark their knives with the country of origin. This seemed to encourage the collectors, and knife collecting became an interest of a large group of people. All types of knives are collected, from top quality twentieth–century examples to old bone– or pearl–handled knives in excellent condition.

KNIFE, Akron Zeppelin, Aluminum, Pocket	65.00
Bone Handle, Sheath	13.00
Bowie, Hunting, Case, Germany	30.00
Bowie, Stag Grips, Clip Point	85.00
Bread, Mother–of–Pearl Handle, 11 1/2 In.	16.00
Case, No. 61011	70.00
Case, Pocket, Kansas City Royals, Champions, Presentation Box, 1985	750.00
Clinch, Blacksmith's, Made From Rasp, 4 3/4 In.	18.00
Cooper, Chamfering, Signed Barton, Rochester	60.00
Cutrite, Pocket, 4 Blade	12.00
Dagger, Bone, Brass Blade, Bone Grip, Carved Seated Figure, Japan	70.00
Dagger, Congolese, Steel Blade, Hide–Covered Scabbard	140.00
Dagger, Sudanese, Belt, Leather Scabbard, Reptile Skin Terminals	155.00
Dagger, Tetela, Stepped Tapered Cylindrical Pommel, c.1860	240.00
Dirk, Engraved Blade, Ivory Handle	200.00
Glass, Blue	12.00
Hunter Fine–Blended Whiskey, 2 1/2 In.	18.00
Hunting, Bowie, With Scabbard	45.00
Hunting, Shapleigh	55.00
Inlaid Brewing, Spokane, Preprohibition	125.00
Jack, 10K Gold, Monogram	29.00
Jack, Remington	20.00
Jack, Stockyard Advertising	25.00
Kutmaster	25.00
Paring, McConkey Hatchery, 7 1/2 In.	15.00
Pen, Figural, Baseball Bat, Babe Ruth Signed, Marbelized	45.00
Pen, N. E. S. W., Climate Detour, Bone	10.00
Pen, Winchester, Red–Gold Boot Shape, 3 3/8 In.	75.00
Pocket, Cattaraugus, Horn Handle, 2 Blades, 3 In.	40.00
Pocket, Curtiss Candy, Baby Ruth, Marked Remington	105.00
Pocket, Dutch Military	12.00
Pocket, Edward VIII, Coronation, 1937	25.00
Pocket, Figural, Car, Brass	10.00
Pocket, Figural, Plane, Brass	10.00
Pocket, Figural, Train Engine, Brass	10.00
Pocket, Figural, Truck, Brass	10.00
Pocket, German Savings Bank, Davenport Iowa, 1909, Sterling Silver	45.00
Pocket, Hammer Brand, 2 In.	9.00
Pocket, Home Insurance Co., Sterling Switchblade, North Wind Design	90.00
Pocket, Imperial Sunshine Biscuits	35.00
Pocket, Lady's Leg, West End Brewing Co., Utica, N. Y.	95.00
Pocket, Nude Marilyn Monroe On Handle, Package	25.00
Pocket, S. S. Columbus	125.00

Pocket, Scout, Horn With Ring For Chain, 1 1/2 In.	30.00
Pocket, Shatt & Morgan Riggers, Bone Handles	50.00
Pocket, Traveler's Insurance Co., Train Design, Silver	85.00
Pocket, White House Coffee	35.00
Pocket, White–Gold Filled, Green Inlaid For Watch Chain, Victorian	20.00
Pruning, Case	35.00
Pruning, M. Klein	16.00
Race, Folding Blade, Brass, Timber Scribe	40.00
Remington, No. R. 7284, Masonic	85.00
Skinning, Blacksmith Riveted Tiger–Maple Handle, W. Nash, 11 In.	95.00
Steak, Camillus, Bone Handle, Holder, Set of 6	28.00
Winchester, No. 2211	50.00
Wolf Milling Co.	40.00
Zeppelin	35.00

KNOWLES, TAYLOR & KNOWLES, see KTK; Lotus Ware

KOCH   The name *Koch* is signed on the front of a series of plates decorated with fruit, vegetables, animals, or birds. The dishes date from the 1910 to 1930 period and were probably decorated in Germany.

KOCH, Plate, Apple	20.00
Plate, Apple, 9 In.	65.00
Plate, Grape	20.00
Plate, Peach, 9 In.	65.00
Shaker, Grape	85.00

KOREAN WARE, see Sumida

Ш **KOSTA**   Kosta is the oldest Swedish glass factory, founded in 1742. During the 1920s through the 1950s, many pieces of original design were made at the factory. The firm is still working.

KOSTA, Bowl, Amethyst, Clear, 4 1/2 In.	*Illus*	220.00
Bowl, Black Spirals, Blue, 3 In.	*Illus*	550.00
Bowl, Blue On Green Spirals, 6 3/4 In.	*Illus*	468.00
Bowl, Cranberry, White Grid, 3 1/2 In.	*Illus*	165.00
Bowl, Diamond, Crystal, Pink, White Spirals, 3 1/2 In.		140.00
Decanter, Etched Geometrics, 13 In.		500.00
Vase, Amber, Facet Cut, Pedestal, Signed, 8 In.		98.00
Vase, Amber, Facet Cut, Signed		75.00
Vase, Black Stripes, Lindstrand, 8 In.		350.00
Vase, Etched Tree Branches, 11 In.		95.00
Vase, Internal Black Line, Spiral Twist, c.1955, 12 7/8 In.		660.00
Vase, Stylized City Skyline, c.1955, 15 In.		3190.00

K.P.M   Most dealers and collectors use the term *KPM* to refer to Berlin porcelain, but the same initials were used alone and in combination with other symbols by several German porcelain makers. They include the Konigliche Porzellan Manufaktur of Berlin, initials used in mark, 1823–1847; Meissen, 1723–1724 only; Krister Porzellan

Kosta, Bowl, Blue On Green Spirals, 6 3/4 In.   *Kosta, Bowl, Amethyst, Clear, 4 1/2 In.*

Kosta, Bowl, Black Spirals, Blue, 3 In.   *Kosta, Bowl, Cranberry, White Grid, 3 1/2 In.*

KPM   Manufaktur in Waldenburg, after 1831; Kranichfelder Porzellan Manufaktur in Kranichfeld, after 1903; and the Kister Porzellan Manufaktur in Scheibe, after 1838.

KPM, Ashtray, Medallion of Masks Smoking, White, 4 3/4 In.	35.00
Bowl, Cherub's Faces, 2 Handles, Head Knop Cover	715.00
Bowl, Child's, Maxim, 1880, 8 1/4 In.	65.00
Bowl, Pink Roses, Handles, Oval, 8 1/2 x 12 In.	125.00
Bowl, Scattered Flowers, Rope Handles, 5 In.	40.00
Chocolate Pot, Shaded Blue Floral, Gold	125.00
Clock, Single Cherub, Butterflies & Flowers, c.1900, 21 In. ....*Illus*	1200.00
Cup & Saucer, Angel Amid Clouds, Gilt Floral Ground, 4 In.	75.00
Figurine, Cherub, With Eagle, 6 In.	650.00
Figurine, Classical Goddess With Basket of Fruit, Marked, 6 1/2 In.	175.00
Figurine, Jupiter, 5 1/4 In.	500.00

KPM, LITHOPHANE, see also Lithophane

Lithophane, Plaque, Girl Carrying Child, Leading Lamb, 4 3/4 x 6 In.	150.00
Plaque, Daphne, Blind Girl, Crown of Laurel Leaves, Signed, 8 1/2 In.	6600.00
Plaque, Daphne, Oval, Marked, 10 1/2 x 8 3/4 In.	5225.00
Plaque, Daphne, The Blind Girl, Signed Wagner, 8 1/2 In. ....*Illus*	6600.00
Plaque, Girl Angel On Rocks, 5 x 7 In.	4500.00
Plaque, Goodnight, Woman, With Candle, Signed, R. Eno, 10 x 7 1/2 In.	4675.00
Plaque, Madonna & Child, Gilt Frame, 7 3/4 x 5 1/2 In.	775.00
Plaque, Madonna, Simulating Rafael, Frame, 13 In.	3410.00
Plaque, Magdalene, Rocky Landscape, Reading, Frame, 18 1/2 x 11 In.	8800.00
Plaque, Men Playing Cards, Transfer, Marquetry Frame, 10 x 7 In.	385.00
Plaque, Ruth, Flowing Gown, Sheaf of Wheat, Marked, Framed, 9 x 6 In.	2750.00
Plaque, Ruth, Profile, In Wheat Field, Sceptre Mark, 13 In.	6050.00
Plaque, Voluptuous Maiden, Reading, Oval, Scrollwork Frame, 1870s	1650.00
Plaque, Woman, Elaborate Jeweled Headdress, Marked, 7 In.	1750.00
Plaque, Woman, Holding Vase With Flowers, Signed Ullman, 10 x 7 1/4 In.	4675.00
Plaque, Woman, Reading Letter, 8 1/4 x 6 In. ....*Illus*	4500.00
Plaque, Woman, Seated, White Veil & Dress, Sceptre Mark, 10 1/4 In.	4125.00
Plaque, Young Girl, Ruffled Collar, Oval, Marked, 6 3/4 In.	665.00
Plaque, Young Man, Woman & Child, Garden Setting, Frame, 24 1/2 x 28 In.	880.00
Plaque, Young Woman, Eastern Dress, Marked, Frame, 9 1/4 x 6 1/4 In.	5775.00
Plaque, Young Woman, Flowing Tresses, Flower At Top, c.1900, 4 In.	1870.00
Plaque, Young Woman, Shultz, Marked, 10 x 7 1/2 In.	7700.00
Plate, King Friedrich Wilhelm III Portrait, 19th Century, 9 3/4 In.	65.00
Tile, Young Woman, Erbluht, 5 x 3 3/4 In. ....*Illus*	1600.00
Tile, Young Woman, Oriental Robe, Cockatoo, Marked, 9 1/2 x 6 1/2 In.	6380.00

KPM, Clock, Single Cherub,
Butterflies & Flowers, c.1900, 21 In.

◆◆◆◆◆◆◆◆◆◆◆◆◆◆◆◆◆◆◆◆◆◆

A hair dryer set for cool can be used to blow the dust off very ornate pieces of porcelain.

◆◆◆◆◆◆◆◆◆◆◆◆◆◆◆◆◆◆◆◆◆◆

KPM, Plaque, Daphne,   KPM, Plaque, Woman,   KPM, Tile, Young Woman,
The Blind Girl,   Reading Letter, 8 1/4 x 6 In. Erbluht, 5 x 3 3/4 In.
Signed Wagner, 8 1/2 In.

Urn, Cover, Floral Finial, Bust of Woman Handles, 22 In. 995.00
Vase, Chinese Style, Gilt Trim, Blue & White, c.1900, 12 1/2 In., Pair 885.00
Vase, Peach Crystaline Glaze, 5 1/2 In. 175.00

K.T.&K.
CHINA

KTK are the initials of the Knowles, Taylor & Knowles Company of East Liverpool, Ohio, founded by Isaac W. Knowles in 1853. The company made many types of utilitarian wares, hotel china, and dinnerwares. They made the fine bone china known as Lotus Ware from 1891 to 1896. The company merged with American Ceramic Corporation in 1928. It closed in 1934. Lotus Ware is listed in its own category in this book.

KTK, Bowl, Applied Designs, Impressed Leaves, Twig Handles, 13 In. 2400.00
Chocolate Pot, Gold Leaves & Lattice Base, Marked, 9 In., Pair 240.00
Chocolate Pot, Hand–Painted Poppies, 9 In. 135.00
Cookie Jar, Yellow–Swirled Body, Blue Flowers, Marked 82.50
Ewer, Petal–Form Mouth, Gilt Handles, Turquoise, Marked, 10 1/4 In. 1100.00
Jug, Whiskey, Expressly For Medicinal Use 35.00
Tea Set, Child's, Rose, 11 Piece 55.00
Teapot, Gilt Outlined Leaves & Wildflowers, Marked, 8 1/2 In. 195.00

Any items relating to the Ku Klux Klan are now collected because of their historic importance. Literature, robes, and memorabilia are available. The Klan is still in existence, so new material is found.

KU KLUX KLAN, Booklet, KKK Exposed, 1920s 15.00
Knife, Pocket 25.00
Order Form, Ordering Robe 7.00
Outfit, Cone–Shaped Headgear, 1920s 250.00
Parade Tag, Portland, Maine, 1926 .... 15.00
Petition For Citizenship, Invisible Empire 12.00
White Book, Kloran 45.00

Kutani ware is a Japanese porcelain made after the mid–seventeenth century. Most of the pieces found today are nineteenth century. Collectors often use the term *kutani* to refer to just the later, colorful pieces decorated with red, gold, and black pictures of warriors, animals, and birds.

KUTANI, Chocolate Set, Scenic, Portrait Medallions, 6 Piece 300.00
Dish, Cover, Thousand–Faces Design, Signed, 15 x 11 5/8 In. 2750.00
Figure, Buddha, Green Robe, Phoenix & Dragons, 13 In. ....*Illus* 115.00
Figure, Buddhist Monk, Blue Robe, Phoenix Birds, 1880, 17 In. 1095.00
Figurine, Beggar On Rock, Scratching Back, c.1920, 7 1/4 In. 195.00

Kutani, Figure, Buddha, Green Robe,
Phoenix & Dragons, 13 In.

Kutani, Vase, Geishas In Garden, Ocher,
Gold, 13 1/4 In., Pair

Foo Dog, Forelegs On Pierced Ball, Porcelain, 6 1/2 In., Pair 125.00
Jardiniere, Mountain–Village Scenes Allover, Marked, 10 x 12 In. 715.00
Platter, Scholar Riding Horned Animal, Fish Form, 16 1/2 In. 440.00
Tea Set, Thousand Flowers, 3 Piece 75.00
Tea Set, Thousand Flowers, Rose & Lavender, 3 Piece 125.00
Teapot, Scenic, Figures, Potbellied, Red Mark, 8 In. 595.00
Vase, Floral & Geometric, Crane & Cherry Blossom, 40 3/4 In. 1150.00
Vase, Geishas In Garden, Ocher, Gold, 13 1/4 In., Pair ....*Illus* 300.00
Vase, Reserves of Birds Amid Flowering Trees, 22 In., Pair 1100.00

Lacquer is a type of varnish. Collectors are most interested in the Chinese and Japanese lacquer wares made from the Japanese varnish tree. Lacquer wares are made from wood coated with many coats of lacquer. Sometimes the piece is carved or decorated with ivory or metal inlay.

LACQUER, Box, Music, Scenic, Jewelry Section Lights, Mirrors, 1950s, Pair 110.00
Box, Sewing, Claw Feet, Chinese Export, Large 950.00
Bucket, Rice, Dragon & Figural Design, Flat Cover, Chinese, 17 In. 132.00
Inro, Gold Rooster, 2 Hens, Landcape, Koma Kyuhaku Saku, 4 Case 5000.00
Inro, Mother–of–Pearl & Metal Butterflies, Gold, 4 Case 3500.00
Manju, Rabbit & Flowers, Mother–of–Pearl Inlay, Gold, Shibayamasaku 1750.00
Panel, Oriental, Black, Applied Composition Figure, 36 x 12 In., Pr. 50.00
Panel, Story of Ben–Kei, Ivory Overlay, Signed Hozan, 51 x 36 In. 650.00
Screen, Ivory, Mother–of–Pearl, Pierced Crest, Chinese, 70 x 58 In. 300.00
Vase, Mother–of–Pearl, Flowers, Birds, Black 65.00
LADY HEAD VASE, see Head Vase

Lalique glass was made by Rene Lalique in Paris, France, between the 1890s and his death in 1945. The glass was molded, pressed, and engraved in Art Nouveau and Art Deco styles. Pieces were marked with the signature *R. Lalique.* Lalique glass is still being made. Pieces made after 1945 bear the mark *Lalique.*

LALIQUE, Ashtray, Feuilles, Overlapping Leaves, Oval, Signed, 1928, 6 7/8 In. 880.00
Bottle, Atomizer, Fleurettes, Signed 395.00
Bottle, Scent, Classical Woman, Frosted, 6 In. 295.00
Bowl, Carved & Knobbed Frosted Stem, Smoke Amber, Signed, 8 In. 235.00
Bowl, Chicoree, 9 1/2 In. 625.00
Bowl, Chiens No. 1, Running Dog, Domical, Signed, c.1928, 9 3/8 In. 1520.00
Bowl, Dandelions, Leaves From Center To Rim, Signed, 9 1/4 In. 450.00
Bowl, Dauphins, Fish, Stylized Waves, Signed, c.1932, 9 3/8 In. 1215.00
Bowl, Frosted Oak Leaves, Clear Base, 18 In. 695.00
Bowl, Frosted Roses Entwined Branches, Clear Ground, 9 3/4 x 3 In. 475.00
Bowl, Nemours, Tiers of Flowerheads, Signed, c.1932, 10 In. 1225.00
Bowl, Pinsons, Finch In Circular Sections, Signed, 9 1/4 In. 335.00
Box, Chanteclair, Black Glass, Stylized Wheat Design, 4 1/4 In. 9900.00
Box, Clusters of Florets On Handle of Cover, Signed, 6 1/4 x 4 In. 850.00
Box, Cover, Birds, Berries, Branches, Charcoal, Signed, 1932, 5 1/4 In. 2000.00

Box, Cover, Florets Finial, Floret Clusters, Signed, 4 x 6 1/4 In.	850.00
Box, Hinged Cover, Intaglio Nude, Knees Drawn Up, Signed, 2 1/4 In.	395.00
Cherub, Enfants, Pair	575.00
Clock, Marly, Enameled Lily–of–The–Valley, Signed, c.1932, 6 3/4 In.	5225.00
Clock, Silvered–Metal Face, Demilune, 6 x 8 1/2 In.	2750.00
Coaster, Wine, Sepia Enamel Patina, Sister Odile, Marked, 6 1/4 In.	440.00
Compote, Black Fish Eyes, Smoky, 10 In.	3500.00
Compote, St. Denis, First Bishop of Paris, 1932	3000.00
Decanter, Frosted, 4 Sides, Teardrop Shape, Stopper, 19 1/2 In., Pr.	6380.00
Dish, Ice Cream, Green Doves, 4 Piece	475.00
Dish, Seaweed, Opalescent, 10 In.	325.00
Figurine, Buffalo, Paper Label, 5 In.	400.00
Figurine, Lion, 8 In.	335.00
Figurine, Madonna, Crystal & Blue, 9 1/4 In.	1150.00
Figurine, Nude Maiden, Seated Pan In Vineyard, Signed, 5 1/4 In.	495.00
Figurine, Nude, Half Turning, Square Plinth, 12 In.	885.00
Figurine, Rooster, Paper Label, Signed, 10 In.	2000.00
Figurine, Statuette Drapee, Opalescent, Blue Traces, 2 1/2 In.	1500.00
Figurine, Suzanne, Outstretched Arms, Signed, c.1932, 8 3/4 In.	6600.00
Figurine, Thais, Holding Links of Fabric, Signed, c.1925, 8 3/8 In.	9900.00
Hood Ornament, Chrysis, Kneeling Nude, Opalescent, 3 15/16 In.	4000.00
Hood Ornament, Petite Libellule, Dragonfly, Wings Closed, 8 1/4 In.	5500.00
Hood Ornament, Tete De Belier, Ram's Head, Signed, 3 3/4 In.	1215.00
Inkwell, Bubble Style, Opalescent Glass, 7 1/4 In.	175.00
Luminaire, Coq De Jungle, Rooster, Clear Glass, Metal, 18 1/2 In.	9000.00
Luminaire, Gros Poisson Algues, Carp, Clear Glass, Bronze, 15 In.	9900.00
Medallion, Orphelinat Des Armees, Brass, Square, 1 1/2 In.	65.00
Paperweight, Daim, Deer, Signed, 3 x 3 In.	150.00
Paperweight, Partridge, Signed	65.00
Pen Tray, Pheasant, 4 In.	55.00
Pendant, Fioret, Kneeling Nymph, Holes For Cord, Signed, 1 1/4 In.	500.00
Perfume Bottle, 5 Women In Gowns, Amber Patina, Signed, 6 3/4 In.	935.00
Perfume Bottle, Art Deco, Blue, Blue Glass Stopper	475.00
Perfume Bottle, Clairefontaine	120.00
Perfume Bottle, Coeur Joie, 3 3/4 In.	495.00
Perfume Bottle, Dahlia	300.00
Perfume Bottle, Dans La Nuit, Blue, Flat Body, Box, 3 1/4 In.	350.00
Perfume Bottle, Dans La Nuit, Signed, c.1925, 5 1/4 In.	1225.00
Perfume Bottle, Flattened Spherical, Frosted, Stopper, 2 1/2 In.	3750.00
Perfume Bottle, Frosted Maidens, Brass–Toned Lid, Signed, 5 In.	825.00
Perfume Bottle, Knotted Rope Enclosed Glass Cabochons, Signed	550.00
Perfume Bottle, L'Air Du Temps, 5 3/4 In.	650.00
Perfume Bottle, Mystere, Salamanders, Signed, 3 7/8 In.	1875.00
Perfume Bottle, Nude, Pump, 6 1/4 In.	1600.00
Perfume Bottle, Pearls, Blue Wash, Signed, 6 1/2 In.	1250.00
Perfume Bottle, Standing Female Holding Flowers, c.1925, 5 In.	1875.00
Perfume Bottle, Tzigane, 5 1/2 In.	550.00
Plate, Green Leaf, 10 In., Pair	400.00
Platter, Quail Pattern, Overall Frosted Design, 18 In.	385.00
Powder Box, 3 Nudes On Lid, Brown Enamel Patina, Marked, 3 3/4 In.	445.00
Powder Box, Armour Assis, Flowering Vines, Signed, c.1932, 5 1/2 In.	1650.00
Powder Box, Birds In Flight, Tails Form Arcs, Puff, Signed, 3 In.	350.00
Powder Box, Emiliane	395.00
Powder Box, Parakeets, On Branches, Berries, 4 1/4 In.	125.00
Scent Bottle, Amphitrite, Brown Traces, Script Base	3500.00
Scent Bottle, Amphitrite, Green, Mold Signed, 3 3/4 In.	8500.00
Scent Bottle, Anemone Blossoms, Signed, 9 1/2 In.	695.00
Seal, Eagle, Tete D'Aigle	550.00
Tumbler, Embossed Fruit & Leaves, Signed, 4 3/4 In.	295.00
Vase, Aigrettes, Birds In Flight, Signed, c.1932, 9 3/4 In.	1450.00
Vase, Amber Walls, Molded Ducks In Swirling Design, Signed	1650.00
Vase, Amber, Macaws Among Berried Branches, 9 In.	8400.00
Vase, Archers, Band of Nude Male Archers, Signed, c.1932, 10 1/4 In.	4125.00

Vase, Bacchantes, Band of Nude Maidens, Signed, c.1932, 9 3/4 In. 4950.00
Vase, Bacchantes, Cavorting Nude Females, Signed, Modern, 9 1/2 In. 3575.00
Vase, Birches, Deer In Various Poses, Signed, c.1932, 6 3/4 In. 1450.00
Vase, Birds, Clear Swirls Around Body, Frosted, 9 1/2 In. 795.00
Vase, Bouchardon, Garlands, Seated Nudes Handle, Signed, 4 1/4 In. 1325.00
Vase, Ceylon, Pairs of Lovebirds, Mounted As Lamp, 1932, 23 1/2 In. 995.00
Vase, Cogs Et Raisins, Brown Stained, Frosted, 6 1/4 In. 900.00
Vase, Formose, Frosted, Etched Script Mark On Base 1200.00
Vase, Formose, Stylized Swimming Fish, Signed, c.1930, 6 5/8 In. 7150.00
Vase, Leaf & Berry Design, Lavender, Frosted, Signed 1700.00
Vase, Leaves, Veins In High Glass, Signed, 6 1/2 x 6 In. 850.00
Vase, Malesherbes, 4 Tiers of Leaves, Amber, Signed, c.1925, 9 In. 2865.00
Vase, Malines, Silver Rim 595.00
Vase, Marisa, 4 Tiers Undulating Fish, Signed, c.1932, 9 In. 3300.00
Vase, Mermaids, 12 In. 2500.00
Vase, Mistletoe, Berries, Leaves, Signed, 6 3/4 x 7 In. 950.00
Vase, Molded As Coiled Serpent, Signed, 9 1/2 In. 7775.00
Vase, Monnaie De Pape, Amber, Honesty Plant Pods, Marked, 9 1/4 In. 5500.00
Vase, Nude Figures, Signed, 7 In. 2250.00
Vase, Ormeaux, Overlapping Leaves, Signed, c.1932, 6 1/4 In. 1320.00
Vase, Overlapping Leaves, Veins In High Gloss, Signed, 6 1/2 In. 850.00
Vase, Pairs of Love Birds, Ceylon, Signed, c.1921, 9 7/16 In. 5225.00
Vase, Red Molded Case, Signed, 9 1/2 In. ....*Illus* 7750.00
Vase, Rena, White & Gray Leaves, 10 In. 450.00
Vase, Roosters, Feathers Extend To Bottom, Signed, 6 In. 850.00
Vase, Stand–Out Ribs All Around, Continous Leaf Pattern, Signed 500.00
Vase, Undulating Thorny Branches, Signed, c.1932, 9 In. 2475.00
Wine Cooler, Ganymede, Nude Dancing Maidens, Signed, 1950s ....715.00 To 1215.00

Interest is strong in lamps of every type, from the early oil–burning Betty and Phoebe lamps to the recent electric lamps with glass or beaded shades. Fuels used in lamps changed through the years; whale oil (1800–1840), camphene (1828), Argand (1830), lard (1833–1863), turpentine and alcohol (1840s), gas (1850–1879), kerosene (1860), and electricity (1879) are the most common. Other lamps are listed by manufacturer or type of material.

LAMP, Aladdin, Alacite, Gold Pheasant 165.00
Aladdin, Alacite, Wall Pocket 70.00
Aladdin, B–40, Washington Drape, Amber, Complete 95.00
Aladdin, B–42, Beehive, Light Amber, Burner 85.00
Aladdin, B–55, Amber Beta Crystal 75.00

Lalique, Vase, Red Molded Case, Signed, 9 1/2 In.

Aladdin, B–60, Ivory Alacite Art Glass	300.00
Aladdin, B–70, Solitaire, No Burner	700.00
Aladdin, B–75, No Burner, Box	120.00
Aladdin, B–81, With Burner	70.00
Aladdin, B–83, Beehive, Ruby, Burner	240.00 To 325.00
Aladdin, B–88, Vertique, Yellow	425.00
Aladdin, B–88, Vertique, Yellow, No Burner	400.00
Aladdin, B–90, With Burner	150.00
Aladdin, B–104, Corinthian, Ship–O–Lite Wagon Trail West Shade	85.00
Aladdin, B–111, Moonstone, Green	175.00
Aladdin, B–111, Moonstone, Green, Burner	190.00
Aladdin, B–114, Moonstone, White	110.00
Aladdin, B–125, Moonstone, Green Base, White Bowl	95.00
Aladdin, Cincinnati, Cherry Bomb, Shade	75.00
Aladdin, Coleman Shade, 4 Colored Panels	95.00
Aladdin, Coolidge Drape, Finger	275.00
Aladdin, Floral, Lime Ground, Electric, Finials, Large, Pair	45.00
Aladdin, G–18, Electric, Black & Chromium, Lancet Finials	90.00
Aladdin, G–46, Cupid, Blue	72.50
Aladdin, G–50, Frosted White, Original Shade	175.00
Aladdin, G–50, Powder Dish	375.00
Aladdin, G–97, Crystal, Millefleur Finial	155.00
Aladdin, G–124, Velvex, Amber	250.00
Aladdin, G–140, Moonstone, White	175.00
Aladdin, G–168, Amber, Frosted Millifleur Finial, Fluted Shade	375.00
Aladdin, G–324, Finial, Original Shade	25.00
Aladdin, G–333, Dubonnet, Plume Finial	125.00
Aladdin, G–335c, Hoppy, Horsehead	180.00
Aladdin, G–348, World, Original Shade & Finial	175.00
Aladdin, G–375, Dancing Ladies Urn, Alacite	525.00
Aladdin, Gone With The Wind, White Opalescent Spider Web	375.00
Aladdin, Ivory, Embossed Allover Flowers, 4 1/2 In.	50.00
Aladdin, Lincoln Drape, Alacite, Tall	185.00
Aladdin, Lincoln Drape, Short	375.00
Aladdin, M–123, Figurine, Gold Finish, Fleur–De–Lis Finial	80.00
Aladdin, Mother–of–Pearl, Electric, No Shade, 5 x 13 In.	75.00
Aladdin, Nightlight, Hoppy, Bullet	95.00
Aladdin, No. 4, Parlour, Tripod	270.00
Aladdin, No. 6, Nickel, With 301 Shade	150.00
Aladdin, No. 101, Venetian, Green, A Burner	85.00
Aladdin, No. 1214N, Plain Shade, Hanging	125.00
Aladdin, No. 1242, Bengal, Red Vase, Burner	230.00
Aladdin, Rayo, Nickel, Tall Chimney	60.00
Aladdin, Simplicity, Gold Luster	145.00
Argand, 1–Arm, Electrified, Brass, c.1820, 17 In.	1210.00
Argand, 1–Arm, Electrified, Early 19th Century, 13 In., Pair	495.00
Argand, 1–Arm, Romeo & Juliet, Etched Shades, Brass	775.00
Argand, 2–Arm, Etched Shades, Electrified, Gilt & Bronzed	715.00
Argand, 2–Arm, Glass Globes, Electrified, 17 1/2 In., Pair	495.00
Argand, 2–Arm, Period Shades	1435.00
Argand, 2–Arm, Silver Plate, Pierced Gallery, 19th Century, 19 In.	4200.00
Argand, 4–Arm, Bronze, Etched Glass Globes, Electrified, 24 In., Pair	7150.00

◆◆

To remove a stubborn stain from the outside of a bottle, try this. Fill
a bucket with soft sand. Push the bottle in and out of the sand, rotate
it, and try to loosen the stain. Then wash in clean water. To remove
a stain inside a bottle, put a handfull of gravel in the bottle and
shake vigorously.

◆◆

Argand, Boar's Head, Cast Bronze, Pair 3520.00
Argand, Bronze, 2–Arm, Etched Glass Shade, Electrified, 17 In., Pair 1100.00
Argand, Bronze, John B. Jones, Boston, Pair 715.00
Argand, Clark, Coit & Cargill, Pair 3250.00
Argand, Cut Shades, Marble Bases, Crystal Pendants, Bronze, 22 In. 1650.00
Argand, Etched & Frosted Shades, Cast Bronze, 11 1/4 In., Pair 3550.00
Argand, Mantel, Etched Glass Shade, Electrified, 12 In., Pair .... 1600.00 To 1760.00
Astral, Cornelius & Co., Marble Base, Electrified, 23 1/4 In. 225.00
Astral, Cornelius, Brass, Ionic Column, Frosted Shade, 1843, 26 In. 600.00
Astral, Electric, Marble & Brass Base, Silk Shade, 31 In. 100.00
Astral, Gilt–Brass Stem, Cut Prisms, Frosted To Clear Shade, 22 In. 500.00
Banquet, Ball Shade, Oil Burning, Signed Handle 325.00
Banquet, Pink Font & Stem, Embossed Design, Brass Base, 26 In. 1475.00
Banquet, White Shade, Font & Stem, Parker, Electrified, 29 In. 990.00
Betty, Brass Ornament, Tooled Initials, Wrought Iron, 4 1/2 In. 275.00
Betty, Iron, Bullet Hole Side, 18th Century, 3 1/4 x 5 1/2 In. 110.00
Betty, Iron, With Hook & Wick Pick, America 350.00
Betty, Twisted Wire Hanger, Gold Paint, Tin, 4 1/4 In. 85.00
Betty, Wrought Iron, Sliding Wick Cover, Large Hook, Hanging, 4 1/2 In. 550.00
Bicycle, Mathews & Willard Mfg. 135.00
Bouillotte, Louis XV, Gilt Bronze, 3–Light, Scrolled Branches, 31 In. 1925.00
Bouillotte, Louis XVI, Gilt Bronze, 3–Light, Pierced Base, 31 In. 3300.00
Bracket, Swing Away, Reflector & Font 275.00
              LAMP, BRADLEY & HUBBARD, see Bradley & Hubbard, Lamp
Brass & Zinc, Key Wind Forced Draft, Patented 1868, 11 In. 175.00
Candle, Hurricane, White Opalescent, 10 In. 65.00
Carbide, Polished Brass, 31 In. 195.00
Ceiling, Leaded, Red & Green Swag Border, 3 Metal Chains, 15 In. 525.00
Chandelier, 4–Light, Candles, Tin, 13 3/4 In. 525.00
Chandelier, 4–Light, Gas, Colored Jewels, Prisms, Brass, c.1880, 43 In. 1650.00
Chandelier, 5–Light, Electric Candles, Crystal, Prisms, Chain, 26 In. 350.00
Chandelier, 5–Light, Marie Theresa Style, Crystal Swags, 19 In. 67.00
Chandelier, 5–Light, Square Oak Frame, Iron Chains, G. Stickley, c.1907 .... 4300.00
Chandelier, 8–Light, Painted Tole, Scrolls With Dolphin Masks, 36 In. 8800.00
Chandelier, 8–Light, Prisms, Patinated Metal & Crystal, 38 In. 1540.00
Chandelier, 12–Light, Berried Finials, Gilt Bronze, 47 In. 4500.00
Chandelier, 12–Light, Electric Candles, Green Prisms, Chain, 20 In. 175.00
Chandelier, 12–Light, Venetian Glass, Double Foliate Globe, 54 In. 2250.00
Chandelier, 18–Light, Candles, Tin Sockets & Drip Pans, Chain, 28 In. 275.00
Chandelier, Geometric & Foliate Design, Painted Iron, 19 1/2 In. 385.00
Chandelier, Graduated Rows of Prisms, Cut Glass, 16 1/2 x 13 In. 285.00
Chandelier, Grapevine Dripping Clusters of Glass Grapes 3630.00
Chandelier, Green Slag, Oak, 5 Chains, 5 Shades, Square, 34 x 36 In. 550.00
Chandelier, Kerosene, Victorian, Cast Iron, 4–Light 375.00
Chandelier, Leaded, Prairie–School Design, Square, 9 x 20 In. 335.00
Chandelier, Mistletoe Leaves, Branches, Bronze, France, c.1900, 32 In. 550.00
Chandelier, Outset Quadrants, Pierced, Bronze & Glass, Austria, 40 In. 4850.00
Coleman, Quick–Lite, Brass, Electrified, White Shade 175.00
Crusie, Double, Punched Heart Designs On Diamond Crest, 9 5/8 In. 200.00
Crusie, Double, Ram's–Horn Finial, Wrought Iron, 6 1/2 In. 325.00
Crusie, Double, Twisted Hanger, Iron, 7 In. 225.00
Crusie, Double, Wrought Iron, Primitive, Crests, 7 1/2 In. 105.00
Crusie, Double, Wrought Iron, Twisted Hanger, 6 In. 100.00
Crusie, Double, Wrought Iron, Twisted Hanger, Europe, 6 In. 125.00
Egg Candler, Tin, c.1890, 10 3/8 In. 35.00
Electric, 2 Playful Bears, Rocky Base, Bronze, Austria, c.1900, 22 In. 3300.00
Electric, 4–Light, Marble Base, Bronze Feet, Vines Standard, 34 In. 4950.00
Electric, Airplane Shape, Blue, 1935 .... 880.00
Electric, Alabaster, Rebecca At The Well, 44 In. ....*Illus* 4180.00
Electric, Allegorical, Industry & Navigation, Gilt Metal, 16 In., Pair 175.00
Electric, Aluminum, Flat–Top Shade, Adjustable, 16 1/2 In. 137.00
Electric, Amber & White Leaded Shade, Bronze Shaft, Bigelow, 19 In. 3195.00
Electric, Amber Shade, Amethyst Diamonds, Duffner & Kimberly, 22 In. 665.00

Lamp, Electric, Alabaster,   Lamp, Electric, Leaded Glass   Lamp, Electric, Louis Majorelle
Rebecca At The Well, 44 In.   Shade, Lotus, Welkerson, 22 In.   & Daum Nancy, 29 In.

Electric, Art Deco, 3 Graces, Nudes, Shade	60.00
Electric, Art Deco, Brass Base, Brass & Green Slag Shade, 20 In.	285.00
Electric, Art Deco, Bronze Serpent Form, Jeweled Glass Shade, Floor	2650.00
Electric, Art Deco, Bronze, 3 Birds On Ball, 2–Light, O. B. Bach, 26 In.	825.00
Electric, Art Deco, Gilded Metal Base, Alabaster Insert, 12 In., Pair	120.00
Electric, Art Deco, Globe, Paper Litho In Glass, Walnut Base, 12 In. D.	110.00
Electric, Art Glass, 2 Curved Lights, Allover Silver Flakes, 19 In.	165.00
Electric, Bell–Form Marbelized Shade, Roycroft, c.1926, 15 In.	1320.00
Electric, Blond Girl, Standing, China, Green Glass Ball Shade, 4 In.	145.00
Electric, Bridge Table, Wicker, Brass Trim	595.00
Electric, Bridge, Iron, 61 In.	135.00
Electric, Candle, Pierced Brass Shades, 1900s, Pair	175.00
Electric, Candle, Punched Tin	100.00
Electric, Carved Flourite, Amethyst Finial, Chinese, 16 3/4 In.	165.00
Electric, Clock, Art Deco Airplane, Chrome Wings, Cockpit Light, 22 In.	175.00
Electric, Clown, Figural, Hand Painted, 8 In., Pair	65.00
Electric, Colonial Woman & Man, Shade, 12 In., Pair	50.00
Electric, Dancing Harlequin, Ivorene Face, Alabaster Base, 14 In.	275.00
Electric, Dennis The Menace	50.00
Electric, Desk, Pittsburgh, Brass, 3 1/4–In. Gold Art Glass Shade	300.00
Electric, Desk, Teroma–Glass Shade, Lakeside Scene, 15 In.	1760.00
Electric, Desk, Verdelite, Double Knuckle	30.00
Electric, Dirk Van Erp, Beanpot	5500.00
Electric, Dirk Van Erp, Canister, 4–Arm, Copper, Mica Shade, 16 x 12 In.	9350.00
Electric, Eclipse Light, Reverse–Painted Waterfront, 2–Light, 24 In.	775.00
Electric, Elephant, Cast Metal, Black–Marble Base, 17 1/4 In.	175.00
Electric, Emerald Light Jr., No Shade	140.00
Electric, Floor, Combined With Smoke Stand, Nude At Base, 5 Ft.	180.00
Electric, Floor, Goose Neck, Cloisonne, Chrome Sphere, 1930, 57 In.	82.50
Electric, Floral Design, Prisms, Marble Stepped Base, 21 1/2 In.	240.00
Electric, G. Stickley, Joiner's Compass Shape, Glass Shade, 15 In.	4950.00
Electric, Glass Ball, White Flowers, Czechoslovakia	35.00
Electric, Jefferson, Art Deco Reverse–Painted Shade, 1–Light, 20 In.	935.00
Electric, Jefferson, Hexagonal Riverside Scene Shade, 21 1/2 In.	935.00
Electric, Jefferson, Mushroom Shade, Landscape Scene, 20 1/2 In.	1100.00
Electric, Jefferson, Reverse–Painted Scene, Gold–Painted Base	1200.00
Electric, Jefferson, Textured Glass Dome Shade, 21 1/2 In.	1325.00
Electric, Knickerbocker, Raggedy Ann & Andy	35.00
Electric, Leaded Dome Shade, Band of Flowers, c.1915, 23 3/4 In.	1100.00
Electric, Leaded Glass Shade, Lotus, Welkerson, 22 In. ....*Illus*	2200.00
Electric, Leaded, Umbrella Shade, White Panels, Swag & Blossom, 21 In.	385.00

Electric, Leigh Ware, Geometric, Mottled Olive Green, 1930, 15 In. 22.00
Electric, Louis Majorelle & Daum Nancy, 29 In. ....*Illus* 13200.00
Electric, Moe Bridges, 2–Light, Interior Riverscape, Marked, 20 1/4 In. 1325.00
Electric, Moe Bridges, Foliaged Trees, Lakefront, Metal Base, 21 In. 3080.00
Electric, Mushroom Shape, Wicker, Brown, 30 In. 295.00
Electric, Mushroom, Satin Glass, Yellow To Orange Shaded, 20 In. 150.00
Electric, Niagara Falls, Revolving, Heat Activated, 1950s 70.00
Electric, Nude, In Crescent Moon, Metal, Art Deco, Glass Shade 145.00
Electric, Nursery Rhymes, Metal, Wooden, Drum Shape, Colors 65.00
Electric, Nutmeg Burner, Mercury Glass Lining, Cranberry, 8 1/2 In. 350.00
Electric, Patinated Metal, Slag Shade, Laurel Wreath Filigree, 26 In. 250.00
Electric, Phoenix Birds Cut To Yellow, Globular Top, Opaque, 26 In. 195.00
Electric, Pink Flamingos & Seashell, 1950s 20.00
Electric, Pittsburgh, Forest Fire, Reverse Painted, 2 Labels 2900.00
Electric, Pittsburgh, Reverse–Obverse Painted, Winter Scene, 2–Light 1150.00
Electric, Pittsburgh, Sheep, Flowering Trees, 16 In. 950.00
Electric, Plastic, 2 Shades, V Standard, White Plastic, 1953, 31 In. 99.00
Electric, Porcelain, Gray, White, Tiny Rosebuds, New Shades, 12 In., Pr. 75.00
Electric, Porky Pig, Plastic, 19 In. 75.00
Electric, Quezal Type, Double Shades, Wrought Iron Base 700.00
Electric, Reverse Painted, Sailboat Shade, Blue–Green Platform, 17 In. 605.00
Electric, Russel Wright, Torch, Brass Trumpet, Bamboo, 1955, 66 In., Pair 192.00
Electric, Sonneman, Floor, Chrome & Metal, Swing Arm, 63 In. 60.00
Electric, Stickley, Oak, Hammered–Copper Shade, Mica Panels, 22 In. 7700.00
Electric, Student, Green Overlay Shade, Brass, 21 In. 400.00
Electric, Student, Hand–Painted Milk Glass Shade, Brass, 23 In. 325.00
Electric, Swing Arm, Sonneman, Chrome & Metal, 63 In. 65.00
Electric, Television, 2 Siamese Cats, Green Eyes 25.00
Electric, Television, Black Panther 24.00
Electric, Television, Black Wolfhound 28.00
Electric, Television, Glass Ship, Chrome Sails 65.00
Electric, Television, Leaping Stag 10.00
Electric, Television, Nubian, Black, Turbaned 35.00
Electric, Television, Turbaned Nubian, Black Glaze 35.00
Electric, Tulip, Cheuret, Silvered Bronze & Alabaster, 1930, 33 In., Pr. 7700.00
Electric, Verdelite, Desk, Double Knuckle 275.00
Electric, Victorian Couple, Germany, 6 1/2 In., Pair 26.00
Electric, Will Rogers Airplane, Earth Globe, Metal 145.00
Electric, Woman Holding Skirt Off Ground, G. Obiols, Bronze, 27 In. 2200.00
Electric, Woman, With Mandolin, Lavender Shades, White, Germany 55.00
Fairy, Blue Frosted, Ruffled Shade & Base, Crystal, 7 1/4 In. 395.00
Fairy, Burmese, Piecrust Crimps, Clarke Insert 2450.00
Fairy, Burmese, Pyramid, Prunus Blossom, Clarke Insert, 8 1/2 In. 2750.00
Fairy, Clarke, Man's Face, Pyramid, Camphor Glass, England, 1890 .... 395.00
Fairy, Cut Glass, Cobalt Blue Overlay 49.00
Fairy, Diamond–Quilted, Mother–of–Pearl, Clarke Base, Blue, 4 3/4 In. 195.00
Fairy, Dome Shade With Embossed Petal Point Pattern, 10 In. 165.00
Fairy, Lighthouse Shape, Blue, Marked Pantin, 8 In. 335.00
Fairy, Lime Green Diamond–Quilted, Clarke Base, 4 3/4 In. 165.00
Fairy, Mother–of–Pearl Satin Glass, Pink Swirl, Ruffled Base, 5 In. 525.00
Fairy, Pyramid, Mother–of–Pearl Shade, Clarke Inset, 3 3/4 In. 385.00
Fairy, Rainbow Satin Glass 2600.00
Fairy, Verre Moire, Frosted Cranberry, Square Base, 6 x 4 3/4 In. 450.00
Fairy, Verre Moire, Matching Base, Frosted Cranberry, 5 1/2 In. 495.00
Finger, Coin Dot, Foster, White 250.00
Finger, Fringed Curtain 70.00
Finger, New England Centennial 140.00
Finger, Sapphire Blue, Applied Blue Handle, Embossed Floral, 4 3/4 In. 75.00
Finger, Sapphire Blue, Embossed, Applied Blue Handle, 4 3/4 In. 95.00
Finger, Thousand Eye 60.00
Finger, Wheat In Shield 70.00
Finger, White, Clear Polka Dots 425.00
Fluid, Figural Stem, Iron Base, c.1870, 10 3/8 In. 165.00

Fluid, Hinks, Pedestal, White Overlay Cut To Cranberry, Mid–1800s, Pair 350.00
Fluid, Paneled Bull's–Eye, Opaque White Base, c.1860, 9 1/2 In. 82.50
Fluid, Ring Punty, Milk–Glass Base, c.1860, 9 1/2 In. 88.00
Fostoria, Beaded Crinkle, Frosted Font & Globe, c.1890, 18 3/4 In. 412.50
Fostoria, Shade, Striated Green Feathering, Gold Interior, 13 1/2 In. 750.00
Gas, Hanging, Chicago, Brass & Copper, 1899 .... 250.00
Gas, Newel Post, Spelter Woman, Holding Urn, Globe At Top, 1894, 36 In. 770.00
Girandole, 2–Light, Sulton, Pair 467.50
Girandole, 3–Light, 3 Tiers of Shelves, Floral Columns, Giltwood, 5 Ft. 2475.00
Girandole, 5–Light, Sulton, Pair 935.00
Girondale, Gilded Brass Base, Indians, Cut Prisms, 17 3/4 In., 3 Piece 300.00
Gone With The Wind, Cosmos, Blue, Fuchsia, White, Kerosene, 15 In. 150.00
Gone With The Wind, Drape, Red Satin Glass, Miniature 300.00
Gone With The Wind, Grape & Leaf Design, Red Satin Glass, 25 1/2 In. 600.00
Gone With The Wind, Parlour, Late Victorian, Original Shade 180.00
Gone With The Wind, Red Satin Glass, 1930s .... 425.00 To 475.00
Gone With The Wind, Regal Iris, Red Satin Blown Out 125.00
Gone With The Wind, Stag Shade, Forest Scene On Base 1000.00
Gone With The Wind, Sunflower, Red Satin Glass 350.00
Grease, 4 Spouts, On Tramel, Iron, 19 In. 250.00
Grease, Adjustable, Crown Base, Wrought Iron, Chain, 25 1/2 In. 50.00
Grease, Handing, Wrought Iron, European, 5 In. 205.00
Grease, Hanging, Square Pan, Sawtooth Tramel, Iron, 27 1/2 In. 350.00
Grease, Hanging, Triangular Pan, Sawtooth Tramel, 28 1/4 In. 425.00
Grease, Square Pan, Corner Spouts, Iron, 5 x 4 3/4 In. 75.00
Grease, Wrought Iron, Round Open Pan, Twisted Hanger, 9 In. 150.00
Hand, Hobbs Dots, Crimped, c.1880, 5 1/4 In. 247.00
Hand, Lomax, Footed, c.1870, 5 5/8 In. 175.00
Hand, Safety, Perkins & House, Brass, c.1860, 5 In. 385.00
   LAMP, HANDEL, see Handel, Lamp
Hanging, Candle, Cranberry Smoke Bell, Floral Design, 23 1/2 In. 1700.00
Hanging, Leaded–Glass Shade, Wreath & Swag Design, Duffner & Kimberly 660.00
Hanging, Rochester, Brass, Tin Shade 550.00
Hanging, Twist, Cranberry, Complete 290.00
Kerosene, 2–Tier, Milk Glass, Feather, Brass Base 115.00
Kerosene, Aquarius, Vaseline Glass, Small 275.00
Kerosene, Blue Font, White Base, Brass Collar, 11 1/2 In. 125.00
Kerosene, Blue Milk Glass, Brass Base, Dated 1891 .... 105.00
Kerosene, Carriage, Beveled Glass, Red Lens, Tin & Brass, 11 1/2 In. 30.00
Kerosene, Cathedral, Blue Bowl, Amber Base 495.00
Kerosene, Chapman With Diamonds, Milk Glass Base 225.00
Kerosene, Coolidge Drape, Stand 65.00
Kerosene, Dietz, Corporation Street 250.00
Kerosene, Eugenie, Figural, Electrified 75.00
Kerosene, Heart, Bull's–Eye, Fleur–De–Lis Foot, Marble Base, 9 3/4 In. 105.00
Kerosene, Lacemaker's, Inverted Thumbprint, Cranberry, 16 1/4 In. 425.00
Kerosene, Logan, Amber 115.00
Kerosene, Magic Sun, Pat. 1869, Wall, Santa Claus Shade, Brass, Copper 200.00
Kerosene, Overlay, Marble Base, Brass Stem, White To Cranberry, 11 In. 500.00
Kerosene, Peacock Feather, Blue 140.00
Kerosene, Peanut, 8 1/2 In. 90.00
Kerosene, Peanut, Owl & Moon, Etched Chimney 89.00
Kerosene, Perkins & House, Brass 110.00
Kerosene, Petticoat, Lyre & Star, Pewter Collar, Snuffer Cap, 6 3/4 In. 285.00
Kerosene, Ripley, Double Handle 80.00
Kerosene, Riverside, Oval 88.00
Kerosene, Sewing, Peanut 80.00
Kerosene, Student, Mercury, White Vienna Shade, Brass, c.1880, 22 In. 495.00
Kerosene, Swirled–Rib Bands, Crystal, 9 In. 50.00
Kerosene, Teardrop, Eyewinker, Frosted Plume Font, 9 In. 110.00
Kerosene, Three Face, Frosted, Table 165.00
Kerosene, Wagon, Dietz No. 30, 16 x 12 In. 275.00
Kerosene, Webster, Blue 135.00

Kitchen, Pull Down, Milk Glass Shade, Smoke Bell 165.00
Lacemaker's, Cut Circles Ring Font, Clear, 10 In. 325.00
Lacemaker's, Folded Rim, Bulbous Font, Clear Blown, 10 1/2 In. 350.00
Lacemaker's, Pleated & Beaded Stem, 9 In. 225.00
Miner's Teapot, U. S. Tool Co. 75.00
Miner's, American Safety Lamp Co. 275.00
Miner's, Carbide, Hanging, 9 In. 62.00
Miner's, Cast Iron, 5–In. Diam. Round Font, 12–In. Hook 185.00
Miner's, Kohler, Marlboro, Mass 150.00
Miner's, Safety, Permissible, 11 In. 45.00
Miner's, Tin, 2 1/2 In. 65.00
Miner's, Tin, 3 In. 50.00
Miner's, Wolf 200.00
Oil, 2 Gnomes Blowing Bubbles, Figural, Bisque 595.00
Oil, Acanthus Leaf, Brass Standard, Marble Base, 1850s, 11 1/4 In. 412.50
Oil, Americus, Clear Blue Font, Dark Clear Amber Base, c.1890, 15 In. 495.00
Oil, Aquarius, Amber, 10 In. 135.00
Oil, Artichoke, Miniature 625.00
Oil, Atterbury Wave, c.1870, 9 1/4 In. 55.00
Oil, Banquet, Hand–Painted Yellow Roses, Brass Base 190.00
Oil, Bicycle, Majestic Model, Nickel–Plated Brass, c.1900, 7 3/4 In. 180.00
Oil, Blue Glass Base, Frosted Vintage Shade, Blown Glass, 23 In. 160.00
Oil, Blue Japanning, No. 12, Clear Globe, Tin, 14 1/2 In. 45.00
Oil, Boy, Holding Basket, Green Logs, Ceramic, Brass, Chimney, 8 1/2 In. 85.00
Oil, Bradley and Hubbard, Brass, Copper Oil Reserve, Rivet Trim, 17 In. 110.00
Oil, Bull's–Eye, Emerald Green, c.1900, 8 3/8 In. 182.50
Oil, Columbian Coin, Milk Glass 600.00
Oil, Cranberry Opalescent, Sheldon Swirl, 8 In. 350.00
Oil, Cranberry, Daisies, Herringbone, 17 In. 285.00
Oil, Demon Head Design, Chain & Hook, Bronze, Asian, 20 1/2 In. 275.00
Oil, Diamond & Dot Font, Thousand–Eye Base, Amber, 12 In. 225.00
Oil, Diamond Pattern, Ball Base, Acorn Burner, Cranberry, 1877, 9 In. 1100.00
Oil, Diamond–Quilted Satin Glass, Matching Shade, 14 1/2 In. 1140.00
Oil, Double Bull's–Eye, Milk–Glass Base, c.1860, 9 3/4 In. 120.00
Oil, Double, Railway Car, Brass, c.1890, 32 x 30 In. 1320.00
Oil, Egyptian Pattern, Clear & Frosted, c.1880, 11 5/8 In. 335.00
Oil, Floral–Shaped Shade, Prisms, Glass, 21 In., Pair 1100.00
Oil, Gilt–Metal Base, Enameled Design, Milk Glass, Electrified, 37 In. 35.00
Oil, Gothic Arch Font, Hexagonal Base, Brass Collar, 11 In. 135.00
Oil, Green Glass, Electrified 75.00
Oil, Hand, Eyebrow 100.00
Oil, Hand, Log Cabin, Patent 1876 .... 545.00
Oil, Hand, Nutmeg, Green Glass, Brass Frame & Handle, 3 x 6 1/2 In. 140.00
Oil, Hand, Swirled Ribbing At Top, c.1860, 3 3/8 In. 130.00
Oil, Hand, White Opalescent Stripe 450.00
Oil, Hanging, Ruby Hobnail, Brass Fittings, c.1870, 31 In. 275.00
Oil, Heart, Opaque Green, Glass, 8 1/2 In. 325.00
Oil, Lincoln Drape Shade, Cambridge, Miniature 150.00
Oil, Marriage, 2 Fonts, Match Holder Between, Ripley & Co., 13 1/2 In. 695.00
Oil, Melon Sections, Raised Sewing, Sawtooth Top, Cranberry, 18 1/2 In. 850.00
Oil, Metal Base & Bowl, Gold Leaves, Blossoms, Green, 17 1/4 In. 550.00
Oil, Milk–Glass Cased Base, Fired–On Angels, Miniature 220.00
Oil, Milk–Glass Oil Reserves, Flowers, Electrified, 12 In., Pair 187.00
Oil, Nellie Bly, Pink Base & Shade, 9 In. 145.00
Oil, Opalescent Reverse Swirl, White 350.00
Oil, Opaque White, Flowers, Leaves, Brass, c.1880, 6 1/8 In. 450.00
Oil, Opaque White, Tin Handle & Base, c.1880, 2 1/2 In. 27.50
Oil, Owl, Green Paint, Miniature 1650.00
Oil, Paneled Fern, c.1970, 9 3/4 In. 100.00
Oil, Peacock Feather Pattern, Amethyst, 7 1/2 In., Pair 145.00
Oil, Picket, 8 In. 55.00
Oil, Princess Feather, Green 425.00
Oil, Queen of Hearts, Riverside Collar, 7 1/2 In. 125.00

◆◆◆

Be very careful when handling old bottles or medical equipment. The remains of old drugs, even toxic materials, may still cling to the surface. A broken bit of glass or a sliver could let these toxic materials reach your bloodstream.

◆◆◆

Oil, Rib & Pleat, Opaque White, Baroque–Type Base	110.00
Oil, Ring Punty Sawtooth Eye & Leaf, Black Glass, C, 1860, 11 1/2 In.	5225.00
Oil, Sanded Opaque Yellow Font, Opaque White Base, 13 In.	125.00
Oil, Sheldon Swirl, Vaseline Opalescent Reverse–Swirl Font, Glass	225.00
Oil, Sheldon Swirl, White Diagonal–Striped Font, 7 1/8 In.	325.00
Oil, Sheldon Swirl, White Opalescent	400.00
Oil, Silver Plate, English Touchmarks	105.00
Oil, Stepped Pyramid Base, Hollow Knop, c.1835, 12 3/4 In.	302.50
Oil, Thousand Eye, Blur Diamond & Dot Font, Ives Shade, Amber	340.00
Oil, Thousand–Eye Variant, Blue, Clear Base, 13 3/4 In.	275.00
Oil, Three Printie, Double Pewter Burners, Canary, 1840s, 10 1/2 In.	825.00
Oil, Triple Bull's–Eye, Canadian Brass, 1890s, 10 1/4 In.	135.00
Oil, White Opalescent, Seaweed, Mini–Stem	285.00
Oil, White Opalescent, Vertical Polka Dot, Flat Hand	575.00
LAMP, PAIRPOINT, see Pairpoint, Lamp	
Peg, Brass Candlestick, Yellow Overlay, Mushroom Shade, 15 In.	525.00
Peg, Clear Paneled, Fastened With Pewter Chamberstick, 6 3/4 In., Pair	280.00
Peg, Diamond Font Pattern, 5 1/4 In.	60.00
Peg, Diamond Pattern, Brass Holder, Pink Interior, Crystal, 14 1/2 In.	700.00
Peg, Etched Daises & Stem On Ball Shade, Icicle Design, Brass Base	290.00
Peg, Frosted Girl's Head, Butterflies, Flowers, Green, 14 In., Pair	895.00
Peg, Gold Flowers, Leaves & Bows, Cranberry Glass, Brass Stem, 11 In.	375.00
Peg, Gold Scrolls & Trim, Brass Candlestick, Green, 12 1/4 In., Pair	750.00
Peg, Rubena–Frosted Shades, Fern Fronds, Brass Base, 15 1/4 In., Pair	950.00
Peg, Yellow–Overlay Glass, Mushroom Shade, Glass Chimney, Brass, 15 In.	495.00
Perfume, Cockatoo, Porcelain	295.00
Perfume, St. Louis, Red To Frost, Art Deco Cameo, 7 In.	660.00
Perfume, Woman, Germany	42.00
Police, Tin, Bull's–Eye Lens, Brown Japanning, 6 3/4 In.	65.00
Sconce, 1–Light, Brass Wall Plate, Holland, 18th Century, 9 1/2 In.	1980.00
Sconce, 2–Light, Gilt, Pierced Backplate, Stylized, 10 1/4 In., Pair	1450.00
Sconce, 3–Light, Greek Figure With Wings Above, Bronze, c.1880, 4 Piece	7500.00
Sconce, 3–Light, Rococo, Scrolling Acanthus Leaves, Bronze, 15 In., Pair	335.00
Sconce, 3–Light, Scrolled Plate, Voluted Branches, Bronze, 24 In., 4 Pc.	3525.00
Sconce, 3–Light, Tin, Black Paint, 7 In.	300.00
Sconce, 4–Light, Louis XVI, Gilt Bronze, Porcelain Back, 28 In., Pair	1215.00
Sconce, Candle, Tooled Back, Semicircular Crest, Tin, 10 In.	150.00
Sconce, Cut & Stamped Leaf Crest, Painted Black, Tin. 17 In.	1050.00
Sconce, Double, Miller Label	135.00
Sconce, Gilt Bronze, Glass, 3 Sides, F. L. Wright, 13 1/2 x 5 In.	7800.00
Sconce, Polychrome Flowers, Spanish, Wrought Iron, 69 In., Pair	1985.00
Sconce, Punched Tin, Conical, Front Hinge, Yellow Paint, 13 In., Pair	60.00
Sconce, Quezal Gold Shades, Brass, c.1904, 4 1/2 In., Pair	1295.00
Sconce, S–Arm, Gilded Brass, Pair	155.00
Sconce, Scrolled Back Plate, Electrified, Bronze, 21 In., Pair	335.00
Sconce, Sunflowers & Tulips, Iron Candle Prong, Brass, 20 In., Pair	225.00
Sconce, Tombstone–Edge Crest, Mirrored Back, Tin	2100.00
Sewing, Green Paneled, Comes Apart	125.00
Sinumbra, Brass, Frosted Cut–Glass Shade, Prisms, Electrified, 28 In.	1210.00
Sinumbra, Etched–Glass Shade, Prisms, Gilt Bronze & Marble, 30 1/2 In.	1875.00
Skater's, Brass & Tin, Clear Globe, 7 In.	35.00
Skater's, Clear Globe, 7 1/4 In.	40.00

Skater's, Clear Globe, Impressed Ribs, Tin, 6 1/2 In. 100.00
Skater's, Tin, Clear Globe, Jewel, 7 1/8 In. 55.00
Sparking, Loop Pattern, Sandwich Glass, Miniature 120.00
Sparking, Single Spout Burner, Snuffer Cap, Brass, 4 3/4 In. 85.00
Sparking, Whale Oil Burner, Pewter, 2 In. 100.00
Splint Holder, Hand Forged, Twisted Iron, 3-Footed, 18th C., 18 In. 385.00
Star Wars, Blinking Inside Lights, Ceramic 65.00
Street, Kerosene, Dietz Corporation, Post Mounted, c.1890 .... 250.00
Street, Twin Torch-Type Heads, Globes, Cast Iron, 1900, 16 Ft., Pair 3500.00
Student, Electric, Downer Mineral Sperm-Oil Study Lamp, 20 1/4 In. 500.00
Student, Electric, Green Overlay Shade, Brass, 20 3/4 In. 175.00
Student, Electric, Nickel-Plated Brass Frame, Green Shade, 26 In. 300.00
Student, Electric, White Shade, Steel Pole, Brass, 21 1/4 In. 275.00
Student, Kerosene, Double, White Shade, Brass, 29 In. 1275.00
Student, Kerosene, Teal Blue, Insert For Perfection, Pat. Nov. '81 .... 195.00
Student, Wick Knob Marked New Vista, E. M. & Co., Brass, 19 1/2 In. 450.00
Theater Footlight, Mirrored, Adjustable Iron & Sheet Metal, 15 In. 220.00
   LAMP, TIFFANY, see Tiffany, Lamp
Torchere, Candles, Hinged Base, Cranberry Shades, 19 In. 645.00
Torchere, Female Holding Torch, Putti, Electrified, Bronze, 32 In. 1320.00
Torchere, Floor, Bronze, Steuben Etched Shade, 19th Century, Pair 5000.00
Torchere, George III Style, Rosette & Ribbon Rim, Mahogany, 64 In. 1100.00
Wall Bracket, Mercury Reflector, Cast Iron 70.00
Whale Oil, Beveled Front Glass, Pierced Vent Top, Tin, 8 3/4 In. 135.00
Whale Oil, Boiler Inspector's, Oval Font, Burner, 14 1/2 In. 10.00
Whale Oil, Brass 149.00
Whale Oil, Double Spouts, Bull's-Eye & Fleur-De-Lis, Pair 650.00
Whale Oil, Glass, Tin, Police Inscribed Chimney, 16 In. 605.00
Whale Oil, Tin, Brass, Fancy Reflector, Pennsylvania, 6 In. 85.00
Whale Oil, Yale & Curtis, Pewter, 7 In. 200.00

A lantern is a special type of lighting device. It has a light source, usually a candle, totally hidden inside the walls of the lantern. Light is seen through holes or glass sections.

LANTERN, 5-Light, Within Gilt-Bronze Cage, Glazed Panels, 27 In. 2200.00
Adam-Westlake, G. T. W. 40.00
Adlake, No. 3-48 .... 40.00
Amico, Bunny Shape, Box 25.00
Barn, Hinged Door & Glass Panels, Mortised Pine Frame, 11 In. 175.00
Barn, Mortised Wooden Frame, Tin Top & Bottom, 13 1/2 In. 275.00
Brass, 3 Red Glass Sides, Fluted, Handle, Sterling Candle, 6 1/2 In. 77.00
Candle, Brown Japanning, Pierced Star, Ring Handle, 11 1/2 In. 150.00
Candle, Clear Globe, J. Fleming, Tin, 10 In. 80.00
Candle, Clear Globe, Wire Guard, Tin, 11 1/4 In. 45.00
Candle, Clear Pressed Globe, Tin, Ring Handle, 11 In. 275.00
Candle, Conical Top, Wire Guards, Cylindrical, Tin, 11 3/4 In. 225.00
Candle, Paul Revere Type, Pierced Tin, 5 1/2 x 16 In. 225.00
Candle, Revere Type, Ring Handle, Punched Tin, 12 1/2 In. 75.00
Clear Blown Globe, Pierced Tin Top, Tin, Black Repaint, 10 In. 200.00
Coal Oil, Archer & Pancoast, Pyramid Shape, Tin & Glass, Wire Bail 175.00
Conductor's, 2-Color Globe, Brass 450.00
Copper, Slag Glass Panels, Shop of Crafters, c.1906, 13 In. 1875.00
Dietz, Bell Systam 35.00
Dietz, Farm, Blizzard 16.00
Dietz, Fireman's, Brass, Dated 1906 .... 350.00
Dietz, Little Giant 35.00
Dietz, Little Wizard, Blue Globe, 1918 .... 45.00
Dietz, Vesta, Navy Deck, 1909 .... 95.00
Garden, Lotus Finial, Bird & Floral Design, Japanese, 87 In. 2200.00
Hall, 12 Ribs At Base, White Rim, 3 Handles, Amethyst, 11 1/2 In. 230.00
Ham, Voting Booth 75.00
Kerosene, Brass, Round Globe, 14 1/2 In. 325.00
Kerosene, E. J. Buckholt, Engine Co. No. 5, Brass, Electrified, 14 In. 100.00

Luck–E–Lite, No. 25	45.00
Meyrose & Co., Queen Style, Brass, Clear Globe	240.00
Moorish Arched Panels, Pierced Galleries, Brass, 1850s, 32 In.	1650.00
New York Central, Clear Glass	25.00
Palace, Pagoda Top & Base, Japan, c.1850, 39 In.	1500.00
Paul Revere Type, Punched Tin, Green Paint, Ring, 13 In.	55.00
Paul Revere Type, Punched Tin, Ring Handle, 12 1/2 In.	80.00
Porch, Iron Frame, Textured Amber Glass Panels, G. Stickley, 15 In.	779.00
Prison Guard's, Bull's–Eye	265.00
Rayo, Red Globe, Brass	20.00
Skater's, Dietz	70.00
Skating, Cobalt Blue Chimney	85.00
Tin, Strap Handle Above Conical Ventilated Top, Glass, 18 In.	990.00

Le Verre Francais is one of the many types of cameo glass made in France. The glass was made by the C. Schneider factory in Epinay–sur–Seine from 1920 to 1933. It is a mottled glass, usually decorated with floral designs, and bears the incised signature *Le Verre Francais.*

LE VERRE FRANCAIS, Bowl, Stems, Thorn–Covered Seed Pods, 5 1/2 x 11 In.	865.00
Box, Cover, Scrolling Leaves, Signed, c.1925, 3 1/2 In.	1100.00
Ewer, Stylized Leaves, Streaked, Marked, 1920, 14 3/4 In.	1450.00
Lamp, Domical Shade, Stylized Bellflowers, 1925, 16 In.	4950.00
Lamp, Shade, Pendent Fuchsia, Iron Mount, 1925, 15 5/8 In.	5500.00
Perfume Bottle, Molded Fruits, Ovoid, 10 1/2 In.	135.00
Vase, Art Deco, Cut To Yellow, Signed, 17 In.	1300.00
Vase, Blue, Yellow, Orange, Cameo, 18 In., Pair ....*Illus*	2700.00
Vase, Circles & Flowers Over Brickwork, c.1925, 14 In.	1100.00
Vase, Flowers, Blue, Orange Overlay, 12 In. ....*Illus*	900.00
Vase, Fuchsia Blossoms, Leaves, Signed, c.1925, 17 5/8 In.	2750.00
Vase, Geometric Blossoms, Signed, c.1925, 22 7/8 In.	2550.00
Vase, Geometric Curves & Lines, Ovoid, c.1925, 21 1/2 In.	8900.00
Vase, Japanese Lantern, Brown & Orange To Yellow, 16 In.	1500.00
Vase, Lady Slippers & Grasses, Signed, 23 5/8 In.	3850.00
Vase, Mottled Yellow, Orange To Brown Overlay, 6 1/2 In.	355.00
Vase, Orange, Yellow, Brown, 12 In. ....*Illus*	1210.00
Vase, Pink Mushrooms, Red Overlay, 9 In. ....*Illus*	900.00
Vase, Roses & Leaves, Signed, c.1925, 16 3/8 In.	2300.00
Vase, Stylized Butterflies, Signed, c.1920, 12 1/2 In.	1750.00
Vase, Stylized Flowerhead Panels, Gray, 1920, 23 1/4 In.	3850.00
Vase, Stylized Fruiting Leaves, Signed, 1925, 12 5/8 In.	1650.00

Le Verre Francais, Vase, Blue, Yellow, Orange, Cameo, 18 In., Pair

Le Verre Francais, Vase, Pink Mushrooms, Red Overlay, 9 In. Le Verre Francais, Vase, Flowers, Blue, Orange Overlay, 12 In.

Le Verre Francais, Vase, Orange, Yellow, Brown, 12 In.

Vase, Stylized Fungi, Brickwork Borders, 1925, 12 1/2 In. 1775.00

Leather is tanned animal hide and it has been used to make decorative and useful objects for centuries. Leather objects must be carefully preserved with proper humidity and oiling or the leather will deteriorate and crack. This damage cannot be repaired.

LEATHER, Chaps, Blacksmith's 200.00
   Holster, Gun, Left–Handed 30.00
   Jacket & Hat, Indian Scout's, Buckskin, 1800s 3500.00
   Mailbag 22.50
   Saddle Bags, U. S. Cavalry, Rock Island Arsenal, 1918 .... 75.00
   Saddle, Heiser, 1930s 850.00
   Saddle, Leather, Silver Ornaments, Burgundy Patina, L. White, Texas 715.00
   Saddle, Matching Martingale, Hess & Hopkins, Tooled, Brass Studded 475.00
   Saddle, Officer's, McClellan, Brass Pommel, 1880s 225.00
   Saddle, Porter, 1940s 925.00
   Saddle, Roping, Stamped King Ranch, Kingsville, Texas 365.00
   Saddle, Western, Tooled, Horse's Head, Burgundy, L. White, 30 In. 715.00
   Sidesaddle, Red–Carpet Seat, Tulip Designs, Decorative Stitching 10.00
   Spurs, Black & Iron With Silver Inlay, Pair 75.00
   Suitcase, Alligator, 5 Cut–Glass Bottles, Sterling Tops 1500.00

LEEDS POTTERY   Leeds pottery was made at Leeds, Yorkshire, England, from 1774 to 1878. Most Leeds ware was not marked. Early Leeds pieces had distinctive twisted handles with a greenish glaze on part of the creamy ware. Later ware often had blue borders on the creamy pottery.

LEEDS, Bowl, Prince & Princess William V of Orange, 5 In. 825.00
   Plate, American Eagle, Shield Breast, Green Rim, 8 In. 385.00
   Plate, Animal Center Medallion, Landscape, Piecrust Rim, 8 1/4 In. 225.00
   Plate, Baptismal Scene, Inscribed Den Doop, 9 3/4 In. 2550.00
   Plate, Lady of Kevelaar On Horseback, Inscription, 9 7/8 In. 2300.00
   Plate, Prince & Princess William V of Orange, 9 1/2 In. 3025.00
   Plate, Prince & Princess William V of Orange, Inscription, 10 In. 1300.00
   Teapot, Blue, 18th Century, Miniature 9625.00
   Teapot, Floral Knob, Sliding Lid, Floral & Figural Design, 9 1/4 In. 275.00
   Teapot, Prince & Princess William V of Orange, Floral Handle, 4 In. 3510.00
   Teapot, Solid Border King's Rose, 6 1/2 In. 250.00
   Teapot, Solid Strawberry Border, Leaves & Vines On Body, 6 7/8 In. 440.00
   Vase, Reticulated Panels, Flaring Hexagonal Form, Marked, 6 1/4 In. 745.00

The Geo. Zoltan Lefton Company has imported porcelains to be sold in America since 1940. The pieces are often marked with the Lefton name. The firm is still in business. The company mark has changed through the years; but because marks have been used for long periods of time, they are of little help in dating an object.

LEFTON, Bank, Billiken, 7 In. 30.00
   Cologne Bottle, Tray, Lavender & White, Porcelain 45.00
   Cookie Jar, Santa Claus 85.00
   Cookie Jar, Santa Claus, Standing 88.00
   Cookie Jar, Woman's Head, 1950s 38.00
   Figurine, Baby, Red Hearts On Bib, Bisque, Pair 35.00
   Figurine, Cupped Hands, Roses On Cuff, Pink, 6 1/4 x 3 1/2 In. 45.00
   Figurine, Elegant Girl, Hat & Hat Box, Hand Painted, 1957, 4 1/2 In. 25.00
   Figurine, Kewpie, Lying On Floor, 4 1/2 In. 40.00
   Figurine, Peacock 24.00
   Figurine, Standing, Pants Down, Kewpie 40.00
   Head Vase, African Girl 26.00
   Plaque, Boy & Girl 20.00

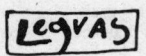

Legras was founded in 1864 by Auguste Legras at St. Denis, France. It is best known for cameo glass and enamel–decorated glass with Art Nouveau designs. Legras merged with Pantin in 1920 and became the Verreries et Cristalleries de St. Denis et de Pantin Reunies.

LEGRAS, Biscuit Jar, Enameled	475.00
Bowl, Enameled Winter–Forest Scene, Signed, 4 In.	335.00
Pin Dish, Winter Scene, Signed, 4 1/2 In.	400.00
Salt, Enameled Winter Scene, Signed, c.1920, 1 In., 4 Piece	1980.00
Salt, Winter Landscape, Snow On Ground, Enameled, c.1920, 1 In., 4 Pc.	2000.00
Vase, Barrel Shape, Scenic Design, Mountains & Foliage, Signed, 8 In.	975.00
Vase, Bottle Shape, Allover Grape Leaves, Burgundy, 9 In.	500.00
Vase, Cut Vines & Berries, Pink, Green & Browns, Signed, 4 3/4 In.	575.00
Vase, Flowers, Coral Shaded To Yellow Frost, Signed, 9 In.	275.00
Vase, Frieze of 4 Birds In Flight, Brown Enamel, Signed, 21 In.	1540.00
Vase, Frosted Ice Ground, Cameo & Enamel, Signed, 8 1/2 In.	875.00
Vase, Grape Leaves, Tendrilled Vines, Signed, c.1915, 15 3/4 In.	1650.00
Vase, Mountain Landscape, Enameled, Signed, c.1910, 11 3/4 In., Pair	1540.00
Vase, Mountain Scene, Square Top, Signed, 13 In.	1595.00
Vase, Red Leaves & Cherries, Frosted Ground, Signed, 10 1/4 In.	490.00
Vase, Reddish, Purple, Ivy, Pink Frost, 16 In.	2300.00
Vase, Scenic, Half Barren Trees, Blue & Green Ground, 5 1/2 In.	950.00
Vase, Scenic, Trees, Mountains, Streams, 10 1/4 In.	1250.00
Vase, Stick, Scene of Majestic Pines, Signed, 7 1/2 In.	335.00
Vase, Stream, Green Shrubs, Trees, Orange Interior, Signed, 4 In.	4500.00
Vase, Winter Scene, Reverse Trumpet Shape, Signed, 16 In.	850.00

Walter Scott Lenox and Jonathan Cox founded the Ceramic Art Company in Trenton, New Jersey, in 1889. In 1906, Lenox left and started his own company. The company makes a porcelain that is similar to Irish Belleek. The marks used by the firm have changed through the years and collectors prefer the earlier examples.

LENOX, see also Ceramic Art Co.

LENOX, Base, Portrait, Silver Designs Over Porcelain, 9 1/4 In.	1870.00
Box, White Leaf Design, Green Wreath Mark, 3 1/2 x 4 3/4 In.	65.00
Cake Plate, Cream, Gold, Tab Handle, Square, 10 In.	45.00
Candleholder, Serenade, Pair	85.00
Candlestick, Dolphin, Gold Trim, Marked, 9 1/2 In., Pair	75.00
Creamer, Kingsley	85.00
Cup & Saucer, Burgundy, Demitasse, Set of 6	150.00
Cup & Saucer, Christie	30.00
Cup & Saucer, Tuxedo	35.00
Desk Set, Holder, Pen & Pencil, Sheaffer	95.00
Dinner Set, Grenoble, Ivory, Service For 10	1100.00
Dish, Swan, White, Green Mark, 4 In.	35.00
Figurine, Bird, Seated, Pink, 2 1/2 In.	45.00
Figurine, Penguin, Wings Out, Ivory, 4 1/2 In.	120.00
Figurine, Rapunzel, 8 1/2 In.	115.00
Gravy Boat, Christie	85.00
Mug, 5 In.	100.00
Penholder, With Pen, Sheaffer	98.00
Place Setting, Imperial	75.00
Plate, 1970 Advertising, 4 1/4 In.	13.00
Plate, Cream, Gold, Green Mark, 8 1/4 In.	10.00
Plate, Dinner, Annapolis Blue	30.00
Plate, Peach Tree, Sterling Silver Frame, 9 1/2 In.	65.00
Platter, Christie, 16 In.	95.00
Platter, Kingsley, 16 In.	175.00
Salt, Shell & Seaweed, Cream, Oval, Black Mark, 12 Piece	150.00
Setting For 12, Cretan, 63 Piece	775.00
Stein, Golf, In Position, Driver, Hand Painted, 1900, 1/2 Liter	2660.00
Stein, Golf, Putting, Caddy On 9th Hole, Sterling, 1900, 1/2 Liter	2600.00

Stein, Golfer Scene	2310.00
Stein, Golfer, Gorham Lid & Rims, Blue, c.1900	3850.00
Sugar, Kingsley	95.00
Swan, Open, Pink, Gold, 5 In.	25.00
Toby Jug, William Penn, 7 In.	135.00
Vase, Acanthus Leaf, Green Mark, 8 1/2 In., Pair	165.00
Vase, Black, Gold Seahorse, 11 1/2 In.	220.00
Vase, Dipped Pink, Handles, Green Mark, 7 1/2 In.	45.00
Vase, Gold Rim, 4 1/2 x 10 1/2 In.	95.00

Letter openers have been used since the eighteenth century. Ivory and silver were favored by the well–to–do. In the late–nineteenth century, the letter opener was popular as an advertising giveaway and many were made of metal or celluloid. Brass openers with figural handles were also popular.

LETTER OPENER, Art Deco, Motto, U. S. S. Steel, Irvin Works, Dec. 15, 1938	10.00
Bulldog's Head, Figural, With Sword & Chains, 6 1/2 In.	20.00
Cherub, Figural, Brass	65.00
DeLaval Cream Separators, Brass	30.00
Figural, Anaconda Copper & Brass, Arrowhead	14.00
Fuller Brush Man	7.00
Gulf Oil	10.00
Harley Co., Solid Brass	30.00
Howco Fishing Tackle, Celluloid	80.00
Mechanics Savings Bank, Manchester, N. H., Bronze	18.00
Nabisco Uneeda Biscuit	80.00
Nude, Chrome Plated, 11 In.	13.00
Nude, Clear Lucite	20.00
Slicker Boy, 1920s	46.00
Whale Bone	45.00
Zeith Furnace Co., Tin	50.00

The Libbey Glass Company has made glass of many types since 1888. Libbey made cut glass and tablewares that are collected today. The stemwares of the 1930s and 1940s are once again in style. The Toledo, Ohio, firm was purchased by Owens–Illinois in 1935 and is still working under the name *Libbey* as a division of that company.

LIBBEY, see also Amberina; Cut Glass; Maize

LIBBEY, Basket, Star & Feather, Triple Notched Handle, Signed, 16 In.	850.00
Bonbon, Amberina, 6–Pointed Rim, Signed, 1 1/2 x 7 In.	585.00
Bonbon, Wavy 6–Pointed Rim, Fuchsia, Signed, 7 In.	585.00
Bowl, Aztec, Signed, 8 In.	2650.00
Bowl, Chain of Hobstars Alternating With Fans, Sawtooth Rim, 9 In.	195.00
Bowl, Cut Flowers & Thistles, Serrated Rim, Signed, 8 In.	225.00
Bowl, Fine–Lined Cut Leaves, Floral Border, Sawtooth Rim, 8 In.	195.00
Bowl, Lovebirds, Wisteria Pattern, Crosshatch Border, Signed, 8 In.	450.00
Bowl, Nash, Clear, Cranberry Thread, Diamond Optic, 13 In.	275.00
Bowl, Radiant, Signed, 9 In.	195.00
Carafe, Harvard, 7 1/4 In.	195.00
Castor, Pickle, Raised Swirls Design, Amberina Insert, Footed Frame	245.00
Celery, Maize, White & Green Leaves	200.00
Cocktail, Kangaroo Stem, Opalescent	150.00
Cocktail, Kangaroo Stem, Signed	95.00
Compote, Brilliant Period, Teardrop Stem, Signed, 6 x 5 1/2 In.	360.00
Compote, Silhouette, Jumbo Elephant Stem, Signed, 11 x 7 1/2 In.	600.00
Decanter, Colonna, Signed, 8 1/2 In.	845.00
Decanter, Russian Pattern, Amberina, 7 1/2 In.	1210.00
Dish, Puritana, Oval	595.00
Ewer, Inverted Thumbprint, Blue, Amber Handle, 10 1/4 In.	125.00
Flower Center, Empress, Faceted Neck, Signed, 6 1/4 x 10 1/2 In.	550.00
Perfume Bottle, Hobstar & Snowflake, Faceted Stopper, Signed	250.00
Perfume Bottle, Intaglio, Peacock On Branches, Signed, 7 1/2 In.	700.00
Perfume Bottle, Optic Narrow Panels, Amberina, Signed, 6 5/8 In.	695.00

Pitcher, Aztec, Signed, 12 In.	7250.00
Pitcher, Harvard, Cut In Handle, 7 1/2 In.	395.00
Pitcher, Russian Pattern, Thumbprint Handle, Amberina, 12 In.	2200.00
Pitcher, Sonora, 11 1/2 In.	675.00
Pitcher, Wedgemere, 10 1/2 In.	4250.00
Salad Bowl, Ellsmere, Signed, 1901, 12 In.	1850.00
Sherbet, Rabbit, Signed	70.00
Sherry, Monkey Stem, Opalescent	100.00
Tumbler, Hobstars & Fans, Signed, 6 Piece	235.00
Vase, Brilliant Period, Hobstars & Hobnails, Signed, 17 1/4 In.	3080.00
Wine, Princess, Cut Glass, 4 In.	70.00

Cigarettes became popular in the late–nineteenth century and with the cigarette came matches and cigarette lighters. All types of lighters are collected, from solid gold to the first of the recent disposable lighters. Most examples found were made after 1940.

LIGHTER, Atlantic Gasoline	14.00
Capital Brand, Bottle Shape, 1912	90.00
Cigar, Blaine	350.00
Cigar, Gretchen, Louis Ash Co., Brass Trim, Sheet Metal, 7 3/4 In.	350.00
Cigar, Ivory Inlays	15.00
Cigar, Midland	325.00
Cigar, Patinated Copper, Silver Mounted, Gorham, 5 In.	605.00
Cigar, Teapot Shape, Dragon Handle, Mixed Metal, Gorham	600.00
Elephant, Figural	85.00
Elgin, Cigarette Case Combo, Deco, Magic Action Lite, Box	40.00
Elgin, With Cigarette Case	25.00
Evans, Attached To Cigarette Case	20.00
Evans, Horsehead	15.00
H & H Corned Beef & Raritan Frankfurters	35.00
Hamm's Beer	35.00
Hancock Oil Co.	10.00
Inset Watch, 1928	250.00
Jell–O, Musical	32.00
Knight, Figural	25.00
Outboard Motor, Swank	125.00
Parker, Nude, Table Model	35.00
Pepsi–Cola, Bottle Shape	27.50
Pepsi–Cola, Musical, Box	125.00
Pinup Girl	18.00
Pipe, Nimrod	10.00
Pistol, Occupied Japan	25.00
Redilite, Flying–A, Illustrated Box, 1950s	10.00
Regal Beer, Bottle Shape	35.00
Ronson, Crown, Table	30.00
Ronson, Cupids	20.00
Ronson, Diana	18.00
Ronson, Mayfair, Table	20.00
Ronson, Pencil	75.00
Ronson, Pencil, Chrome	21.00
Ronson, Queen Anne, Silver Plate	16.00
Royal Crown Cola, Bottle Shape	19.50
Royaliter, Art Deco	16.00
Stag, Mr. Magoo On Reverse, Box	15.00

◆◆◆

Avoid flies. They leave droppings on mirrors, pictures and chandeliers. Flyspecks on pictures can be carefully removed with a knife blade. Glass can be washed.

◆◆◆

Stock Ticker, Edison	75.00
Storz, Box, Matching Pencil	26.00
Table, Dunhill, Silver Plate, Monogrammed, 4 1/4 In.	55.00
Weisner, Rhinestones, Box	75.00
Windproof, Men Fishing	10.00
Windproof, Men Golfing	10.00
Windproof, Men Hunting	10.00
World War II Bullet, Comet	4.00
Zippo, Canada	10.00
Zippo, Kent Cigarette, Kent Crest, 1950s	3.00

Lightning rod balls are collected for their variety of shape and color. These glass balls were at the center of the rod that was attached to the roof of a house or barn to avoid lightning damage.

LIGHTNING ROD, Ball, Amethyst	8.00
Ball, Black, Hawkeye	25.00
Ball, Cobalt, National	18.00
Ball, Light Purple Glaze	110.00
Ball, Mercury, Gold	25.00
Ball, Mercury, Silver	25.00
Ball, Milk Glass, National	15.00
Ball, Swirl, Opalescent White	15.00

 Limoges porcelain has been made in Limoges, France, since the mid–nineteenth century. Fine porcelains were made by many factories including Haviland, Ahrenfeldt, Guerin, Pouyat, Elite, and others. Modern porcelains are being made at Limoges and the word *Limoges* as part of the mark is not an indication of age. Haviland is listed as a separate category in this book.

LIMOGES, Berry Set, Overall Rose Design, Gilt Borders, 13 Piece	82.50
Bowl, Flowers & Leaves, Enamel On Copper, c.1925, 7 1/4 In.	1760.00
Butter, Cover, Floral & Gold Design, Small	95.00
Cake Plate, Grapes, Gold Trim, Open Handles, 12 In.	75.00
Candlestick, Gold & Pastel Art Deco Design, 5 In., Pair	95.00
Chocolate Set, Coronet, 4 Cups & Saucer, 11 In.	325.00
Chocolate Set, Tiny Rose Garlands Encircling, 21 Piece	350.00
Cider Set, Hand–Painted Clusters, Grapes, Leaves, Tray, 16 In., 5 Pc.	210.00
Dresser Set, Hair Receiver, Powder Jar, Candlestick, Blue Flowers	150.00
Fish Set, 12 Plates, Platter, c.1900	390.00
Fish Set, Gold & Scalloped Border, Seaweed, Platter, 24 In., 9 Piece	495.00
Fish Set, Gold Rim, Blue Ground, Platter, 8 Plates, Marked	595.00
Fish Set, Hand Painted, 24 x 10–In. Platter, 9 Piece	495.00
Hatpin Holder, Floral, Handpainted	65.00
Humidor, Pinecones, Yellow, Coral & Brown, 6 1/2 In.	75.00
Ice Cream Set, Blue Flowers, Pink Rosebuds, Gold Trim	425.00
Ice Cream, Dish, Green, Floral, 8 In.	60.00
Jardiniere, Roses & Purple Flowers, Floral Baroque Feet, 5 x 9 In.	275.00
Oyster Plate, Tiffany & Co., 9 In.	85.00
Pitcher, 14 1/2 In. Pair ....*Illus*	357.00
Pitcher, Cider, Allover Fruit & Leaves, Hand Painted	45.00
Pitcher, Lemonade, Marked	160.00
Pitcher, Painted Poinsettias, Dragon Handle, Signed, 14 1/2 In.	88.00
Plaque, 4 Kittens, In A Row, Gilt & Wood Frame, 5 3/8 x 7 5/8 In.	1000.00
Plaque, American Soldiers, Cannon, Stone Bridge, 13 In.	295.00
Plaque, Coronet, Deer	145.00
Plaque, Coronet, Monk	145.00
Plaque, Fish, Gold Rococo Trim, Pierced, 10 1/4 In.	75.00
Plaque, Game, Scalloped Gold Rococo Border, Signed, 13 1/4 In.	295.00
Plaque, U. S. Army Soldiers, Flags, Cannon, Burning Bridge, 13 In.	375.00
Plaque, U. S. Cavalry Soldiers, Rococo Border, 13 In.	285.00
Plate, 2 Game Birds, Gold Rococo Edge, Marked, 12 1/4 In.	295.00
Plate, Fruit Design, Signed, 13 3/4 In.	150.00
Plate, Game Birds, Gold Rococo Rim, Marked, 12 1/4 In.	295.00

Limoges, Pitcher, 14 1/2 In. Pair   Limoges, Punch Bowl, 14 1/2 In.

Plate, Large Dog Head, Signed Coudert, 1906, 10 In. 95.00
Platter, Ears of White & Yellow Corn, Brown Ground, 9 1/2 x 13 In. 75.00
Platter, Game Birds, Gold Edge & Handles, 9 1/2 x 13 3/4 In. 425.00
Platter, Woodson, 10 In. 100.00
Platter, Yellow & Orange Roses, Round, 13 3/4 In. 145.00
Punch Bowl, 14 1/2 In. ....*Illus* 440.00
Punch Bowl, Birds & Flowers, Grapes & Leaves Inside, 12 1/2 In. 350.00
Punch Bowl, Grapes & Leaves, Trusemanes & Vogt, c.1880, 16 1/2 In. 450.00
Tankard, Art Nouveau Peacocks, Cream Ground, Tri–Handled 125.00
Tankard, Hand Painted Purple Berries & Vines, Green Border, 11 In. 195.00
Tankard, Monk, Signed, 14 7/8 In. 250.00
Tile, European Man & Woman, Resting Child, 12 x 8 In. 665.00
Tray, Center Castle, River, Rowboats, Open Handles, 9 x 6 In. 125.00
Tray, Couple Center, Hand Painted, Oval, Framed, 1848, 15 x 13 In. 375.00
Tray, Dresser, Hand Painted Flowers, Gold On White, Round, 9 1/2 In. 35.00
Tray, Dresser, Pink Roses, 8 x 12 In. 35.00
Tray, Floral Center, Green & Gold Reticulated Rim, 13 1/4 In. 85.00
Tray, Turtle Shape, 1800s Man & Lady, Marked, 15 x 13 In. 375.00
Tureen, Child's, Blue Flowers, Stand, 7 In. 95.00
Vase, Allover Grape, Enameled, Teak Base, P. Bonnand, 1906, 6 In. 825.00
Vase, Angels & Roses, Gold Handles, E. Ryland, 9 1/2 In. 350.00
Vase, Floral Design, Gilt Rim, Baluster Form, 22 In. 300.00
Vase, Hand–Painted Acorns, Gold Trim, Signed, 7 1/2 In. .... 45.00 To 95.00
Vase, Hand–Painted Birds In Flowering Trees, Signed, 12 1/2 In. 125.00
Vase, Overlapping Circles, Enamel On Copper, Signed, 1925, 6 3/4 In. 665.00
Vase, Pink Magnolias, Double Entwined Handles, Cream, 12 1/2 In. 235.00
Vase, Yellow & Brown Birds, Flowering Trees, Signed, 12 1/2 In. 125.00

In 1927, Charles Lindbergh, the aviator, became the first man to make a nonstop solo flight across the Atlantic Ocean. He was a national hero. In 1932, his son was kidnapped and murdered, and Lindbergh was again the center of public interest. He died in 1974. All types of Lindbergh memorabilia are collected.

LINDBERGH, Badge, Commemorates New York To Paris Flight, 1927 .... 85.00
Cap, Soda Jerk, Lindbergh's Plane 45.00
Cigar Label, World's Greatest Flyer, Large 16.00
Cover, Time Magazine, 1939 .... 30.00
Game, Lucky Lindy, Instructions 35.00
Medal, Gold Plated, 1931, 3 In. 125.00
Photograph, Lindbergh In Front of S. S. L, Framed, 18 x 12 3/4 In. 350.00
Toy, Airplane, Lindy, Iron, 4 In. 125.00
Watch & Fob, Pocket, Spirit of St. Louis Etched On Face 575.00

Liverpool, Pitcher, True–Blooded Yankee, Ship, 7 1/2 In.

◆◆◆◆◆◆◆◆◆◆◆◆◆◆◆◆◆◆◆◆◆◆◆◆◆◆◆◆

It is easy to glue pieces of broken china. Use a new fast–setting but not instant glue. Position the pieces correctly, then use tape to hold the parts together. If the piece needs special support, lean it in a suitable position in a box filled with sand.

◆◆◆◆◆◆◆◆◆◆◆◆◆◆◆◆◆◆◆◆◆◆◆◆◆◆◆◆

Lithophanes are porcelain pictures made by casting clay in layers of various thicknesses. When a piece is held to the light, a picture of light and shadow is seen through it. Most lithophanes date from the 1825–1875 period. A few are still being made. Many lithophanes sold today were originally panels for lampshades.

LITHOPHANE, 2 Children, On Each Side of Fence, 5 1/8 x 4 1/4 In.	145.00
Escape of Fairies, KPM, 4 1/2 x 6 In.	175.00
Mother & Child, Under Heavy Cloud, 8 1/4 x 6 1/2 In.	55.00
Mother Washing Babies, Hands In Bowl, 5 1/4 x 5 In.	35.00
Older Sister Reading, 2 Seated Boys, 5 1/4 x 5 In.	135.00
Seated Mother With Daughter, Teaching To Sew, 5 1/4 x 5 In.	130.00
Shade, Genessee Falls Scene, Mother, 5 Sides, 6 3/4 x 9 1/2 In.	550.00
Shade, Various Monument & River Scenes, 5 Sides, 9 In.	650.00
Spanish Woman, Child Reaching Toward Her, 5 1/4 x 5 In.	135.00
Stein, 1st Pioneer Battalion, Figural Lid, 11 1/2 In.	385.00
Stein, 23rd Infantry, 8th Company, Saargemund, Pewter Lid, 11 In.	330.00
Stein, Mother & Child In Base, Hand Painted Pink & Florals	300.00
Woman In Museum, Cherub, People In Background, 5 1/4 In.	375.00
Young Girl Seated On Donkey, Pushed By Boy, 5 1/4 x 5 In.	135.00

Liverpool, England, was the site of several pottery and porcelain factories from 1716 to 1785. Some earthenware was made with transfer decorations. Sadler and Green made print–decorated wares from 1756. Many of the pieces were made for the American market and feature patriotic emblems, such as eagles, flags, and other special–interest motifs.

LIVERPOOL, Bowl, Black Transfer, Ship With British Flag, 2 1/2 x 5 In.	467.50
Coffeepot, Yellow Chinoiserie Transfer, Brown Glaze, 11 In.	330.00
Creamer, Yellow Chinoiserie Transfer, Brown Glaze, 5 1/2 In.	165.00
Cup & Saucer, Handleless, Washington, His Country's Father, 6 Pc.	300.00
Mug, Black Transfer, An East View of Iron Bridge, 5 7/8 In.	125.00
Mug, Black Transfer, True–Blooded Yankee, Ship, 6 1/4 In.	800.00
Mug, England, Early 19th Century, 3 5/8 In.	605.00
Pitcher, 2 Hunt Scenes, 1 Intellectual Arts, 9 7/8 In.	525.00
Pitcher, American Ship, Jack Spritsail, Black Transfer, 8 3/8 In.	75.00
Pitcher, Frigates Constellation & L'Insurgent, 6 3/4 In.	1550.00
Pitcher, George Washington, Lattice Rim, c.1800, 6 3/4 In., Pair	2475.00
Pitcher, Masonic Designs	400.00
Pitcher, Peace & Prosperity, Black Transfer, 8 1/8 In.	300.00
Pitcher, Polychrome Lemons & Green Leaves, Red Ribbon, 13 In.	895.00
Pitcher, Portrait of Commodore Perry, Full Dress, 9 1/4 In.	3550.00
Pitcher, Ship Transfer, Eagle On Reverse, Creamware, 1800, 10 In.	2100.00
Pitcher, True–Blooded Yankee, Ship, 7 1/2 In. ....*Illus*	1045.00
Pitcher, Union of French & American Republics, 9 1/4 In.	5175.00
Pitcher, Washington & Lafayette Transfer, Creamware, 5 In.	525.00
Pitcher, Yellow Chinoiserie Transfer, Brown Glaze, 7 3/4 In.	195.00

Teapot, Oriental Figures, Flocks of Birds, Insects, 5 1/2 In., Pr. 440.00

Juan, Jose, and Vicente Lladro opened a ceramics workshop in Almacera, Spain, in 1951. They soon began making figurines in a distinctive, elongated style. In 1958 the factory moved to Tabernes Blanques, Spain. The company makes stoneware and porcelain vases and figurines in limited and nonlimited editions.

LLADRO, Figurine, Boy With Lamb, 6 In. 65.00
Figurine, Boy With Pony, No. 1460 .... 750.00
Figurine, Clown With Violin, No. 1126 .... 2350.00
Figurine, Doves, No. 1335 .... 1500.00
Figurine, Dutch Girl, No. 4860 .... 250.00
Figurine, Flower Song .... 400.00 To 450.00
Figurine, Free As A Butterfly, No. 1483 .... 425.00
Figurine, Hunters, No. 1048 .... 1875.00
Figurine, Little Gardner, No. 4726 .... 450.00
Figurine, Little Pals, Box 2000.00
Figurine, Little Traveler .... 750.00 To 1000.00
Figurine, Lolita, No. 2078 .... 600.00
Figurine, Lovers From Verona, No. 1250 .... 1450.00
Figurine, Male Tennis Player, No. 1426 .... 225.00
Figurine, My Buddy 175.00
Figurine, Othello and Desdemona, No. 1145 .... 3000.00
Figurine, School Days .... 300.00 To 450.00
Figurine, Sleeping Nymph, No. 1401 .... 575.00
Figurine, Spring Bouquets .... 450.00 To 600.00
Figurine, Valencian Couple On Horseback, No. 4648 .... 1050.00
Figurine, Venus and Cupid, No. 1392 .... 1375.00
Group, Boy Seated On Donkey, 17 In. 55.00
Group, Girl With Umbrella, Under Bush, Picking Daisies, 11 3/4 In. 210.00

Locke Art is a trademark found on glass of the early–twentieth century. Joseph Locke worked at many English and American firms. He designed and etched his own glass in Pittsburgh, Pennsylvania, starting in the 1880s. Some pieces were marked *Joe Locke,* but most were marked with the words *Locke Art.* The mark is hidden in the pattern on the glass.

LOCKE ART, Pitcher Set, Acid–Etched Floral Design, 10 Goblets, 11 Piece 480.00
Tumbler, Rose, Signed, 4 1/4 In. 95.00
Vase, Daisies & Leaves, Bisque Finish, Pate–Sur–Pate, 9 In. 600.00

Johann Loetz bought a glassworks in Austria in 1840. He died in 1848 and his widow ran the company; then in 1879, his grandson took over. Loetz glass was varied. Most collectors recognize the iridescent gold glass similar to Tiffany, but many other types were made. The firm closed during World War II.

LOETZ, Biscuit Jar, Pinched Walls, Silver–Plated Cover & Handle, 7 In. 355.00

Loetz, Bowl, Lobed–Shell Form,
Variegated Red & Gold, 10 In.

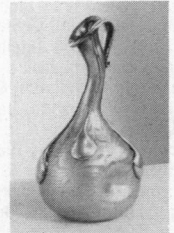

Loetz, Vase, Silver Overlay, Gold,
Iridescent Blue, 9 In.

Loetz, Dish, Iridescent   Loetz, Vase, Iridescent   Loetz, Vase, Iridescent
Gold & Blue, 13 In.   Blue–Green, 8 In.   Green, Bronze Mounted,
                                                        9 1/2 In., Pair

Bottle, Purple Streaks, Iridescent Body 325.00
Bowl, 8 Sides, Textured Scattered Ash, Green, Gold Trim, 7 1/2 In. 375.00
Bowl, Blue Pulled Feather, Yellow Iridescent, Spherical, 4 1/4 In. 7560.00
Bowl, Large Green Blossom, Claret Border, Deep, 1930, 14 In. 2000.00
Bowl, Lobed–Shell Form, Variegated Red & Gold, 10 In. ....*Illus* 165.00
Bowl, Oil Spot, 12 In. 450.00
Bowl, Ruffled, Fuchsia, Metal Base, Signed, 12 1/2 In. 475.00
Candlestick, Purple & Green Threading, Sterling Collar, 7 In., Pair 525.00
Compote, Glass Scarabs, Silver Base, Ruffled, 10 In. 600.00
Compote, Reverse Dimples, Pink, Brass Stand, 10 In. 400.00
Compote, Scarabs, Silver Base, Signed, 12 x 12 In. 550.00
Cornucopia, Floral Pedestal, Silver–Plated Base, 10 x 8 In. 250.00
Dish, Iridescent Gold & Blue, 13 In. ....*Illus* 495.00
Dish, Sweetmeat, Blown Out & Ribbed, Cranberry 330.00
Ewer, Silver–Plated Handle, Signed, 10 In. 295.00
Iridescent Spotted Surface, Platform Foot, 6 1/2 In. 665.00
Jar, Brown Webbing, Ruffled, 3 1/2 In. 175.00
Lamp, Boudoir, Oil Spot Shade, 4–Prong Metal Base, 15 In. 660.00
Lamp, Sterling Overlay, Iridescent, 6 3/4 In. 500.00
Loving Cup, Silver Overlay, 11 In. 8250.00
Perfume Bottle, Blue Oil Spot, Gold Acorn Screw–On Top, Signed 1045.00
Shade, Red Spotting, Alligator Finish, Green, 2 x 3 In., Pair 350.00
Torchere, Ruffled Feather Shade, Iron, Brass, 10 In., Pair 2800.00
Vase, Allover Branch & Buds, Flared Top, Signed, 10 1/2 In. 450.00
Vase, Amber Craquelure Texture, Amber Zigzags, c.1900, 5 3/4 In. 990.00
Vase, Amethyst, Green & Silver Between Clear Crystal, 8 1/4 In. 2000.00
Vase, Applied Globs of Glass Running Down Sides, Signed, 8 In. 1500.00
Vase, Art Nouveau, Reserve of Irises, Sterling Overlay, 12 In. 825.00
Vase, Blown Out, Swirls, Pink, 7 1/2 In. 385.00
Vase, Blue & Green, Lotus Flower Sterling Overlay, 11 In. 3520.00
Vase, Blue Iridescent, Flattened Sphere, Double Gourd Neck, 4 In. 3080.00
Vase, Blue Loopings & Trailings, Brown Base, c.1900, 10 In. 6600.00
Vase, Blue Oil Spots, On Blue Ground, V–Shaped Top, Signed, 12 In. 5000.00
Vase, Blue Raindrop Design, Ruffled Top, 3 Clear Ball Feet, 5 In. 335.00
Vase, Blue Swirls On Gold Ground, Signed, 13 In. 260.00
Vase, Bottle Shape, Random Threading Iridescent Green, 9 3/4 In. 145.00
Vase, Crackle Glass, Spherical Body, Ring Foot, c.1900, 5 In. 385.00
Vase, Crimped Top, Green Iridescent, 11 In. 250.00
Vase, Deep Pink, Cranberry Flecks, Peacock Feather, 10 In. 950.00
Vase, Double Gourd Form, Oil Spottings, c.1900, 8 7/8 In. 880.00
Vase, Everted Rim, Oil–Spot Iridescence, Signed, 6 In. 950.00

◆◆◆

You can date an old bottle from the spelling of the word Pittsburgh. From 1891 to 1911 the "h" was removed by the United States Board of Geographic names. The old spelling was resumed because of complaints from those who lived in Pittsburg.

◆◆◆

Vase, Everted Trefoil Rim, Pitted Texture, Twisted Shape, 9 1/2 In.	1450.00
Vase, Gold Oil Spots, Green Ground, 7 x 7 In.	250.00
Vase, Gold Spotted, Amber Body, Oval, Signed, 5 1/4 In.	330.00
Vase, Gold, Purple, Blue, Twisted Root Form, 3 Flowers, 9 In.	358.00
Vase, Green Iridescent, Raised Gilt, Foliate & Floral, 5 In.	100.00
Vase, Green, Gold, Purple, Iridescent, Pinched Body, 9 In.	195.00
Vase, Green, Iridescent–Gold Coiled Snake Around, Cylindrical, 8 In.	1540.00
Vase, Green, Pink Interior, Sterling Floral Casing, 4 1/2 In.	550.00
Vase, Grotesque Shape, Iridescent, Bronze Mounted, 8 In.	1500.00
Vase, Internal Layers of Silver & Metallic Swirls, 5 1/2 In.	1760.00
Vase, Iridescent Blue Oil Spot, Footed, Cylindrical, 10 1/4 In.	2000.00
Vase, Iridescent Blue–Green, 8 In. _____*Illus*	495.00
Vase, Iridescent Gold, Applied Blue Handles, Bottle Shape, 7 In.	335.00
Vase, Iridescent Gold, Leaf–Shape Green Feet, 9 1/2 In.	850.00
Vase, Iridescent Green, Bronze Mounted, 9 1/2 In., Pair _____*Illus*	715.00
Vase, Iridescent Green, Gold, Purple, Swirled, Pinched Body, 9 In.	295.00
Vase, Lily–of–The–Valley Blossoms, Silver Overlay, 4 1/2 In.	330.00
Vase, Maroon, Salmon, Cream & Gold Iridescent, Double Gourd, 4 3/4 In.	2420.00
Vase, Oil–Spot Design, Pinched, Oviform, Signed, 6 In.	950.00
Vase, Oil–Spot Design, Urn Shape, Blue, Signed, 5 1/2 In.	1050.00
Vase, Pinched Lip, Swirled & Spotted Design, Ovoid, 7 1/2 In.	2800.00
Vase, Pinched Neck, Ruffled Lip, Gold Iridescence, 7 In.	450.00
Vase, Raised Gilt, Foliate & Floral Design, 5 In.	110.00
Vase, Silver Overlay, Gold, Iridescent Blue, 9 In. _____*Illus*	4675.00
Vase, Silver Overlay, Pinched Top, Ruffled Lip, c.1900, 9 1/8 In.	660.00
Vase, Silvery Blue & Yellow Loopings, Trailings, c.1900, 9 3/4 In.	1650.00
Vase, Silvery Blue & Yellow Loopings, Trailings, c.1900, 8 1/2 In.	2850.00
Vase, Silvery Blue Oil Spotting, Lily Tendrils, c.1900, 6 In.	1430.00
Vase, Spotted Gold Surface, Diagonally Swirled Stripes, 5 1/4 In.	412.50
Vase, Sprays of Wildflowers, Butterfly, Signed, c.1910, 13 3/4 In.	1430.00
Vase, Stick, Pulled Feather of Platinum & Black, 5 In.	625.00
Vase, Stick, Scrolled Siver Overlay, Green, 4 In.	192.50
Vase, Trefoil Lip, Blue & Purple Drippings, Signed, c.1902, 5 7/8 In.	7700.00
Vase, Triple Gourd Shape, Art Nouveau, Encircled By Blue Snake, 9 In.	665.00
Vase, Twisted Neck, 3 Openings Near Center, 17 In.	3300.00
Vase, Twisted–Bottle Shape, Iridescent Spun Design, Signed, 10 In.	410.00
Vase, Yellow Crackled Ground, Silver Overlay, 5 In.	250.00
Vase, Yellow Ground, Silver Blue Iridescent Spot, Oviform, 6 3/4 In.	3850.00
Vase, Yellow Rim, Iridescent Blue Oil Spot, Chalice Form, 10 1/2 In.	4180.00

 The Lone Ranger is a fictional character introduced on the radio in 1932. Over three thousand shows were produced before the series ended in 1954. In 1938, the first Lone Ranger movie was made. Television shows were started in 1949 and are still seen on some stations. The Lone Ranger appears on many products and was even the name of a restaurant chain for several years.

LONE RANGER, Assembly Kit, Plastic, Aurora, Box	25.00
Atom Bomb Ring	45.00
Badge, Chief Scout	200.00
Badge, Jr. Deputy	19.00
Badge, Safety Scout, 1930s	40.00
Belt	30.00

Big Little Book, 1967 .... 25.00
Big Little Book, Whitman, 1968 .... 8.00
Binoculars, Box 125.00
Blotter, Ranger On Silver, Safety Bond Bread, Colorful, 8 In. 20.00
Book, Coloring, 1953 .... 20.00
Book, Coloring, Whitman, Wrapper, 1950s 18.00
Book, Pop–Up 10.00
Booklet, How Lone Ranger Captured Silver, 1936, 7 Pages 65.00
Brush, Decal, 1940s .... 25.00 To 49.00
Bullet With Compass In End 40.00
Cap Gun, Rifle, Winchester, 1963 .... 190.00
Card, Membership, Lone Ranger Peace Patrol 16.00
Chaps 35.00
Comic Book, Lone Ranger Family Restaurant, 1960s, 5 x 7 In. 5.00
Costume, Box, 1977 .... 15.00
Costume, Tonto, Box 175.00
Coupon, Cone, 1940 .... 23.00
Cutouts, Merita Bread, Complete 150.00
Figure, Lone Ranger & Tonto, Barclay 50.00
Figurine, Carnival Chalk, 16 In. 55.00
Figurine, Chalkware, 14 1/2 In. 45.00
First Aid Kit, Tin, 1938 .... 60.00
Frontier Town, 71 Buildings, Maps, Cheerios, 1948 .... 1149.00
Game, Board, 1980 .... 8.00
Game, Dart, With Gun, Marx, 1938 .... 145.00
Game, Parker Brothers, 1938 .... 55.00
Game, Silver Bullets, Board, 1955 .... 30.00
Game, Target, Marx, Stand, Tin, Large 125.00
Guitar, Cardboard & Wood, Jefferson Co., Box 98.00
Guitar, Lone Ranger & Tonto, Orange, Images, Jefferson Mfg. 95.00
Guitar, Wooden, Original Case, 1940 .... 200.00
Gun, Water, Figural 20.00
Hairbrush .... 40.00 To 85.00
Hat, Sailor's 85.00
Holder, Toothbrush 85.00
Knife, Pocket 50.00
Lamp, Chalkware 100.00
Lantern 12.50
Lunch Box, 1954 .... 165.00
Lunch Box, 1980 .... 25.00
Mask, Wheaties 18.00
Official Outfit, Vest, Chaps, Box 115.00
Pedometer .... 20.00 To 25.00
Pencil, Official Silver Bullet, Metal, Lone Ranger ....*Illus*   5.00
Pencil, Silver Bullet 18.00
Pin, Pony Contest 7.00
Poster, Advertising Six–Gun Ring, 17 x 21 In. 125.00
Prairie Wagon, 4 In L, Gabriel, Box 50.00
Puppet, Push–Up, Wooden 125.00
Puzzle, Lone Ranger & Tonto, 1974 .... 7.00
Puzzle, Whitman, 1965, 11 x 15 In. 12.00
Range Rider 250.00
Record Album 15.00
Record, Box, Set of 4 .... 75.00
Record, Radio Program, Coke, 1972, Unopened 12.50
Ring, Atomic Bomb .... 65.00 To 75.00
Ring, Filmstrip .... 45.00 To 95.00
Ring, Flashlight .... 50.00 To 95.00
Ring, Saddle, With Film 115.00
Ring, Six–Shooter .... 75.00 To 90.00
School Bag, Raised Plastic Bust of Masked Man, Vinyl, 1950s 120.00
Shirt, Vest, Chaps, 1940s 150.00
Silver Bullet, Sold With Gum Balls, 1950, 12 Piece 24.00

Silver Bullet, With Compass	35.00
Silver, Prospector Disguise, Burro, Tools, Gabriel	50.00
Snow Dome	115.00
Soap, Tonto, Box, 1940s	45.00
Target Board, 1939	175.00
Target, Double, With Stand, Gun, Box	120.00
Target, Lithographed Tin, Marx	68.00
Target, Lithographed Tin, Marx, Box	120.00
Tent, Box	175.00
Toy, Lone Ranger On Silver, Tin, Litho, Windup, Marx .... 425.00 To	450.00
Viewer, Acme, Films, Box	95.00
Watch, New Haven, Pocket, 1939	350.00
Wristwatch, 1939	250.00
Guitar	75.00
Paint Book	85.00
Pedometer	75.00
Viewer, Movie, Box	75.00

The Longwy Workshop of Longwy, France, first made ceramic wares in 1798. The workshop is still in business. Most of the ceramic pieces found today are glazed with many colors to resemble cloisonne or other enameled metal. The factory used a variety of marks.

LONGWY, Bowl, Floral, Art Deco, Blue, Turquoise Interior, Hexagonal, 5 In.	90.00
Bowl, Overall Floral Design, Crackle Exterior, Turquoise, 6 In.	110.00
Box, Red, Blue, Yellow, 4 In.	250.00
Candlestick, Griffin Shape, Pottery & Bronze, 8 In., Pair	145.00
Candlestick, Ornate Brass Mounts, 8 1/2 In., Pair	90.00
Candlestick, Shape of Griffins, Bronze, 8 In., Pair	195.00
Charger, Egret, 12 In. .... 185.00 To	350.00
Charger, Firebirds, Flowers On Branches, 15 In. .... 450.00 To	750.00
Charger, La Belle Epogue, 15 In.	450.00
Charger, La Diligence, 15 In.	450.00
Dish, Floral, 8 Sides, 5 In.	75.00
Dish, Florals, Electric Blue, 4 1/2 In.	85.00
Dish, Star Shape, Floral, Cobalt Blue Ground, 5 In.	15.00
Lighter, Cigar, Counter, Brass Fittings, Cloisonne	300.00
Owl, Primavera Style, 5 1/2 In.	75.00
Plaque, 3 Herons, Art Deco Floral Border, Signed AK, 14 1/2 In.	400.00
Plate, Floral, 12 In.	115.00
Tray, 11 1/2 In.	85.00
Tray, Fan, 5 1/4 In.	80.00
Tray, Tile In Brass Mount, 12 x 12 In.	200.00
Vase, Multicolored Floral Designs, Turquoise Ground, 5 3/4 In., Pair	357.50

LONHUDA The Lonhuda Pottery Company of Steubenville, Ohio, was organized in 1892 by William Long, W. H. Hunter, and Alfred Day. Brown underglaze slip–decorated pottery was made. The firm closed in 1896. The company used many marks; the earliest included the letters *LPCO.*

LONHUDA, Vase, Fish Design, 8 In.	475.00
Vase, Floral, 5 1/2 In.	135.00
Vase, Green Leaves, Raised Decoration, 8 In.	165.00

Lotus Ware was made by the Knowles, Taylor & Knowles Company of East Liverpool, Ohio, from 1890 to 1900. Lotus Ware is a thin, Belleek–like porcelain. It was sometimes decorated outside the factory. Other types of ceramics that were made by the Knowles, Taylor & Knowles Company are listed under *KTK.*

LOTUS WARE, Bowl, Center, Painted Floral, Gilt Handles & Rim, 9 In. D.	495.00
Bowl, Center, Ruffled Rim, Applied Handles, White, 11 In. D.	385.00
Bowl, Flowering Prunus On Branches, Beaded Rim, 4 1/2 In.	275.00
Bowl, Gadrooned Scrolled Designs, Beaded Trim, Marked, 4 1/2 In.	330.00

Bowl, Globular, White, Ruffled Beaded Rim, 4 1/2 In. H. 110.00
Bowl, Ovoid, White, Jeweled Raised Medallions, 4 1/4 In. 300.00
Bowl, Ovoid, White, Pink Matte Overglaze, Gilt 357.00
Bowl, Raised Jeweled Medallion, Pinched Ovoid, 6 1/4 In. 330.00
Bowl, Triangular Patterns, Fishnet Design, White, 1/2 In. 275.00
Clock Case, Oval Medallions, Prunus Branches, Marked, 7 3/8 In. 3520.00
Clock Case, Prunus Branches, Beaded Swags, 3 7/8 In. 715.00
Compote, Interior Floral Sprays, Ruffled Rim, Marked, 9 3/4 In. 385.00
Dish, Cover, Lily Pad, Domed Leaf Cover, Bud Handle, 6 In. D. 2640.00
Dish, Shell, Scallop, Gilt & Pink Floral, Branch Feet, 8 In. D. 302.00
Dish, Shell, Scallop, Painted Ships At Sea, 8 In. D. 385.00
Dish, Shell, Scallop, Pink, Floral, 3 Branch Feet, 8 In. D. 330.00
Ewer, Blue, Pink & Purple Flowers, Gilt, 9 1/2 In. ....*Illus* 385.00
Ewer, Bulbous, White, Applied Floral Branch, 7 In. 880.00
Ewer, White Flowers & Leaves, Pale Green, 1/2 In. 1210.00
Ewer, Yellow Matte Glaze, Pink Flowers, Gilt, 6 In. ....*Illus* 192.00
Jar, Cover, Cylindrical, White, Fishnet Panels, 6 1/2 In. 385.00
Jar, Cover, Fishnet Design, Gilt Floral, Marked, 7 In. 330.00
Jar, Cover, Globular, Painted Flowers, Gilt, 5 1/4 In. 143.00
Jar, Cover, Potpourri, Gadrooned Forms, Beaded, Marked, 7 1/2 In. 880.00
Jar, Cover, Potpourri, Scrolled Designs, Beaded Rim, 6 1/4 In. 770.00
Jar, Potpourri, Jeweled Swags, White, 7 1/4 In. ....*Illus* 2310.00
Jug, Milk, Squat, Bulbous, Pink, Roses, Gilt, Dated Dec. 25, 1900 .... 247.00
Jug, Milk, White, Textured Leaves, 4 1/2 In. 220.00
Jug, Milk, White, Triangular Fishnet, 5 In. 137.00
Jug, Milk, Yellow Ground, Butterflies & Nymph, 5 In. 275.00
Match Holder, Floral & Scroll, White, 3 7/8 In. 715.00
Pitcher, All White, Twig Handle, 5 x 7 1/2 In. 175.00
Pitcher, Chrysanthemum, White Fluted, 6 3/4 In. ....*Illus* 165.00
Sugar & Creamer, Ovoid, Pale Blue & Ecru, Gilt, 2 1/2 In. 110.00
Sugar, Cover, Shaped Medallions Each Side, Pink Roses, Marked 880.00
Tea Set, Wildflowers, Gilt Trim, Marked, 3 Piece 495.00
Tea Set, Wildflowers, White, Blue, Purple, 4 1/2 In. 495.00
Teapot, Tapering, White, Floral Sprays, Gilt, 8 1/2 In. 247.00
Teapot, Tapering, White, Molded Decoration, 8 1/2 In. 110.00
Teapot, Tapering, White, Raised Gilt Decoration, 8 1/2 In. 137.00
Urn, Raised Jeweled Design In White, 15 In. 4620.00
Vase, Applied Flower & Leaves, 9 3/4 In. ....*Illus* 935.00
Vase, Applied Leaves & Flowers, Marked, 7 1/2 In. 990.00
Vase, Bowl Shape, Ruffled Mouth, Applied Chain Forms, 7 1/2 In. 1100.00
Vase, Bud, Baluster, Dark Green, Applied Floral, 6 In. 1045.00
Vase, Bud, Baluster, Pale Green, Applied Floral, 6 In. 550.00
Vase, Bulbous, Pale Green, Applied White Floral, 10 In. 1045.00
Vase, Double Gourd, White, Painted Flowers & Leaves, 8 1/4 In. 385.00
Vase, Florals, Flask Form, Pale Green, Marked, 8 1/4 In. 1045.00
Vase, Floriform, Cylindrical, White, Gilt Leaf Base, 8 3/4 In. 330.00
Vase, Floriform, Cylindrical, White, Leaf–Form Base, 8 In. 412.00

Lotus Ware, Ewer, Blue,
Pink & Purple Flowers, Gilt, 9 1/2 In.

Lotus Ware, Jar, Potpourri, Jeweled Swags,
White, 7 1/4 In.

Lotus Ware, Vase, Psyche, Gilt Border,
14 1/2 In.

Lotus Ware, Vase, Applied Flower & Leaves,
9 3/4 In.

Lotus Ware, Ewer, Yellow Matte Glaze,
Pink Flowers, Gilt, 6 In.

Lotus Ware, Pitcher, Chrysanthemum,
White Fluted, 6 3/4 In.

Vase, Floriform, Cylindrical, Yellow Matte Glaze, 8 1/4 In. 467.00
Vase, Flower & Leaf Design, Petal Foot, Marked, 9 3/4 In. 1760.00
Vase, Globular Body, Slim Neck, Handles, White, 9 In. H. 165.00
Vase, Lazy Susan Flowers, Dark Green, 7 3/4 In. 1875.00
Vase, Pale Green Flowers, Dark Green, 7 1/2 In. 990.00
Vase, Pale Green Flowers, Dark Green, 9 3/4 In. 1765.00
Vase, Presentation, White, Jeweled Designs, 10 1/4 In. 5720.00
Vase, Psyche, Gilt Border, 14 1/2 In. ....*Illus* 2640.00

J.&J.G.LOW Low art tiles were made by the J. and J. G. Low Art Tile Works of Chelsea, Massachusetts, from 1877 to 1902. A variety of art and other tiles were made. Some of the tiles were made by a process called *natural,* some were hand–modeled, and some made mechanically.

LOW, Tile, Abraham Lincoln, George Washington, Green, 4 x 6 In. 185.00
Tile, Ivy, 3 x 6 In. 55.00
Tile, Old Man's Face, 6 In. 200.00
Tile, Scene of Men Plowing Field, Frame, 6 Tiles, 12 x 36 In. 440.00
Tile, Sheep, Haystacks, Green, 18 x 10 In. 700.00
LOY–NEL–ART, see McCoy

Lunch pails and lunch boxes have been used to carry lunches to school or work since the nineteenth century. Today, most collectors want either early tobacco advertising boxes or children's lunch boxes made since the 1930s. The original Thermos bottle must be inside the children's boxes for the collector to consider them complete.

LUNCH BOX, Adam 12 .... 65.00 To 95.00
Addams Family 100.00
Addams Family, No Thermos 40.00
Aladdin, Plaid 3.00
America On Parade 25.00
Annie Oakley .... 145.00 To 175.00
Archies, 1969 .... 45.00 To 55.00
Astronaut, Domed, Space Scene, 1960s .... 150.00 To 195.00
Atom Ant, 1966 .... 125.00
Atom Ant, No Thermos, 1966 .... 48.00
Atomic Sub, 1960–1963 .... 45.00
Barbie & Francie, Vinyl, 1966–1970 .... 50.00
Barbie & Midge, Vinyl, 1965–1966 .... 100.00 To 175.00
Barbie & Midge, Vinyl, No Thermos, 1965–1966 .... 45.00 To 50.00
Barbie, Vinyl, 1962 .... 75.00
Barbie, Vinyl, Blue, Yellow Trim, 1971 .... 95.00
Batman, 1966–1967 .... 100.00
Battle Kit, 1965–1966 .... 65.00
Battlestar Galactica, 1979 .... 32.00 To 40.00
Battlestar Galactica, No Thermos, 1979 .... 17.00
Beatles, Blue, 1966–1967 .... 150.00
Bedknobs & Broomsticks, 1972 .... 35.00
Bee Gees, Barry Gibb, 1979 .... 30.00
Bee Gees, Maurice Gibb, 1979 .... 15.00
Beverly Hillbillies, 1963–1965 .... 55.00 To 85.00
Bionic Woman, 1977 .... 12.00 To 25.00
Blondie, 1969 .... 60.00 To 100.00
Blondie, No Thermos, 1969 .... 40.00 To 75.00
Bonanza, 4 Cartwrights, Brown Trim, 1963 .... 50.00
Bonanza, Green, 1963–1964 .... 40.00
Bozo, Dome .... 95.00 To 135.00
Brave Eagle, 1957–1958 .... 145.00 To 175.00
Bread Loaf 400.00
Buccaneer, 1957–1958 .... 225.00 To 350.00
Bugaloos, 1971 .... 45.00
Burley Boy Tobacco 550.00
Cable Car, 1962 .... 400.00

Campus Queen, 1967 .... 30.00
Captain Kangaroo, Vinyl, 1964–1966 .... 400.00
Care Bears, 1984–1985 .... 20.00 To 35.00
Casey Jones, 1960–1961 .... 95.00
Charlies's Angels, 1978 .... 16.00
Chitty Chitty Bang Bang, 1969 .... 45.00 To 95.00
Chuck Wagon, 1958–1960 ....95.00 To 165.00
Clash of The Titans, 1981 .... 20.00 To 30.00
Close Encounters, 1978 .... 40.00
Cowboy In Africa, 1968 .... 130.00 To 195.00
Cracker Jack, 1979 .... 30.00
Daniel Boone, 1950s .... 65.00 To 95.00
Daniel Boone, 1965 .... 28.00
Denim Diner, Dog Picture, Dome, 1975–1977 .... 25.00
Dixie Kid Cut Plug 450.00
Dixie Queen Tobacco, 8 x 14 In. 175.00
Donnie & Marie Osmond, Vinyl, 1977–1978 .... 125.00
Dr. Doolittle 85.00
Dr. Seuss, 1970–1971 ....60.00 To 110.00
Drag Strip, 1975–1977 .... 25.00
Dukes of Hazzard, 1978 .... 10.00
E. T., 1983 .... 30.00
Early West Pony Express, 1982–1984 .... 18.00 To 40.00
Emergency, Dome, 1977 .... 75.00
Emergency, Square, 1974 .... 35.00
Empire Strikes Back, 1980 .... 10.00
Evel Knievel, 1974 .... 30.00
Fall Guy, 1981 .... 15.00
Family Affair, 1969 .... 50.00 To 75.00
Fat Albert .... 35.00 To 45.00
Fireball XL5, 1964–1965 .... 65.00 To 95.00
Firefighter .... 65.00 To 85.00
Flintstone & Dino, 1973 .... 25.00 To 50.00
Flintstones, 1962 .... 95.00
Flipper, 1966–1968 .... 60.00
Flying Nun, 1968–1969 .... 150.00
Fritos Corn Chips, 1975 .... 50.00 To 95.00
G. I. Joe, 1967 .... 35.00
G. I. Joe, 1987 .... 75.00
Gentle Ben, 1968 .... 100.00
George Washington Cut Plug, Tin Lithograph, 6 In. 55.00
Get Smart, 1966 .... 50.00 To 85.00
Ghostland 35.00
Go Go 350.00
Gomer Pyle, 1966 .... 30.00 To 80.00
Green Hornet, 1967 .... 40.00 To 90.00
Green Turtle Tobacco 300.00
Gremlins 25.00
Grizzly Adams, Dome, 1977 .... 45.00 To 75.00
Grizzly Adams, No Thermos, 1975 .... 22.00
Guns of Will Sonnet, Thermos, 1968 .... 110.00
Gunsmoke, 1959 .... 60.00
Gunsmoke, 1972 .... 95.00
Gunsmoke, No Thermos, 1973 .... 20.00
Handbag Tobacco .... 15.00 To 25.00
Happy Days, 1977 .... 12.00 To 35.00
Hardy Boys, 1978–1979 .... 45.00
Harlem Globetrotters, 1971 .... 45.00
Harlem Globetrotters, No Thermos, 1971 .... 20.00
Hector Heathcoat, 1964 .... 25.00 To 30.00
Hee Haw, 1970 .... 30.00
Hogan's Heroes, Dome Top, Vinyl, 1966 .... 210.00 To 300.00
Hopalong Cassidy, Full Face, Square Decal, 1951 .... 70.00

Hopalong Cassidy, Lithograph TV Screen, 1954 .... 100.00
Hot Wheels 20.00
How The West Was Won, 1979 .... 12.00 To 35.00
Huckleberry Hound, 1961 .... 35.00 To 75.00
Hulk, 1979 .... 40.00
Inch High Detective 35.00
Indiana Jones 13.00
It's About Time, 1967 .... 500.00
Jet Patrol 65.00
Jetsons, 1963 .... 550.00 To 600.00
Joe Palooka, 1948 .... 55.00 To 99.00
Johnny Lightning 35.00
Jungle Book 40.00
Kelloggs 25.00
Kewtie Pie, Vinyl 85.00
King Kong, 1977 .... 20.00 To 35.00
Kiss, 1970 .... 45.00 To 65.00
Kit Carson, Davy Crockett 225.00
Knight Rider, 1984–1985 .... 12.00 To 35.00
Kung Fu, 1974 .... 15.00 To 40.00
Land of The Giants, 1969–1970 .... 45.00 To 85.00
Lassie, 1961–1963 .... 45.00
Laugh–In, 1968 .... 35.00 To 95.00
Lawman, 1960s .... 30.00 To 75.00
Little House On The Prairie, 1979 .... 25.00
Little Red Riding Hood, Ohio Art, 1982–1984 .... 13.00
Looney Tunes, 1959 .... 120.00 To 250.00
Lost In Space, Dome Top, Vinyl .... 100.00 To 335.00
Love & Peace 27.50
Ludwig Von Drake, 1962 .... 75.00
Magic of Lassie, 1979 .... 20.00
Marvel Super Heroes 20.00
Mary Poppins, 1965 .... 30.00
Masters of The Universe, 1983 .... 15.00
Monroes, 1967 .... 45.00
Moon Landing, 1968–1969 .... 35.00
Mork & Mindy, 1978 .... 20.00 To 30.00
Movie Monsters, 1980 .... 35.00
Munsters, Dome Top, 1965–1966 .... 100.00
Muppets 25.00
Muppets, 1978–1979 .... 10.00
Nancy Drew, 1978 .... 70.00
Orbit 100.00
Orphan Annie, Fisher–Price, 1979 .... 15.00
Pac Man .... 10.00 To 30.00
Partridge Family, 1971 .... 25.00 To 40.00
Peanuts, Charlie At Tree, 1956 .... 16.00 To 20.00
Peanuts, Red, Vinyl, 1969–1970 .... 60.00
Pedro Tobacco 50.00
Pee–Wee's Playhouse 20.00
Penny Post Tobacco 175.00
Peter Pan, 1969 .... 500.00
Pets 'N' Pals, 1962 .... 40.00
Pigs In Space, Muppets, 1979–1980 .... 25.00
Pink Panther, Vinyl 75.00
Pinocchio, Round, 1940 .... 30.00 To 45.00
Planet of The Apes, 1975 .... 50.00
Play Ball, Game On Reverse, 1969–1972 .... 35.00
Porky's Lunch Wagon, Dome, 1959–1961 .... 135.00 To 225.00
Puff 'N' Stuff 25.00
Raggedy Ann & Raggedy Andy, 1973–1976 .... 18.00
Rambo, 1986–1987 .... 17.00
Rat Patrol, 1967 .... 50.00 To 85.00

Red Barn, Closed Door, 1957 .... 95.00
Red Barn, Open Door, 1958–1960 .... 50.00
Return of The Jedi, 1983 .... 17.00
Rice Krispies, Snap, Crackle & Pop 16.00
Road Runner, 1970–1973 ....25.00 To 30.00
Robin Hood, 1956 ....120.00 To 165.00
Robin Hood, No Thermos, 1956 .... 15.00
Ronald McDonald, 1983 .... 20.00
Ronald McDonald, Sheriff 10.00
Rough Riders 35.00
S. W. A. T., 1975 .... 10.00
Satelite, 1959–1962 .... 55.00
School Bus, Disney, Dome Top 20.00
Scooby Doo, 1973–1976 .... 35.00
Secret Agent, 1968–1969 .... 45.00
See America 90.00
Sesame Street ....20.00 To 27.50
Snoopy's Dog House ....35.00 To 40.00
Snow White, With Game ....15.00 To 35.00
Space 1999, 1975 ....30.00 To 45.00
Space Cadet, Blue, 1952–1953 .... 200.00
Star Trek, 1968–1969 .... 50.00
Star Wars, 1977 ....15.00 To 45.00
Steve Canyon, 1959 .... 195.00
Strawberry Shortcake, 1980–1981 .... 10.00
Super Friends, 1977–1979 ....45.00 To 100.00
Tammy & Pepper 100.00
Tarzan, 1967 ....30.00 To 70.00
Tiger Chewing Tobacco, Blue 125.00
Tiger Chewing Tobacco, Red 65.00
Trigger, 1956 .... 60.00
Twiggy, 1967 .... 55.00
U. S. Mail, Dome Top, 1969–1976 .... 27.00
U. S. Space Corps, 1961 .... 385.00
UFO, 1973 ....60.00 To 150.00
Underdog, 1974 .... 1600.00
Union Commander, George Washington 390.00
Volkswagen Bus, 1960s ....400.00 To 450.00
Voyage To Sea, 1967 .... 125.00
Waltons, 1974–1975 ....18.00 To 45.00
Warrick & Brown Tobacco 40.00
Welcome Back Kotter, 1977 .... 20.00
Wild Bill Hickok & Jingles, 1955 .... 85.00
Wild Wild West, 1969 ....30.00 To 85.00
Wonder Woman, Vinyl, 1978–1979 ....75.00 To 130.00
Worker Cut Plug 63.00
Yellow Submarine, 1969 ....360.00 To 450.00
Yogi Bear & Friends, 1963 ....75.00 To 125.00
Zorro, Black Rim, 1958–1959 .... 80.00
LUNCH PAIL, Central Union Cut Plug, Tin 28.00
Dixie Kid Cut Plug, Tin Lithograph, 7 3/4 In. 192.50
Fashion Cut Plug, Tin Lithograph, 8 In. 230.00
Handbag Cut Plug, Tin Lithograph, 7 In. 82.50
Just Suits Plug Tobacco, Tin Lithograph, 7 3/4 In. 65.00

◆◆

Fishing line is strong and almost invisible and can be used to tie
fragile items to a base or wall. This will prevent damage from earth-
quake, 2–year–olds, and dogs with wagging tails.

◆◆

Miner's, Gray	48.00
Patterson Seal Cut Plug	30.00
Pedro Smoking Tobacco, Tin Lithograph, 7 3/4 In.	135.00
Pinocchio, Red, 1938	195.00
Winner Cut Plug, Tin Lithograph, 7 3/4 In.	385.00

K 👑 G
Luneville

Luneville, a French faience factory, was established in 1731 by Jacques Chambrette. It is best known for its fine biscuit figures and groups and for large faience dogs and lions. The early pieces were unmarked. The firm was acquired by Keller and Guerin and is still working.

LUNEVILLE, Bowl, Raised Leaf Design, Roses In Panels, Green Ground, 16 In.	1200.00
Pitcher, Birds, Insects, Flowers, Rope Handle, 8 In.	150.00
Pitcher, Insects, Birds, Rope Handle, 8 In.	175.00
Plate, Floral, 10 In.	35.00
Plate, Rooster, Spatter Edge	50.00

Lusterware was meant to resemble copper, silver, or gold. It has been used since the sixteenth century. Most of the luster found today was made during the nineteenth century. The metallic glazes are applied on pottery. The finished color depends on the combination of the clay color and the glaze.

LUSTER, Blue, Cup & Saucer, Czechoslovakia	6.00
Canary, Mug, LaFayette & Washington, Black Transfer, 2 5/8 In.	800.00
Canary, Pitcher, Mask, Orange & Black Enamel, 5 3/4 In.	200.00
Canary, Pitcher, Silver Luster Floral, 5 1/2 In.	175.00
Canary, Pitcher, Wellington & Nelson, Brown Transfer, 5 5/8 In.	450.00
Canary, Waste Bowl, Classically Attired Woman, Children, 4 3/4 In.	300.00
Canary, Waste Bowl, Floral Design, 3 1/4 x 6 1/4 In.	400.00
Copper, Coffeepot, Flower Finial, Child's	95.00
Copper, Creamer, Child's, Flower Band	195.00
Copper, Creamer, White Vintage Band, Purple Floral Band, 4 1/4 In.	45.00
Copper, Creamer, Woman & Child At Desk, 4 7/8 In.	165.00
Copper, Creamer, Woman & Child With Badminton Rackets, 8 3/4 In.	300.00
Copper, Cup & Saucer, Child's, Handleless, Lily of The Valley	125.00
Copper, Goblet, Bands of Rose Over Cream, 4 1/2 In.	45.00
Copper, Mug	50.00
Copper, Pitcher, Basket of Flowers, Bearded Man Spout, 6 In.	95.00
Copper, Pitcher, Cobalt Blue Bands, 4 1/4 In.	50.00
Copper, Pitcher, Floral Band, 4 1/2 In.	45.00
Copper, Pitcher, Green Band, Embossed Figures, Mask Spout, 4 1/4 In.	90.00

Luster, Copper, Pitcher, Red, Lafayette & Cornwallis, c.1810, 9 In.

Copper, Pitcher, Miniature 33.00
Copper, Pitcher, Red, Lafayette & Cornwallis, c.1810, 9 In. ....*Illus* 1925.00
Copper, Pitcher, Squared Panels, Enameled Flowers, 6 In. 85.00
Copper, Pitcher, White Reserves, Red–Transfer Scenes, 8 3/4 In. 300.00
Copper, Pitcher, Yellow Band, Polychrome Enamel Scenes, 6 3/4 In. 125.00
LUSTER, COPPER, TEA LEAF, see Tea Leaf Ironstone
Copper, Tea Set, Blue Trim, Gibson, England, 20th Century, 4 Piece 225.00
Copper, Tea Set, Cream Body, Pink Luster Rims, Shorthose, 8 Piece 550.00
Copper, Teapot, Eagle Handle, Luster Stylized Leaf Design, 5 3/4 In. 250.00
Copper, Tumbler, Tan Panel, Floral Design 75.00
LUSTER, FAIRYLAND, see Wedgwood
Ink, Cup & Saucer, Bird Handle That Is Whistle, Child's 125.00
Pink & Purple, Pitcher, House Design, 4 3/4 In. 60.00
Pink & Purple, Pitcher, Hunt Scenes, Basket Weave, Enamel, 5 1/2 In. 90.00
Pink & Purple, Pitcher, Ribs, Floral Rim With House, 4 3/4 In. 50.00
Pink, Creamer, Roses In Pink Luster Amid Grapes, Vines, 4 5/8 In. 303.00
Pink, Cup & Saucer, Vintage Band, Red & Yellow Ochre Enamel 15.00
Pink, Jug, Hunt Scene, Multicolored Transfer, 5 1/4 In. 145.00
Pink, Pitcher & Bowl, Red Roses, Green Leaves, Miniature 110.00
Pink, Pot–De–Creme, Leaf & Vine, Ram's Head Handles, 5 1/2 In. 45.00
Pink, Shaving Mug 40.00
Pink, Sugar & Creamer, Flowers 35.00
Pink, Teapot, 2–Cup 65.00
Pink, Teapot, House Pattern, Staffordshire, Large 125.00
Purple, Tea Set, Child's, Germany 150.00
Silver, Pitcher, Floral, Birds, 4 3/8 In. 60.00
Silver, Pitcher, Grapes & Leaves, Bulbous, England, 3 1/2 In. 35.00
Silver, Pitcher, Mask, 3 Faces, Polychrome Enamel, 5 1/2 In. 50.00
Silver, Teapot, Embossed Design, Birdlike Handle, 6 7/8 In. 25.00
Silver, Toby Shaker, Brown Body, 5 1/4 In. 25.00
LUSTER, SUNDERLAND, see Sunderland

Lustre Art Glass Company was founded in Long Island, New York, in 1920 by Conrad Vahlsing and Paul Frank. The company made lampshades and globes that are almost indistinguishable from those made by Quezal. Most of the shades made by the company were unmarked.

LUSTRE ART, Shade, Marigold 125.00
Shade, Snakeskin Pattern, Green & Gold, Signed, 5 Piece 750.00

Lustres are mantel decorations, or pedestal vases, with many hanging glass prisms. The name really refers to the prisms, and it is proper to refer to a single glass prism as a lustre. Either spelling, luster or lustre, is correct.

LUSTRES, Cranberry & Gold, 10 Cut–Glass Prisms, 12 1/4 In. 275.00
Lead Crystal, Prisms, 14 In., Pair 450.00
Mantel, Bristol Glass, Crystal Drops, Sapphire Blue, 7 1/2 In. 245.00
Officer Portraits, Glass Globe, Czarist Russian Mark, Pair 900.00
Pink Overlay, Double Row of Prisms, White Dots, 15 1/2 In., Pair 850.00

Nicolas Lutz worked at the Boston and Sandwich Glass Company from 1869 to 1888. He made delicate and intricate threaded glass of several colors. Other similar wares made by other makers are now known by the generic name *Lutz*.

LUTZ, Cup & Saucer, Pink, Gold, Blue Threading, Diagonal, Demitasse 400.00
Vase, Latticinio, Pink Threading For Spiral Effect, 13 In. 875.00

Petrus Regout established the De Sphinx pottery in Maastricht, Holland, in 1836. The firm was noted for its transfer–printed earthenware. Many factories in Maastricht are still making ceramics.

MAASTRICHT, Bowl, Oriental Scene, Orange, Luster, 8 In. 40.00
Bowl, Spatter Floral Design, 1 3/8 x 7 3/8 In. 45.00
Plate, Abbey, 9 In. 22.00

Majolica, Charger, Satyr, Nymphs, 23 1/2 In.   *Majolica, Pedestal, Bear, Standing, Green,*
Purple, 40 In.

Plate, Flowers, Orange, Blue, 10 In.	25.00
Plate, Green Leaves, Flowers, 11 In.	55.00
Platter, Flowers, Orange, Blue, 15 In.	65.00

Maize glass was made by W. L. Libbey & Son Company of Toledo, Ohio, after 1889. The glass resembled an ear of corn. The leaves were usually green, but some pieces were made with blue or red leaves. The kernels of *corn* were light yellow, white, or light green.

MAIZE, Bowl, Green Leaf Design, Libbey, c.1895, 8 In.	330.00
Celery Vase, Amber Staining On Kernels, 7 In.	550.00
Celery Vase, Libbey	145.00
Celery Vase, Rows of Kernels of Corn, 6 1/2 In.	165.00
Celery, White, Green Stain, Libbey	95.00
Condiment Set, Handled Frame, Libbey, 3 Piece	225.00
Cruet, Blue Leaves, Stopper	225.00
Pitcher, Barrel Shape, Blue Husks, Strap Handle, 8 3/4 In.	585.00
Pitcher, Water, Blue Husks, Amber Kernels, Libbey	575.00
Pitcher, Water, Green Husks, Strap Handle, White, Libbey	245.00
Tumbler, Green Leaves, Gold Trim, Libbey	155.00
Tumbler, Pink	50.00
Waste Bowl, Yellow Husks	155.00

Majolica is a general term for any pottery glazed with an opaque tin enamel that conceals the color of the clay body. It has been made since the fourteenth century. Today's collector is most likely to find Victorian majolica. The heavy, colorful ware is rarely marked. Some famous makers include Wedgwood; Minton; Griffen, Smith and Hill (marked *Etruscan*); and Chesapeake Pottery (marked *Avalon* or *Clifton*).

MAJOLICA, Bank, Gourd, Marked	200.00
Basket, Intertwined Fruit & Vine Design, 10 1/2 x 15 1/2 In.	35.00
Bowl, Fish Shape, Signed, 8 In.	30.00
Bowl, Shell & Seaweed, 8 In.	250.00
Bread Tray, Corn	210.00
Bust, Man, Woman, 18th–Century French Dress, Marked, 15 In., Pair	225.00
Butter Chip, Butterfly, Fielding	60.00
Butter Chip, Floral Shell, Cobalt Blue	80.00
Butter Chip, Lily Pond, Etruscan, 3 Piece	120.00
Butter, Cover, Hand With Corn	295.00
Butter, Cover, Pond Lily	295.00
Cachepot, Muticolored Floral & Leaf Design, 3 In., Pair	88.00
Cake Set, Birds On Limbs, Relief Leaves, Zells, 6, 8, 11 In., 8 Pc.	250.00
Cake Stand, Blue & Green, White & Rose Buds	150.00
Card Holder, Boy, Standing, Holds Large Tray, 18 In.	750.00
Charger, Angels Night Scene, Pink, Aqua & Cream, 16 In.	110.00
Charger, Multicolored Oriental Design, 17th Century, 13 1/4 In.	610.00
Charger, Satyr, Nymphs, 23 1/2 In. ....*Illus*	475.00

Cheese Keeper, Blackberries On Bark, Holdcroft 2800.00
Cheese Keeper, Strawberry Flowers, George Jones 1800.00
Cheese Keeper, Strawberry Flowers, Picket Fence, George Jones 2400.00
Cheese Stand, Branch Handles, Molded Apple Blossoms, G. Jones 1000.00
Cheese Stand, Cover, Stilton, Vines, Blossoms, c.1875, 10 1/4 In. 1200.00
Cigar Holder, Ashtray, Indian, Standing, Figural, 6 1/2 IIN. 95.00
Compote, Begonia Leaf Colors, Pedestal, 10 In. 230.00
Compote, Figural Animals Around Stem, George Jones, Pair 5060.00
Compote, Shell, Dolphin, Cobalt Blue, Holdcroft, 18 In. 2500.00
Cup & Saucer, Cottage Pattern 45.00
Dish, Stilton Cheese, Molded Primrose Body, Turquoise Ground 950.00
Ewer, Blue Flowers, Leaves, Twig Handle, 12 In. 250.00
Figurine, Bird, On Leafy Perch, 12 1/4 In. 195.00
Figurine, Black Girl, Reclining On Stomach, 3 x 5 1/2 In. 95.00
Flower Bowl, Boat Shape, Pink Lilies, Brown Ground, 10 In. 225.00
Flowerpot, Pinecone, 5 x 4 In. 100.00
Game Dish, Liner, Minton 3200.00
Holder, Cigarette & Match, Black Child Playing Mandolin 125.00
Humidor, Clown, 6 1/2 In. 260.00
Humidor, Fisherman's Head, 4 1/2 In. 65.00
Humidor, Motorist's, Man Wearing Goggles, Cigar, 6 In. 225.00
Humidor, Pinecone, 3 Cones, Green, Yellow & Brown, 7 In. 145.00
Jardiniere, Peacock At Fountain, Brown, 7 1/2 In. 35.00
Match Holder, Cow, Lying On Leaf 450.00
Match Holder, Indian Chief, Seated 375.00
Match Holder, Striker, Beaded, Green, Brown, Tans, 3 1/4 x 5 In. 78.00
Match Holder, Striker, Black Boy, Seated, With Watermelon 275.00
Match Holder, Striker, Black Man, On Leaf 250.00
Match Holder, Striker, Wedgwood 135.00
Pedestal, Bear, Standing, Green, Purple, 40 In. ....*Illus* 2200.00
Pie Dish, Dead Game On Cover, Liner, c.1860, 13 1/2 In. 1325.00
Pitcher, Basket Weave & Floral, Green Inside, 7 In. 125.00
Pitcher, Bird & Fan, English 195.00
Pitcher, Bird & Fan, Rose To Green, 7 In. 80.00
Pitcher, Bird, Cattail Handle, Holdcroft, 6 1/4 x 5 1/2 In. 175.00
Pitcher, Blue Leaves, Grapes, Gold Gargoyles, 7 1/2 In. 85.00
Pitcher, Bowl, Leaves, Berries, 6 In. 60.00
Pitcher, Bowl, Leaves, Strawberries, 6 In. 60.00
Pitcher, Brown Bark, Blackberries, Leaves & Flowers, 7 1/2 In. 150.00
Pitcher, Colored Fans, Triangular, 1880s, 8 In. 265.00
Pitcher, Corn Pattern, Metal Top, 6 In. 45.00
Pitcher, Corn, Lavendar, 5 In. 30.00
Pitcher, Cover, Basketweave & Flower, 5 1/4 In. 65.00
Pitcher, Flower, 3 Recessed Panels, Baroque Base, 14 In. 280.00
Pitcher, Game, Hound Handle 375.00
Pitcher, Greek Key, Fan, Lotus Blossom, 2 Sizes, Pair 595.00
Pitcher, Green & Yellow Corn, Small 50.00
Pitcher, Ivory, Floral, Turquoise Interior, Handle, 8 In. 75.00
Pitcher, Lily-of-The-Valley, 7 In. 25.00
Pitcher, Molded Flower, 3 Panels Outlined In Blue, 14 In. 280.00
Pitcher, Mottled Browns, Yellow Flowers & Leaves, Squat, 5 1/2 In. 35.00
Pitcher, Mottled, Cat Handle 650.00
Pitcher, Owl Form, c.1900, 11 In. 290.00
Pitcher, Parrot, 12 In. 180.00
Pitcher, Pineapple, 8 1/2 In. 135.00
Pitcher, Stork In Rushes, Holdcroft 1050.00
Pitcher, Trout 60.00
Planter, Acorn 30.00
Planter, Ornate Floral, Square 180.00
Planter, Tree Trunk, Branches, Nest of Birds Front, 10 In. 725.00
Planter, Wall, Horn Shape, Elephant & Palm Leaves 28.00
Plaque, Bird Center, Surrounded By Flowers, Marked, 13 In., Pair 610.00
Plate, Asparagus, Drained 225.00

Plate, Blackberries, Turquoise Ground, Tell	30.00
Plate, Cauliflower, Rose Border, Etruscan, 9 In.	135.00
Plate, Deer & Dog, 8 In.	70.00
Plate, Dog Chasing Deer, Fleur–De–Lis Border, 8 In.	75.00
Plate, Green Leaf Center, 7 1/2 In.	125.00
Plate, Leaf With Acorns, Handle, Green, Yellow, Brown, 13 In.	95.00
Plate, Leaf, White, Peach, Handle, 12 In.	95.00
Plate, Lettuce Leaf, 8 In.	15.00
Plate, Lizard, Palissy, 10 In.	275.00
Plate, Pond Lily, Turquoise & Yellow Florals, 1869, 8 3/4 In.	48.50
Plate, Reticulated Border, Brown, Green, Wedgwood, 8 1/2 In., 6 Pc.	775.00
Plate, Serpent & Crab, Palissy, 10 In.	275.00
Plate, Shaggy Dog, 11 In.	125.00
Plate, Starfish, Etruscan, 9 In.	75.00
Platter, Lettuce Leaf, Round, 12 In.	130.00
Platter, Maple Leaf, Twig Handles, 8 1/2 In.	75.00
Platter, Strawberry & Bow, 14 In.	325.00
Salt & Pepper, 4 1/2 In.	90.00
Server, Strawberry, George Jones, Pair	2750.00
Spittoon, Water Lily, Etruscan	575.00
Strawberry Server, George Jones, 3 Piece	1600.00 To 2200.00
Sugar & Creamer, Strawberry	115.00
Sugar, Brown Flying Geese, Yellow Basket Weave Bottom	175.00
Sugar, Cover, Berry Finial, Leaves, Berries	70.00
Syrup, Bird & Iris	495.00
Syrup, Metal Lid, Pink Flowers, Butterfly	125.00
Tankard, Baroque Style, Green, Blue, Pink, Pewter Top	295.00
Teapot, Monkey, 1874	2400.00
Teapot, Owl	225.00
Teapot, Shell & Seaweed	595.00
Teapot, Shell Finial, Albino Shell & Seaweed, 5 1/2 In.	340.00
Tray, Figural, Fish, 20 In.	110.00
Tray, Leaf, Blue Base, Brown Top, 14 In.	145.00
Tureen, Corn, Ear of Corn On Lid, 8 In.	275.00
Urn, Snake Handles, Baluster, Italy, 20 In., Pair	110.00
Vase, Bird, 5 In.	265.00
Vase, Chinese Figures, Lanterns, Serpent Handles, WS & S, 9 In.	225.00
Vase, Chinese Woman, Scene, 12 In.	125.00
Vase, Cupid In White Relief, Black Ground, George Jones, 6 In.	495.00
Vase, Cutouts, Open Handles, Blue Ground, 13 In.	95.00
Vase, Figural, Shepherdess, Sheep	55.00
Vase, Fish, Pink Interior, 11 In.	195.00
Vase, Flowers, Rococo, Deep Rose, 13 3/4 In., Pair	400.00
Vase, Girl, Wooden Shoes, Bowl of Fish, Multicolored, 11 1/2 In.	185.00
Vase, Monkey Design, 2 Handles	150.00
Vase, Morning Glories, Stem Handles, 6 1/2 In.	75.00
Vase, Oriental Man, 6 In.	35.00
Vase, Polychrome Floral & Fern, 11 In.	240.00
Vase, Serpent Handles, Palissy, 10 In.	375.00

 Maps of all types have been collected for centuries. The earliest known printed maps were made in 1478. The first printed street map showed London in 1559. The first road maps for use by drivers of automobiles were made in 1901. Collectors buy maps that were pages of old books, as well as the multifolded road maps popular in this century.

MAP, Africa, Relief Cartography, K. Wenschow GmbH, Germany, 39 x 55 In.	35.00
Alabama, Tanner's Atlas, 1839, 13 1/2 x 17 1/2 In.	60.00
Alaska, Capt. E. F. Glenn, Military Expedition Route, 1898, 12 x 30 In.	40.00
Alaska, Coast Survey, Paper, c.1910, 30 x 40 In.	8.50
Alaska, Eldridge, Geo. & Robt. Muldrow, 20 x 26 In.	25.00
Alaska, Geodetic Survey, Paper, c.1910, 30 x 40 In.	8.50
America, Hand Colored, Engraved, Framed, 22 1/4 x 25 1/2 In.	300.00

◆◆

Light can damage many types of antiques. Furniture finish will fade, textiles and paper fade or darken. Light will also weaken wood and fabric.

◆◆

Atlas, Rand McNally, 1890	75.00
Atlas, State of Indiana, 1876	35.00
Atlas, World, Crams Family, 1887	95.00
Auto, Michigan, Garage, Hotels, Etc., 1918	15.00
Baltimore, Mitchell's Atlas, 1860, 15 3/4 x 13 In.	45.00
California, Inset San Francisco, Border, Colored, 1860, 13 x 16 In.	110.00
Case, Cylindrical, Leather Handle, Tin, 26 In.	25.00
Celestial, American, Wilson & Sons, Mahogany Tripod Base, 36 1/2 In.	1320.00
Civil War, Alabama, Color, West Miss. Army, 1865, 17 x 28 In.	125.00
Connecticut, Hand Drawn, Mary E. Hotchkiss, April 1, 1829	495.00
Dakota Territory, 1884, 24 x 19 In.	15.00
Delaware, Maryland, 5 Vignettes, Johnson & Browning, 1861, 13 x 16 In.	60.00
Detroit, Michigan, 1872, 18 x 20 1/2 In.	75.00
East & West Hemipshere, Watercolor, Ink, H. P. Gilman, 1819, 44 x 29 In.	550.00
Florida, Mitchell's Atlas, 1860, 15 3/4 x 13 In.	45.00
Globe, Cary, Mahogany, Cabriole Legs, 1810, 28 x 18 In.	1980.00
Globe, Celestial, W. & Th. Bardin, Ltd., Mahogany Stand, c.1800, 44 In.	3850.00
Globe, Replogle, 1940s, 12 In.	55.00
Globe, Terrestrial, Gilman Jaslin, c.1860	2530.00
Iowa, Hypsography of N. E. Iowa, Color, U. S. G. S., McGee, 1889, 15 x 17 In.	12.50
Motoring, Scandinavia & Finland, Foldout, Color, c.1920	4.00
New England, Road, Sunoco, Illustrated, 22 x 28 In.	4.00
New Map of The Terraquerous Globe, English, Frame, 20 1/2 x 15 1/4 In.	550.00
New York City, Atlas, Bromley, 40 Double Page Street Maps, 22 x 17 In.	525.00
North Carolina, Discovery, Frame, 1937, Pair	300.00
North Carolina, Rand McNally, Indexed, Pocket, 78 Pages	18.00
Ohio, Each County Individually Colored, 1842, 12 x 13 In.	120.00
Ohio, Engraved, Frame, Printed By John Melish, 1815, 13 3/4 x 12 In.	175.00
Ohio, Hand Colored, John Kilbourne, Columbus, Ohio, 1822, 32 x 31 In.	650.00
Oklahoma, 1893	25.00
Pennsylvania, Canals, Railroads, Tanner, Phila., Framed, 14 1/2 x 17 In.	95.00
Pennsylvania, Engraved, Hand Colored, Colton, N. Y., 1855, 14 1/2 x 17 In.	25.00
Road From London To Dover, Colored, Engraved, 1678, 16 x 20 1/2 In.	200.00
State of Ohio, Department of Interior, Engraved, 1866, 18 1/4 x 20 In.	150.00
Streetcar Route, Minneapolis, 1891	30.00
United States, Engraved, 1832, 11 1/4 x 17 In.	55.00
War Department, Survey of Railroad Routes	45.00

 Marble is used in many ways on antiques. Marble tops are popular for tables because they resist stains and damage. Listed here are marble carvings, large or small figurines, and groups of people or animals that have been a special art form since the time of the ancient Greeks. Reproductions, especially of large Victorian groups, are being made of a mixture using marble dust. These are very difficult to detect and collectors should be careful. Other carvings are listed under Alabaster.

MARBLE CARVING, 3 Graces, Back To Back, Paw Foot Base, White, 22 In.	240.00
Allegorical, Mercy, Right Hand On Breast, 25 1/2 In.	2750.00
Bird Bath, Baluster Pedestal, Octagonal Plinth, 29 x 27 In.	1760.00
Bird, Attacking Lizard, Faux Marble Pedestal, 35 In.	7700.00
Bust, Child, Ivory Pedestal, C. B. Iveys, Fecit Romae, 39 In.	1850.00
Bust, Classical, F. Vichi, 25 In.	2640.00
Bust, Classical, Turned Head, 21 In.	3300.00
Bust, Diana, Head Turned To Dexter, G. Tomguinetti, 26 In.	5500.00

Marble Carving, Bust, Pink Veined,
Signed J. V., 20 1/2 In.

♦ ♦

Marble is porous and will absorb
water vapors into the stone up to
six inches deep. Airborne pollu-
tants will also be absorbed; and
eventually, when the marble
dries, the dirt will erode or stain
the surface of the marble. Avoid
humidity.

♦ ♦

Bust, Joan of Arc, 15 x 15 In.	650.00
Bust, Napoleon, 1860–80	4500.00
Bust, Pink Veined, Signed J. V., 20 1/2 In. ....*Illus*	3000.00
Bust, Woman, M. Planet, 1902, 27 In.	440.00
Bust, Woman, Peaked Hat, Alabaster Robe, Pochini, 17 In.	605.00
Column, Louis XV, Fluted, France, c.1770, Pair	1500.00
Female Nude Torso, Wood Plinth, Barky, 16 In. .... 500.00 To	550.00
Gentleman, Standing, 47 In.	4125.00
Goat, Mythological, 1/2 Goat, 1/2 Sea Urchin, 40 In., Pair	4180.00
Group, Kneeling Girl, Putto, Pedestal, Lombardi, 31 In.	7150.00
Nymph & Putto, Painted Wooden Base, 27 In.	2750.00
Nymph, A. Batacchi, Late 19th Century, 29 In.	3300.00
Urn, Foliate Band, Masks, Bronze Mounted, 18 In., Pair	3575.00

The game of marbles has been popular since the days of the ancient
Romans. American children were able to buy marbles by the mid–
eighteenth century. Dutch glazed clay marbles were least expensive.
Glazed pottery marbles, attributed to the Bennington potteries in
Vermont, were of a better quality. Marbles made of pink marble
were also available by the 1830s. Glass marbles seem to have been
made later. By 1880, Samuel C. Dyke of South Akron, Ohio, was
making clay marbles and The National Onyx Marble Company was
making marbles of onyx. The Navarre Glass Marble Company of
Navarre, Ohio, and M. B. Mishler of Ravenna, Ohio, made the glass
marbles. Ohio remained the center of the marble industry and the
Akron–made Akro Agate brand became nationally known. The most
expensive marbles collected today are the sulphides. These are glass
marbles with frosted white figures in the center.

MARBLE, Bennington, Blue, 1 In.	12.00
Bennington, Brown, 1 7/16 In.	10.00
Carving, Peyre, Nymph, Standing, Nude, White, 20th Century, 27 1/4 In.	3520.00
Clambroth, White, Red Lines, 1 7/8 In.	375.00
General Grant, Bennington Marble, Pee–Wee Size	145.00
Gold Mica, 1 7/8 In.	450.00
Goldstone, 7/8 In.	45.00
Lutz, 2 In.	600.00
Onionskin, Blue & White Swirl, 1 7/8 In.	140.00
Purple Mica, 5/8 In.	85.00
Salazar, Moon & Star, 1 1/4 In.	45.00
Sulphide, Bear, Standing, Clear, 1 3/4 In.	90.00
Sulphide, Bust of Jenny Lind, 1 3/8 In.	1600.00
Sulphide, Dog, Standing	75.00
Sulphide, Girl In Upside–Down Chair, 1 5/8 In.	900.00
Sulphide, Goat, 1 3/4 In.	10.00
Sulphide, Little Boy Blue, 2 In.	280.00
Sulphide, Rooster, 1 3/4 In.	4000.00
Sulphide, Rooster, 2 3/8 In.	240.00

Sulphide, Woman In Dress, 1 1/4 In. 900.00

The Marblehead Pottery was founded in 1905 by Dr. J. Hall as a rehabilitative program for the patients of a Marblehead, Massachusetts, sanitarium. Two years later it was separated from the sanitarium and it continued operations until 1936. Many of the pieces were decorated with marine motifs.

MARBLEHEAD, Basket, Hanging, Blue Matte, 4 x 5 In.	155.00
Basket, Hanging, Lavender Matte, 4 x 5 In.	155.00
Basket, Hanging, Ribbed, Green Gloss Glaze, 5 1/2 In.	155.00
Bowl, Dark Blue Flecks, Matte Green, 2 x 4 1/2 In.	195.00
Bowl, Dark Blue, 4 1/2 In.	145.00
Bowl, Exterior Glaze, Gray Interior, Marked, 9 1/4 In.	165.00
Bowl, Green Over Pink Gloss Glaze, 8 1/2 In.	195.00
Bowl, Pink Matte, 6 In.	195.00
Bowl, Purple, Blue Interior, 5 In.	125.00
Tile, Oak Tree & Marsh Scene, Brown, Tan, Green & Yellow, 6 In.	3100.00
Tile, Sailing Ship, Blue & White, 5 In.	450.00
Vase, 2 Bands of Checkerboard Design, c.1915, 8 3/8 In.	1750.00
Vase, Alternating Elongated Trees & Circles, Marked, 6 3/8 In.	1350.00
Vase, Black Stylized Flowers & Leaves, Gray–Green Ground, 7 In.	4650.00
Vase, Blue Glaze, Bulbous, 5 In.	85.00
Vase, Blue, 12 In.	450.00
Vase, Blue, 6 In.	265.00
Vase, Bud, Gray & Blue, 5 1/2 In.	135.00
Vase, Deep Blue, Signed, 4 1/2 x 3 1/2 In.	275.00
Vase, Flared, Matte Brown Outside, Orange Inside, 6 In.	275.00
Vase, Green & Ocher Glaze, Swollen Cylindrical, 1908, 7 1/16 In.	225.00
Vase, Moth Border, Blue Stippled Ground, c.1910, 6 3/4 In.	2090.00
Vase, Painted Stylized Floral, c.1915, 3 1/4 In.	1110.00
Vase, Repeating Flowers & Arched Branches, Speckled, 3 3/4 In.	2200.00
Vase, Repeating Parrots On Branches, Marked, 7 In.	1775.00
Vase, Repeating Stylized Branches, Marked, c.1915, 4 1/2 In.	885.00
Vase, Seahorses, Amidst Underwater Vegetation	6050.00
Vase, Straight Cylinder, Blue, 4 1/2 In.	165.00
Vase, Stylized Floral, Gray–Green Ground, 5 1/4 In.	1100.00
Vase, Stylized Floral, Speckled Ground, Marked, 5 1/4 In.	715.00
Vase, Stylized Floral, Speckled Ground, Marked, 7 In.	1750.00
Vase, Stylized Floral, Stippled Glaze, Marked, c.1915, 3 1/4 In.	1225.00
Vase, Stylized Gray Poppy Pod & Leaves, Pebbly Ground, 7 In.	1100.00
Vase, Stylized Trees Around, Yellow, Baggs & Tutt, 4 1/4 In.	3850.00
Vase, Swollen Cylinder, Blue Matte, 5 1/2 In.	165.00
Wall Pocket, Brown, Cream Gloss Glaze, 5 1/2 In.	175.00
Wall Pocket, Green Gloss Glaze, 5 In.	175.00

Martinware is a salt–glazed stoneware made by the Martin Brothers of Middlesex, England, between 1873 and 1915. Many figural jugs and vases were made by the three brothers. Of special interest are the fanciful birds, usually made with removable heads.

MARTIN BROTHERS, Bird, Head Removable, Grotesque, 14 In.	10000.00
Bird, Wooden Base, Comic, Salt Glaze, 10 5/8 In.	9350.00
Jug, Face, Grotesque, 1898, 9 In.	5000.00
Vase, Animals, Birds, Sgraffito, 9 1/2 In.	2000.00
Vase, Birds On Each Side, 1893, 8 1/2 In.	8000.00

Mary Gregory glass is identified by a characteristic white figure painted on dark glass. It was made from 1870 to 1910. The name refers to any glass decorated with a white silhouette figure and not just to the Sandwich glass originally painted by Miss Mary Gregory. Many reproductions have been made and there are new pieces being sold in gift shops today.

MARY GREGORY, Beaker, Tumbler, Male & Female Blowing Horn, Clear, Cranberry	159.00
Bottle, Barber, Tennis Scene, Cobalt, 8 1/4 In., Pr. ....*Illus*	350.00

Bottle, Dresser, Girl, Butterflies In Hand, Pink, 7 1/2 In.	985.00
Bottle, Water, Girl, Butterfly, Rubina Paneled, 7 1/2 In.	195.00
Bowl, Pedestal, Cherub Base, Amethyst, Square, 9 1/2 In.	1100.00
Box, Boy With Flowers, Sapphire Blue, 3 1/2 In.	350.00
Box, Hinged Cover, Girl In Garden, Holding Flower, 2 In.	195.00
Box, Hinged Cover, Girl, Angel Wings, 3 1/2 x 2 3/4 In.	195.00
Box, Hinged Cover, Woman & Bouquet, Cobalt Blue, 3 1/2 In.	465.00
Box, Hinged Cover, Young Boy, Lime Green, 3 3/4 In.	225.00
Carafe, Clear, Figure of Boy, 7 In.	148.00
Carafe, Water, Boy, Crystal, 7 In.	65.00
Card Holder, Girl, Crimped Fan, White, 9 x 9 1/2 In.	565.00
Cruet, Boy In Forest Meadow, Hollow Stopper, Crystal, 8 In.	192.50
Cruet, Boy In Knickers, Smelling Flower, Sapphire Blue, 8 In.	380.00
Cruet, Boy, 3–Petal Top, Ball Stopper, Amber, 9 1/2 In.	265.00
Cruet, Green, 6 1/2 In., Pair	250.00
Decanter, Blue, 6 Shot Glasses, 11 1/2 In.	195.00
Decanter, Green, White Enameled Girl, 12 In.	250.00
Decanter, Mushroom Stopper, Man In Frock Coat, Cranberry	245.00
Decanter, Young Woman, Swan In Water, Cranberry, 9 1/2 In.	425.00
Epergne, Enamel Design, Plated Metal Ormolu, 22 In.	685.00
Erui, Cranberry, Venice Scene, Canal	143.00
Goblet, Girl With Hat, Cranberry, Clear Footed, 4 3/4 In.	110.00
Jam Jar, Girl, Brass Bail & Cover, Cranberry, 4 1/2 In.	170.00
Jar, Apple Stem Cover, Boy With Fern, Spoon, 6 In.	305.00
Jar, Cobalt Blue, Figure of Boy, Cover, 4 In.	275.00
Jar, Necessaire, Cranberry, Twisted–Brass Form, Girl, 4 In.	275.00
Lamp, Fairy, Child, Ribbons & Curls, Green	85.00
Lamp, Girl Holding Parrot, Black Amethyst, 7 In.	315.00
Mug, Boy, Girl, Facing Pair, Amber, Barrel Shape, 4 In., Pair	165.00
Mug, Single Handle, Figure of Boy	66.00
Patch Box, Boy With Hat, Cranberry, 2 1/2 In.	175.00
Pitcher, Boy Catching Butterflies, Petal Top, Blue, 9 1/2 In.	195.00
Pitcher, Boy With Rake, Girl With Apples, Blue, 10 In.	350.00
Pitcher, Cranberry, Clear Handle, Girl With Flute, 10 In.	220.00
Pitcher, Girl Amid Foliage, Scalloped Top, 8 1/2 In.	175.00
Pitcher, Girl With Flute, Clear Handle, Cranberry, 10 In.	220.00
Pitcher, Horse & Man, Blowing Bugle, Amethyst, 14 1/4 In.	195.00
Pitcher, Water, Deep Blue, Ruffled, Reeded Handle	195.00
Pitcher, Water, Girl, Gold Trim, Amber Handle, Olive, 10 3/4 In.	375.00
Pitcher, Water, Girl, Sapphire Blue, 10 In.	275.00
Pitcher, White Girl, Sapphire Blue, 10 7/8 In.	230.00
Pitcher, Young Woman, Amber Handle, Teal Blue, 10 1/2 In.	445.00
Powder Box, Boy, Sapphire Blue, 3 In.	295.00
Powder Box, Girl On Lid, Metal Fittings, Red, 5 In.	585.00
Powder Box, Hinged Cover, Boy In Garden, 3 x 3 In.	195.00
Powder Jar, Boy On Lid, Cobalt Blue, 3 In.	192.50
Toothpick, Inverted Thumbprint, Girl Leaning On Cross, Amber	245.00

Mary Gregory, Bottle, Barber, Tennis Scene, Cobalt, 8 1/4 In., Pr.

Tumbler, Boy, Foliage, Cranberry Glass, 2 In. 110.00
Tumbler, Girl, With Hat, White Enameling, Cranberry, 4 In. 85.00
Tumbler, Juice, Boy With Flower, Cranberry 95.00
Vase, Black Ground, Boy & Girl, 6 In., Pair 250.00
Vase, Boy & Girl, Black Ground, 5 1/4 In., Pair 250.00
Vase, Boy Blowing Horn, Crimped Rim, Cranberry, 4 1/2 In. 125.00
Vase, Boy Carrying Bowl of Flowers, Green, 11 1/8 In. 225.00
Vase, Boy Under Tree, Girl, Black Amethyst, 11 7/8 In. 450.00
Vase, Boy With Butterfly Net, Sapphire Blue, 10 In. 225.00
Vase, Bud, Cobalt, Girl With Flower, Bulbous Base, 5 In. 135.00
Vase, Bud, Lime Green Paneled 95.00
Vase, Cobalt, Cylinder, 12 In., Pair 240.00
Vase, Facing Figures, Cranberry, 12 In., Pair 7a75.00
Vase, Facing Pair, Boy & Girl, Cranberry, 4 3/4 In., Pair 245.00
Vase, Girl Blowing Horn, Fluted Rim, Emerald Green, 8 In. 135.00
Vase, Girl Dancing, Tinted Features, Emerald Green, 6 3/4 In. 130.00
Vase, Girl Holding Bouquet, Ruffled, Sapphire Blue, 6 3/4 In. 165.00
Vase, Girl On Swing Near Tree, Amber, 13 In., Pair 445.00
Vase, Girl On Swing, Amber To Topaz, 12 In., Pair 685.00
Vase, Girl On Tiptoe, Green, Cylinder, 6 x 1 3/4 In. 90.00
Vase, Girl Picking Apples, Sapphire Blue, 12 In. 255.00
Vase, Girl Sitting On Tree Branch, Pink, 11 7/8 In. 225.00
Vase, Girl With Balloon In White, Cobalt Blue, 4 1/2 In. 85.00
Vase, Girl With Balloon, Scalloped, Amber, 10 1/2 In. 225.00
Vase, Girl With Handkerchief, Snail Handles, Green, 11 1/2 In. 295.00
Vase, Girl With Parasol, Cranberry, 8 1/2 In. 225.00
Vase, Girl, Basket of Flowers, Cobalt Blue, Ruffled, 4 3/4 In. 195.00
Vase, Lady, Satin Chartreuse, Pyramid, 7 In. 138.00
Vase, Pyramid, Cranberry, Children Catching Butterfly, 13 In. 585.00
Vase, Pyramid, Lime Green, Lovely Woman, Flared, 7 In. 165.00
Vase, Ruffled, Boy Carrying Tray of Flowers, Green, 11 1/8 In. 235.00
Vase, White To Deep Blue, Gold Trim, Girl, Butterfly, 7 In. 138.00
Vase, Young Girl, White Enameling, Cranberry, 5 3/4 In. 125.00
MASONIC, see Fraternal

Massier pottery is iridescent French art pottery made by Clement Massier in Golfe–Juan, France, in the late–nineteenth and early–twentieth centuries. It has an iridescent metallic luster glaze that resembles the Weller Sicard pottery glaze. Most pieces are marked *J. Massier.*

MASSIER, Vase, Cloverleaf Design, 5 1/2 In. 275.00
Vase, Red–Purple Iridescent, Gold Overglaze, 14 1/2 In. ....*Illus* 1300.00

Large wooden matches were used in the nineteenth and twentieth centuries for a variety of purposes. The kitchen stove and the fireplace or furnace had to be lit regularly. One type of match

Massier, Vase, Red–Purple Iridescent,
Gold Overglaze, 14 1/2 In.

Matt Morgan, Bottle, Incised D. R., 6 In.

holder was made to hang on the wall, another was designed to be kept on a tabletop. Of special interest today are match holders that have advertisements as part of the design.

MATCH HOLDER, American Brew Co., Rochester, N. Y., Eagle, Shield, Stoneware	175.00
Bacchus Face, Cast Iron	80.00
Baseball Player, Book, Bronzed	25.00
Bertolli Italina Olive Oil, Plaster of Paris, 6 1/4 In.	55.00
Bible, Glass	40.00
Boot, Amber Glass, With Striker	36.00
Boot, Amethyst Glass, Wall	40.00
Bull Dog Cut Plug	385.00
Ceresota Flour Boy, Figural, Wall	300.00
Ceresota Flour, Tin .... 200.00 To	350.00
Columbia Flour	200.00
Crystal Spring Brewing Co., Stoneware	275.00
Daisy & Button, Wall Mounted, Glass, Amber, c.1870, 5 1/8 In.	385.00
DeLaval Cream Separators, Die Cut Metal Separator, Wall	225.00
Double Pocket, Crest Shape, Tin	14.00
Dr Pepper .... 55.00 To	60.00
Dr. Hoffman's Red Drops, Tin, Wall	65.00
Dr. Shoop's	150.00
Dubonnet Wine, Pottery	13.00
Ellwood Steel Fences	95.00
Emerson's Foot Ease Powder, Small Boy	95.00
Figural, Girl Feeding Rooster, China	65.00
Figural, White Fluffy Dog, Porcelain, Strike On Side, 3 In.	70.00
Frisco Line R.R., Telephone Shape, Wall Mount	400.00
Frog, Hinged Cover, Yellow Eyes, Cast Iron, Green, Wall, 4 In.	65.00
George Washington Hatchet, Brass, Figural, Wall	95.00
Hanging, A. E. Sonnedecket Coal Dealer & 10 Cent Barn, Tin	70.00
Hanging, Cast Iron, 1872, Wall	32.00
Hanging, Dockash Stove Factory, Tin, Wall	55.00
Hanging, Word Matches On Front, Blue, Japanned, Tin, Wall, 3 In.	50.00
Hatchet, Nickel Over Iron, 1908	35.00
Indian, Beaded, Wall, 1917	25.00
Indian, Wooden, Striker, Wall	25.00
Kitchen, Kay As Co.	25.00
Kool, Tin, 1 Cent	47.50
Little Boy, With Dog, Elbogen, c.1890, 4 x 5 In.	125.00
Moxie, Die Cut Metal, Bottle Shape, Wall	300.00
New Process Gas Ranges	85.00
Othello Range	150.00
Phillip Morris, Tin Litho, Little Johnny Pictured, Wall	85.00
Pig, Pink, Striker, German	55.00
Satchel Shape, Milk Glass	55.00
Sharples Cream Separators, Wall	200.00
Shoe, Mouse, Bronze	50.00
Shoe, Woman's, Mounted On Gold Leaf, Cast Iron, 4 1/2 x 5 In.	95.00
Shoe, Woman's, Striking Surface On Sole, 3 x 6 In.	50.00
Standing Donkey, Pack Basket, Cast Iron, c.1865, 4 1/2 x 5 In.	110.00
Woman's Dress Shoe, Daisy & Button, Amber, 5 3/4 x 3 In.	49.00

Early matches were made with phosphorus and could ignite unexpectedly. Match safes were designed to be carried in the pocket. The matches were safely stored in the tightly closed container. Examples were made in sterling silver, plated silver, or other metals. The English call these *vesta boxes*.

MATCH SAFE, Allover Engraved, Sterling Silver, Hallmark	58.00
Allover Leaves, Sterling Silver, English	95.00
Book, Compartment For Postage Stamps, English, Silver Plate	100.00
Bowler Bros. Brewery	75.00
Brass, Fancy	20.00

Bundle Tied With Rope, Figural, Silver Plate	90.00
Clothiers, 237 Mercer St., New York, Metal	55.00
Columbian Exposition, Administration Building, Nickel On Brass	145.00
English Bulldog	90.00
Flowers, Scrolls, Capitol Building, Sterling, Pre–1900	65.00
Harding Memorial, Ohio	17.50
International Tailoring, Nickel Over Brass	55.00
Meyer Bros., Clinton, Indiana, Christmas, 1911	22.50
Monkey, Figural, Pocket	235.00
Nude & Cattails, Swan & Lake On Reverse, Nickel Plated	45.00
Ornate, Silver, German	40.00
Park Sherman Co., Ever Dry, Springfield, Ill.	40.00
Schlitz Beer	55.00
Sterling Silver, Art Nouveau	70.00
United Cigars, Copper, Holds Book Matches	12.50
Washington, D. C., Capitol & White House, Celluloid	55.00
White Rock, Striker, 1910s	45.00
Wildton, Cover	25.00
Windmill Design, Wooden Lithograph, Dutch	28.00
Winged Nude, On Diagonal Stripes, German Silver, 2 1/2 In.	70.00
Woodrow Wilson, Old White House, 2 1/2 In.	45.00

Matsu–no–ke was a type of applied decoration for glass patented by Frederick Carder in 1922. There is clear evidence that pieces were made before that date at the Steuben glassworks. Stevens & Williams of England also made an applied decoration by the same name.

MATSU–NO–KE, Vase, Flowers, Scroll Feet, Cranberry, 7 1/8 In.	675.00
Vase, Frilled Top, Crystal Leaves, Flowers, Cranberry, 7 7/8 In.	675.00

Matt Morgan, an English artist, was making pottery in Cincinnati, Ohio, by 1883. His pieces were decorated to resemble Moorish wares. Incised designs and colors were applied to raised panels on the pottery. Shiny or matte glazes were used. The company lasted only a few years.

MATT MORGAN, Bottle, Incised D. R., 6 In. ....*Illus*	550.00
Vase, Pillow, Forest Scene, No. 281, 14 1/2 x 12 1/2 In.	4675.00
Vase, Raised White Flowers, Green Leaves, Marked, 5 1/2 In.	66.00
Vase, Red Body, Bamboo & Flying Bird, 4 1/2 In.	440.00

McCoy pottery is made in Roseville, Ohio. The J. W. McCoy Pottery was founded in 1899. It became the Brush McCoy Pottery Company in 1911. The name changed to the Brush Pottery in 1925. The word *Brush* was usually included in the mark on their pieces. The Nelson McCoy Sanitary and Stoneware Company, a different firm, was founded in Roseville, Ohio, in 1910. The firm made art pottery after 1926. In 1933 it became the Nelson McCoy Pottery. Pieces marked *McCoy* were made by the Nelson McCoy Company.

MCCOY, Bank, Seaman	35.00
Bowl, Green Leaves, Red Flowers, Brown, Loy–Nel–Art, 12 In.	275.00
Cookie Jar, Apple	21.50 To 30.00
Cookie Jar, Bananas	45.00
Cookie Jar, Barn	258.00
Cookie Jar, Barnum's Animals, Animal Cookie Box, Clown	165.00 To 275.00
Cookie Jar, Basket of Eggs	40.00
Cookie Jar, Basket of Strawberries	45.00

◆◆

Put a rubber collar on the faucet spout over the sink. This may save you from breaking a piece of glass or china you are washing.

◆◆

Cookie Jar, Basket of Strawberries 35.00
Cookie Jar, Bobby Baker .... 30.00 To 50.00
Cookie Jar, Boy On Football 90.00
Cookie Jar, Bronze Teakettle, Stationary Bail 30.00
Cookie Jar, Brown, With Drip Glaze 22.50
Cookie Jar, Bugs Bunny Cylinder ....75.00 To 100.00
Cookie Jar, Caboose ....70.00 To 150.00
Cookie Jar, Chiffonier 45.00
Cookie Jar, Chilly Willy 30.00
Cookie Jar, Chipmunk 95.00
Cookie Jar, Christmas Tree .... 360.00 To 580.00
Cookie Jar, Circus Horse ....50.00 To 155.00
Cookie Jar, Clown In Barrel .... 65.00 To 75.00
Cookie Jar, Clown, Bust 45.00
Cookie Jar, Coffee Grinder .... 20.00 To 25.00
Cookie Jar, Cookie Barrel .... 12.00 To 30.00
Cookie Jar, Cookie Boy ....55.00 To 125.00
Cookie Jar, Cookie Cabin .... 40.00 To 55.00
Cookie Jar, Cookie House 65.00
Cookie Jar, Cookie Log 35.00
Cookie Jar, Cookstove, Black .... 20.00 To 35.00
Cookie Jar, Cookstove, White .... 20.00 To 32.50
Cookie Jar, Covered Wagon .... 40.00 To 75.00
Cookie Jar, Dalmatians In Rocking Chair .... 175.00 To 350.00
Cookie Jar, Davy Crockett .... 135.00 To 375.00
Cookie Jar, Duck On Basketweave 45.00
Cookie Jar, Early American Milk Can 40.00
Cookie Jar, Elephant 185.00
Cookie Jar, Engine, Black ....45.00 To 110.00
Cookie Jar, Engine, Yellow 135.00
Cookie Jar, Fireplace 65.00
Cookie Jar, Friendship .... 69.00 To 85.00
Cookie Jar, Friendship 7 ....90.00 To 175.00
Cookie Jar, Frontier Family .... 45.00 To 48.00
Cookie Jar, Globe 210.00
Cookie Jar, Grandfather Clock 55.00
Cookie Jar, Granny .... 45.00 To 55.00
Cookie Jar, Happy Face .... 20.00 To 40.00
Cookie Jar, Have A Happy Day 20.00
Cookie Jar, Hen On Nest 40.00
Cookie Jar, Hobby Horse ....60.00 To 112.00
Cookie Jar, Hocus Rabbit 17.50
Cookie Jar, Honey Bear .... 30.00 To 45.00
Cookie Jar, Hot–Air Balloon 20.00
Cookie Jar, Indian .... 195.00 To 255.00
Cookie Jar, Jack-O'-Lantern 450.00
Cookie Jar, Kangaroo, Blue .... 140.00 To 195.00
Cookie Jar, Kangaroo, Tan 250.00
Cookie Jar, Keebler Treehouse .... 30.00 To 45.00
Cookie Jar, Kookie Kettle 25.00
Cookie Jar, Lamp On Basketweave .... 25.00 To 45.00
Cookie Jar, Leprechaun 350.00
Cookie Jar, Lollipop 40.00
Cookie Jar, Mammy ....65.00 To 125.00
Cookie Jar, Mammy With Cauliflower 250.00
Cookie Jar, Mammy, 1948 .... 140.00
Cookie Jar, Mother Goose ....90.00 To 120.00
Cookie Jar, Mr. & Mrs. Owl .... 50.00 To 95.00
Cookie Jar, Pepper, Green 45.00
Cookie Jar, Picnic Basket 40.00
Cookie Jar, Popeye Cylinder 75.00
Cookie Jar, Pot Belly Stove 35.00
Cookie Jar, Puppy With Sign .... 39.00 To 65.00

Cookie Jar, Quaker Oats	210.00
Cookie Jar, Snoopy	100.00 To 145.00
Cookie Jar, Snow Bear	30.00 To 65.00
Cookie Jar, Squirrel On Stump	35.00
Cookie Jar, Strawberry	25.00 To 40.00
Cookie Jar, Tepee	125.00 To 225.00
Cookie Jar, Thinking Puppy	20.00 To 30.00
Cookie Jar, Touring Car	50.00
Cookie Jar, Tudor Cookie House	90.00
Cookie Jar, Turkey	135.00 To 200.00
Cookie Jar, Two Kittens In Low Basket	250.00
Cookie Jar, Upside Down Bear	75.00
Cookie Jar, W. C. Fields	120.00 To 135.00
Cookie Jar, Wedding Jar	30.00 To 49.00
Cookie Jar, Windmill, Blue	50.00
Cookie Jar, Winking Pig	100.00 To 188.00
Cookie Jar, Wishing Well	40.00
Cookie Jar, World Globe	188.00 To 195.00
Cookie Jar, Wren House	75.00 To 85.00
Cookie Jar, Yosemite Sam, Warner Bros., 1971	225.00
Creamer & Sugar, Daisy, Green, Brown	18.00
Figurine, Dutch Shoe	8.00
Flowerpot, Smiley	4.50
Flowerpot, Vista, Green	10.00
Jardiniere, Rosewood, 9 In.	75.00
Lamp, Black Panther	45.00
Mug, Grapeware, 1926	15.00
Mug, Smiley	4.50
Pitcher, Corn	75.00
Planter, Alligator	16.00 To 26.00
Planter, Bear, Hugging Tree	20.00
Planter, Blossom Time, Yellow	5.00
Planter, Dog, Tan	15.00
Planter, Duck, White	9.00
Planter, Dutch Shoe, Blue	8.00
Planter, Frog, Figural	7.00
Planter, Grist Mill, Gold Letters & Trim	16.00
Planter, Scotty	8.00
Planter, Spinning Wheel, Brown	12.50
Planter, Springwood, Pink, 3–Footed, 6 In.	6.00
Planter, Springwood, White Flowers, Pink Matte, Footed	6.00
Planter, Turtle	14.00 To 18.00
Planter, Uncle Sam, White	12.00
Planter, Wishing Well, Green	6.50
Sprinkler, Turtle	25.00
Stein, Beer, Schlitz, No. 9616	15.00
Stein, Cover, Hunt Scene	30.00
Sugar & Creamer, Elsie & Elmer	65.00
Tankard, Barrel, Shield Mark, 1926	40.00
Teapot, Cat, Figural	35.00
Vase, Double Tulip, Pair	35.00
Vase, Flowers, Brown, Loy–Nel–Art, 1905, 9 In.	150.00
Vase, Harmony, Blue, 8 In.	5.00
Vase, Hyacinth, Pink	16.00
Vase, Jetwood, Tree Scene, Marked Brush McCoy, 12 In.	450.00
Vase, Shoe Shape, Glossy Blue & Green Drip, Aqua, 9 In.	10.00
Vase, Tulip, Yellow, Double	25.00
Wall Pocket, Butterfly, Vase Shape	12.00
Wall Pocket, Flower	12.00
Wall Pocket, Violin	18.00
Water Cooler, Chuck Wagon	195.00
Water Set, Buccaneer, Mugs, 7 Piece	95.00

Medical, Chest, Medicine, Portable,
Inlaid Mahogany, 13 1/2 In.

◆◆◆◆◆◆◆◆◆◆◆◆◆◆◆◆◆◆◆◆◆◆◆◆

For a pollution–free glass
cleaner use a mixture of white
vinegar and water.

◆◆◆◆◆◆◆◆◆◆◆◆◆◆◆◆◆◆◆◆◆◆◆◆

PRESCUT

The McKee name has been associated with various glass enterprises
in the United States since 1836, including J. & F. McKee (1850),
Bryce, McKee & Co. (1850 to 1854), McKee and Brothers (1865),
and National Glass Co. (1899). In 1903, the McKee Glass Company
was formed in Jeanette, Pennsylvania. It became McKee Division of
the Thatcher Glass Co. in 1951 and was bought out by the Jeanette
Corporation in 1961. Pressed glass, kitchenwares, and tablewares
were produced.

MCKEE, see also Custard Glass

MCKEE, Champagne, Rock Crystal, Red	22.00
Coaster, Bottom's Up	12.00
Compote, Crowsfoot, Yale	30.00
Creamer & Sugar	22.00
Pan, Loaf, Jade, 5 x 8 In.	10.00
Pepper Shaker, Roman Arches, Black	4.00
Pitcher, Measuring, Custard, 2 Cup	15.00
Plate, Rock Crystal, Red, 6 3/4 In.	10.00
Plate, Rock Crystal, Silver–Flashed Bottom, 10 1/2 In.	28.00
Salt, Rabbit & Chickens, Moon & Star Top	30.00
Saltshaker, Roman Arches, White	6.00
Tumble–Up, Jade Green	70.00
Vase, Nudes In Relief, Footed, Green, 8 1/2 In.	85.00
Wine, Colonial, Green	40.00
Wine, Rock Crystal, Red, 4 Oz.	22.00
Wine, Sunken Buttons, Blue	38.00

MECHANICAL BANK, see Bank, Mechanical

All types of equipment used by doctors or hospitals are included in
this section. Medical office furniture, operating tools, microscopes,
thermometers, and other paraphernalia used by doctors are included.
Medicine bottles are listed under Bottle. There are related
collectibles listed under Dental.

MEDICAL, Bedpan, White Porcelain, Unused, 1930s, Box	32.00
Bleeder, 2 Blade, Revolutionary War	80.00
Bleeder, Brass, Blade Spring Loaded	295.00
Bleeder, Double Edge Blade, Bone Handle, 1860s, 2 1/2 x 4 In.	75.00
Bleeder, Gold	150.00
Bleeder, Spring Loaded	295.00
Book, Sajou's Analytic Cyclopedia, Practical Medicine, 12 Volumes	110.00
Bottle, Hot Water, Embossed Nursery Rhyme, Box	25.00
Cabinet, Apothecary, Counter Top, 41 Drawers, 24 x 18 In.	390.00
Cabinet, Dr. Daniels Veterinary, Tin Front	1300.00
Cabinet, Humphrey's Remedies, Match Symptoms To Numbers, 38 Slots	375.00
Cabinet, Prescription, Hercules, 6 Drawers	35.00
Case, Apothecary, 24 Drawers, Brass Pulls, 11 1/2 x 28 3/4 In.	1300.00
Chest, 8 Drawers. Apothecary, Iron Pulls, Poplar, 18 x 23 In.	750.00

Chest, Apothecary, 8 Drawers, Porcelain Pulls, Pine, 26 3/4 x 39 In. 550.00
Chest, Apothecary, Brown Sponged Graining, 16 Drawers, Birch 2350.00
Chest, Apothecary, Painted To Simulate Maple, Burl Walnut, 46 In. 6250.00
Chest, Medicine, Drawer, Mahogany, Bottles, 14 x 16 In. 2100.00
Chest, Medicine, Portable, Inlaid Mahogany, 13 1/2 In. ....*Illus* 2300.00
Cooling Board, Mortician's, B. F. Gleason, N. Y., Patent 1881 .... 265.00
Dispenser, Mahogany, Metal, 20 In. 330.00
Dr. Miles Liver Pills 7.00
Drill Set, Brain, Dovetailed Box 400.00
Enema Can, Porcelain, Paper Label 16.00
Eyecup, Clear, Ribbed 12.00
Eyecup, Glasco, Pedestal 10.00
Eyecup, John Bull, Clear, 1917 .... 12.00 To 17.50
Eyecup, John Bull, Green 65.00
Eyecup, Stippled Band, Base Rim 12.00
Eyecup, Vaseline 18.00
Eyecup, Woltra, Flint, Box 20.00
Feeder, Hygienic, Open Ends, Boat Shape 35.00
Fleam Bleeder, Horn 145.00
Fleam Knife 75.00
Hearing Aid, Horn Shape, Tin 110.00
Instrument, 2 Glass Tubes, Adjustable Frame, 19 3/4 In. 300.00
Jar, Leeches, Ceramic, 8 1/2 In. 425.00
Kit, Ultra–Violet, Doctor's, Blue & White Glass, Case 100.00
Microscope, Brass, Ernst Leitz, Wetzlar, 170 mm To 250 mm 165.00
Mirror, Optometrist's, Triple, Counter 35.00
Muscle Developer, Mills, Oak Case 1150.00
Nasal Doucher, Glass, Box, Early 1900s 25.00
Phrenology Head, Baby's 1250.00
Pill Roller, Brass & Walnut, 12 Size, 13 1/2 In. 210.00
Prescription Slip, Reedley Drug Co., Reedley, Ca., 1904, 5 1/2 In. 4.50
Saddlebag, Leather, Apothecary Samples 480.00
Skeleton, Human 1250.00
Spectroscope & Arc Lamp, With Attachments, Pre–1930 .... 600.00
Suppository Maker, Pharmacy, No Handle 96.00
Surgeon's Kit, Army, Henry Levensaler, 8 Maine Volunteers, Wooden 700.00
Surgical Suction & Pressure Pump, Nickel Plated, Wooden Case, 1920 .... 100.00
Table, Examining, Leather Top, Beaded, Large Fluted Oak Legs, 1880 .... 600.00
Table, Undertaker's, Cooling, Oak & Canvas 30.00

Meerschaum pipes and other pieces of carved meerschaum, a soft mineral, date from the nineteenth century to the present.

MEERSCHAUM, Pipe, Black Person, Sterling Band, Amber Stem, 6 1/4 In. 412.00
Pipe, Dog, Case, Miniature 65.00
Pipe, Fashionable Woman, Sterling Band, Amber Stem, 5 1/2 In. 175.00
Pipe, Group of Revelers Around Floral Base 6600.00
Pipe, Horse, Amber Stem 85.00
Pipe, Indian Chief, Full Headdress, Amber Stem, 3 1/8 In. 310.00
Pipe, Oriental Sailor & Compass, Amber Stem, 3 1/4 In. 145.00
Pipe, Pack of Playful Fox Kits, Fitted Case, 3 x 8 In. 165.00
Pipe, Risque Nude, Amber Stem, Case, 10 In. 410.00
Pipe, Sultan Head Bowl, 13 1/2 In. 110.00

Meissen is a town in Germany where porcelain has been made since 1710. Any china made in the town can be called Meissen, although the famous Meissen factory made the finest porcelains of the area. The crossed swords mark of the great Meissen factory has been copied by many other firms in Germany and other parts of the world.

MEISSEN, Beaker & Saucer, Chinese Woman Holding Birdcage, c.1725, 3 In. 3300.00
Bowl, Cover, Floral Sprig Handle On Domed Cover, 1750s, 7 In. 880.00
Bowl, Gold & White Rose Design, Cobalt Ground, Marked, 12 3/8 In. 165.00
Bowl, Portrait Center, Pink & Gold Rim, Crossed Swords, 12 3/8 In. 175.00

Meissen, Figurine, Winter, Bearded Man, Naked, Cloak, 8 7/8 In.

Meissen, Group, Winter, Gray–Bearded Man, Cupid, 10 5/16 In.

Meissen, Group, Allegorical, 2 Cupids, c.1755, 5 5/8 In.

Bust, Child, Floral Bonnet, Feather & Bow, Marked, 6 In.	440.00
Bust, Child, Floral Corsage, Headdress, Marked, 6 In.	495.00
Bust, Young Girl, Double Mark	1500.00
Cake Stand, Floral, Crossed Swords, 13 1/4 x 4 1/4 In.	115.00
Candelabra, 2–Light, Eagle Behind Female Figure, 14 7/8 In.	880.00
Candle Snuffer, Gold Knob Finial, Floral Border	150.00
Candlestick, Rose & White, Gilt, Marked, c.1880, 12 In., Pair	125.00
Charger, Floral Center & Border, Gilt, Marked, 11 3/4 In.	220.00
Chess Set, Marine Life, Max Esser, 1925	4750.00
Clock, Desk, Fusee Works, Polychrome, 18th Century, 3 In.	1500.00
Coffee & Tea Set, Dragon, c.1895, Service For 8, 29 Piece	3750.00
Coffeepot, Floral, Gilt Trim, 10 In.	200.00
Cup & Saucer, Floral, With Buildings & Gilt, Crossed Swords	50.00
Desk Set, Tray, Sander, Ink Pot, Blue Floral, White, Gilt Trim, 3 Pc.	175.00
Dish, 4–Section Design, Gilt, Crossed Swords, Square, 10 3/4 In.	200.00
Dish, Rose, Foliate, Gilt Scrolling, 10 In.	250.00 To 275.00
Ewer, Figure of The Wind, Goddess, Three Cherubs, 24 In. ....*Illus*	3000.00
Ewer, Neptune & Juno, Flattened Oviform, 26 1/2 In., Pair	8800.00
Figurine, Athena, Spear, Head of Medusa On Shield, Marked, 5 5/8 In.	440.00
Figurine, Ballerina, Miniature	195.00
Figurine, Boy With Rake, Girl With Basket, Marked, 6 In., Pair	410.00
Figurine, Cherub On Skull, Crossed Swords, 7 In.	1000.00
Figurine, Child, Toy Horse, Newspaper Hat Dated 1905, 6 5/8 In.	650.00
Figurine, Child, With Dog, Crossed Swords, 6 1/4 In.	650.00
Figurine, Cupid, Fettered, 7 1/4 In.	750.00
Figurine, Cupid, Hand Painted, On Plinth, Marked, 7 1/2 In.	715.00
Figurine, Cupid, Holding Garland of Flowers, c.1890, 3 1/4 In.	325.00
Figurine, Dancing Girl, M 415, 10 In.	595.00
Figurine, Horse Trainer, Holding Reins, Marked, 10 In.	330.00
Figurine, Hunchback, With Staff, 5 1/2 In.	325.00
Figurine, Man & Woman, Crossed Swords Mark, 28 In., Pair ....*Illus*	7700.00

Meissen, Ewer, Figure of The Wind, Goddess, Three Cherubs, 24 In.

Meissen, Figurine, Man & Woman, Crossed Swords Mark, 28 In., Pair

Meissen, Tureen, Floral, Cherubs Cover, 15 In.

* *

Rubber cement solvent, available at art supply and office supply
stores, has many uses. Put a few drops on a paper towel and rub off
ink smudges, adhesive tape glue, and label glue from glass or
porcelains.

* *

Figurine, Pair of Shoes, Cherubs, Crossed Swords, 5 5/8 In., Pair	1000.00
Figurine, Regal Woman In Chair, Gray Hair, Miniature	295.00
Figurine, Standing Allegorical Woman, With Bird, Marked, 11 In.	715.00
Figurine, Wind, Child Holding Bird, To Place In Cage, Marked, 5 In.	660.00
Figurine, Winter, Bearded Man, Naked, Cloak, 8 7/8 In. ....*Illus*	1300.00
Figurine, Woman & Man, In Chair, Miniature	230.00
Gravy Boat, Ladle, Underplate, Double Handle, Floral Swirling	110.00
Group, Allegorical, 2 Cupids, c.1755, 5 5/8 In. ....*Illus*	1100.00
Group, Cherub Gardener, Crossed Swords, 4 3/4 In.	300.00
Group, Children Working Wine Press, Various Poses, Marked, 13 In.	2750.00
Group, Children, Playing In Classical Ruins, 10 3/4 In.	425.00
Group, Europa and The Bull, 12 In.	2000.00
Group, Harlequin Family, Marked, 7 1/4 In.	1870.00
Group, Putti Feeding Grapes To Billy Goat, c.1850, 6 In.	495.00
Group, Putti With Rabbit, 4 3/4 In.	275.00
Group, Shepherd & Shepherdess Lovers, Marked, 7 1/2 In.	1870.00
Group, Winter, Gray–Bearded Man, Cupid, 10 5/16 In. ....*Illus*	885.00
Mirror, Cherub, Flowers, Hanging, Crossed Swords, 9 In.	600.00
Plaque, 18th–Century Couple, Bisque, 1930, 11 x 13 In.	65.00
Plate, Birds & Flowers, Marked, 10 In., 8 Piece	1750.00
Plate, Fowls & Birds Center, Bugs & Beetles On Edge, Marked, 9 In.	275.00
Plate, Leaf Shape, Blue, Gold, White, Marked, 9 3/4 In. .... 185.00 To	195.00
Plate, Leaf–On–Leaf Pattern, Cobalt Blue, White & Gold, 9 3/4 In.	185.00
Plate, Multicolored Floral, Insect Design, Scroll & Lattice, 8 In.	775.00
Plate, Scalloped, Floral, Crossed Swords, 10 3/8 In.	145.00
Plate, Weave Pattern, Fruit Centers, 9 3/4 In., 12 Piece	935.00
Platter, Birds & Flowers, Marked, 10 3/4 x 15 In.	1320.00
Platter, Birds & Flowers, Marked, 12 x 17 In.	1210.00
Platter, Birds & Flowers, Marked, 13 x 10 1/2 In.	665.00
Salt, Double, Center Figure Holding Florets, Marked, 5 3/4 In., Pair	935.00
Salt, Figural, 2 Turks, 2 Maidens, Holding Bowls, 7 In., 4 Piece	2100.00
Sauce Boat, Floral, Gilt, Crossed Swords, 10 1/4 In.	150.00
Stein, Hand–Painted Scene, Applied Flower & Leaves, 1900, 1 Liter	1750.00
Tea Set, Floral & Insect Design, Crossed Sword, 7 Piece	1400.00
Tea Set, Gold On Embossed Green Design, Marked, Small, 3 Piece	490.00
Tray, Floral Bouquet, S–Scroll Rim, Shell Corner, 15 1/2 In.	440.00
Tureen, Floral, Cherubs Cover, 15 In. ....*Illus*	2000.00
Urn, Double–Scroll Handles, Rose Cluster, Gilt Banded, 19 In.	775.00
Urn, Palace, Domed Pierced Cover, Encrusted With Flowers, 31 In.	935.00
Vase, Trumpet Shape, Green Ivy, 5 1/2 In.	125.00
Waste Bowl, Puce & Gold Florals, 5 5/8 In.	350.00

Mercury, or silvered, glass was first made in the 1850s. It lost favor
for a while but became popular again about 1910. It looks like a
piece of silver.

MERCURY GLASS, Candlestick, 8 In., Pair	130.00
Compote, 8 In.	45.00
Compote, Vintage Design	30.00
Dish, Leaf	10.00
Eggcup	15.00
Mug, Child's, Christmas, Green	45.00
Tieback, Embossed Flower, Pewter Fittings, 3 1/2 In., Pair	65.00

The Merrimac Pottery Company was founded by Thomas Nickerson in Newburyport, Massachusetts, in 1902. The company made art pottery, garden pottery, and reproductions of Roman pottery. The pottery burned to the ground in 1908.

MERRIMAC, Bowl, Flaring To Angled Shoulder, Matte Green, Speckled, 6 In.	275.00
Bowl, Pink, Crackled, Squat, 2 1/4 x 5 In.	192.00
Bowl, Stylized Blossoms, Lily Pads, Dark Green, 5 1/4 x 8 1/2 In.	1540.00
Vase, Stylized Broad Leaves & Buds, Green Matte Glaze, 6 x 5 In.	880.00

Mettlach, Germany, is a city where the Villeroy and Boch factories worked. Steins from the firm are known as Mettlach steins. They date from about 1842. PUG means *painted under glaze*. The steins can be dated from the marks on the bottom which include a date–number code. Other pieces may be listed in the Villeroy & Boch category.

METTLACH, Beaker, No. 1134/2327, 1/4 Liter, Couple At Feast, PUG	110.00
Beaker, No. 1179/2327, 1/4 Liter, Gesang, PUG	87.00
Coaster, No. 2818, Smoker Toasting, Verse, 4 1/2 In.	237.00
Mug, Hire's Root Beer, Boy With Bib	175.00
Mug, Minneapolis Brewing	125.00
Mug, South Bend Brewing Assoc., Factory Scene	220.00
Pitcher, No. 1513, Scene of Couples Dancing, Warth, 6 1/4 In.	305.00
Pitcher, No. 7012, Nude Figures, Blue Ground, 12 In.	650.00
Plaque, 2 Boys, One With Flute, One With Mandolin, 1898, 10 In.	635.00
Plaque, No. 1004/167, Berlin Castle, PUG, 15 In.	260.00
Plaque, No. 1607, Woman Carrying Baskets of Fruit, 1885, 12 In.	525.00
Plaque, No. 2442, Cameo, Trojan Warriors In Boat, 1899, 19 In.	1250.00
Plaque, No. 5036, Hannover, 17 1/2 In.	225.00
Plaque, No. 7045, Phanolith, Young Man & Maiden, 15 1/2 x 8 In.	330.00
Plate, No. 2960, Art Nouveau, Etched, 15 In.	87.00
Punch Bowl, No. 2087, 8 Liter, Underplate, Dancing People, 15 In.	1150.00
Punch Bowl, No. 2280/1005, 2 Liter, King, Gnomes At Wine Press	375.00
Punch Bowl, No. 2633/1089, 7 2/5 Liter, Dancing Scene	100.00
Stein, No. 1037, 1/2 Liter, Man Drinking	134.00
Stein, No. 1076, 1/2 Liter, Skeet Shooters, PUG	375.00
Stein, No. 1132, 1/2 Liter, Fiddler & Dancing Crocodile	585.00
Stein, No. 1191, Cavalier On Horseback, 19 In. *Illus*	550.00
Stein, No. 1338, 1 1/10 Liter, Floral	300.00 To 325.00
Stein, No. 1396, 1/2 Liter, Drinking Nymph	425.00
Stein, No. 1526, 1/2 Liter, Woman, Foliage, Stag	225.00
Stein, No. 1650, 1 Liter, Tapestry, Hunter With Knapsack	365.00
Stein, No. 1734, 2 1/10 Liter, Lovers	1050.00 To 1150.00
Stein, No. 1740, 1/4 Liter, Applied Hopps Buds & Vines, Verse	116.00
Stein, No. 1905, 1/2 Liter, Regimental Guard	385.00
Stein, No. 1909, 1/2 Liter, Walsheim Tavern, Art Deco	150.00
Stein, No. 1916, 2 1/4 Liter, Tavern Scene, Pewter Lid *Illus*	1320.00

Mettlach, Stein, No. 1191, Cavalier On Horseback, 19 In.
Mettlach, Stein, No. 1916, 2 1/4 Liter, Tavern Scene, Pewter Lid
Mettlach, Stein, No. 2692, 2 Liter, Musician, Pewter Lid
Mettlach, Stein, No. 2270, 2 Liter, Women & Soldier, Pewter Lid

Mettlach, Stein, No. 2038, 3 4/5 Liter, Town of Rodenstein
Mettlach, Stein, No. 2796, 3 Liter, Scene of Heidelberg

Stein, No. 2035, 1/2 Liter, Bacchus 425.00
Stein, No. 2038, 3 4/5 Liter, Town of Rodenstein ....*Illus* 2500.00
Stein, No. 2077, 3/10 Liter, Coat of Arms, Blue, Inlaid Lid 110.00
Stein, No. 2204, 1 Liter, Blue Max, Prussian 800.00
Stein, No. 2270, 2 Liter, Women & Soldier, Pewter Lid ....*Illus* 880.00
Stein, No. 2278, 1/2 Liter, Men In Sporting Event, Pewter Lid 330.00
Stein, No. 2358, 1/2 Liter, Drink & Dance Scene, Ear of Corn On Lid 219.00
Stein, No. 2481, 1 2/5 Liter, Hildebrand Aiding Wounded Knights 880.00
Stein, No. 2692, 2 Liter, Musician, Pewter Lid ....*Illus* 1320.00
Stein, No. 2715, 1/2 Liter, Cameo, Couples Dancing, Pewter Lid 578.00
Stein, No. 2796, 3 Liter, Scene of Heidelberg ....*Illus* 650.00
Stein, No. 2882, 1/2 Liter, Thirsty Rider, Marked, 9 1/2 In. 880.00
Stein, No. 2931, 1/2 Liter, Verse, Man & Woman 175.00
Stein, No. 2956, 3 1/10 Liter, Bowling Scene 700.00
Stein, No. 5022, 1 Liter, Rural Scene 1201.00
Stein, No. 5024, 1 Liter, Faience, Floral, Fancy Pewter Mounts 936.00
Tobacco Jar, No. 3025, Elf, King 395.00
Tumbler, Fisherman .... 58.00 To 65.00
Urn, No. 7077, Last Event, Persian Blue, Ivory Greek Gods 800.00
Vase, No. 2242, Classical Maidens, Birds, Signed, 14 In., Pair 800.00

 Milk glass was named for its milky white color. It was first made in England during the 1700s. The height of its popularity in the United States was from 1870 to 1880. It is now correct to refer to some colored glass as blue milk glass, black milk glass, etc. Reproductions of milk glass are being made and sold in many stores.

MILK GLASS, see also Cosmos; Vallerysthal

MILK GLASS, Bell, White Smoke, 7 1/2 In. 15.00
Bottle, Matador 85.00
Bottle, Whiskey, Red Lettering, Old Homestead Bourbon, 1/2 Pt. 195.00
Bowl, Acanthus, Melon, Atterbury 75.00
Bowl, Carolina Dogwood, Marigold 295.00
Bread Plate, Basket Weave, Motto, Pat. June 30, 1874 .... 65.00
Butter, Cover, Daisy & Button, Lacy Edge 50.00
Butter, Cover, Sawtooth, Flint .... 75.00 To 85.00
Butter, Cover, Sugar & Creamer, Gold Trim, Guttate 135.00
Can, Sprinkling, Blue, Cover, 4 In. 85.00
Candlestick, Dolphin, 4 1/8 In., Pair 15.00
Candy Box, Cover, Heart Shape, 3 Sections, 1950s 45.00
Compote, Basket Weave, Scalloped, Low Standard, Pat. 1874, 9 In. 50.00
Compote, Cover, Waffle, Green 145.00
Cracker Jar, Cover, Tree of Life, Olive Green 185.00
Creamer, Holly With Cord & Tassel 65.00
Creamer, Lacy Dewdrop 15.00
Creamer, Minerva 45.00
Creamer, Paneled Wheat 30.00
Cruet, Apple Blossom, Blue Neck 90.00
Darner, Ribbed Handle 68.00
Dish, American Eagle Cover 85.00
Dish, American Hen Cover 30.00
Dish, Bird & Strawberry Cover, Footed, 5 In. 35.00
Dish, Bull's Head Cover 165.00
Dish, Cat Cover, 1889 .... 130.00
Dish, Cat Cover, On Lacy Base, Blue, Blue Eyes 95.00
Dish, Cat Cover, On Ribbed Base 65.00
Dish, Chicks On Egg Cover, Basket Weave Base, 6 1/2 x 6 1/2 In. 150.00
Dish, Crouching Fox Cover, Oval, 8 x 6 1/2 In. 160.00
Dish, Dewey Cover 32.00
Dish, Dolphin Cover, Blue 30.00
Dish, Duck On Basket Weave Cover 95.00
Dish, Eagle On Nest, Westmoreland, 1970–80 .... 45.00
Dish, Football, Cover 90.00
Dish, Hen Cover, Flaccus 140.00

Dish, Hen On Nest, Hazel Atlas 12.50
Dish, Lamb On Basket Weave Cover 65.00
Dish, Maine Cover 65.00
Dish, Mother Eagle Cover 500.00
Dish, Pekingese Dog Cover 475.00
Dish, Pineapple Cover 95.00
Dish, Rabbit Cover, 1886 .... 175.00
Dish, Reclining Fox Cover, Glass Eyes, 6 1/2 x 8 In. 160.00
Dish, Robin On Nest Cover 110.00
Dish, Rooster Cover, Red Comb, Yellow Feet 35.00
Dish, Rooster On Nest, Large 45.00
Dish, Squirrel On Acorn Cover 165.00
Dish, Squirrel On Acorn, Blue 32.00
Dish, Swan Cover, Glass Eyes 145.00
Dresser Set, Raised Florals, 2 Cologne Bottles, 2 Boxes, Tray 135.00
Eggcup, Double, Leaf Garland, 4 Piece 95.00
Epergne, Hand-Painted Flowers, American, 1880, 14 x 10 In. 350.00
Figurine, Cat In Shoe, 4 In. 15.00
Fruit Bowl, Lattice Rim, 9 1/2 In. 60.00
Goblet, Etched Birds & Roses 35.00
Goblet, Etched Lily-of-The-Valley 22.00
Goblet, Owl & Possum 80.00
Guttate, Butter, Cover, Pink 125.00
Guttate, Table Set, Gold Trim, 4 Piece 325.00
Hat, Panama 45.00
Hat, Uncle Sam's, Philadelphia Expo, 36 Stars, 1876, 2 1/2 In. 150.00
Holder, Calling Card, Hand, Holding Fan, Standing 26.00
Jar, Apothecary, Viking, Stopper 65.00
Jar, Eagle 95.00
Jar, Owl 110.00
Jug, Mephistopheles 75.00
Jug, Topeka, Kansas, 2-Tone, Miniature 30.00
Kittens, Plate 45.00
Lamp, Art Nouveau, Draped Nude 125.00
Lamp, Floral Transfer, Umbrella Shade, Pair 165.00
Lamp, Heart Finger 95.00
Lamp, Owl, Green Paint, Miniature 1775.00
Match Holder, Grape & Leaf 25.00
Match Holder, Grape Panel 18.00
Match Holder, Indian Head, White 110.00
Mug, Liberty Bell, 2 In. 180.00
Mug, Mephistopheles 35.00
Mustard, Bull's Head, White 125.00
Nappy, Maple Leaf 12.00
Pin Tray, Full Figure Rabbit, 5 5/8 x 3 3/4 In. 35.00
Pitcher, Diamond, c.1860, 6 1/2 In. 55.00
Pitcher, Owl, 7 1/4 In. .... 110.00 To 155.00
Pitcher, Water, Beaded Circle, Applied Handle 68.00
Pitcher, Water, Royal Oak, Applied Handle, Pink Neck 200.00
Plate, 3 Owls, Dated 1901 .... 30.00
Plate, Little Red Hen 49.00
Plate, Owl Lovers 55.00
Plate, Robert Burns, Thistle Border, 10 In. 55.00
Platter, Rock of Ages 125.00
Powder Box, Blown-Out Flowers, Woman, Victorian, Square 90.00
Powder Jar, Fluting & Shells 12.00
Powder Jar, Heart Shape, Victorian, On Tray 95.00
Punch Bowl, Nursery Rhyme 125.00
Punch Cup, Nursery Rhyme 35.00
Punch Set, Paneled Grape, Bowl, Base, Ladle, 12 Cups 675.00
Ray, Scrolls, Flowers, With Loving Easter Thoughts, 10 x 6 In. 45.00
Relish, Daisy & Button, Heart Shape, Lillie In Center 32.00
Rose Bowl, Doric Border, Westmoreland, 6 1/2 In. 28.00

Salt & Pepper, Brass, Farberware 35.00
Sauce, Crossed Fern, Footed 12.00
Shade, Hanging, 14 In. 55.00
Spooner, Blackberry 75.00
Spooner, Swan 35.00
Sprinkling Can, Metal Bail 85.00
Sugar & Creamer, 10 x 5–In. Tray, Brass, Farberware 55.00
Sugar Shaker, Pinched Center, Hand Painted Flowers 60.00
Sugar Shaker, Wild Iris 45.00
Sugar, Cover, Gothic Arch 225.00
Sugar, Cover, Ribbed Lacy Edge, Millard 55.00
Sugar, Cover, Sawtooth, Flint 65.00
Syrup, Banded Shells, 5 3/8 In. 65.00
Syrup, Daisy & Palm, Original Top 65.00
Syrup, Leaf Mold .... 210.00 To 255.00
Syrup, Netted Oak, Gold Paint 85.00
Syrup, Scroll 25.00
Table Set, Guttate, Gold Trim, 4 Piece 285.00
Tea Set, Doll's, c.1920, 7 Piece 50.00
Toothpick, Boy In Knickers 23.00
Toothpick, Bundled Cigars 12.00
Toothpick, Vermont, Decal 55.00
Tray, Water, Stippled Forget–Me–Not, Flamingo, Foliage Center 125.00
Tray, With Loving Easter Thoughts, Gold Trim, Scrolls, 10 In. 45.00
Vase, Victorian, Flowers & Castle, Tapestry Design, 7 1/4 In. 135.00

Millefiori means, literally, a thousand flowers. It is a type of glasswork popular in paperweights. Many small flowerlike pieces of glass are grouped together to form a design.

MILLEFIORI, Box, Domed Cover, Ormolu Hinge, 5 3/8 In. 250.00
Rose Bowl, Art Glass 149.00
Salt, White Loops, Crystal Skirt, 3 In. 95.00
Toothpick, Fluted, 2 1/2 In. 35.00
Toothpick, Octagon Shape 95.00

Minton china has been made in the Staffordshire region of England from 1793 to the present. The firm became part of the Royal Doulton Tableware Group in 1968, but the wares continued to be marked *Minton.* Many marks have been used. The one shown dates from about 1873 to 1891, when the word *England* was added.

MINTON, Butter, Cover, Goat Finial, Musical Instruments Border, 1867 .... 7000.00
Dish, Sweetmeat, Boy & Girl Holding Basket, Pair 2800.00
Figurine, Vintage With Basket, S, Majolica, 1864, 15 1/2 In. 2650.00
Game Plate, Majolica, 1868, 14 In. ....*Illus* 1430.00
Group, Three Graces, Parian 1600.00
Plate, Embossed Bust of Shakespeare, Salt Glaze, 12 3/4 In. 30.00
Plate, Gilt Border Design, Green & Ivory Ground, 10 1/2 In., 12 Pc. 360.00
Plate, Multicolored Geometric & Floral Design, 10 1/4 In., 8 Piece 70.00
Tile, Bird & Nest, 6 x 6 In. 20.00
Tile, Cow In Cowshed, William Wise, Brown & White, 1879, 6 x 6 In. 95.00
Tile, Nursing Mother In Field, Twisted–Wire Frame, Dated 1876 .... 125.00
Tile, Romeo & Juliet, Act II, Scene II, J. Smith, c.1873, 6 x 6 In. 95.00
Tile, Scenic, Hingham, Mass. 29.00
Tile, Swan With Cygnet, Framed, 6 x 6 In. 210.00
Underplate, Flow Blue, Rust, Pate–Sur–Pate Sides, 1867, 8 In. 75.00
Vase, Lily of The Valley, Biscuit Blossoms, c.1830, 5 In., Pair 1925.00
Vase, Lily of The Valley, Scroll–Edge Base, c.1860, 4 7/8 In., Pair 1100.00
Wine Cooler, Majolica, c.1865, 14 In. ....*Illus* 2640.00
     MIRROR, see Furniture, Mirror

Mocha, Jug, Blue &
Olive Stripes, 8 In.

Mocha, Jug, Tree & Dot,
Banded & Impressed, 8 1/4 In.

Mocha, Jug, White Curving
Lines On Brown, 6 3/4 In.

 Mochaware is an English–made product that was sold in America during the early 1800s. It is a heavy pottery with pale coffee–and–cream coloring. Designs of blue, brown, green, orange, black, or white were added to the pottery.

MOCHA, Bowl, Black Seaweed Design, Green Ribs At Rim, 3 1/2 x 7 1/4 In.	250.00
Bowl, Earthworm On White Band, Stripes, Vertical Rib Band, 7 3/8 In.	125.00
Bowl, Embossed Green Band, Black Seaweed, 6 1/4 In.	450.00
Bowl, Marbelized Design, Embossed Green Band, 2 1/4 x 4 3/8 In.	650.00
Chamber Pot, Cat's–Eye Design, Leaf Handle, 8 x 9 In.	500.00
Crock, Butter, Seaweed Design	175.00
Cup & Saucer, Black Seaweed, Beige Ground, White Interior	400.00
Cup & Saucer, Handleless, Seaweed Designs On Orange Ground	1300.00
Jug, Blue & Green Striped Design, 8 In.	275.00
Jug, Blue & Olive Stripes, 8 In. *Illus*	275.00
Jug, Dot & Wave Pattern In White, Banded, 7 In.	385.00
Jug, Dot Pattern, Brown & White, White Underglaze, 7 In.	1100.00
Jug, Tree & Dot, Banded & Impressed, 8 1/4 In. *Illus*	2530.00
Jug, White Curving Lines On Brown, 6 3/4 In. *Illus*	880.00
Mug, Black Seaweed On Blue Band, 4 3/4 In.	150.00
Mug, Black Seaweed On Tan Band, 6 1/4 In.	75.00
Mug, Blue Band, Alternating Black Stripes, 1830–40, 6 1/4 In.	325.00
Mug, Blue Seaweed Band, Brown Band Border, 3 x 4 In.	475.00
Mug, Checkerboard Pattern, Smoke Design, 6 In.	775.00
Mug, Cider, Blue Band, c.1860, 5 3/4 In.	395.00
Mug, Cover, Stripes, Black Seaweed, Leaf Handle, 4 3/8 In.	700.00
Mug, Gray Band, Blue Stripes, Leaf Handle, 2 5/8 In.	40.00
Mug, Green Seaweed Design, White Band, 3 3/4 In.	150.00
Mustard, Blue Bands, Cat's–Eye & Stripes, 3 7/8 In.	1200.00
Mustard, Cover, Earthworm Design, Stripes, Leaf Handle, 2 1/4 In.	375.00
Mustard, Gray Band, Black Seaweed Stripes, 2 In.	35.00

Minton, Game Plate, Majolica, 1868, 14 In.

Minton, Wine Cooler, Majolica, c.1865, 14 In.

Pitcher, Black Seaweed Design, Blue Ribs, Leaf Handle, 6 7/8 In. 400.00
Pitcher, Blue Worming Band, Brown Ground, 6 In. 990.00
Pitcher, Brown Seaweed Design, Embossed Leaf Handle, 7 3/8 In. 1100.00
Pitcher, Cat's-Eye Design, Leaf Garland, Leaf Spout & Handles, 8 In. 875.00
Pitcher, Earthworm Design, Ecru & Sienna Ground, 8 In. 1650.00
Pitcher, Embossed Horizontal Ribs, Green Rim Band, 4 1/4 In. 85.00
Pitcher, Floral Seaweed, Banded 795.00
Pitcher, Herringbone Bands, Cat's Eye & Earthworm, Leaf Handle, 7 In. 1450.00
Pitcher, Orange & White Cat's Eye & Worming, Brown Ground, 7 In. 715.00
Potty, Child's, Seaweed, Band 175.00
Salt, Footed, Blue Seaweed Design, 2 1/8 In. 275.00
Shaker, Black Seaweed Design, Gray Band, 4 1/4 In. 200.00
Shaker, Embossed Green Band, Stripes, Foliage Design, 4 In. 800.00
Shaker, Green Stripe, Bands & Stripes of White, 4 1/4 In. 700.00
Teapot, Marbelized Brown, Embossed Blue Ribs, 4 7/8 In. 1025.00
Waste Bowl, Earthworm Design On White Band, Stripes, 6 1/4 In. 800.00
Waste Bowl, Earthworm Design, Green Rim, Brown Stripes, 5 1/4 In. 700.00

Monmouth Pottery Company started working in Monmouth, Illinois, in 1892. The pottery made a variety of utilitarian wares. They became part of Western Stoneware Company in 1906. The maple leaf mark was used until 1930. If the word *Co.* appears as part of the mark, the piece was made before 1906.

MONMOUTH, Cookie Jar, Cookie Jug .... 20.00 To 25.00
Figurine, Pig, Brown Glaze, Label, 7 1/2 In. 400.00
Pitcher, Shell Pattern, Brown, 6 In. 22.00
    MONT JOYE, see Mt. Joye

William Moorcroft managed the art pottery department for James MacIntyre & Company of England from 1898 to 1913. In 1913, he started his own company, Moorcroft Pottery, in Burslem, England. He died in 1945, but the company continues. The earlier wares are similar to those made today, but color and marking will help indicate the age.

MOORCROFT, Bowl, Blue Exterior, Orchids & White Flowers, Interior, 7 3/8 In. 375.00
Bowl, Deep Purple Pansies, Blue & Green Ring, 9 In. 615.00
Bowl, Mauve, Yellow Freesia, Green Ground, c.1935, 8 In. 310.00
Bowl, Pomegranate & Grape Exterior, 7 In. 475.00
Bowl, Purple & Yellow Flowers, Olive Green, Label, 5 3/4 In. 110.00
Bowl, Red & Yellow Orchid, Green & Blue, Label, 4 1/4 In. 83.50
Bowl, Spanish Design, c.1910, 6 1/4 In. 975.00
Box, Cover, Red & Yellow Hibiscus, 6 In. 250.00
Candlestick, Cobalt Blue, Pink & Yellow Floral, 3 3/8 In., Pair 65.00
Candlestick, Pomegranate, c.1918, 7 1/8 In., Pair 675.00
Compote, Dahlias, Olive Green, Marked, 7 x 3 1/2 In. 104.50
Ginger Jar, Multicolored Dahlias, Cobalt Blue, Signed, 6 In. 425.00
Potpourri, Cover, Pomegranate & Pansy, c.1905, 5 In. 1100.00
Vase, Assorted Flowers, Blue-Green, Marked, 4 1/4 In. 82.50
Vase, Berry & Leaves, Blues & Creams, Signed, c.1935, 9 3/4 In. 665.00
Vase, Clematis, Flambe Glaze, 5 In. 325.00
Vase, Cornflowers, Red, Brown & Green, c.1913, 8 1/2 In. 2300.00
Vase, Floral, 5 In. 125.00
Vase, Florian Design of Tulips, MacIntyre, c.1903, 7 1/4 In. 1000.00
Vase, Florian Ware, Shades of Blue, Raised Slip, 7 In. 885.00
Vase, Forget-Me-Nots, Cream Ground, MacIntyre, 8 1/8 In. 750.00
Vase, Fruit, Blue, Squatty, 3 1/2 In. 165.00
Vase, Grape & Leaf, c.1930, 12 1/2 In. 975.00
Vase, Indigo Blue, Apples & Blueberries, 8 In. ....*Illus* 220.00
Vase, Iris, Green Leaf Design, Blue Ground, Signed, 1915, 8 1/2 In. 1200.00
Vase, Mushroom, Blue & Green Ground, 4 In. 550.00
Vase, Orange Hibiscus, Green Ground, 7 In. 250.00
Vase, Orchid Design, Blue-Green, Stamped, 4 In. 110.00
Vase, Pomegranate & Pansy, Signed, c.1915, 8 1/4 In. 995.00

Moorcroft, Vase, Red, Purple, Flowers, Green, Blue Underglaze, 8 In.
Moorcroft, Vase, Indigo Blue, Apples & Blueberries, 8 In.

Vase, Pomegranate & Pansy, Signed, c.1925, 4 3/4 In.	192.00
Vase, Pomegranate Design, c.1920, 4 1/4 In.	355.00
Vase, Pomegranate, c.1913, 8 In.	325.00
Vase, Pomegranate, c.1913, Marked, 7 1/8 In., Pair	675.00
Vase, Poppies, Art Pottery, 4 1/2 In.	65.00
Vase, Raspberry–Colored Pansies, Cobalt Blue, Signed	885.00
Vase, Red Poppies, Blue Forget–Me–Nots, White Ground, 6 In.	1350.00
Vase, Red, Purple, Flowers, Green, Blue Underglaze, 8 In. ....*Illus*	286.00
Vase, Spanish Design, Orchid On Blue Ground, 6 3/4 x 8 In.	495.00
Vase, Stick, Poppy Design, Green, Marked, 3 1/4 In.	55.00
Vase, Various Flowers, Cobalt Blue, Signed In Green, 7 1/2 In.	357.00

Some types of Japanese pottery and porcelain are decorated with a special type of raised decoration known as moriage. Sometimes pieces of clay were shaped by hand and applied to the item; sometimes the clay was squeezed from a tube in the way we apply cake frosting. One type of moriage is called dragonware and is listed under that name.

MORIAGE, Ashtray, Flowers Around Rim, Building In Center, 5 In.	65.00
Bowl, Marbelized Medallions, Beading, Scalloped, Footed, 8 In.	189.00
Bowl, Marbelized Medallions, Jeweling, Footed, 8 In.	165.00
Box, Floral Reserve On Cover, Reserves On Box, 2 x 4 In.	110.00
Cup & Saucer, Flowers, Purple, Burgundy, Lavender, Pinks, Demitasse	48.00
Ewer, Grape Clusters Over Orchids, Dark Green Ground, 8 In.	225.00
Jar, Tobacco, Colorful, 7 In.	225.00
Pitcher, Net Over Rose Ground, Beading, 6 1/4 In.	55.00
Plaque, Fronds & Pods, Pierced, 8 1/2 I.	185.00
Sugar & Creamer, Gray Daisies, Lavender & Blue Ground	185.00
Teapot, Daisies	450.00
Vase, Flowers, Blue–Green Ground, Wishbone Handles, 9 1/2 In.	195.00
Vase, Red, Yellow & Red Roses, Bottle Shape, 10 In.	175.00

◆◆

Sunlight and heat can harm most antiques. Wood, paper, textiles, glass, ivory, leather, and many other organic materials will discolor, fade, or crack. Cover sunny windows with blinds or curtains or apply a sun–filtering plastic coating to the windows. These coatings can be found at hardware and window stores, or installed by special companies listed in the Yellow Pages. Information is available from museums or art conservators.

◆◆

The Mosaic Tile Company of Zanesville, Ohio, was started by Karl Langerbeck and Herman Mueller in 1894. Many types of plain and ornamental tiles were made until 1959. The company closed in 1967. The company also made some ashtrays, bookends, and related gift wares. Most pieces are marked with the entwined MTC monogram.

MOSAIC TILE CO., Ashtray–Matchbox Holder, Gray 10.00
  Cookie Jar, Mammy .... 289.00 To 400.00
  Figurine, Black Bear 125.00
  Plaque, Viking Ship, Denmark, 48 1/2 x 12 1/2 In. 250.00

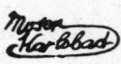

Moser glass is made by Ludwig Moser und Sohne, a Bohemian glasshouse founded in 1857. Art Nouveau–type glassware and iridescent glassware were made. The most famous Moser glass is decorated with heavy enameling in gold and bright colors. The firm is still working in Czechoslovakia. Few pieces of Moser glass are marked.

MOSER, Bell, Cranberry, Signed 250.00
  Bottle, Floral Design, Wide Body, Tapered Neck, 6 1/2 In. 605.00
  Bowl, Cut–Back Gilded Floral Border, Amethyst Footed, Signed, 6 In. 245.00
  Bowl, Figures of Fish Each Side, Malachite, Signed, 8 1/2 In. 425.00
  Bowl, Fish & Aquatic Plants, Stump Feet, Loop Handles, 8 In. 230.00
  Bowl, Gold Band At Top, Blue & Clear Jewels, Signed, 8 3/4 In. 995.00
  Box, Cover, Gold Gladiators, Green, 3 In. 150.00
  Box, Dresser, Blue Glass, Gold Design, Bronze Frame, Miniature 350.00
  Candlestick, Panel Cut, Hollow Balusters, Signed, 10 1/2 In., Pair 465.00
  Cruet, Cranberry, Signed 800.00
  Cruet, Deep Ruby, Gold Oak Leaves, Acorns, 10 In. 1370.00
  Cruet, Enameled Floral Design, Amber Foot, Blue Body, 7 1/2 In. 550.00
  Cruet, Floral, Green, Gold Trim, Signed 495.00
  Decanter Set, Girl & Boy Lovers, Lake, Hills, Gold & Silver, 7 Piece 550.00
  Decanter, Enameled, Overall Gold, Cut Stopper, Cranberry, Signed 300.00
  Decanter, Overall Oak Leaves, Steeple Stopper, Cranberry, 17 In. 1200.00
  Goblet, Sherry, Gold & White Beading, Knobbed Stem, Signed, 4 1/4 In. 195.00
  Mug, Overlaid & Padded, Blossom Leaf & Stem, Angled Handle, Signed 995.00
  Perfume Bottle, Art Nouveau, Malachite, Leaf Design, 14 In. 450.00
  Perfume Bottle, Band of Warriors At Center, Signed, 4 1/4 In. 450.00
  Perfume Bottle, Enameled Oak Leaves, Luster Acorns, Cranberry, 5 In. 395.00
  Pitcher, Fern Fronds, Bird & Insects, Salamander Handle, 11 3/4 In. 2530.00
  Pitcher, Gold Scale Pattern, Green Snake Handle, 12 In. 675.00
  Pitcher, Lemonade, Peacock Design, Hand Painted, 1870–80 .... 950.00
  Salt & Pepper, Signed Alexander 130.00
  Salt & Pepper, Turquoise Spangle Glass, Enameled Fish, Pewter Tops 325.00
  Tray, Fish Around Growth of Coral, Enameled, 4 Feet, 15 In. 320.00
  Tumbler, Arabesque–Like Medallions, Sapphire Blue, Signed, 3 7/8 In. 435.00
  Tumbler, Clear To Coral, Engraved Tree With Squirrel, 4 1/2 In. 135.00
  Vase, 4 Seminude Women, Polished Ribbed Panels, Malachite, 10 In. 750.00
  Vase, Covered With Gold Leaves, Aqua To Blue–Green, 25 In. 975.00
  Vase, Cranberry, Coralene Design, Gold Trim, Signed, 13 In. 2380.00
  Vase, Double Layer of Flowers, Buds, Crystal, Signed, 11 3/4 In. 3500.00
  Vase, Elephants Under Palm Trees, Ovoid, Signed, c.1925, 11 3/8 In. 1760.00
  Vase, Enameled Floral Design, Aqua Blue, Signed, 11 In. 295.00
  Vase, Enameled Flower, Gold Scrollwork, Topaz To Clear, 10 1/2 In. 395.00
  Vase, Enameled, Intaglio Clouds & Flowers, Signed, 14 In. ....*Illus* 1600.00
  Vase, Gold & Enamel Top & Dots, Signed, 12 In. 585.00
  Vase, Gold Floral, Enameled, Blue, Signed, 10 In. 495.00
  Vase, Gold Intaglio Warriors, Paneled, 14 In. 450.00
  Vase, Gold Leaves, White Outline, Blue Dots, Woodland Scene, 5 In. 165.00
  Vase, Gold Scrolls, Enameled Flowers, Birds, Glass Buds, 10 1/2 In. 765.00
  Vase, Green & Orange Cameo Flowers, Marquetry, Signed, 7 In. 1900.00
  Vase, Green, Signed, 9 1/2 In. 350.00
  Vase, Malachite, Seminude Women Each Corner, 4 Sides, 7 x 10 In. 750.00
  Vase, Multicolored Fern Design, 7 In. 685.00

Vase, Pulled Up To Points, Flying Insects, White Spatter, 12 1/2 In. 700.00
Vase, Purple To Clear, Cut Design, Flower & Stem, Gold Rim, 4 In. 90.00
Vase, Seaweed & Fish, Sapphire Blue, 8 1/4 In. 525.00
Vase, Trumpet, Oak Leaf & Acorn, Gilt & Polychrome Enamel, 11 1/4 In. 2530.00

Moss rose china was made by many firms from 1808 to 1900. It has a typical moss rose pictured as the design. The plant is not as popular now as it was in Victorian gardens, so the fuzz-covered bud is unfamiliar to most collectors. The dishes were usually decorated with pink and green flowers.

MOSS ROSE, Bowl, 8 In. 50.00
   Egg Cup 7.00
   Mug, Meakin 35.00
   Pitcher & Bowl Set, Meakin, 6 Piece 250.00
   Plate, 10 In. 20.00
   Plate, Knowles, Taylor and Knowles, 8 In. 20.00
   Plate, Powell & Bishop, 9 In. 18.00
   Plate, Rosenthal, 8 In. 75.00
   Sugar 45.00
   Tea Set, Child's, Box, 29 Piece 250.00
   Tea Set, Child's, Teapot, Creamer, Sugar, 4 Cups, Saucers 55.00
   Teapot, T & V, 8 1/2 In. 45.00

Mother-of-pearl glass, or pearl satin glass, was first made in the 1850s in England and in Massachusetts. It was a special type of mold-blown satin glass with air bubbles in the glass, giving it a pearlized color. It has been reproduced. Mother-of-pearl shell objects are listed under Pearl.

MOTHER-OF-PEARL, Ball, Rainbow Diamond-Quilted, White Lining, 5 1/4 In. 995.00
   Basket, Herringbone, Wishbone Handle, 5 1/2 In. 320.00
   Bowl, Crimped Rim, Yellow Coralene Seaweed Design, 3 In. 247.00
   Bride's Bowl, Diamond-Quilted, Blue, 3 3/8 x 10 1/2 In. 375.00
   Creamer, Gold-To-White Coin Spot, Dimpled, 5 1/2 In. 325.00
   Creamer, Pinched Sides, Tricorner Mouth, 5 1/2 In. 325.00
   Cruet, Frosted, Clear Knob Stopper, 8 1/4 In. 585.00
   Fairy Lamp, Blue, Swirl, Cup Base, 4 5/8 In. 325.00
   Finger Bowl, Diamond-Quilted, Cream Lining 915.00
   Jam Jar, Blue Herringbone, Enamel Floral, 4 3/4 In. 275.00
   Lamp, Peg, Rainbow Diamond-Quilted, Metal Clips, 6 In. 650.00
   Mustard, Raindrop Pattern, Pewter Lid, 3 In. 375.00
   Pitcher, Water, Frosted Handle, Square Body, 9 In. 485.00
   Plate, White Peacock-Eye, Ladybugs, Gold Edge, 6 1/2 In. 585.00
   Toothpick, Diamond-Quilted, Apricot To Blue, Ruffled, 2 In. 225.00
   Tumbler, Diamond-Quilted, Enameled Daises, Green Foliage 265.00
   Tumbler, Yellow Herringbone, Floral, 3 7/8 In. 225.00
   Vase, Amberina Swirl, 7 1/2 x 5 1/2 In. 675.00
   Vase, Blue Diamond-Quilted, Floral, 4 3/4 In. 195.00

Moser, Vase, Enameled, Intaglio Clouds & Flowers, Signed, 14 In.

Motorcycle, Scott, Flying Squirrel, 1939,

Vase, Diamond–Quilted, Frosted Ball Feet, Stipes, 5 1/4 In.	995.00
Vase, Diamond–Quilted, Multicolored Exterior, 6 3/8 In.	850.00
Vase, Diamond–Quilted, Satin Glass, 10 1/2 In.	275.00
Vase, Dimpled Body, Crimped Rim, Blue, 8 1/4 In.	220.00
Vase, Gold Flowers & Leaves, 3 In.	505.00
Vase, Herringbone, Amber Handles, Blue, 9 3/4 In., Pair	650.00
Vase, Melon Sections, Medallions, 9 1/2 In.	445.00
Vase, Pink Herringbone, Frosted Handles, 7 1/2 In.	225.00
Vase, Rainbow Diamond–Quilted, White Lining, 6 1/4 In.	950.00
Vase, Ruffled, Flowers With Yellow Buds, 7 1/4 In.	495.00

Motorcyles of all types are being collected today. Examples can be found that date back to the early years of the twentieth century.

MOTORCYCLE, Henderson, Goulding, Sidecar, 1925	17600.00
Humber, England, 1922	8800.00
Indian, Single Cylinder, 1919	8250.00
Powerplus, Red, 1920	6050.00
Scott, Flying Squirrel, 1939 ....*Illus*	6100.00

MOUNT WASHINGTON, see Mt. Washington
MOUSTACHE CUP, see Mustache Cup

 Mt. Joye is an enameled cameo glass made in the late nineteenth and the twentieth centuries by Saint–Hilaire Touvier de Varraux and Co. of Pantin, France. This same company made De Vez glass. Pieces were usually decorated with enameling. Most pieces are not marked.

MT. JOYE, Bowl, Gray Texture, White, Yellow, Green Flower, 6 In. ....*Illus*	400.00
Lamp, Banquet, Cameo Shade, Rainbow Crystal Font, 28 In.	1600.00
Planter, Green Leaves, Gold, 7 1/2 In.	275.00
Vase, Banjo Shape, Hammered Ground, Green & Gilt Leaves, 13 1/2 In.	975.00
Vase, Cameo, Green, Purple, Gold, Red Thistles, 11 1/2 In. ....*Illus*	1200.00

Mt. Joye, Bowl, Gray Texture, White, Yellow, Green Flower, 6 In.
Mt. Joye, Vase, Cameo, Green, Purple, Gold, Red Thistles, 11 1/2 In.

Vase, Cameo, Leaves, Seed Pods, 20 In	1200.00
Vase, Chrysanthemums, Leaves, Signed, c.1910, 15 5/8 In.	935.00
Vase, Enameled Floral & Dragonfly Design, Green & Gold, 8 1/2 In.	575.00
Vase, Enameled Leaves, Chrysanthemums, Gold, Green, 8 In.	350.00
Vase, Gold–Enameled Chestnut & Leaves, Ruffled Neck, 5 In.	225.00
Vase, Pink Iris On Dark Green Satin, 7 1/2 In.	395.00
Vase, White Daisies On Green, Gold Band, 14 1/2 In.	295.00

The Mt. Washington Glass Works started in 1837 in South Boston, Massachusetts. In 1869 the company moved to New Bedford, Massachusetts. Many types of art glass were made there to the 1890s. Amberina, Burmese, Crown Milano, cut glass, Peachblow, and Royal Flemish are each listed in their own sections.

MT. WASHINGTON, Basket, Rainbow, Ruffled, Tufts Holder, 10 3/4 In.	440.00
Biscuit Jar, Apple Blossoms, Wild Roses, 8 1/2 In.	1500.00
Biscuit Jar, Ribbed Panels, Double–Ring Top, 8 1/2 In.	450.00
Box, Cover, Lusterless, Hand Painted Pansies, Scrolls, 6 In.	550.00
Bride's Basket, Pink Case, Opal Glass	975.00
Bride's Bowl, Eagle & Floral, Coral On Ivory	850.00
Castor, Pickle, Pink & White Flowers, Albertine	1120.00
Condiment Set, Cruet, Salt & Pepper, Pairpoint Holder	1485.00
Cracker Jar, Gold Spider Mums, Marked M. W., Square, 7 1/2 In.	355.00
Cruet, Blossoms, Faceted Stopper, 6 3/4 In.	885.00
Dish, Sweetmeat, Cover, Albertine, Gold Holly Leaves, Jewels	50.00
Flower Arranger, Mushroom Shape, Yellow, Pink Roses, Cover	250.00
Flower Frog, Mushroom	245.00
Flower Frog, Mushroom, Blue, Lavender Forget–Me–Nots	225.00
Lamp, Banquet, Pansies, Brass Base, Victor Burner, 17 1/4 In.	1950.00
Lamp, Kerosene, Hand Painted Guba Ducks, 32 In.	7900.00
Lamp, Kerosene, Lava Glass, Brass Fittings, Metal Base, 15 In.	935.00
Lamp, Oil, 1880	950.00
Lamp, Pink Cut To Opaque White, Cameo Portrait, 16 1/4 In.	485.00
Lamp, Purple Pansies, Gold Scrolls, Electric, 17 1/2 In.	465.00
Lamp, Student, Electric, Crown Milano Shade, 19 In.	825.00
Muffineer, White–Enameled Asters, Egg Shape, 4 In.	147.00
Mustard, Burmese, Hinged Lid, Metal Collar, Marked 1334	285.00
Plate, Yellow Chrysanthemums, White Satin, 10 In.	40.00
Punch Cup, Napoli, Palmer Cox Brownies, Cat, 5, 3 1/4 In.	2250.00
Rose Bowl, Pansies, Blue Ground, Numbered, 5 1/2 In.	565.00
Salt & Pepper	75.00
Salt & Pepper, Enameled, Egg, Pewter Top	125.00
Salt & Pepper, Melon Shape, Violets, Pansies	67.50
Salt & Pepper, Pink Florals, Gold Stripes, 6 Panels	225.00
Saltshaker, Chick	285.00
Sugar & Creamer, Lava Glass	3750.00
Sugar & Creamer, Painted Floral Design, 2 3/4 In.	110.00
Sugar Shaker, Apricot To Pale Yellow	265.00
Sugar Shaker, Egg Shape, Blossoms & Shadow Leaves, Metal Cap	135.00
Sugar Shaker, Egg, Allover Beaded Flowers	1285.00
Sugar Shaker, Ostrich Egg, Pewter Pronged Lid, Mums	350.00
Toothpick, Brownie Policeman Holding Brownie On Front	550.00
Toothpick, Hand Painted, 2 1/8 In.	110.00
Toothpick, Tricorner Shape, Blue–Gray To Rose	750.00
Tumbler, Enameled Flowers & Design, Opaque, 3 3/4 In.	165.00
Vase, Butterflies & Daisy, 11 In.	265.00
Vase, Fireglow, Florals, 10 1/2 In.	125.00
Vase, Jack–In–The–Pulpit, Pink Upper Section, 8 1/2 In.	750.00
Vase, Stick, Oak Leaf & Blue Dot, 1880s, 10 In.	1750.00

Mud figures are small Chinese pottery figures made in the twentieth century. The figures usually represent workers, scholars, farmers, or merchants. Other pieces are trees, houses, and similar parts of the landscape. The figures have unglazed faces and hands but glazed clothing. They were originally made for fish tanks or planters. Mud figures were of little interest and brought low prices until the 1980s. When the prices rose, reproductions appeared.

MUD FIGURE, Boy Fishing	55.00
Elder, Sitting, Legs Crossed, Fish On Line, 4 In.	68.00
Lamp, Attached Vase, Red Cloth Shade, China, 10 In.	185.00
Man With Urn, 8 In.	45.00
Man, Green & Blue Robe, Black Beard, China, 9 3/4 In.	175.00
Old Man Seated On Stump, 6 In.	55.00
Old Man With Fish, Red, Brown, 6 In.	55.00
Old Man With Yoke and Buckets	75.00

Mulberry ware was made in the Staffordshire district of England from about 1850 to 1860. The dishes were decorated with a transfer design of a reddish brown, now called *mulberry*. Many of the patterns are similar to those used for flow blue and other Staffordshire transfer wares.

MULBERRY, Coffeepot, Rhone Scene, Podmore	375.00
Creamer, Panama, Challinor	175.00
Cup & Saucer, Handleless, Chusan	55.00
Cup & Saucer, Handleless, Pelew	55.00
Cup & Saucer, Handleless, Wreath	55.00
Cup Plate, Corean, P. W. & Co., c.1850	40.00
Gravy Boat, Panama, Challinor	150.00
Plate, Boston, 10 In.	45.00
Plate, Corean, 9 3/4 In.	60.00
Plate, Corean, Podmore & Walker, 9 1/4 In.	45.00
Plate, Music, 6 In.	30.00
Plate, Washington Vase, 9 In.	50.00
Platter, Chusan, P. H. & Co., 17 In.	185.00
Platter, Rhone Scenery, 13 1/2 In.	100.00
Platter, Rhone Scenery, 15 3/4 In.	100.00
Platter, Scinde, Walker, 15 1/2 In.	150.00
Platter, Vincennes, 15 1/2 In.	165.00
Sugar, Cover, Hyson	150.00
Teapot, Corea, Clementson	275.00
Teapot, Cyprus	295.00
Teapot, Jeddo, W. Adams	375.00
Tureen, Soup, Rhone Scenery	295.00

Muller Freres, French for Muller Brothers, made cameo and other glass from the early 1900s to the late 1930s. Their factory was first located in Luneville, then in nearby Croismaire, France. Pieces were usually marked with the company name.

MULLER FRERES, Chandelier, 5-Light, Gilt Metal, Shades, Signed, c.1900, 33 In.	775.00
Chandelier, Stylized Birds, Iron Frame, Pink, c.1925, 36 In.	2300.00
Lamp, Figural, Egret, Marble Plinth, Glass, Chapelle, 14 In.	8800.00
Lamp, Landscape, Gilt-Metal Mounts, Signed, c.1920, 10 1/2 In.	775.00
Lamp, Panels of Stylized Flowers, Gilt Metal, c.1930, 35 In.	1650.00
Lamp, Yellow, Orange, Cobalt, 9 In. ....*Illus*	3300.00
Night-Light, Scarab, 6-Legged Bronze Base, Signed, 8 3/4 In.	2250.00
Vase, Alsatian Mountains, Conifers, Signed, c.1920, 11 In.	5500.00
Vase, Anemones, Plum & Mauve, Blue Frosted, Cameo, 9 1/4 In.	7150.00
Vase, Blossoms, Claret, Red Frosted, Spherical, 7 3/4 In.	3850.00
Vase, Coiling Serpent Attacking Eagle, Signed, c.1910, 12 In.	4500.00
Vase, Full-Blown Peony Blossoms, Signed, c.1920, 10 1/4 In.	3025.00
Vase, Hydrangea Blossoms, Leaves, Signed, c.1920, 10 7/8 In.	2475.00
Vase, Mottled Design, Flaring Neck, Signed, 8 1/4 In.	795.00
Vase, Orange, Blue Design, Flaring Neck, Signed, 8 In.	725.00
Vase, Rhododendron Blossoms, Signed, c.1920, 5 3/4 In.	3025.00
Vase, Winter Trees, Yellow To Purple, Signed, 4 1/2 In.	2975.00

Muller Freres, Lamp, Yellow, Orange, Cobalt, 9 In.

◆◆◆

You and your antiques may have different ideas about ideal temperature and humidity. Bronzes and photographs like 40% humidity, stone carvings and oil paintings like 50%, wooden pieces and paper prefer 55%. The level, whatever you choose, should be constant. It can be measured by a hygrometer you will be able to find at a hardware store.

◆◆◆

MUNCIE

The Muncie Clay Products Company was established by Charles Benham in Muncie, Indiana, in 1922. The company made pottery for the florist and gift shop trade. The company closed by 1939. Pieces are marked with the name *Muncie* or just with a system of numbers and letters like *1A*.

MUNCIE, Lamp, Aqua, Phoenix, Molded Lovebirds	160.00
Vase, Green To Caramel, Tapered, 1930s, 7 In.	45.00
Vase, Green To Pink, 6 In.	45.00

MURANO, see Venetian Glass

Music boxes and musical instruments are listed in this section. Phonograph records, jukeboxes, phonographs, and sheet music are listed in other sections in this book.

MUSIC, Accordion, Monarch, Fancy, 1880s	95.00
Accordion, Red Mother–of–Pearl Type, Child's, 1950s	45.00
Accordion, Trafficanty, Mother–of–Pearl Inlay, Case	115.00
Autoharp, Hand Painted Flowers, West Germany	95.00
Automaton, 2 Singing Birds, Cage	1800.00
Automaton, Birds Singing & Flying, Clock In Base, French, 24 In.	2310.00
Automaton, Black Warrior, On Camel, Carrying Spear, c.1870	4500.00
Automaton, Feather–Covered Bird In Wire Cage, Key Wind, 22 In.	800.00
Automaton, Singing Bird, Cage, France, 11 In.	300.00
Automaton, Singing Bird, Cage, Germany, 11 In.	225.00
Automaton, Singing Birds, Domed Brass Cage, French, 20 In.	2420.00
Automaton, Stage, Turkish Tightrope Dancer, Clock Top, Swiss, 18 In.	6600.00
Band Box, Chicago Coin	2800.00
Banjo, Silvertone, 5 String	30.00
Box, 3 Butterflies, 3 Bells, English Madrigals, England, 12 x 19 In.	1545.00
Box, Capitol, Violin Pipes, A Rolls, Tabletop Model	7500.00
Box, Criterion, Double Comb, Upright Oak Case	9800.00
Box, Criterion, Hotel, Quartersawn Oak, 30 Steel Discs	9075.00
Box, Cylinder, Swiss, 12 Tunes, Late 19th Century, 8 x 30 x 12 1/2 In.	1650.00
Box, Edison, Maroon Gem, Original Finish	1250.00

Box, Home, Gem–Roller Organ, Papers, Box, 4 Cobs 600.00
Box, Mandolin, Paillard, 8 Tunes, Inlaid Case, 11–In. Cylinder 900.00
Box, Mermod Freres, Cylinder, 8 Tunes, Change–Repeat Lever 1200.00
Box, Merry–Go–Round, Bisque Head Riders, Hide–Covered Ponies, Germany 935.00
Box, Murry–Spinx, 1 Comb, Coin–Operated 5 Cent, 14 Regina Discs 2985.00
Box, Paillard Excelsior, 6 Tunes, Cylinder, Mahogany, 43 x 13 x 15 In. 7500.00
Box, Polyfone, Wooden, 80 Metal Discs 800.00
Box, Regina, 52312, Mahogany, Double Comb, 20 Discs, 19 x 21 x 12 In. 5225.00
Box, Regina, Double Comb, 10 Discs, 15 1/2 In. 3000.00
Box, Regina, Double Comb, Serpentine Case, Tabletop, 5 1/2 In. 6200.00
Box, Regina, No. 11A, Mahogany, 15 1/2 In. 4750.00
Box, Regina, Style 50, Banjo Attachment, 30 Discs, c.1880, 21 x 18 In. 2400.00
Box, Regina, Tabletop, Bells, 26–In. Discs 4500.00
Box, Regina, Tabletop, Doublecomb, Serpentine Case, Discs 6200.00
Box, Regina, Under Cabinet 7750.00
Box, Stella, Grand, Tabletop, Stand, Oak, 17 1/4 In. 4500.00
Box, Stella, Model 168, 16 Discs 3000.00
Box, Stella, Storage Drawer, 20 Discs, 17 1/4 In. 6230.00
Box, Stella, Table Model, Inlaid Case, Base Cabinet 6800.00
Box, Swiss, 19–In Cylinder, 2 Combs, 12 Tunes, Walnut, Queen Anne Legs 4510.00
Box, Swiss, 6 Tunes, Rosewood, 11 3/4 X5 3/4 x 5 3/4 In. 465.00
Box, Symphonion Disc, Coin–Operated 3000.00
Box, Symphonion, Double Comb, Rosewood, 15 Discs, 1900 .... 6600.00
Box, Waxed Reclining Putto, Eyes Open & Close As Playing, Italy 250.00
Box, Weber, 6 Tunes, String Inlay, Rosewood, 6 x 17 1/2 In. 600.00
Concertina, Tanzbar, Roll Frame, Trackers, Reeds, Hexagonal Bedplate 165.00
Drum, Mt. Pleasant Martial Band, Pa., Glass Plate Top, 27 1/2 In. 150.00
Drum, Polychrome Eagle, Banner, T. S. B., 15 1/4 x 17 In. 1200.00
Drum, Temple, Red Lacquered, Chinese, 6 Ft., Pair 1595.00
Drum, Zebra Skin, Double Handles, 15 x 16 In. 330.00
Drumstick, Curly Maple, Leather–Covered Heads, 13 In., Pair 85.00
Figurine, Dog, Nipper, RCA, Papier-Mache, 38 In. 500.00
Flute, Ivory Fittings, Wooden, Leather Case 50.00
Graphophone, Columbia, AH 1150.00
Guitar, Fender, Lap, 6 Steel Strings, No. 0197, Leather & Wood Case 250.00
Harmonica, Comet, Hohner, Case 60.00
Harmonica, Hohner Goliath, 48 Reeds, Box, 1895 .... 28.00
Harmonica, Hohner, Tremolo 60.00
Harmonica, Hoosier Boy, Herb Shriner 50.00
Harmonica, Koch, Chromatic 165.00
Harmonica, Pee–Wee, Occupied Japan, 1 1/4 In. 10.00
Harmonica, The Song Bird, Holtz, Cardinal Pictured On Box 20.00
Harp, Dodd, London, Plume & Ram's Head Top, Gilt Gesso, Painted, 67 In. 1300.00
Harp, Gerard Mengers, Paris 2200.00
Harp, Lyon & Healy, Gilt Column, Painted Sound Chamber, 1920s, 70 In. 5500.00
Harp, Parcel–Gilt & Ebonized, 1880s, 5 Ft. 1 In. 3025.00
Hurdy–Gurdy, Crank 3960.00
Jukebox, Wurlitzer 1015, Coin Gear 8500.00
Mandolin, Musikalia Lyre, Italy 400.00
Melodeon, Rosewood, Matching Stool 500.00
Nickelodeon, Chicago, Quartersawn Oak, Stained–Glass Windows 6500.00
Nickelodeon, Coinola, Cupid, 1915 .... 8500.00
Nickelodeon, Cremona, Model B 8400.00
Nickelodeon, Englehart, Semi–Orchestrion 3500.00
Nickelodeon, Peerless, Model D 6500.00
Nickelodeon, Western Electric, Mascot 8000.00
Nickelodeon, Wurlitzer, Keyboard Style, 1912 .... 7500.00
Nickelodeon, Wurlitzer, Style DX, Violin & Flute Pipes 9250.00
Organ, A. B. Chase, Pump, Carved Walnut, Beveled Mirror, Shelves. c.1880 .... 3200.00
Organ, Aeolian, Duo-Art, 13 Ranks, Chimes, 10 Rolls 9750.00
Organ, Aeolian, Duo-Art, Pipe, 13 Ranks, Chimes, Harp, Bench, 9 Rolls 9750.00
Organ, Aeolian, Duo-Art, Pipe, Reproducing, Large Harp, 10 Rolls 9750.00
Organ, Aeolian, Player, Style 1500 .... 6000.00

Organ, Chautauqua, Roller, 18 Rolls	695.00
Organ, Eastlake, Pump, Walnut	2500.00
Organ, Estey, Reed, Modernistic Case, 1930s	200.00
Organ, Field, Liberty, 1920	195.00
Organ, Fratti, Barrel, Mexican Tunes, Berlin, Early 1900s	7500.00
Organ, Gem, Black	850.00
Organ, Gem, Roller, 12 Musical Cobs	1500.00
Organ, Gem, Roller, 13 Cobs, Desk Top	1500.00
Organ, Gem, Roller, 8 Cobs	500.00
Organ, Gem, Roller, Desk Top, 13 Cobs	1500.00
Organ, Melville Clark, Apollophone, Pump & Electric, Figured Walnut	3500.00
Organ, Moline, Pump, Reed, 1892	425.00
Organ, Monarch, Golden Oak, Reed, 1903	800.00
Organ, Monkey, 5 Wooden Rolls	1600.00
Organ, Monkey, Reed–Type	3800.00
Organ, Peerless Pump, Oak, Spoon Carved	950.00
Organ, Peerless, Pump, Spoon Carved	950.00
Organ, Seeburg, Style E, Oak, Xylophone	7500.00
Organ, Shinek, Monkey, 26 Keys, 63 Pipes, 4 Ranks	4500.00 To 5800.00
Organ, Thomas, Color Glo, Bench, Electronic	600.00
Organ, Wilcox–White Pneumatic Symphony, Player, 14 Stops, Oak	5000.00
Organ, Wurlitzer, Band, 150 Rolls	500.00
Piano, A. B. Chase, Grand, Player, Tiger Stripe Mahogany, 1915	7500.00
Piano, Aeolian, Orchestrelle, Style V	8750.00
Piano, Ampico, Player, Upright, Marshall & Wendell, 20 Rolls	3900.00
Piano, Arlington Piano Co., Grand, Square, Rosewood, 37 x 40 x 76 In.	415.00
Piano, Arthur P. Griggs, Player, Oak Case, 850 Rolls	3500.00
Piano, Baby Grand, Barbs, Bird's–Eye Maple Case, c.1850, 5 Ft. 6 In.	600.00
Piano, Barrel, 6 Tunes, Spain	675.00
Piano, Barrel, Scenes Painted On Front, Electric Lamps, France	3500.00
Piano, Chickering, Baby Grand, Ebonized Finish, c.1900, 75 1/4 In.	1545.00
Piano, Chickering, Grand, c.1830	3500.00
Piano, Chickering, Grand, Square, Rosewood Case, 1853	2000.00
Piano, Coinola, Cupid	8500.00
Piano, Coinola, Plays Mandolin, Leaded Front, Wooden Cabinet, 5 Rolls	7500.00
Piano, Criterion, 13 Discs, Duplex Combs, Oak, Restored, 15 3/4 In.	3950.00
Piano, Drum, Empress, Electric	7500.00
Piano, Hallet & Davis, Grand, Rosewood, Square, 1879	3500.00
Piano, Hallet & Davis, Player, Art Case, Bench, 5 Ft. 8 In.	2500.00
Piano, Hazelton Bros., Grand, Matching Bench	8500.00
Piano, Knabe, Baby Grand, White Lacquered & Plexiglass, 40 In.	3300.00
Piano, M. Welte & Sons, Upright, Player, 18 Red Rolls	5000.00
Piano, Marshall & Wendall, Ampico Player, 30 Rolls, Reconditioned	4500.00
Piano, Marshall & Wendell, Ampico, 5 Ft. 2 In.	5900.00
Piano, Marshall & Wendell, Ampico, Model B, Art Case	4900.00
Piano, Marshall & Wendell, Ampico, Upright, Restored, 20 Rolls	3900.00
Piano, Marshall & Wendell, Player, Extra Rolls, 1931	5900.00
Piano, Mason & Hamlin, Ampico, Bench & Rolls	6500.00
Piano, Mason & Hamlin, Grand, 5 Ft.	3000.00
Piano, Mason & Hamlin, Grand, Mahogany, 1950, 5 Ft.	6000.00
Piano, Mason & Hamlin, Grand, Pianocorder System, Walnut, 5 Ft. 8 In.	5000.00
Piano, Mason & Hamlin, Louis XV, 5 Ft. 4 In.	8500.00
Piano, Mason & Hamlin, Model B, Ampico, Walnut Case	9700.00

◆◆

Never throw out your plate's original box or papers. They add to the resale value. Your homeowner's insurance doesn't cover your plates or figurines. You will need a Fine Art's policy with a breakage clause.

◆◆

Piano, Mason & Hamlin, Reproducing, 200 Tapes, 1973 .... 5000.00
Piano, Ohio Valley Piano Co., Grand, Square, 9876 .... 2500.00
Piano, Orchestrion, Leaded Glass Front, Coin–Operated 5500.00
Piano, Palestina, Player, Inside Works Visible, Bench 650.00
Piano, Phillips Duca, Player, Top Loader, Ebony Finish, 350 Rolls 7500.00
Piano, Pieyel, Spinet, Music Stand, Candle Slides, Rosewood, 93 In. 1540.00
Piano, Regina, Player, Sublima, Mandolin, 3 Rolls 6500.00
Piano, Schultz, Grand, Bench, Carved Art Case, Aria Devina Action 8500.00
Piano, Schultz, Grand, Carved, Aria Divinia Action, 28 Recordo Rolls 8500.00
Piano, Seeburg L, Player 7500.00
Piano, Seeburg, Player, Model E, Xylophone, 10 Rolls 7500.00
Piano, Sohmer, Grand, Rosewood, Square 4200.00
Piano, Spinet, Victorian, Ebony & Ivory Keys, Pierced Harp, Rosewood 335.00
Piano, Steck, Grand, Electric Player, Aeolian Movement, 100 Rolls 2900.00
Piano, Steinway, Baby Grand, Ebony & Ivory Keys, Ebony, 55 x 58 In. 6100.00
Piano, Steinway, Duo–Art, Grand, Player 7950.00
Piano, Steinway, Grand, Player, Duo–Art Case, 57 In. 9000.00
Piano, Steinway, Grand, Square, Rosewood Case, c.1873 .... 6500.00
Piano, Steinway, Pump, Model 65/88 .... 9500.00
Piano, Steinway, Upright, Art Case, Rosewood, 1877 .... 2750.00
Piano, Steinway, Upright, Rosewood Case 2750.00
Piano, Weber, Player, Electric, Upright, Stripped 750.00
Pianocorder, Mason–Hamlin, Upright 4800.00
Pionola, Weber, Foot Pumped, Upright, 65 & 88 Note Rolls, 1910 .... 7500.00
Reproducer, Victor Concert 185.00
Tambura, Case 195.00
Trombone, Collegiate, Silver, Holt 57.00
Violin, Yuke, Original Case 85.00
Zither, Menzenhauer, Patent 1894 .... 65.00

The mustache cup was popular from 1850 to 1900 when the large, flowing mustache was in style. A ledge of china or silver held the hair out of the liquid in the cup. This kept the mustache tidy and also kept the mustache wax from melting. Left–handed mustache cups are rare but are being reproduced.

MUSTACHE CUP, 3 Elves, Frog & Flying Insect On Wall, Porcelain, 3 1/2 In. 65.00
Floral Design, Left Handed, France 65.00
Occupational, Buggy Driver, Gentleman, Buggy, Homer H. Conn 475.00
Occupational, Salesman, Arm Holding Calling Card, Gold Name 295.00
Saucer, Child Catching Butterflies 60.00
Yankee Girl Chewing Tobacco, Brown Glaze 135.00

MZ Austria is the wording on a mark used by Moritz Zdekauer on porcelains made at his works from about 1900. The firm worked in the town of Alt–Rohlau, Austria. The pieces were decorated with lavish floral patterns and overglaze gold decoration. Full sets of dishes were made as well as vases, toilet sets, and other wares.

MZ AUSTRIA, Berry Bowl, Gold Ruffled Inside Rim, Footed 60.00
Powder Box & Hair Receiver, Violets, Hand Painted 125.00
Salt & Pepper 5.00
Soup, Dish, Pink Roses 56.00

Nailsea glass was made in the Bristol district in England from 1788 to 1873. It was made by many different factories, not just the Nailsea Glass House. Many pieces were made with loopings of either white or colored glass as decoration.

NAILSEA, Flask, Pocket, White Looping, Cranberry, 7 3/4 In. 180.00
Lamp, Fairy, Tri–Formed Base 1200.00
Vase, Turquoise Looping, White, 5 1/2 In. 45.00

NAKARA   Nakara is a trade name for a white glassware made about 1900 by the C. F. Monroe Company of Meriden, Connecticut. It was decorated in pastel colors. The glass was very similar to another

Nanking, Tureen, Village Scene, c.1800,
14 In.

glass made by the company called *Wave Crest*. The company closed
in 1916. Boxes for use on a dressing table are the most commonly
found Nakara pieces. The mark is not found on every piece.

NAKARA, Bonbon, Pink Flowers, Blue Ground, 6 3/4 In.	385.00
Box, Applied Petal Flowers, Octagonal, Peach Ground, 6 1/4 In.	1055.00
Box, Cherubs On Cover, Raised Dots, Blue, 3 3/4 In.	350.00
Box, Dark & Light Blue, Pink Flowers, White Dot Trim, 5 In.	435.00
Box, Hinged Cover, Light Blue, Hexagonal, 4 In.	275.00
Box, Jewelry, Pink Flowers, Green Ground, Silk Lining, Marked	365.00
Hair Receiver, Autumn Leaves, Blue, Square, 4 1/2 In.	485.00
Humidor, Ashtray On Top	575.00
Tray, Pin, Yellow Trim, White Dots, Pink, 4 3/4 In.	260.00
Vase, Blue, Burmese Shading, Enameled Orchids, 11 In.	965.00
Vase, Ormolu Handle & Feet, 13 In.	690.00

Nanking is a type of blue–and–white porcelain made in Canton,
China, since the late–eighteenth century. It is very similar to
Canton, which is listed under its own name in this book. Both
Nanking and Canton are part of a larger group now called *Chinese
Export* porcelain. Nanking has a spear–and–post border and may
have gold decoration.

NANKING, Bowl, Platter, Landscape, Trees, Floral & Butterfly Border, 14 In.	358.00
Dish, Cover, Embossed Finial, Boar's Head Handles, 7 1/2 In.	200.00
Dish, Scene of Bridge, Bamboo & Foliage, Oval, 1850s, 12 In.	325.00
Jug, Cider, Foo Dog Finial, Intertwined Handle, 10 1/2 In.	700.00
Mug, Intertwined Handle, Floral Ends, 4 1/4 In.	125.00
Platter, 14 In.	1500.00
Platter, Octagon, Deep, 14 In.	850.00
Platter, Oval, Drainage Holes, 12 1/2 In.	150.00
Tureen, Village Scene, c.1800, 14 In. ....*Illus*	350.00

Napkin rings were in fashion from 1869 to about 1900. They were
made of silver, porcelain, wood, and other materials. They are still
being made today. The most popular rings with collectors are the
figural napkin rings of silver plate. Small, realistic figures were made
to hold the ring. Good and poor reproductions of the more
expensive rings are now being made and collectors must be very
careful, especially when buying any of the Kate Greenaway rings.

NAPKIN RING, China, Hand Painted Violets	30.00
Figural, 2 Eagles, Silver Plate	70.00
Figural, Angel, Pulling Sled	195.00
Figural, Baby Boy, Crawling, William Rogers	165.00
Figural, Bear, Standing, Yosemite Souvenir, Silver Plate	65.00
Figural, Begging Dog In Front of Ring, Reed & Barton	125.00
Figural, Bird Pulling Ring, Ball Feet, Meriden	95.00
Figural, Boy Feeding Dog, Sterling	275.00

Figural, Boy Sitting, Reading, Simpson Hall, Miller 165.00
Figural, Bull On Oval Base, Etched Ring, Knickerbocker Silver 185.00
Figural, Cat, Silver Plate 120.00
Figural, Cherub Reading Book 135.00
Figural, Chick, Wishbone, Best Wishes, Silver Plate 45.00
Figural, Child On See–Saw, Sterling Silver 25.00
Figural, Clown On Back, Feet In Air Balancing Ring, Bronze 125.00
Figural, Cow, Silver Plate 350.00
Figural, Dogs In Dog Houses, Silver Plate 135.00
Figural, Egyptian Woman Kneeling In Front of Ring, Sterling 225.00
Figural, Fan With 2 Butterflies 135.00
Figural, Kate Greenaway Bow, Begging Dog 260.00
Figural, Leopard, Beside Ring 195.00
Figural, Lily Pad, Silver, Meridian 85.00
Figural, Lion, Ring In Back 180.00
Figural, Poodle, Etched Ring, Back Legs On Table 165.00
Figural, Prancing Horse, Pulling Cart, Wheels Revolve 295.00
Figural, Reindeer, Pulling Wheeled Cart, Sterling 350.00
Figural, Seated Cherub With Wings 135.00
Figural, Shepherd Dog, Seated, Tufts ....95.00 To 165.00
Figural, Squirrel, Sitting On Log, With Acorns 305.00
Figural, Turtle, Pulling Book, Movable Wheels 275.00

NASH   Nash glass was made in Corona, New York, after 1919 by Arthur Nash and his sons. He worked at the Webb factory in England and for the Tiffany Glassworks in the United States.

NASH, Decanter, Chain–Type Design, Green Chintz Swags, Signed, 16 In., Pair 750.00
Vase, Broken Thread, Pink, Diamond Mold, 8 1/2 In. 185.00

Nautical antiques are listed in this section. Any of the many objects that were made or used by the seafaring trade, including ship parts, models, and tools, are included. Other pieces may be found listed under Scrimshaw.

NAUTICAL, Bell, Matching Barometer, Waterbury 495.00
Bell, Ship's, U. S. Navy, c.1940, 9 x 10 In. 165.00
Bevel, Carpenter's, Rosewood, Brass, J. Rabone & Sons 75.00
Binnacle, Brass Claw Feet, Wood & Brass 1210.00
Binnacle, With Ritchie Compass, Steel, c.1860, 10 In. 110.00
Bowl, Lusitania 175.00
Button, U. S. Battleship Massachusetts, Celluloid, Pin, 1 1/4 In. 30.00
Card, Playing, Eastern Steamship Line, Box 10.00
Chest, Merchant's, Marked J. Clemens, New York, No. 5 .... 285.00
Chest, Sea, Oak, Iron Hardware, Brass Lock, Lethbridge, 1957, 54 In. 175.00
Chronometer, Harrison & Co., No. 10731, Mahogany Box, 4 3/4 In. 1100.00
Chronometer, Mahogany Box, Silvered Dial, Germany, 5 3/4 In. 1650.00
Chronometer, Mahogany, Brass Bound, William White, No. 3125, 5 In. 1200.00
Clock, Seamaster, Brass, Key Wind 195.00
Clock, Seth Thomas, Brass, Key Wind 250.00
Clock, Seth Thomas, Chimes, Watch Bell, Nickel Over Brass 400.00
Clock, Seth Thomas, Outside Bell 550.00
Clock, United, Electric 95.00
Compass, Marine, Encased, 20 In. 166.00
Compass, Riggs & Brother, Phila., Wooden, Glass, 6 3/4 x 10 In. 195.00
Compass, Ship's, From Whale Bark, Peru, Box 1100.00
Compass, With Sundial, Marine, Brass, B. N. Y. V. Co., Case, '73 & '74 .... 1350.00
Diorama, Clipper Ship Kate O'Connor, 20 3/4 x 40 In. 455.00
Figurehead, Commodore Perry, c.1822 .... 5600.00
Figurehead, Knight, Small 4125.00
Fog Horn, Hand Pumped, Brass 253.00
Folder, Furness Bermuda Line, Rates & Sailings, 1935 .... 20.00
Instrument, Backstaff, Quadrant, Ebony, Boxwood Scales, Ivory Inlay 5500.00
Lamp, Signal, Kerosene 37.50
Lantern, Blue Curved Glass, Interior Reflector, c.1900, 11 In. 225.00

Lantern, Boat, Metal, Red, Green Faceted Lights, 19th Century, 7 In. 55.00
Lantern, Gresnel Shade, Brass, c.1880, 8 1/8 In. 35.00
Lantern, Wilcox, Crittendom & Co., Brass, 10 1/2 In. 220.00
Log, Recorded Bearing, Distance & Speed, Mechanical 1760.00
Manifest, Ship Josephine, Bound From Liverpool For N. Y., 1839 .... 10.00
Manifest, Ship North America, New York To Liverpool, 1838 .... 10.00
Model, 2–Masted Sailing Ship, 29 x 27 In. 200.00
Model, 3–Masted Schooner, Glass Case, Framed, Miniature 220.00
Model, 3–Masted Ship, Wooden, Spain, 19 3/4 In. 95.00
Model, 4–Masted Schooner, S. M. Brume 650.00
Model, Destroyer U. S. S. Preston, Glass Case, 31 1/2 In. 335.00
Model, Fishing Boat, Wood & Metal, Polychrome Paint, 50 In. 480.00
Model, French Prisoner of War, Bone Hull, 19 x 31 In. 6600.00
Model, Half, Sailing Ship, Carved, Painted, 12 1/2 x 37 1/2 In. 715.00
Model, Half–Hull Ship, On Board, Pine, 34 In. 50.00
Model, Island Queen, Rigging & Life Boats, Painted Metal, 43 In. 495.00
Model, Island Queen, Sidewheeler 525.00
Model, Normandie, Glass Case, 32 1/2 In. 605.00
Model, Schooner Victor, Plank On Frame Construction, 19th Century 7500.00
Model, W. E. Morrill, 3–Masted Ship, By Condemned Murderer, 1888 .... 2000.00
Model, Whaleship, Baleen, Bone & Walrus Ivory, Case, 2 Ft. 2530.00
Octant, Long Radial Arms, 14 In. 385.00
Octant, Long Radial Arms, 26 In. 4125.00
Propeller, Liberty Motor, Lang Products Co., Mahogany, 100 In. 665.00
Quarter Board, Ship's, Chattanooga 300.00
Scull, Rowing, Balliol College, Oxford, 11 Ft. 7 In. 605.00
Sea Chest, Camphorwood, Canvas, JFS Stenciled On Front 192.50
Search Lights, Brass, Iron Brackets, 11 In., Pair 50.00
Sextant, 7 Colored Shades, Hoppe, London, Brass, 8 5/8 In. 305.00
Ship's Model, Isle De France, Wood, Brass, 1895, 85 x 12 In. 5500.00
Sign, SS Imperator, Hamburg American Line, Metal, 1911, 40 x 30 In. 775.00
Spoon, S. S. Minnekahda, Enameled 15.00
Steering Station, Oak Stand, Clipper Ship, 19th Century 2200.00
Telescope, Floor Standing, Sighting Scope, Optics, 44 In. 1980.00
Telescope, Navy, Aidade, Oak Box 125.00
Telescope, Round Weighted Foot, Brass, c.1850, 15 In. 115.00
Telescope, Single Draw, Closed 6 Ft. 4400.00
Telescope, Surveying, C. L. Berger & Sons, Brass, 9 1/2 x 18 In. 302.00
Tip Tray, Cunard Line, Aquatania 145.00
Valentine, Sailor's, White & Pink Shells, Mahogany Case 3080.00
Washstand, Painted, Bird's–Eye Maple, Lower Shelf, 1830 .... 475.00
Wheel, Sailing Ship, Mahogany, 66 In. 610.00
Wheel, Ship's, Maine Lobster Boat, Iron, Wooden, 16 In. 55.00

Small ivory, wood, metal, or porcelain pieces were used as buttons on the end of the cord that held a Japanese money pouch. These were called *netsuke*. The earliest date from the sixteenth century. Many are miniature, carved works of art.

NETSUKE, Bone, Skeleton, Beating Bell Drum, Signed, 1 1/4 In. 110.00
Boxwood, 2 Children, Seated, Clinging To Each, 1 1/2 In. 302.00
Boxwood, Man, Seated, Holding Fan, Signed, 1 3/4 In. 605.00
Ivory, 2 Boys Holding A Baby, 2 In. 90.00

◆◆◆

You can check to see if the light intensity is too strong for your antique pictures and fabrics. Take a light meter used with a camera and check the exposure values (EV) and lux. Maximum level for watercolors, paper, and other easily damaged items is 50 lux. Glass, stone, and metal is safe up to 300 lux.

◆◆◆

Ivory, 2 Sumo Wrestlers, 2 In. 110.00
Ivory, 3 Love Positions, Erotica, 2 In. 158.00
Ivory, 3 Women Taking Bath, 1 1/2 In. 85.00
Ivory, 9 Masks, Ball Form, Signed, Shugyoku, 1 3/4 In. 605.00
Ivory, Ape, Seated On A Sack, 18th Century 550.00
Ivory, Boar Tooth, Woman, Holding A Whisk, 19th Century 600.00
Ivory, Boy, Catching Fish, 1 1/2 In. 78.00
Ivory, Boy, On Dragon, 1 1/2 In. 88.00
Ivory, Boy, Sitting On Duck, 1 1/2 In. 85.00
Ivory, Buddha, With Boy, Standing, 3 In. 275.00
Ivory, Buddha, With Staff & Hu–Lu, 4 In. 220.00
Ivory, Chinese Zodiac, 12 Animals, 3 1/2 In. 390.00
Ivory, Comedian Face Mask, 2 In. 78.00
Ivory, Cowboy, With Buffalo, 1 1/2 In. 98.00
Ivory, Daikoku & Ebisu, Standing At A Mill, Tomochika 650.00
Ivory, Dragon, Emerging From Clamshell, Inlaid Eyes 175.00
Ivory, Dutchman, Short Coat, Feather–Topped Hat, Curly Locks 4750.00
Ivory, Fisherman, Seated, Blowfish, 1 1/2 In. 357.00
Ivory, Fisherman, Seated, Blowfish, Signed Nobuchika, 2 In. 359.00
Ivory, Fruit Bough, 3 Dimensional, Leaves, Flowers, Signed, 2 In. 1045.00
Ivory, Fruit Bough, National Himotoshi, Ryuheisai, 2 1/16 In. 1045.00
Ivory, Happy Family With Fish, 3 In. 230.00
Ivory, Happy Monk With Fan, 1 1/2 In. 110.00
Ivory, Hippopotamus, 4 In. 180.00
Ivory, Immortal Horse, 2 1/2 In. 158.00
Ivory, Japanese Lady, With Umbrella, 2 In. 72.00
Ivory, Japanese Scholar, With Hat, 2 1/2 In. 150.00
Ivory, Jurojin, 19th Century 2500.00
Ivory, Lion, Sitting, 1 1/2 In. 90.00
Ivory, Longevity, With Bird & Staff, 6 In. 350.00
Ivory, Longevity, With Boy, 2 In. 98.00
Ivory, Longevity, With Turtle & Hu–Lu, 3 In. 275.00
Ivory, Man, Eating With Chopsticks, 1 1/2 In. 90.00
Ivory, Man, With Reclining Elephant, Hidemasa, 19th Century 1250.00
Ivory, Mask, Akame & Otafuku, Signed Shinsui 450.00
Ivory, Monk, With Bat, 1 1/2 In. 85.00
Ivory, Monkey, Seated, Holding Fruit, Signed Kaigyoku, 1 1/2 In. 1320.00
Ivory, Mother & Baby, On Horse, 4 In. 138.00
Ivory, Nine Masks, Shugyoku, 1 3/4 In. 605.00
Ivory, Nude Lady, In Tub, 2 In. 98.00
Ivory, Nude Lady, With Jellyfish, 1 1/2 In. 85.00
Ivory, Old Man, Cutting Toe Nails, 2 In. 210.00
Ivory, Old Man, Playing With Monkey, 2 In. 85.00
Ivory, Old Man, With Horn & Rat, 1 1/2 In. 78.00
Ivory, Owl, Sitting On Tree, 3 In. 180.00
Ivory, Puppy, Playing With A Roof Tile, Tomochika, 19th Century 875.00
Ivory, Rabbit Sitting On Turtle's Back, Signed 32.00
Ivory, Rabbit, Sitting On Turtle's Back, Signed, Small 32.00
Ivory, Rhinoceros, Male, 4 In. 180.00
Ivory, Rich Man, Dog & Hu–Lu, 6 1/5 In. 330.00
Ivory, Scholar, On Giant Fish, 2 In. 98.00
Ivory, Scholar, With Brush & Paper, 5 In. 330.00
Ivory, Shishi, With Ball, Seated On A Table, 19th Century 1500.00
Ivory, Skull, 1 7/8 In. 135.00
Ivory, Tengu, Masatsugu, Early 19th Century 4000.00
Ivory, Turtle, On Lily Pad, Signed 45.00
Ivory, Two Dogs, Heads Resting On Other's Back, 19th Century 2000.00
Ivory, Two Puppies, Ransui 550.00
Ivory, Wife On Husband, Erotica, 2 1/2 In. 195.00
Ivory, Wolf, Monkey Beneath Its Front Legs, Mitsuhide 1500.00
Ivory, Wolf, Tomotada, 19th Century 2500.00
Walrus Ivory, Skull, 1 1/2 In. 85.00
Wood, 3 Chestnuts, Inlaid Ivory Worm, Insects, 18th Century, 2 In. 550.00

Wood, Beetle, Signed	75.00
Wood, Boar, Reclining, Toyomasa, 19th Century	1250.00
Wood, Boy, Seated, Playing Bekkanko, Miwa	900.00
Wood, Elephant, Seizan, 19th Century	3000.00
Wood, Karako On Shishi, Late 18th Century	1500.00
Wood, Karako, Seated, Holding A Coin, 19th Century	775.00
Wood, Mask, Okame, Signed Shuzan	850.00
Wood, Monkey, Eating Bamboo, Ebony, Juichi	500.00
Wood, Oceanographic, Figure Holding Pot With Coral, 3 1/4 In.	225.00
Wood, Octopus, Emerging From Pot, 19th Century, 2 In.	4000.00
Wood, Octopus, Emerging From Shell, 2 In.	4400.00
Wood, Octopus, Emerging From Shell–Encrusted Pot, 2 In.	4400.00
Wood, Samurai & Friend, Minkoku, 19th Century, 1 7/8 In.	2500.00
Wood, Shinto Priest & 2 Priests, Pair	175.00
Wood, Snake, Shinzan	2500.00
Wood, Tiger, Seated, Kokei, c.1800	4000.00

New Hall Porcelain Manufactory was started at Newhall, Shelton, Staffordshire, England, in 1782. Simple decorated wares were made. Between 1810 and 1825, the factory made a glassy bone porcelain sometimes marked with the factory name. Do not confuse New Hall porcelain with the pieces made by the New Hall Pottery Company, Ltd., a twentieth–century firm.

NEW HALL, Bowl, Chinese Figures, Red, Blue, 8 In.	125.00
Cup & Saucer, Flowers, Orange, Blue	85.00
Cup & Saucer, Orange, Gold Triangles	100.00

The New Martinsville Glass Manufacturing Company was established in 1901 in New Martinsville, West Virginia. It was bought and renamed the Viking Glass Company in 1944 and is still producing fine glasswares.

NEW MARTINSVILLE, Bookends, Elephant	175.00
Bookends, Nautilus	35.00
Bowl, 2 Sections, Handle, 6 In.	12.00
Bowl, Ruffled, Peach Blow, 8 1/2 In.	95.00
Butter, Cover, Radiance, Sterling Deposit Grapes	75.00
Cake Stand, Radiance, Gorham Base	89.00
Console Set, Swan, Amber, 5 1/2–In. Candlesticks	60.00
Cordial, Moondrops, Amber	10.00
Cordial, Radiance, Amber	10.00
Decanter, Moondrops, Cobalt, Clear Fan Stopper, 6 Piece	120.00
Decanter, Poppy, Amber, Clear Fan Stopper	35.00
Figurine, Bear, Baby	40.00 To 48.00
Figurine, Bear, Papa	130.00
Figurine, Chick	14.00
Figurine, Rooster, 7 In.	32.00 To 60.00
Figurine, Squirrel	30.00
Figurine, Wolfhound	70.00
Moonstone, Tumbler, Amber, 8 Piece	50.00
Pitcher, Moondrops, Amber, 8 1/2 In.	75.00
Punch Cup, Radiance, Blue	11.00
Punch Set, Radiance, Black, 7 Piece	250.00
Sugar & Creamer, Ruby, Miniature	28.00
Vase, Radiance, Crimped Top, Black, 12 In.	155.00

Newcomb Pottery was founded by Ellsworth and William Woodward at Sophie Newcomb College, New Orleans, Louisiana, in 1896. The work continued through the 1940s. Pieces of this art pottery are marked with the printed letters *NC* and often have the incised initials of the artist as well. Most pieces have a matte glaze and incised decoration.

NEWCOMB, Bowl, Cherokee Rose, Hilda Blank, c.1919, 4 1/2 x 4 1/4 In.	1000.00
Bowl, Entwined Irises & Vines, Sadie Irvine, 1914, 8 1/2 In.	875.00

Bowl, Iris Entwined Vine At Bottom, Sadie Irvine, 1914, 8 1/2 In. 950.00
Bowl, Pink Daffodils, Dark Blue Ground, H. Bailey, 3 1/2 x 8 In. 110.00
Bowl, Sadie Irvine, 1915, 3 x 8 1/2 In. 635.00
Candlestick, Band of Open Flowers, A. F. Simpson, 1910, 6 7/8 In. 825.00
Creamer, 4–Color Floral, Henrietta Bailey, 1910 .... 950.00
Creamer, Abstract Design, 2 1/2 In. 328.00
Creamer, Carved Florals, Henrietta Bailey, 1910, 2 1/2 In. 950.00
Inkwell, Stylized Serpentine Black Design, Cream, 2 1/2 x 4 In. 990.00
Mug, Yellow Dandelions, Cream Ground, Base Saying, S. B. Levy, 6 In. 2750.00
Pot, 2 Live Oaks, Full Moon, Blue Matte Glaze, KG, 1933, 4 3/4 In. 1650.00
Pot, 2 Live Oaks, Full Moon, Henrietta Bailey, 1921, 4 1/4 In. 1650.00
Vase, 2 Handles, Incised Line Design, Baluster, J. M., 17 1/2 In. 2640.00
Vase, 4 Handles, Stylized Design, C. Littlejohn, 1905, 4 1/4 In. 880.00
Vase, Blue Bayou Trees, Light Blue, S. Irvine, Bulbous, 8 1/2 In. 4400.00
Vase, Blue Iris, Spiked Leaves, Blue Ground, A. Roman, 7 1/2 In. 8800.00
Vase, Floral, Blue Ground, Henrietta Bailey, 7 1/4 In. .... 1450.00 To 2200.00
Vase, Incised & Painted, Glossy, Marked, c.1905, 9 3/4 In. 2860.00
Vase, Incised Floral Design, Henrietta Bailey, 1929, 6 1/2 In. 1765.00
Vase, Incised Stylized Irises, Henrietta Bailey, 1908, 6 1/2 In. 2150.00
Vase, Iris, Henrietta Bailey 4070.00
Vase, Louisiana Iris, Leaves, Henrietta Bailey, 1919, 8 1/2 In. 4070.00
Vase, Matte Blue, J. M., 6 In. 475.00
Vase, Moon Shining Through Trees, Spanish Moss, Signed, 6 1/2 In. 2350.00
Vase, Open Petaled Flowers, C. Littlejohn, 1905, 5 1/2 In. 1100.00
Vase, Pine Trees, Moon, 1918, 8 In. 4500.00
Vase, Spanish Moss, Marked, 1910s, 6 1/4 In. 1350.00

Niloak Pottery (Kaolin spelled backward) was made at the Hyten
Brothers Pottery in Benton, Arkansas, between 1909 and 1946.
Although the factory did make cast and molded wares, collectors
are most interested in the marbelized art pottery line made of
colored swirls of clay. It was called *Mission Ware.*

NILOAK, Candlestick, Marbelized, 8 x 6 In., Pair 260.00
 Candlestick, Marbelized, 9 In. 125.00
 Candlestick, Marbelized, Blue, Brown & Cream, 8 1/2 In. 125.00
 Cookie Jar, Marbelized, Blue, Brown & Cream, 8 1/2 In. 795.00
 Ewer, Eagle & Star 30.00
 Pitcher, Geometric Floral Design, Square 45.00
 Pitcher, Marbelized Blue, 7 In. 27.50
 Planter, Camel 20.00
 Planter, Polar Bear 10.00
 Planter, Squirrel, Green 12.00
 Vase, Cluster of Leaves, Pink To Blue, 3 In. 12.00
 Vase, Marbelized, 2 1/2 In. 50.00
 Vase, Marbelized, 14 1/2 In. 325.00
 Vase, Marbelized, 5 Colors, 8 1/2 In. 110.00
 Vase, Marbelized, Blue, 6 In. 60.00
 Vase, Marbelized, Brown, 6 1/2 In. 65.00
 Vase, Marbelized, Bulbous Bottom, Corset Top, 8 In. 125.00
 Vase, Marbelized, Cylindrical, 8 In. 90.00
 Vase, Marbelized, Gourd, 6 In. 45.00
 Vase, Marbelized, Wide Rim, 6 1/2 In. 75.00

Nippon–marked porcelain was made in Japan from 1891 to 1921.
Nippon is the Japanese word for *Japan.* A few firms continued to
use the word *Nippon* on ceramics after 1921 as a part of the
company name more than as an identification of the country of
origin. More pieces marked Nippon will be found in the
Dragonware, Moriage, and Noritake sections.

NIPPON, Ashtray, Indian Chieftain, Beaded 125.00
 Berry Set, Gold Beaded, 7 Piece 285.00
 Beverage Set, Grape Design, 5 Piece 150.00
 Bowl, Daises Inside, Gold Band, 3–Footed, 6 In. 35.00

Bowl, Hand Painted, Floral Trim, Cover, Green Mark, 7 1/2 x 4 1/2 In.	85.00
Box, Jewelry, Stylized Moriage Chrysanthemums, Square, 5 In.	115.00
Cake Plate, Winged Dragon, Pierced Handles, Marked, 11 In.	65.00
Cake Set, Gold & Black Border, 7 Piece	125.00
Cake Set, Pink Floral Border, 7 Piece	125.00
Candlestick, Allover Lavender Violet Flowers, Cream, 9 In., Pair	325.00
Charger, Egyptian Boat, Buildings, Gold Trim, 11 1/2 In.	110.00
Cheese Dish, 2 Swans In Water	115.00
Chocolate Pot, Hand Painted, Rosenthal Vase, 10 1/2 In.	88.00
Chocolate Pot, Moriage, Dragon, Beaded, Signed, 10 In.	195.00
Chocolate Pot, Scenic, Gold Gilt Design Top & Bottom, Signed, 10 In.	75.00
Chocolate Set, Cobalt & Gold	595.00
Chocolate Set, Cobalt Blue, 6 Cups & Saucers	1400.00
Chocolate Set, Floral, Cobalt Blue, 13 Piece	350.00
Chocolate Set, Palm Trees, Beaded, 7 Piece	235.00
Coaster, Gouda Style, Flowers, Brown, Orange, Green Wreath, 6 Piece	100.00
Compote, Cottage In Woods, Gold Filigree Border, 9 1/2 In., 2 Piece	300.00
Compote, Pink Hibiscus, 5 x 8 In.	95.00
Cruet, Bisque	350.00
Dish, Black & Gold Scenic On White, Center Handle, 6 3/4 In.	17.00
Dish, Cheese, Slant Top, Roses, Gold On White	95.00
Dish, Egyptian Lady, Blue, Red, Yellow, Cream Ground, Signed, 8 In.	125.00
Dish, Floral, Gold, Tricornered, 3 Handle, Marked, 7 In.	35.00
Doll, Bisque, Jointed, 4 In.	75.00
Ewer, Aqua, Purple Chrysanthemums, 10 In.	95.00
Fernery, Lake Scene, Footed, Square	40.00
Hair Receiver, Pink Rosebuds, Gold, 3-Footed	87.50
Hatpin Holder, Maple Leaf, Gold, 5 In.	55.00
Humidor, Blown-Out Camel & Rider	675.00
Humidor, Lion & Lioness, Marked, 5 1/4 In.	225.00
Humidor, Man On Camel, Tan, Brown Ground, 9 In.	980.00
Humidor, Moriage	525.00
Humidor, Skull, Moriage Decor, Marked	145.00
Jug, Whiskey, Scene	450.00
Lemonade Set, Hand Painted Pink Roses, 5 Piece	135.00
Match Holder, Dragon Design, Hanging, M In Wreath, 4 1/2 In.	45.00
Mug, Boating Scene, Green Mark	48.00
Mustard, Attached Liner, Pink Flowers, Gold	60.00
Mustard, Gold & Pink Roses, Cobalt Blue, 3 Piece	40.00
Nut Dish, Nut & Landscape, Footed, 4 Piece	50.00
Nut Dish, Nuts, Autumn Leaves, Oval, 6 Piece	55.00
Nut Set, Handpainted, Large Bowl, 7 1/2 In.	55.00
Pitcher, Gold Pattern	120.00
Pitcher, Milk, Stylized Flowers, Yellow Ground, 10 1/2 In.	150.00
Plaque, 2 Lions, Blown Out, 10 1/2 In.	750.00
Plaque, Fruit Scene, Green Wreath, 11 In.	100.00
Plaque, Stag, 10 3/4 In.	500.00

Nippon, Tea Set, 16 Piece

Plate, 2 Squirrels Gathering Pinecones, 7 1/2 In. 115.00
Plate, Florals, Gold Beading, Green Wreath Mark, 10 1/2 In. 80.00
Plate, Flying Geese, 10 In. 65.00
Punch Bowl, Stand, Floral Medallion, Handles, Paw Feet 300.00
Smoke Set, Windmill, 3 Piece 150.00
Sugar & Creamer, Egyptian Sailboats, Palm Trees, Green Wreath 75.00
Sugar & Creamer, Egyptian Sailboats, Palm Trees, Jeweled Rim, Marked 85.00
Sugar Shaker, Cobalt Blue, Gold 85.00
Tankard, Allover Design, Roses, Black Grapes, Raised Gold, 10 1/2 In. 195.00
Tankard, Cobalt Blue, Scene 375.00
Tea Set, 16 Piece ....*Illus* 77.00
Tea Set, Floral, 15 Piece 295.00
Tea Set, Gaudy, Gold Beading, Reds, Gold, Green, Signed, 3 Piece 250.00
Tea Set, Gold, Cake Plate, Service For 6 .... 595.00
Tea Set, Swans In Flight, Aqua Ground, Marked, 6 In. 310.00
Tea Strainer, 2 Piece 50.00
Teapot, Hand Painted Pastel Florals, Gold 45.00
Teapot, Scene, Individual, Marked 45.00
Teapot, Swans In Marsh 75.00
Toast Rack 125.00
Toothpick, Figural Dog, Amber, Top Hat 75.00
Toothpick, Trees, Lake 47.50
Tray, Dresser, Pink & Fuchsia Roses, Gold Trim, Marked, 10 x 7 In. 35.00
Tray, Sunset, Camels & Trees, Border, 9 1/4 In. 85.00
Tray, Trellis, Leaves & Berries, 10 1/4 In. 45.00
Tureen, Cover, Florals In Medallions, Butterflies, Marked, 11 1/2 In. 145.00
Urn, Cover, Floral, 14 In. 550.00
Vase, Allover Gold Gilt, Blue Enamel Dots, Pink Roses, 6 2/3 In. 150.00
Vase, Art Deco Landscape, Trees, Gold & Green Leaves, Marked, 10 In. 175.00
Vase, Basket Form, Gold Ground, Stippled, 7 1/2 x 6 3/4 In. 285.00
Vase, Birds In Flight, Moriage Neck, Handles, Base, Green M, 8 1/2 In. 255.00
Vase, Cobalt & Gold Floral, 7 In. 165.00
Vase, Cobalt Blue Scene, 18 In., Pair 1700.00
Vase, Egyptian, 8 1/4 In. 225.00
Vase, Enamel Glaze Resembling Pottery, 8 1/2 In. 195.00
Vase, Farm Scene, 10 In. 150.00
Vase, Flower, Swan, Trees, Lake, Hexagon, Green Wreath, 11 1/2 In. 250.00
Vase, Forest & Stream Scene, Double Handles, Blue Wreath, 14 1/2 In. 450.00
Vase, Overall Gold Beading, Red Poppies, Blue Mark, 8 In. 95.00
Vase, Poinsettias, 2 Handle, 8 In. 65.00
Vase, Queen Louise Portrait, 12 In. 900.00
Vase, Rising Sun, Forget–Me–Nots, Gold Trim, 5 In. 15.00
Vase, Roses, Black & Red Trim, 2 Handles, Marked 55.00
Vase, Roses, Gold, Handles, Nishiki, 13 In. 95.00
Vase, Ruffled, Gold Loop Handles, Poppies, Gold Stems, 12 In. 125.00

Nodders, or nodding figures, or pagods, are porcelain figures with heads and hands that are attached to wires. Any slight movement causes the parts to move up and down. They were made in many countries during the eighteenth and nineteenth centuries. A few Art Deco designs are also known. Copies are being made.

NODDER, Ashtray, Boy, In Bowler Hat, Die Cast 70.00
 Ashtray, Lady On Couch, Legs & Fan Move, Ceramic 45.00
 Ashtray, Woman On Bed, Legs Move 38.00
 Baseball Player, Japan 24.00
 Baseball, Brewers, Gold 75.00
 Baseball, Twins, Blue 75.00
 Beachcomber Man, Head & Legs Move, Bisque, Occupied Japan 135.00
 Ben Casey, 1960s 40.00
 Big Tex 75.00
 Black Boy, Bisque 110.00
 Black Man, Papier–Mache Head, Chalk Body, 11 In. 2000.00
 Black Sambo, Straw Hat 45.00

◆◆◆

If you have an old piano, beware of moths. They sometimes infest the interior fabrics.

◆◆◆

Black Woman, Nods Head, Watermelon Slice, Salt & Pepper	100.00
Blond Oriental Woman, Sitting, Fan, Bisque, 5 1/4 x 3 In.	165.00
Boy & Girl, Gold, Red, Germany, Pair	75.00
Chicken, Papier–Mache	15.00
Chickens, With Chick Lid	55.00
Children Kissing	25.00
Chinese Man & Woman, Head & Fan Nod, Bisque	240.00
Colonel Sanders	75.00
Dennydimwit	165.00
Devil	20.00
Dog, Boxer	35.00
Dog, Papier–Mache	12.00
Donald Duck, Papier–Mache	22.00
Donkey	6.50
Donkey, Celluloid	55.00
Dutch Boy & Girl	25.00
Golfer, Japan	24.00
Hawaiian Boy & Girl, Kissing, Papier–Mache, Japan	35.00
Hobo, Green Coat, Bottle In Pocket, In Chair, Bisque, 3 1/2 In.	210.00
Hula Girl	15.00
Hula, Tiny	25.00
Indian Boy	10.00
Lucy, of Peanuts Comic Strip	15.00
Man & Woman, Colonial Clothes, Eyeglasses, Bisque, Germany, Pair	100.00
Mandarin, Regency, Plaster, Swirling Dragons On Robe, 11 In.	1650.00
Mickey Mouse, Papier–Mache	200.00
Monkey, Red Cap	20.00
Oriental Family	6.50
Oriental Man, Hands, Head & Tongue Nod, Bisque, Porcelain, Germany	125.00
Oriental Man, Standing, Carrying 2 Pink Baskets, Pottery, 4 1/2 In.	150.00
Santa Claus	135.00
Santa Claus, Windup, 5 In.	35.00
Shriner	65.00
Spaceman, 1950–1960	35.00
Tiger	25.00
Walking Pigs	85.00
Woman, Full–Bodied, Surface Cracks, 8 In.	145.00
Woodpecker, Picks Up Matches, Striking Surface, Iron, 1865, 4 1/2 In.	100.00
Zero, From Beetle Bailey	75.00

Noritake–marked porcelain was made in Japan after 1904 by Nippon Toki Kaisha. The best–known Noritake pieces are marked with the M in a wreath for the Morimura Brothers, a New York City distributing company. This mark was used until 1941. Another famous Noritake china was made for the Larkin Soap Company from 1916 through the 1930s. This dinnerware, decorated with azaleas, was sold or given away as a premium. There may be some helpful price information in the Nippon category since prices are comparable.

NORITAKE, Ashtray, Figural, Clown, Art Deco	150.00
Ashtray, Figural, Girl In Harlequin Suit	200.00
Ashtray, Figural, Tramp	1000.00
Bowl, Arabian River Scene, Gold & Blue Trim, 11 In.	75.00
Bowl, Azalea, 7 In.	22.00
Bowl, Azalea, 10 In.	35.00

Bowl, Azalea, Footed, 4 1/2 In.	35.00
Bowl, Flowers, Birds, Gold Rim, 8 In.	100.00
Bowl, Tree In Meadow, 2 Handles, 7 1/2 In.	15.00
Box, Cat Handle On Lid, 5 In.	125.00
Box, Clown, Blue Polka Dots, 5 1/2 In.	160.00
Box, Elephant, Howdah, 6 1/2 In.	225.00
Box, Powder Puff, Art Deco Woman	85.00
Butter Tub, 3 Piece	32.00
Butter Tub, Insert, Azalea	70.00
Cake Plate, Tree In Meadow	30.00
Card Holder, Golfer On Side	60.00
Casserole, Cover, Azalea, Gold Finial	450.00
Celery Tray, Azalea, Closed Handles	275.00
Celery, Swans, House, Lake, Trees, Sunset Sky, Handle	15.00
Chocolate Set, White, Gold Tracery Bands, 21 Piece	175.00
Coffeepot, Cover, Scheherazade	48.00
Coffeepot, Demi, Tree In Meadow	185.00
Condiment Set, Gold, Blue, Parrots, 6 Piece	35.00
Condiment Set, Tree In Meadow, 5 Piece	24.00 To 35.00
Creamer, Azalea	50.00
Cruet, Azalea	18.00
Cup & Saucer, Ardis	13.00
Cup & Saucer, Azalea	25.00
Cup & Saucer, Daphne	8.00
Cup, Mother-of-Pearl	5.00
Dealer Sign	95.00
Dessert Set, Azalea, 14 Piece	120.00
Dish, Lemon, Blown-Out Lemon	52.00
Egg, Easter, 1971	55.00
Eggcup, Azalea	35.00
Figurine, Colonial Lady With Fan, 6 1/2 In.	95.00
Gravy Boat, Azalea	45.00
Gravy Boat, Baroda	20.00
Gravy Boat, Daphne	25.00
Inkwell, Cover, Figural, Woman	250.00
Jam Jar, Azalea	85.00
Jam Jar, Locust	95.00
Match Holder, Polar Bear	100.00
Mustard Jar, Azalea	45.00
Plate, Azalea, 10 In.	20.00
Plate, Azalea, 8 In.	15.00
Plate, Flowers, Blue, Black, Orange, 10 In.	17.50
Plate, Lemon, Gold, Red M	20.00
Plate, Lemon, Orange, Green, Red M	20.00
Platter, Azalea, 14 In.	90.00
Powder Box, Peacock On Cover, Blue Luster, Signed	45.00
Punch Bowl, Peacocks	750.00
Relish, Azalea, Hand Painted	30.00
Salt & Pepper, Tree In Meadow	10.00
Salt Dip, Swan, Figural	20.00
Salt Dip, Swan, Matching Spoon	25.00
Shaving Mug, House On Lake Scenes, Signed	35.00
Snack Set, Japanese Lanterns, Red Mark, 8 Sets	175.00
Spoon Holder, Roses, Leaves, Gold Trim	55.00
Sugar & Creamer, Azalea	22.50
Sugar & Creamer, Open, Azalea	100.00
Sugar & Creamer, Strawberry Set, Tree In Meadow	70.00
Sugar, Cover, Berries 'N Such	8.00
Sugar, Cover, Daphne	10.00
Sugar, Heather, No Lid	6.00
Tea Set, Child's, Tree In Meadow, 1940s, 23 Piece	175.00
Teapot, Azalea	125.00
Teapot, Azalea, 6 In.	95.00

Toast Rack, Bird Finial	75.00
Toothpick, Azalea	85.00
Vase, Fan, Tree In The Meadow, Marked	55.00
Vase, Floral, 2 Handles, Light & Dark Blue, Green Wreath, 11 In.	225.00
Vase, Royal Blue, Gold & Enamel Design, 10 In.	375.00
Vase, Tree In Meadow, 8 In.	40.00
Vase, Tulips, Leaves, 5 1/2 In.	185.00
Wall Pocket, Bees, 5 3/4 In.	95.00

The Norse Pottery Company started in Edgerton, Wisconsin, in 1903. In 1904 the company moved to Rockford, Illinois. The company made a black pottery which resembled early bronze relics of the Scandinavian countries. The firm went out of business in 1913.

NORSE, Bowl, Black, Scroll Design, 6 In.	150.00
Bowl, Sunburst Design, Snake Handles, 8 In.	200.00

The North Dakota School of Mines was established in 1892 at the University of North Dakota. A ceramic course was included and pieces were made from the clays found in the region. Students at the university made pieces from 1909 to 1949. Although very early pieces were marked *U.N.D.*, most pieces were stamped with the university seal.

NORTH DAKOTA SCHOOL OF MINES, Ashtray, Forest Green, Triangular, 5 In.	40.00
Bowl, Matte Mauve, Glossy Interior, 8 1/2 In.	125.00
Bowl, Striated Brown, Rust Interior, 8 In.	85.00
Candleholder, Holly Shape, Gloss, Pair	45.00
Coaster, Parent's Day, 1932	80.00
Honey Jar, Bee Lid, Strawberrys, 4 In.	110.00
Paperweight, Parents' Day, 1939, 3 1/2 In.	30.00
Paperweight, Rebekah Lodge, Green, 3 1/2 In.	40.00
Plate, Brownish Mauve, Rolled Edge, 7 5/8 In.	35.00
Pot, Green, 2 1/2 In.	38.00
Pot, Green, Miniature	35.00
Rose Bowl, Blue, Ribbed Opening, 2 1/2 In.	35.00
Rose Bowl, Sandy Color, 2 1/2 In.	40.00
Tile, Blue & White, Square, 3 1/4 In.	40.00
Vase, Gold To Rose, 6 In.	85.00
Vase, Green To Brown, Penelope Thomson, 9 In.	425.00
Vase, Light Blue, Geometrical, 4 In.	35.00
Vase, Matte Green, 1926, 8 1/2 In.	90.00
Vase, Mr. Obocell	95.00
Vase, Oxen & Wagon, M. Cable, 6 1/2 In.	450.00
Vase, Plowman, Brown Shades, 4 3/4 In.	575.00
Vase, Ribbed Green, Hand Thrown, 5 In.	98.00
Vase, Rose To Gray, MHM, '26, 6 x 7 In.	95.00
Vase, Terra–Cotta, Bottle Shape, 7 1/2 In.	130.00

The Harry Northwood Glass Company was founded by Harry Northwood, a glassmaker who worked for Hobbs, Brockunier and Company, La Belle Glass Company, and Buckeye Glass Company before founding his own firm. He opened one factory in Indiana, Pennsylvania, in 1896, and another in Wheeling, West Virginia, in 1902. Northwood closed when Mr. Northwood died in 1923. Many types of glass were made, including carnival, custard, goofus, and pressed. The underlined N mark was used on some pieces.

NORTHWOOD, Berry Bowl, Leaf Umbrella, Mauve, 7 Piece	385.00
Berry Set, Grape & Gothic, 6 Piece	35.00
Berry Set, Inverted Fan & Feather, Emerald, Gold, 7 Piece	340.00
Berry Set, Peach, Green, Gold Trim, 7 Piece	150.00
Berry Set, Regal, Green, Gold, 7 Piece	140.00
Bowl, Amethyst, Basketweave, Carnival Glass, Scalloped, 8 1/2 In.	80.00
Bowl, Beads, Bowl, Green, 7 In.	53.00

Bowl, Pillar Optic, Cranberry Opalescent, 11 In. 110.00
Bowl, Poppy Scroll, Purple, 7 In. 40.00
Bowl, Shell & Wildrose, Green Opalescent, 3–Footed, 7 1/2 In. 35.00
Bushel Basket, Blue, Carnival Glass, Signed 125.00
Butter, Cover, Grape & Cable, Purple 175.00
Butter, Cover, Paneled Holly, White, Red Berries, Green Leaves 125.00
Compote, Fern, Carnival Glass, Green 70.00
Compote, Hearts & Flowers, White, Iridescent 195.00
Cruet, Leaf Umbrella, Faceted Stopper, Cranberry 395.00
Cruet, Parian Swirl, Cranberry 195.00
Cup, Grape & Cable, Green 35.00
Pitcher, Water, 3–Tier Coin Spot, Cranberry 365.00
Pitcher, Water, Leaf Umbrella, Yellow, Clear Frosted Handle 425.00
Pitcher, Water, Regent, Green, Gold Trim 110.00
Plate, Grape, Nutmeg Stained, 8 In. 30.00
Plate, Strawberry, Green 175.00
Punch Set, Grape & Cable, 10 Piece 1000.00
Sauce, Argonaut Shell, Opalescent, Footed 39.00
Spooner, Argonaut Shell, Opalescent Blue 125.00
Spooner, Wild Bouquet 122.00
Sugar Shaker, Leaf Mold, Blue Frosted 185.00
Sugar, Cover, Intaglio, Blue 175.00
Table Set, Diamond Maple Leaf, Cobalt Blue, Gold, 4 Piece 850.00
Table Set, Golden Peach, Green, Gold, 4 Piece 265.00
Tumbler, American Beauty Rose 22.00
Tumbler, Drapery, Blue 45.00
Tumbler, Flute, Marigold 35.00
Tumbler, Memphis 25.00
Tumbler, Peach Pattern, Green, Gold 35.00
Tumbler, Water Lily & Cattails, Dark Aqua Opalescent 25.00
Vase, Tree Trunk, Squatty 1600.00
Water Set, Golden Peach, Green, Gold, 7 Piece 355.00
Water Set, Leaf Mold, Mica, 7 Piece 780.00
Water Set, Leaf Umbrella, Cranberry, 7 Piece 595.00
Water Set, Leaf Umbrella, Mauve, 7 Piece 730.00

Nu–Art was a trademark registered by the Imperial Glass Company of Bellaire, Ohio, about 1920.

NU–ART, Ashtray, Bulldog 125.00
Lamp, Nude, Kneeling, Frosted Shade 300.00
Lamp, Nude, Sitting On Pillar, Ball Shade 265.00
Plate, Chrysanthemum, White 975.00

Nutcrackers of many types have been used through the centuries. At first the nutcracker was a fancy hammer; but by the nineteenth century, many elaborate and ingenious types were made. Levers, screws, and hammer adaptations were the most popular. Because nutcrackers are still useful, they are still being made, some in the old styles.

NUTCRACKER, Alligator, Brass 35.00
Cow, Cast Iron 17.00
Demon Form, Bronze, India, 1890s, 9 1/2 In. 50.00
Dog, 12 In. 25.00
Dog, Black, Defined Hair, Cast Iron, Harper Supply, 13 x 6 In. 130.00
Dog, Collie, Cast Iron, 1920 .... 45.00
Dog, Retriever, Cast Iron 6.00
Dog, Tail Is Handle, Althoff Co., Chicago, Cast Iron, 1915 .... 125.00
Dog, Victorian, Iron, Gold Paint, 11 x 6 In. 55.00
Eagle, Brass 25.00
Elephant 17.00
Elephant, Full–Bodied 78.00
Squirrel, Cast Iron, In Wooden Bowl 35.00
Woman's Legs, Brass 36.00

NYMPHENBURG, see Royal Nymphenburg

The words *Occupied Japan* were used on pottery, porcelain, toys, and other goods made during the American occupation of Japan after World War II, from 1945 to 1952. Collectors now search for these pieces. The items were made for export.

OCCUPIED JAPAN, Ashtray, Duck	12.00
Ashtray, Hat, Cowboy's, Metal	8.00
Bride & Groom, Bisque, 3 3/4 In., Pair	30.00
Cup & Saucer, Cherries	20.00
Cup & Saucer, Flowers	18.00
Doll, Twins, Dressed, Bisque, 6 In., Pair	70.00
Figurine, 2 Pelicans, Black Base, 6 x 4 1/2 x 3 In.	60.00
Figurine, Black Cat	12.00
Figurine, Boy, Holding Kitten, Dog, 4 In.	8.00
Figurine, Boy, Hummel Type, Empty Pockets, Dog, 4 3/4 In.	10.00
Figurine, Boy, Seated On Fence, Playing Horn, 4 In.	10.00
Figurine, Buxom Woman, Seated, Blue & Pink Dress, 4 1/2 In.	18.00
Figurine, Chariot & Grecian Figure, 2 Horses, Bisque, Andrea	225.00
Figurine, Child, Unicorn Pulling Shell, Ardalt, 9 1/2 In.	20.00
Figurine, Circus Tricycle, Box	50.00
Figurine, Clown, Leaning On Drum, 4 In.	45.00
Figurine, Clown, Riding Donkey, 5 In.	65.00
Figurine, Colonial Couple, Maruyama, 3 1/2 In., Pair	17.50
Figurine, Colonial Couple, Orator, 6 In., Pair	33.00
Figurine, Colonial Couple, Seated, Maruyama, 3 1/2 In., Pair	30.00
Figurine, Colonial Man, 4 In.	18.00
Figurine, Colonial Man, Bisque, 10 1/4 In.	60.00
Figurine, Colonial Woman, 4 In.	18.00
Figurine, Cowboy, 2 Lambs, 3 1/2 In.	8.00
Figurine, Dancing Girl, Hands Behind Head, 5 In.	12.00
Figurine, Dancing Girl, Holding Skirt, Hand Painted, 4 In.	10.00
Figurine, Dog, Lying, T In Circle Mark, 4 1/2 In.	8.00
Figurine, Dutch Boy, 3 In.	12.00
Figurine, Elephant	8.00
Figurine, Girl, Carrying Umbrella, 4 1/2 In.	8.00
Figurine, Girl, Hummel Style, Basket, Mouse, 5 1/2 In.	20.00
Figurine, Girl, Seated On Fence, 4 In.	8.00
Figurine, Man, With Mandolin	45.00
Figurine, Shepherd & Shepherdess, Hand Painted, 12 In., Pair	125.00
Figurine, Woman, Full Lace Dress & Bonnet	40.00
Lamp, Figural, Woman	50.00
Lamp, Love Couple, Seated, White, Shade, 11 1/2 In., Pair	200.00
Pin, Bird Shape, Celluloid, 2 1/4 In.	9.00
Pin, Bluebird	18.00
Pin, Woman & Elf	12.00
Planter, Birdhouse, 2 Birds, 3 1/2 In.	10.00
Planter, Elephant & Cart	10.00
Planter, Madonna, Blue Veil, Blond, 6 In.	30.00
Planter, Parrot, 6 In.	28.00
Planter, Shell, Baby Duck Inside	35.00
Plaque, Colonial Figures, Bisque, Hand Painted, Pair	45.00
Plaque, Woman, Bisque, Chase	20.00
Plate, 3 Muses, Reticulated, Scalloped, 9 1/4 In.	55.00
Plate, Floral, Domed Base, Hokutosha, 5 x 3 3/4 In.	15.00
Plate, Pastoral Lovers, Gold Beading, Pierced, 9 1/4 In., Pr.	55.00
Ragtime Band, Box, 6 Piece	30.00
Salt & Pepper, Tray, Metal	10.00
Shelf Sitter, Boy Fishing	18.00
Sugar & Creamer, Lily of The Valley	24.00
Sugar Bowl, Tomato	18.00
Teapot, Spout To Handle, Cover, 5 3/4 In.	25.00
Teapot, Tomato, 4 1/2 In.	45.00

Toby Jug, General MacArthur	65.00
Vase, Cover, Swirl, Pottery	95.00
Vase, Wedgwood Type, 5 1/4 In.	25.00
Wall Pocket, 3 Flying Ducks	35.00

George E. Ohr, a true eccentric, made pottery in Biloxi, Mississippi, between 1883 and 1918. The pottery was made of very thin clay that was twisted, folded, and dented into odd, graceful shapes. Some pieces were lifelike models of hats, animal heads, or even a potato. Some pieces were decorated with folded clay *snakes.* Although reproductions would be almost impossible to make, there have been some reworked pieces appearing on the market. These have been reglazed, or snakes and other embellishments have been added.

OHR, Bank, Lip Shape, Coin Slot Top, Green & Pink Mottled Glaze, 8 1/4 In.	1980.00
Bank, Potato Shape, Brown, Yellow Butter, Marked, 5 x 3 In.	550.00
Bowl, Asymmetrical Ruffled Rim, Gunmetal Over Brown, Marked, 5 In.	525.00
Bowl, Crimped Rim, Medium Brown Glaze, Black Metal Flakes, 2 x 5 In.	660.00
Bowl, Folded, 8 In.	750.00
Bowl, Gunmetal Glaze, Signed, Dated, 3 In.	590.00
Bowl, Gunmetal Glaze, Twisted Shoulder, Pinched & Ruffled, 3 1/4 In.	1980.00
Bowl, Lavender, Green & Blue Mottled Glaze, Squat, Dimpled, 2 3/4 In.	2860.00
Candleholder, Mottled Green, Signed	1200.00
Cup, Folded, 6 In.	750.00
Lamp, Fat, Duck Head Form, Signed, 4 In.	350.00
Mug, Puzzle, Green Glaze, Script Signed	650.00
Penholder, Panther's Head, Square Flat Base, Green Glaze, 4 1/2 x 3 In.	605.00
Pitcher, Blue–Green Glaze, Folded Cutout Handle, Cylindrical, 4 7/8 In.	2860.00
Pot, Crimped Top To Bottom, Gun Metal, 3 1/2 x 2 3/4 In.	650.00
Urn, White, Green & Blue Flecks & Drips, Signed, 2 1/2 x 5 In.	500.00
Vase, Brown–Green, Jagged Rim, 3 x 3 In.	225.00
Vase, Cave, 4 In.	700.00
Vase, Dark Speckled Green Glaze, 2 Spaghetti–Type Handles, 9 x 5 In.	4950.00
Vase, Deep Cobalt Glaze, 2 Kinked Handles, Twisted Neck, 10 x 6 1/2 In.	6600.00
Vase, Gunmetal, 3 In.	550.00
Vase, Metallic Black, Smooth & Dimpled, Bulbous, Flared Foot, 8 In.	3850.00
Vase, Mottled Mustard & Moss Green Metallic Glaze, Cylindrical, 7 In.	5500.00
Vase, Mottled Olive Green Glaze, Marked, c.1898, 4 In.	440.00
Vase, Mustard & Brown Dappled Glaze, Bulbous, 5 1/4 In.	2640.00
Vase, Mustard Glaze, Trailing Design, Bulbous, 4 1/4 In.	2200.00
Vase, Olive Green & Brown Dappled, Oviform, Twisted Neck, 4 3/4 In.	6050.00
Vase, Olive Green, Dark Green, Brown, Ovoid, 1910, 3 1/2 In.	465.00
Vase, Oviform, Gunmetal Glaze, Marked, c.1898, 3 1/2 In.	105.00
Vase, Oxblood, Green & Blue Dappled Glaze, Waisted Bulbous, 4 In.	4950.00
Vase, Rose Glaze, Green Vertical & Dot Design, 2 Ear Handles, 6 1/4 In.	6600.00
Vase, Rose, Green, Burgundy, Blue & Yellow Flambes, Bulbous Base, 7 In.	2640.00
Vase, Squat Goblet Form, Glossy Ochre Glaze, Marked, c.1891, 3 1/4 In.	165.00

OLD IVORY 84

Old Ivory china was made in Silesia, Germany, at the end of the nineteenth century. It is often marked with a crown and the word *Silesia.* Some pieces are also marked with the words *Old Ivory.* The pattern numbers appear on the base of each piece.

OLD IVORY, Berry Set, No. 16, Silesia, 7 Piece	150.00 To 225.00
Bowl, No. 11, Silesia, 10 In.	85.00
Bowl, No. 32, Silesia, 9 1/2 In.	120.00
Bowl, No. 63, Pink, Roses, Silesia, 10 In.	165.00
Bowl, No. 73, Silesia, 9 1/2 In.	125.00
Bowl, No. 75, Silesia, 9 1/2 In.	80.00 To 85.00
Bowl, Oyster, No. 16, Silesia	175.00
Bowl, Vegetable, Silesia, Round, 9 1/2 In.	125.00
Butter Chip, No. 28, Silesia	85.00 To 95.00
Cake Plate, No. 84, Silesia, 10 In.	95.00 To 110.00
Cake Set, No. 4, Silesia	250.00
Cake Set, No. 12, Silesia, 7 Piece	375.00

Celery Dish, No. 84	65.00
Charger, No. 16, Silesia, 13 In.	175.00
Chocolate Pot, No. 84, Silesia	285.00
Chocolate Pot, Thistle	210.00
Chocolate Set, No. 16, Silesia, 13 Piece	595.00 To 650.00
Chop Plate, No. 15	185.00
Cracker Jar, No. 16, Silesia, Squatty	350.00 To 375.00
Cracker Jar, No. 200, Silesia	275.00
Creamer	27.00
Cup & Saucer, Chocolate, No. 33	65.00
Cup & Saucer, No. 33, Silesia	55.00
Mustard, No. 84, Silesia	195.00
Oyster Bowl, No. 16, Silesia	175.00
Plate, 8 In.	20.00
Plate, No. 12, Silesia, 7 1/2 In.	85.00
Plate, No. 124, 6 Sides, Silesia, 8 3/4 In.	85.00
Plate, No. 75, Silesia, 6 In.	15.00
Platter, No. 16	375.00
Rose Bowl, No. 16, Silesia, Fluted	175.00
Salt & Pepper, No. 16, Silesia	125.00
Sugar & Creamer, No. 12, Silesia	165.00
Sugar & Creamer, No. 16, Silesia	135.00
Sugar Shaker, No. 84	395.00
Tile, Tea, No. 15, Silesia	175.00 To 185.00
Toothpick, No. 15, Silesia	250.00
Toothpick, No. 75, Silesia	250.00

OLD SLEEPY EYE, see Sleepy Eye

 Onion pattern, originally named *bulb pattern,* is a white ware decorated with cobalt blue or pink. Although it is commonly associated with Meissen, other companies made the pattern in the late–nineteenth and the twentieth centuries. A rare type is called *red bud* because there are added red accents on the blue-and-white dishes.

ONION, Bottle, Oil & Vinegar, Germany	125.00
Bowl, Rosenthal, 9 In.	575.00
Cup & Saucer, Soup, Double Handle, Marked Meissen, 4 Sets	198.00
Dish, Fruit, Leaf, Handle, Meissen	95.00
Dish, Leaf, Handle, Crossed Swords, 3 1/2 In.	76.00
Knife Set, Dinner, 9 3/4 In., 12 Piece	225.00
Luncheon Set, Meissen, Partial Set, 33 Piece	302.00
Mustache Cup & Saucer, Blue, 1890s	95.00
Platter, Floral Interior, Meissen, 17 1/2 x 23 1/4 In.	330.00
Salt Dip, Meissen	50.00
Saucer, Meissen, 4 In.	45.00
Sugar, Cover, Meissen Form, Thurn, Kloesterle, 3 In.	65.00
Tureen, Red, Crossed Swords, 12 1/2 In.	500.00

 Opalescent glass is translucent glass that has the tones of the opal gemstone. It originated in England in the 1870s and is often found in pressed glassware made in Victorian times. Opalescent glass was first made in America in 1897 at the Northwood glassworks in Indiana, Pennsylvania. Some dealers use the terms *opaline* and *opalescent* for any of these translucent wares.

OPALESCENT, see also Northwood; Pressed Glass; Spanish Lace

OPALESCENT, Banana Boat, Swirling Maize, Cranberry	100.00
Basket, Bushel, White, 8 Sides	130.00
Basket, Diamond–Quilted, Applied Flowers, Vaseline, 7 1/2 In.	200.00
Basket, Random Thorns, Crystal Rim, Base & Handle, 7 3/4 In.	260.00
Berry Bowl, Seaweed, Blue, 5 In.	42.00
Berry Set, Inverted Fan & Feather, White, 7 Piece	245.00
Berry Set, Petal & Fan, Peach, 7 Piece	450.00
Biscuit Jar, William & Mary, England, 7 1/2 In.	295.00

Boat, Base, Victorian, Dated 1886 .... 195.00
Bowl, Blue, 6–Petal Lotus Blossom 110.00
Bowl, Green, Higgins, 12 1/4 In. 100.00
Bowl, Hobnail, Ruffled, Vaseline, 11 In. 85.00
Bowl, Wheel & Block, Crystal, Goofus Trim, 9 1/2 In. 32.50
Bowl, Wreath & Shell, Vaseline, 8 In. 95.00
Bride's Bowl, Daisy Scroll 125.00
Bride's Bowl, Dogwood Flowers, Enamel Stamens & Stems, 12 In. 145.00
Butter, Cover, Diamond Spearhead, Cobalt Blue 435.00
Butter, Cover, Fluted Scroll, Vaseline 175.00
Butter, Cover, Jefferson's Idyll, Blue 350.00
Butter, Cover, Reverse Swirl, Blue 125.00
Butter, Cover, Swag With Brackets, Green 125.00
Butter, Fluted Scroll, Blue 215.00
Celery, Blue 85.00
Celery, Diamond Spearhead, Cobalt Blue 110.00
Celery, Opalescent Network, Pastel Ground, 6 3/4 In. 325.00
Celery, Wreath & Shell, Vaseline .... 155.00 To 175.00
Compote, Hearts & Flowers, Aqua 625.00
Compote, Jelly, Seedpod, Blue, Gold Trim 28.00
Compote, Jelly, Swag With Brackets 47.50
Compote, Squirrel & Acorn, Green 95.00
Creamer, Beatty Swirl, Blue 75.00
Creamer, Frosted Leaf & Basketweave 135.00
Creamer, Jewel & Flower, Blue 70.00
Creamer, Palm Beach, Blue 45.00
Creamer, Swag With Brackets, Green 50.00
Cruet, Alaska, Blue 250.00
Cruet, Daisy & Fern, White 45.00
Cruet, Daisy & Fern, White, Faceted Stopper 110.00
Cruet, Ribbed Lattice, Blue 185.00
Cruet, Ringneck Coin Spot, Blue 295.00
Cruet, Seaweed, Blue 245.00
Cruet, Silver–Plated Spring Lid, Clear Handle, Cranberry 265.00
Cruet, Wild Bouquet, Blue 275.00
Dish, Cheese, Cover, Swirl, Cranberry 350.00
Dish, Many Loops, Green 20.00
Dish, Pickle, Poppy, White 620.00
Finger Bowl, Buckeye Lattice, Cranberry 90.00
Finger Bowl, Expanded Diamond, Green–Blue To Blue, 6 Sides 75.00
Finger Bowl, Lattice, Cranberry 135.00
Lamp, Snowflake, Cranberry, Miniature 1200.00
Lemonade Set, Light Blue, Tropical Design, 5 Piece 95.00
Muffineer, Leaf Umbrella, Mauve 295.00
Mug, Singing Birds, Aqua 925.00
Mustard, Striped, Yellow, Hinged Cover 55.00
Nappy, Leaf Rays, Peach 55.00
Nappy, Sea Spray, Handle, 5 In. 25.00
Pitcher Set, Maiden Blush, Galloway, 5 Piece 495.00
Pitcher, Daisy & Fern, Blue 195.00
Pitcher, Daisy & Fern, Cranberry 495.00
Pitcher, Grapes & Leaves, Lined, Plated Holder, 5 In. 85.00
Pitcher, Swirling Maize, Cranberry 495.00
Pitcher, Water, Blue, Swirl, Bulbous, Flat Squared Ruffled Mouth 175.00

◆◆

Never stop a music box in the middle of a tune. If the box is later moved, it is more likely to damage the spikes on the cylinder if not at the end of a song.

◆◆

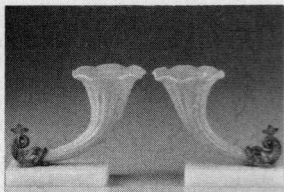

Opalescent, Vase, Blue, Bronze,
Dolphin Marble Base, 7 In., Pair

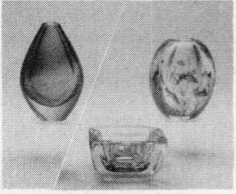

Orrefors, Vase, Ariel, Blue Crosshatching, 8 In.
Orrefors, Bowl, Green & Black Fish, E. Hald, 3 In.
Orrefors, Vase, Green & Black Fish, E. Hald, 6 In.

Pitcher, Water, Dahlia, Blue	185.00
Pitcher, Water, Daisy & Fern, Cranberry, Ball Shaped	225.00
Pitcher, Water, Regal, White	95.00
Pitcher, Water, Ringneck Stripe, Cranberry	495.00
Pitcher, Water, Swirl, White	70.00
Pitcher, Water, White	95.00
Rose Bowl, Leaf Chalice, Pedestal, Blue	45.00
Saltshaker, Crisscross, Cranberry	145.00
Spittoon, Frolicking Bears, Aqua, ICGA Souvenir	75.00
Spittoon, Frolicking Bears, Vaseline, ICGA Souvenir	75.00
Spooner, Bubble Lattice, Cranberry	135.00
Spooner, Diamond & Spear, Vaseline	45.00
Spooner, Palm Beach, Blue	50.00
Spooner, Stippled Leaf & Basketweave, Blue	75.00
Spooner, Swag With Brackets, Green	50.00
Spooner, Vaseline, Crimped, 4 1/4 In.	55.00
Sugar Shaker, Daisy & Fern, Netted Apple Blossom, Cranberry	245.00
Sugar Shaker, Flint	75.00
Sugar Shaker, Swirl, White	95.00
Sugar Shaker, Windows Swirled, White	165.00
Sugar, Cover, Daisy & Button, Blue	40.00
Sugar, Cover, Swag With Bracket, Vaseline	125.00
Sugar, Open, Diamond Optic, Vaseline, 4 3/8 In.	55.00
Swan, Green	35.00
Syrup, Flat Flower, Blue	195.00
Syrup, Grape & Leaf, Green	195.00
Syrup, Leaf Umbrella, Yellow	495.00
Syrup, Ring Neck, Spatter, Cranberry	195.00
Table Set, Alabama, Ruby Stain	495.00
Table Set, Palm Beach, Blue, 4 Piece	435.00
Table Set, Panel Holly, Clear, Gold, 4 Piece	385.00
Table Set, Swag With Brackets, Vaseline, 3 Piece	295.00
Table Set, Swag With Brackets, Vaseline, 4 Piece	475.00
Table Set, Tacoma, Amber Stain	475.00
Table Set, Wreath & Shell, White, Enamel, 4 Piece	375.00
Toothpick, Beatty Ribbed, Blue	20.00
Toothpick, Diamond Spearhead, Green	50.00
Toothpick, Diamond Spearhead, Vaseline	65.00
Toothpick, Idyll, Blue	225.00
Toothpick, Iris With Meander, Blue	75.00 To 87.50
Toothpick, Iris With Meander, Green	55.00
Toothpick, Paneled Sprig, White	45.00
Toothpick, Ribbed Lattice, Blue	135.00
Toothpick, Swirled Windows, Cranberry	225.00
Toothpick, Windows, White	95.00
Toothpick, Wreath & Shell, Blue	295.00 To 300.00
Tray, Sanibel, Yellow, 8 1/2 In.	48.00

Tumbler, Blue, Spangled, Sanded Gold Flower & Leaves, 3 5/8 In. 50.00
Tumbler, Daisy & Fern, Cranberry 50.00
Tumbler, Jeweled Heart, Blue 65.00
Tumbler, Jeweled Heart, Green 30.00
Tumbler, Paneled Holly, White 42.50
Tumbler, Poinsettia, Blue 70.00
Tumbler, Poinsettia, Cranberry 85.00
Tumbler, Regal, Blue, 4 Piece 185.00
Tumbler, Stork & Rushes, White 65.00
Tumbler, Wild Bouquet, Green 110.00
Vase, Blue, Bronze, Dolphin Marble Base, 7 In., Pair ....*Illus* 715.00
Vase, Cranberry, Ruffled, 8 In. 95.00
Vase, Double Key, Blue, 6 In. 95.00
Vase, Horse Chestnut, English, Vaseline, 8 1/2 In. 260.00
Vase, Jack-In-The-Pulpit, Petal Top, Enamel Inside, 13 1/2 In. 260.00
Vase, Piasa Bird, Blue 40.00
Vase, Piasa Bird, White 35.00
Vase, Swirl, Green Flowers, Amber Stems, Cranberry, 8 In. 320.00
Vase, Swirling Maize, Cranberry, 11 In. 350.00
Vase, Tree Trunk, Blue, Northwood, Pair 85.00
Water Lily & Cattails, Bowl, Amethyst, 10 1/2 x 11 1/2 In. 58.00
Water Lily & Cattails, Pitcher, Water, Frosted 195.00
Water Set, Alaska, Blue, 7 Piece 385.00
Water Set, Argo Shell, Clear, 7 Piece 310.00
Water Set, Drapery, Blue, Gold, 7 Piece 410.00
Water Set, Everglades, Blue, 7 Piece 695.00
Water Set, Everglades, Clear, Gold, 7 Piece 525.00
Water Set, Iris With Meander, Vaseline, 7 Piece 650.00
Water Set, Iris, Blue, 7 Piece .... 695.00 To 835.00
Water Set, Jeweled Heart, Blue, 7 Piece 625.00
Water Set, Lily & Cattails, Blue, 7 Piece 195.00
Water Set, Regal, Green, 7 Piece 565.00
Water Set, Reverse Swirl, Blue, 7 Piece 295.00
Water Set, Wreath & Shell, Blue, 7 Piece .... 650.00 To 850.00

Opaline, or opal glass, was made in white, green, and other colors. The glass had a matte surface and a lack of transparency. It was often gilded or painted. It was a popular mid-nineteenth-century European glassware.

OPALINE, Box, Hinged Cover, White, Cobalt & Orange, Brass Feet, 4 In. 148.00
Box, Hinged Lid, Pink, Scrolls, Country Scene, 1 3/4 x 2 1/2 In. 95.00
Pitcher, Blue, Gold & Yellow Flowers, Leaves, 2 1/8 In. 58.00
Ring Tree, Blue, Gold-White Trim, France, 2 1/2 In. 45.00
Vase, Allover Gold, Yellow Design, Blue, France, 3 1/4 In. 40.00
Vase, Indian Design, 10 In. 37.50
Vase, Iris, Pink, Burgundy, Tall 50.00

The stage is a long way from some of the seats at a play or an opera, so the patrons sometimes carried special opera glasses in the nineteenth and early twentieth centuries. Mother-of-pearl was a popular decoration.

OPERA GLASSES, Abalone Shell & Gilded Brass, Audemair, Paris, Leather Case 85.00
Abalone-Shell Cased, French Chevalier, Paris, 4 x 2 1/4 In. 75.00
Aluminum & Mother-of-Pearl Frame, Birds, Insects, Case 495.00
Enameled Design, Cherub, Fleur-De-Lis, France 995.00
Mother-of-Pearl, Brass, Case, Signed LeMarie, Paris 75.00
Mother-of-Pearl, Brass, LeMaire De Paris 105.00
Mother-of-Pearl, Folding Handle, France 135.00
Mother-of-Pearl, French 58.00
Mother-of-Pearl, Gilt Brass, Iris, Paris, Leather Case 45.00
Mother-of-Pearl, Theodore B. Starr, N. Y., Case 75.00
Platinum & Diamond Bands, Cartier, Red Leather Case, c.1920 .... 9500.00
Silver, Peacock Design In Relief 30.00

 Little Orphan Annie first appeared in the comics in 1924. The redheaded girl and her friends have been on the radio and are still on the comic pages. A Broadway musical show and a movie in the 1980s made Annie popular again and many toys, dishes, and other memorabilia are being made.

ORPHAN ANNIE, Book, Annie & The Gila Monster Gang, Copyright 1934, '38, '44 .... 25.00
Book, Bucking The World, Hardcover, 1929 .... 35.00
Book, Comic, Popped Wheat, 1938, 16 Pages 15.00
Book, Life & Hard Times of Little Orphan Annie, H. Gray, 1935 .... 45.00
Book, Little Orphan Annie, Whitman, 1944 .... 23.00
Certificate, Membership, Secret Guard 35.00
Cupboard, Annie's Cookery, Plastic, 24–Piece Play Set, Box 35.00
Cutout Toys, Sandy, Grunts The Pig, Pee Wee The Elephant 125.00
Decoder, 1935 .... 32.00
Decoder, Manuals 100.00
Doll, Celluloid, Jointed, 8 In. 170.00
Doll, Knickerbocker, Box, 1982, 5 In. 12.00
Doll, Oilcloth 95.00
Game, Treasure Hunt, Ovaltine 25.00
Light Bulb, Christmas 60.00
Limousine, Annie, Knickerbocker, Box 20.00
Lunch Box, Aladdin, 1982 .... 20.00
Mug, China 30.00
Mug, Ovaltine, Beetleware .... 18.00 To 30.00
Ovaltine Treasure Hunt Game, 1933 .... 45.00
Pastry Set 65.00
Puzzle, Sandy, Annie, Warbucks & Punjab, Jaymar 22.00
Shake–Up Mug, Green, Orange Top 35.00
Toy, Sandy, Windup, Tin Litho, Marx 85.00
Wristwatch, Harold Gray 95.00

The Orrefors Glassworks, located in the Swedish province of Smaaland, was established in 1898. The company is still making glass for use on the table or as decorations. There is renewed interest in the glass made in the modern styles of the 1940s and 1950s. Most vases and decorative pieces are signed with the etched name.

ORREFORS, Ashtray, Etched, Frosted Nude Center, 6 Sides, 7 1/2 In. 165.00
Bowl, Blue–Gray 175.00
Bowl, Concentric Overlapping Circles, Signed, 5 1/2 In. 140.00
Bowl, Green & Black Fish, E. Hald, 3 In. ....*Illus* 550.00
Bowl, Man Lying On Galloping Horse, Chased By Dogs, Signed, 9 In. 225.00
Bowl, Red 195.00
Bowl, Thousands Windows, 5 In. 150.00
Bowl, Thousands Windows, 7 1/4 In. 200.00
Candleholder, Eden, Pair .... 55.00 To 75.00
Cigar Jar, Ashtray, Gray, Individual 24.00
Cordial Set, Etched & Frosted Design, Stemmed Wines, 14 Piece 550.00
Goblet, Etched Design On Cup & Part of Stem, S. Palmquist, 8 In. 550.00
Plate, Notre Dame Cathedral, 1970 .... 50.00
Plate, Westminster Abbey, 1971 .... 50.00
Sugar & Creamer, Signed 45.00
Vase, Ariel, Blue Crosshatching, 8 In. ....*Illus* 990.00
Vase, Ariel, Ruby Stripes & Clear Bubbles Interior, Signed, 6 In. 1045.00
Vase, Engraved Dancing Girls, Art Nouveau, Signed, 10 /2 In. 400.00
Vase, Engraved, Signed, 8 In. 150.00
Vase, Fish Design, Monochromatic Fish Interior, Signed, 4 3/4 In. 465.00
Vase, Green & Black Fish, E. Hald, 6 In. ....*Illus* 825.00
Vase, Green, Brown, Signed Eduard Hald, 209L, 6 In. 400.00
Vase, Heavy Wall, Marine Design Inside, 6 1/2 In. 825.00
Vase, Oval Thumbprints, Teardrop Shape, Signed, 11 In. 170.00
Vase, Selena Smoke, P. Pomquist, 7 In. 85.00

Vase, St. Francis, Kneeling, Flying Birds, Signed, 8 In.	225.00
Vase, Stylized Geometric Design, Black Lines, 10 1/4 In.	135.00
Vase, Teardrop Form, Heavy Wall, Crosshatch Design, Signed, 8 In.	1000.00

Ott & Brewer Company operated the Etruria Pottery at Trenton, New Jersey, from 1863 to 1893. They started making belleek in 1882. The firm used a variety of marks that incorporated the initials O & B.

OTT & BREWER, Basket, Thorn Handle, 1870s	950.00
Chocolate Pot, Blue Flowers, White Ground, Marked	185.00
Creamer, Scalloped, Florals, Thumbprint Base, Branch Handle	200.00
Tray, Gold–Paste Orchid, Gilt Feet, Ruffled, Square, 8 1/4 In.	395.00
Tumbler, Blue Interior, Signed	163.00

The four Overbeck sisters started a pottery in Cambridge City, Indiana, in 1911. They made all types of vases, each one-of-a-kind. Small, hand-modeled figurines are the most popular pieces with today's collectors. The factory continued until 1955 when the last of the four sisters died.

OVERBECK, Candlestick, Blue, Handle	40.00
Figurine, Baby Birds, 4 1/2 In.	525.00
Figurine, Camel, 4 1/2 In.	300.00
Figurine, Dutch Girl, 4 In.	155.00
Figurine, Man In Hat, Cane, 5 In.	155.00
Figurine, Two Victorian Women, 5 In.	450.00
Vase, 3 Vertical Bands, Geometric Design, Marked, c.1915, 4 1/2 In.	522.00
Vase, Flying Birds, White, Blue, 6 In.	900.00

Owens Pottery was made in Zanesville, Ohio, from 1891 to 1928. The first art pottery was made after 1896. Utopian Ware, Cyrano, Navarre, Feroza, and Henri Deux were made. Pieces were usually marked with a form of the name *Owens*. About 1907, the firm began to make tile and discontinued the art pottery wares.

OWENS, Bowl, Lotus, Japanese–Style Pink Floral, Blue To Ivory, 3 1/2 In.	160.00
Jardiniere, Utopian, Chrysanthemums, Pedestal, 27 1/2 In.	450.00
Pitcher, Utopian, Pansy, 3–Footed, 5 1/2 In.	192.00
Vase, Aborigine, Bulbous, 5 x 7 In.	165.00
Vase, Bud, Utopian, Holly Berries, Leaves, 4 In.	70.00
Vase, Cyrano, Ivory & Light Blue, Black Ground, 3–Footed, 6 1/2 In.	40.00
Vase, Floral, Burnt Orange & Green Ground, Terrell, 12 1/2 In.	220.00
Vase, Utopian, 12 In.	260.00
Vase, Utopian, Autumn Leaves, Pinched Sides, 6 3/4 In.	495.00
Vase, Utopian, Bird Portrait, Floral Reverse, 12 1/2 In.	295.00
Vase, Utopian, Chrysanthemums, Fall Colors, Signed S. T., 13 1/2 In.	200.00
Vase, Utopian, Clover Design, 4 In.	95.00
Vase, Utopian, Handles, 7 x 4 1/2 In.	145.00
Vase, Utopian, Orange Poppy & Bud, 8 3/4 In.	120.00
Vase, Utopian, Swirled, Clover, Artist FMD, 4 In.	192.00
Vase, Utopian, Yellow Violets, Artist E. B., 4 1/4 In.	165.00

Oyster plates were popular from the 1880s. Each course at dinner was served in a special dish. The oyster plate had indentations shaped like oysters. Usually six oysters were held on a plate. There is no greater value to a plate with more oysters although that myth continues to haunt antiques dealers. There are other plates for shellfish including cockle plates and whelk plates. The appropriately shaped indentations are part of the design of these dishes.

OYSTER PLATE, Cobalt Blue, Gold Border, Germany, Square, 8 3/4 In.	145.00
Floral, Foliate & Gilt Design, Haviland, 7 3/4 In., 12 Piece	495.00
Gaudy Dutch	350.00
Shell Shape, Turquoise, Majolica, 9 In.	295.00

Paden City Glass Manufacturing Company was established in 1916 at Paden City, West Virginia. It is best known for glasswares but also produced a pottery line. The firm closed in 1951.

PADEN CITY, Bowl, Caliente, Tangerine, 10 In. 12.00
  Bread Plate, Ivy 2.00
  Cup & Saucer, Ivy 5.00
  Dinner Set, Shennandoah Ware, Extra Serving Pieces, 82 Piece 375.00
  Figurine, Pheasant 95.00
  Figurine, Polar Bear 50.00
  Figurine, Rooster, Blue 32.50
  Mayonnaise, Liner, Gazebo Etch 48.00
  Mayonnaise, Nora Bird, Pink, Footed 38.00
  Pitcher Set, Line No. 991, Amber, 8 Goblets 125.00
  Plate, Dinner, Ivy 6.00
  Plate, Garden Path, 9 In. 2.50
  Plate, Tab Handle, Loden Green, Maroon, Square, 10 In. 10.00
  Sugar & Creamer, Cupid, Pink 175.00
  Toothpick 24.00
  Tray, Oval, 11 In. 150.00

The paintings listed in this book are not works by major artists but rather decorative paintings on ivory, board, or glass that would be of interest to the average collector. To learn the value of an oil painting by a listed artist you must contact an expert in that area.

PAINTING, Oil On Board, Pearl of Orr's Island, Hathaway, Framed, 14 In. 3300.00
  Oil On Board, Still Life of Lemons, Wenzell, Frame, 16 x 20 In. 550.00
  Oil On Canvas, Alpine Landscape, Gilt Frame, 20 3/4 x 29 3/4 In. 70.00
  Oil On Canvas, American Ship, Brig Turk, Frame, 23 1/2 x 30 In. 3200.00
  Oil On Canvas, Boy Fishing, 19 3/4 x 28 1/4 In. 200.00
  Oil On Canvas, Boy, Holding Book, Framed, 19th Century, 20 x 16 In. 450.00
  Oil On Canvas, Child In Blue Dress, Oval, 15 3/4 x 12 3/4 In. 300.00
  Oil On Canvas, Child, Blue, Hobbyhorse, Burl Frame, 24 x 20 In. 935.00
  Oil On Canvas, Court Scene, H. Airens, Frame, 43 x 52 In. 2640.00
  Oil On Canvas, Duck, Chicks, Pond, Gilt Frame, 10 3/4 x 16 In. 200.00
  Oil On Canvas, Findochtie, Moray Firth, Gyrth Russell, 15 x 21 In. 1045.00
  Oil On Canvas, French Landscape, Myron Barlow, 32 x 36 In. 880.00
  Oil On Canvas, Gentleman, Frock Coat, Gilt Frame, 35 1/2 x 30 In. 700.00
  Oil On Canvas, Girl In Red Dress, Book At Feet, 15 1/2 x 12 In. 1540.00
  Oil On Canvas, Girl, Crocheting Bag, Frame, 21 3/4 x 18 3/4 In. 450.00
  Oil On Canvas, Handsome Dandy, R. Street, 1835, 29 1/2 x 25 In. 3850.00
  Oil On Canvas, Kitten In Sewing Basket, 4 1/2 x 5 1/2 In. 880.00
  Oil On Canvas, Landscape, Corn Shocks, Frame, 26 x 20 1/2 In. 140.00
  Oil On Canvas, Landscape, Hunter Shooting, 27 1/4 x 32 3/4 In. 250.00
  Oil On Canvas, Landscape, Mountains, Lake, Frame, 21 3/4 x 31 In. 100.00
  Oil On Canvas, Man, Glasses In Hand, Framed, 1847, 39 x 32 In. 700.00
  Oil On Canvas, Mifflinburg Covered Bridge, U. S., 22 x 28 In. 165.00
  Oil On Canvas, Mountain Landscape, Sheep, Frame, 11 1/2 x 14 In. 225.00
  Oil On Canvas, Old Woman, Lace Bonnet, Frame, 27 1/4 x 23 1/4 In. 450.00
  Oil On Canvas, Ships At Sea, American School, Frame, 16 x 20 In. 275.00
  Oil On Canvas, Ships, Rocky Coast, Gilt Frame, 14 1/2 x 20 1/2 In. 150.00
  Oil On Canvas, Trees, Mountains, Cattle, Frame, 30 1/2 x 35 1/4 In. 2000.00
  Oil On Canvas, Washington & Family, Frame, 31 3/4 x 41 1/2 In. 2200.00
  Oil On Canvas, Woman, Pink Lacy Hat, Frame, 19 1/4 x 16 In. 350.00
  Oil On Canvas, Woman, Wearing Cameo, Unsigned, Framed, 18 x 23 In. 475.00
  Oil On Canvas, Young Gentleman, Frockcoat, 35 1/2 x 30 1/2 In. 1650.00
  Oil On Ivory, Young Man Portrait, 4 1/4 x 3 1/2 In. 715.00
  Oil On Paper, Farm Building, Man, Horses, Stream, 18 1/2 x 18 In. 250.00
  On Academy Board, Girl Portrait, Frame, 12 x 9 In. 75.00
  On Academy Board, Landscape, Shadow Box, 12 1/2 x 16 1/2 In. 435.00
  On Academy Board, Peasant Girl At Toilet, 13 1/2 x 11 1/2 In. 250.00
  On Academy Board, Seascape, Fishing Boats, 13 3/4 x 23 1/4 In. 95.00
  On Academy Board, Still Life, Fruits, Frame, 12 1/2 x 16 1/2 In. 155.00

◆◆◆

Never, never wash an oil painting; it will dull the colors and may damage the canvas. Never rub an oil polish on an oil painting; it will darken with age. Never try to remove dust with a vacuum cleaner; it may also remove bits of paint.

◆◆◆

On Canvas, 18th–Century Gaming Scene, Framed, 20 x 24 In.	600.00
On Canvas, Adam & Eve, Folk Art, B. C. Moment, Framed, 20 x 24 In.	750.00
On Canvas, Boy With Banjo, Bird's–Eye Frame, 28 1/4 x 24 In.	950.00
On Canvas, British Ship Ben Venue, Gold Frame, 34 1/4 x 44 In.	2500.00
On Canvas, Child, Nettie Valentine, February 1871, 24 x 20 In.	2000.00
On Canvas, Child, Ornate Long Dress, Framed, England, 31 x 27 In.	7200.00
On Canvas, Clipper Ship Beech Bank, Lai Fong, 1898, 34 x 54 In.	7700.00
On Canvas, Cottage, Trees, Hunter, Frame, 19 1/2 x 23 1/2 In.	1600.00
On Canvas, Forest Scene, Brook, Gilt Frame, 24 3/4 x 18 1/2 In.	200.00
On Canvas, Landscape, Lake, Mountain, Trees, Frame, 28 x 32 1/2 In.	750.00
On Canvas, Old Woman, White Bonnet, Glasses, Framed, 35 x 30 In.	325.00
On Canvas, Peasant Girl, Pink Bonnet, Basket, 11 3/4 x 9 1/4 In.	75.00
On Canvas, Still Life of Peaches, Gilt Frame, 13 1/2 x 16 3/4 In.	350.00
On Canvas, Street Jewelry Vendor, Women, Oval, London, 18 x 22 In.	1100.00
On Canvas, Woman, Lace Bonnet, Ruff, Gilt Frame, 40 x 36 In.	600.00
On Canvas, Young Child With Dog, American School, 47 3/8 x 36 In.	7700.00
On Canvas, Young Nobleman, Duke of York, Frame, 33 1/2 x 28 In.	500.00
On Canvas, Young Nobleman, Modern Frame, England, 33 x 28 1/2 In.	700.00
On Ivory, Bearded Gentleman, Newspaper On Lap, 6 x 4 7/8 In.	325.00
On Ivory, Boy, Cromwell, Oval, Ornate Brass Frame, Miniature	1400.00
On Ivory, Child Holding Apple, Luigi Bernieri, 1927, Miniature	100.00
On Ivory, Child, Checked Costume, Black Hat, J. W. Stock, Miniature	1870.00
On Ivory, Dandy In Frock Coat, Gilt Brass Frame, c.1790, Miniature	165.00
On Ivory, Duchesse De Devonshire, Dumont, 4 3/4 x 3 3/4 In.	50.00
On Ivory, French Interior, Brass Frame, 6 x 7 In.	125.00
On Ivory, Gentleman, 18th–Century Attire, Marquetry Inlaid Frame	245.00
On Ivory, Lola Montez, Bouille Frame, 3 1/2 x 2 1/2 In.	175.00
On Ivory, Lord Nelson & Lady Hamilton, Square Ground, 4 In., 2 Pc.	695.00
On Ivory, Mother & Child, Metal Frame, c.1880, 5 x 3 3/4 In.	195.00
On Ivory, Portrait of Bowman, January, 1850, 6 x 5 1/4 In.	275.00
On Ivory, Quaker Woman & Man, Watercolor, 2 7/8 x 2 1/2 In., Pair	3960.00
On Ivory, Watercolor, Gentleman, Brass Frame, 2 7/8 x 2 1/2 In.	275.00
On Ivory, Watercolor, Gentleman, Oval Case, Miniature	185.00
On Ivory, Watercolor, Oval Portraits, Woman, Bonnet, 6 1/2 x 5 In.	150.00
On Ivory, Watercolor, Profile of Young Woman, 5 3/8 x 4 7/8 In.	650.00
On Ivory, Watercolor, Young Man, Oval Frame, 4 3/8 x 3 7/8 In.	525.00
On Ivory, Watercolor, Young Woman, Frame, 1 1/2 x 1 3/4 In.	220.00
On Ivory, Woman In Black, Dated Oct. 2, 1877, 3 x 2 1/4 In.	280.00
On Ivory, Woman In Blue, Brass Frame, 1 3/4 x 2 1/4 In.	285.00
On Ivory, Woman In Victorian Attire, Wooden Frame, Miniature	175.00
On Ivory, Woman Portrait, Gilt, Lock of Hair, 2 3/4 x 2 3/8 In.	250.00
On Ivory, Woman, La Biane, 2 7/8 x 3 3/8 In.	65.00
On Ivory, Young Man Portrait, Brass, Lock of Hair, 2 5/8 x 2 In.	520.00
On Ivory, Young Man, Blue Coat, Oval, Frame, c.1790, Miniature	220.00
On Ivory, Young Man, Feathered Hair, Reverse Opalescent, Miniature	800.00
On Oilcloth, Pheasant & Quail, Framed, 39 x 40 In.	100.00
On Oilcloth, Rooster, Chick & Bird, Framed, 36 x 29 In.	185.00
On Panel, Bearded Man, Fur Collar, Ornate Gilt Frame, 19 x 17 In.	600.00
On Panel, European Scene, Children, 16 1/2 x 21 In.	275.00
On Panel, Portrait, Young Man, 18 1/4 x 14 1/4 In.	250.00
On Panel, Portrait, Young Man, Framed, 11 x 9 In.	375.00
On Paper, 2–Headed Eagle, Watercolor, 1825, 9 x 11 In.	375.00

On Paper, Black, In Chains, Abolish Slavery, 1857	450.00
On Paper, Charcoal, Cave, Ohio, M. J. Stephan, 13 x 17 In. ....*Illus*	605.00
On Paper, Gentleman, Black & White Watercolor, 6 3/8 x 5 1/2 In.	55.00
On Paper, George Washington, Watercolor, 10 x 12 In.	575.00
On Paper, Honorable Cassius M. Clay, 1845, 8 x 7 In. ....*Illus*	2420.00
On Paper, Portrait, Man, Hat & Gloves In Hand, 18 x 13 1/2 In.	550.00
On Paper, Sailor's Valentine, Watercolor, J. Martin, 1862	575.00
On Paper, Watercolor & Ink, View of West Point, 15 x 20 1/2 In.	1210.00
On Paper, Watercolor, Amish Village, Hattie K. Brunner, 10 x 14 In.	1705.00
On Paper, Watercolor, Liberty Bust, Lion Hilt Sword, 9 x 7 In.	5775.00
On Paper, Watercolor, Man & Woman, Seated, 8 3/4 x 7 5/8 In., Pair	1000.00
On Paper, Watercolor, Sandy Dunes, Sydney J. Yard, 13 3/4 x 19 In.	7150.00
On Paper, Watercolor, Winter Landscape, H. K. Brunner, 14 x 18 In.	800.00
On Paper, Watercolor, Woman, Ermine Stole, 16 x 13 1/2 In.	500.00
On Paper, Young Man, Brass Trimmed Frame, 5 3/4 x 4 3/4 In.	150.00
On Plywood, Quail Woman, M. Tolliver, 1915, 17 x 11 In.	200.00
On Porcelain, Blossoms, Birds, Oriental, Ornate Carved Frame, 18 In	150.00
On Porcelain, Cupid, Brass Flower & Leaf Frame, 8 1/2 x 6 3/4 In.	325.00
On Porcelain, Girl's Portrait, Mademoiselle Lebrun, 4 1/2 x 4 In.	175.00
On Porcelain, Woman, Curly Hair, Classical Gown, Oval, 5 3/4 In.	295.00
On Porcelain, Woman, Signed Wagner, Oval, Miniature	650.00
On Porcelain, Youth & Maiden, Ornate White Metal Frame, 4 3/4 In.	55.00
On Velvet, Parrot On Box, P. C., 10th Mo. 4th, 1828, 10 3/4 x 8 In.	600.00
On Velvet, Theorem, Basket of Fruit & Foliage, 14 1/2 x 18 In.	750.00
On Velvet, Theorem, Basket of Fruit, 9 1/2 x 12 1/2 In.	1320.00
On Velvet, Theorem, Basket of Fruit, Frame, 18 1/4 x 22 1/4 In.	5250.00
On Velvet, Theorem, Buildings, Deer, Frame, 12 1/4 x 13 1/8 In.	4800.00
On Velvet, Theorem, Floral, Frame, 18 1/2 x 22 1/4 In.	400.00
On Velvet, Theorem, Parrot On Vine, Basket of Fruit, 22 x 26 In.	3050.00
On Velvet, Theorem, Pot of Flowers, J. N. Boyer, 14 x 12 1/4 In.	500.00
On Velvet, Theorem, Rooster, Tulip, Ellinger, Frame, 8 x 9 1/2 In.	400.00
On Velvet, Theorem, Stylized Compote, Fruit, Frame, 14 3/4 x 17 In.	3500.00
On Velvet, Watercolor, Mourning Scene, J. Bacon, 1807 ....*Illus*	2300.00
Reverse On Glass, Bearded Man In Tomb, 11 3/4 x 14 3/4 In.	55.00
Reverse On Glass, Bride, Frame, 11 7/8 x 9 1/2 In.	550.00
Reverse On Glass, Cottages, Lake Scene, Frame, 21 1/2 x 17 1/2 In.	65.00
Reverse On Glass, George Washington, Frame, 11 7/8 x 9 3/8 In.	1400.00
Reverse On Glass, Gold Frame, Oval, Small, Pair	100.00
Reverse On Glass, Jesus, Beardless, Frame, 11 5/8 x 9 1/8 In.	35.00
Reverse On Glass, Panel, Girl, Field, Evan's Westbrook Co., 9 In.	195.00
Reverse On Glass, Silhouette, Man, H. Gibbs, Framed, 5 7/8 x 5 In.	125.00

Painting, On Paper, Charcoal, Cave, Ohio, M. J. Stephan, 13 x 17 In.

Painting, On Paper, Honorable Cassius M. Clay, 1845, 8 x 7 In.

Painting, On Velvet, Watercolor, Mourning Scene, J. Bacon, 1807

Reverse On Glass, Young Woman, Flowered Hat, Frame, 12 x 9 1/4 In. 375.00

The Pairpoint Manufacturing Company started in 1880 in New Bedford, Massachusetts. It soon joined with the glassworks nearby and made glass, silver plated pieces, and lamps. Reverse–painted glass shades and molded shades known as *puffies* were part of the production until the 1930s. The company reorganized and changed its name several times but is still working today. Items listed here are glass or glass and metal. Silver–plated pieces are listed under Silver Plate.

PAIRPOINT, Biscuit Jar, Hydrangeas On Leafy Branch, Marked 440.00
Biscuit Jar, Melon Ribbed, Gold Floral, Green Ground, Marked 550.00
Biscuit Jar, Paneled, Colored Pansies, Marked 385.00
Biscuit Jar, Raised Gold Spider Mums, Apricot Ground, Square 550.00
Bowl, Engraved Vintage, Bubble Ball Connector, Green, 12 In. 155.00
Box, Collar & Cuff, Puffy Glass 950.00
Box, Hinged Cover, Scrolled Border, Metal Frame, 4 x 6 3/4 In. 665.00
Candlestick, Cut Glass, Adelaid Pattern, Red–Amber, 12 In., Pair 250.00
Candlestick, Flattened Bobeche Rims, Cobalt Blue, 16 In., Pair 275.00
Candlestick, Veneti Design, Red & White Spiral Threading, 12 In. 435.00
Compote, Engraved Gainsborough, Crystal, 7 1/2 x 8 1/2 In. 135.00
Compote, Etched Grapes & Leaves, Amber Base, Clear Stem, 8 In. 165.00
Compote, Gainsborough, Clear, 7 1/2 x 8 1/2 In. 135.00
Console, Grape, Amber, 16 In. 235.00
Lamp, Art Nouveau, Orchid, c.1890, 18 1/2 In. 5500.00
Lamp, Berkley Shade, Robin Hood Design On Base, 21 In. 2200.00
Lamp, Blossoms, Hummingbirds, Patinated Metal, 22 1/2 In. 2400.00
Lamp, Boudoir, Silver Base, Vaseline Stem, 18 In., Pair .... 450.00 To 650.00
Lamp, Chipped–Ice Shade, Coralene Trees, 22 In. 950.00
Lamp, Draped Cherub, Metal Base, Pineapple Finial, 14 In. 275.00
Lamp, Floral Shade, Controlled Air Bubble, 8 Sided Base 2500.00
Lamp, Oil, Orchid, Green Font, Blown Chimney, 1890s, 18 1/2 In. 6050.00
Lamp, Parrots, Flowers, Textured Glass, 18 In. 8500.00
Lamp, Puffy Hollyhocks, 9 In. 3500.00
Lamp, Puffy Pansy, Silvered–Metal Base, Signed, 18 3/4 In. 7150.00
Lamp, Puffy Reverse Painted Shade, Metal, Signed, 14 1/2 In. 1985.00
Lamp, Puffy Tulip, Brass Base, c.1915, 14 In. 4500.00
Lamp, Puffy, 6 Butterflies, 6 In. 3250.00
Lamp, Puffy, Marked Shade 2300.00
Lamp, Puffy, Peony, Square Shade, 18 In. 6000.00
Lamp, Puffy, Vaseline Glass Base, Florals, 8 In. 925.00
Lamp, Reverse Painted Country Landscape, c.1915, 17 1/4 In. 880.00
Lamp, Reverse Painted Puffy Nautilus Shade, 1915, 19 In. 3300.00
Lamp, Reverse Painted Scenic Shade, c.1915, 22 In. 2475.00
Lamp, Reverse Painted Sea Gull Shade, c.1915, 25 1/4 In. 7150.00
Lamp, Reverse Painted Seascape, Dolphin Standard, 15 1/2 In. 3575.00
Lamp, Reverse Painted Shade, Chipped Ice, Camel Scene, 16 In. 8500.00
Lamp, Reverse Painted Shade, Durand, 16 In. ....*Illus* 3080.00
Lamp, Reverse Painted Shade, Hurricane, Yellow, Walnut Base 450.00
Lamp, Reverse Painted Shade, Jungle Bird, 18 In. 4495.00
Lamp, Reverse Painted Shade, London Bridge, Textured, 20 1/2 In. 1870.00
Lamp, Reverse Painted Shade, Metal Base, Signed, 14 1/2 In. 2100.00
Lamp, Reverse Painted Shade, Trees, 11 In. ....*Illus* 2640.00
Lamp, Reverse Painted, Flanged Edge Shade, 1920 .... 5800.00
Lamp, Reverse Painted, Jade, Orange, Purple, Blue, 16 In. ....*Illus* 3300.00
Lamp, Roses, Tulip Form Base, 10 In. ....*Illus* 12100.00
Lamp, Seagull, Scenic, Copley Shade, Seascape, Signed, 23 In. 4500.00
Lamp, Table, Reverse Painted French Scenic Shade, Signed, 16 In. 3410.00
Lustre, Vintage, Hollow Stem, 10 Prisms, 11 In. 220.00
Orange Bowl, Scalloped, Beaded, Interior Florals, 1894, 10 1/2 In. 85.00
Powder Box, Acid–Etched Flower & Leaf Design, 4 In. 165.00
Salt & Pepper, Baroque Scrolls, Ribbed, Pewter Tops 80.00
Shade, Grapes & Lattice, Mary 31, 1910, 10 x 9 In. 1800.00

Pairpoint, Lamp,   Pairpoint, Lamp,.   Pairpoint, Lamp,   Pairpoint, Lamp,
Reverse Painted Shade, Reverse Painted Shade, Reverse Painted, Jade,   Roses, Tulip Form
Durand, 16 In.   Trees, 11 In.   Orange, Purple, Blue, 16 In.   Base, 10 In.

Urn, Bubble–Ball Connector, Foot Flares To Rim, Blue, 13 In. 235.00
Vase, Butterfly On Web, 12 In. 195.00
Vase, Colias, Urn Shape, Flower Cut Into Base, 8 1/2 x 19 1/2 In. 325.00
Vase, Cranberry & Crystal, 11 1/2 In. 175.00
Vase, Sailing Galleon, Wavy Sea, c.1900, 6 In. 485.00
Vase, Trumpet, Controlled Bubble Sphere At Foot, Amber, 12 In. 95.00
PALMER COX, BROWNIES, see Brownies

The first paper dolls were probably the pantins, or jumping jacks,
made in eighteenth–century Europe. By the 1880s, sheets of printed
paper dolls and clothes were being made. The first paper doll books
were made in the 1920s. Collectors prefer uncut sheets or books or
boxed sets of paper dolls. Prices are about half as much if the pages
have been cut.

PAPER DOLL, American Beauties, White House Ladies, 1951, Uncut 75.00
Amos 'N' Andy, Pepsodent, Framed, Uncut 215.00
Ann Sheridan, Cut 15.00
Ann Southern, Cut 20.00
Annie Oakley, 1956, Uncut 100.00
Ballerina, Lace & Pearl Outfit, Germany, 1880, 13 In. 49.00
Bandstand, 1958, Uncut 6.00
Barbie & Ken, Suitcase Box, 1962, Cut 10.00
Barbie, Whitman, 1962, Uncut 100.00
Betsy McCall, Bluebirds, 1962, Uncut 12.00
Betsy McCall, Finds Treasure, 1966, Uncut 8.00
Betsy McCall, Wonderful Christmas, 1964, Uncut 10.00
Betsy McCall, Writes From Holland, 1969, Uncut 7.00
Betty Bonnett's Mother & Father, Uncut 25.00
Betty Grable, Whitman, Uncut 1946.00
Blondie, Pink Suit, Dagwood, Folded Arms, Cut 25.00
Blondie, Whitman, 1954, Uncut 55.00
Bonnie Blue, 2 Pages of Movie Costumes, By Pat Stall 25.00
Captain Marvel, Jr., Ski Jump, 1946, Uncut 40.00
Carmen Mirando, Cut 85.00
Charlie's Angels, Jill, 1977, Box 45.00
Charming, Saalfield, Illustrated By Lucille Wallace, 1958 .... 20.00
Chatty Cathy, 1964, Uncut 15.00
Dodi, From My 3 Sons, Uncut 30.00
Dollhouse, 1920s, Uncut 18.00
Dolls From The Land of Make Believe, Hall Brothers, 16 Dolls 80.00
Dolls of The Nations Album, Hall Brothers, 1948 .... 80.00
Douglas Fairbanks, 1921, Uncut 75.00
Dude Ranch, 1950s 20.00
Elizabeth Taylor, Folder, Cut 11.00
Family Affair 10.00
First Family, Ronald & Nancy Reagan, Uncut 15.00
Flying Marvels, Fawcett Publishing, Uncut 90.00

Flying Nun, Unpunched, Saalfield, 1969 .... 75.00
Gene Tierney, Cut 35.00
Gloria Jean, 1940, Uncut 150.00
Gloria Jean, Green Suit, 6 Outfits 16.00
Gloria Jean, Striped Suit 19.00
Greer Garson, Cut 40.00
Gulliver's Travels 20.00
Ice Show, 17 Skaters 25.00
Jane Arden, 1930s, Cut 45.00
Jeanette MacDonald, 2 Dolls, 36 Outfits, Merrill, 1941 .... 50.00
Jinny, Carol & Patsy, Samuel Lowe Co., Uncut, 1944 .... 12.00
Judy Garland, Cut 85.00
Lana Turner, Cut 35.00
Lennon Sisters 15.00
Lettie Lanes Father, 1909, Uncut 14.00
Little Lulu, 1973, Uncut 35.00
Little Sister, 1963, Box 5.00
Loraine Day, Saalfield, 1953, Uncut 40.00
Lost Horizon, Uncut 15.00
Mae West, 4 Pages of Movie Outfits, Satch La Valley 25.00
Magic Mary, Magnetic, Bradley, Box, 1940s 12.50
Maple–Flake Cereal, Premium, Cardboard, 1911, Uncut 65.00
Mary Pickford, 1921, Uncut 75.00
Nanny & The Professor, Juliet Mills, Cut 4.00
None–Such Mincemeat, Late 1800s 24.00
Norma Talmadge, 1921, Uncut 75.00
Oklahoma, Storybook, 1965, Uncut 60.00
Our Gang, Queen Holden, Whitman, 1921, Uncut 343.00
Our Soldier Boys, Arnold Print Works, 6 Dolls, 1892, Uncut 350.00
Patty Duke, Whitman 25.00
Pebbles, Wonder Books, 1974, Uncut 45.00
Princess Diana & Charles, Have A Baby 35.00
Prom Time, 1962, Uncut 6.00
Quaker Puffed Rice Or Wheat, Movie Stars, Mailer, Set of 8, 1936 .... 75.00
Raggedy Ann, Box, 1941, Uncut 90.00
Roy Rogers & Dale Evans, Horse, Whitman, 1950, Cut 40.00
Shirley Temple, Uncut 250.00
Statuette, 1950s, Uncut 5.00
That Girl, Uncut 30.00
Tillie The Toiler, Whitman, 1942, Uncut 115.00
Tricia Nixon, Standup, With White House Game 25.00
Tyrone Power & Linda Darnell, Cut 55.00
Uncle Mose, Envelope, 1949, Uncut 65.00
Wartime Armed Forces, Men & Women 35.00
Wedding Party, 1950s, Uncut 20.00
Western Boy & Girl, 2 Horses, Cut 45.00
White House First Ladies, 1955, Uncut 50.00
Zorro, 3–D, Original Package 35.00

Paper collectibles, including almanacs, catalogs, children's books, stock certificates, and other paper ephemera, are listed here. Paper calendars are listed separately under Calendar Paper.

PAPER, Almanac, Ayer's, 1893 .... 7.00
Almanac, Dr. Kilmer's Swamp Root, 1936 .... 4.00
Almanac, Dr. Miles Laboratories, 1935 .... 5.00
Almanac, Hartman Magazine of Health, 1903 .... 20.00
Almanac, Kellogg's, Housewife's, 1938 .... 10.00
Almanac, Massachusetts Bay, Daniel George, 1775 .... 225.00
Almanac, Poor Will's, Philadelphia, 1835 .... 7.00
Bill of Lading, Wells Fargo, From Virginia City, 1870 .... 65.00
Book, Better Little Book, Tarzan, Edgar Rice Burroughs 12.50
Book, Big Little Book, David Copperfield, W. C. Fields 14.00
Book, Big Little Book, Jaragu of The Jungle, Rex Beach 15.00

Book, Big Little Book, Mickey Mouse & The Dude Ranch Bandits, 1943 .... 35.00
Book, Big Little Book, Mickey Mouse, Mail Pilot, 1933 .... 75.00
Book, Big Little Book, Tailspin Tommy & Lost Transport 30.00
Book, Big Little Book, Treasure Island, Jackie Cooper 14.00
Book, Color–By–Number, Barbie, Mattel, c.1962, 11 x 13 In. 15.00
Book, Coloring, Skeezix, 1929 .... 18.00
Book, Comic, Felix The Cat, McLoughlin Bros., 1931 .... 65.00
Book, Receipt, Wells Fargo, 1908 .... 7.00
Bookplate, Penna. German, Catharina, 1771, Framed, 5 3/4 x 3 1/8 In. 100.00
Catalog, 1989 Butterfield Auction, Fine Saddles, Bits & Spurs 30.00
Catalog, Banner Tailoring Co., Fall & Winter, Hard Cover, 1917–18 .... 245.00
Catalog, Colt Firearms, 1933, 40 Pages 65.00
Catalog, Coward Shoes, 1899, 64 Pages 30.00
Catalog, Dent Hardware Co., Fullerton, Pa., 1910, 7 x 10 In., 39 Pages 30.00
Catalog, FAO Schwartz, Christmas, 1958 .... 60.00
Catalog, Gibson Art Co., Toys, 1924, 16 Pages 25.00
Catalog, H. B. Smith Machine Co., Highwheels, Accessories, 1886, 37 Pg. 210.00
Catalog, Hitching's Supply Book, Greenhouses, 123 Pages, 1917 .... 12.00
Catalog, J. C. Penney, Spring–Summer, 1964 .... 30.00
Catalog, J. C. Penney, Spring–Summer, 1970 .... 25.00
Catalog, John Deere, Equipment, 1945 .... 15.00
Catalog, Jung Seeds, 1936, 66 Pages 10.00
Catalog, Kresge's Radio & Buyer's Guide, 1927–1928, 32 Pages 25.00
Catalog, Lake Erie Female Seminary, 1883–1884 .... 10.00
Catalog, Lane Bryant, Summer, 1948 .... 14.00
Catalog, Lufkin Tool, 1940s 18.50
Catalog, Marshall Field & Co., Holiday, 1890–1891, 9 1/2 x 12 In. 550.00
Catalog, Marshall Field, 1908 .... 95.00
Catalog, Montgomery Ward, Christmas, 1951 .... 40.00
Catalog, Montgomery Ward, Christmas, 1953 .... 65.00
Catalog, Montgomery Ward, Fall & Winter, 1924 .... 37.50
Catalog, Montgomery Ward, No. 89, 1918 .... 100.00
Catalog, Montgomery Ward, Wallpaper Samples, 1950, 82 Pages 35.00
Catalog, Peter Henderson & Co. Seed, 1907, 188 Pages 15.00
Catalog, Pittston Stove Co., Pittston, Pa., 1895, 57 Pages 20.00
Catalog, Saddles & Saddle Makers of Porteville, Ca., 17 Pages 15.00
Catalog, Sears & Roebuck, Children's & Baby's Needs, 1921 .... 25.00
Catalog, Sears Roebuck, Shoe Fashions, 1922, 8 x 11 In. 15.00
Catalog, Sears, Christams, 1977 .... 20.00
Catalog, Sears, Christmas, 1946 .... 65.00
Catalog, Sears, Christmas, 1959 .... 40.00
Catalog, Sears, Fall–Winter, 1934 .... 60.00
Catalog, Sears, Fall–Winter, 1943–44 .... 26.00
Catalog, Sears, Spring–Summer, 1933 .... 60.00
Catalog, Sears, Spring–Summer, 1941 .... 28.00
Catalog, Sears, Spring–Summer, 1976 .... 15.00
Catalog, Spiegel, Christmas, 1947 .... 40.00
Catalog, Spiegel, Christmas, 1954 .... 65.00
Catalog, Spiegel, Fall & Winter, 1941, 663 Pages, 10 x 14 In. 35.00
Catalog, Stanton McDonald Wright Drawing, Christmas Decoration, 1946 .... 25.00
Catalog, Trade, Northern Furniture Co., No. 40, 20 Pages, 1920–30 .... 55.00
Catalog, Wallpaper, Montgomery Ward, 1940 .... 15.00
Catalog, Walter A. Wood Co., Farm Machinery, 1914, 48 Pages 14.00
Catalog, Winchester Repeating Arms, No. 81, 1919, 213 Pages 100.00
Catalog, Winchester, 1962 .... 30.00
Catalog, Winchester–Western, Sporting Arms & Ammunition, 1967 .... 5.00
Deed, Dallas County, Penna., Dated 1830, Frame, 17 1/2 x 21 1/2 In. 7.50
Deed, Hand Written, Parchment, Folded, England, 1868, 23 1/2 x 30 In. 25.00
Easter Basket, Foldout Eggs, Dated 1925 .... 35.00
Fraktur, Bird With Snake In Corner, Georg Tib, 1763, 7 5/8 x 12 In. 2950.00
Fraktur, Birds In Trees, Anna Doe, Frame, 1808, 12 1/2 x 10 1/4 In. 1100.00
Fraktur, Birth, Abraham Kinig, 1786, Magdelena, 1783, 16 1/2 x 11 In. 1350.00
Fraktur, Birth, Angel, Northampton County, 1801, Frame, 15 3/4 x 19 In. 1650.00

Do not mount old maps, prints, etc., on cardboard. The acid in the cardboard causes stains. Use an all rag board (an art store can help).

Paper, Fraktur, Miss Selina Jones,
Poem To Muses, 1830, 8 x 5 In.

Fraktur, Birth, Barbara Eschlemann, Frame, 1777, 10 x 12 In.	1300.00
Fraktur, Birth, Bucks County, German & English, Frame, 16 x 18 In.	975.00
Fraktur, Birth, Chester County, F. Krebs, 1800, 15 1/2 x 18 In.	550.00
Fraktur, Birth, Geburts Und Taufschein, 1843, 21 3/4 x 17 1/2 In.	85.00
Fraktur, Birth, Geburts Und Taufschein, Berks County, 1852, 20 3/4 In.	165.00
Fraktur, Birth, Heart, Cherubs, Berks County, 1811, 16 x 19 In.	300.00
Fraktur, Birth, Jacob Wetzel, Floral, 1795, 17 1/2 x 14 3/4 In.	510.00
Fraktur, Birth, Jonathan Trautmann, 1819, Frame, 12 3/8 x 16 In.	2950.00
Fraktur, Birth, Pen, Ink, Watercolor, 1795, Frame, 16 3/4 x 19 3/4 In.	550.00
Fraktur, Certificate of Birth & Baptism, 1853, 12 1/4 x 9 3/4 In.	400.00
Fraktur, Certificate, Anna Marie Enig, March, 1810, 10 3/4 x 8 3/4 In.	400.00
Fraktur, Family Record, Johan Adam Eyre	5800.00
Fraktur, Miss Selina Jones, Poem To Muses, 1830, 8 x 5 In. ....*Illus*	880.00
Fraktur, Path To Heaven & Hell, Lancaster, Pa., Frame, 15 x 19 In.	200.00
Fraktur, Penna. German, Magdalena Millerin, 1808, Frame, 14 x 10 In.	425.00
Indenture, Lancaster, Penna., 1817	45.00
Invitation, Columbian Expo, Dedication of Buildings, Oct. 20, 22, 1892	25.00
Letter, Miner's, Montana, Meeting With A Woman On Train, Dated 1896	150.00
License, Hunting, Nonresident Alien, Pennsylvania, 1931	1500.00
Mailer, Tournament of Roses, Pictorial, 1938	15.00
Menu, Waldorf Astoria, Cugat Playing, 1939	10.00
Playbill, Camelot, Richard Burton & Julie Andrews, NYC, 1961	20.00
Program, Camille, Herberty Stock Co., Jessica Miner, 1900	12.00
Program, Circus, King Brothers, 1953	12.00
Program, Ice Capades, 1944	45.00
Program, Ice Capades, First, 1940	40.00
Program, Ticket Stub, Jazz Singer, Al Jolson, Warner Theater, N. Y.	850.00
Punch–Out, Animals, Whitman, 1930, 22 Piece	38.00
Punch–Out, Kitchen, Living Room, Bath, Furnishings, Whitman, 250 Piece	85.00
Punchboard, Professional Charley, 25 Cent	325.00
Stock Certificate, Sheep Mountain & 10 Mile Mining Co., Colo., 1881	90.00
Stock Certificate, Tombstone Consolidated Mines, Ariz. Terr., 1902	100.00
Stock Certificate, Universal Aerial Navigation Company, 1902	80.00
Stock, Hartford & Conn. Western Railroad Co., Late–1800s, 8 x 9 In.	20.00
Stock, Pittsburgh & Lake Erie Railroad Co., Cancelled, 1926	15.00
Valentine, Boy With Sailboat, Foldout, Die Cut, 8 In.	12.00
Valentine, Dog Pulling Boy In Cart, Movable, With Hankie, 7 In.	25.00

A heavy odor from smoke or mildew lowers the value of a collection of paper.

Paperweights must have first appeared along with paper in ancient Egypt. Today's collectors search for every type from the very expensive French weights of the nineteenth century to the modern artist weights or advertising pieces. The glass tops of the paperweights sometimes have been nicked or scratched and this type of damage can be removed by polishing. Some serious collectors think this type of repair is an alteration and will not buy a repolished weight; others think it is an acceptable technique of restoration that does not change the value. Baccarat paperweights are listed separately under Baccarat.

PAPERWEIGHT, Advertising, Bear Tire Company, Line Up With Bear, Iron, 1920	55.00
Advertising, Dutch Boy Paint, Raised Relief of Boy	35.00
Advertising, Huylin's Chocolate, Gibson–Type Lady, Metal, 4 In.	109.00
Advertising, Hylins Chocolate, Gibson–Type Woman, Metal, 4 In.	109.00
Advertising, Oil Well, Oil Well Supply Co., Lead	45.00
Advertising, Paine Webber & Co., 50th Anniversary, Bronze, 1930	42.00
Advertising, Pope Bicycle	45.00
Advertising, Puritan Coke, Pilgrim Figure, Brass	185.00
Advertising, Sandell Beer Pumps & Coolers, Brass	35.00
Advertising, Schmidt's Beer, Metal Barrel, 2 In.	15.00
Advertising, Skippy Peanut Butter, Brass	25.00
Advertising, Strobl Pottery, Cincinnati, Ohio, Matte Green	90.00
Agricultural Building, Square, Glass, 1893, 3 In.	45.00
Ayotte, Yellow Chrysanthemums, 3 Buds & Petals	900.00
Ayotte, Yellow–Breasted Warbler, Rainbow, Clear, 2 7/8 In.	385.00
Banford, Blue & White Complex Flower, Bud, Clear, 3 1/2 In.	400.00
Banford, Yellow & Ruby Flowers, Complex Cane, Muslin, 4 In.	1200.00
Barney Google	35.00
Beaver Stove Works	30.00
Bird, Cast Iron, 2 3/4 In.	300.00
Bohemian, Amber Flash, White Floral Bouquet, 2 1/2 In.	385.00
Caithness, Charisma, Purple Shades, Petal–Like, Clear Ground	175.00
Chicago Bears, Chrome, 1933, 1 1/2 In.	75.00
Choko, Yellow–Striped Green Lizard, On Dahlia, 3 1/16 In.	770.00
Clichy, 1–Rose Center, Meandering Chain & Canes, 3 1/4 In.	2400.00
Clichy, Blue & White Swirl, Pastry Mold Center Cane, 2 3/8 In.	1350.00
Clichy, Checkerboard Canes, Spaced Millefiori, 2 5/8 In.	1650.00
Clichy, Concentric, Cane Center, 8 White Roses Around, 2 In.	575.00
Clichy, Concentric, Green Edelweiss, 2 Roses, Clear, 1 3/4 In.	825.00
Clichy, Millefiori, White Roses, Scarlet Ground, 2 3/4 In.	1650.00
Clichy, Red, White & Blue Candy Cane, Large	300.00
Clichy, Trefoil 50 Cane Garlands, Muslin Ground, 3 In.	900.00
D'Albret, Columbus, 1966	90.00
D'Albret, Paul Revere, 1969	90.00
Dog, Floppy Ears, Cast Iron	20.00
Father Christmas Inside, Crystal Ball, Wood Base, 5 In.	150.00
Frog, Cast Iron, 5 In.	45.00
Frog, Human Penis, Cast Iron, 3 x 3 In.	285.00
Hacker, Salamander, Realistic Sandy Ground, 2 11/16 In.	990.00
Harrie, Rainbow Swirl, White & Black Casings, 4 1/4 In.	170.00
Harris, Blown & Cut Apple, Red & White Apple, Seeds, 3 1/2 In.	130.00
Harris, Swirl, Aqua, Pink & White Pastel Shades, 2 1/2 In.	80.00
Holland America Line	28.00
Home Sweet Home	48.00
J. & D. Trabucco, 4 Flowers & Leaves, Clear Relief, Frosted	350.00
J. & D. Trabucco, Blue Rose, Sculptured Design, Frosted Ground	350.00
Kaziun, Cameo Portrait, Heart With K Canes, Gilt Frame, 2 In.	825.00
Kaziun, Gold–Flecked Turquoise, Blossom, Marked, 2 1/4 In.	305.00
Kaziun, Pansy, Bud, Gold Insect, Azure Transparent, 2 1/4 In.	800.00
Kaziun, Red Rose, Clear Ground, Pedestal, 3 In.	1430.00
Kaziun, Silhoutte, Woman, Ponytail, Yellow Ground, 2 1/16 In.	1100.00
Kaziun, Twisted Rose, Bud, Green Stem, Blue, Marked, 2 1/4 In.	440.00

Kosta, Cameo, Sweden 125.00
Labino, Bubble, Green Abstract, Silver Veiling, 2 15/16 In. 1430.00
Lewis, Pansy, Green Leaves, White Canes, Crimped, 2 3/8 In. 303.00
Merry Christmas 40.00
Military Hat, 1920, 3 In. 25.00
Milleville, Umbrella Mushroom, Pink Chips, Footed, 3 3/4 In. 385.00
Mt. St. Helens, Glass 39.00
Multicolored Floral Design, Colorless Body, 7 3/8 In. 320.00
New England, Concentric Millefiori, Off–Center, 2 9/16 In. 468.00
New England, Concentric, Latticinio, Blue Cane, 2 1/2 In. 350.00
Nude Girl, Lying, Silver Plate 35.00
Olympics, Heavy Brass, 1960s 25.00
Perthshire, Bouquet, Red & White Overlay, Square, 3 1/8 In. 825.00
Perthshire, Dragonfly, Gold Aventurine, Latticinio, 2 7/16 In. 275.00
Pinchbeck, Medallion, Village Celebration, Gold, 3 7/8 In. 770.00
Pinchbeck, Woman & Men Scene, Silveroid, Leaf Bower, 2 3/4 In. 660.00
Rosenfeld, 2 Zinnia, 2 Buds, Light Blue Transparent, 3 1/8 In. 400.00
Ruby Flash, Calendar, 1912 .... 45.00
Sandwich, Blue Poinsettia, Bubble Petals, Clear, 2 7/8 In. 1045.00
Sandwich, Broken Candy, End–of–Day, Bubbles, Clear, 2 13/16 In. 770.00
Sandwich, Light Blue Flower, Red, White & Blue Jasper, 3 In. 900.00
Sandwich, Poinsettia, Blue Ground 340.00
Sandwich, Red Poinsettia, Red, White & Blue Jasper, 2 7/8 In. 880.00
Sandwich, Weedflower, 2 Dotted & 2 Striped Petals, 3 In. 850.00
Smith, Bird of Paradise, Clear Ground, 3 1/4 In. 450.00
Snow Dome, Chimney Rock, S. C., Bear, Glass, 3 Tiered Base 20.00
Snow Dome, General MacArthur 29.00
Snow Dome, Lady Lighting The Fireplace, Large 25.00
Snow Dome, Man Carrying Lantern & Lunch Box 12.00
Sommerville, 2 Pink & 2 Blue Flowers, Clear, 3 15/16 In. 715.00
St. Louis, Cane Bouquet, Amber Flash Diamond Ground, 2 3/4 In. 990.00
St. Louis, Concentric Circles, 4 Flowers, Animals In Center 600.00
St. Louis, Fruit, Swirling White Latticinio Ground, 3 In. 1210.00
St. Louis, Jasper Panels, Pie Wedges, Multicolored, 3 3/16 In. 990.00
St. Louis, King St. Louis, Sulphide, Cobalt Ground, 2 3/4 In. 440.00
St. Louis, Latticinio Cup, Concentric Millefiore, 3 3/4 In. 880.00
St. Louis, Madonna, Child, Sulphide, Translucent Blue, 2 3/8 In. 605.00
St. Louis, Mixed Fruit, Latticinio Basket, 2 5/16 In. 660.00
St. Louis, Red Honeycomb Millefiori, Clear Centers, 2 3/4 In. 430.00
St. Louis, Sulphide, Jimmy Carter, Faceted, Blue Ground 200.00
St. Louis, White Latticinio, Star Center Canes 330.00
St. Louis, White Pompon, Green Aventurine Ground, 2 9/16 In. 2750.00
Stankard, Jacob's Ladder, Lavender Blossoms, Clear, 3 1/16 In. 1320.00
Stankard, Pink Trailing Arbutus, Clear Ground, 3 3/16 In. 2200.00
Stankard, Pink Wild Rose, Yellow Stamens, Clear, 2 7/8 In. 1210.00
Steuben, Crystal, Stars & Stripes, c.1976, 2 3/4 In. 130.00
Tarsitano, Stylized Dahlia, Bouquet, Clear, 2 3/4 In. 990.00
Whitefriars, Blue & White Cane, White Cog Canes, 3 3/4 In. 275.00
Whitefriars, Concentric Millefiori, Off–Center, 3 1/16 In. 440.00
Whitefriars, Concentric Millefiori, Red, White, Blue, 3 7/16 In. 468.00
Whitefriars, Green & White Cane, Rows of Canes, 2 1/2 In. 175.00
Woman's Hand, Figural, Brass, 3 1/2 In. 12.00
Ysart, 2 White Mice, With Cheese, Clear On Brown 895.00
Ysart, Magnum Butterfly, Branch, Blossoms, Black, 3 3/4 In. 1650.00
Ysart, Parrot, Brown Branch, Blue & White Jasper, 3 1/16 In. 935.00

 Papier-mache is made from paper mixed with glue, chalk, and other ingredients, then molded and baked. It becomes very hard and can be painted. Boxes, trays, and furniture were made of papier-mache. Some of the nineteenth-century pieces were decorated with mother-of-pearl.

PAPIER–MACHE, see also Furniture
PAPIER–MACHE, Bank, Scotty 25.00

Parian, Figurine, Gilt Decorated,
German-Style, 22 In., Pair

Paris, Vase, Relief Lily Pads, Portraits, 18 In.,
Pair

Birdhouse, 1920	75.00
Box, Wig, Girl In Bonnet, 7 x 5 In.	125.00
Bull Terrier, Articulated Head	440.00
Card Case, Mother-of-Pearl Inlay, England, 1860	250.00
Chicken, Polychrome, Wooden Base, 3 1/4 In.	5.00
Cow, Black & White, 11 x 15 1/2 In.	175.00
Easter Egg, Decoupage, 4 x 8 In., 4 Piece	120.00
Easter Egg, Resurrection, Cathedral of St. Basil, Russia	4070.00
Easter Egg, Victorian Scene of Women Strolling In Park	75.00
Egg, Children Playing Scenes, Paper Lace Inside Rim, Germany	20.00
Elephant	20.00
Owl, Gray Cover, Large	40.00
Rhinoceros, Full-Bodied, Painted, Ochre & Brown, 26 x 48 In.	165.00
Tray, Columbian Exposition, Machinery Hall, Black & Gold	125.00
Tray, Mother-of-Pearl & Painted Floral, c.1880, 25 1/2 In.	385.00
Tray, On Stand, Mother-of-Pearl, Scalloped, 18 x 33 x 25 In.	2475.00

PARASOL, see Umbrella

Parian is a fine-grained, hard-paste porcelain named for the marble it resembles. It was first made in England in 1846 and gained in favor in the United States about 1860. Figures, tea sets, vases, and other items were made of Parian at many English and American factories.

PARIAN, Bust, Aristotle, Bird's-Eye Veneer Frame, 11 5/8 x 9 1/4 In.	40.00
Bust, Clytie	165.00
Bust, George Washington, 5 In.	35.00
Bust, Leonardo Da Vinci, Bird's-Eye Frame, 11 5/8 x 9 1/4 In.	45.00
Bust, Lord Byron, E. W. Wyons, 15 In.	500.00
Bust, Maiden, Garland In Hair, Black Pedestal, 16 In.	165.00
Bust, May Queen, Ceramic & Crystal Palace Art Union, 1868, 13 In.	110.00
Bust, Tasso, Bird's-Eye Veneer Frame, 11 5/8 x 9 1/4 In.	45.00
Bust, Wagner, Robinson & Leadbeater, 7 7/8 x 1 1/4 x 4 1/2 In.	175.00
Figurine, Apollo, 12 In.	220.00
Figurine, Gilt Decorated, German-Style, 22 In., Pair ....*Illus*	300.00
Figurine, Nude, Draped Body, Butterfly On Shoulder, c.1920, 14 In.	125.00
Figurine, Swan, Small	25.00
Figurine, Three Graces, 13 1/4 In.	220.00
Figurine, Woman & Man, Bringing In The Wheat, 11 In.	100.00
Figurine, Young Apollo, 18 In.	220.00
Lamp, 2-Winged Caryatids, 16 In.	265.00
Pitcher, Cascade Pattern, United States Pottery Co., 10 In.	150.00
Pitcher, Eagles, Heads Form 3 Spouts, Flagstaff Handle, 9 In.	375.00
Syrup, Pewter Lid, Figure of Washington, 5 3/4 In.	35.00

Vieux Paris, or Old Paris, is porcelain ware that is known to have been made in Paris in the eighteenth or early–nineteenth century. These porcelains have no identifying mark but can be identified by the whiteness of the porcelain and the lines and decorations.

PARIS, Creamer, Ornithological, Cardinal Dominiquain De Louisiane, 6 In.	880.00
Dessert Set, Floral Center, Gold & Maroon Border, Tray & 24 Plates	2600.00
Fruit Cooler, Cover, Sprigs of Flowers, c.1785, 11 7/8 In. Pair	2475.00
Humidor, Eagle Finial, Painted Mountain Scene, 19th Century	155.00
Inkwell, Nautilus Shape	245.00
Jar, Apothecary, Winged Mythological Women, Pair	412.00
Pitcher & Plate, White Medallions With Flowers, Gold Trim, 10 In.	325.00
Planter, Floral Design, Gilt Trim, Oval, 18 In.	550.00
Relish, Scalloped, Gold Trim, c.1850	125.00
Tea Tray, Center Roses, Green & Gold Border, 18 1/4 x 13 In.	150.00
Vase, Butterfly, 20 1/4 In.	440.00
Vase, Campana Form, Country Scenes, Mask Handles, 10 In., Pair	440.00
Vase, Cover, Hand Painted Putti & Garden, c.1930, 16 In.	1540.00
Vase, Flair, Floral & Gilt Design, c.1850, 8 1/4 In.	110.00
Vase, Flair, Floral & Gilt, c.1850, 9 3/4 In.	170.00
Vase, French Scenes, Polychrome Paint, Converted To Lamp, 14 In., Pair	4025.00
Vase, Neo–Persian Style, Floral Cartouches, Pink Ground, 16 In.	245.00
Vase, Oriental Figures, Stylized Trees & Insects, 13 1/4 In., Pair	440.00
Vase, Relief Lily Pads, Portraits, 18 In., Pair ....*Illus*	1200.00
Vase, Urn Form, Landscape Scenes, Sphinxes Handles, Lamp, 14 In., Pair	935.00
Wash Set, Anneau D'Or, c.1850, 7 Piece	3300.00

Pate–de–verre is an ancient technique in which glass is made by blending and refining powdered glass of different colors into molds. The process was revived by French glassmakers, especially Galle, around the end of the nineteenth century.

PATE–DE–VERRE, Lamp, Purple, Green, G. Argy–Rousseau, 11 1/2 In. ......*Illus*	1000.00
Paperweight, Sea Nymph, Mottled Green Leaf, Daum, 6 3/4 In.	4400.00
Plate Set, Four Seasons, Daum Nancy, 1940, 4 Piece	495.00

Pate–sur–pate means paste on paste. The design was made by painting layers of slip on the ceramic piece until a relief decoration was formed. The method was developed at the Sevres factory in France about 1850. It became even more famous at the English Minton factory about 1870. It has since been used by many potters to make both pottery and porcelain wares.

PATE–SUR–PATE, Box, Medallion of Cupids With Lyres On Cloud, 4 1/4 x 4 In.	185.00
Oil Lamp, Putti & Ferns In Relief, England, 1870s, 12 1/4	415.00
Plaque, Stork Eating Frogs, 19th Century, 17 In.	330.00
Plate, Wild Rose, Salmon Ground, Gilt Tracery Edge, 9 In.	175.00
Tile, Gentleman's Portrait, Sherwin & Cotton, 9 x 6 In.	100.00
Vase, Celadon Green Ground, Figure of Woman, 8 1/2 In.	325.00
Vase, Nude, White Veils, Blue Ground, Germany, 4 1/2 In.	145.00
Vase, Pillow, Black Cupid Chasing Butterfly, G. Jones, 6 In.	525.00
Vase, Prunus Blossoms, Birds, Celadon Ground, Lenox, 9 1/4 In.	175.00
Vase, Woman In Flimsy Gown, Basket On Head, 8 1/2 In.	375.00

Paul Revere pottery was made at several locations in and around Boston, Massachusetts, between 1906 and 1942. The pottery was operated as a settlement house program for teenaged girls. Many pieces were signed *S.E.G.* for Saturday Evening Girls. The artists concentrated on children's dishes and tiles. Decorations were outlined in black and filled with color.

PAUL REVERE POTTERY, Bowl, Band of Trees & Hills, Green, SG, 5 x 12 In.	2200.00
Bowl, Colored Bands, SEG, F. Levine, c.1909, 6 In.	445.00
Bowl, Green Drip Glaze, 7 1/2 In.	200.00
Candletick, Blue, For Hurricane Shade, 7 1/2 x 4 In.	165.00
Dish, Band of 5 Mice, SEG, 1909, 5 3/8 In.	385.00

Mug, Motto, Roosters, Loop Handle, SEG, Label, 5 In. 605.00
Pitcher, Milk, Turquoise Glaze, Fanny Levine, 1923 .... 82.50
Pitcher, Motto, Band of Roosters, Marked, 9 3/4 In. 2420.00
Plate, Duck, Monroe, Blue Border, 2–26, 7 1/2 In. 275.00
Saucer, Swirl Glaze, Blue–Green, 6 In. 150.00
Tea Set, Blue Iris, Blue, Tan, Marked AM 1912, 3 Piece 2640.00
Tile, Band of Landscape, Fanny Levine, 1918, 5 1/2 In. 220.00
Tile, Landscape, Fanny Levine, c.1925, 5 5/8 In. 275.00
Vase, Band of Trees, SEG, Marked, 4 1/4 In. 1045.00
Vase, Blue, 6 1/2 In. 100.00
Vase, Bud, Pear Shape, Turquoise, Green Drip, 6 1/2 In. 145.00
Vase, Incised Band of Trees, Label, 1920s, 8 1/2 In. 2530.00
Vase, Incised Band of Tulips, SEG, Marked, 6 3/4 In. 357.00
Vase, Painted Band of Birds, Marked, 10 1/2 In. 935.00
Vase, Painted Band of Lotus Flowers, Marked, 4 3/4 In. .:............................... 220.00
Vase, Swollen Cylindrical Form, Marked S. E. G., 10 In. 275.00
Vase, White, Label, 5 In. 125.00

Peachblow glass originated about 1883 at Hobbs, Brockunier and Company of Wheeling, West Virginia. It is a glass that shades from yellow to peach. It was lined with white glass. New England peachblow is a one–layer glass shading from red to white. Mt. Washington peachblow shades from pink to blue. Reproductions of all types of peachblow have been made. Some are poor and easy to identify as copies, others are very accurate reproductions and could fool the unwary.

PEACHBLOW, Bowl, Tricorner, Pink To Blue–Gray, Mt. Washington, 5 x 2 1/2 In. 1285.00
Celery, New England, Scalloped Edge, Square Top, 4 3/4 In. 450.00
Cruet, Amber Faceted Stopper, Twisted Handle 750.00
Cruet, Curved Handle, Flated Lip, White Interior, 5 In. 715.00
Cruet, Wheeling, Satin Finish 1350.00
Figure, Pear, New England 75.00
PEACHBLOW, GUNDERSON, see Gunderson
Pear, New England 147.00
Pear, Wheeling, 4 In. 500.00
Pear, Wheeling, Butter Cream One Side, Blush Other Side, 4 In. 500.00
Pitcher, Applied Amber Thorn Handle, Leaves, 8 In. 395.00
Pitcher, Water, Custard Handle, Design 2000.00
Pitcher, Wheeling, Claret, Mahogany To Fuchsia To Cream, 10 In. 2250.00
Pitcher, Wheeling, Yellow To Rose Shaded, 12 In. 170.00
Rose Bowl, New England, 7–Crimp Top, 2 1/2 x 2 7/8 In. 325.00
Rose Bowl, Wild Rose, World's Fair, 1893, 3 1/4 x 4 In. 675.00
Sherbet, Berries, Mt. Washington, 2 1/2 In. 577.50
Sock Darner 25.00
Toothpick, New England, Squared Top 450.00
Tumbler, Water, New England, Raspberry, 3 3/4 In. 325.00
Tumbler, Water, Wheeling, White Lining, 3 7/8 In. 325.00

Pate–De–Verre, Lamp, Purple, Green,
G. Argy–Rousseau, 11 1/2 In.

Peachblow, Vase, Gargoyles,
Fuchsia To White, Amber Holder, 10 In.

Tumbler, Wheeling, Satin Finish 485.00
Vase, Banjo, 6 3/4 In. 285.00
Vase, Bud, Small 55.00
Vase, Crimp, Gunderson, 6 1/4 x 4 In. 140.00
Vase, Enameled Red Cherries, Green Leaves, Rococo, 10 In., Pair 650.00
Vase, Flying Duck Over Flowers, Marked, 8 3/4 In. 640.00
Vase, Gargoyles, Fuchsia To White, Amber Holder, 10 In. ....*Illus* 825.00
Vase, Lily, 10 In. 950.00
Vase, Lily, New England, Wafer Base, 10 In. 950.00
Vase, New England, Crimson Upper Half, White Wafer Base, 12 In. 985.00
Vase, Pink To Cranberry Shaded, Small 95.00
Vase, Wheeling, Morgan, Griffin Holder, Fuchsia To Amber 1650.00
  PEACHBLOW, WEBB, see Webb Peachblow

Listed under Pearl are items made of the natural mother–of–pearl from shells. The glassware known as mother–of–pearl is listed by that name. Opera glasses made with natural pearl shell are listed under Opera Glasses. Natural pearl has been used to decorate furniture and small utilitarian objects for centuries.

PEARL, Box, Pietra Dura Inset On Lid, Rosewood, 5 x 8 In. 265.00
Buckle, Belt, Slightly Curved, 2 1/2 In. 10.00
Button Hook, Steel Hook, 1900 .... 15.00
Case, Calling Card, c.1890 .... 45.00
Knife & Fork, Plated Blades, Landers Frary & Clark, 24 Piece 490.00
Serving Fork, Carved Handle, Silver Tines, c.1895 .... 65.00
Woman's Portrait, On Case, Green Velvet, 3 1/2 x 3 In. 35.00

Peking glass is a Chinese cameo glass first made popular in the eighteenth century. The Chinese have continued to make this layered glass in the old manner, and many new pieces are now available that could confuse the average buyer.

PEKING GLASS, Bottle, Snuff, Figure of Climbing Monkey, 2 1/2 In. 220.00
Bottle, Snuff, Wild Flowers Rising Past Mushrooms, 2 1/2 In. 175.00
Bowl, Green To Opaque White Cut, Bird, Grain, Stand, 7 x 3 In. 375.00
Perfume Bottle, Silver Fittings, Red, c.1900, 3 1/2 In. 115.00
Vase, Birds, Plum Branches, White Ground, Baluster, 6 In., Pair 440.00
Vase, Cameo, Blue Dragons, Pink Scrolls On White, 4 1/2 In. 935.00
Vase, Carved Crane & Leaves, White Ground, 8 In. 245.00
Vase, Cobalt Bird In Flight, Trees, Flowers, White, 8 In. 350.00
Vase, Flared Rim, Ducks, Flowers, Red To White, 8 1/2 In. 550.00
Vase, Flowers & Rockery, Baluster Form, c.1885, 5 1/2 In. 67.50
Vase, Horizontal Bands of Lotus Petals, Mallet, 8 In., Pr. 8000.00
Vase, Leaves & Berries, Chinese Red, White, c.1920, 9 In. 300.00
Vase, Red Cameo On Milk White, c.1900, 9 In. 290.00
Vase, Tropical Fish, Lotus Pond, Baluster Shape, 13 In. 750.00

Peloton glass is a European glass with small threads of colored glass rolled onto the surface of clear or colored glass. It is sometimes called spaghetti, or shredded coconut, glass. Most pieces found today were made in the nineteenth century.

PELOTON, Bowl, Colored Spaghetti Strands, Silver Plated Wire Frame, 7 In. 385.00
Dish, Sweetmeat, Ribbed, White Interior, Plated Lid & Handle 565.00
Rose Bowl, Wishbone Feet, 6–Crimp Top, Pink Ground, 2 3/4 In. 225.00
Vase, Threading, White, Clear Rigaree Top, 6 Petal Feet, 3 3/4 In. 258.00
Vase, Tricorner Folded–Over Top, Coconut Strings, 4 1/4 In. 295.00
Vase, Tricorner, White–Ribbed Ground, Coconut Strings, 4 3/4 In. 350.00

The first steel pen point was made in England in 1780 to replace the hand–cut quill as a writing instrument. It was 100 years before the commercial pen was a common item. The fountain pen was invented in the 1830s but was not made in quantity until the 1880s. All types of old pens are collected.

PEN & PENCIL, Chanel No. 5, 14K Gold 30.00

◆◆◆

Advertising card collectors should be careful how the cards are displayed. Don't use the photo albums with plastic envelopes and a sticky cardboard backing (sometimes called "magnetic" albums). The cards will stick and the backs will be ruined. Pure pharmacy acetone, carefully dripped under the corner of the card will help free it with minimal damage. Do not use nail polish remover.

◆◆◆

Conklin, Black & Gold	125.00
Duofold	125.00
Eversharp Skyline, Maroon, Gold Filled Caps, Box	85.00
Jefferson, Brown, Gold Ripple, Gold Point	150.00
Parker 51, Special	85.00
Wahl Eversharp, Black & Pearl, Roller Clip, Gold Seal	325.00
Wahl, Woman's, Gold Filled, Box	55.00
Waterman, Box	20.00
PEN, Conklin, No. 30, Black Rubber, 1903	70.00
Conklin, Wooden, With Brass Printing Block	10.00
Desk, Signed Wahl	40.00
Eclipse, Maroon	40.00
Esterbrook, With Holder	11.00
European, Cartridge, Sterling Silver, Gold Trim	85.00
Fountain, Hanging Loop, Gold Trim, Black, 3 In.	20.00
Fountain, Sheaffer, White Dot, Marbelized Black & Yellow	400.00
Majestic, Fountain, Leaf Green Pyralin	15.00
Morrison, Ball Point, Sterling Filigree	30.00
Park Row, Fountain, 14–Gold Tips, Box, 2 Piece	395.00
Parker Duofold	75.00
Parker, Lucky Curve, Push–Button Fill, 1917	85.00
Pen Wipe Doll, Black Pigtails, Red Felt Dress, 1865, 7 1/2 In.	150.00
Sheaffer, 14K–Gold Point	15.00
Sheaffer, Clip, White Dot	30.00
Sheaffer, Desk Set, Art Deco	20.00
Sheaffer, Desk, Onyx Holder	45.00
Sheaffer, Lifetime	20.00
Sheaffer, Lifetime, Desk	30.00
Sheaffer, Red	10.00
Sheaffer, Tuck–A–Way, Blue, Box	25.00
Waterman, Gold Filled, Filigree	120.00
Waterman, Marked, c.1890	450.00
Waterman, Ripple, Box	50.00

The pencil was invented, so it is said, in 1565. The eraser was not added to the pencil until 1858. The automatic pencil was invented in 1863. Collectors today want advertising pencils or automatic pencils of unusual design. Boxes and sharpeners for pencils are also collected.

PENCIL SHARPENER, Baker's Chocolate Lady	35.00
Baker's Chocolate, Girl, Metal	110.00
Block, Bakelite	65.00
Boston, Self–Feeder, No Move	30.00
Charlie The Tuna, Box	25.00
Charlie The Tuna, Electric	50.00
Pinocchio, Figural	125.00
Tank, Bakelite, Decals	43.00
U. S. Army Plane, Green Bakelite, 1940s	18.00
Upright, Red Bakelite	25.00
World Globe, Colorful, Germany	25.00

PENCIL, 14K Gold, Hand Chased, Retractible, Jewel Top, 16 gms. 245.00
  Automatic, Figural, Blackamoor, Bakelite 75.00
  Borden's Ice Cream, Mechanical, Elsie Picture 45.00
  Bullet, Harley & Ranger Bikes 20.00
  Case, Ben Casey 20.00
  Clip, Morton's Salt 6.00
  Eversharp, Eagle Automatic, Box, 10 1/2 In. 25.00
  Holder, Golf Ball, Bronzed 30.00
  Mechanical, Bat Shape, Ralph Kiner, 16 In. 65.00
  Mechanical, Borden's Ice Cream, Elsie The Cow Picture 45.00
  Mechanical, NuGrape Soda, Catalin Plastic, 1920s 18.50
  Mechanical, Rummy Soda, 1940s 18.50
  Mechanical, Sheaffer, Jade Marble, Gold Filled 100.00
  Parker Duofold Deluxe, Green & Pearl, 1930 .... 60.00
  Parker, Challenger, Mechanical, Marbelized Green Jade 45.00
  Parker, Vacumatic, 1940s 18.00
  Wahl–Eversharp, Gold Filled, Ring At Top 35.00
  Wahl–Eversharp, Mechanical 10.00
  Wahl–Eversharp, Woman's, Gold Filled 40.00

Pennsbury Pottery   The Pennsbury Pottery worked in Morrisville, Pennsylvania, from 1950 to 1971. Full sets of dinnerware were made as well as many decorative items. Pieces are marked with the name of the factory.

PENNSBURY, Ashtray, Amish Couple .... 15.00 To 25.00
  Ashtray, Rooster 25.00
  Ashtray, Such A Schmoozer 35.00
  Bowl, Pretzel, Sweet Adelaine 45.00
  Canister Set, Red Rooster, 4 Piece 370.00
  Canister Set, Rooster, Flour, Sugar & Coffee 250.00
  Coaster, Doylestown Trust 22.00
  Cookie Jar, Amish Scene 98.00
  Cookie Jar, Chicken 60.00
  Creamer, Tulip, Advertising, 4 In. 25.00
  Cup, Rooster, Red 14.00
  Mug, Beer, Eagle, 5 In. 35.00
  Mug, Sweet Adeline, 5 In. 35.00
  Pitcher & Bowl, Rooster .... 40.00 To 45.00
  Pitcher, Amish Couple, 6 In. 35.00
  Pitcher, Black Rooster, 4 In. 35.00
  Pitcher, Eagle, 6 In. 42.00
  Pitcher, Rooster, 5 In. 28.00
  Pitcher, Rooster, Black, 4 In. 35.00
  Pitcher, Sweet Adeline, 7 1/2 In. 85.00
  Plaque, Eagle, 21 In. 48.00
  Plaque, Harvest, Round, 6 In. 30.00
  Plaque, Kissing Over Cow 50.00
  Plaque, Pennsylvania R.R. 1856 Tiger, Locomotive 45.00
  Plate, Barber 12.00
  Plate, Christmas, 1971 .... 28.00 To 35.00
  Plate, Yuletide, 1970 .... 30.00
  Salt & Pepper, Rooster, Black 26.00
  Soup, Dish, Rooster 16.00
  Sugar & Creamer, Red Rooster 50.00
  Wall Pocket, Bust of Woman 125.00

PEPSI·COLA   Pepsi-Cola, the drink and the name, was invented in 1898 but was not trademarked until 1903. The logo was changed from an elaborate script to the modern block letters in the 1970 Pepsi label. All types of advertising memorabilia are collected and reproductions are being made.

PEPSI–COLA, Bag, Bottle, 1930s 25.00
  Bank, Vending Machine, Plastic 95.00
  Blotter, Pepsi & Pete 60.00

Bottle Cap, Cardboard, Encased In Plastic	47.50
Bottle Opener, 5 Cents	40.00
Bottle Opener, Bottle Shape, Double Dot Logo	28.00
Bottle, Fountain Syrup, 1940	18.00
Can, 75th Anniversary	9.00
Clock, Round	150.00
Clock, Wall, 1940s	275.00 To 350.00
Coin–Operated Machine, Vendolator, 10 Cent, 12 Oz. Bottles	3000.00
Cup, Daisy Duck, Milk Glass, 4 In.	4.00
Dispenser, Radio, Box	550.00
Door Push Bar, Iron, 1960s	95.00
Door Push, Wrought Iron & Tin	115.00
Drum, Cover, 1941	195.00
Lighter, Metal	35.00
Menu Board, Art Deco, 1940s	250.00
Pen, Bottle Clip	165.00
Pen, Bottle Shaped Clip, Logo On Top & Bottom, 1937	200.00
Pen, Fountain, Bottle Clip	165.00
Pen, Fountain, Box	150.00
Pitcher, Tiffany Style, Red Enameled, Blue Top & Base, 8 1/8 In.	53.00
Rack, Wire	22.50
Radio, Bottle Shape, 1930s, 23 In.	450.00
Record, Voice of Your Man In Service, Package, World War II	75.00
Salt & Pepper	10.00 To 15.00
Sign, Bottle Cap, Tin, 1950s	125.00
Sign, Drink Pepsi–Cola, Bottle Cap, Square, 3 Ft.	60.00
String Holder, Tin, 1930s	375.00
Thermometer, Have A Pepsi	58.00
Thermometer, Round	45.00
Thermometer, Say Pepsi Please, Tin, 1960s	50.00
Thermometer, With Bottle Cap, Yellow, Embossed, 1960s	95.00
Tip Tray, Black & Red Rose Floral	20.00
Tip Tray, Evervess	36.00
Tray, 1940s	75.00
Tray, Bottles Buried In Ice Cubes, Square	25.00
Tray, Mirrored, Bamboo Frame, 1960	35.00
Tray, Woman At Bar, c.1909	2500.00
Truck, Buddy L, Wooden	1100.00
Tumbler, Bugs Bunny, Looney Tunes Series, 1979, 6 In.	4.00
Tumbler, Donald Duck, White Enameled, 6 In.	7.00
Tumbler, Hot Sam, Logo	45.00
Tumbler, Mickey Mouse, Picnic, 1970s, 6 In.	12.00
Tumbler, Pepsi Super–Hero, Logo, Tomart, 14 Piece	140.00
Tumbler, Popeye's Fried Chicken, Brutus Thru Years, 5 5/8 In.	6.00
Tumbler, Red Logo Over White, Syrup Line, 10 Oz., 5 1/8 In.	11.00
Tumbler, Ringling Bros. Barnum & Bailey, 1975, 6 1/4 In.	12.00
Tumbler, Super Heroes	8.00
Vending Machine, Cooler, Vendolater, Model 81, 10 Cents, c.1955	2500.00

Cut glass, pressed glass, art glass, silver, metal, enamel, and even plastic or porcelain perfume bottles have been made. Although the small bottle to hold perfume was first made before the time of ancient Egypt, it is the nineteenth– and twentieth–century examples that interest today's collector. Examples with the atomizer top marked *DeVilbiss* are listed under that name. Glass or porcelain examples will be found under the appropriate name such as Lalique, Czechoslovakia, etc.

PERFUME BOTTLE, 20 Carats, Dana, Contents, 1933	55.00
Ambre D'Orsay, Classical Maidens, Black, Lalique, 5 1/4 In.	1980.00
Art Deco Face, Goo–Goo Eyes, Milk Glass, 1920s, 3 In.	35.00
Babs Yesteryear	50.00
Belle De Jour, Dorsay, 4 1/2 In.	135.00
Blue Grass, Elizabeth Arden, Crystal, 1930s	10.00

Blue Opaline, Allover Gold, White, Red Design, France, 5 In. 58.00
Blue, Cut Glass, Enameled Atomizer 125.00
Bristol, Pink, Gold Branch Design, Stopper, 10 1/8 In. 135.00
Bull's–Eye & Punty, Apple Green, Cut Stopper, 3 1/4 In. 340.00
Cheveliar De La Nuit, Black Glass, 4 1/2 In. 195.00
Cobalt Blue, Gold Mica Allover, Stopper, 3 1/2 In. 60.00
Cranberry, Cut Glass 95.00
Crown Devon, Hill's Devon Garden, Not Opened, Box 90.00
Cut Glass, Laydown, Brilliant, Sterling Lid, 3 1/2 In. 95.00
Cut Glass, Pump Type, England, 5 In. 75.00
Cut Glass, Red, Sterling Repousse Flip Back Cap, Stopper 255.00
Daisy & Button, Blue 185.00
Danger, Ciro, Contents, Box 85.00
Desert Flower 4.50
Diamond Panel Cut Glass, Gold & Silver Mica, 3 1/4 In. 225.00
Diamond Quilted, Mother–of–Pearl, Blue, 5 In. 355.00
Double, Laydown, Hinged In Middle, Diamond Panel, 5 1/4 In. 220.00
Enameled Romantic Scene, Ovoid, Lobmyer, 4 3/4 In. 385.00
Etched Man Under Palm Tree, Mexican Silver, 1 1/4 In. 40.00
Evening In Paris 8.00
Fern & Bamboo Leaves, Ivory, Sterling Cap, 3 3/4 In. 355.00
Floral & Basket, Frosted Ground, St. Louis, 2 1/4 In. 295.00
Frenzy, Cordey, Contents, Box, 1930s 65.00
Gold Trim Stopper, Craquelle, Cranberry, 4 1/2 In. 88.00
Gold Water, For Americans, Box 15.00
Golliwog, Figural 600.00
Golliwog, Large 375.00
Green Cut Panels, Laydown, France 145.00
Green, Black Glass Ribs, Czechoslovakia, 1930s, 4 In., 4 Pc. 225.00
Green, Double–Ended, 5 1/4 In. 250.00
Hoyt's, Germany 20.00
L'Heure Bleue, Guerlain, Contents, Box, 1930s 85.00
Lantern, Tappan's Sweet Bye–Bye Bouquet, Winter Scene, 1882 .... 65.00
Le Jade, Roger & Gallet, 3 3/4 In. 250.00
Lucretia Vanderbilt, Blue 385.00
Lydia Pinkham, Metal, Pocket 50.00
Mais Oui, Bourjois, Contents, Box, 1938 .... 35.00
Malachite, Art Glass, Pan & Dancers, 6 In. 250.00
Marilyn Monroe 12.00
Mickey Mouse & Donald Duck, Glass, Pair 45.00
Millefiori, 7 Portrait Canes, Venice, 1830–40 .... 425.00
New Horizons, Ciro, Box, 1941 .... 45.00
Parfum Orloff 50.00
Park & Tilford Lilac Cologne 8.00
Pear Shape, Chased Cap, 2–Color Gold Mount, Pairs, c.1790 .... 1650.00
Pink Satin Glass, Original Stopper 45.00
Prince Matchiabelli, Gold Crown 22.00
Ralphael's Replique, 3 1/4 In. 175.00
Risque, Leigh, Contents, 1926 .... 35.00
Schiaparelli, Frosted, Metalic Pink Cap 65.00
Schiaparelli, Sleeping, 6 1/4 In. 75.00
Secret De Suzanne, Contents, Box, 1930s 55.00
Shalimar, Baccarat, Box 70.00
Shoe Shape, Original Label 27.50
Shulton, Box, Unused 35.00
Silver Feathers, Pedestal, Lundberg, 6 In. 145.00
Silver, Mexico 30.00
Soir De Paris, Bourjois, Cobalt Blue, 1930s 25.00
St. Clair, Blue & White Flowers 75.00
Swirl Pattern, White & Orange Flowers, 4 1/2 In. 160.00
Tempest, Lelong, Box 50.00
Three Silent Messengers, Lentheric, Box, 1940 .... 45.00
Tic Toc, Babs Creation, Dome 45.00

Tweed, Lentheric, Contents, Box, 1935 .... 20.00

Peters & Reed Pottery Company of Zanesville, Ohio, was founded by John D. Peters and Adam Reed in 1897. Chromal, Landsun, Montene, Pereco, and Persian are some of the art lines that were made. The company became Zane Pottery in 1920, Gonder Pottery in 1941, and closed in 1957. Peters & Reed was unmarked.

PETERS & REED, Bowl, Ereco, 5 In. 65.00
Bowl, Moss Aztec, 4 x 5 In. 140.00
Bowl, Stylized Branches, Matte Green Glaze, 3 1/2 x 9 In. 247.00
Ewer, Floral Garland, Brown High Gloss Ground, 4 3/4 In. 20.00
Figurine, Cat, Seated 375.00
Jug, Cobbler, Musician & Gentleman With Umbrella, 4 1/2 In. 35.00
Jug, Rembrandt Portraits, 4 In. 25.00
Mug, Sprig of Lincoln & Washington, Standard Glaze, 7 In. 115.00
Planter, Moss Aztec, Nude Figures 120.00
Stand, Umbrella, Moss Aztec, Grecian Women Panels 225.00
Tankard Set, Embossed Grapes, 2 Steins, 17–In. Tankard 155.00
Vase, Blue Over Green, 6 In. 95.00
Vase, Bud, Florentine, Double, 7 In. 35.00
Vase, Bud, Wilse Blue, 6 Sides, 6 In. 25.00
Vase, Chromal, 8 In. 125.00
Vase, Drip Line, 4 In. 50.00
Vase, Floral, Clover–Shaped Opening, 3 Footed, 4 In. 20.00
Vase, Landsun, 8 In. 30.00
Vase, Marbelized, 11 In. 70.00
Vase, Mirror Black, Hexagon, 9 In. 40.00
Vase, Roses, Buds, Chamberstick–Style, 7 1/2 In. 30.00
Wall Pocket, Moss Aztec, Grape Design, 8 In. 60.00
Wall Pocket, Moss Aztec, Nude Woman, 9 In. 80.00
  PETRUS REGOUT, see Maastricht

The Pewabic Pottery was founded by Mary Chase Perry Stratton in 1903 in Detroit, Michigan. The company made many types of art pottery including pieces with matte green glaze and an iridescent crystalline glaze. The company continued working until the death of Mary Stratton in 1961. It was reactivated by Michigan State University in 1968.

PEWABIC, Ashtray, Pink & Green, Triangular 100.00
Bowl, Black Iridescent, 3 3/4 x 8 In. 750.00
Bowl, Metallic Brown–Rose Luster, Turquoise Inside, 3 x 8 3/4 In. 350.00
Charger, Turquoise, Gray & Green Flambe, Iridescent, 14 1/2 In. 800.00
Paperweight, Raised Skyline, Impressed, G. F. W. C., Detroit, 1939 .... 150.00
Planter, Lavender Exterior, Turquoise Interior, 1 3/4 x 9 1/2 In. 350.00
Plate, Apple & Leaf Design Rim, Iridescent Glaze, 10 3/8 In. 275.00
Plate, Apple & Leaf Design, Multicolored Ground, 10 In. 250.00
Plate, Running Rabbit Border, Glaze Craquelure, 10 1/2 In. 440.00
Radiator Cover, Green To Gray, Iridescent Glaze, 6 x 6 In. 132.00
Tile, Bactrain Camel & Calf, Mottled Blue Glaze, Square, 6 In. 55.00
Tile, Elephant Train, Marked, Square, 8 In. 55.00
Tile, United States Seal, Copper Glaze, 7 1/2 x 7 1/2 In. 330.00
Tile, Wayne State University, 1868, Round, 5 1/2 In. 225.00
Vase, Blue Dripping, Iridescent Glaze, 2 1/2 In. .... 250.00 To 295.00
Vase, Blue Feather & Gold Luster, Royal Blue Ground, 11 1/2 In. 1980.00
Vase, Gold & Purple Glaze, 2 In. 70.00
Vase, Gold & Purple Glaze, Cylindrical Form, 1 7/8 In. 70.00
Vase, Gold Luster, Rolled Rim, Baluster, 5 1/4 x 3 1/2 In. 522.00
Vase, Iridescent Yellow & Green Glaze, Flared Neck, 4 3/4 In. 415.00
Vase, Light Blue–Gray Over Dark Blue, Bulbous, 4 1/2 x 5 1/2 In. 775.00
Vase, Yellow & Green Glaze, 5 In. 375.00

Pewter is a metal alloy of tin and lead. Some of the pewter made after 1840 has a slightly different composition and is called *Britannia metal*. This later type of pewter was worked by machine; the earlier pieces were made by hand. In the 1920s pewter came back into fashion and pieces were often marked *Genuine Pewter*. Eighteenth-, nineteenth-, and twentieth-century examples are listed here.

PEWTER, Basin, H. N. Rust, 2 x 8 In.	650.00
Basin, London, 9 1/4 x 2 1/2 In.	175.00
Basin, Nathaniel Austin, Boston, 2 x 8 In.	600.00
Basin, Samuel Danforth, 2 x 8 In.	225.00
Basin, Thomas Danforth, Boardman, 1 3/4 x 7 1/4 In.	300.00
Basin, Thomas Danforth, Boardman, Conn., 8 In.	205.00
Basin, Thomas Danforth, Early 19th Century, 12 In.	550.00
Beaker, Griswold, 4 In.	1320.00
Bed Warmer, Oval	125.00
Bedpan, Screw On Handle, D. Curtiss, Early 19th Century, 16 In.	110.00
Bedpan, Thomas Danforth, Boardman, Conn., 11 1/2 In.	200.00
Bowl, Baptismal, Footed, 3 1/8 x 5 1/4 In.	135.00
Bowl, Footed, London, 5 x 2 3/4 In., 4 Piece	300.00
Bowl, Footed, Silver Plate, Floral Engraved, 5 7/8 x 3 5/8 In.	110.00
Box, Engraved Scenes, Divided, Rectangular, Oriental, 6 In.	95.00
Candlestick, 3–Light, 2 1/2 In.	30.00
Candlestick, Baluster Form, Flagg & Homan, c.1850, 7 In., Pair	600.00
Candlestick, Figural, Servant With Tray Supports Socket, 11 In., Pr.	1650.00
Candlestick, Flagg & Homan, Cincinnati, Ohio, 2 1/8 In., Pair	265.00
Candlestick, Fuller & Smith, 8 3/8 In.	75.00
Candlestick, Punch–Up, 9 3/8 In., Pair	600.00
Candlestick, Telescoping, 7 5/8 In., Pair	50.00
Candlestick, Tulip Candlesocket, Baluster Stem, Ohio, 8 In., Pair	275.00
Charger, Angel Touchmarks, 14 In.	15.00
Charger, Charles White Leigh, London, 14 3/4 In.	300.00
Charger, Continental, Rim Engraved A. H., 1749, 14 In.	150.00
Charger, Engraved Initials, John Ansell, London, 1732, 14 In.	250.00
Charger, H. & R. Joseph, England, 12 1/4 In.	115.00
Charger, Marked London, 15 3/4 In.	125.00
Charger, Nathaniel Austin, Charleston, Mass., 13 1/2 In.	450.00
Charger, Norwich Scroll, John Danforth, 12 1/4 In.	100.00
Charger, Richard King, London, 16 1/2 In.	375.00
Charger, Samuel Ellis, 13 1/4 In.	125.00
Charger, Samuel Ellis, 18 In.	225.00
Charger, Samuel Hamlin, 11 1/2 In.	300.00
Charger, Samuel Hamlin, 13 1/2 In.	600.00
Charger, Thomas Badger, Boston, 13 3/8 In.	650.00
Charger, Townsend & Compton, England, 13 1/2 In.	120.00
Charger, Townsend & Griffin, 13 1/4 In.	100.00
Charger, Woods, Waterford, England, 17 In.	440.00
Coffee Set, Sellew & Co., c.1860, 3 Piece	750.00
Coffee Urn, Wooden Finial, Feet & Handle, Europe, 4 3/4 In.	175.00
Coffeepot, Ashbil Griswold, Meriden, Conn., 1802, 12 In.	625.00
Coffeepot, Floral Finial, Floral Engraving, Homan & Co., 8 1/4 In.	120.00
Coffeepot, J. Munson, 19th Century, 11 1/2 In.	220.00
Coffeepot, James Dixon, 11 7/8 In.	120.00
Coffeepot, Pear Shape, Wishbone Handle, Sellew & Co., 1840, 10 In.	385.00
Coffeepot, Roswell Gleason, 10 3/4 In.	90.00
Coffeepot, Roswell Gleason, 11 In.	275.00
Coffeepot, Sellew & Co., 11 In.	95.00
Coffeepot, Serpentine Spout, H. C. Wilcox, c.1850, 8 1/2 In.	137.00
Coffeepot, Serpentine Spout, Sellew & Co., 11 1/4 In.	330.00
Cuspidor, 4 7/8 In.	400.00
Dish, Deep, Reed Rim, 13 3/4 In.	220.00
Flagon, Continental, 8 3/4 In.	590.00

Flagon, Continental, 11 In.	800.00
Flagon, Continental, Engraved Name & Date, 1697, 13 3/4 In.	250.00
Flagon, Double Litre, F. Boulaget, 10 3/4 In.	200.00
Flagon, Embossed Eagle, Head Spout, Inscribed, 1872–1897, 13 3/8 In.	285.00
Flagon, J. Boardman	2800.00
Flagon, Large A On Rim, 11 1/4 In.	1150.00
Flagon, Smith & Feltman, Albany, 12 In.	350.00
Flagon, Tooled Handle & Ball Thumbpiece, Continental, 12 3/4 In.	95.00
Ink Stand, Hinged Lids, Fitted Interior, 4 3/4 x 6 3/4 In.	125.00
Inkwell, Lid, Ceramic Insert, Wide Flat Base, 6 7/8 In.	85.00
Jar, Pale Jade Insert In Cover Handle, Chinese, 5 3/8 In.	35.00
Ladle, 12 1/2 In.	75.00
Ladle, Punch, John Yates, 13 1/2 In.	140.00
Lamp, Chamber, Brass & Tin Whale Oil Burner, F. Porter, 6 In.	425.00
Lamp, Fluid Burner, Capen & Molineux, New York, 7 3/4 In.	200.00
Lamp, Fluid, Endicott & Summer, N. Y., 6 5/8 In.	500.00
Lamp, Jacob Whitmore, 7 7/8 In.	130.00
Lamp, Sparking, 1 Spout, Brass Burner, Snuffer Cap, 4 In.	85.00
Lamp, Sparking, Saucer Base, Snuffer, 4 1/2 In.	125.00
Lamp, Spout, Lift–Out Font, 9 1/4 In.	125.00
Measure, Bellied, Mason's Arms, England, 4 3/4 In., 4 Piece	260.00
Measure, Handleless, English, 1/2 Pint, 5 In.	40.00
Measure, Tankard, English, 4 In.	75.00
Measure, Tankard, Thomas Danforth III, 6 In.	325.00
Measures, James Yates, 1/4 Gill To 1 Gal., 2 In. To 10 In.	1600.00
Mold, Candle, 12–Tube, Pine Frame, 14 In.	225.00
Mold, Chocolate, Foxy Grandpa	100.00
Mold, Ice Cream, Bell, Cupid & Ribbons	43.00
Mold, Ice Cream, Cannon, Banquet Size	50.00
Mold, Ice Cream, Chicken, Banquet Size	110.00
Mold, Ice Cream, Chinaman, E & Co., N. Y., 3 7/8 In.	22.50
Mold, Ice Cream, Chrysanthemum, 5 3/4 In.	40.00
Mold, Ice Cream, Cow, 4 In.	40.00
Mold, Ice Cream, Donkey	82.00 To 85.00

◆◆

Bugs, unfortunately, also like collections! Flies stain paper; cock–roaches eat paper and books; silverfish and firebrat damage paper, leather, fabrics; moths and carpet beetles eat upholstery, stuffed animals, furs, and fabrics; termites eat wood, paper, and parts of rugs; powder post beetles and dry wood termites eat wood. Use proper sprays, check often for damage, hire professional exterminators if you have a serious problem.

◆◆

Pewter, Pitcher, Cover, Roswell Gleason,
1830–50, 1 Gal., 12 In.

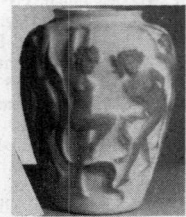

Phoenix, Vase, Dancing Nudes, 12 1/2 In.

Mold, Ice Cream, Duck, 4 1/4 In. 47.00
Mold, Ice Cream, Easter Lily 55.00
Mold, Ice Cream, Engagement Ring 35.00
Mold, Ice Cream, Flag, S & Co., 4 In. 35.00
Mold, Ice Cream, Foxy Grandpa, 5 In. 100.00
Mold, Ice Cream, Heart 22.00
Mold, Ice Cream, Jack of Diamonds 70.00
Mold, Ice Cream, Lady's Slipper 70.00
Mold, Ice Cream, Mother, E. & Co., Oval, 4 1/2 x 4 1/2 In. 40.00
Mold, Ice Cream, Oval Compote, E. & C. D., 4 Sections, 11 3/4 In. 35.00
Mold, Ice Cream, Palmer Cox Brownie, Hinged, 2 Piece, 5 In. 100.00
Mold, Ice Cream, Rose, 4 1/4 In. 37.00
Mold, Ice Cream, Santa Claus, 5 In. 45.00
Mold, Ice Cream, Swan, 3 Sections, Added Brass Feet, 9 In. 55.00
Mold, Ice Cream, Tulip, 4 In. 35.00
Mold, Ice Cream, Valentine, Envelope Shape, 1896, 4 5/8 In. 70.00
Mold, Ice Cream, Witch On Broom, 5 5/8 In. 121.00
Mold, Ice Cream, Witch Riding Broom, Big Nose, Ugly Face 12.00
Nativity Set, 9 Piece 65.00
Pipe Rest, Paperweight, Clipper Ship 25.00
Pitcher, Barrel Shape, Cast Ear Handle, England, 5 1/8 In. 160.00
Pitcher, Bellied Side Spout, Cast Ear Handle, James Yates, 6 5/8 In. 50.00
Pitcher, Cover, J. D. Locke, New York, c.1840, 9 3/4 In. 605.00
Pitcher, Cover, Roswell Gleason, 1830–50, 1 Gal., 12 In. ....*Illus* 1450.00
Pitcher, Hinged Lid, Homan & Co., Cincinnati, 12 In. 415.00
Pitcher, Ovoid Form, D. Curtiss, 9 3/4 In. 550.00
Pitcher, Turned Finial, Acanthus Handle, Sellew & Co., c.1830 .... 550.00
Pitcher, Water, Boardman & Hart, New York, 8 In. 325.00
Pitcher, Water, Boardman & Hart, Ovoid, J. P. M. Monogram, 6 In. 305.00
Plate, 3 Angels, Fein Zinn, Marked, 9 1/2 In. 35.00
Plate, Ashbil Griswold, Conn., 7 7/8 In. 250.00
Plate, B. Barns, Phila., 7 7/8 In. .... 200.00 To 235.00
Plate, Calder, Provid., 8 3/8 In. 375.00
Plate, F. Bassett, N. Y., 9 In. 350.00
Plate, Fen Church St. London, 8 1/4 In. 50.00
Plate, G. Lightner, Baltimore, 7 7/8 In. 225.00
Plate, Gershon Jones, 8 3/8 In. 375.00
Plate, In God We Trust, David Melville, 8 1/4 In. 350.00
Plate, Initials Stamped In Rim, Thomas Badger, Boston, 7 3/4 In. 300.00
Plate, Initials Stamped In Rin, John Skinner, 9 1/8 In. 400.00
Plate, Jacob Eggleston, 8 In. 325.00
Plate, John Danforth, 7 3/4 In. 375.00
Plate, Joseph Belcher, 8 In. 650.00
Plate, London, 9 1/4 In., Pair 90.00
Plate, Marked Luno, 7 In. 20.00
Plate, Richard Austin, 7 7/8 In. 175.00
Plate, S. Kilbourn, Baltimore, 7 3/4 In. 325.00
Plate, Samuel Danforth, 7 7/8 In. .... 300.00 To 325.00
Plate, Samuel Hamlin, 11 1/2 In. 225.00
Plate, Scalloped, Continental, 8 1/2 In., 6 Piece 90.00
Plate, Thomas & Townsend, Compton, London, 7 5/8 In. 125.00
Plate, Thomas Badger, 8 1/2 In. 125.00
Plate, Thomas Danforth III, 7 3/4 In. 325.00
Plate, Thomas Danforth, Boardman, 9 1/2 In. 105.00
Plate, W. Billings, Providence, Rhode Island, 7 7/8 In. 350.00
Plate, William Danforth, 8 In. 325.00
Platter, Domed Leaf Cover, Kayserzinn, 8 x 21 In. 440.00
Platter, Scalloped, Coat of Arms Rim, Edward York, 17 1/2 In. 170.00
Porringer, Cast Crown Handle, Marked W. W., 4 3/4 In. 325.00
Porringer, Cast Flowered Handle, 5 1/4 In. 85.00
Porringer, Gersham Jones 1320.00
Porringer, S. Hamlin Sr. 1100.00
Salt, Spoon, Viking Shop 17.50

Sauce Boat, Underplate, Kayserzinn, 7 In.	95.00
Server, Nekrassoff, Triangular	60.00
Soup, Dish, Angel Touchmarks, 8 1/4 In., Pair	20.00
Soup, Dish, Engraved M. E. P. 1736, Continental, 10 1/4 In.	75.00
Soup, Dish, Foliage, Griffon, Continental, 10 In.	55.00
Soup, Dish, Francis Piggot, London, 9 3/4 In.	150.00
Spoon, Fiddleback Handles, Marked, 8 1/2 In., 6 Piece	30.00
Spoon, Shell Handles, Marked C. P., 8 1/2 In., 4 Piece	90.00
Sugar & Creamer, Crescent	35.00
Sugar, Acorn Finial, Cast Ear Handles, 6 1/4 In.	200.00
Sugar, Acorn Finial, Cast Ear Handles, Sellew & Co., 7 In.	400.00
Sugar, Nautilus Shell Shape, 5 In.	25.00
Syrup, Cast Floral Finial, Homan & Co., Cincinnati, 7 3/4 In.	475.00
Syrup, Underplate, Wallace	55.00
Tankard Mug, Engraved Berries & Foliage, Europe, 5 1/2 In.	35.00
Tankard, Domed Cover, Banded Base, 7 In.	275.00
Tankard, Domed Cover, Openwork Thumb Latch, 18th Century, 8 In.	305.00
Tankard, Domed Lid, Scrolled Handle, Marked John Will, c.1760, 7 In.	9350.00
Tankard, Engraved Monogram, Ear Handle, England, 6 5/8 In.	110.00
Tankard, James Moyes, Edinburgh, 1860, 1 Pt.	165.00
Tea Caddy, England, 6 1/2 In.	155.00
Tea Set, 3 1/4–In. Teapot, 15 Piece	145.00
Tea Set, Flag & Homan, Cincinnati, Ohio, 3 Piece	75.00
Teapot, Best Britannia Metal, 7 5/8 In.	40.00
Teapot, Boardman & Hart, New York, 7 In.	235.00
Teapot, Calder, Providence 12, 9 1/8 In.	150.00
Teapot, Domed Cover, Wishbone Handle, C. Curtiss, 7 In.	440.00
Teapot, E. Smith, 7 1/4 In.	225.00
Teapot, Ebonized Foliate Handle, J. Fisher, 9 1/2 In.	110.00
Teapot, Engraved Designs, Bust of Woman, Homan & Co., 8 In.	25.00
Teapot, Finial Shape, Flower Like, 1840, 9 In.	175.00
Teapot, Flower Finial, James Dixon, 5 3/4 In.	45.00
Teapot, Flower Finial, Sellew & Co., 9 3/8 In.	300.00
Teapot, G. Richardson, 7 5/8 In.	350.00
Teapot, J. Danforth, No. 4, 6 5/8 In.	2000.00
Teapot, J. B. Woodbury, 7 In.	250.00
Teapot, Morey & Smith Warrented, 9 In.	50.00
Teapot, Paneled, Wooden Handle & Finial, Roswell Gleason, 10 1/8 In.	200.00
Teapot, Putnam, Massachusetts, 8 5/8 In.	85.00
Teapot, Queen Anne, S. Ellis, 1740	1700.00
Teapot, R. Dunham, 7 5/8 In.	275.00
Teapot, R. Gleason, 8 1/2 In.	275.00
Teapot, Roswell Gleason	445.00
Teapot, Savage, Middletown, Conn., 6 1/4 In.	100.00
Teapot, Savage, Middletown, Conn., 7 7/8 In.	125.00
Teapot, Sellew & Co., Cincinnati, 6 1/2 In.	115.00
Teapot, Simpson & Benham, N. Y., 8 In.	175.00
Teapot, Smith & Co., 7 5/8 In.	250.00
Teapot, T. S. Derby, 9 1/4 In.	125.00
Teapot, Thomas Danforth & Samuel Boardman, 7 In.	500.00
Teapot, Tudric, Carved Macassar Handle, Liberty & Co.	250.00
Teapot, Wm. McQuailkin	90.00
Teapot, Wooden Finial, J. Danforth No. 5, 7 1/4 In.	275.00
Tray, Art Nouveau, Flowers & Butterfly, 11 3/4 x 8 1/4 In.	65.00
Tray, Card, Antlered Deer Center, 4 1/4 x 5 In.	58.00
Tray, Pheasant, Art Nouveau, Kayserzinn, 24 In.	325.00
Urn, Melon Ribbed, Brass Spigot, Wooden Finial, Ivory Trim, 12 In.	90.00
Vase, Nouveau Style Sea Monster, Bust of Bismark, Kayserzinn, 12 In.	275.00
Wine Pot, Temple Lion Finial, Chinese, 7 1/2 In.	145.00

Phoenix Bird, or Flying Phoenix, is the name given to a blue–and–white kitchenware popular between 1900 and World War II. A variant is known as Flying Turkey. Most of this dinnerware was made in Japan for sale in the dime stores in America. It is still being made.

PHOENIX BIRD, Bowl, Rice, Cover 85.00
Coffeepot, Blue and White, Nippon 85.00
Salt & Pepper .... 15.00 To 25.00
Sugar, 2 3/4 In. 20.00
Sugar, Cover 18.50
Sugar, Cover, Turkey, 3 3/4 In. 14.00
Teapot, 2 3/4 In. 45.00

Phoenix Glass Company was founded in 1880 in Pennsylvania. The firm made commercial products such as lampshades, bottles, and glassware. Collectors today are interested in the sculptured glassware made by the company from the 1930s until the mid–1950s. The company is still working.

PHOENIX, Lamp, Table, Reverse Painted Shade, Art Nouveau Base, 18 In. 995.00
Platter, Jonquil, Frosted, Yellow Flowers 120.00
Vase, Aqua Leaves, Orange Berries, 10 In. 80.00
Vase, Bluebirds Flying, Fruit Trees, Onion Shape, 9 In. 225.00
Vase, Brown Hummingbird, Peach Flowers, Blue Leaves, 6 In. 85.00
Vase, Dancing Nudes & Pan, Cream Ground, 11 In. 385.00
Vase, Dancing Nudes, 12 1/2 In. ....*Illus* 357.00
Vase, Dogwood, Blue Flowers, Frosted White, 10 1/2 In. 150.00
Vase, Fairy, Star Flowers, Art Deco, Milk Glass, 7 In. 125.00
Vase, Fan Shape, Grasshoppers, Custard Glass, 8 1/4 In. 150.00
Vase, Frosted Cosmos, White Ground, 7 1/2 In. 80.00
Vase, Gold Fish, Rectangular, 9 In. 155.00
Vase, Madonna Head, Blue & White, 10 1/2 In. 185.00
Vase, Pinecone, 3 Colors, 7 In. 95.00
Vase, Sculptured Double Birds, Vaseline Ground, 10 1/2 In. 260.00
Vase, Thistle, Mother–of–Pearl Flowers, Dark Gray Ground, 18 In. 525.00
Vase, Thistle, Mother–of–Pearl Flowers, Label, 18 In. 500.00
Vase, Thistle, Pearlized, Red Ground, 18 In. 375.00
Vase, Turquoise & White, Floral, 6 In. 63.00
Vase, Yellow Peonies, Green Leaves, Frosted White, 12 1/2 In. 175.00

The tin cases that held phonograph needles are collected today by music and phonograph enthusiasts and advertising addicts. The tins are very small, about 2 inches across, and often have attractive graphic designs lithographed on the tin.

PHONOGRAPH NEEDLE, Box, Victor 15.00
Tin, Columbia 12.00
Tin, KE Brand, Orange, Black 15.00
Tin, RCA Victor 22.00

The phonograph, invented by Thomas Edison in the 1880s, has been made by many firms. This section also includes other items associated with the phonograph. Jukeboxes and records are listed in their own sections.

PHONOGRAPH, Amberola, Edison, Oak Case 210.00
Busy Bee, Disc Type 450.00
Edison, Amberola 415.00
Edison, Amberola, No. 30–225883, Built–In Horn Case, Oak, Signed 240.00
Edison, Brass Horn, Small Horn 350.00
Edison, Cylinder, Horn, Oak 320.00
Edison, Home, Type D 375.00
Edison, Model 444909, Large Horn, Patent Oct. 3, 1905 .... 135.00
Edison, No. 494844, Stop Mechanism, Language Cylinder 275.00
Edison, Standard, Model C, Oak Case, c.1905, 10 x 11 In. 825.00

Edison, Table, Red Metallic Morning Glory Horn	1000.00
Endlessgraph Mfg., Lamp, Fairy, Floppy Hat–Type Shade, 1900	4800.00
Graphonola, Columbia, Regent, Table Top, Oak	800.00
Graphophone, Columbia	155.00
Lindstrom, Child's, Model 777, Records, Electric	125.00
Nickelodeon, Wurlitzer No. 1, Keyboard Style, 1912	7500.00
Radio, Victor, Electrola, No. 26	250.00
RCA Victor Special, Aluminum, Metal, J. Vassos, 1935, 8 x 15 In.	3410.00
Standard Edison, Horn, 18 Cylinders	950.00
Terrophon	300.00
Victor, Orthophonics, Type 8, Gold Oak Cabinet	750.00
Victrola, RCA, Wooden Cabinet, Blue Amplifier, 1930s	950.00
Victrola, Talking Machine	1050.00

 The first photograph was a view from a window in France taken in 1826. The commercially successful photograph started with the daguerreotype introduced in 1839. Today all sorts of photographs and photographic equipment are collected. Albums were popular in Victorian times. Cartes de visite, popular after 1854, were mounted on 2 1/2– by 4–inch cardboard. Cabinet cards were introduced in 1866. These were mounted on cards 4 1/4 x 6 1/2 inches. Stereo views are listed under Stereo Card.

PHOTOGRAPHY, Ambrotype, 2 Men Gambling, Cigar, At Table, 1850s, 1/2 Plate	413.00
Ambrotype, 6 People Next To Great Falls of Niagara	385.00
Ambrotype, Cabinetmaker, Tools, 1850s, 1/6 Plate	605.00
Ambrotype, Child With Doll, Holds Hat, 1850, 2 3/4 x 3 1/4 In.	95.00
Ambrotype, Father & Son, Gutta–Percha Case, Floral, 1/4 Plate	65.00
Ambrotype, Mother Holding Infant, Double Sided, 1/4 Plate	300.00
Cabinet Card, 2 Girls, With Woman's Portrait On Large Easel	15.00
Cabinet Card, Albino Princess, Wendt	25.00
Cabinet Card, Balloon Ascension	85.00
Cabinet Card, Edwin Booth	35.00
Cabinet Card, Herbert Barrett, Midget, Wendt	25.00
Cabinet Card, Horse–Drawn Wagon, Grocery Store, Interior, 1900s	150.00
Cabinet Card, Ice Carnival, St. Paul, Minn., 186, 6 x 4 In.	27.50
Cabinet Card, Ice Skating Party	35.00
Cabinet Card, J. J. Corbett	125.00
Cabinet Card, Major Anton, Eisenmann	35.00
Cabinet Card, Man Holding Pistol & Night Stick	35.00
Cabinet Card, Man, Military Uniform, Studio, 1885, 4 x 6 1/2 In.	11.50
Cabinet Card, Midget Group, Eisenmann	25.00
Cabinet Card, Naval Vessel, 1880s	25.00
Cabinet Card, Peter Jackson, Black Fighter	125.00
Cabinet Card, Sitting Bull, Seated With Peace Pipe, 1882	330.00
Camera, Bausch & Lomb, Unicum Ray No. 7, 1891, 14 In.	250.00
Camera, Brownie 2A, Folding Autographic, Kodak, 1913	20.00
Camera, Brownie, 2A, Box	8.00
Camera, Brownie, Autographic, No. 2C	15.00
Camera, Brownie, Autographic, No. 3A, Folding	50.00
Camera, Brownie, Hawkeye, Box	6.00
Camera, Cinemaster, Model G8	22.50
Camera, Conley, Folding Plate, 5 x 7 In.	90.00
Camera, Coronet, Stereo, 1950s	67.50
Camera, Eastman Kodak Co., Pre–1900s	500.00
Camera, Eastman, No. 2A, Hawkeye	25.00
Camera, Emson, Miniature	45.00
Camera, Graflex, Crown View, 4 x 5 In.	215.00
Camera, Hawkeye, No. 2, Folding, Box	75.00
Camera, Kodak, Century 2, Box, Wooden, Tripod, Folmer Div., 1910	275.00
Camera, Kodak, Century, Box, On Tripod	345.00
Camera, Kodak, Rainbow Hawkeye, Folding	35.00
Camera, Mick–A–Matic, Box	75.00
Camera, Movie, Minolta, 8 mm Fast Speed Lens	140.00

Camera, Polaroid Land, Model 95, Brown & Chromed Metal, 1952	55.00
Camera, Polaroid, No. 800, Wink Light, Leather Case	25.00
Camera, Rohkor, 1930s, 3 x 5 In.	75.00
Camera, View, E. & H. T. Anthony & Co., New York	575.00
Carte De Visite, Album, Civil War Officers, Generals, 80 Piece	660.00
Carte De Visite, Brigadier General Anderson, Civil War	30.00
Carte De Visite, Civil War Soldier, Kady Brownell, Pair	146.00
Carte De Visite, Civil War, Leading Period Dignitaries	7150.00
Carte De Visite, Deep–Sea Diver, 1860s	35.00
Carte De Visite, Man With Corkscrew & Champagne Set, 1860s	35.00
Carte De Visite, Ned Bunline	250.00
Carte De Visite, Overland Mail Station, Ft. Concho, Texas, 1860	65.00
Carte De Visite, Photographer Next To Camera, Full Length	275.00
Carte De Visite, Young Buffalo Bill, 1860s	100.00
Daguerreotype, Black Nursemaid, White Girl, 1840s, 1/4 Plate	440.00
Daguerreotype, Child With Wooden Doll, 2 x 2 1/2 In.	65.00
Daguerreotype, Family Portrait, Tinted, J. Gurney, 1840s, Plate	1760.00
Daguerreotype, Man's Portrait, M. Brady, Velvet Case, 1/2 Plate	330.00
Daguerreotype, Military Officer, Full–Dress Uniform	1650.00
Daguerreotype, Portrait of Union Soldier, Gutta Percha Case	65.00
Daguerreotype, Quaker Woman	45.00
Daguerreotype, Unidentified Man, Leather Case, Civil War	715.00
Daguerreotype, Young Girl With Doll, c.1845, 2 3/4 x 3 1/4 In.	145.00
Ferrotype, Double, Civil War Soldier	467.50
Ferrotype, Single, Civil War Soldier	77.00
Film Tank, Exposure Scale, Negative Frames, Kodak, 1926	50.00
Kinematoscope, 5 Slides, Box, 1900, Germany	185.00
Lamp, Dark Room, Ruby Glass Panels, Tin, 8 3/4 In.	38.50
Photograph, 11 Musicians, Instruments, 1910, 3 1/2 x 4 1/2 In.	22.50
Photograph, Captain James Otis & Company A, Oval, 1862	550.00
Photograph, Caucasian Captain, Chinese Crew, c.1930, 19 x 8 In.	32.50
Photograph, Child's, Our Darling, Mourning Shadow Box, Large	165.00
Photograph, Chinese Couple, 4 Small Children, c.1928	37.50
Photograph, Mae West, Signed	275.00
Photograph, Mattullath Mfg. Co., Cooperage, 1882, 8 1/2 In.	67.50
Photograph, Pasadena Rose Bowl Parade, 1920, 7 x 10 3/4 In.	45.00
Photograph, Portia Law School, Boston, 1928, 24 x 15 In.	25.00
Photograph, Sabbathday Lake & Canterbury Shakers, 1897	750.00
Photograph, Studio, Teenage Boy & Girl, With Bicycles, 1900	5.00
Pitcher, Measure, Eastman Kodak, 24 Oz.	25.00
Portrait Attachment, Kodak, Gold Tin, Gold, Glass Lens	18.00
Scrapbook, Cannon Mills, Steichen, c.1933, 13 x 4 1/2 In.	440.00
Talbotype, George Bernard Shaw, Lunch Date At His Home, 1928	220.00
Tintype, 2 Seated Indians, Plains Attire, 1 White Man	715.00
Tintype, Child On Tricycle, Period Costume	45.00
Tintype, Indians With Bows & Arrows, Colored	2200.00
Tintype, Union Sergeant, c.1861, 3 1/2 x 3 1/2 In.	250.00
Tintype, Union Soldier, H. M. Goddard, Currier & Ives Case	770.00
Tintype, Union Soldier, Musket, Case, 3 In.	125.00
Tintype, Woman, Trade–Cloth Shawl, Northern Plains, 3 3/4 In.	192.50
Tintype, Young Boy With Rocking Horse, c.1860, 2 1/2 x 4 In.	120.00
Tintype, Young Man, Oval Mounted, 1900, 1 3/4 x 2 3/4 In.	15.00

 About 1880, the well–decorated home had a shawl on the piano. Bisque piano babies were designed to help hold the shawl in place. They range in size from 6 to 18 inches. Most of the figures were made in Germany. Reproductions are being made. Other piano babies are listed under manufacturers' names.

PIANO BABY, Crawling, Frilly Gown, Blue Bow, 6 In.	210.00
Dog & Pacifier, 5 In.	95.00
Dutch Boy, Seated, Leaning On Basket, Heubach, Large	350.00
Figurine, Boy, Holding Apple, Girl, Hand To Mouth, 12 In., Pair	110.00
Leaning On Elbow, White Underwear, 8 In.	350.00

◆◆

Date business cards and other advertising from telephone numbers.
Numbers were first used in 1878. The seven digit number was in use
by the 1940s, less than seven digits dates the card from 1878 to the
1940s.

◆◆

Lying With Pug Dog, Bisque, 10 In.	135.00
Sitting On Crossed Leg, Knee & Hand Up, 9 In.	55.00
Sitting, Arms Up, Nude, 5 In.	90.00

Pickard China Company was started in 1898 by Wilder Pickard. Hand–painted designs were used on china purchased from other sources. In the 1930s, the company began to make its own china wares in Chicago, Illinois. The company now makes many types of porcelains including a successful line of limited edition collector plates.

PICKARD, Bowl, Bachelor Buttons, Footed, Gold Trim, 8 In.	85.00
Bowl, Gooseberry & Leaf Design, Signed, 5 In.	75.00
Bowl, Scrolling Figural Handles, Gold Encrusted, 12 1/2 In.	45.00
Bowl, Shallow, 7 1/2 In.	40.00
Candy Dish, Gold, Handle, 7 In.	45.00
Pitcher, Gold & Beaded Design, Gold Handle, Signed	225.00
Pitcher, Hand Painted Grapes, Black With Gold, Handle, 10 In.	195.00
Pitcher, Water, Autumn Leaves, Wheat, Ornate Handle, 1905–10	255.00
Plate, Nut Design, Shades of Brown & Tan, Signed, 8 1/2 In.	145.00
Sugar & Creamer, Aura Argental Linear, Signed	165.00
Sugar & Creamer, Deserted Garden	200.00
Sugar & Creamer, Gold Over Flowers	100.00
Sugar & Creamer, Multicolored Floral Bands, Ovoid, Signed	95.00
Sugar & Creamer, Pink, Blue, Orange Florals, Marked	80.00
Tankard, Gold Design, Purple Grund	45.00
Tobacco Jar, Monk Portrait, 1910 Mark	75.00
Vase, Forest & Mountain Lake Scene, Gold Top & Handles, 7 In.	175.00
Vase, Garden Trees, Roses, Gold Band, Signed, 10 In.	496.00
Vase, Green, Gray & Lavender Trees, 8 In.	470.00
Vase, Rose Arbor Upper Half, Hanging Roses Lower Half, 5 1/4 In.	245.00
Vase, Scenic, Matte Finish, Challinor, 9 In.	425.00
Vase, Scenic, Matte, Signed, 10 In.	495.00

PICTURE FRAME, see Furniture, Frame

Silhouettes and small decorative pictures are listed here. Some other types of pictures are listed under Print or Painting.

PICTURE, Beadwork, Charles II, Catherine, Braganza, 1660, 11 1/2 x 16 In.	7160.00
Calligraphy, Cat, Black Ink, E. B., Framed, 30 3/4 x 26 3/4 In.	450.00
Charcoal On Paper, Work Horse, N. W. Wineland, 28 x 34 In.	1600.00
Collage, Fruit Compote, Printed Paper, Framed, 18 1/4 x 16 1/4 In.	110.00
Cut Paper, Memorial With Tombs, Trees, Gilt Frame, 6 14 x 6 7/8 In.	325.00
Diorama, 2 Kabuki Dolls, Black Lacquer Base, 6 x 10 1/2 x 12 In.	30.00
Diorama, 2–Masted Ship, Flying American Flag, 14 1/4 x 18 1/4 In.	325.00
Diorama, 3 Dimensional, Washington, Velvet Ground, 16 x 12 In.	759.00
Diorama, 3–Masted Ship, Flying American Flag, 19 3/4 x 27 1/2 In.	325.00
Diorama, Farmyard, People, Animals, Wood, Paper, Moss, 18 x 13 In.	435.00
Diorama, Shells, Moss, Painted Litho, Framed, France, 13 x 18 In., Pr.	300.00
Embossed Paper, Peacock & Cock Pheasant, 1750, 11 1/2 x 9 In., Pair	8250.00
Felt, Peter Pan & Tinkerbell	28.00
Hair Wreath, Several Shades, Frame, c.1870, 11 x 12 In.	245.00
Needlepoint, Lady, Holding Rifle, Hunt Clothes, Framed, 11 x 14 In.	250.00
Needlepoint, Shepherd & Shepherdess, Landscape, Wool, 21 x 20 In.	1650.00

Needlework, Allegorical Scene, Silk, Frame, 16 x 18 3/4 In.	750.00
Needlework, Moses, In Bullrushes, Other Scene, Framed, 18 x 14 In.	1925.00
Pastel On Sandpaper, Girl In Red, Dog, Demmesey, Framed, 11 x 9 In.	990.00
Pen & Ink, Bird Nest In Flowering Tree, Framed, 1876, 17 x 15 In.	175.00
Pencil Drawing On Paper, Profile, Man & Woman, 4 1/8 x 4 1/8 In.	400.00
Penwipe, Figure, Head & Hand, Cloth Costume, Framed, 10 1/2 x 8 In.	125.00
Polychrome Wax, J. Wedgwood's Doctor, Shadow Box Frame, 7 x 6 In.	500.00
Retablo, Anthony With Jesus, South America, 10 x 14 In.	250.00
Retablo, Blessed Virgin, New Mexico	2860.00
Retablo, St. Joseph, Child, Jose Rafael Aragon, 1836–50	6600.00
Retablo, St. Raymond Nonatus, New Mexico	1980.00
Retablo, Virgin With Christ Child, South America, 10 x 14 In.	250.00
Shadowbox, Butterflies, Flowers Under Glass, Burl Walnut Framed	35.00
Silhouette, 14 Bust Student, Friends School, Peale Museum Artists	3410.00
Silhouette, Alphonso Taft, R. Cummings, 1840, 4 1/4 x 3 1/4 In.	525.00
Silhouette, Bearded Gentleman, Brass Frame, 4 3/4 x 3 3/4 In.	200.00
Silhouette, Benjamin Franklin, Paul Jones, 4 1/2 x 3 1/2 In., Pair	550.00
Silhouette, Eglomise, Young Man, Frame, 5 3/8 x 4 5/8 In.	275.00
Silhouette, Elya, Wife of J. Goddard, c.1880, 5 3/8 x 6 3/8 In.	185.00
Silhouette, Girl With Book, Gilt Frame, 11 3/8 x 9 1/4 In.	250.00
Silhouette, Man & Woman Bust, Whitcomb, Pair	440.00
Silhouette, Man, Brass Frame, Bowen, 1810, 2 3/4 In.	300.00
Silhouette, Man, Gilt–Trim Frame, 6 1/4 x 5 In.	75.00
Silhouette, Man, Masonic Devices, J. W., Framed, 4 1/4 x 6 5/8 In.	825.00
Silhouette, Man, Oval Gutta–Percha Frame, 5 3/4 x 5 1/4 In.	45.00
Silhouette, Man, Reverse Painted, Convex Glass, 4 1/2 In.	200.00
Silhouette, Mary Had A Little Lamb, 5 x 4 In.	7.50
Silhouette, Mother, Daughter, Painted, Adolphe, Framed, 6 1/2 In., Pr.	400.00
Silhouette, Old Man, Hollow Cut, Frame, 6 x 5 In.	45.00
Silhouette, Sam'l Brooks Family, J. Sartain, 1864, 16 x 19 In.	1400.00
Silhouette, The Return, Family of 4, Martin Griffing, 1847	6600.00
Silhouette, William Seward, Signed R. Cummings, 1835, 3 x 2 In.	525.00
Silhouette, Woman & Man, Gilt Highlights, Framed, 6 3/8 In., Pair	300.00
Silhouette, Woman With Banner, Gilt Frame, 5 5/8 x 4 3/8 In.	185.00
Silhouette, Woman, Umbrella, Edouart Fecit, 1840, Framed, 12 x 10 In.	1000.00
Silhouette, Women, Historical Dress, F. S. Campbell, 1900, 26 In., Pr.	775.00
Silhouette, Young Man & Woman, Hollow Cut, 5 5/8 x 4 5/8 In., Pair	350.00
Silhouette, Young Man, Full Length, Frame, 11 1/2 x 7 3/8 In.	350.00
Silhouette, Young Man, Hollow Cut, Crayon Hair, Framed, 5 x 4 In.	50.00
Silhouette, Young Man, Ink, Gold–Painted Frame, 3 7/8 x 3 In.	60.00
Silhouette, Young Man, J. T., Nov. 1844, 4 3/4 x 3 3/4 In.	200.00
Silhouette, Young Man, Jas. B. Ardery, Frame, 5 1/4 x 4 7/8 In.	125.00
Silhouette, Young Man, Sailor Outfit, 1813, Silver–Gilt Frame, 8 In.	975.00
Silhouette, Young Woman With Bouquet, Frame, 12 3/8 x 9 1/2 In.	350.00
Silhouette, Young Woman, Abigail Good, 1846, 11 5/8 x 9 5/8 In.	250.00
Silhouette, Young Woman, Black–Lacquered Frame, 6 5/8 x 5 3/4 In.	65.00
Silhouette, Young Woman, Brass Frame, 4 7/8 x 4 1/8 In.	425.00
Silhouette, Young Woman, Peale's Museum, Frame, 5 3/4 x 4 3/4 In.	125.00
Straw Work, Port Scene, English, Framed, 27 x 19 In.	825.00
Straw Work, Ships In Port, 16 x 25 In.	330.00
Stumpwork, Charles I & Henrietta, Framed, 1645, 7 3/4 x 11 3/4 In.	7150.00
Stumpwork, Charles II, Family Scenes, 1650, 5 1/2 In., Pair	1980.00
Stumpwork, Floral Scene, Late–19th Century, England	250.00
Stumpwork, King & Queen, Camel At Top, Framed, 13 1/2 x 17 In.	3630.00
Theorem, Fruit, Foliage, Eglomise Glass Matte, 21 1/2 x 22 1/2 In.	350.00
Theorem, Memorial, Morris Family, Vermont, Framed, 20 x 21 1/2 In.	2200.00
Theorem, Memorial, Woman, Monument, Watercolor, Framed, 13 x 16 In.	410.00
Tinfoil, My House Serves The Lord, Framed, Germany	65.00
Tinsel, Vase of Flowers, White Ground, 13 x 11 In.	300.00

The Pigeon Forge Pottery was started in Pigeon Forge, Tennessee, in 1946. Red clay found near the pottery was used to make the pieces. Molded or thrown pottery with matte glaze and slip decoration was made. The pottery is still working.

PIGEON FORGE, Pitcher, Flowers, Brown, 5 1/2 In.	25.00
Sugar, Creamer & Teapot, Dogwood	25.00

The Pilkington Tile and Pottery Company was established in 1892 in England. The company made small pottery wares like buttons and hatpin heads but soon started decorating vases purchased from other potteries. By 1903, the company had discovered an opalescent glaze that became popular on the Lancastrian pottery line. The manufacture of pottery ended in 1937 but decorating continued until 1948.

PILKINGTON, Tile, Sgraffito Vegetables, Frame, Square, 6 In., Pair	110.00
Vase, Rolled Rim Neck, Shades of Green, 4 In.	35.00

The pincushion doll is not really a doll and often was not even a pincushion. The top half of the doll was made of porcelain. The edge of the half–doll was made with several small holes for thread, and the doll was stitched to a fabric body with a voluminous skirt. The finished figure was used to cover a hot pot of tea, a powder box, a pincushion, a whiskbroom, or a lamp. They were made in sizes from less than an inch to over 9 inches high. Most date from the early 1900s to the 1950s.

PINCUSHION DOLL, Arms Extended, 3 Feathers In Hair, 5 In.	250.00
Arms Up To Blue Hat	65.00
Bisque, Silver Hair, Arms Extended, 3 In.	55.00
Blue Blouse, Arms Extended, 3 1/4 In.	40.00
Brown–Spotted Blouse, Green Tie, Large Hat, 2 3/4 In.	40.00
Child, Long Blond Curls	50.00
Cone–Shaped Hat, Tassel On Top, Germany, 1 1/2 In.	35.00
Face Looking Down, Arms Extended	350.00
Flapper, Head On Heart Pillow	35.00
Lacemaker, Primitive, 7 1/2 In.	55.00
Powder–Puff Cover, Germany	38.00
Princess De Lamballi, Snuffbox In Hand	400.00
Roses In Hair, Capez Shell Skirt, 12 In.	170.00
Senorita, 8 1/2 In.	75.00
Spanish Woman, Mantilla, Arms Extended	100.00
PINK SLAG, see Slag, Pink	

Pipes have been popular since tobacco was introduced to Europe by Sir Walter Raleigh. Meerschaum pipes are listed under Meerschaum.

PIPE, Bearded & Hooded Man, Silver Ferule, Amber Stem, 7 1/2 In.	440.00
Black & Red Stone, 2 Pewter Bands, Beaded Stem	600.00
Boar's Head, Amber Stem, Fitted Case, 9 In.	1210.00
Briar, American Eagle Crest, May 11, 1862, 5 x 3 In.	155.00
Briar, Built–In Lighter	35.00
Briar, Carved, Ornate Brass Design	12.50
Briar, Sterling–Filigree Design On Bowl & Shank	50.00
Buffalo Head, Ivory Horns, Carved	35.00
Cavalier, Gold–Filled Ferule, Amber Stem, Fitted Case, 5 In.	137.50
Chip Carved, Lid	35.00
Christopher Columbus, Head, Carved	40.00
Grapes & Leaves, Carved	35.00
Head of Devil, Red Horns, Carved	45.00
Ivory, Gold Inlay, Case, 1890s	67.00
North African Man, Wearing Fez, Amber Ferule & Stem, Case, 6 1/2 In.	275.00
Nude Woman With Bellflower, Amber Stem, Case, 7 In.	165.00
Reclining Nude, Amber Stem, Case, 9 In.	360.00
Romeo & Juliet, Inscribed Silver Ferule, Amber Stem, Case, 9 1/2 In.	1210.00

Sherlock Holmes Type, Carved Designs, Metal Edge & Lid	30.00
Skull, Amber Stem, Fitted Case, 6 In.	220.00
Wolf's Head, Metal Ferule, Amber Stem, Fitted Case, 7 In.	220.00

Pirkenhammer is a porcelain manufactory started in 1802 by Friedrich Holke and J. G. Lilst. It was located in Bohemia, now Brezova, Czechoslovakia. The company made tablewares usually decorated with views and flowers. Lithophanes were also made. The mark of the crossed hammers is easy to remember as the Pirkenhammer symbol.

PIRKENHAMMER, Cup & Saucer, Cherubs, Gold	50.00
Teapot, Shaped Like Fat Woman, Red, Blue, 7 In.	175.00
Vase, Snake Handles, 8 In.	150.00

Pisgah pottery pieces that are marked *Pisgah Forest Pottery* were made in North Carolina from 1926. The pottery was started by Walter R. Stephen in 1914, and after his death in 1941, the pottery continued in operation. The most famous types of Pisgah Forest ware are the cameo type with designs made of raised glaze and the turquoise crackle glaze wares.

PISGAH FOREST, Bowl-Vase, Mottled Green & Blue, Pink Interior, 3 1/2 In.	15.00
Creamer, Green, Pink, Crazed, 3 1/2 In.	7.50
Ginger Jar, 1942	60.00
Lamp, Factory, Blue, With Fittings, 1925, 10 x 7 In.	75.00
Sugar & Creamer, Blue & Pink	25.00
Sugar & Creamer, Cover	100.00
Sugar & Creamer, Turquoise & Pink, 1943	35.00
Vase, Blue, 8 1/2 In.	95.00
Vase, Crackle, 2 Colors, 7 1/2 In.	150.00
Vase, Crackle, Blue, 4 1/2 In.	55.00

Planters Nut and Chocolate Company was started in Wilkes-Barre, Pennsylvania, in 1906. The Mr. Peanut figure was adopted as a trademark in 1916. National advertising for Planters Peanuts started in 1918. The company was acquired by Standard Brands, Inc., in 1961. Some of the Mr. Peanut jars and other memorabilia have been reproduced and, of course, new items are being made.

PLANTERS PEANUTS, Ad, Newspaper, Color, 1931, Full Page	60.00
Bank, Plastic, Red, 8 1/2 In. .... 15.00 To 18.00	
Belt, Gold Mr. Peanut Buckle, Box	28.00
Book, Coloring, Mr. Peanut & Smokey The Bear, 1973	20.00
Bracelet	15.00
Cap, Golf	18.00
Cap, Ski, Knit	18.00
Container, Papier-Mache, 12 In.	195.00
Cookie Cutter, Mr. Peanut, Red	22.00
Dish, Die Cast	15.00
Doll, Mr. Peanut, Cloth, 21 In.	16.00
Envelope, Mr. Peanut Pennant, The Nickel Lunch, Unused	10.00
Game, Dart Board, Mr. Peanut	125.00
Jar, 6 Sides, Embossed Cover, Yellow	95.00
Jar, 75th Anniversary	12.00
Jar, Football	235.00
Jar, General Store	140.00
Jar, Peanut Butter, Jumbo, 1 Lb.	8.00
Jar, Peanut Corners	340.00
Jar, Pennant, Peanut Lid	185.00
Jar, Yellow, 6 Sides, Embossed Lid	95.00
Lunch Box, Mr. Peanut, 1965	35.00
Mr. Peanut, Cloth	15.00
Mr. Peanut, Figure, Papier-Mache, 24 In. ....*Illus*	3080.00
Mug, Figural, Plastic, Green	15.00
Mug, Mr. Peanut's Head Shape, Plastic, Blue, 1950s	28.00

Planters Peanuts, Mr. Peanut, Figure,
Papier–Mache, 24 In.

◆◆◆◆◆◆◆◆◆◆◆◆◆◆◆◆◆◆◆◆◆◆◆◆

If you display your collection at a library, museum, or commercial store, do not let the display include your street address or city name. It is best if you don't even include your name. A display is an open invitation to a thief. Be sure the collection will be guarded and fully insured.

◆◆◆◆◆◆◆◆◆◆◆◆◆◆◆◆◆◆◆◆◆◆◆◆

Nodder, Mr. Peanut, Lego	65.00
Nut Chopper, 1944	28.00
Nut Dish Set, 1 Large & 4 Small	25.00
Nut Dish Set, Mr. Peanut, World's Fair, 1934, 5 Piece	30.00
Old King Cole, Papier–Mache, 24 In.	3380.00
Paint Book, U. S. Historical & Educational, 1949	24.00
Peanut Butter Maker, Mr. Peanut, Box	22.00
Pedal Car	195.00
Pencil, Figural Top	18.00
Pencil, Mechanical, Yellow & Blue, Cello Wrap	10.00
Pencil, Mr. Peanut, Mechanical	15.00 To 20.00
Pin, 1939 World's Fair	25.00
Pin, Mr. Peanut, Plastic, 1950s, 1 In.	5.00
Punchboard	50.00
Puzzle, Just Nuts About Mr. Peanut, 18 x 23 1/2 In.	35.00
Radio, Can, Cocktail Nuts	45.00
Radio, Figural, 1980s	33.00
Raft, Rubberized Canvas, Inflatable, 2 1/2 x 6 Ft.	75.00
Salt & Pepper, Mr. Peanut, Celluloid, U. S. A.	18.00
Salt & Pepper, Mr. Peanut, Chromed Plastic	20.00
Scoop, Tin, Blue, 5 Cents	110.00
Sign, Wooden, Mr. Peanut, 5 Cents A Bag	600.00
Spoon, Plastic, Blue	15.00
Spoon, Slotted, Plastic, Red	6.00 To 9.00
Tape Measure & Key Chain	20.00
Tape Measure, Key Chain	20.00
Tie, Maroon, Box	45.00
Tin, Lithographed Label, 9 1/2 In.	60.00
Tin, Mr. Peanut, Red Pennant, Black, Blue, 5 Lb.	95.00
Tin, Nut Chopper On Top	22.00
Tin, Salted–In–Shell, Cover, 10 Lb.	775.00
Watch, Mr. Peanut	32.00

Plated amberina was patented June 15, 1886, by Joseph Lock and made by the New England Glass Company. It is similar in color to amberina, but is characterized by a cream colored or chartreuse lining (never white) and small ridges or ribs on the outside.

PLATED AMBERINA, Punch Cup, Ribbed, 9 Panels, Amber Handle	2250.00

Plique-a-jour is an enameling process. The enamel is laid between thin raised metal lines and heated. The finished piece has transparent enamel held between the thin metal wires. It is different from cloisonne because it is transparent.

PLIQUE–A–JOUR, Bowl, Enamel Bird & Flowers, Flared Rim, 6 In.	275.00
Bowl, Multicolored Flowers, c.1900, Japanese, 4 In.	3850.00
Dragon Boat, Compote Form, Inset Panels, 3 x 5 In.	250.00
Vase, Multicolored Flowers & Leaves, 5 1/2 In.	465.00

All types of political memorabilia are collected, from buttons to banners. Items related to presidential candidates are the most popular, but collectors also search for material related to state and local offices. Many reproductions have been made.

POLITICAL, Ashtray, Eisenhower & Halleck, 1962, Square	18.50
Ax, Parade, Red, White & Blue Paint, Wooden, 30 In.	25.00
Ballot Box, Marbles, Post 5 G. A. R., Pa., Apr. 11, 1881, 13 x 11 In.	1760.00
Banner, Eisenhower, Nixon, Campaign, Red, White & Blue, 1952	50.00
Banner, Nixon, Agnew	23.00
Banner, Smith For President, Cloth	475.00
Bumper Sticker, Anderson For President	1.00
Bumper Sticker, Dukakis	1.00
Bumper Sticker, Reagan, Bush, '84	1.00
Bumper Sticker, Robert C. Byrd For President	13.50
Button, American Choice, Goldwater, Picture, Celluloid,	10.00
Button, Arrow Shape, Anti L. B. Johnson, 1968	11.50
Button, Barry Goldwater, For President, 1 3/4 In.	4.00
Button, Cox Sure, Blue	75.00
Button, Cranston For President, Picture At Top	2.00
Button, CWA For Carter, Mondale, 1980, Pictures Both Men	2.00
Button, Dewey, Warren, Letters On Blue, Red & White Lower Stripes	8.00
Button, Eisenhower, Red, White & Blue Ribbon, 1 3/4 In.	7.00
Button, Flasher, Goldwater In '64, Black & White	5.00
Button, Franklin D. Roosevelt, Celluloid	85.00
Button, George Washington, Eagle & Star Within Border	2000.00
Button, George Washington, Long Live The President, Brass	600.00
Button, Harding, Red Rim, Celluloid	7.00
Button, Jesse Jackson, For President, Picture Center	2.00
Button, Kefauver For President, Red, White & Blue, Celluloid	7.00
Button, Kennedy, Fulbright	18.50
Button, Kentucky Delegate For Carter, Mondale, State Map	5.00
Button, LaFollete, Lithograph Tin	28.50
Button, Lyndon B. Johnson, Gold, 1964, 1 3/4 In.	4.00
Button, M. L. King & Ralph Abernathy, 1968, 3 1/2 In.	30.00
Button, McGovern & Shriver, Jugate, 1972	70.00
Button, McKinley & Roosevelt, Jugate, Flag Draped, 7/8 In.	20.00
Button, McKinley, Picture, Celluloid	10.00
Button, McKinley, Shield Shape	10.00
Button, Richard M. Nixon, For President, 1 3/4 In.	4.00
Button, Roosevelt Goodbye, Hello Willkie, Running Elephant, 1940	18.00
Button, Snoopy For President, Celluloid	5.00
Button, Tennesseans For Jimmy Carter, Picture Center	10.00
Button, Truman & Stevenson, My Dollar Went Democratic, Tab	5.00
Button, Truman, Porch For Dewey	12.00
Button, We Don't Want Eleanor Either	8.00
Button, Wilke For President	13.00
Button, Wilson, War In Europe, Peace In America	26.50
Button, Youth For Quayle, 2 In.	27.50
Cabinet Photograph, Grover Cleveland	14.00
Cabinet Photograph, James G. Blaine, For President, 1884	22.50
Cabinet Photograph, Theodore Roosevelt, Colonel Volunteers	30.00
Calendar, Perpetual, General Pershing, Center Picture, Round	85.00
Canteen, G. A. R.	49.50
Card, Elect John W. Davis, Printed Both Sides, 3 1/2 x 5 1/2 In.	30.00
Card, Vote Straight Democratic, Stevenson & Sparkman, Michigan	17.50
Cigar, Bubble Gum, Win With Dick, Photograph On Box, 24 Piece	35.00
Cigar, Campaign, Woodrow Wilson, Oversized	36.50
Clock, Bartender, F. D. R., Man of The Hour, Animated	175.00
Coloring Book, J. F. Kennedy, Unused	26.50
Cup, Picnic, Quayle, Senate, Blue	9.00
Doll, George Washington, Paper & Cloth, 11 In.	495.00

Doll, Spiro Agnew, Inflatable, Taiwan, 24 In.	11.00
Flag, Benjamin Harrison & Levi Morton, Silk, 1888	150.00
Flyer, Trick Under Stevenson Picture, Treat Under Ike's, 6 In.	12.50
Fob, Mechanical, McKinley, 4 Changing Windows, Brass	95.00
Folder, Barry Goldwater & Social Security, 4 Page	7.50
Folder, Goldwater, Air Force Uniform, Message To Veterans, 4 Page	7.50
Folder, Wallace, Red, White & Blue, 6 Page	7.50
Hat, Campaign, John F. Kennedy	22.00
Hat, Coattail, L. B. Johnson, Harker, Kizer, Indiana, 1964	17.50
Hat, He's Allright–The Same Old Hat, Harrison, Glass	150.00
Hat, I Like Ike, Paper, 1956	20.00
Inaugural Ticket, Program, Reagan & Bush, 1981	15.00
Jugate Medallion, Cleveland & Hendricks, Blaine & Logan, 1884	325.00
Key Ring, Carter	6.00
Lighter, Cigarette, J. F. K.	10.00
Mug, Beer, Franklin D. Roosevelt, New Deal	28.00
Mug, Beer, Prohibition's Repeal, Crystal, 5 In.	55.00
Mug, Eisenhower Profile	26.00
Mug, Reagan, Myers, Coattail, 1982	13.00
Needle Case, Pictures of Hoover & Curtis, 3 x 4 3/4 In.	24.00
Notebook, Pocket, Garfield & Arthur On Back, 3 1/4 x 5 In.	35.00
Painting, Uncle Sam, I Remembered The Maine, 2–15–98, 20 x 25 In.	935.00
Paperweight, Wendell Willkie	110.00
Parade Torch, End Pivots To Maintain Level, 60 In.	315.00
Pencil, Hoover For President, Bust End	17.00
Pennant, Nixon	8.50
Pennant, Nixon & Agnew, Presidential Inauguration, 1973, 28 In.	25.00
Pin, Lapel, Bull Moose, Brass, 1912, 1 1/2 In.	22.50
Pin, McGovern For Senate, Tab Clip	9.00
Pin, Truman, Barkley	30.00
Plate, Eisenhower, 1st Birthday In White House, Box, 1953	35.00
Plate, Reagan, Bush, Joe St. Clair, 1900	35.00
Plate, Republican Convention, Florida, 1968	40.00
Pledge Card, Landon, Knox, 1936	8.00
Poll Card, E. R. A. In '76, Vote Socialist Workers	2.00
Poll Card, Vote Row B, McGovern, Shriver	2.00
Postcard, Bryant, Taft, 1908	38.50
Postcard, J. F. Kennedy & Jackie, Oversized	10.00
Postcard, NASA, John Glenn Autograph	17.50
Postcard, Taft, Sherman, Nation's Choice, Jugate, 1908	15.00
Poster, Jesse Jackson, U. S. Senate, For Statehood, Picture	15.00
Poster, Landon, Knox, Deeds Not Deficits, Both Pictured	5.00
Poster, LBJ For U. S. A., Johnson's Picture, 1964, 12 x 21 In.	23.00
Poster, Lincoln's Funeral, Wednesday, April 19, 1865, 9 x 6 In.	825.00
Poster, McGovern, Shriver, One World, Lithograph	16.50
Poster, Proclamation, Woodrow Wilson, Census, 1920, 14 x 11 In.	40.00
Poster, Trial of Richard Wilson, Black Judge, 1880, 12 x 10 In.	245.00
Poster, Vote Stassen, He Cared Enough To Come	5.00
Reel, For Viewmaster, Eisenhower Inauguration	6.00
Ribbon, Massachusetts Temperance Union, Silk, Black & White	43.00
Ribbon, Memorial, Henry Clay, Silk, 1825, 7 3/4 In.	75.00
Salt & Pepper, Coattail, Nixon, Lamkin, 1972	18.00
Scarf, Benjamin Harrison & Levi P. Morton, Dated 1888	145.00
Song Sheet, Our Presidential Chair, Woodrow Wilson, 1912	20.00

◆◆◆

Do not use scotch tape or other sticky tapes on paper. Even if the tape is removed, the paper will eventually discolor from the contact with the glue.

◆◆◆

Stickpin, Figural, Goldbug 30.00
Stickpin, Nixon, Stop Kickin' My Dawg Around 35.00
Stud, Taft 10.00
Thimble, Herbert Hoover, Campaign 15.00
Toby, Al Smith, Ceramic, 7 In. 79.00
Toby, Al Smith, Facsimile Signature On Base 100.00
Toby, Taft, Germany, 5 In. 115.00
Tumbler, John F. Kennedy, Vanderburgh County, Indiana 26.00
Tumbler, Wendell L. Willkie, Acceptance, Aug. 17, 1940, 4 5/8 In. 22.00
Watch Fob, Bryan & Kern, 1908 .... 30.00
Watch Fob, Roosevelt & Fairbanks, 1904 On Brass Plate 125.00
Watch Fob, Taft & Sherman, 1909 .... 85.00
Watch Fob, Taft & Sherman, Bust 30.00
Watch Fob, Taft, Bust 25.00
Window Sticker, Hi, I'm A Neighbor For Nixon 3.00
Window Sticker, Nixon, California State Map Outline, 1962 .... 10.00
Window Sticker, Roosevelt, Red, White & Blue 14.00
Window Sticker, Willkie, McNary, Capitol Dome 3.00
Window Sticker, Young Republicans For Willkie, Shield Shape 14.00

Pomona glass is a clear glass with a soft amber border decorated with pale blue or rose–colored flowers and leaves. The colors are very, very pale. The background of the glass is covered with a network of fine lines. It was made from 1885 to 1888 by the New England Glass Company. First grind was made from April 1885 to June 1886. It was made by cutting a wax surface on the glass, then dipping it in acid. Second grind was a less expensive method of acid etching that was then developed.

POMONA, Bowl, Mint, Cornflower, 1st Grind, Ruffled Rim, 3 1/4 x 6 In. 330.00
Candlestick, Clear Twisted Stem, Green, Marked, 12 In., Pair 610.00
Finger Bowl, 10 Fluted Sides, Rivulet Design, 2nd Grind, 5 1/2 In. 145.00
Punch Cup, 1st Grind 20.00
Punch Cup, 1st Grind, 6 Piece 365.00
Sugar & Creamer, Ruffled Edges, Amber Stain On Handles, 1st Grind 585.00
Toothpick, Applied Rigaree, Tapered Shape 75.00
Toothpick, Barrel Shape 45.00
Tumbler, 2nd Grind, 6 Piece 198.00
Tumbler, Blueberry, Gold Leaves, Amber Stained, 2nd Grind, 3 3/4 In. 175.00
Tumbler, Cornflowers, 2nd Grind, 3 1/4 In. 150.00
Tumbler, Fish & Seaweed, 2nd Grind, 3 3/4 In. 100.00
PONTYPOOL, see Tole

Popeye was introduced to the Thimble Theater comic strip in 1929. The character became a favorite of readers. In 1932, an animated cartoon featuring Popeye was made by Paramount Studios. The cartoon series continued and became even more popular when the old movies were used on television starting in the 1950s. The full–length movie with Robin Williams as Popeye was made in 1980.

POPEYE, Bank, American Bisque 310.00
Bank, Dime, 5 Characters Pictured, 1929 .... 99.00
Bank, Popeye's Head, Ceramic 300.00
Box, Chalk 22.00
Can, Spinach, 1958 .... 10.00
Cel, Bluto, Sneering, Closeup, Matted 325.00
Cel, Popeye In Spotlight, Hand Painted, Matted, 1960s 450.00
Colorforms, Popeye The Weatherman, 1959 .... 45.00
Comic Book, No. 10069–405 .... 6.00
Cookie Jar, American Bisque .... 520.00 To 750.00
Cookie Jar, McCoy 100.00
Cookie Jar, Olive Oyl, American Bisque 900.00
Crayon Set 15.00
Display, Olive, Wimpy, Jiggs, 1953, King Features, 6 x 10 In. 125.00
Doll, Hard Rubber Face & Arms, 1960s 35.00

Doll, Squeak, Vinyl, 1979, 9 In.	15.00
Doll, Walker, Papier–Mache, Wooden Feet, 1929, 5 1/2 In.	195.00
Doll, Wimpy, Squeeky Squeeze, King Features	125.00
Figure, Popeye The Thinker, Chalkware, 1929, 6 In.	95.00
Figure, Popeye's Fried Chicken, Rubber, 1980, Set of 5, 2 In.	10.00
Figure, Popeye, Wooden, Jointed, 1930s	150.00
Game, Juggler, For Hand	50.00
Game, Pipe Toss, 1935	45.00
Game, Popeye The Champ, Marx, Box	2300.00
Game, Rescue, Puzzle–Game, 1934, Einson–Freeman, 7 In.	225.00
Game, Ring Toss, Box	65.00
Game, Rope Ring, Popeye & Olive Oyl, 1930s	120.00
Game, Target, Tin, Tall, 1935	175.00
Kazoo, Pipe	40.00
Knife, Pocket, Red	65.00
Little Big Book	6.00
Lunch Box, Thermos, 1964	60.00 To 75.00
Marionette, Olive Oyl, Gund, 12 In.	65.00
Paint Box, Tin	12.00
Paint Set, 1933	35.00
Parrot Cage, Tin Lithograph, 8 1/2 In.	220.00
Patch, Iron–On, 1947	20.00
Pen	10.00
Phonograph, Emerson	30.00
Pilot, Tin, Mechanical, Airplane, 7 In.	825.00
Pipe, Kazoo, 1934	19.00 To 70.00
Poster, Cartoon, 1950, 27 x 41 In.	475.00
Poster, Movie, 1950s	85.00
Puppet, Olive Oyl, Gund	65.00
Puppet, Popeye & Olive Oyl, Gund	260.00
Record, Popeye Son & Story, Popeye Shaped Cardboard Sleeve	20.00
Ring, Post Toasties, Wrapper	25.00
Roller Skates, Box	2800.00
Salt & Pepper, Nodder, Popeye & Olive Oyl, 1950s, 4 3/4 In.	90.00
Salt & Pepper, Popeye & Olive Oyl, Porcelain, 1950s, 6 In.	100.00
Salt & Pepper, Popeye & Olive Oyl, Vandor, 1980	28.00
Spinach Can, 1958	15.00
Toothpick	25.00
Toy, Blowing Bubbles, Battery Operated, Box	3000.00
Toy, Car, Olive Being Kidnapped, Popeye, Pull Toy, Paper Lithograph	550.00
Toy, Carrying Parrot Cages, Windup, Tin	135.00
Toy, Jack–In–The–Box, Head Comes Out of Can of Spinach	200.00
Toy, Popeye & Olive Oyl, Dancer, Mechanical, Tin, 9 In.	600.00
Toy, Popeye & Wimpy Walk–A–Way, Marx, Box, 1960s	75.00
Toy, Popeye Bag Puncher, Windup, Tinplate, Chien, 9 3/4 In., Box	4840.00
Toy, Popeye Express, Mechanical, Tin Lithograph, 8 1/2 In.	270.00
Toy, Popeye, In Rowboat, Moves Back & Forth, Tinplate, Hoge, 1935	6050.00
Toy, Popeye, With Parrot, Tin Lithograph, Windup	625.00
Toy, Spinach Patrol, Hubley	575.00
Walker, Slant Board	95.00
Wristwatch, Box	35.00
Wristwatch, Bradley	145.00

Major porcelain factories are listed in this book under the factory name. This section lists pieces that are by the less well-known factories.

PORCELAIN, Basket, Reticulated, Rose Florettes, Ropework Foot, 10 1/2 In.	440.00
Bottle, French Priest, Hat Stopper, Robj, 10 1/4 In.	335.00
Bottle, Hot Water, Rose Mandarin, Courtyard Scenes, 14 3/4 In.	415.00
Bottle, Napoleon, Cocked Hat Stopper, Robj, 10 1/4 In.	335.00
Bowl, Arabian Figures, Castle, Hand Painted, 1905, 7 3/4 x 4 In.	125.00
Bowl, Center, Sevres Type, Floral, Geometric, 12 In.	275.00
Bowl, Fish, Diaper & Rain Border, River Landscape, Chinese, 28 In.	6820.00

Bowl, Jewel Like Polychrome Enameling, Oriental, 9 x 12 3/4 In. 65.00
Bowl, Pastel Floral Enameling, Russia, Red Mark, 7 1/4 In. 70.00
Box, Florals, Turquoise Ground, Gold Trim, France, 1925, 5 1/4 In. 245.00
Box, Hairpin, Pink & White, 2 x 4 In. 40.00
Cachepot, Underdish, Enameled 100 Butterflies, Chinese, 9 1/2 In. 385.00
Candleholder, Figural, 2–Light, Putti Or Cupid, Sitzendorf, 1890 .... 150.00
Compote, Bronze Neptune Support, Pierced Shell, 17 In. 1100.00
Cracker Jar, Allover Floral, Cream Ground, Silver Plated, 7 In. 150.00
Creamer, Ram's Head, Austria 25.00
Cup & Saucer, Handleless, Brown Landscape, Tucker 2500.00
Cup & Saucer, Handleless, Landscapes, Houses, Black Silk Screen 150.00
Cup & Saucer, Handleless, Pink & Purple House, English 25.00
Dish, Sweetmeat, 3 Scallop Shells, Floral, Bow, 1760–65, 7 In. 1550.00
Dresser Set, Allover Pink Flowers & Leaves, Germany, 3 Piece 125.00
Dresser Set, Hand Painted Floral, 6 Piece 325.00
Easter Egg, Birds, Flowers, Christ Is Risen, Russia, 4 1/4 In. 385.00
Easter Egg, White Body, Gilded Imperial Monogram, Russia 1100.00
Egg, Cyrillic Imperial Monogram, Russian, 1880s, 4 1/8 In. 1100.00
Figurine, 18th–Century Woman, Lace, Fan, Alka, Germany, 5 1/2 In. 85.00
Figurine, Beggar Lady, With Musical Vagabond, Germany, 7 In. 245.00
Figurine, Chinese Foo Dogs, Green & Brown, 9 1/2 In., Pair 95.00
Figurine, Dandy, Reading, Listening, Germany, 6 In., Pair 75.00
Figurine, Dragon, Scaly, Red Nose, On Blue Waves, China, 9 x 18 In. 250.00
Figurine, Girl, Grain–Filled Apron, Frankenthal, 1784, 5 1/2 In. 1650.00
Figurine, Hound, Seated, 4 1/4 In. 95.00
Figurine, Man In Floral Coat, Girl, Castanet, Sitzendorf, 10 In. 650.00
Figurine, Monkey Band, Each Playing Instrument, Sitzendorf, 9 Pc. 850.00
Figurine, Mustached Man, Brown Tunic, Popov, Russia, 8 1/2 In. 2420.00
Figurine, Polar Bear, Sitzendorf 290.00
Figurine, Sculptress, Woman In Toga, Man's Bust, Germany, 8 In. 250.00
Figurine, Spring, Red Dress, Hat At Side, Paragon, 7 1/2 In. 165.00
Figurine, Stork Dressed As Doctor, Top Hat, 7 x 2 1/2 In. 95.00
Figurine, The Importance of Being Earnest, Swansea, 8 1/2 In. 330.00
Figurine, Woman, Blue Outfit, Fur Trim, Roses, Germany, 8 1/2 In. 100.00
Figurine, Woman, Riding Habit, Jumping Stallion, Lera, Ps. 17 In. 450.00
Group, 12–Piece Monkey Band, Germany, c.1900, 5 1/2 In. 495.00
Group, Family In 18th–Century Dress, Germany, 15 x 21 In. 550.00
Group, Man & Woman Playing Chess, Ludwigsburg, 8 1/4 x 5 x 7 In. 60.00
Group, Monkey Band, Different Instruments, Sitzendorf, 6 In. 850.00
Group, Roman Festival, Seated Woman, Man, Maids, Sitzendorf, 15 In. 1950.00
Group, Woman, Child, Cradle, Putti, Flower Base, Germany, 8 1/2 In. 495.00
Holder, Place Card, Floral Sprays, Germany, 4 In., 12 Piece 120.00
Jar, Allover Secret Designs, Yellow Glaze, Chien Lung, 5 1/2 In. 395.00
Jar, Applied Fruit Cover, Crown Mark, Germany, 5 7/8 x 3 1/2 In. 105.00
Jar, Tobacco, Elegant Woman's Head, Germany 40.00
Pitcher, Floral Sprigs, Gilt Trim, American, 7 1/2 In. 175.00
Pitcher, Hexagonal Paneled, Floral Sprays, Gilt Trim, 8 1/2 In. 165.00
Pitcher, Stylized Design, Gold & Teal, L. Olson, 7 3/4 In. 220.00
Planter, With Stand, Scrolling Lotus Design, Chinese, 9 In., Pair 665.00
Plaque, Cupid & Maiden, Mythological Scene 605.00
Plaque, Monk Plucking A Goose, German, Wagner, c.1900, 7 x 5 In. 605.00
Plaque, Seminude Fairy, On Edge of Cliff, Gold Frame, 7 x 5 In. 2420.00
Plaque, Ships, Low Country, Framed, Continental, 12 1/2 x 10 In. 330.00
Plaque, Thread of Life, 19th Century 2090.00
Plaque, Woman Beside Water, Cherubs, Oval, Germany, 7 x 5 1/2 In. 2475.00
Plate, Center Finch & Peacock, Gilded Scrolls, Russia, 8 7/8 In. 770.00
Plate, Dog Portrait, Cream, Green & Blue, Pierced, Austria, 13 In. 225.00
Plate, Gilt & Polychrome Floral, W. Tucker, 1826, 6 1/8 In., 6 Pc. 3300.00
Plate, Gilt–Rim Design, Tucker, 6 1/4 In. 275.00
Plate, Oriental, Floral Enameling, 8 3/4 In., Pair 170.00
Platter, Rose Mandarin, Blue Bat & Bird Border, 12 1/2 x 15 In. 3400.00
Pot Pourri, Gilt–Bronze Mount, Domed Cover, Ring Handles, 18 In. 3850.00
Stand, Kettle, Hand Painted Landscape, Gilt Rim, 6 1/2 In. 40.00

Sugar, Cover, Swan Finial & Handles, Blue & Yellow Flowers 12.50
Teapot, Roof & Chimney Cover, Large 30.00
Tray, Serving, Red & Green Floral, Malmaison, Austria, 11 1/2 In. 25.00
Urn, Cobalt & Gilt Floral, Cover, 13 1/2 In., Pair 130.00
Urn, Floral Enameling, Gilt, Beige, Satyr Handles, 9 In., Pair 290.00
Urn, Ormolu Mounted, Chinese–Style Painted, France, 18 In., Pair 220.00
Vase, Camel, Palm Tree Scene, Bohemian, 1905, 3 3/4 x 4 In. 45.00
Vase, Center Medallion, Figures, French, c.1810, 9 1/2 In., Pair 1100.00
Vase, Couple In 18th–Century Dress, Lake Scene, C. A. C., 12 In. 95.00
Vase, Floral & Butterflies, Ming Dynasty, Signed, 18 1/2 In. 1650.00
Vase, Floral Enameling, Blue Underglaze, Oriental, 17 3/4 In. 300.00
Vase, Geometric Design, Double Handles, Robert Hanke, 13 1/8 In. 165.00
Vase, Rose Mandarin, Raised Lizards, Foo Dog Handles, 9 1/4 In. 445.00
Vase, Roses Transfer, 10 In. 24.00
Vase, Sprays of White Flowers, Butterflies, Gustavsberg, 16 In. 650.00
Vase, Victorian Woman, With Flowers, Austria, 6 In. 45.00
Vase, White Crystalline, University City, 4 1/2 In. 475.00

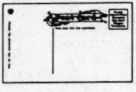

Postcards were first legally permitted in Austria on October 1, 1869. The United States passed postal regulations allowing the card in 1872. Most of the picture postcards collected today date after 1910. The amount of postage can help to date a card. The years the rates changed and the rates are: 1872 (1 cent), 1917 (2 cents), 1919 (1 cent), 1925 (2 cents), 1928 (1 cent), 1952 (2 cents), 1959 (3 cents), 1963 (4 cents), 1968 (5 cents), 1973 (8 cents), 1975 (7 cents), 1976 (9 cents), 1978 (10 cents), 1981 (12 cents), 1981 (13 cents), 1985 (14 cents), 1988 (15 cents), 1991 (19 cents).

POSTCARD, Air View of Olympic Swimming Stadium, Los Angeles, 1932 .... 6.00
Album, Philippines, China, Japan, Hawaii, 280 Views 375.00
Black Man Chained To Chair, Other Man Holds Tooth, 1907 .... 30.00
Boys Shooting Marbles, 1915 .... 18.00
Broadmoor 65.00
Buffalo Bill & His Show, 1910, 6 Piece 36.00
Bufflo Brewery, 21st Street, Sacramento, Ca., Factory 24.50
Catholic Church, Honolulu, 1910 .... 3.50
Chinese Laundry Worker, Words Are Poor Means To Express, 1906 .... 25.00
Chinese Scenes, This Is Not A Laundry Ticket, 1908 .... 16.00
Christmas, Skippy, 1932 .... 20.00
Coon Chicken Inn 30.00
Cracker Jack 22.00
Cunard Liner, Mauretania, 1908 .... 7.50
Davenport's Restaurant, Interior View, 1906 .... 4.00
Dick & Bros., Quincy Brewing Co., Factory 22.50
Fat Man On Scale, Never Worry Card, Poem, 1908, Unused 7.50
Gay's Lion Farm, El Monte, California, c.1930 .... 6.00
Grap Zeppelin 15.00
Harley–Davidson 20.00
Indian Motorcycle, Hendee Mfg. Factory, Springfield, Mass. 12.50
Iowa Falls, Street Scene, Model T Car 10.00
Jefferson, Dated 1899 .... 7.00
Laurel & Hardy, Poster Type, 1950, 5 x 8 In. 8.50
Lillian Russell, Photograph 22.00
Luther Burbank's Home, Santa Rosa, Ca., 1915 .... 6.50
Maggie & Jiggs, 6 Different Scenes 50.00
Marilyn Monroe, Pinup, 3 Different Poses, 3 Piece 25.00
Mechanical, Valentine, Signed Clapsaddle 26.00
Mountain, Floral Design, Red Swastika, Color, 1911 .... 5.00
Moxie, 1908 .... 55.00
Opium Den, Chinese Men, Pipes, Color, c.1902 .... 22.50
Panama Pacific Exposition, Chinese Child, 1915 .... 12.50
People In Victorian Era Bathing Suits, Atlantic City, 1908 .... 8.50
Phantom, King Comics, Colored 15.00
Photograph, Anna Pavlova 10.00

President Wilson, Flags, Submission Never Speech, Patriotic, 1917 .... 10.00
Ruder Brewing Co., Factory 30.00
S. Dakota National Guard Baseball Team, 1916–18, Photograph 95.00
Santa Claus, Reindeer, Germany, 1910, 3 Piece 12.00
Sectional Bookcases, Globe–Wernicke Co., Color 10.00
Self Portrait, Artist Yun Gee, Message, Signed, 1940 .... 65.00
Sharples Separator Co., Woman With Cow, Milk To Husband & Child 15.00
St. Patrick's, 1910, 12 Piece 25.00
St. Paul's Church, Augusta, Ga., 1906 .... 4.00
Stewardess, TWA 8.00
Stratoliner, TWA 5.00
Street Scene, Chinatown, San Francisco, Linen, 1939 .... 4.00
Sunkist Crate, Oranges, Label, Linen, 1939, Unused 6.00
Tournament of Roses, Folder, 1946 .... 6.00
TWA, Stewardess In Blue Uniform, 1 Cent 30.00
Wheat Harvest, View of Fields, Moscow, Idaho, 1930 .... 3.50
Woman's Face, Human Hair, Gold Leaf Accents, c.1900 .... 35.00

 Posters have informed the public about news and entertainment events since ancient times. Nineteenth–century advertising or theatrical posters and twentieth–century movie and war posters are of special interest today. The price is determined by the artist, the condition, and the rarity. Other posters are listed under Political, World War I, and World War II.

POSTER, 3 Faces East, J. Goudal, R. Ames, Cecil B. DeMille, 1926, 27 x 41 In. 375.00
Alaska, Kent Taylor, John Carradine, Monogram, 1944, 27 x 41 In. 150.00
Alice In Wonderland, 1951, 41 x 27 In. 880.00
America's First Union Label Union Hand Made Cigar, 11 x 4 In. 4.50
Americans All, Howard Chandler Christy, 39 x 27 In. 75.00
An American In Paris, Gene Kelly, 1951, 14 x 22 In. 45.00
Anna Dickinson, Women's Rights Lecturer, As Hamlet, 80 1/2 x 37 In. 195.00
Anthony Adverse, Frederic March, Warner Bros., 1936, 27 x 41 In. 475.00
Black Crook, Scenes, 2 Color Panels, 24 x 30 In. 715.00
Blackstone The Magician, 14 x 22 In. 75.00
Born Yesterday, Judy Holiday, 1950, 14 x 22 In. 25.00
Buffalo Bill's Wild West, Riders of The World, 1907, 26 x 37 In. 1100.00
Bull Durham, Framed Under Glass, Dated 1932, Framed, 14 x 19 In. 1200.00
Campus Confessions, Betty Grable, Paramount, 1938, 27 x 41 In. 450.00
Death of M. V. S. Jackson, Poem On Silk, 10 1/2 x 6 In. 770.00
Dr. B. J. Kendall's Tonic, Blood Purifier, Pink Paper, 24 x 5 In. 15.00
Duke Ellington, Sophisticated Ladies, 22 x 14 In. 22.00
Dupont, Infallible, Waterproof, Smokeless, 2 Mallard Ducks, 1909 .... 850.00
Fighting Bob Acres, The Rivals, Linen, Wooden Rollers, 104 x 60 In. 137.50
Fly With The Marines, Eagle, Airplane In Mouth, 1942, 28 x 40 In. 45.00
Fourth Liberty Loan War Bonds, Early 20th Century, 56 x 36 In. 305.00
General Dynamics, Servodynamics, c.1956, 35 x 50 In. 450.00
Gold Dust Washing Powder, N. K Fairbank Co., 27 x 14 In. 6600.00
Grand Union Tea, Little Girls, Christmas Morning, 1894, 28 x 13 In. 440.00
Halfway To Heaven, B. Rogers, J. Arthur, Paramount, 1925, 27 x 41 In. 275.00
Harper's February, People Reading Books, Edward Penfield, 1897 .... 4500.00
Heart of A Peddler, Unicorn Films, 1918, 40 x 80 In. 250.00
Hindenburg, Sets Record, Ocean Flight, Photograph, 11 x 16 1/2 In. 50.00
Hoaglan Bros. Circus, Kalamazoo, Chariot Scene, 28 1/2 x 42 In. 50.00
Hong Kong, Ronald Reagan, 1951, 14 x 22 In. 50.00
Hurry Home With Famous Narragansett Ale, Bottle, 1937, 30 x 15 In. 150.00
Independence Theatre, Pizarro Or Death of Rolla 110.00
Indianapolis 500, May 30, 1936, Wilbur Shaw's Racer, 11 x 16 1/2 In. 25.00
International Squadron, Reagan, Warner Bros., 1941, 27 x 41 In. 450.00
Joe Louis Shapes Up For Fight With Max Schmeling, 11 x 16 1/2 In. 17.00
Keystone Comedy, Mack Sennett, A Royal Rogue, 1917, 27 x 41 In. 500.00
Ladies of The Big House, Sylvia Sidney, 1931, 14 x 22 In. 50.00
Lillie, Masterpiece Theatre, Silkscreen, 3 Ft. 10 In. x 2 Ft. 6 In. 38.50
Little Eva's Temptation, Crossing Ice, Color, 28 1/2 x 20 In. 335.00

Louisa, Ronald Reagan, 1950, 14 x 22 In.	50.00
M. Burkhardt Brewing Co., Akron, Ohio, Frame, 14 x 20 In.	50.00
Magic Yeast, Child In Aladdin Costume, Waving Wand, 19 1/2 x 14 In.	150.00
Man Called Flintstone, 41 x 27 In.	65.00
Medicine Show, Clifton Comedy Co., Full Color, c.1915, 30 x 20 In.	300.00
Mennen's Talcum Powder, Frame, 9 x 13 In.	280.00
Mennen's Toilet Powder, Woman With Umbrella, 9 1/2 x 13 In.	22.00
Miller Bros., Arlington, 101 Ranch, Wild West, 1914, 20 x 30 In.	462.00
Minstrel, Greater Sheesley Shows, 28 x 42 In.	385.00
Monaco–Monte Carlo, Alphonse, Seated Maiden, 1897, 43 x 28 In.	9900.00
Montana Frank, Wild West Show, 1910	375.00
N. R. A. Member, We Do Our Part, c.1934, 10 x 14 In.	85.00
New Home Sewing Machine, Wooden Rollers Each End, 19 1/2 x 26 In.	165.00
Old Master Coffee, Frame, 14 x 19 1/2 In.	285.00
Opera, Louise, George Rochegrosse, c.1900, 25 x 35 In.	350.00
Othello, Stafford & Co., With Desdemona, c.1905, 30 x 20 In.	125.00
Our Town, Evelyn Varden & Tom Fadden, 1938, 40 x 24 In.	195.00
Paul Whiteman, King of Jazz, Bevy of Show Girls, 38 x 56 In.	4950.00
Pawnee Bill's Historic Wild West, 1894, 27 1/2 x 37 In.	1320.00
Peck's Bad Boy, Atkinson Comedy Company, Scenes, 24 x 36 In.	315.00
Pendleton Roundup, 1951, 15 x 38 In.	85.00
Philip Morris, Johnny Between Packs, 1930s, 18 x 23 In.	60.00
Prince Albert, Man & Pocket Tin, 1935, 10 x 21 In.	12.00
Red Star Dynamite, New York Powder Co., Canvas, 29 1/2 x 36 In.	137.00
Redford's Celebrated Tobacco, Plantation, c.1925, 25 x 20 In.	150.00
Richard III, Black & White, October, 1974, 42 x 30 In.	11.00
Ringling Bros., & Barnum & Bailey, Giraffes, 1944, 28 x 21 In.	245.00
Ringling Brothers Circus, Frame, 25 x 37 In.	250.00
Rolling Stones, American Tour, Jet Plane, 1972, 25 x 38 In.	65.00
Rumpole of The Bailey, PBS Mystery Theater, c.1960, 46 x 30 In.	95.00
Satin Skin Powder, Detroit, Michigan, Frame, 44 x 29 1/2 In.	165.00
Sesquicentennial, Beautiful Lady, Flags, 1926, 9 1/2 Tapers To 5 In.	50.00
Sharples Tubular Separator, c.1910, 28 1/2 x 42 1/2 In.	465.00
Sherlock Holmes, Crucifer of Blood, 22 x 14 In.	65.00
St. Patricks Day March, 4 Cohans, Frame, Lithograph, 43 x 18 In.	1760.00
Stillwell Ham, Hannibal, Missouri, Cardboard, 11 x 14 In.	45.00
Thomas Bicycle, 4 People On Tandum Bicycle, 42 x 14 In.	935.00
Thurston, Devil Imps On Shoulders, c.1920, 26 x 41 In.	575.00
Two For The Road, Audrey Hepburn	55.00
Uncle Tom's Cabin, Witherell & Davis Traveling Co., 26 x 30 In.	375.00
United Nations, Hands Digging Earth, 1947, 18 x 24 In.	200.00
Valley of The Dolls, 1967	137.00
Vote For Woman Suffrage, c.1915, 19 x 24 In.	175.00
We've Made A Monkey Out of You, Hitler, 1940s, 15 x 20 In.	30.00
Winchester, Dogs On Point, Metal Bands, 30 1/2 x 16 1/2 In.	412.50
World War II, Keep Him Free, Eagle & Bi–Wing Planes	175.00
World War II, Liberty, Be Prepared, J. C. Lyndecker	220.00
Yeast Foam, Metal Bands, 10 x 15 In.	27.50

A potlid is just that, a lid for a pot. Transfer–printed potlids had their heyday from the 1840s to the early 1900s. The English Staffordshire potteries made ceramic containers with decorative lids for bear's grease, shrimp or meat paste, cold cream, and toothpaste. Printed advertising and pictures of historical events, portraits of famous people, or scenic views were designed in black and white or color. Reproductions have been made. The most famous potlids were made by Pratt and are listed in that section.

POTLID, Bazin Genuine Beef Marrow, Blue	450.00
Bears Grease, Ross & Sons, Marked Genuine Bears Grease	1265.00
Liston's Extract of Beef, 2 In.	125.00
Samuel Horn's Lowell Soap, Picture of Scottish Lad, Black Transfer	457.00
Scene of People, Horse, Carriages, Crystal Palace, London	495.00
Seat of Duke of Wellington, Strathfieldsaye	275.00

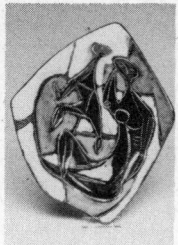

Pottery, Bowl, Black Glaze, Asymmetrical,
Italy, 12 1/2 In.

Pottery, Figurine, Lion, Brown, Yellow,
England, 19th C., 8 x 12 In.

If you are moving or if you are storing paper collectibles and pictures
for a long period of time, remember that extreme changes of temperature are damaging. Air trapped inside a picture frame may con-
dense and cause moisture damage.

The Rivals 240.00

 Pottery and porcelain are different. Pottery is opaque; you can't see
through it. Porcelain is translucent. If you hold a porcelain dish in
front of a strong light you will see the light through the dish.
Porcelain is colder to the touch. Pottery is softer and easier to break
and will stain more easily because it is porous. Porcelain is thinner,
lighter, and more durable. Majolica, faience, and stoneware are all
pottery. Many types of pottery are listed in this book under the
factory name.

POTTERY, Ashtray, Goat, Great Northern	95.00
Ashtray, Sculptured Daisy, Poppy Trail, Metlox	20.00
Beanpot, Trivet, Cover, Handle, Old Hickory, Buryrus, Ohio	65.00
Biscuit Jar, Tuquoise & Brown Floral, Creamware, Ear Handles, Don	95.00
Bottle, Squirrel, Green Glaze, Moravian	2450.00
Bottle, Teddy Bear, Reading Book, Coat & Tie, 4 7/8 In.	110.00
Bowl, 2 Wild Horses, High Foot, W. H. Diederich, c.1925, 14 3/4 In.	3850.00
Bowl, Amber Glaze, Wire Bands At Rim, Buff, 8 1/2 In.	150.00
Bowl, Black Glaze, Asymmetrical, Italy, 12 1/2 In. ....*Illus*	80.00
Bowl, Interior Peacocks & Foliage, Islamic, 12th Century, 7 In.	170.00
Bowl, Tin Glazed Earthenware, W. H. Diederick, c.1925, 14 1/4 In.	7150.00
Bowl, Tom & Jerry, Homer Laughlin, Set of 4	40.00
Bowl, Vegetable, Cover, Georgian, Off–White, Gold Trim, H. Laughlin	16.00
Bowl, Woman's Head Center, Bjorn Wynblad, 1951, 4 1/2 In.	125.00
Box, Cigarette, Poppy, Ashtrays, Blue Ridge	90.00
Box, Cigarette, Ship, Ashtrays, Blue Ridge	100.00
Butter, Cover, Cattail, 1 Lb.	10.00
Canister Set, Poppy Trail, Provincial Rooster, Metlox	175.00
Carafe, Juice, Turquoise, Metlox	20.00
Cheese Dish, Cover, Floral, Cream Ground, England, 7 1/4 x 9 1/4 In.	118.00
Churn, Superior Sanitary, Metal Frame	360.00
Cider Set, D. F. Haynes & Son, 5 Piece	125.00
Coffeepot, Brown Metallic Glaze, Ribbed Strap Handle, 10 1/4 In.	70.00
Coffeepot, Fruit, Purinton	25.00
Coffeepot, George & Martha, ABC	20.00
Coffeepot, Pink Greenaway–Type Girl, Jackfield Type, Enameled	155.00
Coffeepot, Sculptured Daisy, Poppy Trail, Metlox	50.00

Coffeepot, Weathervane, E. M. Knowles	35.00
Creamer, Bluebell Bouquet, Blue Ridge	6.00
Cup & Saucer, Poppy Trail, Sculptured Grape	14.00
Cup & Saucer, Virginia Rose, Homer Laughlin	5.00
Cup, Apple, Purinton	6.00
Cup, Brittany, Blue Ridge, Demitasse	29.50
Cuspidor, Flint Enamel, Etruria Works, England, 1852, 7 1/2 In.	325.00
Eggcup, Crab Apple, Blue Ridge	10.50
Figurine, Arthur, Brayton	38.00
Figurine, Cat, Black & White, Blue Trim, Agateware, 4 In.	800.00
Figurine, Cat, Black Spots, White Clay, Chinese, 6 1/2 In.	75.00
Figurine, Chinese Boy & Girl, Brad Keeler	35.00
Figurine, Dog, Blue Sponging, Yellow Eyes, Ohio, 6 1/2 In.	700.00
Figurine, Dog, Brown Spots, Unglazed Biscuit, White, Ohio, 7 1/4 In.	355.00
Figurine, Dog, Seated, Dark Brown Glaze, Gray Clay, 8 5/8 In.	75.00
Figurine, Dog, Seated, White Slip, Brown Spots, 9 1/4 In.	65.00
Figurine, Dutch Girl, Brayton	28.00
Figurine, Girl, Knitting Sock, Brayton	32.00
Figurine, Julia Ray, Brayton	38.00
Figurine, Lion, Brown, Yellow, England, 19th C., 8 x 12 In. ....*Illus*	495.00
Figurine, Peacock, Blue, Brayton, 8 In.	65.00
Figurine, Peasant Woman, Brayton	45.00
Figurine, Sally, Brayton	15.00
Figurine, Swan, Canuck, 4 1/2 In.	10.00
Figurine, Victorian Children, Adult Clothes, Hennecke, 10 In., Pr.	84.00
Figurine, Woman, On Carousel Horse, Bjorn Wynblad, 11 x 10 In.	225.00
Flowerpot, Titusville, Attached Plate, Green, White Glaze, 6 In.	15.00
Garden Seat, Elephant, Overall Floral Design, 22 1/2 In.	175.00
Gravy Boat, Attached Liner, Coronado, Franciscan	25.00
Grill Plate, Rose, Western Design	8.00
Group, Cocktails For 2, Allerton Hotel, Burr Abbott, 20th Century	88.00
Group, Couple In Evening Dress, Burr Abbott, 20th Century	88.00
Group, Perusing Menu, 3 People At Table, B. Abbott, 20th Century	99.00
Jar, Green Ash Glaze, Ear & Shoulder Handles, David Meaders, 8 In.	25.00
Jar, Running Green Ash Glaze, Ear Handles, Southern Pottery, 17 In.	300.00
Jardiniere, Muted Blues, Wine, Green, Cream Ground, 32 x 14 In., Pr.	1200.00
Jug, Citro, Thirst Quencher, 5 Cents, Handle, 1 Gal.	95.00
Jug, Whiskey, Music Box, 1900s	100.00
Mug, Aqua, Catalina, 4 In.	22.00
Pie Baker, Mardi Gras, Blue Ridge	25.00
Pie Plate, Tulip, Pink, Green, Yellow Slip, Moravian, 1973, 10 In.	95.00
Pitcher, Betsy, Blue Ridge	98.00
Pitcher, Chick, Blue Ridge, 5 1/2 In.	25.00
Pitcher, Eagles & Floral Rim, Albany Slip, M. Tyler, 10 3/4 In.	400.00
Pitcher, Egyptian, Bulbous, Haynes Ware, 6 3/4 In.	55.00
Pitcher, Fan & Scroll, Insert, Blue Ground, Fielding, Small	125.00
Pitcher, Floral Design, Brown Brushed Slip, New Geneva, 9 5/8 In.	650.00
Pitcher, Floral Design, Brushed Slip, New Geneva, 5 3/4 In.	675.00
Pitcher, Floral Design, Brushed Slip, New Geneva, 6 1/2 In.	525.00
Pitcher, Hummingbird, Gold Ground, Eureka Pottey	120.00
Pitcher, Hunt Scene, Green Matte Glaze, Hound Handle, Ohio, 10 In.	200.00
Pitcher, Jan, Blue Ridge	89.00
Pitcher, Juice, Turquoise, Wooden Handle, Metlox	18.00
Pitcher, Landing of Gen. Lafayette, American Pottery Co., 9 In.	5100.00
Pitcher, Milk, Shenandoah, Turquoise & White	100.00
Pitcher, Raised Fruit, Blue Ridge, 7 1/2 In.	25.00
Pitcher, Virginia Rose, Blue Ridge	60.00
Pitcher, White, Cobridge	32.00
Pitcher, Yellow Glaze Scrolling, Brighton, 9 1/4 In.	660.00
Planter, Double, Woman, Fan, On Couch, California Pottery	25.00
Planter, Fawn, Leaping, Figural, Cliftwood, Label, 8 In.	8.00
Planter, Sculptured Daisy, Poppy Trail, Metlox, 14 In.	18.00
Plaque & Planter Set, Blackamoor, Brayton, 22 In., 2 Piece	125.00

Plate, Currier & Ives, Winter In The Country 22.00
Plate, Dinner, Apple, Purinton 8.00
Plate, Dinner, Luray, Pink 7.00
Plate, Dinner, Poppy Trail, Sculptured Grape 10.00
Plate, Dinner, Virginia Rose, Homer Laughlin 5.00
Plate, Dinner, Wild Strawberry, Blue Ridge 15.00
Plate, Fruit Punch, Blue Ridge, 9 In. 7.50
Plate, German Emperor's Yacht, Meteor, Launch, Onondago, 1902, 10 In. 70.00
Plate, Gladding McBean, Red, 10 1/2 In. 15.00
Plate, LuRay, 9 1/2 In. 7.00
Plate, Ribbon, White, Flower Center, Cutout Design Rim, 7 In. 45.00
Plate, Spotted Wolf, D. F. Haynes & Son 275.00
Plate, Tulips, Blue Ridge, 11 1/2 In. 30.00
Platter, Luray, Pink, 13 In. 8.00
Pot, Carved Design, Iowa State College, Dunbar, 1922, 3 x 6 1/2 In. 550.00
Relish, Deep Shell, Blue Ridge 39.00
Salt & Pepper, Stove-Shaped Grease Jar, Mammy & Chef, Blue, Gold 125.00
Salt & Pepper, Virginia Rose, Homer Laughlin 17.50
Soup Dish, Poppy Trail, Provincial Rooster 14.00
Sugar & Creamer, Cover, Autumn, Franciscan 30.00
Sugar & Creamer, Cover, Normandy Plaid, Purinton 15.00
Tankard, Cinderella & Prince, Shaded Brown, W. H. Tatler, 12 1/2 In. 110.00
Tankard, Indian Portrait, Usona Goodwin 150.00
Teapot, Apple, 1 Cup 9.00
Teapot, Dachshund, Erphila 65.00
Teapot, Dogwood, Homer Laughlin 20.00
Teapot, Gladding McBean, Dark Purple, 8 In. 45.00
Teapot, Lavender, Tin Lid, Daisy Design 176.00
Teapot, Whig Rose, Blue Ridge 48.00
Tobacco Jar, Egyptian Design, Japanese Faces, Japan, 1905, 7 In. 125.00
Tom & Jerry Set, Covered Bowl, Pastel, 8 Cups, Metlox 55.00
Tray, Maple Leaf Handle, Grape Cluster, Blue Ridge 40.00
Urn, Floral Design, Trenton, 12 In., Pair 750.00
Urn, Mustard Glaze, Handles, 5 Gal. 90.00
Vase, Burgundy Drip Glaze To Rust, Concentric Rings Base, 16 In. 110.00
Vase, Cactus Flower, Catalina, 7 3/4 In. 65.00
Vase, Catalina, Oxblood, Flared, 6 In. 46.00
Vase, Laguna Beach, Brown & Gree Leaves, Coalpotter, 8 1/4 In. 25.00
Vase, Mood Indigo, Blue Ridge 95.00
Vase, Sea Dragon On Waves, Handle, Artist Otto, 14 In. 200.00
Vase, Speckled High Gloss, Jamestowne, 5 1/4 In. 65.00
Vase, Swimming Rainbow Trout Design, Rick Wisecarver, 7 x 9 In. 225.00
Vase, Turquoise Blue, White Interior, Handles, Catalina, 5 3/4 In. 125.00
Vase, Young Male Hunter, Forester & Sons, c.1890, 9 In. 195.00

Powder flasks and powder horns were made to hold the gunpowder used in antique firearms. The early examples were made of horn or wood; later ones were of copper or brass.

POWDER FLASK, Eagle Powder, Duck Shooting, Dupont Label, Tin, 6 In. 65.00
POWDER HORN, Engraved Eagle, Fish, Ship & 1870, 6 1/2 In. 55.00
Engraved Lion & Unicorn, Man Shooting, Fort Pitt, 12 In. 1900.00
Geometric Design, Albert J. Houghton, Feb. 27, 1874, 15 In. 450.00
Geometric Designs, Uriah Amsden, 1746, 9 1/4 In. 800.00
Naps of Rivers & Forts, Samuel Holborn, 1756, 10 1/2 In. 950.00
Neptune & Wife, Birds, For John Kilbun, Sep. 28, 1757, 9 In. 695.00
New York Map, Hudson, Niagara, 16 In. ....Illus 2650.00
Scrimshaw, Signed James Larkin, Pepperel, 1812 .... 1250.00
Turtle, Deer, Fish Etched, Signed James Larkin Pepperell, 1812 .... 1265.00
Wrought Iron Chain, 16 In., Pair 45.00

PRATT
FENTON
Pratt ware means two different things. It was an early Staffordshire pottery, cream-colored with colored decorations, made by Felix Pratt during the late eighteenth century. There was also Pratt ware

made with transfer designs during the mid–nineteenth century in Fenton, England. Reproductions of the transfer–printed Pratt are being made.

PRATT, Bank, House Shape, 5 1/8 In.	135.00
Bank, House, Slot In Roof, Figures At Side, Faces In Windows, 5 In.	600.00
Creamer, Hunt Scenes, 4 7/8 In.	175.00
Creamer, Scenes of Children At Play, 4 3/4 In.	250.00
Figurine, Bear, Polychrome Color, 3 1/2 In.	600.00
Figurine, Fall, Woman With Sickle, Child With Wheat	1300.00
Figurine, Lion, 4 In.	900.00
Group, Harvest, Figures, 9 1/4 In.	1430.00
Jar, Design On Lid, Shakespeare's House, 4 In.	65.00
Jar, Snuff, Wild Boar Hunt Scene, Blue Glazed Earthenware, 4 In.	38.00
Pitcher, Relief Busts, Floral Designs, 7 1/2 In.	400.00
Pitcher, Scenes of Children In Heart Medallion, 7 1/4 In.	250.00
Plate, Transfer Scene With Cathedral, Marked, 8 5/8 In.	45.00
Platter, Blind Fiddler, Marked, 12 In.	99.00
Potlid, Cherry Toothpaste, Patronized By The Queen, J. Cosnell Co.	85.00
Potlid, Dr. Johnson, 4 1/4 In.	25.00
Potlid, Pegwell Bay, 4 1/4 In.	25.00
Spill, Triple, Bull Terrier Baiting Bull, c.1790, 7 15/16 In.	2475.00
Sugar, Cover, Swan Finial, Medallion of Woman & Child, 5 3/4 In.	400.00
Tea Caddy, Comic Characters, 4 Colors, Soft Paste, 4 3/4 In.	235.00
Teapot, Grecian Figures	160.00
Vase, Finger, Leaves & Flowers, 4 Colors, 7 In.	950.00
Wall Pocket, Putto, Quiver of Arrows, c.1805, 9 5/16 In., Pair	3300.00

Pressed glass was first made in the United States in the 1820s after the invention of glass pressing machines. Hundreds of patterns of pressed glass were made in complete table settings. Although the Boston and Sandwich Works was the most famous of the pressed glass factories, there were about sixteen other factories making pressed glass from 1830 to 1850, and still more from 1850 to 1900, when pressed glass reached its greatest popularity. It is now being widely reproduced. The pattern names used in this listing are based on the information in the book *Pressed Glass in America* by John and Elizabeth Welker. There may be pieces of pressed glass listed in this book in other sections. See Lamp, Ruby, Sandwich, and Souvenir.

PRESSED GLASS, Bartlett Pear, Sugar & Creamer	90.00

100–LEAVED ROSE, see Hundred Leaved Rose
1000–EYE, see Thousand Eye
101, see One–Hundred–One
8–0–8, see Eight–0–Eight
ACANTHUS, see Ribbed Palm
ACME, see Butterfly With Spray

Powder Horn, New York Map, Hudson, Niagara, 16 In.

Pressed glass, Actress   *Pressed glass,*   *Pressed glass,*   *Pressed glass,*
                           Amberette   *Artichoke, frosted*   *Ashburton*

Acme Swirl, Goblet	12.00
Acorn In Wreath, Goblet	57.50
ACORN MEDALLION, BEADED, see Beaded Acorn Medallion	
Acorn, Sugar, Open	50.00
Actress, Bowl, Footed, 6 In.	30.00
Actress, Bread Plate	95.00
Actress, Bread Plate, Miss Neilson	80.00
Actress, Butter, Lotta On Cover, Davenport & Neilson	247.00
Actress, Celery Vase, Pinafore Scene, 9 In.	155.00
Actress, Celery Vase, Pinafore Scene, Frosted, 9 In.	250.00
Actress, Compote, Cover, 8 In.	125.00
Actress, Compote, Cover, Annie Pixley, Maude Granger, Frosted	120.00
Actress, Creamer	57.50
Actress, Creamer, Large	100.00
Actress, Goblet	75.00 To 85.00
Actress, Jam Jar	67.50 To 125.00
Actress, Pitcher, Davenport & Neilson, 6 1/2 In.	60.00
Actress, Pitcher, Water, Maggie Mitchell, Adelaide Neilson	385.00
Actress, Relish, Adelaide Neilson, Frosted, 8 x 5 In.	50.00
Actress, Relish, Maggie Mitchell, 7 x 4 1/2 In.	82.50
Actress, Relish, Maude Granger, Frosted, 9 x 5 3/4 In.	88.00
Actress, Saucer, Footed	12.50
Actress, Spooner	90.00
Actress, Spooner, Maude Granger, Mary Anderson, 6 1/2 In.	50.00
Actress, Sugar & Creamer	120.00
Actress, Sugar, Kate Claxton & Lotta, 9 In.	88.00 To 100.00
ADMIRAL DEWEY, see Spanish American	
Adonis, Celery	27.50
Adonis, Compote	25.00
Adonis, Compote, High Standard	45.00
Adonis, Creamer	18.50
Adonis, Plate, 10 In.	12.50 To 35.00
Adonis, Relish	9.50
Aegis, Pitcher, Water	47.50
Alabama, Butter Cover, Ruby Stained	135.00
Alabama, Butter, Cover	50.00
Alaska, Berry Set, Blue Opalescent, 7 Piece	345.00
Alaska, Creamer, Vaseline	55.00 To 95.00
Alaska, Creamer, Yellow	160.00
Alaska, Pitcher, Vaseline	250.00
Alaska, Pitcher, Water, Blue Opalescent, Design	450.00

Alaska, Pitcher, Water, Enamel Flowers, Blue Opalescent 395.00
Alaska, Pitcher, Water, Enameled Flowers, Vaseline 450.00
Alaska, Saltshaker, Flowers, Blue 85.00
Alaska, Saltshaker, White & Opalescent 37.50
Alaska, Spooner, Vaseline .... 45.00 To 60.00
Alaska, Table Set, Blue Opalescent, 4 Piece 545.00
Albany, Butter, Cover, Ruby Stained 145.00
Albany, Goblet 14.00
Albany, Spooner 45.00
Alligator Scales, Goblet 45.00
Amazon, Creamer 37.50
Amazon, Goblet 22.50
Amberette, Pitcher, Milk, Amber Panels 285.00
Amberette, Pitcher, Water, Amber Panels 255.00
Amberette, Platter, Celery Dish, 11 1/4 x 9 In. 145.00
Amberette, Tumbler, Water, Frosted, 4 In. 135.00
Ambidextrous, Spooner 25.00
Anthemion, Pitcher, Water 38.00
Apollo, Cake Stand, 9 In. 47.00
Apollo, Creamer, Etched 57.50
Apollo, Goblet, Frosted 47.50
Apollo, Syrup, Etched 95.00
Arched Leaf, Goblet 60.00
Arched Ovals, Saltshaker 32.50
Argonaut Shell, Berry Set, Blue Opalescent, 7 Piece 465.00
Argonaut Shell, Pitcher, Water, Blue Opalescent 375.00
Argus, Creamer, Flint 98.00
Argus, Eggcup, Flint 55.00
    ARROWHEAD IN OVAL, see Style
Art, Banana Boat 100.00
Art, Banana Stand .... 75.00 To 97.50
Art, Butter, Cover 45.00
Art, Cake Stand .... 55.00 To 58.00
Art, Celery 48.00
Art, Compote, Cover, 8 In. 97.50
Art, Creamer 40.00
Art, Pitcher, Red Flashed 135.00
Art, Pitcher, Water, Bulbous 82.50
Art, Sauce, Etched, Flat, 4 1/2 In. 18.50
Artichoke, Goblet, Frosted 35.00
Artichoke, Saltshaker, Frosted 22.00

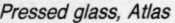

Pressed glass, Atlas   Pressed glass, Austrian   Pressed glass, Barberry

Ashburton, Cordial, Flint 39.00
Ashburton, Creamer 250.00
Ashburton, Eggcup, Flint 55.00
Ashburton, Tumbler, Flint 60.00
Ashburton, Whiskey, Handle, Flint 125.00
Atlanta, Butter, Cover Etched, Square 75.00
Atlanta, Compote, Cover, 5 In. 95.00
Atlanta, Compote, Cover, 6 In. 95.00
Atlanta, Creamer 47.50
Atlanta, Sugar, Cover, Etched 145.00
Atlas, Toothpick, Etched 22.50
Aurora, Goblet 35.00
Aurora, Wine 22.50
Austrian, Berry Bowl, 8 In. 47.50
Austrian, Bowl, 7 1/4 In. 42.50
Austrian, Compote, 8 1/2 In. 67.50
Austrian, Creamer 25.00
Austrian, Goblet .... 40.00 To 55.00
Austrian, Rose Bowl 47.50
Austrian, Sugar, Cover, Individual 24.50
Austrian, Table Set, Gold Trim, 4 Piece 225.00
Austrian, Tumbler 32.50
Austrian, Vase, 6 1/2 In. 42.50
Austrian, Wine .... 42.50 To 47.50
Aztec, Cruet 48.00
    BABY THUMBPRINT, see Dakota
    BALDER, see Pennsylvania
    BALKY MULE, see Currier & Ives
Ball & Swirl, Spooner 21.00
Baltimore Pear, Bowl, 5 In. 25.00
Baltimore Pear, Cake Stand 60.00
Baltimore Pear, Table Set, 4 Piece 135.00
Banded Buckle, Goblet 28.00
    BANDED PORTLAND, when flashed with pink, is sometimes called *Maiden Blush.*
Banded Portland, Cologne Bottle, 3 In. 55.00
Banded Portland, Compote, Cover, 8 In. 110.00
Banded Portland, Cup 12.50
Banded Portland, Goblet 175.00
Banded Portland, Tankard, Water 245.00
Banded Portland, Vase, Bud, Enameled 60.00
Banded Star, Compote, Cover, 6 In. 48.00
    BAR & DIAMOND, see Kokomo
Barberry, Butter, Cover 65.00
Barberry, Cake Stand, 11 In. 110.00
Barberry, Celery 32.50
Barberry, Celery Vase 65.00
Barberry, Compote, Cover, 8 In. 77.50
Barberry, Compote, High Stand and Cover, 9 In. 140.00
Barberry, Plate, 6 In. 28.00
    BARLEY & OATS, see Wheat & Barley
    BARLEY & WHEAT, see Wheat & Barley
Barley, Plate, 6 In. 27.50

◆◆◆

Never store old paper collectibles in ordinary cardboard boxes or plastic bags. Buy the acid free boxes and mylar wrapping film that is approved for long term storage. Many picture framing and supply stores will have these items.

◆◆◆

Barred Forget–Me–Not, Bowl, Handle, 6 x 9 In.	27.50
Barred Forget–Me–Not, Compote, Cover, 8 In.	62.50
Barred Forget–Me–Not, Plate, Handles, 9 In.	27.50
Barred Oval, Goblet	35.00
BARRELED BLOCK, see Red Block	
Bartlett Pear, Pitcher, Water	110.00
Basket Weave, Goblet, Blue	28.00
Basket Weave, Pitcher, Water, Vaseline	68.00
Bead Column, Compote, Cover, High Standard, 6 In.	45.00
Bead Column, Goblet	25.00
Bead Swag, Butter, Cover, White Flower	125.00
Bead Swag, Spooner, White Flower	37.50
Beaded Acorn Medallion, Eggcup	25.00
Beaded Acorn Medallion, Spooner	25.00
Beaded Acorn, Goblet	35.00
BEADED BULL'S–EYE & DRAPE, see Alabama	
Beaded Dart Band, Goblet	11.00
BEADED DEWDROP, see Wisconsin	
Beaded Grape Medallion, Celery	45.00
Beaded Grape Medallion, Compote, Cover, 8 In.	95.00
Beaded Grape Medallion, Goblet	30.00
Beaded Grape, Bowl, Cover, Square, 7 In.	85.00
Beaded Grape, Cake Stand, Green, High Standard, 9 In.	70.00
Beaded Grape, Creamer	50.00
Beaded Grape, Cruet, Green	77.50 To 95.00
Beaded Grape, Saltshaker	33.00
Beaded Grape, Sugar & Creamer, Green	90.00
Beaded Grape, Sugar, Cover	60.00
Beaded Grape, Toothpick	18.00
Beaded Loop, Butter, Cover	45.00
Beaded Loop, Salt & Pepper	42.50
Beaded Loop, Sauce, Small	7.00
Beaded Loop, Tumbler	55.00
Beaded Mirror, Plate, 8 In.	27.50
Beaded Scroll, Cruet, Green	225.00
Beaded Swirl & Disc, Berry Bowl, 8 3/4 In.	50.00
Beaded Swirl, Salt & Pepper	22.50
Beaded Swirl, Table Set, 4 Piece	175.00
Beaded Swirl, Table Set, Green, Gold Trim	375.00
Bear Climber, Goblet, Etched	115.00
BEARDED HEAD, see Viking	
BEARDED MAN, see Queen Anne	
Beehive, Dish, Lacy, Octagonal, 9 3/4 In.	65.00
Bellflower Double Vine, Bread Plate	25.00
Bellflower, Compote, Flint, 8 In.	75.00
Bellflower, Eggcup	40.00
Bellflower, Eggcup, Flint	40.00

Pressed glass, Barred Oval

Pressed glass,
Beaded Grape Medallion

Pressed glass, Bellflower

Pressed glass,   Pressed glass, Buckle   Pressed glass,   Pressed glass,
Bethlehem Star   Bull's–Eye & Daisy   Bull's-Eye & Fan

Bellflower, Goblet	40.00
Bellflower, Goblet, Knob Stem, Rayed Base	53.00
Bellflower, Spooner, Flint	35.00 To 40.00
Bellflower, Sugar, Cover, Double Vine	125.00
Bellflower, Tumbler	120.00
Bellflower, Whiskey, 3 In.	175.00
Bellflower, Wine	95.00
Bellflower, Wine, Knob Stem	150.00
Belmont, Butter, Pedestal, Cover	68.00
BENT BUCKLE, see New Hampshire	
Berry Cluster, Butter, Cover	28.00
Berry Cluster, Creamer	38.00
Berry Cluster, Spooner	25.00 To 32.00
Bethlehem Star, Compote, Jelly, Cover	47.50
Bethlehem Star, Spooner	17.00
Bethlehem Star, Sugar & Creamer, Cover	52.50
Bethlehem Star, Sugar, Large	22.00
BEVELED DIAMOND & STAR, see Albany	
Beveled Star, Compote, Jelly, Green	55.00
Beveled Star, Table Set, Amber, Flint, 4 Piece	250.00
Big Button, Cruet, Ruby Stained Stopper, Small	135.00
Big Button, Sugar, Cover, Individual	125.00
Birch Leaf, Goblet	28.50
Bird & Strawberry Table Set, 4 Piece	250.00
Bird & Strawberry, Berry Set, 8 Piece	150.00
Bird & Strawberry, Cake Stand	40.00 To 75.00
Bird & Strawberry, Compote, 5 7/8 In.	70.00
Bird & Strawberry, Compote, Cover	85.00
Bird & Strawberry, Compote, Jelly, Cover	125.00
Bird & Strawberry, Punch Cup	18.00
Bird & Strawberry, Relish, Heart Shape	45.00
Bird & Strawberry, Sauce, Footed, 4 1/8 In.	25.00
BIRD IN RING, see Grace	
Birds In Swamp, Goblet, Amber	82.50
Blackberry Band, Spooner	25.00
Blaze, Goblet	48.00
Blaze, Wine, Flint	42.50
Bleeding Heart, Cake Stand, 11 1/4 In.	145.00
Bleeding Heart, Goblet	25.00
Bleeding Heart, Mug, 3 1/4 In.	65.00
Bleeding Heart, Spooner	25.00
Bleeding Heart, Sugar	30.00
Bleeding Heart, Sugar, Cover	85.00
BLOCK & FAN, see Romeo	
BLOCK & FINE CUT, see Fine Cut & Block	
BLOCK & LATTICE, see Big Button	
Block & Panel, Saltshaker	25.00

Block, Bowl, Flint, 11 In.	60.00
Block, Celery Vase, Pedestal, 10 1/2 In.	325.00
Blocked Thumbprint, Tumbler, Ruby Stained	26.00
BLUEBIRD, see Bird & Strawberry	
Bohemian, Berry Bowl, Boat Shaped, Green	47.50
Bohemian, Berry Bowl, Master, Cranberry, Gold Trim	150.00
Bohemian, Creamer, Frosted, Green & Rose Flowers	55.00 To 65.00
Bohemian, Creamer, Green, Individual	22.50 To 27.50
Bohemian, Mug, Rose Leaves, Gilded	70.00
Bohemian, Pitcher, Rose, Gold Trim	195.00 To 225.00
Bohemian, Tumbler, Frosted, Red Flowers	42.50
Bordered Ellipse, Mug	25.00
Bosc Pear, Spooner	18.00
Bowtie, Goblet	68.00
Box–In–Box, Creamer, Hand Painted, Ruby Flashed	50.00
Box–In–Box, Relish	27.50
Box–In–Box, Tumbler, Ruby Stained	42.50
Brazen Shield, Tumbler, Cobalt Blue	50.00
Britannic, Butter, Cover, Ruby Stained	125.00
Britannic, Spooner, Ruby Stained	48.00
Broken Column, Bowl, Rectangular, 5 1/2 x 8 In.	27.50
Broken Column, Cake Stand	42.50
Broken Column, Celery	32.50
Broken Column, Compote, Ruby Stained, 7 x 6 1/2 In.	235.00
Broken Column, Cracker Jar, Cover	45.00
Broken Column, Cruet	48.50 To 60.00
Broken Column, Cup, Blue	95.00
Broken Column, Goblet	40.00
Broken Column, Relish, Ruby Stained	60.00
Broken Column, Saltshaker	35.00
Broken Column, Saucer, 4 1/2 In.	14.50
BROUGHTON, see Pattee Cross	
BRYCE, see Ribbon Candy	
BUCKET, see Oaken Bucket	
Buckle With Shield, Goblet	11.00
Buckle, Salt, Master	27.50
Buckle, Tumbler	85.00
Budded Ivy, Spooner	15.00
Bulging Loops, Cruet, Pink	225.00
Bulging Loops, Pitcher, White Interior, Pink Frosted Handle	225.00
Bulging Loops, Salt & Pepper, Ruby	175.00
Bulging Loops, Toothpick, Green	55.00
Bull's–Eye & Bar, Eggcup, Flint	125.00
Bull's–Eye & Daisy, Creamer, Gold Trim	75.00
Bull's–Eye & Daisy, Sugar, Cover, Gold Trim	100.00
Bull's–Eye & Daisy, Sugar, Large	30.00
Bull's–Eye & Daisy, Wine, Amethyst Stained	38.00
Bull's–Eye & Fan, Cake Stand, 10 In.	23.50
Bull's–Eye & Fan, Toothpick	22.50
Bull's–Eye & Fleur–De–Lis, Goblet, Flint	100.00
Bull's–Eye & Spearhead, Wine	12.00 To 20.00
Bull's–Eye Band, Cake Stand, 9 1/2 In.	55.00
Bull's–Eye Band, Creamer	67.50
Bull's–Eye Band, Goblet	45.00 To 65.00
Bull's–Eye Variant, Wine	12.00
Bull's–Eye With Diamond Point, Compote, Flint, 8 1/2 In.	150.00
Bull's–Eye With Diamond Point, Goblet	35.00
Bull's–Eye With Diamond, Goblet	27.00
Bull's–Eye, Butter, Cover, Gold Trim	150.00
Bull's–Eye, Goblet	110.00
Bull's–Eye, Goblet, Knob Stem	70.00
Bullet Emblem, Sugar, Cover	275.00
Bunker Hill, Bread Plate	60.00 To 95.00

BUTTERFLY & FAN, see Grace

Butterfly Handles, Celery Vase	45.00
Butterfly With Spray, Sugar, Cover	62.50
Butterfly, Butter, Handle, Finial Cover, Frosted Band	125.00
Butterfly, Jam Jar, Frosted Band	45.00
Button Arches, Creamer	30.00
Button Arches, Creamer, Sandusky, Ohio	44.00
Button Arches, Mug, Child's, Cranberry Top, Pine Island	22.00
Button Arches, Mug, Cranberry Top, 1908	22.00
Button Arches, Spooner, Ruby Stained, Clear Band	62.50
Button Arches, Sugar, Cover, Ruby Stained	85.00
Button Arches, Tumbler, Frosted Band, Ruby Stained	45.00
Button Arches, Tumbler, Ruby Stained	37.50 To 42.50
Button Band, Compote, Cover, 13 In.	165.00
Button Panel, Carafe, Gilded	38.00
Button Panel, Punch Set, Bowl, Stand, 8 Cups	195.00
Button Panel, Salt & Pepper, Gilded	38.00
Buttressed Loop, Sugar & Creamer, Yellow	65.00
Buzz Saw, Punch Set, Child's, 8 Piece	60.00
Buzz Star, Butter, Cover, Child's	25.00
Buzz Star, Punch Set, Child's, 6 Piece	60.00
Buzz Star, Spooner	20.00
Buzz Star, Toothpick	22.50
Cabbage Leaf, Compote, High Standard, Frosted	250.00
Cabbage Leaf, Creamer, Frosted	175.00
Cabbage Leaf, Sugar, Rabbit Heads On Lid, Frosted, Clear Foot	200.00
Cabbage Rose, Cake Salver	45.00
Cabbage Rose, Cake Stand, 9 In.	45.00
Cabbage Rose, Compote, Cover, Strawberry Finial	80.00
Cabbage Rose, Sauce, Flat, 4 In.	15.00
Cabbage Rose, Spooner	35.00
Cabbage Rose, Tumbler	55.00
Cable, Goblet, Flint	70.00
Cable, Spooner, Flint	32.00
Cactus, Cruet, Chocolate	165.00

CALIFORNIA, see Beaded Grape
CAMEO, see Profile & Sprig

Canadian, Butter, Cover	65.00
Canadian, Compote, Cover, 8 In.	110.00
Canadian, Pitcher, Water	110.00
Canadian, Plate, 10 In.	38.00 To 40.00
Canadian, Plate, 6 In.	32.00
Canadian, Plate, Handles, 10 In.	65.00
Canadian, Wine	38.00 To 42.50
Canary, Cake Stand, Flint, 10 1/4 In.	65.00

Pressed glass,
Bull's–Eye with
Diamond Point

Pressed glass,
Button Arches

Pressed glass,
Cabbage Rose

Pressed glass, Cable

Pressed glass, Cathedral   *Pressed glass, Celtic*   *Pressed glass, Chain & Shield*

The pressed glass pattern sometimes called Candlewick is properly named Banded Raindrop. There is also a pattern called *Candlewick* which has been made by Imperial Glass Corporation since 1936. It is listed in this book under Imperial, Candlewick.

CANDY RIBBON, see Ribbon Candy
Cane & Rosette, Celery 35.00
Cane, Creamer 25.00
Cane, Pitcher, Amber 60.00
Cane, Pitcher, Water, Amber 85.00
Cane, Pitcher, Water, Blue 58.00
Cane, Spooner, Amber 42.00
Cantilever Band, Goblet 22.00
Cape Cod, Goblet 35.00
Cape Cod, Plate, Handles, 10 In. 45.00
Capitol Building, Goblet 35.00
CARDINAL, see Cardinal Bird
Cardinal Bird, Creamer 30.00
Cardinal Bird, Goblet 32.50
Cardinal Bird, Spooner 35.00
Cardinal Bird, Sugar, Cover 40.00
CARMEN, see Paneled Diamond & Finecut
Carolina, Compote, Cover, Crimped Edge, 13 1/2 In. 125.00
Cathedral, Bowl, 6 In. 14.50
Cathedral, Goblet, Amber .... 36.50 To 37.50
Cathedral, Spooner 32.00
Cathedral, Sugar, Cover, Amethyst 75.00
Cathedral, Wine 18.50
Cathedral, Wine, Amber .... 27.50 To 37.50
Celtic Cross, Compote, Square, 11 1/2 In. 70.00
Celtic Cross, Creamer, Etched 35.00
Celtic Cross, Spooner, Etched 35.00
CENTENNIAL, see also Liberty Bell; Washington Centennial
Centennial, Goblet .... 40.00 To 45.00
CERES, see Profile & Sprig
Chain & Shield, Goblet 18.00
CHAIN WITH DIAMONDS, see Washington Centennial
Chain With Star, Compote, Cover 50.00
Chain With Star, Creamer 25.00
Chain With Star, Goblet 25.00
Chain With Star, Pitcher, Water 55.00

Pressed glass, Classic

Pressed glass,
Columbian Coin

Pressed glass,
Deer & Dog

◆◆

Never store pictures or books in damp cellars or basements. Try to
keep the humidity below 70 degrees, preferably around 50 degrees.
Never frame pictures directly against glass. Use a mat. Keep prints
away from strong direct light.

◆◆

Chain With Star, Spooner	22.00
Chain With Star, Sugar	20.00
Chain With Star, Sugar, Open	27.00
Chain With Star, Wine	28.00
Chain, Spooner	20.00
Chain, Sugar, Cover	40.00
Champion, Sugar, Cover, Gold Trim	55.00
Champion, Toothpick	18.00
Chandelier, Compote, 7 In.	55.00
Chastity, Spooner	24.00
Checkerboard, Tankard, Water	35.00
Chrysanthemum, Butter, Cover, Swirl, Blue Opalescent	125.00
Chrysanthemum, Celery, Base Swirl, Blue Opalescent	80.00
CHURCH WINDOWS, see Tulip Petals	
Circle & Swag, Bowl, 10 In.	25.00
Circled Scroll, Cruet, Clear Stopper, Blue Opalescent	175.00
Classic, Butter, Cover, Log Feet	260.00
Classic, Celery	110.00 To 165.00
Classic, Compote, Log Feet, 8 In.	128.00
Classic, Creamer, Log Feet	130.00 To 175.00
Classic, Pitcher, Water, Log Feet	350.00
Classic, Spooner, Log Feet	85.00 To 125.00
Classic, Sugar, Cover, Log Feet	225.00
Clear Block, Creamer	18.00
Coachman's Cape, Wine	22.50
Coin & Dewdrop, Goblet	11.00
COIN SPOT, see also U.S. Coin Spot Category	
Colonial, Spooner	60.00
Colorado, Bowl, Green, Footed, Gold Medallion, 9 In.	40.00
Colorado, Bowl, Green, Gold Trim, 9 In.	35.00
Colorado, Butter, Cover, Blue, Gold Trim	245.00
Colorado, Candy Dish, Green, Handle	32.00
Colorado, Compote, Green, 6 1/2 In.	22.00
Colorado, Creamer, Crystal	35.00
Colorado, Creamer, Green, Gold Trim, Large	45.00
Colorado, Creamer, Green, Gold Trim, Souvenir, Individual	20.00
Colorado, Mug, Souvenir, Harrisville, N. Y., Ruby Stained	16.00

Colorado, Sugar, Cover, Green, Gold Trim 85.00
Colorado, Table Set, Green, Gold Trim, 4 Piece .... 305.00 To 325.00
Colorado, Toothpick, Blue 60.00
Colorado, Toothpick, Blue, Gold Trim 40.00
Colorado, Toothpick, Green 27.50
Colorado, Toothpick, Green, Gold Trim 30.00
Colorado, Tumbler, Green, Gold Trim 32.50
Colorado, Violet Bowl, Blue, Gold Trim ....85.00 To 140.00
Columbia, Pitcher, Water, Vaseline Opalescent 200.00
Columbian Coin, Celery Vase, Frosted 110.00
Columbian Coin, Cruet, Stopper, Frosted 125.00
Columbian Coin, Goblet, Frosted 145.00
Columbian Coin, Sugar, Cover 85.00
Columbian Exposition, Goblet 23.00
 COMPACT, see Snail
Constitution, Bread Plate 60.00
Cord & Tassel, Goblet .... 35.00 To 45.00
Cord & Tassel, Spooner .... 35.00 To 40.00
Cord & Tassel, Wine 40.00
Cord Drapery, Cake Stand, Green, 10 In. 225.00
Cord Drapery, Creamer, Blue 85.00
Cord Drapery, Pitcher, Water 65.00
Cord Drapery, Pitcher, Water, Green 195.00
Cordova, Syrup 45.00
Cordova, Toothpick, Green 45.00
Cornell, Creamer, Gold Trim 18.00
Cornell, Syrup 37.50
Cornell, Toothpick, Green 45.00
Cornucopia, Celery 45.00
Cornucopia, Goblet 22.50
Cornucopia, Pitcher, Water 45.00
Cornucopia, Sugar, Cover 45.00
Corona, Toothpick 49.00
 COSMOS, see Cosmos Category
Cottage, Bowl, 7 x 9 In. 24.50
Cottage, Cake Stand, 10 In. 37.50
Cottage, Creamer 28.00
Cottage, Goblet 18.50
Cottage, Goblet, Amber .... 40.00 To 45.00
Cottage, Goblet, Blue 60.00
Cottage, Plate, 10 In. 42.50
 CRANE, see Stork
Crescent & Fan, Spooner 15.00
Croesus, Berry Bowl, Green, Master 100.00
Croesus, Berry Saucer, Green, Gold Trim 45.00
Croesus, Butter, Cover, Amethyst, Gold Trim 185.00
Croesus, Butter, Cover, Green 165.00
Croesus, Butter, Cover, Green, Gold Trim 170.00
Croesus, Celery Vase 260.00
Croesus, Creamer, Green, 4 In. 150.00
Croesus, Cruet .... 100.00 To 120.00
Croesus, Cruet, Amethyst 70.00
Croesus, Cruet, Green, Gold Trim 245.00
Croesus, Pitcher, Water, Green 175.00
Croesus, Relish 50.00
Croesus, Sugar, Cover 75.00
Croesus, Sugar, Cover, Amethyst 150.00
Croesus, Sugar, Cover, Amethyst, Gold Trim 160.00
Croesus, Sugar, Cover, Green, Gold Trim .... 150.00 To 225.00
Croesus, Table Set, Amethyst, 4 Piece 325.00
Croesus, Table Set, Amethyst, Gold Trim, 4 Piece .... 600.00 To 625.00
Croesus, Toothpick, Green, Gold Trim 50.00
Croesus, Tumbler, Green, Gold Trim .... 50.00 To 55.00

◆◆

Date Mickey Mouse from his appearance. He has changed in the 60 years since his introduction in "Steamboat Willie." Originally, he didn't have pupils in his eyes. His legs were like pipe cleaners, now they have shape. He had a neck and white inside his ears in his middle years, but none when young or old. His nose has gotten shorter and more tilted.

◆◆

Croesus, Tumbler, Water, Gold Trim, 4 In.	70.00
Croesus, Water Set, Amethyst, 6 Piece	300.00
Croesus, Water Set, Green, 6 Piece	450.00
Croesus, Water Set, Green, Gold Trim, 7 Piece	545.00
Crossbar, Goblet, Flint	25.00
Crossed Ovals, Creamer	20.00
Crowfoot, Compote, Open	30.00
Crowfoot, Creamer	45.00
Crowfoot, Spooner	15.00 To 30.00
CROWN JEWELS, see Chandelier; Queen's Necklace	
Crystal Wedding, Celery, Frosted	45.00
Crystal Wedding, Creamer	115.00
Crystal Wedding, Goblet, Fern Etched	85.00
Crystal Wedding, Spooner	100.00
Crystal Wedding, Sugar, Cover	135.00
Crystal Wedding, Sugar, Cover, Frosted	75.00
CUBE WITH FAN, see Pineapple & Fan	
Cube, Decanter	40.00
CUPID & PSYCHE, see Psyche & Cupid	
Cupid & Venus, Bowl, 9 1/2 In.	50.00
Cupid & Venus, Bread Plate, Amber	135.00
Cupid & Venus, Bread Plate, Vaseline	135.00
Cupid & Venus, Celery	40.00
Cupid & Venus, Pitcher	200.00
Cupid & Venus, Pitcher, Milk	55.00 To 90.00
Cupid & Venus, Sauce, Footed, 4 In.	9.00
Cupid & Venus, Table Set, 3 Piece	130.00
Currant, Butter, Cover	57.50
Currant, Cake Stand, 11 In.	57.50
Currant, Creamer	42.00
Currant, Eggcup, Footed	20.00
Currant, Spooner	25.00
Currier & Ives, Bowl, Oval, Amber, 10 In.	65.00
Currier & Ives, Goblet	14.00 To 35.00
Currier & Ives, Pitcher, Water	45.00 To 70.00
Currier & Ives, Pitcher, Water, Amber	90.00 To 105.00
Currier & Ives, Salt & Pepper	65.00
Currier & Ives, Syrup, Blue	132.50
Currier & Ives, Syrup, Dated Cover	175.00
Currier & Ives, Water Set, 5 Piece	200.00
Curtain, Cake Stand, 9 In.	47.50
Curtain, Salt & Pepper	77.50
Cut Log, Compote, Jelly	24.00
Cut Log, Creamer, 5 In.	30.00
Cut Log, Cruet	45.00 To 80.00
Cut Log, Goblet	48.00
Cut Log, Pitcher	90.00
Cut Log, Tumbler	35.00
Cut Log, Wine	25.00
Czarina, Pickle Castor	145.00

Czarina, Wine 17.50
DAISIES IN OVAL PANELS, see Bull's–Eye & Fan
Daisy & Button With Crossbar, Compote, Blue, Standard, 7 In. 85.00
Daisy & Button With Crossbar, Spooner 25.00
DAISY & BUTTON WITH OVAL PANELS, see Hartley
Daisy & Button With V–Ornament, Bowl, Blue, 8 In. 40.00
Daisy & Button With V–Ornament, Celery Vase, Amber 37.50
Daisy & Button With V–Ornament, Toothpick, Vaseline 15.00
DAISY & BUTTON, see also Paneled Daisy & Button
Daisy & Button, Berry Set, Sapphire Blue, 7 Piece 90.00
Daisy & Button, Canoe, Amber, 12 In. 45.00
Daisy & Button, Carafe, Water, Stopper 45.00
Daisy & Button, Dish, Pickle, Boat–Shaped 39.50
Daisy & Button, Ice Tub, Amber, 6 3/4 x 4 1/2 In. 70.00
Daisy & Button, Sugar Shaker, Green, Silver Top, 5 3/4 In. 40.00
Daisy & Button, Tumbler 20.00
Daisy & Button, Tumbler, Pink Narcissus 20.00
Daisy & Scroll, Water Set, 7 Piece .... 65.00 To 80.00
Daisy In Square, Cruet 55.00
Daisy With Button Band, Spooner 30.00
Daisy With Button Crossbar, Creamer 38.00
Daisy With Button Crossbar, Pitcher, Water 85.00
Daisy With Button With Crossbar, Bread Plate, Rectangular 38.00
Daisy With Button With Crossbar, Pitcher, Amber 90.00
Dakota, Butter, Cover 40.00
Dakota, Butter, Cover, Ruffled Base 115.00
Dakota, Celery Vase 35.00
Dakota, Celery, Vase, Etched 47.50
Dakota, Compote, Jelly, Fern & Berry Etched 45.00
Dakota, Creamer, Etched 42.50
Dakota, Goblet, Fern & Berry, Etched .... 25.00 To 38.50
Dakota, Goblet, Ruby Stain, Etched 95.00
Dakota, Pitcher, Milk, Fern & Berry, Etched .... 80.00 To 90.00
Dakota, Pitcher, Water, Ruby Stained 145.00
Dakota, Tumbler, Ruby Stained 45.00
Dakota, Wine, Ruby Stain .... 45.00 To 55.00
Dalton, Punch Cup 40.00
Dart, Compote, Jelly 13.50
Dart, Pitcher, Water 30.00
Dart, Saltshaker 22.50
Deer & Dog, Butter, Cover, Etched 125.00
Deer & Dog, Celery, Vase 135.00
Deer & Dog, Celery, Vase, Etched 75.00
Deer & Dog, Compote, Cover, Frosted Dog Finial, 8 x 6 In. 182.00
Deer & Dog, Compote, Cover, Oval, 7 x 9 In. 135.00
Deer & Oak Tree, Pitcher, Water .... 195.00 To 200.00
Deer & Pine Tree, Bread Plate .... 42.00 To 50.00
Deer & Pine Tree, Bread Plate, Amber .... 95.00 To 100.00
Deer & Pine Tree, Butter, Cover 70.00
Deer & Pine Tree, Celery Vase 80.00
Deer & Pine Tree, Mug, Blue, Child's 55.00
Deer & Pine Tree, Pitcher, Water 145.00
Deer & Pine Tree, Waste Bowl 110.00
Deflating Balloon, Goblet 14.00
Delaware, Berry Set, Boat–Shaped Master, Green, 6 Piece 180.00
Delaware, Bowl, Green, Gold Trim, Octagonal, 9 In. .... 40.00 To 45.00
Delaware, Butter, Cover, Green 135.00
Delaware, Creamer 20.00
Delaware, Sugar & Creamer, Green 135.00
Delaware, Sugar & Creamer, Rose, Gold Trim 185.00
Delaware, Tankard, Green, Gold Trim 89.00
Delaware, Toothpick 45.00
Delaware, Toothpick, Green, Gold Trim .... 65.00 To 73.00

Delaware, Toothpick, Rose Flowers, Gold Trim 50.00
Delaware, Toothpick, Rose, Gold Trim 75.00
Delaware, Water Set, Green, Gold Trim, 7 Piece 600.00
Dewdrop In Points, Compote, Cover, 7 In. 47.50
Dewdrop In Points, Plate, 9 In. 20.00
    DEWEY, see also Spanish American
Dewey, Butter, Cover, Amber 72.50
Dewey, Creamer, Amber 135.00
Dewey, Cruet 64.00
Dewey, Pitcher, Water .... 75.00 To 80.00
Dewey, Pitcher, Water, Amber 125.00
Diamond Bridges, Sugar, Frosted, Cover 295.00
    DIAMOND HORSESHOE, see Aurora
Diamond In Diamond, Spooner 15.00
    DIAMOND MEDALLION, see Grand
Diamond Point Loop, Creamer, Blue 50.00
Diamond Point Loop, Spooner, Blue 50.00
Diamond Point, Champagne, Flint 125.00
Diamond Point, Compote, 8 1/2 In. 50.00
Diamond Point, Compote, Flint, 8 1/2 In. 40.00
Diamond Point, Goblet 60.00
Diamond Point, Jam Jar, Scalloped, Cover 28.00
Diamond Point, Pitcher, Flint, 9 1/8 In. 325.00
Diamond Point, Tumbler, Flint 110.00
    DIAMOND PRISMS, see also Albany
Diamond Quilted, Berry Bowl, Amethyst, 8 In. 48.00
Diamond Quilted, Goblet, Vaseline 35.00
Diamond Quilted, Tumbler, Amber 28.00
Diamond Spearhead, Bowl, Vaseline Opalescent, 9 1/2 In. 50.00
Diamond Spearhead, Compote, Jelly, Vaseline Opalescent 75.00
Diamond Spearhead, Goblet, Vaseline Opalescent 125.00
Diamond Spearhead, Pitcher, Cobalt Blue Opalescent, 7 In. 235.00
Diamond Sunburst, Compote, Cover, 7 In. 45.00
Diamond Sunburst, Spooner 15.00
Diamond Thumbprint, Bottle, Bar 225.00
Diamond Thumbprint, Butter, Cover 200.00
Diamond Thumbprint, Candy Jar, Cover, Flint, 8 7/8 In. 90.00
Diamond Thumbprint, Champagne 350.00
Diamond Thumbprint, Goblet, Flint 450.00
Diamond Thumbprint, Pitcher, Water 500.00
Diamond Thumbprint, Whiskey 145.00
Diamond Thumbprint, Whiskey, Handle 300.00
Diamond Thumbprint, Wine 235.00
Dice & Block, Cruet 55.00
Dickinson, Spooner, Flint 45.00
Divided Hearts, Celery, Pedestal 55.00
Dolphin, Compote, Frosted, 6 In. 67.50

Pressed glass,   *Pressed glass,*   *Pressed glass,*   *Pressed glass,*
Diamond Point   *Diamond Thumbprint*   *Double Ribbon*   *Egg in Sand*

Dolphin, Compote, Frosted, 8 In.	55.00
Dolphin, Toothpick, Amber	40.00
DORIC, see Feather	
Dotted Loop, Goblet	14.00
Double Arch, Goblet	25.00
Double Circle, Salt & Pepper, Blue	100.00
DOUBLE DAISY, see Rosette Band	
Double Leaf & Dart, Goblet	11.00
DOUBLE LOOP, see Ribbon Candy	
Double Ribbon, Bread Plate, Frosted	45.00
Double Ribbon, Butter, Cover, Frosted	65.00
Double Ribbon, Compote, Open, Low, 7 x 5 In.	35.00
Double Ribbon, Creamer	45.00
Double Ribbon, Spooner, Frosted	35.00
DOUBLE VINE, see Bellflower Double Vine	
Doyle's 500, Creamer, Child's, Amber	55.00
Doyle's 500, Spooner, Child's, Amber	65.00
Doyle's 500, Tray, Child's, Blue	35.00
Dragon, Sugar	55.00
Drapery, Plate, 6 In.	22.50
Drapery, Table Set, Blue Opalescent, Gold Trim, 4 Piece	380.00
Drapery, Water Set, 7 Piece	325.00
Drum, Creamer, Child's	45.00
Drum, Spooner	45.00
Drum, Sugar, Cover, Cannon Finial	195.00
Duchess, Creamer, Green, Gold Trim	95.00
Duchess, Sauce, Green, Gold	55.00
EARL, see Spirea Band	
Egg In Sand, Bread Plate	25.00
Egg In Sand, Creamer	25.00
Egg In Sand, Pitcher, Water	32.50
Egg In Sand, Pitcher, Water, Amber	70.00
Egg In Sand, Relish, 5 x 9 In.	20.00
Egg In Sand, Spooner, Blue	35.00
Egg In Sand, Tumbler, Amber	33.00
Egyptian, Bread Plate, Cleopatra	42.50 To 55.00
Egyptian, Bread Plate, Salt Lake Temple	248.00
Egyptian, Celery	90.00
Egyptian, Creamer	37.50
Egyptian, Goblet	32.50 To 40.00
Egyptian, Pitcher, Water	175.00
Egyptian, Relish	15.00 To 20.00
Egyptian, Spooner	27.50
Egyptian, Table Set, 4 Piece	225.00
Eight–O–Eight, Plate, 5 1/4 In.	18.50
Eight–O–Eight, Wine	32.50
Elephant Toes, Tumbler	15.00
Elephant Toes, Water Set, Rose, Gold Trim, 7 Piece	295.00
Ellipse, Spooner, Flint, 5 3/8 In.	30.00
Elongated Honeycomb, Goblet	35.00
Emerald Green Herringbone, Butter, Cover	55.00
Emerald Green Herringbone, Goblet	18.00
Emerald Green Herringbone, Sugar, Cover	50.00
Empress, Bowl, Green, 8 In.	72.50
Empress, Butter, Cover, Etched	57.50
Empress, Celery Vase, Green	125.00
Empress, Punch Cup, Green Foot	35.00
Empress, Saltshaker, Green, Gold Trim	67.50
Empress, Spooner, Green, Gold Trim	62.50
Empress, Table Set, Green, Gold Trim, 4 Piece	700.00
Empress, Water Set, Green, Gold Trim, 7 Piece	750.00
Esther, Berry Set, Green, 7 Piece	290.00
Esther, Butter, Cover, Green	145.00

Esther, Compote, Cover, 8 In. 95.00
Esther, Compote, Jelly, Green 45.00
Esther, Cracker Jar, Amber, Cover 225.00
Esther, Creamer, Green 115.00
Esther, Goblet, Ruby Stained 55.00
Esther, Sauce 23.00
Esther, Spooner 32.50
Esther, Sugar, Cover, Green, Gold Trim 115.00
Esther, Toothpick, Green 65.00
Esther, Toothpick, Green, Gold Trim 55.00
Esther, Tumbler, Green, Gold Trim 50.00
    ETCHED DAKOTA, see Dakota
Eureka, Bread Plate 30.00
Eureka, Wine, Flint, 1860s 40.00
Everglades, Berry Set, Blue Opalescent, 6 Piece 180.00
Excelsior, Goblet 60.00
Eyewinker, Butter 75.00
Eyewinker, Saltshaker, Original Lid 65.00
Eyewinker, Syrup 100.00
    FAGOT, see Vera
Falcon Strawberry, Toothpick 8.00
Fan & Flute, Sauce, Footed, Ruby Stained, 4 In. 35.00
Fan & Flute, Tumbler, Ruby Stained 38.50
Fancy Arches, Table Set, 4 Piece 85.00
Fancy Cut, Tumbler, Child's 15.00
Fancy Loop, Tumbler, Green, Gold Trim 45.00
Fancy Loop, Wine, Gold Trim 55.00
Feather Duster, Spooner 20.00
Feather, Butter, Cover 42.50
Feather, Cake Stand, 11 In. .... 68.00 To 78.00
Feather, Cake Stand, 9 1/2 In. .... 27.50 To 48.00
Feather, Cake Stand, Green, 9 1/2 In. 150.00
Feather, Compote, Jelly 22.50
Feather, Cruet, Stopper, Green 250.00
Feather, Pitcher, Water 48.00
Feather, Pitcher, Water, 5 Goblets 300.00
Feather, Plate, 10 In. 40.00
Feather, Table Set, 4 Piece 160.00
Feather, Tumbler 35.00
Feather, Wine 45.00
    FESTOON & GRAPE, see Grape & Festoon
Festoon, Bowl, 8 In. 22.50
Fickle Block, Lamp, Finger 60.00
File, Creamer 20.00
Findlay 19, Goblet 38.00
Fine Cut & Block, Creamer, Amber 40.00
Fine Cut & Block, Eggcup .... 30.00 To 32.00

Pressed glass,   Pressed glass,   Pressed glass, Flattened   Pressed glass,
Excelsior   Fine Cut   Diamond & Sunburst   Frosted Eagle

Fine Cut & Block, Punch Bowl, 10 x 8 1/2 In.	125.00
Fine Cut & Block, Table Set, 4 Piece	345.00
Fine Cut & Block, Wine, Amber Blocks	45.00 To 48.00
Fine Cut & Block, Wine, Blue Blocks	50.00
FINE CUT & FEATHER, see Feather	
Fine Rib, Sugar, Cover, Flint	172.50
Fish Scale, Cake Stand, 8 1/2 In.	19.50
Fish Scale, Compote, Jelly	10.00
Fish Scale, Goblet	30.00
Fish Scale, Plate, 8 In.	45.00
Fish Scale, Sauce, Small	7.00
Flamingo Habitat, Compote, 5 In.	35.00
Flamingo Habitat, Compote, Cover, 8 In.	67.50
Flamingo Habitat, Goblet	22.50
Flamingo, Bowl Set, 3 Piece	75.00
Flat Diamond & Panel, Pitcher, Water, Flint	250.00
Flat Diamond & Panel, Wine, Flint	85.00
Flat Diamond, Creamer	15.00
Flattened Diamond & Sunburst, Punch Bowl, Child's	27.50
Fleur–De–Lis & Drape, Mustard, Cover	38.00
Fleur–De–Lis & Tassel, Goblet	23.00
Fleur–De–Lis, Mug, Child's, Ruby Stained	25.00
Fleur–De–Lis, Mug, Ruby Stained	36.00
Flora, Creamer, Blue	85.00
Floral Panel, Table Set, Gold Wash, 4 Piece	250.00
Florette, Spooner, Pink	50.00
Florida Palm, Compote	20.00
FLORIDA, see Emerald Green Herringbone; Sunken Primrose	
FLORODORA, see Bohemian	
Flower & Pleat, Celery Vase, Ruby Stained	125.00
Flower Band, Sugar, Cover, Love Birds, Frosted	145.00
FLOWER FLANGE, see Dewey	
Flower Medallion, Goblet	35.00
FLOWER PANELED CANE, see Cane & Rosette	
Flower Pot, Creamer	27.50
Flower Pot, Saltshaker	32.50
Flute, Eggcup, Flint	25.00
Fluted Scrolls, Table Set, Vaseline Opalescent, 4 Piece	385.00
FLYING ROBIN, see Hummingbird	
Flying Stork, Compote, Cover	140.00
Four Petal, Sugar, Cover, Flint	62.50
Four Row Honeycomb, Celery	25.00
FROSTED PATTERNS, see also under name of main pattern	
Frosted Artichoke, Bowl Set, 9 In., 9 Piece	325.00
Frosted Artichoke, Bowl, 9 In.	55.00 To 125.00
Frosted Artichoke, Butter	175.00
Frosted Artichoke, Nappy, Handle	60.00
Frosted Artichoke, Vase, Celery	160.00
FROSTED CRANE, see Frosted Stork	
Frosted Double Ribbon, Bread Plate	60.00
Frosted Eagle, Butter	225.00
FROSTED FLOWER BAND, see Flower Band, Frosted	

◆◆◆

To remove the musty odor from old books, try this. Leather covered books should be wiped with a mixture of equal parts alcohol and water. The pages of the books should be warmed. Stand the books on edge, open them and blow–dry them with a portable hair dryer on high heat.

◆◆◆

Frosted Fruits, Pitcher, Water 95.00
Frosted Leaf, Creamer 120.00
Frosted Leaf, Goblet, Flint 110.00
Frosted Leaf, Spooner, Flint 95.00
Frosted Leaf, Sugar 100.00
    FROSTED LION, see Lion, Frosted
Frosted Owls, Sugar, Cover, Etched 50.00
    FROSTED ROMAN KEY, see Roman Key, Frosted
Frosted Stork, Bowl, Iowa City, 7 In. 65.00
Fuchsia, Goblet 65.00
Gaelic, Goblet, Rose & Green, Gold Trim 32.50
Galloway, Butter, Cover 50.00
Galloway, Compote, 6 1/2 In. 35.00
Galloway, Goblet 85.00
Garden Fruits, Sugar & Creamer 95.00
Garfield Stars, Bread Plate, 6 In. 40.00
Garfield Stars, Bread Plate, We Mourn, Dated 75.00
Geneva, Pitcher, Water, Green, Gold Trim 80.00
Geneva, Spooner 32.00
Geneva, Spooner, Green, Gold Trim 95.00
George Peabody, Cup & Saucer 145.00
George Peabody, Saucer 47.50
Giant Prism, Goblet 85.00
Girl With Fan, Goblet .... 75.00 To 95.00
Gladstone, Saucer 42.50
Goat's Head, Sugar 57.50
Gonterman Swirl, Berry Set, Amber, Frosted, 7 Piece 195.00
    GOOD LUCK, see Horseshoe
Gothic Arch, Sugar, Cover, Flint, 5 1/2 In. 25.00
Gothic Arch, Sugar, Cover, Flint, 7 1/2 In. 65.00
Gothic Windows, Creamer 25.00
Gothic, Goblet, Flint 50.00
Grace, Creamer, Footed 100.00
Grace, Spooner 48.50
Grand, Cake Stand, 9 1/2 In. 25.00
Grand, Goblet 18.00
Grand, Wine 35.00
Grape & Festoon, Compote, High Stand, Cover 140.00
Grape & Festoon, Goblet 23.00
Grape Band, Goblet 30.00
Grape Band, Spooner 25.00
    GRAPE, see also Beaded Grape; Beaded Grape Medallion; Magnet &
    Grape; Paneled Grape
Grape, Punch Cup, Twig Handle 22.00
Grasshopper, Butter, Cover, Etched 70.00
Greek Key, Goblet, Buttermilk 45.00
Greek Key, Plate, 5 1/2 In. 18.50
Gridley, Pitcher, Water .... 105.00 To 135.00
Hairpin With Thumbprint, Goblet 48.00
Hairpin, Cup Plate 40.00
Hairpin, Eggcup 25.00
Halley's Comet, Pitcher, Water 85.00
Halley's Comet, Wine 35.00
Hamilton, Compote, Flint, 8 In. 47.50
Hand, Celery 65.00
Hand, Compote, Open, 9 x 7 1/2 In. 35.00
Hand, Jam Jar 45.00
Hand, Tumbler 55.00
Harp, Cake Stand, Blue 22.00
Hartley, Goblet, Blue 35.00
Harvard Yard, Saltshaker 18.00
Hawaiian Pineapple, Goblet .... 85.00 To 125.00
Heart & Thumbprint, Creamer 25.00

Pressed glass,
Grape & Festoon

Pressed glass,
Hairpin with Rayed Base

Pressed glass,
Hamilton

Pressed glass, Harp

Pressed glass, Holly

Pressed glass,
Horn of Plenty

Pressed glass,
Inverted Fern

Pressed glass,
Jeweled Heart

Heart Band, Mug, Columbus, Ohio, 1907	25.00 To 30.00
Heart Band, Sugar	25.00
Heart In Sand, Creamer	14.50
Heart Stem, Celery, Amber	175.00
Heart Stem, Compote, Cover, 7 In.	65.00 To 85.00
Heart With Thumbprint, Banana Boat	110.00 To 165.00
Heart With Thumbprint, Compote, Pedestal, 7 1/2 In.	145.00
Heart With Thumbprint, Goblet	48.00 To 65.00
Heart With Thumbprint, Ice Bucket	85.00
Heart With Thumbprint, Plate, 12 In.	65.00
Heart With Thumbprint, Plate, 6 In.	22.50
Heart With Thumbprint, Rose Bowl, 3 1/2 In.	55.00
Heart With Thumbprint, Syrup, Pewter Lid	100.00 To 120.00
Heart With Thumbprint, Tray, 8 x 4 1/2 In.	28.50
Heart With Thumbprint, Tumbler, Water	75.00
Heavy Drape, Butter, Cover, Clear, Cranberry Flashed	55.00
Heavy Jewel, Tray, 14 x 8 In.	20.00
Heron & Peacock, Mug	110.00
Heron, Pitcher, Water	195.00
Heron, Spooner, Blue	35.00
Heron, Sugar, Cover	85.00
Herringbone, Plate, Up–Turned Corners, Green, 9 In.	32.50
Herringbone, Tumbler, Green	22.50
Herringbone, Water Set, Green, 7 Piece	185.00
Hexagon Block, Pitcher, Water	75.00
Hexagon Block, Wine, Amber Stained, Pair	85.00
Hickman, Creamer	12.00
HOBNAIL & BARS, see Barred Hobnail	
Hobnail With Fan, Goblet	11.00
Holly Leaves, Goblet	45.00
Holly, Compote, Cover, 9 In.	175.00

Homestead, Banana Boat, Rolled Edge	20.00
Homestead, Banana Bowl, Rolled Rim	30.00
Homestead, Creamer, Etched	21.00
Homestead, Spooner, Etched	21.00
Honeycomb, Compote, Flint, 8 In.	50.00
Honeycomb, Compote, Short Pedestal, Flint, 9 1/2 In.	75.00
Honeycomb, Jar, Cover, Cut & Etched, 1850s	57.00
Honeycomb, Lamp, Kerosene, 8 In.	80.00
Honeycomb, Mustard, Cover, Spoon, Flint, 4 3/16 In.	55.00
Honeycomb, Pitcher, Water, Blue	125.00
Honeycomb, Salt & Pepper	75.00
Honeycomb, Spooner	23.00
Honeycomb, Syrup, Pewter Lid, Strap Handle, Flint	195.00
Honeycomb, Vase, Flint, 9 7/8 In.	45.00
Horizontal Threads, Spooner	25.00
Horizontal Threads, Toothpick	20.00
Horn of Plenty, Compote, Flint, 7 In.	110.00
Horn of Plenty, Compote, Scalloped, 7 3/8 In.	100.00
Horn of Plenty, Lamp, Oil, 1860, 10 1/4 In.	185.00
Horn of Plenty, Pitcher, Water, Flint	200.00
Horn of Plenty, Spill, Gold Trim, Flint	125.00
Horn of Plenty, Sugar & Creamer, Cover, Flint	325.00
Horn of Plenty, Sugar & Creamer, Flint	150.00
Horn of Plenty, Sugar, Cover, Flint	125.00
Horsehead Medallion, Celery	35.00
Horseshoe Stem, Cake Stand, 8 In.	65.00
Horseshoe, Bread Plate	50.00
Horseshoe, Cake Stand, 8 In.	65.00
Horseshoe, Celery Vase	67.50
Horseshoe, Cheese Dish	275.00
Horseshoe, Compote, 8 x 11 In.	150.00
Horseshoe, Compote, Cover	60.00
Horseshoe, Creamer	30.00 To 47.50
Horseshoe, Goblet, Knob Stem	25.00
Horseshoe, Goblet, Plain Stem	20.00
Horseshoe, Pitcher, Milk	55.00
Horseshoe, Pitcher, Water	95.00 To 110.00
Horseshoe, Spooner	20.00
Horseshoe, Sugar	30.00
Huber, Spooner, Flint, 5 1/4 In.	28.50
HUCKLE, see Feather Duster	
Hummingbird, Celery	50.00
Hummingbird, Pitcher	85.00
Hummingbird, Tumbler, Amber	68.00
Hummingbird, Wine	55.00
Hundred–Leaved Rose, Pitcher, Water	30.00
Ibex, Goblet, Flint	65.00
Icicle With Loops, Goblet	48.00
IDA, see Sheraton	
Idyll, Pitcher, Water, Green Opalescent, Gold Trim	150.00
Illinois, Doughnut Stand, Square, 4 1/4 x 7 1/2 In.	55.00
Illinois, Tankard, Silver Lip	130.00
Illinois, Toothpick	25.00 To 37.50
INDIANA SWIRL, see Feather	
Intaglio, Creamer, Blue Opalescent	35.00
Intaglio, Spooner, Blue Opalescent	52.00
Intaglio, Spooner, Green Opalescent, Gold Trim	60.00
Intaglio, Sugar & Creamer, Blue Opalescent	135.00
Inverted Fan & Feather, Tumbler, Green	22.00
Inverted Fern, Goblet	35.00 To 37.50
Inverted Fern, Honey, Individual, 3 1/2 In.	25.00
Inverted Fern, Spooner	50.00
Inverted Fern, Sugar, Cover	47.50

Inverted Strawberry, Tumbler, Blue, Gold Trim, 4 In. 40.00
Inverted Thistle, Spooner, Green Satin, Bird 35.00
Inverted Thumbprint & Star, Goblet, Vaseline 32.50
Inverted Thumbprint, Creamer, Blue, Reeded Handle, 5 In. 32.00
Inverted Thumbprint, Pitcher, Water, Blue, Clear Handle 195.00
Ionia, Bread Plate 25.00
Ionia, Goblet 11.00
Iris With Meander, Pitcher, Water, Amethyst 80.00
Iris With Meander, Plate, Blue Opalescent, 7 In. 40.00
Jacob's Ladder, Bowl, Serving, Oval, 3 Piece 55.00
Jacob's Ladder, Cruet, Maltese Cross Stopper ....45.00 To 125.00
Jacob's Ladder, Salt, Footed 22.50
Jefferson's Optic, Sugar, Cover, Hand Painted, Amethyst 75.00
Jefferson's Optic, Toothpick 21.00
Jefferson's Optic, Toothpick, Green .... 32.50 To 47.50
Jewel & Dewdrop, Bread Plate 55.00
Jewel & Dewdrop, Compote, Jelly 32.50
Jewel & Dewdrop, Doughnut Stand 65.00
Jewel & Dewdrop, Pitcher, Water 60.00
Jewel & Dewdrop, Toothpick 45.00
Jewel & Dewdrop, Tumbler 50.00
    JEWEL & FESTOON, see Loop & Jewel
Jewel Band, Creamer 32.50
Jeweled Heart, Creamer, Blue 40.00
Jeweled Heart, Tumbler, Blue 75.00
    JEWELED MOON & STAR, see Moon & Star Variant; Moon & Star
Jeweled Pendants, Creamer 15.00
    JOB'S TEARS, see Art
    JUBILEE, see Hickman
Jumbo, Castor Base 45.00
Jumbo, Castor Set 185.00
Jumbo, Spoon Rack ....275.00 To 425.00
    KAMONI, see Pennsylvania
    KANSAS, see Jewel & Dewdrop
King's 500, Cup, Blue 30.00
King's 500, Sugar, Cover, Blue 95.00
    KING'S CROWN, see also Ruby Thumbprint
King's Crown, Compote 35.00
King's Crown, Compote, High Standard, 7 In. 75.00
King's Crown, Cordial 20.00
King's Crown, Goblet, Souvenir, Cobalt Blue 110.00

Pressed glass, Jumbo

Pressed glass,
Leaf & Dart

Pressed glass, Liberty Bell

King's Crown, Saltshaker 22.00
King's Crown, Toothpick, Ruby Stained 27.00
   KLONDIKE, see Amberette
Knights of Labor, Mug 50.00
Kokomo, Syrup, Spring Lid 35.00
   LACY SPIRAL, see Colossus
Ladder With Diamond, Toothpick 30.00
Late Block, Creamer 15.00
Late Block, Tumbler 25.00
Late Block, Tumbler, Ruby Stained 42.50
   LATE THISTLE, see Inverted Thistle
   LATTICE & OVAL PANELS, see Flat Diamond & Panel
Leaf & Dart, Goblet .... 28.50 To 39.00
Leaf & Dart, Tumbler, Footed 20.00
Leaf & Flower, Celery Vase, Amber Stained, Frosted 65.00
Leaf & Star, Wind 18.00
Leaf & Umbrella, Sauce, Mauve, 4 In. 65.00
Leaf Medallion, Creamer, Cobalt Blue 50.00
Leaf Mold, Salt & Pepper, Pink & White Spatter, Mica 150.00
Lean Queen, Toothpick, Monticello, Minn. 26.50
Liberty Bell, Bread Plate, 10 In. .... 40.00 To 60.00
Liberty Bell, Butter, Cover 120.00
Liberty Bell, Creamer, Reeded Handle 125.00
Liberty Bell, Lamp, Finger, Dated Collar, 1876 Centennial 250.00
Liberty Bell, Spooner .... 40.00 To 65.00
Liberty Bell, Sugar, Cover .... 85.00 To 110.00
Liberty Bell, Sugar, Creamer & Spooner 545.00
Lily-of-The-Valley, Bowl, Oval, 8 In. 32.50
Lily-of-The-Valley, Celery 40.00
Lily-of-The-Valley, Creamer, Footed 35.00
Lincoln Drape, Compote, Flint, 6 In. 30.00
Lincoln Drape, Compote, Flint, 7 1/2 In. 87.50
Lined Smocking, Goblet 48.00
Lion In The Jungle, Goblet, Etched 75.00
Lion With Cable, Sugar, Cover 40.00
   LION'S LEG, see Alaska
Lion, Bread Plate, Frosted .... 45.00 To 80.00
Lion, Celery Vase, Frosted 85.00
Lion, Compote, Cover, Frosted, Lion Head Finial, 8 In. 115.00
Lion, Compote, Frosted, 7 In. 90.00
Lion, Compote, Jelly, Open, Frosted 43.00
Lion, Creamer, Child's .... 40.00 To 48.00
Lion, Creamer, Child's, Frosted 80.00
Lion, Creamer, Frosted 40.00
Lion, Eggcup .... 75.00 To 95.00
Lion, Eggcup, Frosted .... 95.00 To 145.00
Lion, Jam Jar 75.00

*Pressed glass,
Lily-of-the-Valley*

*Pressed glass,
Lincoln Drape*

*Pressed glass,
Mitered Diamond*

*Pressed glass,
Moon & Star*

◆◆◆

To remove trade cards from album pages, first try soaking the pages in a mixture of 2 gallons of warm water and one cup of white vinegar. If this fails, put the album in the freezer overnight, then drop into the vinegar water in the morning. If the glue is made of flour paste, the cards come off, or can be loosened in 20 minutes. Rinse the cards in clear warm water and rub off the remains of glue with a soft wet towel. Sounds like a good system, but check the album to be sure there are no inked names or other wanted information that might wash off.

◆◆◆

Lion, Jam Jar, Frosted	135.00
Lion, Jam Jar, Rampant Lion Finial	125.00
Lion, Sauce, Frosted	75.00
Lion, Spooner, Frosted	45.00
Lion, Table Set, Child's, 4 Piece	375.00
LIPPMAN, see Flat Diamond	
Little River, Jam Jar	67.50
Log Cabin, Butter, Cover	225.00 To 295.00
Log Cabin, Compote, Cover, 10 1/2 In.	350.00
Log Cabin, Compote, Cover, 4 3/4 In.	210.00
Log Cabin, Sugar & Creamer, Cover	225.00
Loop & Block, Creamer, Ruby Stained	55.00
Loop & Dart With Round Ornaments, Butter, Cover	77.50
Loop & Dart With Round Ornaments, Celery, Flint	47.50
Loop & Dart With Round Ornaments, Compote, Cover, 6 1/4 In.	87.50
Loop & Dart With Round Ornaments, Compote, Cover, 8 In.	77.50
Loop & Dart With Round Ornaments, Eggcup	22.50
Loop & Dart With Round Ornaments, Goblet	32.50
Loop & Dart, Eggcup	24.50
Loop & Dart, Goblet	39.00
Loop & Dart, Spooner	28.00
Loop & Jewel, Butter, Cover	38.00
Loop & Petal, Candlestick, Yellow, 6 7/8 In.	225.00
Loop & Petal, Sugar, Cover, Flint, 8 1/4 In.	75.00
Loop & Pillar, Bottle, Bar	100.00
Loop With Dewdrop, Goblet	25.00
LOOP WITH STIPPLED PANELS, see Texas	
LOOP, see also Seneca Loop	
Loop, Compote, Cover, Flint, 10 x 7 1/4 In.	45.00
Loop, Compote, Flint, 8 x 8 In.	125.00
Loop, Goblet	32.00
Loop, Lamp, Oil, Double Burner, Amethyst, 11 3/4 In.	1320.00

◆◆◆

Be careful about displaying paperweights or other heavy objects on glass shelves. With each new purchase you add more weight to the display shelf, until one day there is a crash and the shelf and weights are damaged. It may seem safe for years, but a slight jar from a slamming door may be enough to cause the glass to crack. We also add a word of warning about wall hung shelves on metal strips. These develop "creep" and after several years may pull loose at the top and eventually collapse.

◆◆◆

LOOPS & DROPS, see New Jersey
Lorraine, Tumbler 25.00
Lotus, Bread Plate 45.00
Lotus, Salt Dip, Pink 12.00
Louis XV, Saucer, Green, Gold Trim 37.50
Lozenges, Sugar, Plain Rim 20.00
Lucere, Table Set, 4 Piece 95.00
Lustre Rose, Tumbler, Green, Gold Trim, 6 Piece 120.00
Madison, Goblet 57.00
Magnet & Grape, Goblet, Flint 75.00
MAIDEN BLUSH, see Banded Portland
Maple Leaf, Bowl, Cover, Footed, Yellow 85.00
Maple Leaf, Bowl, Footed, Yellow 52.00
Maple Leaf, Compote, Cover, Log Feet, Yellow, 7 In. 95.00
Maple Leaf, Table Set, Blue, Gold Trim, 3 Piece 215.00
Marquisette, Goblet 28.00
Marsh Fern, Cake Stand, Pink 40.00
Maryland, Tumbler 30.00
Mascotte, Compote, Cover, Low Standard, 7 In. 22.50
Mascotte, Creamer, Etched 40.00
Mascotte, Goblet, Etched 42.50
Mascotte, Sugar, Cover, Etched 45.00
Masonic, Creamer 32.50
Massachusetts, Bowl, Scalloped Squared Top, 6 In. 17.50
Massachusetts, Cup & Saucer, State Seal, Mayflower, Violets 25.00
Massachusetts, Goblet 50.00
Massachusetts, Jug, Rum, 5 In. 84.00
Massachusetts, Toothpick 40.00
Massachusetts, Toothpick, Applied Filigree 58.00
Massachusetts, Tumbler 25.00
Massachusetts, Wine 45.00
McKinley, Bread Plate, It Is God's Way 20.00
McKinley, Cup, Cover 65.00
Medallion Sunburst, Cruet, Blown 45.00
Medallion, Cake Plate, Pedestal, 10 In. 55.00
Medallion, Pitcher, Water, Amber 75.00
Medallion, Pitcher, Water, Blue 60.00
Medallion, Wine 12.00
Menagerie, Mustard, Bear 150.00
Menagerie, Spooner, Amber 60.00
Michigan, Tumbler 35.00
Minerva, Bread Plate, Mars .... 42.00 To 60.00
Minerva, Goblet 90.00
Minerva, Pitcher, Water 80.00
Minerva, Platter, Oval 80.00
Minerva, Spooner 40.00
Minnesota, Carafe, Water 45.00
Minnesota, Table Set, Gold Trim, 4 Piece 275.00
Minnesota, Toothpick 32.00
Mirror & Fan, Wine .... 12.00 To 20.00
Missouri, Bowl, Green, 9 In. 39.00
Missouri, Cake Stand, 10 In. 42.50
Missouri, Doughnut Stand 27.50
Missouri, Sugar, Cover 45.00
Mitered Bars, Goblet 20.00
MITERED DIAMOND POINTS, see Mitered Bars
Mitered Diamond, Pitcher, Water, Amber 55.00
Monkey, Sugar 90.00
Moon & Star, Celery .... 40.00 To 45.00
Moon & Star, Celery, Enameled 72.50
Moon & Star, Compote, 8 In. 32.50
Moon & Star, Creamer 47.50
Moon & Star, Lamp, Hand, Brass Collar, 2 7/8 In. 85.00

Pressed glass, New England Pineapple	Pressed glass, Open Rose	Pressed glass, Ostrich Looking at the Moon	Pressed glass, Paneled Diamond & Flowers

Moon & Star, Pitcher, Tooled Lip, Flint, 6 1/2 In.	450.00
Moon & Star, Relish	17.00
MOON & STORK, see Ostrich Looking At The Moon	
Nail, Goblet, Etched	65.00
Nail, Wine	60.00
Nailhead, Celery Vase	75.00
Nailhead, Orange Bowl, Notched, 8 1/2 In.	225.00
Naturalistic Blackberry, Goblet	23.00
NAUTILUS, see Argonaut Shell	
Nestor, Butter, Cover, Blue, Gold Trim	125.00
Nestor, Toothpick, Amethyst	75.00
Netted Oak, Syrup	27.50
Nevada, Biscuit Jar	47.50
Nevada, Spooner, Gold Trim	27.50
Nevada, Sugar, Cover, Gold Trim	32.50
New England Centennial, Goblet	245.00
New England Centennial, Goblet, Amethyst, White Flowers	120.00
New England Pineapple, Creamer, Flint	77.50
New England Pineapple, Decanter, Flint, 10 In.	200.00
New England Pineapple, Eggcup, Flint	42.00
New England Pineapple, Goblet	85.00
New England Pineapple, Whiskey, Flint, 3 In.	225.00
New Hampshire, Cruet	40.00
New Jersey, Bowl, 9 In.	20.00
New Jersey, Goblet, Gold Washed	32.50
New Jersey, Pitcher, Water	47.50
New Jersey, Toothpick	15.00
Nicotiana, Goblet	28.00
Notched Oval, Celery Vase	32.50
Notched Oval, Pitcher, Water, Gold Trim	57.50
Nova Scotia Crown, Compote, Open, 7 1/2 In.	125.00
Nugget, Pitcher, Water, Deep Blue	250.00
Nursery Tales, Butter, Cover, Child's	58.00 To 65.00
Nursery Tales, Creamer, Child's	35.00 To 45.00
Nursery Tales, Cup, Child's	15.00
Nursery Tales, Cup, Child's, 6 Piece	125.00
Nursery Tales, Dish, Feeding, Divided, Matching Cup	22.50
Nursery Tales, Plate, Child's, Blue & White Enameled, 8 In.	35.00
Nursery Tales, Spooner, Child's	50.00
Nursery Tales, Table Set, Child's, 4 Piece	250.00
Nursery Tales, Tumbler, Child's	20.00
O'Hara's Diamond, Pitcher, Water	30.00
Oak Leaf Band, Celery	50.00
Oak Leaf, Compote, Cover, Acorn Finial, 7 1/2 In.	125.00
Oaken Bucket, Butter, Cover, Amber	40.00
Oaken Bucket, Creamer, Amethyst	70.00
Oaken Bucket, Pitcher	95.00

Oaken Bucket, Pitcher, Amber 55.00
Oaken Bucket, Pitcher, Amethyst 195.00
Ohio, Goblet, Etched 35.00
Ohio, Table Set, 4 Piece 175.00
OLD ABE, see Frosted Eagle
Old State House, Bread Plate, Blue, Round, 12 1/2 In. 225.00
Old Statehouse, Bread Plate, Round, 12 1/2 In. 65.00
One–Hundred–One, Bread Plate, 9 1/2 In. 62.50
One–Hundred–One, Bread Plate, Agricultural Center, 11 In. 45.00
One–Hundred–One, Butter, Cover 55.00
One–Hundred–One, Celery Dish 30.00
One–Hundred–One, Celery Vase 47.50
One–Hundred–One, Goblet, Amber 35.00
One–Hundred–One, Plate, 7 In. 22.50
One–Hundred–One, Relish 16.50
One–Hundred–One, Spooner 50.00
One–Hundred–One, Toothpick, Blue Opaque 70.00
One–Hundred–One, Toothpick, Green 85.00
One–Hundred–One, Water Set, 7 Piece 295.00
ONE–O–ONE, see One–Hundred–One
ONE–THOUSAND EYE, see Thousand Eye
Open Plaid, Spooner 9.50
Open Rose, Creamer 35.00
Open Rose, Eggcup 24.50
Open Rose, Sauce, Small 7.00
Orange Tree, Mug 45.00
OREGON, see also Beaded Loop; Skilton
Oregon, Butter, Cover .... 35.00 To 40.00
Oregon, Goblet .... 20.00 To 35.00
Oregon, Pitcher, Milk 30.00
Oregon, Pitcher, Water 45.00
Oregon, Toothpick 60.00
Orinda, Toothpick 35.00
ORION, see Cathedral
Ostrich Looking At The Moon, Goblet .... 50.00 To 82.50
Oval Star, Table Set, Child's, 4 Piece 110.00
Overall Lattice, Sugar, Cover 75.00
OWL, see Bull's–Eye with Diamond Points
Owl In Horseshoe, Goblet 90.00
Paddlewheel, Toothpick 25.00
Palm & Scroll, Wine, Green 32.00
Palm Beach, Table Set, Red, Green & Gold On Clear, 4 Piece 380.00
Palm Stub, Goblet 35.00
Palmette, Celery 55.00
Palmette, Cup Plate 45.00
Palmette, Relish 17.50
Palmette, Sauce, Small 7.00
Palmette, Sugar 22.50
Paneled 44, Berry Bowl, Footed, Platinum Stained 110.00
Paneled 44, Goblet, Rose Stained 65.00
Paneled 44, Pitcher, Platinum Stained, 1/2 Gal. 155.00
Paneled 44, Sauce, Platinum Stained .... 12.50 To 15.00
Paneled 44, Tumbler, Platinum Stained 40.00
Paneled Cherry, Toothpick 35.00
Paneled Daisy & Button, Bread Plate, Green 35.00
Paneled Daisy & Button, Spooner, Amber 35.00
Paneled Dewdrop, Celery Vase 35.00
Paneled Dewdrop, Jam Jar 80.00
Paneled Diamond & Finecut, Creamer 32.00
Paneled Diamond & Flowers, Goblet 50.00
Paneled Finecut, Saltshaker, Amber 37.50
Paneled Forget–Me–Not, Bread Plate, Handle, 11 In. 25.00
Paneled Forget–Me–Not, Celery 28.50

| Pressed glass,
Paneled Nightshade | Pressed glass,
Paneled Wheat | Pressed glass,
Parrot & Fan | Pressed glass,
Pennsylvania |

Paneled Forget–Me–Not, Goblet .... 35.00 To 45.00
Paneled Forget–Me–Not, Relish, 8 In. 45.00
Paneled Grape, Custard Cup 12.00
Paneled Heather, Goblet 27.50
Paneled Heather, Sugar, Cover, Serrated Rim 22.00
Paneled Julep, Goblet 18.00
Paneled Nightshade, Goblet 23.00
Paneled Ovals, Goblet 85.00
Paneled Palm, Creamer .... 17.00 To 20.00
Paneled Smocking, Pitcher, Water, Amber Stained, Gold Trim 65.00
Paneled Thistle, Cake Stand, 9 In. 30.00
Paneled Thistle, Compote, 6 1/2 x 8 In. 25.00
Paneled Thistle, Cruet 40.00
Paneled Thistle, Honey, Marked 60.00
Paneled Thistle, Spooner, Blue 35.00
Paneled Thumbprint, Butter, Cover, Green 85.00
Paneled Waffle, Vase, Wafer Joins Stem & Bowl, Flint, 9 In. 65.00
Paneled Wheat, Spooner 25.00
Paneled, Nightshade, Goblet 25.00
Pansy, Toothpick, Blue 45.00
Parachute, Pitcher 60.00
Parrot & Fan, Goblet .... 45.00 To 65.00
Pattee Cross, Pitcher, Gold Trim, Child's 48.00
Pattee Cross, Pitcher, Water, Child's 35.00
Pattee Cross, Tumbler 15.00
Pattee Cross, Vase, 8 In. 27.00
Pavonia, Butter, Cover, Maple Leaf Etched 95.00
Pavonia, Celery Vase, Etched 42.50
Pavonia, Compote, Cover, Etched, 7 In. 125.00
Pavonia, Goblet, Etched 25.00
Pavonia, Goblet, Maple Leaf Etched 42.50
Pavonia, Pitcher, Water 37.50
Pavonia, Pitcher, Water, Ruby Stain 145.00
Pavonia, Spooner, Footed 45.00
Pavonia, Sugar, Etched 45.00
Pavonia, Tankard, Water, Ruby Stained, Etched 150.00
Pavonia, Tumbler, Etched, Ruby Stained 45.00
Pavonia, Tumbler, Ruby Stained .... 37.50 To 48.50
Pavonia, Water Set, Ruby Stained, Etched, 6 Piece 135.00
Peacock Feathers, Bowl, 9 In. 55.00
Peacock Feathers, Bowl, Oval, 5 1/4 x 12 In. 12.50
Peacock Feathers, Butter, Cover 35.00
Peacock Feathers, Sugar, Cover 34.50
    PEACOCK'S EYE, see Peacock Feathers
    PEAR, see Bartlett Pear
Peerless, Sugar, Cover 50.00
    PENNSYLVANIA, see also Hand

Pennsylvania, Creamer, Child's .... 20.00 To 25.00
Pennsylvania, Cup, Gold Trim 18.50
Pennsylvania, Goblet 18.50
Pennsylvania, Spooner & Creamer, Child's, Green 145.00
Pennsylvania, Table Set, 4 Piece 195.00
Pennsylvania, Table Set, 4 Piece, Child's 175.00
Pennsylvania, Table Set, Gilt, Child's, 4 Piece 250.00
Pennsylvania, Table Set, Gold Trim, 4 Piece, Miniature 275.00
Pennsylvania, Toothpick, Green 38.00
Pennsylvania, Wine 10.00
Pennsylvania, Wine, Gold Trim 20.00
Persian, Goblet 23.00
Petalled Medallion, Sugar & Creamer 70.00
Petticoat, Compote, 6 In. 20.00
Petticoat, Table Set, Vaseline, Gold Trim, 4 Piece 365.00
Pheasant, Compote, Cover, Oval, Frosted 140.00
Philadelphia Centennial, Goblet .... 30.00 To 35.00
  PILLAR & BULL'S–EYE, see Thistle
Pillar, Goblet 85.00
Pillow Encircled, Sugar, Cover, Ruby Stained 125.00
Pillow Encircled, Tumbler, Ruby Stained, Etched 38.50
  PINAFORE, see Actress
Pineapple & Fan, Rose Bowl 28.00
Pioneer's Victoria, Celery, Ruby Stained 85.00
Pioneer's Victoria, Tumbler, Ruby Stained 42.50
Pioneer's Victoria, Tumbler, Ruby Stained, Etch 48.50
Pittsburg, Goblet 40.00
Pleat & Panel, Celery Vase 38.00
Pleat & Panel, Creamer 35.00
Pleat & Panel, Goblet .... 25.00 To 27.50
Pleat & Panel, Plate, 7 In. 18.00
Pleat & Panel, Sauce, Footed 12.50
Pleat Band, Bowl, 6 In. 20.00
Plume, Spooner 19.00
Pogo Stick, Bowl, 9 1/2 In. 25.00
Pogo Stick, Cup & Saucer 40.00
Poinsettia, Pitcher, Water, Blue Opalescent 165.00
Poinsettia, Sugar Shaker 255.00
Poinsettia, Tankard, Water, Blue Opalescent 185.00
Poinsettia, Water Set, Blue, 7 Piece 450.00
Pointed Cube, Wine .... 13.00 To 20.00
Pointed Jewels, Goblet 18.00
  POINTED PANEL DAISY & BUTTON, see Paneled Daisy & Button
Polar Bear, Goblet 150.00
Polar Bear, Water, Tray 125.00
Polar Bear, Water, Tray, Frosted 265.00
Popcorn, Creamer, Ears 27.50
Popcorn, Goblet 48.00
  PORTLAND WITH DIAMOND POINT BAND, see Banded Portland
Portland, Butter, Cover, Gold Flashed 47.50
Portland, Goblet 27.50
Portland, Spooner 27.50
  POTTED PLANT, see Flower Pot
Powder & Shot, Castor Set, 5 Bottles, Pewter Frame 250.00
Powder & Shot, Creamer 95.00
Powder & Shot, Goblet, Flint 55.00
  PRAYER RUG, see Horseshoe
Pressed Diamond, Salt & Pepper, Blue 47.50
Pressed Diamond, Tumbler, Blue 28.50
Pressed Leaf, Eggcup 12.00
Pressed Leaf, Flint 15.00
Pressed Leaf, Goblet 18.00
Princess Feather, Butter, Cover 50.00

Princess Feather, Celery 32.50
Princess Feather, Compote, Cover, 8 In. 95.00
Princess Feather, Plate, 6 In. 27.50
Princess Feather, Plate, 9 In. 32.50
Princess Feather, Plate, Amber, 7 In. 225.00
Princess Feather, Spooner 22.50
Printed Hobnail, Pitcher 40.00
Priscilla, Bowl, 10 In. 38.00
Priscilla, Toothpick .... 27.50 To 35.00
Prism With Diamond Points, Creamer 40.00
Prism With Diamond Points, Cruet 82.50
Prism, Bowl, Pedestal, Flint, 8 In. 60.00
Prism, Goblet 48.00
Prize, Banana Stand 125.00
Prize, Berry Bowl, 8 In. 28.50
Prize, Toothpick 45.00
Profile & Sprig, Mug, Turquoise 55.00
Psyche & Cupid, Goblet 47.50
Quartered Block, Lamp, Finger 75.00
Queen Anne, Butter, Cover 50.00
Queen Anne, Sugar, Large 50.00
Queen's Necklace, Toothpick 60.00
Queen's Necklace, Wine 12.50
Quilted Phlox, Salt & Pepper 25.00
Quilted Phlox, Sugar Shaker, Blue 90.00
Ranson, Cruet, Vaseline, Gold Trim 225.00
Ranson, Toothpick, Vaseline 65.00
Reardon, Goblet 32.50
Red Block, Butter, Cover 75.00
Red Block, Butter, Cover, Handles 95.00
Red Block, Goblet, 8 Piece 240.00
Red Block, Saltshaker, Opalescent 80.00
Red Block, Spooner 30.00
    REGENT, see Leaf Medallion
Reverse Swirl, Celery Vase 150.00
Reverse Swirl, Tumbler, Opalescent Blue, 6 Piece 275.00
    REVERSE TORPEDO, see Bull's-Eye Band
Ribbed Acorn, Compote, Bellflower Base 75.00
Ribbed Grape, Compote, Flint, 5 x 8 In. 40.00
Ribbed Grape, Goblet, Flint 62.50
Ribbed Ivy, Champagne 225.00
Ribbed Palm, Eggcup 35.00
Ribbed Palm, Pitcher, 9 1/4 In. 350.00
Ribbed Palm, Spooner .... 30.00 To 35.00
Ribbed Palm, Sugar & Creamer, Flint 40.00
Ribbon Candy, Spooner 30.00
Ribbon, Butter, Cover 80.00

Pressed glass, Pleat & Panel   Pressed glass, Princess Feather   Pressed glass, Profile & Sprig   Pressed glass, Psyche & Cupid

Pressed glass, Romeo   Pressed glass, Rose in Snow   Pressed glass, Sandwich Star

Rising Sun, Pitcher	50.00
Rising Sun, Vase, Rose Stained	35.00
Rising Sun, Wine, Rose Stained	25.00 To 30.00
Roanoke Star, Goblet	23.00
Roanoke, Berry Set, 7 Piece	125.00
Roanoke, Creamer	22.00
ROCHELLE, see Princess Feather	
Rock Crystal, Pitcher, Water, 2 Qt.	60.00
Roman Cross, Creamer	15.00
Roman Cross, Goblet	18.00
Roman Key With Ribs, Goblet, Frosted, Flint	45.00
Roman Key, Goblet, Frosted	40.00 To 42.50
Roman Rosette, Cordial	47.50
Romeo, Cracker Jar, Cover	50.00
Romeo, Saucer, Ruby Stain, 3 3/4 In.	25.00
Romeo, Wine	55.00
Rooster, Butter, Cover, Child's	235.00
Rooster, Creamer, Child's	75.00
Rose In Snow, Cake Stand, 9 In.	95.00
Rose In Snow, Creamer	35.00 To 50.00
Rose In Snow, Plate	26.00
Rose In Snow, Relish, Divided	95.00
Rose In Snow, Sauce	12.00
Rose In Snow, Tumbler	37.50 To 55.00
Rose Sprig, Goblet, Blue	55.00
Rose Sprig, Relish, Amber	45.00
Rose Sprig, Relish, Blue	45.00
Rose, Spooner, Blue	35.00
Rosette & Palms, Butter, Cover	47.50
Rosette & Palms, Saltshaker	27.50
Rosette & Palms, Sugar, Cover	47.50

Pressed glass,
Ribbon Candy

Pressed glass,
Roman Cross

Pressed glass,
Roman Rosette

Pressed glass,
Sawtooth

Pressed glass,
Shell & Jewel

Pressed glass,
Shell & Tassel

Pressed glass,
Shrine

Rosette & Palms, Wine	18.50
Rosette Band, Sugar, Cover, Creamer & Spooner	64.50
ROSETTE MEDALLION, see Feather Duster	
Royal Ivy, Pitcher, Water, Rainbow	245.00 To 295.00
Royal Ivy, Spooner	85.00
Royal Ivy, Table Set, Rubina, Frosted, 4 Piece	725.00
Royal Ivy, Toothpick, Frosted	47.50
Royal Ivy, Tumbler, Rubina	73.00
Royal Ivy, Water Set, Clear To Cranberry, 7 Piece	295.00
Royal Oak, Butter, Cover, Frosted, Square	95.00
Royal Oak, Butter, Cover, Rubina, Frosted	175.00
Royal Oak, Sugar Shaker, Frosted	192.50
Royal Oak, Table Set, Clear To Cranberry, 4 Piece	585.00
Royal Oak, Water Set, Clear To Cranberry, 7 Piece	595.00
RUBY THUMBPRINT, see also King's Crown	
Ruby Thumbprint, Goblet	42.00
Ruby Thumbprint, Pitcher, Milk	95.00
Ruby Thumbprint, Sugar & Creamer, Individual	75.00
Rustic, Compote, Cover, Twig Finial	60.00
S–Repeat, Table Set, Green, 4 Piece	375.00
Sandwich Ivy, Celery	35.00
Sandwich Star, Spooner, 5 In.	17.50
SAWTOOTH BAND, see Amazon	
Sawtooth, Compote, Flint, 9 1/2 In.	100.00
Sawtooth, Goblet, Knob Stem, Flint	16.00
Sawtooth, Sugar, Flint	32.50
Sawtooth, Wine, Flint	25.00
Saxon, Toothpick, Ruby Flashed	13.50
Scalloped Swirl, Creamer, Green, Individual	30.00
SCALLOPED TAPE, see Jewel Band	
Scroll & Flower, Cookie Server	26.00
Scroll With Acanthus, Compote, Jelly, Green Opalescent	45.00
Scroll With Cane Band, Compote, High Standard	100.00
Scroll With Cane Band, Toothpick, Gold Trim	25.50
Scroll With Flowers, Creamer	15.00
Scroll With Flowers, Jam Jar, Cover	55.00
Scroll With Flowers, Pitcher, Milk	75.00
Scroll With Flowers, Salt, Handle	28.50
Seashell, Creamer, Etched	45.00
Seed Pod, Sugar, Cover, Green, Gold Trim	95.00
Seed Pod, Table Set, Green & Gold, 4 Piece	395.00
Selby, Goblet	11.00
Seneca Loop, Syrup, Dated Pewter Lid, Flint	125.00
Sequoia, Wine	25.00
Sheaf & Diamond, Compote, 7 1/2 In.	50.00
Shell & Jewel, Pitcher	35.00
Shell & Jewel, Pitcher, Water	65.00

Shell & Jewel, Sauce, Small 7.00
Shell & Tassel, Bowl, Amber, 5 1/2 x 10 In. 90.00
Shell & Tassel, Goblet 70.00
Shell & Tassel, Oyster Plate 225.00
Shell & Tassel, Salt & Pepper 250.00
Shell & Tassel, Spooner 45.00
Sheraton, Wine 22.50
    SHOSHONE, see Victor
Shrine, Pitcher, Beer, Gal. 200.00
Simple Scroll, Toothpick, Amethyst, Gold Trim 45.00
Single Rose, Cookie Jar 65.00
Single Rose, Pitcher, Water 85.00
Single Rose, Tankard, Water 95.00
Six Panel Finecut, Bowl, 8 In. 27.50
Six Panel Finecut, Cake Stand, Amber Stained, 10 In. 65.00
Six Panel Finecut, Saucer 18.00
Skilton, Butter, Cover, Ruby Stained 97.50
Skilton, Spooner, Ruby Stained 44.50
Skilton, Sugar, Cover, Ruby Stained 82.50
Slashed Swirl, Creamer 17.50
Snail, Butter, Cover .... 72.50 To 80.00
Snail, Creamer 37.50
Snail, Cup 32.50
Snail, Rose Bowl 32.50
Snail, Saltshaker 37.50
Snail, Saltshaker, Ruby Stained 50.00
Snail, Sugar, Cover 52.50
Snail, Table Set, 4 Piece 200.00
Snake Drape, Goblet 18.00
Snow Drop, Sauce 25.00
Spanish American, Lamp 220.00
Spanish American, Sugar, Cover, 1895 .... 125.00
Spanish American, Vase, Amber, 5 3/4 In. 30.00
    SPANISH COIN, see Columbian Coin
Spearpoint Band, Toothpick, Ruby Stained 62.50
Spearpoint Band, Tumbler, Frosted Band, Ruby Stained 42.50
Spirea Band, Goblet, Amber 32.50
Spirea Band, Spooner, Amber 24.00
Spirea Band, Wine, Amber 22.50
Spirea Band, Wine, Blue 55.00
Spooner & Creamer, Child's, Green 125.00
Sprig, Sauce, Green 15.00
Square Fuchsia, Butter, Cover 45.00
Square Fuchsia, Goblet 35.00
Square Fuchsia, Goblet, Etched 30.00
Square Fuchsia, Pitcher, Water, Blue 145.00
Square Fuchsia, Plate, Amber, 10 In. 85.00
Square Fuchsia, Plate, Handles, 9 In. 22.50
Square Fuchsia, Wine 35.00
Squat Pineapple, Bowl, Green, 9 In. 30.00
Squirrel In Bower, Creamer 85.00
Squirrel In Bower, Sauce 25.00
Squirrel, Pitcher, Water 85.00
Squirrel, Sauce, Scalloped, Footed, 4 1/2 In. 55.00
    STAR & PUNTY, see Moon & Star
Star & Rib, Table Set, Blue, 4 Piece 275.00
    STAR BAND, see Bosworth
Star In Bull's-Eye, Goblet 22.50
Star In Honeycomb, Goblet 39.00
Star Rosetted, Bread Plate, A Good Mother 65.00
Star Rosetted, Plate, Blue, 7 In. 12.00
Star, Cake Stand, 9 3/4 In. 95.00
Star, Table Set, Vaseline, Ruby Stained, 4 Piece 275.00

Starred Cosmos, Water Set, 6 Piece 95.00
Stars & Stripes, Tumbler, Blue, 3 5/8 In. 110.00
Stars & Stripes, Vase, Bud, Blue, Opalescent, 7 In. 165.00
Stars & Stripes, Vase, Bud, Red, 7 In. 220.00
    STAYMAN, see Rustic
Stippled Cherry, Bread Plate, 10 In. 25.00
Stippled Cherry, Butter, Cover, Pink 25.00
Stippled Dart & Balls, Goblet, Ring Stem 28.50
Stippled Double Loop, Goblet .... 37.50 To 42.50
Stippled Forget–Me–Not, Goblet 22.50
Stippled Forget–Me–Not, Pitcher, Water 85.00
Stippled Grape & Festoon, Goblet .... 30.00 To 35.00
Stippled Grape & Festoon, Pitcher, Water Set, 7 Piece 135.00
Stippled Ivy, Celery, Flint 60.00
Stippled Medallion, Eggcup 25.00
Stippled Medallion, Goblet, Flint 30.00
Stippled Sandbur, Goblet 18.00
    STIPPLED STAR VARIANT, see Stippled Sandbur
    STORK LOOKING AT THE MOON, see Ostrich Looking At The Moon
Stork, Creamer 47.50
Stork, Jam Jar 450.00
Stork, Spooner, Frosted 47.50
Strawberry & Fan Variant, Compote, 9 In. 125.00
Strawberry, Spooner 30.00
Strawberry, Sugar 35.00
Style, Creamer, Child's 20.00
Style, Table Set, Child's, 4 Piece 95.00
Sunbeam, Toothpick, Blue, Gold Trim 95.00
Sunk Daisy, Toothpick, Gold Trim 17.00
Sunk Honeycomb, Cake Stand 110.00
Sunk Honeycomb, Creamer, Ruby Stained 57.50
Sunk Honeycomb, Mug 30.00
Sunk Honeycomb, Saltshaker, Ruby Stained 37.50
Sunk Honeycomb, Tumbler, Ruby Stained, Etched 32.50
Sunken Buttons, Celery 35.00
Sunken Primrose, Salt & Pepper 65.00
    SUNRISE, see Rising Sun
Swag With Brackets, Butter, Cover, Green 110.00
Swag With Brackets, Sugar, Cover, Green Opalescent 75.00
Swan, Celery, Etched 40.00
Swan, Creamer 44.00
Swan, Sugar & Creamer, Cover 67.50
Swan, Syrup, Etched 50.00
Sweetheart, Lamp, Finger, Frosted Hearts 135.00
Sweetheart, Spooner, Child's 15.00
Sweetheart, Sugar & Creamer, Child's 40.00
Sweetheart, Sugar, Cover, Child's 20.00

Pressed glass,
Squirrel

Pressed glass,
Strawberry

Pressed glass, Tandem
Diamonds & Thumbprint

Pressed glass,
Thistle

Swirl & Diamond, Pitcher, Water, Ruby Stain 195.00
Swirl & Panel, Toothpick 16.00
Tacoma, Celery, Amber Stained 62.50
Tacoma, Water Set, Ruby Stained, 6 Piece 465.00
Tandem Bicycle, Celery 35.00
Tandem Diamonds & Thumbprint, Goblet 25.00
Tarentum's Buttressed Sunburst, Berry Set, Ruby, 7 Piece 195.00
Tarentum's Manhattan, Tumbler 40.00
TEARDROP, see Teardrop & Thumbprint
Teardrop & Cracked Ice, Spooner 25.00
Teardrop & Tassel, Butter, Cover .... 57.50 To 65.00
Teardrop & Tassel, Sugar & Creamer, Cover, White Opaque 125.00
Teardrop & Thumbprint, Creamer, Cobalt 67.50
Tennessee, Mug 35.00
Tennessee, Mug, Frosted, Gilt Trim 50.00
Tepee, Salt & Pepper 22.50
TEXAS BULL'S-EYE, see Bull's-Eye Variant
Texas Star, Creamer 30.00
Texas, Creamer 18.50
Texas, Cruet, Stopper 150.00
Texas, Tumbler 110.00
Texas, Vase, Scalloped Top, 9 In. 45.00
Thistle Shield, Goblet 23.00
Thistle, Bottle, Bar, Flint 60.00
Thistle, Dish, Scrolled Flower, 6 In. 10.00
Thistle, Goblet .... 35.00 To 80.00
Thousand Eye, Compote, Amber 30.00
Thousand Eye, Goblet, Amber 20.00
Thousand Eye, Goblet, Blue 18.00
Thousand Eye, Salt & Pepper 75.00
Thousand Eye, Saucer, Amber, Frosted 12.50
Thousand Eye, Spooner, Stem, Amber 52.50
Threaded, Eggcup 24.50
Three Birds, Pitcher, Water 125.00
Three Face, Bowl, Cable Edge, 8 1/2 In. 125.00
Three Face, Butter, Cover 150.00
Three Face, Cake Stand, 9 In. 165.00
Three Face, Cake Stand, 10 In. .... 210.00 To 275.00
Three Face, Champagne, 5 1/2 In. 150.00
Three Face, Compote, Cover, 8 1/2 In. .... 165.00 To 325.00
Three Face, Creamer 135.00
Three Face, Saltshaker 45.00
Three Face, Spooner 50.00
Three Face, Sugar, Cover 140.00
THREE GRACES, see also Three Face
Three Graces, Bread Plate, 10 In. 45.00
Three Graces, Bread Plate, Patent Date 1875 .... 55.00
Three Graces, Goblet 185.00
Three Graces, Lamp, Oil, Frosted Base 225.00
Three Graces, Plate 35.00
Three Panel, Berry Bowl, 10 In. 45.00
Three Panel, Bread Plate, Scalloped Rim, 10 In. 25.00
Three Panel, Creamer, Amber 40.00
Three Panel, Creamer, Vaseline 45.00
Three Panel, Mug, Amber 15.00
Three Panel, Spooner, Vaseline 40.00
Three Presidents, Bread Plate .... 50.00 To 110.00
THREE SISTERS, see Three Face
Thrush & Apple Blossoms, Wine 50.00
Thumbprint, Compote, Flint, 12 x 14 3/4 In. 700.00
Thumbprint, Compote, Flint, 7 1/4 x 9 In. 55.00
Thumbprint, Pitcher, Milk 80.00
Thumbprint, Sugar, Cover, 8 5/8 In. 35.00

◆◆

Don't display photographs in direct sunlight. If labeling the back of a
picture use a pencil or china marker, not a felt–tipped pen. Don't use
scotch tape, staples, or paper clips. Don't mount in a sticky photo
album. Don't store in an area with rapid temperature or humidity
changes.

◆◆

Tic–Tac–Toe, Goblet	18.00
TIDY, see Rustic	
Tiny Lion, Butter, Cover, Cable Base, Frosted	85.00
Tiny Lion, Compote, Cover, 7 1/2 In.	95.00
Tiny Lion, Spooner, Etched	65.00
Tiny Lion, Sugar, Cover, Cable Base, Frosted	75.00
TOBIN, see Leaf & Star	
Tokyo, Berry Bowl, Master, Green Opalescent	40.00
Tokyo, Cruet, Clear Stopper, Green Opalescent	150.00
Tokyo, Sugar, Cover, Blue, Gold Trim	75.00
Tokyo, Sugar, Cover, Green	90.00
Tokyo, Water Set, Blue, 7 Piece	645.00
Torpedo, Cruet	55.00
Torpedo, Goblet	40.00
Torpedo, Lamp, Finger	70.00
Torpedo, Pitcher, Water	65.00 To 85.00
Torpedo, Syrup	65.00
Torpedo, Syrup, Ruby Stained	160.00
Tree of Life, Compote, 5 3/4 x 5 1/2 In.	48.00
Tree of Life, Goblet, Flint	50.00
Trophy, Toothpick, Denton, Texas	12.50
Truncated Cube, Toothpick, Ruby Stained	30.00
Tulip & Honeycomb, Butter, Cover, Child's	35.00
Tulip & Honeycomb, Creamer, Child's	20.00
Tulip & Honeycomb, Spooner, Child's	20.00
Tulip Petals, Butter, Cover	125.00
Tulip Petals, Toothpick, Child's	21.00
Tulip With Sawtooth, Tumbler	50.00
Tulip With Sawtooth, Wine	12.00

Pressed glass,
Three Face

Pressed glass,
Thumbprint

Pressed glass,
Tree of Life

Pressed glass, U.S. Coin

◆◆◆◆◆◆◆◆◆◆◆◆◆◆◆◆◆◆◆◆◆◆◆

The early 1840s were the time of the pressed–glass table settings. The early patterns were simple, with heavy loops or ribbed effects. The 1870s meant more elaborate naturalistic patterns. Clear and frosted patterns with figures were in style during the 1870s. Overall patterns that were slightly geometric in feeling were in style by 1880, as were patterns such as Daisy and Button and Hobnail. Colored patterns became popular after the Civil War.

◆◆◆◆◆◆◆◆◆◆◆◆◆◆◆◆◆◆◆◆◆◆◆

Twin Snowshoes, Toothpick	45.00
TWINKLE STAR, see Utah	
Two Panel, Compote, Open, Vaseline	45.00
Two Panel, Water Set, Blue, 7 Piece	295.00
Two Panel, Wine, Green	45.00
U. S. Coin, Compote, Frosted Coins, 6 In.	550.00
U. S. Coin, Toothpick, Frosted Coins	70.00
U. S. Coin, Tumbler, Coin In Base	190.00
U. S. Coin, Bread Plate, Quarters & Half Dollars, 1892	270.00
U. S. Coin, Butter, Cover, Dollars & Half Dollars, Frosted	450.00
U. S. Coin, Cake Plate, 1 Dollar, 6 1/2 x 10 In.	330.00
U. S. Coin, Compote, 50 Cents, 5 1/2 x 7 In.	357.00
U. S. Coin, Compote, 9 3/4 In.	425.00
U. S. Coin, Compote, Cover	365.00
U. S. Coin, Compote, Frosted, 10 1/2 x 7 In.	450.00
U. S. Coin, Cruet	600.00
U. S. Coin, Goblet, 50 Cents, 6 3/4 In.	513.00
U. S. Coin, Jar, Cover, 50 Cents, 7 In.	385.00
U. S. Coin, Lamp, Frosted Stem, 1892	795.00
U. S. Coin, Lamp, Oil, 50 Cents, 11 1/2 In.	523.00
U. S. Coin, Pitcher, Water, 1 Dollar, 7 1/2 In.	660.00
U. S. Coin, Pitcher, Water, 50 Cents, 8 1/4 In.	495.00
U. S. Coin, Toothpick, On Plate, 1 Dollar, 8 In.	633.00
U. S. Rib, Butter, Cover, Green, Gold Trim	125.00
Urn, Toothpick	45.00
Utah, Goblet	38.50
Utah, Pitcher, Water, Frosted Flower	48.50
Valencia, Pitcher, Water	145.00
Vera, Compote, 7 1/4 In.	45.00
Vermont, Goblet, Green, Gold Trim	575.50
Vermont, Pitcher, Water, Amber Stained	100.00
Vermont, Salt & Pepper, Green, Gold Trim	125.00
Vermont, Spooner, Flower Rim, Gold Trim	65.00
Vermont, Toothpick, Green, Gold Trim	34.50 To 65.00
Vermont, Tumbler	65.00
Vermont, Tumbler, Green, Gold Trim	55.00
Victor, Butter, Cover, Gold Trim	95.00
Victor, Cake Stand, Green	40.00
Victor, Cruet	45.00
Victor, Toothpick	40.00
Viking, Apothecary Jar	65.00

Pressed glass,   Pressed glass,   Pressed glass,   Pressed glass,
Waffle & Thumbprint   Washington Centennial   Westward Ho   Wildflower

Viking, Butter, Cover, Frosted	85.00
Viking, Celery Vase	45.00
Viking, Compote, Cover, 9 In.	120.00
Viking, Creamer	50.00
Viking, Sugar, Cover	65.00
Waffle & Thumbprint, Goblet	48.00
Waffle & Thumbprint, Wine, Flint	95.00
Waffle, Celery, Flint	48.00
Waffle, Goblet	50.00
Waffle, Sugar, Cover, Flint	95.00
Washington Centennial, Goblet	39.00
Washington Centennial, Sugar, Cover	70.00
Water Lily, Bowl, Cattails, Amethyst Opalescent, Square	75.00
Wedding Bells, Spooner, Rose Stained	28.00
Wedding Bells, Toothpick, Rose Stained	22.00
Wedding Bells, Wine, Rose Stained	55.00
Westward Ho, Compote, 8 In.	125.00
Westward Ho, Compote, Cover, 4 In.	100.00
Westward Ho, Compote, Cover, Oval	200.00
Westward Ho, Jam Jar	195.00
Wheat & Barley, Spooner	12.00
Wheat & Barley, Tumbler, Amber	40.00
WHIRLIGIG, see Buzz Star	
Wild Bouquet, Syrup	95.00
Wildflower, Celery, Amber	34.00 To 45.00
Wildflower, Creamer, Amber	33.00
Wildflower, Goblet, Green	55.00
Wildflower, Pitcher, Water	85.00
Wildflower, Plate, Blue, Square, 10 In.	45.00
Wildflower, Spooner	25.00
Wildflower, Tumbler, Amber	40.00
Wildflower, Tumbler, Green	20.00
Willow Oak, Cake Stand, Amber, 10 In.	60.00
Willow Oak, Celery Vase	95.00
Willow Oak, Celery, Vase, Blue	95.00
Willow Oak, Compote, Cover, 6 In.	46.50
Willow Oak, Creamer	30.00
Willow Oak, Creamer, Blue	65.00
Willow Oak, Goblet	28.00
Willow Oak, Goblet, Amber	35.00
Willow Oak, Table Set, 4 Piece	300.00
Willow Oak, Table Set, Amber, 4 Piece	300.00 To 350.00
Windflower, Eggcup	32.50
Windflower, Spooner	28.00
Wisconsin, Bonbon, Handle, 4 In.	22.50
Wisconsin, Butter, Cover	87.50
Wisconsin, Cake Stand, 8 1/2 In.	42.50

Wisconsin, Celery 47.50
Wisconsin, Compote, 8 In. 32.50
Wisconsin, Relish 20.00
Wishbone, Goblet, Flint 125.00
    WOODEN PAIL, see Oaken Bucket
Wreath & Shell, Butter, Cover 95.00
Wreath & Shell, Butter, Cover, Blue Opalescent 190.00
Wreath & Shell, Butter, Vaseline, Cover 165.00
Wreath & Shell, Cracker Jar, Cover, Blue Opalescent 625.00
Wreath & Shell, Rose Bowl, Blue Opalescent 65.00
Wreath & Shell, Spooner, Blue Opalescent 95.00
Wreath & Shell, Spooner, Opalescent 40.00
Wreath & Shell, Spooner, Vaseline Opalescent 55.00
Wreath & Shell, Sugar, Cover, Blue Opalescent 135.00
Wreath & Shell, Sugar, Cover, Vaseline Opalescent .... 75.00 To 85.00
Wreath & Shell, Toothpick, Vaseline 195.00
Wyoming, Butter, Cover 95.00
Wyoming, Creamer, Cover 85.00
Wyoming, Pitcher, Water 95.00
Wyoming, Wine 125.00
X–Ray, Saltshaker 18.50
X–Ray, Saucer, Green, Gold Trim 22.50
    YALE, see Crowfoot
York Herringbone, Tumbler, Ruby Stained, Etched 47.50
Yutec, Sugar & Creamer, Cover, American Indian Design 45.00
Zanesville, Toothpick, Frosted, Enameled Design 57.50
Zipper Slash, Toothpick, Ruby Stained, Souvenir 25.00
Zipper, Cruet 50.00
Zipper, Saltshaker 45.00

 Print, in this listing, means any of many printed images produced on paper by one of the more common methods, such as lithography. The prints listed here are of interest primarily to the antiques collector, not the fine arts collector. Many of these prints were originally part of books. Other prints will be found in the sections headed Advertising, Currier & Ives, and Poster.

PRINT, Armstrong, Black Lace, 16 x 20 In. 30.00
  Armstrong, Double Orange, 20 x 20 In. 30.00

        Audubon bird prints were originally issued as part of books printed from 1826 to 1854. They were issued in two sizes, 26 1/2 in. by 39 1/2 in. and 11 in. by 7 in. The quadrupeds were issued in 28 in. by 22 in. size prints. Later editions of the Audubon books were done in many sizes and reprints of the books in the original size were also made. The bird pictures have been so popular they have been copied in myriad sizes by both old and new printing methods. This list includes originals and later copies because Audubon prints of all ages are sold in antiques shops.

Audubon, American Cross Fox, Shadow Box Frame, 1843, 25 x 31 1/4 In. 200.00
Audubon, Arkansas Goldfinch, Birds of America, 10 3/8 x 6 7/8 In. 105.00
Audubon, Canada Otter, Framed, 27 x 32 In. 200.00
Audubon, Common American Skunk, Frame, 15 3/4 x 12 3/4 In. 75.00
Audubon, Kentucky Flycatching Warbler, Curly Maple Frame, 16 7/8 In. 85.00
Audubon, Little American Brown Weasel, Frame, 21 1/2 x 27 1/2 In. 200.00
Audubon, Soft Haired Squirrel, 17 x 14 In. 45.00
Audubon, Tawny Weasel, Hand Colored, Frame, 27 x 32 In. 300.00
Baillie, Moses, Frame, 10 x 15 In. 50.00
Balthafar, View of Notre Dame, 10 x 15 In. 110.00
Barchus, Sunset On Mount Hood, 14 x 36 In. 1850.00
Big Elk, Chief of Omahas, With Peace Medal, Frame, 21 x 18 In. 100.00
Bishop, Friends, Signed, 1942, 8 5/8 x 4 1/8 In. 1100.00
Bishop, Two Girls Sitting In Union Square Fountain, 1936, 5 x 5 In. 2500.00
Bogue, Hunt, Pheasant, Framed 18.00

Boileau, Peggy, Frame, 23 x 16 In.	175.00
Burton, View of Boston In 1848, Framed, 19 3/4 x 44 1/2 In.	1650.00
Corbett, Cleaning Day, Matted, 12 x 9 In.	25.00
Corbett, Mending Day, Matted, 12 x 9 In.	30.00
Curtis, Vanishing Race, Gold Tone, 8 x 10 In.	1150.00
Eagle Fire Engine No. 13, Frame, Nov. 1825, 9 x 11 In.	75.00
Farny, Indian Camp, Hand Colored, Gilt Frame, '98, 14 x 10 1/4 In.	60.00
Fisher, 6 Moments In A Girl's Life, Matted, Framed	125.00
Fox, Departure of Columbus, 16 x 18 In.	275.00
Fox, Dreamland, Large	110.00
Fox, Fallen Monarch	45.00
Fox, First Raising of Stars & Stripes At Valley Forge	45.00
Fox, Good Ship Adventure	65.00
Fox, Heart's Desire	85.00
Fox, Nature's Beauty, Framed	80.00
Fox, Nature's Sublime Grandeur, 14 x 18 In.	50.00
Fox, Path To The Valley, 10 x 16 In.	60.00
Fox, Perfect Day, 14 x 18 In.	65.00
Fox, Poppies	48.00
Fox, Poppies, 14 x 20 In.	50.00
Fox, Sunset Dreams, Framed	80.00
Georgetown, Vessels At Potomac Wharf, J. Stobart, 18 x 26 1/2 In.	440.00
Giotto's Chapel, Arundel, Victorian, Framed, 22 1/2 x 25 1/2 In.	192.50
Godey, 2 Fashion Figures, Color, 1880s, 7 x 10 In.	25.00
Gutmann, A Little Bit of Heaven	50.00 To 70.00
Gutmann, Awakening, Signed, Framed	68.00
Gutmann, Baby In Bed, With Stuffed Teddy Bear, Framed, 8 x 10 In.	75.00
Gutmann, Child Eating, Frame, 19 1/2 x 16 1/2 In.	45.00
Gutmann, Chuckles, 8 x 11 In.	21.00
Gutmann, Fairest of The Flowers	150.00
Gutmann, Friendly Enemies, 11 x 14 In.	50.00 To 55.00
Gutmann, Good Morning	80.00
Gutmann, Good Night, No. 613, 1911, 14 x 20 In.	75.00
Gutmann, Homebuilders	90.00
Gutmann, In Port of Dreams, No. 214, 11 x 14 In.	85.00
Gutmann, In Slumberland	50.00
Gutmann, Little Bit of Heaven, No. 850, 18 3/4 x 14 In.	125.00
Gutmann, Little Boy Blue	50.00
Gutmann, Little Jack Horner	50.00
Gutmann, Love's Blossom, 14 x 11 In.	50.00
Gutmann, Love's Blossom, 1927	125.00
Gutmann, Message of The Roses	125.00
Gutmann, Miss Flirt, 11 x 14 In.	40.00
Gutmann, Nitey Nite	75.00
Gutmann, Seeing, No. 211, 11 x 14 In.	50.00
Gutmann, Sweet Innocence, 1915	125.00
Gutmann, Symphony	125.00
Gutmann, Thank You God, 21 x 14 In.	65.00
Gutmann, To Love & To Cherish	150.00
Gutmann, Winged Aureole, Framed, 19 x 14 In.	115.00
Harrison, Girl With Cat, 1908	40.00
Hill & Smith, Philadelphia, From Girard College, 1850, 23 x 39 In.	4200.00
Humphrey, A Busy Day	25.00
Humphrey, Boy Golfer, Framed, 1887	145.00
Icart, After The Raid, Signed, c.1917, Frame	4125.00
Icart, Angry Steed, 1917, 10 1/2 x 16 1/2 In.	2000.00
Icart, Apple Girl, 1928	195.00
Icart, Apple Girl, c.1928, 18 x 22 In.	245.00
Icart, Attic, Watercolor	2500.00
Icart, Autumn Leaves, 1926, 17 x 21 In.	3960.00
Icart, Autumn, 1928, 6 1/2 x 9 In.	2475.00
Icart, Bathers, 1926, 17 x 24 1/2 In.	4290.00
Icart, Bathing Beauties, 1931, 17 1/4 x 25 1/2 In.	5500.00

Icart, Bewilderment, 1920, 15 1/4 x 18 1/8 In.	1760.00
Icart, Bird of Prey, 1918, 13 x 18 3/4 In.	2475.00
Icart, Birds of July, 1926, 13 x 17 In.	4950.00
Icart, Black Fan, 1931, 16 x 21 In.	5000.00
Icart, Blossom Time, 1926, 14 x 19 In.	2700.00
Icart, Blue Buddha, 1924, 16 x 21 In.	3025.00
Icart, Broken Jug, 1922, 13 x 18 In.	2300.00
Icart, Butterfly, 1914, 11 x 19 In.	2520.00
Icart, Carmen, Signed, Frame, 21 1/8 x 14 1/8 In.	1980.00
Icart, Casanova, c.1920, 20 1/4 x 13 1/4 In.	1875.00
Icart, Casanova, Signed, Frame, 1928, 21 x 14 1/8 In.	2420.00
Icart, Casanova, Signed, Frame, 1928, 21 x 14 In.	2200.00
Icart, Charm of Montmartre, 1932, 14 x 20 In.	3300.00
Icart, Chilly One, Signed, 1924, 17 1/2 x 11 7/8 In.	2860.00
Icart, Coursing II, Signed, Frame, c.1929, 15 1/2 x 25 In.	7700.00
Icart, Dancer, 1931, 15 x 19 In.	9400.00
Icart, Delila, Signed, Frame, 1929, 21 1/8 x 14 1/4 In.	2530.00
Icart, Eve	3200.00
Icart, Faust, Signed, Frame, 21 1/2 x 13 1/2 In.	2090.00
Icart, Fishing, Menu Cover, Signed, 7 5/8 x 5 7/8 In.	660.00
Icart, Fountain, 1936, 8 x 20 In.	9400.00
Icart, Illusions, Double Matted & Framed, 10 1/2 x 17 In.	70.00
Icart, Intimacy, Signed, Frame, 15 3/4 x 18 3/4 In.	2640.00
Icart, Invitation, Signed, Frame, 1924, 17 1/2 x 11 3/4 In.	2860.00
Icart, Japanese Garden	1800.00
Icart, Joan of Arc, 1929, 15 x 21 In.	5200.00
Icart, Kiss of The Motherland, 1917, 11 x 19 In.	3700.00
Icart, Kiss of The Motherland, Signed, c.1917, 19 1/2 x 11 3/4 In.	3850.00
Icart, Kittens, 1925, 16 x 21 In.	4200.00
Icart, Kittens, Signed, 1923, 14 3/4 x 19 1/4 In.	4125.00
Icart, La Cage Rouge, Frame, c.1929, 18 x 14 In.	3850.00
Icart, La Lettre, 1928, 18 x 22 In.	95.00
Icart, La Vie Des Seins, Signed, Frame, c.1945, 10 x 18 In.	1650.00
Icart, Lady of The Camellias, Signed, 16 x 14 In.	305.00
Icart, Laziness, Signed, Frame, 1925, 15 3/4 x 19 3/4 In.	2640.00
Icart, Lemon Tree, Signed, c.1923, 18 x 12 1/4 In.	1200.00
Icart, Lilies, Drypoint Etched, 36 x 26 1/2 In.	7500.00
Icart, Louise, Signed, Frame, 1927, 21 x 14 1/8 In.	2585.00
Icart, Love's Blossom, 1937, 17 x 25 In.	9200.00
Icart, Monte Carlo, Litho	300.00
Icart, Montmartre, Signed, 20 1/2 x 14 In.	1875.00
Icart, My Model, Signed, 1933, 21 x 16 1/2 In.	3300.00
Icart, Paris Flowers, Signed, Frame, 1930, 15 3/4 x 19 5/8 In.	2860.00
Icart, Red Riding Hood, Signed, 1927, 21 1/8 x 14 1/8 In.	3300.00
Icart, Seated Lady With Parasol, Signed, 1948, 19 3/8 x 15 5/8 In.	3100.00
Icart, Sleeping Beauty, Signed, c.1927, 16 x 19 1/2 In.	2900.00
Icart, Speed, Engraving	5000.00
Icart, Speed, Stamp, 1929, 25 x 15 1/2 In.	6050.00
Icart, Temptation	3500.00
Icart, The Coach, Signed, Frame, c.1948, 22 1/8 x 18 3/8 In.	2310.00
Icart, The Four Seasons, Matted & Framed, Set of 4	375.00
Icart, Venus In The Waves, Signed	65.00
Icart, Vitesse, 1929, 25 x 15 In.	6050.00
Icart, Vitesse/Speed, Signed, Frame, c.1933, 15 1/2 x 25 In.	7150.00
Icart, Waltz Echos, Signed, c.1940, 19 5/8 x 19 1/4 In.	6000.00
Icart, White Underwear, c.1925, 15 1/2 x 19 1/2 In.	4500.00
Icart, White Wings, Signed, Frame, 17 3/8 x 12 1/2 In.	3520.00
Icart, Woman With Braids, Signed, 17 3/4 x 13 1/8 In.	2750.00
Innis, Autumn Oaks, Framed, 1825–94	50.00
Jansen, Champ	25.00

Japanese woodblock prints are listed as follows: Print, Japanese, name of artist, title or description, type, and size. Dealers use the following terms: Tate-e is a vertical composition. Yoko-e is a horizontal composition. The words Aiban (13 by 9 inches), Chuban (10 by 7 1/2 inches), Hosoban (12 by 6 inches), Oban (15 by 10 inches), and Koban (7 by 4 inches) denote size. Modern versions of some of these prints have been made.

Japanese, Beauty On The Veranda, 11 x 7 In. ....*Illus*	77.00
Japanese, Eisan, Sunset On The Verandah, c.1820, 15 1/4 x 10 In.	5000.00
Japanese, Eishi, 100 Poems By 100 Poets, c.1790, 15 1/4 x 10 1/4 In.	9000.00
Japanese, Hiroshi Yoshida, Glimpse of Ueno Park, 9 3/4 x 14 3/4 In.	935.00
Japanese, Hiroshi Yoshida, In A Temple Yard, 9 3/4 x 14 3/4 In.	632.00
Japanese, Hiroshi Yoshida, Yozahura In Rain, 9 3/4 x 14 3/4 In.	660.00
Japanese, Hiroshige, 53 Stations of Tokaido, 1840, 9 1/4 x 14 1/4 In.	225.00
Japanese, Hiroshige, Winter Scenes, Triptych, 1840, 15 x 10 In., 3 Pc.	625.00
Japanese, Horie, Impression of Arc, 1990, 26 1/4 x 33 1/4 In.	450.00
Japanese, Inagaki, Cat Waking Up, Framed, 1955, 23 x 16 3/4 In.	715.00
Japanese, Kiyonaga, Iris Flower, c.1775, 12 1/2 x 8 1/2 In.	5000.00
Japanese, Kiyoshi Saito, 2 Cats, Frolicking Butterfly, 15 x 10 In.	245.00
Japanese, Kiyoshi Saito, Landscape, Buildings, 10 1/4 x 15 1/4 In.	215.00
Japanese, Komoda Haruki, Snowy Mountain, Ink, 50 5/8 x 16 3/4 In.	80.00
Japanese, Koryusai, Courtesan Mitsuharu, c.1770, 14 3/4 x 9 3/4 In.	5000.00
Japanese, Koryusai, Hussy, c.1800, 15 1/4 x 10 1/4 In.	5000.00
Japanese, Kunisada, Ichikawa Danjuro, c.1830, 14 1/2 x 9 3/4 In.	800.00
Japanese, Kunisada, Matsumoto Koshiro, c.1830, 14 1/2 x 9 3/4 In.	800.00
Japanese, Kuniteru, Triptych, Figures, Landscape, 14 1/4 x 9 3/4 In.	475.00
Japanese, Kuniyoshi, 100 Popular Heroes of Suikoden, c.1828	1800.00
Japanese, Kuniyoshi, Mirror of Loyal Retainers, 1857, 14 1/2 x 9 In.	800.00
Japanese, Kuniyoshi, Rainstorm, 1840, 10 3/4 x 15 1/4 In.	225.00
Japanese, Mt. Fuji, Matted & Framed, 16 1/4 x 20 1/4 In.	100.00
Japanese, Nakayama, Girl With Sunflower, 1957, 27 x 19 1/4 In.	900.00
Japanese, Sadanobu III, Warrior On Black Horse, 17 1/2 x 11 3/4 In.	105.00
Japanese, Sadanobu III, Warrior On White Horse, 17 1/2 x 11 3/4 In.	105.00
Japanese, Shiro, Ikebana, 1945, 15 1/2 x 10 3/4 In.	340.00
Japanese, Shiro, Shitomae In Snow, c.1950, 15 1/2 x 10 3/4 In.	340.00
Japanese, Shodo, Peony, c.1950, 15 1/2 x 10 3/4 In.	150.00
Japanese, Shodo, Yellow Rose, c.1950, 15 1/2 x 10 3/4 In.	150.00
Japanese, Tokuriki, Nude, 1974, 12 3/4 x 19 3/4 In.	700.00
Japanese, Toyokuni III, Momoi Wakasanosuke, 1859, 14 1/4 x 9 3/4 In.	700.00
Japanese, Toyokuni III, Tsuchiya Jiemon, 1860, 13 3/4 x 9 3/4 In.	700.00

◆ ◆

Spray glass cleaner on a cloth, then wipe the glass on a framed print. Do not spray the glass because the liquid may drip and stain the mat or print.

◆ ◆

Print, Japanese, Beauty On The Veranda,
11 x 7 In.

Japanese, Toyokuni, Iwai Hanshiro, c.1810, 14 1/2 x 9 1/4 In. 1600.00
Japanese, Toyokuni, Suketakaya Takasuke, c.1810, 14 1/2 x 10 In. 1600.00
Japanese, Utamaro, Birds In Water, 10 1/8 x 15 1/8 In. 50.00
Japanese, Utamaro, Woman, In Mirror, 15 1/2 x 10 1/2 In. 225.00
Japanese, Yoshida, A Glimpse of Ueno Park, Signed, 9 x 14 In. 935.00
Japanese, Yoshida, In A Temple Yard, Signed, 9 x 14 In. 632.00
Japanese, Yoshida, Yozahur In Rain, Signed, 9 x 14 In. 660.00
Japanese, Yoshiharu, Mirror of Suikoden Heroes, 1856, 14 1/4 x 9 In. 900.00
Japanese, Yoshitoshi, 100 Views of The Moon, 1855, 14 x 9 3/4 In. 900.00
Japanese, Yoshitoshi, Moon At Chikubujima, 1886, 13 3/4 x 9 1/4 In. 900.00
Japanese, Yoshitsuya, Crossing Lake On Horse, 1864, 14 x 9 1/2 In. 800.00
Kellogg & Comstock, Tree of Temperance, Framed, 16 3/4 x 12 1/4 In. 65.00
Kellogg, Tree, Representing Evil & Good, Frame, 17 x 13 In., Pair 420.00
Lehman, Girard College, Main Building, 1835, Framed, 7 5/8 x 11 In. 850.00
Lehman, Great Elm Tree of Shackumaxon, Kensington, 1829 .... 2400.00
Margaret J. Patterson, Woodcut, Tree Scene, Color, Framed, 7 x 10 In. 880.00
Monkey, Hand Colored, 18th Century, Framed, 14 x 10 In., Pair 350.00
Mozert, My Dream Girl, 28 x 22 In. 30.00
Nast, Ringing In The Air, Santa Claus Ringing Bells 90.00
Nast, Santa, Decorating Large Christmas Tree, 1880s, 9 x 8 In. 75.00

> Wallace Nutting is known for his pictures, furniture, and books.
> Nutting *prints* are actually hand–colored photographs issued from
> 1900 to 1941. There are over 10,000 different titles.

Nutting, Barre Brook, Large 115.00
Nutting, Between Elm & Birch, 11 x 14 In. 80.00
Nutting, Happy Valley Road, 13 x 16 In. 85.00
Nutting, May Countryside, 1910, 18 x 15 In. 135.00
Nutting, May Countryside, Dated 1910, 9 1/2 x 7 1/2 In. 135.00
Nutting, Red, White & Blue, Large 95.00
Nutting, Returning From A Walk 187.00
Nutting, Tending The Fire 195.00
Nutting, Weaving A Straw Hat, 1916 .... 150.00

> Maxfield Frederick Parrish was an illustrator who lived from 1870
> to 1966. He is best known as a designer of magazine covers, posters,
> calendars, and advertisements. All Parrish prints are wanted by
> collectors.

Parrish, Circe's Place, 9 x 11 In. 90.00
Parrish, Daybreak, Frame, 7 x 11 In. 75.00
Parrish, Daybreak, Frame, Large 195.00
Parrish, Dreaming, Frame, Small 35.00
Parrish, Falls By Moonlight, 8 1/2 x 11 In. 95.00
Parrish, Garden of Allan, Original Frame, 15 x 30 In. 175.00
Parrish, Hilltop, Large 850.00
Parrish, Land of Make Believe 295.00
Parrish, Moonlight, Small 250.00
Parrish, Old King Cole, Frame 950.00
Parrish, Royal Gorge, Frame, 15 x 20 In. 250.00
Parrish, Sheltering Oaks, 16 x 19 In. 65.00
Parrish, Twilight, Frame, 9 x 12 In. 45.00
Parrish, Under Summer Skies, 16 x 19 In. 65.00
Parrish, Venetian Lamplighter, Small Folio 195.00
Parrish, Venetian, Large 850.00
Parrish, Wild Geese, 11 1/2 x 8 1/2 In. 165.00
Paul De Longpre, Roses, Color, Matted, 1903, 14 x 10 1/2 In. 50.00

◆◆

If the photograph album you buy smells like plastic, don't take it. The
fumes will eventually destroy the pictures.

◆◆

Peter Hurd, Pennsylvania Quaker, Black & White, Framed, 9/70, 24 In.	150.00
Phillips, Fade–Away Girl, Book Plate, 1910	18.00
Remington, Bronco Buster, Black & White, 1957	25.00
Remington, Western Portfolio, Color, 1956, 8 Piece	95.00
Roadrunner, Folk Art, Color, Life Size	65.00
Roseland, Mammy In Chair, Fireplace, 2 Girls Watching, 20 x 28 In.	750.00
Roseland, Mammy In Front of Fireplace, 1 Girl Watching, 20 x 28 In.	750.00
Ruthven, Canada Geese, Color, Signed, Matted & Framed	185.00
Ruthven, Wood Ducks & Ruddy Duck, Framed, 38 x 31 & 20 x 26 In., Pr.	180.00
Timberlake, Day In The Sun, Matted, Framed	200.00
Timberlake, Lake Snow At Riverwood, Matted, Framed	1150.00
Timberlake, Morning Sun, Matted, Framed	250.00
Trip Down The Harbour, Colored, Framed, Large	660.00
Vargas, Legacy Girl, 26 x 36 In.	60.00
Vargas, Sleepy Time Gal, 26 x 38 In.	60.00
Victorian Angel, Tear Drop Shape, Lithograph, 33 x 18 In.	125.00
Weir, Who Are You?, Terrier Looking In Mirror, 1887, 5 3/4 x 8 In.	42.50
Women In Grecian Drape, Garden Scene, Framed, 1920s	40.00

How to carry a handkerchief and lipstick is a problem today for every woman, including the Queen of England. The purse has been recognizable since the eighteenth century. Leather and needlework purses were preferred. Beaded purses became popular in the nineteenth century, went out of style, but are again in use. Mesh purses date from the 1880s and are still being made.

PURSE, Allover Black Beads, Rhinestones On Opening, Melon Shape	145.00
Alumesh, Whiting & Davis	28.00
Armadillo Skin	150.00
Art Nouveau, German Silver, Chain Mesh	70.00
Beaded, Black & Crystal, Filigree Spiderweb Frame	65.00
Beaded, Black, Silver Running Through, 1920–30, Small	35.00
Beaded, Black, Tulip Design, Hand Made, 1930s, 4 x 6 In.	25.00
Beaded, Celluloid, Flowers, Brown, Pink, French, 6 x 5 In. *Illus*	90.00
Beaded, Evening, Geometric Design, Tassels, 4 1/2 In.	33.00
Beaded, Evening, Velvet, Blue–Green Tassle, 12 In. *Illus*	99.00
Beaded, Flower Design	225.00
Beaded, Green Stones, 14K Gold, Tiffany, 8 x 6 In. *Illus*	685.00
Beaded, Lilac, Greek Key Top, Velvet Handle, 1920s, 5 1/2 x 8 In.	55.00
Beaded, Mesh, Bead Tassels, French, 1930s, 8 1/2 In.	45.00
Beaded, Multicolored Flowers, Fringed, Germany, 1920s, 6 x 8 In.	125.00
Beaded, Peacock, Beaded Fringe, Large	75.00

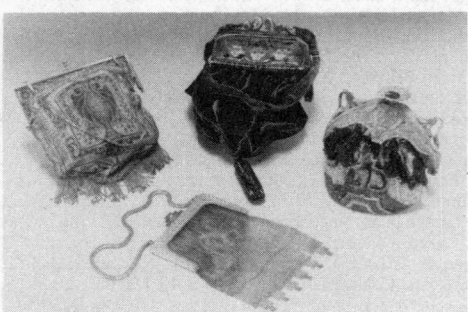

Purse, Beaded, Green Stones, 14K Gold, Tiffany, 8 x 6 In.

Purse, Beaded, Evening, Velvet, Blue–Green Tassle, 12 In.

Purse, Mesh, Pyramid Fringe, Rose, Green, Whiting & Davis

Purse, Beaded, Celluloid, Flowers, Brown, Pink, French, 6 x 5 In.

Beaded, Turquoise, Pewter Intertwined, Czechoslovakia, 8 x 6 In. 150.00
Black, Gold Clasp, Print Lining, Shoulder Chain 40.00
Change, Woven Basket of Flowers, Metal Frame & Clasp, 1834, 3 1/2 In. 120.00
Child's, Brown Leather Bag, Silver Frame & Locks, 1880 .... 65.00
Child's, Duck, Gold Silk 45.00
Child's, Foxy Grandpa, Leather 45.00
Child's, Mesh, Painted, Worn Clasp, 4 In. 14.00
Child's, White Linen, Hankie Inside 18.00
Cloth, Rhinestones, Expandable Top, Germany 12.00
Clutch, Art Deco Leather Pouch, Bakelite Frame, Amber Rhinestones 25.00
Clutch, Black Velvet, Silver & Gold Metallic Thread Design, India 95.00
Clutch, Clear Lucite, Rhinestones, White Marbelized, 1950s 20.00
Clutch, Suede, Sterling & Chrysoprase Accents, Austria 275.00
Coin, Inset Turquoise & Pearls On Bail, Gold, 2 1/2 In. 395.00
Coin, Mother-of-Pearl, Red Accordian Interior, No Chain, 4 In. 15.00
Coin, Rods Suspending Mesh Bag, Gold Beads, Pierced Fob, Yellow Gold 105.00
Coin, Rods Suspending Mesh Bag, Yellow Gold, Pierced Fob 95.00
Coin, Silver & Gold Foil Design, Floral Medallion, Enameled, c.1840 .... 75.00
Crocheted, Beige 22.00
Doll's, Gold Mesh, Victorian 27.00
Doll's, Mesh, Victorian, Silver Plated 45.00
Evening Bag, Beaded Rose, Green, Fringed, Looped Base, 1920s, 3 1/2 In. 45.00
Evening Bag, Clutch, White Beaded, Floral, Belgium, 1950s, 8 x 5 In. 45.00
Evening Bag, Gold Plated, Basketweave Design, Side Compartment, 1950s 50.00
Evening, Gold Sequins, Bugle Beads, Shoulder Chain, Oval, 1960s 35.00
Lace, Black Knit, Pink Satin Lined, 1915 .... 50.00
Leather, Hand Tooled 60.00
Linen, Arts & Crafts 50.00
Man's, Flame Stitch, Lined With Rings, Drawstring, 5 x 7 In. 350.00
Mesh & Celluloid, Whiting & Davis, Art Deco, Signed 37.50
Mesh, Cream, Whiting & Davis, Gold Frame, 1940s 25.00
Mesh, Depicts Charlie Chaplin, Whiting & Davis 260.00
Mesh, Evening, Silver, Germany 30.00
Mesh, Fringe, Black & Silver, Medallion, 4 x 8 In. 65.00
Mesh, Gold, Whiting & Davis 60.00
Mesh, Gold, Woman's Name Engraved On Frame, Embossed Floral, 1908 .... 95.00
Mesh, Pyramid Fringe, Rose, Green, Whiting & Davis ....*Illus* 195.00
Mesh, Silver, Silver Bead Fringe, Germany 65.00
Mesh, Silver, Whiting & Davis, 1930s 40.00
Mesh, Whiting & Davis, Art Deco, Black On Gold, 7 1/2 x 5 In. 95.00
Mesh, Whiting & Davis, Art Deco, Emerald & Gold Beaded, Mesh Handle 125.00
Mesh, Whiting & Davis, Charcoal & Dove Gray, Silver Frame, 5 x 7 In. 225.00
Mother-of-Pearl, Carved, 3 In. 50.00
Needlepoint, 2 Birds, Gold Floss On Linen, Snap Closure, 5 1/2 In. 135.00
Petit Point, Engraved Gold Frame, Onyx Clasp, 5 x 7 In. 65.00
Petit Point, Fitted, Chain Handle, 1940s 90.00
Pocket, Fabric, Worn Under Skirt, Reach Through Slit In Skirt 1400.00
Pouch, Brass & Copper, On Chain, 2 1/2 x 2 1/2 In. 25.00
Silk, Black, 14K Gold Fittings 140.00
Silk, Black, Clear Crystal Clasp 25.00
Sterling & Leather, Fitted With Change Purse, GHJ, c.1903 .... 605.00
Taffeta, Black, Pouch, Schiaparelli, Embroidered Pink, Pink Handles 38.00
Tapestry, Seed Pearls, Cultured Pearl Clasp, Gold Tubing, 5 x 7 In. 175.00
Velvet, Green, Silver Thread Embroidery, English, 15 3/4 x 11 1/2 In. 300.00

Quezal   Quezal glass was made from 1901 to 1920 by Martin Bach, Sr., in Brooklyn, New York. Other glassware by other firms, such as Loetz, Steuben, and Tiffany, resembles this gold-colored iridescent glass. After Martin Bach's death in 1920, his son continued the manufacture of a similar glass under the name *Lustre Art Glass.*

QUEZAL, Bowl, Ribbed, Iridescent, 4 x 3 3/4 In. 88.00
Candelabra, 4 Candle Lights, Center Shade, Glass & Brass Plateau 1150.00
Candlestick, King Tut, Iridescent Design, Signed, 9 3/4 In., Pair 1045.00

Quezal, Vase,
Blue Swirl Design,
Gold, 6 1/2 In.

Quezal, Vase,
Hearts, White,
Threading, 8 1/2 In.

◆◆◆◆◆◆◆◆◆◆◆◆◆◆◆◆◆◆◆◆◆◆◆◆
Never use bleach on luster
decorated pottery. It will destroy
the luster effect.
◆◆◆◆◆◆◆◆◆◆◆◆◆◆◆◆◆◆◆◆◆◆◆◆

Candy Dish, Gold Iridescent, Signed	195.00
Lamp, Gold Vines, Green Holly Leaves, Shade, Signed, 17 In.	3195.00
Sconce, Gold & Green Full Feather Shades, Pair	2500.00
Shade, Double Blue Hooked Feather, Pair	400.00
Shade, Gold Snakeskin	95.00
Shade, Iridescent Gold, Ribbed, 1904, 4 1/2 In., 4 Piece	795.00
Shade, Paperweight, White Feather, Encased In Clear Glass, Signed	375.00
Shade, Pull-Ups In Green & Gold, Stalagtite, 11 x 4 In.	575.00
Shade, Pulled Feather, Gold Interior, 2-In. Fitting	185.00
Vase, Applied Gold Disk Base, Gold Lined, Linear Designs, 8 In.	1200.00
Vase, Blue Swirl Design, Gold, 6 1/2 In. ....*Illus*	1000.00
Vase, Blue, Green & Purple, Reflecting Gold, Signed, 6 1/2 In.	450.00
Vase, Bluish Gold Flared Rim, Pedestal Base, Signed, 6 In.	1155.00
Vase, Gold Interior, Footed, 3 1/4 x 4 In.	850.00
Vase, Hearts, White, Threading, 8 1/2 In. ....*Illus*	665.00
Vase, Jack-In-The-Pulpit, Green Feathering, 1905-20, 13 1/2 In.	6100.00
Vase, Paneled Fold-Down Rim, Signed, 3 1/2 In.	495.00
Vase, Ruffled Rim, Signed, Iridescent, 7 1/2 In.	350.00

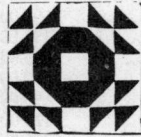

Quilts have been made since the seventeenth century. Early textiles were very precious and every scrap was saved to be reused. A quilt is a combination of fabrics joined to a filler and a backing by small stitched designs known as quilting. An appliqued quilt has pieces stitched to the top of a large piece of background fabric. A patchwork, or pieced, quilt is made of many small pieces stitched together. Embroidery can be added to either type.

QUILT, Amish, 2 Diamonds On Blue Ground, Lavender Border, 30 x 48 In.	150.00
Amish, Diamond-In-The-Square, Pieced & Quilted, Square, 75 1/2 In.	1550.00
Amish, Fan Pattern, Feather Stitching, Cotton Sateen, 81 x 77 In.	715.00
Amish, Friendship, 1810, 8-Point Stars, Stitched Names, 76 x 61 In.	950.00
Amish, Patchwork, Bar Pattern, Meandering Border, 47 1/2 x 49 In.	600.00
Amish, Patchwork, Hand Quilted, Machine Sewn, 30 x 45 In.	225.00
Amish, Patchwork, Lightning Bolt, Wool, Corduroy, F. Detweller, 1940	350.00
Amish, Patchwork, Open Bar, Cube Quilting, c.1930, 80 x 80 In.	5200.00
Amish, Patchwork, Pinwheel Design, Red Calico Back, 80 x 82 In.	215.00
Amish, Patchwork, Primary Color, 4-Patch Variation, 1920s, 74 x 70 In.	2640.00
Amish, Patchwork, Stripes, Reversible, Margaret Mengle, 77 x 91 In.	700.00
Amish, Patchwork, Velvet Border, Geometric Squares, Doll's, c.1880	75.00
Appliqued, 12 Tulips, 6 Red Squares, Scalloped Edge, 72 x 90 In.	325.00
Appliqued, 4 Stylized Eagles, 82 x 82 In.	1050.00
Appliqued, Album, Embroidery, Beads, Braid, 80 x 94 In.	2200.00
Appliqued, Album, Flowers In Pots, Calico, 88 x 90 In.	700.00
Appliqued, Apple Trees & Birds, Embroidered Stems, 79 x 92 In.	400.00
Appliqued, Basket of Tulips, West Hope, Ohio, 1882, 70 x 88 In.	550.00
Appliqued, Bear Paw, Pink, Blue & Yellow Calico, Doll's, 15 x 18 In.	25.00
Appliqued, Carolina Lily, Red, Olive, On White, Machine Sewn, 88 In.	275.00
Appliqued, Eagle & Flower, White Ground, 1930s, 94 x 80 In.	750.00

*Quilt, Appliqued, Green, Mustard,
Statira Pease, 1856, 70 x 72 In.*

*Quilt, Patchwork, Log Cabin, Satin,
39 x 68 In.*

Appliqued, Floral Medallions, Embroidered Berries, 92 x 94 In.	750.00
Appliqued, Geometric Floral & Musical Instruments, 1896, 66 x 80 In.	357.00
Appliqued, Green, Mustard, Statira Pease, 1856, 70 x 72 In. ....*Illus*	775.00
Appliqued, Hearts & Spades, Calico, c.1880, 77 x 85 In.	1430.00
Appliqued, Large Floral, Brown & Red Print, 80 x 84 In.	600.00
Appliqued, Lavender Fans, Crib, 38 In.	98.00
Appliqued, Log Cabin, Prints & Calico, Pennsylvania, 88 x 90	695.00
Appliqued, Princess Feather, Quilted Whig Rose Corners, 80 x 88 In.	2860.00
Appliqued, Rose Pattern Within Floral Border, 1854, 92 x 96 In.	3850.00
Appliqued, Squares of Maker's Name, 1846, 1847, 87 x 102 In.	750.00
Appliqued, Stylized 4-Part Tulips, 82 x 86 In.	200.00
Appliqued, Stylized Floral Design, Yellow On White, 63 x 83 In.	450.00
Appliqued, Stylized Floral, Green Calico, Solid Red, 100 x 100 In.	800.00
Appliqued, Stylized Floral, Green, Red & Goldenrod, 88 x 88 In.	450.00
Appliqued, Stylized Floral, Scalloped Edges, 90 x 104 In.	300.00
Appliqued, Stylized Flowers In Squares, Tree Border, 86 x 102 In.	825.00
Appliqued, Stylized Tulip & Oak Leaf Design, White, 90 x 92 In.	1700.00
Appliqued, Stylized Tulip Medallions, 78 x 92 In.	200.00
Appliqued, Sunflower Stars, Floral Border, 84 x 86 In.	3600.00
Appliqued, Sunflowers, Border Stripes, White Ground, 78 x 94 In.	350.00
Appliqued, Urns of Stylized Flowers, 72 x 82 In.	185.00
Crazy Album, Black, Appliqued Circles, Presentation, 1929, 80 x 89 In.	450.00
Crazy, Patchwork, 88 Rectangles, Ohio Counties, 75 x 80 In.	200.00
Crazy, Patchwork, American Flag In Corner, 72 x 60 In.	330.00
Crazy, Patchwork, Embroidered & Beaded, 1891, 24 1/2 x 24 In.	880.00
Crazy, Patchwork, Mennonite, Purple Border, 76 x 80 In.	115.00
Crazy, Patchwork, Silk & Velvet, Embroidered, 54 x 40 1/2 In.	2200.00
Crazy, Patchwork, Silks, Satins, Feather Stitched, 60 x 76 In.	135.00
Crazy, Patchwork, Star, Calico, Late 19th Century, 81 x 86 In.	550.00
Crazy, Velvet, Silk, Tobacco Cloth, Feather Stitched, 64 x 84 In.	80.00
Patchwork, 16 Patch, Indigo Blue & White Calico, 76 x 84 In.	175.00

Patchwork, Album, Floral, Pictorial & Geometric, Cotton, 84 x 84 In.	3080.00
Patchwork, Alternating Bars of Black Silk, Embroidered, 53 x 56 In.	95.00
Patchwork, Appliqued, Original Pattern, Ohio, Dated 1856, 85 x 87 In.	3600.00
Patchwork, Appliqued, Star of Bethlehem Variant, 74 x 76 In.	385.00
Patchwork, Baltimore Album, Sarah Alter Delaney, 100 x 100 In.	5225.00
Patchwork, Basket of Flowers, Navy, Appliqued, 80 x 82 In.	990.00
Patchwork, Basket, Trapunto, Blue & White, 1860, 76 1/2 x 79 In.	2090.00
Patchwork, Bear Claw, Wool, Blue Plaid, Green, Salmon, 83 x 85 In.	85.00
Patchwork, Bear's Paw, Orange On White, 79 x 82 In.	95.00
Patchwork, Blue & White, 88 x 94 In.	225.00
Patchwork, Blue & White, Scalloped, Crib	400.00
Patchwork, Bow Tie, Indigo & White, 1890–1910, 80 1/2 x 88 In.	750.00
Patchwork, Carpenter's Square, 1880–1900, 79 x 79 In.	7425.00
Patchwork, Cathedral Window, 62 x 72 In.	265.00
Patchwork, Center Medallion, Scrolls, Floral, White, 70 x 70 In.	400.00
Patchwork, Century of Progress, Embroidered, 1933, 88 x 84 In.	2475.00
Patchwork, Chain & Cross, Red & White, 72 x 80 In.	350.00
Patchwork, Child's, Bow Tie Squares, Reds, Browns, White Ground, 42 In.	200.00
Patchwork, Circle & Grid Figure, Reversal Design, 68 x 78 In.	225.00
Patchwork, Concentric Diamonds, Prints & Solids, 82 x 88 In.	225.00
Patchwork, Concentric Squares, Quilted Hearts, 22 1/2 x 22 1/2 In.	160.00
Patchwork, Delectable Mountain With Swallow, 1850s, 48 x 47 In.	1320.00
Patchwork, Diamond In Square Center, White On White, 66 x 72 In.	350.00
Patchwork, Doll's, Knotted, 17 x 25 In.	20.00
Patchwork, Double Wedding Ring, Multicolored, Top Only, 76 x 92 In.	50.00
Patchwork, Dresden Plate, 72 x 90 In.	200.00
Patchwork, Dresden Plate, Multicolors, 70 x 84 In.	150.00
Patchwork, Dresden Plate, Prints, 70 x 84 In.	175.00
Patchwork, Dresden Plate, Prints, 76 x 92 In.	575.00
Patchwork, Drunkard's Path, Calico, 86 x 88 In.	265.00
Patchwork, Drunkard's Path, Goldenrod Calico On White, 70 x 84 In.	200.00
Patchwork, Feathered Star, Blue & White Calico, 45 x 33 In.	1760.90
Patchwork, Flower Basket, Blue & White, 76 x 80 In.	195.00
Patchwork, Flying Geese, Blue & White, 61 x 92 In.	175.00
Patchwork, Garden Walk, Pastel, Scalloped Edge, Kentucky, 80 x 83 In.	425.00
Patchwork, German Baptist, Blue & Black, Wool, c.1875, 42 x 35 In.	950.00
Patchwork, Goose In The Pond, Pinwheel Quilting, 1915, 71 x 78 In.	1100.00
Patchwork, Goose In The Pond, Red & White Cotton, c.1920, 76 x 76 In.	1100.00
Patchwork, Green & Yellow Calico, Solid Red, 76 x 79 In.	400.00
Patchwork, Hawaiian, Orange, White, Palm Stalk Corners, 122 x 100 In.	2200.00
Patchwork, Horses & Cowboys Pattern, Embroidered, Muslin, 96 x 73 In.	1760.00
Patchwork, House, Blue, Floral Print, 48 x 79 In.	475.00
Patchwork, Irish Chain, Pink & Green Calico, 74 x 84 In.	200.00
Patchwork, Large Star, Multicolored Print, Calico, Border, 72 x 72 In.	300.00
Patchwork, Lightning, Red & Yellow Calico, 72 x 80 In.	300.00
Patchwork, Lilies of The Nile Basket, White Ground, 78 x 66 In.	250.00
Patchwork, Log Cabin Type, Printed & Solid Silks, 78 x 78 In.	65.00
Patchwork, Log Cabin, Blue, Rose & Gold, 80 x 84 In.	325.00
Patchwork, Log Cabin, c.1900, Crib, 35 x 28 In.	195.00
Patchwork, Log Cabin, Diamond Pattern, Ohio, 1880s, 61 x 78 In.	6875.00
Patchwork, Log Cabin, Multicolored Prints, 72 x 78 In.	600.00
Patchwork, Log Cabin, Multicolored Prints, 75 x 75 In.	750.00
Patchwork, Log Cabin, Red Wool, 70 x 70 In.	150.00
Patchwork, Log Cabin, Satin, 39 x 68 In. *Illus*	500.00
Patchwork, Log Cabin, Silks, Green, Brown, Black, Crib, 35 x 28 In.	195.00
Patchwork, Lone Star, Solid Colors On White, 34 x 34 In.	425.00
Patchwork, Maltese Cross, Red & White, 76 x 88 In.	250.00
Patchwork, Mennonite, Indigo & Red Calico, c.1880, 27 x 24 In.	850.00
Patchwork, Moon & Stars, Rose, Pink & White, c.1910, 80 x 60 In.	250.00
Patchwork, Mosaic, 78 x 78 In.	210.00
Patchwork, Nine Patch Variant, White On Light Blue, 68 x 68 In.	400.00
Patchwork, Nine Patch, 62 x 70 In.	125.00
Patchwork, Nine Patch, c.1910, 88 x 88 In.	265.00

◆◆

Never touch the surface of a daguerrotype or an ambrotype. The
perspiration will stain the image.

◆◆

Patchwork, Nine Patch, Irish Chain Border, 88 x 88 In.	125.00
Patchwork, Nine Patch, Small Crosses, Brown, Blue, Red, 77 x 78 In.	425.00
Patchwork, Ocean Waves, Multicolored, White Ground, 79 x 79 In.	300.00
Patchwork, Ohio Star, Frog Center, 1800s, 61 x 72 In.	950.00
Patchwork, Optical Tumbling Blocks, Deer, Trees, c.1880, 72 x 54 In.	5225.00
Patchwork, Orange Peel, White Ground, 76 x 86 In.	165.00
Patchwork, Peter & Paul, Brown & White, 78 x 90 In.	410.00
Patchwork, Pieced Cotton, Saw–Tooth, Red, White, Crib, 42 x 36 In.	4180.00
Patchwork, Pineapple Pattern, Blue & White Calico, 76 x 78 In.	300.00
Patchwork, Pineapple, Printed Cotton Patches, 19th C., 84 x 88 In.	550.00
Patchwork, Pinwheel, Blue & White, Homespun Back, 70 x 78 In.	150.00
Patchwork, Pinwheel, White, Red & Blue, 79 1/2 x 70 1/2 In.	330.00
Patchwork, Pinwheels & Squares, Pink & White, 74 x 86 In.	150.00
Patchwork, Political, Harrison, Morton Campaign, 80 x 76 In.	7000.00
Patchwork, Princess Feather, Calico On White Ground, 87 x 85 In.	2700.00
Patchwork, Red & Ecru, White Ground, 73 x 87 In.	175.00
Patchwork, Red Print, White, 72 x 72 In.	285.00
Patchwork, Rob Peter, Pay Paul, Red & Yellow, 70 x 82 In.	110.00
Patchwork, Sampler, Penciled Names, Olive Brown Fabric, 65 x 78 In.	550.00
Patchwork, School House, Green & Multicolored, Square, 93 In.	470.00
Patchwork, School House, Multicolor Prints, Green Grid, 80 x 88 In.	150.00
Patchwork, Single Star, Feather Quilted Circles, 80 x 82 In.	400.00
Patchwork, Snowflakes, Pink Gingham, 82 x 70 In.	450.00
Patchwork, Spirit of St. Louis, 25 Airplanes, 1928, 74 x 80 In.	565.00
Patchwork, Square Blocks, Multicolored Prints & Solids, 83 x 88 In.	170.00
Patchwork, Star Designs, Ecru Ground, 77 x 89 In.	200.00
Patchwork, Star Pattern, Khaki Squares, Dated 1882, 67 x 82 In.	225.00
Patchwork, Star, Calico, Gingham Back, 69 1/2 x 88 1/2 In.	225.00
Patchwork, Star, Calico, Reversible, Calico Bars On Back, 88 x 88 In.	850.00
Patchwork, Star, Green & White, 72 x 88 In.	85.00
Patchwork, Star, Red Calico, Solid Green, 68 x 82 In.	325.00
Patchwork, Stars, Suns, Rising Suns, Red Calico, 101 x 101 In.	2300.00
Patchwork, Stuff–Work, Lady of The Lake, C. A. C. & W. F. I., 72 x 84 In.	2970.00
Patchwork, Sunbonnet Babies, Embroidered, Pink, White, 78 x 78 In.	105.00
Patchwork, Sunburst, Triple Band Border, 19th Century, 78 x 88 In.	610.00
Patchwork, Tiny White Star Print, Navy, 70 x 85 In.	550.00
Patchwork, Triangular Designs, Blue & White Calico, 82 x 90 In.	550.00
Patchwork, Tulip, Diamond Quilting, c.1860, 100 x 100 In.	1700.00
Patchwork, Tumbling Block, Checked Border, 74 x 86 In.	450.00
Patchwork, Tumbling Block, Red & White, Dark Blue Ground, 68 x 82 In.	345.00
Patchwork, Tumbling Blocks & Stars, Silk, Cotton, 76 x 84 In.	1760.00
Patchwork, Twelve Mariner's Compass, White Ground, 72 x 98 In.	150.00
Patchwork, Twenty Baskets, 70 x 84 In.	200.00
Patchwork, Twenty–Five Stars, Calico, 80 x 80 In.	450.00
Patchwork, Twenty–Five Stars, Pinwheel Centers, 78 x 80 In.	350.00
Patchwork, Washington's Plume, Mennonite, c.1870, 77 x 76 1/2 In.	7150.00
Patchwork, Wild Goose Chase, Pink & White, 74 x 90 In.	200.00
Patchwork, Yo–Yo, Pastel Colors, 81 x 95 In.	375.00
Patchwork, Zigzag Design, Blue & White, 74 x 86 In.	465.00
Patchwork, Zigzag Stars, Blue Calico, White Ground, 70 x 76 In.	200.00

Tin–glazed, hand–painted pottery has been made in Quimper,
France, since the late seventeenth century. The earliest firm, founded
in 1685 by Jean Baptiste Bousquet, was known as HB Quimper.
Another firm, founded in 1772 by Francois Eloury, was known as

Porquier. The third firm, founded by Guillaume Dumaine in 1778, was known as HR or Henriot Quimper. All three firms made similar pottery decorated with designs of Breton peasants and sea and flower motifs. The Eloury (Porquier) and Dumaine (Henriot) firms merged in 1913. Bousquet (HB) merged with the others in 1968. The group was sold to a United States family in 1984. The American holding company is Quimper Faience Inc., located in Stonington, Connecticut. The French firm has been called Societe Nouvelle des Faienceries de Quimper HB Henriot since March 1984.

QUIMPER, Bookends, Art Deco, Bagpipe Players, Green Lustered, Signed, 7 In.	385.00
Bottle, Snuff, Laydown, Woman & Man On Reverse, 2 1/2 In.	125.00
Bowl, Peasant Man, Blue Sponged Handles	45.00
Bowl, Peasant Man, Yellow Ground, Handle, 2 1/2 In.	35.00
Bowl, Peasant Woman, Scalloped, Pierced, Marked, 6 1/2 In.	50.00
Butter Chip, Peasant Woman, Cobalt Border, 4 1/2 x 3 1/2 In.	10.00
Butter, Cover, Croisille, Star Shape, 9 In.	365.00
Candlestick, Flowers, Peasant Woman, Marked, 5 1/2 In.	230.00
Candlestick, Serpent & Dolphin, Pair	1300.00
Creamer, Floral, 5 In.	55.00
Cup & Saucer, Peasant Woman On Cup, Marked	20.00
Figure, Shoe, White, Peasant Woman, Marked, 2 1/2 In.	25.00
Figure, Shoe, Yellow, Peasant Man, Marked, 3 1/2 In.	35.00
Figurine, Dancing Figures, Double, Signed Micheau Vernez	350.00
Figurine, Peasant, Sitting, Lady With Basket, Signed Nicot	275.00
Figurine, Sailor, French, 4 In.	155.00
Figurine, St. Anne, Marked, 6 3/8 In.	170.00
Figurine, St. Vierge, Marked, 3 1/2 In.	82.00
Inkwell, Cover, Colored, Oblong, Insert, 4 In.	450.00
Inkwell, Heart Shape, Cover, Insert, 3 In.	295.00
Jardiniere, Swan	550.00
Jug, Puzzle, Openwork Rim, Blue Handle, Motto, 6 In.	200.00
Liquor Set, Breton Border, Tray, 8 Piece	210.00
Plate, Peasant Man, Blue & Yellow Ring Border, Marked, 8 In.	20.00
Plate, Peasant Woman, Shaped Rim, Signed, 9 3/4 In.	145.00
Salt, Swan, Double, Marked	85.00
Sauceboat, Duck	190.00
Shoes, Attached, Center Handle, 3 1/2 In.	65.00
Sugar & Creamer, Peasant 65.00 To	80.00
Sugar & Creamer, Peasant Woman, Blue Spooned Handles	65.00
Sugar & Creamer, Yellow & Blue Bands, Herriot	142.00
Vase, Blue & Gold Bands, Ajonc & Coral Bells	195.00
Vase, Pink Quintal, Signed, 5 1/2 In.	235.00
Wall Pocket, Peasant Man, 7 x 5 3/4 In.	295.00

RADURA. Radford pottery was made by Alfred Radford in Broadway, Virginia, Tiffin and Zanesville, Ohio, and Clarksburg, West Virginia, from 1891 until 1912. Jasperware, Ruko, Thera, Radura, and Velvety Art Ware were made. The jasperware resembles the famous Wedgwood ware of the same name.

RADFORD, Vase, Abraham Lincoln, Eagle, 8 In.	350.00
Vase, Angels, Pink, Drip Glaze, 17 In.	275.00
Vase, Lady With Flowers, Grapes, No. 59, 4 In.	210.00

The first radio broadcast receiving sets were sold in New York City in 1910. They were used to pick up the experimental broadcasts of the day. The first commercial radios were made by Westinghouse Company for listeners of the experimental shows on KDKA Pittsburgh in 1920. Collectors today are interested in all early radios, especially those made of Bakelite plastic or decorated with blue mirrors.

RADIO, Admiral, Portable, Tubes, Turquoise Leather & Chrome	40.00
Atlas, Figural, Battery, Transistor	25.00

Atwater Kent, Cathedral, Heterodyne	100.00
Atwater Kent, Cathedral, Model 82, 16 x 19 In.	130.00
Atwater Kent, Separate Speaker, Metal Case, 1920s	85.00
Bakelite, Glass Front, Painted Numerals, 1950s	55.00
Bakelite, Headboard Light, 1930s	95.00
Bendix, 2 Colors	467.00
Bottle, Heinz Catsup, Box	45.00
Catalin, No. 520, 1946	250.00
Catalin, Portable, Red	21.00
Charlie Tuna	35.00
Cheeseburger	30.00 To 35.00
Chevron, Beer Can Size	40.00
Crosley, Art Deco, Green & Gold	90.00
Crosley, Art Deco, Red & Gold, 1940s	85.00
Crosley, Art Deco, Red, 1940s	70.00
Crosley, Cathedral, Model 157	225.00
Crosley, Model 11, Brown	18.00
Crosley, Model 51, With Head Set	150.00
Crosley, Model 515–55, Art Deco Cutout Front, Cherry, Refinished	75.00
Crosley, Pup	250.00
Crosley, Super 6 AM Shortwave, Police Band, 1930s	65.00
Crosley, Wigit	300.00
Crystal, Headphones	20.00
Crystal, Pocket	20.00
Emerson, Bakelite, 6 1/2 x 5 In.	35.00
Emerson, Brown Bakelite	25.00
Emerson, Catalin, Model 400, Butterscotch With Brown & White Grill	400.00
Emerson, Catalin, Model 520, 1946	265.00
Emerson, Model 520	325.00
Emerson, Patriot, Butterscotch & Brown	400.00
Emerson, Transistor, Bakelite, Portable, 1950s	55.00
Erla, Cabinet, 18 In.	83.00
Fada, Bakelite, 2 Colors	775.00
Fada, Bullet, Butterscotch	600.00
Fada, Butterscotch	550.00
Fada, Catalin, Model 700, Light Green	650.00
Fada, Model 60V	290.00
Garod, Commander	800.00
Garod, Model 6AU–1, Wrap–Around Grill, Butterscotch	950.00
General Electric, Doll	625.00
General Electric, Model 622, Plastic, 1941, Tortoiseshell	1350.00
General Electric, Model 622, Plastic, Tortoiseshell Color, 1941	1350.00
General Electric, Tombstone, Wood	95.00
Ghostbusters	35.00
Globe, Navigator	450.00
Grigsby–Grunow, Hinds Co., Bakelite Speaker Horn	85.00
Hallicrafter, Sky Challenger	70.00
Hamburger Helper	30.00
Hawaiian Punch	45.00
Ivory, Westinghouse	20.00
Knight Rider, Kit, Box	25.00
Kollerola, Coin–Operated, Hotel, Wood	245.00
Majestic, Black Celluloid Horn Speaker	100.00
Metrodyne, Speaker, 1 Dial	475.00
Motorola, Diplomat	25.00
Motorola, Diplomat, Model 65L2	25.00
Motorola, No. 5R1	30.00
Motorola, Transistor	35.00
Music Master	375.00
Packard–Bell, Model 100A, Red Bakelite	18.00
Pasin Man	45.00
Peanut, Jimmy Carter	35.00 To 75.00
Philco, AM Shortwave, 1920s	125.00

Philco, Bakelite, Model 48–460 .... 35.00
Philco, Cathedral 300.00
Philco, Cathedral, Model 60 .... 175.00
Philco, Ivory Bakelite Trim, 1930s 75.00
Philco, With Record Player, Model 49–1401, Wood, 1946 .... 200.00
Philco, With Record Player, Wooden Cabinet, 1947 .... 100.00
Pizza Hut, Box 40.00
Radiola III–A, Type RL, Speaker, Pat. 1922 .... 125.00
Raggedy Ann & Andy, 2 Dimensional 25.00
Raisin Man, Am/Fm, Box 35.00
RCA, Model 1X2, Off White 10.00
RCA, Model 6–BX–8A, Dinner Bucket, Plastic 35.00
RCA, Oriental 175.00
RCA, Tombstone, Model 118 .... 125.00
RCA, Tombstone, Model 6T 125.00
Santa Maria Ship 25.00
Sentinel, Carmel Marbelized 75.00
Sentinel, Model 312, Battery Or Current, Double Grill Speaker 195.00
Short Wave, Air Castle, Model 711, Wood 15.00
Smurf's Head, Box 20.00
Snow White, 1938 .... 1200.00
Sparton, 3–Band, Wood 35.00
Sparton, Blue Mirror Center, Chrome Framed Dial, 15 x 14 1/4 In. 1700.00
Sparton, Bluebird, America 4600.00
Sparton, Bluebird, Blue Mirrors, Canada, 1933 .... 9500.00
Sparton, Chrome Frame, Blue Mirror Glass, W. D. Teague, 1936, 15 In. ... 1870.00
Sparton, Model 558, 4 Knob, America 4250.00
Sparton, Model 5A116, White Bakelite 85.00
Stewart–Warner, Porto–Bar, Brown Bakelite, Cream Trim, 1935, 23 In. 93.00
Stomberg–Carlson, Wood, Table Model, 1940s 75.00
T–Bird, Transistor 28.00
Tony The Tiger, Figural 35.00
Tube Tester, Hickock, Instruction Book 75.00
Westinghouse, Reddish Brown Plastic, 1950s 25.00
Zenith, 5 Band, Art Deco, Table Model, c.1931 .... 150.00
Zenith, Holiday, No. 5G0032, Maroon 75.00
Zenith, Model 622F 45.00
Zenith, With Phonograph, Bakelite, Cobra Head Arm 145.00
Zenith, Wood 120.00

Railroad enthusiasts collect any train memorabilia. Everything is wanted, from oilcans to whole train cars. The Chessie system has a store that sells many reproductions of their old dinnerware and uniforms.

RAILROAD, Ashtray, Goat, Great Northern ....95.000 To 125.000
Badge, Baggage Agent, Metal 40.00
Badge, Hat, Conductor's, Brass 40.00
Bell, Locomotive, Brass, Cradle & Yoke, 17 x 17 In. 800.00
Bell, On Frame, 16 In. 248.00
Bond, Las Vegas & Hot Springs Electric Railroad, N. M. Terr., 1903 .... 130.00
Booklet, Rhymes of The Rail, C. J. Byrne, Illustrated, 30 Pages 15.00
Bowl, Union Pacific, Challenger, 5 In. 20.00
Bowl, Union Pacific, Harriman, 5 1/2 In. 30.00
Broadside, Maine Central Railroad, Trip Ad., 1927, 9 x 21 In. 24.00
Brochure, B & O R.R., Century of Progress Expo., 1934 .... 33.00
Brochure, Lewis & Clark Expo., Great Northern Railway, 1905 .... 40.00
Bucket, Collapsible, Canvas, Rock Island R.R. 25.00
Butter Pat, Adobe, Santa Fe 8.00
Butter Pat, California Poppy, Santa Fe 18.50
Can, Kerosene, Union Pacific 25.00
Chamber Pot, Central Pacific R.R., Brass 25.00
Cigar Box, Northwestern R.R. 29.00
Coat Hanger, GM & O, Mobile, Ala., Wooden 10.00

Coffeepot, Atchison, Topeka & Santa Fe, Poppies 125.00
Cup & Saucer, Baltimore & Ohio, Blue, White, Lamberton, Demitasse 98.00
Cup & Saucer, Chicago, Milwaukee, St. Paul & Pacific R.R. 85.00
Cup, Coffee, Union Pacific, Desert Flower 30.00
Cup, Tea, Union Pacific, Desert Flower 30.00
Cuspidor, Soo Lines, Graniteware, Brown 175.00
First Aid Box, Erie R. R, Small 35.00
First Aid Kit, Pennsylvania R.R., Red Tin 25.00
Hand Cart, Velocipede, Northern Pacific Railroad, 1883 .... 7500.00
Hat, Conductor's, Maine Central 88.00
Hat, Conductor's, N. Y., N. H., & H. R.R., Navy Blue 440.00
Hat, Conductor's, New York, New Haven & Hartford, Black 66.00
Hat, Conductor's, Pennsylvania R.R. 90.00
Headlight, Incandescent, Imperial 247.50
Lamp, Caboose, Wall Bracket, Complete 155.00
Lamp, Maine Central R.R., Whale Oil, Fixed Engraved Globe 302.50
Lamp, Pennsylvania R.R., Electrified 15.00
Lamp, Union Carbide, No. A 75.00
Lantern, A. T. & S. F., Amber Globe 75.00
Lantern, Adams 95.00
Lantern, Adams, Pennsylvania R.R. 50.00
Lantern, Adlake Reliable, GNRY, Safety Always, Clear 175.00
Lantern, Adlake, CNW, Embossed, Tall 90.00
Lantern, Adlake, Great Northern, Safety Always, 5 3/8 In. 125.00
Lantern, Adlake, IC, Embossed, Tall 85.00
Lantern, Adlake, No. 300, Blue Globe 75.00
Lantern, Adlake, No. 300, Clear Globe 55.00
Lantern, Armspear, N. & W., Clear Globe, 1925 .... 40.00
Lantern, Brass, Green, Clear Globe 550.00
Lantern, Burlington Route 55.00
Lantern, Burlington Route, Cobalt Blue Logo Globe 395.00
Lantern, Caboose, Mounting Bracket, Smoke Hood 33.00
Lantern, Conductor's, Nickeled Brass 250.00
Lantern, Dietz, No. 6, New York Central, Red Globe 60.00
Lantern, Dressel, Pennsylvania R.R. In Keystone On Top 60.00
Lantern, Dressel, Pennsylvania R.R., Clear Globe 70.00
Lantern, Green Over Clear Globe, Brass 550.00
Lantern, Hand, 4–Light, 14 In. 90.00
Lantern, Hand, Adams & Westlake, Half Green, Half Clear Globe 687.50
Lantern, Hand, Baltimore & Ohio, High Globe 75.00
Lantern, Hand, Embossed AT & SF, Red Globe, 4 In. 75.00
Lantern, Hand, Embossed I. C. R.R., Red Globe, 5 In. 125.00
Lantern, Hartford R.R., Red Globe, Embossed 50.00
Lantern, IC, Adlake, Clear Globe, Short 40.00
Lantern, Inspector's, Dietz 65.00
Lantern, Inspector's, Dietz, New York Central, Logo, 11 In. 71.50
Lantern, Kerosene, Green Cast Letters, 1880s 850.00
Lantern, Mopac 150.00
Lantern, New York Central, Red 75.00
Lantern, New York, New Haven & Hartford R.R. 30.00
Lantern, Pennsylvania R.R. 17.50
Lantern, Rock Island R.R. 40.00
Lantern, Switch, Adams & Westlake, 2 Amber, 2 Blue Lenses 60.50
Lantern, Switch, Kerosene, Etched Globe, N. Y., N. H. & H. R.R. 78.00
Lantern, Switch, Kerosene, Red Globe, Pennsylvania R.R. 60.00
Lantern, Switch, L & N 80.00
Lantern, Wall Bracket, Lehigh Valley R.R., Marked 50.00
Lantern, Watchman's, Copper Clad, Bull's–Eye Lens, 12 In. 125.00
Lantern, Westlake 95.00
Light, Signal, Aluminum Cased 9.00
Lighter, Commemorate Retired Steam Locomotive, 1959 .... 30.00
Lock, Southern Pacific R.R., Solid Brass, No. 117 .... 45.00
Map, Southern Pacific R.R., Color, 1932, 19 1/2 x 30 In. 15.00

Menu, Oyster Shape, B & O R.R., Die–Cut, Early 1930s 24.00
Paperweight, Central of Georgia 25.00
Paperweight, Missouri–Pacific R.R. 55.00
Payroll Document, J. L. & S. Railroad, Stamp, 1859, 3 1/2 x 5 1/2 In. 17.50
Perpetual Calendar, Missouri–Pacific R.R., Diesel Engine Picture 150.00
Plaque, Missouri–Pacific R.R., Admiral Byrd, Bronze 50.00
Plate, AT & SF, Adobe, 9 In. 50.00
Plate, Baltimore & Ohio, Potomac Valley, 1827–1927, 8 1/2 In. 85.00
Plate, Baltimore & Ohio, Thomas Viaduct, 6 3/4 In. 35.00
Plate, Harper's Ferry, Blue & White, Lamberton China, 8 In. 110.00
Plate, Maroon Rim, Gold Trim, Marked AP, 10 1/2 In. 150.00
Plate, New York Central, Mohawk, 10 In. .... 60.00 To 75.00
Plate, Union Pacific R.R., Challenger, 6 1/4 In. 20.00
Plate, Union Pacific R.R., Challenger, 9 1/2 In. 35.00
Plate, Union Pacific, Desert Flower, 5 1/2 In. 25.00
Platter, Denver & Rio Grande, Prospector, 12 In. 75.00
Platter, Nickel Plate Road, Oval, 12 In. 85.00
Platter, Pullman, Oval, 13 In. 85.00
Platter, Rio Grande, Prospector, 12 In. 60.00
Platter, Union Pacific, Challenger, Oval, 8 In. 30.00
Platter, Union Pacific, Desert Flower, Oval, 9 1/2 In. 50.00
Platter, Union Pacific, Oval, 8 In. 35.00
Postcard, Santa Fe R.R., World War II 6.50
Postcard, Welcome Arch, Union Depot, Denver, Colorado, 1910 .... 5.00
Poster, Pennsylvania R.R., New York Invites You, 25 x 39 In. 110.00
Print, Santa Fe, At The Water Hole, Logo, 1942 .... 40.00
Route List, Cotton Belt, Officers, Stations, Agents, 25 Pages, 1904 .... 50.00
Saucer, Union Pacific, Challenger, 5 1/4 In. 15.00
Scale, Railway Express 80.00
Signal Lock, Illinois Central Signal, Brass 20.00
Signal Switch, Glass Sides, c.1920 .... 35.00
Spittoon, Pullman Co., Nickel 50.00
Spittoon, Union Pacific, Steam Engine Each Side, Brass, 12 In. 225.00
Spoon, Northwest Pacific R.R., Souvenir 38.00
Steps, Conductor's, Pullman 110.00
Syrup, Great Northern Railway, Attached Saucer, Silver Plate 575.00
Thermometer, Sante Fe, Porcelain, 13 x 3 In. 65.00
Ticket Punch, Conductor's 35.00
Ticket, Trolley Car, July 27, 1917, Passenger Checks 15.00
Timetable, Rock Island, 1912 .... 10.00
Token, Elmyra R.R. 35.00
Token, Union Pacific, Alcoa Aluminum 60.00
Torch, Baltimore & Ohio 35.00
Tumbler, Louisville & Eastern, Yellow Flyer 25.00
Tumbler, Pennsylvania R.R., Brown & White Train, Logo, 4 3/8 In. 9.00
Tumbler, Santa Fe, White Enameled, 3 7/8 In. 9.00
Tumbler, Soo Line, Red Logo, 1885–1985, 5 1/4 In. 39.00
Uniform, Brakeman's, C & O, Hat, Coat, Vest & Pants 600.00
Uniform, Conductor's, Frisco R.R. 140.00
Velocipede Handcart, Track Inspector's, SD & AE, 1898 .... 5000.00
Whistle, Caboose, Brass 55.00
Whistle, Steam, Lunenheimer 225.00
Wrench, Flat, Marked CPR, Yellow, 18 In. 25.00

The razor was used in ancient Egypt and subsequently wherever shaving was in fashion. The metal razor used in America until about 1870 was made in Sheffield, England. After 1870, machine–made hollow–ground razors were made in Germany or America. Plastic or bone handles were popular. The razor was often sold in a set of seven, one for each day of the week. The set was often kept by the barber who shaved the well–to–do man each day in the shop.

RAZOR, Blade, Broadway Double Edge 5.00
Blade, Golf Club & Flag, Red & Green Wrapper, Dated 1933 .... 3.00

Blade, Majestic, Single Edge 6.00
Darwin, Holds & Sharpens Blades, Built–In Strop, Chrome Case 125.00
Gillette, Brass, Leather Case 15.00
Hodgson & Co., Hinged Steel Blade, Tortoiseshell Case, 6 1/8 In. 110.00
Hone, Keen Kutter, Box 40.00
Keen Kutter, Bone Handle 150.00
Kewpir, Woman's, Case 12.00
Kewtie, Aqua, Case, Miniature 12.00
Pacific Safety, Hollow Handle, Holds Septic Pencils 15.00
Rolls, Box 25.00
Schick, Brass Case 22.50
Sharpener, Kriss–Kross, Hand Crank, Box, 1920s 10.00
Sharpener, Strand, Safety 12.00
Shermack Safety, Woman's Round Head Razor, Pat. 1934, Box 12.00
Star Brand Safety, Government Issue, Box, World War II 12.00
Straight Razor, Red Devil Tobacco Blade 18.00
Straight, Benz, Berlin Airlift On Blade 40.00
Straight, Blue Diamond 45.00
Straight, C–Mono 40.00
Straight, Double Duck, Gold Edge 55.00
Straight, Green 8.00
Straight, Keen Kutter 17.50
Straight, Mozart Special, Case 40.00
Straight, Peacock 40.00
Straight, Red Imperial, Case 32.00
Straight, Small, For Mustaches 37.50
Straight, Sterling, Art Nouveau, J. Engstrom, Paris, Lacquer Case, 1878 .... 300.00
Straight, Winchester, No. 8626 .... 75.00
Strop, E. E. Monson 18.00
Strop, Ingersoll, Outfit 12.00
Strop, Silver Plate 225.00
Strop, Traveller's, Howard Strop Co., No. 262, Leather Case 25.00
Woman's, Round Shape, Silver Box, 1930s 35.00

Reamers, or juice squeezers, have been known since 1767, although most of those collected today date from the twentieth century. Figural reamers are among the most prized.

REAMER, Blue Delphite, Swirl 35.00
Child's, Glass 18.00
Clown, Sunrise Design On Bottom 35.00
Crisscross, Cobalt Blue 295.00
Duck, Figural 20.00
Duck, Figural, Ceramic, Japan 40.00
Eastley, Cobalt Blue 65.00
Green, Depression Glass 15.00
Green, Large 15.00
Handy–Andy, Crystal Measuring Cup 30.00
Lemon, Figural, Japan 20.00
Little Old Lady, Ceramic, Japan 55.00

◆◆

When storing tintype pictures, first dust them carefully with a soft brush. Put each one in a separate acid–free envelope with the image side away from the envelope seam. Label the envelope with pencil or india ink before inserting the tintype. Do not flex or bend the tintype because it might crack. If the tintype is mounted in an old cardboard mat or daguerreotype case, keep it in the case and then store in the envelope.

◆◆

Monkey Face, Ceramic, Japan, 1920	90.00
Sunkist, Jadite	18.00
Sunkist, White Milk Glass	20.00
Swirl, Pink, Finger Handle	18.00
Toby, Figural, 1 Piece	89.00

The cylinder–shaped phonograph record for use with the early Edison phonograph was made about 1889. Disc records were first made by 1894; the double–sided disc by 1904. The high–fidelity records were first issued in 1944, the first vinyl disc in 1946, the first stereo record in 1958. The 78 RPM became the standard in 1926 but was discontinued in 1957. In 1932, the first 33 1/3 RPM was made but was not sold commercially until 1948. In 1949, the 45 RPM was introduced.

RECORD, Army Airforce Band, Balling Field, World War II, 78 RPM	60.00
Berliner Disk	47.50
Cylinder, Brown Wax	25.00
Doctor Who, BBC, 2 Records Set	40.00
Glenn Miller, Vol. II, Commemorative Set, 45 RPM, Case, History, 15 Pc.	50.00
Golden Walzes, Bill Vaughn, LP	2.00
Jerry Lewis, Cinderella, Dot	25.00
Jerry Mahoney Club Songs, 45 RPM, Sleeve, 1950s	30.00
Jim & Tammy Baker, Building On The Rock, Sincord, 1975	40.00
Let It Rock, Chuck Berry	14.00
Pledge of Allegiance, Red Skelton, Paper	15.00

The Red Wing Pottery of Red Wing, Minnesota, was a firm started in 1878. The company first made utilitarian pottery. In the 1920s art pottery was made. Many dinner sets and vases were made before the company closed in 1967. Rumrill pottery was made for George Rumrill by the Red Wing Pottery and other firms. It was sold in the 1930s. For more information, see *Kovels' Depression Glass & American Dinnerware Price List.*

RED WING, Ashtray, Arrowhead, Brown	115.00
Ashtray, Canoe	110.00
Ashtray, Commemorative, General Electric	35.00
Ashtray, Duck	25.00
Ashtray, Gypsy Trail	25.00
Ashtray, Minnesota Twins, World Series, 1965	60.00
Ashtray, Red Wing	195.00
Bean Pot, Bail Handle, 1 Gal.	60.00
Bean Pot, Little Store On The Corner, C. L. Carlson, Minn.	330.00
Beater Jar, Advertising	85.00 To 125.00
Beater Jar, Gray Line	175.00
Beater Jar, Montevideo, Marked	175.00
Beater Jar, Seefeldt's Grocery, Hustisford, Wisc.	75.00
Beater Jar, Semon's Fair Store, Athens, Wisc.	95.00
Bowl, Blossom Time, Square, 8 1/2 In.	8.00
Bowl, Blue, Rust & Cream Spongeware, Signed, 7 In.	65.00
Bowl, Cap, 7 In.	70.00
Bowl, Cereal, Random Harvest	7.00
Bowl, Grayline, 5 In.	225.00
Bowl, Manitowoc Marine Grocery, Blue Saffron Sponge, 11 In.	135.00
Bowl, Salad, Hamm	175.00
Bowl, Serving, Hamm	40.00
Bowl, Vegetable, Zinnia, 8 1/2 In.	9.00
Bread Plate, Capistrano	2.50
Butter, 1 Qt.	60.00
Butter, Bobwhite	33.00
Butter, Cover, Land 'O Lakes	140.00
Butter, Round Up	150.00 To 225.00
Candlestick, Pair	15.00
Casserole, Bobwhite, Small	20.00

Casserole, Gray Line 185.00
Casserole, Rooster, Yellow, Large 130.00
Casserole, White, Minnesota Advertising 65.00
Churn, Advertising, Table Condiments 800.00
Churn, Birch Leaf, Signed, 3 Gal. 225.00
Churn, Cover, Dasher, Dated 1914, 4 Gal. 175.00
Clock Plate, Bob White 30.00
Clock, Mammy ....95.00 To 250.00
Cookie Jar, Baker, Beige .... 35.00 To 43.00
Cookie Jar, Baker, Yellow ....75.00 To 120.00
Cookie Jar, Blue Monk 48.00
Cookie Jar, Bobwhite 65.00
Cookie Jar, Carousel, Colored Animals, White Base .... 197.00 To 228.00
Cookie Jar, Cattail, Brown 90.00
Cookie Jar, Chef .... 55.00 To 65.00
Cookie Jar, Cylinder, Speckled, Floral, Poem 25.00
Cookie Jar, Dutch Girl .... 47.00 To 65.00
Cookie Jar, Dutch Girl, Yellow .... 50.00 To 60.00
Cookie Jar, Dutch People, Aqua 68.00
Cookie Jar, Gray Line, Cover 150.00
Cookie Jar, Jack Frost 295.00
Cookie Jar, King of Tarts, Hat, Blue With Black Trim 210.00
Cookie Jar, King of Tarts, Multicolor 220.00
Cookie Jar, King of Tarts, Pink .... 210.00 To 565.00
Cooler, Bobwhite, Cover, Spigot 270.00
Creamer, Zinnia 8.00
Crock, Butter, Cover, Blue & Gray 150.00
Crock, Butter, St. Cloud, Advertising, 3 Lb. 125.00
Crock, Cobalt Butterfly, Salt Glaze, 20 Gal. 85.00
Crock, Large Wing, 1 Gal. 325.00
Cruet, Bobwhite, Stand 125.00
Dish, Candy, White, 7 In. 6.00
Figurine, Bulldog, Brown 500.00
Flowerpot, Attached Saucer, Cobalt Blue 18.00
Gravy Boat, Bobwhite 45.00
Jar, Butter, Low, No. 10, Signed 225.00
Jar, No. 3, Cover, Handle, Gray Line 325.00
Jar, Packing, Bail, No. 10 .... 45.00
Jar, Pantry, Lid, Lomas, Tuckwood & Wchuette, 5 Lb. 215.00
Jar, Preserve, Ball Lock, 5 Gal. 85.00
Jar, Refrigerator, Squat, Signed, 6 In. 90.00
Jardiniere 12.00
Jug, Albany Slip, Bird Marking, 1/2 Gal. 80.00
Jug, Albany Slip, Bird Marking, 2 Gal. 90.00
Jug, Beehive, Albany Slip, 5 Gal. 575.00
Jug, Beehive, Albany Slip, RWS Co. On Handle, 5 Gal. 725.00
Jug, Beehive, Colfax, Advertising, 5 Gal. 1250.00
Jug, Beehive, Sangcura Sprudel Water, Texas, 5 Gal. 595.00
Jug, Large Wing, 6 Gal. 175.00
Jug, Moose Convention, Miniature 430.00
Jug, Nicollet Hotel, Miniature 295.00
Jug, Syrup, Smith, 1/2 Pt. 125.00
Mug, Bobwhite 40.00
Mug, Bobwhite, Pair 85.00
Mug, Bratwursthaus, Marked 85.00
Mug, Verse 1400.00
Pail, Butter, Blue Band 150.00
Pitcher & Bowl, Lily, Blue & White 450.00
Pitcher, Bobwhite, 12 In. 30.00
Pitcher, Cherry Band, 8 1/2 In. 80.00
Pitcher, Cherry Band, 8 1/2 In. 70.00
Pitcher, Cherry Band, Manitowoc, Wisc. 225.00
Pitcher, Floral, Ivory, Large 20.00

Pitcher, Gray Line, Advertising 225.00
Pitcher, Lady With Harp, 8 In. 100.00
Pitcher, Tampico 30.00
Planter, Deer, Frog, No. 520, 16 In. 23.00
Planter, Free Form, Turquoise & Brown Spatter, 10 1/2 In. 8.00
Planter, Leaf Border, Pink & Brown, Gray Interior, 7 1/2 In. 6.00
Planter, Salt Box, Blue Edge 15.00
Planter, Sgraffito Swan On Pond, Sewer Pipe Co. 225.00
Plate, Dinner, Bobwhite 8.00
Plate, Dinner, Zinnia 8.00
Platter & Double Iron Warmer, Smart Set, Pattern Handles, 20 In. 115.00
Platter, Capistrano, 13 1/2 In. 13.00
Platter, Village Green, 13 In. 15.00
Relish, Pitchfork 85.00
Service For 8, Lute Song, Service Pieces 250.00
Soup, Dish, Provincial, Lug 20.00
Stand, Christmas Tree 275.00
Success Filter 295.00
Sugar & Creamer, Bobwhite 35.00
Sugar & Creamer, Zinnia 10.00
Sugar, Cover, Tampico 3.50
Teapot, Katrina 35.00
Teapot, Western Round Up 150.00
Tidbit, 2 Tiers, Floral Design 15.00
Toothpick, Man, Union Stoneware 195.00
Tray, A. Miller, Wines & Liquors, Minn. 340.00
Vase, Acorns & Leaves 65.00
Vase, Black, 6 In. 10.00
Vase, Lion, 7 1/2 In. 110.00
Vase, Raised Abstract Designs, Blue, 11 In. 80.00
Vase, Turquoise, Black Speckles, 12 In. 30.00
Water Cooler, Cover, 3 Gal. 150.00
Water Cooler, Cover, Blue Band, 3 Gal. 310.00
Water Cooler, Cover, Hand Turned, 3 Gal. 2100.00
Water Cooler, Stand, Tampico 250.00

Redware is a hard, red stoneware that originated in the late 1600s and continues to be made. The term is also used to describe any common clay pottery that is reddish in color.

REDWARE, Bank, A Present From Nod Hill, Egg Shaped, Knob Handle, 5 In. 15.00
Bank, Acorn, Brown Fleck Glaze, 4 In. 5.00
Bottle, Pinched Neck, Speckled Glaze, 7 1/2 In. 260.00
Bowl, Coggled Rim, Yellow Slip Interior, Brown Polka Dots, 14 In. 2300.00
Bowl, Coggled Rim, Yellow Slip, Sgraffito Bird, 7 7/8 In. 625.00
Bowl, Dark Brown Sponging, Footed, 3 1/8 x 6 1/8 In. 75.00
Bowl, Dated 1890, England, 7 x 17 In. 700.00
Bowl, Milk, Greenish Amber Interior Glaze, 3 1/4 x 17 1/4 In. 150.00
Bowl, Mixing, Off–White Irregular Slip, 4 x 10 In. 150.00
Bowl, Orange Ground, Rim Spout, Ribbed Handle, 5 x 9 1/2 In. 175.00
Bowl, Outwardly Tapering, Brown Mottled Rim, 14 1/2 In. 965.00
Bowl, Stylized Tulip, 11 In. 2100.00
Bowl, White Slip Stripes, Running Brown, 2 1/4 x 7 1/4 In. 425.00
Bowl, Yellow Glazed Interior, 18 1/4 x 8 1/2 In. 155.00
Bowl, Yellow Slip Design, 2 3/4 x 7 1/4 In. 30.00
Bowl, Yellow Slip Design, Wavy Lines & Dots, 2 x 7 1/4 In. 325.00
Bowl, Yellow Slip Interior, Brown Polka Dotted Bird, 14 In. 2300.00
Bust, Black Man, Dark Brown, Yarn Hair & Beard, Beaded, 4 3/4 In. 200.00
Butter Stamp, Flower, Leaves, 3 x 4 In. 285.00
Butter Tub, Multi–Glaze, Mid 19th Century, 8 1/2 In. 625.00
Candleholder, 3–Light, Adam & Eve, Serpent In Apple Tree, 12 In. 675.00
Charger, Coggled Rim, Yellow & Orange Slip, 11 In. 1200.00
Charger, Coggled Rim, Yellow Slip Design, 12 1/4 In. 700.00
Charger, Green & Yellow Slip Design, 13 In. 4950.00

Charger, Stylized Tulip Design, Brown Glazed Ground, 11 1/4 In. 2100.00
Creamer, Yellow Slip Design, 3 3/4 In. 45.00
Crock, Cover, 8 In. 120.00
Crock, Cream Glaze, New York State Potter, 10 1/2 In. 750.00
Crock, Red Mottled Glaze, 11 1/2 In. 137.00
Cup, Brown Splotched Glaze, Strap Handle, 3 In. 85.00
Dish, Black Splotches, 3 x 6 In. 175.00
Dish, Brown Splotches, Rim Handles, 6 1/4 In. 325.00
Dish, Yellow Slip Design, 7 1/4 In. 125.00
Figurine, Dog, Seated, Open Front Legs, Tooled Coat, 8 3/4 In. 450.00
Figurine, Eagle, Conical Plinth, Yellow Beak, 4 1/2 In. 525.00
Figurine, Lion, P. Ipsen 380, Unglazed, 4 3/4 In. 100.00
Flowerpot, Attached Saucer, John Bell, Waynesboro, 6 In. 300.00
Flowerpot, Spattered Glaze, Finger Crimped Rim, 6 In. 90.00
Jar, Amber Glaze, Brown Flecks, Egg Shaped, 13 In. 60.00
Jar, Brown Flecks, Brownish Amber, Egg Shaped, 10 In. 300.00
Jar, Canning, G. N. Fulton, Manganese Splotches, Signed 1000.00
Jar, Canning, Mottled Dark Green Glaze, 10 3/4 In. 65.00
Jar, Cream Slip, Egg Shape, 7 1/4 In. 35.00
Jar, Dark Brown, Applied Handles, Wavy Lines, Egg Shaped, 12 1/2 In. 165.00
Jar, Ear Handles, Incised Wavy Lines, Decoupage, Egg Shaped, 11 In. 35.00
Jar, Incised Lines, Vertical Brown Brush Marks, Clear Glaze, 10 In. 175.00
Jar, Preserve, Amber Glaze, Dark Brown Spots, 10 1/4 In. 95.00
Jar, Sponged Design, Tooled Line At Midpoint, 5 In. 125.00
Jar, Storage, Cover, Manganese Splotches, 6 1/2 In. 660.00
Jar, Tooled Line At Shoulder, Side Spout, Strap Handle, 6 3/4 In. 225.00
Jar, Tooled Lines, Amber Glaze, Egg Shaped, 5 3/8 In. 1000.00
Jar, Tooled Lines, Brown Splotches On Red, Egg Shape, 10 In. 325.00
Jug, Applied Lug Handle, Mottled Glaze, New England, 10 1/2 In. 2310.00
Jug, Black Spotted Glaze, Strap Handle, Egg Shaped, 6 3/8 In. 1100.00
Jug, Greenish Glaze, Amber Spots, 14 1/4 In. 400.00
Jug, Manganese Splotches, 19th Century, Egg Shaped, 10 1/2 In. 2100.00
Jug, Mottled Brown Glaze, Ribbed Strap Handle, 7 3/4 In. 155.00
Jug, Strap Handle, Running Glaze, Lyndeboro Pottery, 7 1/4 In. 350.00
Lamp, Turnip, Green Glaze, 4 7/8 In. 95.00
Loaf Pan, Yellow Slip Design, 3 1/2 x 14 x 17 In. 485.00
Milk Pan, Albany Brown Glaze, Round, Early 1800s, 17 x 4 In. 195.00
Mold, Butter, Stylized Tulip, 4 1/8 In. 450.00
Mold, Cake, Lamb Shape 1500.00
Mold, Food, Coiled Fish, Amber Glaze, 10 1/2 x 11 1/4 In. 225.00
Mold, Food, Turk's Head, Brown Dots On Rim, 4 1/2 x 9 In. 40.00
Mold, Food, Turk's Head, Dark Brown Glaze, 4 1/2 In. 45.00
Mold, Food, Turk's Head, Yellow Amber Glaze, Brown Flecks, 9 7/8 In. 185.00
Mug, Brown Sponging, Ribbed Strap Handle, 6 1/2 In. 800.00
Ornament, Mantel, Dog, Sitting, Brown Glaze, 12 In. 275.00
Pie Plate, Coggled Rim, 3 Line Design, 8 In. 350.00
Pie Plate, Coggled Rim, 3 Line Yellow Slip Design, 10 3/4 In. 150.00
Pie Plate, Coggled Rim, Floral, German Inscription, 10 5/8 In. 175.00
Pie Plate, Coggled Rim, Yellow Slip Wavy Line, 8 3/4 In. 170.00
Pie Plate, Coggled Rim, Yellow Wavy Line, 9 1/2 In. 125.00
Pie Plate, Sunflower, Benjamin Bergey, 13 In. 9350.00
Pie Plate, Yellow Slip Design, 10 In. 1430.00
Pitcher, Black Shiny Glaze, 6 1/4 In. 55.00
Pitcher, Blue Green Mottled Glaze, 10 1/4 In. 150.00
Pitcher, Brown Splotches Glaze, Strap Handle, 4 In. 150.00
Pitcher, Brown Splotches Glaze, Strap Handle, 5 1/2 In. 225.00
Pitcher, Face, 8 In. 80.00
Pitcher, Milk, Brown Glaze, 6 In. 16.00
Pitcher, Shenandoah Valley, Multiglaze, 9 1/2 In. 1800.00
Pitcher, Shenandoah, Embossed Bands, Tooled Rim, 10 3/4 In. 500.00
Pitcher, Spatter Glaze, Isaac Good, Zigler Pottery, 1873–74 .... 9000.00
Pitcher, White Slip, Running Green & Brown, Shenandoah, 10 1/2 In. 1350.00
Pitcher, Yellow Rim, Brown Interior, England, 8 1/2 In. 185.00

Pitcher, Yellow Slip Design, 8 In.	35.00
Pitcher, Yellow Slip Design, Green Highlights, 7 In.	60.00
Pitcher, Yellow Slip Design, Signed Rdo De Alba, 6 In.	20.00
Pitcher, Yellow Slip, Brown Splotches, Handle, 7 1/2 In.	355.00
Plaque, Ram, Initials L. B. 1976, 9 x 12 In.	250.00
Plate, Sgraffito, Lester Breininger, 1974, 12 1/4 In.	115.00
Plate, Yellow Slip, Green & Brown Glaze, Orange Ground, 10 1/4 In.	200.00
Pot, Dome Top, Tooled Design, Embossed Leaf Handle, 11 1/4 In.	150.00
Pot, Incised Design, Ruffled Rim, c.1910, 4 1/2 In.	190.00
Sconce, Candle, Wheel Turned, Base Socket, 6 1/2 In.	350.00
Spittoon, Fancy	90.00
Tea Caddy, Yellow Slip & Manganese, Heart & Floral, 6 In.	3200.00
Tub, Open Rim Handles, Greenish Glaze, 3 3/4 x 7 1/2 In.	200.00
Tumbler, Black Sponged Rim, 3 1/8 In.	125.00
Vase, Brown Spots, Yellow Glaze, Isaac Good	9000.00
Wash Bowl & Soap Dish, White Slip, Running Glaze, 16 In.	800.00

REGOUT, see Maastricht

Richard was the mark used on acid–etched cameo glass vases, bowls, night–lights, and lamps made in Lorraine, France, during the 1920s. The pieces were very similar to the other French cameo glasswares made by Daum, Galle, and others.

RICHARD, Lamp, Domical Shade, Village, Oasis, Signed, c.1920, 12 1/2 In.	3850.00
Perfume Bottle, Raspberry Leaves, Flowers, Pink, Signed, 7 In.	650.00
Vase, Alsatian River Landscape, House, Signed, c.1920, 9 7/8 In.	1320.00
Vase, Blue Flowers, Leaves & Vines, 4 1/2 In.	500.00
Vase, Flamingos, Chartreuse, Brown & Burnt Orange, Signed, 5 7/8 In.	1000.00
Vase, Lakeside Villa, Amethyst Overlay, Frosted, Signed, 7 In.	410.00
Vase, Purple On Orange, Floral, Butterfly, 11 3/4 In. ....*Illus*	445.00
Vase, Purple Trees & Mountains, Yellow Ground, Signed, 14 In.	1925.00

Ridgway pottery has been made in the Staffordshire district in England since 1808 by a series of companies with the name Ridgway. The transfer–design dinner sets are the most widely known product. They are still being made. Other pieces of Ridgway are listed under Flow Blue.

RIDGWAY, Biscuit Jar, Rattan Handle, Brown, 6 1/2 In.	235.00
Dessert Set, Shamrock, Floral & Gold Design, 17 Piece	1500.00
Fish Set, Platter & 5 Plates	325.00
Jug, Full Body & Head of Pan, Pipes Forms Handle, c.1840, 9 1/2 In.	350.00
Plaque, Coaching Days, In A Snow Drift, 12 In.	135.00
Plaque, Coaching Days, Taking Up The Mails, 12 In.	135.00
Platter, Grecian, Green, 13 In.	35.00
Tea Caddy, Square, Brown, 5 3/4 In.	155.00

A rifle is a firearm that has a rifled bore and that is intended to be fired from the shoulder. Other firearms are listed under Gun.

A glass vase or bowl can be cleaned with a damp cloth. Try not to put the glass in a sink filled with water. Hitting the glass on a faucet or the sink is a common cause of breakage.

Richard, Vase, Purple On Orange, Floral,
Butterfly, 11 3/4 In.

RIFLE, Air, Winchester, No. 423 .... 85.00
   Kentucky, Long, Tiger Maple Stock, 55 In. 465.00
   Meriden, Model 10, 22 Gauge, Wood Stock, 35 1/2 In. 69.50
   Musket, Austrian, 1861 .... 250.00
   Musket, Tower, Flintlock, 1776 .... 835.00
   Percussion, Curly Maple, Brass, Griffiths & Siebert, 57 1/2 In. 770.00
   Percussion, Curly Maple, Brass, Marked D. Loomis, Dayton, Ohio, 53 In. 705.00
   Percussion, Curly Maple, Brass, Marked Griffiths, Cincinnati, 58 In. 440.00
   Percussion, Maple, Brass, Marked J. O. Stutsman, Dayton, Ohio, 53 In. 495.00
   Percussion, Revolving, Arms Mfg. Co., Colt's Pat., 498, 50 1/2 In. 3740.00
   Pneumatic, Poacher's, Plain Half Stock, 19th Century 130.00
   Remington, Model 700, . 30–06 Gauge, Scope 220.00
   Stevens, Crack Shot 130.00
   Winchester, M94, Golden Spike, 30–30 .... 340.00

Riviera dinnerware was made by the Homer Laughlin Co. of Newell, West Virginia, from 1938 to 1950. The pattern was similar in coloring and in mood to Fiesta and Harlequin. The Riviera plates and cup handles were square. For more information, see *Kovels' Depression Glass & American Dinnerware Price List.*

RIVIERA, Butter, Mauve, 1/4 Lb. 85.00
   Butter, Red, 1/4 Lb. 75.00
   Butter, Yellow, 1/4 Lb. 85.00
   Butter, Yellow, 1/2 Lb. 25.00
   Casserole, Cover, Ivory 80.00
   Casserole, Cover, Red 60.00
   Creamer, Red 8.00
   Creamer, Yellow 6.00
   Jug, Disk, Mauve Blue .... 120.00 To 185.00
   Nappy, Yellow, 9 In. 16.00
   Saltshaker, Ivory 5.00
   Saltshaker, Red 8.00
   Sugar & Creamer, Cover, Light Green 20.00
   Teapot, Cover, Yellow 65.00
   Teapot, Light Green 55.00

Roblin Art Pottery was founded in 1898 by Alexander W. Robertson and Linna Irelan in San Francisco, California. The pottery closed in 1906. The firm made faience with green, tan, dull blue, or gray glazes. Decorations were usually animal shapes. Some red clay pieces were made.

ROBLIN, Vase, Speckled Glaze, Dark Green, 4 In. 350.00
   Vase, Unglazed, Red Clay, 4 1/2 In. 200.00

Rockingham, in the United States, is a brown glazed pottery with a tortoiseshell–like glaze. It was made from 1840 to 1900 by many American potteries. Mottled brown Rockingham wares were first made in England at the Rockingham factory. Other types of ceramics were also made by the English firm.

ROCKINGHAM, Bed Pan, 16 3/4 In. 10.00
   Bottle, Coachman, Embossed 1849, Speck of Green, 10 3/8 In. 700.00
   Bottle, Gin, Mermaid 200.00
   Bottle, Gin, Potato 135.00
   Bottle, Toby .... 25.00 To 45.00
   Bowl, 3 x 11 3/4 In. 50.00
   Bowl, Embossed Exterior, 5 x 10 1/2 In. 65.00
   Bowl, Leaf Design, Fire Proof, J. E. Jeffords & Co., 11 1/2 In. 175.00
   Bowl, Mixing, 4 5/8 x 10 5/8 In. 50.00
   Bowl, Skim Milk, 12 In. 135.00
   Coffeepot, Rebecca At Well 25.00
   Dish, Soap, Embossed Leaf Lip Design, Oblong, 8 1/8 In. 40.00
   Dish, Soap, Round, 5 1/2 In. 65.00

◆◆

Furniture with marquetry designs is always expensive. Best are pieces
made of walnut, then mahogany, then oak. Flower marquetry designs
are more common than bird or insect designs.

◆◆

Figurine, Dog, Seated, 10 1/4 In.	175.00
Figurine, John Liston, Marked, 1826, 6 1/4 In.	550.00
Figurine, Lion, Rectangular Base, 9 1/2 In.	600.00
Figurine, Lion, Recumbent, Glazed, 15 x 9 1/2 In.	1045.00
Figurine, Spaniel, Glazed, 1830s	742.50
Figurine, Spaniel, On Shaped Base, Glazed, 11 In.	165.00
Flask, Book, Flint Enamel, 5 3/4 In.	950.00
Flask, Embossed Floral, 7 In.	100.00
Flask, Embossed Morning Glories, 7 3/8 In.	85.00
Flask, Figural, Mermaid, 7 3/4 In.	45.00
Flask, Shoe, 6 5/8 In.	100.00
Foot Warmer, 13 In.	350.00
Frame, Picture, Glazed, Oval, 9 1/2 x 8 1/2 In.	247.00
Inkwell, Lady's Shoe, 3–Hole, Brown & Yellow, 5 In.	220.00
Inkwell, Shoe Shape, 3 1/8 In.	75.00
Jar, Acorn Finial, Embossed Handles, 11 1/2 In.	215.00
Jar, Cover, 5 x 5 1/2 In.	65.00
Jar, Cover, Embossed Rope Bands, 4 x 5 In.	25.00
Jar, Cover, Left Handles, 8 x 8 In.	85.00
Pie Plate, 10 In.	70.00
Pie Plate, Mottled Brown & Yellow, 7 1/2 In.	20.00
Pitcher, 5 3/8 In.	40.00
Pitcher, Cover, Embossed Classical Foliage, 10 1/2 In.	75.00
Pitcher, Daniel Boone, Marked	85.00
Pitcher, Embossed Hunt Scene, 8 5/8 In.	45.00
Pitcher, Embossed Hunt Scene, 9 1/4 In.	145.00
Pitcher, Embossed Scene of Cupid & Psyche, 7 5/8 In.	75.00
Pitcher, Figural, Man's Head, 8 1/4 In.	75.00
Pitcher, Fox Handle, Hunt Scene, 7 In.	135.00 To 150.00
Pitcher, Hound Handle, Embossed Hanging Game, 9 1/4 In.	120.00
Pitcher, Hound Handle, Embossed Hunt Scene, 10 3/4 In.	650.00
Pitcher, Hound Handle, Embossed Hunt Scene, 11 In.	1700.00
Pitcher, Hound Handle, Hunt Scene, 9 3/4 In.	1100.00
Pitcher, Paneled, 10 1/2 In.	135.00
Pitcher, Solid Dark, 11 In.	88.00
Pitcher, Squat, 3 5/8 In.	45.00
Soap Dish, 3 1/4 x 5 1/4 In.	35.00
Soap Dish, Embossed Foliage, 4 x 5 1/2 In.	155.00
Soap Dish, Leaves & Panels, 6 In.	60.00
Soap Dish, Round, 4 In.	80.00
Sugar, Cover, 5 7/8 In.	285.00
Teapot, Rebecca At The Well, 8 In.	45.00

ROGERS, see John Rogers

Rookwood pottery was made in Cincinnati, Ohio, from 1880 to
1960. All of this art pottery is marked, most with the famous flame
mark. The R is reversed and placed back to back with the letter P.
Flames surround the letters. After 1900, a Roman numeral was
added to the mark to indicate the year. The name and some of the
molds were purchased in 1984; new items will be clearly marked.

ROOKWOOD, Ashtray, Fish Shape, Ivory	35.00 To 45.00
Ashtray, Mustard, Matte	35.00

Ashtray, Nude Woman, Bronze	75.00
Ashtray, Sallie Toohey, 1928	165.00
Basket, Floral, Gold Ground, Signed AMB, 4 1/2 x 6 3/4 In.	325.00
Bookends, Collie, White	225.00
Bookends, Crow, 1920	195.00
Bookends, Dutch Boy & Girl	325.00
Bookends, Girl On Bench, Pink & Gray	165.00 To 190.00
Bookends, Laughing Girl, 1924	140.00
Bookends, Panther	285.00
Bookends, Peacock, Green, Rose, No. 2445, Dated 1930	195.00
Bookends, Rook Among Branches, Gray, Marked, 5 x 5 1/4 In.	220.00
Bookends, Rook, Olive, 1931	100.00
Bookends, Ships, Blue	175.00
Bookends, St. Francis, Fox & Dove	90.00
Bottle, 3 Wise Men & Woman In Oriental Dress, 7 3/4 In., Pair	2750.00
Bowl, Brown & Tan Mottled, Lorinda Epply, 1930, 9 1/2 In.	195.00
Bowl, Stylized Flower Heads & Lines, Marked, 1914, 11 In.	440.00
Bowl, Turtles, Swimming, Green Glaze, Shirayamadani, 1887, 5 x 7 In.	2300.00
Bowl, Wild Roses, White, Standard Glaze, 1891, 4 3/4 In.	275.00
Candlestick, Olive Green, Twisted Handles, 1922, Pair	275.00
Chocolate Pot, Limoges–Type, Frogs, Spiders, Brown, Nichols, 12 In.	1350.00
Creamer, Floral, Standard Glaze, 3 x 4 In.	150.00
Ewer, Blue & Yellow, 1892, 7 1/2 In. ....*Illus*	220.00
Ewer, Branch & Blossoms, 1907, 5 1/2 In.	225.00
Ewer, Demarest, 1900, 5 In.	395.00
Ewer, Hibiscus, Standard Glaze, Rose Fechheimer, 1899, 6 1/4 In.	330.00
Ewer, Limoges–Style Glaze, Anchor Mark, 9 1/2 In. ....*Illus*	385.00
Ewer, Serrated Leaves, Berry Clusters, Valentien, 1891, 19 5/8 In.	2530.00
Ewer, Standard Glaze, Carl Schmidt, 1899, 12 1/2 In.	550.00
Figurine, Dog, Seated, 6 In.	275.00
Figurine, Elephant, Ivory, Matte, c.1936, 4 x 4 1/8 In.	55.00
Figurine, Girl, Signed, 1930, 6 1/2 In.	185.00
Figurine, Witch's Shoe, Black, Cinnamon, 1922, 14 x 9 In.	250.00
Ginger Jar, Apple Blossoms, Blue–Gray, Lenore Asbury, 1918, 12 In.	775.00
Inkwell & Pen Tray, Sphinx Fitted With Well, 1920, 9 x 8 1/2 In.	275.00
Inkwell, Water Lily, Green Ground, Insert, Ed Diers, 1901, 4 In.	225.00
Jar, Ginger, Birds of Paradise, Emerald, Cover, E. T. Hurley, 14 In.	2875.00
Jar, Orange Poppies, Amelia Browne Sprague, 1897, 12 In. ....*Illus*	880.00
Jardiniere, Magnolia, Bisque To Gold To Blue, Valentien, 16 In.	2650.00
Jug, Big Tree's Sister Kiowa, Constance A. Baker, 1899, 7 1/2 In.	2640.00
Jug, Japanese Design, Birds, Branches, A. Valentien, 1883, 4 3/4 In.	225.00
Jug, White Swan, Crow, Edward Hurley, 1900, 7 1/2 In.	2420.00
Lamp, Fluid, Yellow Roses, Globular Top, Thin Flared Base, 20 In.	1320.00
Lamp, Leaf & Berry Carving, Shirayamadani, 1903, 14 In.	1925.00
Lamp, Open Flowers, Sea Green Glaze, Metal Base, 1930, 22 1/2 In.	275.00
Mug, Blue Carved, 3 Handles, Green Matte, C. A. D., 1907, 7 In.	330.00
Mug, Figural, Owl Perched Amid Leaves, Acorns On Handle, c.1906	770.00

Rookwood, Ewer, Blue & Yellow, 1892, 7 1/2 In.
Rookwood, Stein, Jefferson Portrait, M. A. Daly, 1896, 9 1/2 In.
Rookwood, Ewer, Limoges–Style Glaze, Anchor Mark, 9 1/2 In.

Rookwood, Jar, Orange
Poppies, Amelia Browne
Sprague, 1897, 12 In.

Rookwood, Mug, Spotted Jack
Rabbit Crow, 3 Handles,
E. Brain, c.1899

Rookwood, Vase, The Man,
c.1900, 8 3/4 In.

Rookwood, Vase, Conquering
Bear, Sioux, 9 In.

Rookwood, Stein, Clara Chapman Newton,
1881, 11 1/2 In.
Rookwood, Stein, Marked E. T. K., 1882,
9 1/2 In.

Rookwood, Vase, Mary Madeline Nourse,
1895, 8 3/4 In.

Mug, Figural, Owl, Perched In Oak Tree, Branch Handle, 5 In.		255.00
Mug, Indian Brave, Sadie Markland, 1898, 5 In.		3000.00
Mug, Indian White Thunder, Brown Glaze Over Yellow, 5 In.		3000.00
Mug, Portrait, Chief White Man, 3 Handles, A. D. Sehon, 7 3/4 In.		3410.00
Mug, Portrait, Truesdale, Indian, 1892, 5 In.		1760.00
Mug, Puzzle, Frederick Sturgis Laurence, 1899, 5 In.		1155.00
Mug, Spotted Jack Rabbit Crow, 3 Handles, E. Brain, c.1899	*Illus*	2200.00
Paperweight, Bear, Dark Brown, 1923, 4 1/4 In.		200.00
Paperweight, Burro, Standing, Ivory, Matte, 1945, 6 In.		100.00
Paperweight, Cat, Crouching, Green, Brown Glaze, 1937, 2 1/2 In.		150.00
Paperweight, Duckling		175.00
Paperweight, Frog, Green Glaze, c.1912		110.00
Pitcher, 2 Elves On A Log, Tricornered, 4 1/4 In.		1400.00
Pitcher, Berries, 3–Cornered Lip, 1893, 4 In.		575.00
Pitcher, Flight of Swallows, M. M. Nourse, 1895, 8 3/4 In.		1650.00
Pitcher, Portrait of Sleeping Bear, Grace Young, 1899, 14 1/4 In.		5500.00
Pitcher, Shirayamadani, 1891		2950.00
Plaque, Black Foliage, Tan Lioness, Signed, 1902, 18 1/2 In.		650.00
Plaque, Fall Forest Scene, Blue, Cream Ground, E. Diers, 5 x 8 In.		2090.00
Plaque, Green Poplar Trees, Cream To Blue, L. Epply, 7 1/2 In.		1760.00
Plaque, Inlet, Blue Trees, Foliage, Cream, E. T. Hurley, 8 x 5 In.		1550.00
Plaque, Sampans In Harbor Scene, Carl Schmidt, 1920, 8 x 6 In.		2650.00
Plaque, Winter Morning, Vellum, Lorinda Epply, 8 x 10 In.		4400.00
Plaque, Woodland River Scene, Fred Rothenbusch, 1922, 8 x 6 In.		2640.00
Plate, Child's, Leaves, Berries, 4 In.		25.00
Plate, Molded Water Lilies, 7 In.		65.00
Rose Bowl, Pansies, White, High Glaze, E. T. Hurley, 1899		550.00
Rose Bowl, Yellow Wild Roses, Swirled, Jeannette Swing, 7 1/2 In.		192.00
Shoe, Witch's, Black & Cinnamon, 1922, 14 x 9 In.		175.00
Sign, Matte Glaze, 1924, 4 x 13 1/4 In.		1100.00
Stein, Clara Chapman Newton, 1881, 11 1/2 In.	*Illus*	825.00

Stein, Geo. Wiedemann Brewing Co., Inc., Pewter Lid, 1/2 Liter 578.00
Stein, Jefferson Portrait, M. A. Daly, 1896, 9 1/2 In. ....*Illus* 7700.00
Stein, Marked E. T. K., 1882, 9 1/2 In. ....*Illus* 605.00
Sugar & Creamer, Turquoise 95.00
Tankard, 1885 .... 225.00
Teapot, Sailboat, 1912 .... 350.00
Tile, Center 3 Trees, Surrounded By 20 Pale Trees, 23 Piece 3850.00
Tile, Faience, Grapes 195.00
Tile, Girl, Long Bouffant Skirt, 1919 .... 210.00
Tile, Grapes 165.00
Tile, Parrot & Floral, Square, 1919, 5 1/2 In. 192.00
Tile, Pinecone, 6 In. 45.00
Tray, Rook, Blue, Matte, 1929, 4 x 8 In. 135.00
Vase, 3 Vertical Rectangles, Moss Green Glaze, 7 In. 100.00
Vase, Angled Shoulder, Matte Glaze, 1918, 9 1/8 In. 825.00
Vase, Art Nouveau, Glazed Blue Green, Matte, 1912, 7 1/2 In. 105.00
Vase, Band of Pink Apple Blossoms, Vellum, 1910, 8 3/4 In. 467.50
Vase, Bats Around Top, Gun Metal Production 185.00
Vase, Berry & Pods, Standard Glaze, E. N. Lincoln, 1904, 5 1/2 In. 275.00
Vase, Black–Eyed Susans, Standard Glaze, Bulbous, Wilcox, 6 3/4 In. 110.00
Vase, Blue & Green Designs, Lorinda Epply, 1921, 8 3/4 In. 825.00
Vase, Blue Violets, Blue Vellum, F. Rothenbusch, 1931, 4 1/2 In. 495.00
Vase, Bluebird, Matte, 1934, 5 In. 38.00
Vase, C. Steinle, 1913 .... 350.00
Vase, Carved Design, C. S. Todd, 1914, 3 3/4 In. 240.00
Vase, Cavalier Portrait, Grace Young, 1902, 11 1/2 In. 4125.00
Vase, Clusters of Berries, Leaves, Marked, c.1928, 14 3/8 In. 1325.00
Vase, Conquering Bear, Sioux, 9 In. ....*Illus* 5600.00
Vase, Cranberry To Purple, Peacock Feathers, Todd, 7 1/2 In. 595.00
Vase, Daffodils, Standard, Narrow Neck, Sallie E. Coyne, 10 3/4 In. 1155.00
Vase, Dahlias, Wax Matte, Elizabeth Lincoln, 1928, 5 3/4 In. 400.00
Vase, Dancing Nymph, Maroon Exterior, Green Interior, 13 1/4 In. 500.00
Vase, Decorated With Violets, Shaded Blue Ground, 4 In. 335.00
Vase, Deep Pink Poppy, Black Outline, Brown Bisque, Sax, 8 1/2 In. 4675.00
Vase, Fan, Blue Ribbed, 1928, 7 1/2 In. 137.00
Vase, Floral Design, Ed Diers, 1913, 8 1/2 In. 1375.00
Vase, Floral Vellum, 1912, 6 1/2 In. 425.00
Vase, Florals, Brown, Wax Finish, Bulbous, K. J., 1923, 6 In. 385.00
Vase, Floriform, Dark Blue, Speckled Turquoise Interior, 7 1/4 In. 120.00
Vase, Glazed Amber, Painted Thistles, Laura Lindeman, 1905, 6 In. 165.00
Vase, Gold–Brown Pansies, Sea Green, C. A. Baker, 8 1/2 x 3 3/4 In. 1650.00
Vase, Greek Key, Blue–Green, L. M. C. 10–1–02, 7 In. 225.00
Vase, Green Calla Lilies, Gold Outlined, Black Interior, 6 In. 235.00
Vase, Green Design, Sara Sax, 7 In. 285.00
Vase, Green Exterior, Apricot Interior, 7 In. 50.00
Vase, Hand Painted, Wax Matte Glaze, c.1912, 4 x 5 1/2 In. 550.00
Vase, Iris Glaze, 2 Dragonflies, C. Schmidt, 9 5/8 In. 4850.00
Vase, Iris, Cream To Green To Black, Glazed, 1904, 11 x 5 1/2 In. 2875.00
Vase, Irises On Brown Ground, Matthew Daly, Ovoid, 13 1/2 In. 1200.00
Vase, Lady Godiva, Horse, High Glaze, Jens Jensen, 1932, 8 1/2 In. 4025.00
Vase, Leaves & Berries, E. N. L. Lincoln, Marked, 11 In. 335.00
Vase, Light Blue Stylized Blossoms, Peach, Chas. Todd, 13 1/2 In. 715.00
Vase, Lily of The Valley, White, Mary Nourse, 1893, 5 1/4 In. 880.00
Vase, Mary Madeline Nourse, 1895, 8 3/4 In. ....*Illus* 1650.00
Vase, Molded Swans, Blue Vellum, 1918, 3 In. 225.00
Vase, Mushrooms On Tall Stalks, Handles, CPM, 1900, 4 1/2 x 5 In. 350.00
Vase, Olive Branches, Yellow Interior, A. Sprague, 1903, 7 1/4 In. 390.00
Vase, Open Daffodils, Yellow Shaded To Green, 1910, 9 1/2 In. 302.00
Vase, Oriental Design, Stylized Flowers, Marked, 1887, 5 1/2 In. 1650.00
Vase, Pink Clover, Blue Vellum Glaze, C. Lindeman, 1906, 7 1/4 In. 550.00
Vase, Pink Glaze, Flaring Neck, 5 1/2 In. 77.00
Vase, Portrait, 3 Fingers Cheyenne, E. Hurley, 1899, 9 In. 2530.00
Vase, Portrait, The Man, Assinboin, G. Young, 1900, 8 3/4 In. 2200.00

Vase, Purple Blossoms, Branches, 1950, 14 In. 450.00
Vase, Red Mottled Floral, Cream Ground, E. T. Hurley, 1933, 7 In. 990.00
Vase, Rook On Stump, Blue, Dated 1928, 6 1/2 In. 75.00
Vase, Roosters, Tiger's–Eye Glaze, Harriet E. Wilcox, 9 1/2 In. 2090.00
Vase, Salmon, Yellow Azalea, Green To Brown, Matt Daly, 1895, 15 In. 3960.00
Vase, Scenic Vellum Sunset, 1915, 7 1/2 In. 1085.00
Vase, Scenic Vellum, 10 In. 4675.00
Vase, Scenic Vellum, 1914, 12 In. 2400.00
Vase, Scenic Vellum, Band of Landscape, 1912, 9 In. 1540.00
Vase, Scenic Vellum, Sallie Coyne, 1920, 5 3/4 In. 850.00
Vase, Standard Glaze, Constance Baker, 1897, 8 In. 250.00
Vase, Swollen Form, Spiderwort With Leaves, E. N. L. Lincoln, 8 In. 245.00
Vase, The Man, c.1900, 8 3/4 In. ....*Illus* 2200.00
Vase, Trees & Lake, Sallie Coyne, 1920, 5 1/2 In. 775.00
Vase, Tulips, Green, Gray To Cream, A. R. Valentien, 12 1/2 In. 4950.00
Vase, Violets On Blue Ground, Sallie E. Coyne, Ovoid, 4 In. 330.00
Vase, Violets, Standard Glaze, Carolyn Stegner, 1896, 6 1/4 In. 330.00
Vase, Wax Matte, Louise Abel, Blue, 6 In. 450.00
Vase, White Clouds, Black, Bisque Ground, L. Holtkamp, 6 x 5 In. 247.00
Vase, White Magnolias, Cream To Gray–Blue, Sara Sax, 10 1/4 In. 1875.00
Vase, Yellow Berry & Leafy Branch, Albert Pons, 1906, 6 In. 445.00
Vase, Yellow Blossoms, Chocolate To Gold, Shirayamadani, 8 3/4 In. 1980.00
Vase, Yellow Mums, Iris Glaze, Ed Diers, 1902, 5 1/2 In. 715.00
Vase, Yellow Tulips, Brown, Reverse Corset, S. E. Coyne, 10 1/2 In. 1650.00
Vase, Yellow Tulips, Iris Glaze, Ovoid, 1901, 9 In. 825.00
Vase, Yellow, 1922, 7 In. 75.00
Vase, Yellow, High Gloss, 6 In. 40.00
Vase, Yellow, Palm Tree, 1921, 6 1/2 In. 50.00
Vase, Yellow, Raised Flower, 1948 .... 50.00
Wall Pocket, Oak Leaves 185.00
Wall Pocket, Peacock Feather, Turquoise, 1915, 11 In. 165.00

ROSALINE, see Steuben

Rose bowls were popular during the 1880s. Rose petals were kept in the open bowl to add fragrance to a room, a popular idea in a time of limited personal hygiene. The glass bowls were made with crimped tops, which kept the petals inside. Many types of Victorian art glass were made into rose bowls.

ROSE BOWL, Basket Shape, Flowers, Twisted Amber Handle, Cream, 7 5/8 In. 195.00
Black Satin, Tiffin, Large 145.00
Blue Satin Glass, Black & White Flower Sprays, 9–Crimp 100.00
Coralene, Pink Overlay, Amber Feet, 6–Crimp, 3 In. 375.00
Pink Shaded, White Interior, 17–In. Circumference 90.00
Satin Glass, Yellow, Shell Design 80.00

Rose Canton china is similar to Rose Medallion, except no people are pictured in the decoration. It was made during the nineteenth and twentieth centuries in greens, pinks, and other colors.

ROSE CANTON, Brush Box, Cover, Enamel Floral, Butterly & Bird, 7 In. 412.00
Plate, Central Bird, Flowers & Butterflies, 8 3/4 In., Pair 195.00
Platter, c.1860, 16 In. 1600.00

Rose Medallion china was made in China during the nineteenth and twentieth centuries. It is a distinctive design picturing people, flowers, birds, and butterflies. Pieces are colored in greens, pinks, and other colors.

ROSE MEDALLION, Bowl, 1840–50, 9 1/2 x 4 7/8 In. 1950.00
Bowl, Petal Rim, 8 In. 35.00
Bowl, Pierced, Oval, Conforming Tray, 11 In. 1045.00
Bowl, Trophies of Birds, Garden Scene, 10 In. 550.00
Bowl, Underplate, Reticulated, 11 In. 1895.00
Candlestick, Floral & Figural Panels, 6 In., Pair 335.00
Candlestick, Floral & Figural Reserves, 6 3/4 In., Pair 715.00

Cuspidor, Floral & Figural Panels, Flaring Rim, 7 5/8 In. 465.00
Dish, Cover, Floral & Butterfly Design, 11 In., Pair 1325.00
Dish, Cover, Geometric & Butterfly Design, Oval, 11 In., Pair 1200.00
Dish, Serving, Cover, 9 In. 125.00
Fish Tank, c.1860 .... 1600.00
Jar, Cover, Cylindrical, 12 1/2 In. 125.00
Lamp, Kerosene, Cylinder, Brass Base, Electrified, 12 In. 660.00
Mug, Floral & Figural Panels, Twisted Handle, 5 3/4 In. 465.00
Plate, Square, 6 In. 20.00
Platter, 14 1/2 In. 325.00
Platter, Scenes of Figures, Pierced Insert, 15 In. 1210.00
Punch Bowl, 19th Century, 5 1/4 x 13 1/2 In. 935.00
Punch Bowl, Figure & Bird Panels, 5 1/2 x 13 In. ....*Illus* 825.00
Punch Bowl, Floral & Figural Panels, 1880s, 14 5/8 In. 1100.00
Tea Set, Fitted Basket, 1850s, 8 In., 3 Piece 110.00
Tea Set, Wicker Basket, Pre-1900s 450.00
Teapot, Marked Japanese Porcelain, 5 3/4 In. 45.00
Vase, Alternating Figural & Floral Reserves, 12 1/2 In. 135.00
Vase, Bird & Floral Design, Bottle Form, 10 In., Pair 550.00
Vase, Cylindrical, Bird & Floral Panels, 9 In. 150.00
Vase, Lizard Each Side, Foo Dog Handles, 13 3/4 In., Pair 660.00
Wash Basin, Figural & Floral Reserves, 5 1/4 x 16 In. 445.00
    ROSE O'NEILL, see Kewpie

Rose Tapestry porcelain was made by the Royal Bayreuth factory of Tettau, Germany, during the late nineteenth century. The surface of the porcelain was pressed against a coarse fabric while it was still damp, and the impressions remained on the finished porcelain. It looks and feels like a textured cloth. Very skillful reproductions are being made that even include a variation of the Royal Bayreuth mark, so be careful when buying.

ROSE TAPESTRY, Basket, Blue Mark, 5 In. 295.00
Basket, Braided Handle, Scalloped Rim 450.00
Basket, Scalloped Swag of Gold Flowers, Oval, 6 x 5 In. 395.00
Basket, Swing Handle, Blue Mark, 4 1/4 In. 295.00
Bonbon, Circle of Roses Around Rim, Roses In Center 195.00
Box, Trinket, Blue Mark, 3 1/2 In. 345.00
Box, Trinket, Colonial Couple, Blue Mark, 2 1/4 x 3 1/2 In. 235.00
Creamer, Pinched Spout, 3-Color Roses, 3 3/4 In. .... 210.00 To 295.00
Creamer, Tankard Shape, Pinched Spout, 3 3/4 In. 250.00
Hair Receiver, Footed, Marked 255.00
Hair Receiver, Goat .... 325.00 To 350.00
Hair Receiver, Goat, Marked 275.00
Match Holder, Bust of Woman, Shading Eyes, Blue Mark 395.00
Nappy, Clover Shape, Ring Handle, Blue Mark 295.00
Pitcher, Pinched Spout, Scenic 210.00
Pitcher, Pink Roses, 5 3/4 In. 420.00

Rose Medallion, Punch Bowl,
Figure & Bird Panels, 5 1/2 x 13 In.

◆◆◆◆◆◆◆◆◆◆◆◆◆◆◆◆◆◆◆◆◆◆

Be careful when burning candles in glass candlesticks. If the candle burns too low, the hot wax and flame may break the glass.

◆◆◆◆◆◆◆◆◆◆◆◆◆◆◆◆◆◆◆◆◆◆

Pitcher, Scene of 3 Sheep, 3 3/4 In.	295.00
Ring Box, Cover, Courting Couple, Oval, Marked, 3 3/4 x 2 In.	235.00
Shoe, Woman's, Original Laces	350.00
Toothpick, Handle, Footed, Blue Mark	495.00
Tray, Dresser, Courting Couple, Pastel, 7 x 9 In.	475.00
Tray, Dresser, Portrait, Marked, 11 1/2 x 8 1/4 In.	325.00
Tray, Handles, Oval, Blue Mark, 7 3/4 x 4 1/4 In.	225.00
Vase, Blue Mark, 4 1/4 In.	195.00
Vase, Forest & Gazebo, 4 In.	220.00

Rosemeade Pottery of Wahpeton, North Dakota, worked from 1940 to 1961. The pottery was operated by Laura A. Taylor and her husband, R.I. Hughes. The company was also known as the Wahpeton Pottery Company. Art pottery and commercial wares were made.

ROSEMEADE, Bank, Buffalo	145.00 To 245.00
Bell, Peacock	145.00
Figurine, Bear	25.00
Figurine, Buffalo, White Clay	150.00
Figurine, Coyote Pups, Pair	175.00
Figurine, Golden Pheasants	125.00
Figurine, Howling Coyote	250.00
Figurine, International Peace Garden	100.00
Figurine, Montana Goat	200.00
Figurine, Pheasant	45.00
Figurine, Pheasants, Tail Down	45.00
Figurine, Roadrunners	145.00
Figurine, Roosters, Fighting	95.00
Figurine, Swordfish	100.00
Flower Frog, Duck	35.00
Jar, Strawberry, Pink, 6 In.	300.00
Lamp, TV, Panther, 10 In.	750.00
Planter, White Dove	230.00
Plaque, Pike	125.00
Salt & Pepper, Chihuahua Dogs	85.00
Salt & Pepper, Cucumbers	30.00
Salt & Pepper, Deer, Jumping	60.00
Salt & Pepper, Deer, Lying	75.00
Salt & Pepper, Dog's Head	18.50
Salt & Pepper, Dog, Chow, Blue	18.50
Salt & Pepper, Dog, English Setters	18.50
Salt & Pepper, Dog, Scotty	18.50
Salt & Pepper, Mice	18.50
Salt & Pepper, Ox Heads	65.00
Salt & Pepper, Raccoons	80.00
Salt & Pepper, Roadrunners	60.00
Salt & Pepper, Skunk	15.00
Spoon Rest, Apple	35.00

MARKE

Rosenthal porcelain was made at the factory established in Selb, Bavaria, in 1880. The factory is still making fine-quality tablewares and figurines. A series of Christmas plates was made from 1910. Other limited edition plates have been made since 1971.

ROSENTHAL, Bowl, Acorns, Leaves, Gold Feet, 1885 Mark, 8 x 4 In.	85.00
Bowl, Bavaria, Singed, 10 In.	35.00
Figurine, Birl Holding Flowers In Front of Deer, 7 In.	325.00

◆◆

Worcestershire sauce is a good brass polish.

◆◆

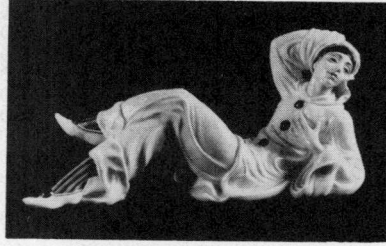

Rosenthal, Figurine, Pierrot, Reclining

◆◆◆◆◆◆◆◆◆◆◆◆◆◆◆◆◆◆◆◆◆◆

Always wash antique china in a sink lined with a rubber mat or towels. This helps prevent chipping. Wash one piece at a time. Rinse and let it air dry. If you suspect a piece has been repaired, do not wash it. Clean with a soft brush dampened in a solution of ammonia and water.

◆◆◆◆◆◆◆◆◆◆◆◆◆◆◆◆◆◆◆◆◆◆

Figurine, Colt	9.00
Figurine, Dachshund, Standing, Round Base, 8 In.	295.00
Figurine, Dog, Scotty, White, Fritz Heindenreich, 6 1/2 In.	225.00
Figurine, Hounds, Attacking Deer, T. Karner	225.00
Figurine, Nefertiti Bust, 11 In.	175.00
Figurine, Pierrot, Reclining ....*Illus*	250.00
Figurine, Princess & Frog, Pastels, Gold, 11 In. ....295.00 To	385.00
Figurine, Rooster, Double, Stand, Lying, 5 In.	98.00
Figurine, Siamese Cat, Lying	125.00
Gravy Boat, Greenblume	40.00
Group, Princess and Frog, Ferdinand Liebermann, 9 In.	65.00
Lighter, Cigarette, Table, 8 In.	12.00
Plate, Dessert, Rose Border, Gold Interior Rim, Set of 6	115.00
Plate, Plaza Scene, Sterling Rims, 12 In.	95.00
Platter, Chop, Shadow Rose	45.00
Platter, Greenblume, 15 In.	48.00
Platter, Roses, Ivory, Sterling Rim, 12 In.	55.00
Relish, Pink Wild Roses, Pastel Shaded, Gold Rim, Donatello Shape	20.00
Vase, Dancing Nude, 8 In.	60.00
Vase, Girl With Flower Basket, Bush, Gold Trim, 13 1/2 In.	250.00
Vase, Magic Flute, White, Bjorn Wiinblad, 6 In.	60.00
Vase, Polychrome Floral Design, 9 7/8 In.	45.00

Roseville U.S.A. The Roseville Pottery Company was organized in Roseville, Ohio, in 1890. Another plant was opened in Zanesville, Ohio, in 1898. Many types of pottery were made until 1954. Early wares include sgraffito, Olympic, and Rozane. Later lines were often made with molded decorations, especially flowers and fruit. Pieces are marked *Roseville*.

ROSEVILLE, Ashtray, Bushberry, Green ....75.00 To	100.00
Ashtray, Hyde Park ....15.00 To	20.00
Ashtray, Hyde Park, Green & Brown	15.00
Ashtray, Magnolia, Blue	50.00
Ashtray, Magnolia, Brown	67.00
Ashtray, Morning Glory, Green, 10 In.	575.00
Ashtray, Morning Glory, White, 4 In.	200.00
Ashtray, Morning Glory, White, 8 In.	325.00
Ashtray, Pine Cone, Blue	115.00
Ashtray, Pine Cone, Brown	135.00
Ashtray, Zephyr Lily, Green	45.00
Bank, Dog, 1900s	125.00
Bank, Piggy, Early 1900s, Small	70.00
Basket, Apple Blossom, Blue, 10 In.	150.00
Basket, Bittersweet, Green, 10 In.	175.00
Basket, Bleeding Heart, Blue, 8 In. ....115.00 To	160.00
Basket, Bleeding Heart, Green, 10 In.	125.00
Basket, Bushberry, Brown, 6 1/2 In.	80.00
Basket, Bushberry, Brown, 8 In.	90.00

Basket, Bushberry, Green, 10 In. 75.00
Basket, Clematis, Green, 7 In. 70.00
Basket, Columbine, 8 In. 110.00
Basket, Columbine, 12 In. 125.00
Basket, Gardenia, Gray, 10 In. .... 100.00 To 125.00
Basket, Hanging, Apple Blossom 90.00
Basket, Hanging, Bushberry, Blue 325.00
Basket, Hanging, Dahlrose 175.00
Basket, Hanging, Gardenia 75.00
Basket, Hanging, Moss, Original Chains 325.00
Basket, Hanging, Mostique 145.00
Basket, Hanging, Pine Cone 125.00
Basket, Hanging, Rozane, Allover Florals, Ivory, 1917 .... 125.00
Basket, Hanging, Silhouette, Red 100.00
Basket, Hanging, Snowberry .... 95.00 To 115.00
Basket, Hanging, White Rose, Blue 95.00
Basket, Imperial I, 6 In. 150.00
Basket, Ixia, Green, 10 In. .... 160.00 To 175.00
Basket, Magnolia, Blue, 8 In. 95.00
Basket, Magnolia, Brown, 8 In. 85.00
Basket, Ming Tree, 12 In. 175.00
Basket, Pine Cone, Boat Shape, Blue, 10 In. 450.00
Basket, Silhouette, Burgundy, 10 In. .... 85.00 To 160.00
Basket, Silhouette, Turquoise, 8 In. 85.00
Basket, Silhouette, White, 8 In. 85.00
Basket, Snowberry, 7 In. .... 78.00 To 85.00
Basket, Vista, 10 In. 110.00
Basket, White Rose, Blue, 8 In. 105.00
Basket, Wincraft, 12 In. 80.00
Basket, Zephyr Lily, Brown & Green, 10 In. 145.00
Basket, Zephyr Lily, Brown & Green, 8 In. 97.00
Basket, Zephyr Lily, Dark Green, 8 In. 65.00
Basket, Zephyr Lily, Hanging, Blue 150.00
Bookends, Bittersweet 70.00
Bookends, Freesia, Green 35.00
Bookends, Gardenia .... 95.00 To 135.00
Bookends, Magnolia, Blue 95.00
Bookends, Magnolia, Brown 135.00
Bookends, Peony 85.00
Bookends, Pine Cone, Brown .... 40.00 To 175.00
Bookends, Snowberry .... 95.00 To 125.00
Bookends, White Rose, Pink 125.00
Bookends, Wincraft, Blue 20.00
Bowl, Baneda, Flat, Pink, 8 In. 175.00
Bowl, Baneda, Green, 11 In. 250.00
Bowl, Baneda, Pink, 8 In. 175.00
Bowl, Bittersweet, Green, 5 In. 60.00
Bowl, Blackberry, 8 In. .... 195.00 To 225.00
Bowl, Bleeding Heart, Pink, 14 In. 85.00
Bowl, Bushberry, 14 In. 185.00
Bowl, Bushberry, Green, 4 In. 60.00
Bowl, Chicks, Orange Band, Green Band & Chicks Inside, 6 1/2 In. 300.00
Bowl, Clematis, Blue, 10 In. 50.00
Bowl, Clematis, Brown, 10 In. 75.00
Bowl, Corinthian, 7 In. .... 30.00 To 40.00
Bowl, Dogwood, 10 In. .... 95.00 To 125.00
Bowl, Donatello, 10 1/2 In. 150.00
Bowl, Donatello, Rolled Rim, 10 In. 75.00
Bowl, Ferella, Red, 4 1/2 In. 115.00
Bowl, Ferella, Rose, With Flower Frog, 9 1/2 In. 350.00
Bowl, Flower Frog, Ferella, Red, 10 In. 425.00
Bowl, Fuchsia, 5 In. 95.00
Bowl, Jonquil, 12 In. 160.00

Bowl, Jonquil, Brown, 6 In.	125.00
Bowl, Laurel, 7 In.	110.00
Bowl, Mock Orange, 4 In.	55.00
Bowl, Peony, 6 In.	30.00
Bowl, Pine Cone, Green, 5 In.	25.00
Bowl, Primrose, Red, 5 In.	55.00
Bowl, Raymor, 9 In.	15.00
Bowl, Raymor, Divided	29.00
Bowl, Rosecraft, 6 In.	20.00
Bowl, Rosecraft, Black, 8 In.	20.00
Bowl, Thorn Apple, 9 In.	65.00
Bowl, Topeo, Green, 2 1/2 x 7 1/2 In.	90.00
Bowl, Water Lily, Handles, Blue Ground, 5 In.	50.00 To 55.00
Bowl, Waterlily, Pink Flowers, Blue, Handles, 5 In.	50.00
Bowl, White Rose, Pink, 4 In.	40.00
Bowl, Wincraft, Brown, 10 In.	75.00
Box, Cigarette, Hyde Park, Green	27.50
Candleholder, Pine Cone, Green, 2 1/4 In.	45.00
Candlestick, Apple Blossom, Green	27.50
Candlestick, Cherry Blossom, Tan	245.00
Candlestick, Chloron	55.00
Candlestick, Clematis, Blue, Pair	12.00
Candlestick, Columbine, Pink, 2 1/2 In.	70.00
Candlestick, Creamware	115.00
Candlestick, Donatello, 8 In.	35.00
Candlestick, Florentine, Dark Brown, 10 1/2 In., Pair	70.00
Candlestick, Mock Orange, Green, 2 In.	65.00
Candlestick, Peony, Yellow, 2 In.	55.00
Candlestick, Primrose, Blue, Pair	75.00
Candlestick, Silhouette, Borwn, Pair	55.00
Candlestick, Wincraft, Blue	55.00
Casserole, Cover, Raymor, 14 In.	45.00
Celery, Raymor, Gray	8.00
Cider Set, Bushberry, Blue	825.00
Cider Set, Magnolia, Green, 7 Piece	450.00
Coffeepot, Raymor, Swinging, Gray, 3 Piece	225.00
Compote, Bittersweet, Yellow	40.00
Compote, Ferella, 4 In.	325.00
Conch Shell, Foxglove, Blue	80.00
Conch Shell, Peony, Large	150.00
Console Set, Baneda, Green, 3 x 11 In., 3 Piece	465.00
Console Set, Clematis, 3 Piece	75.00
Console, Apple Blossom, Pink	65.00
Console, Bushberry, 10 In.	100.00
Console, Bushberry, Green, 10 In.	120.00
Console, Clematis, Green, 14 In.	75.00
Console, Magnolia, Brown, 12 In.	95.00
Console, Magnolia, Green	82.00
Console, Morning Glory, White, 4 1/2 x 10 1/2 In.	200.00
Console, Peony, Pink, Green, 6 In.	75.00
Console, Snowberry, Pink, 6 In.	58.00
Console, Wisteria, 12 In.	275.00
Console, Zephyr Lily, Brown & Green, 12 In.	95.00
Cookie Jar, Freesia, Tangerine	265.00
Cookie Jar, Magnolia, Blue	165.00
Cookie Jar, Magnolia, Green	135.00 To 250.00
Cookie Jar, Peony, Pink	650.00
Cookie Jar, Water Lily, Blue	250.00
Cookie Jar, Zephyr Lily, Brown	165.00
Cornucopia, Apple Blossom, Pink, 6 In.	55.00
Cornucopia, Magnolia, Brown, 6 In.	444.00
Cornucopia, Peony, Green, Pair	95.00
Cornucopia, Pine Cone, Green, 6 In.	67.00

Cornucopia, Primrose, Red, 6 In. 55.00
Cornucopia, Silhouette .... 35.00 To 40.00
Cornucopia, Wincraft, 8 In. 65.00
Cornucopia, Zephyr Lily, 8 In. 50.00
Creamer, Apple Blossom 45.00
Creamer, Child's, Fat Puppy, Side Pour 189.00
Creamer, Child's, Standing Rabbit, 3 In. 65.00
Creamer, Medallion 65.00
Cruet, Freesia, Green, 6 In. 55.00
Cup & Saucer, Velmoss II, Green, 2 1/2 In. 50.00
Cuspidor, Rozane, 1917 .... 150.00
Desk Set, Raymor, 3 Piece 125.00
Ewer, Apple Blossom, Pink, 8 In. ....65.00 To 145.00
Ewer, Bleeding Heart, Blue, 6 In. 85.00
Ewer, Bleeding Heart, Blue, 10 In. ....75.00 To 165.00
Ewer, Clematis, Green, 15 In. 220.00
Ewer, Cosmos, 10 In. .... 135.00 To 160.00
Ewer, Foxglove, Flower Shape, 6 1/2 In. 125.00
Ewer, Freesia, Blue, 15 In. 250.00
Ewer, Freesia, Brown, 6 In. 95.00
Ewer, Freesia, Green, 15 In. 230.00
Ewer, Gardenia, Seafoam, 15 In. 295.00
Ewer, Iris, Blue, 10 In. 160.00
Ewer, Iris, Brown, 10 In. 165.00
Ewer, Magnolia, Brown, 10 In. 115.00
Ewer, Magnolia, Green, 10 In. 85.00
Ewer, Pine Cone, Brown, 10 In. 290.00
Ewer, Poppy, Pink, 10 In. .... 125.00 To 145.00
Ewer, Silhouette, Red, 10 In. 85.00
Ewer, Snowberry, Blue, 15 In. 67.00
Ewer, Snowberry, Brown, 10 In. ....95.00 To 140.00
Ewer, Water Lily, Blue & White, 6 In. 100.00
Ewer, Water Lily, Blue & White, 15 In. 300.00
Ewer, Water Lily, Brown, 6 In. .... 75.00 To 85.00
Ewer, White Rose, Blue, 10 In. 265.00
Ewer, Zephyr Lily 42.50
Ewer, Zephyr Lily, Blue, 10 In. 185.00
Ewer, Zephyr Lily, Green, 6 In. 22.00
Ferrella, Brown, 6 In. 265.00
Florane, Wall Pocket, 9 In. 145.00
Florentine, Jardiniere, 5 1/4 x 7 In. 65.00
Flower Frog, Bleeding Heart, Pink 55.00
Flower Frog, Blue 32.00
Flower Frog, Ixia, Green 50.00
Flower Frog, Magnolia, Green 50.00
Flower Frog, Peony, Gold 45.00
Flower Frog, Peony, Green 28.00
Flower Frog, Pink & Gray 50.00
Flower Frog, Thorn Apple, Pink 45.00
Flower Frog, Tuscany, Pink 20.00
Flower Frog, Water Lily, Blue 45.00
Flower Frog, Water Lily, Brown 45.00
Flower Frog, White Rose, Green 50.00
Flowerpot, Apple Blossom, Blue, 5 In. 85.00
Flowerpot, Cosmos, Blue, Saucer 125.00
Flowerpot, Donatello, Saucer, 6 1/2 In. 95.00
Flowerpot, Futura, Striated Blue, Green & Yellow, 4 In. 275.00
Flowerpot, Pine Cone, Blue, Sauce 275.00
Flowerpot, Pine Cone, Brown 60.00
Flowerpot, Primrose, Saucer 165.00
Flowerpot, Snowberry, Blue 50.00
Flowerpot, Snowberry, Pink, Saucer 85.00
Flowerpot, White, Matte, 4 In. 50.00

Humidor, Dutch	120.00
Humidor, Indian	550.00
Jardiniere, Apple Blossom, Green, Pedestal	825.00
Jardiniere, Apple Blossom, Pink, 6 In.	115.00
Jardiniere, Baneda, 4 1/2 In.	125.00
Jardiniere, Baneda, Green, Pedestal, 8 In.	2000.00
Jardiniere, Corinthian, 9 x 12 In.	160.00
Jardiniere, Dahlrose, 10 1/2 In.	65.00
Jardiniere, Dogwood I, 9 1/2 x 13 1/2 In.	150.00
Jardiniere, Donatello, Pedestal, 28 In.	395.00
Jardiniere, Florane, Ivory, 8 In.	80.00
Jardiniere, Freesia, Blue, Pedestal, 8 In.	500.00
Jardiniere, Freesia, Brown, Pedestal, 24 1/2 In.	550.00
Jardiniere, Freesia, Green, 6 In.	40.00
Jardiniere, Futura, 13 1/2 In.	385.00
Jardiniere, Magnolia, Green, Pedestal, 10 In.	650.00
Jardiniere, Pedestal, Poppy, Blue, 26 In.	1250.00
Jardiniere, Pine Cone, Blue, 3 In.	125.00
Jardiniere, Pine Cone, Blue, 5 In.	180.00
Jardiniere, Pine Cone, Brown, 10 In.	495.00
Jardiniere, Poppy, Green, 6 1/2 In.	97.00
Jardiniere, Primrose, Red, 6 In.	125.00
Jardiniere, Rozane, 1917, 10 In.	850.00
Jardiniere, Sylvan, 7 1/2 In.	395.00
Jardiniere, Vista, 7 In.	300.00 To 350.00
Jardiniere, Wisteria, Brown, 5 In.	235.00 To 245.00
Lamp, Angel Wing Design, Custard, Rust	275.00
Lamp, Blue–Green	195.00
Lamp, Carnelian, Blue Drip Design, Over Pink, 2 Handles, 12 In.	275.00
Lamp, Kerosene, Aztec, Slate Blue, Geometric, 11 In.	175.00
Lamp, Leaf Form, Tan, Olive, 10 1/2 In.	250.00
Lamp, Oil, Egypto	475.00
Lamp, Orian, Solid Blues, Crystals, 12 1/2 In.	295.00
Letter Holder, Rozane, Signed Meyers, Flowers Underglaze	250.00
Mixing Bowl, Orange & Tan, 11 1/2 x 6 3/4 In.	75.00
Mug, Bushberry	54.00
Mug, Indian, Creamware	175.00
Mug, Magnolia, Brown, 3 In.	45.00
Mug, Moose, Creamware	70.00
Mug, Peony, Green	45.00
Nut Dish, Pine Cone, Blue	145.00
Pedestal, Green, 16 1/2 In.	200.00
Pedestal, Peony, Mostique, Gray	150.00
Pie Bird, Pocket, Bushberry, Brown	175.00
Pitcher, Aztec, 5 1/4 In.	175.00 To 300.00
Pitcher, Chloron, 11 In.	295.00
Pitcher, Cider, Bushberry, Green, 6 Mugs	900.00
Pitcher, Cider, Magnolia	120.00 To 145.00
Pitcher, Foxglove, Blue, 6 1/2 In.	115.00
Pitcher, Freesia, Brown, 10 In.	140.00
Pitcher, Milk, Flowers, Gold Spatter	65.00
Pitcher, Pine Cone, Green, 10 1/2 In.	295.00
Pitcher, Pine Cone, Ice Lip, Blue, 8 In.	350.00 To 525.00
Pitcher, Pine Cone, Ice Lip, Brown	400.00
Pitcher, Pine Cone, Ice Lip, Green	275.00
Pitcher, Utility Ware, Green Band, 7 x 11 In.	40.00
Pitcher, White Rose, Green	125.00
Planter, Artwood, 8 In.	45.00
Planter, Gardenia, Green, 8 In.	40.00
Planter, Silhouette, Aqua, 14 In.	55.00
Planter, Silhouette, Double, Rust, 9 In.	85.00
Planter, Silhouette, Green, 10 In.	20.00
Planter, Silhouette, Rust, 10 In.	38.00

◆◆◆

If you hang your quilt like a picture, rotate it once a year and hang it from the opposite end to avoid too much stress on the fabric.

◆◆◆

Planter, Silhouette, White, 10 In.	38.00
Planter, Thornapple, Pink	88.00
Plate, Child's, 3 Chicks, 7 1/2 In.	125.00
Plate, Child's, 5 Chicks, 7 1/2 In.	70.00
Plate, Child's, Duck With Hat, 8 In.	100.00
Plate, Dinner, Raymor	8.50
Punch Bowl, Pine Cone	825.00
Rose Bowl, Primrose, Blue, 4 In.	65.00
Rose Bowl, Topeo, Blue, 8 1/2 In.	125.00
Rose Bowl, White Rose, Pink, 4 In.	40.00
Strawberry Pot, Earlam, Tan To Lilac, 8 In.	375.00
Sugar & Creamer, Forget–Me–Not, Pink	185.00
Sugar & Creamer, Magnolia, Blue	70.00
Sugar & Creamer, Persian	95.00 To 115.00
Sugar & Creamer, Zephyr Lily	90.00
Tankard, Elks, 11 1/2 In.	150.00
Tankard, Futura, 2 Handles, 6 In.	190.00
Tea Set, Clematis, Brown, 3 Piece	150.00 To 175.00
Tea Set, Landscape, 3 Piece	250.00
Tea Set, Mock Orange, Green	380.00
Tea Set, White Rose, Brown, Green	220.00 To 285.00
Tea Set, White Rose, Pink, Green	300.00
Tray, Pine Cone, Double Handles, Brown, 13 In.	225.00
Tray, Pine Cone, Green	140.00
Tumbler, Pine Cone, 5 In., 6 Piece	1350.00
Tumbler, Pine Cone, Brown	150.00
Umbrella Stand, Dogwood	450.00
Umbrella Stand, Florentine, Brown	375.00
Umbrella Stand, Majolica, Art Nouveau Woman, 26 1/2 In.	575.00
Umbrella Stand, Mostique	475.00
Umbrella Stand, Pine Cone, Blue	2700.00
Umbrella Stand, Rozane, 1917	525.00
Urn, Blackberry, 6 In.	240.00
Urn, Bleeding Heart, Blue, 4 In.	65.00
Urn, Bushberry, Green, 6 In.	120.00
Urn, Carnelian II, Bulbous, Purple & Rose, 8 x 9 In.	160.00
Urn, Carnelian II, Pink, 5 In.	220.00
Urn, Cover, Volpato, Crazed Ivory	175.00
Urn, Earlam, Tan & Lavender, 4 1/2 In.	65.00
Urn, Falline, 6 In.	395.00
Urn, Moss, Pink, 4 In.	65.00
Urn, Pine Cone, Blue, 5 In.	245.00
Urn, Pine Cone, Blue, 7 In.	265.00 To 270.00
Urn, Sunflower, 5 In.	225.00
Urn, Sunflower, 7 In.	390.00
Urn, Velmoss II, Green, 5 In.	60.00
Vase, Apple Blossom, Green, 7 In.	75.00
Vase, Apple Blossom, Pink, 9 In.	88.00
Vase, Apple Blossom, Pink, 15 1/2 In.	270.00
Vase, Aztec, 6 1/2 In.	195.00
Vase, Aztec, 8 In.	150.00
Vase, Aztec, 9 In.	265.00
Vase, Aztec, 11 1/2 In.	165.00
Vase, Baneda, 4 1/2 In.	200.00
Vase, Baneda, 5 1/2 In.	185.00

Vase, Baneda, 6 In. 145.00
Vase, Baneda, 7 In. 295.00
Vase, Baneda, 8 In. 335.00
Vase, Baneda, 9 In. 200.00
Vase, Baneda, 12 In. 600.00
Vase, Bittersweet, Green, Double 65.00
Vase, Blackberry, 4 In. .... 195.00 To 295.00
Vase, Blackberry, 6 In. .... 200.00 To 270.00
Vase, Bleeding Heart, Green, 15 In. 325.00
Vase, Bud, Apple Blossom, Green, 7 In. 30.00
Vase, Bud, Bittersweet, Gray, 7 In. 35.00
Vase, Bud, Carnelian II 39.50
Vase, Bud, Dahlrose, Triple, 6 In. 60.00
Vase, Bud, Florentine, Double, Brown, 7 In. 50.00
Vase, Bud, Freesia 45.00
Vase, Bud, Moderne, Two Tone, 7 In. 22.00
Vase, Bud, Pine Cone, Brown, 7 In. 105.00
Vase, Bud, Zephyr Lily, Green 35.00
Vase, Bushberry, Blue, 6 In. .... 49.00 To 75.00
Vase, Bushberry, Green, 14 1/2 In. 225.00
Vase, Carnelian II, Green, 10 In. 185.00
Vase, Carnelian, 18 1/2 In. 185.00
Vase, Carnelian, Pillow, Red & Purple 75.00
Vase, Cherry Blossom, 5 In. 150.00
Vase, Clematis, Autumn Brown, 12 In. 195.00
Vase, Clematis, Blue, 6 In. 35.00
Vase, Clematis, Brown, 15 In. 160.00
Vase, Clematis, Green, 6 In. 40.00
Vase, Clematis, Plum Colored Flowers, Orange Centers, 7 In. 675.00
Vase, Columbine, Blue, 12 In. 195.00
Vase, Columbine, Pink, 3 In. 22.00
Vase, Columbine, Pink, 30 In. 1100.00
Vase, Corinthian, 6 In. 55.00
Vase, Cosmos, Blue, 3 In. 25.00
Vase, Cremona, Pink, 8 In. 145.00
Vase, Crocus, Greenish Gray, Melon Design, 7 In. 250.00
Vase, Dahlrose, 6 In. 125.00
Vase, Dahlrose, 10 In. 130.00
Vase, Della Robbia, 11 In. 2000.00
Vase, Donatello, 12 In. 395.00
Vase, Earlam, 7 In. 125.00
Vase, Experimental Nude, 4 Panels, Small Handles, 12 In. 2000.00
Vase, Falline, Brown, 8 In. 200.00
Vase, Falline, Brown, Horn Shape, 8 In. 395.00
Vase, Ferella, Brown, 9 In. .... 345.00 To 360.00
Vase, Florane, Ruffled, Green, 14 In. 55.00
Vase, Foxglove, Blue, 10 In. 125.00
Vase, Foxglove, Green To Pink, 2 Handles, 7 1/4 In. 75.00
Vase, Freesia, Green, 10 In. 75.00
Vase, Freesia, Green, 18 In. 255.00
Vase, Fuchsia, Brown, 9 In. 155.00
Vase, Fuchsia, Brown, 10 In. 215.00
Vase, Fudji, 11 In. 2500.00
Vase, Futura, Brown, 5 In. 275.00
Vase, Futura, Mauve, Thistle Stems, 8 In. 200.00
Vase, Gardenia, 12 In. 150.00
Vase, Imperial I, 8 In. 70.00
Vase, Imperial I, 12 In. 250.00
Vase, Imperial II, 8 In. 275.00
Vase, Iris, Blue, 9 In. 225.00
Vase, Iris, Pink, 3 1/2 x 5 1/2 In. 35.00
Vase, Iris, Pink, 4 In. 30.00
Vase, Ixia, Pink, 10 1/2 In. .... 75.00 To 95.00

Vase, Ixia, Red & Green, 8 In. 75.00
Vase, Ixia, Red & Green, 10 In. 125.00
Vase, Jonquil, 4 In. 65.00
Vase, La Rose, 7 In. .... 45.00 To 75.00
Vase, Laurel, 10 In. 160.00
Vase, Luffa, Brown, 5 In. 85.00
Vase, Luffa, Brown, 7 1/2 In. 90.00
Vase, Luffa, Brown, 13 In. .... 300.00 To 330.00
Vase, Luffa, Green, 7 1/4 In. 30.00
Vase, Magnolia, Blue, 14 In. 200.00
Vase, Magnolia, Brown, 6 In. 57.00
Vase, Mayfair, Maroon, 8 In. 45.00
Vase, Ming Tree, White, 10 In. 95.00
Vase, Mock Orange, Green, 6 In. 65.00
Vase, Moderne, 7 In. 40.00
Vase, Monticello, Brown, 5 In. 135.00
Vase, Monticello, Green, 5 In. 150.00
Vase, Morning Glory, Green, 10 In. 325.00
Vase, Morning Glory, White, 6 In. ....95.00 To 155.00
Vase, Morning Glory, White, 10 In. 300.00
Vase, Moss, Pink, 6 1/2 In. 75.00
Vase, Mostique, 6 In. 30.00
Vase, Mostique, 9 In. 55.00
Vase, Mostique, 10 In. ....75.00 To 195.00
Vase, Mostique, 12 In. 135.00
Vase, Nude Paneled, Brown, Fan Shape 295.00
Vase, Panels of Nudes, 10 In. 575.00
Vase, Pauleo, Green, 18 In. 1350.00
Vase, Peony, Yellow, 4 In. 25.00
Vase, Pillow, Pine Cone, 2 Handles 125.00
Vase, Pillow, Pine Cone, Blue, 9 In. 650.00
Vase, Pine Cone, Blue Glaze, Slant Fan Shape, 6 In. 60.00
Vase, Pine Cone, Blue, 8 In. 75.00
Vase, Pine Cone, Brown, 7 In. 135.00
Vase, Pine Cone, Brown, 10 1/2 In. 275.00
Vase, Poppy, Green, 8 In. 110.00
Vase, Primrose, Fan Shape, 8 In. 95.00
Vase, Primrose, Pink, 7 In. 135.00
Vase, Primrose, Tan, 10 In. 125.00
Vase, Rozane Royal, Dog & Pheasant, 8 1/2 In. ....*Illus* 330.00
Vase, Rozane Royal, Red & White Poppies, W. Myers, 13 3/4 In. 2310.00
Vase, Rozane, Pansies, 8 In. 110.00
Vase, Rozane, Stick, Clover, Dark Ground, 8 In. 203.00
Vase, Rozane, W. Myers, 9 1/2 In. 150.00
Vase, Russco, Gold, 6 In. 80.00
Vase, Russco, Green, 7 In. 95.00
Vase, Silhouette Nude, Turquoise, Fan Shape 225.00

Roseville, Vase, Rozane Royal,
Dog & Pheasant, 8 1/2 In.

◆◆◆◆◆◆◆◆◆◆◆◆◆◆◆◆◆◆◆◆◆◆◆

China can be washed in warm
water with mild soap suds. The
addition of ammonia to the water
will add that extra sparkle.

◆◆◆◆◆◆◆◆◆◆◆◆◆◆◆◆◆◆◆◆◆◆◆

Vase, Silhouette, Nude Shape 125.00
Vase, Snowberry, Brown, Handles, 8 In. 55.00
Vase, Snowberry, Green, 4 In. .... 35.00 To 50.00
Vase, Snowberry, Green, 12 1/2 In. 65.00
Vase, Sunflower, 5 In. 175.00
Vase, Sunflower, 10 In. 575.00
Vase, Teasel, Pink, 9 In. 65.00
Vase, Thorn Apple, Blue, 8 In. 95.00
Vase, Thorn Apple, Brown, 6 In. .... 45.00 To 75.00
Vase, Thorn Apple, Pink, 4 In. 50.00
Vase, Topeo, Blue, 6 1/2 In. 150.00
Vase, Topeo, Red, 6 In. 70.00
Vase, Tourmaline, 6 In. 50.00
Vase, Tourmaline, 7 1/2 In. 150.00
Vase, Tourmaline, 8 In. 55.00
Vase, Tuscany, Pink, 8 In. 55.00
Vase, Velmoss, Blue, 7 In. 45.00
Vase, Velmoss, Green, 5 In. 65.00
Vase, Vista, 14 In. 325.00
Vase, Vista, 1920, 12 In. 65.00
Vase, Water Lily, Blue, 7 In. 45.00
Vase, Water Lily, Brown, 12 In. 95.00
Vase, Water Lily, Pink, 8 In. 75.00
Vase, White Rose, Green, 8 1/2 In. 135.00
Vase, White Rose, Pink, 7 In. 85.00
Vase, White Rose, Pink, 9 In. 120.00
Vase, White Rose, Pink, 12 1/2 In. 150.00
Vase, Wincraft, Blue, 10 In. 75.00
Vase, Windsor, Blue Flowers, 8 In. 280.00
Vase, Windsor, Garlands, Rust, 10 In. 300.00
Vase, Windsor, Geometric, Blue, 7 In. 275.00
Vase, Winecraft, Pine Cone, Green, 6 In. 30.00
Vase, Wisteria, Brown, 8 In. 180.00
Vase, Zephyr Lily, Green, 7 In. 65.00
Vase, Zephyr Lily, Green, 8 1/2 In. 55.00
Vase, Zephyr Lily, Green, 15 In. 230.00
Vase, Zephyr Lily, Green, 4 In. 60.00
Wall Pocket, Apple Blossom .... 120.00 To 155.00
Wall Pocket, Bucket 385.00
Wall Pocket, Carnelian I 95.00
Wall Pocket, Clematis, Blue 75.00
Wall Pocket, Corinthian 70.00
Wall Pocket, Egypto, Cherubs, Fan Shape, Marked, 8 In. 450.00
Wall Pocket, Ferella, Red 750.00
Wall Pocket, Florane .... 75.00 To 145.00
Wall Pocket, Florentine, 9 1/2 In. 95.00
Wall Pocket, Florentine, 12 In. 125.00
Wall Pocket, Iris 265.00
Wall Pocket, La Rose, 8 In. 95.00
Wall Pocket, Magnolia 125.00
Wall Pocket, Nude, Green, 7 1/2 In. 450.00
Wall Pocket, Orion 450.00
Wall Pocket, Pine Cone, Blue, Double 200.00
Wall Pocket, Rosecraft, 9 In. 150.00
Wall Pocket, Snowberry, Green 80.00
Wall Pocket, Tuscany, Sticker .... 110.00 To 135.00
Wall Pocket, Velmoss, Green .... 185.00 To 279.00
Wall Pocket, Zephyr Lily, Blue .... 85.00 To 140.00
Window Box, Apple Blossom, Blue, 12 In. 95.00
Window Box, Dahlrose, 16 In. 225.00
Window Box, Orian, Red, 15 In. 195.00
Window Box, Pine Cone, Blue, 8 In. 180.00
Window Box, Pine Cone, Brown, 12 In. .... 150.00 To 200.00

Window Box, Pine Cone, Green, 12 In. 295.00
Window Box, Sunflower 275.00

Rowland & Marsellus Company is the mark used by a New York importing firm working from 1890 to 1933. It has been suggested that the pieces were made in England by British Anchor Pottery, Sampson Hancock, Royal Fenton, and others. Many American views were made. Of special interest to collectors are the rolled edge, blue and white plates.

ROWLAND & MARSELLUS, Cup & Saucer, Building, Bridge, Large, Blue 50.00
Plate, Asbury Park, Rolled Edge, 10 In. 50.00
Plate, Atlantic City, Blue, 10 1/2 In. 45.00
Plate, Charles Dickens, Blue, 10 In. 50.00
Plate, Garfield Memorial, Cleveland, Ohio, Rolled Edge 45.00
Plate, Indian, 10 In. 110.00
Plate, Indianapolis, Rolled Edge, 10 In. 40.00
Plate, Mt. Ranier, Rolled Edge 55.00
Plate, Robert Burns, Rolled Edge 55.00
Plate, Tower, Rolled Edge, Blue, 8 1/2 In. 90.00

Roy Rogers was born in 1911 in Cincinnati, Ohio. In the 1930s, he made a living as a singer; and in 1935, his group started work at a Los Angeles radio station. He appeared in his first movie in 1937. From 1952 to 1957, he made 101 television shows. Roy Rogers memorabilia is collected, including items from the Roy Rogers restaurants.

ROY ROGERS, Bank, Book, Cast Metal, Pair 68.00
Bank, Statue 200.00
Bank, Trigger, Metal 65.00
Bank, Western Boot, Tin 28.00
Bedspread ....95.00 To 125.00
Billfold 45.00
Binoculars 45.00
Binoculars, Box 60.00
Book, Annual 36.00
Book, Coloring, Roy & Dale Evans 10.00
Book, Coloring, Roy, Trigger, Bullet 30.00
Book, King of The Cowboys, Whitman 18.00
Book, Paint 16.00
Boots, Rubber 145.00
Bow & Arrow Set 85.00
Briefcase ....45.00 To 55.00
Button, Pinback, Dale Evans, Lithograph, Post's, 1953 .... 20.00
Camera, Roy & Trigger ....45.00 To 65.00
Cards, Playing 55.00
Chaps, Cowboy, Tag, Roy Rogers Facsimile Signed, 1940s 75.00
Chuckwagon Set, Box 200.00
Chuckwagon, Fix-It, Nellybell Jeep, Box 165.00
Clock, Alarm, Animated, Tan, Lux 150.00
Costume, Chaps & Vest 175.00
Costume, Dale Evans, Cowgirl, Box ....150.00 To 175.00
Crayon Set, Colorful Box 95.00
Cuff Links & Tie Bar, Display Card ....25.00 To 27.00
Decal, King of The Cowboys, Meyercord, 1952, 6 1/4 x 8 In. 22.50
Dinner Set, Western, Ideal, Service For 4, Box 110.00
Figurine, Dale Evans, With Horse, Hartland 45.00
Figurine, Trigger, Glass, 1950s 145.00
Flashlight, Roy & Trigger, Signal Siren 35.00
Game, Gabby Hayes Target, Box 100.00
Game, Horseshoes, Box 35.00
Game, Rodeo 30.00
Game, Tim Holt Target, Box 55.00
Guitar, Jefferson, Box 85.00

Guitar, Roy & Trigger, 1950s	95.00
Gun & Holster Set	65.00
Gun, Cap, Cast Iron	95.00
Gun, Cap, G. H. On Handle	75.00
Harmonica, Package	85.00
Hat, Felt	47.00 To 85.00
Holster Set, Box	275.00
Horseshoe Set	85.00 To 100.00
Iron On Transfer, 8 x 10 In.	18.00
Jacket, Leather Suede, Box	400.00
Jacket, Leather, Fringed, Size 6, Label	150.00
Lamp, Dale Evans, Desk, 13 In.	170.00
Lamp, Trigger	185.00
Lantern, Tin	50.00 To 95.00
Lucky Horseshoe, Rubber	27.50
Lunch Box, 8 Scenes	90.00
Lunch Box, Chow Wagon	165.00
Lunch Box, Dale & Roy, 1953	225.00
Lunch Box, Dale Evans	60.00
Lunch Box, Mineral City, Marx	27.50
Lunch Box, Saddlebag, Tan, 1960	150.00 To 325.00
Lunch Box, Trigger	115.00 To 150.00
Lunch Box, Vinyl	200.00 To 330.00
Lunch Pail, Chow Wagon, 1958	225.00
Lunch Pail, Roy & Dale Evans, Metal, Blue Band, 1954	80.00
Lunch Pail, Roy & Dale Evans, Metal, Red Band, 1954	80.00
Lunch Pail, Trigger	105.00
Marbles, Trigger	21.00
Mug, Red, Plastic	20.00
Nodder	165.00
Paint Set, Roy's Picture On Carrying Case, 1941	145.00
Paper Dolls, Dale Evans, Uncut	75.00
Paper Dolls, Roy & Dale Evans, 1947, Uncut	110.00
Pendant, Dale Evans, Horseshoe	12.00
Phone, Wall, Battery Operated	45.00
Phone, Wall, Plastic	65.00
Pin, Picture of Roy, 1940s	20.00
Pin, Roy Roger's Saddle	32.50
Pin, Sheriff	32.50
Play Set, Mineral City, Marx	225.00
Play Set, Rodeo Ranch	100.00 To 300.00
Poster, Springtime In The Sierras, Movie	125.00
Pup Tent, Cloth, Hettrick Mfg. Co.	45.00
Puzzle	20.00 To 25.00
Record Player, With Trigger	250.00
Reel, For Viewmaster, Roy & Trigger	12.00
Rifle, Cap, Plastic, Marx, 25 In.	95.00
Rifle, Fires Caps, Plastic, Marx, Box	150.00
Ring, Branding Iron	45.00
Ring, Microscope	75.00 To 90.00
Road Decoder & Manual, 1938	85.00
Rodeo Ranch Play Set	95.00
Sheet Music, I Dream of Jeannie, Dale Evans, 1939	6.00
Song Book, Jamboree	30.00
Target Game, Gabby Hayes, Box	100.00
Telephone	40.00
Telephone, Box	225.00
Telescope	25.00
Tent, Box	150.00
Thermos, Blue Sky, Roy & Dale Evans	50.00
Token, Good Luck Trigger	12.00
Toothbrush, Badge of Merit Tag, 1950s	25.00
Toy, Double R Ranch Set, Box, Marx	160.00

Wallet, Leather, Zipper	65.00
Wrist Set, Package	45.00
Wristwatch Flasher	125.00
Wristwatch, Dale Evans ....85.00 To 125.00	
Wristwatch, Toy, Jewelry On Card	65.00
Yoyo, Display Box, 3 Piece	100.00

The Royal Bayreuth factory was founded in Tettau, Bavaria, in 1794. It has continued to modern times. The marks have changed through the years. A stylized crest, the name *Royal Bayreuth,* and the word *Bavaria* appear in slightly different forms from 1870 to about 1919. Later dishes may include the words *U.S. Zone,* the year of the issue, or the word *Germany* instead of *Bavaria.*

ROYAL BAYREUTH, see also Rose Tapestry; Sand Babies; Snow Babies; Sunbonnet Babies

ROYAL BAYREUTH, Ashtray, Clown, Signed	210.00
Ashtray, Devil	60.00
Ashtray, Hunt Scene	65.00
Ashtray, Red Devil, Handle, Blue Mark	145.00
Ashtray, Riding To Hounds, Gold Trim, Triangular, 5 1/2 In.	85.00
Bell, Dutch Children Playing	225.00
Bowl, Lobster, Blue Mark, 4 x 8 In. .... 160.00 To 185.00	
Bowl, Salad, Lobster	175.00
Bowl, Salad, Lobster & Leaves	225.00
Bowl, Salad, Tomato, 9 1/2 In.	115.00
Bowl, Salad, Tomato, Footed, 8 In.	295.00
Box, Cover, Woman & Man Scene, Brown, Green Mark, 1 1/2 In.	65.00
Box, Pink, Hand Painted Flowers	40.00
Box, Trinket, Cover, Christmas Cactus, 3 1/2 In. .... 275.00 To 325.00	
Box, Trinket, Cows Scene	100.00
Cake Plate, Pink Roses, Gold Handles, Blue Mark, 11 In.	95.00
Candleholder, Clown, Orange, Blue Mark, 3 1/2 In.	195.00
Candy Dish, Lobster, Blue Mark, 5 x 3 In.	125.00
Chamberstick, 2 Men Playing Instruments, Marked	210.00
Charger, Lobster & Leaves	225.00
Chocolate Pot, Poppy, 3 Cups	650.00
Clock, Gray, Floral, Marked	225.00
Coffeepot, Barnyard Scene, Signed, Demitasse, 6 3/4 In.	70.00
Cracker Jar, Pearlized White Grape	450.00
Cracker Jar, Poppy	325.00
Cracker Jar, Shell	475.00
Creamer, Alligator	285.00
Creamer, Apple, Marked	125.00
Creamer, Band of Black & White Key Trim, 4 1/4 In.	65.00
Creamer, Bellringer	295.00
Creamer, Bird of Paradise	230.00
Creamer, Boar	45.00
Creamer, Bull, Black	165.00
Creamer, Bull, Brown	225.00
Creamer, Bull, Gray	210.00
Creamer, Bull, Red	260.00
Creamer, Butterfly, Signed	165.00
Creamer, Cat Handle	245.00
Creamer, Cat, Black	95.00

◆◆

The playing surface of phonograph records should never be touched by a bare hand. The records should be stored vertically and packed to prevent warping. Keep away from extremes of heat or cold.

◆◆

Creamer, Chimpanzee 450.00
Creamer, Clown .... 150.00 To 155.00
Creamer, Coachman .... 175.00 To 180.00
Creamer, Crow 115.00
Creamer, Dachshund ....75.00 To 225.00
Creamer, Elk, Blue Mark 125.00
Creamer, Fish Head 115.00
Creamer, Flounder, Blue Mark 295.00
Creamer, Fox 750.00
Creamer, Frog, Green 155.00
Creamer, Girl With A Basket, Signed 120.00
Creamer, Girl With A Pitcher 395.00
Creamer, Goat, Marked 200.00
Creamer, Grape, White Mother-of-Pearl 110.00
Creamer, Horse Head 750.00
Creamer, Kangaroo ....*Illus* 725.00
Creamer, Lamplighter .... 140.00 To 243.00
Creamer, Lemon 210.00
Creamer, Man In The Mountain 150.00
Creamer, Monkey 350.00
Creamer, Mother-of-Pearl Grape 125.00
Creamer, Mountain Goat 165.00
Creamer, Parakeet 195.00
Creamer, Pelican .... 110.00 To 140.00
Creamer, Penguin .... 325.00 To 395.00
Creamer, Poodle, Black 135.00
Creamer, Poodle, Gray 210.00
Creamer, Poppy, Red, Green Handle & Foot, Blue Mark, 2 In. 75.00
Creamer, Robin .... 100.00 To 145.00
Creamer, Rooster, Black 210.00
Creamer, Rooster, White .... 210.00 To 260.00
Creamer, Santa Claus 1195.00
Creamer, Seal .... 225.00 To 245.00
Creamer, Shell, Green Mark 60.00
Creamer, Shell, Wildwood, Commemorative 60.00
Creamer, Snake 595.00
Creamer, St. Bernard 115.00
Creamer, Strawberry ....95.00 To 180.00
Creamer, Turtle, 2 3/4 In. 450.00
Creamer, Water Buffalo, Black 95.00
Dish, Cheese, Children Playing, Slanted Top, Miniature 225.00
Dish, Soap, Dutch Children 60.00
Dutch Shoe, Pink Roses, Pansies, Forget-Me-Nots, Signed 250.00
Hair Receiver, Pink Roses, 3 Gold Feet, Blue Mark, 3 In. 78.00
Hatpin Holder, Swimming Swans In Lake, Sunset, Blue Mark 245.00
Humidor, Gorilla 495.00
Match Holder, Hanging, Red Clown, Marked 325.00

Royal Bayreuth, Creamer, Kangaroo

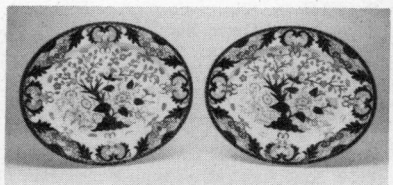

Royal Crown Derby, Platter, Tree of Life,
1877–89, 19 In., Pair

Match Holder, Wall, Devil & Cards	185.00
Mug, Beer, Elk, Blue Mark	425.00
Mug, Beer, Marked	295.00
Mug, Tavern Scene, Blue Mark, 5 In.	50.00
Mustard, Grape, Luster, Signed	70.00
Mustard, Grape, Pearlized	75.00
Mustard, Grape, White Satin, Spoon	115.00
Nut Dish, Poppy, White Satin	30.00
Pin Tray, Dutch Children, Pier, Blue Mark, 3 3/4 x 5 3/4 In.	42.00
Pipe Holder, Girl With Ducks, Gold Trim, Marked, 4 In.	195.00
Pitcher, Apple, 6 In.	448.00
Pitcher, Apple, 7 1/2 In. .... 490.00 To	510.00
Pitcher, Bellringer, 7 1/2 In. .... 550.00 To	1015.00
Pitcher, Coachman, 7 In.	700.00
Pitcher, Corinthian, Yellow Flowers, Red Bands, 5 In.	95.00
Pitcher, Devil & Cards, Blue Mark, 7 1/4 In.	425.00
Pitcher, Duck, 6 1/2 In.	550.00
Pitcher, Eagle, 6 1/4 In.	695.00
Pitcher, Elk, 5 In.	195.00
Pitcher, Face, Leaves Form Body, Gray, Gold Outlines, 5 In.	148.00
Pitcher, Fishing Scene, 2 Anglers Fishing From Boat, 4 In.	90.00
Pitcher, Fishing Scene, 2 Anglers Fishing From Boat, 6 In.	165.00
Pitcher, Grape, Mother-of-Pearl, 6 In.	395.00
Pitcher, Lamplighter, 6 In.	1075.00
Pitcher, Lobster, 7 In.	425.00
Pitcher, Lobster, Blue Mark, 7 In.	225.00
Pitcher, Lobster, Orange, Green Handle, Marked, 7 In.	175.00
Pitcher, Mouse, 7 1/4 In.	1395.00
Pitcher, Poppy, Red, Blue Mark, 4 1/2 In.	225.00
Pitcher, Santa Claus, 6 1/4 In.	1495.00
Pitcher, Seal, 6 In.	895.00
Pitcher, Snake, 6 1/4 In.	1995.00
Pitcher, Tomato, 6 1/4 In.	350.00
Pitcher, Water, Devil & Cards	495.00
Pitcher, Wide Mouth, Yellow Roses On Green, Gold Trim	150.00
Planter, Boy With Turkey, Handle, Large	100.00
Plate, Nursery Rhyme, Jack In The Beanstalk, 6 1/2 In.	75.00
Salt & Pepper, Corinthian, Mythological Figures, Marked	110.00
Salt & Pepper, Lobster	125.00
Salt & Pepper, Pepper	85.00
Shoe, High Button, White Top, Black Bottom, Gold Buckle	145.00
Stein, Chinoiserie Man, Smoking Pipe, 1880s, 9 1/4 In.	990.00
Stein, Elk, Blue Mark	395.00
Stein, Faience, Pewter Knobbed Lid, 1 Liter	1040.00
String Holder, Rooster, Blue Mark	245.00
Sugar & Creamer, Britanny Girls, Flying Gull	90.00
Sugar & Creamer, Corinthian, Classical Figures	75.00
Sugar & Creamer, Cover, Tomato	175.00
Sugar & Creamer, Grape, Mother-of-Pearl	250.00
Sugar & Creamer, Hunting Scene	115.00
Sugar & Creamer, Turtle, Blue Mark	895.00
Sugar, Cover, Elk	295.00
Sugar, Cover, Grape, Purple	85.00
Sugar, Lobster	115.00
Teapot, Child's, Girl & Dog	65.00
Teapot, Grape, Luster	225.00
Teapot, Poppy, Red	275.00
Toothpick, Girl & Dog, 3 Handles	135.00
Toothpick, Kettle Shape, Handle	110.00
Vase, Arab Scene, Silver Rim, Footed, Blue Mark, 3 1/4 In.	50.00
Vase, Bands of Yellow Flowers, Figures, 4 1/2 In.	75.00
Vase, Brown To Burnt Orange To Brown, Deer Scene, 8 1/2 In.	90.00
Vase, Nymph of The Sea, 9 In.	795.00

Vase, Pastoral Scene, Trumpet, Blue Mark, 7 In.	85.00
Vase, Peasant Woman, Sheep, 3 Handles, Blue Mark, 3 1/2 In.	50.00
Vase, Scenic, Gold Wedding Ring Handles, Scalloped, 7 In.	195.00
Vase, Soccer Scene, Bulbous, Blue Mark, 7 In.	295.00
Vase, Tavern Scene, 2 Handles, 6 1/2 In.	195.00
Vase, Trumpet, Pastoral Scene, Blue Mark, 7 In.	85.00
Vase, Woman Carrying Baskets, Blue Mark, 5 1/2 In.	35.00
Wall Pocket, Grape, Green Leaves, Blue Mark, 9 In.	210.00
Wall Pocket, Grape, Pearlized White	375.00
Watering Can, Little Jack Horner, Miniature	425.00

Royal Bonn is the nineteenth– and twentieth–century trade name for the Bonn China Manufactory. It was established in 1755 in Bonn, Germany. A general line of porcelain was made. Many marks were used, most including the name *Bonn*, the initials *FM* and a crown.

ROYAL BONN, Vase, Animal Head Handles, Pear Shape, Marked FM, 1890, 14 In.	350.00
Vase, Bird & Iris, 12 In.	85.00
Vase, Exotic Flowers, Textured Black Matte, 12 1/4 In.	450.00
Vase, Purple & Yellow Irises, Gold Handles, 7 1/2 In.	135.00
Vase, Red, Green, Ivory & Gold Roses, Bulbous, 4 1/2 In., Pair	145.00
Vase, Roses, 8 1/2 In.	110.00

Royal Copenhagen porcelain and pottery have been made in Denmark since 1772. The Christmas plate series started in 1908. The figurines with pale blue and gray glazes have remained popular in this century and are still being made. Many other old and new style porcelains are made today.

ROYAL COPENHAGEN, Ashtray, Blue & White, Square, 5 1/2 In.	35.00
Bowl, Woman, Holding Fish Center, Crackleware, 7 In.	45.00
Figurine, Amager Girl, Knitting, No. 1314	175.00
Figurine, Australian Wren, No. 1315, 4 In.	150.00
Figurine, Boxer, No. 1069, 6 In.	250.00
Figurine, Boy With Calves, No. 1858	350.00
Figurine, Boy With Umbrella, No. 3556	200.00
Figurine, Cairn Terrier, No. 1149	145.00
Figurine, Cat, White, 5 In.	60.00
Figurine, Children Reading, No. 1567	140.00
Figurine, Ermine On Log, No. 1121, 9 1/2 In.	195.00
Figurine, Faun On Tortoise	150.00
Figurine, Faun With Bear, No. 648	325.00
Figurine, Faun With Crow, No. 2113	375.00
Figurine, Faun With Parrot, No. 752	325.00
Figurine, Faun With Snake, No. 1712	200.00
Figurine, Girl, Knitting, 9 In.	250.00
Figurine, Goose Girl, No. 527, 9 1/2 In.	225.00
Figurine, Hunter, Seated, Gun, Dog, 8 1/2 In.	265.00
Figurine, Kitten, No. 2506	70.00
Figurine, Lovebirds, 8 In.	130.00
Figurine, Mermaid, No. 4431	495.00
Figurine, Newsboy, No. 2148, 8 In.	150.00
Figurine, Owl, No. 1741, 3 1/2 In.	65.00
Figurine, Owl, No. 2999c	95.00
Figurine, Pan On Goat, No. 1228	175.00
Figurine, Robin, No. 1235, Head Cocked, Berry Base, 8 In.	195.00
Figurine, Robin, No. 2238, 1 1/2 In.	35.00
Figurine, Scotty, No. 3162	85.00
Figurine, Seal, No. 1441	115.00
Figurine, Spilt Milk, No. 2246, c.1948, 6 1/2 In.	248.00
Figurine, Standing Girl, Holding Book, No. 922, 7 In.	150.00
Figurine, Striped Cat, Raised Tail, No. 1108, 8 In.	265.00
Figurine, Wave & Rock, No. 1132	1500.00
Figurine, Woman, Baby, Terra–Cotta, Kedegaard, 7 In.	260.00
Figurine, Young Satyrs, 4 3/4 In., Pair	130.00

Lamp, Harbor Scene, Hafnia Metropolis Celebrinna, 11 In.	150.00
Plate, Christmas, 1913	90.00
Plate, Christmas, 1915	75.00
Plate, Christmas, 1919	85.00
Plate, Christmas, 1953	75.00
Plate, Christmas, 1954	135.00
Plate, Christmas, 1959	75.00
Plate, Christmas, 1962	170.00
Plate, Christmas, 1965	60.00
Plate, Christmas, 1967	30.00
Plate, Christmas, 1969	35.00
Plate, Christmas, 1970	15.00
Plate, Christmas, 1972	75.00
Plate, Christmas, 1975	14.00
Plate, Christmas, 1977	75.00
Plate, Christmas, 1978	80.00
Plate, Christmas, 1987	32.00 To 35.00
Plate, Flora Danica, Reticulated Border, 10 In., 12 Piece	6050.00
Plate, Mother's Day, 1971	20.00
Plate, Mother's Day, 1977	10.00
Plate, Mother's Day, 1984	20.00
Teapot, Acorn Finial, Flowers, Palmetto Leaves, 10 In.	60.00
Tray, Lobster, Fish Center	175.00
Vase, Abstract, 3 Colors, 11 In.	200.00
Vase, Border of Cows, Horns Form Ring Handles, 14 1/2 In.	1545.00
Vase, Cactus, Crackleware, 7 In.	85.00
Vase, Floral, 4 Colors, 8 In.	185.00
Vase, Iris, Bluebird, 1959, 5 In.	60.00
Vase, White Porcelain, Cover, Milkmaid Design, 7 In.	68.00

Royal Copley china was made by the Spaulding China Company of Sebring, Ohio, from 1939 to 1960. The figural planters and the small figurines, especially those with Art Deco designs, are of great collector interest.

ROYAL COPLEY, Bank, Piggy	20.00
Candy Dish, Hummingbird	25.00
Figurine, Bear, With Lollipop	30.00
Figurine, Bear, With Mandolin	35.00
Figurine, Bird On House	45.00
Figurine, Blackamoor, Pair	38.00
Figurine, Doe's Head & Fawn, 8 1/2 In.	23.00
Figurine, Duck, Signed A. Priola	49.50
Figurine, Hummingbird, On Flower	12.50
Figurine, Kingfisher, 5 3/4 In.	12.00
Figurine, Macaw	45.00
Head Vase, Black	20.00
Planter, Bear	22.00
Planter, Cat, Resting	39.50
Planter, Elephant, Small	45.00
Planter, Horse, 5 1/2 In.	18.00
Vase, African Head	20.00
Vase, Wall, Pirate's Head	22.00
Wall Pocket, Black, Turban	35.00

Royal Crown Derby Company, Ltd., was established in England in 1876. There is a complex family tree that includes the Derby, Crown Derby, Worcester, and Royal Crown Derby porcelains. The Royal Crown Derby mark includes the name and a crown. The words *Made in England* were used after 1921.

ROYAL CROWN DERBY, Bowl, Golden Aves, Octagonal, 8 1/2 In.	800.00
Breakfast Set, Posies, Box	90.00
Candlestick, Golden Waves, 10 1/2 In., Pair	1200.00
Creamer, Imari	150.00

Cup & Saucer, Imari	100.00
Cup & Saucer, Imari, Demitasse	85.00
Dish, Imari, Square, 10 1/2 In.	50.00
Loving Cup, Australian Bicentenary, Presentation Box	325.00
Pitcher, Oriental Garden, Pagoda, Flying Birds, 6 In.	286.00
Plate, Imari, 7 In.	75.00
Platter, Tree of Life, 1877–89, 19 In., Pair ....*Illus*	900.00
Sugar, Cover, Imari	175.00
Teapot, Imari, Signed, 2 3/4 x 2 1/2 In.	110.00
Vase, Flowers On Upper Section, Handles, 8 1/2 In.	1600.00
Vase, Flowers, Handles, Signed, 8 1/2 In.	2600.00
Vase, Gold Morning Glories, Vine, Knob Handles, 9 In.	250.00
Vase, Imari, 4 In.	295.00

Royal Doulton is the name used on Doulton and Company pottery made from 1902 to the present. Doulton and Company of England was founded in 1853. Pieces made before 1902 are listed in this book under Doulton. Royal Doulton collectors search for the out–of–production figurines, character jugs, and series wares.

ROYAL DOULTON, Animal, Airdale Terrior With Pheasant, HN 1022	400.00
Animal, Brown Bear, HN 2659	275.00
Animal, Cat, Flambe	350.00
Animal, Cat, Persian, White, HN 2539	150.00
Animal, Collie, Ashstead Applause, HN 1057	258.00
Animal, Dachshund, Standing, K 17	45.00
Animal, Dog, With Brown Ball, HN 1103	50.00
Animal, Dog, With Plate, HN 1158	60.00
Animal, Dog, Yawning, HN 1099	50.00
Animal, Elephant, Flambe	145.00
Animal, Elephant, Flambe, A Mark	80.00
Animal, Great Horned Owl, On Limb, Flambe, 12 1/4 In.	675.00
Animal, Rhinoceros, Half–Seated, Flambe, 17 In.	950.00
Animal, Snowy Owl, HN 2670	1500.00
Animal, Tiger, Flambe, Black Stripes, 6 1/2 x 14 1/4 In.	950.00
Animal, Tiger, Flambe, Crouching, Signed, 9 1/4 In.	400.00
Ash Pot, Sairey Gamp	125.00
Ashtray, Dutch People, 3 Men In Scene, Marked, 3 5/8 In.	35.00
Ashtray, John Barleycorn	120.00
Biscuit Jar, Bunches of Flowers, Silver Fittings, 7 3/4 In.	175.00
Biscuit Jar, Scenic, Sheep, 6 In.	295.00
Bottle, Old Crow	200.00
Bowl, Isaac Walton, Hand Painted, Deep, Large	235.00
Bowl, Norbury, Flow Blue, 16 1/2 In.	225.00
Bowl, Shakespeare Ware, Portia, 7 1/2 In.	48.00
Bowl, Shakespeare Ware, Romeo, 7 1/2 In.	48.00
Bowl, Shakespeare Ware, Wolsey, 7 1/2 In.	48.00
Candlestick, Isaac Walton, 4 Anglers, 6 1/2 In.	355.00

Character jugs are the modeled head and shoulders of the subject. They are made in four sizes: large, 5 1/4 to 7 inches; small, 3 1/4 to 4 inches; miniature, 2 1/4 to 2 1/2 inches; and tiny, 1 1/4 inches. Toby jugs depict a seated, full figure.

Character Jug, 'Ard of 'Earing, Miniature	1015.00
Character Jug, 'Arriet, Large	295.00
Character Jug, 'Arriet, Tiny	250.00
Character Jug, 'Arry, Miniature	55.00
Character Jug, 'Arry, Tiny .... 175.00 To 200.00	
Character Jug, Anne Boleyn, Large	85.00
Character Jug, Apothecary, Large ....75.00 To 125.00	
Character Jug, Apothecary, Miniature	35.00
Character Jug, Athos, Large	85.00
Character Jug, Auld Mac, Large	65.00
Character Jug, Auld Mac, Small ....*Illus*	80.00

Royal Doulton,	*Royal Doulton,*	*Royal Doulton,*	*Royal Doulton,*
Character Jug,	*Character Jug,*	*Character Jug,*	*Character Jug,*
Beefeater, Small	*Auld Mac, Small*	*Cavalier, Small*	*Dick Turpin, Small*

◆◆

Clean your rug the old–fashioned way. Put it face down in clean snow. After a short while, gently shake the snow off. You will be surprised at the dirt that is removed.

◆◆

Character Jug, Auld Mac, Tiny	250.00
Character Jug, Bacchus, Large	125.00
Character Jug, Beefeater, Miniature	55.00
Character Jug, Beefeater, Small ....*Illus*	80.00
Character Jug, Blacksmith, Large	75.00
Character Jug, Bootmaker, Large	90.00
Character Jug, Captain Ahab, Large ....90.00 To	125.00
Character Jug, Captain Hook, Large .... 395.00 To	425.00
Character Jug, Captain Hook, Small	265.00
Character Jug, Cardinal, Large	135.00
Character Jug, Cavalier, Large	115.00
Character Jug, Cavalier, Small ....*Illus*	90.00
Character Jug, Clown, White Hair, Large .... 650.00 To	975.00
Character Jug, Dick Turpin, Large .... 133.00 To	150.00
Character Jug, Dick Turpin, Small ....*Illus*	80.00
Character Jug, Don Quixote, Large	45.00
Character Jug, Drake, Large	165.00
Character Jug, Falconer, Large	70.00
Character Jug, Falstaff, Large	160.00
Character Jug, Fat Boy, Tiny	110.00
Character Jug, Fortune Teller, Large	260.00
Character Jug, Fortune Teller, Miniature	295.00
Character Jug, Friar Tuck, Large	400.00
Character Jug, Gardener, Large	145.00
Character Jug, George Washington, Large	120.00
Character Jug, Gladiator, Large .... 475.00 To	550.00
Character Jug, Golfer, Large .... 70.00 To	85.00
Character Jug, Gondolier, Small	380.00
Character Jug, Gone Away, Large	38.00
Character Jug, Gone Away, Small	45.00
Character Jug, Gunsmith, Large	97.00
Character Jug, Henry Morgan, Large	75.00
Character Jug, Henry VIII, Large	95.00
Character Jug, Henry VIII, Miniature	42.00
Character Jug, Jarge, Large	295.00
Character Jug, Jester, Small	75.00
Character Jug, John Barleycorn, Miniature	60.00
Character Jug, John Barleycorn, Small	75.00

Character Jug, John Peel, A Mark, Small 50.00
Character Jug, John Peel, Large 130.00
Character Jug, John Peel, Miniature 47.00
Character Jug, John Peel, Tiny .... 160.00 To 275.00
Character Jug, Johnny Appleseed, Large 300.00
Character Jug, Lord Nelson, Large 300.00
Character Jug, Lumberjack, Large 90.00
Character Jug, Mad Hatter, Large .... 110.00 To 150.00
Character Jug, Mephistopheles, Large 1750.00
Character Jug, Mikado, Large 500.00
Character Jug, Mr. Pickwick, Small 65.00
Character Jug, Mr. Pickwick, Tiny 250.00
Character Jug, North American Indian, Large 125.00
Character Jug, North American Indian, Small 75.00
Character Jug, Old Charley, Small 70.00
Character Jug, Old Charley, Tiny .... 85.00 To 110.00
Character Jug, Old King Cole, A Mark, Large 280.00
Character Jug, Old King Cole, Large .... 240.00 To 245.00
Character Jug, Pied Piper, Large 85.00
Character Jug, Porthos, Large 125.00
Character Jug, Punch & Judy Man, Miniature 285.00
Character Jug, Regency Beau, Large 850.00
Character Jug, Robin Hood, Large .... 126.00 To 140.00
Character Jug, Robin Hood, Miniature 65.00
Character Jug, Robinson Crusoe, Large 90.00
Character Jug, Robinson Crusoe, Small 45.00
Character Jug, Sairey Gamp, A Mark, Miniature 55.00
Character Jug, Sairey Gamp, Large 160.00
Character Jug, Sairey Gamp, Miniature 40.00
Character Jug, Sairey Gamp, Small 60.00
Character Jug, Sairey Gamp, Tiny 95.00
Character Jug, Samuel Johnson, Large 260.00
Character Jug, Scaramouche, Small 375.00
Character Jug, Sergeant Buz Fuz, Small 125.00
Character Jug, Simon The Cellarer, Small 60.00
Character Jug, Simple Simon, Large 500.00
Character Jug, Smuggler, Small 77.00
Character Jug, Tam O'Shanter, Large .... 95.00 To 100.00
Character Jug, Toby Philpots, Miniature 38.00
Character Jug, Tony Weller, Large 135.00
Character Jug, Touchstone, Large .... 190.00 To 300.00
Character Jug, Town Crier, Large 221.00
Character Jug, Uncle Tom Cobbleigh, Large .... 395.00 To 445.00
Character Jug, Veteran Motorist, Small 66.00
Character Jug, Walrus & Carpenter, Large .... 90.00 To 110.00
Character Jug, William Shakespeare, Large 88.00
Child's Set, Bunnykins, 4 Piece 65.00
Chocolate Pot, Floral 160.00
Chop Plate, Long John Silver, Parrot, Men, 13 1/2 In. 165.00
Chop Plate, Tony Weller, Whip On Plate, Marked, 13 1/2 In. 165.00
Coffeepot, Arab Merchants, With Wares, 3 3/4 In. 145.00
Coffeepot, Moorish Gate Series, Marked, 6 3/4 In. 145.00
Compote, Sunset Cottage Scene, Marked, 5 3/8 In. 165.00
Creamer, Mr. Pickwick 65.00
Creamer, Stoneware 65.00
Cup & Saucer, Chivalry 95.00
Cup & Saucer, Plate, Brambly Hedge Summer, 1983, 3 Piece 42.00
Cup & Saucer, Ravenswood 20.00
Cup, Bunnykins, 2 Handles 20.00
Cuspidor, Landscape & Windmill, Greens & Browns 150.00
Dinner Set, Dickensware, 20 Piece 835.00
Eggcup, Bunnykins 15.00
Figurine, A'courting, HN 2004 .... 325.00 To 450.00

Figurine, Abdullah, HN 2104 .... 395.00 To 425.00
Figurine, Adrienne, HN 2152 .... 110.00
Figurine, Affection, HN 2236 .... 120.00 To 121.00
Figurine, Afternoon Tea, HN 1747 .... 250.00 To 300.00
Figurine, All Aboard, HN 2940 .... 150.00
Figurine, Antoinette, HN 2326 .... 75.00 To 100.00
Figurine, Apple Maid, HN 2160 .... 310.00
Figurine, Ascot, HN 2356 .... 231.00
Figurine, Auctioneer, HN 2988 .... 165.00 To 265.00
Figurine, Autumn Breezes, HN 1913 .... 195.00
Figurine, Autumn Breezes, HN 1934 .... 125.00 To 175.00
Figurine, Balinese Dancer, HN 2808 .... 525.00
Figurine, Ballerina, HN 2116 .... 120.00 To 255.00
Figurine, Balloon Man, HN 1954 .... 235.00
Figurine, Bather, HN 687 .... 750.00
Figurine, Bedtime Story, HN 2059 .... 245.00 To 246.00
Figurine, Belle O' The Ball, HN 1997 .... 275.00
Figurine, Belle, HN 754 .... 550.00 To 720.00
Figurine, Belle, HN 2340 .... 60.00
Figurine, Bess, HN 2002 .... 220.00
Figurine, Biddy Penny Farthing, HN 1843 .... 190.00
Figurine, Blacksmith of Williamsburg, HN 2240 .... 175.00
Figurine, Blithe Morning, HN 2021 .... 90.00
Figurine, Blithe Morning, HN 2065 .... 125.00
Figurine, Bluebeard, HN 2105 .... 345.00
Figurine, Breton Dancer, HN 2383 .... 625.00
Figurine, Bride, HN 2873 .... 110.00
Figurine, Bridesmaid, HN 2148 .... 231.00
Figurine, Bunny, HN 2214 .... 130.00
Figurine, Calumet, HN 2068 .... 525.00
Figurine, Camille, HN 1586 .... 550.00
Figurine, Captain Cook, HN 2889 .... 275.00
Figurine, Captain MacHeath, HN 464 .... 625.00
Figurine, Cellist, HN 2226 .... 300.00
Figurine, Centurion, HN 2726 .... 110.00 To 165.00
Figurine, Charlotte, HN 2421 .... 75.00
Figurine, Chief, HN 2892 .... 200.00
Figurine, China Repairer, HN 2943 .... 145.00 To 165.00
Figurine, Christmas Morn, HN 1992 .... 188.00
Figurine, Christmas Parcels, HN 2851 .... 232.00
Figurine, Clarissa, HN 1525 .... 295.00
Figurine, Clemency, HN 1634 .... 795.00
Figurine, Cleopatra, HN 2868 .... 900.00 To 1200.00
Figurine, Clockmaker, HN 2279 .... 200.00 To 250.00
Figurine, Clown, HN 2890 .... 30.00
Figurine, Cobbler, HN 1705 .... 295.00 To 475.00
Figurine, Cobbler, HN 1706 .... 235.00
Figurine, Cookie, HN 2218 .... 145.00
Figurine, Coppelia, HN 2115 .... 450.00
Figurine, Craftsman, HN 2284 .... 415.00
Figurine, Cymbals, HN 2699 .... 425.00
Figurine, Daffy Down Dilly, HN 1712 .... 240.00
Figurine, Daydreams, HN 1731 .... 120.00

●●

If you have a vinyl doll with dirt or pencil marks on the head or body, try this. Wrap the doll so that only the marked part shows. Rub the mark with a solid vegetable shortening and put the doll in the sun for the day. Try this for several days and the mark should disappear.

●●

Figurine, Deidre, HN 2020	225.00
Figurine, Detective, HN 2359	250.00
Figurine, Dimity, HN 2169	275.00
Figurine, Dorcas, HN 1558	320.00
Figurine, Dulcinea, HN 1419	1595.00
Figurine, Easter Day, HN 1976	450.00 To 475.00
Figurine, Easter Day, HN 2039	290.00
Figurine, Ermine Coat, HN 1981	200.00
Figurine, Esmeralda, HN 2168	235.00
Figurine, Evelyn, HN 1622	795.00
Figurine, Eventide, HN 2814	195.00
Figurine, Fair Maiden, HN 2211	118.00
Figurine, Fairyspell, HN 2979	70.00
Figurine, Fat Boy, HN 2096	250.00
Figurine, Fiona, HN 1933	875.00
Figurine, Flora, HN 2349	270.00
Figurine, Flower Seller's Children, HN 1342	340.00 To 455.00
Figurine, Flute, HN 2483	800.00
Figurine, Foaming Quart, HN 2162	77.00
Figurine, Fortune Teller, HN 2159	295.00 To 425.00
Figurine, Forty Winks, HN 1974	185.00
Figurine, Forty Winks, HN 1974	195.00
Figurine, Gaffer, HN 2053	450.00
Figurine, Gay Morning, HN 2135	195.00
Figurine, Genevieve, HN 1962	145.00
Figurine, Genie, HN 2989	185.00
Figurine, Giselle, HN 2139	345.00
Figurine, Good Catch, HN 2258	130.00
Figurine, Good Morning, HN 2671	195.00 To 250.00
Figurine, Gossips, HN 2025	340.00 To 355.00
Figurine, Grandma, HN 2052	266.00
Figurine, Granny's Shawl, HN 1647	325.00
Figurine, Griselda, HN 1993	225.00 To 495.00
Figurine, Gypsy Dance, HN 2157	470.00 To 695.00
Figurine, Gypsy Dance, HN 2230	250.00
Figurine, Happy Anniversary, HN 3097	196.00
Figurine, Helmsman, HN 2499	220.00
Figurine, Herminia, HN 1646	500.00 To 705.00
Figurine, Honey, HN 1909	615.00
Figurine, Ibrahim, HN 2095	450.00
Figurine, Indian Brave, HN 2376	1300.00 To 1430.00
Figurine, Invitation, HN 2170	115.00
Figurine, Jacqueline, HN 2001	525.00
Figurine, Janet, HN 1916	205.00
Figurine, Janine, HN 2461	195.00
Figurine, Jersey Milkmaid, HN 2057	195.00 To 245.00
Figurine, Jester, HN 2016	285.00
Figurine, Judith, HN 2089	395.00
Figurine, Julia, HN 2705	165.00
Figurine, June, HN 2027	365.00
Figurine, Karen, HN 1994	395.00
Figurine, Ko–Ko & Yum–Yum, HN 2898, 2899, Pair	1300.00
Figurine, Ko–Ko, HN 2898	650.00
Figurine, Lady Anne Nevill, HN 2006	615.00
Figurine, Lady April, HN 1958	260.00
Figurine, Lady Charmian, HN 1948	120.00
Figurine, Lady Charmian, HN 1949	140.00 To 220.00
Figurine, Lady Clare, HN 1465	775.00
Figurine, Lady From Williamsburg, HN 2228	150.00
Figurine, Ladybird, HN 1638	1395.00
Figurine, Lambing Time, HN 1890	130.00
Figurine, Lambing, HN 1890	140.00
Figurine, Leisure Hour, HN 2055	435.00

Figurine, Lily, HN 1798 .... 88.00
Figurine, Lion On A Rock, HN 2641 .... 1600.00
Figurine, Little Boy Blue, HN 2062 .... 115.00 To 116.00
Figurine, Little Bridesmaid, HN 1433 .... 140.00
Figurine, Lobster Man, HN 2317 .... 210.00
Figurine, Lord Oliver As Richard III, HN 2881 .... 250.00
Figurine, Lucy Lockett, HN 524 .... 475.00
Figurine, Lunchtime, HN 2485 .... 195.00
Figurine, Lyric, HN 2757 .... 75.00
Figurine, Margaret of Anjou, HN 2012 .... 575.00
Figurine, Margery, HN 1413 .... 510.00
Figurine, Marguerite, HN 1928 .... 295.00
Figurine, Market Day, HN 1991 .... 240.00 To 275.00
Figurine, Mary Had A Little Lamb, HN 2048 ....75.00 To 133.00
Figurine, Mary Jane, HN 1990 .... 235.00
Figurine, Masquerade, HN 2259 ...., 215.00
Figurine, Master Sweep, HN 2205 .... 495.00
Figurine, Master, HN 2325 .... 189.00 To 200.00
Figurine, Maureen, HN 1770 .... 225.00 To 275.00
Figurine, Mayor, HN 2280 .... 395.00
Figurine, Maytime, HN 2113 .... 275.00
Figurine, Memories, HN 2030 .... 235.00 To 325.00
Figurine, Mendicant, HN 1365 .... 185.00 To 200.00
Figurine, Mermaid, HN 97 .... 600.00
Figurine, Midinette, HN 2090 .... 170.00
Figurine, Midsummer Noon, HN 1899 .... 595.00
Figurine, Millicent, HN 1715 .... 530.00
Figurine, Minuet, HN 2019 .... 295.00
Figurine, Mirabel, HN 1743 .... 890.00
Figurine, Miranda, Hn 1819 .... 581.00
Figurine, Miss Fortune, HN 1897 .... 150.00 To 165.00
Figurine, Miss Muffet, HN 1937 .... 182.00 To 235.00
Figurine, Monica, HN 1467 .... 115.00
Figurine, Mr. Micawber, HN 2097 .... 225.00
Figurine, My Pretty Maid, HN 2064 .... 335.00
Figurine, Nanny, HN 2221 .... 65.00
Figurine, News Vendor, HN 2891 .... 150.00
Figurine, Nicola, HN 2839 .... 325.00
Figurine, Noelle, HN 2179 .... 375.00
Figurine, Old Meg, HN 2494 .... 195.00
Figurine, Olga, HN 2463 .... 275.00
Figurine, Omar Khayyam, HN 2247 .... 145.00 To 175.00
Figurine, Orange Lady, HN 1759 .... 220.00 To 225.00
Figurine, Orange Lady, HN 1953 .... 165.00 To 231.00
Figurine, Orange Seller, HN 1325 .... 975.00
Figurine, Paisley Shawl, HN 1988 .... 145.00
Figurine, Palio, HN 2428 .... 5000.00
Figurine, Pantalettes, HN 1362 .... 295.00 To 425.00
Figurine, Pearly Boy, HN 1547 .... 375.00
Figurine, Pecksniff, HN 2098 .... 225.00
Figurine, Peggy, HN 2038 .... 90.00
Figurine, Penelope, HN 1901 .... 198.00
Figurine, Philippine Dancer, HN 2439 .... 700.00
Figurine, Pinkie, HN 1552 .... 475.00
Figurine, Pirate King, HN 2901 .... 325.00
Figurine, Pirouette, HN 2216 .... 195.00
Figurine, Polish Dancer, HN 2836 .... 750.00
Figurine, Polly Peachum, HN 698 .... 290.00
Figurine, Pretty Polly, HN 2768 .... 140.00
Figurine, Pride & Joy, HN 2945 .... 275.00
Figurine, Prince Phillip, HN 2386 .... 345.00
Figurine, Priscilla, HN 1337 .... 365.00
Figurine, Prized Possessions, HN 2942 .... 525.00 To 575.00

Figurine, Professor, HN 2281 .... 135.00 To 275.00
Figurine, Punch & Judy Man, HN 2765 .... 275.00 To 280.00
Figurine, Puppetmaker, HN 2253 .... 400.00
Figurine, Reflections, HN 1821 .... 850.00
Figurine, Reverie, HN 2306 .... 195.00 To 225.00
Figurine, Roseanna, HN 1926 .... 140.00 To 280.00
Figurine, Rosebud, HN 1983 .... 325.00 To 595.00
Figurine, Rowena, HN 2077 .... 510.00
Figurine, Royal Governor's Cook, HN 2233 .... 330.00 To 395.00
Figurine, Sabbath Morn, HN 1982 .... 240.00
Figurine, Samantha, HN 2954 .... 70.00
Figurine, Sea Sprite, HN 2191 .... 265.00 To 335.00
Figurine, Seafarer, HN 2455 .... 200.00
Figurine, Serenade, HN 2753 .... 75.00
Figurine, Shore Leave, HN 2254 .... 200.00
Figurine, Silks and Ribbons, HN 2017 .... 168.00
Figurine, Sleeping Beauty, HN 3079 .... 170.00 To 195.00
Figurine, Sleepy Darling, HN 2953 .... 150.00 To 195.00
Figurine, Song of Sea, HN 2729 .... 210.00
Figurine, Southern Belle, HN 2229 .... 225.00
Figurine, Spanish Flamenco Dancer, HN 2831 .... 1200.00
Figurine, Spring Flowers, HN 1807 .... 235.00
Figurine, Spring Flowers, HN 1945 .... 513.00
Figurine, St. George, HN 2051 .... 385.00
Figurine, St. George, HN 2067 .... 1300.00
Figurine, Stephanie, HN 2807 .... 140.00
Figurine, Sunday Morning, HN 2184 .... 375.00
Figurine, Sunshine Girl, HN 1344 .... 2223.00
Figurine, Sweet & Twenty, HN 1298 .... 195.00 To 235.00
Figurine, Sweet Anne, M 5 .... 250.00
Figurine, Sweet Lavender, HN 1373 .... 675.00
Figurine, Sweet Suzy, HN 1918 .... 750.00
Figurine, Taking Things Easy, HN 2677 .... 125.00 To 210.00
Figurine, Tall Story, HN 2248 .... 180.00
Figurine, Teenager, HN 2203 .... 210.00
Figurine, Thanks Doc, HN 2731 .... 270.00
Figurine, This Little Pig, HN 1793 .... 30.00 To 35.00
Figurine, This Little Pig, HN 1794 .... 325.00
Figurine, Tinker Bell, HN 1677 .... 87.00
Figurine, Top O' The Hill, HN 1834 .... 50.00
Figurine, Top O' The Hill, HN 1849 .... 216.00
Figurine, Town Crier, HN 2119 .... 230.00 To 285.00
Figurine, Toymaker, HN 2250 .... 235.00 To 270.00
Figurine, Two–A–Penny, HN 1359 .... 650.00
Figurine, Uncle Ned, HN 2094 .... 300.00
Figurine, Vanessa, HN 1836 .... 750.00
Figurine, Veneta, HN 2722 .... 110.00
Figurine, Viking, HN 2375 .... 250.00 To 280.00
Figurine, Wardrobe Mistress, HN 2145 .... 425.00
Figurine, Wayfarer, HN 2362 .... 175.00
Figurine, Wee Willie Winkie, HN 2050 .... 150.00
Figurine, Willy–Won't He, HN 2150 .... 375.00
Figurine, Wintertime, HN 3060 .... 225.00
Figurine, Young Master, HN 2872 .... 195.00
Figurine, Young Miss Nightingale, HN 2010 .... 684.00
Figurine, Yum–Yum, HN 2899 .... 650.00
Humidor, Isaac Walton, 3 Anglers, Inscription, 6 1/2 In. 605.00
Jardiniere, Welsh Ladies, Going To Church, Marked, 8 1/2 In. 335.00
Jug, Sea Shanty, Sailor & His Girl, Verses, 6 5/8 In. 145.00
Liquor Container, Rip Van Winkle 110.00
Match Holder, Isaac Walton, Signed Noke 325.00
Mug, Bowl & Plate Set, Bunnykins, 1978, 3 Piece 35.00
Mug, Dutch Girls, Yellow & Green Trim, 2 In. 40.00

Mug, Elk, Dickensware	225.00
Mug, Hamlet, Large	90.00
Mug, Isaac Walton, Rod In Hand, Inscription, D 6829, 8 In.	523.00
Mug, Minstrels, Instrument Border, 3 1/4 In.	65.00
Music Box, Jogger, Bunnykins, DB37	30.00
Pitcher, 2 Girls Under Tree, Gilt Handle, Green	225.00
Pitcher, Blue & White, Horseshoe Framing, 2 Doe, Stag, 9 In.	350.00
Pitcher, Floral, Turquoise Jeweling, Cream, Burslem	195.00
Pitcher, Motor Series, Room For One, 6 In.	175.00
Pitcher, Oliver Twist, Square	145.00
Pitcher, Pickwick's Papers, White Hart Inn	150.00
Plate, Admiral, Black Mark	75.00
Plate, Balloon Seller, D 6655	100.00
Plate, Chusan, Flow Blue, 10 1/4 In.	15.00
Plate, Coaching Days	90.00
Plate, Dicken's Portrait Rack	110.00
Plate, Doctor, Black Mark	75.00
Plate, English Game Fish Scenes, Signed, 9 In., 12 Piece	1320.00
Plate, Fishing, Reel, Edward Vom Hofe, No. 360, Handmade	6050.00
Plate, Floral Pattern, 1920s, 4 Piece	300.00
Plate, Game, Blue & White	90.00
Plate, Harvesting, Rustic England, Square	75.00
Plate, Hot Air Ballooning, 10 In.	135.00
Plate, Johnson At The Cheshire Cheese, 13 In.	90.00
Plate, Old Balloon Seller, D 6649	100.00
Plate, Squire, 10 1/2 In.	45.00
Platter, Dick Swiveller, Oval, 18 In.	175.00
Punch Set, Dickensware, Signed, Noke, 8 Cups, 14 1/2 In.	950.00
Sugar & Creamer, Cambridge	45.00
Tankard, Christmas, 1971	50.00
Tankard, Christmas, 1976	70.00
Tankard, Christmas, 1979	65.00
Tea Set, Dickensware, Teapot, 12 Cups & Saucers	625.00
Teapot, Cambridge	125.00
Teapot, Gold Lace, 9 1/2 In.	95.00
Teapot, Melon Ribbed, White, Gold Handle & Finial, Pre–1930	45.00
Teapot, Sugar & Creamer, Sairey Gamp	2000.00
Teapot, White Flowers, Gold Trim, Cobalt Blue	85.00
Tobacco Jar, Old Charley	1950.00
Tobacco Jar, Paddy	1250.00
Toby Jug, Falstaff, Large	85.00 To 105.00
Toby Jug, Happy John, Large	100.00
Toby Jug, Old Charley, Large	180.00
Toby Jug, Sherlock Holmes, Large	100.00
Toby Jug, Sir Winston Churchill, 5 1/2 In.	35.00
Toby Jug, Sir Winston Churchill, 9 In.	95.00
Toothpick, Issac Walton, Signed	98.00
Tray, Flower Seller	50.00
Tray, Red & Pink Poppies, Green Lion Mark, 7 1/4 x 8 1/2 In.	175.00
Tray, Robin Hood	15.00
Tray, Zunday Zmocks, Man In High Hat, Marked, 5 x 11 In.	85.00
Trivet, Old Moreton	45.00
Vase, Babe In Woods, Flow Blue, Woman & Child	235.00
Vase, Dunolly Castle, Landscape, Gold Trim, Marked, 4 3/8 In.	165.00
Vase, Fox Hunt Scene, 2 1/4 In.	50.00
Vase, Green Reserves, Stylized Flowers, Bulbous, Blue, 16 In.	350.00
Vase, Isaac Walton, 3 Anglers With Rod & Reel, 10 In.	715.00
Vase, Pillow, Monk, Dickensware, 2nd Line	425.00
Vase, Tapestry, White & Aqua Flowers, Gold Trim, 10 1/4 In.	245.00
Vase, Veined Sung, 6 In.	300.00
Wall Vase, Old Charley	2500.00
Water Cooler, Purolator	125.00

 The Duxer Porzellanmanufaktur was founded in Dux, Bohemia, in 1860 by E. Eichler. By the turn of the century, the firm specialized in porcelain statuary and busts of Art Nouveau–style maidens, large porcelain figures, and ornate vases with three-dimensional figures climbing on the sides. The firm is still in business.

ROYAL DUX, Bowl, Art Nouveau, Florals, 2 Scantily Clad Maidens, 13 x 19 In. 775.00
Bowl, Centerpiece, Maiden & Cherubs Hold Up Bowl, Marked, 20 In. 1150.00
Bowl, Upright Boy & Girl At Ends, Marked, 10 1/4 In. 250.00
Bust, Caesar, Gold Shirt, Floral Toga, Marked, 9 In. 350.00
Bust, Girl, Art Deco, Marked, 6 1/2 In. 215.00
Ewer, Gold Design, Leaves & Fruits, Marked, Green, 5 1/2 In. 185.00
Ewer, Green, Moss To Light Green, Leaves, Fruits, 5 In. 185.00
Ewer, Leaves & Fruits, Gold Design, Marked, 5 1/2 In. 185.00
Figurine, 2 Children With Baskets, Marked, 8 3/4 In. 425.00
Figurine, Arab On Camel, Marked, 20 In. 1500.00
Figurine, Cockatoo, 17 In. 165.00
Figurine, Cockatoo, Marked, 16 1/2 In. 160.00
Figurine, Colonial Couple, Man In Coat, Girl In Dress, 11 1/2 In. 1150.00
Figurine, Dove, Pink Triangle Mark 130.00
Figurine, Elephant, Pink Triangle Mark, 8 1/4 x 11 1/2 In. 135.00
Figurine, Flower Bowl, Kneeling Girl, Pouring Water, 9 1/2 In. 650.00
Figurine, German Shepherd, Pink Triangle Mark, 8 3/4 In. 45.00
Figurine, Lion, Pink Mark 195.00
Figurine, Male Water Carrier, Triangle Mark, 20 In. 975.00
Figurine, Man, Water Jug, & Woman, Carrying Fish, 1900, 24 In., Pair 1650.00
Figurine, Mother Holding Child, Marked, 8 1/2 In. 375.00
Figurine, Nude Woman, Matte, 8 In. 150.00
Figurine, Nude Woman, Sitting With Butterfly, 9 In. 135.00
Figurine, Nude, Seated 8 In. 165.00
Figurine, Nude, Seated, Marked, 8 In. 145.00
Figurine, Nude, Seated, White, 6 In. 85.00
Figurine, Nude, Seated, White, 10 In. 225.00
Figurine, Rebecca At Well, Pink Triangle Mark, 8 1/2 x 17 In. 950.00
Figurine, Roman Woman, Pink Triangle Mark, 10 In. .... 130.00 To 190.00
Figurine, Russian Wolfhound 45.00
Figurine, Tiger, Marked, 12 In. 200.00
Figurine, Water Carrier, Man, Marked, 20 In. 695.00
Figurine, Wolf Chasing Deer 110.00
Figurine, Woman, No. 15386, Peach 195.00
Powder Jar, Figure of Woman Seated On Top, Cobalt Blue, Gold 595.00
Vase, Art Nouveau, Likeness of Woman, 14 1/4 In. 210.00
Vase, Figural, Girl, Baroque Floral Top, Marked, 12 In., Pair 1250.00
Vase, Maiden, Turned Head, Grape Leaves, Fruit, Signed, 25 In. 995.00
Vase, Woman, Floral Design, Signed, 17 In. 700.00

◆◆

One moth can lay 300 eggs. Each egg will hatch into a larva that eats 15 times its body weight in wool. If you see a single flying moth, you probably have a family. Look under rugs regularly for signs of damage, tunnels, or tufts of wool. If you find any, have all of your carpets and rugs cleaned. Remove any jute padding. Spray baseboards and moldings for insects. Have all your own woolen clothes dry cleaned. Do all of this at the same time to be sure to find all of the larvae or eggs.

◆◆

Royal Flemish glass was made during the late 1880s in New Bedford, Massachusetts, by the Mt. Washington Glass Works. It is a colored satin glass decorated with dark colors and raised gold designs. The glass was patented in 1894. It was supposed to resemble stained glass windows.

ROYAL FLEMISH, Biscuit Jar, Gold Enamel, Spiral Designs, 8 In. 935.00
  Jar, Flowers, Frosted Glass, 6 In. ....*Illus* 850.00
  Pitcher, Marine Design, Rope Handle, 8 1/2 In. 2200.00
  Vase, Gold Enamel, Signed, 14 1/2 In. ....*Illus* 2750.00
    ROYAL HAEGER, see Haeger
    ROYAL IVY, see Pressed Glass, Royal Ivy

The Nymphenburg porcelain factory was established at Neudeck–ob–der–Au, Germany, in 1753 and moved to Nymphenburg in 1761. The company is still in existence. Modern marks used by the firm known as Royal Nymphenburg include a checkered shield topped by a crown, a crowned *CT* with the year, and a contemporary shield mark on reproductions of eighteenth–century porcelain.

ROYAL NYMPHENBURG, Beaker, Topographical, Figures In Park, c.1860, 4 3/4 In.   1100.00
  Bowl, Centerpiece, Floral, Gold, Green Band, 10 In. 413.00
  Bowl, Serving, Floral, Gold, Green Band, 10 In. 320.00
  Cake Plate, Floral, Gold, Green Band, 13 In. 330.00
  Casserole, Pineapple Finial, Loop Handles, 9 x 10 In. 495.00
  Chop Plate, Floral, Gold, Green Band, 14 In. 358.00

Royal Flemish, Jar, Flowers, Frosted Glass, 6 In.

Royal Flemish, Vase, Gold Enamel, Signed, 14 1/2 In.

Royal Nymphenburg, Vase, Venus, Nymphs, Cream, 19 In.

Royal Worcester, Figurine, Cairo Water Carriers, 1883, 21 In., Pair   Royal Worcester, Figurine, Eastern Water Carriers, 1877, 17 In., Pair

Cup & Saucer, Art Deco Floral Design, After Dinner	35.00
Dinner Set, White, Purple, Basketweave Border, 30 Piece	350.00
Dish, Entree, Fruit, Gold, Green Band, Cover, Handle, 9 In.	600.00
Figurine, Bear, On Back, Chewing Paw, Neuhauser, 5 In.	185.00
Figurine, Bird, Blue Tit, White Tree Stump, 5 In.	85.00
Figurine, Deer, Lying On Side, 4 x 3 3/4 In.	95.00
Figurine, Horse, White, 8 In.	95.00
Plate, Dinner, Floral, Gold, Green Band, 10 In., Set of 6	550.00
Plate, Luncheon, Floral, Gold, Green Band, 9 In., Set of 8	600.00
Plate, Salad, Floral, Gold, Green Band, 8 In., Set of 10	660.00
Platter, Floral, Gold, Green Band, Oval, 15 In.	385.00
Platter, Floral, Gold, Green Band, Oval, 16 1/2 In.	375.00
Platter, Floral, Gold, Green Band, Oval, 18 In.	358.00
Relish, Shell Form, Scrolled Handle, Green Band, 8 In.	195.00
Soup, Floral, Gold, Green Band, 9 In., Set of 10	880.00
Tea Set, Grisaill Landscapes, Blue, Gilt, 6 Piece	550.00
Tureen, Fruit Finial, Scrolled Handle, Green Band, Gold	2200.00
Vase, Venus, Nymphs, Cream, 19 In. ....*Illus*	1430.00

ROYAL OAK, see Pressed Glass, Royal Oak
ROYAL RUDOLSTADT, see Rudolstadt
ROYAL VIENNA, see Beehive

Worcester porcelains were made in Worcester, England, from about 1751. The firm went through many different periods and name changes. It became the Worcester Royal Porcelain Company, Ltd., in 1862. Today collectors call the porcelains made after 1862 *Royal Worcester.* In 1976, the firm merged with W. T. Copeland to become Royal Worcester Spode. Some early products of the factory are listed under Worcester.

ROYAL WORCESTER, Biscuit Jar, Cobalt Leaves On White Bamboo Ground, 7 In.	355.00
Bowl, Grape Leaves Over Basket Weave Ground, 1884, 9 In.	335.00
Box, Pin, Yellow To Peach, Gold Scroll, Purple Mark, 4 In.	85.00
Butter Dish, Floral Design, Pinecone Interior, c.1890	525.00
Candle Snuffer, Monk	85.00
Candlestick, Coiled Horn, Ivory, Gold Outlines, c.1889	175.00
Candlestick, Kate Greenaway Boy, Signed, 1887, 10 1/2 In.	450.00
Cracker Jar, Melon Rib, Floral, Marked	325.00
Creamer, Wren In Leaves, Twig Stem, Signed, 3 In.	35.00
Cup & Saucer, Kent, Fluted, Dated 1937, 12 Piece	100.00
Dish, Maple Leaf Form, Flower Clusters, 1887, 9 1/4 In.	175.00
Ewer, Gold & Brown, Reticulated Neck, Handle, 8 In.	350.00
Ewer, Hand Painted Floral Sprigs, Gold Handle, 7 In., Pair	350.00
Ewer, Salamander Handle, 1886, 7 In.	195.00
Figurine, Ballet Dancer, No. 3192, 11 In.	175.00
Figurine, Bird, Outstretched Wings, 6 Cupids Heads, 8 In.	350.00
Figurine, Birds, Blue Tit, 3 1/2 In.	40.00
Figurine, Bridesmaid, No. 3224	275.00
Figurine, Bridesmaid, No. 3225	275.00
Figurine, Brigideen Indian, No. 1243, Pair	750.00
Figurine, Broom Girl, 5 3/4 In.	185.00
Figurine, Cairo Water Carriers, 1883, 21 In., Pair ....*Illus*	1650.00
Figurine, Dairy Shorthorn Bull	750.00
Figurine, December, No. 3458, 6 1/2 In.	295.00
Figurine, Eastern Water Carriers, 1877, 17 In., Pr. .... *Illus*	2200.00
Figurine, February	250.00
Figurine, Grandmother's Dress	120.00
Figurine, Indigo Bunting In Blackberry Sprays, 9 In.	335.00
Figurine, Kneeling Woman, Urn, Signed, c.1900, 5 1/2 In.	400.00
Figurine, Lark Sparrow, Wooden Base, Case, 1966, 6 5/8 In.	200.00
Figurine, Mockingbirds, 10 1/4 In., Pair	495.00
Figurine, Monday's Child	89.00
Figurine, Monday's Child, No Flower	195.00
Figurine, Oven Birds With Crested Iris, Lady Slipper, 1957	900.00

Royal Worcester, Figurine, Palomino Stallion, No. 160, 9 In.

Royal Worcester, Pitcher, Elephant Head Handle, Ivory, 8 In.

Royal Worcester, Vase, Lug Handle, Blue Flowers, Ivory, 9 In.

Royal Worcester, Vase, Ivory, Thistles, Pitcher Form, 8 In.

Figurine, Palomino Stallion, No. 160, 9 In. ....*Illus*	300.00
Figurine, Parakeet, 7 In.	88.50
Figurine, Parakeet, No. 3087, 6 1/4 In.	45.00
Figurine, Scarlet Tanagers & White Oak, 1956	700.00
Figurine, Sleepy Boy	70.00
Figurine, Tuesday's Child	250.00
Figurine, Water Carriers, 1 Man, 1 Woman, c.1900, Pair	600.00
Figurine, Yankee, Beige & Brown, c.1881, 7 In.	300.00
Figurine, Yellow Throats & Water Hyacinth, 1958	700.00
Jug, Owl On Branch, Serpentine Handle, c.1885, 11 1/4 In.	930.00
Pin Box, Green Scrolls, Gold Trim, Oval, 2 1/2 x 4 In.	95.00
Pitcher, Cantaloupe Form, Vine Handle, 1889, 9 3/4 In.	360.00
Pitcher, Elephant Head Handle, Ivory, 8 In. ....*Illus*	175.00
Pitcher, Floral, 5 In.	65.00
Pitcher, Floral, Cream Ground, 5 1/2 In.	75.00
Pitcher, Signed, c.1887, 4 1/2 In.	75.00
Plaque, Portrait, English Nobleman, 1865 Mark, 17 In.	975.00
Plate, Flowers, Scalloped Gold Rim, Ribbed, 7 3/8 In., Pair	100.00
Salt, Salamander On Side, Head Above Top, Square, 2 In.	350.00
Sugar & Creamer, Green Serpent Handles & Base, 3 1/2 In.	195.00
Vase, Black–Faced Sheep, Cream, Reticulated Base, 6 In.	165.00
Vase, Florals, Gold Trim, Cream Ground, c.1903, 6 1/8 In.	165.00
Vase, Florals, Gold Twig Handles, Marked, 5 1/4 In., Pair	385.00
Vase, Flowers & Butterflies, Marked, 1883, 14 In., Pair	1100.00
Vase, Flowers Surrounded By Gilt Leaves, Handle, 13 In.	1015.00
Vase, Flowers, Ivory Enameled, Gilt, 13 In.	1020.00
Vase, Gilt Trim & Handles, Bottle Shape, Marked, 13 1/2 In.	605.00
Vase, Ivory, Thistles, Pitcher Form, 8 In. ....*Illus*	175.00
Vase, Ivoryware Dragon, Flowering Branches, Marked, 12 In.	335.00
Vase, Lug Handle, Blue Flowers, Ivory, 9 In. ....*Illus*	220.00
Vase, Pheasants, Stinton, 4 In., Pair	895.00
Vase, Pierced, Cranes & Prunus, 7 1/4 In., Pair	440.00
Vase, Shell Form, Roman Gold Trim, 1888, 8 1/2 In.	450.00
Wall Pocket, Orchid, 1883 Mark, 8 In.	675.00

Roycroft products were made by the Roycrofter community of East Aurora, New York, in the late–nineteenth and early–twentieth centuries. The community was founded by Elbert Hubbard, famous philosopher, writer, and artist. The workshops owned by the community made furniture, metalware, leatherwork, embroidery, and jewelry. A printshop produced many signs, books, and the magazines that promoted the sayings of Elbert Hubbard. Furniture by the Roycroft community is listed in the furniture section.

ROYCROFT, Bookends, Bird Design, Signed	125.00
Bookends, Engraved Owl	395.00
Bookends, Flower On Hammered Ground, Cutout Center, 8 1/2 x 6 In.	195.00
Bookends, Hammered Copper, Ring & Linear Design, Marked, 5 1/4 In.	195.00

Bookends, Owl, Central Medallion, Logo, 4 x 6 1/4 In. 165.00
Bookends, Owl, Copper, Planished Background, 4 x 6 1/2 In., Pair 195.00
Bookends, Scrolled Ends, Dark Patina, No. 340, 4 1/8 x 6 1/2 In. 225.00
Bookends, Stylized Flower, Copper, 5 1/2 In. 150.00
Bowl, Nut, 3–Footed, Scoop With Curved Handle, 7 1/4–In. Bowl, 2 Pc. 550.00
Box, Verde Green Patina, Leaf–Form Brass Handles, 5 x 10 In. 1200.00
Candelabrum, 3 Bobeches On Long Brass Strip, Footed, 3 x 20 In. 415.00
Candelabrum, 3–Light, Twisted Standard, Signed, 20 In., Pair 1325.00
Candlestick, Brass Stem, Marked, 9 1/2 In., Pair 445.00
Candlestick, Floral Base, Cupped Bobeche, 8 x 3 1/2 In., Pr. 605.00
Candlestick, Hammered Copper, Twisted Stem, Marked, Pair 695.00
Candlestick, Princess, Cupped Bobeche, Square Stem, 7 1/2 In., Pair 550.00
Centerpiece, Copper, Rolled Rim, 3 Dimple Footed, Orb, 10 3/4 In. 1450.00
Desk Set, Hammered Copper, 7 Piece 125.00
Dish, Fern 8250.00
Humidor, Hammered Copper, 5 In. 250.00
Jug, 5 In. 55.00
Lamp, Ceiling, Copper & Glass, Conical, 3 Chains, Orb, 26 x 17 In. 8250.00
Lamp, Desk, Original Patina 1925.00
Lamp, Flared Rim, 3 Curving Handles, Signed, 9 1/2 In. 110.00
Lamp, Hammered Copper, Mica, Domed Strap Hinges Shade, 15 x 10 In. 1450.00
Lamp, Table, Bell–Form Marbelized Shade, c.1926, 15 In. 1325.00
Nut Bowl, Spoon, Silver On Copper, 2 1/4 x 6 In. 150.00
Nut Dish, Hammered, Center Design, Dark Patina, 4 In. 85.00
Nut Set, Spoon, 6 Piece 325.00
Smoking Set, Humidor, Match Holder, Ashtrays, 13 x 9–In. Tray 935.00
Telephone, Copper, Pyramid Base, American Tel & Tel Co., 12 In. 1750.00
Vase, Bud, Glass Insert, 8 In. 125.00
Vase, Matte Green Over Copper, Flat Base, Thin Neck, 16 x 9 In. 1100.00
Vase, Nickel Silver Cutout On Copper 850.00
Vase, Silver Washed, Verre De Soie Insert, 1926, 6 In. 275.00
Walking Stick, Tapering Form, Leather Thong, Logo, 1903, 35 In. 215.00
    ROZANE, see Roseville

> Rozenburg worked at The Hague, Holland, from 1890 to 1914. The
> most important pieces were earthenware made in the early–twentieth
> century with pale–colored Art Nouveau designs.

ROZENBURG, Jug, Art Nouveau Design, Butterflies, Floral, Green, Blue, 7 In. 500.00
Vase, Art Nouveau Pomegranates, High Gloss, Signed KE, 4 3/4 In. 200.00

R. R. P.
R. U.S.A.
ROVILLE.

> *RRP* is the mark used by the firm of Robinson–Ransbottom. It is
> not a mark of the more famous Roseville Pottery. The Ransbottom
> brothers started a started a pottery in 1900 in Ironspot, Ohio. In
> 1920, they merged with the Robinson Clay Product Company of
> Akron, Ohio, to become Robinson–Ransbottom. The factory is still
> working.

RRP, Ashtray, Factory Anniversary, 1951 .... 15.00
Cookie Jar, Brownie .... 120.00 To 125.00
Cookie Jar, Cow Jumped Over The Moon 70.00
Cookie Jar, Cow Jumped Over The Moon, Gold Trim 55.00
Cookie Jar, Dutch Girl, Blue, Yellow 76.00
Cookie Jar, Man's Head, Christmas Party, 1960s 110.00
Cookie Jar, Old King Cole .... 210.00 To 460.00
Cookie Jar, Oscar 85.00
Cookie Jar, Peter, Peter Pumpkin Eater ....85.00 To 150.00
Cookie Jar, Pig Sheriff 115.00
Cookie Jar, Pig, Yellow Hat 35.00
Cookie Jar, Pirate 105.00
Cookie Jar, Preacher 110.00
Cookie Jar, Wise Bird 35.00
Cookie Jar, Wise Bird, Gold Trim ....80.00 To 125.00
Cookie Jar, World War II Soldier .... 240.00 To 350.00
Pitcher, Raised Cows, Blue, 8 In. 47.50

◆◆◆

Oriental rugs should be vacuumed once a week and have an expert
cleaning and mothproofing once a year, if in a heavy traffic area.

◆◆◆

Pitcher, Raised Flowers, Brown, 8 In.	45.00

Porcelain with a variety of *RS Germany* marks was made at the
Tillowitz, Germany, factory of Reinhold Schlegelmilch from about
1869 until about 1956. It was sold decorated and undecorated. The
Schlegelmilch family made porcelains marked in many ways. See
also ES Germany, RS Poland, RS Prussia, RS Silesia, RS Suhl, and
RS Tillowitz.

RS GERMANY, Berry Set, Pink Magnolias, Luster Finish, 7 Piece	255.00
Bowl, Blue & Ivory Flowers, 10 1/4 In.	125.00
Bowl, Florals, 4 Footed, Oval	40.00
Bowl, Roses, Violets, Gray Shaded, 2 Pierced Handles, 10 x 9 In.	65.00
Chocolate Pot, Blue, Soft Green Trim	235.00
Condensed Milk Holder, Lid, Underplate, Floral On White, 5 In.	150.00
Cracker Jar, White Floral	80.00
Match Holder, Wall, Roses, Striker	100.00
Mustard, Floral Design, Spoon, 3 In.	85.00
Plate, Clusters of Violets, Foliage, Green, Gold, Marked, 8 In.	50.00
Plate, Felicitas, 7 In.	40.00
Plate, Gibson Girl	75.00
Powder Shaker, Floral Design, Gold Trim, 5 In.	185.00
Sugar & Creamer, Ring of Roses, White Ground, 3 In.	45.00
Tankard, Poppy & Berry, Signed, 11 In.	185.00
Tray, Hummingbird & Bird of Paradise, Blue Mark, 7 x 16 In.	1100.00

The *RS Poland (German)* mark was used by the Reinhold
Schlegelmilch factory at Tillowitz from about 1945 to 1956. This is
one of many of the RS of the RS marks used. See also ES
Germany, RS Germany, RS Prussia, RS Silesia, RS Suhl, and RS
Tillowitz.

RS POLAND, Planter, Band of Pink Flowers, Gold Trim, 6 3/4 x 6 1/2 In.	235.00
Server, Center Handle, Lavender & Pink Roses, 8 x 11 In.	515.00
Vase, Cottage, Woman, Sheep, Gold Rim, 10 In.	650.00
Vase, Crowned Crane, 3 1/2 In.	800.00
Vase, Mill Scene, Gold Rim, 10 In.	650.00

RS Prussia appears in several marks used on porcelain before 1915.
Two brothers used the same basic marks. Erdmann Schlegelmilch
opened a factory in 1861 in Suhl, Germany; his brother Reinhold
started his porcelain works in Tillowitz, Germany, in 1869. See also
ES Germany, RS Germany, RS Poland, RS Silesia, RS Suhl, and
RS Tillowitz.

RS PRUSSIA, Basket, White Flowers, Gold Trim, Oval, Marked, 7 In.	75.00
Bell, White Ground, Green Bridal Trim, 4 In.	195.00
Berry Set, Pink Roses, Signed, 7 Piece	450.00
Berry Set, Snowballs & Roses, Red Mark, 7 Piece	350.00
Berry Set, Swan, Icicle Mold, 7 Piece	875.00
Bowl, 5 Dome Sections, Roses, Footed, 10 1/2 In.	435.00
Bowl, Blown-Out Carnations, Pink & Yellow Roses, 14 3/4 In.	895.00
Bowl, Blown-Out, 2 Swans, Flowers, Red Mark, 11 In.	500.00
Bowl, Cabbage Mold, Pink Roses Interior, Red Mark, Large	350.00
Bowl, Cabbage Mold, Purple & Green Iridescent Leaves, Roses	350.00
Bowl, Cabbage, 10 In.	400.00
Bowl, Countess Anna Potocka, Allover Gold Flowers, 10 1/2 In.	1295.00
Bowl, Girl Watering Flowers, Pink Roses, Violet Mold, 10 1/2 In.	225.00

Bowl, Grape Mold, 10 1/2 In. 285.00
Bowl, Lily, Green, White & Beige, 11 In. 260.00
Bowl, Maple Leaves, Berries, Red Mark, 10 In. 160.00
Bowl, Masted Ship Scene, Oval, 13 x 19 In. 915.00
Bowl, Mill Scene, Castle Scene, Pair 1775.00
Bowl, Multicolored Asters On Rim, Lilacs Center, 10 In. 145.00
Bowl, Pink & Red Roses, Violet Mold Edge, Red Mark, 10 In. 98.00
Bowl, Pink Flowers, Gold, 10 1/2 In. 55.00
Bowl, Pink Poppies, Floral Design, Cobalt, Brown, 10 In. 855.00
Bowl, Poppies, Red Rim, Marked, 10 In. 195.00
Bowl, Sheepherder Scene, 10 In. 755.00
Bowl, Sunflower, Tiffany Trim, 9 x 3 In. 350.00
Bowl, Wild Roses, Scalloped Edge, Red Mark, 9 1/2 In. 185.00
Bowl, Yellow, Pink Roses, Shaded Ground, 10 In. 150.00
Butter Chip, Dogwood Blossoms, Green Pearlized Luster 35.00
Cake Plate, Basket of Roses, Pearl Luster, 10 1/2 In. 275.00
Cake Plate, Dice Players 1275.00
Cake Plate, Hydrangeas, Shaded Green Ground, 11 In. 75.00
Cake Plate, Lilies of The Valley, Open Handles, 12 In. 250.00
Cake Plate, Man In The Mountain, Medallion Mold, 10 1/2 In. 695.00
Cake Plate, Melon Eaters, 10 In. 375.00
Cake Plate, Melon Eaters, Open Handles, Red Mark, 10 1/2 In. 875.00
Cake Plate, Mill Scene, Browns 650.00
Cake Plate, Swallows, Chickens, Water With Lilies, 10 In. 1010.00
Cake Plate, Swan Scene, Satin Finish, 12 In. 550.00
Cake Plate, Swan Scene, Satin, Mold 301 .... 450.00
Celery, Lily 225.00
Celery, Snowballs & Roses, Gold Border, 12 x 6 In. 135.00
Celery, Snowballs & Roses, Red Mark, 12 x 6 In. 110.00
Celery, Spring Season, Red Mark 2000.00
Celery, Yellow With Roses 175.00
Chocolate Pot, Red Mark, 10 In. 225.00
Chocolate Pot, Snowball & Leaf Design, Red Mark, 10 1/2 In. 325.00
Chocolate Pot, Sunflower Mold 325.00
Chocolate Pot, Swans & Evergreens, Red Mark, 9 1/2 In. 895.00
Chocolate Set, Red Mark, 9 Piece 450.00
Coffeepot, Roses, Serpent Head Spout, Red Mark, 1 1/2 Cup 350.00
Cracker Jar, Beaded Rim & Feet, Wild Roses, Gold Trim, Red Mark .. 285.00
Cracker Jar, Cover, Ornate Floral, Gold Trim, 8-Footed 350.00
Cracker Jar, Dogwood Blossoms, Pearlized Luster, Marked, 8 In. ... 275.00
Cracker Jar, Laurel Chain Mold, Poppies, Daisies, Red Mark, 9 In. ... 295.00
Cracker Jar, Roses, Leaf Mold Top of Curled Feet, Red Mark 275.00
Cracker Jar, Scalloped, Curled Feet, Pink Flowers, Red Mark 275.00
Creamer, Quiet Cove, Boat, Red Mark 135.00
Cup & Saucer, Footed, Demitasse 100.00
Cup & Saucer, Satin Finish Lilacs, Pedestal 125.00
Cup & Saucer, Swans, Pine Trees 195.00
Cup & Saucer, White Lily, Aqua Trim, Tiffany Band 55.00
Fernery, Swans 550.00
Fruit Bowl, Raised Iris, Pierced Handles, Iridescent Luster 440.00
Hatpin Holder, Crowned Crane 575.00
Hatpin Holder, Floral, Gold Trim, Red Mark 145.00
Mustache Cup, Cascade of Roses, Gold Trim, Marked 185.00
Mustache Cup, Florals, Red Mark 195.00
Mustard, Blackberry Design, Spoon, Red Mark 180.00
Mustard, Ladle, Green Ground, White Floral Design 165.00
Pitcher, Cider, Point & Clover Mold, Marked 475.00
Plaque, Mill Scene, Green Ground, 11 1/4 In. 710.00
Plaque, Mill Scene, Tapestry, 8 3/4 In. 650.00
Plate, Colonial, Red Mark, 9 In. 1095.00
Plate, Lily With Maidenhair Fern, 9 In. 195.00
Plate, Madame Recamier, Red Mark, 7 1/2 In. 850.00
Plate, Melon Eaters, Jewel & Ribbon Mold, Keyhole, 6 In. 495.00

Plate, Melon Eaters, Point & Clover Mold, 6 In. 485.00
Plate, Queen Louise, Steeple Mark, 10 In. 925.00
Plate, Rose, 8 In. 65.00
Plate, Scalloped, Embossed Floral Rim, Red Jeweled, 7 1/2 In. 90.00
Plate, Spring Season, 9 In. 1250.00
Plate, Victorian Apple Girl, Red Mark, 9 In. 1785.00
Sugar & Creamer, Floating Lilies, Pedestal, Red Mark 175.00
Sugar & Creamer, Maple Leaves, Berries, Red Mark 160.00
Sugar & Creamer, Mill Scene, Signed 300.00
Sugar & Creamer, Roses 295.00
Sugar & Creamer, Sheepherder, Pedestal, Red Mark 625.00
Sugar Shaker, Portrait of Colonial Couple, Red Mark 350.00
Sugar, Stippled Floral Mold, Cover, Red Mark 75.00
Tankard, Castle Scene, Browns 2300.00
Tankard, Mill Scene 650.00
Tea Set, Cottage Scene, Browns, Red Mark, 3 Piece 1295.00
Tea Set, Spooner, Clusters of Pink Roses, Satin Finish 615.00
Tea Set, Surreal Dogwood, Pedestal, Marked, 3 Piece 350.00
Toothpick, Castle Scene, Double Handle, 2 1/2 In. 295.00
Tray, Dice Players, Jeweled, Red Mark, 11 3/4 x 7 3/4 In. 1980.00
Tray, Dresser, Barnyard Scene, Red Mark 2400.00
Tray, Turkeys, Icicle Mold, Red Mark, 11 1/2 x 7 1/2 In. 595.00
Vase, Dog, Pointer, 12 In. 500.00
Vase, Farmyard Scene, Birds Overhead, 11 1/2 In. 975.00
Vase, Gold Tapestry Ground, Pink Roses, Marked, 9 In. 325.00
Vase, Hummingbirds, Brown, Footed, Red Mark, 6 In. 2200.00
Vase, Man In Mountain, Red Mark, 7 1/2 In. 595.00
Vase, Night Watch Scene, 10 In. 885.00
Vase, Portrait, Pink, 9 In. 375.00
Vase, Sheepherder Scene, Red Mark 800.00
Vase, Winter Lady Medallion, Scalloped, Pearl Luster, 11 In. 1250.00
Vase, Woman Scene, Green Ground, Handle, Lebrun, 10 1/4 In. 495.00
Vase, Woman With Dog, Red Mark 550.00

The *RS Silesia* mark appears on porcelain made at the Reinhold Schlegelmilch factory in Tillowitz, Germany, during the 1930s. The Schlegelmilch family made porcelains marked in many ways. See also ES Germany, RS Germany, RS Poland, RS Prussia, RS Suhl, and RS Tillowitz.

RS SILESIA, Sugar & Creamer, Pink, Yellow Roses 50.00
Vase, Roses, Gold Handles, 9 In. 250.00

RS Suhl was a mark used by the Erdmann Schlegelmilch factory in Suhl, Germany, in the early 1900s. The Schlegelmilch family made porcelains in many places. See also ES Germany, RS Germany, RS Poland, RS Prussia, RS Silesia, and RS Tillowitz.

RS SUHL, Vase, Melon Eaters, 9 In. 815.00
Vase, Napoleon Scene, 5 In. 275.00
Vase, White Floral Spray, Pale Green, Gold Handles, 8 In. 130.00

The *RS Tillowitz* mark was used by the Reinhold Schlegelmilch factory at Tillowitz in the 1930s and 1940s. Table services and ornamental pieces were made. See also ES Germany, RS Germany, RS Poland, RS Prussia, RS Silesia, and RS Suhl.

RS TILLOWITZ, Bowl, White Flowers, Green Ground, 9 1/4 In. 45.00
Charger, Rose Design, 12 In. 55.00
Smoking Set, Cigarette & Match Holder, Pine Cones, 3 Piece 125.00

Rubena Verde is a Victorian glassware that was shaded from red to green. It was first made by Hobbs, Brockunier and Company of Wheeling, West Virginia, about 1890.

RUBENA VERDE, Biscuit Jar, Gold Sprays, Silver Plate, 7 In. 185.00
Bride's Bowl, Ruffled Rim, Multicolored Floral, 12 1/2 In. 365.00

Butter	375.00
Cake Stand, Spirea Band, Blue	95.00
Epergne, Single	375.00
Pitcher, Inverted Thumbprint, Blown, c.1880	450.00
Pitcher, Milk, Hobnail, 5 1/2 In.	95.00
Pitcher, Water, Hobnail	350.00
Punch Cup, Inverted Thumbprint	65.00
Syrup, Hobnail	850.00
Tumbler, Hobnail, 10 Rows, 4 In.	165.00
Vase, Squared Crystal Rim, Spiraling Design, 10 1/4 In.	190.00

Rubena is a glassware that shades from red to clear. It was first made by George Duncan and Sons of Pittsburgh, Pennsylvania, about 1885. This coloring was used on many types of glassware. The pressed glass patterns of Royal Ivy and Royal Oak are listed under Pressed Glass.

RUBENA, Lamp, Hall, Optic Opal, Brass Frame	250.00
Pitcher, Swirl, Opalescent	495.00
Pitcher, Water, Hobnail, Frosted	350.00
Tumbler, Hobnail, Opalescent	49.00
Water Set, Oriental Poppy, Blue, Gold, 7 Piece	565.00

Ruby glass is the dark red color of the precious gemstone known as a ruby. It was a popular Victorian color that never went completely out of style. The glass was shaped by many different processes to make many different types of ruby glass. There was a revival of interest in the 1940s when modern shaped ruby table glassware became fashionable. Sometimes the red color is added to clear glass by a process called flashing or staining. Flashed glass is clear glass dipped in a colored glass, then pressed or cut. Stained glass has color painted on a clear glass. Then it is refired so the stain fuses with the glass. Pieces of glass colored in this way are indicated by the word *stained* in the description.

RUBY GLASS, see also Cranberry Glass; Pressed Glass; Souvenir

RUBY GLASS, Figurine, Elephant, 1927	75.00
Figurine, Piglet, Imperial, 1960s	5.00
Lamp, Pittsburgh Lamp Co., Late 1800s	400.00
Pitcher, Clear Applied Handle, Pontil, 7 In.	40.00
Sugar Shaker, Bulging Loop	250.00
Tumbler & Soap Dish, Brass Stand, 2 Piece	12.50

Rudolstadt was a faience factory in the Thuringia region of Germany from 1720 to about 1791. In 1854, Ernst Bohne began working in the area. From about 1887 to 1918, the New York and Rudolstadt Pottery made decorated porcelain marked with the RW and crown familiar to collectors. This porcelain was imported by Lewis Straus and Sons of New York, which later became Nathan Straus and Sons. The word *Royal* was included in their import mark. Collectors often call it *Royal Rudolstadt*. Late-nineteenth- and early-twentieth-century pieces are most commonly found today.

RUDOLSTADT, see also Kewpie

RUDOLSTADT, Bonbon, 2 Handles	20.00
Cake Plate, Roses, Open Handles, 10 1/2 In.	70.00
Dish, Baby, Happy Face	100.00
Figurine, Young Man Holding Bouquet of Flowers, 9 In.	65.00
Group, Girl & Boy, Sitting On Bench, Cream, Beige & Gold	195.00
Group, Woman Sitting On Bench, Holding Jug, Signed, 8 1/2 In.	175.00
Pitcher, 4 Kewpies, Rose O'Neill	280.00
Plate, Roses, 8 1/4 In.	38.00
Relish, Figural, Grape	40.00
Sugar, Figural, Rose	45.00
Syrup & Underplate, Floral Design	75.00
Vase, Branch Handles, Flowers, Gold Trim, Marked, 11 1/2 In.	145.00

◆◆◆◆◆◆◆◆◆◆◆◆◆◆◆◆◆◆◆◆◆◆

The material used to make repairs is warmer to the touch than
the porcelain. Feel the surface of
a figurine to see if there are unseen repairs.

◆◆◆◆◆◆◆◆◆◆◆◆◆◆◆◆◆◆◆◆◆◆

Rudolstadt, Vase, Portrait, Dragon Handles,
Matte Yellow, 12 In.

Vase, Floral Panels, Seminude Maiden Handles, 14 In. 550.00
Vase, Portrait, Dragon Handles, Matte Yellow, 12 In. ....*Illus* 330.00
Wall Pocket, Birds Back To Back, Blue Enameled, 1900, 9 3/4 In. 230.00

Rugs have been used in the American home since the seventeenth
century. The Oriental rug of that time was often used on a table,
not on the floor. Rag rugs, hooked rugs, and braided rugs were
made by housewives from scraps of material.

RUG, Afghan Beluchistan, Animals, Flat & Pile Design, 2 Ft. x 5 Ft. 8 In. 250.00
Afshar, Joined Hooked Diamonds, Rust Field, 4 Ft. 9 In. x 3ft. 3 In. 1100.00
Agra, Overall Floral & Stylized Design, White Field, 9 x 12 Ft. 495.00
Anatolian, 2 Ft. 10 In. x 4 Ft. 3 In. 100.00
Anatolian, 2 Ft. 9 In. x 4 Ft. 3 In. 95.00
Anatolian, Central Medallion, 3 Ft. 8 In. x 5 Ft. 11 In. 175.00
Anatolian, Mercerized Cotton, 1920s, 5 Ft. 8 In. x 4 Ft. 2 In. 440.00
Anatolian, Yastik, Hooked Diamond, Rust, 2 Ft. 10 In. x L Ft. 8 In. 220.00
Ardebil, 8 Ft. 6 In. x 12 Ft. 5 In. 1540.00
Aubusson, Central Floral Bouquet, c.1880, 13 Ft. 8 In. x 10 Ft. 10 In. 9900.00
Aubusson, Flowering Branches, Birds, c.1875, 11 Ft. 9 In. x 7 Ft. 8 In. 9900.00
Aushak, Floral Tracery, Angora, c.1900, 15 Ft. 3 In. x 13 Ft. 3 In. 8800.00
Bahktiari, Center Medallion, Red Ground, 5 Ft. 3 In. x 8 Ft. 8 In. 335.00
Bahktiari, Ivory Medallion, Brown Field, 10 Ft. x 5 Ft. 2 In. 385.00
Baluch, Columns of Ashik Forms, 4 Ft. 4 In. x 2 Ft. 11 In. 660.00
Baluch, Flatweave Sofreh, Zigzag Border, Brown, 7 Ft. x 2 Ft. 4 In. 330.00
Baluch, Prayer, Tree of Life, Camel Field, 5 Ft. 5 In. x 3 Ft. 2 In. 440.00
Baluchistan, 3 Ft. 3 In. x 5 Ft. 6 In. 125.00
Beluchistan, Sofreh, Serrated Medallions, 4 Ft. 5 In. x 4 Ft. 2 In. 1045.00
Bergama, 4 Ft. 7 In. x 6 Ft. 3 In. 385.00
Bergama, Stepped Hexagonal Medallion, 4 Ft. 2 In. x 3 Ft. 4 In. 995.00
Beshir, Rows of 7 Geometric Medallions, 10 x 8 Ft. 250.00
Beshir, Stripes At Top & Bottom, 15 Ft. 6 In. x 7 Ft. 10 In. 7700.00
Bibikabad, Central Floral Medallion, 8 Ft. 10 In. x 11 Ft. 7 In. 275.00
Bidjar, Allover Floral & Foliate, 17 Ft. 9 In. x 11 Ft. 1 In. 8800.00
Bidjar, Central Hexagonal Medallion, Floral Border, 9 x 13 Ft. 440.00
Bidjar, Herati Pattern, Floral & Leaf Border, 9 Ft. 2 In. x 4 Ft. 6 In. 2640.00
Bidjar, Ivory Herati–Filled Medallions, 7 Ft. 7 In. x 5 Ft. 1 In. 1650.00
Bidjar, Overall Lobed Diamonds, c.1900, 11 Ft. 6 In. x 11 Ft. 5 In. 4125.00
Bidjar, Pendant Medallion, Herati Field, 8 Ft. 10 In. x 5 Ft. 4 In. 5500.00
Bidjar, Quarter Pendant Medallions, 6 Ft. 1 In. x 4 Ft. 2200.00
Bokhara, 3 Ft. 2 In. x 3 Ft. 9 In. 700.00
Bokhara, 4 Ft. 6 In. x 6 Ft. 2 In. 500.00
Bokhara, 4 Ft. 7 In. x 5 Ft. 10 In. 300.00
Bokhara, Pakistan, 2 Ft. 9 In. x 6 Ft. 8 In. 475.00
Bokhara, Princess, 3 Ft. 8 In. x 4 Ft. 1 In. 250.00
Bokhara, Symmetrical Medallions, Diamond Border, 5 x 8 Ft. 275.00
Cabistan, 3 Ft. 9 In. x 5 Ft. 6 In. 1350.00
Carabash, Rows of Boteh, Slant Leaf Border, 8 Ft. 6 In. x 3 Ft. 6 In. 1650.00

Caucasian, Medallions, Rust, Geometric Motifs, 6 Ft. 5 In. x 4 Ft. 3 In. 715.00
Causasian, Central Stepped Medallions, 6 Ft. 5 In. x 4 Ft. 3 In. 715.00
Chinese, 2 Concentric Circles, Peony Blossoms, 11 Ft. 6 In. x 9 Ft. 755.00
Chinese, Art Deco, 10 x 17 Ft. 3000.00
Chinese, Birds, Vines, Cream, 7 Ft. 10 In. x 4 Ft. 1 In. ....*Illus* 1300.00
Chinese, Blue Dragons, 8 Ft. x 11 Ft. 7 In. 7250.00
Chinese, Central Ying-Yang Roundel, c.1840, 4 Ft. 3 In. x 2 Ft. 2 In. 2200.00
Chinese, Clouds, Vases Flanked By Peacocks, 9 Ft. 8 In. x 8 Ft. 990.00
Chinese, Dragon & Bat Center Medallion, Peking, 11 Ft. 6 In. x 8 Ft. 1320.00
Chinese, Dragon, Coiled To Form Medallion, 8 Ft. 6 In. x 5 Ft. 10 In. 1540.00
Chinese, Flowering Branches, 1920s, 11 Ft. 4 In. x 8 Ft. 10 In. 4510.00
Chinese, Ivory, Geometric Border, Navy, 8 x 9 Ft. 500.00
Chinese, Junk Floating Among Flowering Shrubs, 14 x 11 Ft. 1650.00
Chinese, Maze-Work, Grimacing Bats, Cream, 5 Ft. 9 In. x 6 Ft. 2 In. 2750.00
Chinese, Peony-Formed Roundel Reserves, c.1900, 5 Ft. 8 In. x 2 Ft. 1100.00
Continental, Geometric Devices, Wool, 1935, 8 Ft. 11 In. x 12 Ft. 2200.00
Darjazine, 3 Ft. 6 In. x 5 Ft. 6 In. 1150.00
Dhurrie, Concentric Stepped Polygons, 10 Ft. 3 In. x 21 Ft. 8 In. 330.00
Dorosch, Rows of Floral Boteh, c.1900, 8 Ft. 5 In. x 4 Ft. 11 In. 4950.00
Doumac, Dragon Design, 10 Ft. x 8 Ft. 2 In. 4675.00
Drugget, Allover Triangles, Trapezoid, 10 Ft. 4 In. x 7 Ft. 8 In. 412.00
Drugget, Large Green Squares, Camel, Arts & Crafts, 10 x 11 1/2 Ft. 1210.00
Embroidered, Crewel, Floral, Beige Ground, Wool, 45 x 65 In. 130.00
Ersari, 3 Columns Gulli-Guls, Diamond, Border, 11 Ft. 8 In. x 8 Ft. 2 In. 880.00
Ersari, 3 Rows Ersari Guls, c.1880, 9 Ft. x 7 Ft. 6 In. 7420.00
Felt Diamonds, Leaf Shapes, Woven Gold Ground, 22 x 37 In. 200.00
Fereghan, 4 Ft. 2 In. x 6 Ft. 3 In. 1665.00
Fereghan, Floral Lattice Overall, c.1885, 6 Ft. 8 In. x 4 Ft. 1 In. 8250.00
French, Art Deco, Ivan Da Silva Bruhns Design, c.1935, 8 x 12 Ft. 1980.00
Gorovan, 8 Ft. 12 In. x 12 Ft. 1 In. 4900.00
Grenfell, Hooked, 2 Eskimos On Sled, Pulled By Dogs, 2 x 3 Ft. ....*Illus* 440.00
Hamadan, 2 Ft. 1 In. x 2 Ft. 9 In. 85.00
Handwoven, Art Deco, Grid, Polygons, Floral, 4 Ft. 2 In. x 8 Ft. 9 In. 192.00
Hereke, Mughal Design, 9 Ft. 4 In. x 6 Ft. 9 In. 4500.00
Hereke, Silk, Floral Blue Border, 2 Ft. 6 In. x 4 Ft. 6 In. ....*Illus* 2100.00
Hereke, Vine & Floral, Geometric Border, 9 Ft. 6 In. x 6 Ft. 6 In. 550.00
Heriz, 8 Lobed Medallion, Flowerhead Border, 11 Ft. 9 In. x 8 Ft. 11 In. 4500.00
Heriz, Geometric Floral Design, c.1920, 10 Ft. 3 In. x 7 Ft. 1 In. 1320.00
Heriz, Open Brick Field, c.1900, 5 Ft. 10 In. x 4 Ft. 9 In. 3575.00
Heriz, Overall Herati Design, 13 Ft. 2 In. x 9 Ft. 6 In. 4500.00
Heriz, Overall Herati Design, Hexagon Border, 4 Ft. 6 In. x 2 Ft. 8 In. 610.00

Rug, Chinese, Birds, Vines, Cream,
7 Ft. 10 In. x 4 Ft. 1 In.

Rug, Grenfell, Hooked, 2 Eskimos On Sled,
Pulled By Dogs, 2 x 3 Ft.

Rug, Hereke, Silk,
Floral Blue Border,
2 Ft. 6 In. x 4 Ft. 6 In.

Rug, Kazak,
Turtleback Medallion,
Green, Red, Blue, 4 x 7 Ft.

Rug, Turkish,
Prayer, Silk, c.1850,
4 Ft. 9 In. x 7 Ft.

Heriz, Overall Palmettes, Rosettes, Navy Border, 12 Ft. 2 In. x 9 Ft. 4950.00
Homud Asmalyk, Vine Filled Reserves, 4 Ft. x 2 Ft. 5 In. 1650.00
Hooked, 2 Chickens On Field of Tulips, American, 26 1/2 x 55 In. 610.00
Hooked, 2 Ducks On Pond, Flanked By Tulips & Trees, 22 x 51 1/2 In. 412.50
Hooked, 2 Stylized Chickens, Gray Ground, 23 x 40 In. 150.00
Hooked, 2 Swans, Scalloped Border, Yarn, 20 x 32 In. 35.00
Hooked, 6 Egg Shapes, Striations of Green & Brown, 58 x 50 1/2 In. 170.00
Hooked, Acorns, Beige Ground, Floral Border, 1888, 26 1/2 x 36 In. 100.00
Hooked, Airedale, Multicolored Ground, 24 x 37 In. 110.00
Hooked, American Eagle, 34 x 45 1/2 In. 65.00
Hooked, American Pictorial, Flowering Tree, c.1930, 27 1/2 x 61 In. 2420.00
Hooked, American Ship At Sea, Blue, Rope Border, 37 x 58 In. 495.00
Hooked, Animal, Striped Gray Ground, Floral Border, 20 1/2 x 35 In. 115.00
Hooked, Aquatic Forms, Mauve, Ecru, Beige Field, 1950, 97 x 58 In. 385.00
Hooked, Beaver On Branch, Half Circle, Off–White Ground, 17 x 37 In. 395.00
Hooked, Black Dog, Sawtooth Border, Cream & Tan Ground, 30 In. 1500.00
Hooked, Checkerboard, Herringbone Border, Multicolored, 36 x 55 1/2 In. 302.50
Hooked, Circle Design, Flowers & Geometrics, 33 x 34 In. 75.00
Hooked, Cow Jumped Over The Moon, c.1930, 30 x 44 In. 1100.00
Hooked, Deer, Colorful Border, Edward Sand Frost, 28 1/2 x 52 In. 200.00
Hooked, Dog On Rug, Edward Frost, 23 x 44 1/2 In. 400.00
Hooked, Eagle With Olive Branch, E Pluribus Unum, 42 1/2 x 32 In. 150.00
Hooked, Eagle, Olive Branch, Arrows, Tan, Brown, White Ground, 46 x 35 In. 350.00
Hooked, Floral Center, Foliage Border, Cotton & Wool, 142 x 110 In. 3850.00
Hooked, Floral Design, Gray Ground, Black Border, 28 x 38 In. 85.00
Hooked, Floral Design, Leaf Border, Beige Ground, 50 x 84 In. 850.00
Hooked, Floral Design, Maroon Ground, 26 x 37 In. 25.00
Hooked, Floral, Cattails On Oval, Brown Border, 24 x 35 In. 85.00
Hooked, Floral, Colors, Centennial, 1776–1876, 37 x 57 In. 375.00
Hooked, Floral, Stylized Leaf Border, Gray Ground, 26 x 48 1/2 In. 115.00
Hooked, Flowers, Hand & Flag, Leaf Scroll Border, 36 x 88 In. 700.00

Hooked, Flowers, Made By Ann Hand, Chester, N. J., 1943, 30 x 52 In.	45.00
Hooked, Frog & Waterlily, 23 1/2 x 37 In.	85.00
Hooked, Geometric Design, Red & White, 18 x 70 In.	550.00
Hooked, Grenfell, Ship, Bright Colors, Mat	358.00
Hooked, Horse & Buggy, Corner Bouquets, 24 x 46 In.	245.00
Hooked, Leaves, Butterflies, Blues & Grays, 32 x 53 In.	150.00
Hooked, Multicolored Basket of Fruit, Foliage Border, 32 x 57 In.	170.00
Hooked, Multicolored Stripe Design, 29 x 57 In.	725.00
Hooked, Old Woman In The Shoe, Martha Louise, c.1930, 53 x 36 In.	1500.00
Hooked, Overall Bird, Floral & Geometrics, Portugal, 12 x 15 Ft.	412.50
Hooked, Peaceable Kingdom, 24 x 36 1/2 In.	200.00
Hooked, Rag & Yarn, Floral Design, Beige Ground, 35 x 56 In.	200.00
Hooked, Rag, Stylized Ivy, Bright Colors, 32 x 62 In.	50.00
Hooked, Raised Center, Waldoboro, Maine, 22 x 38 1/2 In.	245.00
Hooked, Reindeer Pulling Rescue Sled, 2 Figures, 27 1/2 x 38 1/2 In.	450.00
Hooked, Rose Design, 4 Rows of 9 Squares, 1880s, 4 Ft. 6 In. x 9 Ft.	88.00
Hooked, Runner, Floral Sprigs & Cherry Branches, Scrolls, 143 x 26 In.	935.00
Hooked, Running Horse In Shades of Red, Stylized Plants, 31 x 53 In.	1600.00
Hooked, Sailboat, Grenfell Labrador Industries, 10 1/2 x 14 In.	200.00
Hooked, Semicircular, Welcome, Black Border, 29 1/2 x 42 1/2 In.	400.00
Hooked, Sheared, Stagecoach & 4 Horses, 26 1/2 x 51 In.	125.00
Hooked, Spray of Flowers Reserve, Floral Vine Around, 39 1/2 x 64 In.	357.00
Hooked, Stag With Oak Leaf, Acorn Border, 33 1/2 x 59 In.	200.00
Hooked, Star Center, Stylized Flowers & Diamond Border, 21 x 34 In.	85.00
Hooked, Star, Teal Blue Ground, Border Stripes, 35 1/2 x 48 In.	375.00
Hooked, Stylized Floral Design, Beige Ground, 34 x 54 In.	250.00
Hooked, Stylized Floral Medallions, Abstract Leaf Design, 29 x 64 In.	85.00
Hooked, Stylized Floral, 22 x 22 1/2 In.	225.00
Hooked, Stylized Floral, Oval, 22 1/2 x 37 In.	105.00
Hooked, Tan Ground, Light Red, Orange & Green, 38 1/2 x 79 In.	290.00
Hooked, Trellis, Blossoms, Peach Field, Border, 13 Ft. 1 In. x 7 Ft. 1 In.	6600.00
Hooked, Tulip, Gray Medallion, Blue Ground, 23 x 35 In.	125.00
Hooked, Whimsical Horse, Autumnal Colors, 40 1/2 x 33 1/2 In.	1500.00
Hooked, Winter Scene, House & Barn, Walnut Frame, 22 x 36 In.	195.00
Hooked, Yarn, Floral Design, Soft Colors, 26 x 56 In.	50.00
Hooked, Yarn, White Cat, Blue & Pink Cushion, Brown Ground, 18 x 33 In.	55.00
Indo–Chinese, Floral Roundel, c.1900, 18 Ft. 1 In. x 11 Ft. 11 In.	5225.00
Indo–Chinese, Throw, Gold, Floral, Scrolling, Pink, Green, Blue, 2 x 4 Ft.	90.00
Iranian, Floral Design, 2 Ft. 10 In. x 11 Ft.	350.00
Isparta, 8 Ft. x 9 Ft. 8 In.	880.00
Isphahan, Arabesque Lobed Medallion, 1920s, 5 Ft. 3 In. x 3 Ft. 5 In.	2310.00
Isphahan, Floral Trellis Medallion, 7 Ft. 2 In. x 4 Ft. 10 In.	3850.00
Isphahan, Multicolored Silk Warps, 7 Ft. 1 In. x 4 Ft. 10 In.	8250.00
Isphahan, Split–Leaf Arabesque Field, 1920, 5 Ft. 3 In. x 3 Ft. 6 In.	2420.00
Isphahan, Tree of Life, 13 Ft. 10 In. x 9 Ft. 8 In.	4400.00
Joshaqan, Central Stepped Diamond Medallion, 25 Ft. 8 In. x 14 Ft.	3850.00
Joshaqan, Step–Diamond Medallions, c.1900, 5 Ft. 2 In. x 3 Ft. 7 In.	2750.00
Karabagh, 3 x 5 Ft.	775.00
Karabagh, 5 Ft. 2 In. x 8 Ft. 2 In.	3520.00
Karachopf Kazak, Ram's Horns, Flowerheads, 6 Ft. 3 In. x 5 Ft. 6 In.	1430.00
Karagashli, Afshan Medallions, 5 Ft. 6 In. x 3 Ft. 7 In.	4675.00
Karagashli, Serrated Diamond Medallions, 6 Ft. 5 In. x 3 Ft. 3 In.	3740.00
Karagashli, Serrated Palmette Medallions, 3 Ft. 11 In. x 2 Ft. 7 In.	3850.00
Kashan, 4 Ft. 4 In. x 6 Ft. 9 In.	3000.00

◆◆◆

Tea stains on rugs can be removed with soda water, red wine stains with white wine, grease with a solvent. Gum should be hardened with an ice cube, then scraped off.

◆◆◆

Kashan, 4 Ft. 5 In. x 6 Ft. 11 In., Pair 6050.00
Kashan, Flowering Shrubs, c.1900, 19 Ft. 2 In. x 8 Ft. 1 In. 3300.00
Kashan, Geometric & Foliate Design Overall, 10 Ft. 6 In. x 13 Ft. 4 In. 9350.00
Kashan, Medallion Inset, Vase of Blossoms, 6 Ft. 8 In. x 4 Ft. 5 In. 2200.00
Kashan, Silk, 1930, 4 Ft. 2 In. x 6 Ft. 8 In. 5500.00
Kashan, Silk, 3 Ft. 4 In. x 5 Ft. 5700.00
Kasvin, Scalloped, Medallions, Vine Border, 12 Ft. 2 In. x 8 Ft. 10 In. 6050.00
Kazak, Checkerboard Arches, 7 Ft. 11 In. x 5 Ft. 8800.00
Kazak, Cloudband–Filled Medallions, c.1885, 7 Ft. 8 In. x 3 Ft. 7 In. 2200.00
Kazak, Floral Design, Ivory & Red, c.1880, 4 Ft. 4 In. x 3 Ft. 7 In. 1540.00
Kazak, Hexagonal Medallions, 6 Ft. 7 In. x 3 Ft. 6 In. 5500.00
Kazak, Staggered Shield Rows, Brick Red Field, 11 Ft. x 3 Ft. 5 In. 1430.00
Kazak, Turtleback Medallion, Green, Red, Blue, 4 x 7 Ft. ....*Illus* 3300.00
Kazak, Zigzag Cartouche, 2 Central Medallions, 10 Ft. x 5 Ft. 7 In. 550.00
Khamseh, 6 Ft. 2 In. x 6 Ft. 4125.00
Khilim, Geometric Designs, 5 Ft. 1 In. x 7 Ft. 1 In. 305.00
Khilim, Latched Diamonds Overall, c.1880, 9 Ft. 8 In. x 5 Ft. 1100.00
Khorossan, Anchored Medallion, Cream Field, 13 Ft. 1 In. x 10 Ft. 8 In. 9900.00
Kirman, 10 Ft. 1 In. x 20 Ft. 3 In. 5600.00
Kirman, 17 Ft. x 15 Ft. 11 In. 6000.00
Kirman, 1940, 10 Ft. 9 In. x 15 Ft. 4 In. 8000.00
Kirman, 8 Ft. 6 In. x 12 Ft. 1900.00
Kirman, Circular Floral Medallion, 12 Ft. 6 In. x 8 Ft. 8 In. 1430.00
Kirman, Floral Design, Cranberry Field, 13 Ft. 6 In. x 9 Ft. 11 In. 8800.00
Kirman, Geometric & Foliate Design, Cranberry, 9 Ft. 8 In. x 12 Ft. 3850.00
Kirman, Gold, Geometric, Floral Foliage, Blue, Rose, Ivory, 9 x 14 Ft. 5500.00
Kirman, Ivory Ground, 3 Ft. 11 In. x 5 Ft. 10 In. 525.00
Kirman, Ivory, Multicolored Geometric, Floral, Blue, Green, 3 x 5 Ft. 300.00
Kirman, Overall Palmettes, Floral Sprays, 11 Ft. 8 In. x 9 Ft. 2970.00
Kirman, Wine Red Ground, Some Bleeding, 12 x 16 Ft. 1200.00
Konya, Cruciform Medallions, c.1875, 11 Ft. 10 In. x 3 Ft. 9 In. 1210.00
Kuba, Flowering Shrub Rows, Gold Field, 3 Ft. 10 In. x 2 Ft. 11 In. 935.00
Kuba, Geometric Designs, c.1900, 8 Ft. 6 In. x 4 Ft. 2860.00
Kuba, Rows of Blossoms, Blue Border, c.1885, 5 Ft. 3 In. x 2 Ft. 10 In. 2860.00
Kuba, Serrated Medallions Overall, 8 Ft. 5 In. x 5 Ft. 4 In. 2200.00
Kula, Turkish, 2 Ft. 10 In. x 11 Ft. 3 In. 425.00
Kurdish, 2 Ft. 9 In. x 4 Ft. 100.00
Kurdish, Abrashed Blue Field, Hooked Hexagons, 6 Ft. 8 In. x 4 Ft. 4 In. 1100.00
Kurdish, Tribal, Late 19th Century, 3 x 4 Ft. 775.00
Lava Kirman, Center Floral Medallion, 12 Ft. 8 In. x 10 Ft. 5 In. 660.00
Lillihan, 3 Ft. 4 In. x 4 Ft. 8 In. 225.00
Lillihan, 4 Floral Medallions, Blossoming Shrubs, 6 Ft. 6 In. x 5 Ft. 990.00
Mahal, 10 Ft. 10 In. x 14 Ft. 11 In. 3900.00
Mahal, 10 Ft. 3 In. x 15 Ft. 4 In. 1325.00
Mahal, 12 x 15 Ft. 9600.00
Mahal, 4 Ft. x 6 Ft. 7 In. 275.00
Mahal, Central Floral Medallion, 9 Ft. 10 In. x 5 Ft. 5500.00
Mahal, Overall Animals, Vines & Palmettes, 11 Ft. 6 In. x 8 Ft. 7 In. 3300.00
Mahal, Overall Floral Vines, 11 Ft. 10 In. x 10 Ft. 5 In. 7700.00
Mahal, Overall Palmettes, Vines, 11 Ft. 6 In. x 8 Ft. 8 In. 1100.00
Mahal, Palmettes & Floral Vinery, c.1880, 13 Ft. 9 In. x 10 Ft. 4675.00
Mahal, Polychrome Herati, c.1900, 12 Ft. 2 In. x 7 Ft. 10 In. 4400.00
Mahal, Polychrome Palmettes, Vines, 11 Ft. 7 In. x 9 Ft. 6600.00
Nain, Floral–Filled Field, Silk Warp, c.1920, 7 Ft. 6 In. x 5 Ft. 2200.00
Nain, Overall Vine & Floral, Silk & Wool, 8 Ft. 8 In. x 5 Ft. 5 In. 2420.00
Navajo, Allover Diamond, Lightning, Hunting Scene, Red, Brown, 6 x 8 Ft. 3850.00
Needlepoint, Continental, c.1900, 9 Ft. 11 In. x 7 Ft. 5 In. 8800.00
Needlepoint, Floral Spray–Filled Squares, 14 Ft. x 7 Ft. 10 In. 990.00
Needlepoint, French, Trefoil Design, c.1900, 9 Ft. 1 In. x 7 Ft. 1 In. 3300.00
Needlepoint, Ivy & Acanthus Leaves, c.1900, 13 Ft. 9 In. x 13 Ft. 9 In. 7700.00
Needlepoint, Mandarin Scrolled Cartouche, French, 10 Ft. 5 In. x 6 Ft. 4950.00
Needlepoint, Overall Floral, Portuguese, 20 Ft. 1 In. x 10 Ft. 9 In. 4290.00
Oriental, Floral Geometric, Camel, Blue Border, 3 Ft. 3 In. x 5 Ft. 9 In. 275.00

Oriental, Map, Turkish Territory, 1967, 3 Ft. 10 In. x 6 Ft. 9 In. 5500.00
Oushak, Medallions, Floral Tracery, 18th Century, 15 Ft. 6 In. x 10 Ft. 4125.00
Persian, Central Vine, Guard Borders, 3 Ft. 1 In. x 7 Ft. 3 In. 440.00
Persian, Deep Wine–Red Ground, 5 Ft. 1 In. x 6 Ft. 3 In. 575.00
Persian, Diamond Medallion, Boteh Field, 4 Ft. 8 In. x 8 Ft. 8 In. 4675.00
Qashqa'I, Blue Stepped Cartouche, 3 Medallions, 6 Ft. 8 In. x 5 Ft. 550.00
Qashquai, Pole Medallions, Rosettes, Dark Blue, 9 Ft. 7 In. x 5 Ft. 2 In. 330.00
Qashquai, Star Rosettes, Dark Blue, Border, 9 Ft. 2 In. x 5 Ft. 1100.00
Rag, 4 Red Strips, Shades of Brown, Penn., 12 Ft. 4 In. x 15 Ft. 6 In. 980.00
Rag, Runner, Cotton, Gray, Tan, Black, Red, Amana Colonies, 14 x 33 In. 125.00
Rag, Runner, Striped Pattern, Red, Blue, Olive, Yellow, Brown, 75 x 220 In. 275.00
Sarouk, Brick Lobed Medallion, c.1900, 11 Ft. 10 In. x 8 Ft. 7 In. 8800.00
Sarouk, Circular Medallions, Floral Sprays, 5 Ft. 2 In. x 3 Ft. 6 In. 1000.00
Sarouk, Floral Medallion, Floral Border, 11 Ft. 4 In. x 9 Ft. 1 In. 5500.00
Sarouk, Floral Pattern, Double Floral Border, 11 Ft. 6 In. x 8 Ft. 6 In. 1100.00
Sarouk, Floral Sprays, Palmette Meander Border, 5 Ft. x 3 Ft. 6 In. 825.00
Sarouk, Overall Floral & Vine, 4 Ft. 9 In. x 3 Ft. 5 In. 330.00
Sarouk, Palmette & Floral Spray Field, 16 Ft. 7 In. x 11 Ft. 4000.00
Sarouk, Palmette & Trellising Vine Field, 11 Ft. 9 In. x 8 Ft. 9 In. 4000.00
Sarouk, Raspberry Field, Detached Floral Sprays, 77 x 50 In. 1430.00
Sarouk, Throw, 2 Ft. 5 In. x 4 Ft. 375.00
Senneh, Boteh Design, c.1870, 4 Ft. 1 1/2 In. x 6 Ft. 2 In. 9350.00
Senneh, Concentric Medallions, Herati Design, 4 Ft. 10 In. x 3 Ft. 8 In. 995.00
Senneh, Herati Design, Red Turtle Main Border, 6 Ft. 2 In. x 4 Ft. 4 In. 1435.00
Senneh, Multicolored Warps, 8 Ft. 2 In. x 4 Ft. 11 In. 9900.00
Serab, 3 Hexagonal Medallions, 6 Ft. 6 In. x 3 Ft. 445.00
Serab, Center Diamond Medallions, c.1890, 3 Ft. 6in. x 15 Ft. 8 In. 1045.00
Serebend, 3 Ft. 6 In. x 6 Ft. 725.00
Serebend, 4 Ft. 4 In. x 5 Ft. 10 In. 325.00
Serebend, Iranian, 6 Ft. 10 In. x 8 Ft. 10 In. 900.00
Sevas, Strap–Work Medallion, c.1925, 12 Ft. 10 In. x 10 Ft. 10 In. 7705.00
Seychour, Cabbage Roses Overall, c.1875, 5 Ft. 6 In. x 3 Ft. 10 In. 2860.00
Shiraz, 4 Ft. x 5 Ft. 2 In. 1825.00
Shiraz, 5 Ft. x 6 Ft. 9 In. 850.00
Shirvan, 3 Blue Medallions On Madder Field, 6 Ft. 7 In. x 3 Ft. 11 In. 2860.00
Shirvan, 3 Lesghi Stars, Geometric Border, 4 Ft. 8 In. x 3 Ft. 6 In. 1430.00
Shirvan, 3 Sections With Lesghi Stars, 5 Ft. 6 In. x 3 Ft. 8 In. 1765.00
Shirvan, Blue, Red & Beige, 59 x 42 In. 3300.00
Shirvan, Geometric & Foliate Design, Maroon, 3 Ft. 7 In. x 7 Ft. 2 In. 1650.00
Shirvan, Geometric Medallions, 6 Ft. 10 In. x 3 Ft. 10 In. 1985.00
Shirvan, Human Flanked By Lions, 5 Ft. 4 In. x 4 Ft. 5 In. 6325.00
Soumac, Stylized Dragon Design, c.1875, 10 Ft. 10 In. x 7 Ft. 3080.00
South Caucasian, Hooked Medallions, Blue Field, 9 Ft. 9 In. x 3 Ft. 715.00
Spanish, Art Deco, Stylized Flowerheads, 17 Ft. 7 In. x 16 Ft. 7 In. 7700.00
Sparta, Floral & Foliate Design, Burgundy, 9 Ft. 9 In. x 13 Ft. 9 In. 880.00
Sultanabad, Herati–Filled Field, 11 Ft. 6 In. x 12 Ft. 9 In. 8525.00
Tabriz, Center Medallion, Floral Vine Border, 8 Ft. 4 In. x 11 Ft. 5 In. 385.00
Tabriz, Finely Woven, 2 Ft. 7 In. x 3 Ft. 7 In. 1225.00
Tabriz, Gold & Blue Medallion, Vines, 9 Ft. 8 In. x 6 Ft. 10 In. 1100.00
Tabriz, Hunting Pattern, 3 Ft. 7 In. x 5 Ft. 10 In. 1300.00
Tabriz, Lobed Medallions, Silk, c.1900, 6 Ft. 5 In. x 4 Ft. 5 In. 9350.00
Tan & White Hounds Scene, Black Ground, 1900, 38 x 25 In. 295.00
Teheran, Floral Medallion, Floral Field, 1900, 7 Ft. 2 In. x 4 Ft. 7 In. 1870.00
Tekke, 8 Columns Guls, Dark Rust Field, Border, 4 Ft. 4 In. x 3 Ft. 5 In. 220.00
Tekke, Geometric & Floral Design, Maroon, 3 Ft. 6 In. x 4 Ft. 6 In. 580.00
Tekke, Vertical Rows of Guls, c.1875, 9 Ft. 4 In. x 6 Ft. 7 In. 2750.00
Turkish, Prayer, Silk, c.1850, 4 Ft. 9 In. x 7 Ft. ....*Illus* 600.00
Turkoman, Handmade, Red, Deep Blue Ground, 4 Ft. x 6 Ft. 2 In. 325.00
White Primitive Ducks, Gray Sky, Aqua Water, 1920–30, 24 x 36 In. 275.00
Wool, Art Deco, Geometric & Curvilinear, Mid–20th Century, 9 x 12 Ft. 1210.00
Yomud, Ensi, Guls, Stepped Rosette Borders, Brown, 5 Ft. 11 In. x 4 Ft. 522.00
Yomud, Stylized Floral & Animal Design, 56 Ft. 10 In. 2860.00
Yuruk, Hooked & Rosettes, Linked Octagon Border, 6 Ft. 6 In. x 4 Ft. 220.00

Yuruk, Shaped Oval Design, Stylized Border, 4 Ft. x 6 Ft. 6 In. 275.00

Rumrill Pottery was designed by George Rumrill of Little Rock, Arkansas. From 1930 to 1933, it was produced by the Red Wing Pottery of Red Wing, Minnesota. In 1938, production was transferred to the Shawnee Pottery in Zanesville, Ohio. Production ceased in the 1940s.

RUMRILL, Candleholder, Nude Seated On Turtle, With Cornucopia, 10 1/2 In. 135.00
Rocket Ship, Brown, Cream Interior, 8 In. 50.00
Vase, Art Deco, Handles Form Circle, 7 In. 35.00
Vase, Blue, 10 1/2 In. 25.00
Vase, Double Cornucopia, Aqua 25.00
Vase, Embossed, Green, 6 In. 16.00
Vase, Fan Shape, Graduated Ball Handles, 9 x 10 In. 25.00
Vase, Handles, Blue, 11 In. 35.00
Vase, Shaded Green, Handle, 7 In. 20.00

Ruskin is a British art pottery of the twentieth century. The Ruskin Pottery was started by William Howson Taylor; his name was used as the mark until about 1899. The factory, at West Smethwick, Birmingham, England, stopped making new pieces in 1933 but continued to glaze and sell the remaining wares until 1935. The art pottery is noted for the exceptional glazes.

RUSKIN, Bowl, Deep Red, Gray Speckled Interior, 1933, 9 1/2 In. Diam. 1710.00
Bowl, Mottled Pink, 8 In. 120.00
Dish, Mottled Purple, Green, Deep Red, c.1920, 9 1/2 In. Diam. 1390.00
Vase, Cylindrical, Everted Foot, Red, Purple, Gray, 1926, 12 1/4 In. 2560.00
Vase, Cylindrical, Flared Foot, Everted Rim, Red, 1926, 14 1/2 In. 2560.00
Vase, Cylindrical, Flared Foot, Red, Purple, Green, 1920, 14 3/4 In. 3840.00

Russel Wright designed dinnerwares in modern shapes for many companies. Iroquois China Company, Harker China Company, Steubenville Pottery, and Justin Tharaud and Sons made dishes marked *Russel Wright.* The Steubenville wares, first made in 1938, are the most common today. This section lists the dinnerwares and other pieces by Wright. He was a designer of domestic and industrial wares, including furniture, aluminum, radios, interiors, and glassware. For more information, see *Kovels' Depression Glass & American Dinnerware Price List.*

RUSSEL WRIGHT, Bowl, American Modern, Seafoam, 6 1/4 In. 3.50
Bowl, Iroquois, Avocado, 5 In. 4.00
Bowl, Iroquois, Avocado, 8 In. 10.00
Bowl, Iroquois, Ice Blue, 8 In. 15.00
Bowl, Iroquois, Pink, Redesigned, 5 1/2 In. 3.00
Bowl, Salad, Iroquois, Blue 16.00
Bowl, Vegetable, American Modern, Coral 10.00
Bowl, Vegetable, Cover, American Modern, Chartreuse 28.00
Bowl, Vegetable, Iroquois, Nutmeg, Divided, 10 In. 28.00
Butter, Cover, Chutney 125.00
Butter, Cover, Iroquois, Avocado 40.00
Butter, Cover, Iroquois, Blue 55.00
Butter, Cover, Iroquois, White 45.00
Butter, Iroquois, Avocado 45.00
Carafe, Iroquois, Avocado 75.00
Casserole, Iroquois, Blue, Cover 32.00
Casserole, Iroquois, Green 25.00
Celery Dish, American Modern, Coral 18.00
Chop Plate, American Modern, Chartreuse 20.00
Clock, Coral 50.00
Clock, Harker 48.00
Creamer, American Modern, Seafoam 10.00
Creamer, Iroquois, Avocado 7.00
Creamer, Iroquois, Ice Blue 8.00

Cup & Saucer, American Modern, Chartreuse, Demitasse	25.00
Cup & Saucer, Iroquois, Charcoal	6.00
Cup & Tray Snack Sets, Wood Leaf, 8 Piece	96.00
Cup, American Modern, Coral	5.00
Flatware, Stainless Steel, 45 Piece	1500.00
Gravy Boat, American Modern, Chartreuse	17.50
Hen, Chocolate, 7 In.	25.00
Pitcher, Water, Iroquois, Nutmeg	55.00
Plate, Dinner, American Modern, Coral	6.00
Plate, Dinner, Iroquois, Apricot	7.00
Plate, Dinner, Iroquois, Charcoal	7.00
Plate, Iroquois, Oyster Gray	7.00
Platter, Iroquois, Avocado	15.00
Salt & Pepper, American Modern, Chartreuse	12.00
Sauce Boat, Iroquois, Underplate, Oyster Gray	20.00
Sugar & Creamer, American Modern, Chartreuse	12.50
Sugar & Creamer, Stacking, Iroquois	15.00
Sugar, Cover, American Modern, Coral	13.00
Sugar, Open, American Modern, Seafoam	7.00
Sugar, Open, American Modern, White	4.00
Teapot, American Modern, Coral	70.00
Teapot, American Modern, Gray	55.00
Teapot, Iroquois, Yellow	80.00
Vase, Pinched Form, Yellow, Green Interior, Bauer, 6 1/2 In.	350.00

SABINO FRANCE

Sabino

France

Sabino glass was made in the 1920s and 1930s in Paris, France. Founded by Marius-Ernest Sabino, the firm was noted for Art Deco lamps, vases, figurines, and animals in clear, colored, and opalescent glass. Production stopped during World War II but resumed in the 1960s with the manufacture of nude figurines and small opalescent glass animals. The new pieces are a slightly different color and can be recognized.

SABINO, Figurine, Woman, Long Flowing Hair, Signed, 7 In.	245.00
Lamp, Pinecone Panels, Silvered Metal Support, Signed, 1930, 22 In.	1320.00
Vase, Molded Frieze of Draped Nude Women, Signed, 14 In.	550.00
Vase, Nude, Flowing Hair, 6 1/2 In.	145.00
Vase, Stylized Fish-Like Design, Green Wash, Signed, 8 1/2 In.	1100.00

Salopian ware was made by the Caughley factory of England during the eighteenth century. The early pieces were blue and white with some colored decorations. Another ware called *Salopian* today is a tableware decorated with color transfers. This ware was made during the late-nineteenth century.

SALOPIAN, Bowl, Milkmaid & Cow, 7 3/4 In.	220.00
Bowl, Nut, Fisherman Pattern, Leaf Form, 2 3/4 In., Pair	305.00
Creamer, Deer & Cottage, 3 In.	45.00
Cup & Saucer, Deer, Blue, Black, Yellow & Green	250.00
Cup & Saucer, Handleless, Black & White Floral	85.00
Cup & Saucer, Handleless, Black Floral Transfer, Enameling	75.00
Cup & Saucer, Handleless, Brown Transfer, Enameling	150.00
Cup & Saucer, Handleless, Eagle & Shield, Floral Border	255.00
Cup & Saucer, Handleless, Oriental Scenes	25.00
Cup & Saucer, Handleless, Oriental Transfer, Caughley, S Mark	100.00
Cup & Saucer, Handleless, Youth & Sheep	75.00
Cup & Saucer, Historical, South Carolina Pattern	115.00
Dish, Fisherman Pattern, Oval, 10 1/4 In.	335.00
Eye Bath, Fisherman Pattern, 18th Century, 1 7/8 In.	550.00
Pitcher, Embossed Designs, Mask Spout, Marked With 5, 5 7/8 In.	500.00
Pitcher, Milk, Fisherman Pattern, Facial Relief Spout, 7 1/2 In.	495.00
Plate, Deer, Floral Border, 7 1/4 In.	100.00
Plate, Fisherman Pattern, Piecrust Rim, 7 7/8 In., 9 Piece	665.00
Platter, Fisherman Pattern, Oval, 18th Century, 9 1/4 In.	195.00
Strainer, Egg, Fisherman Pattern, Leaf & Vine Handle, 4 In., Pair	330.00

Strainer, Egg, Fisherman Pattern, Leaf Handle, 3 3/4 In., 3 Piece	445.00
Sugar, Shepherd & Maiden Scene, Stubbs, 4 7/8 In.	70.00
Tea Caddy, Fisherman Pattern, Cylindrical, 4 1/4 In.	335.00
Teapot, Scenes of Milkmaids, 5 3/8 In.	125.00
Waste Bowl, Britannia Scene, Embossed Ribs, 5 In.	105.00

Matched sets of salt and pepper shakers were first used in the nineteenth century. Collectors are primarily interested in figural examples made after World War I. Huggies are pairs of shakers which appear to embrace each other. Many salt and pepper shakers are listed in other categories and can be located through the index at the back of this book.

SALT & PEPPER, Accent, In Rack, 1950s	12.00
Amish Boy & Girl, Cast Iron	10.00
Apple In Basket	12.00
Bambi, Ceramic, 1940s	30.00
Baseball & Glove, 4 In.	20.00
Bear	45.00
Bear, Huggie, Yellow, Van Tellingen	18.00
Bear, Huggies, Pink, Van Tellingen	12.00
Bears, On Tree	8.00
Black & White Boys, On Raft	39.50
Black Boy & Dog, Huggies	48.00
Black Cat, Japan	12.50
Black Clown, Teapot Shape	20.00
Black Mammy & Chef, 4 1/4 In.	50.00
Black Mammy & Chef, 8 1/4 In.	148.00
Black Mammy & Chef, Japan, 5 1/2 In.	50.00
Black Porter, With Suitcases	75.00
Blue Bonnet Sue	25.00
Boot & Creel	12.00
Boston Bulldogs, Dressed In Sweaters	12.00
Bowling Ball & Pin	12.00
Bunny, Huggies, Green, Van Tellingen	12.00
Bylas Grocery, Arizona	12.00
Cabbage Rose, Amber	26.00 To 28.00
Cat, Orange, Bavarian	32.00
Chicken & Fox	10.00
Christmas Tree, Porcelain	25.00
Clown	12.00
Cow & Milk Pail	12.00
Deer Horn, Story, Wyoming	13.00
Dick Tracy, Chalkware	50.00
Dog & Fire Hydrant	15.00
Donkey & Hay Carrier	15.00
Egg & Skillet	12.00
Elephant	45.00
Elephant Teapots	15.00
Elephant, Standing	12.00
Eskimo, Porcelain	10.00
Fireman Hat & Boots	10.00
Fish, Ceramic Arts	25.00
Fish, Nodder	25.00
Friar Tuck, Marked B	40.00
Fruit, Purinton	15.00
Gas Pumps, Phillips 66, Orange	18.00
Geisha Girls, Triangular Shape, Red Trim	15.00
Giraffe, Long Neck	10.00 To 15.00
Giraffe, Twisted Neck	23.00
Greyhound's Head, Rosemeade, Paper Label	55.00
Hand & Corn	69.00
Handgun, Metal	20.00
Hen & Rooster, Japan	11.00

Horsehead, Stylized, Pink, Marked Hollywood Bowl, 3 In. 18.00
Humpty Dumpty 15.00
Ice Box, Milk Glass 85.00
Indian Boy & Girl 10.00
Indian Chiefs 15.00
Japanese Couple 12.00
Jonah In Whale 20.00
Kayo, Glass 30.00
Kewpie, Japan 35.00
Kewpie, With Turkeys, Action 750.00
Kitten & Ball of Yarn, Meows 20.00
Lighter & Cigarettes 12.00
Lion & Tamer 15.00
Little America, Wyoming, Souvenir, Indian Style 32.00
Little Sprout 25.00
Maid & Butler, 4 3/4 In. 65.00
Marilyn Monroe .... 19.50 To 30.00
Mary & Lamb, Huggies, Van Tellingen .... 18.00 To 23.00
Mason Jars, Box 25.00
Mermaid & Sailor, Huggies, Van Tellingen .... 65.00 To 95.00
Monitor Top, Milk Glass 55.00
Monkey 45.00
Nipper, RCA, Lenox 45.00
Oriental Children, Ceramic Arts Studio, 3 In. 22.00
Outhouse & Catalog 12.00
Pebbles & Bam Bam 15.00
Peek–A–Boo, Van Tellingen, Small 59.50
Pig 45.00
Pillsbury Doughboy .... 18.00 To 40.00
Pluto, Ceramic, Walt Disney, 1940s 28.00
Pop–Up Toaster, Chrome, Box 20.00
Praying Girls, Dressed In Pink 15.00
Range, Purinton 15.00
Rat In Cheese 15.00
RCA Nipper & Horn, Green Ceramic, c.1940, 3 1/2 In. 50.00
RCA Nipper, Plastic, 1950, Box 15.00
Roaster & Turkey 12.00
Rocketship 10.00
. Scarecrows, On Wire Fence 12.00
Seahorses 12.00
Skull, Nodder 25.00
Smokey The Bear .... 15.00 To 65.00
Squirt, Soda Bottle .... 6.50 To 15.00
Stagecoach 12.00
Steins, Elk Scene 12.00
Tappan Chefs 15.00
Toaster .... 9.50 To 18.00
Tropical Fish 15.00
Veggie People 6.00
Venus Di Milo 15.00
Walruses 10.00
Westinghouse Washer & Dryer, Celluloid, 1950s .... 10.00 To 32.00
Willie & Millie, Penguins, F & F 14.00
Wizard of Oz 19.50
Wolf & Little Red Riding Hood 15.00

Salt glaze has a grayish white, pitted, orange–peel–textured surface.
It is a method of decoration that has been used since the eighteenth
century. Salt–glazed pieces are still being made.

SALT GLAZE, Butter Tub, Cover, Foliate Scrolling, 1760, 4 13/16 In. 1650.00
Castor, Star & Dot Diaperwork, c.1760, 5 9/16 In. 1100.00
Churn, Blue Floral, Marked, 6 Gal. 275.00
Coffeepot, Ridged Rim, Serpent Spout, c.1760, 8 7/16 In. 7700.00

◆◆◆◆◆◆◆◆◆◆◆◆◆◆◆◆◆◆◆◆◆

An unglazed rim on the bottom
of a plate usually indicates it was
made before 1850.

◆◆◆◆◆◆◆◆◆◆◆◆◆◆◆◆◆◆◆◆◆◆◆◆

Salt Glaze, Pitcher, Apostle, Gothic Revival,
England, 10 3/8 In.

◆◆◆

Outdoor bronze sculptures need special care. Wash with soap,
water, and a little ammonia to remove oil and dirt. Then rinse, dry,
and rub with a cloth dipped in olive oil or boiled linseed oil. Rub with
a dry cloth to remove extra oil. Outdoor bronzes should be oiled several times a year.

◆◆◆

Creamer, Embossed Floral, Eros In Center Circle, 3 7/8 In.	125.00
Crock, A. W. Eddy & Co., Macomb, Ill., 8 Gal.	95.00
Crock, Butter, Embossed Deer & Hunter	200.00
Crock, Cobalt Blue Flowers, Brown Lining, RW, 3 Gal.	125.00
Crock, Double P, Minnesota Stoneware Co., 3 Gal.	500.00
Crock, E. T. Miller & Sons, Alexandria, Va., Cobalt, 1 1/2 Gal.	575.00
Dish, Pickle, Heart Shape, Foliate Scrolls, 1745, 4 1/8 In., Pair	1375.00
Figurine, Gentleman, Tricorn, Greatcoat, 1745, 3 5/8 In.	2750.00
Jar, Pantry, Cover, Incised R.R. Stoneware Co., 2 Gal.	675.00
Jug, Chicago Advertising In Cobalt Blue, 1 Gal.	325.00
Jug, Milk, 16 Vignettes of Hunt, Camel Rider, c.1745, 4 5/16 In.	885.00
Jug, Plummer Thompson & Co., French Lick, Indiana, 2 Gal.	65.00
Jug, Seligohn & Co., Chicago, Signed RWS Co., 1 Gal.	675.00
Jug, Universe, Embossed Medallions, People, Animals, 9 5/8 In.	295.00
Mold, Jelly, Sun Face, 1750, 3 7/8 In.	1350.00
Pitcher, Apostle, Gothic Revival, England, 10 3/8 In. ....*Illus*	225.00
Pitcher, Falstaff In Laundry Basket, Trees, Turner, 8 1/8 In.	130.00
Pitcher, Grapes & Leaves, Branches Form Handle, Brown, 8 In.	375.00
Pitcher, Milk, Grape Leaf, Cobridge, Pewter Lid, 1800s	150.00
Plate, Armorial, Royal Arms, Foliate Fronds, c.1760, 9 1/8 In.	3575.00
Plate, King of Prussia, Frederick The Great, c.1756, 9 5/16 In.	550.00
Plate, Reticulated Rim, 9 3/4 In.	300.00
Sauceboat, Naked Chinese Boy, Paw Feet, c.1750, 6 7/8 In.	1925.00
Teapot, Camel, Pleated Saddle Blanket, Howdah, c.1745, 5 3/8 In.	7800.00
Teapot, Flowering Plants, Bird On Front, 1745, Miniature	1100.00
Teapot, House, 3 Story, Serpent's Head Spout, 1745, 5 5/16 In.	1650.00
Teapot, Scallop Shells, Dolphins, 1740, 5 1/4 In.	3850.00
Teapot, Woman & Child Finial, Scenes With Figures, 6 1/2 In.	175.00

ABCDE Samplers were made in America from the early 1700s. The best
examples were made from 1790 to 1840. Long, narrow samplers are
usually older than square ones. Early samplers just had stitching or
alphabets. The later examples had numerals, borders, and pictorial
decorations. Those with mottoes are mid–Victorian.

SAMPLER, Adam & Eve, Angels, Mary Day, 8 Years, 1799, 18 1/2 x 14 3/4 In. 300.00

Alphabet, —Beth Stokes, In 16th Year, 11 1/2 x 9 3/4 In. 225.00
Alphabet, Amalia Klipstein, 1848, 10 x 12 1/2 In. 412.50
Alphabet, Ann Bentley, Age 12, Done For David & Ann Snell, 1825 .... 895.00
Alphabet, Homespun, Flowers, Birds, Framed, 21 3/4 x 8 In. 275.00
Alphabet, Homespun, House Scene, Amorena D. T. Roberts, 1823, 20 In. 650.00
Alphabet, Homespun, Linen, Strawberry Border, Frame, 12 3/4 x 11 In. 300.00
Alphabet, Leaf Border, Green Tones, Signed & Dated 1836 .... 1250.00
Alphabet, Linen, Silk Threads, Sally Goss, Framed, 11 1/2 x 16 In. 1760.00
Alphabet, Maria Shea, 26 August 1845, Linen, Framed 495.00
Alphabet, Mary McClatchie, 1842, 12 x 9 In. 220.00
Alphabet, Mathilda Manmom, 1877, 11 1/2 x 8 1/2 In. 145.00
Alphabet, Numbers, 1853, 7 x 9 In. 165.00
Alphabet, Plants, Marilda Martha Baker, 1771, 14 x 11 1/2 In. 385.00
Alphabet, Polychrome Threads, Linen Ground, 15 1/2 x 12 1/2 In. 1650.00
Alphabet, Red Stitching, 1881, Framed, 15 x 15 In. 275.00
Alphabet, Several Styles, Homespun, Name, 1750, 18 1/2 x 9 1/4 In. 500.00
Alphabet, Verse, Border, Betsey Gifford, 20 3/4 x 17 3/4 In. 375.00
Alphabet, Verse, Emily Inbraham, Linen, Silk, 10 3/4 x 16 In. 770.00
Alphabet, Verse, Margaret Ann Pearsall, Aged 13, 1838, 17 x 16 In. 775.00
Alphabet, Verse, Sarah G. Vail, 9 Years, 1836, 28 1/4 x 22 5/8 In. 1750.00
Alphabet, Waynesville School, Homespun, Wool Floss, 18 x 20 In. 775.00
Basket of Flowers, Elizabeth Kline, 1821, 12 1/2 x 16 1/2 In. 4000.00
Center House, Motto, Mary Dinton, December 28, 1814, 13 1/2 x 13 In. 220.00
Cross & Tent Stitch, Birds, Animals, Gentleman, 16 1/4 x 12 In. 2860.00
Cross–Stitch, House, Trees, Birds, Needlepoint, 18 1/8 x 10 1/4 In. 500.00
Cross–Stitch, Linen, Harriet Wetmore, Canfield, March 6, 1827, Small 2200.00
Eagle In Wreath, Hannah Closson, Aged 13, AD 1825, 30 3/4 x 24 In. 1550.00
Emancipation, Wool, We's Free, We Is, 1879 .... 1000.00
Family Record, Mary W. Bellows, Mass., Silk, 1821, 19 1/2 x 16 In. 4125.00
Family Record, Rudulph Family, Births 1794–1826, 16 x 11 3/4 In. 350.00
Floral Border, Hundon School, Elizabeth Golding, 1817, 11 3/4 In. 375.00
Floral, Architectural, Anna Worsnop, Framed, 1830, 26 x 26 In. 137.00
Flowers Around Verse, Cynthia Ray, 7 Years, 1823, 16 x 17 1/2 In. 1025.00
Flowers, Louiza Thompson, George Ward, 1819, 22 1/4 x 17 1/2 In. 550.00
Framed House, Trees, Birds, Lily, Age 4, 1886, 8 x 12 In. 85.00
Homespun Linen, Ann Rebecca Carlson, 1822, Framed, 20 x 12 3/4 In. 950.00
Homespun, Ann Forde, March 13, 1848, Aged 9 Years, Square, 20 3/8 In. 450.00
Homespun, Birds, People, Framed, M. S., Age 12, 1797, 20 x 16 In. 600.00
Homespun, Elizabeth Fearby Acomb, 1785, 17 3/4 x 11 1/2 In. 575.00
Homespun, Family of Robert & Hannah Fosgate, 1831, 22 1/2 x 20 In. 150.00
Homespun, Family Record, Louisa Webb, No. 16, 1827, Square, 22 1/2 In. 375.00
Homespun, Julia Mary Newton, November 26, 1835, 18 5/8 x 15 3/4 In. 450.00
Homespun, Marion McDonald, Finished August 1873, Framed, 14 In. Sq. 400.00
Homespun, Mary Pollard, Nine & Half, 1740, 19 1/2 x 14 In. 325.00
Homespun, Red Stitching, Elizabeth Hunter, 1856, 9 3/4 x 11 1/4 In. 485.00
Homespun, Sarah Gill Bedale, 9 Years, 1800, 18 5/8 x 18 1/8 In. 700.00
Homespun, Verse, Janet Fisher, Aged 12, 1839, Frame, 19 x 14 1/2 In. 375.00
Homespun, Wool Needlepoint, Margaret Johnston, 20 3/4 x 21 1/2 In. 1000.00
House, Trees, Birds, Elizabeth Baldwin, 1800, Framed, 15 x 15 In. 660.00
House, Trees, Flowers, Prayer, 1830, 16 x 16 In. ....*Illus* 2200.00
Linen, Abigail Bush, 10th Year, Novb. 6th AD 1807, 18 x 15 1/2 In. 10000.00
Linen, Elizabeth Yarmalls, 13th Year, Framed, 15 3/8 x 12 1/2 In. 800.00
Linen, Lydia Mitchell, Nine Partners, 1810, 12 1/2 x 12 3/4 In. 2550.00
Linen, Silk Threads, Sally Goss, 11 1/2 x 15 3/4 In. 1600.00
Linen, Silk, Sally Harrington's Work, 1808, Framed, 25 x 19 1/2 In. 2310.00
Needlepoint, Animals, Flowers, Large A, Barn Frame, 24 x 26 In. 150.00
Needlepoint, Geometric & Floral Blocks, 14 x 10 1/2 In. 330.00
Needlepoint, Pot of Flowers, R. T., 1892, 7 x 10 In. 100.00
Needlepoint, Vase, Flowers, Animals, Framed, 21 3/4 x 23 1/4 In. 400.00
Organdy, Silk Thread, House, Mariah Reeder, 1831, 17 x 21 In. 5500.00
Petit Point On Silk, Caroline Crumpton, 20 1/2 x 16 In. 950.00
Religious Verse, Ann Wright, At Age 12, 1823, 17 1/2 x 19 3/8 In. 395.00
Religious Verse, Mary, 9 Years of Age, Warwick, 1804, Framed 1500.00

Silk, Sarah Elizabeth Wright, Aged 18 Years, 1821, 15 3/4 x 17 In. 1210.00
Strawberry Border, Margaret McIntosh, Framed, 17 1/2 x 12 In. 400.00
Trees, Animals, House, Cathie Firgall, Aged 11, Framed, 18 x 14 In. 500.00
Trees, Dog, Louisa Eastes, Born December 18th, 1812, 17 3/8 x 10 In. 275.00
Verse, Eliza Ann Peters, 8 Years, January 9————, Framed, 18 x 18 In. 300.00
Verse, Eliza Thurstan's, Novb. 4th, 1803, 8 3/4 x 8 In. 1025.00
Verse, Hannah Bond, Her Work 1837, Framed, 18 1/2 x 19 1/2 In. 1750.00
Verse, Rosanna Campbell, Born 24 January 1820, 18 1/2 x 13 1/2 In. 225.00
Vining Border, B. Veyssie, F. Veyssie, Wool On Cotton, 21 x 22 In. 300.00
Vining Border, Sarah McCortney, 14th Year, 1804, 23 1/2 x 21 In. 2600.00
Wool, On Punched Paper, Hattie L. Cooley 1879, 23 1/2 x 32 1/2 In. 350.00

Samson and Company, a French firm specializing in the reproduction of collectible wares of many countries and periods, was founded in Paris in the early–nineteenth century. Chelsea, Meissen, Famille Verte, and Chinese Export porcelain are some of the wares that have been reproduced by the company. The firm uses a variety of marks on the reproductions. It is still in operation.

SAMSON, Cup & Saucer, c.1840 .... 495.00
   Garniture, Oriental Figures, Porcelain & Tole, 15 3/4 In., 3 Piece 7700.00
   Tea Caddy, Gilt Sterling Lid 595.00
   Vase, Cover, Baluster Form, 1880s, 10 In., Pair 465.00

Sand Babies were used as decorations on a line of children's dishes made by the Royal Bayreuth China Company. The children are playing at the seaside. Collectors use the names *Sand Babies* and *Beach Babies* interchangeably.

SAND BABIES, Inkwell, Skipping Rope, Blue Mark, 3 Piece 325.00
   Sugar & Creamer, Signed 200.00

Sampler, House, Trees, Flowers, Prayer,
1830, 16 x 16 In.

◆ ◆ ◆ ◆ ◆ ◆ ◆ ◆ ◆ ◆ ◆ ◆ ◆ ◆ ◆ ◆ ◆ ◆ ◆ ◆

If you want to remove a grease stain from silk, wool, or paper, cover it with grated chalk. Cover the chalk with a piece of a brown paper bag. Set a warm iron on the paper. Repeat if necessary. Be sure the iron is not hot enough to scorch the paper.

◆ ◆ ◆ ◆ ◆ ◆ ◆ ◆ ◆ ◆ ◆ ◆ ◆ ◆ ◆ ◆ ◆ ◆ ◆ ◆

Sandwich Glass, Candlestick,
Clambroth, c.1840,
7 1/2 In., Pair

Sandwich Glass, Vase,
Clambroth, Cobalt Snake,
10 In., Pair

Satin Glass, Creamer,
Rainbow Quilted, 4 3/4 In.

Sandwich glass is any one of the myriad types of glass made by the Boston and Sandwich Glass Works in Sandwich, Massachusetts, between 1825 and 1888. It is often very difficult to be sure whether a piece was really made at the Sandwich factory because so many types were made there and similar pieces were made at other glass factories.

SANDWICH GLASS, see also Pressed Glass, etc.

SANDWICH GLASS, Bowl, Woman, Medallions, Octagonal, 9 7/8 In.	175.00
Candlestick, Clambroth, c.1840, 7 1/2 In., Pair ....*Illus*	385.00
Candlestick, Yellow, Square Base, Pair	1200.00
Cigar Holder, Pink Cut To White, Ovals & Circles, 2 5/8 In.	225.00
Compote, Loop, 9 x 11 1/2 In.	325.00
Honey Casket, Undertray, Gothic Arch	750.00
Newel–Post Knob, Jade Green, Pair	650.00
Pitcher, Cranberry To Clear Overshot	125.00
Pitcher, Inverted Thumbprint, Twisted Rope Handle, 7 In.	265.00
Plate, Lacy Plaid, 8 In.	75.00
Salt Dish, Eagles & Ships, Round	395.00
Salt, Boat Shape, Cobalt Blue, Signed	350.00
Salt, Boat Shape, Lafayette	295.00
Sauce, Roman Rosette, Opalescent, 4 In.	45.00
Sugar, Cover, Gothic Arch, Clambroth	240.00
Tie–Back, Pewter Stem, Amberina, 3 1/2 In., Pair	72.00
Tureen, Sapphire Blue, Child's	450.00
Vase, Clambroth, Cobalt Snake, 10 In., Pair ....*Illus*	358.00
Vase, Swirl, Rounded Corners, Opaque Overlay, 7 1/2 In.	195.00
Vase, Yellow Swirl, Square, Flared Rim, Opaque Overlay, 8 In.	195.00

Utzschneider and Company, a porcelain factory, made ceramics in Sarreguemines, Lorraine, France, from 1770. Transfer–printed wares and majolica were made in the nineteenth century. The nineteenth-century pieces, most often found today, usually had colorful transfer–printed decorations showing peasants in local costumes.

SARREGUEMINES, Basket, Rose & Leaf	240.00
Cake Plate, Basketweave & Vine, Dark Green, 9 1/2 In.	25.00
Character Mug, Pitcher Form, 8 1/2 In.	225.00
Cup & Saucer, Orange Cup, Leafy Saucer	35.00
Oyster Plate, 6 Gray & Coral Wells, 9 1/2 In.	75.00
Pitcher, Toby Shape, 6 3/4 In.	
Plate, Mars, Transfer, 7 1/2 In.	45.00
Plate, November, Transfer, 7 1/2 In.	45.00
Platter, Fruit On Gold Leaves, 10 In.	55.00
Platter, Fruit On Gold Leaves, 12 In.	70.00
Tureen, Gourd Shape, Attached Leaf Tray, 12 1/2 In.	45.00
Vase, Gold, Brown Glaze, Bowling Pin Shape, 6 In.	25.00

Sascha Brastoff made decorative accessories, ceramics, enamels on copper, and plastics of his own design. He headed a factory, Sascha Brastoff of California, Inc., in West Los Angeles, from 1953 until about 1973.

SASCHA BRASTOFF, Bowl, Huskie Dog, Blue, 6 In.	60.00
Plaque, Enamel, Horse, Pink, 9 In.	1150.00
Plaque, Enamels, Leaves, Flowers, Gold, Green, 12 In.	50.00
Tea Set, Pink, Silver, 3 Piece	185.00

Satin glass is a late–nineteenth–century art glass. It has a dull finish that is caused by a hydrofluoric acid vapor treatment. Satin glass was made in many colors and sometimes had applied decorations. Satin glass is also listed by factory name or in the Mother–of–pearl category in this book.

SATIN GLASS, Bowl, Pink, Blue Forget–Me–Nots, Ruffled, Ormolu Mount, 3 In.	165.00
Box, Cuff, Painted Design	225.00

Centerpiece, Plateau & Twist Candlesticks, Blue, 4 Piece 65.00
Compote, Cover, Pink, Dolphin Footed, Westmoreland 35.00
Cookie Jar, Cover, Fleurette, Pink, 6 1/4 In. 225.00
Creamer, Pink, Diamond–Quilted, White Inside, Handle, 5 1/4 In. 595.00
Creamer, Rainbow Quilted, 4 3/4 In. ....*Illus* 605.00
Dish, Sweetmeat, Diamond–Quilted, Stationary Handle, 7 1/2 In. 490.00
Epergne, Ruffled Bowl, Lily, Orange To Vaseline, 14 1/2 In. 395.00
Ewer, Beaded Drape, Metal Top & Base, Blue, 19 In. 165.00
Ewer, Melon Sections, Leaves, Foliage, Birds, Blue, 10 3/4 In. 145.00
Jar, Sweetmeat, Shell & Seaweed, Pink, Silver Plated Rim & Lid 15.00
Lemonade Set, Rainbow–Quilted, Pink, Blue & Yellow, 5 Piece 1100.00
Pitcher, Rainbow–Quilted, Fluted Handle, 7 3/4 In. 935.00
Rose Bowl, Blue Overlay, Egg Shape, White Lining, 6 3/8 In. 135.00
Rose Bowl, Cut Velvet, Diamond–Quilted, Rose Pink, 3 3/8 In. 195.00
Rose Bowl, Enameled Yellow Flowers & Leaves, 5 1/2 x 6 In. 250.00
Rose Bowl, Indented Swirl, White Lining, Blue, 3 1/4 In. 85.00
Rose Bowl, Petal Feet, Pansies, White Lining, Oval, 5 1/2 In. 135.00
Rose Bowl, Yellow, Shell & Seaweed, 8–Crimp, White Lining, 5 In. 195.00
Sugar & Creamer, Pink, Fleurette, Silver Cover, 3 3/4 In 245.00
Syrup, Hand Painted Rooster, Yellow Handle, Chrome 15.00
Tumbler, Green Opaque, Mottled, Gold, 3 3/4 In. 650.00
Vase, Aqua, Raindrop Pattern, 7 1/4 In. 155.00
Vase, Classical Robed Figures, Gillinder, Marked Cameo, 8 In. 600.00
Vase, Cut Velvet, Diamond Quilted, White Lining, 4 1/2 In., Pr. 195.00
Vase, Gold & Enamel Floral, Tapered, Marked P. K., 4 1/2 In., Pr. 247.00
Vase, Yellow Wheat, Coralene Design, Pink To Frosted, 6 In. 275.00
    SATIN GLASS, WEBB, see Webb

Satsuma is a Japanese pottery with a distinctive creamy beige crackled glaze. Most of the pieces were decorated with blue, red, green, orange, or gold. Almost all the Satsuma found today was made after 1860. During World War I, Americans could not buy undecorated European porcelains. Women who liked to make hand–painted porcelains at home began to decorate plain Satsuma. These pieces are known today as *American Satsuma.*

SATSUMA, Bowl, Interior & Exterior Florals, Millefiore, Marked, 10 In. 225.00
Bowl, Takarabune In Parade Interior, Butterflies Exterior, 5 In. 1320.00
Bowl, Women In Varied Scenes, Red, Gold Rim, 13 In. 225.00
Ewer, White Mums, Orange & Yellow Ground, c.1870, 5 1/2 In. 75.00
Figurine, Eagle, Perched, Wings Back, Rockwork Base, 11 In. 885.00
Figurine, Quan Yin, 1880s, 14 1/4 In. 1540.00
Figurine, Quan Yin, On Platform, Elephant Legs, Moriaga 95.00
Hatpin, Oriental Scenery, Gold Outlining, Steel Shank, 10 In. 195.00
Incense Burner, Panels of Various Castes, Signed, 3 1/2 x 4 In. 1100.00
Jar, Band of Children At Play Between Floral Borders, 3 1/2 In. 2860.00
Jar, Cover, Figural Finial, Battle Scene, 23 In. 135.00
Jar, Cover, Frieze of Figures In Landscape, c.1885, 5 1/2 In. 175.00
Jar, Dog & Lion Handles, Cover 68.00
Jardiniere, Figural & Floral Reserves, Early 20th Century, 10 In. 305.00
Napkin Ring, Butterflies 285.00
Planter, Scotty Dog, Moriaga 95.00
Punch Bowl, 8 Samurai Interior, Geishas Exterior, Dai Nihon, 12 In. 4125.00
Rose Jar, Multicolored Landscape & Geometric Design, 6 3/4 In. 65.00
Sake Pot, Figural Scenes, Blue Ground, Signed, 5 In. 1000.00
Salt, Floral, 2 1/2 In. 68.00
Tea Set, Molded Serpent & Figural Design, Globular, 15 Piece 250.00
Tea Set, Pheasants, 3 Piece 195.00
Teapot, Coiled Snake On Cover, Dragon Spout & Handle, 4 1/2 In. 440.00
Teapot, Squat Form, Signed 935.00
Urn, Palace, Butterfly & Tied Tassel Handles, 44 1/2 In., Pair 1045.00
Urn, Samurai, Geisha, Blue Ground, 8 1/2 In. ....*Illus* 400.00
Vase, Arahats & Quan Yin, Haloes, Trail, Baluster, 1910, 6 x 12 In. 450.00
Vase, Chrysanthemums On Red Ground, Ovoid, 16 In. 220.00

Satsuma, Urn, Samurai,   Satsuma, Vase, Scholar, Children, Tassel Handles, 12 In., Pair
Geisha, Blue Ground, 8 1/2 In.   Satsuma, Water Pail, Scholar & Arahat, Geometric, 14 1/2 In.

Vase, Crane, Gold Pebble Clouds, Signed, 12 In., Pair	1250.00
Vase, Domed Cover, Everted Rim, Gilt Designs, Signed, 18 In.	1870.00
Vase, Dragon Around Neck & Body, Gold Halos, Marked, 6 In.	495.00
Vase, Figural & Floral Reserves On Cloud, Ovoid, 31 In.	210.00
Vase, Figural Reserves, Ovoid, Mounted As Lamp, 12 In., Pair	350.00
Vase, Figures of Rakan & Kannon, Encircling Dragon, 5 In.	275.00
Vase, Geometric Enameled, Figural Medallions, Bulbous, 17 In.	180.00
Vase, Mallet Form, Figures of Seated Samurai, 1880s, Pair	550.00
Vase, Pierced Top, Countryside Scenes, Double Handles, 4 In.	880.00
Vase, Polychrome Enamel Floral & Bamboo, Shosai, 14 In.	610.00
Vase, Rows of Flowers, Signed, Early 20th Century, 8 1/2 In., Pair	335.00
Vase, Samurai Warrior Each Side, Blown Out, 12 1/2 In.	145.00
Vase, Scholar, Children, Tassel Handles, 12 In., Pair ....*Illus*	600.00
Vase, Sprays of Leaves, Short Neck, Signed, 10 3/4 In.	885.00
Vase, Thousand Faces, Lion Mask Handles, Signed, 5 In.	275.00
Vase, Thousand Faces, Overall Gilt, Signed, 12 In.	550.00
Water Pail, Scholar & Arahat, Geometric, 14 1/2 In. ....*Illus*	650.00

Special scales have been made to weigh everything from babies to gold. Collectors search for all types. Most popular are small gold-dust scales and special grocery scales.

SCALE, Ainsworth & Sons, Gold Miner's	295.00
Analytical, Balance, Mahogany Case, 18 In.	185.00
Baby, 30 Lbs. By Ounces	11.00
Baby, Wicker	40.00
Baird & Tatlock, Gold Miner's	350.00
Balance, Candy, Brass Scoop	125.00
Balance, Rectangular Wooden Case, 2 Brass Trays, 18 1/2 x 7 1/2 In.	110.00
Balance, Walnut–Like, Weighs Diamonds, 1912	275.00
Balance, Wrought Iron, 27 x 35 In.	350.00
Bathroom, Art Deco, Cast Iron	60.00 To 75.00
Brass Fixtures & Trays, Wooden Base, London, 19th Century, 30 In.	605.00
Caille Bros., George Washington	5500.00
Chatillon, Milk, 30 Lbs.	60.00
Cotton, Set	15.00
Dectogram, Brass Trays & Weights, Cast Iron	85.00
Dring & Fage, Lbs. Per Bushel, London, Brass & Steel, Mahogany Box	165.00
Fairbanks Morris, Candy, Scoop, Iron & Brass, 1 1/2 Lb.	75.00
Fairbanks, Gold Assaying, Brass, c.1880	1870.00
Gold Miner's, California Gold Rush Type, Brass Bed	1200.00
Gold Miner's, Village Scene On Oval Box, 6 1/2 In.	135.00
Hanging, Brass, Round, Large	85.00
Hide, Crab Shape, Iron, Brass Dial	95.00
Howe, Grain, 1880s	75.00
Ideal, Postal	22.00
Jacobs, Candy, Weights, Pedestal	145.00
Jiffyway, Egg	15.00

Schneider, Vase, Gray, Mottled & Streaked, Signed, 14 3/4 In.

Schneider, Compote, Red–Orange, Black, Yellow Swirl Design, 4 In.

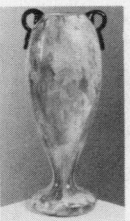

Schneider, Vase, Orange & White Glass, Black Handles, 17 In.

Kitchen, Graniteware	295.00
Landers, Frary & Clark, Household	25.00
Lumber, Paddle Shape, 2 Sides, Hand Stamped, 1/4 x 2 3/4 x 30 1/2 In.	45.00
National, 1 Cent, 1890s	1900.00
O'Haus Triple Beam, 2610 Grams	25.00
Peerless, Lollipop, Low Base	1000.00
Pelouze, Candy, Scoop, 2 Lb., Cast Iron	85.00 To 120.00
Pennsylvania Scale Mfg., Circular Spring Balance, Hanging	160.00
Postal, Set of Weights, English, Brass, 19th Century, 5 In.	110.00
Produce, Los Angeles, Large	40.00
Sears Roebuck, Family, 1906 Model, With Pan	45.00
Toledo, Candy, 5 Lb.	145.00
Toledo, Candy, Scoop, 5 Lb.	145.00
Triner, Candy, 1 Lb.	32.00
Triner, Candy, Scoop, 1 Lb.	32.50
Triner, Scoop, 1 Lb.	30.00
Watling Jr., Lock & Key, Porcelain Finish, 1 Cent	350.00
Winchester, Lbs. Per Bushel, Brass & Steel	135.00

Schafer & Vater, makers of small ceramic items, are best known for their amusing figurals. The factory was located in Volkstedt–Rudolstadt, Germany, from 1890 to 1962. Some pieces are marked with the crown and R mark, but many are unmarked.

SCHAFER & VATER, Ash Holder, Cigar, Bald Man, Mouth Open, 5 1/4 In.	150.00
Basket, Pink Jasper, White Cameo Bust of Lady, 5 In.	55.00
Bottle, Man Holding Pig, Blue, Signed, 9 1/2 In.	150.00
Box, Cover, Sphinx Head, Tan Ground, 3 x 3 In.	135.00
Chamberstick, Woman's–Head Cameo, Pink	75.00
Creamer, Children's Faces Front & Back	85.00
Creamer, Clown With Mandolin, 3 1/2 In.	135.00
Creamer, Devil, 3 1/2 In.	85.00
Ewer, White Frogs, Dancing, Blue Ground, Marked	125.00
Figurine, Dog, Sucking Pacifier, Baby Crying	95.00
Figurine, Man, Sitting On Keg, What We Want, Signed	95.00
Figurine, Scotsman, of Course I've Pants Ye Fool	135.00
Hair Receiver, Lady's–Head Cameos, Greens, Beige, Bisque	45.00
Hair Receiver, Woman & Child	115.00

◆◆◆

There is a modern safe way to hang an antique Oriental rug on the wall. Put a strip of two–inch–wide Velcro on a strip of wood. Mount the wood on the wall. Hang the rug directly on the Velcro. The rug will stay in place and can be pulled loose to be cleaned.

◆◆◆

Hatpin Holder, Lady's Head, Urn Style, 5 1/2 In.	135.00
Hatpin Holder, Woman's Profile, Jasperware, 5 In.	125.00
Inkwell, Nodder, Big Mouthed Baby, 3 1/2 In.	138.00
Napkin Ring, Japanese Geisha, Dark Blue	75.00
Pitcher, Figural, Black Face, Watermelon Mouth	135.00
Powder Box, Woman's Face On Lid, Pink & Green, 3 3/4 In.	110.00
Rose Bowl, Cupids, Musicians, Birds, Pink	90.00
Vase, Medallion of 2 Women, Jewels, Handles, 6 In.	145.00

Schneider

Schneider Glassworks was founded in 1903 at Epinay–sur–Seine, France, by Charles and Ernest Schneider. Art glass was made between 1903 and 1930. The company still produces clear crystal glass.

SCHNEIDER, Bowl, Frosted & Lavender, Footed, 9 In.	350.00
Christmas Tree, Solid, 8 In.	50.00
Compote, Mottled Pink & White To Blue, Black Base, 6 x 7 In.	385.00
Compote, Red–Orange, Black, Yellow Swirl Design, 4 In. ....*Illus*	990.00
Compote, Transparent Blue On Zebra Base, 7 x 12 In.	1100.00
Ewer, White, Orange Overlay, Purple Handle, Oviform, 15 1/2 In.	1100.00
Vase, 2 Salamanders, Dragonflies, Rocky Ground, Signed, 10 In.	1980.00
Vase, Blown Into Geometric Iron Frame, Signed, c.1920, 8 1/4 In.	885.00
Vase, Gray, Mottled & Streaked, Signed, 14 3/4 In. ....*Illus*	1045.00
Vase, Intertwining Branches, Oranges, Signed, c.1925, 23 In.	3025.00
Vase, Mottled Pink, Random Air Bubbles, Signed, c.1920, 13 3/4 In.	1650.00
Vase, Mottled Pink, Thick Walls, Signed, c.1925, 14 3/4 In.	935.00
Vase, Mottled, Ovoid, Double Handles, 15 3/4 In.	660.00
Vase, Orange & White Glass, Black Handles, 17 In. ....*Illus*	1100.00
Vase, Orange, Mauve & Purple Waves, Bulbous, Handles, 12 3/4 In.	1875.00
Vase, Pale Blue, Crimped Orange Appliques, Baluster, 15 1/2 In.	2450.00
Vase, Randomly Mixed Crystal, Air Bubbles Throughout, 8 3/4 In.	765.00
Vase, Royal Blue Threading, Mottled, Flared Rim, Signed, 11 In.	1045.00
Vase, Squared Neck, Hemispherical Handles, Signed, c.1925, 13 In.	1760.00
Vase, Stylized Poppy Blossoms, Signed, c.1930, 7 3/4 In.	8800.00

Scientific instruments of all kinds are included in this category. Other categories such as barometer, binoculars, dental, nautical, medical, and thermometer may also price scientific apparatus.

SCIENTIFIC INSTRUMENT, Chronometer, Marine, 2–Day, J. Bruce & Sons, 1900	1430.00
Measuring, Steam Compression, Oak, Brass, 6 x 16 In.	195.00
Telescope, 4 Lenses, Mahogany Case, 30 3/4 In.	1650.00
Telescope, Brass, Negretti & Zambra, 21 In.	770.00

Scrimshaw is bone or ivory or whale's teeth carved by sailors and others for entertainment during the sailing–ship days. Some scrimshaw was carved as early as 1800. There are modern scrimshanders making pieces today on bone, ivory, or plastic.

SCRIMSHAW, see also Ivory, Nautical

SCRIMSHAW, Ivory, Ship, Clouds, Gulls, 4 1/2 In.	32.00
Ornament, Whale, Ebony, Nautilus Shell, 1850, 16 x 15 x 4 1/2 In.	3080.00
Powder Horn, Indian With War Club, Signed Gottfried Halfen, 1847	165.00
Swift, Provence, In Scrimshaw Box	6000.00
Tooth, Whale, King George, Queen Elizabeth	650.00
Tooth, Whale, Sailing Ship, Iceberg, Bust of Man, 1863, 6 In.	305.00
Tooth, Whale, Ship	4750.00
Tooth, Whale, Spread Eagle, E. Pluribus Unum, Whaling Scene, 9 In.	2090.00
Tooth, Whale, Whaling Scene, Neptune On Reverse	8250.00
Toy, Whalebone & Whale Ivory, Gears Activate Women, 6 3/4 In.	2450.00

Prescott W. Baston

Prescott W. Baston made the first Sebastian miniatures in 1938 in Marblehead, Massachusetts. More than 400 different designs have been made and collectors search for the out–of–production models. The mark may say *Copr. P. W. Baston U.S.A.,* or *P. W. Baston, U.S.A.,* or *Prescott W. Baston.* Sometimes a paper label was used.

SEBASTIAN MINIATURES, 3 Kittens, Jello	475.00
Baker's Dozen	32.00
Betsy Trotwood	75.00
Boy & Girl Skaters	60.00
Brown's Savin' Sandy	125.00
Coronado's Wife	25.00
Falstaff, Marblehead	165.00
Family Picnic	20.00
George Washington, Cannon, Signed ....75.00 To 100.00	
Judge Thatcher	45.00
Little Mother, No. 6231	55.00
Mark Twain's Home, Hannibal, Missouri	700.00
Martha Washington	30.00
Mr. Obocell	175.00
Old Woman In The Shoe, Jello	475.00
Photographer	29.50
Pilgrims	65.00
Sailing Days, Pair	45.00
Santa Claus, 1949	50.00
Thomas Jefferson	45.00
Thomas Jefferson, Marblehead	85.00
Tom Sawyer, Marblehead	25.00

SEG, see Paul Revere Pottery

Sevres porcelain has been made in Sevres, France, since 1769. Many copies of the famous ware have been made. The name originally referred to the works of the Royal Porcelain factory. The name now includes any of the wares made in the town of Sevres, France. The entwined lines with a center letter used as the mark is one of the most forged marks in antiques. Be very careful to identify Sevres by quality, not just by mark.

SEVRES, Box, Jewelry, Young Woman & Man On Lid, Fishing, Marked, 6 x 7 In.	1000.00
Box, Ormolu Cover, Leaf Swags, Porcelain Grip, 8 1/2 In.	550.00
Bust, Marie Antoinette, Bisque, 1890s, 17 1/2 In.	495.00
Cake Stand, Deep Blue, Mottled Blue–Green, Bronze Mountings, Low	150.00
Centerpiece, Gilt Bronze, Beads, Portraits, Pierced, 17 1/2 In.	1925.00
Centerpiece, Putti, With Carriage, Gilt, Pink Ground, 10 1/2 In.	7150.00
Cup & Saucer, Pink, Gold Trim, Garlands, Blue Ribbons	85.00
Cup, Portrait, Jewels, Cover, Saucer, Cobalt Scallops, 6 In.	550.00
Dish, Sprays & Sprigs of Flowers, c.1750, 9 15/16 In.	2100.00
Figurine, Dancing Couple, Floral Dress, Green Trousers, 11 x 12 In.	1650.00
Figurine, Monkey Band, 13 Piece	1500.00
Figurine, Woman With Basket of Flowers, Cherub At Feet, 25 1/2 In.	1650.00
Planter, 2 Young Lovers, Scrolling Handles, Gilt Border, 6 1/2 In.	330.00
Plaque, Courting Scene, Mahogany Frame, 15 1/4 x 21 1/2 In., Pair	775.00
Platter, Military Camp Scene, Cobalt Blue Border, Gilt, 13 1/4 In.	605.00
Tray, Porcelain Plaque, Champleve Mount, 21 In. ....*Illus*	2700.00

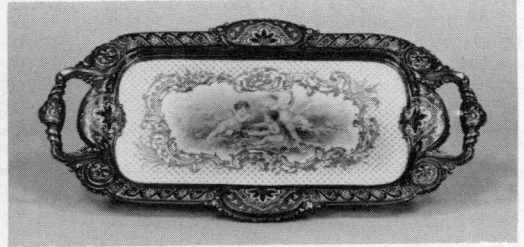

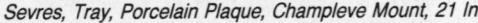

Sevres, Tray, Porcelain Plaque, Champleve Mount, 21 In.

Sevres, Urn, Landscape and Couple, Signed Mela, 31 1/2 In.

Sewer Tile, Figurine, Bird,
Signed EJE, 9 1/2 In.

Sewer Tile, Figurine, Lion,
Signed EJE, 6 1/2 X 9 In.

Sewer Tile, Figurine, Spaniel,
Signed, 10 1/2 In.

Urn, Cover, Woman In Period Dress, Signed, 8 In.	295.00
Urn, Figural Landscape, Applied Mounts, 14 In.	250.00
Urn, Garden Scene, Young Woman & Cherub, Grape Finial, 34 1/2 In.	4400.00
Urn, Gilt Bronze Cupid, Leaf Handles, Bronze Mounted, 35 In.	665.00
Urn, Landscape and Couple, Signed Mela, 31 1/2 In. ....*Illus*	1900.00
Urn, Pearl, Rose Ground, Maiden, Putti, Signed, Cover, 15 In. .	990.00
Urn, Pineapple Finial, Gilt Bronze Beading, Landscape, 35 In.	4620.00
Vase, Gilt–Bronze Mounted, Scrolled Handles, Blue Celeste, 23 In.	3300.00
Vase, Napoleonic Battle Scene, Ovoid, Domed Cover, 31 In., Pair	9350.00
Vase, Oxblood Glaze, Striated Navy Over Rose, Cylindrical, 15 In.	110.00
Vase, Royal Blue To Light Blue, Classical Baluster, 12 In.	150.00
Vase, Splotches of Yellow, Turquoise & Blue Glaze, Signed, 10 In.	220.00

Sewer tile figures were made by workers at the sewer tile and pipe factories in the Ohio area during the late nineteenth and early twentieth centuries. Figurines, small vases, and cemetery vases were favored. Often the finished vase was a piece of the original pipe with added decorations and markings. All types of sewer tile work are now considered folk art by collectors.

SEWER TILE, Bank, Pig, 9 In.	225.00
Bird, On Tree Stump, Signed EJE, 9 1/2 In.	467.00
Birdhouse, 7 1/2 In.	100.00
Colander, Impressed Crest, Akron, Ohio, 9 In.	75.00
Dog, 6 In.	55.00
Dog, Reclining, Paint Traces, 7 3/4 In.	115.00
Dog, Seated, 11 1/4 In.	75.00
Dog, Seated, Signed E. J. E., 11 In.	460.00
Dog, Spaniel, Seated, E. J. E., 10 1/2 In.	225.00
Dog, Tooled Detail, Traces of White, 7 3/4 In.	150.00
Doorstop, Book Shape, Embossed Inscription, 9 1/2 In.	225.00
Doorstop, Dog, Buff, Brown, c.1870, 11 x 8 In.	200.00
Doorstop, Lion, Stalking, Iowa	200.00
Figurine, Bird, Signed EJE, 9 1/2 In. ....*Illus*	467.00
Figurine, Lion, Signed EJE, 6 1/2 x 9 In. ....*Illus*	105.00
Figurine, Spaniel, Signed, 10 1/2 In. ....*Illus*	1320.00
Gorilla, Open Mouth, 14 1/2 In.	10.00
Laboratory Vessel, U. S. Stoneware Co., Akron, Oh., 16 1/2 In.	105.00
Lamp Base, 8 3/4 In.	25.00
Lamp, Tree Shape, 21 In.	85.00
Lion, Initials M. F. C., 12 3/4 In.	55.00
Lion, Orange Over Gold & Silver Paint, 10–20–27, 9 In.	350.00
Lion, Reclining On Plinth, Signed EJE, 6 1/2 x 9 In.	105.00
Lion, Scalloped Base, R. Germain, 1890, 9 1/4 In.	200.00
Owl, 14 1/2 In.	200.00
Owl, Perched On Tree Stump, 14 In.	220.00
Spaniel, Seated, Staffordshire Style, Signed EJE, 10 1/2 In.	1350.00
Tobacco Jar, Tree Bark Texture, Protruding Branch Nubs, 10 In.	55.00

Sewing, Box, 3 Tiers, 2 Drawers,
Signed Lydia Crosby, 1847, 9 In.
Sewing, Box, Ivory Finials, 9 In.
Sewing, Box, 3 Tiers, 2 Drawers,
Pincushion, 9 In.

Sewing, Box, Oak,
2 Drawers, 12 In.

Sewing, Box, Spool Rack,
2 Tiers, Blue, 2 Drawers,
21 1/4 In.
Sewing, Box, Wooden, Metal
Holders, 2 Drawers, 20 1/2 In.

Toothpick, Tree Trunk, Marked What Cheer, Brown, 3 In. 65.00

> All types of sewing equipment are collected, from sewing birds that held the cloth to old wooden spools.

SEWING, Basket, Bentwood, Pine, Red, Black & Yellow Design, Cover, 11 3/4 In. 265.00
Basket, Brown Wicker, Square 15.00
Bird, Brass, Clamp, 1800s, 4 x 5 1/2 In. 220.00
Bird, Clamp Inlaid With Ivory & Abalone, Mirror, 3 1/2 In. 1320.00
Bird, Heart Thumbpiece, Iron, 4 1/4 In. 135.00
Bird, Red Plush Pincushion, Worn Silver Finish, 4 1/2 In. 115.00
Bird, Victorian, Stand, Thimble & 2 Spool Holders, 6 In. 175.00
Bobbin, Lace, Ivory 36.00
Box, 3 Tiers, 2 Drawers, Pincushion, 9 In. ....*Illus*   110.00
Box, 3 Tiers, 2 Drawers, Signed Lydia Crosby, 1847, 9 In. ....*Illus*   99.00
Box, Carved & Turned, Lidded Compartment, Turned Legs, 11 In. 110.00
Box, Geometric Inlay, 1 Large & 3 Small Drawers, Mahogany, 15 In. 225.00
Box, Hinged Compartments, Center Pincushion, Rosewood 95.00
Box, Interior Tray, Inlaid Trim, 14 1/4 In. 175.00
Box, Ivory Eyelets, Hardwood & Mahogany, 6 1/2 In. 65.00
Box, Ivory Finials, 9 In. ....*Illus*   429.00
Box, Oak, 2 Drawers, 12 In. ....*Illus*   110.00
Box, On Stand, Regency, Loop Handle, Penwork, 1820, 33 x 9 3/4 In. 885.00
Box, On Tripod Stand, Lacquered, Chinese Export, c.1835, Pair 4200.00
Box, Ring–Turned Pedestal, 4 Drawers, Spool Rack, 25 3/4 In. 775.00
Box, Spool Rack, 2 Tiers, Blue, 2 Drawers, 21 1/4 In. ....*Illus*   140.00
Box, Spool, 2 Tiers, 18 Grommets, Pincushion Top, 8 x 9 In. 165.00
Box, Tin, Fitted Tray, Brass Bail Handle, Red Paint Traces, 14 In. 110.00
Box, Wooden, 2 Compartments, Ivory Finial, Pullout Mirror, 9 In. 429.00
Box, Wooden, 3 Tiers, 3 Compartments, Lydia Crosby, Dated 1847, 9 In. 99.00
Box, Wooden, Metal Holders, 2 Drawers, 20 1/2 In. ....*Illus*   135.00
    SEWING, CABINET, SPOOL, see Advertising, Cabinet, Spool
Cabinet, Walnut, Victorian, 2 Doors, Gothic Style Back 150.00
Caddy, Spool, Celluloid, Blue 8.00
Caddy, Spool, Eyelets For Thread, Walnut, 8 3/4 In. 135.00
Case, Lyre Shape, French, c.1850 ....   500.00
Darner, Sock, Striped Tiger Maple, Handle, 1 Piece, 6 1/2 In. 95.00
Darner, Sterling, Webster 145.00
Darning Egg, Sterling Silver, Black Wood, Ornate Handle 68.00
Dress Form, Wire 125.00
Embroidery Clamp, Hemmarker, Wooden, 15 1/2 In., 2 Piece 11.00
Embroidery, Clamp, Sycamore, Horn Hoop 110.00

Hem Gauge, Holly 145.00
Hem Gauge, October 2, 1894 .... 50.00
Hem Stitching Machine, Singer, 1920s 1250.00
Kit, G. E. Mini Vacuum 28.00
Kit, Iron Mines, Hibbing, Minn. ....8.00 To 15.00
Kit, Victorian, Tole, Implements, c.1880 .... 275.00
Machine, Pinking, Hand Operated, Black, Gold Trim 85.00
Machine, Singer, Featherweight, Model 221, Attachments 400.00
Machine, Singer, Featherweight, Model 221, Case .... 150.00 To 210.00
Machine, Singer, Treadle 125.00
Machine, Stitchwell 40.00
Needle Book, Cameron Cash Grocery, Hannibal, Mo., Woman Front 12.50
Needle Book, Food Fair 8.00
Needle Case & Bobbin, Boye, Metal, Round, 16 In. 75.00
Needle Case, Butterfly, Avery 475.00
Needle Case, Fold–Out, Beatrice, 1870s 350.00
Needle Case, Fulton Trouser Co., Paper, Calendar Inside, 1904 .... 10.00
Needle Case, Gilt 95.00
Needles, Dix & Rands, Japan, 12 Packs 10.00
Oil Can, Singer Sewing Machine 12.00
Pattern, Doll, McCall's, 3 Fashions 42.00
SEWING, PINCUSHION DOLL, see Pincushion Doll
Pincushion, Apple, Celluloid 35.00
Pincushion, Beadwork, Victorian, 9 x 7 In. 48.00
Pincushion, Black Man, Large Dice 40.00
Pincushion, Child On Heart Pillow 45.00
Pincushion, Cowrie Shell 18.00
Pincushion, Dress Form, Tape In Base, Thimble Top 55.00
Pincushion, Dutch Boy 10.00
Pincushion, Elephant 10.00
Pincushion, Elephant, Sitting, Silver Plate 40.00
Pincushion, Leather, Black Alligatored, 4 Velvet Pads, Birds, 9 In. 195.00
Pincushion, Mammy's Head, Cloth 8.00
Pincushion, Pheasant, Metal 65.00
Pincushion, Pillow Shape, Velvet, Flowers, 4 1/4 x 5 1/2 In. 105.00
Pincushion, Red Wood Cover, Cast Iron Base, 4 1/2 In. 20.00
Pincushion, Rotating World 15.00
Pincushion, Shoe Shape, Carved Wood, Polychrome Paint, 11 In. 25.00
Pincushion, Shoe, Ornate Brass 30.00
Pincushion, Strawberry, Green Felt Hull, Red Velvet, 1880s, 3 x 5 In. 85.00
Pincushion, Swan, Brass 18.00
Pincushion, Thread Holder, Mammy 27.00
Pincushion, Turkish Shoe 22.00
Pincushion, Woman's Shoe, Brass, 3 1/2 In. 20.00
Punch Gauge, Sterling Silver, Floral Design 60.00
Quilting Frame, Sawbuck Base, 31 1/2 x 56 In. 175.00
Scissors, Souvenir, Washington, D. C., 1900 .... 95.00
Seam Ripper, Pat. May 22, 1900 .... 14.00
Sewing Bird, Heart Clamp, Pat. 1853 .... 175.00
Sharpener, Scissors, Magnetic 85.00
SEWING, SPOOL CABINET, see Advertising, Cabinet, Spool
Spool Holder, Pincushion, Turned Wood, 18 1/2 In 440.00
Spool Holder, Rotating, Cast Iron, Pincushion–Holder Top, 1870 .... 125.00
Spool Stand, Pincushion, Bird's–Eye Maple, Walnut, 2 Drawers, 8 In. 193.00
Stand, 3 Tiers, Bird's–Eye Maple, 9 3/4 In. 270.00
Stand, Multitiered, Revolving Thread Holder, 12 In. 495.00
Stand, Pincushion, Turned & Molded Wood, Pyramid, Mirror, 12 In. 165.00
Swift, Tabletop, Natural Patina, 11 3/4 In. 35.00
Tape Measure, Atlas 15.00
Tape Measure, Black Man's Head, Cigarette In Mouth Is Tab 55.00
Tape Measure, Bradley Walking Plow 35.00
Tape Measure, Brass Owl, Stainless Steel, Germany 55.00
Tape Measure, Clock, As Tape Is Pulled Hands Move, 1 1/4 In. 55.00

◆◆

A photoelectric cell can be put into an existing exterior light to turn the light on at dusk, off at dawn. Another kind of adaptor will turn a light on when there is motion in your yard.

◆◆

Tape Measure, Colgate Fab Soap, Celluloid, Soap Box	15.00
Tape Measure, Fish, Celluloid	30.00
Tape Measure, General Electric, Celluloid, Pictures Refrigerator	25.00
Tape Measure, Golfer, Celluloid, 2 In.	65.00
Tape Measure, Hoover Vacuum, 1950s	30.00
Tape Measure, Indian Woman, Blanket Around Shoulders	30.00
Tape Measure, John Deere, Celluloid	25.00
Tape Measure, Lydia Pinkham	35.00
Tape Measure, Lydia Pinkham, Celluloid, Portrait Front	80.00
Tape Measure, Pig In Boot, Celluloid	48.00
Tape Measure, Pincushion, Chicken	12.00
Tape Measure, Pink Pig With Baby Pig, Celluloid	65.00
Tape Measure, Policeman, Celluloid	40.00
Tape Measure, Puppy, Pull Tail, Glass Eyes	95.00
Tape Measure, Spindle	45.00
Tape Measure, Windmill, Celluloid	30.00 To 38.00
Tatting Shuttle, Lydia Pinkham, Portrait Top, Advertising Bottom	100.00
Thimble & Spool Holder, Greenaway Girl, Bronzed	35.00
Thimble Case, Mauchline Tartan Ware	100.00
Thimble Holder, Brass, Ornate, Austria	35.00
Thimble Holder, Crocheted Hat	10.00
Thimble Holder, Felt Hat	12.00
Thimble Holder, Thimble, Sweetgrass, Sterling Silver	45.00
Thimble, 14K Gold–Lined Case	125.00
Thimble, Onkins Laundry, Aluminum Color	5.00
Thimble, Red Glass, Cola Advertising	25.00
Thimble, Round Oak Ranges & Furnaces, Blue Band	35.00
Thimble, Sterling Silver, House Scene	30.00
Thread Caddy, Ebonized Trim, Turned Hardwood, 9 1/2 In.	90.00
Yarn Winder, Oak, Handmade Wood Gears, Pegs, Counter	450.00

Shaker–produced items are characterized by simplicity, functionalism, and orderliness. There were many Shaker communities in America from the eighteenth century to the present day. The religious order made furniture, small wooden pieces, and packaged medicines, herbs, and jellies to sell to *outsiders*. Other useful objects were made for use by members of the community. Shaker furniture is listed in this book under Furniture.

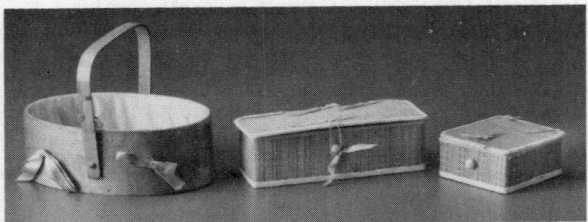

Shaker, Basket, Serving,   *Shaker, Box, Sewing,*   *Shaker, Box, Sewing,*
Splint, Sabbathday Lake, 7 In.   *Sabbathday Lake,*   *Sabbathday Lake,*
                                         2 1/2 x 7 In.   *3 1/2 x 3 1/2 In.*

SHAKER, Almanac, 1886, Predictions, Chronological Events, 32 Pages .... 60.00 To 85.00
  Basket, Gathering, Black Ash, Square, Signed Seed Shop, 24 In. 605.00
  Basket, Pincushion Top, Hinged Lid, S. A. W., Date 1814, 4 1/2 In. 650.00
  Basket, Pink Ribbon, 10 In. 35.00
  Basket, Serving, Splint, Sabbathday Lake, 7 In. ....*Illus* 660.00
  Basket, Sewing, White Liner, Woven Splint, Rim Handles, 12 In. 145.00
  Basket, Splint, Cover, Signed Denison, Rectangular, 12 In. 330.00
  Bonnet, Blue Ribbon, Liner 225.00
  Bonnet, Red Ribbon 145.00
  Book Press, Enfield, Conn. 775.00
  Box Set, Oval, Graduated, Natural Varnish, 2 3/4 To 13 1/2 In., 6 Pc. 2200.00
  Box, 1–Finger, Red & Black Graining, Oval, 5 3/4 In. 425.00
  Box, 2–Finger, All Natural, 7 3/4 In. 200.00
  Box, 2–Finger, Painted Top, 11 1/2 In. 300.00
  Box, 3–Finger, Copper Tacks, Yellow Paint, 5 1/2 In. 250.00
  Box, 4–Finger, Fitted Cover, Canterbury, Oval, 8 1/4 In. 605.00
  Box, Cinnamon Red, 8 3/4 In. 990.00
  Box, Copper Fasteners, Wooden Pinned, 1 x 2 1/2 x 3 1/2 In. 330.00
  Box, Finger Construction, Copper Tacks, D. C. Wilson, c.1875, 4 In. 225.00
  Box, Harvard Type, Copper Tacks, Paint Traces, Oval, 6 1/4 In. 165.00
  Box, Pumpkin Orange, 5 3/4 In. 2200.00
  Box, Sabbathday Lake, Mahogany, Rosewood & Figured Maple, 11 In. 45.00
  Box, Seed, 2 Divided & Hinged Lids, Curly Maple, 38 1/4 In. 750.00
  Box, Seed, Paper Label 1100.00
  Box, Sewing, 2 Drawers, Thread Caddy, Pincushion, Cherry, 8 3/4 In. 160.00
  Box, Sewing, Blue Damask Lining, Accessories, Bentwood, 6 3/4 In. 400.00
  Box, Sewing, Sabbathday Lake, 2 1/2 x 7 In. ....*Illus* 220.00
  Box, Sewing, Sabbathday Lake, 3 1/2 x 3 1/2 In. ....*Illus* 159.00
  Box, Sewing, Sabbathday Lake, Wallpaper & Cloth Lined, 11 1/4 In. 115.00
  Box, Storage, Blue Paint 770.00
  Box, Winnow, 1830 .... 685.00
  Broadside, Shaker's Dried Sweet Corn, Color 1900.00
  Brush, Multicolored, 14 1/21 In. 175.00
  Butter Tub, Turquoise Paint, 2 Iron Wraps, c.1830, Pine, 10 1/2 In. 9000.00
  Dibbler Board, Hand–Hewn Pegs, 12 Pins, 67 In. 130.00
  Dipper, Maple, 19th Century, 7 1/4 In. 500.00
  Dipper, Maple, 19th Century, 7 x 6 In. 550.00
    SHAKER, FURINITURE, see Furniture
  Hanger, Cloak 95.00
  Hanger, Wooden, Curved Design, EJ Paper Label, 13 In. 150.00
  Loom, New Lebanon, Signed Sister Sarah Neale 3575.00
  Measure, Mt. Lebanon, N. Y. 175.00
  Pen Wipe, Doll's 85.00
  Pie Lifter, Wire, Wooden Handle, 13 1/2 In. 55.00
  Rack, Drying, Pine, Rose Paint Over Mustard, 37 In. 2310.00
  Rolling Pin, Enfield 145.00
  Shuttle, Weaving 110.00
  Stove, Cast Iron, Enfield, N. H. 1100.00
  Sunbonnet, Woven Poplar, Paper Label, No. 8, On Stand, 10 In. 135.00
  Swift, Cup Top, Table Mount, Hancock, Mass., Elder Thomas Damon 600.00

Shaving mugs were popular from 1860 to 1900. Many types were made, including occupational mugs featuring pictures of men's jobs. There were scuttle mugs, silver plated mugs, glass–lined mugs, and others.

SHAVING MUG, Cat's Head, Red & Gold Trim, Script Name George, China 150.00
  Civil War Veteran, Victory Medal Dated 1861–66 .... 395.00
  Columbian Exposition, Machinery Hall, Ceramic 175.00
  Fraternal, United American Machinists, T–Square, Calipers 165.00
  Occupational, Artist, Palette, Paints & Brushes, Name In Gold 365.00
  Occupational, Banjo Player, 1870s 350.00
  Occupational, Bartender, 2 Customers, Name 195.00
  Occupational, Bartender, C. F. C. Foster, Customers At Bar 412.50

Occupational, Bartender, Customer In Bowler Hat, Gold Name 650.00
Occupational, Bartender, Customers, Crates of Bottles 450.00
Occupational, Baseball Player, Lew Jones, Hat, Glove 1210.00
Occupational, Brick Maker, Working At Table 1050.00
Occupational, Bridge Builder, Mountain, Gold Lettering, 1890 .... 265.00
Occupational, Coachman, Man In Top Hat, Lantern, Gold Name 595.00
Occupational, Farmer & Cow, Name In Gold 1200.00
Occupational, Farmer Driving Horses, Blue Flowers, Gold Trim 175.00
Occupational, Farmer, Milk Can, Cows In Pasture, Name, Vienna 195.00
Occupational, Firefighter's Equipment, 2 Men, Cobalt Blue 250.00
Occupational, Judge Stanley In Gold 150.00
Occupational, Machine Operator, Koken 750.00
Occupational, Stone Mason, JD Gross 770.00
Rhinoceros Head, Victorian 125.00

The Shawnee Pottery was started in Zanesville, Ohio, in 1935. The
company made vases, novelty ware, flowerpots, figurines,
dinnerwares, and cookie jars. Shawnee produced pottery for George
Rumrill during the late 1930s. The company stopped working in
1961.

SHAWNEE, Bank, Bulldog 65.00
Bank, Smiley 135.00
Bank, Tumbling Bear .... 55.00 To 75.00
Basket, Oriental 5.00
Bowl, Corn King, 6 1/2 In. 25.00
Bowl, Mixing, Corn King, Set of 3 .... 45.00
Butter, Cover, Corn King .... 36.00 To 42.00
Casserole, Corn King, 11 1/2 In. 48.00
Casserole, Corn King, Cover .... 40.00 To 45.00
Cookie Jar & Bank, Winnie Pig 175.00
Cookie Jar, Amish Hearts & Flowers 85.00
Cookie Jar, Basket of Fruit 75.00
Cookie Jar, Drummer Boy, Gold Trim 450.00
Cookie Jar, Dutch Boy, Blue Pants .... 45.00 To 65.00
Cookie Jar, Dutch Girl 185.00
Cookie Jar, Dutch Girl, Gold Trim .... 125.00 To 140.00
Cookie Jar, Dutch Girl, Named Cooky 170.00
Cookie Jar, Dutch Girl, With Tulip 70.00
Cookie Jar, Dutch Girl, Yellow Shirt 30.00
Cookie Jar, Elephant, Pink 48.00
Cookie Jar, Farmer Pig, With Tulips 95.00
Cookie Jar, Great Northern Dutch Boy 149.00
Cookie Jar, Great Northern Dutch Girl 149.00
Cookie Jar, Mugsy .... 130.00 To 185.00
Cookie Jar, Owl .... 50.00 To 57.00
Cookie Jar, Puss 'N Boots .... 60.00 To 85.00
Cookie Jar, Puss 'N Boots, Decals, Gold Trim 145.00
Cookie Jar, Sailor Boy .... 40.00 To 75.00
Cookie Jar, Salt & Peppers, Owl, 3 Piece 100.00
Cookie Jar, Smiley Pig, Green Clovers 125.00
Cookie Jar, Smiley Pig, Red–Orange Collar 70.00
Cookie Jar, Winking Owl 75.00
Cookie Jar, Winking Owl, Gold Trim .... 60.00 To 105.00
Cookie Jar, Winnie Pig, Green Collar .... 70.00 To 100.00
Cookie Jar, Yellow, With Flowers, Hexagon Shape 25.00
Creamer, Cat 20.00
Creamer, Corn King .... 15.00 To 18.00
Creamer, Elephant .... 15.00 To 16.00
Creamer, Elephant, Gold Deal 75.00
Creamer, Smiley Pig, Red Scarf, Clover Bud 45.00
Creamer, Smiley Pig, Yellow, Blue Bib 35.00
Darner, Woman, Label 18.00
Figurine, Baby Shoe, Blue 5.00

Figurine, Boy At Stump	8.00
Figurine, Elf On Shoe	8.00
Figurine, Gazelle, Black	40.00
Jug, Corn King	15.00
Mug, Corn King	30.00
Mug, Pistol Grip Handle, Hershey Park, Pa., 5 In.	27.00
Pitcher, Bopeep, Gold Trim & Flowers	85.00
Pitcher, Bopeep, Lavender Bonnet	60.00
Pitcher, Bopeep, White	75.00
Pitcher, Chanticleer Rooster	45.00
Pitcher, Corn King	45.00
Pitcher, Little Boy Blue	65.00
Pitcher, Smiley, Large	45.00
Planter, 4 Birds, Perched, Glazed	18.00
Planter, Bicycle For Two	15.00
Planter, Bow Knot	14.00
Planter, Boy, At High Stump	9.00
Planter, Clown	8.00
Planter, Crib	10.00
Planter, Deer	12.00
Planter, Doe & Fawn, Green Base	85.00
Planter, Doe & Fawn, Yellow & Green	6.00
Planter, Duck, Pulling Cart	8.00
Planter, Dutch Children At Well	15.00
Planter, Elephant, White	8.00
Planter, Elf On Shoe	8.00
Planter, Elf's Shoe, Gold Trim	10.00
Planter, Fawn, Black	7.00 To 15.00
Planter, Gazelle's Head, Black, 10 In.	17.00
Planter, Giraffe	22.00
Planter, Horse, Red	19.00
Planter, Little Skunk, Green	9.50
Planter, Little Skunk, Pink	9.50
Planter, Man Pushing Cart, Rum Carioca Advertising	25.00
Planter, Piano, Green	10.00
Planter, Polynesian Girl	16.00
Planter, Pump	12.00
Planter, Pup, Yellow, On Shoe	10.00
Planter, Squirrel, Pulling Nut	11.00
Planter, Toy Horse	14.00
Planter, Wagon, Covered, Bronze	18.00
Planter, Wheelbarrow	14.00
Planter, Windmill	12.00
Plate, Amish Sayings & Pictures, 9 In.	15.00
Plate, Corn King, 10 In.	15.00 To 28.00
Relish, Corn King, 4 Sections	20.00 To 22.00
Salt & Pepper, Cat	20.00
Salt & Pepper, Chanticleer	18.00
Salt & Pepper, Corn King, Large	17.00 To 32.00
Salt & Pepper, Corn King, Small	10.00 To 12.00
Salt & Pepper, Dutch Boy & Girl	10.00 To 25.00
Salt & Pepper, Milk Can	5.00
Salt & Pepper, Mugsy, Large	35.00 To 59.00
Salt & Pepper, Mugsy, Small	20.00 To 25.00
Salt & Pepper, Owl	10.00
Salt & Pepper, Puss 'N Boots	20.00
Salt & Pepper, Rooster, Large	13.00
Salt & Pepper, Sailor Boy, Gold Trim	25.00
Salt & Pepper, Smiley Pig	15.00 To 20.00
Salt & Pepper, Smiley Pig, Burgundy Scarf	30.00
Salt & Pepper, Smiley, Green, Large	35.00
Salt & Pepper, Smiley, Red, Large	35.00
Salt & Pepper, Winking Owl	12.00 To 15.00

Salt Box, Lid, Embossed Flowers, Buff Color 45.00
Shaker, Corn King, Large 20.00
Shaker, Corn King, Small 12.00
Shaker, Flower Lady 7.00
Shaker, Mugsy, Large 20.00
Sugar & Creamer, Corn King, Cover 45.00
Sugar Shaker, Corn Queen, White 45.00
Sugar, Corn King 20.00
Sugar, Corn Queen 25.00
Sugar, Cover, Corn King 20.00
Sugar, Cover, Corn Queen, White 30.00
Sugar, Kitty 15.00
Sugar, Pig 15.00
Sugar, Water Bucket 28.00
Teapot, Corn King, Individual 75.00
Teapot, Corn Queen 45.00
Teapot, Daisy, Pink 20.00
Teapot, Granny Ann .... 45.00 To 60.00
Teapot, Old Lady 90.00
Teapot, Tom, Tom, The Piper's Son .... 35.00 To 60.00
Teapot, Tulip 20.00
Vase, Bud, Yellow 5.00
Vase, Dolphin, Beige 14.00
Vase, Ivy 35.00
Vase, Pink, 10 In. 8.00
Vase, Tulip 8.00
Vase, Wall, Telephone 12.00
Wall Pocket, Girl & Doll 15.00

The Shearwater pottery is a family business started by Mr. and Mrs. G. W. Anderson, Sr., and their three sons. The local Ocean Springs, Mississippi, clays were used to make the wares in the 1930s. The company is still in business.

SHEARWATER, Bowl, Blue Drip Over Brown, 5 1/2 In. 50.00
Bowl, Lily Pad, Reticulated, Green & Gun Metal, Squat, 4 x 8 In. 752.00

Sheet music from the past centuries is now collected. The favorites are examples with covers featuring artistic or historic pictures. Early sheet music covers were lithographed but by the 1900s photographic reproductions were used. The early music was larger than more recent sheets and you must watch out for examples that were trimmed to fit in a twentieth-century piano bench.

SHEET MUSIC, 11th Hour Melody, Blacks, Al Hibbler Cover, 1958 .... 20.00
Alexander, Don't You Love Your Baby No More?, Blacks, 1910 .... 32.50
Andy Gump 40.00
Aunt Jemima Pancakes, 1925 .... 25.00
Barney Google, Barney & Spark Plug On Cover, 1923 .... 35.00
Barney Google, Barney On Spark Plug, 1923 .... 20.00
Barney Google, Operatic Edition, 1923 .... 25.00
Book, Army, Navy & Marines, Andrews Sisters, 64 Pgs., 9 x 12 In. 17.50
Book, Joy To The World, Sacred Songs, 1878 .... 12.50
Book, Old Time Ballads & Cowboys Songs, Loye Pack, 1930s 15.00
Bromo Seltzer, Early 1900 .... 9.00
Can't Help But Falling In Love, Elvis Presley 25.00
Captain Lindy of The U. S. A., 1927 .... 25.00
Carry Me Back To Old Virginny, Bland, 1906 .... 10.00
Cherry Pink & Apple Blossom White, Jane Russell On Cover 12.00
Down On The Levee, 6 Pages, 1912 .... 125.00
Down The Trail of The Old Dirt Road 9.50
Gentlemen Prefer Blondes, Marilyn Monroe 30.00
Gold Dust Twins, Forster Music Publisher, 10 3/4 x 13 3/4 In. 55.00
Gone With The Wind, 1937 .... 28.00
Home On The Range, 1932 .... 8.50

I Want My Mammy, Eddie Canter, 1921	23.00
I'm A Long Way From Tipperary	9.50
Just Like Washington Crossed The Delaware	9.50
Keep A Little Blue Star, Heart Design, 1944	12.50
Love Is A Song, Bambi	25.00
MacArthur The Man, Picture On Cover, 1942	15.00
Mammy's Lullaby, Night Scene, 1908	35.00
Maple Leaf Rag, Scott Joplin, 1899	65.00
Morning Song, By Mozart, 9 x 13 In.	65.00
Movie, Bus Stop, Marilyn Monroe Photo, 1956	40.00
Old Crow Rag, Crow Design, 1909	17.50
Paper Doll, Mills Brothers, Cutout Paper Doll, 1953	22.00
Perfect Song, Amos 'N Andy, 1929	25.00
R & H Beer, Staten Island, N. Y., 1941	20.00
Short'nin' Bread, Mammy Scene, 1920	40.00
Silver Wings In The Moonlight, Clarence Fuhrman Picture, 1943	12.50
Skippy	25.00
Someday They're Coming Home Again	9.50
Space Patrol	35.00
Spirit of France, E. T. Paull, 1919	25.00
Summer Madness, Autographed, Salvatore Billeci, 1943	15.00
Sunday, Monday Or Always, Dixie, Bing Crosby, D. Lamour, 1943	28.50
There's A Star Spangled Banner Waving Somewhere, 1942	10.00
There's No One But You, Rita Hayworth On Cover	20.00
Tumbling Tumbleweeds	7.50
Wreck of The Titanic, Clipping of Capt. Smith	82.50

SHEFFIELD, see Silver–English; Silver Plate

The name *Shelley* first appeared on English ceramics about 1912. The Foley China Works started in England in 1860. Joseph Ball Shelley joined the company in 1862 and became a partner in 1872. Percy Shelley joined the firm in 1881. The company went through a series of name changes and in 1910 the then Foley China Company became Shelley China. In 1929 it became Shelley Potteries. The company was acquired in 1966 by Allied English Potteries, then merged with the Doulton group in 1971. The name *Shelley* was put into use again in 1980.

SHELLEY, Butter, Cover, White, Gold Design	60.00
Cake Plate, Rosebud, 6 Flutes	68.00
Coffeepot, 6 Flutes, 6 1/2 In.	128.00
Cup & Saucer, Begonia, After Dinner	38.00
Cup & Saucer, Blue Rock	30.00
Cup & Saucer, Coffee, Dainty White	35.00
Cup & Saucer, Daffodil Time	40.00
Cup & Saucer, Dainty Blue	42.00
Cup & Saucer, Hedgerow Pattern	40.00
Cup & Saucer, Melody, Allover Floral, Green	42.00
Cup & Saucer, Pink & Blue, Gold Trim, 12 Scallops, After Dinner	38.00
Cup & Saucer, Thistle	30.00
Cup & Saucer, White, Gold Design	35.00
Cup & Saucer, Wildflowers, Demitasse	40.00
Dish, Crested, Ruffled, 6 In.	32.00
Eggcup, Linear Design, White–Gold Trim	35.00
Place Setting, Shell, Pink, 3 Piece	85.00
Plate, Bramble, 6 1/2 In.	12.00
Plate, Bridal Rose, 8 1/4 In.	20.00
Plate, Chelsea, 7 In.	12.00
Plate, Dainty White, 6 In.	15.00
Plate, Regency, Small	14.00
Plate, Rosebud, 6 In.	15.00
Saucer, Blue Rock, After Dinner	10.00
Saucer, Bramble	8.00
Saucer, Wildflowers, Oleander Shape	8.00

Soap Dish, Butterfly Design, 3 Piece 75.00
Sugar & Creamer, Allover Floral, Yellow, Miniature 30.00
Sugar & Creamer, Rosebud 45.00
Vase, Cloisonne Design, Blue, 5 In. 32.50

 Shirley Temple, the famous movie star, was born in 1928. She made her first movie in 1932. Thousands of items picturing Shirley have been and still are being made. Shirley Temple dolls were first made in 1934 by Ideal Toy Company. Millions of Shirley Temple cobalt blue glass dishes were made by Hazel Atlas Glass Company and U.S. Glass Company from 1934 to 1942. They were given away as premiums for Wheaties and Bisquick. A bowl, mug, and pitcher were made as a breakfast set. Some pieces were decorated with the picture of a very young Shirley, others used a picture of Shirley in her 1936 *Captain January* costume. Although collectors refer to a cobalt creamer it is actually the 4 1/2 inch high milk pitcher from the breakfast set. Many of these items are being reproduced today.

SHIRLEY TEMPLE, Ad, Photo, Quaker Puffed Wheat 6.00
Book, 6th Birthday, Paper Dolls, Puzzles, Toys, Uncut 65.00
Book, Big Little Book, Rebel 45.00
Book, Birthday, Paper Dolls, Toys, Etc. 95.00
Book, How I Raised Shirley Temple, Told To M. Sharon, 1935 .... 50.00
Book, Stories That Never Grow Old, Photograph On Back, 1958 .... 12.00
Booklet, Story of My Life, Premium, 1934 .... 40.00
Bowl, Cobalt Blue 25.00
Buggy, Doll's, Wooden, Dark Blue, Decals, Name On 3 Wheels 400.00
Cake Topper, Happy Birthday 75.00
Card, Arcade, 1970s, Set of 6 Different 3.00
Doll, 15 In. 230.00
Doll, 1950s, 36 In. 1250.00
Doll, 1950s, Original Box & Pin 235.00
Doll, 1984, 36 In. 325.00
Doll, All Original, 1972, 16 In. 55.00
Doll, Captain January, Ideal, Box 85.00
Doll, Captain January, Ideal, Box, 1982, 12 In. 45.00
Doll, Composition, 13 In. 285.00
Doll, Composition, Blond Wig, Open Mouth, Ideal, 17 In. 82.00
Doll, Composition, Ideal, 20 In. 225.00
Doll, Cowboy Clothes, 1930s, 11 In. 875.00
Doll, Dressed, Photo Pin, 18 In. 200.00
Doll, Ideal, 1972 .... 90.00
Doll, Original Clothes, 1957, 12 In. 95.00
Doll, Pink Organdy Dress, 1930s, 18 In. 750.00
Doll, Sailor Clothes, 1930s, 15 In. 675.00
Doll, Sleep Eyes, Open Mouth, Sailor Dress, Ideal, 12 In. 49.50
Doll, Vinyl, 1972, 16 In. 65.00
Fountain Pen, Brown, Glittery Gold Threads 65.00
Mirror, Pocket 25.00
Paper Doll, Polly & Molly, Fancy Dress, 1943, Uncut 30.00
Paper Dolls, Cut 35.00
Paper Dolls, Teen Age, Cut 65.00
Photograph, Merry Christmas, 1934 .... 45.00
Pitcher, Cobalt Blue .... 30.00 To 35.00
Pitcher, Cobalt Blue, 4 1/2 In. 10.00
Poster, Blue Bird, Nigel Bruce, Fox, 1940, 27 x 41 In. 1000.00
Poster, Happy New Year, Clock Face, 1937, 11 x 16 1/2 In. 50.00

◆◆◆

Beware of fire. Never put a heavy object on top of an extension cord. Never put the cord under a rug.

◆◆◆

Poster, Rebecca of Sunnybrook Farm, Fox, 27 x 4 1/2 In.	975.00
Poster, Wee Willie Winkie, Fox, 1937, 27 x 41 In.	1350.00
Print, Drink Milk Daily, 1938, 8 x 10 In.	8.00
Trade Card, Adventure In Baltimore, 2 Poses, Color	35.00

SHRINER, see Fraternal

Silver deposit glass was made during the late–nineteenth and early–0twentieth centuries. Solid sterling silver was applied to the glass by a chemical method so that a cutout design of silver metal appeared against a clear or colored glass. It is sometimes called silver overlay.

SILVER DEPOSIT, Bottle, Blue, Scrolled Overlay, 8 In.	75.00
Mug, Brown, Flowers, 6 In.	75.00
Vase, Black Amethyst, Parrot, Marked, Black Amethyst, Large	455.00
Vase, Black Amethyst, Roll–Over Rim, c.1930, 5 x 8 In.	55.00

Listed in this section are many of the current and out–of–production silver and silver plated flatware patterns made in the past eighty years. Other silver is listed under Silver–American, Silver–English, etc. Most silver flatware sets that are missing a few pieces can be completed through the help of one of the many silver matching services listed in *Kovels' Guide to Selling Your Antiques & Collectibles.*

SILVER FLATWARE PLATED, Adam, Olive Spoon, Pierced, Community	5.00
Alhambra, Dinner Fork, Community	3.00
American Beauty Rose, Knife, Holmes & Edwards	12.00
Arbutus, Dinner Knife	40.00
Avalon, Sugar Tongs, Community, 1903	20.00
Berkshire, Cold Meat Fork	25.00
Berkshire, Cream Ladle, 1847 Rogers	18.00
Berkshire, Sugar Tongs, 1847 Rogers	30.00
Bird of Paradise, Baby Spoon, Community	2.00
Brides Bouquet, Chipped Beef Fork	45.00
Carnation, Cream Ladle, 1847 Rogers	18.00
Carnation, Individual Butter	20.00
Charter Oak, Bouillon Spoon, 1847 Rogers	18.00
Charter Oak, Bread Knife	195.00
Charter Oak, Fruit Spoon, 1847 Rogers	20.00
Charter Oak, Salad Fork	18.00
Columbia, Pastry Server	25.00
Columbia, Salad Fork	18.00
Coronation, Baby Spoon & Fork, Community	8.00
Coronation, Carving Set, 2 Piece	46.00
Daffodil, Dinner Fork	6.50
Daffodil, Dinner Knife	7.50
Daffodil, Teaspoon	3.25
Eternally Yours, Iced Teaspoon	14.50
Eternally Yours, Service For 6, Rogers, 45 Piece	150.00
First Love, Berry Spoon, 1847 Rogers	25.00
First Love, Carving Set, 2 Piece	46.00
First Love, Meat Fork	14.00
First Love, Olive Fork	8.00
Floral, Salad Fork	12.00
Floral, Spreader	16.00
Floral, Teaspoon	7.00
Grenoble, Demitasse Spoon, Community	6.00
Grosvenor, Cold Meat Fork, Community	4.00
Grosvenor, Cream Ladle, Community	6.00
Grosvenor, Sugar Tongs, Community	20.00
Hanover, Fish Fork	8.00
Hanover, Mustard Ladle	65.00
Holly, Soup Ladle	45.00
Isabella, Cold Meat Fork	21.00
Jubilee, Carving Set, Rogers, 2 Piece	45.00

Jubilee, Soup Spoon, Oval, Rogers	4.50
Jubilee, Teaspoon, Rogers	3.50
La Vigne, Grapefruit Spoon	16.00
La Vigne, Salad Fork	24.00
La Vigne, Sugar Tongs	55.00
Laurel Mist, Berry Spoon, Rogers	18.00
Laurel Mist, Gravy Ladle, Rogers	15.00
Laurel Mist, Salad Fork, Rogers	8.00
Laurel Mist, Tablespoon, Rogers	9.00
Leilani, Teaspoon, Rogers	6.00
Melrose, Cheese Scoop, Wm. Rogers	20.00
Melrose, Jam Spoon, Wm. Rogers	15.00
Milady, Bonbon Spoon, Community	2.00
Modern Art, Egg Spoon	30.00
Moselle, Baby Spoon, Curved Handle	90.00
Moselle, Berry Spoon	35.00
Moselle, Cold Meat Fork	71.00
Moselle, Food Pusher	90.00
Moselle, Pickle Fork, Long Handle	85.00
Mystic, Cold Meat Fork	24.00
Nenuphar, Berry Fork	40.00
New Century, Meat Fork, Small, Community	3.00
Old Colony, Cake Lifter, Rogers	45.00
Old Colony, Chipped Beef Fork, Rogers	17.00
Old Colony, Ice Cream Fork	30.00
Old Colony, Soup Spoon, Round, Community	2.00
Old Colony, Tomato Server, Rogers	15.00
Orange Blossom, Cocktail Fork	9.00
Orange Blossom, Iced Tea Spoon	20.00
Orange Blossom, Sugar Tongs	60.00
Oxford, Pastry Server	12.00
Persian, Fish Knife	25.00
Remembrance, Iced Tea Spoon, 1847 Rogers	10.00
Remembrance, Steak Carving Set, 1847 Rogers	65.00
Rochambeau, Cold Meat Fork, International	20.00
Rochambeau, Soup Spoon, Oval, International	8.00
Rochambeau, Teaspoon, International	7.00
Rochambeau, Vegetable Spoon, Pierced, International	12.00
Savoy, Cake Fork	16.00
Shelburne, Meat Fork, Gorham	12.00
Shelburne, Pastry Fork, Gorham	10.00
Springtime, Iced Tea Spoon, Rogers	7.50
Springtime, Seafood Fork, Rogers	5.00
Springtime, Soup Spoon, Oval, Rogers	7.00
Springtime, Tomato Server, Rogers	18.00
Thistle, Iced Tea Spoon, Rogers & Bros.	15.00
Thistle, Salad Fork	28.00
Tiger Lily, Fork, Reed & Barton	7.00
Tiger Lily, Meat Fork, Reed & Barton	20.00
Tudor, Cucumber Server	25.00
Tudor, Knife, Rogers & Hamilton	8.00
Vesta, Knife, Hollow Handle	9.00
Vesta, Punch Ladle	75.00
Vintage, Berry Spoon	32.00
Vintage, Bouillon Spoon	18.00
Vintage, Cocktail Fork	18.00
Vintage, Ice Cream Fork	75.00
Vintage, Pastry Fork	38.00
Vintage, Tomato Server	80.00
Yale, Soup Ladle	75.00
SILVER FLATWARE STERLING, 1776, Sugar Spoon, Gorham	60.00
Aegean Weave, Luncheon Setting, Wallace, 4 Piece	75.00
Afterglow, Salad Fork, Oneida	20.00

Afterglow, Teaspoon, Oneida	14.00
Albermale, Ice Cream Fork, Gorham	17.00
Alexandra, Gravy Ladle, Lunt	70.00
America, Dessert Spoon, Wallace	15.00
Angelique, Luncheon Setting, International, 4 Pc.	70.00
Antique, Luncheon Setting, Wallace, 4 Piece	65.00
Arlington, Tablespoon, Towle	60.00
Autumn Leaves, Luncheon Setting, R & B, 4 Piece	75.00
Baronial, Citrus Spoon, Gorham	25.00
Bridal Rose, Butter Pick, Alvin	110.00
Bridal Rose, Cold Meat Fork, Alvin	90.00
Bridal Rose, Dinner Fork, Alvin	55.00
Bridal Rose, Dinner Knife, Alvin	65.00
Bridal Rose, Sardine Fork, Alvin	85.00
Bridal Rose, Sugar Tongs, Alvin	95.00
Bridal Veil, Cream Soup Spoon, International	18.00
Bridal Veil, Salad Fork, International	20.00
Buckingham, Cold Meat Fork, Gorham	35.00
Buttercup, Cheese Scoop, Gorham	250.00
Buttercup, Pastry Fork, Gorham	32.00
Buttercup, Serving Spoon, Gorham	50.00
Calvert, Salad Fork, Kirk	18.00
Cambridge, Dessert Spoon, Gorham	15.00
Candlelight, Citrus Spoon, Towle	21.00
Candlelight, Cream Soup Spoon, Towle	19.00
Candlelight, Ice Cream Fork, Towle	23.00
Candlelight, Lemon Fork, Towle	15.00
Candlelight, Napkin Clip, Towle	16.00
Celeste, Bonbon Spoon, Gorham	21.00
Celeste, Napkin Clip, Gorham	16.00
Celeste, Olive Fork, Gorham	11.00
Celeste, Sugar Spoon, Gorham	13.00
Celeste, Teaspoon, Gorham	12.00
Century, Dinner Fork, Dominick & Haff	20.00
Chambord, Salad Fork, Reed & Barton	15.00
Champlain, Service For 8, Amston, 48 Piece	984.00
Chantilly, Asparagus Fork, Gorham	495.00
Chantilly, Butter Knife, Gorham	15.00
Chantilly, Salad Fork, Gorham	25.00
Chantilly, Seafood Fork, Gorham	18.00
Chantilly, Service For 8, Gorham, 51 Piece	795.00
Chantilly, Soup Ladle, Gorham	295.00 To 325.00
Chantilly, Soup Spoon, Gorham	18.00
Chapel Bells, Baked Potato Server, Alvin	33.00
Chapel Bells, Cream Soup Spoon, Alvin	10.00
Chapel Bells, Service For 8, Alvin, 48 Piece	968.00
Chased Romantique, Butter Knife, Alvin	11.00
Chased Romantique, Cake Breaker, Alvin	29.00
Chased Romantique, Dessert Spoon, Alvin	15.00
Chased Romantique, Gumbo Soup Spoon, Alvin	19.00
Chased Romantique, Ice Cream Fork, Alvin	15.00
Chased Romantique, Iced Tea Spoon, Alvin	18.00
Chateau Rose, Pie Server, Alvin	29.00
Chateau Rose, Salad Fork, Alvin	19.00
Chatham, Citrus Spoon, Durgin	13.00
Chatham, Olive Fork, Durgin	20.00
Chatham, Serving Spoon, Durgin	41.00
Cheryl, Luncheon Setting, Kirk, 4 Piece	100.00
Chippendale, Jelly Server, Lunt	22.00
Chippendale, Sugar Spoon, Towle	18.00
Chrysanthemum, Cracker Scoop, Durgin	400.00
Chrysanthemum, Ladle, Gorham, 11 In.	250.00
Classic Rose, Jam Server, Reed & Barton	20.00

Classic Rose, Luncheon Setting, R & B, 4 Piece	75.00
Classic Rose, Teaspoon, Reed & Barton	13.00
Classique, Cheese Server, Gorham	18.00
Cluny, Fork & Spoon, Gorham	465.00
Colbert, Teaspoon, Frank Smith	9.00
Colonial, Demitasse Teaspoon, Gorham	25.00
Colonial, Gravy Ladle, Gorham	150.00
Commonwealth, Citrus Spoon, Watson	9.00
Contessina, Fork, Towle	18.00
Contessina, Knife, Towle	18.00
Corsage, Luncheon Setting, Stieff, 4 Piece	90.00
Corsage, Youth Fork, Stieff	18.00
Cottage, Teaspoon, Gorham	30.00
Da Vinci, Dinner Fork, Reed & Barton	15.00
Damask Rose, Service For 12, Oneida, 64 Piece	895.00
Devonshire, Coffee Spoon, International	12.00
Devonshire, Sugar Tongs, International	14.00
Duke of Windsor, Luncheon Fork, Manchester	15.00
Egyptian, Berry Spoon, Gorham	375.00
Egyptian, Ice Cream Server, Gorham	475.00
Empire, Berry Spoon, Durgin	125.00
Empire, Luncheon Fork, Whiting	12.50
Empire, Meat Fork, Towle	34.00
Empire, Olive Spoon, Whiting	39.00
English King, Butter Knife, Tiffany	35.00
English King, Child's Spoon, Gorham	100.00
Etiquette, Bouillon Spoon, Watson	15.00
Etruscan, Fork, Gorham	15.00
Etruscan, Fruit Spoon, Gorham	13.00
Etruscan, Ice Cream Fork, Gorham	16.00
Fairfax, Citrus Spoon, Durgin	18.00 To 22.00
Fairfax, Service For 12, Durgin, 48 Piece	1188.00
Fairfax, Steak Knife, Durgin	24.00
Fairfax, Tablespoon, Durgin	39.00
Floral Lace, Service For 12, Lunt, 61 Piece	1400.00
Fontainebleau, Fork, Gorham	35.00
Francis I, Cheese Scoop, Reed & Barton	120.00
Francis I, Chocolate Spoon, Reed & Barton	50.00
Francis I, Food Pusher, Reed & Barton	50.00
Francis I, Fork, Reed & Barton, 7 In.	35.00
Francis I, Ice Cream Slice, Reed & Barton	495.00
Francis I, Jelly Trowel, Pierced, Reed & Barton	380.00
Francis I, Mustard Ladle, Reed & Barton	95.00
Francis I, Punch Ladle, Reed & Barton	695.00
Francis I, Sandwich Tongs, Reed & Barton	180.00
Francis I, Tea Strainer, Reed & Barton	495.00
Francis I, Vegetable Fork, Pierced, Reed & Barton	395.00
French Provincial, Pickle Fork, Towle	12.00
French Provincial, Tablespoon, Towle	30.00
French Provincial, Teaspoon, Towle	12.00
Frontenac, Aspargus Fork, International	395.00
Frontenac, Ice Cream Spoon, International	42.00
Frontenac, Olive Fork, Long, International	95.00
Frontenac, Olive Spoon, International	88.00
Gadroonette, Teaspoon, Manchester	9.00
Georgian Maid, Pastry Fork, International	10.00
Georgian Maid, Teaspoon, International	8.00
Governor's Lady, Service For 8, Gorham, 40 Piece	816.00
Grape, Salad Set, Dominick & Haff	495.00
Hamilton, Teaspoon, Alvin	8.00
Heiress, Teaspoon, Oneida	9.00
Hepplewhite, Demitasse Spoon, Reed & Barton	8.00
Hepplewhite, Sauce Ladle, Reed & Barton	30.00

Hepplewhite, Serving Fork, Reed & Barton 75.00
Hindostanee, Teaspoon, Gorham 48.00
Imperial Chrysanthemum, Berry Spoon, Gorham 75.00
Intermezzo, Dinner Fork, National 15.00
Irian, Dinner Fork, Wallace 28.00
Irian, Soup Spoon, Wallace 28.00
Iris, Butter Pick, Durgin 135.00
Iris, Gravy Ladle, Durgin 295.00
Iris, Sardine Fork, Durgin 195.00
Iris, Soup Ladle, Durgin 650.00
Japanese, Nut Pick, Gorham, 8 Piece 85.00
Joan of Arc, Cocktail Fork, International 22.00
Joan of Arc, Salad Fork, International 26.00
Joan of Arc, Sugar Shell, International 32.00
Joan of Arc, Tomato Server, International 75.00
Juliet, Demitasse Spoon, Wallace 8.00
King Cedric, Iced Tea Spoon, Oneida 15.00
King Edward, Salad Set, Whiting 350.00
King George, Salad Server, Gorham, Pair 520.00
King Richard, Dinner Set, Towle, 91 Piece 2200.00
King, Fish Slice, Dominick & Haff 150.00
La Parisienne, Serving Spoon, Reed & Barton 85.00
La Reine, Strawberry Fork, Reed & Barton, 6 Pc. 150.00
Labors of Cupid, Punch Ladle, Dominick & Haff 1900.00
Labors of Cupid, Salad Set, D & H .... 595.00 To 650.00
Lady Baltimore, Fish Fork, Whiting 75.00
Lady Diana, Service For 12, Towle, 48 Piece 960.00
Lafayette, Seafood Fork, Towle 8.00
Lancaster, Lettuce Fork, Gorham 75.00
Lancaster, Luncheon Fork, Gorham 12.00
Lancaster, Tablespoon, Gorham 25.00
Lancaster, Teaspoon, Gorham 7.00
Layfayette, Teaspoon, Towle .... 8.00 To 9.00
Lenore, Cocktail Fork, Manchester 15.00
Les Cinq Fleurs, Dinner Knife, Reed & Barton 37.50
Les Cinq Fleurs, Luncheon Fork, Reed & Barton 24.00
Les Cinq Fleurs, Master Butter, Reed & Barton 39.00
Les Cinq Fleurs, Salad Fork, Reed & Barton 45.00
Les Cinq Fleurs, Teaspoon, Reed & Barton 14.00
Lily of The Valley, Mustard, Whiting 135.00
Lily of The Valley, Nut Spoon, Whiting 65.00
Lily of The Valley, Tablespoon, Whiting 69.00
Lily, Berry Spoon, Whiting 300.00
Lily, Bonbon Spoon, Whiting 110.00
Lily, Cheese Scoop, Whiting 450.00
Lily, Jelly Spoon, Whiting 150.00
Lily, Salad Set, Whiting 795.00
Lily, Tablespoon, Whiting 77.00
Lily, Teaspoon, Whiting 30.00
Lion, Sugar Spoon, Frank Smith 235.00
Louis XV, Caddy Spoon, Whiting 125.00
Louis XV, Cucumber Server, Whiting 65.00
Louis XV, Dinner Fork, Whiting 20.00
Louis XV, Fork, Whiting 14.00
Louis XV, Lemonade Muddler, Whiting 75.00
Louis XV, Lettuce Fork, Whiting 55.00
Louis XV, Olive Spoon, Pierced, Whiting 110.00
Louis XV, Serving Spoon, Whiting 125.00
Louis XV, Soup Ladle, Whiting 195.00
Louis XV, Teaspoon, Whiting 12.00
Louis XV, Teaspoon, Whiting, 5 1/4 In. 13.00
Luxembourg, Ice Cream Spoon, Gorham 30.00
Madame Morris, Luncheon Fork, Whiting 22.00

◆◆

Go outside and try to read your house numbers from the street. If
you can't read them, get new, larger ones. Police responding to an
emergency must be able to see the numbers in your address.

◆◆

Madame Royale, Citrus Spoon, Durgin	34.00
Madeira, Salad Fork, Towle	22.00
Madeira, Teaspoon, Towle	11.00
Madrigal, Pickle Fork, Lunt	24.00
Madrigal, Sugar Spoon, Lunt	22.00
Madrigal, Teaspoon, Lunt	15.00
Margaret Rose, Cream Soup Spoon, National	18.00
Margaret Rose, Dinner Knife, National	24.00
Margaret Rose, Teaspoon, National	15.00
Marlborough, Lemon Fork, Reed & Barton	17.00
Marlborough, Luncheon Knife, Whiting	15.00
Marlborough, Teaspoon, Reed & Barton	17.00
Mary Chilton, Luncheon Fork, Towle	24.00
Mary Chilton, Service For 8, Towle, 58 Piece	975.00
Mary Chilton, Soup Spoon, Oval, Towle	24.00
Mazarin, Claret Ladle, Dominic & Haff	75.00
Mazarin, Sugar Sifter, Dominic & Haff	95.00
Meadow Rose, Carving Set, Wallace	125.00
Meadow Rose, Cream Soup Spoon, Wallace	24.00
Meadow Rose, Tablespoon, Wallace	46.00
Medallion, Berry Spoon, Cutout & Etched, Gorham	475.00
Medallion, Berry Spoon, Gorham	275.00
Melrose, Jelly Server, Gorham	30.00
Melrose, Place Setting, Gorham, 8 Piece	87.00
Melrose, Salad Serving Fork, Gorham	90.00
Melrose, Service For 8, Gorham, 56 Piece	1300.00
Melrose, Sugar Spoon, Gorham	27.00
Milan, Sugar Shell, Gorham	29.00
Minuet, Dinner Knife, International	10.00
Minuet, Lemon Fork, International	6.00
Minuet, Luncheon Fork, International	21.00
Minuet, Salad Fork, International	10.00 To 20.00
Minuet, Spreader, International	8.00
Minuet, Teaspoon, International	6.00
Modern Victorian, Butter Spreader, Flat, Lunt	14.00
Modern Victorian, Luncheon Fork, Lunt	22.00
Modern Victorian, Pickle Fork, Lunt	24.00
Modern Victorian, Teaspoon, Lunt	16.00
Monticello, Baby Spoon, International	16.00
Monticello, Mustard Ladle, Lunt	55.00
Monticello, Olive Spoon, Lunt	39.00
Monticello, Sugar Spoon, International	20.00
Moonglow, Tablespoon, International	40.00
Mt. Vernon, Fork, Lunt	17.00 To 18.00
Mt. Vernon, Knife, Lunt	16.00
Mt. Vernon, Service For 12, Lunt, 80 Piece	1745.00
Newcastle, Dessert Spoon, Gorham	20.00
Norfolk, Fork, Gorham	38.00
Norfolk, Tablespoon, Gorham	36.00
Old Colonial, Asparagus Fork, Towle	575.00
Old Colonial, Gravy Ladle, Towle	55.00
Old French, Fruit Knife, Gorham	21.00
Old French, Teaspoon, Gorham	13.00
Old Master, Dinner Fork, Towle	35.00

Old Master, Teaspoon, Towle 16.00
Old Mirror, Butter Spreader, Towle 15.00
Old Mirror, Teaspoon, Towle 14.00
Old Newbury, Luncheon Fork, Towle 15.00
Old Newbury, Soup Spoon, Oval, Towle 11.00
Old Newbury, Teaspoon, Towle, 5 5/8 In. 8.00
Old Orange Blossom, Teaspoon, Alvin, 12 Piece 175.00
Olympian, Dessert Spoon, Tiffany 78.00
Orchid Elegance, Service For 8, Wallace, 48 Piece 1600.00
Orient, Luncheon Fork, Alvin 25.00
Pantheon, Tablespoon, International 33.00
Pilgrim, Dessert Spoon, Frank Smith 15.00
Plymouth, Olive Spoon, Pierced, Gorham 25.00
Poppy, Teaspoon, Gorham 18.50
Prelude, Service For 12, International, 64 Piece 1095.00
Princess Patricia, 8 Place, Durgin, 64 Piece 2200.00
Princess, Luncheon Knife, Manchester 15.00
Rapallo, Service For 8, Lunt, 48 Piece 760.00
Raphael, Teaspoon, Alvin 90.00
Renaissance Scroll, Service For 12, 88 Piece 1000.00
Repousse, Service For 8, Kirk, 47 Piece 1225.00
Repousse, Serving Fork, 5 Prongs, Kirk, 9 1/4 In. 185.00
Repousse, Toothpick, Kirk 40.00
Rococo, Cream Ladle, Dominick & Haff 55.00
Rococo, Dessert Spoon, Dominick & Haff 15.00
Rococo, Pastry Fork, Dominick & Haff, 12 Piece 480.00
Romantique, Service For 12, Alvin, 72 Piece 1440.00
Romantique, Teaspoon, Alvin 12.00
Rosalind, Oyster Fork, International 30.00
Rose, Ice Cream Fork, Wallace 24.00
Saxon Stag, Serving Spoon, Gorham, c.1855, Pair 550.00
Sea Rose, Sugar Spoon, Gorham 14.00
Sea Rose, Teaspoon, Gorham 13.00
Seville, Salad Fork, Towle 11.00
Silver Rhythm, Luncheon Knife, International 17.00
Silver Rhythm, Sugar Spoon, International 15.00
Silver Rhythm, Teaspoon, International 14.00
Skylark, Gravy Ladle, Kirk 50.00
Skylark, Salad Fork, Kirk 24.00
Skylark, Tea Spoon, Kirk 55.00
Sonja, Service For 8, International, 40 Piece 768.00
Spanish Baroque, Luncheon Knife, Reed & Barton 24.00
Spanish Baroque, Place Setting, R & B, 10 Piece 80.00
Spanish Baroque, Teaspoon, Reed & Barton 14.00
Spanish Lace, Salad Fork, Wallace 20.00
St. Cloud, Ice Cream Knife, Gorham 345.00
St. Cloud, Teaspoon, Gorham 30.00
Strasbourg, Beef Fork, Gorham 65.00
Strasbourg, Dinner Fork, Gorham 22.00
Strasbourg, Dinner Knife, Gorham 16.00
Strasbourg, Fork, Gorham 30.00
Strasbourg, Gravy Ladle, Gorham 55.00
Strasbourg, Nut Spoon, Gorham 32.00
Strasbourg, Salad Set, Gorham, 2 Piece 155.00
Strasbourg, Sardine Fork, Gorham 48.00
Strasbourg, Seafood Fork, Gorham 22.00
Strasbourg, Sugar Spoon, Gorham 20.00
Strasbourg, Teaspoon, Gorham 12.00
Stratford, Teaspoon, International 9.00
Stuart, Spoon, Gold Washed Bowl, Towle 40.00
Talisman Rose, Luncheon Knife, Whiting 13.00
Talisman Rose, Service For 12, Whiting, 60 Piece 1308.00
Tara, Luncheon Fork, Reed & Barton 28.00

Tara, Pie Server, Reed & Barton 24.00
Tara, Teaspoon, Reed & Barton .... 15.00 To 16.00
Trianon, Cream Soup Spoon, International 18.00
Tulip, Grapefruit Spoon, Durgin 22.00
Versailles, Dessert Spoon, Gorham 26.00
Versailles, Luncheon Fork, Gorham 35.00
Victoria, Fork, Whiting, 6 7/8 In. 10.00
Victoria, Knife, Whiting, 9 1/2 In. 13.00
Victoria, Service For 12, Whiting, 65 Piece 1375.00
Violet, Olive Fork, Wallace 30.00
Violet, Olive Spoon & Fork Set, Whiting 95.00
Virginia Carvel, Tablespoon, Towle 28.00
Virginian, Luncheon Knife, Oneida 20.00
Virginian, Salad Fork, Oneida 24.00
Waltz of Spring, Place Setting, Wallace, 8 Piece 90.00
Waltz of Spring, Sugar Spoon, Wallace 35.00
Wave Edge, Vegetable Spoon, Tiffany 75.00
Waverly, Egg Spoon, Wallace 25.00
Waverly, Ice Cream Fork, Wallace 25.00
Waverly, Lettuce Fork, Wallace 42.00
Waverly, Pusher, Wallace 50.00
Waverly, Sugar Sifter, Wallace 110.00
William & Mary, Coffee Spoon, Lunt 11.00
William & Mary, Lemon Fork, Lunt 11.00
William & Mary, Sugar Spoon, Lunt 14.00

Silver plate is not solid silver. It is a ware made of a metal, such as nickel or copper, that is covered with a thin coating of silver. The letters *EPNS* are often found on American and English silver plated wares. Sheffield silver is a type of silver plate.

SILVER PLATE, Basket, Repousse, Panels of Fruit, c.1870, 11 1/2 In. 187.00
Bowl, Center, Staffordshire Pattern, Reed & Barton, 15 1/2 In. 140.00
Bowl, Fruit, Openwork, Pairpoint, Dark Green Glass Liner 90.00
Bowl, Raised Grape & Leaves, Pairpoint, 9 1/2 x 5 1/2 x 5 In. 95.00
Box, Sardine, Etched Glass Insert, 8 In. 220.00
Butter, Cover, Cow & Maiden Inside, Wilcox, 7 x 9 In. 225.00
Cake Basket, Footed, Florals, Tufts 50.00
Cake Stand, Cutout Geometrics, Gallery, Pairpoint, 9 1/2 In. 110.00
Candelabrum, 3–Light Scroll Arms, Sheffield, 19 1/2 In., Pair 175.00
Candelabrum, 3–Light, Removable Arms, Convert To Candlesticks 825.00
Candelabrum, 3–Light, Sheffield, 1930s, 24 1/2 In., Pair 495.00
Candlesnuffer & Tray, Sheffield, 9 In. 395.00
Candlestick, 2–Light, Child Holding Stem, Pair 195.00
Candlestick, Rib Molded Rim, M. Boulton, 11 1/4 In., 4 Piece 1500.00
Card Receiver, Figural Kate Greenaway Girl & Dog On Top 190.00
Castor Set, Revolving, Gothic 1150.00
Champagne Bucket, Regency Style, 7 1/2 In. 187.00
Cocktail Shaker, Hammered, Tail Feathers Form Handle, Wallace 4950.00
Coffee & Tea Set, Cube, T. W. & S. Leicester, c.1925, 6 Piece 1650.00
Compote, Beaded & Scrolled Base, Medallions of Busts, 9 In. 525.00
Compote, Center, Allover Raised Fruit & Floral, Meriden, 8 In. 125.00
Compote, Indians Hunting Buffalo, Reed & Barton, c.1875 .... 165.00
Compote, Raised Fruit & Floral Overall, Meriden, 8 In. 137.50
Cup, Child's, Alphabet 22.00
Cup, Humpty Dumpty, c.1910 .... 25.00
Cup, Wine Taster's, Snake Handle, Duck's Head 40.00
Dish, Serving, Pierced Oval Form, Garrard Sheffield, 18 In. 160.00
Dish, Vegetable, Cover, Chased Acanthus Design, Irish, c.1900 .... 110.00
Epergne, England, 1910 .... 630.00
Epergne, George II, Irish Style, Lion Masks, 31 3/4 In. 3300.00
Epergne, Victorian, 4 Wide–Mouth Flutes 895.00
Garniture, Classical Revival, Goldsmiths & Silversmiths Co. 2475.00
Holder, Calling Card, Cupid In Boat 40.00

Holy Water Font, The Assumption, German, c.1900, 13 In. 225.00
Ice Bucket, Engraved Polar Bear, Icebergs, Pairpoint, 5 In. 175.00
Ice Bucket, Engraved Vintage Pattern, Pairpoint, 7 x 6 In. 175.00
Inkstand, Double Ram's Horn, Walker & Hall, 21 In. 1800.00
Kettle, Cannonball, Brass Footed, England, 18th Century 1042.00
Kettle, Hot Water, Scroll, Floral & Foliate Design, 11 1/2 In. 130.00
Kettle, Hot Wine, Barrel, Finial Cover, Sheffield, 16 In. 2750.00
Kettle, Stand, Foliage, Inverted Pear Shape, c.1870, 17 In. 385.00
Mirror, Plateau, Cut Rosettes In Circle, Victorian, 18 In. 185.00
    SILVER PLATE, NAPKIN RING, see Napkin Ring
Pitcher, Hammered, Dragonfly & Flowers, Rogers, 10 1/4 In. 110.00
Punch Bowl, Underplate, Ladle, William Rogers 100.00
Rattle & Teething Ring, Figural, Teddy Bear 98.00
Server, Lazy Susan, Fitted With Containers, England, 25 In. 2975.00
    SILVER PLATE, SPOON, SOUVENIR, see Souvenir, Spoon, Silver Plate
Tea & Coffee Set, Bright Cutting, Pairpoint, 5 Piece 220.00
Tea & Coffee Set, Tray, Oneida Community, 13 Piece 1000.00
Tea Set, Bright Cut, James Tufts, 19th Century, 4 Piece 150.00
Tea Set, Heraldic Crest, Gilt Interiors, Sheffield, 3 Piece 440.00
Tea Set, Heritage Pattern, Rogers Bros., 5 Piece 335.00
Tea Set, Remembrance, Rogers, 5 Piece 475.00
Tea Strainer, Hampden, Rogers, 1916 .... 15.00
Teaball, Teapot Shape, Underplate 45.00
Teapot & Spoon Holder, Brite-Cut Flowers, Rogers 1883 .... 80.00
Toast Rack, England, 1870 .... 230.00
Tray, Calling Card, Oak Branches, Butterfly, Tufts, 7 x 9 In. 235.00
Tray, Engraved Design, Cherub Handles, American, c.1870, 27 In. 405.00
Tray, Floral Design, Etched Center, Scrolled Feet, 27 In. 130.00
Tray, Gadrooned, Acanthus & Floral Handles, Sheffield, 31 In. 1045.00
Tray, Loop Handles, Gadrooned Border, Sheffield, 28 1/2 In. 110.00
Tray, Pierced Border, Shellwork, 2 Handles, Sheffield, 29 In. 1350.00
Tray, Pierced Gallery, Incised Acanthus Leaf, 20 1/4 In. 137.50
Tureen, Cow's Handle & Finial, Reed & Barton ....*Illus* 500.00
Tureen, Soup, Cover, Bombe, Oval, Sheffield, 1830, 15 1/4 In. 2860.00
Urn, Sheffield, Scroll Handle, Acanthus Leaf & Gadroon, 13 In. 375.00
Vase, Art Nouveau, Relief Maiden & Water Nymph, c.1900, 22 In. 1760.00
Wagon, 4 Wheels, Attached Bowls, 13 x 3 In. 45.00
Wine Cooler, Compana Form, Rococo Ornament, Sheffield, 10 In. 2310.00
    SILVER, SHEFFIELD, see Silver Plate; Silver–English

The silver listed in this book is subdivided by country. Silver–American is the first listing, followed by Silver–Austrian, Silver–Canadian, Silver–Chinese, Silver–Danish, etc. There are also other pieces of silver and silver plate listed under special categories.

SILVER–AMERICAN, see also Napkin Ring; Silver Plate; Silver Flatware; Silver–Sterling; Tiffany Silver
SILVER–AMERICAN, Beaker, Coin, S. Best, 1790, 3 1/8 In. 5060.00

Silver Plate, Tureen, Cow's Handle & Finial,
Reed & Barton

Silver–American, Bowl, Bud & Vine Border, Marshall Field, 10 In.

Silver–American, Cup, Gothic, Coin, c.1850
Silver–American, Jug, Cream, Repousse, Coin, T. E. Co., c.1855
Silver–American, Cup, Coin, Footed, 1850–1855
Silver–American, Cup, Coin, Cylindrical

Bell, Old Florentine Bell, Ivory Handle, Gorham, 6 In.	300.00
Berry Spoon, Ivory Handle, Whiting, 10 In.	450.00
Bowl & Tongs, Condiment, Hollowed Fruit Form, Gorham, 1906	715.00
Bowl, 3 Curved Feet, Flared, Gebelein, 2 1/8 x 6 In.	165.00
Bowl, Bud & Vine Border, Marshall Field, 10 In. ....*Illus*	700.00
Bowl, Chrysanthemum Blossoms, Black, Starr & Frost, 11 In.	495.00
Bowl, Everted Foliate Rim, Gorham, 1906	350.00
Bowl, Everted Rim, Grapevine Pierced, Mauser, c.1900, 5 In.	5250.00
Bowl, Flared Rim, Chased Floral & Lime, Arthur Stone, 8 In.	1100.00
Bowl, Floral & Vintage Design, S. Kirk & Son, 10 3/4 In.	1850.00
Bowl, Flowering Branches, Galt & Bros., c.1900, 11 3/8 In.	1980.00
Bowl, Fluted Panels, Handles, Kalo Shop, c.1915, 8 5/8 In.	1320.00
Bowl, Footed, Monogrammed, Arthur Stone, 5 1/4 In.	550.00
Bowl, Fruit, Floral Repousse, F. Smith, 8 1/2 In.	440.00
Bowl, Hammered Pierced Oval, Crystal Liner, Shreve, 5 In.	305.00
Bowl, Hammered, 4 Plaques, R. Wallace, 2 x 4 5/8 In.	110.00
Bowl, Monogrammed, Frank W. Smith Silver Co., 9 3/4 In.	137.50
Bowl, Pierced & Chased Florals, Fuchs & Beiderhase, 10 In.	305.00
Bowl, Pierced With Lilies, Mauser, 12 In.	550.00
Bowl, Pinched 5 Sections, Arthur Stone, c.1918, 9 5/8 In.	440.00
Bowl, Repousse, 1920s, 13 x 10 In.	695.00
Bowl, Repousse, Rosebuds & Daisies, J. Caldwell, 7 In.	175.00
Bowl, Scrolls, Hammered, Lebkuecher, c.1925, 9 1/2 In.	495.00
Bowl, Swags & Cartouche Rim, Black, Starr & Frost, c.1920	412.00
Bread Tray, Chased Flowers, Everted Rim, Stieff, 13 In.	660.00
Bread Tray, Chased Flowers, Kirk, c.1930, 12 1/2 In.	275.00
Bread Tray, Foliate Spirals, Gorham, 15 In.	275.00
Buckle, Belt, Unger Bros.	125.00
Butter Knife, Floral Pattern, J. E. Caldwell, Master, c.1870	65.00
Butter, Cover, Floral Design, Lows, Ball & Co., 4 1/2 In.	475.00
Butter, Cover, Griffin Feet, Engraved Design	975.00
Butter, Cover, Plantation, Starr & Gorham, 7 x 3 In.	70.00
Cake Basket, Wood & Hughes, c.1845, 15 1/2 x 7 1/8 In.	1550.00
Cake Plate, Pierced Oak Leaf, Acorns, Gorham, c.1900, 9 In.	495.00
Candelabrum, 3–Arm, Frank Whiting, 14 In., Pair	450.00
Candelabrum, 5–Light, Art Mfg. Co., 1930s, 16 In.	695.00
Candelabrum, 5–Light, Foliate Pendants, Wallace, 16 In.	1710.00
Candlestick, Cylindrical, Curved Base, Towle, 8 3/8 In., Pr.	137.00
Carving Set, Swedish Modern, Allan Adler, 12 & 10 In., Pair	165.00
Case, Cigarette, Elgin, Box	65.00
Case, Cigarette, Elgin, Embossed Floral Border	70.00
Caster, Pierced Cover, Elias Pelletreau, 1760, 3 1/4 In.	3850.00
Centerpiece, Coin Silver, Handles, Gorham, 1850, 9 x 8 In.	850.00
Chalice, Kuchler & Himmel, Inscribed Hook, Ladder, c.1852	3400.00
Coaster, Wine, Theodore Starr, Treen Bottom, 6 In.	495.00
Coffee & Tea Set, Dominick & Hall, 7 Piece	4250.00
Coffee & Tea Set, Spaulding & Co., 4 Piece	1800.00

Coffee Set, Baroque, Wallace 3100.00
Coffee Set, Grapevines, Hammered, Gorham, c.1905, 4 Piece 2800.00
Coffee Set, Louis XIV, Tray, Gorham, 4 Piece 650.00
Coffeepot, Chased Foliage, Durgin, 11 In. 385.00
Coffeepot, Paneled Design, Black, Starr & Frost 165.00
Coffeepot, Pointed Finial, Spot-Hammered, Dominick & Haff 2450.00
Coffeepot, Serpentine Spout, George I. Welles, c.1800 .... 1350.00
Compote, Flowers, Scrolls, Black, Starr & Frost, 11 In., Pair 2530.00
Compote, Foliage, Grotesque Masks, Gorham, 10 5/8 In. 715.00
Compote, Pierced Borders, Lebkuecher & Co., 8 In. 110.00
Cream Ladle, E. Robinson, Rhode Island, c.1815 .... 75.00
Creamer, Faceted Body, Geradus Boyce, c.1840, 7 In. 275.00
Creamer, Helmet Form, McFee & Reeder, c.1796, 7 In. 550.00
Creamer, J. B. Jones, Boston, c.1825, 6 In. 295.00
Creamer, W. Whetcroft, Pear Shape, Lyre Handle, Hoofed Feet 1600.00
Crumber, Hall & Hewson, Albany, N. Y., c.1819 .... 135.00
Cup, Coin, Cylindrical ....*Illus* 190.00
Cup, Coin, Footed, 1850-1855 ....*Illus* 125.00
Cup, Cover, Greek Key Band, Medallions, Albert Coles, 9 In. 335.00
Cup, Gothic, Coin, c.1850 ....*Illus* 275.00
Cup, Inverted Pear Shape, Domed Cover, Handles, Howard 6700.00
Cup, Julep, Banded & Beaded Rim, 1840-1850, 4 In. 445.00
Cup, Julep, Coin, Abbott Bailey & Co., 3 1/2 In. 665.00
Cup, Julep, Coin, Banded, Cartouche, Willey & Co., 3 1/2 In. 605.00
Cup, Julep, Coin, Banded, Scovil & Willey, 1818, 3 1/2 In. 413.00
Cup, Julep, Coin, Cartouche, E. & D. Kinsey, 1840-50, 3 1/2 In. 275.00
Cup, Julep, Coin, Clark, 1850, 4 In., Pr. 1375.00
Cup, Julep, Coin, MPR Monogram, Eli. C. Garner, 1840, 3 1/2 In. 495.00
Cup, Julep, Coin, Robert Best & Co., 3 In. 2300.00
Cup, Julep, Coin, Scovill, 1836, 4 In. 440.00
Cup, Julep, Coin, William Wilson McGrew, Gorham, 4 In. 242.00
Cup, Julep, John J. Bamp, 1829, 3 1/4 In. 577.00
Cup, Tubular Side Spout, W. S. Nichols, c.1821, 2 3/8 In. 1650.00
Demitasse Set, Royal Danish, International, 3 Piece 550.00
Desk Set, Blotter, Box, Tray, Greek Key Border, Gorham, 3 Pc. 165.00
Dish, Chafing, Scrolled Rim, Reed & Barton, 10 1/2 In. 1540.00
Dish, Cover, Chased Design, Oblong, 1919, Gorham 440.00
Dish, Repousse Floral Border, S. Kirk, Oval, 7 3/8 x 10 In. 225.00
Dish, Shell Shape, Gorham, 4 1/2 In., 12 Piece 660.00
Dish, Shell Shape, Gorham, 9 1/4 In. 250.00
Dish, Vegetable, Cover, Oval, Reed & Barton, Pair 610.00
Dresser Set, Engraved Floral, Webster Co., c.1920, 12 Piece 395.00
Egg Cruet, 8 Cups, Georg Sharp, 11 1/4 x 10 In. 2900.00
Entree Dish, George Sharp, c.1850, 11 1/2 x 8 3/8 In., Pair 3500.00
Epergne, 4-Light, Theodore B. Starr, c.1900 .... 4000.00
Epergne, Trumpet Form, Theodore B. Starr, c.1900, 15 In. 4400.00
Ewer, Crosby, Morse & Foss, c.1850, 14 In. 825.00
Fish Fork, Geo. W. Shiebler, Applied Fish, Seaweed, 11 Pc. 550.00
Fish Set, King Pattern, Bailey & Kitchen, Box, 2 Piece 465.00
Fork, Hyde & Goodrich, New Orleans, 10 Piece 800.00
Fork, Serving, 3 Tines, Randall, ST Initials, 8 In. 55.00
Fruit Stand, S. Kirk & Son, Hand Decorated 575.00
Glue Pot, Theo. B. Starr, c.1912 .... 300.00
Goblet, Monogram, Tall, Gorham, 6 1/2 In. 75.00
Gravy Boat, Stand, Chased, Martele, Gorham, c.1900, 9 In. 7425.00
Gravy Ladle, Fiddle Thread, Gorham, c.1850 .... 85.00
Ice Tongs, Spring-Form, 2 Mask Medallions, Gorham, c.1870 .... 1210.00
Jug, Cream, Repousse, Coin, T. E. Co., c.1855 ....*Illus* 125.00
Jug, Milk, John Taylor, Jr., & Horace S. Hinsdale, c.1820 .... 440.00
Ladle, Bright Cut, Edward & David Kinsey, c.1845, 12 In. 525.00
Ladle, Coin, Cottage, Gorham, 1861, Large 200.00
Ladle, Coin, Hazen, Scovil & Willey, Set of 3 ....*Illus* 525.00
Ladle, Coin, NB Monogram, Scovil & Co. ....*Illus* 495.00

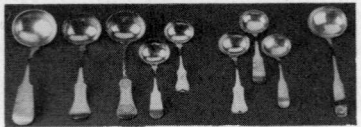

Silver-American, Ladle, Coin, NB Monogram, Scovil & Co.

Silver-American, Ladle, Fiddle Back, Coin, C. & JH Plant, c.1850

Silver-American, Ladle, Floral, Coin, E. & D. Kinsey Co., c.1845

Silver-American, Ladle, Eagles & Shields, Coin, 8 1/2 In., Pair

Silver-American, Ladle, Coin, Hazen, Scovil & Willey, Set of 3

Silver-American, Ladle, Shell Handle, Coin, C. Burnett, c.1795

Ladle, Eagles & Shields, Coin, 8 1/2 In., Pair ....*Illus*   445.00
Ladle, Fiddle Back Handle, David Kinsey, c.1850, 12 In. 465.00
Ladle, Fiddle Back, Coin, C. & JH Plant, c.1850 ....*Illus*   470.00
Ladle, Fiddle Thread, Hyde & Goodrich, 10 7/8 In. 595.00
Ladle, Floral, Coin, E. & D. Kinsey Co., c.1845 ....*Illus*   525.00
Ladle, Louis Muh, New Orleans, 13 1/4 In. 650.00
Ladle, Punch, Engraved Flowers, S. Kirk & Son. 14 1/2 In. 355.00
Ladle, Punch, Isaac Hutton, Bright Cut, c.1800, 14 1/4 In. 715.00
Ladle, Shell Handle, Coin, C. Burnett, c.1795 ....*Illus*   550.00
Ladle, Soup, Bright Cut, J. Anthony, Jr., 1785, 13 3/4 In. 1870.00
Ladle, Willey & Co., 19th Century, 12 3/4 In. 330.00
Mug, Baby's, Engine Turned, Engraved Design, Wood & Hughes 195.00
Mug, Baby's, Engraved Design, Gorham 235.00
Mug, Bird On Branch, Reserve In Beak, Durgin, 3 5/8 In. 1100.00
Mug, Engraved Monogram, Marked G & H., 2 7/8 In. 275.00
Olive Fork, Pear & Bacall, c.1850 ....   125.00
Pen Tray, Arthur Stone, Pinched Ends, 8 1/4 x 3 1/4 In. 665.00
Pen Wiper, S. Kirk & Sons 110.00
Pendant, Kalo, Lily of The Valley, 2 1/2 In. 385.00
Pill Box, Frederick Davis 65.00
Pitcher, Beaded Rim, Marked Boston & Coin, 1850, 18 1/8 In. 1045.00
Pitcher, Chased Foliage, Mauser, c.1880 ....   770.00
Pitcher, Coin, Robert Smith, 1820, 13 In. ....*Illus*   1980.00
Pitcher, Fluted Glass, Silver Mounted, Gorham, 10 3/8 In. 880.00
Pitcher, Lobed Lower Body, W. B. Heyer, c.1825, 14 In. 1650.00

Silver-American, Pitcher, Coin, Silver-American, Pitcher, Water, Silver-American, Sugar, Coin, Robert Smith, 1820, 13 In. Coin, Bull's Head Handle, 10 In. Abraham Palmer, 1850, 10 In.

Pitcher, Neoclassical Design, Goodnow & Jenks, 13 1/2 In. 775.00
Pitcher, Presentation, Fletcher & Gardiner, 1811, 7 In. 4400.00
Pitcher, Renaissance Revival, Coin, David Kinsey, 11 In. 1870.00
Pitcher, Rococo Cartouches, Wilcox & Evertsen, c.1895 .... 715.00
Pitcher, Stieff, Baltimore, c.1900, 9 In. 1045.00
Pitcher, Stylized Leaves, Flowers, Gorham, 1883, 10 7/8 In. 1870.00
Pitcher, Water, Baluster, Spot Hammered, De Matteo, 11 In. 3520.00
Pitcher, Water, Bright Cut Foliage, Gorham, c.1860, 13 In. 385.00
Pitcher, Water, Coin Silver, Lincoln & Reed, 12 1/2 In. 1100.00
Pitcher, Water, Coin, Bull's Head Handle, 10 In. ....*Illus* 1875.00
Pitcher, Water, David Kinsey, Classical Portrait, 11 In. 1870.00
Pitcher, Water, Floral & Scroll Design, Dominick & Haff 935.00
Pitcher, Water, Hammered, Kalo, 9 In. 1500.00
Pitcher, Water, Robert E. Smith, c.1820, 13 In. 1980.00
Pitcher, Water, Weidlich 650.00
Plate, Chased Flowers, Jenkins & Jenkins, 13 In. 825.00
Plate, Coin, Presentation, 1849, E. & D. Kinsey, 10 1/2 In. 1100.00
Plate, Dominick & Haff, Dragonflies, Foliage, 9 In. 550.00
Porringer, Benjamin Burt, 18th Century, 6 1/2 In. 1760.00
Porringer, Cast Cherubs, Gorham, c.1865, 5 5/8 In. 1750.00
Porringer, Child's, Lincoln & Reed, Boston, Mass, c.1840 .... 475.00
Porringer, Jacob Hurd, Early 19th Century, 5 In. 1760.00
Porringer, Jones, Lows & Ball, Boston, Mass., c.1835 .... 975.00
Porringer, William Homes, Jr., Boston, c.1780, 5 1/8 In. 2100.00
Punch Bowl, Art Deco, Presentation, Meriden, 1939, 10 In. 750.00
Punch Bowl, Patinated Bronze Base, 1910, Gorham, 12 3/8 In. 3520.00
Relish, Scroll Gadrooned Border, Reed & Barton, 14 1/2 In. 88.00
Ruler, Floral Design, Straight Edge, Kirk & Son 225.00
Salt Shovel, Hyde & Goodrich, c.1860, 4 Piece 385.00
Salt Spoon, Beggs & Smith, Louisville, Kentucky, c.1840 .... 35.00
Salt Spoon, Farrington & Hunnewell, Boston, c.1850, Pair 45.00
Salt Spoon, J. Shoemaker, Philadelphia, c.1790 .... 75.00
Salt Spoon, J. Targee, New York City, c.1815 .... 45.00
Salt Spoon, J. Vernon, New York City, c.1790 .... 95.00
Salt Spoon, Jenny Lind, Squire & Lander, N. Y. City, c.1850 .... 21.00
Salt Spoon, Meadows & Co., Philadelphia, c.1840, Pair 45.00
Salt, 3 In. 295.00
Salt, Lion Heads, Footed, Wood & Hughes, Pair 300.00
Salt, Open, Myer Myers, New York, c.1775, 1 7/8 x 2 3/8 In. 2085.00
Salt, Reeded Rim, Marked FRR, S. F. CAL., 2 1/2 In., Pair 550.00
Sauce Boat, Crosby & Morse, Boston, c.1860, 8 1/4 In. 1550.00
Sauce Boat, William Gale, New York, 1855 .... 565.00
Sauceboat, Beaded Border, Ford & Tupper, c.1865, 7 In., Pair 1320.00
Sauceboat, Beaded Rim, Scroll Handle, c.1850, Gorham 550.00
Scoop, Berry, Twisted Stem, John L. Westervelt, 8 3/4 In. 110.00
Scoop, Cheese, Mouse & Moon Handle, Whiting 605.00
Scoop, Cracker, Head Handle, Lyre Design, Gorham, 9 1/4 In. 770.00
Serving Fork, Pierced Thistle Design, Arthur Stone 357.50
Serving Set, Starlit Pattern, Fork & Spoon, Allan Adler 192.50
Serving Spoon, Grape, Arthur Stone, 9 1/4 In. 357.50
Shaker, Banded, Scroll Handle, Edward Winslow, 3 1/4 In. 1815.00
Shaker, Domical Cover, Urn Shape, Arthur Stone, 4 In., 4 Pc. 465.00
Silent Butler, Domed Hinged Lid, Oval, Crichton Bros. 165.00
Spoon & Fork, Christmas, Gold Plated, 1925, A. Michelsen 90.00

◆◆◆

In snowy weather make tracks both in and out of your door. One set
of tracks leaving the house is an invitation to an intruder. Or perhaps
you could walk out of the house backwards.

◆◆◆

Spoon, Art Deco, Erickson, Scalloped Handle, 11 1/2 In. 125.00
Spoon, Coffee, Paul Revere, Jr., Marked P PR, 5 In. 715.00
Spoon, Engraved Monogram, Marked Revere, 8 3/4 In., Pair 1800.00
Spoon, Stuffing, Marked G. D., Tooled Handle, 12 1/8 In. 175.00
Spoon, Word Buzette On Front, E. & D. Kinsey, c.1837 .... 125.00
Sugar & Creamer, Cover, Anthony Rasch, Marked, c.1820 .... 600.00
Sugar & Creamer, Cover, Eoff & Conner, c.1834, 6 In. 380.00
Sugar & Creamer, Cover, Joseph Shoemaker, 7 3/8 & 10 In. 2700.00
Sugar & Creamer, Cover, Wm. G. Forbes, 1840s, 6 & 5 In. 495.00
Sugar & Creamer, Kalo 770.00
Sugar & Creamer, Lucy Albert, E. & D. Kinsey, c.1845 .... 2420.00
Sugar & Creamer, Pinched Square Form, Floral, Whiting 88.50
Sugar Shell, Fiddle Shell, R. & W. Wilson, c.1840 .... 75.00
Sugar Tongs, Bright Cut, Acorn Ends, John Lynch, 6 3/8 In. 200.00
Sugar, Coin, Abraham Palmer, 1850, 10 In. ....*Illus* 2860.00
Sugar, Cover, Christof C. Kuchler, c.1850, 5 3/4 x 6 In. 3650.00
Tablespoon, A. Dubois, N. J. & Penna., c.1790 .... 175.00
Tablespoon, B. Woodcock, Delaware, Upturned Front, c.1760 .... 350.00
Tablespoon, Bird Back, J. Letellier, c.1790 .... 175.00
Tablespoon, Bright Cut, J. Musgrave, Philadelphia, c.1790 .... 175.00
Tablespoon, C. Hellebush, Engraved W, 8 1/8 In., 3 Piece 105.00
Tablespoon, Coin Silver, Johnson & Reat, Oval End, c.1805 .... 275.00
Tablespoon, Coin Silver, Monogram, Duhme & Co., 6 Piece 120.00
Tablespoon, Fiddle Back, Steele & Crocker, 1841, 6 Piece 465.00
Tablespoon, Fiddle Form, S. Garman, 19th Century, 8 3/4 In. 35.00
Tablespoon, Fiddle Head, Lows, Ball & Co., c.1845, 6 Piece 295.00
Tablespoon, G. Haversticker, 1805, 6 Piece 925.00
Tablespoon, J. Clarke, R. I., Rattail, c.1730 .... 395.00
Tablespoon, J. Cluett, New York, c.1750 .... 350.00
Tablespoon, J. Gibbs, Providence, R. I., c.1760 .... 325.00
Tablespoon, J. Trott, Jr., Norwich, New London, Conn., 1780 .... 175.00
Tablespoon, J. Watts, Fiddle Thread, c.1840, 6 Piece 295.00
Tablespoon, Jacob Hurd, c.1730, 8 In. 330.00
Tablespoon, Jeremiah Dummer, Chased Foliage On Back, 7 In. 2090.00
Tablespoon, Philip Syng, Sr., c.1725, 8 In. 440.00
Tablespoon, R. Humphreys, Del. & Phila., c.1765 .... 375.00
Tablespoon, S. Vernon, Newport, R. I., c.1715 .... 750.00
Tazza, Greek Revival, Female Busts Handles, Gorham, 7 In. 605.00
Tea & Coffee Set, Chrysanthemums, 1880, Shiebler, 5 Piece 2430.00
Tea & Coffee Set, Floral, Alvin, 6 Piece ....*Illus* 1650.00
Tea & Coffee Set, Hot Water Kettle, Fluted, Gorham, 6 Piece 1760.00
Tea & Coffee Set, Pear Shape, Monogram, Wallace, 7 Piece 1870.00
Tea & Coffee Set, Scrolled Leaves, Whiting, 1914, 6 Piece 6325.00
Tea & Coffee Set, Whiting, 5 Piece 4510.00
Tea Ball, Teapot Shape, Chain, Attleboro, Mass. 60.00
Tea Caddy, Spoon, Stylized Leaf Bowl, Curved Handle, Pratt 110.00
Tea Set, Fruit Finials, B. Gardiner, c.1830, 3 Piece 2420.00

Silver–American, Tea & Coffee Set, Floral,
Alvin, 6 Piece

Silver–American, Teapot, Sugar, Coin,
Edward Kinsey, 1840

Tea Set, Jones, Lows & Ball, Marked, 3 Piece 1100.00
Tea Set, Presentation, Grapes, Vines, Forbes, c.1851, 3 Piece 1350.00
Tea Set, Stodder & Frobisher, Boston, 1816-25, Teapot, 9 In. 2450.00
Tea Strainer, Bowl Is Poppy, Floral Handle, Alvin 250.00
Tea Urn, Lows, Ball & Co., Boston, c.1840, 13 x 11 In. 1650.00
Teapot, Apple Shape, Bell Finial, J. Burt, 1735, 5 In. 7700.00
Teapot, Sugar, Coin, Edward Kinsey, 1840 ....*Illus* 4400.00
Teaspoon, Coin Silver, D. B. Anderson, Monogrammed, 6 Piece 78.00
Teaspoon, Gennetta & Osborne, 6 1/8 In., 6 Piece 55.00
Teaspoon, J. S. Heald, 6 Piece 150.00
Teaspoon, N. Dodge, Rhode Island, Coffin End, c.1810, 5 Pc. 185.00
Teaspoon, Palmer & Bachelder, 1830s, 6 Piece 1765.00
Tongs, Bright Cut Fronds, General James Wolf, 6 1/2 In. 195.00
Tongs, Christopher Tuthill, Philadelphia, c.1730 .... 75.00
Toothpick, Band of Repousse Flowers, Stieff 50.00
Toothpick, Prelude, International 40.00
Tray, Art Nouveau Floral, Barbour Silver Co., 14 1/4 In. 715.00
Tray, Cupid, Drawn Bow, Theodore Starr, 1905, 10 3/4 In. 600.00
Tray, Flared Edge, Stamped Logo, Porter Blanchard, 11 In. 275.00
Tray, Pinched Rim, Oval Well, Kalo, 21 1/2 x 13 In. 550.00
Tray, Reeded Rim, Shreve, Crump & Low, 12 In. 715.00
Tray, Renaissance Style Chasing, Redlich, 14 1/2 I. 220.00
Tray, Royal Danish, Handles, 1949, International, 12 In. 187.00
Tray, Swags & Ribbons, Serpentine Rim, Gorham, 1901, 20 In. 995.00
Trophy Cup, Flower & Scrolls, Martele, 1900, 9 1/2 In. 4620.00
Trophy Vase, Mermaids, Inscriptions, Whiting, 1887, 15 In. 4950.00
Tureen, Lobed Cover, Foliate Handles, Gorham, 13 1/2 In. 2200.00
Tureen, Scrollwork On Rims, Whiting, c.1900, 15 1/2 In. 1875.00
Vase, Everted Rim, Chased Flowers, Leaves, Martele, 10 In. 3520.00
Vase, Everted Rim, Flowers, Leaves, Martele, 1900, 15 3/4 In. 4400.00
Vase, Flowering Clematis Vine, Black, Starr & Frost, 14 In. 3100.00
Vase, Fluted Body, Flowers, Martele, c.1910, 11 3/8 In. 4180.00
Vase, Fluted Mouth, Floral Design, Arthur Stone, 5 1/4 In. 385.00
Vase, Trumpet, Greek Key Border, Dominick & Haff, 18 In. 220.00
Vinaigrette, Striped Design, W. Lee, c.1812, 1 1/8 In. 195.00
Yo-Yo, Gorham, Scroll Work 125.00
SILVER-AUSTRIAN, Bowl, Undulating Sides, W. Werkstatte, c.1920, 11 3/4 In. 9900.00
Candle Snuffer, Vienna, 1823 .... 375.00
Candlestick, Foliate & Interlaced Design, 13 In., Pair 715.00
Candlestick, Octagonal, Lion Mask Feet, 16 3/4 In., Pair 3550.00
Cigar Cutter, Bear Head, Glass Eyes, c.1870, 4 1/2 In., Pair 525.00
Dish, Vegetable, Cover, Stand, J. C. Klinkosch, 11 In., Pr. 4200.00
Flatware Set, Floral Swags, Reeded Borders, 1900, 193 Piece 6600.00
Plate, Arms & Coronet, J. C. Klinkosch, 9 7/8 In., 12 Piece 5250.00
Plate, Cake, Pierced Rim, Augsburg Hallmarks, 10 In., Pair 610.00
Tazza, Mythological, Wings Support, c.1885, 8 3/4 In. 4400.00
SILVER-CANADIAN, Tea & Coffee Set, Squat Melon Shape, Floral, Birks, 4 Piece 1225.00
Wine Taster, Shell Thumbpiece, Ring Handle, 1770, 3 1/2 In. 2200.00
SILVER-CHINESE, Basket, Swing Handle, Miniature 100.00
Cocktail Set, Dragons, Shaker, 12 Beakers, Stand 1210.00
Egg Set, Wirework Stand, 6 Cups & Spoons, KHC, 8 In. 2860.00
Figure, Covered Wagon, Horse, Miniature ....*Illus* 100.00
Figure, Rickshaw, Miniature ....*Illus* 60.00
Jug, Repousse Dragon, Flowers, Flared Rim, 4 1/2 In. 55.00
Punch Bowl, Dragon Handles & Feet, Chased Flowers, Shells 6600.00
Salt, Figural, Laden Rickshaw, Glass Lined, 6 1/2 In., Pair 275.00
Vase, Incised Design & Landscape, S Mark, c.1900, 10 In. 525.00
SILVER-CONTINENTAL, Box, Singing Bird, Enameled Flowers, c.1900, 3 3/4 In. 3850.00
Cigarette Case, Enameled Maid On Lid, 1900, 3 3/8 In. 2090.00
Cigarette Case, Enameled Nude On Lid, c.1900, 3 1/2 In. 880.00
Figure, Sedan Chair, Miniature ....*Illus* 200.00
Open Salt & Pepper Shaker, Shell Form, Pedestal, 2 Sets 1450.00
Plateau Mirror, Art Nouveau, 1900, 20 1/2 x 14 1/4 In. 1550.00

Silver–Chinese,
Figure, Rickshaw,
Miniature

Silver–Continental,
Figure, Sedan Chair,
Miniature

Silver–Chinese, Figure,
Covered Wagon,
Horse, Miniature

Silver–Sterling, Figurine,
Cherub, Floral,
Baskets, Miniature

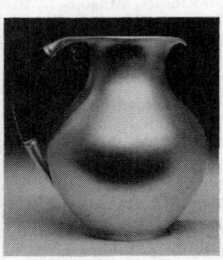

Silver–Danish, Bowl, Berry
Design, Georg Jensen, 7 1/2 In.

Silver–Danish, Centerpiece,
Berry Design, G. Jensen,
14 3/4 In.

Silver–Danish, Pitcher, Water,
Ebony Handle, Georg Jensen

Snuffbox, Quatrefoil Seascape, Enameled, c.1900	525.00
Tray, Anthemion Pierced Rim, Marked, c.1900, 21 1/2 In.	880.00
SILVER–DANISH, Bowl, Berry Design, Georg Jensen, 7 1/2 In. ....*Illus*	2800.00
Bowl, Molded Rim, J. Holm, 14 1/2 In.	330.00
Bowl, Serving, J. Holm, 13 In.	175.00
Candelabrum, Arcing Leaf–Form Arms, Georg Jensen, 6 In., Pr.	3850.00
Candleholder, 3–Lite, Dragsted	165.00
Carving Set, Acanthus, Georg Jensen	395.00
Centerpiece, Berry Design, George Jensen, 14 3/4 In. .... *Illus*	6600.00
Compote, Georg Jensen, 10 1/2 x 9 3/4 In.	2900.00
Compote, Vintage Pattern, Georg Jensen, 5 1/8 In., Pair	1650.00
Cup, Cover, Applied Jeweled Lions, Michelsen, 1906, 16 1/2 In.	3080.00
Flask, Woman's, Unger Bros.	550.00
Iced Tea Spoon, Acorn, Georg Jensen	75.00
Lamp, Table, Neoclassical, Laurel Garland, 1883	775.00
Letter Opener, Acorn, Georg Jensen	148.00
Meat Fork, 3 Tines, Blossom, Georg Jensen	195.00
Pickle Fork, Georg Jensen	75.00
Pitcher, Hammered, Carved Squash Blossom, Georg Jensen	1765.00
Pitcher, Water, Ebony Handle, Georg Jensen ....*Illus*	1900.00
Pitcher, Water, No. 432A, Hammered, Georg Jensen, 9 In.	2200.00
Place Setting, Acorn, Georg Jensen, 4 Piece	200.00
Platter, Double Fish Form Handles, George Jensen, 10 3/4 In.	825.00
Platter, Fish, Banded Reed & Foliate Border, 24 1/2 In.	550.00
Punch Bowl, Grape & Vine Design, Michelsen, 1912, 12 In.	1550.00
Salt & Pepper, Bud Design, Urn Shape, Georg Jensen	195.00
Salt, Acanthus, Enameled Inside, Spoon, Georg Jensen, 12 Piece	1225.00
Serving Dish Set, Molded Brim, Beaded, Georg Jensen, 3 Piece	4950.00
Spoon & Fork, Christmas, Gold Plated, 1946, A. Michelsen	85.00
Spoon & Fork, Christmas, Gold Plated, 1949, A. Michelsen	85.00
Spoon, Black Boy, Sitting On Cotton Bale, Banjo, Demitasse	20.00

Spoon, Leaf & Berry Form Handle, 5 1/2 In.	195.00
Spoon, Tea Caddy, Acorn, Georg Jensen	125.00
Sugar Spoon, Acanthus, Georg Jensen	90.00
Sugar Tongs, Scissor Type, Cactus, Georg Jensen	175.00
Tea Set, Leaf & Bud Finial, Georg Jensen, 1930, 3 Piece	1430.00
Tray, Rococo Style, Engraved Crest, Michelsen, 1920, 28 In.	2200.00
Tureen, Cover, Acanthus Form Handles, Michelsen, 17 In.	2970.00
SILVER–DUTCH, Basket, Scroll & Floral Open Work, Lion Paw Feet, c.1900	385.00
Box, Tobacco, Engraved Scene, Marked, 1880s, 4 1/4 In.	330.00
Creamer, Cow, Late 19th Century, 5 1/4 In., Pair	1650.00
Salver, Leaves, 4 Bracket Feet, R. Memeling, Square, 8 In.	2750.00
Tea Caddy Spoon, Farm Scene, Farm Boy Handle	68.00
Tea Caddy Spoon, Flowers & Flying Bird	125.00
Tea Caddy, Reeded Cover, Figures In Tavern Scene, 5 1/2 In.	470.00
Tea Set, Gilt, Oval Vase, Mother–of–Pearl Handles, 1807, 5 Pc.	5500.00
Tea Set, Renaissance Revival Designs, c.1880, 3 Piece	995.00

English silver is marked with a series of four or five small hallmarks. The standing lion mark is the most commonly seen sterling quality mark. The other marks indicate the city of origin, the maker, and the year of manufacture. These dates can be verified in many good books on silver.

SILVER–ENGLISH, Bowl, 3–Footed, Geo. Mathuin, Mid–18th Century ......*Illus*	900.00
Bun Warmer, Folding, Sheffield, c.1860 ......*Illus*	650.00
Caddy Spoon, Enameled Celtic Design, A. Knox, 4 1/2 In.	990.00
Candelabrum, 4–Light, Husk Swags, Beaded, Elkington, Pair	5500.00
Candlestick, George III, William Cafe, 1758, 9 In., Pair	4400.00
Card Case, Scott Memorial, Scrolls, W. & E. Turnpenny, 1845	525.00
Centerpiece, Hemispherical, Pedestal, Sheffield, 11 5/8 In.	2450.00
Coaster, George III, William Abdy, 4 1/4 In., Pair	1850.00
Coffeepot, Charles Wright, Acanthus Spout, 1773, 12 In.	3550.00
Coffeepot, Daniel Smith, c.1780	1750.00
Coffeepot, John Rowe, 1798	3600.00
Creamer, George III, Peter & Anne Bateman, 5 1/4 In.	250.00
Cup, Scroll & Floral Repousse, Robert Harper, 9 In.	425.00
Desk, Miniature ......*Illus*	150.00
Dish, Vegetable, Cover, Divided	65.00
Epergne, 5 Baskets, Festoons, Victorian, London, 1892, 14 In.	7700.00
Ewer, Domed Cover, Richard Gurney & Co., 1759, 8 In.	1650.00
Frame, William Comyns, London, 1901	695.00
Humidor, 30 Signatures, 3 1/2 x 5 1/2 x 9 In.	275.00
Inkstand, James Bradbury & Son	1350.00
Jug, Claret, Animal Frieze, Masks, S. Smith, 1856, 13 1/2 In.	2850.00
Kettle, Lampstand, George I Style, James Robinson, 14 In.	3300.00
Ladle, George III, Hester Bateman	577.50
Ladle, Hester Bateman, 1788–89, 12 3/4 In.	515.00
Manicure Set, Original Fitted Box, c.1900, 5 Pc.	100.00

Silver–English, Bowl, 3–Footed, Geo. Mathuin, Mid–18th Century

Silver–English, Bun Warmer, Folding, Sheffield, c.1860

Silver–English, Tray, George III, John Edwards, 1780s

Marrow Scoop, Elias Cachaart, 8 1/4 In. 220.00
Marrow Scoop, Hester Bateman, Hallmark For 1780–81 .... 385.00
Mote Spoon, Rattail, T. Mann, c.1720 .... 450.00
Mug, Children of Seasons, Reily & Storer, 4 1/2 In., Pair 2420.00
Plate, Engraved Crest, Crown Over Arm, 1754, 9 1/2 In., 8 Pc. 4250.00
Porringer, Benjamin Burt, 8 1/4 In. 1100.00
Punch Set, Hemispherical Bowl, C. J. Vander, 36 Bell Cups 9350.00
Salt, Shell Form Bowl, Dolphin Feet, H. Archer, 1864, Pair 225.00
Salver, George I Style, Coat of Arms, James Robinson, 18 In. 4070.00
Salver, Shell & Scroll Border, J. Sanders, c.1750, 6 1/4 In. 415.00
Salver, Vintage Pattern, Storr, Mortimer & Hunt, 1852 .... 3740.00
Skimmer Spoon, Bar Along Bowl, GS Over TH, 1794, 11 3/4 In. 650.00
Spoon, Bright Cut, Gilt Bowl, Bateman, 1808 .... 375.00
Spoon, Charles II, London, 1681 .... 440.00
Straining Spoon, CS Over TH, 1794, 12 In. 650.00
Stuffing Spoon, George III, S. Hennell, 1811, 12 1/2 In. 275.00
Stuffing Spoon, Shell Design On Front, WG, 1827 .... 495.00
Stuffing Spoon, William Eley & William Fearn 137.50
Sugar Basket, Solomon Hougham, London, 1799, 7 1/2 Oz. 850.00
Sugar Shaker, Repousse Scenes, 1840, 6 In. 595.00
Sugar Tongs, Pierced Design, Hester Bateman, c.1778 .... 145.00
Sugar, Cover, Samuel Herbet, London, 1760 .... 3400.00
Sugar, Inverted Pear Form, Crichton Brothers, 4 1/4 In. 345.00
Table Set, Cherubs, Garlands, Miniature, 5 Piece 895.00
Tablespoon, Gilt Pattern In Bowl, Bateman, 1808, 9 1/8 In. 375.00
Tablespoon, William IV, Fiddle, James Beebe, 1832, Pair 115.00
Tankard, Hinged Cover, George II, Richard Bayley, 7 In. 4840.00
Tea & Coffee Set, Baluster, C. S. Harris & Sons, 1929, 6 Pc. 7700.00
Tea & Coffee Set, George IV, Rocaille, J. E. Terrey, 4 Piece 2750.00
Tea & Coffee Set, Globular, Flower Swags, Sissons, 4 Piece 5500.00
Tea Caddy Spoon, Bust of Wadsworth On Handle 275.00
Tea Caddy, George III, Pineapple Finial, J. Schofield, 1799 .... 330.00
Tea Set, Crespin Fuller, 1798, 4 Piece 5800.00
Teapot, Chased Rococo Floral Design, 1781–82, 5 1/4 In. 500.00
Teapot, Mahogany Finial & Handle, George III, TH–JT 330.00
Teapot, Regency, Globular Form, R. Peppin, 1823–24 .... 330.00
Teapot, Treen Finial, Charles Aldridge & Henry Green, 5 In. 605.00
Teapot, Treen Finial, William Bennett, 1800, 6 3/4 In. 1875.00
Toast Rack, Birmingham, 1926 .... 135.00
Toast Rack, Loop Handle, 7 Arched Sections, 1853, 5 1/2 In. 187.00
Tray, George III, John Edwards, 1780s ....*Illus* 1200.00
Tray, Tea, George III Style, Gadroon, Oval, J. S. Hunt, 30 In. 4125.00
Tray, Tea, Raised Rim, Rod Handles, Mappin & Webb, 25 3/4 In. 2850.00
Tureen, Soup, Cover, Shells, Leaves, c.1820, 16 In. ....*Illus* 2300.00
Urn, Wm. Holmes, c.1776, 21 In. ....*Illus* 2400.00
Vinaigrette, Acorns & Oak Leaves, S. Pemberton, c.1790 .... 335.00
Waiter, George III, Thomas Wallis, 6 x 4 1/2 In. 415.00

Silver–English, Tureen, Soup, Cover,   *Silver–English, Urn, Wm.*   *Silver–French, Jug, Claret,*
Shells, Leaves, c.1820, 16 In.   *Holmes, c.1776, 21 In.*   *Swirl, Pear Shape, 10 In.*

Silver–French, Tea & Coffee Set, Cylindrical, c.1930, 3 Piece

◆◆

Protect your home and antiques from theft. Use a timer on your lights at all times, even when you are at home. This will set a pattern of certain lights going on and off each day. When you are away, the house will appear to have normal activity. If possible, when you are away, park a car near the front of the house. The car will block your driveway so a burglar cannot load up through your garage. Have someone keep your trash cans filled. This will help to make the house look occupied. Keep the grass mowed. Stop your mail and paper deliveries.

◆◆

SILVER–EUROPEAN, Box, Pill, Fish Shape, Red Stone Eye, 5 5/8 In. 275.00
SILVER–FRENCH, Box, Pill, Carriage Pulled By Tropical Bird, 2 x 4 1/2 In. 1545.00
   Candlestick, Fluted Vase Shape, Jean Hannier, 8 1/4 In. 2100.00
   Coffeepot, Pear Shape, 3 Hoof Feet, Side Cover, L. S., 9 In. 3200.00
   Coffeepot, Vase Shape, Hinged Cover, N. Fauconnier, 10 1/4 In. 4400.00
   Desk Seal, Medieval Knight Form, Bloodstone, 1860, 4 1/4 In. 2100.00
   Dish, Serving, Cover, Foliate Finial, Globular Body, 6 1/2 In. 1875.00
   Dish, Shell Shape, Thomas Germain Style, 8 1/8 In., 4 Piece 8250.00
   Ewer, Chased, Shellwork Borders, Scroll Handle, Odiot, 13 In. 5225.00
   Jug, Claret, Rococo, Inverted Pear Shape, Marked EL, 12 In. 2550.00
   Jug, Claret, Swirl, Pear Shape, 10 In. ....*Illus* 1050.00
   Rattle, Ivory Teething Ring, Handle, De Versailles, 1900s 155.00
   Salt, Open, Shell Bowls, Dolphin Stems, 3 1/2 In., 6 Piece 8500.00
   Sauce Pan, Mid 19th Century, 13 In. 600.00
   Snuffbox, Mid 19th Century, 2 5/8 In. 250.00
   Tea & Coffee Set, Cylindrical, c.1930, 3 Piece ....*Illus* 3850.00
   Tea & Coffee Set, Fluted Pear Shape, Marked L. B., 6 Piece 5225.00
   Tray, Card, Chased Leaves, Maker AD, 1870s, 8 In. 305.00
   Tureen, Soup, Domed Cover, Liner, Bombe, Trophies, 13 3/4 In. 7150.00
SILVER–GERMAN, Basket, Flower, Swing Handle, Quartrefoil Bowl, 13 In. 3410.00
   Bonbon, Ribbons & Swags, Cut Glass Insert, 4 In. 470.00
   Bowl, Openwork, Cherubs, Floral, Large ....*Illus* 1000.00
   Bowl, Pierced Sides, Augsburg, 18th Century, 8 1/2 In. 775.00
   Bowl, Repousse, Floral Band, Masks, 6 In., Pair ....*Illus* 2800.00
   Box, Cigarette, Stag On Front, Signed 45.00
   Box, Rococo Scenes, c.1880, 6 1/4 In. 550.00
   Candelabrum, 3–Light, Scroll Design, A. H. Heidelberg, 9 In. 330.00
   Candelabrum, 4–Light, Empire, W. C. Hessenberg & Son, 22 In. 5775.00
   Candlestick, Hexagonal, 3 Paw Feet, Mark S., 9 In., Pair 1650.00
   Centerpiece, Parcel Gilt, Caryatids Handles, Oval, 22 3/4 In. 4950.00

Silver-German, Wager Cup, Man & Woman, 1890, 10 1/2 In., Pair; Silver-German, Figurine, Knight, British Royal Arms, 8 In., Pair

Silver–German, Nef, Nersheimer, 3 Masts, Sailors, 1928, 22 1/2 In.

Centerpiece, Swan Shape, Georg Roth & Co., 1900, 17 1/2 In.	4450.00
Coaster, Bottle, Openwork, Grapes & Vines, Pair	1900.00
Coffee Set, Ivory Rings, Solid, Grimminger, 1945	5000.00
Compote, Neptune Holding Bowl	1000.00
Cup, Cover, Allegorical Scene, H. Bohm, c.1885, 18 1/4 In.	8800.00
Cup, Stirrup, Open Jawed Boar's Head Shape, Chased, 6 1/4 In.	1450.00
Figurine, Knight, British Royal Arms, 8 In., Pair ....*Illus*	3525.00
Jug, Claret, Art Nouveau Iris, F. J. Schroder, 1900, 13 1/2 In.	1320.00
Ladle, Punch, c.1900, 14 1/2 In.	137.50
Nef, Nersheimer, 3 Masts, Sailors, 1928, 22 1/2 In. ....*Illus*	6875.00
Tea & Coffee Set, Applied Cupids, Ovoid, Schleissner, 5 Piece	7150.00
Tea & Coffee Set, Pear Shape, Gothic Arch & Scroll, 4 Piece	3300.00
Tray, Applied Floral Repousse, P. Bruckman & Sohne, 20 In.	605.00
Tray, Figural Scene, Scroll Rim, c.1880, 12 In.	825.00
Urn, Cover, Ram's Head Handles, Schleissner, 1900, 16 3/4 In.	3300.00
Vase, Floral Swag Above C–Scroll Ground, 14 1/2 In.	330.00
Wager Cup, Man & Woman, 1890, 10 1/2 In., Pair ....*Illus*	4675.00
Wine Cooler, Elegant Couples, 18th Century Clothes, 9 In.	3850.00
SILVER–IRISH, Dish Ring, Chinoiserie Design, John Graham, Dublin, 1760	3600.00
Ladle, Hallmark For 1800, 15 In.	385.00
Sauceboat, George III, Hoof Feet, Wm. Haney, c.1780, 7 1/2 In.	660.00
Spoon, Dessert, King, J. Scott, Dublin, 1818, Pair	145.00
Sugar, Chased Flowers & Scrolls, Wm. Townsend, 6 1/2 In.	935.00
Tea Caddy Spoon, Hand Hammered, Feather Edge, Dublin, 1973	95.00
Teaspoon, Fiddle Thread, Hallmark For 1883, 10 Piece	170.00
SILVER–ITALIAN, Candlestick, Fluted Vase Form, 10 In., Pair	5225.00
Candlestick, Gilt, Domed Base, Arms, Coronets, 8 1/8 In. Pair	6600.00
Tazza, Figural David & Judith Stems, G. Accarisi, 8 In., Pair	3575.00
SILVER–JAPANESE, Bowl, Bombe Form, Applied Dragon, 19th Century, 12 1/4 In.	2640.00
Tea Set, Globular, Dragon Design, SM Mark, 5 Piece	3575.00
Teapot, Applied Panels, Signed, 4 In., Pair ....*Illus*	1100.00

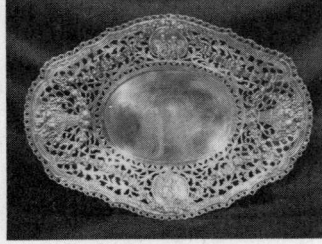

Silver–German, Bowl, Openwork, Cherubs, Floral, Large

Silver–German, Bowl, Repousse, Floral Band, Masks, 6 In., Pair

Teapot, Incised Diaper, Globular, 5 In. 1980.00
SILVER–MEXICAN, Bowl, 3 Vertical Handles, Spratling, 6 x 3 In. 550.00
  Bowl, Fluted, Milton, Juarez, 13 In. 110.00
  Bowl, Half–Spherical Form, Avanti, 5 1/2 In., Pair 125.00
  Box, Cigarette, Butterflies, Abalone, Copper, Taxco, 8 In. 1500.00
  Box, Cover, Wood, Brass, Copper Designs, Sigi, 6 x 3 In. 250.00
  Bread Tray, Fluted, Scrolled Rim, c.1920 .... 220.00
  Candlestick, Inverted Cone, Spratling, 7 In., Pair 800.00
  Cheese Knife, Rosewood Handle, Spratling, 5 1/2 In. 175.00
  Dish, Openwork, 3 Scooped Feet, Spratling, 2 In. 400.00
  Flatware Set, Aguilar, 10 Serving Pieces 5000.00
  Matchbook Holder, Copper Strike, Silver, Hector Aguilar 210.00
  Monstrance, Rococo, Cross Top, Gilt, F. A. Y Cobos, 21 1/4 In. 7700.00
  Pitcher, Foliate Pierced Base, Scroll Handle, 8 1/2 In. 137.00
  Pitcher, Water, Scrolled Handle, Ovoid Body, 11 In. 198.00
  Plate, Petal Border, Gadrooned Rim, JFR, 8 1/2 In., 6 Piece 305.00
  Salt & Pepper, Abstract Trim, Handles, Feet, Salvador 275.00
  Tea & Coffee Set, Coffeepot, 10 In., 3 Piece 745.00
  Tea & Coffee Set, Melon Form, Floral Accents, 6 Piece 2300.00
  Tea Set, Taxco, 6 Piece 2100.00
  Tray, Raised Borders, Square, 11 1/4 In. 120.00
SILVER–NORWEGIAN, Spoon, Enameled, Rococo Scroll, Floral, 4 9/16 In., Pair... 385.00
SILVER–PERSIAN, Vase, Repousse, Foliage, Building & Woman, Marked, 8 1/4 In. 625.00
SILVER–PORTUGUESE, Cup, Baroque, Bell Shape, Domed Pedestal, 13 1/4 In. 4180.00
  Pitcher, Wine, Scroll & Fluted Design, 10 1/4 In. 1375.00
  Teapot, Serpent Head Spout, Wood Handle, DCBC, 8 1/4 In. 1760.00
  Toothpick, Clown, Poodle, Leaf Chased Base, 4 5/8 In. 2875.00
  Toothpick, Indian Form, JPC, Oporto, 1825, 11 3/8 In. 4500.00
  Toothpick, Whippet, On Openwork Base, Lisbon, 5 3/4 In. 2300.00

Russian silver is marked with the cyrillic, or Russian, alphabet. The numbers 84, 88, or 91 indicate the silver content. Russian silver may be higher or lower than sterling standard. Other marks indicate maker, assayer, or city of manufacture. Many pieces of silver made in Russia are decorated with enamel. Faberge pieces are listed in their own section.

SILVER–RUSSIAN, Beaker, Frieze of Figures On Horseback, D. Shelaputin, 1875 .... 3300.00
  Beaker, Molded Border, Efim Sidorov, 1837, 3 1/4 In. 885.00
  Bowl, Enameled Flowers, Gilded Interior, c.1900, 4 1/4 In. 2300.00
  Box, Money, Barrel Shape, My Bank Account, c.1885, 3 1/2 In. 825.00
  Cake Basket, Enameled Flowers, Swing Handle, Alexaev, 1895 .... 3575.00
  Cake Basket, Trompe l'oeil, Khlebnikov, 1886, 16 7/8 In. 2200.00
  Case, Cigar, Enameled, Andrei Gragin, c.1885, 4 1/2 In. 1925.00
  Chalice, Saviour & Mother of God, c.1900, 10 7/8 In. 2750.00
  Creamer, Enameled Swans, Foliage, K. Konov, c.1910, 3 1/2 In. 2200.00
  Cup, Vodka ....40.00 To 100.00
  Cup, Vodka, Chased Shellwork, Scrolls, 18th Century, 12 Piece 4675.00

Silver–Japanese, Teapot, Applied Panels,
Signed, 4 In., Pair

Silver–Sterling, Dish, Serving, Poppies,
Mt. Vernon, 15 In.

Dessert Spoon, Enamel Floral On Bowl & Handle, 6 Piece	495.00
Egg, Floral Design, Gold Wash Ground & Interior, 4 In.	3850.00
Figurine, Rabbit, Crouched, Red Glass Eyes, 1908, 4 In., Pair	885.00
Flask, Scent, Enameled Flowers, Semyonova, c.1900, 2 3/4 In.	3575.00
Flask, Scent, Enameled Foliage, c.1900, 4 3/4 In.	1650.00
Group, Troika, Men In Sleigh, Marble Base, Sazikov, 6 In.	2420.00
Holder, Tea Glass, Simulates Woodgrain, 1880, 5 1/2 In.	1325.00
Jug, Kvass, Chased Birchbark, Marked, 1868, 4 In.	665.00
Kovsh, Enameled Vegetables, Ruckert, c.1910, 5 1/2 In.	2975.00
Medal, Czar's Portrait, Cyrillic Inscription, c.1890	115.00
Punch Bowl, Enameled Panels of Dragons, Agafonov, c.1900	5775.00
Salt Chair, Hinged Seat, Enameled, c.1910, 3 3/8 In., Pair	4625.00
Sherbet, Translucent Interior, Enameled Armorials, c.1900	1100.00
Snuffbox, Hinged Top, Scrolled Roses, Wigglework, 3 1/2 In.	275.00
Sugar Basket, Enameled Birds, Foliage, Lubavin, c.1885, 5 In.	1760.00
Tablespoon, 1884	75.00
Tea Set, Enameled Foliage, G. Sbitnev, c.1910, 3 Piece	4070.00
Tea Set, Trompe l'oeil Woven Design, S. Prokhorov, 3 Piece	1650.00
Teaspoon, Enameled, Ovchinnikov, c.1910, 12 Piece	2090.00
Tumbler, Scenic, 2 3/4 In.	135.00
Vase, Pictorial, Enameled Figures, c.1900, 5 1/4 In.	7700.00
SILVER–SCOTTISH, Biscuit Box, Chasing & Repousse, Edward & Sons	2200.00
Ladle, Sauce, George IV, Scalloped Bowl, Elias Cachart, Pair	335.00
Mug, S–Scroll Handle With Leaf Grip, A. Kincaid, c.1730	3850.00
Teapot, Foliate Finial, Edward Lathian, 1745, 6 1/2 In.	3080.00
SILVER–SOUTH AMERICAN, Brazier, 4 Monopod Support, 2–Handled Insert, 30 In.	4125.00
Frame, Strapwork & Flowers, Mirror, 52 1/2 In.	8800.00
SILVER–SPANISH, Candlestick, Fluted Circular, Baluster, Noble, 8 3/8 In., Pr.	7150.00
Cistern, Basin, Applied Ram's Heads Sides, 20 x 13 In.	6600.00

 Sterling silver is made with 925 parts silver out of 1,000 parts of metal. The word *sterling* is a quality guarantee used in the United States after about 1860. The word was used much earlier in England and Ireland. Pieces listed here are not identified by country. Other pieces of sterling quality silver are listed under Silver–American, Silver–English, etc.

SILVER–STERLING, Box, Jewel, Repousse, Wooden, 8 x 5 x 3 In.	495.00
Box, Pill, Enameled Crest, P. Hertz, 1 1/8 In.	55.00
Brush & Mirror, Art Deco	55.00
Brush, Floral Design, Victorian	50.00
Case, Card, Bird Each Side, Gold Inlay, Chain, Box	240.00
Case, Card, Bright Cut Engraving, 3 3/4 In.	115.00
Case, Card, Engraved Foliage, Monogram, 3 5/8 In.	95.00
Case, Card, Machine Engraving, Carrie, Marked, 3 1/2 In.	75.00
Case, Eyeglass, Velvet Lined	50.00
Case, Playing Card, Enameled Hearts, Clubs, 3 3/4 In.	150.00
Coaster, In Caddy, 2 5/8 In., Set of 6	24.00
Cup & Saucer, Lenox Insert, Demitasse, 6 Piece	162.00
Dish, Serving, Poppies, Mt. Vernon, 15 In. ....*Illus*	485.00
Dresser Set, Art Nouveau, 5 Piece	895.00
Dresser Set, Floral, Hand Mirror, Buffer, Comb, Monogrammed	95.00
Figurine, Cherub, Floral, Baskets, Miniature ....*Illus*	90.00
Figurine, Coach, Horses, Amethyst, Pearl, c.1885	3850.00
Fork, Baby's, Little Boy Blue	15.00
Ladle, Punch, Engraved Handle, 1930, 14 In.	325.00
Loving Cup, Serpentine Brim, Seaweed Swags, c.1889, 9 In.	2430.00
Marrow Scoop, Mother–of–Pearl Handle	45.00
Mug, Shaving, Victorian, Flowers, Bird, c.1880	325.00
Pill Box, Hinged Cover, Neck Ring, Gold Interior, 1 3/8 In.	130.00
Pitcher, Water, Arts & Crafts, Bombe Form, c.1920, 9 In.	2475.00
Punch Bowl, Hammered, Bud Design, L. Huemer, c.1920	1100.00
Rattle, With Whistle, Mother–of–Pearl	150.00
Rose Bowl, Applied Borders of Roses, Monogrammed, 14 In.	3575.00

Salt & Pepper, Towle, 4 3/4 In. 32.50
Salt Dish, Blue Liner, Pair 495.00
Salt, Rococo, Oval Bowl, Dragon Handles, 2 Spoons, 1900, Pair 330.00
    **SILVER–STERLING, SPOON, SOUVENIR, see Souvenir, Spoon, Sterling
    Silver**
Tea Caddy Spoon, Celtic Designs, Pointed Bowl 125.00
Tea Kettle Set, Melon Shape, Creighton Brothers, 4 Piece 2640.00
Tea Maker, Hinged, Lid, Spoon, 6 1/4 In. 35.00
Tea Set, H Monogram, D & H, Pedestal Pot, Tray, 4 Piece 800.00
Teapot, Floral Repousse, Engraved, Monogram, 8 1/2 In. 675.00
Tumbler, Overlay, Monogram 60.00
Vase, Trumpet, Iris, Stems, Footed, Marked, 15 In. 3870.00
Yo–Yo 150.00
SILVER–SWEDEN, Cup, Cover, Horn, Silver Mounts, Enameled Flowers, 10 1/4 In. 3025.00

Sinclaire cut glass was made by H. P. Sinclaire and Company of Corning, New York, between 1905 and 1929. He cut glass made at other factories until until 1920. Pieces were made of crystal as well as amber, blue, green, or ruby glass. Only a small percentage of Sinclaire glass is marked with the S in a wreath.

SINCLAIRE, Bowl, Rock Crystal, Leaves, Flowers 550.00
Box, Powder, Intaglio 175.00
Candlestick, Rose Color, Engraved Flowers, Signed, 3 1/2 In., Pair 145.00
Candlestick, White Rim, Black Jade, Signed, 9 In. 95.00
Clock, Diamonds & Silver Threads Pattern, 5 x 3 3/4 In. 685.00
Finger Bowl, Underplate, Cut Glass 70.00
Loving Cup, Rock Crystal, 10 In. 550.00
Sugar & Creamer, Etched Floral 160.00
Teapot, Carnation, Unpolished Intaglio, Signed 2200.00
Tray, Snowflake & Holly, Signed, Round, 12 1/2 In. 3500.00
Tray, Stars & Pillars, Signed, 13 In. 3850.00
Vase, Band of Hobstars, Tapering St. Louis Diamond, 14 In. 550.00
Vase, Diamond & Silver Threads, 30 In., 3 Piece 4000.00
Vase, Engraved Grapes & Maple Leaves, Handles With Rings, 8 In. 275.00

Slag glass resembles a marble cake. It can be streaked with different colors. There were many types made from about 1880. Pink slag was an American Victorian product of unknown origin. Purple and blue slag were made in American and English factories. Red slag is a very late–Victorian and twentieth–century glass. Other colors are known but are of less importance to the collector.

SLAG, Blue, Eyecup 15.00
    SLAG, CARAMEL, see Chocolate Glass
Green, Cruet 35.00
Green, Eyecup 15.00
Green, Shade, Streaked & Mottled, Geometric Design, 18 In. 410.00
Pink, Butter, Cover, Inverted Fan & Feather 950.00
Pink, Compote, Inverted Fan & Feather 425.00
Pink, Compote, Jelly, Inverted Fan & Feather 525.00
Pink, Cruet, Inverted Fan & Feather 1250.00
Pink, Eyecup 15.00
Pink, Pitcher, Water, Inverted Fan & Feather 1450.00
Pink, Punch Cup, Inverted Fan & Feather 265.00
Pink, Sauce, Inverted Fan & Feather 225.00
Pink, Toothpick, Inverted Fan & Feather 850.00
Pink, Tumbler 485.00
Pink, Tumbler, Water, Inverted Fan & Feather, 4 In. 350.00
Purple, Cake Stand, 10 In. 120.00
Purple, Cat On Basket, Westmoreland 40.00
Purple, Celery Vase, Jewel Pattern, 8 3/4 In. 87.50
Purple, Compote, Jelly 48.00
Purple, Dish, Chicken Cover, 5 In. 15.00
Purple, Dish, Eagle Cover, 8 In. 160.00

Purple, Dish, Fox Cover, 8 In. 160.00
Purple, Figurine, Indian, 4 In. 35.00
Purple, Pitcher, Raised Cherries, 5 In. 75.00
Purple, Spooner, Oval Medallion 100.00
Purple, Spooner, Scroll With Acanthus 45.00
Purple, Sugar & Creamer, Owl, Glass Eyes 60.00
Purple, Sugar, Cover, Tree of Life 150.00
Red, Candlestick & Bowl Set, Northwood, 3 Piece 150.00
Red, Rose Bowl, Imperial, 9 1/4 In. 125.00

Sleepy Eye collectors look for anything bearing the image of the 19th–century Indian chief with the drooping eyelid. The Sleepy Eye Milling Co., Sleepy Eye, Minnesota, used his portrait in advertising from 1883 to 1921. It offered many premiums, including stoneware and pottery steins, crocks, bowls, mugs, and pitchers, all decorated with the famous profile of the Indian. The pottery was popular and was made by Western Stoneware and other potteries long after the flour mill went out of business in 1921. Reproductions of the pitchers are being made today. The original pitchers came in only five sizes: 4 in., 5 1/4 in., 6 1/2 in., 8 in., and 9 in. The Sleepy Eye image was also used by companies unrelated to the flour mill.

SLEEPY EYE, Butter Crock 500.00
Cookbook, Shape of Loaf of Bread 230.00
Cookbook, Sleepy Eye Milling Co., Indian 45.00
Crock Salt, Butter, Blue & Gray, 6 1/2 In. Diam. .... 350.00 To 550.00
Display, Counter, Indian, Die–Cut Tin, Stand–Up 6250.00
Fan, Indian Chief, Die Cut, Advertising, 1900 .... 180.00
Fan, Tassle, Framed ....95.00 To 110.00
Flour Sack, Brown Paper, St. Louis 140.00
Flour Sack, Logo, Blue & White, Framed, 11 x 11 In. 75.00
Mug, 6 Piece 900.00
Mug, Blue & White, Marked, 4 1/4 In. 145.00
Mug, Blue & White, Marked, 4 3/4 In. 165.00
Paperweight, Bronzed Head 140.00
Pillow Cover, President Monroe 350.00
Pitcher, Indian, Brown & Green, 1 Qt. .... 230.00 To 400.00
Pitcher, No. 1, Blue & White, 4 In. 175.00
Pitcher, No. 1, Blue On White, 4 In. 170.00
Pitcher, No. 2, Blue & White, 5 In. .... 110.00 To 250.00
Pitcher, No. 3, Blue & Gray, 6 1/2 In. 225.00
Pitcher, No. 3, Blue & White, 6 1/2 In. ....95.00 To 225.00
Pitcher, No. 4, Blue & White, 8 In. .... 155.00 To 190.00
Pitcher, No. 4, Blue On Cream, 8 In. 275.00
Pitcher, No. 5, Blue & Gray, 9 In. 255.00
Pitcher, No. 5, Blue & White, 9 In. 225.00
Pitcher, No. 5, Brown & Off–White, 9 In. 925.00
Plate, Miniature 15.00
Salt Bowl, Weir .... 450.00 To 500.00
Sign, Flour & Cereals Free, Die Cut, Tin, 9 3/4 x 13 1/4 In. 6875.00
Spoon 90.00
Stein, Blue & White, Weir, 7 3/4 In. 325.00
Stein, Blue On Gray 675.00
Stein, Brown & Gold 875.00
Sugar Bowl, 3 In. .... 275.00 To 400.00
Thermometer, Cut–Out Brass 250.00
Thimble 200.00
Vase, Cattails, Blue & Gray, 9 In. 425.00
Vase, Flemish Indian & Cattails 325.00
    SLOT MACHINE, see Coin–Operated Machine

Smith Brothers glass was made after 1878. Alfred and Harry Smith had worked for the Mt. Washington Glass Company in New Bedford, Massachusetts, for seven years before going into their own shop. They made many pieces with enamel decoration.

SMITH BROTHERS, Biscuit Jar, Melon Ribbed, Gold Butterfly & Blossoms	522.00
Biscuit Jar, Oriental Style Floral, Silver Plated Mount	88.00
Cookie Jar, Spider Mums, Leaves, Gold Flowers, Signed	825.00
Perfume Bottle, Carnations Outlined In Gold, Marked	595.00
Perfume Bottle, Gold Daisies, Blue Leaves, Melon, 5 1/2 In.	165.00
Powder Box, Melon Ribbed, Iris Blossoms, Gold Leaves, 4 In.	335.00
Sugar & Creamer, Ribbed, Flowers, Plated Fittings	415.00
Sugar & Creamer, Silver Plated Spout & Collar	435.00
Sweetmeat, Cover, Melon Ribbed, Gold Outlined Florals	295.00
Syrup, Melon Ribbed, Swags of Daisies, Metal Lid, 5 1/4 In.	485.00
Vase, Blue Floral, Gold Gilt Design, Signed, 6 3/4 In.	525.00
Vase, Canteen Shape, Wisteria, Gold Leaves, Signed, 8 1/2 In.	1250.00
Vase, Florals, Dark Gray Ground, 10 1/2 In.	150.00
Vase, Japanese Style, Birds In Branch, 8 In.	45.00
Vase, Pansies, Gold Tracery, Bead Trim, Marked, 6 x 4 In.	225.00
Vase, Swirl Mold, Enameled Daisies, Marked, 7 In.	565.00
Vase, Tropical Bird, Palm Tree Branch, Signed, 6 In.	550.00

Snow Babies, made from bisque and spattered with glitter sand, were first manufactured in 1864 by Hertwig and Company of Thuringia. Other German and Japanese companies copied the Hertwig designs. Originally, Snow Babies were made of candy and used as Christmas decorations. There are also Snow Babies tablewares made by Royal Bayreuth. Copies of the small Snow Babies figurines are being made today and can easily confuse the collector.

SNOW BABIES, Creamer, Gold Trim, Squat	90.00
Tea Cup, Blue Mark	50.00
Tea Tile, Royal Bayreuth, 6 In.	90.00
Vase, Brown Ground, 3 1/4 In.	100.00
SNUFF BOTTLE, see Bottle, Snuff	

Taking snuff was popular long before cigarettes became available. The snuff was kept in a small box. The gentleman or lady would take a small pinch of the ground tobacco or snuff in the fingers, then sniff it and sneeze. Snuffboxes were made of many materials, including gold, silver, enameled metal, and wood. Most snuffboxes date from the late–eighteenth or early–nineteenth centuries.

SNUFFBOX, Burl, 3 1/2 In.	175.00
Carved Floral Cover, Carved Horn, Brass Edges, c.1820, 3 3/4 In.	425.00
Coin Silver, W. C., Scrolls, Oval, 3 x 3 5/8 In.	175.00
Enameled Band of Flowers, Swiss, c.1830, 3 3/8 In.	3850.00
Enameled Border, Basket of Flowers, Gold, Swiss, 3 1/8 In.	5500.00
Enameled Leaves, Gold, Swiss, c.1810, 3 1/2 In.	4500.00
Foliage On Matted Ground, 3–Color Gold, Paris, 1788, 3 1/4 In.	4500.00
Heart Shape, 3 Sections, Hook & Eye Fastener, Brass, 1800s	85.00
Hinged Cover, Bright Cut Engraving, Shoe Shape, Pewter, 4 1/8 In.	250.00
Hinged Lid, Briarwood, Silver Wheels, Rawlings & Summer, 10 In.	5150.00
Italian Mosaic Cover, Swiss, Gold, c.1830, 3 1/4 In.	9950.00
Painting On Ivory Set In Top, Tortoiseshell	400.00
Pocketwatch Shape, Hunting Scene, Metal, 3 1/4 In.	40.00
Red & Gold Cover, Louis XV, 2–Color Gold, Garbe, 1762, 2 3/4 In.	9350.00
Shoe Shape, Copper Tacks In Sole, Leather, 4 1/4 In.	165.00

Soapstone is a mineral that was used for foot warmers or griddles because of its heat-retaining properties. Soapstone was carved into figurines and bowls in many countries in the nineteenth and twentieth centuries. Most of the soapstone seen today is from China or Japan. It is still being carved in the old styles.

SOAPSTONE, Bookends, Urn & Flowers, 5 x 6 1/2 In.	70.00
Container, Monkey & Bat, 3 In.	65.00
Container, Water, Lotus, 3 In.	45.00
Figure, Seal, With Food Dog, 7 In.	20.00
Figurine, Black Rabbit, With Orange Spotted Rabbit, 4 In.	45.00
Figurine, Foo Dog, 8 In., Pair	55.00
Figurine, Sage, Carved Black Base, 6 In.	110.00
Figurine, Woman, Alabaster Bust, Hands & Shoes, Fiaschi, 33 In.	1760.00
Jar, Mounted As Lamp, Green, Silk Shade, Jade Finial, 31 In.	175.00
Lamp, Figural, Silk Shade, 21 In.	395.00
Lamp, Spout, 7 1/2 In.	55.00
Urn, Cover, Foo Lion Finial, Foo Dog Design, 9 1/2 In.	35.00
Vase, White, Carved, Base, China, 1900, 8 3/4 In.	125.00

Soft paste is a name for a type of pottery. Although it looks very much like porcelain, it is a chemically different material. Most of the soft-paste wares were made in the early nineteenth century. Other pieces may be listed under Gaudy Dutch or Leeds.

SOFT PASTE, Bowl, Floral Design, 4 Colors, 4 x 9 In.	500.00
Coffeepot, King's Rose, Green & Yellow Flowers, 10 1/2 In.	330.00
Coffeepot, Red Grapes, Pink Luster Roses & Vines, 11 1/2 In.	55.00
Creamer, Brown Floral Transfer With Birds, 3 1/8 In.	25.00
Creamer, Floral Design, 3 Colors, 3 5/8 In.	150.00
Creamer, Floral Design, 3 Colors, Stripes, 3 1/8 In.	105.00
Creamer, Gaudy Floral, Ribbed Handle, Leaf Ends, 3 5/8 In.	250.00
Creamer, Peafowl In Tree, 5 Colors, 4 1/4 In.	500.00
Creamer, Tulip Design, 3 3/8 In.	500.00
Cup & Saucer, Gold Sprig	90.00
Cup & Saucer, Handleless, Black Transfer of Mill	65.00
Cup & Saucer, Handleless, Gaudy Floral	115.00
Mug, Foliage Design, Silver Luster Resist, 2 5/8 In.	125.00
Pitcher, Farmer's Tools, Horse, Cow, James Farr, 1803, 7 7/8 In.	2600.00
Pitcher, Gaudy Floral, Embossed Leaf Handle, 6 7/8 In.	525.00
Pitcher, Sheaf & Farm Tools Design, 5 Colors, 6 5/8 In.	400.00
Plate, Eagle In 5 Colors, Green Feather Rim, 10 In.	450.00
Plate, Feather Edge, Peafowl, Sponged Tree, 8 1/8 In.	400.00
Plate, Floral Design, 4 Colors, Scalloped Rim, 8 1/4 In.	150.00
Plate, Floral Design, Green Edge, Octagonal, 6 5/8 In.	1400.00
Plate, Green Feather Edge, Peafowl, Sponged Tree, 7 3/8 In.	550.00
Plate, King's Rose, Pink Border, 7 1/2 In.	125.00
Platter, Oriental Design, Insert, 15 In.	95.00
Soup, Dish, Green Feather Rim, Floral At 4 Corners, 8 1/8 In.	160.00
Sugar Shaker, Stick Spatter	65.00
Sugar, Gaudy Floral, Acorn Finial, 6 In.	200.00
Sugar, Gaudy Floral, Blue & White, 4 1/2 In.	125.00

◆◆

Safety tips: If garage windows are painted, burglars won't be able to tell if cars are home or not. Use translucent paint to get light in the closed garage, if it has an entrance to your house. Mailboxes large enough to conceal several days' mail make daily pickup unnecessary. Don't put your name on signs outside your house. Install large windows; burglars avoid shattering them because of noise.

◆◆

Tea Bowl & Saucer, Tea Drinkers, Blue, Signed	70.00
Teapot, Black Transfer, Oriental Scenery, 5 1/2 In.	400.00
Teapot, Gaudy Floral, Miniature	750.00
Teapot, Leeds Floral Design, 5 Colors, 6 In.	200.00

What could be more fun than to bring home a souvenir of a trip? Our ancestors enjoyed the same thing and souvenirs were made for almost every location. Most of the souvenir pottery and porcelain pieces of the nineteenth century were made in England or Germany, even if the picture showed a North American scene. In the twentieth century, the souvenir china business seems to have gone to the manufacturers in Japan, Taiwan, Hong Kong, England, and America. Another popular souvenir item is the souvenir spoon, made of sterling or silver plate. These are usually made in the country pictured on the spoon.

SOUVENIR, see also Coronation; World's Fair

SOUVENIR, Ashtray, Boeing No. 247 Airplane, 1934	200.00
Ashtray, Las Vegas, Miniature Roulette Wheel Base	15.00
Ashtray, Le Lido, Black & Rust Gondola, Limoges	30.00
Ashtray, Maxim's, Red Bellhop & Umbrella, Haviland	35.00
Ashtray, Mirabelle Restaurant, London, Rosenthal	35.00
Badge, Silk Flag Ribbon, Woman's Relief Corps, 1890s	30.00
Cufflinks, Miss America Pageant, Sterling	17.00
Cup, Colorado, Green	35.00
Dish, Heart, 6 Lakes, Michigan, Ruby Stain, Scroll Border	20.00
Dish, Heart, Garden of Gods, Cobalt Flashed Gold, Wheelock, 3 In.	22.00
Dish, Panama Canal	25.00
Glass Dome, Atlanta Expo, Cotton Inside, Dated 1895	250.00
Goblet, Cranberry Stain, Chambersburg, Pa., Dum Clavum Teneam, 1906	40.00
Goblet, Double Beaded Band, Seattle, Wa., Ruby Stain	65.00
Key, Pretzel Handle, Reading, Pa., Prezel Capital, World, Iron, Large	35.00
Knife, Glass, Treasure Island, Box, Marked 1939	40.00
Life Preserver, S. S. Florida, Miami–Havanna, Miniature	45.00
Map, Hollywood Star's Homes, 1963, 23 x 19 In.	10.00
Mirror, Joan Blondell Picture, Auto	20.00
Mug, Child's, H. M. S. Pinafore	25.00
Mug, Gettysburg, Drum & Eagle, Ruby Flashed, Gold Trim, 1913	45.00
Mug, Katie Flaherty, Green, Gold	25.00
Mug, Mother 1903, Lacy Medallion, Ruby Stained	28.00
Pin, Zeppelin, 1930	45.00
Pitcher, Chicago Midland Club, Silver	100.00
Pitcher, Conneaut Lake, Pressed Glass	52.00
Pitcher, Ruby Flashed, McFarland, July 21, 1900, 3 In.	38.00
Pitcher, Ruby Stained, Woodstock, Ill., 4 In.	18.00
Pitcher, Water, Hammered Silver, Edgewater Beach Hotel, Heavy	120.00
Plaque, Lincoln, Louisiana Purchase Exposition, Weller, 1904	50.00
Plate, Columbo Expo, Machinery Bldg., Blue, White, 1893, 8 1/2 In.	32.00
Plate, Kentucky Derby, 1964	16.00
Plate, Mirror Lake Inn, Lake Placid, Adirondacks, Scene, B. Heiges	35.00
Plate, Panama Canal, Scene, 9 In.	39.00
Plate, Pittsburg Commandery, 28th Triennial, 1901, Cobalt Blue	55.00
Plate, Point Loma Lighthouse, 1900s	85.00
Plate, Texas Centennial, Wedgwood, Alamo Scene	135.00
Shell, Carved, Coney Island, 1900	25.00
Shoe, Memorial University, Picture, China, Germany	17.50
Spoon, Brass, Century of Progress	9.00
Spoon, Sterling Silver, Alaska, Husky Dog & Pups	54.00
Spoon, Sterling Silver, Alaska, Juneau	47.50
Spoon, Sterling Silver, Alaska, Mendenhall's Glacier	47.50
Spoon, Sterling Silver, Atlantic City, N. J.	28.00
Spoon, Sterling Silver, Baptist Church, Iowa	35.00
Spoon, Sterling Silver, Carlisle, Kentucky	25.00
Spoon, Sterling Silver, Carlsbad Caverns, Totem Poles	28.50

Spoon, Sterling Silver, Century of Progress, 1934	18.00
Spoon, Sterling Silver, Courthouse, Iowa	38.00
Spoon, Sterling Silver, Deer Lodge, Montana	38.00
Spoon, Sterling Silver, Elks Home, Ft. Worth	15.00
Spoon, Sterling Silver, Ellsworth College, Iowa Falls	38.00
Spoon, Sterling Silver, Enameled, Statue of Liberty Bowl	42.00
Spoon, Sterling Silver, Home of Andrew Jackson	14.00
Spoon, Sterling Silver, Honolulu, Pineapple, Cut–Out Handle	30.00
Spoon, Sterling Silver, Humboldt Library, Iowa	35.00
Spoon, Sterling Silver, Kansas, Sunflower, Capitol In Bowl	30.00
Spoon, Sterling Silver, Kentucky, Bust of Daniel Boone	37.50
Spoon, Sterling Silver, Kentucky, Daniel Boone Cabin	42.50
Spoon, Sterling Silver, Kentucky, Henry Clay Monument	42.50
Spoon, Sterling Silver, Kentucky, Old Kentucky Home, Floral Back	37.50
Spoon, Sterling Silver, Mackinac Island, Michigan, Indian Chief	30.00
Spoon, Sterling Silver, Maine, Courthouse	27.50
Spoon, Sterling Silver, Maine, Forest Scene	27.50
Spoon, Sterling Silver, Maine, Golfers	27.50
Spoon, Sterling Silver, Maine, State Seal	27.50
Spoon, Sterling Silver, Mason City, Iowa	25.00
Spoon, Sterling Silver, Mexico, Eagle & Wreath Bowl	22.50
Spoon, Sterling Silver, Montana, Cowboy	40.00
Spoon, Sterling Silver, Morgan, Public School, Minn., Indian Handle	50.00
Spoon, Sterling Silver, New Orleans, Enameled Cathedral	50.00
Spoon, Sterling Silver, New York, World's Fair, 1939, Floral Back	56.50
Spoon, Sterling Silver, Niagara Falls	13.00
Spoon, Sterling Silver, Niagara, Indian Head	30.00
Spoon, Sterling Silver, Pan American Exposition Tower, 1901	25.00
Spoon, Sterling Silver, Panama Exposition, 1915	60.00
Spoon, Sterling Silver, Panama Pacific Exposition, 1915	20.00
Spoon, Sterling Silver, Plateville, State Normal School, Wisconsin	38.00
Spoon, Sterling Silver, Prospector, Cut–Out Donkey Handle	35.00
Spoon, Sterling Silver, Rich Hill, Missouri	12.00
Spoon, Sterling Silver, Santa Monica	15.00
Spoon, Sterling Silver, Skagway, Alaska	32.00
Spoon, Sterling Silver, St. Louis, City Seal Adopted 1823	37.50
Spoon, Sterling Silver, St. Louis, Columbus Monument	37.50
Spoon, Sterling Silver, St. Louis, East Bridge	37.50
Spoon, Sterling Silver, University of Nebraska, Ornate, Watson	35.00
Spoon, Sterling Silver, Waterloo, Iowa	26.00
Spoon, Sterling Silver, West Virginia, Men With Picks & Shovels	30.00
Spoon, Sterling Silver, Windmill Handle, 8 In.	25.00
Spoon, Sterling Silver, World's Fair, 1893	30.00
Spoon, Sterling Silver, World's Fair, 1964, Teapot On Handle	30.00
Stickpin, Frying Pan, With Buffalo Head, Pan–American Expo., 1901	36.00
Stickpin, National Education Association, New York, 1916	20.00
Swizzle Stick, Don Ho, Hawaii, Red	6.00
Swizzle Stick, Hotel Marquette, St. Louis, Cobalt Blue Glass	12.50
Swizzle Stick, Stork Club, Cobalt Blue Glass	12.00
Tie Tack, St. Louis Cardinals, 14K Gold	18.00
Tumbler, Baltimore Orioles, Mike Boddicker, 1959, Orange, 6 1/8 In.	4.00
Tumbler, Cincinnati Reds, Reds Take It, 1, 2, 3, 1975, 5 1/2 In.	2.00
Tumbler, Golf, Archer of Advisory Staff, Wilson Logo, 3 3/4 In.	2.00
Tumbler, Indianapolis 500, 1971	12.00
Tumbler, Kentucky Derby, 1964	15.00
Tumbler, Kentucky Derby, 1973	10.00
Tumbler, Kentucky Derby, Churchill Downs, Frosted, 1940–50, 5 In.	66.00
Wine, Hubbleton, Wisc., Custard Glass	45.00

 Spangle glass is multicolored glass made from odds and ends of colored glass rods. It includes metallic flakes of mica covered with gold, silver, nickel, or copper. Spangle glass is usually cased with a thin layer of clear glass over the multicolored layer.

SPANGLE GLASS, see also Vasa Murrhina

SPANGLE GLASS, Cruet, Silver Mica Flakes, White Mottling, Clear Stopper	235.00
Pitcher, Mica Flakes, Amber Handle, 6 In.	125.00
Pitcher, Square Top, Amber Shell Handle, 5 In.	275.00
Rose Bowl, Mica Flecks Between Blue Exterior, 3 3/4 In.	95.00
Tumbler, Inverted Thumbprint, Orange, White, 3 3/4 In.	45.00
Vase, Cherries, Leaf Rigaree, Gold Mica Flecks, 8 1/2 In.	550.00
Vase, Gold Mica, Pink Cased, Ruffled, Cherries, 8 1/2 In.	450.00
Vase, Ruffled, Clear Glass Footed	75.00

Spanish lace is a type of Victorian glass that has a white lace design. Blue, yellow, cranberry, or clear glass was made with this distinctive white pattern. It was made in England and the United States after 1885. Copies are being made.

SPANISH LACE, Cracker Jar, Cranberry	675.00
Pitcher, Water, Blue	110.00
Pitcher, Water, Blue Opalescent Handle, Blue	195.00
Rose Bowl, Opalescent White	35.00
Sugar	40.00
Sugar Shaker, Brass Plated Top, Bulbous, 4 1/2 In.	85.00
Sugar Shaker, Cranberry	165.00
Sugar, Cover, Blue	75.00
Syrup, Blue	130.00
Tumbler, Cranberry Opalescent	95.00
Vase, Canary, 6 1/2 In.	65.00
Vase, Cranberry, 11 In.	595.00
Water Bottle, Silver Plated Top, Yellow	195.00
Water Set, 9 Piece	235.00

Spatter glass is a multicolored glass made from many small pieces of different colored glass. It is sometimes called *End-Of-Day* glass. It is still being made.

SPATTER GLASS, Basket, Pin, Aqua, Brown, White, Thorn Handle, 8 In.	250.00
Basket, Thorn Handle, Blue, White & Brown, 7 1/2 In.	165.00
Bowl, Rock Island Lumber Co., Blue, Rust, Cream, 9 In.	65.00
Pitcher, Cranberry, Frosted, Swirl, Frosted Handle, 5 1/2 In.	145.00
Salt, Cylinder, Maroon, Pink, White Ground, 3 In.	125.00
Vase, Enameled Daisies, Clear Handle, 3 Petal Top, 12 In.	125.00

The creamware or soft-paste dinnerware decorated with spatter designs in color is called, of course, spatterware. The earliest pieces were made in the late-eighteenth century, but most of the spatterware found today was made from about 1800 to 1850 or is a late-nineteenth- and twentieth-century form of kitchen crockery that has added spatter designs. The early spatterware was made in the Staffordshire district of England for sale in America. The later kitchen type is an American product.

SPATTERWARE, Bowl, Castle, 2 Sided Circular, 13 1/2 In.	248.00
Bowl, Vegetable, Scalloped Rim, Blue & White Sponge, 9 In.	125.00
Box, Dove Shape, Blue & Pink, 8 In.	330.00
Center Bowl, Eagle & Shield, Blue, Footed, Handles, 6 x 10 In.	523.00
Center Bowl, Rose, Blue Banded, Octagonal, 11 In.	495.00
Coffeepot, Blue & White, Cover	35.00
Coffeepot, Blue, Flared, Faceted Foot, Scroll Handle, 10 3/4 In.	330.00
Coffeepot, Tulip, Yellow, Octagonal, 8 In.	2310.00
Creamer, Blue, Miniature	15.00
Creamer, Cluster of Buds, Red & Blue, Bulbous, 3 3/8 In.	220.00
Creamer, Fort, Blue Paneled, 6 1/8 In.	800.00
Creamer, Part Flower, Red & Blue, 4 In.	250.00
Creamer, Peafowl, Thumbprint, 4 In.	150.00
Creamer, Rainbow & Leaf, Red, Green, Amber, 3 3/4 In.	605.00
Creamer, Red Dots, 4 In.	155.00
Creamer, Rose & Bud, Blue, 4 In.	200.00

Creamer, Rose, Octagonal, Blue, 5 1/2 In. 413.00
Creamer, Schoolhouse, Bulbous, Red, Green 1980.00
Creamer, Townhouse, Black, Blue, Red, Purple 2860.00
Creamer, Tulip, Yellow, Octagonal, James Edwards, 4 3/4 In. 990.00
Creamer, Tulip, Yellow, Squared Octagonal, 4 3/4 In. 1650.00
Creamer, Windmill, Red, Blue, Yellow, 4 5/8 In. 1430.00
Crock, Pastry, Draped Windows, Lid, Bail 165.00
Cup & Saucer, Eagle In Flight, Yellow, 2 1/2 x 5 7/8 In. 775.00
Cup & Saucer, Gooney Bird, Blue Green, Purple, Black 798.00
Cup & Saucer, Handleless, Fort Pattern, Blue 125.00
Cup & Saucer, Handleless, Peafowl, Red 225.00
Cup & Saucer, Handleless, Red & Green Thistle 250.00
Cup & Saucer, Handleless, Tulip, Blue 175.00
Cup & Saucer, Rainbow, Red, Black, Green, 2 1/2 x 4 1/2 In. 3300.00
Cup & Saucer, Shield With Stars, Red, Blue 1100.00
Cup & Saucer, Star, Blue, Red, Green 413.00
Cup & Saucer, Star, Border, 2 3/4 x 5 3/4 In. 413.00
Cup, Fish, Red, Green, Black, 4 In. 2420.00
Cup, Handleless, Black & Green, Miniature 75.00
Cup, Peafowl, George, 3 1/4 In. 1025.00
Dish, Serving, Thistle, Octagonal, Yellow Border, 10 3/8 In. 1045.00
Dish, Serving, Thistle, Yellow Border, Octagonal, 9 1/8 In. 3080.00
Dish, Umbrella Flower, Purple, Blue, Green, Deep, 10 3/8 In. 2090.00
Honey Pot, Schoolhouse, Blue, 5 1/2 In. 6820.00
Jug, Tulip, Pink & Red, Yellow Spatter, 7 1/4 In. ....*Illus* 885.00
Mug, Peafowl, Blue, 2 1/2 In. 425.00
Mug, Peafowl, Cream, Inscription, 4 3/4 In. 55.00
Mug, Peafowl, Yellow, Blue, Red, Inscription, Miniature, 2 1/2 In. 1018.00
Mug, Pheasant, Peafowl In Red, Yellow, Blue, 5 1/8 In. 660.00
Pitcher, Castle, Octagonal, Black, Red, Green, Blue, 11 In. 1870.00
Pitcher, Rainbow, Bulbous Middle, Scroll Handle, 8 1/4 In. 880.00
Pitcher, Rainbow, Octagonal, Blue Handle & Base, 8 7/8 In. 2530.00
Pitcher, Rainbow, Paneled, Bulbous Middle, 9 3/4 In. 2090.00
Pitcher, Rooster, Cream, Bulbous, W. Kazmer, 7 In. 66.00
Pitcher, Rose Design, Red, 8 5/8 In. 125.00
Pitcher, Tulip, Leaves, Yellow Spatter, 8 1/2 In. ....*Illus* 1650.00
Plate, Acorn & Oak Leaf, Blue, 9 3/8 In. 550.00
Plate, Acorn, Purple, 9 3/8 In. 800.00
Plate, Bird On A Fence, Creamware, c.1785–1790, 7 7/8 In. 1320.00
Plate, Bird On A Fence, Creamware, c.1785–1790, 8 1/4 In. 1045.00
Plate, Blue Peafowl, Red, 8 1/8 In. 300.00
Plate, Castle, Brown, Red, Green, Blue, 9 5/8 In. 880.00
Plate, Clover Flower, Green, Red, Black, 9 1/2 In. 880.00
Plate, Cowboy & Horse, Red Transfer, Red, 9 1/2 In. 100.00
Plate, Crisscross, Blue, Red, 9 3/4 In. 825.00
Plate, Eagle In Flight, Blue Border, 8 1/4 In. 275.00
Plate, Fort, Blue, 9 3/4 In. 650.00
Plate, Morning Glory, Blue, Black, Green, Yellow 1210.00
Plate, Parrot, Red, Green, Blue, 7 1/4 In. 743.00
Plate, Peafowl & Three–Color Rainbow, 8 1/4 In. 1870.00
Plate, Peafowl In Tree, Blue, Adams, 10 1/2 In. 525.00
Plate, Peafowl, 9 1/2 In. 500.00
Plate, Peafowl, Blue Border, 10 7/8 In. 990.00
Plate, Peafowl, Blue, 9 1/2 In. 475.00
Plate, Peafowl, Blue, 9 3/4 In. 225.00
Plate, Peafowl, Blue, 9 5/8 In. 475.00
Plate, Peafowl, Blue, Yellow, Red, 9 1/2 In. 3850.00
Plate, Peafowl, Blue, Yellow, Red, Purple, 9 1/2 In. 1045.00
Plate, Peafowl, Light Blue, P. W. & Co., 8 5/8 In. 100.00
Plate, Peafowl, Red, 10 In. 275.00
Plate, Peafowl, Red, 7 5/8 In. 55.00
Plate, Peafowl, Red, 8 3/4 In. .... 400.00 To 425.00
Plate, Peafowl, Red, 9 1/4 In. 450.00

Spatterware, Pitcher, Tulip, Leaves,
Yellow Spatter, 8 1/2 In.
Spatterware, Sugar, Cover, Thistle,
Leaves, Hexagonal, 8 In.
Spatterware, Jug, Tulip, Pink & Red,
Yellow Spatter, 7 1/4 In.

Spatterware, Plate, Rabbit,
10 In.

Spatterware, Platter, Tulip,
18 In.

Plate, Peafowl, Red, Yellow, Green, Blue, 10 7/8 In.	990.00
Plate, Pineapple, Purple, Black, Green, Blue, 8 In.	2970.00
Plate, Pomegranate, Blue Border, 9 1/2 In.	550.00
Plate, Rabbit, 10 In. ....*Illus*	850.00
Plate, Rainbow, Bull's-Eye Center, Blue & Green, 9 1/2 In.	600.00
Plate, Rainbow, Bull's-Eye Center, Red & Green, 9 3/8 In.	270.00
Plate, Rainbow, Scalloped	1540.00
Plate, Red Stick, Flowers, Dotted Leaves, Staffordshire, 6 In.	42.00
Plate, Rooster, Red, 8 In.	210.00
Plate, Rose, Blue, 9 3/8 In.	275.00
Plate, Schoolhouse, Pearl Stoneware, 8 1/8 In.	95.00
Plate, Schoolhouse, Red, 8 3/8 In. .... 1000.00 To	1600.00
Plate, Schoolhouse, Red, 9 1/2 In.	175.00
Plate, Schoolhouse, Red, Green, 10 3/8 In.	2860.00
Plate, Schoolhouse, Red, Green, Blue, 10 1/4 In.	1870.00
Plate, Thistle, Red, Yellow, Green, 9 3/4 In.	990.00
Plate, Tulip, Blue Border, 9 7/8 In.	495.00
Plate, Tulip, Blue, Purple, Green, 9 1/4 In.	660.00
Plate, Tulip, Red, Green, Yellow, 8 3/4 In.	1700.00
Platter, Blue & White Sponge, 12 3/4 In.	200.00
Platter, Blue Transfer, Eagle & Shield, Purple, 15 1/2 In.	250.00
Platter, Eagle & Shield, Blue, Red, 17 3/4 In.	550.00
Platter, Thistle, Octagonal, Red, Green, Yellow, 10 In.	3630.00
Platter, Thistle, Yellow Border, Octagonal, 14 1/2 In.	8360.00
Platter, Tulip, 18 In. ....*Illus*	4840.00
Reindeer, Red Ground, Blue Border, 9 In.	990.00
Salt, Butterfly, Wooden Lid, Blue & White	85.00
Serving Dish, Thistle, Octagonal, Red, Green, Yellow, 9 1/8 In.	3080.00
Sugar Shaker, Ringneck, Cranberry	95.00
Sugar, Cover, 2 Men On A Raft, Blue, Bulbous, 4 1/4 In.	995.00
Sugar, Cover, Alternating Black & Yellow Stripe, 3 3/4 In.	2860.00
Sugar, Cover, Cluster of Buds, Bulbous, 4 1/2 In.	110.00
Sugar, Cover, Parrot, Blue, Globular, 4 In.	995.00
Sugar, Cover, Parrot, Globular, 5 In.	225.00
Sugar, Cover, Thistle, Leaves, Hexagonal, 8 In. ....*Illus*	3600.00
Sugar, Covered, Windmill, Red, Black, Green, Blue, 4 In.	660.00
Sugar, Fort, Blue, 8 1/2 In.	275.00
Sugar, Open, Tulip, Yellow, 5 1/8 In.	935.00
Sugar, Rooster In Blue, Red, Yellow & Black, 4 5/8 In.	65.00
Sugar, Tulip, Open, Wide-Flaring, 5 1/2 In.	358.00
Tea Set, Child's, Blue & White, 11 Piece	250.00
Teapot, 2-Tone, Rose Design, 6 In.	350.00
Teapot, Blue & Green, 5 1/2 In.	85.00
Teapot, Dove, Globular, Blue, Yellow, Green, Blue, 6 1/4 In.	415.00
Teapot, Miniature, Townhouse, Black, Blue, Red, Purple, 4 In.	2310.00
Teapot, Peafowl In Blue, Red, Green & Black, 8 1/2 In.	100.00
Teapot, Peafowl, Blue, 8 1/2 In.	400.00

◆◆◆

The best burglary protection is a dog. Inmates from three Ohio prisons were surveyed and said timed lights, deadbolt locks, and alarms are deterrents; but the thing most avoided by a professional thief is a noisy dog.

◆◆◆

Teapot, Rose, 10 1/2 In.	550.00
Teapot, Schoolhouse, 9 In.	3410.00
Teapot, Schoolhouse, Red, Blue, Yellow, 6 In.	1100.00
Tray, Yellow, White, 18 In.	64.00
Tureen, Covered, Castle, Yellow, Brown, Red, Green, Blue, 8 In.	4620.00

Spelter is a synonym for a zinc alloy. Figurines, candlesticks, and other pieces were made of spelter and given a bronze or painted finish. The metal has been used since about the 1860s to make statues, tablewares, and lamps that resemble bronze. Spelter is soft and breaks easily. To test for spelter, scratch the base of the piece. Bronze is solid; spelter will show a silvery scratch.

SPELTER, Bust, Girl, Les Cersis, Signed, 4 1/2 In.	250.00
Figurine, Horse, 5 x 7 In.	65.00
Figurine, Milton, 14 In.	70.00
Lamp, Boudoir, Slag Glass Shade, 15 In.	120.00
Lamp, Figural, Frosted Glass Flame Shade, 17 1/2 In., Pair	87.50
Salt & Pepper, Indian, 3 In.	25.00
Torchere, Warrior, Victorian, c.1885 ....*Illus*	850.00

The old spinning wheel in the corner has been the symbol of earlier times for the past 100 years. Although spinning wheels date back to medieval times, the ones found today are rarely more than 200 years old. Because the style of the spinning wheel changed very little, it is often impossible to place an exact date on a wheel.

SPINNING WHEEL, American, 40 In.	235.00
Flax	95.00
Flax, Complete	675.00
Flax, Shaker, Cherry, Oak Platform, Ivory Bushings	685.00
Original Paint	500.00
Original Spools, American, Oak, 74 x 61 In.	220.00
Shaker, Wooden Wheel Stamped D. M., 1743–26	990.00
Turned & Chip Carved, Oak, 34 1/2 In.	95.00

Spode pottery, porcelain, and bone china were made by the Stoke-on-Trent factory of England founded by Josiah Spode about 1770. The firm became Copeland and Garrett from 1833 to 1847, then W.

Spelter, Torchere, Warrior, Victorian, c.1885

Spode, Vase, Oriental Garden,
Scroll Handles, 10 3/16 In.

Stone-China

T. Copeland or W. T. Copeland and Sons until 1976. It then became Royal Worcester Spode Ltd. The word *Spode* appears on many pieces made by the factories. Most collectors include all the wares under the more familiar name of Spode. Porcelains are listed in this book by the name that appears on the piece.

SPODE, see also Copeland; Copeland Spode

Spongeware is very similar to spatterware in appearance. The designs were applied to the ceramics by daubing the color on with a sponge or cloth. Many collectors do not differentiate between

---

A vase that is drilled for a lamp, even if the hole for the wiring is original, is worth 30% to 50% of the value of the same vase without a hole.

spongeware and spatterware and use the names interchangeably. Modern pottery is being made to resemble the old spongeware, but careful examination will show it is new.

SPONGEWARE, Bowl, Blue & White Stick, 14 In. 495.00
Bowl, Blue & White, Bail, Wooden Handle, 8 1/2 x 4 In. 175.00
Bowl, Blue, Rust, Cream, Geneva, Iowa, 7 In. 120.00
Bowl, General Store, Blue, Rust, Cream, Geneva, Iowa 125.00
Bowl, Yellow, 12 In. 95.00
Cookie Jar, Red & Blue 127.00
Crock, Butter, Butter In Blue, 4 x 5 1/2 In. 190.00
Crock, Butter, Draped Windows, Cover, Bail, Tan & Blue 185.00
Crock, Butter, Embossed Cows, Pasture, Black, White, 1 Lb. 225.00
Cuspidor, Blue & White Sponge, 7 3/4 In. 20.00
Dish, Soap, Blue & White 50.00
Dish, Soap, Blue–Gray 210.00
Dish, Vegetable, Blue On White, c.1870, 9 x 8 x 2 In. 185.00
Pitcher, Barrel, Green, Yellow, Brown, 7 1/2 In. 90.00
Pitcher, Beige & Blue On White, 10 In. 125.00
Pitcher, Blue & White, Spatter, 9 In. 175.00
Pitcher, Embossed Swastika, 6 1/2 In. 175.00
Pitcher, Farmer's Coop, Jackson, Minn. 4 1/2 In. 75.00
Pitcher, Milk, Black & White, 7 1/2 In. 185.00
Pitcher, Wayside Cheese, Brockmann Proprietor, 4 1/2 In. 75.00
Slop Jar, Cover, Blue & White 235.00
Stand, Umbrella, Late 19th Century, 21 In. 550.00
Tea Set, Child's, Blue, 11 Piece 265.00
Teapot, Brown, Green, Cream 135.00
Vase, Black & White, 6 1/2 In. 20.00

Sporting goods, equipment, brochures, and related items are listed here. Other sections of interest are Bicycle; Card, Baseball; Fishing; Gun; Rifle; Sword; and Toy.

SPORTS, Baseball, Ball, Autographed, Babe Ruth .... 1200.00 To 1980.00
Baseball, Ball, Autographed, Brooklyn Dodgers, 23 Signatures, 1955 .... 1760.00
Baseball, Ball, Autographed, Brooklyn Dodgers, 26 Signatures, 1952 .... 2000.00
Baseball, Ball, Autographed, Cleveland Indians Team, 1954 .... 110.00
Baseball, Ball, Autographed, Cy Young, June 6th, 1931, Box 2475.00
Baseball, Ball, Autographed, Don Drysdale 18.00
Baseball, Ball, Autographed, Frank Robinson 25.00
Baseball, Ball, Autographed, Hall of Famers, 11 Signatures 2000.00
Baseball, Ball, Autographed, Joe Morgan 18.00
Baseball, Ball, Autographed, Kansas City Royals, 20 Signatures 75.00
Baseball, Ball, Autographed, Signed By 1975 Pirate Team 150.00
Baseball, Ball, Autographed, St. Louis Browns, 22 Signatures, 1952 .... 1500.00
Baseball, Ball, Autographed, Yankees, 26 Signatures, 1947 .... 2000.00
Baseball, Ball, Babe Ruth, 700th Home Run, Team Signatures 1934 .... 9350.00
Baseball, Ball, Seams On Outside, 1915 .... 30.00
Baseball, Ball, Wiffle, Pete Rose & Jerry Koosman, Box, 1960s 45.00
Baseball, Bank, Ball Shaped, National Baseball Hall of Fame, Glass 25.00
Baseball, Bat, Autographed By Ernie Banks 95.00
Baseball, Bat, Boy's Special, Louisville Bat Co. 7.00
Baseball, Bat, Honus Wagner, Black Tape, Stamped Wagner, c.1903 .... 3575.00
Baseball, Bat, Louisville Slugger, Carl Yastrzemski, Miniature 55.00
Baseball, Bobbing Head, Chicago Cub, White Square Base 125.00
Baseball, Button, Brooklyn Dodgers, Pinback, 1950s, 1 3/4 In. 10.00
Baseball, Button, Warren Spahn, Pinback, 1963, 2 In. 35.00
Baseball, Catcher's Mitt, Winchester 110.00
Baseball, Coaster, Gil Hodges 15.00
Baseball, Desk Set, 1923 Anniversary Yankee Stadium, Ruth Autograph 1320.00
Baseball, Figurine, Joe Dimaggio, Gartlan, Autographed 750.00
Baseball, Game, Board, Field, Walter Johnson Autograph, 10 x 14 In. 715.00
Baseball, Glove, Larry Sherry, Wilson, Dated 1941, Box 125.00

Baseball, Glove, Warren Spahn 10.00
Baseball, Glove, Winchester, 3 Signatures 300.00
Baseball, Guide, Spaulding, No Front Cover, 1888 .... 145.00
Baseball, Hat, Autographed, Pete Rose 395.00
Baseball, Jacket, Warm–Up, Brooklyn Dodgers, Blue, Dick Fisher, 1950 .... 660.00
Baseball, Jersey, Reggie Jackson, Oakland As, Number On Back 345.00
Baseball, Jersey, Willie Mays, Team Name, Number, 1989 .... 345.00
Baseball, Mitt, Catcher's, Wilson 8.00
Baseball, Mug, Beer, Pete Rose's Career Hit Record 25.00
Baseball, Mug, Dodgers Win Pennant, 1963 .... 15.00
Baseball, Photograph, Iron Sides, Team, Albumen, 1880s, 10 x 13 In. 165.00
Baseball, Picture, Babe Ruth, Autograph, Idol of America, 4 x 4 In. 550.00
Baseball, Picture, New York Giants Team, 1951 .... 40.00
Baseball, Picture, Ralph Kiner, On Dugout Steps, 1949 .... 25.00
Baseball, Pin, Dizzy Dean, Winner's 15.00
Baseball, Plate, Bob Feller, Dem Bums 75.00
Baseball, Plate, Mickey Mantle, Signed 195.00
Baseball, Plate, Ted Williams, Signed 125.00
Baseball, Program, All Star, Cleveland, Unscored, 1935 .... 220.00
Baseball, Program, All Star, St. Louis, Scored, 1940 .... 220.00
Baseball, Program, Cardinals At New York, Scored, 1928 .... 1210.00
Baseball, Program, Cubs At New York, Unscored, 1932 .... 935.00
Baseball, Program, Giants & Yankees, World Series, Autographed, 1936 .... 1210.00
Baseball, Program, Yankees & Giants, World Series, 1951 .... 75.00
Baseball, Program, Yankees At St. Louis, Babe Ruth Autograph, 1926 .... 1430.00
Baseball, Ring, 1972 World Series, 14K, White Stone, Charlie O. Finley 2450.00
Baseball, Shirt, Brooklyn Dodger, C. Dressen, Flannel, Size 42, 1952 .... 3025.00
Baseball, Uniform, Brooklyn Dodger, Bobby Bragan, Satin, No. 2, 1940 .... 5500.00
Baseball, Uniform, Brooklyn Dodger, George Shubar 1150.00
Basketball, Ball, Autographed, Lakers, c.1988 .... 605.00
Basketball, Jersey, Curly Neal, Harlem Globetrotters 1250.00
Basketball, Trophy, Full Figure, 1929 .... 40.00
Billiards, Table, Brunswick, Model VIP, Regulation Size, Accessories 950.00
Billiards, Table, Brunswick, Union League, Carved Oak 4000.00
Billiards, Ball, Ivory, Box, 3 Piece 75.00
Boxing, Button, Joe Louis, Brown Bomber, 1914–1981, 3 1/2 In. 12.50
Boxing, Clock, Joe Louis, Cast Metal 125.00
Boxing, Glove, Autographed, Floyd Patterson & Ingemar Johanson 90.00
Boxing, Glove, Autographed, Muhammad Ali 90.00
Boxing, Photograph, Young Ray Robinson, Sepia, 1939, 5 x 3 In. 25.00
Boxing, Picture, Autographed, Kid Mack, 1927 .... 25.00
Darts, Quackenbush 65.00
Football, Ball, Autographed, Joe Montana 100.00
Football, Ball, Autographed, Senators, 1954 .... 85.00
Football, Ball, Autographed, Unitas 85.00
Football, Helmet, Arkansas Razor Backs, Hogs On Front 200.00
Football, Helmet, Cleveland Browns, Size 7 1/8 .... 200.00
Football, Helmet, Leather, Wilson Sporting, Knute Rockne Endorsed 100.00
Football, Helmet, New England Patriots 200.00
Football, Jersey, Roger Staubach, Dallas Cowboys, Letter 3250.00
Football, Pants, Padded 35.00
Football, Picture, Fold–Out, Rose Bowl, Souvenir, 16 Pictures, 1925 .... 15.00
Football, Pin, Homecoming, Illinois Vs. Michigan, 1925 .... 45.00
Football, Pin, Homecoming, Iowa Vs. Minnesota, 1979 .... 8.00
Golf, Bag, Tripod, Bussey Patent 1430.00
Golf, Ball, Black Diamond, Worthington Rubber Co., 1915–1930 .... 20.00
Golf, Ball, Hawthorne, Square Mesh Pattern, c.1920 .... 20.00
Golf, Ball, Penfold, Spades Dimple, Display Box, 1940–1960 .... 25.00
Golf, Ball, Texaco, 3 Piece 20.00
Golf, Ball, Wilson, Cheero Square Mesh Pattern, 1920–1930 .... 25.00
Golf, Bookends, Golfer In Sandtrap, Titled Profanity, Bronze 125.00
Golf, Caddy Bag, Built–In Wheels, Wicker, c.1925 .... 1485.00
Golf, Club Starter Set, Wilson Junior, 3 Clubs, 1920–1930 .... 150.00

Golf, Club, 2 Iron, Woman's, Bamboo Shaft, BTN, 1920	35.00
Golf, Club, Brassie, Aberdeen, Wood, 1910–1920	45.00
Golf, Club, Brassie, Bone Insert, Burkey Bilt, c.1910	75.00
Golf, Club, Driver Mashie, Slazenger & Sons, c.1903	450.00
Golf, Club, Driver, Black Fiber Insert, W. Leith, c.1920	125.00
Golf, Club, Driver, Sweny Patent	3850.00
Golf, Club, Driver, Wilson, Wood, 1910–20	75.00
Golf, Club, Driver, Wood, Juvenile, William Burke, c.1914	75.00
Golf, Club, Driving Niblick, Spalding	2090.00
Golf, Club, Iron, Juvenile, C. C. Chatell & Co., c.1900	65.00
Golf, Club, Left–Handed, MacGregor, Iron, 1920	200.00
Golf, Club, Lofter, Lunn & Co., London, c.1890	150.00
Golf, Club, Lofting Mashie, Iron, B. G. I., c.1897	75.00
Golf, Club, Louise Suggs, L. P. G. A., MacGregor Boxes	2750.00
Golf, Club, Mashie, Abercrombie & Fitch, Iron, 1920–1930	50.00
Golf, Club, Mashie, Iron, Ayres, 1890s	225.00
Golf, Club, Mashie, Mono Metl, Abercombie & Fitch, c.1920	50.00
Golf, Club, Mashie, Sharpe's Patent	525.00
Golf, Club, Mid–Iron, Jim Harnett, c.1920	50.00
Golf, Club, Niblick, Beckley Ralston, Iron	50.00
Golf, Club, Niblick, Cardinal Dreadnought, Hendry & Bishop, c.1910	225.00
Golf, Club, Putter, Amby Dex, Aluminum Mallet Head, 1910	550.00
Golf, Club, Putter, Amby Dex, c.1910	550.00
Golf, Club, Putter, Brass Headed Blade, Edinboro, c.1900	75.00
Golf, Club, Putter, Otto Hackbarth	550.00
Golf, Club, Putter, Split Forked Hosel, Hackbarth, Otto, c.1915	550.00
Golf, Club, Putter, Winchester	130.00
Golf, Club, Spalding, Wooden Shaft	16.00
Golf, Club, Wood, No. 2, David Anderson, c.1910	95.00
Golf, Club, Wood, No. 3, Winchester	135.00
Golf, Counter, Strokes, Wrist–Type	14.00
Golf, Loving Cup, Ohio Golf Championship, 1920, Sterling, 9 1/2 In.	100.00
Golf, Pen & Pencil, To Walter Hagen By Duke & Duchess of Windsor	2310.00
Golf, Print, 18th At Pebble Beach, Sportsman's Gallery, 20 x 16 In.	35.00
Golf, Print, Fore, Golfer In Knickers, A. B. Frost, 1971, 10 x 13 In.	75.00
Golf, Texaco, Man & Woman Walking To Tee, Sign, 9 x 12 In.	75.00
Golf, Trophy, Full Figure, Silver Plate, 1932	58.00
Golf, Vase, Florida Senior Golf Association, Etched Crystal	50.00
Hockey, Jersey, Bob Joyce, Boston Bruins, White	350.00
Hockey, Jersey, Errol Rouse, Minnesota North Stars, Green Mesh	200.00
Hockey, Jersy, Autographed, Bobby Hull, Chicago Black Hawks	150.00
Hockey, Stick, Autographed, Gordie Howe	70.00
Horse Racing, Glass, Kentucky Derby, 1955	25.00
Horse Racing, Glass, Kentucky Derby, 1971	10.00
Horse Racing, Glass, Kentucky Derby, 1975	9.00
Horse Racing, Glass, Kentucky Derby, 1977	10.00
Horse Racing, Glass, Kentucky Derby, 1981	9.00
Horse Racing, Glass, Kentucky Derby, 1984	9.00
Horse Racing, Mug, Willie Shoemaker	15.00
Hunting, Goose Call, Ohman	15.00
Hunting, License, Ontario, Nonresident, Oilcloth, 1943, 6 x 9 1/4 In.	30.00
Hunting, Poster, No Hunting, Trapping, Middleboro Gunning Club, 1930s	12.00
Pool, Ball Set, Cue, 1920–30s, 15 Balls	45.00
Pool, Level, For Table, Mahogany, Brass, Wooden Case, 15 In.	95.00
Pool, Table, Brunswick Jewel, 1890	4500.00
Pool, Table, Brunswick Arcade, 1890	4500.00
Pool, Table, Brunswick, Leather Pockets, Cue Sticks & Holder, 1920	3000.00
Pool, Table, Brunswick, Rosewood Rails, Inlaid Mahogany Legs, 1927	2200.00
Skating, Program, Petty Ice Capades, 1947	20.00
Skating, Skates, Ice, Child's, Wooden, Steel Blades, 8 In.	75.00
Skating, Skates, Ice, Gold Paint, Wrought Iron, 12 1/2 In.	300.00
Skating, Skates, Ice, Sonja Henie, White, 1938	185.00
Skating, Skates, Roller, Ball Bearings, Leather Strap, Key	17.50

Skating, Skates, Roller, Winchester	45.00
Skating, Skates, Sonja Henie, Box, Signature On Skates, 1938	60.00
Target, Ball, Blue Perth	110.00
Target, Ball, Embossed Bogardus 187, Amber	185.00
Target, For Winchester Air Rifle, Paper, 3 3/4 x 4 3/4 In., 5 Piece	20.00
Tennis, Racket, Gonzales Signature	22.00
Trap, Score Pad, Peters Duvrock Trap, 9 1/2 x 12 In.	3.00

Pottery and porcelain have been made in the Staffordshire district in England since the 1700s. Hundreds of kilns are still working in the area. Thousands of types of pottery and porcelain have been made in the many factories that worked and still work in the area. Some of the most famous factories have been listed separately, such as Adams, Davenport, Ridgway, Rowland & Marsellus, Royal Doulton, Royal Worcester, Spode, Wedgwood, and others. Some Staffordshire pieces are listed under sections like Fairing, Flow Blue, Shaving Mug, etc.

STAFFORDSHIRE, see also Flow Blue; Mulberry

STAFFORDSHIRE, Ashtray, Country Scene, 5 In.	10.00
Bank, Cottage, Enameling, 5 In.	150.00
Bank, Dog	85.00
Basket, Chestnut, Lattice Body, Sprig Handles, 1830s, 9 In.	275.00
Bone Dish, Grecian	7.00
Bowl, Copper Luster, Paneled, Scenes & Flowers, c.1825, 5 In.	135.00
Bowl, Cover, Blue Transfer, Palestine, 11 In.	45.00
Bowl, Fairmont Near Philadelphia, Eagle Border, 13 In.	5610.00
Bowl, Fisherman & Family, Tray, 12 3/8 In.	550.00
Bowl, Imari Pattern, 18th Century, 4 3/4 In.	1540.00
Bowl, Male & Female Figures Exterior, Salt Glaze, 9 3/4 In.	6600.00
Bowl, Vegetable, Cover, Grecian	35.00
Box, Button, Jeb Stuart Standing By Horse, 5 x 4 In.	225.00
Box, Castle Scene On Oval Top, Brass Mounted, 1790, 1 3/4 In.	195.00
Box, Cover, Letter Mirror Back	75.00
Box, George Washington Beside Horse On Cover	85.00
Bust, George Washington, 1880s, 8 In.	305.00
Bust, George Washington, Polychrome Enamel, 8 In.	425.00
Candle Snuffer, Mme. Vestris, Mr. Mathews, 1830, 5 1/2 In., Pr.	225.00
Chimney Piece, Woman, Horseback, Polychrome, Gilt, 11 1/4 In.	125.00
Coffeepot, Cover, Creamware, Black Transfer, Tea Party, 10 In.	250.00
Coffeepot, Strawberry, Vine Border, 10 1/2 In. ....*Illus*	165.00
Compote, Brown Oriental Transfer, Hong, 8 1/4 In.	45.00
Creamer, Boy Fishing, 5 7/8 In.	200.00
Creamer, Canary Ware, Cabbage Roses & Leaves, 3 3/4 In.	715.00
Creamer, Canary Ware, Flowers & Leaves, 3 7/8 In.	410.00
Creamer, Dark Blue Transfer, Basket of Flowers, Stevenson	125.00
Creamer, Embossed Scenes of 2 Men On Barrels, 4 In.	25.00
Creamer, Floral Design, Gaudy, 3 1/2 In.	35.00
Creamer, Franklin's Tomb, c.1840	405.00
Creamer, Strawberry, Vine Border, 3 1/2 In. ....*Illus*	330.00
Cup & Saucer, Blue & White Floral, Late 18th Century, Pair	600.00
Cup Plate, 2 Sailboats, Rowboat, Shell Border, 4 5/8 In.	165.00
Cup Plate, Battery, New York, 3 3/4 In.	250.00
Cup Plate, Black, LaFayette, Washington, 3 3/4 In.	600.00
Cup Plate, Constant Dropping Wears Away Stones, 4 5/8 In.	65.00
Cup Plate, Dark Blue, Seashells, Stubbs, 4 1/8 In.	185.00
Cup Plate, Holiday Street Theatre, Baltimore, 3 1/2 In.	170.00
Cup Plate, Indian Chief's, Brown Transfer, 3 In.	125.00
Cup Plate, Kite Flying, Light Blue Transfer, 3 1/2 In.	85.00
Cup Plate, View Near Sandy Hill, Dark Brown, Clews, 3 7/8 In.	85.00
Cup, Stirrup, Fox Head, 1780, 5 1/2 In.	1375.00
Cup, Stirrup, Hound's Head Form, 1830s, 4 1/4 In.	1210.00
Cup, White, Gray Ground, Raised Floral, Handle	75.00
Dish, Cheese, Agate Pattern	3500.00

Staffordshire, Sugar, Strawberry, Vine Border, 6 5/8 In.
Staffordshire, Coffeepot, Strawberry, Vine Border, 10 1/2 In.
Staffordshire, Creamer, Strawberry, Vine Border, 3 1/2 In.

Staffordshire, Figurine, Horse,
Tom King, 10 1/2 In.
Staffordshire, Figurine,
Vivandiere, 12 In.

Dish, Commodore MacDonnough's Victory, Leaf Shape		5610.00
Dish, Hen Cover, Basketweave Base, Grass, Red Comb, 6 1/2 In.		245.00
Dish, Hen On Basket Cover, 6 x 7 In.		245.00
Dish, Hen On Basket, White, 7 1/2 x 6 1/4 x 8 In.		325.00
Dish, Hen On Nest Cover, 4 In.		140.00
Dish, Hen On Nest, Cover, 9 In.		250.00
Dish, Hen With Chicks On Nest Cover, 9 1/2 In.		175.00
Dish, Hen With Chicks On Nest Cover, 10 3/4 In.		400.00
Dish, Leaf, Press Molded, Manganese & Green Metallic Oxide		4200.00
Dish, Oriental, Dark Blue Transfer, Wood, 11 3/4 In.		275.00
Dish, Saint Paul's Chapel, N. Y., Leaf Shape, 5 In.		3500.00
Dish, Serving, Escape of Mouse, Clews, 12 1/4 In.		600.00
Figurine, Bird On Rocky Perch, 4 3/4 In.		145.00
Figurine, Cat, Enameling, 6 7/8 In., Pair		700.00
Figurine, Dog, Gold Spots, Chain, White, 8 1/2 In.		125.00
Figurine, Elephant of Siam At Wombwell's Menagerie		357.50
Figurine, Exchange No Robbery, 6 1/2 In.		225.00
Figurine, Falstaff, 10 In.		995.00
Figurine, Greyhound, Enameling, Pair		500.00

◆◆◆

Think about security when you landscape your house. Cut bushes
low under windows. Don't plant trees or bushes near doors where
prowlers could hide. Place decorative lights in the yard to illuminate
windows and doors. You might try the early 19th–century style of
landscaping in the midwest farm areas—no shrubbery plantings, but
flowers were near the house.

◆◆◆

Staffordshire, Figurine, Lion, Yellow Glaze,
c.1825, 9 In.

Staffordshire, Figurine, Spaniel,
Copper Luster Spots, 8 In., Pair
Staffordshire, Figurine, Spaniel,
Brown & Black Patches, 8 In.

Figurine, Horse, Tom King, 10 1/2 In. ....*Illus*	138.00
Figurine, Iago & Othello, 12 In.	1100.00
Figurine, Lady Macbeth, 8 1/4 In.	550.00
Figurine, Lady Macbeth, 10 In.	135.00
Figurine, Lion Tamer From Kentucky, 10 1/2 In.	445.00
Figurine, Lion, Pinning Napoleon III To Ground, 9 In.	510.00
Figurine, Lion, Yellow Glaze, c.1825, 9 In. ....*Illus*	1375.00
Figurine, Little Red Riding Hood, 4 In.	165.00
Figurine, Little Red Riding Hood, 7 In.	210.00
Figurine, Love, Law & Physics, 7 1/4 In.	1000.00
Figurine, Lovers In Bower, 8 In.	575.00
Figurine, Man & Woman, Tree, 4 3/8 In.	200.00
Figurine, Minerva, With Helmet, Torch & Quiver, 8 In.	355.00
Figurine, Mother Goose, c.1828, 6 In.	660.00
Figurine, Mrs. Gamp, 6 1/2 In.	145.00
Figurine, Neptune, 9 1/2 In.	225.00
Figurine, Neptune, Pearlware, 1780, 10 7/8 In.	1000.00
Figurine, Pecksniff, 7 In.	145.00
Figurine, Pizarro, 12 In.	385.00
Figurine, Poodle With Bird, 4 In.	70.00
Figurine, Queen Victoria & Prince of Wales, 17 1/2 In., Pair	450.00
Figurine, Ram & Ewe With Lambs, 5 3/4 In.	1100.00
Figurine, Ram & Lamb, Tree, 4 3/4 In.	300.00
Figurine, Richard III, 10 In.	1045.00
Figurine, Rollo, 7 In.	165.00
Figurine, Rubini, 1860, 10 In.	2100.00
Figurine, Shepherd Boy, Enameling, 4 3/4 In.	200.00
Figurine, Shylock, 7 1/4 In.	550.00
Figurine, Spaniel, Brown & Black Patches, 8 In. ....*Illus*	55.00
Figurine, Spaniel, Copper Luster Spots, 8 In., Pair ....*Illus*	247.00
Figurine, Spaniel, Gilt Collar, 1860s, 10 In., Pair	300.00
Figurine, T'would Puzzle A Conjuror, 6 1/4 In.	880.00
Figurine, T'would Puzzle A Conjuror, 8 1/4 In.	1100.00
Figurine, Tam O'Shanter & Souter Johnny, c.1844, 4 3/4 In.	450.00
Figurine, Vivandiere, 12 In. ....*Illus*	192.00
Figurine, Whippets, Standing, Rabbit In Mouth, 10 3/4 In., Pr.	305.00
Figurine, Widow With Child, 9 In.	300.00
Figurine, Widow, 9 1/2 In.	155.00
Figurine, Winter's Tale, 11 3/4 In.	495.00
Figurine, Winter, Man, Ice Skating Stance, 7 3/8 In.	225.00
Figurine, Woman With Bow & Arrow, Tree, 7 1/4 In.	55.00
Figurine, Woman With Cornucopia, 11 In.	275.00
Figurine, Woman With Fruit Basket, 5 1/2 In.	125.00
Figurine, Woman With Sprinkling Can, Tree, 5 1/4 In.	225.00
Figurine, Zebra, c.1860, 12 1/2 In.	445.00
Group, Darby & Joan, Flesh Features, 11 1/8 In.	350.00
Group, Darby & Joan, Pink, Blue & Black Trim, 11 1/8 In.	350.00
Incense Burner, House Shape, Polychrome, 4 3/8 In.	225.00
Inkwell, Bird's Nest, With Bird & Eggs, 3 In.	225.00
Inkwell, House Shape, Polychrome, 3 1/4 In.	85.00
Jug, Canary Ware, Charity & Faith, Silver Luster, 6 1/2 In.	495.00
Jug, Canary Ware, Pugilistic Transfer, 5 In.	2090.00
Jug, Fight Between Tom Cribb & Tom Molinaux, Luster, 6 In.	495.00
Jug, Flower Basket Pattern, Serpent Handle, Gaudy, 6 In.	140.00
Jug, Flowers, Green Overglaze, Lion's Head Spout, 7 In.	45.00
Jug, Giraffes, Blue & White, 7 In.	150.00
Jug, King Henry III Kneeling, Copper Luster, 5 In.	165.00
Jug, Major General Brown At Niagara, Pink Rim, 5 3/4 In.	3300.00
Jug, Pearlware, 6 3/4 In.	66.00
Jug, Portrait of Pike, Captain Hull, Pink Luster, 6 3/4 In.	3410.00
Jug, Wasp Boarding Frolic, Constitution's Escape, 6 1/4 In.	2090.00
Mug, 2 Children, Cat & Dog, Brown Transfer, 2 1/2 In.	30.00
Mug, Black Transfer, Precepts That Never Die	145.00

Staffordshire, Pitcher, 2 Boxers,
Black Transfer, 8 1/2 In.

Staffordshire, Tureen, Turk, With Camel,
Blue & White, 12 In.

Mug, Boys At Play, Bluish Gray Transfer, 2 1/4 In. 55.00
Mug, Child's, Country Scenes, Black Transfer, Pink Luster Rim 100.00
Mug, Child's, Dr. Franklin Maxims 135.00
Mug, Pearlware, 5 3/4 In. 330.00
Mug, Tavern Scenes, Frog, 5 In. 70.00
Mustard, Domed Cover, Lafayette At Castle Garden, 1819, 3 In. 1980.00
Pen Holder, Reclining Greyhound, c.1850, 4 1/2 In. 145.00
Pitcher, 2 Boxers, Black Transfer, 8 1/2 In. ....*Illus* 415.00
Pitcher, Canary Ware, Red Cabbage Roses, Leaves, 7 In. 1375.00
Pitcher, Canary Ware, Red Grapes, Green Leaves, 6 1/2 In. 715.00
Pitcher, Cartouche of Oriental Courtyard Scene, 4 1/4 In. 110.00
Pitcher, Cottage, Enameling, 6 3/8 In. 65.00
Pitcher, Esplanade & Castle Garden, Almshouse, 8 1/4 In. 880.00
Pitcher, Floral In Underglaze, Green Enamel, 9 In. 200.00
Pitcher, Gravy, Saucer, Mulberry Shades 60.00
Pitcher, Green, Bright Yellow, Burleigh Ware, Handle, 8 In. 185.00
Pitcher, Hunter & 2 Dogs, Silver Luster Rim, 5 3/4 In. 770.00
Pitcher, Lafayette At Franklin's Tomb, Blue, 7 1/2 In. 440.00
Pitcher, Pearlware, Flowers, Trailing Vines, 7 1/2 In. 550.00
Pitcher, Pearlware, Stylized Florals, Brown Handle, 8 In. 550.00
Pitcher, Seed Pods On Branch, Shaped Rim, 5 3/4 In. 330.00
Plate, ABC Rim, Sad Bulldog Center, My Face Is My Fortune 125.00
Plate, America Independence, Clews, c.1840, 10 1/2 In. 550.00
Plate, American Marine, Ship, Lifeboat, Sailor, 9 In. 40.00
Plate, Arms of Rhode Island 450.00
Plate, B & O Railroad, Shell Border, 10 1/4 In. .... 470.00 To 715.00
Plate, Boston, Blue & White, 10 In. 55.00
Plate, Boy & 2 Dogs, Purple Luster Rim, Octagonal, 5 5/8 In. 85.00
Plate, British Views, Dark Blue Transfer, 9 3/4 In. 45.00
Plate, Brown Transfer, Floral, Wood & Sons, 9 1/4 In. 225.00
Plate, Canary Ware, Cabbage Rose, Molded Border, 10 In. 3410.00
Plate, Canary Ware, Central Rose, Molded Rim, 6 3/4 In. 1100.00
Plate, Canova, Red & Green Transfer, 10 1/2 In. 45.00
Plate, Capital, Washington, Stevenson, 10 In. 305.00
Plate, City Hall, New York, Ridgway, 9 7/8 In. 225.00
Plate, City of Albany, New York, c.1830, 10 In. 440.00
Plate, Commodore MacDonnough's Victory, 9 1/4 In. 250.00
Plate, Commodore MacDonnough's Victory, 10 1/4 In. 550.00
Plate, Courthouse, Baltimore, 8 5/8 In. 425.00
Plate, Dark Blue Transfer, Fisherman By Stream, 7 3/4 In. 150.00
Plate, Dark Blue Transfer, Quadrupeds, 10 1/4 In. 100.00
Plate, Dark Blue, A Winter View of Pittsfield, 6 3/4 In. 375.00
Plate, Dark Blue, Landing of Gen. LaFayette, 10 In. 225.00
Plate, Employ Time Well Center, Green Transfer, 7 3/4 In. 65.00
Plate, English Scene With Fishermen, Dark Blue, Adams, 9 In. 65.00
Plate, Fall of Montmorenci Near Quebec, Wood, 8 3/8 In. 300.00
Plate, Grecian, 9 In. 15.00

Plate, Green Transfer, Peace On Earth, 10 1/2 In. 30.00
Plate, Hancock House, Boston, Dark Brown, 8 In. 75.00
Plate, Harvard College, 10 1/8 In. 300.00
Plate, Hospital, Boston, Stevenson, 8 7/8 In. 250.00
Plate, Knighthood Conferred On Don Quixote, 10 In. 175.00
Plate, LaFayette, Washington, Eagle, Red Transfer, 10 1/8 In. 925.00
Plate, Landing of General LaFayette, Clews, 9 In. 250.00
Plate, Liberty, Philadelphia, 8 1/2 In. 225.00
Plate, Library, Philadelphia, Ridgway, Blue, 8 1/4 In. 225.00
Plate, Marina, 14–Sided Rim, Pink, 9 1/2 In. 35.00
Plate, Medium Blue, Farmyard Scene & Beehive, 10 1/4 In. 135.00
Plate, New York Battery, Stevenson, Blue, 7 7/8 In. 250.00
Plate, Oriental Scene, Medium Blue, 10 3/8 In. 65.00
Plate, Park Theater, New York, 10 In. 275.00
Plate, Peace & Plenty, Dark Blue, Marked Clews, 8 7/8 In. 275.00
Plate, Peace On Earth, Red Transfer, 6 3/4 In. 85.00
Plate, Peace, Plenty, Clews, 10 1/4 In. 425.00
Plate, Pine Orchard House, Catskill Mountains, c.1840, 10 In. 495.00
Plate, Quebec, Retailer's Label, Neff Warton, 9 In. 275.00
Plate, Robinson Crusoe, Black Transfer, Octagonal, 5 3/4 In. 75.00
Plate, Shell Design, Stubbs, 8 5/8 In. 135.00
Plate, Union Line, Seashell Border, Enoch Wood, 10 1/2 In. 247.00
Plate, Valentine From Wilkie's Designs, 10 In. 225.00
Plate, View of Catskill Mountain House, Jacksons, 10 1/2 In. 35.00
Plate, View of Liverpool, 10 In. 300.00
Plate, Winter View of Pittsfield, Mass., Clews, 8 3/4 In. 155.00
Plate, Woman With Lyre, Embossed Border, 5 In. 50.00
Platter, Dark Blue, Cornwall Terrace, Regent Park, 19 1/4 In. 650.00
Platter, Maryland State Seal, T. Mayer, 1830, 12 1/2 x 15 In. 3850.00
Platter, Medium Blue, Country Squire & Hunting Dog, 15 In. 300.00
Platter, Polychrome Floral Design, Gaudy, Marked, 12 3/4 In. 300.00
Platter, Sidon, Red Transfer, 19 3/4 In. 225.00
Shaker, Floral Garland, Black Stripe, Gaudy, 3 7/8 In. 185.00
Soap Dish, Purple Transfer, Ivy Pattern, Acorn Finial 85.00
Soup, Dish, Dark Blue, Landing of LaFayette, Clews, 9 7/8 In. 295.00
Soup, Dish, Medium Blue, Hunter & Dog, 10 1/4 In. 95.00
Soup, Dish, Table Rock, Niagara, E. Wood, 10 1/4 In. 175.00
Sugar, Cover, Franklin's Tomb, c.1840 .... 357.50
Sugar, Floral, Gaudy, 5 5/8 In. 95.00
Sugar, MacDonnough's Victory, Dark Blue, 6 7/8 In. 350.00
Sugar, Strawberry, Vine Border, 6 5/8 In. ....*Illus* 77.00
Tea Set, Strawberry Luster, 23 Piece 2400.00
Teapot, Black Stripes & Sprig Design, 7 In. 25.00
Teapot, Columbia, Blue Transfer, Paneled, 9 In. 45.00
Teapot, Lafayette At Franklin's Tomb, Enoch Wood 850.00
Teapot, Neptune, Dark Blue Transfer, Clews, 7 1/2 In. 275.00
Teapot, Red Striping, Polychrome Floral, 7 In. 95.00
Teapot, Tortoiseshell Ware, c.1760, 4 5/16 In. 775.00
STAFFORDSHIRE, TOBY JUG, see Toby Jug
Toddy Plate, Winter View, Pittsfield, Mass., Clews, 4 5/8 In. 475.00
Tureen, Form of Doves Seated On Nest, 6 In., Pair 660.00
Tureen, Gravy, Passaic Falls, New Jersey, c.1830 .... 1045.00
Tureen, Reverse Stenciling, Fleur–De–Lis Handles, 15 In. 825.00
Tureen, River Scene, Floral & Grape Rim, c.1850, 9 x 13 In. 880.00
Tureen, Sauce, Underplate, Venetian Gardens, Brown, 7 3/4 In. 35.00
Tureen, Tray, Brown Transfer, Royal Jasmine, 8 1/2 In. 45.00
Tureen, Turk, With Camel, Blue & White, 12 In. ....*Illus* 850.00
Vase, Pig & Duck, Girl At Bridge, Red Interior, 9 In. 235.00
Watch Holder, 2 Figures & Hound, c.1880, 12 In. 85.00
Watch Holder, Man & Woman Form, Fitted With 6–Jewel Watch 100.00

The Fulper Pottery had a long history that entwined with the Stangl Pottery in 1910 when Johann Martin Stangl started work. He bought into the firm in 1913, became president in 1926, and in 1929 changed the company name to Stangl Pottery. The pottery made dinnerwares and a line of limited–edition bird figurines. The company went out of business in 1972.

STANGL, Ashtray, Antique Gold	18.00 To 30.00
Ashtray, Colonial Silver	20.00
Ashtray, Pheasant	12.00
Ashtray, Quail, Oval, Large	25.00
Ashtray, Rainbow Trout	22.00
Basket, Rose, Thorn Handle	250.00
Beer Set, Happy Days Are Here Again, 5 Piece	495.00
Bird, Bird of Paradise, No. 3408	80.00 To 125.00
Bird, Blue Jay, No. 3456	45.00
Bird, Blue–Headed Vireo, No. 3448	68.00 To 75.00
Bird, Bluebird, No. 3276	100.00
Bird, Bluebirds, No. 3276D	110.00 To 185.00
Bird, Broadtail Hummingbird, No. 3626	90.00 To 150.00
Bird, Cardinal, No. 3444	75.00
Bird, Cardinal, No. 3596	60.00
Bird, Cerulean Warbler, No. 3456	80.00
Bird, Chickadees, No. 3581	135.00 To 175.00
Bird, Cock Pheasant, No. 3492	170.00
Bird, Cockatoo, No. 3405	65.00
Bird, Cockatoo, No. 3580	125.00 To 165.00
Bird, Cockatoo, No. 3584	200.00
Bird, Cockatoos, No. 3405D	135.00
Bird, Flying Duck, No. 3443	175.00 To 300.00
Bird, Goldfinches, No. 3635	145.00 To 230.00
Bird, Gray Cardinal, No. 3596	65.00
Bird, Grosbeak, No. 3813	75.00
Bird, Hummingbird, No. 3585	50.00
Bird, Hummingbirds, No. 3599D	375.00
Bird, Indigo Bunting, No. 3589	95.00
Bird, Kentucky Warbler, No. 3598	35.00 To 65.00
Bird, Keywest Quail Dove, No. 3454	225.00
Bird, Kingfisher, No. 3406	30.00 To 90.00
Bird, Kingfishers, No. 3406D	125.00
Bird, Lovebird, No. 3400	45.00
Bird, Nuthatch, No. 3593	50.00
Bird, Oriole, No. 3402	45.00 To 75.00
Bird, Orioles, No. 3402D	75.00
Bird, Painted Bunting, No. 3452	90.00
Bird, Parakeets, No. 3582D	125.00 To 140.00
Bird, Parrot, No. 3449	100.00
Bird, Parula Warbler, No. 3583	45.00 To 80.00
Bird, Prothonatary Warbler, No. 3447	60.00 To 90.00
Bird, Redstarts, No. 3490D	210.00
Bird, Reiffers Hummingbird, No. 3628	90.00
Bird, Rivoli Hummingbird, No. 3627	110.00
Bird, Titmouse, No. 3592	65.00
Bird, Wilson's Warbler	48.00
Bird, Wren, No. 3401	65.00
Bird, Wrens, No. 3401D	150.00
Bowl, Antique Gold, 7 In.	9.00
Bowl, Artware, Tulip	25.00
Bowl, Bamboo, 8 In.	6.50
Bowl, Blueberry, 5 1/2 In.	5.00
Bowl, Flower, Colonial Silver	15.00
Bowl, Fruit, Fruit & Flowers	5.00
Bowl, Magnolia, 8 In.	22.00

Bowl, Nut, Spun Gold, Handle	8.00
Bowl, Rainbow, Pelican Flower Frog, Set	150.00
Bowl, Salad, Garland, 12 In.	27.50
Bowl, Shell, Antique Gold	18.00
Bowl, Tulip, Antique Gold	20.00
Bowl, Vegetable, Divided, Fruit & Flowers, Oval	15.00
Box, Cigarette, Cover, Orioles	25.00
Box, Cigarette, Terra Rose, Cover, Yellow Tulip	10.00
Bread Plate, Thistle	4.00
Butter, Corn, Green	15.00
Cake Plate, Sculptured Fruit, Pedestal	17.00
Candlestick, Antique Gold, Pair	20.00
Candlestick, Colonial, Blue, 3 1/4 In.	8.00
Candlestick, Granada Gold	8.00
Candlestick, Terra Rose, Pair	20.00
Candy Dish, Cover, Antique Gold	20.00
Candy, Cover, Granada Gold	25.00
Casserole, Handle, Red Cherry	9.00
Chop Plate, Magnolia, 12 In.	22.00
Clock, Dogwood, White	35.00
Clock, Kitchen, Rooster, Battery Operated	45.00
Coaster, Apple Delight, Bittersweet	5.50
Coaster, Garden Flower	5.50
Coffee Warmer, Golden Harvest	18.00
Coffeepot, Golden Grape	45.00
Coffeepot, Town & Country, Green Spatter	55.00
Compote, Antique Gold	15.00
Cup & Saucer, Bamboo	4.00
Cup & Saucer, Bittersweet	8.00
Cup & Saucer, Blue Daisy ....5.50 To	11.00
Cup & Saucer, Fruit	7.50
Cup & Saucer, Fruit & Flowers	15.00
Cup & Saucer, Golden Harvest	10.00
Cup & Saucer, Orchard Song	18.00
Cup & Saucer, Star Flower	18.00
Cup & Saucer, Thistle	11.00
Cup Plate, Star Flower, 5 In.	5.00
Cup, Blue Daisy	8.00
Cup, Golden Harvest	8.00
Cup, Kiddieware, ABC, Letter D In Design	20.00
Dinner Set, Green Spatterware, 12 Place Settings	255.00
Dish, Apple, Antique Gold	15.00
Dish, Feeding, Divided, ABC's	55.00
Dish, Feeding, Kiddieware, 3 Little Pigs	55.00
Eggcup, Magnolia	12.50
Gravy Boat, Magnolia	22.00
Gravy Boat, Stand, Golden Blossom	7.00
Horn of Plenty, Antique Gold	60.00
Mug, Blue Daisy	8.00
Mug, Country Garden, Pink Flowers	12.50
Pitcher, Antique Gold, 12 In.	30.00
Pitcher, Terra Rose, 1 Qt.	17.50
Plate, Americana, 7 In.	7.00
Plate, Americana, 8 In.	8.00
Plate, Bamboo, 10 In.	5.00
Plate, Bittersweet, 5 In.	5.00
Plate, Blue Daisy, 10 In.	10.00
Plate, Blueberry, 9 In.	7.50
Plate, Country Garden, 6 In.	5.00
Plate, Festival, 6 In.	6.00
Plate, Fruit & Flowers, 8 In.	5.00
Plate, Fruit, 6 In.	4.50
Plate, Golden Blossom, 6 In.	3.00

◆◆◆

When you cancel your paper before you leave on a trip, do not tell why you want the paper stopped. Call to restart it when you return.

◆◆◆

Plate, Golden Blossom, 8 In.	7.00
Plate, Golden Grape, 10 In.	9.00
Plate, Magnolia, 6 In.	6.00
Plate, Magnolia, 10 In.	10.00
Plate, Maple Whirl, 10 In.	10.00
Plate, Orchard Song, 10 In.	10.00
Plate, Prelude, 6 In.	6.00
Plate, Prelude, 10 In.	10.00
Plate, Rooster, Hanging, 6 In.	15.00
Plate, Star Flower, 10 In.	10.00
Plate, Terra Rose, 8 In.	9.50
Plate, Thistle, 5 In.	5.00
Punch Cup, Holly	22.50
Relish, Country Garden	22.00
Relish, Orchard Song, Brass Handle	10.00
Salt & Pepper, Celery & Butter, Thistle, 4 Piece	20.00
Salt & Pepper, Magnolia	15.00
Sandwich Server, Country Garden, Handle, 10 In.	15.00
Sandwich Server, Golden Grape, Handle, 10 In.	20.00
Sandwich Server, Terra Rose, Handle, 10 In.	17.50 To 30.00
Sauce, Chickory	4.00
Saucer, Americana, 5 3/4 In.	6.00
Saucer, Americana, 6 1/2 In.	5.00
Saucer, Apple Delight, 6 In.	3.00
Saucer, Fruit, Brown Edge	5.00
Saucer, Fruit, Yellow Edge	5.00
Saucer, Golden Harvest	6.00
Soup, Dish, Americana, Liner, Green	8.00
Soup, Dish, Americana, Orange	7.00
Soup, Dish, Magnolia	36.00
Soup, Dish, Star Flower, Lug	10.00
Sugar, Cover, Terra Rose, Blue Tulip	8.00
Sugar, Garland	12.00
Sugar, Golden Harvest	9.00
Teapot, Terra Rose	47.50
Tray, Leaf, Antique Gold	20.00
Vase, Granada Gold, 8 In.	15.00
Vase, Leaf, Terra Rose, 6 In.	8.00
Vase, Redware, Pink & Brown, 8 In.	25.00
Vase, Terra Rose, Yellow, Handles, Paper Label, 3 In.	5.00
Wig Stand, Paper Label, 14 1/2 In.	160.00

 Steins have been used by beer and ale drinkers for over 500 years. They have been made of ivory, porcelain, stoneware, faience, silver, pewter, wood, or glass in sizes up to nine gallons. Although some were made by Meissen, Capo–di–Monte, and other famous factories, most were made in Germany. The words *Geschutz* or *Musterschutz* on a stein are the German words for patented or registered design, not company names. Steins are still being made in the old styles.

STEIN, Alabama Brewing Co., Etched Glass, A Logo, 3 3/8 In.	127.00
Alpine Tavern Crowd, Happy Dancer, Pottery, Pewter Lid, 1/2 Liter	148.00
American Society of Mechanical Engineers, Stoneware, Ringer, 1 Liter	462.00
Anheuser–Busch, Ft. Collins Brewery, Pewter	300.00
Artillery Shell, Pewter, Iron Cross Medal, 1914, 1/2 Liter	462.00
Avon, Car Classics, 1910 Stanley Steamer, 1982, 5 In.	4.00

Avon, Cattle Driver 21.00
Bartholomay Rochester Beer & Ale, Glass, 4 In. 30.00
Bismarck, Porcelain, Mustershutz, 1/2 Liter 576.00
Blown & Cut Pattern, Pedestal, Glass, Steeple Pewter Lid, 3/10 Liter 69.00
Budweiser, Chicago, Our Kind of Town, 1982 .... 120.00
Budweiser, King of Beers, Red, Gold Band Top, 2 3/4 In. 9.00
Cavalier & Maid, Enameled, Pewter Hinged Lid, 1/2 Liter, 6 7/8 In. 325.00
Comical Fat Man, Curl In Cigar Holder, Stoneware, Ringer, 1/2 Liter 284.00
Cornflower, Alpine Couple At Home, Porcelain, Pewter Lid, 1/2 Liter 289.00
Dwarf Sitting On Pewter Lid, Hobnail, Mold Blown, 1/2 Liter 116.00
Fred Miller Brewing Co., Milwaukee, Etched, 3 1/2 In. 28.00
Gabelsberger Brau, Munchen Brewery, Pottery, Pewter Lid, 1 Liter 1155.00
Gerz, Golfer Scene, Stoneware 3960.00
High-Wheeled Bicycle, Lithophane, Man Falling Into Woman's Arms 445.00
Hopps & Malt Design, Art Nouveau, Pewter, Germany, 1905, 1/2 Liter 127.00
Judge, Pouring Wisdom In Lawyer's Head, Stoneware, Ringer, 1/2 Liter 284.00
Knight's Head, Bearded, Dumler & Breiden, 1/2 Liter 424.00
Leinenkugel Beer, Since 1867, Indian Maiden, 7 1/2 In. 39.00
Lowenbrau, Munchen Brewery, Pottery, Pewter Lid, 1/2 Liter 116.00
Man With Pipe, Pottery, Pewter Lid, 1/2 Liter 300.00
    STEIN, METTLACH, see Mettlach, Stein
Military, German Coat of Arms, 4 Kingdoms, Pottery, 1/2 Liter 295.00
Monk, Grinning, Stoneware, 1/2 Liter 318.00
Monk, Noritake 20.00
Monk, Red Robe, Porcelain, 1/2 Liter 321.00
Monk, Wine Cellar, Pewter Lid, Manning Bowman & Co., 1900, 1/2 Liter 185.00
Monkey, Dressed, Top Hat, Pottery, Japan, 1/2 Liter 21.00
Mozart, 1/2 Liter, Bisque 525.00
Munich Child, Hooded Figure, 1902, 1/2 Liter ....*Illus* 200.00
Munich Maid, Green-Amber Glass, Verse, 1/2 Liter 208.00
Munich Maid, Greetings From Munich, Pewter Lid, Pauson, 1/2 Liter 127.00
Mythological Scene, Royal Vienna Type, Cat On Red Lid, 1/2 Liter 1386.00
Nazi, Antiaircraft Gun, Swastika Flag, Enameled Transfer, 1/2 Liter 924.00
Nazi, Machine Gunner, Swastika, Stoneware, Enameled, 1/2 Liter 723.00
Occupational, Baker, Emil Meier, Darmstadt, 1901, 1/2 Liter 309.00
Office Suds, Cartoon, Utica Beer, 1950s, 1/2 Liter 87.00
Old Man, Pouring & Drinking From Keg, Germany, Cobalt, 19 In. 225.00
Old Milwaukee Beer 73.00
Owl, Bird In Beak, Rodent In Claws, Stoneware, 1/2 Liter 491.00
Pick Albert Hotel, Chicago, Glass 35.00
Red, Over Clear Overlay Glass, Circles Lid, 1/2 Liter 520.00
Regimental, 109 Infantry, Porcelain, Germany, 1903-1905 .... 403.00
Regimental, 20th Infantry, 11 1/2 In. ....*Illus* 357.00
Regimental, Horse & Rider Finial, Eagle Thumblift, Porcelain, 12 In. 139.00
Regimental, Lithophane of Soldier's Farewell, 12 In. ....*Illus* 440.00
Regimental, Lithophane, 1st Pioneer Battalion, 11 1/2 In. ....*Illus* 357.00
Regimental, ULAN 2nd Guards, Pottery, Germany, 1903-1906 .... 400.00

Stein, Regimental, Lithophane
of Soldier's Farewell, 12 In.

Stein, Munich Child,   Stein, Regimental, 20th   Stein, Regimental, Lithophane,
Hooded Figure, 1902, 1/2 Liter   Infantry, 11 1/2 In.   1st Pioneer Battalion, 11 1/2 In.

Rollicking Cherubs & Prosit, Pewter Lid, Germany, 7 1/2 In. 65.00
Schlitz 25th Anniversary Commemorative 75.00
Skull, Porcelain, E. Bohne, 1/4 Liter 289.00
Soccer Scene, Verse Around Base, Pottery, 3/4 Liter 173.00
Squirrel Handle, Occupied Japan 15.00
Star of David, 1 Liter 200.00
Stoneware, Scenes of Revelry, Vines, Term Handle, Germany, 11 3/4 In. 155.00
Stroh's Beer, Detroit, White Pebbled Glass, 3 5/8 In. 46.00
Strohs Heritage III 18.00
Tavern Scene, Gray Salt Glaze & Cobalt Blue, Pewter Lid, 13 1/4 In. 45.00
Val Blatz Brewing Co., Milwaukee Beer, Glass, 3 5/8 In. 22.00
Victorian Hunt Scene, Pewter Lid, 12 In. 250.00
Wedding, Biedermeier, Blown Glass, Enameled, Inscribed 1852, 1 Liter 202.00
Wedding, Biedermeier, Blown Glass, Enameled, Pewter Lid, 1800, 1 Liter 785.00

Stereo cards that were made for stereopticon viewers became
popular after 1840. Two almost identical pictures were mounted on
a stiff cardboard backing so that, when viewed through a
stereoscope, a three-dimensional picture could be seen. Value is
determined by maker and by the subject. These cards were made in
quantity through the 1930s.

STEREO CARD, Among The Chrysanthemums, R. Y. Young 10.00
Corps of Engineers, USA, Expedition of 1874 .... 132.00
Gathering Iris, R. Y. Young 10.00
Hero of Gettysburg, Taylor & Huntington 20.00
Mt. Clark, Sierra, Nevada, J. P. Soule 10.00
Photographique En France, 1933 .... 30.00
San Francisco Quake, Homeless Amid Former Wealth, 1906 .... 12.00
Steamer, Providence, W. C. Schultzberg 12.00
Stoddard Next To Camera, Ft. Wm. Henry Hotel, Mirrored 175.00
World War I Troops, Shops, Etc., 18 Piece 48.00

The stereoscope, or stereopticon, was used for viewing stereo cards.
The hand viewer was invented by Oliver Wendell Holmes, although
more complicated table models were used before his was produced
in 1859.

STEREOSCOPE, Keystone, Bausch & Lomb Lens, Wooden Frame, 1904 .... 350.00
Removable Standard, JA & O, Patent 1872 .... 395.00
STERLING SILVER, see Silver-Sterling

Steuben glass was made at the Steuben Glass Works of Corning,
New York. The factory, founded by Frederick Carder and T. C.
Hawkes, Sr., was purchased by the Corning Glass Company. They
continued to make glass called *Steuben*. Many types of art glass
were made at Steuben. The firm is still making exceptional quality
glass but it is clear, modern-style glass.

STEUBEN, see also Aurene; Cluthra
STEUBEN, Bonbon, Cover, Alabaster Foot & Knob, 6 1/2 x 6 In. 650.00
Bowl, Alabaster Overlaid With Green Jade, Floral Border, 8 In. 335.00
Bowl, Base Mounted On 4 Swirled Drops, 13 1/4 In. 340.00
Bowl, Black Stringing, Reeded 175.00
Bowl, Blue Calcite, Label, 8 In. 1045.00
Bowl, Calcite With Gold, Aurene Interior, Footed, 1 1/2 x 6 In. 250.00
Bowl, Calcite With Gold, Aurene Interior, Footed, 3 x 8 In. 425.00
Bowl, Crystal, 4 Applied Lobe Feet, 10 In. 300.00
Bowl, Fan Shape, Footed & Scalloped, Ribbed Rim, Signed, 12 In. 385.00
Bowl, Flared, Tapers To Small Foot, Gold, Green, Signed, 12 In 357.50
Bowl, Free Form, Wavy Shell, Ring Foot, 14 1/2 x 10 x 6 In. 175.00
Bowl, Frieze of Gazelle, Etched Crystal, Signed, 7 1/4 In. 6975.00
Bowl, Goblet Shape, Fold-Over Lip, 7 1/8 x 8 1/4 In. 850.00
Bowl, Gold Aurene On Calcite, 12 In. 260.00
Bowl, Gold On Calcite, 8 In. 300.00
Bowl, Gold On Calcite, Ringed With Pale Pink, 12 In. 250.00

Bowl, Grotesque, Ivrene, 11 1/2 x 7 In. 450.00
Bowl, Jade, Alabaster Base, Signed, 12 In. 425.00
Bowl, Rose Base, 3 Green Prunts, Green, Marked, 9 1/2 In. 400.00
Bowl, Scrolled Feet, 8 In., Pair 440.00
Candlestick, 3 Rings, Trapped Bubble In Stem, 4 1/2 In., 3 Piece 357.00
Candlestick, Amber Twisted Around Clear Hollow Stem, 10 In., Pair 425.00
Candlestick, Jade, 18 In., Pair 1200.00
Candlestick, Swirl, Celeste Blue, Signed, 10 In. 250.00
Candlestick, Teardrop Center, Single Light, Signed, 5 In. 355.00
Candlestick, Teardrop Shafts, Pedestal Base, 14 1/2 In., Pair 4180.00
Candlestick, Teardrop, Baluster, F. B. Sellew, 1937, 9 In., Pair 750.00
Candlestick, Teardrop, Domed Feet, F. B. Sellew, 1937, 9 In., Pair 825.00
Candlestick, Twisted, Crystal, Single 75.00
Candy Dish, Cover, Alabaster Leaf, Jade, 6 In. 82.00
Cocktail, Teardrop Stem, Set of 8 .... 360.00
Compote, Fleur-De-Lis, Footed, Yellow & Jade, 4 1/2 x 7 In. 225.00
Compote, Gold Aurene On Calcite, Flattened Rim, Pedestal, 9 3/4 In. 305.00
Compote, Pink & Clambroth, Pedestal, Cover 165.00
Compote, Red Threading On Crystal, 7 In. 225.00
Compote, Ribbed Bowl, Waved Rim, Calcite, Aurene, 5 1/2 In. 495.00
Compote, Rosaline & Alabaster, 2 1/2 x 6 1/4 In. 295.00
Compote, Twisted Stem, Waffle Pontils, Pomona Green, 7 In., Pair 250.00
Console Set, Amethyst, Clear, 10-In. Candlesticks ....975.00 To 1050.00
Console Set, Applied Green Threads, Signed, 3 Piece 250.00
Cornucopia, Ivrene, 7 In. 325.00
Dish, Applied Side Lobe, 6 1/2 In. 110.00
Ewer, Ruffled, Apricot Spangles, 7 1/4 In. 125.00
Figurine, Elephant, Ivory, 5 1/2 In. 950.00
Figurine, Guardian Angel, Gold Halo, 6 In. ....600.00 To 660.00
Figurine, Horsehead, 4 1/2 In. 285.00
Figurine, Horsehead, 5 In. 215.00
Figurine, Nude, Kneeling, Black Jade 1250.00
Finger Bowl, Underplate, Celeste Blue, Fleur-De-Lis Mark 200.00
Finger Bowl, Underplate, Ruffled Rim, Gold 440.00
Globe, Ivrene, ABC Schoolhouse, Raised Fleur-De-Lis, 9 In. 345.00
Goblet, Braided Stem, 7 In. 75.00
Goblet, Conical, Twisted Alabaster Stem, Jade, 7 In., 6 Piece 440.00
Goblet, Green Cut To Clear Thistle, Fleur-De-Lis, Signed 250.00
Goblet, Pink Reeding, Crystal, 8 1/2 In., Pair 225.00
Goblet, Pink Stem, Opalescent 350.00
Goblet, Twist Stem, Opalescent 145.00
Ice Bucket, Green Jade, Alabaster Threading, Signed, 6 1/4 In. 325.00
Lamp, Fairy, Verre Moire, Crystal 145.00
Lamp, Pulled Feather Design, Double Shade, Signed, 17 1/2 In. 825.00
Martini Glass, Conical Form, Inverted Conical Stem, 4 In., 8 Piece 198.00
Martini Glass, Teardrop, Flared, Cone Base, 3 3/4 In., 8 Pc. 330.00
Nappy, Rosaline, Alabaster Handle, Ground Pontil, 4 1/2 x 5 1/2 In. 325.00
Newel-Post Knob, Rosaline & Alabaster, Metal Mount, 7 1/2 In. 550.00
Paperweight, Stars & Stripes, c.1976, 2 3/4 In. 145.00
Paperweight, White Swirled, Center Teardrop, Crystal, Signed, 1988 .... 395.00
Parfait, Stem, Rosaline & Alabaster, 6 1/2 In. 125.00
Perfume Bottle, Flower Top, Amber Stem At Top, 12 1/2 In. 725.00
Pitcher, Crystal, Applied Handles, 10 In. 135.00
Plaque, Thomas Edison, 1928, 8 1/2 x 6 1/2 In. 650.00
Plate, Amethyst, 8 1/4 In. 22.00
Plate, Bird Design, 10 In., Set of 12 .... 4400.00
Plate, Verre De Soie, Raised Outer Rim, 8 1/2 In. 200.00
Salt, Verre De Soie 150.00
Shade, Green Leaf & Vine, Calcite 250.00
Shade, White Calcite, Green-Gold Hearts, Gold Aurene, 4 1/2 In. 125.00
Sugar & Creamer, Black Threading, Bristol Yellow, Signed 375.00
Tazza, Arched Supports, Round Base, 4 3/4 x 10 1/4 In. 275.00
Tazza, Shallow Bowl, On Full Arched Supports, Base, 10 x 4 3/4 In. 250.00

Vase, Applied Leaf Decorations, Rose Quartz, 10 1/2 In. ....*Illus* 1300.00
Vase, Applied Scrolling Lobes, Flared, Crystal, 6 3/4 In. 140.00
Vase, Blue, Aurene, 2 1/2 In. 675.00
Vase, Bud, Jadite, 1 Prong, White Base 500.00
Vase, Diamond–Quilted, Threaded, Bristol Yellow, Signed, 7 1/2 In. 185.00
Vase, Engraved Gazelle, Signed, Dated 1936, 7 1/4 In. 775.00
Vase, Flared Swirl Form, Selenium Ruby, Marked, 7 In. 385.00
Vase, Flying Gouba Ducks, Trees, Black Jade, 10 In. 3500.00
Vase, Gold Aurene & Ivrene, Triple Stem, 6 In. 425.00
Vase, Grotesque, 4–Ribbed Body, Marked, 6 3/4 x 12 In. 195.00
Vase, Ivrene, Panelled, 5 In. 350.00
Vase, Overall Etched Dragons, Stylized Swirls, 16 1/4 In., Pair 1870.00
Vase, Paneled, Dark Blue Jade, Signed, 8 In. 1800.00
Vase, Paneled, Ivrene, Signed, 5 In. 285.00
Vase, Ribbed Jade, Fan Shape, Alabaster Ball Stem & Foot, 8 1/2 In. 250.00
Vase, Rosaline & Chrysanthemum, Acid Cut Back, 14 In. 1300.00
Vase, Rosaline, Pink Jade On Cupped Alabaster Pedestal, 7 1/4 In. 935.00
Vase, Selenium, 7 1/2 In. 695.00
Vase, Self Reeding To Top, Cylindrical, Green, Signed, 8 In. 165.00
Vase, Silverina Airtrap, Amethyst, 9 In. 850.00
Vase, Stamford Pattern, Gazelles, Ivory, Signed, c.1925, 10 1/4 In. 1540.00
Vase, Trailing Vines, Millefiori, 3 1/2 In. 1870.00
Vase, Trapped Air Bubbles, Pink & Lavender, Ovoid, Signed, 4 In. 825.00
Vase, Triple Lily, Floriform, Silvery Iridescence, 12 1/2 In. 1875.00
Vase, Triple, Jade, Alabaster Base, Cupped, Signed, 10 1/2 In. 550.00
Vase, Trumpet, Calcite, Gold Aurene Interior, 6 x 5 In. 310.00

Stevengraphs are woven pictures made like fancy ribbons. They were manufactured by Thomas Stevens of Coventry, England, and became popular in 1862. Most are marked *Woven in silk by Thomas Stevens* or were mounted on a cardboard that tells the story of the Stevengraph. Other similar ribbon pictures have been made in England and Germany.

STEVENGRAPH, Bookmark, Late Lamented Pres., Tassel, Frame, 10 In. 225.00
　Bookmark, Washington, Philadelphia Centennial ....65.00 To 100.00
　Crystal Palace, Matted, Late–1800s, Small 150.00
　Dick Turpin's Ride, 1739, Small 300.00
　Grace Darling, Matted, Late–1800s, Small 325.00
　Lady Godiva Procession, Matted, Late–1800s, Small 450.00
　Present Time 150.00
　Robert Burns 135.00
　The Meet, Framed 250.00

Stevens & Williams of Stourbridge, England, made many types of glass, including layered, etched, cameo, and art glass, between the 1830s and 1930s. Some pieces are signed *S & W*. Many pieces are decorated with flowers, leaves, and other designs based on nature.

*Steuben, Vase, Applied Leaf Decorations,
Rose Quartz, 10 1/2 In.*

◆ ◆

For emergency repairs to chipped pottery, try coloring the spot with a wax crayon or oil paint. It will look a little better.

◆ ◆

STEVENS & WILLIAMS, Basket, Blackthorn Flowers, Cream Lining, Blue, 9 In. 750.00
   Basket, Crimped Amber Rim, Enameled Florals, 6 x 9 In. 250.00
   Bowl, Alternating Colored Swirls, 4 1/2 In. 645.00
   Bowl, Carved Trailing Stems, Butterfly, Marked, 5 In. 880.00
   Bowl, Gold Swirl, Blue Lining, 5 3/8 In. 850.00
   Epergne, 3 Bowls, Rigaree, Mirrored Base, 7 1/2 In. 935.00
   Ewer, Internal Pulled Red & Yellow Design, 13 1/4 In. 660.00
   Lamp, Applied Fruit, 22 In. 2100.00
   Lamp, Applied Fruit, Pink Opaline 4100.00
   Lamp, Fairy, Ruffled Rim, Stripes, Clarke Cup, 6 In. 815.00
   Pitcher, Swirl, Blue & White, Clear Handle, 5 1/2 In. 115.00
   Rose Bowl, Arabesque 195.00
   Rose Bowl, Scalloped, Yellow Lining, Clear Feet, 6 In. 625.00
   Sherbet, Underplate, Cherries, Blue, Clear, 4 7/8 In. 325.00
   Toothpick, Green Cut To Clear, Sterling Rim 350.00
   Vase, 3 Amber Ruffled Leaves, Opaque Cream, 7 1/2 In. 225.00
   Vase, 5–Petaled Blossoms, Red–Orange, Signed, 7 In. 1980.00
   Vase, Apple Blossoms, Buds, Branches, Gourd Form, 12 In. 2425.00
   Vase, Apple Blossoms, Green & Amber Leaves, 6 In. 255.00
   Vase, Applied Flowers, Leaves, Amber Feet, 7 1/4 In. 450.00
   Vase, Applied Fruit, Amber Feet & Handles, 9 3/4 In. 550.00
   Vase, Applied Ruffled Leaf, Cream, 6 5/8 In. 145.00
   Vase, Art Nouveau Water Lilies, Amber Bee, Signed, 6 In. 100.00
   Vase, Band of Scroll & Blossom, Signed, 1885, 3 1/4 In. 1870.00
   Vase, Jack–In–The–Pulpit, Pink, Flowers, 6 In. 165.00
   Vase, Layers of Red & Pink, Zigzag Stripes, 9 1/2 In. 725.00
   Vase, Mother–of–Pearl, White Lining, 11 In. 265.00
   Vase, Multicolor Swirl Design, Floral, Signed, 13 In. 325.00
   Vase, Pink Cherries, Wishbone Feet, Handle, 6 1/2 In. 145.00
   Vase, Rainbow Swirl, Trefoil Crimped Top, 6 3/4 In. 485.00
   Vase, Ruffled Applied Leaves, Coral Overlay, 11 3/4 In. 395.00
   Vase, Ruffled Applied Leaves, Rose Lined, 7 1/2 In. 225.00
   Vase, Ruffled, Opalescent Swirl Stripes, Birds, 12 In. 185.00
   Vase, Swirled Ribs, Overlapping Ribbons, 6 3/4 In. 485.00
   Vase, Yellow & Opaque Rose, Green Leaves, Double Bud 260.00

Henry William Stiegel, a colorful immigrant to the colonies, started his first factory in Pennsylvania in 1763. He remained in business until 1774. Glassware was made in a style popular in Europe at that time and was similar to the glass of many other makers. It was made of clear or colored glass and was decorated with enamel colors, mold blown designs, or etching. It is almost impossible to be sure a piece was made by Stiegel, so the knowing collector now refers to this glass as Stiegel type.

STIEGEL TYPE, Beaker, Animals, Shields & Flowers, 1700s 950.00
   Decanter, Animals, Shields & Flowers, 1700s 2500.00
   Goblet, Animals, Shields & Flowers, 1700s 600.00
   Salt, Double Ogee Form, Honeycomb Over Diamonds, Blue, 3 In. 165.00
   Vigil Light, Amber 200.00

The Stockton Terra Cotta Company was started in Stockton, California, in 1891. The art pottery called Rekston was made after 1897. The company burned in 1902 and was never reopened.

STOCKTON, Bowl, Brown, Flowers, 6 In. 85.00
   Mug, Brown, Flowers, 5 In. 465.00

Stoneware is a coarse, glazed, and fired potter's ceramic that is used to make crocks, jugs, bowls, etc. It is often decorated with cobalt blue decorations. Stoneware is still being made.

STONEWARE, Barrel, Menlo Root Beer, White 605.00
   Batter Jar, Brown Albany Slip, Wooden Cork, 11 In. 45.00
   Batter Jar, Brown Glaze, Tin Cap & Bail, 11 In. 175.00
   Batter Jar, Cobalt Blue Floral Spray, H. Smith & Co., 2 Gal. 2900.00

Batter Jar, Stenciled Reppert, Greensboro, Pa., 1 Gal.	2500.00
Batter Jug, Wire Handle, Yellowish Amber Salt Glaze, 8 In.	75.00
Batter Pail, Basketweave	195.00
Batter Pail, Cowden & Wilcox, Design Front & Back, 4 Qt.	935.00
Batter Pail, Even R. Jones, Design On Front & Back, 4 Qt.	740.00
Batter Pail, Pine Tree, Tin Cap, New York, Small	355.00
Batter Pitcher, Tin Spout Cover, Wire Bail, Wood Handle	175.00
Bean Pot, Blue & White	95.00
Bean Pot, Robin's–Egg Blue	25.00
Beater Bowl, Western Pottery Co.	68.00
Beater Jar, 3 Blue Bands	35.00
Beater Jar, Blue Ring, Gray	50.00
Birdhouse, White Hall	135.00
Bottle, 2–Tone Gray Salt, Blue, J. Melvin, 1854, 9 3/4 In.	105.00
Bottle, Arnold, London, Spout	20.00
Bottle, Hot Water, Blue	50.00
Bottle, Hot Water, Leaf Design, Blue & White Glaze	975.00
Bottle, Pure Old Rye, Pig	250.00
Bottle, Whiskey, Klein Bros. & Hyman, Cincinnati, Ohio	125.00
Bowl, Boone Dairy Products, Blue, Gray, 1928, 7 In.	60.00
Bowl, Compliments of Maribel Grain Co., Blue & White	85.00
Bowl, Delft Blue, 4 In.	65.00
Bowl, Feather, Blue & White, Large	85.00
Bowl, Gadroon Arches, Blue & White, 8 In.	100.00
Bowl, Geneva, Iowa, Blue, Rust & Cream Sponge, 7 In.	120.00
Bowl, Peoria Pottery, Brown, 10 In.	15.00
Bowl, Pierron Pottery Co., 4 In.	350.00
Bowl, Rosemont, Minn., 8 In.	175.00
Butter, Cover, Good Luck, Blue & White	125.00
Canister, Sugar, Blue & White	195.00
Canister, Tea, Cover, Basketweave, Blue & White	235.00
Canteen, Bardwell's Root Beer, 2 Deer On Reverse, 11 In.	412.50
Canteen, GAR, Heinricks Pottery, 1900	230.00
Canteen, I. Brickman & Co., Montgomery, Alabama, Brown, 1 Gal.	225.00
Canteen, Rochester, Whites, Utica, Miniature	155.00
Casserole, Cover, 4 1/2 In.	305.00
Casserole, Cover, Pierpoint, South Dakota, 7 1/4 In.	205.00
Cheese Bell, Cover, Cow Figure Finial, Whites, Utica	385.00
Chicken Waterer, White Hall, 1/2 Gal	35.00
Churn, Design, Brewster & Halm, Havana, N. Y., 5 Gal.	550.00
Churn, Floral Design, No. 5, Cobalt Blue Slip, 17 In.	145.00
Churn, Flower, No. 6, Wooden Lid & Dasher, Ovoid, 17 1/2 In.	120.00
Churn, Harrington, Bold Snowflake With Face, 4 Gal.	8500.00
Churn, Hood Handles, I. Thomas, Kentucky, Dated 1837, 2 Gal.	2640.00
Churn, J. C. Waelde, North Bay, Cobalt Wash, 4 Gal.	3520.00
Churn, Minnesota Stoneware, Co., 3 Gal.	475.00
Churn, Salt Glaze, Minnesota Stoneware Co., 3 Gal.	475.00
Churn, Western, Blue Floral Design, 3 Gal.	285.00
Churn, Wooden Lid & Dasher, Cobalt Blue 3, 15 1/2 In.	950.00
Colander, Beige, Thick Rim	140.00
Cooler, Bardwell's, Patent Pending, Root Beer, White's, Utica	1430.00
Cooler, Barrel Shape, Bands, Cobalt Blue, 1863, 15 1/4 In.	400.00

Clean silver with any acceptable commercial polish. Don't use household scouring powder on silver, no matter how stubborn the spot may be. Use a tarnish–retarding silver polish to keep your silver clean. It will not harm old solid or plated wares. Do not use "instant" silver polishes.

Cooler, Barrel Shape, Embossed Bands, Floral Design, 16 3/8 In. 450.00
Cooler, Cover, Cherub, 5 Gal. 700.00
Cooler, Grande Vin De Chateau Maison, Spigot 55.00
Cooler, Hastings & Belding, Diana With Her Dogs 1925.00
Cooler, Minnesota Stoneware Co., 8 Gal. 2300.00
Cooler, Radium Ore Revigator Co., Patent 1912 .... 175.00
Cooler, Stag & Trees 325.00
Cooler, Water, Cobalt, A. Stedman & R. Frederick, 1825–35, 17 In. 357.00
Cooler, Whiteways Devon Cider, Brass Spigot, 3 Gal. 125.00
Creamer, Arc & Leaf 45.00
Crock, Albert Deutsch, Star Liquor House, Akron, Ohio, 1/2 Gal. 135.00
Crock, Argillo Works, Carbon Cliff, Illinois, 6 Gal. 350.00
Crock, Bennington, Deer Design, Ears, 1 1/2 Gal. 4250.00
Crock, Bird On Branch, Ears, 2 Gal. 365.00
Crock, Bird On Floral Branch, W. Roberts, 6 Gal. 935.00
Crock, Bird On Stump, Even R. Jones, 5 Gal. 475.00
Crock, Blue Daisy & Leaves Allover Front, Burger & Lang, 5 Gal. 395.00
Crock, Brushed Cobalt Blue Design, With 3, 10 1/2 In. 175.00
Crock, Butter, Butterfly 95.00
Crock, Butter, Draped Windows, Tan & Blue 165.00
Crock, Butter, F. H. Cowden, Harrisburg, Albany Slip, 5 x 9 1/4 In. 175.00
Crock, Butter, Lambrechts, 1 Lb. 35.00
Crock, Butter, Peacock At The Fountain, Nurock 175.00
Crock, Butter, Robinson Clay Products Co., 6 x 9 1/2 In. 105.00
Crock, Butter, Stenciled Label, Hamilton & Jones, 7 x 11 In. 375.00
Crock, Butter, Willow Farm, 2 Lb. 40.00
Crock, Butterfly, Wood Handle, Bail, Blue & White 98.00
Crock, Buttermilk, Roman Key Design, Spigot, White's, 4 Gal. 495.00
Crock, Cake, Even R. Jones, 2 Gal. 445.00
Crock, Cobalt Blue Bird, 11 1/2 In. 330.00
Crock, Cobalt Blue Design, White & Wood, 3 Gal., 11 1/4 In. 825.00
Crock, Cobalt Blue Label, Jas. Benjamin, Cinni., Ohio, 13 1/2 In. 65.00
Crock, Cobalt Target Bottom, Minnesota Stoneware Co., 2 Gal. 65.00
Crock, Combined Insecticide & Fungicide, Stamp, Bowker's Poison 82.50
Crock, Cover, Blue & White, Bread Or Cake, 12 1/2 x 7 1/2 In. 250.00
Crock, Cover, Blue & White, Embossed Vintage, 9 1/2 In. 100.00
Crock, Dean, Eley & Robertson, Druggists, Birmingham, Ala., 2 Gal. 85.00
Crock, Diamond Stickline Paste, Cover, 1 Gal. 90.00
Crock, Dog Holding Basket, S. Hart, Fulton, N. Y., 4 Gal. 2200.00
Crock, Dotted Bird, Large Flying Insects, A. O. Whitemore, 5 Gal. 2820.00
Crock, Eagle, W. E. Warner, West Troy, 4 Gal. 1760.00
Crock, F. Norton & Co., Blue Slip Floral, 9 In. 110.00
Crock, F. K. Norton, Worcester, Mass., Bird On Branch, 7 1/2 In. 165.00
Crock, Fairmont's Cottage Cheese, Blue Letters 57.50
Crock, Fantail Bird On Branch, White's, 2 Gal. 495.00
Crock, Floral Design, Cobalt Blue Slip, 13 1/2 In. 115.00
Crock, Floral, Cobalt Blue, Norton & Fenton, No. 3, 10 1/2 In. 135.00
Crock, Geo. N. Fulton, 1881, 3 1/4 In. 3000.00
Crock, Grapes, Ballard, 3 Gal. 242.00
Crock, H. C. Warner, Zanesville, Ohio, 1 Gal. 140.00
Crock, Hanson & VanWinkle Acid Co., Chicago, 15 Gal. 155.00
Crock, House Design, N. Y. Stoneware Co., 4 Gal. 3400.00
Crock, Ice Water, Western Pottery, Denver, 8 Gal. 110.00
Crock, Jack Daniels, Distillery, 1/2 Gal. 235.00
Crock, Jack Daniels, Hunter, 1 Gal. 145.00
Crock, Jack Daniels, No. 7, 1 Gal. 265.00
Crock, Jas. Hamilton & Co., Greensboro, Pa., Eagle, Tulip, 20 Gal. 2000.00
Crock, John Burger, Rochester, N. Y., 2 Ears, 1 Gal. 35.00
Crock, John Waugh, Jr., 2 Gal., 11 1/2 In. 385.00
Crock, Lamson & Swasey, Portland, Me., 2, Birds On Branch, 8 In. 375.00
Crock, Lid, Blue Floral & Leaf, Remmey, 17 In. 1485.00
Crock, Montclair Cantaloupes, Paper Label, 5 Lb. 93.50
Crock, N. Clark Jr., Athens, N. Y., 2, Blue Flower, 8 3/4 In. 200.00

Crock, N. Clark, Large Raven, Branches, 4 Gal.	3750.00
Crock, Norton & Fenton, Bennington, Vt., Cobalt Design, 12 1/2 In.	192.50
Crock, O. L. & A. K. Ballard, Cobalt Bird On Sprig, 1856–72, 5 Gal.	935.00
Crock, Pecking Chicken, 3 Gal.	825.00
Crock, Pickle, L. A. Budlong, Chicago, Ill., 2 Gal.	80.00
Crock, Polka Dot Bird, Cobalt Blue Slip, Impressed 3, 10 1/2 In.	400.00
Crock, R. Kean & Co., Barrow Street, N. Y.	155.00
Crock, Riedinger & Caire, Cobalt Bird On Stump, c.1850, 4 Gal.	550.00
Crock, Riedinger & Caire, Cobalt Birds, c.1850, 6 Gal.	1320.00
Crock, Riedinger & Caire, Poughkeepsie, N. Y., c.1850, 13 In.	1200.00
Crock, Sanfords Ink, Advertising	45.00
Crock, Stenciled Label In Wreath, Norwich Pottery Works, 13 In.	75.00
Crock, Stenciled Leaf, 6 Gal.	95.00
Crock, Stylized Man's Face, Brown Glaze, Pam Meaders, c.1920	298.00
Crock, T. F. Reppert, 5 Gal.	275.00
Crock, Tapered Sides, J. Weaver 5, Cobalt Blue Quillwork, 14 In.	150.00
Crock, Triple Floral Design, Blue At Handles, Wm. Moyer, 2 Gal.	465.00
Crock, Water, Salutaris Water Co., London	90.00
Cup, Measuring, Blue & White	395.00
Cuspidor, Peacock	295.00 To 325.00
Cuspidor, Polka Dot Letters, Elm Park Hotel, 7 1/4 In.	1100.00
Dispenser, Buttermilk, Butter Churn Shape	550.00
Filter, Water, Empire, Central N. Y., Pottery, Utica, 9 1/2 In.	132.00
Flask, Utica Commandery No. 3, Sep. 4, 1900 Reverse, 2 3/4 In.	407.00
Flowerpot, 4 Designs, New York Stoneware Co., 2 Gal.	995.00
Fruit, Banana, Polychrome Paint, 5 1/4 In.	11.00
Fruit, Large Bunch of Grapes, Polychrome Yellow	15.00
Fruit, Peach, Original Paint, 2 1/2 In., 3 Piece	105.00
Humidor, Serpent Finial On Cover, Word Cigars On Side, 5 1/2 In.	357.50
Inkstand, Embossed Rails & Balusters, 6 3/4 In.	250.00
Jar, 2 Birds On Branches, J. Norton & Co., 15 In.	1100.00
Jar, 4 Horizontal Cobalt Blue Stripes, Ovoid, 6 5/8 In.	150.00
Jar, Blue Foliage, Impressed 4, Shoulder Handles, Ovoid, 14 In.	450.00
Jar, Blue Label & Handle, I. M. Mead & Co., 3, 12 1/2 In.	80.00
Jar, C. Crolius, New York, Open Handles, Blue Swags, 11 1/2 In.	400.00
Jar, C. Hermann's Co., Milwaukee, Brown, 1 Qt.	45.00
Jar, Canning, Bailed, 5 Gal.	170.00
Jar, Canning, Bierbower & Co., Stoves & Tinware, Ky., 8 1/2 In.	300.00
Jar, Canning, Blue Leaf Design, Gray Salt Glaze, 8 1/4 In.	105.00
Jar, Canning, Cobalt Blue Apples & Grapes, Ovoid, 13 In.	200.00
Jar, Canning, Cobalt Blue Foliage At Shoulder, 8 7/8 In.	245.00
Jar, Canning, Cobalt Blue Label With 2–In. Wreath, 11 3/4 In.	75.00
Jar, Canning, Cobalt Blue Label, Hamilton & Jones, 9 3/4 In.	150.00
Jar, Canning, Cobalt Blue Straight & Wavy Lines, 7 1/8 In.	155.00
Jar, Canning, Freehand Label, Jas. Hamilton & Co., 9 3/4 In.	200.00
Jar, Canning, Stenciled Label, Hamilton & Jones, 6 3/4 In.	375.00
Jar, Canning, Stenciled Label, Hamilton & Jones, 9 3/4 In.	200.00
Jar, Canning, Stenciled Label, Hamilton & Jones, 10 In.	150.00
Jar, Canning, Stenciled Label, Williams & Reppert, 10 In.	105.00
Jar, Canning, T. F. Reppert, Greensboro, Pa., 9 3/4 In.	185.00
Jar, Canning, Williams & Reppert, Greensboro, Pa., 10 In.	115.00
Jar, Charlestown, 3 Hearts, Applied Handles, Ovoid, 15 In.	330.00
Jar, Cobalt Blue Design, Stripe, Flower & 2, 10 3/4 In.	210.00
Jar, Cobalt Blue Floral, Handles, Ovoid, 14 In.	175.00
Jar, Cobalt Blue Quill Work Floral, Ovoid, 13 1/2 In.	140.00
Jar, Cobalt Blue Tulip, Liminier 4, 13 1/4 In.	150.00
Jar, Cortland 2, Cobalt Blue Floral Design, 10 1/2 In.	375.00
Jar, Cover, Basketweave, Cloves	200.00
Jar, Cover, Basketweave, Nutmeg	250.00
Jar, Cover, Malted Beef, 6 In.	577.50
Jar, Floral Design, Blue At Handles, Cowden & Wilcox, 2 Gal.	605.00
Jar, Freehand Label, T. F. Reppert, Greensboro, Pa., 19 3/4 In.	1075.00
Jar, Hamilton & Jones Star Pottery, Greensboro, Pa., 15 In.	725.00

Jar, Handle, Tan Albany Slip, S. L. Pewtress & Co., 8 3/8 In. 30.00
Jar, Incised 4, N. C. Clark, Parkersburg, 14 In. 55.00
Jar, Japanese & Dutch Scenes, D. Albright, 1928, 12 In. 100.00
Jar, Julius Norton, No. 2, Ovoid, 10 3/8 In. 45.00
Jar, Label Peach With Flower In Cobalt Blue, 12 1/2 In. 500.00
Jar, McKenzie & Jackson, Beaver, Pa., Blue At Handles, 10 3/4 In. 150.00
Jar, No. 6, Yellow Glaze, 15 1/2 In. 40.00
Jar, Pickling, Blue Flower, 2 Gal. 175.00
Jar, Preserving, Weyman & Bro., Pittsburgh, Pa., 9 1/2 In. 375.00
Jar, Stenciled & Freehand Label, Williams & Reppert, 5, 16 In. 175.00
Jar, Stenciled Cobalt Blue, Greensboro, Pa, 13 In. 150.00
Jar, Storage, R. T. Williams, New Geneva, Pa., 5 Gal. 450.00
Jar, Storage, Western Stoneware Co., Wire Bail, Cover, 1/2 Gal. 35.00
Jar, Triple Floral, Cowden & Wilcox, 2 Gal. 550.00
Jar, Williams & Reppert, Greensboro, Pa., Eagle, 20 1/2 In. 1000.00
Jug, Acorn Design, Cobalt Blue, G. N. F. 1800.00
Jug, Archery Lesson, Turner White, England, c.1795, 8 1/4 In. 250.00
Jug, Bayless, McCarthey & Co., Ovoid, 3 Gal. 675.00
Jug, Beehive, Birch Leaf, Black Leaves, 3 Gal. 225.00
Jug, Beehive, Union Stoneware, 5 Gal. 250.00
Jug, Blue Floral, N. Clark Jr., 2 Gal. 350.00
Jug, Brown Glaze Drips, E. S. & B., 11 In. 75.00
Jug, Charles H. Slack Grocer, Brown Top, White 300.00
Jug, Clark & Fox, Athens #2, Tooled Lines At Shoulder, 13 In. 250.00
Jug, Cobalt Blue Bird & Flower, Washington, Michigan, 20 In. 700.00
Jug, Cobalt Blue Circles, Dots & Swags, Top Handle, 3 Gal. 1250.00
Jug, Cobalt Blue Floral Design, Ottman Bros. & Co., 15 1/2 In. 225.00
Jug, Cobalt Blue Floral, Harrington & Burger, 2 Gal. 850.00
Jug, Cobalt Blue Floral, J. W. Perkins & Co., 4 Gal., 17 1/2 In. 440.00
Jug, Cobalt Blue Slip Floral Design, S. Risley, 14 In. 150.00
Jug, Cobalt Blue Tulip, Straight & Wavy Lines, No. 2, 14 1/2 In. 350.00
Jug, Cowden & Wilcox Centennial, Shield, Dates 1776–1876, 4 Gal. 8800.00
Jug, Cowden & Wilcox, Centennial, Dated 1876, 4 Gal. 9680.00
Jug, Cowden & Wilcox, Harrisburg, Pa., Ovoid, 16 3/4 In. 700.00
Jug, Detrick Distilling Co., Dayton, Ohio, Motto, 5 In. 67.50
Jug, Dragonfly, N. Clark Jr., 2 Gal, ... 375.00
Jug, E. & L. P. Norton, Cobalt, 1858–81, 13 In. 105.00
Jug, E. Purdy 2, Brushed With Blue, Ovoid, 13 1/2 In. 225.00
Jug, E. L. Anderson Distilling Co., Newport, Ky., 1 Gal. 110.00
Jug, Emands & Co., Cobalt Bird On Branch, 3 Gal., 17 In. 275.00
Jug, Fantail Bird, Haxston Ottman & Co., 4 Gal. 775.00
Jug, Field, 2 Handles, 15 Gal. 125.00
Jug, Floral, No. 3, Quill & Brush Work, J. Shepard Jr., 15 1/2 In. 200.00
Jug, Ft. Dodge, Iowa, Tate Liquors, Sioux Falls, S. D., Miniature 450.00
Jug, Goodwin & Webster, Daubs of Blue, Ovoid, 11 1/4 In. 100.00
Jug, Gray, Deep Blue Poppy, H. Weston, Honesdale, Pa., 2 Gal. 350.00
Jug, Green Ash Glaze, Tooled Lines, Strap Handle, 16 3/4 In. 95.00
Jug, Hollyhocks, White, 4 Gal. 425.00
Jug, I. L. Lyons & Co., New Orleans, Brown Top, 2 Gal. 90.00
Jug, J. & E. Norton, Stylized Cobalt Blue Quill Work, 11 In. 550.00
Jug, J. & S. Hart, Oswego Falls, Cobalt Slip, Ovoid, 12 3/4 In. 250.00
Jug, J. Fisher For J. Patrzykowski, Buffalo, N. Y., Blue 145.00
Jug, J. Norton & Co., Cobalt Blue Bird, 10 3/4 In. 550.00
Jug, J. Norton & Co., No. 2, 14 In. 775.00
Jug, J. S. Taft, Keene, N. H., Cobalt Bird On Sprig, 5 Gal. 19 In. 220.00
Jug, J. T. Doores Distillers & Wholesalers, Bowling Green, Ky. 90.00
Jug, J. W. Allen, Fancy & Staple Groceries, Kentucky, 2 Gal. 125.00
Jug, James Yaugn, Georgia, Green Ash Glaze, 12 1/4 In. 275.00
Jug, Jas. Benjamin Stoneware Depot, Stenciled Label, 13 In. 65.00
Jug, Julius Norton, Bennington, Blue Impressed Label, 11 1/2 In. 65.00
Jug, Keystone Rye, Klein Bros., Cincinnati, Gold Letters, 1 Qt. 65.00
Jug, L. D. Addison, Old Breckenridge, Kentucky, 1/2 Gal. 85.00
Jug, L. P. Hoosley, Canton, Miss., 3 Gal. 75.00

◆◆◆◆◆◆◆◆◆◆◆◆◆◆◆◆◆◆◆◆◆◆◆◆

Glue broken china with an invisible mending cement that is waterproof.

◆◆◆◆◆◆◆◆◆◆◆◆◆◆◆◆◆◆◆◆◆◆◆◆

*Stoneware, Jug, W. Hart, Ogdensburg, Horse,
3 Gal.*

Jug, Lewin Mercantile, Denver, Co., 1 Gal.	95.00
Jug, Los Angeles Wine Co., Blue Banded Shoulder, 1 Qt.	650.00
Jug, Louis Abel, Chicago, Fancy, 1/2 Gal.	145.00
Jug, Man–In–The–Moon, Cowden & Wilcox, 2 Gal.	2585.00
Jug, N. Clark, Rooster, Cartoon, Gen. Grant For President, 2 Gal.	1700.00
Jug, No. 2 In Blue Quill Work, West Troy Pottery, 13 1/4 In.	325.00
Jug, Old Joe Sour Mash Whiskey, McBray, Anderson County, Ky.	95.00
Jug, P. H. Smith, Chocolate Brown Albany Slip, Ovoid, 11 1/2 In.	35.00
Jug, Parrot On Branch, J. Norton & Co., Cobalt Blue, 11 1/4 In.	450.00
Jug, Petty's Tonic, Sioux City, Iowa, Pig, 3 Gal.	185.00
Jug, Polka–Dotted Bird On Double Flower, W. Roberts, 2 Gal.	1430.00
Jug, Pouring Lip Spout, A. K. Ballard, No. 2, 12 In.	500.00
Jug, Radam's Microbe Killer	180.00
Jug, Rose Distiller, Atlanta, 2 Gal.	125.00
Jug, S. Purdy 2, Splash of Blue, 13 1/2 In.	100.00
Jug, Sam's Saloon, Brown Top, 1 Qt.	450.00
Jug, Snow Brand Horseradish, Brown Top, Wide Mouth, 1 Gal.	300.00
Jug, Spotted Bird, Nathan Clark Jr.	700.00
Jug, Star Shaped Leaves, Sibb J. Beighel, Unity, Pa., 11 1/4 In.	275.00
Jug, Steuben County Wine Co., Chicago, Ill., 5 Gal.	465.00
Jug, Stylized 4 Bloom Flowers, James Collins, No. 4, 18 In.	450.00
Jug, Stylized Bird, L. Norton & Son, Ovoid, 11 1/4 In.	2700.00
Jug, Stylized Cobalt Floral, O. L. & A. K. Ballard, Vt., 14 1/4 In.	255.00
Jug, Stylized Floral Design, Whites, Utica, 2, 14 In.	325.00
Jug, Stylized Floral, Cobalt Blue, F. B. Norton, No. 2, 13 1/2 In.	200.00
Jug, Stylized Floral, E. & L. P. Norton, Cobalt Blue, 13 1/4 In.	150.00
Jug, Stylized Foliage, Frank B. Norton, 14 1/4 In.	300.00
Jug, To–Kalon Wine Co., Black Birch Leaves, 5 Gal.	1000.00
Jug, Tom Keller Rye, Utica, N. Y., 1 Qt.	98.00
Jug, W. Hart, Ogdensburg, Horse, 3 Gal. ....*Illus*	5200.00
Jug, W. Roberts, Binghamton, N. Y., Polkadot Bird, 18 1/4 In.	900.00
Jug, Wauconda Springs, Advertising, 5 Gal.	145.00
Jug, West Troy Pottery 2, Leopard On Leaf, Quill Work, 13 3/4 In.	3150.00
Jug, Whiskey, A. P. Gizzard	50.00
Jug, Whiskey, Weideman, Tavern Scene	30.00
Jug, White, Bluebird On Branch, Utica, 2 Gal.	425.00
Meat Pounder, Wildflower	250.00
Meat Tenderizer, Wildflower, B & W	190.00
Mixing Bowl, Dark Blue & Rust, 7 x 3 1/2 In.	65.00
Mold, Sturgeon Fish, Legs, Red Slip, 4 x 16 In.	225.00
Mug, 3 Men At A Barrel, Whites, Utica, 5 1/4 In.	308.00
Mug, Berry's Famous Root Beer, 4 1/4 In.	120.00
Mug, Bezirks Turnfest, New York, CNY Pottery, 5 In.	210.00
Mug, Embossed Stripes, Blue Design, John Wygand, N. Y., 5 5/8 In.	135.00
Mug, Grape On Trellis, Blue & White	75.00
Mug, Pan–American Exposition, Whites, Utica, 1901, 5 1/2 In.	385.00
Mug, Rochester Brewing, Stamped 20, 5 1/2 In.	253.00

Pitcher & Bowl, Fishscale & Rose 375.00
Pitcher & Bowl, Fishscale & Wild Rose 150.00
Pitcher, 6 Tulips, Pennsylvania, 6 Qt. 905.00
Pitcher, A. J. Bailey, Blue & Gray, Leaf & Scroll 195.00
Pitcher, Apricots, Blue & White 100.00
Pitcher, Basket Weave, Gold Flowers 200.00
Pitcher, Blue Design, Blue At Handle, Pennsylvania, 4 Qt. 795.00
Pitcher, Blue Design, Remmey, 2 Gal. 2700.00
Pitcher, Brown Albany Slip, 11 3/4 In. 45.00
Pitcher, Brown, 2 Qt. 25.00
Pitcher, Brushed Cobalt Design, E. Bishop, Ohio 2, 13 1/2 In. 200.00
Pitcher, Cattail, Blue & White, 8 In. .... 100.00 To 185.00
Pitcher, Chain Link, Blue Inside & Out, 1 Pt. 20.00
Pitcher, Cherry Cluster, B & W 290.00
Pitcher, Child's, Grapevine With Ovals, 2 In. 55.00
Pitcher, Cobalt Blue Accents, Whites, Utica, c.1890, 9 3/4 In. 185.00
Pitcher, Cobalt Blue Floral, 10 3/8 In. 700.00
Pitcher, Coffman–Zigler Pottery, 1832 On Top 5300.00
Pitcher, Cow, Blue, Gray, 9 In. 145.00
Pitcher, Cow, Blue, White, 8 In. 300.00
Pitcher, Cow, Green & Cream, 9 In. 95.00
Pitcher, Cow, Green, Ivory, 7 In. 85.00
Pitcher, Doe & Fawn, Blue & White, 8 In. 175.00
Pitcher, Eagle, Shield With Arrows, Blue & White, 9 In. 275.00
Pitcher, Edelweiss, Whites, Utica, 9 In. 295.00
Pitcher, Floral Design, Cobalt Blue, Ovoid, 9 In. 425.00
Pitcher, Floral, Date 1832, Zigler Coffman, 9 In. 5300.00
Pitcher, Flying Bird, Blue & White, 8 In. 575.00
Pitcher, G. N. Fulton, Manganese Design, 8 In. 2750.00
Pitcher, Good Luck, Blue, White, 7 In. 190.00
Pitcher, Good Luck, Blue, White, 8 In. 150.00
Pitcher, Grape & Leaf Band, John B. Tayler, 8 In. 125.00
Pitcher, Grapes With Rickrack, 8 In. 115.00
Pitcher, Grapes, Green, 8 In. 65.00
Pitcher, Green & Tan, 6 In. 225.00
Pitcher, Hunter & Stag Scene, Blue & White 220.00
Pitcher, Indian, Blue & White, 8 In. 195.00
Pitcher, John Burger, Spout, Grapes, 1 Gal. 3500.00
Pitcher, Kissing Dutch Children, B & W, 9 In. 158.00
Pitcher, Makek's Grocery, 2 Qt. 225.00
Pitcher, Oval Medallion, Bearded Men, Dog's Head, 10 3/4 In. 85.00
Pitcher, Pewter Lid, Bardwell Root Beer, 10 In. 1595.00
Pitcher, Pewter Lid, Serpent Handle, Mask Spout, 15 In. 880.00
Pitcher, Sipe Nichols & Co., No. 2, Cobalt Blue Floral, 12 3/4 In. 1000.00
Pitcher, Sponge Band, Spiegelhoff's, Burlington, Wis., 1 Qt. 145.00
Pitcher, Stenciled Label, Hamilton & Jones, 10 3/4 In. 1100.00
Pitcher, Stenciled Label, Williams & Reppert, 10 1/2 In. 1200.00
Pitcher, Swan, Brown, 8 In. 85.00
Pitcher, Swirl, Blue & White, 9 In. 145.00
Pitcher, Tavern, Men Around Barrel, Hugo Bilhardt, 1894, 11 In. 302.50
Pitcher, Tooled Lines, Mark In Circle 1 1/2, Ovoid, 12 1/4 In. 700.00
Pitcher, Tree Bark, Leaves, Bust of Girl & Man, 8 1/4 In. 75.00
Pitcher, Tree Bark, Leaves, Drinking Scene, Blue & White, 8 In. 85.00
Pitcher, W. K. Richardson, Leominster, Mass., 10 3/4 In. 550.00
Pitcher, Williams and Reppert, Greensboro, Pa. 2, 13 In. 1400.00
Plate, Dinner, Blue & White, Sealforth 6.00
Pot, Baked Beans, Boston, Blue & White 235.00
Roaster, Blue & White, Cover 125.00
Rolling Pin, Advertising, Blue & White 200.00
Rolling Pin, Wild Flower 235.00
Salt & Pepper, Sponge Cream, Brown & Green 65.00
Salt Bowl, Come Again, Buss, Rockham S. D. 95.00
Salt Box, Hanging, Western 315.00

Salt Crock, Butterfly, Blue & White	85.00
Soap Dish, Rose Decal, Blue & White	65.00
Teapot, Chocolate Brown Glaze, Raised Dotting Design	35.00
Teapot, Horizontal Bands On Spout, Red, Seal Mark, 7 In.	357.00
Toothbrush Holder, Fishscale, Blue & White	65.00
Umbrella Stand, Blue	125.00
Urn, Painted Red, c.1910, 32 x 18 In.	55.00
Vase, Gourd Form, Applied Salamander, Flambe, As Lamp, 10 In.	275.00
Vase, Hyacinth, Tan, Brown Glaze Interior, 1870, Bulbous, 8 1/2 In.	65.00
Wash Set, Rose Decal, Blue & White, 6 Piece	550.00
Whistle, Bird Form, Glazed	88.00

Most items found in an old store are listed under advertising in this book. Store fixtures, cases, cutters, and other items that have no advertising as part of the decoration are listed here.

STORE, see also Advertising

STORE, Barrel, Pickle, Wooden, Bail Handle, Yellow & Red Paint, 12 In.	195.00
Bench, Jeweler's, Oak, Rolltop	1800.00
Bin, Poplar, Red Stain, Lift Lid, Divided, 50 x 22 x 27 In.	350.00
Bin, Seed, 18 Glass Front Drawers, Oak, 6 x 3 x 2 Ft.	4000.00
Cabinet, Spool, Oak, 4 Drawers, 19th Century, 43 x 25 x 15 In.	495.00
Carrier, Fish, Tin, N. Y.	22.50
Case, Counter Top, Wood, Glass Screen Back, Green, 1920	75.00
Chair, Shoe Shine, Wire	950.00
Check Writer, Todd, 1919	20.00
Chest, Apothecary, Brown Paint, 68 3/4 x 24 1/4 x 12 In.	2090.00
Cooler, Walk-In, McCray, Oak, Glass & Porcelain Front, Large	500.00
Cooler, Walk-In, McCray, Oak, Mirror Center, Porcelain, 10 x 8 Ft.	1000.00
Counter, Display, Newberry's 5 & 10 Cent Store	45.00
Crate, Shipping, Log Cabin Syrup, Rope Handles, Graphics, Wooden	145.00
Cupboard, Pine, 3 Paneled Doors, 6 Drawers With Locks, 49 1/2 In.	850.00
Dispenser, Iced Tea, Restaurant, Teapot Shape, Lid, Spigot, Large	165.00
Dispenser, Wrapping Paper	35.00
Display Rack, Revolving, Postcard	35.00
Display, Counter Top, Miss Peepy, 1950	20.00
Display, Pen, Large	35.00
Flour Sifter, Bakery, Wooden Frame, Large	20.00
Gambling Wheel, Mirrored, Wood, On Iron Stand, Mason & Co., c.1926	5500.00
Holder, Ice Cream Cone, Single, Blue Glass	145.00
Holder, Necklace, Counter Top, Brass, Revolves	60.00
Machine, Hot Nuts, Electric, Blinking Lights, Metal Base	185.00
Mannequin, Child's Underwear, Cloth Arms, Painted Face & Hair, 28 In.	50.00
Measure, Bartender's, With Bottle Opener, Brass	12.00
Meat Slicer, Cast Iron, Pat. 1861	85.00
Push Cart, Street Vendor, 1800s	145.00
Rack, Bakery, Removable Shelves, Red Over Black, 63 1/2 In.	525.00
Safe, On Wheels, 24 x 36 In., 1880s	700.00
Soda Fountain, Marble, 1880s	8500.00
Stool, Shoe Fitting, Bentwood	55.00
Tobacco Cutter, Abercrombie & Co., Royal Standard Havana, Iron	467.00
Tobacco Cutter, Brown & Williams, Iron	70.00
Tobacco Cutter, Finzer Bros., Louisville, Kentucky, Iron	45.00
Tobacco Cutter, Horse Shape, Metal Wrap On Handle, Iron, 7 1/4 In.	55.00
Tobacco Cutter, Roger Iron Co., Plain, Iron	100.00
Vault Alarm, American Bank, Cherry Cabinet, 2 Clocks, 1908, 69 In.	3500.00

Stoves have been used in America for heating since the eighteenth century and for cooking since the nineteenth century. Most types of wood, coal, gas, kerosene, and even some electric stoves are collected.

STOVE, Cook, Chambers, Cast Iron, 1940s	500.00
Cook, Detroit Jewel, Broiler Under Oven, Black Iron, 35 x 25 1/4 In.	275.00
Cook, Magic Chef, Gas, Cream, Blue-Gray Top, American Stove Co., 1940s	2000.00

◆◆◆

Felt gives off hydrogen sulphide which tarnishes silver. Do not use felt liners in drawers or felt bags to store silver unless they are the specially treated tarnish preventative cloths.

◆◆◆

Fireplace, Ornate, Enameled, Gas	58.00
Griddle, Wrought Iron Range Co.	17.50
Home Comfort, Wood Burning, 1864	4500.00
Ornament, Doe–Wah–Jack, Full Figural, Metal, 12 In.	130.00
Parlor, Beacon Universal, Nickel Trim, Crown, Pat. 1907	975.00
Parlor, Charter Oak, Green & Cream	250.00
Parlor, Florence, Hot Blast, Wood Burning, No. 53	1000.00
Parlor, Neoclassical Style, 2 Smokestacks, Stanley's No. 2	110.00
Parlor, Oak, E–16, Round	995.00
Parlor, Universal, Warming Closet, Gas, Coal, Wood	985.00
Plate, Fireback, Arched Panels, Hearts & Tulips, Cast Iron, 22 In.	1200.00
Plate, Fireback, Classical Bust In Laural Wreath, Cast Iron, 27 In.	6200.00
Potbellied, Grey Iron Casting Co., Mt. Joy, Pa., Sample	310.00
Riya Stove Company, Salesman's Sample	100.00
Wick, Blue Bird Oil	6.50

STRAWBERRY, see Soft Paste

Stretch glass is named for the strange stretch marks in the glass. It was made by many glass companies in the United States from about 1900 to the 1920s. It is iridescent. Most American stretch glass is molded; most European pieces are blown and may have a pontil mark.

STRETCH GLASS, Cake Server, Green, Center Handle	18.00
Candleholder, Green, 10 In., Pair	35.00
Candy Dish, Cover, Paneled, Footed, Blue	30.00
Candy Dish, Cover, Yellow, Low	15.00
Plate, Laurel Leaf, Green Edge, 8 In.	12.00
Ring Holder, Yellow, Enameled Bottom, 5 In. Diam.	25.00

A cameo of unglazed white porcelain was encased in transparent glass to produce a sulphide. The technique was patented in 1819 in France and has been used ever since for paperweights, decanters, tumblers, and other type of glassware. Paperweights are listed in their own section.

SULPHIDE, Medallion, Cleveland, Speckled, 3 1/2 In.	195.00
Tumbler, Cased, Molded, 3 1/2 In.	440.00
Tumbler, Cased, Molded, Cutting, Foil Back Flower, 4 In.	825.00
Tumbler, Figure, Military Man, Cased	600.00
Tumbler, Figure, Military Man, Cased, Heavy Pressing, 4 In.	750.00

Sumida, or Sumida Gawa, is a Japanese pottery. The pieces collected by that name today were made about 1895 to 1970. There has been much confusion about the name of this ware, and it is often called *Korean Pottery* or *Poo ware*. Most pieces have a very heavy orange–red, blue, or green glaze, with raised three-dimensional figures as decorations.

SUMIDA, Basket, Monkey, Dog Handle, Rock–Like Sides	200.00
Bowl, Carved Peony Foliage, Conical, Celadon, 7 In.	2200.00
Bowl, Children On Rim, Red–Orange Glaze, 6 In. Diameter	250.00
Humidor, Cover, 2 Figures On Front, Figure Finial, Signed, 6 In.	335.00
Mug, Boy Chasing Bird, 4 In.	85.00
Tankard, Monkey Climbing Rocks On Side, 12 In.	350.00
Tankard, Tigers In Relief, Blue–Green Glaze, 12 1/2 In.	595.00
Vase, Ring Handles, Drip Glaze, Green, Red, Pink, 7 In.	200.00

Sunbonnet Babies were first introduced in 1902 in the *Sunbonnet Babies Primer.* The stories were by Eulalie Osgood Grover, illustrated by Bertha Corbett. The children's faces were completely hidden by the sunbonnets. The children had been pictured in black and white before this time, but the color pictures in the book were immediately successful. The Royal Bayreuth China Company made a full line of children's dishes decorated with the Sunbonnet Babies. Some Sunbonnet Babies plates have been reproduced but are clearly marked.

SUNBONNET BABIES, Bowl, Fruit, Washing & Hanging, 9 3/4 In.	525.00
Box, Hand Burned	45.00
Chamberstick, Fishing Scene, Shieldback, Blue Mark	495.00
Creamer, Fishing, Mug Shape, Blue Mark, 3 1/2 In.	165.00
Dish, Feeding, Babies Fishing, Blue Mark, 7 1/2 In.	235.00
Dish, Mending, Fluted, Gold Trim, 6 In.	140.00
Figurine, Set of 7	560.00
Hair Receiver, Cleaning, Blue Mark	285.00
Inkwell, Running, Blue Mark	325.00
Nappy, Mending, Handle, Blue Mark, 6 In.	185.00
Plate, Candy For My Mandy	43.00
Rose Bowl, Cleaning	280.00
Tea Set, Fishing, Blue Mark, 4 Piece	425.00
Teapot, Fishing, 4 In.	495.00
Toothpick, Cleaning, 3 Handles, Blue Mark	395.00

Sunderland luster is a name given to a special type of pink luster made by Leeds, Newcastle, and other English firms during the nineteenth century. The luster glaze is metallic and glossy and appears to have bubbles in it. Other pieces of luster are listed in the luster section.

SUNDERLAND, Bowl, Black Transfer, Sailor's Farewell, Pink Luster, 6 7/8 In.	145.00
Jar, Forget–Me–Not, West View of Cast Iron Bridge, 3 x 5 In.	55.00
Jar, Sailor's Tear, West View of Cast Iron Bridge, 4 5/8 In.	85.00
Jug, Enterprise & Boxer, U. S. & Macedonian, Pink, 4 3/8 In.	1980.00
Mustard, Cover, 4 In.	150.00
Pitcher, MacDonough's Victory, Leaf Handle, 1814, 9 1/2 In.	4400.00
Pitcher, Perry's Victory, Insignia Under Spout, 9 In.	1210.00
Pitcher, Sailor's Farewell, Pink Luster, Black, 4 5/8 In.	125.00
Plaque, Black Transfer, Pink & Copper Luster, 7 3/4 x 8 3/4 In.	300.00
Plaque, Black Transfer, Pink Luster, C. C. & Co., 6 3/4 In.	175.00
Plate, Center Portrait of Pike, Yellow Band, c.1820, 10 In.	2100.00
Salt, Cloud Pattern, Footed, Master	42.00 To 45.00
Vase, Embossed Design, Pink Luster, Polychrome Enamel, 6 3/4 In.	175.00

Superman was created by two seventeen–year–olds in 1938. The first issue of *Action* comics had the strip. Superman remains popular and became the hero of a radio show in 1940, cartoons in the 1940s, a television series, and several major movies.

SUPERMAN, Art Set, Paint By Numbers, Touch of Velvet, 1966, Hasbro	85.00
Bank, Dime Register	150.00
Belt Buckle, Metal, 1960s	18.00
Book, Bicentennial, Comic Type, 1976	12.00
Book, Coloring	10.00
Book, Comic, 3–D	350.00
Book, Leather, Dust Jacket, First Book	950.00
Booklet, Comic, Premium, Sugar Smacks, 1955	45.00
Cake Decoration Set, 1978, 6 Piece	2.00
Card Set, Movie Scenes, 1966	60.00
Christmas Crackers, Hovell, 1982	35.00
Container, Plastic, Avon, 1978	15.00
Display, Advertising, Paper, Die Cut, 1940s	125.00
Doll, 1978	20.00

Figure, Elastic, Stretched, Pulled, Squeezed, Mego, 12 In. 85.00
Game, Calling Superman, 1945 .... 115.00
Game, Cards, 1966 .... 15.00
Game, Hasbro, 1975 .... 55.00
Gun, Squirt .... 20.00 To 65.00
Hood Ornament, Chrome, 1940s 3000.00
Krypton Ray Gun Set, Box 850.00
Krypton Rocket, Box 250.00
Lunch Box, 1967 .... 125.00 To 175.00
Lunch Box, 1978 .... 15.00
Marionette, Display, 1978, Box 125.00
Pennant, 1966 .... 40.00
Pin, Lapel, Figural, Superman, Cloisonne, DC Comics, 1940, 1/2 In. 12.00
Pin, Superman of America, Chains Around Chest, 1940s 60.00
Pistol, Cinematic, Directions, Daisy, Box 450.00
Poster, Superman & The Mole Men, Movie, 1951 .... 150.00
Puppet, Ideal, 1965 .... 30.00 To 85.00
Record Player 125.00
Record, Radio Program, Coke, 1972, Unopened 12.50
Ring, Black Jet Airplane, Kellogg's Pep 200.00
Stamp & Card, Junior Defense League of America, 1940s 20.00
Tank, Tin Lithograph, Linemar 1045.00
Tumbler, Pepsi–Cola, 1976, 6 1/4 In. 16.00
TV Guide, George Reeves As Superman Cover, Sept. 25, 1953 .... 400.00
Viewer, Acme, Original Card, 1955 .... 110.00
Wallet .... 15.00 To 20.00
Wristwatch, 1939 .... 275.00
Wristwatch, 1960s 40.00
Wristwatch, Black Band, D. C. Comics, 1977 .... 50.00

 In 1933, the Kraft Food Company began to market cheese spreads in decorated, reusable glass tumblers. These were called *Swankyswigs.* They were discontinued from 1941 to 1946, then made again from 1947 to 1958. Then plain glasses were used for most of the cheese, although a few special decorated Swankyswigs have been made since that time. A complete list of prices can be found in *Kovels' Price Guide to Depression Glass & American Dinnerware.*

SWANKYSWIG, Antique, Black .... 1.75 To 2.50
Antique, Brown 2.50
Band No. 1, Red & Black .... 1.50 To 2.00
Band No. 2, Red & Black 2.50
Bustlin' Betsy, Blue 2.00
Bustlin' Betsy, Red 2.00
Carnival, Blue .... 3.00 To 4.00
Carnival, Green .... 4.00 To 6.00
Checkerboard, Red 2.00
Cornflower No. 1, Light Blue 2.00
Forget–Me–Not, Light Blue 1.75
Forget–Me–Not, Red 1.75
Kiddie Cup, Green 2.00
Kiddie Cup, Orange 2.00
Kiddie, Green 2.00
Petal Star, 50 Year Anniversary 1.50
Posy Cornflower No. 1, Light Blue 2.00
Red Circle and Dot, 3 1/2 In. 3.50
Sailboat No. 1, Blue 12.00
Sailboat No. 2, Green 12.00
Sailboat, Blue 12.00
Texas Centennial, Blue 23.00
Tulip No. 1, Dark Blue 3.00
Tulip No. 3, Dark Blue 2.50
Tulip No. 3, Yellow 2.00

All types of swords are of interest to collectors. The military dress sword with elaborate handle is probably the most wanted. Be sure to display swords in a safe way, out of reach of children.

SWORD, Bayonet, Dress, Lukas Stroebele, Oct. 1912, World War I	150.00
Bone, Hand Carved, Korean Figures	450.00
Civil War, Alfred L. Tuner, Pierced Counterguard, War Issue	660.00
Dress, Lion Figural Handle, Paste Jewel Eyes, 36 In.	135.00
European, Horn Grip, Pierced Shell Guard, Brass Mounts	245.00
Executioner's, 2-Hand Grip, c.1880	625.00
Figure of Man & Elephant On Handle, Sheath, Japan, 27 In.	605.00
Infantry Officer's, F. W. Widmann, Philadelphia, 1835, 36 1/2 In.	2950.00
Ivory Handle, Acanthus Design, American Eagle, Japan, 36 In.	470.00
Saber, Civil War	175.00
U. S. Artillery Officer's, Eagle On Globe, Gold Overlay Grip, c.1820	850.00

Syracuse is a trademark used by the Onondaga Pottery of Syracuse, New York. The company was established in 1871. It is still working. The name became the Syracuse China Company in 1966. It is known for fine dinnerware and restaurant china.

SYRACUSE, Bread Plate, Lady Mary	12.00
Creamer, Forget-Me-Not	20.00
Cup & Saucer, Bracelet	30.00
Cup & Saucer, Lady Mary	30.00
Cup & Saucer, Victoria	22.00
Gravy Boat, Victoria	50.00
Plate, Forget-Me-Not, 9 1/2 In.	20.00
Plate, Gold Band, 8 In.	20.00
Plate, Victoria, 9 1/2 In.	18.00
Platter, Lady Mary, 12 In.	35.00
Soup, Dish, Old Ivory	15.00
Sugar, Cover, Forget-Me-Not	25.00
TAPESTRY, PORCELAIN, see Rose Tapestry	

A tea caddy is a small box made to hold tea leaves. In the eighteenth century, tea was very expensive and it was stored under lock and key. The first tea caddies were made with locks. By the nineteenth century, tea was more plentiful and the tea caddy was larger. Often there were two sections, one for green tea, one for black tea.

TEA CADDY, Brass Bale, Bombay, Mahogany, 10 1/4 In.	450.00
Brass Borders, Brass Insets, Stepped Lid, Laburnum, 7 In.	935.00
Burl Yew Wood, Paneled Dome-Hinged Cover, 6 1/2 In.	550.00
Burl Yew Wood, Stepped-Wing Top, Paw Feet, 6 1/2 In.	440.00
Chinese Export, Serpent Feet, Pewter Insert, Small	1450.00
Fruitwood, Pear Shape, Escutcheon & Key, Foil Lined, 6 3/4 In.	1545.00
George III, Pear Form, 6 In.	715.00
George III, Pear Form, Red Stain Stem Traces, 1800, 7 1/2 In.	3300.00
George III, Silver Mounted Ivory, 10-Sided, c.1800, 6 In.	880.00
Inlaid Figured Wood, Hexagonal Quillwork, Brass Ring Handle	400.00
Inlaid Mother-of-Pearl, Tortoiseshell Veneer, Cover, 6 1/2 In.	550.00
Lacquer, 2 Lidded Interior Compartments, Black, 14 In.	1000.00
Mahogany Veneer, Brass Inlay, No Lock, 5 1/4 In.	150.00
Mahogany, 3 Sections & Lids, Mixing Spoon, England, 9 3/4 In.	225.00
Pewter, Brass Design, Chinese Marking, 5 1/2 In.	55.00
Prince & Princess William V of Orange, Leeds, 2 3/4 In.	2750.00
Prince & Princess William V of Orange, Leeds, 5 1/4 In.	3080.00
Red Flowers & Bird, Gold Leaves, Cover, Marcolini, c.1775, 5 In.	115.00
Regency, Ivory-Inlaid Tortoiseshell, 2 Wells, 5 1/2 x 7 In.	1540.00
Regency, Rosewood, Ivory-Inlaid Design, Rosewood, c.1825, 13 In.	165.00
Rosewood Medallions On Lid, Mahogany On Pine, 10 3/4 In.	175.00
Royal Worcester, Hand Painted Bluebells, 4 In.	295.00
Serpentine Case, Tortoiseshell, 4 1/2 x 7 In.	770.00

Sheraton, Mahogany, Holly Stringing, Shell Inlaid, 1790 .... 1325.00
Silver On Copper, Sheffield, 4 1/4 In. 120.00
Silver Plate, Scroll Repousse, Birmingham, 1906, 3 3/4 In. 120.00
Silver, Applied Floral Design, Pedestal, Reed & Barton 280.00
Silver, Rococo Floral Design, Peter & Ann Bateman, 5 7/8 In. 750.00
Soft Paste, Blue Floral, 5 3/4 In. 145.00
Sterling, Slip–On Lid, Enameled Foliage, Russia, 1892, 4 1/2 In. 2640.00
Tole, Black Paint, Floral Design, 8 In. 85.00
Tole, Red, Yellow Bird, 5 In. 4300.00
Tortoiseshell Veneer, 2 Inner Lids, Brass Ball Feet, 6 1/2 In. 550.00
Tortoiseshell, Domed Case, Ivory Bun Feet, 6 In. 465.00
Tortoiseshell, Hinged Lid, Silver Finial, Square Body, 5 1/2 In. 385.00
Tortoiseshell, Rectangular Case, Silver Ball Feet, 4 1/2 In. 825.00
Wedgwood, Tricolor, Classical Figures, 5 1/4 In. 1395.00
William IV, Rosewood & Burl Elm Panels, 6 1/4 In. 660.00
Wooden, Pear Shape 695.00

There was a superstition that it was lucky if a whole tea leaf unfolded at the bottom of your cup. This idea was translated into the pattern of dishes known as *tea leaf.* The earliest was probably made by Anthony Shaw in 1856. At least 30 English, several Scottish, and about 20 American potteries made Tea Leaf. The tea leaf was always a luster glaze on early wares, although now some pieces are made with a brown tea leaf.

TEA LEAF IRONSTONE, Bowl, Square, Meakin, 8 1/2 In. 50.00
Bowl, Square, Meakin, 9 1/4 In. 60.00
Jam Jar 15.00
Platter, Meakin, 10 x 14 In. 55.00
Platter, Small 50.00
Soap Dish, Square, Powell & Bishop 110.00
Teapot, Pinwheel, Octagonal 150.00
Tureen, Cover 55.00

Teco is the mark used on the art pottery line made by the American Terra Cotta and Ceramic Company of Terra Cotta and Chicago, Illinois. The company was an offshoot of the firm founded by William D. Gates in 1881. The Teco line was first made in 1885 but was not sold commercially until 1902. It continued in production until 1922. Over 500 designs were made in a variety of colors, shapes, and glazes. The company closed in 1930.

TECO, Bookends, Gargoyle, Ivory 300.00
Bowl, Green, 4 Buttress Legs, White Glaze Interior, 1910, 6 In. 4620.00
Cuspidor, Woman's, Stoneware 200.00
Jardiniere, Green, Flared, Squares & Lines Around Collar, 7 5/8 In. 1650.00
Matchbox, Cover, No. 384 .... 350.00
Pitcher, Aventurine, 8 In. 265.00
Pot, Green, 4–Sided, 15 In. 6100.00
Urn, Indian Chiefs, Fleur–De–Lis Diaper, Molded Handles, 27 1/4 In. 7700.00
Vase, Basket Weave Neck, Green Matte Glaze, Tulips, 1910, 10 In. 1650.00
Vase, Buff Matte, Blade–Shaped Leaves, Cylindrical Neck, 12 1/4 In. 1045.00
Vase, Buttressed, Brown, 7 1/2 In. 685.00
Vase, Crimson Metallic Glaze, Experimental, 11 1/2 In. 850.00
Vase, Gray High Gloss, Experimental Glaze, 11 In. 350.00
Vase, Green Matte Glaze, 4 Buttressed Handles, Oval, Flared, 5 x 2 In. 495.00
Vase, Green Matte Glaze, Amphora Seated, 4 Buttresses, 9 7/8 In. 4400.00
Vase, Green Matte Glaze, Triple Gourd, 4 Buttress Supports, 13 In. 7700.00
Vase, Green Matte, 4 Buttressed Handles, Bulbous, Flared Neck, 7 In. 1210.00
Vase, Green Matte, Circular Base, Long Tapered Neck, 13 x 4 3/4 In. 715.00
Vase, Green Matte, Stepped–In Neck, 2 Buttressed Handles, 11 1/2 In. 1350.00
Vase, Green, 2 Square Handles, 7 In. 795.00
Vase, Green, 4 Handles, Green, 11 1/2 In. 2500.00
Vase, Green, 4 Sides, 15 In. 6050.00
Vase, Green, Flared, 6 Applied Lily Leaves, 1910, 10 1/4 In. 4400.00

Vase, High Glaze Over Metallic Burgundy Glaze, 11 1/2 In. 575.00
Vase, Metallic Glaze, 11 In. 3575.00
Vase, Mustard Matte, Knob At Top, Bulbous Bottom, Long Neck, 5 In. 475.00
Vase, Pink Matte, 3 Flared Feet, Bulbous, Cylindrical Neck, 9 x 6 In. 660.00
Vase, Pumpkin Matte, Cylindrical Neck, 4 Angular Handles, 8 x 6 In. 2200.00
Vase, Veined Green Glaze, 10 1/2 In. 1950.00
Wall Pocket, Green, Gray Glaze 550.00
Wall Pocket, Indian Designs, Matte Green 750.00

The first teddy bear was a cuddly toy said to be inspired by a hunting trip made by Teddy Roosevelt in 1902. Morris and Rose Michtom started selling their stuffed bears as *Teddy bears* and the name stayed. The Michtoms founded the Ideal Novelty and Toy Company. The German version of the teddy bear was made about the same time by the Steiff Company. There are many types of teddy bears and all are collected. The old ones are being reproduced.

TEDDY BEAR, Bello–Jolie, Yolanda 1000.00
Button Eyes, Red Suit, c.1910, 11 1/2 In. 245.00
Gold Plush, Long Snout, Jointed, Hump, Kapok & Straw, 23 In. 209.00
Gold, Electric Eye, Jointed Shoulders, Straw Stuffed, 22 In. 375.00
Golden Plush Mohair, Jointed, Excelsior Stuffing, 20 1/2 In. 137.50
Green Overalls, Tyrolean Felt Hat, Long Nose, Brown, Large 95.00
Gund, Bubba, Baby, Pink Snowsuit 60.00
Haircloth, Straw Stuffed, Button Eyes, Articulated Limbs, 13 In. 110.00
Hermann, Jointed, Straw Stuffed, Hump Backed 225.00
Ideal, Honey, Shoebutton Eyes, 14 In. 325.00
Ideal, Mohair, Humpback, Leather Collar, Lock, Jointed, 1925 .... 600.00
John Wright, Pooh, 20 In. 375.00
Knickerbocker, Cindy Bear, Yogi's Girlfriend, Plush, 1959, 18 In. 80.00
Kodiak, Fur Cover, Bass Viol Animated Music Box 1870.00
Nisbet, Tan Mohair, John Bull's Deli, 80th Birthday, 25 In. 99.00
Schuco, Gold Mohair, 2 3/4 In. 100.00
Steiff, Baby Ophelia, White, Net Tutu, M. D. Clise, 1986, 11 In. 99.00
Steiff, Baby, Open Mouth, Button, U. S. Zone, 11 In. 985.00
Steiff, Bear Tea Party, Box 450.00
Steiff, Blond Mohair, Jointed, Original Buggy, 19 1/4 In. 250.00
Steiff, Button, Tan, 16 In. 460.00
Steiff, Button, Tan, 21 In. 475.00
Steiff, Dark Brown, Jointed, Black Eyes, 6 In. 93.00
Steiff, Gold Mohair, 17 In. 430.00
Steiff, Gold, Button, 8 In. 300.00
Steiff, Gold, Chest Tag, 1940s, 8 In. 350.00
Steiff, Mama & Baby, Signed, 2 Piece 500.00
Steiff, Mohair, Fully Jointed, Embroidered Muzzle, 1950s, 11 In. 440.00
Steiff, On Wheels, Growler, 48 In. 4180.00
Steiff, Papa Bear, Signed, 10 In. 800.00
Steiff, Polar Bear, Chest Tag, 1950s, 5 In. 135.00
Steiff, Somersault 275.00
Steiff, Strong, Cream, 26 In. 450.00
Steiff, Tan, Straw Stuffed, Long Nose, 1930–40, 10 In. 350.00
Steiff, Ullu, Button & Chest Tag, 1970s, 8 In. 140.00
Straw Stuffed, Jointed Arms & Legs, Glass Eyes, Wool, 14 In. 100.00
Straw Stuffed, Jointed, Glass Eyes, Stitched Eyebrows, 22 In. 180.00
Twyford, Fully Jointed, Mohair, Squeaker, 10 In. 75.00

The first telephone may have been made in Havana, Cuba, in 1849, but it was not patented. The first publicly demonstrated phone was used in Frankfurt, Germany, in 1860. The phone made by Alexander Graham Bell was shown at the Centennial Exhibition in Philadelphia in 1876, but it was not until 1877 that the first private phones were installed. Collectors today want all types of old phones, phone parts, and advertising.

TELEPHONE, 7–Up Can 25.00
  Army, World War II 40.00
  Booth, Pay, Seat, Shelf & Light, Wooden, 1930s 850.00
  Booth, Red, England, Cast Iron, 8 1/2 Ft. 2500.00
  Candlestick, Black 40.00
  Candlestick, Display, Brass, Composition, 24 1/2 In. 2640.00
  Candlestick, Kellogg 95.00
  Candlestick, Swedish–American Tel. Co., Chicago, Brass, 11 1/2 In. 185.00
  Candlestick, Western Electric 90.00
  Candlestick, Working Box 125.00
  Charlie Tuna, Starkist, Pushpad Built–In Base, 1987 .... 66.00
  Crest Toothpaste Man, 1980s, Box .... 55.00 To 65.00
  Desk, Stromberg–Carlson, Pink, Rebuilt, 1950s 30.00
  Desk, Western Electric, Oak Box 125.00
  First Aid, Pocket Case, Bell System, 1940s 12.00
  Heinz Catsup Bottle 35.00
  Pay Phone, 3 Slot 150.00
  Pay Phone, Black, 1950s 147.00
  Reveille–Bell, Philadelpia, 1905 .... 35.00
  Switch Board, Hotel, Small 125.00
  Tetley Tea Man, Stand, Base, Canada, 10 1/2 In. 85.00
  Wall, Oak, Long 175.00
  Wall, Western Electric, Oak 150.00

Although the first television transmission took place in England in 1925, collectors find few sets which pre–date 1946. The first sets had only five channels, but by 1949 the additional VHF channels were included. The first color television set became available in 1951.

TELEVISION, Philco, 1958 .... 895.00
  RCA Victor, c.1940 .... 300.00
  Zenith, Console, Color, Remote Control, 1960s, 27 x 33 1/2 In. 120.00

Teplitz refers to art pottery manufactured by a number of companies in the Teplitz–Turn area of Bohemia during the late nineteenth and early twentieth centuries. The Amphora Porcelain Works and the Alexandra Works were two of these companies.

TEPLITZ, Bust, Green Collar, Pink Bowl, Feathers In Hair, 8 In. 757.00
  Ewer, Art Nouveau, 9 In. 250.00
  Ewer, Blue & Gold Flowers, Cream Ground, 6 1/2 In. 50.00
  Ewer, Waterlilies Handles, Mauve, Sponged Gold Ground, 1892, 13 In. 1500.00
  Figurine, Lioness, Amphora, 10 In. 165.00
  Figurine, Reclining Girl On Rock, 2 Baskets, c.1905, 19 In. 675.00
  Goblet, Engraved Fox Hunt Scene, Hand Blown 95.00
  Humidor, Figural, Amphora, 11 In. 450.00
  Humidor, Owls, 9 In. 175.00
  Lamp, Hand Painted Woman, 12 In. 400.00
  Pitcher, Arab, Colorful Robes, 6 1/2 In. 120.00
  Planter, Boy Figure At Side Holding Basket, 12 1/2 x 11 In. 595.00
  Urn, Cover, Hand Painted Woman, Flowers, Whallis, 10 1/2 In. 285.00
  Urn, Tan To Cream To Tan, Gold Scroll Center, 2 Handles, 10 In. 95.00
  Vase, 2 Parrots On Branch, Flowers, Circles, Brown, Marked, 7 In. 100.00
  Vase, 3 Boys Carry Woven Baskets, Amphora, c.1905, 9 In. 495.00
  Vase, Artist, 5 1/2 In. 95.00

◆◆◆

If there is goldwash in the bright cut silver design, the wash is a later addition. Victorian pieces were made with bright cutting against the gold to show the design in two colors.

◆◆

Terra–Cotta, Figurine, Conch Shell, Putto,
Dolphin, 21 In.

◆◆◆◆◆◆◆◆◆◆◆◆◆◆◆◆◆◆◆◆◆◆◆◆

Condition, size, and small details
determine the value of political
buttons. To be sure the description is accurate for buying, selling, or insurance, just put the
buttons on the glass top of a
photocopy machine. Get copies
of both the front and the back.

◆◆◆◆◆◆◆◆◆◆◆◆◆◆◆◆◆◆◆◆◆◆◆◆

Vase, Bird, Flowers, High Glaze, Matte Ground, 7 In.	85.00
Vase, Blown–Out Flowers, Serpent Encircles Neck, Marked, 17 In.	650.00
Vase, Blue–Gold Flowers, Cream Ground, 11 In.	150.00
Vase, Enameled Potted Trees, Geometric Flowers, Cylindrical, 14 In.	285.00
Vase, Enameled Woman Water Carrier, 5 1/2 In.	95.00
Vase, Eskimo, Kayak, Stellmacher, 6 In.	190.00
Vase, Floral Basket, 2 Salamander, Bulbous Top, Red Mark, 8 x 10 In.	350.00
Vase, Floral Encrusted Vines, Blue–Green Ground, 9 In.	245.00
Vase, Flowers, Open Handles, 10 In.	150.00
Vase, Girl Bouncing Ball, Bulbous, Matte Green, 3 1/2 In.	75.00
Vase, Girl, Moon, 5 In.	85.00
Vase, Green, Blue & White Girl Bouncing Ball, 4 In.	75.00
Vase, Matte Brown, Impressed Mark, 7 In. ....*Illus*	99.00
Vase, Mottled Tan, Cobalt Flowers, 8 1/2 In.	225.00
Vase, Multicolored Poppies, Enameled Centers & Stems, 13 In.	185.00
Vase, Nursery Rhyme, Little Jack Horner, Marked, 6 In.	250.00
Vase, Owl Perched On Oak Branch, Amphora, c.1905, 12 3/4 In.	660.00
Vase, Pheasant In Full Relief, Expanded Lip, Amphora, c.1900, 16 In.	440.00
Vase, Spider Webs, Moths, Glass Cabochons, Amphora, c.1905, 12 In.	1760.00
Vase, Stylized Flowers, Blue Trim, Center Band, Marked, 6 1/4 In.	175.00

Terra–cotta is a special type of pottery. It ranges from pale orange
to dark reddish–brown in color. The color comes from the clay,
which is fired but not always glazed in the finished piece.

TERRA–COTTA, Bust, Renaissance Woman, M. Strozzi, Marble Plinth, 19 In.	275.00
Figurine, 2 Men, 2 Women, Clothes, France, 1920, 8 1/2 In., 4 Pc.	195.00
Figurine, Conch Shell, Putto, Dolphin, 21 In. ....*Illus*	770.00
Figurine, Girl & Two Kittens, William Zorach, 12 1/2 In.	1875.00
Figurine, Horse & Rider, Straw Glaze, T'ang Dynasty, 10 In.	1750.00
Figurine, Mother & Child, William Zorach, 6 1/8 In.	2420.00
Jardiniere, Garden, 23 In., Pair	3025.00

◆◆◆◆◆◆◆◆◆◆◆◆◆◆◆◆◆◆◆◆◆◆◆◆

Stains on porcelains can be
removed by soaking in a mixture
of two tablespoons of Polident
denture cleaner in a quart of
tepid water.

◆◆◆◆◆◆◆◆◆◆◆◆◆◆◆◆◆◆◆◆◆◆◆◆

Teplitz, Vase, Matte Brown, Impressed Mark,
7 In.

◆◆◆

If your doll's body leaks sawdust, try patching the hole by putting a few drops of clear glue in the hole. If the hole is too large, patch it with a piece of muslin or kid cut from an old glove. Cut a circular patch, glue in place.

◆◆◆

Nodder, Japanese Man's Head, Startled By Frog, 5 1/2 In.	88.00
Teapot, Embossed Ribbing, Ribbed Strap Handle, 5 5/8 In.	375.00
Teapot, Enamel Dragon On Side & Handle, China, 1920s, 8 In.	195.00
Urn, Allegorical Figural Band, Ram's Head Handles, 30 In.	2530.00
Urn, Basket-Weave Design, Lion Mask Handles, 1780s, 26 In.	5500.00
Vase, Embossed Design, Gilt, Oriental, 18 1/2 In.	35.00

Textile includes many types of printed textiles, table and household linens, and clothing. Some other textiles will be found under Clothing, Coverlet, Rug, Quilt, etc.

TEXTILE, Backpack, Revolutionary War	725.00
Bedspread, Blue & White Plaid, Loosely Woven Cotton, 74 x 82 In.	115.00
Bedspread, Carolina Lily, Appliqued & Embroidered, 88 x 90 In.	2750.00
Bedspread, Crocheted, Scalloped Stitch Edge & Bottom, 88 x 104 In.	100.00
Bedspread, Embroidered Geometric Flora & Foliate, 80 x 70 In.	880.00
Bedspread, Embroidered Wreath, Flowers, Black Wool, 50 x 52 In.	125.00
Bedspread, Embroidered, Barberry Trackler, 1836, 84 x 96 In.	625.00
Bedspread, Paneled, Seaweed Center, 1780s, 87 1/2 x 93 In.	5225.00
Bedspread, Popcorn Star, Crocheted, White, 96 x 108 In.	150.00
Bedspread, Popcorn, Crocheted, 88 x 92 In.	85.00
Bedspread, Scattered Flowers, Stenciled, 1810, 92 x 94 In.	6600.00
Bedspread, Taffeta, Roses On White Ground, Full Size	25.00
Bedspread, Trapunto, White On White, Flowers In Circle, 88 x 94 In.	900.00
Bell Pull, Victorian, Needlepoint, Bronze Mounts	155.00
Blanket, Baby's, Pink, Briboro Products Box, 1940s	25.00
Blanket, Blue, Red & White Plaid, Center Seam, 68 x 80 In.	50.00
Blanket, Crooked Path Pattern, Wool, Norwegian, 69 x 49 In.	135.00
Blanket, Embroidered Stylized Flowers, Wool, 92 x 94 In.	770.00
Blanket, Lap, Sigma Phi Episilon, 1930	22.00
Blanket, Linen & Wool Tabby Weave, Indigo, White, 72 x 90 In., Pair	650.00
Bolster Cover, Navy Blue & White Plaid, 19 x 58 1/2 In.	155.00
Centerpiece, White Cotton Center, Crocheted Edge, Round, 24 In.	35.00
Cushion, Marriage, Red, Blue & Yellow, Sweden, c.1850	1100.00
Drapery, Floral Crewelwork, 19th Century, 89 x 69 In., Pair	1875.00
Flag, U. S., 48 Stars, Metal Holder, Box, 1940s, 3 3/4 x 5 In.	15.00
Handkerchief, Printed Memorial Hall Art Gallery, 1776-1876	50.00
Knapsack, Mexican War, Geo. S. Stone, Otter River, Mass.	352.00
Knapsack, Mexican War, Single Pouch, 1840s	1045.00
Mat, Chinese, Sculpted Floral Design, Lavender Ground, 2 x 3 Ft.	170.00
Mat, Hooked, Landscape With House, 10 x 12 In.	35.00
Pajama Bag, Walrus, Steiff	550.00
Panel, Hooked, Eagle & Shield, Brown Velvet, 28 x 33 1/2 In.	170.00
Panel, My Flag & Flower, Needlework, Frame, 22 1/2 x 23 1/2 In.	75.00
Panel, Needlepoint, Figures In Landscape, 33 1/2 x 25 In.	415.00
Panel, Needlepoint, Scene of Man, Woman & Child, 17 1/2 x 15 In.	125.00
Panel, Needlework, Shepherd, 1 Sheep, Floral Border, America, Framed	880.00
Panel, Shield Shape, Medallion, Woman & Dog, Frame, 23 1/2 x 17 In.	50.00
Panel, Woven Silk, Dutch Scene, Louis Leloir, Framed, 7 3/4 x 11 In.	45.00
Picture, Mother & Child, Embroidered, Oval, c.1810, 8 x 6 In.	660.00
Picture, Mourning, Silk Embroidered, Thomas Family, 17 1/4 x 22 In.	7425.00
Pillow Cover, Needlepoint, Father Time, Wool, England, 21 x 19 In.	3850.00
Pillowcase, Cotton, White On White, Embroidered, Crocheted, Pair	25.00

Pillowcase, Madeira, Pair 40.00
Robe, Lap, Sleigh, Horsehair 67.50
Runner, Battenburg Lace, Lacy Design, 17 x 54 In. 125.00
Scarf, Buffet, Battenburg, Grapes, 65 x 16 In. 140.00
Scarf, Piano, Ecru Silk, Embroidered, Fringed 75.00
Shawl, Hand-Knotted Fringe, Square, 60 In. 45.00
Shawl, Orange Silk, Embroidered, Yellow & Cream, Fringed, 1921, Italy 500.00
Shawl, Paisley, Olive, Plum & Putty, Wool & Silk, 67 x 63 In. 410.00
Stair Kicker & Tread Set, Needlework, American Flag & Emblem 525.00
Tablecloth, Battenburg Lace, Center Hearts, Grapes, Round, 65 In. 250.00
Tablecloth, Battenburg Lace, Drawn Work Center, Round, 33 In. 165.00
Tablecloth, Battenburg Lace, Grapes, Round, 64 In. 225.00
Tablecloth, Battenburg Lace, Round, 1900s, 48 In. 300.00
Tablecloth, Battenburg Lace, Square, 32 In. 70.00
Tablecloth, Battenburg Lace, White, Round, 1900s, 68 In. 400.00
Tablecloth, Embroidered, Chinese Linen, 12 Napkins, 96 x 67 In. 525.00
Tablecloth, Italian, Point De Venise, Needle Lace, 60 x 96 In. 395.00
Tablecloth, Lace, China, 92 x 64 In. 45.00
Tablecloth, Madeira Style, Ecru, 8 Napkins, 68 x 88 In. 50.00
Tablecloth, Spider Webs Allover, Hand Crocheted, Ecru, 76 x 54 In. 95.00
Tablecloth, White Linen, Filet Crocheted, Inserts, 64 x 51 In. 55.00
Tablelcoth, Cotton, Embroidered, Geometric, Europe, 54 x 54 In. 49.50
Tapestry, Aubusson, Landscape, 7 Ft. 9 In. x 4 Ft. 11 In. 3520.00
Tapestry, Aubusson, Landscape, Birds, 4 Ft. 6 In. x 7 Ft. 10 In. 2100.00
Tapestry, Central Urn, Flowers, 1870s, 4 Ft. 6 In. x 3 Ft. 4 In. 3740.00
Tapestry, Crowned Boar's Head, Field Flowers, Birds, 41 x 75 In. 451.00
Tapestry, Dog, Classical Ruins, Forest, Brussels, 99 x 64 In. 2640.00
Tapestry, Egrets In Forest Scene, 40 x 66 In. ....*Illus* 425.00
Tapestry, Embroidered, Animals, Birds, c.1938, 5 Ft. 9 In. x 7 Ft. 5500.00
Tapestry, Figures At Banquet, Woman With Horse, Needlepoint, 93 In. 1200.00
Tapestry, Figures In Landscape, Belgium, 48 x 68 In. 75.00
Tapestry, Floral, Large Cherub Border, Faded, 74 x 77 In. 195.00
Tapestry, Garden, Flower Border, Brussels, 7 Ft. 9 In. x 6 Ft. 2640.00
Tapestry, Gothic Style, 2 Couples, Flemish 5500.00
Tapestry, Lover Crowned, Fragonard, 1830s, 54 x 36 In. 135.00
Tapestry, Maiden, Musicians, Flemish, 3 Ft. 8 In. x 6 Ft. 9 In. 4950.00
Tapestry, Man & Woman, 18th-Century Dress, French, 53 x 69 In. 1100.00
Tapestry, Venice Scene, Delicate Colors, 56 1/2 x 20 In. 85.00
Valence, Aubusson, Pair of Doves, Trailing Flowers, 32 x 92 In. 825.00
Wall Hanging, E. Pluribus Unum, Embroidered Silk, 26 1/2 x 32 In. 660.00

Textile, Tapestry, Egrets In Forest Scene,
40 x 66 In.

♦ ♦

Moths can damage stored textiles. Use moth crystals such as paradichlorobenzene. The vapors are heavier than air so the crystals must be placed above the textiles, preferably in small cloth bags suspended from the ceiling.

♦ ♦

The thermometer was invented in 1731. It measures temperature of either water or air. All kinds of thermometers are collected, but those with advertising messages are the most popular.

THERMOMETER, Barometric, Mahogany, Arched Crest, Door, c.1860, 37 In.	2640.00
Barq's, Picture of Bottle	85.00
Bear Us In Mind, Indians, Bear, Calif., Framed, Tin, 1930s	35.00
Bireley's, 1947	45.00 To 68.50
Bubble Up, With Cap	35.00
Cheer–Up, Round	40.00
Clark Bars, Enameled Lithograph, Candy In Clock Design, 18 In.	100.00
Clark Bars, Wooden	250.00
Coca–Cola	48.00
Crushie, Tin	95.00
Dairy, Floating, Case	18.00
Dental Scotch Snuff, 6 1/2 x 16 In.	35.00
Desk, Pie–Eyed Mickey Mouse & Pluto, Tin Lithograph	350.00
Desk, Rococo Style, Gilt Bronze, Cherub Figure	78.00
Doan's, Wooden	65.00
Dr Pepper, 1930s	250.00
Fish Shape, We've Landed Some Big Ones, Brass	30.00
Friedman–Shelby, Red Goose Shoes, 1915	150.00
Gaines Dog Meal, Tin	75.00
Gulf, Orange, Blue, White, Tin, 1940s, 5 x 20 In.	185.00
Hardy's Salt, Color, Round	125.00
Hires Root Beer, Die Cut Bottle	55.00 To 85.00
Inez Ruki, Produce Picture, 1955 Calendar	25.00
International Tailoring Co., Picture of Lion, Wooden, 22 In.	155.00
Jim Beam, Tin, 25 1/2 x 10 In.	45.00
Kemp's Milk, Figural, Milk Carton, Weather Forecaster	20.00
Kentucky Club Pipe Tobacco, Tin	70.00
Kentucky Club Tobacco	55.00
Key To New York, Pat. Aug. 25, 1925, 8 1/2 In.	23.00
Lube King Motor Oil	100.00
Mail Pouch Tobacco, Porcelain, 38 x 8 In.	90.00
Mail Pouch Tobacco, Tin, 9 x 3 In.	35.00
Mail Pouch, Wood Frame, 5 In.	550.00
Marathon Gas, With Runner, Tin	75.00
Metal, Marilyn Monroe, Dress Flaring Up, Metal, Package, 13 In.	95.00
Michelin Tires, Electroplated, 1960s, 10 In.	95.00
Morton Salt, Tin, 15 x 5 In.	35.00
Nesbitt's, Professor Picture	73.00
Norway Antifreeze, Porcelain, 26 x 10 In.	395.00
Packard Automobiles	65.00
Prestone Antifreeze	95.00
RCA Victor, T. V. Backed By Factory Service, 1955, 16 x 6 In.	50.00
Royal Crown Cola, 13 1/2 In.	50.00 To 55.00
Royal Crown Cola, Tin, 28 In.	45.00
Royal Scarlet Food Products	175.00
Sauer's Box	130.00
Sphinx Base, Gilded, Brass, 9 In.	45.00
Stephenson Union Suits, Enameled Porcelain	132.00
Suncrest, With Bottle	30.00
Tracto Weather Station, Box	75.00
Triple XXX Root Beer	65.00
Ward's Vitamin Bread, Enamel, 20 1/2 x 8 1/2 In.	165.00
Woolsey Paint, Tin, 26 In.	30.00

Tiffany glass was made by Louis Comfort Tiffany, the American glass designer who worked from about 1879 to 1933. His work included iridescent glass, Art Nouveau styles of design, and original contemporary styles. He was also noted for his stained glass windows, his unusual lamps, bronze work, pottery, and silver. Other

types of Tiffany are listed under Tiffany Pottery, Tiffany Silver, or at the end of this section under Tiffany. The famous Tiffany lamps are under Tiffany, Lamp. Reproductions of some types of Tiffany are being made. Tiffany jewelry is listed in the jewelry and wristwatch sections.

TIFFANY GLASS, Bonbon, Short Pedestal Base, Gold Iridescence, 4 3/4 In.	275.00
Bonbon, Stretched Rim, Amber Stem, Ruffled, Signed, 4 1/2 In.	467.50
Bowl, Floriform, Gold, Cupped Disk Foot, Signed, 4 1/2 In.	770.00
Bowl, Grotesque, Paperweight, 8 In.	3500.00
Bowl, Herringbone, 16 Ribs, Amber, Gold, Oval, 2 1/4 x 6 In.	445.00
Bowl, Intaglio Cut, Blue Leaf & Vine Border, 6 1/4 In.	1765.00
Bowl, Lily Pad Design, Double Flower Frog, Signed, 10 1/4 In.	1550.00
Bowl, Opalescent Star Pattern, Stretch Rim, Signed, 8 In.	670.00
Bowl, Raised Paneled Sides, Monogrammed, 8 1/2 In.	470.00
Bowl, Ruffled Rim, Center Well, Signed, 2 x 4 1/2 In.	650.00
Candlestick, Favrile, Gold, Oval Top, 3 3/4 In., Pair	2800.00
Candlestick, Flared, Collared Pedestal, Pastel, 3 1/2 In.	305.00
Compote, Gold–Amber, Overall Iridized, Signed, 6 In.	550.00
Compote, Iridescent Pale Green, Flared Shape, 7 1/2 In.	467.50
Compote, Pulled Feather Design, Favrile, 4 3/4 In.	1250.00
Compote, Ruffled, Engraved Leaves & Vines Interior, 6 In.	750.00
Cordial, Bluish Gold, Stemmed, Signed, 5 In.	300.00
Creamer, Violet Rim, Opaque To Yellow Handle, 3 1/4 In.	650.00
Decanter, Snail Design, Phantom Green Luster, Signed, 10 In.	1150.00
Dish, Gold Center, Pink & Red, Scalloped Rim, Signed, 5 In.	995.00
Dish, Peacock & Pulled Feather Design, Signed, 6 1/4 In.	2650.00
Dish, Ribbed, Gold Interior, Green Exterior, Signed, 4 1/4 In.	357.50
Finger Bowl, Gold	375.00
Finger Bowl, Pinched Scalloped Rim, Flower Shape, 4 In.	385.00
Finger Bowl, Ruffled, Iridescent Blue & Gold, 2 1/2 x 5 In.	467.50
Flower Frog, 2 Rows of Loops For Flowers, Blue, 2 1/4 In.	250.00
Flower Frog, 2 Tiers of Loops, Cylindrical Base, 7 In.	357.50
Goblet, Floriform, Green Petal On Cream, 8 In.	950.00
Goblet, Tortoiseshell, Agate	4800.00
Paperweight, Vase, Hearts & Flowers, 3 In.	4000.00
Perfume Bottle, Dimpled, Scallop Flare–Out, Signed, 6 In.	1500.00
Perfume Bottle, Favrile, Bulbous, Button Stopper, Signed	950.00
Perfume Bottle, Gold Sphere, Green Leaf & Vine, 4 1/4 In.	165.00
Plate, Green Pastel, Favrile, Signed, 8 1/2 In.	335.00
Plate, Peacock Eye, Small	2100.00
Salt, Favrile, Gold Iridescent, Ruffled, Signed	200.00
Salt, Ruffled & Crimped Edge, Gold, Signed, 2 1/2 In, 8 Piece	880.00
Salt, Ruffled Rim, Gold, Signed, 2 3/4 In.	195.00
Shade, Lily, 8–Ribbed Flower Form, Signed, 4 1/2 In., 3 Piece	2145.00
Sugar Bowl & Creamer, C–Scroll Handles, Blue, Marked	1450.00
Tazza, Stretched Glass Rim, Stem, Signed, 5 x 12 In.	2800.00
Tumbler, Juice, Iridescent Gold, Hooked Design, Signed, 4 In.	355.00
Tumbler, Phantom Luster, Applied Threads, Signed, 4 In.	200.00
Vase, 3 Gold Pulled Designs, Red, Signed, 3 3/4 In.	4675.00
Vase, Agata, Signed L. C. T., 7 In.	3800.00
Vase, Blend of Yellow & Orange, Signed, 10 In.	2800.00
Vase, Blue Enamel Insets, Flared Cut Rim, Blue, 19 1/4 In.	3575.00
Vase, Bud, Green & Gold Pulled Feather, 4 In.	850.00
Vase, Bulbous Neck, Squat Body, Iridescent, c.1917, 4 3/4 In.	1650.00
Vase, Dimpled, Gold, Signed, 3 In.	440.00
Vase, Double Gourd Form, Favrile, Signed, 12 1/4 In.	1650.00
Vase, Egyptian Collar, Paper Label, Signed, 10 In.	5225.00
Vase, Enameled Leaves & Vines, Gold, Signed, 2 1/2 In.	1450.00
Vase, Favrile, Blue Base, Stand–Out Ribs, Signed, 4 1/4 In.	2000.00
Vase, Favrile, Gold Floriform, 4 1/2 In.	750.00
Vase, Favrile, Gold, Pedestal, Ruffled, 4 3/4 In.	950.00
Vase, Favrile, Trumpet, Blue, Bronze Holder, Signed, 12 In.	1950.00

Vase, Fishnet Design, Multicolor Highlights, Signed, 5 In. 2750.00
Vase, Floriform, Rust, Green, 10 In. 4250.00
Vase, Flower Form, Pulled Leaves, Ribbed Base, Signed, 6 In. 7650.00
Vase, Gold Cypriote, Free–Form, 3 1/2 In. 3750.00
Vase, Gold Iridescent, Enameled, Gilt Bronze Holder, 16 In. 1000.00
Vase, Gold Pulled Design, Opalescent Top, Tapered, 4 1/2 In. 1980.00
Vase, Gold Swirls Over Custard Glass, Round, 6 In. 3000.00
Vase, Gold Swirls, Blue Highlights, Marked, 4 x 3 1/2 In. 1025.00
Vase, Gold Vines, Millefiori Flowers, Signed, 8 In. 2500.00
Vase, Gold Waves At Shoulder, Footed, Signed, 2 3/4 In. 1980.00
Vase, Gourd Shape, Gold, 8 1/4 In. 800.00
Vase, Grecian Urn, Amber, Label, Signed, 3 7/8 In. 575.00
Vase, Green Hearts, Blue Iridescence, 6 1/2 In. 1950.00
Vase, Green Ivy, Flared, 12 In. 1650.00
Vase, Green Leaves & Vines, Signed, 5 1/2 In. 1320.00
Vase, Green, Pulled Leaves On Gold Base, Signed, 11 In. 4400.00
Vase, Jack–In–The–Pulpit, Flattened Face, c.1909, 19 1/8 In. 2310.00
Vase, Jack–In–The–Pulpit, Twisted Stem, Gold 2300.00
Vase, Marbelized Surface, 8 Panels, Faceted Agate, 8 1/2 In. 1100.00
Vase, Overlaid Blue Pulled Feather, Marked, Label, 2 1/2 In. 7250.00
Vase, Pulled Feather, White Ground, Gold & Green, 4 1/2 In. 850.00
Vase, Raised Pads Extending From Base Into Body, 3 1/2 In. 495.00
Vase, Ribbed Body, Knob Bottom, Signed, 8 1/4 In. 1100.00
Vase, Ruffled Raised Rim, 4 Pulled Feet, Signed, 4 In. 260.00
Vase, Ruffled Top, Pedestal Foot, Gold Iridescent, 11 In. 1875.00
Vase, Salmon Body On Clear Knob Stem & Base, Signed, 9 In. 825.00
Vase, Trumpet, Bronze Base, Blue Aurene, Signed, 15 In. 1795.00
Vase, Trumpet, Gold Ribbed, Signed, 17 In. 1100.00
Vase, Trumpet, Pulled Feather Fluted Top, Signed, 21 In. 9500.00
Vase, White Millefiori Canes Interior, Signed, 2 5/8 In. 2860.00
Wine, Favrile, Gold, Pulled Dimpled Design, 3 1/2 In., 6 Piece 3135.00
Wine, Flower Form, Stepped, Favrile, Aqua, Signed, 7 1/4 In. 550.00

TIFFANY POTTERY, Jar, Cover, Branch of Magnolia Blossoms, Signed, 9 1/4 In. 3025.00
Jug, Corn, Pulled Spout, Husk Handle, 10 1/2 x 4 1/2 In. 1200.00
Pitcher, Cat–o'nine–Tails, Glazed Green, Signed, 12 1/2 In. 2000.00
Tile Panel, Leaf, Blossom Design, Signed & Dated, 9 Piece 665.00
Vase, All Glazed, 3 Handles, Signed, 9 In. 1500.00
Vase, Berry Clusters, Green Glaze, Signed, c.1910, 2 In. 1200.00
Vase, Blossoms On Branches, Unglazed, Signed, 4 In. 750.00
Vase, Branches, Mottled Glaze, Signed, c.1910, 6 1/4 In. 1550.00
Vase, Center Hanging Pods, Fully Glazed, Signed, 6 1/2 In. 2000.00
Vase, Glazed, Raised Leaves, Tan Glaze, Signed, 4 3/4 In. 1500.00
Vase, Green Drippings, All Glazed, Stand–Up Collar, 6 In. 1500.00
Vase, Leaves Top To Center, Unglazed, Signed, 3 1/2 In. 750.00
Vase, Pods, Branches, Overlapping Leaves, Signed, 12 1/4 In. 1100.00
Vase, Poppies Going To Seed, Bronze, 9 1/2 In. 2100.00
Vase, Raised Leaves, Branches Form Top Rim, Signed, 8 In. 2000.00
Vase, Sumac Leaves & Berries, Glazed, c.1910, 9 7/8 In. 1875.00
Vase, Unglazed Outside, Tulip Blossoms, Signed, 6 1/2 In. 2500.00
Vase, Unglazed, Blossoms, Raised Branches, Signed, 4 In. 750.00
Vase, Veined Leaves, Overlapping Stems, Signed, 4 3/4 In. 1500.00
TIFFANY SILVER, Asparagus Tongs, With 8 Individual Tongs, St. Dunstan 1700.00
Bell, Dinner, Enameled, Applied Leaves, Pods, 1880s, 3 3/4 In. 5500.00
Bottle, Christening, Destroyer Hull, At Bath Iron Works 1320.00
Bowl, Raised Paneled Sides, Monogrammed, 8 1/2 In. 465.00
Bowl, Rim Roses, Pierced Scrolled Reserves, 1902, 14 1/2 In. 3500.00
Bowl, Scalloped Everted Rim, Pierced Woodbine, 1907, 9 In. 770.00
Butter Knife, Wave Edge, Flat, 6 Piece 210.00
Centerpiece, Angled Rim, Tapered Supports, 1956, 18 3/4 In. 4400.00
Centerpiece, Chrysanthemum, 8 Supports, 1891, 14 1/2 In. 5500.00
Coffee Urn, Stand, Basketweave Design, 1938–1947, 15 In. 8250.00
Cold Meat Fork, Grapevine, Fluted Bowl, 9 In. 330.00

◆◆◆

When polishing silver, first remove all detachable parts like handles or finials. Rest the silver piece in your lap, never on the table or other hard surface. Polish by rubbing in circles. If there are wooden handles or other parts, these should be waxed when the silver is cleaned.

◆◆◆

Cream Ladle, Blackberry	475.00
Dish, Cover, Chrysanthemum, Loop Finials, 1891, 12 In., Pair	7700.00
Dish, Geometric Center, Dogwood Blossoms, c.1910, 12 1/2 In.	1760.00
Dish, Triangular, Convex Sides, 3–Footed, Monogram, 9 In.	137.00
Fish Set, Richelieu, Knife & Fork	440.00
Flashlight, Pencil Type	65.00
Fork, Luncheon, Shell & Thread	50.00
Gravy Ladle, Audubon	335.00
Ice Tongs, Persian	850.00
Ice Tongs, Persian, Claw Tip, 1872, 9 1/4 In.	665.00
Inkwell, Cover, Foliage & Horizontal Bars, 1904, 7 1/2 In.	2550.00
Inkwell, Putti & Swags, c.1891, 1 1/2 In.	605.00
Ladle, King's Pattern	632.50
Marrow Scoop, English King	550.00
Match Safe, Hinged Lid, Crab, Octopus, Engraved, 2 5/8 In.	88.00
Pancake Server, Renaissance	450.00
Pitcher, Hinged Lid, Chased Barrel Staves, Hoops, 9 3/4 In.	6050.00
Plate, Art Nouveau, 1890s, 7 In.	850.00
Platter, Crest Over Initials, Oval, 1870, 22 In.	2750.00
Porringer, Repousse, c.1895	797.50
Salt Spoon, Gold Wash, Green Cloth Holder, Label, 6 Piece	165.00
Salt, Guilloche Border, Ram's Head Feet, Marked, 3 In., Pair	770.00
Sandwich Tongs, English King	650.00
Serving Spoon, Broomcorn, Gilt Bowl Formed As Shell, 9 In.	330.00
Shell, 3 Footed, Small, Pair	90.00
Shoehorn, Cherub & Floral	125.00
Soap Box, Signed	250.00
Soup Ladle, Audubon	110.00
Soup Ladle, English King	850.00
Stuffing Spoon, English King	750.00
Sugar Spoon, Faneuil	30.00
Tea & Coffee Set, Flowers, Foliage, c.1860, 3 Piece	1650.00
Tea & Coffee Set, Globular, Mid Banding, 1891, 7 Piece	4620.00
Tea Infuser Spoon, English King	350.00
Tray, Chippendale Style, Footed, 1891–1902, 20 1/2 In.	4720.00
Tureen, Soup, Cover, Ribbons & Flowerheads, 1865, 12 1/2 In.	3300.00
Vase, Bud, Everted Rim, 1907–38, 8 In.	335.00
Vase, Chased Ram's Head Handles, c.1875, 8 In.	715.00
Vase, Flaring Rim & Foot, Ovoid, Signed, 20 In.	6380.00
Vase, Lion's Paw Feet, Gilt Liner, 1902, 11 1/2 In.	4400.00

> Tiffany objects made from a mixture of materials, such as bronze and glass boxes, are listed here. Tiffany lamps are included in this section.

TIFFANY, Andirons, Scenic Tile Insets, Bronze	2640.00
Blotter Ends, Zodiac, Pair	450.00
Blotter, Rocker, Zodiac	250.00
Book Rack, Pine Needle, Bronze & Glass, Signed, Extends To 24 In.	1200.00
Bookends, 15 Yellow & Blue Faceted Jewels, Bronze, 5 1/4 In.	775.00
Bookends, Grapevine, Amber Slag Glass, Bronze, 5 1/2 In.	700.00
Bookends, Horsehead, Dark Patina, Bronze, Signed, 5 x 5 3/4 In.	650.00

Tiffany, Candlestick,
Favrile Glass Shade,
Signed L. C. T., 12 In.

Tiffany, Lamp, Acorn,
Patinated Bronze Urn, 16 In.

Tiffany, Lamp, Bronze,
Pebble Shade, Signed J. Meyer,
12 In.

Bookends, Oriental Design, Inset Jewels, Bronze, Signed, 5 1/2 In. 1200.00
Bookends, Venetian, 14K Gold Plated, Row of Minks, Bronze, Signed 650.00
Bookends, Zodiac, Bronze 750.00
Box, Stamp, American Indian, 3 Sections, Bronze 295.00
Box, Stamp, Zodiac, Bronze .... 190.00 To 200.00
Bronze, Desk Set, Enameled, Zodiac, 5 Piece 1200.00
Brush, Floral Repousse, Ring Handle 550.00
Candelabrum, 3 Arms, Paw Feet, Bronze, 1900–1918, 11 3/8 In., Pair 1325.00
Candelabrum, 6 Arms, Foliate Terminal, Bronze, 1918–1928, 10 In., Pr. 2000.00
Candelabrum, Beaded Design, Glass & Bronze, Signed, 17 1/2 In. 1435.00
Candleholder, 2–Light, 16 Green Cabochons, Bronze, Marked, 9 In. 1450.00
Candleholder, Bobeche Insert In Urn Holder, Marked, 17 In. 1215.00
Candlestick, Favrile Glass Shade, Signed L. C. T., 12 In. ....*Illus* 1650.00
Cane, Rosewood, 18K Gold Trim, Marked 190.00
Card Tray, Grapevine, Green Glass, Bronze Frame, 3 x 2 3/4 In. 250.00
Chest, Jewel, Bronze Body, Arches & Squares, Lined, Signed, 3 x 8 In. 2000.00
Clock, Art Deco, Chrome Base, Green Glass, 8–Day, 5 x 11 In. 275.00
Clock, Desk, Venetian, Beehive Form, Gilt Bronze, 1851, 5 3/4 In. 1200.00
Clock, Desk, Venetian, Gilt Bronze, Signed, 1918, 3 In. 1650.00
Clock, Enamel & Bronze Frame, Bronze Ball Feet, Signed, 5 1/2 In. 1200.00
Clock, Tall Case, Moon Dial, Weights & Pendulum 3300.00
Clock, Travel, Red Leather Case 125.00
Desk Set, Bookmark, Signed, 1902–1918, 12 Piece 2750.00
Desk Set, Grape Vine & Pinecone, Bronze & Slag Glass, 5 Piece 1430.00
Desk Set, Venetian, Marked, Gilt Bronze, 6 Piece 1320.00
Desk Set, Zodiac, Bronze, 1899–1928, Signed, 7 Piece 1200.00
Dish, Dragonflies Amid Leaves & Vines Center, Bronze, 7 3/4 In. 450.00
Dish, Nut, Scallop Pattern Divides Dish Into 6 Sections, 4 1/4 In. 225.00
Figurine, Indian, Hammer & Knife, Bronze, 6 1/4 In. 345.00
Frame, Abalone Discs, Floral Design, Bronze, Signed, 10 1/4 x 5 In. 2800.00
Frame, Picture, Zodiac, Bronze, Signed, 1928, 8 1/4 x 7 1/8 In. 935.00
Frame, Pine Needle, Amber Slag Glass, Bronze, Signed, 8 1/2 x 6 In. 2200.00
Garniture, Onyx & Gilt Bronze, Time & Strike, 13 1/2 In., 3 Piece 605.00
Hand Mirror, Grapevine Pattern, Bronze, Curved Handle, Signed 1800.00
Holder, Note Pad, Venetian, Gold Dore Finish, 7 1/2 x 4 1/2 In. 357.00
Inkstand, Bookmark, Octagonal, Gold Dore, Marked, 4 1/4 x 2 3/4 In. 625.00
Inkwell, Adam Pattern, Gold Dore Finish, Bronze, Signed, 4 x 3 In. 250.00
Inkwell, Bookmark, Bronze 750.00
Inkwell, Gilt Bronze, Treasure Chest Form, Double, Signed, 5 x 3 In. 465.00
Inkwell, Glass Mosaic & Bronze, c.1900, 2 1/4 In. 3525.00
Inkwell, Hinged Lid, Grapevine, Ball Feet, Glass & Bronze, 4 1/8 In. 445.00

Tiffany, Lamp, Floor, Bronze,   Tiffany, Lamp, Student,   Tiffany, Vase, Bronze & Glass,
Bamboo Style, 54 In.   Blue Favrile Shades, 20 In.   13 In.

Inkwell, Pine Needle, Mottled Glass Insert, Bronze	400.00
Inkwell, Turtleback & Jewel, Bronze Frame, Signed	2500.00
Inkwell, Zodiac	195.00 To 400.00
Inkwell, Zodiac, Large	900.00
Lamp, Abalone Discs, Bronze Base, Curved Arm, Bronze, Signed, 9 In.	3200.00
Lamp, Acorn, Patinated Bronze Urn, 16 In. ....*Illus*	8580.00
Lamp, Adjustable Harp Top, Bronze & Glass, Signed, 57 In.	6500.00
Lamp, Amber & Gold Pulled Feather, Double Gourd Shade, 17 1/4 In.	1100.00
Lamp, Arabian, Applied Prunts, Bronze, Signed, 15 In.	6325.00
Lamp, Bronze, Pebble Shade, Signed J. Meyer, 12 In. ....*Illus*	2640.00
Lamp, Candle, 14K Gold Filigree Shade, Glass Base, Signed	220.00
Lamp, Candle, Art Glass Shade, Bronze Base	3650.00
Lamp, Candle, Blue Base, Silver Shade, Beads, 12 In.	950.00
Lamp, Candle, Bronze Base, Art Glass Shade, 12 In.	3650.00
Lamp, Candle, Damascene Shade, Pulled Feather Design, 17 In.	1900.00
Lamp, Candle, Favrile, Twisted Ribbed Body, Signed, 13 In.	2200.00
Lamp, Candle, Gold & Silver In Base & Shade, Blue, Signed, 14 In.	6000.00
Lamp, Candle, Pine Needle Shades, Bronze Base, Signed, 23 In.	1800.00
Lamp, Candle, Tulip Shade, Bronze Base, Signed, 14 3/4 In.	2200.00
Lamp, Counterbalance, White Damascene, Bronze, Signed, 14 In.	4070.00
Lamp, Curling Lines In Domical Shade, Bronze, 1920, 4 Ft. 6 3/4 In.	1100.00
Lamp, Damascene Shade, 5 Legs, 4 Ft. 8 In.	6500.00
Lamp, Damascene Shade, Swivel Socket, Bronze, Signed, 55 In.	7700.00
Lamp, Domical Shade, Pivoting, Bronze, 1928, 4 Ft. 6 3/4 In.	1650.00
Lamp, Double Curved Arms, Counterweight, Bronze Base, Signed, 18 In.	6800.00
Lamp, Favrile Glass Base, Swirl Pattern Shade, Signed, 15 In.	3800.00
Lamp, Favrile Glass, Bronze, Domical Green Shade, 4 Ft. 8 In.	6600.00
Lamp, Feather Pull Design Shade, 4 Arms, Bronze, Favrile, 22 In.	9000.00
Lamp, Floor, Bronze, Bamboo Style, 54 In. ....*Illus*	4290.00
Lamp, Gold Shade With Green Leaves & Vine, Signed, 15 In.	7150.00
Lamp, Gold Wire Mesh, Glass Jewels, Bronze Finial, Signed, 25 In.	5500.00
Lamp, Green Damascene Shade, Adjustable Bronze Harp, 22 In.	5500.00
Lamp, Green Favrile Shade, 15 In.	750.00
Lamp, Ivy Leaf, Bronze Base & Arms, Signed, 16 x 12 In.	7500.00
Lamp, Jeweled Wire Mesh, Blossoms, Bronze Base, Signed, 12 In.	1600.00
Lamp, Liberty Bell, Bronze Base, Side Posts Join At Top, 14 1/2 In.	6000.00
Lamp, Linenfold, Gold Favrile Glass Panels, Signed, 14 In.	2310.00
Lamp, Nautilus Shell, Bronze, 13 In.	1650.00
Lamp, Nautilus, Adjustable Shade, Bronze Double Stem, 14 In.	6600.00
Lamp, Nautilus, Favrile Glass As Seashell, Bronze, Signed, 14 In.	7150.00
Lamp, Nautilus, Leaded Shade, Bronze Base, Signed, 13 In.	7500.00
Lamp, Nautilus, Shell Form Shade, Bronze Shaft, Signed, 15 In.	7150.00
Lamp, Pomegranate, Emerald Green Ground, Bronze, Signed, 21 In.	9500.00
Lamp, Slag Domed Shade, Brass Base, Electric, c.1910, 22 1/2 In.	7950.00
Lamp, Spider Finial, 3 Socket, Amber & Green, Bronze, 18 In.	10450.00
Lamp, Student, Blue Favrile Shades, 20 In. ....*Illus*	5500.00
Lamp, Student, Damascene Shade	5700.00

Lamp, Student, Harvard, Double, Maroon Case Glass Shades 6500.00
Lamp, Turtleback, Adjustable, Gold Dore, Bronze, 11 1/4 In. 2860.00
Lamp, Zodiac, Bell-Shaped Shade, Green Feather, Signed, 13 1/2 In. 3000.00
Letter Opener, Abalone, Iridescent Discs, 10 In. 250.00
Letter Opener, Crab 80.00
Letter Opener, Grapevine, Amber Slag Glass In Handle, Signed, 9 In. 250.00
Letter Opener, Pine Needle, Amber Slag Glass In Handle, 9 In. 1500.00
Letter Opener, Spanish, Pattern Both Sides, Signed, 8 3/4 In. 250.00
Letter Rack, 2 Compartments, Bronze & Abalone 650.00
Letter Rack, Grapevine, Bronze Over Green Glass, Signed, 12 1/2 In. 715.00
Magnifying Glass, Gold Dore 650.00
Match Holder, Zodiac, Bronze, 4 In. 225.00
Night Light, Scarab, Bronze .... 1200.00 To 1750.00
Paperweight, Crouching Lion, Bronze, Marked, 4 In. 467.50
Paperweight, Lion, Bronze 775.00
Paperweight, Reclining Lion, Gilt Finish, Bronze, Signed, 5 In. 495.00
Planter, Grapevine, Amber Slag Glass, Bronze Liner, 10 1/4 In. 1500.00
Plate, Man Carrying Large Stone, Signed, Bronze, 7 In. 850.00
Purse, Mesh, 14K Gold, Sapphires, Diamonds .... *Illus* 3300.00
Sconce, 2 Arms, Domed Wall Plate, Bronze, 1920, 10 1/4 In. 550.00
Silver, Fork, Olive, English King Pattern 85.00
Silver, Paperweight, Elongated Rectangular, 10 x 2 In. 384.00
Stamp Box, Zodiac, Gilt 295.00
Tray, Abalone, Bronze, Gold Dore Finish, Marked, Round, 14 1/4 In. 1045.00
Tray, Gold Dore, Twisted Rope Design On Rim, Bronze, 8 1/4 In. 150.00
Tray, Raised Entwined Line Design Border, Bronze, 8 x 10 In. 475.00
Trivet, Cypriote Glass Mounted In Bronze Frame, Square, 6 1/4 In. 850.00
Vase Bud, Cherub Holder, Gold, 12 In. 1500.00
Vase, Bronze & Glass, 13 In. .... *Illus* 3300.00
Vase, Stand-Out Ribs Around Body, Ruffled Top, Signed, 10 3/4 In. 2100.00
Vase, Trumpet, Gold Ribbed, Gold Dore Base, Signed 1650.00

The Tiffin Glass Company of Tiffin, Ohio, was a subsidiary of the United States Glass Co. of Pittsburgh, Pennsylvania, in 1892. The U.S. Glass Co. went bankrupt in 1963, and the Tiffin plant employees purchased the building and the inventory. They continued running it from 1963 to 1966, when it was sold to Continental Can Company. In 1969, it was sold to Interpace; and in 1980, it was closed. The black satin glass, made from 1923 to 1926, and the stemware of the last twenty years are the best-known products.

TIFFIN, Bowl, Twilight, 5 1/4 In. 30.00
Bowl, Twilight, Crimped, 10 1/2 In. 115.00
Candlestick, Blown, Pair 75.00
Candlestick, Desert Red, 2-Light, Pair 85.00
Candy Jar, Cover, Twilight, 9 In. 185.00
Champagne, Fuchsia 18.00
Claret, Canterbury, Citron 17.50

Tiffany, Purse, Mesh, 14K Gold, Sapphires, Diamonds

♦♦♦♦♦♦♦♦♦♦♦♦♦♦♦♦♦♦♦♦♦♦♦♦

Gemstones are colder to the touch than glass. Colored gems like emeralds, rubies, and sapphires should not appear scratched. If there are scratches, the "stone" is probably colored glass.

♦♦♦♦♦♦♦♦♦♦♦♦♦♦♦♦♦♦♦♦♦♦♦♦

Cocktail, Byzantine, 5 1/4 In., 8 Piece	60.00
Cocktail, Fuchsia	18.00
Cocktail, Oyster, Flanders, Pink	40.00
Compote, Cheese, Sylvan, Green	15.00
Cordial, June Light	17.00
Cordial, Kilarny, Green	20.00
Creamer, Cerise, Footed	25.00
Cup & Saucer, Flanders	35.00
Cup & Saucer, Rosalind, Yellow	35.00
Decanter, Cadena, Stopper, Yellow	225.00
Dish, Mayonnaise, Flanders	25.00
Goblet, Claret, Pink	22.50
Goblet, Water, Cherokee Rose .... 18.00 To	24.00
Goblet, Water, Fontaine, Pink	40.00
Goblet, Water, Persian Pheasant	35.00
Goblet, Water, Rambling Rose	23.00
Pitcher, Water, Classic	375.00
Plate, Byzantine, 10 1/2 In.	35.00
Plate, Cerise, 12 In.	45.00
Plate, Empire Twilight, 8 In.	17.50
Plate, Flanders, Pink, 8 In.	17.50
Plate, Flanders, Yellow, 10 1/2 In.	35.00
Plate, Fontaine, Green, 8 In.	15.00
Plate, June Night, 8 In.	15.00
Plate, Rosalind, Yellow, 10 1/2 In.	35.00
Plate, Wisteria, 8 In.	16.00
Relish, Rambling Rose, 3 Sections, Round	17.50
Sherbet, Canterbury, Citron, Stemmed	12.50
Sherbet, Flying Nun, Green	25.00
Sugar & Creamer, Cherokee Rose	45.00
Sugar & Creamer, Tray, Cerise	95.00
Sugar & Creamer, Twilight	125.00
Sugar, Flying Nun, Green	85.00
Tumbler, Iced Tea, Canterbury, Citron	15.00
Tumbler, Iced Tea, Classic, Green Trim	45.00
Tumbler, Iced Tea, Flanders, Yellow	24.00
Tumbler, Juice, Cardelia, Yellow, Footed	15.00
Tumbler, Juice, Cherokee Rose	27.50
Tumbler, Juice, Classic, Footed	35.00
Tumbler, Juice, Fontaine, Green	30.00
Tumbler, June Night, Footed, 6 In.	10.00
Vase, Bud, Cerise, 10 1/2 In.	45.00
Vase, Flanders, Pink, 8 In.	195.00
Vase, Poppy, Black Satin, 9 In.	50.00
Vasel, Signed C. King, 9 1/4 In.	98.00
Water Set, Amber, 7 Piece	150.00
Wine, Cardella	17.50
Wine, Classic, Green Trim	50.00
Wine, Persian Pheasant	35.00
Wine, Psyche	50.00

Tiles have been used in most countries of the world as a sturdy building material for floors, roofs, fireplace surrounds, and surface toppings. Many of the American tiles are listed in this book under the factory name.

TILE, Annual, Jones McDufee & Stratton	45.00
Calendar, 1922	35.00
California Faience, 5 Colors, 6 In.	350.00
Cityscape, Wood & Linen Frame, Harris Strong, Square, 10 1/2 In.	95.00
Duck & Frog, Incised & Painted, C. Purdee Works, 4 3/8 In.	250.00
Embossed Swan, U. S. E. T. Co., 3 x 3 In.	18.00
Farmhouse, Woman & Chickens, Sepia, 6 In.	45.00
Flowers, Volkmar	47.00

Hunter Scene, Providential, 3 Piece 450.00
Luxfer Glass Prism, Frank Lloyd Wright, Prairie School Era 15.00
Man & Woman, Elizabethan Clothes, 1882, J. & J. G. Low, 8 1/4 In., Pair 330.00
Man On Horse, India 65.00
Man Shooting A Bow, India 65.00
Mercer, Bounty, 3 x 3 In. 70.00
Multicolored Floral, Bird, Inscription, Persia, 11 x 12 In. 825.00
Pedagogue, Man's Profile, Glasses, Blue–Green, J. & J. G. Low, 8 In. 385.00
Portrait, McKinley 40.00
Raised Peacock, Grape & Foliate Design, Persia, 11 1/2 x 5 7/8 In. 365.00
Reclining Nude, Hand Painted, Blues, Yellows, Italy, Framed, 43 x 21 In. 2800.00
Red Dragon Center, Green & Red Slag, Square, 4 In. 200.00
Sailboats, Linen Frame, Harris Strong, 8 In. 45.00
Sailing Ships, Windmills, Blue, Pilkington 25.00
Ship, Hand Painted, English Registry Mark, Framed, 9 1/4 x 9 1/4 In. 70.00
Water Lilies, Peach & Green, California Art Tiles, 4 x 4 In. 60.00

Tin has been used to make household containers in America since the seventeenth century. The first tin utensils were brought from Europe; but by 1798, tin plate was imported and local tinsmiths made the wares. Painted tin is called *tole* and is listed separately. Some tin kitchen items may be found listed under Kitchen. The lithographed tin containers used to hold food and tobacco are listed under Advertising, Tin.

TINWARE, Basket, Open Lattice Weave, Traces of Red, 8 1/4 x 16 1/4 In. 100.00
Candleholder, Crimped, Saucer Base, Flat Ring Handle, c.1840, 5 In. 75.00
Coffeepot, Pewter Handle, Lid & Spout, R. Dunham, 9 1/2 In. 85.00
Coffeepot, Pewter Handle, Lid & Spout, Stamped Mark, 11 1/4 In. 60.00
Coffeepot, Punched Potted Tulip, Hinged Lid, 11 In. ....*Illus* 1540.00
Coffeepot, Punchwork, Potted Tulips, Brass Finial, 11 In. 1400.00
Coffeepot, Spread Winged Eagle, Flag, Tulips, Swag Border, c.1830 .... 2700.00
Coffeepot, Straight Spout, Tapered, Handcrafted, 9 In. 79.00
Comb Case, Mirror, Embossed Floral, 9 x 9 In. 65.00
Foot Warmer, Pierced, Wooden Frame, Circular Design, 7 1/2 x 9 In. 165.00
Horn, Baker's, 56 In. 35.00
Measure, Wrap–Around Lip, Strap Handle, 1 Qt. 12.00
Mold, Candle, 3 Tube 65.00
Mold, Candle, 6 Tube 85.00
Mold, Candle, 6 Tube, Fanned, Ear Handle, 10 1/4 In. 75.00
Mold, Candle, 10 Tube, 10 3/4 In. 65.00
Mold, Candle, 12 Tube, 11 In. 125.00
Mold, Candle, 12 Tube, Fitted As Lamp, 10 1/2 In. 75.00
Mold, Candle, 12 Tube, Lantern Shape, Ring Handle, 15 In. 450.00
Mold, Candle, 12 Tube, Tubular Legs, 12 In. 105.00
Mold, Candle, 24 Tube, 10 1/2 In. 125.00
Mold, Candle, 24 Tube, 11 1/4 In. 125.00

Tinware, Coffeepot, Punched Potted Tulip,
Hinged Lid, 11 In.

Tinware, Urn, Baluster Form,
Pointed Obelisk Finial, 70 In.

Tole, Box, Deed, Red Ground,
Stylized Flowers, 6 1/4 x 9 1/2 In.

Tole, Coffeepot, Black
Ground, 19th Century,
10 3/4 In.

Tole, Coffeepot, Red
Ground, 19th Century,
10 1/2 In.

Mold, Candle, 24 Tube, Pewter, Poplar Case, 8 1/4 x 22 In.		2300.00
Mold, Candle, 24 Tube, Pine Frame		1100.00
Mold, Candle, 36 Tube, J. Walker, Pine Frame, 11 1/4 x 12 1/2 In.		350.00
Mold, Chocolate, Rabbit, 2 Parts, 7 In.		30.00
Mold, Pudding, Melon Shape, 2 Piece		28.00
Pail, Dinner		37.50
Pan, Muffin, 12 Separate Joined, Sunburst Bottom, 8 x 11 1/2 In.		85.00
Planter, Hanging, 24 Candle Holders, Insert & Chain, 6 1/4 In.		25.00
Scoop, Cranberry, 10 1/2 In.		45.00
Skimmer, Round, Pierced, 9–In. Hollow Handle, Ring Top, 5 1/2 In.		44.00
Tea Set, Child's, Copper Color, Polished, Mass., Salesman's Sample		155.00
Urn, Baluster Form, Pointed Obelisk Finial, 70 In.	*Illus*	450.00

TOBACCO CUTTER, see Advertising, Tobacco Cutter

Because tobacco needs special conditions of humidity and air, it has
been stored in special containers since the eighteenth century. The
tobacco jar is often made in fanciful shapes.

TOBACCO JAR, Boar Finial, Blue Frosted		150.00
Boy, Leaning On Tree Stump, Bisque, Austria		175.00
Cat Head Finial Knob, Mice & Rats Running Around Body of Jar		175.00
Cover, Tree Stump, Branch Handles, 1920, 7 1/4 In.		125.00
Dachshund, Man Smoking Pipe		48.00
Frog, Smoking Pipe		48.00
Men & Dogs, Raised Figures, Hunt Scene, Royal Doulton, 5 In.		125.00
Monkey, Pipe In Mouth		95.00

The toby jug is a very special form of pitcher. It is shaped like the
full figure of a man or woman. A pitcher that shows just the top
half of a person is not correctly called a toby. More examples of
toby jugs can be found under Royal Doulton and other factory
names.

◆◆◆

The blue Staffordshire patterns were the earliest, with both black and
blue transfer designs used during the eighteenth century. Pink,
green, or brown transfer designs were used about 1820, and the
combination of several colors began about 1820.

◆◆◆

TOBY JUG, Bennington Type, Removable Top 325.00
Cover, Pearlware, Tricorn, Loop Handle, Staffordshire, 1770, 9 In. 1100.00
Douglas MacArthur, Occupied Japan 75.00
Indian Chief 22.00
Staffordshire, Semi–Transparent Glazes, Sponging, Cover, 10 In. 1050.00
Washington, Bisque, Homer Laughlin, 2 In. 30.00

Tole is painted tin. It is sometimes called *japanned ware, pontypool,* or *toleware.* Most nineteenth–century tole is painted with an orange–red or black background and multicolored decorations. Many recent versions of toleware are made and sold.

TOLE, see also Tinware
TOLE, Birdhouse, Garden Pavilion Type, Cupola, Chimneys, White Paint 475.00
Bowl, Design Inside & Out, 12 In. 70.00
Box, Candle, Hanging, Black, 11 3/4 In. 200.00
Box, Deed, Black, Polychrome Floral, Dome Top, 8 3/4 In. 150.00
Box, Deed, Brown Japanning, Floral Design, Dome Top, 9 1/2 In. 500.00
Box, Deed, Brown Japanning, Stenciled Floral, Gilt, 9 1/4 In. 85.00
Box, Deed, Floral Design, Star Design, Dome Top, 9 In. 500.00
Box, Deed, Polychrome Floral, Black Paint, 9 In. 500.00
Box, Deed, Polychrome Floral, Black Paint, Dome Top, Brass Handle, 9 In. 250.00
Box, Deed, Red Ground, Stylized Flowers, 6 1/4 x 9 1/2 In. ....*Illus* 1980.00
Box, Deed, Stenciled Floral, Embossed Cover, Brass Handle, 9 1/2 In. 45.00
Box, Dome Top, Open–Worked Slots In Base, 9 1/4 In. 85.00
Box, Floral, Initials J. W. On Lift Cover, Brass Bail Handle, 14 In. 450.00
Box, Red Background, 19th C. 1100.00
Box, Spice, Cover, 6 Removable Compartments, 9 1/2 In. 45.00
Canister, Tea, Floral Design, Red Paint, 5 1/4 In. 375.00
Canister, Tea, Picture of Sharpshooters Aiming Through Knees 467.50
Coffeepot, American Prize, Iron Handle, Brew Liner, 13 In. 68.00
Coffeepot, Black Ground, 19th Century, 10 3/4 In. ....*Illus* 3080.00
Coffeepot, Floral Design, Dark Brown Japanning, 10 1/2 In. 1200.00
Coffeepot, Floral, Red Paint, 10 In. 75.00
Coffeepot, Polychrome Floral, Black Paint, 10 1/2 In. 425.00
Coffeepot, Red Ground, 19th Century, 10 1/2 In. ....*Illus* 3300.00
Coffeepot, Side Spout, Floral Design, Dark Brown Japanning, 8 3/4 In. 1450.00
Container, Lid, Painted Leaves, Flowers & Birds, 3 1/4 In. 245.00
Creamer, Hinged Lid, Floral Design, 4 1/8 In. 475.00
Creamer, Hinged Lid, Floral Design, Mottled Japanning, 4 1/8 In. 675.00
Egg, Boy Kicking A Ball, 1910 .... 20.00
Food Warmer, Whale Oil, Brown Japanning, Gilt Floral, 8 1/4 In. 225.00
Lamp, Bracket, Hanging, Black Smoked Design, Red Striping 555.00
Lamp, Miniature 95.00
Lunch Box, Hinged Lid, 3 Inner Sections, Lift–Out Center, 12 1/4 In. 250.00
Match Box, Trefoil Crest, Brown Japanning, Floral, Crimped, 7 1/4 In. 50.00
Pencil Box, Jackie Coogan, Red 30.00
Sugar, Floral Design, 2–Tone Red Paint, 3 3/4 In. 200.00
Tea Caddy, Yellow & Red Flowers, Black Ground 175.00
Teapot, Floral Design, Dark Brown Japanning, 10 1/2 In. 1400.00
Tray, 6 Colors On Black, 11 x 11 In. 65.00
Tray, Bamboo Turned Stand, Lobed Rim, Gilt Highlights, 19 x 23 In. 440.00
Tray, Cluster of Fruit Amid Flowers, Pierced Hand Grips, Stand 2640.00
Tray, Gilt & Bronze Stenciling, Stand 1400.00
Tray, Gold Floral Design, Black Ground, 19th Century, 16 1/4 x 12 In. 35.00
Tray, Stylized Florals, Gold Highlights & Tracery, 30 x 20 In. 155.00
Tray, Victorian, Abalone Inlay On Black Ground, 29 1/2 In. 315.00
Urn, Cottages & Wooded Scene, Paw Feet, Continental, Square, 7 In., Pair 1750.00
Urn, Gold Design, Black Ground, Pair, 14 In. 990.00
Urn, Mantle, Pastoral Landscape, Swan Neck Handles, 8 1/2 In., Pair 2860.00
Watering Can, Green Paint, 4 In. 85.00

Tom Mix was born in 1880 and died in 1940. He was the hero of over 100 silent movies from 1910 to 1929, and 25 sound films from 1929 to 1935. There was a Ralston Tom Mix radio show from 1933 to 1950, but the original Tom Mix was not in the show. Tom Mix comics were published from 1942 to 1953.

TOM MIX, Arrow, Lucite	50.00
Belt Buckle, Ralston Championship	65.00
Book, Big Little Book, Fighting Cowboys	25.00
Book, Big Little Book, Range War	30.00
Boots, Box	350.00
Bowl, Ralston, Straight Shooter	32.00
Bracelet, Identification	25.00
Bullet Telescope, Manual	95.00
Cigar Label, Picture	10.00
Compass, Magnifier, Glow-In-Dark	60.00
Compass, Magnifier, Plastic, 1947	45.00
Compass, Straight Shooter, Ralston	65.00
Decoder, Six-Shooter	55.00
Gun, Glow-In-The-Dark, Arrowhead Compass, Whistle	95.00
Initial Ring	150.00
Manual, Life of Tom Mix, Ralston, Envelope, 1933, 5 x 7 In.	153.00
Parachute, Rocket	125.00
Periscope	75.00
Pocket Knife, Tony	325.00
Ring, Look Around	75.00 To 85.00
Ring, Magnet	65.00 To 85.00
Ring, Tiger Eye	200.00 To 250.00
Signal Set, Postal Telegraph, Ralston	75.00
Spinner, Good Luck	35.00
Spurs	37.50 To 75.00
Sun Watch	100.00
Telegraph	75.00
Telescope, Bullet, With Bird Call	50.00
Watch	295.00
Watch Fob, Gold Ore	45.00 To 50.00
Western Theater	125.00
Wrist Cuffs & Spurs, Glow-In-The-Dark, Box	125.00
Wristwatch, Ralston, 1983	275.00

Tools of all sorts are listed here, but most are related to industry. Other tools will be found listed under Iron; Kitchen; Tinware; and Wooden.

TOOL, Adze, Cooper's, Marked Collins, 3-In. Blade	40.00
Adze, Gutter, Hand Wrought, 30-In. Handle	67.50
Anvil, Jeweler's, Small	25.00
Apple Peeler, Industrial Type, Bonanza Goodell Co., N. H.	88.00
Auger, Turned Curly Maple Handle, 17 In.	25.00
Ax, Boy's, Winchester, Hickory Handle, 28 In.	90.00
Ax, Broad, Collins Axe, Pennsylvania, Bicentennial, 1976, 12-In. Blade	200.00
Ax, Broad, Goosewing	250.00
Ax, Camp, Marble Safety Axe Co., 11 1/2 In.	125.00
Ax, Goosewing, G. Rohrbach, Kutztown, Pa., 13 1/2-In. Blade	300.00
Ax, Marble No. 5, Safety	138.00
Ax, Marble, No. 9, Sheath	170.00
Ax, Side, Cooper's, W. Wright	55.00
Battery Tester, W. C. Fields, Red Nose, On Card	15.00
Bean Sorter, A. S. Clough, Meredith Village, N. H.	225.00
Bench Vise, Harness Maker's, Blue, Weathered Seat, 44 1/2 In.	55.00
Bench, Cobbler's, Pine, 19th Century, 42 x 15 1/2 x 14 In.	70.00
Bench, Leather Worker's	80.00
Bit Brace, Thomas Turner, Sheffield, Brass Framed Ebony, 1823	525.00
Blow Torch, Craftsman, Brass	25.00

Book Press, 1 Drawer, Wooden Screw Press, Curly Birch, 52 x 24 3/4 In. 550.00
Book Press, Hand Operated, Table Top, A. L. Swett Co., N. Y. 85.00
Boring Auger, Timber, Miller's Fall, Nonadjustable 121.00
Bow Drill 320.00
Box, Feed, Slant Lid, Old Red Stained, Dovetailed Wood 220.00
Box, Stanley, Dark Oak, Label On Lid, 4 1/2 x 11 x 25 In. 55.00
Brace, Corner Bit, Millers Falls 49.50
Brace, Drill, Corner, Millers Falls 30.00
Brace, Keen Kutter, Krio, 6–In. Swing 24.50
Brace, Yankee, North Bros., No. 2101 .... 30.00
Bung Borer, Cooper's, Diameters Etched In Face, To 2 1/4 In. 35.00
Calipers, Bow, P. Lowentraut, Newark, N. J., 6 In. 15.00
Calipers, L. S. Starrett, 8 1/2 In. 10.00
Calipers, Leg Shape, 2 In. 100.00
Canteen, Red Paint, Extra Wide Bands, 18th Century, 8 1/2 x 9 1/2 In. 575.00
Case, Watchmaker's, Oak, 20 Drawers, Compartments, Bottles, 8 x 16 In. 390.00
Chart, Stanley Tools Educ. Dept., How To Use, Wooden Stand, 10 Piece 60.00
Check Writer, Protectograph, 1912 .... 75.00
Chest, Pine, Painted, Leather Handles, With Tools, 40 x 18 x 19 1/2 In. 275.00
Chest, Tools, Painted Body, Leather Handles, Pine, 19 1/2 x 40 x 18 In. 305.00
Chisel Set, Stanley No. 50, Everlasting, 1/4, 1/2 & 3/4 In., 3 Piece 45.00
Chisel, Turning, Riverside, 2–In. Skew 35.00
Cider Press, Wooden, Buckeye, Thomas & Mast, Ohio, Pat. Feb. 6, '64 .... 50.00
Cigarette Roller, Box, 1930s 25.00
Clamp, Curly Maple, Stamped No. 17, 20 In. 85.00
Clamp, Quilting, Wooden, 33 In., 4 Piece 60.00
Clippers, Hand, Oster, Model 110 .... 17.00
Cobbler's Bench, 5 Drawers, Gallery Back, Pine, 42 3/4 In. 600.00
Coin Changer, Brandt, Complete 100.00
Combination Saw Set & Screwdriver, W. H. Clay, Cheffield, 1918 .... 6.00
Compass, Cooper's, Hand Forged 55.00
Compass, Drafting, Eagle, Box 7.50
Compass, U. S. Army, All Brass, Dated 1918 .... 50.00
Compass–Divider, Eagle, Box, 1894 .... 22.00
Corn Dryer, Iron 15.00
Corn Husker, Steel, Leather, Signed Boss, 4 1/2 In. 12.00
Cradle, Grain 65.00
Croze, Cooper's, Carved Plate, Speckled Burl, 15 In. 350.00
Croze, Saw Tooth, Cooper's, 20 x 6 1/2 In. 35.00
Cuber, Plug Tobacco, Wooden 20.00
Divider, W. Marples & Sons, England, 3/4–In. Wood Screw Box 35.00
Drill, Pump, With Bit, 6 1/2–In. Iron Flywheel, 24 In. 275.00
Dryer, Seed Corn, 10 Prongs 15.00
Dug Lock, Keen Kutter, Santa Fe 20.00
Duplicating Apparatus, Neo–Cyclostyle, Gestetner, Oak, 20th Century 75.00
Egg Tester, Reeves Rigling, Tin, Kerosene Lamp, Identifies Rotten Eggs 250.00
Emery Wheel, Chain Driven 25.00
Engine, Gasoline, John Deere, 1 Cylinder 650.00
Eyelet Fastener, Bates 40.00
Fanning Mill, Belts & Screens, Salesman's Sample 500.00
Feeder, Chicken, Metal 6.00
Flax Wheel, Red & Black Design 275.00
Fork, Hay, Wooden, 3 Prongs 150.00
Gauge, Butt, Stanley, No. 93, S. & W. Hart Logo 45.00
Gauge, Butt, Stanley, No. 95, Box 25.00
Gauge, Marking, Stanley, No. 265, Boxwood 55.00
Gauge, Mortise, Inlaid Brass & Steel, Rosewood, 7 In. 25.00
Glass Cutter, Karelson, N. Y., Brass, Wood Handle 18.00
Grain Measure, Bell–Metal, Pontifex Sons & Wood, 1826, 3 Piece 3300.00
Grinder, Corn, Marvin & Smith Co., Marked Factory No. 1 & Otis, 1880s 185.00
Hammer, Claw, Keen Kutter, Chrome Polished Head, 13 In. 34.50
Hammer, Filemaker's, Ash Handle, Weights 7 1/2 Lbs. 375.00
Hammer, Sayer's, Henry Disston, Phil., 2 1/2 Lbs. 45.00

Hammer, Spike, Railroad 27.50
Hasp, Barn, Wrought Iron, 8 To 15 1/2 In., 6 Piece 40.00
Hat Stretcher, Electric, Amco 75.00
Hatchet, Dark Colored Compass Designed Backboard, 7 1/4 x 29 1/2 In. 65.00
Hatchet, Half, William Beatty & Son, Cow Trademark 45.00
Hatchet, Keen Kutter 27.50
Hatchet, Nail Claw, Bridgeport Hdw., Conn., Iron Strapped Handle 45.00
Hay Cutter, Keen Kutter 75.00
Hay Fork, Wooden .... 100.00 To 125.00
Hay Hook, Wooden 6.00
Hone Block, Oil Stone, Shapening Knifes, Pine, 1820, Hole, 12 1/2 In. 65.00
Horse Anchor, Cast Iron, Round 8.00
Horse Anchor, Cast Iron, Square 4.00
Horse Brush, U. S. Cavalry 12.50
Ice Tongs, Iron, 10 Lbs., 28 In. 30.00
Ice Tongs, Union Ice Co. 12.00
Iron, Burning, Blacksmith's, Double Ended, Forged, 31 In. 45.00
Iron, Cauterizing, Blacksmith's, 12 1/2 In. 18.00
Jack, Conestoga Wagon, Iron & Wood, Dated 1832, 20 In. 100.00
Jack, Conestoga Wagon, Iron Band, 1793 .... 125.00
Jack, Plane, Winchester, No. 3010 .... 115.00
Jack, Wagon, Handmade, Wood & Forged Iron 145.00
Jack, Wagon, Wood & Iron, C. G., 1758 .... 150.00
Jigsaw, Treadle, The Star In Black Paint, Red Racing Stripe 275.00
Knife, Chamfer, Cooper's, Wooden Handle, Right–Handed, 15 In. 28.00
Ladder, For Picking Apples, 10 Ft. 89.00
Ladder, Pine, 66 In. 105.00
Lathe, Jeweler's 550.00
Lathe, Metal, Sers, Atlas, Stand, Milling Attachment, 12 x 24 In. 700.00
Level, Davis, Verticle & Horizontal Bubbles, Spindle Design 825.00
Level, Fitted Brass & Mahogany Case, L. L. Davis, 12 In. 395.00
Level, Goodell–Pratt, Brass Bound Mahogany, 18 In. 98.00
Level, Inclinometer, Mantle, No. 1, L. L. Davis 245.00
Level, Machinist, W. Lund Colne, Germany, Bronze, Leather Case 115.00
Level, Stanley No. 96, Brass Bound, Rosewood, Pat. 1891, 28 In. 105.00
Level, Stratton Bros., No. 10, Brass Bound, Rosewood, 8 In. 300.00
Level, Winchester, Brass & Walnut 65.00
Level, Winchester, No. 9825, 28 In. 50.00
Lever, Starrett, Cast Iron 46.00
Loom, Weaving, 4–Harness, 1900s, Floor Size 200.00
Micrometer Set, Inside, Starrett, No. 823C, 4 To 24 In. 125.00
Mimeograph Machine, Edison For A. B. Dick, Wooden Hinged Lid, 1880 .... 75.00
Mold, Candle, 29 Tube, Bench, Primitive, Black Paint, Design, 22 1/2 In. 275.00
Molder, Crown, A. B. Senbey Bros., Louisville, Ky. 525.00
Motor, Unison, 3 Horsepower 265.00
Nibbler, AEGG, Model KN 3. 25, Metal Workers, 12 Gal. 400.00
Niddy–Noddy, Mahogany 72.00
Oiler, Metal Spout, Danville, Indiana, Pat. 1922 .... 20.00
Pail, Water, Canvas, Military 25.00
Pedometer, Switzerland 65.00
Pipe Wrench, Keen Kutter, 7–In. Square 22.50
Plane, Badger, E. Preston & Sons, Beech 45.00
Plane, Barrel, Cooper's, Charles Buck 55.00
Plane, Bench, Applewood, 1861 Each End, 3 x 17 1/2 In. 35.00
Plane, Bench, Hazard Knowles, 1827 .... 80.00
Plane, Block, Coffin Shape, Rosewood, 8 1/2 In. 58.00
Plane, Block, Stanley, No. 120 .... 10.00
Plane, Chamfer, E. Preston, Beech Sliding Box 98.00
Plane, Chamfer, Stanley, No. 72 .... 110.00
Plane, Chariot, Brass, Oak Wedge, 1 3/8 x 3 1/4 In. 150.00
Plane, Chariot, Steel, Shaped Walnut Wedge, Brass Restraint, 4 1/2 In. 155.00
Plane, Chariot, Walnut Wedge, J. Howarths, Scotland, 2 1/8 x 1 3/4 In. 135.00
Plane, Circular, Stanley No. 20, Nickel Plated, Pat. Apr. 19, '92 .... 110.00

Plane, Compass, Stanley Victor No. 20 .... 77.00
Plane, Compass, Stanley, No. 20 1/2 .... 115.00
Plane, Corebox, Elisha W. Lewis, Phila., 1866 .... 150.00
Plane, Crown Molding, Iron, Dated 1814 .... 600.00
Plane, Crown Molding, Ohio Tool, 6 1/2 In. 700.00
Plane, Dado, Auburn Tool Co., No. 177, 7/8 In. 28.00
Plane, Dado, Shipwright's, Ohio Tool, 15 In. 68.00
Plane, Jack, Boston Metallic 275.00
Plane, Jack, Winchester No. 3010, Pre-1926, 14 In. .... 75.00 To 80.00
Plane, Keen Kutter, No. KK6C 60.00
Plane, Keen Kutter, Steel, 14 In. 30.00
Plane, Low Angle Miter, Alexander Mathieson, Scotland, 9 x 2 1/8 In. 155.00
Plane, Metallic Plane, Throat Adjustment, Palmer Storkes Pat., 15 In. 185.00
Plane, Miller's, Iron, 4 Cutters 6000.00
Plane, Plow, 1/4 In., Ohio Tool Co., Rosewood, 11 3/4 In. 225.00
Plane, Plow, 3/8 In., Abbot & Co., Adjustable Fence, 11 1/2 In. 40.00
Plane, Plow, Bridled, Wedge Cut In Handle 275.00
Plane, Plow, Sandusky, Brass Fence Trim 600.00
Plane, Plow, Siegley No. 2, No Blades 150.00
Plane, Plow, Stanley No. 45, 15 Cutters 85.00
Plane, Rabbet, J. Poppin, N. Y., Rosewood Insets, Brass 250.00
Plane, Rabbet, Rosewood, 15 3/4 In. 35.00
Plane, Rabbet, Stanley, No. 190 .... 19.00
Plane, Router, Stanley, No. 71, Nickel Plate 30.00
Plane, Sash, Adjustable, Auburn Tool Co., No. 165, Box 35.00
Plane, Sash, Joshia King, Adjustable 44.00
Plane, Scaper, Stanley No. 85, Pat. 4/1/05 .... 600.00
Plane, Scrub, Stanley, No. 40 .... 30.00 To 40.00
Plane, Smoothing, Union No. 21, Wood Bottom, Pat. Oct. 22, 1888 .... 110.00
Plane, Stanley No. 45, 4 Cutters, 1908 .... 42.00
Plane, Stanley, Multipurpose, No. 46, Adjustable, 3 Racks of Blades, Box 55.00
Plane, Stanley, No. 97 .... 300.00
Plane, Tongue, 1/4 In., Beech, Schaeffer & Cobb, 13 3/4 In. 45.00
Plane, Transition, Stanley, No. 2, Short Knob 22.00
Plane, Trim, Stanley No. 95 .... 125.00
Plane, Violin Maker's 2 In. 50.00
Plane, Weatherstripping, Sandusky Tool, All Metal 72.00
Plane, Window Mullion, Beech, Casey & Co., 9 1/2 In. 55.00
Plane, Wood Bottom, Sargent, No. 3426 .... 55.00
Plane, Zenith, No. Z604-C 50.00
Pliers, Crimping, Hercule, No. 2 .... 26.00
Pliers, Crimping, Metal Grip Handles, Steel Teeth 15.00
Pliers, Electrician's 10.00
Pliers, Flat Nose, Keen Kutter 18.00
Plumb Bob, Brass, Screw Top, Short, Fat 20.00
Post Grinder, Dumore, No. 14-011 .... 450.00
Pounce Sander, Pierced Star In Flared Top, 3 x 3 1/2 In. 85.00
Pounce Sander, Pinstriping Bands, Maple, c.1810 .... 130.00
Powder Gun, Acme, Handles, Bellows, Insecticide, Potato Implement Co. 28.00
Press, Lard 27.50
Printing Press, Monarch Jr. Marking System, Wooden Base, 1920, 9 In. 210.00
Rake, Wooden, 34 1/2 In. 100.00
Reamer, Tapan, B & S, No. 12 .... 40.00
Roller, Log, Right Angle Hook, Ram's Horn Curls At Handle, 26 In. 165.00
Rose Petal Press, Polychrome Design, Brass Finial, Lead, 7 3/8 In. 65.00
Router, Coachmaker's, Brass Faced, Old Hickory, 16 In. 40.00
Router, Double Pistol, Coachmaker's, Beech, 19 In. 145.00
Router, Fenced Grooving, Coachmaker's, Ash, 15 In. 45.00
Rug Beater, Wicker 28.00
Rule, Boxwood, Stanley No. 36 1/2 .... 16.00
Rule, Engineer's, Keuffel Essert, 2 Levels, Compasses, Sight, 12 In. 175.00
Rule, Lufkin, No. 1206, Brass End, Folding 15.00
Rule, Stanley No. 68, Sweetheart Logo, Compl. of J. A. Thompson & Sons 20.00

◆◆

Never use an antique stove before it has been restored and inspected by a qualified stove dealer or repair service. A damaged stove may explode or burn and cause serious injury.

◆◆

Rule, Stanley, Brass Trim, Contour Joint, 2 Ft.	18.00
Rule, Stanley, No. 54, Brass Bound, 4–Fold, Inch & Metric Scales, 2 Ft.	25.00
Rule, Stanley, No. 87, Ivory, Silver Bound, Arch Joint	395.00
Saw, Crosscut, Beech	25.00
Saw, Hack, Rail Cutting, Sterling, 22 x 11 3/4 In.	45.00
Saw, Ice	18.00
Saw, Miter Box, Craftsman, Chrome Edge, 11 Teeth Per Inch, 26 In.	35.00
Saw, Pruning, Disston, Model D24, Copper Handle, Beech Grip	35.00
Scoop, Blueberry, Tin, Wooden Handle, W. W. Small, Me., 1914, 8 x 10 In.	67.00
Scoop, Cranberry, Wooden, Large	45.00
Scraper, Cabinet, Stanley, No. 83	75.00
Scribe, No. 90, Stanley	20.00
Seed Cleaner, Clipper, Tabletop, Atferrell & Co.	1450.00
Shears, Pruning, Chrome Plated, Logo In Center, Keen Kutter	55.00
Shears, Tailor's, W. Greaves & Co., Newark, N. J., 12 1/2 In.	20.00
Shovel, Grain, Curly Maple, Faded Name On Back of Handle, 42 In.	1000.00
Skimmer, Maple Syrup, Pierced Star & Circle, Copper, Penna., 5 x 10 In.	87.00
Slick, Carpenter's, New Haven Tool, No. 66, 3–In. Blade	67.00
Slick, Replaced Handle, 3 1/2 x 33 In.	67.50
Slide Rule, Keuffel & Esser, Pat. 1900	37.50
Smoker, Bee, Red Leather Bellows, Tin	35.00
Smoothing Board, Carved Foliage Scrolls, Lion Handle, 30 In.	600.00
Smoothing Board, Floral Design, Heart, Green Paint, 24 1/4 In.	125.00
Smoothing Board, Fruit Wood, Edge Inlay, Initials B., St., 1894, 23 In.	75.00
Smoothing Board, Stippled Designs, Stylized Horse Handle, 23 In.	250.00
Smoothing Board, Wood Bottom, Union, No. 21	170.00
Speednut Wrench, Cockran, 8 In.	16.00
Spelk, Primitively Design, Leather Trap–Door Top, Handle, 20 1/2 In.	130.00
Spokeshave, Matheison, Decal, Boxwood	22.00
Spokeshave, Stanley, No. 151, 2 Screw Adjustments, Iron, 10 In.	25.00
Spring Winder, Brass & Steel, 8 3/4 In.	75.00
Square, Combination, Starrett, Center Finder, Protractor, Box	75.00
Square, Lufkin, Model 2504R	50.00
Stand, Cobbler's, Shoe Repair, Cast Iron	35.00
Stencil, Running Deer, Foliage, White Metal, Wooden Frame, 8 x 10 In.	55.00
Stretcher, Collar, Man's, Wooden	15.00
Stretcher, Curtain, Pine	22.00
Stretcher, Sock, Wooden, Long, Pair	30.00
Swift, Table Clamp, Dark Brown Finish, 21 In.	55.00
T–Level, Oak, Side Braces, Pegged 23 x 18 In.	195.00
T–Level, Stanley, All Metal, Stippled, Pat. 7/14/08	15.00
Thread Winder, Turned Wood, Pullout Drawer, 12 1/2 x 13 In.	121.00
Timing Machine, Watch, Jeweler's	650.00
Tongs, Pipe, Iron, 8 In.	100.00
Tool Set, Staking, Jeweler's	150.00
Treadmill, Dog, For Churn	500.00
Turning Machine, Dowl & Rod, Stanley No. 77, All Cutters	545.00
Vise, Harness Marker's	185.00
Vise, Miter, Marsh, Marked, Patent Information	75.00
Vise, Saw, Wall Mount, Cam Operated, Wentworth's, 10 1/2 In.	25.00
Wagon Wheel, Farm, Set of 4	280.00
Wheel, Foot Pedal Power, April 14, 1896	110.00
Wheelbarrow, Wooden Spoked Front Wheel, Green Paint, Wood	195.00
Wire Gauge, Brass & Steel, 6 In.	35.00

Witchit, Adjustable, For Rounding Pegs	100.00
Wool Winder, 2 Adjustable Reels, Triangular Base, Oak & Walnut, 48 In.	175.00
Wrench, Alligator, Adjustable, 8 3/4 In.	35.00
Wrench, Basin, Trimo, 10 In.	30.00
Wrench, Crescent, Marked Foreign, 6 In.	52.00
Wrench, Open End, Winchester, No. 1152	60.00
Wrench, Polly, No. 91, Gellman Mfg. Co., 9 In.	18.00
Yarn Winder	110.00
Yarn Winder, Floor, Various Hardwoods, Chip Carved, 42 1/2 In.	75.00
Yarn Winder, Horizontal Shaft, Counting Mechanism, 35 x 27 In.	110.00
Yarn Winder, Large	100.00
Yarn Winder, Niddy Noddy, Half Skein, 9 In.	150.00
Yarn Winder, Turned & Chip Carved, Hard & Soft Wood, 33 In.	150.00

Toothpick holders are sometimes called *toothpicks* by collectors. The variously shaped containers made to hold the small wooden toothpicks are of glass, china, or metal. Most of the toothpick holders are Victorian.

TOOTHPICK, 6 Points, Scalloped, Clear, Gold Top	35.00
Barrel, Mineral Water, Glenwood Springs, Colo.	45.00
Bear, Standing, Red Stone Eyes, Head Tilts Back, Bronze, 3 In.	175.00
Beggar's Hand, Pig & Pot, Boston Baked Beans, Blue Opaque	25.00
Blocked Thumbprint Band, Clarinda, World's Fair, 1933	22.00
Cat, Bag, Umbrella, Bisque, Germany	50.00
Colorado, Green, Gold	30.00
Coon Chicken Inn	150.00
Cranberry Overlay, 3 Handles, Sterling Trim	325.00
Croesus, Purple, Gold Trim	90.00
Crystal, Art Deco, Cut Glass, Enameled Black Bands, 2 1/2 In.	65.00
Crystal, Sterling Base	20.00
Depression Glass, Green	25.00
Dog, Hat, Cobalt Blue	65.00
Elephant Head, Clear	48.00
Embossed Leaves & Flowers, Pairpoint, Silver Plate	40.00
Fan & Feather, Signed Joe St. Clair	45.00
Figural, Bloomers, Long Underwear	85.00
Figural, Candlestick, Curled Handle, Sapphire Blue	95.00
Figural, Dog, Next To Top Hat, Blue Glass	85.00
Figural, Golfer	295.00
Figural, Hedgehog, Porcupine, Silver Plate, Meriden	75.00
Figural, Soldier, Sailor, Spanish–American War, Preparedness	145.00
Florette, Frosted Pink & White	55.00
Griffin, Brass	325.00
Hobnail, Opalescent White	28.00
Indian Head	45.00
Ladders With Diamond, Clear, Gold Top	32.00
Majestic, Clear	30.00
Milk Glass, Scalloped, Ornate, Gold	20.00
Mug, Marshalltown, Iowa, Ruby Flash	18.00
Owl, Sitting Beside Holder, Silver Plate	30.00
Pressed Glass, Green, Gold Trim, Stemmed, Souvenir, 4 In., Pair	65.00
Pretty Maid, Clear	45.00
Punty Band, Soo St. Marie, Michigan, Custard Glass	45.00
Rosemeade, Pheasant, Signed	26.00
Ruby Flashed, Newton, Iowa	17.50
Santa Claus, Pewter	25.00
Spinning Star	24.00
Sterling Silver & Crystal, Repousse, Whiting	26.00
Sunk Honeycomb, Souvenir, 1897, Katie Casino	38.00
Woodpecker, Log	10.00
Woodpecker, Metal, Grabber	12.00

Tortoiseshell, Bowl, Warrior, Geisha, Serpent,
21 In.

Tortoiseshell, Box, Ivory Feet, Inlaid,
9 3/4 x 15 3/4 In.

TORQUAY

Torquay is the name given to ceramics by several potteries working near Torquay, England, from 1870 until 1962. Until about 1900, the potteries used local red clay to make classical style art pottery vases and figurines. Then they turned to making souvenir wares. Items were dipped in colored slip and decorated with painted slip and sgraffito designs. They often had mottos or proverbs, and scenes of cottages, ships, birds, or flowers. The *Scandy* design was a symmetrical arrangement of brush strokes and spots done in colored slips. Potteries included Watcombe Pottery (1870–1962); Torquay Terra–Cotta Company (1875–1905); Aller Vale (1881–1924); Torquay Pottery (1908–1940); and Longpark (1883–1957).

TORQUAY, Bowl, Cottage, 6 In.	30.00
Cache Pot, Cottage, Motto Ware, 3 In.	18.00
Creamer, Cottage, Satsuma, Motto Ware	25.00
Creamer, Miniature	40.00
Cup & Saucer, Cottage Scene, Oversize	125.00
Dish, Jam, Cottage, Motto Ware, Watcombe	40.00
Eggcup, Watcombe	20.00
Hatpin Holder	75.00
Jardiniere, Pheasant, Blue Ground, 5 1/4 x 6 1/4 In.	160.00
Pitcher, Cottage, Motto Ware, 2 1/2 In.	15.00
Plate, May You Live As Long As You Want and Never Want, 9 In.	220.00
Relish, 3 Sections, Loop Handle, Cloverleaf, 9 In.	45.00
Teapot, 5 1/4 In.	50.00
Teapot, Scandy	80.00
Tile, Iron, Scandy	150.00
Vase, Blue Heather, 8 In.	85.00
Vase, Peaches, Black Ground, 10 In.	125.00
Vase, Sculptured Grapes, Ruffled, High Gloss, 13 1/2 In.	15.00

◆◆◆

If the teddy bear needs washing, do it very carefully. First vacuum the fur, then mix water and liquid detergent and brush the detergent through the fur. Dry with a towel, then a hair dryer on low. Let dry completely, comb with a dog comb.

◆◆◆

Tortoiseshell glass was made during the 1800s and after by the Sandwich Glass Works of Massachusetts and some firms in Germany. Tortoiseshell glass is, of course, named for its resemblance to real shell from a tortoise. It has been reproduced.

TORTOISESHELL GLASS, Pitcher, Red Design, Clear Handle, Crimped Rim, 9 In.	175.00
Vase, Crimped Top, 10 In.	175.00
Vase, Curved Foot, 8 In.	100.00

The shell of the tortoise has been used as inlay and to make small decorative objects since the seventeenth century. Some species of tortoise are now on the endangered species list, and objects made from these shells cannot be sold legally.

TORTOISESHELL, Bowl, Warrior, Geisha, Serpent, 21 In. ....*Illus*	300.00
Box, Ivory Feet, Inlaid, 9 3/4 x 15 3/4 In. ....*Illus*	2200.00
Box, Sewing, Trimmed In Ivory, England, c.1900	1000.00
Case, Calling Card, Inlaid Ivory, 3 3/4 In.	85.00
Case, Card, Nacre Inlay, 3 3/4 In.	65.00
Case, Gilded Landscape & Eagle, Oriental	165.00
Case, Jewelry, Expandable, 3 Compartments	375.00
Casket, Jewel, Allover Mother-of-Pearl Inlaid, 19th Century	1705.00
Comb, Ornate Carved, 1900s	15.00
Desk Set, Silver, Victorian, William Comyns, 1895-1896, 4 Pc.	4675.00
Hair Receiver, Gold, Large	15.00
Mirror, Queen Anne, Green Felt Borders, 36 1/2 x 25 1/2 In.	1100.00
Napkin Ring, Lily Pad	85.00
Pitcher, Ribbed Body, Crimped Rim, Clear Handle, 9 x 8 In.	250.00
Shoehorn, Child's, Velvet Box	25.00
Tea Caddy, Serpentine, 2 Interior, Lids, Ivory Trim	1320.00

Toys are designed to entice children; and today, they have attracted new interest among adults who are still children at heart. All types of toys are collected. Tin toys, iron toys, battery operated toys, and many others are collected by specialists. Dolls, Games, Teddy Bears, and Bicycles are listed under their own categories. Other toys may be found under company or celebrity names.

TOY, Accordion, Hobner Mignon, 8 In.	95.00
Acrobat, Pinocchio, Windup, Marx	210.00
Adam, Tin Lithograph, Hand Painted, Lehmann, 8 In.	1815.00
Adding Machine, Tin, Wolverine	23.00
Airplane, Aero-Smurf, Biplane, Yellow, Die Cast, Ertl	6.00
Airplane, Air France, Tin Lithograph, 6 Motors	950.00
Airplane, America, Single Engine, Cast Iron, Hubley, 17-In. Wingspan	4500.00
Airplane, American Airliner, Marx, 27 In.	135.00
Airplane, American Airlines, DC-3, Tin, 21 1/2 In.	65.00
Airplane, American Airlines, Prop, Wheels, Stewardess, Battery, 1950	375.00
Airplane, American Eagle, World War II Fighter, Hubley, 11 In.	175.00
Airplane, Army Scout	1350.00
Airplane, Army, Tin, Mechanical Fighter, Marx, 7 In.	140.00
Airplane, Biplane, Painted Pressed Steel, 16 In.	525.00
Airplane, Biplane, Spiral Gravity Tower, Red & Yellow Paint	1540.00
Airplane, Bomber, Mechanical, Tin Lithograph, Marx, 14 In.	99.00
Airplane, Bomber, Windup, Marx, 18 In. Wing Span	295.00
Airplane, Capitol Airlines, Strato Cruiser, Linemar, Battery Operated	150.00
Airplane, Clockwork Props, 6 Propellors, Tinplate, Jep, 21 In.	522.00
Airplane, Delta Wing Jet, Hubley	75.00
Airplane, Girard, Windup, Gray & Yellow, 10-In. Wing Span	650.00
Airplane, Helicopter, Fix All, Marx	500.00
Airplane, Helicopter, Police, Britain, No. 9611	13.50
Airplane, Helicopter, Toy Town, Windup, Chein	95.00
Airplane, Helicopter, U-Turn, Tin, Box, 5 In.	18.00
Airplane, Helicopter, Windup, Box	30.00
Airplane, Lockheed Dirius	925.00

Airplane, Loop The Loop, Car Moves Up & Down, McDowell Mfg. Co., 12 In. 65.00
Airplane, Mail, Popping Pistons, Keystone 900.00
Airplane, Mail, Windup, Tin Lithograph, Marx, 13 In. 225.00
Airplane, Marble Shooter 145.00
Airplane, Marx, 1940s, 27 In. 285.00
Airplane, Mechanical, Paya, Tin Lithograph, 12 In. 176.00
Airplane, Messerschmitt 400.00
Airplane, Navy Fighter, Tin, Windup, Japan, Box 65.00
Airplane, Northwest Airliner, 20 In. 295.00
Airplane, P–38 Fighter, Camouflage Paint, Hubley, 12 1/2–In. Wingspan 165.00
Airplane, Pan–Am Clipper, Wyandotte, 13–In. Wingspan 195.00
Airplane, Pan–Am DC–8, Friction Wheels, Japan, 15–In. Wingspan 150.00
Airplane, Passenger, Alps, Lithograph, Friction, Japan, 11 In. 187.00
Airplane, Penny Toy, Spring Activated, Aeronautical Roundabout, 6 In. 302.00
Airplane, Police Patrol, Tin, Japan, Box, 13 In. 165.00
Airplane, Roll Over, Windup, Forward & Reverse, Marx, 1920s, 5 1/2 In. 445.00
Airplane, Sea, Mercury 95.00
Airplane, Snow Skids, Rotating Prop, Tootsietoy, 4 In. 75.00
Airplane, Spirit of St. Louis, Friction, Tin Lithograph, 1930s, Japan 390.00
Airplane, Steel Craft 475.00
Airplane, Tri–Motor, Katz, 26 1/2–In. Wingspan 2400.00
Airplane, TWA, Biplane, 4 Engine, Windup, Marx, 18 In. 365.00
Airport, American Airlines, With Airplanes, Wyandotte, 1930s 250.00
Airport, Marx, 1930s, Box 120.00
Airport, Sky Way City, Marx 75.00
Ajax, Tin Lithograph, Cloth, Lehmann, 9 1/2 In. 1870.00
Alabama Coon Jigger, Tin Lithograph, Windup, Lehmann 350.00
Allie Gator, Fisher–Price, No. 653 ....   40.00
Alligator, Clockwork, Snapper, Metal 3575.00
Alligator, Windup, Germany, 1930s 250.00
Ambulance, Army, Die Cast, Britain 165.00

Toy, Taxi, Amos & Andy, Tin Lithograph,
Marx, 8 In.

Toy, Bus, Royal Bus Line, Tin Lithograph,
10 In.

Toy, Car, Leaping Lena, Tin Lithograph,
Strauss, 8 In.

Toy, Ambulance, Tin Lithograph, Marx, 10 In.

Ambulance, Cast Iron, Kenton, 1910 .... 1650.00
Ambulance, Keystone Military, Oversized 1210.00
Ambulance, Tin Lithograph, Marx, 10 In. ....*Illus* 303.00
Ambulance, Wyandotte, 11 In. 110.00
Amos & Andy, Walkers, Tin Lithograph, Windup, Marx 1300.00
Ampol, 3 Wheels, 2 People, Parasol, Tin Lithograph, Lehmann, 6 In. 825.00
Anxious Bride, Tin Lithograph, Hand Painted, Lehmann, 9 In. 2200.00
Architectural Bricks, Purple Seal, Wooden Box 50.00
Ark, 18 Animals, Converse, c.1910, 22 In. 695.00
Army Training Center Playset, Marx, Box 90.00
Army Wagon, Field Kitchen, Horse Drawn, Hausser 450.00
Artillery Piece, 4 Horses, 2 Riders, Heyde, 1940s 195.00
Autobus, Double Decker, Tin Lithograph, Lehmann, 8 In. 660.00
B. O. Plenty, Mechanical, Tin Lithograph, Marx, 8 1/2 In. ....*Illus* 176.00
Baby, Crawling, Ives, 1893 .... 2200.00
Badge, Marshall, Wyatt Earp, Tin, 1957 .... 16.00
Badge, Melvin Purvis, Junior G–Man 25.00
Baker & Chimney Sweep, Tin Lithograph, Painted, Lehmann, 5 1/2 In. 4290.00
Balky Mule, Dressed, Tin Litho, Windup, Lehmann, 7 1/2 In. .... 110.00 To 175.00
Balky Mule, With Clown, Windup, Lehmann, 1913 .... 475.00
Ball, Poll Parrot Shoes, Rubber, 1930s 20.00
Banjo Player, Black, Clockwork, Stomps Feet, Plays Banjo, Germany, 7 In. 550.00
Bar M Ranch, Playset, Marx 65.00
Barn, Wooden Lithograph, Stanchions, Wooden Animals 165.00
Barnacle Bill, Windup, Chein 250.00
Bartender, Spinning Eyes 75.00
Basket, Easter, Nursery Rhyme Figures, Tin, Chein 24.00
Bat, Boy's, Winchester 110.00
Batmobile, Batboat On Trailer, Corgi 125.00
Battleship, Clockwork, Tin Lithograph, Kellerman, c.1935, 14 In. 330.00
Battleship, Flywheel, Tin Lithograph, Germany, 12 In. 297.00
Battleship, Hess 700.00
Battleship, Painted Tin Lithograph, Windup, Bing Leipzig, 11 In. 800.00
Battleship, St. Vincent, Tin Lithograph, Box, Lehmann, 13 1/2 In. 2310.00
Battleship, Tin, Hand Painted, Germany, 10 In. 880.00

TOY, BEAR, see also Teddy Bear

Bear, Balloon Blowing, Battery Operated, Box 125.00
Bear, Dancing, Windup, Eyes To Side, 9 1/2 In. 135.00
Bear, Holding Coke Bottle 245.00
Bear, Knitting, Windup, Germany, Box 95.00
Bear, Maxwell Coffee, Battery Operated, Box .... 130.00 To 195.00
Bear, Picnic, Windup 45.00
Bear, Skating, Santa, Battery 25.00
Bear, Walking, Celluloid, Windup 85.00
Bear, Walking, Growling, Windup, Germany 70.00
Bear, Windup, Clockwork Mechanism, Rabbit Fur, 3 x 5 x 10 In. 495.00
Beaver, Mohair, Steiff, 1950–1960, 9 In. 75.00

Toy, B. O. Plenty, Mechanical, Tin Lithograph, Marx, 8 1/2 In.

Toy, Cap Gun, Nickel Plated, Uncle Sam & Admiral Dewey, 1899

Toy, G. I. Joe & K–9 Pups, Mechanical, Unique Art, 9 In.

Toy, Grasshopper, Movable, Noisemaker, Hubley, 9 In.

Bed, Doll's, Canopy, Dotted Swiss Extras, F. A. O. Schwartz, 1940, 34 In. 190.00
Bed, Doll's, Counterpane & Bolster, Maple, 10 x 16 1/4 In. 75.00
Bed, Doll's, Enameled Blue Metal, 26 In. 65.00
Bed, Doll's, Oak 45.00
Bed, Doll's, Red Robin 15.00
Bed, Doll's, Rope, Cannonball, Blanket Roll, Red Paint 280.00
Bed, Doll's, Rope, Red Paint, 1800, 10 1/2 x 16 x 25 In. 495.00
Bed, Doll's, Spindle, Iron 45.00
Bedroom Suite, Doll's, Accessories, Oak 125.00
Bell, Eagle, Painted Cast Iron, American, 6 In. 825.00
Bell, Elephant, American, Cast Iron, 6 In. 385.00
Bell, Harold Lloyd 450.00
Bell, Monkey & Coconut, American, Cast Iron, 6 In. 525.00
Bell, Wild Mule Jack, American, Painted Cast Iron, 8 In. 295.00
Bench, Doll's, Oak Bentwood, 13 In. 275.00
Bengal Tiger, Wheels, Hard Plastic, Movable Mouth, Marx 32.00
    TOY, BICYCLE, see Bicycle
Bicyclist, Man, Tin, Hand Painted, France, 8 In. 1430.00
Bird, Blue Bonnet, Steiff, Movable Wings, 1950s 200.00
Bird, Chirping, In Cage, Automated, Germany, 11 1/2 In. 275.00
Bird, Flying, Mechanical, Tin & Paper Lithograph, Lehmann, 7 1/2 In. 990.00
Black Jigger, Tin Lithograph 295.00
Black Walker, Windup, Marx, 1920s 350.00
Blackboard, Free Standing 20.00
Blocks, Anchor, Instructions & Layouts, Richter, No. 7, Box 82.50
Blocks, Architectural, Wood, Painted, Box 50.00
Blocks, Building, Architectural, Wooden Box, Unused, 1910 .... 65.00
Blocks, Building, Union, No. 5, Stone Blocks, Metal Bridge Spans, Box 82.50
Blocks, Building, Victorian, Multirace Children Chromo, Germany 55.00
Blocks, Santa Claus Cubes, Lithograph On Wood, McLoughlin, Box 4400.00
Blocks, Village, Wooden, For Train Set, Keystone, Box 45.00
Blushing Frankenstein, Battery Operated, Original Box 250.00
Blushing Willy, Battery Operated 95.00
Boat, Arnold Ocean Liner, 1930s, 11 In. 495.00
Boat, Cruiser, Warship, Clockwork & Steam Driven, Bing 2200.00
Boat, Destroyer, Clockwork & Steam Driven, Bing 2860.00
Boat, Flying, Friction, Box 33.00
Boat, Gun, Spanish American War, Wheels, Sheet Metal, 1890s, 15 In. 130.00
Boat, Gunboat, Carette, 1920s, 10 In. 245.00
Boat, Luxury Liner, Tin, Friction, Marx, Box 195.00
Boat, Missouri Battleship, Friction, Tin, Sparus, Box 65.00
Boat, Ocean Liner, 3 Funnels, Clockwork, Carette, c.1912, 12 3/8 In. 1100.00
Boat, Ocean Liner, Painted Wood & Tin, Wolverine 50.00
Boat, Ocean Liner, Plastic, Windup, Tin Stacks, Lehmann, Box 45.00
Boat, Ocean Liner, Whirlygig, Tin Lithograph, Airplanes, CKO, Box, 9 In. 1200.00
Boat, Paddle Wheel, Tin, Hand Painted, Stenciled, Bing, 8 In. 990.00
Boat, Paddle, Mississippi, Whistling, Battery Operated, Japan 155.00
Boat, Pedal, American National Chandler, 1923 .... 2100.00
Boat, Revenue Cutter, Clockwork, Steel, Chrome Guns, 1930s, 20 3/4 In. 305.00
Boat, River Queen, Battery Operated, Tin, Japan, 14 In. 110.00
Boat, Sailboat, Flywheel, Tin Lithograph, Paper Sail, Germany, 9 1/2 In. 121.00
Boat, Sailboat, Yankee Clipper, Box, 21 In. 39.00
Boat, Speed, Tin Lithograph, Canopy, Solid Mahogany, Key Wind, 1930s 80.00
Boat, Speed, Wolverine, Clockwork 176.00
Boat, Speedo, Tin, Windup 52.00
Boat, Steam Engine, Tin, 2 Turrets Shoot Black Powder, On Wheels, 1890s 3400.00
Boat, Submarine, Clockwork, Flags, Rudder, Booklet, Bing, 11 5/8 In. 275.00
Boat, Submarine, Power, Kenner, 13 In. 35.00
Boat, Submarine, Skipjack, Plastic, Box 35.00
Boat, Submarine, Tin, Japan, 12 In. 40.00
Boat, Texaco, Box 85.00
Boat, Torpedo, Steam Powered, Bing, c.1910 .... 1980.00
Boat, Tug, Neptune, Battery Operated, Tin, Japan, 15 In. 125.00

Boat, Tug, Pulling Two Barges, Painted Tin, Windup, Germany, Box 375.00
Boat, U. S. Ship Liner, Battery Operated, Tin, 14 In. 120.00
Boat, Warship Whipple, Marklin, Clockwork 4070.00
Boat, Windup, Lionel, No. 43, Stand 355.00
Boat, Zoom Zoom, Battery Operated, Japan 95.00
Bombu The Monk, Windup, Unique Art, Box 155.00
Bop Bag, Joe Palooka 40.00
Box, Circus Wagon, 1940s 125.00
Box, Shape of Railroad Freight Car, Smith Miller 400.00
Boxer, Mechanical, Cloth Covered, 8 In. 880.00
Boxers, Knockout Champs, Windup, Marx, Box 925.00
Boxers, Knockout Prize Fighters, Windup, Strauss 400.00
Boy On Horse Bell, Nickel Plated, Steel Pull Along, 6 1/2 In. 88.00
Boy On Tricycle, Windup, Japan 950.00
Boy With Cart, Stenciled & Tin Lithograph, Rico, 5 In. 220.00
Bricks, Building, Auburn, Box, 740 Piece 30.00
Bricks, Building, Container, Instructions, M. I. Toys 45.00
Bubble–Blowing Boy, Battery Operated, Japan 91.00
Bubble–Blowing Elephant, Battery Operated, Box 90.00
Bubble–Blower, Fox Magicina, Battery Operated, Box 375.00
Bubble–Blowing Musician, Bobs Head, Sways, Toots, Plastic, Pattery 200.00
Bucking Bronco, Cowboy On Horse, Celluloid, Windup, 1950s, Japan 60.00
Bucking Bronco, Painted Tin, Lehmann, 8 In. 257.00
Bucky Burro, Pulltoy, Driver, Fisher–Price 125.00
Bug, Windup, Tin, Lehmann, 4 In. 50.00
Bulldozer, Bump & Turn Action, Battery Operated, Flashing Lights, Box 250.00
Bulldozer, Junior, 4 Actions, Box 110.00
Bunny, Picnic, Battery, Original Box 75.00
Bunny, Telephone, Battery Operated 225.00
Burger Chef, Box 145.00
Bus, 5 Windows, Cast Iron, 1920s 80.00
Bus, American Delux, Pressed Steel, Friction, Rubber Tires, 26 In. 725.00
Bus, American Van Lines, Windup, Cream, Red, Marx, Box, 13 1/2 In. 140.00
Bus, Double Decker, Advertising Gordon Gin, Tin Lithograph, 10 In. 175.00
Bus, Greyhound, Buddy–L 285.00
Bus, Greyhound, Tin, Friction, Japan, Scenicruiser, 13 In. 85.00
Bus, Greyhound, Tin, Japan 65.00
Bus, Greyhound, Tootsietoy, 6 In. 50.00
Bus, Interstate, Windup, Strauss 385.00
Bus, Lone Star, Double Decker, England 35.00
Bus, Motor, Buddy–L, No. 208, 28 In. 2300.00
Bus, Observation Coach, Dinky 75.00
Bus, Observation, Metlox, 6 In. 225.00
Bus, Omnibus, Tin Lithograph, Burnett, 14 1/2 In. 1450.00
Bus, Royal Bus Line, Tin Lithograph, 10 In. ....*Illus* 575.00
Bus, School, Wooden Wheels, Metal, Hubley 85.00
Bus, Sightseeing, Arcade, 1933 .... 200.00
Bus, Sightseeing, Battery Operated, Tin. Japan, 1960s, 14 In. 125.00
Bus, Speedway, Push–Down Motor, Steel, Wolverine 40.00
Bus, Yellow, Chein Jr 250.00
Busy Box, Gabriel, Fisher–Price 25.00
Butter & Egg Man, Tin Lithograph, Windup, Marx 800.00
Cab Carriage, Wooden, Joe Ellis, 1860–70 .... 1100.00
Cabin Dancers, Crank, Musical, Black Figures, D. A. Buck 3300.00
Cabinet, Kitchen, Art Deco Design, Blue, Label, Dubuque, Iowa, 1920s 85.00
Cable Car, San Francisco, Friction 55.00
Cackling Chicken, Tin, Baldwin Mfg. 45.00
Cackling Hen, Fisher–Price, No. 120 .... 40.00
Calliope Set, Teddy Driver, 5 Cars, Steiff 2750.00
Calliope, Circus, Steiff, Box 1350.00
Calliope, Lion Wagon & Driver, Steiff 1200.00
Camel, 2 Humps, Schoenhut 350.00
Camel, Walking, Tin, Windup, c.1900 .... 150.00

Cannon, Firecracker, Cast Iron, Kilgore 90.00
Cannon, Made To Fire, Cast Iron, 21 In. 40.00
Cannon, Nazi, Lineol 425.00
Cannon, On 4–Wheeled Carriage, Red & Black, Sheet Metal, 18 In. 50.00
Cannon, Tootsietoy, 1 1/2 In. 10.00
Cap Bomb, Yellow Kid 150.00
Cap Gun, America, 1873 .... 425.00
Cap Gun, Atomic Disintegrator, Spring Magazine Release, Hubley, 8 In. 275.00
Cap Gun, Big Scout 65.00
Cap Gun, Black Boy & Bear 2200.00
Cap Gun, Border Patrol 45.00
Cap Gun, Buc–A–Roo, Cast Iron, Box 58.00
Cap Gun, Buck, Kilgore, Box 75.00
Cap Gun, Buffalo Bill, 7 3/4 In. 60.00
Cap Gun, Cast Steel, Nickel Finish, Dick, 4 1/8 In. 17.50
Cap Gun, Circle K, 6 Shooter 35.00
Cap Gun, Colt 1887 Pistol 60.00
Cap Gun, Colt Detective Special, Hubley 12.00
Cap Gun, Cowboy Jr., Hubley, Box 90.00
Cap Gun, Cowboy, Hubley 40.00
Cap Gun, Coyote, With Holster 25.00
Cap Gun, Daisy, No. 4 .... 20.00
Cap Gun, Derringer, Hubley 17.50
Cap Gun, Disintegrator Atomic 72.00
Cap Gun, Fanner 50, Bullet Loading, Mattel, Box 150.00
Cap Gun, Frontier, Smoker, Box 75.00
Cap Gun, Hawkeye 30.00
Cap Gun, Kilgore, Machine Gun, 1938 .... 125.00
Cap Gun, Lion's Head, 1887 .... 330.00
Cap Gun, Mark II, Nicols Stallion 100.00
Cap Gun, Monkey, Seated, With Coconut, Explodes When Triggered 410.00
Cap Gun, Mountie, Automatic, Kilgore, Box, 1950s, 6 In. 45.00
Cap Gun, Mustang 500, Nichols, Box 215.00
Cap Gun, National, 5 In. 7.50
Cap Gun, Nichals Stallion 38, With Bullets 90.00
Cap Gun, Nickel Plated, Uncle Sam & Admiral Dewey, 1899 ....*Illus* 7800.00
Cap Gun, O. M. 30.00
Cap Gun, Pal, Leather Holster, 6 In. 20.00
Cap Gun, Peace Maker 32.00
Cap Gun, Pioneer, Silver Finish, Lever–Magazine, Hubley, Box, 10 In. 145.00
Cap Gun, Pony Boy 6.00
Cap Gun, Punch & Judy 1100.00
Cap Gun, Ranger, 1950s 25.00
Cap Gun, Ric–O–Shaw, Hubley 45.00
Cap Gun, Rin Tin Tin, Bronzed Finish 120.00
Cap Gun, Rodeo, White Handles, Hubley, Box 55.00
Cap Gun, Sheriff, Stevens, Box 125:00
Cap Gun, Spitfire, Cast Iron 65.00
Cap Gun, Stallion 32, Box 135.00
Cap Gun, Stallion, Nichols, Box 350.00
Cap Gun, Texan, Hubley, 38 Cap, Leather Holster 25.00
Cap Gun, Texas Jr., Hubley, Box 125.00
Cap Gun, Train Mounted On Barrel 115.00
Cap Gun, Trooper, Hubley .... 20.00 To 35.00
Cap Gun, Victor 265.00
Cap Gun, Western Pioneer, Leather Holster & Belt, Box, 1950s 25.00
Cap Gun, Winner, Cast Iron 45.00
Cap Gun, Wyatt Earp, Buntline Special 175.00
Car, Armoured Command, Dinky Toys 50.00
Car, Battery Operated Headlamps, Clockwork, Germany, c.1935, 15 In. 385.00
Car, Beverly Hillbillies, Plastic, Orignal Box, Ideal, 23 In. 675.00
Car, Bluebird Daytona, Tootsietoy 50.00
Car, Cadillac, 1959, Gold Fins, Tin, Bandai, 11 1/2 In. 275.00

Car, Chain–Driven, Sheet Steel & Wooden 3250.00
Car, Chevrolet, AMT Electric, Remote Control, 1953, Box 175.00
Car, Chevrolet, Police, 1961, Ichiko, Box, 6 In. 85.00
Car, Chevy, Fire Chief, Malibu, Box 200.00
Car, Chrysler Airflow, Hubley, Cast Iron, 4 1/2 In. 150.00
Car, Clown, Tin Lithograph, Unique Art, 7 In. 275.00
Car, Convertible, Fix–It, Ideal, Box 90.00
Car, Convertible, Marx, 11 In. 25.00
Car, Convertible, Retractable Top, Wyandotte, Sheet Metal, 13 In. 285.00
Car, Corvette, 1960, Cragstan, Tin Lithograph 75.00
Car, Corvette, Battery Operated, 1968 .... 70.00
Car, Corvette, Cox, Box 245.00
Car, Corvette, Friction, Tin, Box 22.00
Car, Cougar, White, Battery Operated, Tin, Bandai 165.00
Car, Coupe, Clockwork, Kingsbury, 12 1/2 In. 907.00
Car, Coupe, Fliver, Buddy L 1295.00
Car, Coupe, Mercedes, Motex 1088, Red & White, Shuco 495.00
Car, Coupe, Red, Painted Cast Iron, Arcade, 5 In. 77.00
Car, Coupe, Rumble Seat, Wyandotte, 8 In. 145.00
Car, Coupe, Windup, Tin, Blue & Yellow, Metroy, England 185.00
Car, Crazy Dan, Windup, Marx, Tin 35.00
Car, Dandy Cadillac Convertible, 1929 Model 68.00
Car, Dick Tracy, Siren, Linemar, Box 150.00
Car, Dipsy, Marx, Box 1700.00
Car, Dodge'Em Carnival, Girl Driver, Box 115.00
Car, Dodge'Em, Driver, Windup, Tin 55.00
Car, Estate Wagon, Toytown, Wyandotte, 21 In. 275.00
Car, Fastback, Red Pressed Steel, Windup, Nylint 145.00
Car, Faux–Cabriolet, Clockwork, Battery–Operated Lamps, Tipp, 22 In. 4125.00
Car, Fiat, Tootsietoy 20.00
Car, Figure 8, Windup 60.00
Car, Fire Chief, Hoge 350.00
Car, Fire Chief, Red Working Lights, Marx 200.00
Car, Flintmobile, Flintstones, Rubber Band Powered, 2 x 3 x 4 In. 12.00
Car, Fliver, Spare Wheel, Buddy L, 12 In. 750.00
Car, Ford, Fairlane, White & Green, Plastic, Friction, 1957, Box 300.00
Car, Ford, Mantra, Windup, Schuco, 10 In. 98.00
Car, Ford, Model T, Buddy L 1150.00
Car, Ford, Model T, Movable Parts, Hubley 100.00
Car, Ford, Model T, Windup, Woman Driver, 4 Door, Bing, 6 1/2 In. 445.00
Car, Ford, Old Timer, Windup, Schuco, Box, 7 In. 65.00
Car, Ford, Sedan, 1937, 12 In. 350.00
Car, Ford, Sedan, Kingsbury, 1937, 12 In. 350.00
Car, Ford, Stock, 1956, Tin, Japan, Box, 10 1/2 In. 150.00
Car, Ford, T–Bird, Bubble Top, Tin, Japan, Box 250.00
Car, Friction, Tin Wheels, Signed TM Co., 1950s 60.00
Car, Funny Flivver, Tin Lithograph, Marx, 7 In. 297.00
Car, Gama, Schuco 100.00
Car, Grand Prix, 1964, GP, AMT 40.00
Car, Grand Prix, Cox, Box 245.00
Car, Huckleberry Hound, Friction, Marx 225.00
Car, Indy Racer, Black Jaguar, Marusan Toys, 12 In. 150.00
Car, Jaguar, Cabriolet, Red, Burago 35.00
Car, Jalopy, Marx, Windup, Tin Driver, Motor Sparks, Crank, Box .... 225.00 To 275.00
Car, Jalopy, Rubber Wheels, Friction, Tin 40.00
Car, Kiddie, Dog Shape, Wooden, Yellow, Red & Black Trim, Stylized, 25 In. 500.00
Car, Kingsbury Airflow, Windup, Battery–Operated Lights, 14 In. 900.00
Car, Kojack Buick, 1976, Corgi, 6 In. 45.00
Car, Leaping Lena, Tin Lithograph, Strauss, 8 In. ....*Illus* 154.00
Car, Limousine, Airport, Tin, Friction, Japan 40.00
Car, Limousine, Carette, Tin Litho, Clockwork, Battery–Powered Headlamp 3300.00
Car, Limousine, Tin Lithograph, Painted, Bing, 7 In. 330.00
Car, Magico, Windup, Red Seats, White, Shuco 440.00

Car, Milton Berle, Tin Lithograph, Marx, 6 In. 165.00
Car, Mystery, With Camera, Pathe News 2195.00
Car, Nifty Highway Henry, Tin Lithograph, Windup, 10 In. 3500.00
Car, Oldsmobile, Surrey Top, Friction, Bandai, 1900s 100.00
Car, Police, Battery Operated, Japan, 1960s 45.00
Car, Police, Tin, Cortland, 9 In. 85.00
Car, Pontiac, 1964, GTO, AMT 135.00
Car, Porsche 356, Prototype, Windup & Battery Operated, Germany, 1950 .... 1600.00
Car, Porsche, 911, Battery Operated, Remote Control, Bandai, Box 50.00
Car, Racing Set, Dodge Charger Road Race, 1967 .... 95.00
Car, Racing, Arrow, Dooling, Powered 1895.00
Car, Racing, Bluebird, Kingsbury 1980.00
Car, Racing, Camaro, Taiyo, 10 In. 60.00
Car, Racing, Camaro, Z28, Battery Operated, Box 75.00
Car, Racing, Dick Dastardly, Comic Car, Corgie 90.00
Car, Racing, Driver, Rubber Tires, Painted Tinplate, Marklin, 11 In. 660.00
Car, Racing, Hubley, Cast Iron 175.00
Car, Racing, Marx, Windup 60.00
Car, Racing, McCoy Powered, Dooling .... 1495.00 To 2295.00
Car, Racing, Mercedes, Painted Tin, Rubber Tires, Windup, Marklin 500.00
Car, Racing, Mustang, Battery Operated, Box .... 55.00 To 65.00
Car, Racing, Porsche, Rally, Battery Operated, Box 85.00
Car, Racing, Timbledrome, 9 In. 230.00
Car, Racing, Tin Lithograph, Pull Rod Action, Elnee, 1930s, 11 In. 195.00
Car, Racing, White Rubber Wheels, Hubley, 7 In. 185.00
Car, Radio 4012, Windup, Schuco, Box 462.00
Car, Rocket Racer, Marx, 1930s 300.00
Car, Rolls Royce, Carbriolet, Keywind, Tinplate, Wells, 9 In. 357.50
Car, Rolls Royce, Friction, Rubber Tires, Linemar, 5 In. 115.00
Car, Sedan, Bing, Tin Lithograph, Germany, 6 In. 330.00
Car, Sedan, Electric Lights, Wyandote, 9 1/2 In. 95.00
Car, Sedan, Model A, Arcade, Cast Iron, Orange, 6 3/4 In. 1320.00
Car, Shaking Antique, Craston, Box 180.00
Car, Sheriff, Driver, Turns Siren, Battery Operated 275.00
Car, Sports, Schuco Tacho Examico, Windup, Tin, 1940s, 6 1/2 In. 300.00
Car, Sportsman's Convertible, 2-Way Top, Wyandotte, Box, 12 1/4 In. 375.00
Car, Studebaker, Commander, Dinky, France 75.00
Car, Stutz, Driver, Windup, Orange & Red, Marx 200.00
Car, Tin Lizzie, Marx 225.00
Car, Tin Lizzie, Strauss 245.00
Car, Touring, 4 Doors, Friction, Black Rubber Tires, Linemar, 5 1/2 In. 115.00
Car, Touring, 4 Passengers, Georges Carette No. 50, 1900s 5170.00
Car, Touring, Clockwork, Tin, Germany 400.00
Car, Touring, Dayton Group, Friction, 16 In. 695.00
Car, Touring, Friction, Wood, Tin & Cast Iron, 7 3/4 In. 350.00
Car, Touring, Tin Lithograph, Friction, Germany, 5 1/2 In. 357.00
Car, Touring, Tin Lithograph, Germany, 9 In. 137.00
Car, Touring, Windup, Tin Lithograph, Spoked Wheels, c.1912, 12 1/4 In. 6050.00
Car, Transport, Wyandotte 65.00
Car, Uncle Wiggly, Marx 357.00
Car, Visible V-8 Engine, Battery Operated, Renwal 75.00
Car, Volkswagen, Friction, 1950s, Japan 45.00
Car, Volvo, Police Department, Keywind 18.00
Car, Whoopee, 4 College Students, Witty Slogans, Reverses, Marx, 1946 .... 265.00
Car, Wienermobile, Oscar Mayer 125.00
Car, Winnebago, Barbie 65.00
Car, X, With Driver, Windup, Tin, Box, Occupied Japan 150.00
Carousel, Airship, Keywind, Tin, Germany, Box, Early 1900s 3300.00
Carousel, Electric, 2 Tiers, Papier-Mache Horses, 1920s, 36 x 42 In. 3245.00
Carousel, Music Box, Tin Lithograph, Plastic Figures, Mattel 95.00
Carousel, Rocket Shape, Cars Revolve, Windup, Tin Lithograph, Germany 115.00
Carousel, Sail Away, Musical, Unique Art 280.00
Carousel, Wolverine, 1930s .... 650.00 To 700.00

Carpet Sweeper, Bissel, Ohio Art 10.00
Carpet Sweeper, Little Gem, Bissell 20.00
Carpet Sweeper, Little Handy, Tin Lithograph 45.00
Carpet Sweeper, Little Queen, Bissell, 1940s 40.00
Carpet Sweeper, Little Susy 12.50
Carpet Sweeper, Premier 35.00
Carpet Sweeper, Susy Goose 11.00
Carriage, Doll's, All-Metal Products 65.00
Carriage, Doll's, Black Fringed Surrey, Joel Elis 550.00
Carriage, Doll's, Cinderella's, Bliss 1700.00
Carriage, Doll's, Hood, Metal 30.00
Carriage, Doll's, Leatherette 15.00
Carriage, Doll's, South Bend Toy Co., 1920s 165.00
Carriage, Doll's, Stenciled Body, Convertible Cloth Top, Spoke Wheels 330.00
Carriage, Doll's, Victorian, Bentwood Construction, Wooden Wheels 310.00
Carriage, Doll's, Victorian, Leather Canopy, Wooden Wheels, Red Cushions 715.00
Carriage, Doll's, Victorian, Wire 200.00
Carriage, Doll's, Wicker, Convertible Top, Steinfed, 1920s, 32 1/2 In. 225.00
Carriage, Doll's, Wicker, Hood, Green 90.00
Carriage, Doll's, Wicker, Lloyd Looms, 1917 .... 185.00
Carriage, Doll's, Wicker, Opera Windows 190.00
Cart, Blackman In Seat, Pulled By Ostrich, Windup, Tin, Lehmann 625.00
Cart, Canted Sides, Wooden Wheels, Metal Tires, Pull Handle, 34 In. 305.00
Cart, Goat, Yellow Kid, Cast Iron 192.50
Cart, Grocery, Metal, 1930s 98.00
Cart, Sand & Gravel, 2 Horses, Kenton, 1946 .... 325.00
Case, Carrying, Rudolph Reindeer, 1950s 25.00
Cash Register, Fisher-Price 25.00
Cash Register, Tin, Red 55.00
Cash Register, Tom Thumb 22.00
Cash Register, Tom Thumb, Box 32.00
Cat & Ball, Lever Drive, Tin, 7 In. 125.00
Cat & Ball, Windup, Tin, Marx, 5 1/2 In. 55.00
Cat, Embroidered Face & Paws, Lays Flat, 10 In. 65.00
Cat, Fluffy, Sitting, Blue Tip Fur, Button, Steiff, 11 In. 1250.00
Cat, Painted Wood, Painted Eyes, Schoenhut 275.00
Cat, Pip-Squeak, Cloth Covered Bellows, Papier-Mache, 5 1/4 In. 85.00
Cat, Pushing Ball, Straw Stuffed, Keywind 125.00
Cat, Squeak, Composition, Painted, On Bellows, Late 19th Century, 8 In. 1320.00
Cat, With Ball, Cloth Covered, Windup, Tin, 5 In. 20.00
Caterpillar, Arcade No. 270, Steel, 1920s, 8 1/2 In. 1000.00
Cecil The Sea Serpent, Talking 110.00
Cement Mixer, Britain, No. 9843 .... 11.00
Cement Mixer, Structo, Steel 95.00
Chair, Doll's, Ladderback, Rush Set, Oak, 16 In. 35.00
Chair, Doll's, Ladderback, Woven Splint Seat, 13 In. 90.00
Chair, Doll's, Lounge, Folding, Striped Canvas & Wood 30.00
Chair, Doll's, Oak, Ladderback, Rush Seat, Block Legs, 16 In. 30.00
Chair, Doll's, Twig 20.00
Chair, Doll's, White, Homemade, 10 3/4 In. 70.00
Chalkboard, Wooden Frame, 15 x 19 In. 15.00
Charlie Chimp, Windup, Japan, Charlie Does Hula 45.00
Charlie Weaver, Battery Operated 75.00
Chemistry Set, Gilbert, 1936 .... 95.00
Chemistry Set, Mr. Wizard's Experiments, 1970 .... 25.00
Chemistry Set, Skillcraft, No. PM130, Box 55.00
Cherry Cook, Celluloid, Windup, Occupied Japan 42.00
Chest, Doll's, Empire Style, Pine, Dark Finish, 9 1/2 In. 50.00
Chest, Doll's, Pine, Old Red Paint, Whittled Crest, 4 Drawers, 12 In. 275.00
Chest, Drawers, Original Paint, 1890–1900 .... 275.00
Chicken In Cage, Mechanical, Wooden Cage, Feathered Chicken, 10 In. 195.00
Chicken Snatcher, Tin Lithograph, Germany, 7 In. 1450.00
Chicken, Clucking, Baldwin, Tin, Lays Marbles, Wyandotte 35.00

Chicken, Egg Laying, Mechanical, Feather, Papier–Mache, 5 Eggs, Germany 750.00
Child On Swing, Windup, Celluloid, Red Costume, 18 In. 130.00
Chimes, 3–Face, Silver Flashed, Twig Base, Push Toy, Watrous, 6 In. 88.00
Chimpanzee, Tan Mohair, Jointed, Glass Eyes, Button, Steiff, 1930s, 11 In. 137.50
Choo–Choo, Fisher–Price, No. 215 .... 45.00
Choo–Choo, Keebler, Miniature, Box 59.00
Choo–Choo, Windup, Hat Moves Up & Down, Whistle 45.00
Circus Set, Tent, Animals, Performers, Schoenhut, 21 Piece 2800.00
Circus Train, Engine, 2 Cars, Clown, Animals, Fisher–Price 35.00
Circus Train, No. 991, Fisher–Price 25.00
Circus Wagon, 2 Bears, Steiff 400.00
Circus Wagon, 6 Opening Cages, Metal Sheels, c.1900, 15 1/2 x 18 In. 675.00
Circus Wagon, Hill Climber, Driver, Lions, Dayton–Hill, Cast Iron 650.00
Circus Wagon, Overland, 2 Horses, Riders, Driver, Cast Iron, 14 In. 450.00
Circus Wagon, Overland, 6 Musicians, Kenton, 15 In. 650.00
Circus, Bear Pulling Toy, Tin, Steel, Wolverine, 10 In. 130.00
Circus, Mignot, 3 Tiered, Tin Lithograph, Box, 30 Piece 795.00
Circus, Overland, With Bear, Kenton, Cast Iron, 14 In. 450.00
Clock Radio, 3 Mice On Clock, Turn Dial, Fisher–Price 20.00
Clock, Talking, Fisher–Price 55.00
Clothespin Set, Doll's, Box, 1940s 12.00
Clothespin Set, Little Lulu, Box 85.00
Clothespin Set, Little Miss Clothesline, Original Card 9.00
Clothespins, Bag, Doll's, 33 Piece 22.00
Clown, Barrel Walker, Tin Lithograph, Windup, Box 900.00
Clown, Clockwork, Balancing On Chairs, Striped Costume, c.1890, 10 In. 1320.00
Clown, Doing Handstands, Windup, Chein 145.00
Clown, Dressed As Duck, Riding Trike, Tin Lithograph, Windup, Germany 95.00
Clown, Drummer, Cloth Dress, Plaster, Clockwork, 27 In. 350.00
Clown, Jumping, Bozo, 1960, Kohner 35.00
Clown, Lion Jumps Hoop, Windup, Tin 145.00
Clown, Nodder, Glass Eyes, German, 28 In. 1100.00
Clown, Riding Bucking Horse, Pull, Wood, S. A. Smith Mfg. Co., 12 1/2 In. 375.00
Clown, Skating, Tin, Windup 295.00
Clown, Tumbling, Windup, Japan, 6 1/2 In. 135.00
Clownie, Steiff, 1950s, 14 In. 150.00
Coal Cart, Drawn By 2 Wooden Horses, Ride–On, Wood, 31 In. 495.00
Coffee Set, Doll's, Little Red Riding Hood, Tin, Ohio Arts, 4 Piece 25.00
Coloring Set, Kit Carson, Saddlebag 75.00
Coloring Set, U. N. C. L. E., Box, 1965 .... 65.00
Combat Engineer Construction Set, Hasbro 15.00
Concertina, Cardstock Ends, Wood Grip, Paper Bellows, c.1880, 6 1/4 In. 60.00
Construction Set, American Skyline, Elgo, Box, 1940s 25.00
Coon Jigger, Strauss, Box 775.00
Coronation Coach, George VI & Elizabeth, 8 Horses, Britain, No. 1470 .... 335.00
Couch, Fainting, Doll's, 21 In. 230.00
Cow, Mohair, Steiff, 1950–60, 4 In. 60.00
Cow, Pull, Hide Covered, Platform, Metal Wheels, 19 5/8 In. 300.00
Cow, Straw Stuffed Fabric, Metal Base, Wheels, 19 In. 305.00
Cowboy, Celluloid, On Tin Horse, Windup, Box, 6 x 6 In. 125.00
Cowboy, On Donkey, Windup, Japan 35.00
Cowboy, On Horse, Moving Arm & Gun, Rotating Lasso, Windup 175.00
Cowboy, On Horse, Windup, Japan 180.00
Cowboy, Outfit, Rifle, 2 Cap Guns, Spurs, Wristcuffs, Carnell, 1960, Box 250.00
Cowboy, Set, Diecast, Box, Crescent 60.00
Cowboy, With Gun On Horse, Celuloid, Windup, 1950s, Japan 100.00
Crabby Lobster, Original Tag, Steiff, 7 In. 175.00
Cradle, Doll's, Basket Woven, Husk Filled Mattress, Tulip Rockers 172.00
Cradle, Doll's, Heart Cut–Outs, Poplar, 22 3/4 In. 195.00
Cradle, Doll's, Hooded, Poplar, Brown Finish, 14 In. 120.00
Cradle, Doll's, Hooded, Rockers, Pine, 12 3/4 In. 115.00
Cradle, Doll's, Mission Style, Walnut, c.1920 .... 125.00
Cradle, Doll's, Slat Sides, Ball Trim, Wooden 22.50

◆◆◆

Do not dry clean white fabric dresses. They tend to turn yellow. If possible, remove any rusty metal snaps or hooks, then boil the dress about 15 minutes in a weak solution of water and dry bleach. Dry naturally, not in a dryer, then iron.

◆◆◆

Cradle, Doll's, Splint	110.00
Crap Shooter, Cragstan, Battery Operated	95.00
Croquet Set, Trixy Toy, Inside Type, Complete	28.00
Cub, Sleeping, Speckled Beige & Brown, Wiskers, Steiff, 1950s, 9 In.	44.00
Cupboard, Doll's, Pine, Dark Green	25.00
Cupboard, Doll's, Step Back, Open Top, 2 Doors, Handmade, 15 x 10 x 26 In	325.00
Cutlery Set, Spoons, Original Card, 6 Piece	15.00
Daisy, Jolly Drumming Duck, Battery Operated	225.00
Dancing Couple, Windup, Celluloid, Occupied Japan	70.00
Dancing Merry Chimp, Battery, Original Box	130.00
Dancing Senorita, Bakelite, Irwin Corp, Windup	55.00
Daredevil, Tin Lithograph, Lehmann, 7 1/2 In.	198.00
Dart Board, Major League Baseball, Metallic, Cardboard Envelope, 1950s	44.00
Dart Board, Tim Holt, Box	225.00
Dart, Space Patrol Gun	65.00
Dennis The Menace, Battery, Original	275.00
Dennis The Menace, Wooden, Pull String Arms & Legs Move, 6 In.	85.00
Derrik, Construction, Wooden Wheels, Buddy L, 24 In.	165.00
Dice Cage, Chuck–A–Luck, Box, 11 In.	40.00
Dinner Set, Ohio Art, Tin, 18 Piece	46.00
Dino The Dinosaur, Fred Riding On Top, Battery, 1962, Marx, 12 x 18 In.	290.00
Dinosaur, Plastic, 1972	30.00
Dinosaur, Steiff	650.00
Dippee Bug, Pull Toy, Rubber, Colorful, Box	40.00
Dirigible, Graf–Zeppelin, Tippco, c.1935	1430.00
Dirigible, Small Cast Man, Cardboard Propeller, Windup, Tin, 8 In.	375.00
Dish Set, Cinderella, Mirro Aluminum, Box, 27 Piece	65.00
Doctor's Cart, Painted, Cast Iron, Doctor, Horse, 10 In.	295.00
Dog, Begging Poodle, Windup, Occupied Japan	65.00
Dog, Bulldog, On Platform, Cast Iron Wheels, Button, Steiff, 14 In.	395.00
Dog, Bulldog, Papier–Mache, Nodding Head, Growls When Pull Chain	467.00
Dog, Bulldog, Papier–Mache, Pull Toy, Nodding Head, France, 17 1/2 In.	600.00
Dog, Cockie, Steiff, Tag, 1950s, 4 In.	65.00
Dog, Drinking Milk, Battery Operated	55.00
Dog, Flipo The Jumping, Back Flip, Lands On Hind Feet, 3 1/2 In.	145.00
Dog, German Shepherd, Pull Ring Activates Voice Box, Steiff, 23 In.	150.00
Dog, Happy Doggie, Windup, T. N. Japan, Box, 1950s	65.00
Dog, Happy Pup, Windup, Box	25.00
Dog, Itchy, Celluloid, Windup, Box	125.00
Dog, Scotty, Windup, Runs In Circles, Schuco, 5 In.	135.00
TOY, DOLL, see Doll	
Dollhouse, 2 Bedrooms, Dining Room, Living Room, Tootsietoy, No. 12	1400.00
Dollhouse, 2 Story, Wood, c.1910, 31 x 25 In.	275.00
Dollhouse, 4 Rooms, Tabletop, McLoughlin, Folds For Storage, c.1893	650.00
Dollhouse, Bathroom, Tin Lithograph, Germany, c.1915, 14 1/2 In.	450.00
Dollhouse, Bliss, 9 1/2 In.	795.00
Dollhouse, Celmet Products, Cardboard, Envelope, 1923, 16 x 8 x 9 In.	45.00
Dollhouse, Cottage, Wooden, Polychrome Paint, Asphalt Shingles, 29 In.	375.00
Dollhouse, Dream House, Barbie's, 1962	65.00
Dollhouse, Furniture, 3 Tufted Armchairs, Sofa, Red Paint, Cast Iron	295.00
Dollhouse, Furniture, Alarm Clock, Metal, Germany	38.00
Dollhouse, Furniture, Armoire, Shackman	20.00

Dollhouse, Furniture, Bathroom, Cast Iron, 3 Piece 75.00
Dollhouse, Furniture, Bedside Table, Cindy, Marx 12.00
Dollhouse, Furniture, Boston Rocker, Shackman 15.00
Dollhouse, Furniture, Chair, Metal, Germany 28.00
Dollhouse, Furniture, Cook Stove, Royal, Cast Iron 22.50
Dollhouse, Furniture, Couch, 2 Chairs, Leatherette 110.00
Dollhouse, Furniture, Cupboard, Yellow Paint, Hardwoods, 14 In. 95.00
Dollhouse, Furniture, Deacon's Bench, Shackman 20.00
Dollhouse, Furniture, Desk, Rolltop 30.00
Dollhouse, Furniture, Electric Fan, Metal, France 48.00
Dollhouse, Furniture, Grand Piano, Petite Princess, 9 Piece 65.00
Dollhouse, Furniture, Hutch, Washing Machine, Mangle, Cast Iron, Arcade 275.00
Dollhouse, Furniture, Kitchen & Dinette, Penny Brite, Carton, 1963 .... 125.00
Dollhouse, Furniture, Kitchen Wall Unit, Tin Lithograph, Marx, 25 In. 155.00
Dollhouse, Furniture, Kitchen, Drawers, Equipment, Germany, 1920s 375.00
Dollhouse, Furniture, Kitchen, Tootsietoy, Box, 1930s 110.00
Dollhouse, Furniture, Living Room Set, ABC, Bliss 375.00
Dollhouse, Furniture, Luggage, Metal, Germany, 2 Piece 38.00
Dollhouse, Furniture, Mother, Father, Clock, Dustpan, Stool, Renwal 38.00
Dollhouse, Furniture, Parlour Set, French, 1875 .... 1575.00
Dollhouse, Furniture, Piano, Bench, Sofa, Chairs, Table, Bliss, 10 Piece 350.00
Dollhouse, Furniture, Piano, Bliss 150.00
Dollhouse, Furniture, Range, Cindy, Marx 10.00
Dollhouse, Furniture, Refrigerator & Desk, Renwal 15.00
Dollhouse, Furniture, Sewing Machine, France 48.00
Dollhouse, Furniture, Snow White, Refrigerator, Stove, Sink, Wolverine 95.00
Dollhouse, Furniture, Stove, Royal, Cast Iron, 4 1/4 In. 115.00
Dollhouse, Furniture, Stove, Sink & Toilet, Marx 25.00
Dollhouse, Furniture, Swing, Slatted, Wood 40.00
Dollhouse, Furniture, Table, Pie Crust Rim, Oval, Cast Iron 20.00
Dollhouse, Furniture, Vanity, Cindy, Marx 12.00
Dollhouse, Furniture, Wall Oven, Cindy, Marx 8.00
Dollhouse, Furniture, Wardrobe, Cindy, Marx 15.00
Dollhouse, Grimm's & Leeds, 1903 .... 275.00
Dollhouse, Log Cabin, Shingled Roof, Painted, 24 In. 250.00
Dollhouse, Paper Cover, 30 Glass Windows, Front Opens, 45 1/2 In. 750.00
Dollhouse, Paper Lithograph On Wood, Bliss, 2 Floors, 17 3/4 In 1210.00
Dollhouse, Sterns & Lyons, Box, 1881 .... 650.00
Dollhouse, Sunshine Family, Box 30.00
Dollhouse, Tin, With Disney Nursery Furniture, Marx 80.00
Dollhouse, Tin, With Plastic Furniture 50.00
Dollhouse, Victorian, American, 1800s 1250.00
Dolly's Nursing & Bath Set, Box 38.00
Donkey, Floppy, Steiff, 22 In. 75.00
Donkey, Pull Toy, Papier–Mache, Nodding Head, Gray Paint, 10 1/2 In. 225.00
Dresser, Doll's, Glove Boxes, Oak 178.00
Dresser, Empire, Key 325.00
Drinking Captain, Battery Operated 120.00
Drum Major, Tin, Wolverine 250.00
Drum, Gulliver's Travels, Tin, 1939 .... 50.00 To 100.00
Drum, Moon Mullins Painting, 23 In. 125.00
Drum, Ohio Art, 6 1/2 In. 22.00
Drum, Yankee Doodle Dandy Candy, Tin Lithograph, 5 1/2 In. 110.00
Drummer Boy, Moving Eyes, Battery Operated, Marx, 1930s 195.00
Drummer Boy, Tin Lithograph, Windup, Box, Marx 900.00
Drummer, Mad Russian, Windup, Marx, Box, 7 In. 100.00
Drummer, Panda, Clockwork, Rubber Head, Tin, 4 1/2 In. 35.00
Drumming Major, Tin, Wolverine, Windup 95.00
Drying Rack, Doll Clothes, Wooden, Folding, c.1880, 11 1/2 x 8 x 10 In. 85.00
Duck, Mamma & 3 Babies, Wobbling, Wood, Fisher–Price 175.00
Duck, Swimming, Windup, Haji 40.00
Duck, Waddles, Windup, Sailor Suit, Chein, 1930 .... 80.00
Duck, Windup, Chein 20.00

Ducky Cart, Mattel, Box	25.00
Ears, Dr. Spock, On Card, 1976	12.00
Earthmover, Dopeke	145.00
Electrol Fox Dog, 1960s, Steiff, 5 In.	325.00
Elephant, Blue Headdress, Pink, Sun Rubber Co.	10.00
Elephant, Bubble Blowing, Battery, Box	120.00
Elephant, Circus, Battery Operated, Box, 1950s	250.00
Elephant, Circus, Pedals Trike, Windup, Germany	115.00
Elephant, Jumbo No. 780, Fisher–Price	75.00
Elephant, On Wheels, Steiff, Early 1900	525.00
Elephant, Plush, Walks, Ears, Legs, Head Move, 5 In.	75.00
Elephant, Tan Mohair, Ear Button, Steiff, 3 3/4 x 5 In.	75.00
Elephant, Wooden, Pull Toy, Wheels, Gray & White, Blanket, 9 In.	85.00
Elsie, Wooden, Dance Toy	85.00
Emergency Medical Kit, The Rookies	16.00
Erector Set, Gilbert, No. 6 1/2, Electric, Book, 1948	90.00
Erector Set, Gilbert, No. 10 1/2, Carousel	245.00
Erector Set, Gilbert, No. 10053, Rocket Launcher	80.00
Erector Set, Mecanno 3X, Builds Train	145.00
Fainting Couch, Doll's, 17 In.	30.00
Farm Animal Set, Paper Lithograph, Milton Bradley, Box, 1940s	100.00
Farm Wagon, Scale Model, Painted, Stenciled, Feed Sacks, Barrels, 30 In.	275.00
Farm Wagon, With Horse & Driver, Windup, Wolverine	55.00
Farm, With House, Barn, Animals, People, Fence, Wooden, 2 5/8–In. Pieces	175.00
Farmer, Pushing Cart, Windup, Girard, Tin	185.00
Felix The Cat, Jointed, Leather Ears, Label, Schoenhut, Wooden, 4 In.	225.00
Felix The Cat, White Face, Leather Arms, Papier-Mache, 1927, 12 In.	425.00
Ferdinand The Bull, Tin, Windup, Marx	165.00 To 250.00
Ferris Wheel, Carette, 1890s	5800.00
Ferris Wheel, Chein	300.00
Finnegan, Windup, Unique Art	150.00
Fire Department, Fire Truck & Equipment, Wyandotte, Box	150.00
Fire Patrol Wagon, 2 Horses, 4 Firemen, Cast Iron, 18 In.	2200.00
Fire Pumper, 2 Horses, Driver, Cast Iron, 9 In.	125.00
Fire Pumper, Cast Iron & Brass, Weeden, Early 1900s	2200.00
Fire Pumper, Friction, Wood, Cast Iron & Sheet Metal, 11 1/4 In.	65.00
Fire Pumper, Pressed Steel, Painted, 14 In.	550.00
Fire Pumper, Richter & Co., Box	900.00
Fire Station, Tin, Cortland	45.00
Fire Truck, 2 Celluloid Firemen, Battery Operated, Marx, 12 In.	95.00
Fire Truck, 6 Wheels, Fisher–Price, Large	20.00
Fire Truck, Aerial, Buddy L	450.00
Fire Truck, Aerial, Ladders, Brass Bell, Buddy L, 1920s, 39 In.	925.00
Fire Truck, Cast Iron, Ladder, Kenton, 22 1/4 In.	1150.00
Fire Truck, Doepke, 29 In.	75.00
Fire Truck, GMC, Buddy L, 12 In.	95.00
Fire Truck, Hook & Ladder, Buddy L, 30 In.	75.00
Fire Truck, Hook & Ladder, Diecast, Rubber Tires, Hubley, 18 In.	100.00
Fire Truck, Hook & Ladder, Iron, 33 In. ....*Illus*	550.00
Fire Truck, Hook & Ladder, Structo, 1940s, 36 In.	85.00
Fire Truck, Hook & Ladder, Structo, 32 In.	50.00
Fire Truck, Hubley, No. 468	80.00
Fire Truck, Jack–Like Lever, Pressed Metal, Kingsbury, 1930, 23 1/2 In.	375.00
Fire Truck, Kingsbury, Rubber Tires, 18 In.	200.00
Fire Truck, Ladder, Cast Iron, Hubley, 5 1/2 In.	55.00
Fire Truck, Mechanical, Painted, Germany, 11 In.	55.00
Fire Truck, Pontiac, Arcade, Cast Iron, 7 In.	355.00
Fire Truck, Tonka, 1950, 32 In.	230.00
Fire Truck, Wyandotte, 28 In.	180.00
Fire Wagon, Horse Drawn, Cast Iron, 1910, 15 In.	185.00
Fire Wagon, Patrol, 4 Ringing Fireman, 1 Driver, 2 Horses, Ives	1700.00
Firehouse, Mechanical, Tin & Iron, 10 x 13 1/4 In. ....*Illus*	1760.00
Firehouse, Tin Lithograph, Wyandotte, 1930s, 6 1/2 x 8 In.	195.00

Toy, Firehouse, Mechanical, Tin & Iron,
10 x 13 1/4 In.

Toy, Fire Truck, Hook & Ladder, Iron, 33 In.

Fireman, Climbing, Windup, Marx, Box	195.00 To 285.00
Fish Bowl, Mechanical Plunger, Germany, Tin, 4 In.	40.00
Fishing Outfit, Gabby Hayes, Carry All, Complete, Metal Case	300.00
Fishing Polar Bear, Catches Fish, Magnetized Pole, Battery	160.00
Flashlight, Alligator Shape	15.00
Flashlight, Atomix Pistol, Rex Mars, Marx, Box	155.00
Flashlight, Captain Ray-O-Vac, Comic Book, Box	55.00
Flashlight, Optic Ozan & Magic Lantern, Box	110.00
Flashlight, Sgt. Preston, Secret 2-Way Signal	30.00
Flippo, Tin Lithograph, Marx	50.00
Fly, Hinged Wings, Traces of Gold, Cast Iron, 4 1/2 In.	25.00
Flying Saucer, Astronaut, Light, Siren, Japan, 7 1/2 In.	99.00
Fort Apache, Marx, Box	40.00
Fort Apache, Set, Sears Heritage	50.00
Fox Chasing Goose, Clockwork, Flapping Wings, Tin, Germany, 10 1/8 In.	660.00
Fox, Magician, Windup	325.00
Fox, Standing, Mohair, Steiff, Pre-1958, 3 In.	75.00
Foxy Alphabet Board	45.00
Fred Flintstone On Dino, Windup	375.00
Fred Flintstone's Bedrock Band, Battery Operated, Hanna Barbera, 1962	375.00
Freight Station, Tin Lithograph, Wired, Ives, No. 115, Box, 10 1/2 In.	715.00
Friendship Space Capsule, Cranstan, 1950s	120.00
Frisbee, Star Trek, 1967	40.00
Funland Tea Cup Ride, Battery Operated	125.00
G. I. Joe & K-9 Pups, Mechanical, Unique Art, 9 In. ....*Illus*	110.00
G. I. Joe Jouncing Jeep	150.00
G. I. Joe Training Center	70.00
Gabby Duck, Fisher-Price, No. 767	35.00
TOY, GAME, see Game	
Garage, Automatic Car Wash, Car, Windup, Tin, Marx	225.00
Garage, Automatic, Tin, Windup Family Car, Marx	165.00
Garage, Clapboard Siding, Shingle Roof, Hinged Doors, Wooden, 7 x 11 In.	55.00
Garage, Keystone, Fiberboard	22.00
Gee-Tar, Yogi Bear, Box	65.00
Giraffe, Pull Toy, Wooden, Tick Tock, 9 1/2 x 16 In.	135.00
Giraffe, Steiff, Open Mouth, 5 Ft.	1450.00
Giraffe, Twill Covered, Glass Eyes, Papier-Mache, Clockwork, 31 3/4 In.	335.00
Girl, With Hoola Hoop, Tin, Working Condition	75.00
Globe, Tin Lithograph, Rand McNally, 1950s, 11 x 8 In.	125.00
Gloves, Mr. Jinx, Huckleberry Hound	30.00
Gloves, Zorro	25.00

Goat Drawn Wagon, Tin Lithograph, Germany, 8 1/4 In. 75.00
Going To The Fair, Friction, Tin Lithograph, Lehmann, 6 1/2 In. 1260.00
Gold Detector, Terry & Pirates 70.00
Golden Goose, Windup, Tin Lithograph, Marx, 1930s 40.00
Golf Set, Indoor, Female Golfer, Booklet, Score Card, Ball, Schoenhut 475.00
Goose, Pull, Articulated Head, Green Platform, Penny Toy, 3 1/2 In. 302.00
Gorilla, Growling, Mohair & Celluloid 130.00
Gorilla, King Louie, Paper Label, Ear Button, Steiff, 11 In. 85.00
Grader, Road, Structo 55.00
Graf Zeppelin, Steel Craft, Sheet Metal, 30 1/2 In. 240.00
Grandpa Munster, Remco 150.00
Grasshopper, Movable, Noisemaker, Hubley, 9 In. ....*Illus* 355.00
Groundhog, Mohair, Steiff, 1950–60, 7 In. 50.00
Gun & Holster Set, Deputy Dawg, Halco 35.00
Gun & Holster Set, Wagon Train, Double Set, Major Adams On Holster, Box 300.00
Gun & Holster Set, Wild Bill Hickock & Jingles, Box 150.00
Gun Set, Double Holster, Wrist Cuffs, Hubley, Box 110.00
Gun Set, Matt Dillon, Gunsmoke Guns, Halco 500.00
Gun Set, Tall Man, Double Leather Holster, Hubley, Box 275.00
Gun, BB, Buck Jones, Daisy, No. 107 .... 135.00
Gun, Bubble, Outer Space, 1950s, Box 35.00
Gun, Bull's–Eye Band Shooter, H & H Novelty, Cleveland, Ohio 25.00
Gun, Cork, King & Markham, 17 In. 25.00
Gun, Flintlock Jr., Hubley, Box 35.00
Gun, Flip Special, Used By Rifleman, Hubley 275.00
Gun, For Your Eyes Only, Crescent, 1981, 7 In. 80.00
Gun, Holster, Girl From U. N. C. L. E., 1966, Lonestar, Box 120.00
Gun, Kilgore, Cast Iron, 1925 .... 34.00
Gun, Lunar Landing, Prototype, Marx 260.00
Gun, Midgie Beretta, James Bond 007, 1960s, 3 1/2 In. 95.00
Gun, Pellet, Smith & Wesson 100.00
Gun, Pioneer, Hubley 125.00
Gun, Pistol, Clicker, Red Ranger 24.00
Gun, Pop, Cork, Daisy 20.00
Gun, Pop, Red Ryder, Double Barrel 75.00
Gun, Ray, Hydrogen, Space Patrol .... 135.00 To 150.00
Gun, Ray, Space Patrol, Hydrogen, Ring 150.00
Gun, Red Fox Missile Launching, Hubley 85.00
Gun, Rubber Band, Repeating, Kingston Prod. Co., 12 In. 45.00
Gun, Secret Ray, Captain Video, Instructions, Box 150.00
Gun, Shoot–N–Shell, Mattel, Box 300.00
Gun, Shoots A Dart, Pressed Metal, Wyandotte, c.1935, 7 1/2 In. 60.00
Gun, Snub Nose . 38, Mattel, Box 200.00
Gun, Space Landing Craft, Apollo Eagle, Tin, Plastic, Japan, 9 1/2 In. 88.00
Gun, Space Patrol Cosmic Ray Protector, In Pack 225.00
Gun, Space, Battery Operated, Adjustable Sound Control, Daisy, 20 In. 125.00
Gun, Space, Take–Apart Puzzle, Key Chain 15.00
Gun, Squirt, Daiby, Metal 30.00
Gun, Squirt, DIA 35.00
Gun, Squirt, Hand Grip, Plastic 5.00
Gun, Squirt, Planet of The Apes, Head Shape 20.00
Gun, Wyatt Earp, Holster, Box 175.00
Hand Car, Hoky Poky, Wyandotte 225.00
Hanson Cab, With Horse, Driver & Passenger, Kenton, Box, Iron, 15 3/4 In. 280.00
Hay Wagon, Horse Drawn, S. A. Smith, c.1900, 12 In. 625.00
Hay Wagon, Stenciled Label, Steiff 48851, Metal Fittings, 37 In. 325.00
Headshrinker Kit, Witch Doctor 100.00
Helmet, Bubble, Space Patrol, Collar 950.00
Hen, Cackling, Fisher–Price 30.00
Hi–Jinx Clown, Monkey, Battery Operated 275.00
Highchair, Doll's, Wood, 1940s 38.00
Hike–O–Meter, Wheaties, Original Mailer 45.00
Hippopotamus, Schoenhut 475.00

Toy, Lion, Lying, Glass Eyes, Steiff, 16 In.   *Toy, Horse, Standing, Brown Horsehair,*
12 In.

Hobbyhorse, Wooden, White, Applied Harness, Hair, Saddle, 1917, 46 In.	275.00
Hobbyhorse, Leather Saddle & Stirrups, Red Painted Rocker, 1917, 46 In.	305.00
Hobbyhorse, Painted, Saddle, 1840-50	1895.00
Hobbyhorse, Wooden, Iron Tipped Wooden Wheel, Leather Strap, 44 In.	125.00
Hobo Clown, Accordion Player, Cymbal Playing Monkey, Battery Operated	165.00
Horn, Birds Tending Nest On Branch, Celluloid, 5 3/4 In.	35.00
Horse & Cart, Pull, Gibbs, Wood, Wire, Sheet Metal & Cast Iron, 7 In.	40.00
Horse & Cart, Pull, Sheet Steel, Silver Horse, Leather Ear, Blue, 27 In.	900.00
Horse & Rider, Tin Lithograph, Windup, Germany	175.00
Horse, Circus, Schoenhut, Brown	165.00
Horse, Circus, Schoenhut, White	195.00
Horse, Dapple Gray, Plaster, Wood Legs, Ears, Hair Tail, Pull Toy, 10 In.	145.00
Horse, Ladder Wagon, Pull Toy, 2 Drivers, Tin, Painted, 22 1/2 In.	8300.00
Horse, On Wheels, Dapple Gray Paint, Wooden, 44 In.	450.00
Horse, Pinto, Pull, On Wheels	160.00
Horse, Pull Toy, Hide Covered, Leather Harness, Wooden Platform, 10 In.	440.00
Horse, Pull Toy, Painted Tin, Hull & Stafford, 1880s, 7 In.	385.00
Horse, Pull Toy, Polomino, Felt, Glass Eyes, Wood Frame, Tin Wheels	115.00
Horse, Pull Toy, Wooden Base, Casters, Early 20th Century, 25 x 26 In.	175.00
Horse, Pull Toy, Wooden Platform, Iron Wheels	985.00
Horse, Pulling Iron Sulky, Full-Bodied Tin, 4 1/2 x 9 1/2 In.	260.00
Horse, Red & Black Saddle, Chestnut Repaint, 38 In.	225.00
Horse, Rocking Glider, White & Dapple Gray, Glass Eyes, 52 In.	6300.00
Horse, Rocking, Apaloosa, Horsehide Cover, Leather Saddle, c.1880, 36 In.	3025.00
Horse, Rocking, Carved & Painted, Leather Saddle, 19th Century	880.00
Horse, Rocking, Green Repaint, Red Striping, 32 In.	750.00
Horse, Rocking, Hide Cover, White Horsehair Mane, Black Tail, 73 In.	800.00
Horse, Rocking, Papier-Mache, Wooden Frame, Green Over Red, 45 x 33 In.	130.00
Horse, Rocking, Prancing Position, Hide Cover, Horse Hair, Glass Eyes	2900.00
Horse, Rocking, Running Deer Painted On Platform, 29 1/2 x 48 3/4 In.	3600.00
Horse, Rocking, Stationary Base, Dapple Gray Paint, 35 In.	600.00
Horse, Rocking, Stuffed Straw Body, Leather Saddle, 30 In.	215.00
Horse, Rocking, Stuffed, Rocking Mechanism, Green Paint	1600.00
Horse, Rocking, Wooden Silhouette, Upholstered Seat, Painted, 32 In.	125.00
Horse, Rocking, Wooden, Composition, Cowhide Cover, Platform, 36 x 33 In.	250.00
Horse, Rocking, Wooden, Red & White, Black Mane, Iron Stirrups, 46 In.	775.00
Horse, Standing, Brown Horsehair, 12 In. ....*Illus*	190.00
Horse, Stylized, Wooden, Small Head, White, Brown Hooves, 12 3/4 In.	425.00
Horse, Windup, Metal, Leather Tail, Occupied Japan, 5 In.	40.00
Horse-Drawn Wagon, Amish Style Driver, Lancaster Toys, 8 In.	125.00
Horse-Drawn Wagon, Yankee Notions, George Brown, Stenciled Name	2970.00
Horses & Buckboard, Pull Toy, Tin, 12 1/4 In.	500.00
Horses, Cart, Pull Toy, Driver & Passenger, Wooden, Painted, 12 In.	150.00
House, Hollywood Bungalow, Awnings, Garage, Marx, Tin, Celluloid, 1935	265.00
Humpheymobile, House, On 2 Wheels, Tin Plate, Keywind, Wyandotte	880.00
Humpty Dumpty, Pull, Hands Rotate As It Moves, Fisher-Price	20.00
Hurdy Gurdy, Tin Lithograph, Plays Music, Converse, c.1900	335.00

Hy–Que, Amazing Monkey, 6 Actions, Rosko, 1960s, 17 In. 350.00
Ice Cream Vendor, Windup, China, 4 1/2 In. 50.00
Ice Cream Vendor, Windup, Occupied Japan 165.00
Ice Truck, Buddy L, Black, Yellow & Red, 26 In. 1430.00
Indian, Nutty, Drummer, Windup, Marx 35.00
Iron & Board, Doll's 40.00
Iron, Dolly Dell, Chrome 27.50
Iron, Double Heart Shape, Figural Step Down, Cast Iron, 3 1/2 In. 295.00
Iron, Electric, Wolverine, Box 15.00
Iron, Sunny Suzy, Wolverine 10.00
Ironing Board, Folding Metal Legs, Saginaw 25.00
Ironing Board, Little Bo–Peep, Wolverine, Metal 25.00
Ironing Board, Padded Mat 65.00
Ironing Board, Sunnie Miss, Ohio Art 25.00
Ironing Board, Wall Mount, 14 x 5 In. 50.00
Ironing Board, Wooden, Dated 1943 .... 30.00
Jack–In–The–Box, Clown, Papier–Mache, 5 x 5 In. 300.00
Jack–In–The–Box, Mickey Mouse, 1958 .... 70.00
Jackson Park Trolley, Wood, Paper Litho, Horse–Drawn Trolley, 28 In. 3400.00
Jalopy, Trikauto Mechanical Wonder, Strauss, Tin, Windup, 1920s 400.00
James Bond Accessory Pack, Loose–Scuba Tank, Spear Gun 30.00
Jeep, Jumping, Tin Lithograph, Marx, 5 1/2 In. 99.00
Jeep, Tonka, Blue 35.00
Jigger, Black, Keywind, Painted Composition & Wood, Dressed Figure 2200.00
Jockey Bell, Nickel Plated, Watrous, 7 In. 176.00
Jockey, Horse, On Platform, Painted Tin, 9 1/2 In. 440.00
Jocko, The Climbing Monkey, Box 100.00
Joe Penner, Tin Lithograph, Marx, 8 In. 209.00
Joker, Billiken, Windup, Japan, Box 125.00
Joker, Squirt Head, England, 4 In. 25.00
Jolly Chimp, Battery Operated 65.00
Jolly Daddy, Smoking Elephant, Battery Operated, Japan, Box 175.00
Jonah & Whale, Jonah Pops In & Out As Pulled, Cast Iron, 5 15/16 In. 550.00
Josie T6 Cow, Box, Battery 265.00
Jumping Jack, Clown Head, Wooden Body, Composition, Painted, 18 In. 105.00
Jumping Jack, On Stick, Plume On Hat, Wood, 24 In. 250.00
Jumping Jack, Painted Face, 8 1/2 In. 85.00
Jungle Jumbo, Battery Operated, Original Box 450.00
Jungle Man, Spear, Tin, Marx 225.00
Kadi, 2 Queued Chinese Porters, Baggage Litter, Windup, Lehmann 742.00
Kaleidoscope, Claremont, New Hampshire, Cardboard & Brass, 13 1/2 In. 610.00
Kaleidoscope, Glass Bits, Canes & Vials, Brass Turning Ring, C. G. Bus 522.50
Kaleidoscope, Ship's Wheel Style, Brush 475.00
Kamera, Kookie, Ideal Toy Co., 1968 .... 35.00
Katzenjammer Kids, Cast Iron, Heine Driving, Mama Spanking, 12 In. 2800.00
Kiddie Grocery Store, Counter, 8 Sample Packages, Box 245.00
King Arthur Sword & Shield, Tin, Marx 50.00
Kitchen Range, Wolverine 40.00
Kitchen Set, Tin, Coppertone, Breadbox, Cake, Cookie Jar, Canister, 5 Pc. 15.00
Kitchen Set, Wooden, Washtub, Bowls, Masher, 13 Piece 35.00
Kitchen Tool Set, Mother's Little Helper, Box, 1923, 5 Piece 70.00
Kitty, Fishing, Battery Operated, No Fish, Japan 250.00
Kraft Cameraman, T.V. Show, Plastic, Yellow, Black, 1950s 150.00

◆◆

Restoration of an old dollhouse should be restrained. Wash it, repair the structural problems, repaint as little as possible, and redecorate with appropriate old wallpaper fabrics and paint colors.

◆◆

Lady Driver, Woman In Cart, Tin Lithograph, Germany, 4 1/2 In.	357.00
Lamb, Painted Wood, Glass Eye, Schoenhut	250.00
Lamb, Pull, Wooden Wheels, 1880	140.00
Lamb, Sleeping, White Plush, Embroidered Mouth & Nose, Steiff, 13 In.	55.00
Land Pouch, Sgt. Preston, Instruction Sheet	75.00
Land Rover, Britain, No. 9512	12.50
Landing of Columbus, American, Cast Iron, 7 1/2 In.	380.00
Lassie & Her Pups Playset, In Bag	45.00
Lassie, Stuffed, 1965	45.00
Laundry Box, Contains Clothespins, Doll Size, Verse On Box	55.00
Laundry Tub, Picture Around Outside	15.00
Leopard, Baby, Steiff, Paper Label, 8 1/2 In.	150.00
Leopard, Steiff, Paper Label, 11 1/2 In.	250.00
Li'l Abner's Dogpatch Band, Windup, Tin, 1948	425.00 To 650.00
Lila Coach, Windup, Lehmann	1815.00
Lindstrom Betty, Tin Lithograph, Windup	50.00
Lion, Lying, Glass Eyes, Steiff, 16 In. ....*Illus*	110.00
Lion, Painted Eye, Schoenhut	75.00
Lion, Plush, Mechanical, Mouth Opens & Closes, 5 1/2 In.	95.00
Lion, Roaring, Windup, Box, Occupied Japan, 7 x 4 In.	90.00
Little Snoopy, Fisher–Price	15.00
Loader, Aerial Sand, Red, Tonka, 20 x 25 In.	400.00
Log Set, Log Cabin, Box	20.00
Lorry, Searchlight, Pre–War, Dinky Toys	225.00
MacGregor Scotsman, Battery Operated, Box	125.00
Magic Kit, Mandrake The Magician, Carrying Case, 1949	250.00
Magic Mirror, Paper Lithograph, Wood Box, 22 Pictures, 10 In.	1540.00
Man On Bicycle, Papier–Mache Figure, Steel Bicycle, 23 1/4 In.	1600.00
Manure Spreader, McCormick Deering, Arcade	250.00
Marble Set, Weather–Bird Shoes, Glass, Mesh Sack, 18 Piece	7.00
Mask, Hans, of Katzenjammer Kids, Molded	24.00
Mask, King Bombo, Ceresota Flour, Paper, 1939	10.00
Mask, Mandrake The Magician, Molded	30.00
Mask, Zorro, Secret Sight	35.00
Massey–Ferguson Loader, Corgi, 1960s	65.00
Matthews Wild Animal Circus Wagon, Wooden, Red, Yellow & Black, 15 In.	55.00
Maxwell, Coffeetime Bear, Bear Pours Coffee, Cup, Drinks, Battery	250.00
Meat Grinder, Cast Iron, Marked Pony	45.00
Merry–Go–Round, Automaton, 4 Bisque–Headed Children, Germany, 11 In.	935.00
Merry–Go–Round, Cloth Top, 8 Horses, 4 Boats, Clockwork, Gunthermann	2100.00
Merry–Go–Round, Wolverine, Tin	700.00
Merrymakers Band, Marx, Box, 1929	1500.00
Mexican Dancer, Windup, Bakelite, Irwin Corp.	45.00
Microscope, Gilbert, Box, 1952, 16 In.	17.00
Microscope, Gilbert, No. 8, Box, 1938	50.00
Microscope, Gilbert, Wooden Box, 1939	45.00
Microscope, Skilcraft, Metal Case	20.00
Microscope, Space Patrol	165.00
Mighty Kong, Battery Operated, Original Box, Marx	800.00
Mighty Mouse, Squeaker, Terrytune, Box	65.00
Milk Wagon, Driver, Cloth–Covered Horse, Schoenhut	5100.00
Milk Wagon, Supplee & Fairmount Farms, Cloth–Covered Horse, 25 In.	6050.00
Miracle Monkey, Eden Toy, Box	35.00
Model Kit, 20 Mule Team, Death Valley Days, Box	45.00
Model Kit, Apollo II, Columbia, Eagle Model, Box	40.00
Model Kit, Bonanza, Ben, Joe, Hoss, Plastic, Revell, 1966, 10 In.	165.00
Model Kit, Car, El Camino, 1960	35.00
Model Kit, Cosmorana, Planetarium, Sky Screen, Renwal, 1963	800.00
Model Kit, Dr. Seuss, Tingo, 1959	40.00
Model Kit, Frankenstein, Glo–In–The–Dark, Aurora	65.00
Model Kit, Jaws, The Movie, Box	85.00
Model Kit, Model T, MPC, Box	20.00
Model Kit, Mummy, Aurora, Box	40.00

Model Kit, Phantom of The Opera, Glo–In–The–Dark, Aurora, 1973 .... 75.00
Model Kit, Pickup Truck, 1960 .... 35.00
Model Kit, Robin, Boy Wonder, Box 85.00
Model Shooting Gallery, Windup, Tin, Wyandotte, 11 x 14 1/4 In. 115.00
Money & Palm Tree, Tin, Unique Art, Box 140.00
Monkey, Acrobatic, Ride Cycles Around Circus Ring, Windup, Wyandotte 375.00
Monkey, Acrobatic, Windup, Box, 1960 .... 35.00
Monkey, Balloon Blowing, Battery Operated 90.00
Monkey, Bellhop, Yes–No 350.00
Monkey, Bombo, Acrobat, Windup, Tin, Unique Art 125.00
Monkey, Bubble Blowing, Battery Operated, Box 105.00
Monkey, Climbing, On String, Marx, 1930s, Windup 95.00
Monkey, Combing Hair, Japan, Windup 20.00
Monkey, Going Up & Down Palm Tree, Tin, Emporium Specialty Co. 125.00
Monkey, Holding Binoculars, Snake In Basket, 5 In. ....*Illus* 275.00
Monkey, Jocko, Steiff, Ear Tag 75.00
Monkey, Mechanical, Playing Cymbals & Drum, West Germany, 9 In. 88.00
Monkey, Mechanical, Tips Hat, Tin, Chein 110.00
Monkey, Seesaw, Tin Lithograph, Windup 225.00
Monkey, Skipping, Battery Operated, Box 90.00
Monkey, Steiff, 14 1/2 In. 45.00
Monkey, With Violin, Windup, Schuco 185.00
Monkey, Yes–No, Gold, 18 In. 75.00
Moon Mullins, Wooden, Jointed, Box, 5 In. 120.00
Motor Coach, Tin Lithograph, Painted, Lehmann, 5 In. 242.00
Motorcycle Cop, Mechanical, Siren, Tin Lithograph, Marx, 8 1/4 In. 143.00
Motorcycle Policeman, Auburn, Cast Iron 45.00
Motorcycle, Arnold Mac, Box 950.00
Motorcycle, Cast Iron, Hubley, 4 In. 65.00
Motorcycle, Driver, Champion, White Rubber Wheels, Cast Iron, 7 In. 175.00
Motorcycle, Harley, Friction, Tin, Japan, Box, 1950s, 5 In. 495.00
Motorcycle, Harley–Davidson, Friction Motor, TN of Japan, 1958 .... 75.00
Motorcycle, Indian, Rider, Cast Iron 750.00
Motorcycle, Patrol, Hubley, Green 695.00
Motorcycle, Police, Sidecar, Hubley 935.00
Motorcycle, Police, Tin, Japan, 6 In. 135.00
Motorcycle, Rider, Patrol, Cast Iron, 6 1/2 In. 275.00
Motorcycle, Schuco 275.00
Motorcycle, Siren, Marx 190.00
Motorcycle, Windup, Tecnofix, Germany 175.00
Motorcycle, Windup, Tin, Arnold, Box, 8 In. 695.00
Motorcyclist, Boy, Tin Lithograph, Germany, 8 In. 1210.00
Mouse Shaving Cat, Windup, Japan 80.00
Movie Projector, Cragstan 60.00
Mr. Machine, 1970 .... 20.00
Mule, Pulling Coach, Driver Seated Up Behind, Cast Iron, 12 In. 633.00
Mumbo Electric Band, Battery Operated 125.00

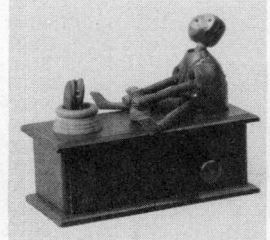

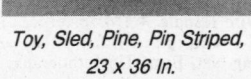

Toy, Monkey, Holding Binoculars,   *Toy, Sled, Pine, Pin Striped,*   *Toy, Pedal Car, Comet,*
Snake In Basket, 5 In.   *23 x 36 In.*   *Halford, English, c.1928*

Toy, Pail, U. S. Sea Side,
Wood & Bail Handle, 6 1/2 In.

Toy, Pail, Ocean Grove, Roses,
Wood & Bail Handle, 5 1/2 In.

Toy, Pail, Sea Side, Beach, Blimp,
Plane & Boats, Wire Handle, 5 In.

Toy, Pail, Sea Side,
Embossed Tin Lithograph, 6 In.

Music Box, 2 Children, With Snowman, Round, Small	95.00
Music Box, Egg, Tin, Mattel, 1950s	15.00
Mystery Police Cycle, Windup, Marx	150.00
Native On Alligator, Windup, Chein	100.00
Naughty Boy, Windup, Tin, Lehmann	425.00
Nipper, Plush, Stuffed, 1950s	150.00
Noah's Ark, 18 Animals, Bright Polychrome Paint, 10 In.	225.00
Noah's Ark, Pull Toy, Wooden, Mr. & Mrs. Noah, Animals, 12 x 4 x 8 In.	495.00
Noah's Ark, United States Baking Co., Wooden, Paper, 9 In.	95.00
Nursing Kit, Doll's, Box	25.00
Nutty Mad Indian, Battery Operated	120.00
Nutty Nibs, Battery Operated, Linemar, Marx	800.00
NW Century Cycle, Tin Lithograph, Painted, Lehmann, 5 In.	225.00
Office Skyscraper, With Furniture, Metal	100.00
Organ, Coronet, 1 Roll	175.00
Organ, Mechanical, Tin, Crank, Birds, Music Scroll, Germany, 1800s	100.00
Organ, Melody Player, Chein, 1 Roll	95.00
Ostrich Cart, Girl, Tin Lithograph, G & K, Germany, 9 In.	1540.00
Ostrich, Painted Eye, Schoenhut	275.00
Outboard Motor, Evina, Japan, Miniature	85.00
Owl, Wittie, Steiff, Small	165.00
Ox Cart, Hubley	95.00
Paddy On Pig, Windup, Lehmann	1750.00
Pail, 3 Little Pigs, Chein, 3 1/2 In.	40.00
Pail, Boy & Girl Fishing, Tin, 8 In.	25.00
Pail, Boy, Chicken & Lamb, 5 In.	20.00
Pail, Coney Island, Tin Lithograph	150.00
Pail, Cowboy, Steer, 5 In.	20.00
Pail, Dutch Children, Planes, Wire Handle, 4 1/4 In.	44.00
Pail, Girl, Sailboat, Ohio Art, 4 1/4 In.	55.00
Pail, Girls, Boys, Shovels, Fishing Net, Boat, Tin Lithograph, 4 In.	45.00

Pail, Little Red Riding Hood, Ohio Art, 7 1/2 In. .... 20.00 To 35.00
Pail, Mickey Garden, Tin, 5 In. 55.00
Pail, Ocean Grove, Roses, Wood & Bail Handle, 5 1/2 In. ....*Illus* 187.00
Pail, Peter Rabbit 40.00
Pail, Sea Side, Beach, Blimp, Plane & Boats, Wire Handle, 5 In. ....*Illus* 149.00
Pail, Sea Side, Embossed Tin Lithograph, 6 In. ....*Illus* 33.00
Pail, Sunnylane Pops, Woolworth Co., 4 In. 25.00
Pail, U. S. Sea Side, Wood & Bail Handle, 6 1/2 In. ....*Illus* 148.00
Pail, Zeppelin & Airplanes, Tin Lithograph, 1930s 60.00
Paint By Number Set, Maverick, Box, Garner Photo, Unused 125.00
Paint By Number Set, Zorro, Box, Unused 100.00
Paint Set, Oil, The Rifleman, Cardboard Village, 1960, Box 135.00
Panda, Steiff, 1950s, 8 In. 495.00
Panther, Black Mohair Plush, Green Eyes, Straw & Kapok, Steiff, 30 In. 220.00
Paper Village, Accessories, McLoughlin Bros., Box, 1890s 325.00
Parrot, Pete, Battery Operated, Tin Lithograph, Cloth, Lights Up 300.00
Patrol Wagon, Hubley 770.00
Pedal Airplane, 1940 .... 2200.00
Pedal Airplane, 1950 .... 135.00
Pedal Airplane, Steel Craft Pursuit, World War II Type 2500.00
Pedal Boat, Steerable, Eureka Brevete, Drance, 8 Ft. 500.00
Pedal Car, Alpha Romeo, Milano Racer, Marked CIJ, 21 In. 3482.50
Pedal Car, American National Air Mail, 1926 .... 4700.00
Pedal Car, Caterpillar Dozer 1500.00
Pedal Car, Caterpillar Tractor 5500.00
Pedal Car, Champion, Blue, Wide 500.00
Pedal Car, Champion, Coke 500.00
Pedal Car, Champion, Murray, Light Blue 375.00
Pedal Car, Chevrolet, 1936, Steelcraft 2500.00
Pedal Car, Chevrolet, 1937, Red, White & Black 2255.00
Pedal Car, Chevrolet, 1956 .... 8500.00
Pedal Car, Comet, Halford, English, c.1928 ....*Illus* 1100.00
Pedal Car, Corvette, 1957 .... 1500.00
Pedal Car, Doser 1500.00
Pedal Car, Earth Mover, Yellow 350.00
Pedal Car, Essex, 1922 .... 1750.00
Pedal Car, Fire Engine, AMF, No. 508 .... 200.00
Pedal Car, Fire Engine, Original Paint, 1950s 135.00
Pedal Car, Fire Truck, Hook 'N Ladder, BMC, 1950s 450.00
Pedal Car, Fire Truck, Murray, 1960s 200.00
Pedal Car, Fire Truck, Sportcraft 85.00
Pedal Car, Forbedo, Electric Lights, Air–Inflated Tires, Germany 475.00
Pedal Car, Ford, 1934 .... 1650.00
Pedal Car, Ford, 1937 .... 550.00
Pedal Car, Ford, 1937, V–8, Skippy 750.00
Pedal Car, Ford, 1938, Tin, Gendron, 2–Tone Green, Souped Up 2695.00
Pedal Car, Hot Rod 450.00
Pedal Car, Jeep, 1950s 150.00
Pedal Car, Kidillac, Continental Kit, Garton 450.00
Pedal Car, Kidillac, Red 350.00
Pedal Car, Kissel 1500.00
Pedal Car, Lincoln, 1934 .... 12900.00
Pedal Car, Lincoln, 1956 .... 250.00
Pedal Car, Murray Comet, 1950 .... 470.00
Pedal Car, Mustang 180.00
Pedal Car, Packard 700.00
Pedal Car, Packard, Gendron 4400.00
Pedal Car, Pierce Locomotive, Hand Crank, Wire, Rubber, Tin 1760.00
Pedal Car, Pontiac, 1948 .... 300.00
Pedal Car, Pontiac, 1948, Station Wagon 650.00
Pedal Car, Pontiac, 1956 .... 7500.00
Pedal Car, Roadster, Chain Drive, Sheet Steel & Wood, c.1900 .... 4125.00
Pedal Car, Studebaker, Fire Chief, No. 5, White Lettering, Red 225.00

Pedal Car, T–Bird, Murray	175.00
Pedal Car, Tervedo, Shell Sticker, Germany	925.00
Pedal Car, Torpedo	650.00
Pedal Car, Tractor, Caterpillar, D–4	5000.00
Pedal Car, Tractor, Framall 560, Red, Beige Decals	250.00
Pedal Car, Tractor, John Deere, Lawn & Garden	250.00
Pedal Car, Tractor, Murray, 1950s	175.00
Pedal Car, Truck, Mac	1400.00
Pedal Car, Truck, Pontiac, 1948	500.00
Pedal Car, Winston Cup	325.00
Pedal Car, Yellow Cab, AMF	175.00
Pedometer, Sgt. Preston, Mailer, Instructions	40.00
Pelican, No Fish, Fisher–Price	80.00
Pencil Box, Comic Character, Skippy	60.00
Penguin, Windup, Chein	40.00
Penguin, Windup, Papier–Mache	175.00
Pennsylvania Engine, Tootsietoy, No. 5435, Hard White Tires	23.00
Periscope, Tank, M4A1	25.00
Piano, 22 Keys, Schoenhut	185.00
Piano, Baby Grand, Fold–Down Top, 18 Keys, Schoenhut	175.00
Piano, Baby Grand, Tin, Marx, With Piano–Shaped Music Books	70.00
Piano, Bliss, Lithograph	165.00 To 200.00
Piano, Bo–Peep & Sheep, Animated	65.00
Piano, Grand, Wooden Keys, Schoenhut, 1920s	325.00
Piano, Jaymar, 25 Keys	125.00
Piano, Player, Chein, 8 Rolls	375.00
Piano, Player, Fisher–Price, 8 Muppets	45.00
Pig Cart, Musicians, Painted Tin, Clockwork, Gunthermann, 16 In.	900.00
Piggy The Cook, Battery Operated, Japan	160.00
Pinball, Deep Sea Dive, Marx, 7 In.	8.00
Pinky Pig, Fisher–Price	80.00
Pinocchio, Multi Products	230.00
Pip–Squeak, Bird & Butterfly, Pull	235.00
Pip–Squeak, Child Riding Rooster, Papier–Mache, 3 3/4 In.	50.00
Pip–Squeak, House With Chickens & Ducks, Wood, Papier–Mache, 4 1/2 In.	350.00
Pip–Squeak, Peafowl, White Polka Dots, Papier–Mache, 5 3/4 In.	250.00
Pip–Squeak, Rooster, Spring Legs, Papier–Mache, 6 In.	65.00
Pip–Squeak, Rooster, Spring Legs, Polychrome Paint, Papier–Mache, 8 In.	250.00
Pip–Squeak, Rooster, Wooden Bellows, Papier–Mache, 6 1/2 In.	75.00
Pip–Squeak, Seated Dog, Polychrome Trim, Papier–Mache, 4 3/8 In.	45.00
Pirate Ship, Captain Kidd, Battery Operated, Original Box	210.00
Play Set, Battleground	60.00
Playful Cat, Windup, With Ball, Occupied Japan	65.00
Playing Mice, Tin, Painted, Lehmann, 15 In.	330.00
Pluto, Mytic Action, Marx, 1939, 8 1/4 In.	210.00
Pogo Set, Walt Kelly, 1969, 6 Piece	45.00
Pokey, Laddie's Pal, Stuffed	45.00
Polar Bear, Button, Label, Steiff, 1950s, 11 In.	85.00
Polar Bear, Fishing, Battery Operated, Cragstan, Box	225.00
Pollack's Toy Theater, Cardboard Lithograph, 40 Piece	550.00
Poodle, Riding, Steiff, 1950s	750.00
Poodle, Steiff, Black, 1960	95.00
Pool Player, Kiko, Man Shooting Pool, Lithograph, Germany, 6 In.	660.00
Pool Player, Tin Lithograph, Windup	325.00
Pool Table Set, Dollhouse	50.00
Pop Gun, Rifle, Double Barrel, Sling, Metal & Wood, Wyandotte, 28 In.	30.00
Pop Gun, Shoots A Cork, String At Trigger, Little Daisy, 16 1/2 In.	150.00
Popeye & Parrots, Windup, Tin, Marx	375.00
Porky Pig, Rotating Umbrella, Tin, Marx, 1939	250.00
Porter, Red Cap, Marx, 1930s	395.00
Porter, Tin Lithograph, Windup, Porter, Germany	100.00
Power Dozer, Linemar, Box, 1950s	45.00
Prancy Pony, Fisher–Price, Pull Toy	25.00

◆◆

If you have old laces and ribbons, press them by pulling them over a
warm electric light bulb. Limp lace can be washed, then sprayed
with starch or sizing. Lace can be colored by a quick dip in tea.

◆◆

Prince Valiant Castle Fort, Marx	175.00
Printing Press, Metal, Acessories, Instructions, Box, 1950	35.00
Printing Set, Favorite Funnies	30.00
Projector, Give A Show, Kenner, 112 Slides, 1963	60.00
Projector, Magic Lantern, 10 Glass Slides, Tin, 9 3/4 In.	40.00
Projectoscope, Space Patrol, With Filmstrip	100.00
Pull–A–Tune, Fisher–Price, 1920s	25.00
Pump, Punching Bag, Joe Palooka	19.00
Punching Bag, Joe Palooka, Floor Standing	185.00
Punchout Kite, Herman & Katnip, Book Unfolds Into Kite, 1960, Saalfield	35.00
Purse, Doll's, Tiny Blue Beads, Drawstring, Miniature	55.00
Puzzle, Stack–Egg, Wooden, Oriental	45.00
Queen's Coronation State Coach Set, Britains, No. 1470	595.00
Quiz Machine, Arithmetic, Wolverine, Tin	38.00
Rabbit, On Tricycle, Windup, Tin	35.00
Rabbit, Painted Wood, Painted Eye, Schoenhut	200.00
Racer's Bell, Nickel Plated, 10 In.	198.00
Radcycle, Painted & Tin Lithograph, Windup, Mars, Lehmann	1800.00
Radio & Clock, Hickory Dickory Dock, Fisher–Price	25.00
Radio, Snoopy, Sing–A–Long	12.00
Radio, Space Capsule, Box	15.00
Radio, Tony The Tiger	37.00
Range Rider, Windup, Japan	65.00
Rapid Transit, Pressed Steel, Friction, Trolley, 21 In.	450.00
Rattle, Baby's, Wooden, Cloth, 4 Metal Balls, 6 In.	40.00
Rattle, Telephone, Plakie, Box	22.00
Record Player, Beany & Cecil	75.00
Record Player, Cabinet, Bing Crosby	475.00
Record Player, Ding Dong School, 45 RPM, Miss Frances	75.00
Record Player, Happy Days, Picture of Fonz	12.00
Record Player, Little Wonder Records, Windup, Floor Model	550.00
Red Ryder Target, Complete, Box	39.00
Refrigerator, Nassau	13.00
Reindeer, Painted Wood, Leather, Antlers, Ears, Tail, Glass Eye, Schoenhut	175.00
Rifle, 6 Shooter, Colt, Mattel	500.00
Rifle, Atomic, Tom Corbett	125.00
Rifle, Ranch Rifle, Repeater, Plastic, Marx	35.00
Ring, Barbie, Rhinestones, Box	50.00
Ring, Sky King, Magnifier	60.00
Ring, Sky King, Radar	200.00
Ring, Sky King, Writing	65.00
Ring–A–Ling Circus, Tin Lithograph, Marx, 8 1/2 In.	797.00
Ring–A–Ling Circus, Windup, Tin, Marx, 7 3/4 In.	400.00
Ringmaster, Painted Wood, Schoenhut	100.00
Riverboat, Cast Iron, Wilkins, c.1910	135.00
Road Grader, Nickel Plated Blade, Kenton	240.00
Roadside Rest Service Station, Laurel & Hardy, At Counter, Marx, 1935	775.00
Robot, Astronaut, Shoots Guns, Rotates, Tin	175.00
Robot, Attacking Martian, Battery Operated	50.00
Robot, Batman, Windup, Tin, Billiken, Box	165.00
Robot, Big Max, Battery Operated, Picks Up From Conveyor Belt, 1960s	400.00
Robot, Boxing, Roc 'Em–soc 'Em, Box, Pair	65.00 To 125.00
Robot, Bulldozer–Cultivator, Friction, Tin, Marusan, Box, 6 In.	500.00
Robot, Captain Robot, Windup, Korea	25.00

Robot, King, Bump & Go Lights, Battery Operated, Moving Feet, 10 In. 40.00
Robot, Laughing, Marx 50.00
Robot, Lost In Space, Box, 1977, 10 In. .... 85.00 To 95.00
Robot, Machine Guns In Chest, Walks, Battery Operated, 1950, 12 In. 345.00
Robot, Maria, Battery Operated, Masudaya, 16 In. 95.00
Robot, Mighty Robot, Green, Box 135.00
Robot, Moon Astronaut 500.00
Robot, Mystery Moonman, Silver, Cragston 850.00
Robot, Piston 185.00
Robot, Plante, Windup, Tin Lithograph, Sparking Action 500.00
Robot, Radical, Cragston, Box 1100.00
Robot, Robby The Robot, Tin Lithograph, Plastic, Rubber, 1956, 13 In. 1600.00
Robot, Robert, Talking, Ideal 65.00
Robot, Rotate–O–Matic 200.00
Robot, Shooting Astronaut Attack, Tin, Japan, 11 In. ....*Illus* 15.00
Robot, Silver Warrior, Plastic, Hong Kong, 10 In. ....*Illus* 20.00
Robot, Space Attack, Tin & Plastic, Japan, 9 In. 45.00
Robot, Space Explorer, Battery Operated, Box 195.00
Robot, Space Fighter 95.00
Robot, Sparky, Green, Windup 60.00
Robot, Sparky, Windup, Tin, Gray, Maroon Feet, 5 3/4 In. 400.00
Robot, Super, Battery Operated, Tin, Japan, 1960s, Box 150.00
Robot, T. V. Spaceman, Battery Operated 375.00
Robot, Tin, Linemar 275.00
Robot, Tin, Plastic, Battery, Japan, 11 In. ....*Illus* 33.00
Robot, Video, Tin, Plastic, Japan, 10 In. 25.00
Robot, Zoomer, Japan 435.00
Rock 'N' Roll Monkey, Battery Operated, Box, Alps 175.00
Rocker, Doll's, Bentwood, Handmade 17.50
Rocker, Doll's, Ladder Back, Arms, Splint Seat, 14 In. 120.00
Rocket Fighter, Marx 275.00
Rocket Ship, G–Man Pursuit, Tin Lithograph, Color 90.00
Rocket Ship, Windup, Ron Corbett, Marx 275.00
Rocket Shop, Jupiter, Friction, Japan, Box 65.00
Roll Over Cat, Box, Marx 45.00
Roller Coaster, 2 Cars, Tin, Chein, 1960s 175.00
Roller Coaster, Battery Operated, Original Box 100.00
Roller Coaster, Jet, Wolverine 160.00
Roller Skating Waiter, Windup, Tin Lithograph, 7 In. 350.00
Rolly Polly Teddy, Fisher–Price 20.00
Rooster, Bellows Squeak, Polychrome Paint, Chalkware, 4 1/2 In. 295.00
Rooster, Lays Eggs, Wyandotte, Tin, 1930s 55.00
Rooster, Painted Tin, Pull Toy, 19th Century, 4 5/8 In. 250.00
Ruff, Dennis Menace's Dog, Squeeze Toy 25.00
Sailor, Movable Arms & Legs, Polychrome Paint, Wooden, 2 3/4 In., 4 Pc. 130.00
Sailor, Plays Drums, Windup, Tin, Germany 295.00
Sailor, Plays Guitar, Windup, Tin, Germany 295.00

Toy, Robot, Silver Warrior, Plastic,
Hong Kong, 10 In.
Toy, Robot, Tin, Plastic, Battery, Japan, 11 In.

◆◆◆◆◆◆◆◆◆◆◆◆◆◆◆◆◆◆◆◆◆◆◆◆

Take batteries with you to the
toy sales if you plan to buy a
battery operated toy. Check to
see if the toy really works.

◆◆◆◆◆◆◆◆◆◆◆◆◆◆◆◆◆◆◆◆◆◆◆◆

Sailor, Tin, Painted, Cloth, Lehmann, 7 1/2 In. 385.00
Salad Set, Little Sweetheart, Original Box, 14 Piece 35.00
San The Shaving Man, Battery Operated, Original Box 150.00
Sand Loader, Buddy L, 17 In. 125.00
Sand, Dutch Mill, Box, MAC, No. 26 .... 475.00
Sand, Tick Tock Clock, Box 65.00
Scarab, Buddy L 450.00
School Bag, Jock Mahoney, Ranger Rider 150.00
Scooter, Kiddy Car-Go, Playskool, Wood 95.00
Scooter, Painted Red & White, 32 1/2 x 41 In. 110.00
Scooter, Sears 25.00
Scottish Jigger, Windup, Ives 2200.00
Seal, Circus, Acrobat, Tin, Windup, Japan, Box 40.00
Seal, Pull Toy, Schoenhut 350.00
Seal, Sparky, Battery Operated, Linemar 75.00
Seal, Tin, Hand Painted, Bell, Lehmann, 7 In. 137.00
Seal, Windup, Lehmann, 7 1/2 In. 150.00
Seaplane, Tin Lithograph, Windup, Chein, Box 175.00
Seesaw, Girl & Boy, Clockwork, Ives, Papier-Mache, Metal 2310.00
Seesaw, Rabbit & Boy, Windup, Japan, Box 235.00
Service Station, Roadside Rest, Pumps, Globes, Laurel & Hardy, Marx, 1938 .... 700.00
Service Station, Superior, 14 x 25 In. 35.00
Settee & Rocker, Doll's, Bentwood, Thonet 225.00
Sewing Machine, Betsy Ross 40.00
Sewing Machine, Casige, British Zone, Germany .... 45.00 To 75.00
Sewing Machine, Gateway, Instructions, Metal 35.00
Sewing Machine, Holly Hobbie 10.00
Sewing Machine, Kay and Ee, Instructions 65.00
Sewing Machine, Kay and Ee, Red, Box 24.00
Sewing Machine, Litle Mother, Clamp, Red Metal, 7 1/2 In. 58.00
Sewing Machine, Little Betty, England 45.00
Sewing Machine, Little Comfort Improved, Dated 1897 .... 125.00
Sewing Machine, Little Modiste 35.00
Sewing Machine, Red, Gateway Engineering, 8 1/2 x 4 1/2 x 7 In. 25.00
Sewing Machine, Sew-E-Z, Battery Operated 35.00
Sewing Machine, Sewmaster, Metal, Blue, Red Roses 87.00
Sewing Machine, Singer 59.00
Sewing Machine, U. S. Zone Germany, Box 40.00
Sewing Machine, Vulcan, Box 50.00
Sheep, Baby Putz, Wooly Coats, Wood Stakes, 2 1/4 In. 18.00
Sheep, Pull Toy, Skin Covering, Glass Eyes, Voice Box, 18 1/2 In. 900.00
Sheep, Wooden Base, Pull Toy, White Repaint, Early 20th Century, 35 In. 200.00
Sheep, Wooly Coat, Pink Ribbon Collar, Wood & Papier-Mache, 3 1/2 In. 55.00
Shoeshine Joe, Battery Operated 60.00
Shoot-A-Loop, Tin, Marbles, Wolverine 25.00
Shooting Gallery, Jungle Eyes, Metal, Ohio Art 55.00
Shooting Gallery, Mechanical, Wyandotte, Box, 1930s 500.00
Shooting Gallery, Posse, Wyandotte, Box 225.00
Shooting Gallery, Target Spins, Tin 20.00
Showboat, Battery Operated, 1950 .... 165.00
Showboat, Remco, 1962 .... 50.00
Siamese Twins, Squeak, Rubber, Adult Jointed Twins, 1870s 189.00
Signal Scope, With Whistle, Sky King 85.00
Sink, Bo-Peep 6.00
Ski Boy, Chein 260.00
Ski Ride, Battery Operated, Chein, Box 425.00
Skier, Boy, Windup, Tin, Chein 150.00
Skier, Skirolf, Tin Lithograph, Lehmann 4700.00
Sky Ranger, Unique Art 315.00
Slate, Large 65.00
Slate, Small 24.00
Sled, Flexible Flyer, Family Size 28.50
Sled, Go-Devil Coaster, 1 Runner, Picture of Black Boy, 34 3/4 In. 225.00

Sled, Green Paint, Floral Design, Metal Runners, Wood, 16 In. 425.00
Sled, Hand Painted Wood, Metal Runners, 20th Century, 31 1/2 In. 145.00
Sled, Oak Runners, Brass Side Supports 247.00
Sled, Painted Design In Red, Green & Gold, 19th Century, 4 Ft. 375.00
Sled, Painted, Iron & Wood, Sheffield Mfg. Co., 40 In. 88.00
Sled, Pennsylvania Stump Jumper 30.00
Sled, Pine, Pin Striped, 23 x 36 In. ....*Illus* 605.00
Sled, Red Paint, Stenciled Floral Design, Paris Mfg. Co., No. 63 .... 93.50
Sled, Red Striping, 4 Persons, Oak & Metal, 100 In. 137.50
Sled, Red, Black & Gold Stenciled Design, Gooseneck Runners 1000.00
Sled, Red, Black Stork, Marked Ruth Lane Hill, Dec. 25, 1904, 35 In. 390.00
Sled, Runners Inscribed Village Romp, Painted Design, Pine, 13 1/4 In. 7500.00
Sled, Seat Marked Boy Scout, 2 Runner, Painted, 24 In. 175.00
Sled, Shooting Star, Green, Stenciled Sides & Top 450.00
Sled, Steel Frame, Wooden Top, Painted Design, 36 In. 145.00
Sled, Toddler's, Rounded Front Runners, Name Lillian Painted On Top 945.00
Sled, Village Romp, Shaped Seat, Oval American Flag, 52 1/4 In. 8250.00
Sled, White Pin Striping, Green, Iron Runners, American, 35 1/2 In. 1100.00
Sled, Wooden, Green Paint, Metal Trim, Cast Iron Swan's Heads, 37 In. 325.00
Sled, Wooden, Steel Overlay On Runners 500.00
Sled, Wooden, Varnish, Polychrome Sailboat Design, 45 In. 175.00
Sleeping Baby Bear, Opens Eyes, Sits Up, Stretches, Battery Operated 150.00
Smokey The Bear, Bobbin Head, Figural 95.00
Smokey The Bear, Vinyl Face, Ideal, 16 In. 25.00
Snoopy, On Skate Board, Battery Operated, Box 75.00
Soccer Player, Mechanical, Kicking, Tin Lithograph, Germany, 8 In. 412.00
Soldier, 10 Marching Band, 14 Marching Pieces, Elastolin, Set 450.00
Soldier, Banner Bearer of Bourbon, Courtenay 1210.00
Soldier, Bedouin Arabs, 5 Tribesmen, Horses, Britains, Box, 1930s 195.00
Soldier, Belgian Cavalry, Halt Review, Britains, c.1940 .... 335.00
Soldier, British Hussas, Mounted, Heyde, c.1935 .... 885.00
Soldier, Coldstream Guards, Britains, No. 120, Box, 1930s, 8 Piece 225.00
Soldier, Colour Part of Irish Guards, Blenheim, Box 525.00
Soldier, Confederate, Astride Horse, Windup, Tin 55.00
Soldier, Curassiers, Britains, No. 138, Box, 10 Piece 190.00
Soldier, Egyptian Camel Corps, Britains, Set In Box, c.1935 .... 775.00
Soldier, Egyptian Infantry, At Attention, Britians, No. 117, Box, 8 Piece 445.00
Soldier, French Napoleonic Guards of Honor, Mignot, Box 385.00
Soldier, Gordon Highlanders, Britains, Box, c.1940 .... 185.00
Soldier, Gordon Highlanders, Kneeling, Firing, Britains, No. 157, 1930s 275.00
Soldier, Grenadier Guards, Marching, Britains, No. 312, Box, 7 Piece 225.00
Soldier, Gurkha Rifles, Marching, Britains, Whisstock Box, c.1935 .... 445.00
Soldier, Italian Bersagliere, Britains, Box 175.00
Soldier, Napoleonic Coach, 4–Horse Team, Mignot–Lucotte, c.1950 .... 660.00
Soldier, Prussian Cavalry Mounted Band, c.1930 .... 550.00
Soldier, Prussian Infantry Encampment, Box 495.00
Soldier, Prussian Infantry, Mignot, Box, c.1950 .... 175.00
Soldier, Royal Artillery Gunners, Britains, Whisstock Box, c.1940 .... 495.00
Soldier, Royal Dublin Fussauers, In Khaki, Pith Helmets, Britains, 8 Pc. 415.00
Soldier, Royal Welsh Fusilers, No. 74, Goat Mascot, Britains, Box 225.00
Soldier, Saxon Infantry of The Line, 1890–1914, Heyde 775.00
Soldier, Sentry Box, Britains, 4 Piece 52.00
Soldier, South African Defense Forces, Britains, Box, 8 Piece 4125.00
Soldier, South African Mounted Infantry, Britains 3300.00
Soldier, Third Hussars, Trotting Horses, Britains, Box, 1930s 355.00
Soldier, Zouves, Charging, Britains, No. 142, Box, 1930s, 8 Piece 305.00
Space 1999 Model Kit, Sealed 30.00
Space Capsule, Battery Operated, Tin, Japan, 7 In. 110.00
Space Capsule, S4, Friction, Japan, 6 1/2 In. 250.00
Space Capsule, Tin Lithograph, Battery, 9 1/2 In. 132.00
Space Patrol Diplomatic Pouch 250.00
Space Patrol Phones, Box, Instructions 150.00
Space Ship, NASA Apollo, Attached Flying Astronaut, Box 195.00

Space Ship, Whale, Windup, Tin, Sparks, Moving Eyes, Flapping Ears, 9 In.	950.00
Spark Plug, Bathtub, Pull Toy, AC Spark Plugs	135.00
Sparkler, Buster Keaton, Tinplate, Spanish Isla, 1925	3300.00
Sparkplug, Barney Google's Horse, 1924, Germany, 1924, 9 In.	4950.00
Speedboat, Tin Lithograph, Windup, Lindstrom, 12 In. .... 75.00 To 95.00	
Speedway Set, 2 Windup Sedans, Figure 8 Tin Track, Marx, 1937	450.00
Spiral Speedway, 16 Sections of Track, Automatic Toy Co., 1955, Box	125.00
Sprinkling Can, Panda Bear, Ohio Art	22.00
Spy–O–Graph, Drawing Set, Viewer, Sketch Sheets, Box	120.00
Squirrel, Friction, Tail Twitches	12.00
Star Wars, Wicket The Ewok Magic Transfer Set, Box	25.00
Station Wagon, Isinglass Windows, Decals, Wood, Buddy L, 18 1/2 In.	350.00
Station, Gas Pumps, Tin Lithograph, Marx, 9 In.	176.00
Steam Roller, Key Wind, Tin Lithograph, U. S. Zone, 8 In.	215.00
Steam Shovel, Red & Black, Keystone, 20 In.	115.00
Steam Shovel, Sturditoy, 20 In.	200.00
Stereo Camera & Viewer, Lionel Linex	85.00
Stethoscope, Dr. Kildare, Box	25.00
Stove, Buck's Jr, No. 2	1000.00
Stove, Cook, Empire	22.00
Stove, Cook, Passion Flower, Scantlin & Sons	750.00
Stove, Eagle, Oven, 6 Lids, Coal Door, Iron Grates, 18 1/2 x 15 In.	325.00
Stove, Little Lady, Electric, Brown, Empire	30.00
Stove, Perfection, Shelves, Stove Pipe, 8 3/4 x 10 In.	250.00
Stove, Snow White, Wolverine	20.00
Stroller, Baby, Blondie & Dagwood, Tin Lithograph, Bells In Wheels	110.00
Stroller, Doll's, Ohio Art, Tin, 19 1/2 In.	40.00
Stroller, Doll's, Tin Lithograph, Teddies, 1940s, Large	52.00
Stroller, Susan, Eegee, 20 In.	60.00
Strutting Turkey, Windup, U. S. Zone	95.00
Stuntcar, With Pop–Up Man, Friction, Tin Lithograph, Box	300.00
Submarine Kit, Polaris Nuclear, Box	30.00
Submarine, Dives, Surfaces, Battery, Schuco	165.00
Submarine, Diving, Battery Operated, Linemar	125.00
Submarine, Diving, Wolverine, No Key	175.00
Submarine, Electric, Battery Operated, Schuco, Box	165.00
Submarine, Kellogg's, Powder, Box	95.00
Submarine, Power, Kenner, 13 In.	35.00
Suitcase, 3 Bears, Black, Brown Trim, Handle, 1930–40, 7 x 7 1/2 In.	77.00
Sulky, Doll's, Wire Wheels	125.00
Super Circus Set, Marx	325.00
Super Circus Set, Sears Heritage	300.00
Supermarket, Tin, Miniatures On Shelves, Wolverine, 1950s	150.00
Susy, Bouncing Ball, Box, Japan	85.00
Tambourine, Judy Canova, Tin	20.00
Tank, Arnold, 5 In.	95.00
Tank, Cast Iron, Arcade	165.00
Tank, Doughboy Pops Out, Turret Turns, Tin Lithograph, Marx, 9 In.	140.00
Tank, Lever Action, Tin Lithograph, Japan, Cragstan	100.00
Tank, Pop–Up Army Man Shooting, Marx	295.00
Tank, Rollover, Superman, Windup, Tin, Marx, 4 In.	360.00
Tank, Sparking, Marx, Box	125.00
Tank, Windup, Karl Bubb	1800.00
Tank, Windup, Turnover, Marx, Box	125.00
Tank, World War II, Key Wind, Changes Directions, Marx, 10 In.	175.00
Tanker Truck, Mobil Gasoline, Battery Operated, Box, 16 In.	195.00
Tanker, Dairy, Tootsietoy	95.00
Target Set, I Spy	80.00
Target, Bull's–Eye, Knickerbocker	5.00
Tarzan, Battery, Original Box, San	675.00
Taxi, Amos & Andy, Tin Lithograph, Marx, 8 In. ....*Illus*	523.00
Taxi, Checker, Windup, Courtland	55.00
Taxi, Door Opens, Light Blinks, Meter Turns, Battery Operated, Japan, Box	150.00

Taxi, Fresh Air, Windup, Tin, Marx, 8 1/4 In. 400.00
Taxi, Friction, Bandai, 1950s 100.00
Taxi, Hand Painted, Bing, Germany, 8 1/2 In. 990.00
Taxi, Open Air, Marx 950.00
Taxi, Yellow, Rubber Tires, Arcade, 8 In. .... 900.00 To 925.00
Tea Cart, Doll's, White Rubber Tires, Ohio Art, 1930s 35.00
Tea Kettle, Cast Iron, Wagner 140.00
Tea Set, Blue Willow, Japan, Box, 13 Piece 200.00
Tea Set, Blue Willow, Occupied Japan, 17 Piece 175.00
Tea Set, Bunny Birthday, Tin, Ohio Art, 7 Piece 30.00
Tea Set, Chiquita, J. Pressman, Cobalt Blue, Box, 12 Piece 145.00
Tea Set, Cinderella, Happynak, Box, 15 Piece 310.00
Tea Set, Cinderella, Tin, Ohio Art, 9 Piece 30.00
Tea Set, Doll's, Blue Floral Transfer, Ironstone, 11 Piece 185.00
Tea Set, Doll's, Milk Glass, 1920s 60.00
Tea Set, Doll's, Porcelain, Cream Luster, Design, Occupied Japan, 9 Piece 55.00
Tea Set, Doll's, Wreath & Bow Design, Green, Gold, Purple, 1910, 12 Piece 95.00
Tea Set, Kids With Cats, Ohio Art, 8 Piece 25.00
Tea Set, Kittens & Mittens, Aluminum, 21 Piece 60.00
Tea Set, Little Hostess, Bluebird, Box, 13 Piece 75.00
Tea Set, Little Red Riding Hood, Plastic, 13 Piece 65.00
Tea Set, Pink Roses, Japan, Box 42.00
Tea Set, Pumpkin, Small 40.00
Tea Set, Snow White & 7 Dwarfs, Marx, 24 Piece 145.00
Tea Set, Steiff, Box, 15 Piece 60.00
Tea Set, Teddy Bear, Steiff 375.00
     TOY, TEDDY BEAR, see also Teddy Bear
Teddy Bear, Drummer, Battery Operated 65.00
Teddy Bear, Standing, In Black Boot, Red, White, Glass Eyes, Fisher–Price 30.00
Teddy Bear, Walking, Windup, Tag, Irwin Darling, 1930s, 11 In. 195.00
Teddy Silo, 1950s, Fisher–Price 75.00
Teeter–Totter Boy & Girl, Painted Tin Plate, Gibb's 150.00
Teeter–Totter, Busy Mike, Tin, J. Chein 125.00
Telephone, Atom Boy, Yonezawa, Battery, Japan, 12 In. 200.00
Telephone, Darth Vader, Figural, Box 125.00
Telephone, Gerber Talk–Back Phone, Box 8.00
Telephone, Gong Bell, Red, Dial 90.00
Telephone, Speed Phone, Tin, Dial & Bell 30.00
Theatre, Poolock's, Paper Lithograph, Scenery, Figures, 16 x 15 In. 1100.00
Thingmaker Fang 'N Claw Kit, Mattel, 1967 .... 65.00
Threshing Machine, Gray & White, Red Trim, Arcade, Cast Iron, 10 In. 300.00
Tick Tock Clock, Sand Toy, Box 60.00
Tidy Tim, Tin Lithograph, Marx, 8 In. 412.00
Tiger, Baby, Seated, Steiff, 4 1/4 In. 215.00
Tiger, Bengali, Prowling, Growling, Battery Operated, Marx, Box 98.00
Tiger, Ear Button, Steiff, 8 In. 20.00
Tiger, On Wheels, Orange Mohair, Green Plastic Eyes, Steiff, 30 x 18 In. 450.00
Tiger, Painted Wood, Glass Eyes, Schoenhut 75.00
Tinkling Trolley, Battery Operated 250.00
Tip Toe Turtle, Fisher–Price 17.00
Toaster, Excel Electric Co. 50.00
Toilet Set, Doll's, Celluloid, Brush, Comb, Mirror & Receiver, Box 150.00
Tool Chest, Elite, Early 1900s 85.00
Toonerville Trolly, Windup 975.00
Toot Toot Train, Pull Toy, Fisher–Price .... 15.00 To 20.00
Toot Toot Turtle, Fisher–Price No. 773 .... 12.00
Top, Gyroscope 15.00
Toto The Acrobat, Marx, Box .... 350.00 To 480.00
Tractor Set, Wooden, Peter Mar, 1941, 60 In., 4 Piece 235.00
Tractor, Allis Chalmers, Model C, 1950 .... 95.00
Tractor, Ertl, Box 20.00
Tractor, Farm, Marx, Tin Driver 95.00
Tractor, Farm, Trailer, Gama, 16 In. 195.00

Tractor, Farm, With Trailer, Campbell's, Ertl 28.00
Tractor, Fordson, Iron, 4 1/4 In. 90.00
Tractor, John Deer, No. 20, Restored 250.00
Tractor, John Deere, No. 440, Industrial 395.00
Tractor, Load Lift, Box 55.00
Tractor, Massey Ferguson, Model 1150, Aluminum, Ertl, Box, 10 In. 650.00
Tractor, McCormack Deering, Rubber Wheels, Cast Iron, Arcade 380.00
Tractor, Mighty, Fisher–Price No. 629 .... 22.00
Tractor, Oliver, Super 55, Box 1000.00
Tractor, Sparkling, Driver, Windup, Marx 195.00
Tractor, Wooden Wheels, 4 In. 165.00
Trailer, Travel, Ford Falcon, Box 325.00
Train Set, American Flyer, Pennsy. Torpedo Locomotive, Tender, 4 Cars 247.00
Train Set, Ives, Halloween, Orange & Black Roofs, Brass, 3 Cars, Box 4400.00
Train Set, Ives, Standard Gauge, 1 Car, Caboose, Tracks, Switches 395.00
Train Set, Lionel, City of Portland, Box 325.00
Train Set, Lionel, No. 37, Original Box 400.00
Train Set, Lionel, No. 33, Dark Olive, Red Trim, 4 Cars 385.00
Train Set, Lionel, No. 42, Dark Olive, 7 Cars 330.00
Train Set, Lionel, No. 154, Dark Green, 3 Cars 385.00
Train Set, Lionel, Transformer, Track, 4 Cars, 1960s 25.00
Train Set, Marklin, Adler–Eagle Centennial, 0 Gauge, Painted Tin 5500.00
Train Set, Marx, Tin Lithograph, New York Central, 1960 .... 175.00
Train Set, Unique Art, Windup, Box 385.00
Train, Althof Bergmann, Locomotive, Clockwork, Painted Tin, c.1874 .... 1430.00
Train, American Flyer, Standard Gauge, Electric 500.00
Train, Bing, Cast Iron Locomotive, Windup, 2 Tin Lithograph Cars 165.00
Train, Bing, Torpedo, With Black, Red & White Tender 192.00
Train, Buddy L, Industrial, 5 Cars, 12 Tracks, Pressed Steel 800.00
Train, Buddy L, Steam Engine & Tender, 1921 .... 2500.00
Train, Caboose, Deluxe, Brass Rail On Cupola, Ladders 95.00
Train, Car, Lionel, Pullman, No. 6440 .... 45.00
Train, Engine, Friction, Wood & Cast Iron, 13 In. 85.00
Train, Fisher–Price, Circus, Cars, Engine, Toots, Animals, Engineer 45.00
Train, Floor, Painted Cast Iron, American, 23 In., 4 Piece 295.00
Train, Ives, 6 Tin Cars, Caboose, 14 Sections of Track, Windup, Iron 325.00
Train, KTM, Locomotive & Tender, 20th Century Limited, Box 392.00
Train, Lionel, 2 Locomotives, Remote Control Switches, Track, 9 Cars 600.00
Train, Lionel, Box Car, No. 2814, Orange, Tuscan, Black, Rubber 700.00
Train, Lionel, Bridge No. 106, Box, 3 Piece 75.00
Train, Lionel, Engine, HO 75.00
Train, Lionel, Floodlight Tower No. 92, Painted Tin 50.00
Train, Lionel, Fueling Station No. 415, Box 175.00
Train, Lionel, New York Central Line, Pullman, Observation, Motor Car 385.00
Train, Lionel, No. 50, Gang Car, Box 65.00
Train, Lionel, No. 212, Marine Engine, Power 120.00
Train, Lionel, No. 215, Tanker, Pea Green 165.00
Train, Lionel, No. 3462, Milk Car, Operating, Box 25.00
Train, Lionel, No. 384, Locomotive & Tender, Box 400.00
Train, Lionel, No. 627, Diesel 145.00
Train, Lionel, No. 632A, Diesel 175.00
Train, Lionel, No. 6475B, Pickle Vat Car 60.00
Train, Lionel, Round House, 1932 .... 1210.00
Train, Lionel, Side Loader, Coal Car, Cattle Car, Crane Car 275.00

◆◆◆

To remove rust spots from washable textiles, try Grandma's remedy: boil the fabric in a solution of four teaspoons of cream of tartar in one pint of water.

◆◆◆

Train, Lionel, Steam Engine & Tender, O Gauge, 1939 .... 185.00
Train, Locomotive & Pullman Car, Pressed Metal, 1920s 465.00
Train, Locomotive, Sparkling, Friction, Japan 45.00
Train, Locomotive, With Pullman Car, Pressed Metal, 1920s 495.00
Train, Marx, Electric, Switches, Tracks, O Gauge, 1930, 7 Cars 150.00
Train, Marx, Engine, 4 Cars, New York Central, Tin Lithograph, 1960, 5 Pc. 175.00
Train, Marx, Engine, HO, 1960s, 10 Cars, No Track 165.00
Train, Marx, Honeymoon Express, Tin Lithograph, Windup 75.00
Train, Marx, Railroad Station, Glendale Depot, Accessories, Tin, 1930s 175.00
Train, Marx, Windup, Commodore Vanderbilt, Track 185.00
Train, Merchandise Car, Trucks 55.00
Train, MH Nuremburg, Locomotive, Clockwork, Reversing Automatic Engine 1127.00
Train, Overland Flyer, Tin, 4 Cars, Some Track 20.00
Train, Penny Toy, Tin, Engine & 4 Cars, 1930s 150.00
Train, President Special, Engine With 3 Cars, 1926 .... 900.00
Train, Sante Fe Express, Tin, Friction 75.00
Train, Schieble, Hill Climber, Engine & Tender, 1920s 700.00
Train, Shilling Electric, Battery, Box 30.00
Train, Tank Car, 1000, 000 Gallon Marking 85.00
Train, Windup Engine, Passenger Car, Marked J. A. J., 9 In., 2 Piece 125.00
Trapeze, Swinging Donald Duck, Windup, Celluloid, Box 2500.00
Trash Can, Laugh–In, Pictures The Stars 35.00
Tricycle, Horse, Polychromed Wood & Iron, Hand Driven 2000.00
Tricycle, Jr. Toy Corp., Purple 175.00
Trolley Car, Safety Car Fenders, Patent Model, F. DeFontes, 1894, 19 In. 7150.00
Trolley, Converse, 1910 .... 300.00
Trolley, Floral Design, Passengers, Gold & Maroon Paint, Tin, 15 In. 225.00
Trolley, Hillclimber, c.1920 .... 295.00
Trolley, Jackson Park, Horse Drawn, Paper Lithograph 3100.00
Trolley, Pinstripes, Pressed Steel, c.1900, 22 In. 350.00
Trolley, Powell & Mason Streets, Tin, 10 Figures, Windup 75.00
Trolley, Sandy Andy Railway, Tin, Bell Rings, Wolverine, 13 1/2 In. 225.00
Trolley, Windup, Marx No. 200, 1920s, 9 In. 495.00
Truck, 6 Wheels, Driver, Fisher–Price 30.00
Truck, Alps Army, 1936, 10 In. 75.00
Truck, Ambulance, Keystone, Pressed Steel 1495.00
Truck, Ambulance, Wyandotte 185.00
Truck, American Express Railroad, Wire Sides, Keystone, 26 1/2 In. 775.00
Truck, Army Cargo, Tin, Chein, 1920s, 8 In. 345.00
Truck, Army Supply Corps., Buddy L 95.00
Truck, Army Transport, Buddy L, Box 475.00
Truck, Army, Buddy L, 1940s, 20 In. 175.00
Truck, Army, Marx, 20 In. 35.00
Truck, Army, Rubber Tires, Lumar, Box, Large 150.00
Truck, Artillery, Kingsbury, 14 In. .... 265.00 To 295.00
Truck, Auto Haulaway, Structo, 20 In. 125.00
Truck, Bell Telephone, Hubley, 1940, 12 In. .... 65.00 To 85.00
Truck, Brinks, Buddy L, 14 In. 60.00
Truck, Bucket Loader, Doepke 70.00
Truck, Carnation Milk, Tonka 130.00
Truck, Cement Mixer, Buddy L, Oversized 577.00
Truck, Chrome Wheels, Arcade, Cast Iron, 7 In. 400.00
Truck, Coal, Automatic Dumping, Forward & Reverse, Tin, Battery, Marx 125.00
Truck, Coca–Cola, Friction, Linemar 125.00
Truck, Coca–Cola, Yellow, Buddy L 198.00
Truck, Coca–Cola, Yellow, Marx, 20 In. 330.00
Truck, Cortland Storage & Moving Co., Windup 65.00
Truck, Daily News, Linemar 65.00
Truck, Delivery, EHE & Co., Windup, Tin, Lehmann 875.00
Truck, Delivery, Express Line, Buddy L, Sheet Metal, 25 In. 810.00
Truck, Dispatch, Green & Gray, Structo, Box 125.00
Truck, Dumont T. V., Tin 600.00
Truck, Dump, 1930–1940, Marx, 4 1/2 In. 60.00

Truck, Dump, Battery–Operated Headlights, Girard, 1930s, 10 In. 150.00
Truck, Dump, Buddy L, Chain Hoist, 24 In. 330.00
Truck, Dump, Hydraulic, Structo, 1950s 18.00
Truck, Dump, Keystone, 26 In. 350.00
Truck, Dump, Loader On Front, Wyandotte 65.00
Truck, Dump, Mack, Decals, Arcade, 12 In. 1200.00
Truck, Dump, Red & Green, Wyandotte, 11 In. 35.00
Truck, Dump, Ride–Em, Keystone, Label, 1934 .... 395.00
Truck, Dump, Rider, Buddy L, Box 725.00
Truck, Dump, Steel, Structo, 1940s 85.00
Truck, Dump, Turner, 26 In. 295.00
Truck, Dump, Wooden Wheels, Chrome Bumper, 1940s, 9 1/2 In. 45.00
Truck, Dump, Wyandotte, 6 In. 35.00
Truck, Farm Supply, Buddy L, 1940s, 21 In. 175.00
Truck, Ford Model T, Open Bed, Buddy L, c.1923, 12 In. 495.00
Truck, Freight Carrier Van, Buddy L, 1940s 72.50
Truck, Freightways Transport, Japan, Box 20.00
Truck, Garbage, Structo, 1940s 185.00
Truck, Grocery, Marx, Cardboard Boxes, Tinplate & Plastic, 14 1/2 In. 165.00
Truck, Gulf, Bright Orange, Metal, 1940s, 6 In. 65.00
Truck, Haul–Away, Tin, Wyandotte, 8 1/2 In. 125.00
Truck, Hi–Way Express, Pressed–Steel, Marx 175.00
Truck, Hook & Ladder, Double Team Driver & Tillerman, Cast Iron, 26 In. 525.00
Truck, Hydraulic Dump, Buddy L 625.00
Truck, Hydraulic Pole Digger, Derrick, 1950 Dodge, Box, 6 1/2 In. 75.00
Truck, Hydraulic, Tonka 75.00
Truck, Ice Delivery, Red, Black, Canvas Cover On Bed, Buddy L, 25 1/2 In. 1525.00
Truck, Ice, Ice Blocks & Tongs, Arcade 695.00
Truck, International Wrecker, Cast Iron, Arcade, 11 In. 1100.00
Truck, Keystone Railway Express, Screen Side, Black, Green, Red, 26 In. 495.00
Truck, Lazy Day Farm, Tin 95.00
Truck, Loader, Pressed Steel, Painted, Crank Action, Keystone, 17 In. 110.00
Truck, Mail, Keystone, 26 In. 750.00
Truck, Mail, U. S., Keystone, 26 1/2 In. 1400.00
Truck, Military, Tin Lithograph, Driver, Germany, 6 In. 352.00
Truck, Milk, 14 Bottles, Buddy L, 17 In. 90.00
Truck, Mr. Mail Express, Buddy L 375.00
Truck, Nazi Artillery, Tippco, 12 In. 495.00
Truck, North American Van Lines, Windup, Marx, 1940s .... 180.00 To 185.00
Truck, Open Bed, Model T Ford, Steelplate, Black, Buddy L, 12 In. 495.00
Truck, Oven Fresh Bread & Cake, Japan 95.00
Truck, Parcel Post, U. S. Mail, Crank 605.00
Truck, Pickup, Camper, Tonka, 1962, Box 90.00
Truck, Pickup, Chevrolet, Friction, Japan, 1960s, Box 65.00
Truck, Pickup, Revell, 1950s, Box 55.00
Truck, Pumper, Painted Cast Iron, Nickel Plated, Kenton, 8 In. 325.00
Truck, Pumper, Tonka, 1950s 175.00
Truck, Railway Express Agency, Wrigley Spearmint Chewing Gum, Buddy L 685.00
Truck, Railway Express, Hubley, Cast Iron 235.00
Truck, Repair, Bell Telephone, Tin, 1940s, Japan 250.00
Truck, Rocket Launching, Ideal, Box 150.00
Truck, Rubber Tips, Tin, Turner, 26 In. 195.00
Truck, Sandloader, Buddy L 295.00
Truck, Sanitation, Marx, 1940s .... 135.00 To 210.00
Truck, Semi, With Car Carrier, Wyandotte 35.00
Truck, Sit–N–Ride, Buddy L 60.00
Truck, Stake, Model A, Arcade, Iron Wheels 85.00
Truck, Standard Oil, Cast Iron 2255.00
Truck, State Highway, Crane, Tonka 125.00
Truck, Steer, Dumps, Black Top, Red Frame, Iron Wheels, Kelmit, 26 In. 2200.00
Truck, Sunshine Biscuits, Metalcraft, 12 1/2 In. 475.00
Truck, Tank, Buddy L, Black, Green, & Red Paint, 26 In. 1320.00
Truck, Tow, Allstate, Linemar 40.00

Truck, Tow, Hubley .... 29.50 To 35.00
Truck, Tractor Trailer, Britain, No. 9434 .... 10.00
Truck, U. S. Guided Missile, Marx 50.00
Truck, U. S. Mail, Keystone, 26 In. 850.00
Truck, Van, Coast To Coast, Tootsietoy, Box. 9 In. 70.00
Truck, Van, Delivery, Pure Milk, Keystone, Kingsbury Windup, Cast Iron 425.00
Truck, Wrecker, Structo 85.00
Truck, Wrecker, White Wall Tires, Green & White, Hubley, 11 1/2 In. 40.00
Trunk, Doll's, Flat Top, Plaid Paper Over Wood, Tray 95.00
Tunnel, Lincoln Tunnel, Unique Art 125.00
Turtle, Pull, Papier–Mache 48.00
Turtle, Tin Lithograph, Windup, Original Box, Chein 200.00
Turtle, Windup, Chein, 1940s 135.00
Turtle, Windup, Tin, Occupied Japan 65.00
Tut Tut, Painted & Tin Lithograph, Windup, Lehmann 1250.00
Typewriter, Junior Dial, Marx 30.00
Typewriter, Marx, Wolverine, Tin 25.00
Typewriter, Remington, White Metal, 2 7/8 In. 10.00
Typewriter, Simplex, Box .... 28.00 To 30.00
Typewriter, Tom Thumb, Box .... 35.00 To 40.00
Typist, Vinyl Secretary, Tin Lithograph, Japan, 8 In. 140.00
Umbrella, Wizard of Oz 32.00
Uncle Sam & John Bull, Gravity See–Saw, Tin Lithograph, 8 In. 130.00
Uncle Sam, String Toy, Tin Lithograph, 8 1/4 In. 330.00
Vacuum Cleaner, Hoover, Box 35.00
Velocipede, Horse Figure With Handles For Steering, c.1880 .... 6875.00
Viewmaster Reels, Star Trek 60.00
Viewmaster, Bakelite, Sawyer, Box, 1950s 20.00
Waffle Iron, Stover Jr. 60.00
Waffle Iron, Wagner 60.00
Wagon, Blue Streak Coaster, Wooden, Steel Wheels, Alligatored, 34 In. 40.00
Wagon, Coaster, Sherwood 225.00
Wagon, Express, Wire Wheels, Red Paint, 12 In. 375.00
Wagon, Express, Wood, Wire & Sheet Steel, Wire Tongue, 12 1/4 In. 375.00
Wagon, Fender Skirts, Red 200.00
Wagon, Flying Coaster, Original Wheels 90.00
Wagon, Greyhound Bus, Dog Logo On Side, Early 1940s 125.00
Wagon, McCormick Deering, Running Gear, Arcade 65.00
Wagon, Painted Farm Scenes, Green Paint, Wooden Spokes 2800.00
Wagon, Pioneer Express 925.00
Wagon, Playboy 225.00
Wagon, Sherwood Express, Wood Spoked Wheels 440.00
Wagon, Stewart Hardware, Indiana, Penn., Spoked Wheels, Wooden 650.00
Wagon, Streak–O–Lite 275.00
Wagon, Wooden, Original Stencil, Red Trim, Varnish, 26 1/2 In. 850.00
Walking Down Broadway, Couple, Rack & Pinion Drive, Tin, Lehmann, 6 In. 2200.00
Wallet, Barbie, With Coin Holder, Mattel, c.1961 .... 25.00
Wallet, Gunsmoke, Vinyl 25.00
Wallet, Zorro 25.00
Waltzing Doll, Celluloid Head, Cloth Dress, Lehmann, 9 1/2 In. 1815.00
Washboard & Washtub, Wooden, Blue Metal Bands, 10 In., Pair 55.00
Washboard, 2 In 1 Junior Carolina Washboard 35.00
Washboard, Glass, Marked Crystal 37.00
Washboard, Little Housekeeper, Stenciled 16.00
Washboard, Wolverine 10.00
Washer & Dryer, Blue, Tin Lithograph, Marx 250.00
Washing Machine, Hand Crank, Tub–Type, Tinplate, 1925 .... 145.00
Washing Machine, Sunny Suzy, Wolverine 95.00
Washing Machine, With Wringer, Red Metal 98.00
Washtub, Doll's, Oval, Tin & Brass 35.00
Washtub, Ohio Art, 7 In. 10.00
Water Tower, Buddy L, 43 In. 600.00
Water Wagon, Double Team, Gold Striped Barrel, Tin, 9 x 22 In. 3300.00

If you have a large exposed window, put up glass shelves, fill them with inexpensive, colorful bottles. A burglar would have to break all of it, with accompanying noise, to get in.

Tramp Art, Sewing Box,
2 Heart–Shaped Pincushions, 4 x 15 In.

Water Wagon, Drawn By Pair of Horses, Painted Tin, 1870s	3300.00
Wheelbarrow, Victory, Wooden, 1940s	65.00
Wheelbarrow, Walnut, Dark Finish, 23 In.	85.00
Whirligig, Minstrels & Pig, Windup, Japan	450.00
Whistle, Dragnet, Jack Webb, Plastic	7.00
Whistle, Fish Shape, Tin	5.00
Whistle, Jack Webb, Dragnet	35.00
Wild Boar Baby, Steiff, 11 In.	75.00
Wilma Flintstone, In Car, Corgie, Box	16.00
Winky Dink, Magic T. V. Kit	20.00
Woodpecker, Mysterious, Tin, Marx	20.00
Wristwatch, Gone With The Wind, 1940s	20.00
Xylophone, Pinky Lee, Box	125.00
Xylophone, Pinocchio, Box	250.00
Xylophone, Tiny Teddy, Fisher–Price	20.00
Yellow Goat Cart, Painted Cast Iron, Nickel Plated, 7 1/2 In.	425.00
Yo–Yo, Crushy Ski–Top, Orange Crush, 1930s	85.00
Yo–Yo, Duncan, Champion, Metal	45.00
Yo–Yo, Fred Flintstone Head	10.00
Yo–Yo, General Lee Tires, Duncan	35.00
Yo–Yo, Life Savers	15.00
Yo–Yo, Oklahoma Weiner's Pride, Wooden	15.00
Zebra, Pull Toy, Straw Stuffed, Glass Eyes, Rubber Wheels, 13 x 7 In.	165.00
Zebra, Schoenhut	450.00
Zeppelin, Cast Iron, 5 In.	100.00
Zeppelin, EPL–1, Lehmann, Box	1525.00
Zeppelin, Windup, Buffalo Toy Co., 1920s	550.00
Zig–Zag, Tin Lithograph, Hand Painted, Lehmann, 5 In.	715.00

Tramp art is a form of folk art made since the Civil War. It is usually made from chip–carved cigar boxes. Examples range from small boxes and picture frames to full–sized pieces of furniture.

TRAMP ART, Box, Applied Gilt Brass, 13 1/2 In.	65.00
Box, Footed, Old Varnish, 11 1/2 x 8 x 9 1/2 In.	265.00
Box, Jewelry, Lift Top, 2 Drawers, 9 x 6 x 5 In.	170.00
Box, Rectangular, 1910	85.00
Box, Sewing, Pincushion & Spool Holder	55.00
Box, Storage, Hinged, Turret Forms, Dark Green, 9 x 7 In.	135.00
Box, Walnut, Red Fabric Interior, 6 x 13 In.	303.00
Cigar Box, Young Trumos, 1883	85.00
Clock Case, Gothic Style, Lighted Windows, 1934	775.00
Desk, 2 Small Over 2 Longer Drawers, Carved & Pierced	300.00
Dresser, Oval Mirror, 3 Drawers, Marble Top, Miniature	675.00
Frame, Teardrop Shape, 10 x 8 In.	125.00
Music Stand, 1890–1900	325.00
Pagoda, c.1910, 14 x 18 x 15 In.	145.00
Sewing Box, 2 Heart–Shaped Pincushions, 4 x 15 In. ....*Illus*	193.00

Animal traps may be handmade. One of the most unusual is the mousetrap made so that when the mouse entered the trap, it was hit on the head with a mallet. Other traps were commercially manufactured and often are marked with the name of the manufacturer. Many traps were designed to be as humane as possible, and they would trap the live animal so it could be released in the woods.

TRAP, Kodiak Bear, No. 6, Marked H In Pan	275.00
Mouse, Dead Fall, Dome Shape, c.1820	350.00
Mouse, Double, Wooden Trapezoid, Wire Grids Both Sides, Spring Handle	120.00
Mouse, Tin, Wooden	70.00
Mouse, Victor Black Cat Choker	11.00

TREEN, see Wooden

Trench art is a form of folk art made by soldiers. Metal casings from bullets and mortar shells were cut and decorated to form useful objects such as vases.

TRENCH ART, Lamp, Artillery Shells On Stainless Discs, Oak Base, 30 In.	300.00
Model, Airplane, Fuselages Are .30–Caliber Cartridges, Bullets	35.00
Plane, Fighter, World War I, Cartridges Cases, Buttons	80.00
Shell, Flowers, Argonne, World War I, Large	50.00
Shell, Vase, Brass Casing, Hammered Pattern, World War I, 12 In.	85.00
Shell, Vase, Fluted, Punched Floral, World War I, 13 In., Pair	125.00
Shell, Vase, Nude, World War I, Dated 1914	70.00

Trivets are now used to hold hot dishes. Most trivets of the late–nineteenth and early–twentieth centuries were made to hold hot irons. Iron or brass reproductions are being made of many of the old styles.

TRIVET, 2 Hearts, Handle, 3 Legs, Cast Iron	38.00
Brass, Punch Engraved Date 1826, 10 5/8 In.	65.00
Brass, Standing, 18th Century	295.00
Brass, Tea Table Shape, Reticulated Vintage Top	150.00
Child's, For Toy Iron, 3 3/4 In.	20.00
Flatiron Shape, Iron, Royal/W, Footed, 7 1/2 In.	20.00
Foliage Design, Paw Feet, Brass, England, 5 1/2 x 10 In.	65.00
Footman, Pierced Design, Brass	27.50
Fox & Tree, Pierced, Brass & Iron	25.00
General George Washington, Iron	145.00
Griswold, 5–Footed, Fancy, Round, 7 In.	50.00
Heart Shape, For Dutch Oven Kettle, Forged Iron, 5 In.	85.00
Heart, Iron	110.00
Horseshoe, Good Luck, Cast Iron, Pat'd 1885, 4 7/8 In.	75.00
Horseshoe, Laced Boots, 3–Footed, Iron, 5 1/2 x 6 In.	650.00
Indian, Cast Iron	15.00
Isle of Man, Brass	15.00
Open Hearts & Circle Center, Cast Iron, 18th Century, 4 1/2 In.	140.00
Peace & Plenty, Brass	22.50
Pierced, Brass & Iron	20.00
Reticulated Design, Brass, 11 3/8 In.	65.00
Reticulated Top, Tooling, Brass, 7 1/2 x 5 1/4 In.	95.00
Sadiron, Diamond Shape, Cast Iron, Letter T Inside, 4 x 6 1/2 In.	39.00
Smoothing Iron, Cast Iron, C. Gefrorer & Son, Philadelphia, Pa.	20.00
Smoothing Iron, Cast Iron, Colebrookdale Iron Co., Pottstown, Pa.	20.00
Spinning Star, Iron	192.00
Stars, Brass, 8 1/2 In.	25.00
State of Texas, Old Blue Paint, Cast Iron	45.00
Word Erie In Center, Footed, Elliptical, Cast Iron, 7 In.	250.00

Trunks of many types were made. The nineteenth–century sea chest was often handmade of unpainted wood. Brass–fitted camphorwood chests were brought back from the Orient. Leather–covered trunks were popular from the late–eighteenth to mid–nineteenth centuries. By 1895, trunks were covered with canvas or decorated sheet metal. Embossed metal coverings were used from 1870 to 1910. By 1925, trunks were covered with vulcanized fiber or undecorated metal.

TRUNK, Arabia, Leather Top, Intricate Brass Tack Design, Brass, 56 x 24 In.	1800.00
Brass Bound, Camphorwood, 40 In.	330.00
Brown & Black Leather Cover, Brass Tacks, 12 1/4 In.	75.00
Brown & Mustard Vinegar Design, Softwood, 24 In.	3410.00
Chinese Export, Camphorwood, Black, Bright Nail Heads Design, 1810–20	995.00
Chinese Export, Leather, Brass Bound, Studs Look Like Tassels, 3 Ft.	3025.00
Dome Top, Fitted Interior, Till, 4 Drawers, Pine, 35 In.	175.00
Dome Top, Red Flame Graining, Iron Lock, Pine & Poplar, 35 1/2 In.	175.00
Immigrant's, Dome Top, Pine, Red, Strap Hinges, 36 In.	275.00
Immigrant's, Dome Top, Pine, Traces of Blue, Iron Strapping, 30 In.	225.00
Immigrant's, Dovetailed, Iron Bound, Pine, 48 In.	175.00
Immigrant's, Pine, Green, German Inscription, 1828, 47 In.	475.00
Immigrant's, Stylized Floral, Strap Hinges, Pine, 47 In.	150.00
Immigrant's, Till, Black Graining, Pine, 27 In.	85.00
Iron Hinges & Lock, Korea, Pine, 24 In.	605.00
Leather Bound, Brass Tacks, Iron Lock, Red Trim, Black, 11 1/4 In.	140.00
Norwegian, Original Paint, Dated 1855	950.00
Steamer, Domed Hinged Top, Oak Bound Tin, 23 x 28 x 18 In.	88.00
Woven Leather Strips, Geometric Design, Spanish, Iron Mounts, 20 In.	900.00

Tuthill The Tuthill Cut Glass Company of Middletown, New York, worked from 1902 to 1923. Of special interest are the finely cut pieces of stemware and tableware.

TUTHILL, Bowl, Primrose, 8 In.	240.00
Bowl, Rex, Signed, 8 In.	2450.00
Compote, Intaglio, Rolled Over Edge, Signed, 8 1/2 In.	400.00
Fernery, Brilliant Cut Stars & Fans, Signed, 7 1/2 In.	295.00
Pitcher, Cut Stars, 8 1/2 In.	325.00
Relish, Poppy & Geometric, Signed, 9 x 4 In.	450.00
Vase, Geometric Cutting & Engraving, Corset Shape, 10 In.	275.00
Vase, Geometric Cutting & Engraving, Cylinder Shape, 10 In.	485.00
Vase, Lily, Signed, 4 In.	195.00
Vase, Overall Continous Chrysanthemum Design, Signed, 18 1/4 In.	775.00

The first successful typewriter was made by Sholes and Glidden in 1874. Collectors divide typewriters into two main classifications: the index machine, which has a pointer and a dial for letter selection, and the keyboard machine, most commonly seen today.

TYPEWRITER, Blickensderfer, No. 6	110.00
Blickensderfer, No. 7, Oak Case	125.00
Corona, No. 3, Folding, Small	35.00
Corona, Portable, 1917	25.00 To 45.00
Hammond Multiplex	95.00 To 110.00
Hammond Multiplex, Folding	50.00
Oliver, No. 5	110.00
Oliver, No. 9	55.00 To 95.00
Remington, Porto–Rite, Portable, 2–Tone Green	195.00

Uhl Pottery
hand turned
since 1849
Huntingburg Ind
Uhl pottery was made in Evansville, Indiana, in 1854. The pottery moved to Huntingburg, Indiana, in 1908. Stoneware and glazed pottery were made until the mid–1940s.

UHL, Ashtray, Cannelton Sewer Pipe Co., Telephone 774, White	275.00
Bowl, Tulips, Brown	35.00
Canteen, Blue, Small	70.00
Jug, Canteen Shape, Blue	40.00
Jug, Prunella, Brown & White	20.00
Mug, No. 16, Tan	12.00
Pitcher, Blue & White Sponge, Marked, 9 1/2 In.	550.00

Union Porcelain Works, Pitcher,
Chinese Gambler, Blue, 9 5/8 In.
Union Porcelain Works, Cup & Saucer,
Liberty, Justice, Hermes, C. 1880

Cups are best stored by hanging them on cup hooks. Stacking cups inside each other can cause chipping.

Try Grandma's solution to yellowing fabrics. She used bluing in the next to last rinse to cover the slight yellowing of age. Bluing is still sold at the supermarket.

Pitcher, Grape & Leaf Band, Marked, 7 In.	85.00
Pitcher, Grape, Squat	150.00
Pitcher, Incised Cable, 5 1/2 In.	225.00
Potlid, Blue, 7 1/2 In.	45.00
Sports, Baseball	65.00
Syrup, Cover, Blue	350.00
Urn, 5 Incised Tulips, Off–White, 5 x 6 In.	200.00
Vase, Wheat, 5 In.	235.00
Water Cooler, Cover, Polar Bear, Green, 6 Gal.	495.00

The first known umbrella was owned by King Louis XIII of France in 1637. The earliest umbrellas were sunshades, not designed to be used in the rain. The umbrella was embellished and redesigned many times. In 1852, the fluted steel rib style was developed and that has remained the most useful style.

UMBRELLA, Black Lacquer, Red Parchment, Wooden Handle & Spokes, Full Size	25.00
Black, Ornate Mother–of–Pearl & Gold Tone Handle, Large	60.00
Carved Horn Handle	125.00
Child's, Beaded Black Silk, Carved Bone Handle	50.00
Paper, Ornate, Huge	45.00
Paper, Purple, 8 In.	5.00
Parasol, Black Brocade, Floral Lining, Wood Handle, 1880	90.00
Parasol, Black Satin, Folding Handle, Tilt Top, Pinked, Civil War	75.00
Parasol, Black Silk, Ruffled Edge, Embroidered, Ebony Handle, 1890	90.00
Parasol, Geisha Canned Food, 1940s, 29 In.	35.00
Parasol, Green & Rose Brocade, Ivory Finial, Folding, 1820s	50.00
Parasol, White Linen, Wood Handle, 1919	75.00
White Eyelet, Victorian	65.00
Woman's, Parasol, White, Embroidered, 1910	60.00

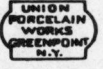

The Union Porcelain Works was established at Greenpoint, New York, in 1848 by Charles Cartlidge. The company went through a series of ownership changes and finally closed in the early 1900s. The company made a fine quality white porcelain that was often decorated in clear, bright colors.

UNION PORCELAIN WORKS, Cup & Saucer, Liberty, Justice, Hermes, c.1880 .... *Illus*	2860.00
Oyster Plate, 1881, 8 1/2 In.	225.00
Pitcher, Chinese Gambler, Blue, 9 5/8 In. ....*Illus*	4100.00

Stein, Inlaid Lid, 3 Men Drinking, Jetter Brewery 225.00
UNIVERSITY OF NORTH DAKOTA, see North Dakota School of Mines

Val St. Lambert Cristalleries of Belgium was founded by Messieurs Kemlin and Lelievre in 1825. The company is still in operation. All types of table glassware and decorative glassware were made. Pieces were often decorated with cut designs.

VAL ST. LAMBERT, Box, Cover, Berries On Vines Climbing Overall, 5 In. 1100.00
Compote, Signed, Crystal, 6 x 8 1/2 In. 225.00
Paperweight, Silhouette Cane, Canes Around, 1920s, 1 1/2 In. 125.00
Perfume Bottle & Powder Jar, Signed 175.00
Perfume Bottle, Blue Stopper, Pattern, Sapphire Blue, 5 In. 88.00
Plate, Multiple Roses & Leaves, Gray Ground, 9 In. 350.00
Plate, Van Dyck, Great Masters, Crystal 14.50
Plate, Van Gogh, Great Masters, Crystal 14.50
Tazza, Red, Clear Stem, Signed, 6 In. ....*Illus* 140.00
Vase, Amethyst Plants, Cameo, 10 In. ....*Illus* 700.00
Vase, Amethyst, Crystal, Roman Figures, Signed, 10 In. 325.00
Vase, Art Deco, Taupe, 8 1/2 In. 165.00
Vase, Berries, Clear, Frosted Pinks, 9 3/4 In. ....*Illus* 550.00
Vase, Roman Figures On Frosted Band, Amethyst, 10 3/4 In. 325.00
Vase, Sailboat & Trees, Frosted, Amethyst, Signed, 9 7/9 In. 1900.00

Vallerysthal Glassworks was founded in 1836 in Lorraine, France. In 1854 the firm became Klenglin et Cie. It made table and decorative glass, opaline, cameo, and art glass. A line of covered, pressed glass animal dishes was made in the nineteenth century. The firm is still working.

VALLERYSTHAL, Dish, Hen Cover, Milk Glass, 5 In. 50.00
Dish, Hen Cover, Opaque Blue, 5 In. 55.00
Dish, Setter With Gun Cover, Milk Glass 95.00
Dish, Squirrel Cover, Crystal & Amber 60.00
Hen, Milk Glass, Signed, 5 In. 50.00
Vase, Lavender Grapes & Leaves, Red To Clear, 3 x 4 In. 750.00
Vase, Random Blossoms, Leaves, Gilt, Signed, c.1900, 6 3/4 In. 1100.00

Van Briggle Pottery was made by Artus Van Briggle in Colorado Springs, Colorado, after 1901. Van Briggle had been a decorator at the Rookwood Pottery of Cincinnati, Ohio. He died in 1904. His

*Val St. Lambert, Tazza,
Red, Clear Stem,
Signed, 6 In.*

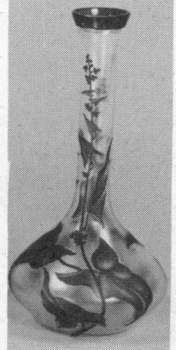

*Val St. Lambert, Vase,
Amethyst Plants,
Cameo, 10 In.*

*Val St. Lambert, Vase,
Berries, Clear,
Frosted Pinks, 9 3/4 In.*

wares usually had modeled relief decorations and a soft, dull glaze. The pottery is still working and still making some of the original designs.

VAN BRIGGLE, Bookends, Maroon	135.00
Bookends, Owl, Blue–Green	160.00
Bookends, Owl, Mt. Craig, Brown, 1919	150.00
Bookends, Puppy	185.00
Bookends, Ram, 2–Tone Blue	235.00
Bookends, Squirrel, Mulberry	90.00
Bowl, Blue Dragonfly Flower Frog, 8 3/8 In.	75.00
Bowl, Mermaid & Fish, Turtle Frog, Turquoise, 15 In.	250.00
Bowl, Persian Rose, 8 In.	40.00
Bowl, Siren of The Sea, Shell Frog, Turquoise, 14 In.	275.00 To 300.00
Bowl, Tulips, Turquoise, 8 1/2 In.	40.00
Bowl, Wine, Leaf Design, Dated 1916, 6 In.	225.00
Bust, Girl With Book, Brown, 1920, 6 1/2 In.	160.000 To 225.000
Candleholder, Ming, Turquoise, 1930, Pair	90.00
Conch Shell, Maroon, 12 In.	70.00
Figurine, Elephant, Rose, 1940s Glaze, 4 In.	85.00
Figurine, Elephant, White, 7 3/4 In.	75.00
Figurine, Indian Girl, Grinding Corn, Turquoise, Signed, 8 In.	120.00
Figurine, Indian Maiden, Grinding Corn, White Bisque, Signed	150.00
Figurine, Unicorn, Turquoise, 10 In.	50.00
Flower Frog, Duck, Turquoise	35.00
Flower Frog, Turquoise, 4 1/2 x 3 In.	25.00
Jug, Black, Anna, 9 1/2 In.	32.00
Lamp, Conch, 17 In.	85.00
Lamp, Galloping Horse, Turquoise	175.00
Lamp, Turquoise, Butterfly Shade, Natural Glaze Crackle, 1930s	165.00
Night Light, Owl, Maroon, Handle	195.00
Paperweight, Elephant	50.00
Pink–Red Glaze, Stylized Floral Panels, Conical, 10 1/8 In.	1650.00
Pitcher, Ming Blue, 7 1/2 In.	58.00
Pitcher, Sprigs, Black Glaze, Mottled Gray Lip, 12 In.	75.00
Planter, Blue, Dark Blue Swan, 9 In.	45.00
Planter, Cowboy Boot	21.00
Plaque, Indian Bust, Big Buffalo, Oval, Turquoise, 6 In.	50.00
Plate, Leaf Shape, Brown Glaze, 1971, 9 In.	20.00
Pot, Pinecone, Frothy Green, c.1908, 5 x 9 In.	1500.00
Rose Bowl, Mt. Craig, Brown, 4 In.	85.00

Van Briggle, Vase, Green Matte, Blue Overglaze, 20 In.

◆ ◆

The pattern numbers on Van Briggle pottery can help date a piece. Numbers below 899 were used before 1912. AA alone was used before 1920, AA–USA was used from 1922 to 1929.

◆ ◆

Rose Bowl, Persian Rose, Butterflies, 3 1/2 In. 65.00
Shell, Conch, Turquoise, 9 In. 35.00
Teapot, Blue, 1920s 250.00
Urn, Rust Brown, 1905, 5 x 7 In. 120.00
Vase, 3 Nude Women, Outstretched Arms, Support Drapery, 11 In. 250.00
Vase, Allover Leaf & Thistle, Mauve Glaze, Gourd, 8 1/2 In. 2100.00
Vase, Blue, 1904, 11 In. 575.00
Vase, Butterfly, Green, Brown, 3 In. 35.00
Vase, Clover, Marked, 5 In. 65.00
Vase, Crocus, Feathered Brown To Ocher, 1904, 4 x 4 1/2 In. 550.00
Vase, Curdled Blue Over Cream, 1918, 10 In. 600.00
Vase, Geese Heads, Green–Black Glaze, Short Baluster, 6 1/4 In. 3300.00
Vase, Green Matte, Blue Overglaze, 20 In. ....*Illus* 660.00
Vase, Indian Head, Burgundy, 1920s, 11 In. 340.00
Vase, Iris, Ming Turquoise Glaze, 13 1/2 In. 50.00
Vase, Leaf Design, Honey Brown, 1915, 4 1/2 In. 225.00
Vase, Lorelei, Blue Tones, Signed Z, 1970, 11 In. .... 195.00 To 350.00
Vase, Lorelei, Off–White, Marked, 10 1/2 In. 185.00
Vase, Lorelei, Woman Figure Wrapped Around, Burgundy, 9 1/2 In. 665.00
Vase, Molded Floral Design, Semi–Matte Glaze, c.1904, 8 1/2 In. 935.00
Vase, Moth, Dated 1918, 2 1/2 In. 200.00
Vase, Mt. Craig, Leaves, Panels, Brown, 12 1/2 In. 140.00
Vase, Narcissi, Matte Green Glaze, c.1904, 9 5/8 In. 775.00
Vase, Persian Rose, Tulip Shape, 3 1/2 In. 25.00
Vase, Poppies & Pods, Maroon, 7 3/4 In. 275.00
Vase, Red, Blue Dragonflies, 8 In. 285.00
Vase, Relief Cranes, Turquoise Matte Glaze, TE, 16 3/4 In. 600.00
Vase, Repeated Daisies, Blue On Turquoise Matte, 12 1/2 In. 257.00
Vase, Repeated Stylized Flowers, Blue, Turquoise, 5 1/2 In. 235.00
Vase, Shell, Wine, Marked 45.00
Vase, Striated Brown Matte Glaze, Ovoid, c.1909, 9 3/4 In. 250.00
Vase, Turquoise Yucca Blossoms, Foliage, c.1920, 14 In. 400.00
Vase, Whiplash, Stylized Leaves, Pea Green, 1904, 12 1/2 In. 1760.00
Vase, Yucca, Turquoise, 6 In. 135.00
Wall Pocket, Persian Rose, Colorado Springs, 7 3/4 In. 70.00

Vasa Murrhina is the name of a glassware made by the Vasa
Murrhina Art Glass Company of Sandwich, Massachusetts, about
1884. The glassware was transparent and was embedded with small
pieces of colored glass and metallic flakes. Some of the pieces were
cased. The same type of glass was made in England. Collectors often
confuse Vasa Murrhina glass with aventurine, spatter, or spangle
glass. There is much confusion about what actually was made by the
Vasa Murrhina factory.

VASA MURRHINA, see also Spangle Glass
VASA MURRHINA, Bride's Bowl, Mica Flecking, Butterscotch, V Handle, 13 In. 550.00
Ewer, White Lining, Clear Handle, Silver Spangles, 9 3/8 In. 135.00
Lamp, Finger, Alternating Stripes, Mica Flakes, 5 1/2 In. 195.00
Rose Bowl, 8–Crimp Top, Mica Flakes, 3 3/4 x 4 1/8 In. 100.00
Rose Bowl, 8–Crimp Top, Mica Flakes, Blue & White, 3 1/4 In. 88.00
Rose Bowl, Beige, Red Spatter, Swirled Mica Flakes, 3 3/8 In. 110.00
Vase, Crimped Ruffled Top, Red Ground, Silver Mica, 7 1/2 In. 175.00
Vase, Mica Flakes, White Lining, Orange Overlay, 8 3/8 In. 125.00
Vase, Swirl, Mica Flecking, Cranberry Interior, 10 In. 145.00

Vaseline glass is a greenish–yellow glassware resembling petroleum
jelly. Some vaseline glass is still being made in old and new styles.
Pressed glass of the 1870s was often made of vaseline–colored glass.
Some pieces of vaseline glass may also be listed under Pressed Glass
in this book.

VASELINE GLASS, Basket, Amber Thorny Handle, 2 Pink Flowers, 8 1/2 In. 245.00
Basket, Crimped & Ruffled Rim, Yellow Handle, 12 x 12 In. 150.00
Basket, Flowers, Opalescent, Amber Thorn Handle, 8 1/2 In. 245.00

Basket, Pressed Cherry, Applied Handle, 5 x 4 In.	65.00
Berry Bowl Set, Child's	65.00
Berry Bowl, Lacy Daisy	65.00
Berry Set, Gold, 5 Piece	125.00
Bowl, Hobnail, Ruffled, Opalescent, 4 1/2 x 9 1/2 In	90.00
Bowl, Swan	25.00
Bread Tray, Diamond Center, Frosted Leaf Rim, 13 In.	90.00
Candleholder, Opalescent, Pair	35.00
Celery Vase, Petticoat Pattern	225.00
Compote, Engraved Vintage Pattern	135.00
Compote, Fruit	59.00
Compote, Opalescent	45.00
Cruet, Alaska, Opalescent	245.00
Eyecup	25.00
Fairy Lamp	65.00
Hand Mirror	49.00
Lamp, Leaf Mold, Miniature	245.00
Mug, Kitten	25.00
Pedestal, Clark's Teabury Gum	48.00
Reamer	49.00
Rose Bowl, Fern & Daisy	65.00
Salt Dip, Tulip	25.00
Toothpick, Fan & Feather	25.00
Toothpick, Inverted Thumbprint, Barrel Shape	110.00
Toothpick, S Repeat	25.00
Toothpick, Witch's Pot	25.00
Tray, Chick, Miniature	25.00
Tumbler	25.00
Water Set, Leaf Mold, 7 Piece	665.00
Wine	25.00

Venetian glass has been made near Venice, Italy, from the thirteenth to the twentieth century. Thin, colored glass with applied decoration is favored, although many other types have been made. Collectors have recently become interested in the Art Deco and fifties designs. Glass was made on the Venetian island of Murano from 1291. The output dwindled in the late seventeenth century, but began to flourish again in the 1850s. Some of the old techniques of glassmaking were revived and firms today make traditional designs and original modern glass. Since 1981, the name *Murano* may only be used on glass made on Murano Island. Other pieces of Italian glass may be found in the Contemporary Glass and Veneni sections of this book.

VENETIAN GLASS, Ashtray, Blue, Silver Mica, Murano	20.00
Ashtray, Green & Yellow, Silver Mica, Murano	20.00
Candleholder, Blue Jeweled Knobs, Pink, 10 In.	100.00
Candlestick, Dolphin, Gold Flecks, Berry Prunting, 5 In., Pr.	45.00
Compote, White Latticinio Stripe, Dolphin Stem, 6 In.	120.00
Figurine, Rooster, Gold, Red, 8 In., Murano	40.00
Jewel Box, Frosted Orange, Brass Hinged, Murano	295.00
Lemonade Set, Hand Painted Flowers, Frosted & Green, 6 Pc.	150.00
Obelisk, Red & Blue Horizontal Stripes, 9 In.	375.00
Perfume Bottle, Red & Gold Striped, 6 In.	225.00
Plate, Gold Flecked, Gold, 9 In.	54.00
Sculpture, Freeform, Clear, Seguso, 26 1/2 In.	1650.00
Tray, Ribbon Etched, Courting Scene, Dolphin Handles, Murano	275.00
Vase, Asymmetric, Polychrome Patchwork, AVEM, 1960s, 15 In.	4400.00
Vase, Black Spirals, Red Zigzags, Footed, c.1960, 7 3/4 In.	9690.00
Vase, Bulbous, Yellow Rim, Gold Speckled, Barover & Toso	75.00
Vase, Cylinder, Murrhine, E. Barovier, c.1956, 10 In.	10560.00
Vase, Double, Black, Millefiori, A. Nason, c.1960, 15 1/2 In.	5280.00
Vase, Ovoid, Blue Carved Surface, Barbini, c.1962, 10 In.	7925.00
Vase, Pointed Top, Murrhine, AVEM, Ferro, 1953, 19 1/2 In.	7750.00

Vase, Red, Clear, Gold Flecks, 11 1/2 In., Pair	110.00
Vase, Rotellati Series, E. Barovier, c.1970, 12 In.	3080.00
Vase, Sideri Series, E. Barovier, 1967, 13 1/4 In.	4400.00
Vase, Split, Millefiori Canes, Pink, Crystal Casing, 12 In.	64.00
Vase, Squashed Body, Elongated Spout, Toso, c.1954, 10 In.	5280.00

venini
mmarano
ITALIA

Paolo Venini established a glass factory in Murano, Italy, in 1925. He is best known for pieces of modern design, including the famous *handkerchief* vase. The company is still working. Other pieces of Italian glass may be found in the Contemporary Glass and Venetian Glass sections of this book.

VENINI, Bottle, Tessuto, Narrow Body, Thin Neck, Scarpa, c.1955, 9 1/4 In.	2290.00
Bowl, Cut Corners, Folded Inward, Trapped Air Bubbles, 15 x 10 In.	715.00
Candlestick, Black Glass, Signed, Paper Label, 4 In.	50.00
Figurine, Musician Playing Instrument, c.1950, 9 To 9 1/2 In., 4 Pc.	1320.00
Fruit Bowl, Gray, 15 In.	725.00
Hour Glass, Blue & Green, 7 In.	575.00
Vase, Flattened Oval, Patchwork, Red, Blue, Green, Bianconi, 8 1/4 In.	8250.00
Vase, Free Form, Iridescent Red, Signed, 6 3/4 In.	1325.00
Vase, Handkerchief, Striped Colors & Clear, 8 1/2 In.	850.00
Vase, Occhi, Ovoid, Narrow Neck, Blown Glass, Murrino, c.1960, 6 In.	6170.00

Verlys

Verlys glass was made in France after 1931. It was made in the United States from 1935 to 1951. The glass is either blown or molded. The American glass is signed with a diamond–point–scratched name, but the French pieces are marked with a molded signature. The designs resemble those used by Lalique.

VERLYS, Bowl, Birds & Bees, Signed, 11 1/2 In.	135.00
Bowl, Child & Lamb, Signed, 1944, 13 In.	195.00
Bowl, Coral, Thistle, 11 3/4 In.	125.00
Bowl, Poppy, Frosted, Signed, 14 In.	159.00
Charger, Water Lily, 13 1/2 In.	125.00
Console, Sculptured Poppies, Frosted, Signed, 14 In.	155.00
Trivet, Opalescent Fish, Oval, 12 In.	275.00
Vase, Autumn & Spring Figures In Relief, Signed, 8 1/4 In.	225.00
Vase, Blown–Out Flowers, Frosted & Clear, 7 In.	175.00
Vase, Mermaids, Flowing Hair, Sea Creatures, Signed, 1925, 10 5/8 In.	1325.00
Vase, Overall Raised Rose Blossoms, 7 1/2 In.	110.00
Vase, Sunflower, Flared Flattened Rim, Topaz, Ovoid, Signed, 9 In.	660.00

VERNON
MONTICITO

Vernon Potteries, Ltd., started in Vernon, California, in 1931. It became Vernon Kilns by 1948. The company made dinnerware and figurines until it closed in 1958. Collectors search for the brightly colored dinnerware and the pieces designed by Rockwell Kent, Walt Disney, and Don Blanding. For more information, see *Kovels' Depression Glass & American Dinnerware Price List.*

VERNON KILNS, Ashtray, Galloping Goose, Rio Grande R.R.	40.00
Bowl, Brown–Eyed Susan, 9 In.	12.00
Bowl, Cover, Beverly, Melinda Shape, Oval, 9 In.	45.00
Bowl, Salamina, Pewter Frame With Handles, 9 1/2 In.	200.00
Bowl, Tab Handle, May Flower	2.00
Bowl, Vegetable, May Flower, Round	7.50
Bowl, Winged Nymph, 12 In.	265.00
Casserole, Cover, Homespun	17.00
Chop Plate, Homespun, 12 In.	10.00
Chop Plate, Organdie, 12 In.	10.00
Console Set, Hawaiian Flowers, Blue, 3 Piece	95.00
Creamer, Hawaiian Flowers, Blue	22.00
Cup & Saucer, Brown–Eyed Susan, After Dinner	10.00
Cup & Saucer, Homespun	4.50
Cup & Saucer, Monument Valley, Ariz., After Dinner	14.00
Cup & Saucer, Organdie	4.50
Figurine, Ballet Elephant	400.00

Pitcher, Organdie	18.00
Plate, Anniston, Ala., 11 In.	12.00
Plate, Baker's Chocolate, 10 In.	45.00
Plate, Bits of Old England, 8 1/2 In.	15.00
Plate, Bits of The Old West, 8 1/2 In.	20.00
Plate, Brown–Eyed Susan, 10 In.	7.00
Plate, Chicago Railroad Fair, 1949, 10 3/8 In.	40.00
Plate, Eisenhower & Nixon, Colored, 10 1/2 In.	50.00
Plate, Florida	10.00
Plate, Lei Lani, 14 In.	55.00
Plate, Moby Dick, 9 In.	45.00
Plate, Our America, Sternwheeler, Signed, 6 1/2 In.	10.00
Plate, Pennsylvania Turnpike	5.00
Plate, Salamina, 9 1/2 In.	55.00 To 95.00
Plate, Santa Rosa, Calif.	5.00
Plate, St. Louis, 10 1/2 In.	18.00
Plate, Stage Arrival, 8 1/2 In.	20.00
Plate, State of Texas, 9 In.	10.00
Platter, Brown–Eyed Susan, 11 In.	8.00
Platter, Raffia, Chartreuse, Oval, 11 In.	5.00
Salt & Pepper, Homespun	8.00
Salt & Pepper, Mushroom, Disney Fantasia, c.1941	185.00
Teapot, Kansas, Yellow, Gold Trim	125.00
Teapot, Tweed	35.00
Tidbit, Brown–Eyed Susan	17.50
Tumbler, Ultra California, Pink	10.00
Vase, Pink Flowers, Pair	25.00

Verre de soie glass was first made by Frederick Carder at the Steuben Glass Works from about 1905 to 1930. It is an iridescent glass of soft white or very, very pale green. The name means glass of silk, and it does resemble silk. Other factories have made verre de soie, and some of the English examples were made of different colors. Verre de soie is an art glass and is not related to the iridescent, pressed, white Carnival glass mistakenly called by its name.

VERRE DE SOIE, see also Steuben

VERRE DE SOIE, Cruet, Double Spouted, Engraved Florals, 7 1/2 In.	185.00
Goblet, Bell Form, Iridescent Finish, 6 In., 9 Piece	495.00
Perfume Bottle, Roselaine Dipper, Steuben, 5 In.	525.00
Vase, Corset, Steuben, 6 1/4 x 3 3/4 In.	120.00

Vienna Art plates are round metal serving trays produced at the turn of the century. The designs, copied from Royal Vienna porcelain plates, usually featured a portrait of a woman encircled by a wide, ornate border. Many were used as advertising or promotional items and were produced in Coshocton, Ohio, by J. F. Meeks Tuscarora Advertising Co. and H. D. Beach's Standard Advertising Co.

VIENNA ART, Plate, Semi–Nude Woman, Maroon Border	45.00
Plate, Statue In Garden, Beige	55.00
Plate, Woman With Urn	55.00
Plate, Woman, Floral Border, Green	45.00

VIENNA, see Beehive

◆◆◆

Use a clean plant mister to dampen old fabrics for ironing. Mist the cloth then roll it and wrap it in a towel for a few hours so the moisture will be absorbed into the threads.

◆◆◆

The Villeroy & Boch Pottery of Mettlach was founded in 1841. The firm made many types of pottery, including the famous Mettlach steins. It is confusing for the collector because although Villeroy and Boch made most of its pieces in the city of Mettlach, Germany, they also had factories in other locations. There is a dating code impressed on the bottom of most pieces that makes it possible to determine the age of the piece.

VILLEROY & BOCH, see also Mettlach

VILLEROY & BOCH, Beaker, Bowl	58.00
Coffepot, Blue & White, Bulbous Bottom, 1900, 10 In.	145.00
Plaque, Wallerfangen Boats, Mecury Mark, 10 1/4 In.	65.00
Stein, No. 1370, 1/2 Liter	175.00

VOLKMAR Corona N.Y

Volkmar pottery was made by Charles Volkmar of New York from 1879 to about 1911. He was associated with several firms, including the Volkmar Ceramic Company, Volkmar and Cory, and Charles Volkmar and Son. Volkmar had been a painter, and his designs often look like oil paintings drawn on pottery.

VOLKMAR, Charger, Blue & White, 11 In.	185.00
Vase, Blue, White, Green, 10 In.	500.00

Volkstedt was a soft-paste porcelain manufactory started in 1760 by Georg Heinrich Macheleid at Volkstedt, Thuringia. Volkstedt-Rudolstadt was a porcelain factory started at Volkstedt-Rudolstadt by Beyer and Bock in 1890. Most pieces seen in shops today are from the later factory.

VOLKSTEDT, Figurine, Chess Game, Table & Pieces, Man, Woman, 6 x 9 In.	850.00
Figurine, Rook, 7 In.	125.00
Group, Wedding March, Bride & Groom, 7 x 13 In.	1250.00
Plaque, Cherubs, Green Jasperware, White Floral Frame, 9 x 10 In.	450.00
Vase, Art Nouveau Form, Applied Fish, Lizard & Angel, 8 1/2 In.	55.00
WAHPETON POTTERY, see Rosemeade	

WALLACE NUTTING photographs are listed under Print, Nutting. His reproduction furniture is listed under Furniture.

Frederich Walrath was a potter who worked in New York City, Rochester, New York, and at the Newcomb Pottery in New Orleans, Louisiana. He died in 1920. Pieces listed here are from his Rochester period.

WALRATH, Vase, Art Nouveau, Floral Design, Signed, 7 3/4 In.	1870.00
Vase, Flared, Green, Blue, 6 In.	750.00
Vase, Vegetal Green Matte, Over Burgundy, Flared, 1907, 5 x 3 In.	577.00
WALT DISNEY, see Disneyana	
WALTER, see A. Walter	

Warwick china was made in Wheeling, West Virginia, in a pottery working from 1887 to 1951. Many pieces were made with hand painted or decal decorations. The most familiar Warwick has a shaded brown background. The name *Warwick* is part of the mark and sometimes the word *IOGA* is also included.

WARWICK, Cheese Saver, Violets, Green, Lily of The Valley Scrolls	75.00
Ewer, Oak Leaves & Acorns, Green Glaze, IOGA, 10 In.	95.00
Mug, B. P. O. E.	72.00
Mug, Fisherman, 1910	55.00 To 60.00
Mug, Monk	95.00
Stein, B. P. O. E., IOGA	45.00
Tankard, Brown, Poppy, 10 1/2 In.	140.00
Tankard, Elk Picture, B. P. O. E., 13 In.	90.00
Tankard, Portrait, Cardinal, Bar Handle, 10 1/2 In.	145.00
Vase, Aladdin Style Handles, Floral Both Sides, IOGA, 7 1/2 In.	75.00
Vase, Brown, Floral, Thelma, 11 In.	130.00
Vase, Flowers & Stems, 4 In.	70.00

Vase, Full–Faced Woman, Cascading Hair, Twig Handles, 10 1/2 In. 145.00
Vase, Loga Twig, Gypsy With Shawl 165.00
Vase, Profile of Woman With Red Roses, Twig Handles, 12 In. 145.00
Vase, Woman Portrait, Ringlet Hair, Headband, Square Handles, 10 In. 150.00
Vase, Woman, Pearls In Hair, Star Medallion On Ear, 10 1/2 In. 145.00

Watch fobs were worn on watch chains. They were popular during Victorian times and after. Many styles, especially advertising designs, are still made today.

WATCH FOB, Adams Leaning Machinery 45.00
Adolph Hitler, Brass, Dated 1943 .... 22.50
Allis–Chalmers, Tractor 75.00
American Bakery & Confectionery Workers, Enameled 25.00
Anheuser Beer, Enameled A & Flag 125.00
Ashland, Kentucky, Coal 15.00
Atlantic City Seal, 1854 .... 35.00
Attached Strap, Bullet, Flag Says Protect The Flag, 1910s 61.00
Banigan Condoms .... 35.00 To 45.00
Birdsell Clover & Alfalfa Hullers, Threshing Machine, Bronze 75.00
Block Electrical Cutting Machines 35.00
Broadcasting Suits For Boys 75.00
Brotherhood of Eagles, Pink Gold, Fob With Ivory Elk's Teeth 150.00
Brotherhood of Locomotive, Fireman & Engineers 40.00
Bucyrus Erie, Brass, c.1912 .... 30.00
Bull Durham 75.00
Carnelian, Child With Grapes, Perched On Bear, 14K Gold 330.00
Caterpillar 25.00
CNR, Locomotive 25.00
Compass 65.00
Dead Shot, Winchester 125.00
Delmont Watches 45.00
Diamond Edge Shapleigh 50.00
Dr Pepper 85.00
Drink Chero–Cola 40.00
Elk's Tooth, Large 35.00
Finck & Co., Railroad Overalls, Celluloid, Train 85.00
Goldsmith's Sporting Goods, Baseball Shape 150.00
Green River Whiskey 55.00
Harley Davidson 27.50
Hatchet Shape, Centennial, 1876 .... 50.00
Hughes Tool 45.00
Intaglio Roman Soldier Head, Square Carnelian, Yellow Gold 65.00
K. C. Southern Golden Spike Anniversary, 1897–1947 .... 47.00
Kellogg's Toasted Corn Flakes 75.00
Keystone Watch Case Co., 1893 Exposition 22.50
Martin–Senour Paints, Celluloid Insert 75.00
Massey Harris Farm Equipment 70.00
McCaws Washing Powder, Celluloid Insert 75.00

◆◆

Good tips for care of Fiesta and any other heavy, color–glazed dishes of the 1930s. Bauer is oven safe for baking—up to 350 degrees. Do not use in a microwave. Do not use on a direct flame. Do not wash in an automatic dishwasher. The detergent may discolor the glaze. Do not scour. Store with felt between stacked plates to avoid scratching. Early 1930 to 1942 dishes used a lead in the glazing, so do not use scratched dishes with acidic foods. Lead poisoning is possible with prolonged use.

◆◆

McKinley Monument	17.50
Michigan Power Shovel	28.00
Munson Warm–Air Furnaces	35.00
Nashville National Building Dedication, Enameled	40.00
National Sportsman, Gillette Tires	45.00
National Sportsman, Magazine	35.00
National Thresher's Assoc., Enameled	60.00
Newark, N. J., 250th Anniversary, Enameled Pilgrims, 1916	35.00
Northwestern Hide & Fur Co.	150.00
Omaha Bee News, Newsboy	30.00
Ox Tobacco, Ox Picture, Celluloid, Flink Tobacco Co.	95.00
Padlock Trousers, Lock Shape	45.00
Pierce Arrow, Enameled Arrowhead	85.00
S. Silberman & Son Fur Co.	150.00
Samuel Rosenthal & Bros., Boy Holding Up Britches, Copper, 1890 ..	30.00
San Francisco Earthquake, 1906	25.00
Sante Fe Railroad	135.00
Shell Oil Co.	85.00
T. P. A., 27th Annual Convention, Enclosed Compass, 1917	20.00
Taggart's Bread	25.00
Trainman, Chain	68.00
U. S. Gypsum, 1928	20.00
U. S. Master Brewers Assoc., 1911	50.00
West Pennsylvania Volunteer Firemen, Aluminum, Strap, 1926	25.00
Woodmen Accident Assoc., Home Office, Lincoln, Enameled Brass	30.00
Wright & Ditson, Baseball	95.00
Yellow Gold, Intaglio Cut, Black Onyx	65.00

The pocket watch was important in Victorian times because it was not until World War I that the wristwatch was used. All types of watches are collected: silver, gold, or plated. Watches are listed by company name or by style. Pocket watches are listed here. Wristwatches are listed in their own category.

WATCH, A. Lange & Sohne, Pocket, Hunter Case, 18K Gold, Cord Bezels, c.1880	2475.00
Boston Watch Co., Hunting Case, Gold Filled	200.00
Bradley, Smokey, Box	195.00
C. H. Meylan, Platinum, 21 Jewels, Black Bezels, Size 16	695.00
Carriage, Key Wind, Fusee, Sterling Silver Case, Chain, Fob	2950.00
Cartier, Openface, 18 Jewels, Silvered Dial, c.1900	2750.00
Charles Taylor & Son, Knights Jousting, Key Wind, 18K Gold	2500.00
Coin, 1907 U. S. 20 Dollar Gold Piece, 18K Yellow Gold, Jeweled	1210.00
Duber, Hunting, John Hancock Model, Lever Set, 1960s	200.00
Eberhard, Quarter Repeating Chronograph, 18K Gold, c.1900	1760.00
Elgin, 21 Jewel, Hunting Case	250.00
Elgin, 5–Position Adjustment, 19 Jewels, Lever Set	200.00
Elgin, Art Deco, Black & Chrome .... 65.00 To	85.00
Elgin, Coin Silver Case, Key Wind & Set, 1887	185.00
Elgin, Colored Dial, Hunting Case, 15 Jewels, Rose Gold	275.00
Elgin, Culver, Railroad, Keywind	150.00
Elgin, Diamond, 14K Gold	395.00
Elgin, Hunting Case, Gold, 1897	350.00
Elgin, Keywind, Coin Silver Case	375.00
Elgin, Scenic Hunting Case, 14K Gold, 1970s	160.00
Elgin, Silver Dial, 14K Gold	270.00
Elgin, Timer, Black Dial, Nickel, 1/4 Seconds, U. S. Army Air Corp	100.00
Elgin, Woman's, Hunting Case, Bird & Flowers, 14K Gold, 1888	350.00
Elgin, Woman's, Hunting Case, Coin Silver, Keywind, c.1881	200.00
Elgin, Woman's, Hunting Case, Gold	240.00
Ford, 1960	85.00
Fred Nicoud, Jeweled Movement, Enamel Dial, Hunting Case, 18K Gold	525.00
Gruen, Woman's, 8–Sided, Shadowbox Effect, Gold Numerals, 14K Gold	500.00
Hamilton, 16 Jewel, Grade 933, Sterling Silver, Low Serial Number	750.00
Hamilton, 16 Jewel, Hunting Case, Sterling, H. G. Smith .... 650.00 To	900.00

Hamilton, 19 Jewel, Eagle & American Flag On Case .... 175.00 To 225.00
Hamilton, 23 Jewel, 14K Gold 375.00
Hamilton, 23 Jewel, Gold Jewel Setting 285.00
Hamilton, 23 Jewel, Train, Pocket 350.00
Hamilton, Glass Back Display Case, Nickel 100.00
Hamilton, Military, Black Dial, Sweep Second Hand, Yellow Gold 150.00
Hamilton, Railroad Special, Model 9992B 200.00
Hamilton, Sea–Lectric II, Steel, 1st Model, Battery 200.00
Hampden, 21 Jewel, Duber 25 Hunting Case, John Hancock Model 175.00
Hampden, 21 Jewel, Lever Set, John Hancock Model 200.00
Hampden, General Stark, Hunting Case, Engraved 250.00
Hampden, Wm. McKinley Model, Dueber Case, Railroad Grade 70.00
Howard, Hunting Case, Gold 290.00
Hunting Case, 18K Gold, Chronometer Invicta, Roadster Picture, 1900 .... 2860.00
Hunting Case, Double Dial Calendar, 18K Gold, Roman Numerals, 1900 .... 2090.00
Hunting Case, Gold, Mock Pendulum, 1850 .... 2200.00
Illinois, 2–Tone Gun Metal 20.00
Illinois, 21 Jewel, 2–Colored Dial, 14K Gold 325.00
Illinois, 21 Jewel, Railroad, Burlington 200.00
Illinois, Bunn Special, 21 Jewel, Pocket, c.1872 .... 225.00
Illinois, Bunn Special, 60 Hour, 10K Gold Filled 330.00
Illinois, Bunn Special, Gold Cap Jewels, 23 Jewel, 14K White Gold 700.00
Illinois, Bunn Special, Silver Case, Chain 200.00
Illinois, Bunn, Railroad, Base Metal 200.00
Illinois, Coin Silver Hunting Case, Name Dial, 1876 .... 150.00
Illinois, Glass Back Display Case, Nickel 65.00
Illinois, Key Wind, Set, c.1872, Pocket 175.00
Illinois, Lincoln Train On Reverse, Adjusted To 5 Positions 250.00
Illinois, Woman's, Hunting Case, 14K Gold 135.00
Illinois, Woman's, Hunting, Deer Scene, 14K Gold, 1887 .... 650.00
Illnois, Key Wind & Set, 1872 .... 200.00
Imperial Eagle On Cover, Enameled Dial, Pavel Buhre, c.1900 .... 3300.00
Ingersoll, Dollar, New York To Paris Airplane On Dial 150.00
J. Assmann, Gold Hunting Case, Scroll Work With Acorns, c.1880 .... 6100.00
J. Stoddart, Keywind, Enamel Dial, Hunting Case, Fitted Box, c.1872 .... 660.00
J. Watson, Silver, Dated 1861 .... 425.00
James Picard, Portrait of Woman On Face, 18K Gold 1485.00
John C. Heppert, 21 Ruby Jewels, Railroad, Lever Set 250.00
Langined, Open Face Design, Second Hand, 18K Yellow Gold 335.00
Lapel, Marcasite, Silver 175.00
LH & Co., 14K Gold, Hunting, Lighthouse Design, Size 6 .... 649.00
Longines, 17 Jewel, 14K Gold 225.00
Longines, Hunting Case, Minute Repeating, 18K Gold, 1900 .... 5225.00
Moonphase Calendar, Gunmetal, Porcelain Dial, Filigree Hands 349.00
Movado, Calendar, Day, Date, Second Hand, 14K Gold, 1940s 995.00
New York Watch, World's Exhibition, Hunting, Size 16 .... 649.00
Opera, Waltham, 1908 .... 95.00
P. A. Merckel, Repeating, Gilt Verge Movement, Vari–Color, 1780 .... 3100.00
Patek Philippe, 18 Jewel, Open Face, 18K Gold, Regulator, 1955 .... 2200.00
Patek Philippe, 18K Pink Rose Gold, Repouse Style 3000.00
Patek Philippe, Open Face, Platinum, Diamond, 14K White Gold Chain 6050.00
Patek Philippe, Porcelain Enamel Dial, 18K Gold, Open Face 2495.00
Piaget, Baton Numerals, Folds Into 10 Dollar U. S. Gold Piece 3100.00
Poitevin Geneva, 21 Jewel, Straight Line Escapement, 18K Gold 625.00
Poitevin, 21 Jewel, Straight Line Escapement, 18K Gold 700.00
Rolex, 2 Tone 14K Gold Bezel & Crown, Perpetual, Chronograph, 1950s 1000.00
Seth Thomas, Porcelain Dial, 2–Tone Gold, Signed 90.00
South Bend, 21 Jewel, Colored Dial, 14K Gold Case, 1960s .... 185.00 To 200.00
South Bend, 21 Jewel, Open Face, Gold Case, c.1913 .... 200.00
Swiss, 1/4 Hour Repeater, 14K Gold 1400.00
Swiss, Colsen Incabloc, 17 Jewel, Train On Reverse, 10K Gold 110.00
Thomas Wagstaffe, Open Face, Gold Case, c.1770 .... 2300.00
Tiffany, Chronograph, Silver Over Gold Case, 1 Button, Pocket 399.00

Watch, Waltham, Pocket, Hunting Case, 14K Gold

◆ ◆

If you are having antique jewelry repaired, be sure the jeweler uses old stones. New ones are cut differently and will seem brighter. Pearls and turquoise change color with age.

◆ ◆

Tiffany, Open Face, 18K Gold, Enameled, Arabic Numerals, 1900	5775.00
Tiffany, Open Face, Repeating, 18K Gold, Arabic Numerals, 1930	4950.00
Tiffany, Pocket, 19 Jewels, Thin	444.00
Tiffany, Victorian, Jeweled Nickel Movement, Enamel Face, Hunting	825.00
Tourbillon, Open Face, Gun-Metal Case, Roman Numerals, 1900	2860.00
Tremont, Key Wind, Coin Silver Case	350.00
U. S. Royal, Golf Ball, 1950s	95.00
Ulysse Nardin, Hunting, 18K Gold, Chronograph, Register, Monogram, 1900	2100.00
Ulysse Nardin, Hunting, 18K Gold, Repeating, Chronograph, Register, 189	6600.00
Vacheron & Constantin, Woman's, Open Face, 18K Gold, Enamel, 1900	2530.00
Vacheron, 8 Jewel, White Enamel Dial, Cylinder Movement, Hunting Case	330.00
Waltham, 21 Jewel, Railroad, 10K Rolled Gold Plate	275.00
Waltham, 23 Jewel, Yellow Gold Filled, Porcelain Dial	425.00
Waltham, Broadway, Key Wind, Silveride Case	65.00
Waltham, Hunting, 14K Gold	800.00
Waltham, Key Wind, Coin Silver Case	225.00
Waltham, Key Wind, Gold, Key	200.00
Waltham, Nickel Movement, Enamel Dial, 14K Gold	330.00
Waltham, Pocket, Hunting Case, 14K Gold ....*Illus*	287.00
Waltham, Railroad Inspector, Name, Silverore, Porcelain Dial, Pocket	149.00
Waltham, Railroad, Open Face, Gold Hinges, Coin Silver	100.00
Waltham, Van Guard, Diamond Cap Jewels	300.00
Washington, 17 Jewel, Liberty Bell, Hunting, Gold Filled	899.00
Woman's, Hunter Case, Jeweled Movement, Blue & Gold Numbers	825.00

Waterford-type glass resembles the famous glass made from 1783 to 1851 in the Waterford Glass Works in Ireland. It is a clear glass that was often decorated by cutting. Modern glass is being made again in Waterford, Ireland, and is marketed under the name *Waterford*.

WATERFORD, Bell, No. 200	150.00
Brandy Snifter, Alana, 8 In.	412.00
Decanter, Alana, Round, Flat Cut Stopper	165.00
Girondole, 4 Scrolled Candle Arms, Prisms, Electric, 27 In.	110.00
Goblet, Lismore, 12 Piece	400.00
Goblet, Wine, Alana, Set of 8	358.00
Salt & Pepper, Pedestal, Signed, 6 In.	138.00
Tureen, Cover, Relief Diamond, Oval Underplate, 11 In.	137.50
Vase, Bud, Trumpet Form, 7 In.	110.00
Vase, Cut Flowers, 8 1/2 In.	425.00

The Watt family bought the Globe pottery of Crooksville, Ohio, in 1922. They made pottery mixing bowls and dishes of the type made by Globe. In 1935 they changed the production and made the pieces with the freehand decorations that are popular with collectors today. Apple, Starflower, Rooster, Red & Blue Tulip, and Autumn Foliage are the best-known patterns. Apple, the most popular pattern, can

◆◆

Fresh air and limited sunlight are good for fabrics. Cotton and linen should be washed once a year, even if stored in a drawer, because dirt will cause damage. Dry clean wool and silk if cleaning is needed. Protect fabrics from moths with the usual precautions. Paradichlorobenzine will do the job.

◆◆

be dated from the leaves. Originally, the apples had three leaves; after 1958 two leaves were used. The plant closed in 1965. For more information, see *Kovels' Depression Glass & American Dinnerware Price List.*

WATT, Baker, Cover, Starflower, No. 96, Wire Stand	60.00
Bean Pot, Apple, No. 21, Open	35.00
Berry Bowl, Starflower, 4 Piece	50.00
Bowl, Apple, No. 5	15.00
Bowl, Apple, No. 6	15.00 To 30.00
Bowl, Apple, No. 7	20.00
Bowl, Apple, No. 8	65.00
Bowl, Apple, No. 63	30.00
Bowl, Apple, No. 65	50.00 To 56.00
Bowl, Apple, No. 73	50.00
Bowl, Blue & Pink Stripes, 5 In.	25.00
Bowl, Mixing, Apple, 4 Piece	95.00
Bowl, Mixing, Autumn Foliage	22.00
Bowl, Phillips 66, No. 7	37.00
Bowl, Starflower, No. 7	25.00
Canister Set, Lazy Susan	48.00
Casserole, Cover, Starflower No. 18	16.00
Creamer, Apple, Advertising	45.00
Dispenser, Iced Tea	150.00
Mug, Apple	95.00 To 100.00
Pie Plate, Apple	115.00
Pie Plate, Apple, Advertising	55.00 To 65.00
Pie Plate, Autumn Foliage	35.00
Pie Plate, Starflower	35.00
Pitcher, Apple, No. 15	22.00 To 45.00
Pitcher, Apple, No. 16	50.00
Pitcher, Apple, No. 16, Advertising	60.00
Pitcher, Apple, No. 17	125.00 To 139.00
Pitcher, Christmas, 1955, No. 15	45.00
Pitcher, Starflower, No. 15	10.00 To 19.00
Pitcher, Starflower, No. 16	38.00 To 42.00
Pitcher, Tulip, No. 16	55.00
Plate, Apple, No. 105	80.00
Salt & Pepper, Apple	55.00
Salt & Pepper, Apple, Hourglass	152.00
Salt & Pepper, Starflower	45.00 To 75.00

WAVE CREST WARE

Wave Crest glass is a white glassware manufactured by the Pairpoint Manufacturing Company of New Bedford, Massachusetts, and some French factories. It was decorated by the C. F. Monroe Company of Meriden, Connecticut. The glass was painted in pastel colors and decorated with flowers. The name *Wave Crest* was used after 1898.

WAVE CREST, Biscuit Jar, Pink & Lavender Flowers, Blue Ground, 10 1/2 In.	885.00
Biscuit Jar, Wild Roses On Top Half, White Enamel Dots, 10 In.	460.00
Box, Blown–Out Dahlia Cover, Satin Lined, 2 3/4 x 4 1/2 In.	495.00
Box, Blue Flowers, Brass Handles, 4 3/4 In.	150.00

Box, Cigar, Egg Crate, Blue Florals, Square, 6 1/2 In. 825.00
Box, Collars & Cuffs, Blown–Out, Wild Rose Design, 7 1/4 In. 550.00
Box, Collars & Cuffs, Rococo, Gold Highlights, 6 x 7 In. 975.00
Box, Daises, Blue Border, Lavender Outlined, 7 1/4 In. 765.00
Box, Egg Crate, Pink Iris, Square, 5 In. 350.00
Box, Glove, Dark Green Ground, 5 1/2 x 10 In. 1750.00
Box, Green, Blue Florals, Lined, 8 In. 850.00
Box, Jewelery, Hinged Cover, Lined, Scrolled Medallion, 5 x 4 In. 475.00
Box, Landscape Scene Lid, Helmschmied Swirl, Gilt Metal, 7 In. 1000.00
Box, Pink Scrolls, Blue & White Forget-Me-Nots, 6 In. 585.00
Box, Rococo Embossed Panels, Pink, Dainty Florals, Marked, 6 In. 895.00
Box, Swirl, Lilacs, Yellow, Green & White, 7 In. 950.00
Box, Trinket, American Flags Crossed Over Laurel Wreath, 3 In. 195.00
Box, Yellow To Cream, Floral, Helmschmied Swirl, Round, 7 In. 450.00
Carafe, Blue Blossoms, Signed, 8 1/4 In. 845.00
Carafe, Blue Blossoms, Swirled, Impressed Signature, 8 1/4 In. 845.00
Cruet, Winged Female Bust On Handle 385.00
Hair Receiver, Pale Pink, Blue Flowers, 3 1/2 In. 310.00
Humidor, Bronze Cover, Monk On Front, Pipe On Back, 6 In. 200.00
Humidor, Cigar, Blue & Pink Wild Roses, Blue, 6 In. 640.00
Jar, Powder, Hinged Cover, Applied Flowers & Leaves 185.00
Jar, Woman, Standing In Garden 300.00
Jardiniere, Flowers, Pink & White, Cupid Head Border, 9 3/4 In. 795.00
Match Holder & Ashtray, Indian Design 750.00
Pencil Holder, Indian Chief, Ormolu Band At Neck & Base 750.00
Pin Dish, Blown–Out, Collar & Handles 125.00
Pin Dish, Blue & White Flowers, Brass Rim, 4 In. 85.00
Pin Dish, Brass Mounted, 4 1/4 In. 45.00
Pin Dish, Metal Ormolu Mounting, Signed, 3 1/2 In. 115.00
Pin Dish, Ormolu Rim, Handles 110.00
Pitcher, Water, Raindrop Pattern, Rainbow, Footed 595.00
Plaque, Pink Water Lilies, Cattails In Background, 12 x 11 In. 1225.00
Salt & Pepper, Erie Twist, Pewter Tops, 2 3/4 In. 185.00
Salt & Pepper, Swirl, Blue Flowers, Pink At Top, 2 1/2 In. 175.00
Salt & Pepper, Swirl, Enamel Asters, Beige Swirls, 2 3/4 In. 185.00
Salt & Pepper, Tulip 115.00
Saltshaker, Tulip Pattern, Rose Blossoms, Pewter Top 85.00
Sugar & Creamer, Birds On Wood Fence, Twisted Metal Handles 225.00
Sugar, Cover, Swirl, Daisies 145.00
Syrup, Silver–Plated Cover, 3 1/2 In. 165.00
Toothpick, Floral Design, Gilt Metal Base 225.00
Toothpick, Painted Daisy, Red Banner Mark 235.00
Tray, Raised Scrolling, Apple Blossoms, 6 1/2 x 4 3/4 In. 425.00
Vase, Blue Satin Ground, Pink Orchids, White Beading, 11 In. 950.00
Vase, Blue To Ivory, Florals, 7 In. 135.00
Vase, Embossing Outlined In Pink Luster, Dotted Rim, 6 1/2 In. 295.00
Vase, Floral Design, Ormolu Mounted, 17 In. 1500.00
Vase, Flowers, Handles, 7 In. 325.00
Vase, Ormolu Top, 4 1/2 In. 550.00
Vase, Violets On Cream, 6 3/8 In. 260.00

The earliest American weather vanes were used in seventeenth–century Boston. The direction of the wind was an indication of coming weather, important to the seafaring and farming communities. By the mid–nineteenth century, commercial weather vanes were made of metal. Today's collectors often consider weather vanes to be examples of folk art, even though they may not have been handmade.

WEATHER VANE, American Flag, Sheet Metal, 13 Stars, 15 In. 2750.00
Angel, Wreath & Broken Horn, Tin 1045.00
Automobile, Sheet Metal, Silhouette, Man Driver, 35 In. 1320.00
Banner, Copper, Gold Leaf Traces 1050.00
Banner, Iron Star & Arrow, Cast Bronze, 71 In. 2000.00

Bird & Horse, Wood, Tin, Red & White, Trotting, 38 In.	275.00
Blacksmith, Sheet Metal, Raised Hammer, 48 In.	550.00
Bull's–Eye Propeller, Sheet Metal, Arrow Tail, 32 In.	220.00
Centaur, Sheet Metal, 61 x 76 In.	3300.00
Cock, 3–Dimensional, Copper, Flat Tail, 15 In.	1760.00
Cock, On Arrow, Copper, Contemporary, 23 In.	175.00
Cow, Copper, Late–19th Century, 28 x 39 In.	550.00
Cow, Embossed Zinc, Iron Arrow, Red Paint, Gilt, 31 In.	145.00
Cow, Horns, Pendant Tail, Copper, c.1875, 28 1/2 In.	3850.00
Cow, Standing, Original Black & White Paint, 1900	1950.00
De Kalb, Ear of Corn, Green Wings	80.00
Dexter, Copper, Cushing & White, Verdigris, 19 x 43 1/2 In.	4675.00
Eagle, Raised Wings, On Arrow, Copper, 26 1/2 In.	300.00
Fish, Sheet Metal, 28 In.	248.00
Flying Goose, Laminated Body, Plywood Core, 59 x 42 In.	1250.00
Gamecock, Copper, 19th Century, 26 In.	825.00
Gamecock, Full–Bodied, Copper, On Arrow, 26 In.	1550.00
Grasshopper, Full–Bodied, Copper, Contemporary, 34 1/2 In.	375.00
Horse & Jockey, Running, Copper, Zinc, 33 In.	7150.00
Horse & Rider, Carved Pine, Black, 17 1/2 x 35 In.	2750.00
Horse & Sulky, Rod & Directionals, Copper, Contemporary	105.00
Horse, Full–Bodied, Gilt Tin, 10 x 9 In.	125.00
Horse, Index, J. Howard & Co., Late 19th Century, 18 In.	4450.00
Horse, Iron Support Bars, Sheet Iron, 24 x 21 1/2 In.	2075.00
Horse, Prancing, Copper & Zinc, American, 1880s, 25 x 35 In.	1980.00
Horse, Prancing, Gilt Metal Cast Head, c.1885, 26 In.	3300.00
Horse, Prancing, Silhouette, Sheet Metal, Silver, 15 x 18 In.	550.00
Horse, Racing, Molded Copper, American, 19th Century, 32 In.	3300.00
Horse, Red Paint, Iron, 34 x 26 In.	325.00
Horse, Running, Copper & Zinc, A. L. Jewell & Co., 28 x 16 In.	2000.00
Horse, Running, Copper Body, Zinc Head, Gold Leaf, Fiske, 28 In.	1750.00
Horse, Running, Copper, Full–Bodied	550.00
Horse, Running, Flattened Body, On Iron Arrow, 10 x 8 In.	550.00
Horse, Running, Full–Bodied, Copper & Zinc, 61 x 42 In.	4950.00
Horse, Running, Full–Bodied, Copper, Col. Atchen, 20 1/2 In.	7425.00
Horse, Running, Hollow Body, Bullet Holes, Copper, 29 1/2 In.	200.00
Horse, Running, Hollow Copper Body, Cast Iron Head, 28 In.	850.00
Horse, Running, Hollow Copper, Zinc Head, Bullet Holes, 29 In.	850.00
Horse, Running, Hollow Copper, Zinc Head, Gilt, 26 In.	1000.00
Horse, Running, Hollow Embossed Tin, Red Paint, 14 1/4 In.	95.00
Horse, Running, Hollow Zinc Body, 32 In.	200.00
Horse, Running, Sheet Zinc, Original Paint, Early 20th Century	295.00
Horse, Running, Silhouette, Sheet Metal, Stand, 27 x 77 In.	245.00
Horse, Running, Smuggler, Copper, W. A. Snow Co., 32 In.	445.00
Horse, Standing, Sheet Metal, Anno 1887, 20 In.	825.00
Horse, Trotting, Kennebec Valley	2860.00
Jockey, Horse, Hollow Copper, Lacquer, Rod, Directional, 64 In.	500.00
Peacock, Copper & Lead, 19th Century, 31 In.	7000.00
Rooster Silhouette, Sheet Iron, Yellow & Black, 16 1/2 In.	300.00
Rooster, Above 4 Arms, Painted Metal, 23 In.	145.00
Rooster, Amethyst Globe	275.00
Rooster, Copper, Small	2200.00
Rooster, Copper, Zinc, Silhouette, Yellow, 17 In.	490.00
Rooster, Full–Bodied, On Ball, Copper	2100.00
Rooster, Full–Bodied, Red Paint	2100.00
Rooster, Gilded Sheet Zinc, Full–Bodied, 27 x 25 In.	2750.00
Rooster, Half Round, Copper	425.00
Rooster, Hollow Copper, Gilt Traces, Bullet Holes, 13 In.	625.00
Rooster, Hollow Zinc, Cast Iron & Tin, 25 In.	350.00
Rooster, Ornate Arrow, Zinc, 3–D, 9 x 7 In., 23–In. Arrow	175.00
Rooster, Sheet Iron, Traces of Old Red, Yellow & Black	850.00
Rooster, Silhouette, Gold Repaint, Sheet Metal, 22 3/4 In.	125.00
Rooster, Silhouette, Sheet Iron, 29 1/2 In.	400.00

*Weather Vane, Simple Simon, Dog,
Howard Johnson, 48 X 54 In.*

Rooster, Silhouette, Sheet Iron, Yellow & Black, 16 1/2 In. 300.00
Rooster, Silhouette, Sheet Metal, Worn Old Paint, 33 In. 350.00
Rooster, Silhouette, White & Polychrome Paint, 17 In. 25.00
Rooster, Zinc, Sheet Steel Tail, Red & White Traces, 24 In. 1075.00
Running Horse, Copper Body, Zinc Head, Fiske, 1800s 1750.00
Sailboat, Directions, Copper, 37 x 26 1/2 In. 445.00
Shooting Star, Haley's Comet, 5 Point, New Moon, 44 In. 1325.00
Simple Simon, Dog, Howard Johnson, 48 x 54 In. ....*Illus* 775.00
Smuggler, Running Horse, 41 In. 3500.00
Snake, Coiled, Forked Tongue, Wood, 18 In. 248.00
Star, Square Frame 875.00
Steam Locomotive, Silhouette, Sheet Metal, 20 1/2 In. 500.00
Steamship, Polychromed Wood, Green, White, 2 Masts, 26 In. 445.00
Whale, Wooden, Black & Red Paint, Weathered, 6 1/2 x 23 In. 522.00

Webb Webb glass was made by Thomas Webb & Sons of Stourbridge,
England. Many types of art and cameo glass were made by them
during the Victorian era. The factory is still producing glass. Webb
Burmese and Webb Peachblow are special colored glasswares of the
Victorian period.

WEBB BURMESE, Bowl, Collared 6–Sided Top, Green Leaves, Grapes, 3 1/2 In. 325.00
Bowl, Ivory, Folded–In Scallops, Signed, 2 x 4 1/2 In. 385.00
Fairy Lamp, Clarke Base, 5 x 3 3/4 In. 225.00
Fairy Lamp, Matching Folded–In Base, Red Flowers, 6 In. 1250.00
Fairy Lamp, Pink To Yellow, Clarke Base, 5 In. 225.00
Fairy Lamp, Shading To Lavender Rim, Ruffled Base, 6 In. 835.00
Perfume Bottle, Purple Flowers, Sterling Top, 3 1/2 In. 695.00
Rose Bowl, Green Leaves, Red Bud Flowers, 2 1/2 In. 325.00
Rose Bowl, Joined 4 Bowls, Berry Prunts On Ends, 9 5/8 In. 595.00
Toothpick, Berry 450.00
Vase, 6–Sided Top, 5–Petal Flowers, Leaves, 3 3/8 In. 310.00
Vase, 6–Sided Top, Grape Leaves, Rose Grapes, 3 1/4 In. 365.00
Vase, Bottle Shape, Green Leaves, Marked, 10 In. 1050.00
Vase, Bud Flowers, Green & Brown Leaves, Signed, 8 In. 695.00
Vase, Buds & Green Leaves, 8 1/4 In. 750.00
Vase, Flower Petal Top, Bunch of Grapes, Leaves, 3 1/4 In. 395.00
Vase, Flower Petal Top, Signed, 2 7/8 In. 225.00
Vase, Flowering Vines, Birds Each Side, Pair 5230.00
Vase, Glossy Finish, Scalloped Rim, 2 1/2 In. 385.00
Vase, Gold Over Star Shaped Top, Signed, 3 3/8 In. 225.00
Vase, Red Buds, Green & Brown Leaves, Signed, 8 In. 695.00

Vase, Ruffled, 5–Petal Flowers, Leaves, 4 3/8 In. 325.00
WEBB PEACHBLOW, Biscuit Jar, Gold Branches & Flowers, Butterfly On Back 1470.00
  Rose Bowl, 8–Crimp Top, Cream Lining, 2 3/4/ x 3 In. 225.00
  Vase, Berry Pontil, Branch Feet, Crystal Flowers, 11 3/4 In. 650.00
  Vase, Gold & Silver Leaves & Flowers, Butterfly, 4 1/4 In. 350.00
  Vase, Gold Branches & Prunus Blossoms, Butterfly, 9 1/4 In. 495.00
  Vase, Gold Flowers & Leaves, Cream Lining, 8 1/4 In. 395.00
  Vase, Gold Prunus & Bee, Cream Lining, 6 1/4 In. 450.00
  Vase, Gold Prunus & Bee, Cream Lining, 9 1/2 In. 495.00
  Vase, Yellow Seaweed, Coralene Decoration, 5 1/2 In. 385.00
WEBB, Biscuit Jar, Flowering Leafage, Metal Frame 880.00
  Bowl Vase, Gold Floral, Butterfly, 3 Crystal Feet, Pale Green, 5 In. 395.00
  Bowl, Apple Blossoms, Buds, Branches, Floral Border, Marked, 5 1/2 In. 1980.00
  Bowl, Blown–Out, Scalloped, Elephant Head Metal Holder, 8 In. 1500.00
  Bowl, Citron & White Leaves, Vines, Butterfly, Sterling Rim, 8 1/4 In. 2500.00
  Bowl, Diamond–Quilted, Clear Handles, Chartreuse, 10 In. 385.00
  Bowl, Multi–Layered, Dahlia–Like Blossoms, Marked, 2 3/4 x 5 1/2 In. 2750.00
  Custard Cup & Underplate, Moire Crystal, Foliage, Flowers, Butterfly 600.00
  Ewer, Etched Fauna & Wildlife, Vermeil Mounted, Handle, 10 1/2 In. 3300.00
  Ewer, Mother–of–Pearl, Raindrop, Frosted Handle, 8 In. 215.00
  Fairy Lamp, Leaf & Flower Design, Clarke Base, 4 In. 245.00
  Jar, Sweetmeat, Flower & Acorn, Berry & Leaf, Satin Glass, 1880s 1125.00
  Jug, Claret, Holly Leaf, Cameo Cut, 7 1/2 In. 250.00
  Lamp, Butterfly, Green, Brass Finger Loop, Miniature 375.00
  Lamp, Kerosene, Enameled Birds & Flowers, Cut Glass Shade, 24 In., Pair 2900.00
  Perfume Bottle, Carved Florabunda Roses, Buds, Butterfly, 7 1/2 In. 5100.00
  Perfume Bottle, Coin Gold Design, Screw Top, 5 In. 465.00
  Perfume Bottle, Cut Allover Apple Blossoms, Ball Cover, Silver Rim 2750.00
  Perfume Bottle, Layered With White, Cameo Cut, Bulbous, 7 1/2 In. 4600.00
  Perfume Bottle, Robin's Egg Blue 950.00
  Perfume Bottle, Tricolor, Morning Glory Blossoms, 4 1/4 In. 1875.00

Webb, Perfume Bottle,   *Webb, Vase, Cameo,*   *Webb, Vase,*   *Webb, Vase, Poppies,*
Yellow Overlaid With   *Lilies, Foliage, Deep* *Geranium, Buds, Leaves,*   *Red, 8 1/2 In.*
White, 3 1/2 In.   *Red, White, 5 1/2 In.*   *Frosted Yellow,*
                                    Red, White, 9 In.

Perfume Bottle, White Over Red, Carved Blossoms, Buds, Butterfly, 6 In. 3525.00
Perfume Bottle, Yellow Overlaid With White, 3 1/2 In. ....*Illus* 4290.00
Pitcher, Mother-of-Pearl, Herringbone, Square Mouth, Rose, 4 1/2 In. 245.00
Rose Bowl, Stylized Daisy & Scroll, Simulated Ivory, Marked, 2 1/2 In, ... 550.00
Tumbler, Variety of Blossoms, Grasses, Flared, Mauve, Signed, 3 1/4 In. 2300.00
Vase Burmese, Queensware, 5-Petaled Flowers, Handles, 5 In. 695.00
Vase, Berry Clusters, Yellow Overlaid With Red, Marked, 6 1/4 In. 2640.00
Vase, Blossom & Leafy Sprig, Linear Borders, Marked, 4 In. 1450.00
Vase, Blossoms & Butterfly, Overlay Cut As Leaves, 6 1/4 In. 1325.00
Vase, Bowl Shape, Gold Floral & Butterfly, Crystal Feet, 5 x 5 In. 395.00
Vase, Butterfly & Flowers, White Satin Glass, Gold Leaves, 3 1/2 In. 70.00
Vase, Cameo, Flared Rim, Honeysuckle Motif, Elongated Neck, 14 1/2 In. 6050.00
Vase, Cameo, Lilies, Foliage, Deep Red, White, 5 1/2 In. ....*Illus* 1200.00
Vase, Coralene Floral, Butterflies, Diamond-Quilted, Signed, 11 In. 725.00
Vase, Coralene, 6 In. 335.00
Vase, Enameled Birds & Flowers, Butterscotch To White, 7 x 5 1/2 In. 295.00
Vase, Floral Design, 4 In. 800.00
Vase, Geranium, Buds, Leaves, Frosted Yellow, Red, White, 9 In. ....*Illus* 2750.00
Vase, Gold & Silver Enameling, Green & Clear Jewels, Ovoid, 4 1/2 In. 300.00
Vase, Gold Flowers, Coral Overlay, White Lining, Signed, 9 In. 350.00
Vase, Hand Painted Gold Floral, 8 In. 400.00
Vase, Honeycomb Mother-of-Pearl, White Interior, 10 x 5 In. 650.00
Vase, Ivory Colored Allover Blossom & Vine, Marked, 6 3/4 In. 1430.00
Vase, Morning Glory Design, Cornflower Blue, Marked, 3 1/4 In. 770.00
Vase, Narcissus, White On Citron, 5 In. 950.00
Vase, Passion Flowers & Bee, Blue Ground, Cameo, 8 In. 2000.00
Vase, Pillow, Aquatic Plants, Dragonfly, Birds, Gold Handles, 7 1/2 In. 3900.00
Vase, Poppies, Red, 8 1/2 In. ....*Illus* 3080.00
Vase, Teardrop Form, Flowers, Dragonflies, Cranberry Red, 15 In. 990.00
Vase, Tulips, Cobalt Blue, Crystal Ground, 9 1/4 In. 515.00

WEDGWOOD Josiah Wedgwood, although considered a cripple by his brother and forbidden to work at the family business, founded one of the world's most successful potteries. The pottery was founded in England in 1759. A large variety of wares has been made, including the well-known jasperware, basalt, creamware, and even a limited amount of porcelain. There are two kinds of jasperware. One is made from two colors of clay, the other is made from one color clay with a color dip to create the contrast in design. The firm is still in business.

WEDGWOOD, Biscuit Jar, Creamware, Footed, 6 In. 50.00
Biscuit Jar, Jasperware, Acorn Cover, Yellow & White, 5 In. 475.00
Biscuit Jar, Jasperware, Classical Ladies, Plated Mounts, 6 In. 150.00
Biscuit Jar, Jasperware, Green & White, Silver Fittings 195.00
Biscuit Jar, Jasperware, Plated Cover, Rim & Feet, Blue, 6 1/2 In. 150.00
Biscuit Jar, Jasperware, White Figures, Lavender Bands, 9 In. 925.00
Bottle, Barber, Jasperware, Tricolor, 10 In. 2250.00
Bowl, Black Basalt, Geometric Patterns, Marked, 7 1/8 x 9 In. 935.00
Bowl, Dragon Luster, 9 1/2 In. 495.00
Bowl, Dragon Luster, Celestial Dragons, Marked, 8 7/8 In. 520.00
Bowl, Embossed Rim, Ram's Head Handles, Etruria, 9 3/4 In. 40.00
Bowl, Fairyland Luster, Birds In Flight, Orange, 10 In. ....*Illus* 550.00
Bowl, Fairyland Luster, Butterfly, Peacocks, Cobalt Interior, 7 In. 325.00
Bowl, Fairyland Luster, Dana-Castle On A Road, c.1920, 10 7/8 In. 1000.00
Bowl, Fairyland Luster, Garden of Paradise, c.1920, 8 1/16 In. 3300.00
Bowl, Fairyland Luster, Imperial, Mermaid, c.1920, 10 7/8 In. 2200.00
Bowl, Fairyland Luster, Rhino, 2 1/4 x 3 1/2 In. 175.00
Bowl, Fairyland Luster, Smoke Ribbons Interior, 8 1/2 In. 2710.00
Bowl, Jasperware, Dancing Hours, Black & White, 9 3/4 In. 395.00
Bowl, Lahore Luster, Indian Warriors, Camel, Birds, 1920, 8 3/4 In. 5775.00
Box, Jasperware, Heart Shape, Blue, Flowers, 3 Figures, 4 1/2 In. 115.00
Box, Lilac Cover, Acorn Finial, 6 In. 495.00
Bust, George II, Black Basalt, c.1785, 9 3/16 In. 1200.00
Bust, Mercury, Black Basalt, Marked, 17 In. 1100.00

Bust, Prior, Black Basalt, Marked, 11 1/2 In.	750.00
Bust, Rousseau, Black Basalt, Fur Hat, Cloak, 6 1/16 In.	665.00
Bust, Shakespeare, Black Basalt, Head Turned Slightly, 12 3/8 In.	775.00
Butter Chip, Shell & Seaweed Design, Majolica	70.00
Candlestick, Dolphin Stem, Leaf Sconce, c.1875, 9 1/2 In., Pair	935.00
Cracker Jar, Blue & White Classic Figures, Woman, Cherub	145.00
Creamer, Black Bassalt, c.1900, 6 In.	65.00
Creamer, Terra–Cotta, Enameled Florals	115.00
Cup & Saucer, Alpine Pink, Demitasse, 12 Sets	75.00
Cup & Saucer, Appledore	40.00
Cup & Saucer, Drabware, Can Shape, Copper Luster Floral, 12 Piece	95.00
Cup & Saucer, Ivanhoe	25.00
Cup & Saucer, Patrician	18.00
Cup & Saucer, Williamsburg Husk	40.00
Figurine, Hercules, Black, 12 In.	360.00
Figurine, Polar Bear, Creamware, c.1927, 7 x 10 In.	395.00
Figurine, Raven, Black Basalt, 4 1/2 In.	165.00
Figurine, Sleeping Boy, Nude, On Blanket, Black Basalt, 4 1/2 In.	935.00
Fruit Set, Floral, Foliate, Fruit & Cornucopia Design, 15 Piece	300.00
Game Dish, Insert, Majolica, 8 1/2 x 5 1/2 In.	1400.00
Gravy Boat, Williamsburg Husk	65.00
Jam Jar, Figures, Goat, Lamb, Silver Plate, 3 3/4 x 3 1/4 In.	90.00
Jar, Cover, 2 Ashtrays, Queensware, Pink Grapes, White, Square, 3 In.	200.00
Jug, Jasperware, Queen Victoria Jubilee, Blue, 1897	375.00
Jug, Roger Williams, 1886	350.00
Lamp, Oil, Leaves, Beaded Trim, Black Basalt, Marked, 5 1/2 In.	525.00
Matchbox, Jasperware, Striker In Lid, Green	60.00
Pitcher, Bird & Fan, Majolica, 5 In.	325.00
Pitcher, Jasperware, Dark Blue, White Design, Signed, 6 1/2 In.	125.00
Plaque, 7 Graces, Gold Frame, 13 1/2 x 6 In.	475.00
Plate, Anticipation Is Rather Dangerous, E. Lessore, 9 1/2 In.	375.00
Plate, Buns!Buns!Buns!, Scenic, E. Lessore, 1863, 9 1/2 In.	375.00
Plate, Columbia Univ. Buildings, Blue, 1932, 11 In., 12 Piece	325.00
Plate, Etruria Seashell	65.00
Plate, Fruit & Flower, Sterling Silver Frame, 1900, 10 1/2 In.	75.00
Plate, Grape Leaf, Majolica, 8 3/4 In.	200.00
Plate, Ivanhoe, Flow Blue, 10 In.	45.00 To 95.00
Plate, Ivanhoe, Rebecca	47.50
Plate, Ivanhoe, Wamby & Gurch The Swineherd	95.00

◆◆

To restore old tools, wash wood with Murphy's oil soap, dry, sand
with steel wool, apply two coats of Minwax or other oil, then use
paste wax and buff. Clean metal parts, then coat with clear lacquer.

◆◆

*Wedgwood, Bowl, Fairyland Luster,   Wedgwood, Urn, Dolphin   Wedgwood, Vase, Classical
Birds In Flight, Orange, 10 In.   Supports, Jeweled, 12 3/4 In.   Figures, 2 Handles, Blue & White*

Plate, King & Queen of Diamonds, Verse, Marked, Pair 80.00
Plate, Shell, Cream, Set of 5 .... 50.00
Plate, University of Michigan, 10 1/4 In., 6 Piece 100.00
Plate, Washington & Lee 25.00
Plate, Wellesley 18.00
Plate, West Point, 1931, 10 1/2 In. .\. 35.00
Plate, Williams College, Blue, Large 65.00
Plate, Williamsburg Husk 30.00
Platter, Grape Leaf, Cobalt Blue, Majolica 600.00
Punch Bowl, Fairyland Luster, Poplar Trees, c.1920, 11 In. 3025.00
Salt Dip, Creamware, Master 30.00
Saucer, Black Basalt, Encaustic Design, 1780s, 6 1/2 In. 885.00
Server, Leaf, Melon 27.50
Server, Pancake, Cover, Blue, Landscape, 1903 .... 65.00
Sugar, Cover, Black Basalt, Leaf Border, Medallion On Sides 305.00
Tea Caddy, Jasperware, Classical Figures, Tricolor, 1800, 5 3/4 In. 1375.00
Teapot, Jasperware, Olive Green, 4 1/2 x 7 1/2 In. 150.00
Tile, Month & Year, Scenes of Youths, c.1880, 6 x 6 In., 12 Piece 885.00
Tray, Fairyland Luster, Fairy Gondola, c.1920, 13 1/4 In. 3650.00
Tray, Lavender, Oval, 10 x 7 1/2 In. 125.00
Urn, Cover, Dancing Female Figures, 3 Color, 10 1/2 In. 1000.00
Urn, Cover, Dancing Hours, Green & White, 7 In., Pair 450.00
Urn, Cover, Jasperware, Green & White, 8 1/4 In. 595.00
Urn, Dolphin Supports, Jeweled, 12 3/4 In. .... *Illus* 1600.00
Vase, Black & White Jasper, Classical Figures, c.1880, 10 3/16 In. 2750.00
Vase, Black Basalt, Double-Spouted, Seated Putto, 6 11/16 In. 1650.00
Vase, Butterfly Luster, Orange, Green Interior, 8 1/2 x 5 7/8 In. 995.00
Vase, Classical Figures, 2 Handles, Blue & White .... *Illus* 2000.00
Vase, Cover, Dancing Hours, Satyr Handles, 1886, 8 3/4 In. 715.00
Vase, Cover, Fairyland Luster, Ghostly Wood, c.1920, 15 In. 3875.00
Vase, Cover, Marbelized & Speckled, Handles, Bentley, c.1775, 9 In. 1100.00
Vase, Dragon Luster, Blue, Mottled Green Interior, 8 1/2 In., Pair 1200.00
Vase, Dragon Luster, Gold, Mottled Blue Ground, Marked, 10 In. 340.00
Vase, Fairyland Luster, Butterflies, Ivory, Orange, 4-Footed, 5 In. 175.00
Vase, Fairyland Luster, Dana, c.1920, 7 11/16 In. 3025.00
Vase, Fairyland Luster, Roches, c.1925, 11 1/2 In. 650.00
Vase, Gilt Paste, Daisies & Primroses, c.1875, 9 7/8 In. 2475.00
Vase, Grecian Style, Basalt, Handle, 1800 .... 9800.00
Vase, Hummingbird Luster, 4 In. 275.00
Vase, Portland, Phrygian Capital, c.1839 .... 2900.00

LOUWELSA
WELLER
Weller pottery was first made in 1873 in Fultonham, Ohio. The firm moved to Zanesville, Ohio, in 1882. Art wares were first made in 1893. Hundreds of lines of pottery were made, including Louwelsa, Eocean, Dickens, and Sicardo, before the pottery closed in 1948.

WELLER, Basket, Double, Sabrinian, 7 In. 95.00
Basket, Hanging, Souevo 125.00
Basket, Hanging, Woodcraft, Fox 250.00
Basket, Sabrinian, 7 In. ....•.............. 160.00
Basket, Silvertone, 13 In. 200.00
Basket, Warwick, Mottled, Strawberries, 7 1/2 In. 247.00
Bowl & Mug, Cereal, Rabbit, Birds, Signed 65.00
Bowl, Frog & Lily Pads, Coppertone 295.00
Bowl, Pond Lilies In Relief, 7 In. 62.00
Bowl, Sea Gulls, Nest of Eggs, Flower Frog 395.00
Bowl, Souevo, 4 x 5 In. 155.00
Bowl, Wild Rose, Shallow, 3-Footed, Blue, 7 1/2 In. 28.50
Box, Cover, Sicard, Clover Blossoms, Magenta To Green, 6 x 9 In. 2420.00
Bucket, Woodrose, c.1920, 15 In. 295.00
Candleholder, Louwelsa, Pansies, 7 3/8 In. 198.00
Candlestick, Glendale, Pair 225.00
Centerpiece, Woodcraft, Handled Log Shape, Green & Brown, 9 1/2 In. 105.00
Cider Set, Crackle Glaze, Purple Grapes On Vine, Marked, 7 Piece 440.00

Weller, Pitcher & Mug, Crackle Glaze

Clock, Louwelsa, Daffodil, Painted Floral Dial, 9 3/4 In.	935.00
Console Set, Lavonia, Basketweave Flower Arranger, 4 Piece	60.00
Console, Roma, 7 x 16 In.	125.00
Cornucopia, Sydonia, Blue, 8 In.	25.00
Cuspidor, Brown	165.00
Dish, Powder, Cover, Cameo, Lavender, Green & Blue, 4 1/2 x 5 1/2 In.	350.00
Ewer, Lonhuda	165.00
Ewer, Louwelsa, Nasturtium, Signed M, 9 1/2 In.	275.00
Ewer, Louwelsa, Orange Floral, Signed AD, 12 1/2 In.	165.00
Ewer, Louwelsa, Pansies, 6 1/2 In.	90.00
Ewer, Louwelsa, Trefoil	150.00
Ewer, Oak Leaf, Blue, 8 1/2 In.	55.00
Ewer, Oak Leaf, Green, 14 In.	95.00
Ewer, Sabrinian, 10 1/2 In.	195.00 To 210.00
Figurine, Bluebird, On Apple Tree Stump, Brighton, 7 1/2 In.	375.00
Figurine, Buffalo, Dickota, 3 1/2 x 3 7/8 In.	135.00
Figurine, Dutch Lady, Dickens Ware, 9 1/2 In.	350.00
Figurine, Goose Boy, White, 9 In.	135.00
Figurine, Kingfisher, Brighton	89.00
Figurine, Kneeling Woman, Muskota	85.00
Flower Frog, Lavonia, Vines & Flowers, Pink	25.00
Flower Frog, Lobster	25.00
Flowerpot, Breton Green, 4 In.	40.00
Frog, Coppertone, Holding Water Lily	125.00
Humidor, Roma	85.00
Humidor, Woodcraft, Squirrel On Top of Acorn, 9 In.	225.00
Inkwell, Figural, Turtle, Frog Handle	340.00
Jardiniere, Base, Cretone, Flowers, Cream	150.00
Jardiniere, Cats Stalking Canaries, Roses, 9 In.	235.00
Jardiniere, Roma	135.00
Jug, Aurelian, Blackberries & Leaves, C. Minnie Terry, 7 1/2 In.	495.00
Jug, Hunter, Incised Fish & Currents, Mottled Green, 5 3/4 In.	275.00
Jug, Louwelsa, Blackberry, 6 1/2 In.	302.00
Jug, Louwelsa, Currants, 6 1/4 In.	160.00
Mug, Floral, Dickens Ware, 5 In.	110.00
Mug, Indian, Creamware	60.00
Paperweight, St. Louis Exposition, 1904	95.00
Piggy Bank, Corky	25.00
Pitcher & Mug, Crackle Glaze ....*Illus*	440.00
Pitcher, Blossom, Green, 12 In.	75.00
Pitcher, Dickens Ware II, Dolphin–Shaped Handle, 12 1/2 In.	225.00
Pitcher, Louwelsa, Yellow Roses On Brown, 9 1/4 In.	100.00
Pitcher, Marvo, Green, 8 In.	90.00 To 110.00
Pitcher, Panel of Kingfisher, Flower Rosettes, 8 x 3 1/2 In.	250.00
Pitcher, Panella, Blue	45.00
Pitcher, Shaded Cream Rose, Signed Burgess, 12 In. ....*Illus*	550.00
Pitcher, Zona, Kingfisher, High Gloss	140.00

Weller, Pitcher, Shaded Cream
Rose, Signed Burgess, 12 In.

Weller, Vase, Turquoise, Salmon,
Upjohn & Mull, 1902, 17 1/2 In.

Planter, Dachshund, 8 1/2 In. 55.00
Planter, Duck 35.00
Planter, Elephant, Cactus, Rust 85.00
Planter, Ethel, Creamware, 11 In. 70.00
Planter, Penguin 35.00
Planter, Rabbit 35.00
Planter, Woodcraft, Fox 150.00
Planter, Woodcraft, Little Fox, Molded Twigs, 5 1/2 In. 125.00
Plaque, Apache, 1905, 9 3/4 In. ....*Illus* 1765.00
Plate, Zona, 9 1/2 In. 20.00
Stein, Monk, Seated, Table, Praying, Dickens Ware II, Signed, 5 1/2 In. 175.00
Strawberry Pot, Greora, 9 In. .... 65.00 To 95.00
Tankard, Aurelian, Signed 625.00
Tankard, Floretta, Grape, Standard Glaze, 14 In. 175.00
Tankard, Grape, 14 In. 175.00
Tankard, Indian Portrait, J. B. Owens, 17 In. 2600.00
Tankard, Louwelsa, Monk In Red Cloak, Minnie Mitchell, 12 In. 1250.00
Tile, Coppertone 75.00
Toby, Golfer, Dickens Ware, 4 1/2 In. 275.00
Umbrella Stand, Claywood, Incised Rooster 1150.00
Umbrella Stand, Full Indian Headdress, Signed, 23 In. 5500.00
Umbrella Stand, Jap Birdimal, 1904 .... 3000.00
Umbrella Stand, Sicard, Iridescent, 22 In. 800.00
Umbrella Stand, Tulips & Sunflowers, Green Glaze, 20 1/2 In. 412.00
Umbrella Stand, Woodcraft, 21 In. 750.00
Urn, Sicard, Iridescent Copper Glaze, 9 x 9 In. ....*Illus* 825.00
Vase, Ardsley, Fan, 8 In. 55.00
Vase, Aurelian, 3–Footed, Clover–Shaped Opening, 4 In. 150.00
Vase, Aurelian, Marked, 10 1/2 In. 40.00
Vase, Aurelian, Yellow Carnations, 13 In. 302.00
Vase, Aurora, Orange & Rust Thistles, 8 In. 425.00

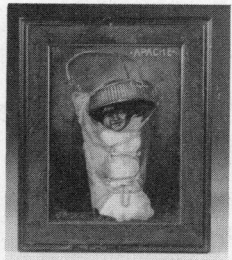

Weller, Plaque, Apache, 1905, 9 3/4 In.

◆◆◆◆◆◆◆◆◆◆◆◆◆◆◆◆◆◆◆◆◆◆◆

Iridescent pottery like Sicardo
should be carefully cleaned.
Wash in mild detergent and
water. Rinse, dry by buffing vigorously with dry, fluffy towels.
Then polish with a silver cloth as
if it were made of metal. Buff
again with a clean towel.

◆◆◆◆◆◆◆◆◆◆◆◆◆◆◆◆◆◆◆◆◆◆◆

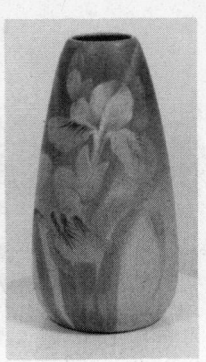

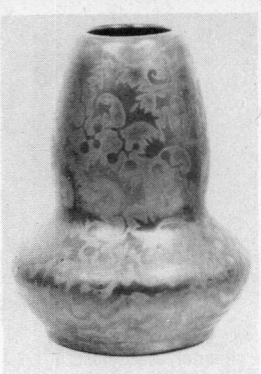

Weller, Vase, Sicard,
Iridescent Purple, 8 1/2 In.
Weller, Urn, Sicard, Iridescent
Copper Glaze, 9 X 9 In.

Weller, Vase,
Hudson, Iris, Blue, 11 1/2 In.

Weller, Vase,
Sicard, Foliate, 6 1/2 In.

Vase, Barcelona, 3 Handles, 10 In.	150.00
Vase, Barcelona, 6 In.	90.00
Vase, Bedford, Glossy, 8 In.	50.00
Vase, Blo'red, 8 In.	75.00
Vase, Blue Ware, Dancing Female, Grecian Toga, 10 1/4 In.	110.00
Vase, Blue Ware, Grecian Woman Dancing, 11 In.	203.00
Vase, Bodies of 2 Women, Textured Matte Green Glaze, 13 x 4 1/2 In.	1750.00
Vase, Bonito, Dorothy England, 7 In.	85.00
Vase, Bonito, Hand Painted Flowers, 4 1/2 In.	35.00
Vase, Bud, Double, Woodcraft, 7 3/4 In.	44.00
Vase, Bud, Louwelsa, Floral, 4 In.	50.00
Vase, Bud, Roma, 7 In.	121.00
Vase, Bud, Woodcraft, 10 In.	65.00
Vase, Bud, Woodcraft, 7 1/2 In.	40.00
Vase, Chengtu, Marked, 8 In.	50.00
Vase, Chief Wolf Robe, Dickens Ware II, 10 In.	700.00
Vase, Coppertone, Flared, Lily Pads, 10 In.	125.00
Vase, Copra, Floral, 10 In.	125.00
Vase, Dancing Satyrs, Vintage Designs, Marked, 13 In.	440.00
Vase, Double Gourd Form, Dragonflies Form Handles, Marked, 4 1/4 In.	465.00
Vase, Eocean, Rose, Pink Roses At Top, 6 In.	195.00
Vase, Etna, 11 In.	175.00 To 205.00
Vase, Etna, Mums, Blue, Cream, 11 1/2 In.	385.00
Vase, Etna, Pink Wild Roses, 9 1/4 In.	137.00
Vase, Faience, Geisha, Standing, Stylized Trees, Signed MP, 12 In.	950.00
Vase, Flemish, Blue, 7 In.	60.00
Vase, Flemish, Lily Pads & Floral, 6 In.	85.00
Vase, Floral, Dorothy England, 6 1/2 In.	225.00
Vase, Floretta, Grape Clusters, Tricornered, 6 1/2 In.	125.00
Vase, Floretta, Red Strawberries, 12 In.	75.00
Vase, Floretta, Strawberry Design, 9 1/4 In.	357.00
Vase, Forest, 13 In.	165.00
Vase, Frog Shaped Handles, Green Glaze, 7 In.	250.00
Vase, Gold Swirl, Pinecone Design, Cylinder, 9 In.	770.00
Vase, Grape Cluster, Buckeye Lake, Gold Trim, Signed, 9 In.	175.00
Vase, Greora, Cylindrical, 9 x 6 In.	72.00
Vase, Hudson, 2 Arabs, Camels, 13 1/2 In.	1100.00
Vase, Hudson, 2 Long-Tailed Birds, White, Paper Label, 13 In.	375.00
Vase, Hudson, Berry Design, Hester Pillsbury, 6 1/2 In.	245.00
Vase, Hudson, Bulbous, Pink Azaleas, 5 1/2 In.	385.00
Vase, Hudson, Clematis, 15 In.	1500.00

Vase, Hudson, Daffodils, 10 In. 195.00
Vase, Hudson, Dark Blue, Pink–Blue Berries, Cylinder, 8 1/2 In. 165.00
Vase, Hudson, Dorothy England Langhead, 1915–36, 7 In. 265.00
Vase, Hudson, Floral, C. Leffler, 7 1/2 In. 522.00
Vase, Hudson, Iris, Blue, 11 1/2 In. ....*Illus* 165.00
Vase, Hudson, Raised Flowers, Cylinder, 9 3/4 In. 165.00
Vase, Hudson, Raspberry & Leaves, 11 In. 250.00
Vase, Indian Jack Red Cloud, Marked, 10 1/2 In. 1600.00
Vase, Iridescent Flowers, Marked, c.1904, 6 1/2 In. 550.00
Vase, Iris, Tan, 12 1/2 In. 70.00
Vase, Juneau, 6 1/2 In. 58.00
Vase, LaSa, Oasis, 6 1/2 In. 495.00
Vase, LaSa, Scenic, 7 1/2 In. 200.00
Vase, LaSa, Scenic, 11 In. 700.00
Vase, LaSa, Trees & Mountains, 5 1/4 In. 245.00
Vase, LeMar, Buck & Trees, White Streaks, 8 1/2 In. .... 80.00 To 95.00
Vase, Lonhuda, Cherry Blossoms, 3–Footed, Boat Shape 385.00
Vase, Louwelsa, Buttercups, Squatty, 5 1/2 In. 155.00
Vase, Louwelsa, Floral, 5 In. 105.00
Vase, Louwelsa, Floral, Green, 8 1/4 In. 275.00
Vase, Louwelsa, Gooseberries, Squatty, 9 In. 330.00
Vase, Louwelsa, Lybarger, c.1899, 16 In. 745.00
Vase, Louwelsa, Pansies, 3 Handles, Footed, Signed, 6 In. 375.00
Vase, Louwelsa, Triangular, 4 In. 95.00
Vase, Lustre, Gray, 5 In. .... 45.00 To 55.00
Vase, Malvern, 7 In. 47.50
Vase, Mountain & Lake Scene, 5 1/2 In. 440.00
Vase, Patra, Mottled Design, 7 In. 66.00
Vase, Patricia, Green, 18 In. 150.00
Vase, Peacock, Pink Roses, Rose Flared Rim, M. T., 16 In. 2200.00
Vase, Pillow, Louwelsa, Raspberries, 7 In. 181.00
Vase, Pillow, Portrait, Ta–Wits–Nen–Ute, 4–Footed, 12 1/4 In. 990.00
Vase, Roma, Atlantic Panels, 10 In. 35.00
Vase, Rosemont, Bluebird On Each Side, Black, 10 1/2 In. 155.00
Vase, Rosemont, Cardinals On Glassy Black, 9 1/4 In. 350.00
Vase, Sabrinian, Seahorse Handles, 12 In. 215.00
Vase, Sabrinian, Square Shell, 4 x 5 In. .... 55.00 To 75.00
Vase, Seagulls, Flying, Dickens Ware II, Blue & Brown, 7 1/2 In. 225.00
Vase, Sicard, 7 In. 500.00
Vase, Sicard, Foliate, 6 1/2 In. ....*Illus* 445.00
Vase, Sicard, Gold Leaves & Berries, Purple, Bulbous, 13 3/4 In. 880.00
Vase, Sicard, Gold–Green Lilies, Purple–Red Ground, 14 1/2 In. 1650.00
Vase, Sicard, Green & Magenta, 7 In. 375.00
Vase, Sicard, Iridescent Copper Glaze, 9 In. 660.00
Vase, Sicard, Iridescent Purple, 8 1/2 In. ....*Illus* 935.00
Vase, Sicard, Lavender Luster, Stem Flowers, 6 In. 385.00
Vase, Sicard, Peacock Feather Design, 14 In. 1925.00
Vase, Sicard, Seaweed, Cylinder, 5 1/2 In. 605.00
Vase, Sicard, Shoulder Handles, 14 In. 2000.00
Vase, Silvertone, 9 1/2 In. 145.00
Vase, Silvertone, Grapes, 7 1/2 In. 80.00
Vase, Silvertone, Handle, 9 1/2 In. 165.00
Vase, Silvertone, Raised Tulip Tree, 8 1/4 In. 137.00
Vase, Souevo, Indian, 3 3/4 In. 165.00
Vase, Sydonia, Shell Shape, Embossed Leaves On Base, 7 1/2 In. 33.00
Vase, Turada, 7 In. 210.00
Vase, Turkis, 5 In. 25.00
Vase, Turquoise, Salmon, Upjohn & Mull, 1902, 17 1/2 In. ....*Illus* 1800.00
Vase, Umbrella, Flaring Loops In Green Matte, Loop Handle, 7 1/2 In. 235.00
Vase, Velva, Brown, 4 In. 45.00
Vase, Woodcraft, 4 Climbing Squirrels, Leaves, Acorns, 11 In. 400.00
Vase, Woodcraft, Dogwood Blossoms, 8 1/2 In. 35.00
Vase, Zona, Green, 6 In. 70.00

Wall Pocket, Girl, Kneeling, 5 In.	125.00
Wall Pocket, Hobart Girl, 12 In.	245.00
Wall Pocket, Owl, 10 In.	225.00
Wall Pocket, Pearl, 8 In.	95.00
Wall Pocket, Woodcraft, Squirrel	120.00 To 225.00
Window Box, Forest, 15 In.	250.00

Wemyss ware was made by Robert Heron in Kirkaldy, Scotland, from 1850 to 1929.

WEMYSS, Bank, Maroon, Green Flowers, 5 In.	95.00
Pig, 6 In.	85.00

Thomas J. Wheatley worked with the founders of the art pottery movement in Cincinnati, Ohio, including M. Louise McLaughlin of the Rookwood Pottery. In 1880, he established his own pottery. Wheatley Pottery was purchased by the Cambridge Tile Manufacturing Company in 1927.

WHEATLEY, Basket, Moon Shape, Green Limoges Style Glaze, Flowers, 8 In.	375.00
Vase, Buds, Leaves, Mustard Yellow, 9 In.	895.00
Vase, Green Matte	1430.00
Vase, Raised Leaves, Green Matte Glaze, 10 In.	1400.00

Whieldon was a potter in England who worked alone and with Josiah Wedgwood in eighteenth–century England. Whieldon made many pieces in natural shapes, like cauliflowers or cabbages. The tortoiseshell glazed pieces are known as *clouded ware.*

WHIELDON, Plate, Black Tortoiseshell Glaze, 9 1/2 In.	375.00 To 400.00
Plate, Brown Tortoiseshell Glaze, Octagonal, 9 3/8 In.	400.00
Plate, Brown Tortoiseshell Glaze, Octagonal, Embossed Rim, 9 In.	450.00
Plate, Multicolored Tortoiseshell Glaze, 10 In.	600.00
Soup, Dish, Black Tortoiseshell Glaze, 9 1/4 In.	500.00
Tray, Embossed Flowers, Black Tortoiseshell Glaze, 8 x 9 In.	1375.00

Willets Manufacturing Company of Trenton, New Jersey, worked from 1879. The company made belleek in the late 1880s and 1890s in shapes similar to those used by the Irish Belleek factory. They stopped working about 1912. Pieces were marked with a variety of marks, all including the name Willets.

WILLETS, Chalice, Monk Smoking Cigar, 12 In.	275.00
Cup & Saucer, Embossed, Tiny Green Enamel & Gold Flowers, Marked	95.00
Hatpin Holder, Raised Floral, Green Leaves, Signed, Dated 1911	150.00
Mug, Hand Painted Brown Elk	75.00
Mug, Hand Painted Windmill Scene	75.00
Vase, Forest Scene, 7 In.	175.00
Vase, Forest Scene, Bulbous, 6 1/2 In.	425.00
Vase, Landscape, Hunting Dogs, 15 1/2 In.	1300.00

WILLOW, see Blue Willow

Stained glass and beveled glass windows were popular additions to houses during the late nineteenth and early twentieth centuries. The old windows became popular with collectors in the 1970s; today, old and new examples are seen.

WINDOW, Bow, Abstract Floral, Clear & Slag Glass, Leaded, 51 x 24 In.	165.00
Central Woman, Ode To September, 1880–90, 5 1/2 Ft.	5600.00
Geometric & Fleur–De–Lis, Slag & Textured, 77 x 27 1/2 In., Pair	880.00
Geometric Design, Blue & Purple, 30 x 24 In.	175.00
Ice Cream, Leaded, Oak Frame, 24 x 33 In.	1750.00
Keyhole Shape, Stained Glass, Molding Intact, 64 In.	300.00
Leaded & Stained, 3 Birds Reserve, Framed, c.1900, 18 1/2 x 27 In.	885.00
Leaded, Architectural Rigging Design, F. L. Wright, 72 x 4 In.	6600.00
Leaded, Green Slag Border, Pink, Medallions, Framed, 1915, 22 x 40 In.	275.00
Leaded, Slag & Colored Glass Panels, Arched, 33 In.	110.00
Leaded, Slag & Textured Glass, Geometric Designs, Mosaic Style	385.00

◆◆◆

Musty odors in trunks seem to be a constant problem. Try this system. Fill the trunk with wrinkled, crushed newspaper, close the lid for a week, remove and replace the papers and repeat the process until the musty odor is gone. This system also helps with car interiors for tobacco odors, musty books if kept in a closed paper bag, and suitcases.

◆◆◆

Leaded, Slag & Textured, Tulip Design, 68 x 36 1/2 In.	935.00
Leaded, Slag Glass, Art Nouveau Floral Design, 65 x 44 1/2 In.	330.00
Leaded, Slag Glass, White, Green, Blue & Purple Floral, 45 x 29 In.	2450.00
Little Girl, Walking With Lamb, 33 1/2 x 22 In.	55.00
Stained Glass, Budweiser–Faust, Eagle Logo	4950.00
Transom, Slag Glass, Floral Design, Center Number 77, 52 x 22 In.	412.50

Wood carvings and wooden pieces are listed separately in this book. There are also wooden pieces found in other sections, such as Kitchen.

WOOD CARVING, Bear, On Platform, Carrying Large Fish Over Shoulder, Brown	115.00
Beauty & The Beast, Dog Under Woman's Legs, Painted, 16 In.	270.00
Beaver, Half–Round, On Branches, 1910s, 38 In.	2750.00
Bird, Stylized, Turned Base, Green, Red, Yellow & Blue, 7 In.	2500.00
Bird, Stylized, Turned Base, Red, Yellow & Green, 9 In.	3500.00
Bird, Worn Silver Gilt, Red, Gold, Hanging, 11 1/4–In. Wingspan	110.00
Bowl, Cylindrical, Lizard Legs, Cameroon, Africa, 12 In.	100.00
Box, Conestoga Wagon, Iron Fittings, Chip Carved Edge, 12 In.	1025.00
Buffalo, With Rider, Carved Wooden Stand, Oriental, 13 In.	75.00
Bust, Blackamoor, Smiling Woman, Earrings, 15 In., Pair	3300.00
Bust, Man & Woman, Old Patina, 9 1/2 In., Pair	18.00
Bust, Richard Nixon, Pine, Colored Hair, Eyes & Eyebrows, 1963	150.00
Cardinal, Driftwood, Wire Legs, J. Washington, '37, 8 3/4 In.	30.00
Cardinal, Wooden Base, 7 In.	55.00
Cat, In Boot, Hardwood, Ivory Teeth, Emory Papp, Oh., 3 5/8 In.	65.00
Chess Set, Wooden Box	45.00
Chicken, 7 In., Pair ....*Illus*	330.00
Chicken, 8 In., Pair ....*Illus*	1210.00
Conductor, Primitive, Movable Arms & Mouth, 11 1/2 In.	175.00
Cow & Bull, Primitive, Painted, 8 In., Pair	400.00
Crucifix, Walnut, 20 In.	50.00
Diorama, Ships, British Flags, Other Materials, 16 x 34 In.	420.00
Eagle & Shield, Red, White & Blue, J. H. Bellamy, 20 x 55 In.	5500.00
Eagle, Lectern, Standing, Pine, On Base	225.00
Eagle, Pine, Wall Mount, Orange Shellac, Pre–1940, 28 x 15 In.	585.00
Eagle, Rock Pile Plinth, Dark Finish, 12–In. Wingspan, 8 In.	37.50
Eagle, Standing Over Dead Deer, 1870s, 35 In.	3300.00
Horse, Rearing, Free Standing, Painted, 44 x 51 In.	425.00
Horse, Red Pigment, Ch'ing Dynasty, 18th Century, 10 In.	350.00
Lamb, Resting On Book, 1 Piece, 10 1/2 x 8 1/2 In.	250.00
Lion, 43 x 63 In.	2300.00
Lion, Oak, Varnish, Ivory Eyes, Horn Teeth, 8 3/4 In.	125.00
Male, Standing, Upper Volta, Africa, 30 In.	68.00
Man, Stylized, Large Hat, 2–Tone Finish, 12 In.	450.00
Mary & Child, Polychromed, Gilt, 9 1/2 In.	120.00
Mask, Boar, Movable Jaw, Leather Ears, Black, Guatemala, 8 In.	15.00
Mask, Buffalo, Cameroon, Africa, 24 In.	75.00
Mask, Face, Lobed Hair, Baule, Africa, 9 In.	65.00
Mask, Face, Slit Eyes, Triangular Form, Gabon, Africa, 32 In.	175.00
Model, Geo. Washington's Private Carriage, Worn Paint, 23 In.	90.00

Panel, Gilded, Lacquered Frame, Oriental, 31 1/2 x 16 3/4 In. 55.00
Pigeon, On Branch, For Wall, Painted, Glass Eyes, 13 1/2 In. 305.00
Saint, Painted Robe, Spanish Colonial, 15 1/2 In. 275.00
Shore Bird, Primitive, Inserted Bill, Modern Base, 10 In. 125.00
Slavic Woman, Sol A. Bauer, 1957, 37 1/2 In. 935.00
Soldier, Ohio Militia, Worn Polychrome Paint, 67 1/2 In. 550.00
Spoon Rack, Oak, Ornate, Old Finish, Europe, 14 1/2 In. 65.00
Stag's Head, Real Antlers, On Wood Plaque, c.1870, 24 x 19 In. 1430.00
Tray, Sculptured Fruit & Leaves Each End, Michel, 18 x 8 In. 400.00
Virgin of The Assumption, Standing On Cloud, Spain, 32 In. 525.00
Wall Hanging, Angel, Wings, Polychrome Chalk Paint, 17 In. 325.00

Wood was used for many containers and tools used in the early home. Small wooden pieces are called *treenware* in England, but the term *woodenware* is more common in the United States.

WOODEN, see also Advertising; Kitchen; Tool
WOODEN, Apple, Wooden Tea Set Inside, China, 1935s 75.00
Barrel, Cover, Iron Bands, Quartersawn Oak, 28 In. 200.00
Book Rack, Mission Oak, Clover Cutouts 40.00
Bowl, American Ash, Speckled Burl, 18th Century, 6 1/2 In. 570.00
Bowl, Bird's-Eye Maple, Walnut Handles, Carved Acorns 30.00
Bowl, Burl, Circular, Molded Edge, 19th Century, 15 In. 770.00
Bowl, Burl, Dark Green Paint Traces, 4 3/4 In. 550.00
Bowl, Burl, Molded Rim, Incised Lines At Sides, 18th Century, 19 In. 665.00
Bowl, Burl, Old Dark Finish, 11 1/2 x 5 3/4 In. 800.00
Bowl, Burl, Round, 3 x 13 In. 795.00
Bowl, Burl, Slot Handles, 20 In. 2400.00
Bowl, Burl, Tab End Handle, 5 x 11 x 14 In. 400.00
Bowl, Butter, Burl, Natural, 14 3/4 In. 550.00
Bowl, Cover, Red Sponged Paint On Yellow Ground, Poplar, 10 3/4 In. 20.00
Bowl, Primitive, Combination Handle & Spout Each End, 26 In. 75.00
Bowl, Round, 18th Century, 8 1/2 x 9 x 1 3/4 In. 130.00
Bowl, Scrubbed Interior, Old Red Exterior, 2 Hanging Hole, 20 In. 250.00
Bowl, Worn Interior, Yellow Exterior, 21 In. 175.00
Box, Apple, Original Paint, 3 In. 45.00
Box, Cover, Imitation Bird's-Eye Maple Graining, 10 In. 150.00
Box, Knife, Federal, Inlaid Urns, Flowers, Mahogany, c.1800, 28 In. 1870.00
Box, Knife, George III, Urn Form, Inlaid Mahogany, 24 In., Pair 1760.00
Box, Knife, Lift Lid, Urn Shape, Inlay, Mahogany, Pair 2500.00
Box, Tobacco, Fish Shape, 5 7/8 In. 175.00
Bucket, Ears Support Swivel Bentwood Handle, Metal Bands, 10 In. 105.00

Wood Carving, Chicken, 8 In., Pair   *Wood Carving, Chicken, 7 In., Pair*

Bucket, Metal Bands, Wire Bale, Wooden Handle, 4 1/2 In. 500.00
Bucket, Stave Constructed, Bands, Hinged Lid, Red, Stenciled, 15 In. 145.00
Bucket, Stave Constructed, Wooden Lid On String Fastener, 13 In. 135.00
Bucket, Stave, Wire Bands, Green Repaint, 3 Draining Holes, 10 In. 20.00
Bucket, Sugar, Cover, Galvanized Metal Lower Band, Wire Bale, 8 In. 130.00
Bucket, Sugar, Cover, Stave Constructed, Branded Saratoga, 11 3/4 In. 105.00
Bucket, Sugar, Stave Constructed, White Paint Over Gray, 14 In. 190.00
Bucket, Sugar, Stave Constructed, Wire Bale, Old Finish, 7 1/2 In. 75.00
Carrier, Cover, Bentwood, Wire Bale Handle, Old Finish, 11 1/2 In. 85.00
Casket, William & Mary, Walnut, Brass, Hinged, 7 x 11 In. 3575.00
Coffin, Black Paint, Gold Stenciled 15.00
Comb Case, Victorian, Original Mirror 195.00
Comb Case, Walnut, Rabbit Design 165.00
Compote, Traces of Green Paint, 4 1/4 x 5 1/4 In. ....*Illus* 110.00
Dipper, Burl, 11 1/4 In. 80.00
Door Wedge, Black Boy, Black Girl 88.00
Easel, Artist's, Ball & Stick Design 165.00
Firkin, Child's 80.00
Frame, Curly Maple, Beveled, 14 1/2 x 17 3/4 In., Pair 90.00
Frame, Neutral Galuchat, Tapezoidal Base, 1925, 8 7/8 x 6 7/8 In. 245.00
Goblet, Variegated Pattern, Footed, Pease–Brown, 5 In. ....*Illus* 140.00
Hanger, Clothes, Wall, 8 Arms, No. Girard, Penna. 32.00
Jar, Cover, Red Sponging Design, Poplar, 9 1/2 In. 275.00
Jar, Cover, Red Sponging, Poplar, 6 1/4 In. 425.00
Jar, Cover, Turned Foot, 5 In. ....*Illus* 55.00
Jar, Cover, Urn–Form Finial, 4 1/4 In. ....*Illus* 220.00
Jar, Cylinder, Covered, 6 In. ....*Illus* 220.00
Jar, D. M. Pease, 6 1/2 In. ....*Illus* 605.00
Jar, Flat Cover, Finial, Pease Type, 6 In. 220.00
Jar, Iron & Wood Handle, Paper Label, D. M. Pease 605.00
Jar, Turned Finial, Paper Label, James Brown, 4 1/4 In. 300.00
Keg, Cover, Laced Wooden Bands, Black Paint, 29 x 28 1/2 In. 95.00
Ladle, Beer, German Slogan Painted On Handle, 1874, 7 3/8 x 32 In. 625.00
Lazy Susan, Turned Base, Dish Turned Top, Mahogany, 17 In. 85.00
Mask, Tribal, Ivory Coast, Orange & White 269.00
Measure, Grain, Old Red, Bentwood, 12 1/4 In. 75.00
Ornament, Wall, Star, Stairway On Moon, 1940s, 2 Piece 35.00
Pail, Green & Brown Sponging, 19th Century, 4 1/2 x 5 5/8 In. 715.00
Peg Board, Brown Patina, Pine, Walnut Pegs, 39 3/4 In. 145.00
Sander, Pounce, Black Pinstriping, Wooden, c.1810, 2 3/4 In. 140.00
Sander, Pounce, Pierced Concave Top, Maple, c.1810, 3 1/4 In. 85.00
Scoop, Cranberry, Long Handle, 43 1/2 In. 125.00
Scoop, Cranberry, Poplar, Blue Paint, Steel Teeth, 18 1/2 In. 100.00
Scoop, Long Shallow Bowl, Ash, 16 3/4 In. 45.00
Seeder Bow, Walking, Rawhide String Turns Wheel, Primitive 95.00
Shoe Shine Box, Metal Shoe Last 30.00
Sign, Red Numeral 11, Yellow & White Striping, Oval, 22 x 43 1/2 In. 425.00

Wooden, Jar, Cylinder, Covered, 6 In.
Wooden, Jar, D. M. Pease, 6 1/2 In.
Wooden, Compote, Traces of Green Paint,
4 1/4 x 5 1/4 In.

Wooden, Goblet, Variegated Pattern, Footed,
Pease–Brown, 5 In.
Wooden, Jar, Cover, Turned Foot, 5 In.
Wooden, Jar, Cover, Urn–Form Finial, 4 1/4 In.

Tub, Stave Constructed, Iron Bands, Cutout Handles, 11 1/2 In. 150.00
Urn, Acorn Finial, Inlaid Walnut & Satinwood, 26 3/4 In., Pair 3850.00
Urn, Cutlery, Inlaid Herringbone Bands, Mahogany, 24 In., Pair 4675.00
Vessel, Drinking, Bird Form, 1870, Unpainted, Wisc., 9 1/2 In. 650.00
Wall Pocket, Hanging, Wire Nail Construction, 21 x 11 In. 450.00

Worcester porcelains were made in Worcester, England, from 1751. The firm went through many name changes and eventually, in 1862, became The Royal Worcester Porcelain Company Ltd. Collectors often refer to Dr. Wall, Barr, Flight, and other names that indicate time periods and artists at the factory. It became part of Royal Worcester Spode Ltd. in 1976.

WORCESTER, see also Royal Worcester
WORCESTER, Biscuit Jar, Hop Flowers & Leaves, Gold Trim, Silver Fittings 350.00
Creamer, Fisherman, Scroll Handle, 4 1/2 In. 275.00
Cup & Saucer, Oriental Floral Design, Blue Mark 150.00
Dish, Sweetmeat, Figure of Girl, Green Mark, 7 1/2 In. 250.00
Pitcher, Milk, Fisherman, Gilt Highlights, 4 1/2 In. 195.00
Sauceboat, Fringed Tree Pattern, 1755–1760, 8 3/4 In., Pair 770.00
Sugar, Cover, Fisherman, Floral Handle, 5 1/2 In. 225.00
Tea Caddy, Fisherman, Cylindrical, 4 5/8 In. 635.00
Teapot, Fisherman, Flower Finial, 5 1/2 In. 495.00
Wash Bowl, Fisherman, Gilt String Highlights, 6 In. 210.00

Souvenirs of World War I and World War II are collected today. Be careful not to store anything that includes live ammunition. Your local police station will tell you how to dispose of the explosives. See also Gun, Sword, and Trench Art.

WORLD WAR I, Ammunition Drum, Aircraft Machine Gun, 8 In. Diam. 150.00
Bomb, Aerial, Tear-Drop Shape, 14 In. 110.00
Book, History of World War I, Francis March, Photos 13.00
Boots, Aviator's Moccasin Type, Strap Buckle Closure 275.00
Campaign Hat 35.00
Cap, Overseas, 103rd Aero Squadron, Captains' Bars 632.00
Card, Christmas, Flag, Eagle, Uncle Sam, Color, Gibson, 5 In. 7.50
Card, Window, U. S. Food Adm. Membership, 1918, 6 x 9 In. 20.00
Coat, Flying, Leather, British Made For United States 2150.00
Coat, Uniform, Aviation Signal Corps, Khaki Wool 193.00
Coat, Uniform, Rickenbacker Squadron, Olive Drab Gabardine 775.00
Face Mask, Full, Aviator's, Leather, Silk Lining 95.00
Field Phone, Military, Oak Case, Metal Handset, 1917 .... 45.00
Goggles, Pilot's, Flat Yellow Lenses 165.00
Helmet, Crash, Flight, Neck Flap, French 1000.00
Helmet, Flight, German Air Service, Black Leather 800.00
Helmet, Flight, Leather, Simulated Suede Liner 175.00
Helmet, Flight, Leather, Suede Lining In Crown, Face Shield 300.00
Jacket, Flight, U. S. Navy G–1 .... 852.00
Mess Kit, Air Corps, Oval Aluminum, Folding Handle, 8 1/4 In. 36.00
Microphone, Aircraft, Worn On Leg Or Chest 20.00
Photograph, Signal Corps, Gen. Pershing & King George, 5 Pc. 10.00
Pistol, Colt 45, Commemorative, Aeuse–Argonne, Automatic 475.00
Pistol, Colt 45, Commemorative, Battle of Belleau Wood 550.00
Pistol, Colt 45, Commemorative, Battle of Chateau–Thierry 550.00
Pistol, Colt 45, Commemorative, Second Battle of The Marne 550.00
Poster, Americans All, Christy 95.00
Poster, Aviator Picture, Brussels International Air Show, Pair 1000.00
Poster, Colored Man Is No Slacker, Scene, Framed, 14 x 18 In. 145.00
Poster, Help Fill The War Chest 50.00
Poster, I Want You For The Navy, Woman, Coat, 1917, 27 x 41 In. 900.00
Poster, Victory, Liberty Loan 65.00
Poster, War Bond, Framed 175.00
Uniform, 168th Aero Squadron, Coat, Trousers & Cap 155.00
Uniform, Air Service Sergeant's, Heavy–Weight Wool 125.00

WORLD WAR II, 10 National Puzzle, Box, 1943 .... 11.00
  Album, Postcard, Photo, Sailors On USS Idaho, Alaska, Honolulu 25.00
  Arm Band, Nazi, Cloth 77.00
  Bank, Keep 'Em Sailing, Dime Register, Battleship Litho 100.00
  Belt & Buckle, Hitler Youth 30.00
  Book, Cutout, Girls In Uniform, 6 Uncut Pages, Military Groups 75.00
  Book, History, Armed Services Memorial Edition, 1945 .... 15.00
  Book, Victory Gardening, Signal Gasoline, 1943, 32 Pages 8.50
  Booklet, Uncle Sam Wants It To Last, Gas Equipment, 14 Pages 4.00
  Boots, Flying, Fleece, Lace–Up Rear 50.00
  Box, Cigarette, Aluminum, Alpha–Switzerland, USS Wasp Logo 65.00
  Bracelet, Charm, U. S. Navy Charms 30.00
  Cap, Overseas, 10th Air Force Patch, Olive Gabardine 40.00
  Card, Birthday, GI, Girlie Print Inside, Rolf Armstrong, Unused 17.50
  Card, Christmas, GI, From England, Sign Says To Berlin, 1943 .... 10.00
  Card, Punch Board, Hitler, Red, White & Blue, 1940s 15.00
  Currency, Nazi Concentration Camp, 1943 .... 6.00
  Dagger, Nazi 150.00
  Dagger, Youth's, Blade Marked RXM 35.00
  Field Binoculars, Case, Japan 125.00
  Figure, Pregnant Woman, Kilroy Was Here, Bakelite, 3 1/2 In. 22.00
  Flag, Nazi, 9 x 6 1/2 Ft. 165.00
  Flight Suit, Army Air Force, Zipper Front, Olive Gabardine 103.00
  Flight Suit, Full Body, Japan 305.00
  Flight Suit, High Altitude, Luftwaffe 100.00
  Flight Suit, Zipper Front, AAF Insignia On Shoulder 130.00
  Hat, Visor, Airman's, Olive Wool, Leather Visor 25.00
  Headset, Bomber Type, Oval Ear Pads, Jack At End of Cord 72.00
  Headset, Bomber, Rubber Earphones, Suede Pads 60.00
  Helmet, Air Force Parade, Worn On V–E Day In England 125.00
  Helmet, Leather, America 80.00
  Helmet, Leather, Germany 80.00
  Holder, Ration Book, Simulated Leather, Eagle, 5 x 7 In. 8.50
  Insignia Guide, Army, Navy, Rotating Wheel, Wonder Bread, 1942 .... 22.00
  Jacket, 64th Bomb Squadron, Painted Plane On Back 665.00
  Jacket, 530th Bomb Squadron 975.00
  Jacket, 552nd Bomber Squadron, Painted Insignia 880.00
  Jacket, A–2, Bombing Missions Recorded On Back 1331.00
  Jacket, Aircraft's Name, LIBERTY BELL–E 2000.00
  Jacket, Fighting Hell Cats, Silk–Screened Insignia 1000.00
  Jacket, Flight, B–26 Marauder, Painted Shark Mouth 1100.00
  Jacket, Flight, Leather, Painted B–17 Plane On Back 1250.00
  Jacket, Flight, Leather, Scotch Grain Texture 406.00
  Jacket, Jolly Rogers, Black Pirates, South West Pacific 1540.00
  Jacket, Leather, 7th Bombardment Group 1331.00
  Knife, Hitler Youth, Marked, Dated 1937 .... 65.00
  Knife, Nazi Youth Corps, Swastika On Handle, Sheath 95.00
  Letter, Prisoner At Buchenwald, Camp Stationery, Censor Stamp 300.00
  Map, Escape, Aviators, Printed In Color On Silk, 20 x 27 In. 30.00
  Map, Escape, Silk, Square, 29 In. 50.00
  Map, Germany & Invasion Fronts, Red Swastika Corners, 41 In. 12.50
  Mask, Oxygen, Continuous Flow, Rebreather Diluter Type 88.00
  Mirror, Hand, Remember Pearl Harbor 25.00
  Mirror, Nazi, Pocket 780.00
  Parachute, Luftwaffe, August, 1942 .... 1290.00
  Photograph, Hitler, Sterling Frame 3600.00
  Pin, 6th Savings Bond, Blue & White Figure Bond Logo, 1940s 5.00
  Pin, Flag, Remember Pearl Harbor 45.00
  Plaque, Blue Star, Metal, For Window, 6 1/2 x 4 1/2 In. 11.00
  Postcard, Hanging, Tassels, American Eagle, All Nation Flags 10.00
  Postcard, Hawaiian Buffalo, APO San Fran., Censor Stamp, 1943 .... 6.50
  Poster, Buy U. S. War Savings Bonds, Flag, 1942, 21 x 11 In. 10.00
  Poster, Nazi Agent, Conrad Veldt, Ann Ayars, MGM, 27 x 41 In. 175.00

Poster, Prelude To War, US Army Signal Corps, 27 x 41 In.	225.00
Range Finder, Size & Shape of Hand Mirror, Instructions, 1943	15.00
Ration Book, Leather, Many Tokens	12.50
Spyglass, U. S. Navy, Buships, Oak Case, 1942	500.00
Tunic, Sergeant's, Balloon Section, Khaki, Eagle Buttons	335.00
Uniform, Air Force, Medals & Accessory Pieces	40.00
Warning Device, Civil Defense Gas Attack, Wooden	5.00
Water Bag, Canvas, Marked, 1942	25.00
Wings, Command Pilot, Sterling	125.00

Souvenirs of all world's fairs are collected. The first fair was the Great Exhibition of 1851 in London. Other important exhibitions and fairs include Philadelphia, 1876 (Centennial); Chicago, 1893 (World's Columbian); Buffalo, 1901 (Pan–American); St. Louis, 1904 (Louisiana Purchase); San Francisco, 1915 (Panama–Pacific); Philadelphia, 1926 (Sesquicentennial); Chicago, 1933 (Century of Progress); Cleveland, 1936 (Great Lakes); San Francisco, 1939 (Golden Gate International); New York, 1939 (World of Tomorrow); Seattle, 1962 (Century 21); New York, 1964 (World's Fair); Montreal, 1967 (Man and His World); and Knoxville, 1982 (Energy Expo). Memorabilia of fairs include directories, pictures, fabrics, ceramics, etc.

WORLD'S FAIR, Ashtray, 1933, Chicago, Chrysler Motors, Brass	12.00
Ashtray, 1933, Chicago, Chrysler Motors, Copper	15.00
Ashtray, 1933, Chicago, Graniteware, Yellow & Navy, Logo	45.00
Ashtray, 1939, New York, Brass, Blue Ball Insert	25.00
Badge, 1901, Buffalo, Women Shaking Handles, Celluloid	15.00
Bank, 1939, New York, Remington Typewriter, Cast Aluminum	45.00
Book, Flip, 1939, New York, Bromo Seltzer	20.00 To 60.00
Bookmark, 1904, St. Louis, Leather	20.00
Bookmark, 1933, Chicago	7.50
Bottle, 1939, New York, Milk Glass, 9 In.	30.00
Bottle, 1962, Seattle, Space Needle, Beam	14.00
Box, 1933, Chicago, Button, Stretch Penny, Century of Progress	20.00
Bracelet, 1939, New York, Railroad Building, Box	12.00
Candy Container, 1939, New York, Flying Saucer Shape, Metal	25.00
Cane, 1933, Chicago, Beer Barrel Handle	50.00
Card, Playing, 1893, Chicago, Landing Scene, Half of Box	50.00
Card, Playing, 1933, Chicago	30.00
Card, Playing, 1939, New York	45.00
Cards, Playing, 1933, Chicago, Sealed	25.00
Clothes Brush, 1933, Chicago, Parrot's Head	45.00
Compact, 1939, New York	75.00
Globe, 1933, Chicago	29.50
Gyroscope, 1933, Chicago, Box	15.00
Inkwell, 1904, St. Louis, Glass & Brass	95.00
Key, 1933, Chicago, 8 1/2 In.	29.00
Knife, 1939, New York, Vitex, Pink Glass, Box	20.00
Lighter, Cigarette, 1962, Seattle, Space Needle, 10 1/2 In.	25.00
Map, 1939, New York, DeCamp Bus Co., Color	8.00
Map, Grounds, 1935, San Diego, 16 x 11 In.	15.00
Match Holder, 1939, New York, Tin	75.00
Medal, 1904, St. Louis, Gold Wash Bronze	45.00
Medal, 1939, New York, Official Executive Committee, Oval	28.00
Medallion, 1933, Chicago, Zettler, 2 1/2 In.	55.00
Mirror, 1939, New York, Pittsburgh Glass Co.	35.00
Mug, 1904, St. Louis, Ruby Flash	26.00
Mug, 1933, Chicago, Columbus–Washington, Pressed Glass	45.00
Napkin Ring, 1933, Chicago, 2 1/4 In.	55.00
Nappy, 1939, New York, Multicolored, Handle, 6 In.	20.00
Paperweight, 1876, Philadelphia, Building In Relief, Glass	125.00
Paperweight, 1893, Chicago, Fisheries Bldg., Glass	24.00
Paperweight, 1893, Chicago, Vienna, Glass	45.00

Pin, 1939, New York, I Have Seen The Future 35.00
Pin, 1939, New York, Lapel, Logo & Date 12.00
Pin, 1939, New York, Original Card 50.00
Pincushion Shoe, 1939, New York 25.00
Plate, 1893, Chicago, Gold Floral Center, Script Words, 5 In. 135.00
Plate, 1904, St. Louis, Festival Hall, Goofus Glass 50.00
Plate, 1904, St. Louis, Weller 70.00
Pocket Knife, 1933, Chicago, Mickey Mouse On Handle 60.00
Postcard, 1904, St. Louis, Palace of Machinery, Hold To Light 60.00
Radio, 1939, Flyer Wagon, New York 150.00
Rain Bonnet, 1964, New York 3.00
Razor Blade, 1893, Chicago, Bone Handle, Imperial Co. 50.00
Ring, Flicker, 1964, New York 2.00
Salt & Pepper, 1939, New York, Ship, Metal 25.00
Salt & Pepper, 1939, New York, Trylon & Perisphere, Plastic 20.00
Scarf, 1939, New York 15.00
Spoon, 1893, Chicago, Souvenir 20.00
Spoon, 1904, Portland, Silver Plate 35.00
Spoon, 1933, Chicago, Sterling Silver 13.00
Spoon, 1962, Seattle 7.00
Stick Pin, 1901, Buffalo, Frying Pan, Metal 12.00
Sugar & Creamer, 1962, Seattle, Miniature 20.00
Tapestry, 1933, Chicago, Skyscraper, Log Cabin, Metallic, 17 Ft. 45.00
Tapestry, 1939, San Francisco 28.00
Teaspoon, 1901, Buffalo, Electric Tower 20.00
Thermometer, 1904, St. Louis, Hammer Shape 25.00
Thermometer, 1933, Chicago, Golden Temple, Framed .... 22.00 To 28.00
Thermometer, 1939, San Francisco, Clock Type 35.00
Ticket, 1893, Chicago, Columbus, Lincoln, 4 Piece 40.00
Tip Tray, 1893, Chicago 35.00
Token, 1933, Chicago, Brass 10.00
Token, 1964, New York 15.00
Tray Set, 1967, Montreal, Pictures, Metal, 5 x 7 In., 5 Piece 12.50
Tray, 1939, New York, Orange & Blue, 16 x 8 In. 45.00
Tray, 1964, New York, GM Futurama, Glass, Box 20.00
Tumbler, 1933, Chicago, Etched, Administration Build 49.00
Tumbler, 1962, Seattle, Boulevards of The World, Glass 12.00
Tumbler, 1962, Seattle, Frosted Glass, Century 21, 6 5/8 In. 6.00
Tumbler, 1964, New York 8.00
Tumbler, 1982, Knoxville 5.00
Umbrella, 1933, Chicago 32.00
Vase, 1904, St. Louis, Cobalt Blue, Glass 30.00
Viewbook, 1933, Chicago, Official Pictures 20.00
Walking Stick, 1939, New York, Logo 45.00
Watch Fob, 1933, Century of Progress 25.00

The wristwatch came into use during World War I. Pocket watches are listed in the watch category. Wristwatches are listed here by manufacturer or as advertising or character watches.

WRISTWATCH, 3 Stooges, Box 65.00
    Abra, Art Deco, 18K White Gold, 17 Jewel, Flower On Face & Band 650.00

✦✦

The word "Wedgewood" is found on china that was not made by the famous factory of Josiah Wedgwood. William Smith and Company of Stockton on Tees, England, made a cream–colored ware marked "Wedgewood" from 1826 to 1848. The mark was a deliberate attempt to mislead the public and to misrepresent the china as that of the more famous factory.

✦✦

Accutron, Man's, Sweep Second Hand 100.00
Advertising, 7–Up, Leather Band 35.00
Advertising, Charlie Tuna, 1977, Box 75.00
Advertising, Chevrolet, Radiator Grill Shape, 1927 .... 599.00
Advertising, Hamm Beer 40.00
Advertising, Hartford Ins. Co., Stag Has Moving Eyes 110.00
Advertising, Hawaiian Punch, Windup, Box 65.00
Advertising, Holly Hobbie, Bradley 15.00
Advertising, Keebler Elf, Box 65.00
Advertising, Kellogg's, Box 85.00
Advertising, Kool Aid, 1950s 125.00
Advertising, McDonald, Card 5.00
Advertising, Ritz Cracker 400.00
Advertising, Spearmint, On Card 40.00
Advertising, Sugar Bear Cereal, Shifting Eyes 65.00
Alf, Black Band, Digital, Hong Kong 12.00
Audemars Piguet, 18K Gold, 18 Jewel, Square Case, 1945 .... 1540.00
Audemars Piguet, 18K Gold, Oval Bracelet, Tiger–Eye Numerals 2200.00
Babe Ruth, 18K Gold, Estango, White Face 4950.00
Bueche–Girod, 18K Gold, Oval Dial, Sapphire Crystal, Oval 2420.00
Bulgari, Silvered Dial, Folds Into 20 Dollar Gold Coin 4400.00
Bulova, Accutron, Spaceview, Model 214 .... 175.00
Bulova, Computron 150.00
Bulova, Watertite, Dancing Girl, Pink Gold, Box 600.00
Bulova, Woman's, 14K White Gold, 16 Jewel, Fancy Dial, 1820 .... 110.00
Bulova, Woman's, 14K White Gold, 17 Jewels, Diamonds 160.00
Bulova, Woman's, 8 Diamonds 185.00
Bulova, Woman's, Diamonds, 23 Jewels, 14K Gold 595.00
Cabbage Patch Kids, Yellow Band, Hong Kong 10.00
Cartier, 18K Gold Tank, 19 Jewel, Roman Numerals, 1935 .... 6600.00
Cartier, 18K Gold, Octagonal Stepped Case, Lever Movement 3300.00
Cartier, 18k Gold, Self–Winding, Santos Bracelet, Oval Case 7425.00
Cartier, Woman's, 18K Gold, 17 Jewels, Vendome, Black Numerals 2750.00
Cartier, Woman's, 18K Gold, Santos, Roman Dial, Square Case, 1970 .... 2750.00
Character, Big Bad Wolf, Steel, Animated, Eyes Move Back & Forth 999.00
Character, Bugs Bunny, Original Band 325.00
Character, Buzzy The Crow, Red Hat, Multicolor, Sweep Second 99.00
Character, Capt. Kirk, Mego 45.00
Character, Cinderella, Bradley Time 25.00
Character, Clingon, Box, Mego 55.00
Character, Evel Knievel 8.00
Character, Fess Parker, Box 50.00
Character, Fred Flintstone, Box, 1972 .... 230.00
Character, J. R., From Dallas, Box 75.00
Character, Jackie Gleason, Black Band, For Showtime, Hong Kong 75.00
Character, Jerry Lewis, Box .... 65.00 To 75.00
Character, Lost In Space, Box 50.00
Character, Mary Marvel, Box 225.00
Character, Million Dollar Man 60.00
Character, Mohammad Ali, Box 70.00
Character, Mummy, Hands & Eyes Glow, Mego 125.00
Character, New York Yankees 250.00
Character, Pebbles, 1972 .... 170.00
Character, Porky Pig 225.00
Character, Return of Jedi, Box 75.00
Character, Road Runner, Black Band, Legs Move, Quartz, Armitron 30.00
Character, Roger Rabbit, Silhouette, Shiraka, 1987 .... 50.00
Character, Ronald McDonald 45.00
Character, Snoopy, Bradley 20.00
Character, Snoopy, Doghouse Box 165.00
Character, Space Patrol 165.00
Character, Spiro Agnew, Dirty Time Co. 50.00
Character, Spock, Mego 45.00

Character, Tarzan, Mego, Box	135.00
Character, Tom & Jerry	55.00
Elgin, Art Deco, Chain Band, Round Dial In Square Case	175.00
Elgin, Art Deco, Mermaid & Seahorse, 14K White Gold	225.00
Elgin, Woman's, 14K White Gold, 17 Jewels, Tonneau Case, 1930s	110.00
Elgin, Yellow Gold	95.00
Girard Perregaux, 14K Gold, Bracelet	245.00
Girard Perregaux, Woman's, 14K Yellow Gold, Nurse's	225.00
Gruen, 17 Jewel, Pink Face, Bicolor Gold Expandable Bracelet	715.00
Gruen, Curvex, Man's, Rose Gold Filled	250.00
Gruen, Curvex, Round Case, Rectangular Movement, Masonic Dial	350.00
Gruen, Curvex, Veri-Thin, Yellow Gold Filled	165.00
Hamilton, Woman's, 14K White Gold, 17 Jewel, Diamond, Square Case	60.00
Invicta, 18K Gold, Curved, Elongated, Art Deco, Thin	599.00
Jules Jurgensen, 18K Gold, Rectangular, Matte Finish	200.00
LeCoultre, 10K Gold Filled, Alarm	400.00
LeCoultre, 14K Gold Case, Memovox, Gold Filled Band	250.00
LeCoultre, 18K Gold, Mystery, Enameled Bezel, c.1950	2750.00
LeCoultre, Futurmatic, Teardop Lugs, Yellow Gold Filled	600.00
LeCoultre, Gold Filled, Grasshopper	799.00
Longines, Black Face, No Hour Marked, Diamond At Midnight	90.00
Longines, Woman's, 14K Gold, Gold Band	175.00
Lord Elgin, 14K Gold, Pontiac, 1950s	299.00
Lord Elgin, Mystery, Yellow Gold Filled	259.00
Movado, Calendar, Moon Phases, 17 Jewels, Gold, c.1940	4620.00
Movado, Stainless Steel, Calendar, Moon Phases, Low Gold, 1950	2860.00
Movado, Woman's, 14K Gold, 1950s	550.00
Omega, Man's, Seamaster Automatic Calendar, Second Hand	300.00
Omega, Woman's, 18K Yellow Gold, Oval Face, Rope Design	200.00
Patek Philippe, 18 Jewel, 18K Gold, Black Dial, c.1940	3300.00
Patek Philippe, 18 Jewel, 18K Gold, Champagne Round Case, 1940	3850.00
Patek Philippe, 18 Jewel, 18K Gold, Mesh Bracelet, Oval, 1966	4750.00
Patek Philippe, 18 Jewel, 18K Gold, Oblong, c.1970	2750.00
Patek Philippe, 18 Jewel, 18K Gold, Ultra-Thin	4125.00
Patek Philippe, 18 Jewel, Cushion Form, Gold Dial	185.00
Patek Philippe, 18 Jewel, Pink Gold, 8 Adjustments, c.1946	3960.00
Patek Philippe, 18 Jewel, Silvered Dial, c.1937	5500.00
Patek Philippe, Woman's, 18 Jewel, 18K Gold, Rectangular Case	2200.00
Patek Philippe, Woman's, 18K White Gold, Mesh Bracelet, 1925	2530.00
Patek Phillippe, 18 Jewel, Silvered Dial, c.1937	5000.00
Paul Valette, Woman's, 18K White Gold, Cloisonne, Rectangular	499.00
Piaget, Woman's, Diamonds & Pearls, c.1930	2310.00
Pilot's, Waltham, Sterling, Assymetrical Lugs, World War I	499.00
Quartz Chronograph, For Your Eyes Only, Digital, Box, 1981	95.00
Rolex Oyster, Woman's, 18K Gold, Self-Winding, Sweep Seconds	1800.00
Rolex Tudor, 17 Jewel, Cushion Shape, Yellow Filled Gold	795.00
Rolex, 17 Jewel, 18K Pink Gold, Enamel Numerals, 1935	4125.00
Rolex, 17 Jewel, Chronometer, Pink Gold, Signed, c.1945	2250.00
Rolex, Cosmograph, Registers & Tachomete, Silvered Dial, c.1968	7975.00
Rolex, Cosmograph, Stainless Steel, Chronograph, 1970	6600.00
Rolex, Oyster, 14K Gold, Perpetual, Silvered Dial, c.1950	4100.00
Rolex, Oyster, 14K Gold, Self-Winding, Rolex Buckle, 1945	4400.00
Rolex, Oyster, No. 18, Bubble Back, Solid Gold, 1940s	4000.00
Rolex, Oyster, Woman's, 18K Gold, Self-Winding, Jubilee Bracelet	6100.00
Rolex, Woman's, 18K Gold, Handwind, Diamond Dial, Mesh Bracelet	440.00
Rolex, Woman's, Tank Style Case, White Gold Filled	250.00
U. S. Civil Air Patrol, Yellow Gold Filled, Sweep Seconds	199.00
Universal, 18K Gold, Moon Phase Calendar, Window, 1945	2750.00
Vacheron & Constantin, 18K Gold, 17 Jewel, c.1950	1980.00
Vacheron & Constantin, 18K White Gold, 17 Jewel, Mesh Bracelet	3190.00
Waltham, Art Deco, Enameled Design On Bezel, Rectangular	299.00
Waltham, Military Style, Porcelain Dial, Oval	100.00
Waltham, Ruby Model, Porcelain Dial, Orchid On Case Back	200.00

Wristwatch, Woman's, Platinum, Diamonds, Sapphires, 1930

Wittnauer, Aviator's, Steel, Sweep Seconds, Rotating Bezel, Weems	599.00
Wittnauer, Calendar, Red Face	75.00
Woman's, Platinum, Diamonds, Sapphires, 1930 ....*Illus*	1815.00
Woman's, Tiffany, 18K Gold, Wolf Tooth Wind, Porcelain Dial	1495.00
Wyler, 14K Gold, 3 Diamonds, Black Dial, 1940s	225.00
Zorro, Cellophane On Hat, Box, 1957	425.00

Yellowware is a heavy earthenware made of a yellowish clay. It varies in color from light yellow to orange–yellow. Many nineteenth– and twentieth–century kitchen bowls and jugs were made of yellowware. It was made in England and in the United States. Another form of pottery that is sometimes classed as yellowware is listed in this book under Mocha.

YELLOWWARE, Bank, Pig, Black & Brown Sponging, Amber Glaze, 3 3/4 In.	105.00
Beater Jar, Fenton, Iowa	45.00
Bottle, Pig	375.00
Bowl, 12 1/4 In.	36.00
Bowl, 14 x 7 In.	49.00
Bowl, Brown Bands, Marked 120, 14 1/2 In.	67.50
Bowl, Cover, Blue Sponging, White Interior, Wire Bale, 12 3/4 In.	150.00
Bowl, Girl With Watering Can, 5 x 9 In.	55.00
Bowl, Kitty Logo	40.00
Bowl, Label, Sharpe's Warranted Fire Proof, 3 3/8 x 13 In.	70.00
Bowl, Milk, Unglazed Exterior, 6 3/4 x 17 In.	125.00
Bowl, Seaweed Design, 5 3/4 x 3 In.	95.00
Crock, 3 Brown Bands, 5 In.	25.00
Crock, Butter, Cover, Dark Blue Stripes, 7 1/4 x 4 In.	95.00
Crock, Butter, Elsie The Cow	85.00
Dish, Baking, Vintage & Vegetables, Glazed Insert, 11 1/2 In.	195.00
Dish, Vegetable, Bennett & Brothers, Octagonal, 12 3/8 In.	475.00
Dog Dish	15.00
Figurine, Cat, Seated, Free Standing Front Legs, 11 3/8 In.	2000.00
Jar, Canning, 7 1/4 In.	65.00
Jar, Cover, Tan & White Stripes, 6 x 8 In.	35.00
Jug, John Haig's Whisky, Black Sponged, 4 x 4 In.	95.00
Match Holder & Strike Shoe	93.00
Measurer, Green & Brown Spoke Design, Morton Pottery, 5 In.	95.00
Mixing Bowl, Blue Bands	15.00
Mold, Corn, Oval, 7 In. .... 50.00 To	70.00
Mold, Food	67.50
Mold, Pinwheel, Miniature	85.00
Mold, Wheat Pattern, Octagon	75.00
Mug, 2 Blue Bands, Marked Buckey Pure	30.00
Mug, Roosevelt, New Deal	65.00
Mug, White Stripes, 2 3/4 In.	175.00
Nesting Bowls, White Bands, 10 To 14 In., 4 Piece	260.00
Pan, Milk, 3 x 11 1/2 In.	60.00

Pitcher, Advertising, 1 Pt. 39.00
Pitcher, Barrel Shape, Blue Band, 4 1/2 In. 65.00
Pitcher, Brown Sponging, Embossed Arches, 5 1/2 In. 25.00
Pitcher, Embossed Swastikas, Brown & Blue Sponging, 6 1/2 In. 105.00
Pitcher, Hunt Scene 125.00
Pitcher, Milk, Water Lilies, Trees, Green 35.00
Pitcher, Paneled Floral Designs, Norton & Fenton, 10 In. 250.00
Pitcher, Pint 30.00

Zane Pottery was founded in 1921 by Adam Reed and Harry McClelland in South Zanesville, Ohio, at the old Peters and Reed Building. Zane pottery is very similar to Peters and Reed pottery, but it is usually marked. The factory was sold in 1941 to Lawton Gonder.

ZANE, Basket, Hanging, Moss Aztec 65.00
Vase, Brown, Blue–Black Drip Glaze 85.00

The Zanesville Art Pottery was founded in 1900 by David Schmidt in Zanesville, Ohio. The firm made faience umbrella stands, jardinieres, and pedestals. The company closed in 1962. Many pieces are marked with just the words *La Moro.*

ZANESVILLE, Tile, Woman, Man, Blue, Green, Tan, 6 x 18 In. 285.00
Vase, Brown, Green Leaves, La Moro, 8 In. 275.00

Zsolnay pottery was made in Hungary after 1862 and was characterized by Persian, Art Nouveau, or Hungarian motifs. A series of new Zsolnay figurines with green–gold luster finish is available in many shops today. Early Zsolnay was not marked; but by 1878, the tower trademark was used.

ZSOLNAY, Bowl, Basket Shape, Reticulated, Floral, Bronze Cupid Base 2200.00
Bowl, Reticulated, Gold, Burgundy & Blue, Square, 6 In. 95.00
Figurine, Chickadee, Hand Painted, Green, Stamp, 4 1/2 In. 85.00
Group, Sparrows, 4 Colors, Marked, 4 1/2 In. 60.00
Jardiniere, Overall Florals, Oval Body, 16 In. 412.00
Pitcher, Puzzle, Flowers & Insects, Loop Handle, Signed, 8 In. 369.00
Pitcher, Puzzle, Yellow Ground, Flowers, Insects, Signed, 8 In. 369.00
Tile, Multicolored With Gold, Square, 5 In. 75.00
Vase, Iridescent Purple & Gold, 2 Handles, 8 In. 375.00
Vase, Mottled Blue & Green Glaze, Baluster Form, 4 1/2 In. 165.00
Vase, Pastel Flowers, Reticulated, 2 Handles, 4 Claw Feet, 9 3/4 In. 450.00
Vase, Purple Iridescent, Melon Ribbed, Marked, 6 In. 330.00
Vase, Purple, Gold, Red Iridescent, 7 1/2 In. 850.00

The following index is computer generated, making it as complete as possible. References in uppercase letters are category listings. Lowercase entries refer to pages of the book where other pieces of that type can be found. There is also an internal indexing system used in the text, so if you look for a Kewpie doll in the "Doll" section you will be told it is in the "Kewpie" section. There is additional information about where to find prices of pieces similar to yours at the end of many paragraphs.

This index is computer generated, making it as complete as possible. References in uppercase letters are category listings. Lowercase entries refer to pages of the book where other pieces of that type can be found. There is also an internal indexing system used in the text, so if you look for a Kewpie doll in the "Doll" section you will be told it is in the "Kewpie" section. There is additional information about where to find prices of pieces similar to yours at the end of many paragraphs.

THE KOVELS' LIBRARY

American Country Furniture 1780–1875

Over 700 close-up photographs identify styles, construction, woods, finishes, hardware, and other details. All the information you need to be an expert on American country furniture. Special sections on Pennsylvania, Shaker furniture, spool furniture and furniture construction, plus an illustrated glossary of accessories and terms.
54668 X $14.95 paper

Dictionary of Marks—Pottery and Porcelain (1580–1880)

A classic in the field, the *Dictionary of Marks* is a comprehensive guide to more than 5,000 American and European pottery and porcelain marks. It shows at a glance the geographical location of the factory, family name or manufacturer's name, type of ware, color of mark, and the date the mark was used.

001411 $10.95 hardcover

Kovels' New Dictionary of Marks—Pottery and Porcelain
1850 TO THE PRESENT

Kovels' New Dictionary of Marks provides the quickest and easiest way to identify more than 3,500 American, European, and Oriental marks. The perfect companion to the Kovels' original best seller, *The Dictionary of Marks—Pottery and Porcelain,* this is the most comprehensive reference for nineteenth- and twentieth-century marks. Together, the two volumes are an indispensable guide to the porcelain and pottery marks of the last four centuries.

559145 $17.95 hardcover